…ki Shikibu, …le of Genji; …ikibu (diary)

…court poetry; …manuscript

**…00 CE**

**1100 CE** — Kamo no Chōmei (*An Account of My Hermitage*); Tales of the Heike

**1175 CE** — Farīd al-Dīn Attar; Marie de France

**1300 CE** — Marco Polo; Dante

**1350 CE** — Ibn Battutah; *The Thousand and One Nights* manuscript

**1400 CE** — Japanese Nō plays; Chaucer; Christine de Pizan

**1600 CE** — Wu Cheng'en; Cervantes; Shakespeare; Popul Vuh manuscript

**1690 CE** — Matsuo Basho; Madame de Sévigné; Cao Xueqin

**1750 CE** — *Dream of the Red Chamber*

**1800 CE** — Jane Austen; Fredrich Hölderlin

**1850 CE** — Fyodor Dostoyevsky; Emily Dickinson; Walt Whitman

**1900 CE** — Natsume Sōseki

**1920 CE** — Virginia Woolf; Franz Kafka; T.S. Eliot

**1940 CE** — Ding Ling; Anna Akhmatova; Jorge Luis Borges; William Faulkner

**1950—present** — Léopold Senghor; Pablo Neruda; Toni Morrison; Wislawa Szymborska; Kawabata Yasunari; Abe Kōbō; Ōba Minako

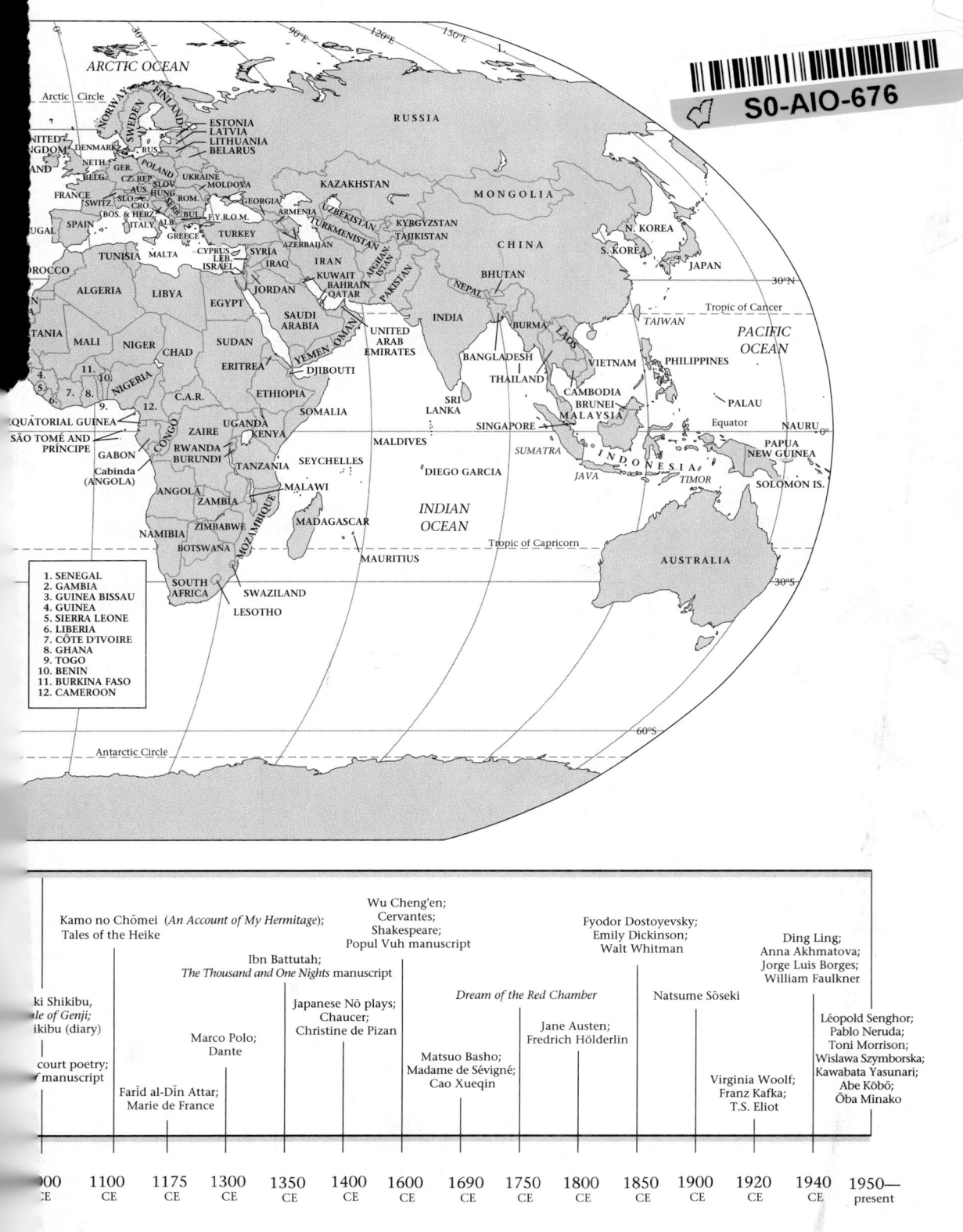

# The World of Literature

Louise Westling
Stephen Durrant
James W. Earl
Stephen Kohl
Anne Laskaya
Steven Shankman

*of the University of Oregon*

PRENTICE HALL, Upper Saddle River, NJ 07458

Library of Congress Cataloging-in-Publication Data

The world of literature / Louise Westling . . . [et al.].
p. cm.
Includes index.
ISBN 0-13-439159-4 (alk. paper)
1. Literature—Collections. I. Westling, Louise Hutchings.
PN6014.W6275 1999
808.8—dc21 98-36416
CIP

Editorial Director: Charlyce Jones Owen
Acquisition Editor: Carrie Brandon
Editorial Assistant: Gianna Caradonna
AVP, Director of Manufacturing and Production: Barbara Kittle
Senior Managing Editor: Bonnie Biller
Production Liaison: Fran Russello
Project Manager: Linda B. Pawelchak
Manufacturing Manager: Nick Sklitsis
Prepress and Manufacturing Buyer: Mary Ann Gloriande
Creative Design Director: Leslie Osher
Interior Design: Nancy Camuso-Wells
Cover Design: Nancy Camuso-Wells
Cover Art: World Map from Mercator Atlas Showing Terra Australia, 1595. Royal Geographical Society, London/Bridgeman Art Library, London. Copyright Superstock, Inc.
Director, Image Resource Center: Lori Morris-Nantz
Photo Research Supervisor: Melinda Lee Reo
Image Permission Supervisor: Kay Dellosa
Photo Researcher: Francelle Carapetyan
Electronic Art Creation: Mirella Signoretto
Marketing Manager: Susan Brekka

Acknowledgments may be found on pp. 2230–2244, which constitute an extension of this copyright page.

This book was set in 10/12 New Baskerville by Lithokraft II and was printed and bound by Courier Companies, Inc. The cover was printed by Phoenix Color Corp.



Printed in the United States of America
10 9 8 7 6 5 4 3 2 1

ISBN 0-13-439159-4

Prentice-Hall International (UK) Limited, *London*
Prentice-Hall of Australia Pty. Limited, *Sydney*
Prentice-Hall Canada Inc., *Toronto*
Prentice-Hall Hispanoamericana, S.A., *Mexico*
Prentice-Hall of India Private Limited, *New Delhi*
Prentice-Hall of Japan, Inc., *Tokyo*
Simon & Schuster Asia Pte. Ltd., *Singapore*
Editora Prentice-Hall do Brasil, Ltda., *Rio de Janeiro*

# Brief Contents

# Contents

# Preface

After four years of working together in remarkable good humor, the editors of *The World of Literature* would like to acknowledge the pleasures of our close collaboration. All six of us were part of a National Endowment for the Humanities summer institute in 1992 that was devoted to integrating Asian materials into the general humanities curriculum. We owe much to Esther Jacobson, director of that NEH institute, who adroitly shaped a month's interdisciplinary work for some twenty-five colleagues in the University of Oregon College of Arts and Sciences. Lectures from distinguished visiting scholars of Asian literature and art, as well as from several of our own faculty, a very heavy reading schedule, and seminar discussions exploring intersections of Asian and European traditions taught all participants how fruitful a global cultural perspective can be. A follow-up NEH Study Grant for College Teachers enabled Anne Laskaya to further explore Islamic literature the next year.

*The World of Literature* has grown out of the interdisciplinary teaching we have all been doing since the 1992 institute. John Moseley, Provost and Vice President for Academic Affairs of the University of Oregon, has supported our project from the beginning; and without the institutional resources he made available, we could never have begun such an undertaking. The Center for Asian Pacific Studies and the International Studies Program at the University of Oregon have also been important backers from the beginning. We owe a large debt to the UO English Department, which has provided space and staff support all through the project. In particular we wish to thank Marilyn Reid, Diane Hunsaker, Mike Stamm, Lynn Rossi, and Chris Hitt. We are grateful to our colleague George Wickes for contributing important editorial guidance, as well as two introductions and the selections from Madame de Sévigné. The UO Center for Asian Pacific Studies has also provided space and other support for the project. Both the Oregon Humanities Center and the UO Medieval Studies Program have supported our interdisciplinary work with various programmatic emphases. Clearly our anthology is a child of many ongoing humanistic programs at our university.

We owe the inception of our anthology to Tony English, then of Macmillan Publishers, who suggested the project to us when he learned of our desire for a truly global world literature anthology at a time when there really was no viable text available. Since the project moved to Prentice Hall, we have had the wise guidance of a succession of editors from Tony English to Nancy Perry and then to Carrie Brandon. All have supported our conception of the project and have been excellent guides for our work. We also wish to thank Linda Pawelchak for heroic management of the production process and Francelle Carapetyan for her work on illustrations.

We would like to acknowledge the contributions of the following reviewers:

Michael Atkinson
University of Cincinnati

Susan Beck
University of Wisconsin, River Falls

Paula Berggren
City University of New York, Bernard M. Baruch College

Eleni Coundouriotos
University of Connecticut, Storrs

Brian Doherty
University of Texas, Austin

Alistair Duckworth
University of Florida, Gainesville

David Ferris
Yale University

Brewster E. Fitz
Oklahoma State University

Leo K. Fong
University of Nevada at Las Vegas

John Gottcent
University of Southern Indiana

Donald Gray
Indiana University, Bloomington

Karen Hatch
California State University, Chico

Stuart Hirschberg
Rutgers University, Newark

Jeffrey Hoeper
Arkansas State University

Dennis Hoilman
Ball State University

Michael Johman
University of Louisville

Anna Joy
Scaramento City College

Gene Koppel
University of Arizona, Tucson

Larry Labin
Virginia Commonwealth University

Beth Madison
West Virginia University

Gregory Mason
Gustavus Adolphus College

Ronald D. Morrison
Moorhead State University

Alan Nagel
University of Iowa

Eric Nye
University of Wyoming

William Naufftus
Winthrop University

Lynn Risser
Texas Wesleyan University

Paul Trout
Montana State University

Ulrich Wicks
University of Maine, Orono

Carmen Wong
John Tyler Community College

Finally we wish to thank our partners, children, and friends who have put up with our world literature obsessions and seemingly endless work on the anthology during the past four years.

*The Editors*

# Introduction

THE SIX EDITORS OF THIS BOOK, EACH A SPECIALIST IN A DIFFERENT AREA OF world literature, have discussed and debated its contents for several years, learning from each other every step of the way. Among the things we agree on are the pressing need for such a book, and also the difficulty of making the particular selection of texts that will please most teachers. This is a new kind of book for a new kind of course, and many experienced teachers will find they need to adapt somewhat to the new situation. The rewards, however, are great. We hope others will find the prospect of teaching *global* literature as inviting and exciting as we have, but first we invite you to consider the challenges of assembling an anthology for this new kind of course.

We are in sore need of a fresh approach to the world's literature, but the literature of the world is so vast as to stagger the imaginations of any team of editors. How can the subject be taught most effectively in one year? What are the goals of such a course? What tiny percentage of the available texts are the finest, the most important, the best translated, and the most useful for the purpose? Deciding what to teach in the traditional Western Literature course was hard enough, even though we had inherited a familiar canon, and long experience had made the pedagogical goals seem obvious and achievable. Now that we can choose from all the world's riches, the prospect is far more daunting. Students and teachers alike deserve a rationale for the choices we have made, the results of long and stimulating conversations among colleagues.

The time for a global approach to world literature has obviously arrived. Today's students are not content to survey the Western classics, and it is not enough to add a few Eastern classics into the old syllabus. Whole worlds of literature are commonly ignored in "world literature" courses—Egyptian and Persian, Medieval Latin and Arabic, Scandinavian and Eastern European, Indian and African, pre-Columbian and Latin American, Southeast Asian, and many others. Here on the verge of the twenty-first century we can no longer dismiss any of them as unworthy of our awareness. They are parts of the great tapestry of world literature, which has been woven globally from the beginning—far more globally than most of us have realized.

We are not speaking of the *literatures* of the world, but the *literature* of the world. Through the Ancient and Middle Periods as well as the Modern, some of the most diverse and seemingly disparate cultures of the world were in steady if indirect contact and developed in relation to each other. Chinese silks have been found in ancient Greek and Celtic tombs, and Arabic coins somehow found their way to medieval Iceland; Greek artisans produced the earliest Buddhist sculptures in India, and Buddhist statues have turned up in the Viking graves of medieval Sweden. Genghis Khan's Mongol empire extended westward into the modern Czech Republic and south into Arabia. Trade routes for silk and spices linked China to Western Europe through Russia, India, Persia, Arabia, Egypt, Turkey, and Greece. Today our understanding of these connections is hampered mostly by the difficulty of any one scholar mastering all the languages involved and all the disciplines needed to reassemble this vast puzzle. Our ancestors were better traveled, more cosmopolitan, and more multicultural than we realized—in some ways more so than we ourselves are.

In addition to geographical movements and the diffusion of culture from place to place, there are also large patterns—so large they may go unnoticed—in the human enterprise as it has been carried on around the world. These patterns include the discovery and spread of writing and its effects on society; the origins of "literature" in religion, myth, and oral storytelling; the distinction between sacred and secular texts, and between official and vernacular languages, often tied to gender and class; the invention of printing and the ever-widening effects of literacy; the tension between urban and agricultural groups; and the forging of ethnic and cultural identities, and efforts to reach beyond them. We see familiar parallels and contrasts when different peoples grapple in their different contexts and languages with the inescapable realities of human life—time and change, youth, gender, love and sex, family, power and necessity, government, the private and the public, cultural difference, body and mind, spirit and religion, justice, good and evil, war and suffering, age and death. In addition to the history of particular cultural interactions, then, there are many bases for significant comparison between literatures we usually think of in terms of their differences.

While wrestling with the immense library of texts that history has bequeathed to us, the editors have also struggled with the problem of defining the concept "literature." Editors of other anthologies will have other definitions, the most common these days being that literature consists of any and all written texts of cultural importance. As a group, however, the six of us believe that there is a more precisely definable category of the "literary," and that certain texts are more literary than others—in spite of the fact that different cultures have defined this quality differently, and literary experience has taken innumerable forms around the world.

Many texts depend almost entirely on their immediate cultural contexts for significant appreciation. We understand them only with an extreme historical effort, patiently reconstructing their original functions and meanings as their creators and original audiences might have understood them. Legal and commercial records are an obvious example. They are seldom if ever considered as art, and with few exceptions have little or no aesthetic value, no matter how great their practical value. They belong, we might say, to humanity's short-term memory and now are of more interest to the historian than the general reader or the literary critic.

On the other hand, there are some texts, from all cultures and all periods, that have the ability to surprise us by seeming to transcend their original contexts. They reach out through the centuries and around the world to startle us at our reading desks with their power—against all odds, even before we have begun our historical researches. Modern readers respond to such texts in strong, sometimes unexpected ways, guided in large part by the aesthetic principles that their cultures have developed precisely for the purpose of shaping readers' responses.

How could we expect the ancient Sumerian Descent of Inanna to make sense to us, torn as it is from its nearly primordial setting four thousand years ago in the lost liturgy of a fertility cult in a barely imaginable Mesopotamia? In spite of our ignorance and incredulity, however, we are struck by this text's awesome dramatic force. It makes the hair on the back of our necks stand up. Its stylized, symbolic characters; its stark, ritualized dialogue; its escalating, hypnotic repetitions; the release of tension in sheer horror when Inanna is suddenly impaled—these same techniques have been used to similar effect in Greek tragedies, medieval morality plays, and contemporary films. There is something universal in this text's terrible beauty, and its power to move us.

Why are we so moved by the hymns of the ancient Indian Rig Veda? They were composed to accompany long-lost religious rituals, and their fastidiously precise recitation in Sanskrit was intended to maintain the world's very existence. Why, when stripped of their ritual setting and the belief system that was their reason for being, stripped even of their original language, do they still radiate such aesthetic and religious power? In this case, as in the case of the Inanna poems, it is clear that no matter how modern the world has become, human beings still possess powerful, nearly instinctive responses to the language of myth, which these texts present in amazingly pure form.

The idea that literature has a universal content, and that there are enduring principles of literary form, is at least as old as Aristotle. The validity of our "transhistorical" readings is not a modern, much less a postmodern, idea; it is a classic idea, perhaps a natural one, that has managed to survive countless cultural changes and intellectual fashions. It is, one might say, the way people read. In making our selections, therefore, we have considered each text's ability to reach out to a naive reader across time and space as a first measure of its literariness. By this principle, many texts of undisputed historical importance have not been included in this book. The Laws of Hammurabi, the Rosetta Stone, the Buddhist *Pillar Edicts of Ashoka,* St. Benedict's *Rule for Monks,* the works of Galileo, Darwin, and Freud—these may all be literary to some degree, but their chief claims on our attention are historical and intellectual, not artistic. Likewise, we have included many texts that are not always treated as literature—the Indian Vimalakīrti Sutra, Plato's *Symposium,* the letters of Abelard and Heloise, *The Travels of Marco Polo,* and *The Travels of Ibn Battuta.* By their style and content, by their beautiful language and crafted narratives, these texts almost inevitably produce wide-eyed amazement in thoughtful readers today, touching even those with little or no particular historical knowledge.

If these texts speak so well for themselves, then why does each require a historical introduction? We have kept our introductions to a minimum, but they are intended to be helpful. There are many kinds of reading, and interpretation benefits from all of them, as they build on each other. Historical and transhistorical interpretations are equally important. Our initial untutored response to a text like The Descent of Inanna can never be retracted or nullified, but it can be sharpened by greater awareness of the text's historical dimensions. A reader coming to the Chinese *Book of Songs*, for example, can find immediate personal resonances in the simple depictions of common human experiences and emotions like love or loneliness—the subjects of popular culture in every age. Today most readers find these simple themes the most compelling aspect of the songs, even after some study. Study reveals, however, that in China the *Book of Songs* has long been associated with Confucius; and though this attribution is dubious, it is likely that many of the individual songs were originally selected to be part of the *Book of Songs* because of their practical Confucianism. That is, they reject the older mythological and religious thought that remains in other texts from the same period, like the *Songs of the South*. In fact, for most of their long Confucian history, the poems of the *Book of Songs* were read in China as political allegories of China's heroic age, the Zhou dynasty, and used in that regard as part of the required curriculum for civil service examinations.

There is little point in rejecting as irrelevant either the traditional Confucian readings of the songs or our own instinctive ones, although they were arrived at by different methods for different purposes, and appear mutually exclusive. Each possesses, or has possessed, cultural power in different times and settings. Besides, no matter how strained the Confucian readings of the songs may seem to modern Western readers, they profoundly influenced later literature, for at some point Chinese poets began writing love songs according to these interpretive conventions, expecting them to be interpreted as political allegories.

We can compare this complex case from China with the biblical Song of Songs, or the Indian Rig Veda, both of which underwent similar transformations of interpretation over the millennia. Today most readers of the Song of Songs find its poetry highly erotic. It is now normally read as an anthology of ancient Middle Eastern courtship and marriage songs. In this light, traditional Jewish and Christian allegorical readings of it, in which the groom is understood as God, Christ, or the king, and the bride Israel, the Church, or the human soul, seem curious at best, in spite of their ancient authority. It is important to remember, however, that the traditional readings, no matter how curious they seem now, deeply influenced medieval love poetry, which is often allegorical in the same way. In medieval love poems, lovers commonly represent Christ and the human soul (as in the English poems included here, *Quia amore langueo* and the *Corpus Christi Carol*). Under the influence of the Song of Songs, then, erotic and religious love became metaphors for each other in Western literature. The ancient reading, artificial and counter-intuitive as it may seem, complements the modern one, allowing us to understand how the poetry of love and religion has developed over the intervening centuries.

There is nothing too surprising in our editorial conviction that some texts are great literature, and that literary texts can be understood in more ways than one at the same time. These are old ideas. However, we can hardly overstate the changes to the humanities implied by the true globalization of literary study represented in this book. Specialization and professionalization have dominated university life in recent decades. For all their benefits, these trends have stifled and sometimes killed certain kinds of excitement that once characterized the life of letters, which depended on expanding rather than limiting horizons. In the classroom, expertise is our greatest strength, but also our greatest weakness. Teachers have to explore new areas in their classrooms and in their research year after year, or students will be led into smaller and smaller pockets of specialized learning—a common complaint in universities today. Our best hope for this anthology is that our students and our colleagues will share in the thrill that we have found in exploring new materials as we prepared it.

The tremendous wealth of the Western tradition from Homer to Virginia Woolf is actually but one day in the week; and today's trends and innovations are only a blip on the screen when seen in historical perspective. Nothing written today can cancel or eclipse the literary achievements of the past, and the greatest achievements of our own literature do not diminish those in other languages. It does not require a lifetime to become acquainted with this larger context. A significant portion of it can be contained in a single book on one's shelf and can be absorbed by occasional reading as well as in a college course.

We have tried not to forge a new canon of "essential" or "classic" texts. There must be a high degree of arbitrariness in any selection this small from a stock so great. We have tried always to think of the practicalities of teaching a year-long introduction to world literature, choosing texts that resonate with each other, from culture to culture and age to age, displaying the rich diversity of the world's literature within the structure of a reasonably unified syllabus. Other anthologies include more texts. We have tried not to overwhelm the student or the teacher, but we have included enough texts to construct many different possible syllabi.

For example, the dramas included here, from Greece, India, China, and Japan, as well as those by Shakespeare and Beckett, would themselves provide an exciting term's reading. So would the sacred texts, including Inanna, the Bible, the Qur'an and Ibn Ishaq's Life of the Prophet, the Rig Veda and the Bhagavad-Gītā, the Life of Buddha and the Lotus Sutra, the Dao de jing, and many, many others. And so would the literature of love, including the Chinese *Book of Songs;* the biblical Song of Songs; Plato's *Symposium;* Virgil's, Ovid's, and Christine de Pizan's accounts of Dido and Aeneas; the Sanskrit poems of Vidyakara; the novels, diaries, and poetry of medieval Japan; the letters of Abelard and Heloise; Provençal poems; the works of Marie de France, Petrarch, and others, right up to the poems of Baudelaire and Neruda. Literature by and about women could form another exciting course; literature of travel and cultural connection another; and of course a straightforward chronological survey could embrace many of these themes.

Our choice of texts becomes less obvious and more arbitrary as we move from the Ancient to the Middle and then to the Modern Period, as the number of possibilities increases exponentially. It should be especially obvious that the modern selections do not constitute a canon, since scores of great writers and great works are conspicuously absent. Every reader opening this book for the first time will find a few favorites missing. The modern works that have been included, however, tend to work well together and work well with earlier texts. In the end, no matter what has been omitted, everything that has been included will be found to possess extraordinary literary merit and will reward new readers well.

For more than a year we debated the book's organization. Every solution has obvious flaws, but in the end we decided on the division into Ancient, Middle, and Modern Periods. This division corresponds roughly to the conventional periodization of European literature (though what we call the Middle Period extends well past the European Middle Ages). This division may at first seem arbitrary when applied to Arabic and Asian literature, but in fact unexpected synchronies make the three-period division more natural than one might expect. In India and China, for example, deep breaks with ancient tradition were caused by the spread of Buddhism in the second century CE, corresponding roughly to the spread of Christianity in the West. Indian tradition took another turn with the arrival of Muslim rule in the thirteenth century, and Chinese and Japanese tradition with the arrival of European missionaries in the sixteenth and seventeenth. It was during these centuries that the Renaissance brought deep changes to Europe, too. So there are ways of discussing, if not exactly explaining, the roughly simultaneous appearance of, say, female mysticism in Europe, Arabia, and India in the Middle Period (Hildegard of Bingen, Rabe'a al-'Adawiya, and Mīrābāī), or the development of romance literature in Europe and Japan at the same time (the personal accounts of Heloise and Izumi Shikibu, the fictions of Marie de France and Murasaki Shikibu).

An almost inevitable result of the tripartite division, however, is the sense it sometimes produces that the Middle Period has no particular definition beyond separating the Ancient and Modern. The European Middle Ages have suffered from this prejudice ever since Renaissance humanists invented the concept, and we certainly do not want to see it expanded to include the rest of the world. Still, in the end, it seems better to study the several literatures of each period together, rather than each regional literature separately from its beginnings to the present, for that would only sustain the false isolation of Europe, Africa, the Middle East, India, China, Japan, and the New World that this book is trying to overcome.

Something should be said about the fact that most of the texts in this book appear in translation. As intercultural a project as the book is, it has obviously been carried out in English, by English-speaking scholars, primarily for North American students. We have tried to find texts that represent different cultural, aesthetic, and linguistic worlds, but no doubt there is a bias toward what is most accessible in English. We have consistently preferred texts that translate well over ones that do not, and poetic translations over literal ones. To illustrate this problem, we have included separate discussions of the translation of Homer (pp. 430–488), The Chinese *Book of Songs* (p. 295), Confucius (p. 317), and Bashō (p. 1240). In the process, important texts have been omitted, and readers who know the texts in their original languages will of course note that some of their most distinctive literary features and meanings have vanished in translation.

Even the best English translation of a Chinese poem is an English poem. Interestingly, the Chinese classics most likely to electrify modern American readers may not be the ones Chinese readers most admire. There is no way to escape the influence of our Western education completely, and of course we respond most immediately to poems of other cultures when they resonate with themes familiar from our own. Arthur Waley's beautiful translation of the *Bones of Zhuangzi* by Zhang Heng is a stunning case in point: Chinese readers are sometimes puzzled by this poem's special appeal to Western readers.

It should also be obvious that the Chinese four-character line of the *Book of Songs* cannot be experienced in an alphabetic language, any more than Egyptian hieroglyphs or Mayan pictograms can. Nor can the intricacy of Greek syntax be captured in an English rendition of Pindar, nor the aesthetic effect of Virgil's word order, nor the rich fabric of wordplay in the Hebrew Bible, nor the use of different languages in the classical Indian drama of Kalidasa, nor the lack of pronouns in the Japanese novel, nor the subtlety of *haiku,* nor the elegant rhetorical periods of Heloise's Latin prose, nor the compression and formal precision of Old Norse poetry, nor even, closer to home, the magical fluidity of Baudelaire's French line. Reading in translation is largely an act of faith.

These cultural, historical, and linguistic limitations notwithstanding, the experience of these texts in the best English translations will still open whole new worlds of mental experience for thoughtful readers. Then, with further reading, we can learn to appreciate them more, some even in their original languages. In the end, we must do what we can to respect the other cultures of the world, or we have no right to expect them to respect us. Even more, we must do what we can to respect the past, or we have no right to expect the future to care about us and the world culture in which we are immersed and that we are struggling daily to understand and improve.

# *part 1*

# *Ancient Literature*

THE WORLD OF LITERATURE AS PRESENTED IN THE PAGES OF THIS ANTHOLOGY is a world of written words. But the world of writing is surrounded by a vast oral universe. Long before any poem or story was transformed into marks on bricks, bamboo strips, or papyrus rolls, songs were sung and stories were told. In fact, within the long span of human existence, the appearance of writing is fairly recent and has become a general part of human experience only in the last few centuries.

Whether the startling idea that human speech could be reduced to visible marks occurred only once and diffused throughout the world or emerged independently in two or possibly three different places is impossible to know with certainty. We do know that writing first appeared in Sumer, along the Tigris and Euphrates Rivers, during the last centuries of the fourth millennium BCE and was seen in Egypt within several centuries. These early scripts, like those of China, which are first attested fifteen hundred years later, were basically systems of word writing in which each graph represented, sometimes pictographically or ideographically, an entire word. Another written script, that of the Harappans who lived along the Indus River, is preserved on seals from as early as 2500 BCE, but it has not been deciphered and belongs to a civilization that was eventually overwhelmed by the Indo-Europeans in the second millennium BCE. Around 1800 BCE, an alphabet was created among the Phoenicians along the eastern shores of the Mediterranean Sea and spread, by different lines of influence, to the Greek and Latin languages toward the west and to Hebrew, Arabic, and Sanskrit toward the east. Quite far removed from all of this, and probably independent of the earlier scripts of Eurasia and Africa, a hieroglyphic script appeared, perhaps as early as the first century BCE, among the Mayans in America.

In none of these cases was writing first used to record literary texts. Perhaps the bond joining the song and the story with living performance was too strong or too sacred to be broken easily. It was a huge step, we might presume, to the startling notion that one could reduce a living art to visible marks and transfer something of the experience of oral performance to a person in a distant place or in a later age.

Rarely do we feel more strongly the mystery of the transfer of literary response across time and space than when we read texts from the ancient world. They speak to us from thousands of years ago and from cultural worlds that we can scarcely imagine. Yet they still speak with astounding power and relevance. And we believe, sometimes wrongly, but perhaps sometimes rightly, that we understand the minds and the hearts that produced them.

The *quality* of literature, unlike our knowledge of the stars or of the human body, has not necessarily improved with time. Literary forms might become more elaborate and complex, and the nuance of the written word might grow ever more subtle and sophisticated as texts pile up through the ages, but is there a more moving confrontation with death than the Sumerian *Epic of Gilgamesh?* A more powerful expression of the eternal tension between rest and quest than the Greek *Odyssey?* A more charming evocation of first love than in some of the poems of the Chinese *Book of Songs?* Perhaps the appeal of these ancient texts, and so many others included here, comes from the fact that they were produced in an age when the mysterious power of the written text to convey the most fundamental human concerns had only recently been discovered.

As literature passes from the spoken word into the realm of writing, it begins to accumulate in ways that speech alone never can. Literary history begins to unfold as texts take on a certain shape and are left for others, often much later, to contemplate and build on. While the literatures of the civilizations of antiquity influenced one another in ways we can sometimes trace, and in other ways that remain hidden from our excavations, the literary history of each civilization follows its own course. Literature first appears among the Sumerians and the Indians in sacred hymns tied closely to religious ritual, among the Greeks in the form of epics, and among the Chinese in relatively secular songs. Still, there are moments in the history of ancient literature when common interests arise in quite different places at roughly the same time. In no instance is this more striking than in the two or three centuries Karl Jaspers has called the "Axial Age," a time between roughly 700 and 400 BCE when a new philosophical inclination swept across the ancient world. In India this is the time of the Upanishads and of Gautama Buddha, in Greece the time of the pre-Socratic philosophers, in Israel the age of the prophets, and in China the period of Confucius and Laozi. Why such concern with religious and philosophical thought arose in these cultures at approximately the same time is not entirely understood, but many texts that still shape our ideas and our behavior derive from this age, one we have tried to represent amply in this anthology.

In the literature of each civilization represented here, the rhythmic and undeniably formal language of poetry plays a central role. It is a universal phenomenon. Poetry bears witness to the power of the rhythms of song and ritual as well as to the appeal of games, where the goal is always to play within the formal confines of an elaborate set of rules. It is a puzzle worth pondering over, that with a few exceptions literary art emerged first in poetry rather than in the prose that modern readers are likely to consider more normal and natural. If history is any guide, there is nothing particularly "normal" or "natural" about the short story or the novel, no matter how obvious they may seem today, whereas poetry seems to be as natural as the human pulse.

# Ancient Mesopotamia and Egypt

The oldest literature known to us is that of ancient Sumer, an agricultural civilization that developed around 3500 BCE in the fertile alluvial plain between the Tigris and Euphrates Rivers in what is now Iraq. The Sumerians were busy traders and agricultural engineers, the creators of large walled cities and complex social and political systems. Their commercial activities connected them with the civilization of the Indus Valley as well as with other parts of Mesopotamia—Syria, Anatolia, the Iranian plain, Afghanistan, southern Arabia, Bahrain, and Egypt.

Although people have probably used symbolic visual codes for thirty thousand years or more, no decipherable writings have been found to predate the cuneiform records pressed in clay tablets that Sumerian scribes began to make in large numbers toward the end of the fourth millennium BCE. This cuneiform writing was created by pressing the wedge-shaped end of a reed into damp clay tablets that were then dried in the sun. The earliest tablets were commercial records and lists of commodities, but by 2500 BCE there were Sumerian historical records in the form of king lists; and by the turn of the millennium a whole tradition of hymns and poetic narratives was being produced, putting into written form oral traditions that probably go back many centuries before writing was developed. Sumerian literature established themes and stories that lived on for two thousand years, as civilizations succeeded each other in the region. Many Mesopotamian themes and stories eventually passed into European culture through Greek literature and the Hebrew Bible. Thus, for example, hymns to the Sumerian fertility goddess Inanna find expression in Babylonian poems dedicated to Ishtar, which are later echoed in sacred hymns to Greek and Roman deities like Demeter or Ceres and Artemis or Diana. Some of their language may also be echoed in the beautiful Song of Songs of the Hebrew Bible. The earliest known epic is the story of Gilgamesh, in which the heroic themes of self-definition, quest, and combat define patterns repeated in the Homeric epics, Virgil's *Aeneid,* the Old English *Beowulf,* and many other European epic tales, right down to our own time in novels such as Joyce's *Ulysses* and films such as *Star Wars.*

The mighty civilization of ancient Egypt developed around the same time as that of Mesopotamia. It too was made possible by the development of agriculture on fertile alluvial lands irrigated by regular flooding. The Egyptians developed a hieroglyphic mode of writing not long after the Sumerian invention of cuneiform script. From as early as 3100 BCE the Egyptians were recording their spoken language in the form of elaborate pictographic symbols. A rich variety of Egyptian writings from the Old Kingdom (c. 2685–2180 BCE) through the New Kingdom (c. 1567–1090 BCE) is found in papyrus scrolls, temple carvings, and wall paintings in the monumental tombs and pyramids that have made Egyptian civilization so famous in our time. As in the case of Mesopotamian writing, much of what survives from ancient Egypt consists of business correspondence, legal matters, and addresses to monarchs and to other public officials. However, narrative works, moral teachings, and semiphilosophical or spiritual exercises appear in prose we would consider "literary." A good deal of religious poetry has also survived, as well as love poetry of a charming lightness and lyrical intimacy.

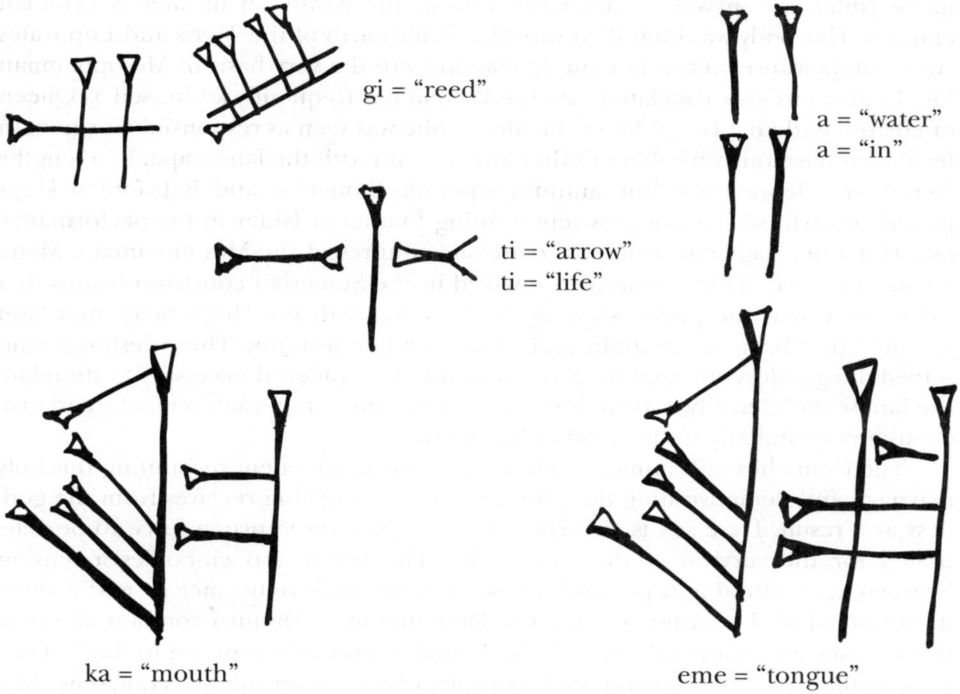


# Cuneiform Writing

The Sumerians contributed the first known writing system to civilization, and it spread among the peoples throughout their region of Mesopotamia. "Cuneiform" means "wedge shaped," referring to the marks made with a reed stylus on damp clay tablets. Originally the script was a series of pictographic signs used by temple priests to keep records of economic activities, but gradually it evolved into a phonetic system of writing for much wider communication. Many thousands of inscribed tablets have been excavated from the buried ruins of ancient Sumerian cities, but these represent only a small fraction of what still remains to be discovered in the "tells" or archaeological mounds scattered over modern Iraq. Scholars have been working for fifty years to decipher the more than five thousand literary tablets and fragments that have been discovered so far. Sumerian literature includes a rich store of myths, epics, hymns, and wisdom texts inscribed in these wedge-shaped signs.

## The Descent of Inanna (c. 2000 BCE)

The goddess Inanna was the central fertility deity of ancient Sumer, and under the name Ishtar she served a similar function in the pantheon of later Babylonian empires. Her body was identified with the fertile earth of the Tigris and Euphrates river valleys whose cultivation and irrigation were the very basis of Mesopotamian life. Inanna was also associated with the sky and was frequently addressed as Queen of Heaven and First Daughter of the Moon. She was seen as responsible for human fertility in harmony with that of other animals and with the landscape. In a lengthy New Year celebration at the autumn equinox, Sumerian and Babylonian kings joined annually with a priestess representing Inanna or Ishtar in the performance of a ritual marriage common in the archaic cultures of the Mesopotamian/Mediterranean world. This ceremony is invoked in the Sumerian courtship hymns that follow, in which the goddess's body is identified with the "high field" and "wet ground" that bring forth grain and plants for her servants. The priestesses who served the goddess engaged in sacred sexual acts considered necessary to stimulate the landscape's fertility and vitalize the human community each year. Human procreation was similarly understood to be sacred.

The Courtship of Inanna and Dumuzi is a narrative poem recounting this holy marriage and demonstrating the protection the young king receives from the goddess as a result. Here sex is a subject of the highest reverence, a force to be celebrated for the survival of the community. The poem also embodies a tension between agricultural and pastoral life, seen in Inanna's reluctance to wed a shepherd instead of the farmer she prefers. Descriptions of Dumuzi combine the symbolism associated with both ways of life. A similar tension is depicted in the Hebrew Bible in the rivalry of Cain and Abel—a rivalry with a less harmonious outcome than the erotic reconciliation of Inanna and Dumuzi. Israel defined itself as a pastoral nation, whereas Sumer was both pastoral and agricultural, but primarily agricultural.

The Descent of Inanna is a heroic journey to the land of the dead. Sumerian religious tradition identified the king with a vegetation god whose annual sacrifice, death, resurrection, and reunion with his wife parallel the dying of plants in the hot, dry summer season, followed by the return of vegetation in the winter rainy season. Once Inanna is trapped in the underworld, her only chance for release is the substitution of another victim. Rather than sacrifice her faithful servant or her sons, she gives over her husband Dumuzi. Later, however, she joins her mother-in-law and sister-in-law in grieving over Dumuzi's fate. This lament for the dead king is preserved on clay tablets dating from 2000 BCE, and variations on this popular theme are found throughout Mesopotamia, down to late Babylonian laments of Ishtar for Tammuz.

In the Sumerian version included here, Dumuzi's sister's grief moves Inanna to arrange a compromise by which Dumuzi's place in the underworld is taken for half the year by his sister. This arrangement creates an oscillating male and female descent into the underworld and ascent into life, paralleling the seasonal cycle of death and rebirth. This pattern is modified in the Greek story of Demeter and Persephone, and in the traditions associated with the god Dionysos (or Bacchus).

One can also compare the combination of an exuberantly sexual creation story with a journey to the land of death in the ancient Japanese *Kojiki* (pp. 1063–1071).

The Sumerian poems to Inanna are recorded on cuneiform tablets about four thousand years old.

## *from The Courtship of Inanna and Dumuzi*

*Translated by Samuel Noah Kramer*

The brother spoke to his younger sister.
The Sun God, Utu, spoke to Inanna, saying:
"Young Lady, the flax in its fullness is lovely.
Inanna, the grain is glistening in the furrow.
I will hoe it for you. I will bring it to you.
A piece of linen, big or small, is always needed.
Inanna, I will bring it to you."

* * *

"Brother, after you've brought my bridal sheet to me,
Who will go to bed with me?
Utu, who will go to bed with me?"

"Sister, your bridegroom will go to bed with you.
He who was born from a fertile womb,
He who was conceived on the sacred marriage throne,
Dumuzi, the shepherd! He will go to bed with you."

Inanna spoke:
"No, brother!
The man of my heart works the hoe.
The farmer! He is the man of my heart!
He gathers the grain into great heaps.
He brings the grain regularly into my storehouses."

Utu spoke:
"Sister, marry the shepherd.
Why are you unwilling?
His cream is good; his milk is good.
Whatever he touches shines brightly.
Inanna, marry Dumuzi.

You who adorn yourself with the agate necklace of fertility,
Why are you unwilling?
Dumuzi will share his rich cream with you.

You who are meant to be the king's protector,
Why are you unwilling?"

Inanna spoke:
"The shepherd! I will not marry the shepherd!
His clothes are coarse; his wool is rough.
I will marry the farmer.
The farmer grows flax for my clothes.
The farmer grows barley for my table."

Dumuzi spoke:
"Why do you speak about the farmer?
Why do you speak about him?
If he gives you black flour,
I will give you black wool.
If he gives you white flour,
I will give you white wool.
If he gives you beer,
I will give you sweet milk.
If he gives you bread,
I will give you honey cheese.
I will give the farmer my leftover cream.
I will give the farmer my leftover milk.
Why do you speak about the farmer?
What does he have more than I do?"

Inanna spoke:
"Shepherd, without my mother, Ningal, you'd be driven away,
Without my grandmother, Ningikuga, you'd be driven into
the steppes,
Without my father, Nanna, you'd have no roof,
Without my brother, Utu—"

Dumuzi spoke:
"Inanna, do not start a quarrel.
My father, Enki, is as good as your father, Nanna.
My mother, Sirtur, is as good as your mother, Ningal.
My sister, Geshtinanna, is as good as yours.
Queen of the palace, let us talk it over.

Inanna, let us sit and speak together.
I am as good as Utu.
Enki is as good as Nanna.
Sirtur is as good as Ningal.
Queen of the palace, let us talk it over."

The word they had spoken
Was a word of desire.
From the starting of the quarrel
Came the lovers' desire.

The shepherd went to the royal house with cream.
Dumuzi went to the royal house with milk.
Before the door, he called out:
"Open the house, My Lady, open the house!"

Inanna ran to Ningal, the mother who bore her.
Ningal counseled her daughter, saying:
"My child, the young man will be your father.
My daughter, the young man will be your mother.
He will treat you like a father.
He will care for you like a mother.
Open the house, My Lady, open the house!"

Inanna, at her mother's command,
Bathed and anointed herself with scented oil.
She covered her body with the royal white robe.
She readied her dowry.
She arranged her precious lapis beads around her neck.
She took her seal in her hand.

Dumuzi waited expectantly.
Inanna opened the door for him.
Inside the house she shone before him
Like the light of the moon.

Dumuzi looked at her joyously.
He pressed his neck close against hers.
He kissed her.

Inanna spoke:
"What I tell you
Let the singer weave into song.
What I tell you,
Let it flow from ear to mouth,
Let it pass from old to young:
My vulva, the horn,
The Boat of Heaven,
Is full of eagerness like the young moon.
My untilled land lies fallow.

As for me, Inanna,
Who will plow my vulva?
Who will plow my high field?
Who will plow my wet ground?

As for me, the young woman,
Who will plow my vulva?
Who will station the ox there?
Who will plow my vulva?"

Dumuzi replied:
"Great Lady, the king will plow your vulva.
I, Dumuzi the King, will plow your vulva."

Inanna:
"Then plow my vulva, man of my heart!
Plow my vulva!"

At the king's lap stood the rising cedar.
Plants grew high by their side.
Grains grew high by their side.
Gardens flourished luxuriantly.

Inanna sang:
"He has sprouted; he has burgeoned;
He is lettuce planted by the water.
He is the one my womb loves best.

My well-stocked garden of the plain,
My barley growing high in its furrow,
My apple tree which bears fruit up to its crown,
He is lettuce planted by the water.

My honey-man, my honey-man sweetens me always.
My lord, the honey-man of the gods,
He is the one my womb loves best.
His hand is honey, his foot is honey,
He sweetens me always.

My eager impetuous caresser of the navel,
My caresser of the soft thighs,
He is the one my womb loves best,
He is lettuce planted by the water."

Dumuzi sang:
"O Lady, your breast is your field.
Inanna, your breast is your field.
Your broad field pours out plants.

Your broad field pours out grain.
Water flows from on high for your servant.
Bread flows from on high for your servant.
Pour it out for me, Inanna.
I will drink all you offer."

Inanna sang:
"Make your milk sweet and thick, my bridegroom.
My shepherd, I will drink your fresh milk.
Wild bull, Dumuzi, make your milk sweet and thick.
I will drink your fresh milk.

Let the milk of the goat flow in my sheepfold.
Fill my holy churn with honey cheese.
Lord Dumuzi, I will drink your fresh milk.

My husband, I will guard my sheepfold for you.
I will watch over your house of life, the storehouse,
The shining quivering place which delights Sumer—
The house which decides the fates of the land,
The house which gives the breath of life to the people.
I, the queen of the palace, will watch over your house."

Dumuzi spoke:
"My sister, I would go with you to my garden.
Inanna, I would go with you to my garden.
I would go with you to my orchard.
I would go with you to my apple tree.
There I would plant the sweet, honey-covered seed."

Inanna spoke:
"He brought me into his garden.
My brother, Dumuzi, brought me into his garden.
I strolled with him among the standing trees,
I stood with him among the fallen trees,
By an apple tree I knelt as is proper.

Before my brother coming in song,
Who rose to me out of the poplar leaves,
Who came to me in the midday heat,
Before my lord Dumuzi,
I poured out plants from my womb.
I placed plants before him,
I poured out plants before him.
I placed grain before him,
I poured out grain before him.
I poured out grain from my womb."

* * *

The Queen of Heaven,
The heroic woman, greater than her mother,
Who was presented the *me* by Enki,
Inanna, the First Daughter of the Moon,
Decreed the fate of Dumuzi:
"In battle I am your leader,
In combat I am your armor-bearer,
In the assembly I am your advocate,
On the campaign I am your inspiration.
You, the chosen shepherd of the holy shrine,
You, the king, the faithful provider of Uruk,
You, the light of An's great shrine,
In all ways you are fit:

To hold your head high on the lofty dais,
To sit on the lapis lazuli throne,
To cover your head with the holy crown,
To wear long clothes on your body,
To bind yourself with the garments of kingship,
To carry the mace and sword,
To guide straight the long bow and arrow,
To fasten the throw-stick and sling at your side,
To race on the road with the holy sceptre in your hand,
And the holy sandals on your feet,
To prance on the holy breast like a lapis lazuli calf.

You, the sprinter, the chosen shepherd,
In all ways you are fit.
May your heart enjoy long days.

That which An has determined for you—may it not be altered.
That which Enlil has granted—may it not be changed.
You are the favorite of Ningal.
Inanna holds you dear."

## *from The Descent of Inanna*

### From the Great Above to the Great Below

From the Great Above she opened her ear to the Great Below.
From the Great Above the goddess opened her ear to the Great Below.
From the Great Above Inanna opened her ear to the Great Below.

My Lady abandoned heaven and earth to descend to the underworld.
Inanna abandoned heaven and earth to descend to the underworld.
She abandoned her office of holy priestess to descend to the
underworld.

In Uruk she abandoned her temple to descend to the underworld.
In Badtibira she abandoned her temple to descend to the
underworld.
In Zabalam she abandoned her temple to descend to the
underworld.
In Adab she abandoned her temple to descend to the underworld.
In Nippur she abandoned her temple to descend to the underworld.
In Kish she abandoned her temple to descend to the underworld.
In Akkad she abandoned her temple to descend to the underworld.

She gathered together the seven *me.*
She took them into her hands.
With the *me* in her possession, she prepared herself:

She placed the *shugurra,* the crown of the steppe, on her head.
She arranged the dark locks of hair across her forehead.
She tied the small lapis beads around her neck,
Let the double strand of beads fall to her breast,
And wrapped the royal robe around her body.
She daubed her eyes with ointment called "Let him come, Let him
come,"
Bound the breastplate called "Come, man, come!" around her chest,
Slipped the gold ring over her wrist,
And took the lapis measuring rod and line in her hand.

Inanna set out for the underworld.
Ninshubur, her faithful servant, went with her.
Inanna spoke to her, saying:
"Ninshubur, my constant support,
My *sukkal* who gives me wise advice,
My warrior who fights by my side,
I am descending to the *kur,* to the underworld.
If I do not return,
Set up a lament for me by the ruins.
Beat the drum for me in the assembly places.
Circle the houses of the gods.
Tear at your eyes, at your mouth, at your thighs.
Dress yourself in a single garment like a beggar.
Go to Nippur, to the temple of Enlil.

When you enter his holy shrine, cry out:
'O Father Enlil, do not let your daughter
Be put to death in the underworld.
Do not let your bright silver
Be covered with the dust of the underworld.
Do not let your precious lapis
Be broken into stone for the stoneworker.
Do not let your fragrant boxwood
Be cut into wood for the woodworker.
Do not let the holy priestess of heaven
Be put to death in the underworld.'

If Enlil will not help you,
Go to Ur, to the temple of Nanna.
Weep before Father Nanna.
If Nanna will not help you,
Go to Eridu, to the temple of Enki.
Weep before Father Enki.
Father Enki, the God of Wisdom, knows the food of life,
He knows the water of life;
He knows the secrets.
Surely he will not let me die."

Inanna continued on her way to the underworld.
Then she stopped and said:
"Go now, Ninshubur—
Do not forget the words I have commanded you."

When Inanna arrived at the outer gates of the underworld,
She knocked loudly.

She cried out in a fierce voice:
"Open the door, gatekeeper!
Open the door, Neti!
I alone would enter!"

Neti, the chief gatekeeper of the *kur,* asked:
"Who are you?"

She answered:
"I am Inanna, Queen of Heaven,
On my way to the East."

Neti said:
"If you are truly Inanna, Queen of Heaven,
On your way to the East,

Why has your heart led you on the road
From which no traveler returns?"

Inanna answered:
"Because . . . of my older sister, Ereshkigal,
Her husband, Gugalanna, the Bull of Heaven, has died.
I have come to witness the funeral rites.
Let the beer of his funeral rites be poured into the cup.
Let it be done."

Neti spoke:
"Stay here, Inanna, I will speak to my queen.
I will give her your message."

Neti, the chief gatekeeper of the *kur,*
Entered the palace of Ereshkigal, the Queen of the Underworld,
and said:
"My queen, a maid
As tall as heaven,
As wide as the earth,
As strong as the foundations of the city wall,
Waits outside the palace gates.

She has gathered together the seven *me.*
She has taken them into her hands.
With the *me* in her possession, she has prepared herself:

On her head she wears the *shugurra,* the crown of the steppe.
Across her forehead her dark locks of hair are carefully
arranged.
Around her neck she wears the small lapis beads.
At her breast she wears the double strand of beads.
Her body is wrapped with the royal robe.
Her eyes are daubed with the ointment called, 'Let him come,
let him come.'
Around her chest she wears the breastplate called, 'Come, man,
come!'
On her wrist she wears the gold ring.
In her hand she carries the lapis measuring rod and line."

When Ereshkigal heard this,
She slapped her thigh and bit her lip.
She took the matter into her heart and dwelt on it.
Then she spoke:
"Come, Neti, my chief gatekeeper of the *kur.*
Heed my words:

Bolt the seven gates of the underworld.
Then, one by one, open each gate a crack.
Let Inanna enter.
As she enters, remove her royal garments.
Let the holy priestess of heaven enter bowed low."

Neti heeded the words of his queen.
He bolted the seven gates of the underworld.
Then he opened the outer gate.
He said to the maid:
"Come, Inanna, enter."

When she entered the first gate,
From her head, the *shugurra,* the crown of the steppe, was removed.

Inanna asked:
"What is this?"

She was told:
"Quiet, Inanna, the ways of the underworld are perfect.
They may not be questioned."

When she entered the second gate,
From her neck the small lapis beads were removed.

Inanna asked:
"What is this?"

She was told:
"Quiet, Inanna, the ways of the underworld are perfect.
They may not be questioned."

When she entered the third gate,
From her breast the double strand of beads was removed.

Inanna asked:
"What is this?"

She was told:
"Quiet, Inanna, the ways of the underworld are perfect.
They may not be questioned."

When she entered the fourth gate,
From her chest the breastplate called "Come, man, come!" was removed.

Inanna asked:
"What is this?"

She was told:
"Quiet, Inanna, the ways of the underworld are perfect.
They may not be questioned."

When she entered the fifth gate,
From her wrist the gold ring was removed.

Inanna asked:
"What is this?"

She was told:
"Quiet, Inanna, the ways of the underworld are perfect.
They may not be questioned."

When she entered the sixth gate,
From her hand the lapis measuring rod and line was removed.

Inanna asked:
"What is this?"

She was told:
"Quiet, Inanna, the ways of the underworld are perfect.
They may not be questioned."

When she entered the seventh gate,
From her body the royal robe was removed.

Inanna asked:
"What is this?"

She was told:
"Quiet, Inanna, the ways of the underworld are perfect.
They may not be questioned."

Naked and bowed low, Inanna entered the throne room.
Ereshkigal rose from her throne.
Inanna started toward the throne.
The Annuna, the judges of the underworld, surrounded her.
They passed judgment against her.

Then Ereshkigal fastened on Inanna the eye of death.
She spoke against her the word of wrath.
She uttered against her the cry of guilt.

She struck her.

Inanna was turned into a corpse,
A piece of rotting meat,
And was hung from a hook on the wall.

When, after three days and three nights, Inanna had not returned,
Ninshubur set up a lament for her by the ruins.
She beat the drum for her in the assembly places.
She circled the houses of the gods.
She tore at her eyes; she tore at her mouth; she tore at her thighs.
She dressed herself in a single garment like a beggar.
Alone, she set out for Nippur and the temple of Enlil.

* * *

*[Ninshubur travels to the temples of both Enlil and Nanna, imploring them to rescue their daughter Inanna, but both refuse angrily, saying:*

*"My daughter craved the Great Above.*
*Inanna craved the Great Below.*
*She who receives the* me *of the underworld does not return.*
*She who goes to the Dark City stays there."]*

Ninshubur went to Eridu and the temple of Enki.
When she entered the holy shrine,
She cried out:
"O Father Enki, do not let your daughter
Be put to death in the underworld.
Do not let your bright silver
Be covered with the dust of the underworld.
Do not let your precious lapis
Be broken into stone for the stoneworker.
Do not let your fragrant boxwood
Be cut into wood for the woodworker.
Do not let the holy priestess of heaven
Be put to death in the underworld."

Father Enki said:
"What has happened?
What has my daughter done?
Inanna! Queen of All the Lands! Holy Priestess of Heaven!
What has happened?
I am troubled. I am grieved."

From under his fingernail Father Enki brought forth dirt.

He fashioned the dirt into a *kurgarra,* a creature neither male nor female.
From under the fingernail of his other hand he brought forth dirt.
He fashioned the dirt into a *galatur,* a creature neither male nor female.
He gave the food of life to the *kurgarra.*
He gave the water of life to the *galatur.*
Enki spoke to the *kurgarra* and *galatur,* saying:
"Go to the underworld,
Enter the door like flies.
Ereshkigal, the Queen of the Underworld, is moaning
With the cries of a woman about to give birth.
No linen is spread over her body.
Her breasts are uncovered.
Her hair swirls about her head like leeks.
When she cries, 'Oh! Oh! My inside!'
Cry also, 'Oh! Oh! Your inside!'
When she cries, 'Oh! Oh! My outside!'
Cry also, 'Oh! Oh! Your outside!'
The queen will be pleased.
She will offer you a gift.
Ask her only for the corpse that hangs from the hook on the wall.
One of you will sprinkle the food of life on it.
The other will sprinkle the water of life.
Inanna will arise."

The *kurgarra* and the *galatur* heeded Enki's words.
They set out for the underworld.
Like flies, they slipped through the cracks of the gates.
They entered the throne room of the Queen of the Underworld.
No linen was spread over her body.
Her breasts were uncovered.
Her hair swirled around her head like leeks.

Ereshkigal was moaning:
"Oh! Oh! My inside!"

They moaned:
"Oh! Oh! Your inside!"

She moaned:
"Ohhhh! Oh! My outside!"

They moaned:
"Ohhhh! Oh! Your outside!"

She groaned:
"Oh! Oh! My belly!"

They groaned:
"Oh! Oh! Your belly!"

She groaned:
"Oh! Ohhhh! My back!!"

They groaned:
"Oh! Ohhhh! Your back!!"

She sighed:
"Ah! Ah! My heart!"

They sighed:
"Ah! Ah! Your heart!"

She sighed:
"Ah! Ahhhh! My liver!"

They sighed:
"Ah! Ahhhh! Your liver!"

Ereshkigal stopped.
She looked at them.
She asked:
"Who are you,
Moaning—groaning—sighing with me?
If you are gods, I will bless you.
If you are mortals, I will give you a gift.
I will give you the water-gift, the river in its fullness."

The *kurgarra* and *galatur* answered:
"We do not wish it."

Ereshkigal said:
"I will give you the grain-gift, the fields in harvest."

The *kurgarra* and *galatur* said:
"We do not wish it."

Ereshkigal said:
"Speak then! What do you wish?"

They answered:

"We wish only the corpse that hangs from the hook on the wall."

Ereshkigal said:
"The corpse belongs to Inanna."

They said:
"Whether it belongs to our queen,
Whether it belongs to our king,
That is what we wish."

The corpse was given to them.

The *kurgarra* sprinkled the food of life on the corpse.
The *galatur* sprinkled the water of life on the corpse.
Inanna arose. . . .

Inanna was about to ascend from the underworld
When the Annuna, the judges of the underworld, seized her.
They said:
"No one ascends from the underworld unmarked.
If Inanna wishes to return from the underworld,
She must provide someone in her place."

As Inanna ascended from the underworld,
The *galla,* the demons of the underworld, clung to her side.
The *galla* were demons who know no food, who know no drink,
Who eat no offerings, who drink no libations,
Who accept no gifts.
They enjoy no lovemaking.
They have no sweet children to kiss.
They tear the wife from the husband's arms,
They tear the child from the father's knees,
They steal the bride from her marriage home.

The demons clung to Inanna.
The small *galla* who accompanied Inanna
Were like reeds the size of low picket fences.
The large *galla* who accompanied Inanna
Were like reeds the size of high picket fences.

The one who walked in front of Inanna was not a minister,
Yet he carried a sceptre.
The one who walked behind her was not a warrior,
Yet he carried a mace.
Ninshubur, dressed in a soiled sackcloth,

Waited outside the palace gates.
When she saw Inanna
Surrounded by the *galla,*
She threw herself in the dust at Inanna's feet.

The *galla* said:
"Walk on, Inanna,
We will take Ninshubur in your place."

Inanna cried:
"No! Ninshubur is my constant support.
She is my *sukkal* who gives me wise advice.
She is my warrior who fights by my side.
She did not forget my words.

She set up a lament for me by the ruins.
She beat the drum for me at the assembly places.
She circled the houses of the gods.
She tore at her eyes, at her mouth, at her thighs.
She dressed herself in a single garment like a beggar.

Alone, she set out for Nippur and the temple of Enlil.
She went to Ur and the temple of Nanna.
She went to Eridu and the temple of Enki.
Because of her, my life was saved.
I will never give Ninshubur to you."

The *galla* said:
"Walk on, Inanna,
We will accompany you to Umma."
In Umma, at the holy shrine,
Shara, the son of Inanna, was dressed in a soiled sackcloth.
When he saw Inanna
Surrounded by the *galla,*
He threw himself in the dust at her feet.

The *galla* said:
"Walk on to your city, Inanna,
We will take Shara in your place."

Inanna cried:
"No! Not Shara!
He is my son who sings hymns to me.
He is my son who cuts my nails and smooths my hair.
I will never give Shara to you."

The *galla* said:
"Walk on, Inanna,
We will accompany you to Badtibira."

In Badtibira, at the holy shrine,
Lulal, the son of Inanna, was dressed in a soiled sackcloth.
When he saw Inanna
Surrounded by the *galla*,
He threw himself in the dust at her feet.

The *galla* said:
"Walk on to your city, Inanna,
We will take Lulal in your place."

Inanna cried:
"Not Lulal! He is my son.
He is a leader among men.
He is my right arm. He is my left arm.
I will never give Lulal to you."

The *galla* said:
"Walk on to your city, Inanna.
We will go with you to the big apple tree in Uruk."

In Uruk, by the big apple tree,
Dumuzi, the husband of Inanna, was dressed in his shining *me*-garments.
He sat on his magnificent throne; (he did not move).

The *galla* seized him by his thighs.
They poured milk out of his seven churns.
They broke the reed pipe which the shepherd was playing.

Inanna fastened on Dumuzi the eye of death.
She spoke against him the word of wrath.
She uttered against him the cry of guilt:
*"Take him! Take Dumuzi away!"*

The *galla*, who know no food, who know no drink,
Who eat no offerings, who drink no libations,
Who accept no gifts, seized Dumuzi.
They made him stand up; they made him sit down.
They beat the husband of Inanna.
They gashed him with axes.

Dumuzi let out a wail.
He raised his hands to heaven to Utu, the God of Justice, and beseeched him:
"O Utu, you are my brother-in-law,
I am the husband of your sister.
I brought cream to your mother's house,
I brought milk to Ningal's house.
I am the one who carried food to the holy shrine.
I am the one who brought wedding gifts to Uruk.
I am the one who danced on the holy knees, the knees of Inanna.

Utu, you who are a just god, a merciful god,
Change my hands into the hands of a snake.
Change my feet into the feet of a snake.
Let me escape from my demons;
Do not let them hold me."

The merciful Utu accepted Dumuzi's tears.
He changed the hands of Dumuzi into snake hands.
He changed the feet of Dumuzi into snake feet.
Dumuzi escaped from his demons.
They could not hold him. . . .

*[Other tablets record a prophetic dream of Dumuzi which anticipates his capture, and a story of his sister Geshtinanna's attempt to save him when the* galla *track him down and bear him away to the underworld.]*

## The Return

A lament was raised in the city:
"My Lady weeps bitterly for her young husband.
Inanna weeps bitterly for her young husband.
Woe for her husband! Woe for her young love!
Woe for her house! Woe for her city!

Dumuzi was taken captive in Uruk.
He will no longer bathe in Eridu.
He will no longer soap himself at the holy shrine.
He will no longer treat the mother of Inanna as his mother.
He will no longer perform his sweet task
Among the maidens of the city.

He will no longer compete with the young men of the city.
He will no longer raise his sword higher than the *kurgarra* priests.
Great is the grief of those who mourn for Dumuzi."

Inanna wept for Dumuzi:
"Gone is my husband, my sweet husband.
Gone is my love, my sweet love.
My beloved has been taken from the city.
O, you flies of the steppe,
My beloved bridegroom has been taken from me
Before I could wrap him with a proper shroud.

The wild bull lives no more.
The shepherd, the wild bull lives no more.
Dumuzi, the wild bull, lives no more.

I ask the hills and valleys:
'Where is my husband?'
I say to them:
'I can no longer bring him food.
I can no longer serve him drink.'

The jackal lies down in his bed.
The raven dwells in his sheepfold.
You ask me about his reed pipe?
The wind must play it for him.
You ask me about his sweet songs?
The wind must sing them for him."

Sirtur, the mother of Dumuzi, wept for her son:
"My heart plays the reed pipe of mourning.
Once my boy wandered so freely on the steppe,
Now he is captive.
Once Dumuzi wandered so freely on the steppe,
Now he is bound.

The ewe gives up her lamb.
The goat gives up her kid.
My heart plays the reed pipe of mourning.

O treacherous steppe!
In the place where he once said
'My mother will ask for me,'
Now he cannot move his hands.
He cannot move his feet.

My heart plays the reed pipe of mourning.
I would go to him,
I would see my child."

The mother walked to the desolate place.
Sirtur walked to where Dumuzi lay.
She looked at the slain wild bull.
She looked into his face. She said:
    "My child, the face is yours.
    The spirit has fled."

There is mourning in the house.
There is grief in the inner chambers.

The sister wandered about the city, weeping for her brother.
Geshtinanna wandered about the city, weeping for Dumuzi:
    "O my brother! Who is your sister?
    I am your sister.
    O Dumuzi! Who is your mother?
    I am your mother.

    The day that dawns for you will also dawn for me.
    The day that you will see I will also see.

    I would find my brother! I would comfort him!
    I would share his fate!"

When she saw the sister's grief,
When Inanna saw the grief of Geshtinanna,
She spoke to her gently:
    "Your brother's house is no more.
    Dumuzi has been carried away by the *galla.*
    I would take you to him,
    But I do not know the place."

Then a fly appeared.
The holy fly circled the air above Inanna's head and spoke:
    "If I tell you where Dumuzi is,
    What will you give me?"

Inanna said:
    "If you tell me,
    I will let you frequent the beer-houses and taverns.
    I will let you dwell among the talk of the wise ones.
    I will let you dwell among the songs of the minstrels."

The fly spoke:
    "Lift your eyes to the edges of the steppe,
    Lift your eyes to Arali.

There you will find Geshtinanna's brother,
There you will find the shepherd Dumuzi."

Inanna and Geshtinanna went to the edges of the steppe.
They found Dumuzi weeping.
Inanna took Dumuzi by the hand and said:
"You will go to the underworld
Half the year.
Your sister, since she has asked,
Will go the other half.
On the day you are called,
That day you will be taken.
On the day Geshtinanna is called,
That day you will be set free."

Inanna placed Dumuzi in the hands of the eternal.

*Holy Ereshkigal! Great is your renown!*
*Holy Ereshkigal! I sing your praises!*

Take off your holy crown from your head!
Take off your *me*-garment from your body!
Let your royal sceptre fall to the ground!
Take off your holy sandals from your feet!
Naked, you go with us!"

The *galla* seized Dumuzi.
They surrounded him.
They bound his hands. They bound his neck.

The churn was silent. No milk was poured.
The cup was shattered. Dumuzi was no more.
The sheepfold was given to the winds.

## THE EPIC OF GILGAMESH (1800–1600 BCE)

*Compiled by N. K. Sandars*

Gilgamesh was a historical Sumerian king of Uruk (c. 2700 BCE). A number of mythic tales gathered around his name over the centuries following his death. Stories about Gilgamesh were so popular that they were revised and passed down for more than two thousand years, from the Sumerians through the Semitic cultures of the Mesopotamian region and into the Indo-European language of the Hittite kingdom of Anatolia (modern Turkey). The Gilgamesh story cycle was as widespread in its day as story cycles about the Trojan War and the Court of King Arthur were in later ages.

Versions of *The Epic of Gilgamesh* have been found in Syrian, Canaanite, and Babylonian texts, presenting many variations on its themes. These were gradually combined into a single epic narrative in the Akkadian language of Babylon during the first millennium BCE. The epic was then lost and forgotten under desert sands for thousands of years until its clay tablets were rediscovered by British archeologists in the nineteenth century.

The Babylonian Gilgamesh epic combines earlier, sometimes unrelated, materials into a single narrative that emphasizes the relationship of Gilgamesh and his friend Enkidu. Enkidu is carefully presented as a primitive double or mirror for the hero king. The bond between the two friends comes to replace both Gilgamesh's relation to Ishtar (the Babylonian name for Inanna) and Enkidu's intimacy with the wilderness. The two men turn their energies outward toward adventure and conquest, away from the community and its reproductive cycles in harmony with the landscape and the feminine. In the process they triumph over the monstrous Humbaba, guardian of the Great Cedar Forest that was probably located in the Zagros Mountains. Although their first reaction to the forest and its guardian is one of awe, the young heroes kill Humbaba and cut down the sacred trees. The cost of this heroic achievement is tragedy and irreparable loss, for Enkidu is also a double of Humbaba, and his vital powers are related to wild creatures and the landscape. Enkidu dies, and Gilgamesh's grief for him sets up a theme that will be echoed in Homer's *Iliad,* in Achilles's mourning for his dear friend Patroclus. Arrogant defiance of the goddess and the sacred beasts and land also brings inescapable doom for Gilgamesh that no cyclical renewal can reverse. The epic records an alienation from the harmony of the human and natural worlds depicted in the Inanna poems. It is also one of the most powerful meditations on the problem of death in world literature. Gilgamesh's quest for immortality finally ends with the realization, a realization we all must face, that death awaits us all.

The following selection is a composite prose version based on the Standard Babylonian Text from the library of seventh-century BCE Assyrian King Assurbanipal, supplemented by materials from much earlier (c. 2000 BCE) Sumerian versions of the epic.

## Prologue

### Gilgamesh King in Uruk

I will proclaim to the world the deeds of Gilgamesh. This was the man to whom all things were known; this was the king who knew the countries of the world. He was wise, he saw mysteries and knew secret things, he brought us a tale of the days before the flood. He went on a long journey, was weary, worn-out with labour, returning he rested, he engraved on a stone the whole story.

When the gods created Gilgamesh they gave him a perfect body. Shamash the glorious sun endowed him with beauty, Adad the god of the storm endowed him with courage, the great gods made his beauty perfect, surpassing all others, terrifying like a great wild bull. Two thirds they made him god and one third man.

In Uruk he built walls, a great rampart, and the temple of blessed Eanna for the god of the firmament Anu, and for Ishtar the goddess of love. Look at it still today: the outer wall where the cornice runs, it shines with the brilliance of copper; and the inner wall, it has no equal. Touch the threshold, it is ancient. Approach Eanna the dwelling of Ishtar, our lady of love and war, the like of which no latter-day king, no man alive can equal. Climb upon the wall of Uruk; walk along it, I say; regard the foundation terrace and examine the masonry: is it not burnt brick and good? The seven sages laid the foundations.

## I

### The Coming of Enkidu

Gilgamesh went abroad in the world, but he met with none who could withstand his arms till he came to Uruk. But the men of Uruk muttered in their houses, 'Gilgamesh sounds the tocsin for his amusement, his arrogance has no bounds by day or night. No son is left with his father, for Gilgamesh takes them all, even the children; yet the king should be a shepherd to his people. His lust leaves no virgin to her lover, neither the warrior's daughter nor the wife of the noble; yet this is the shepherd of the city, wise, comely, and resolute.'

The gods heard their lament, the gods of heaven cried to the Lord of Uruk, to Anu the god of Uruk: 'A goddess made him, strong as a savage bull, none can withstand his arms. No son is left with his father, for Gilgamesh takes them all; and is this the king, the shepherd of his people? His lust leaves no virgin to her lover, neither the warrior's daughter nor the wife of the noble.' When Anu had heard their lamentation the gods cried to Aruru, the goddess of creation, 'You made him, O Aruru, now create his equal; let it be as like him as his own reflection, his second self, stormy heart for stormy heart. Let them contend together and leave Uruk in quiet.'

So the goddess conceived an image in her mind, and it was of the stuff of Anu of the firmament. She dipped her hands in water and pinched off clay, she let it fall in the wilderness, and noble Enkidu was created. There was virtue in him of the god of war, of Ninurta himself. His body was rough, he had long hair like a woman's; it waved like the hair of Nisaba, the goddess of corn. His body was covered with matted hair like Samuqan's, the god of cattle. He was innocent of mankind; he knew nothing of the cultivated land.

Enkidu ate grass in the hills with the gazelle and lurked with wild beasts at the water-holes; he had joy of the water with the herds of wild game. But there was a trapper who met him one day face to face at the drinking-hole, for the wild game had entered his territory. On three days he met him face to face, and the trapper was frozen with fear. He went back to his house with the game that he had caught, and he was dumb, benumbed with terror. His face was altered like that of one who has made a long journey. With awe in his heart he spoke to his father: 'Father, there is a man, unlike any other, who comes down from the hills. He is the strongest in the world, he is like an immortal from heaven. He ranges over the hills with wild beasts and eats grass; he ranges through your land and comes down to the wells. I am afraid and dare not go near him. He fills in the pits which I dig and tears up my traps set for the game; he helps the beasts to escape and now they slip through my fingers.'

His father opened his mouth and said to the trapper, 'My son, in Uruk lives

Gilgamesh; no one has ever prevailed against him, he is strong as a star from heaven. Go to Uruk, find Gilgamesh, extol the strength of this wild man. Ask him to give you a harlot, a wanton from the temple of love; return with her, and let her woman's power overpower this man. When next he comes down to drink at the wells she will be there, stripped naked; and when he sees her beckoning he will embrace her, and then the wild beasts will reject him.'

So the trapper set out on his journey to Uruk and addressed himself to Gilgamesh saying, 'A man unlike any other is roaming now in the pastures; he is as strong as a star from heaven and I am afraid to approach him. He helps the wild game to escape; he fills in my pits and pulls up my traps.' Gilgamesh said, 'Trapper, go back, take with you a harlot, a child of pleasure. At the drinking-hole she will strip, and when he sees her beckoning he will embrace her and the game of the wilderness will surely reject him.'

Now the trapper returned, taking the harlot with him. After a three days' journey they came to the drinking-hole, and there they sat down; the harlot and the trapper sat facing one another and waited for the game to come. For the first day and for the second day the two sat waiting, but on the third day the herds came; they came down to drink and Enkidu was with them. The small wild creatures of the plains were glad of the water, and Enkidu with them, who ate grass with the gazelle and was born in the hills; and she saw him, the savage man, come from far-off in the hills. The trapper spoke to her: 'There he is. Now, woman, make your breasts bare, have no shame, do not delay but welcome his love. Let him see you naked, let him possess your body. When he comes near uncover yourself and lie with him; teach him, the savage man, your woman's art, for when he murmurs love to you the wild beasts that shared his life in the hills will reject him.'

She was not ashamed to take him, she made herself naked and welcomed his eagerness; as he lay on her murmuring love she taught him the woman's art. For six days and seven nights they lay together, for Enkidu had forgotten his home in the hills; but when he was satisfied he went back to the wild beasts. Then, when the gazelle saw him, they bolted away; when the wild creatures saw him they fled. Enkidu would have followed, but his body was bound as though with a cord, his knees gave way when he started to run, his swiftness was gone. And now the wild creatures had all fled away; Enkidu was grown weak, for wisdom was in him, and the thoughts of a man were in his heart. So he returned and sat down at the woman's feet, and listened intently to what she said. 'You are wise, Enkidu, and now you have become like a god. Why do you want to run wild with the beasts in the hills? Come with me. I will take you to strong-walled Uruk, to the blessed temple of Ishtar and of Anu, of love and of heaven: there Gilgamesh lives, who is very strong, and like a wild bull he lords it over men.'

When she had spoken Enkidu was pleased; he longed for a comrade, for one who would understand his heart. 'Come, woman, and take me to that holy temple, to the house of Anu and of Ishtar, and to the place where Gilgamesh lords it over the people. I will challenge him boldly, I will cry out aloud in Uruk, "I am the strongest here, I have come to change the old order, I am he who was born in the hills, I am he who is strongest of all."'

She said, 'Let us go, and let him see your face. I know very well where Gilgamesh is in great Uruk. O Enkidu, there all the people are dressed in their gorgeous robes, every day is holiday, the young men and the girls are wonderful to see. How sweet they smell! All the great ones are roused from their beds. O Enkidu, you who love life, I will show you Gilgamesh, a man of many moods; you shall look at him well in his radiant manhood. His body is perfect in strength and maturity; he never rests by night or day. He is stronger than you, so leave your boasting. Shamash the glorious sun has given favours to Gilgamesh, and Anu of the heavens, and Enlil, and Ea the wise has given him deep understanding. I tell you, even before you have left the wilderness, Gilgamesh will know in his dreams that you are coming.'

Now Gilgamesh got up to tell his dream to his mother, Ninsun, one of the wise gods. 'Mother, last night I had a dream. I was full of joy, the young heroes were round me and I walked through the night under the stars of the firmament, and one, a meteor of the stuff of Anu, fell down from heaven. I tried to lift it but it proved too heavy. All the people of Uruk came round to see it, the common people jostled and the nobles thronged to kiss its feet; and to me its attraction was like the love of woman. They helped me, I braced my forehead and I raised it with thongs and brought it to you, and you yourself pronounced it my brother.'

Then Ninsun, who is well-beloved and wise, said to Gilgamesh, 'This star of heaven which descended like a meteor from the sky; which you tried to lift, but found too heavy, when you tried to move it it would not budge, and so you brought it to my feet; I made it for you, a goad and spur, and you were drawn as though to a woman. This is the strong comrade, the one who brings help to his friend in his need. He is the strongest of wild creatures, the stuff of Anu; born in the grass-lands and the wild hills reared him; when you see him you will be glad; you will love him as a woman and he will never forsake you. This is the meaning of the dream.'

Gilgamesh said, 'Mother, I dreamed a second dream. In the streets of strong-walled Uruk there lay an axe; the shape of it was strange and the people thronged round. I saw it and was glad. I bent down, deeply drawn towards it; I loved it like a woman and wore it at my side.' Ninsun answered, 'That axe, which you saw, which drew you so powerfully like love of a woman, that is the comrade whom I give you, and he will come in his strength like one of the host of heaven. He is the brave companion who rescues his friend in necessity.' Gilgamesh said to his mother, 'A friend, a counsellor has come to me from Enlil, and now I shall befriend and counsel him.' So Gilgamesh told his dreams; and the harlot retold them to Enkidu.

And now she said to Enkidu, 'When I look at you you have become like a god. Why do you yearn to run wild again with the beasts in the hills? Get up from the ground, the bed of a shepherd.' He listened to her words with care. It was good advice that she gave. She divided her clothing in two and with the one half she clothed him and with the other herself; and holding his hand she led him like a child to the sheepfolds, into the shepherds' tents. There all the shepherds crowded round to see him, they put down bread in front of him, but Enkidu could only suck the milk of wild animals. He fumbled and gaped, at a loss what to do or how he should eat the bread and drink the strong wine. Then the woman said, 'Enkidu, eat bread, it is the staff of life; drink the wine, it is the custom of the land.' So he ate till he was full and drank strong wine, seven goblets. He became merry, his heart exulted and his face shone. He rubbed down the matted hair of his body and anointed himself with oil. Enkidu had become a man; but when he had put on man's clothing he appeared like a bridegroom. He took arms to hunt the lion so that the shepherds could rest at night. He caught wolves and lions and the herdsmen lay down in peace; for Enkidu was their watchman, that strong man who had no rival.

He was merry living with the shepherds, till one day lifting his eyes he saw a man approaching. He said to the harlot, 'Woman, fetch that man here. Why has he come? I wish to know his name.' She went and called the man saying, 'Sir, where are you going on this weary journey?' The man answered, saying to Enkidu, 'Gilgamesh has gone into the marriage-house and shut out the people. He does strange things in Uruk, the city of great streets. At the roll of the drum work begins for the men, and work for the women. Gilgamesh the king is about to celebrate marriage with the Queen of Love, and he still demands to be first with the bride, the king to be first and the husband to follow, for that was ordained by the gods from his birth, from the time the umbilical cord was cut. But now the drums roll for the choice of the bride and the city groans.' At these words Enkidu turned white in the face. 'I will go to the place where Gilgamesh lords it over the people, I will challenge him boldly, and I will cry aloud in Uruk, "I have come to change the old order, for I am the strongest here."'

Now Enkidu strode in front and the woman followed behind. He entered Uruk, that great market, and all the folk thronged round him where he stood in the street in strong-walled Uruk. The people jostled; speaking of him they said, 'He is the spit of Gilgamesh.' 'He is shorter.' 'He is bigger of bone.' 'This is the one who was reared on the milk of wild beasts. His is the greatest strength.' The men rejoiced: 'Now Gilgamesh has met his match. This great one, this hero whose beauty is like a god, he is a match even for Gilgamesh.'

In Uruk the bridal bed was made, fit for the goddess of love. The bride waited for the bridegroom, but in the night Gilgamesh got up and came to the house. Then Enkidu stepped out, he stood in the street and blocked the way. Mighty Gilgamesh came on and Enkidu met him at the gate. He put out his foot and prevented Gilgamesh from entering the house, so they grappled, holding each other like bulls. They broke the doorposts and the walls shook, they snorted like bulls locked together. They shattered the doorposts and the walls shook. Gilgamesh bent his knee with his foot planted on the ground and with a turn Enkidu was thrown. Then immediately his fury died. When Enkidu was thrown he said to Gilgamesh, 'There is not another like you in the world. Ninsun, who is as strong as a wild ox in the byre, she was the mother who bore you, and now you are raised above all men, and Enlil has given you the kingship, for your strength surpasses the strength of men.' So Enkidu and Gilgamesh embraced and their friendship was sealed.

## 2

### The Forest Journey

Enlil of the mountain, the father of the gods, had decreed the destiny of Gilgamesh. So Gilgamesh dreamed and Enkidu said, 'The meaning of the dream is this. The father of the gods has given you kingship, such is your destiny, everlasting life is not your destiny. Because of this do not be sad at heart, do not be grieved or oppressed. He has given you power to bind and to loose, to be the darkness and the light of mankind. He has given you unexampled supremacy over the people, victory in battle from which no fugitive returns, in forays and assaults from which there is no going back. But do not abuse this power, deal justly with your servants in the palace, deal justly before Shamash.'

The eyes of Enkidu were full of tears and his heart was sick. He sighed bitterly and Gilgamesh met his eye and said, 'My friend, why do you sigh so bitterly?' But Enkidu opened his mouth and said, 'I am weak, my arms have lost their strength, the cry of sorrow sticks in my throat, I am oppressed by idleness.' It was then that the lord Gilgamesh turned his thoughts to the Country of the Living; on the Land of Cedars the lord Gilgamesh reflected. He said to his servant Enkidu, 'I have not established my name stamped on bricks as my destiny decreed; therefore I will go to the country where the cedar is felled. I will set up my name in the place where the names of famous men are written, and where no man's name is written yet I will raise a monument to the gods. Because of the evil that is in the land, we will go to the forest and destroy the evil; for in the forest lives Humbaba whose name is "Hugeness", a ferocious giant.' But Enkidu sighed bitterly and said, 'When I went with the wild beasts ranging through the wilderness I discovered the forest; its length is ten thousand leagues in every direction. Enlil has appointed Humbaba to guard it and armed him in sevenfold terrors, terrible to all flesh is Humbaba. When he roars it is like the torrent of the storm, his breath is like fire, and his jaws are death itself. He guards the cedars so well that when the wild heifer stirs in the forest, though she is sixty leagues distant, he hears her. What man would willingly walk into that country and explore its depths? I tell you, weakness overpowers whoever goes near it: it is not an equal struggle when one fights with Humbaba; he is a great warrior, a battering-ram. Gilgamesh, the watchman of the forest never sleeps.'

Gilgamesh replied: 'Where is the man who can clamber to heaven? Only the gods live for ever with glorious Shamash, but as for us men, our days are numbered, our occupations are a breath of wind. How is this, already you are afraid! I will go first although I am your lord, and you may safely call out, "Forward, there is nothing to fear!" Then if I fall I leave behind me a name that endures; men will say of me, "Gilgamesh has fallen in fight with ferocious Humbaba." Long after the child has been born in my house, they will say it, and remember.' Enkidu spoke again to Gilgamesh, 'O my lord, if you will enter that country, go first to the hero Shamash, tell the Sun God, for the land is his. The country where the cedar is cut belongs to Shamash.'

Gilgamesh took up a kid, white without spot, and a brown one with it;

he held them against his breast, and he carried them into the presence of the sun. He took in his hand his silver sceptre and he said to glorious Shamash, 'I am going to that country, O Shamash, I am going; my hands supplicate, so let it be well with my soul and bring me back to the quay of Uruk. Grant, I beseech, your protection, and let the omen be good.' Glorious Shamash answered, 'Gilgamesh, you are strong, but what is the Country of the Living to you?'

'O Shamash, hear me, hear me, Shamash, let my voice be heard. Here in the city man dies oppressed at heart, man perishes with despair in his heart. I have looked over the wall and I see the bodies floating on the river, and that will be my lot also. Indeed I know it is so, for whoever is tallest among men cannot reach the heavens, and the greatest cannot encompass the earth. Therefore I would enter that country: because I have not established my name stamped on brick as my destiny decreed, I will go to the country where the cedar is cut. I will set up my name where the names of famous men are written; and where no man's name is written I will raise a monument to the gods.' The tears ran down his face and he said, 'Alas, it is a long journey that I must take to the Land of Humbaba. If this enterprise is not to be accomplished, why did you move me, Shamash, with the restless desire to perform it? How can I succeed if you will not succour me? If I die in that country I will die without rancour, but if I return I will make a glorious offering of gifts and of praise to Shamash.'

So Shamash accepted the sacrifice of his tears; like the compassionate man he showed him mercy. He appointed strong allies for Gilgamesh, sons of one mother, and stationed them in the mountain caves. The great winds he appointed: the north wind, the whirlwind, the storm and the icy wind, the tempest and the scorching wind. Like vipers, like dragons, like a scorching fire, like a serpent that freezes the heart, a destroying flood and the lightning's fork, such were they and Gilgamesh rejoiced.

He went to the forge and said, 'I will give orders to the armourers; they shall cast us our weapons while we watch them.' So they gave orders to the armourers and the craftsmen sat down in conference. They went into the groves of the plain and cut willow and box-wood; they cast for them axes of nine score pounds, and great swords they cast with blades of six score pounds each one, with pommels and hilts of thirty pounds. They cast for Gilgamesh the axe 'Might of Heroes' and the bow of Anshan; and Gilgamesh was armed and Enkidu; and the weight of the arms they carried was thirty score pounds.

The people collected and the counsellors in the streets and in the market-place of Uruk; they came through the gate of seven bolts and Gilgamesh spoke to them in the market-place: 'I, Gilgamesh, go to see that creature of whom such things are spoken, the rumour of whose name fills the world. I will conquer him in his cedar wood and show the strength of the sons of Uruk, all the world shall know of it. I am committed to this enterprise: to climb the mountain, to cut down the cedar, and leave behind me an enduring name.' The counsellors of Uruk, the great market, answered him, 'Gilgamesh, you are young, your courage carries you too far, you cannot know what this enterprise means which you plan. We have heard that Humbaba is not like men who die, his weapons are such that none can stand against them; the forest stretches for ten thousand leagues in every direction; who would willingly go down to explore its depths? As for Humbaba, when he roars it is like the torrent of the storm, his breath is like fire and his jaws are death itself. Why do you crave to do this thing, Gilgamesh? It is no equal struggle when one fights with Humbaba, that battering-ram.'

When he heard these words of the counsellors Gilgamesh looked at his friend and laughed, 'How shall I answer them; shall I say I am afraid of Humbaba, I will sit at home all the rest of my days?' Then Gilgamesh opened his mouth again and said to Enkidu, 'My friend, let us go to the Great Palace, to Egalmah, and stand before Ninsun the queen. Ninsun is wise with deep knowledge, she will give us counsel for the road we must go.' They took each other by the hand as they went to Egalmah, and they went to Ninsun the great queen. Gilgamesh approached, he entered the palace and spoke to Ninsun. 'Ninsun, will you listen to me; I have a long journey to go, to the Land of Humbaba, I must travel an unknown road and fight a strange battle. From the day I go until I return, till I reach the cedar forest and destroy the evil which Shamash abhors, pray for me to Shamash.'

Ninsun went into her room, she put on a dress becoming to her body, she put on jewels to make her breast beautiful, she placed a tiara on her head and her skirts swept the ground. Then she went up to the altar of the Sun, standing upon the roof of the palace; she burnt incense and lifted her arms to Shamash as the smoke ascended: 'O Shamash, why did you give this restless heart to Gilgamesh, my son; why did you give it? You have moved him and now he sets out on a long journey to the Land of Humbaba, to travel an unknown road and fight a strange battle. Therefore from the day that he goes till the day he returns, until he reaches the cedar forest, until he kills Humbaba and destroys the evil thing which you, Shamash, abhor, do not forget him; but let the dawn, Aya, your dear bride, remind you always, and when day is done give him to the watchman of the night to keep him from harm.' Then Ninsun the mother of Gilgamesh extinguished the incense, and she called to Enkidu with this exhortation: 'Strong Enkidu, you are not the child of my body, but I will receive you as my adopted son; you are my other child like the foundlings they bring to the temple. Serve Gilgamesh as a foundling serves the temple and the priestess who reared him. In the presence of my women, my votaries and hierophants, I declare it.' Then she placed the amulet for a pledge round his neck, and she said to him, 'I entrust my son to you; bring him back to me safely.'

And now they brought to them the weapons, they put in their hands the great swords in their golden scabbards, and the bow and the quiver. Gilgamesh took the axe, he slung the quiver from his shoulder, and the bow of Anshan, and buckled the sword to his belt; and so they were armed and ready for the journey. Now all the people came and pressed on them and said, 'When will you return to the city?' The counsellors blessed Gilgamesh and warned him, 'Do not trust too much in your own strength, be watchful, restrain your blows at first. The one who goes in front protects his companion; the good guide who knows the way guards his friend. Let Enkidu lead the way, he knows the road to the forest, he has seen Humbaba and is experienced in battles; let him press first into the passes, let him be watchful and look to himself. Let Enkidu protect his friend, and guard his companion, and bring him safe through the pitfalls of the road. We, the counsellors of Uruk entrust our king to you, O Enkidu; bring him back safely to us.' Again to Gilgamesh they said, 'May Shamash give you your heart's desire, may he let you see with your eyes the thing accomplished which your lips have spoken; may he open a path for you where it is blocked, and a road for your feet to tread. May he open the mountains for your crossing, and may the nighttime bring you the blessings of night, and Lugulbanda, your guardian god, stand beside you for victory. May you have victory in the battle as though you fought with a child. Wash your feet in the river of Humbaba to which you are journeying; in the evening dig a well, and let there always be pure water in your water-skin. Offer cold water to Shamash and do not forget Lugulbanda.'

Then Enkidu opened his mouth and said, 'Forward, there is nothing to fear. Follow me, for I know the place where Humbaba lives and the paths where he walks. Let the counsellors go back. Here is no cause for fear.' When the counsellors heard this they sped the hero on his way. 'Go, Gilgamesh, may your guardian god protect you on the road and bring you safely back to the quay of Uruk.'

After twenty leagues they broke their fast; after another thirty leagues they stopped for the night. Fifty leagues they walked in one day; in three days they had walked as much as a journey of a month and two weeks. They crossed seven mountains before they came to the gate of the forest. Then Enkidu called out to Gilgamesh, 'Do not go down into the forest; when I opened the gate my hand lost its strength.' Gilgamesh answered him, 'Dear friend, do not speak like a coward. Have we got the better of so many dangers and travelled so far, to turn back at last? You, who are tried in wars and battles, hold close to me now and you will feel no fear of death; keep beside me and your weakness will pass, the trembling will leave your hand. Would my friend rather stay behind? No, we will go down together into the heart of the forest. Let your courage be roused by the battle to come; forget death and follow me, a man resolute in action, but one who is not foolhardy. When two go together each will protect himself and shield his companion, and if they fall they leave an enduring name.'

Together they went down into the forest and they came to the green mountain. There they stood still, they were struck dumb; they stood still and gazed at the forest. They saw the height of the cedar, they saw the way into the forest and the track where Humbaba was used to walk. The way was broad and the going was good. They gazed at the mountain of cedars, the dwelling-place of the gods and the throne of Ishtar. The hugeness of the cedar rose in front of the mountain, its shade was beautiful, full of comfort; mountain and glade were green with brushwood.

There Gilgamesh dug a well before the setting sun. He went up the mountain and poured out fine meal on the ground and said, 'O mountain, dwelling of the gods, bring me a favourable dream.' Then they took each other by the hand and lay down to sleep; and sleep that flows from the night lapped over them. Gilgamesh dreamed, and at midnight sleep left him, and he told his dream to his friend. 'Enkidu, what was it that woke me if you did not? My friend, I have dreamed a dream. Get up, look at the mountain precipice. The sleep that the gods sent me is broken. Ah, my friend, what a dream I have had! Terror and confusion; I seized hold of a wild bull in the wilderness. It bellowed and beat up the dust till the whole sky was dark, my arm was seized and my tongue bitten. I fell back on my knee; then someone refreshed me with water from his water-skin.'

Enkidu said, 'Dear friend, the god to whom we are travelling is no wild bull, though his form is mysterious. That wild bull which you saw is Shamash the Protector; in our moment of peril he will take our hands. The one who gave water from his water-skin, that is your own god who cares for your good name, your Lugulbanda. United with him, together we will accomplish a work the fame of which will never die.'

Gilgamesh said, 'I dreamed again. We stood in a deep gorge of the mountain, and beside it we two were like the smallest of swamp flies; and suddenly the mountain fell, it struck me and caught my feet from under me. Then came an intolerable light blazing out, and in it was one whose grace and whose beauty were greater than the beauty of this world. He pulled me out from under the mountain, he gave me water to drink and my heart was comforted, and he set my feet on the ground.'

Then Enkidu the child of the plains said, 'Let us go down from the mountain and talk this thing over together.' He said to Gilgamesh the young god, 'Your dream is good, your dream is excellent, the mountain which you saw is Humbaba. Now, surely, we will seize and kill him, and throw his body down as the mountain fell on the plain.'

The next day after twenty leagues they broke their fast, and after another thirty they stopped for the night. They dug a well before the sun had set and Gilgamesh ascended the mountain. He poured out fine meal on the ground and said, 'O mountain, dwelling of the gods, send a dream for Enkidu, make him a favourable dream.' The mountain fashioned a dream for Enkidu; it came, an ominous dream; a cold shower passed over him, it caused him to cower like the mountain barley under a storm of rain. But Gilgamesh sat with his chin on his knees till the sleep which flows over all mankind lapped over him. Then, at midnight, sleep left him; he got up and said to his friend, 'Did you call me, or why did I wake? Did you touch me, or why am I terrified? Did not some god pass by, for my limbs are numb with fear? My friend, I saw a third dream and this dream was altogether frightful. The heavens roared and the earth roared again, daylight failed and darkness fell, lightnings flashed, fire blazed out, the clouds lowered, they rained down death. Then the brightness departed, the fire went out, and all was turned to ashes fallen about us. Let us go down from the mountain and talk this over, and consider what we should do.'

When they had come down from the mountain Gilgamesh seized the axe in his hand: he felled the cedar. When Humbaba heard the noise far off he was enraged; he cried out, 'Who is this that has violated my woods and cut down my cedar?' But glorious Shamash called to them out of heaven, 'Go forward, do not be afraid.' But now

Gilgamesh was overcome by weakness, for sleep had seized him suddenly, a profound sleep held him; he lay on the ground, stretched out speechless, as though in a dream. When Enkidu touched him he did not rise, when he spoke to him he did not reply. 'O Gilgamesh, Lord of the plain of Kullab, the world grows dark, the shadows have spread over it, now is the glimmer of dusk. Shamash has departed, his bright head is quenched in the bosom of his mother Ningal. O Gilgamesh, how long will you lie like this, asleep? Never let the mother who gave you birth be forced in mourning into the city square.'

At length Gilgamesh heard him; he put on his breastplate, 'The Voice of Heroes,' of thirty shekels' weight; he put it on as though it had been a light garment that he carried, and it covered him altogether. He straddled the earth like a bull that snuffs the ground and his teeth were clenched. 'By the life of my mother Ninsun who gave me birth, and by the life of my father, divine Lugulbanda, let me live to be the wonder of my mother, as when she nursed me on her lap.' A second time he said to him, 'By the life of Ninsun my mother who gave me birth, and by the life of my father, divine Lugulbanda, until we have fought this man, if man he is, this god, if god he is, the way that I took to the Country of the Living will not turn back to the city.'

Then Enkidu, the faithful companion, pleaded, answering him, 'O my lord, you do not know this monster and that is the reason you are not afraid. I who know him, I am terrified. His teeth are dragon's fangs, his countenance is like a lion, his charge is the rushing of the flood, with his look he crushes alike the trees of the forest and reeds in the swamp. O my Lord, you may go on if you choose into this land, but I will go back to the city. I will tell the lady your mother all your glorious deeds till she shouts for joy: and then I will tell the death that followed till she weeps for bitterness.' But Gilgamesh said, 'Immolation and sacrifice are not yet for me, the boat of the dead shall not go down, nor the three-ply cloth be cut for my shrouding. Not yet will my people be desolate, nor the pyre be lit in my house and my dwelling burnt on the fire. Today, give me your aid and you shall have mine: what then can go amiss with us two? All living creatures born of the flesh shall sit at last in the boat of the West, and when it sinks, when the boat of Magilum sinks, they are gone; but we shall go forward and fix our eyes on this monster. If your heart is fearful throw away fear; if there is terror in it throw away terror. Take your axe in your hand and attack. He who leaves the fight unfinished is not at peace.'

Humbaba came out from his strong house of cedar. Then Enkidu called out, 'O Gilgamesh, remember now your boasts in Uruk. Forward, attack, son of Uruk, there is nothing to fear.' When he heard these words his courage rallied; he answered, 'Make haste, close in, if the watchman is there do not let him escape to the woods where he will vanish. He has put on the first of his seven splendours but not yet the other six, let us trap him before he is armed.' Like a raging wild bull he snuffed the ground; the watchman of the woods turned full of threatenings, he cried out. Humbaba came from his strong house of cedar. He nodded his head and shook it, menacing Gilgamesh; and on him he fastened his eye, the eye of death. Then Gilgamesh called to Shamash and his tears were flowing, 'O glorious Shamash, I have followed the road you commanded but now if you send no succour how shall I escape?' Glorious Shamash heard his prayer and he summoned the great wind, the north wind, the whirlwind, the storm and the icy wind, the tempest and the scorching wind; they came like dragons, like a scorching fire, like a serpent that freezes the heart, a destroying flood and the lightning's fork. The eight winds rose up against Humbaba, they beat against his eyes; he was gripped, unable to go forward or back. Gilgamesh shouted, 'By the life of Ninsun my mother and divine Lugulbanda my father, in the Country of the Living, in this Land I have discovered your dwelling; my weak arms and my small weapons I have brought to this Land against you, and now I will enter your house.'

So he felled the first cedar and they cut the branches and laid them at the foot of the mountain. At the first stroke Humbaba blazed out, but still they advanced. They felled seven cedars and cut and bound the branches and laid them at the foot of the mountain, and seven times Humbaba loosed his glory on them. As the seventh blaze died out they reached his lair. He slapped his thigh in scorn. He approached like a noble wild bull roped on the mountain, a warrior whose elbows are bound together. The tears started to his eyes and he was pale, 'Gilgamesh, let me speak. I have never known a mother, no, nor a father who reared me. I was born of the mountain, he reared me, and Enlil made me the keeper of this forest. Let me go free, Gilgamesh, and I will be your servant, you shall be my lord; all the trees of the forest that I tended on the mountain shall be yours. I will cut them down and build you a palace.' He took him by the hand and led him to his house, so that the heart of Gilgamesh was moved with compassion. He swore by the heavenly life, by the earthly life, by the underworld itself: 'O Enkidu, should not the snared bird return to its nest and the captive man return to his mother's arms?' Enkidu answered, 'The strongest of men will fall to fate if he has no judgement. Namtar, the evil fate that knows no distinction between men, will devour him. If the snared bird returns to its nest, if the captive man returns to his mother's arms, then you my friend will never return to the city where the mother is waiting who gave you birth. He will bar the mountain road against you, and make the pathways impassable.'

Humbaba said, 'Enkidu, what you have spoken is evil: you, a hireling, dependent for your bread! In envy and for fear of a rival you have spoken evil words.' Enkidu said, 'Do not listen, Gilgamesh: this Humbaba must die. Kill Humbaba first and his servants after.' But Gilgamesh said, 'If we touch him the blaze and the glory of light will be put out in confusion, the glory and glamour will vanish, its rays will be quenched.' Enkidu said to Gilgamesh, 'Not so, my friend. First entrap the bird, and where shall the chicks run then? Afterwards we can search out the glory and the glamour, when the chicks run distracted through the grass.'

Gilgamesh listened to the word of his companion, he took the axe in his hand, he drew the sword from his belt, and he struck Humbaba with a thrust of the sword to the neck, and Enkidu his comrade struck the second blow. At the third blow Humbaba fell. Then there followed confusion for this was the guardian of the forest whom they had felled to the ground. For as far as two leagues the cedars shivered when Enkidu felled the watcher of the forest, he at whose voice Hermon and Lebanon used to tremble. Now the mountains were moved and all the hills, for the guardian of the forest was killed. They attacked the cedars, the seven splendours of Humbaba were extinguished. So they pressed on into the forest bearing the sword of eight talents. They uncovered the sacred dwellings of the Anunnaki and while Gilgamesh felled the first of the trees of the forest Enkidu cleared their roots as far as the banks of Euphrates. They set Humbaba before the gods, before Enlil; they kissed the ground and dropped the shroud and set the head before him. When he saw the head of Humbaba, Enlil raged at them. 'Why did you do this thing? From henceforth may the fire be on your faces, may it eat the bread that you eat, may it drink where you drink.' Then Enlil took again the blaze and the seven splendours that had been Humbaba's: he gave the first to the river, and he gave to the lion, to the stone of execration, to the mountain and to the dreaded daughter of the Queen of Hell.

O Gilgamesh, king and conqueror of the dreadful blaze; wild bull who plunders the mountain, who crosses the sea, glory to him; and from the brave the greater glory is Enki's!

## 3

### Ishtar and Gilgamesh, and the Death of Enkidu

Gilgamesh washed out his long locks and cleaned his weapons; he flung back his hair from his shoulders; he threw off his stained clothes and changed them for new. He put on his royal robes and made them fast. When Gilgamesh had put on the crown, glorious Ishtar lifted her eyes, seeing the beauty of Gilgamesh. She said, 'Come to me Gilgamesh, and be my bridegroom; grant me seed of your body, let me be your bride and you shall be my husband. I will harness for you a chariot of lapis lazuli and of gold, with wheels of gold and horns of copper; and you shall have mighty demons of the storm for draft-mules. When you enter our house in the fragrance of cedar-wood, threshold and throne will kiss your feet. Kings, rulers, and princes will bow down before you; they shall bring you tribute from the mountains and the plain. Your ewes shall drop twins and your goats triplets; your pack-ass shall outrun mules; your oxen shall have no rivals, and your chariot horses shall be famous far-off for their swiftness.'

Gilgamesh opened his mouth and answered glorious Ishtar, 'If I take you in marriage, what gifts can I give in return? What ointments and clothing for your body? I would gladly give you bread and all sorts of food fit for a god. I would give you wine to drink fit for a queen. I would pour out barley to stuff your granary; but as for making you my wife—that I will not. How would it go with me? Your lovers have found you like a brazier which smoulders in the cold, a backdoor which keeps out neither squall of wind nor storm, a castle which crushes the garrison, pitch that blackens the bearer, a water-skin that chafes the carrier, a stone which falls from the parapet, a battering-ram turned back from the enemy, a sandal that trips the wearer. Which of your lovers did you ever love for ever? What shepherd of yours has pleased you for all time? Listen to me while I tell the tale of your lovers. There was Tammuz, the lover of your youth, for him you decreed wailing, year after year. You loved the many-coloured roller, but still you struck and broke his wing; now in the grove he sits and cries, "kappi, kappi, my wing, my wing." You have loved the lion tremendous in strength: seven pits you dug for him, and seven. You have loved the stallion magnificent in battle, and for him you decreed whip and spur and a thong, to gallop seven leagues by force and to muddy the water before he drinks; and for his mother Silili lamentations. You have loved the shepherd of the flock; he made meal-cake for you day after day, he killed kids for your sake. You struck and turned him into a wolf; now his own herd-boys chase him away, his own hounds worry his flanks. And did you not love Ishullanu, the gardener of your father's palm-grove? He brought you baskets filled with dates without end; every day he loaded your table. Then you turned your eyes on him and said, "Dearest Ishullanu, come here to me, let us enjoy your manhood, come forward and take me, I am yours." Ishullanu answered, "What are you asking from me? My mother has baked and I have eaten; why should I come to such as you for food that is tainted and rotten? For when was a screen of rushes sufficient protection from frosts?" But when you had heard his answer you struck him. He was changed to a blind mole deep in the earth, one whose desire is always beyond his reach. And if you and I should be lovers, should not I be served in the same fashion as all these others whom you loved once?'

When Ishtar heard this she fell into a bitter rage, she went up to high heaven. Her tears poured down in front of her father Anu, and Antum her mother. She said, 'My father, Gilgamesh has heaped insults on me, he has told over all my abominable behaviour, my foul and hideous acts.' Anu opened his mouth and said, 'Are you a father of gods? Did not you quarrel with Gilgamesh the king, so now he has related your abominable behaviour, your foul and hideous acts.'

Ishtar opened her mouth and said again, 'My father, give me the Bull of Heaven to destroy Gilgamesh. Fill Gilgamesh, I say, with arrogance to his destruction; but if you refuse to give me the Bull of Heaven I will break in the doors of hell and smash the bolts; there will be confusion of people, those above with those from the lower depths. I shall bring up the dead to eat food like the living; and the hosts of dead will outnumber the living.' Anu said to great Ishtar, 'If I do what you desire there will be seven years of drought throughout Uruk when corn will be seedless husks. Have you saved grain enough for the people and grass for the cattle?' Ishtar replied. 'I have saved grain for the people, grass for the cattle; for seven years of seedless husks there is grain and there is grass enough.'

When Anu heard what Ishtar had said he gave her the Bull of Heaven to lead by the halter down to Uruk. When they reached the gates of Uruk the Bull went to the river; with his first snort cracks opened in the earth and a hundred young men fell down to death. With his second snort cracks opened and two hundred fell down to death. With his third snort cracks opened, Enkidu doubled over but instantly recovered, he dodged aside and leapt on the Bull and seized it by the horns. The Bull of Heaven foamed in his face, it brushed him with the thick of its tail. Enkidu cried to Gilgamesh, 'My friend, we boasted that we would leave enduring names behind us. Now thrust in your sword between the nape and the horns.' So Gilgamesh followed the Bull, he seized the thick of its tail, he thrust the sword between the nape and the horns and slew the Bull. When they had killed the Bull of Heaven they cut out its heart and gave it to Shamash, and the brothers rested.

But Ishtar rose up and mounted the great wall of Uruk; she sprang on to the tower and uttered a curse: 'Woe to Gilgamesh, for he has scorned me in killing the Bull of Heaven.' When Enkidu heard these words he tore out the Bull's right thigh and tossed it in her face saying, 'If could lay my hands on you, it is this I should do to you, and lash the entrails to your side.' Then Ishtar called together her people, the dancing and singing girls, the prostitutes of the temple, the courtesans. Over the thigh of the Bull of Heaven she set up lamentation.

But Gilgamesh called the smiths and the armourers, all of them together. They admired the immensity of the horns. They were plated with lapis lazuli two fingers thick. They were thirty pounds each in weight, and their capacity in oil was six measures, which he gave to his guardian god, Lugulbanda. But he carried the horns into the palace and hung them on the wall. Then they washed their hands in Euphrates, they embraced each other and went away. They drove through the streets of Uruk where the heroes were gathered to see them, and Gilgamesh called to the singing girls, 'Who is most glorious of the heroes, who is most eminent among men?' 'Gilgamesh is the most glorious of heroes, Gilgamesh is most eminent among men.' And now there was feasting, and celebrations and joy in the palace, till the heroes lay down saying, 'Now we will rest for the night.'

When the daylight came Enkidu got up and cried to Gilgamesh, 'O my brother, such a dream I had last night. Anu, Enlil, Ea and heavenly Shamash took counsel together, and Anu said to Enlil, "Because they have killed the Bull of Heaven, and because they have killed Humbaba who guarded the Cedar Mountain one of the two must die." Then glorious Shamash answered the hero Enlil, "It was by your command they killed the Bull of Heaven, and killed Humbaba, and must Enkidu die although innocent?" Enlil flung round in rage at glorious Shamash, "You dare to say this, you who went about with them every day like one of themselves!"'

So Enkidu lay stretched out before Gilgamesh; his tears ran down in streams and he said to Gilgamesh, 'O my brother, so dear as you are to me, brother, yet they will take me from you.' Again he said, 'I must sit down on the threshold of the dead and never again will I see my dear brother with my eyes.'

While Enkidu lay alone in his sickness he cursed the gate as though it was living flesh, 'You there, wood of the gate, dull and insensible, witless, I searched for you over twenty leagues until I saw the towering cedar. There is no wood like you in our land. Seventy-two cubits high and twenty-four wide, the pivot and the ferrule and the jambs are perfect. A master craftsman from Nippur has made you; but O, if I had known the conclusion! If I had known that this was all the good that would come of it, I would have raised the axe and split you into little pieces and set up here a gate of wattle instead. Ah, if only some future king had brought you here, or some god had fashioned you. Let him obliterate my name and write his own, and the curse fall on him instead of on Enkidu.'

With the first brightening of dawn Enkidu raised his head and wept before the Sun God, in the brilliance of the sunlight his tears streamed down. 'Sun God, I beseech you, about that vile Trapper, that Trapper of nothing because of whom I was to catch less than my comrade; let him catch least, make his game scarce, make him feeble, taking the smaller of every share, let his quarry escape from his nets.'

When he had cursed the Trapper to his heart's content he turned on the harlot. He was roused to curse her also. 'As for you, woman, with a great curse I curse you! I will promise you a destiny to all eternity. My curse shall come on you soon and sudden. You shall be without a roof for your commerce, for you shall not keep house with other girls in the tavern, but do your business in places fouled by the vomit of the drunkard. Your hire will be potter's earth, your thievings will be flung into the hovel, you will sit at the cross-roads in the dust of the potter's quarter, you will make your bed on the dunghill at night, and by day take your stand in the wall's shadow. Brambles and thorns will tear your feet, the drunk and the dry will strike your cheek and your mouth will ache. Let you be stripped of your purple dyes, for I too once in the wilderness with my wife had all the treasure I wished.'

When Shamash heard the words of Enkidu he called to him from heaven: 'Enkidu, why are you cursing the woman, the mistress who taught you to eat bread fit for gods and drink wine of kings? She who put upon you a magnificent garment, did she not give you glorious Gilgamesh for your companion, and has not Gilgamesh, your own brother, made you rest on a royal bed and recline on a couch at his left hand? He has made the princes of the earth kiss your feet, and now all the people of Uruk lament and wail over you. When you are dead he will let his hair grow long for your sake, he will wear a lion's pelt and wander through the desert.'

When Enkidu heard glorious Shamash his angry heart grew quiet, he called back the curse and said, 'Woman, I promise you another destiny. The mouth which cursed you shall bless you! Kings, princes and nobles shall adore you. On your account a man though twelve miles off will clap his hand to his thigh and his hair will twitch. For you he will undo his belt and open his treasure and you shall have your desire; lapis lazuli, gold and carnelian from the heap in the treasury. A ring for your hand and a robe shall be yours. The priest will lead you into the presence of the gods. On your account a wife, a mother of seven, was forsaken.'

As Enkidu slept alone in his sickness, in bitterness of spirit he poured out his heart to his friend. 'It was I who cut down the cedar, I who levelled the forest, I who slew Humbaba and now see what has become of me. Listen, my friend, this is the dream I dreamed last night. The heavens roared, and earth rumbled back an answer; between them stood I before an awful being, the sombre-faced man-bird; he had directed on me his purpose. His was a vampire face, his foot was a lion's foot, his hand was an eagle's talon. He fell on me and his claws were in my hair, he held me fast and I smothered; then he transformed me so that my arms became wings covered with feathers. He turned his stare towards me, and he led me away to the palace of Irkalla, the Queen of Darkness, to the house from which none who enters ever returns, down the road from which there is no coming back.

'There is the house whose people sit in darkness; dust is their food and clay their meat. They are clothed like birds with wings for covering, they see no light, they sit in darkness. I entered the house of dust and I saw the kings of the earth, their crowns put away for ever; rulers and princes, all those who once wore kingly crowns and ruled the world in the days of old. They who had stood in the place of the gods like Anu and Enlil, stood now like servants to fetch baked meats in the house of dust, to carry cooked meat and cold water from the water-skin. In the house of dust which I entered were high priests and acolytes, priests of the incantation and of ecstasy; there were servers of the temple, and there was Etana, that king of Kish whom the eagle carried to heaven in the days of old. I saw also Samuqan, god of cattle, and there was Ereshkigal the Queen of the Underworld; and Belit-Sheri squatted in front of her, she who is recorder of the gods and keeps the book of death. She held a tablet from which she read. She raised her head, she saw me and spoke: "Who has brought this one here?" Then I awoke like a man drained of blood who wanders alone in a waste of rushes; like one whom the bailiff has seized and his heart pounds with terror.'

Gilgamesh had peeled off his clothes, he listened to his words and wept quick tears, Gilgamesh listened and his tears flowed. He opened his mouth and spoke to Enkidu: 'Who is there in strong-walled Uruk who has wisdom like this? Strange things have been spoken, why does your heart speak strangely? The dream was marvellous but the terror was great; we must treasure the dream whatever the terror; for the dream has shown that misery comes at last to the healthy man, the end of life is sorrow.' And Gilgamesh lamented, 'Now I will pray to the great gods, for my friend had an ominous dream.'

This day on which Enkidu dreamed came to an end and he lay stricken with sickness. One whole day he lay on his bed and his suffering increased. He said to Gilgamesh, the friend on whose account he had left the wilderness, 'Once I ran for you, for the water of life, and I now have nothing.' A second day he lay on his bed and Gilgamesh watched over him but the sickness increased. A third day he lay on his bed, he called out to Gilgamesh, rousing him up. Now he was weak and his eyes were blind with weeping. Ten days he lay and his suffering increased, eleven and twelve days he lay on his bed of pain. Then he called to Gilgamesh, 'My friend, the great goddess cursed me and I must die in shame. I shall not die like a man fallen in battle; I feared to fall, but happy is the man who falls in the battle, for I must die in shame.' And Gilgamesh wept over Enkidu. With the first light of dawn he raised his voice and said to the counsellors of Uruk:

'Hear me, great ones of Uruk,
I weep for Enkidu, my friend,
Bitterly moaning like a woman
mourning,
I weep for my brother.
O Enkidu, my brother,
Your were the axe at my side,
My hand's strength, the sword in
my belt,
The shield before me,
A glorious robe, my fairest
ornament;
An evil Fate has robbed me.
The wild ass and the gazelle

That were father and mother,
All long-tailed creatures that nourished you
Weep for you,
All the wild things of the plain and pastures;
The paths that you loved in the forest of cedars
Night and day murmur.
Let the great ones of strong-walled Uruk
Weep for you;
Let the finger of blessing
Be stretched out in mourning;
Enkidu, young brother. Hark,
There is an echo through all the country
Like a mother mourning.
Weep all the paths where we walked together;
And the beasts we hunted, the bear and hyena,
Tiger and panther, leopard and lion,
The stag and the ibex, the bull and the doe.
The river along whose banks we used to walk,
Weeps for you,
Ula of Elam and dear Euphrates
Where once we drew water for the water-skins.
The mountain we climbed where we slew the Watchman,
Weeps for you.
The warriors of strong-walled Uruk
Where the Bull of Heaven was killed,
Weep for you.
All the people of Eridu
Weep for you Enkidu.
Those who brought grain for your eating
Mourn for you now;
Who rubbed oil on your back
Mourn for you now;
Who poured beer for your drinking
Mourn for you now.
The harlot who anointed you with fragrant ointment
Laments for you now;
The women of the palace, who brought you a wife,
A chosen ring of good advice,
Lament for you now.
And the young men your brothers
As though they were women
Go long-haired in mourning.
What is this sleep which holds you now?
You are lost in the dark and cannot hear me.'

He touched his heart but it did not beat, nor did he lift his eyes again. When Gilgamesh touched his heart it did not beat. So Gilgamesh laid a veil, as one veils the bride, over his friend. He began to rage like a lion, like a lioness robbed of her whelps. This way and that he paced round the bed, he tore out his hair and strewed it around. He dragged off his splendid robes and flung them down as though they were abominations.

In the first light of dawn Gilgamesh cried out, 'I made you rest on a royal bed, you reclined on a couch at my left hand, the princes of the earth kissed your feet. I will cause all the people of Uruk to weep over you and raise the dirge of the dead. The joyful people will stoop with sorrow; and when you have gone to the earth I will let my hair grow long for your sake, I will wander through the wilderness in the skin of a lion.' The next day also, in the first light, Gilgamesh lamented; seven days and seven nights he wept for Enkidu, until the worm fastened on him. Only then he gave him up to the earth, for the Anunnaki, the judges, had seized him.

Then Gilgamesh issued a proclamation through the land, he summoned them all, the coppersmiths, the goldsmiths, the stone-workers, and commanded them, 'Make a statue of my friend.' The statue was fashioned with a great weight of lapis lazuli for the breast and of gold for the body. A table of hard-wood was set out, and on it a bowl of carnelian filled with honey, and a bowl of lapis lazuli filled with butter. These he exposed and offered to the Sun; and weeping he went away.

## 4

### The Search for Everlasting Life

Bitterly Gilgamesh wept for his friend Enkidu; he wandered over the wilderness as a hunter, he roamed over the plains; in his bitterness he cried, 'How can I rest, how can I be at peace? Despair is in my heart. What my brother is now, that shall I be when I am dead. Because I am afraid of death I will go as best I can to find Utnapishtim whom they call the Faraway, for he has entered the assembly of the gods.' So Gilgamesh travelled over the wilderness, he wandered over the grasslands, a long journey, in search of Utnapishtim, whom the gods took after the deluge; and they set him to live in the land of Dilmun, in the garden of the sun; and to him alone of men they gave everlasting life.

At night when he came to the mountain passes Gilgamesh prayed: 'In these mountain passes long ago I saw lions, I was afraid and I lifted my eyes to the moon; I prayed and my prayers went up to the gods, so now, O moon god Sin, protect me.' When he had prayed he lay down to sleep, until he was woken from out of a dream. He saw the lions round him glorying in life; then he took his axe in his hand, he drew his sword from his belt, and he fell upon them like an arrow from the string, and struck and destroyed and scattered them.

So at length Gilgamesh came to Mashu, the great mountains about which he had heard many things, which guard the rising and the setting sun. Its twin peaks are as high as the wall of heaven and its paps reach down to the underworld. At its gate the Scorpions stand guard, half man and half dragon; their glory is terrifying, their stare strikes death into men, their shimmering halo sweeps the mountains that guard the rising sun. When Gilgamesh saw them he shielded his eyes for the length of a moment only; then he took courage and approached. When they saw him so undismayed the Man-Scorpion called to his mate, 'This one who comes to us now is flesh of the gods.' The mate of the Man-Scorpion answered, 'Two thirds is god but one third is man.'

Then he called to the man Gilgamesh, he called to the child of the gods: 'Why have you come so great a journey; for what have you travelled so far, crossing the dangerous waters; tell me the reason for your coming?' Gilgamesh answered, 'For Enkidu; I loved him dearly, together we endured all kinds of hardships; on his account I have come, for the common lot of man has taken him. I have wept for him day and night, I would not give up his body for burial, I thought my friend would come back because of my weeping. Since he went, my life is nothing; that is why I have travelled here in search of Utnapishtim my father; for men say he has entered the assembly of the gods, and has found everlasting life. I have a desire to question him concerning the living and the dead.' The Man-Scorpion opened his mouth and said, speaking to Gilgamesh, 'No man born of woman has done what you have asked, no mortal man has gone into the mountain; the length of it is twelve leagues of darkness; in it there is no light, but the heart is oppressed with darkness. From the rising of the sun to the setting of the sun there is no light.' Gilgamesh said, 'Although I should go in sorrow and in pain, with sighing and with weeping, still I must go. Open the gate of the mountain.' And the Man-Scorpion said, 'Go, Gilgamesh, I permit you to pass through the mountain of Mashu and through the high ranges; may your feet carry you safely home. The gate of the mountain is open.'

When Gilgamesh heard this he did as the Man-Scorpion had said, he followed the sun's road to his rising, through the mountain. When he had gone one league the darkness became thick around him, for there was no light, he could see nothing ahead and nothing behind him. After two leagues the darkness was thick and there was no light, he could see nothing ahead and nothing behind him. After three leagues the darkness was thick, and there was no light, he could see nothing ahead and nothing behind him. After four leagues the darkness was thick and there was no light, he could see nothing ahead and nothing behind him. At the end of five leagues the darkness was thick and there was no light, he could see nothing ahead and nothing behind him. At the end of six leagues the darkness was thick and there was no light, he could see nothing ahead and nothing behind him. When he had gone seven leagues the darkness was thick and there was no light, he could see nothing ahead and nothing behind him. When he had gone eight leagues Gilgamesh gave a great cry, for the darkness was thick and he could see nothing ahead and nothing behind him. After nine leagues he felt the north wind on his face, but the darkness was thick and there was no light, he could see nothing ahead and nothing behind him. After ten leagues the end was near. After eleven leagues the dawn light appeared. At the end of twelve leagues the sun streamed out.

There was the garden of the gods; all round him stood bushes bearing gems. Seeing it he went down at once, for there was fruit of carnelian with the vine hanging from it, beautiful to look at; lapis lazuli leaves hung thick with fruit, sweet to see. For thorns and thistles there were haematite and rare stones, agate, and pearls from out of the sea. While Gilgamesh walked in the garden by the edge of the sea Shamash saw him, and he saw that he was dressed in the skins of animals and ate their flesh. He was distressed, and he spoke and said, 'No mortal man has gone this way before, nor will, as long as the winds drive over the sea.' And to Gilgamesh he said, 'You will never find the life for which you are searching.' Gilgamesh said to glorious Shamash, 'Now that I have toiled and strayed so far over the wilderness, am I to sleep, and let the earth cover my head for ever? Let my eyes see the sun until they are dazzled with looking. Although I am no better than a dead man, still let me see the light of the sun.'

Beside the sea she lives, the woman of the vine, the maker of wine; Siduri sits in the garden at the edge of the sea, with the golden bowl and the golden vats that the gods gave her. She is covered with a veil; and where she sits she sees Gilgamesh coming towards her, wearing skins, the flesh of the gods in his body, but despair in his heart, and his face like the face of one who has made a long journey. She looked, and as she scanned the distance she said in her own heart, 'Surely this is some felon; where is he going now?' And she barred her gate against him with the cross-bar and shot home the bolt. But Gilgamesh, hearing the sound of the bolt, threw up his head and lodged his foot in the gate; he called to her, 'Young woman, maker of wine, why do you bolt your door; what did you see that made you bar your gate? I will break in your door and burst in your gate, for I am Gilgamesh who seized and killed the Bull of Heaven, I killed the watchman of the cedar forest, I overthrew Humbaba who lived in the forest, and I killed the lions in the passes of the mountain.'

Then Siduri said to him, 'If you are that Gilgamesh who seized and killed the Bull of Heaven, who killed the watchman of the cedar forest, who overthrew Humbaba that lived in the forest, and killed the lions in the passes of the mountain, why are your cheeks so starved and why is your face so drawn? Why is despair in your heart and your face like the face of one who has made a long journey? Yes, why is your face burned from heat and cold, and why do you come here wandering over the pastures in search of the wind?'

Gilgamesh answered her, 'And why should not my cheeks be starved and my face drawn? Despair is in my heart and my face is the face of one who has made a long journey, it was burned with heat and with cold. Why should I not wander over the pastures in search of the wind? My friend, my younger brother, he who hunted the wild ass of the wilderness and the panther of the plains, my friend, my younger brother who seized and killed the Bull of Heaven and overthrew Humbaba in the cedar forest, my friend who was very dear to me and who endured dangers beside me, Enkidu my brother, whom I loved, the end of mortality has overtaken him. I wept for him seven days and nights till the worm fastened on him. Because of my brother I am afraid of death, because of my brother I stray through the wilderness and cannot rest. But now, young woman, maker of wine, since I have seen your face do not let me see the face of death which I dread so much.'

She answered, 'Gilgamesh, where are you hurrying to? You will never find that life for which you are looking. When the gods created man they allotted to him death, but life they retained in their own keeping. As for you, Gilgamesh, fill your belly with good things; day and night, night and day, dance and be merry, feast and rejoice. Let your clothes be fresh, bathe yourself in water, cherish the little child that holds your hand, and make your wife happy in your embrace; for this too is the lot of man.'

But Gilgamesh said to Siduri, the young woman, 'How can I be silent, how can I rest, when Enkidu whom I love is dust, and I too shall die and be laid in the earth. You live by the sea-shore and look into the heart of it; young woman, tell me now, which is the way to Utnapishtim, the son of Ubara-Tutu? What directions are there for the passage; give me, oh, give me directions. I will cross the Ocean if it is possible; if it is not I will wander still farther in the wilderness.' The wine-maker said to him, 'Gilgamesh, there is no crossing the Ocean; whoever has come, since the days of old, has not been able to pass that sea. The Sun in his glory crosses the Ocean, but who beside Shamash has ever crossed it? The place and the passage are difficult, and the waters of death are deep which flow between. Gilgamesh, how will you cross the Ocean? When you come to the waters of death what will you do? But Gilgamesh, down in the woods you will find Urshanabi, the ferryman of Utnapishtim; with him are the holy things, the things of stone. He is fashioning the serpent prow of the boat. Look at him well, and if it is possible, perhaps you will cross the waters with him; but if it is not possible, then you must go back.'

When Gilgamesh heard this he was seized with anger. He took his axe in his hand, and his dagger from his belt. He crept forward and he fell on them like a javelin. Then he went into the forest and sat down. Urshanabi saw the dagger flash and heard the axe, and he beat his head, for Gilgamesh had shattered the tackle of the boat in his rage. Urshanabi said to him, 'Tell me, what is your name? I am Urshanabi, the ferryman of Utnapishtim the Faraway.' He replied to him, 'Gilgamesh is my name, I am from Uruk, from the house of Anu.' Then Urshanabi said to him, 'Why are your cheeks so starved and your face drawn? Why is despair in your heart and your face like the face of one who has made a long journey; yes, why is your face burned with heat and with cold, and why do you come here wandering over the pastures in search of the wind?'

Gilgamesh said to him, 'Why should not my cheeks be starved and my face drawn? Despair is in my heart, and my face is the face of one who has made a long journey. I was burned with heat and with cold. Why should I not wander over the pastures? My friend, my younger brother who seized and killed the Bull of Heaven, and overthrew Humbaba in the cedar forest, my friend who was very dear to me, and who endured dangers beside me, Enkidu my brother whom I loved, the end of mortality has overtaken him. I wept for him seven days and nights till the worm fastened on him. Because of my brother I am afraid of death, because of my brother I stray through the wilderness. His fate lies heavy upon me. How can I be silent, how can I rest? He is dust and I too shall die and be laid in the earth for ever. I am afraid of death, therefore, Urshanabi, tell me which is the road to Utnapishtim? If it is possible I will cross the waters of death; if not I will wander still farther through the wilderness.'

Urshanabi said to him, 'Gilgamesh, your own hands have prevented you from crossing the Ocean; when you destroyed the tackle of the boat you destroyed its safety.' Then the two of them talked it over and Gilgamesh said, 'Why are you so angry with me, Urshanabi, for you yourself cross the sea by day and night, at all seasons you cross it.' 'Gilgamesh, those things you destroyed, their property is to carry me over the water, to prevent the waters of death from touching me. It was for this reason that I preserved them, but you have destroyed them, and the *urnu* snakes with them. But now, go into the forest, Gilgamesh; with your axe cut poles, one hundred and twenty, cut them sixty cubits long, paint them with bitumen, set on them ferrules and bring them back.'

When Gilgamesh heard this he went into the forest, he cut poles one hundred and twenty; he cut them sixty cubits long, he painted them with bitumen, he set on them ferrules, and he brought them to Urshanabi. Then they boarded the boat, Gilgamesh and Urshanabi together, launching it out on the waves of Ocean. For three days they ran on as it were a journey of a month and fifteen days, and at last Urshanabi brought the boat to the waters of death. Then Urshanabi said to Gilgamesh, 'Press on, take a pole and thrust it in, but do not let your hands touch the waters. Gilgamesh, take a second pole, take a third, take a fourth pole. Now, Gilgamesh, take a fifth, take a sixth and seventh pole. Gilgamesh, take an eighth, and ninth, a tenth pole. Gilgamesh, take an eleventh, take a twelfth pole.' After one hundred and twenty thrusts Gilgamesh had used the last pole. Then he stripped himself, he held up his arms for a mast and his covering for a sail. So Urshanabi the ferryman brought Gilgamesh to Utnapishtim, whom they call the Faraway, who lives in Dilmun at the place of the sun's transit, eastward of the mountain. To him alone of men the gods had given everlasting life.

Now Utnapishtim, where he lay at ease, looked into the distance and he said in his heart, musing to himself, 'Why does the boat sail here without tackle and mast; why are the sacred stones destroyed, and why does the master not sail the boat? That man who comes is none of mine; where I look I see a man whose body is covered with skins of beasts. Who is this who walks up the shore behind Urshanabi, for surely he is no man of mine?' So Utnapishtim looked at him and said, 'What is your name, you who come here wearing the skins of beasts, with your cheeks starved and your face drawn? Where are you hurrying to now? For what reason have you made this great journey, crossing the seas whose passage is difficult? Tell me the reason for your coming.'

He replied, 'Gilgamesh is my name. I am from Uruk, from the house of Anu.' Then Utnapishtim said to him, 'If you are Gilgamesh, why are your cheeks so starved and your face drawn? Why is despair in your heart and your face like the face of one who has made a long journey? Yes, why is your face burned with heat and cold; and why do you come here, wandering over the wilderness in search of the wind?'

Gilgamesh said to him, 'Why should not my cheeks be starved and my face drawn? Despair is in my heart and my face is the face of one who has made a long journey. It was burned with heat and with cold. Why should I not wander over the pastures? My friend, my younger brother who seized and killed the Bull of Heaven and overthrew Humbaba in the cedar forest, my friend who was very dear to me and endured dangers beside me, Enkidu, my brother whom I loved, the end of mortality has overtaken him. I wept for him seven days and nights till the worm fastened on him. Because of my brother I am afraid of death; because of my brother I stray through the wilderness. His fate lies heavy upon me. How can I be silent, how can I rest? He is dust and I shall die also and be laid in the earth for ever.' Again Gilgamesh said, speaking to Utnapishtim, 'It is to see Utnapishtim whom we call the Faraway that I have come this journey. For this I have wandered over the world, I have crossed many difficult ranges, I have crossed the seas, I have wearied myself with travelling; my joints are aching, and I have lost acquaintance with sleep which is sweet. My clothes were worn out before I came to the house of Siduri. I have killed the bear and hyena, the lion and panther, the tiger, the stag and the ibex, all sorts of wild game and the small creatures of the pastures. I ate their flesh and I wore their skins; and that was how I came to the gate of the young woman, the maker of wine, who barred her gate of pitch and bitumen against me. But from her I had news of the journey; so then I came to Urshanabi the ferryman, and with him I crossed over the waters of death. Oh, father Utnapishtim, you who have entered the assembly of the gods, I wish to question you concerning the living and the dead, how shall I find the life for which I am searching?'

Utnapishtim said, 'There is no permanence. Do we build a house to stand for ever, do we seal a contract to hold for all time? Do brothers divide an inheritance to keep for ever, does the flood-time of rivers endure? It is only the nymph of the dragon-fly who sheds her larva and sees the sun in his glory. From the days of old there is no permanence. The sleeping and the dead, how alike they are, they are like a painted death. What is there between the master and the servant when both have fulfilled their doom? When the Anunnaki, the judges, come together, and Mammetun the mother of destinies, together they decree the fates of men. Life and death they allot but the day of death they do not disclose.'

Then Gilgamesh said to Utnapishtim the Faraway, 'I look at you now, Utnapishtim, and your appearance is no different from mine; there is nothing strange in your features. I thought I should find you like a hero prepared for battle, but you lie here taking your ease on your back. Tell me truly, how was it that you came to enter the company of the gods and to possess everlasting life?' Utnapishtim said to Gilgamesh, 'I will reveal to you a mystery, I will tell you a secret of the gods.'

## 5

### The Story of the Flood

'You know the city Shurrupak, it stands on the banks of Euphrates? That city grew old and the gods that were in it were old. There was Anu, lord of the firmament, their father, and warrior Enlil their counsellor, Ninurta the helper, and Ennugi watcher over canals; and with them also was Ea. In those days the world teemed, the people multiplied, the world bellowed like a wild bull, and the great god was aroused by the clamour. Enlil heard the clamour and he said to the gods in council, "The uproar of mankind is intolerable and sleep is no longer possible by reason of the babel." So the gods agreed to exterminate mankind. Enlil did this, but Ea because of his oath warned me in a dream. He whispered their words to my house of reeds, "Reed-house, reed- house! Wall, O wall, hearken reed-house, wall reflect; O man of Shurrupak, son of Ubara-Tutu; tear down your house and build a boat, abandon possessions and look for life, despise worldly goods and save your soul alive. Tear down your house, I say, and build a boat. These are the measurements of the barque as you shall build her: let her beam equal her length, let her deck be roofed like the vault that covers the abyss; then take up into the boat the seed of all living creatures."

'When I had understood I said to my lord, "Behold, what you have commanded I will honour and perform, but how shall I answer the people, the city, the elders?" Then Ea opened his mouth and said to me, his servant, "Tell them this: I have learnt that Enlil is wrathful against me, I dare no longer walk in his land nor live in his city; I will go down to the Gulf to dwell with Ea my lord. But on you he will rain down abundance, rare fish and shy wild-fowl, a rich harvest-tide. In the evening the rider of the storm will bring you wheat in torrents."

'In the first light of dawn all my household gathered round me, the children brought pitch and the men whatever was necessary. On the fifth day I laid the keel and the ribs, then I made fast the planking. The ground-space was one acre, each side of the deck measured one hundred and twenty cubits, making a square. I built six decks below, seven in all, I divided them into nine sections with bulkheads between. I drove in wedges where needed, I saw to the punt-poles, and laid in supplies. The carriers brought oil in baskets, I poured pitch into the furnace and asphalt and oil; more oil was consumed in caulking, and more again the master of the boat took into his stores. I slaughtered bullocks for the people and every day I killed sheep. I gave the shipwrights wine to drink as though it were river water, raw wine and red wine and oil and white wine. There was feasting then as there is at the time of the New Year's festival; I myself anointed my head. On the seventh day the boat was complete.

'Then was the launching full of difficulty; there was shifting of ballast above and below till two thirds was submerged. I loaded into her all that I had of gold and of living things, my family, my kin, the beast of the field both wild and tame, and all the craftsmen. I sent them on board, for the time that Shamash had ordained was already fulfilled when he said, "In the evening, when the rider of the storm sends down the destroying rain, enter the boat and batten her down." The time was fulfilled, the evening came, the rider of the storm sent down the rain. I looked out at the weather and it was terrible, so I too boarded the boat and battened her down. All was now complete, the battening and the caulking; so I handed the tiller to Puzur-Amurri the steersman, with the navigation and the care of the whole boat.

'With the first light of dawn a black cloud came from the horizon; it thundered within where Adad, lord of the storm was riding. In front over hill and plain Shullat and Hanish, heralds of the storm, led on. Then the gods of the abyss rose up; Nergal pulled out the dams of the nether waters, Ninurta the war-lord threw down the dykes, and the seven judges of hell, the Annunaki, raised their torches, lighting the land with their livid flame. A stupor of despair went up to heaven when the god of the storm turned daylight to darkness, when he smashed the land like a cup. One whole day the tempest raged, gathering fury as it went, it poured over the people like the tides of battle; a man could not see his brother nor the people be seen from heaven. Even the gods were terrified at the flood, they fled to the highest heaven, the firmament of Anu; they crouched against the walls, cowering like curs. Then Ishtar the sweet-voiced Queen of Heaven cried out like a woman in travail: "Alas the days of old are turned to dust because I commanded evil; why did I command this evil in the council of all the gods? I commanded wars to destroy the people, but are they not my people, for I brought them forth? Now like the spawn of fish they float in the ocean." The great gods of heaven and of hell wept, they covered their mouths.

'For six days and six nights the winds blew, torrent and tempest and flood overwhelmed the world, tempest and flood raged together like warring hosts. When the seventh day dawned the storm from the south subsided, the sea grew calm, the flood was stilled; I looked at the face of the world and there was silence, all mankind was turned to clay. The surface of the sea stretched as flat as a roof-top; I opened a hatch and the light fell on my face. Then I bowed low, I sat down and I wept, the tears streamed down my face, for on every side was the waste of water. I looked for land in vain, but fourteen leagues distant there appeared a mountain, and there the boat grounded; on the mountain of Nisir the boat held fast, she held fast and did not budge. One day she held, and a second day on the mountain of Nisir she held fast and did not budge. A third day, and a fourth day she held fast on the mountain and did not budge; a fifth day and a sixth day she held fast on the mountain. When the seventh day dawned I loosed a dove and let her go. She flew away, but finding no resting-place she returned. Then I loosed a swallow, and she flew away but finding no resting-place she returned. I loosed a raven, she saw that the waters had retreated, she ate, she flew around, she cawed, and she did not come back. Then I threw everything open to the four winds, I made a sacrifice and poured out a libation on the mountain top. Seven and again seven cauldrons I set up on their stands, I heaped up wood and cane and cedar and myrtle. When the gods smelled the sweet savour, they gathered like flies over the sacrifice. Then, at last, Ishtar also came, she lifted her necklace with the jewels of heaven that once Anu had made to please her. "O you gods here present, by the lapis lazuli round my neck I shall remember these days as I remember the jewels of my throat; these last days I shall not forget. Let all the gods gather round the sacrifice, except Enlil. He shall not approach this offering, for without reflection he brought the flood; he consigned my people to destruction."

'When Enlil had come, when he saw the boat, he was wrath and swelled with anger at the gods, the host of heaven, "Has any of these mortals escaped? Not one was to have survived the destruction." Then the god of the wells and canals Ninurta opened his mouth and said to the warrior Enlil, "Who is there of the gods that can devise without Ea? It is Ea alone who knows all things." Then Ea opened his mouth and spoke to warrior Enlil, "Wisest of gods, hero Enlil, how could you so senselessly bring down the flood?

Lay upon the sinner his sin,
Lay upon the transgressor his
transgression,
Punish him a little when he breaks
loose,
Do not drive him too hard or he
perishes;
Would that a lion had ravaged
mankind
Rather than the flood,
Would that a wolf had ravaged
mankind
Rather than the flood,
Would that famine had wasted the
world
Rather than the flood,
Would that pestilence had wasted
mankind
Rather than the flood.

It was not I that revealed the secret of the gods; the wise man learned it in a dream. Now take your counsel what shall be done with him."

'Then Enlil went up into the boat, he took me by the hand and my wife and made us enter the boat and kneel down on either side, he standing between us. He touched our foreheads to bless us saying, "In time past Utnapishtim was a mortal man; henceforth he and his wife shall live in the distance at the mouth of the rivers." Thus it was that the gods took me and placed me here to live in the distance, at the mouth of the rivers.'

## 6

### The Return

Utnapishtim said, 'As for you, Gilgamesh, who will assemble the gods for your sake, so that you may find that life for which you are searching? But if you wish, come and put it to the test: only prevail against sleep for six days and seven nights.' But while Gilgamesh sat there resting on his haunches, a mist of sleep like soft wool teased from the fleece drifted over him, and Utnapishtim said to his wife, 'Look at him now, the strong man who would have everlasting life, even now the mists of sleep are drifting over him.' His wife replied, 'Touch the man to wake him, so that he may return to his own land in peace, going back through the gate by which he came.' Utnapishtim said to his wife, 'All men are deceivers, even you he will attempt to deceive; therefore bake loaves of bread, each day one loaf, and put it beside his head; and make a mark on the wall to number the days he has slept.'

So she baked loaves of bread, each day one loaf, and put it beside his head, and she marked on the wall the days that he slept; and there came a day when the first loaf was hard, the second loaf was like leather, the third was soggy, the crust of the fourth had mould, the fifth was mildewed, the sixth was fresh, and the seventh was still on the embers. Then Utnapishtim touched him and he woke. Gilgamesh said to Utnapishtim the Faraway, 'I hardly slept when you touched and roused me.' But Utnapishtim said, 'Count these loaves and learn how many days you slept, for your first is hard, your second like leather, your third is soggy, the crust of your fourth has mould, your fifth is mildewed, your sixth is fresh and your seventh was still over the glowing embers when I touched and woke you.' Gilgamesh said, 'What shall I do, O Utnapishtim, where shall I go? Already the thief in the night has hold of my limbs, death inhabits my room; wherever my foot rests, there I find death.'

Then Utnapishtim spoke to Urshanabi the ferryman: 'Woe to you Urshanabi, now and for ever more you have become hateful to this harbourage; it is not for you, nor for you are the crossings of this sea. Go now, banished from the shore. But this man before whom you walked, bringing him here, whose body is covered with foulness and the grace of whose limbs has been spoiled by wild skins, take him to the washing-place. There he shall wash his long hair clean as snow in the water, he shall throw off his skins and let the sea carry them away, and the beauty of his body shall be shown, the fillet on his forehead shall be renewed, and he shall be given clothes to cover his nakedness. Till he reaches his own city and his journey is accomplished, these clothes will show no sign of age, they will wear like a new garment.' So Urshanabi took Gilgamesh and led him to the washing-place, he washed his long hair as clean as snow in the water, he threw off his skins, which the sea carried away, and showed the beauty of his body. He renewed the fillet on his forehead, and to cover his nakedness gave him clothes which would show no sign of age, but would wear like a new garment till he reached his own city, and his journey was accomplished.

Then Gilgamesh and Urshanabi launched the boat on to the water and boarded it, and they made ready to sail away; but the wife of Utnapishtim the Faraway said to him, 'Gilgamesh came here wearied out, he is worn out; what will you give him to carry him back to his own country?' So Utnapishtim spoke, and Gilgamesh took a pole and brought the boat in to the bank. 'Gilgamesh, you came here a man wearied out, you have worn yourself out; what shall I give you to carry you back to your own country? Gilgamesh, I shall reveal a secret thing, it is a mystery of the gods that I am telling you. There is a plant that grows under the water, it has a prickle like a thorn, like a rose; it will wound your hands, but if you succeed in taking it, then your hands will hold that which restores his lost youth to a man.'

When Gilgamesh heard this he opened the sluices so that a sweet-water current might carry him out to the deepest channel; he tied heavy stones to his feet and they dragged him down to the water-bed. There he saw the plant growing; although it pricked him he took it in his hands; then he cut the heavy stones from his feet, and the sea carried him and threw him on to the shore. Gilgamesh said to Urshanabi the ferryman, 'Come here, and see this marvellous plant. By its virtue a man may win back all his former strength. I will take it to Uruk of the strong walls; there I will give it to the old men to eat. Its name shall be "The Old Men Are Young Again"; and at last I shall eat it myself and have back all my lost youth.' So Gilgamesh returned by the gate through which he had come, Gilgamesh and Urshanabi went together. They travelled their twenty leagues and then they broke their fast; after thirty leagues they stopped for the night.

Gilgamesh saw a well of cool water and he went down and bathed; but deep in the pool there was lying a serpent, and the serpent sensed the sweetness of the flower. It rose out of the water and snatched it away, and immediately it sloughed its skin and returned to the well. Then Gilgamesh sat down and wept, the tears ran down his face, and he took the hand of Urshanabi; 'O Urshanabi, was it for this that I toiled with my hands, is it for this I have wrung out my heart's blood? For myself I have gained nothing; not I but the beast of the earth has joy of it now. Already the stream has carried it twenty leagues back to the channels where I found it. I found a sign and now I have lost it. Let us leave the boat on the bank and go.'

After twenty leagues they broke their fast, after thirty leagues they stopped for the night; in three days they had walked as much as a journey of a month and fifteen days. When the journey was accomplished they arrived at Uruk, the strong-walled city. Gilgamesh spoke to him, to Urshanabi the ferryman, 'Urshanabi, climb up on to the wall of Uruk, inspect its foundation terrace, and examine well the brickwork; see if it is not of burnt bricks; and did not the seven wise men lay these foundations? One third of the whole is city, one third is garden, and one third is field, with the precinct of the goddess Ishtar. These parts and the precinct are all Uruk.'

This too was the work of Gilgamesh, the king, who knew the countries of the world. He was wise, he saw mysteries and knew secret things, he brought us a tale of the days before the flood. He went a long journey, was weary, worn out with labour, and returning engraved on a stone the whole story.

## 7

### The Death of Gilgamesh

The destiny was fulfilled which the father of the gods, Enlil of the mountain, had decreed for Gilgamesh: 'In nether-earth the darkness will show him a light: of mankind, all that are known, none will leave a monument for generations to come to compare with his. The heroes, the wise men, like the new moon have their waxing and waning. Men will say, "Who has ever ruled with might and with power like him?" As in the dark month, the month of shadows, so without him there is no light. O Gilgamesh, this was the meaning of your dream. You were given the kingship, such was your destiny, everlasting life was not your destiny. Because of this do not be sad at heart, do not be grieved or oppressed; he has given you power to bind and to loose, to be the darkness and the light of mankind. He has given unexampled supremacy over the people, victory in battle from which no fugitive returns, in forays and assaults from which there is no going back. But do not abuse this power, deal justly with your servants in the palace, deal justly before the face of the Sun.'

The king has laid himself down
 and will not rise again,
The Lord of Kullab will not rise
 again;
He overcame evil, he will not
 come again;
Though he was strong of arm he
 will not rise again;
He had wisdom and a comely face,
 he will not come again;
He is gone into the mountain, he
 will not come again;
On the bed of fate he lies, he will
 not rise again,
From the couch of many colours
 he will not come again.

The people of the city, great and small, are not silent; they lift up the lament, all men of flesh and blood lift up the lament. Fate has spoken; like a hooked fish he lies stretched on the bed, like a gazelle that is caught in a noose. Inhuman Namtar is heavy upon him, Namtar that has neither hand nor foot, that drinks no water and eats no meat.

For Gilgamesh, son of Ninsun, they weighed out their offerings; his dear wife, his son, his concubine, his musicians, his jester, and all his household; his servants, his stewards, all who lived in the palace weighed out their offerings for Gilgamesh the son of Ninsun, the heart of Uruk. They weighed out their offerings to Ereshkigal, the Queen of Death, and to all the gods of the dead. To Namtar, who is fate, they weighed out the offering. Bread for Neti the Keeper of the Gate, bread for Ningizzida the god of the serpent, the lord of the Tree of Life; for Dumuzi also, the young shepherd, for Enki and Ninki, for Endukugga and Nindukugga, for Enmul and Ninmul, all the ancestral gods, forbears of Enlil. A feast for

Shulpae the god of feasting. For Samuqan, god of the herds, for the mother Ninhursag, and the gods of creation in the place of creation, for the host of heaven, priest and priestess weighed out the offering of the dead.

Gilgamesh, the son of Ninsun, lies in the tomb. At the place of offerings he weighed the bread-offering, at the place of libation he poured out the wine. In those days the lord Gilgamesh departed, the son of Ninsun, the king, peerless, without an equal among men, who did not neglect Enlil his master. O Gilgamesh, lord of Kullab, great is thy praise.

## Glossary of Names

A short description of the gods and of other persons and places mentioned in the Epic will be found in this Glossary. The gods were credited at different times with a variety of attributes and characteristics, sometimes contradictory; only such as are relevant to the material of the Gilgamesh Epic are given here. Cross-references to other entries in the Glossary are indicated by means of italics.

ADAD: Storm-, rain-, and weather-god.

ANUNNAKI: Usually gods of the underworld, judges of the dead and offspring of *Anu.*

ANSHAN: A district of Elam in southwest Persia; probably the source of supplies of wood for making bows. Gilgamesh has a 'bow of Anshan.'

ANTUM: Wife of *Anu.*

ANU: Sumerian An; father of gods, and god of the firmament, the 'great above.' In the Sumerian cosmogony there was, first of all, the primeval sea, from which was born the cosmic mountain consisting of heaven, 'An,' and earth, 'Ki'; they were separated by *Enlil,* then An carried off the heavens, and Enlil the earth. Anu later retreated more and more into the background; he had an important temple in Uruk.

APSU: The Abyss; the primeval waters under the earth; in the later mythology of the *Enuma Elish,* more particularly the sweet water which mingled with the bitter waters of the sea and with a third watery element, perhaps cloud, from which the first gods were engendered. The waters of Apsu were thought of as held immobile underground by the 'spell' of *Ea* in a death-like sleep.

ARURU: A goddess of creation, she created *Enkidu* from clay in the image of *Anu.*

AYA: The dawn, the bride of the Sun God *Shamash.*

BELIT-SHERI: Scribe and recorder of the underworld gods.

BULL OF HEAVEN: A personification of drought created by *Anu* for *Ishtar.*

DILMUN: The Sumerian paradise, perhaps the Persian Gulf, sometimes described as 'the place where the sun rises' and 'the Land of the Living'; the scene of a Sumerian creation myth and the place where the deified Sumerian hero of the flood, Ziusudra, was taken by the gods to live for ever.

DUMUZI: The Sumerian form of *Tammuz;* a god of vegetation and fertility, and so of the underworld, also called 'the Shepherd' and 'lord of the sheepfolds'. As the companion of *Ningizzida* 'to all eternity' he stands at the gate of heaven. In the

Sumerian 'Descent of Inanna' he is the husband of the goddess Inanna, the Sumerian counterpart of *Ishtar.* According to the Sumerian King-List Gilgamesh was descended from 'Dumuzi a shepherd.'

EA: Sumerian Enki; god of the sweet waters, also of wisdom, a patron of arts and one of the creators of mankind, towards whom he is usually well-disposed. The chief god of Eridu, where he had a temple, he lived 'in the deep'; his ancestry is uncertain, but he was probably a child of *Anu.*

EANNA: The temple precinct in Uruk sacred to *Anu* and *Ishtar.*

EGALMAH: The 'Great Palace' in Uruk, the home of the goddess *Ninsun,* the mother of Gilgamesh.

ENDUKUGGA: With *Nindukugga,* Sumerian gods living in the underworld; parents of *Enlil.*

ENKIDU: Moulded by *Aruru,* goddess of creation, out of clay in the image and 'of the essence of *Anu,*' the sky-god, and of *Ninurta* the war-god. The companion of Gilgamesh, he is wild or natural man; he was later considered a patron or god of animals and may have been the hero of another cycle.

ENLIL: God of earth, wind, and the universal air, ultimately spirit; the executive of *Anu.* In the Sumerian cosmogony he was born of the union of An heaven, and *Ki* earth. These he separated, and he then carried off earth as his portion. In later times he supplanted *Anu* as chief god. He was the patron of the city of Nippur.

ENMUL: See *Endukugga.*

ENNUGI: God of irrigation and inspector of canals.

ENUMA ELISH: The Semitic creation epic which describes the creation of the gods, the defeat of the powers of chaos by the young god Marduk, and the creation of man from the blood of Kingu, the defeated champion of chaos. The title is taken from the first words of the epic 'When on high.'

ERESHKIGAL: The Queen of the underworld, a counterpart of Persephone; probably once a sky-goddess. In the Sumerian cosmogony she was carried off to the underworld after the separation of heaven and earth.

ETANA: Legendary king of Kish who reigned after the flood; in the epic which bears his name he was carried to heaven on the back of an eagle.

GILGAMESH: The hero of the Epic; son of the goddess *Ninsun* and of a priest of *Kullab,* fifth king of Uruk after the flood, famous as a great builder and as a judge of the dead. A cycle of epic poems has collected round his name.

HANISH: A divine herald of storm and bad weather.

HUMBABA: Also Huwawa; a guardian of the cedar forest who opposes Gilgamesh and is killed by him and *Enkidu.* A nature divinity, perhaps an Anatolian, Elamite, or Syrian god.

IGIGI: Collective name for the great gods of heaven.

IRKALLA: Another name for *Ereshkigal,* the Queen of the underworld.

ISHTAR: Sumerian Inanna; the goddess of love and fertility, also goddess of war, called the Queen of Heaven. She is the daughter of *Anu* and patroness of *Uruk,* where she has a temple.

ISHULLANA: The gardener of Anu, once loved by Ishtar whom he rejected;

he was turned by her into a mole or frog.

KI: The earth.

KULLAB: Part of *Uruk.*

LUGULBANDA: Third king of the post-diluvian dynasty of Uruk, a god and shepherd, and hero of a cycle of Sumerian poems; protector of Gilgamesh.

MAGAN: A land to the west of Mesopotamia, sometimes Egypt or Arabia, and sometimes the land of the dead, the underworld.

MAGILUM: Uncertain meaning, perhaps 'the boat of the dead.'

MAMMETUM: Ancestral goddess responsible for destinies.

MAN-SCORPION: Guardian, with a similar female monster, of the mountain into which the sun descends at nightfall. Shown on sealings and ivory inlays as a figure with the upper part of the body human and the lower part ending in a scorpion's tail. According to the *Enuma Elish* created by the primeval waters in order to fight the gods.

MASHU: The word means 'twins' in the Akkadian language. A mountain with twin peaks into which the sun descends at nightfall and from which it returns at dawn. Sometimes thought of as Lebanon and Anti-Lebanon.

NAMTAR: Fate, destiny in its evil aspect; pictured as a demon of the underworld, also a messenger and chief minister of *Ereshkigal;* a bringer of disease and pestilence.

NEDU: See *Neti.*

NERGAL: Underworld god, sometimes the husband of *Ereshkigal,* he is the subject of an Akkadian poem which describes his translation from heaven to the underworld; plague-god.

NETI: The Sumerian form of Nedu, the chief gate-keeper in the underworld.

NINDUKUGGA: With *Endukugga,* parental gods living in the underworld.

NINGAL: Wife of the Moon God and mother of the Sun.

NINGIRSU: An earlier form of *Ninurta;* god of irrigation and fertility, he had a field near Lagash where all sorts of plants flourished; he was the child of a she-goat.

NINGIZZIDA: Also Gizzida; a fertility god, addressed as 'Lord of the Tree of Life'; sometimes he is a serpent with human head, but later he was a god of healing and magic; the companion of *Tammuz,* with whom he stood at the gate of heaven.

NINHURSAG: Sumerian mother-goddess; one of the four principal Sumerian gods with An, *Enlil,* and Enki; sometimes the wife of Enki, she created all vegetation. The name means 'the Mother'; she is also called 'Nintu,' lady of birth, and *Ki,* the earth.

NINKI: The 'mother' of *Enlil,* probably a form of Ninhursag.

NINLIL: Goddess of heaven, earth, and air and in one aspect of the underworld; wife of *Enlil* and mother of the Moon; worshipped with Enlil in Nippur.

NINSUN: The mother of Gilgamesh, a minor goddess whose house was in Uruk; she was noted for wisdom, and was the wife of *Lugulbanda.*

NINURTA: The later form of *Ningirsu;* a warrior and god of war, a herald, the south wind, and god of wells and irrigation. According to one poem he once dammed up the bitter waters of the underworld and conquered various monsters.

NISABA: Goddess of grain.

NISIR: Probably means 'Mountain of Salvation'; sometimes identified with the Pir Oman Gudrun range south of the lower Zab, or with the biblical Ararat north of Lake Van.

PUZUR-AMURRI: The steersman of *Utnapishtim* during the flood.

SAMUQAN: God of cattle.

SEVEN SAGES: Wise men who brought civilization to the seven oldest cities of Mesopotamia.

SHAMASH: Sumerian Utu; the sun; for the Sumerians he was principally the judge and law-giver with some fertility attributes. For the Semites he was also a victorious warrior, the god of wisdom, the son of *Sin*, and 'greater than his father.' He was the husband and brother of *Ishtar.* He is represented with the saw with which he cuts decisions. In the poems 'Shamash' may mean the god, or simply the sun.

SHULLAT: A divine herald of storm and of bad weather.

SHULPAE: A god who presided over feasts and feasting.

SHURRUPAK: Modern Fara, eighteen miles north-west of Uruk; one of the oldest cities of Mesopotamia, and one of the five named by the Sumerians as having existed before the flood. The home of the hero of the flood story.

SIDURI: The divine wine-maker and brewer; she lives on the shore of the sea (perhaps the Mediterranean), in the garden of the sun. Her name in the Hurrian language means 'young woman' and she may be a form of *Ishtar.*

SILILI: The mother of the stallion; a divine mare?

SIN: Sumerian Nanna, the moon. The chief Sumerian astral deity, the father of Utu-*Shamash,* the sun, and of *Ishtar.* His parents were *Enlil* and *Ninlil.* His chief temple was in Ur.

TAMMUZ: Sumerian *Dumuzi;* the dying god of vegetation, bewailed by *Ishtar,* the subject of laments and litanies. In an Akkadian poem Ishtar descends to the underworld in search of her young husband Tammuz; but in the Sumerian poem on which this is based it is Inanna herself who is responsible for sending Dumuzi to the underworld because of his pride and as a hostage for her own safe return.

UBARA-TUTU: A king of *Shurrupak* and father of *Utnapishtim.* The only king of Kish named in the prediluvian King-List, apart from Utnapishtim.

URSHANABI: Old Babylonian Sursunabu; the boatman of *Utnapishtim* who ferries daily across the waters of death which divide the garden of the sun from the paradise where Utnapishtim lives for ever (the Sumerian *Dilmun*). By accepting Gilgamesh as a passenger he forfeits this right, and accompanies Gilgamesh back to Uruk instead.

URUK: Biblical Erech, modern Warka, in southern Babylonia between Fara (*Shurrupak*) and Ur. Shown by excavation to have been an important city from very early times, with great temples to the gods *Anu* and *Ishtar.* Traditionally the enemy of the city of Kish, and after the flood the seat of a dynasty of kings, among whom Gilgamesh was the fifth and most famous.

UTNAPISHTIM: Old Babylonian Utanapishtim, Sumerian Ziusudra; in the Sumerian poems he is a wise king and priest of *Shurrupak;* in the Akkadian sources he is a wise citizen of Shurrupak. He is the son of Ubara-Tutu, and his name is usually translated, 'He Who Saw Life.' He is the protégé of the god *Ea,* by whose connivance he survives the flood, with his family and with 'the seed of all living creatures'; afterwards he is taken by the gods to live for ever at 'the mouth of the rivers' and given the epithet 'Faraway'; or according to the Sumerians he lives in *Dilmun* where the sun rises.

## Appendix: Sources

The main sources for this version of the Epic have already been given. . . . Full bibliographies will be found in *Ancient Near Eastern Texts Relating to the Old Testament,* edited by James B. Pritchard, and *Gilgameš et sa légende,* Cahiers du Groupe François-Thureau-Dangin, and in the *Reallexikon der Assyriologie;* what follows here is a short note on the distribution of the material between the different tablets.

(i) The Sumerian poem 'Gilgamesh and the Land of the Living'; text from fourteen tablets found at Nippur, one at Kish, and two of unknown provenance, giving 175 lines extant. All date from the first half of the second millennium. The following incidents are covered: the friendship of the Lord Gilgamesh and his servant Enkidu, the need to set up a lasting name, entreaty of Utu (Shamash), who appoints supernatural helpers, arming of Gilgamesh and Enkidu, departure with fifty companions, felling of the cedar, Gilgamesh overcome with weakness, dusk on the mountain, dialogue with Enkidu, Huwawa (Humbaba) found in his house, Gilgamesh uproots trees, goes to the house of Huwawa who pleads for his life and is refused on the advice of Enkidu, Huwawa is killed and his body presented to a furious Enlil. Here the Sumerian text breaks off.

(ii) The Sumerian 'Death of Gilgamesh' is still very fragmentary and it is not clear what is its relation to the other Gilgamesh poems, and especially to 'Gilgamesh and the Land of the Living'. The text followed here is taken from the three tablets found at Nippur, dated to the first half of the second millennium. Two fragments, 'A' and 'B', give Enlil's 'Destiny' of Gilgamesh, and the lament for the dead king and account of the funeral offerings; but recently Professor Kramer has identified other fragments which indicate that the 'Death' was inscribed on a tablet with at least 450 lines.

(iii) Old Babylonian versions, dating from the first dynasty of Babylon, first half of the second millennium: the so-called 'Pennsylvania Tablet' gives the coming of Enkidu and the dreams of Gilgamesh concerning him. The 'Yale Tablet' has the preparation for the forest journey up to the departure from Uruk. The 'Meissner' fragment, from Sippar, gives the Siduri episode and the meeting with the ferryman Sursunabu (Urshanabi). An independent publication of the Old Babylonian material was made by M. Jastrow and A.T. Clay in 1920 as *An Old Babylonian Version of the Epic of Gilgamesh.* Recently another Old Babylonian fragment from Tell Iščali has been published by T. Bauer (see now *Ancient Near Eastern Texts referring to the Old Testament*). It deals with the death of Humbaba and does not differ from the Sumerian account so much as do the later Akkadian versions. From the Ur tablets in the British Museum (UET VI), we now have a slightly fuller Middle Babylonian version of Enkidu's sickness: C.J. Gadd, *Iraq,* 28, 1966, 105–21 and Old Babylonian fragments (published by A.R. Millard, *Iraq,* 26, 1964, 99) provide some additions to Tablet IX.

(iv) Hittite version, from tablets found at Boghazköy in central Anatolia, dated to the middle of the second millennium; these contain fragments of the description of Gilgamesh and of his endowments, the forest episode with the felling of the cedar, Enkidu's dream when he is sick and dying, and part of the journey to find Utnapishtim with the Siduri incident and the meeting with Urshanabi. From this point the story appears to diverge widely from other versions. The translation was published by J. Friedrich in the *Zeitschrift für Assyriologie,* 39, 1929, and H. Otten, *Instanbuler Mitteilungen* 8, 1958, 93–125. Another fragment from the Hittite tablets from Boghazköy (KUB VIII, 48, 1924) published now by R. Stefanini, *Journal of Near Eastern Studies,* 28, 1968, gives a slightly different version of the Council of Gods in Enkidu's deathbed dream.

(v) A Hurrian language fragment, also from Boghazköy, gives part of the journey to Utnapishtim. It was published in the *Zeitschrift für Assyriologie,* 35, 1923.

(vi) Semitic versions. An Akkadian version was used in the Hittite Empire and fragments have been found at Boghazköy; but the fullest of all versions is the Assyrian. Originally it was written on twelve tablets of six columns and approximately three hundred lines to each tablet; parts of all twelve still exist. Nearly all are from the palace library at Nineveh, and are seventh century B.C. Based on earlier material, these cover all the incidents of the story up to the return from the search for Utnapishtim. The material is divided as follows: Tablet I, the descriptions of Gilgamesh and of Enkidu up to the end of Gilgamesh's second dream concerning Enkidu. Tablet II, very fragmentary, probably covered the encounter of Gilgamesh and Enkidu and the first mention of the cedar forest. Tablet III, also very fragmentary, probably has Gilgamesh's interviews with the counsellors, with Ninsun, and the commission to Enkidu. Tablet IV, of which only a few lines survive, probably covered the journey to the forest and the arrival at the gate. Tablet V had the description of the forest, the dreams on the mountain, and probably the meeting with and killing of Humbaba. Tablet VI had the encounter of Gilgamesh and Ishtar, the incident of the Bull of Heaven, and the beginning of Enkidu's sickness. Tablet VII had Enkidu's sickness continued, his dreams and death. Tablet VIII had the lament over Enkidu and probably a description of the funeral. Tablet IX covers Gilgamesh's journey to find Utnapishtim up to the meeting with Siduri. Tablet X covers the Siduri incident, Urshanabi, and the finding of Utnapishtim. Tablet XI is the fullest and best preserved of all, with over three hundred extant lines. It describes the Deluge, the testings of Gilgamesh, and his return to Uruk. There is no death of Gilgamesh in the Assyrian recension, and the twelfth and last tablet recounts a separate incident, an alternative to the death of Enkidu as recounted in Tablet VII. Tablet XII is a direct translation from a Sumerian original, which has also survived in part. The relationship between the two has been discussed by Prof. Kramer in the *Journal of the American Oriental Society*, 64, 1944; and by several writers, especially L. Matouš in *Gilgameš et sa légende.*

(vii) The Sultantepe Akkadian fragment. This was excavated by Mr Seton Lloyd and Bay Nuri Gökçe in 1951. Two one-column tablets were found, one a fragment with Enkidu's sickness, and the other with Gilgamesh's lament over Enkidu; and probably also a description of the funeral, and the statue of Enkidu raised by Gilgamesh. Although very short, both fragments fill gaps in the Nineveh recension from which they differ slightly, and Dr Gurney, who has published them in the *Journal of Cuneiform Studies,* 8, 1954, and *Anatolian Studies,* II, 1952, thinks they are schoolboys' work with characteristic mistakes.

## Poetry of Ancient Egypt (1900–1090 BCE)

Ancient Egypt had a continuous literary tradition for more than two thousand years, using hieroglyphs right into the fourth century CE. Scholars have recently discovered that most Egyptian literature is written in verse, and like other ancient literature it is primarily religious in orientation. Ancient cultures saw the world as permeated by the sacred.

Ancient Egyptian verse is dominated by the couplet form, each couplet comprising a verse sentence. Couplets could be combined into triplets and quatrains, but the basic unit remained a two-line sentence. Egyptian poets often engaged in wordplay, used much imagery, and employed sound repetition as a unifying device. Because they did not write vowel sounds, however, and because their language is no longer spoken, we cannot recover the sound of their poetry.

The Egyptian literary works that have survived in carvings on monuments, paintings in tombs and on funerary objects, and on papyrus scrolls lack the grandiose scope of Mesopotamian works like *The Epic of Gilgamesh.* Nevertheless, many narratives of a more modest character have come down to us. They are more like folk tales or short stories, sometimes with a ritualistic quality that implies a relationship to religious or philosophical practices. *The Tale of the Shipwrecked Sailor* has an interesting framed structure that shows that narrative techniques often regarded as modern are actually very ancient.

Religious hymns are numerous among Egyptian literary remains. Perhaps the best known is the *Hymn to the Sun* by the Pharoah Akhenaton (c. 1375 BCE), which reflects Akhenaton's radical effort to make the sun god Aton (or Aten) the sole deity, replacing the traditional polytheistic pantheon of Egyptian religion.

Egyptian love poetry takes the form of short lyrics of amazingly fresh and seemingly modern tone. These poems are often presented as dialogues between a girl and a boy, expressing longing, eagerness to be together, and delight in the beloved's beauty. The poetry is remarkably secular and personal when compared with the Sumerian courtship poems involving Inanna and Dumuzi from the same general time period. Common themes of Egyptian love poetry often recur in later lyrics of the Eastern Mediterranean area—for example in Hebrew and Arabic poems about lovers parting at daybreak, a young woman daring to seek out her love in public, or a young man frustrated by a closed door.

# Egyptian Writing System

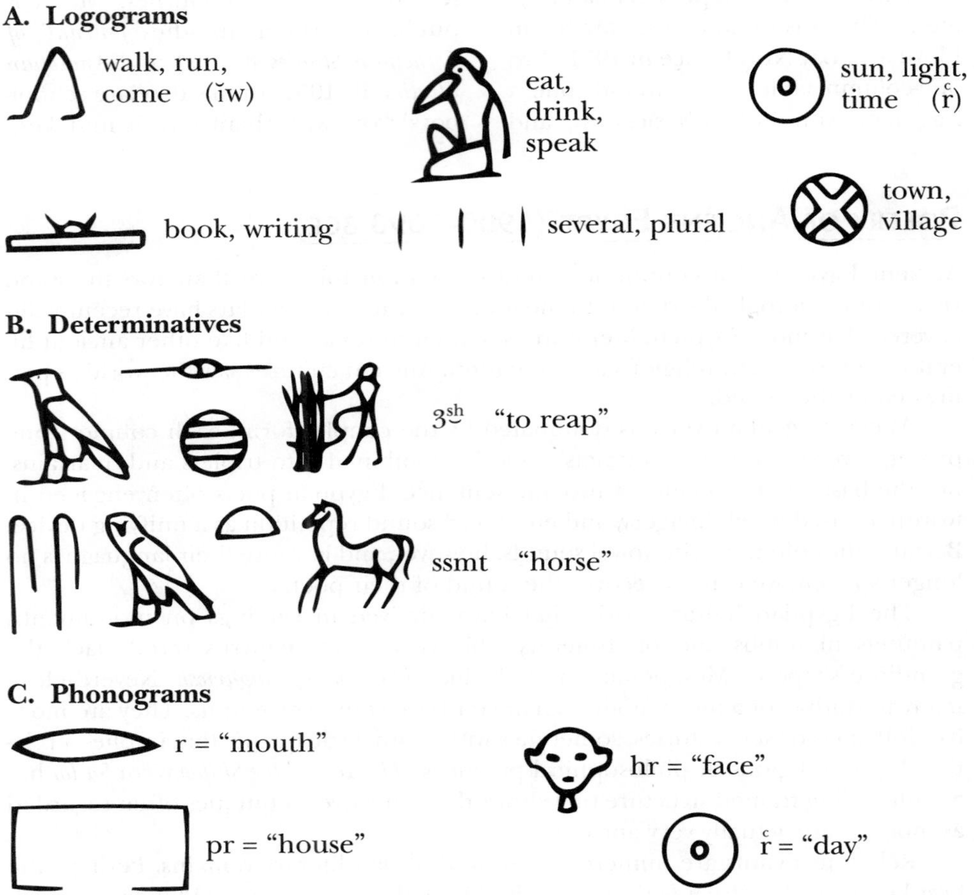


The Egyptian writing system contains three main types of signs, each serving a different purpose. The first is the *logogram,* which equals a complete word. The second is the *determinative,* which helps to indicate a word's precise meaning. The third is the *phonogram,* which represents a sound. The hieroglyphic script was more than just a writing system, because the Egyptians thought of it as the "divine words" closely related to art. Both were considered sacred and magical.

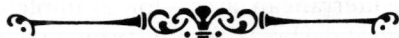

## *from Hymn to the Sun*

*Translated by John A. Wilson*

When thou settest in the western horizon,
    The land is in darkness as if in death.
Men sleep in a room with heads wrapped up,
    And no eye sees another.
Though all their goods under their heads be stolen,
    Yet would they not perceive it.
Every lion comes forth from his den,
    And all creeping things sting.
Darkness is a shroud and the earth is still,
    For he who made them rests in his horizon.

At daybreak, when thou risest on the horizon,
    When thou shinest as the sun disk by day,
Thou drivest away darkness and givest thy rays;
    Then the Two Lands are in daily festivity:
Men awake and stand upon their feet,
    For thou hast raised them up.
They wash their bodies and take their clothing,
    Their arms raised in praise at thy appearing.
And all the world, they do their work. . . .

How manifold it is,
    What thou hast made!
    It is hidden from the face of man.
Thou sole god, without thy like,
    Thou didst create the world after thy desire,
    Whilst thou wert alone:
All mankind, cattle and wild beasts,
    Whatever goes by foot upon the earth,
    Whatever flies on high with wings. . . .

The world came into being by thy hand,
    According as thou didst make them all.
When thou hast risen they live,
    When thou settest then they die.
Thou art lifetime thy own self,
    For we live only through thee.
Eyes are fixed on beauty until thou settest,
    All work is laid aside when thou settest in the west.
But when thou risest again,
    Then everything is made to flourish. . . .

## *The Tale of the Shipwrecked Sailor*

*Translated by John L. Foster*

Be hale of heart, my leader!
    Look, we have come through!
The mallet has been taken, the mooring peg struck in,
    the forward rope secured upon the land;
Thanksgiving has been offered, god is praised,
    each man embraces his companion.
Your crew has come back safely,
    there are no losses to our expedition
Though we traversed the northern marches of Wawat
    and skirted Senmut fortress.
Just look at us, we are successfully returned—
    this is our country; we are home!

Now, hear me out, my leader;
    I am a man who never stretches truth:
Purify yourself, pour water on your fingers!
    Thereafter you can answer what is put to you
That you address the King staunch-hearted,
    responding with no hesitation.
The mouth of a man can save him;
    speech can soften an angry face. . . .

        —Well, never mind.
You do whatever in the world you want, then;
        it gets to be a bother, talking to you!

But let me tell you just a little story, a bit like this,
    which happened once upon a time to me.
I was traveling to the region of the royal mines
    and had descended to the Great Green Sea
In a grand two-hundred-foot-long vessel
    (its width was seventy feet from rail to rail),
The crew within it, one hundred twenty
    of the finest men in Egypt:
Let them see only sky, let them see land,
    braver were their hearts than lions;
They could foretell a storm before its coming,
    foul weather before ever it occurred.

A storm came up—with us on the open sea—
    and no chance for us to reach harbor;

The wind grew sharp and made a constant moaning,
and there were hungry fourteen-foot-high waves!
A piece of wood of some sort hit me,
and then the ship was dead.
Of all those fine men, not a one survived.

Then I was carried to a desert island
by a swell of the Great Green Sea.
I spent three days alone,
my heart my sole companion;
I nested in the shelter of a covering tree
and hugged the shadows.
Finally, I stretched my legs
in order to discover what to eat;
And I found figs and grapes there
and every sort of tasty greens,
And sycamore figs, and notched figs,
and cucumbers that looked cared for,
And fish, and birds—
there was nothing that that island did not have!
Then I filled myself past satisfaction,
spilling and dropping the abundance in my arms.
I shaped a fire drill, and made a fire,
and gave burnt offering to the gods.

Then I heard a sound as of approaching storm,
and I assumed it was another Great Green Sea wave—
trees were breaking, ground was quaking—
I bared my face
and found it was a serpent coming my way:
The thing was over fifty huge feet long!
its beard hung down a yard,
Its flesh was gilt,
its eyebrows lapis lazuli;
and it reared up in front.

It bared its mouth at me—
I lying prone in fear and trembling—
and spoke:
"What brings you? brings you?
Little man, what brings you?
If you delay to tell me
what brings you to this isle,
I promise that you shortly shall be ashes—
become like something that has never been."

"Though you just spoke to me,
I am not all quite here to hear it;
I am, I know, before you
but hardly know myself."

Then he put me in his mouth
and took me to his place of residence
And set me down again without ill-treatment:
I still was whole—no bites were out of me.
He bared his mouth once more,
I on my belly on the ground before him,
and said:
"What brings you? brings you?
Little man, what brings you
To this island of the Great Green Sea
with shores as changing as the shifty waves?"

This time I told him all about it,
my arms raised humbly in his presence,
saying:
"I was traveling to the region of the royal mines
on an errand of the King
In a grand two-hundred-foot-long vessel
(its width was seventy feet from rail to rail),
The crew within it, one hundred twenty
of the finest men in Egypt:
Let them see only sky, let them see land,
braver were their hearts than lions;
They could foretell a storm before its coming,
foul weather before ever it occurred.
Each in his heart was steadier,
his arm more powerful, than his companion—
there was no sluggard in the lot!

"A storm came up—with us on the open sea—
and no chance for us to reach harbor;
The wind grew sharp and made a constant moaning,
and there were hungry fourteen-foot-high waves!
A piece of wood of some sort hit me,
and then the ship was dead.
Of those fine men, not one survived, except for me—
see, down here, beside you.
Then I was carried to this desert island
by a swell of the Great Green Sea."

Then he said to me,
"Fear not, fear not!
My little man, you must not pale your face so—
you have reached me!
Look, God has let you live
that he might bring you to this phantom isle.
There is nothing that it does not have,
it is full of every fine and lovely thing!

"Now, you are going to spend one month, and then another,
until you finish four months on this island.
Then a ship will come from Egypt
with sailors in it whom you know
That you may go with them toward home
and die in your own city.
What joy for one who lives to tell the things he has been through
when the suffering is over!

"But let me tell you just a little story, a bit like yours,
which happened on this very isle while I was here
living with companions and my children
in one great extended family.
We totaled five and seventy persons,
consisting of my offspring, relatives, and friends
(I cannot bear to dwell on a small daughter
brought to me through prayer):

"A star fell
and they were gone, gone up in flame.
It happened when I could not be there . . . all burned . . .
and I not even with them.
I wanted to be dead instead of them
after finding them a heap of tangled corpses.

"If you have courage, steel your heart
that you may fill your arms with children,
And kiss your wife,
and see your home.
Believe me, it is better than all else
when you are back again
and dwell within the bosom of your friends."

Now I was lying stretched out on the ground,
and I touched head to earth before him in respect:

"Let me say something to you:
let me chronicle your glories for my King,
cause him to be acquainted with your highness;
Let me arrange to have them bring you precious ointments,
balsam, spices, perfumes, sacred oils,
The finest temple incense
that thrills the nostrils of each god;
Let me relate all that has happened to me
as well as what I know at first hand of your power
So they may properly praise God for your existence
before the courts and councils of the Land;
Let me kill bulls to burn as offerings to you
and wring the necks of birds;
Let me have them bring the fleet
heaped with the fabled wealth of Egypt—
As one does for any god much loved by men
who lives in a far country dimly known."

He laughed at me for what I told him—
wrongly, to his way of thinking—
saying:
"Yours is no great supply of myrrh
though it happens you have incense;
Why, I myself rule Punt,
the myrrh from there is mine.
And that poor sacred oil you spoke of bringing—
it is the main thing on this island!
Now, you in due time will remove from here
nevermore to see my island
which shall turn to trackless sea."

At last the ship arrived
just as he had foretold.
I climbed a lofty tree
and recognized the sailors in the ship
And went running to report it,
but he already knew.

Then he said to me,
"Fare well, fare well, my little man, off to your home
to see your children.
Make my name a proverb in your city;
my reputation rests with you."

I placed myself upon the ground,
my arms raised gratefully to him.

Then he collected me a cargo
of myrrh, the sacred oil, perfumes, spices,
*Tishepes*-spices, kohl, Punt perfume, giraffe tails,
great lumps of incense, elephant tusks,
Hounds, long- and short-tailed monkeys, and every helpful thing;
and I loaded all of it onto the ship.
I placed myself upon the ground again
giving praise to God for him.

Then he said to me,
"You shall reach your native land in two months time
To fill your arms with children
and grow young again at home until you die."
Then I descended to the shore near where the ship was.
I hailed the crew
And offered thanks beside the sea to the Lord of the Isle;
and those on board did likewise.

It was a voyage that we then made northwards
toward the royal city of the King;
And we arrived home after two months,
just as he had said.
Then I entered to my Sovereign
and presented him these gifts
which I had fetched him from the island.
He offered thanks to God for my existence
before the courts and councils of the Land;
And I was made a royal Follower
and given two hundred servants.
Just look at me, once I touched land!
and after seeing all that I had seen!

Now, let what I have told sink in, my leader—
you know, things people say can help you!"

Then he replied,
"Don't try to play the expert, friend.
Does one give water to a sacrificial bird
the morning of its execution day?"

# *The Debate Between a Man Tired of Life and His Soul*

*Translated by John L. Foster*

*[The beginning of this poem from 2000–1800 BCE is lost, but in the surviving fragment, the soul counsels a dispirited man who is in some ways similar to Job of the Hebrew scriptures.]*

## I

"The tongues of the gods, they do not speak amiss,
they make no special cases."

## II

*I opened my mouth to my soul*
*that I might answer what it had said:*

"This is more than I can bear just now!
—my soul could find no time for me!
It is beyond belief
—as if I should hesitate to do the deed!
Let my soul not disappear like this, not flutter off,
but let it take its stand beside me—
Or never shall it have the chance
to wrap my person in its stifling bonds;
And for all its twitter, never
shall it escape the Day of Reckoning.

"O all you gods,
see how my soul defames me!
I will not listen to it ever
as I drag my way toward dissolution;
For it will not help me do the death by fire—
myself the victim, who shall no more suffer.

"Let it be near me on the Day of Reckoning!
Let it stand tall on that side yonder
as one who shares my joy!
Yet this the very soul that rushes off, it vanishes,
to separate itself from death.
My foolish soul is going to ease the pains of living, is it?
Keep me from death until I come to it by nature?

"No! make the West sweet for me now!
Is there not pain and suffering enough?

—That is the stuff of life: a troubled journey, a circuit of the sun;
even the trees decay and fall.

"O tread you down upon injustice,
end my helplessness!
Judge me, O Thoth, you who can soothe the gods;
defend, O Khonsu, me, a teller of the truth;
Hear, O Re, my speaking, you who command the skyship;
defend me, O Anubis, in the holy hall of judgment—
Because my need is heavy in the scale,
and it has raised the pan of sweetness out of reach.
Preserve, O gods, the quiet center of my being!"

## III

*What my soul said to me:*

"You are no man at all!
Are you even alive?
How full you are of your complaints of life
like a man of means preaching to passersby!
Things sink down to ruin. Well, save yourself by getting up!
There are no bonds on you as of some prisoner whining,
'I shall get even with you:
and you, your name shall die!
Life! That is the place of fluttering down,
heart's own desire, the district of the West
. . . after a troubled crossing.'"

## IV

*[I continued:]*

"If my soul, my foolish brother, would only listen,
its wish would be like mine;
And it would perch most blest at my right hand,
reaching the West like one who has a pyramid
towering for after-generations over his grave.

"And I would wave the sacred fan above your listless form
that you attract another soul to join you, weary one;
And I would wave the fan again, then say the spell,
so you might lure a different, fiery soul;
I would find drink from inshore eddies, raise up food,
beguile some other hungry soul to stay with you.
But if you keep me back from death this way,
I promise you no peace in the West forever!

"Be still, my soul, my brother,
  until a successor comes with offerings
To stand at the tomb on burial day
  and deck a bed in the city of God."

## V

*Then my soul opened its mouth to me*
  *that it might answer what I had said:*

"Your graveyard thoughts bring sadness to the heart,
  and tears, feeding our misery;
That is what shovels a man into his house
  dug in the rock on the high hill:
There, there is no more coming forth for you
  to see the sunny days,
Or workmen crafting their buildings in granite,
  putting last touches on pyramids,
Or the beauties of the monuments,
  or where builders fashion altars for the gods:
You are emptied and drear, like those without motion
  dead on the riverbank, no one caring:
Water laps at their backs,
  the sun does its work,
    and, lips in the current, fish whisper to them.

"Now listen to me—
  pay some attention to what people say:
    Spend your days happily! Forget your troubles!

"There was a man, and he farmed his plot of land;
  and he was loading his harvest into a ship
    for the voyage to his accounting, which drew near.
And he saw coming a night of wind and weather
  so that he was watchful of the ship, waiting for day,
While he dreamed of life with his wife and children
  who had perished on the Lake of Death
    on a dark night, with crocodiles.
And after he was pondering there some time,
  he shaped the silence into words, saying,
'I have not wept that mother yonder—
  for her there is no returning from the West,
    no more than any who have lived on earth.
But let me mourn the children, killed in her womb,
  who saw the face of Death ere ever they were born.'

"There was another man, and he wanted his evening meat;
and there was his wife, saying,
'There will be bread.'
And he went outdoors to fume awhile
and then go back inside
Behaving like a better person
(his wife was wise to his ways).
Yet he never really listened to her,
so the death demons came and carried him off."

## VI

*I opened my mouth to my soul*
*that I might answer what it had said:*

### i

"How my name stinks because of you
more than the stink of bird dung on a summer's day
under a burning sky.
How my name stinks because of you
more than the catch of fish on a good angling day
under a burning sky.
How my name stinks because of you
more than the stench of marsh birds on the hummocks
filthy with waterfowl.
How my name stinks because of you
more than the fishermen's smell at runnels of swamps
after they have been fishing.
How my name stinks because of you
more than the reek of crocodiles sunning on sandbanks
alive with their crocodile kind.
How my name stinks because of you
more than the wife about whom lies
are told to her wedded husband.
How my name stinks because of you
more than the able youth of whom they falsely say
that he is prisoner of everything he should despise.
How my name stinks because of you
more than the crocodile's cove, where the fool taunts him
careful his back is turned.

### ii

"Who is there to talk to today?
Brothers are evil;
the friends of today, they do not love us.

Who is there to talk to today?
    Hearts are rapacious;
        each man covets his neighbor's goods.
Who is there to talk to today?
    Gentleness is dead;
        brute strength bears down on everyone.
Who is there to talk to today?
    Men are proud of the evil they do;
        good everywhere falls defeated.
Who is there to talk to today?
    A man is maddened by evil fortune;
        the sad injustice moves all to laughter.
Who is there to talk to today?
    Robbery, plundering;
        each man a predator on his companion.
Who is there to talk to today?
    The malefactor masks as best friend;
        the trusted brother turns into an enemy.
Who is there to talk to today?
    There is no thought for tradition;
        no one nurturing decency these days.
Who is there to talk to today?
    Brother betray;
        they take to strangers, not men of integrity.
Who is there to talk to today?
    Faces are wiped out;
        each, high or low, fighting all others.
Who is there to talk to today?
    Hearts are selfish and slick;
        no heart to lean on.
Who is there to talk to today?
    There are no righteous men;
        earth is abandoned to evil.
Who is there to talk to today?
    Emptiness in trusted friends;
        blind ignorance to life that brings wisdom.
Who is there to talk to today?
    No man of satisfied mind;
        one to walk quietly with does not exist.
Who is there to talk to today?
    I am bowed too low with my misery
        lacking someone to share the thoughts in my heart.
Who is there to talk to today?
    Wrongdoing beats on the earth,
        and of it there is no end.

iii

"So death is before me now—
the healthy state of sick man—
like coming out in the air after suffering.
So death is before me now
like the fragrance of myrrh
or sailing at ease on a breezy day.
So death is before me now
like aroma of flowers,
like being drunk in a promised land.
So death is before me now
like the breath of a new Inundation,
like coming home from a long expedition.
So death is before me now
like a clearing sky,
like understanding what perplexed us before.
So death is before me now
like one longing to see his home
after long years in prison.

iv

"But to be one who is over there
with living God
fighting evil for Him who made him!
But to be one who is over there
erect in the skyship
offering choice gifts to the temples!
But to be one who is over there!
One who finally, perfectly knows!
And he shall never be kept from approaching great God
whenever he would speak!"

## VII

*What my soul said to me:*

"Put your murmuring aside now.

"O you who belong to me, my brother,
must you be sacrificed upon the flaming altar?
Friend, fight on the side of life!
Say to me, 'Love me *here!*'
Put thoughts of the West behind you!
Love! yes, love, indeed,
So that you may in due time reach the West,
may touch your body gently to the earth;

And I shall flutter down beside you
    when you are weary of the world at last.
        Then shall we two be fellow citizens together."

## *The Song of the Harper*

*Translated by John A. Wilson*

Generations pass away and others remain
    Since the time of the forefathers.
The gods who lived of old rest in their pyramids,
    As also the blessed dead, buried in their pyramids.
And men who once built houses—
    Their places are no more.
    See what has become of them!
I have heard the words of Imhotep and Hordedef,
    Those whose sayings men repeat so much—
    But what are their places now?
Their walls are crumbled down,
    And their places are no more,
    As though they had never been!

There is none who returns from over there,
    That he may tell us how they fare,
    That he may tell us what they need,
That he may still our hearts,
    Until we too travel to the place where they have gone.

So give your desires free play,
    To let your heart forget the funeral rites for you,
    And follow your desire as long as you live.
Put myrrh upon your head
    And don clothing of fine linen.
    Be anointed with true marvels of god's gift.
Give increase to the good things of yours,
    Nor let your heart be weary,
    Follow your desire and your good.
Fulfill your needs upon earth
    After the command of your heart,
    Until there come for you that day of mourning.
The Weary of Heart will not hear their lamentation,
    Nor does wailing save a man's heart from the underworld.

Make holiday, and do not lag therein—
See, no man can take his property with him!
See, none who departs comes back again!

## Selected Love Poems

### *"The voice of the swallow"*

*Translated by John A. Wilson*

The voice of the swallow speaks and says:
    "Day is breaking—where will you go?"
O bird, you shall not distract me,
    For I have found my loved one in his bed,
And my heart is more than glad
    When he said to me:
"I shall not go afar off,
    But my hand is in your hand,
And I shall stroll about,
    Being with you in every pleasant place."
So he makes me the foremost of maidens,
    And he injures not my heart.

### *"The little sycamore"*

*Translated by William Kelly Simpson*

The little sycamore,
which she planted with her hand,
sends forth its words to speak.

The flowers [of its stalks]
[are like] an inundation of honey;
beautiful it is, and its branches shine
more verdant [than the grass].

It is laden with the ripeness of notched figs,
redder than carnelian,
like turquoise its leaves,
like glass its bark.

Its wood is like the color of green feldspar,
its sap like the *besbes* opiate;
it brings near whoever is not under it,
for its shade cools the breeze.

It sends a message by the hand of a girl,
the gardener's daughter;
it makes her hurry to the lady love:
come, spend a minute among the maidens.

The country celebrates its day.
Below me is an arbor and a hideaway;
my gardeners are joyful
like children at the sight of you.

Send your servants ahead of you
supplied with their cooking gear;
I am heady when hastening to you
without having a drink.

These servants of yours
come with their stuffs,
bringing beer of every sort,
all kinds of kneaded dough for beer,
heady wine of yesterday and today,
all kinds of fruit for enjoyment.

Come spend the day happily,
tomorrow and the day after tomorrow, for three days,
seated in my shade,

Her friend is on her right.
She gets him drunk
while doing what he says;
and the wine cellar is disordered in drunkenness,
as she stays with her lover.

She has ample room beneath me,
the lady love as she paces;
I am discreet
and will not say that I have seen their discourse.

## *"Lover excites my desire with his voice"*

*Translated by William Kelly Simpson*

Lover excites my desire with his voice,
he gets a sickness to seize me,
for though he is a neighbor to my mother's house,
I know not how to go to him.
Is my mother good to restrict me so?
Leave off seeing her!

My heart is troubled whenever he is thought of:
his love possesses me.

See, he is mindless,
yet I am like him.

He does not know my lust to embrace him,
or that he could write my mother.
Lover, I am given over to you
by the Golden Goddess of womankind.

Come to me that I can see your perfection;
my father and my mother will be glad.
All men with one accord rejoice for you,
rejoice they for you, Lover.

## *"I passed by the precinct of his house"*

*Translated by William Kelly Simpson*

I passed by the precinct of his house,
I found his door ajar,
the lover standing by his mother,
with him his brothers and sisters.

Love of him captures the heart
of all who walk the road.
Handsome guy, no one like him,
a lover of perfect taste.

He stares me out when I walk by,
and all alone I cry for joy;
how happy in my delight
with the lover in my sight.

If only mother knew my wish,
she would have gone inside by now.
O, Golden Goddess, place him in her heart too,
then I'll rush off to the lover.

I'll kiss him in front of his crowd,
I'll not be ashamed because of the women.
But I'll be happy at their finding out
that you know me this well.

I'll make festivals for my Goddess,
my heart trembles to come forth,
and to let me look over the lover tonight.
How happy, how happy is this passing by.

## *"Seven days have passed"*

*Translated by William Kelly Simpson*

Seven days have passed, and I've not seen my lady love;
a sickness has shot through me.
I have become sluggish,
I have forgotten my own body.

If the best surgeons come to me,
my heart will not be comforted with their remedies.
And the prescription sellers, there's no help through them;
my sickness will not be cut out.

Telling me "she's come" is what will bring me back to life.
It's only her name which will raise me up.
It's the coming and going of her letters
which will bring my heart to life.

To me the lady love is more remedial than any potion;
she's better than the whole Compendium.
My only salvation is her coming inside.
Seeing her, then I'm well.

When she opens her eyes my body is young,
when she speaks I'll grow strong,
when I embrace her she drives off evil from me.
But by now the days of her absence amount to Seven.

## *"Please come quick"*

*Translated by William Kelly Simpson*

Please come quick to the lady love
like a gazelle
running in the desert
its feet are wounded
its limbs are exhausted
fear penetrates its body

the hunters are after it
the hounds are with them
they cannot see
because of the dust

its sees its rest place like a ⌜mirage⌝
it takes a canal as its road.

Before you have kissed your hand four times,
you shall have reached her hideaway
as you chase the lady love.

For it is the Golden Goddess
who has set her aside for you, friend.

## *"How well the lady knows to cast the noose"*

*Translated by William Kelly Simpson*

How well the lady knows to cast the noose
yet still escape the cattle tax.

With her hair she throws lassoes at me,
with her eyes she catches me,
with her necklace entangles me
and with her seal ring brands me.

## *"See what the lady has done to me!"*

*Translated by William Kelly Simpson*

See what the lady has done to me!
Faugh! Shall I keep silent for her sake?

She made me stand at the door of her house
while she went inside.
She didn't say to me, come in, young man,
but deaf to me remained tonight.

# The Hebrew Bible

The power exerted by the Hebrew Bible and the Christian New Testament over the millennia can hardly be exaggerated. The three world religions rooted in the Bible—Judaism, Christianity, and Islam—today embody the cultural values of more than half of humanity. It should not be surprising, then, that the literary qualities of the Bible are extraordinary. Over the centuries, interpreting the Bible has been the lifetime work of some of the world's greatest scholars. The delight and inspiration that the Bible has also brought to millions of ordinary readers is due in part to its great poetry and exciting narratives, its dazzling styles and literary techniques, the influence of which is seen in the literatures of later centuries, especially in Europe, the Americas, and the Islamic world.

The Hebrew Bible (called by Christians the "Old Testament") consists of hundreds of documents compiled by the Jewish people over the course of the first millennium BCE. In some ways it is a literary anthology: it contains myths, legends and folktales, a heroic epic, laws, historical narratives and romances, philosophy and ethical literature, political allegories, preaching and social commentaries, love lyrics, hymns, and much more. It is first of all a book of the Jewish religion, but much of it is surprisingly secular. In the portions included here, for example, God plays no explicit role in the beautiful stories of Joseph or Ruth, or in the love lyrics of The Song of Songs; Job and Ecclesiastes seem almost antireligious in their skepticism.

Early in their history the Jews distinguished themselves from their cultural neighbors in the ancient Middle East by not having kings and by refusing to worship images of gods in temples. Instead, they believed in only one god, who is transcendent (i.e., exists beyond the earthly world) and cannot be represented, and who governs the people in place of a king. A single god living nowhere in particular may seem like a simple idea to us and highly appropriate for a nomadic people always on the move, but the concept of a hidden unity behind the multiplicity of experience was unique in the world of ancient religion and has had far-reaching consequences for religious thought. Centuries later that concept was inherited by Christianity and blended with Greek philosophy to form the foundation of Western religion. A similar development was seen in the East, where the underlying unity of the world first expounded in the Vedic literature of India was absorbed by Buddhism and became a guiding principle of Eastern religious thought.

The legends of Genesis occasionally imagine God as appearing to human beings, and even as having a remarkably human personality; after his appearance to Moses on Mount Sinai, however, God operates more remotely as a hidden principle of history itself. The physical symbol of this transcendent, unrepresentable god was an empty throne (the "ark of the covenant"), which the Jewish people carried from place to place for centuries. Around the year 1020 BCE, the Jews, up till then a loosely knit group of twelve tribes, joined together to overthrow the Canaanites and found the kingdom of Israel. Their second king was David, who brought the ark to Jerusalem, where his son Solomon built a temple for it. From the very beginning of the kingdom, however, the priesthood and later the prophets were sharply critical of state power. The kings of Israel were nothing like the god-kings of Egypt and Mesopotamia.

The earliest biblical narratives were written as these profound changes were overtaking Jewish tradition. The transition from a pastoral culture to a settled urban civilization (which resembled the life of their Mesopotamian neighbors in many ways) was deeply traumatic to the people of Israel and produced a historical literature that openly explored some of the most fundamental questions of ancient society, such as the nature of kingship and power, the relation of religion to the state, and the necessary constraints upon individual desire that are required for a civilized life.

Whereas other ancient cultures told myths about their gods (as in The Descent of Inanna), the Jews wrote "sacred history," in which God manifests himself in the patterns of historical events. This history begins in Genesis with the familiar stories of Adam and Eve, Cain and Abel, the Tower of Babel, and Noah and the Flood—legends of the origins of all humanity. Though today these are among the best-known biblical stories, they are virtually never referred to in the rest of the Hebrew Bible, indicating perhaps that they were not considered historical in the same sense as that which follows them.

A careful reading of Genesis, with its repetitions, variations, and inconsistencies, reveals that it is woven of several literary strands written at different times for different purposes. One example is the two versions of the Creation, first the account of the seven days and then the story of Adam and Eve. The styles, themes, and the depictions of God in these two accounts could hardly be more different. The first is highly formal and abstract and builds to an explanation of the ritual observance of the Sabbath; the second is a charming tale about good and evil in which God appears in quite human form. In the first, animals are created on the fifth day, man and woman on the sixth; in the second, God first creates man, then animals, then woman. Complications like these arise from the composite nature of the biblical text and make biblical interpretation extremely complex and controversial. The very concept of "literary criticism" was born in the so-called "higher criticism" of the Bible during the nineteenth century.

With the stories of the patriarchs Abraham, Isaac, and Jacob, the particular history of the Jewish people begins. Offshoots of the family tree give birth to neighboring cultures, most of them traditional enemies of Israel. The stories of wives and concubines, half-sons and rejected brothers, not only brilliantly depict the ancient patriarchal family in all its fierce complexity, but also are political allegories of the peoples of the ancient Middle East. The twelve tribes of Israel are said to descend from the twelve sons of a single ancestor, Jacob (or Israel). The story of Joseph and his eleven brothers, a unified romance with beautifully conceived characters, also portrays the complex relations among the twelve tribes of Israel at the time of its writing centuries later.

Although Abraham, Isaac, and Jacob inhabit the land that would one day become Israel, the story of Joseph explains how the tribes came to invade and conquer the land after escaping from slavery in Egypt. Their liberation from slavery and return to their homeland under Moses, and the land's reconquest under Joshua, is a heroic epic of national origins. The story became a model of history for the ancient Jews and retains its original power today. Not only is it fundamental to the origins of the modern state of Israel, but it has a universal resonance; when Martin Luther King cried "Let my people go!" he was invoking Exodus as the epic of oppressed peoples everywhere.

The unified kingdom of Israel under David and Solomon lasted less than a century, then divided. The later books of the Hebrew Bible are best understood in light of the fates of these two kingdoms. The northern kingdom was destroyed in the eighth century BCE by the Assyrians; the Babylonians conquered the southern kingdom in the sixth, destroying the temple at Jerusalem and taking the Jews into captivity in Babylon. Biblical writers of the period saw this new exile as a repetition of the Egyptian one and predicted a new exodus. In fact, the exiles returned to their homeland within half a century.

For many writers, though, Israel's suffering during this time undermined the notions of the chosen people, sacred history, and God's justice. Job is a poetic meditation on the loss of these comforting beliefs, asking how God could allow the innocent to suffer. The answer, such as it is, is that God is unknowable. Like many biblical texts, Job transcends its original historical setting by exploring an enduring and universal theme. It is often compared to Greek tragedy, which treats many of the same themes, though in a quite different way.

The process by which the various books of the Hebrew Bible became approved and ordered as a single, official, unchangeable text—the process of "canonization"—was very gradual, stretching from the seventh to the first centuries BCE. A century later, Christianity appeared, first as a Jewish sect, but then quickly reaching out to the non-Jewish peoples of the Roman Empire. The Christian scriptures, or "New Testament," were conceived as a continuation of the Hebrew Bible, but they were written in Greek for a wider audience. Though Christianity came to occupy quite a different cultural world than Judaism, a European rather than Middle Eastern one, the New Testament must be read with the Hebrew Bible in mind. In this anthology, New Testament texts are included with the literature of the Greek and Roman world (pp. 692–716), but it seems appropriate to remark on their relation to the Hebrew Bible here.

The four Gospels treat the life of Jesus as a recapitulation or fulfillment of Israel's sacred history. The exodus is reenacted yet again, not only in Jesus' flight to Egypt and return right after his birth, but also in his forty-day fast in the wilderness, which echoes Israel's forty-year exodus in the wilderness, and yet once more in the timing of Jesus' death with the Passover, the night when Israel escaped from bondage in Egypt. In biblical interpretation the elaborate system of such parallels is known as "typology." In the Middle Ages typology would become a common way of structuring historical and fictional narratives, as if all history could be interpreted in terms of biblical references.

Biblical history, unlike mythology, flows in one direction toward a fulfillment in the future, rather than turning in cycles with the seasons—though the elaborate patterns of sacred history do repeat and expand from age to age as time progresses. Our modern sense of linear time, aiming at some future fulfillment, is ultimately derived from the Hebrew Bible. That is only one example of the ways in which the Bible has exerted influence over world history.

## GENESIS

The Book of Genesis evolved out of ancient oral traditions and is woven from several documents that were written down and revised from 1000 to 300 BCE. The word "genesis," or origins, was first applied to this material in the third century BCE by Greek translators. In Hebrew, the book is titled *Ber'sht,* meaning "at the beginning of" or "when," which is the first word of the text. Genesis is the first book of sacred scriptures for both Jews and Christians and has striking narrative and linguistic parallels with other Middle Eastern literature. The word "Eden," for example, appears in ancient Sumerian texts meaning "plain" or "steppe," and the rivers of Paradise mentioned in Genesis actually converge near the Persian Gulf, once home to the great cities of Sumeria. The biblical Flood story has a close parallel in *Gilgamesh* (see pp. 61–64), and the tree of life, the serpent, and the Tower of Babel in Genesis are prominent in other ancient Mesopotamian texts.

Genesis begins with two creation stories: the first, Genesis 1:1–2:3 (which names God *Elohim*) places heaven at its center and explains the origin of the Sabbath law (the seventh day of the week as a day of rest); the second (which names God *Yahweh*) runs from 2:4 to 3:24 and places earth and man at the center. This second account locates the origin of human suffering in Adam's and Eve's disobedience of God's command not to eat fruit from the Tree of Knowledge of Good and Evil.

Although presented as a loss, the "fall" from innocence allows Adam and Eve to commence a human line that will lead to Noah and then on to the great patriarchs of Israel. Their son, Cain, who slays his brother Abel in Genesis 4, further contaminates humanity with yet another primal sin. The conflict between the two brothers depicts the age-old strife between agricultural and pastoral ways of life and offers the first evidence of sacrifices made to God. Genealogies here, and elsewhere in the Bible, are important and are typical of much ancient literature; they have parallels in ancient Sumerian king lists, in warrior lists in the Turkish *Dede Korkut,* and in the king lists of the ancient Iranian *Shāh-nāmah,* and in the Japanese *Kojiki.*

Genesis 6–9 records a flood narrative, a story found in various forms throughout world literature. Whereas *Gilgamesh,* for example, attributes the flood to a whimsical act on the part of the gods, Genesis constructs the flood as punishment. Genesis 6:18 has a uniquely Jewish slant on the flood, identifying it as the first covenantal (contractual) agreement between God and humanity, thereby beginning a series of covenants that characterize the relationship between God and Israel throughout the Bible.

The genealogy of the patriarchs moves through several generations to Abraham and his wife Sarah (21:1–21 and 22:1–18). Abraham, having been chosen by God to establish his people in a land called Canaan, has already been cast in the biblical narrative as a leader and as a person with a unique relationship with God. Abraham's willingness to sacrifice his promised son, which would seem to undo his covenant with God, paradoxically confirms the strength of the covenant and ensures his heirs' right to the Promised Land. The testing scene is brilliantly orchestrated with narrative details and with ominous silences (what is not said), and it reveals a very complex relationship with God, whose motives are incomprehensible and whose actions appear contradictory and absurd.

Genesis 37–50 tells the story of Isaac's son Jacob (also called Israel), and his twelve sons. Like protagonists in mythical narrative, Joseph endures a figurative death and emerges from his imprisonment to interpret dreams, prophesy the future, and restore order, but the story is told in a charming naturalistic style that might be termed "*romance.*" The long-delayed recognition scene, when Joseph finally reveals himself to his brothers, is highly dramatic, moving, and comic at the same time. It is never explained exactly why Joseph delays so long, but we do learn in the end that the plot's many conflicts, betrayals, and secrets have really been God's way of saving Israel from famine. By the end of Genesis, God is working in strange ways indeed. History—even an intensely personal history like this one—turns out to be the expression of God's underlying will.

The following selections from Genesis are from the Revised Standard Version.

## *Chs. 1–4 [Creation]*

**1** In the beginning when God created the heavens and the earth, 2the earth was a formless void and darkness covered the face of the deep, while a wind from God swept over the face of the waters. 3Then God said, "Let there be light"; and there was light. 4And God saw that the light was good; and God separated the light from the darkness. 5God called the light Day, and the darkness he called Night. And there was evening and there was morning, the first day.

6And God said, "Let there be a dome in the midst of the waters, and let it separate the waters from the waters." 7So God made the dome and separated the waters that were under the dome from the waters that were above the dome. And it was so. 8God called the dome Sky. And there was evening and there was morning, the second day.

9And God said, "Let the waters under the sky be gathered together into one place, and let the dry land appear." And it was so. 10God called the dry land Earth, and the waters that were gathered together he called Seas. And God saw that it was good. 11Then God said, "Let the earth put forth vegetation: plants yielding seed, and fruit trees of every kind on earth that bear fruit with the seed in it." And it was so. 12The earth brought forth vegetation: plants yielding seed of every kind, and trees of every kind bearing fruit with the seed in it. And God saw that it was good. 13And there was evening and there was morning, the third day.

14And God said, "Let there be lights in the dome of the sky to separate the day from the night; and let them be for signs and for seasons and for days and years, 15and let them be lights in the dome of the sky to give light upon the earth." And it was so. 16God made the two great lights—the greater light to rule the day and the lesser light to rule the night—and the stars. 17God set them in the dome of the sky to give light upon the earth, 18to rule over the day and over the night, and to separate the light from the darkness. And God saw that it was good. 19And there was evening and there was morning, the fourth day.

20And God said, "Let the waters bring forth swarms of living creatures, and let birds fly above the earth across the dome of the sky." 21So God created the great sea monsters and every living creature that moves, of every kind, with which the waters swarm, and every winged bird of every kind. And God saw that it was good. 22God blessed them, saying, "Be fruitful and multiply and fill the waters in the seas, and let birds multiply on the earth." 23And there was evening and there was morning, the fifth day.

24And God said, "Let the earth bring forth living creatures of every kind: cattle and creeping things and wild animals of the earth of every kind."

And it was so. [25]God made the wild animals of the earth of every kind, and the cattle of every kind, and everything that creeps upon the ground of every kind. And God saw that it was good.

[26]Then God said, "Let us make humankind in our image, according to our likeness; and let them have dominion over the fish of the sea, and over the birds of the air, and over the cattle, and over all the wild animals of the earth, and over every creeping thing that creeps upon the earth."

> [27]So God created humankind in
> his image,
> in the image of God he created
> them;
> male and female he created them.

[28]God blessed them, and God said to them, "Be fruitful and multiply, and fill the earth and subdue it; and have dominion over the fish of the sea and over the birds of the air and over every living thing that moves upon the earth." [29]God said, "See, I have given you every plant yielding seed that is upon the face of all the earth, and every tree with seed in its fruit; you shall have them for food. [30]And to every beast of the earth, and to every bird of the air, and to everything that creeps on the earth, everything that has the breath of life, I have given every green plant for food." And it was so. [31]God saw everything that he had made, and indeed, it was very good. And there was evening and there was morning, the sixth day.

**2** Thus the heavens and the earth were finished, and all their multitude. [2]And on the seventh day God finished the work that he had done, and he rested on the seventh day from all the work that he had done. [3]So God blessed the seventh day and hallowed it, because on it God rested from all the work that he had done in creation.

[4]These are the generations of the heavens and the earth when they were created.

In the day that the LORD God made the earth and the heavens, [5]when no plant of the field was yet in the earth and no herb of the field had yet sprung up—for the LORD God had not caused it to rain upon the earth, and there was no one to till the ground; [6]but a stream would rise from the earth, and water the whole face of the ground— [7]then the LORD God formed man from the dust of the ground, and breathed into his nostrils the breath of life; and the man became a living being. [8]And the LORD God planted a garden in Eden, in the east; and there he put the man whom he had formed. [9]Out of the ground the LORD God made to grow every tree that is pleasant to the sight and good for food, the tree of life also in the midst of the garden, and the tree of the knowledge of good and evil.

[10]A river flows out of Eden to water the garden, and from there it divides and becomes four branches. [11]The name of the first is Pishon; it is the one that flows around the whole land of Havilah, where there is gold; [12]and the gold of that land is good; bdellium and onyx stone are there. [13]The name of the second river is Gihon; it is the one that flows around the whole land of Cush. [14]The name of the third river is Tigris, which flows east of Assyria. And the fourth river is the Euphrates.

[15]The LORD God took the man and put him in the garden of Eden to till it and keep it. [16]And the LORD God commanded the man, "You may freely eat of every tree of the garden; [17]but of the tree of the knowledge of good and evil

you shall not eat, for in the day that you eat of it you shall die."

[18]Then the LORD God said, "It is not good that the man should be alone; I will make him a helper as his partner." [19]So out of the ground the LORD God formed every animal of the field and every bird of the air, and brought them to the man to see what he would call them; and whatever the man called every living creature, that was its name. [20]The man gave names to all cattle, and to the birds of the air, and to every animal of the field; but for the man there was not found a helper as his partner. [21]So the LORD God caused a deep sleep to fall upon the man, and he slept; then he took one of his ribs and closed up its place with flesh. [22]And the rib that the LORD God had taken from the man he made into a woman and brought her to the man. [23]Then the man said,

> "This at last is bone of my bones
> and flesh of my flesh;
> this one shall be called Woman,
> for out of Man this one was
> taken."

[24]Therefore a man leaves his father and his mother and clings to his wife, and they become one flesh. [25]And the man and his wife were both naked, and were not ashamed.

**3** Now the serpent was more crafty than any other wild animal that the LORD God had made. He said to the woman, "Did God say, 'You shall not eat from any tree in the garden'?" [2]The woman said to the serpent, "We may eat of the fruit of the trees in the garden; [3]but God said, 'You shall not eat of the fruit of the tree that is in the middle of the garden, nor shall you touch it, or you shall die.'" [4]But the serpent said to the woman, "You will not die; [5]for God knows that when you eat of it your eyes will be opened, and you will be like God, knowing good and evil." [6]So when the woman saw that the tree was good for food, and that it was a delight to the eyes, and that the tree was to be desired to make one wise, she took of its fruit and ate; and she also gave some to her husband, who was with her, and he ate. [7]Then the eyes of both were opened, and they knew that they were naked; and they sewed fig leaves together and made loincloths for themselves.

[8]They heard the sound of the LORD God walking in the garden at the time of the evening breeze, and the man and his wife hid themselves from the presence of the LORD God among the trees of the garden. [9]But the LORD God called to the man, and said to him, "Where are you?" [10]He said, "I heard the sound of you in the garden, and I was afraid, because I was naked; and I hid myself." [11]He said, "Who told you that you were naked? Have you eaten from the tree of which I commanded you not to eat?" [12]The man said, "The woman whom you gave to be with me, she gave me fruit from the tree, and I ate." [13]Then the LORD God said to the woman, "What is this that you have done?" The woman said, "The serpent tricked me, and I ate." [14]The LORD God said to the serpent,

> "Because you have done this,
> cursed are you among all
> animals
> and among all wild creatures;
> upon your belly you shall go,
> and dust you shall eat
> all the days of your life.
> [15]I will put enmity between you
> and the woman,
> and between your offspring
> and hers;

he will strike your head,
and you will strike his heel."
[16]To the woman he said,
"I will greatly increase your pangs
in childbearing;
in pain you shall bring forth
children,
yet your desire shall be for your
husband,
and he shall rule over you."
[17]And to the man he said,
"Because you have listened to the
voice of your wife,
and have eaten of the tree
about which I commanded you,
'You shall not eat of it,'
cursed is the ground because of
you;
in toil you shall eat of it all the
days of your life;
[18]thorns and thistles it shall bring
forth for you;
and you shall eat the plants of
the field.
[19]By the sweat of your face you
shall eat bread
until you return to the ground,
for out of it you were taken;
you are dust,
and to dust you shall return."

[20]The man named his wife Eve,
because she was the mother of all living.
[21]And the LORD God made garments of
skins for the man and for his wife, and
clothed them.

[22]Then the LORD God said, "See,
the man has become like one of us,
knowing good and evil; and now, he
might reach out his hand and take also
from the tree of life, and eat, and live
forever"—[23]therefore the LORD God
sent him forth from the garden of
Eden, to till the ground from which he
was taken. [24]He drove out the man;
and at the east of the garden of Eden
he placed the cherubim, and a sword
flaming and turning to guard the way
to the tree of life.

**4** Now the man knew his wife Eve, and
she conceived and bore Cain, saying,
"I have produced a man with the help of
the LORD." [2]Next she bore his brother
Abel. Now Abel was a keeper of sheep,
and Cain a tiller of the ground. [3]In
the course of time Cain brought to the
LORD an offering of the fruit of the
ground, [4]and Abel for his part brought
of the firstlings of his flock, their fat portions. And the LORD had regard for Abel
and his offering, [5]but for Cain and his
offering he had no regard. So Cain was
very angry, and his countenance fell.
[6]The LORD said to Cain, "Why are you
angry, and why has your countenance
fallen? [7]If you do well, will you not be
accepted? And if you do not do well, sin
is lurking at the door; its desire is for
you, but you must master it."

[8]Cain said to his brother Abel, "Let
us go out to the field." And when they
were in the field, Cain rose up against
his brother Abel, and killed him. [9]Then
the LORD said to Cain, "Where is your
brother Abel?" He said, "I do not know;
am I my brother's keeper?" [10]And the
LORD said, "What have you done?
Listen; your brother's blood is crying
out to me from the ground! [11]And now
you are cursed from the ground, which
has opened its mouth to receive your
brother's blood from your hand.
[12]When you till the ground, it will no
longer yield to you its strength; you will
be a fugitive and a wanderer on the
earth." [13]Cain said to the LORD, "My
punishment is greater than I can bear!
[14]Today you have driven me away from
the soil, and I shall be hidden from your
face; I shall be a fugitive and a wanderer
on the earth, and anyone who meets me

may kill me." [15]Then the Lord said to him, "Not so! Whoever kills Cain will suffer a sevenfold vengeance." And the LORD put a mark on Cain, so that no one who came upon him would kill him. [16]Then Cain went away from the presence of the LORD, and settled in the land of Nod, east of Eden.

[17]Cain knew his wife, and she conceived and bore Enoch; and he built a city, and named it Enoch after his son Enoch. [18]To Enoch was born Irad; and Irad was the father of Mehujael, and Mehujael the father of Methushael, and Methushael the father of Lamech. [19]Lamech took two wives; the name of the one was Adah, and the name of the other Zillah. [20]Adah bore Jabal; he was the ancestor of those who live in tents and have livestock. [21]His brother's name was Jubal; he was the ancestor of all those who play the lyre and pipe. [22]Zillah bore Tubal-cain, who made all kinds of bronze and iron tools. The sister of Tubal-cain was Naamah.

[23]Lamech said to his wives:
"Adah and Zillah, hear my voice;
you wives of Lamech, listen to
 what I say:
I have killed a man for wounding
 me,
a young man for striking me.
[24]If Cain is avenged sevenfold, truly
 Lamech seventy-sevenfold."

[25]Adam knew his wife again, and she bore a son and named him Seth, for she said, "God has appointed for me another child instead of Abel, because Cain killed him." [26]To Seth also a son was born, and he named him Enosh. At that time people began to invoke the name of the LORD.

## *Chs. 6–9 [The Flood]*

**6** When people began to multiply on the face of the ground, and daughters were born to them, [2]the sons of God saw that they were fair; and they took wives for themselves of all that they chose. [3]Then the LORD said, "My spirit shall not abide in mortals forever, for they are flesh; their days shall be one hundred twenty years." [4]The Nephilim were on the earth in those days—and also afterward—when the sons of God went in to the daughters of humans, who bore children to them. These were the heroes that were of old, warriors of renown.

[5]The LORD saw that the wickedness of humankind was great in the earth, and that every inclination of the thoughts of their hearts was only evil continually. [6]And the LORD was sorry that he had made humankind on the earth, and it grieved him to his heart. [7]So the LORD said, "I will blot out from the earth the human beings I have created—people together with animals and creeping things and birds of the air, for I am sorry that I have made them." [8]But Noah found favor in the sight of the LORD.

[9]These are the descendants of Noah. Noah was a righteous man, blameless in his generation; Noah walked with God. [10]And Noah had three sons, Shem, Ham, and Japheth.

[11]Now the earth was corrupt in God's sight, and the earth was filled with violence. [12]And God saw that the earth was corrupt; for all flesh had corrupted its ways upon the earth. [13]And God said to Noah, "I have determined to make an end of all flesh, for the earth is filled with violence because of them; now I

am going to destroy them along with
the earth. [14]Make yourself an ark of
cypress wood; make rooms in the ark,
and cover it inside and out with pitch.
[15]This is how you are to make it: the
length of the ark three hundred cubits,
its width fifty cubits, and its height
thirty cubits. [16]Make a roof for the ark,
and finish it to a cubit above; and put
the door of the ark in its side; make it
with lower, second, and third decks.
[17]For my part, I am going to bring a
flood of waters on the earth, to destroy
from under heaven all flesh in which is
the breath of life; everything that is on
the earth shall die. [18]But I will establish
my covenant with you; and you shall
come into the ark, you, your sons, your
wife, and your sons' wives with you.
[19]And of every living thing, of all flesh,
you shall bring two of every kind into
the ark, to keep them alive with you;
they shall be male and female. [20]Of the
birds according to their kinds, and of
the animals according to their kinds, of
every creeping thing of the ground
according to its kind, two of every kind
shall come in to you, to keep them
alive. [21]Also take with you every kind of
food that is eaten, and store it up; and
it shall serve as food for you and for
them." [22]Noah did this; he did all that
God commanded him.

**7** Then the LORD said to Noah, "Go
into the ark, you and all your household, for I have seen that you alone are
righteous before me in this generation.
[2]Take with you seven pairs of all clean
animals, the male and its mate; and a
pair of the animals that are not clean,
the male and its mate; [3]and seven pairs
of the birds of the air also, male and
female, to keep their kind alive on the
face of all the earth. [4]For in seven days
I will send rain on the earth for forty
days and forty nights; and every living
thing that I have made I will blot out
from the face of the ground." [5]And
Noah did all that the LORD had commanded him.

[6]Noah was six hundred years old
when the flood of waters came on the
earth. [7]And Noah with his sons and his
wife and his sons' wives went into the
ark to escape the waters of the flood.
[8]Of clean animals, and of animals that
are not clean, and of birds, and of everything that creeps on the ground, [9]two
and two, male and female, went into the
ark with Noah, as God had commanded
Noah. [10]And after seven days the waters
of the flood came on the earth.

[11]In the six hundredth year of Noah's
life, in the second month, on the seventeenth day of the month, on that day
all the fountains of the great deep burst
forth, and the windows of the heavens
were opened. [12]The rain fell on the
earth forty days and forty nights. [13]On
the very same day Noah with his sons,
Shem and Ham and Japheth, and
Noah's wife and the three wives of his
sons entered the ark, [14]they and every
wild animal of every kind, and all domestic animals of every kind, and every
creeping thing that creeps on the earth,
and every bird of every kind—every
bird, every winged creature. [15]They went
into the ark with Noah, two and two of
all flesh in which there was the breath
of life. [16]And those that entered, male
and female of all flesh, went in as God
had commanded him; and the LORD
shut him in.

[17]The flood continued forty days on
the earth; and the waters increased, and
bore up the ark, and it rose high above
the earth. [18]The waters swelled and
increased greatly on the earth; and the
ark floated on the face of the waters.
[19]The waters swelled so mightily on the

earth that all the high mountains under
the whole heaven were covered; [20]the
waters swelled above the mountains,
covering them fifteen cubits deep.
[21]And all flesh died that moved on the
earth, birds, domestic animals, wild animals, all swarming creatures that swarm
on the earth, and all human beings;
[22]everything on dry land in whose nostrils was the breath of life died. [23]He
blotted out every living thing that was
on the face of the ground, human
beings and animals and creeping things
and birds of the air; they were blotted
out from the earth. Only Noah was left,
and those that were with him in the ark.
[24]And the waters swelled on the earth
for one hundred fifty days.

**8** But God remembered Noah and all
the wild animals and all the domestic
animals that were with him in the ark.
And God made a wind blow over the
earth, and the waters subsided; [2]the
fountains of the deep and the windows
of the heavens were closed, the rain
from the heavens was restrained, [3]and
the waters gradually receded from the
earth. At the end of one hundred fifty
days the waters had abated; [4]and in the
seventh month, on the seventeenth day
of the month, the ark came to rest on
the mountains of Ararat. [5]The waters
continued to abate until the tenth
month; in the tenth month, on the first
day of the month, the tops of the
mountains appeared.

[6]At the end of forty days Noah
opened the window of the ark that he
had made [7]and sent out the raven; and
it went to and fro until the waters were
dried up from the earth. [8]Then he sent
out the dove from him, to see if the
waters had subsided from the face of
the ground; [9]but the dove found no
place to set its foot, and it returned to
him to the ark, for the waters were still
on the face of the whole earth. So he
put out his hand and took it and
brought it into the ark with him. [10]He
waited another seven days, and again
he sent out the dove from the ark; [11]and
the dove came back to him in the
evening, and there in its beak was a
freshly plucked olive leaf; so Noah
knew that the waters had subsided from
the earth. [12]Then he waited another
seven days, and sent out the dove; and
it did not return to him any more.

[13]In the six hundred first year, in
the first month, the first day of the
month, the waters were dried up from
the earth; and Noah removed the covering of the ark, and looked, and saw
that the face of the ground was drying.
[14]In the second month, on the twenty-
seventh day of the month, the earth was
dry. [15]Then God said to Noah, [16]"Go out
of the ark, you and your wife, and your
sons and your sons' wives with you.
[17]Bring out with you every living thing
that is with you of all flesh—birds and
animals and every creeping thing that
creeps on the earth—so that they may
abound on the earth, and be fruitful
and multiply on the earth." [18]So Noah
went out with his sons and his wife and
his sons' wives. [19]And every animal,
every creeping thing, and every bird,
everything that moves on the earth,
went out of the ark by families.

[20]Then Noah built an altar to the
LORD, and took of every clean animal
and of every clean bird, and offered
burnt offerings on the altar. [21]And when
the LORD smelled the pleasing odor,
the LORD said in his heart, "I will never
again curse the ground because of
humankind, for the inclination of the
human heart is evil from youth; nor will
I ever again destroy every living creature as I have done.

22As long as the earth endures,
seedtime and harvest, cold and
heat,
summer and winter, day and night,
shall not cease."

**9** God blessed Noah and his sons, and
said to them, "Be fruitful and multiply,
and fill the earth. 2The fear and dread
of you shall rest on every animal of the
earth, and on every bird of the air, on
everything that creeps on the ground,
and on all the fish of the sea; into your
hand they are delivered. 3Every moving
thing that lives shall be food for you;
and just as I gave you the green plants,
I give you everything. 4Only, you shall
not eat flesh with its life, that is, its
blood. 5For your own lifeblood I will
surely require a reckoning: from every
animal I will require it and from
human beings, each one for the blood
of another, I will require a reckoning
for human life.

6Whoever sheds the blood of a
human,
by a human shall that person's
blood be shed;
for in his own image
God made humankind.

7And you, be fruitful and multiply,
abound on the earth and multiply in it."
8Then God said to Noah and to his
sons with him, 9"As for me, I am establishing my covenant with you and your
descendants after you, 10and with every
living creature that is with you, the
birds, the domestic animals, and every
animal of the earth with you, as many as
came out of the ark. 11I establish my
covenant with you, that never again
shall all flesh be cut off by the waters of
a flood, and never again shall there be
a flood to destroy the earth." 12God said,
"This is the sign of the covenant that I
make between me and you and every living creature that is with you, for all
future generations: 13I have set my bow
in the clouds, and it shall be a sign of
the covenant between me and the
earth. 14When I bring clouds over the
earth and the bow is seen in the clouds,
15I will remember my covenant that is
between me and you and every living
creature of all flesh; and the waters
shall never again become a flood to
destroy all flesh. 16When the bow is in
the clouds, I will see it and remember
the everlasting covenant between God
and every living creature of all flesh
that is on the earth." 17God said to
Noah, "This is the sign of the covenant
that I have established between me and
all flesh that is on the earth."
18The sons of Noah who went out of
the ark were Shem, Ham, and Japheth.
Ham was the father of Canaan. 19These
three were the sons of Noah; and from
these the whole earth was peopled.
20Noah, a man of the soil, was the
first to plant a vineyard. 21He drank some
of the wine and became drunk, and he
lay uncovered in his tent. 22And Ham,
the father of Canaan, saw the nakedness
of his father, and told his two brothers
outside. 23Then Shem and Japheth took
a garment, laid it on both their shoulders, and walked backward and covered
the nakedness of their father; their faces
were turned away, and they did not see
their father's nakedness. 24When Noah
awoke from his wine and knew what his
youngest son had done to him, 25he said,

"Cursed be Canaan;
lowest of slaves shall he be to his
brothers."
26He also said,
"Blessed by the LORD my God be
Shem;
and let Canaan be his slave.

27May God make space for
  Japheth,
and let him live in the tents of
  Shem;
and let Canaan be his slave."

28After the flood Noah lived three hundred fifty years. 29All the days of Noah were nine hundred fifty years; and he died.

## *Chs. 21–22 [Abraham and Isaac]*

**21** The LORD dealt with Sarah as he had said, and the LORD did for Sarah as he had promised. 2Sarah conceived and bore Abraham a son in his old age, at the time of which God had spoken to him. 3Abraham gave the name Isaac to his son whom Sarah bore him. 4And Abraham circumcised his son Isaac when he was eight days old, as God had commanded him. 5Abraham was a hundred years old when his son Isaac was born to him. 6Now Sarah said, "God has brought laughter for me; everyone who hears will laugh with me." 7And she said, "Who would ever have said to Abraham that Sarah would nurse children? Yet I have borne him a son in his old age."

8The child grew, and was weaned; and Abraham made a great feast on the day that Isaac was weaned. 9But Sarah saw the son of Hagar the Egyptian, whom she had borne to Abraham, playing with her son Isaac. 10So she said to Abraham, "Cast out this slave woman with her son; for the son of this slave woman shall not inherit along with my son Isaac." 11The matter was very distressing to Abraham on account of his son. 12But God said to Abraham, "Do not be distressed because of the boy and because of your slave woman; whatever Sarah says to you, do as she tells you, for it is through Isaac that offspring shall be named for you. 13As for the son of the slave woman, I will make a nation of him also, because he is your offspring." 14So Abraham rose early in the morning, and took bread and a skin of water, and gave it to Hagar, putting it on her shoulder, along with the child, and sent her away. And she departed, and wandered about in the wilderness of Beer-sheba.

15When the water in the skin was gone, she cast the child under one of the bushes. 16Then she went and sat down opposite him a good way off, about the distance of a bowshot; for she said, "Do not let me look on the death of the child." And as she sat opposite him, she lifted up her voice and wept. 17And God heard the voice of the boy; and the angel of God called to Hagar from heaven, and said to her, "What troubles you, Hagar? Do not be afraid; for God has heard the voice of the boy where he is. 18Come, lift up the boy and hold him fast with your hand, for I will make a great nation of him." 19Then God opened her eyes and she saw a well of water. She went, and filled the skin with water, and gave the boy a drink.

20God was with the boy, and he grew up; he lived in the wilderness, and became an expert with the bow. 21He lived in the wilderness of Paran; and his mother got a wife for him from the land of Egypt.

**22** After these things God tested Abraham. He said to him, "Abraham!" And he said, "Here I am." 2He said, "Take your son, your only son Isaac, whom you love, and go to the land of Moriah, and offer him there as a burnt offering on one of the mountains that I shall show you.” 3So Abraham rose early in the morning, saddled his donkey, and took two of his young men with him, and his son Isaac; he cut the wood for the burnt offering, and set out and went to the place in the distance that God had shown him. 4On the third day Abraham looked up and saw the place far away. 5Then Abraham said to his young men, “Stay here with the donkey; the boy and I will go over there; we will worship, and then we will come back to you.” 6Abraham took the wood of the burnt offering and laid it on his son Isaac, and he himself carried the fire and the knife. So the two of them walked on together. 7Isaac said to his father Abraham, “Father!” And he said, “Here I am, my son.” He said, “The fire and the wood are here, but where is the lamb for a burnt offering?” 8Abraham said, “God himself will provide the lamb for a burnt offering, my son.” So the two of them walked on together.

9When they came to the place that God had shown him, Abraham built an altar there and laid the wood in order. He bound his son Isaac, and laid him on the altar, on top of the wood. 10Then Abraham reached out his hand and took the knife to kill his son. 11But the angel of the LORD called to him from heaven, and said, “Abraham, Abraham!” And he said, “Here I am.” 12He said, “Do not lay your hand on the boy or do anything to him; for now I know that you fear God, since you have not withheld your son, your only son, from me.” 13And Abraham looked up and saw a ram, caught in a thicket by its horns. Abraham went and took the ram and offered it up as a burnt offering instead of his son. 14So Abraham called that place “The LORD will provide”; as it is said to this day, “On the mount of the LORD it shall be provided.”

15The angel of the LORD called to Abraham a second time from heaven, 16and said, “By myself I have sworn, says the LORD: Because you have done this, and have not withheld your son, your only son, 17I will indeed bless you, and I will make your offspring as numerous as the stars of heaven and as the sand that is on the seashore. And your offspring shall possess the gate of their enemies, 18and by your offspring shall all the nations of the earth gain blessing for themselves, because you have obeyed my voice.”

## *Chs. 37–50 [The Story of Joseph]*

**37** Jacob settled in the land where his father had lived as an alien, the land of Canaan. 2This is the story of the family of Jacob.

Joseph, being seventeen years old, was shepherding the flock with his brothers; he was a helper to the sons of Bilhah and Zilpah, his father’s wives; and Joseph brought a bad report of them to their father. 3Now Israel loved Joseph more than any other of his children, because he was the son of his old age; and he had made him a long robe with sleeves. 4But when his brothers saw that their father loved him more than all his brothers, they hated him, and could not speak peaceably to him.

5Once Joseph had a dream, and when he told it to his brothers, they hated him even more. 6He said to them, “Listen to this dream that I dreamed. 7There we were, binding sheaves in the field. Suddenly my sheaf rose and stood upright; then your sheaves gathered around it, and bowed down to my sheaf.” 8His brothers said to him, “Are you indeed to reign over us? Are you indeed to have dominion over us?" So they hated him even more because of his dreams and his words.

[9]He had another dream, and told it to his brothers, saying, "Look, I have had another dream: the sun, the moon, and eleven stars were bowing down to me." [10]But when he told it to his father and to his brothers, his father rebuked him, and said to him, "What kind of dream is this that you have had? Shall we indeed come, I and your mother and your brothers, and bow to the ground before you?" [11]So his brothers were jealous of him, but his father kept the matter in mind.

[12]Now his brothers went to pasture their father's flock near Shechem. [13]And Israel said to Joseph, "Are not your brothers pasturing the flock at Shechem? Come, I will send you to them." He answered, "Here I am." [14]So he said to him, "Go now, see if it is well with your brothers and with the flock; and bring word back to me." So he sent him from the valley of Hebron.

He came to Shechem, [15]and a man found him wandering in the fields; the man asked him, "What are you seeking?" [16]"I am seeking my brothers," he said; "tell me, please, where they are pasturing the flock." [17]The man said, "They have gone away, for I heard them say, 'Let us go to Dothan.'" So Joseph went after his brothers, and found them at Dothan. [18]They saw him from a distance, and before he came near to them, they conspired to kill him. [19]They said to one another, "Here comes this dreamer. [20]Come now, let us kill him and throw him into one of the pits; then we shall say that a wild animal has devoured him, and we shall see what will become of his dreams." [21]But when Reuben heard it, he delivered him out of their hands, saying, "Let us not take his life." [22]Reuben said to them, "Shed no blood; throw him into this pit here in the wilderness, but lay no hand on him"—that he might rescue him out of their hand and restore him to his father. [23]So when Joseph came to his brothers, they stripped him of his robe, the long robe with sleeves that he wore; [24]and they took him and threw him into a pit. The pit was empty; there was no water in it.

[25]Then they sat down to eat; and looking up they saw a caravan of Ishmaelites coming from Gilead, with their camels carrying gum, balm, and resin, on their way to carry it down to Egypt. [26]Then Judah said to his brothers, "What profit is it if we kill our brother and conceal his blood? [27]Come, let us sell him to the Ishmaelites, and not lay our hands on him, for he is our brother, our own flesh." And his brothers agreed. [28]When some Midianite traders passed by, they drew Joseph up, lifting him out of the pit, and sold him to the Ishmaelites for twenty pieces of silver. And they took Joseph to Egypt.

[29]When Reuben returned to the pit and saw that Joseph was not in the pit, he tore his clothes. [30]He returned to his brothers, and said, "The boy is gone; and I, where can I turn?" [31]Then they took Joseph's robe, slaughtered a goat, and dipped the robe in the blood. [32]They had the long robe with sleeves taken to their father, and they said, "This we have found; see now whether it is your son's robe or not." [33]He recognized it, and said, "It is my son's robe! A wild animal has devoured him; Joseph is without doubt torn to pieces." [34]Then Jacob tore his garments, and put sackcloth on his loins, and mourned for his son many days. [35]All his sons and all his daughters sought to comfort him;

but he refused to be comforted, and said, "No, I shall go down to Sheol to my son, mourning." Thus his father bewailed him. [36]Meanwhile the Midianites had sold him in Egypt to Potiphar, one of Pharaoh's officials, the captain of the guard.

**38** It happened at that time that Judah went down from his brothers and settled near a certain Adullamite whose name was Hirah. [2]There Judah saw the daughter of a certain Canaanite whose name was Shua; he married her and went in to her. [3]She conceived and bore a son; and he named him Er. [4]Again she conceived and bore a son whom she named Onan. [5]Yet again she bore a son, and she named him Shelah. She was in Chezib when she bore him. [6]Judah took a wife for Er his firstborn; her name was Tamar. [7]But Er, Judah's firstborn, was wicked in the sight of the LORD, and the LORD put him to death. [8]Then Judah said to Onan, "Go in to your brother's wife and perform the duty of a brother-in-law to her; raise up offspring for your brother." [9]But since Onan knew that the offspring would not be his, he spilled his semen on the ground whenever he went in to his brother's wife, so that he would not give offspring to his brother. [10]What he did was displeasing in the sight of the LORD, and he put him to death also. [11]Then Judah said to his daughter-in-law Tamar, "Remain a widow in your father's house until my son Shelah grows up"—for he feared that he too would die, like his brothers. So Tamar went to live in her father's house.

[12]In course of time the wife of Judah, Shua's daughter, died; when Judah's time of mourning was over, he went up to Timnah to his sheepshearers, he and his friend Hirah the Adullamite. [13]When Tamar was told, "Your father-in-law is going up to Timnah to shear his sheep," [14]she put off her widow's garments, put on a veil, wrapped herself up, and sat down at the entrance to Enaim, which is on the road to Timnah. She saw that Shelah was grown up, yet she had not been given to him in marriage. [15]When Judah saw her, he thought her to be a prostitute, for she had covered her face. [16]He went over to her at the road side, and said, "Come, let me come in to you," for he did not know that she was his daughter-in-law. She said, "What will you give me, that you may come in to me?" [17]He answered, "I will send you a kid from the flock." And she said, "Only if you give me a pledge, until you send it." [18]He said, "What pledge shall I give you?" She replied, "Your signet and your cord, and the staff that is in your hand." So he gave them to her, and went in to her, and she conceived by him. [19]Then she got up and went away, and taking off her veil she put on the garments of her widowhood.

[20]When Judah sent the kid by his friend the Adullamite, to recover the pledge from the woman, he could not find her. [21]He asked the townspeople, "Where is the temple prostitute who was at Enaim by the wayside?" But they said, "No prostitute has been here." [22]So he returned to Judah, and said, "I have not found her; moreover the townspeople said, 'No prostitute has been here.'" [23]Judah replied, "Let her keep the things as her own, otherwise we will be laughed at; you see, I sent this kid, and you could not find her."

[24]About three months later Judah was told, "Your daughter-in-law Tamar has played the whore; moreover she is pregnant as a result of whoredom." And Judah said, "Bring her out, and let her be burned." [25]As she was being

brought out, she sent word to her father-in-law, "It was the owner of these who made me pregnant." And she said, "Take note, please, whose these are, the signet and the cord and the staff." [26]Then Judah acknowledged them and said, "She is more in the right than I, since I did not give her to my son Shelah." And he did not lie with her again.

[27]When the time of her delivery came, there were twins in her womb. [28]While she was in labor, one put out a hand; and the midwife took and bound on his hand a crimson thread, saying, "This one came out first." [29]But just then he drew back his hand, and out came his brother; and she said, "What a breach you have made for yourself!" Therefore he was named Perez. [30]Afterward his brother came out with the crimson thread on his hand; and he was named Zerah.

**39** Now Joseph was taken down to Egypt, and Potiphar, an officer of Pharaoh, the captain of the guard, an Egyptian, bought him from the Ishmaelites who had brought him down there. [2]The LORD was with Joseph, and he became a successful man; he was in the house of his Egyptian master. [3]His master saw that the LORD was with him, and that the LORD caused all that he did to prosper in his hands. [4]So Joseph found favor in his sight and attended him; he made him overseer of his house and put him in charge of all that he had. [5]From the time that he made him overseer in his house and over all that he had, the LORD blessed the Egyptian's house for Joseph's sake; the blessing of the LORD was on all that he had, in house and field. [6]So he left all that he had in Joseph's charge; and, with him there, he had no concern for anything but the food that he ate.

Now Joseph was handsome and good-looking. [7]And after a time his master's wife cast her eyes on Joseph and said, "Lie with me." [8]But he refused and said to his master's wife, "Look, with me here, my master has no concern about anything in the house, and he has put everything that he has in my hand. [9]He is not greater in this house than I am, nor has he kept back anything from me except yourself, because you are his wife. How then could I do this great wickedness and sin against God?" [10]And although she spoke to Joseph day after day, he would not consent to lie beside her or to be with her. [11]One day, however, when he went into the house to do his work, and while no one else was in the house, [12]she caught hold of his garment, saying, "Lie with me!" But he left his garment in her hand, and fled and ran outside. [13]When she saw that he had left his garment in her hand and had fled outside, [14]she called out to the members of her household and said to them, "See, my husband has brought among us a Hebrew to insult us! He came in to me to lie with me, and I cried out with a loud voice; [15]and when he heard me raise my voice and cry out, he left his garment beside me, and fled outside." [16]Then she kept his garment by her until his master came home, [17]and she told him the same story, saying, "The Hebrew servant, whom you have brought among us, came in to me to insult me;[18] but as soon as I raised my voice and cried out, he left his garment beside me, and fled outside."

[19]When his master heard the words that his wife spoke to him, saying, "This is the way your servant treated me," he

became enraged. [20]And Joseph's master took him and put him into the prison, the place where the king's prisoners were confined; he remained there in prison. [21]But the LORD was with Joseph and showed him steadfast love; he gave him favor in the sight of the chief jailer. [22]The chief jailer committed to Joseph's care all the prisoners who were in the prison, and whatever was done there, he was the one who did it. [23]The chief jailer paid no heed to anything that was in Joseph's care, because the LORD was with him; and whatever he did, the LORD made it prosper.

**40** Some time after this, the cupbearer of the king of Egypt and his baker offended their lord the king of Egypt. [2]Pharaoh was angry with his two officers, the chief cupbearer and the chief baker, [3]and he put them in custody in the house of the captain of the guard, in the prison where Joseph was confined. [4]The captain of the guard charged Joseph with them, and he waited on them; and they continued for some time in custody. [5]One night they both dreamed—the cupbearer and the baker of the king of Egypt, who were confined in the prison—each his own dream, and each dream with its own meaning. [6]When Joseph came to them in the morning, he saw that they were troubled. [7]So he asked Pharaoh's officers, who were with him in custody in his master's house, "Why are your faces downcast today?" [8]They said to him, "We have had dreams, and there is no one to interpret them." And Joseph said to them, "Do not interpretations belong to God? Please tell them to me."

[9]So the chief cupbearer told his dream to Joseph, and said to him, "In my dream there was a vine before me, [10]and on the vine there were three branches. As soon as it budded, its blossoms came out and the clusters ripened into grapes. [11]Pharaoh's cup was in my hand; and I took the grapes and pressed them into Pharaoh's cup, and placed the cup in Pharaoh's hand." [12]Then Joseph said to him, "This is its interpretation: the three branches are three days; [13]within three days Pharaoh will lift up your head and restore you to your office; and you shall place Pharaoh's cup in his hand, just as you used to do when you were his cupbearer. [14]But remember me when it is well with you; please do me the kindness to make mention of me to Pharaoh, and so get me out of this place. [15]For in fact I was stolen out of the land of the Hebrews; and here also I have done nothing that they should have put me into the dungeon."

[16]When the chief baker saw that the interpretation was favorable, he said to Joseph, "I also had a dream: there were three cake baskets on my head, [17]and in the uppermost basket there were all sorts of baked food for Pharaoh, but the birds were eating it out of the basket on my head." [18]And Joseph answered, "This is its interpretation: the three baskets are three days; [19]within three days Pharaoh will lift up your head—from you!—and hang you on a pole; and the birds will eat the flesh from you."

[20]On the third day, which was Pharaoh's birthday, he made a feast for all his servants, and lifted up the head of the chief cupbearer and the head of the chief baker among his servants. [21]He restored the chief cupbearer to his cupbearing, and he placed the cup in Pharaoh's hand; [22]but the chief baker he hanged, just as Joseph had interpreted

to them. 13Yet the chief cupbearer did not remember Joseph, but forgot him.

**41** After two whole years, Pharaoh dreamed that he was standing by the Nile, 2and there came up out of the Nile seven sleek and fat cows, and they grazed in the reed grass. 3Then seven other cows, ugly and thin, came up out of the Nile after them, and stood by the other cows on the bank of the Nile. 4The ugly and thin cows ate up the seven sleek and fat cows. And Pharaoh awoke. 5Then he fell asleep and dreamed a second time; seven ears of grain, plump and good, were growing on one stalk. 6Then seven ears, thin and blighted by the east wind, sprouted after them. 7The thin ears swallowed up the seven plump and full ears. Pharaoh awoke, and it was a dream. 8In the morning his spirit was troubled; so he sent and called for all the magicians of Egypt and all its wise men. Pharaoh told them his dreams, but there was no one who could interpret them to Pharaoh.

9Then the chief cupbearer said to Pharaoh, "I remember my faults today. 10Once Pharaoh was angry with his servants, and put me and the chief baker in custody in the house of the captain of the guard. 11We dreamed on the same night, he and I, each having a dream with its own meaning. 12A young Hebrew was there with us, a servant of the captain of the guard. When we told him, he interpreted our dreams to us, giving an interpretation to each according to his dream. 13As he interpreted to us, so it turned out; I was restored to my office, and the baker was hanged."

14Then Pharaoh sent for Joseph, and he was hurriedly brought out of the dungeon. When he had shaved himself and changed his clothes, he came in before Pharaoh. 15And Pharaoh said to Joseph, "I have had a dream, and there is no one who can interpret it. I have heard it said of you that when you hear a dream you can interpret it." 16Joseph answered Pharaoh, "It is not I; God will give Pharaoh a favorable answer." 17Then Pharaoh said to Joseph, "In my dream I was standing on the banks of the Nile; 18and seven cows, fat and sleek, came up out of the Nile and fed in the reed grass. 19Then seven other cows came up after them, poor, very ugly, and thin. Never had I seen such ugly ones in all the land of Egypt. 20The thin and ugly cows ate up the first seven fat cows, 21but when they had eaten them no one would have known that they had done so, for they were still as ugly as before. Then I awoke. 22I fell asleep a second time and I saw in my dream seven ears of grain, full and good, growing on one stalk, 23and seven ears, withered, thin, and blighted by the east wind, sprouting after them; 24and the thin ears swallowed up the seven good ears. But when I told it to the magicians, there was no one who could explain it to me."

25Then Joseph said to Pharaoh, "Pharaoh's dreams are one and the same; God has revealed to Pharaoh what he is about to do. 26The seven good cows are seven years, and the seven good ears are seven years; the dreams are one. 27The seven lean and ugly cows that came up after them are seven years, as are the seven empty ears blighted by the east wind. They are seven years of famine. 28It is as I told Pharaoh; God has shown to Pharaoh what he is about to do. 29There will come seven years of great plenty throughout all the land of Egypt. 30After them there will arise seven years of famine, and all the plenty will be forgotten in the land of Egypt; the famine will consume the land. 31The

plenty will no longer be known in
the land because of the famine that will
follow, for it will be very grievous. [32]And
the doubling of Pharaoh's dream
means that the thing is fixed by God,
and God will shortly bring it about.
[33]Now therefore let Pharaoh select a
man who is discerning and wise, and set
him over the land of Egypt. [34] Let Pharaoh proceed to appoint overseers over
the land, and take one-fifth of the produce of the land of Egypt during
the seven plenteous years. [35]Let them
gather all the food of these good years
that are coming, and lay up grain under
the authority of Pharaoh for food in the
cities, and let them keep it. [36]That food
shall be a reserve for the land against
the seven years of famine that are to
befall the land of Egypt, so that the land
may not perish through the famine."

[37]The proposal pleased Pharaoh
and all his servants. [38]Pharaoh said to
his servants, "Can we find anyone else
like this—one in whom is the spirit of
God?" [39]So Pharaoh said to Joseph,
"Since God has shown you all this,
there is no one so discerning and wise
as you. [40]You shall be over my house,
and all my people shall order themselves as you command; only with
regard to the throne will I be greater
than you." [41]And Pharaoh said to
Joseph, "See, I have set you over all the
land of Egypt." [42]Removing his signet
ring from his hand, Pharaoh put it on
Joseph's hand; he arrayed him in garments of fine linen, and put a gold
chain around his neck. [43]He had him
ride in the chariot of his second-
in-command; and they cried out in
front of him, "Bow the knee!" Thus he
set him over all the land of Egypt.
[44]Moreover Pharaoh said to Joseph, "I
am Pharaoh, and without your consent
no one shall lift up hand or foot in all
the land of Egypt." [45]Pharaoh gave
Joseph the name Zaphenath-paneah;
and he gave him Asenath daughter of
Potiphera, priest of On, as his wife.
Thus Joseph gained authority over the
land of Egypt.

[46]Joseph was thirty years old when
he entered the service of Pharaoh king
of Egypt. And Joseph went out from
the presence of Pharaoh, and went
through all the land of Egypt. [47]During
the seven plenteous years the earth produced abundantly. [48]He gathered up all
the food of the seven years when there
was plenty in the land of Egypt, and
stored up food in the cities; he stored
up in every city the food from the fields
around it. [49]So Joseph stored up grain
in such abundance—like the sand of
the sea—that he stopped measuring it;
it was beyond measure.

[50]Before the years of famine came,
Joseph had two sons, whom Asenath
daughter of Potiphera, priest of On,
bore to him. [51]Joseph named the firstborn Manasseh, "For," he said, "God has
made me forget all my hardship and all
my father's house." [52]The second he
named Ephraim, "For God has made me
fruitful in the land of my misfortunes."

[53]The seven years of plenty that prevailed in the land of Egypt came to an
end; [54]and the seven years of famine
began to come, just as Joseph had said.
There was famine in every country, but
throughout the land of Egypt there was
bread. [55]When all the land of Egypt was
famished, the people cried to Pharaoh
for bread. Pharaoh said to all the
Egyptians, "Go to Joseph; what he says
to you, do." [56]And since the famine had
spread over all the land, Joseph opened
all the storehouses, and sold to the
Egyptians, for the famine was severe in
the land of Egypt. [57]Moreover, all the
world came to Joseph in Egypt to buy

grain, because the famine became severe throughout the world.

**42** When Jacob learned that there was grain in Egypt, he said to his sons, "Why do you keep looking at one another? [2]I have heard," he said, "that there is grain in Egypt; go down and buy grain for us there, that we may live and not die." [3]So ten of Joseph's brothers went down to buy grain in Egypt. [4]But Jacob did not send Joseph's brother Benjamin with his brothers, for he feared that harm might come to him. [5]Thus the sons of Israel were among the other people who came to buy grain, for the famine had reached the land of Canaan.

[6]Now Joseph was governor over the land; it was he who sold to all the people of the land. And Joseph's brothers came and bowed themselves before him with their faces to the ground. [7]When Joseph saw his brothers, he recognized them, but he treated them like strangers and spoke harshly to them. "Where do you come from?" he said. They said, "From the land of Canaan, to buy food." [8]Although Joseph had recognized his brothers, they did not recognize him. [9]Joseph also remembered the dreams that he had dreamed about them. He said to them, "You are spies; you have come to see the nakedness of the land!" [10]They said to him, "No, my lord; your servants have come to buy food. [11]We are all sons of one man; we are honest men; your servants have never been spies." [12]But he said to them, "No, you have come to see the nakedness of the land!" [13]They said, "We, your servants, are twelve brothers, the sons of a certain man in the land of Canaan; the youngest, however, is now with our father, and one is no more." [14]But Joseph said to them, "It is just as I have said to you; you are spies! [15]Here is how you shall be tested: as Pharaoh lives, you shall not leave this place unless your youngest brother comes here! [16]Let one of you go and bring your brother, while the rest of you remain in prison, in order that your words may be tested, whether there is truth in you; or else, as Pharaoh lives, surely you are spies." [17]And he put them all together in prison for three days.

[18]On the third day Joseph said to them, "Do this and you will live, for I fear God: [19]if you are honest men, let one of your brothers stay here where you are imprisoned. The rest of you shall go and carry grain for the famine of your households, [20]and bring your youngest brother to me. Thus your words will be verified, and you shall not die." And they agreed to do so. [21]They said to one another, "Alas, we are paying the penalty for what we did to our brother; we saw his anguish when he pleaded with us, but we would not listen. That is why this anguish has come upon us." [22]Then Reuben answered them, "Did I not tell you not to wrong the boy? But you would not listen. So now there comes a reckoning for his blood." [23]They did not know that Joseph understood them, since he spoke with them through an interpreter. [24]He turned away from them and wept; then he returned and spoke to them. And he picked out Simeon and had him bound before their eyes. [25]Joseph then gave orders to fill their bags with grain, to return every man's money to his sack, and to give them provisions for their journey. This was done for them.

[26]They loaded their donkeys with their grain, and departed. [27]When one of them opened his sack to give his donkey fodder at the lodging place, he saw his money at the top of the sack. [28]He said to his brothers, "My money

has been put back; here it is in my sack!" At this they lost heart and turned trembling to one another, saying, "What is this that God has done to us?"

29When they came to their father Jacob in the land of Canaan, they told him all that had happened to them, saying, 30"The man, the lord of the land, spoke harshly to us, and charged us with spying on the land. 31But we said to him, 'We are honest men, we are not spies. 32We are twelve brothers, sons of our father; one is no more, and the youngest is now with our father in the land of Canaan.' 33Then the man, the lord of the land, said to us, 'By this I shall know that you are honest men: leave one of your brothers with me, take grain for the famine of your households, and go your way. 34Bring your youngest brother to me, and I shall know that you are not spies but honest men. Then I will release your brother to you, and you may trade in the land.'"

35As they were emptying their sacks, there in each one's sack was his bag of money. When they and their father saw their bundles of money, they were dismayed. 36And their father Jacob said to them, "I am the one you have bereaved of children: Joseph is no more, and Simeon is no more, and now you would take Benjamin. All this has happened to me!" 37Then Reuben said to his father, "You may kill my two sons if I do not bring him back to you. Put him in my hands, and I will bring him back to you." 38But he said, "My son shall not go down with you, for his brother is dead, and he alone is left. If harm should come to him on the journey that you are to make, you would bring down my gray hairs with sorrow to Sheol."

**43** Now the famine was severe in the land. 2And when they had eaten up the grain that they had brought from Egypt, their father said to them, "Go again, buy us a little more food." 3But Judah said to him, "The man solemnly warned us, saying, 'You shall not see my face unless your brother is with you.' 4If you will send our brother with us, we will go down and buy you food; 5but if you will not send him, we will not go down, for the man said to us, 'You shall not see my face, unless your brother is with you.'" 6Israel said, "Why did you treat me so badly as to tell the man that you had another brother?" 7They replied, "The man questioned us carefully about ourselves and our kindred, saying, 'Is your father still alive? Have you another brother?' What we told him was in answer to these questions. Could we in any way know that he would say, 'Bring your brother down'?" 8Then Judah said to his father Israel, "Send the boy with me, and let us be on our way, so that we may live and not die—you and we and also our little ones. 9I myself will be surety for him; you can hold me accountable for him. If I do not bring him back to you and set him before you, then let me bear the blame forever. 10If we had not delayed, we would now have returned twice."

11Then their father Israel said to them, "If it must be so, then do this: take some of the choice fruits of the land in your bags, and carry them down as a present to the man—a little balm and a little honey, gum, resin, pistachio nuts, and almonds. 12Take double the money with you. Carry back with you the money that was returned in the top of your sacks; perhaps it was an oversight. 13Take your brother also, and be on your way again to the man; 14may God Almighty grant you mercy before the man, so that he may send back your other brother and Benjamin. As for me, if I am bereaved of my children, I am bereaved." 15So the men took the present, and they took double the money with them, as well as Benjamin. Then they went on their way down to Egypt, and stood before Joseph.

16When Joseph saw Benjamin with them, he said to the steward of his house, "Bring the men into the house, and slaughter an animal and make ready, for the men are to dine with me at noon." 17The man did as Joseph said, and brought the men to Joseph's house. 18Now the men were afraid because they were brought to Joseph's house, and they said, "It is because of the money, replaced in our sacks the first time, that we have been brought in, so that he may have an opportunity to fall upon us, to make slaves of us and take our donkeys." 19So they went up to the steward of Joseph's house and spoke with him at the entrance to the house. 20They said, "Oh, my lord, we came down the first time to buy food; 21and when we came to the lodging place we opened our sacks, and there was each one's money in the top of his sack, our money in full weight. So we have brought it back with us. 22Moreover we have brought down with us additional money to buy food. We do not know who put our money in our sacks." 23He replied, "Rest assured, do not be afraid; your God and the God of your father must have put treasure in your sacks for you; I received your money." Then he brought Simeon out to them. 24When the steward had brought the men into Joseph's house, and given them water, and they had washed their feet, and when he had given their donkeys fodder, 25they made the present ready for Joseph's coming at noon, for they had heard that they would dine there.

26When Joseph came home, they brought him the present that they had carried into the house, and bowed to the ground before him. 27He inquired about their welfare, and said, "Is your father well, the old man of whom you spoke? Is he still alive?" 28They said, "Your servant our father is well; he is still alive." And they bowed their heads and did obeisance. 29Then he looked up and saw his brother Benjamin, his mother's son, and said, "Is this your youngest brother, of whom you spoke to me? God be gracious to you, my son!" 30With that, Joseph hurried out, because he was overcome with affection for his brother, and he was about to weep. So he went into a private room and wept there. 31Then he washed his face and came out; and controlling himself he said, "Serve the meal." 32They served him by himself, and them by themselves, and the Egyptians who ate with him by themselves, because the Egyptians could not eat with the Hebrews, for that is an abomination to the Egyptians. 33When they were seated before him, the firstborn according to his birthright and the youngest according to his youth, the men looked at one another in amazement. 34Portions were taken to them from Joseph's table, but Benjamin's portion was five times as much as any of theirs. So they drank and were merry with him.

**44** Then he commanded the steward of his house, "Fill the men's sacks with food, as much as they can carry, and put each man's money in the top of his sack. 2Put my cup, the silver cup, in the top of the sack of the youngest, with his money for the grain." And he did as Joseph told him. 3As soon as the morning was light, the men were sent away with their donkeys. 4When they had gone only a short distance from the city, Joseph said to his steward, "Go, follow after the men; and when you overtake them, say to them, 'Why have you returned evil for good? Why have you stolen my silver cup? 5Is it not from this that my lord drinks? Does he not indeed use it for divination? You have done wrong in doing this.'"

6When he overtook them, he repeated these words to them. 7They said to him, "Why does my lord speak such words as these? Far be it from your servants that they should do such a thing! 8Look, the money that we found at the top of our sacks, we brought back to you from the land of Canaan; why then would we steal silver or gold from your lord's house? 9Should it be found with any one of your servants, let him die; moreover the rest of us will become my lord's slaves." 10He said, "Even so; in accordance with your words, let it be: he with whom it is found shall become my slave, but the rest of you shall go free." 11Then each one quickly lowered his sack to the ground, and each opened his sack. 12He searched, beginning with the eldest and ending with the youngest; and the cup was found in Benjamin's sack. 13At this they tore their clothes. Then each one loaded his donkey, and they returned to the city.

14Judah and his brothers came to Joseph's house while he was still there; and they fell to the ground before him. 15Joseph said to them, "What deed is this that you have done? Do you not know that one such as I can practice divination?" 16And Judah said, "What can we say to my lord? What can we speak? How can we clear ourselves? God has found out the guilt of your servants; here we are then, my lord's slaves, both we and also the one in whose possession the cup has been found." 17But he said, "Far be it from me that I should do so! Only the one in whose possession the cup was found shall be my slave; but as for you, go up in peace to your father."

18Then Judah stepped up to him and said, "O my lord, let your servant please speak a word in my lord's ears, and do not be angry with your servant; for you are like Pharaoh himself. 19My lord asked his servants, saying, 'Have you a father or a brother?' 20And we said to my lord, 'We have a father, an old man, and a young brother, the child of his old age. His brother is dead; he alone is left of his mother's children, and his father loves him.' 21Then you said to your servants, 'Bring him down to me, so that I may set my eyes on him.' 22We said to my lord, 'The boy cannot leave his father, for if he should leave his father, his father would die.' 23Then you said to your servants, 'Unless your youngest brother comes down with you, you shall see my face no more.' 24When we went back to your servant my father we told him the words of my lord. 25And when our father said, 'Go again, buy us a little food,' 26we said, 'We cannot go down. Only if our youngest brother goes with us, will we go down; for we cannot see the man's face unless our youngest brother is with us.' 27Then your servant my father said to us, 'You know that my wife bore me two sons; 28one left me, and I said, Surely he has been torn to pieces; and I have never seen him since. 29If you take this one also from me, and harm comes to him, you will bring down my gray hairs in sorrow to Sheol.' 30Now therefore, when I come to your servant my father and the boy is not with us, then, as his life is bound up in the boy's life, 31when he sees that the boy is not with us, he will die; and your servants will bring down the gray hairs of your servant our father with sorrow to Sheol. 32For your servant became surety for the boy to my father, saying, 'If I do not bring him back to you, then I will bear the blame in the sight of my father all my life.' 33Now therefore, please let your servant remain as a slave to my lord in place of the boy; and let the boy go back with his brothers. 34For how can I go back to my father if the boy is not with me? I fear to see the suffering that would come upon my father."

**45** Then Joseph could no longer control himself before all those who stood by him, and he cried out, "Send everyone away from me." So no one stayed with him when Joseph made himself known to his brothers. 2And he wept so loudly that the Egyptians heard it, and the household of Pharaoh heard it. 3Joseph said to his brothers, "I am Joseph. Is my father still alive?" But his brothers could not answer him, so dismayed were they at his presence.

4Then Joseph said to his brothers, "Come closer to me." And they came closer. He said, "I am your brother, Joseph, whom you sold into Egypt. 5And now do not be distressed, or angry with yourselves, because you sold me here; for God sent me before you to preserve life. 6For the famine has been in the land these two years; and there are five more years in which there will be neither plowing nor harvest. 7God sent me before you to preserve for you a remnant on earth, and to keep alive for you many survivors. 8So it was not you who sent me here, but God; he has made me a father to Pharaoh, and lord of all his house and ruler over all the land of Egypt. 9Hurry and go up to my father and say to him, 'Thus says your son Joseph, God has made me lord of all Egypt; come down to me, do not delay. 10You shall settle in the land of Goshen, and you shall be near me, you and your children and your children's children, as well as your flocks, your herds, and all that you have. 11I will provide for you there—since there are five more years of famine to come—so that you and your household, and all that you have, will not come to poverty.' 12And now your eyes and the eyes of my brother Benjamin see that it is my own mouth that speaks to you. 13You must tell my father how greatly I am honored in Egypt, and all that you have seen. Hurry and bring my father down here." 14Then he fell upon his brother Benjamin's neck and wept, while Benjamin wept upon his neck. 15And he kissed all his brothers and wept upon them; and after that his brothers talked with him.

16When the report was heard in Pharaoh's house, "Joseph's brothers have come," Pharaoh and his servants were pleased. 17Pharaoh said to Joseph, "Say to your brothers, 'Do this: load your animals and go back to the land of Canaan. 18Take your father and your households and come to me, so that I may give you the best of the land of Egypt, and you may enjoy the fat of the land.' 19You are further charged to say, 'Do this: take wagons from the land of Egypt for your little ones and for your wives, and bring your father, and come. 20Give no thought to your possessions, for the best of all the land of Egypt is yours.'"

21The sons of Israel did so. Joseph gave them wagons according to the instruction of Pharaoh, and he gave them provisions for the journey. 22To each one of them he gave a set of

garments; but to Benjamin he gave
three hundred pieces of silver and five
sets of garments. 23To his father he sent
the following: ten donkeys loaded with
the good things of Egypt, and ten female
donkeys loaded with grain, bread, and
provision for his father on the journey.
24Then he sent his brothers on their way,
and as they were leaving he said to them,
"Do not quarrel along the way."

25So they went up out of Egypt and
came to their father Jacob in the land
of Canaan. 26And they told him, "Joseph
is still alive! He is even ruler over all the
land of Egypt." He was stunned; he
could not believe them. 27But when they
told him all the words of Joseph that he
had said to them, and when he saw the
wagons that Joseph had sent to carry
him, the spirit of their father Jacob
revived. 28Israel said, "Enough! My son
Joseph is still alive. I must go and see
him before I die."

**46** When Israel set out on his journey
with all that he had and came to Beer-
sheba, he offered sacrifices to the God
of his father Isaac. 2God spoke to Israel
in visions of the night, and said, "Jacob,
Jacob." And he said, "Here I am."
3Then he said, "I am God, the God of
your father; do not be afraid to go
down to Egypt, for I will make of you a
great nation there. 4I myself will go
down with you to Egypt, and I will also
bring you up again; and Joseph's own
hand shall close your eyes."

5Then Jacob set out from Beer-
sheba; and the sons of Israel carried
their father Jacob, their little ones, and
their wives, in the wagons that Pharaoh
had sent to carry him. 6They also took
their livestock and the goods that they
had acquired in the land of Canaan,
and they came into Egypt, Jacob and all
his offspring with him, 7his sons, and his
sons' sons with him, his daughters, and
his sons' daughters; all his offspring he
brought with him into Egypt.

8Now these are the names of the
Israelites, Jacob and his offspring, who
came to Egypt. Reuben, Jacob's firstborn, 9and the children of Reuben:
Hanoch, Pallu, Hezron, and Carmi.

28Israel sent Judah ahead to Joseph
to lead the way before him into
Goshen. When they came to the land of
Goshen, 29Joseph made ready his chariot and went up to meet his father
Israel in Goshen. He presented himself
to him, fell on his neck, and wept on his
neck a good while. 30Israel said to
Joseph, "I can die now, having seen for
myself that you are still alive." 31Joseph
said to his brothers and to his father's
household, "I will go up and tell Pharaoh, and will say to him, 'My brothers
and my father's household, who were in
the land of Canaan, have come to me.
32The men are shepherds, for they have
been keepers of livestock; and they
have brought their flocks, and their
herds, and all that they have.' 33When
Pharaoh calls you, and says, 'What is
your occupation?' 34you shall say, 'Your
servants have been keepers of livestock
from our youth even until now, both we
and our ancestors'—in order that you
may settle in the land of Goshen,
because all shepherds are abhorrent to
the Egyptians."

**47** So Joseph went and told Pharaoh,
"My father and my brothers, with their
flocks and herds and all that they pos-
sess, have come from the land of
Canaan; they are now in the land of
Goshen." 2From among his brothers he
took five men and presented them to
Pharaoh. 3Pharaoh said to his brothers,
"What is your occupation?" And they
said to Pharaoh, "Your servants are

shepherds, as our ancestors were." [4]They
said to Pharaoh, "We have come to
reside as aliens in the land; for there is
no pasture for your servants' flocks
because the famine is severe in the land
of Canaan. Now, we ask you, let your servants settle in the land of Goshen."
[5]Then Pharaoh said to Joseph, "Your
father and your brothers have come to
you. [6]The land of Egypt is before you;
settle your father and your brothers in
the best part of the land; let them live in
the land of Goshen; and if you know that
there are capable men among them, put
them in charge of my livestock."

[7]Then Joseph brought in his father
Jacob, and presented him before
Pharaoh, and Jacob blessed Pharaoh.
[8]Pharaoh said to Jacob, "How many are
the years of your life?" [9]Jacob said to
Pharaoh, "The years of my earthly
sojourn are one hundred thirty; few
and hard have been the years of my life.
They do not compare with the years of
the life of my ancestors during their
long sojourn." [10]Then Jacob blessed
Pharaoh, and went out from the presence of Pharaoh. [11]Joseph settled his
father and his brothers, and granted
them a holding in the land of Egypt, in
the best part of the land, in the land of
Rameses, as Pharaoh had instructed.
[12]And Joseph provided his father, his
brothers, and all his father's household
with food, according to the number of
their dependents.

[13]Now there was no food in all the
land, for the famine was very severe.
The land of Egypt and the land of
Canaan languished because of the
famine. [14]Joseph collected all the money
to be found in the land of Egypt and in
the land of Canaan, in exchange for the
grain that they bought; and Joseph
brought the money into Pharaoh's
house. [15]When the money from the land
of Egypt and from the land of Canaan
was spent, all the Egyptians came to
Joseph, and said, "Give us food! Why
should we die before your eyes? For our
money is gone." [16]And Joseph answered,
"Give me your livestock, and I will give
you food in exchange for your livestock, if your money is gone." [17]So they
brought their livestock to Joseph; and
Joseph gave them food in exchange for
the horses, the flocks, the herds, and the
donkeys. That year he supplied them
with food in exchange for all their livestock. [18]When that year was ended, they
came to him the following year, and said
to him, "We can not hide from my lord
that our money is all spent; and the
herds of cattle are my lord's. There is
nothing left in the sight of my lord but
our bodies and our lands. [19]Shall we die
before your eyes, both we and our land?
Buy us and our land in exchange for
food. We with our land will become
slaves to Pharaoh; just give us seed, so
that we may live and not die, and that
the land may not become desolate."

[20]So Joseph bought all the land of
Egypt for Pharaoh. All the Egyptians
sold their fields, because the famine
was severe upon them; and the land
became Pharaoh's. [21]As for the people,
he made slaves of them from one end
of Egypt to the other. [22]Only the land of
the priests he did not buy; for the
priests had a fixed allowance from
Pharaoh, and lived on the allowance
that Pharaoh gave them; therefore they
did not sell their land. [23]Then Joseph
said to the people, "Now that I have this
day bought you and your land for Pharaoh, here is seed for you; sow the land.
[24]And at the harvests you shall give
one-fifth to Pharaoh, and four-fifths
shall be your own, as seed for the field
and as food for yourselves and your
households, and as food for your little

ones." 25They said, "You have saved our
lives; may it please my lord, we will be
slaves to Pharaoh." 26So Joseph made it a
statute concerning the land of Egypt,
and it stands to this day, that Pharaoh
should have the fifth. The land of the
priests alone did not become Pharaoh's.

27Thus Israel settled in the land of
Egypt, in the region of Goshen; and
they gained possessions in it, and were
fruitful and multiplied exceedingly.
28Jacob lived in the land of Egypt seventeen years; so the days of Jacob, the
years of his life, were one hundred
forty-seven years.

29When the time of Israel's death
drew near, he called his son Joseph and
said to him, "If I have found favor with
you, put your hand under my thigh and
promise to deal loyally and truly with
me. Do not bury me in Egypt. 30When I
lie down with my ancestors, carry me
out of Egypt and bury me in their burial place." He answered, "I will do as
you have said." 31And he said, "Swear to
me"; and he swore to him. Then Israel
bowed himself on the head of his bed.

**48** After this Joseph was told, "Your
father is ill." So he took with him his
two sons, Manasseh and Ephraim.
2When Jacob was told, "Your son Joseph
has come to you," he summoned his
strength and sat up in bed. 3And
Jacob said to Joseph, "God Almighty
appeared to me at Luz in the land
of Canaan, and he blessed me, 4and
said to me, 'I am going to make you
fruitful and increase your numbers; I
will make of you a company of peoples,
and will give this land to your offspring
after you for a perpetual holding.'
5Therefore your two sons, who were
born to you in the land of Egypt before
I came to you in Egypt, are now mine;
Ephraim and Manasseh shall be mine,
just as Reuben and Simeon are. 6As for
the offspring born to you after them,
they shall be yours. They shall be
recorded under the names of their
brothers with regard to their inheritance. 7For when I came from Paddan,
Rachel, alas, died in the land of Canaan
on the way, while there was still some
distance to go to Ephrath; and I buried
her there on the way to Ephrath" (that
is, Bethlehem).

8When Israel saw Joseph's sons, he
said, "Who are these?" 9Joseph said to
his father, "They are my sons, whom
God has given me here." And he said,
"Bring them to me, please, that I may
bless them." 10Now the eyes of Israel
were dim with age, and he could not
see well. So Joseph brought them near
him; and he kissed them and embraced
them. 11Israel said to Joseph, "I did not
expect to see your face; and here God
has let me see your children also."
12Then Joseph removed them from his
father's knees, and he bowed himself
with his face to the earth. 13Joseph took
them both, Ephraim in his right hand
toward Israel's left, and Manasseh in his
left hand toward Israel's right, and
brought them near him. 14But Israel
stretched out his right hand and laid
it on the head of Ephraim, who was the
younger, and his left hand on the head
of Manasseh, crossing his hands, for
Manasseh was the firstborn. 15He
blessed Joseph, and said,

> "The God before whom my
> ancestors Abraham and
> Isaac walked,
> the God who has been my
> shepherd all my life to this day,
> 16the angel who has redeemed me
> from all harm, bless the boys;
> and in them let my name be
> perpetuated, and the name

of my ancestors Abraham
and Isaac;
and let them grow into a
multitude on the earth."

17 When Joseph saw that his father
laid his right hand on the head of
Ephraim, it displeased him; so he took
his father's hand, to remove it from
Ephraim's head to Manasseh's head.
18 Joseph said to his father, "Not so, my
father! Since this one is the firstborn,
put your right hand on his head." 19 But
his father refused, and said, "I know, my
son, I know; he also shall become a people, and he also shall be great. Nevertheless his younger brother shall be
greater than he, and his offspring shall
become a multitude of nations." 20 So he
blessed them that day, saying,

"By you Israel will invoke blessings,
saying,
'God make you like Ephraim and
like Manasseh.'"

So he put Ephraim ahead of Manasseh.
21 Then Israel said to Joseph, "I am
about to die, but God will be with you
and will bring you again to the land of
your ancestors. 22 I now give to you one
portion more than to your brothers,
the portion that I took from the hand
of the Amorites with my sword and with
my bow."

**49** Then Jacob called his sons, and said: "Gather around, that I may tell you what will happen to you in days to come.

2 Assemble and hear, O sons of
Jacob;
listen to Israel your father.

3 Reuben, you are my firstborn,
my might and the first fruits
of my vigor,
excelling in rank and excelling in
power.
4 Unstable as water, you shall no
longer excel
because you went up onto your
father's bed;
then you defiled it—you went
up onto my couch!

5 Simeon and Levi are brothers;
weapons of violence are their
swords.
6 May I never come into their
council;
may I not be joined to their
company—
for in their anger they killed
men,
and at their whim they hamstrung
oxen.
7 Cursed be their anger, for it is
fierce,
and their wrath, for it is cruel!
I will divide them in Jacob, and
scatter them in Israel.

8 Judah, your brothers shall praise
you;
your hand shall be on the neck of
your enemies;
your father's sons shall bow down
before you.
9 Judah is a lion's whelp; from the
prey, my son, you have gone up.
He crouches down, he stretches
out like a lion,
like a lioness—who dares rouse
him up?
10 The scepter shall not depart
from Judah,
nor the ruler's staff from between
his feet,
until tribute comes to him; and
the obedience of the peoples
is his.

[11]Binding his foal to the vine
and his donkey's colt to the
choice vine,
he washes his garments in wine and
his robe in the blood of grapes;
[12]his eyes are darker than wine,
and his teeth whiter than milk.

[13]Zebulun shall settle at the shore
of the sea;
he shall be a haven for ships,
and his border shall be at Sidon.

[14]Issachar is a strong donkey,
lying down between the sheepfolds;
[15]he saw that a resting place was
good,
and that the land was pleasant;
so he bowed his shoulder to the
burden,
and became a slave at forced labor.

[16]Dan shall judge his people
as one of the tribes of Israel.
[17]Dan shall be a snake by the
roadside,
a viper along the path,
that bites the horse's heels
so that its rider falls backward.

[18]I wait for your salvation, O Lord.

[19]Gad shall be raided by raiders,
but he shall raid at their heels.

[20]Asher's food shall be rich,
and he shall provide royal
delicacies.

[21]Naphtali is a doe let loose
that bears lovely fawns.

[22]Joseph is a fruitful bough,
a fruitful bough by a spring;
his branches run over the wall.

[23]The archers fiercely attacked him;
they shot at him and pressed him
hard.
[24]Yet his bow remained taut,
and his arms were made agile
by the hands of the Mighty One of
Jacob,
by the name of the Shepherd, the
Rock of Israel,
[25]by the God of your father, who
will help you,
by the Almighty who will bless you
with blessings of heaven above,
blessings of the deep that lies
beneath,
blessings of the breasts and of the
womb.
[26]The blessings of your father
are stronger than the blessings
of the eternal mountains,
the bounties of the everlasting
hills;
may they be on the head of
Joseph,
on the brow of him who was set
apart from his brothers.

Benjamin is a ravenous wolf,
in the morning devouring the
prey,
and at evening dividing the
spoil."

[28]All these are the twelve tribes of
Israel, and this is what their father said
to them when he blessed them, blessing each one of them with a suitable
blessing.
[29]Then he charged them, saying to
them, "I am about to be gathered to
my people. Bury me with my ancestors—in the cave in the field of Ephron
the Hittite, [30]in the cave in the field at
Machpelah, near Mamre, in the land
of Canaan, in the field that Abraham

bought from Ephron the Hittite as a burial site. [31]There Abraham and his wife Sarah were buried; there Isaac and his wife Rebekah were buried; and there I buried Leah— [32]the field and the cave that is in it were purchased from the Hittites." [33]When Jacob ended his charge to his sons, he drew up his feet into the bed, breathed his last, and was gathered to his people.

**50** Then Joseph threw himself on his father's face and wept over him and kissed him. [2]Joseph commanded the physicians in his service to embalm his father. So the physicians embalmed Israel; [3]they spent forty days in doing this, for that is the time required for embalming. And the Egyptians wept for him seventy days.

[4]When the days of weeping for him were past, Joseph addressed the household of Pharaoh, "If now I have found favor with you, please speak to Pharaoh as follows: [5]My father made me swear an oath; he said, 'I am about to die. In the tomb that I hewed out for myself in the land of Canaan, there you shall bury me.' Now therefore let me go up, so that I may bury my father; then I will return." [6]Pharaoh answered, "Go up, and bury your father, as he made you swear to do."

[7]So Joseph went up to bury his father. With him went up all the servants of Pharaoh, the elders of his household, and all the elders of the land of Egypt, [8]as well as all the household of Joseph, his brothers, and his father's household. Only their children, their flocks, and their herds were left in the land of Goshen. [9]Both chariots and charioteers went up with him. It was a very great company. [10]When they came to the threshing floor of Atad, which is beyond the Jordan, they held there a very great and sorrowful lamentation; and he observed a time of mourning for his father seven days. [11]When the Canaanite inhabitants of the land saw the mourning on the threshing floor of Atad, they said, "This is a grievous mourning on the part of the Egyptians." Therefore the place was named Abel-mizraim; it is beyond the Jordan. [12]Thus his sons did for him as he had instructed them. [13]They carried him to the land of Canaan and buried him in the cave of the field at Machpelah, the field near Mamre, which Abraham bought as a burial site from Ephron the Hittite. [14]After he had buried his father, Joseph returned to Egypt with his brothers and all who had gone up with him to bury his father.

[15]Realizing that their father was dead, Joseph's brothers said, "What if Joseph still bears a grudge against us and pays us back in full for all the wrong that we did to him?" [16]So they approached Joseph, saying, "Your father gave this instruction before he died, [17]'Say to Joseph: I beg you, forgive the crime of your brothers and the wrong they did in harming you.' Now therefore please forgive the crime of the servants of the God of your father." Joseph wept when they spoke to him. [18]Then his brothers also wept, fell down before him, and said, "We are here as your slaves." [19]But Joseph said to them, "Do not be afraid! Am I in the place of God? [20]Even though you intended to do harm to me, God intended it for good, in order to preserve a numerous people, as he is doing today. [21]So have no fear; I myself will provide for you and your little ones." In this way he reassured them, speaking kindly to them.

[22]So Joseph remained in Egypt, he and his father's household; and Joseph lived one hundred ten years. [23]Joseph saw Ephraim's children of the third

generation; the children of Machir son of Manasseh were also born on Joseph's knees.

24Then Joseph said to his brothers, "I am about to die; but God will surely come to you, and bring you up out of this land to the land that he swore to Abraham, to Isaac, and to Jacob." 25So Joseph made the Israelites swear, saying, "When God comes to you, you shall carry up my bones from here." 26And Joseph died, being one hundred ten years old; he was embalmed and placed in a coffin in Egypt.

## EXODUS

The first five books of the Bible are called the Pentateuch, the "five vessels or books," and are traditionally attributed to Moses. Exodus is the second of these books. It tells the story of the deliverance of the Jews from centuries of slavery in Egypt, their pilgrimage to Sinai, and their covenant with God. It was probably composed around the ninth century BCE but refers to events occurring several centuries earlier, in the nineteenth Egyptian dynasty (c. 1350–1200 BCE).

As we have seen, one of the distinctive qualities of the Jewish tradition is its conception of God as radically transcendent, that is, as existing beyond the earthly world. This idea set Israel apart from the empires of the Near East, such as Egypt, with their divine kings. Egyptian civilization drew its authority from the correspondences it developed between its political organization and the natural rhythms of the cosmos. The Jews' experience of the radically transcendent nature of the divine is symbolized in the dramatic episode in which God reveals himself to Moses miraculously through a burning bush. The revelation comes suddenly and unexpectedly, as Moses is tending his father-in-law's sheep. In the Greek experience, as articulated by the philosophers Plato and Aristotle, the divine is actively sought by the enquirer; the emphasis is upon the search and the movement upwards. In the case of Moses, however, the divine is experienced as reaching down and finding the person who may well have his or her mind on other things.

For the Jews, the revelation on Mount Sinai marked a turning point that conferred upon history itself a sacred dimension that is not characteristic of the cosmological empires of the Middle East. In the second of the Ten Commandments, Yahweh insists that the divine must not be represented in images: "You shall not make for yourself an idol, whether in the form of anything that is in heaven above, or that is on the earth beneath, or that is in the water underneath the earth." This commandment amounts to a ban on representational art in general. The idea that the divine cannot be represented, and that nothing may represent the divine, set Israel apart from its Middle Eastern and Mediterranean neighbors—though interestingly, early Buddhism (from the fifth to the first centuries BCE) shares the same idea, as does Islam much later. When Moses finds the Jews worshipping the image of a golden calf (ch. 32), he angrily throws to the ground the tablets on which the commandments are inscribed.

Like Aeneas in Virgil's epic, *The Aeneid,* Moses is at first a reluctant hero who is bemused and astonished to find himself chosen as the founder of his nation.

These selections from Exodus are from the new Revised Standard Version.

## *Chs. 1–3 [Birth of Moses, the Burning Bush]*

**1** These are the names of the sons of Israel who came to Egypt with Jacob, each with his household: [2]Reuben, Simeon, Levi, and Judah, [3]Issachar, Zebulun, and Benjamin, [4]Dan and Naphtali, Gad and Asher. [5]The total number of people born to Jacob was seventy. Joseph was already in Egypt. [6]Then Joseph died, and all his brothers, and that whole generation. [7]But the Israelites were fruitful and prolific; they multiplied and grew exceedingly strong, so that the land was filled with them.

[8]Now a new king arose over Egypt, who did not know Joseph. [9]He said to his people, "Look, the Israelite people are more numerous and more powerful than we. [10]Come, let us deal shrewdly with them, or they will increase and, in the event of war, join our enemies and fight against us and escape from the land." [11]Therefore they set taskmasters over them to oppress them with forced labor. They built supply cities, Pithom and Rameses, for Pharaoh. [12]But the more they were oppressed, the more they multiplied and spread, so that the Egyptians came to dread the Israelites. [13]The Egyptians became ruthless in imposing tasks on the Israelites, [14]and made their lives bitter with hard service in mortar and brick and in every kind of field labor. They were ruthless in all the tasks that they imposed on them.

[15]The king of Egypt said to the Hebrew midwives, one of whom was named Shiphrah and the other Puah, [16]"When you act as midwives to the Hebrew women, and see them on the birthstool, if it is a boy, kill him; but if it is a girl, she shall live." [17]But the midwives feared God; they did not do as the king of Egypt commanded them, but they let the boys live. [18]So the king of Egypt summoned the midwives and said to them, "Why have you done this, and allowed the boys to live?" [19]The midwives said to Pharoah, "Because the Hebrew women are not like the Egyptian women; for they are vigorous and give birth before the midwife comes to them." [20]So God dealt well with the midwives; and the people multiplied and became very strong. [21]And because the midwives feared God, he gave them families. [22]Then Pharaoh commanded all his people, "Every boy that is born to the Hebrews you shall throw into the Nile, but you shall let every girl live."

**2** Now a man from the house of Levi went and married a Levite woman. [2]The woman conceived and bore a son; and when she saw that he was a fine baby, she hid him three months. [3]When she could hide him no longer she got a papyrus basket for him, and plastered it with bitumen and pitch; she put the child in it and placed it among the reeds on the bank of the river. [4]His sister stood at a distance, to see what would happen to him.

[5]The daughter of Pharaoh came down to bathe at the river, while her attendants walked beside the river. She saw the basket among the reeds and sent her maid to bring it. [6]When she opened it, she saw the child. He was crying, and she took pity on him, "This must be one of the Hebrews' children," she said. [7]Then his sister said to Pharaoh's daughter, "Shall I go and get you a nurse from the Hebrew women to nurse the child for you?" [8]Pharaoh's daughter said to her, "Yes." So the girl

went and called the child's mother. [9]Pharaoh's daughter said to her, "Take this child and nurse it for me, and I will give you your wages." So the woman took the child and nursed it. [10]"When the child grew up, she brought him to Pharaoh's daughter, and she took him as her son. She named him Moses, "because," she said, "I drew him out of the water."

[11]One day, after Moses had grown up, he went out to his people and saw their forced labor. He saw an Egyptian beating a Hebrew, one of his kinsfolk. [12]He looked this way and that, and seeing no one he killed the Egyptian and hid him in the sand. [13]When he went out the next day, he saw two Hebrews fighting; and he said to the one who was in the wrong, "Why do you strike your fellow Hebrew?" [14]He answered, "Who made you a ruler and judge over us? Do you mean to kill me as you killed the Egyptian?" Then Moses was afraid and thought, "Surely the thing is known." [15]When Pharaoh heard of it, he sought to kill Moses.

But Moses fled from Pharaoh. He settled in the land of Midian, and sat down by a well. [16]The priest of Midian had seven daughters. They came to draw water, and filled the troughs to water their father's flock. [17]But some shepherds came and drove them away. Moses got up and came to their defense and watered their flock. [18]When they returned to their father Reuel, he said, "How is it that you have came back so soon today?" [19]They said, "An Egyptian helped us against the shepherds; he even drew water for us and watered the flock." [20]He said to his daughters, "Where is he? Why did you leave the man? Invite him to break bread." [21]Moses agreed to stay with the man, and he gave Moses his daughter Zipporah in marriage. [22]She bore a son, and he named him Gershom; for he said, "I have been an alien residing in a foreign land."

[23]After a long time the king of Egypt died. The Israelites groaned under their slavery, and cried out. Out of the slavery their cry for help rose up to God. [24]God heard their groaning, and God remembered his covenant with Abraham, Issac, and Jacob. [25]God looked upon the Israelites, and God took notice of them.

**3** Moses was keeping the flock of his father-in-law Jethro, the priest of Midian; he led his flock beyond the wilderness, and came to Horeb, the mountain of God. [2]There the angel of the LORD appeared to him in a flame of fire out of a bush; he looked, and the bush was blazing, yet it was not consumed. [3]Then Moses said, "I must turn aside and look at this great sight, and see why the bush is not burned up." [4]When the LORD saw that he had turned aside to see, God called to him out of the bush, "Moses, Moses!" And he said, "Here I am." [5]Then he said, "Come no closer! Remove the sandals from your feet, for the place on which you are standing is holy ground." [6]He said further, "I am the God of your father, the God of Abraham, the God of Isaac, and the God of Jacob." And Moses hid his face, for he was afraid to look at God.

[7]Then the LORD said, "I have observed the misery of my people who are in Egypt; I have heard their cry on account of their taskmasters. Indeed, I know their sufferings, [8]and I have come down to deliver them from the Egyptians, and to bring them up out of that land to a good and broad land, a land flowing with milk and honey, to the country of the Canaanites, the Hittites,

the Amorites, the Perizzites, the Hivites, and the Jebusites. [9]The cry of the Israelites has now come to me; I have also seen how the Egyptians oppress them. [10]So come, I will send you to Pharaoh to bring my people, the Israelites, out of Egypt." [11]But Moses said to God, "Who am I that I should go to Pharaoh, and bring the Israelites out of Egypt?" [12]He said, "I will be with you; and this shall be the sign for you that it is I who sent you: when you have brought the people out of Egypt, you shall worship God on this mountain."

[13]But Moses said to God, "If I come to the Israelites and say to them, 'The God of your ancestors has sent me to you,' and they ask me, 'What is his name?' what shall I say to them?" [14]God said to Moses, "I AM WHO I AM." He said further, "Thus you shall say to the Israelites, 'I AM has sent me to you.'" [15]God also said to Moses, "Thus you shall say to the Israelites, 'The LORD, the God of your ancestors, the God of Abraham, the God of Isaac, and the God of Jacob, has sent me to you':

> This is my name forever,
> and this my title for all
> generations.

[16]Go and assemble the elders of Israel, and say to them, 'The LORD, the God of your ancestors, the God of Abraham, of Isaac, and of Jacob, has appeared to me, saying: I have given heed to you and to what has been done to you in Egypt. [17]I declare that I will bring you up out of the misery of Egypt, to the land of the Canaanites, the Hittites, the Amorites, the Perizzites, the Hivites, and the Jebusites, a land flowing with milk and honey.' [18]They will listen to your voice; and you and the elders of Israel shall go to the king of Egypt and say to him, 'The LORD, the God of the Hebrews, has met with us; let us now go a three days' journey into the wilderness, so that we may sacrifice to the LORD our God.' [19]I know, however, that the king of Egypt will not let you go unless compelled by a mighty hand. [20]So I will stretch out my hand and strike Egypt with all my wonders that I will perform in it; after that he will let you go. [21]I will bring this people into such favor with the Egyptians that, when you go, you will not go empty-handed; [22]each woman shall ask her neighbor and any woman living in the neighbor's house for jewelry of silver and of gold, and clothing, and you shall put them on your sons and on your daughters; and so you shall plunder the Egyptians." . . .

## *Chs. 19–20 [The Ten Commandments]*

**19** On the third new moon after the Israelites had gone out of the land of Egypt, on that very day, they came into the wilderness of Sinai. [2]They had journeyed from Rephidim, entered the wilderness of Sinai, and camped in the wilderness; Israel camped there in front of the mountain. [3]Then Moses went up to God; the LORD called to him from the mountain, saying, "Thus you shall say to the house of Jacob, and tell the Israelites: [4]You have seen what I did to the Egyptians, and how I bore you on eagles' wings and brought you to myself. [5]Now therefore, if you obey my voice and keep my covenant, you shall be my treasured possession out of all the peoples. Indeed, the whole earth is mine, [6]but you shall be for me a priestly kingdom and a holy nation. These are

the words that you shall speak to the
Israelites."
7So Moses came, summoned the
elders of the people, and set before
them all these words that the LORD had
commanded him. 8The people all
answered as one: "Everything that the
LORD has spoken we will do." Moses
reported the words of the people to the
LORD. 9Then the LORD said to Moses, "I
am going to come to you in a dense
cloud, in order that the people may
hear when I speak with you and so trust
you ever after."
When Moses had told the words of
the people to the LORD, 10the LORD said
to Moses: "Go to the people and consecrate them today and tomorrow. Have
them wash their clothes 11and prepare
for the third day, because on the third
day the LORD will come down upon
Mount Sinai in the sight of all the people. 12You shall set limits for the people
all around, saying, 'Be careful not to
go up the mountain or to touch the
edge of it. Any who touch the mountain
shall be put to death. 13No hand shall
touch them, but they shall be stoned or
shot with arrows; whether animal or
human being, they shall not live.'
When the trumpet sounds a long blast,
they may go up on the mountain." 14So
Moses went down from the mountain
to the people. He consecrated the people, and they washed their clothes.
15And he said to the people, "Prepare
for the third day; do not go near a
woman."
16On the morning of the third day
there was thunder and lightning, as
well as a thick cloud on the mountain,
and a blast of a trumpet so loud that
all the people who were in the camp
trembled. 17Moses brought the people
out of the camp to meet God. They
took their stand at the foot of the
mountain. 18Now Mount Sinai was
wrapped in smoke, because the LORD
had descended upon it in fire; the
smoke went up like the smoke of a kiln,
while the whole mountain shook violently. 19As the blast of the trumpet grew
louder and louder, Moses would speak
and God would answer him in thunder.
20When the LORD descended upon
Mount Sinai, to the top of the mountain, the LORD summoned Moses to the
top of the mountain, and Moses went
up. 21Then the LORD said to Moses, "Go
down and warn the people not to break
through to the LORD to look; otherwise
many of them will perish. 22Even the
priests who approach the LORD must
consecrate themselves or the LORD will
break out against them." 23Moses said to
the LORD, "The people are not permitted to come up to Mount Sinai; for you
yourself warned us, saying, 'Set limits
around the mountain and keep it
holy.'" 24The LORD said to him, "Go
down, and come up bringing Aaron
with you; but do not let either the
priests or the people break through to
come up to the LORD; otherwise he will
break out against them." 25So Moses
went down to the people and told
them.

**20** Then God spoke all these words:
2I am the LORD your God, who brought
you out of the land of Egypt, out of the
house of slavery; 3you shall have no
other gods before me.
4You shall not make for yourself an
idol, whether in the form of anything
that is in heaven above, or that is on the
earth beneath, or that is in the water
under the earth. 5You shall not bow
down to them or worship them; for
I the LORD your God am a jealous God,
punishing children for the iniquity
of parents, to the third and the fourth

generation of those who reject me, 6but showing steadfast love to the thousandth generation of those who love me and keep my commandments.

7You shall not make wrongful use of the name of the LORD your God, for the LORD will not acquit anyone who misuses his name.

8Remember the sabbath day, and keep it holy. 9Six days you shall labor and do all your work. 10But the seventh day is a sabbath to the LORD your God; you shall not do any work—you, your son or your daughter, your male or female slave, your livestock, or the alien resident in your towns. 11For in six days the LORD made heaven and earth, the sea, and all that is in them, but rested the seventh day; therefore the LORD blessed the sabbath day and consecrated it.

12Honor your father and your mother, so that your days may be long in the land that the LORD your God is giving you.

13You shall not murder.

14You shall not commit adultery.

15You shall not steal.

16You shall not bear false witness against your neighbor.

17You shall not covet your neighbor's house; you shall not covet your neighbor's wife, or male or female slave, or ox, or donkey, or anything that belongs to your neighbor.

18When all the people witnessed the thunder and lightning, the sound of the trumpet, and the mountain smoking, they were afraid and trembled and stood at a distance, 19and said to Moses, "You speak to us, and we will listen; but do not let God speak to us, or we will die." 20Moses said to the people, "Do not be afraid; for God has come only to test you and to put the fear of him upon you so that you do not sin." 21Then the people stood at a distance, while Moses drew near to the thick darkness where God was.

22The LORD said to Moses: Thus you shall say to the Israelites: "You have seen for yourselves that I spoke with you from heaven. 23You shall not make gods of silver alongside me, nor shall you make for yourselves gods of gold. 24You need make for me only an altar of earth and sacrifice on it your burnt offerings and your offerings of well-being, your sheep and your oxen; in every place where I cause my name to be remembered I will come to you and bless you. 25But if you make for me an altar of stone, do not build it of hewn stones; for if you use a chisel upon it you profane it. 26You shall not go up by steps to my altar, so that your nakedness may not be exposed on it." . . .

## *Ch. 32 [The Golden Calf]*

**32** When the people saw that Moses delayed to come down from the mountain, the people gathered around Aaron, and said to him, "Come, make gods for us, who shall go before us; as for this Moses, the man who brought us up out of the land of Egypt, we do not know what has become of him." 2Aaron said to them, "Take off the gold rings that are on the ears of your wives, your sons, and your daughters, and bring them to me." 3So all the people took off the gold rings from their ears, and brought them to Aaron. 4He took the gold from them, formed it in a mold, and cast an image of a calf; and they said, "These are your gods, O Israel, who brought you up out of the land of Egypt!" 5When Aaron saw this, he built an altar before it; and Aaron made proclamation and said, "Tomorrow shall be a festival to the LORD." 6They rose early the next day, and offered burnt offerings and brought sacrifices of well-being; and the people sat down to eat and drink, and rose up to revel.

7The LORD said to Moses, "Go down at once! Your people, whom you brought up out of the land of Egypt, have acted perversely; 8they have been quick to turn aside from the way that I commanded them; they have cast for themselves an image of a calf, and have worshipped it and sacrificed to it, and said, 'These are your gods, O Israel, who brought you up out of the land of Egypt!'" 9The LORD said to Moses, "I have seen this people, how stiff-necked they are. 10Now let me alone, so that my wrath may burn hot against them and I may consume them; and of you I will make a great nation."

11But Moses implored the LORD his God, and said, "O LORD, why does your wrath burn hot against your people, whom you brought out of the land of Egypt with great power and with a mighty hand? 12Why should the Egyptians say, 'It was with evil intent that he brought them out to kill them in the mountains, and to consume them from the face of the earth'? Turn from your fierce wrath; change your mind and do not bring disaster on your people. 13Remember Abraham, Isaac, and Israel, your servants, how you swore to them by your own self, saying to them, 'I will multiply your descendants like the stars of heaven, and all this land that I have promised I will give to your descendants, and they shall inherit it forever.'" 14And the LORD changed his mind about the disaster that he planned to bring on his people.

15Then Moses turned and went down from the mountain, carrying the two tablets of the covenant in his hands, tablets that were written on both sides, written on the front and on the back. 16The tablets were the work of God, and the writing was the writing of God, engraved upon the tablets. 17When Joshua heard the noise of the people as they shouted, he said to Moses, "There is a noise of war in the camp." 18But he said,

"It is not the sound made by
  victors,
or the sound made by losers;
it is the sound of revelers that I
  hear."

19As soon as he came near the camp and saw the calf and the dancing, Moses' anger burned hot, and he threw the tablets from his hands and broke them at the foot of the mountain. 20He took the calf that they had made, burned it with fire, ground it to powder, scattered it on the water, and made the Israelites drink it.

21Moses said to Aaron, "What did this people do to you that you have brought so great a sin upon them?" 22And Aaron said, "Do not let the anger of my lord burn hot; you know the people, that they are bent on evil. 23They said to me, 'Make us gods, who shall go before us; as for this Moses, the man who brought us up out of the land of Egypt, we do not know what has become of him.' 24So I said to them, 'Whoever has gold, take it off'; so they gave it to me, and I threw it into the fire, and out came this calf!"

25When Moses saw that the people were running wild (for Aaron had let them run wild, to the derision of their enemies), 26then Moses stood in the gate of the camp, and said, "Who is on the LORD's side? Come to me!" And all the sons of Levi gathered around him. 27He said to them, "Thus says the LORD, the God of Israel, 'Put your sword on your side, each of you! Go back and

forth from gate to gate throughout the
camp, and each of you kill your
brother, your friend, and your neighbor.'" 28 The sons of Levi did as Moses
commanded, and about three thousand of the people fell on that day.
29 Moses said, "Today you have ordained
yourselves for the service of the LORD,
each one at the cost of a son or a
brother, and so have brought a blessing
on yourselves this day."
30 On the next day Moses said to the
people, "You have sinned a great sin.
But now I will go up to the LORD; perhaps I can make atonement for your
sin." 31 So Moses returned to the LORD
and said, "Alas, this people has sinned a
great sin; they have made for themselves gods of gold. 32 But now, if you will
only forgive their sin—but if not, blot
me out of the book that you have written." 33 But the LORD said to Moses,
"Whoever has sinned against me I will
blot out of my book. 34 But now go, lead
the people to the place about which I
have spoken to you; see, my angel shall
go in front of you. Nevertheless, when
the day comes for punishment, I will
punish them for their sin."
35 Then the LORD sent a plague on
the people, because they made the
calf—the one that Aaron made. . . .

## THE BOOK OF RUTH

The Book of Ruth is a perennial favorite with readers of the Bible; it is a story told in a simple and realistic style, focusing on the daily lives of ordinary people in a small village in ancient Israel. Moreover, it represents the lives of women and constructs them as central to history.

Ruth has long been part of the biblical canon. Although the date of its written form is contested, it probably lies somewhere between 950 and 700 BCE with possible later emendations. Almost two-thirds of the scroll consists of dialogue, making Ruth the biblical text with the highest ratio of dialogue to narrative. Wordplay abounds, much of it lost in translation. In the original Hebrew, puns and verbal echoes—both within the text itself and with other biblical texts—are noticeable, as are assonance, chiasmus, and the repetition of words and phrases. These stylistic features, coupled with a carefully structured narrative that balances scenes, characters, and actions, led the nineteenth-century German writer Goethe to remark that Ruth was the most exquisite "little whole" in the Bible.

In this text, women's journeys and decisions are central to Israel's history, as the genealogy at the very end of the tale suggests. Ruth traverses cultural difference when she marries Naomi's son, and she moves across geographic and religious boundaries when she chooses Naomi's God and returns with her to Judah. Ruth is not a Jew, but a Moabite who is gathered into the Jewish nation—just as the crops are gathered in during the story. She goes into Boaz's fields to glean, offers herself in marriage to him, and ultimately moves from obscurity to historical importance as the great-grandmother of King David, the great hero-king of Jewish history. The marriage practices and legal issues on which the plot turns are not entirely clear, but fortunately the meaning of the story does not depend upon our understanding them completely.

At least since rabbinic times (the third and fourth centuries CE), The Book of Ruth has been recited annually at Shabuoth, a harvest festival that celebrates both food (God's material gift to his people) and Israel's acceptance of the Torah (the Law, God's spiritual gift). This liturgical practice suggests that Ruth's choices, actions, love, and obedience are to be understood in relation to those of the community of Israel. Just as Ruth chooses to accompany Naomi and accept Yahweh as her God, so Israel chooses to enter into a covenantal relationship with Yahweh and follow the Torah. The interconnection of human and divine behavior in the text receives emphasis through word choices in the Hebrew original, which also describe the relationship between God and Israel. One such key covenantal word, *hesed,* means "loyalty" but suggests divine kindliness, or grace, as well. As a sixth-century *midrash* (rabbinic commentary) suggests, "This scroll is not concerned with either purity or defilement, either prohibition or permission. Why then, was it written? To teach you of a magnificent reward given to those who practice and dispense hesed."

As an edifying narrative, Ruth features characters whose actions help preserve the community, who choose to honor and love one another despite misfortune and cultural difference. Ruth's decision to accompany Naomi and take her people as family and Boaz's decision to marry Ruth even though she is a foreigner highlight relationships entered into voluntarily. Instead of tribal connections that require obligation and reciprocity, the freedom to choose such relationships echoes the covenantal relationship between God and Israel, one in which the community of Israel is chosen by God and in which Israel must continually renew its commitment to Yahweh.

The translation of The Book of Ruth is from the Revised Standard Version.

**1** In the days when the judges ruled,
there was a famine in the land, and a
certain man of Bethlehem in Judah
went to live in the country of Moab,
he and his wife and two sons. [2]The
name of the man was Elimelech and
the name of his wife Naomi, and the
names of his two sons were Mahlon and
Chilion; they were Ephrathites from
Bethlehem in Judah. They went into
the country of Moab and remained
there. [3]But Elimelech, the husband of
Naomi, died, and she was left with her
two sons. [4]These took Moabite wives;
the name of the one was Orpah and the
name of the other Ruth. When they
had lived there about ten years, [5]both
Mahlon and Chilion also died, so that
the woman was left without her two
sons and her husband.

[6]Then she started to return with
her daughters-in-law from the country of Moab, for she had heard in the
country of Moab that the LORD had
considered his people and given them
food. [7]So she set out from the place
where she had been living, she and her
two daughters-in-law, and they went on
their way to go back to the land of
Judah. [8]But Naomi said to her two
daughters-in-law, "Go back each of you
to your mother's house. May the LORD
deal kindly with you, as you have dealt
with the dead and with me. [9]The LORD
grant that you may find security, each
of you in the house of your husband."
Then she kissed them, and they wept
aloud. [10]They said to her, "No, we will
return with you to your people." [11]But
Naomi said, "Turn back, my daughters,
why will you go with me? Do I still have
sons in my womb that they may become
your husbands? [12]Turn back, my daughters, go your way, for I am too old to
have a husband. Even if I thought there
was hope for me, even if I should have

a husband tonight and bear sons,
[13]would you then wait until they were grown? Would you then refrain from marrying? No, my daughters, it has been far more bitter for me than for you, because the hand of the LORD has turned against me." [14]Then they wept aloud again. Orpah kissed her mother-in-law, but Ruth clung to her.

[15]So she said, "See, your sister-in-law has gone back to her people and to her gods; return after your sister-in-law."
[16]But Ruth said,

"Do not press me to leave you
or to turn back from following you!
Where you go, I will go;
Where you lodge, I will lodge;
your people shall be my people,
and your God my God.
[17]Where you die, I will die—
there will I be buried.
May the LORD do thus and so to me,
and more as well,
if even death parts me from you!"

[18]When Naomi saw that she was determined to go with her, she said no more to her.

[19]So the two of them went on until they came to Bethlehem. When they came to Bethlehem, the whole town was stirred because of them; and the women said, "Is this Naomi?" [20]She said to them,

"Call me no longer Naomi,
call me Mara,
for the Almighty has dealt
bitterly with me.
[21]I went away full,
but the LORD has brought me back
empty;
why call me Naomi
when the LORD has dealt harshly
with me,
and the Almighty has brought
calamity upon me?"

[22]So Naomi returned together with Ruth the Moabite, her daughter-in-law, who came back with her from the country of Moab. They came to Bethlehem at the beginning of the barley harvest.

**2** Now Naomi had a kinsman on her husband's side, a prominent rich man, of the family of Elimelech, whose name was Boaz. [2]And Ruth the Moabite said to Naomi, "Let me go to the field and glean among the ears of grain, behind someone in whose sight I may find favor." She said to her, "Go, my daughter." [3]So she went. She came and gleaned in the field behind the reapers. As it happened, she came to the part of the field belonging to Boaz, who was of the family of Elimelech. [4]Just then Boaz came from Bethlehem. He said to the reapers, "The LORD be with you." They answered, "The LORD bless you." [5]Then Boaz said to his servant who was in charge of the reapers, "To whom does this young woman belong?" [6]The servant who was in charge of the reapers answered, "She is the Moabite who came back with Naomi from the country of Moab. [7]She said, 'Please, let me glean and gather among the sheaves behind the reapers.' So she came, and she has been on her feet from early this morning until now, without resting even for a moment."

[8]Then Boaz said to Ruth, "Now listen, my daughter, do not go to glean in another field or leave this one, but keep close to my young women. [9]Keep your eyes on the field that is being reaped, and follow behind them. I have ordered the young men not to bother you. If you get thirsty, go to the vessels and drink from what the young men have drawn." [10]Then she fell prostrate, with her face to the ground, and said to him, "Why have I found favor in your

sight, that you should take notice of me, when I am a foreigner?" [11]But Boaz answered her, "All that you have done for your mother-in-law since the death of your husband has been fully told me, and how you left your father and mother and your native land and came to a people that you did not know before. [12]May the LORD reward you for your deeds, and may you have a full reward from the LORD, the God of Israel, under whose wings you have come for refuge!" [13]Then she said, "May I continue to find favor in your sight, my lord, for you have comforted me and spoken kindly to your servant, even though I am not one of your servants."

[14]At mealtime Boaz said to her, "Come here, and eat some of this bread, and dip your morsel in the sour wine." So she sat beside the reapers, and he heaped up for her some parched grain. She ate until she was satisfied, and she had some left over. [15]When she got up to glean, Boaz instructed his young men, "Let her glean even among the standing sheaves, and do not reproach her. [16]You must also pull out some handfuls for her from the bundles, and leave them for her to glean, and do not rebuke her."

[17]So she gleaned in the field until evening. Then she beat out what she had gleaned, and it was about an ephah of barley. [18]She picked it up and came into the town, and her mother-in-law saw how much she had gleaned. Then she took out and gave her what was left over after she herself had been satisfied. [19]Her mother-in-law said to her, "Where did you glean today? And where have you worked? Blessed be the man who took notice of you." So she told her mother-in-law with whom she had worked, and said, "The name of the man with whom I worked today is Boaz." [20]Then Naomi said to her daughter-in-law, "Blessed be he by the LORD, whose kindness has not forsaken the living or the dead!" Naomi also said to her, "The man is a relative of ours, one of our nearest kin." [21]Then Ruth the Moabite said, "He even said to me, 'Stay close by my servants, until they have finished all my harvest.'" [22]Naomi said to Ruth, her daughter-in-law, "It is better, my daughter, that you go out with his young women, otherwise you might be bothered in another field." [23]So she stayed close to the young women of Boaz, gleaning until the end of the barley and wheat harvests; and she lived with her mother-in-law.

**3** Naomi her mother-in-law said to her, "My daughter, I need to seek some security for you, so that it may be well with you. [2]Now here is our kinsman Boaz, with whose young women you have been working. See, he is winnowing barley tonight at the threshing floor. [3]Now wash and anoint yourself, and put on your best clothes and go down to the threshing floor; but do not make yourself known to the man until he has finished eating and drinking. [4]When he lies down, observe the place where he lies; then, go and uncover his feet and lie down; and he will tell you what to do." [5]She said to her, "All that you tell me I will do."

[6]So she went down to the threshing floor and did just as her mother-in-law had instructed her. [7]When Boaz had eaten and drunk, and he was in a contented mood, he went to lie down at the end of the heap of grain. Then she came stealthily and uncovered his feet, and lay down. At midnight the man was startled, and turned over, and there, lying at his feet, was a woman! [9]He said, "Who are you?" And she answered, "I am Ruth, your servant; spread your

cloak over your servant, for you are
next-of-kin." [10]He said, "May you be
blessed by the LORD, my daughter;
this last instance of your loyalty is
better than the first; you have not gone
after young men, whether poor or rich.
[11]And now, my daughter, do not be
afraid, I will do for you all that you ask,
for all the assembly of my people know
that you are a worthy woman. [12]But now,
though it is true that I am a near kinsman, there is another kinsman more
closely related than I. [13]Remain this
night, and in the morning, if he will
act as next-of-kin for you, good; let him
do it. If he is not willing to act as
next-of-kin for you, then, as the LORD
lives, I will act as next-of-kin for you. Lie
down until the morning."

[14]So she lay at his feet until morning, but got up before one person
could recognize another; for he said,
"It must not be known that the woman
came to the threshing floor." [15]Then he
said, "Bring the cloak you are wearing
and hold it out." So she held it, and he
measured out six measures of barley,
and put it on her back; then he went
into the city. [16]She came to her
mother-in-law, who said, "How did
things go with you, my daughter?"
Then she told her all that the man had
done for her, [17]saying, "He gave me
these six measures of barley, for he said,
'Do not go back to your mother-in-law
empty-handed.'" [18]She replied, "Wait,
my daughter, until you learn how the
matter turns out, for the man will not
rest, but will settle the matter today."

**4** No sooner had Boaz gone up to the
gate and sat down there than the
next-of-kin, of whom Boaz had spoken,
came passing by. So Boaz said, "Come
over, friend; sit down here." And he
went over and sat down. [2]Then Boaz
took ten men of the elders of the city,
and said, "Sit down here"; so they sat
down. [3]He then said to the next-of-kin,
"Naomi, who has come back from the
country of Moab, is selling the parcel of
land that belonged to our kinsman
Elimelech. [4]So I thought I would tell
you of it, and say: Buy it in the presence
of those sitting here, and in the presence of the elders of my people. If you
will redeem it, redeem it; but if you will
not, tell me, so that I may know; for
there is no one prior to you to redeem
it, and I come after you." So he said, "I
will redeem it." [5]Then Boaz said, "The
day you acquire the field from the hand
of Naomi, you are also acquiring Ruth
the Moabite, the widow of the dead
man, to maintain the dead man's name
on his inheritance." [6]At this, the next-
of-kin said, "I cannot redeem it for
myself without damaging my own
inheritance. Take my right of redemption yourself, for I cannot redeem it."

[7]Now this was the custom in former
times in Israel concerning redeeming
and exchanging: to confirm a transaction, the one took off a sandal and gave
it to the other; this was the manner of
attesting in Israel. [8]So when the next-
of-kin said to Boaz, "Acquire it for yourself," he took off his sandal. [9]Then Boaz
said to the elders and all the people,
"Today you are witnesses that I have
acquired from the hand of Naomi all
that belonged to Elimelech and all that
belonged to Chilion and Mahlon. [10]I
have also acquired Ruth the Moabite,
the wife of Mahlon, to be my wife, to
maintain the dead man's name on his
inheritance, in order that the name of
the dead may not be cut off from his
kindred and from the gate of his native
place; today you are witnesses." [11]Then
all the people who were at the gate,
along with the elders, said, "We are

witnesses. May the LORD make the
woman who is coming into your house
like Rachel and Leah, who together
built up the house of Israel. May you
produce children in Ephrathah and
bestow a name in Bethlehem; [12]and,
through the children that the LORD will
give you by this young woman, may your
house be like the house of Perez, whom
Tamar bore to Judah."

[13]So Boaz took Ruth and she
became his wife. When they came
together, the LORD made her conceive,
and she bore a son. [14]Then the women
said to Naomi, "Blessed be the LORD,
who has not left you this day without
next-of-kin; and may his name be
renowned in Israel! [15]He shall be to you
a restorer of life and a nourisher of
your old age; for your daughter-in-law
who loves you, who is more to you than
seven sons, has borne him." [16]Then
Naomi took the child and laid him in
her bosom, and became his nurse.
[17]The women of the neighborhood gave
him a name, saying, "A son has been
born to Naomi." They named him
Obed; he became the father of Jesse,
the father of David.

[18]Now these are the descendants
of Perez: Perez became the father of
Hezron, [19]Hezron of Ram, Ram of
Amminadab, [20]Amminadab of Nahshon,
Nahshon of Salmon, [21]Salmon of Boaz,
Boaz of Obed, [22]Obed of Jesse, and Jesse
of David.

## THE BOOK OF JOB

The Book of Job consists of at least two parts: a prose folk tale (most of the first two chapters and most of the final one) and some forty chapters of poetry inserted into this prose setting. The theme of the folk tale is fairly straightforward, but profound: God accepts Satan's wager that Job cannot withstand a test of his faith, and Job lives up to God's expectation. Job asserts that if God can give, God can also take away; such changes in fortune have no bearing on his faith. Job is never told about the wager and draws no theological conclusions from his experience. In the end God rewards Job doubly for his steadfastness, confirming Israel's traditional belief that God rewards goodness; but Job has importantly demonstrated that humanity's goodness does not depend upon the promise of a reward.

Inserted into this short tale, as if to explore its implications, is a series of dialogues between Job and three "friends," plus a disquisition by a fourth (perhaps a separate insertion), and a long concluding speech by God. The debate asks from different angles whether Job's suffering does not really destroy Israel's long-held belief that God protects the just and punishes the wicked. Here Job is by no means patient; he is angry and sometimes blasphemous. He steadfastly (and correctly) denies that he has sinned, which seems to this point to be Israel's only rationale for suffering. The poet offers no substitute rationale, except to say that God can do what he wants, does not answer to human reason, and cannot be understood. The poem was probably written after the national trauma of the Babylonian exile (586–539 BCE) shattered Israel's secure faith in its sacred history.

Though the two parts of the book are apparently irreconcilable, the effect of their being joined is thematically powerful. During the brilliant and impassioned debate about the meaning of Job's suffering, the reader already knows the answer—that it is the result of nothing more than a wager. This dramatic irony (the reader knowing more than the characters) undermines the debate in a disturbing way, for no matter what the characters say, it is never really to the point.

Included here are the prose frame and the final five chapters, including God's speech from the whirlwind. In its concentrated attempt to express the inexpressible, this last speech is one of the most sublime poems in all of world literature. Surprisingly, in the account of the Creation as God tells it here, man plays virtually no role—a radical revision of Genesis, where the world was made for man, and man was made in God's image. In contrast, Job represents man as disillusioned, pitifully unable to understand God or the world, and unimportant in the big picture. Negative as this vision is, however, Job never contemplates suicide or questions the existence of God.

As a dramatic representation of fundamental problems of being human, The Book of Job is often compared to Greek tragedy. Jewish culture was hellenized after Alexander the Great conquered Palestine in 332 BCE, so it is possible that the work was influenced by Greek tragedy, though this cannot be proved. Among the other texts in this anthology, Samuel Beckett's modern drama *Happy Days* grapples most directly with the themes of Job.

The translation of The Book of Job is from the Revised Standard Version.

## *Chs. 1–2 [God's Wager]*

**1** There was once a man in the land of Uz whose name was Job. That man was blameless and upright, one who feared God and turned away from evil. [2]There were born to him seven sons and three daughters. [3]He had seven thousand sheep, three thousand camels, five hundred yoke of oxen, five hundred donkeys, and very many servants; so that this man was the greatest of all the people of the east. [4]His sons used to go and hold feasts in one another's houses in turn; and they would send and invite their three sisters to eat and drink with them. [5]And when the feast days had run their course, Job would send and sanctify them, and he would rise early in the morning and offer burnt offerings according to the number of them all; for Job said, "It may be that my children have sinned, and cursed God in their hearts." This is what Job always did.

[6]One day the heavenly beings came to present themselves before the LORD, and Satan also came among them. [7]The LORD said to Satan, "Where have you come from?" Satan answered the LORD, "From going to and fro on the earth, and from walking up and down on it." [8]The LORD said to Satan, "Have you considered my servant Job? There is no one like him on the earth, a blameless and upright man who fears God and turns away from evil." [9]Then Satan answered the LORD, "Does Job fear God for nothing? [10]Have you not put a fence around him and his house and all that he has, on every side? You have blessed the work of his hands, and his possessions have increased in the land. [11]But stretch out your hand now, and touch all that he has, and he will curse you to your face." [12]The LORD said to Satan, "Very well, all that he has is in your power; only do not stretch out your hand against him!" So Satan went out from the presence of the LORD.

13One day when his sons and daughters were eating and drinking wine in the eldest brother's house, 14a messenger came to Job and said, "The oxen were plowing and the donkeys were feeding beside them, 15and the Sabeans fell on them and carried them off, and killed the servants with the edge of the sword; I alone have escaped to tell you." 16While he was still speaking, another came and said, "The fire of God fell from heaven and burned up the sheep and the servants, and consumed them; I alone have escaped to tell you." 17While he was still speaking, another came and said, "The Chaldeans formed three columns, made a raid on the camels and carried them off, and killed the servants with the edge of the sword; I alone have escaped to tell you." 18While he was still speaking, another came and said, "Your sons and daughters were eating and drinking wine in their eldest brother's house, 19and suddenly a great wind came across the desert, struck the four corners of the house, and it fell on the young people, and they are dead; I alone have escaped to tell you."

20Then Job arose, tore his robe, shaved his head, and fell on the ground and worshiped. 21He said, "Naked I came from my mother's womb, and naked shall I return there; the LORD gave, and the LORD has taken away; blessed be the name of the LORD."

22In all this Job did not sin or charge God with wrong-doing.

**2** One day the heavenly beings came to present themselves before the LORD, and Satan also came among them to present himself before the LORD. 2The LORD said to Satan, "Where have you come from?" Satan answered the LORD, "From going to and fro on the earth, and from walking up and down on it." 3The LORD said to Satan, "Have you considered my servant Job? There is no one like him on the earth, a blameless and upright man who fears God and turns away from evil. He still persists in his integrity, although you incited me against him, to destroy him for no reason." 4Then Satan answered the LORD, "Skin for skin! All that people have they will give to save their lives. 5But stretch out your hand now and touch his bone and his flesh, and he will curse you to your face." 6The LORD said to Satan, "Very well, he is in your power; only spare his life."

7So Satan went out from the presence of the LORD, and inflicted loathsome sores on Job from the sole of his foot to the crown of his head. 8Job took a potsherd with which to scrape himself, and sat among the ashes.

9Then his wife said to him, "Do you still persist in your integrity? Curse God, and die." 10But he said to her, "You speak as any foolish woman would speak. Shall we receive the good at the hand of God, and not receive the bad?" In all this Job did not sin with his lips.

11Now when Job's three friends heard of all these troubles that had come upon him, each of them set out from his home—Eliphaz the Temanite, Bildad the Shuhite, and Zophar the Naamathite. They met together to go and console and comfort him. 12When they saw him from a distance, they did not recognize him, and they raised their voices and wept aloud; they tore their robes and threw dust in the air upon their heads. 13They sat with him on the ground seven days and seven nights, and no one spoke a word to him, for they saw that his suffering was very great.

## Chs. 38–42 [God Speaks from the Whirlwind]

38 Then the LORD answered Job
out of the whirlwind:
2"Who is this that darkens counsel
by words without knowledge?
3Gird up your loins like a man,
I will question you, and you shall
declare to me.

4"Where were you when I laid the
foundation of the earth?
Tell me, if you have
understanding.
5Who determined its
measurements—surely you know!
Or who stretched the line upon it?
6On what were its bases sunk,
or who laid its cornerstone
7when the morning stars sang
together
and all the heavenly beings
shouted for joy?

8Or who shut in the sea with doors
when it burst out from the womb?—
9when I made the clouds its
garment,
and thick darkness its swaddling
band,
10and prescribed bounds for it,
and set bars and doors,
11and said, 'Thus far shall you
come, and no farther,
and here shall your proud waves
be stopped'?

12"Have you commanded the
morning since your days began,
and caused the dawn to know its
place,
13so that it might take hold of the
skirts of the earth,
and the wicked be shaken out
of it?
14It is changed like clay under the
seal,
and it is dyed like a garment.
15Light is withheld from the wicked,
and their uplifted arm is broken.

16"Have you entered into the
springs of the sea,
or walked in the recesses of the
deep?
17Have the gates of death been
revealed to you,
or have you seen the gates of deep
darkness?
18Have you comprehended the
expanse of the earth?
Declare, if you know all this.

19"Where is the way to the dwelling
of light,
and where is the place of darkness,
20that you may take it to its
territory
and that you may discern the
paths to its home?
21Surely you know, for you were
born then,
and the number of your days is
great!

22"Have you entered the
storehouses of the snow,
or have you seen the storehouses
of the hail,
23which I have reserved for the
time of trouble,
for the day of battle and war?
24What is the way to the place
where the light is distributed,
or where the east wind is
scattered upon the earth?

25"Who has cut a channel for the
torrents of rain,
and a way for the thunderbolt,
26to bring rain on a land where no
one lives,

on the desert, which is empty of
human life,
27to satisfy the waste and desolate
land,
and to make the ground put forth
grass?

28"Has the rain a father,
or who has begotten the drops
of dew?
29From whose womb did the ice
come forth,
and who has given birth to the
hoarfrost of heaven?
30The waters become hard like
stone,
and the face of the deep is frozen.

31"Can you bind the chains of the
Pleiades,
or loose the cords of Orion?
32Can you lead forth the Mazzaroth
in their season,
or can you guide the Bear with its
children?
33Do you know the ordinances of
the heavens?
Can you establish their rule on the
earth?

34"Can you lift up your voice to the
clouds,
so that a flood of waters may cover
you?
35Can you send forth lightnings, so
that they may go
and say to you, 'Here we are'?
36Who has put wisdom in the
inward parts,
or given understanding to the
mind?
37Who has the wisdom to number
the clouds?
Or who can tilt the waterskins of
the heavens,
38when the dust runs into a mass
and the clods cling together?

39"Can you hunt the prey for the
lion,
or satisfy the appetite of the young
lions,
40when they crouch in their dens,
or lie in wait in their covert?
41Who provides for the raven its
prey,
when its young ones cry to God,
and wander about for lack of
food?

**39** "Do you know when the
mountain goats give birth?
Do you observe the calving of the
deer?
2Can you number the months that
they fulfill,
and do you know the time when
they give birth,
3when they crouch to give birth to
their offspring,
and are delivered of their young?
4Their young ones become strong,
they grow up in the open;
they go forth, and do not return
to them.

5"Who has let the wild ass go free?
Who has loosed the bonds of the
swift ass,
6to which I have given the steppe
for its home,
the salt land for its dwelling
place?
7It scorns the tumult of the city;
it does not hear the shouts of the
driver.
8It ranges the mountains as its
pasture,
and it searches after every green
thing.

9"Is the wild ox willing to serve
you?
Will it spend the night at your
crib?

10 Can you tie it in the furrow with ropes,
or will it harrow the valleys after you?
11 Will you depend on it because its strength is great,
and will you hand over your labor to it?
12 Do you have faith in it that it will return,
and bring your grain to your threshing floor?

13 "The ostrich's wings flap wildly,
though its pinions lack plumage.
14 For it leaves its eggs to the earth,
and lets them be warmed on the ground,
15 forgetting that a foot may crush them,
and that a wild animal may trample them.
16 It deals cruelly with its young, as if they were not its own;
though its labor should be in vain, yet it has no fear;
17 because God has made it forget wisdom,
and given it no share in understanding.
18 When it spreads its plumes aloft,
it laughs at the horse and its rider.

19 "Do you give the horse its might?
Do you clothe its neck with mane?
20 Do you make it leap like the locust?
Its majestic snorting is terrible.
21 It paws violently, exults mightily;
it goes out to meet the weapons.
22 It laughs at fear, and is not dismayed;
it does not turn back from the sword.
23 Upon it rattle the quiver,
the flashing spear, and the javelin.
24 With fierceness and rage it swallows the ground;
it cannot stand still at the sound of the trumpet.
25 When the trumpet sounds, it says 'Aha!'
From a distance it smells the battle,
the thunder of the captains, and the shouting.

26 "Is it by your wisdom that the hawk soars,
and spreads its wings toward the south?
27 Is it at your command that the eagle mounts up
and makes its nest on high?
28 It lives on the rock and makes its home
in the fastness of the rocky crag.
29 From there it spies the prey;
its eyes see it from far away.
30 Its young ones suck up blood;
and where the slain are, there it is."

**40** And the LORD said to Job:
2 "Shall a faultfinder contend with the Almighty?
Anyone who argues with God must respond."

3 Then Job answered the Lord:
4 "See, I am of small account; what shall I answer you?
I lay my hand on my mouth.
5 I have spoken once, and I will not answer;
twice, but will proceed no further."

6 Then the Lord answered Job out of the whirlwind:

7"Gird up your loins like a man;
I will question you, and you
declare to me.
8Will you even put me in the
wrong?
Will you condemn me that you
may be justified?
9Have you an arm like God,
and can you thunder with a voice
like his?

10"Deck yourself with majesty and
dignity;
clothe yourself with glory and
splendor.
11Pour out the overflowings of your
anger,
and look on all who are proud,
and abase them.
12Look on all who are proud, and
bring them low;
tread down the wicked where they
stand.
13Hide them all in the dust
together;
bind their faces in the world
below.
14Then I will also acknowledge to
you
that your own right hand can give
you victory.

15"Look at Behemoth,
which I made just as I made you;
it eats grass like an ox.
16Its strength is in its loins,
and its power in the muscles of its
belly.
17It makes its tail stiff like a cedar;
the sinews of its thighs are knit
together.
18Its bones are tubes of bronze,
its limbs like bars of iron.
19"It is the first of the great acts of
God—
only its Maker can approach it
with the sword.
20For the mountains yield food for it
where all the wild animals play.
21Under the lotus plants it lies,
in the covert of the reeds and in
the marsh.
22The lotus trees cover it for
shade;
the willows of the wadi
surround it.
23Even if the river is turbulent, it is
not frightened;
it is confident though Jordan
rushes against its mouth.
24Can one take it with hooks
or pierce its nose with a snare?

**41** "Can you draw out Leviathan
with a fishhook,
or press down its tongue with a
cord?
2Can you put a rope in its nose,
or pierce its jaw with a hook?
3Will it make many supplications
to you?
Will it speak soft words to you?
4Will it make a covenant with you
to be taken as your servant
forever?
5Will you play with it as with a
bird,
or will you put it on leash for your
girls?
6Will traders bargain over it?
Will they divide it up among the
merchants?
7Can you fill its skin with
harpoons,
or its head with fishing spears?
8Lay hands on it;
think of the battle; you will not do
it again!
9Any hope of capturing it will be
disappointed;

were not even the gods
overwhelmed at the sight of it?
10No one is so fierce as to dare to
stir it up.
Who can stand before it?
11Who can confront it and be safe?
—under the whole heaven, who?

12"I will not keep silence
concerning its limbs,
or its mighty strength, or its
splendid frame.
13Who can strip off its outer
garment?
Who can penetrate its double coat
of mail?
14Who can open the doors of its
face?
There is terror all around its teeth.
15Its back is made of shields in
rows,
shut up closely as with a seal.
16One is so near to another
that no air can come between
them.
17They are joined one to another;
they clasp each other and cannot
be separated.
18Its sneezes flash forth light,
and its eyes are like the eyelids of
the dawn.
19From its mouth go flaming
torches;
sparks of fire leap out.
20Out of its nostrils comes smoke,
as from a boiling pot and burning
rushes.
21Its breath kindles coals,
and a flame comes out of its
mouth.
22In its neck abides strength,
and terror dances before it.
23The folds of its flesh cling
together;
it is firmly cast and immovable.
24Its heart is as hard as stone,
as hard as the lower millstone.
25When it raises itself up the gods
are afraid;
at the crashing they are beside
themselves.
26Though the sword reaches it, it
does not avail,
nor does the spear, the dart, or
the javelin.
27It counts iron as straw,
and bronze as rotten wood.
28The arrow cannot make it flee;
slingstones, for it, are turned to
chaff.
29Clubs are counted as chaff;
it laughs at the rattle of javelins.
30Its underparts are like sharp
potsherds;
it spreads itself like a threshing
sledge on the mire.
31It makes the deep boil like a pot;
it makes the sea like a pot of
ointment.
32It leaves a shining wake behind it;
one would think the deep to be
white-haired.
33On earth it has no equal,
a creature without fear.
34It surveys everything that is lofty;
it is king over all that are proud."

**42** Then Job answered the Lord:
2"I know that you can do all things,
and that no purpose of yours can
be thwarted.
3'Who is this that hides counsel
without knowledge?'
Therefore I have uttered what I
did not understand,
things too wonderful for me,
which I did not know.
4'Hear, and I will speak;
I will question you, and you
declare to me.'

5I had heard of you by the hearing
of the ear,
but now my eye sees you;
6therefore I despise myself,
and repent in dust and ashes."

7After the LORD had spoken these
words to Job, the LORD said to Eliphaz
the Temanite: "My wrath is kindled
against you and against your two
friends; for you have not spoken of me
what is right, as my servant Job has.
8Now therefore take seven bulls and
seven rams, and go to my servant Job,
and offer up for yourselves a burnt offering; and my servant Job shall pray for
you, for I will accept his prayer not to
deal with you according to your folly; for
you have not spoken of me what is right,
as my servant Job has done." 9So Eliphaz
the Temanite and Bildad the Shuhite
and Zophar the Naamathite went and
did what the LORD had told them; and
the LORD accepted Job's prayer.

10And the LORD restored the fortunes of Job when he had prayed for his
friends; and the LORD gave Job twice as
much as he had before. 11Then there
came to him all his brothers and sisters
and all who had known him before,
and they ate bread with him in his
house; they showed him sympathy
and comforted him for all the evil
that the LORD had brought upon him;
and each of them gave him a piece
of money and gold ring. 12The LORD
blessed the latter days of Job more than
his beginning; and he had fourteen
thousand sheep, six thousand camels,
a thousand yoke of oxen, and a thousand donkeys. 13He also had seven sons
and three daughters. 14He named the
first Jemimah, the second Keziah, and
the third Keren-happuch. 15In all the
land there were no women so beautiful
as Job's daughters; and their father
gave them an inheritance along with
their brothers. 16After this Job lived one
hundred and forty years, and saw his
children, and his children's children,
four generations. 17And Job died, old
and full of days.

## THE PSALMS

The English term "psalm" comes from the Greek *psalmos,* meaning "a song sung with musical accompaniment." In Hebrew, the original language of the Psalms, they are called *tehillim,* "praises." Frequent references within the Psalms themselves provide evidence that they were indeed sung with accompaniment, but little is now known about the nature of ancient Jewish music or the original performance of these songs.

By the fourth century BCE, headings had been added to most of the one hundred fifty Psalms, suggesting authors and historical settings. These headings attribute many of the Psalms to King David (tenth century BCE), a tradition that has profoundly shaped the way some pieces, particularly the laments (see Psalm 51), have been read. Most modern scholars agree that the information given in the headings is questionable. They disagree, however, as to whether the Psalms derive from individual poets reflecting upon their own personal experience or from a community of poets charged with providing liturgy to the faithful. Perhaps a useful comparison is a modern Christian hymnbook that contains a great variety of religious songs chosen for their usefulness to the faithful under various circumstances. Even if David did not write the Psalms, it is interesting that Israel considered poetry to be one of the most desirable talents of an ideal king.

Dating the composition of the Psalms is also difficult. Some may have been written as early as the last years of the tenth century BCE, while others obviously date from the Babylonian captivity (586–539 BCE—see Psalm 137). Thus, the Psalms are roughly contemporary with two other anthologies of ancient poetry to which they can be productively compared, the Chinese *Book of Songs* (pp. 295–317) and the Indian Rig Veda (pp. 176–182).

The most obvious poetic feature of the Psalms, as of Hebrew poetry generally, is the abundant use of parallelism (repetition with variation), a feature that can be preserved quite well in translation:

> Whither shall I go from thy spirit?
>   or whither shall I flee from thy presence?
> If I ascend up into heaven, thou art there:
>   if I make my bed in hell, behold thou art there. (139:8–9)

The Psalms also often display what has been called an "envelope structure." That is, they contain structurally or thematically similar lines repeated in a fashion that encloses what comes between. This device is exemplified in Psalm 8, where the same line ("O Lord our Lord, how excellent is thy name in all the earth") begins and ends the poem. Such a feature can become quite elaborate, with envelopes inside envelopes. The Psalms also follow metric patterns, but these can be difficult to identify with precision, so specialists prefer to speak simply of their rhythm.

The Psalms, like the Vedas, are poetic distillations of one of the world's great religious traditions. They have inspired and sustained vast communities of readers. But like much great religious literature, the Psalms are not always easily appreciated or understood, for they derive from a spiritual piety and devotion that can seem quite distant from our more skeptical and cynical age. Many of the Psalms are poems praising God, some written in an extremely lofty tone (see Psalm 104) and some in a startlingly intimate tone (see Psalm 23); others are songs of supplication that come from a soul racked with an almost unfathomable guilt (see Psalm 51); and still others mingle a tone of deep distress with a desire for revenge that can startle and disturb the modern reader. Who can read Psalm 137, for example, without being alternately sympathetic with the plight of the exile who cannot "sing the Lord's song in a strange land," and horrified at that same exile's wish to dash the children of his captors "against the stones"? It is perhaps this mingling of such strong and seemingly incompatible emotions, expressed so directly and unabashedly, that enables these poems both to inspire and to trouble readers.

Unlike the other biblical selections in this book, the translation of the Psalms is from the King James Version, made in the seventeenth century. Though the King James Version does not always reflect the formal design of the original, it achieves a poetic power that transforms great Hebrew poetry into great English poetry. The wording of these translations has had a profound impact on subsequent literature in English.

## 8

*To the chief Musician upon Gittith*
*A Psalm of David*

O LORD our Lord,
How excellent is thy name in all the earth!
Who hast set thy glory above the heavens.
Out of the mouth of babes and sucklings hast thou ordained
strength
Because of thine enemies,
That thou mightest still the enemy and the avenger.
When I consider thy heavens, the work of thy fingers,
The moon and the stars, which thou hast ordained;
What is man, that thou art mindful of him?
And the son of man, that thou visitest him?
For thou hast made him a little lower than the angels,
And hast crowned him with glory and honour.
Thou madest him to have dominion over the works of thy hands;
Thou hast put all things under his feet:
All sheep and oxen,
Yea, and the beasts of the field;
The fowl of the air, and the fish of the sea,
And whatsoever passeth through the paths of the seas.
O Lord our Lord, how excellent is thy name in all the earth!

## 23

*A Psalm of David*

The Lord is my shepherd; I shall not want.
He maketh me to lie down in green pastures:
He leadeth me beside the still waters.
He restoreth my soul:
He leadeth me in the paths of righteousness for his name's sake.
Yea, though I walk through the valley of the shadow of death,
I will fear no evil: for thou art with me;
Thy rod and thy staff they comfort me.
Thou preparest a table before me in the presence of
mine enemies:
Thou anointest my head with oil; my cup runneth over.
Surely goodness and mercy shall follow me all the days of my life:
And I will dwell in the house of the Lord for ever.

## 24

*A Psalm of David*

The earth is the Lord's, and the fulness thereof;
The world, and they that dwell therein.
For he hath founded it upon the seas,
And established it upon the floods.
Who shall ascend into the hill of the Lord?
Or who shall stand in his holy place?
He that hath clean hands, and a pure heart;
Who hath not lifted up his soul unto vanity,
Nor sworn deceitfully.
He shall receive the blessing from the Lord,
And righteousness from the God of his salvation.
This is the generation of them that seek him,
That seek thy face, O Jacob. *Selah.*
Lift up your heads, O ye gates;
And be ye lift up, ye everlasting doors;
And the King of glory shall come in.
Who is this King of glory?
The Lord strong and mighty,
The Lord mighty in battle.
Lift up your heads, O ye gates;
Even lift them up, ye everlasting doors;
And the King of glory shall come in.
Who is this King of glory?
The Lord of hosts, he is the King of glory. *Selah.*

## 36

*To the chief Musician*
*A Psalm of David the servant of the Lord*

The transgression of the wicked saith within my heart,
That there is no fear of God before his eyes.
For he flattereth himself in his own eyes,
Until his iniquity be found to be hateful.
The words of his mouth are iniquity and deceit:
He hath left off to be wise, and to do good.
He deviseth mischief upon his bed;
He setteth himself in a way that is not good;
He abhorreth not evil.
Thy mercy, O Lord, is in the heavens;
And thy faithfulness reacheth unto the clouds.
Thy righteousness is like the great mountains;
Thy judgments are a great deep:

O Lord, thou preservest man and beast.
How excellent is thy lovingkindness, O God!
Therefore the children of men put their trust under the shadow
of thy wings.
They shall be abundantly satisfied with the fatness of thy house;
And thou shalt make them drink of the river of thy pleasures.
For with thee is the fountain of life:
In thy light shall we see light.
O continue thy lovingkindness unto them that know thee;
And thy righteousness to the upright in heart.
Let not the foot of pride come against me,
And let not the hand of the wicked remove me.
There are the workers of iniquity fallen:
They are cast down, and shall not be able to rise.

## 51

*To the chief Musician*
*A Psalm of David*
*When Nathan the prophet came unto him, after he had gone in to Bath-sheba*

Have mercy upon me, O God, according to thy lovingkindness:
According unto the multitude of thy tender mercies blot out my
transgressions.
Wash me throughly from mine iniquity,
And cleanse me from my sin.
For I acknowledge my transgressions:
And my sin is ever before me.
Against thee, thee only, have I sinned,
And done this evil in thy sight:
That thou mightest be justified when thou speakest,
And be clear when thou judgest.
Behold, I was shapen in iniquity;
And in sin did my mother conceive me.
Behold, thou desirest truth in the inward parts:
And in the hidden part thou shalt make me to know wisdom.
Purge me with hyssop, and I shall be clean:
Wash me, and I shall be whiter than snow.
Make me to hear joy and gladness;
That the bones which thou hast broken may rejoice.
Hide thy face from my sins,
And blot out all mine iniquities.
Create in me a clean heart, O God;
And renew a right spirit within me.
Cast me not away from thy presence;

And take not thy holy spirit from me.
Restore unto me the joy of thy salvation;
And uphold me with thy free spirit.
Then will I teach transgressors thy ways;
And sinners shall be converted unto thee.
Deliver me from bloodguiltiness, O God, thou God of
 my salvation:
And my tongue shall sing aloud of thy righteousness.
O Lord, open thou my lips;
And my mouth shall shew forth thy praise.
For thou desirest not sacrifice; else would I give it:
Thou delightest not in burnt offering.
The sacrifices of God are a broken spirit:
A broken and a contrite heart, O God, thou wilt not despise.
Do good in thy good pleasure unto Zion:
Build thou the walls of Jerusalem.
Then shalt thou be pleased with the sacrifices of righteousness,
 with burnt offering and whole burnt offering:
Then shall they offer bullocks upon thine altar.

## *104*

Bless the Lord, O my soul.
O Lord my God, thou art very great;
Thou art clothed with honour and majesty.
Who coverest thyself with light as with a garment:
Who stretchest out the heavens like a curtain:
Who layeth the beams of his chambers in the waters:
Who maketh the clouds his chariot:
Who walketh upon the wings of the wind:
Who maketh his angels spirits;
His ministers a flaming fire:
Who laid the foundations of the earth,
That it should not be removed for ever.
Thou coveredst it with the deep as with a garment:
The waters stood above the mountains.
At thy rebuke they fled;
At the voice of thy thunder they hasted away.
They go up by the mountains; they go down by the valleys
Unto the place which thou hast founded for them.
Thou hast set a bound that they may not pass over;
That they turn not again to cover the earth.
He sendeth the springs into the valleys,
Which run among the hills.
They give drink to every beast of the field:
The wild asses quench their thirst.

By them shall the fowls of the heaven have their habitation,
Which sing among the branches.
He watereth the hills from his chambers:
The earth is satisfied with the fruit of thy works.
He causeth the grass to grow for the cattle,
And herb for the service of man:
That he may bring forth food out of the earth;
And wine that maketh glad the heart of man,
And oil to make his face to shine,
And bread which strengtheneth man's heart.
The trees of the Lord are full of sap;
The cedars of Lebanon, which he hath planted;
Where the birds make their nests:
As for the stork, the fir trees are her house.
The high hills are a refuge for the wild goats;
And the rocks for the conies.
He appointed the moon for seasons:
The sun knoweth his going down.
Thou makest darkness, and it is night:
Wherein all the beasts of the forest do creep forth.
The young lions roar after their prey,
And seek their meat from God.
The sun ariseth, they gather themselves together,
And lay them down in their dens.
Man goeth forth unto his work
And to his labour until the evening.
O Lord, how manifold are thy works!
In wisdom hast thou made them all:
The earth is full of thy riches.
So is this great and wide sea,
Wherein are things creeping innumerable,
Both small and great beasts.
There go the ships:
There is that leviathan, whom thou hast made to play therein.
These wait all upon thee;
That thou mayest give them their meat in due season.
That thou givest them they gather:
Thou openest thine hand, they are filled with good.
Thou hidest thy face, they are troubled:
Thou takest away their breath, they die,
And return to their dust.
Thou sendest forth thy spirit, they are created:
And thou renewest the face of the earth.
The glory of the Lord shall endure for ever:
The Lord shall rejoice in his works.
He looketh on the earth, and it trembleth:

He toucheth the hills, and they smoke.
I will sing unto the Lord as long as I live:
I will sing praise to my God while I have my being.
My meditation of him shall be sweet:
I will be glad in the Lord.
Let the sinners be consumed out of the earth,
And let the wicked be no more.
Bless thou the Lord, O my soul.
Praise ye the Lord.

## 137

By the rivers of Babylon, there we sat down, yea, we wept,
When we remembered Zion.
We hanged our harps
Upon the willows in the midst thereof.
For there they that carried us away captive required of us a song;
And they that wasted us required of us mirth,
Saying, Sing us one of the songs of Zion.
How shall we sing the Lord's song
In a strange land?
If I forget thee, O Jerusalem,
Let my right hand forget her cunning.
If I do not remember thee,
Let my tongue cleave to the roof of my mouth;
If I prefer not Jerusalem above my chief joy.
Remember, O Lord, the children of Edom in the day
of Jerusalem;
Who said, Rase it, rase it, even to the foundation thereof.
O daughter of Babylon, who art to be destroyed;
Happy shall he be, that rewardeth thee
As thou hast served us.
Happy shall he be, that taketh
And dasheth thy little ones against the stones.

## 139

*To the chief Musician*
*A Psalm of David*

O Lord, thou hast searched me, and known me.
Thou knowest my downsitting and mine uprising,
Thou understandest my thought afar off.
Thou compassest my path and my lying down,
And art acquainted with all my ways.
For there is not a word in my tongue,

But, lo, O Lord, thou knowest it altogether.
Thou hast beset me behind and before,
And laid thine hand upon me.
Such knowledge is too wonderful for me;
It is high, I cannot attain unto it.
Whither shall I go from thy spirit?
Or whither shall I flee from thy presence?
If I ascend up into heaven, thou art there:
If I make my bed in hell, behold, thou art there.
If I take the wings of the morning,
And dwell in the uttermost parts of the sea;
Even there shall thy hand lead me,
And thy right hand shall hold me.
If I say, Surely the darkness shall cover me;
Even the night shall be light about me.
Yea, the darkness hideth not from thee;
But the night shineth as the day:
The darkness and the light are both alike to thee.
For thou hast possessed my reins:
Thou hast covered me in my mother's womb.
I will praise thee; for I am fearfully and wonderfully made:
Marvellous are thy works;
And that my soul knoweth right well.
My substance was not hid from thee,
When I was made in secret,
And curiously wrought in the lowest parts of the earth.
Thine eyes did see my substance, yet being unperfect;
And in thy book all my members were written,
Which in continuance were fashioned, when as yet there was
none of them.
How precious also are thy thoughts unto me, O God!
How great is the sum of them!
If I should count them, they are more in number than the sand:
When I awake, I am still with thee.
Surely thou wilt slay the wicked, O God:
Depart from me therefore, ye bloody men.
For they speak against thee wickedly,
And thine enemies take thy name in vain.
Do not I hate them, O Lord, that hate thee?
And am not I grieved with those that rise up against thee?
I hate them with perfect hatred:
I count them mine enemies.
Search me, O God, and know my heart:
Try me, and know my thoughts:
And see if there be any wicked way in me,
And lead me in the way everlasting.

## 150

Praise ye the Lord.
Praise God in his sanctuary:
Praise him in the firmament of his power.
Praise him for his mighty acts:
Praise him according to his excellent greatness.
Praise him with the sound of the trumpet:
Praise him with the psaltery and harp.
Praise him with the timbrel and dance:
Praise him with stringed instruments and organs.
Praise him upon the loud cymbals:
Praise him upon the high sounding cymbals.
Let every thing that hath breath praise the Lord.
Praise ye the Lord.

## ECCLESIASTES

Ecclesiastes injects a note of radical skepticism into the biblical worldview. The book reflects the discrepancy between our longing for an ordered and rational world on the one hand, and reality as we actually experience it on the other. Recognizing that we live in a world characterized by apparently meaningless change, the book provides a guide to finding satisfaction and contentment in spite of uncertainty.

The term "ecclesiastes" ("churchman" in Greek) is a medieval translation of the Hebrew *Qoheleth,* which might better be rendered the "Teacher" in English. The author is traditionally thought to be Solomon, but scholars think the work was probably written in the third century BCE. Whoever he is, Qoheleth looks at the world he lives in and raises the question of meaning: what is the purpose of pleasure, wealth, work, or wisdom? He skeptically reminds us that the only thing we know for certain is that death comes to us all, no matter how we live our lives, and that in the end "all is vanity and chasing after wind." Furthermore, experience teaches us that right and wrong behavior are rewarded and punished arbitrarily: "The race is not to the swift, nor the battle to the strong . . . but time and chance happen to them all." God may have a plan and an order for the world, but it is known only to him; in practical terms, the world we know is absurd. But Qoheleth insists that we should not despair, even if we cannot grasp the purpose of existence or fathom the will of God, nor should we be discouraged by the apparent futility of life. Instead, we are encouraged to savor the moment, to enjoy what is, and to find satisfaction in immediate existence: "This is what I have seen to be good: it is fitting to eat and drink and find enjoyment in all the toil with which one toils under the sun for the few days of the life God gives us; for this is our lot." This notion is found in the work of other ancient authors, too, notably Horace (*Odes* 1.11), who coined for it the phrase *carpe diem* ("seize the day").

By arguing that chance determines everything, Qoheleth rejects the value of the intellect and rejects as well any confidence in the benevolence of the hand of God. Ecclesiastes is in this sense profoundly practical and realistic in its recommendations of acceptance of the world and temperance in our enjoyment of it. Qoheleth argues that all human endeavor, even religious devotion, should be practiced in moderation, and that good people and satisfaction can be found in everyday life. Like many other writers in both Europe and Asia, he counsels that we should stop fretting about questions of ultimate purpose and meaning and simply live each moment in the fullness of experience.

Although the underlying tone of Ecclesiastes is one of resignation, recognition of the absurdity of the world does not free us from moral responsibility. Though the picture he paints of life is grim, the Teacher advises us to accept the full range of life's experiences as they come to us, live in the fear of God, cherish wisdom, and strive to do good—though with no hope of reward. It must be admitted that the exact nature of his advice is debated by scholars. Some commentators suggest that the book is influenced by Greek philosophy; others have seen a resemblance to *The Epic of Gilgamesh,* which also deals with the ephemerality of life, happiness, and fame.

The translation of Ecclesiastes is from the Revised Standard Version.

**1** The words of the Teacher, the son of David, king in Jerusalem.
2 Vanity of vanities, says the Teacher,
vanity of vanities! All is vanity.
3 What do people gain from all the toil
at which they toil under the sun?
4 A generation goes, and a generation comes,
but the earth remains forever.
5 The sun rises and the sun goes down,
and hurries to the place where it rises.
6 The wind blows to the south,
and goes around to the north;
round and round goes the wind,
and on its circuits the wind returns.
7 All streams run to the sea,
but the sea is not full;
to the place where the streams flow,
there they continue to flow.
8 All things are wearisome;
more than one can express;
the eye is not satisfied with seeing,
or the ear filled with hearing.
9 What has been is what will be,
and what has been done is what will be done;
there is nothing new under the sun.
10 Is there a thing of which it is said,
"See, this is new"?
It has already been,
in the ages before us.
11 The people of long ago are not remembered,
nor will there be any remembrance
of people yet to come
by those who come after them.

12 I, the Teacher, when king over
Israel in Jerusalem, 13 applied my mind to
seek and to search out by wisdom all that
is done under heaven; it is an unhappy
business that God has given to human
beings to be busy with. 14 I saw all the
deeds that are done under the sun; and
see, all is vanity and a chasing after wind.

> 15 What is crooked cannot be made
> straight,
> and what is lacking cannot be
> counted.

16 I said to myself, "I have acquired great wisdom, surpassing all who were over Jerusalem before me; and my mind has had great experience of wisdom and knowledge." 17 And I applied my mind to know wisdom and to know madness and folly. I perceived that this also is but a chasing after wind.

> 18 For in much wisdom is much
> vexation,
> and those who increase knowledge
> increase sorrow.

**2** I said to myself, "Come now, I will make a test of pleasure; enjoy yourself." But again, this also was vanity. 2 I said of laughter, "It is mad," and of pleasure, "What use is it?" 3 I searched with my mind how to cheer my body with wine—my mind still guiding me with wisdom—and how to lay hold on folly, until I might see what was good for mortals to do under heaven during the few days of their life. 4 I made great works; I built houses and planted vineyards for myself; 5 I made myself gardens and parks, and planted in them all kinds of fruit trees. 6 I made myself pools from which to water the forest of growing trees. 7 I bought male and female slaves, and had slaves who were born in my house; I also had great possessions of herds and flocks, more than any who had been before me in Jerusalem. 8 I also gathered for myself silver and gold and the treasure of kings and of the provinces; I got singers, both men and women, and delights of the flesh, and many concubines.

9 So I became great and surpassed all who were before me in Jerusalem; also my wisdom remained with me. 10 Whatever my eyes desired I did not keep from them; I kept my heart from no pleasure, for my heart found pleasure in all my toil, and this was my reward for all my toil. 11 Then I considered all that my hands had done and the toil I had spent in doing it, and again, all was vanity and a chasing after wind, and there was nothing to be gained under the sun.

12 So I turned to consider wisdom and madness and folly; for what can the one do who comes after the king? Only what has already been done. 13 Then I saw that wisdom excels folly as light excels darkness.

> 14 The wise have eyes in their head,
> but fools walk in darkness.

Yet I perceived that the same fate befalls all of them. 15 Then I said to myself, "What happens to the fool will happen to me also; why then have I been so very wise?" And I said to myself that this also is vanity. 16 For there is no enduring remembrance of the wise or of fools, seeing that in the days to come all will have been long forgotten. How can the wise die just like fools? 17 So I hated life, because what is done under the sun was grievous to me; for all is vanity and a chasing after wind.

18 I hated all my toil in which I had toiled under the sun, seeing that I must leave it to those who come after me 19—and who knows whether they will be wise or foolish? Yet they will be master of all for which I toiled and used my wisdom under the sun. This also is vanity. 20 So I turned and gave my heart up to despair concerning all the toil of my labors under the sun, 21 because sometimes one who has toiled with wisdom and knowledge and skill must leave all to be enjoyed by another who did not

toil for it. This also is vanity and a great
evil. [22]What do mortals get from all the
toil and strain with which they toil
under the sun? [23]For all their days are
full of pain, and their work is a vexation; even at night their minds do not
rest. This also is vanity.
[24]There is nothing better for mortals than to eat and drink, and find
enjoyment in their toil. This also, I saw,
is from the hand of God; [25]for apart
from him who can eat or who can have
enjoyment? For to the one who pleases
him God gives wisdom and knowledge
and joy; but to the sinner he gives the
work of gathering and heaping, only to
give to one who pleases God. This also
is vanity and a chasing after wind.

**3** For everything there is a season, and
a time for every matter under heaven:

[2]a time to be born, and a time to die;
a time to plant, and a time to
pluck up what is planted;
[3]a time to kill, and a time to heal;
a time to break down, and a time
to build up;
[4]a time to weep, and a time to
laugh;
a time to mourn, and a time to
dance;
[5]a time to throw away stones, and
a time to gather stones
together;
a time to embrace, and a time to
refrain from embracing;
[6]a time to seek, and a time to lose;
a time to keep, and a time to
throw away;
[7]a time to tear, and a time to sew;
a time to keep silence, and a time
to speak;
[8]a time to love, and a time to hate;
a time for war, and a time for
peace.

[9]What gain have the workers from
their toil? [10]I have seen the business that
God has given to everyone to be busy
with. [11]He has made everything suitable
for its time; moreover he has put a sense
of past and future into their minds, yet
they cannot find out what God has done
from the beginning to the end. [12]I know
that there is nothing better for them
than to be happy and enjoy themselves
as long as they live; [13] moreover, it is
God's gift that all should eat and drink
and take pleasure in all their toil. [14]I
know that whatever God does endures
forever; nothing can be added to it, nor
anything taken from it; God has done
this, so that all should stand in awe
before him. [15]That which is, already has
been; that which is to be, already is; and
God seeks out what has gone by.
[16]Moreover I saw under the sun that
in the place of justice, wickedness was
there, and in the place of righteousness,
wickedness was there as well. [17]I said in
my heart, God will judge the righteous
and the wicked, for he has appointed a
time for every matter, and for every
work. [18]I said in my heart with regard to
human beings that God is testing them
to show that they are but animals. [19]For
the fate of humans and the fate of animals is the same; as one dies, so dies the
other. They all have the same breath,
and humans have no advantage over the
animals; for all is vanity. [20]All go to one
place; all are from the dust, and all turn
to dust again. [21]Who knows whether the
human spirit goes upward and the spirit
of animals goes downward to the earth?
[22]So I saw that there is nothing better
than that all should enjoy their work, for
that is their lot; who can bring them to
see what will be after them?

**4** Again I saw all the oppressions that
are practiced under the sun. Look, the

tears of the oppressed—with no one to comfort them! On the side of their oppressors there was power—with no one to comfort them. 2And I thought the dead, who have already died, more fortunate than the living, who are still alive; 3but better than both is the one who has not yet been, and has not seen the evil deeds that are done under the sun.

4Then I saw that all toil and all skill in work come from one person's envy of another. This also is vanity and a chasing after wind.

> 5Fools fold their hands
> and consume their own flesh.
> 6Better is a handful with quiet
> than two handfuls with toil,
> and a chasing after wind.

7Again, I saw vanity under the sun: the case of solitary individuals, without sons or brothers; yet there is no end to all their toil, and their eyes are never satisfied with riches. "For whom am I toiling," they ask, "and depriving myself of pleasure?" This also is vanity and an unhappy business.

9Two are better than one, because they have a good reward for their toil. 10For if they fall, one will lift up the other; but woe to one who is alone and falls and does not have another to help. 11Again, if two lie together, they keep warm; but how can one keep warm alone? 12And though one might prevail against another, two will withstand one. A threefold cord is not quickly broken.

13Better is a poor but wise youth than an old but foolish king, who will no longer take advice. 14One can indeed come out of prison to reign, even though born poor in the kingdom. 15I saw all the living who, moving about under the sun, follow that youth who replaced the king; 16there was no end to all those people whom he led. Yet those who come later will not rejoice in him. Surely this also is vanity and a chasing after wind.

**5** Guard your steps when you go to the house of God; to draw near to listen is better than the sacrifice offered by fools; for they do not know how to keep from doing evil. 2Never be rash with your mouth, nor let your heart be quick to utter a word before God, for God is in heaven, and you upon earth; therefore let your words be few.

3For dreams come with many cares, and a fool's voice with many words.

4When you make a vow to God, do not delay fulfilling it; for he has no pleasure in fools. Fulfill what you vow. 5It is better that you should not vow than that you should vow and not fulfill it. 6Do not let your mouth lead you into sin, and do not say before the messenger that it was a mistake; why should God be angry at your words, and destroy the work of your hands?

7With many dreams come vanities and a multitude of words; but fear God.

8If you see in a province the oppression of the poor and the violation of justice and right, do not be amazed at the matter; for the high official is watched by a higher, and there are yet higher ones over them. 9But all things considered, this is an advantage for a land: a king for a plowed field.

10The lover of money will not be satisfied with money; nor the lover of wealth, with gain. This also is vanity.

11When goods increase, those who eat them increase; and what gain has their owner but to see them with his eyes?

12Sweet is the sleep of laborers, whether they eat little or much; but the surfeit of the rich will not let them sleep.

13There is a grievous ill that I have
seen under the sun: riches were kept
by their owners to their hurt, 14and
those riches were lost in a bad venture;
though they are parents of children,
they have nothing in their hands. 15As
they came from their mother's womb,
so they shall go again, naked as they
came; they shall take nothing for their
toil, which they may carry away with
their hands. 16This also is a grievous ill:
just as they came, so shall they go; and
what gain do they have from toiling for
the wind? 17Besides, all their days they
eat in darkness, in much vexation and
sickness and resentment.

18This is what I have seen to be
good: it is fitting to eat and drink and
find enjoyment in all the toil with
which one toils under the sun the few
days of the life God gives us; for this is
our lot. 19Likewise all to whom God
gives wealth and possessions and whom
he enables to enjoy them, and to accept
their lot and find enjoyment in their
toil—this is the gift of God. 20For they
will scarcely brood over the days of
their lives, because God keeps them
occupied with the joy of their hearts.

**6** There is an evil that I have seen
under the sun, and it lies heavy
upon humankind: 2those to whom God
gives wealth, possessions, and honor, so
that they lack nothing of all that they
desire, yet God does not enable them
to enjoy these things, but a stranger
enjoys them. This is vanity; it is a grievous ill. 3A man may beget a hundred
children, and live many years; but however many are the days of his years, if he
does not enjoy life's good things, or has
no burial, I say that a stillborn child is
better off than he. 4For it comes into
vanity and goes into darkness, and in
darkness its name is covered; 5moreover
it has not seen the sun or known anything; yet it finds rest rather than he.
6Even though he should live a thousand
years twice over, yet enjoy no good—do
not all go to one place?

7All human toil is for the mouth, yet
the appetite is not satisfied. 8For what
advantage have the wise over fools? And
what do the poor have who know how to
conduct themselves before the living?
9Better is the sight of the eyes than the
wandering of desire; this also is vanity
and a chasing after wind.

10Whatever has come to be has
already been named, and it is known
what human beings are, and that they
are not able to dispute with those who
are stronger. 11The more words, the
more vanity, so how is one the better?
12For who knows what is good for mortals while they live the few days of their
vain life, which they pass like a shadow?
For who can tell them what will be after
them under the sun?

**7** A good name is better than
precious ointment,
and the day of death, than the
day of birth.
2It is better to go to the house of
mourning
than to go to the house of
feasting:
for this is the end of everyone,
and the living will lay it to
heart.
3Sorrow is better than laughter,
for by sadness of countenance
the heart is made glad.
4The heart of the wise is in the
house of mourning;
but the heart of fools is in the
house of mirth.
5It is better to hear the rebuke of
the wise
than to hear the song of fools.

6 For like the crackling of thorns
under a pot,
so is the laughter of fools;
this also is vanity.
7 Surely oppression makes the wise
foolish,
and a bribe corrupts the heart.
8 Better is the end of a thing than
its beginning;
the patient in spirit are better
than the proud in spirit.
9 Do not be quick to anger,
for anger lodges in the bosom
of fools.
10 Do not say, "Why were the former
days better than these?"
For it is not from wisdom that you
ask this.
11 Wisdom is as good as an
inheritance,
an advantage to those who see
the sun.
12 For the protection of wisdom is
like the protection of money,
and the advantage of knowledge
is that wisdom gives life to the
one who possesses it.
13 Consider the work of God;
who can make straight what he
has made crooked?

14 In the day of prosperity be joyful,
and in the day of adversity consider;
God has made the one as well as the
other, so that mortals may not find out
anything that will come after them.

15 In my vain life I have seen everything; there are righteous people who
perish in their righteousness, and there
are wicked people who prolong their
life in their evil-doing. 16 Do not be too
righteous, and do not act too wise; why
should you destroy yourself? 17 Do not
be too wicked, and do not be a fool;
why should you die before your time?
18 It is good that you should take hold of
the one, without letting go of the other;
for the one who fears God shall succeed
with both.

19 Wisdom gives strength to the wise
more than ten rulers that are in a city.

20 Surely there is no one on earth so
righteous as to do good without ever
sinning.

21 Do not give heed to everything
that people say, or you may hear your
servant cursing you; 22 your heart knows
that many times you have yourself
cursed others.

23 All this I have tested by wisdom; I
said, "I will be wise," but it was far from
me. 24 That which is, is far off, and deep,
very deep; who can find it out? 25 I
turned my mind to know and to search
out and to seek wisdom and the sum of
things, and to know that wickedness is
folly and that foolishness is madness. 26 I
found more bitter than death the
woman who is a trap, whose heart is
snares and nets, whose hands are fetters; one who pleases God escapes her,
but the sinner is taken by her. 27 See, this
is what I found, says the Teacher, adding
one thing to another to find the sum,
28 which my mind has sought repeatedly,
but I have not found. One man among
a thousand I found, but a woman
among all these I have not found. 29 See,
this alone I found, that God made
human beings straightforward, but they
have devised many schemes.

**8** Who is like the wise man?
And who knows the
interpretation of a thing?
Wisdom makes one's face shine,
and the hardness of one's
countenance is changed.

2 Keep the king's command because
of your sacred oath. 3 Do not be terrified; go from his presence, do not delay

when the matter is unpleasant, for he
does whatever he pleases. 4For the word
of the king is powerful, and who can
say to him, "What are you doing?"
5Whoever obeys a command will meet
no harm, and the wise mind will know
the time and way. 6For every matter has
its time and way, although the troubles
of mortals lie heavy upon them.
7Indeed, they do not know what is to be,
for who can tell them how it will be?
8No one has power over the wind to
restrain the wind, or power over the
day of death; there is no discharge
from the battle, nor does wickedness
deliver those who practice it. 9All this I
observed, applying my mind to all that
is done under the sun, while one person exercises authority over another to
the other's hurt.

10Then I saw the wicked buried;
they used to go in and out of the holy
place, and were praised in the city
where they had done such things. This
also is vanity. 11Because sentence against
an evil deed is not executed speedily,
the human heart is fully set to do evil.
12Though sinners do evil a hundred
times and prolong their lives, yet I
know that it will be well with those who
fear God, because they stand in fear
before him, 13but it will not be well with
the wicked, neither will they prolong
their days like a shadow, because they
do not stand in fear before God.

14There is a vanity that takes place
on earth, that there are righteous people who are treated according to the
conduct of the wicked, and there are
wicked people who are treated according to the conduct of the righteous. I
said that this also is vanity. 15So I commend enjoyment, for there is nothing
better for people under the sun than to
eat, and drink, and enjoy themselves,
for this will go with them in their toil
through the days of life that God gives
them under the sun.

16When I applied my mind to know
wisdom, and to see the business that is
done on earth, how one's eyes see sleep
neither day nor night, 17then I saw all
the work of God, that no one can find
out what is happening under the sun.
However much they may toil in seeking, they will not find it out; even
though those who are wise claim to
know, they cannot find it out.

**9** All this I laid to heart, examining it
all, how the righteous and the wise and
their deeds are in the hand of God;
whether it is love or hate one does not
know. Everything that confronts them
2is vanity, since the same fate comes to
all, to the righteous and the wicked,
to the good and the evil, to the clean
and the unclean, to those who sacrifice and those who do not sacrifice. As
are the good, so are the sinners; those
who swear are like those who shun an
oath. 3This is an evil in all that happens
under the sun, that the same fate comes
to everyone. Moreover, the hearts of all
are full of evil; madness is in their hearts
while they live, and after that they go to
the dead. 4But whoever is joined with all
the living has hope, for a living dog is
better than a dead lion. 5The living
know that they will die, but the dead
know nothing; they have no more
reward, and even the memory of them
is lost. 6Their love and their hate and
their envy have already perished; never
again will they have any share in all that
happens under the sun.

7Go, eat your bread with enjoyment, and drink your wine with a merry
heart; for God has long ago approved
what you do. 8Let your garments always
be white; do not let oil be lacking on
your head.

[9]Enjoy life with the wife whom you love, all the days of your vain life that are given you under the sun, because that is your portion in life and in your toil at which you toil under the sun. [10]Whatever your hand finds to do, do with your might; for there is no work or thought or knowledge or wisdom in Sheol, to which you are going.

[11]Again I saw that under the sun the race is not to the swift, nor the battle to the strong, nor bread to the wise, nor riches to the intelligent, nor favor to the skillful; but time and chance happen to them all. [12]For no one can anticipate the time of disaster. Like fish taken in a cruel net, and like birds caught in a snare, so mortals are snared at a time of calamity, when it suddenly falls upon them.

[13]I have also seen this example of wisdom under the sun, and it seemed great to me. [14]There was a little city with few people in it. A great king came against it and besieged it, building great siegeworks against it. [15]Now there was found in it a poor wise man, and he by his wisdom delivered the city. Yet no one remembered that poor man. [16]So I said, "Wisdom is better than might; yet the poor man's wisdom is despised, and his words are not heeded."

[17]The quiet words of the wise are
more to be heeded
than the shouting of a ruler
among fools.
[18]Wisdom is better than weapons
of war,
but one bungler destroys much
good.

**10** Dead flies make the perfumer's
ointment give off a foul odor;
so a little folly outweighs
wisdom and honor.
[2]The heart of the wise inclines to
the right,
but the heart of a fool to the left.
[3]Even when fools walk on the
road, they lack sense,
and show to everyone that they
are fools.
[4]If the anger of the ruler rises
against you, do not leave
your post,
for calmness will undo great
offenses.

[5]There is an evil that I have seen under the sun, as great an error as if it proceeded from the ruler: [6]folly is set in many high places, and the rich sit in a low place. [7]I have seen slaves on horseback, and princes walking on foot like slaves.

[8]Whoever digs a pit will fall into it;
and whoever breaks through a wall
will be bitten by a snake.
[9]Whoever quarries stones will be
hurt by them;
and whoever splits logs will be
endangered by them.
[10]If the iron is blunt, and one does
not whet the edge,
then more strength must be
exerted;
but wisdom helps one to succeed.
[11]If the snake bites before it is
charmed,
there is no advantage in a
charmer.

[12]Words spoken by the wise bring
them favor,
but the lips of fools consume
them.
[13]The words of their mouths begin
in foolishness,
and their talk ends in wicked
madness;

[14]yet fools talk on and on.
No one knows what is to happen,
and who can tell anyone what
the future holds?
[15]The toil of fools wears them out,
for they do not even know the way
to town.

[16]Alas for you, O land, when your
king is a servant,
and your princes feast in the
morning!
[17]Happy are you, O land, when
your king is a nobleman,
and your princes feast at the
proper time—
for strength, and not for
drunkenness!
[18]Through sloth the roof sinks in,
and through indolence the house
leaks.
[19]Feasts are made for laughter;
wine gladdens life,
and money meets every need.
[20]Do not curse the king, even in
your thoughts,
or curse the rich, even in your
bedroom;
for a bird of the air may carry
your voice,
or some winged creature tell the
matter.

**11** Send out your bread upon the
waters,
for after many days you will get
it back.
[2]Divide your means seven ways, or
even eight,
for you do not know what disaster
may happen on earth.
[3]When clouds are full,
they empty rain on the earth;
whether a tree falls to the south or
to the north,
in the place where the tree falls,
there it will lie.
[4]Whoever observes the wind will
not sow;
and whoever regards the clouds
will not reap.

[5]Just as you do not know how the breath comes to the bones in the mother's womb, so you do not know the work of God, who makes everything.

[6]In the morning sow your seed, and at evening do not let your hands be idle; for you do not know which will prosper, this or that, or whether both alike will be good.

[7]Light is sweet, and it is pleasant for the eyes to see the sun.

[8]Even those who live many years should rejoice in them all; yet let them remember that the days of darkness will be many. All that comes is vanity.

[9]Rejoice, young man, while you are young, and let your heart cheer you in the days of your youth. Follow the inclination of your heart and the desire of your eyes, but know that for all these things God will bring you into judgment.

[10]Banish anxiety from your mind, and put away pain from your body; for youth and the dawn of life are vanity.

**12** Remember your creator in the days of your youth, before the days of trouble come, and the years draw near when you will say, "I have no pleasure in
them"; [2]before the sun and the light and
the moon and the stars are darkened
and the clouds return with the rain; [3]in
the day when the guards of the house tremble, and the strong men are bent, and the women who grind cease working because they are few, and those who look through the windows see dimly;

[4]when the doors on the street are shut, and the sound of the grinding is low, and one rises up at the sound of a bird, and all the daughters of song are brought low; [5]when one is afraid of heights, and terrors are in the road; the almond tree blossoms, the grasshopper drags itself along and desire fails; because all must go to their eternal home, and the mourners will go about the streets; [6]before the silver cord is snapped, and the golden bowl is broken, and the pitcher is broken at the fountain, and the wheel broken at the cistern, [7]and the dust returns to the earth as it was, and the breath returns to God who gave it. [8]Vanity of vanities, says the Teacher; all is vanity.

[9]Besides being wise, the Teacher also taught the people knowledge, weighing and studying and arranging many proverbs. [10]The Teacher sought to find pleasing words, and he wrote words of truth plainly.

[11]The sayings of the wise are like goads, and like nails firmly fixed are the collected sayings that are given by one shepherd. [12]Of anything beyond these, my child, beware. Of making many books there is no end, and much study is a weariness of the flesh.

[13]The end of the matter; all has been heard. Fear God, and keep his commandments; for that is the whole duty of everyone. [14]For God will bring every deed into judgment, including every secret thing, whether good or evil.

## The Song of Songs

The Song of Songs (often attributed to Israel's King Solomon, and therefore sometimes called The Song of Solomon) is one of the most beloved bodies of poetry in the Judeo-Christian world. As love poetry it is close in many ways to the Egyptian love poetry included in this anthology (pp. 89–93). This kinship should not be surprising in view of the people of Israel's long sojourn in the land of Egypt and the close geographical relationship between the two nations. The Song of Songs has been interpreted in widely different ways for the past twenty-five hundred years, but its appeal comes mostly from its literal meaning as joyous erotic lyric poetry.

Jewish tradition interprets the relation between the lovers as symbolic of the relation between God and his people, or between the king and Israel. Christian tradition adapts that interpretation to signify the relation between Christ and his Church or the human soul. Modern literary historians see the poems instead as a secularized version of the poetry of Middle Eastern fertility cults, like the Sumerian Courtship of Inanna and Dumuzi, which celebrates an annual fertility ritual. In the simplest literary terms the Song of Songs is a graceful dialogue between two lovers and a chorus, containing a number of abrupt transitions from section to section. It is perhaps best understood as a cycle of traditional courtship and wedding songs with a wide range of possible connotations.

The dialogue form is reminiscent of Egyptian love poetry, as are the garden settings and the sensuous intimacy evoked through vivid scenes. Common specific elements are the comparison of the young man to a gazelle, reference to the young woman as "my sister," and the young woman's eagerness to rush out into the streets in search of her lover. Although the pain of yearning and separation is mentioned, the poems emphasize the joy of youthful passion and lovemaking.

In spite of the strong literal meanings, it is easy to see the basis of the traditional allegorical readings as well. The young man is repeatedly referred to as king, and the famous descriptions of his beloved's body are composed of long strings of striking similes in which she is compared to features of the geography, landscape, and pastoral life of Israel. Perhaps this imagery is a residue of the poems' fertility-cult origins; certainly on this level the poems seem also to celebrate the king's love for his nation, his land, and his people—all in the form of charming courtship and wedding songs.

The translation of The Song of Songs is from the Revised Standard Version.

**1** The Song of Songs, which is Solomon's.

[2]Let him kiss me with the kisses of his mouth!
For your love is better than wine,
[3]your anointing oils are fragrant,
your name is perfume poured out;
therefore the maidens love you.
[4]Draw me after you, let us make haste.
The king has brought me into his chambers.
We will exult and rejoice in you;
we will extol your love more than wine;
rightly do they love you.

[5]I am black and beautiful,
O daughters of Jerusalem,
like the tents of Kedar,
like the curtains of Solomon.
[6]Do not gaze at me because I am dark,
because the sun has gazed on me.
My mother's sons were angry with me;
they made me keeper of the vineyards,
but my own vineyard I have not kept!
[7]Tell me, you whom my soul loves,
where you pasture your flock,
where you make it lie down at noon;
for why should I be like one who is veiled
beside the flocks of your companions?

[8]If you do not know,
O fairest among women,
follow the tracks of the flock,
and pasture your kids
beside the shepherds' tents.

[9]I compare you, my love,
to a mare among Pharaoh's chariots.
[10]Your cheeks are comely with ornaments,
your neck with strings of jewels.
[11]We will make you ornaments of gold,
studded with silver.

[12]While the king was on his couch,
my nard gave forth its fragrance.
[13]My beloved is to me a bag of myrrh
that lies between my breasts.
[14]My beloved is to me a cluster of henna blossoms
in the vineyards of En-gedi.

[15]Ah, you are beautiful, my love;
ah, you are beautiful;
your eyes are doves.

16 Ah, you are beautiful, my
beloved, truly lovely.
Our couch is green;
17 the beams of our house are cedar,
our rafters are pine.

2 I am a rose of Sharon,
a lily of the valleys.

2 As a lily among brambles,
so is my love among maidens.

3 As an apple tree among the trees
of the wood,
so is my beloved among young
men.
With great delight I sat in his
shadow,
and his fruit was sweet to my taste.
4 He brought me to the banqueting
house,
and his intention toward me was
love.
5 Sustain me with raisins,
refresh me with apples;
for I am faint with love.
6 O that his left hand were under
my head,
and that his right hand
embraced me!
7 I adjure you, O daughters of
Jerusalem,
by the gazelles or the wild does:
do not stir up or awaken love
until it is ready!

8 The voice of my beloved!
Look, he comes,
leaping upon the mountains,
bounding over the hills.
9 My beloved is like a gazelle
or a young stag.
Look, there he stands
behind our wall,
gazing in at the windows,
looking through the lattice.
10 My beloved speaks and says to me:
"Arise, my love, my fair one,
and come away;
11 for now the winter is past,
the rain is over and gone.
12 The flowers appear on the earth;
the time of singing has come,
and the voice of the turtledove
is heard in our land.
13 The fig tree puts forth its figs,
and the vines are in blossom;
they give forth fragrance.
Arise, my love, my fair one,
and come away.
14 O my dove, in the clefts of the
rock,
in the covert of the cliff,
let me see your face,
let me hear your voice;
for your voice is sweet,
and your face is lovely.
15 Catch us the foxes,
the little foxes,
that ruin the vineyards—
for our vineyards are in
blossom."

16 My beloved is mine and I am his;
he pastures his flock among the
lilies.
17 Until the day breathes
and the shadows flee,
turn, my beloved, be like a gazelle
or a young stag on the cleft
mountains.

3 Upon my bed at night
I sought him whom my soul loves;
I sought him, but found him not;
I called him, but he gave no
answer.
2 "I will rise now and go about the
city,
in the streets and in the squares;
I will seek him whom my soul loves."
I sought him, but found him not.

[3]The sentinels found me,
as they went about in the city.
"Have you seen him whom my
soul loves?"
[4]Scarcely had I passed them,
when I found him whom my soul
loves.
I held him, and would not let
him go
until I brought him into my
mother's house,
and into the chamber of her that
conceived me.
[5]I adjure you, O daughters of
Jerusalem,
by the gazelles or the wild does:
do not stir up or awaken love
until it is ready!

[6]What is that coming up from the
wilderness,
like a column of smoke,
perfumed with myrrh and
frankincense,
with all the fragrant powders of
the merchant?
[7]Look, it is the litter of Solomon!
Around it are sixty mighty men
of the mighty men of Israel,
[8]all equipped with swords
and expert in war,
each with his sword at his thigh
because of alarms by night.
[9]King Solomon made himself a
palanquin
from the wood of Lebanon.
[10]He made its posts of silver,
its back of gold, its seat of
purple;
its interior was inlaid with love.
Daughters of Jerusalem,
[11]come out.
Look, O daughters of Zion,
at King Solomon,
at the crown with which his
mother crowned him
on the day of his wedding,
on the day of the gladness of his
heart.

**4** How beautiful you are, my love,
how very beautiful!
Your eyes are doves
behind your veil.
Your hair is like a flock of goats,
moving down the slopes of Gilead.
[2]Your teeth are like a flock of
shorn ewes
that have come up from the
washing,
all of which bear twins,
and not one among them is
bereaved.
[3]Your lips are like a crimson
thread,
and your mouth is lovely.
Your checks are like halves of a
pomegranate
behind your veil.
[4]Your neck is like the tower of
David,
built in courses;
on it hang a thousand bucklers,
all of them shields of warriors.
[5]Your two breasts are like two
fawns,
twins of a gazelle,
that feed among the lilies.
[6]Until the day breathes
and the shadows flee,
I will hasten to the mountain of
myrrh
and the hill of frankincense.
[7]You are altogether beautiful, my
love;
there is no flaw in you.
[8]Come with me from Lebanon, my
bride;
come with me from Lebanon.
Depart from the peak of Amana,
from the peak of Senir and
Hermon,

from the dens of lions,
from the mountains of leopards.

9You have ravished my heart, my
sister, my bride,
you have ravished my heart with a
glance of your eyes,
with one jewel of your necklace.
10How sweet is your love, my sister,
my bride!
how much better is your love than
wine,
and the fragrance of your oils than
any spice!
11Your lips distill nectar, my bride;
honey and milk are under your
tongue;
the scent of your garments is like
the scent of Lebanon.
12A garden locked is my sister, my
bride,
a garden locked, a fountain
sealed.
13Your channel is an orchard of
pomegranates
with all choicest fruits,
henna with nard,
14nard and saffron, calamus and
cinnamon,
with all trees of frankincense,
myrrh and aloes,
with all chief spices—
15a garden fountain, a well of living
water,
and flowing streams from
Lebanon.

16Awake, O north wind,
and come, O south wind!
Blow upon my garden
that its fragrance may be wafted
abroad.
Let my beloved come to his
garden,
and eat its choicest fruits.

5 I come to my garden, my sister,
my bride;
I gather my myrrh with my spice,
I eat my honeycomb with my
honey,
I drink my wine with my milk.

Eat, friends, drink,
and be drunk with love.

2I slept, but my heart was awake.
Listen! my beloved is knocking.
"Open to me, my sister, my love,
my dove, my perfect one;
for my head is wet with dew,
my locks with the drops of the
night."
3I had put off my garment;
how could I put it on again?
I had bathed my feet;
how could I soil them?
4My beloved thrust his hand into
the opening,
and my inmost being yearned for
him.
5I arose to open to my beloved,
and my hands dripped with myrrh,
my fingers with liquid myrrh,
upon the handles of the bolt.
6I opened to my beloved,
but my beloved had turned and
was gone.
My soul failed me when he spoke.
I sought him, but did not find him;
I called him, but he gave no answer.
7Making their rounds in the city
the sentinels found me;
they beat me, they wounded me,
they took away my mantle,
those sentinels of the walls.
8I adjure you, O daughters of
Jerusalem,
if you find my beloved,
tell him this:
I am faint with love.

9 What is your beloved more than
another beloved,
O fairest among women?
What is your beloved more than
another beloved,
that you thus adjure us?

10 My beloved is all radiant and
ruddy,
distinguished among ten
thousand.
11 His head is the finest gold;
his locks are wavy,
black as a raven.
12 His eyes are like doves
beside springs of water,
bathed in milk,
fitly set.
13 His cheeks are like beds of spices,
yielding fragrance.
His lips are lilies,
distilling liquid myrrh.
14 His arms are rounded gold,
set with jewels.
His body is ivory work,
encrusted with sapphires.
15 His legs are alabaster columns,
set upon bases of gold.
His appearance is like Lebanon,
choice as the cedars.
16 His speech is most sweet,
and he is altogether desirable.
This is my beloved and this is my
friend,
O daughters of Jerusalem.

**6** Where has your beloved gone,
O fairest among women?
Which way has your beloved turned,
that we may seek him with you?

2 My beloved has gone down to his
garden,
to the beds of spices,
to pasture his flock in the gardens,
and to gather lilies.
3 I am my beloved's and my
beloved is mine;
he pastures his flock among the
lilies.

4 You are beautiful as Tirzah, my
love,
comely as Jerusalem,
terrible as an army with banners.
5 Turn away your eyes from me,
for they overwhelm me!
Your hair is like a flock of goats,
moving down the slopes of Gilead.
6 Your teeth are like a flock of ewes,
that have come up from the
washing;
all of them bear twins,
and not one among them is
bereaved.
7 Your cheeks are like halves of a
pomegranate
behind your veil.
8 There are sixty queens and eighty
concubines,
and maidens without number.
9 My dove, my perfect one, is the
only one,
the darling of her mother,
flawless to her that bore her.
The maidens saw her and called
her happy;
the queens and concubines also,
and they praised her.
10 "Who is this that looks forth like
the dawn,
fair as the moon, bright as the sun,
terrible as an army with banners?"

11 I went down to the nut orchard,
to look at the blossoms of the
valley,
to see whether the vines had
budded,

whether the pomegranates were in bloom.
[12]Before I was aware, my fancy set me
in a chariot beside my prince.

[13]Return, return, O Shulammite!
Return, return, that we may look upon you.

Why should you look upon the Shulammite,
as upon a dance before two armies?
7 How graceful are your feet in sandals,
O queenly maiden!
Your rounded thighs are like jewels,
the work of a master hand.
[2]Your navel is a rounded bowl
that never lacks mixed wine.
Your belly is a heap of wheat,
encircled with lilies.
[3]Your two breasts are like two fawns,
twins of a gazelle.
[4]Your neck is like an ivory tower.
Your eyes are pools in Heshbon,
by the gate of Bath-rabbim.
Your nose is like a tower of Lebanon,
overlooking Damascus.
[5]Your head crowns you like Carmel,
and your flowing locks are like purple;
a king is held captive in the tresses.

[6]How fair and pleasant you are,
O loved one, delectable maiden!
[7]You are stately as a palm tree,
and your breasts are like its clusters.
[8]I say I will climb the palm tree
and lay hold of its branches.
Oh, may your breasts be like clusters of the vine,
and the scent of your breath like apples,
[9]and your kisses like the best wine
that goes down smoothly,
gliding over lips and teeth.

[10]I am my beloved's,
and his desire is for me.
[11]Come, my beloved,
let us go forth into the fields,
and lodge in the villages;
[12]let us go out early to the vineyards,
and see whether the vines have budded,
whether the grape blossoms have opened
and the pomegranates are in bloom.
There I will give you my love.
[13]The mandrakes give forth fragrance,
and over our doors are all choice fruits,
new as well as old,
which I have laid up for you,
O my beloved.

8 O that you were like a brother to me,
who nursed at my mother's breast!
If I met you outside, I would kiss you,
and no one would despise me.
[2]I would lead you and bring you
into the house of my mother,
and into the chamber of the one who bore me.
I would give you spiced wine to drink,
the juice of my pomegranates.
[3]O that his left hand were under my head,

and that his right hand embraced
me!
4 I adjure you, O daughters of
Jerusalem,
do not stir up or awaken love
until it is ready!

5 Who is that coming up from the
wilderness,
leaning upon her beloved?

Under the apple tree I awakened
you.
There your mother was in labor
with you;
there she who bore you was in
labor.
6 Set me as a seal upon your heart,
as a seal upon your arm;
for love is strong as death,
passion fierce as the grave.
Its flashes are flashes of fire,
a raging flame.
7 Many waters cannot quench love,
neither can floods drown it.
If one offered for love
all the wealth of his house,
it would be utterly scorned.

8 We have a little sister,
and she has no breasts.
What shall we do for our sister,
on the day when she is spoken for?
9 If she is a wall,
we will build upon her a
battlement of silver;
but if she is a door,
we will enclose her with boards of
cedar.
10 I was a wall,
and my breasts were like towers;
then I was in his eyes
as one who brings peace.
11 Solomon had a vineyard at
Baal-hamon;
he entrusted the vineyard to
keepers;
each one was to bring for its fruit
a thousand pieces of silver.
12 My vineyard, my very own, is for
myself;
you, O Solomon, may have the
thousand,
and the keepers of the fruit two
hundred!

13 O you who dwell in the gardens,
my companions are listening for
your voice;
let me hear it.

14 Make haste, my beloved,
and be like a gazelle
or a young stag
upon the mountains of spices!

# Ancient India

India is often regarded as a vast, colorful, and baffling bazaar of religious beliefs, languages, and political affiliations, and yet Indians themselves speak of the homogeneity of their culture. This sense of unity derives from ancient Sanskrit literature, which has provided a common basis for the subsequent diversity of India's religious and literary traditions.

The Sanskrit literature of ancient India reaches back thirty-five hundred years to the time of the Aryan invasion of the subcontinent. From this tumultuous era came the birth of a literary tradition, as the indigenous culture of the Indus valley and that of the Aryans, an Indo-European people invading from the north, came into conflict and eventually merged. The Vedic hymns of the Aryan invaders established a foundation for poetry, literature, religion, and philosophy that would be amplified and developed through later centuries. Although not as old as the earliest surviving cuneiform and hieroglyphic texts of the ancient Near East, these hymns provide an organized and comprehensive picture of the social and religious life of India at the very dawn of literacy. While we cannot know today whether the hymns were later enacted as rituals, or whether the rituals came first and were described by the hymns, it is clear that from an early age a highly sophisticated literary language existed in India. Because of the importance of ritual and incantation, coupled with the belief that the word is sacred and that the hymns are the breath of the Supreme Being (*Brahman*), the Vedas may have endured unchanged orally for centuries before being put into writing. Subsequent Indian literature has also been considered an expression of the divine, even when it deals with secular affairs and is used for mundane purposes.

The sacred myth of the Rig Veda, the earliest collection of hymns, recounts the deeds of Indra, the chief god and progenitor of the world. The ideas expressed in elliptical, poetic form in the Vedic hymns were later elaborated and explicated in a series of philosophical treatises known as the Upanishads. The Vedic period lasted for a thousand years, from 1500 BCE to about 500 BCE, when Sanskrit became formalized as a literary language. At the end of this Vedic period we see the composition of India's two great epic poems, the *Mahābhārata* and the *Rāmāyana.* These vast works are encyclopedic in nature, incorporating within themselves the religious doctrines and social concepts of Indian culture. The *Mahābhārata* includes the complete text of the Bhagavad-Gītā, a religious treatise of the first century BCE. These epics provide not only a summing up and an elaboration of the earlier literary traditions, but they also provide the basis for much of the literature that followed. So vast and inclusive are these epics that the Indians have a saying, "What is found here may be found elsewhere; what is not here is not anywhere."

Hinduism is an amorphous religion with no single prophet or religious leader and no single doctrine shared by all believers, but its principles are embodied in the Vedas, the Upanishads, and the two epics. One of the most prominent tenets shared by all Hindus is the notion of dharma, or duty. Dharma demands that a person know and perform the appropriate duties for his or her station in life. The emphasis upon knowing one's place in the total context of society implies that not all people are equal, a belief embodied in India's elaborate caste system. Those of Aryan ancestry, known as Brāhmans, occupy the top caste. One's dharma takes precedence over one's personal desires. Sometimes people must act in ways that are distasteful or repellent to them, as when Arjuna must go to war against his relatives in the *Mahābhārata,* or when Rama must reject his faithful wife Sita in the *Rāmāyana.* If these heroes did not do these things, they would violate their dharma with grievous consequences to themselves, their families, society, and the world. An example of what consequences can follow from defying one's dharma can be seen in the case of the old emperor in the Japanese *Tale of Genji* (pp. 1100–1131).

Beginning around 500 BCE there was a period of disruption in Indian culture that may be characterized in several ways. From the outside came a series of invasions, including that of Alexander the Great, that left behind a permanent Greek influence. Internally, a period of religious debate challenged the orthodoxy of Hinduism. Chief among these religious alternatives was Buddhism, which drew much from the Hindu tradition even as it rebelled against it. Unlike the amorphous Hinduism, Buddhism bases its doctrines on the teachings of a single, enlightened figure, Gautama Buddha. Another difference between these two religions is that the early Buddhist canon was not written in classical Sanskrit, but in Pali, a vernacular form of Sanskrit that developed parallel to the Sanskrit tradition. In terms of doctrine as well, Buddhism differs substantially from Hindu orthodoxy by emphasizing the concept of the transmigration of souls, a belief not found in the early Vedic texts, although it develops within Hinduism shortly thereafter. Associated with the transmigration of the soul in both Buddhism and later Hinduism is the idea of *karma,* the notion that our actions in this life have consequences that determine the quality of our next life. In both religious traditions, the ultimate goal is not simply to improve the quality of one's future lives, but to escape the wheel of reincarnation altogether. In Buddhism this means entering the state of *nirvāna*. In Hinduism it means merging with the world-soul.

Hinduism teaches that one's goal is to know one's dharma, that is, one's caste, position, and duty. We find this expressed in the Bhagavad-Gītā when Krishna explains to Arjuna that he must fulfill his caste duty, regardless of the personal suffering he will endure as a result. The Hindu, therefore, seeks to perfect identity as it is defined by dharma. Buddhism, on the other hand, teaches that existence inevitably entails suffering and that suffering arises from excessive attachment to the things of this ephemeral and transitory world.

In the third century BCE the Mauryan emperor Ashoka converted to Buddhism and campaigned to spread the new religion throughout India, setting up inscribed stone pillars that survive to this day. By the beginning of the Common Era, the two chief characteristics of Indian culture, the caste system and the idea of the transmigration of the soul, had become firmly entrenched. Hinduism and Buddhism carried on a dialogue that led to significant borrowing and mingling on both sides. At the same time, Buddhism began to atrophy in India even while its evangelists were spreading its doctrines to both East and Southeast Asia, where Buddhism had endured. Hinduism, meanwhile, flourished in India and reached its full flower during the Gupta dynasty (320–467 CE).

The influence of Sanskrit writing has been widespread both within and without India. Sanskrit literature was discovered by Europeans in the eighteenth century and had a profound influence on the modern study of mythology, religion, and literature. The surprising discovery that Sanskrit is related to Greek and Latin stimulated the birth of modern philology and linguistics. Goethe was deeply influenced by Sanskrit writings, while Schopenhauer discovered in the Upanishads the basis for a meaningful philosophical system. Ralph Waldo Emerson and Henry David Thoreau were the original "Boston Brahmins," whose theories of transcendentalism were inspired by Indian philosophy, especially the Bhagavad-Gītā. T.S. Eliot and Aldous Huxley were profoundly moved by their reading of ancient Indian texts; the Irish poet William Butler Yeats translated the Upanishads into English verse; and at the very dawning of the nuclear age J. Robert Oppenheimer was inspired by the ominous power of the first nuclear explosion to utter a quotation from the Bhagavad-Gītā.

The wisdom of Indian literature and religion was carried to China and Japan through the efforts of Chinese pilgrims such as Xuan Zang and Indian evangelists such as Kumarajiva, who dedicated themselves to translating the Buddhist scriptures into Chinese. Bodhidarma carried the teachings of Zen Buddhism across Central Asia to China. These teachings subsequently reached Japan and formed an important foundation for Japanese culture. Many of the Buddhist texts transmitted to China were subsequently lost in India and were later translated back into Sanskrit from the Chinese (for example the Vimalakīrti Sutra, pp. 260–265). Other travelers brought Indian epics and court poetry to Southeast Asia, where they have had an enduring influence.

## FROM THE RIG VEDA (C. 1500 BCE)

Excepting the earliest Mesopotamian and Egyptian texts, the Indian Vedas ("revelations" or "wisdom") are the oldest surviving literature of humanity. They are the oldest texts in the Indo-European language family, predating Homer by several centuries. The Aryan (or Brāhmanic) people, related to the settlers of Europe, invaded the Indus valley around 2000 BCE. Their sacred texts, in particular the Rig Veda, a collection of more than a thousand hymns, date to around 1500 BCE but may have been transmitted orally for many centuries before that. They are composed in classical Sanskrit, in tightly structured verse forms that must be learned without deviation or improvisation, ensuring an unchanging oral transmission. The Vedas were an *oral* literature, therefore, but not an *oral-formulaic* one like Homer's epics; they were strictly memorized rather than composed in performance.

The culture of the Brāhmans is shrouded in mystery, despite the large literature they left behind. They did not record their history and left no archeological remains. Their scriptures reveal an agricultural people ruled by kings and a priestly class, worshiping a pantheon of divinities not unlike those of Greece and Rome. Vedic religion was organized around recitation of the Vedas in fire-sacrifices involving the use of a sacred drug, soma, which cannot now be identified. Brāhmanism is the ancestor of present-day Hinduism, which still recognizes the superiority of the Brāhman caste in today's Indian society.

The poems of the Rig Veda are unlike other poetry in several ways. They are intended for chanting and calculated to have a deep psychological effect when recited correctly. They are "hymns of power." Their correct recitation is actually thought to sustain the world. Brahman, the Sanskrit word for "universe" or "Supreme Being," also means "breath," as in speech. The language of the hymns has been carefully crafted to produce many levels of meaning simultaneously (scientific, philosophical, theological, psychological, linguistic, spiritual, historical, and mathematical). The hymns reveal, as few texts can, the richness, beauty, and profundity of ancient humanity's mythical-religious perception of the universe. The poems included here are not quaintly antique, but awesome in their antiquity, even for modern readers, and even in translation.

The Hymn of Man expresses the identity of the microcosm and macrocosm, of man with the universe; the Hymn of Creation is startling for its skepticism about the creation it describes; A Psalm of Vasishtha can be compared to the Psalms of the Hebrew Bible; the Hymn of the Thoughts of Men, in the voice of a boy, shows an unexpected sense of humor; the Hymn to Purification addresses the divine drink, soma. These selections range from the purely philosophical—"In nonbeing lay the bond of being"—to the gorgeously mythological:

> Blessed, bearing the sun, the eye of the Gods,
> Leading her white horse, magnificent to see,
> Dawn reveals herself, arrayed in beams of light,
> And with boundless glory she transforms the world.

## Hymn of Creation (X.129)

*Translated by Jean LeMée*

Neither nonbeing nor being was as yet,
Neither was airy space nor heavens beyond;
What was enveloped? And where? Sheltered by whom?
And was there water? Bottomless, unfathomed?

Neither was there death nor immortality,
Nor was there any sign then of night or day;
Totally windless, by itself, the One breathed;
Beyond that, indeed, nothing whatever was.

In the Principle darkness concealed darkness;
Undifferentiated surge was this whole world.
The pregnant point covered by the form matrix,
From conscious fervor, mightily, brought forth the One.

In the Principle, thereupon, rose desire,
Which of consciousness was the primeval seed.
Then the wise, searching within their hearts, perceived
That in nonbeing lay the bond of being.

Stretched crosswise was their line, a ray of glory.
Was there a below? And was there an above?
There were sowers of seeds and forces of might:
Potency from beneath and from on high the Will.

Who really knows, who could hear proclaim
Whence this creation flows, where is its origin?
With this great surge the Gods made their appearance.
Who therefore knows from where it did arise?

This flow of creation, from where it did arise,
Whether it was ordered or was not,
He, the Observer, in the highest heaven,
He alone knows, unless . . . He knows it not.

## Hymn of Man (X.90)

*Translated by Jean LeMée*

Man indeed is this Universe,
What has been and what is to come,
Master of immortality,
When He rises through nourishment.

So great is His majesty, yet
Man, the Person, is still greater:
All beings are a part of Him,
Three parts are immortal in Heaven.

With three parts of Himself, Man rose.
The other part was reborn here.
From here on all sides He advanced
Toward what feeds and does not feed.

From Him came the Source of Radiance,
From the Source of Radiance came Man.
Born, He was master of the Earth,
From east to west, from high to low.

When, with man as their offering,
The Gods performed the sacrifice,
Spring was the oil of sacrifice,
Summer its fuel, autumn its gift.

That sacrifice, blessed on the straw,
Was Man, born in the beginning:
Gods sacrificed by means of Him.
So did the seers and the saints.

From that act of total giving
Drops of oil were collected:
Beasts of the wind were created,
And those of woods and villages.

From that act of total giving
Recited and sung hymns were born.
Rhythms were also born from that.
From that arose holy mantras.

From that horses were given birth
And all beasts with two rows of teeth.
Cattle as well were born from that.
From that were born all goats and sheep.

When they divided Man, the Person,
How were parts distributed?
What became of his mouth and arms?
What did they call his thighs and feet?

His mouth was the Man of the Word,
Into the Prince His arms were made.

While His thighs produced the People,
His feet gave birth to the Servant.

The moon was produced from His mind.
Out of His eye the sun was born,
Lightning and fire came from His mouth
And from His breath the wind was born.

From his navel came aerial space;
The sky evolved from His head;
From feet—earth; from ears—directions.
Thus the worlds were regulated.

Seven were the surrounding sheaths,
Thrice seven the prepared firebrands,
When the Gods, offering sacrifice,
Bound Man as sacrificial beast.

By sacrifice Gods sacrificed to sacrifice.
These were the earliest established principles.
The Mighty Ones in this way reached perfect bliss,
Where dwell the Gods, Ancients who made straight the Way.

## *Hymn to the Dawn (VII.77)*

*Translated by Jean LeMée*

Like a youthful maiden, Dawn shines brightly forth,
Stirring to motion every living creature.
Divine fire was kindled for the use of men;
Dawn created light, driving away the dark.

Sending out her beams, she rose up facing all,
In brilliant robes, resplendent, radiating—
Golden-colored and glorious to behold,
Mother of plenty, mistress of the days she shone.

Blessed, bearing the sun, the eye of the Gods,
Leading her white horse, magnificent to see,
Dawn reveals herself, arrayed in beams of light,
And with boundless glory she transforms the world.

O fair one, banish the enemy with light!
And prepare for us broad pastures free from fear!
Ward off hatred, bring us your priceless treasure!
O bountiful, shower blessings on the singer!

Illumine us with your glorious splendor,
O divine Dawn! Enrich and lengthen our lives,
O Goddess full of grace! Grant us fulfillment
And cows, horses, and chariots in abundance!

O Daughter of Heaven, Dawn of noble birth,
Whom the men of glory celebrate in hymns,
Establish in us wealth sublime and mighty!
O Gods, protect us always with your blessings!

## *A Psalm of Vasishtha to the Lord of Lords (VII.86)*

*Translated by Jean LeMée*

Wise are the works of Him Who with His Glory
Thrust apart the two great worlds and held them there.
He raised on high the sublime vault of Heaven
And the radiant Sun, and stretched the Earth beneath.

While communing with myself, alone, I ask:
O when shall I dwell with the great Lord of Lords?
Will He accept my gift with joy, not anger?
With mind at peace, when shall I see His Mercy?

I ask, Supreme Lord, wishing to know my sin;
I seek out the pure in heart to question them.
The enlightened always give the same reply:
In truth the Lord Himself is angry with you.

O Lord of Lords, what was my chief transgression
That makes You punish a singer of Your praise?
Tell me, Mighty One, from Whom nothing is hid,
That purified I soon may kneel and adore You.

Release us from the misdeeds of our fathers,
Release us from those we committed ourselves,
Release Vasishtha, O King, as a cattle thief,
Or as a calf is released from his fetters.

It was not my own will, but malice itself,
O Lord—gambling, drink, anger, and carelessness.
The older man leads the younger one astray
And even sleep does not prevent transgression.

Like a slave I will serve the bountiful Lord,
Blameless, I will serve the Compassionate One.

The gentle Lord has enlightened the simple
And in His wisdom drives greedy men to wealth.

Let this song of praise, O invincible Lord,
Come to Your attention, close to Your heart.
Peace be with us, peace with us in rest and work!
O Gods, protect us always with Your blessings!

## *Hymn of the Thoughts of Men (IX.112)*

*Translated by Jean LeMée*

Our thoughts wander in all directions
And many are the ways of men:
The cartwright hopes for accidents,
The physician for the cripple,
And the priest for a rich patron.
For the sake of Spirit, O Mind,
Let go of all these wandering thoughts!

With his dry grass and feather fan
And all his tools of fashioned stone,
The blacksmith seeks day after day
The customer endowed with gold.
For the sake of Spirit, O Mind,
Let go of all these wandering thoughts!

I'm a singer, father's a doctor,
Mother grinds flour with a millstone.
Our thoughts all turn upon profit
And cowlike we all plod along.
For the sake of Spirit, O Mind,
Let go of all these wandering thoughts!

The horse would draw a swift carriage,
The entertainer a good laugh,
The penis seeks a hairy slot
And the frog seeks a stagnant pond.
For the sake of Spirit, O Mind,
Let go of all these wandering thoughts!

## *Hymn of Purification (IX.60)*

*Translated by Jean LeMée*

Oh sing a song, a song of praise
To the clear and swiftly flowing
Drop of crystal with a thousand eyes.

It is you with a thousand eyes,
It is you with a thousand ways
That they purified with the sieve.

Swiftly ran the drop of crystal
Streaming through the sieve and rushing into the jars,
Finding its way to Indra's heart.

For Indra's sake, O nectar!
Be purified, quick-flowing one.
Bring us the seed of abundance.

## THE UPANISHADS (6TH CENT. BCE)

At the end of the Vedic period, starting around 600 BCE, the Upanishads were composed as speculative treatises on the Vedas. The work of many authors, and without systematic doctrine, the Upanishads as a group seem to revolt against the rigidity of Vedic religion. They are more philosophical than ritualistic, focusing on various means of self-fulfillment or enlightenment rather than on the religious formalism of the Vedas. They are often "literary" in the way Plato's dialogues might be said to be literary, although their style and teachings are unlike anything in the European tradition. Many of the most memorable passages of the Upanishads take narrative or dialogue form; but their extreme repetitiveness, which suits the purposes of Indian philosophical meditation, may surprise Western readers. Nevertheless, the beauty of the Upanishads has impressed Western readers for centuries.

Some of the more philosophical hymns of the Rig Veda, like the Hymn of Man and the skeptical Hymn of Creation, are explored deeply in the Upanishads. Whereas the Vedas portray a world teeming with divinities, the Upanishads explore the essential unity of the universe. The unity of the self (*Ātman*) and the universe (Brahman) is perhaps their most fundamental doctrine. The oneness of the universe (Brahman) is utterly transcendent, but it can be perceived in meditation as immanent in the oneness of the self (Ātman). The difficulty of understanding this identification is the subject of the following two selections from Chāndogya Upanishad.

In the first selection, the god Indra requires one hundred and one years to achieve understanding—not because the truth is so complex, but precisely because it is so simple. In the second, Shevetaketu learns the truth by means of simple demonstrations with clay, a fig, and salt water. In both cases, the understanding being sought cannot be found in language. The Upanishads undermine the use of language as power found in Vedic ritual. In this respect, too, Indian philosophy differs from that of Europe, where (with some notable exceptions) language and truth are generally identified with each other. The Gospel of John, for example, a Greek text, identifies the Word (*Logos*) with God.

## *from Chāndogya Upaniṣad*

*Translated by Royal Weiler*

### 8.7–12 passim

"The Self [*ātman*] who is free from evil, free from old age, free from death, free from grief, free from hunger, free from thirst, whose desire is the Real [*satya,* or truth], whose intention is the Real—he should be sought after, he should be desired to be comprehended. He obtains all worlds and all desires, who, having found out that Self, knows him." Thus, indeed, did the god Prajāpati speak. Verily, the gods and the demons both heard this. They said among themselves: "Aha! Let us seek after that Self—the Self, having sought after whom one obtains all worlds and all desires." Then Indra from among the gods went forth unto Prajāpati, and Virochana from among the demons. Indeed, without communicating with each other, those two came into the presence of Prajāpati with sacrificial fuel in hand [i.e., as students willing to serve their preceptor]. For thirty-two years the two lived under Prajāpati the disciplined life of a student of sacred knowledge [*brahmacarya*]. Then Prajāpati asked them: "Desiring what, have you lived the disciplined life of a student of sacred knowledge under me?" They said: "'The Self, who is free from evil, free from old age, free from death, free from grief, free from hunger, free from thirst, whose desire is the Real, whose intention is the Real—he should be sought after, he should be desired to be comprehended. He obtains all worlds and all desires, who, having found out that Self, knows him.' These, people declare to be the venerable master's words. Desiring him [the Self] have we lived the student's life under you." Prajāpati said to them: "That Purusha who is seen in the eye—he is the Self [*ātman*]," said he. "That is the immortal, the fearless; that is Brahman." "But this one, Sir, who is perceived in water and in a mirror—who is he?" Prajāpati replied: "The same one, indeed, is perceived in all these." "Having looked at yourself in a pan of water, whatever you do not comprehend of the Self, tell that to me," said Prajāpati. They looked at themselves in the pan of water. Prajāpati asked them: "What do you see?" They replied: "We see here, Sir, our own selves in entirety, the very reproduction of our forms, as it were, correct to the hairs and nails." Then Prajāpati said to them: "Having become well ornamented, well dressed, and refined, look at yourselves in a pan of water." Having become well ornamented, well dressed, and refined, they looked at themselves in a pan of water. Thereupon Prajāpati asked them: "What do you see?" They replied: "Just as we ourselves here are, Sir, well ornamented, well dressed, and refined. . . ." "That is the Self," said he. "That is the immortal, the fearless; that is Brahman." Then they went away with a tranquil heart. Having looked at them, Prajāpati said to himself: "They are going away without having realized, without having found out the Self. Whosoever will accept this doctrine as final, be they gods or demons, they shall perish." Then Virochana, verily, with a tranquil heart, went to the demons and declared to them that doctrine, namely: One's self [one's bodily self] alone is to be made happy here; one's self is to be served. Making oneself alone happy here, serving oneself, does one obtain both worlds, this world and the one beyond. Therefore, here, even now, they say of one who is not a giver, who has no faith, who does not offer sacrifices, that he is, indeed, a demon; for this is the doctrine of the demons. They adorn the body of the deceased with perfumes, flowers, etc., which they have begged, with dress and with ornaments, for they think they will thereby win the yonder world.

But then Indra, even before reaching the gods, saw this danger: "Just as, indeed, the bodily self becomes well ornamented when this body is well ornamented, well dressed when this body is well dressed, and refined when this body is refined, even so that one becomes blind when this body is blind, lame when this body is lame, and maimed when this body is maimed. The bodily Self, verily, perishes immediately after the perishing of this body. I see no good in this." With sacrificial fuel in hand, he again came back to Prajāpati. [Indra states his objection to Prajāpati, who admits its truth and asks him to live as a student under him for another thirty-two years.] Indra lived a student's life under Prajāpati for another thirty-two years. Then, Prajāpati said to him: "He who moves about happy in a dream—he is Self," said he. "That is the immortal, the fearless; that is Brahman." Thereupon, with a tranquil heart, Indra went away.

But then, even before reaching the gods, he saw this danger: "Now, even though this body is blind, the Self in the dream condition does not become blind; even though this body is lame, he does not become lame; indeed, he does not suffer any defect through the defect of this body. He is not slain with the slaying of this body. He does not become lame with the lameness of this body. Nevertheless, they, as it were, kill him; they, as it were, unclothe him. He, as it were, becomes the experiencer of what is not agreeable; he, as it were, even weeps. I see no good in this." [Again Indra returns to Prajāpati with his objection. The latter admits its truth but asks Indra to be his student for another thirty-two years.] Then Prajāpati said to him: "Now, when one is sound asleep, composed, serene, and knows no dream—that is the Self," said he. "That is the immortal, the fearless; that is Brahman." Thereupon, with a tranquil heart, Indra went away.

But then, even before reaching the gods, he saw this danger: "Assuredly, this Self in the deep sleep condition does not, indeed, now know himself in the form: "I am he"; nor indeed does he know these things here. He, as it were, becomes one who has gone to annihilation. I see no good in this." [Indra once more returns to Prajāpati, who promises to tell him the final truth after another five years of studenthood.] Indra lived a student's life under Prajāpati for another five years. The total number of these years thus came to one hundred and one; thus it is that people say that, verily, for one hundred and one years Maghavan [Indra, the Rewarder] lived under Prajāpati the disciplined life of a student of sacred knowledge. Then Prajāpati said to him: "O Maghavan, mortal, indeed, is this body; it is taken over by death. But it is the basis of that deathless, bodiless Self. Verily, the Self, when embodied, is taken over by pleasure and pain. Verily, there is no freedom from pleasure and pain for one who is associated with the body. The wind is bodiless; cloud, lightning, thunder—these are bodiless. Now as these, having risen up from yonder space and having reached the highest light, appear each with its own form, even so this serene Self, having risen up from this body and having reached the highest light, appears with its own form. That Self is the Supreme Person [*uttama puruṣa*].

## 6.1–3, 12–14, *passim*

There, verily, was Shvetaketu, the son of Uddālaka Āruni. To him his father said: "O Shvetaketu, live the disciplined life of a student of sacred knowledge [*brahmacarya*]. No one, indeed, my dear, belonging to our family, is unlearned in the Veda and remains a brāhman only by family connections." He [Shvetaketu], then, having approached a teacher at the age of twelve and having studied all the Vedas, returned at the age of twenty-four, conceited, thinking himself to be learned, stiff. To him his father said: "O Shvetaketu, since, my dear, you are now conceited, think yourself to be learned, and have become stiff, did you also ask for that instruction whereby what has been unheard becomes heard, what has been unthought of becomes thought of, what has been uncomprehended becomes comprehended?" "Of what sort, indeed, Sir, is that instruction?" asked Shvetaketu. "Just as, my dear, through the comprehension of one lump of clay all that is made of clay would become comprehended—for the modification is occasioned only on account of a convention of speech, it is only a name, whereas clay as such alone is the reality. Just as, my dear, through the comprehension of one ingot of iron all that is made of iron would become comprehended—for the modification is occasioned only on account of a convention of speech, it is only a name, whereas iron as such alone is the reality. . . . So, my dear, is that instruction." "Now, verily, those venerable teachers did not know this; for, if they had known it, why would they not have told me?" said Shvetaketu. "Nevertheless, may the venerable sir tell it to me." "So be it, my dear," said he.

"In the beginning, my dear, this world was just being [*sat*], one only, without a second. Some people, no doubt, say: 'In the beginning, verily, this world was just nonbeing [*asat*], one only, without a second; from that nonbeing, being was produced.' But how, indeed, my dear, could it be so?" said he. "How could being be produced from nonbeing? On the contrary, my dear, in the beginning this world was being alone, one only, without a second. Being thought to itself: 'May I be many; may I procreate.' It produced fire. That fire thought to itself: 'May I be many, may I procreate.' It produced water. Therefore, whenever a person grieves or perspires, then it is from fire [heat] alone that water is produced. That water thought to itself: 'May I be many; may I procreate.' It produced food. Therefore, whenever it rains, then there is abundant food; it is from water alone that food for eating is produced. . . . That divinity [Being] thought to itself: 'Well, having entered into these three divinities [fire, water, and food] by means of this living Self, let me develop names and forms. Let me make each one of them tripartite.'

That divinity, accordingly, having entered into those three divinities by means of this living Self, developed names and forms. . . . It made each one of them tripartite. . . ."

"Bring hither a fig from there." "Here it is, sir." "Break it." "It is broken, sir." "What do you see there?" "These extremely fine seeds, sir." "Of these, please break one." "It is broken, sir." "What do you see there?" "Nothing at all, sir." Then he said, to Shvetaketu: "Verily, my dear, that subtle essence which you do not perceive—from that very essence, indeed, my dear, does this great fig tree thus arise. Believe me, my dear, that which is the subtle essence—this whole world has that essence for its Self; that is the Real [*satya,* truth]; that is the Self; that [subtle essence] art thou, Shvetaketu." "Still further may the venerable sir instruct me." "So be it, my dear," said he.

"Having put this salt in the water, come to me in the morning." He did so. Then the father said to him: "That salt which you put in the water last evening—please bring it hither." Although he looked for it, he did not find it, for it was completely dissolved. "Please take a sip of water from this end," said the father. "How is it?" "Salt." "Take a sip from the middle," said he. "How is it?" "Salt." "Take a sip from that end," said he. "How is it?" "Salt." "Throw it away and come to me." Shvetaketu did so thinking to himself: "That salt, though unperceived, still persists in the water." Then Āruni said to him: "Verily, my dear, you do not perceive Being in this world; but it is, indeed, here only: That which is the subtle essence—this whole world has that essence for its Self. That is the Real. That is the Self. That art thou, Shvetaketu." "Still further may the venerable sir instruct me." "So be it, my dear," said he.

"Just as, my dear, having led away a person from Gandhāra with his eyes bandaged, one might then abandon him in a place where there are no human beings; and as that person would there drift about toward the east or the north or the south: 'I have been led away here with my eyes bandaged, I have been abandoned here with my eyes bandaged'; then as, having released his bandage, one might tell him: 'In that direction lies Gandhāra; go in that direction.' Thereupon he, becoming wise and sensible, would, by asking his way from village to village, certainly reach Gandhāra. Even so does one who has a teacher here know: 'I shall remain here [in this phenomenal world] only as long as I shall not be released from the bonds of ignorance. Then I shall reach my home.'"

## FROM THE RĀMĀYANA OF VĀLMIKĪ (C. 500 BCE)

*Translated by Hari Prasad Shastri*

The *Rāmāyana* of Vālmikī represents an ancient oral tradition first written down some 500 years BCE. Shorter than its fellow Indian epic, the *Mahābhārata,* its more tightly focused narrative is perhaps the most popular and enduring work of Indian literature. The author, Vālmikī, is widely considered to be India's first poet known to us by name. Whereas the epic was originally written in formal and poetic Sanskrit, versions of the *Rāmāyana* exist in every major vernacular language of

South Asia, and adaptations are found in narrative, song, and drama throughout Southeast and East Asia. Even today this heroic epic provides material for film, television, and comic books as well as numerous variations, translations, and adaptations. The range and endurance of the *Rāmāyana*'s popularity owes much to the fact that it speaks to all the major bases of Indian culture. As a work of art it is considered to be the source of Indian poetry; as a religious text, it affirms the principles of morality set forth by the major Indian religious traditions; and as a social text, it serves as a guide for the consideration of proper behavior.

The central thrust of the story has to do with the ascendance of Ravana, the embodiment of evil, in the world. Enjoying the protection of magic spells, he is invulnerable to the power of both deities and demons. At the request of the other gods, Vishnu incarnates himself on earth in the form of a mortal man, Rama, to combat this evil. As the manifestation of Vishnu, Rama is compelled always to be virtuous and correct in maintaining his integrity, or dharma. Born the eldest son of good King Dasartha, Rama is cheated out of his right to the throne in a palace intrigue. Uncomplaining, he accepts fourteen years of exile in the forest, where he constantly improves the world by ridding it of a variety of demons and other forces of chaos.

As if exile were not bad enough, while Rama is in the forest his wife Sita is abducted by the evil Ravana and carried away to the island fortress of Lanka. In the subsequent quest to retrieve his wife, Rama seeks the help of bears, led by Jabavan, and of monkeys, led by the monkey hero Hanuman. With the special help of Hanuman, Rama invades Lanka, destroys Ravana's army, and in single combat kills Ravana. After Sita has been rescued, however, Rama repudiates her on the ground that she has lived in the household of another man and is therefore not a suitable wife. Sita proves her innocence in a test by fire.

Returning to the city of Ayodhya, Rama claims his rightful position as king. He rules virtuously and wisely for many years, but when rumors once more begin to circulate that Sita was unchaste while a prisoner of Ravana, Rama bows to public pressure and repudiates her again. Although he knows she is innocent (and pregnant), he casts her into exile at the hermitage of the poet-sage Vālmikī. There she bears twin sons, Lava and Kusa, who memorize the *Rāmāyana* and eventually appear at Rama's court to recite it. Moved by this account of his own life, Rama recalls Sita to Ayodhya and agrees to reinstate her as his consort if she will publicly swear that she has always been faithful to him. Declaring that she has already proved her innocence in a test by fire and fulfilled her duty as a wife by producing sons, she refuses to be tried a second time for the same alleged crime. Instead she returns to the arms of her mother, the earth goddess, and is swallowed up by the earth.

The selections presented here depict Rama as a righteous warrior defeating his enemies and as a virtuous king subordinating his own wishes to the will of the community he represents. Rama's choices, however unpleasant they may sometimes be, are made to maintain his dharma. Sita, whose name means "furrow," also maintains the dharma of her own integrity by refusing to prove her virtue every time someone questions it.

Structurally, the epic is interesting because it forms a complete circle. Vālmikī's name proclaims him to be the "first poet." He hears the story of Rama and recasts it in the form of poetry, which he then teaches to Lava and Kusa. They recite the story of his own life to their father Rama. As a work that explores the definitions and scope of heroic action, the *Rāmāyana* can be compared to the *Iliad* of Homer and to the Japanese *Tales of the Heike.* A hero who enlists animals to assist him in his quest is also found in Wu Cheng'en's *Monkey.*

## *Yuddha Kanda*

*Chs. 100–120 passim [Sita's Rescue and Trial]*

### Chapter 100

*Rama and Ravana fight with magic Weapons*

Beholding Mahodara and Mahaparshwa slain and, despite his great strength, the valiant Virupaksha also struck down, a great rage seized Ravana, who urged on his charioteer with these words:—

"By slaying Rama and Lakshmana I shall remove that double scourge, the cause of the slaughter of my faithful adherents and the siege of the city. In the fight I shall cut down Rama, that tree of which Sita is the flower and the fruit, whose branches are Sugriva, Jambavan, Kumuda, Nala, also Dvivida, Mainda, Angada, Gandhamadana, Hanuman, Sushena and all the leading monkeys."

Thereupon that mighty car-warrior, who caused the ten regions to resound, drove rapidly on Raghava with his chariot, and the earth, with its rivers, mountains and woods, trembled with the uproar, and the lions, gazelles and birds that inhabited it were seized with terror.

Then Ravana employed a dark and magic weapon that was formidable and terrifying and with it he consumed the monkeys, who fled hither and thither. Amidst the dust raised by their battalions, for they were unable to endure that weapon created by Brahma himself, Raghava, seeing those countless divisions taking refuge in innumerable places, pursued by Ravana's powerful shafts, stood ready waiting.

Meanwhile that Tiger among the Titans, having routed the army of monkeys, beheld Rama standing there unconquered with his brother Lakshmana, like unto Vasava with Vishnu, and Rama seemed to touch the sky as it were as he stretched his great bow and those heroes with eyes as large as lotus petals were long-armed and the conquerors of their foes.

From his side the extremely illustrious and valiant Rama, who was accompanied by Saumitri, seeing Ravana overwhelming the monkeys in the fight, joyfully took hold of the centre of his bow and immediately began to bend that excellent weapon that was stout and sonorous, riving the earth as it were.

At the sound of Ravana's loosing a myriad arrows and Rama stretching his bow, the titans fell to the ground in their hundreds! Thereafter Ravana, coming within a bow's length of the two princes, resembled Rahu in the presence of the sun and moon. Desiring to be the first to enter into combat, Lakshmana with his sharp arrows, having placed them on his bow, loosed his shafts resembling flames of fire. Hardly had that archer let fly his darts into the air than the extremely energetic Ravana stayed them in their course, severing one with one, three with three and ten with ten, thus demonstrating his lightness of hand. Leaping over Saumitri, that triumphant warrior, Ravana approached Rama in the conflict, who stood ready like unto an unscalable mountain. Bearing down on Raghava, his eyes red with anger, the Lord of the Titans loosed a rain of shafts upon him but, with the aid of his sharp arrows, Raghava severed those innumerable darts that flamed in formidable wise and resembled venomous snakes.

Thereafter Raghava struck Ravana with redoubled blows and Ravana struck Raghava and they riddled each other with a hail of varied and penetrating missiles and, for a long time, described marvellous circles round each other from left to right, overwhelming each other with swift arrows, each remaining undefeated. And all beings were seized with terror witnessing that desperate duel between those two redoubtable bowmen, the equals of Yama and Antaka. The sky was covered with clouds riven by lightning flashes and the firmament became, as it were, pierced with holes by a rain of whirling arrows of extreme velocity, possessing sharp points, adorned with heron's plumes. With their darts, they first obscured the sky as when the sun withdraws behind the Astachala Mountains and two great clouds suddenly appear.

Thereafter, between those two warriors, each seeking to slay the other, an incomparable and unimaginable struggle ensued like unto the duel between Vritra and Vasava. Both were furnished with excellent bows, both were skilled warriors, both brought exceptional knowledge in the science of arms to the fight. In all their manoeuvrings they were followed by a stream of shafts as the waves in two oceans that are whipped up by a tempest.

Then, with a skilful hand, Ravana, the Destroyer of the Worlds, aiming at Rama's forehead, loosed a formidable succession of iron shafts from his bow, which Rama received unmoved on his head like a garland of lotus leaves. Thereupon, reciting a sacred formula, arming himself with Rudra's weapon and choosing a large number of spears, full of wrath, the illustrious Raghava bent his bow and with force let fly those weapons in rapid succession against that Indra of Titans but those darts fell without breaking through the armour of Ravana, who, like an immense cloud, remained unmoved.

Then Rama, skilled in the use of arms, struck Ravana afresh on the forehead, as he stood in his chariot, with arrows to which he had joined a miraculous weapon, and it appeared as if five-headed serpents in the form of darts were penetrating hissing into the earth repelled by Ravana whom they sought to devour. Thereupon, having rendered Raghava's weapon void, Ravana, in a transport of rage, armed himself in his turn with the dreadful Asura weapon which he loosed joined to sharp and terrible arrows with huge points, having the heads of lions, tigers, herons, geese, vultures, falcons, jackals and wolves or resembling serpents with five heads. Others had the heads of donkeys, boars, dogs, cocks, aquatic monsters and venomous reptiles and those sharp arrows were the creation of his magic power. Struck by the Asuric shafts, that lion among the Raghus, he who resembled the God of Fire himself, responded with the Agneya Dart that was full of power and to it he joined arrows of every kind with points that burnt like fire and which resembled suns, planets and stars in hue or great meteors like unto flaming tongues. Those formidable missiles belonging to Ravana striking against those loosed by Rama, disintegrated in space and were annihilated in their thousands.

Thereupon all the valiant monkeys with Sugriva at their head, able to change their form at will, beholding the titan's weapon destroyed by Rama of imperishable karma, let forth joyous acclamations and made a circle round him.

Then the magnanimous son of Dasaratha, the descendant of Raghu, having destroyed that weapon discharged by Ravana's own arm, was filled with felicity, whilst the leaders of the monkeys joyfully paid homage to him.

## Chapter 101

*Ravana flees from Rama*

His weapon having been destroyed, Ravana, the King of the Titans, whose fury was redoubled, in his wrath instantly produced another; and he loosed the fearful Rudra Weapon, forged by Maya, on Raghava. Thereafter, from his bow, innumerable spears, maces, flaming bars hard as diamond, mallets, hammers, chains and spiked clubs, like unto fiery thunderbolts, issued forth like the tempests at the dissolution of the worlds.

Then the glorious Raghava, most skilled in the knowledge of excellent shafts, that warrior of great renown, broke that weapon with the aid of the marvellous Gandharva Dart, and when it was shattered by the magnanimous Raghava, Ravana, his eyes red with fury, loosed his Solar Weapon whereupon huge and brilliant discs issued from the bow of the skilful Dashagriva of redoubtable courage, which, falling, lit up the sky on every side and the four quarters were consumed by the fall of those flaming missiles that resembled the sun, moon and stars.

With a mass of arrows Raghava destroyed those discs and darts loosed by Ravana in the fore-front of the battle and, seeing his weapon broken, Ravana, the Lord of the Titans with ten arrows struck Rama in his vital parts. Struck by ten shafts that Ravana had discharged from his great bow, the exceedingly energetic Raghava did not flinch and, in his turn, that victorious prince, in the height of anger, pierced Ravana in all his limbs with the aid of innumerable darts.

At that instant, the younger brother of Raghava, the valiant Lakshmana, slayer of hostile warriors, armed himself with seven arrows and, with those exceedingly swift shafts, that illustrious prince severed Ravana's standard in many places, which bore the image of a man's head. With a single arrow, the fortunate Lakshmana of immense vigour, cut off the head adorned with brilliant earrings of the titan who drove the chariot, and with five sharp arrows severed the bow resembling the trunk of an elephant that belonged to the King of the Titans.

Thereafter Bibishana, bounding forward, with his mace slew Ravana's beautiful horses that were as tall as hills and resembled a dark cloud in hue, whereupon Dashagriva, leaping quickly from his car, the steeds of which having been slain, was filled with exceeding wrath against his brother and that powerful and spirited monarch loosed a flaming spear on Bibishana like unto a thunderbolt, but ere it reached its target, Lakshmana severed it with three arrows, whereupon a great cheer arose amongst the monkeys in that formidable struggle, and that spear, wreathed in gold, fell down shattered in three fragments like unto a great meteor falling from the sky amidst a shower of flaming sparks.

Then the titan, that mighty Ravana of wicked soul, armed himself with another superior and tested spear which Death himself would have found hard to resist and which was of immense size and shone with its own effulgence. Brandished with violence by the mighty Ravana of perverse soul it gave out a lurid gleam so that it appeared like forked lightning.

Meanwhile the valiant Lakshmana, perceiving that Bibishana stood in peril of his life, placed himself quickly in front of him and that hero, stretching his bow, with a rain of darts riddled Ravana, who stood waiting to discharge the weapon he held in his hand. Under the shower of arrows with which the courageous Saumitri overwhelmed him, thus frustrating his design, the titan no longer thought of striking him in return. Seeing that he had preserved his brother's life, Ravana, who was standing before him, addressed him thus:—

"O Thou whose strength renders thee arrogant, since thou hast preserved this titan, my spear shall fall on thee; having pierced thine heart, this bloodstained weapon that mine arm, equal to an iron bar, will hurl at thee will rob thee of thy life's breath and return to my hand."

Thus did Ravana, speak and in a paroxysm of rage, levelling that pick adorned with eight extremely loud bells, created magically by Maya, that was infallible, the slayer of its foes, the splendour of which flamed up as it were, hurled it at Lakshmana with a mighty shout. Loosed with terrible violence and a sound of thunder, that spear fell with force on Lakshmana in the forefront of the battle.

Then Raghava sought to mitigate the power of that weapon and said:—

"May good fortune attend Lakshmana! May this mortal impact be rendered void!"

Released by the enraged titan on that indomitable hero, the spear which resembled a venomous snake, falling with extreme violence, penetrated his great chest and so brilliant was it that it appeared like the tongue of the King of the Serpents. Loosed with force by Ravana, that spear penetrated deep into the body of Lakshmana who, with his heart pierced, fell on the earth.

Beholding Lakshmana in that condition, near to whom he stood, the extremely powerful Raghava, full of solicitude for his brother, felt his heart stricken, but after an instant's reflection, his eyes welling with tears, enraged as is Pavaka at the dissolution of the world, he thought—'This is not the time for lamentation' and thereafter he entered once more into the fearful conflict, resolved to make a supreme attempt to slay Ravana.

His eyes fixed on his brother, Rama saw how he had been pierced with a spear in the great fight and was covered with blood, resembling a mountain with its reptiles. And the most vigorous of monkeys sought to draw out that weapon loosed by the mighty Ravana, overwhelmed though they were by a hail of shafts discharged by the King of the Titans; the spear, however, having passed through Saumitri's body had penetrated into the earth. Then Rama, with his powerful hands seized hold of that spear and, in his wrath, snapped it, throwing the fragments to a great distance and, as he drew it out, Ravana penetrated his every limb with his shafts that pierced to his very marrow. Ignoring these darts, Rama embraced Lakshmana and said to Hanuman and that mighty Monkey Sugriva:—

"Ye foremost of the monkeys, gather round Lakshmana! O King of the Monkeys, the time has come for me to manifest my prowess! For long I have sought this occasion! May the wicked Dashagriva of infamous exploits perish! My longing resembles that of the Chatak bird on beholding the clouds at the end of summer. Ere long, I swear to thee either Ravana or Rama will cease to exist in the world! Ye shall be witness thereof! The loss of the kingdom, my sojourn in the forest and my wanderings in the woods of Dandaka, the insult offered to Vaidehi, my encounter with the titans, the great and terrible misfortune that has visited me, this torment resembling hell will be wiped out this day when I slay Ravana on the battlefield! He on whose account I took the army of monkeys in my train, having installed Sugriva, when I had slain Bali in the open field, and on whose account I crossed the ocean, having thrown a bridge over it, that wretch to-day has come within my range of vision and shall therefore cease to live. Appearing before me, Ravana cannot survive any more than one who comes into the presence of a serpent whose glance is poisonous or a snake falling under Vainateya's gaze. Be tranquil witnesses of my combat with Ravana, O Invincible Ones, Foremost of the Monkeys; seat yourselves on the brow of the mountain. To-day in this duel, the Three Worlds with the Gandharvas, the Siddhas and Charanas will recognize Rama's attributes! I shall accomplish a feat that the world with all beings who move or do not move, as also the Gods, will recount as long as the earth exists!"

Speaking thus Rama began to discharge his penetrating shafts embellished with gold at Dashagriva. From his side, Ravana, like a cloud from which the rain falls, showered down arrows and clubs with violence on Rama. And a mighty uproar arose when, in order to slay each other, those marvellous arrows were loosed by Rama and Ravana. Severed and scattered, the shafts with flaming points discharged by Rama and Ravana fell from the sky on the earth, and the twanging of their bows, causing great terror amongst all beings, was astonishing to hear. Then that amazing hail of missiles, that the mighty hero let fly in continuous streams from his burning bow, overwhelmed Ravana who, terrified, took to flight like a great cloud driven before the tempest.

## Chapter 102

*Lakshmana's miraculous Recovery*

Seeing the courageous Lakshmana lying on the battlefield drenched in blood, struck down by the spear discharged by the mighty Ravana, Rama entered into a terrible duel with that cruel titan whom he overwhelmed with a hail of arrows. Then he addressed Sushena and said:—

"The valiant Lakshmana, struck down by the ruthless Ravana, is writhing like a serpent, filling me with anguish! When I behold that hero, dearer to me than life itself, how, in mine affliction, can I find the strength to fight? If my brother, who is endowed with auspicious marks, that proud warrior, returns to the five elements, of what use is life or prosperity to me? My prowess is ebbing away as it were and my bow seems to be falling from my grasp; mine arrows are blunted, mine eyes blinded with tears, my limbs are heavy as when one is overcome by sleep, my thoughts wander and I long to die! In this extreme misfortune in which I am plunged, weeping, my mind distracted on seeing my brother, who is emitting inarticulate cries, lying in the dust of the battlefield, brought low by the wicked Ravana, a prey to suffering and seriously wounded in his vital parts, even victory cannot bring me felicity, O Hero. If the moon is hidden from sight what delight can it give? Of what use is it to fight? What purpose is served by living? The combat has no longer any meaning since Lakshmana is lying dead in the forefront of the battle. As that illustrious warrior followed me when I retired to the forest so will I follow him now to the abode of death.

"Ever affectionate to his kinsfolk, he was undeviatingly devoted to me; I was led to this pass by the titans who have made use of magic in the fight. Wives may be found everywhere and everywhere one may meet with friends but I see no place where one could find so dear a brother. Without Lakshmana of what use will it be for me to rule over a kingdom, O Invincible Warrior? What shall I say to Sumitra who loves her son so tenderly? I shall not be able to endure the reproaches with which she will address me. What shall I say to my mother Kaushalya or even to Kaikeyi? What answer shall I give to Bharata and the exceedingly powerful Shatrughna? Having gone with him to the forest, how can I return without him? Better were it to die than suffer the censure of my family. What sin did I commit in a former life that my virtuous brother is now lying dead before mine eyes? O My Brother, O Foremost of Men, O First of Heroes, O Prince, why, forsaking me, wilt thou repair to the other regions? How comes it that thou dost not answer me who am lamenting? Rise, look about thee, why dost thou remain lying there? Witness my grief with thine own eyes! In my despair, be my comforter, O Long-armed Warrior, overwhelmed as I am with anguish, wandering distracted amidst the woods and mountains."

As Rama was speaking thus, overwhelmed with affliction, Sushena, in order to comfort him, addressed these well-considered words to him:—

"O Tiger among Men, abandon this idea that causes thee pain, this thought that pierces thine heart as a javelin in the forefront of the battle. Nay, Lakshmana, the enhancer of prosperity, has not rejoined the five elements for his features have not changed nor is he pale, rather is his countenance serene and handsome! Observe how the palms of his hands resemble the petals of a lotus and his eyes are bright. Those who appear thus have not yielded up their lives, O Lord of all Men! Do not grieve O Hero, Conqueror of thy Foes, Lakshmana lives, and the proofs are the multiple beatings of his heart united with his sighs even though his body lies stretched on the earth."

Thus spoke the extremely sagacious Sushena to Raghava and thereafter he addressed that great monkey, Hanuman, who stood near and said:—

"O Friend, go quickly, repair to the Mountain Mahodaya! Formerly thou hast heard of it from Jambavan, O Warrior! On the southern peak grow curative herbs, the plants named Vishalyakarani, Savarnyakarani, Samjivakarani and also Samdhani of great virtue. Bring them back, O Warrior, in order to revive that hero, Lakshmana."

At these words, Hanuman repaired to the Mountain of Herbs but there he became anxious, for that illustrious monkey could not recognize those remedial plants. Then the thought came to Maruti, whose strength was immeasurable, 'I will carry back the peak of the mountain for it is on the summit that the auspicious herbs are growing, at least I infer so from what Sushena has said. If I return without having picked the Vishalyakarani, the loss of time will prove fatal and a great misfortune will follow.'

Reflecting thus, the mighty Hanuman hastened on his way and when he reached that high mountain, he shook the summit three times and having broken it off, balanced it, with its multitudinous trees in full flower of varying fragrance, in his two hands. Thereafter, like a dark cloud charged with rain, that monkey sprang into the air carrying the mountain peak and returned in great haste setting it down and, having rested awhile, he said to Sushena:—

"I am not conversant with the medicinal plants, O Bull among Monkeys, here is the whole summit which I have brought to thee!"

At these words of the son of Pavana, Sushena, the foremost of the monkeys, having uprooted the herb, took hold of it and there was great amazement among the monkeys witnessing Hanuman's feat which even the Gods themselves could only have accomplished with difficulty.

Then the foremost of monkeys, Sushena, having crushed that herb, held it to Lakshmana's nostrils and on inhaling it that prince, the scourge of his foes, who was riddled with arrows, instantly rose from the ground released from the darts and his sufferings. Meanwhile the monkeys beholding him standing erect cried out 'Excellent! Excellent!' and, full of joy, paid homage to him.

Then Rama, the slayer of his foes, said to Lakshmana:—

"Come, Come!" and, embracing him, pressed him close to his heart, his eyes wet with tears. Thereafter, having embraced him, Raghava said to Saumitri:— "O Hero, what good fortune to see thee return from the dead! Nay, assuredly neither life nor Sita nor victory had any attraction for me; in sooth what reason had I for living since thou hadst returned to the five elements?"

Then Lakshmana, pained, answered the magnanimous Raghava who had spoken thus and, in a voice trembling with emotion, said:—

"Bound by thy vow, O Thou who hast truth for thy prowess, it does not become thee to utter such cowardly words! Nay, those who speak with sincerity do not render a promise void and the proof they give is the fulfilment of their vow! Thou shouldst not give way to despair on mine account, O Irreproachable Hero! Mayest thou redeem thy word by Ravana's death this day. Nay, when he comes within the range of thy shafts, thine adversary must not return alive, as a great elephant may not live when he falls under the sharp tooth of a roaring lion. I desire to see that wretch perish ere the orb of the day withdraws behind the Astachala Mountain, his task accomplished. If thou seekest the death of Ravana on the battlefield, if thou wishest to fulfil thy duty and if thou dost aspire to re-capture the princess, O Illustrious Hero, do what I tell thee without delay."

* * *

## Chapter 104

*Rama arraigns Ravana and reproaches him for his Misdeeds*

Grievously wounded by the wrathful Kakutstha, Ravana, that proud warrior fell into a great rage. His eyes flaming with anger, that titan raised his bow in a paroxysm of fury and in that great combat, overwhelmed Raghava with blows. Like unto a heavy shower, Ravana deluged Rama as clouds fill a pond. Drowned in a rain of arrows loosed from the titan's bow in the fight, Kakutstha stood firm like unto a mighty mountain.

Then that hero, resolute in combat, with his shafts deflected the succession of darts which fell upon him like unto the rays of the sun. Thereafter, with a skilled hand, the ranger of the night, in fury, struck the breast of the magnanimous Raghava with thousands of darts and the elder brother of Lakshmana, covered with blood, looked like a huge Kimshuka Tree in flower in the forest. His wrath roused by the wounds he had received, the exceedingly powerful Kakutstha armed himself with shafts the lustre of which resembled the sun's at the end of the world period; and Rama and Ravana, both transported with anger, became invisible to each other on the battlefield that was darkened by their shafts.

Thereafter at the height of fury, the valiant son of Dasaratha addressed his adversary in these mocking and ironic words:—

"Having carried away my consort against her will in Janasthana, imposing on her ignorance, thou art verily no hero! Bearing away by force, Vaidehi who was wandering forlornly in the great forest far from me, thou thinkest 'I am a great hero!' Because thou hast molested other women who were without a protector, which is the act of a coward, thou deemest thyself to be a hero, O Valiant One! O Thou who hast overthrown the ramparts of duty, O Arrogant Wretch of fickle nature, in thine insolence, thou hast invited death into thine house, saying 'I am a hero!' Is it in the role of the valiant brother of Dhanada that thou, grown presumptuous on account of power, hast accomplished this memorable, great and glorious exploit? Thou shalt presently receive a fitting recompense for this infamous act. O Wretch, in thine own estimation, thinking to thyself 'I am a hero,' thou wast not ashamed to bear Sita away like a thief. Had I been there when thou didst affront Vaidehi, handling her so brutally, I should have dispatched thee to rejoin thy brother Khara by striking thee down with my shafts. By good fortune, O Insensate One, thou art now before me; to-day with my penetrating darts, I shall hurl thee into Yama's abode. To-day thy head with its dazzling earrings, severed by my weapon, shall roll in the dust on the battlefield where the wild beasts will devour it. Vultures will swoop on thy breast when thou art lying stretched on the earth, O Ravana, and will drink the blood greedily that flows from the wounds inflicted by my sharp arrows. To-day pricked by my shafts, lying without life, birds of prey will tear out thine entrails as eagles destroy serpents!"

Speaking thus, the valiant Rama, scourge of his foes, covered that Indra among Titans, who stood near, with a hail of arrows, and his courage, strength and martial ardour in loosing his shafts was redoubled. Then all the celestial weapons belonging to Raghava, versed in the Science of the Self, presented themselves before him and, in his joy, that illustrious hero felt the dexterity of his touch increase.

On these auspicious signs appearing of themselves, Rama, the Destroyer of the Titans, attacked Ravana himself with increasing violence.

* * *

## Chapter 109

*The Duel continues*

Witnessing the combat between Rama and Ravana, all beings were struck with amazement and those two warriors, assuming a dreadful aspect in the struggle, highly enraged, determined on mutual slaughter and, in their excellent cars, bore down on each other. Thereupon their drivers, parading their skill as charioteers, advanced, circled and manoeuvred in various ways. In their rapid course and swift evolutions, those two marvellous chariots ranged the battlefield, whilst the two warriors discharged countless shafts on each other, like unto clouds letting loose their showers.

Having displayed their immeasurable resource in the use of weapons, those two champions halted face to face, chariot shaft to chariot shaft, their horses' heads touching, their standards intertwined. Then Rama loosed four sharp arrows, driving back Ravana's four spirited steeds and he, furious on beholding them retreat, let fly his penetrating shafts on Raghava.

That hero, however, grievously wounded by the mighty Dashagriva, manifested neither agitation nor emotion and again the Ten-necked One discharged his shafts, that resounded like thunder, aiming at the charioteer of that God who bears the Thunderbolt; and he struck Matali with his arrows with great force without being able to disturb him in any way or cause him to falter. Nevertheless Raghava, indignant at the affront offered to Matali more than if it had been directed at himself, with the aid of a succession of darts, decided to humble his adversary, and the valiant Raghava discharged twenty, thirty, sixty and thereafter hundreds and thousands of shafts on his rival's chariot.

On his side, Ravana, the Lord of the Titans, standing in his car, enraged, overwhelmed Rama with an avalanche of maces and clubs and the struggle became more desperate causing the hair to stand on end.

At the sound of the maces, clubs and axes and the loosing of plumed arrows, the seven seas were agitated and the tumult of the oceans sowed terror in the Danavas and Pannagas in their thousands, in the depths of hell. The earth shook with its mountains, forests and jungles; the orb of day lost its brilliance and the wind ceased to blow. Devas, Gandharvas, Siddhas and Paramarishis were wrought up with anxiety as also the Kinneras and Great Serpents.

"May good fortune attend the cows and brahmins! May all the worlds endure forever! May Raghava emerge triumphant in his combat with Ravana, the King of the Titans!"

Offering up these prayers, the Devas accompanied by hosts of Rishis witnessed that duel between Rama and Ravana, a spectacle that caused the hair to stand on end, and the hosts of the Gandharvas and Apsaras, watching that indescribable struggle, cried out:—"The sky resembles the sea and the sea the sky, but the fight between Rama and Ravana resembles nought but itself!"

Thus did they speak on beholding the combat between Rama and Ravana. In his rage, the Long-armed Warrior, the increaser of the glory of the Raghus, Rama, placed an arrow, like unto a venomous reptile, on his bow and cut off one of Ravana's heads, whereupon that glorious head, adorned with sparkling earrings, rolled on the earth in the presence of the Three Worlds. Nevertheless another, equal to the former, grew immediately and Rama, with a steady hand, dexterously sundered the second head with his shafts. Hardly was it eliminated when another head appeared which was severed once more by Rama's darts like unto thunderbolts. Thereafter he struck off a hundred more, being unable to bring Ravana low, and that hero, conversant with every weapon, he the increaser of Kaushalya's delight, who had made use of innumerable missiles, reflected:—

'These were the shafts by the help of which I slew Maricha, Khara, and Dushana as also Viradha in the Krauncha Wood and Kabandha in the Dandaka Forest; these were the shafts wherewith I transfixed the Sala Trees and the mountains and Bali and with which I agitated the ocean! All these weapons found their target, how is it that they have so little power over Ravana?'

Absorbed though he was in his reflections, Raghava, without ceasing from action, let loose a shower of arrows on the breast of his adversary. On his side, Ravana, the Lord of the Titans, standing in his chariot, enraged, overwhelmed Rama with an avalanche of maces and clubs. Thus the fearful and desperate conflict, causing the hair to stand on end, continued in the air and on the ground and thereafter on the summit of the mountain.

Devas, Danavas, Yakshas, Pisachas, Uragas and Rakshasas watched the dreadful combat that lasted seven days and neither by night nor day for a single hour did Rama and Ravana cease from fighting and the son of Dasaratha and the Indra of the Titans continued to struggle thus. Then the magnanimous charioteer of the King of the Gods, beholding no sign of Raghava gaining the victory, addressed him rapidly in the following words.

## Chapter 110

*The Death of Ravana*

At that moment, Matali sought to recall Raghava's thoughts, saying:—"How is it that thou dost act in regard to Ravana as if thou wert unaware of thine own powers? In order to bring about his end, discharge Brahma's Weapon upon him, O Lord! Foretold by the Gods, the hour of his doom is at hand!"

Prompted by Matali, Rama took up a flaming shaft that was hissing like a viper, formerly bestowed on him by the magnanimous and powerful Sage Agastya. A gift of the Grandsire, that weapon never missed its target and it had been created of yore by Brahma for Indra and bestowed on the King of the Gods for the conquest of the Three Worlds. In its wings was the wind, in its point the fire and the sun, in its haft space, and, in size, it resembled the Mountains Meru and Mandara. With its marvellous point, haft and gilding, it was composed of the essence of all the elements and was as resplendent as the sun. Resembling the Fire of Time enveloped in smoke, it was like unto an enormous snake and was capable of riving men, elephants, horses, gateways, bars and even rocks. Dreadful to behold, covered with blood from countless victims, coated with their flesh and of the temper of lightning, it emitted a thunderous sound. The disperser of hosts, it created universal alarm, and hissing like a great serpent, it was exceedingly formidable. In war, it was the provider of nourishment to herons, vultures, cranes and hordes of jackals; it was a form of death itself, the sower of terror, the delight of the monkeys, the scourge of the titans and its wings were composed of innumerable brightly coloured plumes, like unto Garuda's.

That marvellous and powerful shaft that was to destroy the titan was the object of terror to the worlds, the remover of the fear of the supporters of the Ikshvakus, the depriver of the glory of the foe, and it filled Rama with delight. Having charged it with the sacred formula, the valiant Rama of indescribable prowess placed that excellent weapon on his bow according to the method prescribed by the Veda and, when he made ready, all beings were seized with terror and the earth shook. Enraged, he stretched his bow with force and, deploying his whole strength, discharged that weapon, the destroyer of the vital parts, on Ravana, and that irresistible shaft like unto lightning, irrevocable as fate, loosed by the arm of one equal to the God who bears the Thunderbolt, struck Ravana's breast. Loosed with exceeding force, that missile, the supreme destroyer, pierced the breast of the wicked-hearted titan and, covered with blood, that fatal dart having extinguished his vital breaths, buried itself in the earth. Thereafter, having slain Ravana, that shaft, stained with blood which dripped therefrom, its purpose accomplished, returned submissively to the quiver.

And Dashagriva, who had been struck down suddenly, let his bow and arrow fall from his hand as he yielded up his breath. Bereft of life, that Indra of the Nairritas of redoubtable valour and great renown, fell from his chariot as Vritra when struck by Indra's thunderbolt.

Seeing him stretched on the ground, the rangers of the night who had escaped the carnage, struck with terror, their sovereign being slain, fled in all directions and, from every side, the monkeys who, in the presence of the dead Dashagriva had assumed a victorious air, hurled themselves upon them, armed with trees. Harassed by the monkey divisions, the titans, terror-stricken, took refuge in Lanka and, having lost their lord, in despair, gave way to tears.

In the ranks of the monkeys, however, there arose cries of joy and shouts of triumph proclaiming Raghava's victory and Ravana's defeat, and the skies re-echoed to the music of the drums beaten by the Gods. A rain of flowers fell from heaven on to the earth, covering Raghava's chariot with a ravishing and marvellous shower of blossom. The cry of 'Well done! Well done!' came from the firmament and the celestial voices of the magnanimous Gods were raised in Rama's praise. On the death of that source of terror to all the worlds a great joy filled the Celestial Host as also the Charanas.

The blessed Raghava, by slaying that Bull among the Titans, fulfilled the ambitions of Sugriva, Angada and Bibishana; peace reigned over all; the cardinal points were stilled; the air became pure, the earth ceased to tremble, the wind blew gently and the star of the day regained its full glory.

At that instant, Sugriva, Bibishana and Angada, the foremost of his friends, and Lakshmana also, approached that happy conqueror and joyfully offered him due homage. Rama, the delight of the House of Raghu, surrounded by his adherents on the battlefield, having slain his adversary by his extraordinary power, resembled Mahendra amidst the Celestial Host.

* * *

## Chapter 116

*Rama sends for Sita*

That highly intelligent monkey, having paid obeisance to Rama, whose eyes resembled the petals of a lotus, the most skilled of archers, said to him:—

"It behoveth thee to visit Maithili who is consumed with grief and on account of whom this enterprise, that has been crowned with success, was undertaken. In the distress that overwhelms her, Maithili, her eyes bathed in tears, hearing of thy victory, expressed a desire to behold thee once more. Confiding in me formerly, her glances warm with emotion, she repeated 'I desire to see my lord again!'"

These words of Hanuman instantly evoked thoughts in Rama, the first of men, causing him to shed tears. Sighing deeply, he said to Bibishana standing near, who resembled a cloud:—

"Bring the Princess of Videha, Sita, hither, anointed with celestial unguents, adorned with heavenly jewels, having laved her head; do not delay!"

At these words of Rama, Bibishana hastened to the private apartments to fetch Sita with her attendants. Beholding the unfortunate Maithili, Bibishana, the powerful King of the Titans, paid obeisance to her, raising his joined palms to his forehead, and respectfully addressed her, saying:—

"O Vaidehi, sprinkle thyself with celestial unguents, adorn thyself with divine ornaments and ascend this palanquin! May happiness attend thee! Thy lord desires to see thee!"

Then Vaidehi answered Bibishana who had addressed her thus, saying:—"Without having bathed, I wish to see my consort, O Bibishana."

Hearing this, Bibishana replied:—"It behoveth thee to do what Rama commands!" Whereto the virtuous Maithili, who regarded her husband as a god, filled with conjugal duty, said:—'Be it so!'

Thereupon Sita, her tresses waved, adorned with priceless ornaments, wearing gorgeous raiment, ascended a palanquin borne by those titans accustomed to do so, accompanied by a large escort under Bibishana's command.

And Bibishana approaching that magnanimous hero, who was merged in meditation, bowing down to him, joyfully announced Sita's arrival.

Hearing that his consort, who had dwelt long in the titan's abode, had come, rage, joy and grief overwhelmed Raghava, the slayer of his foes and, beholding Sita in the palanquin, Rama, in order to test her, dissembling his happiness, said to Bibishana:—

"O Supreme Lord of the Titans, O My Friend who ever rejoiced in my victories, bring Vaidehi nearer to me."

At Raghava's command, the righteous Bibishana caused the crowd to disperse, whereupon titans clad in armour, wearing turbans, with drums and bamboo staves in their hands began to move about driving away the warriors, bears, monkeys and titans, who, scattering, stood apart some way off. And as they were being driven away, a tremendous clamour arose resembling the roar of the sea buffeted by the winds.

Seeing them dispersing, whilst confusion was created amongst them, Rama in affection for them, grew indignant at their departure and, highly incensed, with a glance that seemed as if it would consume him, addressed the exceedingly intelligent Bibishana in terms of reproach, saying:—

"Why, disregarding me, dost thou harass them, are they not my people? Her conduct, not raiment, walls, seclusion or other royal prohibitions, are a woman's shield. In times of calamity, peril, war, the Swyamvara or the nuptual ceremony, it is not forbidden to behold a woman unveiled. It is not prohibited to look upon a woman who has fallen into distress and difficulty, above all in my presence. Therefore, leaving the palanquin, let Vaidehi come hither on foot so that the dwellers in the woods may see her at my side."

Hearing Rama's words, Bibishana became thoughtful and conducted Sita to him reverently, whilst Lakshmana, Sugriva and also Hanuman, hearing Rama speak thus, were saddened.

Then Maithili, confused and shrinking within herself, approached her lord accompanied by Bibishana; and it was with astonishment, delight and love that Sita, whose husband was a god, gazed on Rama's gracious appearance, she whose own face was still beautiful. Beholding the countenance of her dearly loved lord, whom she had not seen for so long and which was as radiant as the full moon when it rises, she cast aside all anxiety and her own face became as fair as the immaculate orb of the night.

## Chapter 117

*Rama repudiates Sita*

Beholding Maithili standing humbly beside him, Rama gave expression to the feelings he had concealed in his heart, saying:—

"O Illustrious Princess, I have re-won thee and mine enemy has been defeated on the battlefield; I have accomplished all that fortitude could do; my wrath is appeased; the insult and the one who offered it have both been obliterated by me. To-day my prowess has been manifested, to-day mine exertions have been crowned with success, to-day I have fulfilled my vow and am free. As ordained by destiny the stain of thy separation and thine abduction by that fickle-minded titan has been expunged by me, a mortal. Of what use is great strength to the vacillating, who do not with resolution avenge the insult offered to them?

"To-day Hanuman is plucking the fruit of his glorious exploits, and Sugriva, who is valiant in war and wise in counsel, with his army is reaping the harvest of his exertions! Bibishana too is culling the fruits of his labours, he who cast off a brother, who was devoid of virtue, to come to me."

When Sita heard Rama speak in this wise, her large doe-like eyes filled with tears and, beholding the beloved of his heart standing close to him, Rama, who was apprehensive of public rumour, was torn within himself. Then, in the presence of the monkeys and the titans, he said to Sita, whose eyes were as large as lotus petals, her dark hair plaited, and who was endowed with faultless limbs:—

"What a man should do in order to wipe out an I insult, I have done by slaying Ravana for I guard mine honour jealously! Thou wert re-won as the southern region, inaccessible to man, was re-gained by the pure-souled Agastya through his austerities. Be happy and let it be known that this arduous campaign, so gloriously terminated through the support of my friends, was not undertaken wholly for thy sake. I was careful to wipe out the affront paid to me completely and to avenge the insult offered to mine illustrious House.

"A suspicion has arisen, however, with regard to thy conduct, and thy presence is as painful to me as a lamp to one whose eye is diseased! Henceforth go where it best pleaseth thee, I give thee leave, O Daughter of Janaka. O Lovely One, the ten regions are at thy disposal; I can have nothing more to do with thee! What man of honour would give rein to his passion so far as to permit himself to take back a woman who has dwelt in the house of another? Thou hast been taken into Ravana's lap and he has cast lustful glances on thee; how can I reclaim thee, I who boast of belonging to an illustrious House? The end which I sought in re-conquering thee has been gained; I no longer have any attachment for thee; go where thou desirest! This is the outcome of my reflections, O Lovely One! Turn to Lakshmana or Bharata, Shatrughna, Sugriva or the Titan Bibishana, make thy choice, O Sita, as pleases thee best. Assuredly Ravana, beholding thy ravishing and celestial beauty, will not have respected thy person during the time that thou didst dwell in his abode."

On this, that noble lady, worthy of being addressed in sweet words, hearing that harsh speech from her beloved lord, who for long had surrounded her with every homage, wept bitterly, and she resembled a creeper that has been torn away by the trunk of a great elephant.

## Chapter 118

*Sita's Lamentations; She undergoes the Ordeal by Fire*

Hearing these harsh words from the wrathful Raghava, causing her to tremble, those fearful utterances, which till that time had never been heard by her and were now addressed to her by her lord in the presence of a great multitude, Maithili, the daughter of Janaka, overwhelmed with shame, pierced to the heart by that arrow-like speech, shed abundant tears. Thereafter, wiping her face, she addressed her husband in gentle and faltering accents, saying:—

"Why dost thou address such words to me, O Hero, as a common man addresses an ordinary woman? I swear to thee, O Long-armed Warrior, that my conduct is worthy of thy respect! It is the behaviour of other women that has filled thee with distrust! Relinquish thy doubts since I am known to thee! If my limbs came in contact with another's, it was against my will, O Lord, and not through any inclination on my part; it was brought about by fate. That which is under my control, my heart, has ever remained faithful to thee; my body was at the mercy of another; not being mistress of the situation, what could I do? If despite the proofs of love that I gave thee whilst I lived with thee, I am still a stranger to thee, O Proud Prince, my loss is irrevocable!

"When, in Lanka, thou didst dispatch the great warrior Hanuman to seek me out, why didst thou not repudiate me then? As soon as I had received the tidings that I had been abandoned by thee, I should have yielded up my life in the presence of that monkey, O Hero! Then thou wouldst have been spared useless fatigue on mine account and others lives would not have been sacrificed, nor thine innumerable friends exhausted to no purpose. But thou, O Lion among Men, by giving way to wrath and by thus passing premature judgement on a woman, hast acted like a worthless man.

"I have received my name from Janaka, but my birth was from the earth and thou hast failed to appreciate fully the nobility of my conduct, O Thou who are well acquainted with the nature of others. Thou hast had no reverence for the joining of our hands in my girlhood and mine affectionate nature, all these things hast thou cast behind thee!"

Having spoken thus to Rama, weeping the while, her voice strangled with sobs, Sita addressed the unfortunate Lakshmana, who was overwhelmed with grief, saying:—

"Raise a pyre for me, O Saumitri, this is the only remedy for my misery! These unjust reproaches have destroyed me, I cannot go on living! Publicly renounced by mine husband, who is insensible to my virtue, there is only one redress for me, to undergo the ordeal by fire!"

Hearing Vaidehi's words, Lakshmana, the slayer of hostile warriors, a prey to indignation, consulted Raghava with his glance and by Rama's gestures he understood what was in his heart, whereupon the valiant Saumitri, following his indications, prepared the pyre.

None amongst his friends dared to appeal to Rama, who resembled Death himself, the Destroyer of Time; none dared to speak or even to look upon him.

Thereafter Vaidehi, having circumambulated Rama, who stood with his head bowed, approached the blazing fire and, paying obeisance to the Celestials and brahmins, Maithili, with joined palms, standing before the flames, spoke thus:—

"As my heart has never ceased to be true to Raghava, do thou, O Witness of all Beings, grant me thy protection! As I am pure in conduct, though Rama looks on me as sullied, do thou, O Witness of the Worlds, grant me full protection!"

With these words, Vaidehi circumambulated the pyre and with a fearless heart entered the flames.

And a great multitude were assembled there, amongst which were many children and aged people who witnessed Maithili entering the fire. And, resembling gold that has been melted in the crucible, she threw herself into the blazing flames in the presence of all. That large-eyed lady, entering the fire, who is the Bearer of Sacrificial Offerings, appeared to those who watched her to resemble a golden altar. That fortunate princess entering the fire, which is nourished by oblations, seemed, in the eyes of the Rishis, Devas and Gandharvas, to resemble a sacrificial offering.

Then all the women cried out:—'Alas!' on seeing her, like a stream of butter hallowed by the recitation of mantras, fall into the flames, and she appeared to the Three Worlds, the Gods, the Gandharvas and the Danavas like a goddess smitten by a curse and cast down from heaven into hell. Then, as she entered the flames, a great and terrible cry rose from the titans and the monkeys.

## Chapter 119

*Brahma's Praise of Rama*

Meanwhile the righteous Rama, hearing the lamentation of the masses, afflicted, pondered awhile and his eyes filled with tears.

Then the King Vaishravana and Yama with the Pitris, the Thousand-eyed Lord of the Celestials, Varuna, Lord of the Waters and Mahadeva the blessed Three-eyed God who rides the Bull, as also Brahma the Creator of the World, King of the Learned, all gathered together, having hastened there in their chariots as bright as the sun, coming to the City of Lanka to seek out Rama.

Lifting up their great arms and hands adorned with jewels, they made obeisance with joined palms and the King of the Gods addressing Raghava, said:—

"O Creator of the Universe and foremost of those versed in the spiritual science, how canst thou manifest indifference to Sita falling into the flames? How art thou unaware that thou thyself art the Chief of the Gods? Formerly thou wert the Vasu Ritadhaman, the Progenitor of the Vasus! Thou art the Creator of the Three Worlds, Swyamprabhu, the eighth Rudra and the fifth of the Sadhyas. The Twin Ashwins are thy two ears, the sun and moon thine eyes; these are the forms at the beginning, middle and end of creation in which thou dost appear, O Scourge of Thy Foes; and yet thou dost distrust Vaidehi as if thou wert an ordinary man!"

Thus addressed by the Protector of the Worlds, the Leader of the Gods, Raghava, Lord of Peoples, Foremost of the Pious, answered:—

"I deem myself to be a man, Rama, born of Dasaratha; who then am I in reality? From whence have I come? Let the Grandsire of the World inform me!"

Thus spoke Kakutstha and Brahma, foremost of those who know the truth, addressed him saying:—

"Thou art the great and effulgent God Narayana, the fortunate Lord armed with the discus. Thou art the One-Tusked Boar, the Conqueror of thy Foes in the past and the future. Thou art the imperishable Brahman, Existence Itself, transcending the three divisions of time; Thou art the Law of Righteousness, the Four-armed, the Bearer of the Sharnga Bow; Thou art the Subduer of the senses, the Supreme Purusha; Thou art invincible, Thou art the Holder of the Dagger, Thou art Vishnu, Thou art Krishna and of immeasurable might; Thou art Senani and Gramani, the Controller of passions, the Origin and Dissolution; Thou art Upendra and the Slayer of the Demon Madhu, Thou art the Creator of Indra and Indra Himself; Thou art the Lotus-navelled One; Thou dost bring combat to an end. The great and divine Rishis acknowledge Thee as their refuge and protector. Thou art the Himalayas of a hundred peaks, the Essence of the Vedas, the God of a Hundred Tongues, the Great Bull, Thou thyself art the Creator of the World, Swyamprabhu; Thou art the Refuge and Elder of the Siddhas and Sadhyas; Thou art the Sacrifice, the sacred syllable 'Vashat' and 'Aum', the greatest of the great. None knows thine origin or end or who Thou really art. Thou art manifest in all beings, in the cows and the brahmins; Thou pervadest all regions, the firmament, the mountains and the rivers, Thou, the Thousand-footed God, the Thousand-headed One, Thou of a Thousand Eyes! Thou art the support of all beings and the earth. When the earth is withdrawn, under the form of a great serpent, Thou dost appear on the waters supporting all the worlds and the Gods, Gandharvas and Danavas, O Rama. I am thy heart and the Goddess Saraswati, thy tongue; the Gods are the hairs of Thy body, I, Brahma created them thus. When Thou dost close thine eyes, it is night and when Thou dost open them, it is day. The Vedas are Thy Samskaras; nothing exists apart from thee; the whole universe is Thy body, the earth Thy forbearance; Agni Thy wrath, Soma Thy beneficence, the Shrivatsa Mark, Thy holy symbol.

"Thou didst cover the Three Worlds in three strides; Thou didst bind the terrible Bali and establish Mahendra as King. Sita is Lakshmi and Thou, the God Vishnu, Krishna and Prajapati. It was in order to slay Ravana that Thou didst enter a human body. This task that we entrusted to Thee has been accomplished, O Thou, the foremost of those who observe their duty. Ravana having fallen, do Thou ascend to heaven joyfully! Thy might is irresistible, O Rama, and thine exploits are never fruitless. To behold Thee and offer adoration to Thee is never unprofitable! It is not in vain that men are devoted to Thee on earth. Those who are ever faithful to Thee, attain to Thee who art the primeval Purusha and their desires will be fulfilled in this world and the other worlds. Those who recite this eternal, ancient and traditional theme, transmitted by the Rishis, will never suffer defeat."

## Chapter 120

*Sita is restored to Rama*

Hearing those excellent words uttered by the Grandsire, Vibhabasu, who bore Vaidehi in his lap, having extinguished the pyre, rose up, and that Bearer of Sacrificial Offerings, assuming a corporeal form, stood up and took hold of the daughter of Janaka. Then that youthful woman, beautiful as the dawn, wearing ornaments of refined gold, attired in a red robe, having dark and curly hair, wearing fresh garlands, the irreproachable Vaidehi was restored to Rama by the God of Fire.

Thereafter the Witness of the whole world, Pavaka, addressed Rama, saying:—

"Here is Vaidehi, O Rama, there is no sin in her! Neither by word, feeling or glance has thy lovely consort shown herself to be unworthy of thy noble qualities. Separated from thee, that unfortunate one was borne away against her will in the lonely forest by Ravana, who had grown proud on account of his power. Though imprisoned and closely guarded by titan women in the inner apartments, thou wast ever the focus of her thoughts and her supreme hope. Surrounded by hideous and sinister women, though tempted and threatened, Maithili never gave place in her heart to a single thought for that titan and was solely absorbed in thee. She is pure and without taint, do thou receive Maithili; it is my command that she should not suffer reproach in any way."

These words filled Rama's heart with delight and he, the most eloquent of men, that loyal soul, reflected an instant within himself, his glance full of joy. Then the illustrious, steadfast and exceedingly valiant Rama, the first of virtuous men, hearing those words addressed to him, said to the Chief of the Gods:—

"On account of the people, it was imperative that Sita should pass through this trial by fire; this lovely woman had dwelt in Ravana's inner apartments for a long time. Had I not put the innocence of Janaki to the test, the people would have said:—'Rama, the son of Dasaratha is governed by lust!' It was well known to me that Sita had never given her heart to another and that the daughter of Janaka, Maithili, was ever devoted to me. Ravana was no more able to influence that large-eyed lady, whose chastity was her own protection, than the ocean may pass beyond its bournes. Despite his great perversity, he was unable to approach Maithili even in thought, who was inaccessible to him as a flame. That virtuous woman could never belong to any other than myself for she is to me what the light is to the sun. Her purity is manifest in the Three Worlds; I could no more renounce Maithili, born of Janaka than a hero his honour. It behoveth me to follow your wise and friendly counsel, O Gracious Lords of the World."

Having spoken thus, the victorious and extremely powerful Rama, full of glory, adored for his noble exploits, was re-united with his beloved and experienced the felicity he had merited.

* * *

# Uttara Kanda

## *Chs. 42–47 [Rama and Sita's Marriage]*

### Chapter 42

*The Felicity enjoyed by Rama and Sita*

Having dismissed the Pushpaka Chariot, which was encrusted with gold, the long-armed Rama entered the Ashoka Grove that was rendered beautiful by Sandal, Agallocha, Mango, Tunga and Kalakeya Trees with groves of Devadaru on all sides, whilst Champaka, Aguru, Punnaga, Madhuka, Panasa and Asana Trees adorned it and radiant Parijatras blazed like smokeless fires. Lodhra, Nipa, Arjuna, Naga, Saptaparna, Atimuktaka, Mandara and Kadali Trees screened it with a web of thicket and creepers; Priyangu, Kadamba, Bakula, Jambu, Dadima and Kovidara Trees embellished it on every side with their magnificent flowers, marvellous fruits of celestial fragrances, divine nectar, tender shoots and buds. Heavenly trees of graceful shape, thick with heavy foliage and enchanting blossom were humming with intoxicated bees. Kokilas, Bhringarajas and other birds of varied plumage, their heads crowned with pollen from the Mango Trees, added to the beauty of those marvellous woods. Some of the trees had the brilliance of gold or resembled tongues of flame, others were as dark as collyrium and everywhere only flowers of sweet fragrance and wreaths of blossom of all kinds were to be found.

Pools of various shapes, filled with limpid water on which tufts of flowering lotus and water-lilies floated, were approached by steps made of rubies. Trees in full flower adorned the banks which re-echoed to the call of Datyuhas and Shukas and the cries of geese and swans. That grove was enclosed by flat rocks of differing forms within which were many grassy glades of the sheen of emerald and pearl, and these were adorned by trees rivalling each other in the profusion of their blossom, the earth beneath being heaped with flowers, resembling the sky full of stars, so that it appeared like the garden of Indra or Chaitaratha created by Brahma.

Such was Rama's pastoral retreat with its arbours filled with countless seats and grassy couches inviting one to rest; and the Increaser of Raghu's joy entered that magnificent Ashoka Grove and seated himself on a throne of great splendour which was decorated with innumerable flowers and covered with a carpet of Kusha Grass.

Taking Sita by the hand, Kakutstha gave her delicious wine made of distilled honey to drink, as formerly Purandara had offered to Sachi. Thereafter pure viands and fruits of every kind were brought by servants, whilst lovely Apsaras, skilled in the arts of singing and dancing, began to perform in the Prince's presence and troops of Nymphs and Uragas, surrounded by the Kinneris intoxicated with wine, danced before Kakutstha, and the virtuous Rama, the most captivating of warriors, delighted those ravishing and charming women.

Seated by Vaidehi, he was radiant with splendour and resembled Vasishtha at the side of Arundhati. In this way, in the joy that possessed him, Rama, like unto a God, each day prepared some new delight for Sita, the Princess of Videha, who was like unto the daughter of a Celestial Being.

While Sita and Raghava sported thus for a long time, the flowery season, that yields perpetual enjoyment, passed away and, as those two tasted every kind of felicity, Spring appeared once more. One day, having fulfilled the functions of state, that virtuous Prince returned to his palace where he spent the rest of the day. On her side, Sita, having worshipped the Gods and performed her morning duties, offering her services to all her mothers-in-law without distinction, thereafter adorned herself with marvellous jewels and re-joined Rama, like unto Sachi when re-united with that God of a Thousand Eyes as he returns to his City Trivishtapa.

Beholding his consort glowing with beauty, Raghava experienced an unequalled delight and exclaimed "It is well!" then he addressed the lovely Sita, who resembled a daughter of the Gods, and said:—

"Now, O Vaidehi, that thou dost bear a child in thy womb, what dost thou desire, O Lady of lovely hips? What pleasure can I prepare for thee?"

Smiling, Vaidehi answered Rama, saying:—

"O Raghava, I wish to visit the sacred retreats of the Rishis of rigid penances, who dwell on the banks of the Ganges where they subsist on fruit and roots, and there I will throw myself at their feet, O Lord. O Kakutstha, it is my supreme desire even to pass a night in the hermitage of these ascetics who live on fruit and roots."

Then Rama of imperishable exploits gave her permission to do so, saying:—

"Be at peace, O Vaidehi, to-morrow without fail, thou shalt go there!"

Having answered Maithili, born of Janaka, in this wise, Kakutstha went to the central court surrounded by his friends.

## Chapter 43

*Rama informs himself concerning current Rumours from his Friends*

Having entered there, the King was surrounded by entertaining companions accustomed to the exchange of humorous experiences, Vijaya, Madhumatta, Kashyapa, Mangala, Kula, Suraji, Kaliya, Bhadra, Dantavakra and Sumagadha, and they beguiled the magnanimous Raghava with amusing tales of every kind amidst great merriment.

Raghava, however, during some narrative, enquired of Bhadra, saying:—

"O Bhadra, what do they say of me in the town and country? What do they say of Sita, Bharata and Lakshmana? What do they say of Shatrughna and Kaikeyi our mother? Kings are always the subject of criticism whether they are in the forest or on the throne."

On hearing Rama's enquiry, Bhadra, with joined palms, answered:—

"Amongst the inhabitants of the city, nought but what is good is spoken of thee, O King, above all they tell of thy victory over Dashagriva, whom thou didst slay, O Dear Prince!"

At these words of Bhadra, Raghava said:—

"Tell me all truthfully without reserve, what reports, good or ill, do the people of the city circulate regarding me? When I learn of them, I shall endeavour to do what is meet in the future and eschew what is evil. Tell me all in full confidence without fear. Laying aside every scruple, relate all the rumours current about me in the kingdom!"

Thus exhorted by Raghava, Bhadra, with joined palms, in profound reverence, addressed that mighty hero in measured tones, saying:—

"Hear, O King, what the people are saying, be it good or ill, in the highways, markets, streets, woods and parks—'Rama has achieved the impossible by throwing a bridge over the sea which to our knowledge was never done by his predecessors nor even by the Gods and Danavas together. With his foot-soldiers and cavalry, he has destroyed the invincible Ravana and has made the monkeys, bears and Rakshasas subject to him. Having slain Ravana in the fight and recovered Sita, Raghava, having mastered his anger, has taken his spouse into his house again. What pleasure can his heart experience in possessing Sita, whom Ravana formerly held in his lap, having borne her away by force? How is it that Rama was not filled with aversion for her after she had been taken to Lanka and conducted to the Ashoka Grove, where she was left to the mercy of the titans? We shall now have to countenance the same state of affairs regarding our own wives, since what a king does, his subjects follow!'

"These are the sayings current everywhere among the people of town and country, O King."

At these words, Raghava, stricken with grief, asked, "Is it thus that they speak of me?"

Then all, bowing to the ground in reverence, answered the unfortunate Raghava and said:—

"It is true, O Lord of the Earth!"

Having heard their unanimous testimony, Kakutstha, the Scourge of His Foes, dismissed his companions.

## Chapter 44

*Rama summons his Brothers*

Having dismissed his companions, Raghava began to ponder within himself and thereafter said to the doorkeeper who stood near:—

"Go speedily and seek out the son of Sumitra, Lakshmana of auspicious marks and the fortunate Bharata and the invincible Shatrughna."

At Rama's command, the janitor paid obeisance with joined palms and went to Lakshmana's abode which he entered unchallenged and there, having saluted the magnanimous prince, he said:—

"The King desires to see thee, do thou go to him without delay!"

"It is well!" answered Saumitri and, in obedience to Raghava's command, he ascended a chariot and hastened to the palace. When he had departed, the doorkeeper approached Bharata and, saluting him in a like manner, said:—

"The king respectfully requests thy presence!"

Hearing these instructions issued by Rama, Bharata, rising swiftly from his seat, started out hurriedly on foot. Beholding the virtuous Bharata going away, the messenger speedily approached Shatrughna's abode and, with joined palms, addressed him, saying:—

"Go quickly, O Prince of the Raghus, the king wishes to see thee; Lakshmana has already preceded thee as also the renowned Bharata."

At these words, Shatrughna descended from his throne and, bowing to the ground, went to rejoin Raghava.

Meantime the messenger having returned, paid obeisance to Rama and made it known to him that his brothers had come. Learning of the youthful princes' arrival, Rama, who was deeply troubled, with a downcast mien, sad at heart, said to the doorkeeper:—

"Make haste and usher them into my presence! Mine existence depends on them, they are my very life's breath!"

At this command from that Indra of Men, the princes, attired in white, bowed with joined palms and entered respectfully. On beholding Rama, who resembled the moon in eclipse or the sun that the dusk robs of its splendour, whose eyes were filled with tears and who looked like a lotus bereft of its brilliance, they placed their heads at his feet and then stood silent. Thereupon the mighty Rama, shedding tears, having raised them up, clasped them in his arms and said to them:—

"Be seated! You are my whole wealth, you are my very life! It is with your assistance that I attained a kingdom and now rule, O Princes!"

Thus spoke Kakutstha and all, attentive and deeply moved, wondered what words he might be about to address to them.

## Chapter 45

*Rama commands Lakshmana to take Sita to the Hermitage*

All having taken their places full of sadness, Kakutstha, his features stricken, said to them:—

"Hear me all of you, may good betide you! Do not let your attention wander! This is what people are saying about me concerning Sita! The inhabitants of the city as also those of the country censure me severely and their criticism pierces my heart! I am born in the Race of the illustrious Ikshvakus and Sita belongs to the family of the great-souled Janaka. My Dear Lakshmana, thou knowest how, in the lonely forest, Ravana bore Sita away and that I destroyed him. It was then that the thought came to me regarding the daughter of Janaka, 'How can I bring Sita back to Ayodhya from this place?' Thereupon, in order to re-assure me, Sita entered the fire in my presence and that of the Gods, O Saumitri! Agni, the Bearer of sacrificial offerings, witnessed to Maithili's innocence and Vayu also, who was then journeying through space, and Chandra and Aditya proclaimed it formerly before the Gods and all the Rishis, that the daughter of Janaka was without fault. The Gods and Gandharvas testified to her pure conduct in Lanka, where Mahendra placed the proofs in my hand, further I knew from my own inner being that the illustrious Sita was innocent. It was then that I took her back and returned to Ayodhya. Since then a great sadness, on hearing the censure of the people of town and country, has filled my heart. Whoever it may be, if his ill fame be current in the world, he falls to a lower state, so long as the defamatory rumours exist. Dishonour is condemned by the Gods; honour is revered in the world and, it is on account of fair repute, that great souls act. As for me, so greatly do I fear dishonour that I would renounce my life and you yourselves on its account, O Bulls among Men, how much more therefore is it incumbent on me to separate myself from the daughter of Janaka. See therefore in what an ocean of grief I have fallen! There is no misfortune greater than this! To-morrow, at dawn, O Saumitri, take my chariot with Sumantra as thy charioteer and, causing Sita to ascend it, leave her beyond the confines of the kingdom.

"On the further side of the Ganges, the magnanimous Valmiki has his hermitage of celestial aspect situated by the Tamasa; it is in a solitary spot that thou shouldst leave her, O Thou who art the Joy of the House of Raghu. Go quickly, O Saumitri, and carry out my behest. Do not discuss it in any way; go therefore, O Saumitri, it is not the time for observations. Any resistence on thy part will cause me extreme displeasure. Yea, I swear to thee by my two feet, by my life, that those who seek to make me alter my resolve in any way or oppose my desire, I shall deem to be mine enemies. If you are subject to me and hold me in reverence, then obey me and take Sita away from here this very day. Formerly she appealed to me saying, 'I wish to visit the sacred retreats of the banks of the Ganges', let her wish be fulfilled!"

Having spoken thus, the virtuous Kakutstha, his eyes filled with tears, re-entered his apartments escorted by his brothers, his heart riven with grief, sighing like an elephant.

## Chapter 46

*Lakshmana takes Sita away*

When the night had passed, Lakshmana, with a sad heart and downcast mien, said to Sumantra:—

"O Charioteer, harness swift horses to the most excellent of cars and, by the king's orders, prepare a comfortable and luxurious seat for Sita, she, in accord with the king's wish, under my charge, is to visit the retreats of the great Rishis of pious practices, therefore bring hither the chariot with all speed!"

Then Sumantra saying, "Be it so!" yoked some superb horses to a splendid chariot that was well furnished with cushions and, approaching Saumitri, the heaper of honours on his friends, he said:—

"The car is ready, let what must be accomplished be done, O Lord!"

At these words of Sumantra, Lakshmana re-entered the King's palace and, having approached Sita, that Bull among Men addressed her thus:—

"According to the wish that thou didst express to him, that Lord of Men, the king, has charged me to take thee to the desired retreats. At the request of our sovereign, I will conduct thee without delay to those excellent solitudes of the Rishis on the banks of the Ganges, O Divine Vaidehi. I shall take thee to those hermitages inhabited by the Sages."

At these words of the magnanimous Lakshmana, Vaidehi experienced supreme felicity, so greatly did the thought of the expedition please her and, having furnished herself with costly raiment and jewels of every kind, she prepared to depart, saying:—

"I shall give these jewels as also the excellent robes and various treasures to the wives of the ascetics."

"It is well", said Saumitri, causing Maithili to ascend the chariot and, recollecting Rama's command, he went forward drawn by swift horses.

Thereafter Sita said to Lakshmana, the increaser of prosperity:

"I behold countless inauspicious omens, O Joy of the House of Raghu, observe how my left eye twitches and all my limbs tremble, further my mind is confused and I feel extremely restless whilst all my courage has ebbed away, O Saumitri. The earth appears deserted, O Large-eyed Prince, can thy brother be happy, O Thou who art so devoted to him? May all be well with my mothers-in-law without distinction, O Hero! May all beings in town and country be happy!"

Thus, with joined palms, Sita, the divine Maithili prayed, and Lakshmana listening, bent his head and, though his heart was contracted with grief, he cried in joyous accents, "Mayest thou too be happy!"

Meantime they reached the banks of the Gaumati and rested in a hermitage, and the following day, at dawn, Saumitri, rising, said to the charioteer:—

"Harness the car speedily! To-day, with great strength, I shall bear the waters of the Bhagirathi on my head, as did Tryambaka."

Thus commanded, the driver with joined palms, said to Vaidehi:—

"Mount!" and he gave rein to the horses yoked to the chariot, who were as swift as thought, whereupon she, hearing the voice of the charioteer, ascended that excellent car. Thereafter the large-eyed Sita accompanied by Saumitri and Sumantra reached the Ganges, that destroys all sin and, arriving there at noon, beholding the waters of the Bhagirathi, the unfortunate Lakshmana began to weep openly in his profound distress and the virtuous Sita, in her extreme solicitude, observing Lakshmana's misery, enquired of him, saying:—

"Wherefore art thou groaning? We have reached the banks of the Jahnavi, the object of my desires for a long time and, at the moment of rejoicing, why dost thou cause me pain in this wise, O Lakshmana? O Bull among Men, is thy grief on account of these two days absence from Rama, thou who art ever in attendance on him? Rama is dearer to me than life, O Lakshmana, yet I do not distress myself; do not behave like a child! Let us cross the Ganges and visit the Sages so that I may distribute the raiment and jewels. Having paid homage to the great Rishis, which we owe to them and, passing one day there, we shall return to the city. My heart is impatient to see Rama again, whose eyes are like the petals of a lotus, whose chest is like a lion's, that foremost of men!"

At these words of Sita's, Lakshmana, wiping his beautiful eyes, hailed the ferrymen and they, with joined palms, said "The boat is ready!"

Eager to cross over that splendid river, Lakshmana boarded the skiff, and his mind pre-occupied, took Sita across the Ganges.

## Chapter 47

*Lakshmana tells Sita she has been repudiated*

The younger brother of Raghava, having first assisted Maithili to board it, entered the well-furnished boat ready to depart, thereafter he said to Sumantra, "Wait here with the chariot" and, overcome with grief, he commanded the craft to set sail.

Arriving at the farther bank of the Bhagirathi, Lakshmana, with joined palms, his face bathed in tears, said:—

"A stake has been driven into my heart by the noble and virtuous Rama, which will bring universal censure upon me. Death were better for me this day, verily death would be preferable to the mission on which I am engaged, which the world will condemn. Forgive me and do not impute this offence to me, O Illustrious Princess."

Thereafter, making obeisance, Lakshmana threw himself on the earth. Seeing him weep, paying her homage and calling on death, Maithili, alarmed, said to Lakshmana:—

"What is this? I do not understand anything; tell me the truth, O Lakshmana, why art thou agitated? Is the king well? Tell me the cause of thy grief!"

Thus questioned by Vaidehi, Lakshmana, his heart filled with anguish, with bowed head, choked with sobs, addressed her saying:—

"Having learnt in open council that he was the object of severe censure in the city and country on thine account, O Daughter of Janaka, Rama, his heart riven, returning home told me of it. I am unable to repeat the things spoken in confidence to me, O Queen. Although thou art blameless in mine eyes, the king has repudiated thee. Public condemnation has perturbed him; do not misunderstand the matter, O Goddess. I am to leave thee in the vicinity of the sacred hermitages. The king has commanded me to do so on the pretext of satisfying thy desire. The ascetics' retreats on the banks of the Jahnavi are sacred and enchanting, do not give way to grief, O Lovely One. The foremost of Rishis, the supremely illustrious Sage Valmiki was a great friend of thy sire, King Dasaratha. Taking refuge under the shadow of the feet of that magnanimous One and living in chastity, be happy, O Daughter of Janaka. It is by remaining faithful to thy Lord and practising devotion to Rama in thine heart that thou shalt, by thy conduct, acquire supreme felicity, O Goddess."

## *Uttara Kanda*

### *Chs. 93–99 [Rama Hears the Ramayana]*

#### Chapter 93

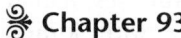

*Valmiki commands Kusha and Lava to recite the Ramayana*

As this most wonderful sacrifice was proceeding, the disciples of Valmiki, that blessed Sage, suddenly came there and, having witnessed the divine festival, admirable to behold, that company of Rishis constructed some comfortable huts a little way off. Innumerable bullock carts full of provisions, with excellent fruit and roots were heaped in Valmiki's charming grove, and thereafter that Sage said to his disciples, Kusha and Lava:—

"Go, and with great enthusiasm sing the Epic Ramayana, cheerfully and carefully, in the sacred enclosures of the Rishis, the dwellings of the brahmins, along the roads and highways and in the residence of princes, and especially it should be sung at the gate of Rama's pavilion, where the sacrifice is taking place and also before the priests.

"Here are savoury fruits of every kind that grow in the mountainous regions, eat and then sing. You will not experience any fatigue, O Dear Ones, on account of these roots and succulent fruits that will preserve the purity of your voices. If Rama, the Lord of the Earth, indicates that you should be heard by the assembled Sages, act accordingly. Each time you will have twenty Sargas to sing, which you have previously learnt from me. Above all, do not entertain the least desire for reward! Of what use is gold to ascetics who live on fruit and roots? If Kakutstha questions you, saying 'Who is your Master?' answer the king in this wise, 'We are both the disciples of the great Sage Valmiki!' Sing without fear to the accompaniment of these stringed instruments of a tone unknown heretofore, that you have tuned sweetly. Sing the poem from the beginning without showing any lack of respect to the king, who is the Father of all beings according to the law.

"To-morrow therefore, at dawn, with a cheerful heart and taking care to sing with sweet voices, accompany yourselves on these stringed instruments of harmonized intervals."

Having repeatedly issued these instructions, that ascetic born of Pracetas, of noble birth, the illustrious Sage Valmiki, became silent.

On receiving the commands of that Sage, the two sons of Maithili humbly answered "We will act in accord with thy behests!" and those Conquerors of Hostile Cities then took their leave.

Those youthful boys allowed the excellent counsels of the Rishi to enter their hearts, as the Ashwins receive the teachings of Bhargava and, eager to put them into practice, they whiled away that auspicious night.

## Chapter 94

*Kusha and Lava chant the Ramayana*

When the dawn appeared, those two youthful ascetics, having bathed and ignited the sacred fire, began to sing, as the Rishi had previously instructed them to do.

Kakutstha listened to that poem, composed by the aged Valmiki, unheard till then, set to music in multiple cadences, accompanied by stringed instruments, in measured rhythm, and, hearing those youthful musicians, Raghava was greatly mystified.

During an interval in the sacrifice, that foremost of monarchs called together the great Sages, Kings, Pundits, Naigamas, aged Grammarians, venerable brahmins and those versed in music, the Twice-born, those learned in omens and the citizens specially instructed in aesthetics, those who had knowledge of metres, words and accents, those who knew the different rhythms and measures, those versed in astronomy, those skilled in the science of sacrifices and rituals and experienced liturgists, those versed in discerning cause and effect, philosophers, scholars, teachers of hymns and legends and the Veda, those conversant with the Vrittas and Sutras, and also singers and dancers.

Thereafter, having assembled them all, Rama ushered in the two singers to that vast and murmuring throng of listeners for his own great pleasure. The two youthful disciples of the Sage began that recitation that unrolled melodiously, like unto the singing of the Gandharvas, nor could the company be sated with listening to so beautiful a song. In their delight, ascetics and great potentates, seemed to consume those musicians with their gaze, whom they looked upon again and again, and the whole assembly having centred its attention upon them, each said to his neighbour:—'Both resemble Rama, like twin representations of the same planet. If they did not wear matted locks and bark robes, we should see no difference between the singers and Raghava!'

As the people of town and country spoke thus, Kusha and Lava, having introduced the first part according to Narada's instructions, continued up to the twentieth Sarga during the afternoon, then Raghava, having heard the twenty Sargas, said to his beloved brother, "Give these two musicians eighteen thousand gold pieces immediately with aught else that they may desire, O Kakutstha!" Thereupon Saumitri instantly offered this to those youthful boys, one after the other, but the great-souled Kusha and Lava would not accept the gold that was presented to them, enquiring in astonishment, "What good is this? Grain, fruit and roots suffice ascetics like ourselves, what should we do with gold or silver in the forest?"

These words amazed all Rama's assistants extremely and, desiring to know the origin of the poem, that illustrious prince enquired of those two disciples of the ascetic, saying:—

"What is this poetical composition? Where is the residence of the sublime author of this great epic? Where is this bull among the ascetics?"

On this enquiry from Raghava, the two disciples of the Sage answered, saying:—

"The blessed Valmiki, who is attending the sacrifice, is the author of the poem in which thine whole life is told. Twenty-four thousand verses and a hundred Upakhyanas have been used by that ascetic, the son of Bhrigu. Five hundred Sargas divided into six Kandas, together with the Uttarakanda, O King, are the work of that magnanimous Rishi, our Guru. Thy conduct, thy circumstances, thine entire life is unrolled with its vicissitudes. If thou desirest it, O King, thou mayest hear it from us in the intervals of the sacrifice, in thy moments of leisure."

Thereafter Rama, accompanied by the Sages and magnanimous monarchs, having heard that melodious chant, returned to the sacrificial pavilion.

That recitation accompanied by Talas and Layas, divided into Sargas in harmonious notes and tones, in which the scansion was stressed by the stringed instruments, was heard by the King from the lips of Kusha and Lava.

## Chapter 95

*Rama sends for Sita*

Surrounded by the ascetics, kings and monkeys, Rama listened during many days to the sublime and wonderful epic, and while the two sons of Sita, Kusha and Lava, were singing, he recognized them. Having reflected deeply, he summoned messengers of virtuous conduct and in the assembly spoke to them of that princess, saying:—

"Go and repeat my words to that Blessed One and say:—

"'If she be irreproachable in her conduct and without sin, then, should she so desire it and has the approval of the Rishi, let her prove her good faith!' Do you then return and inform me concerning this matter. To-morrow at dawn, let Maithili, the daughter of Janaka attest her purity on oath in my presence, before the assembly!"

At this extremely significant command from Raghava, the messengers straightway went to seek out the foremost of the ascetics and, bowing to that Sage, who shone with infinite effulgence, they, with humility, communicated Rama's words to him.

Hearing them, the extremely illustrious ascetic, learning of Rama's wish, said "Be it so! May prosperity attend you!"

Thereafter those royal messengers returned with the Muni's answer and repeated it faithfully to Raghava and he, being informed of the decision of that magnanimous Sage, full of joy, addressed the Rishis and the assembled kings, saying:—

"O Blessed Ones, with your disciples, the kings and their attendants and whosoever may wish to do so, bear witness to the vow that Sita will make!"

These words of the magnanimous Raghava were praised by all the leading Rishis and those mighty kings who addressed the monarch saying:—

"Such conduct is only possible in Thee and is found nowhere else in the world, O Prince!"

Having resolved thus, Raghava, the Scourge of his Foes, said:—

"To-morrow this shall take place," whereupon he dismissed the assembly.

The trial by oath being fixed for the following day, the magnanimous and illustrious Rama gave leave to all the great Sages and Kings to depart.

## Chapter 96

*Valmiki leads Sita before Rama*

When the night had passed, the great descendant of Raghu went to the place of sacrifice to which he had summoned all the Rishis: Vasishtha, Vamadeva, Javali, Kashyapa, Vishvamitra, Dirghatmas and Durvasa of rigid penances, also Poulastya and Shakti, Bhargava, Vamana, Markandeya, Dhirghayus and the highly renowned Maudgalya, Garga, Chyavana, the virtuous Shatananda, the far-famed Bharadwaja, the illustrious Agniputra, Narada, Parvata and Gautama of great glory, all these ascetics and others of austere observances, in great numbers.

Inspired by curiosity, they all assembled, as also the intrepid titans; and the valiant monkeys and kings, intrigued, gathered there in like manner, with the warriors, merchants and thousands of the lower caste. Brahmins of rigid penances arrived from every region and all met together to be present at the taking of the oath by Sita; and that immense multitude stood absolutely motionless, as if turned to stone.

Knowing that all were come, the foremost of Sages immediately approached with Sita following him, her head bowed, her palms joined, choked with sobs, her mind absorbed in Rama.

Beholding Sita walking behind Valmiki, like unto the holy Shruti following in Brahma's footsteps, there arose a great clamour with cries of "Halahala!" from all those who were oppressed with profound sorrow on account of the unfortunate princess. And some cried "Hail, O Rama!" and some "Hail, O Sita!" while the rest acclaimed both. Thereafter, advancing amidst that multitude, the foremost of the ascetics, accompanied by Sita, addressed Raghava, saying:—

"I am Valmiki, and here, O Dasarathi, is Sita of virtuous ways and conduct, who, on account of calumny, was abandoned near mine hermitage, the censure of the people having inspired thee with fear, O Virtuous One! Sita will prove her innocence; it is for thee to issue the command. These two sons of Janaki, twin brothers, invincible heroes, are thy sons also; I speak the truth to thee! I am the tenth son of Pracetas, O joy of the Raghus, I do not recollect ever having uttered a lie; truly these are thy two children. During countless years I have practised asceticism, may I never reap the fruits thereof if Maithili be guilty! I have nothing wherewith to reproach myself regarding thought, word or deed; if Maithili be guilty, may I never gather the fruits thereof! With my five senses and the mind as the sixth, meditating amidst the forest waterfalls, Sita's innocence was revealed to me. That lady of irreproachable and pure conduct, to whom her lord is a God, will give proof of her good faith, O Thou who didst fear public condemnation! O Foremost of Men, here is that lady whom I proclaim to be essentially chaste, I whose vision is divinely illumined and who, though she was supremely dear to thee and her innocence well known, thou didst repudiate when thy spirit was troubled by the censure of the people!"

## Chapter 97

*Sita descends into the Earth*

Thus spoke Valmiki, and Raghava, on seeing that fair-complexioned princess, with joined palms, answered in the presence of the assembly:—

"O Fortunate and virtuous Brahmin, may it be so! I fully concur in thine irreproachable words. This assurance was formerly given to me by Vaidehi in the presence of the Gods and, believing in that oath, I reinstated her in my house, but great indeed was the public condemnation, therefore I sent Maithili away. O Brahmin, though wholly convinced of her innocence, it was from fear of the people that I cast off Sita, do thou pardon me! I acknowledge these twins, Kusha and Lava, to be my sons! I desire to make my peace with the chaste Maithili amidst the assembly."

Hearing of his intention, the foremost of the Gods, led by Brahma, all assembled there to witness Sita's defence, and Adityas, Vasus, Rudras, Vishvadevas, the hosts of the Maruts and all the great Rishis, Nagas, Sadhyas, Suparnas and Siddhas gathered with delight. Beholding the Gods and the Sages, the foremost of men, Raghava, once more affirmed: "I am in agreement with the irreproachable words of the Rishi Valmiki! I wish to be reconciled with the chaste Vaidehi in the presence of this assembly."

The defence of Sita filled all who witnessed it with emotion and, at that moment, Vayu, the foremost of the Gods, sent forth a pure and fragrant breeze to the great delight of the assembly, as formerly in the Golden Age, and, it appeared marvellous to all those people from many lands who experienced it!

Beholding that assembly, Sita, attired in a yellow robe, with joined palms, her head bowed, her eyes lowered, said:—

"If, in thought, I have never dwelt on any but Rama, may the Goddess Madhavi receive me!"

As Vaidehi was still speaking, a miracle took place and, from the earth rose a marvellous celestial throne supported on the heads of Nagas of immeasurable power, their bodies adorned with divine gems. The Goddess Dharani, bidding her welcome, took Maithili in her arms, causing her to be seated on that celestial seat and, while she occupied the throne, a shower of blossoms fell without ceasing from the sky. Then the Gods burst into loud acclamations, crying "Excellent! Excellent! O Sita, thy virtue is supreme!"

From the heavens, the Gods, with delighted hearts, beholding Sita descend into the earth, praised her again and again, and at the place of sacrifice, where all were assembled, Sages, kings and the foremost of men were unable to recover from their astonishment. In the sky, on earth and in the nether regions, all beings, animate and inanimate, Danavas of vast stature and the foremost of the Pannagas cried out in delight, whilst others remained absorbed in their thoughts or gazed on Rama and on Sita in ecstasy. The entire assembly witnessed Sita's descent into the earth and, at that moment, a great tremor passed through the whole world.

## Chapter 98

*Rama's Anger and Grief, Brahma appeases him*

When Vaidehi had descended into the earth, all the monkeys and Sages cried out in Rama's presence, "Excellent! Excellent" but Rama, deeply distressed, supporting himself on a staff employed in the sacrifice, his eyes veiled with tears, his head bowed, was overcome with grief. Sighing again and again, letting fall many tears, a prey to pain and wrath, he said:—

"Beholding Sita, the personification of Shri, vanish in my presence, my soul experiences an agony hitherto unknown. Formerly, when she was in Lanka, on the further side of the vast ocean, I brought her back, how much more easily shall I be able to wrest her from the bosom of the earth! O Goddess Vasuda, give me back my Sita, whom thou retainest, or thou shalt witness my wrath! Thou shouldst know me since thou art assuredly my mother-in-law and Maithili rose from thee when Janaka was following the plough. Therefore let Sita go or open thyself to me that I may dwell with her in Patala or else in Nakaprishtha! Bring back Maithili on whose account I am distraught! If thou failest to return Sita to me in her original form, I shall plough thee up with thy mountains and forests and shall destroy thee so that nothing but water remains!"

Thus spoke Kakutstha, full of wrath and grief, and Brahma, accompanied by the Hosts of the Gods, addressed the son of Raghu, saying:—

"O Rama, virtuous Rama, do not be incensed, recollect thy divine origin and nature, O Scourge of Thy Foes! Assuredly, O Prince, I do not need to remind thee that no-one is superior to thee! Now recall that thou art Vishnu, O Invincible Hero! The chaste and virtuous Sita, who was wholly absorbed in thee formerly, has happily reached the region of the Nagas, by virtue of her ascetic practices. Thou wilt undoubtedly be re-united with her in the Celestial Realm. O Rama, hear, in the assembly, what I relate in this poem, the most beautiful of epics, recited in thine honour, I will make all known to thee in detail, do not doubt it. In this poem of Valmiki all is included from the time of thy birth, O Hero, the good and evil that has visited thee and what will happen in the future. That great poet, O Rama, is wholly devoted to thee, none other is worthy of the honour bestowed by poets save Raghava. Formerly, in company with the Gods, I heard the entire classic; it is divine, marvellously beautiful, true, and the remover of nescience. O Foremost of Men, O Supremely Virtuous Kakutstha, listen to the conclusion of the Ramayana and what concerns the future. Listen now with the Rishis, O Doughty and Illustrious Prince, to the end of this sublime poem entitled 'Uttara'. Assuredly, O Kakutstha, this excellent epilogue may not be heard by any other save thee, who art the supreme Sage, O Hero, O Joy of the House of Raghu."

Having spoken thus, Brahma, the Lord of the Three Worlds, returned to his abode with his followers, the Gods.

Meantime the magnanimous and high-souled Rishis, whose abode was Brahmaloka, at Brahma's command, remained, desirous of hearing 'Uttara kanda' and what should happen to Raghava.

Having listened to the significant words of that God of Gods, the illustrious Rama said to Valmiki:—

"O Blessed One, the Rishis of Brahmaloka desire to listen to 'Uttara kanda' and all that shall happen to me; to-morrow let it be narrated by thee!"

Having resolved thus, Rama sought out Kusha and Lava and, dismissing the company, returned with them to the leaf-thatched hut of the Rishi Valmiki, where he passed the night lamenting for Sita.

## Chapter 99

*The Death of the Queens*

When night had given way to dawn, Rama called together the great ascetics and said to his two sons:—

"Now sing without anxiety," and when those great and magnanimous Sages were seated, Kusha and Lava sang the epilogue to the 'Ramayana.'

Sita, having re-entered the earth, thus proving her fidelity, and the sacrifice being completed, Rama, in the extremity of grief, not beholding Vaidehi, regarded the world as a desert, and he dismissed the kings, bears, monkeys and titans and the host of leading brahmins, having loaded them with treasure.

Taking leave of them, the lotus-eyed Rama, who was ever absorbed in the thought of Sita, returned to Ayodhya. The Joy of the House of Raghu never sought another consort but, in every sacrifice, he set up a golden image of Janaki in her stead. For ten thousand years, Rama performed the Vajamedha Sacrifice and the Vajapeya, ten times more, distributing quantities of gold, and that fortunate One also performed the Agnisthoma, Atiratra and Gosava Sacrifices, giving away abundant charity.

For a long time, the magnanimous Raghava occupied the throne, his heart fixed in his duty; bears, monkeys and titans were subject to his rule and monarchs came daily to pay him homage. Parjanya sent rains in the proper season and it was abundant, the skies were clear, the regions sinless, the city and country abounding in cheerful and satisfied people. None died prematurely nor was there any disease, and in Rama's reign, none were destitute.

After many years however, Rama's aged mother, surrounded by her sons and grandsons, passed away and she was followed by Sumitra and the renowned Kaikeyi, who having performed many righteous acts went to the celestial region, where those happy Ones were re-united with Dasaratha and received the fruit of their merit in heaven.

From time to time, in memory of his mother, Raghava distributed gifts to the brahmins vowed to asceticism, and the virtuous Rama offered up obsequies accompanied by gifts of gems to the Sages and performed incomparable austerities in honour of his ancestors.

Thus thousands of years passed happily during which, with the aid of sacrifices, that prince promoted the execution of duty in all its aspects.

## FROM THE MAHĀBHĀRATA (5TH CENT. BCE–4TH CENT. CE), INCLUDING THE BHAGAVAD-GĪTĀ (1ST CENT. BCE)

The great Indian epic, the *Mahābhārata,* is thought to describe a war that occurred in the Punjab region of northwest India around 1000 BCE. The complete work consists of some 88,000 verses, making it the longest epic in the world. It was compiled between the fifth century BCE and the fourth century CE. Incorporating and elaborating such religious texts as the Bhagavad-Gītā, it became a vast repository of the myth, legend, and philosophy central to Indian culture and history. Although it is clear that the work we have today is the product of many hands, authorship is traditionally ascribed to Vyāsa "the Arranger."

The story tells of the five godlike Pāṇḍava brothers, who are cheated out of their kingdoms by relatives, the Kurus, in a dice game. After thirteen years of exile in the forest, the Pāṇḍavas return and feel compelled to go to war to regain their rightful lands. Wanting to be fair, the god Kṛṣṇa says that he personally will not take up arms in the war but offers to support both sides. The Kurus choose to have Kṛṣṇa's army while the Pāṇḍavas choose Kṛṣṇa himself with his knowledge of strategy and tactics. Kṛṣṇa becomes the charioteer of Arjuna. Before the fighting begins Kṛṣṇa goes to the Kurus in an attempt to settle the matter peacefully, saying that the Pāṇḍavas will be satisfied to receive only five villages to replace their lost kingdoms. The Kurus, however, arrogantly refuse to give up even as much land as would be covered by a pin driven into the earth. War is inevitable.

On the eve of battle, as the two armies are drawn up facing each other, the great Pāṇḍava warrior Arjuna loses heart at the thought of having to kill his kinsmen and expresses his concerns to Kṛṣṇa. Kṛṣṇa argues (in the Bhagavad-Gītā) that virtue consists of doing one's duty without regard for profit or loss, success or failure. In this case, Arjuna's duty, his dharma, is to perform as a warrior to the best of his ability regardless of who his enemy might be.

After many days of bloody battle, Arjuna eventually confronts and kills his half brother Karṇa. In the end, with Kṛṣṇa's help, the Pāṇḍavas achieve victory. The defeated and dying Kuru leader Duryodhana bitterly complains that the Pāṇḍavas have won only by using unfair means through Kṛṣṇa's dishonest tactics. This is hypocritical, since Duryodhana himself has resorted to unfair tactics; indeed, his name itself means something like "Dirty Fighter." The main point, however, is that in performing one's dharma one may sometimes be required to do things that seem repellent.

Having defeated their enemies and regained their kingdoms, the Pāṇḍavas rule for many years. Eventually, they die and ascend the Himalayas to heaven where they are reconciled with their former foes, and the family is once again united and harmonious. All bitterness and resentment are resolved. Although the brothers and their enemies are godlike in heroic stature and embody many divine attributes, they also have many human characteristics. At the end, for example, when Yudhiṣṭhira goes to heaven, he refuses to enter unless his dog is allowed to accompany him.

The Bhagavad-Gītā, which is contained within the *Mahābhārata,* is perhaps the single most beloved text from ancient India, and it has had an enduring impact on the world. It was the inspiration for Mahatma Gandhi's doctrine of nonviolence, for example. Composed in the first century BCE, it offered a liberal and relatively undogmatic Hindu counter-response to Buddhism, providing what many consider India's most universal spiritual message, the performance of correct action without regard for worldly consequences. Three chapters are included here: the first establishes the situation (Arjuna's despair over having to fight his own kin); the second delivers Kṛṣṇa's (Krishna's) first lessons on dharma; the eleventh chapter, perhaps the most memorable of all, is a mystical vision of God's totality.

## *Chs. XXXVI–XLI passim [Kṛṣṇa Arranges a Settlement]*

*Translated by Chakravarthi V. Narasimhan*

### XXXVI

By sending out scouts privately, Duryodhana learnt all that had been done by the Pāṇḍavas. Hearing that Kṛṣṇa was on his way to Dvārakā, he set out for that city, with a modest retinue borne by horses speedy as the wind. Arjuna arrived at Dvārakā, the beautiful city of the Ānartas, on the same day. The two descendants of Kuru, foremost among men, reached Dvārakā at about the same time, and saw Kṛṣṇa asleep. As Kṛṣṇa slept, Duryodhana entered the bedroom and sat on a fine seat near Kṛṣṇa's head. Then entered the great-souled Arjuna; with folded hands he stood near Kṛṣṇa's feet. When Kṛṣṇa awoke, he naturally saw Arjuna first, and Duryodhana only second. He welcomed them both, did them due honours, and then made inquiries as to the occasion for their visit. Duryodhana said smilingly; "It is proper that you should help me in this war, for your friendship with myself and with Arjuna is equal. Our relationship with you is also equally close. Furthermore, today I have come to you first. Our good ancestors always honoured those who came first."

Kṛṣṇa said, "I have not the slightest doubt that you came here first, but I first set eyes on Arjuna. O Duryodhana, since you arrived here first and I saw him first, I shall help both of you. But the holy books say that younger persons should be aided first; therefore I should first assist Arjuna. I have a large army of ten million gopas, each of whom is capable of slaying me, who are known as the Nārāyanas. I shall place this invincible army at the disposal of one party among you; I myself, non-combatant and unarmed, shall take the side of the other. Of these two, O Arjuna, make your choice as you please, since customary law gives you the right of choosing first."

Thus addressed by Kṛṣṇa, Arjuna unhesitatingly chose Kṛṣṇa, who was not to fight in the battle. And Duryodhana for his part chose the whole of that army. Since he had got thousands upon thousands of warriors, even though Kṛṣṇa was lost to him, he was well pleased.

Having obtained the whole army of Kṛṣṇa, Duryodhana went to see Balarāma. He told him why he had come, upon which Balarāma said in reply, "I will not help either you or Arjuna; such is the unalterable conclusion I have reached, after taking into account Kṛṣṇa's views. You are born in the race of Bharata, honoured by all rulers of the earth; go and fight in strict accordance with the code of honour and chivalry."

After Duryodhana's departure, Kṛṣṇa said to Arjuna: "Why have you chosen me, knowing that I shall not take any part in the battle?" "There is no doubt that you can slay them all," said Arjuna. "O foremost among men, I too can slay them all singlehanded. It has been my yearning to have you as my charioteer and it behoves you to fulfil this longfelt desire of mine." Kṛṣṇa replied, "It is but fair that you should compare yourself with me. I shall be your charioteer in fulfilment of your wish."

## XXXVII

Śalya too heard the news and went to help the Pāṇḍavas, surrounded by a large army and accompanied by his sons who were mighty car-warriors. He proceeded by slow marches toward the camp of the Pāṇḍavas, resting his army en route. Duryodhana learned that the great Śalya was coming with a large army and hastened to welcome him in person. He also had pavilions erected in charming spots, ornamented with gems and well decorated, for Śalya's accommodation and in his honour. Well pleased with these attentions, Śalya asked the servants, "Who are the men of Yudhiṣṭhira who built these palaces? Bring them to me. I think it is meet that I reward them."

Duryodhana, who had concealed himself, then appeared before Śalya. On seeing him, Śalya knew that all these attentions came from him. Embracing Duryodhana, he said, "Accept whatever you desire." "May your words come true!" said Duryodhana. "Grant me this auspicious boon. It is proper that you should lead all my armies." "It is done," said Śalya. "Is there anything else?" Duryodhana had no other wish. He took leave of Śalya, and returned to his own city.

Śalya went on to see Yudhiṣṭhira and to inquire what he wished to have done. In the course of time, he reached Upaplavya, and entered the Pāṇḍava encampment, where he spoke about his meeting with Duryodhana, and the great boon he had given because of the attentions he had received.

Yudhiṣṭhira said, "O king, what you have done is good; you have fulfilled a promise made when you were well pleased in the innermost recesses of your heart. I want you to do only one thing for me. You are the best among kings, you are Kṛṣṇa's equal in battle; when the two, Karṇa and Arjuna, riding their chariots, meet in battle, I have no doubt that you will fill the office of Karṇa's charioteer. O king, if you wish me well, you must protect Arjuna, and do whatever is necessary to kill the energy of Karṇa, and whatever is calculated to bring us victory. Though this is improper, yet must you do it, uncle mine!" "O son," replied Śalya, "I shall do what you have asked me to do, and anything else which I can see is for your good." The ruler of Madra, the noble Śalya, then took leave of the sons of Kuṅtī and went with his army to Duryodhana, as he had promised.

## XL

Meanwhile, at the Pāṇḍava camp, Yudhiṣṭhira said to Kṛṣṇa, "Relying on you, O Kṛṣṇa, we have without fear demanded our share of the kingdom from the son of Dhṛtarāṣṭra who is filled with vain pride, as are all his advisers. You have heard what Dhṛtarāṣṭra and his son intend to do. It is exactly as Sañjaya told me. He wants to make peace with us without restoring our kingdom to us; the greedy man, moved by his sinful heart, shows bias towards his own son. We said to him, 'Give us, O sire, five villages or towns where we may live together; for we do not desire the destruction of the Bhāratas.' Even this the wicked-souled son of Dhṛtarāṣṭra does not permit, thinking that he is the sole lord. What is more deplorable than this?"

"Wealth is said to be the best virtue," Yudhiṣṭhira continued. "Everything is established on wealth; and rich men live in this world, while poor men are practically dead. Poverty is a greater danger to a man than death; for it destroys his prosperity, which is the source of his virtue as well as his pleasures. A man who is born poor does not suffer so much as one who, after having enjoyed great prosperity and a life of great happiness, is deprived of it. We have many cousins, and our elders are our allies on both sides. Their slaughter would be extremely sinful. One may well ask: what then is the good of engaging in battle? A Kṣatriya kills another Kṣatriya; a fish lives on another fish; a dog kills another dog. See how each follows his rule of life, O Kṛṣṇa. In all cases war is evil. Who that strikes is not struck in return? Victory and defeat, O Kṛṣṇa, are the same to one who is killed. Defeat is not very much better than death, I think; but he whose side gains victory also surely suffers some loss."

Yudhiṣṭhira asked him, "What then do you think, O Kṛṣṇa, to be appropriate to the occasion? How shall I find a way out without deviating from virtue as well as from worldly good? In such a predicament, whom else but yourself is it proper for us to consult, O best among men?" In reply, Kṛṣṇa said to Yudhiṣṭhira, "For the good of both of you I shall go to the Kuru camp. If I succeed in ensuring peace without sacrificing your interests, then I shall have performed a virtuous and fruitful act."

"As it pleases you, O Kṛṣṇa!" said Yudhiṣṭhira. "May good come out of it! May I see you return from the Kurus with your object gained, and in good health!" Kṛṣṇa said, "Going to the Kurus, I shall seek to make peace without any sacrifice of your interests; and I shall also observe their intentions. After noting the conduct of the sons of Kuru and ascertained their preparations for war, I shall return to make victory yours, O Bhārata."

Having come to know through his spies of the departure of Kṛṣṇa, Dhṛtarāṣṭra said to Bhīṣma, after paying him due honour, "The powerful scion of the Dāśārha race is coming here for the sake of the Pāṇḍavas; he is at all times worthy of our respect and regard. Prepare for his worship and erect pavilions on the way, filled with all needed articles." Then at many places on the way, at spots of great beauty, pavilions were constructed and decked with all kinds of gems. The king sent there comfortable seats, girls, perfumes, ornaments, fine fabrics, excellent viands and drinks, and several kinds of fragrant garlands.

Vidura addressed Dhṛtarāṣṭra, "O king, the five Pāṇḍavas desire only five villages. If you do not give them even those, who will conclude peace? You wish to win over Kṛṣṇa by wealth; and by this means you want to separate him from the Pāṇḍavas. Let me tell you this: he cannot be separated from Arjuna by wealth, or by efforts, or by accusations and complaints against the Pāṇḍavas."

Duryodhana said, "What Vidura has said just now regarding Kṛṣṇa has been truly spoken; for he is firmly attached to the Pāṇḍavas and inseparable from them. Listen to this great idea which I am determined to carry out. I shall imprison Kṛṣṇa, the refuge of the Pāṇḍavas. On his imprisonment, the Vṛṣṇis and the Pāṇḍavas, in fact the whole world, will be at my disposal. Kṛṣṇa will be here tomorrow morning."

Hearing these words of terrible significance, the plan of making Kṛṣṇa a captive, Dhṛtarāṣṭra and his ministers were much pained. Dhṛtarāṣṭra then said to Duryodhana, "Do not say such foolish things, O my son. This is against eternal virtue. Kṛṣṇa is an ambassador, and he is also our kinsman. He has done no wrong to the Kurus. How then is it right that he should be made prisoner?"

Bhīṣma said, "This son of yours, Dhṛtarāṣṭra, has been seized by folly. He chooses evil rather than good, despite the entreaties of his well-wishers. I wish never to listen to the risk-laden words of this sinful and wicked wretch who has abandoned all virtue." Having said these words, the old chief of the Bhāratas, the truthful Bhīṣma, rose in a towering rage and left the court.

## XLI

In honour of Kṛṣṇa the city was well decorated and the streets were adorned with various gems. The people, with their heads bowed low to the ground, were in the streets when Kṛṣṇa entered the city. That lotus-eyed hero entered the ash-coloured palace of Dhṛtarāṣṭra, graced with many buildings. He was duly honoured by Dhṛtarāṣṭra and then came out with the permission of the king. Having exchanged greetings with the Kurus in the assembly, Kṛṣṇa went to the enchanting abode of Vidura. The virtuous Vidura completed the rites of hospitality for Kṛṣṇa, and then asked him about the welfare of the Pāṇḍavas.

After his visit to Vidura, Kṛṣṇa went in the afternoon to visit his aunt Kuntī. Seeing Kṛṣṇa approach, shining like the radiant sun, Kuntī clasped his neck with her arms, and poured forth her lamentations, remembering her sons whom she had not seen for so long.

Kṛṣṇa said to her, "Your sons, along with Draupadī, salute you. They are well and have asked me to inquire about your welfare. You will soon see the Pāṇḍavas, in good health, with all their objects gained, their enemies killed and themselves surrounded by prosperity." Bidding her farewell, and respectfully circumambulating her, the mighty-armed Kṛṣṇa then left for Duryodhana's mansion.

During the night, after he had dined and refreshed himself, Vidura said to him, "O Kṛṣṇa, this mission of yours is not a well-considered act. The sons of Dhṛtarāṣṭra and Karṇa are convinced that the Pāṇḍavas are not capable even of gazing at an army under the leadership of Bhīṣma and Droṇa. The idea of your going and speaking in the midst of all those misguided, impure, and evil-minded men does not please me. All the sons of Dhṛtarāṣṭra have come to the conclusion, O Kṛṣṇa, that they can give battle to Iṅdra himself along with the other gods. Your words, though wise in themselves, will be of no avail against those who are thus inclined, and who follow the dictates of desire and anger."

Kṛṣṇa said, "You have spoken wisely—you have spoken as a man of insight, and even as one friend to another. When there is a dispute between cousins, the wise men say that the friend who does not serve them as a mediator by all his efforts is not a true friend. If I can bring about peace with the Kurus without sacrificing the interests of the Pāṇḍavas, then my conduct will have been meritorious and very significant; and the Kurus will have been freed from the shackles of death."

In such talk the two wise men spent that starlit and beautiful night. At dawn many professional bards and singers endowed with good voices awakened Kṛṣṇa with the sound of conch and cymbal. Duryodhana and Śakuni came to Kṛṣṇa while he was still performing his morning rites, and said the him, "King Dhṛtarāṣṭra has come to the assembly hall, and so have the other Kurus, headed by Bhīṣma and all the rulers of the earth. They are waiting for you, O Kṛṣṇa, as the gods in heaven may await Iṅdra's arrival." Kṛṣṇa received them courteously, and in due course proceeded to the assembly hall.

When all the kings and courtiers had taken their seats and perfect stillness prevailed, Kṛṣṇa said in a voice like a drum, "I have come so that there may be peace between the Kurus and Pāṇḍavas, O Bhārata, without the slaughter of heroes on either side. However, your sons, headed by Duryodhana, are acting impiously, putting behind them all considerations of morality and earthly good. As boys the Pāṇḍavas lost their father and were brought up by you; protect them in accordance with justice, as you would your own sons, O king. The Pāṇḍavas salute you, and have sent you this message: 'At your command our followers and we ourselves have suffered untold misery. We have spent twelve years in banishment in the forest and the thirteenth year in disguise. We did not break our word, truly believing that our father would not break his pledge towards us. The Brāhmanas who accompanied us know this. Therefore abide by your pledge as we have done by ours, O best of the Bhārata race. We have suffered long, and now we desire to get our share of the kingdom.'"

Having given this message, Kṛṣṇa continued, "Restore to the Pāṇḍavas their due share of the ancestral kingdom, and enjoy the blessings of life, along with your sons. As for me, O Bhārata, I desire your welfare as much as that of the others. In the interests of virtue, profit, and happiness, O king, I adjure you not to allow the destruction of your subjects. Restrain your sons, who regard evil as good and good as evil, and who, moved by greed, have gone too far. The Pāṇḍavas are as ready to serve you dutifully as to fight. O king, adopt that course which seems wisest to you."

## *The Bhagavad-Gītā*

### *The First Teaching: Arjuna's Dejection*

*Translated by Barbara Stoler Miller*

*Dhritarashtra*

Sanjaya, tell me what my sons
and the sons of Pandu did when they met,
wanting to battle on the field of Kuru,
on the field of sacred duty?

*Sanjaya*

Your son Duryodhana, the king,
seeing the Pandava forces arrayed,
approached his teacher Drona
and spoke in command.

"My teacher, see
the great Pandava army arrayed
by Drupada's son,
your pupil, intent on revenge.

Here are heroes, mighty archers
equal to Bhima and Arjuna in warfare,
Yuyudhana, Virata, and Drupada,
your sworn foe on his great chariot.

Here too are Dhrishtaketu, Cekitana,
and the brave king of Benares;
Purujit, Kuntibhoja,
and the manly king of the Shibis.

Yudhamanyu is bold,
and Uttamaujas is brave;
the sons of Subhadra and Draupadi
all command great chariots.

Now, honored priest, mark
the superb men on our side
as I tell you the names
of my army's leaders.

They are you and Bhishma,
Karna and Kripa, a victor in battles,
your own son Ashvatthama,
Vikarna, and the son of Somadatta.

Many other heroes also risk
their lives for my sake,
bearing varied weapons
and skilled in the ways of war.

Guarded by Bhishma, the strength
of our army is without limit;
but the strength of their army,
guarded by Bhima, is limited.

In all the movements of battle,
you and your men,
stationed according to plan,
must guard Bhishma well!"

Bhishma, fiery elder of the Kurus,
roared his lion's roar
and blew his conch horn,
exciting Duryodhana's delight.

Conches and kettledrums,
cymbals, tabors, and trumpets
were sounded at once
and the din of tumult arose.

Standing on their great chariot
yoked with white stallions,
Krishna and Arjuna, Pandu's son,
sounded their divine conches.

Krishna blew Pancajanya, won from a demon;
Arjuna blew Devadatta, a gift of the gods;
fierce wolf-bellied Bhima blew Paundra,
his great conch of the east.

Yudhishthira, Kunti's son, the king,
blew Anantavijaya, conch of boundless victory;

his twin brothers Nakula and Sahadeva
blew conches resonant and jewel toned.

The king of Benares, a superb archer,
and Shikhandin on his great chariot,
Drishtadyumna, Virata, and indomitable Satyaki,
all blew their conches.

Drupada, with his five grandsons,
and Subhadra's strong-armed son,
each in his turn blew
their conches, O King.

The noise tore the hearts
of Dhritarashtra's sons,
and tumult echoed
through heaven and earth.

Arjuna, his war flag a rampant monkey,
saw Dhritarashtra's sons assembled
as weapons were ready to clash,
and he lifted his bow.

He told his charioteer:
"Krishna,
halt my chariot
between the armies!

Far enough for me to see
these men who lust for war,
ready to fight with me
in the strain of battle.

I see men gathered here,
eager to fight,
bent on serving the folly
of Dhritarashtra's son."

When Arjuna had spoken,
Krishna halted
their splendid chariot
between the armies.

Facing Bhishma and Drona
and all the great kings,
he said, "Arjuna, see
the Kuru men assembled here!"

Arjuna saw them standing there:
fathers, grandfathers, teachers,
uncles, brothers, sons,
grandsons, and friends.

He surveyed his elders
and companions in both armies,
all his kinsmen
assembled together.

Dejected, filled with strange pity,
he said this:
"Krishna, I see my kinsmen
gathered here, wanting war.

My limbs sink,
my mouth is parched,
my body trembles,
the hair bristles on my flesh.

The magic bow slips
from my hand, my skin burns,
I cannot stand still,
my mind reels.

I see omens of chaos,
Krishna; I see no good
in killing my kinsmen
in battle.

Krishna, I seek no victory,
or kingship or pleasures.
What use to us are kingship,
delights, or life itself?

We sought kingship, delights,
and pleasures for the sake of those
assembled to abandon their lives
and fortunes in battle.

They are teachers, fathers, sons,
and grandfathers, uncles, grandsons,
fathers and brothers of wives,
and other men of our family.

I do not want to kill them
even if I am killed, Krishna;

not for kingship of all three worlds,
much less for the earth!

What joy is there for us, Krishna,
in killing Dhritarashtra's sons?
Evil will haunt us if we kill them,
though their bows are drawn to kill.

Honor forbids us to kill
our cousins, Dhritarashtra's sons;
how can we know happiness
if we kill our own kinsmen?

The greed that distorts their reason
blinds them to the sin they commit
in ruining the family, blinds them
to the crime of betraying friends.

How can we ignore the wisdom
of turning from this evil
when we see the sin
of family destruction, Krishna?

When the family is ruined,
the timeless laws of family duty
perish; and when duty is lost,
chaos overwhelms the family.

In overwhelming chaos, Krishna,
women of the family are corrupted;
and when women are corrupted,
disorder is born in society.

This discord drags the violators
and the family itself to hell;
for ancestors fall when rites
of offering rice and water lapse.

The sins of men who violate
the family create disorder in society
that undermines the constant laws
of caste and family duty.

Krishna, we have heard
that a place in hell
is reserved for men
who undermine family duties.

I lament the great sin
we commit when our greed
for kingship and pleasures
drives us to kill our kinsmen.

If Dhritarashtra's armed sons
kill me in battle when I am unarmed
and offer no resistance,
it will be my reward."

Saying this in the time of war,
Arjuna slumped into the chariot
and laid down his bow and arrows,
his mind tormented by grief.

## *The Second Teaching: Philosophy and Spiritual Discipline*

*Translated by Barbara Stoler Miller*

*Sanjaya*

Arjuna sat dejected,
filled with pity,
his sad eyes blurred by tears.
Krishna gave him counsel.

*Lord Krishna*

Why this cowardice
in time of crisis, Arjuna?
The coward is ignoble, shameful,
foreign to the ways of heaven.

Don't yield to impotence!
It is unnatural in you!
Banish this petty weakness from your heart.
Rise to the fight, Arjuna!

*Arjuna*

Krishna, how can I fight
against Bhishma and Drona
with arrows
when they deserve my worship?

It is better in this world
to beg for scraps of food

than to eat meals
smeared with the blood
of elders I killed
at the height of their power
while their goals
were still desires.

We don't know which weight
is worse to bear—
our conquering them
or their conquering us.
We will not want to live
if we kill
the sons of Dhritarashtra
assembled before us.

The flaw of pity
blights my very being;
conflicting sacred duties
confound my reason.
I ask you to tell me
decisively—Which is better?
I am your pupil.
Teach me what I seek!

I see nothing
that could drive away
the grief
that withers my senses;
even if I won kingdoms
of unrivaled wealth
on earth
and sovereignty over gods.

*Sanjaya*

Arjuna told this
to Krishna—then saying,
"I shall not fight,"
he fell silent.

Mocking him gently,
Krishna gave this counsel
as Arjuna sat dejected,
between the two armies.

*Lord Krishna*

You grieve for those beyond grief,
and you speak words of insight;
but learned men do not grieve
for the dead or the living.

Never have I not existed,
nor you, nor these kings;
and never in the future
shall we cease to exist.

Just as the embodied self
enters childhood, youth, and old age,
so does it enter another body;
this does not confound a steadfast man.

Contacts with matter make us feel
heat and cold, pleasure and pain.
Arjuna, you must learn to endure
fleeting things—they come and go!

When these cannot torment a man,
when suffering and joy are equal
for him and he has courage,
he is fit for immortality.

Nothing of nonbeing comes to be,
nor does being cease to exist;
the boundary between these two
is seen by men who see reality.

Indestructible is the presence
that pervades all this;
no one can destroy
this unchanging reality.

Our bodies are known to end,
but the embodied self is enduring,
indestructible, and immeasurable;
therefore, Arjuna, fight the battle!

He who thinks this self a killer
and he who thinks it killed,
both fail to understand;
it does not kill, nor is it killed.

It is not born,
it does not die;
having been,
it will never not be;
unborn, enduring,
constant, and primordial,
it is not killed
when the body is killed.

Arjuna, when a man knows the self
to be indestructible, enduring, unborn,
unchanging, how does he kill
or cause anyone to kill?

As a man discards
worn-out clothes
to put on new
and different ones,
so the embodied self
discards
its worn-out bodies
to take on other new ones.

Weapons do not cut it,
fire does not burn it,
waters do not wet it,
wind does not wither it.

It cannot be cut or burned;
it cannot be wet or withered;
it is enduring, all-pervasive,
fixed, immovable, and timeless.

It is called unmanifest,
inconceivable, and immutable;
since you know that to be so,
you should not grieve!

If you think of its birth
and death as ever-recurring,
then too, Great Warrior,
you have no cause to grieve!

Death is certain for anyone born,
and birth is certain for the dead;

since the cycle is inevitable,
you have no cause to grieve!

Creatures are unmanifest in origin,
manifest in the midst of life,
and unmanifest again in the end.
Since this is so, why do you lament?

Rarely someone
sees it,
rarely another
speaks it,
rarely anyone
hears it—
even hearing it,
no one really knows it.

The self embodied in the body
of every being is indestructible;
you have no cause to grieve
for all these creatures, Arjuna!

Look to your own duty;
do not tremble before it;
nothing is better for a warrior
than a battle of sacred duty.

The doors of heaven open
for warriors who rejoice
to have a battle like this
thrust on them by chance.

If you fail to wage this war
of sacred duty,
you will abandon your own duty
and fame only to gain evil.

People will tell
of your undying shame,
and for a man of honor
shame is worse than death.

The great chariot warriors will think
you deserted in fear of battle;

you will be despised
by those who held you in esteem.

Your enemies will slander you,
scorning your skill
in so many unspeakable ways—
could any suffering be worse?

If you are killed, you win heaven;
if you triumph, you enjoy the earth;
therefore, Arjuna, stand up
and resolve to fight the battle!

Impartial to joy and suffering,
gain and loss, victory and defeat,
arm yourself for the battle,
lest you fall into evil.

Understanding is defined in terms of philosophy;
now hear it in spiritual discipline.
Armed with this understanding, Arjuna,
you will escape the bondage of action.

No effort in this world
is lost or wasted;
a fragment of sacred duty
saves you from great fear.

This understanding is unique
in its inner core of resolve;
diffuse and pointless are the ways
irresolute men understand.

Undiscerning men who delight
in the tenets of ritual lore
utter florid speech, proclaiming,
"There is nothing else!"

Driven by desire, they strive after heaven
and contrive to win powers and delights,
but their intricate ritual language
bears only the fruit of action in rebirth.

Obsessed with powers and delights,
their reason lost in words,

they do not find in contemplation
this understanding of inner resolve.

Arjuna, the realm of sacred lore
is nature—beyond its triad of qualities,
dualities, and mundane rewards,
be forever lucid, alive to your self.

For the discerning priest,
all of sacred lore
has no more value than a well
when water flows everywhere.

Be intent on action,
not on the fruits of action;
avoid attraction to the fruits
and attachment to inaction!

Perform actions, firm in discipline,
relinquishing attachment;
be impartial to failure and success—
this equanimity is called discipline.

Arjuna, action is far inferior
to the discipline of understanding;
so seek refuge in understanding—pitiful
are men drawn by fruits of action.

Disciplined by understanding,
one abandons both good and evil deeds;
so arm yourself for discipline—
discipline is skill in actions.

Wise men disciplined by understanding
relinquish the fruit born of action;
freed from these bonds of rebirth,
they reach a place beyond decay.

When your understanding passes beyond
the swamp of delusion,
you will be indifferent to all
that is heard in sacred lore.

When your understanding turns
from sacred lore to stand fixed,
immovable in contemplation,
then you will reach discipline.

*Arjuna*

Krishna, what defines a man
deep in contemplation whose insight
and thought are sure? How would he speak?
How would he sit? How would he move?

*Lord Krishna*

When he gives up desires in his mind,
is content with the self within himself,
then he is said to be a man
whose insight is sure, Arjuna.

When suffering does not disturb his mind,
when his craving for pleasures has vanished,
when attraction, fear, and anger are gone,
he is called a sage whose thought is sure.

When he shows no preference
in fortune or misfortune
and neither exults nor hates,
his insight is sure.

When, like a tortoise retracting
its limbs, he withdraws his senses
completely from sensuous objects,
his insight is sure.

Sensuous objects fade
when the embodied self abstains from food;
the taste lingers, but it too fades
in the vision of higher truth.

Even when a man of wisdom
tries to control them, Arjuna,
the bewildering senses
attack his mind with violence.

Controlling them all,
with discipline he should focus on me;
when his senses are under control,
his insight is sure.

Brooding about sensuous objects
makes attachment to them grow;
from attachment desire arises,
from desire anger is born.

From anger comes confusion;
from confusion memory lapses;
from broken memory understanding is lost;
from loss of understanding, he is ruined.

But a man of inner strength
whose senses experience objects
without attraction and hatred,
in self-control, finds serenity.

In serenity, all his sorrows
dissolve;
his reason becomes serene,
his understanding sure.

Without discipline,
he has no understanding or inner power;
without inner power, he has no peace;
and without peace where is joy?

If his mind submits to the play
of the senses,
they drive away insight,
as wind drives a ship on water.

So, Great Warrior, when withdrawal
of the senses
from sense objects is complete,
discernment is firm.

When it is night for all creatures,
a master of restraint is awake;
when they are awake, it is night
for the sage who sees reality.

As the mountainous depths
of the ocean
are unmoved when waters
rush into it,
so the man unmoved
when desires enter him
attains a peace that eludes
the man of many desires.

When he renounces all desires
and acts without craving,

possessiveness,
or individuality, he finds peace.

This the place of the infinite spirit;
achieving it, one is freed from delusion;
abiding in it even at the time of death,
one finds the pure calm of infinity.

## *The Eleventh Teaching: The Vision of Krishna's Totality*

*Translated by Barbara Stoler Miller*

*Arjuna*

To favor me you revealed
the deepest mystery of the self,
and by your words
my delusion is dispelled.

I heard from you in detail
how creatures come to be and die,
Krishna, and about the self
in its immutable greatness.

Just as you have described
yourself, I wish to see your form
in all its majesty,
Krishna, Supreme among Men.

If you think I can see it,
reveal to me
your immutable self,
Krishna, Lord of Discipline.

*Lord Krishna*

Arjuna, see my forms
in hundreds and thousands;
diverse, divine,
of many colors and shapes.

See the sun gods, gods of light,
howling storm gods, twin gods of dawn,
and gods of wind, Arjuna,
wondrous forms not seen before.

Arjuna, see all the universe,
animate and inanimate,
and whatever else you wish to see;
all stands here as one in my body.

But you cannot see me
with your own eye;
I will give you a divine eye to see
the majesty of my discipline.

*Sanjaya*

O King, saying this, Krishna,
the great lord of discipline,
revealed to Arjuna
the true majesty of his form.

It was a multiform, wondrous vision,
with countless mouths and eyes
and celestial ornaments,
brandishing many divine weapons.

Everywhere was boundless divinity
containing all astonishing things,
wearing divine garlands and garments,
annointed with divine perfume.

If the light of a thousand suns
were to rise in the sky at once,
it would be like the light
of that great spirit.

Arjuna saw all the universe
in its many ways and parts,
standing as one in the body
of the god of gods.

Then filled with amazement,
his hair bristling on his flesh,
Arjuna bowed his head to the god,
joined his hands in homage, and spoke.

*Arjuna*

I see the gods
in your body, O God,
and hordes

of varied creatures:
Brahma, the cosmic creator,
on his lotus throne,
all the seers
and celestial serpents.

I see your boundless form
everywhere,
the countless arms,
bellies, mouths, and eyes;
Lord of All,
I see no end,
or middle or beginning
to your totality.

I see you blazing
through the fiery rays
of your crown, mace, and discus,
hard to behold
in the burning light
of fire and sun
that surrounds
your measureless presence.

You are to be known
as supreme eternity,
the deepest treasure
of all that is,
the immutable guardian
of enduring sacred duty;
I think you are
man's timeless spirit.

I see no beginning
or middle or end to you;
only boundless strength
in your endless arms,
the moon and sun in your eyes,
your mouths of consuming flames,
your own brilliance
scorching this universe.

You alone
fill the space
between heaven and earth
and all the directions;

seeing this awesome,
terrible form of yours,
Great Soul,
the three worlds
tremble.

Throngs of gods enter you,
some in their terror
make gestures of homage
to invoke you;
throngs of great sages
and saints
hail you and praise you
in resounding hymns.

Howling storm gods, sun gods,
bright gods, and gods of ritual,
gods of the universe,
twin gods of dawn, wind gods,
vapor-drinking ghosts,
throngs of celestial musicians,
demigods, demons, and saints,
all gaze at you amazed.

Seeing the many mouths
and eyes
of your great form,
its many arms,
thighs, feet,
bellies, and fangs,
the worlds tremble
and so do I.

Vishnu, seeing you brush
the clouds with flames
of countless colors,
your mouths agape,
your huge eyes blazing,
my inner self quakes
and I find no resolve
or tranquility.

Seeing the fangs
protruding
from your mouths
like the fires of time,

I lose my bearings
and I find no refuge;
be gracious, Lord of Gods,
Shelter of the Universe.

All those sons
of the blind king
Dhritarashtra
come accompanied
by troops of kings,
by the generals Bhishma,
Drona, Karna,
and by our battle leaders.

Rushing through
your fangs
into grim
mouths,
some are dangling
from heads
crushed
between your teeth.

As roiling
river waters
stream headlong
toward the sea,
so do these human
heroes enter
into your blazing
mouths.

As moths
in the frenzy
of destruction
fly into a blazing flame,
worlds
in the frenzy
of destruction
enter your mouths.

You lick at the worlds
around you,
devouring them
with flaming mouths;
and your terrible fires

scorch the entire universe,
filling it, Vishnu,
with violent rays.

Tell me—
who are you
in this terrible form?
Homage to you, Best of Gods!
Be gracious! I want to know you
as you are in your beginning.
I do not comprehend
the course of your ways.

*Lord Krishna*

I am time grown old,
creating world destruction,
set in motion
to annihilate the worlds;
even without you,
all these warriors
arrayed in hostile ranks
will cease to exist.

Therefore, arise
and win glory!
Conquer your foes
and fulfill your kingship!
They are already
killed by me.
Be just my instrument,
the archer at my side!

Drona, Bhishma, Jayadratha,
and Karna,
and all the other battle heroes,
are killed by me.
Kill them
without wavering;
fight, and you will conquer
your foes in battle!

*Sanjaya*

Hearing Krishna's words,
Arjuna trembled
under his crown,

and he joined his hands
in reverent homage;
terrified of his fear,
he bowed to Krishna
and stammered in reply.

*Arjuna*

Krishna, the universe
responds
with joy and rapture
to your glory,
terrified demons
flee in far directions,
and saints throng
to bow in homage.

Why should they not bow
in homage to you, Great Soul,
Original Creator,
more venerable than the creator Brahma?
Boundless Lord of Gods,
Shelter of All That Is,
you are eternity,
being, nonbeing, and beyond.

You are the original god,
the primordial spirit of man,
the deepest treasure
of all that is,
knower and what is to be known,
the supreme abode;
you pervade the universe,
Lord of Boundless Form.

You are the gods of wind,
death, fire, and water;
the moon; the lord of life;
and the great ancestor.
Homage to you,
a thousand times homage!
I bow in homage to you
again and yet again.

I bow in homage
before you and behind you;

I bow everywhere
to your omnipresence!
You have boundless strength
and limitless force;
you fulfill
all that you are.

Thinking you a friend,
I boldly said,
"Welcome, Krishna!
Welcome, cousin, friend!"
From negligence,
or through love,
I failed to know
your greatness.

If in jest
I offended you,
alone
or publicly,
at sport, rest,
sitting, or at meals,
I beg your patience,
unfathomable Krishna.

You are father of the world
of animate and inanimate things,
its venerable teacher,
most worthy of worship,
without equal.
Where in all three worlds
is another to match
your extraordinary power?

I bow to you,
I prostrate my body,
I beg you to be gracious,
Worshipful Lord—
as a father to a son,
a friend to a friend,
a lover to a beloved,
O God, bear with me.

I am thrilled,
and yet my mind
trembles with fear
at seeing

what has not been seen before.
Show me, God, the form I know—
be gracious, Lord of Gods,
Shelter of the World.

I want to see you
as before,
with your crown and mace,
and the discus in your hand.
O Thousand-Armed God,
assume the four-armed form
embodied
in your totality.

*Lord Krishna*

To grace you, Arjuna,
I revealed
through self-discipline
my higher form,
which no one but you
has ever beheld—
brilliant, total,
boundless, primal.

Not through sacred lore
or sacrificial ritual
or study or charity,
not by rites
or by terrible penances
can I be seen in this form
in the world of men
bv anyone but you, Great Hero.

Do not tremble
or suffer confusion
from seeing
my horrific form;
your fear dispelled,
your mind full of love,
see my form again
as it was.

*Sanjaya*

Saying this to Arjuna,
Krishna once more
revealed

his intimate form;
resuming his gentle body,
the great spirit
let the terrified hero
regain his breath.

*Arjuna*

Seeing your gentle human form,
Krishna, I recover
my own nature,
and my reason is restored.

*Lord Krishna*

This form you have seen
is rarely revealed;
the gods are constantly craving
for a vision of this form.

Not through sacred lore,
penances, charity, or sacrificial rites
can I be seen in the form
that you saw me.

By devotion alone
can I, as I really am,
be known and seen
and entered into, Arjuna.

Acting only for me, intent on me,
free from attachment,
hostile to no creature, Arjuna,
a man of devotion comes to me.

## *Chs. LXV–LXXIV passim [Battle of Arjuna and Karna]*

*Translated by Chakravarthi V. Narasimhan*

### LXV

The next day was the fourteenth day of battle. In the course of the day's fighting, Aśvatthāmā, filled with rage, rushed furiously against Sātyaki. Thereupon Bhīma's son Ghaṭotkaca rushed at him. He rode on a huge car made of black iron covered with bearskins, and drawn neither by horses nor by elephants, but by bearers resplendent as elephants. He was surrounded by an akṣauhiṇi of fierce-looking rākṣasas armed with lances, heavy clubs, rocks, and trunks of trees. Seeing him advance with uplifted bow, resembling the mace-armed Destroyer himself in the hour of universal dissolution, the opposing kings were struck with fear. As the evening advanced, the rākṣasas became more powerful and threw on the field of battle a thick shower of stones.

Duryodhana said to Karṇa, "O you who are devoted to friends, the hour has come when your help is most needed. O Karṇa, save in battle all my warriors!" Karṇa replied, "If Iṅdra himself were to come hither to save Arjuna, I should quickly vanquish even him, and then slay that son of Pāṇḍu." When Karṇa spoke thus, Kṛpa, the mighty armed son of Śāradvata, smiling the while, addressed him in these words: "Your speech is fair, O Karṇa! If words alone could achieve success, then Duryodhana would be well protected. You boast much, but your prowess or strength is seldom witnessed."

Karṇa replied, "It is true that the Pāṇḍavas cannot be vanquished by the very gods with Iṅdra at their head, nor by the Daityas, the yakṣas, and the rākṣasas. Even so, I will vanquish them with the help of the weapon given me by Iṅdra. You know, O Brāhman, that the dart given by Iṅdra is invincible. With that I will slay the amibidextrous Arjuna in battle."

Meanwhile, in another part of the battle, Somadatta fearlessly attacked Sātyaki, scattering showers of arrows like the clouds pouring torrents of rain. Then Sātyaki let loose a terrible shaft of fiery effulgence, whetted on stone, and fitted with wings of gold. It struck Somadatta on his chest, and pierced him deeply, so that the great car-warrior Somadatta fell down from his car and expired.

Kṛṣṇa said, "I behold Karṇa, O Arjuna, careering in battle like the chief of the celestials himself. There is none else capable of advancing against him in battle, save you and the rākṣasa Ghaṭotkaca. I do not, however, think that the time has come for you to face Karṇa in battle. The blazing dart, resembling a mighty meteor, given him by Iṅdra, and intended for you, is still with him. Let the mighty Ghaṭotkaca proceed against Karṇa, the son of Rādhā. He is the offspring of Bhīma and is equal to a celestial in strength."

Hearing those words of Kṛṣṇa, Arjuna said to the rākṣasa Ghaṭotkaca, "O Ghaṭotkaca, yourself, the long-armed Sātyaki, and Bhīma, the son of Pāṇḍu, these three, in my judgment, are the foremost among all our warriors. Go and attack Karṇa in single combat tonight. The mighty car-warrior Sātyaki will protect your rear." Ghaṭotkaca said, "I am a match for Karṇa, as well as for Droṇa, O Bhārata, or for any illustrious Kṣatriya, however accomplished in weapons. This night I shall fight a battle with Karṇa that will be talked about as long as the world lasts." Having said these words, Ghaṭotkaca rushed against Karṇa in that dreadful fight.

When he saw that frightful rākṣasa advancing against him, Karṇa withstood him smilingly. The clash between Karṇa and the rākṣasa became terrible, resembling that between Iṅdra and the demon Śaṁbara. The air was filled with the sound of twanging bowstrings. Despite his best efforts Karṇa could not prevail over Ghaṭotkaca.

Then Karṇa, seeing the rākṣasa still alive at dead of night, and the Kuru army struck with fear, decided to hurl his dart. Inflamed with rage like a wrathful lion and unable to brook the assaults of Ghaṭotkaca, Karṇa in his desire to kill Ghaṭotkaca took up that foremost of victory-giving and invincible darts, the Śakti weapon. That dart which for years he had kept to kill Arjuna in battle, that foremost of darts which Iṅdra himself had given to Karṇa in exchange for the latter's earrings, that blazing and terrible missile twined with strings and seeming to thirst for blood, that fierce weapon which looked like the very tongue of the Destroyer or the sister of Death himself, that terrible and effulgent dart, Karṇa hurled at the rākṣasa.

Destroying the blazing illusion created by Ghaṭotkaca and piercing right through his breast, that resplendent dart soared aloft in the night and entered a starry constellation in the sky. Ghaṭotkaca, who had fought using diverse weapons against many heroic rākṣasa and human warriors, uttered a terrible roar and fell, deprived of his life by the dart of Iṅdra.

When Ghaṭotkaca was thus killed and lay like a riven mountain, all the Pāṇḍavas were filled with grief and began to shed copious tears. Only Kṛṣṇa was in transports of delight as he embraced Arjuna. He said, "Great is the joy I feel! Listen to me, O Arjuna! This will immediately dispel your sorrow and give you cheer. You know that Karṇa, having shot his Śakti bolt at Ghaṭotkaca, is already slain in battle. The man does not exist in this world that could withstand Karṇa armed with that dart and looking like Kārtikeya in battle. By good luck, his natural armour and his earrings were taken away. By good luck, he has now been deprived also of his infallible dart through Ghaṭotkaca. With his divine weapon, Karṇa was like a bountiful evening cloud, pouring showers of arrows. Without the dart given him by Iṅdra, Karṇa has now become a mere human. There will arise one opportunity for his slaughter, when his car wheels sink in the earth. Availing yourself of that opportunity, and warned by a sign which I will make beforehand, you should slay him when he is in that difficult situation."

## LXVI

As fighting began on the fifteenth day, Yudhiṣṭhira said to Dhṛṣṭadyumna, "Attack Droṇa today. Remember you were born out of the sacrificial fire, clad in mail, and armed with bow and arrows and sword, for the destruction of Droṇa. Cheerfully give him battle, and have no fear."

Meanwhile the Pāñcālas, though suffering great pain, continued to contend in battle against Droṇa. Then Drupada and Virāṭa proceeded against Droṇa, that invincible warrior, who was dominating the field. The three grandsons of Drupada, and those mighty bowmen, the Cedis, also proceeded against Droṇa in that encounter. With three sharp shafts, Droṇa killed the three grandsons of Drupada, who fell lifeless on the ground.

Next Droṇa discharged a couple of well-tempered and broad-headed shafts which dispatched both Drupada and Virāṭa to the abode of Yama. Upon the fall of Virāṭa and Drupada, and the slaughter of the Kekayas, the Cedis, the Matsyas, and the Pāñcālas, as well as those three heroes, the three grandsons of Drupada, the high-souled Dhṛṣṭadyumna was filled with rage and grief, and swore in the midst of all the car-warriors: "Let me lose the merits of all my religious acts if Droṇa should escape alive, or if he should succeed in vanquishing me!"

Meanwhile Droṇa caused great carnage among the Pāñcālas. Seeing the Pāṇḍavas thus afflicted by the shafts of Droṇa and overcome by fear, the wise

Kṛṣṇa who was ever devoted to their welfare said to Arjuna, "This foremost of all car-warriors cannot be vanquished in battle, not even by the very gods with Indra at their head! Hence you must put aside fair means, and adopt some contrivance for gaining victory, so that Droṇa may not slay us all in battle. I think he will cease to fight if his son Aśvatthāmā should fall. Let some man, therefore, tell him that Aśvatthāmā has been slain in battle."

Arjuna did not relish this suggestion of Kṛṣṇa's, though others approved of it. Yudhiṣṭhira himself accepted it very reluctantly. Then the mighty Bhīma, having slain with a mace a huge elephant, named Aśvatthāmā, approached Droṇa on the battlefield, and—not without some embarrassment—exclaimed aloud, "Aśvatthāmā has been slain!"

Meanwhile, Kṛṣṇa grew seriously concerned because Droṇa, foremost of warriors, was capable of sweeping all the Pāṇḍavas off the face of the earth. He said to King Yudhiṣṭhira, "If Droṇa, roused to anger, fights for even half a day, I tell you truly, your army will be annihilated. Save us then from Droṇa! Under such circumstances, falsehood is preferable to truth. By telling a lie to save a life, one is not touched by sin."

Bhīma supported Kṛṣṇa's argument. He said, "Droṇa did not believe my words. To ensure our victory, accept Kṛṣṇa's advice. Tell Droṇa that his son is no more. If you say so, Droṇa will believe you and will never fight thereafter, since you are famed for your truthfulness in the three worlds."

Urged thus by Bhīma and induced by the counsels of Kṛṣṇa, and also because of the inevitability of destiny, Yudhiṣṭhira gave in. Fearing to tell a downright lie, but earnestly desirous of victory, Yudhiṣṭhira added indistinctly that the elephant was slain. Before this, Yudhiṣṭhira's car had stayed at a height of four fingers above the surface of the earth; after he had uttered that lie, his vehicle and animals touched the earth.

Hearing those words of Yudhiṣṭhira's, the mighty car-warrior Droṇa was afflicted with grief for the reported death of his son, and lost all desire to live. Already he was feeling a sense of guilt for fighting against the high-souled Pāṇḍavas. Hearing now of the death of his son, he became deeply depressed and filled with anxiety. Thus, when Dhṛṣṭadyumna approached him, Droṇa had no mind to fight as before.

Seeing that Droṇa was filled with great anxiety and almost deprived of his senses by grief, Dhṛṣṭadyumna, the hero who had been obtained by King Drupada at a great sacrifice from the bearer of sacrificial libations expressly for Droṇa's destruction, rushed at him. He took up a formidable bow and fixed on it a fierce and fiery arrow, resembling a snake of virulent poison, intent on killing Droṇa. But the invincible Droṇa cut off all the weapons, and all the bows of his antagonist, with the sole exception of his mace and sword.

Then Bhīma, in a great rage, approached Droṇa's chariot and deliberately said these words to him: "Wretched are the Brāhmaṇas who, not content with the avocations of their own order, have become well versed in arms, and taken to fighting. But for them the Kṣatriya order would not have been thus exterminated. Nonviolence to all creatures is said to be the highest of all virtues. The Brāhmaṇa is the root of all virtue. You, Droṇa, are supposed to be the best of Brāhmaṇas. And yet you fight, while your son lies dead on the field of battle, unknown to you and behind your back. Yudhiṣṭhira the just has told you this. It behoves you not to doubt this fact."

Thus addressed by Bhīma, Droṇa laid aside his bow. Deciding to give up all his weapons, the virtuous man called for Karṇa, Kṛpa, and Duryodhana. He repeated his son's name loudly. Laying aside his weapons, he sat down on the platform of his car, and devoted himself to yoga. Seizing this opportunity, Dhṛṣṭadyumna took up his sword and, jumping down from his vehicle, rushed quickly against Droṇa, among loud exclamations of woe from all sides.

Droṇa himself remained in a supremely tranquil state. Arjuna pleaded with Dhṛṣṭadyumna, saying, "O son of Drupada, seize the preceptor alive, do not slay him!" All the troops also cried out, "He should not be slain!" Arjuna, in particular, moved by pity, pleaded repeatedly that his life should be spared. Disregarding, however, the protests of Arjuna as well as those of all the kings, Dhṛṣṭadyumna slew Droṇa on the platform of his car.

Upon the fall of Droṇa, the Kaurava [Kuru] warriors, already sorely afflicted by the enemy's arrows, became leaderless. Broken and routed, and filled with grief, they gathered listlessly around Duryodhana, bewailing their loss.

## LXVII

When the mighty bowman Droṇa was slain, the Kaurava host became pale-faced and gloomy. Seeing his own forces standing as if paralysed and lifeless, King Duryodhana said to them, "Relying on the strength of your arms, I have challenged the Pāṇḍavas to this battle. Victory or death is the lot of all warriors. Why wonder then at the fall of Droṇa? Let us resume the fighting in all directions, encouraged by the sight of the lofty-minded Karṇa, the son of Vikartana, mighty bowman and wielder of celestial weapons, who is roving about in the field of battle. Permit me to remind you that it was he who slew Ghaṭotkaca, that creator of illusions, with the indomitable Śakti weapon." Then all those kings, headed by Duryodhana, quickly installed Karṇa as commander in chief, and bathed him according to rites with golden and earthen pitchers of holy water.

As the sixteenth day dawned, Karṇa summoned the Kaurava forces to battle with loud blasts on his conch. He arranged his army in the form of a makara, and proceeded to attack the Pāṇḍavas, desirous of victory. On the Pāṇḍava side, Arjuna, whose car was drawn by white horses, formed a counter-array in the shape of a half-moon.

The day's fighting was marked by many duels, between Bhīma and Aśvatthāmā, Sahadeva and Duhśāsana, Nakula and Karṇa, Ulūka and Yuyutsu, Kṛpa and Dhṛṣṭadyumna, and Śikhaṇḍī and Kṛtavarmā. While they were thus engaged, the sun disappeared behind the western mountains. Then both sides retired from the field and proceeded to their own encampments.

Before the fighting began on the seventeenth day, Karṇa said to Duryodhana, "Today, O king, I will go forth and battle with the famous Pāṇḍava, Arjuna. Either I shall slay that hero, or he shall slay me. You are aware of his energy, weapons, and resources. My bow, known by the name of Vijaya, is the greatest of all weapons. It was made by Viśvakarmā in accordance with

Iṅdra's wishes, and is a celestial and excellent weapon. On this count I believe I am superior to Arjuna."

"Now you must know," continued Karṇa, "in what respect Arjuna is superior to me. Kṛṣṇa, born of the Dāśārha race, who is revered by all people, is the holder of the reins of his horses. He who is verily the creator of the universe thus guards Arjuna's car. On our side Śalya, who is the ornament of all assemblies, is of equal heroism. Should he take over the duties of my charioteer, then victory will surely be yours. Let the irresistible Śalya, therefore, act as my charioteer."

Duryodhana thereupon went to see Śalya. Humbly approaching the Madra prince, he affectionately spoke these words to him: "You have heard what Karṇa has said, namely that he chooses you, foremost of princes, as his charioteer. Therefore, for the destruction of the Pāṇḍavas, and for my own good, be pleased to become Karṇa's charioteer. As that foremost of charioteers, Kṛṣṇa, counsels and protects Arjuna, so should you support Karṇa at all times."

Śalya replied, "You are insulting me, O Duryodhana, or surely you must doubt my loyalty, since you so readily request me to do the work of a charioteer. You praise Karṇa and consider that he is superior to us. But I do not consider him to be my equal in the field of battle. Knowing that I can strike down the enemy, why do you wish to employ me in the office of charioteer to the lowborn Karṇa?"

Duryodhana replied to Śalya with great affection and high respect. Desirous of achieving his main objective, he addressed him in a friendly manner, saying sweetly, "O Śalya, what you say is doubtless true. However, in making this request I have a certain purpose. Even as Karṇa is reckoned to be superior to Arjuna in many ways so are you, in the opinion of the whole world, superior to Kṛṣṇa. As the high-souled Kṛṣṇa is expert in the handling of horses, even so, O Śalya, are you doubly skilled. There is no doubt about it."

Thus flattered, Śalya said, "O Duryodhana! As you tell me that amongst all these troops there is none but myself who is more accomplished than Kṛṣṇa, I am pleased with you. I therefore agree to act as the charioteer of the famous Karṇa while he is engaged in battle with Arjuna, foremost of the Pāṇḍavas. But there is one condition on which I accept your proposal: that I shall give vent in Karṇa's presence to such expressions as I may wish." Duryodhana, who was accompanied by Karṇa, readily accepted this condition, saying, "So be it."

## LXVIII

After Śalya had taken over as his charioteer, Karṇa said to him, "Today I shall fearlessly fight Kṛṣṇa and Arjuna, foremost among all wielders of weapons. My mind is, however, troubled by the curse of Paraśurāma, that best of Brāhmaṇas. In my early days, desirous of obtaining a celestial weapon, I lived with him in the disguise of a Brāhmana. But, O Śalya, in order to benefit Arjuna, Iṅdra, the king of the gods, took on the horrible form of an insect and stung my thigh. Even so, I remained motionless for fear of disturbing my preceptor.

When he woke up, he saw what had happened. He subsequently learnt the deception I had practised on him, and cursed me, that the invocation for the weapon I had obtained by such trickery would not come to my memory at the time of dire need."

"Once while wandering in the forest," Karṇa continued, "I accidentally killed the sacrificial cow of a Brāhmaṇa. Although I offered him seven hundred elephants with large tusks, and many hundreds of male and female slaves, the best of Brāhmaṇas was still not pleased, and although I begged for forgiveness, he said: 'O sūta, what I have prophesied will happen. It cannot be otherwise.' He had said, 'Your wheel shall fall into a hole.' In this battle, while I am fighting, that will be my only fear."

During the fighting on that day there was a dreadful and thrilling battle between Karṇa and the Pāṇḍavas which increased the domain of the god of Death. After that terrible and gory combat only a few of the brave Samśaptakas survived. Then Dhṛṣṭadyumna and the rest of the Pāṇḍavas rushed towards Karṇa and attacked him. As a mountain receives heavy rainfall, so Karṇa received those warriors in battle. Elsewhere on the battlefield Duḥśāsana boldly went up to Bhīma and shot many arrows at him. Bhīma leapt like a lion attacking a deer, and hurried towards him. The struggle that took place between those two, incensed against each other and careless of life, was truly superhuman.

Fighting fiercely, Prince Duḥśāsana achieved many difficult feats in that duel. With a single shaft he cut off Bhīma's bow; with six shafts he pierced Bhīma's driver. Then, without losing a moment, he pierced Bhīma himself with many shafts discharged with great speed and power, while Bhīma hurled his mace at the prince. With that weapon, from a distance of ten bow-lengths, Bhīma forcibly dislodged Duḥśāsana from his car. Struck by the mace, and thrown to the ground, Duḥśāsana began to tremble. His charioteer and all his steeds were slain, and his car too was smashed to pieces by Bhīma's weapon.

Then Bhīma remembered all the hostile acts of Duhśāsana towards the Pāṇḍavas. Jumping down from his car, he stood on the ground, looking steadily on his fallen foe. Drawing his keen-edged sword, and trembling with rage, he placed his foot upon the throat of Duḥśāsana and, ripping open the breast of his enemy, drank his warm lifeblood, little by little. Then, looking at him with wrathful eyes, he said, "I consider the taste of this blood superior to that of my mother's milk, or honey, or ghee, or wine, or excellent water, or milk, or curds, or buttermilk."

All those who stood around Bhīma and saw him drink the blood of Duḥśāsana fled in terror, saying to each other, "This one is no human being!" Bhīma then said, in the hearing of all those heroes, "O wretch among men, here I drink your lifeblood. Abuse us once more now, 'Beast beast,' as you did before!"

Having spoken these words, the victorious Bhīma turned to Kṛṣṇa and Arjuna, and said, "O you heroes, I have accomplished today what I had vowed in respect of Duḥśāsana! I will soon fulfil my other vow by slaying that second sacrificial beast, Duryodhana! I shall kick the head of that evil one with my foot in the presence of the Kauravas, and I shall then obtain peace!" After this speech, Bhīma, drenched with blood, uttered loud shouts and roared with joy, even as the mighty Iṅdra of a thousand eyes after slaying Vṛtra.

## LXIX

Fleeing in the face of Arjuna's onslaught, the broken divisions of the Kauravas saw Arjuna's weapon swelling with energy and careering like lightning. But Karṇa destroyed that fiery weapon of Arjuna with his own weapon of great power which he had obtained from Paraśurāma. The encounter between Arjuna and Karṇa became very fierce. They attacked each other with arrows like two fierce elephants attacking each other with their tusks.

Karṇa then fixed on his bowstring the keen, blazing, and fierce shaft which he had long polished and preserved with the object of destroying Arjuna. Placing in position that shaft of fierce energy and blazing splendour, that venomous weapon which had its origin in the family of Airāvata and which lay within a golden quiver covered by sandal dust, Karṇa aimed it at Arjuna's head. When he saw Karṇa aim that arrow, Śalya said, "O Karṇa, this arrow will not succeed in hitting Arjuna's neck! Aim carefully, and discharge another arrow that may succeed in striking the head of your enemy!" His eyes burning in wrath, Karṇa replied, "O Śalya, Karṇa never aims an arrow twice!"

Thereupon Karṇa carefully let loose that mighty snake in the form of an arrow, which he had worshipped for many long years, saying, "You are slain, O Arjuna!" Seeing the snake aimed by Karṇa, Kṛṣṇa, strongest among the mighty, exerted his whole strength and pressed down Arjuna's chariot with his feet into the earth. When the car itself had sunk into the ground the steeds, too, bent their knees and laid themselves down upon the earth. The arrow then struck and dislodged Arjuna's diadem, that excellent ornament celebrated throughout the earth and the heavens.

The snake said, "O Kṛṣṇa! Know me as one who has been wronged by Arjuna. My enmity towards him stems from his having slain my mother!"

Then Kṛṣṇa said to Arjuna, "Slay that great snake which is your enemy." Thus urged by Kṛṣṇa, Arjuna asked, "Who is this snake that advances of his own accord against me, as if right against the mouth of Garuḍa?" Kṛṣṇa replied, "While you were worshipping the fire-god at the Khāndava forest, this snake was ensconced within his mother's body, which was shattered by your arrows." As the snake took a slanting course across the sky, Arjuna cut it to pieces with six keen shafts, so that it fell down on the earth.

Then, because of the curse of the Brāhmaṇa, Karṇa's chariot wheel fell off, and his car began to reel. At the same time, he forgot the invocation for the weapon he had obtained from Paraśurāma. Unable to endure these calamities, Karṇa waved his arms and began to rail at righteousness, saying, "They that are conversant with virtue say that righteousness protects the righteous! But today righteousness does not save me."

Speaking thus, he shed tears of wrath, and said to Arjuna, "O Pāṇḍava! Spare me for a moment while I extricate my wheel from the earth! You are on your car while I am standing weak and languid on the ground. It is not fair that you should slay me now! You are born in the Kṣatriya order. You are the scion of a high race. Recollect the teachings of righteousness, and give me a moment's time!"

Then, from Arjuna's chariot, Kṛṣṇa said, "It is fortunate, O Karṇa, that you now remember virtue. It is generally true that those who are mean rail at Providence when they are afflicted by distress, but forget their own misdeeds. You and Duryodhana and Duḥśāsana and Śakuni caused Draupadī, clad in a single garment, to be brought into the midst of the assembly. On that occasion, O Karṇa, this virtue of yours was not in evidence! When Śakuni, skilled in dicing, vanquished Yudhiṣṭhira who was unacquainted with it, where was this virtue of yours? Out of covetousness, and relying on Śakuni, you again summoned the Pāṇḍavas to a game of dice. Whither then had this virtue of yours gone?"

When Kṛṣṇa thus taunted Karṇa, Arjuna became filled with rage. Remembering the incidents to which Kṛṣṇa alluded, he blazed with fury and, bent upon Karṇa's speedy destruction, took out of his quiver an excellent weapon. He then fixed on his bow that unrivalled arrow, and charged it with mantras. Drawing his bow Gāṇḍīva, he quickly said, "Let this shaft of mine be a mighty weapon capable of speedily destroying the body and heart of my enemy. If I have ever practised ascetic austerities, gratified my preceptors, and listened to the counsels of well-wishers, let this sharp shaft, so long worshipped by me, slay my enemy Karṇa by that Truth!"

Having uttered these words, Arjuna discharged for the destruction of Karṇa, that terrible shaft, that blazing arrow fierce and efficacious as a rite prescribed in the Atharva of Aṅgiras, and invincible against the god of Death himself in battle. Thus sped by that mighty warrior, the shaft endowed with the energy of the Sun caused all the points of the compass to blaze with light. The head of the commander of the Kaurava army, splendid as the Sun, fell like the Sun disappearing in the blood-red sunset behind the western hills. Cut off by Arjuna's arrow and deprived of life, the tall trunk of Karṇa, with blood gushing from every wound, fell down like the thunder-riven summit of a mountain of red chalk with crimson streams running down its sides after a shower of rain.

Then from the body of the fallen Karṇa a light, passing through the atmosphere, illumined the sky. This wonderful sight was seen by all the warriors on the battlefield. After the heroic Karṇa was thus thrown down and stretched on the earth, pierced with arrows and bathed in blood, Śalya, the king of the Madras, withdrew with Karṇa's car. The Kauravas, afflicted with fear, fled from the field, frequently looking back on Arjuna's lofty standard which blazed in splendour.

## LXXIV

Having regained consciousness, and forgetting his poignant and unbearable pain, Duryodhana began to assail Kṛṣṇa with sharp and bitter words. He said, "O son of Kamsa's slave, it seems to me that you have no shame, for you have forgotten that I was struck down most unfairly in violation of the rules of mace-fighting. You were responsible for this foul play, by reminding Bhīma by a hint about the breaking of my thighs. Do you think I did not mark it when Arjuna under your instructions suggested it by sign to Bhīma?

"You caused the grandsire to be slain by placing Śikhaṇḍī in front. Too, by having an elephant of the name of Aśvatthāmā killed, you made the preceptor Droṇa lay aside his weapons. Do you think that all this is not known to me? Again, when the brave Droṇa was about to be killed by the cruel Dhṛṣṭadyumna, you did not dissuade Dhṛṣṭadyumna!

"The Śakti dart that Karṇa had obtained from Iṅdra as a boon for the destruction of Arjuna was thwarted by you through Ghaṭotkaca. Likewise you caused the powerful Bhūriśravas, with one of his arms cut off, to be slain by Sātyaki while observing the Prāya vow. When Karṇa released the snake for killing Arjuna, you frustrated the object of Aśvasena, the son of Takṣaka, that prince of snakes. Again, when the wheel of Karṇa's car sank in the mire and Karṇa was afflicted by grief and almost defeated, and when he was struggling to free his wheel, you caused Karṇa then to be slain! If your side had fought me and Karṇa, Bhīṣma, and Droṇa by fair means, victory would never have been yours.

"I have obtained that end which Kṣatriyas observant of the duties of their own order look forward to, death in battle. Who then is so fortunate as myself? I have enjoyed pleasures, such as were worthy of the very gods, which could only with difficulty be gained by other kings. I have reached the highest prosperity. Who then is so fortunate as myself? With all my well-wishers, and my younger brothers, I am going to heaven! As for yourselves, with your purposes unfulfilled, and racked with grief, live in this unhappy world!"

After Duryodhana had said these words, a shower of fragrant flowers dropped from the sky. The Gaṅdharvas played on many charming musical instruments. The Apsaras in chorus sang his glory. The Siddhas cried, "Praise be to King Duryodhana!" Sweet and fragrant breezes mildly blew on all sides. All the quarters became clear and the sky looked azure blue. Beholding these auspicious signs and this worship offered to Duryodhana, the Pāṇḍavas, with Kṛṣṇa at their head, were put to shame. Remembering that Bhīṣma, Droṇa, Karṇa, and Bhūriśravas were killed unfairly, they were afflicted with remorse and wept in grief.

Kṛṣṇa, seeing the Pāṇḍavas stricken with remorse, said, "Those four were very great warriors and regarded as atirathas in the world. The very Regents of the Universe could not have killed them in fair fight. Duryodhana too could never have been killed in a fair fight! The same is the case with all those powerful car-warriors led by Bhīṣma. Out of the desire to do you good, I repeatedly applied my illusory powers and caused them to be killed by various means in battle. If I had not adopted such deceitful ways, you would never have been victorious, nor could you have regained your kingdom or your wealth."

He continued, "You should not mind the fact that your enemy has been killed deceitfully. When one is outnumbered by his enemies, then destruction should be brought about by stratagem. The gods themselves, in killing the asuras, have followed the same methods. The way that was followed by the celestials may be followed by all. We have been crowned with success. It is evening, and we had better retire to our tents. O kings, let us all take rest, with our horses and elephants and cars!"

## *Chs. XCV–XCVIII [Yudhiṣṭhira Ascends to Heaven]*

*Translated by Chakravarthi V. Narasimhan*

### XCV

Causing heaven and earth to reverberate, Iṅdra came to Yudhiṣṭhira on a chariot and asked him to ascend it. Seeing his brothers fallen on the earth, and burning with grief, Yudhiṣṭhira said to Iṅdra, "My brothers have all fallen here! They must go with me. Without them I do not wish to go to the celestial region, O lord! The delicate princess Draupadī deserving of every comfort, should also go with us! Please permit this."

"You will behold your brothers in the celestial region." Iṅdra replied. "They have reached there before you. You will see them all there, along with Draupadī. Do not give way to grief, O chief of the Bhāratas! They renounced their human bodies before going there, O king! As for you, it has been ordained that you shall go there in this very body."

Yudhiṣṭhira said, "This dog, O lord, is highly devoted to me. He should go with me. My heart is full of compassion for him." "Today you have acquired immortality and a status equal to mine," replied Iṅdra. "Prosperity and high success attend you, and all the felicities of heaven are open to you. Cast off this dog. There will be no cruelty in doing so."

"O lord of a thousand eyes!" answered Yudhiṣṭhira. "It is extremely difficult for one of virtuous conduct to commit an unrighteous act. I do not wish for prosperity if I have to abandon a creature who is devoted to me." Hearing these words of King Yudhiṣṭhira the just, the dog was transformed into Dharma, the god of Virtue. Well pleased with Yudhiṣṭhira, the deity praised him in a sweet voice. He said, "You are well born, O king of kings, and endued with the intelligence and good conduct of your fathers! You have mercy for all creatures. Just now, out of consideration for the dog which was devoted to you, you renounced the very car of the celestials. Hence, O king, there is no one in heaven to equal you."

Then Dharma, Iṅdra, the maruts, the Aśvins, and other deities, as well as the celestial sages, made Yudhiṣṭhira ascend Iṅdra's car, bound for heaven. Amidst that concourse of celestials, Nārada, foremost of all speakers, and conversant with all the worlds, said these words, "Yudhiṣṭhira has transcended the achievements of all the royal sages who are here. Covering the universe by his fame and splendour and by the nobility of his conduct, he has reached heaven in his own human body! No one else has been known to achieve this."

Hearing these words of Nārada, the righteous King Yudhiṣṭhira saluted the celestials and all the royal sages present, and said, "Happy or miserable, whatever be the region where my brothers are now, I wish to go there. I do not wish to stay anywhere else."

Iṅdra addressed Yudhiṣṭhira, "O king of kings, live in this place, which you have earned by your meritorious deeds. Why do you still cherish human affections?" Yudhiṣṭhira replied, "O conquerer of Daityas, I do not wish to live anywhere, separated from my brothers. I wish to go where they have gone, and where that foremost of women, Draupadī, has gone!"

## XCVI

Though he could not see Draupadī and his brothers anywhere in heaven, Yudhiṣṭhira saw Duryodhana radiant with prosperity and seated on an excellent seat. Thereupon he was suddenly overcome by anger and turned away from the sight. He said, "O you gods, I have no wish to see Duryodhana! I wish to go where my brothers are."

Nārada smilingly told him, "O king of kings! Meet Duryodhana politely now. This is heaven, O king! There can be no enmities here!" Despite Nārada's words, Yudhiṣṭhira persisted in asking about his brothers, saying, "If these eternal regions are reserved for heroes like Duryodhana, that unrighteous and sinful wretch, that man who was the destroyer of friends and of the whole world, that man for whose sake the entire earth was devastated, then I wish to see what regions have been attained by those great heroes, my brothers of high vows, performers of promises, truthful in speech, and distinguished for courage, and by the great Karṇa, by Dhṛṣṭadyumna, by Śātyaki, by the sons of Dhṛṣṭadyumna and those other Kṣatriyas who met with death in the observance of their duties. Where are those kings, O Nārada? I do not see them here, nor Virāṭa nor Drupada nor the other great Kṣatriyas headed by Dhṛṣṭaketu. I wish to see them all, as well as Śikhaṇḍī, the Pāñcāla prince, the sons of Draupadī, and Abhimanyu, who was irresistible in battle."

Addressing the celestials, Yudhiṣṭhira continued, "O foremost of gods! What is heaven to me if I am separated from my brothers? To me, heaven is where those brothers of mine are. This, in my opinion, is not heaven." "If you wish to go there, O son," replied the gods, "go forthwith. If the king of the celestials permits, we are ready to do what you like." Then they told their messenger, "Show Yudhiṣṭhira his friends and kinsmen."

The royal son of Kuṅtī and the celestial messenger went together to where the other Pāṇḍavas were. The heavenly messenger went first, followed by the king. The path was difficult, trodden by men of sinful deeds, and foetid with the stench of corpses. Along that inauspicious path the righteous king went, filled with various thoughts.

Seeing that foul region, Yudhiṣṭhira asked the celestial messenger, "How far must we go along a path like this?" When Yudhiṣṭhira the just spoke to him, the messenger of heaven stopped in his course and replied, "Thus far I have come with you. The dwellers of the celestial region ordered me to stop at this point. If you are tired, O king of kings, you may return with me!"

Yudhiṣṭhira was disconsolate and stupefied by the foul stench. Resolved to return, he retraced his steps. But as the righteous king turned back stricken with sorrow, he heard piteous cries all around: "O son of Dharma, O royal sage, O you of holy birth, O Pāṇḍava, stay a while as a favour to us! At your approach a delightful breeze has begun to blow, bearing the sweet smell of your body. We have been greatly refreshed by this. Remain here, O Bhārata, for some time! As long as you are here tortures cease to afflict us."

From all sides, the king heard these and many other piteous appeals, uttered by persons in distress. The voices of those woebegone and afflicted persons seemed to him to be familiar, although he could not place them. Unable to recognize the voices, Yudhiṣṭhira inquired, "Who are you? Why do you stay here?" In reply, they answered him from all sides, saying, "I am Karṇa!" "I am Bhīma!" "I am Arjuna!" "I am Nakula!" "I am Sahadeva!" "I am Dhṛṣṭadyumna!" "I am Draupadī!" "We are the sons of Draupadī!"

Hearing those painful cries, the royal Yudhiṣṭhira asked himself, "What perverse destiny is this? What are the sins which were committed by those great beings, Karṇa and the sons of Draupadī and the slender-waisted princess of Pāñcāla, that they have been compelled to live in this region of foul smell and great distress? I am not aware of any sin that can be attributed to these persons. By what act of merit has Dhṛtarāṣṭra's son, King Duryodhana, with all his wicked followers, acquired such prosperity?"

Musing thus, Yudhiṣṭhira was filled with righteous indignation, and censured the celestials as well as Dharma himself. Though almost overcome by the foul smell, he told the celestial messenger, "Go back to those whose messenger you are. Tell them that I shall not return to them, but shall stay here since my companionship has brought comfort to these suffering brothers of mine."

### XCVII

King Yudhiṣṭhira had not waited for more than a moment when all the celestials, headed by Iṅdra, appeared. The God of Righteousness, in his embodied form, also came to see Yudhiṣṭhira.

Upon the arrival of those celestials of radiant bodies and noble deeds, the darkness that had enveloped that region immediately disappeared. The tortures afflicting those of sinful deeds were no longer to be seen. The river Vaitaraṇī, the thorny Śalmali, the iron jars, and the terrible boulders of rock also vanished from sight, as did the repulsive corpses which the Kuru king had seen. Then, because of the presence of the celestials, a gentle breeze, bringing with it a pleasant and fragrant odour, pure and delightfully cool, began to blow on that spot.

Iṅdra, the lord of the celestials, consoled Yudhiṣṭhira, saying, "O mighty Yudhiṣṭhira! Join the ranks of the celestials who are pleased with you. These illusions have ended. Hell, O son, should be seen by all kings. There is some good and bad in all things. You once deceived Droṇa concerning his son, and have therefore been shown hell by an act of deception. Like yourself, Bhīma, Arjuna, and Draupadī have reached hell by an act of deception. Your brothers and the other kings who fought on your side have all attained to their respective places. Let the fever of your heart be dispelled! Here is the celestial river, sacred and sanctifying the three worlds. It is called the celestial Gaṅgā. Plunging into it, you will attain your proper place."

## The Vimalakirti Sutra (1st cent. CE)

The Vimalakīrti Sutra appeared in the first century CE, when a new form of Buddhism known as *Mahāyāna* ("the Greater Vehicle") was enjoying rapid growth. Although this *sutra* ("discourse") was subsequently lost in India, it survived in Tibet, China, and Japan. Vimalakīrti's method of argument centers on the resolution of dichotomies, often in nonrational ways. It established a basis for the *Tantric* tradition of Buddhist thought that came to prevail in Tibet and that influenced the development of *Chan* Buddhism in China and, later, of *Zen* (the Japanese equivalent of Chan) Buddhism in Japan. (The older Buddhist tradition, known as *Theravāda,* spread through Sri Lanka and Southeast Asia.)

Vimalakīrti was himself an important figure because he was able to resolve the issue of being both holy and secular, being a part of the world and aloof from it at the same time. In his example we see that it is possible to live successfully in the world and still be an exemplar of virtue. This idea was particularly attractive to Chinese believers, who were often reluctant to renounce home and family in order to devote themselves to religious salvation. Vimalakīrti provides a model for anyone who would meet his or her secular responsibilities while still being true to his or her religious yearnings.

This sutra is also valued because in its brief text it provides a summary of many Mahāyāna doctrines expounded at length and in detail elsewhere. As a literary text, it is easily accessible. When Vimalakīrti falls ill and Sakyamuni asks his disciples to visit him, each in turn refuses, citing an instance in which Vimalakīrti had corrected his teachings and left him speechless. Vimalakīrti is so perceptive and formidable a debater that none of the Buddha's disciples wishes to confront him again. Here we are given a humorous picture of the Buddha's sacred disciples busily evangelizing, but these same followers, it appears, have their doctrines wrong and must have them corrected by the layman Vimalakīrti. The climactic point comes when Mañjuśrī, the most learned and intellectual of the Buddha's disciples, visits Vimalakīrti and engages in a debate on the nature of nonduality, a central tenant of Mahāyāna Buddhism. Several other followers put forward powerful and persuasive arguments, but at the end Mañjuśrī overpowers all others, saying, "all your explanations are themselves dualistic. To know no one teaching, to express nothing, to say nothing, to explain nothing, to announce nothing, to indicate nothing and to designate nothing, that is the entrance to nonduality." He then asks Vimalakīrti for his view on the subject and Vimalakīrti replies with a resounding silence. This, of course, is the most cogent and indeed the only reasonable response, since language itself is separate from the things it signifies. This sound of silence echoes like thunder in medieval Japanese literature—where Kamo no Chōmei, for example (pp. 1132–1141), after arguing the pros and cons of the hermit's life, lapses into silence.

Mahāyāna Buddhism takes the position that anyone might become a Buddha in a future life; those who are bound toward Buddha-hood are *bodhisattvas.* Further, even those who eventually attain Buddha-hood will naturally choose to return to the world to alleviate its suffering, rather than leave it by attaining nirvāna. This sutra argues the bodhisattva ideal that each person should assume responsibility for the salvation of all others. This notion also underlies Japanese Nō theatre, where instead of a protagonist and antagonist locked in conflict and resolution, ending with a victor and vanquished, the two players find their commonality and resolve their conflict by helping each other.

Because it is short, comprehensive, and readable, and because it presents a character who is both a paragon of virtue and an attainable ideal, the Vimalakīrti Sutra has had a profound impact on the shaping of East Asian worldviews.

## *from The Dharma-Door of Nonduality*

*Translated by Robert A.F. Thurmond*

Then, the Licchavi Vimalakīrti asked those bodhisattvas, "Good sirs, please explain how the bodhisattvas enter the Dharma-door of nonduality!"

The bodhisattva Dharmavikurvana declared, "Noble sir, production and destruction are two, but what is not produced and does not occur cannot be destroyed. Thus the attainment of the tolerance of the birthlessness of things is the entrance into nonduality."

The bodhisattva Śrīgandha declared, "'I' and 'mine' are two. If there is no presumption of a self, there will be no possessiveness. Thus, the absence of presumption is the entrance into nonduality."

The bodhisattva Śrīkūṭa declared, "'Defilement' and 'purification' are two. When there is thorough knowledge of defilement, there will be no conceit about purification. The path leading to the complete conquest of all conceit is the entrance into nonduality."

The bodhisattva Bhadrajyotis declared, "'Distraction' and 'attention' are two. When there is no distraction, there will be no attention, no mentation, and no mental intensity. Thus, the absence of mental intensity is the entrance into nonduality."

The bodhisattva Subāhu declared, "'Bodhisattva-spirit' and 'disciple-spirit' are two. When both are seen to resemble an illusory spirit, there is no bodhisattva-spirit, nor any disciple-spirit. Thus, the sameness of natures of spirits is the entrance into nonduality."

The bodhisattva Animiṣa declared, "'Grasping' and 'nongrasping' are two. What is not grasped is not perceived, and what is not perceived is neither presumed nor repudiated. Thus, the inaction and noninvolvement of all things is the entrance into nonduality."

The bodhisattva Sunetra declared, "'Uniqueness' and 'characterlessness' are two. Not to presume or construct something is neither to establish its uniqueness nor to establish its characterlessness. To penetrate the equality of these two is to enter nonduality."

The bodhisattva Tiṣya declared, "'Good' and 'evil' are two. Seeking neither good nor evil, the understanding of the nonduality of the significant and the meaningless is the entrance into nonduality."

The bodhisattva Siṃha declared, "'Sinfulness' and 'sinlessness' are two. By means of the diamond-like wisdom that pierces to the quick, not to be bound or liberated is the entrance into nonduality."

The bodhisattva Siṃhamati declared, "To say, 'This is impure' and 'This is immaculate' makes for duality. One who, attaining equanimity, forms no conception of impurity or immaculateness, yet is not utterly without conception, has equanimity without any attainment of equanimity—he enters the absence of conceptual knots. Thus, he enters into nonduality."

The bodhisattva Śuddhādhimukti declared, "To say, 'This is happiness' and 'That is misery' is dualism. One who is free of all calculations, through the extreme purity of gnosis—his mind is aloof, like empty space; and thus he enters into nonduality."

The bodhisattva Nārāyana declared, "To say, 'This is mundane' and 'That is transcendental' is dualism. This world has the nature of voidness, so there is neither transcendence nor involvement, neither progress nor standstill. Thus, neither to transcend nor to be involved, neither to go nor to stop—this is the entrance into nonduality."

The bodhisattva Dāntamati declared, "'Life' and 'liberation' are dualistic. Having seen the nature of life, one neither belongs to it nor is one utterly liberated from it. Such understanding is the entrance into nonduality."

The bodhisattva Pratyakṣadarśana declared, "'Destructible' and 'indestructible' are dualistic. What is destroyed is ultimately destroyed. What is ultimately destroyed does not become destroyed; hence, it is called 'indestructible.' What is indestructible is instantaneous, and what is instantaneous is indestructible. The experience of such is called 'the entrance into the principle of nonduality.'"

The bodhisattva Parigūḍha declared, "'Self' and 'selflessness' are dualistic. Since the existence of self cannot be perceived, what is there to be made 'selfless'? Thus, the nondualism of the vision of their nature is the entrance into nonduality."

The bodhisattva Vidyuddeva declared, "'Knowledge' and 'ignorance' are dualistic. The natures of ignorance and knowledge are the same, for ignorance is undefined, incalculable, and beyond the sphere of thought. The realization of this is the entrance into nonduality."

The bodhisattva Priyadarśana declared, "Matter itself is void. Voidness does not result from the destruction of matter, but the nature of matter is itself voidness. Therefore, to speak of voidness on the one hand, and of matter, or of sensation, or of intellect, or of motivation, or of consciousness on the other—is entirely dualistic. Consciousness itself is voidness. Voidness does not result from the destruction of consciousness, but the nature of consciousness is itself voidness. Such understanding of the five compulsive aggregates and the knowledge of them as such by means of gnosis is the entrance into nonduality."

The bodhisattva Prabhāketu declared, "To say that the four main elements are one thing and the etheric space-element another is dualistic. The four main elements are themselves the nature of space. The past itself is also the nature of space. The future itself is also the nature of space. Likewise, the present itself is also the nature of space. The gnosis that penetrates the elements in such a way is the entrance into nonduality."

The bodhisattva Pramati declared, "'Eye' and 'form' are dualistic. To understand the eye correctly, and not to have attachment, aversion, or confusion with regard to form—that is called 'peace.' Similarly, 'ear' and 'sound,' 'nose' and 'smell,' 'tongue' and 'taste,' 'body' and 'touch,' and 'mind' and 'phenomena'—all are dualistic. But to know the mind, and to be neither attached, averse, nor confused with regard to phenomena—that is called 'peace.' To live in such peace is to enter into nonduality."

The bodhisattva Akṣayamati declared, "The dedication of generosity for the sake of attaining omniscience is dualistic. The nature of generosity is itself omniscience, and the nature of omniscience itself is total dedication. Likewise, it is dualistic to dedicate morality, tolerance, effort, meditation, and wisdom for the sake of omniscience. Omniscience is the nature of wisdom, and total dedication is the nature of omniscience. Thus, the entrance into this principle of uniqueness is the entrance into nonduality."

The bodhisattva Gambhīramati declared, "It is dualistic to say that voidness is one thing, signlessness another, and wishlessness still another. What is void has no sign. What has no sign has no wish. Where there is no wish there is no process of thought, mind, or consciousness. To see the doors of all liberations in the door of one liberation is the entrance into nonduality."

The bodhisattva Śāntendriya declared, "It is dualistic to say 'Buddha,' 'Dharma,' and 'Śaṅgha.' The Dharma is itself the nature of the Buddha, the Śaṅgha is itself the nature of the Dharma, and all of them are uncompounded. The uncompounded is infinite space, and the processes of all things are equivalent to infinite space. Adjustment to this is the entrance into nonduality."

The bodhisattva Apratihatanetra declared, "It is dualistic to refer to 'aggregates' and to the 'cessation of aggregates.' Aggregates themselves are cessation. Why? The egoistic views of aggregates, being unproduced themselves, do not exist ultimately. Hence such views do not really conceptualize 'These are aggregates' or 'These aggregates cease.' Ultimately, they have no such discriminative constructions and no such conceptualizations. Therefore, such views have themselves the nature of cessation. Nonoccurrence and nondestruction are the entrance into nonduality."

The bodhisattva Suvinīta declared, "Physical, verbal, and mental vows do not exist dualistically. Why? These things have the nature of inactivity. The nature of inactivity of the body is the same as the nature of inactivity of speech, whose nature of inactivity is the same as the nature of inactivity of the mind. It is necessary to know and to understand this fact of the ultimate inactivity of all things, for this knowledge is the entrance into nonduality."

The bodhisattva Puṇyakṣetra declared, "It is dualistic to consider actions meritorious, sinful, or neutral. The non-undertaking of meritorious, sinful, and neutral actions is not dualistic. The intrinsic nature of all such actions is voidness, wherein ultimately there is neither merit, nor sin, nor neutrality, nor action itself. The nonaccomplishment of such actions is the entrance into nonduality."

The bodhisattva Padmavyūha declared, "Dualism is produced from obsession with self, but true understanding of self does not result in dualism. Who thus abides in nonduality is without ideation, and that absence of ideation is the entrance into nonduality."

The bodhisattva Śrīgarbha declared, "Duality is constituted by perceptual manifestation. Nonduality is objectlessness. Therefore, nongrasping and nonrejection is the entrance into nonduality."

The bodhisattva Candrottara declared, "'Darkness' and 'light' are dualistic, but the absence of both darkness and light is nonduality. Why? At the time of absorption in cessation, there is neither darkness nor light, and likewise with the natures of all things. The entrance into this equanimity is the entrance into nonduality."

The bodhisattva Ratnamudrāhasta declared, "It is dualistic to detest the world and to rejoice in liberation, and neither detesting the world nor rejoicing in liberation is nonduality. Why? Liberation can be found where there is bondage, but where there is ultimately no bondage where is there need for liberation? The mendicant who is neither bound nor liberated does not experience any like or any dislike and thus he enters nonduality."

The bodhisattva Maṇikūṭarāja declared, "It is dualistic to speak of good paths and bad paths. One who is on the path is not concerned with good or bad paths. Living in such unconcern, he entertains no concepts of 'path' or 'nonpath.' Understanding the nature of concepts, his mind does not engage in duality. Such is the entrance into nonduality."

The bodhisattva Satyarata declared, "It is dualistic to speak of 'true' and 'false.' When one sees truly, one does not ever see any truth, so how could one see falsehood? Why? One does not see with the physical eye, one sees with the eye of wisdom. And with the wisdom-eye one sees only insofar as there is neither sight nor nonsight. There, where there is neither sight nor nonsight, is the entrance into nonduality."

When the bodhisattvas had given their explanations, they all addressed the crown prince Mañjuśrī: "Mañjuśrī what is the bodhisattva's entrance into nonduality?"

Mañjuśrī replied, "Good sirs, you have all spoken well. Nevertheless, all your explanations are themselves dualistic. To know no one teaching, to express nothing, to say nothing, to explain nothing, to announce nothing, to indicate nothing, and to designate nothing—that is the entrance into nonduality."

Then, the crown prince Mañjuśrī said to the Licchavi Vimalakīrti, "We have all given our own teachings, noble sir. Now, may you elucidate the teaching of the entrance into the principle of nonduality!"

Thereupon, the Licchavi Vimalakīrti kept his silence, saying nothing at all.

The crown prince Mañjuśrī applauded the Licchavi Vimalakīrti: "Excellent! Excellent, noble sir! This is indeed the entrance into the nonduality of the bodhisattvas. Here there is no use for syllables, sounds, and ideas."

When these teachings had been declared, five thousand bodhisattvas entered the door of the Dharma of nonduality and attained tolerance of the birthlessness of things.

## ASVAGHOSHA (1ST CENT. CE)

One of the most admired accounts of the life of the Buddha was written in the first century CE by the Buddhist poet and philosopher Asvaghosha. We know little of the author, but a Chinese Buddhist pilgrim of the seventh century left a description of his influence and the beauty of his text: "He is read far and wide throughout the five Indies and the lands of the southern seas. He clothes in but few words many thoughts and ideas, which so rejoice the reader's heart that he never wearies of the poem. Very profitable also it is to read the poem, for here the noble doctrines are set forth with convenient brevity."

Asvaghosha's Buddha-Karita is preserved in seventeen sections or cantos and is excerpted here to depict the central events of the Buddha's life: his miraculous birth, his youth of privilege and protection, the "four passing sights," the great renunciation, his search for understanding, the enlightenment, and his death and passage into nirvāna. The story has touched the lives of millions of Buddhists and provides a model for all followers. The Buddhist believes that he or she, like Gautama the Buddha, must journey from the illusions of privilege and material comfort to renunciation of the world, to a search after true understanding, and finally to enlightenment and the final escape from the wheel of rebirth.

Asvaghosha's account of the Buddha's life reflects the powerful religious imagination and rich metaphorical texture that characterizes so much great Indian literature. Gautama is no carpenter's son born in a humble stable, like Jesus; he is born Prince Siddhattha, the son of a king, and emerges miraculously from his mother's side. At his birth "the earth, though fastened down by [Himālaya] the monarch of mountains, shook like a ship tossed by the wind; and from a cloudless sky there fell a shower full of lotuses and water-lilies, and perfumed with sandalwood."

The translation provided here is that of E.B. Cowell. It was originally published in the last years of the nineteenth century as part of the *Sacred Books of the East,* a collection that first brought this and many other Asian classics to the attention of the West.

## *from The Buddha-Karita*

*Translated by E.B. Cowell*

### Book I

1. That Arhat is here saluted, who has no counterpart,—who, as bestowing the supreme happiness, surpasses (Brahman) the Creator,—who, as driving away darkness, vanquishes the sun,—and, as dispelling all burning heat, surpasses the beautiful moon.

2. There was a city, the dwelling-place of the great saint Kapila, having its sides surrounded by the beauty of a lofty broad table-land as by a line of clouds, and itself, with its high-soaring palaces, immersed in the sky.

3. By its pure and lofty system of government it, as it were, stole the splendour of the clouds of Mount Kailâsa, and while it bore the clouds which came to it through a mistake, it fulfilled the imagination which had led them thither.

4. In that city, shining with the splendour of gems, darkness like poverty could find no place; prosperity shone resplendently, as with a smile, from the joy of dwelling with such surpassingly excellent citizens.

5. With its festive arbours, its arched gateways and pinnacles, it was radiant with jewels in every dwelling; and unable to find any other rival in the world, it could only feel emulation with its own houses.

6. There the sun, even although he had retired, was unable to scorn the moon-like faces of its women which put the lotuses to shame, and as if from the access of passion, hurried towards the western ocean to enter the (cooling) water.

7. 'Yonder Indra has been utterly annihilated by the people when they saw the glories acquired by the Sâkyas,'—uttering this scoff, the city strove by its banners with gay-fluttering streamers to wipe away every mark of his existence.

8. After mocking the water-lilies even at night by the moonbeams which

rest on its silver pavilions,—by day it assumed the brightness of the lotuses through the sunbeams falling on its golden palaces.

9. A king, by name Suddhodana, of the kindred of the sun, anointed to stand at the head of earth's monarchs,—ruling over the city, adorned it, as a bee-inmate a full-blown lotus.

10. The very best of kings with his train ever near him,—intent on liberality yet devoid of pride; a sovereign, yet with an ever equal eye thrown on all,—of gentle nature and yet with wide-reaching majesty.

11. Falling smitten by his arm in the arena of battle, the lordly elephants of his enemies bowed prostrate with their heads pouring forth quantities of pearls as if they were offering handfuls of flowers in homage.

12. Having dispersed his enemies by his pre-eminent majesty as the sun disperses the gloom of an eclipse, he illuminated his people on every side, showing them the paths which they were to follow.

13. Duty, wealth, and pleasure under his guidance assumed mutually each other's object, but not the outward dress; yet as if they still vied together they shone all the brighter in the glorious career of their triumphant success.

14. He, the monarch of the Sâkyas, of native pre-eminence, but whose actual pre-eminence was brought about by his numberless councillors of exalted wisdom, shone forth all the more gloriously, like the moon amidst the stars shining with a light like its own.

15. To him there was a queen, named Mâyâ, as if free from all deceit (mâyâ)—an effulgence proceeding from his effulgence, like the splendour of the sun when it is free from all the influence of darkness,—a chief queen in the united assembly of all queens.

16. Like a mother to her subjects, intent on their welfare,—devoted to all worthy of reverence like devotion itself, —shining on her lord's family like the goddess of prosperity,—she was the most eminent of goddesses to the whole world.

17. Verily the life of women is always darkness, yet when it encountered her, it shone brilliantly; thus the night does not retain its gloom, when it meets with the radiant crescent of the moon.

18. 'This people, being hard to be roused to wonder in their souls, cannot be influenced by me if I come to them as beyond their senses,'—so saying, Duty abandoned her own subtile nature and made her form visible.

19. Then falling from the host of beings in the Tushita heaven, and illumining the three worlds, the most excellent of Bodhisattvas suddenly entered at a thought into her womb, like the Nâga-king entering the cave of Nandâ.

20. Assuming the form of a huge elephant white like Himâlaya, armed with six tusks, with his face perfumed with flowing ichor, he entered the womb of the queen of king Suddhodana, to destroy the evils of the world.

21. The guardians of the world hastened from heaven to mount watch over the world's one true ruler; thus the moonbeams, though they shine everywhere, are especially bright on Mount Kailâsa.

22. Mâyâ also, holding him in her womb, like a line of clouds holding a lightning-flash, relieved the people

around her from the sufferings of poverty by raining showers of gifts.

23. Then one day by the king's permission the queen, having a great longing in her mind, went with the inmates of the gynaeceum into the garden Lumbinî.

24. As the queen supported herself by a bough which hung laden with a weight of flowers, the Bodhisattva suddenly came forth, cleaving open her womb.

25. At that time the constellation Pushya was auspicious, and from the side of the queen, who was purified by her vow, her son was born for the welfare of the world, without pain and without illness.

26. Like the sun bursting from a cloud in the morning,—so he too, when he was born from his mother's womb, made the world bright like gold, bursting forth with his rays which dispelled the darkness.

27. As soon as he was born the thousand-eyed (Indra) well-pleased took him gently, bright like a golden pillar; and two pure streams of water fell down from heaven upon his head with piles of Mandâra flowers.

28. Carried about by the chief suras, and delighting them with the rays that streamed from his body, he surpassed in beauty the new moon as it rests on a mass of evening clouds.

29. As was Aurva's birth from the thigh, and Prithu's from the hand, and Mândhâtri's, who was like Indra himself, from the forehead, and Kakshîvat's from the upper end of the arm,—thus too was his birth (miraculous).

30. Having thus in due time issued from the womb, he shone as if he had come down from heaven, he who had not been born in the natural way,—he who was born full of wisdom, not foolish,—as if his mind had been purified by countless aeons of contemplation.

31. With glory, fortitude, and beauty he shone like the young sun descended upon the earth; when he was gazed at, though of such surpassing brightness, he attracted all eyes like the moon.

32. With the radiant splendour of his limbs he extinguished like the sun the splendour of the lamps; with his beautiful hue as of precious gold he illuminated all the quarters of space.

33. Unflurried, with the lotus-sign in high relief, far-striding, set down with a stamp,—seven such firm footsteps did he then take,—he who was like the constellation of the seven rishis.

34. 'I am born for supreme knowledge, for the welfare of the world,—thus this is my last birth,'—thus did he of lion gait, gazing at the four quarters, utter a voice full of auspicious meaning.

35. Two streams of water bursting from heaven, bright as the moon's rays, having the power of heat and cold, fell down upon that peerless one's benign head to give refreshment to his body.

36. His body lay on a bed with a royal canopy and a frame shining with gold, and supported by feet of lapis lazuli, and in his honour the yaksha-lords stood round guarding him with golden lotuses in their hands.

37. The gods in homage to the son of Mâyâ, with their heads bowed at his majesty, held up a white umbrella in the sky and muttered the highest blessings on his supreme wisdom.

38. The great dragons in their great thirst for the Law,—they who had had the privilege of waiting on the past Buddhas,—gazing with eyes of intent devotion, fanned him and strewed Mandâra flowers over him.

39. Gladdened through the influence of the birth of the Tathâgata, the gods of pure natures and inhabiting pure abodes were filled with joy, though all passion was extinguished, for the sake of the world drowned in sorrow.

40. When he was born, the earth, though fastened down by (Himâlaya) the monarch of mountains, shook like a ship tossed by the wind; and from a cloudless sky there fell a shower full of lotuses and water-lilies, and perfumed with sandalwood.

41. Pleasant breezes blew soft to the touch, dropping down heavenly garments; the very sun, though still the same, shone with augmented light, and fire gleamed, unstirred, with a gentle lustre.

42. In the north-eastern part of the dwelling a well of pure water appeared of its own accord, wherein the inhabitants of the gynaeceum, filled with wonder, performed their rites as in a sacred bathing-place.

43. Through the troops of heavenly visitants, who came seeking religious merit, the pool itself received strength to behold Buddha, and by means of its trees bearing flowers and perfumes it eagerly offered him worship.

44. The flowering trees at once produced their blossoms, while their fragrance was borne aloft in all directions by the wind, accompanied by the songs of bewildered female bees, while the air was inhaled and absorbed by the many snakes (gathering near).

45. Sometimes there resounded on both sides songs mingled with musical instruments and tabours, and lutes also, drums, tambourines, and the rest,—from women adorned with dancing bracelets.

46. 'That royal law which neither Bhrigu nor Aṅgiras ever made, those two great seers the founders of families, their two sons Sukra and Vrihaspati left revealed at the end.

47. 'Yea, the son of Sarasvatî proclaimed that lost Veda which they had never seen in former ages,—Vyâsa rehearsed that in many forms, which Vasishtha helpless could not compile;

48. 'The voice of Vâlmîki uttered its poetry which the great seer Kyavana could not compose; and that medicine which Atri never invented the wise son of Atri proclaimed after him;

49. 'That Brahmanhood which Kusika never attained,—his son, O king, found out the means to gain it; (so) Sagara made a bound for the ocean, which even the Ikshvâkus had not fixed before him.

50. 'Ganaka attained a power of instructing the twice-born in the rules of Yoga which none other had ever reached; and the famed feats of the grandson of Sûra (Krishna) Sûra and his peers were powerless to accomplish.

51. 'Therefore it is not age nor years which are the criterion; different persons win pre-eminence in the world at different places; those mighty exploits worthy of kings and sages, when left undone by the ancestors, have been done by the sons.'

52. The king, being thus consoled and congratulated by those well-trusted Brahmans, dismissed from his mind all unwelcome suspicion and rose to a still higher degree of joy;

53. And well-pleased he gave to those most excellent of the twice-born rich treasures with all due honour,—'May he become the ruler of the earth according to your words, and may he retire to the woods when he attains old age.'

54. Then having learned by signs and through the power of his penances

this birth of him who was to destroy all birth, the great seer Asita in his thirst for the excellent Law came to the palace of the Sâkya king.

55. Him shining with the glory of sacred knowledge and ascetic observances, the king's own priest,—himself a special student among the students of sacred knowledge,—introduced into the royal palace with all due reverence and respect.

56. He entered into the precincts of the king's gynaeceum, which was all astir with the joy arisen from the birth of the young prince,—grave from his consciousness of power, his pre-eminence in asceticism, and the weight of old age.

57. Then the king, having duly honoured the sage, who was seated in his seat, with water for the feet and an arghya offering, invited him (to speak) with all ceremonies of respect, as did Antideva in olden time to Vasishtha:

58. 'I am indeed fortunate, this my family is the object of high favour, that thou shouldst have come to visit me; be pleased to command what I should do, O benign one; I am thy disciple, be pleased to show thy confidence in me.'

59. The sage, being thus invited by the king, filled with intense feeling as was due, uttered his deep and solemn words, having his large eyes opened wide with wonder:

60. 'This is indeed worthy of thee, great-souled as thou art, fond of guests, liberal and a lover of duty,—that thy mind should be thus kind towards me, in full accordance with thy nature, family, wisdom, and age.

61. 'This is the true way in which those seer-kings of old, rejecting through duty all trivial riches, have ever flung them away as was right,—being poor in outward substance but rich in ascetic endurance.

62. 'But hear now the motive for my coming and rejoice thereat; a heavenly voice has been heard by me in the heavenly path, that thy son has been born for the sake of supreme knowledge.

63. 'Having heard that voice and applied my mind thereto, and having known its truth by signs, I am now come hither, with a longing to see the banner of the Sâkya race, as if it were Indra's banner being set up.'

64. Having heard this address of his, the king, with his steps bewildered with joy, took the prince, who lay on his nurse's side, and showed him to the holy ascetic.

65. Thus the great seer beheld the king's son with wonder,—his foot marked with a wheel, his fingers and toes webbed, with a circle of hair between his eyebrows, and signs of vigour like an elephant.

66. Having beheld him seated on his nurse's side, like the son of Agni (Skanda) seated on Devî's side, he stood with the tears hanging on the ends of his eyelashes, and sighing he looked up towards heaven.

67. But seeing Asita with his eyes thus filled with tears, the king was agitated through his love for his son, and with his hands clasped and his body bowed he thus asked him in a broken voice choked with weeping,

68. 'One whose beauty has little to distinguish it from that of a divine sage, and whose brilliant birth has been so wonderful, and for whom thou hast prophesied a transcendent future,—wherefore, on seeing him, do tears come to thee, O reverend one?

69. 'Is the prince, O holy man, destined to a long life? Surely he cannot be born for my sorrow. I have with difficulty obtained a handful of water,

surely it is not death which comes to drink it.

70. 'Tell me, is the hoard of my fame free from destruction? Is this chief prize of my family secure? Shall I ever depart happily to another life,—I who keep one eye ever awake, even when my son is asleep?

71. 'Surely this young shoot of my family is not born barren, destined only to wither! Speak quickly, my lord, I cannot wait; thou well knowest the love of near kindred for a son.'

72. Knowing the king to be thus agitated through his fear of some impending evil, the sage thus addressed him: 'Let not thy mind, O monarch, be disturbed,—all that I have said is certainly true.

73. 'I have no feeling of fear as to his being subject to change, but I am distressed for mine own disappointment. It is my time to depart, and this child is now born,—he who knows that mystery hard to attain, the means of destroying birth.

74. 'Having forsaken his kingdom, indifferent to all worldly objects, and having attained the highest truth by strenuous efforts, he will shine forth as a sun of knowledge to destroy the darkness of illusion in the world.

75. 'He will deliver by the boat of knowledge the distressed world, borne helplessly along, from the ocean of misery which throws up sickness as its foam, tossing with the waves of old age, and rushing with the dreadful onflow of death.

76. 'The thirsty world of living beings will drink the flowing stream of his Law, bursting forth with the water of wisdom, enclosed by the banks of strong moral rules, delightfully cool with contemplation, and filled with religious vows as with ruddy geese.

77. 'He will proclaim the way of deliverance to those afflicted with sorrow, entangled in objects of sense, and lost in the forest-paths of worldly existence, as to travellers who have lost their way.

78. 'By the rain of the Law he will give gladness to the multitude who are consumed in this world with that fire of desire whose fuel is worldly objects, as a great cloud does with its showers at the end of the hot season.

79. 'He will break open for the escape of living beings that door whose bolt is desire and whose two leaves are ignorance and delusion,—with that excellent blow of the good Law which is so hard to find.

80. 'He, the king of the Law, when he has attained to supreme knowledge, will achieve the deliverance from its bonds of the world now overcome by misery, destitute of every refuge, and enveloped in its own chains of delusion.

81. 'Therefore make no sorrow for him,—that belongs rather, kind sire, to the pitiable world of human beings, who through illusion or the pleasures of desire or intoxication refuse to hear his perfect Law.

82. 'Therefore since I have fallen short of that excellence, though I have accomplished all the stages of contemplation, my life is only a failure; since I have not heard his Law, I count even dwelling in the highest heaven a misfortune.'

83. Having heard these words, the king with his queen and his friends abandoned sorrow and rejoiced; thinking, 'such is this son of mine,' he considered that his excellence was his own.

84. But he let his heart be influenced by the thought, 'he will travel by the noble path,'—he was not in truth

averse to religion, yet still he saw alarm at the prospect of losing his child.

85. Then the sage Asita, having made known the real fate which awaited the prince to the king who was thus disturbed about his son, departed by the way of the wind as he had come, his figure watched reverentially in his flight.

86. Having taken his resolution and having seen the son of his younger sister, the saint, filled with compassion, enjoined him earnestly in all kinds of ways, as if he were his son, to listen to the sage's words and ponder over them.

87. The monarch also, being well-pleased at the birth of a son, having thrown off all those bonds called worldly objects, caused his son to go through the usual birth-ceremonies in a manner worthy of the family.

88. When ten days were fulfilled after his son's birth, with his thoughts kept under restraint, and filled with excessive joy, he offered for his son most elaborate sacrifices to the gods with muttered prayers, oblations, and all kinds of auspicious ceremonies.

89. And he himself gave to the brahmans for his son's welfare cows full of milk, with no traces of infirmity, golden-horned and with strong healthy calves, to the full number of a hundred thousand.

90. Then he, with his soul under strict restraint, having performed all kinds of ceremonies which rejoiced his heart, on a fortunate day, in an auspicious moment, gladly determined to enter his city.

91. Then the queen with her babe having worshipped the gods for good fortune, occupied a costly palanquin made of elephants' tusks, filled with all kinds of white flowers, and blazing with gems.

92. Having made his wife with her child enter first into the city, accompanied by the aged attendants, the king himself also advanced, saluted by the hosts of the citizens, as Indra entering heaven, saluted by the immortals.

93. The Sâkya king, having entered his palace, like Bhava well-pleased at the birth of Kârttikeya, with his face full of joy, gave orders for lavish expenditure, showing all kinds of honour and liberality.

94. Thus at the good fortune of the birth of the king's son, that city surnamed after Kapila, with all the surrounding inhabitants, was full of gladness like the city of the lord of wealth, crowded with heavenly nymphs, at the birth of his son Nalakûvara.

## Book II

1. From the time of the birth of that son of his, who, the true master of himself, was to end all birth and old age, the king increased day by day in wealth, elephants, horses, and friends as a river increases with its influx of waters.

2. Of different kinds of wealth and jewels, and of gold, wrought or unwrought, he found treasures of manifold variety, surpassing even the capacity of his desires.

3. Elephants from Himavat, raging with rut, whom not even princes of elephants like Padma could teach to go round in circles, came without any effort and waited on him.

4. His city was all astir with the crowds of horses, some adorned with various marks and decked with new

golden trappings, others unadorned and with long flowing manes,—suitable alike in strength, gentleness, and costly ornaments.

5. And many fertile cows, with tall calves, gathered in his kingdom, well nourished and happy, gentle and without fierceness, and producing excellent milk.

6. His enemies became indifferent; indifference grew into friendship; his friends became specially united; were there two sides,—one passed into oblivion.

7. Heaven rained in his kingdom in due time and place, with the sound of gentle winds and clouds, and adorned with wreaths of lightning, and without any drawback of showers of stones or thunderbolts.

8. A fruitful crop sprang up according to season, even without the labour of ploughing; and the old plants grew more vigorous in juice and substance.

9. Even at that crisis which threatens danger to the body like the collision of battle, pregnant women brought forth in good health, in safety, and without sickness.

10. And whereas men do not willingly ask from others, even where a surety's property is available,—at that time even one possessed of slender means turned not his face away when solicited.

11. There was no ruin nor murder,—nay, there was not even one ungenerous to his kinsmen, no breaker of obligations, none untruthful nor injurious,—as in the days of Yayâti the son of Nahusha.

12. Those who sought religious merit performed sacred works and made gardens, temples, and hermitages, wells, cisterns, lakes, and groves, having beheld heaven as it were visible before their eyes.

13. The people, delivered from famine, fear, and sickness, dwelt happily as in heaven; and in mutual contentment husband transgressed not against wife, nor wife against husband.

14. None pursued love for mere sensual pleasure; none hoarded wealth for the sake of desires; none practised religious duties for the sake of gaining wealth; none injured living beings for the sake of religious duty.

15. On every side theft and its kindred vices disappeared; his own dominion was in peace and at rest from foreign interference; prosperity and plenty belonged to him, and the cities in his realm were (healthy) like the forests.

16. When that son was born it was in that monarch's kingdom as in the reign of Manu the son of the Sun,—gladness went everywhere and evil perished; right blazed abroad and sin was still.

17. Since at the birth of this son of the king such a universal accomplishment of all objects took place, the king in consequence caused the prince's name to be Sarvârthasiddha.

18. But the queen Mâyâ, having seen the great glory of her new-born son, like some Rishi of the gods, could not sustain the joy which it brought; and that she might not die she went to heaven.

19. Then the queen's sister, with an influence like a mother's, undistinguished from the real mother in her affection or tenderness, brought up as her own son the young prince who was like the offspring of the gods.

20. Then like the young sun on the eastern mountain or the fire when fanned by the wind, the prince gradually

grew in all due perfection, like the moon in the fortnight of brightness.

21. Then they brought him as presents from the houses of his friends costly unguents of sandalwood, and strings of gems exactly like wreaths of plants, and little golden carriages yoked with deer;

22. Ornaments also suitable to his age, and elephants, deer, and horses made of gold, carriages and oxen decked with rich garments, and carts gay with silver and gold.

23. Thus indulged with all sorts of such objects to please the senses as were suitable to his years,—child as he was, he behaved not like a child in gravity, purity, wisdom, and dignity.

24. When he had passed the period of childhood and reached that of middle youth, the young prince learned in a few days the various sciences suitable to his race, which generally took many years to master.

25. But having heard before from the great seer Asita his destined future which was to embrace transcendental happiness, the anxious care of the king of the present Sâkya race turned the prince to sensual pleasures.

26. Then he sought for him from a family of unblemished moral excellence a bride possessed of beauty, modesty, and gentle bearing, of wide-spread glory, Yasodharâ by name, having a name well worthy of her, a very goddess of good fortune.

27. Then after that the prince, beloved of the king his father, he who was like Sanatkumâra, rejoiced in the society of that Sâkya princess as the thousand-eyed (Indra) rejoiced with his bride Sakî.

28. 'He might perchance see some inauspicious sight which could disturb his mind,'—thus reflecting the king had a dwelling prepared for him apart from the busy press in the recesses of the palace.

29. Then he spent his time in those royal apartments, furnished with the delights proper for every season, gaily decorated like heavenly chariots upon the earth, and bright like the clouds of autumn, amidst the splendid musical concerts of singing-women.

30. With the softly-sounding tambourines beaten by the tips of the women's hands, and ornamented with golden rims, and with the dances which were like the dances of the heavenly nymphs, that palace shone like Mount Kailâsa.

31. There the women delighted him with their soft voices, their beautiful pearl-garlands, their playful intoxication, their sweet laughter, and their stolen glances concealed by their brows.

32. Borne in the arms of these women well-skilled in the ways of love, and reckless in the pursuit of pleasure, he fell from the roof of a pavilion and yet reached not the ground, like a holy sage stepping from a heavenly chariot.

## The Great Retirement

Now on a certain day the Future Buddha wished to go to the park, and told his charioteer to make ready the chariot. Accordingly the man brought out a sumptuous and elegant chariot, and adorning it richly, he harnessed to it four state-horses of the Sindhava breed, as white as the petals of the white lotus, and announced to the Future Buddha that everything was ready. And the Future Buddha mounted the chariot, which was like to a palace of the gods, and proceeded towards the park.

"The time for the enlightenment of prince Siddhattha draweth nigh," thought the gods; "we must show him a sign:" and they changed one of their number into a decrepit old man, broken-toothed, gray-haired, crooked and bent of body, leaning on a staff, and trembling, and showed him to the Future Buddha, but so that only he and the charioteer saw him.

Then said the Future Buddha to the charioteer, in the manner related in the Mahāpadāna,—

"Friend, pray, who is this man? Even his hair is not like that of other men." And when he heard the answer, he said, "Shame on birth, since to every one that is born old age must come." And agitated in heart, he thereupon returned and ascended his palace.

"Why has my son returned so quickly?" asked the king.

"Sire, he has seen an old man," was the reply; "and because he has seen an old man, he is about to retire from the world."

"Do you want to kill me, that you say such things? Quickly get ready some plays to be performed before my son. If we can but get him to enjoying pleasure, he will cease to think of retiring from the world." Then the king extended the guard to half a league in each direction.

Again, on a certain day, as the Future Buddha was going to the park, he saw a diseased man whom the gods had fashioned; and having again made inquiry, he returned, agitated in heart, and ascended his palace.

And the king made the same inquiry and gave the same orders as before; and again extending the guard, placed them for three quarters of a league around.

And again on a certain day, as the Future Buddha was going to the park, he saw a dead man whom the gods had fashioned; and having again made inquiry, he returned, agitated in heart, and ascended his palace.

And the king made the same inquiry and gave the same orders as before; and again extending the guard, placed them for a league around.

And again on a certain day, as the Future Buddha was going to the park, he saw a monk, carefully and decently clad, whom the gods had fashioned; and he asked his charioteer, "Pray, who is this man?"

Now although there was no Buddha in the world, and the charioteer had no knowledge of either monks or their good qualities, yet by the power of the gods he was inspired to say, "Sire, this is one who has retired from the world;" and he thereupon proceeded to sound the praises of retirement from the world. The thought of retiring from the world was a pleasing one to the Future Buddha, and this day he went on until he came to the park. The repeaters of the Dīgha, however, say that he went to the park after having seen all the Four Signs on one and the same day.

When he had disported himself there throughout the day, and had bathed in the royal pleasure-tank, he went at sunset and sat down on the royal resting-stone with the intention of adorning himself. Then gathered around him his attendants with diverse-colored cloths, many kinds and styles of ornaments, and with garlands, perfumes, and ointments. At that instant the throne on which Sakka was sitting grew hot. And Sakka, considering who it could be that was desirous of dislodging him, perceived that it was the time of the adornment of a Future Buddha. And addressing Vissakamma, he said,—

"My good Vissakamma, to-night, in the middle watch, prince Siddhattha will go forth on the Great Retirement, and this is his last adorning of himself. Go to the park, and adorn that eminent man with celestial ornaments."

"Very well," said Vissakamma, in assent; and came on the instant, by his superhuman power, into the presence of the Future Buddha. And assuming the guise of a barber, he took from the real barber the turban-cloth, and began to wind it round the Future Buddha's head; but as soon as the Future Buddha felt the touch of his hand, he knew that it was no man, but a god.

Now once round his head took up a thousand cloths, and the fold was like to a circlet of precious stones; the second time round took another thousand cloths, and so on, until ten times round had taken up ten thousand cloths. Now let no one think, "How was it possible to use so many cloths on one small head?" for the very largest of them all had only the size of a sāma-creeper blossom, and the others that of kutumbaka flowers. Thus the Future Buddha's head resembled a kuyyaka blossom twisted about with lotus filaments.

And having adorned himself with great richness,—while adepts in different kinds of tabors and tom-toms were showing their skill, and Brahmans with cries of victory and joy, and bards and poets with propitious words and shouts of praise saluted him,—he mounted his superbly decorated chariot.

At this juncture, Suddhodana the king, having heard that the mother of Rāhula had brought forth a son, sent a messenger, saying, "Announce the glad news to my son."

On hearing the message, the Future Buddha said, "An impediment [rāhula] has been born; a fetter has been born."

"What did my son say?" questioned the king; and when he had heard the answer, he said, "My grandson's name shall be prince Rāhula from this very day."

But the Future Buddha in his splendid chariot entered the city with a pomp and magnificence of glory that enraptured all minds. At the same moment Kisā Gotamī, a virgin of the warrior caste, ascended to the roof of her palace, and beheld the beauty and majesty of the Future Buddha, as he circumambulated the city; and in her pleasure and satisfaction at the sight, she burst forth into this song of joy:—

"Full happy now that mother is,
Full happy now that father is,
Full happy now that woman is,
Who owns this lord so glorious!"

On hearing this, the Future Buddha thought, "In beholding a handsome figure the heart of a mother attains Nirvana, the heart of a father attains Nirvana, the heart of a wife attains Nirvana. This is what she says. But wherein does Nirvana consist?" And to him, whose mind was already averse to passion, the answer came: "When the fire of lust is extinct, that is Nirvana; when the fires of hatred and infatuation are extinct, that is Nirvana; when pride, false belief, and all other passions and torments are extinct, that is Nirvana. She has taught me a good lesson. Certainly, Nirvana is what I am looking for. It behooves me this very day to quit the household life, and to retire from the world in quest of Nirvana. I will send this lady a teacher's fee." And loosening from his neck a pearl necklace worth a hundred thousand pieces of money, he sent it to Kisā Gotamī. And great was her satisfaction at this, for she thought, "Prince Siddhattha has fallen in love with me, and has sent me a present."

And the Future Buddha entered his palace in great splendor, and lay on his couch of state. And straightway richly dressed women, skilled in all manner of dance and song, and beautiful as celestial nymphs, gathered about him with all kinds of musical instruments, and with dance, song, and music they endeavored to please him. But the Future Buddha's aversion to passion did not allow him to take pleasure in the spectacle, and he fell into a brief slumber. And the women, exclaiming, "He for whose sake we should perform has fallen asleep. Of what use is it to weary ourselves any longer?" threw their various instruments on the ground, and lay down. And the lamps fed with sweet-smelling oil continued to burn. And the Future Buddha awoke, and seating himself cross-legged on his couch, perceived these women lying asleep, with their musical instruments scattered about them on the floor,—some with their bodies wet with trickling phlegm and spittle; some grinding their teeth, and muttering and talking in their sleep; some with their mouths open; and some with their dress fallen apart so as plainly to disclose their loathsome nakedness. This great alteration in their appearance still further increased his aversion for sensual pleasures. To him that magnificent apartment, as splendid as the palace of Sakka, began to seem like a cemetery filled with dead bodies impaled and left to rot; and the three modes of existence appeared like houses all ablaze. And breathing forth the solemn utterance, "How oppressive and stifling is it all!" his mind turned ardently to retiring from the world. "It behooves me to go forth on the Great Retirement this very day," said he; and he arose from his couch, and coming near the door, called out,—

"Who's there?"

"Master, it is I, Channa," replied the courtier who had been sleeping with his head on the threshold.

"I wish to go forth on the Great Retirement to-day. Saddle a horse for me."

"Yes, sire." And taking saddle and bridle with him, the courtier started for the stable. There, by the light of lamps fed with sweet-smelling oils, he perceived the mighty steed Kanthaka in his pleasant quarters, under a canopy of cloth beautified with a pattern of jasmine flowers. "This is the one for me to saddle to-day," thought he; and he saddled Kanthaka.

"He is drawing the girth very tight," thought Kanthaka, whilst he was being saddled; "it is not at all as on other days, when I am saddled for rides in the park and the like. It must be that to-day my master wishes to issue forth on the Great Retirement." And in his delight he neighed a loud neigh. And that neigh would have spread through the whole town, had not the gods stopped the sound, and suffered no one to hear it.

Now the Future Buddha, after he had sent Channa on his errand, thought to himself, "I will take just one look at my son;" and, rising from the couch on which he was sitting, he went to the suite of apartments occupied by the mother of Rāhula, and opened the door of her chamber. Within the chamber was burning a lamp fed with sweet-smelling oil, and the mother of Rāhula lay sleeping on a couch strewn deep with jasmine and other flowers, her hand resting on the head of her son. When the Future Buddha reached the threshold, he paused, and gazed at the two from where he stood.

"If I were to raise my wife's hand from off the child's head, and take him up, she would awake, and thus prevent my departure. I will first become a Buddha, and then come back and see my son." So saying, he descended from the palace.

Now that which is said in the Jātaka Commentary, "At that time Rāhula was seven days old," is not found in the other commentaries. Therefore the account above given is to be accepted.

When the Future Buddha had thus descended from the palace, he came near to his horse, and said,—

"My dear Kanthaka, save me now this one night; and then, when thanks to you I have become a Buddha, I will save the world of gods and men." And thereupon he vaulted upon Kanthaka's back.

Now Kanthaka was eighteen cubits long from his neck to his tail, and of corresponding height; he was strong and swift, and white all over like a polished conch-shell. If he neighed or stamped, the sound was so loud as to spread through the whole city; therefore the gods exerted their power, and muffled the sound of his neighing, so that no one heard it; and at every step he took they placed the palms of their hands under his feet.

The Future Buddha rode on the mighty back of the mighty steed, made Channa hold on by the tail, and so arrived at midnight at the great gate of the city.

Now the king, in order that the Future Buddha should not at any time go out of the city without his knowledge, had caused each of the two leaves of the gate to be made so heavy as to need a thousand men to move it. But the Future Buddha had a vigor and a strength that was equal, when reckoned in elephant-power, to the strength of ten thousand million elephants, and, reckoned in man-power, to the strength of a hundred thousand million men.

"If," thought he, "the gate does not open, I will straightway grip tight hold of Kanthaka with my thighs, and, seated as I am on Kanthaka's back, and with Channa holding on by the tail, I will leap up and carry them both with me over the wall, although its height be eighteen cubits."

"If," thought Channa, "the gate is not opened, I will place my master on my shoulder, and tucking Kanthaka under my arm by passing my right hand round him and under his belly, I will leap up and carry them both with me over the wall."

"If," thought Kanthaka, "the gate is not opened, with my master seated as he is on my back, and with Channa holding on by my tail, I will leap up and carry them both with me over the wall."

Now if the gate had not opened, verily one or another of these three persons would have accomplished that whereof he thought; but the divinity that inhabited the gate opened it for them.

At this moment came Māra, with the intention of persuading the Future Buddha to turn back; and standing in the air, he said,—

"Sir, go not forth! For on the seventh day from now the wheel of empire will appear to you, and you shall rule over the four great continents and their two thousand attendant isles. Sir, turn back!"

"Who are you?"

"I am Vasavatti."

"Māra, I knew that the wheel of empire was on the point of appearing to me; but I do not wish for sovereignty. I am about to cause the ten thousand worlds to thunder with my becoming a Buddha."

"I shall catch you," thought Māra, "the very first time you have a lustful, malicious, or unkind thought." And, like an ever-present shadow, he followed after, ever on the watch for some slip.

Thus the Future Buddha, casting away with indifference a universal sovereignty already in his grasp,—spewing it out as if it were but phlegm—departed from the city in great splendor on the full-moon day of the month Āsāḷhī, when the moon was in Libra. And when he had gone out from the city, he became desirous of looking back at it; but no sooner had the thought arisen in his mind, than the broad earth, seeming to fear lest the Great Being might neglect to perform the act of looking back, split and turned round like a potter's wheel. When the Future Buddha had stood a while facing the city and gazing upon it, and had indicated in that place the spot for the "Shrine of the Turning Back of Kanthaka," he turned Kanthaka in the direction in which he meant to go, and proceeded on his way in great honor and exceeding glory.

For they say the deities bore sixty thousand torches in front of him, and sixty thousand behind him, and sixty thousand on the right hand, and sixty thousand on the left hand. Other deities, standing on the rim of the world, bore torches past all numbering; and still other deities, as well as serpents and birds, accompanied him, and did him homage with heavenly perfumes, garlands, sandal-wood powder, and incense. And the sky was as full of coral flowers as it is of pouring water at the height of the rainy season. Celestial choruses were heard; and on every side bands of music played, some of eight instruments, and some of sixty,—sixty-eight hundred thousand instruments in all. It was as when the storm-clouds thunder on the sea, or when the ocean roars against the Yugandhara rocks.

Advancing in this glory, the Future Buddha in one night passed through three kingdoms, and at the end of thirty leagues he came to the river named Anomā.

But was this as far as the horse could go? Certainly not. For he was able to travel round the world from end to end, as it were round the rim of a wheel lying on its hub, and yet get back before breakfast and eat the food prepared for him. But on this occasion the fragrant garlands and other offerings which the gods and the serpents and the birds threw down upon him from the sky buried him up to his haunches; and as he was obliged to drag his body and cut his way through the tangled mass, he was greatly delayed. Hence it was that he went only thirty leagues.

And the Future Buddha, stopping on the river-bank, said to Channa,—

"What is the name of this river?"

"Sire, its name is Anomā [Illustrious]."

"And my retirement from the world shall also be called Anomā," replied the Future Buddha. Saying this, he gave the signal to his horse with his heel; and the horse sprang over the river, which had a breadth of eight usabhas, and landed on the opposite bank. And the Future Buddha, dismounting and standing on the sandy beach that stretched away like a sheet of silver, said to Channa,—

"My good Channa, take these ornaments and Kanthaka and go home. I am about to retire from the world."

"Sire, I also will retire from the world."

Three times the Future Buddha refused him, saying, "It is not for you to retire from the world. Go now!" and made him take the ornaments and Kanthaka.

Next he thought, "These locks of mine are not suited to a monk; but there is no one fit to cut the hair of a Future Buddha. Therefore I will cut them off myself with my sword." And grasping a simitar with his right hand, he seized his top-knot with his left hand, and cut it off, together with the diadem. His hair thus became two finger-breadths in length, and curling to the right, lay close to his head. As long as he lived it remained of that length, and the beard was proportionate. And never again did he have to cut either hair or beard.

Then the Future Buddha seized hold of his top-knot and diadem, and threw them into the air, saying,—

"If I am to become a Buddha, let them stay in the sky; but if not, let them fall to the ground."

The top-knot and jewelled turban mounted for a distance of a league into the air, and there came to a stop. And Sakka, the king of the gods, perceiving them with his divine eye, received them in an appropriate jewelled casket, and established it in the Heaven of the Thirty-three as the "Shrine of the Diadem."

"His hair he cut, so sweet with
many pleasant scents,
This Chief of Men, and high
impelled it towards the sky;
And there god Vāsava, the god
with thousand eyes,
In golden casket caught it, bowing
low his head."

Again the Future Buddha thought, "These garments of mine, made of Benares cloth, are not suited to a monk."

Now the Mahā-Brahma god, Ghaṭīkāra, who had been a friend of his in the time of the Buddha Kassapa, and whose affection for him had not grown old in the long interval since that Buddha, thought to himself,—

"To-day my friend has gone forth on the Great Retirement. I will bring him the requisites of a monk."

"Robes, three in all, the bowl for
alms,
The razor, needle, and the belt,
And water-strainer,—just these
eight
Are needed by th' ecstatic monk."

Taking the above eight requisites of a monk, he gave them to him.

When the Future Buddha had put on this most excellent vesture, the symbol of saintship and of retirement from the world, he dismissed Channa, saying,—

"Channa, go tell my father and my mother from me that I am well."

And Channa did obeisance to the Future Buddha; and keeping his right side towards him, he departed.

But Kanthaka, who had stood listening to the Future Buddha while he was conferring with Channa, was unable to bear his grief at the thought, "I shall never see my master any more." And as he passed out of sight, his heart burst, and he died, and was reborn in the Heaven of the Thirty-three as the god Kanthaka.

At first the grief of Channa had been but single; but now he was oppressed with a second sorrow in the death of Kanthaka, and came weeping and wailing to the city.

## The Great Struggle and the Attainment of Buddhaship

Then the Future Buddha took his noonday rest on the banks of the river, in a grove of sal-trees in full bloom. And at nightfall, at the time the flowers droop on their stalks, he rose up, like a lion when he bestirs himself, and went towards the Bo-tree, along a road which the gods had decked, and which was eight usabhas wide.

The snakes, the fairies, the birds, and other classes of beings did him homage with celestial perfumes, flowers, and other offerings, and celestial choruses poured forth heavenly music; so that the ten thousand worlds were filled with these perfumes, garlands, and shouts of acclaim.

Just then there came from the opposite direction a grasscutter named Sotthiya, and he was carrying grass. And when he saw the Great Being, that he was a holy man, he gave him eight handfuls of grass. The Future Buddha took the grass, and ascending the throne of wisdom, stood on the southern side and faced the north. Instantly the southern half of the world sank, until it seemed to touch the Avīci hell, while the northern half rose to the highest of the heavens.

"Methinks," said the Future Buddha, "this cannot be the place for the attainment of the supreme wisdom;" and walking round the tree with his right side towards it, he came to the western side and faced the east. Then the western half of the world sank, until it seemed to touch the Avīci hell, while the eastern half rose to the highest of the heavens. Wherever, indeed, he stood, the broad earth rose and fell, as though it had been a huge cart-wheel lying on its hub, and some one were treading on the rim.

"Methinks," said the Future Buddha, "this also cannot be the place for the attainment of supreme wisdom;" and walking round the tree with his right side towards it, he came to the northern side and faced the south. Then the northern half of the world sank, until it seemed to touch the Avīci hell, while the southern half rose to the highest of the heavens.

"Methinks," said the Future Buddha, "this also cannot be the place for the attainment of supreme wisdom;" and walking round the tree with his right side towards it, he came to the eastern side and faced the west. Now it is on the eastern side of their Bo-trees that all The Buddhas have sat cross-legged, and that side neither trembles nor quakes.

Then the Great Being, saying to himself, "This is the immovable spot on which all The Buddhas have planted themselves! This is the place for destroying passion's net!" took hold of his handful of grass by one end, and shook it out there. And straightway the blades of grass formed themselves into a seat fourteen cubits long, of such symmetry of shape as not even the most skilful painter or carver could design.

Then the Future Buddha turned his back to the trunk of the Bo-tree and faced the east. And making the mighty resolution, "Let my skin, and sinews, and bones become dry, and welcome! and let all the flesh and blood in my body dry up! but never from this seat will I stir, until I have attained the supreme and absolute wisdom!" he sat himself down cross-legged in an unconquerable position, from which not even the descent of a hundred thunder-bolts at once could have dislodged him.

At this point the god Māra, exclaiming, "Prince Siddhattha is desirous of passing beyond my control, but I will never allow it!" went and announced the news to his army, and sounding the Māra war-cry, drew out for battle. Now Māra's army extended in front of him for twelve leagues, and to the right and to the left for twelve leagues, and in the rear as far as to the confines of the world, and it was nine leagues high. And when it shouted, it made an earthquake-like roaring and rumbling over a space of a thousand leagues. And the god Māra, mounting his elephant, which was a hundred and fifty leagues high, and had the name "Girded-with-mountains," caused a thousand arms to appear on his body, and with these he grasped a variety of weapons. Also in the remainder of that army, no two persons carried the same weapon; and diverse also in their appearances and countenances, the host swept on like a flood to overwhelm the Great Being.

Now deities throughout the ten thousand worlds were busy singing the praises of the Great Being. Sakka, the king of the gods, was blowing the conch-shell Vijayuttara. (This conch, they say, was a hundred and twenty cubits long, and when once it had been filled with wind, it would sound for four months before it stopped.) The great black snake-king sang more than a hundred laudatory verses. And Mahā-Brahma stood holding aloft the white umbrella. But as Māra's army gradually drew near to the throne of wisdom, not one of these gods was able to stand his ground, but each fled straight before him. The black snake-king dived into the ground, and coming to the snake-abode, Mañjerika, which was five hundred leagues in extent, he covered his face with both hands and lay down. Sakka slung his conch-shell Vijayuttara over his back, and took up his position on the rim of the world. Mahā-Brahma left the white umbrella at the end of the world, and fled to his Brahma-abode. Not a single deity was able to stand his ground, and the Great Being was left sitting alone.

Then said Māra to his followers,—

"My friends, Siddhattha, the son of Suddhodana, is far greater than any other man, and we shall never be able to fight him in front. We will attack him from behind."

All the gods had now disappeared, and the Great Being looked around on three sides, and said to himself, "There is no one here." Then looking to the north, he perceived Māra's army coming on like a flood, and said,—

"Here is this multitude exerting all their strength and power against me alone. My mother and father are not here, nor my brother, nor any other relative. But I have these Ten Perfections, like old retainers long cherished at my board. It therefore behooves me to make the Ten Perfections my shield and my sword, and to strike a blow with them that shall destroy this strong array." And he remained sitting, and reflected on the Ten Perfections.

Thereupon the god Māra caused a whirlwind, thinking, "By this will I drive away Siddhattha." Straightway the east wind and all the other different winds began to blow; but although these winds could have torn their way through mountain-peaks half a league, or two leagues, or three leagues high, or have uprooted forest-shrubs and trees, or have reduced to powder and scattered in all directions, villages and towns, yet when they reached the Future Buddha, such was the energy of the Great Being's merit, they lost all power and were not able to cause so much as a fluttering of the edge of his priestly robe.

Then he caused a great rain-storm, saying, "With water will I overwhelm and drown him." And through his mighty power, clouds of a hundred strata, and clouds of a thousand strata arose, and also the other different kinds. And these rained down, until the earth became gullied by the torrents of water which fell, and until the floods had risen over the tops of every forest-tree. But on coming to the Great Being, this mighty inundation was not able to wet his priestly robes as much as a dew-drop would have done.

Then he caused a shower of rocks, in which immense mountain-peaks flew smoking and flaming through the sky. But on reaching the Future Buddha they became celestial bouquets of flowers.

Then he caused a shower of weapons, in which single-edged, and double-edged swords, spears, and arrows flew smoking and flaming through the sky. But on reaching the Future Buddha they became celestial flowers.

Then he caused a shower of live coals, in which live coals as red as kimsuka flowers flew through the sky. But they scattered themselves at the Future Buddha's feet as a shower of celestial flowers.

Then he caused a shower of hot ashes, in which ashes that glowed like fire flew through the sky. But they fell at the Future Buddha's feet as sandal-wood powder.

Then he caused a shower of sand, in which very fine sand flew smoking and flaming through the sky. But it fell at the Future Buddha's feet as celestial flowers.

Then he caused a shower of mud, in which mud flew smoking and flaming through the sky. But it fell at the Future Buddha's feet as celestial ointment.

Then he caused a darkness, thinking, "By this will I frighten Siddhattha, and drive him away." And the darkness became fourfold, and very dense. But on reaching the Future Buddha it disappeared like darkness before the light of the sun.

Māra, being thus unable with these nine storms of wind, rain, rocks, weapons, live coals, hot ashes, sand, mud, and darkness, to drive away the Future Buddha, gave command to his followers, "Look ye now! Why stand ye still? Seize, kill, drive away this prince!" And, arming himself with a discus, and seated upon the shoulders of the elephant "Girded-with-mountains," he drew near the Future Buddha, and said,—

"Siddhattha, arise from this seat! It does not belong to you, but to me."

When the Great Being heard this he said,—

"Māra, you have not fulfilled the Ten Perfections in any of their three grades; nor have you made the five great donations; nor have you striven for knowledge, nor for the welfare of the world, nor for enlightenment. This seat does not belong to you, but to me."

Unable to restrain his fury, the enraged Māra now hurled his discus. But the Great Being reflected on the Ten Perfections, and the discus changed into a canopy of flowers, and remained suspended over his head. Yet they say that this keen-edged discus, when at other times Māra hurled it in anger, would cut through solid stone pillars as if they had been the tips of bamboo shoots. But on this occasion it became a canopy of flowers. Then the followers of Māra began hurling immense mountain-crags, saying, "This will make him get up from his seat and flee." But the Great Being kept his thoughts on the Ten Perfections, and the crags also became wreaths of flowers, and then fell to the ground.

Now the gods meanwhile were standing on the rim of the world, and craning their necks to look, saying,—

"Ah, woe the day! The handsome form of prince Siddhattha will surely be destroyed! What will he do to save himself?"

Then the Great Being, after his assertion that the seat which Future Buddhas had always used on the day of their complete enlightenment belonged to him, continued, and said,—

"Māra, who is witness to your having given donations?"

Said Māra, "All these, as many as you see here, are my witnesses;" and he stretched out his hand in the direction of his army. And instantly from Māra's army came a roar, "I am his witness! I am his witness!" which was like to the roar of an earthquake.

Then said Māra to the Great Being,—

"Siddhattha, who is witness to your having given donations?"

"Your witnesses," replied the Great Being, "are animate beings, and I have no animate witnesses present. However, not to mention the donations which I gave in other existences, the great seven-hundred-fold donation which I gave in my Vessantara existence shall now be testified to by the solid earth, inanimate though she be." And drawing forth his right hand from beneath his priestly robe, he stretched it out towards the mighty earth, and said, "Are you witness, or are you not, to my having given a great seven-hundred-fold donation in my Vessantara existence?"

And the mighty earth thundered, "I bear you witness!" with a hundred, a thousand, a hundred thousand roars, as if to overwhelm the army of Māra.

Now while the Great Being was thus calling to mind the donation he gave in his Vessantara existence, and saying to himself, "Siddhattha, that was a great and excellent donation which you gave," the hundred-and-fifty-league-high elephant "Girded-with-mountains" fell upon his knees before the Great Being. And the followers of Māra fled away in all directions. No two went the same way, but leaving their head-ornaments and their cloaks behind, they fled straight before them.

Then the hosts of the gods, when they saw the army of Māra flee, cried out, "Māra is defeated! Prince Siddhattha has conquered! Let us go celebrate the victory!" And the snakes egging on the snakes, the birds the birds, the deities the deities, and the Brahma-angels the Brahma-angels, they came with perfumes, garlands, and other offerings in their hands to the Great Being on the throne of wisdom. And as they came,—

"The victory now hath this
illustrious Buddha won!
The Wicked One, the Slayer, hath
defeated been!"
Thus round the throne of wisdom
shouted joyously
The bands of snakes their songs of
victory for the Sage;

"The victory now hath this
illustrious Buddha won!
The Wicked One, the Slayer, hath
defeated been!"
Thus round the throne of wisdom
shouted joyously
The flocks of birds their songs of
victory for the Sage;

"The victory now hath this
illustrious Buddha won!
The wicked One, the Slayer, hath
defeated been!"
Thus round the throne of wisdom
shouted joyously
The bands of gods their songs of
victory for the Sage;

"The victory now hath this
illustrious Buddha won!
The Wicked One, the Slayer, hath
defeated been!"
Thus round the throne of wisdom
shouted joyously
The Brahma-angels songs of
victory for the Saint.

And the remaining deities, also, throughout the ten thousand worlds, made offerings of garlands, perfumes, and ointments, and in many a hymn extolled him.

It was before the sun had set that the Great Being thus vanquished the army of Māra. And then, while the Bo-tree in homage rained red, coral-like sprigs upon his priestly robes, he acquired in the first watch of the night the knowledge of previous existences; in the middle watch of the night, the divine eye; and in the last watch of the night, his intellect fathomed Dependent Origination.

Now while he was musing on the twelve terms of Dependent Origination, forwards and backwards, round and back again, the ten thousand worlds quaked twelve times, as far as to their ocean boundaries. And when the Great Being, at the dawning of the day, had thus made the ten thousand worlds thunder with his attainment of omniscience, all these worlds became most gloriously adorned. Flags and banners erected on the eastern rim of the world let their streamers fly to the western rim of the world; likewise those erected on the western rim of the world, to the eastern rim of the world; those erected on the northern rim of the world, to the southern rim of the world; and those erected on the southern rim of the world, to the northern rim of the world; while those erected on the level of the earth let theirs fly until they beat against the Brahma-world; and those of the Brahma-world let theirs hang down to the level of the earth. Throughout the ten thousand worlds the flowering trees bloomed; the fruit trees were weighted down by their burden of fruit; trunk-lotuses bloomed on the trunks of trees; branch-lotuses on the branches of trees; vine-lotuses on the vines; hanging-lotuses in the sky; and stalk-lotuses burst through the rocks and came up by sevens. The system of ten thousand worlds was like a bouquet of flowers sent whirling through the air, or like a thick carpet of flowers; in the intermundane spaces the eight-thousand-league-long hells, which not even the light of seven suns had formerly been able to illumine, were now flooded with radiance; the eighty-four-thousand-league-deep ocean became sweet to the taste; the rivers checked their flowing; the blind from birth received their sight; the deaf from birth their hearing; the cripples from birth the use of their limbs; and the bonds and fetters of captives broke and fell off.

When thus he had attained to omniscience, and was the centre of such unparalleled glory and homage, and so many prodigies were happening about him, he breathed forth that solemn utterance which has never been omitted by any of The Buddhas:

"Through birth and rebirth's
endless round,
Seeking in vain, I hastened on,
To find who framed this edifice.
What misery!—birth incessantly!

"O builder! I've discovered thee!
This fabric thou shalt ne'er rebuild!
Thy rafters all are broken now,
And pointed roof demolished lies!
This mind has demolition reached,
And seen the last of all desire!"

The period of time, therefore, from the existence in the Tusita Heaven to this attainment of omniscience on the throne of wisdom, constitutes the Intermediate Epoch.

## The Death of the Buddha

Then The Blessed One addressed the venerable Ānanda:—

"It may be, Ānanda, that some of you will think, 'The word of The Teacher is a thing of the past; we have now no Teacher.' But that, Ānanda, is not the correct view. The Doctrine and Discipline, Ānanda, which I have taught and enjoined upon you is to be your teacher when I am gone. But whereas now, Ānanda, all the priests address each other with the title of 'brother,' not so must they address each other after I am gone. A senior priest, Ānanda, is to address a junior priest either by his given name, or by his family name, or by the title of 'brother;' a junior priest is to address a senior priest with the title 'reverend sir,' or 'venerable.' If the Order, Ānanda, wish to do so, after I am gone they may abrogate all the lesser and minor precepts. On Channa, Ānanda, after I am gone, the higher penalty is to be inflicted."

"Reverend Sir, what is this higher penalty?'

"Let Channa, Ānanda, say what he likes, he is not to be spoken to nor admonished nor instructed by the priests."

Then The Blessed One addressed the priests:—

"It may be, O priests, that some priest has a doubt or perplexity respecting either The Buddha or the Doctrine or the Order or the Path or the course of conduct. Ask any questions, O priests, and suffer not that afterwards ye feel remorse, saying, 'Our Teacher was present with us, but we failed to ask him all our questions.'"

When he had so spoken, the priests remained silent.

And a second time The Blessed One, and a third time The Blessed One addressed the priests:—

"It may be, O priests, that some priest has a doubt or perplexity respecting either The Buddha or the Doctrine or the Order or the Path or the course of conduct. Ask any question, O priests, and suffer not that afterwards ye feel remorse, saying, 'Our Teacher was present with us, but we failed to ask him all our questions.'"

And a third time the priests remained silent.

Then The Blessed One addressed the priests:—

"It may be, O priests, that it is out of respect to The Teacher that ye ask no questions. Then let each one speak to his friend."

And when he had thus spoken, the priests remained silent.

Then the venerable Ānanda spoke to The Blessed One as follows:—

"It is wonderful, Reverend Sir! It is marvellous, Reverend Sir! Reverend Sir, I have faith to believe that in this congregation of priests not a single priest has a doubt or perplexity respecting either The Buddha or the Doctrine or the Order or the Path or the course of conduct."

"With you, Ānanda, it is a matter of faith, when you say that; but with The Tathāgata, Ānanda, it is a matter of knowledge that in this congregation of priests not a single priest has a doubt or perplexity respecting either The Buddha or the Doctrine or the Order or the Path or the course of conduct. For of all these five hundred priests, Ānanda, the most backward one has become converted, and is not liable to pass into a lower state of existence, but is destined necessarily to attain supreme wisdom."

Then The Blessed One addressed the priests:—

"And now, O priests, I take my leave of you; all the constituents of being are transitory; work out your salvation with diligence."

And this was the last word of The Tathāgata.

Thereupon The Blessed One entered the first trance; and rising from the first trance, he entered the second trance; and rising from the second trance, he entered the third trance; and rising from the third trance, he entered the fourth trance; and rising from the fourth trance, he entered the realm of the infinity of space; and rising from the realm of the infinity of space, he entered the realm of the infinity of consciousness; and rising from the realm of the infinity of consciousness, he entered the realm of nothingness; and rising from the realm of nothingness, he entered the realm of neither perception nor yet non-perception; and rising from the realm of neither perception nor yet non-perception, he arrived at the cessation of perception and sensation.

Thereupon the venerable Ānanda spoke to the venerable Anuruddha as follows:—

"Reverend Anuruddha, The Blessed One has passed into Nirvana."

"Nay, brother Ānanda, The Blessed One has not passed into Nirvana; he has arrived at the cessation of perception and sensation."

Thereupon The Blessed One rising from the cessation of his perception and sensation, entered the realm of neither perception nor yet non-perception; and rising from the realm of neither perception nor yet non-perception, he entered the realm of nothingness; and rising from the realm of nothingness, he entered the realm of the infinity of consciousness; and rising from the realm of the infinity of consciousness, he entered the realm of the infinity of space; and rising from the realm of the infinity of space, he entered the fourth trance; and rising from the fourth trance, he entered the third trance; and rising from the third trance, he entered the second trance;

and rising from the second trance, he entered the first trance; and rising from the first trance, he entered the second trance; and rising from the second trance, he entered the third trance; and rising from the third trance, he entered the fourth trance; and rising from the fourth trance, immediately The Blessed One passed into Nirvana.

# Ancient China

China stepped onto the stage of world history after the first great civilization, Sumer, had passed, Egypt was already in decline, and Indian civilization (or Indian literature, at least) had only recently begun, with the writing down of the Vedas. The earliest written texts in China were oracle inscriptions carved on ox bones and tortoise shells that date from approximately 1400 BCE, nearly two thousand years after the dawn of cuneiform script in Sumeria. By 1200 BCE inscriptions were also being written on ceremonial bronze vessels used in religious ceremonies performed in honor of deceased ancestors. This early script was highly sophisticated, already showing all the formative characteristics of Chinese writing as we know it today, and it must have been the result of a long period of development. In fact, some simple markings on ancient pottery indicate that the time horizon for the beginning of Chinese writing might be pushed back as far as 4000 BCE, but evidence for this remains somewhat ambiguous and inconclusive.

Each Chinese written character represents a single spoken syllable. Since the syllable in early Chinese is almost always a unit of meaning or a word, we might refer to this script as a system of "word writing." Chinese characters originated in simple pictographs and ideographs and, most productively, in the use of certain parts of characters for phonetic value alone (as we might borrow a picture of an eye as a rebus to write the first person pronoun "I"). As time passed, the script was conventionalized and simplified in ways that now mask the origins of the vast majority of written characters. Although some regard this fascinating writing system as cumbersome and difficult to master, it has held great aesthetic appeal to the majority of educated Chinese, who have traditionally counted calligraphy among the most esteemed arts and have considered the visual presentation of a text, particularly poetry, as a critical part of its aesthetic appeal.

The written word was often associated in China with centers of political and ritual control. For much of Chinese history, the state determined the educational curriculum through a complex system of civil service examinations and showed intense concern for what was written and how those writings were read and interpreted. Moreover, most of those who produced literature were members of the civil service bureaucracy, or at least aspired to such status, and had absorbed the Confucian notion that knowledge should be used to promote social and political harmony. Consequently, Chinese literature, from its beginning to the present time, is characterized by strong political or social content, and even attempts at "pure aestheticism" have been interpreted, sometimes quite surprisingly, as veiled political commentary.

Chinese literature, for the most part, was the domain of an elite group of highly educated men. However, alongside this distinguished world of the written text, there existed a rich realm of popular entertainment and oral performance. The relationship in China between elite culture and popular culture was an intimate one. Certain song forms, storytelling techniques, dramatic styles, and other literary features were borrowed from the world of popular culture and incorporated into the literature of the elite. In fact, Chinese scholars have identified a cycle in Chinese literary history that goes something like the following: a song style, to use one example, might be drawn from the common people and become the stylistic foundation of a new poetic form. For a time this new form remains fresh and vibrant, with the art of the poet adding sophistication and beauty to a still strong and rustic expression. Gradually, however, the form becomes further and further detached from its origin and develops an erudition and preciousness that drains it of life and exuberance. At this point, some new form emerges from the common people and the process of literary growth and decay begins again.

The problem with this literary cycle is that it makes use of an organic model of growth and decay to describe literary processes that are surely more complicated than the model allows. Still, it is important to note that the Chinese have typically explained both their literary and political history in precisely such ways. The hold of organic models on the Chinese imagination is not surprising, for from the earliest times China was an agricultural society concerned with the succession of the seasons and the growth, maturation, and inevitable decline of plants and crops. This agricultural way of life was threatened, or so the Chinese always believed, by the nomadic world to the north and northwest. Civilization, to the Chinese, was linked to the tract of land that a family farmed generation after generation; the roaming life of the Turkic and Mongolian herdsmen along the Inner Asian border presented a threat to this settled way of living. Despite occasional military and cultural pressure from peoples along the border, the Chinese remained thoroughly agricultural and much of their culture reflects behavior and ways of thinking that derive from a strong attachment to the land and its cycles.

The same organic model can be seen in the way Chinese mark their history. The past is organized by dynasties, periods during which a single family held the imperial sway. The dynasty, according to the Chinese notion of the dynastic cycle, begins as an energetic and powerful new government that possesses the "mandate of heaven" (*tian ming*), heaven's stamp of approval upon the moral fitness of the dynastic leaders. The government grows, usually in a century or two, to maturity and glory. The high point also marks the beginning of the period of decline, and gradually the government weakens and falls into decay, only to be overthrown and replaced by a new dynasty that begins the cycle again. The Tang dynasty (618–907 CE), for example, is said to have begun its decline with the reign of Xuan Zong (713–763) and his infatuation with the Honored Concubine Yang, a love affair immortalized in Bai Juyi's *Song of Everlasting Sorrow.* Some Chinese have argued that the greatness of high Tang literature, as it is seen in the poetry of Li Bai and Du Fu, results from the fact that their work appears in the "tension of summer," a time when the political world, like the agricultural world, is in full glory but also teeters on the very edge of decline.

The earliest landmarks of Chinese literature appear in the eight centuries of the Zhou dynasty (1045–221 BCE). The founders of the dynasty, Kings Wen and Wu and the Duke of Zhou, Wu's younger brother, were regarded throughout Chinese history as heroes. Confucius and his followers looked to the first century of this dynasty as a utopian time of political order and social harmony. The peace and stability of the early Zhou was as much a creation of later political need as it was an objective historical fact. That need arose initially from discontent over the chaos and conflict that followed the effective end of Zhou power in 771 BCE, when the Zhou court was driven from the area of modern-day Xi'an to the eastern city of Luoyang. Although the Zhou kings continued to reign for another five hundred years, they exercised only the vaguest moral authority, and power gravitated to individual feudatories that quickly became virtually independent states.

The Eastern Zhou dynasty (771–221 BCE), so-named while the capital was at Luoyang, was a prolonged period of frequent wars, great social disruption, and ideological controversy. The unrest of the period finally ceased when one of the competing states, Qin, conquered the others and founded the short-lived Qin dynasty (221–207 BCE). Popular antagonism over immense public works projects such as the Great Wall and the tomb of the First Qin Emperor brought the overthrow of the Qin and its replacement by the Han dynasty (206 BCE–220 CE), one of the longer-lived and most notable dynasties of Chinese history. The Han period was one of political and cultural consolidation. The Han rulers created a highly centralized bureaucratic state government, promoted Confucianism as a state orthodoxy, and initiated a competitive civil service entry system that required mastery of an established canon of texts. Toward the end of the Han a new cultural force, Buddhism, was introduced into China from India. Buddhism was the first major foreign influence on the Chinese cultural landscape. Its appearance marks an important break in Chinese history, so that we might speak of a "pre-Buddhist China" (the China of the "Ancient Period" in this book), and a "Buddhist China" (our "Middle Period").

Although Chinese historians look on the Eastern Zhou as a time of chaos and general unhappiness, they also acknowledge it as one of the liveliest and most important periods for Chinese literature and thought. The earliest and perhaps the greatest work of Zhou literature, the *Book of Songs,* contains at least as many works from the Western as the Eastern Zhou, but it was compiled as a text and gained canonical status during the first centuries of the Eastern Zhou. Moreover, these centuries of disunity were the age of the most significant Chinese thinkers: Confucius, Laozi, Mozi, Mencius, Zhuangzi, Xunzi, Hanfeizi, and many others. In fact, the Chinese refer to the Eastern Zhou as the time of the *zhuzi baijia:* "the many masters and the hundred schools of thought." Of these "hundred schools," Confucianism and Daoism have had the most enduring impact on Chinese civilization.

Confucianism and Daoism can be regarded as complementary philosophies that intertwined so as to fashion the intellectual and literary world of almost every educated person in traditional China. Confucianism was the philosophy of the family and the body politic. It emphasized and justified the hierarchical nature of society and treated duty and ritual behavior as essential to the maintenance of order and harmony; it looked to the past, to tradition, to teachers and fathers as sources of authority for human behavior and for social organization. Daoism, on the other hand, was the philosophy of the individual and of private life—sometimes, indeed, the philosophy of the outcast or the recluse. It valued spontaneity and, at least in the case of the philosopher Zhuangzi, the relativity and thus conditional character of all social institutions and even of language itself. Daoism taught that we should turn back to the untainted vision and joyous action of the newborn child—the person unspoiled by tradition and education. These two ways of thought functioned as a *yin* and *yang* in many Chinese lives—that is, as a kind of complementary duality in which each way, that of Confucianism and that of Daoism, had its season and its place.

Beyond the rational, pragmatic world of Confucianism and the rhapsodic, imaginative world of Daoism was another realm, that of supernatural belief and fascination for the "curious," things that Confucius himself "did not discuss." Glimpses of this world are seen in the soaring, shaman- inspired *On Encountering Sorrow,* and in Mozi's attack on a growing skepticism that he thought undermined all morality. Chinese literature, as we shall see in several of the texts in this anthology, is as much inspired by the supernatural and by the fantastic world of popular belief as by Confucian and Daoist this-worldliness.

In addition to poetry and what the Chinese would call the "texts of the masters," texts that we would describe as "philosophy" or "wisdom literature," narrative also appears in the time of the Eastern Zhou. Chinese narrative begins with the writing of history and remains profoundly engaged with history at least until the rise of the novel many centuries later. This does not mean that pure fiction was not produced, but rather that history was revered in China and became the dominant paradigm against which all narrative was evaluated and criticized. Even when the novel appeared much later, it was called in Chinese "petty talk" (*xiaoshuo*), a label that emphasized its status as not quite worthy of serious consideration.

The literature of the Han dynasty reflected the political mood of consolidation and organization. Sima Qian produced in these years the first comprehensive history of China. His vast historical text, *Records of the Historian,* helped create the notion of a unified Chinese culture that derived from a common ancestry of mythical emperors and sage-kings. The Qin and Han, according to his vision, had simply reasserted a unity that had existed long before. And Han dynasty philosophers, though sometimes proclaiming themselves as Daoists or Confucians, reflected a spirit of synthesis.

The world of ancient China developed without any major outside influence—at least without any influence we can easily trace on the pages of history. This was soon to change. The arrival of Buddhism during the first centuries of the common era posed a challenge to the indigenous traditions of the Ancient Period. The Buddhist bridge from the great civilization of India enriched China spiritually, intellectually, and artistically. China was never quite the same again.

*Note on romanization of Chinese:* There are two different systems for romanizing Chinese in use in this volume—Pinyin and Wade-Giles. All introductions and several of the readings are in the now standard Pinyin system. However, certain readings are in Wade-Giles romanization. Where confusion might result, we have provided the alternative romanization in parentheses.

# Chinese Writing

**1.** 聞古而知新可以為師矣 (*Analects* 1.15)

**2.** *Wen gu er zhi xin. ke yi wei shi yi!*

**3.** "[Warming up] [old] [and] [understanding] [new] [can] [thereby] [act as] [teacher] [indeed].

**4.** "If one reviews the old and understands the new, one can act as a teacher!"

In line 1, above, we give the Chinese text of a famous passage from the Confucian *Analects,* a text that probably derives from sometime in the fourth century BCE but purports to transmit many sayings and teachings of Confucius (551–479 BCE). The Chinese characters are written in a modern form, which derives from an imperial "script reform" that took place in the last decades of the third century BCE. Although many Chinese characters descend from pictographic representations of actual things, the script by the classical period has moved so far from that original foundation that virtually no character can be understood simply by scrutinizing its shape. Each Chinese character represents one syllable. Since the syllable in classical Chinese typically corresponds to a word, classical Chinese has sometimes been called a "monosyllabic language." Although this characterization is for the most part accurate, there are some compound words that cannot be broken down into meaningful syllables (e.g., *hudie* "butterfly"). However, the romanized version of the text above, presented in line 2, and the literal translation in line 3, wherein the meaning of each character is bracketed, demonstrate that in this example each character/syllable can be assigned a meaning, or, as linguists would say, each character here is a "morpheme." Scholars of Chinese are often asked, "How many different characters are there in Chinese?" Or, "How many characters do you have to know to read Chinese?" A standard, comprehensive dictionary of Chinese defines about forty-seven thousand different characters. No reader of Chinese knows anywhere near this number, just as no reader of English knows anywhere near the total number of words in *Webster's Unabridged Dictionary.* A good knowledge of three to four thousand characters is sufficient to read almost all texts. But, as is the case with careful readers of English, a dictionary is best kept close at hand!

## FROM THE BOOK OF SONGS (SHI JING) (1000–600 BCE)

*Translated by Arthur Waley; Steven Shankman (no. 23)*

The *Book of Songs* (*Shi jing*), a collection of 305 poems, is the earliest major work of Chinese literature. Although the individual poems that compose this collection are difficult to date precisely, most probably come from the period between 1000 and 600 BCE, a time that saw both the height of Zhou dynastic power and its subsequent decline. According to an early tradition, Confucius (551–479 BCE) edited the *Book of Songs* from a much larger body of poetry that existed in his time. Most scholars today doubt this tradition, but certainly Confucius knew these poems and taught them to his students. Several centuries after Confucius, the *Book of Songs* was included among the canonical "Five Classics" (along with the *Book of Historical Documents,* the *Book of Changes, Spring and Autumn Annals,* and the *Records of Ritual*) and was memorized by all educated Chinese for nearly two thousand years. Hence, the influence of this text on subsequent Chinese literature has been enormous.

The individual pieces in the *Book of Songs* are thematically varied but share a common poetic form. They were originally sung as part of a now lost musical tradition and were probably shaped to some degree by the structure of that early music. A four-character line predominates throughout. Since each character is read as a single syllable and usually corresponds to a single word in the fundamentally monosyllabic language of ancient China, the line is extremely brief and compact. Rhyme is also common. Indeed, Chinese poetry is unusual among the world's poetic traditions in employing extensive rhyme from its very beginnings.

Most of the poems in the *Book of Songs* are anonymous, but early Chinese interpreters ascribed the poems to important historical figures known from other sources and then typically read them as either direct or indirect commentary on specific political events from the past. The purpose of such an interpretive strategy was to draw the poems into a Confucian world that emphasized the importance of history and the need for art to play an essentially didactic role. Today most scholars reject this view and regard the poems as deriving from a rich tradition of song that was by no means confined to famous historical figures or even the aristocratic class. Certainly the poems reflect a people who lived very close to the natural world and used imagery from that world in a highly evocative way. In fact, many of the poems open with a nature image that seems to set the mood or scene for what follows. Also, many are narrated in the voices of women. Although later Chinese male poets sometimes impersonate a female speaker, these early works might actually have been composed by women singers and poets.

We have selected thirty-one pieces for inclusion here. Most are relatively brief poems with such common themes as love (nos. 1, 42, 93, 143), the desire for offspring (5), conjugal unhappiness (29, 58), the rapid passage of time (20, 115), lost friendship (81), and the cruelty of war (185, 234). The last three pieces are longer dynastic odes that sing praises to King Wen (c.1100 BCE), a founder of the Zhou dynasty (235, 241) and tell the myth of Jiang Yuan and Hou Ji (245), the original ancestors of the Zhou people.

The poems are numbered here according to their traditional "Mao" sequence. Mao (c.180 BCE) was an early editor and commentator on the *Book of Songs*. His edition of the poems became standard. Translation of these terse poems, composed with words whose meanings are often difficult to recover, is always a challenge. The selections provided here are translated by Arthur Waley, with the exception of poem 23, which is translated by Steven Shankman and preserves the four-syllable line and the rhyming structure of the original. Other translations (for example those of Karlgren) are more literal than Waley; some are less literal though perhaps more artful (those of Pound), while yet others try to capture the rhyme of the original (those of Xu).

# TRANSLATING THE *BOOK OF SONGS*

Translating the Chinese *Book of Songs* presents a number of formidable challenges. First among these is the extreme difficulty of the original Chinese, which scholars call "preclassical" because it predates the era of the great philosophical and historical texts of the fifth through first centuries BCE. In addition, these poems, as we have noted, are written in an extremely brief four-syllable line, virtually impossible to emulate in English, and are typically rhymed. There have been several complete translations of the *Book of Songs,* each quite different from the other. We invite the reader to compare three other translations of poem 81 with the version by Arthur Waley we have included. The first is a highly conservative prose translation of the Swedish philologist and sinologist Bernhard Karlgren. What one immediately notes from his translation is that the moving interpretation of Waley—that is, "friendship takes time to overcome"—is problematic. The second translation comes from James Legge, a nineteenth-century translator who attempted to replicate the rhyme of the original, something Waley ignored. The third translation is from the great poet Ezra Pound (see pp. 2168–2173), who did not read Chinese but adapted his versions from those of such sinologists as Karlgren, Waley, and Legge:

***Karlgren:*** 1. I go along the great road, I grasp your sleeve; do not hate me, do not brusque an old friend. 2. I go along the great road, I grasp your hand; do not reject me, do not brusque a loving friend.

(*Bulletin of the Museum of Far Eastern Antiquities,* Vol. 16 [1949], p. 1944.)

***Legge:***

Along the great highway,
I hold you by the cuff.
O spurn me not, I pray,
Nor break old friendship off.

Along the highway worn,
I hold your hand in mine.
Do not as vile me scorn;
Your love I can't resign.

(*The She King or The Book of Poetry* [London: Trubner & Co, 1876], p. 193.)

***Pound:***

I plucked your sleeve by the way, that you should pause.
Cast not an old friend off without cause.

That a hand's clasp in a high road could thee move:
Scorn not an old friend's love.

(*The Classic Anthology as Defined by Confucius* [Cambridge: Harvard University Press, 1954], p. 40.)

## 1: "'Fair, fair,' cry the ospreys"

'Fair, fair,' cry the ospreys
On the island in the river.
Lovely is this noble lady,
Fit bride for our lord.

In patches grows the water mallow;
To left and right one must seek it.
Shy was this noble lady;
Day and night he sought her.

Sought her and could not get her;
Day and night he grieved.
Long thoughts, oh, long unhappy thoughts,
Now on his back, now tossing on to his side.

In patches grows the water mallow;
To left and right one must gather it.
Shy is this noble lady;
With great zithern and little we hearten her.

## 5: "The locusts' wings say 'throng throng'"

The locusts' wings say 'throng, throng';
Well may your sons and grandsons
Be a host innumerable.

The locusts' wings say 'bind, bind';
Well may your sons and grandsons
Continue in an endless line.

The locusts' wings say 'join, join';
Well may your sons and grandsons
Be forever at one.

## 20: "Plop fall the plums; but there are still seven"

Plop fall the plums; but there are still seven.
Let those gentlemen that would court me
Come while it is lucky!

Plop fall the plums; there are still three.
Let any gentleman that would court me
Come before it is too late!

Plop fall the plums; in shallow baskets we lay them.
Any gentleman who would court me
Had better speak while there is time.

## 23: "Fields show dead deer"

Fields show dead deer.
White reeds wrap her.
Spring draws girl near.
White knight clasps her.

In the thick brush
A dead deer—hush!—
Bound in white rush.
Jade girl was such.

"Slowly, gently, Oh!
Touch my sash not, No!
Should the dog bark, Oh!"

## 26: "Tossed is that cypress boat"

Tossed is that cypress boat,
Wave-tossed it floats.
My heart is in turmoil, I cannot sleep.
But secret is my grief.
Wine I have, all things needful
For play, for sport.

My heart is not a mirror,
To reflect what others will.
Brothers too I have;
I cannot be snatched away.
But lo, when I told them of my plight
I found that they were angry with me.

My heart is not a stone;
It cannot be rolled.
My heart is not a mat;
It cannot be folded away.
I have borne myself correctly
In rites more than can be numbered.

My sad heart is consumed, I am harassed
By a host of small men.

I have borne vexations very many,
Received insults not few.
In the still of night I brood upon it;
In the waking hours I rend my breast.

O sun, ah, moon,
Why are you changed and dim?
Sorrow clings to me
Like an unwashed dress.
In the still of night I brood upon it,
Long to take wing and fly away.

## 29: "O sun, ah, moon"

O Sun, ah, moon
That shine upon the earth below,
A man like this
Will not stand firm to the end.
How can such a one be true?
Better if he had never noticed me.

O sun, ah, moon
That cover the earth below,
A man like this
Will not deal kindly to the end.
How can such a one be true?
Better if he had not requited me.

O sun, ah, moon
That rise out of the east,
A man like this,
Of whom no good word is said,
How can he be true?
I wish I could forget him.

O sun, ah, moon
That from the east do rise,
Heigh, father! Ho, mother,
You have nurtured me to no good end.
How should he be true?
He requited me, but did not follow-up.

## 30: "Wild and windy was the day"

Wild and windy was the day;
You looked at me and laughed,

But the jest was cruel, and the laughter mocking.
My heart within is sore.

There was a great sandstorm that day;
Kindly you made as though to come,
Yet neither came nor went away.
Long, long my thoughts.

A great wind and darkness;
Day after day it is dark.
I lie awake, cannot sleep,
And gasp with longing.

Dreary, dreary the gloom;
The thunder growls.
I lie awake, cannot sleep,
And am destroyed with longing.

## 32: "When a gentle wind from the south"

When a gentle wind from the south
Blows to the heart of those thorn-bushes
The heart of the thorn-bushes is freshened;
But our mother had only grief and care.

A gentle wind from the south
Blows on that brushwood of the thorn-tree.
Our mother was wise and kind;
But among us is no good man.

Yonder is a cold spring
Under the burgh of Hsün.
There were sons, seven men;
Yet their mother had only grief and care.

Pretty is that yellow oriole
And pleasant its tune.
There were sons, seven men,
Yet none could soothe his mother's heart.

## 40: "I go out at the northern gate"

I go out at the northern gate;
Deep is my grief.
I am utterly poverty-stricken and destitute;
Yet no one heeds my misfortunes.
Well, all is over now.

No doubt it was Heaven's doing,
So what's the good of talking about it?

The king's business came my way;
Government business of every sort was put upon me.
When I came in from outside
The people of the house all turned on me and scolded me.
Well, it's over now.
No doubt it was Heaven's doing,
So what's the good of talking about it?

The king's business was all piled upon me;
Government business of every sort was laid upon me.
When I came in from outside
The people of the house all turned upon me and abused me.
Well, it's over now.
No doubt it was Heaven's doing,
So what's the good of talking about it?

## 41: "Cold blows the northern wind"

Cold blows the northern wind,
Thick falls the snow.
Be kind to me, love me,
Take my hand and go with me.
Yet she lingers, yet she havers!
There is no time to lose.

The north wind whistles,
Whirls the falling snow.
Be kind to me, love me,
Take my hand and go home with me.
Yet she lingers, yet she havers!
There is no time to lose.

Nothing is redder than the fox,
Nothing blacker than the crow.
Be kind to me, love me,
Take my hand and ride with me.
Yet she lingers, yet she havers!
There is no time to lose.

## 42: "Of fair girls the loveliest"

Of fair girls the loveliest
Was to meet me at the corner of the Wall.

But she hides and will not show herself;
I scratch my head, pace up and down.

Of fair girls the prettiest
Gave me a red flute.
The flush of that red flute
Is pleasure at the girl's beauty.

She has been in the pastures and brought for me rush-wool,
Very beautiful and rare.
It is not you that are beautiful;
But you were given by a lovely girl.

## 45: "Unsteady is that cypress boat"

Unsteady is that cypress boat
In the middle of the river.
His two locks looped over his brow
He swore that truly he was my comrade,
And till death would love no other.
Oh, mother, ah, Heaven,
That a man could be so false!

Unsteady is that boat of cypress-wood
By that river's side.
His two locks looped over his brow
He swore that truly he was my mate,
And till death would not fail me.
Oh, mother, ah, Heaven,
That a man could be so false!

## 58: "We thought you were a simple peasant"

We thought you were a simple peasant
Bringing cloth to exchange for thread.
But you had not come to buy thread;
You had come to arrange about me.
You were escorted across the Ch'i
As far as Beacon Hill.
'It is not I who want to put it off;
But you have no proper match-maker.
Please do not be angry;
Let us fix on autumn as the time.'

I climbed that high wall
To catch a glimpse of Fu-kuan,
And when I could not see Fu-kuan

My tears fell flood on flood.
At last I caught sight of Fu-kuan,
And how gaily I laughed and talked!
You consulted your yarrow-stalks
And their patterns showed nothing unlucky.
You came with your cart
And moved me and my dowry.

Before the mulberry-tree sheds its leaves,
How soft and glossy they are!
O dove, turtle-dove,
Do not eat the mulberries!
O ladies, ladies,
Do not take your pleasure with men.
For a man to take his pleasure
Is a thing that may be condoned.
That a girl should take her pleasure
Cannot be condoned.

The mulberry leaves have fallen
All yellow and seared.
Since I came to you,
Three years I have eaten poverty.
The waters of the Ch'i were in flood;
They wetted the curtains of the carriage.
It was not I who was at fault;
It is you who have altered your ways,
It is you who are unfaithful,
Whose favours are cast this way and that.

Three years I was your wife.
I never neglected my work.
I rose early and went to bed late;
Never did I idle.
First you took to finding fault with me,
Then you became rough with me.
My brothers disowned me;
'Ho, ho,' they laughed.
And when I think calmly over it,
I see that it was I who brought all this upon myself.

I swore to grow old along with you;
I am old, and have got nothing from you but trouble.
The Ch'i has its banks,
The swamp has its sides;
With hair looped and ribboned

How gaily you talked and laughed,
And how solemnly you swore to be true,
So that I never thought there could be a change.
No, of a change I never thought;
And that *this* should be the end!

## 61: "Who says that the River is broad"

Who says that the River is broad?
On a single reed you could cross it.
Who says that Sung is far away?
By standing on tip-toe I can see it.

Who says that the River is broad?
There is not room in it even for a skiff.
Who says that Sung is far away?
It could not take you so much as a morning.

## 69: "In the midst of the valley is motherwort"

In the midst of the valley is motherwort
All withered and dry.
A girl on her own,
Bitterly she sobs,
Bitterly she sobs,
Faced with man's unkindness.

In the midst of the valley is motherwort
All withered and seared.
A girl on her own,
Long she sighs,
Long she sighs,
Faced with man's wickedness.

In the midst of the valley is motherwort
All withered and parched.
A girl on her own,
In anguish she weeps,
In anguish she weeps;
But what does grief avail?

## 76: "I beg of you, Chung Tzu"

I beg of you, Chung Tzu,
Do not climb into our homestead,
Do not break the willows we have planted.
Not that I mind about the willows,

But I am afraid of my father and mother.
Chung Tzu I dearly love;
But of what my father and mother say
Indeed I am afraid.

I beg of you, Chung Tzu,
Do not climb over our wall,
Do not break the mulberry-trees we have planted.
Not that I mind about the mulberry-trees,
But I am afraid of my brothers.
Chung Tzu I dearly love;
But of what my brothers say
Indeed I am afraid.

I beg of you, Chung Tzu,
Do not climb into our garden,
Do not break the hard-wood we have planted.
Not that I mind about the hard-wood,
But I am afraid of what people will say.
Chung Tzu I dearly love;
But of all that people will say
Indeed I am afraid.

## 81: "If along the highroad"

If along the highroad
I caught hold of your sleeve,
Do not hate me;
Old ways take time to overcome.

If along the highroad
I caught hold of your hand,
Do not be angry with me;
Friendship takes time to overcome.

## 92: "Even the rising waters"

Even the rising waters
Will not carry off thorn-faggots that are well bound.
Brothers while life lasts
Are you and I.
Do not believe what people say;
People are certainly deceiving you.

Even the rising waters
Will not carry off firewood that is well tied.

Brothers while life lasts
Are we two men.
Do not believe what people say;
People are certainly not to be believed.

## 93: "Outside the Eastern Gate"

Outside the Eastern Gate
Are girls many as the clouds;
But though they are many as clouds
There is none on whom my heart dwells.
White jacket and grey scarf
Alone could cure my woe.

Beyond the Gate Tower
Are girls lovely as rush-wool;
But though they are lovely as rush-wool
There is none with whom my heart bides.
White jacket and madder skirt
Alone could bring me joy.

## 104: "In the wicker fish-trap by the bridge"

In the wicker fish-trap by the bridge
Are fish, both bream and roach.
A lady of Ch'i goes to be married;
Her escort is like a trail of clouds.

In the wicker fish-trap by the bridge
Are fish, both bream and tench.
A lady of Ch'i goes to be married;
Her escort is thick as rain.

In the wicker fish-trap by the bridge
The fish glide free.
A lady of Ch'i goes to be married;
Her escort is like a river.

## 110: "I climb that wooded hill"

I climb that wooded hill
And look towards where my father is.
My father is saying, 'Alas, my son is on service;
Day and night he knows no rest.
Grant that he is being careful of himself,
So that he may come back and not be left behind!'

I climb that bare hill
And look towards where my mother is.
My mother is saying, 'Alas, my young one is on service;
Day and night he gets no sleep.
Grant that he is being careful of himself,
So that he may come back, and not be cast away.'

I climb that ridge
And look towards where my elder brother is.
My brother is saying, 'Alas, my young brother is on service;
Day and night he toils.
Grant that he is being careful of himself,
So that he may come back and not die.'

## 115: "On the mountain is the thorn-elm"

On the mountain is the thorn-elm;
On the low ground the white elm-tree.
You have long robes,
But do not sweep or trail them.
You have carriages and horses,
But do not gallop or race them.
When you are dead
Someone else will enjoy them.

On the mountain is the cedrela;
On the low ground the privet.
You have courtyard and house,
But you do not sprinkle or sweep them.
You have bells and drums,
But you do not play on them, beat them.
When you are dead
Someone else will treasure them.

On the mountain is the varnish-tree;
On the low ground the chestnut.
You have wine and meat;
Why do you not daily play your zithern,
And perhaps once in a way be merry,
Once in a way sit up late?
When you are dead
Someone else will enter into your house.

## 143: "A moon rising white"

A moon rising white
Is the beauty of my lovely one.

Ah, the tenderness, the grace!
Heart's pain consumes me.

A moon rising bright
Is the fairness of my lovely one.
Ah, the gentle softness!
Heart's pain wounds me.

A moon rising in splendour
Is the beauty of my lovely one.
Ah, the delicate yielding!
Heart's pain torments me.

## 166: "May Heaven guard and keep you"

May Heaven guard and keep you
In great security,
Make you staunch and hale;
What blessing not vouchsafed?
Give you much increase,
Send nothing but abundance.

May Heaven guard and keep you,
Cause your grain to prosper,
Send you nothing that is not good.
May you receive from Heaven a hundred boons,
May Heaven send down to you blessings so many
That the day is not long enough for them all.

May Heaven guard and keep you,
Cause there to be nothing in which you do not rise higher,
Like the mountains, like the uplands,
Like the ridges, the great ranges,
Like a stream coming down in flood;
In nothing not increased.

Lucky and pure are your viands of sacrifice
That you use in filial offering,
Offerings of invocation, gift-offerings, offering in dishes and offering of first-fruits
To dukes and former kings.
Those sovereigns say: 'We give you
Myriad years of life, days unending.'

The Spirits are good,
They will give you many blessings.

The common people are contented,
For daily they have their drink and food.
The thronging herd, the many clans—
All side with you in deeds of power.

To be like the moon advancing to its full,
Like the sun climbing the sky,
Like the everlastingness of the southern hills,
Without failing or falling,
Like the pine-tree, the cypress in their verdure—
All these blessings may you receive!

## 185: "Minister of War"

Minister of War,
We are the king's claws and fangs.
Why should you roll us on from misery to misery,
Giving us no place to stop in or take rest?

Minister of War,
We are the king's claws and teeth.
Why should you roll us from misery to misery,
Giving us no place to come to and stay?

## 201: "Zip, zip the valley wind"

Zip, zip the valley wind!
Nothing but wind and rain.
In days of peril, in days of dread
It was always 'I and you.'
Now in time of peace, of happiness,
You have cast me aside.

Zip, zip the valley wind!
Nothing but wind and duststorms.
In days of peril, in days of dread
You put me in your bosom.
Now in time of peace, of happiness
You throw me away like slop-water.

Zip, zip the valley wind
Across the rocky hills.
No grass but is dying,
No tree but is wilting.
You forget my great merits,
Remember only my small faults.

## 230: "Tender and pretty are the yellow orioles"

Tender and pretty are the yellow orioles
Perching on the side of the hill.
The way is long;
I am so tired. What will become of me?
'Let him have a drink, let him have some food,
Give him a lesson, scold him,
But bid that hind coach
Call to him and pick him up.'

Tender and pretty are the yellow orioles
Perching on the corner of the hill.
How dare I shirk marching?
But I fear I cannot keep up.
'Let him have a drink, let him have some food,
Give him a lesson, scold him,
But bid that hind coach
Call to him and pick him up.'

Tender and pretty are the yellow orioles
Perching on the side of the hill.
How dare I shirk marching?
But I fear I shall not hold out.
'Let him have a drink, let him have some food,
Give him a lesson, scold him,
But bid that hind coach
Call to him and pick him up.'

## 234: "What plant is not faded?"

What plant is not faded?
What day do we not march?
What man is not taken
To defend the four bounds?

What plant is not wilting?
What man is not taken from his wife?
Alas for us soldiers,
Treated as though we were not fellow-men!

Are we buffaloes, are we tigers
That our home should be these desolate wilds?
Alas for us soldiers,
Neither by day nor night can we rest!

The fox bumps and drags
Through the tall, thick grass.
Inch by inch move our barrows
As we push them along the track.

## 235: "King Wên is on high"

King Wên is on high;
Oh, he shines in Heaven!
Chou is an old people,
But its charge is new.
The land of Chou became illustrious,
Blessed by God's charge.
King Wên ascends and descends
On God's left hand, on His right.

Very diligent was King Wên,
His high fame does not cease;
He spread his bounties in Chou,
And now in his grandsons and sons,
In his grandsons and sons
The stem has branched
Into manifold generations,
And all the knights of Chou
Are glorious in their generation.

Glorious in their generation,
And their counsels well pondered.
Mighty were the many knights
That brought this kingdom to its birth.
This kingdom well they bore;
They were the prop of Chou.
Splendid were those many knights
Who gave comfort to Wên the king.

August is Wên the king;
Oh, to be reverenced in his glittering light!
Mighty the charge that Heaven gave him.
The grandsons and sons of the Shang,
Shang's grandsons and sons,
Their hosts were innumerable.
But God on high gave His command,
And by Chou they were subdued.

By Chou they were subdued;
Heaven's charge is not for ever.

The knights of Yin, big and little,
Made libations and offerings at the capital;
What they did was to make libations
Dressed in skirted robe and close cap.
O chosen servants of the king,
May you never thus shame your ancestors!

May you never shame your ancestors,
But rather tend their inward power,
That for ever you may be linked to Heaven's charge
And bring to yourselves many blessings.
Before Yin lost its army
It was well linked to God above.
In Yin you should see as in a mirror
That Heaven's high charge is hard to keep.

The charge is not easy to keep.
Do not bring ruin on yourselves.
Send forth everywhere the light of your good fame;
Consider what Heaven did to the Yin.
High Heaven does its business
Without sound, without smell.
Make King Wên your example,
In whom all the peoples put their trust.

## 241: "God on high in sovereign might"

God on high in sovereign might
Looked down majestically,
Gazed down upon the four quarters,
Examining the ills of the people.
Already in two kingdoms
The governance had been all awry;
Then every land
He tested and surveyed.
God on high examined them
And hated the laxity of their rule.
So he turned his gaze to the west
And here made his dwelling-place.

Cleared them, moved them,
The dead trees, the fallen trunks;
Trimmed them, levelled them,
The clumps and stumps;
Opened them, cleft them,
The tamarisk woods, the stave-tree woods;

Pulled them up, cut them back,
The wild mulberries, the cudranias.
God shifted his bright Power;
To fixed customs and rules he gave a path.
Heaven set up for itself a counterpart on earth;
Its charge was firmly awarded.

God examined his hills.
The oak-trees were uprooted,
The pines and cypresses were cleared.
God made a land, made a counterpart,
Beginning with T'ai-po and Wang Chi.
Now this Wang Chi
Was of heart accommodating and friendly,
Friendly to his elder brother,
So that his luck was strong.
Great were the gifts that were bestowed upon him,
Blessings he received and no disasters,
Utterly he swayed the whole land.

Then came King Wên;
God set right measure to his thoughts,
Spread abroad his fair fame;
His power was very bright,
Very bright and very good.
Well he led, well lorded,
Was king over this great land.
Well he followed, well obeyed,
Obeyed—did King Wên.
His power was without flaw.
Having received God's blessing
He handed it down to grandsons and sons.

God said to King Wên:
'This is no time to be idle,
No time to indulge in your desires.
You must be first to seize the high places.
The people of Mi are in revolt.
They have dared to oppose the great kingdom.
They have invaded Yüan and Kung.'
The king blazed forth his anger;
He marshalled his armies,
To check the foe he marched to Lü,
He secured the safety of Chou,
He united all under Heaven.

They drew near to the capital,
Attacking from the borders of Yüan.
They began to climb our high ridges;
But never did they marshal their forces on our hills,
Our hills or slopes,
Never did they drink out of our wells,
Our wells, our pools.
The king made his dwelling in the foothills and plains,
Dwelt in the southern slopes of Mount Ch'i,
On the shores of the River Wei,
Pattern to all the myriad lands,
King of his subject peoples.

God said to King Wên,
'I am moved by your bright power.
Your high renown has not made you put on proud airs,
Your greatness has not made you change former ways,
You do not try to be clever or knowing,
But follow God's precepts.'
God said to King Wên,
'Take counsel with your partner states,
Unite with your brothers young and old,
And with your scaling ladders and siege-platforms
Attack the castles of Ch'ung.'

The siege-platforms trembled,
The walls of Ch'ung towered high.
The culprits were bound quietly,
Ears were cut off peacefully.
He made the sacrifice to Heaven and the sacrifice of propitiation.
He annexed the spirits of the land, he secured continuance of the
ancestral sacrifices,
And none anywhere dared affront him.
The siege-platforms shook,
So high were the walls of Ch'ung.
He attacked, he harried,
He cut off, he destroyed.
None anywhere dared oppose him.

## 245: "She who in the beginning gave birth to the people"

She who in the beginning gave birth to the people,
This was Chiang Yüan.
How did she give birth to the people?
Well she sacrificed and prayed

That she might no longer be childless.
She trod on the big toe of God's footprint,
Was accepted and got what she desired.
Then in reverence, then in awe
She gave birth, she nurtured;
And this was Hou Chi.

Indeed, she had fulfilled her months,
And her first-born came like a lamb
With no bursting or rending,
With no hurt or harm.
To make manifest His magic power
God on high gave her ease.
So blessed were her sacrifice and prayer
That easily she bore her child.

Indeed, they put it in a narrow lane;
But oxen and sheep tenderly cherished it.
Indeed, they put it in a far-off wood;
But it chanced that woodcutters came to this wood.
Indeed, they put it on the cold ice;
But the birds covered it with their wings.
The birds at last went away,
And Hou Chi began to wail.

Truly far and wide
His voice was very loud.
Then sure enough he began to crawl;
Well he straddled, well he reared,
To reach food for his mouth.
He planted large beans;
His beans grew fat and tall.
His paddy-lines were close set,
His hemp and wheat grew thick,
His young gourds teemed.

Truly Hou Chi's husbandry
Followed the way that had been shown.
He cleared away the thick grass,
He planted the yellow crop.
It failed nowhere, it grew thick,
It was heavy, it was tall,
It sprouted, it eared,
It was firm and good,
It nodded, it hung—
He made house and home in T'ai.

Indeed, the lucky grains were sent down to us,
The black millet, the double-kernelled,
Millet pink-sprouted and white.
Far and wide the black and the double-kernelled
He reaped and acred;
Far and wide the millet pink and white
He carried in his arms, he bore on his back,
Brought them home, and created the sacrifice.

Indeed, what are they, our sacrifices?
We pound the grain, we bale it out,
We sift, we tread,
We wash it—soak, soak;
We boil it all steamy.
Then with due care, due thought
We gather southernwood, make offering of fat,
Take lambs for the rite of expiation,
We roast, we broil,
To give a start to the coming year.

High we load the stands,
The stands of wood and of earthenware.
As soon as the smell rises
God on high is very pleased:
'What smell is this, so strong and good?'
Hou-chi founded the sacrifices,
And without blemish or flaw
They have gone on till now.

## Confucius (551–479 BCE)

Confucius (551–479 BCE) was the single most influential Chinese thinker. He was born in a time of political and social turmoil when the Zhou (Chou) dynasty kings had become little more than figureheads, and real power had shifted to the ruling families of competing states. Many of the older hereditary aristocrats had also begun to lose influence as the ruling families strove to undermine the power of their rivals. Confucius, who descended from an old family of declining status and grew up in the relatively small state of Lu, looked back to the early Zhou dynasty as a golden age when wise kings presided over a unified and relatively peaceful China. His goal was to serve his state in a way that would help restore the good government of the past, but he was not particularly successful in political life. He eventually left Lu and traveled throughout China seeking influence in a series of feudal states other than his own. He was highly successful as a teacher, however, and gradually gathered a group of followers who were to have considerable influence themselves and were to keep his intellectual tradition alive. He spent the last years of his life back in his native state of Lu teaching. According to a now largely discounted tradition, he also edited the series of texts that were later known as the "Five Classics" (the *Book of Songs,* the *Book of Historical Documents,* the *Book of Changes, Spring and Autumn Annals,* and the *Records of Ritual*). Confucius is remembered mainly as a teacher—the first great teacher in a civilization in which teachers came to be held in the highest esteem.

Confucius probably played no role in the collection of the *Analects* (*Lun yu*) or "Sayings." Several compilations of his teachings and those of his early disciples appeared within the century after the Master's death, and these were eventually edited as the *Analects.* This text consists of relatively short sayings, dialogues, and descriptions of Confucius and his disciples. Although passages on a particular topic sometimes appear in proximity to each other, the organization of the text is often quite loose. The current text is made up of twenty chapters and consists of several different layers. Chapters three to eight may constitute the earliest core; chapters one and two and ten to fifteen form a second layer; and chapters sixteen to twenty are the most recent in origin. Though the precise history of the text may now be of interest only to specialists, the entire *Analects* was read and memorized by many throughout the course of Chinese history as an authoritative mirror of Confucius' actual teachings. We have therefore made a selection of passages from across the entire work.

Confucius, above all, was a student and a teacher. The *Analects* open with the Master proclaiming the "pleasure" of "having learned something" (1.1), and his own short self-description begins with the statement that "at fifteen I set my heart on learning" (2.4). Elsewhere he says that he can "teach without growing weary" (5.2, 7.34). What Confucius studied and taught was essentially a knowledge of the history and literature of the past. In fact, he proudly describes himself as one who "transmits" and "does not innovate" (7.1). He wished to preserve a cultural tradition that he believed was in decline and threatened with extinction. To regard the Master's voice as only a conservative one, however, is to oversimplify. In addition to emphasizing the importance of the formal ritual behavior (*li*) he inherited from the older aristocracy, he spoke frequently of "benevolence" (*ren*). Confucius apparently wanted to revive tradition by filling older social and ritual forms—forms that had often become quite empty—with a new humanistic spirit: "What can a man do with the rites," he asks, "who is not benevolent?" (3.3). He also wished to create a new "gentleman" (*junzi*) who was not necessarily high-born, as the Chinese term implies, but who was, above all, a model of moral behavior dedicated to "helping others realize what is good in them" (12.16).

Despite the Master's own subtly complex and humane attitudes, the voice of Confucius was used most frequently in China to buttress the authority of rulers, parents, men, and the past. There is, indeed, much in the *Analects* to sustain such a reading. Nevertheless, the book remains a repository of ancient wisdom that can repeatedly surprise and inspire, particularly as it is read and reread at different stages of one's life.

No English translation of the *Analects* can possibly capture the compactness of the original. For example, the fourteen Chinese syllables (and hence written characters) of 1.16 take three times as many English syllables in the reliable translation of D.C. Lau included here. Moreover, the parallelism, rhythm, and general verbal power of the classical Chinese text, qualities that have endeared the *Analects* to generations of Chinese readers, also tend to disappear as the text is rendered into English.

## *from The Analects*

*Translated by D.C. Lau*

**1.1** The Master said, 'Is it not a pleasure, having learned something, to try it out at due intervals? Is it not a joy to have friends come from afar? Is it not gentlemanly not to take offence when others fail to appreciate your abilities?'

**1.2** Yu Tzu said, 'It is rare for a man whose character is such that he is good as a son and obedient as a young man to have the inclination to transgress against his superiors; it is unheard of for one who has no such inclination to be inclined to start a rebellion. The gentleman devotes his efforts to the roots, for once the roots are established, the Way will grow therefrom. Being good as a son and obedient as a young man is, perhaps, the root of a man's character.'

**1.3** The Master said, 'It is rare, indeed, for a man with cunning words and an ingratiating face to be benevolent.'

**1.4** Tseng Tzu said, 'Every day I examine myself on three counts. In what I have undertaken on another's behalf, have I failed to do my best? In my dealings with my friends have I failed to be trustworthy in what I say? Have I passed on to others anything that I have not tried out myself?'

**1.5** The Master said, 'In guiding a state of a thousand chariots, approach your duties with reverence and be trustworthy in what you say; avoid excesses in expenditure and love your fellow men; employ the labour of the common people only in the right seasons.'

**1.6** The Master said, 'A young man should be a good son at home and an obedient young man abroad, sparing of speech but trustworthy in what he says, and should love the multitude at large but cultivate the friendship of his fellow men. If he has any energy to spare from such action, let him devote it to making himself cultivated.'

**1.7** Tzu-hsia said, 'I would grant that a man has received instruction who appreciates men of excellence where other men appreciate beautiful women, who exerts himself to the utmost in the service of his parents and offers his person to the service of his lord, and who, in his dealings with his friends, is trustworthy in what he says, even though he may say that he has never been taught.'

**1.8** The Master said, 'A gentleman who lacks gravity does not inspire awe. A gentleman who studies is unlikely to be inflexible.

'Make it your guiding principle to do your best for others and to be trustworthy in what you say. Do not accept as friend anyone who is not as good as you.

'When you make a mistake, do not be afraid of mending your ways.'

**1.9** Tseng Tzu said, 'Conduct the funeral of your parents with meticulous care and let not sacrifices to your remote ancestors be forgotten, and the virtue of the common people will incline towards fullness.'

**1.11** The Master said, 'Observe what a man has in mind to do when his father is living, and then observe what he does when his father is dead. If, for three years, he makes no changes to his father's ways, he can be said to be a good son.'

**1.12** Yu Tzu said, 'Of the things brought about by the rites, harmony is the most valuable. Of the ways of the Former Kings, this is the most beautiful, and is followed alike in matters great and small, yet this will not always work: to aim always at harmony without regulating it by the rites simply because one knows only about harmony will not, in fact, work.'

**1.14** The Master said, 'The gentleman seeks neither a full belly nor a comfortable home. He is quick in action but cautious in speech. He goes to men possessed of the Way to be put right. Such a man can be described as eager to learn.'

**1.16** The Master said, 'It is not the failure of others to appreciate your abilities that should trouble you, but rather your failure to appreciate theirs.'

**2.1** The Master said, 'The rule of virtue can be compared to the Pole Star which commands the homage of the multitude of stars without leaving its place.'

**2.2** The Master said, 'The *Odes* are three hundred in number. They can be summed up in one phrase,

Swerving not from the right path.'

**2.3** The Master said, 'Guide them by edicts, keep them in line with punishments, and the common people will stay out of trouble but will have no sense of shame. Guide them by virtue, keep them in line with the rites, and they will, besides having a sense of shame, reform themselves.'

**2.4** The Master said, 'At fifteen I set my heart on learning; at thirty I took my stand; at forty I came to be free from doubts; at fifty I understood the Decree of Heaven; at sixty my ear was atuned; at seventy I followed my heart's desire without overstepping the line.'

**2.6** Meng Wu Po asked about being filial. The Master said, 'Give your father and mother no other cause for anxiety than illness.'

**2.7** Tzu-yu asked about being filial. The Master said, 'Nowadays for a man to be filial means no more than that he is able to provide his parents with food. Even hounds and horses are, in some way, provided with food. If a man shows no reverence, where is the difference?'

**2.9** The Master asked, 'I can speak to Hui all day without his disagreeing with me in any way. Thus he would seem to be stupid. However, when I take a closer look at what he does in private after he has withdrawn from my presence, I discover that it does, in fact, throw light on what I said. Hui is not stupid after all.'

**2.10** The Master said, 'Look at the means a man employs, observe the path he takes and examine where he feels at home. In what way is a man's true character hidden from view? In what way is a man's true character hidden from view?'

**2.11** The Master said, 'A man is worthy of being a teacher who gets to know what is new by keeping fresh in his mind what he is already familiar with.'

**2.13** Tzu-kung asked about the gentleman. The Master said, 'He puts his words into action before allowing his words to follow his action.'

**2.15** The Master said, 'If one learns from others but does not think, one will be bewildered. If, on the other hand, one thinks but does not learn from others, one will be in peril.'

**2.17** The Master said, 'Yu, shall I tell you what it is to know. To say you know when you know, and to say you do not when you do not, that is knowledge.'

**2.18** Tzu-chang was studying with an eye to an official career. The Master said, 'Use your ears widely but leave out what is doubtful; repeat the rest with caution and you will make few mistakes. Use your eyes widely and leave out what is hazardous; put the rest into practice with caution and you will have few regrets. When in your speech you make few mistakes and in your action you have few regrets, an official career will follow as a matter of course.'

**2.24** The Master said, 'To offer sacrifice to the spirit of an ancestor not one's own is obsequious.

'Faced with what is right, to leave it undone shows a lack of courage.'

**3.3** The Master said, 'What can a man do with the rites who is not benevolent? What can a man do with music who is not benevolent?'

**3.4** Lin Fang asked about the basis of the rites. The Master said, 'A noble question indeed! With the rites, it is better to err on the side of frugality than on the side of extravagance; in mourning, it is better to err on the side of grief than on the side of formality.'

**3.7** The Master said, 'There is no contention between gentlemen. The nearest to it is, perhaps, archery. In archery they bow and make way for one another as they go up and on coming down they drink together. Even the way they contend is gentlemanly.'

**3.12** 'Sacrifice as if present' is taken to mean 'sacrifice to the gods as if the gods were present.'

The Master, however, said, 'Unless I take part in a sacrifice, it is as if I did not sacrifice.'

**3.15** When the Master went inside the Grand Temple, he asked questions about everything. Someone remarked, 'Who said that the son of the man from Tsou understood the rites? When he went inside the Grand Temple, he asked questions about everything.'

The Master, on hearing of this, said, 'The asking of questions is in itself the correct rite.'

**3.26** The Master said, 'What can I find worthy of note in a man who is lacking in tolerance when in high position, in reverence when performing the rites and in sorrow when in mourning?'

**4.1** The Master said, 'Of neighborhoods benevolence is the most beautiful. How can the man be considered wise who, when he has the choice, does not settle in benevolence?'

**4.2** The Master said, 'One who is not benevolent cannot remain long in straitened circumstances, nor can he remain long in easy circumstances.

'The benevolent man is attracted to benevolence because he feels at home in it. The wise man is attracted to benevolence because he finds it to his advantage.'

**4.3** The Master said, 'It is only the benevolent man who is capable of liking or disliking other men.'

**4.4** The Master said, 'If a man sets his heart on benevolence, he will be free from evil.'

**4.5** The Master said, 'Wealth and high station are what men desire but unless I got them in the right way I would not remain in them. Poverty and low station are what men dislike, but even if I did not get them in the right way I would not try to escape from them.

'If the gentleman forsakes benevolence, in what way can he make a name for himself? The gentleman never deserts benevolence, not even for as long as it takes to eat a meal. If he hurries and stumbles one may be sure that it is in benevolence that he does so.'

**4.6** The Master said, 'I have never met a man who finds benevolence attractive or a man who finds unbenevolence repulsive. A man who finds benevolence attractive cannot be surpassed. A man who finds unbenevolence repulsive can, perhaps, be counted as benevolent, for he would not allow what is not benevolent to contaminate his person.

'Is there a man who, for the space of a single day, is able to devote all his strength to benevolence? I have not come across such a man whose strength proves insufficient for the task. There must be such cases of insufficient strength, only I have not come across them.'

**4.9** The Master said, 'There is no point in seeking the views of a Gentleman, who, though he sets his heart on the Way, is ashamed of poor food and poor clothes.'

**4.10** The Master said, 'In his dealings with the world the gentleman is not invariably for or against anything. He is on the side of what is moral.'

**4.11** The Master said, 'While the gentleman cherishes benign rule, the small man cherishes his native land. While the gentleman cherishes a respect for the law, the small man cherishes generous treatment.'

**4.12** The Master said, 'If one is guided by profit in one's actions, one will incur much ill will.'

**4.14** The Master said, 'Do not worry because you have no official position. Worry about your qualifications. Do not worry because no one appreciates your abilities. Seek to be worthy of appreciation.'

**4.16** The Master said, 'The gentleman understands what is moral. The small man understands what is profitable.'

**4.17** The Master said, 'When you meet someone better than yourself, turn your thoughts to becoming his equal. When you meet someone not as good as you are, look within and examine your own self.'

**4.18** The Master said, 'In serving your father and mother you ought to dissuade them from doing wrong in the gentlest way. If you see your advice being ignored, you should not become disobedient but remain reverent. You should not complain even if in so doing you wear yourself out.'

**4.19** The Master said, 'While your parents are alive, you should not go too far afield in your travels. If you do, your whereabouts should always be known.'

**4.20** The Master said, 'If, for three years, a man makes no changes to his father's ways, he can be said to be a good son.'

**4.21** The Master said, 'A man should not be ignorant of the age of his father and mother. It is a matter, on the one hand, for rejoicing and, on the other, for anxiety.'

**4.22** The Master said, 'In antiquity men were loath to speak. This was because they counted it shameful if their person failed to keep up with their words.'

**4.24** The Master said, 'The gentleman desires to be halting in speech but quick in action.'

**5.5** Someone said, 'Yung is benevolent but does not have a facile tongue.'

The Master said, 'What need is there for him to have a facile tongue? For a man quick with a retort there are frequent occasions on which he will incur the hatred of others. I cannot say whether Yung is benevolent or not, but what need is there for him to have a facile tongue?'

**5.10** Tsai Yü was in bed in the daytime. The Master said, 'A piece of rotten wood cannot be carved, nor can a wall of dried dung be trowelled. As far as Yü is concerned what is the use of condemning him?' The Master added, 'I used to take on trust a man's deeds after having listened to his words. Now having listened to a man's words I go on to observe his deeds. It was on account of Yü that I have changed in this respect.'

**5.15** Tzu-kung asked, 'Why was K'ung Wen Tzu called "wen"?'

The Master said, 'He was quick and eager to learn: he was not ashamed to seek the advice of those who were beneath him in station. That is why he was called "wen".'

**5.16** The Master said of Tzu-ch'an that he had the way of the gentleman on four counts: he was respectful in the manner he conducted himself; he was reverent in the service of his lord; in caring for the common people, he was generous and, in employing their services, he was just.

**5.25** The Master said, 'Cunning words, an ingratiating face and utter servility, these things Tso-ch'iu Ming found shameful. I, too, find them shameful. To be friendly towards someone while concealing one's hostility, this Tso-ch'iu Ming found shameful. I, too, find it shameful.'

**5.26** Yen Yüan and Chi-lu were in attendance. The Master said, 'I suggest you each tell me what it is you have set your hearts on.'

Tzu-lu said, 'I should like to share my carriage and horses, clothes and furs with my friends, and to have no regrets even if they become worn.'

Yen Yüan said, 'I should like never to boast of my own goodness and never to impose onerous tasks upon others.'

Tzu-lu said, 'I should like to hear what you have set your heart on.'

The Master said, 'To bring peace to the old, to have trust in my friends, and to cherish the young.'

**5.27** The Master said, 'I suppose I should give up hope. I have yet to meet the man who, on seeing his own errors, is able to take himself to task inwardly.'

**5.28** The Master said, 'In a hamlet of ten households, there are bound to be those who are my equal in doing their best for others and in being trustworthy in what they say, but they are unlikely to be as eager to learn as I am.'

**6.3** When Duke Ai asked which of his disciples was eager to learn, Confucius answered, 'There was one Yen Hui who was eager to learn. He did not vent his anger upon an innocent person, nor did he make the same mistake twice. Unfortunately his allotted span was a short one and he died. Now there is no one. No one eager to learn has come to my notice.'

**6.7** The Master said, 'In his heart for three months at a time Hui does not lapse from benevolence. The others attain benevolence merely by fits and starts.'

**6.11** The Master said, 'How admirable Hui is! Living in a mean dwelling on a bowlful of rice and a ladleful of water is a hardship most men would find intolerable, but Hui does not allow this to affect his joy. How admirable Hui is!'

**6.12** Jan Ch'iu said, 'It is not that I am not pleased with your way, but rather that my strength gives out.' The Master said, 'A man whose strength gives out collapses along the course. In your case you set the limits beforehand.'

**6.18** The Master said, 'When there is a preponderance of native substance over acquired refinement, the result will be churlishness. When there is a preponderance of acquired refinement over native substance, the result will be pedantry. Only a well-balanced admixture of these two will result in gentlemanliness.'

**6.20** The Master said, 'To be fond of something is better than merely to know it, and to find joy in it is better than merely to be fond of it.'

**6.22** Fan Ch'ih asked about wisdom. The Master said, 'To work for the things the common people have a right to and to keep one's distance from the gods and spirits while showing them reverence can be called wisdom.'

Fan Ch'ih asked about benevolence. The Master said, 'The benevolent man reaps the benefit only after overcoming difficulties. That can be called benevolence.'

**6.23** The Master said, 'The wise find joy in water; the benevolent find joy in mountains. The wise are active; the benevolent are still. The wise are joyful; the benevolent are long-lived.'

**6.27** The Master said, 'The gentleman widely versed in culture but brought back to essentials by the rites can, I suppose, be relied upon not to turn against what he stood for.'

**6.30** Tzu-kung said, 'If there were a man who gave extensively to the common people and brought help to the multitude, what would you think of him? Could he be called benevolent?'

The Master said, 'It is no longer a matter of benevolence with such a man. If you must describe him, "sage" is, perhaps, the right word. Even Yao and Shun would have found it difficult to accomplish as much. Now, on the other hand, a benevolent man helps others to take their stand in so far as he himself wishes to take his stand, and gets others there in so far as he himself wishes to get there. The ability to take as analogy what is near at hand can be called the method of benevolence.'

**7.1** The Master said, 'I transmit but do not innovate; I am truthful in what I say and devoted to antiquity. I venture to compare myself to our Old P'eng.'

**7.2** The Master said, 'Quietly to store up knowledge in my mind, to learn without flagging, to teach without growing weary, these present me with no difficulties.'

**7.3** The Master said, 'It is these things that cause me concern: failure to cultivate virtue, failure to go more deeply into what I have learned, inability, when I am told what is right, to move to where it is, and inability to reform myself when I have defects.'

**7.6** The Master said, 'I set my heart on the Way, base myself on virtue, lean upon benevolence for support and take my recreation in the arts.'

**7.8** The Master said, 'I never enlighten anyone who has not been driven to distraction by trying to understand a difficulty or who has not got into a frenzy trying to put his ideas into words.

'When I have pointed out one corner of a square to anyone and he does not come back with the other three, I will not point it out to him a second time.'

**7.11** The Master said to Yen Yüan, 'Only you and I have the ability to go forward when employed and to stay out of sight when set aside.'

Tzu-lu said, 'If you were leading the Three Armies whom would you take with you?'

The Master said, 'I would not take with me anyone who would try to fight a tiger with his bare hands or to walk across the River and die in the process without regrets. If I took anyone it would have to be a man who, when faced with a task, was fearful of failure and who, while fond of making plans, was capable of successful execution.'

**7.14** The Master heard the *shao* in Ch'i and for three months did not notice the taste of the meat he ate. He said, 'I never dreamt that the joys of music could reach such heights.'

**7.16** The Master said, 'In the eating of coarse rice and the drinking of water, the using of one's elbow for a pillow, joy is to be found. Wealth and rank attained through immoral means have as much to do with me as passing clouds.'

**7.17** The Master said, 'Grant me a few more years so that I may study at the age of fifty and [*6*] I shall be free from major errors.'

**7.19** The Governor of She asked Tzu-lu about Confucius. Tzu-lu did not answer. The Master said, 'Why did you not simply say something to this effect: he is the sort of man who forgets to eat when he tries to solve a problem that has been driving him to distraction, who is so full of joy that he forgets his worries and who does not notice the onset of old age?'

**7.20** The Master said, 'I was not born with knowledge but, being fond of antiquity, I am quick to seek it.'

**7.21** The topics the Master did not speak of were prodigies, force, disorder and gods.

**7.22** The Master said, 'Even when walking in the company of two other men, I am bound to be able to learn from them. The good points of the one I copy; the bad points of the other I correct in myself.'

**7.24** The Master said, 'My friends, do you think I am secretive? There is nothing which I hide from you. There is nothing I do which I do not share with you, my friends. There is Ch'iu for you.'

**7.25** The Master instructs under four heads: culture, moral conduct, doing one's best and being trustworthy in what one says.

**7.26** The Master said, 'I have no hopes of meeting a sage. I would be content if I met someone who is a gentleman.'

The Master said, 'I have no hopes of meeting a good man. I would be content if I met someone who has constancy. It is hard for a man to have constancy who claims to have when he is wanting, to be full when he is empty and to be comfortable when he is in straitened circumstances.'

**7.28** The Master said, 'There are presumably men who innovate without possessing knowledge, but that is not a fault I have. I use my ears widely and follow what is good in what I have heard; I use my eyes widely and retain what I have seen in my mind. This constitutes a lower level of knowledge.'

**7.30** The Master said, 'Is benevolence really far away? No sooner do I desire it than it is here.'

**7.33** The Master said, 'In unstinted effort I can compare with others, but in being a practising gentleman I have had, as yet, no success.'

**7.34** The Master said, 'How dare I claim to be a sage or a benevolent man? Perhaps it might be said of me that I learn without flagging and teach without growing weary.' Kung-hsi Hua said, 'This is precisely where we disciples are unable to learn from your example.'

**7.35** The Master was seriously ill. Tzu-lu asked permission to offer a prayer. The Master said, 'Was such a thing ever done?' Tzu-lu said, 'Yes, it was. The prayer offered was as follows: pray thus to the gods above and below.' The Master said, 'In that case, I have long been offering my prayers.'

**7.36** The Master said, 'Extravagance means ostentation, frugality means shabbiness. I would rather be shabby than ostentatious.'

**7.37** The Master said, 'The gentleman is easy of mind, while the small man is always full of anxiety.'

**7.38** The Master is cordial yet stern, awe-inspiring yet not fierce, and respectful yet at ease.

**8.2** The Master said, 'Unless a man has the spirit of the rites, in being respectful he will wear himself out, in being careful he will become timid, in having courage he will become unruly, and in being forthright he will become intolerant.

'When the gentleman feels profound affection for his parents, the common people will be stirred to benevolence. When he does not forget friends of long standing, the common people will not shirk their obligations to other people.'

**8.7** Tseng Tzu said, 'A Gentleman must be strong and resolute, for his burden is heavy and the road is long. He takes benevolence as his burden. Is that not heavy? Only with death does the road come to an end. Is that not long?'

**8.8** The Master said, 'Be stimulated by the *Odes,* take your stand on the rites and be perfected by music.'

**8.9** The Master said, 'The common people can be made to follow a path but not to understand it.'

**8.10** The Master said, 'Being fond of courage while detesting poverty will lead men to unruly behaviour. Excessive detestation of men who are not benevolent will provoke them to unruly behaviour.'

**8.11** The Master said, 'Even with a man as gifted as the Duke of Chou, if he was arrogant and miserly, then the rest of his qualities would not be worthy of admiration.'

**8.12** The Master said, 'It is not easy to find a man who can study for three years without thinking about earning a salary.'

**8.13** The Master said, 'Have the firm faith to devote yourself to learning, and abide to the death in the good way. Enter not a state that is in peril; stay not in a state that is in danger. Show yourself when the Way prevails in the Empire, but hide yourself when it does not. It is a shameful matter to be poor and humble when the Way prevails in the state. Equally, it is a shameful matter to be rich and noble when the Way falls into disuse in the state.'

**8.14** The Master said, 'Do not concern yourself with matters of government unless they are the responsibility of your office.'

**8.16** The Master said, 'Men who reject discipline and yet are not straight, men who are ignorant and yet not cautious, men who are devoid of ability and yet not trustworthy are quite beyond my understanding.'

**8.17** The Master said, 'Even with a man who urges himself on in his studies as though he was losing ground, my fear is still that he may not make it in time.'

**8.21** The Master said, 'With Yü I can find no fault. He ate and drank the meanest fare while making offerings to ancestral spirits and gods with the utmost devotion proper to a descendant. He wore coarse clothes while sparing no splendour in his robes and caps on sacrificial occasions. He lived in lowly dwellings while devoting all his energy to the building of irrigation canals. With Yü I can find no fault.'

**9.4** There were four things the Master refused to have anything to do with: he refused to entertain conjectures or insist on certainty; he refused to be inflexible or to be egotistical.

**9.8** The Master said, 'Do I possess knowledge? No, I do not. A rustic put a question to me and my mind was a complete blank. I kept hammering at the two sides of the question until I got everything out of it.'

**9.9** The Master said, 'The Phoenix does not appear nor does the River offer up its Chart. I am done for.'

**9.10** When the Master encountered men who were in mourning or in ceremonial cap and robes or were blind, he would, on seeing them, rise to his feet, even though they were younger than he was, and, on passing them, would quicken his step.

**9.11** Yen Yüan, heaving a sigh, said, 'The more I look up at it the higher it appears. The more I bore into it the harder it becomes. I see it before me. Suddenly it is behind me.

'The Master is good at leading one on step by step. He broadens me with culture and brings me back to essentials by means of the rites. I cannot give up even if I wanted to, but, having done all I can, it seems to rise sheer above me and I have no way of going after it, however much I may want to.'

**9.16** The Master said, 'To serve high officials when abroad, and my elders when at home, in arranging funerals not to dare to spare myself, and to be able to hold my drink—these are trifles that give me no trouble.'

**9.17** While standing by a river, the Master said, 'What passes away is, perhaps, like this. Day and night it never lets up.'

**9.18** The Master said, 'I have yet to meet the man who is as fond of virtue as he is of beauty in women.'

**9.19** The Master said, 'As in the case of making a mound, if, before the very last basketful, I stop, then I shall have stopped. As in the case of levelling the ground, if, though tipping only one basketful, I am going forward, then I shall be making progress.'

**9.23** The Master said, 'It is fitting that we should hold the young in awe. How do we know that the generations to come will not be the equal of the present? Only when a man reaches the age of forty or fifty without distinguishing himself in any way can one say, I suppose, that he does not deserve to be held in awe.'

**9.24** The Master said, 'One cannot but give assent to exemplary words, but what is important is that one should rectify oneself. One cannot but be pleased with tactful words, but what is important is that one should reform oneself. I can do nothing with the man who gives assent but does not rectify himself or the man who is pleased but does not reform himself.'

**9.25** The Master said, 'Make it your guiding principle to do your best for others and to be trustworthy in what you say. Do not accept as friend anyone who is not as good as you. When you make a mistake do not be afraid of mending your ways.'

**9.26** The Master said, 'The Three Armies can be deprived of their commanding officer, but even a common man cannot be deprived of his purpose.'

**9.28** The Master said, 'Only when the cold season comes is the point brought home that the pine and the cypress are the last to lose their leaves.'

**9.29** The Master said, 'The man of wisdom is never in two minds; the man of benevolence never worries; the man of courage is never afraid.'

**11.12** Chi-lu asked how the spirits of the dead and the gods should be served. The Master said, 'You are not able even to serve man. How can you serve the spirits?'

'May I ask about death?'

'You do not understand even life. How can you understand death?'

**11.16** Tzu-kung asked, 'Who is superior, Shih or Shang?' The Master said, 'Shih overshoots the mark; Shang falls short.'

'Does that mean that Shih is in fact better?'

The Master said, 'There is little to choose between overshooting the mark and falling short.'

**12.1** Yen Yüan asked about benevolence. The Master said, 'To return to the observance of the rites through overcoming the self constitutes benevolence.

If for a single day a man could return to the observance of the rites through overcoming himself, then the whole Empire would consider benevolence to be his. However, the practice of benevolence depends on oneself alone, and not on others.'

Yen Yüan said, 'I should like you to list the items.' The Master said, 'Do not look unless it is in accordance with the rites; do not listen unless it is in accordance with the rites; do not speak unless it is in accordance with the rites; do not move unless it is in accordance with the rites.'

Yen Yüan said, 'Though I am not quick, I shall direct my efforts towards what you have said.'

**12.5** Ssu-ma Niu appeared worried, saying, 'All men have brothers. I alone have none.' Tzu-hsia said, 'I have heard it said: life and death are a matter of Destiny; wealth and honour depend on Heaven. The gentleman is reverent and does nothing amiss, is respectful towards others and observant of the rites, and all within the Four Seas are his brothers. What need is there for the gentleman to worry about not having any brothers?'

**12.7** Tzu-kung asked about government. The Master said, 'Give them enough food, give them enough arms, and the common people will have trust in you.'

Tzu-kung said, 'If one had to give up one of these three, which should one give up first?'

'Give up arms.'

Tzu-kung said, 'If one had to give up one of the remaining two, which should one give up first?'

'Give up food. Death has always been with us since the beginning of time, but when there is no trust, the common people will have nothing to stand on.'

**12.11** Duke Ching of Ch'i asked Confucius about government. Confucius answered, 'Let the ruler be a ruler, the subject a subject, the father a father, the son a son.' The Duke said, 'Splendid! Truly, if the ruler be not a ruler, the subject not a subject, the father not a father, the son not a son, then even if there be grain, would I get to eat it?'

**12.13** The Master said, 'In hearing litigation, I am no different from any other man. But if you insist on a difference, it is, perhaps, that I try to get the parties not to resort to litigation in the first place.'

**12.16** The Master said, 'The gentleman helps others to realize what is good in them; he does not help them to realize what is bad in them. The small man does the opposite.'

**12.19** Chi K'ang Tzu asked Confucius about government, saying, 'What would you think if, in order to move closer to those who possess the Way, I were to kill those who do not follow the Way?'

Confucius answered, 'In administering your government, what need is there for you to kill? Just desire the good yourself and the common people will be good. The virtue of the gentleman is like wind; the virtue of the small man is like grass. Let the wind blow over the grass and it is sure to bend.'

**13.2** While he was steward to the Chi Family, Chung-kung asked about government. The Master said, 'Set an example for your officials to follow; show leniency towards minor offenders; and promote men of talent.'

'How does one recognize men of talent to promote?'

The Master said, 'Promote those you do recognize. Do you suppose others will allow those you fail to recognize to be passed over?'

**13.5** The Master said, 'If a man who knows the three hundred *Odes* by heart fails when given administrative responsibilities and proves incapable of exercising his own initiative when sent to foreign states, then what use are the *Odes* to him, however many he may have learned?'

**13.23** The Master said, 'The gentleman agrees with others without being an echo. The small man echoes without being in agreement.'

**13.24** Tzu-kung asked, '"All in the village like him." What do you think of that?'

The Master said, 'That is not enough.'

'"All in the village dislike him." What do you think of that?'

The Master said, 'That is not enough either. "Those in his village who are good like him and those who are bad dislike him." That would be better.'

**13.26** The Master said, 'The gentleman is at ease without being arrogant; the small man is arrogant without being at ease.'

**13.27** The Master said, 'Unbending strength, resoluteness, simplicity and reticence are close to benevolence.'

**14.4** The Master said, 'A man of virtue is sure to be the author of memorable sayings, but the author of memorable sayings is not necessarily virtuous. A benevolent man is sure to possess courage, but a courageous man does not necessarily possess benevolence.'

**14.7** The Master said, 'Can you love anyone without making him work hard? Can you do your best for anyone without educating him?'

**14.10** The Master said, 'It is more difficult not to complain of injustice when poor than not to behave with arrogance when rich.'

**14.24** The Master said, 'Men of antiquity studied to improve themselves; men today study to impress others.'

**14.28** The Master said, 'There are three things constantly on the lips of the gentleman none of which I have succeeded in following: "A man of benevolence never worries; a man of wisdom is never in two minds; a man of courage is never afraid."' Tzu-kung said, 'What the Master has just quoted is a description of himself.'

**14.30** The Master said, 'It is not the failure of others to appreciate your abilities that should trouble you, but rather your own lack of them.'

**14.34** Someone said,

> 'Repay an injury with a good turn.

What do you think of this saying?'

The Master said, 'What, then, do you repay a good turn with? You repay an injury with straightness, but you repay a good turn with a good turn.'

**14.38** Tzu-lu put up for the night at the Stone Gate. The gatekeeper said, 'Where have you come from?' Tzu-lu said, 'From the K'ung family.' 'Is that the K'ung who keeps working towards a goal the realization of which he knows to be hopeless?'

**15.8** The Master said, 'To fail to speak to a man who is capable of benefiting is to let a man go to waste. To speak to a man who is incapable of benefiting is to let one's words go to waste. A wise man lets neither men nor words go to waste.'

**15.12** The Master said, 'He who gives no thought to difficulties in the future is sure to be beset by worries much closer at hand.'

**15.15** The Master said, 'If one sets strict standards for oneself and makes allowances for others when making demands on them, one will stay clear of ill will.'

**15.16** The Master said, 'There is nothing I can do with a man who is not constantly saying, "What am I to do? What am I to do?"'

**15.17** The Master said, 'It is quite a remarkable feat for a group of men who are together all day long merely to indulge themselves in acts of petty cleverness without ever touching on the subject of morality in their conversation!'

**15.20** The Master said, 'The gentleman hates not leaving behind a name when he is gone.'

**15.21** The Master said, 'What the gentleman seeks, he seeks within himself; what the small man seeks, he seeks in others.'

**15.23** The Master said, 'The gentleman does not recommend a man on account of what he says, neither does he dismiss what is said on account of the speaker.'

**15.24** Tzu-kung asked, 'Is there a single word which can be a guide to conduct throughout one's life?' The Master said, 'It is perhaps the word "*shu*". Do not impose on others what you yourself do not desire.'

**15.31** The Master said, 'I once spent all day thinking without taking food and all night thinking without going to bed, but I found that I gained nothing from it. It would have been better for me to have spent the time in learning.'

**15.38** The Master said, 'In serving one's lord, one should approach one's duties with reverence and consider one's pay as of secondary importance.'

**15.41** The Master said, 'It is enough that the language one uses gets the point across.'

**16.6** Confucius said, 'When in attendance upon a gentleman one is liable to three errors. To speak before being spoken to by the gentleman is rash; not to speak when spoken to by him is to be evasive; to speak without observing the expression on his face is to be blind.'

**16.7** Confucius said, 'There are three things the gentleman should guard against. In youth when the blood and *ch'i* are still unsettled he should guard against the attraction of feminine beauty. In the prime of life when the blood and *ch'i* have become unyielding, he should guard against bellicosity. In old age when the blood and *ch'i* have declined, he should guard against acquisitiveness.'

**17.2** The Master said, 'Men are close to one another by nature. They diverge as a result of repeated practice.'

**17.3** The Master said, 'It is only the most intelligent and the most stupid who are not susceptible to change.'

**17.6** Tzu-chang asked Confucius about benevolence. Confucius said, 'There are five things and whoever is capable of putting them into practice in the Empire is certainly "benevolent".'

'May I ask what they are?'

'They are respectfulness, tolerance, trustworthiness in word, quickness and generosity. If a man is respectful he will not be treated with insolence. If he is tolerant he will win the multitude. If he is trustworthy in word his fellow men will entrust him with responsibility. If he is quick he will achieve results. If he is generous he will be good enough to be put in a position over his fellow men.'

**17.9** The Master said, 'Why is it none of you, my young friends, study the *Odes?* An apt quotation from the *Odes* may serve to stimulate the imagination, to show one's breeding, to smooth over difficulties in a group and to give expression to complaints.

'Inside the family there is the serving of one's father; outside, there is the serving of one's lord; there is also the acquiring of a wide knowledge of the names of birds and beasts, plants and trees.'

**17.23** Tzu-lu said, 'Does the gentleman consider courage a supreme quality?' The Master said, 'For the gentleman it is morality that is supreme. Possessed of courage but devoid of morality, a gentleman will make trouble while a small man will be a brigand.'

**19.8** Tzu-hsia said, 'When the small man makes a mistake, he is sure to gloss over it.'

**19.9** Tzu-hsia said, 'In the three following situations the gentleman gives a different impression. From a distance he appears formal; when approached, he appears cordial; in speech he appears stern.'

## LAOZI (TRAD. C. 520 BCE)

Everything about Laozi (Lao Tzu) and the small classic *Dao de jing* (*Tao te ching,* sometimes translated as "The Way and Its Power") is mysterious. First of all, we do not know precisely who Laozi (literally, "The Old Master") was or when he lived. An early Chinese tradition makes him an older contemporary of Confucius (551–479 BCE) and claims that Confucius went to the state of Zhou, where Laozi worked in the archives, to ask him about ritual. By the time of the great historian Sima Qian (145–87? BCE), other traditions placed Laozi well after the lifetime of Confucius, so that Sima could only conclude that "none in our generation know what is correct and what is not [concerning Laozi]." The distinguished modern scholar D.C. Lau, who produced the translation of the *Dao de jing* presented here, concludes that "there is no certain evidence that he was a historical figure."

The *Dao de jing* is unique in early Chinese literature. The Chinese, from earliest times, have been keenly aware of history and typically provide their texts with a historical context, either real or imagined. The *Dao de jing* makes no reference to specific persons or events. It seems to float outside the world of time, a world in which most Chinese writers remain firmly and contentedly embedded. While some would date the text as early as 500 BCE, others believe, with strong evidence, that it is of much later origin, perhaps as late as the last decades of the fourth century BCE or even the first decades of the third century.

But the mystery goes deeper than this. Why would someone who proclaims the inadequacy of words (chs. 1 and 56) and who would discard learning as useless (chs. 20 and 46) write a book in the first place? By the *Dao de jing*'s own standards, anything it says, since it must be said in words, can only be a distortion of the truth. This is the dilemma in which mystics invariably find themselves—forced to proclaim in words a message that cannot be contained in words. An early Chinese tradition removes the dilemma by claiming that Laozi wrote the *Dao de jing* because he was required to do so. As he was leaving China and wandering away into the "shifting sands" toward the west, this tradition maintains, a "keeper of the pass" would not let him depart until he had written down his wisdom. The price Laozi paid to leave China, according to this account, was the *Dao de jing*.

Central to this mysterious and often enigmatic text is the notion of the *dao,* most often translated into English as "the Way." Dao literally means "a path" or "a road," and in the works of other early Chinese thinkers, including Confucius himself, it means "doctrine" or "teaching"—that is, the path one must walk in order to reach correct understanding and proper behavior. The *Dao de jing,* however, rejects any dao that can be expressed in words. It advocates instead a more mystical dao, one that transcends the categories of thought and language and is perceived in "that which is naturally so" (ch. 25). Whatever one makes of the dao, certain themes recur throughout the text: the advantage of yielding, of taking "the lower position"; the benefit of returning to simplicity, to the "uncarved block," to the "breast of the mother"; and the disaster of excessive desire and the ironic way in which sermonizing appears at precisely the moment when moral substance is on the wane.

The great popularity of the *Dao de jing,* both in China and in the West, where new translations appear almost every year, is due in large measure to its haunting poetic beauty. Much of the text is rhymed and it is clearly rhythmical; the imagery is vivid and powerful. The *Dao de jing* is, first and foremost, a great work of literature that has inspired not just the Chinese people but many Westerners as well. While mystery still surrounds the text, it continues to strike a responsive chord in readers of the most varied cultural and philosophical backgrounds.

Of the more than eighty English translations of the *Dao de jing* available, we have selected a new version by D.C. Lau. His translation has the benefit of using the most recent manuscript discoveries of the text, the Mawangdui manuscripts, which date from the first half of the second century BCE and were unearthed in 1973 near Changsha in Hunan Province. In these manuscripts, the text begins with what we give as chapter 39, and follows a somewhat different order from the traditional versions. To facilitate cross-reference with other translations, we have restored the traditional order.

## from Dao de jing

*Translated by D.C. Lau*

### 1

The way can be spoken of,
But it will not be the constant way;
The name can be named,
But it will not be the constant name.
The nameless was the beginning of the myriad creatures;

The named was the mother of the myriad creatures.
Hence constantly rid yourself of desires in order to observe its subtlety;
But constantly allow yourself to have desires in order to observe what it is after.
These two have the same origin but differ in name.
They are both called dark,
Darkness upon darkness
The gateway to all that is subtle.

## 2

The whole world knows the beautiful as the beautiful, and
this is only the ugly; it knows the good as the good and this is, indeed, the bad.
Something and Nothing producing each other;
The difficult and the easy complementing each other;
The long and the short off-setting each other;
The high and the low filling out each other;
Note and sound harmonizing with each other;
Before and after following each other—
These are in accordance with what is constant.
Hence the sage dwells in the deed that consists in taking no action and practises the teaching that uses no words.
It makes the myriad creatures without being their initiator,
It benefits them without exacting any gratitude for this;
It accomplishes its task without claiming any merit for this.
It is because it lays no claim to merit
That its merit never deserts it.

## 3

Not to honour men of excellence will keep the people from contention; not to value goods that are hard to come by will keep the people from theft; not to display what is desirable will keep the people from being unsettled.
Hence in his rule, the sage empties their minds but fills their bellies, weakens their purpose but strengthens their bones.
He constantly keeps the people innocent of knowledge and free from desire, and causes the clever not to dare.
He simply takes no action and everything is in order.

## 4

The way is empty, yet when used there is something that does not make it full.
Deep, it is like the ancestor of the myriad creatures.
Blunt the sharpness;
Untangle the knots;

Soften the glare;
Follow along old wheel tracks.
Darkly visible, it only seems as if it were there.
I know not whose son it is.
It images the forefather of God.

## 6

The spirit of the valley never dies;
This is called the dark female.
The entry into the dark female
Is called the root of heaven and earth.
Tenuous, it seems as if it were there,
Yet use will never exhaust it.

## 8

That which is most good is like water. It is because water is not only good at benefiting the myriad creatures but also vies to dwell in the place detested by the multitude that it comes close to the way.

In a dwelling it is the site that is valued;
In quality of mind it is depth that is valued;
In giving it is being like heaven that is valued;
In speech it is good faith that is valued;
In government it is order that is valued;
In affairs it is ability that is valued;
In action it is timeliness that is valued.

It is because it does not contend that it is never at fault.

## 10

When carrying on your head your perplexed bodily soul can
you hold in your arms the One
And not let go?
In concentrating your breath can you become as supple
As a babe?
Can you polish your dark mirror
And leave no blemish?
In loving the people and bringing life to the state
Are you capable of not resorting to knowledge?
When the gates of heaven open and shut
Are you capable of keeping to the role of the female?
When your discernment penetrates the four quarters
Are you capable of not resorting to knowledge?
It gives them life and rears them.
It gives them life without claiming to possess them;
It is the steward yet exercises no authority over them.
Such is called dark virtue.

## 15

Of old he who was well versed in the way
Was minutely subtle, mysteriously comprehending,
And too profound to be known.
It is because he could not be known
That he can only be given a makeshift description:
    Tentative, as if wading through water in winter,
    Hesitant, as if in fear of his neighbours;
    Formal like a guest;
    Falling apart like thawing ice;
    Thick like the uncarved block;
    Murky like muddy water,
    Immense like a valley.
    The muddy, being stilled, slowly becomes limpid,
    The settled, being stirred, slowly comes to life.
    He who treasures this way
    Desires not to be full.
    It is because he desires not to be full
    That he is able to be worn and incomplete.

## 16

I attain the utmost emptiness;
I keep to extreme stillness.
The myriad creatures all rise together
And I watch thereby their return.
The teeming creatures
All return to their separate roots.
Returning to one's roots is known as stillness.
Stillness is what is called returning to one's destiny.
Returning to one's destiny is normal.
Knowledge of the normal is discernment.
Not to know the normal is to be without basis.
To innovate without basis bodes ill.
To know the normal is to be tolerant.
Tolerance leads to impartiality,
Impartiality to kingliness,
Kingliness to heaven,
Heaven to the way,
The way to perpetuity,
And to the end of one's days one will meet with no danger.

## 18

Thus when the great way falls into disuse
There are benevolence and rectitude;
When cleverness emerges

There is great hypocrisy;
When the six relations are at variance
There are the filial;
When the state is benighted
There are true subjects.

## 19

Exterminate the sage, discard the wise,
And the people will benefit a hundredfold;
Exterminate benevolence, discard rectitude,
And the people will return to being filial;
Exterminate ingenuity, discard profit,
And there will be no more thieves and bandits.

Concerning these three sayings,

It is thought that the text leaves yet something to be desired
And there should, therefore, be something to which it is attached:
Exhibit the unadorned and embrace the uncarved block,
Have little thought of self and as few desires as possible.

## 20

Exterminate learning and there will no longer be worries.
Between yea and nay
How much difference is there?
Between the beautiful and the ugly
How great is the distance?
He whom others fear
Ought also to fear others.
Waxing, it has not reached its limit.
The multitude are joyous
As if partaking of the *t' ai lao* offering
While going on a terrace in spring.
I alone am inactive and reveal no signs,
Like a baby that has not yet learned to smile,
Listless as though with no home to go back to.
The multitude all have more than enough.
I alone am in want.
Mine is the mind of a fool—how blank!
Vulgar men are clear.
I alone am drowsy.
Vulgar men miss nothing.
I alone am muddled.
Unbounded, like the sea;
Limitless, as if there is nowhere to stop.
The multitude all have a purpose.

I alone am foolish and uncouth.
I want to be different from all others
In valuing being fed by the mother.

## 21

In his every movement a man of great virtue
Follows the way and the way only.
As a thing the way is
Shadowy, indistinct.
Indistinct and shadowy,
Yet within it is an image;
Shadowy and indistinct,
Yet within it is a substance.
Dim and dark,
Yet within it is an essence.
This essence is quite genuine,
And within it is something that can be tested.
From the present back to antiquity
Its name never deserted it.

By means of it one goes along with the fathers of the multitude. How do I know that the fathers of the multitude are like that? By means of this.

## 22

Bowed down then whole;
Warped then true;
Hollow then full;
Worn then new;
A little then benefited;
A lot then perplexed.

Hence the sage grasps the One and is the shepherd of the empire.

He does not display himself, and so is conspicuous;
He does not show himself, and so is manifest;
He does not boast of himself, and so has merit;
He does not brag about it, and so is able to endure.

It is because he does not contend that no one is in a position to contend with him.

The way the ancients had it, 'Whole through being bowed down', is as true a saying as can be. Truly, it enables one to hand it back whole.

## 23

To use words but rarely
Is to be natural.

A gusty wind cannot last all morning, and a violent downpour cannot last all day. Who is it that produces these? Heaven and earth. If even heaven and earth cannot make them go on for long, much less can man.

Hence in his pursuit, a man of the way conforms to the way; a man of virtue conforms to virtue; a man of loss conforms to loss. To him who conforms to virtue the way gives virtue; to him who conforms to loss the way gives loss.

## 24

He who blows cannot stand.
He who displays himself is not conspicuous;
He who shows himself is not manifest;
He who boasts of himself will have no merit;
He who brags about himself will not endure.

From the point of view of the way these are 'excessive food and excrescent conduct'. As there are things that detest these, a man of ambition does not abide therein.

## 25

There is a thing confusedly formed,
Born before heaven and earth.
Silent and void
It stands alone and does not change,
Goes round and does not weary.
It is capable of being the mother of heaven and earth.
As yet I do not know its name.
I style it 'the way'.
I give it the makeshift name of 'great'.
Being great, it is described as receding,
Receding, it is described as far away,
Being far away, it is described as turning back.

The way is great; heaven is great; earth is great, and the king is great. Within the realm there are four greats and the king counts as one.

Man models himself on earth,
Earth on heaven,
Heaven on the way,
And the way on that which is naturally so.

## 28

Know the male
But keep to the role of the female
And be a ravine to the empire.
If you are a ravine to the empire,
The constant virtue will not desert you.

When the constant virtue does not desert you,
You will again return to being a babe.
Know the white
But keep to the role of the sullied.
And be a valley to the empire.
If you are a valley to the empire,
The constant virtue will be sufficient.
When the constant virtue is sufficient,
You will again return to being the uncarved block.
Know the white
But keep to the role of the black
And be a model to the empire.
If you are a model to the empire,
The constant virtue will not deviate.
When the constant virtue does not deviate,
You will again return to the infinite.

When the uncarved block shatters it becomes vessels. When the sage is employed he becomes the chief of the officials.

Now the greatest cutting
Never severs.

## 31

Arms are instruments of ill omen. There are things that detest them. Hence a man of ambition does not abide therein. The gentleman gives precedence to the left when at home, but to the right when he goes to war. Thus arms are not the instruments of the gentleman. Arms are instruments of ill omen. When one has no alternative but to use them, it is best to do so without relish. One should not glorify them. If one glorifies them this is to exult in the killing of men. Now one who exults in the killing of men will not have his way in the empire.

Hence in celebrations precedence is given to the left; in funerals precedence is given to the right. Hence a lieutenant's place is on the left; the general's place is on the right. That is to say it is funeral rites that are observed. When men are killed in great numbers, one should look on them with sorrow. When one is victorious in war, this calls for the observance of funeral rites.

## 32

The way is constantly nameless.
Though the uncarved block is small
No one in the world dare treat it as a subject.
Should lords and princes be able to hold fast to it
The myriad creatures will submit of their own accord,
Heaven and earth will unite and send down sweet dew,

And the people will be equitable though no one so decrees.
Then only when it is cut are there names.
Once there are names
One should know it was time to stop.
Knowing when to stop is the way to be free from danger.

The way in distracting the empire is similar to the case of a small valley in relation to the River and the Sea.

## 33

He who knows others is clever;
He who knows himself has discernment.
He who overcomes others has force;
He who overcomes himself has strength.
He who knows contentment is rich;
He who perseveres in action has purpose.
Not to lose one's station is to endure;
Not to be forgotten when dead is long lived.

## 34

The way is broad, reaching left as well as right.
Having accomplished the task and having done the work it does not
assume the name of owner.

The myriad creatures turn to it yet it does not act as their master. Thus in so far as it is constantly without desire it can be named amongst the small; but in so far as it does not act as their master when the myriad creatures turn to it, it can be named amongst the great. Hence the sage succeeds in becoming great because he makes no attempt to be great. It is for this reason that he succeeds in becoming great.

## 36

If you would have a thing shrink,
You must first stretch it;
If you would have a thing weakened,
You must first strengthen it;
If you would desert a thing,
You must first be its ally.
If you would take from a thing,
You must first give to it.
This is called faint enlightenment:
The submissive and weak will overcome the unyielding and
strong.
The fish must not be allowed to leave the deep;
The instruments of power in a state must not be revealed to others.

## 37

The way is constantly nameless,
But should lords and princes be able to hold fast to it,
The myriad creatures will be transformed of their own accord.
After they are transformed should they desire to rise
I shall press them down with the weight of the nameless
uncarved block.
When they are pressed down with the weight of the nameless
uncarved block,
They will not desire;
When they do not desire and are still,
Heaven and earth will be proper of their own accord.

## 38

The man of superior virtue is not virtuous and that is why he has virtue. The man of inferior virtue does not lapse from virtue and that is why he has no virtue. The man of superior virtue resorts to no action, nor has he any ulterior motive for action. The man of superior benevolence acts but has no ulterior motive for his action. The man of superior rectitude acts and has an ulterior motive for his action as well. The man superior in the observance of the rites acts, but when no one responds to his action rolls up his sleeves and resorts to dragging by force.

Hence when the way was lost there was virtue; when virtue was lost there was benevolence; when benevolence was lost there was rectitude; when rectitude was lost there were the rites.

Now the rites are the wearing thin of conscientiousness and good
faith
And the beginning of disorder;
Foreknowledge is the flowery embellishment of the way
And the beginning of folly.

Hence a great man abides in the thick not in the thin, in the fruit not in the flower.

Hence he discards the one and takes the other.

## 39

Of old, these came to possess the One:

Heaven possessed the One and became thereby limpid;
Earth possessed the One and became thereby settled;
Gods possessed the One and became thereby potent;
The valley possessed the One and became thereby full;
Lords and princes possessed the One and became thereby leaders of
the empire.

But when this is pushed to the utmost,

It will mean that not knowing when to stop in being
limpid heaven will split;
It will mean that not knowing when to stop in being
settled earth will sink;
It will mean that not knowing when to stop in being
potent gods will get spent;
It will mean that not knowing when to stop in being
full the valley will run dry;
It will mean that not knowing when to stop in being
noble the high lords and princes will fall.

Hence it is necessarily the case that the noble has as its root the humble and the high has as its foundation the low. Now this is why lords and princes refer to themselves as 'solitary', 'desolate' and 'hapless'. This is the humble as root, is it not?

Thus the highest renown is without renown.
Hence wishing not to be one among many like jade,
Nor to be aloof like stone.

## 40

Reversal is the movement of the way;
Weakness is the use of the way.

The creatures in the world are born from Something, and Something from Nothing.

## 42

The way begets one; one begets two; two begets three, three begets the myriad creatures.

The myriad creatures carry on their backs the *yin* and hold in their arms the *yang*, taking the *ch'i* in between as harmony.

The only names detested by the world are 'solitary', 'desolate' and 'hapless', yet princes and lords use them to name themselves.

Thus a thing is sometimes added to by being diminished and diminished by being added to.

Thus what others teach I also, after due consideration, teach others.

Thus as the violent do not come to a natural end, I take this as my preceptor.

## 43

The most submissive thing in the world can ride roughshod over the most unyielding in the world—that which is without substance entering that which has no gaps.

That is why I know the benefit of taking action. The teaching that uses no words, the benefit of taking no action, these are beyond the understanding of all but a very few in the world.

## 45

Great perfection seems chipped,
Yet use will not wear it out;
Great fullness seems empty,
Yet use will not drain it;
Great straightness seems bent;
Great skill seems awkward;
Great surplus seems deficient;
Great eloquence seems tongue-tied.

Restlessness overcomes the cold; stillness overcomes the heat.

Limpid and still,
One can be a leader in the empire.

## 46

When the way prevails in the empire, fleet-footed horses are relegated to providing manure for the fields; when the way does not prevail in the empire, war-horses breed on the border.

There is no crime greater than being desirable;
There is no disaster greater than not being content;
There is no misfortune more painful than being covetous:

Hence in knowing the sufficiency of being content, one will constantly have sufficient.

## 47

By not setting foot outside the door
One knows the whole world;
By not looking out of the window
One knows the way of heaven.
The further one goes
The less one knows.
Hence the sage knows without having to stir,
Identifies without having to see [it],
Accomplishes without having to do it.

## 48

One who pursues learning makes gains every day; one who gets to hear about the way makes losses every day. One loses and loses until one takes no action. One takes no action nor does one have any ulterior motive for action. If your wish is to gain the empire you should constantly refrain from meddling. By the time you meddle, you are not equal to the task of gaining the empire.

## 51

The way gives them life
And virtue rears them;
Things take shape
And vessels are formed.

Hence the myriad creatures all revere the way and honor virtue. The way in being revered, and virtue in being honored are constantly so of themselves without anyone bestowing nobility on them.

The way gives them life and rears them,
Brings them up and accomplishes them,
Brings them to fruition and maturity,
Feeds and shelters them.
It gives them life without claiming to possess them;
It benefits them yet exacts no gratitude for this;
It is the steward yet exercises no authority over them.
Such is called dark virtue.

## 52

The world had that from which it began
And this is taken as the mother of the world.
After you have got the mother
You can in turn know the son.
After you have known the son
Go back to abiding by the mother,
And to the end of your days you will not meet with danger.
Block the openings,
Shut the doors,
And all your life you will not run dry.
Unblock the openings,
Add to your affairs,
And to the end of your days you will be beyond help.
To see the small is called discernment;
To abide by the submissive is called strength.
Use the light
But give up the discernment.
Bring not misfortune upon yourself.
This is known as following the norm.

## 56

One who knows does not say it; one who says does not know it.

Block the openings,
Shut the doors,

Soften the glare,
Follow along old wheel tracks;
Blunt the point,
Untangle the knots.

This is known as dark identity.

Thus you cannot get close to it, nor can you keep it at arm's length; you cannot bestow benefit on it, nor can you do it harm; you cannot ennoble it, nor can you debase it.

Hence it is the most valued in the empire.

## 58

When the government is muddled,
The people are dull;
When the government misses nothing,
The state is decisive.
It is on disaster that good fortune perches;
It is beneath good fortune that disaster crouches.

Who knows the limit? Does the straightforward not exist?

But the straightforward changes once again into the crafty, and the good changes once again into the monstrous. Indeed, it is long since men were perplexed.

Hence square-edged but does not scrape,
Having corners but does not jab,
Spread out but does not encroach on others,
Shining but does not dazzle.

## 59

In ruling over men and in serving heaven, there is nothing like being sparing.
It is because a man is sparing
That he can follow the way from the start;
Following the way from the start is what is called accumulating an abundance of virtue;
Accumulating an abundance of virtue he overcomes everything he meets;
When he overcomes everything he meets, no one will know his limit;
When no one knows his limit;
He can possess a state.
When he possesses the mother of a state
He can then endure.
This is called the way of deep roots and firm stems by which one lives to see a good many more days.

## 61

A large state is the lower reaches of a river—the female of the world. In the intercourse of the world, the female always gets the better of the male by stillness. It is because of her stillness that it is fitting for her to take the lower position.

Hence the large state, by taking the lower position, annexes the small state;
The small state, by taking the lower position, is annexed by the large state.
Thus the one, by taking the lower position, annexes;
The other, by taking the lower position, is annexed.
Thus all that the large state wants is to take the other under its wing;
All that the small state wants is to have its services accepted by the other.
Now if they both get their desire,
It is fitting that the large should take the lower position.

## 64

It is easy to maintain a situation while it is still secure;
It is easy to deal with a situation before symptoms develop;
It is easy to break a thing when it is yet brittle;
It is easy to disperse a thing when it is yet minute.
Deal with a thing while it is still nothing;
Keep a thing in order before disorder sets in.
A tree that can fill a man's embrace
Grows from a downy tip;
A terrace nine storeys high
Rises from hodfuls of earth;
A height of a thousand yards
Starts from underneath one's feet.

He who does anything will ruin it; he who holds will lose it. Hence the sage, because he does nothing, never ruins anything; and, because he does not hold, loses nothing. In their enterprises the people constantly ruin them when on the verge of success.

Thus it is said,

Be as careful at the end as at the beginning
And there will be no ruined enterprises.
Hence the sage desires not to desire
And does not value goods that are hard to come by;
Learns not to learn
And turns back where the multitude has overshot the mark;
Is able to help the myriad creatures to be natural and yet dare not do it.

### 66

The reason why the River and the Sea are able to be king of the hundred valleys is that they are good at humbling themselves before them. Hence they are able to be king of the hundred valleys.

> Hence the sage, in desiring to rule over the people,
> Of necessity, in his words, humbles himself before them,
> And, in desiring to lead the people,
> Of necessity, in his person, follows behind them.

Thus the sage takes his place in front of the people yet they do not find him an obstruction, takes his place over the people yet they do not find him a burden. The whole empire supports him joyfully without ever tiring of doing so.

Is it not because he is without contention that no one in the empire is in a position to contend with him?

### 70

My words are very easy to understand and very easy to put into practice, yet amongst men there is no one who is able to understand them and there is no one who is able to put them into practice.

Words have an ancestor and affairs have a sovereign.

It is because men are ignorant that they fail to understand me.

> When those who understand me are few,
> Then I shall be highly valued.

Hence the sage, while clad in homespun, conceals on his person a piece of priceless jade.

### 71

> To know yet to think that one does not know is the best;
> Not to know yet to think that one knows will put one in difficulty.

That the sage meets with no difficulty is because he is alive to difficulty. That is why he meets with no difficulty.

### 75

> That men are hungry
> Is because too many live off the taxes.
> That is why they are hungry.
> That the people are not in good order
> Is because those in authority have ulterior motives for their actions.
> That is why they are not in good order.
> That the common people treat death lightly

Is because they set too much store by life.
That is why they treat death lightly.

It is precisely the man that has no use for life who is wiser than him that values life.

## 76

A man is supple and weak when alive, but hard and stiff when dead. The myriad creatures and grass and trees are pliant and fragile when alive, but dried and shrivelled when dead. Thus it is said, the hard and the strong are the comrades of death; the supple and the weak are the comrades of life.

Hence a weapon that is strong will not vanquish;
A tree that is strong will come to its end;
Thus the strong and big takes the lower position;
The supple and weak takes the upper position.

## 78

In the world there is nothing more submissive and weak than water. Yet for attacking that which is unyielding and strong nothing can take precedence over it. This is because there is nothing that can take its place.

The weak overcomes the unbending,
And the submissive overcomes the strong,
This everyone in the world knows yet no one can put it into practice.

Hence in the words of the sage,

One who takes on himself the abuse hurled against the state
Is called a ruler worthy of offering sacrifices to the gods of earth
 and millet;
One who takes on himself the calamities of the state
Is called a king worthy of dominion over the entire empire.

Straightforward words seem paradoxical.

## 80

Reduce the size and population of the state. Ensure that even though there are tools ten times or a hundred times better than those of other men the people will not use them; ensure also that they will look on death as a grave matter and give migration a wide berth.

They have ships and carts but will not go on them; they have armour and weapons but will have no occasion to make a show of them.

Bring it about that the people will return to the use of the knotted rope,

Will find relish in their food,
And beauty in their clothes,

Will be happy in the way they live
And be content in their abode.

Though adjoining states are within sight of one another, and the sound of dogs barking and cocks crowing in one state can be heard in another, yet the people of one state will grow old and die without having had any dealings with those of another.

### 81

Truthful words are not beautiful; beautiful words are not truthful.

He who knows has no wide learning; he who has wide learning does not know.

He who is good does not have much; he who has much is not good.

The sage has no hoard. Having bestowed all he has on others, he has yet more; having given all he has to others, he is richer still.

Hence the way of heaven does not harm but benefits; the way of man does not contend but is bountiful.

## ZHUANGZI (369?–286? BCE)

Laozi and Zhuangzi (Chuang Tzu) are the two great Daoist philosophers of early China. Although Laozi is much better known and more often translated in the West, Zhuangzi is the more accessible of the two. Very little is known of Zhuangzi except that he seems to have been very much a part of the lively philosophical discussions of the last century of the Zhou dynasty, a time when the growing sense of political and social crisis fostered an array of quite different intellectual responses.

Laozi and Zhuangzi present a strong contrast in both style and content. While Laozi's style is terse and remote, Zhuangzi is expansive, amusing, and very engaging. Laozi belongs to a world of aphorism, paradox, and poetry; Zhuangzi, although quite capable of poetry himself, is primarily a storyteller and a master of the humorous anecdote. Laozi presents the dao as a mysterious tool of power, but Zhuangzi regards harmony with the dao as the way to freedom—in his case, a very radical freedom.

*On the Equality of Things* belongs to the oldest layer of Zhuangzi's thirty-three chapter text and, unlike many of the other chapters, is thought to be by Zhuangzi himself. It is, among other things, a bold and sometimes amusing attack on convention and conviction. Language and disputation, the knowledge and authority of the wise men of the past—even the confidence that we are now alive and awake rather than dead or dreaming—are questioned and undermined in this chapter. Zhuangzi may be a playful skeptic, who can question himself as well as others ("I do not know whether what I have said is really saying something or not"), but his writings challenge us to examine our most fundamental beliefs.

Zhuangzi would never have presented himself as a systematic philosopher. Indeed, system is anathema to his thinking. He should, instead, be read and enjoyed as a literary figure who often pushes the classical Chinese language to its very limits as he roams freely and somewhat haphazardly in the world of ideas.

## On the Equality of Things

*Translated by Victor Mair*

*The Great Clod, a metaphor for the Earth and the Way, is introduced. An extended discussion of self and other, right and wrong, affirmation and denial, ensues. Transcendent knowledge goes beyond all such dichotomies.*

### 1

Sir Motley of Southurb sat leaning against his low table. He looked up to heaven and exhaled slowly. Disembodied, he seemed bereft of soul. Sir Wanderer of Countenance Complete, who stood in attendance before him, asked, "How can we explain this? Can the body really be made to become like withered wood? Can the mind really be made to become like dead ashes? The one who is leaning against the table now is not the one who was formerly leaning against the table."

"Indeed," said Sir Motley, "your question is a good one, Yen. Just now, I lost myself. Can you understand this? You may have heard the pipes of man, but not the pipes of earth. You may have heard the pipes of earth, but not the pipes of heaven."

"I venture," said Sir Wanderer, "to ask their secret."

"The Great Clod," said Sir Motley, "emits a vital breath called the wind. If it doesn't blow, nothing happens. Once it starts to blow, however, myriad hollows begin to howl. Have you not heard its moaning? The clefts and crevasses of the towering mountains, the hollows and cavities of huge trees a hundred spans around: they are like nostrils, like mouths, like ears, like sockets, like cups, like mortars, or like the depressions that form puddles and pools. The wind blowing over them makes the sound of rushing water, whizzing arrows, shouting, breathing, calling, crying, laughing, gnashing. The wind in front sings *aiee* and the wind that follows sings *wouu*. A light breeze evokes a small response; a powerful gale brings forth a mighty chorus. When the blast dies down, then all the hollows are silent. Have you not seen the leaves that quiver with tingling reverberations?"

"The pipes of earth," said Sir Wanderer, "are none other than all of the hollows you have described. The pipes of man are bamboo tubes arrayed in series. I venture to ask what the pipes of heaven are."

"As for the pipes of heaven," said Sir Motley, "the myriad sounds produced by the blowing of the wind are different, yet all it does is elicit the natural propensities of the hollows themselves. What need is there for something else to stimulate them?"

## 2

Great knowledge is expansive;
Small knowledge is cramped.

Great speech blazes brilliantly;
Small speech is mere
garrulousness.

When people sleep, their souls are confused; when they awake, their bodies feel all out of joint.

Their contacts turn into conflicts,
Each day involves them in mental
strife.

They become indecisive, dissembling, secretive.

Small fears disturb them;
Great fears incapacitate them.

Some there are who express themselves as swiftly as the release of a crossbow mechanism, which is to say that they arbitrate right and wrong. Others hold fast as though to a sworn covenant, which is to say they are waiting for victory. Some there are whose decline is like autumn or winter, which describes their dissolution day by day. Others are so immersed in activity that they cannot be revitalized. Some become so weary that they are as though sealed up in an envelope, which describes their senility. Their minds are so near to death that they cannot be rejuvenated.

Pleasure and anger; sorrow and joy; worry and regret; vacillation and trepidation; diffidence and abandon; openness and affectedness. These are all like musical sounds from empty tubes, like fungi produced from mere vapors. Day and night they alternate within us, but no one knows whence they arise. Enough! Enough! The instant one grasps *this,* one understands whence they arise!

## 3

"If there were no 'other,' there would be no 'I.' If there were no 'I,' there would be nothing to apprehend the 'other.'" This is near the mark, but I do not know what causes it to be so. It seems as though there is a True Ruler, but there is no particular evidence for Her. We may have faith in Her ability to function, but cannot see Her form. She has attributes but is without form.

The hundred bones, the nine orifices, and the six viscera are all complete within my body. With which am *I* most closely identified? Do you favor all of them equally? Or are there those to which you are partial? Assuming that you treat them equally, do you take them all to be your servants? If so, are your servants incapable of controlling each other? Or do they take turns being lord and subject among themselves? If not, do they have a True Lord over them all? Whether or not we succeed in specifying His attributes has neither positive nor negative effect upon the truth of the Lord.

Once we have received our complete physical form, we remain conscious of it while we await extinction. In our strife and friction with other things, we gallop forward on our course unable to stop. Is this not sad? We toil our whole life without seeing any results. We deplete ourselves with wearisome labor, but don't know what it all adds up to. Isn't this lamentable? There are those who say that at least we are not dead, but what's the good of it? Our physical form decays and with it the mind likewise. May we not say that this is the most lamentable of all? Is human life really so deluded as this? Am I the only one who is so deluded? Are there some individuals who are not deluded?

## 4

If we follow our prejudices and take them as our guide, who will not have such a guide? Why should only those who are intelligent make such mental choices for themselves? The foolish do the same thing. If one claims that right and wrong exist before they are established in the mind, that is like saying one sets out for Viet today but arrived there yesterday. To do so is to make something out of nothing. Even Holy Yü couldn't make something out of nothing. How could I alone do so?

## 5

Speech is not merely the blowing of air. Speech is intended to say something, but what is spoken may not necessarily be valid. If it is not valid, has anything actually been spoken? Or has speech never actually occurred? We may consider speech to be distinct from the chirps of hatchlings, but is there really any difference between them?

How has the Way become so obscured that there are true and false? How has speech become so obscured that there are right and wrong? Could it be that the Way has gone off and is no longer present? Could it be that speech is present but has lost its ability to validate? The Way is obscured by partial achievements; speech is obscured by eloquent verbiage. Thus there are controversies between Confucians and Mohists over what's right and what's wrong. They invariably affirm what their opponents deny and deny what their opponents affirm. If one wishes to affirm what others deny and deny what others affirm, nothing is better than lucidity.

Everything is "that" in relation to other things and "this" in relation to itself. We may not be able to see things from the standpoint of "that," but we can understand them from the standpoint of "this." Therefore, it may be said that "that" derives from "this" and that "this" is dependent upon "that." Such is the notion of the cogenesis of "this" and "that." Nonetheless, from the moment of birth death begins simultaneously, and from the moment of death birth begins simultaneously. Every affirmation is a denial of something else, and every denial is an affirmation of something else. "This" and "that" are mutually dependent; right and wrong are also mutually dependent. For this reason, the sage does not subscribe to [the view of absolute opposites] but sees things in the light of nature, accepting "this" for what it is.

"This" is also "that"; "that" is also "this." "This" implies a concept of right and wrong; "that" also implies a concept of right and wrong. But is there really a "this" and a "that"? Or is there really no "this" and no "that"? Where "this" and "that" cease to be opposites, there lies the pivot of the Way. Only when the pivot is located in the center of the circle of things can we respond to their infinite transformations. The transformations of "right" are infinite and so are the transformations of "wrong." Therefore, it is said that nothing is better for responding to them than lucidity.

## 6

To use a finger as a metaphor for the nonfingerness of a finger is not as good as using nonfingerness as a metaphor for the nonfingerness of a finger. To use a horse as a metaphor for the nonhorseness of a horse is not as good as using nonhorseness as a metaphor for the nonhorseness of a horse. Heaven and earth are the same as a finger; the myriad things are the same as a horse.

Affirmation lies in our affirming; denial lies in our denying. A way comes into being through our walking upon it; a thing is so because people say that it is. Why are things so? They are so because we declare them to be so. Why are things not so? They are not so because we declare them to be not so. All things are possessed of that which we may say is so; all things are possessed of that which we may affirm. There is no thing that is not so; there is no thing that is not affirmable.

Thus, whether it be a tiny blade of grass or a mighty pillar, a hideous leper or beauteous Hsi Shih, no matter how peculiar or fantastic, through the Way they all become one. To split something up is to create something else; to create something is to destroy something else. But for things in general, there is neither creation nor destruction, for they all revert to join in Unity.

Only the perceptive understand that all things join in Unity. For this reason they do not use things themselves but lodge in commonality. . . . It is all a result of their understanding the mutual dependence of "this" and "that." To have achieved this understanding but not be conscious of why it is so is called "The Way."

To weary the spiritual intelligence by trying to unify things without knowing that they are already identical is called "three in the morning." Why is this called "three in the morning"? Once upon a time, there was a monkey keeper who was feeding little chestnuts to his charges. "I'll give you three in the morning and four in the evening," he told them. All the monkeys were angry. "All right, then," said the keeper, "I'll give you four in the morning and three in the evening." All the monkeys were happy with this arrangement. Without adversely affecting either the name or the reality of the amount that he fed them, the keeper acted in accordance with the feelings of the monkeys. He too recognized the mutual dependence of "this" and "that." Consequently, the sage harmonizes the right and wrong of things and rests at the center of the celestial potter's wheel. This is called "dual procession."

## 7

The knowledge of the ancients attained the ultimate. What was the ultimacy that it attained? They realized that there was a stage before there were things. This is the ultimacy they had attained, the utmost to which nothing can be added.

Next, there were those who recognized that there were things, but that there was a stage before which things were distinguished. Next, there were those who recognized that there were distinctions among things, but that there was a stage before there was right and wrong. Now, the manifestation of right and wrong is what diminishes the Way. What causes the diminution is what leads to the creation of preferences. But, after all, are there really diminution and creation? Or are there, after all, really no diminution and creation? That there are diminution and creation may be seen from clansman Chao's playing the lute. That there are no diminution and creation may be seen from clansman Chao's not playing the lute. Chao Wen played the lute, Maestro K'uang beat the rhythm with a stick, and Master Hui commented philosophically beneath a parasol tree. The knowledge of these three masters was virtually complete, so they practiced it till the end of their lives. However, they believed that they were different from others in what they were fond of and wished to enlighten others about their fondness. Yet, try as they may to enlighten them, others were not to be enlightened. Thus one of them ended his life in muddle-headed discussions of "hard" and "white." And Chao Wen's son carried on his father's career his whole life without any accomplishment. If this can be called accomplishment even I, who am without accomplishment, can be called accomplished. But if this cannot be called accomplishment, neither I nor anything else is accomplished. Therefore, the sage endeavors to get rid of bewildering flamboyance. For this reason, he does not use things himself, but lodges in commonality. This is called "using lucidity."

## 8

Now I have something to say here. I do not know whether or not what I have to say is of the same category as "this." But, whether it is of the *same* category or not, like them it is *a* category, thus in the end it is no different from "that." Nevertheless, let me try to explain myself.

There is beginning. There is a time before beginning. There is a time before the time before beginning. There is being. There is nonbeing. There is a stage before nonbeing. There is a stage before the stage before nonbeing. Suddenly there is being and nonbeing. Still, as for being and nonbeing, I do not know which is really being and which is nonbeing. Now I have just said something, but I do not know whether what I have said is really saying something or not.

There is nothing under heaven larger than the tip of a downy hair at the end of autumn, but Mount T'ai is small. There is no greater longevity than that of a child who dies in infancy, but Progenitor P'eng died young. Heaven and earth were born together with me and the myriad things are one with me. Since all things are one, how can there be anything to talk about? But since I have already *said* that all things are one, how can there be nothing to talk about? One and speech makes two, two and one makes three. Continuing on in this fashion, even the cleverest mathematician couldn't keep up, how much less an ordinary person! Therefore, if in proceeding from nonbeing to being we arrive at three, how much farther we shall reach when proceeding from being to being. We need not proceed at all if we understand the mutual dependence of "this" and "that."

## 9

The Way has never been divided up, speech has never been constant. It's all because of "this" that there are demarcations. Let me explain what I mean by demarcations. There are left and right, discussions and deliberations, analyses and disputes, arguments and altercations. These are the eight types of demarcative assertions. The sages set aside without discussion what lies beyond the world. The sages discuss what lies within the world, but do not deliberate upon it. As for annals and other records of the statesmanship of the former kings, the sages deliberate over them but will not dispute about them. Therefore, wherever there is analysis, something is left unanalyzed. Wherever there is dispute, something is left undisputed. You may ask, "How can this be?" The sages embrace all things, but ordinary people dispute over them to show off to each other. Therefore it is said, wherever there is dispute, something is left unseen.

The great Way is ineffable, great disputation is speechless, great humaneness is inhumane, great honesty is immodest, and great bravery is not aggressive. The way that displays itself is not the Way. Speech that is disputatious fails to achieve its aims. Humaneness that is constant cannot go around. Honesty that is aloof will not be trusted. Bravery that is aggressive will not succeed. One who does not abandon these five precepts will be more or less headed in the right direction.

Therefore, she who knows to stop at what she does not know has attained the ultimate. Who knows the disputation that is without words and the Way that cannot be walked upon? If one can have knowledge of them, this is called the Treasury of Heaven. You may pour into it, but it never fills; you may dip from it, but it never empties; and you never know where it comes from. This is called the Inner Light.

## 10

Long ago, Yao inquired of Shun, "Wishing to make a punitive attack against Tsung, K'uai, and Hsü'ao, I sit on my throne feeling all preoccupied. Why is this so?"

"The rulers of these three states," said Shun, "are still living primitively amidst brambles and bushes. Why are you preoccupied? Of old, ten suns appeared simultaneously, illuminating the myriad things. How much more should a ruler like yourself, whose virtue excels that of the sun, be able to tolerate other rulers!"

## 11

Gnaw Gap inquired of Princely Scion, "Do you know wherein all things agree?"

"How could I know that?"

"Do you know what you don't know?"

"How could I know that?"

"Well, then, is it possible to know anything at all?"

"How could I know that? Nonetheless, I'll try to say something about it. How can we know that what I call knowledge is not really ignorance? How can we know that what I call ignorance is not really knowledge? But let me try to ask you a few questions. If people sleep in damp places, they develop lumbago or even partial paralysis. But would the same thing happen if a loach did so? If people dwell in trees, they will tremble with vertigo. But would the same thing happen if a gibbon did so? Of these three, which knows the proper place to dwell? People eat meat, deer eat grass, giant centipedes savor snakes, hawks and crows relish mice. Of these four, which knows the proper food to eat? Gibbons go for gibbons, buck mates with doe, loaches cavort with fish. Mao Ch'iang and Hsi Shih were considered by men to be beautiful, but if fish took one look at them they would dive into the depths, if birds saw them they would fly high into the sky, if deer saw them they would run away pell-mell. Of these four, which knows the correct standard of beauty for all under heaven? As I see it, the principle of humaneness and righteousness, the paths of right and wrong, are inextricably confused. How would I be able to distinguish among them?"

"If you," asked Gnaw Gap, "do not know the difference between benefit and harm, does the ultimate man likewise not know the difference between them?"

"The ultimate man is spiritous," said Princely Scion. "If the great marshes were set on fire, he would not feel hot. If the rivers turned to ice, he would not feel cold. If violent thunder split the mountains, he would not be injured. If whirlwinds lashed the seas, he would not be frightened. Such being the case, he rides the clouds, mounts the sun and moon, and wanders beyond the four seas. Since not even life and death have any transforming effect upon him, how much less do benefit and harm?"

## 12

"I have heard from Confucius," said Master Timid Magpie, enquiring of Master Tall Tree, "that the sage does not involve himself in worldly affairs. He does not go after gain, nor does he avoid harm. He does not take pleasure in seeking, nor does he get bogged down in formalistic ways. He speaks without saying anything; he says something without speaking. Instead, he wanders beyond the dust of the mundane world. Confucius thinks this is a vague description of the sage, but I think that it is the working of the wondrous Way. What do you think of it, my master?"

"Even the Yellow Emperor would be perplexed by hearing these things," said Master Tall Tree. "How is Hillock capable of understanding them? It seems that you, too, are overly hasty in forming an estimate. You're counting your chickens before they're hatched, drooling over roast owl at the sight of a crossbow pellet.

"Let me say a few careless words to you and you listen carelessly, all right? The sage can lean against the sun and moon and tuck the universe under his arm because he melds things into a whole,

> Sets aside obfuscation,
> And is indifferent to baseness and
>     honor.
> The mass of men are all
>     hustle-bustle;
> The sage is slow and simple.

He combines myriad years
Into a single purity.
Thus does he treat the myriad
things,
And thereby gathers them
together.

"How do I know that love of life is not a delusion? How do I know that fear of death is not like being a homeless waif who does not know the way home? When the state of Chin first got Pretty Li, the daughter of the border warden of Ai, she wept till her robe was soaked with tears. But after she arrived at the king's residence, shared his fine bed, and could eat the tender meats of his table, she regretted that she had ever wept. How do I know that the dead may not regret their former lust for life?

"Someone who dreams of drinking wine at a cheerful banquet may wake up crying the next morning. Someone who dreams of crying may go off the next morning to enjoy the sport of the hunt. When we are in the midst of a dream, we do not know it's a dream. Sometimes we may even try to interpret our dreams while we are dreaming, but then we awake and realize it was a dream. Only after one is greatly awakened does one realize that it was all a great dream, while the fool thinks that he is awake and presumptuously aware. 'My excellent lord!' 'Oh, thou humble shepherd!' How perverse they are!

"Both Confucius and you are dreaming, and I too am dreaming when I say that you are dreaming. This sort of language may be called enigmatic, but after myriad generations there may appear a great sage who will know how to explain it and he will appear as though overnight.

"Suppose that you and I have a dispute. If you beat me and I lose to you, does that mean you're really right and I'm really wrong? If I beat you and you lose to me, does that mean I'm really right and you're really wrong? Is one of us right and the other wrong? Or are both of us right and both of us wrong? Neither you nor I can know, and others are even more in the dark. Whom shall we have decide the matter? Shall we have someone who agrees with you decide it? Since he agrees with you, how can he decide fairly? Shall we have someone who agrees with me decide it? Since he agrees with me, how can he decide fairly? Shall we have someone who differs with both of us decide it? Since he differs with both of us, how can he make a decision? Shall we have someone who agrees with both of us decide it? Since he agrees with both of us, how can he make a decision? Given that neither you nor I, nor another person, can know how to decide, shall we wait for still another?

"Whether the alternating voices of disputation are relative to each other or not, they may be harmonized within the framework of nature and allowed to follow their own effusive elaboration so they may live out their years. What does 'harmonized within the framework of nature' mean? I would say, 'Right may be not right, so may be not so. If right were really right, then right would be distinct from not right, and there would be no dispute. If so were really so, then so would be distinct from not so and there would be no dispute. Forget how many years there are in a lifespan, forget righteousness. If you ramble in the realm of infinity, you will reside in the realm of infinity."

### 13

Penumbra inquired of Shadow, saying, "One moment you move and the next moment you stand still; one moment you're seated and the next moment you get up. Why are you so lacking in constancy?"

Shadow said, "Must I depend on something else to be what I am? If so, must what I depend upon in turn depend upon something else to be what it is? Must I depend upon the scales of a snake's belly or the forewings of a cicada? How can I tell why I am what I am? How can I tell why I'm not what I'm not?"

### 14

Once upon a time Chuang Chou dreamed that he was a butterfly, a butterfly flitting about happily enjoying himself. He didn't know that he was Chou. Suddenly he awoke and was palpably Chou. He did not know whether he was Chou who had dreamed of being a butterfly or a butterfly dreaming that he was Chou. Now, there must be a difference between Chou and the butterfly. This is called the transformation of things.

## Mozi (489?–406? BCE)

Ancient Chinese literature contains a considerable amount of philosophical debate concerning what happens after death and whether or not ghosts exist. Confucius himself showed reluctance to speculate on these issues (see *Analects* 7.21 and 11.12, see pp. 325, 328), but many of his later followers seem to have held decidedly skeptical opinions on the supernatural. The philosopher Mozi (Mo Tzu), who probably studied among the Confucians early in his life but then broke away to form his own school, reacted strongly to the growing skepticism of his time. He argued that ghosts do indeed exist and that, furthermore, only a belief in ghosts and supernatural retribution can keep humans from crime and immorality. His essay, *Shedding Light on Ghosts,* relies almost exclusively upon testimony from the records of the past to support his views.

Mozi is the first Chinese philosopher whose ideas are presented in a sustained essay form—a form that stands in contrast to the short statements and brief dialogues of the *Analects.* Almost all of the essays identified with Mozi seem to respond to, and usually disagree with, ideas circulating among the disciples of Confucius. For example, Mozi was against musical performances, extravagant burials, and love that showed partiality toward one's own parents. He favored equal treatment of all, economy in expenditures, and "identifying with superiors," the latter a doctrine that he used to justify a highly centralized and authoritarian form of government.

We know that late in the Zhou dynasty "the followers of Mozi filled the empire," but by the end of the first century of the Han era this school of thought had essentially disappeared. Subsequently Mozi's ideas exerted very little influence on Chinese thought.

## *Shedding Light on Ghosts*

*Translated by Laura E. Hess*

Mozi said, "Since the time when the sage kings of the Three Dynasties of antiquity passed away, the world has lost its sense of propriety and the feudal lords have ruled by force. Lords and vassals, and superiors and inferiors are not kind and loyal. Fathers and sons, and younger and older brothers are not compassionate and filial, deferential and caring, and upright and fine. Officials do not diligently attend to government affairs and the common people do not diligently do their work. The people are wanton and violent, and steal and rebel. Robbers and bandits pursue innocent people on roads and paths with weapons and blades, poisons and drugs, and water and fire, and seize people's carriages and horses, and garments and furs, for their own profit. These conditions all started with the passing of the sage kings of antiquity, whereupon the world fell into a state of chaos."

What is the reason for this? It is all the result of people doubting the existence of ghosts and spirits, and not understanding the ability of ghosts and spirits to reward the worthy and punish the violent. Now if the people of the world all believed in the ability of ghosts and spirits to reward the worthy and punish the violent, then how could the world ever possibly fall into a state of chaos?

Now those who insist that ghosts do not exist claim, "Of course there are no such things as ghosts and spirits!" From dawn until dusk they preach this doctrine to the world, confusing the masses and causing them to doubt the existence of ghosts and spirits. Thus the world has fallen into a state of chaos. Therefore Mozi said, "Now the kings, dukes, great men, officers, and gentlemen of the world wish to promote profit and eliminate harm. Although they believe that they cannot conclusively investigate the question of the existence of ghosts and spirits, were they to undertake such an investigation, they would soon realize the necessity of it." This being the case, then let us now look into this question.

On what grounds shall we base our argument? Mozi said, "One ascertains whether something exists by taking the testimony of the ears and eyes of the masses as the standard. If someone has heard or seen something, then we must believe that it exists. If no one has heard or seen it, then we must believe that it does not exist. If this is so, then why not try going to a district or village and making some inquiries? If from antiquity up until the present, from the birth of mankind on, there have been people who have seen the forms of ghosts and spirits and heard their sounds, then how can we say that ghosts and spirits do not exist? But if no one has heard or seen them, then how can we say that ghosts and spirits exist?"

Now those who insist that ghosts do not exist say, "Countless people in the world have claimed to have seen or heard ghosts and spirits, but what evidence is there for this?"

Mozi said, "If we rely on what the masses have jointly seen and heard, then Du Bo of antiquity is such an example. Although King Xuan of Zhou killed his vassal Du Bo, Du Bo was innocent.

Du Bo said, 'Although my lord kills me, I am innocent. If the dead lack consciousness, then this will be the end of the matter. But if the dead possess consciousness, then I will definitely cause my lord to know this before three years pass.' In the third year, King Xuan of Zhou met with the feudal lords and went hunting at Putian. His entourage of several hundred chariots and several thousand attendants filled the fields. In the middle of the day, Du Bo appeared, riding a plain chariot drawn by a white horse, wearing a vermilion robe and cap, carrying a vermilion bow and clasping a vermilion arrow. He chased after King Xuan of Zhou and shot him in his chariot, piercing his heart and breaking his spine. Struck down in his chariot, the king slumped over his quiver and died. At the time, all the Zhou attendants saw this and all those at a distance heard of it, and it was recorded in the Zhou annals. Rulers used it to instruct their vassals and fathers used it to admonish their sons, saying, 'Be careful and cautious! Those who kill the innocent will surely incur misfortune. The scheming of ghosts and spirits is urgent and swift like this.' If we examine the question of the existence of ghosts and spirits using the account in this text, then how can we possibly doubt their existence?"

"It is not only the account in this text that proves this. Once long ago when Duke Mu of Zheng was in the temple during the day, a spirit entered the door and stood at his left. It had a human face, a bird's body, plain clothing with three slits, and a stern and dignified appearance. Seeing it, Duke Mu of Zheng started to flee in fear. The spirit said, 'In appreciation of your enlightened virtue, God has sent me to bestow upon you an additional nineteen years of longevity. God will cause your state to flourish and prosper, and your descendants to be numerous and not lose possession of the state.' Duke Mu of Zheng bowed twice, then kowtowed, saying, 'May I ask your name?' The spirit said, 'I am Gou Mang.' If we accept what Duke Mu of Zheng saw as evidence, then how can we possibly doubt the existence of ghosts and spirits?"

"It is not only the account in this text that proves this. Long ago, although Duke Jian of Yan killed his vassal Zhuang Ziyi, Zhuang Ziyi was innocent. Zhuang Ziyi said, 'Although my sovereign kills me, I am innocent. If the dead lack consciousness, then this will be the end of the matter. But if the dead possess consciousness, then I will definitely cause my lord to know this before three years pass.' A year later, Duke Jian of Yan was setting off for an excursion to the grasslands. Yan's grasslands are comparable to the altars for the gods of soil and grain in Qi, Sanglin in Song, and Yunmeng in Chu. They are a place where men and women hold ritual observances. In the daytime, when Duke Jian of Yan was setting off for an excursion to the grasslands, Zhuang Ziyi appeared, shouldering a vermilion staff, and struck down the duke in his chariot. At this time, all the Yan attendants saw this and all those at a distance heard of it, and it was recorded in the Yan annals. The feudal lords have handed the story down, saying, 'Those who kill the innocent will surely incur misfortune. The punishment of ghosts and spirits is urgent and swift like this.' If we examine the question of the existence of ghosts and spirits using the account in this text, then how can we possibly doubt their existence?"

"It is not only the account in this text that proves this. Long ago, during the time of Lord Wen of Song, whose name was Bao, there was a vassal named Prayermaster Guangu. Once when Guangu was offering a sacrifice to those deceased who lacked descendants, a spellmaster appeared, wielding a pole. The spellmaster came out and spoke with Guangu, saying, 'Guangu, why is it that the jade tablets and discs do not fulfill the standard, the offerings of wine and millet are impure, the sacrificial animals are not flawless and fat, and the ritual seasonal banquets are being mistimed? Was it you who did this or was it Bao?' Guangu said, 'Bao is but an infant still in swaddling clothes. How could he possibly have known about this? It is I, the official and vassal Guangu, who is solely responsible.' The spellmaster raised his pole and beat Guangu, prostrating him on the altar. At this time, all the Song attendants saw this and all those at a distance heard of it, and it was recorded in the Song annals. The feudal lords have handed down the story, saying, 'The punishment of ghosts and spirits reaches those who are not respectful and cautious when offering sacrifices, and is urgent and swift like this.' If we examine the question of the existence of ghosts and spirits using the account in this text, then how can we possibly doubt their existence?"

"It is not only the account in this text that proves this. Long ago, during the reign of Lord Zhuang of Qi, there were two men named Wang Liguo and Zhong Lijiao. They had been involved in a lawsuit for three years, but the case still had not been decided. The Lord of Qi was reluctant to kill them, fearing they might be innocent. He was reluctant to acquit them, fearing that he might release the guilty party. He therefore had these men provide a sheep and swear an oath at Qi's sacred altar for the god of soil. The two men agreed to take a blood oath. The sheep's throat was then slit and its blood sprinkled on the altar. Wang Liguo's defense was read all the way through, but when Zhong Lijiao's defense had been read only halfway through, the sheep arose and butted him, breaking his leg. The spirit of the ancestral hall came forth and beat him, prostrating him on the altar. At this time, all the Qi attendants saw this and all those at a distance heard of it, and it was recorded in the Qi annals. The feudal lords have handed down the story, saying, 'The punishment of ghosts and spirits reaches all those who do not take oaths sincerely, and is urgent and swift like this.' If we examine the question of the existence of ghosts and spirits using the account in this text, then how can we possibly doubt their existence?"

Therefore Mozi said, "Even in deep valleys, vast forests, secluded streams, and places without people, one must conduct oneself properly because ghosts and spirits are always watching."

Now those who insist that ghosts do not exist say, "How can the testimony of the ears and eyes of the masses be sufficient to settle doubts? How can those who desire to become esteemed gentlemen possibly rely on the testimony of the ears and eyes of the masses?"

Mozi said, "If one does not consider the testimony of the ears and eyes of the masses to be sufficiently trustworthy, are such men as the sage kings of the Three Dynasties of antiquity, namely Yao, Shun, Yu, Tang, Wen and Wu, sufficiently trustworthy? All those who are above average would certainly agree that the sage kings of the Three Dynasties of antiquity are sufficiently trustworthy. If the sage kings of the

Three Dynasties of antiquity are sufficiently trustworthy, then let us now try to look respectfully at their deeds."

"Long ago, after King Wu had defeated the state of Yin and punished its ruler Zhou, he ordered the feudal lords to divide up the sacrificial duties, saying, 'Order near relatives to take charge of the inner sacrifices and distant relatives to take charge of the outer sacrifices.' Thus clearly King Wu believed in the existence of ghosts and spirits, since he ordered the feudal lords to divide up the sacrifices after he had defeated Yin and punished Zhou. If ghosts and spirits did not exist, then why would he have divided up the sacrifices?"

"It is not only the deeds of King Wu that prove the existence of ghosts and spirits. Long ago, the sage kings invariably distributed rewards before the ancestors and held executions before the altar for the god of soil. Why did they distribute rewards before the ancestors? To report the equitability of the division of rewards. Why did they hold executions in front of the altar for the god of soil? To report the justness of hearings."

"It is not only the account in this text that proves the existence of ghosts and spirits. Long ago, on the day when the sage kings of the Three Dynasties of Xia, Shang and Zhou initially established their nations and laid out their capitals, they invariably selected a site for the principal altar of the nation and built an ancestral temple there. They would select long, lush trees and plant them at the altar. They would select the most compassionate and filial, upright and fine among the nation's elders, and appoint them prayermasters and ceremonial masters. They would select the best, plumpest, and most pure-colored among the six kinds of domestic animals and use them as sacrificial victims. They would select shining, sparkling jade tablets and discs, and designate these valuables as the standard. They would select the most fragrant and golden of the five grains, and use them for offertory wine and millet, which meant that the quality of the offerings varied with the harvest. In this way, when the sage kings of antiquity ruled the world, they always gave priority to ghosts and spirits, and only afterwards attended to the affairs of the people. Therefore it was said that the operations of government offices must give priority to ensuring that the necessary sacrificial vessels and robes were stocked in the state treasuries, that prayermasters and civil authorities must be established at the court, and that sacrificial animals must not be permitted to mix with their original flocks. Since the government of the sage kings of antiquity was like this, they must have believed in the existence of ghosts and spirits."

"The sage kings of antiquity were greatly concerned with properly serving ghosts and spirits. They feared that in later ages their descendants would not understand this, so they recorded it on bamboo and silk so it would be handed down to posterity. They feared that the bamboo and silk would rot and be lost, and that their descendants would not learn of it, so they incised it on plates and bowls and engraved it on metal and stone as well. They also feared that in later ages their descendants would not revere ghosts and spirits and hence fail to obtain blessings. Therefore every foot of silk and every fascicle of text containing the writings of the former kings and the words of the sages tell repeatedly of the existence of numerous ghosts and spirits.

Why did the sage kings do this? Because they considered it to be of the utmost importance." Now those who insist that ghosts and spirits do not exist and claim that there are no such things are rejecting the beliefs of the sage kings. This is surely not the way of a true gentleman!

Now those who insist that ghosts do not exist claim, "Not a single foot of silk or a single fascicle of text containing the writings of the former kings tells repeatedly of the existence of numerous ghosts and spirits. What text has such things?"

Mozi said, "Such things can be found in the '*Greater Elegentiae,*' which is a Zhou dynasty text. It says,

> King Wen is located above.
> Brilliant is he in the heavens!
> Although Zhou is an old nation,
> its mandate is new indeed!
> Isn't Zhou illustrious! Wasn't the
> divine mandate timely!
> King Wen ascends and descends.
> He stands at the left and right
> of God.
> Solemn and majestic is King Wen!
> His fine reputation is
> never-ending.

If ghosts and spirits did not exist, then how could King Wen have possibly 'stood at the left and the right of God' after his death? This is evidence from Zhou texts for the existence of ghosts."

"If references to ghosts can be found only in Zhou dynasty texts, but not in Shang dynasty texts, then this still would not be sufficient evidence. Now let us examine a Shang text, which says,

> Alas! In the time in antiquity when the Xia rulers had not yet suffered misfortune, among the various beasts and insects, and even the flying birds, there was none that did not follow the proper way. Thus how could those with human faces dare to diverge in their hearts? Even the ghosts and spirits of the mountains and rivers did not dare to be restless.

Those who were respectful and trustworthy were able to maintain harmony in the world and security in the land below. None of the ghosts and spirits of the mountains and rivers dared to be restless, because they were assisting the Xia dynasty founder Yu. This is evidence from Shang texts for the existence of ghosts."

"If references to ghosts can be found only in Shang dynasty texts, but not in Xia dynasty texts, then this still would not be sufficient evidence. Now let us examine the 'Declaration of Yu,' which is a Xia text. It says,

> There was a great battle at Gan. The king thereupon summoned his six attendants and issued a declaration to the central army, saying: 'Clansman Hu has violated the five elements and discarded the three established calendars. Heaven will therefore terminate his mandate.' He also said, 'At noon today, I will vie with Clansman Hu for the mandate of the day. Ministers and commonfolk, realize that I am not acting because I desire these lands and cities, but rather because I am respectfully carrying out the punishment of Heaven. If those of you on the left do not attack on the left and those of you on the right do not attack on the right, you will be disobeying my orders. If you charioteers fail to manage your horses properly, you will be disobeying my orders. Rewards will be distributed before the ancestors

and executions will be held before the altar for the god of the soil.'

Why were rewards distributed before the ancestors? To report the equitability of the division of rewards. Why were executions held before the altar for the god of the soil? To report the justness of hearings. Thus the sage kings of antiquity must have believed that ghosts and spirits rewarded the worthy and punished the violent. This is why they invariably distributed rewards before the ancestors and held executions before the altar for the god of the soil. This is evidence from Xia texts for the existence of ghosts."

"Thus first Xia dynasty texts, then later Shang and Zhou dynasty texts, tell repeatedly of the existence of numerous ghosts and spirits. Why is this? It is because the sage kings were concerned about such matters. If we examine the question of the existence of ghosts and spirits using the accounts in these texts, then how can we possibly doubt their existence?"

"It is said that in antiquity on the auspicious day of *ding mao,* the Zhou people prayed, presented offerings to the altar for the god of the soil, sacrificed to the four directions, and worshipped their ancestors in the hope of prolonging their lives. If ghosts and spirits did not exist, then how could the Zhou people have hoped to prolong their lives?"

Therefore Mozi said, "If ghosts and spirits can in fact reward the worthy and punish the violent, why not make this a fundamental part of national policy and proclaim it to the state and people? It would be an effective way to rule the nation and benefit the people. Ghosts and spirits will see when government officials are dishonest and when men and women do not maintain the proper separation of the sexes. Ghosts and spirits will see when people are wanton and violent, and steal and rebel, and when robbers and bandits pursue innocent people on roads with weapons and blades, poisons and drugs, and water and fire, and seize people's carriages and horses, and garments and furs, for their own profit. Therefore government officials will not dare to be dishonest. When they see goodness, they will not dare to withhold rewards. When they see violence, they will not dare to withhold punishment. People will no longer be wanton and violent, and steal and rebel, nor will robbers and bandits pursue innocent people on roads with weapons and blades, poisons and drugs, and water and fire, and seize carriages and horses, and garments and furs, for their own profit. Thus the world will be well ordered. The watchful eyes of ghosts and spirits cannot be avoided. Ghosts and spirits are invariably watching, even in dark and secluded places, vast grasslands, mountain forests and deep valleys. The punishment of ghosts and spirits cannot be evaded. It invariably overcomes even wealth, nobility, great numbers, daring, might, solid armor, and sharp weapons."

"If you do not believe this, then consider that long ago King Jie of the Xia dynasty was honored as the Son of Heaven and possessed the wealth of the empire. Above he maligned Heaven and insulted ghosts. Below he despised and endangered the people of the empire. Therefore Heaven dispatched Tang to carry out its enlightened punishment. Tang took nine chariots and proceeded in the Aviary Formation and the Wild Goose March. Mounting a great carriage, Tang attacked and scattered the Xia forces, entered the outskirts of the capital and captured Tuichi Daxi with his own hands. Long ago King Jie of the Xia dynasty was not only honored as the Son of Heaven and possessed the wealth of the empire, but he also had in his service the courageous Tuichi Daxi, who could rip apart live rhinoceroses and tigers and kill people with just a flick of his finger. The corpses of the millions of people he had killed utterly filled the grasslands and hills. Yet Jie could not obstruct the punishment of ghosts and spirits, even with Tuichi Daxi. This is why I said that the punishment of ghosts and spirits cannot be evaded, even with wealth, nobility, great numbers, daring, might, solid armor, and sharp weapons."

"Moreover, this is not the only such example. Long ago King Zhou of the Yin dynasty was honored as the Son of Heaven and possessed the wealth of the empire. Above he maligned Heaven and insulted ghosts. Below he despised and endangered the people of the empire. He cast aside the elderly, tormented young children, tortured the innocent, and cut apart the bellies of pregnant women. The commoners, widowers and widows wept and wailed, but lacked a recourse. Therefore Heaven dispatched King Wu to carry out its enlightened punishment. King Wu took one hundred select chariots and four hundred brave warriors. After reviewing his troops, King Wu fought the Yin forces in the fields of Mu and captured Fei Zhong and E Lai with his hands. Hordes of people deserted and fled. King Wu pursued them and entered the palace. He decapitated Zhou, hanging his head from a red ring and covering it with a white banner, thereby executing him on behalf of the feudal lords. Long ago King Zhou of the Yin dynasty was not only honored as the Son of Heaven and possessed the wealth of the empire, but he also had in his service the courageous and strong Fei Zhong, E Lai, and Duke of Chong, whose name was Hu, who could all kill people with just a flick of their fingers. The corpses of the millions of people they had killed utterly filled the grasslands and hills. Yet Zhou could not obstruct the punishment of ghosts and spirits, even with these men. This is why I said that the punishment of ghosts and spirits cannot be evaded, even with wealth, nobility, great numbers, daring, might, solid armor, and sharp weapons."

"Moreover, Qin Ai speaks of this, saying, 'No favorable act is too insignificant. No destruction of a clan is too great.' This means that ghosts and spirits do not consider any act too insignificant to reward or too great to punish."

Now those who insist that ghosts do not exist claim, "If something fails to benefit one's parents and instead harms them, then isn't one being unfilial?"

Mozi said, "The ghosts of antiquity and the present consist of celestial ghosts, ghosts and spirits of the mountains and waters, and ghosts of those who have died. Now there have been cases of children predeceasing their fathers and younger brothers predeceasing their older brothers. Even so, the world says, 'Those who are born first die first.' Thus it should be one's parents and older siblings who die first."

"Now we should prepare offertory wine and millet, and be respectful and conscientious about sacrifices and rituals. If ghosts and spirits really do exist, then isn't it highly beneficial to provide one's parents and older siblings with food and drink? If ghosts and spirits really do not exist, then it would seem that one is wasting the offertory wine and millet. Yet rather than wasting the provisions and simply dumping them into backwaters and gullies, instead clan members and villagers can always drink and eat together. Even if ghosts and spirits really do not exist, this can still be a way to bring people together for a celebration and be friendly with the villagers."

Now those who insist that ghosts do not exist claim, "Of course there are no such things as ghosts and spirits! Thus there is no need to spend any money on offertory wine and millet or sacrificial animals. It is not that we begrudge the cost of these things, but rather what good would it do for us?" This violates both the writings of the sage kings and the behavior of filial sons, yet those who make these claims strive to be the esteemed officials of the world. This is certainly not the way an esteemed official acts!"

Therefore Mozi said, "Now when I offer a sacrifice, I am not simply dumping the offerings into backwaters and gullies. Above, it is a way to seek the spiritual blessings of ghosts. Below, it is a way to bring people together for a celebration and be friendly with the villagers. If spirits exist, then my parents and brothers are fed. Thus isn't this beneficial to the entire world?"

Therefore, Mozi said, "If the kings, dukes, great men, officers, and gentlemen of the world desire to promote profit and eliminate harm, they must believe in the existence of ghosts and spirits and revere and acknowledge them accordingly. This is the way of the sage kings."

## Qu Yuan (340?–278 BCE)

Around 300 BCE a new style of poetry emerged from the southern Chinese state of Chu, a state centered on the Yangtze River. This new poetry is associated with Qu Yuan, the first great Chinese poet we know by name. Qu Yuan's poems, and those of several others who lived during the two centuries after his death and who followed in his tradition, are anthologized in a collection entitled *Songs of the South* (*Chuci* or *Ch'u Tz'u*).

Qu Yuan's longest and most important poem, *On Encountering Sorrow* (*Li sao*), which we include here, has always been read as an autobiographical statement. Qu Yuan was a minister in the court of Chu and advised his ruler to resist the growing power of the rival state of Qin, which was located to Chu's northwest. Other ministers, who favored a pro-Qin policy, criticized Qu Yuan and eventually persuaded the king of Chu to banish him to the far south. Disconsolate over being slandered and estranged from his king, Qu Yuan committed suicide by plunging into the Milo River. Subsequent history made him a prototype of the loyal minister unfairly attacked by lesser men. In *On Encountering Sorrow,* Qu Yuan raises political frustration and alienation to high art. Drawing on a Chu magical tradition of spiritual encounters between shamans and the deities they worship, Qu Yuan transforms his experience into cosmic drama as he soars into the clouds in pursuit of a divine tryst that never quite takes place.

At least so the poem has been read. But such a straightforward autobiographical reading of *On Encountering Sorrow* hardly explains the power it has exerted on twenty centuries of Chinese readers. The enduring popularity of this piece surely derives in part from the fact that it transcends the individual experience of one poet. It appeals to the widely experienced feeling that we never quite get the admiration we deserve, and that the most desired assignations constantly elude us.

Stylistically, *On Encountering Sorrow* differs radically from its northern Chinese forerunners found in the *Book of Songs*. First of all, and most obviously, it is much longer and vastly more complex than any poem in the *Book of Songs*. Second, the poetic line in this piece and all other pieces in *Songs of the South* is longer than the brief four-syllable line of its northern predecessors and probably reflects the emergence of a new and much more languorous musical style. Third, the poem is replete with lush nature imagery and references to mythology and popular religious belief. Although it can be mined for its rich religious and symbolic content, the poem can also be read and appreciated without a detailed knowledge of its many obscure references.

## *On Encountering Sorrow (Li sao)*

*Translated by David Hawkes*

Scion of the high lord Gao Yang,
Bo Yong was my father's name.
When She Ti pointed to the first month of the year,
On the day *geng-yin* I passed from the womb.
My father, seeing the aspect of my nativity,
Took omens to give me an auspicious name.
The name he gave me was True Exemplar;
The title he gave me was Divine Balance.

Having from birth this inward beauty,
I added to it fair outward adornment:
I dressed in selinea and shady angelica,
And twined autumn orchids to make a garland.
Swiftly I sped as in fearful pursuit,
Afraid Time would race on and leave me behind.
In the morning I gathered the angelica on the mountains;
In the evening I plucked the sedges of the islets.

The days and months hurried on, never delaying;
Springs and autumns sped by in endless alternation:
And I thought how the trees and flowers were fading and falling,
And feared that my Fairest's beauty would fade too.
'Gather the flower of youth and cast out the impure!
Why will you not change the error of your ways?

I have harnessed brave coursers for you to gallop forth with:
Come, let me go before and show you the way!

'The three kings of old were most pure and perfect:
Then indeed fragrant flowers had their proper place.
They brought together pepper and cinnamon;
All the most-prized blossoms were woven in their garlands.
Glorious and great were those two, Yao and Shun,
Because they had kept their feet on the right path.
And how great was the folly of Jie and Zhòu,
Who hastened by crooked paths, and so came to grief.

'The fools enjoy their careless pleasure,
But their way is dark and leads to danger.
I have no fear for the peril of my own person,
But only lest the chariot of my lord should be dashed.
I hurried about your chariot in attendance,
Leading you in the tracks of the kings of old.'
But the Fragrant One refused to examine my true feelings:
He lent ear instead to slander, and raged against me.

How well I know that loyalty brings disaster;
Yet I will endure: I cannot give it up.
I called on the ninefold heaven to be my witness,
And all for the sake of the Fair One, and no other.
There once was a time when he spoke with me in frankness;
But then he repented and was of another mind.
I do not care, on my own count, about this divorcement,
But it grieves me to find the Fair One so inconstant.

I had tended many an acre of orchids,
And planted a hundred rods of melilotus;
I had raised sweet lichens and the cart-halting flower,
And asarums mingled with fragrant angelica,
And hoped that when leaf and stem were in their full prime,
When the time had come, I could reap a fine harvest.
Though famine should pinch me, it is small matter;
But I grieve that all my blossoms should waste in rank weeds.

All others press forward in greed and gluttony,
No surfeit satiating their demands:
Forgiving themselves, but harshly judging others;
Each fretting his heart away in envy and malice.
Madly they rush in the covetous chase,
But not after that which *my* heart sets store by.

For old age comes creeping and soon will be upon me,
And I fear I shall not leave behind an enduring name.

In the mornings I drank the dew that fell from the magnolia;
At evening ate the petals that dropped from chrysanthemums.
If only my mind can be truly beautiful,
It matters nothing that I often faint for famine.
I pulled up roots to bind the valerian
And thread the castor plant's fallen clusters with;
I trimmed sprays of cassia for plaiting melilotus,
And knotted the lithe, light trails of ivy.

I take my fashion from the good men of old:
A garb unlike that which the rude world cares for;
Though it may not accord with present-day manners,
I will follow the pattern that Peng Xian has left.
Heaving a long sigh, I brush away my tears,
Sad that man's life should be so beset with hardship.
Though goodness and beauty were my bit and bridle,
I was slandered in the morning and cast off the same evening.

Yet, though cast off, I would wear my orchid girdle;
I would pluck some angelicas to add to its beauty;
For this it is that my heart takes most delight in,
And though I died nine times, I should not regret it.
What I regret is the Fair One's waywardness,
That never once stops to ask what is in men's minds.
All your ladies were jealous of my delicate beauty;
In their spiteful chattering they said I was a wanton.

Truly this generation are cunning artificers,
From square and compass turn their eyes and change the true
measurement,
Disregard the ruled line to follow their crooked fancies;
To emulate in flattery is their only rule.
But I am sick and sad at heart and stand irresolute:
I alone am at a loss in this generation.
Yet I would rather quickly die and meet dissolution
Before I ever would consent to ape *their* behaviour.

Eagles do not flock like birds of lesser species;
So it has ever been since the olden time.
How can the round and square ever fit together?
How can different ways of life ever be reconciled?
Yet humbling one's spirit and curbing one's pride,
Bearing blame humbly and enduring insults,

But keeping pure and spotless and dying in righteousness:
Such conduct was greatly prized by the wise men of old.

Repenting, therefore, that I had not conned the way more
closely,
I halted, intending to turn back again—
To turn about my chariot and retrace my road
Before I had advanced too far along the path of folly.
I walked my horses through the marsh's orchid-covered margin;
I galloped to the hill of pepper-trees and rested there.
I could not go in to him for fear of meeting trouble,
And so, retired, I would once more fashion my former raiment.

I made a coat of lotus and water-chestnut leaves,
And gathered lotus petals to make myself a skirt.
I will no longer care that no one understands me,
As long as I can keep the sweet fragrance of my mind.
Higher still the hat now that towered on my head,
And longer the girdle that dangled from my waist.
Fragrant and foul mingle in confusion,
But my inner brightness has remained undimmed.

Suddenly I turned back and let my eyes wander.
I resolved to go and visit all the world's quarters.
My garland's crowded blossoms, mixed in fair confusion,
Wafted the sweetness of their fragrance far and wide.
All men have something in their lives that gives them pleasure:
With me the love of beauty is my constant joy.
I could not change this, even if my body were dismembered;
For how could dismemberment ever hurt my mind?

My Nü Xu was fearful and clung to me imploringly,
Lifting her voice up in expostulation:
'Gun in his stubbornness took no thought for his life
And perished, as result, on the moor of Feather Mountain.
Why be so lofty, with your passion for purity?
Why must you alone have such delicate adornment?
Thorns, king-grass, curly-ear hold the place of power:
But you must needs stand apart and not speak them fair.

'You cannot go from door to door convincing everybody;
No one can say, "See, look into my mind!"
Others band together and like to have companions:
Why must you be so aloof? Why not heed my counsel?'
But I look to the wise men of old for my guidance.
So sighing, with a full heart, I bore her upbraidings

And crossing the Yuan and Xiang, I journeyed southwards
Till I came to where Chong Hua was and made my plaint to him.

'Singing the Nine Songs and dancing the Nine Changes,
Qi of Xia made revelry and knew no restraint,
Taking no thought for the troubles that would follow:
And so his five sons fell out, brother against brother.
Yi loved idle roaming and hunting to distraction,
And took delight in shooting at the mighty foxes.
But foolish dissipation has seldom a good end:
And Han Zhuo covetously took his master's wife.

'Zhuo's son, Jiao, put on his strong armour
And wreaked his wild will without any restraint.
The days passed in pleasure; far he forgot himself,
Till his head came tumbling down from his shoulders.
Jie of Xia all his days was a king most unnatural,
And so he came finally to meet with calamity.
Zhòu cut up and salted the bodies of his ministers;
And so the days were numbered of the House of Yin.

'Tang of Shang and Yu of Xia were reverent and respectful;
The House of Zhou chose the true way without error,
Raising up the virtuous and able men to government,
Following the straight line without fear or favor.
High God in Heaven knows no partiality;
He looks for the virtuous and makes them his ministers.
For only the wise and good can ever flourish
If it is given them to possess the earth.

'I have looked back into the past and forward to later ages,
Examining the outcomes of men's different designs.
Where is the unrighteous man who could be trusted?
Where is the wicked man whose service could be used?
Though I stand at the pit's mouth and death yawns before me,
I still feel no regret at the course I have chosen.
Straightening the handle, regardless of the socket's shape:
For that crime the good men of old were hacked in pieces.'

Many a heavy sigh I heaved in my despair,
Grieving that I was born in such an unlucky time.
I plucked soft lotus petals to wipe my welling tears
That fell down in rivers and wet my coat front.
I knelt on my outspread skirts and poured my plaint out,
And the righteousness within me was clearly manifest.
I yoked a team of jade dragons to a phoenix-figured car
And waited for the wind to come, to soar up on my journey.

I started out in the morning on my way from Cang-wu;
By evening I had arrived at the Hanging Garden.
I wanted to stay a while in those fairy precincts,
But the swift-moving sun was dipping to the west.
I ordered Xi He to stay the sun-steeds' gallop,
To stand over Yan-zi mountain and not go in;
For the road was so far and so distant was my journey,
And I wanted to go up and down, seeking my heart's desire.

I watered my dragon steeds at the Pool of Heaven,
And tied their reins up to the Fu-sang tree.
I broke a sprig of the Ruo tree to strike the sun with:
First I would roam a little for my enjoyment.
I sent Wang Shu ahead to ride before me;
The Wind God went behind as my outrider;
The Bird of Heaven gave notice of my comings;
The Thunder God warned me when all was not ready.

I caused my phoenixes to mount on their pinions
And fly ever onward by night and by day.
The whirlwinds gathered and came out to meet me,
Leading clouds and rainbows, to give me welcome.
In wild confusion, now joined and now parted,
Upwards and downwards rushed the glittering train.
I asked Heaven's porter to open up for me;
But he leant across Heaven's gate and eyed me churlishly.

The day was getting dark and drawing to its close.
Knotting orchids, I waited in indecision.
The muddy, impure world, so undiscriminating,
Seeks always to hide beauty, out of jealousy.
I decided when morning came to cross the White Water,
And climbed the peak of Lang-feng, and there tied up my steeds.
Then I looked about me and suddenly burst out weeping,
Because on that high hill there was no fair lady.

'Here I am, suddenly, in this House of Spring.
I have broken off a jasper branch to add to my girdle.
Before the jasper flowers have shed their bright petals,
I shall look for a maiden below to give it to.'
So I made Feng Long ride off on a cloud
To seek out the dwelling-place of the lady Fu Fei.
I took off my girdle as a pledge of my suit to her,
And ordered Lame Beauty to be the go-between.

Many were the hurried meetings and partings:
All wills and caprices, she was hard to woo.

In the evenings she went to lodge in the Qiong-shi mountain;
In the mornings she washed her hair in the Wei-pan stream.
With proud disdain she guarded her beauty,
Passing each day in idle, wanton pleasures.
Though fair she may be, she lacks all seemliness:
Come! I'll have none of her; let us search elsewhere!

I looked all around over the earth's four quarters,
Circling the heavens till at last I alighted.
I gazed on a jade tower's glittering splendour
And spied the lovely daughter of the Lord of Song.
I sent off the magpie to pay my court to her,
But the magpie told me that my suit had gone amiss.
The magpie flew off with noisy chatterings.
I hate him for an idle, knavish fellow.

My mind was irresolute and wavering;
I wanted to go, and yet I could not.
Already the phoenix had taken his present,
And I feared that Gao Xin would get there before me.
I wanted to go far away, but had nowhere to go to:
Where could I wander to look for amusement?
Before they were married to Prince Shao Kang,
Lord Yu's two daughters were there for the wooing.

But my pleader was weak and my matchmaker stupid,
And I feared that this suit, too, would not be successful.
For the world is impure and envious of the able,
Eager to hide men's good and make much of their ill.
Deep in the palace, unapproachable,
The wise king slumbers and will not be awakened.
That the thoughts in my breast should all go unuttered—
How can I endure this until I end my days?

I searched for the holy plant and twigs of bamboo,
And ordered Ling Fen to make divination for me.
He said, 'Beauty is always bound to find its mate:
Who that was truly fair was ever without lovers?
Think of the vastness of the wide world:
Here is not the only place where you can find your lady.
Go farther afield,' he said, 'and do not be faint-hearted.
What woman seeking handsome mate could ever refuse you?

'What place on earth does not boast some fragrant flower?
Why need you always cleave to your old home?
The world today is blinded with its own folly:

You cannot make people see the virtue inside you.
Most people's loathings and likings are different,
Only these men here are not as others are;
For they wear mugwort and cram their waistbands with it,
But the lovely valley orchid they deem unfit to wear.

'Since beauty of flower, then, and of shrub escapes them,
What chance has a rarest jewel of gaining recognition?
They gather up muck to stuff their perfume bags with;
The spicy pepper-plant they say has got no scent at all.'
I wanted to follow Ling Fen's auspicious oracle,
But I faltered and could not make my mind up.
I heard that Wu Xian was descending in the evening,
So I lay in wait with offerings of peppered rice-balls.

The spirits came like a dense cloud descending,
And the host of Doubting Mountain came crowding to meet him.
His godhead was manifested by a blaze of radiance,
And he addressed me in these auspicious words:
'To and fro in the earth you must everywhere wander,
Seeking one whose thoughts are of your own measure.
Tang and Yu sought sincerely for the right helpers;
So Yi Yin and Gao Yao worked well with their princes.

'As long as your soul within is beautiful,
What need have you of a matchmaker?
Yue laboured as a builder, pounding earth at Fu-yan,
Yet Wu Ding employed him without a second thought.
Lü Wang wielded the butcher's knife at Zhao-ge,
But King Wen met him and raised him up on high.
Ning Qi sang as he fed his ox at evening;
Duke Huan of Qi heard him and took him as his minister.

'Gather the flower of youth before it is too late,
While the good season is still not yet over.
Beware lest the shrike sound his note before the equinox,
Causing all the flowers to lose their fine fragrance.'
How splendid the glitter of my jasper girdle!
But the crowd make a dark screen, masking its beauty.
And I fear that my enemies, who never can be trusted,
Will break it out of spiteful jealousy.

The age is disordered in a tumult of changing:
How can I tarry much longer among them?
Orchid and iris have lost all their fragrance;
Flag and melilotus have changed into straw.

Why have all the fragrant flowers of days gone by
Now all transformed themselves into worthless mugwort?
What other reason can there be for this
But that they all have no more care for beauty?

I thought that orchid was one to be trusted,
But he proved a sham, bent only on pleasing his masters.
He overcame his goodness and conformed to evil counsels:
He no more deserves to rank with fragrant flowers.
Pepper is all wagging tongue and lives only for slander;
And even stinking dogwood seeks to fill a perfume bag.
Since they only seek advancement and labour for position,
What fragrance have they deserving our respect?

Since, then, the world's way is to drift the way the tide runs,
Who can stay the same and not change with all the rest?
Seeing the behaviour of orchid and pepper-flower,
What can be expected of cart-halt and selinea?
They have cast off their beauty and come to this:
Only my garland is left to treasure.
Its penetrating perfume does not easily desert it,
And even to this day its fragrance has not faded.

I will follow my natural bent and please myself;
I will go off wandering to look for a lady.
While my adornment is in its pristine beauty
I will travel around looking both high and low.
Since Ling Fen had given me a favourable oracle,
I picked an auspicious day to start my journey on.
I broke a branch of jasper to take for my meat,
And ground fine jasper meal for my journey's provisions.

'Harness winged dragons to be my coursers;
Let my chariot be of fine work of jade and ivory!
How can I live with men whose hearts are strangers to me?
I am going a far journey to be away from them.'
I took the way that led towards the Kun-lun mountain:
A long, long road with many a turning in it.
The cloud-embroidered banner flapped its great shade above us;
And the jingling jade yoke-bells tinkled merrily.

I set off at morning from the Ford of Heaven;
At evening I came to the world's western end.
Phoenixes followed me, bearing up my pennants,
Soaring high aloft with majestic wing-beats.
'See, I have come to the Desert of Moving Sands!'
Warily I drove along the banks of the Red Water,

Then, beckoning the water-dragons to make a bridge for me,
I summoned the God of the West to take me over.

So long the road had been and full of difficulties,
I sent word to my escort to take another route,
To wheel around leftwards, skirting Bu-zhou Mountain:
On the shore of the Western Sea we would reassemble.
When we had mustered there, all thousand chariots,
Jade hub to jade hub we galloped on abreast.
My eight dragon steeds flew on with writhing undulations;
My cloud-embroidered banners flapped on the wind.

In vain I tried to curb them, to slacken the swift pace:
The spirits soared high up, far into the distance.
We played the Nine Songs and danced the Shao Dances,
Borrowing the time to make a holiday.
But when I had ascended the splendour of the heavens,
I suddenly caught a glimpse below of my old home.
My groom's heart was heavy and the horses for longing
Arched their heads back and refused to go on.

### Luan

Enough! There are no true men in the state: no one understands me.
Why should I cleave to the city of my birth?
Since none is worthy to work with in making good government,
I shall go and join Peng Xian in the place where he abides.

## Rhyme-Prose (Fu) and Han Dynasty Poetry (206 BCE–220 CE)

The Chinese term *fu* has been variously translated as "prose-poetry," "rhapsody," "verse essay," or "rhyme-prose." Pieces classified in early Chinese sources as *fu* show considerable formal variety, but all mix rhymed sections with prose exposition. Although *fu* tended toward verbal excess and obscurity, some earlier pieces balance descriptive power with heartfelt instruction. Two such pieces are included here. The first *fu*, "On the Wind," is traditionally attributed to Song Yu (Sung Yü) (290?–222 BCE), a southern poet who followed in the tradition of Qu Yuan. His *fu* contrasts the experiences of the rich and the poor and indicates how social class shapes perceptions of even the simplest natural phenomena. The second example, "The Owl" was written by the brilliant scholar Jia Yi (201–169 BCE), who fell into political disgrace and, according to the historian Sima Qian, "cried for more than a year and then died." Unsurprisingly, his *fu* has a somber tone and seeks consolation in a Daoist vision that turns away from the chains of custom to seek peace in stillness and emptiness.

A great variety of poetry was written during the Han dynasty. Some of it was anonymous and probably of folk origin. "Fighting South of the Ramparts" is such a piece and tells of the unhappy fate of those soldiers who "died north of the wall" while fighting against the nomadic peoples of the inner Asian steppes. The theme of conflict with non-Chinese is also found in the poetry of Cai Yan (162?–239? CE). The daughter of a prominent writer, Cai Yan was captured by the Xiongnu, possibly the same people as the Huns of Western history, and was forced to become a consort to their chieftain. After living twelve years among the Xiongnu, Cai Yan returned to China and wrote of her life among the foreigners. "Eighteen Verses Sung to a Tatar Reed Whistle" tells the unhappy story of her capture and the equally unhappy story of her return to China without the two sons she bore among her captors. Although the attribution and date of this poem are subjects of scholarly dispute, we follow tradition in placing it in the Han dynasty.

Finally, we include Zhang Heng's (78–139 CE) masterful poem "The Bones of Chuang Tzu" (i.e., Zhuangzi). The great translator Arthur Waley once called this the "finest of all Chinese poems." Although most Chinese critics would probably disagree with Waley's judgment, it is a moving poem in which the Daoist philosopher Zhuangzi appears to the poet in a dream and reiterates the lesson of his own earlier writings: "How do I know that love of life is not a delusion? How do I know that the fear of death is not like being a homeless waif who does not know the way home?" (see Zhuangzi, p. 358).

## *Song Yu, On the Wind*

*Translated by Burton Watson*

King Hsiang of Ch'u was taking his ease in the Palace of the Orchid Terrace, with his courtiers Sung Yü and Ching Ch'a attending him, when a sudden gust of wind came sweeping in. The king, opening wide the collar of his robe and facing into it, said, "How delightful this wind is! And I and the common people may share it together, may we not?"

But Sung Yü replied, "This wind is for Your Majesty alone. How could the common people have a share in it?"

"The wind," said the king, "is the breath of heaven and earth. Into every corner it unfolds and reaches; without choosing between high or low, exalted or humble, it touches everywhere. What do you mean when you say that this wind is for me alone?"

Sung Yü replied, "I have heard my teacher say that the twisted branches of the lemon tree invite the birds to nest, and hollows and cracks summon the wind. But the breath of the wind differs with the place which it seeks out."

"Tell me," said the king. "Where does the wind come from?"

Sung Yü answered:

"The wind is born from the land
And springs up in the tips of the green duckweed.
It insinuates itself into the valleys
And rages in the canyon mouth,

Skirts the corners of Mount T'ai
And dances beneath the pines and cedars.
Swiftly it flies, whistling and wailing;
Fiercely it splutters its anger.
It crashes with a voice like thunder,
Whirls and tumbles in confusion,
Shaking rocks, striking trees,
Blasting the tangled forest.
Then, when its force is almost spent,
It wavers and disperses,
Thrusting into crevices and rattling door latches.
Clean and clear,
It scatters and rolls away.
Thus it is that this cool, fresh hero wind,
Leaping and bounding up and down,
Climbs over the high wall
And enters deep into palace halls.
With a puff of breath it shakes the leaves and flowers,
Wanders among the cassia and pepper trees,
Or soars over the swift waters.
It buffets the mallow flower,
Sweeps the angelica, touches the spikenard,
Glides over the sweet lichens and lights on willow shoots,
Rambling over the hills
And their scattered host of fragrant flowers.
After this, it wanders into the courtyard,
Ascends the jade hall in the north,
Clambers over gauze curtains,
Passes through the inner apartments,
And so becomes Your Majesty's wind.
When this wind blows on a man,
At once he feels a chill run through him,
And he sighs at its cool freshness.
Clear and gentle,
It cures sickness, dispels drunkenness,
Sharpens the eyes and ears,
Relaxes the body and brings benefit to men.
This is what is called the hero wind of Your Majesty."

"How well you have described it!" exclaimed the king. "But now may I hear about the wind of the common people?" And Sung Yü replied:

"The wind of the common people
Comes whirling from the lanes and alleys,
Poking in the rubbish, stirring up the dust,
Fretting and worrying its way along.
It creeps into holes and knocks on doors,

Scatters sand, blows ashes about,
Muddles in dirt and tosses up bits of filth.
It sidles through hovel windows
And slips into cottage rooms.
When this wind blows on a man,
At once he feels confused and downcast.
Pounded by heat, smothered in dampness,
His heart grows sick and heavy,
And he falls ill and breaks out in a fever.
Where it brushes his lips, sores appear;
It strikes his eyes with blindness.
He stammers and cries out,
Not knowing if he is dead or alive.
This is what is called the lowly wind of the common people."

## *Jia Yi, The Owl*

*Translated by Burton Watson*

In the year *tan-o,*
Fourth month, first month of summer,
The day *kuei-tzu,* when the sun was low in the west,
An owl came to my lodge
And perched on the corner of my mat,
Phlegmatic and fearless.
Secretly wondering the reason
The strange thing had come to roost,
I took out a book to divine it
And the oracle told me its secret:
    "Wild bird enters the hall;
    The master will soon depart."
I asked and importuned the owl,
"Where is it I must go?
Do you bring good luck? Then tell me!
Misfortune? Relate what disaster!
Must I depart so swiftly?
Then speak to me of the hour!"
The owl breathed a sigh,
Raised its head and beat its wings.
Its beak could utter no word,
But let me tell you what it sought to say:
All things alter and change,
Never a moment of ceasing,
Revolving, whirling, and rolling away,
Driven far off and returning again,
Form and breath passing onward,

Like the mutations of a cicada.
Profound, subtle, and illimitable,
Who can finish describing it?
Good luck must be followed by bad,
Bad in turn bow to good.
Sorrow and joy throng the gate,
Weal and woe in the same land.
Wu was powerful and great;
Under Fu-ch'a it sank in defeat.
Yüeh was crushed at K'uai-chi,
But Kou-chien made it an overlord.
Li Ssu, who went forth to greatness, at last
Suffered the five mutilations.
Fu Yüeh was sent into bondage,
Yet Wu Ting made him his aide.
Thus fortune and disaster
Entwine like the strands of a rope.
Fate cannot be told of,
For who shall know its ending?
Water, troubled, runs wild;
The arrow, quick-sped, flies far.
All things, whirling and driving,
Compelling and pushing each other, roll on.
The clouds rise up, the rains come down,
In confusion inextricably joined.
The Great Potter fashions all creatures,
Infinite, boundless, limit unknown.
There is no reckoning Heaven,
Nor divining beforehand the Tao.
The span of life is fated;
Man cannot guess its ending.
Heaven and earth are the furnace,
The workman, the Creator;
His coal is the yin and the yang,
His copper, all things of creation.
Joining, scattering, ebbing and flowing,
Where is there persistence or rule?
A thousand, a myriad mutations,
Lacking an end's beginning.
Suddenly they form a man:
How is this worth taking thought of?
They are transformed again in death:
Should this perplex you?
The witless takes pride in his being,
Scorning others, a lover of self.
The man of wisdom sees vastly

And knows that all things will do.
The covetous run after riches,
The impassioned pursue a fair name;
The proud die struggling for power,
While the people long only to live.
Each drawn and driven onward,
They hurry east and west.
The great man is without bent;
A million changes are as one to him.
The stupid man chained by custom
Suffers like a prisoner bound.
The sage abandons things
And joins himself to the Tao alone,
While the multitudes in delusion
With desire and hate load their hearts.
Limpid and still, the true man
Finds his peace in the Tao alone.
Transcendent, destroying self,
Vast and empty, swift and wild,
He soars on wings of the Tao.
Borne on the flood he sails forth;
He rests on the river islets.
Freeing his body to Fate,
Unpartaking of self,
His life is a floating,
His death a rest.
In stillness like the stillness of deep springs,
Like an unmoored boat drifting aimlessly,
Valuing not the breath of life,
He embraces and drifts with Nothing.
Comprehending Fate and free of sorrow,
The man of virtue heeds no bounds.
Petty matters, weeds and thorns—
What are they to me?

## *Anonymous, Fighting South of the Ramparts*

*Translated by Arthur Waley*

They fought south of the ramparts,
They died north of the wall.
They died in the moors and were not buried.
Their flesh was the food of crows.
'Tell the crows we are not afraid;
We have died in the moors and cannot be buried.
Crows, how can our bodies escape you?'

The waters flowed deep
And the rushes in the pool were dark.
The riders fought and were slain;
Their horses wander neighing.
By the bridge there was a house.
Was it south, was it north?
The harvest was never gathered.
How can we give you your offerings?
You served your Prince faithfully,
Though all in vain.
I think of you, faithful soldiers;
Your service shall not be forgotten.
For in the morning you went out to battle
And at night you did not return.

## *Cai Yan, from 18 Verses Sung to a Tatar Reed Whistle*

*Translated by Kenneth Rexroth and Ling Chung*

### I

I was born in a time of peace,
But later the mandate of Heaven
Was withdrawn from the Han Dynasty.

Heaven was pitiless.
It sent down confusion and separation.
Earth was pitiless.
It brought me to birth in such a time.
War was everywhere. Every road was dangerous.
Soldiers and civilians everywhere
Fleeing death and suffering.
Smoke and dust clouds obscured the land
Overrun by the ruthless Tatar bands.
Our people lost their will power and integrity.
I can never learn the ways of the barbarians.
I am daily subject to violence and insult.
I sing one stanza to my lute and a Tatar horn.
But no one knows my agony and grief.

### II

A Tatar chief forced me to become his wife,
And took me far away to Heaven's edge.
Ten thousand clouds and mountains
Bar my road home,

And whirlwinds of dust and sand
Blow for a thousand miles.
Men here are as savage as giant vipers,
And strut about in armor, snapping their bows.
As I sing the second stanza I almost break the lutestrings.
Will broken, heart broken, I sing to myself.

## VII

The sun sets. The wind moans.
The noise of the Tatar camp rises all around me.
The sorrow of my heart is beyond expression,
But who could I tell it to anyway?
Far across the desert plains,
The beacon fires of the Tatar garrisons
Gleam for ten thousand miles.
It is the custom here to kill the old and weak
And adore the young and vigorous.
They wander seeking new pasture,
And camp for a while behind earth walls.
Cattle and sheep cover the prairie,
Swarming like bees or ants.
When the grass and water are used up,
They mount their horses and drive on their cattle.
The seventh stanza sings of my wandering.
How I hate to live this way!

## XIII

I never believed that in my broken life
The day would come when
Suddenly I could return home.
I embrace and caress my Tatar sons.
Tears wet our clothes.
An envoy from the Han Court
Has come to bring me back,
With four stallions that can run without stopping.
Who can measure the grief of my sons?
They thought I would live and die with them.
Now it is I who must depart.
Sorrow for my boys dims the sun for me.
If we had wings we could fly away together.
I cannot move my feet,
For each step is a step away from them.
My soul is overwhelmed.
As their figures vanish in the distance
Only my love remains.

The thirteenth stanza—
I pick the strings rapidly
But the melody is sad.
No one can know
The sorrow which tears my bowels.

## *Zhang Heng (78–139 CE), The Bones of Chuang Tzu*

*Translated by Arthur Waley*

I, Chang P'ing-Tzu, had traversed the Nine Wilds and seen their wonders,
In the eight continents beheld the ways of Man,
The Sun's procession, the orbit of the Stars,
The surging of the dragon, the soaring of the phoenix in his flight.
In the red desert to the south I sweltered,
And northward waded through the wintry burghs of Yu.
Through the Valley of Darkness to the west I wandered,
And eastward travelled to the Sun's extreme abode,
The stooping Mulberry Tree.

So the seasons sped; weak autumn languished,
A small wind woke the cold.

And now with rearing of rein-horse,
Plunging of the tracer, round I fetched
My high-roofed chariot to westward.
Along the dykes we loitered, past many meadows,
And far away among the dunes and hills.
Suddenly I looked and by the roadside
I saw a man's bones lying in the squelchy earth,
Black rime-frost over him; and I in sorrow spoke
And asked him, saying, 'Dead man, how was it?
Fled you with your friend from famine and for the last grains
Gambled and lost? Was this earth your tomb,
Or did floods carry you from afar? Were you mighty, were you wise,
Were you foolish and poor? A warrior, or a girl?'
Then a wonder came; for out of the silence a voice—
Thin echo only, in no substance was the Spirit seen—
Mysteriously answered, saying, 'I was a man of Sung,
Of the clan of Chuang; Chou was my name.
Beyond the climes of common thought
My reason soared, yet could I not save myself;
For at the last, when the long charter of my years was told,
I too, for all my magic, by Age was brought
To the Black Hill of Death.

Wherefore, O Master, do you question me?'
Then I answered:
'Let me plead for you upon the Five Hill-tops,
Let me pray for you to the Gods of Heaven and the
 Gods of Earth,
That your white bones may arise,
And your limbs be joined anew.
The God of the North shall give me back your ears;
I will scour the Southland for your eyes;
From the sunrise will I wrest your feet;
The West shall yield your heart.
I will set each several organ in its throne;
Each subtle sense will I restore.
Would you not have it so?'
The dead man answered me:
'O Friend, how strange and unacceptable your words!
In death I rest and am at peace; in life, I toiled and strove.
Is the hardness of the winter stream
Better than the melting of spring?
All pride that the body knew,
Was it not lighter than dust?
What Ch'ao and Hsü despised,
What Po-ch'eng fled,
Shall I desire, whom death
Already has hidden in the Eternal Way—
Where Li Chu cannot see me,
Nor Tzū Yeh hear me,
Where neither Yao nor Shan can praise me,
Nor the tyrants Chieh and Hsin condemn me,
Nor wolf nor tiger harm me,
Lance prick me nor sword wound me?
Of the Primal Spirit is my substance; I am a wave
In the river of Darkness and Light.
The Maker of All Things is my Father and Mother,
Heaven is my bed and earth my cushion,
The thunder and lightning are my drum and fan,
The sun and moon my candle and my torch,
The Milky Way my moat, the stars my jewels.
With Nature am I conjoined;
I have no passion, no desire.
Wash me and I shall be no whiter,
Foul me and I shall yet be clean.
I come not, yet am here;
Hasten not, yet am swift.'
The voice stopped, there was silence.

A ghostly light
Faded and expired.
I gazed upon the dead, stared in sorrow and compassion.
Then I called upon my servant that was with me
To tie his silken scarf about those bones
And wrap them in a cloak of sombre dust;
While I, as offering to the soul of this dead man,
Poured my hot tears upon the margin of the road.

## SIMA QIAN (145–86? BCE)

Born in the first century of the Han dynasty, a time when the imperial household was still consolidating its power, Sima Qian (Ssu-ma Ch'ien) followed his father as a court scribe and used his access to official archives in order to complete a vast historical project that his father had begun, a 130-chapter comprehensive history of China entitled *Records of the Historian* (*Shi ji*). Before his project was finished, he was accused of defaming the emperor and was sentenced to castration. After receiving his punishment, he was rehabilitated and spent the last years of his life finishing his great history of China and serving the very emperor who had ordered his castration.

*Records of the Historian* has been much admired for both its historical and literary value. Most of what we know about the first two thousand years of Chinese history is filtered through the writing brush of Sima Qian, who is sometimes called the "Father of Chinese History." The organization of his history, which includes chronological annals, charts, topical essays, and biographies, became the standard in China for all subsequent official dynastic histories. Few later historians, however, were able to achieve the literary power and liveliness of Sima Qian's historical writing.

Sima Qian is important in the Chinese tradition for another reason: he is the first Chinese to write directly and at some length about himself. These autobiographical writings are found in the last chapter of *Records of the Historian* and in a remarkable letter written to an acquaintance, Jen An, which was preserved in a later historical text. A short excerpt from the former and the entire text of the latter begin our selections. In the first piece, Sima Qian tells of the death of his father and of his promise that as "Grand Historian" he would complete the work his father had begun. His filial devotion is challenged and perhaps even compromised by the events reported in the "Letter to Jen An," a colleague who was himself under sentence of death and apparently hoped Sima Qian could intervene on his behalf. Sima Qian uses this letter to tell his own unhappy story of how, several years before, he had been caught in a terrible ethical dilemma. Should he, now that he had to endure public disgrace, nobly take his own life? Or should he be true to his filial obligation and remain alive to complete the history his father had begun?

Perhaps as a result of his own experience, Sima Qian was fascinated by how characters face reversals of fortune, defeat, and ultimately death. Three such accounts are included here. The first, an excerpt from *The Basic Annals of Xiang Yu,* tells of the death of Xiang Yu (Hsiang Yü), a courageous but sometimes cruel and unwise rebel leader who helped overthrow the Qin dynasty, only to be defeated by his rival Liu Bang, the founder of the Han dynasty. Xiang Yu is the prototypical "noble failure," a type much admired in East Asia, who knows defeat is certain but fights to the end and then takes his own life rather than allowing his enemies the satisfaction of killing him themselves. Nie Zheng (Nieh Cheng), the hero of the second piece, also takes his own life, only to be upstaged by a sister who shows amazing courage in identifying her brother's body. Finally, we include the full account of Meng Tian, who was partially responsible for the construction of China's most famous monument, the Great Wall. His biography demonstrates the complexity and danger of the Chinese imperial world and leads us to ask whether he was a loyal victim of political machinations or a man who received just punishment for the cruelty imposed on the many men working on the Great Wall. Alternatively, was he a man brought to his unhappy fate, as he himself claimed, because he had "cut through the earth's arteries" and hence offended the earth itself?

## *Records of the Historian*

### *from Postface*

*Translated by Burton Watson*

Since The Grand Historian was always in charge of astronomical affairs he was not concerned with the governing of the people. He had a son named Ch'ien [Qian]. Ch'ien was born at Lung-men. He plowed and pastured on the sunny side of the hills along the River. At the age of ten he could read the old writings. When he was twenty he traveled south to the Yangtse and Huai rivers [Kiangsu], he climbed Hui-chi and looked for the Cave of Yü [Chekiang], and he saw the Nine Peaks [Honan]. He sailed down the Yüan and Hsiang rivers and in the north forded the Wen and Ssu rivers [Shantung]. He studied the learning of the cities of Ch'i and Lu. He observed the customs and practices inherited from Confucius and took part in the archery contest at Mount I in Tsou. He met with trouble and danger in P'o and Hsüeh and P'eng-ch'eng. Then he passed through Liang and Ch'u and returned home.

After this Ch'ien entered government service as a Lang-chung. He took part in the western expedition to the south of Pa and Shu, marching south as far as Ch'iung, Tse, and K'un-ming. He returned and reported on his mission.

In the same year [110 BCE] the Son of Heaven first performed the Feng Sacrifice for the house of Han. But The Grand Historian [Ssu-ma T'an] was forced to stay behind at Chou-nan and could not take part in the ceremony. He was filled with resentment over this and lay on the point of death.

When his son Ch'ien returned from his mission, he visited his father at the place where he was staying between the Lo and Yellow rivers. The Grand Historian grasped his hand and said, weeping, "Our ancestors were Grand

Historians for the house of Chou. From the most ancient times they were eminent and renowned when in the days of Yü and Hsia they were in charge of astronomical affairs. In later ages our family declined. Will this tradition end with me? If you in turn become Grand Historian, you must continue the work of our ancestors. Now the Son of Heaven, following the tradition of a thousand years, will perform the Feng Sacrifice on Mount T'ai. But I shall not be able to be present. Such is my fate! Such indeed is my fate! After I die, you will become Grand Historian. When you become Grand Historian, you must not forget what I have desired to expound and write. Now filial piety begins with the serving of your parents; next you must serve your sovereign; and finally you must make something of yourself, that your name may go down through the ages for the glory of your father and mother. This is the most important part of filial piety. Everyone praises the Duke of Chou, saying that he was able to set forth in word and song the virtues of King Wen and King Wu, publishing abroad the Odes of Chou and Shao; he set forth the thoughts and ideals of T'ai-wang and Wang Chi, extending his words back to Kung Liu, and paying honor to Hou Chi. After the reigns of Yu and Li the way of the ancient kings fell into disuse, and rites and music declined. Confucius revived the old ways and restored what had been abandoned, expounding the *Odes* and *Documents* and making the *Spring and Autumn Annals*. From that time until today men of learning have taken these as their models. It has now been over four hundred years since the capture of the unicorn. The various feudal states have merged together and the old records and chronicles have become scattered and lost. Now the house of Han has arisen and all the world is united under one rule. I have been Grand Historian, and yet I have failed to set forth a record of all the enlightened rulers and wise lords, the faithful ministers and gentlemen who were ready to die for duty. I am fearful that the historical materials will be neglected and lost. You must remember and think of this!"

Ch'ien bowed his head and wept, saying, "I, your son, am ignorant and unworthy, but I shall endeavor to set forth in full the reports of antiquity which have come down from our ancestors. I shall not dare to be remiss!" . . .

Three years after the death of his father, Ch'ien became Grand Historian. He read the various historical records and the books of the stone rooms and metal caskets.

Five years after this was the first year of the era *T'ai-ch'u*. At dawn on the first day of the eleventh month, the day *chia-tzu* [Dec. 25, 105 BCE], the zenith of winter, the calendar of the heavens was first corrected and set up in the Illustrious Hall. All the spirits received the chronology.

The Grand Historian remarks: "My father used to say to me, 'Five hundred years after the Duke of Chou died Confucius appeared. It has now been five hundred years since the death of Confucius. There must be someone who can succeed to the enlightened ages of the past, who can set right the transmission of the *Book of Changes*, continue the *Spring and Autumn Annals*, and search into the world of the *Odes* and *Documents*, the rites and music.' Was this not his ambition? Was this not his ambition? How can I, his son, dare to neglect his will?"

## *Letter to Jen An (Shao-ch'ing)*

*Translated by J.R. Hightower*

The Grand Historian Ssu-ma Ch'ien [Sima Qian], bowing repeatedly, addresses his worthy friend Shao-ch'ing:

Some time ago you deigned to send me a letter in which you advised me to be concerned for my social contacts and devote myself to the recommendation and advancement of qualified persons. You expressed yourself with considerable vigor, as though you expected I would not follow your advice but would be influenced by the words of the vulgar: I would hardly behave in such a way. I may be a broken hack, but I have still been exposed to the teachings handed down by my elders. However, I see myself as mutilated and disgraced: I am criticized if I act, and where I hope to be helpful I do harm instead. This causes me secret distress, but to whom can I unburden myself? As the proverb says, "For whom do you do it? Who are you going to get to listen to you?" Why was it that Po-ya never again played his lute after Chung Tzu-ch'i died? A gentleman acts on behalf of an understanding friend, as a woman makes herself beautiful for her lover. Someone like me whose virility is lacking could never be a hero, even if he had the endowments of the pearl of Sui and the jade of Pien-ho or conducted himself like Hsü Yu and Po Yi; he would only succeed in being laughed at and put to shame.

I should have answered your letter sooner, but when I got back from the East in the emperor's suite I was very busy. We were seldom together, and then I was so pressed that there was never a moment's time when I could speak my mind. Now you, Shao-ch'ing, are under an accusation whose outcome is uncertain. Weeks and months have passed until we have now reached the end of winter, and I am going to have to accompany the emperor to Yung. I am afraid that that may come to pass which cannot be avoided, and as a result I will never have the chance to give expression to my grievance and explain myself to you. It would mean that the souls of the departed would carry a never-ending burden of secret resentment. Let me say what is on my mind; I hope you will not hold it against me that I have been negligent in leaving your letter so long unanswered.

I have been taught that self-cultivation is the mark of wisdom, that charity is the sign of humanity, that taking and giving is the measure of decency, that a sense of shame is the index of bravery, that making a name for oneself is the end of conduct. A gentleman who practices these five things can entrust his reputation to the world and win a place among outstanding men. On the other hand there is no misfortune so hurtful as cupidity, no grief so painful as disappointment, no conduct so despicable as disgracing one's forebears, no defilement so great as castration. One who has undergone that punishment nowhere counts as a man. This is not just a modern attitude; it has always been so. Formerly when Duke Ling of Wei rode in the same chariot with the eunuch Yung-ch'ü, Confucius left Wei to go to Ch'en; when T'ung-tzu shared the emperor's chariot, Yüan Ssu blushed. It has always been occasion for shame. Even an ordinary fellow never fails to be offended when he has business with a eunuch—how much the more a gentleman of spirit. Though the court today may want men, you surely do not expect one who has submitted to the knife to recommend the worthies of the empire for places?

It has been twenty years since I inherited my father's office and entered the service of the emperor. It occurs to me that during that time I have not been able to demonstrate my loyalty and sincerity or win praise for good advice and outstanding abilities in the service of a wise ruler; nor have I been able to make good defects and omissions, or advance the worthy and talented, or induce wise hermits to serve; nor have I been able to serve in the ranks of the army, attacking walled cities and fighting in the field to win merit by taking an enemy general's head or capturing his banners; nor have I been able to win merit through long and faithful service to rise to high office and handsome salary, to the glory of my family and the benefit of my friends. From my failure in all four of these endeavors it follows that I am prepared to compromise with the times and avoid giving offense, wholly ineffectual for good or ill. Formerly as Great Officer of the third grade I once had the chance to participate in deliberations in a minor capacity. Since I then offered no great plans nor expressed myself freely, would it not be an insult to the court and an affront to my colleagues if now, mutilated, a menial who sweeps floors, a miserable wretch, I should raise my head and stretch my eyebrows to argue right and wrong? Alas, for one like me what is there left to say? What is there left to say?

It is not easy to explain just what happened. When I was young I had no outstanding abilities and I grew up unpraised by my fellow townsmen. Fortunately, however, thanks to my father's service, the emperor made it possible for me to put my inconsiderable abilities at his disposal, and I had access to the court. It seemed to me that one cannot get a good view of the sky carrying a platter on one's head, so I broke off relations with my friends and neglected my family affairs that I might day and night devote all my small abilities wholeheartedly to my official duties and so gain the liking and approval of the ruler. But then came the event when I made my big mistake and everything was changed.

Li Ling and I were both stationed in the palace, but we never had a chance to become friends. Our duties kept us apart; we never shared so much as a cup of wine, let alone enjoyed a closer friendship. But I observed that he conducted himself as no ordinary gentleman. He was filial toward his parents, honest with his colleagues, scrupulous about money, decent in his behavior, yielding in matters of precedence, respectful, moderate, and polite to others. Carried away by his enthusiasm he never thought of himself but was ever there where his country needed him: such was his constant concern. To me he seemed to have the bearing of a national hero. A subject who exposes himself to a thousand deaths without regard for his own single life, and rushes to the defence of his country—that is a great man. That men who had been solely concerned with keeping themselves and their wives and children safe and sound should go out of their way to stir up trouble for him when he had made a single mistake was something that really pained my inmost feelings.

Moreover Li Ling's troops numbered fewer than 5,000 when he led them deep into the territory of the nomads. They marched to the khan's court and dangled the bait in the tiger's mouth. They boldly challenged the fierce barbarians, in the face of an army of a million. For ten days running they fought the khan, killing more than their own number, so that the enemy were unable to retrieve their dead or rescue their wounded. The princes of felts and furs were all terror-stricken; they called on the neighboring lords to draft bowmen, and the whole nation joined to attack and surround Li Ling's troops. For a thousand miles they retreated, fighting as they went, until their arrows were exhausted and the road cut off. The relieving force had not arrived. Dead and wounded lay in heaps. But when Li Ling rallied his men with a cry, his soldiers rose to fight, with streaming tears and bloody faces. They swallowed their tears and brandishing their empty bows braved naked swords. Facing north they fought to the death with the enemy.

Before Li Ling had reached this extremity a messenger brought news to the court and all the lords and princes raised their cups to drink to his success. Some days later the message arrived announcing that he had been defeated. The news so affected the emperor that he found his food tasteless and took no pleasure in holding court. The great ministers were depressed and fearful, not knowing what course to take. When I saw the emperor in great distress of mind, I took no count of my own humble position, but wished to express my honest opinion: that Li Ling had always shared with his men, renouncing the sweet and dividing his short rations, so that he was able to get them to die for him—no famous general of antiquity surpassed him in this. And though he was now involved in defeat, it could be assumed that he intended to do what was right and make good his obligation to China. The situation was past remedying, but the losses he had already inflicted on the Hsiung-nu were such that his renown filled the empire.

I wished to express these ideas but had no way to do so until by chance I was ordered to give an opinion. In these terms I extolled Li Ling's merits, hoping to get the emperor to take a wider view of things and at the same time to undo the charges of his enemies. I did not succeed in making myself clear, and the emperor, in his wisdom, did not understand, suspecting that I was criticizing the Second General Li Kuang-li, who headed the relief column, and that I was indulging in special pleading in behalf of Li Ling. As a result I was turned over to the judges, and despite all my heartfelt sincerity I was unable to justify myself. In the end it was decided that I was guilty of attempting to mislead the emperor.

Being poor, I had insufficient funds to pay a fine in lieu of punishment. None of my friends came to my aid. My colleagues and associates spoke not a word on my behalf. My body is not of wood or stone: and I was alone with my jailors. When one is shut up in the depths of prison is there anyone he can appeal to? You have experienced this yourself, do you think it was otherwise with me?

In giving himself up alive to the Hsiung-nu, Li Ling disgraced his family; in going to the silkworm chamber after his act I became doubly the laughingstock of the empire. Alas, alas! This is not a thing one can easily talk about to the vulgar. My father never earned tally and patent of nobility; as annalist and astrologer I was not far removed from the diviners and invokers, truly the plaything of the emperor, kept like any singing girl or jester, and despised by the world. Had I chosen to submit to the law and let myself be put to death, it would have been no more important than the loss of a single hair from nine oxen, no different from the crushing of an ant. No one would have credited me with dying for a principle; rather they would have thought that I had simply died because I was at my wit's end and my offence allowed no other way out. And why? They would think so because of the occupation in which I established myself.

A man can die only once, and whether death to him is as weighty as Mount T'ai or as light as a feather depends on the reason for which he dies. The most important thing is not to disgrace one's ancestors, the next is not to disgrace one's self, the next not to disgrace one's principles, the next not to disgrace one's manners. Next worse is the disgrace of being put in fetters, the next is to wear a prisoner's garb, the next is to be beaten in the stocks, the next is to have the head shaved and a metal chain fastened around the neck, the next is mutilation, and the very worst disgrace of all is castration. It is said that corporal punishments are not applied to the great officers, implying that an officer cannot but be careful of his integrity. When the fierce tiger is in the depths of the mountain, all animals hold him in fear, but when he falls into a trap he waves his tail and begs for food; this is the end result of curtailing his dignity. Hence if you draw the plan of a jail on the ground, a gentleman will not step inside the figure, nor will he address even the wooden image of a jailor. In this way he shows his determination never to find himself in such a position. But let him cross his hands and feet to receive the bonds, expose his back to receive the whip, and be incarcerated in the barred cell—by then when he sees the jailor he bows his head to the ground and at the sight of his underlings he pants in terror. And why? It is the result of the gradual curtailment of his dignity. If now he claims there has been no disgrace, he is devoid of a sense of shame and wholly unworthy of respect.

Wen Wang was an earl, and yet he was held prisoner in Yu-li; Li Ssu was prime minister and yet was visited with all five punishments; Han Hsin was a prince and yet he was put in the stocks in Ch'en; P'eng Yüeh and Chang Ao each sat on a throne and called himself king, and yet the one was fettered in prison, the other put to death. These were all men of high rank and office and widespread reputation, but when they got into trouble with the law they were unable resolutely to put an end to themselves. It has always been the same: when one lies in the dirt there is no question of his not being disgraced. In the light of these examples, bravery and cowardice are a matter of circumstance, strength and weakness depend on conditions. Once this is understood, there is nothing to be surprised at in their behavior. If by failing to do away with himself before he is in the clutches of the law a man is degraded to the point of being flogged and then wishes to rescue his honor, has he not missed his chance? This is no doubt why the ancients were chary of applying corporal punishment to a great officer.

Now there is no man who does not naturally cling to life and avoid death, love his parents and cherish his wife and children. But the man who is devoted to the right sometimes has no choice but to behave otherwise. I early had the misfortune to lose my father and mother; I had no brothers and was quite alone. You have seen how little my affection for my wife and children deterred me from speaking out. But a brave man will not always die for his honor, and what efforts will not even a coward make in a cause to which he is devoted? I may be a coward and wish to live at the expense of my honor, but I surely know how to act appropriately. Would I have abandoned myself to the ignominy of being tied and bound? Even a miserable slave-girl is capable of putting an end to herself; could you expect less of me, when I had so little choice? If I concealed my feelings and clung to life, burying myself in filth without protest, it was because I could not bear to leave unfinished my deeply cherished project, because I rejected the idea of dying without leaving to posterity my literary work.

In the past there have been innumerable men of wealth and rank whose names died with them; only the outstanding and unusual are known today. It was when King Wen was in prison that he expanded the *Chou yi;* when Confucius was in straits he wrote the *Spring and Autumn Annals;* when Ch'ü Yüan was banished he composed the "Encountering Sorrow"; Tso Ch'iu lost his sight and so we have the *Conversations from the States;* Sun Tzu had his feet chopped off, and *The Art of War* was put together. The general purport of the 300 poems of the *Book of Songs* is the indignation expressed by the sages. All of these men were oppressed in their minds, and, unable to put into action their principles, wrote of the past with their eyes on the future. For example, Tso Ch'iu without sight and Sun Tzu with amputated feet were permanently disabled. They retired to write books in which they expressed their pent-up feelings, hoping to realize themselves in literature, since action was denied them.

I have ventured not to look for more recent models, but with what little literary ability I possess I have brought together the scattered fragments of ancient lore. I studied the events of history and set them down in significant order; I have written 130 chapters in which appears the record of the past—its periods of greatness and decline, of achievement and failure. Further it was my hope, by a thorough comprehension of the workings of affairs divine and human, and a knowledge of the historical process, to create a philosophy of my own. Before my draft was complete this disaster overtook me. It was my concern over my unfinished work that made me submit to the worst of all punishments without showing the rage I felt. When at last I shall have finished my book, I shall store it away in the archives to await the man who will understand it. When it finally becomes known in the world, I shall have paid the debt of my shame; nor will I regret a thousand deaths.

However, this is something I can confide only to a person of intelligence; it would not do to speak of it to the vulgar crowd. When one is in a compromising situation, it is not easy to justify oneself; the world is always ready to misrepresent one's motives. It was in consequence of my speaking out that I met disaster in the first place; were I to make myself doubly a laughingstock in my native place, to the disgrace of my forebears, how could I ever have the face again to visit the grave of my father and my mother? Even after a hundred generations my shame will but be the more. This is what makes my bowels burn within me nine times a day, so that at home I sit in a daze and lost, abroad I know not where I am going. Whenever I think of this shame the sweat drenches the clothes on my back. I am fit only to be a slave guarding the women's apartments: better that I should hide away in the farthest depths of the mountains. Instead I go on as best I can, putting up with whatever treatment is meted out to me, and so complete my degradation.

And now you want me to recommend worthy men for advancement! Is this not rather the last thing in the world I would want to do? Even if I should want to deck myself out with fine words and elegant phrases, it would not help me any against the world's incredulity; it would only bring more shame on me. In short, I can hope for justification only after my death.

In a letter I cannot say everything. What I have written is a crude and general statement of my feelings. Respectfully I bow to you.

## *from Ch. 7: The Basic Annals of Xiang Yu (Hsiang Yü)*

*Translated by Burton Watson*

Hsiang Yü's army had built a walled camp at Kai-hsia, but his soldiers were few and his supplies exhausted. The Han army, joined by the forces of the other leaders, surrounded them with several lines of troops. In the night Hsiang Yü heard the Han armies all about him singing the songs of Ch'u. "Has Han already conquered Ch'u?" he exclaimed in astonishment. "How many men of Ch'u they have with them!" Then he rose in the night and drank within the curtains of his tent. With him were the beautiful lady Yüh, who enjoyed his favor and followed wherever he went, and his famous steed Dapple, which he always rode. Hsiang Yü, filled with passionate sorrow, began to sing sadly, composing this song:

> My strength plucked up the hills,
> My might shadowed the world;
> But the times were against me,
> And Dapple runs no more,
> When Dapple runs no more,
> What then can I do?
> Ah, Yüh, my Yüh,
> What will your fate be?

He sang the song several times through, and Lady Yüh joined her voice with his. Tears streamed down his face, while all those about him wept and were unable to lift their eyes from the ground. Then he mounted his horse and, with some eight hundred brave horsemen under his banner, rode into the night, burst through the encirclement to the south, and galloped away.

Next morning, when the king of Han became aware of what had happened, he ordered his cavalry general Kuan Ying to lead a force of five thousand horsemen in pursuit. Hsiang Yü crossed the Huai River, though by now he had only a hundred or so horsemen still with him. Reaching Yin-ling, he lost his way, and stopped to ask an old farmer for directions. But the farmer deceived him, saying, "Go left!" and when he rode to the left he stumbled into a great swamp, so that the Han troops were able to pursue and overtake him.

Hsiang Yü once more led his men east until they reached Tung-ch'eng. By this time he had only twenty-eight horsemen, while the Han cavalry pursuing him numbered several thousand.

Hsiang Yü, realizing that he could not escape, turned to address his horsemen: "It has been eight years since I first led my army forth. In that time I have fought over seventy battles. Every enemy I faced was destroyed, every one I attacked submitted. Never once did I suffer defeat, until at last I became dictator of the world. But now suddenly I am driven to this desperate position! It is because Heaven would destroy me, not because I have committed any fault in battle. I have resolved to die today. But before I die, I beg to fight bravely and win for you three victories. For your sake I shall break through the enemy's encirclement, cut down their leaders, and sever their banners that you may know it is Heaven which has destroyed me and no fault of mine in arms!" Then he divided his horsemen into four bands and faced them in four directions.

When the Han army had surrounded them several layers deep, Hsiang Yü said to his horsemen, "I will get one of those generals for you!" He ordered his men to gallop in all four directions down the hill on which they were standing, with instructions to meet again on the east side of the hill and divide into three groups. He himself gave a great shout and galloped down the hill. The Han troops scattered before him and he succeeded in cutting down one of their generals. At this time Yang Hsi was leader of the cavalry pursuing Hsiang Yü, but Hsiang Yü roared and glared so fiercely at him that all his men and horses fled in terror some distance to the rear.

Hsiang Yü rejoined his men, who had formed into three groups. The Han army, uncertain which group Hsiang Yü was with, likewise divided into three groups and again surrounded them. Hsiang Yü once more galloped forth and cut down a Han colonel, killing some fifty to a hundred men. When he had gathered his horsemen together a second time, he found that he had lost only two of them. "Did I tell you the truth?" he asked. His men all bowed and replied, "You have done all you said."

Hsiang Yü, who by this time had reached Wu-chiang, was considering whether to cross over to the east side of the Yangtze. The village head of Wu-chiang, who was waiting with a boat on the bank of the river, said to him, "Although the area east of the river is small, it is some thousand miles in breadth and has a population of thirty or forty thousand. It would still be worth ruling. I beg you to make haste and cross over. I am the only one who has a boat, so that when the Han army arrives they will have no way to get across!"

Hsiang Yü laughed and replied, "It is Heaven that is destroying me. What good would it do me to cross the river? Once, with eight thousand sons from the land east of the river, I crossed over and marched west, but today not a single man of them returns. Although their fathers and brothers east of the river should take pity on me and make me their king, how could I bear to face them again? Though they said nothing of it, could I help but feel shame in my heart?" Then he added, "I can see that you are a worthy man. For five years I have ridden this horse, and I have never seen his equal. Again and again he has borne me hundreds of miles in a single day. Since I cannot bear to kill him, I give him to you."

Hsiang Yü then ordered all his men to dismount and proceed on foot, and with their short swords to close in hand-to-hand combat with the enemy. Hsiang Yü alone killed several hundred of the Han men, until he had suffered a dozen wounds. Looking about him, he spied the Han cavalry marshal Lü Ma-t'ung. "We are old friends, are we not?" he asked. Lü Ma-t'ung eyed him carefully and then, pointing him out to Wang Yi, said, "This is Hsiang Yü!"

"I have heard that Han has offered a reward of a thousand catties of gold and a fief of ten thousand households for my head," said Hsiang Yü. "I will do you the favor!" And with this he cut his own throat and died.

Wang Yi seized his head, while the other horsemen trampled over each other in a struggle to get at Hsiang Yü's body, so that twenty or thirty of them were killed. In the end cavalry attendant Yang Hsi, cavalry marshal Lü Ma-t'ung, and attendants Lü Sheng and Yang Wu each succeeded in seizing a limb. When the five of them fitted together the limbs and head, it was found that they were indeed those of Hsiang Yü. Therefore the fief was divided five ways, Lü Ma-t'ung being enfeoffed as marquis of Chung-shui, Wang Yi as marquis of Tu-yen, Yang Hsi as marquis of Ch'ih-ch'üan, Yang Wu as marquis of Wu-fang, and Lü Sheng as marquis of Nieh-yang.

With the death of Hsiang Yü, the entire region of Ch'u surrendered to Han, only Lu refusing to submit. The king of Han set out with the troops of the empire and was about to massacre the inhabitants of Lu. But because Lu had so strictly obeyed the code of honor and had shown its willingness to fight to the death for its acknowledged sovereign, he bore with him the head of Hsiang Yü and, when he showed it to the men of Lu, they forthwith surrendered.

King Huai of Ch'u had first enfeoffed Hsiang Yü as duke of Lu, and Lu was the last place to surrender. Therefore, the king of Han buried Hsiang Yü at Ku-ch'eng with the ceremony appropriate to a duke of Lu. The king proclaimed a period of mourning for him, wept, and then departed. All the various branches of the Hsiang family he spared from execution, and he enfeoffed Hsiang Po as marquis of She-yang. The marquises of T'ao, P'ing-kao, and Hsüan-wu were all members of the Hsiang family who were granted the imperial surname Liu.

## *from Ch. 86: The Memoirs of the Assassins*

*Translated by Gladys and Hsien-yi Yang*

Nieh Cheng [Nie Zheng] was a native of Shenching Village in the district of Chih. Having killed a man, he escaped with his mother and elder sister to Chi where he set up as a butcher. Later Yen Sui of Puyang, who owed allegiance to Marquis Ai of Hann, offended the chief minister Hsia Lui and fled to escape punishment, searching everywhere for a man who would kill Hsia Lui for him. When he reached Chi, he heard that Nieh Cheng was a brave man who was living as a butcher to avoid vengeance. Yen Sui called on him several times, then prepared a feast in honour of Nieh Cheng's mother at which he presented her with a hundred pieces of gold. Amazed by such munificence, Nieh Cheng declined the gift. When Yen Sui insisted he said, "I am blessed with an aged mother. Though I am but a poor stranger in these parts, I am able to supply her daily food and clothing by selling dog meat. Since I can provide for her, I dare not accept your gift."

Yen Sui sent the others away and told Nieh Cheng, "I have an enemy. Reaching Chi after travelling through many states, I heard that you, sir, were a man with a high sense of honor. So I am offering you a hundred gold pieces to supply food and clothing for your mother and to win your friendship. I want no other return."

Nieh Cheng replied, "I have lowered my ambitions and humbled myself to sell meat in the market solely for my mother's sake. While she lives, I cannot promise my services to anyone." He could not be prevailed upon to accept, whereupon Yen Sui took a courteous leave of him.

In due time Nieh Cheng's mother died. After she was buried and the mourning over, Nieh Cheng said, "I am a poor stall-keeper wielding a butcher's cleaver, while Yen Sui is a state minister; yet he came a thousand *li* in his carriage to seek my friendship. I did very little for him, performed no great services to deserve his favour, yet he offered my mother a hundred pieces of gold; and though I did not accept, this shows how well he appreciated me. His longing for revenge made this worthy gentleman place his faith in one so humble and obscure. How, then, can I remain silent? Previously I ignored his overtures for my mother's sake. Now that my mother has died of old age, I must serve this man who appreciates me."

So he went west to Puyang to see Yen Sui and told him, "I refused you before because my mother was still alive, but now she has died of old age. Who is the man on whom you want to take vengeance? I am at your service."

Then Yen Sui told him the whole story, saying, "My enemy is Hsia Lui, chief minister of Hann and uncle of the marquis of Hann. He has many clansmen and his residence is closely guarded. All my attempts to assassinate him have failed. Since you are good enough to help me, I can supply you with chariots, cavalry and men."

"Hann is not far from Uei, and we are going to kill the chief minister who is also the ruler's uncle," said Nieh Cheng. "In these circumstances, too many men would make for trouble and word might get out. Then the whole of Hann would become your enemy and that would be disastrous."

So refusing all assistance, he bid farewell and carrying his sword went alone to the capital of Hann. Hsia Lui, seated in his office, was surrounded by a host of guards and armed attendants; but Nieh Cheng marching straight in and up the steps stabbed the minister to death. The attendants, in utter confusion, were set upon with loud cries by Nieh Cheng, till several dozen of them were laid low. Then he gashed his face, gouged out his eyes and stabbed himself so that his guts spilled out and he died.

Nieh Cheng's corpse was exposed in the market-place in Hann and inquiries were made but no one knew who he was. A reward of a thousand gold pieces was offered for identifying the assassin, but time passed without any news. Then Nieh Cheng's sister Jung heard of Hsia Lui's assassination and the large reward offered for the identification of his unknown assassin, whose corpse had been exposed. "Can this be my brother?" she sobbed. "Ah, how well Yen Sui understood him!"

She went to the market-place in Hann and found that it was indeed he. Falling on the corpse she wept bitterly and cried, "This is Nieh Chen from Shenching Village in Chih!"

The people in the market warned her, "This man savagely murdered our chief minister and the king has offered a thousand gold pieces for his name. Did you not know this? Why do you come to identify him?"

"I knew this," she replied. "But he humbled himself to live as a tradesman in the market because our mother was living and I had no husband. After our mother died and I was married, Yen Sui raised him from his squalor to be his friend. How else could he repay Yen Sui's great kindness? A man should die for a friend who knows his worth. Because I was still alive, he mutilated himself to hide his identity. But how can I, for fear of death, let my noble brother perish unknown?"

This greatly astounded the people in the market. Having called aloud on heaven three times, she wailed in anguish and died beside her brother.

Word of this reached Tsin, Chu, Chi and Wei, and everyone commented, "Not only was Nieh Cheng able, but his sister was a remarkable woman too." Nieh Cheng might never have given his life for Yen Sui had he known that his sister, with her strong resolution, would not balk at his corpse exposed in the market-place and take the long difficult journey to make his name known and perish by his side. Yen Sui certainly was a good judge of character, able to find loyal helpers!

More than two hundred and twenty years after this, and there was the case of Ching Ko in Chin.

## *Ch. 88: The Meaning of Meng Tian*

*Translated by Raymond Dawson*

As for Meng Tian, his forebears were men of Qi. Tian's paternal grandfather, Meng Ao, came from Qi to serve King Zhaoxiang of Qin, and attained the office of senior minister. In the first year of King Zhuangxiang of Qin, Meng Ao became general of Qin, made an assault on Hann and took Chenggao and Xingyang, and established the Sanchuan province. In the second year Meng Ao attacked Zhao and took thirty-seven cities. In the third year of the First Emperor, Meng Ao attacked Hann and took thirteen cities. In the fifth year Meng Ao attacked Wei, took twenty cities, and established Dong province. In the seventh year of the First Emperor, Meng Ao died. Ao's son was called Wu and Wu's son was called Tian. Tian at one time kept legal records and was in charge of the relevant literature. In the twenty-third year of the First Emperor, Meng Wu became an assistant general of Qin and, together with Wang Jian, made an attack on Chu and inflicted a major defeat upon it and killed Xiang Yan. In the twenty-fourth year Meng Wu attacked Chu and took the King of Chu prisoner. Meng Tian's younger brother was Meng Yi.

In the twenty-sixth year of the First Emperor, Meng Tian was able to become a general of Qin on account of the long-term service given by his family. He attacked Qi and inflicted a major defeat upon it, and was appointed Prefect of the Capital. When Qin had unified all under Heaven, Meng Tian was consequently given command of a host of 300,000 to go north and drive out the Rong and Di barbarians and take over the territory to the south of the Yellow River. He built the Great Wall, taking advantage of the lie of the land and making use of the passes. It started from Lintao and went as far as Liaodong, extending more than 10,000 *li.* Crossing the Yellow River, it followed the Yang Mountains and wriggled northwards. His army was exposed to the elements in the field for more than ten years when they were stationed in Shang province, and at this time Meng Tian filled the Xiongnu with terror.

The First Emperor held the Meng family in the highest esteem. Having confidence in them and so entrusting them with responsibility, he regarded them as men of quality. He allowed Meng Yi to be on terms of close intimacy, and he reached the position of senior minister. When he went out, he took him with him in his carriage, and within the palace he was constantly in the imperial presence. Tian was given responsibility for matters outside the capital, but Yi was constantly made to take part in internal planning. They were reputed to be loyal and trustworthy, so that none even of the generals or leading ministers dared to take issue with them in these matters.

Zhao Gao was a distant connection of the various Zhaos. He had several brothers, and all of them were born in the hidden part of the palace. His mother had been condemned to death, and her descendants were to be of low station for generations to come. When the King of Qin heard that Zhao Gao was forceful and well acquainted with the law, he promoted him and made him Director of Palace Coach-houses. Thereupon Gao privately served Prince Huhai and gave him instruction in judicial decisions. When Zhao Gao committed a major crime, the King of Qin ordered Meng Yi to try him at law. Yi did not dare to show partiality, so he condemned Gao to death and removed him from the register of officials, but because of Gao's estimable performance in the conduct of affairs, the Emperor pardoned him and restored his office and rank.

The First Emperor intended to travel throughout the Empire and go via Jiuyuan directly to Ganquan, so he made Meng Tian open up a road from Jiuyuan straight to Ganquan, hollowing out mountains and filling in valleys for 1,800 *li.* The road had not yet been completed when the First Emperor in the winter of the thirty-seventh year went forth on his journey and travelled to Kuaiji. Going along the sea coast, he went north to Langye. When he fell ill on the way, he made Meng Yi return to offer prayers to the mountains and streams. He had not yet got back when the First Emperor passed away on reaching Shaqiu. It was kept a secret, and none of the officials knew. At this time Chief Minister Li Si, Prince Huhai, and Director of Palace Coach-houses Zhao Gao were in constant attendance. Gao had regularly obtained favours from Huhai and wanted him to be set on the throne. He was also resentful that when Meng Yi had tried him at law he had not been in favour of letting him off. Consequently he felt like doing him harm, and so he secretly plotted together with Chief Minister Li Si and Prince Huhai to establish Huhai as crown prince. When the Crown Prince had been established, messengers were sent to bestow death on Prince Fusu and Meng Tian because of their alleged crimes. Even after Fusu was dead, Meng Tian felt suspicious and requested confirmation of it. The messengers handed Meng Tian over to the law officers and replaced him.

The messengers returned and made their report, and when Huhai heard that Fusu was dead he intended to free Meng Tian. But Zhao Gao, fearing that the Meng family would again be treated with honour and be employed on affairs, felt resentful about this.

So when Meng Yi got back, Zhao Gao, making his plans on the pretext of loyalty towards Huhai, intended on this account to wipe out the Meng family. 'Your servant hears that the previous Emperor had long intended to promote a man of quality and set up a crown prince,' he therefore said, 'but Meng Yi had remonstrated and said that this would be improper. But if he was aware that you were a man of quality and yet insisted that you should not be set up, this would be acting disloyally and deluding one's sovereign. In your servant's foolish opinion, the best thing would be to put him to death.' Paying heed, Huhai had Meng Yi put in bonds at Dai. (Previously he had taken Meng Tian prisoner at Yangzhou.) When the announcement of mourning reached Xianyang and the funeral had taken place, the Crown Prince was set up as Second Generation Emperor and Zhao Gao, being admitted to terms of close intimacy, slandered the Meng family day and night, seeking out their crimes and mistakes so as to recommend their impeachment.

Ziying came forward to remonstrate, saying: 'I hear that in ancient times King Qian of Zhao killed his good minister Li Mu and employed Yan Ju, and King Xi of Yan secretly employed the stratagems of Jing Ke and ignored the pact with Qin, and King Jian of Qi killed loyal ministers from ancient families which had given long-standing service and made use of the counsels of Hou Sheng. Each of these three rulers lost their states through changing ancient ways so that disaster befell them. Now the Meng family are important officials and counsellors of Qin and yet our sovereign intends to get rid of them all in a single morning, but your servant humbly considers this to be improper. Your servant hears that it is impossible for one who plans frivolously to govern a state and it is impossible for one who exercises wisdom on his own to preserve his ruler. If you put to death loyal servants and set up people who have nothing to do with integrity, then within the palace this will cause all your servants to lose confidence in each other, and in the field it will cause the purposes of your fighting men to lose their cohesion. Your servant humbly considers this to be improper.'

Huhai did not take any notice, but dispatched the imperial scribe Qu Gong to ride relay and go to Dai and instruct Meng Yi as follows: 'You, minister, made things difficult when our previous sovereign wanted to set up a crown prince. Now the Chief Minister considers that you are disloyal, and that your whole clan is implicated in the crime. But in the kindness of Our heart We bestow death upon you, minister, which is surely extremely gracious. It is for you to give this your consideration!'

'If it is thought that your servant was incapable of grasping the wishes of our previous sovereign,' replied Meng Yi, 'then when he was young he was in his service and obediently received his patronage until he passed away, so it may be said that he knew what he wanted. Or if it is thought that your servant was unaware of the abilities of the Crown Prince, then he went all over the Empire with the Crown Prince in sole attendance, and left all the other princes extremely far behind, so your servant had no doubts. Our previous sovereign's proposal to employ him as crown prince had been building up over several years, so what words would your servant have dared to utter in remonstrance, and what plan would he dare to have devised! It is not that I dare to produce showy verbiage for the purpose of avoiding death and implicate the reputation of our previous sovereign by creating an embarrassment, but I would like you, sir, to devote your thoughts to this, and make sure that the circumstances which cause your servant to be put to death are true. Moreover perfect obedience is what the Way honours, and killing as a punishment is what the Way puts an end to. In former times Duke Mu of Qin died having killed three good men, and charged Baili Xi with a crime although it was not his. Therefore he was given the title of "False". King Zhaoxiang killed Bai Qi, Lord Wuan. King Ping of Chu killed Wu She. Fucha King of Wu killed Wu Zixu. These four rulers all made major mistakes and so all under Heaven regarded them as wrong and thought such rulers were unenlightened, and as such they were recorded by the feudal lords. Therefore it is said that "Those who govern in accordance with the Way do not kill the guiltless and punishment is not inflicted on the innocent." It is up to you, my lord, to take notice!' But the messengers were aware of what Huhai wanted, so they took no notice of Meng Yi's words, and killed him forthwith.

Second Generation also dispatched messengers to go to Yangzhou, with the following instructions for Meng Tian: 'Your errors, my lord, have become numerous, and your younger brother Yi bears a great burden of guilt, so the law has caught up with you.' 'From my grandfather right down to his sons and grandsons,' said Meng Tian, 'their achievements and trustworthiness have been built up in Qin over three generations. Now your servant has been in command of more than 300,000 soldiers, and although he personally is a prisoner, his influence is sufficient to instigate a revolt. But as one who safeguards righteousness although he is aware he is bound to die, he does not dare to disgrace the teachings of his forebears, and in this way he does not forget his former sovereign. In former times when King Cheng of Zhou was first set on the throne and had not yet left his swaddling clothes, Dan Duke of Zhou carried the King on his back to go to court, and ultimately restored order in all under Heaven. When King Cheng had an illness and was in extreme danger, Duke Dan personally cut his finger-nails and sank the parings in the Yellow River. "The King does not yet possess understanding, and it is I who handle affairs," he said. "If there is a crime-engendered disaster, I accept the unfortunate consequences of it." Accordingly he made an account and stored it away in the repository of records, and he may be said to have behaved with good faith. When the time came when the King was able to govern the country, there was a malicious official who said: "Dan Duke of Zhou has long intended to make a rebellion, and if the King is not prepared, there is bound to be a major crisis." The King was consequently furious and Dan Duke of Zhou ran away and fled to Chu. When King Cheng looked in the repository of records, he got hold of the account of the sinking, and so he said, with tears streaming down his face: "Who said that Dan Duke of Zhou intended to make a rebellion?" He killed the one who had said this and restored Dan Duke of Zhou. Thus the *Book of Zhou* says: "One must put them in threes and fives." Now for generations my family has avoided duplicity, so if our affairs are finally in such straits, this is bound to be due to the methods of a wicked minister rebelliously stirring up trouble. That King Cheng made a mistake, but when he restored the situation, he ultimately flourished; but Jie killed Guan Longfeng and Zhou killed Prince Bi Gan, and they did not repent, and when they died their country was destroyed. Your servant therefore says that errors can be remedied and remonstrance can be understood. To examine into threes and fives is the method of supreme sages. All in all, your servant's words have not been for the purpose of seeking to escape from blame. He is about to die because he is making a remonstrance, and he wishes Your Majesty would think about following the Way for the sake of the myriad people.' 'Your servants have received an imperial decree to carry out the law on you, general,' said the messengers, 'and they do not dare to report your words to the Supreme One.' Meng Tian sighed deeply. 'For what am I being blamed by Heaven,' he cried, 'that I should die although I have avoided error?' After a good long while he solemnly said: 'There is a crime for which I certainly ought to die. I built a wall stretching more than 10,000 *li* from Lintao as far as Liaodong, and so in the course of this I surely could not avoid cutting through the earth's arteries. This then is my crime.' And so he swallowed poison and killed himself.

The Grand Historiographer says: 'I have been to the northern border and returned via the direct road. On my journey I observed the ramparts of the Great Wall which Meng Tian built for Qin. He hollowed out the mountains and filled in the valleys and opened up a direct road. To be sure, he showed little concern for the efforts of the people. Qin had only just destroyed the feudal states and the hearts of the people of all under Heaven had not yet been restored to order, and the wounded had not yet been healed; but Tian, although he had become a famous general, did not use this occasion to remonstrate strongly and remedy the distresses of the people, minister to the old and enable the orphans to survive, and strive to cultivate harmony among the masses. Instead he embarked on great enterprises to pander to imperial ambition, so was it not therefore reasonable that both he and his brother should suffer the death penalty? Why in that case should cutting the arteries of the earth be made a crime?'

# Ancient Greece and Rome

At the time Homer began to compose, in the eighth century BCE, Greece was just emerging from its Dark Age, a period that began with the disastrous collapse of Mycenaean civilization in the twelfth century BCE. Once forming a great civilization that traced its cultural roots to the Minoan period (2600–1400 BCE) with its great palaces on the island of Crete, the Hellenic population was by Homer's time scattered among the islands of the eastern Aegean and along the coast of what is now Turkey. Although their cultural origins were Indo-European, the Mycenaeans identified themselves with Minoan Crete, which was not an Indo-European civilization. Traces of this complex cultural mixture can be seen in Hesiod's creation poem, the *Theogony.* Works of literature are often created as acts of resistance against social and spiritual disorder, and Homer composed his epic poems in order to find his bearings in the wake of the Trojan War. His *Iliad* and *Odyssey* have the twofold purpose of honoring the past by recalling it through song and of critically examining what went wrong.

The *Iliad* attributes the collapse of Mycenaean civilization to the pathological behavior of its heroes who fought at Troy and did not achieve a balance between the two requirements of the Homeric hero: to be both a doer of deeds and a speaker of words. The *Odyssey* analyzes the effects of the war on the kingdoms that were deprived of their rulers for more than a decade before they made their return home and restored order. Odysseus was gone from Ithaka for twenty years before he returned. The paradigmatic return-story that haunts Homer in the *Odyssey* is that of Agamemnon, the leader of the Greek army, who returned only to be murdered at the hands of his wife, Clytemnestra, a story that signals a distrust of women ("A bad name/ she gave to womankind, even the best," the shade of Agamemnon observes in the twenty-fourth book of the *Odyssey*). Homer is determined to reverse this attitude through his portrayal of the loyal, intelligent, and charming figure of Penelope. As the same shade declares of Odysseus's "valiant wife," who was "true to her husband's honor and her own": "The very gods themselves will sing her story/ for men on earth." That story is a central thread of the *Odyssey.*

Homer did indeed create a Hellenic consciousness, and his work became the bible of the Greek world. The sort of individualism that we see in the antisocial behavior of Achilles always threatened to destroy the fabric of Greek culture, even as that hero's decision to reenter the battle against the Trojans represents the complementary urge toward social cohesion. The unit of Greek civilization, by the time of the sixth and fifth centuries BCE, was the city-state (*polis*); there were hundreds of these scattered throughout the Hellenic world. The literature from Greece's golden age was the product of a single polis, Athens, with a relatively large population of around one hundred thousand. Greece had always tended toward individualism, in part because of the nature of the land. It was in reality a number of islands with two land masses that were not at all large, especially when compared with ancient China: *Achaea,* which came to be dominated by inventive, democratic, restlessly experimental Athens; and the *Peloponnesus,* which was dominated by the more conservative, cautious, authoritarian Sparta. When faced with an invasion from the Persian Empire to the east, the Greeks managed to come together to resist a common enemy. But soon afterwards individualism reasserted itself and the Greek world became one of warring city-states, a catastrophic outcome that Thucydides analyzed in his history.

For a brief moment under the rule of Pericles, Athens managed to balance individualism and social responsibility, but Pericles fell victim to the terrible plague that decimated Athens. When less restrained and more self-interested leaders, such as Alcibiades, came to power, the spirit of an ambitious individualism ruled the day. Athens was rightly proud of its contributions to the world of knowledge and intellect, but this positive sense of pride soon shaded into *hubris,* "the pride that comes before a fall."

The literary form we call tragedy arose from a cult movement aimed at breaking the grip of aristocratic rule by vesting more power in citizens on the basis of their merit. It warned upwardly mobile Athenian citizens—often believers in the sophist Protagoras's declaration that "man is the measure of all things"—against hubristic pride. Both the tragedies and comedies of fifth-century Athens often set themselves in opposition to the self-confident rationalism epitomized by Pentheus in the *Bakkhai* of Euripides.

Athens, although remarkably democratic by the standards of the ancient world, ultimately did not take well to self-criticism and thereby dug its own grave. In 399 BCE, the courts condemned the philosopher Socrates to death, allegedly because he was corrupting the youth. In reality, the sentence was a defensive gesture designed to silence a man who provoked angry responses by asking uncomfortable questions of those in power who were pompously and dangerously self-satisfied. Or at least this is the view of Plato, who, along with Xenophon, is the only contemporary author who gives us an account of Socrates' trial and conviction. Although we have no reason to disbelieve Plato, we should be clear that what he presents us with is a literary and not a strictly historical account.

With Plato, we move from the world of poetry and myth to the world of philosophy, although Plato never completely abandons myth. His philosophy, like that of Laozi and Zhuangzi in ancient China, is highly poetic. It is true that Plato explicitly exiles the poets from his ideal republic, yet he constantly quotes the poets, and his attitude toward Homer is, finally, not far removed from Confucius's toward the ancient *Books of Songs.* In Greece as in China, philosophy emerged from the insights of poetry, insights that had to be updated in order to respond to the disorder of the times. As the philosophy of Confucius emerged from the disorder of the contending states in the Spring and Autumn Period, so the philosophy of Plato emerged from the period of the Peloponnesian Wars. Thucydides observes the disorder but his brilliant analysis stops short of offering a cure. That cure is offered by Plato, who attempts to view the political problems of his corrupt time from the perspective of the unseen measure that, he believes, informs all our actions. The philosopher (the "lover of wisdom") is the person who becomes conscious of, and is erotically drawn by, a truth beyond the surface of appearances.

After the death of Plato's brilliant pupil Aristotle, who directed his attention toward understanding the dynamic nature of empirical reality in a staggering number of its manifestations, the legacy of Greece took two different courses. First, there were the philosophical schools, beginning with the Academy at which Plato taught, that were to have a profound influence on later thought in the West. Second, there was the political legacy, through Aristotle's pupil Alexander the Great (fourth century BCE), who tried to spread Greek thought through imperial conquest. Society under Alexander was organized very differently from that in Greece during the fifth century BCE. When Aristotle referred to man as a "political animal," he meant a being whose self-definition was inextricably bound to the particular, and rather intimate, form of the Greek city-state. With Alexander, Greek society and culture—now led from Macedonia—entered a bureaucratic and imperialist phase that was to continue, in that age of empire, until Rome assumed control of the whole Mediterranean region.

Rome was founded in 753 BCE, just at the time that the poet (or poets) we call "Homer" was probably putting the *Iliad* and *Odyssey* into the form in which we know these epics today. A small city situated by the river Tiber, Rome was at first dominated by the Etruscans. From the fifth through the first centuries BCE, it slowly came to dominate the entire Italian peninsula. The city vied for control of the Mediterranean world with Carthage, located in northern Africa, during the Punic Wars in the second and third centuries BCE. Rome defeated Carthage in the second century and scored victories in Greece, the Near East, and Spain as well. The period of the Roman Republic ended in the fury of the bitter civil wars to which Virgil often alludes in his *Aeneid.* With his victory in the Battle of Actium in 31 BCE against Antony and Cleopatra, Octavian became the sole ruler of the Roman world, which now controlled the entire Mediterranean. Four years later, Octavian took the title of Augustus, "the revered one," and declared himself emperor. His empire was to last in the West until Rome fell to foreign invaders in 476 CE.

Virgil, in the first book of the *Aeneid,* has Jupiter predict the time and extent of the Roman Empire: to the Romans, Jupiter remarks, "I have granted empire without end." The success of the empire was attributable to the Romans' remarkable administrative skills and to their belief in their fitness to rule. They left a great legacy in the form of Roman law and in magnificently practical architectural feats such as the Pont du Gard, which still regally bestrides the Gardon River in what is now southern France. They were not, however, always successful in offering spiritual comforts to conquered peoples. In the first and second centuries CE, various religions—such as the cult of Isis and Osiris from Egypt and an obscure persecuted sect that later became known as Christianity—attempted to fill this spiritual vacuum. With the conversion of the Emperor Constantine to Christianity in the third century CE, this once-despised religion became the official creed of the Roman Empire, preparing the way for the Christian Middle Ages in Europe.

Greek and Latin literature strictly adhered to the "classical" levels of style: the most lofty literary genres, such as epic and tragedy, were generally composed in a "high" style that was often removed from the realities of everyday life; the "low" style was direct and dealt with the rough-and-tumble actuality of daily experience. In the Greek of the New Testament we find a simplicity of style combined with a sublimity of content that, with the exception of Plato's writings, is rare in classical literature, and would so impress St. Augustine. As Erich Auerbach has argued in his book *Mimesis,* this mixture of the realistic and the sublime demonstrated in early Christian writing created a new aesthetic of literary representation that would deeply influence the literature of the Western Middle Ages.

Compared with Greek writing, Roman literature may strike readers as unoriginal and imitative. This is not totally untrue. When Quintilian, the famous Roman teacher and theorizer of rhetoric, wrote his short history of Greek and Roman literature (first century CE), he was forced to admit that the Romans worked in genres derived from Greek originals. Only satire, Quintilian remarks, is a uniquely Roman invention. Our selections from Roman literature bear out Quintilian's observation. Several of the most famous poems of Catullus, who writes some of the purest and most direct Latin in the language, are in a verse form invented by the brilliant Greek lyric poetess, Sappho. Virgil's *Aeneid* is a rewriting of the Homeric epics. Horace, in his odes, adapts the meters of Greek lyric poetry. Of the Roman poets represented in this anthology, only Ovid can be thought of as cultivating originality for its own sake, and he was often considered—as he was by Quintilian—self-indulgent and undisciplined. If the Greeks are bold, original, and speculative, the "steady Romans"—as Samuel Johnson described them in his eighteenth-century imitation of a Roman satire (*The Vanity of Human Wishes*)—tend to be solid and practical. Readers of this anthology are invited to compare the Roman attitude to Greek literature with that of the Japanese or Korean toward Chinese literature.

Achieving consistency in the transliteration of Greek names is always a problem in an anthology. In our selected texts, we have remained faithful to the conventions chosen by our translators. In our introductions, we have generally adhered to the practice of conventional but not extreme romanization of Greek names (hence "Achilles" rather than "Achilleus"; but "Odysseus" rather than "Ulysses"). Variant spellings have been added in parenthesis for clarification.

## HESIOD (8TH CENT. BCE)

Since the fifth century BCE, readers have wondered whether Hesiod and Homer actually existed, and which of the poetic works ascribed to them were the more ancient. Hesiod refers to a father who had once been a sea-trader and says that he himself was tending sheep on Mt. Helicon when he was called by the Muses to sing about the gods. The notion of the humble shepherd called on by higher powers to sing divine poetry has become a conventional pose imitated throughout European poetry; it is also familiar in the biblical story of David and some of the prophets of the Hebrew Bible. However Hesiod's *Theogony* came to be written, it dates from a very early period in Greek literature, around the same time as the Homeric epics. Unlike a heroic epic, however, the *Theogony* is a creation story assembled from many differing cultural layers and materials. Some of these were pre-Greek religious beliefs concerned with the reproductive powers of the landscape, perhaps related to the earlier Minoan civilization of Crete. Some were stories and religious traditions circulating in Mesopotamia and the whole eastern Mediterranean region. Other traditions had been brought into the northeastern Mediterranean area from as early as 2000 BCE by waves of migrating or invading Indo-Europeans from the steppes north of the Caucasus Mountains. These nomadic peoples also moved into the Indian subcontinent and into Anatolia (now part of Turkey) around the same time. All these cultures have preserved creation stories resembling those in Hesiod's *Theogony*. The Indo-European religious system focused on a pantheon ruled by a sky-god and associated with a horse-riding warrior caste. In the *Theogony* Hesiod attempts to bring together in coherent form the range of creation beliefs resulting from the mingling of peoples during these centuries of movement and change.

As the ritualized invocation to the Muses explains, the *Theogony* attempts to tell of the origin of the world out of Chaos, a neuter void. Gaia, or Earth, is feminine matter that emerges in the form of a disk surrounded by the river Oceanus, the whole floating on vast empty waters. Darkness and night next emerge, but then Earth herself bears Ouranos, or Heaven, who becomes her mate. The birth of their offspring initiates a cycle of bloody battles for succession between fathers and sons that is characteristic of Indo-European myth systems. Kronos (Cronus) attacks and castrates his father Ouranos, then swallows his own children to prevent a repetition of such rebellion, but his wife Rhea flees to Crete to hide her pregnancy before the birth of Zeus. There the divine son is secretly nurtured until he comes of age, frees his brothers, and overthrows his father. Zeus ends the cycle of battles for succession by swallowing his divine children's mother Metis, thus absorbing into himself the reproductive capacities that had been exclusively women's powers before. Athena is later born from his head and Dionysos from his thigh. Aeschylus, at the conclusion of his *Oresteia,* refers to the birth of Athena from the head of Zeus as proof of the superiority of male parentage over the claims of the mother's authority.

Although masculine power struggles dominate the foreground of Hesiod's story, powerful feminine energies surge beneath the surface and occasionally erupt to challenge the divine patriarchy. Zeus swallows the wise goddess Metis because he fears her children, but she remains alive inside him as an advisor. The goddess

Athena thus has a double birth reflecting the absorption of pre-Greek beliefs into an Indo-European belief system. In fact, even Athena's name is not Greek, and the symbols of her cult suggest that she was originally a snake goddess related to the major deity of Minoan Crete—and also to the debased later figure of Medousa (Medusa).

Feminine powers of the earth emerge again and again and are slain by heroic male figures from Zeus and Apollo to Perseus. Similar patterns are central to Sanskrit myth and may record the overthrow of indigenous fertility deities encountered by the Indo-European invaders of the Indian subcontinent. Such monsters haunt many of the narratives of Europe and the Middle East: Eve's encounter with the serpent, the slaying of the Babylonian Tiamat, the Germanic Fafnir, and the dragons of medieval legend slain by St. George and St. Michael are only a few of the most celebrated examples. Asian traditions of benign earth dragons stand in dramatic contrast to these demonic images.

The *Theogony* is an uneven synthesis of disparate mythic traditions from the pre-Greek world, the Indo-European Greek heritage, and eastern Mediterranean materials that had circulated throughout the region for perhaps thousands of years. Other versions of some of the stories to which Hesiod alludes appear in the Homeric epics and surface again in the great tragedies of fifth- and fourth-century Athens; still others are found in Hellenistic and Roman literary works such as Ovid's *Metamorphosis* and *Amores*. The very awkwardness of Hesiod's composition offers fascinating glimpses into the processes of cultural exchange, combination, and conscious structuring that lie at the heart of all literary traditions.

## Theogony

*Translated by Apostolos N. Athanassakis*

Hail, daughters of Zeus! Grant me the gift of lovely song!
Sing the glories of the holy gods to whom death never comes,
the gods born of Gaia and starry Ouranos,
and of those whom dark Night bore, or briny Pontos fostered.
Speak first of how the gods and the earth came into being
and of how the rivers, the boundless sea with its raging swell,
the glittering stars, and the wide sky above were created.
Tell of the gods born of them, the givers of blessings,
how they divided wealth, and each was given his realm,
and how they first gained possession of many-folded Olympos.
Tell me, O Muses who dwell on Olympos, and observe proper order
for each thing as it first came into being.
Chaos was born first and after her came Gaia
the broad-breasted, the firm seat of all
the immortals who hold the peaks of snowy Olympos,
and the misty Tartaros in the depths of broad-pathed earth
and Eros, the fairest of the deathless gods;
he unstrings the limbs and subdues both mind

and sensible thought in the breasts of all gods and all men.
Chaos gave birth to Erebos and black Night;
then Erebos mated with Night and made her pregnant
and she in turn gave birth to Ether and Day.
Gaia now first gave birth to starry Ouranos,
her match in size, to encompass all of her,
and be the firm seat of all the blessed gods.
She gave birth to the tall mountains, enchanting haunts
of the divine nymphs who dwell in the woodlands;
and then she bore Pontos, the barren sea with its raging swell.
All these she bore without mating in sweet love. But then
she did couple with Ouranos to bear deep-eddying Okeanos,
Koios and Kreios, Hyperion and Iapetos,
Theia and Rheia, Themis and Mnemosyne,
as well as gold-wreathed Phoibe and lovely Tethys.
Kronos, the sinuous-minded, was her last-born,
a most fearful child who hated his mighty father.
Then she bore the Kyklopes, haughty in their might,
Brontes, Steropes, and Arges of the strong spirit,
who made and gave to Zeus the crushing thunder.
In all other respects they were like gods,
but they had one eye in the middle of their foreheads;
their name was Kyklopes because of this single
round eye that leered from their foreheads,
and inventive skill and strength and power were in their deeds.
Gaia and Ouranos had three other sons, so great
and mighty that their names are best left unspoken,
Kottos, Briareos, and Gyges, brazen sons all three.
From each one's shoulders a hundred invincible arms
sprang forth, and from each one's shoulders atop the sturdy trunk
there grew no fewer than fifty heads;
and there was matchless strength in their hulking frames.
All these awesome children born of Ouranos and Gaia
hated their own father from the day they were born,
for as soon as each one came from the womb,
Ouranos, with joy in his wicked work, hid it
in Gaia's womb and did not let it return to the light.
Huge Gaia groaned within herself
and in her distress she devised a crafty and evil scheme.
With great haste she produced gray iron
and made a huge sickle and showed it to her children;
then, her heart filled with grief, she rallied them with these words:
"Yours is a reckless father; obey me, if you will,
that we may all punish your father's outrageous deed,
for he was first to plot shameful actions."
So she spoke, and fear gripped them all; not one of them

uttered a sound. Then great, sinuous-minded Kronos
without delay spoke to his prudent mother:
"Mother, this deed I promise you will be done,
since I loathe my dread-named father.
It was he who first plotted shameful actions."
So he spoke, and the heart of giant Earth was cheered.
She made him sit in ambush and placed in his hands
a sharp-toothed sickle and confided in him her entire scheme.
Ouranos came dragging with him the night, longing for Gaia's love,
and he embraced her and lay stretched out upon her.
Then his son reached out from his hiding place and seized him
with his left hand, while with his right he grasped
the huge, long, and sharp-toothed sickle and swiftly hacked off
his father's genitals and tossed them behind him—
and they were not flung from his hand in vain.
Gaia took in all the bloody drops that spattered off,
and as the seasons of the year turned round
she bore the potent Furies and the Giants, immense,
dazzling in their armor, holding long spears in their hands,
and then she bore the Ash Tree Nymphs of the boundless earth.
As soon as Kronos had lopped off the genitals with the sickle
he tossed them from the land into the stormy sea.
And as they were carried by the sea a long time, all around them
white foam rose from the god's flesh, and in this foam a maiden
was nurtured. First she came close to god-haunted Kythera
and from there she went on to reach sea-girt Cyprus.
There this majestic and fair goddess came out, and soft grass
grew all around her soft feet. Both gods and men
call her Aphrodite, foam-born goddess, and fair-wreathed Kythereia;
Aphrodite because she grew out of *aphros,* foam that is,
and Kythereia because she touched land at Kythera.
She is called Kyprogenes, because she was born
in sea-girt Cyprus, and Philommedes, fond of a man's genitals,
because to them she owed her birth. Fair Himeros and Eros
became her companions when she was born and when she joined
the gods.
And here is the power she has had from the start
and her share in the lives of men and deathless gods:
from her come young girls' whispers and smiles and deception
and honey-sweet love and its joyful pleasures.
But the great father Ouranos railed at his own children
and gave them the nickname Titans, Overreachers,
because he said they had, with reckless power, overreached him
to do a monstrous thing that would be avenged some day.
Night gave birth to hideous Moros and black Ker
and then to Death and Sleep and to the brood of Dreams.

After them dark Night, having lain with no one,
gave birth to Momos and painful Oizys
and to the Hesperides, who live beyond renowned Okeanos
and keep the golden apples and the fruit-bearing trees.
She also bore the ruthless Keres and the Moirai,
Klotho, Lachesis, and Atropos, who when men are born
give them their share of things good and bad.
They watch for the transgressions of men and gods,
and the dreadful anger of these goddesses never abates
until wrongdoers are punished with harshness.
Baneful Night bore Nemesis, too, a woe for mortals,
and after her Deception and the Passion of lovers
and destructive Old Age and capricious Strife.
Then loathsome Strife bore Ponos, the bringer of pains,
Oblivion and Famine and the tearful Sorrows,
the Clashes and the Battles and the Manslaughters,
the Quarrels and the Lies and Argument and Counter-Argument,
Lawlessness and Ruin whose ways are all alike,
and Oath, who, more than any other, brings pains on mortals
who of their own accord swear false oaths.
Pontos sired truthful Nereus, his oldest son,
who tells no lies; they call him the old man
because he is honest and gentle and never forgetful
of right, but ever mindful of just and genial thought.
Then Pontos lay with Gaia and sired great Thaumas,
Phorkys the overbearing, and fair-cheeked Keto,
and Eurybie, who in her breast has a heart of iron.
To Nereus and Doris of the lovely hair,
the daughter of Okeanos, the stream surrounding the earth,
a host of godly daughters was born in the barren sea:

* * *

*[a catalog of daughters]*

These were the daughters born to blameless Nereus,
fifty of them, all wise in deeds of perfection.
Thaumas took as his wife Elektra, daughter of Okeanos,
whose stream is deep, and she bore swift Iris
and the lovely-haired Harpies, Aello and Okypete,
who, with fast wings, trail flying birds and windy breezes
as they soar and swoop from high up in the air.
To Phorkys Keto bore the fair-cheeked Graiai,
gray from birth, who are given this name
both by the immortal gods and by men who tread the earth,
well-robed Pemphredo and saffron-cloaked Enyo;

then the Gorgons, who dwell beyond glorious Okeanos
at earth's end, toward night, by the clear-voiced Hesperides,
Sthenno, Euryale, and ill-fated Medousa,
who was mortal; the other two were ageless and immortal.
Dark-maned Poseidon lay with one of these, Medousa,
on a soft meadow strewn with spring flowers.
When Perseus cut off Medousa's head, immense Chrysaor
and the horse Pegasos sprang forth.
His name came from the springs of Ocean by which he was born,
but Chrysaor's from the golden sword he carried in his hand.
Pegasos left the earth, mother of flocks, and flew away
and reached the immortals; he lives in the palace
of Zeus the counselor, to whom he brings thunder and lightning.
Chrysaor then lay with Kallirhoe, daughter of glorious Okeanos,
and sired the three-headed Geryones
whom the might of Herakles slew
beside his shambling oxen at sea-girt Erytheia
on the very day he crossed Ocean's stream
and drove the broad-browed cattle to holy Tiryns.
Then he also slew Orthos and the oxherd Eurytion
out at that misty place, beyond glorious Ocean.
Then Keto bore another invincible monster,
in no way like mortal men or the deathless gods;
yes, in a hollow cave she bore Echidna, divine
and iron-hearted, half fair-cheeked and bright-eyed nymph
and half huge and monstrous snake inside the holy earth,
a snake that strikes swiftly and feeds on living flesh.
Her lair is a cave under a hollow rock,
far from immortal gods and mortal men;
the gods decreed for her a glorious dwelling there.
Arima, beneath the earth, is the stronghold of the grisly Echidna,
the nymph who is immortal and ageless for ever.
They say that this bright-eyed maiden lay in love
with Typhaon, that lawless and dreadful ravisher,
and impregnated by him she bore a harsh-tempered brood.
First she gave birth to Orthos, the dog of Geryones,
and then she bore a stubborn and unspeakable creature,
Kerberos, the fifty-headed dog of Hades, that mighty
and shameless eater of raw flesh, whose bark resounds like bronze.
Her third child was the loathsome Hydra of Lerna,
and she was nurtured by white-armed Hera
whose wrath at mighty Herakles was implacable.
But Herakles, born to Amphitryon as son of Zeus,
together with Iolaos slew her with the merciless bronze blade,
for Athena, leader of the war host, willed it so.
She bore Chimaira, mighty, dreadful, huge,
and fleet-footed, who breathed forth a ceaseless stream of fire.

She had three heads, one of a glowering lion,
another of a goat, and yet another of a savage dragon;
her front was a lion, her back a dragon, and her middle a goat,
and she breathed forth an awesome stream of gleaming fire.
Pegasos and noble Bellerophon slew her.
Orthos covered her, and she bore the destructive Sphinx,
a scourge for the Kadmeans, and then the Lion of Nemea,
who was reared by Hera, the glorious wife of Zeus,
and settled on the hills of Nemea as a scourge to mankind.
There was his abode and from there he preyed on the tribes of men
and lorded it over Apesas and Nemean Tretos,
but the strength of mighty Herakles subdued him.
Keto then lay in love with Phorkys and bore her youngest,
a ghastly snake that guards the all-golden apples,
lurking in his lair in the gloom of earth's vast limits.
This is the brood born of Phorkys and Keto.
Tethys bore to Okeanos the whirling rivers,

* * *

*[a catalog of rivers]*

Okeanos has three thousand slender-ankled daughters—
splendid children of goddesses—who roam in bevies
and haunt the earth and the depths of the waters alike.
And there are as many tumbling and rushing rivers,
all sons of Okeanos and queenly Tethys.
It is hard for a mortal to recite the names of all,
but those who live by them know each of their names.
Theia yielded to Hyperion's love and gave birth
to great Helios and bright Selene and Eos,
who brings light to all the mortals of this earth
and to the immortal gods who rule the wide sky.
Eurybia, the radiant goddess, lay in love with Kreios
and gave birth to great Astraios and to Pallas
and then to Perses, who surpassed all in wisdom.
Eos shared love's bed with Astraios
and bore him the mighty-spirited winds,
bright Zephyros and gusty Boreas and Notos.
After them Eos the early-born brought forth the dawnstar,
Eosphoros, and the glittering stars that crown the heavens.
Styx, the daughter of Okeanos, lay in love with Pallas
and in his mansion gave birth to Zelos and fair-ankled Nike,
and then she bore two illustrious children, Kratos and Bia.
These two have no home apart from Zeus, nor seat
nor path, except the one to which he leads them,
but their place is with Zeus of the roaring thunder.

For this was the will of Styx, the deathless daughter of Ocean,
on the day the Olympian hurler of lightning
called all the immortals to lofty Olympos
and said that he would not wrest away the rights
of those who would fight with him against the Titans
and that each god would retain his previous honors.
He said that those deprived of rights and honors
by Kronos could now lay just claim to them.
On her own father's advice the immortal Styx
and her children were first to come to Olympos.
And Zeus granted her honor and countless gifts
and decreed that the gods should swear great oaths by her
and that her children should dwell with him for ever.
He fulfilled with exactness the promises made to all;
and yet, he is sovereign lord and his power is unchallenged.
Phoibe went to the much longed-for bed of Koios,
and she, a goddess loved by a god, conceived
and gave birth to dark-robed Leto, ever sweet,
gentle to men and to gods who never die,
sweet from the beginning, gentlest of all the Olympians.
She also bore Asteria, whose name brings good luck;
Perses brought her to his great house, to be his dear wife.
There she conceived and bore Hekate, whom Zeus
honored above all others; he gave her dazzling gifts,
a share of the earth and a share of the barren sea.
She was given a place of honor in the starry sky,
and among the deathless gods her rank is high.
For even now, when a mortal propitiates the gods
and, following custom, sacrifices well-chosen victims,
he invokes Hekate, and if she receives his prayers
with favor, then honor goes to him with great ease,
and he is given blessings, because she has power
and a share in all the rights once granted
to the offspring born to Ouranos and Gaia.
The son of Kronos did not use force on her and took away
none of the rights she held under the Titans, those older gods.
The distribution made in the beginning is still the same.
Nor does the goddess have less honor for being an only child;
in fact, she has much more because Zeus honors her,
and her domain extends over land and sky and sea,
and she can greatly aid a man—if this is her wish.
In trials her seat is at the side of illustrious kings,
and in assemblies the man she favors gains distinction.
And when men arm themselves for man-destroying battle,
the goddess always stands beside those she prefers
and gladly grants them victory and glory.

Again, she is a noble goddess when men compete
for athletic prizes, because she stands by them and helps,
and whoever, by force and strength, wins a fair prize,
carries it away with ease and joy and brings his parents glory.
To horsemen, too, when she wishes, she is a noble helper
and to those working out on the stormy and gray sea
who pray to Hekate and to the rumbling Earthshaker.
With ease this glorious goddess grants a great catch of fish
and with ease, if that is her wish, she makes it vanish.
And when she wishes from the heart she can be noble
and, with Hermes, help livestock breed in the stalls,
and swell or thin out herds of cattle and wide-ranging
flocks of goats and thick-wooled sheep.
And even though she was her mother's only child
she has her share of honors among all the gods.
The son of Kronos made her the fostering goddess for all youths
who after her birth saw the light of wakeful Dawn.
A nurturer of youths from the beginning, she holds these honors.
Rheia succumbed to Kronos's love and bore him illustrious children,
Hestia and Demeter and Hera, who walks in golden sandals,
imperious Hades, whose heart knows no mercy
in his subterranean dwelling, and the rumbling Earthshaker,
and Zeus the counselor and father of gods and men,
Zeus under whose thunder the wide earth quivers.
But majestic Kronos kept on swallowing each child
as it moved from the holy womb toward the knees;
his purpose was to prevent any other child of the Sky Dwellers
from holding the kingly office among immortals.
He had learned from Gaia and starry Ouranos
that he, despite his power, was fated
to be subdued by his own son, a victim of his own schemes.
Therefore, he kept no blind watch, but ever wary
he gulped down his own children to Rhea's endless grief.
But as she was about to bear Zeus, father of gods
and men, she begged her own parents,
Gaia, that is, and starry Ouranos,
to contrive such a plan that the birth of her dear child
would go unnoticed and her father's Erinys would take revenge
for the children swallowed by majestic, sinuous-minded Kronos.
And they listened to their dear daughter and granted her wish
and let her know what fate had in store
for King Kronos and his bold-spirited son.
And so they sent her to Lyktos, in the rich land of Crete,
just as she was about to bear the last of her children,
great Zeus, whom huge Gaia would take into her care
on broad Crete, to nourish and foster with tender love.

She carried him swiftly in the darkness of night, and Lyktos was
the first place she reached; she took him in her arms
and hid him inside the god-haunted earth in a cave
lodged deep within a sheer cliff of densely wooded Mount Aigaion.
But to the great Lord Kronos, king of the older gods,
she handed a huge stone wrapped in swaddling clothes.
He took it in his hands and stuffed it into his belly—
the great fool! It never crossed his mind that the stone
was given in place of his son thus saved to become
carefree and invincible, destined to crush him by might of hand,
drive him out of his rule, and become king of the immortals.
The lord's strength and splendid limbs grew swiftly
and, as the year followed its revolving course,
sinuous-minded Kronos was deceived by Gaia's
cunning suggestions to disgorge his own offspring—
overpowered also by the craft and brawn of his own son.
The stone last swallowed was first to come out,
and Zeus set it up on the broad-pathed earth,
at sacred Pytho, under the rocky folds of Parnassos,
forever to be a marvel and a portent for mortal men.
He freed from their wretched bonds his father's brothers,
[Brontes and Steropes and Arges of the bold spirit,]
whom Ouranos, their father, had thrown into chains;
they did not forget the favors he had done them,
and they gave him the thunder and the smoky thunderbolt
and lightning, all of which had lain hidden in the earth.
Trusting in these, he ruled over mortals and immortals.
Iapetos took as his wife the fair-ankled Klymene,
daughter of Okeanos, and shared her bed,
and she bore him Atlas, a son of invincible spirit,
and Menoitios of the towering pride, and Prometheus,
whose mind was labyrinthine and swift, and foolish Epimetheus,
who from the start brought harm to men who toil for bread;
he was first to accept the virgin woman fashioned by far-seeing Zeus,
who with flaming thunderbolt struck Menoitios
and cast him into murky Erebos
for his folly and reckless flaunting of manliness.
By harsh necessity, Atlas supports the broad sky
on his head and unwearying arms,
at the earth's limits, near the clear-voiced Hesperides,
for this is the doom decreed for him by Zeus the counselor.
With shackles and inescapable fetters Zeus riveted Prometheus
on a pillar—Prometheus of the labyrinthine mind;
and he sent a long-winged eagle to swoop on him
and devour the god's liver; but what the long-winged bird ate
in the course of each day grew back and was restored to its full size.

But Herakles, the mighty son of fair-ankled Alkmene,
slew the eagle, drove the evil scourge away
from the son of Iapetos and freed him from his sorry plight,
and did all this obeying the will of Olympian Zeus,
who rules on high, to make the glory of Herakles, child of Thebes,
greater than before over the earth that nurtures many.
Zeus so respected these things and honored his illustrious son
that he quelled the wrath he had nursed against Prometheus,
who had opposed the counsels of Kronos's mighty son.
When the gods and mortal men were settling their accounts
at Mekone, Prometheus cheerfully took a great ox,
carved it up, and set it before Zeus to trick his mind.
He placed meat, entrails, and fat within a hide
and covered them with the ox's tripe,
but with guile he arranged the white bones of the ox,
covered them with glistening fat, and laid them down as an offer.
Then indeed the father of gods and men said to him:
"Son of Iapetos, you outshine all other kings,
but, friend, you have divided with self-serving zeal."
These were the sarcastic words of Zeus, whose counsels never perish,
but Prometheus was a skillful crook and he smiled faintly,
all the while mindful of his cunning scheme,
and said: "Sublime Zeus, highest among the everlasting gods,
choose of the two portions whichever your heart desires."
He spoke with guileful intent, and Zeus, whose counsels never perish,
knew the guile and took note of it; so he pondered evils in his mind
for mortal men, evils he meant to bring on them.
With both hands he took up the white fat,
and spiteful anger rushed through his mind and heart
when he saw the white bones of the ox laid out in deceit.
From that time on the tribes of mortal men on earth
have burned the white bones for the gods on smoky altars.
Then Zeus the cloud-gatherer angrily said:
"Son of Iapetos, no one matches your resourceful wits,
but, friend, your mind is clinging stubbornly to guile."
So Zeus, whose counsels never perish, spoke in anger
and thereafter never forgot that he had been beguiled
and never gave to ash trees the power of unwearying fire
for the good of men who live on this earth,
but the noble son of Iapetos deceived him again
and within a hollowed fennel stalk stole the far-flashing
unwearying fire. This stung the depths of Zeus's mind,
Zeus who roars on high, and filled his heart with anger,
when he saw among mortal men the far-seen flash of fire;
so straightway because of the stolen fire he contrived an evil for men.
The famous lame smith took clay and, through Zeus's counsels,

gave it the shape of a modest maiden.
Athena, the gray-eyed goddess, clothed her and decked her out
with a flashy garment and then with her hands
she hung over her head a fine draping veil, a marvel to behold;
Pallas Athena crowned her head with lovely wreaths
of fresh flowers that had just bloomed in the green meadows.
The famous lame smith placed on her head a crown of gold
fashioned by the skill of his own hands
to please the heart of Zeus the father.
It was a wondrous thing with many intricate designs
of all the dreaded beasts nurtured by land and sea.
Such grace he breathed into the many marvels therein
that they seemed endowed with life and voice.
Once he had finished—not something good but a mixture of good
and bad—he took the maiden before gods and men,
and she delighted in the finery given her by gray-eyed Athena,
daughter of a mighty father. Immortal gods and mortal men
were amazed when they saw this tempting snare
from which men cannot escape. From her comes the fair sex;
yes, wicked womenfolk are her descendants.
They live among mortal men as a nagging burden
and are no good sharers of abject want, but only of wealth.
Men are like swarms of bees clinging to cave roofs
to feed drones that contribute only to malicious deeds;
the bees themselves all day long until sundown
are busy carrying and storing the white wax,
but the drones stay inside in their roofed hives
and cram their bellies full of what others harvest.
So, too, Zeus who roars on high made women
to be an evil for mortal men, helpmates in deeds of harshness.

* * *

When Zeus drove the Titans out of the sky
giant Gaia bore her youngest child, Typhoeus;
goaded by Aphrodite, she lay in love with Tartaros.
The arms of Typhoeus were made for deeds of might,
his legs never wearied, and on his shoulders were
a hundred snake heads, such as fierce dragons have,
and from them licking black tongues darted forth.
And the eyes on all the monstrous heads flashed
from under the brows and cast glances of burning fire;
from all the ghastly heads voices were heard,
weird voices of all kinds. Sometimes they uttered words
that the gods understood, and then again
they bellowed like bulls, proud and fierce

beyond restraint, or they roared like brazen-hearted lions
or—wondrous to hear—their voices sounded like a whelp's bark,
or a strident hiss that echoed through the lofty mountains.
An irreversible deed would have been done that day,
and Typhoeus would have become lord over gods and men,
had not the father of gods and men kept sharp-eyed watch.
He hurled a mighty bolt and its ear-splitting crash
reverberated grimly through the earth and the wide sky above,
through the sea, the streams of Ocean, and through the underworld.
And when the lord moved, massive Olympos shook
and the earth groaned under his indestructible feet,
and the heat of the duel engulfed the violet-dark sea,
heat from Zeus's lightning and thunder, from hurricanes
and from the fire that raged as thunderbolts struck the monster.
The whole earth, the sea, and the sky seethed;
a dread quake arose in the wake of the immortals' charge
and heaving waves rolled up against the shores;
then Hades, lord of the wasted shades below,
and the Titans under Tartaros and around Kronos
shuddered at the unending din and grisly clash.
But now Zeus's strength surged and he grasped his weapons,
thunder and lightning and glowing thunderbolt,
and, lunging from Olympos, he set fire
to all of the hellish monster's gruesome heads.
Then, when Zeus's blows had whipped him to submission,
Typhoeus collapsed, crippled, on the groaning giant earth;
and the flame from the thunder-smitten lord
leaped along the dark and rocky woodlands
of the mountain, and the infernal blast of the flames
set much of the giant earth on fire until it melted
like tin that has been heated by craftsmen
over a well-pierced crucible, or like that strongest metal,
iron, which in mountain woodlands the scorching fire tames
and the craft of Hephaistos melts inside the divine earth.
So melted the earth from the flash of the burning fire,
and Zeus in terrible anger cast Typhoeus into broad Tartaros.

* * *

Zeus, king of the gods, took as his first wife Metis,
a mate wiser than all gods and mortal men.
But when she was about to bear gray-eyed Athena,
then through the schemes of Gaia and starry Ouranos,
he deceived the mind of Metis with guile
and coaxing words, and lodged her in his belly.
Such was their advice, so that of the immortals

none other than Zeus would hold kingly sway.
It was fated that Metis would bear keen-minded children,
first a gray-eyed daughter, Tritogeneia,
who in strength and wisdom would be her father's match,
and then a male child, high-mettled
and destined to rule over gods and men.
But Zeus lodged her in his belly before she did all this,
that she might advise him in matters good and bad.
His second wife was radiant Themis; she bore the Seasons,
Lawfulness and Justice and blooming Peace,
who watch over the works of mortal men,
and also the Fates, to whom wise Zeus allotted high honors.
These are Klotho, Lachesis, and Atropos,
and they give mortals their share of good and evil.
Then Eurynome, Ocean's fair daughter,
bore to Zeus the three Graces, all fair-cheeked,
Aglaia, Euphrosyne, and shapely Thalia;
their alluring eyes glance from under their brows,
and from their eyelids drips desire that unstrings the limbs.
After Zeus slept with Demeter who nurtures many,
she bore white-armed Persephone, whom Aidoneus
snatched away from her mother with the consent of wise Zeus.
Then he fell in love with Mnemosyne the lovely-haired,
who gave birth to the gold-filleted Muses,
lovers, all nine, of feasts and of enchanting song.
Leto lay in love with aegis-bearing Zeus
and gave birth to Apollon and arrow-shooting Artemis,
children comelier than all the other sky-dwellers.
Last of all, Zeus made Hera his buxom-bride,
and she lay in love with the king of gods and men
and bore Hebe and Ares and Eileithyia.
Then from his head he himself bore gray-eyed Athena,
weariless leader of armies, dreaded and mighty goddess,
who stirs men to battle and is thrilled by the clash of arms.

## The Homeric Hymn to Demeter (8th–7th cent. BCE)

*Translated by Apostolos N. Athanassakis*

The mystery cults of the goddess Demeter were so secret in the ancient world that we know almost nothing of their nature, even though they continued to be centrally important religious rituals from the Mycenaean Greek world (c. 1600–1200 BCE) into the late Roman Empire (c. 300 CE). The goddess's temple at Eleusis just south of Athens sits on layers of ruins that go back far earlier than the Greeks, indicating that she may have originally been an indigenous pre-Indo-European fertility deity.

For the Greek world she certainly held that function, presiding over all plant life and thus the ultimate vitality of all living things. A work as late as Euripides' tragedy *The Bakkhai* testifies to the continuing force of this belief. *The Homeric Hymn to Demeter* is the oldest version of the story that explains her powers in a poignant mother-daughter tale of loss and recovery. It is one of many so-called "Homeric" hymns written in the same general period as the *Iliad* and the *Odyssey* or slightly later, but probably not by the author of the Homeric epics. The hymns do, however, share a place in the same aristocratic literary tradition.

The last two syllables of Demeter's name mean "mother" in Greek, and as a corn or grain mother (known as Ceres by the Romans, as in "cereal") was usually paired with a daughter figure or *Korê* ("maiden" in Greek) as the dual aspect of womanhood. The Korê receives the name Persephone after her return from the underworld. The underworld goddess Hecate makes up the third element in the divine trio of maiden, mother, and crone, who are linked with the regenerative powers of the earth. The fertility myth explains the timing of the historical ritual celebrations of Demeter during early autumn and late spring: the *Anthesterion* celebrated the time when Persephone was thought to have been stolen away by Hades, god of the underworld, just before the early summer harvest and the beginning of the long hot, dry season in Greece; her return was celebrated at the *Boedromion,* when the rains brought green to the fields again after the summer drought.

*The Homeric Hymn to Demeter* is one of the most popular stories from the cycle of Greek myths that have continued to be part of the European literary tradition. It has intriguing parallels with ancient Mesopotamian and Egyptian traditions such as the Descent of Inanna. These stories of death and rebirth in the ancient Mediterranean/Mesopotamian world associate the growing, seeding, and dying of plants with the human life cycle, suggesting close involvement with the seasons and the physical environment, and the possibility of renewal in the face of death. *The Hymn to Demeter* is distinctive in its emphasis on the sterility of the earth caused by the wrath of the goddess against the sexual violator of her daughter. Demeter has the power to withhold the vitality of the land until Zeus and Hades relent and restore Persephone.

I begin to sing of lovely-haired Demeter, the goddess august,
of her and her slender-ankled daughter whom Zeus,
far-seeing and loud-thundering, gave to Aidoneus to abduct.
Away from her mother of the golden sword and the splendid fruit
she played with the full-bosomed daughters of Okeanos,
gathering flowers, roses, crocuses, and beautiful violets
all over a soft meadow; irises, too, and hyacinths she picked,
and narcissus, which Gaia, pleasing the All-receiver,
made blossom there, by the will of Zeus, for a girl with a flower's
beauty.
A lure it was, wondrous and radiant, and a marvel to be seen
by immortal gods and mortal men.
A hundred stems of sweet-smelling blossoms
grew from its roots. The wide sky above
and the whole earth and the briny swell of the sea laughed.

She was dazzled and reached out with both hands at once
to take the pretty bauble; Earth with its wide roads gaped
and then over the Nysian field the lord and All-receiver,
the many-named son of Kronos, sprang out upon her with his
    immortal horses.
Against her will he seized her and on his golden chariot
carried her away as she wailed; and she raised a shrill cry,
calling upon father Kronides, the highest and the best.
None of the immortals or of mortal men heard
her voice, not even the olive-trees bearing splendid fruit.
Only the gentle-tempered daughter of Persaios,
Hekate of the shining headband, heard from her cave,
and lord Helios, the splendid son of Hyperion, heard
the maiden calling father Kronides; he sat
apart from the gods away in the temple of prayers,
accepting beautiful sacrifices from mortal men.
By Zeus' counsels, his brother, the All-receiver
and Ruler of Many, Kronos' son of many names,
was carrying her away with his immortal horses, against her will.
So while the goddess looked upon the earth and the starry sky
and the swift-flowing sea teeming with fish
and the rays of the sun and still hoped to see
her loving mother and the races of gods immortal,
hope charmed her great mind, despite her grief.
The peaks of the mountains and the depths of the sea resounded
with her immortal voice, and her mighty mother heard her.
A sharp pain gripped her heart, and she tore
the headband round her divine hair with her own hands.
From both of her shoulders she cast down her dark veil
and rushed like a bird over the nourishing land and the sea,
searching; but none of the gods or mortal men
wanted to tell her the truth and none
of the birds of omen came to her as truthful messenger.
For nine days then all over the earth mighty Deo
roamed about with bright torches in her hands,
and in her sorrow never tasted ambrosia
or nectar sweet to drink, and never bathed her skin.
But when the tenth light-bringing Dawn came to her,
Hekate carrying a light in her hands, met her,
and with loud voice spoke to her and told her the news:
"Mighty Demeter, bringer of seasons and splendid gifts,
which of the heavenly gods or of mortal men
seized Persephone and pierced with sorrow your dear heart?
For I heard a voice but did not see with my eyes
who it was; I am quickly telling you the whole truth."
Thus spoke Hekate. And to her the daughter of lovely-haired Rhea

answered not a word, but with her she sped away
swiftly, holding the bright torches in her hands.
They came to Helios, watcher of gods and men,
and stood near his horses, and the illustrious goddess made a plea:
"Helios, do have respect for me as a goddess, if I ever
cheered your heart and soul by word or deed.
Through the barren ether I heard the shrieking voice
of my daughter famous for her beauty, a sweet flower at birth,
as if she were being overcome by force, but I saw nothing.
And since you do gaze down upon the whole earth
and sea and cast your rays through the bright ether,
tell me truly if you have seen anywhere
what god or even mortal man in my absence
seized by force my dear child and went away."
Thus she spoke and Hyperionides gave her an answer:
"Lady Demeter, daughter of lovely-haired Rhea,
you shall know; for I greatly reverence and pity you
in your grief for your slender-ankled child; no other immortal
is to be blamed save cloud-gathering Zeus
who gave her to Hades, his own brother, to become
his buxom bride. He seized her and with his horses
carried her crying loud down to misty darkness.
But, Goddess, stop your great wailing; you mustn't give
yourself to grief so great and fruitless. Not an unseemly
bridegroom among immortals is Aidoneus, Lord of Many,
your own brother from the same seed; to his share fell
honor when in the beginning a triple division was made,
and he dwells among those over whom his lot made him lord."
With these words, he called upon his horses, and at his command
speedily, like long-winged birds, they drew the swift chariot,
as a pain more awful and savage reached Demeter's soul.
Afterwards, angered with Kronion, lord of black clouds,
she withdrew from the assembly of the gods and from lofty Olympos
and went through the cities of men and the wealth of their labors,
tearing at her fair form for a long time. . . .

*[The goddess journeys to Eleusis, where after disguising herself as an old woman and being employed as a nurse for the king and queen's infant son, she reveals her true nature and persuades the people to build a temple for her worship.]*

Now when they finished the temple and refrained from labor,
each man went to his home, but blond Demeter,
sitting there apart from all the blessed ones,
kept on wasting with longing for her deep-girded daughter.
Onto the much-nourishing earth she brought a year
most dreadful and harsh for men; no seed
in the earth sprouted, for fair-wreathed Demeter concealed it.

In vain the oxen drew many curved plows over the fields,
and in vain did much white barley fall into the ground.
And she would have destroyed the whole race of mortal men
with painful famine and would have deprived
the Olympians of the glorious honor of gifts and sacrifices,
if Zeus had not perceived this and pondered in his mind.
First he sent golden-winged Iris to invite
the lovely-haired Demeter of the fair form.
He spoke to her and she obeyed Zeus, the son of Kronos
and lord
of dark clouds, and ran swiftly mid-way between earth and heaven.
She reached the town of Eleusis rich in sacrifices,
found the dark-veiled Demeter in the temple
and spoke, uttering winged words to her:
"Demeter, Zeus the father, whose wisdom never wanes,
invites you to come among the tribes of the immortal gods.
But come and let not the word of Zeus be unaccomplished."
Thus she spoke begging her, but her mind was not persuaded.
So then again the father sent forth all the blessed
immortal gods. They ran to her, and each in his turn
summoned her and gave her many beautiful gifts
and whatever honors she might want to choose among the
immortals.
But no one could persuade the mind and thought
of the angry goddess who stubbornly spurned their offers.
She said she would never set foot on fragrant Olympos
and never allow the grain in the earth to sprout forth
before seeing with her eyes her fair-faced daughter.
So when loud-thundering, far-seeing Zeus heard this,
he sent Argeiphontes of the golden wand to Erebos.
His mission was to win Hades over with gentle words,
and bring Persephone out of misty darkness
to light and among the gods, so that her mother
might see her with her eyes and desist from anger.
Hermes did not disobey and, leaving his Olympian seat,
with eager speed plunged into the depths of the earth.
He found the lord inside his dwelling,
sitting on his bed with his revered spouse; she was
in many ways reluctant and missed her mother, who far
from the works of the blessed gods was devising a plan.
Mighty Argeiphontes stood near and addressed him:
"Hades, dark-haired lord of those who have perished,
Zeus the father bids you bring noble Persephone
out of Erebos and among the gods, so that her mother,
seeing her with her eyes, may desist from anger

and dreadful wrath against the gods; because she is contemplating
a great scheme to destroy the feeble races of earth-born men,
hiding the seed under the earth and abolishing the honors
of the immortals. Her anger is dreadful, and she does not mingle
with the gods, but apart from them in a fragrant temple
she sits, dwelling in the rocky town of Eleusis."
Thus he spoke and Aidoneus, lord of the nether world,
with smiling brows obeyed the behests of Zeus the king
and speedily gave his command to prudent-minded Persephone:
"Persephone, go to your dark-robed mother,
with a gentle spirit and temper in your breast,
and in no way be more dispirited than the other gods.
I shall not be an unfitting husband among the immortals,
as I am father Zeus' own brother. When you are here
you shall be mistress of everything which lives and moves;
your honors among the immortals shall be the greatest,
and those who wrong you shall always be punished,
if they do not propitiate your spirit with sacrifices,
performing sacred rites and making due offerings."
Thus he spoke and wise Persephone rejoiced
and swiftly sprang up for joy, but he himself
gave her to eat a honey-sweet pomegranate seed,
contriving secretly about her, so that she might not spend
all her days again with dark-robed, revered Demeter.
Aidoneus, Ruler of Many, harnessed nearby
the immortal horses up to the golden chariot.
She mounted the chariot, and next to her mighty Argeiphontes
took the reins and the whip in his own hands
and sped out of the halls, as the horses flew readily.
Soon they reached the end of the long path, and neither
the sea nor the water of rivers nor the grassy glens
and mountain-peaks checked the onrush of the immortal horses,
but they went over all these, traversing the lofty air.
He drove them and then halted near the fragrant temple
where fair-wreathed Demeter stayed. When she saw them,
she rushed as a maenad does, along a shady woodland on the mountains.
Persephone on her part, when she saw the beautiful eyes
of her mother, leaving chariot and horses, leaped down
to run and, throwing her arms around her mother's neck, embraced her.
And as Demeter still held her dear child in her arms,
her mind suspected trickery, and in awful fear she withdrew
from fondling her and forthwith asked her a question:

"Child, when you were below, did you perchance partake
of food? Speak out, that we both may know.
If your answer is no, coming up from loathsome Hades,
you shall dwell both with me and with father Kronion,
lord of dark clouds, honored by all the immortals.
Otherwise, you shall fly and go to the depths of the earth
to dwell there a third of the seasons in the year,
spending two seasons with me and the other immortals.
Whenever the earth blooms with every kind of sweet-smelling
springflower, you shall come up again from misty darkness,
a great wonder for gods and mortal men.
With what trick did the mighty All-receiver deceive you?"
Facing her now, beautiful Persephone replied:
"Surely, Mother, I shall tell you the whole truth.
When Hermes, the helpful swift messenger, came
from father Zeus and the other heavenly dwellers
to fetch me from Erebos, so that seeing me with your eyes
you might desist from your anger and dreadful wrath against the immortals,
I myself sprang up for joy, but Aidoneus slyly placed
in my hands a pomegranate seed, sweet as honey to eat.
Against my will and by force he made me taste of it.
How he abducted me through the shrewd scheming of Kronides,
my father, and rode away carrying me to the depths of the earth
I shall explain and rehearse every point as you are asking.
All of us maidens in a delightful meadow,
Leukippe, Phaino, Electra, Ianthe,
Melite, Iache, Rhodeia, Kallirhoe,
Melobosis, Tyche, Okyrhoe with a face like a flower,
Chryseis, Ianeira, Akaste, Admete,
Rhodope, Plouto, lovely Kalypso,
Styx, Ourania, charming Galaxaura,
battle-stirring Pallas, and arrow-pouring Artemis,
were playing and picking lovely flowers with our hands,
mingling soft crocuses and irises with hyacinths
and the flowers of the rose and lilies, a wonder to the eye,
and the narcissus which the wide earth grows crocus-colored.
So I myself was picking them with joy, but the earth beneath
gave way and from it the mighty lord and All-receiver
leaped out. He carried me under the earth in his golden chariot,
though I resisted and shouted with shrill voice.
I am telling you the whole truth, even though it grieves me."
So then all day long, being one in spirit,
they warmed each other's hearts and minds in many ways

with loving embraces, and an end to sorrow came for their hearts,
as they took joys from each other and gave in return.
Hekate of the shining headband came near them
and many times lovingly touched the daughter of pure Demeter.
From then on this lady became her attendant and follower.
Far-seeing, loud-thundering Zeus sent them a messenger,
Lovely-haired Rhea, to bring her dark-veiled mother
among the races of the gods, promising to give her
whatever honors she might choose among the immortal gods.
With a nod of his head he promised that, as the year revolved,
her daughter could spend one portion of it in the misty darkness
and the other two with her mother and the other immortals.
He spoke and the goddess did not disobey the behests of Zeus.
Speedily she rushed down from the peaks of Olympos
and came to Rharion, lwife-giving udder of the earth
in the past, and then no longer life-giving but lying idle
without a leaf. It was now hiding the white barley
according to the plan of fair-ankled Demeter, but later
the fields would be plumed with long ears of grain,
as the spring waxed, and the rich furrows on the ground
would teem with ears to be bound into sheaves by withies.
There she first landed from the unharvested ether.
Joyfully they beheld each other and rejoiced in their hearts;
and Rhea of the shining headband addressed her thus:
"Come, child! Far-seeing, loud-thundering Zeus invites you
to come among the races of the gods and promises to give you
whatever honors you wish among the immortal gods.
With a nod of his head he promised you that, as the year revolves,
your daughter could spend one portion of it in the misty darkness
and the other two with you and the other immortals.
With a nod of his head he said it would thus be brought to pass.
But obey me, my child! Come and do not nurse
unrelenting anger against Kronion, lord of dark clouds;
Soon make the life-giving seed grow for men."
Thus she spoke and fair-wreathed Demeter did not disobey,
but swiftly made the seed sprout out of the fertile fields.
The whole broad earth teemed with leaves and flowers;
and she went to the kings who administer the laws,
Triptolemos and Diokles, smiter of horses, and mighty Eumolpos
and Keleos, leader of the people, and showed them the
celebration of holy rites, and explained to all,

to Triptolemos, to Polyxeinos and also to Diokles,
the awful mysteries not to be transgressed, violated
or divulged, because the tongue is restrained by reverence for
the gods.
Whoever on this earth has seen these is blessed,
but he who has no part in the holy rites has
another lot as he wastes away in dank darkness.
After the splendid Demeter had counseled the kings in everything,
she and her daughter went to Olympos for the company of the
other gods.
There they dwell beside Zeus who delights in thunder,
commanding awe and reverence; thrice blessed is he
of men on this earth whom they gladly love.
Soon to his great house they send as guest
Ploutos, who brings wealth to mortal men.
But come now, you who dwell in the fragrant town of Eleusis,
sea-girt Paros and rocky Antron,
mighty mistress Deo, bringer of seasons and splendid gifts,
both you and your daughter, beauteous Persephone,
for my song kindly grant me possessions pleasing the heart,
and I shall remember you and another song, too.

## HOMER (8TH CENT. BCE)

As Chinese literature begins with poetry, so does Greek literature, and at approximately the same time. But whereas the Chinese *Book of Songs* (*Shi jing,* 1000–600 BCE) consists of many brief lyrics, the Homeric *Iliad* and *Odyssey* (c. 750 BCE) are long, continuous, and remarkably unified narratives. As with Vālmīki's ancient Indian epic, the *Rāmāyana* (c. 500 BCE), central to the action of the *Iliad* is the abduction of a ruler's wife—in the Greek case, the abduction of Helen, the wife of Menelaus, king of Sparta, by Paris, a prince of Troy. And as the king in the *Rāmāyana* believes that he must test his wife's purity after he wins her back, so Odysseus tests Penelope—and is tested by her in return—in Homer's *Odyssey.*

We are not sure who Homer was or precisely when he lived and composed the great Greek epics, although many scholars seem reasonably content with assigning the *Iliad* and *Odyssey* to the eighth century BCE. Indeed, the name *Homeros* may simply mean "he who does not see," a reference to the wisdom of the poet whose physical blindness is a symbol of superior spiritual insight. Though both epics are attributed to Homer, the *Odyssey* is often assumed to be the later work, but this cannot be established with certainty.

While we may not know who Homer was, we do have a reasonably good idea of why he composed. The poems were sung for a Hellenic society that was once firmly based on the Greek mainland but later dispersed with its active center on the coast of Asia Minor. The events narrated in the poems are a reflection of Achaean society with its center of power in Mycenae. The *Iliad* and *Odyssey* are attempts by a poet or poets of the Hellenic society of the eighth or perhaps late seventh century BCE both to celebrate the glorious history of the Mycenaean Age (c. 1600–1200 BCE) and to analyze why Mycenaean civilization collapsed. The poems thus have a twofold purpose of praise and critique.

In the *Iliad* Homer tells the story of the wrath of Achilles, a key episode within the ranks of the Greek troops toward the end of the ten-year Trojan War that almost resulted in the destruction of the Greeks. The *Odyssey* tells the story of the return of Odysseus from Troy after the war, a journey that took another ten years.

Homer attributes the collapse of Mycenaean civilization in part to the behavior of heroes, such as Achilles and Odysseus, who at crucial moments are misguided by their passions. In the "Embassy to Achilles" (Book 9 of the *Iliad*), Phoenix, Achilles' tutor, relates that it was his goal to train his pupil "to be a speaker of words and a doer of deeds" (1. 443). The ideal of a hero who is accomplished as both a speaker of words and a doer of deeds parallels the ancient Chinese notion of the hero who balances cultural virtue (*wen*) and martial virtue (*wu*). In the *Iliad,* Achilles is a great but flawed hero whose martial valor is unparalleled, but who achieves a balance between his accomplishments as a speaker of words and a doer of deeds only at the end of the poem, after great suffering for which (he realizes) he is largely responsible. The grief that Achilles feels upon the death of his friend Patroclus, and which brings him back from dream to reality, has a remarkable parallel in Gilgamesh's grief for Enkidu in the *Epic of Gilgamesh.*

In the *Odyssey,* even the more naturally prudent Odysseus must learn to master the passions of revenge and gloating that he unleashes in his taunting of the Cyclops in Book 9, which provoke the wrath of Poseidon. In the first half of the *Odyssey,* Odysseus is himself tested; in the second half, he largely tests others. We have included the first book of the *Odyssey,* where we see the destruction visited upon the household of Odysseus by Penelope's suitors in the wake of her husband's twenty-year absence. We then move to Book 5, where we first encounter Odysseus, who had been Kalypso's lover for seven years, now longing for home. In Book 9, Odysseus narrates to the Phaeacians the incident—the hero's blinding of Poseidon's one-eyed son, Polyphemos the Cyclops—that earned him the wrath of Poseidon, who has been preventing the hero from returning home. From Book 12 we have selected Odysseus' narration of the perilously captivating Siren song; from Book 21, the hero's stringing of the bow that earns him the right to marry Penelope. We have included all of Book 23, in which Penelope shows that she is fully Odysseus' intellectual equal; and from Book 24 we have chosen the scene in which Odysseus, for no apparent reason other than a compulsive sense of curiosity, decides to test his grieving father before revealing his identity. Those wishing to read the famous passage about Odysseus' descent to the underworld in Book 9 of the *Odyssey* should consult the first of Ezra Pound's *Cantos,* which we have included in the modern section of this anthology. In this *Canto,* Pound is translating the Greek via a Renaissance Latin translation.

Since the appearance of the work of Milman Parry in 1928, most scholars have been persuaded that Homer composed in an "oral-formulaic" style. That is, Homer was not a "pen poet" but composed poems in blocks of traditional phrases or formulae that he could repeat and improvise upon. Though the poems have come down to us in written form, their style tells us they were perhaps not really composed in writing to be read in a book, but rather orally, for live presentation. Oral style accounts for the many of the poem's features, including frequently repeated phrases and passages. The poems are composed in the long dactylic hexameter line, which has the sweep and power that is appropriate to heroic epic.

# Homer in English Verse

Most of the texts in this anthology are in translation. Robert Frost once called poetry "what gets lost in translation." Translation is an art of compromise. It is impossible, particularly in translating poetry, to bring across every notable artistic effect of the original, but good translators try to be true to the spirit of the authors they are translating. This usually means abandoning a word-for-word rendition, which would sound awkward. While avoiding a pedantic literalness, however, a translator will probably not want to veer in the opposite direction of complete freedom from the original.

Let us look at the opening of the *Iliad* in five different published translations: two famous older versions (George Chapman's Renaissance translation, and Alexander Pope's eighteenth-century version), and three recent attempts by Richmond Lattimore, Robert Fitzgerald, and Robert Fagles. First let us hear how the lines sound in the original Greek—written first in the Greek alphabet, followed by a transliteration into the Roman alphabet:

Μῆνιν ἄειδε, θεά, Πηληϊάδεω Ἀχιλῆος
οὐλομένην, ἣ μυρί' Ἀχαιοῖς ἄλγε' ἔθηκε,
πολλὰς δ' ἰφθίμους ψυχὰς Ἄϊδι προΐαψεν
ἡρώων, αὐτοὺς δὲ ἑλώρια τεῦχε κύνεσσιν
οἰωνοῖσι τε πᾶσι, Διὸς δ' ἐτελείετο βουλή,
ἐξ οὗ δὴ τὰ πρῶτα διαστήτην ἐρίσαντε
Ἀτρεΐδης τε ἄναξ ἀνδρῶν καὶ δῖος Ἀχιλλεύς.

Mēnin aeīde, Theā, Pēleīadēo Achilēos
oūlomenēn, hē mūri' Achaīoīs ālge' ethēke,
pōllās d'īphthīmoūs psūchās Aïdī proiāpsen
hērōōn, aūtoūs de helōria teūche kunēssīn
oīōnoīsi te pāsi, Diōs d'eteleīeto boūlē,
ēx hoū dē tā prōta diāstēten erisānte
Ātreidēs te anāx āndrōn kaī dīos Achīlleūs.

A fairly literal translation sounds like this:

> The wrath of Achilles, son of Peleus—make this your song, Goddess—
> that devastating wrath that brought so much grief to the Achaeans
> and hurled to Hades many mighty souls
> of heroes, and turned their bodies into prey for dogs
> and all kinds of birds, and the decree of Zeus was being brought to its fulfillment;
> begin the song, then, Goddess, from that moment when the quarrel began
> between Atrides, king of men, and brilliant Achilles.

Homer composes in the dactylic hexameter line. There are six ("*hex*" in Greek) feet (hence "hexameter"), which makes it the longest traditional line in Greek poetry and therefore appropriate to the heroic epics that the lines constitute. As in all classical Greek and Latin verse, the lines do not rhyme. The rhythm of the poetic line is created by a pattern of "long" and "short" syllables. These are roughly equivalent to long and short vowels in English, though in Greek a long syllable simply takes longer to pronounce. The basic rhythmic unit is the dactyl, which is a long syllable followed by two short ones (– uu). For a dactylic foot one may substitute a spondee (– –), which consists of two long syllables. In the transliterated lines here we have marked the long syllables with macrons. Each line has one fairly clear break or pause, technically called a "caesura." The caesura usually appears somewhere in the middle of the line, but a great poet like Homer will vary its position so as to avoid a sense of tedious and mechanical regularity.

Now we can look at our five English versions. Poetic rhythm in English is not created by patterns of long and short syllables, but by patterns of stressed (or accented) syllables and unstressed (unaccented) ones. Stressed syllables are usually spoken a bit louder or at a higher pitch than unstressed ones. The basic unit of traditional English meter is the iamb, a stressed syllable followed by an unstressed one, forming an alternating pattern of stresses.

Here, first, is the Renaissance English poet and dramatist, George Chapman (1611):

> Achilles banefull wrath resound, O Goddesse, that imposd
> Infinite sorrowes on the Greekes; and many brave soules losd
> From breasts Heroique: sent them farre, to that invisible cave
> That no light comforts: and their lims, to dogs and vultures gave.
> To all which, Jove's will gave effect; from whom, first strife begunne,
> Betwixt Atrides, king of men; and Thetis' godlike Sonne.

This is a powerful rendition. For Homer's noble dactylic hexameter, Chapman uses the "fourteener," a long, epic-sounding iambic line that consists of fourteen syllables. The lines rhyme, which Homer's do not, but since Chapman's line is so long, the reader almost forgets the ending of the previous line, so the potentially jingling—and hence unheroic to the classical ear—effect of rhyme is muted. Since the line is so long, however, it may seem ponderous in English, especially in a poem of more than twenty thousand lines, such as the *Iliad*. Chapman's translation can be rather free, for example, when he translates the Greek word "Hades" (the underworld) as "that invisible cave/ That no light comforts." Even here, though, Chapman is elaborating on his understanding of the Greek word *Aides,* which literally means "without sight" or "blind."

Here is Pope (1715):

> Achilles' Wrath, to Greece the direful spring
> Of woes unnumber'd, heav'nly Goddess, sing!
> That Wrath which hurl'd to Pluto's gloomy reign
> The Souls of mighty Chiefs untimely slain;
> Whose limbs unbury'd on the naked shore
> Devouring dogs and hungry vultures tore.
> Since Great Achilles and Atrides strove,
> Such was the sov'reign doom, and such the will of Jove!

For the unfailing regularity of Homer's dactylic hexameter Pope substitutes the iambic pentameter used by Milton. There are five ("*pente*" in Greek) iambs in an iambic pentameter line. The rhyming couplets reassure us that this is not ordinary conversation. Since Pope firmly establishes his metrical norm, he is able to depart from it in subtle but telling ways as the occasion demands. Line 8 ("Such was the sov'reign doom, and such the will of Jove"), for example, is a stately Alexandrine (a twelve-syllable, rather than ten-syllable iambic line) that befits its Jovian contents. At times the necessity of rhyme causes Pope to distort his sense somewhat. Readers might, for example, have been spared the awkward metaphor of the "direful spring/ Of woes unnumber'd" in the first line. It is not present in the Greek, and we can suppose that Pope introduced it because he needed a rhyme with "sing" in the following line. But one can justify this metaphor—along with all the rest of Pope's stylistic choices in these lines—in terms of what Pope, following Aristotle, Milton, and the famous eighteenth-century literary critic and arbiter of taste; Joseph Addison, thought of as the traditional means of elevating poetic style.

"The Language of an heroic Poem," Addison wrote in *Spectator* No. 285, "should be both Perspicuous and Sublime." Sublimity is achieved by following Aristotle's advice in *Poetics* XXII, where the poet is told (1) to use bold metaphors; (2) to use "Idioms of other Tongues," including "placing the Adjective after the Substantive, with several other foreign Modes of Speech"; and (3) to lengthen phrases "by the Addition of Words, which may either be inserted or omitted." This is precisely what Pope does in these opening lines: (1) "the direful spring/ Of woes unnumber'd" is a bold metaphor; (2) the phrase "woes unnumber'd" is a Latinate idiom in which the adjective is placed after the noun, and "to Greece the direful spring" is a transposition of words; (3) "heav'nly Goddess," "Pluto's gloomy reign," and "mighty Chiefs" are all examples of "the length'ning of a Phrase by the Addition of Words, which may either be inserted or omitted." Those who object to Pope's translation because it contains such phrases should realize that they are objecting to the traditional means of elevating poetic style as stated by Aristotle in the *Poetics,* as achieved by Milton in *Paradise Lost,* and as restated by Addison in the pages of the *Spectator* in which he tries to account for the power of Milton's style.

To a modern ear, Pope's choice of the couplet might seem to cramp Homer's elevation. This was not necessarily the case in eighteenth-century England, however. To an eighteenth-century ear, it was often difficult to distinguish blank verse (unrhymed iambic pentameter) from prose, and therefore from the prosaic. As the great literary critic Samuel Johnson remarked, "blank verse is verse only to the eye." Through his use of rhyme, Pope could exalt his poetry above the level of ordinary conversation. For what the writer of a sublime epic such as the *Iliad* wants to represent is nature, but nature—to quote Neander in John Dryden's *Essay of Dramatic Poesy* (1668)—"wrought up to an higher pitch." "Heroic rhyme," according to Neander, is nearest this kind of nature, "as being the noblest kind of modern verse." Once this air of distinction is conveyed, moreover, Pope believed that the poet is no longer forced to depart so violently from idiomatic usage, as he believed Milton was forced to do in *Paradise Lost* in order to distinguish his blank verse from prose. We should also not forget that Pope's genius as a poet cannot be separated from his genius as a master of the rhyming couplet. Translators of poetry should also be poets, and poets have their particular strengths.

Here is Richmond Lattimore (1951):

> Sing, goddess, the anger of Peleus' son Achilleus
> and its devastation, which put pains thousandfold upon the Achaians,
> hurled in their multitudes to the house of Hades strong souls
> of heroes, but gave their bodies to be the delicate feasting
> of dogs, of all birds, and the will of Zeus was accomplished
> since that time when first there stood in division of conflict
> Atreus' son the lord of men and brilliant Achilleus.

Lattimore gives us a fairly clear sense of what is going on here, which is one of the consistent virtues of his translation. The principle of Lattimore's line appears to be this: the number of syllables may vary, but there are roughly six beats to a line, and each beat is roughly the equivalent of the number of long syllables—which to the ear of an English speaker are often heard as stresses—in Homer's line. Lattimore's translation, however, for all its great value as a sensitive crib that provides us with a remarkably literal and yet mostly comprehensible line-by-line rendition of the Homeric original, sometimes sounds lumbering and heavy where the Greek is lighter on its feet. When we read Lattimore, we feel we are reading a translation of a poem from a rather remote and archaic language. It is not transparent. We do not feel we are reading an English poem, as we do with Chapman and Pope. The phrase "which put pains thousandfold upon the Achaians," for example, is awkward English.

Now let us look at Robert Fitzgerald's version of these lines (1975):

> Anger be now your song, immortal one,
> Akhilleus' anger, doomed and ruinous,
> that caused the Akhaians loss on bitter loss,
> and crowded brave souls into the undergloom,
> leaving so many dead men—carrion
> for dogs and birds; and the will of Zeus was done.

Begin it when the two men first contending
broke with one another—
the Lord Marshal
Agamémnon, Atreus' son, and Prince Akhilleus.

This is distinguished English poetry. Fitzgerald writes a supple blank verse. It is recognizable as the same iambic pentameter that Milton thought a fit instrument by which to approximate Homer's and Virgil's ancient dactylic hexameter in *Paradise Lost.* The first five lines are perfectly iambic if we allow for elisions—the blending of vowels—in lines three and four ("th'Akhaians" and "th'undergloom"). Other lines are slightly less regular: for example, there is a tri-syllabic foot after the pause in line six ("for dogs and birds; and the will of Zeus was done"). By eighteenth-century standards of English prosody—in fact, by any standards other than contemporary ones—Fitzgerald's pentameter is fairly loose, but it is unmistakeably there. We can understand what is going on, and we know it is not prose.

Finally, here is Robert Fagles's fairly recent version (1990):

Rage—Goddess, sing the rage of Peleus' son Achilles,
murderous, doomed, that cost the Achaeans countless losses,
hurling down to the House of Death so many sturdy souls,
great fighters' souls, but made their bodies carrion,
feasts for the dogs and birds,
and the will of Zeus was moving toward its end.
Begin, Muse, when the two first broke and clashed,
Agamemnon lord of men and brilliant Achilles.

Robert Fagles writes a clear, clean line. It feels heroic, yet it possesses colloquial ease. It is therefore easier to follow the sense in Fagles's translation than in Chapman's or Pope's, and his version does not create a distanced sense that we are reading a translation, as does Lattimore's. Translation, as we said before, is an art of compromise. One makes sacrifices to achieve certain ends. What sacrifices does Fagles make? Homer's Greek line has a clear, formal structure—the dactylic hexameter. Like Bach in his fugues, the Greek poet can perform a seemingly endless number of variations within a strict, ever-recurring pattern. What is the principle of Fagles's line? It has a basically five-beat structure (in lines three, four, six, seven, and eight), though some of the lines have as many as seven beats (the first two lines) or as few as three (line five). Its metrical structure, therefore, is looser than that of Homer, Chapman (who writes in fourteeners), Pope (who writes in rhymed pentameter couplets), and Fitzgerald (who writes in blank verse).

All three modern translations are excellent in different ways. They are struggling to live up to the brilliant original they admire. Readers will have their favorites, but good readers will want to understand what it is that makes these translations different.

## The Odyssey

*Translated by Robert Fagles*

### Book 1: Athena Inspires the Prince

Sing to me of the man, Muse, the man of twists and turns
driven time and again off course, once he had plundered
the hallowed heights of Troy.
Many cities of men he saw and learned their minds,
many pains he suffered, heartsick on the open sea,
fighting to save his life and bring his comrades home.
But he could not save them from disaster, hard as he strove—
the recklessness of their own ways destroyed them all,
the blind fools, they devoured the cattle of the Sun
and the Sungod blotted out the day of their return.
Launch out on his story, Muse, daughter of Zeus,
start from where you will—sing for our time too.
By now,
all the survivors, all who avoided headlong death
were safe at home, escaped the wars and waves.
But one man alone . . .
his heart set on his wife and his return—Calypso,
the bewitching nymph, the lustrous goddess, held him back,
deep in her arching caverns, craving him for a husband.
But then, when the wheeling seasons brought the year around,
that year spun out by the gods when he should reach his home,
Ithaca—though not even there would he be free of trials,
even among his loved ones—then every god took pity,
all except Poseidon. He raged on, seething against
the great Odysseus till he reached his native land.
But now
Poseidon had gone to visit the Ethiopians worlds away,
Ethiopians off at the farthest limits of mankind,
a people split in two, one part where the Sungod sets
and part where the Sungod rises. There Poseidon went
to receive an offering, bulls and rams by the hundred—
far away at the feast the Sea-lord sat and took his pleasure.
But the other gods, at home in Olympian Zeus's halls,
met for full assembly there, and among them now
the father of men and gods was first to speak,
sorely troubled, remembering handsome Aegisthus,
the man Agamemnon's son, renowned Orestes, killed.
Recalling Aegisthus, Zeus harangued the immortal powers:
"Ah how shameless—the way these mortals blame the gods.
From us alone, they say, come all their miseries, yes,
but they themselves, with their own reckless ways,

compound their pains beyond their proper share.
Look at Aegisthus now . . .
above and beyond *his* share he stole Atrides' wife,
he murdered the warlord coming home from Troy
though he knew it meant his own total ruin.
Far in advance we told him so ourselves,
dispatching the guide, the giant-killer Hermes.
'Don't murder the man,' he said, 'don't court his wife.
Beware, revenge will come from Orestes, Agamemnon's son,
that day he comes of age and longs for his native land.'
So Hermes warned, with all the good will in the world,
but would Aegisthus' hardened heart give way?
Now he pays the price—all at a single stroke."

And sparkling-eyed Athena drove the matter home:
"Father, son of Cronus, our high and mighty king,
surely he goes down to a death he earned in full!
Let them all die so, all who do such things.
But my heart breaks for Odysseus,
that seasoned veteran cursed by fate so long—
far from his loved ones still, he suffers torments
off on a wave-washed island rising at the center of the seas.
A dark wooded island, and there a goddess makes her home,
a daughter of Atlas, wicked Titan who sounds the deep
in all its depths, whose shoulders lift on high
the colossal pillars thrusting earth and sky apart.
Atlas' daughter it is who holds Odysseus captive,
luckless man—despite his tears, forever trying
to spellbind his heart with suave, seductive words
and wipe all thought of Ithaca from his mind.
But he, straining for no more than a glimpse
of hearth-smoke drifting up from his own land,
Odysseus longs to die . . .
Olympian Zeus,
have you no care for *him* in your lofty heart?
Did he never win your favor with sacrifices
burned beside the ships on the broad plain of Troy?
Why, Zeus, why so dead set against Odysseus?"

"My child," Zeus who marshals the thunderheads replied,
"what nonsense you let slip through your teeth. Now,
how on earth could I forget Odysseus? Great Odysseus
who excels all men in wisdom, excels in offerings too
he gives the immortal gods who rule the vaulting skies?
No, it's the Earth-Shaker, Poseidon, unappeased,
forever fuming against him for the Cyclops

whose giant eye he blinded: godlike Polyphemus,
towering over all the Cyclops' clans in power.
The nymph Thoosa bore him, daughter of Phorcys,
lord of the barren salt sea—she met Poseidon
once in his vaulted caves and they made love.
And now for his blinded son the earthquake god—
though he won't quite kill Odysseus—
drives him far off course from native land.
But come, all of us here put heads together now,
work out his journey home so Odysseus can return.
Lord Poseidon, I trust, will let his anger go.
How can he stand his ground against the will
of all the gods at once—one god alone?"

Athena, her eyes flashing bright, exulted,
"Father, son of Cronus, our high and mighty king!
If now it really pleases the blissful gods
that wise Odysseus shall return—home at last—
let us dispatch the guide and giant-killer Hermes
down to Ogygia Island, down to announce at once
to the nymph with lovely braids our fixed decree:
Odysseus journeys home—the exile must return!
While I myself go down to Ithaca, rouse his son
to a braver pitch, inspire his heart with courage
to summon the flowing-haired Achaeans to full assembly,
speak his mind to all those suitors, slaughtering on and on
his droves of sheep and shambling longhorn cattle.
Next I will send him off to Sparta and sandy Pylos,
there to learn of his dear father's journey home.
Perhaps he will hear some news and make his name
throughout the mortal world."
So Athena vowed
and under her feet she fastened the supple sandals,
ever-glowing gold, that wing her over the waves
and boundless earth with the rush of gusting winds.
She seized the rugged spear tipped with a bronze point—
weighted, heavy, the massive shaft she wields to break the lines
of heroes the mighty Father's daughter storms against.
And down she swept from Olympus' craggy peaks
and lit on Ithaca, standing tall at Odysseus' gates,
the threshold of his court. Gripping her bronze spear,
she looked for all the world like a stranger now,
like Mentes, lord of the Taphians.
There she found the swaggering suitors, just then
amusing themselves with rolling dice before the doors,

lounging on hides of oxen they had killed themselves.
While heralds and brisk attendants bustled round them,
some at the mixing-bowls, mulling wine and water,
others wiping the tables down with sopping sponges,
setting them out in place, still other servants
jointed and carved the great sides of meat.

First by far to see her was Prince Telemachus,
sitting among the suitors, heart obsessed with grief.
He could almost see his magnificent father, here . . .
in the mind's eye—if only *he* might drop from the clouds
and drive these suitors all in a rout throughout the halls
and regain his pride of place and rule his own domains!
Daydreaming so as he sat among the suitors,
he glimpsed Athena now
and straight to the porch he went, mortified
that a guest might still be standing at the doors.
Pausing beside her there, he clasped her right hand
and relieving her at once of her long bronze spear,
met her with winged words: "Greetings, stranger!
Here in our house you'll find a royal welcome.
Have supper first, then tell us what you need."

He led the way and Pallas Athena followed.
Once in the high-roofed hall, he took her lance
and fixed it firm in a burnished rack against
a sturdy pillar, there where row on row of spears,
embattled Odysseus' spears, stood stacked and waiting.
Then he escorted her to a high, elaborate chair of honor,
over it draped a cloth, and here he placed his guest
with a stool to rest her feet. But for himself
he drew up a low reclining chair beside her,
richly painted, clear of the press of suitors,
concerned his guest, offended by their uproar,
might shrink from food in the midst of such a mob.
He hoped, what's more, to ask him about his long-lost father.
A maid brought water soon in a graceful golden pitcher
and over a silver basin tipped it out
so they might rinse their hands,
then pulled a gleaming table to their side.
A staid housekeeper brought on bread to serve them,
appetizers aplenty too, lavish with her bounty.
A carver lifted platters of meat toward them,
meats of every sort, and set beside them golden cups
and time and again a page came round and poured them wine.

But now the suitors trooped in with all their swagger
and took their seats on low and high-backed chairs.
Heralds poured water over their hands for rinsing,
serving maids brought bread heaped high in trays
and the young men brimmed the mixing-bowls with wine.
They reached out for the good things that lay at hand,
and when they'd put aside desire for food and drink
the suitors set their minds on other pleasures,
song and dancing, all that crowns a feast.
A herald placed an ornate lyre in Phemius' hands,
the bard who always performed among them there;
they forced the man to sing.
A rippling prelude—
and no sooner had he struck up his rousing song
than Telemachus, head close to Athena's sparkling eyes,
spoke low to his guest so no one else could hear:
"Dear stranger, would you be shocked by what I say?
Look at them over there. Not a care in the world,
just lyres and tunes! It's easy for them, all right,
they feed on another's goods and go scot-free—
a man whose white bones lie strewn in the rain somewhere,
rotting away on land or rolling down the ocean's salty swells.
But that man—if they caught sight of him home in Ithaca,
by god, they'd all pray to be faster on their feet
than richer in bars of gold and heavy robes.
But now, no use, he's died a wretched death.
No comfort's left for us . . . not even if
someone, somewhere, says he's coming home.
The day of his return will never dawn.
Enough.
Tell me about yourself now, clearly, point by point.
Who are you? where are you from? your city? your parents?
What sort of vessel brought you? Why did the sailors
land you here in Ithaca? Who did they say they are?
I hardly think you came this way on foot!
And tell me this for a fact—I need to know—
is this your first time here? Or are you a friend of father's,
a guest from the old days? Once, crowds of other men
would come to our house on visits—visitor that he was,
when he walked among the living."
Her eyes glinting,
goddess Athena answered, "My whole story, of course,
I'll tell it point by point. Wise old Anchialus
was my father. My own name is Mentes,
lord of the Taphian men who love their oars.

And here I've come, just now, with ship and crew,
sailing the wine-dark sea to foreign ports of call,
to Temese, out for bronze—our cargo gleaming iron.
Our ship lies moored off farmlands far from town,
riding in Rithron Cove, beneath Mount Nion's woods.
As for the ties between your father and myself,
we've been friends forever, I'm proud to say,
and he would bear me out
if you went and questioned old lord Laertes.
He, I gather, no longer ventures into town
but lives a life of hardship, all to himself,
off on his farmstead with an aged serving-woman
who tends him well, who gives him food and drink
when weariness has taken hold of his withered limbs
from hauling himself along his vineyard's steep slopes.
And now I've come—and why? I heard that he was back . . .
your father, that is. But no, the gods thwart his passage.
Yet I tell you great Odysseus is not dead. He's still alive,
somewhere in this wide world, held captive, out at sea
on a wave-washed island, and hard men, savages,
somehow hold him back against his will.
Wait,
I'll make you a prophecy, one the immortal gods
have planted in my mind—it will come true, I think,
though I am hardly a seer or know the flights of birds.
He won't be gone long from the native land he loves,
not even if iron shackles bind your father down.
He's plotting a way to journey home at last;
he's never at a loss.
But come, please,
tell me about yourself now, point by point.
You're truly Odysseus' son? You've sprung up so!
Uncanny resemblance . . . the head, and the fine eyes—
I see him now. How often we used to meet in the old days
before he embarked for Troy, where other Argive captains,
all the best men, sailed in the long curved ships.
From then to this very day
I've not set eyes on Odysseus or he on me."

And young Telemachus cautiously replied,
"I'll try, my friend, to give you a frank answer.
Mother has always told me I'm his son, it's true,
but I am not so certain. Who, on his own,
has ever really known who gave him life?
Would to god I'd been the son of a happy man

whom old age overtook in the midst of his possessions!
Now, think of the most unlucky mortal ever born—
since you ask me, yes, they say I am his son."

"Still," the clear-eyed goddess reassured him,
"trust me, the gods have not marked out your house
for such an unsung future,
not if Penelope has borne a son like you.
But tell me about all this and spare me nothing.
What's this banqueting, this crowd carousing here?
And what part do you play yourself? Some wedding-feast,
some festival? Hardly a potluck supper, I would say.
How obscenely they lounge and swagger here, look,
gorging in your house. Why, any man of sense
who chanced among them would be outraged,
seeing such behavior."
Ready Telemachus
took her up at once: "Well, my friend,
seeing you want to probe and press the question,
once this house was rich, no doubt, beyond reproach
when the man you mentioned still lived here, at home.
Now the gods have reversed our fortunes with a vengeance—
wiped that man from the earth like no one else before.
I would never have grieved so much about his death
if he'd gone down with comrades off in Troy
or died in the arms of loved ones,
once he had wound down the long coil of war.
Then all united Achaea would have raised his tomb
and he'd have won his son great fame for years to come.
But now the whirlwinds have ripped him away, no fame for him!
He's lost and gone now—out of sight, out of mind—and I . . .
he's left me tears and grief. Nor do I rack my heart
and grieve for him alone. No longer. Now the gods
have invented other miseries to plague me.
Listen.
All the nobles who rule the islands round about,
Dulichion, and Same, and wooded Zacynthus too,
and all who lord it in rocky Ithaca as well—
down to the last man they court my mother,
they lay waste my house! And mother . . .
she neither rejects a marriage she despises
nor can she bear to bring the courting to an end—
while they continue to bleed my household white.
Soon—you wait—they'll grind *me* down as well."
"Shameful!"—
brimming with indignation, Pallas Athena broke out.

"Oh how much you need Odysseus, gone so long—
how *he'd* lay hands on all these brazen suitors!
If only he would appear, now,
at his house's outer gates and take his stand,
armed with his helmet, shield and pair of spears,
as strong as the man I glimpsed that first time
in our own house, drinking wine and reveling there . . .
just come in from Ephyra, visiting Ilus, Mermerus' son.
Odysseus sailed that way, you see, in his swift trim ship,
hunting deadly poison to smear on his arrows' bronze heads.
Ilus refused—he feared the wrath of the everlasting gods—
but father, so fond of him, gave him all he wanted.
If only *that* Odysseus sported with these suitors,
a blood wedding, a quick death would take the lot!
True, but all lies in the lap of the great gods,
whether or not he'll come and pay them back,
here, in his own house.
                    But you, I urge you,
think how to drive these suitors from your halls.
Come now, listen closely. Take my words to heart.
At daybreak summon the island's lords to full assembly,
give your orders to all and call the gods to witness:
tell the suitors to scatter, each to his own place.
As for your mother, if the spirit moves her to marry,
let her go back to her father's house, a man of power.
Her kin will arrange the wedding, provide the gifts,
the array that goes with a daughter dearly loved.
                    For you,
I have some good advice, if only you will accept it.
Fit out a ship with twenty oars, the best in sight,
sail in quest of news of your long-lost father.
Someone may tell you something
or you may catch a rumor straight from Zeus,
rumor that carries news to men like nothing else.
First go down to Pylos, question old King Nestor,
then cross over to Sparta, to red-haired Menelaus,
of all the bronze-armored Achaeans the last man back.
Now, if you hear your father's alive and heading home,
hard-pressed as you are, brave out one more year.
If you hear he's dead, no longer among the living,
then back you come to the native land you love,
raise his grave-mound, build his honors high
with the full funeral rites that he deserves—
and give your mother to another husband.
                    Then,
once you've sealed those matters, seen them through,

think hard, reach down deep in your heart and soul
for a way to kill these suitors in your house,
by stealth or in open combat.
You must not cling to your boyhood any longer—
it's time you were a man. Haven't you heard
what glory Prince Orestes won throughout the world
when he killed that cunning, murderous Aegisthus,
who'd killed his famous father?
And you, my friend—
how tall and handsome I see you now—be brave, you too,
so men to come will sing your praises down the years.
But now I must go back to my swift trim ship
and all my shipmates, chafing there, I'm sure,
waiting for my return. It all rests with you.
Take my words to heart."
"Oh stranger,"
heedful Telemachus replied, "indeed I will.
You've counseled me with so much kindness now,
like a father to a son. I won't forget a word.
But come, stay longer, keen as you are to sail,
so you can bathe and rest and lift your spirits,
then go back to your ship, delighted with a gift,
a prize of honor, something rare and fine
as a keepsake from myself. The kind of gift
a host will give a stranger, friend to friend."

Her eyes glinting, Pallas declined in haste:
"Not now. Don't hold me here. I long to be on my way.
As for the gift—whatever you'd give in kindness—
save it for my return so I can take it home.
Choose something rare and fine, and a good reward
that gift is going to bring you."
With that promise,
off and away Athena the bright-eyed goddess flew
like a bird in soaring flight
but left his spirit filled with nerve and courage,
charged with his father's memory more than ever now.
He felt his senses quicken, overwhelmed with wonder—
this was a god, he knew it well and made at once
for the suitors, a man like a god himself.
Amidst them still
the famous bard sang on, and they sat in silence, listening
as he performed The Achaeans' Journey Home from Troy:
all the blows Athena doomed them to endure.
And now,
from high above in her room and deep in thought,

she caught his inspired strains . . .
Icarius' daughter Penelope, wary and reserved,
and down the steep stair from her chamber she descended,
not alone: two of her women followed close behind.
That radiant woman, once she reached her suitors,
drawing her glistening veil across her cheeks,
paused now where a column propped the sturdy roof,
with one of her loyal handmaids stationed either side.
Suddenly, dissolving in tears and bursting through
the bard's inspired voice, she cried out, "Phemius!
So many other songs you know to hold us spellbound,
works of the gods and men that singers celebrate.
Sing one of those as you sit beside them here
and they drink their wine in silence.
But break off this song—
the unendurable song that always rends the heart inside me . . .
the unforgettable grief, it wounds me most of all!
How I long for my husband—alive in memory, always,
that great man whose fame resounds through Hellas
right to the depths of Argos!"
"Why, mother,"
poised Telemachus put in sharply, "why deny
our devoted bard the chance to entertain us
any way the spirit stirs him on?
Bards are not to blame—
Zeus is to blame. He deals to each and every
laborer on this earth whatever doom he pleases.
Why fault the bard if he sings the Argives' harsh fate?
It's always the latest song, the one that echoes last
in the listeners' ears, that people praise the most.
Courage, mother. Harden your heart, and listen.
Odysseus was scarcely the only one, you know,
whose journey home was blotted out at Troy.
Others, so many others, died there too.
So, mother,
go back to your quarters. Tend to your own tasks,
the distaff and the loom, and keep the women
working hard as well. As for giving orders,
men will see to that, but I most of all:
I hold the reins of power in this house."
Astonished,
she withdrew to her own room. She took to heart
the clear good sense in what her son had said.
Climbing up to the lofty chamber with her women,
she fell to weeping for Odysseus, her beloved husband,
till watchful Athena sealed her eyes with welcome sleep.

But the suitors broke into uproar through the shadowed halls,
all of them lifting prayers to lie beside her, share her bed,
until discreet Telemachus took command: "You suitors
who plague my mother, you, you insolent, overweening . . .
for this evening let us dine and take our pleasure,
no more shouting now. What a fine thing it is
to listen to such a bard as we have here—
the man sings like a god.
But at first light
we all march forth to assembly, take our seats
so I can give my orders and say to you straight out:
You must leave my palace! See to your feasting elsewhere,
devour your own possessions, house to house by turns.
But if you decide the fare is better, richer here,
destroying one man's goods and going scot-free,
all right then, carve away!
But I'll cry out to the everlasting gods in hopes
that Zeus will pay you back with a vengeance—all of you
destroyed in my house while I go scot-free myself!"

So Telemachus declared. And they all bit their lips,
amazed the prince could speak with so much daring.

Eupithes' son Antinous broke their silence:
"Well, Telemachus, only the gods could teach you
to sound so high and mighty! Such brave talk.
I pray that Zeus will never make *you* king of Ithaca,
though your father's crown is no doubt yours by birth."

But cool-headed Telemachus countered firmly:
"Antinous, even though my words may offend you,
I'd be happy to take the crown if Zeus presents it.
You think that nothing worse could befall a man?
It's really not so bad to be a king. All at once
your palace grows in wealth, your honors grow as well.
But there are hosts of other Achaean princes, look—
young and old, crowds of them on our island here—
and any one of the lot might hold the throne,
now great Odysseus is dead . . .
But I'll be lord of my own house and servants,
all that King Odysseus won for me by force."

And now Eurymachus, Polybus' son, stepped in:
"Surely this must lie in the gods' lap, Telemachus—
which Achaean will lord it over seagirt Ithaca.
Do hold on to your own possessions, rule your house.

God forbid that anyone tear your holdings from your hands
while men still live in Ithaca.
                But about your guest,
dear boy, I have some questions. Where does he come from?
Where's his country, his birth, his father's old estates?
Did he bring some news of your father, his return?
Or did he come on business of his own?
How he leapt to his feet and off he went!
No waiting around for proper introductions.
And no mean man, not by the looks of him, I'd say."

"Eurymachus," Telemachus answered shrewdly,
"clearly my father's journey home is lost forever.
I no longer trust in rumors—rumors from the blue—
nor bother with any prophecy, when mother calls
some wizard into the house to ask him questions.
As for the stranger though,
the man's an old family friend, from Taphos,
wise Anchialus' son. He says his name is Mentes,
lord of the Taphian men who love their oars."
                So he said
but deep in his mind he knew the immortal goddess.
Now the suitors turned to dance and song,
to the lovely beat and sway,
waiting for dusk to come upon them there . . .
and the dark night came upon them, lost in pleasure.
Finally, to bed. Each to his own house.
                Telemachus,
off to his bedroom built in the courtyard—
a commanding, lofty room set well apart—
retired too, his spirit swarming with misgivings.
His devoted nurse attended him, bearing a glowing torch,
Eurycleia the daughter of Ops, Pisenor's son.
Laertes had paid a price for the woman years ago,
still in the bloom of youth. He traded twenty oxen,
honored her on a par with his own loyal wife at home
but fearing the queen's anger, never shared her bed.
She was his grandson's escort now and bore a torch,
for she was the one of all the maids who loved
the prince the most—she'd nursed him as a baby.
He spread the doors of his snug, well-made room,
sat down on the bed and pulled his soft shirt off,
tossed it into the old woman's conscientious hands,
and after folding it neatly, patting it smooth,
she hung it up on a peg beside his corded bed,
then padded from the bedroom,

drawing the door shut with the silver hook,
sliding the doorbolt home with its rawhide strap.
There all night long, wrapped in a sheep's warm fleece,
he weighed in his mind the course Athena charted.

## *Book 5: Odysseus—Nymph and Shipwreck: Odysseus Decides*

As Dawn rose up from bed by her lordly mate Tithonus,
bringing light to immortal gods and mortal men,
the gods sat down in council, circling Zeus
the thunder king whose power rules the world.
Athena began, recalling Odysseus to their thoughts,
the goddess deeply moved by the man's long ordeal,
held captive still in the nymph Calypso's house:
"Father Zeus—you other happy gods who never die—
never let any sceptered king be kind and gentle now,
not with all his heart, or set his mind on justice—
no, let him be cruel and always practice outrage.
Think: not one of the people whom he ruled
remembers Odysseus now, that godlike man,
and kindly as a father to his children.
Now
he's left to pine on an island, racked with grief
in the nymph Calypso's house—she holds him there by force.
He has no way to voyage home to his own native land,
no trim ships in reach, no crew to ply the oars
and send him scudding over the sea's broad back.
And now his dear son . . . they plot to kill the boy
on his way back home. Yes, he has sailed off
for news of his father, to holy Pylos first,
then out to the sunny hills of Lacedaemon."

"My child," Zeus who marshals the thunderheads replied,
"what nonsense you let slip through your teeth. Come now,
wasn't the plan your own? You conceived it yourself:
Odysseus shall return and pay the traitors back.
Telemachus? Sail him home with all your skill—
the power is yours, no doubt—
home to his native country all unharmed
while the suitors limp to port, defeated, baffled men."

With those words, Zeus turned to his own son Hermes.
"You are our messenger, Hermes, sent on all our missions.
Announce to the nymph with lovely braids our fixed decree:
Odysseus journeys home—the exile must return.

But not in the convoy of the gods or mortal men.
No, on a lashed, makeshift raft and wrung with pains,
on the twentieth day he will make his landfall, fertile Scheria,
the land of Phaeacians, close kin to the gods themselves,
who with all their hearts will prize him like a god
and send him off in a ship to his own beloved land,
giving him bronze and hoards of gold and robes—
more plunder than he could ever have won from Troy
if Odysseus had returned intact with his fair share.
So his destiny ordains. He shall see his loved ones,
reach his high-roofed house, his native land at last."

So Zeus decreed and the giant-killing guide obeyed at once.
Quickly under his feet he fastened the supple sandals,
ever-glowing gold, that wing him over the waves
and boundless earth with the rush of gusting winds.
He seized the wand that enchants the eyes of men
whenever Hermes wants, or wakes us up from sleep.
That wand in his grip, the powerful giant-killer,
swooping down from Pieria, down the high clear air,
plunged to the sea and skimmed the waves like a tern
that down the deadly gulfs of the barren salt swells
glides and dives for fish,
dipping its beating wings in bursts of spray—
so Hermes skimmed the crests on endless crests.
But once he gained that island worlds apart,
up from the deep-blue sea he climbed to dry land
and strode on till he reached the spacious cave
where the nymph with lovely braids had made her home,
and he found her there inside . . .
A great fire
blazed on the hearth and the smell of cedar
cleanly split and sweetwood burning bright
wafted a cloud of fragrance down the island.
Deep inside she sang, the goddess Calypso, lifting
her breathtaking voice as she glided back and forth
before her loom, her golden shuttle weaving.
Thick, luxuriant woods grew round the cave,
alders and black poplars, pungent cypress too,
and there birds roosted, folding their long wings,
owls and hawks and the spread-beaked ravens of the sea,
black skimmers who make their living off the waves.
And round the mouth of the cavern trailed a vine
laden with clusters, bursting with ripe grapes.
Four springs in a row, bubbling clear and cold,
running side-by-side, took channels left and right.

Soft meadows spreading round were starred with violets,
lush with beds of parsley. Why, even a deathless god
who came upon that place would gaze in wonder,
heart entranced with pleasure. Hermes the guide,
the mighty giant-killer, stood there, spellbound . . .
But once he'd had his fill of marveling at it all
he briskly entered the deep vaulted cavern.
Calypso, lustrous goddess, knew him at once,
as soon as she saw his features face-to-face.
Immortals are never strangers to each other,
no matter how distant one may make her home.
But as for great Odysseus—
Hermes could not find him within the cave.
Off he sat on a headland, weeping there as always,
wrenching his heart with sobs and groans and anguish,
gazing out over the barren sea through blinding tears.
But Calypso, lustrous goddess, questioned Hermes,
seating him on a glistening, polished chair.
"God of the golden wand, why have you come?
A beloved, honored friend,
but it's been so long, your visits much too rare.
Tell me what's on your mind. I'm eager to do it,
whatever I *can* do . . . whatever can be done."

And the goddess drew a table up beside him,
heaped with ambrosia, mixed him deep-red nectar.
Hermes the guide and giant-killer ate and drank.
Once he had dined and fortified himself with food
he launched right in, replying to her questions:
"As one god to another, you ask me why I've come.
I'll tell you the whole story, mince no words—
your wish is my command.
It was Zeus who made me come, no choice of mine.
Who would willingly roam across a salty waste so vast,
so endless? Think: no city of men in sight, and not a soul
to offer the gods a sacrifice and burn the fattest victims.
But there is no way, you know, for another god to thwart
the will of storming Zeus and make it come to nothing.
Zeus claims you keep beside you a most unlucky man,
most harried of all who fought for Priam's Troy
nine years, sacking the city in the tenth,
and then set sail for home.
But voyaging back they outraged Queen Athena
who loosed the gales and pounding seas against them.
There all the rest of his loyal shipmates died
but the wind drove him on, the current bore him here.

Now Zeus commands you to send him off with all good speed:
it is not his fate to die here, far from his own people.
Destiny still ordains that he shall see his loved ones,
reach his high-roofed house, his native land at last."

But lustrous Calypso shuddered at those words
and burst into a flight of indignation. "Hard-hearted
you are, you gods! You unrivaled lords of jealousy—
scandalized when goddesses sleep with mortals,
openly, even when one has made the man her husband.
So when Dawn with her rose-red fingers took Orion,
you gods in your everlasting ease were horrified
till chaste Artemis throned in gold attacked him,
out on Delos, shot him to death with gentle shafts.
And so when Demeter the graceful one with lovely braids
gave way to her passion and made love with Iasion,
bedding down in a furrow plowed three times—
Zeus got wind of it soon enough, I'd say,
and blasted the man to death with flashing bolts.
So now at last, you gods, you train your spite on *me*
for keeping a mortal man beside me. The man I saved,
riding astride his keel-board, all alone, when Zeus
with one hurl of a white-hot bolt had crushed
his racing warship down the wine-dark sea.
There all the rest of his loyal shipmates died
but the wind drove him on, the current bore him here.
And I welcomed him warmly, cherished him, even vowed
to make the man immortal, ageless, all his days . . .
But since there is no way for another god to thwart
the will of storming Zeus and make it come to nothing,
let the man go—if the Almighty insists, commands—
and destroy himself on the barren salt sea!
I'll send him off, but not with any escort.
I have no ships in reach, no crew to ply the oars
and send him scudding over the sea's broad back.
But I will gladly advise him—I'll hide nothing—
so he can reach his native country all unharmed."

And the guide and giant-killer reinforced her words:
"Release him at once, just so. Steer clear of the rage of Zeus!
Or down the years he'll fume and make your life a hell."

With that the powerful giant-killer sped away.
The queenly nymph sought out the great Odysseus—
the commands of Zeus still ringing in her ears—
and found him there on the headland, sitting, still,

weeping, his eyes never dry, his sweet life flowing away
with the tears he wept for his foiled journey home,
since the nymph no longer pleased. In the nights, true,
he'd sleep with her in the arching cave—he had no choice—
unwilling lover alongside lover all too willing . . .
But all his days he'd sit on the rocks and beaches,
wrenching his heart with sobs and groans and anguish,
gazing out over the barren sea through blinding tears.
So coming up to him now, the lustrous goddess ventured,
"No need, my unlucky one, to grieve here any longer,
no, don't waste your life away. Now I am willing,
heart and soul, to send you off at last. Come,
take bronze tools, cut your lengthy timbers,
make them into a broad-beamed raft
and top it off with a half-deck high enough
to sweep you free and clear on the misty seas.
And I myself will stock her with food and water,
ruddy wine to your taste—all to stave off hunger—
give you clothing, send you a stiff following wind
so you can reach your native country all unharmed.
If only the gods are willing. They rule the vaulting skies.
They're stronger than I to plan and drive things home."

Long-enduring Odysseus shuddered at that
and broke out in a sharp flight of protest.
"Passage home? Never. Surely you're plotting
something else, goddess, urging me—in a raft—
to cross the ocean's mighty gulfs. So vast, so full
of danger not even deep-sea ships can make it through,
swift as they are and buoyed up by the winds of Zeus himself.
I won't set foot on a raft until you show good faith,
until you consent to swear, goddess, a binding oath
you'll never plot some new intrigue to harm me!"

He was so intense the lustrous goddess smiled,
stroked him with her hand, savored his name and chided,
"Ah what a wicked man you are, and never at a loss.
What a thing to imagine, what a thing to say!
Earth be my witness now, the vaulting Sky above
and the dark cascading waters of the Styx—I swear
by the greatest, grimmest oath that binds the happy gods:
I will never plot some new intrigue to harm you.
Never. All I have in mind and devise for *you*
are the very plans I'd fashion for myself
if I were in your straits. My every impulse
bends to what is right. Not iron, trust me,
the heart within *my* breast. I am all compassion."

And lustrous Calypso quickly led the way
as he followed in the footsteps of the goddess.
They reached the arching cavern, man and god as one,
and Odysseus took the seat that Hermes just left,
while the nymph set out before him every kind
of food and drink that mortal men will take.
Calypso sat down face-to-face with the king
and the women served her nectar and ambrosia.
They reached out for the good things that lay at hand
and when they'd had their fill of food and drink
the lustrous one took up a new approach. "So then,
royal son of Laertes, Odysseus, man of exploits,
still eager to leave at once and hurry back
to your own home, your beloved native land?
Good luck to you, even so. Farewell!
But if you only knew, down deep, what pains
are fated to fill your cup before you reach that shore,
you'd stay right here, preside in our house with me
and be immortal. Much as you long to see your wife,
the one you pine for all your days . . . and yet
I just might claim to be nothing less than she,
neither in face nor figure. Hardly right, is it,
for mortal woman to rival immortal goddess?
How, in build? in beauty?"
"Ah great goddess,"
worldly Odysseus answered, "don't be angry with me,
please. All that you say is true, how well I know.
Look at my wise Penelope. She falls far short of you,
your beauty, stature. She is mortal after all
and you, you never age or die . . .
Nevertheless I long—I pine, all my days—
to travel home and see the dawn of my return.
And if a god will wreck me yet again on the wine-dark sea,
I can bear that too, with a spirit tempered to endure.
Much have I suffered, labored long and hard by now
in the waves and wars. Add this to the total—
bring the trial on!" . . .

*[Odysseus builds himself a raft and sets sail for Ithaca and home.]*

## Book 9: The One-Eyed Giant's Cave

When Dawn with her lovely locks brought on the third day,
then stepping the masts and hoisting white sails high,
we lounged at the oarlocks, letting wind and helmsmen
keep us true on course . . .
And now, at long last,

I might have reached my native land unscathed,
but just as I doubled Malea's cape, a tide-rip
and the North Wind drove me way off course
careering past Cythera.
Nine whole days
I was borne along by rough, deadly winds
on the fish-infested sea. Then on the tenth
our squadron reached the land of the Lotus-eaters,
people who eat the lotus, mellow fruit and flower.
We disembarked on the coast, drew water there
and crewmen snatched a meal by the swift ships.
Once we'd had our fill of food and drink I sent
a detail ahead, two picked men and a third, a runner,
to scout out who might live there—men like us perhaps,
who live on bread? So off they went and soon enough
they mingled among the natives, Lotus-eaters, Lotus-eaters
who had no notion of killing my companions, not at all,
they simply gave them the lotus to taste instead . . .
Any crewmen who ate the lotus, the honey-sweet fruit,
lost all desire to send a message back, much less return,
their only wish to linger there with the Lotus-eaters,
grazing on lotus, all memory of the journey home
dissolved forever. But *I* brought them back, back
to the hollow ships, and streaming tears—*I* forced them,
hauled them under the rowing benches, lashed them fast
and shouted out commands to my other, steady comrades:
'Quick, no time to lose, embark in the racing ships!'—
so none could eat the lotus, forget the voyage home.
They swung aboard at once, they sat to the oars in ranks
and in rhythm churned the water white with stroke on stroke.

From there we sailed on, our spirits now at a low ebb,
and reached the land of the high and mighty Cyclops,
lawless brutes, who trust so to the everlasting gods
they never plant with their own hands or plow the soil.
Unsown, unplowed, the earth teems with all they need,
wheat, barley and vines, swelled by the rains of Zeus
to yield a big full-bodied wine from clustered grapes.
They have no meeting place for council, no laws either,
no, up on the mountain peaks they live in arching caverns—
each a law to himself, ruling his wives and children,
not a care in the world for any neighbor.
Now,
a level island stretches flat across the harbor,
not close inshore to the Cyclops' coast, not too far out,
thick with woods where the wild goats breed by hundreds.

No trampling of men to start them from their lairs,
no hunters roughing it out on the woody ridges,
stalking quarry, ever raid their haven.
No flocks browse, no plowlands roll with wheat;
unplowed, unsown forever—empty of humankind—
the island just feeds droves of bleating goats.
For the Cyclops have no ships with crimson prows,
no shipwrights there to build them good trim craft
that could sail them out to foreign ports of call
as most men risk the seas to trade with other men.
Such artisans would have made this island too
a decent place to live in . . . No mean spot,
it could bear you any crop you like in season.
The water-meadows along the low foaming shore
run soft and moist, and your vines would never flag.
The land's clear for plowing. Harvest on harvest,
a man could reap a healthy stand of grain—
the subsoil's dark and rich.
There's a snug deep-water harbor there, what's more,
no need for mooring-gear, no anchor-stones to heave,
no cables to make fast. Just beach your keels, ride out
the days till your shipmates' spirit stirs for open sea
and a fair wind blows. And last, at the harbor's head
there's a spring that rushes fresh from beneath a cave
and black poplars flourish round its mouth.
                                                    Well,
here we landed, and surely a god steered us in
through the pitch-black night.
Not that he ever showed himself, with thick fog
swirling around the ships, the moon wrapped in clouds
and not a glimmer stealing through that gloom.
Not one of us glimpsed the island—scanning hard—
or the long combers rolling us slowly toward the coast,
not till our ships had run their keels ashore.
Beaching our vessels smoothly, striking sail,
the crews swung out on the low shelving sand
and there we fell asleep, awaiting Dawn's first light.

When young Dawn with her rose-red fingers shone once more
we all turned out, intrigued to tour the island.
The local nymphs, the daughters of Zeus himself,
flushed mountain-goats so the crews could make their meal.
Quickly we fetched our curved bows and hunting spears
from the ships and, splitting up into three bands,
we started shooting, and soon enough some god
had sent us bags of game to warm our hearts.

A dozen vessels sailed in my command
and to each crew nine goats were shared out
and mine alone took ten. Then all day long
till the sun went down we sat and feasted well
on sides of meat and rounds of heady wine.
The good red stock in our vessels' holds
had not run out, there was still plenty left;
the men had carried off a generous store in jars
when we stormed and sacked the Cicones' holy city.
Now we stared across at the Cyclops' shore, so near
we could even see their smoke, hear their voices,
their bleating sheep and goats . . .
And then when the sun had set and night came on
we lay down and slept at the water's shelving edge.
When young Dawn with her rose-red fingers shone once more
I called a muster briskly, commanding all the hands,
'The rest of you stay here, my friends-in-arms.
I'll go across with my own ship and crew
and probe the natives living over there.
What *are* they—violent, savage, lawless?
or friendly to strangers, god-fearing men?'

With that I boarded ship and told the crew
to embark at once and cast off cables quickly.
They swung aboard, they sat to the oars in ranks
and in rhythm churned the water white with stroke on stroke.
But as soon as we reached the coast I mentioned—no long trip—
we spied a cavern just at the shore, gaping above the surf,
towering, overgrown with laurel. And here big flocks,
sheep and goats, were stalled to spend the nights,
and around its mouth a yard was walled up
with quarried boulders sunk deep in the earth
and enormous pines and oak-trees looming darkly . . .
Here was a giant's lair, in fact, who always pastured
his sheepflocks far afield and never mixed with others.
A grim loner, dead set in his own lawless ways.
Here was a piece of work, by god, a monster
built like no mortal who ever supped on bread,
no, like a shaggy peak, I'd say—a man-mountain
rearing head and shoulders over the world.
Now then,
I told most of my good trusty crew to wait,
to sit tight by the ship and guard her well
while I picked out my dozen finest fighters
and off I went. But I took a skin of wine along,

the ruddy, irresistible wine that Maron gave me once,
Euanthes' son, a priest of Apollo, lord of Ismarus,
because we'd rescued him, his wife and children,
reverent as we were;
he lived, you see, in Apollo's holy grove.
And so in return he gave me splendid gifts,
he handed me seven bars of well-wrought gold,
a mixing-bowl of solid silver, then this wine . . .
He drew it off in generous wine-jars, twelve in all,
all unmixed—and such a bouquet, a drink fit for the gods!
No maid or man of his household knew that secret store,
only himself, his loving wife and a single servant.
Whenever they'd drink the deep-red mellow vintage,
twenty cups of water he'd stir in one of wine
and what an aroma wafted from the bowl—
what magic, what a godsend—
no joy in holding back when *that* was poured!
Filling a great goatskin now, I took this wine,
provisions too in a leather sack. A sudden foreboding
told my fighting spirit I'd soon come up against
some giant clad in power like armor-plate—
a savage deaf to justice, blind to law.

Our party quickly made its way to his cave
but we failed to find our host himself inside;
he was off in his pasture, ranging his sleek flocks.
So we explored his den, gazing wide-eyed at it all,
the large flat racks loaded with drying cheeses,
the folds crowded with young lambs and kids,
split into three groups—here the spring-born,
here mid-yearlings, here the fresh sucklings
off to the side—each sort was penned apart.
And all his vessels, pails and hammered buckets
he used for milking, were brimming full with whey.
From the start my comrades pressed me, pleading hard,
'Let's make away with the cheeses, then come back—
hurry, drive the lambs and kids from the pens
to our swift ship, put out to sea at once!'
But I would not give way—
and how much better it would have been—
not till I saw him, saw what gifts he'd give.
But he proved no lovely sight to my companions.

There we built a fire, set our hands on the cheeses,
offered some to the gods and ate the bulk ourselves

and settled down inside, awaiting his return . . .
And back he came from pasture, late in the day,
herding his flocks home, and lugging a huge load
of good dry logs to fuel his fire at supper.
He flung them down in the cave—a jolting crash—
we scuttled in panic into the deepest dark recess.
And next he drove his sleek flocks into the open vault,
all he'd milk at least, but he left the males outside,
rams and billy goats out in the high-walled yard.
Then to close his door he hoisted overhead
a tremendous, massive slab—
no twenty-two wagons, rugged and four-wheeled,
could budge that boulder off the ground, I tell you,
such an immense stone the monster wedged to block his cave!
Then down he squatted to milk his sheep and bleating goats,
each in order, and put a suckling underneath each dam.
And half of the fresh white milk he curdled quickly,
set it aside in wicker racks to press for cheese,
the other half let stand in pails and buckets,
ready at hand to wash his supper down.
As soon as he'd briskly finished all his chores
he lit his fire and spied us in the blaze and
'Strangers!' he thundered out, 'now who are you?
Where did you sail from, over the running sea-lanes?
Out on a trading spree or roving the waves like pirates,
sea-wolves raiding at will, who risk their lives
to plunder other men?'
                    The hearts inside us shook,
terrified by his rumbling voice and monstrous hulk.
Nevertheless I found the nerve to answer, firmly,
'Men of Achaea we are and bound now from Troy!
Driven far off course by the warring winds,
over the vast gulf of the sea—battling home
on a strange tack, a route that's off the map,
and so we've come to you . . .
so it must please King Zeus's plotting heart.
We're glad to say we're men of Atrides Agamemnon,
whose fame is the proudest thing on earth these days,
so great a city he sacked, such multitudes he killed!
But since we've chanced on you, we're at your knees
in hopes of a warm welcome, even a guest-gift,
the sort that hosts give strangers. That's the custom.
Respect the gods, my friend. We're suppliants—at your mercy!
Zeus of the Strangers guards all guests and suppliants:
strangers are sacred—Zeus will avenge their rights!'

'Stranger,' he grumbled back from his brutal heart,
'you must be a fool, stranger, or come from nowhere,
telling *me* to fear the gods or avoid their wrath!
We Cyclops never blink at Zeus and Zeus's shield
of storm and thunder, or any other blessed god—
we've got more force by far.
I'd never spare you in fear of Zeus's hatred,
you or your comrades here, unless I had the urge.
But tell me, where did you moor your sturdy ship
when you arrived? Up the coast or close in?
I'd just like to know.'
So he laid his trap
but he never caught me, no, wise to the world
I shot back in my crafty way, 'My ship?
Poseidon god of the earthquake smashed my ship,
he drove it against the rocks at your island's far cape,
he dashed it against a cliff as the winds rode us in.
I and the men you see escaped a sudden death.'

Not a word in reply to that, the ruthless brute.
Lurching up, he lunged out with his hands toward my men
and snatching two at once, rapping them on the ground
he knocked them dead like pups—
their brains gushed out all over, soaked the floor—
and ripping them limb from limb to fix his meal
he bolted them down like a mountain-lion, left no scrap,
devoured entrails, flesh and bones, marrow and all!
We flung our arms to Zeus, we wept and cried aloud,
looking on at his grisly work—paralyzed, appalled.
But once the Cyclops had stuffed his enormous gut
with human flesh, washing it down with raw milk,
he slept in his cave, stretched out along his flocks.
And I with my fighting heart, I thought at first
to steal up to him, draw the sharp sword at my hip
and stab his chest where the midriff packs the liver—
I groped for the fatal spot but a fresh thought held me back.
There at a stroke we'd finish off ourselves as well—
how could *we* with our bare hands heave back
that slab he set to block his cavern's gaping maw?
So we lay there groaning, waiting Dawn's first light.

When young Dawn with her rose-red fingers shone once more
the monster relit his fire and milked his handsome ewes,
each in order, putting a suckling underneath each dam,
and as soon as he'd briskly finished all his chores

he snatched up two more men and fixed his meal.
Well-fed, he drove his fat sheep from the cave,
lightly lifting the huge doorslab up and away,
then slipped it back in place
as a hunter flips the lid of his quiver shut.
Piercing whistles—turning his flocks to the hills
he left me there, the heart inside me brooding on revenge:
how could I pay him back? would Athena give me glory?
Here was the plan that struck my mind as best . . .
the Cyclops' great club: there it lay by the pens,
olivewood, full of sap. He'd lopped it off to brandish
once it dried. Looking it over, we judged it big enough
to be the mast of a pitch-black ship with her twenty oars,
a freighter broad in the beam that plows through miles of sea—
so long, so thick it bulked before our eyes. Well,
flanking it now, I chopped off a fathom's length,
rolled it to comrades, told them to plane it down,
and they made the club smooth as I bent and shaved
the tip to a stabbing point. I turned it over
the blazing fire to char it good and hard,
then hid it well, buried deep under the dung
that littered the cavern's floor in thick wet clumps.
And now I ordered my shipmates all to cast lots—
who'd brave it out with me
to hoist our stake and grind it into his eye
when sleep had overcome him? Luck of the draw:
I got the very ones I would have picked myself,
four good men, and I in the lead made five . . .

Nightfall brought him back, herding his woolly sheep
and he quickly drove the sleek flock into the vaulted cavern,
rams and all—none left outside in the walled yard—
his own idea, perhaps, or a god led him on.
Then he hoisted the huge slab to block the door
and squatted to milk his sheep and bleating goats,
each in order, putting a suckling underneath each dam,
and as soon as he'd briskly finished all his chores
he snatched up two more men and fixed his meal.
But this time I lifted a carved wooden bowl,
brimful of my ruddy wine,
and went right up to the Cyclops, enticing,
'Here, Cyclops, try this wine—to top off
the banquet of human flesh you've bolted down!
Judge for yourself what stock our ship had stored.
I brought it here to make you a fine libation,
hoping you would pity me, Cyclops, send me home,

but your rages are insufferable. You barbarian—
how can any man on earth come visit you after *this?*
What you've done outrages all that's right!'

At that he seized the bowl and tossed it off
and the heady wine pleased him immensely—'More'—
he demanded a second bowl—a hearty helping!
And tell me your name now, quickly,
so I can hand my guest a gift to warm *his* heart.
Our soil yields the Cyclops powerful, full-bodied wine
and the rains from Zeus build its strength. But this,
this is nectar, ambrosia—this flows from heaven!'

So he declared. I poured him another fiery bowl—
three bowls I brimmed and three he drank to the last drop,
the fool, and then, when the wine was swirling round his brain,
I approached my host with a cordial, winning word:
'So, you ask me the name I'm known by, Cyclops?
I will tell you. But you must give me a guest-gift
as you've promised. Nobody—that's my name. Nobody—
so my mother and father call me, all my friends.'

But he boomed back at me from his ruthless heart,
'*Nobody?* I'll eat Nobody last of all his friends—
I'll eat the others first! That's my gift to *you!*'
With that
he toppled over, sprawled full-length, flat on his back
and lay there, his massive neck slumping to one side,
and sleep that conquers all overwhelmed him now
as wine came spurting, flooding up from his gullet
with chunks of human flesh—he vomited, blind drunk.
Now, at last, I thrust our stake in a bed of embers
to get it red-hot and rallied all my comrades:
'Courage—no panic, no one hang back now!'
And green as it was, just as the olive stake
was about to catch fire—the glow terrific, yes—
I dragged it from the flames, my men clustering round
as some god breathed enormous courage through us all.
Hoisting high that olive stake with its stabbing point,
straight into the monster's eye they rammed it hard—
I drove my weight on it from above and bored it home
as a shipwright bores his beam with a shipwright's drill
that men below, whipping the strap back and forth, whirl
and the drill keeps twisting faster, never stopping—
So we seized our stake with its fiery tip
and bored it round and round in the giant's eye

till blood came boiling up around that smoking shaft
and the hot blast singed his brow and eyelids round the core
and the broiling eyeball burst—
its crackling roots blazed
and hissed—
as a blacksmith plunges a glowing ax or adze
in an ice-cold bath and the metal screeches steam
and its temper hardens—that's the iron's strength—
so the eye of the Cyclops sizzled round that stake!
He loosed a hideous roar, the rock walls echoed round
and we scuttled back in terror. The monster wrenched the spike
from his eye and out it came with a red geyser of blood—
he flung it aside with frantic hands, and mad with pain
he bellowed out for help from his neighbor Cyclops
living round about in caves on windswept crags.
Hearing his cries, they lumbered up from every side
and hulking round his cavern, asked what ailed him:
'What, Polyphemus, what in the world's the trouble?
Roaring out in the godsent night to rob us of our sleep.
Surely no one's rustling your flocks against your will—
surely no one's trying to kill you now by fraud or force!'

'*Nobody,* friends'—Polyphemus bellowed back from his cave—
'Nobody's killing me now by fraud and not by force!'

'If you're alone,' his friends boomed back at once,
and nobody's trying to overpower you now—look,
it must be a plague sent here by mighty Zeus
and there's no escape from *that.*
You'd better pray to your father, Lord Poseidon.'

They lumbered off, but laughter filled my heart
to think how nobody's name—my great cunning stroke—
had duped them one and all. But the Cyclops there,
still groaning, racked with agony, groped around
for the huge slab, and heaving it from the doorway,
down he sat in the cave's mouth, his arms spread wide,
hoping to catch a comrade stealing out with sheep—
such a blithering fool he took me for!
But I was already plotting . . .
what was the best way out? how could I find
escape from death for my crew, myself as well?
My wits kept weaving, weaving cunning schemes—
life at stake, monstrous death staring us in the face—
till this plan struck my mind as best. That flock,
those well-fed rams with their splendid thick fleece,

sturdy, handsome beasts sporting their dark weight of wool:
I lashed them abreast, quietly, twisting the willow-twigs
the Cyclops slept on—giant, lawless brute—I took them
three by three; each ram in the middle bore a man
while the two rams either side would shield him well.
So three beasts to bear each man, but as for myself?
There was one bellwether ram, the prize of all the flock,
and clutching him by his back, tucked up under
his shaggy belly, there I hung, face upward,
both hands locked in his marvelous deep fleece,
clinging for dear life, my spirit steeled, enduring . . .
So we held on, desperate, waiting Dawn's first light.
As soon
as young Dawn with her rose-red fingers shone once more
the rams went rumbling out of the cave toward pasture,
the ewes kept bleating round the pens, unmilked,
their udders about to burst. Their master now,
heaving in torment, felt the back of each animal
halting before him here, but the idiot never sensed
my men were trussed up under their thick fleecy ribs.
And last of them all came my great ram now, striding out,
weighed down with his dense wool and my deep plots.
Stroking him gently, powerful Polyphemus murmured,
'Dear old ram, why last of the flock to quit the cave?
In the good old days you'd never lag behind the rest—
you with your long marching strides, first by far
of the flock to graze the fresh young grasses,
first by far to reach the rippling streams,
first to turn back home, keen for your fold
when night comes on—but now you're last of all.
And why? Sick at heart for your master's eye
that coward gouged out with his wicked crew?—
only after he'd stunned my wits with wine—
that, that Nobody . . .
who's not escaped his death, I swear, not yet.
Oh if only you thought like *me,* had words like *me*
to tell me where that scoundrel is cringing from my rage!
I'd smash him against the ground, I'd spill his brains—
flooding across my cave—and that would ease my heart
of the pains that good-for-nothing Nobody made me suffer!'

And with that threat he let my ram go free outside.
But soon as we'd got one foot past cave and courtyard,
first I loosed myself from the ram, then loosed my men,
then quickly, glancing back again and again we drove
our flock, good plump beasts with their long shanks,

straight to the ship, and a welcome sight we were
to loyal comrades—we who'd escaped our deaths—
but for all the rest they broke down and wailed.
I cut it short, I stopped each shipmate's cries,
my head tossing, brows frowning, silent signals
to hurry, tumble our fleecy herd on board,
launch out on the open sea!
They swung aboard, they sat to the oars in ranks
and in rhythm churned the water white with stroke on stroke.
But once offshore as far as a man's shout can carry,
I called back to the Cyclops, stinging taunts:
'So, Cyclops, no weak coward it was whose crew
you bent to devour there in your vaulted cave—
you with your brute force! Your filthy crimes
came down on your own head, you shameless cannibal,
daring to eat your guests in your own house—
so Zeus and the other gods have paid you back!'

That made the rage of the monster boil over.
Ripping off the peak of a towering crag, he heaved it
so hard the boulder landed just in front of our dark prow
and a huge swell reared up as the rock went plunging under—
a tidal wave from the open sea. The sudden backwash
drove us landward again, forcing us close inshore
but grabbing a long pole, I thrust us off and away,
tossing my head for dear life, signaling crews
to put their backs in the oars, escape grim death.
They threw themselves in the labor, rowed on fast
but once we'd plowed the breakers twice as far,
again I began to taunt the Cyclops—men around me
trying to check me, calm me, left and right:
'So headstrong—why? Why rile the beast again?'

'That rock he flung in the sea just now, hurling our ship
to shore once more—we thought we'd die on the spot!'

'If he'd caught a sound from one of us, just a moan,
he would have crushed our heads and ship timbers
with one heave of another flashing, jagged rock!'

'Good god, the brute can throw!'
So they begged
but they could not bring my fighting spirit round.
I called back with another burst of anger, 'Cyclops—
if any man on the face of the earth should ask you
who blinded you, shamed you so—say Odysseus,

raider of cities, *he* gouged out your eye,
Laertes' son who makes his home in Ithaca!'

So I vaunted and he groaned back in answer,
'Oh no, no—that prophecy years ago . . .
it all comes home to me with a vengeance now!
We once had a prophet here, a great tall man,
Telemus, Eurymus' son, a master at reading signs,
who grew old in his trade among his fellow-Cyclops.
All this, he warned me, would come to pass someday—
that I'd be blinded here at the hands of one Odysseus.
But I always looked for a handsome giant man to cross my path,
some fighter clad in power like armor-plate, but now,
look what a dwarf, a spineless good-for-nothing,
stuns me with wine, then gouges out my eye!
Come here, Odysseus, let me give you a guest-gift
and urge Poseidon the earthquake god to speed you home.
I am his son and he claims to be my father, true,
and he himself will heal me if he pleases—
no other blessed god, no man can do the work!'
'Heal you!'—
here was my parting shot—'Would to god I could strip you
of life and breath and ship you down to the House of Death
as surely as no one will ever heal your eye,
not even your earthquake god himself!'

But at that he bellowed out to lord Poseidon,
thrusting his arms to the starry skies, and prayed, 'Hear me—
Poseidon, god of the sea-blue mane who rocks the earth!
If I really am your son and you claim to be my father—
come, grant that Odysseus, raider of cities,
Laertes' son who makes his home in Ithaca,
never reaches home. Or if he's fated to see
his people once again and reach his well-built house
and his own native country, let him come home late
and come a broken man—all shipmates lost,
alone in a stranger's ship—
and let him find a world of pain at home!'
So he prayed
and the god of the sea-blue mane Poseidon heard his prayer.
The monster suddenly hoisted a boulder—far larger—
wheeled and heaved it, putting his weight behind it,
massive strength, and the boulder crashed close,
landing just in the wake of our dark stern,
just failing to graze the rudder's bladed edge.
A huge swell reared up as the rock went plunging under,

yes, and the tidal breaker drove us out to our island's
far shore where all my well-decked ships lay moored,
clustered, waiting, and huddled round them, crewmen
sat in anguish, waiting, chafing for our return.
We beached our vessel hard ashore on the sand,
we swung out in the frothing surf ourselves,
and herding Cyclops' sheep from our deep holds
we shared them round so no one, not on my account,
would go deprived of his fair share of spoils.
But the splendid ram—as we meted out the flocks
my friends-in-arms made him my prize of honor,
mine alone, and I slaughtered him on the beach
and burnt his thighs to Cronus' mighty son,
Zeus of the thundercloud who rules the world.
But my sacrifices failed to move the god:
Zeus was still obsessed with plans to destroy
my entire oarswept fleet and loyal crew of comrades.
Now all day long till the sun went down we sat
and feasted on sides of meat and heady wine.
Then when the sun had set and night came on
we lay down and slept at the water's shelving edge.
When young Dawn with her rose-red fingers shone once more
I roused the men straightway, ordering all crews
to man the ships and cast off cables quickly.
They swung aboard at once, they sat to the oars in ranks
and in rhythm churned the water white with stroke on stroke.
And from there we sailed on, glad to escape our death
yet sick at heart for the comrades we had lost.

## Book 12: The Cattle of the Sun: The Sirens' Song

*[After being instructed by the goddess Circe on the proper route home, Odysseus and his crew set sail again.]*

And so we saw to his rites, each step in turn.
Nor did our coming back from Death escape Circe—
she hurried toward us, decked in rich regalia,
handmaids following close with trays of bread
and meats galore and glinting ruddy wine.
And the lustrous goddess, standing in our midst,
hailed us warmly: 'Ah my daring, reckless friends!
You who ventured down to the House of Death alive,
doomed to die twice over—others die just once.
Come, take some food and drink some wine,
rest here the livelong day
and then, tomorrow at daybreak, you must sail.
But I will set you a course and chart each seamark,

so neither on sea nor land will some new trap
ensnare you in trouble, make you suffer more.'

Her foresight won our fighting spirits over.
So all that day till the sun went down we sat
and feasted on sides of meat and heady wine,
and then when the sun had set and night came on
the men lay down to sleep by the ship's stern-cables.
But Circe, taking me by the hand, drew me away
from all my shipmates there and sat me down
and lying beside me probed me for details.
I told her the whole story, start to finish,
then the queenly goddess laid my course:
'Your descent to the dead is over, true,
but listen closely to what I tell you now
and god himself will bring it back to mind.
First you will raise the island of the Sirens,
those creatures who spellbind any man alive,
whoever comes their way. Whoever draws too close,
off guard, and catches the Sirens' voices in the air—
no sailing home for him, no wife rising to meet him,
no happy children beaming up at their father's face.
The high, thrilling song of the Sirens will transfix him,
lolling there in their meadow, round them heaps of corpses
rotting away, rags of skin shriveling on their bones . . .
Race straight past that coast! Soften some beeswax
and stop your shipmates' ears so none can hear,
none of the crew, but if *you* are bent on hearing,
have them tie you hand and foot in the swift ship,
erect at the mast-block, lashed by ropes to the mast
so you can hear the Sirens' song to your heart's content.
But if you plead, commanding your men to set you free,
then they must lash you faster, rope on rope.

But once your crew has rowed you past the Sirens
a choice of routes is yours. I cannot advise you
which to take, or lead you through it all—
you must decide for yourself—
but I can tell you the ways of either course.
On one side beetling cliffs shoot up, and against them
pound the huge roaring breakers of blue-eyed Amphitrite—
the Clashing Rocks they're called by all the blissful gods.
Not even birds can escape them, no, not even the doves
that veer and fly ambrosia home to Father Zeus:
even of those the sheer Rocks always pick off one
and Father wings one more to keep the number up.

No ship of men has ever approached and slipped past—
always some disaster—big timbers and sailors' corpses
whirled away by the waves and lethal blasts of fire.
One ship alone, one deep-sea craft sailed clear,
the *Argo,* sung by the world, when heading home
from Aeetes' shores. And *she* would have crashed
against those giant rocks and sunk at once if Hera,
for love of Jason, had not sped her through.

On the other side loom two enormous crags . . .
One thrusts into the vaulting sky its jagged peak,
hooded round with a dark cloud that never leaves—
no clear bright air can ever bathe its crown,
not even in summer's heat or harvest-time.
No man on earth could scale it, mount its crest,
not even with twenty hands and twenty feet for climbing,
the rock's so smooth, like dressed and burnished stone.
And halfway up that cliffside stands a fog-bound cavern
gaping west toward Erebus, realm of death and darkness—
past it, great Odysseus, you should steer your ship.
No rugged young archer could hit that yawning cave
with a winged arrow shot from off the decks.
Scylla lurks inside it—the yelping horror,
yelping, no louder than any suckling pup
but she's a grisly monster, I assure you.
No one could look on her with any joy,
not even a god who meets her face-to-face . . .
She has twelve legs, all writhing, dangling down
and six long swaying necks, a hideous head on each,
each head barbed with a triple row of fangs, thickset,
packed tight—and armed to the hilt with black death!
Holed up in the cavern's bowels from her waist down
she shoots out her heads, out of that terrifying pit,
angling right from her nest, wildly sweeping the reefs
for dolphins, dogfish or any bigger quarry she can drag
from the thousands Amphitrite spawns in groaning seas.
No mariners yet can boast they've raced their ship
past Scylla's lair without some mortal blow—
with each of her six heads she snatches up
a man from the dark-prowed craft and whisks him off.

The other crag is lower—you will see, Odysseus—
though both lie side-by-side, an arrow-shot apart.
Atop it a great fig-tree rises, shaggy with leaves,
beneath it awesome Charybdis gulps the dark water down.
Three times a day she vomits it up, three times she gulps it down,

that terror! Don't be there when the whirlpool swallows
down—
not even the earthquake god could save you from disaster.
No, hug Scylla's crag—sail on past her—top speed!
Better by far to lose six men and keep your ship
than lose your entire crew.'
'Yes, yes,
but tell me the truth now, goddess,' I protested.
'Deadly Charybdis—can't I possibly cut and run from *her*
and still fight Scylla off when Scylla strikes my men?'

'So stubborn!' the lovely goddess countered.
'Hell-bent yet again on battle and feats of arms?
Can't you bow to the deathless gods themselves?
Scylla's no mortal, she's an immortal devastation,
terrible, savage, wild, no fighting her, no defense—
just flee the creature, that's the only way.
Waste any time, arming for battle beside her rock,
I fear she'll lunge out again with all of her six heads
and seize as many men. No, row for your lives,
invoke Brute Force, I tell you, Scylla's mother—
she spawned her to scourge mankind,
*she* can stop the monster's next attack!

Then you will make the island of Thrinacia . . .
where herds of the Sungod's cattle graze, and fat sheep
and seven herds of oxen, as many sheepflocks, rich and woolly,
fifty head in each. No breeding swells their number,
nor do they ever die. And goddesses herd them on,
nymphs with glinting hair, Phaëthousa, Lampetie,
born to the Sungod Helios by radiant Neaera.
Their queenly mother bred and reared them both
then settled them on the island of Thrinacia—
their homeland seas away—
to guard their father's sheep and longhorn cattle.
Leave the beasts unharmed, your mind set on home,
and you all may still reach Ithaca—bent with hardship,
true—but harm them in any way, and I can see it now:
your ship destroyed, your men destroyed as well!
And even if *you* escape, you'll come home late,
all shipmates lost, and come a broken man.'

At those words Dawn rose on her golden throne
and lustrous Circe made her way back up the island.
I went straight to my ship, commanding all hands
to take to the decks and cast off cables quickly.

They swung aboard at once, they sat to the oars in ranks
and in rhythm churned the water white with stroke on stroke.
And Circe the nymph with glossy braids, the awesome one
who speaks with human voice, sent us a hardy shipmate,
yes, a fresh following wind ruffling up in our wake,
bellying out our sail to drive our blue prow on as we,
securing the running gear from stem to stern, sat back
while the wind and helmsman kept her true on course.
At last, and sore at heart, I told my shipmates,
'Friends . . . it's wrong for only one or two
to know the revelations that lovely Circe
made to me alone. I'll tell you all,
so we can die with our eyes wide open now
or escape our fate and certain death together.
First, she warns, we must steer clear of the Sirens,
their enchanting song, their meadow starred with flowers.
I alone was to hear their voices, so she said,
but you must bind me with tight chafing ropes
so I cannot move a muscle, bound to the spot,
erect at the mast-block, lashed by ropes to the mast.
And if I plead, commanding you to set me free,
then lash me faster, rope on pressing rope.'

So I informed my shipmates point by point,
all the while our trim ship was speeding toward
the Sirens' island, driven on by the brisk wind.
But then—the wind fell in an instant,
all glazed to a dead calm . . .
a mysterious power hushed the heaving swells.
The oarsmen leapt to their feet, struck the sail,
stowed it deep in the hold and sat to the oarlocks,
thrashing with polished oars, frothing the water white.
Now with a sharp sword I sliced an ample wheel of beeswax
down into pieces, kneaded them in my two strong hands
and the wax soon grew soft, worked by my strength
and Helios' burning rays, the sun at high noon,
and I stopped the ears of my comrades one by one.
They bound me hand and foot in the tight ship—
erect at the mast-block, lashed by ropes to the mast—
and rowed and churned the whitecaps stroke on stroke.
We were just offshore as far as a man's shout can carry,
scudding close, when the Sirens sensed at once a ship
was racing past and burst into their high, thrilling song:
'Come closer, famous Odysseus—Achaea's pride and glory—
moor your ship on our coast so you can hear our song!

Never has any sailor passed our shores in his black craft
until he has heard the honeyed voices pouring from our lips,
and once he hears to his heart's content sails on, a wiser man.
We know all the pains that the Greeks and Trojans once endured
on the spreading plain of Troy when the gods willed it so—
all that comes to pass on the fertile earth, we know it all!'

So they sent their ravishing voices out across the air
and the heart inside me throbbed to listen longer.
I signaled the crew with frowns to set me free—
they flung themselves at the oars and rowed on harder,
Perimedes and Eurylochus springing up at once
to bind me faster with rope on chafing rope.
But once we'd left the Sirens fading in our wake,
once we could hear their song no more, their urgent call—
my steadfast crew was quick to remove the wax I'd used
to seal their ears and loosed the bonds that lashed me.

## *Book 21: Odysseus Strings His Bow*

*[Arriving home in Ithaca in disguise, Odysseus prompts his wife to call on her suitors to string her husband's mighty bow. The suitors cannot bend it, but the hero in his disguise as a beggar steps up to try his luck.]*

The cowherd quietly bounded out of the house
to lock the gates of the high-stockaded court.
Under the portico lay a cable, ship's tough gear:
he lashed the gates with this, then slipped back in
and ran and sat on the stool that he'd just left,
eyes riveted on Odysseus.
Now *he* held the bow
in his own hands, turning it over, tip to tip,
testing it, this way, that way . . . fearing worms
had bored through the weapon's horn with the master gone abroad.
A suitor would glance at his neighbor, jeering, taunting,
"Look at our connoisseur of bows!"
"Sly old fox—
maybe he's got bows like it, stored in *his* house."

"That or he's bent on making one himself."

"Look how he twists and turns it in his hands!"

"The clever tramp means trouble—"

"I wish him luck," some cocksure lord chimed in,
"as good as his luck in bending back that weapon!"

So they mocked, but Odysseus, mastermind in action,
once he'd handled the great bow and scanned every inch,
then, like an expert singer skilled at lyre and song—
who strains a string to a new peg with ease,
making the pliant sheep-gut fast at either end—
so with his virtuoso ease Odysseus strung his mighty bow.
Quickly his right hand plucked the string to test its pitch
and under his touch it sang out clear and sharp as a swallow's cry.
Horror swept through the suitors, faces blanching white,
and Zeus cracked the sky with a bolt, his blazing sign,
and the great man who had borne so much rejoiced at last
that the son of cunning Cronus flung that omen down for *him*.
He snatched a winged arrow lying bare on the board—
the rest still bristled deep inside the quiver,
soon to be tasted by all the feasters there.
Setting shaft on the handgrip, drawing the notch
and bowstring back, back . . . right from his stool,
just as he sat but aiming straight and true, he let fly—
and never missing an ax from the first ax-handle
clean on through to the last and out
the shaft with its weighted brazen head shot free!
"My son,"
Odysseus looked to Telemachus and said, "your guest,
sitting here in your house, has not disgraced you.
No missing the mark, look, and no long labor spent
to string the bow. My strength's not broken yet,
not quite so frail as the mocking suitors thought.
But the hour has come to serve our masters right—
supper in broad daylight—then to other revels,
song and dancing, all that crowns a feast."

He paused with a warning nod, and at that sign
Prince Telemachus, son of King Odysseus,
girding his sharp sword on, clamping hand to spear,
took his stand by a chair that flanked his father—
his bronze spearpoint glinting now like fire . . .

## *Book 23: The Great Rooted Bed*

Up to the rooms the old nurse clambered, chuckling all the way,
to tell the queen her husband was here now, home at last.
Her knees bustling, feet shuffling over each other,
till hovering at her mistress' head she spoke:
"Penelope—child—wake up and see for yourself,
with your own eyes, all you dreamed of, all your days!

He's here—Odysseus—he's come home, at long last!
He's killed the suitors, swaggering young brutes
who plagued his house, wolfed his cattle down,
rode roughshod over his son!"

"Dear old nurse," wary Penelope replied,
"the gods have made you mad. They have that power,
putting lunacy into the clearest head around
or setting a half-wit on the path to sense.
They've unhinged you, and you were once so sane.
Why do you mock me?—haven't I wept enough?—
telling such wild stories, interrupting my sleep,
sweet sleep that held me, sealed my eyes just now.
Not once have I slept so soundly since the day
Odysseus sailed away to see that cursed city . . .
*Destroy,* I call it—I hate to say its name!
Now down you go. Back to your own quarters.
If any other woman of mine had come to me,
rousing me out of sleep with such a tale,
I'd have her bundled back to her room in pain.
It's only your old gray head that spares you that!"

"Never"—the fond old nurse kept pressing on—
"dear child, I'd never mock you! No, it's all true,
he's here—Odysseus—he's come home, just as I tell you!
He's the stranger they all manhandled in the hall.
Telemachus knew he was here, for days and days,
but he knew enough to hide his father's plans
so *he* could pay those vipers back in kind!"

Penelope's heart burst in joy, she leapt from bed,
her eyes streaming tears, she hugged the old nurse
and cried out with an eager, winging word,
"Please, dear one, give me the whole story.
If he's really home again, just as you tell me,
how did he get those shameless suitors in his clutches?—
single-handed, braving an army always camped inside."

"I have no idea," the devoted nurse replied.
"I didn't see it, I didn't ask—all I heard
was the choking groans of men cut down in blood.
We crouched in terror—a dark nook of our quarters—
all of us locked tight behind those snug doors
till your boy Telemachus came and called me out—
his father rushed him there to do just that. And then
I found Odysseus in the thick of slaughtered corpses;

there he stood and all around him, over the beaten floor,
the bodies sprawled in heaps, lying one on another . . .
How it would have thrilled your heart to see him—
splattered with bloody filth, a lion with his kill!
And now they're all stacked at the courtyard gates—
he's lit a roaring fire,
he's purifying the house with cleansing fumes
and he's sent me here to bring you back to him.
Follow me down! So now, after all the years of grief,
you two can embark, loving hearts, along the road to joy.
Look, your dreams, put off so long, come true at last—
he's back alive, home at his hearth, and found you,
found his son still here. And all those suitors
who did him wrong, he's paid them back, he has,
right in his own house!"
"Hush, dear woman,"
guarded Penelope cautioned her at once.
"Don't laugh, don't cry in triumph—not yet.
You know how welcome the sight of him would be
to all in the house, and to me most of all
and the son we bore together.
But the story can't be true, not as you tell it,
no, it must be a god who's killed our brazen friends—
up in arms at their outrage, heartbreaking crimes.
They'd no regard for any man on earth—
good or bad—who chanced to come their way. So,
thanks to their reckless work they die their deaths.
Odysseus? Far from Achaea now, he's lost all hope
of coming home . . . he's lost and gone himself."

"Child," the devoted old nurse protested,
"what nonsense you let slip through your teeth.
Here's your husband, warming his hands at his own hearth,
here—and you, you say he'll never come home again,
always the soul of trust! All right, this too—
I'll give you a sign, a proof that's plain as day.
That scar, made years ago by a boar's white tusk—
I spotted the scar myself, when I washed his feet,
and I tried to tell you, ah, but he, the crafty rascal,
clamped his hand on my mouth—I couldn't say a word.
Follow me down now. I'll stake my life on it:
if I am lying to *you*—
kill me with a thousand knives of pain!"

"Dear old nurse," composed Penelope responded,
"deep as you are, my friend, you'll find it hard
to plumb the plans of the everlasting gods.

All the same, let's go and join my son
so I can see the suitors lying dead
and see . . . the one who killed them."
With that thought
Penelope started down from her lofty room, her heart
in turmoil, torn . . . should she keep her distance,
probe her husband? Or rush up to the man at once
and kiss his head and cling to both his hands?
As soon as she stepped across the stone threshold,
slipping in, she took a seat at the closest wall
and radiant in the firelight, faced Odysseus now.
There he sat, leaning against the great central column,
eyes fixed on the ground, waiting, poised for whatever words
his hardy wife might say when she caught sight of him.
A long while she sat in silence . . . numbing wonder
filled her heart as her eyes explored his face.
One moment he seemed . . . Odysseus, to the life—
the next, no, he was not the man she knew,
a huddled mass of rags was all she saw.

"Oh mother," Telemachus reproached her,
"cruel mother, you with your hard heart!
Why do you spurn my father so—why don't you
sit beside him, engage him, ask him questions?
What other wife could have a spirit so unbending?
Holding back from her husband, home at last for *her*
after bearing twenty years of brutal struggle—
your heart was always harder than a rock!"
"My child,"
Penelope, well-aware, explained, "I'm stunned with wonder,
powerless. Cannot speak to him, ask him questions,
look him in the eyes . . . But if he is truly
Odysseus, home at last, make no mistake:
we two will know each other, even better—
we two have secret signs,
known to us both but hidden from the world."

Odysseus, long-enduring, broke into a smile
and turned to his son with pointed, winging words:
"Leave your mother here in the hall to test me
as she will. She soon will know me better.
Now because I am filthy, wear such grimy rags,
she spurns me—your mother still can't bring herself
to believe I am her husband.
But you and I,
put heads together. What's our best defense?
When someone kills a lone man in the realm

who leaves behind him no great band of avengers,
still the killer flees, goodbye to kin and country.
But *we* brought down the best of the island's princes,
the pillars of Ithaca. Weigh it well, I urge you."

"Look to it all yourself now, father," his son
deferred at once. "You are the best on earth,
they say, when it comes to mapping tactics.
No one, no mortal man, can touch you there.
But we're behind you, hearts intent on battle,
nor do I think you'll find us short on courage,
long as our strength will last."
"Then here's our plan,"
the master of tactics said. "I think it's best.
First go and wash, and pull fresh tunics on
and tell the maids in the hall to dress well too.
And let the inspired bard take up his ringing lyre
and lead off for us all a dance so full of heart
that whoever hears the strains outside the gates—
a passerby on the road, a neighbor round about—
will think it's a wedding-feast that's under way.
No news of the suitors' death must spread through town
till we have slipped away to our own estates,
our orchard green with trees. There we'll see
what winning strategy Zeus will hand us then."

They hung on his words and moved to orders smartly.
First they washed and pulled fresh tunics on,
the women arrayed themselves—the inspired bard
struck up his resounding lyre and stirred in all
a desire for dance and song, the lovely lilting beat,
till the great house echoed round to the measured tread
of dancing men in motion, women sashed and lithe.
And whoever heard the strains outside would say,
"A miracle—someone's married the queen at last!"

"One of her hundred suitors."
"That callous woman,
too faithless to keep her lord and master's house
to the bitter end—"
"Till he came sailing home."

So they'd say, blind to what had happened:
the great-hearted Odysseus was home again at last.
The maid Eurynome bathed him, rubbed him down with oil

and drew around him a royal cape and choice tunic too.
And Athena crowned the man with beauty, head to foot,
made him taller to all eyes, his build more massive,
yes, and down from his brow the great goddess
ran his curls like thick hyacinth clusters
full of blooms. As a master craftsman washes
gold over beaten silver—a man the god of fire
and Queen Athena trained in every fine technique—
and finishes off his latest effort, handsome work . . .
so she lavished splendor over his head and shoulders now.
He stepped from his bath, glistening like a god,
and back he went to the seat that he had left
and facing his wife, declared,
"Strange woman! So hard—the gods of Olympus
made you harder than any other woman in the world!
What other wife could have a spirit so unbending?
Holding back from her husband, home at last for *her*
after bearing twenty years of brutal struggle.
Come, nurse, make me a bed, I'll sleep alone.
She has a heart of iron in her breast."
"Strange *man*,"
wary Penelope said. "I'm not so proud, so scornful,
nor am I overwhelmed by your quick change . . .
You look—how well I know—the way he looked,
setting sail from Ithaca years ago
aboard the long-oared ship.
Come, Eurycleia,
move the sturdy bedstead out of our bridal chamber—
that room the master built with his own hands.
Take it out now, sturdy bed that it is,
and spread it deep with fleece,
blankets and lustrous throws to keep him warm."

Putting her husband to the proof—but Odysseus
blazed up in fury, lashing out at his loyal wife:
"Woman—your words, they cut me to the core!
Who could move my bed? Impossible task,
even for some skilled craftsman—unless a god
came down in person, quick to lend a hand,
lifted it out with ease and moved it elsewhere.
Not a man on earth, not even at peak strength,
would find it easy to prise it up and shift it, no,
a great sign, a hallmark lies in its construction.
I know, I built it myself—no one else . . .
There was a branching olive-tree inside our court,
grown to its full prime, the bole like a column, thickset.

Around it I built my bedroom, finished off the walls
with good tight stonework, roofed it over soundly
and added doors, hung well and snugly wedged.
Then I lopped the leafy crown of the olive,
clean-cutting the stump bare from roots up,
planing it round with a bronze smoothing-adze—
I had the skill—I shaped it plumb to the line to make
my bedpost, bored the holes it needed with an auger.
Working from there I built my bed, start to finish,
I gave it ivory inlays, gold and silver fittings,
wove the straps across it, oxhide gleaming red.
There's our secret sign, I tell you, our life story!
Does the bed, my lady, still stand planted firm?—
I don't know—or has someone chopped away
that olive-trunk and hauled our bedstead off?"
Living proof—
Penelope felt her knees go slack, her heart surrender,
recognizing the strong clear signs Odysseus offered.
She dissolved in tears, rushed to Odysseus, flung her arms
around his neck and kissed his head and cried out,
"Odysseus—don't flare up at me now, not you,
always the most understanding man alive!
The gods, it was the gods who sent us sorrow—
they grudged us both a life in each other's arms
from the heady zest of youth to the stoop of old age.
But don't fault me, angry with me now because I failed,
at the first glimpse, to greet you, hold you, so . . .
In my heart of hearts I always cringed with fear
some fraud might come, beguile me with his talk;
the world is full of the sort,
cunning ones who plot their own dark ends.
Remember Helen of Argos, Zeus's daughter—
would *she* have sported so in a stranger's bed
if she had dreamed that Achaea's sons were doomed
to fight and die to bring her home again?
Some god spurred her to do her shameless work.
Not till then did her mind conceive that madness,
blinding madness that caused her anguish, ours as well.
But now, since you have revealed such overwhelming proof—
the secret sign of our bed, which no one's ever seen
but you and I and a single handmaid, Actoris,
the servant my father gave me when I came,
who kept the doors of our room you built so well . . .
you've conquered my heart, my hard heart, at last!"

The more she spoke, the more a deep desire for tears
welled up inside his breast—he wept as he held the wife

he loved, the soul of loyalty, in his arms at last.
Joy, warm as the joy that shipwrecked sailors feel
when they catch sight of land—Poseidon has struck
their well-rigged ship on the open sea with gale winds
and crushing walls of waves, and only a few escape, swimming,
struggling out of the frothing surf to reach the shore,
their bodies crusted with salt but buoyed up with joy
as they plant their feet on solid ground again,
spared a deadly fate. So joyous now to her
the sight of her husband, vivid in her gaze,
that her white arms, embracing his neck
would never for a moment let him go . . .
Dawn with her rose-red fingers might have shone
upon their tears, if with her glinting eyes
Athena had not thought of one more thing.
She held back the night, and night lingered long
at the western edge of the earth, while in the east
she reined in Dawn of the golden throne at Ocean's banks,
commanding her not to yoke the windswift team that brings
men light,
Blaze and Aurora, the young colts that race the Morning on.
Yet now Odysseus, seasoned veteran, said to his wife,
"Dear woman . . . we have still not reached the end
of all our trials. One more labor lies in store—
boundless, laden with danger, great and long,
and I must brave it out from start to finish.
So the ghost of Tiresias prophesied to me,
the day that I went down to the House of Death
to learn our best route home, my comrades' and my own.
But come, let's go to bed, dear woman—at long last
delight in sleep, delight in each other, come!"

"If it's bed you want," reserved Penelope replied,
"it's bed you'll have, whenever the spirit moves,
now that the gods have brought you home again
to native land, your grand and gracious house.
But since you've alluded to it,
since a god has put it in your mind,
please, tell me about this trial still to come.
I'm bound to learn of it later, I am sure—
what's the harm if I hear of it tonight?"
"Still so strange,"
Odysseus, the old master of stories, answered.
"Why again, why force me to tell you all?
Well, tell I shall. I'll hide nothing now.
But little joy it will bring you, I'm afraid,
as little joy for me.

The prophet said
that I must rove through towns on towns of men,
that I must carry a well-planed oar until
I come to a people who know nothing of the sea,
whose food is never seasoned with salt, strangers all
to ships with their crimson prows and long slim oars,
wings that make ships fly. And here is my sign,
he told me, clear, so clear I cannot miss it,
and I will share it with you now . . .
When another traveler falls in with me and calls
that weight across my shoulder a fan to winnow grain,
then, he told me, I must plant my oar in the earth
and sacrifice fine beasts to the lord god of the sea,
Poseidon—a ram, a bull and a ramping wild boar—
then journey home and render noble offerings up
to the deathless gods who rule the vaulting skies,
to all the gods in order.
And at last my own death will steal upon me . . .
a gentle, painless death, far from the sea it comes
to take me down, borne down with the years in ripe old age
with all my people here in blessed peace around me.
All this, the prophet said, will come to pass."

"And so," Penelope said, in her great wisdom,
"if the gods will really grant a happier old age,
there's hope that we'll escape our trials at last."

So husband and wife confided in each other,
while nurse and Eurynome, under the flaring brands,
were making up the bed with coverings deep and soft.
And working briskly, soon as they'd made it snug,
back to her room the old nurse went to sleep
as Eurynome, their attendant, torch in hand,
lighted the royal couple's way to bed and,
leading them to their chamber, slipped away.
Rejoicing in each other, they returned to their bed,
the old familiar place they loved so well.

Now Telemachus, the cowherd and the swineherd
rested their dancing feet and had the women do the same,
and across the shadowed hall the men lay down to sleep.

But the royal couple, once they'd reveled in all
the longed-for joys of love, reveled in each other's stories,
the radiant woman telling of all she'd borne at home,

watching them there, the infernal crowd of suitors
slaughtering herds of cattle and good fat sheep—
while keen to win her hand—
draining the broached vats dry of vintage wine.
And great Odysseus told his wife of all the pains
he had dealt out to other men and all the hardships
he'd endured himself—his story first to last—
and she listened on, enchanted . . .
Sleep never sealed her eyes till all was told.

He launched in with how he fought the Cicones down,
then how he came to the Lotus-eaters' lush green land.
Then all the crimes of the Cyclops and how he paid him back
for the gallant men the monster ate without a qualm—
then how he visited Aeolus, who gave him a hero's welcome
then he sent him off, but the homeward run was not his fate,
not yet—some sudden squalls snatched him away once more
and drove him over the swarming sea, groaning in despair.
Then how he moored at Telepylus, where Laestrygonians
wrecked his fleet and killed his men-at-arms.
He told her of Circe's cunning magic wiles
and how he voyaged down in his long benched ship
to the moldering House of Death, to consult Tiresias,
ghostly seer of Thebes, and he saw old comrades there
and he saw his mother, who bore and reared him as a child.
He told how he caught the Sirens' voices throbbing in the wind
and how he had scudded past the Clashing Rocks, past grim
Charybdis,
past Scylla—whom no rover had ever coasted by, home free—
and how his shipmates slaughtered the cattle of the Sun
and Zeus the king of thunder split his racing ship
with a reeking bolt and killed his hardy comrades,
all his fighting men at a stroke, but he alone
escaped their death at sea. He told how he reached
Ogygia's shores and the nymph Calypso held him back,
deep in her arching caverns, craving him for a husband—
cherished him, vowed to make him immortal, ageless, all his days,
yes, but she never won the heart inside him, never . . .
then how he reached the Phaeacians—heavy sailing there—
who with all their hearts had prized him like a god
and sent him off in a ship to his own beloved land,
giving him bronze and hoards of gold and robes . . .
and that was the last he told her, just as sleep
overcame him . . . sleep loosing his limbs,
slipping the toils of anguish from his mind.

Athena, her eyes afire, had fresh plans.
Once she thought he'd had his heart's content
of love and sleep at his wife's side, straightaway
she roused young Dawn from Ocean's banks to her golden throne
to bring men light and roused Odysseus too, who rose
from his soft bed and advised his wife in parting,
"Dear woman, we both have had our fill of trials.
You in our house, weeping over my journey home,
fraught with storms and torment, true, and I,
pinned down in pain by Zeus and other gods,
for all my desire, blocked from reaching home.
But now that we've arrived at our bed together—
the reunion that we yearned for all those years—
look after the things still left me in our house.
But as for the flocks those brazen suitors plundered,
much I'll recoup myself, making many raids;
the rest our fellow-Ithacans will supply
till all my folds are full of sheep again.
But now I must be off to the upland farm,
our orchard green with trees, to see my father,
good old man weighed down with so much grief for me.
And you, dear woman, sensible as you are,
I would advise you, still . . .
quick as the rising sun the news will spread
of the suitors that I killed inside the house.
So climb to your lofty chamber with your women.
Sit tight there. See no one. Question no one."

He strapped his burnished armor round his shoulders,
roused Telemachus, the cowherd and the swineherd,
and told them to take up weapons honed for battle.
They snapped to commands, harnessed up in bronze,
opened the doors and strode out, Odysseus in the lead.
By now the daylight covered the land, but Pallas,
shrouding them all in darkness,
quickly led the four men out of town.

## *Book 24: Peace: Odysseus Tests His Aged Father, Laertes*

*[After restoring order to his house, Odysseus seeks out his elderly father living simply in the countryside.]*

With that he passed his armor to his men
and in they went at once, his son as well. Odysseus
wandered off, approaching the thriving vineyard, searching,
picking his way down to the great orchard, searching,

but found neither Dolius nor his sons nor any hand.
They'd just gone off, old Dolius in the lead,
to gather stones for a dry retaining wall
to shore the vineyard up. But he did find
his father, alone, on that well-worked plot,
spading round a sapling—clad in filthy rags,
in a patched, unseemly shirt, and round his shins
he had some oxhide leggings strapped, patched too,
to keep from getting scraped, and gloves on his hands
to fight against the thorns, and on his head
he wore a goatskin skullcap
to cultivate his misery that much more . . .
Long-enduring Odysseus, catching sight of him now—
a man worn down with years, his heart racked with sorrow—
halted under a branching pear-tree, paused and wept.
Debating, head and heart, what should he do now?
Kiss and embrace his father, pour out the long tale—
how he had made the journey home to native land—
or probe him first and test him every way?
Torn, mulling it over, this seemed better:
test the old man first,
reproach him with words that cut him to the core.
Convinced, Odysseus went right up to his father.
Laertes was digging round the sapling, head bent low
as his famous offspring hovered over him and began,
"You want no skill, old man, at tending a garden.
All's well-kept here; not one thing in the plot,
no plant, no fig, no pear, no olive, no vine,
not a vegetable, lacks your tender, loving care.
But I must say—and don't be offended now—
your plants are doing better than yourself.
Enough to be stooped with age
but look how squalid you are, those shabby rags.
Surely it's not for sloth your master lets you go to seed.
There's nothing of slave about your build or bearing.
I have eyes: you look like a king to me. The sort
entitled to bathe, sup well, then sleep in a soft bed.
That's the right and pride of you old-timers.
Come now, tell me—in no uncertain terms—
whose slave are you? whose orchard are you tending?
And tell me this—I must be absolutely sure—
this place I've reached, is it truly Ithaca?
Just as that fellow told me, just now . . .
I fell in with him on the road here. Clumsy,
none too friendly, couldn't trouble himself
to hear me out or give me a decent answer

when I asked about a long-lost friend of mine,
whether he's still alive, somewhere in Ithaca,
or dead and gone already, lost in the House of Death.
Do you want to hear his story? Listen. Catch my drift.
I once played host to a man in my own country;
he'd come to my door, the most welcome guest
from foreign parts I ever entertained.
He claimed he came of good Ithacan stock,
said his father was Arcesius' son, Laertes.
So I took the new arrival under my own roof,
I gave him a hero's welcome, treated him in style—
stores in our palace made for princely entertainment.
And I gave my friend some gifts to fit his station,
handed him seven bars of well-wrought gold,
a mixing-bowl of solid silver, etched with flowers,
a dozen cloaks, unlined and light, a dozen rugs
and as many full-cut capes and shirts as well,
and to top it off, four women, perfect beauties
skilled in crafts—he could pick them out himself."

"Stranger," his father answered, weeping softly,
"the land you've reached is the very one you're after,
true, but it's in the grip of reckless, lawless men.
And as for the gifts you showered on your guest,
you gave them all for nothing.
But if you'd found him alive, here in Ithaca,
he would have replied in kind, with gift for gift,
and entertained you warmly before he sent you off.
That's the old custom, when one has led the way.
But tell me, please—in no uncertain terms—
how many years ago did you host the man,
that unfortunate guest of yours, my son . . .
there was a son, or was he all a dream?
That most unlucky man, whom now, I fear,
far from his own soil and those he loves,
the fish have swallowed down on the high seas
or birds and beasts on land have made their meal.
Nor could the ones who bore him—mother, father—
wrap his corpse in a shroud and mourn him deeply.
Nor could his warm, generous wife, so self-possessed,
Penelope, ever keen for her husband on his deathbed,
the fit and proper way, or close his eyes at last.
These are the solemn honors owed the dead.
But tell me your own story—that I'd like to know:
Who are you? where are you from? your city? your parents?

Where does the ship lie moored that brought you here,
your hardy shipmates too? Or did you arrive
as a passenger aboard some stranger's craft
and men who put you ashore have pulled away?"
"The whole tale,"
his crafty son replied, "I'll tell you start to finish.
I come from Roamer-Town, my home's a famous place,
my father's Unsparing, son of old King Pain,
and my name's Man of Strife . . .
I sailed from Sicily, aye, but some ill wind
blew me here, off course—much against my will—
and my ship lies moored off farmlands far from town.
As for Odysseus, well, five years have passed
since he left my house and put my land behind him,
luckless man! But the birds were good as he launched out,
all on the right, and I rejoiced as I sent him off
and he rejoiced in sailing. We had high hopes
we'd meet again as guests, as old friends,
and trade some shining gifts."
At those words
a black cloud of grief came shrouding over Laertes.
Both hands clawing the ground for dirt and grime,
he poured it over his grizzled head, sobbing, in spasms.
Odysseus' heart shuddered, a sudden twinge went shooting up
through his nostrils, watching his dear father struggle . . .
He sprang toward him, kissed him, hugged him, crying,
"Father—I am your son—myself, the man you're seeking,
home after twenty years, on native ground at last!
Hold back your tears, your grief.
Let me tell you the news, but we must hurry—
I've cut the suitors down in our own house,
I've paid them back their outrage, vicious crimes!"
"Odysseus . . ."
Laertes, catching his breath, found words to answer.
"You—you're truly my son, Odysseus, home at last?
Give me a sign, some proof—I must be sure."
"This scar first,"
quick to the mark, his son said, "look at this—
the wound I took from the boar's white tusk
on Mount Parnassus. There you'd sent me, you
and mother, to see her fond old father, Autolycus,
and collect the gifts he vowed to give me, once,
when he came to see us here.
Or these, these trees—
let me tell you the trees you gave me years ago,

here on this well-worked plot . . .
I begged you for everything I saw, a little boy
trailing you through the orchard, picking our way
among these trees, and you named them one by one.
You gave me thirteen pear, ten apple trees
and forty figs—and promised to give me, look,
fifty vinerows, bearing hard on each other's heels,
clusters of grapes year-round at every grade of ripeness,
mellowed as Zeus's seasons weigh them down."
Living proof—
and Laertes' knees went slack, his heart surrendered,
recognizing the strong clear signs Odysseus offered.
He threw his arms around his own dear son, fainting
as hardy great Odysseus hugged him to his heart
until he regained his breath, came back to life
and cried out, "Father Zeus—
you gods of Olympus, you still rule on high
if those suitors have truly paid in blood
for all their reckless outrage! Oh, but now
my heart quakes with fear that all the Ithacans
will come down on us in a pack, at any time,
and rush the alarm through every island town!"

"There's nothing to fear," his canny son replied,
"put it from your mind. Let's make for your lodge
beside the orchard here. I sent Telemachus on ahead,
the cowherd, swineherd too, to fix a hasty meal."

## Sappho (c. 610–c. 580 BCE)

For conveying the felt immediacy of the situations she represents, Sappho's lyric poems are unparalleled in ancient Greece. Homer composes his narrative almost exclusively in the third person. Pindar may speak about himself more often than Homer does, but the Pindaric lyric "I" is largely a public persona performing his function as encomiastic poet (a poet whose aim is to praise). With Sappho, the "I" is more profoundly individualized. In the second poem included here, for example, Sappho says that truth is not a matter of repeating conventional understandings, but the power of subjective experience, particularly of the soul's experience of love, or *eros:*

> Some say a cavalry corps,
> some infantry, some again
> will maintain that the swift oars
> of our fleet are the finest
> sight on dark earth; but I say
> that whatever one loves is.

The word "lesbian" is derived from Lesbos, the island where Sappho may have been born and composed her poems, some of which tell of her passionate attraction to women such as the Anactoria of this poem. Sappho is the only female ancient Greek poet whose work has survived. We know very little for certain about her life.

Like most of Sappho's lyrics, the poems included are composed in what came to be called the Sapphic stanza consisting of three long lines and a short one. The poems were meant to be sung, accompanied by a lyre—hence the term "lyric" poetry. In their immediacy and the transparency of their feeling, Sappho's poems resemble some of the love songs in the ancient Chinese *Book of Songs*.

Except for the first one we have included, all of Sappho's poems have come down to us in fragments. The numbers of the poems refer to the ordering in the standard edition of E. Lobel and Denys Page, *Poetarum Lesbiorum Fragmenta* (Oxford: Oxford University Press, 1955).

## *1: "Bright-throned, undying Aphrodite"*

*Translated by J.V. Cunningham*

Bright-throned, undying Aphrodite,
God's child, manipulator, hear me!
Destroy not with anguish and heartbreak,
    Lady, my spirit,

But come to me here if other times
You ever my voice in the distance
Have heard, and, leaving your father's house,
    Have come, your golden

Chariots yoked, your beautiful swift
Sparrows, dense-winged, spiraling above
The black earth, from th'heavenly aether
    Through the middle air,

And now here. You, of the Lucky Ones,
With a smile on your undying face,
Asked what now is the matter with me?
    Why now do I call?

What do I most wish for myself
In my mad heart? "Who is it I must
Now win over for you? Who, Sappho,
    Is unfair to you?

She who avoids will soon be seeking;
Who gives back gifts will be giving hers;

Who does not love will soon be in love,
    If unwillingly."

Come once more! This hard-to-be-dealt with
Anxiety loosen, and what my
Spirit would have let it have, yourself
    My fellow-soldier.

## *16: To an Army Wife, in Sardis*

*Translated by Mary Barnard*

Some say a cavalry corps,
some infantry, some, again,
will maintain that the swift oars

of our fleet are the finest
sight on dark earth; but I say
that whatever one loves, is.

This is easily proved: did
not Helen—she who had scanned
the flower of the world's manhood—

choose as first among men one
who laid Troy's honor in ruin?
warped to his will, forgetting

love due her own blood, her own
child, she wandered far with him.
So Anactoria, although you

being far away forget us,
the dear sound of your footstep
and light glancing in your eyes

would move me more than glitter
of Lydian horse or armored
tread of mainland infantry.

## *31: "He is, I should say, on a level"*

*Translated by J.V. Cunningham*

He is, I should say, on a level
With deity, the man who sits over

Against you, and attends to the nearby
Sweetness of your voice

And charm of your laughter. I tell you
It frightens the quick heart in my breast.
For, soon as I look at you, there is
No voice left to me,

My tongue has been fractured, a thin fire
Instantly runs underneath my skin.
My eyes cannot see anything, and
My ears re-echo.

I am in a cold sweat, a trembling
Seizes me all over, and, pallid
As range grass, I think I am almost
On the point of death.

## Pindar (c. 522–c. 440 BCE)

Most of Pindar's complete poems that have come down to us are *epinikia,* poems or "odes" in praise of athletes after their victories in the athletic games held at Olympia, Nemea, Delphi, and the Isthmus of Corinth. Athletes from throughout the Greek world competed at these games. The ode itself was usually sung and danced not at the site of the games themselves but in the victor's home town at the time of his return. Pindar was commissioned by a member of the victor's family; he was a professional poet, paid by an aristocratic patron, and virtually every word of each ode was spoken in order to praise the victor and his family. A lesser poet than Pindar would have turned such an ode into an occasion for mere flattery, always a danger in writing encomia. It was Pindar's genius that enabled him to celebrate the occasion by placing the particular victory within the broadest context of human experience.

The moment of victory is celebrated by Pindar as an epiphany. The poet lauds the victor for achieving success largely through his own efforts, but, Pindar insists, the victory could never have been achieved had the moment not been prepared for by the victor's heritage—both immediate and remote—and by the gods themselves. The way in which the poet reminds his audience, at the time of a person's greatest achievement, of the insignificance of the merely human in comparison with the divine, and of the fleeting—but real—quality of human achievement is quintessentially Pindaric. Pindar's odes celebrate that moment when, as he unforgettably says in his eighth Pythian ode, the "godsent brightness" shines briefly upon men (women did not compete in the athletic games).

The metaphorical brilliance and noble austerity of Pindar's language, his imaginative sweep, and his swift transitions have been the envy of many poets in the

Western tradition who have often tried, and almost always failed, to revive and re-create the Pindaric mode.

The brief but very beautiful "Olympian 14" celebrates the victory of Asopichos of Orchomenos in the boys' foot race, c. 488 BCE. It is typically Pindaric in the way it celebrates the victory by concluding with a moving allusion to the reality of death, as we feel the palpable absence of the young boy's dead father, who cannot bask in the glory of his son's victory. The poem is formally atypical in the sense that, unlike "Pythian 3," it is not triadic (i.e., it consists of two rather than three strophes or stanzas). Pindar's victory odes usually feature *strophe, antistrophe,* and *epode* (sometimes translated as "turn," "counterturn," and "stand," referring to the movements of the dancing chorus); the strophe and antistrophe correspond metrically. While "Pythian 3" is formally typical of Pindar's odes, the occasion of the poem—which is not entirely clear—is not a celebration of a recent athletic victory. It is rather a poem of consolation, written to one of Pindar's patrons, Hieron of Syracuse, who is in failing health. In its insistence on, and its powerful exemplification of, the idea that the experience of poetry is valuable in helping to balance the emotions, this ode would certainly have appealed to Confucius, who made similar points about the ancient *Book of Songs.*

## *Olympian 14*

*Translated by Frank J. Nisetich*

You who dwell by the waters of Kaphisos,
in the country where bright colts are bred,
ladies whose tuneful voices
haunt the lanes of glittering Orchomenos
and who guard the Minyans born of old,
hear me, Graces, for I pray:
if anything sweet or delightful
warms the heart of any mortal man,
whether he has beauty, or skill,
or the light of victory shining upon him,
it is your gift.
Even the gods depend on you
and would renounce
ordering the dance and feast
without your favor.
Of all that is done in heaven you have charge.
Seated beside Pythian Apollo,
god of the golden bow, your worship makes
the Olympian father's glory stream forever.

O lady Aglaia! Euphrosyna, lover of song!
Daughters of the strongest god, hear me,
and hear me, Thalia, who delight in music:

look with favor now upon this chorus
stepping lightly.
In Lydian measures and chosen phrases,
I come singing of Asopichos,
because his home,
the city of the Minyan people,
by your blessing
has triumphed at Olympia.
Now go, Echo, go
to the dark walls
of Persephone's house,
bearing the proud announcement to his father,
and when you've found Kleodamos, tell him
how his boy, in the cleft of Pisa's hills
where glory begins its flight, has wreathed his hair
with the radiant wings of victory.

## *Pythian 3*

*Translated by Steven Shankman*

For Hieron, ruler of Syracuse, who is currently in ill health, Pindar offers this Pythian ode, in which Apollo—who is worshiped at Pytho and who is himself a healer—looms large.

*Strophe I*

I wish—were it permissible to utter
The prayer that is on everybody's lips—
That Chiron, son of Kronos and Philyra,
Now were alive; and that this Centaur, beast
Yet friend to men, were ruling still the glens
Of Pelion, as he did when once he reared
Asklepios, gentle maker of those cures
That strengthen limbs and bring relief from pains,
That savior who protects men from disease.

*Antistrophe I*

Before the mother of Asklepios
Had given birth, with Eleithuia's help,
She made the deep descent to Hades' house,
Struck by the golden shafts of Artemis.
It was Apollo's will. Beware the wrath
Of Zeus's children! Phlegyas's daughter
Slighted the god. She yielded to a lover
Without her father's blessing—she who before
Slept with Apollo of the unshorn hair

*Epode I*

And carried his pure seed. She did not wait
For the arrival of the marriage feast
Or for the sound of full-voiced bridal songs,
The sorts of songs young virgins of her age
Like playfully to sing on wedding nights.
She yearned for the remote, as many do.
There is a foolish type of person who,
Scorning familiar things, seeks the exotic,
Hunting elusive prey with empty hopes.

*Strophe 2*

Fair-robed Koronis—she it was who caught
This great infatuation, lying with
A stranger from Arkadia. The Watcher,
Apollo, off in sheep-receiving Pytho,
Watched nonetheless, for his all-knowing mind—
His surest confidant—revealed the truth.
Apollo does not flirt with lies; no god
Or mortal can, with deeds or plots, deceive him.

*Antistrophe 2*

Learning of her liaison with a stranger
And of her lawless treachery, he sent
His sister, raging with resistless might,
Into Lakeria; for the Virgin Goddess
Lived near the banks of the Boebian lake.
The fortune of Koronis now turned tragic.
She perished, and her neighbors shared her fate:
Just so a single spark ignites a forest.

*Epode 2*

But when her kinsmen placed the girl inside
The wooden walls destined to be her pyre,
And the fierce flame of Lord Hephaistos scorched her,
Apollo cried, "I can endure no longer
To allow a child of my own to share
Its mother's grievous death and suffering!"
He spoke, and with a giant step he seized
The child and ripped it from its mother's corpse.
The flaming pyre had cleared a path of light.
Cradling the boy, he trusted him to Chiron
To teach the child the art of medicine.

*Strophe 3*

Those suffering with sores bred by disease,
Or with limbs seared by hoary bronze or bruised
By rocks thrown from afar, or those whose bodies
Were wracked by summer's heat or winter's cold—
All these Asklepios released from pain,
Tending to some with soothing incantations,
Pouring, for others, gentle potions, or
Swathing their limbs with ointments; some required
The surgeon's knife to bring them back to health.

*Antistrophe 3*

But even such expertise can be corrupted.
Gold, with its heady power, now appearing
Tangibly present in his hands, lured on
Asklepios to bring back from the dead
One of death's captives. Then the son of Kronos
With his hands heaved his shafts and seized the life
From both their hearts. His gleaming thunderbolt
Hurled doom. We mortals must seek from the gods
Things suitable to mortal thoughts, aware
Of what is at our feet, what lot is ours.

*Epode 3*

Do not, dear soul, yearn for immortal life
But rather make full use of each resource
Firmly within your reach. Oh, how I wish
Wise Chiron were still living in his cave,
And that my honey-sounding songs could charm
His soul! I would persuade him, even now,
To grant good health to noble men who ail,
To bless them with the gift of a physician,
Namely Asklepios, or Lord Apollo.
I would set sail, across the Ionian sea,
To Arethusa and my Aetnean host

*Strophe 4*

Who rules, as king, over the Syracusans,
Gentle to citizens, to nobles kind,
By strangers loved as if he were their father.
If I had come bringing the double blessings
Of golden health and epinician song
As an adornment to the Pythian wreaths

Of triumph won by famed Pherenikos,
Your horse, at Kirrha once—I then could boast
That I arrived there as a beaming star!

*Antistrophe 4*

But now I wish to pray to Mother Rhea,
Whose godhead maidens often celebrate
With Pan's, at my front door, at evensong.
Since, Hieron, you are well schooled and know
The ancient poets and have learned their lessons,
You know for every blessing the immortals
Mete out two shares of suffering to men.
Fools cannot take such troubles in their stride,
But good men can, turning the fair part outward.

*Epode 4*

Fair fortune follows you. If any man
Is blessed, it is the leader of his people.
No life, however blessed, is free from sorrow.
This maxim holds even for Peleus,
Aiakos' son, and for the godlike Kadmos.
These reached, they say, the bounds of human joy.
They heard the Muses-with-gold-headbands singing
In seven-gated Thebes and on the mountain
When Kadmos wed ox-eyed Harmonia
And Peleus married Thetis, Nereus' daughter.

*Strophe 5*

They banqueted with gods; they saw the lordly
Children of Kronos on their golden thrones;
Received their wedding gifts. By grace of Zeus
Their spirits—sunk by former troubles—soared.
But soon the bitter fate of his three daughters
Robbed Kadmos of his share of joy, although
His daughter Semele was loved by Zeus;

*Antistrophe 5*

And Peleus' son—the only child that Thetis,
A goddess, bore in Phthia—died in battle.
An arrow tore the life from him. His pyre,
Burning, brought cries of sorrow from the Greeks.
If any mortal knows the way of truth,
He knows he should rejoice when life is blessed.
The gusting winds blow one way, then abruptly

Shift their direction. Great prosperity,
With its full weight soon falling from above,
Is not our human lot for very long.

*Epode 5*

I shall be small in small times, great in great ones.
I lovingly shall honor with devotion
The spirit who directs my present fortunes
And I shall make full use of each resource
Firmly within my reach. If God sends wealth,
Then lofty fame may also grace my future.
Nestor and Lykian Sarpedon live
Through famous poems fashioned by skilled craftsmen.
Virtue endures through fabled song, a task
Accomplished with much ease by very few.

## THUCYDIDES (5TH CENT. BCE)

Herodotus (b. 490–480 BCE) was the first Greek historian; his subject was the great conflict between Greece and Persia. The next Greek historian was Thucydides (fifth century BCE), the great analyst of the sources of the epochal upheaval in Hellas that we now call the Peloponnesian War. This is the event that provoked Plato's therapeutic vision of philosophy, just as the political turmoil of the Spring and Autumn (722–481 BCE) and Warring States (403–222 BCE) periods in China engendered Confucius and Laozi.

Thucydides locates the source of the conflict between the two major protagonists in their distinctive characters—the restlessly experimental city of Athens and the more conservative Sparta. The description of the Athenians by the Corinthians, included here, brilliantly captures the rationalist ethos of the Athenians in the fifth century BCE. This description has literary analogues in the Oedipus of Sophocles' *Oedipus the King,* the Pisthetairos of Aristophanes' *The Birds,* and the Odysseus of Sophocles' *Philoctetes.* In Thucydides' portrait we can see the excesses of a typically Western rationalism that persists into our own day. Focusing on the period 431–404 BCE, Thucydides tells the tale of the fall of his noble but flawed protagonist, the city of Athens. We have included those parts of Thucydides' history that trace this tragic downfall. At the outset of the war, democratic Athens flourished under the enlightened leadership of Pericles, but once less responsible leaders, such as Alcibiades, seduced the people, disasters—such as the ill-fated Sicilian expedition—soon followed. Thucydides' descriptions are vivid, and the speeches of his characters are dramatic and believable.

Despite his implicit critique of the excesses of Athenian rationalism, Thucydides himself does not quite escape its orbit. In the first selection included here, it appears that Thucydides, although a historian, has little reverence for the past per se. He considers his own era to be unquestionably the most important in the history of humanity. He believes his method for arriving at historical truth is far superior to that of Homer, who was a mere "poet displaying the exaggeration of his craft"; and he believes it is superior as well as to the method of Herodotus in his *Histories,* an example of "the compositions of chroniclers that are attractive at truth's expense." Thucydides' view of the past stands in stark contrast to that of the Chinese historian Sima Qian (145–86? BCE), whose reverence for the work of his predecessors is profound. Sima Qian underwent the punishment of castration rather than choose the "nobler" alternative of suicide, in order to continue the historical work of his father. Thucydides, in contrast, believes he must—at least figuratively—kill off his fathers in order to establish the legitimacy of his own enterprise.

## *from The Peloponnesian War*

*Translated by Richard Crawley*

### *Book 1, chs. 70–71: Speech of the Corinthians, at the congress of the Peloponnesian confederacy at Sparta, describing the character of the Athenians.*

'We hope that none of you will consider these words of remonstrance to be rather words of hostility; men remonstrate with friends who are in error, reserving accusations for enemies who have wronged them. **[70.]** Besides, we consider that we have as good a right as anyone to point out a neighbour's faults, particularly when we contemplate the great contrast between the two national characters, a contrast of which, as far as we can see, you have little perception, having never yet considered what sort of antagonists you will encounter in the Athenians, how widely, how absolutely different from yourselves. The Athenians are addicted to innovation, and their designs are characterized by swiftness alike in conception and execution; you have a genius for keeping what you have got, accompanied by a total want of invention, and when forced to act you never go far enough. Again, they are adventurous beyond their power, and daring beyond their judgment, and in danger they are sanguine; your wont is to attempt less than is justified by your power, to mistrust even what is sanctioned by your judgment, and to fancy that from danger there is no release. Further, there is promptitude on their side against procrastination on yours; they are never at home, you are never from it: for they hope by their absence to extend their acquisitions, you fear by your advance to endanger what you have left behind. They are swift to follow up a success, and slow to recoil from a reverse. Their bodies they spend ungrudgingly in their country's cause; their intellect they jealously husband to be employed in her service. A scheme unexecuted is with them a positive loss, a successful enterprise a comparative failure. The deficiency created by the miscarriage of an undertaking is soon filled up by fresh hopes; for they alone are enabled to call a thing hoped for a thing got, by the speed with which they act upon their resolutions. Thus they toil on in trouble and danger all the days of their lives, with little opportunity for enjoying, being ever engaged in getting: their only idea of a holiday is to do what the occasion demands, and to them laborious occupation is less of a misfortune than the peace of a quiet life. To describe their character in a word, one might truly say that they were born into the world to take no rest themselves and to give none to others.

**[71.]** 'Such is Athens, your antagonist. And yet, Lacedæmonians, you still delay, and fail to see that peace stays longest with those who are not more careful to use their power justly than to show their determination not to submit to injustice. On the contrary, your ideal of fair dealing is based on the principle that if you do not injure others, you need not risk your own fortunes in preventing others from injuring you. Now you could scarcely have succeeded in such a policy even with a neighbour like yourselves; but in the present instance, as we have just shown, your habits are old-fashioned as compared with theirs. It is the law as in art, so in politics, that improvements ever prevail; and though fixed usages may be best for undisturbed communities, constant necessities of action must be accompanied by the constant improvement of methods. Thus it happens that the vast experience of Athens has carried her further than you on the path of innovation.

'Here, at least, let your procrastination end. For the present, assist your allies and Potidæa in particular, as you promised, by a speedy invasion of Attica, and do not sacrifice friends and kindred to their bitterest enemies, and drive the rest of us in despair to some other alliance. Such a step would not be condemned either by the gods who received our oaths, or by the men who witnessed them. The breach of a treaty cannot be laid to the people whom desertion compels to seek new relations, but to the power that fails to assist its confederate. But if you will only act, we will stand by you; it would be unnatural for us to change, and never should we meet with such a congenial ally. For these reasons choose the right course, and endeavour not to let Peloponnese under your supremacy degenerate from the prestige that it enjoyed under that of your ancestors.'

## *Book I, ch. 84–85: From the speech of Archidamos, the Spartan king, at the same congress—description of the character of the Spartans.*

**[84.]** 'And the slowness and procrastination, the parts of our character that are most assailed by their criticism, need not make you blush. If we undertake the war without preparation, we should by hastening its commencement only delay its conclusion: further, a free and a famous city has through all time been ours. The quality which they condemn is really nothing but a wise moderation; thanks to its possession, we alone do not become insolent in success, and give way less than others in misfortune; we are not carried away by the pleasure of hearing ourselves cheered on to risks which our judgment condemns; nor, if annoyed, are we any the more convinced by attempts to exasperate us by accusation. We are both warlike and wise, and it is our sense of order that makes us so. We are warlike, because self-control contains honor as a chief constituent, and honor bravery. And we are wise, because we are educated with too little learning to despise the laws, and with too severe a self-control to disobey them, and are brought up not to be too knowing in useless matters—such as the knowledge which can give a specious criticism of an enemy's plans in theory, but fails to assail them with equal success in practice—but are taught to consider that the schemes of our enemies are not dissimilar to our own, and that the freaks of chance are not determinable by calculation. In practice we always base our preparations against an enemy on the assumption that his plans are good; indeed, it is right to rest our hopes not on a belief in his blunders, but on the soundness of our provisions. Nor ought we to believe that there is much difference between man and man, but to think that the superiority lies with him who is reared in the severest school.

**[85.]** These practices, then, which our ancestors have delivered to us, and by whose maintenance we have always profited, must not be given up. And we must not be hurried into deciding in a day's brief space a question which concerns many lives and fortunes and many cities, and in which honor is deeply involved—but we must decide calmly. This our strength peculiarly enables us to do."

. . . Such were the words of Archidamos.

## *Book II, chs. 34–46: Pericles' Funeral Oration*

**[34.]** In the same winter the Athenians gave a funeral at the public cost to those who had first fallen in this war. It was a custom of their ancestors, and the manner of it is as follows. Three days before the ceremony, the bones of the dead are laid out in a tent which has been erected; and their friends bring to their relatives such offerings as they please. In the funeral procession cypress coffins are borne on wagons, one for each tribe, the bones of the deceased being placed in the coffin of their tribe. Among these is carried one empty bier decked for the missing, that is, for those whose bodies could not be recovered. Any citizen or stranger who pleases joins in the procession: and the female relatives are there to wail at the burial. The dead are laid in the public sepulchre in the most beautiful suburb of the city, in which those who fall in war are always buried—with the exception of those slain at Marathon, who for their singular and extraordinary valor were interred on the spot where they fell. After the bodies have been laid in the earth, a man chosen by the state, of approved wisdom and eminent reputation, pronounces over them an appropriate panegyric, after which all retire. Such is the manner of the burying; and throughout the whole of the war, whenever the occasion arose, the established custom was observed. Meanwhile these were the first that had fallen, and Pericles, son of Xanthippus, was chosen to pronounce their eulogium. When the proper time arrived, he advanced from the sepulchre to an elevated platform in order to be heard by as many of the crowd as possible, and spoke as follows:

**[35.]** 'Most of my predecessors in this place have commended him who made this speech part of the law, telling us that it is well that it should be delivered at the burial of those who fall in battle. For myself, I should have thought that the worth which had displayed itself in deeds would be sufficiently rewarded by honors also shown by deeds, such as you now see in this funeral prepared at the people's cost. And I could have wished that the reputations of many brave men were not to be imperilled in the mouth of a single individual, to stand or fall according as he spoke well or ill. For it is hard to speak properly upon a subject where it is even difficult to convince your hearers that you are speaking the truth. On the one hand, the friend who is familiar with every fact of the story may think that some point has not been set forth with that fullness which he wishes and knows it to deserve; on the other, he who is a stranger to the matter may be led by envy to suspect exaggeration if he hears anything above his own nature. For men can endure to hear others praised only so long as they can severally persuade themselves of their own ability to equal the actions recounted: when this point is passed, envy comes in and with it incredulity. However, since our ancestors have stamped this custom with their approval, it becomes my duty to obey the law and to try to satisfy your several wishes and opinions as best I may.

**[36.]** 'I shall begin with our ancestors: it is both just and proper that they should have the honor of the first mention on an occasion like the present. They dwelt in the country without break in the succession from generation to generation, and handed it down free to the present time by their valor. And if our more remote ancestors deserve praise, much more do our own fathers, who added to their inheritance the empire which we now possess, and spared no pains to be able to leave their acquisitions to us of the present generation. Lastly, there are few parts of our dominions that have not been augmented by those of us here, who are still more or less in the vigour of life; and the mother country has been furnished by us with everything that can enable her to depend on her own resources whether for war or for peace. That part of our history which tells of the military achievements which gave us our several possessions, or of the ready valor with which either we or our fathers stemmed the tide of Hellenic or foreign aggression, is a theme too familiar to my hearers for me to dilate on, and I shall therefore pass it by. But by what road we reached our position, under what form of government our greatness grew, out of what national habits it sprang—these are subjects which I may pursue before I proceed to my panegyric upon these men; for I think them to be themes upon which on the present occasion a speaker may properly dwell, and to which the whole assemblage, whether citizens or foreigners, may listen with advantage.

**[37.]** 'Our constitution does not copy the laws of neighbouring states; we are rather a pattern to others than imitators ourselves. Its administration favours the many instead of the few; this is why it is called a democracy. If we look to the laws, they afford equal justice to all in their private differences; if to social standing, advancement in public life falls to reputation for capacity, class considerations not being allowed to interfere with merit; nor again does poverty bar the way: if a man is able to serve the state, he is not hindered by the obscurity of his condition. The freedom which we enjoy in our government extends also to our ordinary life. There, far from exercising a jealous surveillance over each other, we do not feel called upon to be angry with our neighbour for doing what he likes, or even to indulge in those injurious looks which cannot fail to be offensive, although they inflict no positive penalty. But all this ease in our private relations does not make us lawless as citizens. Against this fear is our chief safeguard, teaching us to obey the magistrates and the laws, particularly such as regard the protection of the injured, whether they are actually on the statute book, or belong to that code which, although unwritten, yet cannot be broken without acknowledged disgrace.

**[38.]** 'Further, we provide plenty of means for the mind to refresh itself from business. We celebrate games and sacrifices all the year round, and the elegance of our private establishments forms a daily source of pleasure and helps to banish our cares; and the magnitude of our city draws the produce of the world into our harbour, so that to the Athenian the fruits of other countries are as familiar a luxury as those of his own.

**[39.]** 'If we turn to our military policy, there also we differ from our antagonists. We throw open our city to the world, and never by alien acts exclude foreigners from any opportunity of learning or observing, although the eyes of an enemy may occasionally profit by our liberality; we trust less in system and policy than in the native spirit of our citizens; and in education, where our rivals from their very cradles by a painful discipline seek after manliness, at Athens we live exactly as we please, and yet are just as ready to encounter every legitimate danger. In proof of this it may be noticed that the Lacedæmonians do not invade our country alone, but bring with them all their confederates, while we Athenians advance unsupported into the territory of a neighbour, and fighting upon a foreign soil usually vanquish with ease men who are defending their homes. Our united force was never yet encountered by any enemy, because we have at once to attend to our marine and to despatch our citizens by land upon a hundred different services; thus wherever they engage with some such fraction of our strength, a success against a detachment is magnified into a victory over the nation, and a defeat into a reverse suffered at the hands of our entire people. And yet if with habits not of labour but of ease, and courage not of art but of nature, we are still willing to encounter danger, we have the double advantage of escaping the experience of hardships in anticipation and of facing them in the hour of need as fearlessly as those who are never free from them.

'Nor are these the only points in which our city is worthy of admiration.

**[40.]** We cultivate refinement without extravagance and knowledge without effeminacy; wealth we employ more for use than for show, and place the real disgrace of poverty not in owning to the fact but in declining the struggle against it. Our public men have, besides politics, their private affairs to attend to, and our ordinary citizens, though occupied with the pursuits of industry, are still fair judges of public matters; for, unlike any other nation, regarding him who takes no part in these duties not as unambitious but as useless, we Athenians are able to judge at all events if we cannot originate, and instead of looking on discussion as a stumbling-block in the way of action, we think it an indispensable preliminary to any wise action at all. Again, in our enterprises we present the singular spectacle of daring and deliberation, each carried to its highest point, and both united in the same persons, although usually decision is the fruit of ignorance, hesitation of reflection. But the palm of courage will surely be adjudged most justly to those who best know the difference between hardship and pleasure and yet are never tempted to shrink from danger. In generosity we are equally singular, acquiring our friends by conferring, not by receiving, favours. Yet, of course, the doer of the favour is the firmer friend of the two, in order by continued kindness to keep the recipient in his debt, while the debtor feels less keenly from the very consciousness that the return he makes will be a payment, not a free gift. And it is only the Athenians who, fearless of consequences, confer their benefits not from calculations of expediency, but in the confidence of liberality.

**[41.]** 'In short, I say that as a city we are the school of Hellas; and I doubt if the world can produce a man, who where he has only himself to depend upon, is equal to so many emergencies, and graced by so happy a versatility as the Athenian. And that this is no mere boast thrown out for the occasion, but plain matter of fact, the power of the state acquired by these habits proves. For Athens alone of her contemporaries is found when tested to be greater than her reputation, and alone gives no occasion to her assailants to blush at the antagonist by whom they have been worsted, or to her subjects to question her title by merit to rule. Rather, the admiration of the present and succeeding ages will be ours, since we have not left our power without witness, but have shown it by mighty proofs; and far from needing a Homer for our panegyrist, or other of his craft whose verses might charm for the moment only for the impression which they gave to melt at the touch of fact, we have forced every sea and land to be the highway of our daring, and everywhere, whether for evil or for good, have left imperishable monuments behind us. Such is the Athens for which these men, in the assertion of their resolve not to lose her, nobly fought and died; and well may every one of their survivors be ready to suffer in her cause.

**[42.]** 'Indeed if I have dwelt at some length upon the character of our country, it has been to show that our stake in the struggle is not the same as theirs who have no such blessings to lose, and also that the panegyric of the men over whom I am now speaking might be by definite proofs established. That panegyric is now in a great measure complete; for the Athens that I have celebrated is only what the heroism of these and their like have made her, men whose fame, unlike that of most Hellenes, will be found to be only commensurate with their deserts. And if a test of worth be wanted, it is to be found in their closing scene, and this not only in the cases in which it set the final seal upon their merit, but also in those in which it gave the first intimation of their having any. For there is justice in the claim that steadfastness in his country's battles should be as a cloak to cover a man's other imperfections; for the good action has blotted out the bad, and his merit as a citizen more than outweighed his demerits as an individual. But none of these allowed either wealth with its prospect of future enjoyment to unnerve his spirit, or poverty with its hope of a day of freedom and riches to tempt him to shrink from danger. No, holding that vengeance upon their enemies was more to be desired than any personal blessings, and reckoning this to be the most glorious of hazards, they joyfully determined to accept the risk, to make sure of their vengeance and to let their wishes wait; and while committing to hope the uncertainty of final success, in the business before them they thought fit to act boldly and trust in themselves. Thus choosing to die resisting, rather than to live submitting, they fled only from dishonour, but met danger face to face, and after one brief moment, while at the summit of their fortune, escaped, not from their fear, but from their glory.

**[43.]** 'So died these men as became Athenians. You, their survivors, must determine to have as unaltering a resolution in the field, though you may pray that it may have a happier issue. And not contented with ideas derived only from words of the advantages which are bound up with the defence of your country, though these would furnish a valuable text to a speaker even before an audience so alive to them as the present, you must yourselves realize the power of Athens, and feed your eyes upon her from day to day, till love of her fills your hearts; and then when all her greatness shall break upon you, you must reflect that it was by courage, sense of duty, and a keen feeling of honor in action that men were enabled to win all this, and that no personal failure in an enterprise could make them consent to deprive their country of their valour, but they laid it at her feet as the most glorious contribution that they could offer. For this offering of their lives made in common by them all they each of them individually received that renown which never grows old, and for a sepulchre, not so much that in which their bones have been deposited, but that noblest of shrines wherein their glory is laid up to be eternally remembered upon every occasion on which deed or story shall call for its commemoration. For heroes have the whole earth for their tomb; and in lands far from their own, where the column with its epitaph declares it, there is enshrined in every breast a record unwritten with no tablet to preserve it, except that of the heart. These take as your model, and judging happiness to be the fruit of freedom and freedom of valour, never decline the dangers of war. For it is not the miserable that would most justly be unsparing of their lives; these have nothing to hope for: it is rather they to whom continued life may bring reverses as yet unknown, and to whom a fall, if it came, would be most tremendous in its consequences. And surely, to a man of spirit, the degradation of cowardice must be immeasurably more grievous than the unfelt death which strikes him in the midst of his strength and patriotism!

**[44.]** 'Comfort, therefore, not condolence, is what I have to offer to the parents of the dead who may be here. Numberless are the chances to which, as they know, the life of man is subject; but fortunate indeed are they who draw for their lot a death so glorious as that which has caused your mourning, and to whom life has been so exactly measured as to terminate in the happiness in which it has been passed. Still I know that this is a hard saying, especially when those are in question of whom you will constantly be reminded by seeing in the homes of others blessings of which once you also boasted: for grief is felt not so much for the want of what we have never known, as for the loss of that to which we have been long accustomed. Yet you who are still of an age to beget children must bear up in the hope of having others in their stead; not only will they help you to forget those whom you have lost, but will be to the state at once a reinforcement and a security; for never can a fair or just policy be expected of the citizen who does not, like his fellows, bring to the decision the interests and apprehensions of a father. And those of you who have passed your prime must congratulate yourselves with the thought that the best part of your life was fortunate, and that the brief span that remains will be cheered by the fame of the departed. For it is only the love of honour that never grows old; and honour it is, not gain, as some would have it, that rejoices the heart of age and helplessness.

**[45.]** 'Turning to the sons or brothers of the dead, I see an arduous struggle before you. When a man is gone, all are wont to praise him, and should your merit be ever so transcendent, you will still find it difficult not merely to overtake, but even to approach their renown. The living have envy to contend with, while those who are no longer in our path are honored with a goodwill into which rivalry does not enter. On the other hand, if I must say anything on the subject of female excellence to those of you who will now be in widowhood, it will be all comprised in this brief exhortation. Great will be your glory in not falling short of your natural character; and greatest will be hers who is least talked of among the men whether for good or for bad.

**[46.]** 'My task is now finished. I have performed it to the best of my ability, and in words, at least, the requirements of the law are now satisfied. If deeds be in question, those who are here interred have received part of their honours already, and for the rest, their children will be brought up till manhood at the public expense: the state thus offers a valuable prize as the garland of victory in this race of valour, for the reward both of those who have fallen and their survivors. And where the rewards for merit are greatest, there are found the best citizens.

'And now that you have brought to a close your lamentations for your relatives, you may depart.'

## *Book 5, chs. 84–116: The Melian Conference*

**[84.]** The next summer Alcibiades sailed with twenty ships to Argos and seized the suspected persons still left of the Lacedæmonian faction to the number of three hundred, whom the Athenians forthwith lodged in the neighbouring islands of their empire. The Athenians also made an expedition against the isle of Melos with thirty ships of their own, six Chian and two Lesbian vessels, sixteen hundred heavy infantry, three hundred archers, and twenty mounted archers from Athens, and about fifteen hundred heavy infantry from the allies and the islanders. The Melians are a colony of Lacedæmon that would not submit to the Athenians like the other islanders, and at first remained neutral and took no part in the struggle, but afterwards upon the Athenians using violence and plundering their territory, assumed an attitude of open hostility. Cleomedes, son of Lycomedes, and Tisias, son of Tisimachus, the generals, encamping in their territory with the above armament, before doing any harm to their land, sent envoys to negotiate. These the Melians did not bring before the people, but bade them state the object of their mission to the magistrates and the few, upon which the Athenian envoys spoke as follows:

**[85.]** *Athenians:* 'Since the negotiations are not to go on before the people, in order that we may not be able to speak straight on without interruption, and deceive the ears of the multitude by seductive arguments which would pass without refutation (for we know that this is the meaning of our being brought before the few), what if you who sit there were to pursue a method more cautious still! Make no set speech yourselves, but take us up at whatever you do not like, and settle that before going any farther. And first tell us if this proposition of ours suits you.'

**[86.]** The Melian commissioners answered:

*Melians:* 'To the fairness of quietly instructing each other as you propose there is nothing to object; but your military preparations are too far advanced to agree with what you say, as we see you are come to be judges in your own cause, and that all we can reasonably expect from this negotiation is war, if we prove to have right on our side and refuse to submit, and in the contrary case, slavery.'

**[87.]** *Athenians:* 'If you have met to reason about presentiments of the future, or for anything else than to consult for the safety of your state upon the facts that you see before you, we will stop; otherwise we will go on.'

**[88.]** *Melians:* 'It is natural and excusable for men in our position to turn more ways than one both in thought and utterance. However, the question in this conference is, as you say, the safety of our country; and the discussion, if you please, can proceed in the way which you propose.'

**[89.]** *Athenians:* 'For ourselves, we shall not trouble you with specious pretences—either of how we have a right to our empire because we overthrew the Mede, or are now attacking you because of wrong that you have done us—and make a long speech which would not be believed; and in return we hope that you, instead of thinking to influence us by saying that you did not join the Lacedæmonians, although their colonists, or that you have done us no wrong, will aim at what is feasible, holding in view the real sentiments of us both; for you know as well as we do that right, as the world goes, is in question only between equals in power, while the strong do what they can and the weak suffer what they must.'

**[90.]** *Melians:* 'As we think, at any rate, it is expedient—we speak as we are obliged, since you enjoin us to let right alone and talk only of interest—that you should not destroy what is our common protection, the privilege of being allowed in danger to invoke what is fair and right, and even to profit by arguments not strictly valid if they can be made to persuade. And you are as much interested in this as any, as your fall would be a signal for the heaviest vengeance and an example for the world to meditate upon.'

**[91.]** *Athenians:* 'The end of our empire, if end it should, does not frighten us: a rival empire like Lacedæmon, even if Lacedæmon was our real antagonist, is not so terrible to the vanquished as subjects who by themselves attack and overpower their rulers. This, however, is a risk that we are content to take. We will now proceed to show you that we are come here in the interest of our empire, and that we shall say what we are now going to say, for the preservation of your country, as we would fain exercise that empire over you without trouble, and see you preserved for the good of us both.'

**[92.]** *Melians:* 'And how, pray, could it turn out as good for us to serve as for you to rule?'

**[93.]** *Athenians:* 'Because you would have the advantage of submitting before suffering the worst, and we should gain by not destroying you.'

**[94.]** *Melians:* 'So you would not consent to our being neutral, friends instead of enemies, but allies of neither side?'

**[95.]** *Athenians:* 'No; for your hostility cannot so much hurt us as your friendship will be an argument to our subjects of our weakness, and your enmity of our power.'

**[96.]** *Melians:* 'Is that your subjects' idea of equity, to put those who have nothing to do with you in the same category with peoples that are most of them your own colonists, and some conquered rebels?'

**[97.]** *Athenians:* 'As far as right goes they think that one has as much of it as the other, and that if any maintain their independence it is because they are strong, and that if we do not molest them it is because we are afraid; so besides extending our empire we should gain in security by your subjection, the fact that you are islanders and weaker than others rendering it all the more important that you should not succeed in baffling the masters of the sea.'

**[98.]** *Melians:* 'But do you consider that there is no security in the policy which we indicate? For here again if you debar us from talking about justice and invite us to obey your interest, we also must explain ours, and try to persuade you, if the two happen to coincide. How can you avoid making enemies of all existing neutrals who shall look at our case and conclude from it that one day or another you will attack them? And what is this but to make greater the enemies that you have already, and to force others to become so who would otherwise have never thought of it?'

**[99.]** *Athenians:* 'Why, the fact is that continentals generally give us but little alarm; the liberty which they enjoy will long prevent their taking precautions against us; it is rather islanders like yourselves, outside our empire, and subjects smarting under the yoke, who would be the most likely to take a rash step and lead themselves and us into obvious danger.'

**[100.]** *Melians:* 'Well then, if you risk so much to retain your empire, and your subjects to get rid of it, it were surely great baseness and cowardice in us who are still free not to try everything that can be tried before submitting to your yoke.'

**[101.]** *Athenians:* 'Not if you are well advised, the contest not being an equal one, with honour as the prize and shame as the penalty, but a question of self-preservation and of not resisting those who are far stronger than you are.'

**[102.]** *Melians:* 'But we know that the fortune of war is sometimes more impartial than the disproportion of numbers might lead one to suppose; to submit is to give ourselves over to despair, while action still preserves for us a hope that we may stand erect.'

**[103.]** *Athenians:* 'Hope, danger's comforter, may be indulged in by those who have abundant resources, if not without loss at all events without ruin; but its nature is to be extravagant, and those who go so far as to put their all upon the venture see it in its true colours only when they are ruined; but so long as the discovery would enable them to guard against it, it is never found wanting. Let not this be the case with you, who are weak and hang on a single turn of the scale; nor be like the vulgar, who, abandoning such security as human means may still afford, when visible hopes fail them in extremity, turn to invisible, to prophecies and oracles, and other such inventions that delude men with hopes to their destruction.'

**[104.]** *Melians:* 'You may be sure that we are as well aware as you of the difficulty of contending against your power and fortune, unless the terms be equal. But we trust that the gods may grant us fortune as good as yours, since we are just men fighting against unjust, and that what we want in power will be made up by the alliance of the Lacedæmonians, who are bound, if only for very shame, to come to the aid of their kindred. Our confidence, therefore, after all is not so utterly irrational.'

**[105.]** *Athenians:* 'When you speak of the favour of the gods, we may as fairly hope for that as yourselves, neither our pretensions nor our conduct being in any way contrary to what men believe of the gods, or practise among themselves. Of the gods we believe, and of men we know, that by a necessary law of their nature they rule wherever they can. And it is not as if we were the first to make this law, or to act upon it when made: we found it existing before us, and shall leave it to exist for ever after us; all we do is to make use of it, knowing that you and everybody else, having the same power as we have, would do the same as we do. Thus, as far as the gods are concerned, we have no fear and no reason to fear that we shall be at a disadvantage. But when we come to your notion about the Lacedæmonians, which leads you to believe that shame will make them help you, here we bless your simplicity but do not envy your folly. The Lacedæmonians, when their own interests or their country's laws are in question, are the worthiest men alive; of their conduct towards others much might be said, but no clearer idea of it could be given than by shortly saying that of all the men we know they are most conspicuous in considering what is agreeable honourable, and what is expedient just. Such a way of thinking does not promise much for the safety which you now unreasonably count upon.'

**[106.]** *Melians:* 'But it is for this very reason that we now trust to their respect for expediency to prevent them from betraying the Melians, their colonists, and thereby losing the confidence of their friends in Hellas and helping their enemies.'

**[107.]** *Athenians:* 'Then you do not adopt the view that expediency goes with security, while justice and honour cannot be followed without danger; and danger the Lacedæmonians generally court as little as possible.'

**[108.]** *Melians:* 'But we believe that they would be more likely to face even danger for our sake, and with more confidence than for others, as our nearness to Peloponnese makes it easier for them to act, and our common blood insures our fidelity.'

**[109.]** *Athenians:* 'Yes, but what an intending ally trusts to is not the good-will of those who ask his aid, but a decided superiority of power for action; and the Lacedæmonians look to this even more than others. At least, such is their distrust of their home resources that it is only with numerous allies that they attack a neighbour; now is it likely that while we are masters of the sea they will cross over to an island?'

**[110.]** *Melians:* 'But they would have others to send. The Cretan Sea is wide, and it is more difficult for those who command it to intercept others, than for those who wish to elude them to do so safely. And should the Lacedæmonians miscarry in this, they would fall upon your land, and upon those left of your allies whom Brasidas did not reach; and instead of places which are not yours, you will have to fight for your own country and your own confederacy.'

**[111.]** *Athenians:* 'Some diversion of the kind you speak of you may one day experience, only to learn, as others have done, that the Athenians never once yet withdrew from a siege for fear of any. But we are struck by the fact that after saying you would consult for the safety of your country, in all this discussion you have mentioned nothing which men might trust in and think to be saved by. Your strongest arguments depend upon hope and the future, and your actual resources are too scanty, as compared with those arrayed against you, for you to come out victorious. You will therefore show great blindness of judgment, unless, after allowing us to retire, you can find some counsel more prudent than this. You will surely not be caught by that idea of disgrace, which in dangers that are disgraceful, and at the same time too plain to be mistaken, proves so fatal to mankind; since in too many cases the very men that have their eyes perfectly open to what they are rushing into, let the thing called disgrace, by the mere influence of a seductive name, lead them on to a point at which they become so enslaved by the phrase as in fact to fall wilfully into hopeless disaster, and incur disgrace more disgraceful as the companion of error, than when it comes as the result of misfortune. This, if you are well advised, you will guard against; and you will not think it dishonourable to submit to the greatest city in Hellas, when it makes you the moderate offer of becoming its tributary ally, without ceasing to enjoy the country that belongs to you; nor when you have the choice given you between war and security, will you be so blinded as to choose the worse. And it is certain that those who do not yield to their equals, who keep terms with their superiors, and are moderate towards their inferiors, on the whole succeed best. Think over the matter, therefore, after our withdrawal, and reflect once and again that it is for your country that you are consulting, that you have not more than one, and that upon this one deliberation depends its prosperity or ruin.'

**[112.]** The Athenians now withdrew from the conference; and the Melians, left to themselves, came to a decision corresponding with what they had maintained in the discussion, and answered: 'Our resolution, Athenians, is the same as it was at first. We will not in a moment deprive of freedom a city that has been inhabited these seven hundred years; but we put our trust in the fortune by which the gods have preserved it until now, and in the help of men, that is, of the Lacedæmonians; and so we will try and save ourselves. Meanwhile we invite you to allow us to be friends to you and foes to neither party, and to retire from our country after making such a treaty as shall seem fit to us both.'

**[113.]** Such was the answer of the Melians. The Athenians, now departing from the conference, said: 'Well, you alone, as it seems to us, judging from these resolutions, regard what is future as more certain than what is before your eyes, and what is out of sight, in your eagerness, as already coming to pass; and as you have staked most on, and trusted most in, the Lacedæmonians, your fortune, and your hopes, so will you be most completely deceived.'

**[114.]** The Athenian envoys now returned to the army; and the Melians showing no signs of yielding, the generals at once betook themselves to hostilities, and drew a line of circumvallation round the Melians, dividing the work among the different states. Subsequently the Athenians returned with most of their army, leaving behind them a certain number of their own citizens and of the allies to keep guard by land and sea. The force thus left stayed on and besieged the place.

**[115.]** About the same time the Argives invaded the territory of Phlius and lost eighty men cut off in an ambush by the Phliasians and Argive exiles. Meanwhile the Athenians at Pylos took so much plunder from the Lacedæmonians that the latter, although they still refrained from breaking off the treaty and going to war with Athens, yet proclaimed that any of their people that chose might plunder the Athenians. The Corinthians also commenced hostilities with the Athenians for private quarrels of their own; but the rest of the Peloponnesians stayed quiet. Meanwhile the Melians attacked by night and took the part of the Athenian lines over against the market, and killed some of the men, and brought in corn and all else that they could find useful to them, and so returned and kept quiet, while the Athenians took measures to keep better guard in future.

Summer was now over. **[116.]** The next winter the Lacedæmonians intended to invade the Argive territory, but arriving at the frontier found the sacrifices for crossing unfavourable, and went back again. This intention of theirs gave the Argives suspicions of certain of their fellow-citizens, some of whom they arrested; others, however, escaped them. About the same time the Melians again took another part of the Athenian lines which were but feebly garrisoned. Reinforcements afterwards arriving from Athens in consequence, under the command of Philocrates, son of Demeas, the siege was now pressed vigorously; and some treachery taking place inside, the Melians surrendered at discretion to the Athenians, who put to death all the grown men whom they took, and sold the women and children for slaves, and subsequently sent out five hundred colonists and inhabited the place themselves.

## Euripides (c. 485–406 BCE)

The origins of Greek tragedy lay in the festivals in honor of the god Dionysos beginning around 535 BCE. The poet Thespis, the legendary founder of tragedy, appeared at these festivals with a chorus of *tragodoi* or "goat singers." These were so called either because the chorus impersonated goats, or because they danced for a goat (*tragos*) as the prize, or even perhaps because they danced around a sacrificed goat. Out of this form *tragedy* would emerge a generation or so later. Tragic plays were usually performed at festivals, at which three days might be devoted to performances. Tragic poets would compete for prizes, each presenting three tragedies and one "satyr play" (or farcical short piece: Euripides' *Cyclops* is the only satyr play that has survived), which provided less elevated and lighter fare. Athenian tragedies were performed in the theater of the god Dionysos, a central character in the *Bacchae,* at the foot of the Acropolis, which contained magnificent buildings constructed largely during the period of Pericles' leadership. During the golden age of Athenian drama in the fifth century BCE, the plays almost always dealt with issues of critical importance to the city.

When we read a Greek tragedy in translation, we need to realize that we are not experiencing the play as its audience did, for Greek drama was quite a spectacular multimedia affair. The actors wore masks and costumes, and the chorus sang and danced its lines. The dialogue between characters was usually spoken in iambic verse, and the choruses sang elaborate metrical compositions featuring lines of different lengths.

The shocking catastrophe of Euripides' *Bacchae* may bring us closer than any other literary work to the worship of the god Dionysos. Greek tragedy is full of violent death, though it always occurs offstage; but the tearing to pieces of a living man by a group of frenzied women is far more grisly than the usual stuff of tragic climax, especially when the audience learns that the slaughter was led by the man's own mother, who believed she was ripping the flesh of a lion. Even more bizarre is the fact that this young man was the king of Thebes, disguised in women's clothes so that he could spy on the religious mysteries he professed to despise. The world of the Greeks can seem very alien when we consider the plot of the *Bacchae.*

Many theories have been proposed to explain the *Bacchae,* but any satisfactory interpretation must be based on careful evaluation of how the play presents the actions that lead to Pentheus's death and a consideration of what we know about the worship of Dionysos. Central to the religion of Dionysos were the sacraments of *sparagmos* and *omophagia.* Sparagmos is the tearing apart of a live sacrificial animal, and omophagia is the eating of its warm and quivering flesh so that the god's vital force can be absorbed into the worshiper's body. Dionysos is clearly presented in Euripides' play as a god of immensely powerful natural forces outside human control: he can cause an earthquake or lightning; he is associated with growing plants and wild animals; he radiates erotic energy; he can change his shape from human to animal; and he inspires his devotees with disturbing ecstasy and strength. Dionysos is particularly associated with women, through his followers the Maenads or Bacchantes. He inspires ordinary women to leave the restricted spaces of their domestic duties and join dancing throngs in the meadows and on the hillsides.

Their worship is peaceful, according to Euripides, except when profaned by men. That is when events turn violent, and destructive energies are released. The common association of Dionysos (or Bacchus) with wine is only one among the many attributes of this mysterious deity.

Young King Pentheus's obsession with control and his contempt for the god derive from an attitude the Greeks regarded as fatal: hubris, or arrogance. In tragedy after tragedy, this pride causes men to ignore or dismiss good advice from their elders and to lack reverence for the powers beyond human knowledge. The results are always catastrophic. In Pentheus's case, hubris blinds the young man to the prudent counsel of Tiresias and Kadmos and leads him to ridicule his divine visitor and to fail to pay attention to the signs of danger around him. He behaves like a tyrant who tries to use military force to solve social and religious problems. In addition, Pentheus displays a blind rigidity about gender and sexual roles that collapses into giddy transgression when Dionysos tempts him with hints of voyeuristic excitement to spy on the Maenads' activities. Whether or not one agrees with Nietzsche's theories about the play in *The Birth of Tragedy*, in which he defines the central conflict as between Apollonian reason and Dionysian instinct, it is certain that humility and reverence for what the god represents are required for human survival in the Greek world. The strangely beautiful and androgynous young stranger of the play (Dionysos), for all his cruelty and unfeeling character, must be accepted into the community, just as the worship of Dionysos must be performed in order to celebrate disturbing but central connections between humanity and the vital forces of all life. The irony for Pentheus is that his very irreverence leads him to perform the role of sacrificial victim, a double or stand-in for the god.

## *The Bacchae*

*Translated by William Arrowsmith*

### Characters

DIONYSUS (*also called Bromius, Evius, and Bacchus*)
CHORUS OF ASIAN BACCHAE (*followers of Dionysus*)
TEIRESIAS
CADMUS
PENTHEUS
ATTENDANT
FIRST MESSENGER
SECOND MESSENGER
AGAVE
CORYPHAEUS (*chorus leader*)

### Scene:

*Before the royal palace at Thebes. On the left is the way to Cithaeron; on the right, to the city. In the center of the orchestra stands, still smoking, the vine-covered tomb of Semele, mother of Dionysus.*

*Enter Dionysus. He is of soft, even effeminate, appearance. His face is beardless; he is dressed in a fawn-skin and carries a thyrsus (i.e., a stalk of fennel tipped with ivy leaves). On his head he wears a wreath of ivy, and his long blond curls ripple down over his shoulders. Throughout the play he wears a smiling mask.*

DIONYSUS

I am Dionysus, the son of Zeus,
come back to Thebes, this land where I was born.
My mother was Cadmus' daughter, Semele by name,
midwived by fire, delivered by the lightning's
blast.
And here I stand, a god incognito,
disguised as man, beside the stream of Dirce
and the waters of Ismenus. There before the palace
I see my lightning-married mother's grave,
and there upon the ruins of her shattered house
the living fire of Zeus still smolders on
in deathless witness of Hera's violence and rage
against my mother. But Cadmus wins my praise:
he has made this tomb a shrine, sacred to my mother.
It was I who screened her grave with the green
of the clustering vine.
Far behind me lie
those golden-rivered lands, Lydia and Phrygia,
where my journeying began. Overland I went,
across the steppes of Persia where the sun strikes hotly
down, through Bactrian fastness and the grim waste
of Media. Thence to rich Arabia I came;
and so, along all Asia's swarming littoral
of towered cities where Greeks and foreign nations,
mingling, live, my progress made. There
I taught my dances to the feet of living men,
establishing my mysteries and rites
that I might be revealed on earth for what I am:
a god.
And thence to Thebes.
This city, first
in Hellas, now shrills and echoes to my women's cries,
their ecstasy of joy. Here in Thebes
I bound the fawn-skin to the women's flesh and armed
their hands with shafts of ivy. For I have come
to refute that slander spoken by my mother's sisters—
those who least had right to slander her.
They said that Dionysus was no son of Zeus,
but Semele had slept beside a man in love
and fathered off her shame on Zeus—a fraud, they sneered,
contrived by Cadmus to protect his daughter's name.

They said she lied, and Zeus in anger at that lie
blasted her with lightning.
Because of that offense
I have stung them with frenzy, hounded them from home
up to the mountains where they wander, crazed of mind,
and compelled to wear my orgies' livery.
Every woman in Thebes—but the women only—
I drove from home, mad. There they sit,
rich and poor alike, even the daughters of Cadmus,
beneath the silver firs on the roofless rocks.
Like it or not, this city must learn its lesson:
it lacks initiation in my mysteries;
that I shall vindicate my mother Semele
and stand revealed to mortal eyes as the god
she bore to Zeus.
Cadmus the king has abdicated,
leaving his throne and power to his grandson Pentheus;
who now revolts against divinity, in *me;*
thrusts *me* from his offerings; forgets *my* name
in his prayers. Therefore I shall *prove* to him
and every man in Thebes that I am god
indeed. And when my worship is established here,
and all is well, then I shall go my way
and be revealed to other men in other lands.
But if the men of Thebes attempt to force
my Bacchae from the mountainside by threat of arms,
I shall marshal my Maenads and take the field.
To these ends I have laid my deity aside
and go disguised as man.

*(He wheels and calls offstage.)*

On, my women,
women who worship me, women whom I led
out of Asia where Tmolus heaves its rampart
over Lydia!
On, comrades of my progress here!
Come, and with your native Phrygian drum—
Rhea's drum and mine—pound at the palace doors
of Pentheus! Let the city of Thebes behold you,
while I return among Cithaeron's forest glens
where my Bacchae wait and join their whirling dances.

*(Exit Dionysus as the Chorus of Asian Bacchae comes dancing in from the right. They are dressed in fawn-skins, crowned with ivy, and carry thyrsi, timbrels, and flutes.)*

CHORUS

Out of the land of Asia,
down from holy Tmolus,
speeding the service of god,
for Bromius we come!
Hard are the labors of god;
hard, but his service is sweet.
Sweet to serve, sweet to cry:
*Bacchus! Evohé!*
—You on the streets!
—You on the roads!
—Make way!
—Let every mouth be hushed. Let no ill-omened words
profane your tongues.
—Make way! Fall back!
—Hush.
—For now I raise the old, old hymn to Dionysus.

—Blessèd, blessèd are those who know the mysteries of god.
—Blessèd is he who hallows his life in the worship of god,
he whom the spirit of god possesseth, who is one
with those who belong to the holy body of god.
—Blessèd are the dancers and those who are purified,
who dance on the hill in the holy dance of god.
—Blessèd are they who keep the rite of Cybele the Mother.
—Blessèd are the thyrsus-bearers, those who wield in their hands
the holy wand of god.
—Blessèd are those who wear the crown of the ivy of god.
—Blessèd, blessèd are they: Dionysus is their god!

—On, Bacchae, on, you Bacchae,
bear your god in triumph home!
Bear on the god, son of god,
escort your Dionysus home!
Bear him down from Phrygian hill,
attend him through the streets of Hellas!

—So his mother bore him once
in labor bitter; lightning-struck,
forced by fire that flared from Zeus,
consumed, she died, untimely torn,
in childbed dead by blow of light!
Of light the son was born!

—Zeus it was who saved his son;
with speed outrunning mortal eye,

bore him to a private place,
bound the boy with clasps of gold;
in his thigh as in a womb,
concealed his son from Hera's eyes.

—And when the weaving Fates fulfilled the time,
the bull-horned god was born of Zeus. In joy
he crowned his son, set serpents on his head—
wherefrom, in piety, descends to us
the Maenad's writhing crown, her *chevelure*
of snakes.

—O Thebes, nurse of Semele,
crown your hair with ivy!
Grow green with bryony!
Redden with berries! O city,
with boughs of oak and fir,
come dance the dance of god!
Fringe your skins of dappled fawn
with tufts of twisted wool!
Handle with holy care
the violent wand of god!
And let the dance begin!
He is Bromius who runs
*to the mountain!*
*to the mountain!*
where the throng of women waits,
driven from shuttle and loom,
possessed by Dionysus!

—And I praise the holies of Crete,
the caves of the dancing Curetes,
there where Zeus was born,
where helmed in triple tier
around the primal drum
the Corybantes danced. They,
they were the first of all
whose whirling feet kept time
to the strict beat of the taut hide
and the squeal of the wailing flute.
Then from them to Rhea's hands
the holy drum was handed down;
but, stolen by the raving Satyrs,
fell at last to me and now
accompanies the dance
which every other year

celebrates your name:
*Dionysus!*

—He is sweet upon the mountains. He drops to the earth
from the running packs.
He wears the holy fawn-skin. He hunts the wild goat
and kills it.
He delights in the raw flesh.
He runs to the mountains of Phrygia, to the mountains
of Lydia he runs!
He is Bromius who leads us! *Evohé!*

—With milk the earth flows! It flows with wine!
It runs with the nectar of bees!

—Like frankincense in its fragrance
is the blaze of the torch he bears.
Flames float out from his trailing wand
as he runs, as he dances,
kindling the stragglers,
spurring with cries,
and his long curls stream to the wind!

—And he cries, as they cry, *Evohé!*—
On, Bacchae!
On, Bacchae!
Follow, glory of golden Tmolus,
hymning god
with a rumble of drums,
with a cry, *Evohé!* to the Evian god,
with a cry of Phrygian cries,
when the holy flute like honey plays
the sacred song of those who go
*to the mountain!*
*to the mountain!*

—Then, in ecstasy, like a colt by its grazing mother,
the Bacchante runs with flying feet, she leaps!

*(The Chorus remains grouped in two semicircles about the orchestra as Teiresias makes his entrance. He is incongruously dressed in the bacchant's fawn-skin and is crowned with ivy. Old and blind, he uses his thyrsus to tap his way.)*

TEIRESIAS

Ho there, who keeps the gates?
Summon Cadmus—

Cadmus, Agenor's son, the stranger from Sidon
who built the towers of our Thebes.
Go, someone.
Say Teiresias wants him. He will know what errand
brings me, that agreement, age with age, we made
to deck our wands, to dress in skins of fawn
and crown our heads with ivy.

*(Enter Cadmus from the palace. Dressed in Dionysiac costume and bent almost double with age, he is an incongruous and pathetic figure.)*

CADMUS

My old friend,
I knew it must be you when I heard your summons.
For there's a wisdom in his voice that makes
the man of wisdom known.
But here I am,
dressed in the costume of the god, prepared to go.
Insofar as we are able, Teiresias, we must
do honor to this god, for he was born
my daughter's son, who has been revealed to men,
the god, Dionysus.
Where shall we go, where
shall we tread the dance, tossing our white heads
in the dances of god?
Expound to me, Teiresias.
For in such matters you are wise.
Surely
I could dance night and day, untiringly
beating the earth with my thyrsus! And how sweet it is
to forget my old age.

TEIRESIAS

It is the same with me.
I too feel young, young enough to dance.

CADMUS

Good. Shall we take our chariots to the mountain?

TEIRESIAS

Walking would be better. It shows more honor
to the god.

CADMUS

So be it. I shall lead, my old age
conducting yours.

TEIRESIAS

The god will guide us there
with no effort on our part.

CADMUS

Are we the only men
who will dance for Bacchus?

TEIRESIAS

They are all blind.
Only we can see.

CADMUS

But we delay too long.
Here, take my arm.

TEIRESIAS

Link my hand in yours.

CADMUS

I am a man, nothing more. I do not scoff
at heaven.

TEIRESIAS

We do not trifle with divinity.
No, we are the heirs of customs and traditions
hallowed by age and handed down to us
by our fathers. No quibbling logic can topple *them,*
whatever subtleties this clever age invents.
People may say: "Aren't you ashamed? At your age,
going dancing, wreathing your head with ivy?"
Well, I am *not* ashamed. Did the god declare
that just the young or just the old should dance?
No, he desires his honor from all mankind.
He wants no one excluded from his worship.

CADMUS

Because you cannot see, Teiresias, let me be
interpreter for you this once. Here comes
the man to whom I left my throne, Echion's son,
Pentheus, hastening toward the palace. He seems
excited and disturbed. Yes, listen to him.

*(Enter Pentheus from the right. He is a young man of athletic build, dressed in traditional Greek dress; like Dionysus, he is beardless. He enters excitedly, talking to the attendants who accompany him.)*

PENTHEUS

I happened to be away, out of the city,
but reports reached me of some strange mischief here,
stories of our women leaving home to frisk
in mock ecstasies among the thickets on the mountain,
dancing in honor of the latest divinity,
a certain Dionysus, whoever he may be!
In their midst stand bowls brimming with wine.
And then, one by one, the women wander off
to hidden nooks where they serve the lusts of men.
Priestesses of Bacchus they claim they are,
but it's really Aphrodite they adore.
I have captured some of them; my jailers
have locked them away in the safety of our prison.
Those who run at large shall be hunted down
out of the mountains like the animals they are—
yes, my own mother Agave, and Ino
and Autonoë, the mother of Actaeon.
In no time at all I shall have them trapped
in iron nets and stop this obscene disorder.
  I am also told a foreigner has come to Thebes
from Lydia, one of those charlatan magicians,
with long yellow curls smelling of perfumes,
with flushed cheeks and the spells of Aphrodite
in his eyes. His days and nights he spends
with women and girls, dangling before them the joys
of initiation in his mysteries.
But let me bring him underneath that roof
and I'll stop his pounding with his wand and tossing
his head. By god, I'll have his head cut off!
And *this* is the man who claims that Dionysus
is a god and was sewn into the thigh of Zeus,
when, in point of fact, that same blast of lightning
consumed him and his mother both for her lie
that she had lain with Zeus in love. Whoever
this stranger is, aren't such impostures,
such unruliness, worthy of hanging?

*(For the first time he sees Teiresias and Cadmus in their Dionysiac costumes.)*

*What!*
But this is incredible! Teiresias the seer
tricked out in a dappled fawn-skin!
And *you*,
you, my own grandfather, playing at the bacchant
with a wand!

Sir, I shrink to see your old age
so foolish. Shake that ivy off, grandfather!
Now drop that wand. Drop it, I say.

*(He wheels on Teiresias.)*

Aha,
I see: this is *your* doing, Teiresias.
Yes, you want still another god revealed to men
so you can pocket the profits from burnt offerings
and bird-watching. By heaven, only your age
restrains me now from sending you to prison
with those Bacchic women for importing here to Thebes
these filthy mysteries. When once you see
the glint of wine shining at the feasts of women,
then you may be sure the festival is rotten.

CORYPHAEUS

What blasphemy! Stranger, have you no respect
for heaven? For Cadmus who sowed the dragon teeth?
Will the son of Echion disgrace his house?

TEIRESIAS

Give a wise man an honest brief to plead
and his eloquence is no remarkable achievement.
But you are glib; your phrases come rolling out
smoothly on the tongue, as though your words were wise
instead of foolish. The man whose glibness flows
from his conceit of speech declares the thing he is:
a worthless and a stupid citizen.
I tell you,
this god whom you ridicule shall someday have
enormous power and prestige throughout Hellas.
Mankind, young man, possess two supreme blessings.
First of these is the goddess Demeter, or Earth—
whichever name you choose to call her by.
It was she who gave to man his nourishment of grain.
But after her there came the son of Semele,
who matched her present by inventing liquid wine
as his gift to man. For filled with that good gift,
suffering mankind forgets its grief, from it
comes sleep; with it oblivion of the troubles
of the day. There is no other medicine
for misery. And when we pour libations
to the gods, we pour the god of wine himself
that through his intercession man may win
the favor of heaven.

You sneer, do you, at that story
that Dionysus was sewed into the thigh of Zeus?
Let me teach you what that really means. When Zeus
rescued from the thunderbolt his infant son,
he brought him to Olympus. Hera, however,
plotted at heart to hurl the child from heaven.
Like the god he is, Zeus countered her. Breaking off
a tiny fragment of that ether which surrounds the world,
he molded from it a dummy Dionysus.
This he *showed* to Hera, but with time men garbled
the word and said that Dionysus had been *sewed*
into the thigh of Zeus. This was their story,
whereas, in fact, Zeus *showed* the dummy to Hera
and gave it as a hostage for his son.
Moreover,
this is a god of prophecy. His worshippers,
like madmen, are endowed with mantic powers.
For when the god enters the body of a man
he fills him with the breath of prophecy.
Besides,
he has usurped even the functions of warlike Ares.
Thus, at times, you see an army mustered under arms
stricken with panic before it lifts a spear.
This panic comes from Dionysus.
Someday
you shall even see him bounding with his torches
among the crags at Delphi, leaping the pastures
that stretch between the peaks, whirling and waving
his thyrsus: great throughout Hellas.
Mark my words,
Pentheus. Do not be so certain that power
is what matters in the life of man; do not mistake
for wisdom the fantasies of your sick mind.
Welcome the god to Thebes; crown your head;
pour him libations and join his revels.
Dionysus does not, I admit, *compel* a woman
to be chaste. Always and in every case
it is her character and nature that keeps
a woman chaste. But even in the rites of Dionysus,
the chaste woman will not be corrupted.
Think:
you are pleased when men stand outside your doors
and the city glorifies the name of Pentheus.
And so the god: he too delights in glory.
But Cadmus and I, whom you ridicule, will crown
our heads with ivy and join the dances of the god—
an ancient foolish pair perhaps, but dance

we must. Nothing you have said would make me
change my mind or flout the will of heaven.
You are mad, grievously mad, beyond the power
of any drugs to cure, for you are drugged
with madness.

CORYPHAEUS

Apollo would approve your words.
Wisely you honor Bromius: a great god.

CADMUS

My boy,
Teiresias advises well. Your home is here
with us, with our customs and traditions, not
outside, alone. Your mind is distracted now,
and what you think is sheer delirium.
Even if this Dionysus is no god,
as you assert, persuade yourself that he is.
The fiction is a noble one, for Semele will seem
to be the mother of a god, and this confers
no small distinction on our family.
You saw
that dreadful death your cousin Actaeon died
when those man-eating hounds he had raised himself
savaged him and tore his body limb from limb
because he boasted that his prowess in the hunt surpassed
the skill of Artemis.
Do not let his fate be yours.
Here, let me wreathe your head with leaves of ivy.
Then come with us and glorify the god.

PENTHEUS

Take your hands off me! Go worship your Bacchus,
but do not wipe your madness off on me.
By god, I'll make him pay, the man who taught you
this folly of yours.

*(He turns to his attendants.)*

Go, someone, this instant,
to the place where this prophet prophesies.
Pry it up with crowbars, heave it over,
upside down; demolish everything you see.
Throw his fillets out to wind and weather.
*That* will provoke him more than anything.
As for the rest of you, go and scour the city
for that effeminate stranger, the man who infects our women
with this strange disease and pollutes our beds.

And when you take him, clap him in chains
and march him here. He shall die as he deserves—
by being stoned to death. He shall come to rue
his merrymaking here in Thebes.

*(Exeunt attendants.)*

TEIRESIAS

Reckless fool,
you do not know the consequences of your words.
You talked madness before, but this is raving
lunacy!
Cadmus, let us go and pray
for this raving fool and for this city too,
pray to the god that no awful vengeance strike
from heaven.
Take your staff and follow me.
Support me with your hands, and I shall help you too
lest we stumble and fall, a sight of shame,
two old men together.
But go we must,
acknowledging the service that we owe to god,
Bacchus, the son of Zeus.
And yet take care
lest someday your house repent of Pentheus
in its sufferings. I speak not prophecy
but fact. The words of fools finish in folly.

*(Exeunt Teiresias and Cadmus. Pentheus retires into the palace.)*

CHORUS

—Holiness, queen of heaven,
Holiness on golden wing
who hover over earth,
do you hear what Pentheus says?
Do you hear his blasphemy
against the prince of the blessèd,
the god of garlands and banquets,
Bromius, Semele's son?
These blessings he gave:
laughter to the flute
and the loosing of cares
when the shining wine is spilled
at the feast of the gods,
and the wine-bowl casts its sleep
on feasters crowned with ivy.

—A tongue without reins,
defiance, unwisdom—
their end is disaster.
But the life of quiet good,
the wisdom that accepts—
these abide unshaken,
preserving, sustaining
the houses of men.
Far in the air of heaven,
the sons of heaven live.
But they watch the lives of men.
And what passes for wisdom is not;
unwise are those who aspire,
who outrange the limits of man.
Briefly, we live. Briefly,
then die. Wherefore, I say,
he who hunts a glory, he who tracks
some boundless, superhuman dream,
may lose his harvest here and now
and garner death. Such men are mad,
their counsels evil.

—O let me come to Cyprus,
island of Aphrodite,
homes of the loves that cast
their spells on the hearts of men!
Or Paphos where the hundred-
mouthed barbarian river
brings ripeness without rain!
To Pieria, haunt of the Muses,
and the holy hill of Olympus!
O Bromius, leader, god of joy,
Bromius, take me there!
There the lovely Graces go,
and there Desire, and there
the right is mine to worship
as I please.

—The deity, the son of Zeus,
in feast, in festival, delights.
He loves the goddess Peace,
generous of good,
preserver of the young.
To rich and poor he gives
the simple gift of wine,
the gladness of the grape.

But him who scoffs he hates,
and him who mocks his life,
the happiness of those
for whom the day is blessed
but doubly blessed the night;
whose simple wisdom shuns the thoughts
of proud, uncommon men and all
their god-encroaching dreams.
But what the common people do,
the things that simple men believe,
I too believe and do.

*(As Pentheus reappears from the palace, enter from the left several attendants leading Dionysus captive.)*

ATTENDANT

Pentheus, here we are; not empty-handed either.
We captured the quarry you sent us out to catch.
But our prey here was tame: refused to run
or hide, held out his hands as willing as you please,
completely unafraid. His ruddy cheeks were flushed
as though with wine, and he stood there smiling,
making no objection when we roped his hands
and marched him here. It made me feel ashamed.
"Listen, stranger," I said, "I am not to blame.
We act under orders from Pentheus. He ordered
your arrest."
As for those women you clapped in chains
and sent to the dungeon, they're gone, clean away,
went skipping off to the fields crying on their god
Bromius. The chains on their legs snapped apart
by themselves. Untouched by any human hand,
the doors swung wide, opening of their own accord.
Sir, this stranger who has come to Thebes is full
of many miracles. I know no more than that.
The rest is your affair.

PENTHEUS

Untie his hands.
We have him in our net. He may be quick,
but he cannot escape us now, I think.

*(While the servants untie Dionysus' hands, Pentheus attentively scrutinizes his prisoner. Then the servants step back, leaving Pentheus and Dionysus face to face.)*

So,
you *are* attractive, stranger, at least to women—
which explains, I think, your presence here in Thebes.

Your curls are long. You do not wrestle, I take it.
And what fair skin you have—you must take care of it—
no daylight complexion; no, it comes from the night
when you hunt Aphrodite with your beauty.
Now then,
who are you and from where?

DIONYSUS

It is nothing
to boast of and easily told. You have heard, I suppose,
of Mount Tmolus and her flowers?

PENTHEUS

I know the place.
It rings the city of Sardis.

DIONYSUS

I come from there.
My country is Lydia.

PENTHEUS

Who is this god whose worship
you have imported into Hellas?

DIONYSUS

Dionysus, the son of Zeus.
He initiated me.

PENTHEUS

You have some local Zeus
who spawns new gods?

DIONYSUS

He is the same as yours—
the Zeus who married Semele.

PENTHEUS

How did you see him?
In a dream or face to face?

DIONYSUS

Face to face.
He gave me his rites.

PENTHEUS

What form do they take,
these mysteries of yours?

DIONYSUS

It is forbidden
to tell the uninitiate.

PENTHEUS

Tell me the benefits
that those who know your mysteries enjoy.

DIONYSUS

I am forbidden to say. But they are worth knowing.

PENTHEUS

Your answers are designed to make me curious.

DIONYSUS

No:
our mysteries abhor an unbelieving man.

PENTHEUS

You say you saw the god. What form did he assume?

DIONYSUS

Whatever form he wished. The choice was his,
not mine.

PENTHEUS

You evade the question.

DIONYSUS

Talk sense to a fool
and he calls you foolish.

PENTHEUS

Have you introduced your rites
in other cities too? Or is Thebes the first?

DIONYSUS

Foreigners everywhere now dance for Dionysus.

PENTHEUS

They are more ignorant than Greeks.

DIONYSUS

In this matter
they are not. Customs differ.

PENTHEUS

Do you hold your rites
during the day or night?

DIONYSUS

Mostly by night.
The darkness is well suited to devotion.

PENTHEUS

Better suited to lechery and seducing women.

DIONYSUS

You can find debauchery by daylight too.

PENTHEUS

You shall regret these clever answers.

DIONYSUS

And you,
your stupid blasphemies.

PENTHEUS

What a bold bacchant!
You wrestle well—when it comes to words.

DIONYSUS

Tell me,
what punishment do you propose?

PENTHEUS

First of all,
I shall cut off your girlish curls.

DIONYSUS

My hair is holy.
My curls belong to god.

*(Pentheus shears away the god's curls.)*

PENTHEUS

Second, you will surrender
your wand.

DIONYSUS

*You* take it. It belongs to Dionysus.

*(Pentheus takes the thyrsus.)*

PENTHEUS

Last, I shall place you under guard and confine you
in the palace.

DIONYSUS

The god himself will set me free
whenever I wish.

PENTHEUS

You will be with your women in prison
when you call on him for help.

DIONYSUS

He is here now
and sees what I endure from you.

PENTHEUS

Where is he?
I cannot see him.

DIONYSUS

With me. Your blasphemies
have made you blind.

PENTHEUS (*to attendants*)

Seize him. He is mocking me
and Thebes.

DIONYSUS

I give you sober warning, fools:
place no chains on *me*.

PENTHEUS

But *I* say: chain him.
And I am the stronger here.

DIONYSUS

You do not know
the limits of your strength. You do not know
what you do. You do not know who you are.

PENTHEUS

I am Pentheus, the son of Echion and Agave.

DIONYSUS

Pentheus: you shall repent that name.

PENTHEUS

Off with him.
Chain his hands; lock him in the stables by the palace.
Since he desires the darkness, give him what he wants.
Let him dance down there in the dark.

*(As the attendants bind Dionysus' hands, the Chorus beats on its drums with increasing agitation as though to emphasize the sacrilege.)*

As for these women,
your accomplices in making trouble here,

I shall have them sold as slaves or put to work
at my looms. That will silence their drums.

*(Exit Pentheus.)*

DIONYSUS

I go,
though not to suffer, since that cannot be.
But Dionysus whom you outrage by your acts,
who you deny is god, will call you to account.
When you set chains on me, you manacle the god.

*(Exeunt attendants with Dionysus captive.)*

CHORUS

—O Dirce, holy river,
child of Achelöus' water,
yours the springs that welcomed once
divinity, the son of Zeus!
For Zeus the father snatched his son
from deathless flame, crying:
*Dithyrambus, come!*
*Enter my male womb.*
*I name you Bacchus and to Thebes*
*proclaim you by that name.*
But now, O blessèd Dirce,
you banish me when to your banks I come,
crowned with ivy, bringing revels.
O Dirce, why am I rejected?
By the clustered grapes I swear,
by Dionysus' wine,
someday you shall come to know
the name of *Bromius!*

—With fury, with fury, he rages,
Pentheus, son of Echion,
born of the breed of Earth,
spawned by the dragon, whelped by Earth!
Inhuman, a rabid beast,
a giant in wildness raging,
storming, defying the children of heaven.
He has threatened me with bonds
though my body is bound to god.
He cages my comrades with chains;
he has cast them in prison darkness.
O lord, son of Zeus, do you see?
O Dionysus, do you see

how in shackles we are held
unbreakably, in the bonds of oppressors?
Descend from Olympus, lord!
Come, whirl your wand of gold
and quell with death this beast of blood
whose violence abuses man and god
outrageously.

—O lord, where do you wave your wand
among the running companies of god?
There on Nysa, mother of beasts?
There on the ridges of Corycia?
Or there among the forests of Olympus
where Orpheus fingered his lyre
and mustered with music the trees,
mustered the wilderness beasts?
O Pieria, you are blessed!
Evius honors you. He comes to dance,
bringing his Bacchae, fording the race
where Axios runs, bringing his Maenads
whirling over Lydias,
generous father of rivers
and famed for his lovely waters
that fatten a land of good horses.

*(Thunder and lightning. The earth trembles. The Chorus is crazed with fear.)*

DIONYSUS (*from within*)

Ho!
Hear me! Ho, Bacchae!
Ho, Bacchae! Hear my cry!

CHORUS

Who cries?
Who calls me with that cry
of Evius? Where are you, lord?

DIONYSUS

Ho! Again I cry—
the son of Zeus and Semele!

CHORUS

O lord, lord Bromius!
Bromius, come to us now!

DIONYSUS

*Let the earthquake come! Shatter the floor of the world!*

CHORUS

—Look there, how the palace of Pentheus totters.
—Look, the palace is collapsing!
—Dionysus is within. Adore him!
—We adore him!
—Look there!
—Above the pillars, how the great stones
gape and crack!
—Listen. Bromius cries his victory!

DIONYSUS

*Launch the blazing thunderbolt of god! O lightnings,*
*come! Consume with flame the palace of Pentheus!*

*(A burst of lightning flares across the façade of the palace and tongues of flame spurt up from the tomb of Semele. Then a great crash of thunder.)*

CHORUS

Ah,
look how the fire leaps up
on the holy tomb of Semele,
the flame of Zeus of Thunders,
his lightnings, still alive,
blazing where they fell!
Down, Maenads,
fall to the ground in awe! He walks
among the ruins he has made!
He has brought the high house low!
He comes, our god, the son of Zeus!

*(The Chorus falls to the ground in oriental fashion, bowing their heads in the direction of the palace. A hush; then Dionysus appears, lightly picking his way among the rubble. Calm and smiling still, he speaks to the Chorus with a solicitude approaching banter.)*

DIONYSUS

What, women of Asia? Were you so overcome with fright
you fell to the ground? I think then you must have seen
how Bacchus jostled the palace of Pentheus. But come, rise.
Do not be afraid.

CORYPHAEUS

O greatest light of our holy revels,
how glad I am to see your face! Without you I was lost.

DIONYSUS

Did you despair when they led me away to cast me down
in the darkness of Pentheus' prison?

CORYPHAEUS

What else could I do?
Where would I turn for help if something happened to you?
But how did you escape that godless man?

DIONYSUS

With ease.
No effort was required.

CORYPHAEUS

But the manacles on your wrists?

DIONYSUS

There I, in turn, humiliated him, outrage for outrage.
He seemed to think that he was chaining me but never once
so much as touched my hands. He fed on his desires.
Inside the stable he intended as my jail, instead of me,
he found a bull and tried to rope its knees and hooves.
He was panting desperately, biting his lips with his teeth,
his whole body drenched with sweat, while I sat nearby,
quietly watching. But at that moment Bacchus came,
shook the palace and touched his mother's grave with tongues
of fire. Imagining the palace was in flames,
Pentheus went rushing here and there, shouting to his slaves
to bring him water. Every hand was put to work: in vain.
Then, afraid I might escape, he suddenly stopped short,
drew his sword and rushed to the palace. There, it seems,
Bromius had made a shape, a phantom which resembled me,
within the court. Bursting in, Pentheus thrust and stabbed
at that thing of gleaming air as though he thought it me.
And then, once again, the god humiliated him.
He razed the palace to the ground where it lies, shattered
in utter ruin—his reward for my imprisonment.
At that bitter sight, Pentheus dropped his sword, exhausted
by the struggle. A man, a man, and nothing more,
yet he presumed to wage a war with god.
For my part,
I left the palace quietly and made my way outside.
For Pentheus I care nothing.
But judging from the sound
of tramping feet inside the court, I think our man
will soon be here. What, I wonder, will he have to say?
But let him bluster. I shall not be touched to rage.
Wise men know constraint: our passions are controlled.

*(Enter Pentheus, stamping heavily, from the ruined palace.)*

PENTHEUS

But this is mortifying. That stranger, that man
I clapped in irons, has escaped.

*(He catches sight of Dionysus.)*

What! *You?*
Well, what do you have to say for yourself?
How did you escape? Answer me.

DIONYSUS

Your anger
walks too heavily. Tread lightly here.

PENTHEUS

*How did you escape?*

DIONYSUS

Don't you remember?
Someone, I said, would set me free.

PENTHEUS

Someone?
But who? Who is this mysterious someone?

DIONYSUS

[He who makes the grape grow its clusters
for mankind.]

PENTHEUS

A splendid contribution, that.

DIONYSUS

You disparage the gift that is his chiefest glory.

PENTHEUS

[If I catch him here, he will not escape my anger.]
I shall order every gate in every tower
to be bolted tight.

DIONYSUS

And so? Could not a god
hurdle your city walls?

PENTHEUS

You are clever—very—
but not where it counts.

DIONYSUS

Where it counts the most,
there I *am* clever.

*(Enter a messenger, a herdsman from Mount Cithaeron.)*

But hear this messenger
who brings you news from the mountain of Cithaeron.
We shall remain where we are. Do not fear:
we will not run away.

MESSENGER

Pentheus, king of Thebes,
I come from Cithaeron where the gleaming flakes of snow
fall on and on forever—

PENTHEUS

Get to the point.
What is your message, man?

MESSENGER

Sir, I have seen
the holy Maenads, the women who ran barefoot
and crazy from the city, and I wanted to report
to you and Thebes what weird fantastic things,
what miracles and more than miracles,
these women do. But may I speak freely
in my own way and words, or make it short?
I fear the harsh impatience of your nature, sire,
too kingly and too quick to anger.

PENTHEUS

Speak freely.
You have my promise: I shall not punish you.
Displeasure with a man who speaks the truth is wrong.
However, the more terrible this tale of yours,
that much more terrible will be the punishment
I impose upon that man who taught our womenfolk
this strange new magic.

MESSENGER

About that hour
when the sun lets loose its light to warm the earth,
our grazing herds of cows had just begun to climb
the path along the mountain ridge. Suddenly
I saw three companies of dancing women,
one led by Autonoë, the second captained
by your mother Agave, while Ino led the third.

There they lay in the deep sleep of exhaustion,
some resting on boughs of fir, others sleeping
where they fell, here and there among the oak leaves—
but all modestly and soberly, not, as you think,
drunk with wine, nor wandering, led astray
by the music of the flute, to hunt their Aphrodite
through the woods.
But your mother heard the lowing
of our horned herds, and springing to her feet,
gave a great cry to waken them from sleep.
And they too, rubbing the bloom of soft sleep
from their eyes, rose up lightly and straight—
a lovely sight to see: all as one,
the old women and the young and the unmarried girls.
First they let their hair fall loose, down
over their shoulders, and those whose straps had slipped
fastened their skins of fawn with writhing snakes
that licked their cheeks. Breasts swollen with milk,
new mothers who had left their babies behind at home
nestled gazelles and young wolves in their arms,
suckling them. Then they crowned their hair with leaves,
ivy and oak and flowering bryony. One woman
struck her thyrsus against a rock and a fountain
of cool water came bubbling up. Another drove
her fennel in the ground, and where it struck the earth,
at the touch of god, a spring of wine poured out.
Those who wanted milk scratched at the soil
with bare fingers and the white milk came welling up.
Pure honey spurted, streaming, from their wands.
If you had been there and seen these wonders for yourself,
you would have gone down on your knees and prayed
to the god you now deny.
We cowherds and shepherds
gathered in small groups, wondering and arguing
among ourselves at these fantastic things,
the awful miracles those women did.
But then a city fellow with the knack of words
rose to his feet and said: "All you who live
upon the pastures of the mountain, what do you say?
Shall we earn a little favor with King Pentheus
by hunting his mother Agave out of the revels?"
Falling in with his suggestion, we withdrew
and set ourselves in ambush, hidden by the leaves
among the undergrowth. Then at a signal
all the Bacchae whirled their wands for the revels
to begin. With one voice they cried aloud:

"*O Iacchus! Son of Zeus!*" "*O Bromius!*" they cried
until the beasts and all the mountain seemed
wild with divinity. And when they ran,
everything ran with them.
It happened, however,
that Agave ran near the ambush where I lay
concealed. Leaping up, I tried to seize her,
but she gave a cry: "Hounds who run with me,
men are hunting us down! Follow, follow me!
Use your wands for weapons."
At this we fled
and barely missed being torn to pieces by the women.
Unarmed, they swooped down upon the herds of cattle
grazing there on the green of the meadow. And then
you could have seen a single woman with bare hands
tear a fat calf, still bellowing with fright,
in two, while others clawed the heifers to pieces.
There were ribs and cloven hooves scattered everywhere,
and scraps smeared with blood hung from the fir trees.
And bulls, their raging fury gathered in their horns,
lowered their heads to charge, then fell, stumbling
to the earth, pulled down by hordes of women
and stripped of flesh and skin more quickly, sire,
than you could blink your royal eyes. Then,
carried up by their own speed, they flew like birds
across the spreading fields along Asopus' stream
where most of all the ground is good for harvesting.
Like invaders they swooped on Hysiae
and on Erythrae in the foothills of Cithaeron.
Everything in sight they pillaged and destroyed.
They snatched the children from their homes. And when
they piled their plunder on their backs, it stayed in place,
untied. Nothing, neither bronze nor iron,
fell to the dark earth. Flames flickered
in their curls and did not burn them. Then the villagers,
furious at what the women did, took to arms.
And *there,* sire, was something terrible to see.
For the men's spears were pointed and sharp, and yet
drew no blood, whereas the wands the women threw
inflicted wounds. And then the men *ran,*
routed by women! Some god, I say, was with them.
The Bacchae then returned where they had started,
by the springs the god had made, and washed their hands
while the snakes licked away the drops of blood
that dabbled their cheeks.
Whoever this god may be,

sire, welcome him to Thebes. For he is great
in many other ways as well. It was he,
or so they say, who gave to mortal men
the gift of lovely wine by which our suffering
is stopped. And if there is no god of wine,
there is no love, no Aphrodite either,
nor other pleasure left to men.

*(Exit messenger.)*

CORYPHAEUS

I tremble
to speak the words of freedom before the tyrant.
But let the truth be told: there is no god
greater than Dionysus.

PENTHEUS

Like a blazing fire
this Bacchic violence spreads. It comes too close.
We are disgraced, humiliated in the eyes
of Hellas. This is no time for hesitation.

*(He turns to an attendant.)*

You there. Go down quickly to the Electran gates
and order out all heavy-armored infantry;
call up the fastest troops among our cavalry,
the mobile squadrons and the archers. We march
against the Bacchae! Affairs are out of hand
when we tamely endure such conduct in our women.

*(Exit attendant.)*

DIONYSUS

Pentheus, you do not hear, or else you disregard
my words of warning. You have done me wrong,
and yet, in spite of that, I warn you once
again: do not take arms against a god.
Stay quiet here. Bromius will not let you
drive his women from their revels on the mountain.

PENTHEUS

Don't you lecture me. You escaped from prison.
Or shall I punish you again?

DIONYSUS

If I were you,
I would offer him a sacrifice, not rage

and kick against necessity, a man defying
god.

PENTHEUS

I shall give your god the sacrifice
that he deserves. His victims will be his women.
I shall make a great slaughter in the woods of Cithaeron.

DIONYSUS

You will all be routed, shamefully defeated,
when their wands of ivy turn back your shields
of bronze.

PENTHEUS

It is hopeless to wrestle with this man.
Nothing on earth will make him hold his tongue.

DIONYSUS

Friend,
you can still save the situation.

PENTHEUS

How?
By accepting orders from my own slaves?

DIONYSUS

No.
I undertake to lead the women back to Thebes.
Without bloodshed.

PENTHEUS

This is some trap.

DIONYSUS

A trap?
How so, if I save you by my own devices?

PENTHEUS

I know.
You and they have conspired to establish your rites
forever.

DIONYSUS

True, I *have* conspired—with god.

PENTHEUS

Bring my armor, someone. And *you* stop talking.

*(Pentheus strides toward the left, but when he is almost offstage, Dionysus calls imperiously to him.)*

DIONYSUS

*Wait!*
Would you like to *see* their revels on the mountain?

PENTHEUS

I would pay a great sum to see that sight.

DIONYSUS

Why are you so passionately curious?

PENTHEUS

Of course
I'd be sorry to see them drunk—

DIONYSUS

But for all your sorrow,
you'd like very much to see them?

PENTHEUS

Yes, very much.
I could crouch beneath the fir trees, out of sight.

DIONYSUS

But if you try to hide, they may track you down.

PENTHEUS

Your point is well taken. I will go openly.

DIONYSUS

Shall I lead you there now? Are you ready to go?

PENTHEUS

The sooner the better. The loss of even a moment
would be disappointing now.

DIONYSUS

First, however,
you must dress yourself in women's clothes.

PENTHEUS

*What?*
You want *me*, a man, to wear a woman's dress. But why?

DIONYSUS

If they knew you were a man, they would kill you instantly.

PENTHEUS

True. You are an old hand at cunning, I see.

DIONYSUS

Dionysus taught me everything I know.

PENTHEUS

Your advice is to the point. What I fail to see
is what we do.

DIONYSUS

I shall go inside with you
and help you dress.

PENTHEUS

Dress? In a *woman's* dress,
you mean? I would die of shame.

DIONYSUS

Very well.
Then you no longer hanker to see the Maenads?

PENTHEUS

What is this costume I must wear?

DIONYSUS

On your head
I shall set a wig with long curls.

PENTHEUS

And then?

DIONYSUS

Next, robes to your feet and a net for your hair.

PENTHEUS

Yes? Go on.

DIONYSUS

Then a thyrsus for your hand
and a skin of dappled fawn.

PENTHEUS

I could not bear it.
I *cannot* bring myself to dress in women's clothes.

DIONYSUS

Then you must fight the Bacchae. That means bloodshed.

PENTHEUS

Right. First we must go and reconnoiter.

DIONYSUS

Surely a wiser course than that of hunting bad
with worse.

PENTHEUS

But how can we pass through the city
without being seen?

DIONYSUS

We shall take deserted streets.
I will lead the way.

PENTHEUS

Any way you like,
provided those women of Bacchus don't jeer at me.
First, however, I shall ponder your advice,
whether to go or not.

DIONYSUS

Do as you please.
I am ready, whatever you decide.

PENTHEUS

Yes.
Either I shall march with my army to the mountain
or act on your advice.

*(Exit Pentheus into the palace.)*

DIONYSUS

Women, our prey now thrashes
in the net we threw. He shall see the Bacchae
and pay the price with death.
O Dionysus,
now action rests with you. And you are near.
Punish this man. But first distract his wits;
bewilder him with madness. For sane of mind
this man would never wear a woman's dress;
but obsess his soul and he will not refuse.
After those threats with which he was so fierce,
I want him made the laughingstock of Thebes,
paraded through the streets, a woman.
Now
I shall go and costume Pentheus in the clothes
which he must wear to Hades when he dies, butchered
by the hands of his mother. He shall come to know

Dionysus, son of Zeus, consummate god,
most terrible, and yet most gentle, to mankind.

*(Exit Dionysus into the palace.)*

CHORUS

—When shall I dance once more
with bare feet the all-night dances,
tossing my head for joy
in the damp air, in the dew,
as a running fawn might frisk
for the green joy of the wide fields,
free from fear of the hunt,
free from the circling beaters
and the nets of woven mesh
and the hunters hallooing on
their yelping packs? And then, hard pressed,
she sprints with the quickness of wind,
bounding over the marsh, leaping
to frisk, leaping for joy,
gay with the green of the leaves,
to dance for joy in the forest,
to dance where the darkness is deepest,
where no man is.

—What is wisdom? What gift of the gods
is held in honor like this:
to hold your hand victorious
over the heads of those you hate?
Honor is precious forever.

—Slow but unmistakable
the might of the gods moves on.
It punishes that man,
infatuate of soul
and hardened in his pride,
who disregards the gods.
The gods are crafty:
they lie in ambush
a long step of time
to hunt the unholy.
Beyond the old beliefs,
no thought, no act shall go.
Small, small is the cost
to believe in this:
whatever is god is strong;
whatever long time has sanctioned,

that is a law forever;
the law tradition makes
is the law of nature.

—What is wisdom? What gift of the gods
is held in honor like this:
to hold your hand victorious
over the heads of those you hate?
Honor is precious forever.

—Blessèd is he who escapes a storm at sea,
who comes home to his harbor.
—Blessèd is he who emerges from under affliction.
—In various ways one man outraces another in the
race for wealth and power.
—Ten thousand men possess ten thousand hopes.
—A few bear fruit in happiness; the others go awry.
—But he who garners day by day the good of life,
he is happiest. Blessèd is he.

*(Re-enter Dionysus from the palace. At the threshold he turns and calls back to Pentheus.)*

DIONYSUS

Pentheus, if you are still so curious to see
forbidden sights, so bent on evil still,
come out. Let us see you in your woman's dress,
disguised in Maenad clothes so you may go and spy
upon your mother and her company.

*(Enter Pentheus from the palace. He wears a long linen dress which partially conceals his fawn-skin. He carries a thyrsus in his hand; on his head he wears a wig with long blond curls bound by a snood. He is dazed and completely in the power of the god who has now possessed him.)*

Why,
you look exactly like one of the daughters of Cadmus.

PENTHEUS

I seem to see two suns blazing in the heavens.
And now two Thebes, two cities, and each
with seven gates. And you—you are a bull
who walks before me there. Horns have sprouted
from your head. Have you always been a beast?
But now I see a bull.

DIONYSUS

It is the god you see.
Though hostile formerly, he now declares a truce

and goes with us. You see what you could not
when you were blind.

PENTHEUS (*coyly primping*)

Do I look like anyone?
Like Ino or my mother Agave?

DIONYSUS

So much alike
I almost might be seeing one of them. But look:
one of your curls has come loose from under the snood
where I tucked it.

PENTHEUS

It must have worked loose
when I was dancing for joy and shaking my head.

DIONYSUS

Then let me be your maid and tuck it back.
Hold still.

PENTHEUS

Arrange it. I am in your hands
completely.

*(Dionysus tucks the curl back under the snood.)*

DIONYSUS

And now your strap has slipped. Yes,
and your robe hangs askew at the ankles.

PENTHEUS (*bending backward to look*)

I think so.
At least on my right leg. But on the left the hem
lies straight.

DIONYSUS

You will think me the best of friends
when you see to your surprise how chaste the Bacchae are.

PENTHEUS

But to be a real Bacchante, should I hold
the wand in my right hand? Or this way?

DIONYSUS

No.

In your right hand. And raise it as you raise
your right foot. I commend your change of heart.

PENTHEUS

Could I lift Cithaeron up, do you think?
Shoulder the cliffs, Bacchae and all?

DIONYSUS

If you wanted.
Your mind was once unsound, but now you think
as sane men do.

PENTHEUS

Should we take crowbars with us?
Or should I put my shoulder to the cliffs
and heave them up?

DIONYSUS

What? And destroy the haunts
of the nymphs, the holy groves where Pan plays
his woodland pipe?

PENTHEUS

You are right. In any case,
women should not be mastered by brute strength.
I will hide myself beneath the firs instead.

DIONYSUS

You will find all the ambush you deserve,
creeping up to spy on the Maenads.

PENTHEUS

Think.
I can see them already, there among the bushes,
mating like birds, caught in the toils of love.

DIONYSUS

Exactly. This is your mission: you go to watch.
You may surprise them—or they may surprise you.

PENTHEUS

Then lead me through the very heart of Thebes,
since I, alone of all this city, dare to go.

DIONYSUS

You and you alone will suffer for your city.
A great ordeal awaits you. But you are worthy
of your fate. I shall lead you safely there;
someone else shall bring you back.

PENTHEUS

Yes, my mother.

DIONYSUS

An example to all men.

PENTHEUS

It is for that I go.

DIONYSUS

You will be carried home—

PENTHEUS

O luxury!

DIONYSUS

cradled in your mother's arms.

PENTHEUS

You will spoil me.

DIONYSUS

I *mean* to spoil you.

PENTHEUS

I go to my reward.

DIONYSUS

You are an extraordinary young man, and you go
to an extraordinary experience. You shall win
a glory towering to heaven and usurping
god's.

*(Exit Pentheus.)*

Agave and you daughters of Cadmus,
reach out your hands! I bring this young man
to a great ordeal. The victor? Bromius.
Bromius—and I. The rest the event shall show.

*(Exit Dionysus.)*

CHORUS

—Run to the mountain, fleet hounds of madness!
Run, run to the revels of Cadmus' daughters!
Sting them against the man in women's clothes,
the madman who spies on the Maenads, who peers
from behind the rocks, who spies from a vantage!
His mother shall see him first. She will cry
to the Maenads: "Who is this spy who has come

to the mountains to peer at the mountain-revels
of the women of Thebes? What bore him, Bacchae?
This man was born of no woman. Some lioness
give him birth, some one of the Libyan gorgons!"

—O Justice, principle of order, spirit of custom,
come! Be manifest; reveal yourself with a sword!
Stab through the throat that godless man,
the mocker who goes, flouting custom and outraging god!
O Justice, stab the evil earth-born spawn of Echion!

—Uncontrollable, the unbeliever goes,
in spitting rage, rebellious and amok,
madly assaulting the mysteries of god,
profaning the rites of the mother of god.
Against the unassailable he runs, with rage
obsessed. Headlong he runs to death.
For death the gods exact, curbing by that bit
the mouths of men. They humble us with death
that we remember what we are who are not god,
but men. We run to death. Wherefore, I say,
accept, accept:
humility is wise; humility is blest.
But what the world calls wise I do not want.
Elsewhere the chase. I hunt another game,
those great, those manifest, those certain goals,
achieving which, our mortal lives are blest.
Let these things be the quarry of my chase:
purity; humility; an unrebellious soul,
accepting all. Let me go the customary way,
the timeless, honored, beaten path of those who walk
with reverence and awe beneath the sons of heaven.

—O Justice, principle of order, spirit of custom,
come! Be manifest; reveal yourself with a sword!
Stab through the throat that godless man,
the mocker who goes, flouting custom and outraging god!
O Justice, destroy the evil earth-born sprawn of Echion!

—O Dionysus, reveal yourself a bull! Be manifest,
a snake with darting heads, a lion breathing fire!
O Bacchus, come! Come with your smile!
Cast your noose about this man who hunts
your Bacchae! Bring him down, trampled
underfoot by the murderous herd of your Maenads!

*(Enter a messenger from Cithaeron.)*

MESSENGER

How prosperous in Hellas these halls once were,
this house founded by Cadmus, the stranger from Sidon
who sowed the dragon seed in the land of the snake!
I am a slave and nothing more, yet even so
I mourn the fortunes of this fallen house.

CORYPHAEUS

What is it?
Is there news of the Bacchae?

MESSENGER

This is my news:
Pentheus, the son of Echion, is dead.

CORYPHAEUS

All hail to Bromius! Our god is a great god!

MESSENGER

What is this you say, women? You dare to rejoice
at these disasters which destroy this house?

CORYPHAEUS

I am no Greek. I hail my god
in my own way. No longer need I
shrink with fear of prison.

MESSENGER

If you suppose this city is so short of men—

CORYPHAEUS

Dionysus, Dionysus, not Thebes,
has power over me.

MESSENGER

Your feelings might be forgiven, then. But this,
this exultation in disaster—it is not right.

CORYPHAEUS

Tell us how the mocker died.
How was he killed?

MESSENGER

There were three of us in all: Pentheus and I,
attending my master, and that stranger who volunteered
his services as guide. Leaving behind us
the last outlying farms of Thebes, we forded
the Asopus and struck into the barren scrubland
of Cithaeron.

There in a grassy glen we halted,
unmoving, silent, without a word,
so we might see but not be seen. From that vantage,
in a hollow cut from the sheer rock of the cliffs,
a place where water ran and the pines grew dense
with shade, we saw the Maenads sitting, their hands
busily moving at their happy tasks. Some
wound the stalks of their tattered wands with tendrils
of fresh ivy; others, frisking like fillies
newly freed from the painted bridles, chanted
in Bacchic songs, responsively.
But Pentheus—
unhappy man—could not quite see the companies
of women. "Stranger," he said, "from where I stand,
I cannot see these counterfeited Maenads.
But if I climbed that towering fir that overhangs
the banks, then I could see their shameless orgies
better."
And now the stranger worked a miracle.
Reaching for the highest branch of a great fir,
he bent it down, down, down to the dark earth,
till it was curved the way a taut bow bends
or like a rim of wood when forced about the circle
of a wheel. Like that he forced that mountain fir
down to the ground. No mortal could have done it.
Then he seated Pentheus at the highest tip
and with his hands let the trunk rise straightly up,
slowly and gently, lest it throw its rider.
And the tree rose, towering to heaven, with my master
huddled at the top. And now the Maenads saw him
more clearly than he saw them. But barely had they seen,
when the stranger vanished and there came a great voice
out of heaven—Dionysus', it must have been—
crying: "Women, I bring you the man who has mocked
at you and me and at our holy mysteries.
Take vengeance upon him." And as he spoke
a flash of awful fire bound earth and heaven.
The high air hushed, and along the forest glen
the leaves hung still; you could hear no cry of beasts.
The Bacchae heard that voice but missed its words,
and leaping up, they stared, peering everywhere.
Again that voice. And now they knew his cry,
the clear command of god. And breaking loose
like startled doves, through grove and torrent,
over jagged rocks, they flew, their feet maddened
by the breath of god. And when they saw my master

perching in his tree, they climbed a great stone
that towered opposite his perch and showered him
with stones and javelins of fir, while the others
hurled their wands. And yet they missed their target,
poor Pentheus in his perch, barely out of reach
of their eager hands, treed, unable to escape.
Finally they splintered branches from the oaks
and with those bars of wood tried to lever up the tree
by prying at the roots. But every effort failed.
Then Agave cried out: "Maenads, make a circle
about the trunk and grip it with your hands.
Unless we take this climbing beast, he will reveal
the secrets of the god." With that, thousands of hands
tore the fir tree from the earth, and down, down
from his high perch fell Pentheus, tumbling
to the ground, sobbing and screaming as he fell,
for he knew his end was near. His own mother,
like a priestess with her victim, fell upon him
first. But snatching off his wig and snood
so she would recognize his face, he touched her cheeks,
screaming, "*No, no, Mother! I am Pentheus,*
*your own son, the child you bore to Echion!*
*Pity me, spare me, Mother! I have done a wrong,*
*but do not kill your own son for my offense.*"
But she was foaming at the mouth, and her crazed eyes
rolling with frenzy. She was mad, stark mad,
possessed by Bacchus. Ignoring his cries of pity,
she seized his left arm at the wrist; then, planting
her foot upon his chest, she pulled, wrenching away
the arm at the shoulder—not by her own strength,
for the god had put inhuman power in her hands.
Ino, meanwhile, on the other side, was scratching off
his flesh. Then Autonoë and the whole horde
of Bacchae swarmed upon him. Shouts everywhere,
he screaming with what little breath was left,
they shrieking in triumph. One tore off an arm,
another a foot still warm in its shoe. His ribs
were clawed clean of flesh and every hand
was smeared with blood as they played ball with scraps
of Pentheus' body.
The pitiful remains lie scattered,
one piece among the sharp rocks, others
lying lost among the leaves in the depths
of the forest. His mother, picking up his head,
impaled it on her wand. She seems to think it is
some mountain lion's head which she carries in triumph

through the thick of Cithaeron. Leaving her sisters
at the Maenad dances, she is coming here, gloating
over her grisly prize. She calls upon Bacchus:
he is her "fellow-huntsman," "comrade of the chase,
crowned with victory." But all the victory
she carries home is her own grief.
Now,
before Agave returns, let me leave
this scene of sorrow. Humility,
a sense of reverence before the sons of heaven—
of all the prizes that a mortal man might win,
these, I say, are wisest; these are best.

*(Exit Messenger.)*

CHORUS

—We dance to the glory of Bacchus!
We dance to the death of Pentheus,
the death of the spawn of the dragon!
He dressed in woman's dress;
he took the lovely thyrsus;
it waved him down to death,
led by a bull to Hades.
Hail, Bacchae! Hail, women of Thebes!
Your victory is fair, fair the prize,
this famous prize of grief!
Glorious the game! To fold your child
in your arms, streaming with his blood!

CORYPHAEUS

But look: there comes Pentheus' mother, Agave,
running wild-eyed toward the palace.
—Welcome,
welcome to the reveling band of the god of joy!

*(Enter Agave with other Bacchantes. She is covered with blood and carries the head of Pentheus impaled upon her thyrsus.)*

AGAVE

Bacchae of Asia—

CHORUS

Speak, speak.

AGAVE

We bring this branch to the palace,
this fresh-cut spray from the mountains.
Happy was the hunting.

CHORUS

I see.
I welcome our fellow-reveler of god.

AGAVE

The whelp of a wild mountain lion,
and snared by me without a noose.
Look, look at the prize I bring.

CHORUS

Where was he caught?

AGAVE

On Cithaeron—

CHORUS

On Cithaeron?

AGAVE

Our prize was killed.

CHORUS

Who killed him?

AGAVE

I struck him first.
The Maenads call me "Agave the blest."

CHORUS

And then?

AGAVE

Cadmus'—

CHORUS

Cadmus'?

AGAVE

Daughters.
After me, they reached the prey.
After me. Happy was the hunting.

CHORUS

Happy indeed.

AGAVE

Then share my glory,
share the feast.

CHORUS

Share, unhappy woman?

AGAVE

See, the whelp is young and tender.
Beneath the soft mane of its hair,
the down is blooming on the cheeks.

CHORUS

With that mane he *looks* a beast.

AGAVE

Our god is wise. Cunningly, cleverly,
Bacchus the hunter lashed the Maenads
against his prey.

CHORUS

Our king is a hunter.

AGAVE

You praise me now?

CHORUS

I praise you.

AGAVE

The men of Thebes—

CHORUS

And Pentheus, your son?

AGAVE

Will praise his mother. She caught
a great quarry, this lion's cub.

CHORUS

Extraordinary catch.

AGAVE

Extraordinary skill.

CHORUS

You are proud?

AGAVE

Proud and happy.
I have won the trophy of the chase,
a great prize, manifest to all.

CORYPHAEUS

Then, poor woman, show the citizens of Thebes
this great prize, this trophy you have won
in the hunt.

*(Agave proudly exhibits her thyrsus with the head of Pentheus impaled upon the point.)*

AGAVE

You citizens of this towered city,
men of Thebes, behold the trophy of your women's
hunting! *This* is the quarry of our chase, taken
not with nets nor spears of bronze but by the white
and delicate hands of women. What are they worth,
your boastings now and all that uselessness
your armor is, since we, with our bare hands,
captured this quarry and tore its bleeding body
limb from limb?
—But where is my father Cadmus?
He should come. And my son. Where is Pentheus?
Fetch him. I will have him set his ladder up
against the wall and, there upon the beam,
nail the head of this wild lion I have killed
as a trophy of my hunt.

*(Enter Cadmus, followed by attendants who bear upon a bier the dismembered body of Pentheus.)*

CADMUS

Follow me, attendants.
Bear your dreadful burden in and set it down,
there before the palace.

*(The attendants set down the bier.)*

This was Pentheus
whose body, after long and weary searchings
I painfully assembled from Cithaeron's glens
where it lay, scattered in shreds, dismembered
throughout the forest, no two pieces
in a single place.
Old Teiresias and I
had returned to Thebes from the orgies on the mountain
before I learned of this atrocious crime
my daughters did. And so I hurried back
to the mountain to recover the body of this boy
murdered by the Maenads. There among the oaks
I found Aristaeus' wife, the mother of Actaeon,
Autonoë, and with her Ino, both
still stung with madness. But Agave, they said,
was on her way to Thebes, still possessed.

And what they said was true, for there she is,
and not a happy sight.

AGAVE

Now, Father,
yours can be the proudest boast of living men.
For you are now the father of the bravest daughters
in the world. All of your daughters are brave,
but I above the rest. I have left my shuttle
at the loom; I raised my sight to higher things—
to hunting animals with my bare hands.
You see?
Here in my hands I hold the quarry of my chase,
a trophy for our house. Take it, Father, take it.
Glory in my kill and invite your friends to share
the feast of triumph. For you are blest, Father,
by this great deed I have done.

CADMUS

This is a grief
so great it knows no size. I cannot look.
*This* is the awful murder your hands have done.
*This, this* is the noble victim you have slaughtered
to the gods. And to share a feast like this
you now invite all Thebes and me?
O gods,
how terribly I pity you and then myself.
Justly—too, too justly—has lord Bromius,
this god of our own blood, destroyed us all,
every one.

AGAVE

How scowling and crabbed is old age
in men. I hope my son takes after his mother
and wins, as she has done, the laurels of the chase
when he goes hunting with the younger men of Thebes.
But all my son can do is quarrel with god.
He should be scolded, Father, and you are the one
who should scold him. Yes, someone call him out
so he can see his mother's triumph.

CADMUS

Enough. No more.
When you realize the horror you have done,
you shall suffer terribly. But if with luck

your present madness lasts until you die,
you will seem to have, not having, happiness.

AGAVE

Why do you reproach me? Is there something wrong?

CADMUS

First raise your eyes to the heavens.

AGAVE

There.
But why?

CADMUS

Does it look the same as it did before?
Or has it changed?

AGAVE

It seems—somehow—clearer,
brighter than it was before.

CADMUS

Do you still feel
the same flurry inside you?

AGAVE

The same—flurry?
No, I feel—somehow—calmer. I feel as though—
my mind were somehow—changing.

CADMUS

Can you still hear me?
Can you answer clearly?

AGAVE

No. I have forgotten
what we were saying, Father.

CADMUS

Who was your husband?

AGAVE

Echion—a man, they said, born of the dragon seed.

CADMUS

What was the name of the child you bore your husband?

AGAVE

Pentheus.

CADMUS

And whose head do you hold in your hands?

AGAVE (*averting her eyes*)

A lion's head—or so the hunters told me.

CADMUS

Look directly at it. Just a quick glance.

AGAVE

What is it? What am I holding in my hands?

CADMUS

Look more closely still. Study it carefully.

AGAVE

*No!* O gods, I see the greatest grief there is.

CADMUS

Does it look like a lion now?

AGAVE

No, no. It is—
Pentheus' head—I hold—

CADMUS

And mourned by me
before you ever knew.

AGAVE

But *who* killed him?
Why am *I* holding him?

CADMUS

O savage truth,
what a time to come!

AGAVE

For god's sake, speak.
My heart is beating with terror.

CADMUS

*You* killed him.
You and your sisters.

AGAVE

But where was he killed?
Here at home? Where?

CADMUS

He was killed on Cithaeron,
there where the hounds tore Actaeon to pieces.

AGAVE

But why? Why had Pentheus gone to Cithaeron?

CADMUS

He went to your revels to mock the god.

AGAVE

But *we*—
what were we doing on the mountain?

CADMUS

You were mad.
The whole city was possessed.

AGAVE

Now, now I see:
Dionysus has destroyed us all.

CADMUS

You outraged him.
You denied that he was truly god.

AGAVE

Father,
where is my poor boy's body now?

CADMUS

There it is.
I gathered the pieces with great difficulty.

AGAVE

Is his body entire? Has he been laid out well?

CADMUS

[All but the head. The rest is mutilated
horribly.]

AGAVE

But why should Pentheus suffer for my crime?

CADMUS

He, like you, blasphemed the god. And so
the god has brought us all to ruin at one blow,
you, your sisters, and this boy. All our house
the god has utterly destroyed and, with it,

me. For I have no sons left, no male heir;
and I have lived only to see this boy,
this branch of your own body, most horribly
and foully killed.

*(He turns and addresses the corpse.)*

—To you my house looked up.
Child, you were the stay of my house; you were
my daughter's son. Of you this city stood in awe.
No one who once had seen your face dared outrage
the old man, or if he did, you punished him.
Now I must go, a banished and dishonored man—
I, Cadmus the great, who sowed the soldiery
of Thebes and harvested a great harvest. My son,
dearest to me of all men—for even dead,
I count you still the man I love the most—
never again will your hand touch my chin;
no more, child, will you hug me and call me
"Grandfather" and say, "Who is wronging you?
Does anyone trouble you or vex your heart, old man?
Tell me, Grandfather, and I will punish him."
No, now there is grief for me; the mourning
for you; pity for your mother; and for her sisters,
sorrow.
If there is still any mortal man
who despises or defies the gods, let him look
on this boy's death and believe in the gods.

CORYPHAEUS

Cadmus, I pity you. Your daughter's son
has died as he deserved, and yet his death
bears hard on you.

*[At this point there is a break in the manuscript of nearly fifty lines. The following speeches of Agave and Coryphaeus and the first part of Dionysus' speech have been conjecturally reconstructed from fragments and later material which made use of the Bacchae. Lines which can plausibly be assigned to the lacuna are otherwise not indicated. My own inventions are designed, not to complete the speeches, but to effect a transition between the fragments, and are bracketed. . . .—*TRANS.*]*

AGAVE

O Father, now you can see
how everything has changed. I am in anguish now,
tormented, who walked in triumph minutes past,
exulting in my kill. And that prize I carried home
with such pride was my own curse. Upon these hands

I bear the curse of my son's blood. How then
with these accursed hands may I touch his body?
How can I, accursed with such a curse, hold him
to my breast? O gods, what dirge can I sing
[that there might be] a dirge [for every]
broken limb?

* * *

Where is a shroud to cover up his corpse?
O my child, what hands will give you proper care
unless with my own hands I lift my curse?

*(She lifts up one of Pentheus' limbs and asks the help of Cadmus in piecing the body together. She mourns each piece separately before replacing it on the bier.)*

Come, Father. We must restore his head
to this unhappy boy. As best we can, we shall make
him whole again.
—O dearest, dearest face!
Pretty boyish mouth! Now with this veil
I shroud your head, gathering with loving care
these mangled bloody limbs, this flesh I brought
to birth.

* * *

CORYPHAEUS

Let this scene teach those [who see these things:
Dionysus is the son] of Zeus.

*(Above the palace Dionysus appears in epiphany.)*

DIONYSUS

[I am Dionysus,
the son of Zeus, returned to Thebes, revealed,
a god to men.] But the men [of Thebes] blasphemed me.
They slandered me; they said I came of mortal man,
and not content with speaking blasphemies,
[they dared to threaten my person with violence.]
These crimes this people whom I cherished well
did from malice to their benefactor. Therefore,
I now disclose the sufferings in store for them.
Like [enemies], they shall be driven from this city
to other lands; there, submitting to the yoke
of slavery, they shall wear out wretched lives,
captives of war, enduring much indignity.

*(He turns to the corpse of Pentheus.)*

This man has found the death which he deserved,
torn to pieces among the jagged rocks.
You are my witnesses: he came with outrage;
he attempted to chain my hands, abusing me
[and doing what he should least of all have done.]
And therefore he has rightly perished by the hands
of those who should the least of all have murdered him.
What he suffers, he suffers justly.
Upon you,
Agave, and on your sisters I pronounce this doom:
you shall leave this city in expiation
of the murder you have done. You are unclean,
and it would be a sacrilege that murderers
should remain at peace beside the graves [of those
whom they have killed].

*(He turns to Cadmus.)*

* * *

Next I shall disclose the trials
which await this man. You, Cadmus, shall be changed
to a serpent, and your wife, the child of Ares,
immortal Harmonia, shall undergo your doom,
a serpent too. With her, it is your fate
to go a journey in a car drawn on by oxen,
leading behind you a great barbarian host.
For thus decrees the oracle of Zeus.
With a host so huge its numbers cannot be counted,
you shall ravage many cities; but when your army
plunders the shrine of Apollo, its homecoming
shall be perilous and hard. Yet in the end
the god Ares shall save Harmonia and you
and bring you both to live among the blest.
So say I, born of no mortal father,
Dionysus, true son of Zeus. If then,
when you would not, you had muzzled your madness,
you should have an ally now in the son of Zeus.

CADMUS

We implore you, Dionysus. We have done wrong.

DIONYSUS

Too late. When there was time, you did not know me.

CADMUS

We have learned. But your sentence is too harsh.

DIONYSUS

I am a god. I was blasphemed by you.

CADMUS

Gods should be exempt from human passions.

DIONYSUS

Long ago my father Zeus ordained these things.

AGAVE

It is fated, Father. We must go.

DIONYSUS

Why then delay?
For you must go.

CADMUS

Child, to what a dreadful end
have we all come, you and your wretched sisters
and my unhappy self. An old man, I must go
to live a stranger among barbarian peoples, doomed
to lead against Hellas a motley foreign army.
Transformed to serpents, I and my wife,
Harmonia, the child of Ares, we must captain
spearsmen against the tombs and shrines of Hellas.
Never shall my sufferings end; not even
over Acheron shall I have peace.

AGAVE (*embracing Cadmus*)

O Father,
to be banished, to live without you!

CADMUS

Poor child,
like a white swan warding its weak old father,
why do you clasp those white arms about my neck?

AGAVE

But banished! Where shall I go?

CADMUS

I do not know,
my child. Your father can no longer help you.

AGAVE

Farewell, my home! City, farewell.
O bridal bed, banished I go,
in misery, I leave you now.

CADMUS

Go, poor child, seek shelter in Aristaeus' house.

AGAVE

I pity you, Father.

CADMUS

And I pity you, my child,
and I grieve for your poor sisters. I pity them.

AGAVE

Terribly has Dionysus brought
disaster down upon this house.

DIONYSUS

I was terribly blasphemed,
my name dishonored in Thebes.

AGAVE

Farewell, Father.

CADMUS

Farewell to you, unhappy child.
Fare well. But you shall find your faring hard.

*(Exit Cadmus.)*

AGAVE

Lead me, guides, where my sisters wait,
poor sisters of my exile. Let me go
where I shall never see Cithaeron more,
where that accursed hill may not see me,
where I shall find no trace of thyrsus!
That I leave to other Bacchae.

*(Exit Agave with attendants.)*

CHORUS

The gods have many shapes.
The gods bring many things
to their accomplishment.
And what was most expected
has not been accomplished.
But god has found his way
for what no man expected.
So ends the play.

# Plato (427–347 BCE)

Plato's work was a response to the disintegration of Athenian society during the period of the Peloponnesian Wars described by Thucydides. Plato had wanted to be a poet and a politician, but the corruption he saw around him prevented him from pursuing a conventional career. He became instead a "philosopher," that is, a lover of wisdom, and one of the most influential thinkers of the Western world. The modern philosopher Alfred North Whitehead went so far as to say that all of philosophy is a footnote to Plato.

The experience that changed Plato's life was the execution of his mentor Socrates by the Athenian court. Our first selection from Plato is the *Apology*—the defense—that Socrates makes for himself against the trumped-up charge that he was corrupting Athenian youth. For Plato, who includes himself in the audience addressed by Socrates at his trial, the verdict was tantamount to a death sentence issued by Athens against itself. It is interesting to ask how accurate the *Apology* might be as a report of Socrates' trial. It is impossible to tell, because Plato is a great narrative and rhetorical artist who, in all his works, uses the voice of Socrates to express his own ideas. Given this rhetorical posture, it is difficult to know with certainty anything about the historical Socrates from Plato's depictions of him.

In the *Republic,* Plato tries to answer the question, "What is justice?" The imperialist Athenians, as Thucydides represents them in their chilling dialogue with the subject Melians, believed that might makes right: justice is simply the rule of the stronger. Plato resisted this climate of opinion in the *Republic* by seeking to describe the nature of justice and its formative effect on the human soul. His famous "allegory of the cave" in Book VII is meant to illustrate the persuasion of the soul away from mere conventional opinion and peer pressure toward reality. Plato here conducts his investigation by means of a myth. Philosophy, for Plato, never abandons mythic representation; his dialogues are themselves literary works that continuously move between—and preserve the tension between—conceptual analysis and symbolic representation.

The *Symposium* is the report of a witty, urbane, and often fanciful conversation following a banquet celebrating the victory of the poet Agathon in a tragic competition. Each of the participants—one of whom is the comic poet Aristophanes—gives his opinion on the nature of love. The centerpiece of the *Symposium* is the contribution of Socrates, whose discourse on the ladder of love was to have a profound impact on later literature, for example, the love poetry of the European Renaissance. The other dinner guests present set speeches, but Socrates narrates a conversation he once had with the priestess Diotima. Diotima tells Socrates that love (*Eros*) exists in between the mortal and immortal. Eros, the symbol of the philosopher (the lover of wisdom), is the child of Resource and Need and always exists in the tension between knowledge and ignorance. The philosopher is not the master (or mistress) of his or her experience (in the *Republic,* Socrates maintains that both men and women have the capacity to be philosophic rulers); the awareness of incompleteness or need is as fundamental to the philosophical experience as is the sense of being drawn toward fullness. Interestingly, the same idea emerges in the Chinese philosophy of the same period. The Dao de jing (pp. 332–350) similarly symbolizes the neediness of the philosopher in images that convey passivity rather than activity—images such as water, valleys, and the uncarved block.

The complex narrative frame of the *Symposium*—in which Apollodorus tells an unidentified enquirer what he (Apollodorus) had told Glaucon about what Aristodemus, who was actually at the banquet, had told him (Apollodorus)—is a witty testimony to the tentativeness of Plato's assertions about the nature of Being.

The philosopher is precisely the person who lives between ignorance and knowledge and who is wise enough to feel the lack expressed by the exemplary pupil of Confucius: "What am I to do? What am I to do?" (*Analects* 15.16). Daoists too remind us that "The Dao that can be put into words is not the constant Dao" (Dao de jing, ch. 1). The very awareness of need, of the fact that the human mind can never comprehend reality in a purely discursive manner, requires a highly suggestive and poetic means of expression, in Plato's dialogues as well as in Daoism.

## *The Apology*

*Translated by F.J. Church*

### *Characters*

SOCRATES

MELETUS

*Scene—The Court of Justice*

*Socrates.* I do not know what impression my accusers have made upon you, Athenians. But I do know that they nearly made me forget who I was, so persuasive were they. And yet they have scarcely spoken one single word of truth. Of all their many falsehoods, the one which astonished me most was their saying that I was a clever speaker, and that you must be careful not to let me deceive you. I thought that it was most shameless of them not to be ashamed to talk in that way. For as soon as I open my mouth they will be refuted, and I shall prove that I am not a clever speaker in any way at all—unless, indeed, by a clever speaker they mean someone who speaks the truth. If that is their meaning, I agree with them that I am an orator not to be compared with them. My accusers, I repeat, have said little or nothing that is true, but from me you shall hear the whole truth. Certainly you will not hear a speech, Athenians, dressed up, like theirs, with fancy words and phrases. I will say to you what I have to say, without artifice, and I shall use the first words which come to mind, for I believe that what I have to say is just; so let none of you expect anything else. Indeed, my friends, it would hardly be right for me, at my age, to come before you like a schoolboy with his concocted phrases. But there is one thing, Athenians, which I do most earnestly beg and entreat of you. Do not be surprised and do not interrupt with shouts if in my defense I speak in the same way that I am accustomed to speak in the market place, at the tables of the money-changers, where many of you have heard me, and elsewhere. The truth is this: I am more than seventy, and this is the first time that I have ever come before a law court; thus your manner of speech here is quite strange to me. If I had really been a stranger, you would have forgiven me for speaking in the language and the manner of my native country. And so now I ask you to grant me what I think I have a right to claim. Never mind the manner of my speech—it may be superior or it may be inferior to the usual manner. Give your whole attention to the question, whether what I say is just or not? That is what is required of a good judge, as speaking the truth is required of a good orator.

I have to defend myself, Athenians, first against the older false accusations of my old accusers, and then against the more recent ones of my present accusers. For many men have been accusing me to you, and for very many years, who have not spoken a word of truth; and I fear them more than I fear Anytus and his associates, formidable as they are. But, my friends, the others are still more formidable, since they got hold of most of you when you were children and have been more persistent in accusing me untruthfully, persuading you that there is a certain Socrates, a wise man, who speculates about the heavens, who investigates things that are beneath the earth, and who can make the worse argument appear the stronger. These men, Athenians, who spread abroad this report are the accusers whom I fear; for their hearers think that persons who pursue such inquiries never believe in the gods. Besides they are many, their attacks have been going on for a long time, and they spoke to you when you were most ready to believe them, since you were all young, and some of you were children. And there was no one to answer them when they attacked me. The most preposterous thing of all is that I do not even know their names: I cannot tell you who they are except when one happens to be a comic poet. But all the rest who have persuaded you, from motives of resentment and prejudice, and sometimes, it may be, from conviction, are hardest to cope with. For I cannot call any one of them forward in court to cross-examine him. I have, as it were, simply to spar with shadows in my defense, and to put questions which there is no one to answer. I ask you, therefore, to believe that, as I say, I have been attacked by two kinds of accusers—first, by Meletus and his associates, and, then, by those older ones of whom I have spoken. And, with your leave, I will defend myself first against my old accusers, since you heard their accusations first, and they were much more compelling than my present accusers are.

Well, I must make my defense, Athenians, and try in the short time allowed me to remove the prejudice which you have been so long a time acquiring. I hope that I may manage to do this, if it be best for you and for me, and that my defense may be successful; but I am quite aware of the nature of my task, and I know that it is a difficult one. Be the outcome, however, as is pleasing to god, I must obey the law and make my defense.

Let us begin from the beginning, then, and ask what is the accusation that has given rise to the prejudice against me, on which Meletus relied when he brought his indictment. What is the prejudice which my enemies have been spreading about me? I must assume that they are formally accusing me, and read their indictment. It would run somewhat in this fashion: "Socrates is guilty of engaging in inquiries into things beneath the earth and in the heavens, of making the weaker argument appear the stronger, and of teaching others these same things." That is what they say. And in the comedy of Aristophanes you yourselves saw a man called Socrates swinging around in a basket and saying that he walked on air, and sputtering a great deal of nonsense about matters of which I understand nothing at all. I do not mean to disparage that kind of knowledge if there is anyone who is wise about these matters. I trust Meletus may never be able to prosecute me for that. But the truth is, Athenians, I have nothing to do with these matters, and almost all of you are yourselves my witnesses of this. I beg all of you who have ever heard me discussing, and they are many, to inform your neighbors and tell them if any of you have ever heard me discussing such matters at all. That will show you that the other common statements about me are as false as this one.

But the fact is that not one of these is true. And if you have heard that I undertake to educate men, and make money by so doing, that is not true either, though I think that it would be a fine thing to be able to educate men, as Gorgias of Leontini, and Prodicus of Ceos, and Hippias of Elis do. For each of them, my friends, can go into any city, and persuade the young men to leave the society of their fellow citizens, with any of whom they might associate for nothing, and to be only too glad to be allowed to pay money for the privilege of associating with themselves. And I believe that there is another wise man from Paros residing in Athens at this moment. I happened to meet Callias, the son of Hipponicus, a man who has spent more money on sophists than everyone else put together. So I said to him (he has two sons), "Callias, if your two sons had been foals or calves, we could have hired a trainer for them who would have trained them to excel in doing what they are naturally capable of. He would have been either a groom or a farmer. But whom do you intend to take to train them, seeing that they are men? Who understands the excellence which a man and citizen is capable of attaining? I suppose that you must have thought of this, because you have sons. Is there such a person or not?" "Certainly there is," he replied. "Who is he," said I, "and where does he come from, and what is his fee?" "Evenus, Socrates," he replied, "from Paros, five minae." Then I thought that Evenus was a fortunate person if he really understood this art and could teach so cleverly. If I had possessed knowledge of that kind, I should have been conceited and disdainful. But, Athenians, the truth is that I do not possess it.

Perhaps some of you may reply: "But, Socrates, what is the trouble with you? What has given rise to these prejudices against you? You must have been doing something out of the ordinary. All these rumors and reports of you would never have arisen if you had not been doing something different from other men. So tell us what it is, that we may not give our verdict arbitrarily." I think that that is a fair question, and I will try to explain to you what it is that has raised these prejudices against me and given me this reputation. Listen, then. Some of you, perhaps, will think that I am joking, but I assure you that I will tell you the whole truth. I have gained this reputation, Athenians, simply by reason of a certain wisdom. But by what kind of wisdom? It is by just that wisdom which is perhaps human wisdom. In that, it may be, I am really wise. But the men of whom I was speaking just now must be wise in a wisdom which is greater than human wisdom, or else I cannot describe it, for certainly I know nothing of it myself, and if any man says that I do, he lies and speaks to arouse prejudice against me. Do not interrupt me with shouts, Athenians, even if you think that I am boasting. What I am going to say is not my own statement. I will tell you who says it, and he is worthy of your respect. I will bring the god of Delphi to be the witness of my wisdom, if it is wisdom at all, and of its nature. You remember Chaerephon. From youth upwards he was my comrade; and also a partisan of your democracy, sharing your recent exile and returning with you. You remember, too, Chaerephon's character—how impulsive he was in carrying through whatever he took in hand. Once he went to Delphi and ventured to put this question to the oracle—I entreat you again, my friends, not to interrupt me with your shouts—he asked if there was anyone who was wiser than I. The priestess answered that there was no one. Chaerephon himself is dead, but his brother here will witness to what I say.

Now see why I tell you this. I am going to explain to you how the prejudice against me has arisen. When I heard of the oracle I began to reflect: What can the god mean by this riddle? I know very well that I am not wise, even in the smallest degree. Then what can he mean by saying that I am the wisest of men? It cannot be that he is speaking falsely, for he is a god and cannot lie. For a long time I was at a loss to understand his meaning. Then, very reluctantly, I turned to investigate it in this manner: I went to a man who was reputed to be wise, thinking that there, if anywhere, I should prove the answer wrong, and meaning to point out to the oracle its mistake, and to say, "You said that I was the wisest of men, but this man is wiser than I am." So I examined the man—I need not tell you his name, he was a politician—but this was the result, Athenians. When I conversed with him I came to see that, though a great many persons, and most of all he himself, thought that he was wise, yet he was not wise. Then I tried to prove to him that he was not wise, though he fancied that he was. By so doing I made him indignant, and many of the bystanders. So when I went away, I thought to myself, "I am wiser than this man: neither of us knows anything that is really worth knowing, but he thinks that he has knowledge when he has not, while I, having no knowledge, do not think that I have. I seem, at any rate, to be a little wiser than he is on this point: I do not think that I know what I do not know." Next I went to another man who was reputed to be still wiser than the last, with exactly the same result. And there again I made him, and many other men, indignant.

Then I went on to one man after another, realizing that I was arousing indignation every day, which caused me much pain and anxiety. Still I thought that I must set the god's command above everything. So I had to go to every man who seemed to possess any knowledge, and investigate the meaning of the oracle. Athenians, I must tell you the truth; I swear, this was the result of the investigation which I made at the god's command: I found that the men whose reputation for wisdom stood highest were nearly the most lacking in it, while others who were looked down on as common people were much more intelligent. Now I must describe to you the wanderings which I undertook, like Herculean labors, to prove the oracle irrefutable. After the politicians, I went to the poets, tragic, dithyrambic, and others, thinking that there I should find myself manifestly more ignorant than they. So I took up the poems on which I thought that they had spent most pains, and asked them what they meant, hoping at the same time to learn something from them. I am ashamed to tell you the truth, my friends, but I must say it. Almost any one of the bystanders could have talked about the works of these poets better than the poets themselves. So I soon found that it is not by wisdom that the poets create their works, but by a certain instinctive inspiration, like soothsayers and prophets, who say many fine things, but understand nothing of what they say. The poets seemed to me to be in a similar situation. And at the same time I perceived that, because of their poetry, they thought that they were the wisest of men in other matters too, which they were not. So I went away again, thinking that I had the same advantage over the poets that I had over the politicians.

Finally, I went to the artisans, for I knew very well that I possessed no knowledge at all worth speaking of, and I was sure that I should find that they knew many fine things. And in that I was not mistaken. They knew what I did not know, and so far they were wiser than I. But, Athenians, it seemed to me that the skilled artisans had the same failing as the poets. Each of them believed himself to be extremely wise in matters of the greatest importance because he was skillful in his own art: and this presumption of theirs obscured their real wisdom. So I asked myself, on behalf of the oracle, whether I would choose to remain as I was, without either their wisdom or their ignorance, or to possess both, as they did. And I answered to myself and to the oracle that it was better for me to remain as I was.

From this examination, Athenians, has arisen much fierce and bitter indignation, and as a result a great many prejudices about me. People say that I am "a wise man." For the bystanders always think that I am wise myself in any matter wherein I refute another. But, gentlemen, I believe that the god is really wise, and that by this oracle he meant that human wisdom is worth little or nothing. I do not think that he meant that Socrates was wise. He only made use of my name, and took me as an example, as though he would say to men, "He among you is the wisest who, like Socrates, knows that his wisdom is really worth nothing at all." Therefore I still go about testing and examining every man whom I think wise, whether he be a citizen or a stranger, as the god has commanded me. Whenever I find that he is not wise, I point out to him, on the god's behalf, that he is not wise. I am so busy in this pursuit that I have never had leisure to take any part worth mentioning in public matters or to look after my private affairs. I am in great poverty as the result of my service to the god.

Besides this, the young men who follow me about, who are the sons of wealthy persons and have the most leisure, take pleasure in hearing men cross-examined. They often imitate me among themselves; then they try their hands at cross-examining other people. And, I imagine, they find plenty of men who think that they know a great deal when in fact they know little or nothing. Then the persons who are cross-examined get angry with me instead of with themselves, and say that Socrates is an abomination and corrupts the young. When they are asked, "Why, what does he do? What does he teach?" they do not know what to say. Not to seem at a loss, they repeat the stock charges against all philosophers, and allege that he investigates things in the air and under the earth, and that he teaches people to believe in the gods, and to make the worse argument appear the stronger. For, I suppose, they would not like to confess the truth, which is that they are shown up as ignorant pretenders to knowledge that they do not possess. So they have been filling your ears with their bitter prejudices for a long time, for they are ambitious, energetic, and numerous; and they speak vigorously and persuasively against me. Relying on this, Meletus, Anytus, and Lycon have attacked me. Meletus is indignant with me on behalf of the poets, Anytus on behalf of the artisans and politicians, and Lycon on behalf of the orators. And so, as I said at the beginning, I shall be surprised if I am able, in the short time allowed me for my defense, to remove from your minds this prejudice which has grown so strong. What I have told you, Athenians, is the truth: I neither conceal nor do I suppress anything, trivial or important. Yet I know that it is just this outspokenness which rouses indignation. But that is only a proof that my words are true, and that the prejudice against me, and the causes of it, are what I have said. And whether you investigate them now or hereafter, you will find that they are so.

What I have said must suffice as my defense against the charges of my first accusers. I will try next to defend myself against Meletus, that "good patriot," as he calls himself, and my later accusers. Let us assume that they are a new set of accusers, and read their indictment, as we did in the case of the others. It runs thus: Socrates is guilty of corrupting the youth, and of believing not in the gods whom the state believes in, but in other new divinities. Such is the accusation. Let us examine each point in it separately. Meletus says that I am guilty of corrupting the youth. But I say, Athenians, that he is guilty of playing a solemn joke by casually bringing men to trial, and pretending to have a solemn interest in matters to which he has never given a moment's thought. Now I will try to prove to you that this is so.

Come here, Meletus. Is it not a fact that you think it very important that the young should be as good as possible?

*Meletus.* It is.

*Socrates.* Come, then, tell the judges who improves them. You care so much, you must know. You are accusing me, and bringing me to trial, because, as you say, you have discovered that I am the corrupter of the youth. Come now, reveal to the gentlemen who improves them. You see, Meletus, you have nothing to say; you are silent. But don't you think that this is shameful? Is not your silence a conclusive proof of what I say—that you have never cared? Come, tell us, my good man, who makes the young better?

*Mel.* The laws.

*Socr.* That, my friend, is not my question. What man improves the young, who begins by knowing the laws?

*Mel.* The judges here, Socrates.

*Socr.* What do you mean, Meletus? Can they educate the young and improve them?

*Mel.* Certainly.

*Socr.* All of them? Or only some of them?

*Mel.* All of them.

*Socr.* By Hera, that is good news! Such a large supply of benefactors! And do the members of the audience here improve them, or not?

*Mel.* They do.

*Socr.* And do the councilors?

*Mel.* Yes.

*Socr.* Well, then, Meletus, do the members of the assembly corrupt the young or do they again all improve them?

*Mel.* They, too, improve them.

*Socr.* Then all the Athenians, apparently, make the young into good men except me, and I alone corrupt them. Is that your meaning?

*Mel.* Certainly, that is my meaning.

*Socr.* You have discovered me to be most unfortunate. Now tell me: do you think that the same holds good in the case of horses? Does one man do them harm and everyone else improve them? On the contrary, is it not one man only, or a very few—namely, those who are skilled with horses—who can improve them, while the majority of men harm them if they use them and have anything to do with them? Is it not so, Meletus, both with horses and with every other animal? Of course it is, whether you and Anytus say yes or no. The young would certainly be very fortunate if only one man corrupted them, and everyone else did them good. The truth is, Meletus, you prove conclusively that you have never thought about the young in your life. You exhibit your carelessness in not caring for the very matters about which you are prosecuting me.

Now be so good as to tell us, Meletus, is it better to live among good citizens or bad ones? Answer, my friend. I am not asking you at all a difficult question. Do not the bad harm their associates and the good do them good?

*Mel.* Yes.

*Socr.* Is there anyone who would rather be injured than benefited by his companions? Answer, my good man; you are obliged by the law to answer. Does anyone like to be injured?

*Mel.* Certainly not.

*Socr.* Well, then, are you prosecuting me for corrupting the young and making them worse, voluntarily or involuntarily?

*Mel.* For doing it voluntarily.

*Socr.* What, Meletus? Do you mean to say that you, who are so much younger than I, are yet so much wiser than I that you know that bad citizens always do evil, and that good citizens do good, to those with whom they come in contact, while I am so extraordinarily ignorant as not to know that, if I make any of my companions evil, he will probably injure me in some way? And you allege that I do this voluntarily? You will not make me believe that, nor anyone else either, I should think. Either I do not corrupt the young at all or, if I do, I do so involuntarily, so that you are lying in either case. And if I corrupt them involuntarily, the law does not call upon you to prosecute me for an error which is involuntary, but to take me aside privately and reprove and educate me. For, of course, I shall cease from doing wrong involuntarily, as soon as I know that I have been doing wrong. But you avoided associating with me and educating me; instead you bring me up before the court, where the law sends persons, not for education, but for punishment.

The truth is, Athenians, as I said, it is quite clear that Meletus has never cared at all about these matters. However, now tell us, Meletus, how do you say that I corrupt the young? Clearly, according to our indictment, by teaching them not to believe in the gods the state believes in, but other new divinities instead. You mean that I corrupt the young by that teaching, do you not?

*Mel.* Yes, most certainly I mean that.

*Socr.* Then in the name of these gods of whom we are speaking, explain yourself a little more clearly to me and to these gentlemen here. I cannot understand what you mean. Do you mean that I teach the young to believe in some gods, but not in the gods of the state? Do you accuse me of teaching them to believe in strange gods? If that is your meaning, I myself believe in some gods, and my crime is not that of complete atheism. Or do you mean that I do not believe in the gods at all myself, and that I teach other people not to believe in them either?

*Mel.* I mean that you do not believe in the gods in any way whatever.

*Socr.* You amaze me, Meletus! Why do you say that? Do you mean that I believe neither the sun nor the moon to be gods, like other men?

*Mel.* I swear he does not, judges. He says that the sun is a stone, and the moon earth.

*Socr.* My dear Meletus, do you think that you are prosecuting Anaxagoras? You must have a very poor opinion of these men, and think them illiterate, if you imagine that they do not know that the works of Anaxagoras of Clazomenae are full of these doctrines. And so young men learn these things from me, when they can often buy them in the theater for a drachma at most, and laugh at Socrates were he to pretend that these doctrines, which are very peculiar doctrines, too, were his own. But please tell me, do you really think that I do not believe in the gods at all?

*Mel.* Most certainly I do. You are a complete atheist.

*Socr.* No one believes that, Meletus, not even you yourself. It seems to me, Athenians, that Meletus is very insolent and reckless, and that he is prosecuting me simply out of insolence, recklessness, and youthful bravado. For he seems to be testing me, by asking me a riddle that has no answer. "Will this wise Socrates," he says to himself, "see that I am joking and contradicting myself? Or shall I deceive him and everyone else who hears me?" Meletus seems to me to contradict himself in his indictment: it is as if he were to say, "Socrates is guilty of not believing in the gods, but believes in the gods." This is joking.

Now, my friends, let us see why I think that this is his meaning. You must answer me, Meletus, and you, Athenians, must remember the request which I made to you at the start, and not interrupt me with shouts if I talk in my usual manner.

Is there any man, Meletus, who believes in the existence of things pertaining to men and not in the existence of men? Make him answer the question, gentlemen, without these interruptions. Is there any man who believes in the existence of horsemanship and not in the existence of horses? Or in flute playing and not in flute players? There is not, my friend. If you will not answer, I will tell both you and the judges. But you must answer my next question. Is there any man who believes in the existence of divine things and not in the existence of divinities?

*Mel.* There is not.

*Socr.* I am very glad that these gentlemen have managed to extract an answer from you. Well then, you say that I believe in divine things, whether they be old or new, and that I teach others to believe in them. At any rate, according to your statement, I believe in divine things. That you have sworn in your indictment. But if I believe in divine things, I suppose it follows necessarily that I believe in divinities. Is it not so? It is. I assume that you grant that, as you do not answer. But do we not believe that divinities are either gods themselves or the children of the gods? Do you admit that?

*Mel.* I do.

*Socr.* Then you admit that I believe in divinities. Now, if these divinities are gods, then, as I say, you are joking and asking a riddle, and asserting that I do not believe in the gods, and at the same time that I do, since I believe in divinities. But if these divinities are the illegitimate children of the gods, either by the nymphs or by other mothers, as they are said to be, then, I ask, what man could believe in the existence of the children of the gods, and not in the existence of the gods? That would be as absurd as believing in the existence of the offspring of horses and asses, and not in the existence of horses and asses. You must have indicted me in this manner, Meletus, either to test me or because you could not find any act of injustice that you could accuse me of with truth. But you will never contrive to persuade any man with any sense at all that a belief in divine things and things of the gods does not necessarily involve a belief in divinities, and in the gods.

But in truth, Athenians, I do not think that I need say very much to prove that I have not committed the act of injustice for which Meletus is prosecuting me. What I have said is enough to prove that. But be assured it is certainly true, as I have already told you, that I have aroused much indignation. That is what will cause my condemnation if I am condemned; not Meletus nor Anytus either, but that prejudice and resentment of the multitude which have been the destruction of many good men before me, and I think will be so again. There is no prospect that I shall be the last victim.

Perhaps someone will say: "Are you not ashamed, Socrates, of leading a life which is very likely now to cause your death?" I should answer him with justice, and say: "My friend, if you think that a man of any worth at all ought to reckon the chances of life and death when he acts, or that he ought to think of anything but whether he is acting justly or unjustly, and as a good or a bad man would act, you are mistaken. According to you, the demigods who died at Troy would be foolish, and among them Achilles, who thought nothing of danger when the alternative was disgrace. For when his mother—and she was a goddess—addressed him, when he was resolved to slay Hector, in this fashion, 'My son, if you avenge the death of your comrade Patroclus and slay Hector, you will die yourself, for fate awaits you next after Hector.' When he heard this, he scorned danger and death; he feared much more to live a coward and not to avenge his friend. 'Let me punish the evildoer and afterwards die,' he said, 'that I may not remain here by the beaked ships jeered at, encumbering the earth.'" Do you suppose that he thought of danger or of death? For this, Athenians, I believe to be the truth. Wherever a man's station is, whether he has chosen it of his own will, or whether he has been placed at it by his commander, there it is his duty to remain and face the danger without thinking of death or of any other thing except disgrace.

When the generals whom you chose to command me, Athenians, assigned me my station during the battles of Potidaea, Amphipolis, and Delium, I remained where they stationed me and ran the risk of death, like other men. It would be very strange conduct on my part if I were to desert my station now from fear of death or of any other thing when the god has commanded me—as I am persuaded that he has done—to spend my life in searching for wisdom, and in examining myself and others. That would indeed be a very strange thing. Then certainly I might with justice be brought to trial for not believing in the gods, for I should be disobeying the oracle, and fearing death and thinking myself wise when I was not wise. For to fear death, my friends, is only to think ourselves wise without really being wise, for it is to think that we know what we do not know. For no one knows whether death may not be the greatest good that can happen to man. But men fear it as if they knew quite well that it was the greatest of evils. And what is this but that shameful ignorance of thinking that we know what we do not know? In this matter, too, my friends, perhaps I am different from the multitude. And if I were to claim to be at all wiser than others, it would be because, not knowing very much about the other world, I do not think I know. But I do know very well that it is evil and disgraceful to do an unjust act, and to disobey my superior, whether man or god. I will never do what I know to be evil, and shrink in fear from what I do not know to be good or evil. Even if you acquit me now, and do not listen to Anytus' argument that, if I am to be acquitted, I ought never to have been brought to trial at all, and that, as it is, you are bound to put me to death because, as he said, if I escape, all your sons will be utterly corrupted by practicing what Socrates teaches. If you were therefore to say to me, "Socrates, this time we will not listen to Anytus. We will let you go, but on the condition that you give up this investigation of yours, and philosophy. If you are found following these pursuits again, you shall die." I say, if you offered to let me go on these terms, I should reply: "Athenians, I hold you in the highest regard and affection, but I will be persuaded by the god rather than you. As long as I have breath and strength I will not give up philosophy and exhorting you and declaring the truth to every one of you whom I meet, saying, as I am accustomed, 'My good friend, you are a citizen of Athens, a city which is very great and very famous for its wisdom and power—are you not ashamed of caring so much for the making of money and for fame and prestige, when you neither think nor care about wisdom and truth and the improvement of your soul?'" If he disputes my words and says that he does care about these things, I shall not at once release him and go away: I shall question him and cross-examine him and test him. If I think that he has not attained excellence, though he says that he has, I shall reproach him for undervaluing the most valuable things, and overvaluing those that are less valuable. This I shall do to everyone whom I meet, young or old, citizen or stranger, but especially to citizens, since they are more closely related to me. This, you must recognize, the god has commanded me to do. And I think that no greater good has ever befallen you in the state than my service to the god. For I spend my whole life in going about and persuading you all to give your first and greatest care to the improvement of your souls, and not till you have done that to think of your bodies or your wealth. And I tell you that wealth does not bring excellence, but that wealth, and every other good thing which men have, whether in public or in private, comes from excellence. If then I corrupt the youth by this teaching, these things must be harmful. But if any man says that I teach anything else, there is nothing in what he says. And therefore, Athenians, I say, whether you are persuaded by Anytus or not, whether you acquit me or not, I shall not change my way of life; no, not if I have to die for it many times.

Do not interrupt me, Athenians, with your shouts. Remember the request which I made to you, and do not interrupt my words. I think that it will profit you to hear them. I am going to say something more to you, at which you may be inclined to protest, but do not do that. Be sure that if you put me to death, I who am what I have told you that I am, you will do yourselves more harm than me. Meletus and Anytus can do me no harm: that is impossible, for I am sure it is not allowed that a good man be injured by a worse. He may indeed kill me, or drive me into exile, or deprive me of my civil rights. Perhaps Meletus and others think those things great evils. But I do not think so. I think it is a much greater evil to do what he is doing now, and to try to put a man to death unjustly. And now, Athenians, I am not arguing in my own defense at all, as you might expect me to do, but rather in yours in order you may not make a mistake about the gift of the god to you by condemning me. For if you put me to death, you will not easily find another who, if I may use a ludicrous comparison, clings to the state as a sort of gadfly to a horse that is large and well-bred but rather sluggish because of its size, so that it needs to be aroused. It seems to me that the god has attached me like that to the state, for I am constantly alighting upon you at every point to arouse, persuade, and reproach each of you all day long. You will not easily find anyone else, my friends, to fill my place; and if you are persuaded by me, you will spare my life. You are indignant, as drowsy persons are when they are awakened, and, of course, if you are persuaded by Anytus, you could easily kill me with a single blow, and then sleep on undisturbed for the rest of your lives, unless the god in his care for you sends another to arouse you. And you may easily see that it is the god who has given me to your city; for it is not human, the way in which I have neglected all my own interests and allowed my private affairs to be neglected for so many years, while occupying myself unceasingly in your interests, going to each of you privately, like a father or an elder brother, trying to persuade him to care for human excellence. There would have been a reason for it, if I had gained any advantage by this, or if I had been paid for my exhortations; but you see yourselves that my accusers, though they accuse me of everything else without shame, have not had the shamelessness to say that I ever either exacted or demanded payment. To that they have no witness. And I think that I have sufficient witness to the truth of what I say—my poverty.

Perhaps it may seem strange to you that, though I go about giving this advice privately and meddling in others' affairs, yet I do not venture to come forward in the assembly and advise the state. You have often heard me speak of my reason for this, and in many places: it is that I have a certain divine guide, which is what Meletus has caricatured in his indictment. I have had it from childhood. It is a kind of voice which, whenever I hear it, always turns me back from something which I was going to do, but never urges me to act. It is this which forbids me to take part in politics. And I think it does well to forbid me. For, Athenians, it is quite certain that, if I had attempted to take part in politics, I should have perished at once and long ago without doing any good either to you or to myself. And do not be indignant with me for telling the truth. There is no man who will preserve his life for long, either in Athens or elsewhere, if he firmly opposes the multitude, and tries to prevent the commission of much injustice and illegality in the state. He who would really fight for justice must do so as a private citizen, not as a political figure, if he is to preserve his life, even for a short time.

I will prove to you that this is so by very strong evidence, not by mere words, but by what you value more—actions. Listen, then, to what has happened to me, that you may know that there is no man who could make me consent to commit an unjust act from the fear of death, but that I would perish at once rather than give way. What I am going to tell you may be commonplace in the law court; nevertheless, it is true. The only office that I ever held in the state, Athenians, was that of councilor. When you wished to try the ten admirals who did not rescue their men after the battle of Arginusae as a group, which was illegal, as you all came to think afterwards, the executive committee was composed of members of the tribe Antiochis, to which I belong. On that occasion I alone of the committee members opposed your illegal action and gave my vote against you. The orators were ready to impeach me and arrest me; and you were clamoring and urging them on with your shouts. But I thought that I ought to face the danger, with law and justice on my side, rather than join with you in your unjust proposal, from fear of imprisonment or death. That was when the state was democratic. When the oligarchy came in, The Thirty sent for me, with four others, to the council-chamber, and ordered us to bring Leon the Salaminian from Salamis, that they might put him to death. They were in the habit of frequently giving similar orders to many others, wishing to implicate as many as possible in their crimes. But then I again proved, not by mere words, but by my actions, that, if I may speak bluntly, I do not care a straw for death; but that I do care very much indeed about not doing anything unjust or impious. That government with all its power did not terrify me into doing anything unjust. When we left the council-chamber, the other four went over to Salamis and brought Leon across to Athens; I went home. And if the rule of The Thirty had not been overthrown soon afterwards, I should very likely have been put to death for what I did then. Many of you will be my witnesses in this matter.

Now do you think that I could have remained alive all these years if I had taken part in public affairs, and had always maintained the cause of justice like a good man, and had held it a paramount duty, as it is, to do so? Certainly not, Athenians, nor could any other man. But throughout my whole life, both in private and in public, whenever I have had to take part in public affairs, you will find I have always been the same and have never yielded unjustly to anyone; no, not to those whom my enemies falsely assert to have been my pupils. But I was never anyone's teacher. I have never withheld myself from anyone, young or old, who was anxious to hear me converse while I was making my investigation; neither do I converse for payment, and refuse to converse without payment. I am ready to ask questions of rich and poor alike, and if any man wishes to answer me, and then listen to what I have to say, he may. And I cannot justly be charged with causing these men to turn out good or bad, for I never either taught or professed to teach any of them any knowledge whatever. And if any man asserts that he ever learned or heard anything from me in private which everyone else did not hear as well as he, be sure that he does not speak the truth.

Why is it, then, that people delight in spending so much time in my company? You have heard why, Athenians. I told you the whole truth when I said that they delight in hearing me examine persons who think that they are wise when they are not wise. It is certainly very amusing to listen to. And, as I have said, the god has commanded me to examine men, in oracles and in dreams and in every way in which the divine will was ever declared to man. This is the truth, Athenians, and if it were not the truth, it would be easily refuted. For if it were really the case that I have already corrupted some of the young men, and am now corrupting others, surely some of them, finding as they grew older that I had given them bad advice in their youth, would have come forward today to accuse me and take their revenge. Or if they were unwilling to do so themselves, surely their relatives, their fathers or brothers, or others, would, if I had done them any harm, have remembered it and taken their revenge. Certainly I see many of them in court. Here is Crito, of my own district and of my own age, the father of Critobulus; here is Lysanias of Sphettus, the father of Aeschines; here is also Antiphon of Cephisus, the father of Epigenes. Then here are others whose brothers have spent their time in my company—Nicostratus, the son of Theozotides and brother of Theodotus—and Theodotus is dead, so he at least cannot entreat his brother to be silent; here is Paralus, the son of Demodocus and the brother of Theages; here is Adeimantus, the son of Ariston, whose brother is Plato here; and Aeantodorus, whose brother is Aristodorus. And I can name many others to you, some of whom Meletus ought to have called as witnesses in the course of his own speech; but if he forgot to call them then, let him call them now—I will yield the floor to him—and tell us if he has any such evidence. No, on the contrary, my friends, you will find all these men ready to support me, the corrupter who has injured their relatives, as Meletus and Anytus call me. Those of them who have been already corrupted might perhaps have some reason for supporting me, but what reason can their relatives have who are grown up, and who are uncorrupted, except the reason of truth and justice—that they know very well that Meletus is lying, and that I am speaking the truth?

Well, my friends, this, and perhaps more like this, is pretty much all I have to offer in my defense. There may be some one among you who will be indignant when he remembers how, even in a less important trial than this, he begged and entreated the judges, with many tears, to acquit him, and brought forward his children and many of his friends and relatives in court in order to appeal to your feelings; and then finds that I shall do none of these things, though I am in what he would think the supreme danger. Perhaps he will harden himself against me when he notices this; it may make him angry, and he may cast his vote in anger. If it is so with any of you—I do not suppose that it is, but in case it should be so—I think that I should answer him reasonably if I said: "My friend, I have relatives, too, for, in the words of Homer, I am 'not born of an oak or a rock' but of flesh and blood." And so, Athenians, I have relatives, and I have three sons, one of them nearly grown up, and the other two still children. Yet I will not bring any of them forward before you and implore you to acquit me. And why will I do none of these things? It is not from arrogance, Athenians, nor because I lack respect for you—whether or not I can face death bravely is another question—but for my own good name, and for your good name, and for the good name of the whole state. I do not think it right, at my age and with my reputation, to do anything of that kind. Rightly or wrongly, men have made up their minds that in some way Socrates is different from the multitude of men. And it will be shameful if those of you who are thought to excel in wisdom, or in bravery, or in any other excellence, are going to act in this fashion. I have often seen men of reputation behaving in an extraordinary way at their trial, as if they thought it a terrible fate to be killed, and as though they expected to live for ever if you did not put them to death. Such men seem to me to bring shame upon the state, for any stranger would suppose that the best and most eminent Athenians, who are selected by their fellow citizens to hold office, and for other honors, are no better than women. Those of you, Athenians, who have any reputation at all ought not to do these things, and you ought not to allow us to do them. You should show that you will be much more ready to condemn men who make the state ridiculous by these pathetic performances than men who remain quiet.

But apart from the question of reputation, my friends, I do not think that it is right to entreat the judge to acquit us, or to escape condemnation in that way. It is our duty to teach and persuade him. He does not sit to give away justice as a favor, but to pronounce judgment; and he has sworn, not to favor any man whom he would like to favor, but to judge according to law. And, therefore, we ought not to encourage you in the habit of breaking your oaths; and you ought not to allow yourselves to fall into this habit, for then neither you nor we would be acting piously. Therefore, Athenians, do not require me to do these things, for I believe them to be neither good nor just nor pious; especially, do not ask me to do them today when Meletus is prosecuting me for impiety. For were I to be successful and persuade you by my entreaties to break your oaths, I should be clearly teaching you to believe that there are no gods, and I should be simply accusing myself by my defense of not believing in them. But, Athenians, that is very far from the truth. I do believe in the gods as no one of my accusers believes in them; and to you and to the god I commit my cause to be decided as is best for you and for me.

*[He is found guilty by 281 votes to 220.]*

I am not indignant at the verdict which you have given, Athenians, for many reasons. I expected that you would find me guilty; and I am not so much surprised at that as at the numbers of the votes. I certainly never thought that the majority against me would have been so narrow. But now it seems that if only thirty votes had changed sides, I should have escaped. So I think that I have escaped Meletus, as it is; and not only have I escaped him, for it is perfectly clear that if Anytus and Lycon had not come forward to accuse me, too, he would not have obtained the fifth part of the votes, and would have had to pay a fine of a thousand drachmae.

So he proposes death as the penalty. Be it so. And what alternative penalty shall I propose to you, Athenians? What I deserve, of course, must I not? What then do I deserve to pay or to suffer for having determined not to spend my life in ease? I neglected the things which most men value, such as wealth, and family interests, and military commands, and public oratory, and all the civic appointments, and social clubs, and political factions, that there are in Athens; for I thought that I was really too honest a man to preserve my life if I engaged in these affairs. So I did not go where I should have done no good either to you or to myself. I went, instead, to each one of you privately to do him, as I say, the greatest of benefits, and tried to persuade him not to think of his affairs until he had thought of himself and tried to make himself as good and wise as possible, nor to think of the affairs of Athens until he had thought of Athens herself; and to care for other things in the same manner. Then what do I deserve for such a life? Something good, Athenians, if I am really to propose what I deserve; and something good which it would be suitable for me to receive. Then what is a suitable reward to be given to a poor benefactor who requires leisure to exhort you? There is no reward, Athenians, so suitable for him as receiving free meals in the prytaneum. It is a much more suitable reward for him than for any of you who has won a victory at the Olympic games with his horse or his chariots. Such a man only makes you seem happy, but I make you really happy; he is not in want, and I am. So if I am to propose the penalty which I really deserve, I propose this—free meals in the prytaneum.

Perhaps you think me stubborn and arrogant in what I am saying now, as in what I said about the entreaties and tears. It is not so, Athenians. It is rather that I am convinced that I never wronged any man voluntarily, though I cannot persuade you of that, since we have conversed together only a little time. If there were a law at Athens, as there is elsewhere, not to finish a trial of life and death in a single day, I think that I could have persuaded you; but now it is not easy in so short a time to clear myself of great prejudices. But when I am persuaded that I have never wronged any man, I shall certainly not wrong myself, or admit that I deserve to suffer any evil, or propose any evil for myself as a penalty. Why should I? Lest I should suffer the penalty which Meletus proposes when I say that I do not know whether it is a good or an evil? Shall I choose instead of it something which I know to be an evil, and propose that as a penalty? Shall I propose imprisonment? And why should I pass the rest of my days in prison, the slave of successive officials? Or shall I propose a fine, with imprisonment until it is paid? I have told you why I will not do that. I should have to remain in prison, for I have no money to pay a fine with. Shall I then propose exile? Perhaps you would agree to that. Life would indeed be very dear to me if I were unreasonable enough to expect that strangers would cheerfully tolerate my discussions and arguments when you who are my fellow citizens cannot endure them, and have found them so irksome and odious to you that you are seeking now to be relieved of them. No, indeed, Athenians, that is not likely. A fine life I should lead for an old man if I were to withdraw from Athens and pass the rest of my days in wandering from city to city, and continually being expelled. For I know very well that the young men will listen to me wherever I go, as they do here. If I drive them away, they will persuade their elders to expel me; if I do not drive them away, their fathers and other relatives will expel me for their sakes.

Perhaps someone will say, "Why cannot you withdraw from Athens, Socrates, and hold your peace?" It is the most difficult thing in the world to make you understand why I cannot do that. If I say that I cannot hold my peace because that would be to disobey the god, you will think that I am not in earnest and will not believe me. And if I tell you that no greater good can happen to a man than to discuss human excellence every day and the other matters about which you have heard me arguing and examining myself and others, and that an unexamined life is not worth living, then you will believe me still less. But that is so, my friends, though it is not easy to persuade you. And, what is more, I am not accustomed to think that I deserve anything evil. If I had been rich, I would have proposed as large a fine as I could pay: that would have done me no harm. But I am not rich enough to pay a fine unless you are willing to fix it at a sum within my means. Perhaps I could pay you a mina, so I propose that. Plato here, Athenians, and Crito, and Critobulus, and Apollodorus bid me propose thirty minae, and they guarantee its payment. So I propose thirty minae. Their security will be sufficient to you for the money.

*[He is condemned to death.]*

You have not gained very much time, Athenians, and at the price of the slurs of those who wish to revile the state. And they will say that you put Socrates, a wise man, to death. For they will certainly call me wise, whether I am wise or not, when they want to reproach you. If you had waited for a little while, your wishes would have been fulfilled in the course of nature; for you see that I am an old man, far advanced in years, and near to death. I am saying this not to all of you, only to those who have voted for my death. And to them I have something else to say. Perhaps, my friends, you think that I have been convicted because I was wanting in the arguments by which I could have persuaded you to acquit me, if I had thought it right to do or to say anything to escape punishment. It is not so. I have been convicted because I was wanting, not in arguments, but in impudence and shamelessness—because I would not plead before you as you would have liked to hear me plead, or appeal to you with weeping and wailing, or say and do many other things which I maintain are unworthy of me, but which you have been accustomed to from other men. But when I was defending myself, I thought that I ought not to do anything unworthy of a free man because of the danger which I ran, and I have not changed my mind now. I would very much rather defend myself as I did, and die, than as you would have had me do, and live. Both in a lawsuit and in war, there are some things which neither I nor any other man may do in order to escape from death. In battle, a man often sees that he may at least escape from death by throwing down his arms and falling on his knees before the pursuer to beg for his life. And there are many other ways of avoiding death in every danger if a man is willing to say and to do anything. But, my friends, I think that it is a much harder thing to escape from wickedness than from death, for wickedness is swifter than death. And now I, who am old and slow, have been overtaken by the slower pursuer: and my accusers, who are clever and swift, have been overtaken by the swifter pursuer—wickedness. And now I shall go away, sentenced by you to death; they will go away, sentenced by truth to wickedness and injustice. And I abide by this award as well as they. Perhaps it was right for these things to be so. I think that they are fairly balanced.

And now I wish to prophesy to you, Athenians, who have condemned me. For I am going to die, and that is the time when men have most prophetic power. And I prophesy to you who have sentenced me to death that a far more severe punishment than you have inflicted on me will surely overtake you as soon as I am dead. You have done this thing, thinking that you will be relieved from having to give an account of your lives. But I say that the result will be very different. There will be more men who will call you to account, whom I have held back, though you did not recognize it. And they will be harsher toward you than I have been, for they will be younger, and you will be more indignant with them. For if you think that you will restrain men from reproaching you for not living as you should, by putting them to death, you are very much mistaken. That way of escape is neither possible nor honorable. It is much more honorable and much easier not to suppress others, but to make yourselves as good as you can. This is my parting prophecy to you who have condemned me.

With you who have acquitted me I should like to discuss this thing that has happened, while the authorities are busy, and before I go to the place where

I have to die. So, remain with me until I go: there is no reason why we should not talk with each other while it is possible. I wish to explain to you, as my friends, the meaning of what has happened to me. An amazing thing has happened to me, judges—for I am right in calling you judges. The prophetic guide has been constantly with me all through my life till now, opposing me even in trivial matters if I were not going to act rightly. And now you yourselves see what has happened to me—a thing which might be thought, and which is sometimes actually reckoned, the supreme evil. But the divine guide did not oppose me when I was leaving my house in the morning, nor when I was coming up here to the court, nor at any point in my speech when I was going to say anything; though at other times it has often stopped me in the very act of speaking. But now, in this matter, it has never once opposed me, either in my words or my actions. I will tell you what I believe to be the reason. This thing that has come upon me must be a good; and those of us who think that death is an evil must needs be mistaken. I have a clear proof that that is so; for my accustomed guide would certainly have opposed me if I had not been going to meet with something good.

And if we reflect in another way, we shall see that we may well hope that death is a good. For the state of death is one of two things: either the dead man wholly ceases to be and loses all consciousness or, as we are told, it is a change and a migration of the soul to another place. And if death is the absence of all consciousness, and like the sleep of one whose slumbers are unbroken by any dreams, it will be a wonderful gain. For if a man had to select that night in which he slept so soundly that he did not even dream, and had to compare with it all the other nights and days of his life, and then had to say how many days and nights in his life he had spent better and more pleasantly than this night, I think that a private person, nay, even the Great King of Persia himself, would find them easy to count, compared with the others. If that is the nature of death, I for one count it a gain. For then it appears that all time is nothing more than a single night. But if death is a journey to another place, and what we are told is true—that all who have died are there—what good could be greater than this, my judges? Would a journey not be worth taking, at the end of which, in the other world, we should be delivered from the pretended judges here and should find the true judges who are said to sit in judgment below, such as Minos and Rhadamanthus and Aeacus and Triptolemus, and the other demigods who were just in their own lives? Or what would you not give to converse with Orpheus and Musaeus and Hesiod and Homer? I am willing to die many times if this be true. And for my own part I should find it wonderful to meet there Palamedes, and Ajax the son of Telamon, and the other men of old who have died through an unjust judgment, and to compare my experiences with theirs. That I think would be no small pleasure. And, above all, I could spend my time in examining those who are there, as I examine men here, and in finding out which of them is wise, and which of them thinks himself wise when he is not wise. What would we not give, my judges, to be able to examine the leader of the great expedition against Troy, or

Odysseus, or Sisyphus, or countless other men and women whom we could name? It would be an inexpressible happiness to converse with them and to live with them and to examine them. Assuredly there they do not put men to death for doing that. For besides the other ways in which they are happier than we are, they are immortal, at least if what we are told is true.

And you too, judges, must face death hopefully, and believe this one truth, that no evil can happen to a good man, either in life or after death. His affairs are not neglected by the gods; and what has happened to me today has not happened by chance. I am persuaded that it was better for me to die now, and to be released from trouble; and that was the reason why the guide never turned me back. And so I am not at all angry with my accusers or with those who have condemned me to die. Yet it was not with this in mind that they accused me and condemned me, but meaning to do me an injury. So far I may blame them.

Yet I have one request to make of them. When my sons grow up, punish them, my friends, and harass them in the same way that I have harassed you, if they seem to you to care for riches or for any other thing more than excellence; and if they think that they are something when they are really nothing, reproach them, as I have reproached you, for not caring for what they should, and for thinking that they are something when really they are nothing. And if you will do this, I myself and my sons will have received justice from you.

But now the time has come, and we must go away—I to die, and you to live. Which is better is known to the god alone.

## *from The Republic*

*Translated by F.M. Cornford*

### *from Book 7: The Allegory of the Cave*

Next, said I, here is a parable to illustrate the degrees in which our nature may be enlightened or unenlightened. Imagine the condition of men living in a sort of cavernous chamber underground, with an entrance open to the light and a long passage all down the cave. Here they have been from childhood, chained by the leg and also by the neck, so that they cannot move and can see only what is in front of them, because the chains will not let them turn their heads. At some distance higher up is the light of a fire burning behind them; and between the prisoners and the fire is a track with a parapet built along it, like the screen at a puppet-show, which hides the performers while they show their puppets over the top.

I see, said he.

Now behind this parapet imagine persons carrying along various artificial objects, including figures of men and animals in wood or stone or other materials, which project above the parapet. Naturally, some of these persons will be talking, others silent.

It is a strange picture, he said, and a strange sort of prisoners.

Like ourselves, I replied; for in the first place prisoners so confined would have seen nothing of themselves or of one another, except the shadows thrown by the fire-light on the wall of the Cave facing them, would they?

Not if all their lives they had been prevented from moving their heads.

And they would have seen as little of the objects carried past.

Of course.

Now, if they could talk to one another, would they not suppose that their words referred only to those passing shadows which they saw?

Necessarily.

And suppose their prison had an echo from the wall facing them? When one of the people crossing behind them spoke, they could only suppose that the sound came from the shadow passing before their eyes.

No doubt.

In every way, then, such prisoners would recognize as reality nothing but the shadows of those artificial objects.

Inevitably.

Now consider what would happen if their release from the chains and the healing of their unwisdom should come about in this way. Suppose one of them set free and forced suddenly to stand up, turn his head, and walk with eyes lifted to the light; all these movements would be painful, and he would be too dazzled to make out the objects whose shadows he had been used to see. What do you think he would say, if someone told him that what he had formerly seen was meaningless illusion, but now, being somewhat nearer to reality and turned towards more real objects, he was getting a truer view? Suppose further that he were shown the various objects being carried by and were made to say, in reply to questions, what each of them was. Would he not be perplexed and believe the objects now shown him to be not so real as what he formerly saw?

Yes, not nearly so real.

And if he were forced to look at the fire-light itself, would not his eyes ache, so that he would try to escape and turn back to the things which he could see distinctly, convinced that they really were clearer than these other objects now being shown to him?

Yes.

And suppose someone were to drag him away forcibly up the steep and rugged ascent and not let him go until he had hauled him out into the sunlight, would he not suffer pain and vexation at such treatment, and, when he had come out into the light, find his eyes so full of its radiance that he could not see a single one of the things that he was now told were real?

Certainly he would not see them all at once.

He would need, then, to grow accustomed before he could see things in that upper world. At first it would be easiest to make out shadows, and then the images of men and things reflected in water, and later on the things themselves. After that, it would be easier to watch the heavenly bodies and the sky itself by night, looking at the light of the moon and stars rather than the Sun and the Sun's light in the day-time.

Yes, surely.

Last of all, he would be able to look at the Sun and contemplate its nature, not as it appears when reflected in water or any alien medium, but as it is in itself in its own domain.

No doubt.

And now he would begin to draw the conclusion that it is the Sun that produces the seasons and the course of the year and controls everything in the visible world, and moreover is in a way the cause of all that he and his companions used to see.

Clearly he would come at last to that conclusion.

Then if he called to mind his fellow prisoners and what passed for wisdom in his former dwelling-place, he would surely think himself happy in the change and be sorry for them. They may have had a practice of honouring and commending one another, with prizes for the man who had the keenest eye for the passing shadows and the best memory for the order in which they followed or accompanied one another, so that he could make a good guess as to which was going to come next. Would our released prisoner be likely to covet those prizes or to envy the men exalted to honour and power in the Cave? Would he not feel like Homer's Achilles, that he would far sooner 'be on earth as a hired servant in the house of a landless man' or endure anything rather than go back to his old beliefs and live in the old way?

Yes, he would prefer any fate to such a life.

Now imagine what would happen if he went down again to take his former seat in the Cave. Coming suddenly out of the sunlight, his eyes would be filled with darkness. He might be required once more to deliver his opinion on those shadows, in competition with the prisoners who had never been released, while his eyesight was still dim and unsteady; and it might take some time to become used to the darkness. They would laugh at him and say that he had gone up only to come back with his sight ruined; it was worth no one's while even to attempt the ascent. If they could lay hands on the man who was trying to set them free and lead them up, they would kill him.

Yes, they would.

Every feature in this parable, my dear Glaucon, is meant to fit our earlier analysis. The prison dwelling corresponds to the region revealed to us through the sense of sight, and the fire-light within it to the power of the Sun. The ascent to see the things in the upper world you may take as standing for the upward journey of the soul into the region of the intelligible; then you will be in possession of what I surmise, since that is what you wish to be told. Heaven knows whether it is true; but this, at any rate, is how it appears to me.

## *from The Symposium*

*Translated by Suzy Q. Groden*

It happened recently that when I was coming to town from my home in Phalerum, one of my friends, sighting me ahead, called from far away, and having his joke at the same time, said:

Baldy Phalerian! You, Apollodorus! Won't you wait?

So I stopped and waited, and he said:

Apollodorus, I was looking for you just now. I wanted to ask you about that gathering at Agathon's. Those speeches about Love by Socrates and Alcibiades and the others who were there at the dinner, what were they like? Someone else told me what Phoenix, the son of Phillip told him, and he said that you know. He didn't tell it very clearly, though, so I wish you would tell me. It would be quite proper for you to recount the words of your friend. To begin with, he continued, tell me, were you or weren't you there in person at that gathering?

Obviously your narrator wasn't very clear at all, I replied, if you imagine that the party where they talked about Love took place recently, and that I was there.

Oh, I did, he said.

How could I have been, Glaucon? Don't you realize that it is many years now since Agathon moved away from here, and that it is not three years since I became a companion of Socrates, and made it my business to know everything he says and does every day? Before that I was running in circles, acting at random, thinking I was accomplishing something though I was unhappier than anyone, no less than you are now, imagining that anything was more necessary than philosophy.

Stop jeering, he said, just tell me when the party took place.

When we were still children, I said, and Agathon had won the prize with his first tragedy. It was the day after his victory celebrations with his cast.

It does sound like ancient history, he remarked, but who told you? Socrates himself?

Heavens no, I replied, the same fellow who told Phoenix, a certain Aristodemus it was, from Cydathenaeum, the little fellow who's always barefoot—he was there at the party. I think he was one of Socrates' greatest admirers in those days. But then, too, I've asked Socrates himself about the things I heard from that fellow, and his account agrees exactly with what the man said.

Why, then, he asked, don't you tell me? The road we are taking to the city is just right for conversation.

So, you see, we went along, and as we walked we talked about this matter, and that's how it happens, as I said when we began, that I'm not unprepared, and if that's what you need to talk about, we must do so. As far as I'm concerned, any sort of philosophical discussion I have or listen to is immensely enjoyable, apart from its practical benefit. It's when I hear other kinds of talk, particularly the sort you have with the rich and with businessmen that I get angry, and pity you and your friends for thinking that you're accomplishing something when, in fact, you're not doing a thing! I suppose, in turn, you think I'm unhappy, and I suppose you're right; but for my part it's not that I think it of you, I know it for a certainty!

Always the same, Apollodorus. You're always attacking yourself and others. It seems to me that you consider all men utterly wretched, except for Socrates, beginning with yourself. Where you got your nickname 'maniac' I don't know, but you always talk like one—raging against yourself and others—everyone except Socrates!

Oh, my friend, is it so obviously madness and frenzy to think this way about myself, and about you all?

There's no point to our wrangling about this business any more, Apollodorus. Please, why don't you tell me about those speeches, as I asked you?

The very same men who then—no—I would rather try to tell it to you from the beginning, the way that fellow told me.

## Socrates & Aristodemus

He says that he met Socrates coming from the baths, and that he was wearing sandals, a thing the man rarely did. So he asked him where he might be going, so handsomely got up.

To a dinner at Agathon's. I avoided him and the celebration rites yesterday, for fear of the crowd, but I agreed to be present today. I got dressed up like this so that beauty might match beauty. But what about you, he went on, how about it? Would you go to this dinner uninvited?

Oh, he said that he answered, I'll do just as you say.

Then follow, he urged, so that we can corrupt the saying by turning it around, making it go: *To the feasts of a good man the good go uninvited.* On his part, Homer not only dares to corrupt the proverb, he outrages it! He sets Agamemnon up as an outstandingly good man in warfare, with Menelaus the soft warrior. When Agamemnon has made a sacrifice, he makes Menelaus go to the feast uninvited, the lesser to the better.

I listened to this, he said, and answered, I'm afraid that it isn't the way you represent it, Socrates, but Homer's way. The one who is worthless—me—is going to the feast of the wise man, unasked. So be ready to apologize for me, since I wouldn't agree to go without an invitation, unless you were asking me.

*When two,* he quoted, *go together, one is ahead of the other* in planning what we'll say. But let's get going.

The two of them went on talking in that sort of vein as they walked along. But then Socrates drew his thoughts into himself, and he was left behind to make his own way along the road, having ordered the waiting Aristodemus to go on ahead. And when Aristodemus got to Agathon's house, he discovered the door was open, and he said he felt rather foolish. A servant from inside met him immediately and led him to where all the others were reclining and about to dine. Just as soon as Agathon saw him, he said, he exclaimed:

Ah, I say, Aristodemus! It's a good thing, your coming just now to eat with us! Now, if you've come for any other reason, why put it off for another time. I looked for you yesterday in order to invite you, but I didn't find you! But how is it you haven't brought Socrates to us?

And I turned around, he said, but could see nothing of Socrates behind me. I said then that I had actually come with Socrates, since he had invited me there to dinner.

And right you were to do so, he said, but where is he?

He was right behind me just a minute ago—but now I'm wondering, myself, where he can be.

Why don't you see if you can find Socrates? Agathon said to a servant, and bring him to us. And you, Aristodemus, sit down beside Eryximachus.

And so he tells that a servant helped him wash up, so that he might recline at the table, and that another of the servants came with the report that Socrates himself, who had stopped at a neighbor's, was standing outside on his porch; when he was asked to come in, he didn't wish to do so.

How strange, Agathon said. But go on calling him, and don't give up.

No, by all means leave him alone! He has a way of doing this. Sometimes he goes into a trance just where he happens to be standing. He'll come back presently, I know it. Don't move him—let him be!

Well then that's how it'll have to be if you feel that way, he has Agathon say. So, servants, attend to the others. Set things out exactly as you'd like, seeing as no one is directing you (I've never done this before). Make believe that I've been invited to dinner by you, and these other people too. Take care of us, so that we can congratulate you.

After this business, he says, they started to eat without Socrates. Agathon kept ordering someone to go get Socrates, but Aristodemus wouldn't allow it. He didn't linger as long as he usually did, so that when he did arrive they were at most half-way through dinner. Thereupon Agathon—since he happened to be situated at the end, alone—is said to have called:

Here, Socrates, sit by me and eat so by touching you I may partake of some of that wisdom which has come to you on the porch. Clearly you found what you were searching after and have it, or you wouldn't have left there.

And Socrates sat down, remarking: I wish, Agathon, that wisdom were the sort of thing that could flow from the fuller of us to the emptier by our touching one another, the way, for instance, in the case of cups, water flows through wool from the fuller to the emptier. If wisdom were like that I'd value this seat beside you very much. I know I'd be filled with a great deal of very beautiful wisdom from you. My own is paltry and ambiguous, it has the nature of a dream, while yours glistens and is so full and generous. It radiated brilliantly from your youth and came to light just the other day, for a witness of more than thirty thousand Greeks!

You're mocking me, Socrates, Agathon protested. You and I can carry on our arguments about wisdom a little later, and have Dionysus as judge. But for now just apply yourself to dinner.

After this, he relates, Socrates settled down and ate with the others. Their libations were made, the proper devotions were paid to the god, and the other things that are required were done. They turned to the drinking. Then, he tells me, Pausanias began with a speech that went something like this:

Well then, gentlemen, how shall we go about this drinking with the greatest ease? I, for one, announce that I am in a thoroughly wretched state, thanks to yesterday's drinks, and I could use some respite. My guess is you're all in the same condition; you were there yesterday, yourselves. So let's try to find some way to drink without discomfort.

Then Aristophanes declared, It's quite true, what you say, Pausanias. We must find some way of drinking that'll be easy on us. I got pretty well soaked yesterday, too!

Hearing their remarks, Eryximachus, Acoumenus' son, said, What you're saying is quite true, but there's something else to be asked. How does Agathon feel about a resolution to drink?

Not at all, he said, I'm not up to it.

It would be a godsend for us, it seems, he said, for me and Aristodemus and Phaedrus and these fellows, if you strongest ones put a stop to your drinking. We're always the feeble ones. (I leave Socrates out of it, he's fine either way—he'll be satisfied with whichever we do). Then since it seems to me that no one here is eager for any heavy wine-drinking, I will probably be less likely to cause displeasure by speaking the truth about the nature of intoxication. I think that it becomes obvious when one is a doctor, what an evil inebriation is for mankind. I myself don't voluntarily drink beyond a certain limit, and would counsel another person not to either, particularly when he is still hungover from the preceding day.

Well then, here he reports that Phaedrus the Myrrhinousian spoke.

I myself am usually persuaded by you, particularly in medical matters, but in this matter the others, too, would do well to take your counsel.

At this they all agreed not to turn the get-together into an occasion for drunkenness, and to drink only so far as it gave pleasure.

And what's more, went on Eryximachus, now that we've decreed that each man should drink as he wants, and not under compulsion, I propose our bidding farewell to that flute-girl who just came in. She can play for herself, or, if she wants, for the women inside, and leave us to talk with one another today. And I'd like to suggest a topic for discussion, if you agree.

Well, they did all agree, and urged him to make his proposal. And Eryximachus went on.

I will begin my words after the manner of Euripides' Melanippe: *as what I will say isn't my own*—but Phaedrus'. Phaedrus is always complaining to me like this: Isn't it a shame, Eryximachus, he says, that the poets compose hymns and paeans to all the other gods, but to Love, who is so great and venerable a god, not a single poem or song of praise has ever been composed by anyone of all the poets who have ever lived? And then, too, when you review the good philosophers, who write dissertations praising, say, Heracles and others, the way the eminent Prodicus does—this in itself is not so surprising, but I've actually come upon a book in which salt was given fantastic praise for its usefulness, and you could find a lot of other things of the same ilk receiving eulogies. Now while they make up such things with all that enthusiasm, no man to this day has ever tried to sing the praises of Love as befits him! No, they neglect so great a god! To my mind Phaedrus is quite right, and accordingly I'll willingly give in to him and make my contribution, but, in addition, I see this occasion as a fitting one, with us gathered here, to celebrate the god. So then, if you agree too, it might be pleasant for us to spend the time discoursing. I think the best way would be for each of us to make a speech in praise of Love, going around to the right, and to do so as beautifully as possible. Phaedrus should start first, both because he is sitting in the first position, and because he is, as it were, the father of the idea!

No one will vote you down, Eryximachus, remarked Socrates. I certainly could never refuse, since I claim I understand nothing but love-matters, nor should Agathon and Pausanias, nor Aristophanes, who devotes himself entirely to Dionysus and Aphrodite, nor any other of the people I see here. Of course, it's unfair to those of us who are sitting at the end; but if those who come first speak properly and beautifully, we'll be satisfied. But let Phaedrus get started, and good luck to him! Let's have his praise of Love!

To this all the others gave their assent, and commanded Phaedrus to begin. Everyone of them spoke on this subject, but Aristodemus didn't remember every detail, and now I've even forgotten some of what he told me. But I'll tell you what I think to be most memorable from each one's speech.

## Phaedrus

First of all then, as I've said, he describes Phaedrus as starting roughly like this—saying that Love was truly a great god, marvelous to men and gods alike in a lot of different ways, and not the least of these was the matter of his birth:

He is honored as the most ancient among the gods, and here is the proof of it: No one knows or tells anything about the birth of Love, in either prose or poetry. Hesiod does say that in the beginning there was chaos,

*but then, full-breasted Earth, the*
*eternal safe resting*
*place of all things, and Love.*

Both Hesiod and Acusilaus agree that after chaos, Earth and Love came together into being. And Parmenides says of the Beginning:

*First of all was Love, out of all the*
*gods, created.*

So, there is agreement on many sides that Love is the oldest of them all. And as he is the oldest he is the source of the greatest blessings to us. I can't describe any greater blessing to a person in his earlier youth, than a good lover, and to a lover, his young friend. What men must follow for their entire lives if they intend to live beautifully and well, neither family nor public honors, nor wealth, nor anything else, can implant so well as Love.

So I ask, what is this thing? It is the feeling of shame, on the one hand, before shameful deeds, and the desire, on the other, to emulate noble ones. And without these neither a state nor an individual can achieve anything great and noble.

What is more, I say that if one loves a person, and happens to be exposed in a vile act or in cowardly submission to something vile, one would suffer less from being seen by his father or his comrades, or by any other, than by his young friend. In exactly the same way we see how extremely ashamed the beloved is before his lovers if he is observed in some shameful act.

See then, if some device could be invented whereby a state or army could be made into a colony of lovers and their youths, it would be impossible to lead a better life than with these same people shunning all disgrace and striving to earn one another's respect. When they fought others, these lovers would win over all, though they were few, as the saying goes. A man in love would far less willingly be seen deserting his post or surrendering his arms by his young friend than by all the others, and would sooner embrace death. Then, to leave the youth behind, or to fail to rescue him when he was in danger—no one is so low that Love couldn't inspire him with such valor that he would become equal to the greatest of spirits! And frankly, when Homer says that a god *breathed a wrath* into certain of the heroes, he is talking about what Love instills in lovers.

Further, only lovers desire to die for their beloveds, and this is not only true of men, but women as well. Here Pelius' daughter Alcestis provides ample testimony to Greeks in support of my claim, because only she was willing to die in her husband's place, though he had a father and mother. Because she loved, she surpassed them in affection, so much that she rendered these people strangers to their son, relatives in name only. When she had gone through with it her deed seemed so beautiful, not only to men but to the gods, that they granted her the gift which very few of the many who have performed numerous noble acts are given: they brought her soul back from Hades—they admired her deed so. So, even the gods give great honor to earnestness and courage in love. But then again, they sent Orpheus, the son of Oeagrus, away out of Hades without success. They allowed him the shade of the woman for whom he had come but did not give *her* up, because he showed himself weak—he played the cithera—and lacking in the courage to die for his love, the way Alcestis had done, for he contrived to get down to Hades while still alive. It was on account of this that they made him suffer the penalty of death at the hands of women. But they honored Achilles, the son of Thetis, whom they sent to the Islands of the Blessed because, after learning from his mother that he would himself die once he had killed Hector, and that if he didn't kill him he could go home and live to be an old man, he dared to choose to help his lover Patroclus, and having avenged him, not only to die for his sake, but to join in death the friend whose life had ended. The gods were exceedingly pleased by this, and honored him especially, because he had made so much of his friend. Oh, Aeschylus mixes it all up and says that it was Achilles who pursued Patroclus—Achilles!—who was more glorious, not only than Patroclus, but than all of the heroes put together, and still without a beard, because, as Homer says, he was the younger! But, in reality, the gods honor most the virtue that comes in love; they would treasure, would delight in, would benefit a person if, being wooed, he loved his lover, more than he pursued a youth as a lover! A lover is more divine than the youth he loves. He is inspired. Because of this they honored Achilles more than Alcestis, and sent him to the Islands of the Blessed.

So, you see, I assert that of the gods Love is the most ancient, the most honorable and the most benevolent in bestowing virtue and happiness on men, alive and dead.

He reports that Phaedrus gave his speech like that, and after Phaedrus came some others whose speeches he couldn't completely remember. So he skipped over them and came to Pausanias' oration. It began:

## Pausanias

It seems to me, Phaedrus, that this arrangement won't work out well for us, if we are simply supposed to invent talks in praise of Love. It'd be fine if Love were one thing; but it isn't one. And in view of its not being one it would be better, first, to say which form of Love we're supposed to praise. I'm going to try, then, to set this business straight, beginning with a discussion of the specific Love one ought to praise, and then praising the god appropriately.

We all know that Aphrodite is never without Love. And if she were one there would be a single Love. But since there are actually two Aphrodites, it is necessary to assume two Loves as well. And can anyone challenge the notion of the bifold goddess? On one side we have the ancient one, the motherless daughter of Uranos, whom we even call 'Uranian,' or 'celestial.' Then there is the younger one, the child of Zeus and Dione, whom we address as 'Pandemus'—or 'common.' It is necessary to describe Love, too, as 'common' when he is engaged with the younger Aphrodite and as 'celestial' when with the former. One ought to praise all gods, but I'll try to describe the attributes of each of these two separately.

Every action has this about it: of itself its performance is neither good nor bad. It's this way for our behavior now—if we drink or sing or converse —none of these acts is particularly noble, but rather it's how the deed is done that makes the difference. If it is done in a noble manner and properly it becomes noble, and if improperly, ignoble. Thus I say that even loving and Love are not wholly good, nor worthy of praise, but only that loving which urges us toward noble action.

Now the Love of the common Aphrodite is truly common, and works at random; it is this one your average man loves. First of all, such men love women no less than boys; then, whomever they love, it is their bodies rather than their souls; then, it is the shallowest people they can find, wanting only to have them, without any concern for the beauty of the thing or its lack. These people take it as it happens to come, and go to, good or bad. This is the nature of the god who comes from that younger goddess, whose birth partook of a mixture of female and male.

Then there is the Love of the celestial goddess, who does not partake of the female, only of the male; then, she is older and entirely lacks lust. Men who have been inspired by this Love turn to the male, loving what is most vigorous and more intelligent. And anyone would know, even in this matter of love for young boys, those who are purely involved in this love; they don't desire boys until they are beginning to think, just about the same time that the beard is starting to grow. I believe that people who begin at that point to fall in love, are prepared to share their lives completely, even to live together. They are not deceivers who thoughtlessly will take such a boy, and then laugh and turn away to live with another.

But there must be a law against one's loving young boys, so that a great deal of zeal won't be wasted on an uncertainty. It is uncertain what the boys will grow up to be, what evil or good they will end up having in body and soul. And while good men lay down this law for themselves and hold themselves to it, it is necessary to force the vulgar sort of lovers to adhere to it, just the way we force them, as far as we are able, not to make love to our free women. It is this kind who have introduced the disgrace that makes some men go so far as to say that it is low to gratify lovers—but they say this when they regard the sort I'm describing, observing their importunity and unfairness. If the deed were performed decently and it had a sure legality, they could not justly hold it in reproach.

In other cities the law that deals with love-making is easy to understand, it is simply defined. But the one we have here is complicated. Take Elis, for example, and Boeotia, and places where they are not so articulate. It is set down plainly in the law that to give oneself to lovers is a good thing, nor would anyone, young or old, say it was bad. They wouldn't want, I believe, to have to do the job of convincing the boys of it, and pleading an argument, as they are unskilled in speaking. However, in Ionia, and in many other places it is decreed a bad thing, to the extent that they live under barbarians. Since the barbarians live under tyrants this is made a disgrace, as are philosophy and athletics. It isn't expedient, I imagine, for the rulers, if any deep thoughts develop in their subjects, nor strong friendships and comradeships, and actually, all the very things Love delights in engendering. The tyrants have learned this fact from the experience here. The love of Aristogeiton and the affection of Harmodius, when it had grown constant, destroyed their power. So, where it has been held an evil to give oneself to lovers, it is because of the evil of those who made the laws. On the one hand it stems from the arrogance of the rulers, and on the other from the emasculated cowardice of the ruled. However, if it has been ruled by law to be entirely good, this is the case because of an intellectual laziness in the lawmakers. Here, the law that deals with these matters is far better, but as I said before, it's not easy to understand.

Consider that it is said to be better to love openly than secretly, and especially finest to love the highest in mind and the noblest, even when they are uglier than others. Furthermore, one is cheered on marvelously in this love by everybody: one never does anything disgraceful; being won seems a fine thing, and it seems base not to be; and the law grants freedom to a lover who is trying to catch his beloved by doing marvelous deeds to win him praise, while the very same acts, if done by someone pursuing and wanting some other end, would bring the greatest reproach.

If one wanted to get wealth from someone, or to attain an office or some other power, and wanted to use the same methods that lovers use with their youths (making supplications and entreaties in prayers, and swearing oaths and sleeping at their doorsteps, and desiring to perform menial tasks such that no slave would be willing to perform), he would be prevented from acting out this business by his friends and by his enemies alike. The latter would reproach him for his obsequiousness and slavishness, while the former would chastise him and be ashamed over these things. But in a lover who does all these things one sees some grace. He is allowed by law to act without reproach, as if he were performing acts that were thoroughly noble. But what is strangest of all is how the people say that the gods will give pardon to him alone when he swears on oath and then breaks it; for an oath of someone under Aphrodite's rule, they say, doesn't exist—so that both men and gods give complete freedom to the lover, as the law says here.

For this reason a person might well think that it is ruled completely honorable here in this city, both to be a lover, and to be affectionate to lovers. But fathers have appointed tutors for those who are being wooed, so that they won't be allowed to hold intercourse with their lovers, and restrictions are imposed by the tutor to this end, and the boy's comrades and friends reproach him whenever they see this sort of thing taking place, nor do the elders check the reproachers, nor abuse them as speaking out of turn, so that when one has observed such things one would believe rather that this sort of thing is considered execrable here. But I think that this is how it really is: it isn't simple, as I said at the outset, but the granting of one's affection is, of itself, neither a noble thing, nor deplorable. It is a beautiful act if done beautifully, and if lowly, low. It is done basely when one gives one's affections to a base person, and does so in a low manner; when one does so to a good man, and in a noble way, it is done beautifully. The man who is a lover in the common way is base—he loves the body rather than the soul. Nor is he constant, since he loves things which lack constancy. Why, with the flower of the body fading, his favor, too, *disappearing, is gone*—and his many speeches and promises are discredited. But the person who loves the character of a good man endures throughout life, merging with what is lasting.

Now, our law attempts to prove men in a good and accurate way, those to whom one should yield, and those one ought to avoid. By these means it encourages us to pursue some people and flee from others, acting as referee, and making judgments about lover and beloved. That's why it's customarily considered an ignominy to be won quickly. It's so that time might pass, since time does seem to prove most things well. Then, too, it's held a lowness to grant favors on account of wealth and political power, in case one were suffering miserably from fear, lacked endurance, was unable to scorn the benefits of property or political success, or else were yielding in the hope of receiving some benefit. These things seem to lack steadiness and constancy. Besides, genuine friendship will not arise from this kind of relationship. One path, then, is left us by our legal institution, if the darling is to gratify his lover honorably. Just as it is not considered flattery or anything to be ashamed of when lovers want to serve and act like slaves for their beloved youths, so in the same way our law allows one other form of voluntary servility to be kept without shame; and this is when it is done for the sake of virtue.

It is our wont not to consider his willing slavery execrable, or anything to be ashamed of, when a man desires to serve someone and is led by this person to become better, either in wisdom or some other part of virtue. One must combine both conventions—the one concerning pederasty, and this one, which deals with philosophy and other virtues—then one may conclude that it is a good thing for a young boy to yield to an admirer. When the lover and his darling come to one another, and each holds to his own law: the one justly doing any sort of service whatever for his sweetheart, and the other justly complying, in all ways, with the man who is making him wise and good; the former being capable of endowing intellectuality and other virtues, and the latter needing to acquire knowledge; when these principles have coincided at the same point, then and only then is there a nobility in the beloved youth's acquiescing to his lover. In other circumstances, there is none. Furthermore, in this situation, there is no disgrace for a person who is betrayed, whereas in all others, whether one is betrayed or not, the relationship carries with it disgrace. If someone yields to a lover for his wealth and is deceived and receives no money because the lover turns out to be poor, it is still disgraceful. He shows himself to be the sort who will do anything for anyone, if money will result. There is no honor in this. But then, by the same token, if one gives oneself in love to a man whom one supposes to be good, for the sake of growing to be a better person through one's friend's affection, and then is deceived because the man turns out to be evil and lacking in virtue, the deception is just as honorable. One has in all this proven oneself, in that one could utterly adore someone for the sake of becoming a person of deeper virtue. This is a thing of the greatest beauty, and for this reason I feel that to give oneself for the sake of virtue is thoroughly noble. Such love is the love of the heavenly goddess, celestial, and precious to many, both publicly and privately, compelling a lover and the one beloved to show great concern for their virtue. All the other sorts of love are of the other goddess, the earthly one.

And this, he concluded, is my contribution to you, on Love, Phaedrus, and I have just thrown it together!

When Pausanias had *paused* (heh, heh—get it? my professors taught me how to pun like this)—Aristodemus said it was Aristophanes' turn to speak, but it happened that, either because of his eating too much, or for some other reason, he had a fit of hiccupping and was unable to deliver his speech, but said—since Eryximachus the doctor was placed just below him in order:

Eryximachus, be a good fellow and cure my hiccupping, or else speak for me, so that I can stop it.

And Eryximachus replied, Oh, but I'll do both those things. To start with I'll talk in your place, and when you've stopped hiccupping, you can talk in mine. But while I'm speaking, perhaps the hiccups will decide to leave if you hold your breath for a long time, and if they don't, gargle with water. If they are really stubborn, take something that is likely to tickle your nostrils, and sneeze! If you do this once or twice it'll go away, no matter how stubborn it is.

The sooner you speak the better, said Aristophanes, and I'll do what you say. So Eryximachus spoke.

## Eryximachus

Well then, it appears to me to be necessary, since although Pausanias spoke beautifully at the outset, his conclusion was insufficient, it is necessary, I say, for me to attempt to append a conclusion to his argument. To begin with, to say that Love is dichotomous seems to me perfectly valid; but it moves the hearts of men not only toward beautiful human beings but also toward many other things, and is in other things: is in the bodies of all things living, even things that grow in the earth, and, in a word, in everything that exists. This seems, from the medical point of view, to be true; and men in our field have seen how great and wonderful is this god who vibrates in everything, human and divine. I shall begin by talking from this medical point of view because I respect the science so much.

It is the nature of the body to manifest Pausanias' two-fold Love. For health and disease in a body are admittedly different and distinct, and different things desire and love different things. Thus, while desire is one thing in a healthy body, it is another in one diseased. And just as Pausanias said before, it is a beautiful thing for one to yield in love to good men, but base to obscene ones. Then, too, in the body itself, it is fine and even proper to yield to the good and wholesome wants of every body, and this is what is called therapy, but it is bad to yield to the noxious and evil desires. They will be rejected by anyone proficient in the art. For this is what medicine is, to put it summarily, a knowledge of the forces of Love in the body, for being stuffed and emptied out; and a person who can accurately diagnose whether the noble or the vulgar love is functioning in these cases and can interchange them is a master therapist. Thus, by eliminating one love and replacing it with the other, and knowing when to implant love when it ought to be introduced, and when to extract improper desires when they are present, one may be said to be an able practitioner. For one must, as a matter of fact, make the most antagonistic elements in the body friendly and loving to one another. The most antagonistic things are direct opposites: cold to heat, bitter to sweet, dry to moist, and so on, in all such cases. Our forefather Asclepius, who established our profession, knew how to impart love and concord to these things, as these poets here have said and I believe it.

So that medicine, accordingly, is ruled throughout by this god, and so likewise gymnastics and agriculture. In the case of music too, as is perfectly obvious to anyone who has given the slightest thought to these matters, it is just as Heracleitus tried to point out, although he didn't word it very well. For *The one,* he says, *a thing in discord with itself, is drawn into union, just as in the case of the harmony of bow and lyre.* But it is utterly illogical to speak of a harmony in discord, or of its coming out of discordant things. Rather, he seems to be saying in this that by the art of music it is out of things that are discordant *at first,* as treble and bass, that later on a concord develops. But it isn't really out of the *discord* between treble and bass that harmony arises. Harmony is consonance, and consonance a kind of concord. For concord to arise from discord while the elements are discordant is an impossibility. But then again, a kind of variance that is not incapable of reconciliation can be harmonized, as, say, rhythm develops out of the swift and slow, at variance to begin with, but later reconciled. Just as earlier it was medicine, so here it is music that brings the concord to all these cases, implanting a mutual love and harmony; and so, music is a science of love, relating to harmony and rhythm. It is not difficult to recognize the love-forces in this actual establishment of harmony and rhythm, and here it is not the twofold Love that is at work.

But when it becomes necessary in the world of men to apply rhythm and harmony—or composition—what people call 'song writing,' or else when someone makes arrangements of the melodies and meters already composed—which is called 'pedagogy,' then difficulty arises, and there is need for a good craftsman. And here the earlier principle comes up again, that one ought to give oneself to decent men or to those who aren't, but would be made more decent, and to cherish the love of these men, and that this is the noble, heavenly Love, which is of the Muse Urania. On the other hand, that of Polymnia, the mundane kind, one ought to indulge being careful about those with whom one indulges, so that one may reap pleasure for oneself, without taking on any indecency. It is just as in my profession, where one has to exercise great effort to make proper use of the desire men have for good cooking, so that pleasure can be taken without sickness.

Indeed, in music and in medicine, and in all the other instances of human and divine activity as well, so far as is possible one should take careful note of each of the loves. Each will be present.

Since even the arrangement of the seasons of the year is full with both of these Loves, and when the things which I was just talking about happen to occur together through the functioning of the orderly love-force—that is, the hot and the cold, the dry and the wet—they achieve a harmony and synthesis when they occur in due proportion, they appear as purveyors of a good harvest, of well-being to men and other animals and plants, and there is no injustice. But when Love, in pride, becomes too strong in the control of the seasons of the year, there is much destruction and injustice. Plagues love to develop out of just these sorts of things, and many other lawless maladies among flora and fauna, such as hoarfrosts, hailstorms and mildews, arise out of a grasping excessiveness and disorder of these love-forces toward one another.

The knowledge of these love-forces, when it concerns the courses of the stars, and the seasons of the year is called 'astronomy.'

So too all the sacrifices and things over which the art of divination has control—that is, the intercourse that gods and mortals have with one another—concern nothing other than the preservation and cure of Love. For every impiety loves to develop when someone has not gratified the orderly Love, or has, in every affair, honored and revered not him but the other, where one's parents are concerned (whether they're alive or dead), as well as where the gods are concerned. It has been assigned to divination to oversee these forces of love, and treat them; and divination is the craft responsible for the affections that exist between men and gods. It knows the forces of love in men, and draws them toward what is decent and holy.

Thus Love in his totality holds much great, no, in brief, complete power, and the good he accomplishes with moderation and justice among us and among the gods, this is his greatest power, and through this provides us with a complete joy. It is what makes us able to be with one another, and to be the friends of those who are mightier than us, the gods.

Thus, whereas I may well have left out many of the things that can be said in praise of Love, it was not on purpose, of course; but if I have omitted something, it'll be your job, Aristophanes, to complete the picture. However, if you plan to make your encomium to this god in a completely different way, begin your praise, since you've definitely gotten over your hiccups.

Then he said that Aristophanes started to talk and began with: Yes, it has stopped completely, but only after I applied the sneeze treatment to it! I wonder if the regular principle of my body lusts after such blasts and ticklings as there are in sneezing—it honestly stopped completely when I used the sneeze on it!

Aristophanes, m'love, exclaimed Eryximachus, look out for what you say! You're clowning before you begin and forcing me to guard against any foolishness you may talk, when you could speak in peace!

And Aristophanes, laughing, said, Oh you're right, Eryximachus; I unsay all I've said! But don't be so guarded against me—as far as what I'm going to say is concerned, I'm not so much worried that I'll produce a *farce* (*that'd* be a feather in my cap, it's natural to my Muse)—I'm afraid of being ridiculous!

Do you think you can just strike and run, Aristophanes? Speak your piece but be ready to defend yourself. There is a chance that I may be persuaded to let you off.

## Aristophanes

But of course, Eryximachus, said Aristophanes, I'm planning to make my talk rather different from yours and Pausanias'. It seems to me that men don't understand the power of Love at all—if they did, he would have the biggest temples and altars, and people would offer the greatest sacrifices to him. As things stand, nothing like this exists, and he's the greatest of them all! He is the god who loves men most. He helps them and cures them of those things whose cures provide the greatest joy for mankind. So I'll try to get you to realize the power of this god. Then you, in turn, can be the teachers for others.

To begin with, you must grasp the true nature of mankind and its sufferings. Our nature wasn't originally what it is now. No, it was quite different. First of all, there were three kinds of men, not two as now, the male and the female, but also a third kind combining both. We have the name still, but the thing itself has disappeared. The androgyne, separate in name and nature, partook of man and woman both. But the name is used now only as a reproach. Then also people were shaped like complete spheres. Their backs and sides made a circle. They had four hands, with the same number of legs and two faces—completely the same—on top of a circular neck. These two faces were set on opposite sides of one head, with four ears. And there were two sets of sexual parts, and whatever else one imagines goes along with this arrangement.

They walked around quite upright, just as we do today, but in whichever direction they chose, and whenever they got running fast, it was just like acrobats revolving in a circle—legs straight out and somersaulting! But then they had eight limbs to use for support when they were rolling swiftly around in circles! The three sexes were like this: the male was descended, in the beginning, from the sun, and the female from the earth, and the one that partook of both of them came from the moon, because the moon itself partakes of the natures of those two. So these things were globes themselves, you know, and took after their ancestors in the way they got around. In fact, they had terrific power and energy, were arrogant, and assaulted the gods. The story in Homer about Ephialtes and Otus is told of these: how they were set on while ascending to heaven to launch an attack against the gods.

Then Zeus and the other gods went into a huddle over what had to be done about these creatures, but they were baffled. They were not willing to destroy them and obliterate the race with a blast of lightning, like the giants, since their sacrifices and honors would be lost along with mankind. Nor would they swallow this wanton behavior.

Finally, after a tremendous lot of pondering, Zeus said:

I think I have a scheme whereby men may exist yet stop their licentiousness: we'll debilitate them. We'll slice each of them into two, he said, and they shall both be weakened and more useful to us, through the increase in their numbers. And if their wantonness seems to continue and they refuse to buckle under, why, he went on, I'll slice them in two again! They can go around then on one foot, hoppity-hop!

Thus he spoke, and he cut each man in two, the way people cut sorb apples to make preserves (or the way they do eggs with hairs). And for each one he cut, he set Apollo to turning the face and half of the neck around, towards the cut, so that in contemplating his incision a man might be made more orderly. Then he told him to heal them up.

So Apollo turned their heads around, and pulled the skin together from all sides to what is now called the stomach, like we do with round pouches with drawstrings. Leaving the one opening, he made a knot at the middle of the stomach, what they call the navel. He rubbed smooth many other rough spots, and moulded the breast, using the sort of tool shoemakers use on their lasts when they smooth away the side wrinkles. He left a few, though, around the stomach and navel, to serve as a reminder of past sufferings.

Now since the natural form of man had been severed into two parts and each half yearned for its match, when they met, they would throw their arms about one another and get enmeshed together. They yearned to grow together, and because they didn't want to do anything apart from one another, they began to die from hunger and inactivity. Whenever one of the halves died, and one was left, it would hunt around and get itself involved with another, either a hemi-woman—which we now simply call woman—or hemi-man, it might meet. But they were dying off this way, so Zeus, taking pity on them, devised another plan. He set their genitals around in the front (until this time they had had them behind, and they had fertilized and begat, not with one another, but on the ground like grasshoppers). So he set them around, this way, on the front, and that way got them to propagate with one another, with the male's inside the female. On account of this, if a man happened to come to a woman, while they were embracing she would conceive and they'd have a baby. If it happened between two men they'd simply have the pleasure of being together but then they'd stop, and turn to their labors, and pay some attention to the rest of life. So that's how it is, you see, that the love of one another is ingrained in men, ever since that time. It restores his ancient nature to man, and ventures to make one out of two, and heal the human condition.

Each of us, then, is the matching half of a man, because we were sliced like flatfish, and two were made out of one! And everybody carries on an eternal search for his other half. Those among men who are halves cut from the middle sex, the one that was called 'androgyne' in those days, are lovers of women. Lots of philanderers descend from this sort. Then, adultresses and women who are man-crazy come from this same sex. However, women who were sliced from the total woman have no predilection for men. They are strongly drawn to other women, and the "inverts" are derived from this sort. Those who have been cut from the whole male befriend men, and lying with them, and performing acts of love, yield themselves to men. This sort make for the noblest of boys and young men. They have the most courageous natures. The people who speak of these fellows as shameless are wrong. They don't do it out of shamelessness, but courage. It's done in virility and manliness, because they cherish what is like themselves. And here is further proof: the only men of this sort who succeed in public affairs are adults who were like that as boys. When they grow to manhood they take to boys, and it isn't by nature that they take any interest in marriage and family life, but are only pressured into it by convention. It would suffice for them to live with one another without marrying. This sort of man is born to pederasty and eroticism and always welcomes one like himself with open arms.

So that whenever the pederast, or any other sexual type, meets a half that is the same sort, they are overwhelmed with wonder by the affection, the joy of intimacy, and the love. They don't ever want, one might say, to be separated from one another, not even for a second. These people, living their entire lives together like this, wouldn't be able to articulate what it is they want to happen between them. Nor would anyone believe that such a union is only sexual, or that two people who share a mutual love have such a great passion for sex. But clearly there is something else that the soul of each desires, which it is unable to articulate, but it does divine and feel a hint of what it wants.

Imagine Hephaestus standing over them as they were lying together in this embrace, with his tools ready, and he says: 'What is it you want, you humans, to take place between you?' And suppose he addressed them again, as they lay helpless: 'So, do you want to be melded together as much as possible, and not have to leave one another, night or day? If this is what you want, I am willing to join you and weld you into one and the same being. You'll become one self out of two, and you can live as one, with the two of you sharing a life in common as a single being. And when you die, there in Hades, too, instead of two there will be one and you will share death. But look—is this what you want? Will you be satisfied if this should happen?' We know that not a single one of them would refuse such an offer. They would seem to desire nothing else. Everyone would openly acknowledge this as the age-old desire—the coming together and merging with the one they love so the two become one.

The reason for this is that our original nature was to be whole. And to the longing for wholeness the name 'love' has been attached. In the old days, as I've said, we were one; but now, on account of our crime, we have been split up by god (just the way the Arcadians were by the Lacedaemonians). Then, too, there is a fear that if we don't carry on our relationship with the gods in the proper way we'll be cut in two again. Then we'd have to go around mere outlines, and like the bas-relief carvings on pillars, be sawn through the nostrils, like split dice. That's why it behooves everybody to be obedient and worshipful to the gods. That way we can escape these consequences, and have good luck with the power of Love as our leader and marshal. No one should do anything in opposition to him—the man who does act in opposition is hateful to the gods—*we* must be the friends of god. If we are on good terms with him we will find happiness and be able to get together with the very boys we should, which few of us can claim to have done as of now! But I hope Eryximachus won't refute me with ridicule, as if I were talking about Pausanias and Agathon! Oh, I suppose it's true that they have had the experiences I'm referring to, and both have male natures. But really, I'm talking about all men and women. Our race can become happy if we satisfy desire, and if each can find his proper darling and return to his original, natural state. If this is the best thing, then, by necessity, what in our present circumstances comes closest to it is best for now. That is to find a love who is of like mind to oneself. So, really, if we are going to sing the praises of the god who can realize this with all justice, we should sing for Love. He can help us the most at present by drawing each together with his own. And he gives us great hope, that if we offer proper worship to the gods, he can restore us to our original condition, and by his healing, make us happy and joyful!

This, Eryximachus, he said, is my speech on Love, quite different from yours. So, as I begged of you, don't ridicule it, so that we can hear all of the remaining speakers—or I should say both, since only Agathon and Socrates are left.

Oh, I'll go along with you, Eryximachus declared, since your speech delighted me so much. And if I didn't know that Socrates and Agathon were masters of erotica, I would be afraid that they'd be at a loss for words after all the myriad of things that have been said! However, I'm thoroughly confident.

Then Socrates spoke up. That's fine for you, Eryximachus, you did so well. But if you were where I am now, or rather, where I shall be after Agathon has spoken eloquently, you would be quite fearful, exactly as I am now!

You want to bewitch me, Socrates, said Agathon, so that I'll be disturbed by thinking that the audience has great expectations about my eloquence.

I would certainly be forgetful, Agathon, replied Socrates, if knowing your manliness and greatness of mind when you presented yourself on stage with your actors, and faced that great audience squarely without the slightest perturbation, for the production of your work, I believed now that you could be upset by our little group of people.

But Socrates, exclaimed Agathon, Do you think I'm so blown up by the theater that I don't know that anyone with intelligence is more afraid of a few intelligent men than a multitude of fools?

I'd not do you the slightest justice, Agathon, Socrates allowed, if I thought you were naive. I know very well that when you meet people you consider intelligent, you think much more of them than of the masses. But, suppose we aren't like them—after all, we were present there, we made up part of the crowd—but if you were to meet others, wise men, surely you would be ashamed before them if you thought you were actually doing something shameful. . . . Isn't that so?

True enough, he agreed.

But you wouldn't mind before the crowd—if you thought you were doing something shameful?

Phaedrus, he says, broke in here—Agathon, my friend, if you answer

Socrates it won't matter to him any more what happens to our project here, as long as he gets somebody to argue with him—particularly if that body is a beauty to boot! Personally, I'm delighted to listen to Socrates' arguments, but I am responsible for superintending this encomium to Love, and I must receive a speech from each of you. Both of you must pay up and give your dissertations to the god!

Ah, you're quite right, Phaedrus, Agathon declared, and nothing is going to get in the way of my speaking. There'll be plenty of time for me to argue with Socrates later.

## Agathon

First I'd like to say how I should speak, then make my speech. It seems to me that none of the other speakers have praised the god, but have celebrated men for the joys of which the god is the source. About the nature of the one who has bestowed these blessings, no one has spoken. There is one proper mode for every paean, in every case: The nature of the subject of the speech—whoever that may be—and of the things he causes, should succeed in coming through in the speech. So that it seems to me only just to discuss first the nature of the god Love, and then his gifts.

I declare, then, if I may speak without censure or reproach, that of all the gods, those joyful ones, Love is the most joyful, most beautiful, best.

He is so beautiful in that, first, Phaedrus, he is the very youngest of the gods. He himself provides sure proof for this assertion, running for refuge from old age (a quick thing, obviously—it overtakes us far more quickly than it should). Indeed, Love instinctively loathes it, and avoids it even at a distance. On the other hand, he is always with the young, and is so, as well, for the old saying holds well, that like likes like.

Whereas I agree with Phaedrus in many cases, I can't accept that statement that Love is older than Cronos and Iapetus. I say he is the youngest of the gods, and always young, and that the ancient acts of the gods, of which Hesiod and Parmenides tell, were done by Necessity, and not by Love; that is, if those writers tell the truth. They would not have castrated or enchained one another, nor done the many other violent things, if Love had been among them. But affection and peace, by which Love rules the gods, would have prevailed, as they do now.

So, you see, he is young, and tender in his youth. It demands a poet such as Homer to describe the exquisite tenderness of this god. Homer speaks of Delusion as a goddess, and of her tenderness—how tender her feet were—singing:

> *Her feet are tender; for not upon the*
> *earth does*
> *she come, but see, she treads upon the*
> *heads of men.*

There it seems to me this sweetest tenderness is manifest in a beautiful testimony, for she does not tread upon stiff stuff, but upon soft. And in the same way we would employ a testament to the tenderness of Love. For he doesn't come upon the earth, nor, for that matter, upon our heads, which are not at all soft, but it is in the very softest parts of living things that he comes, and lives. In the characters and souls of gods and men he embeds himself, but it should be added, not in all souls. When he finds the character of a person to be hard, he abandons him, but when he finds it soft, he will dwell there.

Thus clinging always, feet and all, in the very softest souls of gentle men, he must surely be the tenderest of things.

Youngest, surely, and tenderest, and in addition, supple in form. He would not be the god who enfolds all things, he would not escape, going in at first, then going out of every heart, if he were stiff.

Of the symmetry and suppleness of his form, his grace provides strong testimony; the grace which all agree Love possesses beyond everyone, for Love without grace is simply a contradiction in terms.

The beauty of his skin shines for the life he lives in flowers. In a body or soul, or anything else that is withered or past its bloom, Love will not stay, but if a place is fragrant and filled with blossoms, there he will stop and stay.

Of the beauties, then, of our god, enough has been said, although there is still much left. But I shall go on to speak of the goodness of Love.

His greatness is that he treats no god or man unjustly, nor is he unjustly treated by any god, or man. He himself does not suffer violence—if acted on at all—violence cannot apply to Love. Nor when he acts, does he act with violence, for in all ways men all serve Love with willing hearts, and the things one does of one's own free will, by voluntary covenant, *the sovereign of our state—the laws*—declares to be just.

And beyond his justice he is filled with temperance. For we define temperance as the control of pleasure and desire, and no pleasure is more powerful than Love. If they are weaker, Love will control and they will be controlled, and controlling pleasures and desires, Love would be especially temperate!

Further, *not even Ares can resist* the courage of Love. Ares doesn't capture Love, but Love—of Aphrodite—does catch Ares, as the story goes. The captor is more powerful than the captured, and if he overcomes one who is braver than all others, he must be the bravest.

Thus, the justice, the temperance and the courage of the god have been described and only his wisdom is left. As far as I am able, I will try not to slight it.

First, that I may honor my art, as Eryximachus did his: our god is a poet, so masterful as to make others poets as well. At least, everyone becomes a poet, *however songless he may have been before,* once Love takes hold of him. Which is fitting for us to take as proof that Love is a gifted poet, in short, of every expressive art. For the things one doesn't have or know about, one can't give another, or teach. And I ask you, who could deny that the creation of all living things is anything but the art of Love, by which all animate things come to be and develop? On the other hand, do we not know that a craftsman for whom this god has been the teacher becomes celebrated and brilliant, while when Love has not taken hold of one, he remains obscure? Archery, certainly, and medicine, and divination, Apollo invented, under the influence of desire and Love, so that he too is a student of Love. So too, the Muses, when they discovered music, and Hephaestus, when he invented the smith's art, and Athene, weaving, and even Zeus, *the government of gods and men.* From which, too, it is obvious that those acts of the gods were contrived when Love was being born—the love, that is, of beauty—because there is nothing ugly about Love. Before this, however, as I said at the outset, the gods did many awful things, or so they say, under the compulsion of Necessity; but then this god was born, and from then on the ability to love beauty has created all the good things that exist for gods and men.

So Love himself seems to me, Phaedrus, the most beautiful and the very best of the gods—and beyond that to be the source of all the other qualities of this type in others. A desire has come over me just now to make up a poem about the way he creates:

> Peace among men, a calm stillness
> to the sea, rest for
> the winds, and for human sorrow,
> sleep.

He empties out feelings of alienation, and fills us with intimacy, brings us together in all such relations with one another as this—in festivals, in dances, at sacrificial rites, where he himself becomes the leader. He bestows gentleness, banishing brutality, loves to give joy while withholding grief, and has a graceful cheerfulness. Wise men may look at him, and the gods find him wonderful. By those who are unhappy he is coveted, by those who have a happy lot, treasured. He is the begetter of delicacy and elegance, wantonness and beneficence, of human desire and yearning. He is concerned with good men, mindless of bad. In misery, in fear, in drunkenness and the affairs of state, shipmate, comrade, and dearest savior, ornament of all gods and men together, most beautiful and highest leader, whom all men must follow, singing sweetly and partaking of the music he sings as he enchants the mind of every god and man.

And this, he concluded, is the speech I offer, Phaedrus, in dedication to the god. It is partly in a light and partly in a serious mode, combined with all the skill I have.

At Agathon's saying this, reported Aristodemus, the people who were there applauded this speech which so became the young man who had given it, as well as the god! Then Socrates spoke, looking at Eryximachus.

Doesn't it seem to you, oh son of Acumenus, he started out, that I wasn't afraid without cause back there, or was I not speaking like a prophet when I predicted that Agathon would talk brilliantly and that I'd be at a complete loss?

Well, said Eryximachus, I agree that you were prophetic in saying that Agathon would speak well; I very much doubt if you are at a loss.

But how, my good friend, Socrates said, could I not be a loss for words—I or anyone else, for that matter, when I'm expected to follow such a beautiful, many-faceted speech as has just been delivered? The rest of it was not quite so amazing, but that part at the end—who, hearing the beauty of those words and phrases, wouldn't have been astounded? I would have run away and escaped from shame when I realized that I would not be able to speak nearly as well, if I'd had somewhere else to go!

The speech reminded me of Gorgias—and I felt exactly like Homer's character. I was afraid that, in his conclusion, Agathon would hold up to me the awesome Gorgias' head, in opposing his oration to mine, and strike me as voiceless as stone! Then I realized how ridiculous it was to have agreed to take my turn along with you in praising Love, and to have said that I was an expert in love-matters, without knowing how one ought to speak in praise. To begin with, I stupidly thought one ought to speak the truth about anything which is being eulogized; and having this as a foundation, the speaker could esteem the most beautiful aspects and present them in the most becoming manner. So I was thinking to myself how really beautifully I would speak, since I knew the truth. But now it looks as if this is not what it means to discuss something "beautifully," but rather one should ascribe the greatest and most beautiful qualities to it, whether it has them or not. If it is false, it doesn't matter. It was arranged beforehand, it seems, that each of us should appear to praise Love, but that we should not really praise him. That's why, I believe, you dredged up all those sayings and applied them to Love, declaring him such and such, and the cause of such and such, so that he could be described as 'most beautiful' and 'best,' and obviously for people who don't know him—for this wouldn't work with people who know, however beautiful and awesome the eulogy may be! But I didn't realize that this was to be the way the praises would be given, and I ignorantly agreed to offer my praises in turn. *The tongue, yes,* as they say, *but not the heart.* Really—I want out! I'll never make a speech of praise that way! I'm not capable of it! If you like, I'm willing to speak only the truth, in my own style, and not in competition with your own dissertations, so that I'm not branded a laughing-stock. So look here, Phaedrus, do you want a speech like this—do you want to listen to an honest description of Love, with the words and phrases of the sentiments expressed in just the form and order that they happen to come along?

Then he said that Phaedrus and the others commanded him to speak in whatever way he felt he had to address them.

But furthermore, he said, allow me to question Agathon a bit, Phaedrus, so that I can come to some agreement with him before I speak.

Oh, I'll give way, answered Phaedrus. Go ahead and question him. And so it was after this sort of stuff that our friend Socrates began at this point.

## Agathon & Socrates

Now, Agathon my friend, it seems to me that you led off your discussion beautifully by saying that it is necessary first to show what the nature of Love is, and then to discuss his works. I thoroughly admire such a beginning. So tell me this about Love please, since the rest of what you said about him was so beautiful and splendid—is Love such as to be the love of something, or of nothing? I'm not asking if it is the love of some mother or father—to ask whether Love is the love of a mother or father would be absurd—but as if I were asking about a father. Is a father the father of someone, or not? You should undoubtedly say to me, if you wanted to answer me properly, that it is of a son or daughter that a father is a father. Or wouldn't you?

Certainly, said Agathon.

And it would be the same for a mother?

They were in agreement about that as well.

But now then, continued Socrates, answer a few more, so that you get a better understanding of what I want. Let me ask you this: a brother—the thing itself, just as it is—is it the brother of someone or not?

He answered that it was.

Is it not, then, the brother of a brother or sister?

Yes.

So try, he went on, and tell me about Love. Is Love the love of nothing or of something?

Surely he is the love of something!

Now think, Socrates urged, of what this may be, and keep it to yourself; but tell me whether he desires this thing of which Love is the love or not?

Oh yes, Agathon replied.

Does he have the thing which he desires and loves, when he desires and loves it, or does he not have it?

He doesn't have it, I would guess, Agathon said.

Then consider, continued Socrates, beyond guessing, whether it isn't necessary for the desiring thing to desire what is lacking, and not to desire it if it isn't lacking? It seems marvelously clear to me, Agathon, that this is necessary. What about you?

It seems that way to me, too, he said.

Good. So, would anyone wish to be great when he was great? Or strong if he were strong?

That would be impossible, from what we've been saying.

Since they would not be lacking that which they were.

True.

For if he were strong, and still should want to be strong, said Socrates, or swift, and wanted to be swift, or healthy, and wanted to be healthy—since one generally thinks in that sort of situation, and in all of the same sorts of cases, that those who are of such and such a nature and possess those same qualities, want the things that they have (I'm inserting this so that we won't deceive ourselves), for these men, Agathon, if you think about it, it is imperative that they have everything, at a given moment, which they have, whether they wish it or not, and who, I ask you, would desire that? But whenever someone says 'I am healthy, and I want to be healthy,' 'I am rich, and I want to be rich,' or 'I desire the very things I have,' we shall say to him, 'you mean, dear fellow, that possessing riches, health and strength, you want to possess them in the future, too, since as far as the present is concerned you have them, desiring it or not.' But look, when you say 'I desire my present belongings,' do you think you're saying anything besides: 'I wish that the things I have now will be provided for me in the future?' Wouldn't he agree?

Certainly, said Agathon.

Then Socrates went on, So there is a love of that which is not present for one, which one doesn't have, namely the existence of those things in the future, preserved, and provided always.

Absolutely, he answered.

Now such a person, and every other person who feels longing, longs for what is not at hand, for what he isn't himself, and for what he lacks, and these are the sorts of thing that desire is of, and Love?

Definitely, he said.

So come, urged Socrates, let us agree on what has been said. Is Love, first of all, anything but the love of things? And further, isn't it of those very things which it needs?

That's right, Agathon agreed.

Indeed, now think back to the things you said about Love in your oration. If you like, I'll remind you. I believe you spoke of the way that the deeds of the gods were initiated because of the love of beautiful things. For there couldn't be a love of ugly things. Didn't you say that?

Yes, I said it, replied Agathon.

And you spoke quite properly, my friend, asserted Socrates. And if this is the case, can Love be the love of anything but beauty, and not ugliness?

He granted that.

Then wasn't it agreed that he loves what he lacks and doesn't have?

Yes, he said.

Love, then, is wanting in beauty, and doesn't have it?

Necessarily.

But what have we here? Would you say that what was wanting in beauty and in no way possesses beauty was beautiful?

Obviously, it isn't.

Are you then still going to agree that Love is beautiful, if that's how it is?

And Agathon declared, I'm afraid, Socrates, that I didn't know what I was talking about.

Oh, but you spoke beautifully, Agathon, he assured him. But tell me a little more. Don't you think of what is good as being beautiful as well?

Yes, I do.

Then again—if Love is lacking in beauty, and the good is beautiful, he must be lacking in goodness as well.

Socrates! he exclaimed, I'm incapable of refuting you, so have it your own way!

The truth, lovely Agathon, Socrates said, you cannot refute, but Socrates is easily refuted.

## Socrates & Diotima

But I'm going to leave you alone now, and give the account concerning Love which I once heard from a woman of Mantinea, Diotima, who was wise about such things and many others as well. It was she who once gave the Athenians a ten-year respite from disease, by getting them to make sacrifices against the plague. She was my teacher about Love, and I shall try to relate for you, using the points on which Agathon and I agreed, in my own words, and as well as I can, what she told me. It is necessary, Agathon, just as you have indicated, for one to define Love first, and describe his nature, and then to go on to his works. I think it would be easiest for me to follow the procedure the foreign woman used when she questioned me then. I was saying to her pretty nearly the same things that you were to me just now, Agathon—that Love was a great god, and was of beautiful things. So she questioned me on these propositions, just the way I've done here, showing that according to my theory he couldn't be either beautiful or good.

How can you say that, Diotima? I demanded. Can Love then be ugly and evil?

But she said, Be quiet! Do you think that whatever isn't beautiful must necessarily be ugly?

Absolutely.

And that anyone who isn't wise, is ignorant? Or don't you realize that there is something in between wisdom and ignorance?

What is that?

Don't you know, she said: having correct opinions without being able to explain them. That isn't knowledge (for how can something without reason be knowledge?) but it's not ignorance, either (if one chances on what really is, how can that be ignorance?). But correct opinion has just this quality: it is between understanding and ignorance.

And I had to agree that there was truth in what she was saying.

Then don't insist on the thing which isn't beautiful being ugly, or on the thing which isn't good being evil. And when you can bring yourself to agree that Love is neither good nor beautiful, it won't be necessary anymore for him to be ugly and evil. Rather he is between these, she said.

But everyone agrees that Love is a great god, I argued.

Do you mean every ignorant one, she countered, or every knowledgeable one?

I mean *everyone!*

Here she laughed. And how, Socrates, can those people agree that he is such a great god; who deny his being a god at all?

Who are they? I asked.

You, she declared, for one, and me for another!

And I demanded, How is that? Socrates said.

It's simple, she continued. Tell me, wouldn't you say that all gods are joyous and beautiful? Or do you presume to deny the beauty and happiness of the gods?

Not I, by god! I exclaimed.

And wouldn't you say that those who are happy are those who have good and beautiful things?

Completely so.

But you have just now agreed that Love, in his want of good and beautiful things, yearns after the things of which he is in need.

Yes, I did agree to that.

But how, I ask you, could he be a god when he hasn't any share of beautiful and good things?

No, that doesn't seem at all possible.

Then you can see, she asserted, that you are ruling Love a nongod?

But, I asked, what is Love then? A mortal?

Not in the least!

But what then?

Like those things we first discussed —he is intermediate between mortal and immortal.

What is such a thing, Diotima?

A great daemon, Socrates. The entire world of the daemonic is intermediate between divinity and mortality.

What power does it possess? I asked.

Interpreting and communicating human affairs to the gods and divine matters to men—the prayers and sacrifices of men, and the commands and responses of the gods. Being in the middle, it fulfills both, and in this way unites the whole with itself. Through this intermediary all divination proceeds, and religious practice involving sacrifices, mystery rites, magical incantations, all enchantments and sorcery. A god doesn't have intercourse with a human being, but all mingling and dialogue between gods and men take place through this intermediary, both in wakefulness and in dreams. One who knows of such things is a daemonic man, while one who is versed in any other skill, be it craft or any handiwork, is just a workman. Actually, there are many of these daemons, and they are of all kinds, and Love is of them.

But his father—who was that? And his mother? I asked.

That's a rather long story to recount, she answered, but I'll tell it to you. When Aphrodite was born, the gods were feasting, a group of them, including the son of Invention, Resource. And when they had dined, Poverty came along begging since there was a party going on. So she stood there at the doors. Now Resource, having gotten quite drunk on nectar—there was no wine then—had gone out to Zeus' little garden, and in his discomfort fallen asleep. Here Poverty schemed, since she herself was without resource, to have a child by Resource; and she lay with him and thereby conceived Love. For this reason Love has been Aphrodite's attendant and servant, because he was conceived on the day of her birth, and at the same time is by nature a lover of beauty because of Aphrodite's being so beautiful.

Therefore, as the son of Resource and Poverty, Love finds himself in this situation: first of all, he is always impoverished, and far from being tender and beautiful, as most people think, he is harsh and rugged, barefoot and homeless; always lying unsheltered on the ground, he is lulled to sleep on doorsteps and in the open roads. Possessing his mother's nature, he is always in need. But, then again, through his father he turns out a schemer for beautiful and good things, is courageous, bold, and intense, an awesome hunter always devising some machination or other, eager for understanding and inventive; he is a lover of wisdom throughout his life, and a brilliant wizard, healer and philosopher!

And so he was born neither immortal nor mortal. In one day, then, when he is happy, he will spring into life, and then will die, but once again be brought back to life through his father's nature! But his power is always ebbing away, so that Love is never utterly at a loss nor completely wealthy. He exists in the middle, between wisdom and ignorance. It is like this: no god desires wisdom or longs to become wise—they are that—nor does anyone else who is wise desire wisdom. But then those who are ignorant don't desire wisdom or long to become wise either. That's exactly the problem with ignorance—a person who lacks beauty and goodness and intelligence seems perfectly satisfactory to himself. A person who doesn't think of himself as lacking anything won't desire what he doesn't think he lacks!

Then who, Diotima, I asked, are the lovers of wisdom, if it's not wise or ignorant men?

It would be obvious, she answered, even to a child, that it is the ones who are intermediate between them both—and Love is one of these. Wisdom is certainly one of the most beautiful things, and Love is the love of what is beautiful. By necessity, then, Love is a lover of wisdom, a philosopher, and as a philosopher, is intermediate between the wise and the ignorant. And the cause of these facts, again, is his birth. Because on the one hand his father was wise and fortunate, while his mother was unwise and resourceless.

This, then, dear Socrates, is the very nature of a daemon. But it's not remarkable that you came to think of Love the way you did. I believe I may infer from what you said that you imagined Love was the beloved, not the loving. For this reason Love appeared to you, I suppose, as utterly beautiful. For, in fact, it is the beloved that is beautiful and delicate, perfect and most blessed. But that which feels love takes a different form, just as I've explained.

And I answered: Amen, you remarkable woman! You put that so well! But if Love is of such a nature, what function does he serve for men?

That's exactly what I shall try to teach you next, Socrates, she said. To begin with, Love's nature and birth are just as I've said, but then too, he is "of beautiful things," as you've put it. But suppose someone were to ask us: 'What is the Love of beautiful things, Socrates and Diotima?' Or, let me state it more clearly: 'If one loves beautiful things, what is this love?'

And I replied that it was that they would become one's own.

But this answer, she went on, demands a further question, such as: 'Once these beautiful things have become a person's, what will he have?'

I have absolutely nothing at hand, I said, to offer as an answer to such a question.

But, she continued, supposing one substituted 'the good' for 'the beautiful' and put the question: 'Look, Socrates, I say to you, what does someone who loves good things love?'

Their becoming his, I answered.

And what does the fellow have who gets these good things?

That's easier, I responded. I can answer that he has joy.

So, she concluded, by the possession of good things, happy people are happy, and there is no longer any need to ask why a man who wishes for happiness, wishes it. Rather, this answer seems to be complete.

Very true, I asserted.

But do you think that such a desire and love are really common to all men, and that they all desire good things for themselves? What do you say?

Yes, I said. It is common to all.

How is it then, Socrates, she asked, that we don't say that all men love, if all men do always love the same things? Rather we say that some men love, while others do not.

I'm puzzled by that myself, I replied.

Don't puzzle over it, she said. What happens is that we take a certain form of love and call that 'love,' which is the name of the whole; and we misuse the names of other things, too.

Like what, I asked.

For instance, you know that *poetry* is very diverse: that the entire process of turning a thing from nonbeing into being, is poetry, that all kinds of work involving all sorts of techniques are poetry, and that the craftsmen who do the work on them are all 'poets.'

This is true.

In the same way you know, she went on, that they aren't all called 'poets,' but have other names, and from the whole of poetry one part is selected—that which is concerned with music and meter—and this is called by the name of the whole. By *poetry* is meant that alone, and those who do this sort of poetry are called 'poets.'

Yes, it's true, I agreed.

So, it's the same way, you see, regarding love. In its generic aspect love is the entire desire for good things, and for the happiness they give,

*most powerful and all ensnaring Love.*

But those who turn to him in his many other aspects, either in trade, or love of gymnastic exercise, or philosophy, these aren't said to be aspects of love, nor are the people called 'lovers.' However, those who go after the one specific aspect, and court it, they get the name of the whole—they are said to be lovers and to love.

It's very likely that what you say is true, I said.

Whereas a person might make up a story, she continued, that those who seek after the other halves of themselves are loving, my own account describes love as being neither of the half nor of the whole, unless it should chance, my friend, to be something good, since men are ready to have their own hands and feet cut off if it seems to them that these things are harmful to them! No one cherishes what is his own for its own sake, I believe, unless one were to call that which belongs to one 'good' and that which is foreign 'evil.' So that what men love is nothing other than the good. Don't you think so?

By god, I do! I exclaimed.

Then, she asked, may we say simply that what men love is the good?

Yes, I agreed.

But then, she said, shouldn't we add that they desire the good to be theirs?

Yes, let that be added.

Then, furthermore, not only to be theirs, but to be so forever?

Yes, add that too.

To put it briefly, love is for the good to always belong to oneself.

Absolutely true! I declared.

Since love is always of this nature, she went on, how is it pursued? How does this zeal and vehemence find its way into actions? How does it actually work? Can you say?

I wouldn't marvel so at you, Diotima, I replied, and at your wisdom, and attend your teachings to learn these very things, if I could.

Then I'll tell you, she assured me. It is procreation in a beautiful thing—of the body and of the soul.

One would need a prophet to comprehend what you're saying.

All right, she responded, I'll put it more clearly. You see, Socrates, all humans are pregnant, physically and spiritually, and when we reach our prime, our nature desires to give birth. Nature is not capable of giving birth in the ugly, but only in the beautiful. Now this is a divine act, and this pregnancy and birth impart immortality to a living being who is mortal. But it is impossible for these things to come about in the unharmonious. The ugly clashes with all that is divine, while beauty is in harmony with it. Therefore the role of the goddess of childbirth is played by beauty. And because of this, whenever something pregnant approaches the beautiful it becomes gentle and pours out gladness both in the begetting and the birth. But whenever it approaches the ugly, it shrinks into itself, sullen and upset. It turns away, is repelled, and refuses to give birth. It holds back and carries the burden of what it has inside itself with pain. In fact, within the pregnant one, who is teeming with life, there is a violent fluttering before the beautiful, through which it will be released from the great pain of childbirth which it has. But love is not, Socrates, she cautioned, a love of the beautiful, as you may believe.

But of what then?

Of giving birth and procreation in the beautiful.

Is that it, then?

Absolutely, she replied. And why is it of giving birth? Because giving birth is the eternal and immortal element in the mortal, and it's necessary to desire immortality along with the good, from what we've agreed—that love is for the good to be eternally one's own. So, really, from this same assumption it necessarily follows that love is of immortality.

All these ideas, then, she taught me, when she would discourse on love. And once she asked,

What do you believe, Socrates, to be the source of this love, this desire? Look—don't you perceive how profoundly it moves all wild beasts, footed and winged, when they desire to procreate? How they all become sick and deranged with love, at first with the desire for intercourse with one another, and then for nourishing their offspring? How the weakest ones are prepared to fight against the strongest, and to die? How these beasts will wear themselves down with hunger so as to feed their children, and to do anything else that's necessary? A person might imagine, she suggested, that human beings do these things out of rationality. But what causes the wild beasts to be so deeply moved by love? What can you say?

And I replied that I didn't know.

She asked then: Do you intend to become a master in matters concerning love when you don't understand these things?

But that's exactly why I came to you, Diotima, as I said before. I realized my need for instruction. Please, explain the cause of these and any other things that arise because of love.

Well, she answered, if you believe that love has the nature we have often agreed on, you shouldn't wonder. In this case the story is the same as that one—mortal nature always seeks as much as it can to exist forever and achieve immortality. But it is able to do this only by means of procreation, its way of always leaving behind another, young one, against old age. It is particularly in this that each living individual is said to be alive and to be itself—just as one is described as oneself and the same person from childhood until becoming old. But in actuality one hasn't any characteristics at all whereby one can be called the same person. One is always becoming a new person, losing things, portions of hair, flesh, bones, blood and all the stuff of the body. And not only in the body. In the soul as well one's habits and character, beliefs, desires, pleasures, pains, fears—none of these things remain the same in anyone—they arise and they die out. But what's even stranger than these facts is that we not only gain knowledge and lose it, so that we don't remain the same people with respect to what we know, but that every single example of knowledge suffers the same thing! For a man is said to study when there is a departing of knowledge. Forgetting is a leaving of knowledge, and study, by implanting new knowledge in place of what has left, saves the memory of it, so that it seems like the same thing. It is in this way that everything mortal is preserved—not by its being utterly the same forever, like the divine, but by what is old and withdrawing leaving behind something else, something new, like itself. It is by this method, Socrates, that the mortal partakes of immortality, she explained, in the body and in all other respects. It is not possible any other way. On account of this, it is not surprising if everything, by nature, honors its own progeny, for in all, the same intensity and love seeks the joy of immortality.

When I heard this argument I was amazed, and said, Is it possible, wise Diotima, that such things are really true?

And she, just like those precious professors, said, Know it well, Socrates! You might be amazed at the unreasonableness of what I've told you if you looked at the ambitions of men, unless you considered how terribly, in their love, they are affected by a desire to acquire a name,

> *and to store away fame for all immortal time,*

and for the sake of this are prepared to run all risks, greater even than those they run for their children: to go through their wealth, to suffer pains of all sorts, and even to sacrifice their lives! Do you imagine, she asked, that Alcestis would have died for Admetus, or Achilles would have sought death for Patroclus, or our own Codrus would have welcomed death for the sake of his children's kingdom, unless they believed that they were securing for themselves *the undying memory of virtue,* which we now hold? Certainly not, she said. I believe they all performed all their renowned deeds for the sake of the immortality of virtue and such a reputation, and the more so to the degree that they are better people. For they desire the immortal. However, those who are prolific, she said, when they are so in body, turn in preference to women and in this way are their lovers, so that through the conception of children they achieve immortality, memory and joy, and they believe that they are *providing all things against a future time* for themselves. But when it's in the soul—for there are some people who are pregnant more in their souls than in their bodies, with things which are fitting for the soul to bear and bring to life. And what is fitting in this way? Thought—and other virtue. Of these things, you see, all poets are progenitors, and those craftsmen who are said to be inventors. And by far the greatest, she asserted, and most beautiful part of thought is that which concerns the ordering of cities and households, whose name is wisdom and justice.

Whenever a person is filled with these things from his youth, so as to be divine in his soul, when he becomes a man he yearns to bring forth and beget, and goes around seeking, I believe, for the beautiful thing in which he can generate. For he cannot generate in an ugly thing. And so, being pregnant with these things, he welcomes beautiful bodies rather than ugly ones, and if he should chance on a soul who has beauty of nature and body, he delights greatly in both together, and immediately indulges in talks with this man about virtue, and about the sort of person that a good man must be, and about what things are properly done by him. He is taking his education in hand. For I believe that when he fastens onto this beautiful person and has intercourse with him, he gives birth to the things he has been carrying up to then, and brings them to life when, present or absent, he thinks about him. He then nurtures what has been conceived together with that person. Such men share an intimacy with one another which is far deeper than one coming from children and enjoy a surer affection, because they have taken part in the creation of more beautiful and immortal progeny! Everyone would choose for himself to give birth to these sorts of children rather than human ones! Men look at Homer and Hesiod and the other great poets and are jealous of the kind of offspring they left behind them, because they are the kind of beings which afford to those men a deathless fame and memory. Or, if you like, she went on, Lycurgus, the savior of Lacedaemonia, and, as it were, all Hellas, left behind such children in Lacedaemonia. And Solon, too, is more honored by you on account of his creation of the laws; and other men too, in many other places, among the Greeks and barbarians alike, men who are the producers of many beautiful works, bringing forth every sort of virtue. Many shrines have been instituted for them because of the sort of children they had, while for the sake of human ones there is not one.

It is these kinds of mysteries about love, Socrates, into which you may perhaps be initiated. I don't know if you are the sort of man to grasp the higher mysteries, the end to which these lead if correctly followed. But, she promised, I'll tell you about them, and I'll not spare any effort on my own part. You must try to follow as best you can.

It is necessary, she asserted, for one who is going to proceed to this goal properly, to begin as a young man by being drawn to the beauty of the body, and if he is being guided properly by his guide, to love the beauty of one body, and for the fruit of this love to be beautiful conversations. But then this man must perceive that the beauty of one particular body is related to the beauty of another body, and if he must pursue beauty of form it is utterly senseless not to consider as one and the same the beauty which exists in all bodies. Once he has understood this, he will become a lover of all beautiful bodies, but he'll despise his lust for the one, and give it up, considering it petty. After this, he will find the beauty that exists in souls more valuable than that in the body, so that when there is decency of soul in someone, although this person may have very little of the bloom of physical beauty, it satisfies him to love him and care for him and to beget with him the sort of conversations that make young men better, so that he is compelled further to contemplate the beauty which exists in daily pursuits, and laws, and to see here too, how each kind of beauty is related, so that he will come to consider physical beauty rather a minor thing. After actions one comes to kinds of knowledge, so that one sees the beauty of the sciences, and gazing now at this vast beauty, one can no longer be the low, petty slave of an isolated instance of beauty, cherishing, like a lackey, the beauty of a young boy, or of some one person, or even of a single activity. One turns and contemplates the greatest beauty; one brings forth many beautiful and magnificent theories and thoughts in a fruitful philosophy, until, growing strong and thriving in this environment, he comprehends a certain single knowledge, which is of this kind of beauty—now you must try, she interjected, to keep your mind with me as well as you can—the man who has been instructed, up to this point, in an understanding of matters of love, looking at beauty in correct and orderly succession, when he comes to the end of these love matters will suddenly behold a thing which is miraculously beautiful by nature! It is this very thing, Socrates, for the sake of which all the earlier hardships were suffered. First of all, it is eternal, and neither comes into being nor perishes, neither waxes nor wanes. Then it is not beautiful in part and ugly in part, nor beautiful at one time and ugly at another, nor beautiful in relation to one thing and ugly in relation to another, nor is it beautiful from one point of view but ugly from another (so that to some it is beautiful while it is ugly to others). Furthermore, the Beautiful will not manifest itself to this man as a face or pair of hands, or any other bodily thing; nor in any proposition, or science, nor as existing anywhere in something else, such as an animal, or the earth or the heavens, or any other thing whatever. It exists by itself in itself, eternally, and in one form only, and all other beautiful things participate in it in such a way that, while they come into being and perish, it does not, nor does it become greater or less, nor is it affected by anything.

So, whenever someone, making his way from these kinds of beauties, through the correct use of his love for boys, begins to behold this, the Beautiful in itself, he has pretty much attained the ultimate end. This is what it means to progress correctly to an understanding of matters of love, or to be brought to it by another: in beginning from these sorts of beauties, to move up constantly for the sake of that beauty (as if he were using the steps of a stair), from one to two, and from two to all beautiful bodies, from beautiful bodies to beautiful acts, from beautiful acts to the beauties of learning, from learning finally to that knowledge which is none other than knowledge of the Beautiful itself, so that he comes to know, in the end, what beauty is. Here above all places, my dear Socrates, said the woman from far-off Mantinea, is the life that is worth living for a man, lived in the contemplation of the Beautiful itself. If you ever do see this, it will seem to you to be very different from the gold or clothing or beautiful boys and youths you now look at with amazement, so that you are ready, like so many others, when you are looking at your darlings and always being with them, to give up eating and drinking (if such a thing were possible), and only gaze on at them and make love! How would it be, let us imagine, if someone could see the Beautiful itself, pure, clear, unmixed—not infected with human flesh and color, and a lot of other mortal nonsense—if he were able to know the divinely Beautiful itself, in its unique form? Do you think, she went on, that the life of a man who could look in that way, who could contemplate that entity, and live with it by means of the proper faculty, would be meaningless? Don't you realize, she asked, that only there, seeing in the way that the Beautiful can be seen, can one stop giving birth to images of virtue, since one no longer holds on to images, but to truth, because one now grasps the truth? He is able to bring forth true virtue, and to nourish it, and hence to be a favorite of the gods, so that if any man can be immortal, it will be he.

So, Phaedrus, and the rest of you, that is what Diotima told me, and I am persuaded. And because I do believe in it I would like to try and persuade others that for a nature like the human one, we cannot easily find a better helper toward the possession of such a life, than Love. That is why I assert that every man ought to honor Love, as I myself do honor him, devoting myself assiduously to matters of love and urging others to do the same. Now and always, I praise the power and courage of Love as much is I can. So, Phaedrus, consider this story, if you will, as my encomium, spoken in praise of Love. If you will not, please call it whatever you are disposed to call it.

When Socrates had finished speaking they applauded, and Aristophanes started to say something about how Socrates, in his speech, had made reference to his own. Then, suddenly, there was a terrific din—a banging on the door that led to the courtyard—like drunkards—and they heard the music of a flute-girl. At this point Agathon called out: Attendants, won't you go and see who it is? If it's one of our friends, invite him in, and if it isn't say we're not drinking, we're all finished.

In no time at all they heard the voice of Alcibiades out in the hall—shouting out loud—extremely drunk—

asking where was Agathon—ordering them to take him to Agathon! So between them they brought him in, with the flute-girl lending support from underneath, with several others of his followers as well, and he stood there at the door, garlanded with ivy and violets in a thick wreath and fillets all about his head in great profusion. And he said:

Gracious Gentlemen: Will you accept this fellow as a drinking partner? I am totally and utterly drunk! Or shall I simply crown Agathon with a wreath—as I came to do—and go away? I couldn't get here yesterday, you see, he continued, so I've come now with these fillets around my head—I want to take them off my own—this brilliant, most beautiful fellow—if I may say it—I want to tie them on his head—you're laughing at me for being drunk like this? You may laugh all you like—all the same, I know perfectly well that I'm talking honestly. But tell me at once!—on the terms I stated—will you drink with me, or not?

Then they all cried out in acclaim, and demanded that he come in and get comfortable, and Agathon called him over. With his people leading him he went in, undid the fillets which had been tied around his head, so that they were over his eyes and he couldn't see Socrates, and sat down beside Agathon—between Socrates and his host (for Socrates had moved aside when he saw Alcibiades). So, he sat down there, embraced and wreathed Agathon. At this point Agathon said: Undo Alcibiades' shoes, young man, so that he can recline at the table, as our third.

Yes, yes, said Alcibiades. But who is the third with us at the table? And at that he turned around and saw Socrates, and seeing him, jumped up and exclaimed: Oh Lord! What have we here? Is it Socrates? Lying in wait for me again? So, you're lying here—like you always do—suddenly appearing wherever I least expect you! Why have you come here now? And why are you lying here, and not beside Aristophanes or someone else who is a clown by choice? How do you contrive to be lying down beside the most beautiful man here?

And here Socrates interjected: Agathon—look! Will you help me? My love for this young man has become no trivial matter. From the very moment I fell in love with him it has ceased being possible for me either to look at or talk to a single good-looking person, but this fellow here becomes jealous of me and envious, and carries on fantastically, reviles me and just barely manages to keep his hands off me! Look—you see—I'm afraid he's going to carry on even now—please reconcile us—or protect me if he tries to be violent—I'm really completely terrified of this fellow's amorous rage!

No, said Alcibiades, there can be no reconciliation between you and me. But I'll take vengeance on you for these things later on. For now, Agathon, he went on, give me some of the fillets so that I can enwreathe this wonderful head here, and then he won't be able to accuse me of having made a garland for you, while he himself, the champion speaker of all—not only just the day before yesterday, like you, but always—I left uncrowned. And as he said this he took the fillets and made a garland for Socrates and then stretched out beside him. And when he had lain back, he spoke: Well, then, gentlemen—you look sober to me. This can't be allowed—you must drink! That's what you've agreed to, just now. So, I proclaim as Master of Revelry (until you've consumed enough) . . . myself! But look here, Agathon, have you got a great huge vessel? Oh, never mind, it's not necessary: Young man! Bring me that wine-cooler there!—he called out, seeing one that held more than a half-gallon. When he had seen to it that this was filled, he first drained it himself, then had it filled again for Socrates, and asserted at the same time: With Socrates, Gentlemen, my trick won't work. However much anyone asks him to drink, he drinks, and he's never the drunker for it. Then, when the boy had poured, Socrates drank.

And Eryximachus said: Is this the way we should behave, Alcibiades? Shouldn't we be saying anything over our cups, or singing? Should we simply gulp it down like sots?

And Alcibiades answered: Ah, Eryximachus, noblest son of a noble, sober sire!—Greetings!

And the same to you, responded Eryximachus. But how shall we do it?

Oh, lets do it the way you want. One must obey you,

> *For a single doctor's worth a parcel of others. . . .*

So command us however you like.

All right then, listen, said Eryximachus. Before you arrived it had been agreed among us that each in turn, going around to the right, would make as fine a speech as he could in praise of the god Love. And all the rest of us have spoken. But since you haven't spoken yet, and have been drinking, it's only just that you make a speech and when you've made your speech, to command Socrates to do whatever you want, and for him to do it to the one on his right, and so on for the others.

Ah, Eryximachus, answered Alcibiades, that sounds fine, but it isn't fair to compare a drunken man's oration with the speeches of sober men, and to expect them to be of equal quality. Besides, my dear, hasn't Socrates convinced you of the things he said just now? Don't you know that everything is the opposite of what he has said? This one—whenever I praise anyone in his presence—a god or another man or whatever, he won't restrain himself from manhandling me!

Why don't you be still? said Socrates.

Oh, by Poseidon! exclaimed Alcibiades, Don't deny that! I won't praise a single other person in your presence.

Well, do it that way, then, urged Eryximachus, if you want. Praise Socrates.

What are you saying? asked Alcibiades. Do you think I should, Eryximachus? Shall I rush at the fellow and chastise him in front of you all?

Look here! cried Socrates, What are you planning? Are you going to praise me with ridicule? What are you going to do?

I shall tell the truth. Will you permit me?

Well, certainly, he said. I'll permit you—I order you—tell the truth!

I can't do it too soon, responded Alcibiades. But please do this—if I say something that isn't true, catch me up right in the middle, if you wish, and say what it is that I'm falsifying. Because I won't falsify anything on purpose. But if I get something I'm remembering mixed up, don't be surprised—it's no easy matter for someone in my condition to give a lucid and orderly account of your strangeness!

## Alcibiades

To praise Socrates, gentlemen, I shall proceed as follows: through similes. He will assume that I'm ridiculing him. But the simile will be for the sake of the truth, not for ridicule. I assert he is most like the Sileni which sit in statuaries' shops—the ones which the craftsmen carve to hold shepherd's pipes or flutes, which, when they are opened into two, turn out to have images of the gods inside. And I shall compare him, too, with the satyr Marsyas.

And you, yourself, Socrates, won't deny that you are like these in looks. But you are like them in other respects besides this—listen: you are an outrageous mocker, are you not? do you deny it? If you don't agree, I can bring witnesses. And aren't you a flutist? A far more fabulous one than he. His lips had the power to bewitch men, in those days, with his instruments, but even now anyone who plays his music on the flute can do the same. I mean, Olympus played the music of Marsyas, his teacher; and whenever a good flutist, or even a paltry flute girl plays his songs, all by themselves, because the songs are divine they can inspire and reveal those who belong to the gods and have received their mysteries. And you are different from him only in that you do this same thing in speech, without instruments. Thus, when we hear anyone else expressing his arguments—even a first rate rhetorician—practically no one gives it a second thought. But when one hears you, or your discourses from someone else—no matter how inept as a speaker—whether it's a woman who hears it or a man or a schoolboy—we are all stupefied and inspired. At least I, my friends, if I wouldn't show myself to be hopelessly drunk, would take an oath on the degree to which I myself have been affected by this man's words, and still suffer now. When I hear him, I am worse than the corybantes—these words of his make my heart throb and tears come pouring out of my eyes; and I see a great many others going through the same things. I've heard Pericles and other good rhetoricians, and I've thought they spoke well; but I never felt this sort of thing, my soul didn't thunder in me, didn't rage at my slavish condition! But I have been affected in this way many times by this Marsyas here, so that it seemed to me that my own life was not worth living! And you can't deny the truth of this, Socrates. Even now, I know perfectly well that if I allowed myself to hear him again, I'd have the same feelings—I wouldn't be able to resist. He compels me to admit that while I am deficient in many respects I still neglect myself, and look to the affairs of Athens. So I force my ears shut as against the Sirens, and run away, in order not to grow old sitting there at his feet! But there is one thing I have felt in his presence, alone among men, a feeling which no one would have believed to be in me—shame before someone. Before him alone I feel ashamed. For I realize within myself that I am powerless to contradict him, and that I ought to do what he commands, but that I turn my back and submit to the honors of the masses. So I flee him, sneaking off like a slave, and when I see him again I am ashamed at the conclusions we came to. Many times I have wished he would cease to exist among men! But if that happened I am sure that I would grieve even more—so that I don't know what to do about the man!

So, these are the effects which the pipings of this Satyr have had on me and many others. But now you'll really see how much he and the creature I've compared him to are alike, and how astonishing his nature really is. You may be sure that not one of you knows him. However, I shall reveal him, since I have already begun. For instance, you see that Socrates is sexually attracted to beautiful men, and is always rapturously following them around? What is more that he is ignorant of everything and knows nothing—that's the pose he affects—now isn't this like the Silenus? Certainly it is. He has donned this nature on the outside exactly like the carved Silenus. But when the inner man is disclosed, would you believe, fellow-drinkers, how much real sense there is in him? You should know that it doesn't matter at all to him whether one is good-looking or not. Why, you couldn't believe to what extent he looks down on that sort of thing; or whether one is wealthy, or has any other honor that may be considered "happiness" by the crowd. He considers all that sort of goods worth nothing, and we ourselves as nothing too—I tell you—and he pretends to be ignorant, and spends his whole life putting people on. I don't know if any one has seen the images in this man when he is in earnest and has exposed his inner self. I actually saw them once, and as a result, he has seemed to me divine, all-golden, exquisite and miraculous. And so, in brief, I must do whatever Socrates may demand of me.

Believing that he was really serious about my beauty, I thought I had a godsend—a rare piece of luck. By gratifying Socrates I would be able to hear all the things he knew—for I really considered my looks a rare treasure. So, with this intention—up to then I was not accustomed to meet him without an attendant—I sent the attendant away and met him alone. I must tell the whole truth before you; but pay close attention, Socrates, and refute me if I distort a single fact! So I met him, my friends, and we were entirely alone; I believed that he would immediately begin to make love to me—and I was happy. But—nothing of the sort happened. He talked to me just the way he always did when we spent the day together, and then he left me and went away! After this I asked him to go to the gymnasium with me and I exercised with him, expecting to get what I wanted this way. So, he exercised with me, and wrestled with me quite often, when no one was around. And what is there to say? It got me nowhere!

Now, since I was accomplishing nothing with this sort of thing, I thought that I should attack the man head-on and not pull back, now that I had set myself to this seriously. I wanted to know, once and for all, what was going on. I invited him to have dinner with me, you know, the way a lover does with plans for his darling. And this too he was reluctant to accept; however, in time I persuaded him. But the first time he came he wanted to leave as soon as he had eaten, and I felt too embarrassed not to let him go. But I made a plan for the next time. After we had eaten, I talked far into the night, and when he wanted to go, I pretended that it was too late, and forced him to stay. So he came to rest on the couch next to me, right where he had eaten, and no one else was sleeping in the room there with us.

Now, I could have told my story perfectly well before anyone up to this point. But from here on you wouldn't catch me telling it except that, while wine and children are truthful (as the saying goes: the wine works without the children!) and then, too, it would seem to me unjust to hide Socrates' magnificent disdain, when I was making a eulogy to him. And yet, I have the same feeling as the man who was bitten by the snake. They say he didn't want to tell anyone what that experience was like unless they had been bitten themselves, since only such a person could understand and forgive him if he ran wild and raved in his agony. And you see I have been bitten by a more painful thing, and in the most painful way that one can be bitten—in the heart, or soul, or whatever else you call it—being stricken and bitten by the words of his philosophy, which hold on more cruelly than the adder in the soul of a young and not ungifted person, whenever they have grasped it, and make him do and say whatever they will! I see here Phaedrus, Agathon, Eryximachus, Pausanias, Aristodemus, Aristophanes—there is no need to mention Socrates himself—and others of the same sort. All of you have had a share of the madness and ecstasy of philosophy. So listen: you must forgive me for the things that happened then, and for the things that are said now. But, the servants and any one else who is ignorant and common—put thick doors over your ears!

So, my friends, when the light was extinguished and the servants were outside, I thought that I ought not be cagey with him, but rather it seemed right to speak freely about this business. So, shaking him, I asked:

Socrates—are you asleep?

Not at all, he answered.

Do you know what I think about all this?

Why, what?

I think, I announced, that you are my only worthy lover, and yet you seem to hesitate even mentioning love to me. And I feel this way: I would consider myself an utter fool not to give you pleasure in this way—as well as in any other way, if you had any need of my property or friends. I want you to know that there is nothing more important to me than becoming as virtuous as possible, and I think I can have no better helper for this than you. Actually, I'd feel far more shame before enlightened people if I didn't give my love to a man like you, than I would before the know-nothings, if I did!

When he had heard what I had to say, he answered in that extremely ironical way he always uses, very characteristically:

My dear Alcibiades, you may not, in fact, be so foolish after all, if what you are saying about me happens to be true and there is some power in me through which you can get to be a better man. You must perceive in me a sort of incredible beauty, but of a kind, I mean, very different from your own good looks. If you have observed this, and have decided to try and have some share of it, that is, make a trade—beauty for beauty—well! You're trying to get for yourself the real thing in beauty, in place of the sham. That's really the old "gold-for-bronze" exchange! But, my happy friend, look sharp, I may fool you, and turn out not to be what you take me for. The vision of the intellect begins to be acute when that of the eye is starting to weaken, and you're far from that, as yet!

When I heard this I said: There is absolutely no difference between the way I feel about things and what I've said. But you yourself must decide what would be best for both of us.

Ah, he said, well put; in the days to come we'll work out these and other matters, and do what seems to us the best thing.

So then, when I heard him say this, and thinking that I'd shot my own words into him like darts and had got to him with what I'd said, I stood, and without letting him say another word wrapped my own gown around him—it was winter, you know. I lay down under his worn cloak, put my arms around him—around this daemonic and truly marvellous man—and stayed by him for the whole night. (And Socrates, you can't say that I'm making up any of this story!) But despite my having done all this, he proved so superior and showed such contempt and laughed me so to scorn for my youth, that he insulted the one thing I really thought was worth anything, Gentlemen of the Jury—for you must be the judges of Socrates' arrogance—realize, then, that when I got up—I swear by every god and goddess—after having slept with Socrates, it had been in no way different from having slept with a father or elder brother!

Now what sort of mood do you imagine I was in after this affair? First of all I considered myself rejected, but then I got to wondering at his nature—his intelligence and manliness. I had come on a man of such wisdom and strength that I would not have believed I could have found him! Whereas I was unable to deprive myself of his company, I was also thoroughly unsuccessful at seducing him. I came to realize that he was far more invulnerable in every way to bribery than Ajax had been to the sword, and in the only area where I had believed he could be overcome, he eluded me! I was really at a loss! I wandered around, enslaved by this man as no one ever was by anyone!

All of this happened to me, you realize, and then, later, there was that campaign that we were both on to Potidaea. There we were mess-mates. Now first of all, not only did he surpass me in his ability to tolerate hardship, but everyone else too! Whenever we were forced to go without food because we were cut off (which often happens on a campaign), everybody else completely lacked endurance. Then, again, when there was plenty, he was the only man who was fully capable of appreciating it. And furthermore, although he didn't want to drink, whenever he was forced into it he beat everybody, and what is most remarkable of all, no man has ever seen Socrates drunk! My guess is that the proof of this is going to be apparent pretty soon.

And then there were his powers of endurance in winter—and the winters there are terrible. He performed other miracles: once, when there was an amazingly hard frost, and there was either no going out at all, or else if you did have to out, you got all dressed to do so by putting on overshoes and then wrapping up the feet in felts and sheepskins. Well, this man went out into that weather with a cloak on, exactly like what he usually wore, and went about on the ice in bare feet, more easily than the other men with their overshoes! The soldiers suspected him of looking down on them.

So that's that. But this thing, too, the great man dared and did while we were on that expedition, and it is well worth hearing. He thought of something, and right there on the spot, from dawn on, he stood fixed, contemplating whatever it was. For as long as the solution didn't come to him, he didn't move; he stuck to his search. It got to be midday, and the men watched this going on and marvelled at him, and told one another about how Socrates had stood there thinking about something since early morning. At last, a group of Ionians, when it had got to be evening, ate, and because it was summer, carried their bedrolls outside, both to sleep where it was cool, and at the same time to keep an eye on him and see if he'd stand there all night too. And he did stand there, until it got to be dawn, and the sun came up. Then he went away, first turning and making a prayer to the sun.

And if you want, there was the fighting. It's quite proper to describe him in this respect, since it was in that battle for which the high commanders gave me the citation that he, of all my men, saved my life! He refused to desert me when I was wounded, and he saved me and my armor too. And Socrates, I did right then and there demand that the commanders dedicate the citation to you, so you shouldn't blame me for what happened, and you can't say I'm lying. But when the generals wanted to give the medal to me just because of my position, you yourself were even more eager than they for me to have it.

And what's more, my friends, it was worth anything to see Socrates when the army was making its retreat, fleeing from Delios. I happened to be present, on horseback, while he was bearing arms. The men were all scattered, and he was making his retreat along with Laches. So I happened along, and seeing him, I shouted at them right away to be brave, and promised I wouldn't leave the two of them. And here I saw Socrates behave even more beautifully than he had at Potidaea. I myself had less to fear, since I was on horseback. First of all, he was much better at keeping cool than Laches. Then I noticed that he marched along exactly the way he does here at home, as you've described it, Aristophanes, with *strutting and tossing of sidelong looks,* slowly looking around at everybody—friend or enemy—making it obvious to all from any distance, that if anybody tried to touch this man, he'd put up one hell of a wild fight! And that was how he and his comrade got away safely. When people act this way in battle no one bothers them; they chase after those who run away helter-skelter.

Now there are many other fabulous things that one might say in praise of Socrates. But while as much could probably be said for his other characteristics, one could probably say them about someone else, and it's his difference from other men, whether ancient or modern, which is his most amazing trait! For what Achilles was like, one could draw a comparison with Brasidas, or others, and then, again, for Pericles, there is Nestor, and Antenor, and others I could mention. And all other great men can be likened to someone; but this man's nature is so peculiar, both in himself and in the things he says, that one could search and never find his like, not among anyone living today, nor among the ancients, unless it is among the ones I say one has to compare him with—no man, certainly, but those Sileni and Satyrs.

Oh—I neglected that at the beginning—the fact that his words remind one very much of the Sileni that get opened up. When you listen to what Socrates says, at first it sounds ridiculous. His arguments are all clothed by words and phrases which are like the hide of an impudent Satyr, for he speaks of millstones and pack-asses, of smithies, shoemaker's shops and tanners, and through all these things seems to be repeating himself over and over, so that any ignorant fool would laugh at the things he says. But if one sees them opened up and penetrates into them, one finds to begin with that they are the only discourses that make any sense; and later that they have a great divinity, that they are filled with the images of virtue, in themselves, and when they are extended to their fullest meaning they encompass everything that it becomes a man to contemplate who is seeking to achieve the beautiful and the good.

That, my friends, is how I choose to praise Socrates. I have found fault with him too, and have mixed into my account to you the things he did to enrage me. I know perfectly well that it's not only to me that he's done these things. There was Charmides, Glaucon's son, and Euthydemus, the son of Diocles, and a whole lot of others, as well, whom this "lover" utterly deceived, getting them to woo him, so that he was more their darling than their lover! I'm addressing myself particularly to you, Agathon, so that you'll not be tricked by him. Since you're being forewarned, you can escape the things we went through, and not be a fool who, as the saying goes, has to learn from his own mistakes.

When Alcibiades had said all this there was some laughter at his candor, because he seemed to be still in love with Socrates. At this point Socrates spoke up.

You seem quite sober to me, Alcibiades. Otherwise you would never have tried to hide your reason for saying all these things with that elaborate roundabout of circumlocution, and then attach it to the conclusion of your speech like an afterthought. As if you weren't saying the whole thing for the sake of setting Agathon and me at odds! You imagine that I have to love you and nobody else, while Agathon has to be loved by no one but you! But you haven't fooled me. That Satyric and Silenus piece of yours was really transparent. Look, dear Agathon, don't let him get away with it. Be prepared, so that he won't split us up.

Then Agathon said, Well, Socrates, what you're saying is probably true. And I take his sitting between you and me to be aimed at separating us from one another. He's not going to succeed, though; if I want to be there beside you, I will.

Certainly, said Socrates, sit down here, beyond me.

My god! said Alcibiades. What I have to go through with this man! He thinks he has to do me one better every time! But at least, you amazing fellow, you should let Agathon sit between us.

But that's impossible! Socrates said. You've just made a speech in praise of me, and I've got to praise the one on my right. So, if Agathon sits beyond you—won't he have to praise me, again, before he gets praised instead by me? But please! my sweet madman, don't begrudge my praising this boy. I really do want to extol him, with all my heart!

Ah-hah! exclaimed Agathon. Alcibiades, there's not a chance that I'd stay where I am! By all means, I'd rather be a migrant, if I can get Socrates to praise me!

That's the way things go, Alcibiades said. It's always the same. When Socrates is around it's impossible for anyone else to have anything to do with the beauties. Notice how ingeniously he found the right argument to persuade this one here to sit beside him!

So Agathon got up and sat beside Socrates. Suddenly there were a lot of revelers at the doors, and finding them open (for someone was just leaving), they marched straight in and joined the people. The place was filled with utter confusion, there wasn't the slightest semblance of order anymore, and they were compelled to consume vast quantities of wine.

Here Aristodemus says that he believes Eryximachus and Phaedrus and some others left, and he himself fell asleep and slept for a long time, it having been the season of long nights, but toward morning, when the cocks were already crowing, he was awakened. When he'd awakened, he saw the others sleeping or gone away, while only Agathon, Aristophanes, and Socrates were left awake and drinking from a great vessel, passing it around from left to right. Socrates was talking to them. Aristodemus says that he can't remember the rest of what was being said (since he'd not been awake for the beginning and was sleepy), but in the main he says that Socrates was forcing them to agree that it was possible for the same man to know how to write comedy and tragedy, and that the skilled tragedian can write comedy as well. Well, they were being forced to agree to all this, but they weren't following it very actively, and were dozing off. Aristophanes dropped off first, and by the time it was fully daylight, Agathon had too. Socrates, when he had seen the two of them off to sleep, got up and went away, and Aristodemus followed, just as always.

When he reached the Lyceum he bathed, and spent the rest of the day just as any other, and when the day was spent that way, and it got to be evening, he went home to rest.

## CATULLUS (84–54 BCE)

In the first century BCE, there emerged in Rome a school of young poets who knew how to adapt Greek meters to Latin, and who startled their elders with their fresh new styles. Gaius Valerius Catullus died in 54 BCE at the age of thirty after a brilliant but short career. One hundred and sixteen of his poems have survived. They include fairly lengthy lyrics on mythological themes, epigrams, and—most famously—love poems. His poems have a stunning immediacy and an erotic explicitness that appear to grow out of the poet's actual relationships with lovers and friends. Catullus's work reflects both the tremendous influence Greek culture had on Rome from the second century BCE onward and the poet's powerful talent for innovation and concise personal expression in a distinctly Roman style and language.

A number of Catullus's poems chronicle a love affair with a woman he calls "Lesbia." In poems 5, 8, and 11, included here, we can see him move from infatuation to disillusionment to bitterness. Number 11 is written in Sapphic stanzas, as is poem 51, his famous adaptation of Sappho's ode 31, "I should say, on a level" (see p. 490). The last stanza departs from Sappho and creates a powerful rhetorical effect as the poet comments on himself. "*Odi et Amo*" ("I hate and I love"), Catullus's best known couplet, is a compressed statement of the interdependence of love and hate. Here, as in poem 51, explorations of personal subjectivity take precedence over the more detached stance of traditionally public Greco-Roman poetry. It is worth noting in regard to this little poem how sometimes an extremely simple statement can become the classic expression of an important feeling or idea and thus qualify as an important work of literature in spite of its seeming obviousness.

## 5: "Come Lesbia mine, let us but live and love"

*Translated by Clarence W. Mendell*

Come Lesbia mine, let us but live and love
And all the tattling tales of gossiping age
Count not a pennyworth. For *suns* may set
And rise again, but *we*, our brief life gone,
Must sleep one long and never ending night.
Give me a thousand kisses, then a hundred,
A second thousand and a hundred more,
A thousand then, another hundred. So,
When we have kissed so *many* thousand times
We'll lose all count, that no malicious soul
Shall know we kissed *so* many thousand times.

## 8: "My poor Catullus, play no more the fool"

*Translated by Clarence W. Mendell*

My poor Catullus, play no more the fool,
And what you see is gone reckon as lost.
The suns shone bright for you in those glad days
When you but followed where your sweetheart led,
That sweetheart loved by you as none shall be.
Those were the days of happy frolickings
That you loved and your sweetheart loved as well.
Now she will have no more. You too give over
Nor follow where she flees. No longer live
In misery but, with stern heart, endure.
Farewell, my love, Catullus now is firm.
But you will grieve when no one pleads with you.
Ah, wretched girl, what life will now be yours!
Who will pursue you? Who will think you fair?
Whom will you love? Who now will call you his?
Whom will you kiss? Whose lips in passion bite?
But, come—tut, tut, Catullus, you be firm.

## 11: "Aurelius and Furius, comrades sworn"

*Translated by Clarence W. Mendell*

Aurelius and Furius, comrades sworn
To follow where Catullus calls—beyond

The farthest Indies or that shadowy shore
Lashed by the eastern sea,

Or if his goal be the Hyrcanians,
The soft Arabians, or the Parthian hordes,
Or those who live where seven-mouthed Nile dyes
The Inland Ocean's blue,

Or should he march across the mighty Alps
To view the monuments of Caesar's pride,
The Gallic Rhine, the northern ocean dread
And Britain's farthest tribes;

Prepared to meet all these and whatsoe'er
Heaven may decree beside—I ask you this:
Only to carry to my sweetheart's ear
Words few nor comforting.

Let her live on with her lewd following
Of lovers numberless whom now she holds
Fast in her toils, loving none faithfully,
Destroying all alike.

Nor let her hope to win my love again
Which by her faithlessness lies withering
Like some frail flower on the meadow's edge
Touched by the passing plow.

## 51: "That man is seen by me as a God's equal"

*Translated by Guy Lee*

That man is seen by me as a God's equal
Or (if it may be said) the Gods' superior,
Who sitting opposite again and again
Watches and hears *you*

Sweetly laughing—which dispossesses poor me
Of all my senses, for no sooner, Lesbia,
Do I look at you than there's no power left me
(Of speech in my mouth,)

But my tongue's paralysed, invisible flame
Courses down through my limbs, with din of their own
My ears are ringing and twin darkness covers
The light of my eyes.

Leisure, Catullus, does not agree with you.
At leisure you're restless, too excitable.
Leisure in the past has ruined rulers and
Prosperous cities.

## *85: "I hate and love. Perhaps you're asking why I do that?"*

*Translated by Guy Lee*

I hate and love. Perhaps you're asking why I do that?
I don't know, but I feel it happening, and am racked.

## VIRGIL (70–19 BCE?)

Arguably the greatest work of Latin literature and one of the most profound classical literary influences on the European Middle Ages and Renaissance, Virgil's *Aeneid* (19 BCE) is a deeply nuanced apology for the goals and aspirations of the Roman Empire founded by Augustus Caesar. Virgil had previously published the *Eclogues* (c. 37 BCE), a set of ten allusive pastoral poems modeled on the Greek poet Theocritus (third century BCE), and the *Georgics* (c. 29 BCE), a resonant and stately poem on farming, in four books, that harks back to Hesiod's *Works and Days* (eighth century BCE).

Virgil looked to Homer as his model for recreating the lofty epic genre, and his *Aeneid* might be viewed as a grand allusion to Homer's epic. Virgil composes in the same meter (dactylic hexameter) and attempts the same huge narrative sweep. In twelve books Virgil tells the story of the founding of Rome out of the ashes of Troy's defeat at the hands of the Greeks. Following the disastrous fall of Troy, the Trojan hero Aeneas makes a westward journey to Italy, where he at first reluctantly, but then with an increasing sense of ineluctable purpose, defeats the native peoples and founds the city of Rome on the banks of the river Tiber. Like Homer's Odysseus, Aeneas is a wanderer, but a wanderer with a clear sense of social purpose. Like Homer's Achilles, Aeneas is a fierce warrior, but his martial exploits are always performed in the context of his social obligations.

The first books tell the story of Juno's anger at Aeneas and of his arrival at Carthage on his journey to Italy. While in Carthage he falls in love with the beautiful and accomplished Queen Dido. Eventually the gods require him to leave her to fulfill his destiny. She is distraught and takes her own life; Aeneas sees the flames of her funeral pyre as he departs for Italy to found Rome. Book 4 is one of the great love stories of the ancient world, and a classic portrayal of the conflict of passion and duty. Aeneas must bear the grief and responsibility of his personal betrayal, even if he is persuaded that fate requires him to leave Dido. The greatness of the *Aeneid* resides in large part in how powerfully Virgil conveys the personal anguish that often accompanies political necessity. Aeneas's reaction to the unforgiving shade of Dido, whom he meets in the underworld in Book 6, conveys this anguish unforgettably. The same theme is portrayed powerfully in the Indian Bhagavad-Gītā (pp. 225–248) and the *Rāmāyana* (pp. 186–219).

The poem ends with the death of Turnus (Book 12), the fiery, Achillean leader of the Italian forces against Aeneas. Aeneas is at first inclined to show him mercy, but when he sees the belt of his great friend Pallas—the belt that Turnus had removed from Pallas's slain body—he slays Turnus. The Romans must not indulge in misdirected compassion if they are to rule the world. Virgil, who had lived through years of civil war, makes a powerful case for the necessity of Roman rule in an uncertain and often barbarous world. At the same time, he manages to register the pain—of both the ruler and the ruled—that he knows must accompany the relentless imposition of political power, even if one believes in the humanitarian claims of such power.

Virgil's Latin beautifully conveys the haunting ambivalences of the poet, but for this very reason the poem does not translate well. Homer generally does translate well, mainly because the Greek poet has his eye firmly on the action as it unfolds. With Virgil, the action is often less important than the poet's nuanced presentation of it. We have chosen Robert Fitzgerald's blank-verse translation because of its sensitivity to the famous Virgilian pathos.

## FROM THE AENEID

*Translated by Robert Fitzgerald*

### *from Book 1: A Fateful Haven*

I sing of warfare and a man at war.
From the sea-coast of Troy in early days
He came to Italy by destiny,
To our Lavinian western shore,
A fugitive, this captain, buffeted
Cruelly on land as on the sea
By blows from powers of the air—behind them
Baleful Juno in her sleepless rage.
And cruel losses were his lot in war,
Till he could found a city and bring home
His gods to Latium, land of the Latin race,
The Alban lords, and the high walls of Rome.
Tell me the causes now, O Muse, how galled
In her divine pride, and how sore at heart
From her old wound, the queen of gods compelled him—
A man apart, devoted to his mission—
To undergo so many perilous days
And enter on so many trials. Can anger
Black as this prey on the minds of heaven?
Tyrian settlers in that ancient time

Held Carthage, on the far shore of the sea,
Set against Italy and Tiber's mouth,
A rich new town, warlike and trained for war.
And Juno, we are told, cared more for Carthage
Than for any walled city of the earth,
More than for Samos, even. There her armor
And chariot were kept, and, fate permitting,
Carthage would be the ruler of the world.
So she intended, and so nursed that power.
But she had heard long since
That generations born of Trojan blood
Would one day overthrow her Tyrian walls,
And from that blood a race would come in time
With ample kingdoms, arrogant in war,
For Libya's ruin: so the Parcae spun.
In fear of this, and holding in memory
The old war she had carried on at Troy
For Argos' sake (the origins of that anger,
That suffering, still rankled: deep within her,
Hidden away, the judgment Paris gave,
Snubbing her loveliness; the race she hated;
The honors given ravished Ganymede),
Saturnian Juno, burning for it all,
Buffeted on the waste of sea those Trojans
Left by the Greeks and pitiless Achilles,
Keeping them far from Latium. For years
They wandered as their destiny drove them on
From one sea to the next: so hard and huge
A task it was to found the Roman people.

## *from Book 2: How They Took the City*

The room fell silent, and all eyes were on him,
As Father Aeneas from his high couch began:

"Sorrow too deep to tell, your majesty,
You order me to feel and tell once more.
How the Danaans leveled in the dust
The splendor of our mourned-forever kingdom—
Heartbreaking things I saw with my own eyes
And was myself a part of. Who could tell them,
Even a Myrmidon or Dolopian
Or ruffian of Ulysses, without tears?
Now, too, the night is well along, with dewfall
Out of heaven, and setting stars weigh down
Our heads toward sleep. But if so great desire

Moves you to hear the tale of our disasters,
Briefly recalled, the final throes of Troy,
However I may shudder at the memory
And shrink again in grief, let me begin.

Knowing their strength broken in warfare, turned
Back by the fates, and years—so many years—
Already slipped away, the Danaan captains
By the divine handicraft of Pallas built
A horse of timber, tall as a hill,
And sheathed its ribs with planking of cut pine.
This they gave out to be an offering
For a safe return by sea, and the word went round
But on the sly they shut inside a company
Chosen from their picked soldiery by lot,
Crowding the vaulted caverns in the dark—
The horse's belly—with men fully armed

Offshore there's a long island, Tenedos,
Famous and rich while Priam's kingdom lasted,
A treacherous anchorage now, and nothing more.
They crossed to this and hid their ships behind it
On the bare shore beyond. We thought they'd gone,
Sailing home to Mycenae before the wind,
So Teucer's town is freed of her long anguish,
Gates thrown wide! And out we go in joy
To see the Dorian campsites, all deserted,
The beach they left behind. Here the Dolopians
Pitched their tents, here cruel Achilles lodged,
There lay the ships, and there, formed up in ranks,
They came inland to fight us. Of our men
One group stood marveling, gaping up to see
The dire gift of the cold unbedded goddess,
The sheer mass of the horse.
                    Thymoetes shouts
It should be hauled inside the walls and moored
High on the citadel—whether by treason
Or just because Troy's fate went that way now.
Capys opposed him; so did the wiser heads:
'Into the sea with it,' they said, 'or burn it,
Build up a bonfire under it,
This trick of the Greeks, a gift no one can trust,
Or cut it open search the hollow belly!'

Contrary notions pulled the crowd apart.
Next thing we knew, in front of everyone,

Laocoön with a great company
Came furiously running from the Height,
And still far off cried out: 'O my poor people,
Men of Troy, what madness has come over you?
Can you believe the enemy truly gone?
A gift from the Danaans, and no ruse?
Is that Ulysses' way, as you have known him?
Achaeans must be hiding in this timber,
Or it was built to butt against our walls,
Peer over them into our houses, pelt
The city from the sky. Some crookedness
Is in this thing. Have no faith in the horse!
Whatever it is, even when Greeks bring gifts
I fear them, gifts and all.'
He broke off then
And rifled his big spear with all his might
Against the horse's flank, the curve of belly.
It stuck there trembling, and the rounded hull
Reverberated groaning at the blow.
If the gods' will had not been sinister,
If our own minds had not been crazed,
He would have made us foul that Argive den
With bloody steel, and Troy would stand today—
O citadel of Priam, towering still!

* * *

Ashes of Ilium!
Flames that consumed my people! Here I swear
That in your downfall I did not avoid
One weapon, one exchange with the Danaans,
And if it had been fated, my own hand
Had earned my death. But we were torn away
From that place—Iphitus and Pelias too,
One slow with age, one wounded by Ulysses,
Called by a clamor at the hall of Priam.
Truly we found here a prodigious fight,
As though there were none elsewhere, not a death
In the whole city: Mars gone berserk, Danaans
In a rush to scale the roof; the gate besieged
By a tortoise shell of overlapping shields.
Ladders clung to the wall, and men strove upward
Before the very doorposts, on the rungs,
Left hand putting the shield up, and the right
Reaching for the cornice. The defenders
Wrenched out upperworks and rooftiles: these

For missiles, as they saw the end, preparing
To fight back even on the edge of death.
And gilded beams, ancestral ornaments,
They rolled down on the heads below. In hall
Others with swords drawn held the entrance way,
Packed there, waiting. Now we plucked up heart
To help the royal house, to give our men
A respite, and to add our strength to theirs,
Though all were beaten. And we had for entrance
A rear door, secret, giving on a passage
Between the palace halls; in other days
Andromachë, poor lady, often used it,
Going alone to see her husband's parents
Or taking Astyanax to his grandfather.
I climbed high on the roof, where hopeless men
Were picking up and throwing futile missiles.
Here was a tower like a promontory
Rising toward the stars above the roof:
All Troy, the Danaan ships, the Achaean camp,
Were visible from this. Now close beside it
With crowbars, where the flooring made loose joints,
We pried it from its bed and pushed it over.
Down with a rending crash in sudden ruin
Wide over the Danaan lines it fell;
But fresh troops moved up, and the rain of stones
With every kind of missile never ceased.

Just at the outer doors of the vestibule
Sprang Pyrrhus, all in bronze and glittering,
As a serpent, hidden swollen underground
By a cold winter, writhes into the light,
On vile grass fed, his old skin cast away,
Renewed and glossy, rolling slippery coils,
With lifted underbelly rearing sunward
And triple tongue a-flicker. Close beside him
Giant Periphas and Automedon,
His armor-bearer, once Achilles' driver,
Besieged the place with all the young of Scyros,
Hurling their torches at the palace roof.
Pyrrhus shouldering forward with an axe
Broke down the stony threshold, forced apart
Hinges and brazen door-jambs, and chopped through
One panel of the door, splitting the oak,
To make a window, a great breach. And there
Before their eyes the inner halls lay open,

The courts of Priam and the ancient kings,
With men-at-arms ranked in the vestibule.
From the interior came sounds of weeping,
Pitiful commotion, wails of women
High-pitched, rising in the formal chambers
To ring against the silent golden stars;
And, through the palace, mothers wild with fright
Ran to and fro or clung to doors and kissed them.
Pyrrhus with his father's brawn stormed on,
No bolts or bars or men availed to stop him:
Under his battering the double doors
Were torn out of their sockets and fell inward.
Sheer force cleared the way: the Greeks broke through
Into the vestibule, cut down the guards,
And made the wide hall seethe with men-at-arms—
A tumult greater than when dykes are burst
And a foaming river, swirling out in flood,
Whelms every parapet and races on
Through fields and over all the lowland plains,
Bearing off pens and cattle. I myself
Saw Neoptolemus furious with blood
In the entrance way, and saw the two Atridae;
Hecuba I saw, and her hundred daughters,
Priam before the altars, with his blood
Drenching the fires that he himself had blessed.
Those fifty bridal chambers, hope of a line
So flourishing; those doorways high and proud,
Adorned with takings of barbaric gold,
Were all brought low: fire had them, or the Greeks.

What was the fate of Priam, you may ask.
Seeing his city captive, seeing his own
Royal portals rent apart, his enemies
In the inner rooms, the old man uselessly
Put on his shoulders, shaking with old age,
Armor unused for years, belted a sword on,
And made for the massed enemy to die.
Under the open sky in a central court
Stood a big altar; near it, a laurel tree
Of great age, leaning over, in deep shade
Embowered the Penatës. At this altar
Hecuba and her daughters, like white doves
Blown down in a black storm, clung together,
Enfolding holy images in their arms.
Now, seeing Priam in a young man's gear,

She called out:
'My poor husband, what mad thought
Drove you to buckle on these weapons?
Where are you trying to go? The time is past
For help like this, for this kind of defending,
Even if my own Hector could be here.
Come to me now: the altar will protect us,
Or else you'll die with us.'
She drew him close,
Heavy with years, and made a place for him
To rest on the consecrated stone.
Now see
Politēs, one of Priam's sons, escaped
From Pyrrhus' butchery and on the run
Through enemies and spears, down colonnades,
Through empty courtyards, wounded. Close behind
Comes Pyrrhus burning for the death-stroke: has him,
Catches him now, and lunges with the spear.
The boy has reached his parents, and before them
Goes down, pouring out his life with blood.
Now Priam, in the very midst of death,
Would neither hold his peace nor spare his anger.

'For what you've done, for what you've dared,' he said,
'If there is care in heaven for atrocity,
May the gods render fitting thanks, reward you
As you deserve. You forced me to look on
At the destruction of my son: defiled
A father's eyes with death. That great Achilles
You claim to be the son of—and you lie—
Was not like you to Priam, his enemy;
To me who threw myself upon his mercy
He showed compunction, gave me back for burial
The bloodless corpse of Hector, and returned me
To my own realm.'
The old man threw his spear
With feeble impact; blocked by the ringing bronze,
It hung there harmless from the jutting boss.
Then Pyrrhus answered:
'You'll report the news
To Pelidēs, my father; don't forget
My sad behavior, the degeneracy
Of Neoptolemus. Now die.'
With this,
To the altar step itself he dragged him trembling,

Slipping in the pooled blood of his son,
And took him by the hair with his left hand.
The sword flashed in his right; up to the hilt
He thrust it in his body.
That was the end
Of Priam's age, the doom that took him off,
With Troy in flames before his eyes, his towers
Headlong fallen—he that in other days
Had ruled in pride so many lands and peoples,
The power of Asia.
On the distant shore
The vast trunk headless lies without a name.

For the first time that night, inhuman shuddering
Took me, head to foot. I stood unmanned,
And my dear father's image came to mind
As our king, just his age, mortally wounded,
Gasped his life away before my eyes.
Creusa came to mind, too, left alone;
The house plundered; danger to little Iulus.
I looked around to take stock of my men,
But all had left me, utterly played out,
Giving their beaten bodies to the fire
Or plunging from the roof.
It came to this,
That I stood there alone. And then I saw
Lurking beyond the doorsill of the Vesta,
In hiding, silent, in that place reserved,
The daughter of Tyndareus. Glare of fires
Lighted my steps this way and that, my eyes
Glancing over the whole scene, everywhere.
That woman, terrified of the Trojans' hate
For the city overthrown, terrified too
Of Danaan vengeance, her abandoned husband's
Anger after years—Helen, that Fury
Both to her own homeland and Troy, had gone
To earth, a hated thing, before the altars.
Now fires blazed up in my own spirit—
A passion to avenge my fallen town
And punish Helen's whorishness.
'Shall this one
Look untouched on Sparta and Mycenae
After her triumph, going like a queen,
And see her home and husband, kin and children,
With Trojan girls for escort, Phrygian slaves?

Must Priam perish by the sword for this?
Troy burn, for this? Dardania's littoral
Be soaked in blood, so many times, for this?
Not by my leave. I know
No glory comes of punishing a woman,
The feat can bring no honor. Still, I'll be
Approved for snuffing out a monstrous life,
For a just sentence carried out. My heart
Will teem with joy in this avenging fire,
And the ashes of my kin will be appeased.'

So ran my thoughts. I turned wildly upon her,
But at that moment, clear, before my eyes—
Never before so clear—in a pure light
Stepping before me, radiant through the night,
My loving mother came: immortal, tall,
And lovely as the lords of heaven know her.
Catching me by the hand, she held me back,
Then with her rose-red mouth reproved me:
'Son,
Why let such suffering goad you on to fury
Past control? Where is your thoughtfulness
For me, for us? Will you not first revisit
The place you left your father, worn and old,
Or find out if your wife, Creusa, lives,
And the young boy, Ascanius—all these
Cut off by Greek troops foraging everywhere?
Had I not cared for them, fire would by now
Have taken them, their blood glutted the sword.
You must not hold the woman of Laconia,
That hated face, the cause of this, nor Paris.
The harsh will of the gods it is, the gods,
That overthrows the splendor of this place
And brings Troy from her height into the dust.
Look over there: I'll tear away the cloud
That curtains you, and films your mortal sight,
The fog around you.—Have no fear of doing
Your mother's will, or balk at obeying her.—
Look: where you see high masonry thrown down,
Stone torn from stone, with billowing smoke and dust,
Neptune is shaking from their beds the walls
That his great trident pried up, undermining,
Toppling the whole city down. And look:
Juno in all her savagery holds
The Scaean Gates, and raging in steel armor
Calls her allied army from the ships.

Up on the citadel—turn, look—Pallas Tritonia
Couched in a stormcloud, lightening, with her Gorgon.
The Father himself empowers the Danaans,
Urges assaulting gods on the defenders.
Away, child; put an end to toiling so.
I shall be near, to see you safely home.'

She hid herself in the deep gloom of night,
And now the dire forms appeared to me
Of great immortals, enemies of Troy.
I knew the end then: Ilium was going down
In fire, the Troy of Neptune going down,
As in high mountains when the countrymen
Have notched an ancient ash, then make their axes
Ring with might and main, chopping away
To fell the tree—ever on the point of falling,
Shaken through all its foliage, and the treetop
Nodding; bit by bit the strokes prevail
Until it gives a final groan at last
And crashes down in ruin from the height.

Now I descended where the goddess guided,
Clear of the flames, and clear of enemies,
For both retired; so gained my father's door,
My ancient home. I looked for him at once,
My first wish being to help him to the mountains;
But with Troy gone he set his face against it,
Not to prolong his life, or suffer exile.

'The rest of you, all in your prime,' he said,
'Make your escape; you are still hale and strong.
If heaven's lords had wished me a longer span
They would have saved this home for me. I call it
More than enough that once before I saw
My city taken and wrecked, and went on living.
Here is my death bed, here. Take leave of me.
Depart now. I'll find death with my sword arm.
The enemy will oblige; they'll come for spoils.
Burial can be dispensed with. All these years
I've lingered in my impotence, at odds
With heaven, since the Father of gods and men
Breathed high winds of thunderbolt upon me
And touched me with his fire.'
He spoke on
In the same vein, inflexible. The rest of us,
Creusa and Ascanius and the servants,

Begged him in tears not to pull down with him
Our lives as well, adding his own dead weight
To the fates' pressure. But he would not budge,
He held to his resolve and to his chair.
I felt swept off again to fight, in misery
Longing for death. What choices now were open,
What chance had I?
'Did you suppose, my father,
That I could tear myself away and leave you?
Unthinkable; how could a father say it?
Now if it please the powers above that nothing
Stand of this great city; if your heart
Is set on adding your own death and ours
To that of Troy, the door's wide open for it:
Pyrrhus will be here, splashed with Priam's blood;
He kills the son before his father's eyes,
The father at the altars.
My dear mother,
Was it for this, through spears and fire, you brought me,
To see the enemy deep in my house,
To see my son, Ascanius, my father,
And near them both, Creusa,
Butchered in one another's blood? My gear,
Men, bring my gear. The last light calls the conquered.
Give me back to the Greeks. Let me take up
The combat once again. We shall not all
Die this day unavenged.'
I buckled on
Swordbelt and blade and slid my left forearm
Into the shield-strap, turning to go out,
But at the door Creusa hugged my knees,
Then held up little Iulus to his father.

'If you are going out to die, take us
To face the whole thing with you. If experience
Leads you to put some hope in weaponry
Such as you now take, guard your own house here.
When you have gone, to whom is Iulus left?
Your father? Wife?—one called that long ago.'

She went on, and her wailing filled the house,
But then a sudden portent came, a marvel:
Amid his parents' hands and their sad faces
A point on Iulus' head seemed to cast light,
A tongue of flame that touched but did not burn him,
Licking his fine hair, playing round his temples.
We, in panic, beat at the flaming hair

And put the sacred fire out with water;
Father Anchises lifted his eyes to heaven
And lifted up his hands, his voice, in joy:

'Omnipotent Jupiter, if prayers affect you,
Look down upon us, that is all I ask,
If by devotion to the gods, we earn it,
Grant us a new sign, and confirm this portent!'
The old man barely finished when it thundered
A loud crack on the left. Out of the sky
Through depths of night a star fell trailing flame
And glided on, turning the night to day.
We watched it pass above the roof and go
To hide its glare, its trace, in Ida's wood;
But still, behind, the luminous furrow shone
And wide zones fumed with sulphur.
Now indeed
My father, overcome, addressed the gods,
And rose in worship of the blessed star.

'Now, now, no more delay. I'll follow you.
Where you conduct me, there I'll be.
Gods of my fathers,
Preserve this house, preserve my grandson. Yours
This portent was. Troy's life is in your power.
I yield. I go as your companion, son.'
Then he was still. We heard the blazing town
Crackle more loudly, felt the scorching heat.

'Then come, dear father. Arms around my neck:
I'll take you on my shoulders, no great weight.
Whatever happens, both will face one danger,
Find one safety. Iulus will come with me,
My wife at a good interval behind.
Servants, give your attention to what I say.
At the gate inland there's a funeral mound
And an old shrine of Ceres the Bereft;
Near it an ancient cypress, kept alive
For many years by our fathers' piety.
By various routes we'll come to that one place.
Father, carry our hearthgods, our Penatës.
It would be wrong for me to handle them—
Just come from such hard fighting, bloody work—
Until I wash myself in running water.'

When I had said this, over my breadth of shoulder
And bent neck, I spread out a lion skin

For tawny cloak and stooped to take his weight.
Then little Iulus put his hand in mine
And came with shorter steps beside his father.
My wife fell in behind. Through shadowed places
On we went, and I, lately unmoved
By any spears thrown, any squads of Greeks,
Felt terror now at every eddy of wind,
Alarm at every sound, alert and worried
Alike for my companion and my burden.
I had got near the gate, and now I thought
We had made it all the way, when suddenly
A noise of running feet came near at hand,
And peering through the gloom ahead, my father
Cried out:
'Run, boy; here they come; I see
Flame light on shields, bronze shining.'
I took fright,
And some unfriendly power, I know not what,
Stole all my addled wits—for as I turned
Aside from the known way, entering a maze
Of pathless places on the run—
Alas,
Creusa, taken from us by grim fate, did she
Linger, or stray, or sink in weariness?
There is no telling. Never would she be
Restored to us. Never did I look back
Or think to look for her, lost as she was,
Until we reached the funeral mound and shrine
Of venerable Ceres. Here at last
All came together, but she was not there;
She alone failed her friends, her child, her husband.
Out of my mind, whom did I not accuse,
What man or god? What crueller loss had I
Beheld, that night the city fell? Ascanius,
My father, and the Teucrian Penatës,
I left in my friends' charge, and hid them well
In a hollow valley.
I turned back alone
Into the city, cinching my bright harness.
Nothing for it but to run the risks
Again, go back again, comb all of Troy,
And put my life in danger as before:
First by the town wall, then the gate, all gloom,
Through which I had come out—and so on backward,
Tracing my own footsteps through the night;
And everywhere my heart misgave me: even

Stillness had its terror. Then to our house,
Thinking she might, just might, have wandered there.
Danaans had got in and filled the place,
And at that instant fire they had set,
Consuming it, went roofward in a blast;
Flames leaped and seethed in heat to the night sky.
I pressed on, to see Priam's hall and tower.
In the bare colonnades of Juno's shrine
Two chosen guards, Phoenix and hard Ulysses,
Kept watch over the plunder. Piled up here
Were treasures of old Troy from every quarter,
Torn out of burning temples: altar tables,
Robes, and golden bowls. Drawn up around them,
Boys and frightened mothers stood in line.
I even dared to call out in the night;
I filled the streets with calling; in my grief
Time after time I groaned and called Creusa,
Frantic, in endless quest from door to door.
Then to my vision her sad wraith appeared—
Creusa's ghost, larger than life, before me.
Chilled to the marrow, I could feel the hair
On my head rise, the voice clot in my throat;
But she spoke out to ease me of my fear:

'What's to be gained by giving way to grief
So madly, my sweet husband? Nothing here
Has come to pass except as heaven willed.
You may not take Creusa with you now;
It was not so ordained, nor does the lord
Of high Olympus give you leave. For you
Long exile waits, and long sea miles to plough.
You shall make landfall on Hesperia
Where Lydian Tiber flows, with gentle pace,
Between rich farmlands, and the years will bear
Glad peace, a kingdom, and a queen for you.
Dismiss these tears for your beloved Creusa.
I shall not see the proud homelands of Myrmidons
Or of Dolopians, or go to serve
Greek ladies, Dardan lady that I am
And daughter-in-law of Venus the divine.
No: the great mother of the gods detains me
Here on these shores. Farewell now; cherish still
Your son and mine.'
With this she left me weeping,
Wishing that I could say so many things,
And faded on the tenuous air. Three times

I tried to put my arms around her neck,
Three times enfolded nothing, as the wraith
Slipped through my fingers, bodiless as wind,
Or like a flitting dream.
So in the end
As night waned I rejoined my company.
And there to my astonishment I found
New refugees in a great crowd: men and women
Gathered for exile, young—pitiful people
Coming from every quarter, minds made up,
With their belongings, for whatever lands
I'd lead them to by sea.
The morning star
Now rose on Ida's ridges, bringing day.
Greeks had secured the city gates. No help
Or hope of help existed.
So I resigned myself, picked up my father,
And turned my face toward the mountain range.

## *from Book 4: The Passion of the Queen*

The queen, for her part, all that evening ached
With longing that her heart's blood fed, a wound
Or inward fire eating her away.
The manhood of the man, his pride of birth,
Came home to her time and again; his looks,
His words remained with her to haunt her mind,
And desire for him gave her no rest.
When Dawn
Swept earth with Phoebus' torch and burned away
Night-gloom and damp, this queen, far gone and ill,
Confided to the sister of her heart:
"My sister Anna, quandaries and dreams
Have come to frighten me—such dreams!
Think what a stranger
Yesterday found lodging in our house:
How princely, how courageous, what a soldier.
I can believe him in the line of gods,
And this is no delusion. Tell-tale fear
Betrays inferior souls. What scenes of war
Fought to the bitter end he pictured for us!
What buffetings awaited him at sea!
Had I not set my face against remarriage
After my first love died and failed me, left me
Barren and bereaved—and sick to death

At the mere thought of torch and bridal bed—
I could perhaps give way in this one case
To frailty. I shall say it: since that time
Sychaeus, my poor husband, met his fate,
And blood my brother shed stained our hearth gods,
This man alone has wrought upon me so
And moved my soul to yield. I recognize
The signs of the old flame, of old desire.
But O chaste life, before I break your laws,
I pray that Earth may open, gape for me
Down to its depth, or the omnipotent
With one stroke blast me to the shades, pale shades
Of Erebus and the deep world of night!
That man who took me to himself in youth
Has taken all my love; may that man keep it,
Hold it forever with him in the tomb."

At this she wept and wet her breast with tears.
But Anna answered:
"Dearer to your sister
Than daylight is, will you wear out your life,
Young as you are, in solitary mourning,
Never to know sweet children, or the crown
Of joy that Venus brings? Do you believe
This matters to the dust, to ghosts in tombs?
Granted no suitors up to now have moved you,
Neither in Libya nor before, in Tyre—
Iarbas you rejected, and the others,
Chieftains bred by the land of Africa
Their triumphs have enriched—will you contend
Even against a welcome love? Have you
Considered in whose lands you settled here?
On one frontier the Gaetulans, their cities,
People invincible in war—with wild
Numidian horsemen, and the offshore banks,
The Syrtës; on the other, desert sands,
Bone-dry, where fierce Barcaean nomads range.
Or need I speak of future wars brought on
From Tyre, and the menace of your brother?
Surely by dispensation of the gods
And backed by Juno's will, the ships from Ilium
Held their course this way on the wind.
Sister,
What a great city you'll see rising here,
And what a kingdom, from this royal match!
With Trojan soldiers as companions in arms

By what exploits will Punic glory grow!
Only ask the indulgence of the gods,
Win them with offerings, give your guests ease,
And contrive reasons for delay, while winter
Gales rage, drenched Orion storms at sea,
And their ships, damaged still, face iron skies."

This counsel fanned the flame, already kindled,
Giving her hesitant sister hope, and set her
Free of scruple. Visiting the shrines
They begged for grace at every altar first,
Then put choice rams and ewes to ritual death
For Ceres Giver of Laws, Father Lyaeus,
Phoebus, and for Juno most of all
Who has the bonds of marriage in her keeping.
Dido herself, splendidly beautiful,
Holding a shallow cup, tips out the wine
On a white shining heifer, between the horns,
Or gravely in the shadow of the gods
Approaches opulent altars. Through the day
She brings new gifts, and when the breasts are opened
Pores over organs, living still, for signs.
Alas, what darkened minds have soothsayers!
What good are shrines and vows to maddened lovers?
The inward fire eats the soft marrow away,
And the internal wound bleeds on in silence.

Unlucky Dido, burning, in her madness
Roamed through all the city, like a doe
Hit by an arrow shot from far away
By a shepherd hunting in the Cretan woods—
Hit by surprise, nor could the hunter see
His flying steel had fixed itself in her;
But though she runs for life through copse and glade
The fatal shaft clings to her side.
Now Dido
Took Aeneas with her among her buildings,
Showed her Sidonian wealth, her walls prepared,
And tried to speak, but in mid-speech grew still.
When the day waned she wanted to repeat
The banquet as before, to hear once more
In her wild need the throes of Ilium,
And once more hung on the narrator's words.
Afterward, when all the guests were gone,
And the dim moon in turn had quenched her light,
And setting stars weighed weariness to sleep,

Alone she mourned in the great empty hall
And pressed her body on the couch he left:
She heard him still, though absent—heard and saw him.
Or she would hold Ascanius in her lap,
Enthralled by him, the image of his father,
As though by this ruse to appease a love
Beyond all telling.
Towers, half-built, rose
No farther; men no longer trained in arms
Or toiled to make harbors and battlements
Impregnable. Projects were broken off,
Laid over, and the menacing huge walls
With cranes unmoving stood against the sky.

As soon as Jove's dear consort saw the lady
Prey to such illness, and her reputation
Standing no longer in the way of passion,
Saturn's daughter said to Venus:
wondrous.
Covered yourself with glory, have you not,
You and your boy, and won such prizes, too.
Divine power is something to remember
If by collusion of two gods one mortal
Woman is brought low.
I am not blind.
Your fear of our new walls has not escaped me,
Fear and mistrust of Carthage at her height.
But how far will it go? What do you hope for,
Being so contentious? Why do we not
Arrange eternal peace and formal marriage?
You have your heart's desire: Dido in love,
Dido consumed with passion to her core.
Why not, then, rule this people side by side
With equal authority? And let the queen
Wait on her Phrygian lord, let her consign
Into your hand her Tyrians as a dowry."

Now Venus knew this talk was all pretence,
All to divert the future power from Italy
To Libya; and she answered:
"Who would be
So mad, so foolish as to shun that prospect
Or prefer war with you? That is, provided
Fortune is on the side of your proposal.
The fates here are perplexing: would one city
Satisfy Jupiter's will for Tyrians

And Trojan exiles? Does he approve
A union and a mingling of these races?
You are his consort: you have every right
To sound him out. Go on, and I'll come, too."

But regal Juno pointedly replied:
"That task will rest with me. Just now, as to
The need of the moment and the way to meet it,
Listen, and I'll explain in a few words.
Aeneas and Dido in her misery
Plan hunting in the forest, when the Titan
Sun comes up with rays to light the world.
While beaters in excitement ring the glens
My gift will be a black raincloud, and hail,
A downpour, and I'll shake heaven with thunder.
The company will scatter, lost in gloom,
As Dido and the Trojan captain come
To one same cavern. I shall be on hand,
And if I can be certain you are willing,
There I shall marry them and call her his.
A wedding, this will be."
Then Cytherëa,
Not disinclined, nodded to Juno's plea,
And smiled at the stratagem now given away.

Dawn came up meanwhile from the Ocean stream,
And in the early sunshine from the gates
Picked huntsmen issued: wide-meshed nets and snares,
Broad spearheads for big game, Massylian horsemen
Trooping with hounds in packs keen on the scent.
But Dido lingered in her hall, as Punic
Nobles waited, and her mettlesome hunter
Stood nearby, cavorting in gold and scarlet,
Champing his foam-flecked bridle. At long last
The queen appeared with courtiers in a crowd,
A short Sidonian cloak edged in embroidery
Caught about her, at her back a quiver
Sheathed in gold, her hair tied up in gold,
And a brooch of gold pinning her scarlet dress.
Phrygians came in her company as well,
And Iulus, joyous at the scene. Resplendent
Above the rest, Aeneas walked to meet her,
To join his retinue with hers. He seemed—
Think of the lord Apollo in the spring
When he leaves wintering in Lycia
By Xanthus torrent, for his mother's isle

Of Delos, to renew the festival;
Around his altars Cretans, Dryopës,
And painted Agathyrsans raise a shout,
But the god walks the Cynthian ridge alone
And smooths his hair, binds it in fronded laurel,
Braids it in gold; and shafts ring on his shoulders.
So elated and swift, Aeneas walked
With sunlit grace upon him.
Soon the hunters,
Riding in company to high pathless hills,
Saw mountain goats shoot down from a rocky peak
And scamper on the ridges; toward the plain
Deer left the slopes, herding in clouds of dust
In flight across the open lands. Alone,
The boy Ascanius, delightedly riding
His eager horse amid the lowland vales,
Outran both goats and deer. Could he only meet
Amid the harmless game some foaming boar,
Or a tawny lion down from the mountainside!

Meanwhile in heaven began a rolling thunder,
And soon the storm broke, pouring rain and hail.
Then Tyrians and Trojans in alarm—
With Venus' Dardan grandson—ran for cover
Here and there in the wilderness, as freshets
Coursed from the high hills.
Now to the self-same cave
Came Dido and the captain of the Trojans.
Primal Earth herself and Nuptial Juno
Opened the ritual, torches of lightning blazed,
High Heaven became witness to the marriage,
And nymphs cried out wild hymns from a mountain top.
That day was the first cause of death, and first
Of sorrow. Dido had no further qualms
As to impressions given and set abroad;
She thought no longer of a secret love
But called it marriage. Thus, under that name,
She hid her fault.
Now in no time at all
Through all the African cities Rumor goes—
Nimble as quicksilver among evils. Rumor
Thrives on motion, stronger for the running,
Lowly at first through fear, then rearing high,
She treads the land and hides her head in cloud.
As people fable it, the Earth, her mother,
Furious against the gods, bore a late sister

To the giants Coeus and Enceladus,
Giving her speed on foot and on the wing:
Monstrous, deformed, titanic. Pinioned, with
An eye beneath for every body feather,
And, strange to say, as many tongues and buzzing
Mouths as eyes, as many pricked-up ears,
By night she flies between the earth and heaven
Shrieking through darkness, and she never turns
Her eye-lids down to sleep. By day she broods,
On the alert, on rooftops or on towers,
Bringing great cities fear, harping on lies
And slander evenhandedly with truth.
In those days Rumor took an evil joy
At filling countrysides with whispers, whispers,
Gossip of what was done, and never done:
How this Aeneas landed, Trojan born,
How Dido in her beauty graced his company,
Then how they reveled all the winter long
Unmindful of the realm, prisoners of lust.

These tales the scabrous goddess put about
On men's lips everywhere. Her twisting course
Took her to King Iarbas, whom she set
Ablaze with anger piled on top of anger.
Son of Jupiter Hammon by a nymph,
A ravished Garamantean, this prince
Had built the god a hundred giant shrines,
A hundred altars, each with holy fires
Alight by night and day, sentries on watch,
The ground enriched by victims' blood, the doors
Festooned with flowering wreaths. Before his altars
King Iarbas, crazed by the raw story,
Stood, they say, amid the Presences,
With supplicating hands, pouring out prayer:
"All powerful Jove, to whom the feasting Moors
At ease on colored couches tip their wine,
Do you see this? Are we then fools to fear you
Throwing down your bolts? Those dazzling fires
Of lightning, are they aimless in the clouds
And rumbling thunder meaningless? This woman
Who turned up in our country and laid down
A tiny city at a price, to whom
I gave a beach to plow—and on my terms—
After refusing to marry me has taken
Aeneas to be master in her realm.
And now Sir Paris with his men, half-men,

His chin and perfumed hair tied up
In a Maeonian bonnet, takes possession.
As for ourselves, here we are bringing gifts
Into these shrines—supposedly your shrines—
Hugging that empty fable."
Pleas like this
From the man clinging to his altars reached
The ears of the Almighty. Now he turned
His eyes upon the queen's town and the lovers
Careless of their good name; then spoke to Mercury,
Assigning him a mission:
"Son, bestir yourself,
Call up the Zephyrs, take to your wings and glide.
Approach the Dardan captain where he tarries
Rapt in Tyrian Carthage, losing sight
Of future towns the fates ordain. Correct him,
Carry my speech to him on the running winds:
No son like this did his enchanting mother
Promise to us, nor such did she deliver
Twice from peril at the hands of Greeks.
He was to be the ruler of Italy,
Potential empire, armorer of war;
To father men from Teucer's noble blood
And bring the whole world under law's dominion.
If glories to be won by deeds like these
Cannot arouse him, if he will not strive
For his own honor, does he begrudge his son,
Ascanius, the high strongholds of Rome?
What has he in mind? What hope, to make him stay
Amid a hostile race, and lose from view
Ausonian progeny, Lavinian lands?
The man should sail: that is the whole point.
Let this be what you tell him, as from me."

He finished and fell silent. Mercury
Made ready to obey the great command
Of his great father, and he first tied on
The golden sandals, winged, that high in air
Transport him over seas or over land
Abreast of gale winds; then he took the wand
With which he summons pale souls out of Orcus
And ushers others to the undergloom,
Lulls men to slumber or awakens them,
And opens dead men's eyes. This wand in hand,
He can drive winds before him, swimming down
Along the stormcloud. Now aloft, he saw

The craggy flanks and crown of patient Atlas,
Giant Atlas, balancing the sky
Upon his peak—his pine-forested head
In vapor cowled, beaten by wind and rain.
Snow lay upon his shoulders, rills cascaded
Down his ancient chin and beard a-bristle,
Caked with ice. Here Mercury of Cyllenë
Hovered first on even wings, then down
He plummeted to sea-level and flew on
Like a low-flying gull that skims the shallows
And rocky coasts where fish ply close inshore.
So, like a gull between the earth and sky,
The progeny of Cyllenë, on the wing
From his maternal grandsire, split the winds
To the sand bars of Libya.
Alighting tiptoe
On the first hutments, there he found Aeneas
Laying foundations for new towers and homes.
He noted well the swordhilt the man wore,
Adorned with yellow jasper; and the cloak
Aglow with Tyrian dye upon his shoulders—
Gifts of the wealthy queen, who had inwoven
Gold thread in the fabric. Mercury
Took him to task at once:
"Is it for you
To lay the stones for Carthage's high walls,
Tame husband that you are, and build their city?
Oblivious of your own world, your own kingdom!
From bright Olympus he that rules the gods
And turns the earth and heaven by his power—
He and no other sent me to you, told me
To bring this message on the running winds:
What have you in mind? What hope, wasting your days
In Libya? If future history's glories
Do not affect you, if you will not strive
For your own honor, think of Ascanius,
Think of the expectations of your heir,
Iulus, to whom the Italian realm, the land
Of Rome, are due."
And Mercury, as he spoke,
Departed from the visual field of mortals
To a great distance, ebbed in subtle air.
Amazed, and shocked to the bottom of his soul
By what his eyes had seen, Aeneas felt
His hackles rise, his voice choke in his throat.
As the sharp admonition and command

From heaven had shaken him awake, he now
Burned only to be gone, to leave that land
Of the sweet life behind. What can he do? How tell
The impassioned queen and hope to win her over?
What opening shall he choose? This way and that
He let his mind dart, testing alternatives,
Running through every one. And as he pondered
This seemed the better tactic: he called in
Mnestheus, Sergestus and stalwart Serestus,
Telling them:
"Get the fleet ready for sea,
But quietly, and collect the men on shore.
Lay in ship stores and gear."
As to the cause
For a change of plan, they were to keep it secret,
Seeing the excellent Dido had no notion,
No warning that such love could be cut short;
He would himself look for the right occasion,
The easiest time to speak, the way to do it.
The Trojans to a man gladly obeyed.

The queen, for her part, felt some plot afoot
Quite soon—for who deceives a woman in love?
She caught wind of a change, being in fear
Of what had seemed her safety. Evil Rumor,
Shameless as before, brought word to her
In her distracted state of ships being rigged
In trim for sailing. Furious, at her wits' end,
She traversed the whole city, all aflame
With rage, like a Bacchantë driven wild
By emblems shaken, when the mountain revels
Of the odd year possess her, when the cry
Of Bacchus rises and Cithaeron calls
All through the shouting night. Thus it turned out
She was the first to speak and charge Aeneas:

"You even hoped to keep me in the dark
As to this outrage, did you, two-faced man,
And slip away in silence? Can our love
Not hold you, can the pledge we gave not hold you,
Can Dido not, now sure to die in pain?
Even in winter weather must you toil
With ships, and fret to launch against high winds
For the open sea? Oh, heartless!
Tell me now,
If you were not in search of alien lands

And new strange homes, if ancient Troy remained,
Would ships put out for Troy on these big seas?
Do you go to get away from me? I beg you,
By these tears, by your own right hand, since I
Have left my wretched self nothing but that—
Yes, by the marriage that we entered on,
If ever I did well and you were grateful
Or found some sweetness in a gift from me,
Have pity now on a declining house!
Put this plan by, I beg you, if a prayer
Is not yet out of place.
Because of you, Libyans and nomad kings
Detest me, my own Tyrians are hostile;
Because of you, I lost my integrity
And that admired name by which alone
I made my way once toward the stars.
                    To whom
Do you abandon me, a dying woman,
Guest that you are—the only name now left
From that of husband? Why do I live on?
Shall I, until my brother Pygmalion comes
To pull my walls down? Or the Gaetulan
Iarbas leads me captive? If at least
There were a child by you for me to care for,
A little one to play in my courtyard
And give me back Aeneas, in spite of all,
I should not feel so utterly defeated,
Utterly bereft."
                    She ended there.
The man by Jove's command held fast his eyes
And fought down the emotion in his heart.
At length he answered:
                    "As for myself, be sure
I never shall deny all you can say,
Your majesty, of what you meant to me.
Never will the memory of Elissa
Stale for me, while I can still remember
My own life, and the spirit rules my body.
As to the event, a few words. Do not think
I meant to be deceitful and slip away.
I never held the torches of a bridegroom,
Never entered upon the pact of marriage.
If Fate permitted me to spend my days
By my own lights, and make the best of things
According to my wishes, first of all
I should look after Troy and the loved relics

Left me of my people. Priam's great hall
Should stand again; I should have restored the tower
Of Pergamum for Trojans in defeat.
But now it is the rich Italian land
Apollo tells me I must make for: Italy,
Named by his oracles. There is my love;
There is my country. If, as a Phoenician,
You are so given to the charms of Carthage,
Libyan city that it is, then tell me,
Why begrudge the Teucrians new lands
For homesteads in Ausonia? Are we not
Entitled, too, to look for realms abroad?
Night never veils the earth in damp and darkness,
Fiery stars never ascend the east,
But in my dreams my father's troubled ghost
Admonishes and frightens me. Then, too,
Each night thoughts come of young Ascanius,
My dear boy wronged, defrauded of his kingdom,
Hesperian lands of destiny. And now
The gods' interpreter, sent by Jove himself—
I swear it by your head and mine—has brought
Commands down through the racing winds! I say
With my own eyes in full daylight I saw him
Entering the building! With my very ears
I drank his message in! So please, no more
Of these appeals that set us both afire.
I sail for Italy not of my own free will."

During all this she had been watching him
With face averted, looking him up and down
In silence, and she burst out raging now:

"No goddess was your mother. Dardanus
Was not the founder of your family.
Liar and cheat! Some rough Caucasian cliff
Begot you on flint. Hyrcanian tigresses
Tendered their teats to you. Why should I palter?
Why still hold back for more indignity?
Sigh, did he, while I wept? Or look at me?
Or yield a tear, or pity her who loved him?
What shall I say first, with so much to say?
The time is past when either supreme Juno
Or the Saturnian father viewed these things
With justice. Faith can never be secure.
I took the man in, thrown up on this coast
In dire need, and in my madness then

Contrived a place for him in my domain,
Rescued his lost fleet, saved his shipmates' lives.
Oh, I am swept away burning by furies!
Now the prophet Apollo, now his oracles,
Now the gods' interpreter, if you please,
Sent down by Jove himself, brings through the air
His formidable commands! What fit employment
For heaven's high powers! What anxieties
To plague serene immortals! I shall not
Detain you or dispute your story. Go,
Go after Italy on the sailing winds,
Look for your kingdom, cross the deepsea swell!
If divine justice counts for anything,
I hope and pray that on some grinding reef
Midway at sea you'll drink your punishment
And call and call on Dido's name!
From far away I shall come after you
With my black fires, and when cold death has parted
Body from soul I shall be everywhere
A shade to haunt you! You will pay for this,
Unconscionable! I shall hear! The news will reach me
Even among the lowest of the dead!"

At this abruptly she broke off and ran
In sickness from his sight and the light of day,
Leaving him at a loss, alarmed, and mute
With all he meant to say. The maids in waiting
Caught her as she swooned and carried her
To bed in her marble chamber.
Duty-bound,
Aeneas, though he struggled with desire
To calm and comfort her in all her pain,
To speak to her and turn her mind from grief,
And though he sighed his heart out, shaken still
With love of her, yet took the course heaven gave him
And went back to the fleet. Then with a will
The Teucrians fell to work and launched the ships
Along the whole shore: slick with tar each hull
Took to the water. Eager to get away,
The sailors brought oar-boughs out of the woods
With leaves still on, and oaken logs unhewn.
Now you could see them issuing from the town
To the water's edge in streams, as when, aware
Of winter, ants will pillage a mound of spelt
To store it in their granary; over fields

The black battalion moves, and through the grass
On a narrow trail they carry off the spoil;
Some put their shoulders to the enormous weight
Of a trundled grain, while some pull stragglers in
And castigate delay; their to-and-fro
Of labor makes the whole track come alive.
At that sight, what were your emotions, Dido?
Sighing how deeply, looking out and down
From your high tower on the seething shore
Where all the harbor filled before your eyes
With bustle and shouts! Unconscionable Love,
To what extremes will you not drive our hearts!
She now felt driven to weep again, again
To move him, if she could, by supplication,
Humbling her pride before her love—to leave
Nothing untried, not to die needlessly.

"Anna, you see the arc of waterfront
All in commotion: they come crowding in
From everywhere. Spread canvas calls for wind,
The happy crews have garlanded the sterns.
If I could brace myself for this great sorrow,
Sister, I can endure it, too. One favor,
Even so, you may perform for me.
Since that deserter chose you for his friend
And trusted you, even with private thoughts,
Since you alone know when he may be reached,
Go, intercede with our proud enemy.
Remind him that I took no oath at Aulis
With Danaans to destroy the Trojan race;
I sent no ship to Pergamum. Never did I
Profane his father Anchisës' dust and shade.
Why will he not allow my prayers to fall
On his unpitying ears? Where is he racing?
Let him bestow one last gift on his mistress:
This, to await fair winds and easier flight.
Now I no longer plead the bond he broke
Of our old marriage, nor do I ask that he
Should live without his dear love, Latium,
Or yield his kingdom. Time is all I beg,
Mere time, a respite and a breathing space
For madness to subside in, while my fortune
Teaches me how to take defeat and grieve.
Pity your sister. This is the end, this favor—
To be repaid with interest when I die."

She pleaded in such terms, and such, in tears,
Her sorrowing sister brought him, time and again.
But no tears moved him, no one's voice would he
Attend to tractably. The fates opposed it;
God's will blocked the man's once kindly ears.
And just as when the north winds from the Alps
This way and that contend among themselves
To tear away an oaktree hale with age,
The wind and tree cry, and the buffeted trunk
Showers high foliage to earth, but holds
On bedrock, for the roots go down as far
Into the underworld as cresting boughs
Go up in heaven's air: just so this captain,
Buffeted by a gale of pleas
This way and that way, dinned all the day long,
Felt their moving power in his great heart,
And yet his will stood fast, tears fell in vain.

On Dido in her desolation now
Terror grew at her fate. She prayed for death,
Being heartsick at the mere sight of heaven.
That she more surely would perform the act
And leave the daylight, now she saw before her
A thing one shudders to recall: on altars
Fuming with incense where she placed her gifts,
The holy water blackened, the spilt wine
Turned into blood and mire. Of this she spoke
To no one, not to her sister even. Then, too,
Within the palace was a marble shrine
Devoted to her onetime lord, a place
She held in wondrous honor, all festooned
With snowy fleeces and green festive boughs.
From this she now thought voices could be heard
And words could be made out, her husband's words,
Calling her, when midnight hushed the earth;
And lonely on the rooftops the night owl
Seemed to lament, in melancholy notes,
Prolonged to a doleful cry. And then, besides,
The riddling words of seers in ancient days,
Foreboding sayings, made her thrill with fear.
In nightmare, fevered, she was hunted down
By pitiless Aeneas, and she seemed
Deserted always, uncompanioned always,
On a long journey, looking for her Tyrians
In desolate landscapes—
as Pentheus gone mad

Sees the oncoming Eumenidës and sees
A double sun and double Thebes appear,
Or as when, hounded on the stage, Orestës
Runs from a mother armed with burning brands,
With serpents hellish black,
And in the doorway squat the Avenging Ones.

So broken in mind by suffering, Dido caught
Her fatal madness and resolved to die.
She pondered time and means, then visiting
Her mournful sister, covered up her plan
With a calm look, a clear and hopeful brow.

"Sister, be glad for me! I've found a way
To bring him back or free me of desire.
Near to the Ocean boundary, near sundown,
The Aethiops' farthest territory lies,
Where giant Atlas turns the sphere of heaven
Studded with burning stars. From there
A priestess of Massylian stock has come;
She had been pointed out to me: custodian
Of that shrine named for daughters of the west,
Hesperidës; and it is she who fed
The dragon, guarding well the holy boughs
With honey dripping slow and drowsy poppy.
Chanting her spells she undertakes to free
What hearts she wills, but to inflict on others
Duress of sad desires; to arrest
The flow of rivers, make the stars move backward,
Call up the spirits of deep Night. You'll see
Earth shift and rumble underfoot and ash trees
Walk down mountainsides. Dearest, I swear
Before the gods and by your own sweet self,
It is against my will that I resort
For weaponry to magic powers. In secret
Build up a pyre in the inner court
Under the open sky, and place upon it
The arms that faithless man left in my chamber,
All his clothing, and the marriage bed
On which I came to grief—solace for me
To annihilate all vestige of the man,
Vile as he is: my priestess shows me this."

While she was speaking, cheek and brow grew pale.
But Anna could not think her sister cloaked
A suicide in these unheard-of rites;

She failed to see how great her madness was
And feared no consequence more grave
Than at Sychaeus' death. So, as commanded,
She made the preparations. For her part,
The queen, seeing the pyre in her inmost court
Erected huge with pitch-pine and sawn ilex,
Hung all the place under the sky with wreaths
And crowned it with funereal cypress boughs.
On the pyre's top she put a sword he left
With clothing, and an effigy on a couch,
Her mind fixed now ahead on what would come.
Around the pyre stood altars, and the priestess,
Hair unbound, called in a voice of thunder
Upon three hundred gods, on Erebus,
On Chaos, and on triple Hecatë,
Three-faced Diana. Then she sprinkled drops
Purportedly from the fountain of Avernus.
Rare herbs were brought out, reaped at the new moon
By scythes of bronze, and juicy with a milk
Of dusky venom; then the rare love-charm
Or caul torn from the brow of a birthing foal
And snatched away before the mother found it.
Dido herself with consecrated grain
In her pure hands, as she went near the altars,
Freed one foot from sandal straps, let fall
Her dress ungirdled, and, now sworn to death,
Called on the gods and stars that knew her fate.
She prayed then to whatever power may care
In comprehending justice for the grief
Of lovers bound unequally by love.

The night had come, and weary in every land
Men's bodies took the boon of peaceful sleep.
The woods and the wild seas had quieted
At that hour when the stars are in mid-course
And every field is still; cattle and birds
With vivid wings that haunt the limpid lakes
Or nest in thickets in the country places
All were asleep under the silent night.
Not, though, the agonized Phoenician queen:
She never slackened into sleep and never
Allowed the tranquil night to rest
Upon her eyelids or within her heart.
Her pain redoubled; love came on again,
Devouring her, and on her bed she tossed
In a great surge of anger.

So awake,
She pressed these questions, musing to herself:

"Look now, what can I do? Turn once again
To the old suitors, only to be laughed at—
Begging a marriage with Numidians
Whom I disdained so often? Then what? Trail
The Ilian ships and follow like a slave
Commands of Trojans? Seeing them so agreeable,
In view of past assistance and relief,
So thoughtful their unshaken gratitude?
Suppose I wished it, who permits or takes
Aboard their proud ships one they so dislike?
Poor lost soul, do you not yet grasp or feel
The treachery of the line of Laömedon?
What then? Am I to go alone, companion
Of the exultant sailors in their flight?
Or shall I set out in their wake, with Tyrians,
With all my crew close at my side, and send
The men I barely tore away from Tyre
To sea again, making them hoist their sails
To more sea-winds? No: die as you deserve,
Give pain quietus with a steel blade.
Sister,
You are the one who gave way to my tears
In the beginning, burdened a mad queen
With sufferings, and thrust me on my enemy.
It was not given me to lead my life
Without new passion, innocently, the way
Wild creatures live, and not to touch these depths.
The vow I took to the ashes of Sychaeus
Was not kept."
So she broke out afresh
In bitter mourning. On his high stem deck
Aeneas, now quite certain of departure,
Everything ready, took the boon of sleep.
In dream the figure of the god returned
With looks reproachful as before: he seemed
Again to warn him, being like Mercury
In every way, in voice, in golden hair,
And in the bloom of youth.
"Son of the goddess,
Sleep away this crisis, can you still?
Do you not see the dangers growing round you,
Madman, from now on? Can you not hear
The offshore westwind blow? The woman hatches

Plots and drastic actions in her heart,
Resolved on death now, whipping herself on
To heights of anger. Will you not be gone
In flight, while flight is still within your power?
Soon you will see the offing boil with ships
And glare with torches; soon again
The waterfront will be alive with fires,
If Dawn comes while you linger in this country.
Ha! Come, break the spell! Woman's a thing
Forever fitful and forever changing."

At this he merged into the darkness. Then
As the abrupt phantom filled him with fear,
Aeneas broke from sleep and roused his crewmen:
"Up, turn out now! Oarsmen, take your thwarts!
Shake out sail! Look here, for the second time
A god from heaven's high air is goading me
To hasten our break away, to cut the cables.
Holy one, whatever god you are,
We go with you, we act on your command
Most happily! Be near, graciously help us,
Make the stars in heaven propitious ones!"

He pulled his sword aflash out of its sheath
And struck at the stern hawser. All the men
Were gripped by his excitement to be gone,
And hauled and hustled. Ships cast off their moorings,
And an array of hulls hid inshore water
As oarsmen churned up foam and swept to sea.

Soon early Dawn, quitting the saffron bed
Of old Tithonus, cast new light on earth,
And as air grew transparent, from her tower
The queen caught sight of ships on the seaward reach
With sails full and the wind astern. She knew
The waterfront now empty, bare of oarsmen.
Beating her lovely breast three times, four times,
And tearing her golden hair,
"O Jupiter,"
She said, "will this man go, will he have mocked
My kingdom, stranger that he was and is?
Will they not snatch up arms and follow him
From every quarter of the town? and dockhands
Tear our ships from moorings? On! Be quick
With torches! Give out arms! Unship the oars!

What am I saying? Where am I? What madness
Takes me out of myself? Dido, poor soul,
Your evil doing has come home to you.
Then was the right time, when you offered him
A royal scepter. See the good faith and honor
Of one they say bears with him everywhere
The hearthgods of his country! One who bore
His father, spent with age, upon his shoulders!
Could I not then have torn him limb from limb
And flung the pieces on the sea? His company,
Even Ascanius could I not have minced
And served up to his father at a feast?
The luck of battle might have been in doubt—
So let it have been! Whom had I to fear,
Being sure to die? I could have carried torches
Into his camp, filled passage ways with flame,
Annihilated father and son and followers
And given my own life on top of all!
O Sun, scanning with flame all works of earth,
And thou, O Juno, witness and go-between
Of my long miseries; and Hecatë,
Screeched for at night at crossroads in the cities;
And thou, avenging Furies, and all gods
On whom Elissa dying may call: take notice,
Overshadow this hell with your high power,
As I deserve, and hear my prayer!
If by necessity that impious wretch
Must find his haven and come safe to land,
If so Jove's destinies require, and this,
His end in view, must stand, yet all the same
When hard beset in war by a brave people,
Forced to go outside his boundaries
And torn from Iulus, let him beg assistance,
Let him see the unmerited deaths of those
Around and with him, and accepting peace
On unjust terms, let him not, even so,
Enjoy his kingdom or the life he longs for,
But fall in battle before his time and lie
Unburied on the sand! This I implore,
This is my last cry, as my last blood flows.
Then, O my Tyrians, besiege with hate
His progeny and all his race to come:
Make this your offering to my dust. No love,
No pact must be between our peoples; No,
But rise up from my bones, avenging spirit!

Harry with fire and sword the Dardan countrymen
Now, or hereafter, at whatever time
The strength will be afforded. Coast with coast
In conflict, I implore, and sea with sea,
And arms with arms: may they contend in war,
Themselves and all the children of their children!"

Now she took thought of one way or another,
At the first chance, to end her hated life,
And briefly spoke to Barcë, who had been
Sychaeus' nurse; her own an urn of ash
Long held in her ancient fatherland.
"Dear nurse,
Tell Sister Anna to come here, and have her
Quickly bedew herself with running water
Before she brings our victims for atonement.
Let her come that way. And you, too, put on
Pure wool around your brows. I have a mind
To carry out that rite to Stygian Jove
That I have readied here, and put an end
To my distress, committing to the flames
The pyre of that miserable Dardan."

At this with an old woman's eagerness
Barcë hurried away. And Dido's heart
Beat wildly at the enormous thing afoot.
She rolled her bloodshot eyes, her quivering cheeks
Were flecked with red as her sick pallor grew
Before her coming death. Into the court
She burst her way, then at her passion's height
She climbed the pyre and bared the Dardan sword—
A gift desired once, for no such need.
Her eyes now on the Trojan clothing there
And the familiar bed, she paused a little,
Weeping a little, mindful, then lay down
And spoke her last words:
"Remnants dear to me
While god and fate allowed it, take this breath
And give me respite from these agonies.
I lived my life out to the very end
And passed the stages Fortune had appointed.
Now my tall shade goes to the under world.
I built a famous town, saw my great walls,
Avenged my husband, made my hostile brother
Pay for his crime. Happy, alas, too happy,
If only the Dardanian keels had never

Beached on our coast." And here she kissed the bed.
"I die unavenged," she said, "but let me die.
This way, this way, a blessed relief to go
Into the undergloom. Let the cold Trojan,
Far at sea, drink in this conflagration
And take with him the omen of my death!"

Amid these words her household people saw her
Crumpled over the steel blade, and the blade
Aflush with red blood, drenched her hands. A scream
Pierced the high chambers. Now through the shocked city
Rumor went rioting, as wails and sobs
With women's outcry echoed in the palace
And heaven's high air gave back the beating din,
As though all Carthage or old Tyre fell
To storming enemies, and, out of hand,
Flames billowed on the roofs of men and gods
Her sister heard and trembling, faint with terror
Lacerating her face, beating her breast,
Ran through the crowd to call the dying queen:

"It came to this, then, sister? You deceived me?
The pyre meant this, altars and fires meant this?
What shall I mourn first, being abandoned? Did you
Scorn your sister's company in death?
You should have called me out to the same fate!
The same blade's edge and hurt, at the same hour,
Should have taken us off. With my own hands
Had I to build this pyre, and had I to call
Upon our country's gods, that in the end
With you placed on it there, O heartless one,
I should be absent? You have put to death
Yourself and me, the people and the fathers
Bred in Sidon, and your own new city.
Give me fresh water, let me bathe her wound
And catch upon my lips any last breath
Hovering over hers."
Now she had climbed
The topmost steps and took her dying sister
Into her arms to cherish, with a sob,
Using her dress to stanch the dark blood flow.
But Dido trying to lift her heavy eyes
Fainted again. Her chest-wound whistled air.
Three times she struggled up on one elbow
And each time fell back on the bed. Her gaze
Went wavering as she looked for heaven's light

And groaned at finding it. Almighty Juno,
Filled with pity for this long ordeal
And difficult passage, now sent Iris down
Out of Olympus to set free
The wrestling spirit from the body's hold.
For since she died, not at her fated span
Nor as she merited, but before her time
Enflamed and driven mad, Proserpina
Had not yet plucked from her the golden hair,
Delivering her to Orcus of the Styx.
So humid Iris through bright heaven flew
On saffron-yellow wings, and in her train
A thousand hues shimmered before the sun.
At Dido's head she came to rest.
"This token
Sacred to Dis I bear away as bidden
And free you from your body."
Saying this,
She cut a lock of hair. Along with it
Her body's warmth fell into dissolution,
And out into the winds her life withdrew.

## *from Book 6: The World Below*

Now voices crying loud were heard at once—
The souls of infants wailing. At the door
Of the sweet life they were to have no part in,
Torn from the breast, a black day took them off
And drowned them all in bitter death. Near these
Were souls falsely accused, condemned to die.
But not without a judge, or jurymen,
Had these souls got their places: Minos reigned
As the presiding judge, moving the urn,
And called a jury of the silent ones
To learn of lives and accusations. Next
Were those sad souls, benighted, who contrived
Their own destruction, and as they hated daylight,
Cast their lives away. How they would wish
In the upper air now to endure the pain
Of poverty and toil! But iron law
Stands in the way, since the drear hateful swamp
Has pinned them down here, and the Styx that winds
Nine times around exerts imprisoning power.
Not far away, spreading on every side,
The Fields of Mourning came in view, so called

Since here are those whom pitiless love consumed
With cruel wasting, hidden on paths apart
By myrtle woodland growing overhead.
In death itself, pain will not let them be.
He saw here Phaedra, Procris, Eriphylë
Sadly showing the wounds her hard son gave;
Evadnë and Pasiphaë, at whose side
Laodamia walked, and Caeneus,
A young man once, a woman now, and turned
Again by fate into the older form.
Among them, with her fatal wound still fresh,
Phoenician Dido wandered the deep wood.
The Trojan captain paused nearby and knew
Her dim form in the dark, as one who sees,
Early in the month, or thinks to have seen, the moon
Rising through cloud, all dim. He wept and spoke
Tenderly to her:
"Dido, so forlorn,
The story then that came to me was true,
That you were out of life, had met your end
By your own hand. Was I, was I the cause?
I swear by heaven's stars, by the high gods,
By any certainty below the earth,
I left your land against my will, my queen.
The gods' commands drove me to do their will,
As now they drive me through this world of shades,
These mouldy waste lands and these depths of night.
And I could not believe that I would hurt you
So terribly by going. Wait a little.
Do not leave my sight.
Am I someone to flee from? The last word
Destiny lets me say to you is this."

Aeneas with such pleas tried to placate
The burning soul, savagely glaring back,
And tears came to his eyes. But she had turned
With gaze fixed on the ground as he spoke on,
Her face no more affected than if she were
Immobile granite or Marpesian stone.
At length she flung away from him and fled,
His enemy still, into the shadowy grove
Where he whose bride she once had been, Sychaeus,
Joined in her sorrows and returned her love.
Aeneas still gazed after her in tears,
Shaken by her ill fate and pitying her.

## *from Book 12: The Fortunes of War (The Death of Turnus)*

Aeneas moved against his enemy
And shook his heavy pine-tree spear. He called
From his hot heart:
"Rearmed now, who so slow?
Why, even now, fall back? The contest here
Is not a race, but fighting to the death
With spear and sword. Take on all shapes there are,
Summon up all your nerve and skill, choose any
Footing, fly among the stars, or hide
In caverned earth—"
The other shook his head,
Saying:
"I do not fear your taunting fury,
Arrogant prince. It is the gods I fear
And Jove my enemy."
He said no more,
But looked around him. Then he saw a stone,
Enormous, ancient, set up there to prevent
Landowners' quarrels. Even a dozen picked men
Such as the earth produces in our day
Could barely lift and shoulder it. He swooped
And wrenched it free, in one hand, then rose up
To his heroic height, ran a few steps,
And tried to hurl the stone against his foe—
But as he bent and as he ran
And as he hefted and propelled the weight
He did not know himself. His knees gave way,
His blood ran cold and froze. The stone itself,
Tumbling through space, fell short and had no impact.

Just as in dreams when the night-swoon of sleep
Weighs on our eyes, it seems we try in vain
To keep on running, try with all our might,
But in the midst of effort faint and fail;
Our tongue is powerless, familiar strength
Will not hold up our body, not a sound
Or word will come: just so with Turnus now:
However bravely he made shift to fight
The immortal fiend blocked and frustrated him.
Flurrying images passed through his mind.
He gazed at the Rutulians, and beyond them,
Gazed at the city, hesitant, in dread.
He trembled now before the poised spear-shaft
And saw no way to escape; he had no force

With which to close, or reach his foe, no chariot
And no sign of the charioteer, his sister.
At a dead loss he stood. Aeneas made
His deadly spear flash in the sun and aimed it,
Narrowing his eyes for a lucky hit.
Then, distant still, he put his body's might
Into the cast. Never a stone that soared
From a wall-battering catapult went humming
Loud as this, nor with so great a crack
Burst ever a bolt of lightning. It flew on
Like a black whirlwind bringing devastation,
Pierced with a crash the rim of sevenfold shield,
Cleared the cuirass' edge, and passed clean through
The middle of Turnus' thigh. Force of the blow
Brought the huge man to earth, his knees buckling,
And a groan swept the Rutulians as they rose,
A groan heard echoing on all sides from all
The mountain range, and echoed by the forests.
The man brought down, brought low, lifted his eyes
And held his right hand out to make his plea:

"Clearly I earned this, and I ask no quarter.
Make the most of your good fortune here.
If you can feel a father's grief—and you, too,
Had such a father in Anchises—then
Let me bespeak your mercy for old age
In Daunus, and return me, or my body,
Stripped, if you will, of life, to my own kin.
You have defeated me. The Ausonians
Have seen me in defeat, spreading my hands.
Lavinia is your bride. But go no further
Out of hatred."
                    Fierce under arms, Aeneas
Looked to and fro, and towered, and stayed his hand
Upon the sword-hilt. Moment by moment now
What Turnus said began to bring him round
From indecision. Then to his glance appeared
The accurst swordbelt surmounting Turnus' shoulder,
Shining with its familiar studs—the strap
Young Pallas wore when Turnus wounded him
And left him dead upon the field; now Turnus
Bore that enemy token on his shoulder—
Enemy still. For when the sight came home to him,
Aeneas raged at the relic of his anguish
Worn by this man as trophy. Blazing up
And terrible in his anger, he called out:

"You in your plunder, torn from one of mine,
Shall I be robbed of you? This wound will come
From Pallas: Pallas makes this offering
And from your criminal blood exacts his due."

He sank his blade in fury in Turnus' chest.
Then all the body slackened in death's chill,
And with a groan for that indignity
His spirit fled into the gloom below.

## Horace (65–8 BCE)

Like Virgil, the poet Horace was on friendly terms with emperor Augustus. His literary patron, Maecenas, was a minister of the emperor. Horace is famous for writing basically two kinds of poetry: conversational poems (satires and epistles) written in dactylic hexameter; and odes, composed in a variety of meters derived from Greek poetry.

His satires (*sermones,* urbane and witty conversations) and epistles are written in a plain style that presents itself as really no different from prose: they are concerned with the problems of everyday living and often present self-revelatory, although restrained, portraits of the poet. His odes span a variety of subjects, from matters of love to matters of state. In these poems, Horace transposes the metrical forms of many Greek poets, such as Sappho, into Latin—new wine in old bottles. Horace is a master artist, and his odes often appear—as Nietzsche memorably observed—as a mosaic of words. In order to achieve his artful effects, Horace used word order in the odes that is often far from the naturalness of prose.

Although Horace enjoyed the favor of the emperor, much of his poetry sings the praises of retirement on his Sabine farm. There he experienced an exhilarating sense of freedom from the concerns of public life and could concentrate on living a simple existence, close to nature and devoted to the reading and writing of poetry. In this emphasis on the joys of private life, Horace resembles the Chinese poet Tao Qian (365–427 CE); see pp. 1003–1008.

We have selected four of Horace's odes. The first is a translation of the poem that contains, in its last line, the famous phrase *carpe diem* ("seize the day"). This translation attempts to simulate the meter of the original Latin. In the second poem, the translator turns Horace's Sapphic verse into English tetrameter. The third selection memorably conveys Horace's hope that his art will withstand the ravages of time and thus achieve a kind of immortality for the poet. The final selection is a poem in which Horace distinguishes his own poetic style from that of Pindar. The poem is a *recusatio,* a refusal to write in the grand Pindaric manner. The poet claims that he could not possibly write like Pindar, and yet he is imitating Pindar at the same time. Horace's description of Pindar's style is actually a defense of his own: if Pindar is the poet of nature, Horace is the poet of art.

As Pindar is the model of the greater, sublime ode in the Western literary tradition, so Horace is the main exemplar of the so-called "lesser," more intimate ode.

His poetry profoundly influenced the Western Renaissance and particularly the neoclassical period (the late seventeenth and eighteenth centuries).

## *from Odes*

### *I. 11: "Don't ask—banish the thought"*

*Translated by Steven Shankman*

Don't ask—banish the thought, we cannot know—what for you, what for me
God sends, Leuconoë, and don't resort, in your despair, to those
Astrological charts. Better to take whatever comes and see
Whether Jupiter adds winters to this, or if this be our last
Winter pounding the sea's wearying force on the opposing rocks.
Be wise: strain wine, and taste; and in this brief stretch of time's course we run,
Trim luxuriant hopes. Even as we speak, envious time is fleeing,
Has fled. Pluck today's flower, placing small faith in an imagined tomorrow.

### *I. 22: "Dear Fuscus"*

*Translated by Steven Shankman*

Dear Fuscus,
He who, blameless, knows
Himself and literary arts
Needs neither Moorish shafts and bows
Nor quivers crammed with poison darts,

Whether he roves through desert sands
Or through the unfriendly, icy caps
Of the Caucasus or eastern lands
That the far-famed Hydaspes laps.

As I was wandering, carefree,
Beyond the bounds of Sabine's wood,
I saw a wolf approach, then flee.
I went on prattling where I stood.

So fierce a monster you won't see
In bellicose Apulia where
The broad oaks thrive; or in dusty
Numidia, that lion's lair!

To frigid plains where not one tree
Is quickened by a summer breeze

Or to those regions banish me,
Where mists and dark sky by degrees

Grimly descend; or should I come
Beneath the Sun Car's falling fire
To unpeopled lands, I still shall strum
"Lalagê" on fair Sappho's lyre.

## *III. 30: "My memorial is done: it will outlast bronze"*

*Translated by Joseph P. Clancy*

My memorial is done: it will outlast bronze,
it is taller than the Pyramids' royal mounds,
and no rain and corrosion, no raging Northwind
can tear it down, nor the innumerable years
in succession, and the transitory ages.
I will not wholly die: the greater part of me
shall escape the goddess of death: I will grow on,
kept alive by posterity's praise. As long as
high priest and silent virgin climb the Capitol,
I will be known where the wild Aufidus thunders,
in the land where water is scarce, whose farmers
Daunus once ruled, a man who rose from poverty,
who led the way, adapting Aeolian song
to Italian verses. Accept the high honors
I have won by your kindness, and graciously crown
my hair, Melpomene, with Apollo's laurel.

## *IV. 2: "Whoever labors to be Pindar's equal"*

*Translated by Joseph P. Clancy*

Whoever labors to be Pindar's equal,
Iulus, mounts on wings that are fastened with wax,
Daedalus-fashion, and will give his name to glittering water.

As a river roars down a mountain, swollen
by showers of rain, spilling over its banks,
so Pindar rages and the deep of his voice pours ever onward,

worthy of the laurel sacred to Apollo,
whether he is tumbling freshly minted words
through frenzied hymns, carried along on meters free and unruly,

whether he is chanting of gods, and kings, offspring of gods, who struck the Centaurs down,

a death they deserved, struck down the fire-breathing
frightful Chimaera,

or is singing of those the palm of Elis
brings home as immortals, boxer or horseman,
and is giving them an honor finer than hundreds of statues,

or else is lamenting a young man, taken
from his weeping bride, exalting his manhood
and courage and golden virtues to the stars, envying dark Death.

Strong is the wind that lofts the swan of Dirce,
as often, Antonius, as he aims for
the cloudy heights. My methods are those of a bee on Matinus,

working hard to gather the sweet-tasting thyme
all about the many groves and the banks of
Tibur's streams, a painstaking minor poet, shaping my lyrics.

You are a bard in the grand manner: you will
celebrate Caesar, wearing the garland he
won, leading in triumph up the sacred hill savage Sygambri;

the Fates and the kind gods have given the world
nothing that is greater or better than he,
nor ever shall, not even if time returned to the golden age.

You will celebrate festivals and public
games for the answer to the city's prayers,
brave Augustus' return, and no lawsuits heard in the Forum.

Then, if something I sing deserves hearing, my
best voice will join in, and "O glorious
sun, worthy of praise," I will gladly chant for Caesar's homecoming.

As you lead the way, "Hail, God of Triumph,"
we shall sing more than once, "Hail, God of Triumph,"
all the citizens, and to the kind gods shall offer our incense.

Your promise is fulfilled with ten bulls and cows,
mine with a tender calf, no longer beside
his mother, growing big on rich grasses to satisfy my vow,

with a forehead that mirrors the crescent light
of a new moon on the third night it rises,
white as snow wherever he has a marking, otherwise tawny.

## Ovid (43 BCE–17 CE)

Ovid's verses were so well known in the Roman empire that first-century graffiti on the walls of Pompeii contain quotations from his work. Since his initial public poetry readings, given when he was probably about seventeen or eighteen years old, Ovid's work has been read and circulated continuously. He has had an immense impact on European culture (and not just on literature), kindling creative responses in such authors as Dante, Petrarch, Chaucer, Boccaccio, Christine de Pizan, Cervantes, Marlowe, Racine, Pope, Goethe, Byron, Keats, Shelley, Tennyson, T.S. Eliot, and Ezra Pound. Rembrandt, Michelangelo, Titian, and other visual artists found his descriptions inspiring. J.S. Bach, Purcell, Handel, Richard Strauss, and Benjamin Britten have set episodes from his narrative poems to music.

Educated in the rhetorical arts so crucial for young men seeking public careers in Augustan Rome, Ovid lived in the capital. His poetic career flourished until he was banished by Augustus in 8 CE because of his connection to a now-obscure scandal. His early poetry, including the *Heroides,* focuses on love. The *Heroides* ("heroines") is a collection of fifteen imaginary verse letters addressed by mythic or legendary women to their lovers. They are remarkably innovative. Ovid reimagines familiar mythological narratives from a woman's point of view and explores female subjectivity, each epistle focusing on the theme of a woman's loss of her lover. Dido's letter to Aeneas (*Heroides* VII) attempts to articulate Dido's grief and looks at the heroic masculine world from the point of view of a woman who has been used and abandoned. Both Heloise's letters to Abelard in the twelfth century (pp. 1233–1244) and Pope's rewriting of them in *Eloisa to Abelard* in the eighteenth (pp. 1867–1876) borrow heavily from the *Heroides,* as does Christine de Pizan (fifteenth century, pp. 1366–1388). Ho Nonshŏrhŏn's sixteenth-century Korean poem *A Woman's Sorrow* (pp. 1197–1199) treats the same theme.

The *Metamorphoses,* a compendium of mythological verse narratives written in the dactylic hexameter of Homer and Virgil, is Ovid's response to the epic. It includes some two hundred fifty stories from Greek and Roman myth and legend, as well as episodes from Roman history. A magnificent storyteller, Ovid presents a plethora of vivid, compelling details, narrated from ever-shifting points of view that create a fragmented and episodic structure. These features of his text, as well as the content of the episodes themselves, stress his main theme, transformation. The creation story that opens Ovid's text is included here, along with the tale of Echo and Narcissus. Ovid's version of creation provides an interesting contrast with the accounts in the Bible, the Indian Rig Veda, Hesiod's *Theogony,* the Japanese *Kojiki,* and the Mayan *Popul Vuh,* all included in this anthology.

## *from Metamorphoses*

*Translated by Allen Mandelbaum*

### *from Book 1*

#### Prologue

My soul would sing of metamorphoses.
But since, o gods, you were the source of these

bodies becoming other bodies, breathe
your breath into my book of changes: may
the song I sing be seamless as its way
weaves from the world's beginning to our day.

## The Creation

Before the sea and lands began to be,
before the sky had mantled every thing,
then all of nature's face was featureless—
what men call chaos: undigested mass
of crude, confused, and scumbled elements,
a heap of seeds that clashed, of things mismatched.
There was no Titan Sun to light the world,
no crescent Moon—no Phoebe—to renew
her slender horns; in the surrounding air,
earth's weight had yet to find its balanced state;
and Amphitrite's arms had not yet stretched
along the farthest margins of the land.
For though the sea and land and air were there,
the land could not be walked upon, the sea
could not be swum, the air was without splendor:
no thing maintained its shape; all were at war;
in one same body cold and hot would battle;
the damp contended with the dry, things hard
with soft, and weighty things with weightless parts.

A god—and nature, now become benign—
ended this strife. He separated sky
and earth, and earth and waves, and he defined
pure air and thicker air. Unraveling
these things from their blind heap, assigning each
its place—distinct—he linked them all in peace.
Fire, the weightless force of heaven's dome,
shot up; it occupied the highest zone.
Just under fire, the light air found its home.
The earth, more dense, attracted elements
more gross; its own mass made it sink below.
And flowing water filled the final space;
it held the solid world in its embrace.
When he—whichever god it was—arrayed
that swarm, aligned, designed, allotted, made
each part into a portion of a whole,
then he, that earth might be symmetrical,
first shaped its sides into a giant ball.
He then commanded seas to stretch beneath
high winds, to swell, to coil, to reach and ring

shorelines and inlets. And he added springs
and lakes and endless marshes and confined
descending streams in banks that slope and twine:
these rivers flow across their own terrains;
their waters sink into the ground or gain
the sea and are received by that wide plain
of freer waters—there, they beat no more
against their banks, but pound the shoals and shores.

At his command, the fields enlarged their reach,
the valleys sank, the woods were clothed with leaves,
and rocky mountains rose. And as the sky
divides into two zones on its right side,
with just as many to the left, to which
the hottest zone is added as a fifth,
the god provided regions that divide
the mass the heavens wrap, and he impressed
as many zones upon the earth. Of these,
the middle zone, because of its fierce heat,
is uninhabitable; and thick snows
cover two outer zones; between them he
aligned two other regions, and to these
he gave a clement climate, mixing heat
and cold. Above, the air extends; and for
as much as earth is heavier than water,
so is the air more ponderous than fire.
He ordered fog and clouds to gather there—
in air—and thunder, which would terrify
the human mind; there, too, the god assigned
the winds that, from colliding clouds, breed lightning.

Yet he who was the world's artificer
did not allow the winds to rule the air
unchecked, set free to riot everywhere.
(But while each wind received a separate tract,
it still is difficult to curb their blasts,
to keep the world, which they would rend, intact:
though they are brothers, they forever clash.)
Eurus retreated toward Aurora's lands,
into the Nabataeans' kingdom and
to Persia, where the rays of morning meet
the mountain crests. And Zephyrus now went
to shorelines warm with sunset, in the west.
To Scythia, beneath the northern Wain,
swept horrid Boreas. Incessant rain

and mists that drench the southlands opposite—
this was the work of Auster. The god placed
above these winds the ether, without weight,
a fluid free of earth's impurity.

No sooner had he set all things within
defining limits than the stars, long hid
beneath the crushing darkness, could begin
to gleam throughout the heavens. That no region
be left without its share of living things,
stars and the forms of gods then occupied
the porch of heaven; and the waters shared
their dwelling with the gleaming fishes; earth
received the beasts, and restless air, the birds.

An animal with higher intellect,
more noble, able—one to rule the rest:
such was the living thing the earth still lacked.
Then man was born. Either the Architect
of All, the author of the universe,
in order to beget a better world,
created man from seed divine—or else
Prometheus, son of Iapetus, made man
by mixing new-made earth with fresh rainwater
(for earth had only recently been set
apart from heaven, and the earth still kept
seeds of the sky—remains of their shared birth);
and when he fashioned man, his mold recalled
the masters of all things, the gods. And while
all other animals are bent, head down,
and fix their gaze upon the ground, to man
he gave a face that is held high; he had
man stand erect, his eyes upon the stars.
So was the earth, which until then had been
so rough and indistinct, transformed: it wore
a thing unknown before—the human form.

## The Four Ages

That first age was an age of gold: no law
and no compulsion then were needed; all
kept faith; the righteous way was freely willed.
There were no penalties that might instill
dark fears, no menaces inscribed upon
bronze tablets; trembling crowds did not implore

the clemency of judges; but, secure,
men lived without defenders. In those times,
upon its native mountain heights, the pine
still stood unfelled; no wood had yet been hauled
down to the limpid waves, that it might sail
to foreign countries; and the only coasts
that mortals knew in that age were their own.
The towns were not yet girded by steep moats;
there were no curving horns of brass, and no
brass trumpets—straight, unbent; there were no swords,
no helmets. No one needed warriors;
the nations lived at peace, in tranquil ease.
Earth of itself—and uncompelled—untouched
by hoes, not torn by ploughshares, offered all
that one might need: men did not have to seek:
they simply gathered mountain strawberries
and the arbutus' fruit and cornel cherries;
and thick upon their prickly stems, blackberries;
and acorns fallen from Jove's sacred tree.
There spring was never-ending. The soft breeze
of tender zephyrs wafted and caressed
the flowers that sprang unplanted, without seed.
The earth, untilled, brought forth abundant yields;
and though they never had lain fallow, fields
were yellow with the heavy stalks of wheat.
And streams of milk and streams of nectar flowed,
and golden honey dripped from the holm oak.

But after Saturn had been banished, sent
down to dark Tartarus, Jove's rule began;
the silver age is what the world knew then—
an age inferior to golden times,
but if compared to tawny bronze, more prized.
Jove curbed the span that spring had had before;
he made the year run through four seasons' course:
the winter, summer, varied fall, and short
springtime. The air was incandescent, parched
by blazing heat—or felt the freezing gusts,
congealing icicles: such heat and frost
as earth had never known before. Men sought—
for the first time—the shelter of a house;
until then, they had made their homes in caves,
dense thickets, and in branches they had heaped
and bound with bark. Now, too, they planted seeds
of wheat in lengthy furrows; and beneath
the heavy weight of yokes, the bullocks groaned.

The third age saw the race of bronze: more prone
to cruelty, more quick to use fierce arms,
but not yet sacrilegious.

What bestowed
its name upon the last age was hard iron.
And this, the worst of ages, suddenly
gave way to every foul impiety;
earth saw the flight of faith and modesty
and truth—and in their place came snares and fraud,
deceit and force and sacrilegious love
of gain. Men spread their sails before the winds,
whose ways the mariner had scarcely learned:
the wooden keels, which once had stood as trunks
upon the mountain slopes, now danced upon
the unfamiliar waves. And now the ground,
which once—just like the sunlight and the air—
had been a common good, one all could share,
was marked and measured by the keen surveyor—
he drew the long confines, the boundaries.
Not only did men ask of earth its wealth,
its harvest crops and foods that nourish us,
they also delved into the bowels of earth:
there they began to dig for what was hid
deep underground beside the shades of Styx:
the treasures that spur men to sacrilege.
And so foul iron and still fouler gold
were brought to light—and war, which fights for both
and, in its bloodstained hands, holds clanging arms.
Men live on plunder; guests cannot trust hosts;
the son-in-law can now betray his own
father-in-law; and even brothers show
scant love and faith. The husband plots the death
of his own wife, and she plots his. And dread
stepmothers ply their fatal poisons; sons
now tally—early on—how many years
their fathers still may live. Now piety
lies vanquished; and the maid Astraea, last
of the immortals, leaves the blood-soaked earth.

## The Giants

And in this age, not even heaven's heights
are safer than the earth. They say the Giants,
striving to gain the kingdom of the sky,
heaped mountain peak on mountain mass, star-high.

Then Jove, almighty Father, hurled his bolts
of lightning, smashed Olympus, and dashed down
Mount Pelion from Mount Ossa. Overwhelmed
by their own bulk, these awesome bodies sprawled;
and Earth soaked up the blood of her dread sons;
and with their blood still warm, she gave their gore
new life: so that the Giants' race might not
be lost without a trace, she gave their shape
to humans whom she fashioned from that blood.
But even this new race despised the gods;
and they were keen for slaughter, bent on force:
it's clear to see that they were born of blood.

## *from Book 3*

### Tiresias

On earth, things followed all of Fate's decrees,
and even twice-born Bacchus' infancy
was passing tranquilly. The story goes
that meanwhile, in his home on high, great Jove,
his spirits warmed by nectar, set aside
his heavy cares and jested pleasantly
with Juno—she was also idle then.
"The pleasure love allots to you," he said,
"is greater than the pleasure given men."
But she contested that. And they agreed
to let Tiresias decide, for he
knew love both as a woman and a man.

Tiresias had once struck with his staff
two huge snakes as they mated in the forest;
for that, he had been changed—a thing of wonder—
from man to woman. Seven autumns passed,
and still that change held fast. But at the eighth,
he came upon those serpents once again.
He said: "If he who strikes you can be changed
into his counter-state, then this time, too,
I'll strike at you." His stout staff dealt a blow;
and he regained the shape he had before,
the shape the Theban had when he was born.

And when he had been summoned to decide
this jesting controversy, he took sides
with Jove. The story goes that Juno grieved
far more than she had any right to do,

more than was seemly in a light dispute.
And she condemned to never-ending night
the judge whose verdict found her in the wrong.
But then almighty Jove (though no god can
undo what any other god has done),
to mitigate Tiresias' penalty,
his loss of sight, gave him the power to see
the future, pairing pain with prophecy.

*from Book 3*

## Narcissus and Echo

Tiresias was famous: far and near,
through all Boeotian towns, they asked the seer
for counsel; none could fault his prophecies.

The first to test him was Liriope,
a nymph the river-god Cephisus had
caught in his current's coils; within his waves
he snared the azure nymph—and had his way.
And when her time had come, that lovely nymph
gave birth to one so handsome that, just born,
he was already worthy of much love:
Narcissus was the name she gave her son.

And when she asked the augur if her boy
would live to see old age, Tiresias
replied: "Yes, if he never knows himself."
For many years his words seemed meaningless;
but then what happened in the end confirmed
their truth: the death Narcissus met when he
was stricken with a singular, strange frenzy.

For when he reached his sixteenth year, Narcissus—
who then seemed boy or man—was loved by many:
both youths and young girls wanted him; but he
had much cold pride within his tender body:
no youth, no girl could ever touch his heart.

One day, as he was driving frightened deer
into his nets, Narcissus met a nymph:
resounding Echo, one whose speech was strange;
for when she heard the words of others, she
could not keep silent, yet she could not be
the first to speak. Then she still had a body—
she was not just a voice. Though talkative,

she used her voice as she still uses it:
of many words her ears have caught, she just
repeats the final part of what she has heard.

It's Juno who had punished Echo so.
Time after time, when Juno might have caught
her Jove philandering on the mountaintops
with young nymphs, Echo, cunningly, would stop
the goddess on her path; she'd talk and talk,
to give her sister nymphs just time enough
to slip away before they were found out.
As soon as Juno had seen through that plot,
she menaced Echo: "From now on you'll not
have much use of the voice that tricked me so."
The threat was followed by the fact. And Echo
can mime no more than the concluding sounds
of any words she's heard.

When Echo saw
Narcissus roaming through the lonely fields,
she was inflamed with love, and—furtively—
she followed in his footsteps. As she drew
still closer, closer, so her longing grew
more keen, more hot—as sulfur, quick to burn,
smeared round a torch's top bursts into flame
when there are other fires close to it.
How often, as she tracked him, did she pray
that she might tempt him with caressing words
and tender pleas. But she cannot begin
to speak: her nature has forbidden this;
and so she waits for what her state permits:
to catch the sounds that she can then give back
with her own voice.

One day, by chance, the boy—
now separated from his faithful friends—
cried out: "Is anyone nearby?" "Nearby,"
was Echo's answering cry. And, stupefied,
he looks around and shouts: "Come! Come!"—and she
calls out, "Come! Come!" to him who'd called. Then he
turns round and, seeing no one, calls again:
"Why do you flee from me?" And the reply
repeats the final sounds of his outcry.
That answer snares him; he persists, calls out:
"Let's meet." And with the happiest reply
that ever was to leave her lips, she cries:

"Let's meet"; then, seconding her words, she rushed
out of the woods, that she might fling her arms
around the neck she longed to clasp. But he
retreats and, fleeing, shouts: "Do not touch me!
Don't cling to me! I'd sooner die than say
I'm yours!"; and Echo answered him: "I'm yours."
So, scorned and spurned, she hides within the woods;
there she, among the trees, conceals her face,
her shame; since then she lives in lonely caves.
But, though repulsed, her love persists; it grows
on grief. She cannot sleep; she wastes away.
The sap has fled her wrinkled, wretched flesh.

Her voice and bones are all that's left; and then
her voice alone: her bones, they say, were turned
to stone. So she is hidden in the woods
and never can be seen on mountain slopes,
though everywhere she can be heard; the power
of sound still lives in her.

And even as
Narcissus had repulsed that nymph, he scorned
the other nymphs of waves and mountains and,
before that, many men. Until, one day,
a youth whom he had spurned was led to pray,
lifting his hands to heaven, pleading: "May
Narcissus fall in love; but once a prey,
may he, too, be denied the prize he craves."

There was a pool whose waters, silverlike,
were gleaming, bright. Its borders had no slime.
No shepherds, no she-goats, no other herds
of cattle heading for the hills disturbed
that pool; its surface never had been stirred
by fallen branch, wild animal, or bird.
Fed by its waters, rich grass ringed its edge,
and hedges served to shield it from the sun.

It's here that, weary from the heat, the chase,
drawn by the beauty of the pool, the place,
face down, Narcissus lies. But while he tries
to quench one thirst, he feels another rise:
he drinks, but he is stricken by the sight
he sees—the image in the pool. He dreams
upon a love that's bodiless: now he
believes that what is but a shade must be

a body. And he gazes in dismay
at his own self; he cannot turn away
his eyes; he does not stir; he is as still
as any statue carved of Parian marble.
Stretched out along the ground, he stares again,
again at the twin stars that are his eyes;
at his fair hair, which can compare with Bacchus'
or with Apollo's; at his beardless cheeks
and at his ivory neck, his splendid mouth,
the pink blush on a face as white as snow;
in sum, he now is struck with wonder by
what's wonderful in him. Unwittingly,
he wants himself; he praises, but his praise
is for himself; he is the seeker and
the sought, the longed-for and the one who longs;
he is the arsonist—and is the scorched.

How many futile kisses did he waste
on the deceptive pool! How often had
he clasped the neck he saw but could not grasp
within the water, where his arms plunged deep!
He knows not what he sees, but what he sees
invites him. Even as the pool deceives
his eyes, it tempts them with delights. But why,
o foolish boy, do you persist? Why try
to grip an image? He does not exist—
the one you love and long for. If you turn
away, he'll fade; the face that you discern
is but a shadow, your reflected form.
That shape has nothing of its own: it comes
with you, with you it stays; it will retreat
when you have gone—if you can ever leave!

But nothing can detach him from that place:
no need for food, no need for rest. He's stretched
along the shaded grass; his eyes are set—
and never sated—on that lying shape.
It is through his own eyes that he will die.
He lifts himself a little, then he cries—
his arms reach toward the trees that ring that site:
"O woods, you are the ones to testify:
among your trees so many lovers hide
their grief. Do you remember anyone
in your long life—those many centuries—
whose love consumed him more than mine wastes me?
I do delight in him; I see him—yet,

although I see and do delight in him,
I cannot find him (love confounds me so!).
And there's another reason for my sorrow:
it's no great sea that sunders him from me,
no endless road, no mountain peak, no town's
high walls with gates shut tight: no, we are kept
apart by nothing but the thinnest stretch
of water. He is keen to be embraced;
my lips reach down: I touch the limpid wave,
and just as often he, with upturned face,
would offer me his mouth. You'd surely say
that we could touch each other, for the space
that separates our love is brief. Come now,
whoever you may be! Why cozen me,
you boy without a peer in all this world!
When I would seek you out, where do you go?
My age, my form don't merit scorn: indeed,
the nymphs were lavish in their love of me.
Your gaze is fond and promising; I stretch
my arms to you, and you reach back in turn. I smile
and you smile, too. And, often, I've seen tears
upon your face just when I've wept, and when
I signal to you, you reply; and I
can see the movement of your lovely lips—
returning words that cannot reach my ears.
Yes, yes, I'm he! I've seen through that deceit:
my image cannot trick me anymore.
I burn with love for my own self: it's I
who light the flames—the flames that scorch me then.
What shall I do? Should I be sought or seek?
But, then, why must I seek? All that I need,
I have: my riches mean my poverty.
If I could just be split from my own body!
The strangest longing in a lover: I
want that which I desire to stand apart
from my own self. My sorrow saps my force;
the time allotted me has been cut short;
I die in my youth's prime, but death is not
a weight; with death my pain will end, and yet
I'd have my love live past my death. Instead,
we two will die together in one breath."

Such were his words. Then he returns, obsessed,
to contemplate the image he had left:
his tears disturb the water; as he weeps,
they fall upon the surface. What he seeks

is darker, dimmer now—as if to flee.
"Where do you go?" he cries. "Do not retreat;
stay here—do not inflict such cruelty.
Let me still gaze at one I cannot touch;
let sight provide the food for my sad love."

As he laments, he tears his tunic's top;
with marble hands he beats his naked chest.
His flesh, once struck, is stained with subtle red;
as apples, white in one part, will display
another crimson part; or just as grapes,
in varied clusters, when they ripen, wear
a purple veil. But when the water clears
and he sees this, it is too much to bear.
Just as blond wax will melt near gentle fire,
or frost will melt beneath the sun, just so
was he undone by love: its hidden flame
consumes Narcissus: now he wastes away.
His color now has gone—that mix of white
and ruddiness; he's lost his sap and strength,
all that has been so beautiful to see:
there's nothing left of the entrancing flesh
that once had won the love of Echo. Yet,
faced with the sight of him, she feels deep pity;
each time he cries "Ah, me!" the nymph repeats
"Ah, me!"; and when he flails his arms and beats
his shoulders, she repeats that hammering.
His final words at the familiar pool,
when once again he gazed into the waves,
were these: "Dear boy, the one I loved in vain!"
And what he said resounded in that place.
And when he cried "Farewell!," "Farewell!" was just
what Echo mimed. He set his tired head
to rest on the green grass. And then dark death
shut fast the eyes that had been captured by
the beauty of their master. Even when
the world below became his home, he still
would stare at his own image in the pool
of Styx. His Naiad sisters, in lament,
as offering for their brother, cropped their hair.
The Dryads also wept. That choir of grief
was joined by Echo as she mimed their sounds.
They had prepared the pyre, the bier, the torches;
but nowhere could they find Narcissus' body:
where it had been, they found instead a flower,
its yellow center circled by white petals.

*from Book 15*

## Epilogue

And now my work is done: no wrath of Jove
nor fire nor sword nor time, which would erode
all things, has power to blot out this poem.
Now, when it wills, the fatal day (which has
only the body in its grasp) can end
my years, however long or short their span.
But, with the better part of me, I'll gain
a place that's higher than the stars: my name,
indelible, eternal, will remain.
And everywhere that Roman power has sway,
in all domains the Latins gain, my lines
will be on people's lips; and through all time—
if poets' prophecies are ever right—
my name and fame are sure: I shall have life.

# *from Heroides*

*Translated by Daryl Hine*

*VII*

## Dido to Aeneas

Here is Dido's swan song: when you've read
My last words, Aeneas, I'll be dead.
Thus when her time has come, abject upon
The riverbank laments the silver swan.
I do not have a hope that you'll be moved
By prayers the god of love has disapproved,
But, having lost my honor, all I had,
The waste of a few words seems not so bad.

You mean to leave me here—you cannot stay—
An offshore wind has blown good faith away,
And having cast off our relationship
For Italy—wherever—you take ship,
Indifferent to Carthage and her new
Ramparts to be ruled henceforth by you.
What's done you shun, and seek what's to be done,
And having sought throughout the world and won
One land, start looking for another one.
But when you've found it, who will give you, then,
Her land to be exploited by strange men?

Another love? Another Dido? Yet
Other engagements, which you will forget?
When will you found another Carthage and
Gaze down upon the throngs at your command?

But even if all this is granted, O
Where will you find a wife who loves you so?
For you I burn with a religious flame,
And day and night repeat Aeneas' name,
Despite ingratitude, indifference—
I'd do without you, had I any sense!
I do not hate Aeneas—I deplore
Your faithfulness but only love you more.
Pity me, Venus, I am your son's bride!
Befriend your brother, Love, so, mollified,
Aeneas will come over to your side,
And I who loved him first, as I aver,
May find in him my passion's cause and cure.

But I delude myself with fantasy,
You and your mother never could agree:
Wild animals, or rocks and stones and trees—
You were born of parents such as these,
Or else the sea which, wind-swept even now,
You make haste to sail on anyhow.
But why such haste? The wind is in the East:
The wintry weather's on my side at least!
It's you I'd sooner owe this respite to,
But wind and wave are less unjust than you.

Am I worth dying for, that you should flee
(Deserving death for your iniquity)
From me across the vast tracts of the sea?
What exorbitant aversion, this—
Once rid of me and death would seem like bliss!
The waves will soon be calmed, the winds subside,
And Triton on his sea-blue horses ride;
O, like the winds, relent! You know you could,
If you were not inflexible as wood.
You've felt the fury of the elements,
Yet trust them despite your sad experience.
The sea invites you to embark, but keeps
Many a grisly secret in its deeps.
Liars should not risk their lives at sea,
A place that penalizes perfidy,
Especially slighted love, for from sea spray

The mother of loves was born, or so they say.
Abandoned, I fear to hurt the one who so
Hurt me, and dread the shipwreck of my foe:
If I must hate you, better alive than dead—
You take the blame for my demise instead!

If overtaken by a hurricane—
God forbid!—what thoughts would fill your brain?
First your falsehoods, every single lie,
And me by your deceit condemned to die;
The ghastly specter of your wife should rise,
Betrayed, befouled with blood, before your eyes:
"Begone!" you'd cry, "though anything you do
Will be no more than I deserve, it's true."
Each thunderbolt you'd think is aimed at you.
For the moment let your rage give way
Like the sea's. The ransom you must pay
For your safe passage is this small delay—
If only for the sake of your small son.
Is not my life enough to have undone?
Has he or have your household gods deserved
To drown, whom once you from the flames preserved?
Or don't you take these sacred objects, or
Your father whom you boast that you once bore
On your shoulders, with you anymore?
Lies, all lies! for you did not commence
With me your meretricious influence.
What was your little darling's mother's fate?
To be abandoned by her heartless mate.
The story moved me. Lead me to the pyre:
My guilt is more unbearable than fire.

And now your gods have left you, it appears,
Adrift on sea and land for seven years.
I took you in when cast up on our shore
And offered you my crown, almost before
A proper introduction, what is more.
Would with such favors you had been content,
Then our relations might look innocent!
That fatal day when we, afraid to brave
A shower of rain, took refuge in a cave,
I heard voices—nymphs', I thought, but these
Were no nymphs, but the Eumenides
Setting their seal upon our destinies.
Outraged honor, do your worst! I go
To my dead husband full of shame and woe.

I keep his statue in a marble shrine
Which leafy boughs and fleecy wool entwine.
Four times I heard the voice that I thought dumb
Forever, whisper softly, "Dido, come!"
No, this devoted widow won't delay;
Only my guilty conscience makes me stay.
Forgive my lapse; my glib seducer could
Make my bad behavior almost good.
His mother, Venus—and the child whom he
Cherished—bespoke respectability.
So I went wrong, for the right reasons, yet
Had he kept faith, I'd nothing to regret.

The same old fate that worried me to death
Pursues me now, unto my dying breath.
My husband was cut down before his time;
My brother reaped the profit of that crime.
Leaving my husband's grave and home I go
Into harsh exile, followed by my foe.
From him and the sea escaped I'm driven to
This foreign shore, which I acquired for you.
I built a town, and round it a long wall,
A challenge to my neighbors one and all.
Fights break out, the natives seek to try
The strength of foreign females such as I;
My half-built town I cannot fortify.
I have a thousand suitors; all demand
Why I have offered someone else my hand.
Give me to one of them, don't hesitate!
In such a farce I would cooperate.
Then there's my wicked brother: having shed
My husband's blood, he'd like to see me dead.

Lay down your gods, polluted by your touch:
Impious hands do not please heaven much.
Your idols might prefer incineration
To being rescued for your veneration.
Perhaps you've left me pregnant and a part
Of you is hidden under Dido's heart?
The wretched babe will share its mother's doom,
Condemned by you before it leaves the womb.
Ascanius' little brother dies with me,
Confounded in one common penalty.

You say you're leaving at a god's command?
I wish he had forbidden you to land
Here upon the Carthaginian strand;

Even with such a guide, you long were lost
Upon the savage ocean, tempest-tossed.
Regaining Troy would hardly be worth all
This trouble, as it stood before its fall.
Instead of Troy you seek the site of Rome,
But if you get there it won't be like home.
When you are old you may obtain somehow
The long-sought country that eludes you now.
Forego your crooked ways, accept my whole
Realm, and my brother's treasure, which I stole.
Transplant your Troy to this more promising
City, and rule here as anointed king.
If you feel warlike and your young son cries
For more triumphant martial exercise,
I have an enemy for you to face:
Both war and peace are native to this place.

By your mother, and your brother too,
And by those Trojan gods that go with you,
(May those you rescued of your countrymen
Prosper, and war not trouble them again;
May your young son with length of days be blest
And your old father's bones at last find rest!),
Please spare this house, which you are master of:
What crime can you impute to me but love?
No hostile Grecian town gave birth to me,
None of my kinsmen was your enemy.
If making me your wife would bring you shame,
Call me your hostess or whatever name
You please—if I am yours it's all the same.
The winds and tides off Africa I know,
And when they will or will not let you go.
When the wind sets fair you shall set sail,
Now seaweed holds your stranded ships in jail.
Let me decide the time, you'll leave some day,
And if you asked I would not let you stay.
Your shipmates need some rest, so does your fleet,
Whose overdue repairs are half-complete.
For favors past and present, and what may
Come of our union yet—more time, I pray,
And as the sea abates and passion grows
Routine, perhaps I'll learn to bear my woes.

Otherwise, I'll take my life, you'll see:
You shall not long enjoy your cruelty.
I wish that you could see me as I write,
Clasping your broadsword to my bosom tight,

My teardrops falling on the naked blade
Which soon instead of tears will drip with blood—
Your gift was thoughtful, given my sad fate.
My burial expenses won't be great.
This weapon's not the first to deal a blow;
The wounds of love already pierce me so.
My sister, Anna, my sad confidante,
The last respects to my remains will grant.
Sychaeus' wife I shall not be described
As, when my epitaph is thus inscribed:
"Aeneas furnished her the motive and
The means, but Dido died by her own hand."

## FROM THE NEW TESTAMENT: THE GOSPEL OF MARK (1ST CENT. CE)

Unlike the Hebrew Bible, the "New Testament" of Christianity was written in Greek. The story of Jesus is told in four biographies, or "Gospels" (from the Old English *godspel,* meaning "good news"). Three of these, Matthew, Mark, and Luke, are called the "synoptic" gospels because they share so much material, but each seems to adapt the story of Jesus for a different audience—Matthew for Jews, Mark for Romans, and Luke for Greeks. Of these, Mark is probably the earliest, written in Rome within three decades of Jesus' death, probably by a follower of the apostle Peter. A fourth gospel, John, differs from the others in its structure and theological complexity. Included here is the entire book of Mark, which can be usefully compared with Asvaghosha's Life of the Buddha (pp. 265–288) and Ibn Ishāq's biography of Muhammad (pp. 761–786).

Like much of the Hebrew Bible, the four Gospels are rhetorically artful but are not intended as works of literature in the modern sense. They aim to strengthen the religious belief of a Christian community and to gather non-Christians into the faith. Their purpose is thus to change readers fundamentally, to dislodge them from their old social connections and install them in a new community. Readers are encouraged to leave their families and to subordinate ties of kinship to a new relationship to Jesus. The early Church aimed at ethnic diversity within a world religion available to all.

The most distinctive literary features of the Gospels are their realism and their plain style. Written in demotic ("popular") dialect rather than aristocratic classical Greek, they recount life among the lower classes and oppressed and marginal groups, including beggars, prostitutes, criminals, tax-collectors, the disabled and insane, as well as soldiers, bureaucrats, fishermen, farmers, and housewives. The classical world had never produced a literature so realistic in this sense, nor would the Middle Ages, at least until Dante. The simplicity and realism of the Gospels made them more easily transferable from culture to culture across Europe than the elite classical culture. The latter required the complete apparatus of Roman government and cultural occupation for it to take root.

The Gospel of Mark frequently mentions persecution and may thus reflect historical circumstance (namely the Roman oppression of early Christian communities);

but this emphasis on persecution and Christ's Passion (the crucifixion) also functions rhetorically as a call for converts to witness to a hostile world. It urges believers to express their Christian faith even in the face of martyrdom, defining the Christian life as one led in imitation of both Christ's ministry and his suffering.

Mark presumably died in Alexandria while ministering to the early Christian community there; he is, consequently, considered the founder of the Egyptian Christian church. A small population of Christians persist in present-day Egypt and commonly refer to the bishop of Alexandria's position as the "cathedra Marci," or the throne of Mark.

The translation of Mark is from the New Revised Standard.

## *Mark*

1 The beginning of the good news of Jesus Christ, the Son of God.

[2]As it is written in the prophet Isaiah,

> "See, I am sending my messenger
> ahead of you,
> who will prepare your way;
> [3]the voice of one crying out in the
> wilderness:
> 'Prepare the way of the Lord,
> make his paths straight,'"

[4]John the baptizer appeared in the wilderness, proclaiming a baptism of repentance for the forgiveness of sins. [5]And people from the whole Judean countryside and all the people of Jerusalem were going out to him, and were baptized by him in the river Jordan, confessing their sins. [6]Now John was clothed with camel's hair, with a leather belt around his waist, and he ate locusts and wild honey. [7]He proclaimed, "The one who is more powerful than I is coming after me; I am not worthy to stoop down and untie the thong of his sandals. [8]I have baptized you with water; but he will baptize you with the Holy Spirit."

[9]In those days Jesus came from Nazareth of Galilee and was baptized by John in the Jordan. [10]And just as he was coming up out of the water, he saw the heavens torn apart and the Spirit descending like a dove on him. [11]And a voice came from heaven, "You are my Son, the Beloved; with you I am well pleased."

[12]And the Spirit immediately drove him out into the wilderness. [13]He was in the wilderness forty days, tempted by Satan; and he was with the wild beasts; and the angels waited on him.

[14]Now after John was arrested, Jesus came to Galilee, proclaiming the good news of God, [15]and saying, "The time is fulfilled, and the kingdom of God has come near; repent, and believe in the good news."

[16]As Jesus passed along the Sea of Galilee, he saw Simon and his brother Andrew casting a net into the sea—for they were fishermen. [17]And Jesus said to them, "Follow me and I will make you fish for people." [18]And immediately they left their nets and followed him. [19]As he went a little farther, he saw James son of Zebedee and his brother John, who were in their boat mending the nets. [20]Immediately he called them; and they left their father Zebedee in the boat with the hired men, and followed him.

[21]They went to Capernaum; and when the sabbath came, he entered the synagogue and taught. [22]They were

astounded at his teaching, for he taught them as one having authority, and not as the scribes. [23]Just then there was in their synagogue a man with an unclean spirit, [24]and he cried out, "What have you to do with us, Jesus of Nazareth? Have you come to destroy us? I know who you are, the Holy One of God." [25]But Jesus rebuked him, saying, "Be silent, and come out of him!" [26]And the unclean spirit, convulsing him and crying with a loud voice, came out of him. [27]They were all amazed, and they kept on asking one another, "What is this? A new teaching—with authority! He commands even the unclean spirits, and they obey him." [28]At once his fame began to spread throughout the surrounding region of Galilee.

[29]As soon as they left the synagogue, they entered the house of Simon and Andrew, with James and John. [30]Now Simon's mother-in-law was in bed with a fever, and they told him about her at once. [31]He came and took her by the hand and lifted her up. Then the fever left her, and she began to serve them.

[32]That evening, at sundown, they brought to him all who were sick or possessed with demons. [33]And the whole city was gathered around the door. [34]And he cured many who were sick with various diseases, and cast out many demons; and he would not permit the demons to speak, because they knew him.

[35]In the morning, while it was still very dark, he got up and went out to a deserted place, and there he prayed. [36]And Simon and his companions hunted for him. [37]When they found him, they said to him, "Everyone is searching for you." [38]He answered, "Let us go on to the neighboring towns, so that I may proclaim the message there also; for that is what I came out to do." [39]And he went throughout Galilee, proclaiming the message in their synagogues and casting out demons.

[40]A leper came to him begging him, and kneeling he said to him, "If you choose, you can make me clean." [41]Moved with pity, Jesus stretched out his hand and touched him, and said to him, "I do choose. Be made clean!" [42]Immediately the leprosy left him, and he was made clean. [43]After sternly warning him he sent him away at once, [44]saying to him, "See that you say nothing to anyone; but go, show yourself to the priest, and offer for your cleansing what Moses commanded, as a testimony to them." [45]But he went out and began to proclaim it freely, and to spread the word, so that Jesus could no longer go into a town openly, but stayed out in the country; and people came to him from every quarter.

**2** When he returned to Capernaum after some days, it was reported that he was at home. [2]So many gathered around that there was no longer room for them, not even in front of the door; and he was speaking the word to them. [3]Then some people came, bringing to him a paralyzed man, carried by four of them. [4]And when they could not bring him to Jesus because of the crowd, they removed the roof above him; and after having dug through it, they let down the mat on which the paralytic lay. [5]When Jesus saw their faith, he said to the paralytic, "Son, your sins are forgiven." [6]Now some of the scribes were sitting there, questioning in their hearts, [7]"Why does this fellow speak in this way? It is blasphemy! Who can forgive sins but God alone?" [8]At once Jesus perceived in his spirit that they were discussing these questions among themselves; and he said to them, "Why do you raise such questions in your hearts? [9]Which is easier, to say to the paralytic, 'Your sins are forgiven,' or to say, 'Stand up and take your mat and walk'? [10]But so that you may know that the Son of Man has authority on earth to forgive sins"—he said to the paralytic—[11]"I say to you, stand up, take your mat and go to your home." [12]And he stood up, and immediately took the mat and went out before all of them; so that they were all amazed and glorified God, saying, "We have never seen anything like this!"

[13]Jesus went out again beside the sea; the whole crowd gathered around him, and he taught them. [14]As he was walking along, he saw Levi son of Alphaeus sitting at the tax booth, and he said to him, "Follow me." And he got up and followed him.

[15]And as he sat at dinner in Levi's house, many tax collectors and sinners were also sitting with Jesus and his disciples—for there were many who followed him. [16]When the scribes of the Pharisees saw that he was eating with sinners and tax collectors, they said to his disciples, "Why does he eat with tax collectors and sinners?" [17]When Jesus heard this, he said to them, "Those who are well have no need of a physician, but those who are sick; I have come to call not the righteous but sinners."

[18]Now John's disciples and the Pharisees were fasting; and people came and said to him, "Why do John's disciples and the disciples of the Pharisees fast, but your disciples do not fast?" [19]Jesus said to them, "The wedding guests cannot fast while the bridegroom is with them, can they? As long as they have the bridegroom with them, they cannot fast. [20]The days will come when the bridegroom is taken away from them, and then they will fast on that day.

[21]"No one sews a piece of unshrunk cloth on an old cloak; otherwise, the patch pulls away from it, the new from the old, and a worse tear is made. [22]And no one puts new wine into old wine skins; otherwise, the wine will burst the skins, and the wine is lost, and so are the skins; but one puts new wine into fresh wineskins."

[23]One sabbath he was going through the grainfields; and as they made their way his disciples began to pluck heads of grain. [24]The Pharisees said to him, "Look, why are they doing what is not lawful on the sabbath?" [25]And he said to them, "Have you never read what David did when he and his companions were hungry and in need of food? [26]He entered the house of God, when Abiathar was high priest, and ate the bread of the Presence, which it is not lawful for any but the priests to eat, and he gave some to his companions." [27]Then he said to them, "The sabbath was made for humankind, and not humankind for the sabbath; [28]so the Son of Man is lord even of the sabbath."

## 3

Again he entered the synagogue, and a man was there who had a withered hand. [2]They watched him to see whether he would cure him on the sabbath, so that they might accuse him. [3]And he said to the man who had the withered hand, "Come forward." [4]Then he said to them, "Is it lawful to do good or to do harm on the sabbath, to save life or to kill?" But they were silent. [5]He looked around at them with anger; he was grieved at their hardness of heart

and said to the man, "Stretch out your
hand." He stretched it out, and his
hand was restored. 6The Pharisees went
out and immediately conspired with
the Herodians against him, how to
destroy him.

7Jesus departed with his disciples to
the sea, and a great multitude from
Galilee followed him; 8hearing all that
he was doing, they came to him in great
numbers from Judea, Jerusalem, Idu-
mea, beyond the Jordan, and the region
around Tyre and Sidon. 9He told his disciples to have a boat ready for him
because of the crowd, so that they would
not crush him; 10for he had cured many,
so that all who had diseases pressed
upon him to touch him. 11Whenever the
unclean spirits saw him, they fell down
before him and shouted, "You are the
Son of God!" 12But he sternly ordered
them not to make him known.

13He went up the mountain and
called to him those whom he wanted,
and they came to him. 14And he
appointed twelve, whom he also named
apostles, to be with him, and to be sent
out to proclaim the message, 15and to
have authority to cast out demons.
16So he appointed the twelve: Simon (to
whom he gave the name Peter); 17James
son of Zebedee and John the brother of
James (to whom he gave the name
Boanerges, that is, Sons of Thunder);
18and Andrew, and Philip, and Bartholo-
mew, and Matthew, and Thomas, and
James son of Alphaeus, and Thaddaeus,
and Simon the Cananaean, 19and Judas
Iscariot, who betrayed him.

Then he went home; 20and the
crowd came together again, so that they
could not even eat. 21When his family
heard it, they went out to restrain him,
for people were saying, "He has gone
out of his mind." 22And the scribes who
came down from Jerusalem said, "He
has Beelzebul, and by the ruler of the
demons he casts out demons." 23And he
called them to him, and spoke to them
in parables, "How can Satan cast out
Satan? 24If a kingdom is divided against
itself, that kingdom cannot stand. 25And
if a house is divided against itself, that
house will not be able to stand. 26And if
Satan has risen up against himself and
is divided, he cannot stand, but his end
has come. 27But no one can enter a
strong man's house and plunder his
property without first tying up the
strong man; then indeed the house can
be plundered.

28"Truly I tell you, people will be
forgiven for their sins and whatever
blasphemies they utter; 29but whoever
blasphemes against the Holy Spirit can
never have forgiveness, but is guilty of
an eternal sin"—30for they had said,
"He has an unclean spirit."

31Then his mother and his brothers
came; and standing outside, they sent
to him and called him. 32A crowd was
sitting around him; and they said to
him, "Your mother and your brothers
and sisters are outside, asking for you."
33And he replied, "Who are my mother
and my brothers?" 34And looking at
those who sat around him, he said,
"Here are my mother and my brothers!
35Whoever does the will of God is my
brother and sister and mother."

4 Again he began to teach beside the
sea. Such a very large crowd gathered around him that he got into a boat
on the sea and sat there, while the
whole crowd was beside the sea on the
land. 2He began to teach them many
things in parables, and in his teaching
he said to them: 3"Listen! A sower went
out to sow. 4And as he sowed, some seed
fell on the path, and the birds came
and ate it up. 5Other seed fell on rocky

ground, where it did not have much soil, and it sprang up quickly, since it had no depth of soil. [6]And when the sun rose, it was scorched; and since it had no root, it withered away. [7]Other seed fell among thorns, and the thorns grew up and choked it, and it yielded no grain. [8]Other seed fell into good soil and brought forth grain, growing up and increasing and yielding thirty and sixty and a hundredfold." [9]And he said, "Let anyone with ears to hear listen!"

[10]When he was alone, those who were around him along with the twelve asked him about the parables. [11]And he said to them, "To you has been given the secret of the kingdom of God, but for those outside, everything comes in parables; [12]in order that

'they may indeed look, but not
perceive,
and may indeed listen, but not
understand;
so that they may not turn again
and be forgiven.'"

[13]And he said to them, "Do you not understand this parable? Then how will you understand all the parables? [14]The sower sows the word. [15]These are the ones on the path where the word is sown: when they hear, Satan immediately comes and takes away the word that is sown in them. [16]And these are the ones sown on rocky ground: when they hear the word, they immediately receive it with joy. [17]But they have no root, and endure only for a while; then, when trouble or persecution arises on account of the word, immediately they fall away. [18]And others are those sown among the thorns: these are the ones who hear the word, [19]but the cares of the world, and the lure of wealth, and the desire for other things come in and choke the word, and it yields nothing. [20]And these are the ones sown on the good soil: they hear the word and accept it and bear fruit, thirty and sixty and a hundredfold."

[21]He said to them, "Is a lamp brought in to be put under the bushel basket, or under the bed, and not on the lampstand? [22]For there is nothing hidden, except to be disclosed; nor is anything secret, except to come to light. [23]Let anyone with ears to hear listen!" [24]And he said to them, "Pay attention to what you hear; the measure you give will be the measure you get, and still more will be given you. [25]For to those who have, more will be given; and from those who have nothing, even what they have will be taken away."

[26]He also said, "The kingdom of God is as if someone would scatter seed on the ground, [27]and would sleep and rise night and day, and the seed would sprout and grow, he does not know how. [28]The earth produces of itself, first the stalk, then the head, then the full grain in the head. [29]But when the grain is ripe, at once he goes in with his sickle, because the harvest has come."

[30]He also said, "With what can we compare the kingdom of God, or what parable will we use for it? [31]It is like a mustard seed, which, when sown upon the ground, is the smallest of all the seeds on earth; [32]yet when it is sown it grows up and becomes the greatest of all shrubs, and puts forth large branches, so that the birds of the air can make nests in its shade."

[33]With many such parables he spoke the word to them, as they were able to hear it; [34]he did not speak to them except in parables, but he explained everything in private to his disciples.

[35]On that day, when evening had come, he said to them, "Let us go

across to the other side." [36]And leaving the crowd behind, they took him with them in the boat, just as he was. Other boats were with him. [37]A great windstorm arose, and the waves beat into the boat, so that the boat was already being swamped. [38]But he was in the stern, asleep on the cushion; and they woke him up and said to him, "Teacher, do you not care that we are perishing?" [39]He woke up and rebuked the wind, and said to the sea, "Peace! Be still!" Then the wind ceased, and there was a dead calm. [40]He said to them, "Why are you afraid? Have you still no faith?" [41]And they were filled with great awe and said to one another, "Who then is this, that even the wind and the sea obey him?"

**5** They came to the other side of the sea, to the country of the Gerasenes. [2]And when he had stepped out of the boat, immediately a man out of the tombs with an unclean spirit met him. [3]He lived among the tombs; and no one could restrain him any more, even with a chain; [4]for he had often been restrained with shackles and chains, but the chains he wrenched apart, and the shackles he broke in pieces; and no one had the strength to subdue him. [5]Night and day among the tombs and on the mountains he was always howling and bruising himself with stones. [6]When he saw Jesus from a distance, he ran and bowed down before him; [7]and he shouted at the top of his voice, "What have you to do with me, Jesus, Son of the Most High God? I adjure you by God, do not torment me." [8]For he had said to him, "Come out of the man, you unclean spirit!" [9]Then Jesus asked him, "What is your name?" He replied, "My name is Legion; for we are many." [10]He begged him earnestly not to send them out of the country. [11]Now there on the hillside a great herd of swine was feeding; [12]and the unclean spirits begged him, "Send us into the swine; let us enter them." [13]So he gave them permission. And the unclean spirits came out and entered the swine; and the herd, numbering about two thousand, rushed down the steep bank into the sea, and were drowned in the sea.

[14]The swineherds ran off and told it in the city and in the country. Then people came to see what it was that had happened. [15]They came to Jesus and saw the demoniac sitting there, clothed and in his right mind, the very man who had had the legion; and they were afraid. [16]Those who had seen what had happened to the demoniac and to the swine reported it. [17]Then they began to beg Jesus to leave their neighborhood. [18]As he was getting into the boat, the man who had been possessed by demons begged him that he might be with him. [19]But Jesus refused, and said to him, "Go home to your friends, and tell them how much the Lord has done for you, and what mercy he has shown you." [20]And he went away and began to proclaim in the Decapolis how much Jesus had done for him; and everyone was amazed.

[21]When Jesus had crossed again in the boat to the other side, a great crowd gathered around him; and he was by the sea. [22]Then one of the leaders of the synagogue named Jairus came and, when he saw him, fell at his feet [23]and begged him repeatedly, "My little daughter is at the point of death. Come and lay your hands on her, so that she may be made well, and live." [24]So he went with him.

And a large crowd followed him and pressed in on him. [25]Now there was a woman who had been suffering from

hemorrhages for twelve years. 26She had
endured much under many physicians,
and had spent all that she had; and she
was no better, but rather grew worse.
27She had heard about Jesus, and came
up behind him in the crowd and
touched his cloak, 28for she said, "If I
but touch his clothes, I will be made
well." 29Immediately her hemorrhage
stopped; and she felt in her body that
she was healed of her disease. 30Immed-
iately aware that power had gone forth
from him, Jesus turned about in the
crowd and said, "Who touched my
clothes?" 31And his disciples said to him,
"You see the crowd pressing in on you;
how can you say, 'Who touched me?'"
32He looked all around to see who had
done it. 33But the woman, knowing what
had happened to her, came in fear and
trembling, fell down before him, and
told him the whole truth. 34He said to
her, "Daughter, your faith has made you
well; go in peace, and be healed of your
disease."

35While he was still speaking, some
people came from the leader's house to
say, "Your daughter is dead. Why trouble the teacher any further?" 36But overhearing what they said, Jesus said to the
leader of the synagogue, "Do not fear,
only believe." 37He allowed no one to
follow him except Peter, James, and
John, the brother of James. 38When they
came to the house of the leader of the
synagogue, he saw a commotion, people weeping and wailing loudly. 39When
he had entered, he said to them, "Why
do you make a commotion and weep?
The child is not dead but sleeping."
40And they laughed at him. Then he put
them all outside, and took the child's
father and mother and those who were
with him, and went in where the child
was. 41He took her by the hand and
said to her, "Talitha cum," which means,
"Little girl, get up!" 42And immediately
the girl got up and began to walk about
(she was twelve years of age). At this
they were overcome with amazement.
43He strictly ordered them that no one
should know this, and told them to give
her something to eat.

6 He left that place and came to his
hometown, and his disciples followed him. 2On the sabbath he began
to teach in the synagogue, and many
who heard him were astounded. They
said, "Where did this man get all this?
What is this wisdom that has been given
to him? What deeds of power are being
done by his hands! 3Is not this the carpenter, the son of Mary and brother of
James and Joses and Judas and Simon,
and are not his sisters here with us?"
And they took offense at him. 4Then
Jesus said to them, "Prophets are not
without honor, except in their hometown, and among their own kin, and in
their own house." 5And he could do no
deed of power there, except that he
laid his hands on a few sick people and
cured them. 6And he was amazed at
their unbelief.

Then he went about among the villages teaching. 7He called the twelve
and began to send them out two by two,
and gave them authority over the
unclean spirits. 8He ordered them to
take nothing for their journey except a
staff; no bread, no bag, no money in
their belts; 9but to wear sandals and not
to put on two tunics. 10He said to them,
"Wherever you enter a house, stay there
until you leave the place. 11If any place
will not welcome you and they refuse to
hear you, as you leave, shake off the
dust that is on your feet as a testimony
against them." 12So they went out and
proclaimed that all should repent.
13They cast out many demons, and

anointed with oil many who were sick and cured them.

14 King Herod heard of it, for Jesus' name had become known. Some were saying, "John the baptizer has been raised from the dead; and for this reason these powers are at work in him." 15 But others said, "It is Elijah." And others said, "It is a prophet, like one of the prophets of old." 16 But when Herod heard of it, he said, "John, whom I beheaded, has been raised."

17 For Herod himself had sent men who arrested John, bound him, and put him in prison on account of Herodias, his brother Philip's wife, because Herod had married her. 18 For John had been telling Herod, "It is not lawful for you to have your brother's wife." 19 And Herodias had a grudge against him, and wanted to kill him. But she could not, 20 for Herod feared John, knowing that he was a righteous and holy man, and he protected him. When he heard him, he was greatly perplexed; and yet he liked to listen to him. 21 But an opportunity came when Herod on his birthday gave a banquet for his courtiers and officers and for the leaders of Galilee. 22 When his daughter Herodias came in and danced, she pleased Herod and his guests; and the king said to the girl, "Ask me for whatever you wish, and I will give it." 23 And he solemnly swore to her, "Whatever you ask me, I will give you, even half of my kingdom." 24 She went out and said to her mother, "What should I ask for?" She replied, "The head of John the baptizer." 25 Immediately she rushed back to the king and requested, "I want you to give me at once the head of John the Baptist on a platter." 26 The king was deeply grieved; yet out of regard for his oaths and for the guests, he did not want to refuse her. 27 Immediately the king sent a soldier of the guard with orders to bring John's head. He went and beheaded him in the prison, 28 brought his head on a platter, and gave it to the girl. Then the girl gave it to her mother. 29 When his disciples heard about it, they came and took his body, and laid it in a tomb.

30 The apostles gathered around Jesus, and told him all that they had done and taught. 31 He said to them, "Come away to a deserted place all by yourselves and rest a while." For many were coming and going, and they had no leisure even to eat. 32 And they went away in the boat to a deserted place by themselves. 33 Now many saw them going and recognized them, and they hurried there on foot from all the towns and arrived ahead of them. 34 As he went ashore, he saw a great crowd; and he had compassion for them, because they were like sheep without a shepherd; and he began to teach them many things. 35 When it grew late, his disciples came to him and said, "This is a deserted place, and the hour is now very late; 36 send them away so that they may go into the surrounding country and villages and buy something for themselves to eat." 37 But he answered them, "You give them something to eat." They said to him, "Are we to go and buy two hundred denarii worth of bread, and give it to them to eat?" 38 And he said to them, "How many loaves have you? Go and see." When they had found out, they said, "Five, and two fish." 39 Then he ordered them to get all the people to sit down in groups on the green grass. 40 So they sat down in groups of hundreds and of fifties. 41 Taking the five loaves and the two fish, he looked up to heaven, and blessed and broke the loaves, and gave them to his disciples to set before the people; and he divided the two fish among

them all. [42]And all ate and were filled;
[43]and they took up twelve baskets full of
broken pieces and of the fish. [44]Those
who had eaten the loaves numbered
five thousand men.

[45]Immediately he made his disciples
get into the boat and go on ahead to
the other side, to Bethsaida, while he
dismissed the crowd. [46]After saying
farewell to them, he went up on the
mountain to pray.

[47]When evening came, the boat was
out on the sea, and he was alone on the
land. [48]When he saw that they were
straining at the oars against an adverse
wind, he came towards them early in
the morning, walking on the sea. He
intended to pass them by. [49]But when
they saw him walking on the sea, they
thought it was a ghost and cried out;
[50]for they all saw him and were terrified.
But immediately he spoke to them and
said, "Take heart, it is I; do not be
afraid." [51]Then he got into the boat with
them and the wind ceased. And they
were utterly astounded, [52]for they did
not understand about the loaves, but
their hearts were hardened.

[53]When they had crossed over, they
came to land at Gennesaret and
moored the boat. [54]When they got out
of the boat, people at once recognized
him, [55]and rushed about that whole
region and began to bring the sick on
mats to wherever they heard he was.
[56]And wherever he went, into villages or
cities or farms, they laid the sick in the
marketplaces, and begged him that
they might touch even the fringe of his
cloak; and all who touched it were
healed.

7 Now when the Pharisees and some
of the scribes who had come from
Jerusalem gathered around him, [2]they
noticed that some of his disciples were
eating with defiled hands, that is, without washing them. [3](For the Pharisees,
and all the Jews, do not eat unless they
thoroughly wash their hands, thus
observing the tradition of the elders;
[4]and they do not eat anything from the
market unless they wash it; and there
are also many other traditions that they
observe, the washing of cups, pots,
and bronze kettles.) [5]So the Pharisees
and the scribes asked him, "Why do
your disciples not live according to the
tradition of the elders, but eat with
defiled hands?" [6]He said to them,
"Isaiah prophesied rightly about you
hypocrites, as it is written,

> 'This people honors me with
> their lips,
> but their hearts are far from me;
> [7]in vain do they worship me,
> teaching human precepts as
> doctrines.'

[8]You abandon the commandment of
God and hold to human tradition."

[9]Then he said to them, "You have a
fine way of rejecting the commandment
of God in order to keep your tradition!
[10]For Moses said, 'Honor your father
and your mother'; and, 'Whoever
speaks evil of father or mother must
surely die.' [11]But you say that if anyone
tells father or mother, 'Whatever support you might have had from me is
Corban' (that is, an offering to God)—
[12]then you no longer permit doing anything for a father or mother, [13]thus making void the word of God through your
tradition that you have handed on. And
you do many things like this."

[14]Then he called the crowd again
and said to them, "Listen to me, all of
you, and understand: [15]there is nothing
outside a person that by going in can
defile, but the things that come out are
what defile."

[17]When he had left the crowd and entered the house, his disciples asked him about the parable. [18]He said to them, "Then do you also fail to understand? Do you not see that whatever goes into a person from outside cannot defile, [19]since it enters, not the heart but the stomach, and goes out into the sewer?" (Thus he declared all foods clean.) [20]And he said, "It is what comes out of a person that defiles. [21]For it is from within, from the human heart, that evil intentions come: fornication, theft, murder, [22]adultery, avarice, wickedness, deceit, licentiousness, envy, slander, pride, folly. [23]All these evil things come from within, and they defile a person."

[24]From there he set out and went away to the region of Tyre. He entered a house and did not want anyone to know he was there. Yet he could not escape notice, [25]but a woman whose little daughter had an unclean spirit immediately heard about him, and she came and bowed down at his feet. [26]Now the woman was a Gentile, of Syrophoenician origin. She begged him to cast the demon out of her daughter. [27]He said to her, "Let the children be fed first, for it is not fair to take the children's food and throw it to the dogs." [28]But she answered him, "Sir, even the dogs under the table eat the children's crumbs." [29]Then he said to her, "For saying that, you may go—the demon has left your daughter." [30]So she went home, found the child lying on the bed, and the demon gone.

[31]Then he returned from the region of Tyre, and went by way of Sidon towards the Sea of Galilee, in the region of the Decapolis. [32]They brought to him a deaf man who had an impediment in his speech; and they begged him to lay his hand on him. [33]He took him aside in private, away from the crowd, and put his fingers into his ears, and he spat and touched his tongue. [34]Then looking up to heaven, he sighed and said to him, "Ephphatha," that is, "Be opened." [35]And immediately his ears were opened, his tongue was released, and he spoke plainly. [36]Then Jesus ordered them to tell no one; but the more he ordered them, the more zealously they proclaimed it. [37]They were astounded beyond measure, saying, "He has done everything well; he even makes the deaf to hear and the mute to speak."

8 In those days when there was again a great crowd without anything to eat, he called his disciples and said to them, [2]"I have compassion for the crowd, because they have been with me now for three days and have nothing to eat. [3]If I send them away hungry to their homes, they will faint on the way—and some of them have come from a great distance." [4]His disciples replied, "How can one feed these people with bread here in the desert?" [5]He asked them, "How many loaves do you have?" They said, "Seven." [6]Then he ordered the crowd to sit down on the ground; and he took the seven loaves, and after giving thanks he broke them and gave them to his disciples to distribute; and they distributed them to the crowd. [7]They had also a few small fish; and after blessing them, he ordered that these too should be distributed. [8]They ate and were filled; and they took up the broken pieces left over, seven baskets full. [9]Now there were about four thousand people. And he sent them away. [10]And immediately he got into the boat with his disciples and went to the district of Dalmanutha.

[11]The Pharisees came and began to argue with him, asking him for a sign from heaven, to test him. [12]And he sighed deeply in his spirit and said,

"Why does this generation ask for a sign? Truly I tell you, no sign will be given to this generation." [13]And he left them, and getting into the boat again, he went across to the other side.

[14]Now the disciples had forgotten to bring any bread; and they had only one loaf with them in the boat. [15]And he cautioned them, saying, "Watch out—beware of the yeast of the Pharisees and the yeast of Herod." [16]They said to one another, "It is because we have no bread." [17]And becoming aware of it, Jesus said to them, "Why are you talking about having no bread? Do you still not perceive or understand? Are your hearts hardened? [18]Do you have eyes, and fail to see? Do you have ears, and fail to hear? And do you not remember? [19]When I broke the five loaves for the five thousand, how many baskets full of broken pieces did you collect?" They said to him, "Twelve." [20]"And the seven for the four thousand, how many baskets full of broken pieces did you collect?" And they said to him, "Seven." [21]Then he said to them, "Do you not yet understand?"

[22]They came to Bethsaida. Some people brought a blind man to him and begged him to touch him. [23]He took the blind man by the hand and led him out of the village; and when he had put saliva on his eyes and laid his hands on him, he asked him, "Can you see anything?" [24]And the man looked up and said, "I can see people, but they look like trees, walking." [25]Then Jesus laid his hands on his eyes again; and he looked intently and his sight was restored, and he saw everything clearly. [26]Then he sent him away to his home, saying, "Do not even go into the village."

[27]Jesus went on with his disciples to the villages of Caesarea Philippi; and on the way he asked his disciples, "Who do people say that I am?" [28]And they answered him, "John the Baptist; and others, Elijah; and still others, one of the prophets." [29]He asked them, "But who do you say that I am?" Peter answered him, "You are the Messiah." [30]And he sternly ordered them not to tell anyone about him.

[31]Then he began to teach them that the Son of Man must undergo great suffering, and be rejected by the elders, the chief priests, and the scribes, and be killed, and after three days rise again. [32]He said all this quite openly. And Peter took him aside and began to rebuke him. [33]But turning and looking at his disciples, he rebuked Peter and said, "Get behind me, Satan! For you are setting your mind not on divine things but on human things."

[34]He called the crowd with his disciples, and said to them, "If any want to become my followers, let them deny themselves and take up their cross and follow me. [35]For those who want to save their life will lose it, and those who lose their life for my sake, and for the sake of the gospel, will save it. [36]For what will it profit them to gain the whole world and forfeit their life? [37]Indeed, what can they give in return for their life? [38]Those who are ashamed of me and of my words in this adulterous and sinful generation, of them the Son of Man will also be ashamed when he comes in the glory of his Father with the holy angels."

9
[1]And he said to them, "Truly I tell you, there are some standing here who will not taste death until they see that the kingdom of God has come with power."

[2]Six days later, Jesus took with him Peter and James and John, and led them up a high mountain apart, by themselves. And he was transfigured

before them, [3]and his clothes became dazzling white, such as no one on earth could bleach them. [4]And there appeared to them Elijah with Moses, who were talking with Jesus. [5]Then Peter said to Jesus, "Rabbi, it is good for us to be here; let us make three dwellings, one for you, one for Moses, and one for Elijah." [6]He did not know what to say, for they were terrified. [7]Then a cloud overshadowed them, and from the cloud there came a voice, "This is my Son, the Beloved; listen to him!" [8]Suddenly when they looked around, they saw no one with them any more, but only Jesus.

[9]As they were coming down the mountain, he ordered them to tell no one about what they had seen, until after the Son of Man had risen from the dead. [10]So they kept the matter to themselves, questioning what this rising from the dead could mean. [11]Then they asked him, "Why do the scribes say that Elijah must come first?" [12]He said to them, "Elijah is indeed coming first to restore all things. How then is it written about the Son of Man, that he is to go through many sufferings and be treated with contempt? [13]But I tell you that Elijah has come, and they did to him whatever they pleased, as it is written about him."

[14]When they came to the disciples, they saw a great crowd around them, and some scribes arguing with them. [15]When the whole crowd saw him, they were immediately overcome with awe, and they ran forward to greet him. [16]He asked them, "What are you arguing about with them?" [17]Someone from the crowd answered him, "Teacher, I brought you my son; he has a spirit that makes him unable to speak; [18]and whenever it seizes him, it dashes him down; and he foams and grinds his teeth and becomes rigid; and I asked your disciples to cast it out, but they could not do so." [19]He answered them, "You faithless generation, how much longer must I be among you? How much longer must I put up with you? Bring him to me." [20]And they brought the boy to him. When the spirit saw him, immediately it convulsed the boy, and he fell on the ground and rolled about, foaming at the mouth. [21]Jesus asked the father, "How long has this been happening to him?" And he said, "From childhood. [22]It has often cast him into the fire and into the water, to destroy him; but if you are able to do anything, have pity on us and help us." [23]Jesus said to him, "If you are able!—All things can be done for the one who believes." [24]Immediately the father of the child cried out, "I believe; help my unbelief!" [25]When Jesus saw that a crowd came running together, he rebuked the unclean spirit, saying to it, "You spirit that keeps this boy from speaking and hearing, I command you, come out of him, and never enter him again!" [26]After crying out and convulsing him terribly, it came out, and the boy was like a corpse, so that most of them said, "He is dead." [27]But Jesus took him by the hand and lifted him up, and he was able to stand. [28]When he had entered the house, his disciples asked him privately, "Why could we not cast it out?" [29]He said to them, "This kind can come out only through prayer."

[30]They went on from there and passed through Galilee. He did not want anyone to know it; [31]for he was teaching his disciples, saying to them, "The Son of Man is to be betrayed into human hands, and they will kill him, and three days after being killed, he will rise again." [32]But they did not

understand what he was saying and
were afraid to ask him.
33Then they came to Capernaum;
and when he was in the house he asked
them, "What were you arguing about
on the way?" 34But they were silent, for
on the way they had argued with one
another who was the greatest. 35He sat
down, called the twelve, and said to
them, "Whoever wants to be first must
be last of all and servant of all." 36Then
he took a little child and put it among
them; and taking it in his arms, he said
to them, 37"Whoever welcomes one
such child in my name welcomes me,
and whoever welcomes me welcomes
not me but the one who sent me."
38John said to him, "Teacher, we saw
someone casting out demons in your
name, and we tried to stop him,
because he was not following us." 39But
Jesus said, "Do not stop him; for no one
who does a deed of power in my name
will be able soon afterward to speak evil
of me. 40Whoever is not against us is for
us. 41For truly I tell you, whoever gives
you a cup of water to drink because you
bear the name of Christ will by no
means lose the reward.
42"If any of you put a stumbling
block before one of these little ones who
believe in me, it would be better for you
if a great millstone were hung around
your neck and you were thrown into the
sea. 43If your hand causes you to stumble, cut it off; it is better for you to enter
life maimed than to have two hands and
to go to hell, to the unquenchable fire.
45And if your foot causes you to stumble,
cut it off; it is better for you to enter
life lame than to have two feet and to be
thrown into hell. 47And if your eye causes
you to stumble, tear it out; it is better
for you to enter the kingdom of God
with one eye than to have two eyes
and to be thrown into hell, 48where
their worm never dies, and the fire is
never quenched.
49"For everyone will be salted with
fire. 50Salt is good; but if salt has lost its
saltiness, how can you season it? Have
salt in yourselves, and be at peace with
one another."

10 He left that place and went to the
region of Judea and beyond the
Jordan. And crowds again gathered
around him; and, as was his custom, he
again taught them.
2Some Pharisees came, and to test
him they asked, "Is it lawful for a man
to divorce his wife?" 3He answered
them, "What did Moses command you?"
4They said, "Moses allowed a man to
write a certificate of dismissal and to
divorce her." 5But Jesus said to them,
"Because of your hardness of heart he
wrote this commandment for you. 6But
from the beginning of creation, 'God
made them male and female.' 7'For this
reason a man shall leave his father and
mother and be joined to his wife, 8and
the two shall become one flesh.' So
they are no longer two, but one flesh.'
9Therefore what God has joined
together, let no one separate."
10Then in the house the disciples
asked him again about this matter.
11He said to them, "Whoever divorces
his wife and marries another commits
adultery against her; 12and if she divorces
her husband and marries another, she
commits adultery."
13People were bringing little children to him in order that he might
touch them; and the disciples spoke
sternly to them. 14But when Jesus saw
this, he was indignant and said to them,
"Let the little children come to me; do
not stop them; for it is to such as these
that the kingdom of God belongs.
15Truly I tell you, whoever does not

receive the kingdom of God as a little child will never enter it." 16And he took them up in his arms, laid his hands on them, and blessed them.

17As he was setting out on a journey, a man ran up and knelt before him, and asked him, "Good Teacher, what must I do to inherit eternal life?" 18Jesus said to him, "Why do you call me good? No one is good but God alone. 19You know the commandments: 'You shall not murder; You shall not commit adultery; You shall not steal; You shall not bear false witness; You shall not defraud; Honor your father and mother.'" 20He said to him, "Teacher, I have kept all these since my youth." 21Jesus, looking at him, loved him and said, "You lack one thing; go, sell what you own, and give the money to the poor, and you will have treasure in heaven; then come, follow me." 22When he heard this, he was shocked and went away grieving, for he had many possessions.

23Then Jesus looked around and said to his disciples, "How hard it will be for those who have wealth to enter the kingdom of God!" 24And the disciples were perplexed at these words. But Jesus said to them again, "Children, how hard it is to enter the kingdom of God! 25It is easier for a camel to go through the eye of a needle than for someone who is rich to enter the kingdom of God." 26They were greatly astounded and said to one another, "Then who can be saved?" 27Jesus looked at them and said, "For mortals it is impossible, but not for God; for God all things are possible."

28Peter began to say to him, "Look, we have left everything and followed you." 29Jesus said, "Truly I tell you, there is no one who has left house or brothers or sisters or mother or father or children or fields, for my sake and for the sake of the good news, 30who will not receive a hundredfold now in this age—houses, brothers and sisters, mothers and children, and fields with persecutions—and in the age to come eternal life. 31But many who are first will be last, and the last will be first."

32They were on the road, going up to Jerusalem, and Jesus was walking ahead of them; they were amazed, and those who followed were afraid. He took the twelve aside again and began to tell them what was to happen to him, 33saying, "See, we are going up to Jerusalem, and the Son of Man will be handed over to the chief priests and the scribes, and they will condemn him to death; then they will hand him over to the Gentiles; 34they will mock him, and spit upon him, and flog him, and kill him; and after three days he will rise again."

35James and John, the sons of Zebedee, came forward to him and said to him, "Teacher, we want you to do for us whatever we ask of you." 36And he said to them, "What is it you want me to do for you?" 37And they said to him, "Grant us to sit, one at your right hand and one at your left, in your glory." 38But Jesus said to them, "You do not know what you are asking. Are you able to drink the cup that I drink, or be baptized with the baptism that I am baptized with?" 39They replied, "We are able." Then Jesus said to them, "The cup that I drink you will drink; and with the baptism with which I am baptized, you will be baptized; 40but to sit at my right hand or at my left is not mine to grant, but it is for those for whom it has been prepared."

41When the ten heard this, they began to be angry with James and John. 42So Jesus called them and said to them, "You know that among the Gentiles those whom they recognize as their

rulers lord it over them, and their great
ones are tyrants over them. 43But it is
not so among you; but whoever wishes
to become great among you must be
your servant, 44and whoever wishes to
be first among you must be slave of all.
45For the Son of Man came not to be
served but to serve, and to give his life
a ransom for many."

46They came to Jericho. As he and
his disciples and a large crowd were
leaving Jericho, Bartimaeus son of
Timaeus, a blind beggar, was sitting by
the roadside. 47When he heard that it
was Jesus of Nazareth, he began to
shout out and say, "Jesus, Son of David,
have mercy on me!" 48Many sternly
ordered him to be quiet, but he cried
out even more loudly, "Son of David,
have mercy on me!" 49Jesus stood still
and said, "Call him here." And they
called the blind man, saying to him,
"Take heart; get up, he is calling you."
50So throwing off his cloak, he sprang
up and came to Jesus. 51Then Jesus said
to him, "What do you want me to do for
you?" The blind man said to him, "My
teacher, let me see again." 52Jesus said
to him, "Go; your faith has made you
well." Immediately he regained his sight
and followed him on the way.

11 When they were approaching
Jerusalem, at Bethphage and
Bethany, near the Mount of Olives, he
sent two of his disciples 2and said to
them, "Go into the village ahead of you,
and immediately as you enter it, you
will find tied there a colt that has never
been ridden; untie it and bring it. 3If
anyone says to you, 'Why are you doing
this?' just say this, 'The Lord needs it
and will send it back here immediately.'" 4They went away and found a
colt tied near a door, outside in the
street. As they were untying it, 5some of
the bystanders said to them, "What are
you doing, untying the colt?" 6They told
them what Jesus had said; and they
allowed them to take it. 7Then they
brought the colt to Jesus and threw
their cloaks on it; and he sat on it.
8Many people spread their cloaks on
the road, and others spread leafy
branches that they had cut in the fields.
9Then those who went ahead and those
who followed were shouting,

"Hosanna!
Blessed is the one who comes in
the name of the Lord!
10Blessed is the coming kingdom
of our ancestor David!
Hosanna in the highest heaven!"

11Then he entered Jerusalem and
went into the temple; and when he had
looked around at everything, as it was
already late, he went out to Bethany
with the twelve.

12On the following day, when they
came from Bethany, he was hungry.
13Seeing in the distance a fig tree in
leaf, he went to see whether perhaps he
would find anything on it. When he
came to it, he found nothing but leaves,
for it was not the season for figs. 14He
said to it, "May no one ever eat fruit
from you again." And his disciples
heard it.

15Then they came to Jerusalem.
And he entered the temple and began
to drive out those who were selling and
those who were buying in the temple,
and he overturned the tables of the
money changers and the seats of those
who sold doves; 16and he would not
allow anyone to carry anything through
the temple. 17He was teaching and saying, "Is it not written,

'My house shall be called a house
of prayer for all the nations'?
But you have made it a den
of robbers."

18And when the chief priests and the
scribes heard it, they kept looking for a
way to kill him; for they were afraid of
him, because the whole crowd was
spellbound by his teaching. 19And when
evening came, Jesus and his disciples
went out of the city.

20In the morning as they passed by,
they saw the fig tree withered away to its
roots. 21Then Peter remembered and
said to him, "Rabbi, look! The fig tree
that you cursed has withered." 22Jesus
answered them, "Have faith in God.
23Truly I tell you, if you say to this mountain, 'Be taken up and thrown into the
sea,' and if you do not doubt in your
heart, but believe that what you say will
come to pass, it will be done for you.
24So I tell you, whatever you ask for in
prayer, believe that you have received it,
and it will be yours.

25"Whenever you stand praying, forgive, if you have anything against anyone; so that your Father in heaven may
also forgive you your trespasses."

27Again they came to Jerusalem. As
he was walking in the temple, the chief
priests, the scribes, and the elders came
to him 28and said, "By what authority
are you doing these things? Who gave
you this authority to do them?" 29Jesus
said to them, "I will ask you one question; answer me, and I will tell you by
what authority I do these things. 30Did
the baptism of John come from heaven,
or was it of human origin? Answer me."
31They argued with one another, "If we
say, 'From heaven,' he will say, 'Why
then did you not believe him?' 32But
shall we say, 'Of human origin'?"—they
were afraid of the crowd, for all
regarded John as truly a prophet. 33So
they answered Jesus, "We do not know."
And Jesus said to them, "Neither will I
tell you by what authority I am doing
these things."

12 Then he began to speak to them
in parables. "A man planted a
vineyard, put a fence around it, dug a
pit for the wine press, and built a watch-
tower; then he leased it to tenants and
went to another country. 2When the
season came, he sent a slave to the tenants to collect from them his share of
the produce of the vineyard. 3But they
seized him, and beat him, and sent him
away empty-handed. 4And again he sent
another slave to them; this one they
beat over the head and insulted. 5Then
he sent another, and that one they
killed. And so it was with many others;
some they beat, and others they killed.
6He had still one other, a beloved son.
Finally he sent him to them, saying,
'They will respect my son.' 7But those
tenants said to one another, 'This is the
heir; come, let us kill him, and the inheritance will be ours.' 8So they seized him,
killed him, and threw him out of the
vineyard. 9What then will the owner of
the vineyard do? He will come and
destroy the tenants and give the vineyard to others. 10Have you not read this
scripture:

> 'The stone that the builders
> rejected
> has become the cornerstone;
> 11this was the Lord's doing,
> and it is amazing in our eyes'?"

12When they realized that he had
told this parable against them, they
wanted to arrest him, but they feared
the crowd. So they left him and went
away.

13Then they sent to him some
Pharisees and some Herodians to trap
him in what he said. 14And they came
and said to him, "Teacher, we know that
you are sincere, and show deference to
no one; for you do not regard people
with partiality, but teach the way of God

in accordance with truth. Is it lawful
to pay taxes to the emperor, or not?
[15]Should we pay them, or should we
not?" But knowing their hypocrisy, he
said to them, "Why are you putting me to
the test? Bring me a denarius and let me
see it." [16]And they brought one. Then
he said to them, "Whose head is this,
and whose title?" They answered, "The
emperor's." [17]Jesus said to them, "Give
to the emperor the things that are
the emperor's, and to God the things
that are God's." And they were utterly
amazed at him.

[18]Some Sadducees, who say there is
no resurrection, came to him and asked
him a question, saying, [19]"Teacher,
Moses wrote for us that 'if a man's
brother dies, leaving a wife but no child,
the man shall marry the widow and raise
up children for his brother.' [20]There
were seven brothers; the first married
and, when he died, left no children;
[21]and the second married her and died,
leaving no children; and the third likewise; [22]none of the seven left children.
Last of all the woman herself died. [23]In
the resurrection whose wife will she be?
For the seven had married her."

[24]Jesus said to them, "Is not this the
reason you are wrong, that you know
neither the scriptures nor the power of
God? [25]For when they rise from the
dead, they neither marry nor are given
in marriage, but are like angels in
heaven. [26]And as for the dead being
raised, have you not read in the book of
Moses, in the story about the bush, how
God said to him, 'I am the God of Abraham, the God of Isaac, and the God of
Jacob'? [27]He is God not of the dead, but
of the living; you are quite wrong."

[28]One of the scribes came near and
heard them disputing with one another,
and seeing that he answered them well,
he asked him, "Which commandment
is the first of all?" [29]Jesus answered, "The
first is, 'Hear, O Israel: the Lord our
God, the Lord is one; [30]you shall love the
Lord your God with all your heart, and
with all your soul, and with all your
mind, and with all your strength.' [31]The
second is this, 'You shall love your
neighbor as yourself.' There is no other
commandment greater than these."
[32]Then the scribe said to him, "You are
right, Teacher; you have truly said that
'he is one, and besides him there is no
other'; [33]and 'to love him with all the
heart, and with all the understanding, and with all the strength,' and
'to love one's neighbor as oneself,'—
this is much more important than all
whole burnt offerings and sacrifices."
[34]When Jesus saw that he answered
wisely, he said to him, "You are not far
from the kingdom of God." After that
no one dared to ask him any question.

[35]While Jesus was teaching in the
temple, he said, "How can the scribes
say that the Messiah is the son of David?
[36]David himself, by the Holy Spirit,
declared,

> 'The Lord said to my Lord,
> "Sit at my right hand,
> until I put your enemies under
> your feet."'

[37]David himself calls him Lord; so how
can he be his son?" And the large
crowd was listening to him with delight.

[38]As he taught, he said, "Beware of
the scribes, who like to walk around in
long robes, and to be greeted with
respect in the marketplaces, [39]and to
have the best seats in the synagogues
and places of honor at banquets! [40]They
devour widows' houses and for the sake
of appearance say long prayers. They
will receive the greater condemnation."

[41]He sat down opposite the treasury, and watched the crowd putting

money into the treasury. Many rich people put in large sums. [42]A poor widow came and put in two small copper coins, which are worth a penny. [43]Then he called his disciples and said to them, "Truly I tell you, this poor widow has put in more than all those who are contributing to the treasury. [44]For all of them have contributed out of their abundance; but she out of her poverty has put in everything she had, all she had to live on."

13

As he came out of the temple, one of his disciples said to him, "Look, Teacher, what large stones and what large buildings!" [2]Then Jesus asked him, "Do you see these great buildings? Not one stone will be left here upon another; all will be thrown down."

[3]When he was sitting on the Mount of Olives opposite the temple, Peter, James, John, and Andrew asked him privately, [4]"Tell us, when will this be, and what will be the sign that all these things are about to be accomplished?" [5]Then Jesus began to say to them, "Beware that no one leads you astray. [6]Many will come in my name and say, 'I am he!' and they will lead many astray. [7]When you hear of wars and rumors of wars, do not be alarmed; this must take place, but the end is still to come. [8]For nation will rise against nation, and kingdom against kingdom; there will be earthquakes in various places; there will be famines. This is but the beginning of the birth pangs.

[9]"As for yourselves, beware; for they will hand you over to councils; and you will be beaten in synagogues; and you will stand before governors and kings because of me, as a testimony to them. [10]And the good news must first be proclaimed to all nations. [11]When they bring you to trial and hand you over, do not worry beforehand about what you are to say; but say whatever is given you at that time, for it is not you who speak, but the Holy Spirit. [12]Brother will betray brother to death, and a father his child, and children will rise against parents and have them put to death; [13]and you will be hated by all because of my name. But the one who endures to the end will be saved.

[14]"But when you see the desolating sacrilege set up where it ought not to be (let the reader understand), then those in Judea must flee to the mountains; [15]the one on the housetop must not go down or enter the house to take anything away; [16]the one in the field must not turn back to get a coat. [17]Woe to those who are pregnant and to those who are nursing infants in those days! [18]Pray that it may not be in winter. [19]For in those days there will be suffering, such as has not been from the beginning of the creation that God created until now, no, and never will be. [20]And if the Lord had not cut short those days, no one would be saved; but for the sake of the elect, whom he chose, he has cut short those days. [21]And if anyone says to you at that time, 'Look! Here is the Messiah!' or 'Look! There he is!'—do not believe it. [22]False messiahs and false prophets will appear and produce signs and omens, to lead astray, if possible, the elect. [23]But be alert; I have already told you everything.

[24]"But in those days, after that suffering,

the sun will be darkened,
and the moon will not give
its light,
[25]and the stars will be falling
from heaven,
and the powers in the heavens
will be shaken.

[26]Then they will see 'the Son of Man
coming in clouds' with great power and
glory. [27]Then he will send out the
angels, and gather his elect from the
four winds, from the ends of the earth
to the ends of heaven.

[28]"From the fig tree learn its lesson:
as soon as its branch becomes tender
and puts forth its leaves, you know that
summer is near. [29]So also, when you see
these things taking place, you know
that he is near, at the very gates. [30]Truly
I tell you, this generation will not pass
away until all these things have taken
place. [31]Heaven and earth will pass
away, but my words will not pass away.

[32]"But about that day or hour no
one knows, neither the angels in
heaven, nor the Son, but only the
Father. [33]Beware, keep alert; for you do
not know when the time will come. [34]It
is like a man going on a journey, when
he leaves home and puts his slaves in
charge, each with his work, and commands the doorkeeper to be on the
watch. [35]Therefore, keep awake—for
you do not know when the master of
the house will come, in the evening, or
at midnight, or at cockcrow, or at dawn,
[36]or else he may find you asleep when
he comes suddenly. [37]And what I say to
you I say to all: Keep awake."

14 It was two days before the Passover and the festival of Unleavened Bread. The chief priests and the
scribes were looking for a way to arrest
Jesus by stealth and kill him; [2]for they
said, "Not during the festival, or there
may be a riot among the people."

[3]While he was at Bethany in the
house of Simon the leper, as he sat at
the table, a woman came with an
alabaster jar of very costly ointment of
nard, and she broke open the jar
and poured the ointment on his head.
[4]But some were there who said to
one another in anger, "Why was the
ointment wasted in this way? [5]For
this ointment could have been sold for
more than three hundred denarii, and
the money given to the poor." And they
scolded her. [6]But Jesus said, "Let her
alone; why do you trouble her? She has
performed a good service for me. [7]For
you always have the poor with you, and
you can show kindness to them whenever you wish; but you will not always
have me. [8]She has done what she could;
she has anointed my body beforehand
for its burial. [9]Truly I tell you, wherever
the good news is proclaimed in the
whole world, what she has done will be
told in remembrance of her."

[10]Then Judas Iscariot, who was one
of the twelve, went to the chief priests
in order to betray him to them. [11]When
they heard it, they were greatly pleased,
and promised to give him money. So he
began to look for an opportunity to
betray him.

[12]On the first day of Unleavened
Bread, when the Passover lamb is sacrificed, his disciples said to him, "Where
do you want us to go and make the
preparations for you to eat the Passover?" [13]So he sent two of his disciples,
saying to them, "Go into the city, and a
man carrying a jar of water will meet
you; follow him, [14]and wherever he
enters, say to the owner of the house,
'The Teacher asks, Where is my guest
room where I may eat the Passover with
my disciples?' [15]He will show you a large
room upstairs, furnished and ready.
Make preparations for us there." [16]So
the disciples set out and went to the
city, and found everything as he had
told them; and they prepared the
Passover meal.

[17]When it was evening, he came
with the twelve. [18]And when they had

taken their places and were eating,
Jesus said, "Truly I tell you, one of you
will betray me, one who is eating with
me." 19 They began to be distressed and
to say to him one after another, "Surely,
not I?" 20 He said to them, "It is one of
the twelve, one who is dipping bread
into the bowl with me. 21 For the Son of
Man goes as it is written of him, but woe
to that one by whom the Son of Man is
betrayed! It would have been better for
that one not to have been born."

22 While they were eating, he took a
loaf of bread, and after blessing it he
broke it, gave it to them, and said,
"Take; this is my body." 23 Then he took
a cup, and after giving thanks he gave it
to them, and all of them drank from it.
24 He said to them, "This is my blood of
the covenant, which is poured out for
many. 25 Truly I tell you, I will never
again drink of the fruit of the vine until
that day when I drink it new in the kingdom of God."

26 When they had sung the hymn,
they went out to the Mount of Olives.
27 And Jesus said to them, "You will all
become deserters; for it is written,

> 'I will strike the shepherd,
> and the sheep will be scattered.'

28 But after I am raised up, I will go
before you to Galilee." 29 Peter said to
him, "Even though all become deserters, I will not." 30 Jesus said to him,
"Truly I tell you, this day, this very
night, before the cock crows twice, you
will deny me three times." 31 But he said
vehemently, "Even though I must die
with you, I will not deny you." And all of
them said the same.

32 They went to a place called
Gethsemane; and he said to his disciples, "Sit here while I pray." 33 He took
with him Peter and James and John,
and began to be distressed and agitated. 34 And he said to them, "I am
deeply grieved, even to death; remain
here, and keep awake." 35 And going a
little farther, he threw himself on the
ground and prayed that, if it were possible, the hour might pass from him.
36 He said, "Abba, Father, for you all
things are possible; remove this cup
from me; yet, not what I want, but what
you want." 37 He came and found them
sleeping; and he said to Peter, "Simon,
are you asleep? Could you not keep
awake one hour? 38 Keep awake and pray
that you may not come into the time
of trial; the spirit indeed is willing,
but the flesh is weak." 39 And again he
went away and prayed, saying the same
words. 40 And once more he came and
found them sleeping, for their eyes
were very heavy; and they did not
know what to say to him. 41 He came a
third time and said to them, "Are you
still sleeping and taking your rest?
Enough! The hour has come; the Son
of Man is betrayed into the hands of
sinners. 42 Get up, let us be going. See,
my betrayer is at hand."

43 Immediately, while he was still
speaking, Judas, one of the twelve,
arrived; and with him there was a crowd
with swords and clubs, from the chief
priests, the scribes, and the elders.
44 Now the betrayer had given them a
sign, saying, "The one I will kiss is the
man; arrest him and lead him away
under guard." 45 So when he came, he
went up to him at once and said,
"Rabbi!" and kissed him. 46 Then they
laid hands on him and arrested him.
47 But one of those who stood near drew
his sword and struck the slave of the
high priest, cutting off his ear. 48 Then
Jesus said to them, "Have you come out
with swords and clubs to arrest me as

though I were a bandit? [49]Day after day
I was with you in the temple teaching,
and you did not arrest me. But let the
scriptures be fufilled." [50]All of them
deserted him and fled.

[51]A certain young man was following
him, wearing nothing but a linen cloth.
They caught hold of him, [52]but he left
the linen cloth and ran off naked.

[53]They took Jesus to the high priest;
and all the chief priests, the elders, and
the scribes were assembled. [54]Peter had
followed him at a distance, right into
the courtyard of the high priest; and he
was sitting with the guards, warming
himself at the fire. [55]Now the chief
priests and the whole council were
looking for testimony against Jesus to
put him to death; but they found none.
[56]For many gave false testimony against
him, and their testimony did not agree.
[57]Some stood up and gave false testimony against him, saying, [58]"We heard
him say, 'I will destroy this temple that
is made with hands, and in three days
I will build another, not made with
hands.'" [59]But even on this point their
testimony did not agree. [60]Then the
high priest stood up before them and
asked Jesus, "Have you no answer?
What is it that they testify against you?"
[61]But he was silent and did not answer.
Again the high priest asked him, "Are
you the Messiah, the Son of the Blessed
One?" [62]Jesus said, "I am: and

'you will see the Son of Man
seated at the right hand of
the Power,'
and 'coming with the clouds
of heaven.'"

[63]Then the high priest tore his clothes
and said, "Why do we still need witnesses? [64]You have heard his blasphemy!
What is your decision?" All of them
condemned him as deserving death.
[65]Some began to spit on him, to blind-
fold him, and to strike him, saying to
him, "Prophesy!" The guards also took
him over and beat him.

[66]While Peter was below in the
courtyard, one of the servant-girls of the
high priest came by. [67]When she saw
Peter warming himself, she stared at
him and said, "You also were with
Jesus, the man from Nazareth." [68]But he
denied it, saying, "I do not know or
understand what you are talking about."
And he went out into the forecourt.
Then the cock crowed. [69]And the servant-
girl, on seeing him, began again to say
to the bystanders, "This man is one of
them." [70]But again he denied it. Then
after a little while the bystanders again
said to Peter, "Certainly you are one of
them; for you are a Galilean." [71]But he
began to curse, and he swore an oath, "I
do not know this man you are talking
about." [72]At that moment the cock
crowed for the second time. Then Peter
remembered that Jesus had said to him,
"Before the cock crows twice, you will
deny me three times." And he broke
down and wept.

15 As soon as it was morning, the
chief priests held a consultation
with the elders and scribes and the
whole council. They bound Jesus, led
him away, and handed him over to
Pilate. [2]Pilate asked him, "Are you the
King of the Jews?" He answered him,
"You say so." [3]Then the chief priests
accused him of many things. [4]Pilate
asked him again, "Have you no answer?
See how many charges they bring
against you." [5]But Jesus made no further reply, so that Pilate was amazed.

[6]Now at the festival he used to
release a prisoner for them, anyone for

whom they asked. [7]Now a man called Barabbas was in prison with the rebels who had committed murder during the insurrection. [8]So the crowd came and began to ask Pilate to do for them according to his custom. [9]Then he answered them, "Do you want me to release for you the King of the Jews?" [10]For he realized that it was out of jealousy that the chief priests had handed him over. [11]But the chief priests stirred up the crowd to have him release Barabbas for them instead. [12]Pilate spoke to them again, "Then what do you wish me to do with the man you call the King of the Jews?" [13]They shouted back, "Crucify him!" [14]Pilate asked them, "Why, what evil has he done?" But they shouted all the more, "Crucify him!" [15]So Pilate, wishing to satisfy the crowd, released Barabbas for them; and after flogging Jesus, he handed him over to be crucified.

[16]Then the soldiers led him into the courtyard of the palace (that is, the governor's headquarters); and they called together the whole cohort. [17]And they clothed him in a purple cloak; and after twisting some thorns into a crown, they put it on him. [18]And they began saluting him, "Hail, King of the Jews!" [19]They struck his head with a reed, spat upon him, and knelt down in homage to him. [20]After mocking him, they stripped him of the purple cloak and put his own clothes on him. Then they led him out to crucify him.

[21]They compelled a passer-by, who was coming in from the country, to carry his cross; it was Simon of Cyrene, the father of Alexander and Rufus. [22]Then they brought Jesus to the place called Golgotha (which means the place of a skull). [23]And they offered him wine mixed with myrrh; but he did not take it. [24]And they crucified him, and divided his clothes among them, casting lots to decide what each should take.

[25]It was nine o'clock in the morning when they crucified him. [26]The inscription of the charge against him read, "The King of the Jews." [27]And with him they crucified two bandits, one on his right and one on his left. [29]Those who passed by derided him, shaking their heads and saying, "Aha! You who would destroy the temple and build it in three days, [30]save yourself, and come down from the cross!" [31]In the same way the chief priests, along with the scribes, were also mocking him among themselves and saying, "He saved others; he cannot save himself. [32]Let the Messiah, the King of Israel, come down from the cross now, so that we may see and believe." Those who were crucified with him also taunted him.

[33]When it was noon, darkness came over the whole land until three in the afternoon. [34]At three o'clock Jesus cried out with a loud voice, "Eloi, Eloi, lema sabachthani?" which means, "My God, my God, why have you forsaken me?" [35]When some of the bystanders heard it, they said, "Listen, he is calling for Elijah." [36]And someone ran, filled a sponge with sour wine, put it on a stick, and gave it to him to drink, saying, "Wait, let us see whether Elijah will come to take him down." [37]Then Jesus gave a loud cry and breathed his last. [38]And the curtain of the temple was torn in two, from top to bottom. [39]Now when the centurion, who stood facing him, saw that in this way he breathed his last, he said, "Truly this man was God's Son!"

[40]There were also women looking on from a distance; among them were Mary Magdalene, and Mary the mother of James the younger and of Joses, and

Salome. 41 These used to follow him and provided for him when he was in Galilee; and there were many other women who had come up with him to Jerusalem.

42 When evening had come, and since it was the day of Preparation, that is, the day before the sabbath, 43 Joseph of Arimathea, a respected member of the council, who was also himself waiting expectantly for the kingdom of God, went boldly to Pilate and asked for the body of Jesus. 44 Then Pilate wondered if he were already dead; and summoning the centurion, he asked him whether he had been dead for some time. 45 When he learned from the centurion that he was dead, he granted the body to Joseph. 46 Then Joseph bought a linen cloth, and taking down the body, wrapped it in the linen cloth, and laid it in a tomb that had been hewn out of the rock. He then rolled a stone against the door of the tomb. 47 Mary Magdalene and Mary the mother of Joses saw where the body was laid.

16 When the sabbath was over, Mary Magdalene, and Mary the mother of James, and Salome bought spices, so that they might go and anoint him. 2 And very early on the first day of the week, when the sun had risen, they went to the tomb. 3 They had been saying to one another, "Who will roll away the stone for us from the entrance to the tomb?" 4 When they looked up, they saw that the stone, which was very large, had already been rolled back. 5 As they entered the tomb, they saw a young man, dressed in a white robe, sitting on the right side; and they were alarmed. 6 But he said to them, "Do not be alarmed; you are looking for Jesus of Nazareth, who was crucified. He has been raised; he is not here. Look, there is the place they laid him. 7 But go, tell his disciples and Peter that he is going ahead of you to Galilee; there you will see him, just as he told you." 8 So they went out and fled from the tomb, for terror and amazement had seized them; and they said nothing to anyone, for they were afraid.

[THE SHORTER ENDING OF MARK]

[[And all that had been commanded them they told briefly to those around Peter. And afterward Jesus himself sent out through them, from east to west, the sacred and imperishable proclamation of eternal salvation.]]

[THE LONGER ENDING OF MARK]

9 [[Now after he rose early on the first day of the week, he appeared first to Mary Magdalene, from whom he had cast out seven demons. 10 She went out and told those who had been with him, while they were mourning and weeping. 11 But when they heard that he was alive and had been seen by her, they would not believe it.

12 After this he appeared in another form to two of them, as they were walking into the country. 13 And they went back and told the rest, but they did not believe them.

14 Later he appeared to the eleven themselves as they were sitting at the table; and he upbraided them for their lack of faith and stubbornness, because they had not believed those who saw him after he had risen. 15 And he said to them, "Go into all the world and proclaim the good news to the whole creation. 16 The one who believes and is baptized will be saved; but the one who does not believe will be condemned. 17 And these signs will accompany those

who believe: by using my name they will cast out demons; they will speak in new tongues; [18]they will pick up snakes in their hands, and if they drink any deadly thing, it will not hurt them; they will lay their hands on the sick, and they will recover."

[19]So then the Lord Jesus, after he had spoken to them, was taken up into heaven and sat down at the right hand of God. [20]And they went out and proclaimed the good news everywhere, while the Lord worked with them and confirmed the message by the signs that accompanied it.]]

*part 2*

# *Literature of the Middle Period*

IT IS A COMMON MISTAKE TO CONSIDER THE MIDDLE PERIOD A DECLINE from the Ancient or an indistinct age awaiting the arrival of the Modern. The conventional three-part historical schema is somewhat artificial and misleading. Writers of the Middle Period did not think of themselves as occupying a mere interruption between two greater ages, and the literature of the period has its own powerful ideas, styles, and historical dynamics that make it equally absorbing to scholars and ordinary readers alike. It is just an unfortunate accident of history that this period has acquired the nondescript name Middle.

Our term "Middle Period" is borrowed from the European term "Middle Ages," or Medieval Period, invented by Renaissance humanists as a disparaging name for the millennium in Europe between the fall of the Roman Empire and the rediscovery of the Greek and Roman classics by Renaissance humanists. Some people still call this millennium the Dark Ages, but the texts presented here should easily dispel that misconception. Hardly a time of cultural stagnation, these centuries were marked by tremendous movement and change around the world.

In this book, the Middle Period extends from the fourth century CE to the seventeenth, which means that in Europe it embraces not only the Middle Ages but the Renaissance as well. Artificial as these boundaries may be, at the beginning of this time span major cultural changes produced deep breaks with ancient traditions. In the West, the decline of the Roman Empire coincided with the rapid spread of Christianity; at the same time in the East, the sudden spread of Buddhism across Asia produced a reorganization of thought and new directions for literature in many languages. The growth of Christianity and Buddhism, and soon afterward of Islam, into "world religions" crossing ethnic and linguistic borders is perhaps the most salient historical feature of the Middle Period as a whole. Most of the literature of this period is religious in tone—more than in the Ancient Period, and much more than in the Modern.

An anthology of world literature is not, of course, an introduction to world religions, and the texts chosen here have not been selected for their value as religious instruction or for the importance of the doctrines they expound. They have been chosen rather for the quality of their literary art. As with Judaism and Hinduism in the Ancient Period, some of the most important texts in these religious traditions have not been included because their importance does not necessarily make them great poetry, narrative, or artful prose. It is possible to appreciate quite deeply the texts we have chosen without possessing the religious faith many of them expect in the reader, and without understanding fully the complex ideas and attitudes that underlie that faith—though of course the greater one's understanding of these, the fuller one's appreciation will be.

Our confidence that great art can transcend cultural differences, however, should not be exaggerated: the most artful texts of widely various cultures and traditions are likely to challenge our notions of what literature is, for each culture has its own notions of what is beautiful and powerful in writing. The Indian dramas of Kālidāsa or the Japanese Nō theatre are likely at first to strike the Western reader raised on Hollywood films as boring, stilted, and pointless. Patience and tolerance are required; appreciation, and finally love, may then follow.

Throughout the Middle Period, Latin, Greek, Sanskrit, and Classical Chinese were maintained as official or sacred languages, but local vernacular languages emerged everywhere as well and grew literary traditions of their own. Indeed, the veritable explosion of vernaculars might be said to be the chief feature of the period's literary history. In general, new vernacular literatures signal the spread of literacy beyond a ruling elite, and the emergence of unofficial traditions gave voice to women and the lower classes. A major exception to this trend is in areas converted to Islam, where the rapid spread of Arabic as an official language tended to significantly modify the vernacular traditions it encountered.

The Middle Period is characterized by vast movements of peoples worldwide. It begins with the invasion of Europe by "barbarians" from Asia, including the Huns and Vandals. When Augustine was born (354 CE), Europe had never heard of the Vandals, but during his lifetime they swept through Europe all the way to Spain, and then east again across North Africa. They were besieging Augustine's city of Hippo in Africa when he died (430 CE). Then they recrossed the Mediterranean to Italy, which they sacked in the wake of the Goths, Germanic "barbarians" who themselves had already conquered Rome in 410 CE. Among the many displaced peoples during this time, the Anglo-Saxons migrated from present-day Germany and Denmark to Britain.

In the seventh and eighth centuries, we see the sudden emergence of major new literary traditions in Northern Europe, the Islamic world, and Japan. In the tenth century, the Vikings of Scandinavia visited the New World and established communities as far away as Russia and Byzantium. In the twelfth century, there was a fruitful mingling of Arab and European cultures in Spain and France, and the Crusades instituted direct contact between Western Europe and the Middle East. Trade grew throughout the period, all the way from Scandinavia to China, through Russia in the north and through Byzantium, Arabia, Persia, and India in the south. In the thirteenth century, the Mongols pushed from China into Europe and the Middle East, extending strong Islamic communities, which had already absorbed Greek and Persian culture, into India and Southeast Asia. Accounts of Marco Polo's and Ibn Battutah's world travels were circulated in the fourteenth century. China and Japan received missions from Europe in the fifteenth and sixteenth centuries, even as Europe was making its first contacts with the civilizations of the New World. Only recently have we come to appreciate that the New World had literary traditions of its own: Mayan civilization extends back to the Ancient Period, and its one surviving epic, *The Popul Vuh,* may be as old as St. Augustine's *Confessions* and Kālidāsa's *Śākuntala.*

By the end of the sixteenth century, the pace of global cultural contact had accelerated to a point that we might conveniently label as "modern." The Modern Period can be defined in part by truly global communication and literature, as virtually all of the world's literary traditions come into contact with each other, clash, combine, and mingle. This process, which may seem to distinguish our own time from the past, is, however, only an extension of the huge global movements of the Middle Period.

# The Middle East of the Middle Period

In the Ancient Period, the Middle East produced great literature in many languages (especially Sumerian, Babylonian, Egyptian, Hebrew, Aramaic, Persian, and Greek) and nurtured two world religions that have flourished into the present, Judaism and Christianity. During the Middle Period, the region offered the world yet another language and literature, namely Arabic, and another major world religion, Islam. This new culture not only came to dominate the entire Middle East but extended itself westward as far as Spain, south through Africa, and eastward as far as Indonesia. The development of both Arabic and Islam in turn led to a renaissance of Persian literature and thought, and the cultural exchange between Persian and Arabic literature enhanced both traditions. So although the years 300 to 1700 are considered a "Middle Period" in world literature, they witness the rise and fall of "classical," "medieval," and "renaissance" eras in Middle Eastern literature.

Important developments include a pre-Islamic heroic age preserved in writing (c. 500–622); an age of expansion and the Islamic world of the Umayyad dynasty (622–750); the Golden Age of Arabic literature under the 'Abbasid dynasty (750–1055); the age of Mongol invasions, including a growth of local dynasties and the flowering of regional literatures, mostly in Arabic (1055–1258); and finally, the rise of the Ottoman empire, which spread across the Middle East from 1258 into the Modern Period.

When Arabic moved into written culture, it did so with a distinctly sixth-century Bedouin inflection, but because the language spread in connection with Islam far beyond Arabia (and because many preeminent writers in the language were not Arab), to speak of "Arabic literature" is to oversimplify the situation. Spreading out from its origin in the nomadic tribes and desert settlements of Arabia across a vast world stage, Arabic literature is a category of writings that extends from Spain to Turkey, from Egypt to Iran, from Arabia and Africa to India and to Southeast Asia. It includes Muslims, Jews, Christians, and writers from other religious groups as well; consequently, distinct cultural and ethnic differences often make generalizations about "Arabic literature" naive or impossible. "Literature" is also a problematic term in the Islamic world, because religious, philosophic, historical, and scientific texts of all kinds were considered equally "literary" within this tradition.

Arabic literature came into its own after the Qur'ān established the importance of the written word in an unprecedented way in the seventh century. Seeking to understand the sacred text's meaning more thoroughly, scholars preserved pre-Islamic verse that had been part of the oral tradition during Muhammad's lifetime. As a result, written Arabic exploded quite suddenly onto the stage of world culture. The *Jāhiliyyah* ("Time of Ignorance") before Islam yielded important information about grammar, vocabulary, and philology that Qur'ānic scholars craved. The earliest extant pre-Islamic poetic forms include the *qit'ah* or "fragment" (a short verse form) and the longer *qasīdah,* or ode, which is classical Arabic's greatest form. The *qasīdah,* like the Homeric hymn of ancient Greece, was highly developed by the time it was first recorded in writing, having evolved over centuries into a sophisticated genre with its own established conventions, themes, and thematic structures.

Poetry of the *Jāhiliyyah* explores the concerns of nomadic peoples. Tribal and kinship loyalties are primary; and the constant motion of nomadic life, with its nostalgia for traces of encampments in the sand and for people and places, and its commitment to remember heroic deeds are common motifs. Camels, horses, palms, tents, pools, sand, and wild animals are frequent images; and poems celebrate gritty heroism, love, beauty, war, and leadership. The odes also mourn the loss of love and life, kin and tribe, losses especially pronounced in a world of intense interdependence set against the challenge of the forbidding desert. Alongside these endorsements of tribal life are poems about treachery, betrayal, thievery, and murder. The most poignant texts for modern readers are probably the poems of exile, some written by outlaws sentenced to extreme isolation and faced with severe ordeals, men who had to create meaningful lives without the help of a human community. Grounded in concrete images of the desert, the *qasīdahs* rarely move into the overtly mythical or spiritual—though it is important to note that because of the Islamic monotheistic religious aims of the compilers, much sacred and mythic verse from the pre-Islamic polytheistic world has probably not survived.

Muhammad's teachings brought a dramatic shift in the ethics and practices of tribal Arabia. Above all, belief in an afterlife obtained by faith and good works subordinated heroism to religious action. Loyalty shifted away from family and tribe to God, and tribal separatism and ethnocentricism were discouraged. As with all great religious teachings, this teaching was, however, often ignored in practice. The growth and spread of Islam and a common language created possibilities for cultural interchange throughout the Middle East and contributed to the great flowering of Arabic literature during the Middle Period. Dramatic evidence of cross-cultural exchange with ancient Greece can be found in the number of Arabic translations and commentaries on Greek philosophic and scientific texts. For hundreds of years, Cairo, Cordova, Damascus, Basra, Nishapour, and Baghdad far outshone the great cities of the European Middle Ages in terms of intellectual and artistic life. The tenth-century Andalusian leader Hakam II, for example, amassed a palace library of 400,000 volumes and founded twenty-seven "public" schools. The religious and cultural centrality of the Qur'ān, the lack of an established clergy, and the abundance of great wealth contributed to literacy levels throughout the Islamic world that exceeded those of Christian Europe.

Considerable cross-cultural exchange and an expansive Islamic empire under the 'Abbasid dynasty led Muslim philosophy and literature to take many forms. Rationalists, materialists, Neoplatonists and mystics gave rise to a tremendously dissonant but vital artistic and intellectual world. Materialists argued that pleasure was the primary purpose of life, and this sentiment echoed through Arabic verse of the Middle Period. Neoplatonists claimed that all things emanate from the oneness of God's mind, that multiplicity is an illusion, and that the soul experiences alienation and separation from the oneness of the universe because it has fallen into matter. This impulse was shared by Sufism, an influential Islamic form of mysticism, which assumed that the particular resonates with allegorical meaning and reaches toward the divine. The literary tradition that evolved from Sufi mysticism is exemplified in the works of the great female mystic Rābi'ah of Basra, the great Egyptian writer Ibn al-Fārid, the prolific Ibn 'Arabī, who was born in Spain but composed most of his verse in Damascus, and the Persian writers Jalāl al-Dīn Rūmī and Farīd al-Dīn Attar.

In Muslim mysticism of the Middle Period, especially from the ninth century onward, a monistic impulse was powerful. Under monism, the soul was often described as verging on identity with God. Spark and fire, part and whole, present and eternity were explained as simply illusions of a reality that is one. (Readers fascinated with this idea will find it expressed in slightly different form in Indian Buddhism, in The Vimalakīrti Sutra [pp. 260–265], and in Chinese Daoism, in Zhuangzi's *On the Equality of Things* [pp. 350–359].) The mystical impulse in Arabic thought created some of the finest poetry in the world. In this poetry, the Sufi (like the Buddhist and the Daoist) struggles to articulate in language an experience that is beyond language. The intuition, or soul, which is set above reason as a bridge to an ecstatic understanding or experience of divinity, makes demands on language that exceed its capacity, but in the effort, language is used in exciting new ways. Erotic verses, drinking poems, parables, and fables are all used allegorically to communicate the desire for, or the experience of, union with God. But mysticism often threatens institutional religion, because it assumes that individuals can perceive God directly, without the mediation of institutions or orthodox practices. For example, the martyr al-Hallāj claimed, "I am He whom I love and He whom I love is I. . . . I am He who drowned the people of Noah. I am the Truth." He was put to death. Somewhat less radical, the poems of Rūmī and Attar attempt to express the veil of illusion that hangs over the material world and human perception, and both men used writing to express the Sufi path toward God.

Islamic Arabic literature is not only a literature of religion and philosophy, however. As learning and literature flourished, a highly ornate and allusion-laden literacy developed, especially around courts and major intellectual centers. This gave rise to new poetic forms like the *ghazal,* a love lyric that reached its canonical form in eleventh- and twelfth-century Persian poets and in numerous Arabic poets from Al-Andalus (Moorish Spain).

Arabic prose has a history of its own. The pre-Islamic Arabian world yielded prose versions of ancient oral tales, both fantastic and historical. They typically record raids and alliances between tribal groups. Individual heroes and their mothers often receive considerable attention, as do heroic battles, fantastic events, and particularly suspenseful episodes. The tales are episodic and expand to include poems delivered at emotionally important moments. This style influenced Ibn Ishāq's *Life of the Prophet,* which includes many poetic passages ascribed to historical figures. Detailed battle scenes abound in both the pre-Islamic prose material and in later Arabic histories and Arabic-Persian fictional narratives. The popular *Thousand and One Nights* and the innumerable romances that gradually emerged as a tremendously popular genre in both Arabic and Persian also belong to this prose tradition. Widespread literacy gave rise to personal writing too, such as letters, essays, and memoirs like Usāmah's *Book of Reflections.* The vast geographic expanses that housed Islam encouraged trade and travel and popularized a genre of literature known as *Rihlah* (the book of travels), most dramatically represented here by the work of Ibn Battutah, who traveled at least 75,000 miles from northwest Africa to Arabia and on to India, China, and present-day Turkey.

The 'Abbasid empire spread itself thinly over a huge geographic expanse, and this, coupled with a tendency to transfer military and even political power to native peoples, left it vulnerable to revolt and invasion. The repeated invasion of Palestine by European crusaders during the twelfth and thirteenth centuries had less impact on the Arabic world than it did on Europe, but Arabic learning and literature slowed considerably in the face of serious invasions by Mongol groups. The first were the Seljuk Turks (the people of the *Dede Korkut*), who swept across northern Islamic regions until they captured the Baghdad Caliphate in 1055. The Turks installed a puppet government in the Caliphate and eventually ruled Persia, Syria, Iraq, and much of Central Asia. After the Seljuks, Mongols under the leadership of Genghis Khan swept across Europe and the Middle East in the thirteenth century. The great Khan's invasion of Muslim territory began in 1219, and by 1258 his son had control of Baghdad. The main Mongol force later withdrew into Persia, converted to Islam, and established its own dynasties.

Tartars, led by one of Ghengis Khan's sons, made yet another invading sweep into northern Islamic areas. These two Mongol invasions may have been relatively brief, but they brought dramatic changes to the Middle East. During just forty years of invasion, many Middle Eastern cities were stripped of their wealth and demolished; any city that resisted was burned and its population annihilated. It has been estimated that the population of Muslims dropped by half as a result of the Mongol and Tartar invasions. Overrun by the nomadic invaders, Persia became less and less attached to the dynasties in Arabia. Mongol dynasties in Persia accentuated Iran's difference from the Arab world, driving a wedge between different population groups and hardening religious differences.

The economically depleted Middle East, separated from Persia, was open to yet one more invasion during the late Middle Period—the Ottoman conquests. The Ottoman Turks, a branch of the Seljuks, gradually conquered most of Central Asia, toppling Constantinople in 1453. They invaded the Balkans, annexed Hungary, and made raids on wealthy Italian cities. By the sixteenth century, they had incorporated parts of Persia, Egypt, Arabia, and Mesopotamia into their empire. At the same time, Western boundaries with Christendom also proved unsustainable; the last remnants of Al-Andalus (Spain) were conquered by Europeans in 1492, the same year Columbus landed in the Americas. European exploration by sea opened new trade routes to the East, bypassing the caravan routes that had sustained Arabia and the Middle East throughout the Middle Period. The innovations and classical refinements that marked the Middle East's literary outpourings during the Middle Period gradually slowed, and traditional Arabic forms reestablished their power and dominance over the less revered texts of the more modern periods.

## THREE QASIDAHS (6TH–7TH CENT.)

*Translated by Suzanne Pinckney Stetkevych*

Of all pre-Islamic Arabic poetry, the *qasīdahs* or "odes" are the most famous and influential. They surfaced in early Islamic written culture, emerging out of an oral poetic tradition reaching back as far as 500 BCE. Twentieth-century Arabic poets still compose in this genre. The *qasīdahs* usually consist of praise, satire, love, and lamentation but can include lengthy descriptions, self-glorification, and aphorisms. Conventional *qasīdahs* feature fifteen to a hundred lines of metered mono-rhyme organized into three sections, which are associatively linked. To approach this material successfully, a reader needs to suspend strictly linear expectations and seek out metaphoric, symbolic, and associational connections among the sections.

The ode typically begins with a *nasīb,* a nostalgic prelude expressing longing for a lover, a place, or a former time. This section also develops a mood, image, or theme, which points to the purpose of the poem. Imru' al-Qays's *nasīb* is considered the greatest in ancient Arabic poetry because of its allusive opening lines (1–6): here the poet tells his riding companions to stop beside the traces of a former campsite where he tearfully recalls the past. The *nasīb* of Labīd (lines 1–21) incorporates a similar scene and features two friends who accompany the poet, a common convention. Some scholars think that ancient Mesopotamian hymns in praise of deities can be heard faintly in the *nasīb* or "love poetry" of the *qasīdah.*

A *takhallus,* the "disengagement" section of the *qasīdah,* tells of a journey, usually with elaborate descriptions of the horse or camel (see Labīd, lines 22–54). Isolated, the poet moves out into the wilderness with only his camel or horse. This section can also articulate a psychological or emotional movement away from the pain expressed in the *nasīb,* as in Imru' al-Qays (lines 7–52), who relates a series of illicit erotic encounters that do not lead the speaker away from loss but back to it, perhaps suggesting that the love affairs of youth will not provide consolation.

The last section, the *gharad* (see Labīd, lines 55–88; al-Qays, lines 53–82), expresses the purpose of the poem. In Labīd's *Mu'allaqah,* the *gharad* praises the poet's tribe. In Imru' al-Qays, the *gharad* is polyvalent, suggesting spiritual enlightenment (the lightning flash), heroic action (the battle), and change (the storm). Al-Qays's poem, like most great *qasīdahs,* weaves images of culture and nature into complex and shifting relationships. The poem suggests a movement from social dissolution and violation (figured in the ruins of communities and the isolated, liminal sexual exploits of the poet) to a restored and renewed world, the storm having brought rain and renewed life to the desert.

The two poems by Imru' al-Qays and Labīd belong in the *Mu'allaqāt,* the most famous collection of *qasīdahs. Mu'allaqāt* means "suspended," referring to the legend that prize-winning poems were hung in the *Ka'bah* (temple) at the conclusion of poetry competitions held regularly in Mecca. Although many *qasīdahs* exist, those in the *Mu'allaqāt* have long been considered the best and are part of Arabic school curricula today. Although the exact list of poems included in this collection of pre-Islamic verse varies from place to place, the collection includes some seven to ten works, and Imru'al-Qays's poem is nearly always regarded as the best of the best.

The *Lāmiyyat al-'Arab* (Arab ode rhyming in "L") by al-Shanfarā is not part of the *Mu'allaqāt,* but its brilliance has long been acknowledged. It belongs to a subgroup of *qasīdahs* called *su'lūk* or "outlaw" odes. Shanfarā himself was a legendary outlaw and murderer who roamed the desert marauding at random after he was apparently disowned even by his own people. He could reputedly outrun an antelope. He is said to have been tricked, captured, and finally slain by a kinsman who called his murderous deed an act of "eating familiar fruit," a description that suggests the sacrificial status of the liminal figure.

Shanfarā's *su'lūk* begins with a rejection of tribal culture and an alliance of wildness, weapons, and self. Like famous outlaw figures in other ancient and medieval texts, the poet rejects what he sees as the weaknesses of society and cultivates the wildness of liminal heroism. As outcast and criminal, he is gradually stripped of all signs of civilization: weapons, wine, food, bathing, and love. He becomes the prey or sacrifice hunted by society. The concluding image of the poet as a long-horned buck circled by parading she-goats echoes the ritualistic circling of fertility idols in pre-Islamic religious rites. He returns to the community of animals, having escaped the hunter; but standing in for a god, he embodies the sacred sacrifice or scapegoat as well.

## *Imru' al-Qays, Mu'allaqah*

**1.** Halt, two friends, and we will weep for the memory of one beloved
And an abode at Siqṭ al-Liwā between al-Dakhūl, then Ḥawmal,

**2.** Then Tūḍiḥ, then al-Miqrāt, whose trace was not effaced
By the two winds weaving over it from south and north.

**3.** You see the droppings of white antelope
Scattered on its outer grounds and lowlands like peppercorns,

**4.** As if I, on the morning that they loaded up their beasts,
Before the tribe's acacia trees, were splitting colocynth.

**5.** My companions, halting there their mounts for me,
Say, Do not perish out of grief, control yourself!

**6.** Surely my cure is tears poured forth;
Then, at a worn-out trace is there a place for weeping?

**7.** [Console yourself] As was your wont before her with Umm al-Ḥuwayrith
And her neighbor at Mount Ma'sal, Umm al-Rabāb!

**8.** When they arose there wafted from them musk as redolent
As the east breeze when it bears the scent of clove.

**9.** Then my eyes, out of ardent love, sent down a flood of tears upon my neck
Till my sword belt was soaked in tears.

**10.** Did you not have many a fine day from them?
And best of all the day at Dārat Juljul?

**11.** And the day when, for the virgins, I hocked my mount,
—What an amazing sight!—they made off with her saddle and its gear!

**12.** Then through the day the virgins tossed her meat,
And her fat like twisted fringes of white Damascus silk.

**13.** And the day I entered the howdah, 'Unayzah's howdah,
Then she said, Woe to you! You'll make me go on foot.

**14.** She kept saying, when the high-sided saddle listed with our weight,
You have hocked my camel, O Imru' al-Qays, So get down!

**15.** Keep going, I said to her, slacken his reins,
But don't drive me away from your twice-to-be-tasted fruit!

**16.** Then many a woman like you, pregnant and nursing,
have I visited by night,
And distracted from her amuleted one-year-old.

**17.** When he cried from behind her, she turned her upper half toward him,
But the half that was beneath me did not budge.

**18.** And one day on a sand dune's back she rebuffed me,
And swore an oath never to be broken.

**19.** O Fāṭimah, don't try me with your teasing,
[Or] if you have resolved to cut me off, then do it gently.

**20.** Are you deluded about me because your love is my slayer
And whatever you command my heart it does?

**21.** If something of my character has hurt you,
Then pull my clothes away from yours, they will slip off.

**22.** Your eyes do not shed tears but to pierce
with your two shafts the pieces of my slaughtered heart.

**23.** Many an "egg" of the curtained quarters, whose tent none dares to seek,
I took my pleasure with her, unhurried.

**24.** I stole past guards to get to her, past clansmen
Eager, could they conceal it, to slay me.

**25.** When the Pleiades spread out across the sky
Like a girdle's spread-out pleats, alternating gold and gems,

**26.** I came when she, before the tent curtain, had shed her clothes for sleep,
And was clad in nothing but an untied shift.

**27.** She said, God's oath! There's no way to dissuade you,
And I don't see the veil lift from your error.

**28.** I led her forth from her tent, walking as she trailed
Over our tracks the train of her gown of figured silk.

**29.** Then, when we had crossed the clan's enclosure
And made our way to a sandy hollow surrounded by long-winding dunes,

**30.** I drew her temples toward me, and she leaned over me
With hollow waist, but plump the place that anklets ring.

**31.** Slender-waisted, white, not flabby,
Her collarbone shone like a polished mirror.

**32.** Now hiding, now baring a cheek long and wide,
She guards herself with the glance of a wild doe at Wajrah with fawn,

**33.** And a neck like the neck of the white antelope,
Not overly long when she raises it, or lacking ornament.

**34.** A head of hair, jet-black, adorns her back,
Luxuriant as a bunch of dates on a cluster-laden palm.

**35.** Some of its locks are secured on top,
While others stray between the plaited and the loose.

**36.** A waist delicate, like a twisted bowstring, trim,
A lower leg like the papyrus reed, well-watered, tender.

**37.** In the forenoon crumbs of musk still deck her bed,
And she, late morning sleeper, still is clad in sleeping gown, ungirded.

**38.** She grasps with fingers, soft, uncalloused, as if they were
The worms of Ẓaby or the supple tooth sticks of the *isḥil* tree.

**39.** When night falls she lights up the dark as if she were
A lamp in the night cell of an anchorite.

**40.** At one like her the staid man gazes with ardor
When she stands in her full stature between woman's gown
and maiden's shift,

**41.** Like the first inviolate bloom, white mixed with yellow,
Nurtured on water limpid and unmuddied by alighting traveler.

**42.** [Grown] men find consolation from the follies of their youth,
But my heart refuses solace for its love for you.

**43.** How many an enemy, quarreling over you,
Not neglectful of advice or of rebuke, did I repel?

**44.** Many a night like the billowing sea let down its veils over me
With all kinds of cares to test me.

**45.** Then I said to it when it stretched out its spine,
Followed with its hindquarters, and heaved its ponderous breast,

**46.** Alas, long night, will you not dispel, revealing dawn,
Though the dawn of day will be no better for me.

**47.** Then, oh what a night you are! as if its stars
Were all bound by tight-twisted ropes to Mount Yadhbul,

**48.** As if the Pleiades were in midcourse suspended
By flaxen cords from obdurate rock.

**49.** And many a waterskin of the clans have I borne its leathern strap
Upon my shoulder, submissive and much traveled.

**50.** And many a riverbed, a bare waste like the belly of an ass, I crossed,
Where the wolf howled like an outcast profligate
with many mouths to feed.

**51.** So when he howled I said to him, Our lot is meager sustenance
If you have not gained wealth, [for I have none].

**52.** Each of us when he acquires a thing, it soon escapes him,
Whoever tills your tilth and mine, it will leave lean.

**53.** I would ride forth early, the birds still in their nests,
On a steed sleek and swift, a shackle for wild game, huge.

**54.** Now wheeling, now charging, advancing, retreating, all at once,
Like a mighty boulder the torrent has washed down from the heights.

**55.** A dark bay from whose back the saddle pad slips,
Like raindrops from hard rock,

**56.** Despite leanness, spirited as if his bursting gallop,
When he seethes with heat, were a cauldron's boil,

**57.** Pouring forth his gallop when, despite fatigue, the coursers
On the hard and trampled plain stir up the dust.

**58.** The slender youth he makes slip from his back,
The robes of the rugged, bulky rider he sends flying out behind,

**59.** Streaming like a boy's button-on-a-string, when he has tightly twisted it
By his hands' successive circling the connecting string.

**60.** He has the flanks of a gazelle fawn, the ostrich's two legs,
The wolf's lope, the fox cub's canter.

**61.** Huge-ribbed, when you look from behind,
a full tail blocks the gap between his legs,
Reaching almost to the ground, not crooked.

**62.** As if when he heads off there were mounted on his rump a stone
A bride pounds perfumes with or on which colocynth is crushed,

**63.** As if the blood of the herd's front-runners upon his throat
Were henna juice upon an old man's combed and hoary head.

**64.** Then there appeared before us an oryx herd as if its cows were virgins
Circling round a sacred stone in long-trained gowns.

**65.** They turned about like alternated onyx beads upon the neck
Of a child nobly uncled in the clan from dam and sire.

**66.** Then he let us catch the herd's lead runners
And outstripped those that lagged in an unbroken cluster.

**67.** One after the other, he hit a bull and cow,
And yet was not awash with sweat.

**68.** Then the meat cooks kept on cooking both meat laid upon the rocks
To roast well-done, and meat quick boiled in cauldrons.

**69.** And our glance, in the evening, almost failed before him,
To whatever spot the eye was raised, dazzled, it dropped.

**70.** All night he remained, his saddle and bridle upon him,
All night he stood beneath my eye, not loosed to graze.

**71.** O friend, do you see the lightning? There is its flash—
Like two hands shining in a high-crowned cumulus!

**72.** Its flash illumining the sky, or like the sudden flare of a monk's lamp,
When, tilting it, he soaks with oil the tightly twisted wick.

**73.** Between Dārij and al-'Udhayb I sat with my companions
to watch the storm,
How distant was the object of my gaze!

**74.** Over Mount Qaṭan, as I read the signs,
the right flank of its downpour falls,
Over Mount al-Sitār, then Mount Yadhbul, falls the left.

**75.** Then in the forenoon it was pouring its water down around Kutayfah,
Overturning the lofty *kanahbal* trees upon their beards.

**76.** It passed its fringes over Mount Qanān,
And drove the white-footed mountain goats down every path.

**77.** In Taymā' it did not leave a single palm trunk standing,
Or a single castle but those built of stone.

**78.** As if Mount Thabīr in the foremost of its rains
Were a tribal chieftain wrapped in a striped cloak,

**79.** As if the peaks of Mount Mujaymir's crest at morning
Ringed with the torrent's dross were the whorl of a spindle,

**80.** It deposited its load on the low-lying desert
Like a Yemeni alighting with his [fabric]-laden bags,

**81.** As if, early in the morning, the songbirds of the valley
Had drunk a morning draught of fine spiced wine,

**82.** As if the wild beasts drowned at evening in its remotest stretches
Were wild onions' plucked-out bulbs.

## *Labīd, Mu'allaqah*

1. Effaced are the abodes, brief encampments and long-settled ones;
At Minā the wilderness has claimed Mount Ghawl and Mount Rijām.
2. The torrent channels of Mount Rayyān, their tracings are laid bare,
Preserved as surely as inscriptions are preserved in rock,
3. Dung-darkened patches over which, since they were peopled, years elapsed,
Their profane months and sacred ones have passed away.
4. They were watered by the rain the spring stars bring,
And on them fell the rain of thunderclouds, downpour and drizzle
5. From each night-faring rain cloud and early morning horizon-darkener
And cloud at forenoon with resounding rumble.
6. The *ayhuqān* thrust up its shoots, and on the two sides of the valley
Gazelles and ostriches have borne their young.
7. Wide-eyed oryx cows, newly-calved, stand above their newborns, motionless,
While on the plain the yearlings in clusters caper.
8. The torrents have exposed the ruins, as if they were
Writings whose texts pens have inscribed anew
9. Or like the tattooer sprinkling lampblack again and yet again
Over hands on which tattoos appear.
10. Then I stopped and questioned them, but how do we question
Mute immortals whose speech is indistinct?
11. Stripped bare where once a folk had dwelled, then one morn departed;
Abandoned lay the trench that ran around the tents,
the *thumām* grass that plugged their holes.
12. The clanswomen departing stirred your longing
when they loaded up their gear,
Then climbed inside their howdah frames with squeaking tents,
13. The howdahs each enclosed with wooden frame, covered by a woolen carpet,
And shaded by fine veil and figured drape,
14. In clusters they departed, as if the howdahs bore the wild cows of Tūḍiḥ
And the white does of Wajrah tenderly inclining over their young.
15. They were urged on, and the mirage dissolved them till they were like
The windings of the riverbed of Bīshah, its tamarisks and boulders.
16. What then do you remember of Nawār when she has gone far off,
And her bonds, both firm and frayed, are cut asunder?
17. A Murrite woman who alit in Fayd,
then dwelled nearby the people of Ḥijāz,
How then could you hope to meet with her again?
18. On the eastward slopes of Ṭayy's two mounts
she alighted, or on Muḥajjir's mount,
Then a lone peak contained her, and its foothills,
19. Then in Ṣuwā'iq if she headed toward the Yemen, so that by now
She is most likely in its Wiḥāf al-Qahr, or in Ṭilkhām.

**20.** Cut off your love from him whose bond is not secure,
For the best binder of affection's bond is he who breaks it.

**21.** Be generous to him who treats you well,
but only the cutting of bonds remains
When affection falters and its foundation fails,

**22.** With a camel mare jaded by journeys that have reduced her to a remnant,
Till she is emaciate of loins and hump.

**23.** When her flesh has dwindled and she is exhausted,
And after great fatigue her leathern shoe thongs are cut through,

**24.** Yet is she as nimble in the reins as if she were a rose-hued cloud,
Rain-emptied, running with the south wind, sprightly.

**25.** Or is she like a she-ass, teats milk-swollen, pregnant by a stallion
white-bellied
And gaunt from repelling rivals, biting them and kicking.

**26.** Much scratched and bitten he mounts with her the hump-backed hills,
Perplexed by his pregnant mate's recalcitrance and cravings.

**27.** Above the jagged heights of Thalabūt he scouts the empty lookout posts,
Fearful of hunters hid behind the roadmarks made of stone.

**28.** Until when winter's six months pass, they live on moisture from the grass,
Long avoiding waterholes, both he and she.

**29.** Then they put their trust in resolution, tightly twisted,
For the success of one's resolve lies in its firmness.

**30.** Then the blades of *buhmā* grass pricked at her pasterns,
And the summer wind picked up, its passing gusts and fiery blasts.

**31.** Back and forth they tugged a flowing train of stirred-up dust
Whose cloud flies up like smoke when the kindling is lit,

**32.** Fanned by the north wind, mixed with the thorny *'arfaj* tree's green wood,
Like the smoke of a mighty blaze with leaping flames.

**33.** Then he continued driving her before him, for it was his custom,
When she strayed or lagged behind, to drive her on ahead.

**34.** They plunged into the middle of a rivulet
And cut through to a brimming spring grown thick with reeds,

**35.** On all sides surrounded by a stand of canes
That shaded it with fallen stalks and stalks still standing.

**36.** Is my camel mare like this or like the oryx cow, her calf the wild beasts' prey,
Who, though among the lead bull's wards, now lagged behind the herd,

**37.** A snub-nosed cow bereft of calf, who mid the stony tracts between the dunes
Does not leave off her roaming and her lowing

**38.** For a calf half-weaned and white, its limbs torn back and forth
By ashen predators who never hunger long.

**39.** They chanced upon it unawares and struck;
Indeed fate's arrows never miss their mark.

40. She waited through the night beneath a cloud
that shed an unremitting rain
And let a ceaseless downpour fall upon the dense-grown dunes.

41. Uninterrupted raindrops fell on her spine's track
In a night whose stars were veiled by clouds.

42. She took shelter in the hollow of a contorted tree
Set apart upon the edges of the dunes whose drift-sand slopes.

43. And in the first watch of the night her lustrous face
Gleamed like the diver's pearl, its string drawn forth.

44. Till, when the dark dispelled and dawn shone forth,
Her hoofs slipped on the early morning's rain-soaked earth.

45. Bewildered, she searched doggedly among Ṣu'ā'id's puddles
Seven full nights coupled with their days.

46. Until, hope's stores exhausted, and udder, once milk-swollen,
Neither from suckling nor weaning now gone dry,

47. She heard with dread the buzz of human voice
That frightened her from unseen side—
For mankind is her bane.

48. Then early in the day she ventured forth, fearing for head and tail,
Dangers from behind and from in front

49. Until when the hunters in despair of bow and arrow
Set on her their rawhide-collared, flop-eared hounds.

50. They overtook her, and she returned their charge
With a horn like a Samharī spear in point and shaft

51. To ward them off, for she knew
If she did not repel them she would die.

52. Fetch was first to fall, smeared all in blood,
Then Blackie was left for dead where he had charged.

53. On this one when sun's shimmerings dance in full forenoon light,
And the hillocks don the cloaks of the mirage

54. I attend my own heart's needs, not neglecting them for fear
that others will think ill of me or rebukers blame me.

55. Did Nawār not know that I am both
He who ties the knots in ropes and he who cuts them?

56. He who leaves a place that does not please him,
Unless his own soul's fate overtakes him there.

57. And don't you know how many a night mild in its weather,
Delightful in its sport and in its revelry,

58. I spent as its convivial, and rushed to many a merchant's banner
When it was raised and the price of wine was high.

59. I paid a dear price for a wine in an aged and darkened wineskin,
Or in a pitch-lined jug, ladled into cups, its seal broken.

**60.** And many a morning draught of a pure wine and a slave girl with a lute,
Plucking with her thumb on its taut strings.

**61.** My first cup I downed before the cock could crow in daybreak
To take a second when its sleepers woke.

**62.** And many a bitter morn of wind and cold I curbed,
When its reins were in the hand of the north wind.

**63.** I defended the tribe, my battle gear borne by a winning courser,
Her reins my sash when I went forth at dawn.

**64.** Then I mounted a lookout post on a narrow, wind-blown peak
Whose dust rose to the banners of the foe

**65.** Until when daylight dipped its hand into the all-concealing night,
And darkness veiled the crotches of each mountain pass,

**66.** To the plain I descended and my mare held erect her neck
Like the date palm's stripped trunk at which the picker's courage falls.

**67.** I spurred her to a speed fit for the ostrich chase,
Until when she was heated through and her bones were nimble,

**68.** Her light leathern saddle slipped, sweat flowed from her neck,
And her saddle girth was soaked with froth.

**69.** She coursed, head held high and thrusting in the bridle, racing headlong
Like a thirsting dove to water when her flock beats urgent wings.

**70.** And many a chief's domed tent, where unknown strangers sojourn,
Its favor hoped for, its displeasure feared,

**71.** Its men burly-necked, lionlike, braced for revenge,
As if they were the Jinn of al-Badī, their feet fixed in the earth.

**72.** Their false claims I denied, their due rights recognized,
And no nobleman among them could vaunt his glory over me.

**73.** And many a *maysir* players' slaughter camel its death I called for
By the fate-sealing arrows whose shafts look all alike,

**74.** Summoning them to a she-camel, barren or with foal,
Her meat bestowed on all whom we have granted refuge.

**75.** Then for the guest and for the foreign refugee, it is as if
They had descended to Tabālah Valley, its lowlands ever green.

**76.** Every indigent woman seeks the refuge of my tent ropes,
Emaciated, rag-clad, like a starved she-camel hobbled
at her master's grave.

**77.** When winter's winds wail back and forth her orphans plunge
Into streams of flowing gravy which my clan crowns with meat.

**78.** When tribal councils gather there is always one of us
Who contends in grave affairs and shoulders them,

**79.** A divider of spoils who gives each clan its due,
Demanding their rights for the worthy, the rights of the worthless refusing

80. Out of superior might; a man munificent, who with his bounty succors,
Openhanded; a winner and plunderer of all that he desires,
81. From a clan whose fathers set for them their law—
For each tribe has its leader and its law.
82. Their honor is not sullied, their deeds not without issue,
For their judgment is not swayed by passion's flights.
83. Be then content, O enemy, with what the sovereign allotted you,
For virtues were allotted us by him who knows them.
84. When trusts were apportioned to the tribes,
The apportioner allotted us the greatest share.
85. He built for us a high-roofed edifice,
To which the tribesmen mount, both youths and full-grown men.
86. They are the first to act when the tribe is stricken;
In war, its horsemen; in disputes, its arbiters.
87. They are a springtime to those that seek refuge
And to indigent women, their food stores exhausted,
while the year stretches long.
88. They form a band so tight that none of them impedes it out of envy,
Nor, out of treachery, leans toward the foe.

## *al-Shanfara, Lamiyyat al-'Arab*

1. Raise, my brothers, the chests of your mounts, set them straight;
As for me, I incline toward another tribe.
2. The provisions have been readied, the night is moonlit,
The mounts strapped and saddled for your journeys' ends.
3. In the land there is for the noble-hearted a place remote from harm;
For him who fears hatred, a refuge.
4. By your life, the earth does not constrain a man who travels by night,
Whether by free will or by force, if he has his wits about him.
5. I have closer kin than you, a wolf, swift and sleek,
A smooth and spotted leopard (smooth speckled snake),
and a long-maned one—a hyena.
6. They are kin among whom a secret, once confided, is not revealed;
Nor is the criminal forsaken for his crimes.
7. Each one is haughty-proud and reckless-brave, except that I,
When the first of the prey appear, am braver.
8. But when hands stretch into the provision bags, I am not the quickest;
For then the greediest clansman is quicker.
9. This is nothing but my more expansive magnanimity,
For the magnanimous man is the most virtuous.

**10.** To recompense the loss of those who do not requite my kindness,
From whom no satisfaction can be sought, I have

**11.** Three companions—an emboldened heart,
A white and polished sword, a slender yellow bow,

**12.** Its smooth back resonant, adorned with ornaments
Suspended from it and with a shoulder strap.

**13.** When an arrow slips from it, it resounds like a she-camel
Afflicted and bereft, moaning and wailing.

**14.** I am not one quick to thirst, pasturing his herds by night,
Whose young camels get no milk,
though their mothers' udders are not bound,

**15.** Nor am I a coward, foul-breathed, clinging to his wife,
Consulting her on his affairs, how should he go about them?

**16.** Nor a startled ostrich, his heart aflutter
As though a sparrow flitted in it.

**17.** Nor am I a good-for-nothing stay-at-home, flirtatious,
Who comes and goes, night and day, perfume-daubed, kohl-painted.

**18.** Nor an old man like a camel tick, more harm than good, bewildered;
Who starts when frightened, in defenseless frenzy.

**19.** I am not a man confused by darkness, when the wayless waste
Confronts the guidance of the confounded fool.

**20.** When the ground, hard and flint-strewn, strikes my hoofs,
Sparks and splinters fly!

**21.** I prolong the length of hunger till I have killed it;
I turn my mind from it and forget it.

**22.** I eat the earth's dust dry, lest any benefactor
Think me indebted to his favor.

**23.** Except that I shun blame, there would be no drink, life giving,
That was not mine nor any food.

**24.** But a bitter soul does not let me remain in blame;
It prods me to move on.

**25.** I writhe around the hollow of my gut,
Like a rope maker twisting his strands, firm and tight.

**26.** Early morning I go out on scanty food, like the thin-hipped wolf,
Led on from waste to waste, dust-colored.

**27.** He goes out in the morning famished, nose to the wind, light-footed,
Swooping down the ends of mountain paths, or loping.

**28.** When his sought-out prey evades him, he calls out,
And others like him, emaciated, return his call.

**29.** Fleshless, white-faced, they are like bare arrows
In a *maysir* player's hands, clattering,

**30.** Or like the agitated queen bee, her swarm astir
From sticks a honey gatherer has flung down from above.

**31.** Wide-mouthed, as if their jaws were splints of branches,
They bare their teeth, ferocious.

**32.** Then he clamored and they clamored on the broad and barren plain,
As if they and he were wailing women, on the heights, bereaved.

**33.** He refrained, and they refrained; he comforted them, and they him;
In their destitution he consoled them and they consoled him, destitute.

**34.** He whined and they whined, then afterwards
he desisted and they desisted;
For endurance, when complaining is of no avail, is better.

**35.** He returned and they returned, hastening ahead of him,
Each despite his hunger, has the kindness to hide it.

**36.** The dark, dust-colored sandgrouse drink my dregs;
After traveling all night in search of water, their brittle ribs rattle.

**37.** I strove and they strove as we raced; then they slackened
And I went ahead, at leisure, rolling up my sleeves.

**38.** Then I turned away from them, and they collapsed at the water hole,
Their chins and crops resting right on it.

**39.** As if the clamor that arose on its two sides and all around
Were from bands of tribal travelers alighting there.

**40.** From all sides they converged on it; it gathered them
As a wayside water hole draws the scattered bunches of the camel herds.

**41.** They gulped down the water hurriedly, and then departed,
As if they were riders with the morning hastening from Uḥāẓah in alarm.

**42.** I am familiar with the earth's face when I take it as my bed
On a firm back raised by desiccated vertebrae.

**43.** For a cushion I take an arm, fleshless, its joints like gambler's bones
When he casts them forth, so they stand out.

**44.** Then if war, the Mother of Dust, is grieved at al-Shanfarā,
Yet her delight in him before was longer.

**45.** I am an outcast hunted by crimes that draw lots for his flesh;
The winner gets the first choice from his carcass.

**46.** Whenever he sleeps, they sleep, wide-eyed,
Quick to harm him, piercing.

**47.** One accustomed to cares that ever return to tend him,
Like quartan fever, or even graver.

**48.** When they come to drink, I disperse them;
But then they regroup coming from above and from below.

**49.** So if you see me, like the snake, the sand's daughter,
Exposed to the sun, weakened, barefoot and shoeless,

**50.** Know that I am the master of endurance; I don its cloth
Like a shirt on a heart like a young wolf's; I am shod with determination.

**51.** I am at times in want, at others, not in need;
He who attains riches is the ambitious man, heedless of his honor.

**52.** I am not impatient over poverty, exposing it,
Nor, overweening, do I exult in riches.

**53.** Intemperance does not scorn my forbearance,
Nor am I to be seen begging, rumormongering.

**54.** Many a cold, ill-omened night when the bow's owner warms himself
By burning it and the arrows of his skill,

**55.** I tramped in the dark and drizzle, my companions
Hunger and cold, fear and trembling.

**56.** I widowed women and orphaned children,
Then returned as I set out, the black night blacker still.

**57.** In the morning, there sat at Ghumayṣā' two bands,
One questioned about me, the other questioning.

**58.** They said, "Our dogs were whimpering in the night."
We said, "Was it a wolf on the prowl or a prowling hyena whelp?"

**59.** "It was but a faint noise, then they went back to sleep."
We replied, "Was it a sandgrouse startled, or a startled hawk?"

**60.** "If it was one of the jinn, then he is a more sinister night visitor;
And if it was a man—men do not act like that!"

**61.** Many a day of the Dog Star, when the heat waves melt,
And the vipers writhe restlessly on the scorching earth,

**62.** I faced straight on, no covering to shield me
Nor any veil, except a tattered cloak,

**63.** And full long hair; when the wind blows
Its matted dreadlocks fly up on all sides, uncombed.

**64.** Long since the touch of balm or delousing,
It is full and caked with filth; for a full year unwashed.

**65.** Many a windswept plain, like the back of a shield, a barren waste,
Its back not to be crossed, on my two legs I crossed.

**66.** I joined its end to its beginning, looking out from a summit,
Now sitting, knees drawn up; Now standing.

**67.** The dust-hued does of mountain goats roamed around me,
As if they were maidens trailing long-trained gowns.

**68.** Toward sunset motionless they stood about me,
as if among the white-footed goats I were
A long-horned buck, heading for the mountain peak, unassailable.

# The Qur'an (651–652)

*Translated by N.J. Dawood*

Like the Hebrew Bible, the New Testament, the Rig Veda, or the Bhagavad-Gītā, the Qur'ān (often anglicized Koran) belongs to that genre of literature we call Scripture. Received by Muslims as the actual words of God (Allah), the Qur'ān is recited as liturgy and memorized as a basis for all knowledge. It consists of visionary material compiled between 610 and 632. The official written version was established a few years later, in 653.

The Qur'ān's centrality to Islam has kept Arabic dialects from splintering off into separate languages, as happened with the Romance languages in Europe, and has made Arabic an international language. All Arabic dialects are written in the same Arabic alphabet, as are Persian, Turkish, Turki (spoken in Russia and Central Asia), Urdu (in Pakistan and India), Swahili (in Eastern Africa), and the Malagasy and Malayan languages. Although spoken Arabic may cause difficulty for interlocutors, written Arabic is easily understood from Morocco to Southeast Asia and from Russia to Africa. The Qur'ān has accomplished this by being the foundational educational text in Muslim communities and by being the authoritative norm for Arabic itself. Its centrality in creating community across an international landscape cannot be underestimated.

According to Islamic doctrine, translating the Qur'ān into any language from the original Arabic is, in itself, a distortion of the word of God. The book is said to be untranslatable. Of course, any translation diminishes our appreciation of the mystery, resonances, allusions, and beauty of the original, but in this case, even reading the text silently is considered (by some) a distortion, for the word "Qur'ān" means "reading" or "recital"; thus, vocalization and utterance are at the heart of the book's significance. (The concept resembles some other sacred texts; the meaning of the Vedas, for example, is also thought to reside in its spoken sounds; see p. 176.)

When Muhammad was first called to communicate divine messages, God said, "Recite in the Name of your Lord." Reciting the text by heart is considered essential for believers; therefore, Islam's Qur'ānic liturgy is always rendered in Arabic, despite the many regional languages comprising the Islamic world. In this way, the Qur'ān's sanctity reinforces Arabic as an international language, something similar to the power of Latin in the Middle Ages or written Chinese, another language that, when written, communicates across large geographic, ethnic, cultural, and language differences.

Although the Qur'ān includes references to some Hebrew and Christian patriarchs and prophets, it is not designed around Judeo-Christian concerns to document history, law, and events. It differs from the New Testament Gospels written by men to record the life and teachings of Jesus Christ, whose bodily presence on earth is the heart of Christian revelation. The Gospels, inspired by the Holy Spirit, give Christian believers access to Christ, who, in turn (in trinitarian belief), is the embodiment of God. In Islam, the Qur'ān is itself a manifestation of the Umm al-Kitab ("Mother of the Book" 43:4), tablets that were copied by Muhammad and that are eternally present in heaven with God. The Qur'ān does not claim to be about truth; it claims to be truth—it does not document or represent anything other than itself. It affirms the absolute oneness of God and denies any divine incarnation. In Sūrah 112, the text reads: "In the Name of God, the Compassionate, the Merciful/Say: 'God is One, the Eternal God. He begot none, nor was He begotten. None is equal to Him.'"

The sacred text is understood to have been revealed to Muhammad over a twenty-three-year period. The prophet Muhammad is believed to have been illiterate; he is understood to be the chosen messenger of God, not the author or one who determined in any way the content of the book. The Qur'ān is considered the word of God speaking through the Arabic of his apostle. Significantly, the name *Muhammad* occurs only four times in the Qur'ān; instead, he is usually called *al-Rasūl,* the one sent with the *risālah,* or message. Although blessed with vision and chosen as Allah's messenger, Muhammad insisted on his role as a mortal and humble instrument:

> I do not tell you that I possess God's treasures or know what is hidden, nor do I claim to be an angel. I follow only that which is revealed to me. . . . I have not the power to acquire benefits or to avert evil from myself, except by the will of God. Had I possessed knowledge of what is hidden, I would have availed myself of much that is good and no harm would have touched me. But I am no more than one who gives warning and news to true believers. (6:50; 7:188)

As a revelation focused on utterance rather than narrative, the Qur'ān does not often move chronologically. Two rare exceptions are the narrative sections concerning Joseph and Noah, which can profitably be compared with the Hebrew versions (pp. 102–106; 107–125). Most of the Qur'ān demands, however, that Western readers suspend usual reading expectations and assumptions. The 114 chapters of the book, known as *Sūrahs,* are organized by length, moving from lengthy early sections (like *The Table*) to extremely short concluding ones (like *Daybreak* or *Men*). The text emphasizes God's last judgment of humanity, portraying this as a time when all humans will stand trial before God to be admitted into heavenly bliss or condemned to eternal punishment in hell. God, considered both all-powerful and just, is to be praised and worshiped as creator of the universe, and believers are to worship nothing but him. Generosity, especially toward the outcast, the weak, the poor, and the orphaned, is also demanded by the faith. Muslims are commanded to obey God (Islam means "submission") and give him prayers of thanks. Fostering a covenantal relationship with God, similar to the one found in both Judaism and Christianity, Islam maintains that God's forgiveness can redeem humans, and it posits a dynamic and vital relationship between humans and the divine. As in biblical literature, the Qur'ān presents a tension between individual free will and divine omnipotence and foreknowledge. It became (and still continues to be) a hotly debated theological issue. The Shi'ite theologian, Ja'far al-Sadiq (c. 750) is said to have concluded that the issue was beyond human understanding; he warned, it is "a deep sea, venture not into it. . . . It is one of Allah's secrets, do not talk about it. . . . He who attempts to seek knowledge of it goes contrary to Allah's command, disputes His sovereignty, and is probing into His secret and His veil."

The Qur'ān's influence on all Arabic literature written after the establishment of Islam is profound, since it constitutes the supreme model for written Arabic. Constructed in rhymed prose, the book set the standard for both poetic and prose forms imitated even today. Although Muhammad was first considered a poet by his contemporaries (since the roles of poet, healer, seer, and priest were indistinguishable in pre-Islamic Arabia), the Prophet was troubled by this way of dismissing or misunderstanding the significance of his work. Consequently and unsurprisingly, the Qur'ān indicts poets and storytellers, moving canonical classical and medieval Arabic literature toward ethical, moral, intellectual, and spiritual concerns and away from fiction and folktale. In an aesthetic highly influenced by religious beliefs, Islamic culture of the Middle Period most often canonized those literary texts that were written securely within the framework of didacticism and faith or those, like the Qasīdahs, which helped scholars read and fully understand the nuances and allusions of Muhammad's Arabic.

## Sūrah 1: The Exordium

*In the Name of God, the Compassionate, the Merciful* 1:1

Praise be to God, Lord of the Universe,
The Compassionate, the Merciful,
Sovereign of the Day of Judgement!
You alone we worship, and to You alone
we turn for help.
Guide us to the straight path,
The path of those whom You have favoured, 1:7
Not of those who have incurred Your wrath,
Nor of those who have gone astray.

## Sūrah 5: The Table

*In the Name of God, the Compassionate, the Merciful*

5:1 Believers, be true to your obligations. It
is lawful for you to eat the flesh of all beasts other than that which is hereby announced to you. Game is forbidden while you are on pilgrimage. God decrees what He will.

Believers, do not violate the rites of God, or the sacred month, or the offerings or their ornaments, or those that repair to the Sacred House seeking God's grace and pleasure. Once your pilgrimage is ended, you shall be free to go hunting.

Do not allow your hatred for those who would debar you from the Holy Mosque to lead you into sin. Help one another in what is good and pious, not in what is wicked and sinful. Have fear of God; God is stern in retribution.

You are forbidden carrion, blood, 5:3
and the flesh of swine; also any flesh dedicated to any other than God. You

are forbidden the flesh of strangled animals and of those beaten or gored to death; of those killed by a fall or mangled by beasts of prey (unless you make it clean by giving the deathstroke yourselves); also of animals sacrificed to idols.

You are forbidden to settle disputes by consulting the Arrows. That is a pernicious practice.

The unbelievers have this day abandoned all hope of vanquishing your religion. Have no fear of them: fear Me.

This day I have perfected your religion for you and completed My favour to you. I have chosen Islām to be your faith.

He that is constrained by hunger to eat of what is forbidden, not intending to commit sin, will find God forgiving and merciful.

5:4 They ask you what is lawful to them. Say: 'All good things are lawful to you, as well as that which you have taught the birds and beasts of prey to catch, training them as God has taught you. Eat of what they catch for you, pronouncing upon it the name of God. And have fear of God: swift is God's reckoning.'

5:5 All good things have this day been made lawful to you. The food of those to whom the book was given [the Jews] is lawful to you, and yours to them.

Lawful to you are the believing women and the free women from among those who were given the Book before you, provided that you give them their dowries and live in honour with them, neither committing fornication nor taking them as mistresses.

He that denies the Faith shall gain nothing from his labours. In the world to come he shall have much to lose.

Believers, when you rise to pray wash your faces and your hands as far as the elbow, and wipe your heads and your feet to the ankle. If you are polluted cleanse yourselves. But if you are sick or travelling the road; or if, when you have just relieved yourselves or had intercourse with women, you can find no water, take some clean sand and rub your hands and faces with it. God does not wish to burden you; He seeks only to purify you and to perfect His favour to you, so that you may give thanks.

Remember God's favour to you, 5:7
and the covenant with which He bound you when you said: 'We hear and obey.' Have fear of God. God knows the innermost thoughts of men.

Believers, fulfil your duties to God and bear true witness. Do not allow your hatred for other men to turn you away from justice. Deal justly; that is nearer to true piety. Have fear of God; God is cognizant of all your actions.

God has promised those that have faith and do good works forgiveness and a rich reward. As for those who disbelieve and deny Our revelations, they are the heirs of Hell.

Believers, remember the favour 5:11
which God bestowed upon you when He restrained the hands of those who sought to harm you. Have fear of God. In God let the faithful put their trust.

God made a covenant with the 5:12
Israelites and raised among them twelve chieftains. God said: 'I shall be with you. If you attend to your prayers and render the alms levy; if you believe in My apostles and assist them and give God a generous loan, I shall forgive you your sins and admit you to gardens watered by running streams. But he that hereafter denies Me shall stray from the right path.'

But because they broke their covenant We laid on them Our curse and hardened their hearts. They have

tampered with words out of their context and forgotten much of what they
were enjoined. You will ever find them
deceitful, except for a few of them. But
pardon them and bear with them. God
loves those who do good.

With those who said they were
Christians We made a covenant also,
but they too have forgotten much of
what they were enjoined. Therefore We
stirred among them enmity and hatred,
which shall endure till the Day of
Resurrection, when God will declare to
them all that they have done.

5:15 People of the Book! Our apostle
has come to reveal to you much of what
you have hidden of the Scriptures, and
to forgive you much. A light has come
to you from God and a glorious book,
with which God will guide to the paths
of peace those that seek to please Him;
He will lead them by His will from darkness to the light; He will guide them to
a straight path.

Unbelievers are those who declare:
'God is the Messiah, the son of Mary.'
Say: 'Who could prevent God, if He so
willed, from destroying the Messiah,
the son of Mary, his mother, and all the
people of the earth? God has sovereignty over the heavens and the earth
and all that lies between them. He creates what He will and God has power
over all things.'

5:18 The Jews and the Christians say:
'We are the children of God and His
loved ones.' Say: 'Why then does He
punish you for your sins? Surely you are
mortals of His own creation. He forgives whom He will and punishes whom
He pleases. God has sovereignty over
the heavens and the earth and all that
lies between them. All shall return to
Him.'

5:19 People of the Book! Our apostle
has come to you with revelations after
an interval during which there were no
apostles, lest you say: 'No one has come
to give us good news or to warn us.'
Now someone has come to give you
good news and to warn you. God has
power over all things.

Bear in mind the words of Moses to
his people. He said: 'Remember, my
people, the favour which God has
bestowed upon you. He has raised up
prophets among you, made you kings,
and given you that which He has given
to no other nation. Enter, my people,
the holy land which God has assigned
for you. Do not turn back, or you shall
be ruined.'

'Moses,' they replied, 'a race of
giants dwells in this land. We will not set
foot in it till they are gone. As soon as
they are gone we will enter.'

Thereupon two God-fearing men
whom God had favoured said: 'Go in to
them through the gates, and when you
have entered you shall surely be victorious. In God put your trust, if you are
true believers.'

But they replied: 'Moses, we will 5:24
not go in so long as *they* are in it. Go,
you and your Lord, and fight. Here we
will stay.'

'Lord,' cried Moses, 'I have none
but myself and my brother. Keep us
apart from these wicked people.'

He replied: 'They shall be forbidden this land for forty years, during
which time they shall wander homeless
on the earth. Do not grieve for these
wicked people.'

Recount to them in all truth the
story of Adam's two sons: how they each
made an offering, and how the offering
of the one was accepted while that of
the other was not. One said: 'I will
surely kill you.' The other replied: 'God
accepts offerings only from the righteous. If you stretch your hand to kill

me, I shall not stretch mine to slay you; for I fear God, Lord of the Universe. I would rather you should add your sin against me to your other sins and thus become an inmate of the Fire. Such is the reward of the wicked.'

5:30 His soul prompted him to slay his
brother; he slew him and thus became
5:31 one of the lost. Then God sent down a
raven, which dug the earth to show him how to bury the naked corpse of his brother. 'Alas!' he cried. 'Have I not strength enough to do as this raven has done and so bury my brother's naked corpse?' And he repented.

That was why We laid it down for the Israelites that whoever killed a human being, except as a punishment for murder or other villainy in the land, shall be looked upon as though he had killed all mankind; and that whoever saved a human life shall be regarded as though he had saved all mankind.

Our apostles brought them veritable proofs: yet it was not long before many of them committed great evils in the land.

Those that make war against God and His apostle and spread disorder in the land shall be put to death or crucified or have their hands and feet cut off on alternate sides, or be banished from the country. They shall be held up to shame in this world and sternly punished in the hereafter: except those that repent before you reduce them. For you must know that God is forgiving and merciful.

5:35 Believers, have fear of God and seek
the right path to Him. Fight valiantly for His cause, so that you may triumph.

As for the unbelievers, if they offered all that the earth contains and as much besides to redeem themselves from the torment of the Day of Resurrection, it shall not be accepted from them. Theirs shall be a woeful punishment.

They will strive to get out of the Fire, but get out of it they shall not: theirs shall be a lasting punishment.

As for the man or woman who is guilty of theft, cut off their hands to punish them for their crimes. That is the punishment enjoined by God. God is mighty and wise. But whoever repents after committing evil, and mends his ways, shall be pardoned by God. God is forgiving and merciful.

Did you not know that God has 5:40
sovereignty over the heavens and the earth? He punishes whom He will and forgives whom He pleases. God has power over all things.

Apostle, do not grieve for those 5:41
who plunge headlong into unbelief; those who say with their tongues: 'We believe,' but have no faith in their hearts, and those Jews who listen to lies and listen to others who have not come to you. They tamper with words out of their context and say: 'If this be given you, accept it; if not, then beware!'

You cannot help a man if God seeks to confound him. Those whose hearts God does not please to purify shall earn disgrace in this world and a grievous punishment in the hereafter.

They listen to falsehoods and practise what is unlawful. If they come to you, give them your judgement or avoid them. If you avoid them they can in no way harm you; but if you do act as their judge, judge them with fairness. God loves those that deal justly.

But how will they come to you for judgement, when they already have the Torah which enshrines God's own judgement? Soon after, they will turn their backs: they are no true believers.

5:44 We have revealed the Torah, in
which there is guidance and light. By it
the prophets who surrendered themselves judged the Jews, and so did the
rabbis and the divines, according to
God's Book which had been committed
to their keeping and to which they
themselves were witnesses.

Have no fear of man; fear Me, and
do not sell My revelations for a paltry
end. Unbelievers are those who do not
judge according to God's revelations.

We decreed for them a life for a
life, an eye for an eye, a nose for a nose,
an ear for an ear, a tooth for a tooth,
and a wound for a wound. But if a man
charitably forbears from retaliation, his
remission shall atone for him. Transgressors are those that do not judge
according to God's revelations.

After them We sent forth Jesus, the
son of Mary, confirming the Torah
already revealed, and gave him the
Gospel in which there is guidance and
light, corroborating what was revealed
before it in the Torah, a guide and an
5:47 admonition to the righteous. Therefore let those who follow the Gospel
judge according to what God has
revealed therein. Evil-doers are those
that do not base their judgements on
God's revelations.

5:48 And to you We have revealed the
Book with the truth. It confirms the
Scriptures which came before it and
stands as a guardian over them. Therefore give judgement among men according to God's revelations and do not yield
to their fancies or swerve from the truth
made known to you.

We have ordained a law and
assigned a path for each of you. Had
God pleased, He could have made of
you one nation: but it is His wish to
prove you by that which He has
bestowed upon you. Vie with each
other in good works, for to God you
shall all return and He will resolve for
you your differences.

Pronounce judgement among them
according to God's revelations and do
not be led by their desires. Take heed
lest they turn you away from a part of
that which God has revealed to you. If
they reject your judgement, know that it
is God's wish to scourge them for their
sins. A great many of mankind are
evil-doers.

Is it pagan laws that they wish to be
judged by? Who is a better judge than
God for men whose faith is firm?

Believers, take neither Jews nor 5:51
Christians for your friends. They are
friends with one another. Whoever of
you seeks their friendship shall become
one of their number. God does not
guide the wrongdoers.

You see the faint-hearted hastening
to woo them. They say: 'We fear lest a
change of fortune should befall us.' But
when God grants you victory or makes
known His will, they shall regret their
secret plans. Then will the faithful say:
'Are these the men who solemnly swore
by God that they would stand with you?'
Their works will come to nothing and
they will lose all.

Believers, if any among you 5:54
renounce the Faith, God will replace
them by others who love Him and are
loved by Him, who are humble towards
the faithful and stern towards the unbelievers, zealous for God's cause and fearless of man's censure. Such is the grace
of God: He bestows it on whom He will.
God is munificent and all-knowing.

Your only protectors are God, His 5:55
apostle, and the faithful: those who
attend to their prayers, render the alms
levy, and kneel down in worship. Those

who seek the protection of God, His apostle, and the faithful must know that God's followers are sure to triumph.

Believers, do not seek the friendship of the infidels and those who were given the Book before you, who have made of your religion a jest and a pastime. Have fear of God, if you are true believers. When you call them to pray, they treat their prayers as a jest and a pastime. This is because they are devoid of understanding.

Say: 'People of the Book, is it not that you hate us only because we believe in God and in what has been revealed to us and to others before, and because most of you are evil-doers?'

Say: 'Shall I tell you who will receive a worse reward from God? Those whom God has cursed and with whom He has been angry, transforming them into apes and swine, and those who serve the devil. Worse is the plight of these, and they have strayed farther from the right path.'

5:61 When they came to you they said: 'We are believers.' Indeed, infidels they came and infidels they departed. God knew best what they concealed.

You see many among them vie with one another in sin and wickedness and practise what is unlawful. Evil is what they do.

Why do their rabbis and divines not forbid them to blaspheme or to practise what is unlawful? Evil indeed are their doings.

5:64 The Jews say: 'God's hand is chained.' May their own hands be chained! May they be cursed for what they say! By no means. His hands are both outstretched: He bestows as He will.

That which is revealed to you from your Lord will surely increase the wickedness and unbelief of many of them. We have stirred among them enmity and hatred, which will endure till the Day of Resurrection. Whenever they kindle the fire of war, God puts it out. They spread evil in the land, but God does not love the evil-doers.

If the People of the Book accept 5:65
the true faith and keep from evil, We will pardon them their sins and admit them to the gardens of delight. If they observe the Torah and the Gospel and what is revealed to them from their Lord, they shall enjoy abundance from above and from beneath.

There are some among them who are righteous men; but there are many among them who do nothing but evil.

Apostle, proclaim what is revealed to you from your Lord; if you do not, you will surely fail to convey His message. God will protect you from all men. God does not guide the unbelievers.

Say: 'People of the Book, you will attain nothing until you observe the Torah and the Gospel and that which is revealed to you from your Lord.'

That which is revealed to you from your Lord will surely increase the wickedness and unbelief of many of them. But do not grieve for the unbelievers.

Believers, Jews, Sabaeans and Christians—whoever believes in God and the Last Day and does what is right—shall have nothing to fear or to regret.

We made a covenant with the 5:70
Israelites and sent forth apostles among them. But whenever an apostle came to them with a message that did not suit their fancies, some they accused of lying and others they put to death. They thought no harm would follow: they were blind and deaf. God turned to them in mercy, but many again were blind and deaf. God is ever watching their actions.

Unbelievers are those that say:
'God is the Messiah, the son of Mary.'
For the Messiah himself said: 'Children
of Israel, serve God, my Lord and your
Lord.' He that worships other gods
besides God, God will deny him Paradise, and Hell shall be his home. None
shall help the evil-doers.

Unbelievers are those that say:
'God is one of three.' There is but one
God. If they do not desist from so saying, those of them that disbelieve shall
be sternly punished.

5:74 Will they not turn to God in repentance and seek forgiveness of Him?
God is forgiving and merciful.

5:75 The Messiah, the son of Mary, was
no more than an apostle: other apostles
passed away before him. His mother
was a saintly woman. They both ate
earthly food.

See how We make plain to them
Our revelations. See how they ignore
the truth.

Say: 'Will you serve instead of
God that which can neither harm nor
help you? God is He who hears all and
knows all.'

Say: 'People of the Book! Do not
transgress the bounds of truth in your
religion. Do not yield to the desires of
those who have erred before; who have
led many astray and have themselves
strayed from the even path.'

Those of the Israelites who disbelieved were cursed by David and Jesus,
the son of Mary, because they rebelled
and committed evil. Nor did they censure themselves for any wrong they did.
Evil were their deeds.

You see many among them making
friends with unbelievers. Evil is that to
which their souls prompt them. They
have incurred the wrath of God and
shall endure eternal torment. Had they
believed in God and the Prophet and
that which is revealed to him, they
would not have befriended them. But
many of them are evil-doers.

You will find that the most implaca- 5:82
ble of men in their enmity to the faithful are the Jews and the pagans, and
that the nearest in affection to them
are those who say: 'We are Christians.'
That is because there are priests and
monks among them; and because they
are free from pride.

When they listen to that which was
revealed to the Apostle, you see their
eyes fill with tears as they recognize its
truth. They say: 'Lord, we believe.
Count us among Your witnesses. Why
should we not believe in God and in
the truth that has come down to us?
Why should we not hope our Lord will
admit us among the righteous?' And
for their words God has rewarded them
with gardens watered by running
streams, where they shall dwell for ever.
Such is the recompense of the righteous. But those that disbelieve and
deny Our revelations shall become the
inmates of Hell.

Believers, do not forbid the whole- 5:87
some things which God made lawful to
you. Do not transgress; God does not
love the transgressors. Eat of the lawful 5:88
and wholesome things which God has
given you. Have fear of God, in whom
you believe.

God will not punish you for that
which is inadvertent in your oaths. But
He will take you to task for the oaths
which you solemnly swear. The penalty
for a broken oath is the feeding of ten
needy men with such food as you normally offer to your own people; or the
clothing of ten needy men; or the freeing of one slave. He that cannot afford
any of these must fast three days. In
this way you shall expiate your broken
oaths. Therefore be true to that which

you have sworn. Thus God makes plain
to you His revelations, so that you may
give thanks.

5:90 Believers, wine and games of chance,
idols and divining arrows, are abominations devised by Satan. Avoid them, so
that you may prosper. Satan seeks to stir
up enmity and hatred among you by
means of wine and gambling, and to
keep you from the remembrance of
God and from your prayers. Will you
not abstain from them?

Obey God, and obey the Apostle.
Beware; if you give no heed, know that
Our apostle's duty is only to give plain
warning.

No blame shall be attached to
those that have embraced the Faith and
done good works in regard to any food
they may have eaten, so long as they
fear God and believe in Him and do
good works; so long as they fear God
and believe in Him; so long as they fear
God and do good works. God loves the
charitable.

Believers, God will put you to the
proof by means of the game which you
can catch with your hands or with your
spears, so that He may know those
who fear Him in their hearts. He that
transgresses hereafter shall be sternly
punished.

5:95 Believers, kill no game while on pilgrimage. He that kills game by design
shall present, as an offering to the
Ka'bah, an animal equivalent to the
one he killed, to be determined by two
just men among you; or he shall, in
expiation, either feed the poor or fast,
so that he may taste the evil consequences of his deed. God has forgiven
what is past; but if anyone relapses into
wrongdoing He will avenge Himself on
him: He is mighty and capable of
revenge.

5:96 Lawful to you is what you catch from
the sea and the sustenance it provides; a
wholesome food, for you and for the sea-
farer. But you are forbidden the game of
the land while you are on pilgrimage.
Have fear of God, before whom you
shall all be assembled.

God has made the Ka'bah, the
Sacred House, the sacred month, and
the sacrificial offerings with their ornaments, eternal values for mankind; so
that you may know God has knowledge
of all that the heavens and the earth
contain; that God has knowledge of all
things.

Know that God is stern in retribution, and that God is forgiving and
merciful.

The duty of the Apostle is only to
give warning. God knows all that you
hide and all that you reveal.

Say: 'Good and evil are not alike,
even though the abundance of evil
may tempt you. Have fear of God, you
men of understanding, so that you may
triumph.'

Believers, do not ask questions 5:101
about things which, if made known to
you, would only pain you; but if you ask
them when the Koran is being revealed,
they shall be made plain to you. God
will pardon you for this; God is forgiving and gracious. Other men inquired
about them before you, only to disbelieve them afterwards.

God demands neither a *bahīrah,* nor
a *sā'ibah,* nor a *wasīlah,* nor a *hāmi.*
[Names given by pagan Arabs to sacrificial animals offered at the Ka'bah.]
The unbelievers invent falsehoods
about God. Most of them are lacking in
judgement.

When it is said to them: 'Come to
that which God has revealed, and to the
Apostle,' they reply: 'Sufficient for us is
the faith we have inherited from our
fathers,' even though their fathers
knew nothing and were not rightly
guided.

5:105 Believers, you are accountable for none but yourselves; he that goes astray cannot harm you if you are on the right path. To God you shall all return, and He will declare to you what you have done.

5:106 Believers, when death approaches you, let two just men from among you act as witnesses when you make your testaments; or two men from another tribe if the calamity of death overtakes you while you are travelling the land. Detain them after prayers, and if you doubt their honesty let them swear by God: 'We will not sell our testimony for any price even to a kinsman. We will not hide the testimony of God; for we should then be evil-doers.' If both prove dishonest, replace them by another pair from among those immediately concerned, and let them both swear by God, saying: 'Our testimony is truer than theirs. We have told no lies, for we should then be wrongdoers.' Thus will they be more likely to bear true witness or to fear that the oaths of others may contradict theirs. Have fear of God and be obedient. God does not guide the evil-doers.

One day God will gather all the
apostles and ask them: 'How were you
received?' They will reply: 'We have no
knowledge. You alone know what is hid-
5:110 den.' God will say: 'Jesus, son of Mary,
remember the favour I have bestowed
on you and on your mother: how I
strengthened you with the Holy Spirit,
so that you preached to men in your
cradle and in the prime of manhood;
how I instructed you in the Book and in
wisdom, in the Torah and in the
Gospel; how by My leave you fashioned
from clay the likeness of a bird and
breathed into it so that, by My leave, it
became a living bird; how, by My leave,
you healed the blind man and the
leper, and by My leave restored the
dead to life; how I protected you from
the Israelites when you had come to
them with clear signs: when those of
them who disbelieved declared: "This is
but plain sorcery"; how when I enjoined
the disciples to believe in Me and in My
apostle they replied: "We believe; bear
witness that we submit."'

'Jesus, son of Mary,' said the disciples, 'can your Lord send down to us from heaven a table spread with food?'

He replied: 'Have fear of God, if you are true believers.'

'We wish to eat of it,' they said, 'so 5:113
that we may reassure our hearts and
know that what you said to us is true,
and that we may be witnesses of it.'

'Lord,' said Jesus, the son of Mary, 5:114
'send down to us from heaven a table
spread with food, that it may mark a
feast for us and for those that will come
after us: a sign from You. Give us our
sustenance; You are the best provider.'

God replied: 'I am sending one to you. But whoever of you disbelieves hereafter shall be punished as no man will ever be punished.'

Then God will say: 'Jesus, son of Mary, did you ever say to mankind: "Worship me and my mother as gods besides God?"'

'Glory to You,' he will answer, 'how could I ever say that to which I have no right? If I had ever said so, You would have surely known it. You know what is in my mind, but I know not what is in Yours. You alone know what is hidden. I told them only what You bade me. I said: "Serve God, my Lord and your Lord." I watched over them while living in their midst, and ever since You took me to Yourself, You have been watching over them. You are the witness of all things. If You punish them, they surely are Your servants; and if You forgive them, surely You are mighty and wise.'

God will say: 'This is the day when their truthfulness will benefit the truthful. They shall for ever dwell in gardens watered by running streams. God is pleased with them, and they are pleased with Him. That is the supreme triumph.'

God has sovereignty over the heav- 5:120
ens and the earth and all that they contain. He has power over all things.

## *Sūrah 12: Joseph*

*In the Name of God, the Compassionate, The Merciful*

12:1 Alif *lām rā'*. These are the verses of the
Glorious Book. We have revealed the
Koran in the Arabic tongue so that you
may grow in understanding.
12:3 In revealing this Koran We will
recount to you the best of narratives,
though before it you were heedless.

Joseph said to his father: 'Father, I dreamt of eleven stars and the sun and the moon; I saw them prostrate themselves before me.'

'My son,' he replied, 'say nothing of this dream to your brothers, lest they plot evil against you: Satan is the sworn enemy of man. You shall be chosen by your Lord. He will teach you to interpret visions, and will perfect His favour to you and to the house of Jacob, as He perfected it to your forefathers Abraham and Isaac before you. Your Lord is all-knowing and wise.'

Surely in Joseph and his brothers there are signs for doubting men.

They said to each other: 'Joseph and his brother are dearer to our father than ourselves, though we are many. Truly, our father is much mistaken. Let us slay Joseph, or cast him away in some far-off land, so that we may have no rivals in our father's love, and after that be honourable men.'

12:10 One of the brothers said: 'Do not
slay Joseph; but, if you must, rather cast
him into a dark pit. Some caravan will
take him up.'

They said to their father: 'Why do you not trust us with Joseph? Surely we wish him well. Send him with us tomorrow, that he may play and enjoy himself. We will take good care of him.'

He replied: 'It would much grieve me to let him go with you; for I fear lest the wolf should eat him when you are off your guard.'

They said: 'If the wolf could eat him despite our number, then we should surely be lost!'

And when they took him with them, they resolved to cast him into a dark pit. We revealed to him Our will, saying: 'You shall tell them of all this when they will not know you.'

At nightfall they returned weeping
to their father. They said: 'We went off 12:17
to compete together, and left Joseph
with our packs. The wolf devoured him.
But you will not believe us, though we
speak the truth.' And they showed him 12:18
their brother's shirt, stained with false
blood.

'No!' he cried. 'Your souls have tempted you to evil. Sweet patience! God alone can help me bear the loss you speak of.'

And a caravan passed by, who sent their water-bearer to the pit. And when he had let down his pail, he cried: 'Rejoice! A boy!'

They concealed him as part of their merchandise. But God knew what they did. They sold him for a trifling price, for a few pieces of silver. They cared nothing for him.

The Egyptian who bought him said to his wife: 'Be kind to him. He may prove useful to us, or we may adopt him as our son.'

Thus We established Joseph in the land, and taught him to interpret dreams. God has power over all things, though most men may not know it. And when he reached maturity We bestowed on him wisdom and knowledge. Thus do We reward the righteous.

12:23 His master's wife attempted to seduce him. She bolted the doors and said: 'Come!'

'God forbid!' he replied. 'My lord has treated me with kindness. Wrongdoers shall never prosper.'

She made for him, and he himself would have succumbed to her had he not seen a sign from his Lord. Thus did We shield him from wantonness, for he was one of Our faithful servants.

They both rushed to the door. She tore his shirt from behind. And at the door they met her husband.

She cried: 'Shall not the man who wished to violate your wife be thrown into prison or sternly punished?'

Joseph said: 'It was she who attempted to seduce me.'

'If his shirt is torn from the front,' said one of her people, 'she is speaking the truth and he is lying. If it is torn from behind, then he is speaking the truth, and she is lying.'

12:28 And when her husband saw that
Joseph's shirt was rent from behind,
he said to her: 'This is but one of
12:29 your tricks. Your cunning is great
indeed! Joseph, say no more about
this. Woman, ask pardon for your sin.
You have done wrong.'

In the city, women were saying: 'The Prince's wife has sought to seduce her servant. She has conceived a passion for him. It is clear that she has gone astray.'

When she heard of their intrigues, she invited them to a banquet prepared at her house. To each she gave a knife, and ordered Joseph to present himself before them. When they saw him, they were amazed at him and cut their hands, exclaiming: 'God preserve us! This is no mortal, but a gracious angel.'

'This is he,' she said, 'on whose account you blamed me. I attempted to seduce him, but he was unyielding. If he declines to do my bidding, he shall be thrown into prison and shall be held in scorn.'

'Lord,' said Joseph, 'sooner would I go to prison than give in to their advances. Shield me from their cunning, or I shall yield to them and lapse into folly.'

His Lord answered his prayer and 12:34
warded off their wiles from him. He
hears all and knows all.

Yet, for all the evidence they had seen, they thought it right to jail him for a time.

Two young men entered the prison with him. One said: 'I dreamt that I was pressing grapes.' And the other: 'I dreamt I was carrying a loaf upon my head, and the birds came and ate of it. Tell us the meaning of these dreams, for we can see you are a man of virtue.'

Joseph replied: 'Whatever food you are provided with, I can divine for you its meaning, even before it reaches you. This knowledge my Lord has given me, for I have left the faith of those that disbelieve in God and deny the life to come. I follow the faith of my forefathers, Abraham, Isaac and Jacob. We will serve no idols besides God.

Such is the grace which God has bestowed on us and on all mankind. Yet most men do not give thanks.

'Fellow prisoners! Are sundry gods better than God, the One who con-
12:40 quers all? Those you serve besides Him are nothing but names which you and your fathers have devised and for which God has revealed no sanction. Judgement rests only with God. He has commanded you to worship none but Him. That is the true faith: yet most men do not know it.

12:41 'Fellow prisoners, one of you will serve his lord with wine. The other will he crucified, and the birds will peck at his head. That is the answer to your question.'

And Joseph said to the prisoner who he knew would be freed: 'Remember me in the presence of your lord.'

But Satan made him forget to mention Joseph to his lord, so that he stayed in prison for several years.

The king said: 'I saw seven fatted cows which seven lean ones devoured; also seven green ears of corn and seven others dry. Tell me the meaning of this vision, my nobles, if you can interpret visions.'

They replied. 'They are but a medley of dreams; nor are we skilled in the interpretation of dreams.'

Thereupon the man who had been freed remembered Joseph after all that time. He said: 'I shall tell you what it means. Give me leave to go.'

12:46 He said to Joseph: 'Tell us, man of truth, of the seven fatted cows which seven lean ones devoured; also of the seven green ears of corn and the other seven which were dry: so that I may go back to my masters and inform them.'

He replied: 'You shall sow for seven consecutive years. Leave in the ear the corn you reap, except a little which you may eat. There shall follow seven hungry years which will consume all but little of what you stored. Then will come a year of abundant rain, in which the people will press the grape.'

The king said: 'Bring this man before me.'

But when the envoy came to him, Joseph said: 'Go back to your master and ask him about the women who cut their hands. My master knows their cunning.'

The king questioned the women, 12:51
saying: 'What made you attempt to seduce Joseph?'

'God forbid!' they replied. 'We know no evil of him.'

'Now the truth must come to light,' said the Prince's wife. 'It was I who attempted to seduce him. He has told the truth.'

'From this,' said Joseph, 'my lord 12:52
will know that I did not betray him in his absence, and that God does not guide the work of the treacherous. Not that I am free from sin: man's soul is prone to evil, except his to whom my Lord has shown mercy. My Lord is forgiving and merciful.'

The king said: 'Bring him before me. I will choose him for my own.'

And when he had spoken with him, the king said: 'You shall henceforth dwell with us, honoured and trusted.'

Joseph said: 'Give me charge of the granaries of the realm. I shall husband them wisely.'

Thus did We establish Joseph in the land, and he dwelt there as he pleased. We bestow Our mercy on whom We will, and shall never deny the righteous their reward. Better is the reward of the hereafter for those who believe in God and keep from evil.

Joseph's brothers arrived and pre- 12:58
sented themselves before him. He recognized them, but they knew him not. And when he had given them their

provisions, he said: 'Bring me your other brother from your father. Do you not see that I give just measure and am the best of hosts? If you refuse to bring him, you shall have no corn, nor shall you come near me again.'

They replied: 'We will endeavour to fetch him from his father. This we will surely do.'

Joseph said to his servants: 'Put their money into their packs, so that they may discover it when they return to their people. Perchance they will come back.'

When they returned to their father, they said: 'Father, corn is henceforth denied us. Send our brother with us and we shall have our measure. We will take good care of him.'

12:64 He replied: 'Am I to trust you with him as I once trusted you with his brother? But God is the best of guardians: and of all those that show mercy He is the most merciful.'

12:65 When they opened their packs, they discovered that their money had been returned to them. 'Father,' they said, 'what more can we desire? Here is our money paid back to us. We will buy provisions for our people, and take good care of our brother. We should receive an extra camel-load; a camel-load should be easy enough.'

He replied: 'I will not send him with you until you promise in God's name to bring him back to me, unless the worst befall you.'

And when they had given him their pledge, he said: 'God is the witness of what we say. My sons, do not enter from one gate; enter from different gates. In no way can I shield you from the might of God; judgement is His alone. In Him I have put my trust. In Him let the faithful put their trust.'

And when they entered as their father bade them, he could in no way shield them from the might of God. It was but a wish in Jacob's soul which he had thus fulfilled. He was possessed of knowledge which We had given him. But most men have no knowledge.

When they went in to Joseph, he 12:69
embraced his brother, and said: 'I am your brother. Do not grieve at what they did.'

And when he had given them their provisions, he hid a drinking-cup in his brother's pack.

Then a crier called out after them: 'Travellers, you are thieves!'

They turned back, and asked: 'What have you lost?'

'We miss the king's drinking-cup,' he replied. 'He that brings it shall have a camel-load of corn. I pledge my word for it.'

'In God's name,' they cried, 'you know we did not come to do evil in this land. We are no thieves.'

The Egyptians said: 'What punishment shall be his who stole it, if you prove to be lying?'

They replied: 'He in whose pack the cup is found shall be your bondsman. Thus do we punish the wrongdoers.'

Joseph searched their bags before 12:76
his brother's, and then took out the cup from his brother's bag.

Thus We directed Joseph. By the king's law he had no right to seize his brother: but God willed otherwise. We exalt in knowledge whom We will: but above those that have knowledge there is One more knowing.

They said: 'If he has stolen—know 12:77
then that a brother of his has committed theft before him.'

But Joseph kept his secret and revealed nothing to them. He said: 'Your deed was worse. God best knows the things you speak of.'

They said: 'Noble prince, this boy has an aged father. Take one of us, instead of him. We can see you are a generous man.'

He replied: 'God forbid that we should take any but the man with whom our property was found: for then we should be unjust.'

When they despaired of him, they
went aside to confer in private. The
eldest said: 'Do you not know that
your father took from you a pledge
in God's name, and that long ago you
did your worst with Joseph? I will
not stir from this land until my father
gives me leave or God makes known to
12:81 me His judgement: He is the best of
judges. Return to your father and say to
him: "Father, your son has committed
theft. We testify only to what we know.
How could we guard against the
unforeseen? Inquire at the city where
we lodged, and from the caravan with
which we travelled. We speak the
truth."'

'No!' cried their father. 'Your souls have tempted you to evil. But I will have sweet patience. God may bring them all to me. He alone is all-knowing and wise.' And he turned away from them, crying: 'Alas for Joseph!' His eyes went white with grief, and he was oppressed with silent sorrow.

His sons exclaimed: 'In God's name, will you not cease to think of Joseph until you ruin your health and die?'

He replied: 'I complain to God of
my sorrow and sadness. God has made
known to me things that you know not.
12:87 Go, my sons, and seek news of Joseph
and his brother. Do not despair of
God's spirit; none but unbelievers
despair of God's spirit.'

12:88 And when they went in to him,
they said: 'Noble prince, we and our
people are scourged with famine. We
have brought but little money. Give us
some corn, and be charitable to us:
God rewards the charitable.'

'Do you know,' he replied, 'what you did to Joseph and his brother? You are surely unaware.'

They cried: 'Can you indeed be Joseph?'

'I am Joseph,' he answered, 'and this is my brother. God has been gracious to us. Those that keep from evil and endure with fortitude, God will not deny them their reward.'

'By the Lord,' they said, 'God has exalted you above us all. We have indeed been guilty.'

He replied: 'None shall reproach you this day. May God forgive you: of all those that show mercy He is the most merciful. Take this shirt of mine and throw it over my father's face: he will recover his sight. Then return to me with all your people.'

When the caravan departed their 12:94
father said: 'I feel the breath of Joseph,
though you will not believe me.'

'In God's name,' said those who heard him, 'it is but your old illusion.'

And when the bearer of good news arrived, he threw Joseph's shirt over the old man's face, and he regained his sight. He said: 'Did I not tell you, God has made known to me what you know not?'

His sons said: 'Father, implore forgiveness for our sins. We have indeed done wrong.'

He replied: 'I shall implore my Lord to forgive you. He is forgiving and merciful.'

And when they went in to Joseph, he embraced his parents and said: 'Welcome to Egypt, safe, if God wills!'

He helped his parents to a couch, 12:100
and they all fell on their knees and
prostrated themselves before him.

'This,' said Joseph to his father, 'is the meaning of my old vision: my Lord has fulfilled it. He has been gracious to me. He has released me from prison, and brought you out of the desert after Satan had stirred up strife between me and my brothers. My Lord is gracious to whom He will. He alone is all-knowing and wise.

12:101 'Lord, You have given me authority and taught me to interpret dreams. Creator of the heavens and the earth, my Guardian in this world and in the hereafter! Allow me to die in submission, and admit me among the righteous.'

That which We have now revealed to you is a tale of the unknown. You were not present when Joseph's brothers conceived their plans and schemed against him. Yet strive as you may, most men will not believe.

You shall demand of them no recompense for this. It is an admonition to all mankind.

Many are the marvels of the heavens and the earth; yet they pass them by and pay no heed to them. The greater part of them believe in God only if they can worship other gods besides Him.

Are they confident that God's scourge will not fall upon them, or that the Hour of Doom will not overtake them unawares, without warning?

Say: 'This is my path. With sure 12:108
knowledge I call on you to have faith in
God, I and all my followers. Glory be to
God! I am no idolater.'

Nor were the apostles whom We sent before you other than mortals inspired by Our will and chosen from among their people.

Have they not travelled the land and seen what was the end of those who disbelieved before them? Better is the world to come for those that keep from evil. Can you not understand?

And when at length Our apostles despaired and thought they were
denied, Our help came down to them,
delivering whom We pleased. The
evil-doers could not be saved from Our 12:111
scourge. Their annals point a moral to
men of understanding.

This is no invented tale, but a confirmation of previous scriptures, an explanation of all things, a guide and a blessing to true believers.

## *from Sūrah 20: Ṭā' Hā'*

*In the Name of God, the Compassionate, the Merciful*

20:115 We made a covenant with Adam, but he forgot, and We found him lacking in steadfastness. And when We said to the angels: 'Prostrate yourselves before Adam,' they all prostrated themselves except Satan, who refused.

'Adam,' We said, 'Satan is an enemy to you and to your wife. Let him not turn you both out of Paradise and plunge you into affliction. Here you shall not hunger or be naked; you shall not thirst, or feel the scorching heat.'

But Satan whispered to him, saying: 'Shall I show you the Tree of Immortality and an everlasting kingdom?'

They both ate of its fruit, so that they saw their nakedness and began to cover themselves with the leaves of the Garden. Thus did Adam disobey his Lord and go astray.

Then his Lord had mercy on him; He relented towards him and rightly guided him.

'Go hence,' He said, 'and may your offspring be enemies to each other. When My guidance is revealed to you, he that follows it shall neither err nor grieve; but he that rejects My warning shall live in woe and come before Us blind on the Day of Resurrection.'

'Lord,' he will say, 'why have You 20:125
brought me blind before You when in my life I was clear-sighted?'

He will answer: 'Just as Our revelations were declared to you and you forgot them, so on this day you are yourself forgotten.'

## *from Sūrah 24: Light*

*In the Name of God, the Compassionate, the Merciful*

24.1 This is a Chapter which We have revealed and sanctioned, proclaiming in it clear revelations, so that you may take heed.

The adulterer and the adulteress shall each be given a hundred lashes. Let no pity for them cause you to disobey God, if you truly believe in God and the Last Day; and let their punishment be witnessed by a number of believers.

The adulterer may marry only an adulteress or an idolatress; and the adulteress may marry only an adulterer or an idolater. True believers are forbidden such marriages.

Those that defame honourable women and cannot produce four witnesses shall be given eighty lashes. Do not accept their testimony ever after, for they are great transgressors—except those among them that afterwards repent and mend their ways. God is forgiving and merciful.

24:6 If a man accuses his wife but has no witnesses except himself, he shall swear four times by God that his charge is true, calling down upon himself the curse of God if he is lying. But if his wife swears four times by God that his charge is false and calls down His curse upon herself if it be true, she shall receive no punishment.

But for God's grace and mercy, His wisdom and forgiveness, this would never have been revealed to you.

Those who invented that slander 24:11
were a number of your own people. Do not regard it as a misfortune, for it has proved an advantage. Each one of them shall be punished according to his crime. As for him who had the greater share in it, his punishment shall be terrible indeed.

When you heard it, why did the 24:12
faithful, men and women, not think well of their own people, and say: 'This is an evident falsehood'? Why did they not produce four witnesses? If they could not produce any witnesses, then they were surely lying in the sight of God.

But for God's grace and mercy towards you in this life and in the hereafter, you would have been sternly punished for what you did. You carried with your tongues and uttered with your mouths what you did not know. You may have thought it a trifle, but in the sight of God it was a grave offence.

When you heard it, why did you not say: 'It is not right for us to speak of this. God forbid! This is a monstrous slander'?

God bids you never to repeat the like, if you are true believers. God makes

plain to you His revelations. He is all-
knowing and wise.

24:19 Those who delight in spreading
slanders against the faithful shall be
sternly punished in this life and in the
hereafter. God knows, but you know not.

But for God's grace and mercy, His
compassion and forgiveness, you would
have long since been punished.

You that are true believers, do not
walk in Satan's footsteps. He that
walks in Satan's footsteps is incited
to indecency and evil. But for God's
grace and mercy, none of you would
have ever been cleansed of sin. God
purifies whom He will; God hears all and
knows all.

Let the rich and honourable
among you not swear to withhold their
gifts from their kindred, the poor, and
those who have fled their homes for the
cause of God. Rather let them pardon
and forgive. Do you not wish God to forgive you? God is forgiving and merciful.

24:23 Those who defame honourable but
careless believing women shall be
cursed in this world and in the here-
24:24 after. Theirs shall be a woeful punishment on the day when their own
tongues, hands, and feet will testify to
what they did. On that day God will
justly requite them. They shall know
that God is the Glorious Truth.

Unclean women are for unclean
men, and unclean men for unclean
women. But good women are for good
men, and good men for good women.
These shall be cleared of calumny; they
shall be shown forgiveness, and a generous provision shall be made for them.

Believers, do not enter the
dwellings of other men until you have
asked their owners' permission and
wished them peace. That will be best
for you. Perchance you will take heed.

If you find no one in them, do not
go in till you are given leave. If you are
refused admission, it is but right that
you should go away. God has knowledge of all your actions.

It shall be no offence for you to
seek shelter in empty dwellings. God
knows what you hide and what you
reveal.

Enjoin believing men to turn their 24:30
eyes away from temptation and to
restrain their carnal desires. This will
make their lives purer. God has knowledge of all their actions.

Enjoin believing women to turn
their eyes away from temptation and to
preserve their chastity; to cover their
adornments (except such as are normally displayed); to draw their veils over
their bosoms and not to reveal their finery except to their husbands, their
fathers, their husbands' fathers, their
sons, their step-sons, their brothers,
their brothers' sons, their sisters' sons,
their women-servants, and their slave-
girls; male attendants lacking in natural
vigour, and children who have no carnal
knowledge of women. And let them not
stamp their feet when walking so as to
reveal their hidden trinkets.

Believers, turn to God in repentance, that you may prosper.

Take in marriage those among you 24:32
who are single and those of your male
and female slaves who are honest. If
they are poor, God will enrich them
from His own abundance. God is
munificent and all-knowing.

Let those who cannot afford to 24:33
marry live in continence until God shall
enrich them. As for those of your slaves
who wish to buy their liberty, free them
if you find in them any promise and
bestow on them a part of the riches
which God has given you.

You shall not force your slave-girls
into prostitution in order that you may
make money, if they wish to preserve
their chastity. If anyone compels them,

God will be forgiving and merciful to them.

We have sent down to you revelations showing you the right path. We have given you an account of those who have gone before you, and an admonition to righteous men.

24:35 God is the light of the heavens and
the earth. His light may be compared to a niche that enshrines a lamp, the lamp within a crystal of star-like brilliance. It is lit from a blessed olive tree neither eastern nor western. Its very oil would almost shine forth, though no fire touched it. Light upon light; God guides to His light whom He will.

God speaks in metaphors to men. God has knowledge of all things.

His light is found in temples which God has sanctioned to be built for the remembrance of His name. In them, morning and evening, His praise is sung by men whom neither trade nor profit can divert from remembering Him, from offering prayers, or from giving alms; who dread the day when men's hearts and eyes shall writhe with anguish; who hope that God will requite them for their noblest deeds and lavish His grace upon them. God gives without measure to whom He will.

As for the unbelievers, their works are like a mirage in a desert. The thirsty traveller thinks it is water, but when he comes near he finds that it is nothing. He finds God there, who pays him back in full. Swift is God's reckoning.

Or like darkness on a bottomless 24:40
ocean spread with clashing billows and overcast with clouds: darkness upon darkness. If he stretches out his hand he can scarcely see it. Indeed the man from whom God withholds His light shall find no light at all.

Do you not see how God is praised 24:41
by those in heaven and those on earth? The very birds praise Him as they wing their flight. He notes the prayers and praises of all His creatures, and has knowledge of all their actions.

It is God who has sovereignty over the heavens and the earth. To Him shall all things return.

Do you not see how God drives the clouds, then gathers and piles them up in masses which pour down torrents of rain? From heaven's mountains He sends down the hail, pelting with it whom He will and turning it away from whom He pleases. The flash of His lightning almost snatches off men's eyes.

He makes the night succeed the day: surely in this there is a lesson for clear-sighted men. . . .

## *Sūrah 71: Noah*

*In the Name of God, the Compassionate, the Merciful*

71:1 We sent forth Noah to his people, say-
ing: 'Give warning to your people before a woeful scourge overtakes them.'

He said: 'My people, I come to warn you plainly. Serve God and fear Him, and obey me. He will forgive you your sins and give you respite for an appointed term. When God's time arrives, none shall put it back. Would that you understood this!'

'Lord,' said Noah, 'day and night I
have pleaded with my people, but my 71:6

pleas have only added to their aver-
71:7 sion. Each time I call on them to seek
Your pardon, they thrust their fingers in
their ears and draw their cloaks over
their heads, persisting in sin and bearing themselves with insolent pride. I
called out loud to them, and appealed
to them in public and in private. "Seek
forgiveness of your Lord," I said. "He is
ever ready to forgive you. He sends
down abundant water from the sky for
you and bestows upon you wealth and
children. He has provided you with gardens and with running brooks. Why do
you deny the greatness of God when He
has made you in gradual stages? Can
you not see how He created the seven
heavens one above the other, placing in
them the moon for a light and the sun
for a lantern? God has brought you
forth from the earth like a plant, and to
the earth He will restore you. Then He
will bring you back afresh. He has made
the earth a vast expanse for you, so that
you may roam its spacious paths."'

And Noah said: 'Lord, my people 71:21
disobey me, and follow those whose
wealth and offspring will only hasten
their perdition. They have devised an
outrageous plot, and said to each
other: "Do not renounce your gods. Do
not forsake Wadd or Suwā' or Yaghūth
or Ya'ūq or Naṣr." [Names of idols.]
They have led numerous men astray.
You surely drive the wrongdoers to further error.'

And because of their sins they were
overwhelmed by the Flood and cast
into the Fire. They found none besides
God to help them.

And Noah said: 'Lord, do not
leave a single unbeliever on the earth.
If You spare them, they will mislead
Your servants and beget none but sinners and unbelievers. Forgive me, Lord,
and forgive my parents and every true 71:28
believer who seeks refuge in my house.
Forgive all the faithful, men and women,
and hasten the destruction of the
wrongdoers.'

## *Sūrah 76: Man*

*In the Name of God, the Compassionate, the Merciful*

76:1 Does there not pass over man a space of
time when his life is a blank [In the
womb]?

We have created man from the
union of the two sexes, so that We may
put him to the proof. We have endowed
him with hearing and sight and, be he
thankful or oblivious of Our favours,
We have shown him the right path.

For the unbelievers We have prepared chains and fetters, and a blazing
Fire. But the righteous shall drink of a
cup tempered at the Camphor Fountain, a gushing spring at which the servants of God will refresh themselves:
they who keep their vows and dread the
far-spread terrors of Judgement-day;
who, though they hold it dear, give sus- 76:8
tenance to the poor man, the orphan,
and the captive, saying: 'We feed you 76:9
for God's sake only; we seek of you neither recompense nor thanks: for we
fear from our Lord a day of anguish
and of woe.'

God will deliver them from the evil
of that day, and make their faces shine
with joy. He will reward them for their
steadfastness with robes of silk and
the delights of Paradise. Reclining
there upon soft couches, they shall feel

neither the scorching heat nor the biting cold. Trees will spread their shade around them, and fruits will hang in clusters over them.

They shall be served with silver dishes, and beakers as large as goblets; silver goblets which they themselves shall measure: and cups brim-full with ginger-flavoured water from a fount called Salsabīl. They shall be attended by boys graced with eternal youth, who to the beholder's eyes will seem like sprinkled pearls. When you gaze upon that scene, you will behold a kingdom blissful and glorious.

They shall be arrayed in garments of fine green silk and rich brocade, and adorned with bracelets of silver. Their
Lord will give them pure nectar to drink.
76:22 Thus shall you be rewarded; your
high endeavours are gratifying to God.

We have made known to you the Koran by gradual revelation; therefore await with patience the judgement of your Lord, and do not yield to the wicked and the unbelieving. Remember the name of your Lord morning and evening; in the night-time worship Him: praise Him all night long.

The unbelievers love this fleeting life too well, and thus prepare for themselves a heavy day of doom. *We* created them, and endowed their limbs and joints with strength; but if We please, We can replace them by other men.

This is indeed an admonition. Let him that will, take the right path to his Lord. Yet you cannot will, except by the
will of God. God is all-knowing and wise.
He is merciful to whom He will: but 76:31
for the wrongdoers He has prepared a
woeful punishment.

## *Sūrah 100: The War Steeds*

*In the Name of God, the Compassionate, the Merciful*

100:1 By the snorting war steeds, which strike
fire with their hoofs as they gallop to the raid at dawn and with a trail of dust split apart a massed army; man is ungrateful to his Lord! To this he himself shall bear witness.

He loves riches with all his heart. But is he not aware that when the dead are thrown out from their graves and
men's hidden thoughts are laid open,
their Lord will on that day have full 100:11
knowledge of them all?

## *Sūrah 101: The Disaster*

*In the Name of God, the Compassionate, the Merciful*

101:1 The Disaster! What is the Disaster?
Would that you knew what the Disaster is!

On that day men shall become like scattered moths and the mountains like tufts of carded wool.

Then he whose scales are heavy shall dwell in bliss; but he whose scales are light, the Abyss shall be his home.

Would that you knew what this is like!

It is a scorching fire. 101:11

## Sūrah 113: Daybreak

*In the Name of God, the Compassionate, the Merciful*

113:1 Say: 'I seek refuge in the Lord of Daybreak from the mischief of His creation; from the mischief of the night when she spreads her darkness; from
the mischief of conjuring witches; from 113:5
the mischief of the envier, when he envies.'

## Sūrah 114: Men

*In the Name of God, the Compassionate, the Merciful*

114:1 Say: 'I seek refuge in the Lord of men, the King of men, the God of men, from the mischief of the slinking prompter
who whispers in the hearts of men; 114:6
from jinn and men.'

## MUHAMMAD IBN ISHAQ (C. 704–C. 767)

*Translated by A. Guillaume*

The earliest surviving biography of Muhammad was written by Ibn Ishāq and has come down to us in an early ninth-century recension. A compilation of history, sayings, anecdotes, genealogies, stories, and poems recalled by a community's collective memory, the biography sets Muhammad's life within a vast stretch of history. It begins by placing the prophet in a line of descent from Adam to Abraham to Ishmael, the son Abraham cast into the desert (see Genesis, pp. 106–107). After recounting the ancient history of Arabia, Ibn Ishāq narrates the birth and life of Muhammad, recording the prophet's visions in the desert, his preaching in Mecca, the gradual development of a community of believers, their exile in Medina, their return to Mecca, and the religious wars that erupted between Muslims and nonbelievers. It concludes with Muhammad's death and burial.

Muhammad, born in Mecca in 570 CE, was orphaned and later raised by his grandfather and uncle, both powerful men in pre-Islamic Mecca. At twenty-five, he married a widow, Khadījah, (spelled Khadīja in Ibn Ishāq's text), in whose caravans he served. For about twenty years, he journeyed on trade routes throughout the Arabian peninsula, and his travels probably took him into both Jewish and Christian communities. In his forties, he began more rigorous spiritual meditation and retreated into the hills and caves outside of Mecca for solitude. In a vision, he was called to warn humanity to worship God alone, repudiate all idols, and prepare for the final day of judgment. Muhammad was frightened at first, bewildered by the vision and voice, doubting their origin. He gradually grew convinced, as the word of God came to him repeatedly. Supported by his first wife, Khadījah, he gained confidence and very gradually began preaching his monotheism in Mecca, praising a transcendent and omnipotent God and warning of a final divine judgment and bodily resurrection. He and his followers were persecuted by powerful priests and aristocrats who found his teachings absurd or threatening. The Meccan community was, at the time, worshiping a pantheon of more than three-hundred pre-Islamic gods and idols. Especially powerful in the pantheon were distant descendents of ancient Sumerian and Babylonian deities: the high god of the Ka'bah in Mecca and his three daughters: al-'Uzzā, a goddess figure akin to Venus and associated with the morning star to whom human sacrifices were still offered in Muhammad's lifetime; al-Lāt, another astral goddess of sacred sanctuaries where trees could not be felled nor living beings wounded or killed; and Manāh, goddess of fate. After a lifetime spent building a spiritual community, preserving a manifestation of God's word on earth (the Qur'ān), providing leadership in the wars for religious survival, and establishing a powerful community, Muhammad died. His daughter Fatīma, his only surviving heir, and her husband Ali provided a succession of spiritual leaders especially revered by Shi'ite Muslims.

The biography compiled by Ibn Ishāq is far more detailed than most accounts of spiritual leaders found in other religious traditions, and it takes great pains to establish the nature of its evidence by identifying its sources. (For comparisons, see the Gospel of Mark, pp. 692–716, and the Asvaghosha's Life of the Buddha, pp. 265–288.) To a Western reader, Ibn Ishāq's narrative seems to have moved its footnotes into the narrative. It is filled with phrases like "Husayn b. 'Abdullah told me. . ." and "al-Zuhrī said," and "Sa'īd b. al-Musayyib from Abū Hurayra told me that . . ." (*Ibn* means "son of" and is often shortened to "b." *Bint* means "daughter of." Because some of these attributions are long, they have occasionally been shortened in our selection.) Both women and men form substantial authoritative voices, and both participate in establishing the history in rather striking contrast to the Gospels (although both the biography and its written sources were obviously compiled by men).

Unlike biographies written in the third person, which tend to erase their collaborative and oral origins, Ibn Ishāq's text embeds *The Life of the Prophet* within a human community; and the life of the community and other figures' lives are recorded and given prominence. Sometimes the text registers the author's doubt about an account or about someone's words. Ibn Ishāq was, apparently, not always certain of the veracity of the eyewitness reports, and a careful, close reading of his text reveals moments when he is more and less convinced by them. The documentary nature of the narrative, though unfamiliar to a Western reader, provides a fascinating written example of the oral beginnings that lie behind numerous ancient and medieval narratives. The documentations also help emphasize the humanity of Muhammad, a key element that distinguishes him from divine figures like Jesus Christ or Buddha. Although miracles are ascribed to him, Muhammad himself said that the Qur'ān was the only miracle, and when his followers were tempted to worship him instead of God, he said, "Exalted be my Lord, I am but a mortal, a messenger" (Qur'ān 17:93). Abu Bakr, the spiritual and political leader of Islam after Muhammad's death, also warned: "If anyone worships Muhammad, Muhammad is dead; if anyone worships Allah, He is alive, immortal." The burdened documentary style of the biography contrasts sharply with the rhapsodic poetic inspirations of the Qur'ān. The selections from *The Life of the Prophet* included here provide only a few episodes of Ibn Ishāq's extensive biography.

## *from The Life of the Prophet*

### What Was Said to Āmina When She Had Conceived the Apostle

It is alleged in popular stories (and only God knows the truth) that Āmina d. Wahb, the mother of God's apostle, used to say when she was pregnant with God's apostle that a voice said to her, 'You are pregnant with the lord of this people and when he is born say, "I put him in the care of the One from the evil of every envier; then call him Muhammad."' As she was pregnant with him she saw a light come forth from her by which she could see the castles of Buṣrā in Syria. . . .

### The Birth of the Apostle and His Suckling

The apostle was born on Monday, 12th Rabī'u'l-awwal, in the year of the elephant. Al-Muṭṭalib b. 'Abdullah who had it from his grandfather Qays b. Makhrama said, 'I and the apostle were born at the same time in the year of the elephant.' . . .

Ṣāliḥ b. Ibrāhīm b. 'Abdu'l-Raḥmān b. 'Auf b. Yaḥyā b. 'Abdullah b. 'Abdu'l-Raḥmān b. Sa'd b. Zurāra al-Anṣārī said that his tribesmen said that Ḥassān b. Thābit said: 'I was a well-grown boy of seven or eight, understanding all that I heard, when I heard a Jew calling out at the top of his voice from the top of a fort in Yathrib "O company of Jews" until they all came together and called out "Confound you, what is the matter?" He answered: "Tonight has risen a star under which Aḥmad is to be born."'

I asked Sa'īd b. 'Abdu'l-Raḥmān b. Ḥassān b. Thābit how old Ḥassān was when the apostle came to Medina and he said he was 60 when the apostle came, he being 53. So Ḥassān heard this when he was seven years old.

After his birth his mother sent to tell his grandfather 'Abdu'l-Muṭṭalib that she had given birth to a boy and asked him to come and look at him. When he came she told him what she had seen when she conceived him and what was said to her and what she was ordered to call him. It is alleged that 'Abdu'l-Muṭṭalib took him before Hubal in the middle of the Ka'ba, where he stood and prayed to Allah thanking him for this gift. Then he brought him out and delivered him to his mother, and he tried to find foster-mothers for him. . . .

Jahm b. Abū Jahm the client of al-Ḥarīth informed me that Ḥalīma the apostle's foster-mother used to say that she went forth from her country with her husband and little son whom she was nursing, among the women of her tribe, in search of other babies to nurse. This was a year of famine when they were destitute. She was riding a dusky she-donkey of hers with an old she-camel which did not yield a drop of milk. They could not sleep the whole night because of the weeping of her hungry child. She had no milk to give him, nor could their she-camel provide a morning draught, but we were hoping for rain and relief. 'I rode upon my donkey which had kept back the other riders through its weakness and emaciation so that it was a nuisance to them. When we reached Mecca, we looked out for foster children, and the apostle of God was offered to everyone of us, and each woman refused him when she was told he was an orphan, because we hoped to get payment from the child's father. We said, "An orphan! and what will his mother and grandfather do?", and so we spurned him because of that. Every woman who came with me got a suckling except me, and when we decided to depart I said to my husband: "By God, I do not like the idea of returning with my friends without a suckling; I will go and take that orphan." He replied, "Do as you please; perhaps God will bless us on his account." So I went and took him for the sole reason that I could not find anyone else. I took him back to my baggage, and as soon as I put him in my bosom, my breasts overflowed with milk which he drank until he was satisfied, as also did his foster-brother. Then both of them slept, whereas before this we could not sleep with him. My husband got up and went to the old she-camel and lo, her udders were full; he milked it and he and I drank of her milk until we were completely satisfied, and we passed a happy night. In the morning my husband said: "Do you know, Ḥalīma, you have taken a blessed creature?" I said, "By God, I hope so." Then we set out and I was riding my she-ass and carrying him with me, and she went at such a pace that the other donkeys could not keep up so that my companions said to me, "Confound you! stop and wait for us. Isn't this the donkey on which you started?" "Certainly it is," I said. They replied, "By God, something extraordinary has happened." Then we came to our dwellings in the Banū Sa'd country and I do not know a country more barren than that.

'When we had him with us my flock used to yield milk in abundance. We milked them and drank while other people had not a drop, nor could they find anything in their animals' udders, so that our people were saying to their shepherds, "Woe to you! send your flock to graze where the daughter of Abū Dhuayb's shepherd goes." Even so, their flocks came back hungry not yielding a drop of milk, while mine had milk in abundance. We ceased not to recognize this bounty as coming from God for a period of two years, when I weaned him. He was growing up as none of the other children grew and by the time he was two he was a well-made child. We brought him to his mother, though we were most anxious to keep him with us because of the blessing which he brought us. I said to her: "I should like you to leave my little boy with me until he becomes a big boy, for I am afraid on his account of the pest in Mecca." We persisted until she sent him back with us.

'Some months after our return he and his brother were with our lambs behind the tents when his brother came running and said to us, "Two men clothed in white have seized that Qurayshī brother of mine and thrown him down and opened up his belly, and are stirring it up." [The Quraysh were a powerful Arab family group who controlled Mecca and the Ka'bah.] We ran towards him and found him standing up with a livid face. We took hold of him and asked him what was the matter. He said, "Two men in white raiment came and threw me down and opened up my belly and searched therein for I know not what." So we took him back to our tent.

'His father said to me, "I am afraid that this child has had a stroke, so take him back to his family before the result appears." So we picked him up and took him to his mother who asked why we had brought him when I had been anxious for his welfare and desirous of keeping him with me. I said to her, "God has let my son live so far and I have done my duty. I am afraid that ill will befall him, so I have brought him back to you as you wished." She asked me what happened and gave me no peace until I told her. When she asked if I feared a demon possessed him, I replied that I did. She answered that no demon had any power over her son who had a great future before him, and then she told how when she was pregnant with him a light went out from her which illumined the castles of Buṣrā in Syria, and that she had borne him with the least difficulty imaginable. When she bore him he put his hands on the ground lifting his head towards the heavens. "Leave him then and go in peace," she said.'

Thaur b. Yazīd from a learned person who I think was Khālid b. Ma'dān al Kalā'ī told me that some of the apostle's companions asked him to tell them about himself. He said: 'I am what Abraham my father prayed for and the good news of my brother Jesus. When my mother was carrying me she saw a light proceeding from her which showed her the castles of Syria. I was suckled among the B. Sa'd b. Bakr, and while I was with a brother of mine behind our tents shepherding the lambs, two men in white raiment came to me with a gold basin full of snow. Then they seized me and opened up my belly, extracted my heart and split it; then they extracted a black drop from it and threw it away; then they washed my heart and my belly with that snow until they had thoroughly cleaned them. Then one said to the other, weigh him against ten of his people; they did so and I outweighed them. Then they weighed me against a hundred and then a thousand, and I outweighed them. He said, "Leave him alone, for by God, if you weighed him against all his people he would outweigh them."'

The apostle of God used to say, There is no prophet but has shepherded a flock. When they said, 'You, too, apostle of God?', he said 'Yes.'

The apostle of God used to say to his companions, 'I am the most Arab of you all. I am of Quraysh, and I was suckled among the B. Sa'd b. Bakr.' It is alleged by some, but God knows the truth, that when his foster-mother brought him to Mecca he escaped her among the crowd while she was taking him to his people. She sought him and could not find him, so she went to 'Abdu'l-Muṭṭalib and said: 'I brought Muhammad tonight and when I was in the upper part of Mecca he escaped me and I don't know where he is.' So 'Abdu'l-Muṭṭalib went to the Ka'ba praying to God to restore him. They assert that Waraqa b. Naufal b. Asad and another man of Quraysh found him and brought him to 'Abdu'l-Muṭṭalib saying, 'We have found this son of yours in the upper part of Mecca.' 'Abdu'l-Muṭṭalib took him and put him on his shoulder as he went round the Ka'ba confiding him to God's protection and praying for him; then he sent him to his mother Āmina.

A learned person told me that what urged his foster-mother to return him to his mother, apart from what she told his mother, was that a number of Abyssinian Christians saw him with her when she brought him back after he had been weaned. They looked at him, asked questions about him, and studied him carefully, then they said to her, 'Let us take this boy, and bring him to our king and our country; for he will have a great future. We know all about him.' The person who told me this alleged that she could hardly get him away from them.

## Āmina Dies and the Apostle Lives with His Grandfather

The apostle lived with his mother Āmina d. Wahb and his grandfather 'Abdu'l-Muṭṭalib in God's care and keeping like a fine plant, God wishing to honour him. When he was six years old his mother Āmina died.

'Abdullah b. Abū Bakr . . . told me that the apostle's mother died in Abwā' between Mecca and Medina on her return from a visit with him to his maternal uncles of B. 'Adīy b. al-Najjār when he was six years old. Thus the apostle was left to his grandfather for whom they made a bed in the shade of the Ka'ba. His sons used to sit round the bed until he came out to it, but none of them sat upon it out of respect for him. The apostle, still a little boy, used to come and sit on it and his uncles would drive him away. When 'Abdu'l-Muṭṭalib saw this he said: 'Let my son alone, for by Allah he has a great future.' Then he would make him sit beside him on his bed and would stroke his back with his hand. It used to please him to see what he did.

* * *

## The Apostle of God Marries Khadīja

Khadīja was a merchant woman of dignity and wealth. She used to hire men to carry merchandise outside the country on a profit-sharing basis, for Quraysh were a people given to commerce. Now when she heard about the prophet's truthfulness, trustworthiness, and honourable character, she sent for him and proposed that he should take her goods to Syria and trade with them, while she would pay him more than she paid others. He was to take a lad of hers called Maysara. The apostle of God accepted the proposal, and the two set forth until they came to Syria.

The apostle stopped in the shade of a tree near a monk's cell, when the monk came up to Maysara and asked who the man was who was resting beneath the tree. He told him that he was of Quraysh, the people who held the sanctuary; and the monk exclaimed: 'None but a prophet ever sat beneath this tree.'

Then the prophet sold the goods he had brought and bought what he wanted to buy and began the return journey to Mecca. The story goes that at the height of noon when the heat was intense as he rode his beast Maysara saw two angels shading the apostle from the sun's rays. When he brought Khadīja her property she sold it and it amounted to double or thereabouts. Maysara for his part told her about the two angels who shaded him and of the monk's words. Now Khadīja was a determined, noble, and intelligent woman possessing the properties with which God willed to honour her. So when Maysara told her these things she sent to the apostle of God and—so the story goes—said: 'O son of my uncle I like you because of our relationship and your high reputation among your people, your trustworthiness and good character and truthfulness.' Then she proposed marriage. Now Khadīja at that time was the best born woman in Quraysh, of the greatest dignity and, too, the richest. All her people were eager to get possession of her wealth if it were possible.

Khadīja was the daughter of Khuwaylid b. Asad b. 'Abdu'l-'Uzzā b. Quṣayy b. Kilāb b. Murra b. Ka'b b. Lu'ayy b. Ghālib b. Fihr. Her mother was Fāṭima d. Zā'ida b. al-Aṣamm b. Rawāḥa b. Ḥajar b. 'Abd b. Ma'īṣ b. 'Āmir b. Lu'ayy b. Ghālib b. Fihr. Her mother was Hāla d. 'Abdu Manāf b. al-Ḥārith b. 'Amr b. Munqidh b. 'Amr b. Ma'īṣ b. 'Āmir b. Lu'ayy b. Ghālib b. Fihr. Hāla's mother was Qilāba d. Su'ayd b. Sa'd b. Sahm b. 'Amr b. Huṣayṣ b. Ka'b b. Lu'ayy b. Ghālib b. Fihr.

The apostle of God told his uncles of Khadīja's proposal, and his uncle Ḥamza b. 'Abdu'l-Muṭṭalib went with him to Khuwaylid b. Asad and asked for her hand and he married her.

She was the mother of all the apostle's children except Ibrāhīm, namely al-Qāsim (whereby he was known as Abu'l-Qāsim); al-Ṭāhir, al-Ṭayyib, Zaynab, Ruqayya, Umm Kulthūm, and Fāṭima.

Al-Qāsim, al-Ṭayyib, and al-Ṭāhir died in paganism. All his daughters lived into Islam, embraced it, and migrated with him to Medina. . . .

## The Prophet's Mission

When Muhammad the apostle of God reached the age of forty God sent him in compassion to mankind, 'as an evangelist to all men.' Now God had made a covenant with every prophet whom he had sent before him that he should believe in him, testify to his truth and help him against his adversaries, and he required of them that they should transmit that to everyone who believed in them, and they carried out their obligations in that respect. God said to Muhammad, 'When God made a covenant with the prophets (He said) this is the scripture and wisdom which I have given you, afterwards an apostle will come confirming what you know that you may believe in him and help him.' He said, 'Do you accept this and take up my burden?' i.e. the burden of my agreement which I have laid upon you. They said, 'We accept it.' He answered, 'Then bear witness and I am a witness with you.' Thus God made a covenant with all the prophets that they should testify to his truth and help him against his adversaries and they transmitted that obligation to those who believed in them among the two monotheistic religions. . . .

Al-Zuhrī related from 'Urwa b. Zubayr that 'Ā'isha told him that when Allah desired to honour Muhammad and have mercy on His servants by means of him, the first sign of prophethood vouchsafed to the apostle was true visions, resembling the brightness of daybreak, which were shown to him in his sleep. And Allah, she said, made him love solitude so that he liked nothing better than to be alone.

'Abdu'l-Malik who had a retentive memory related to me from a certain scholar that the apostle at the time when Allah willed to bestow His grace upon him and endow him with prophethood, would go forth for his affair and journey far afield until he reached the glens of Mecca and the beds of its valleys where no house was in sight; and not a stone or tree that he passed by but would say, 'Peace unto thee, O apostle of Allah.' And the apostle would turn to his right and left and look behind him and he would see naught but trees and stones. Thus he stayed seeing and hearing so long as it pleased Allah that he should stay. Then Gabriel came to him with the gift of God's grace whilst he was on Ḥirā' in the month of Ramaḍān. . . .

Wahb . . . told me that 'Ubayd said to him: Every year during that month the apostle would pray in seclusion and give food to the poor that came to him. And when he completed the month and returned from his seclusion, first of all before entering his house he would go to the Ka'ba and walk round it seven times or as often as it pleased God; then he would go back to his house until in the year when God sent him, in the month of Ramaḍān in which God willed concerning him what He willed of His grace, the apostle set forth to Ḥirā' as was his wont, and his family with him. When it was the night on which God honoured him with his mission and showed mercy on His servants thereby, Gabriel brought him the command of God. 'He came to me,' said the apostle of God, 'while I was asleep, with a coverlet of brocade whereon was some writing, and said, "Read!" I said, "What shall I read?" He pressed me with it so tightly that I thought it was death; then he let me go and said, "Read!" I said, "What shall I read?" He pressed me with it again so that I thought it was death; then he let me go and said "Read!" I said, "What shall I read?" He pressed me with it the third time so that I thought it was death and said "Read!" I said, "What then shall I read?"—and this I said only to deliver myself from him, lest he should do the same to me again. He said:

> "Read in the name of thy Lord
> who created,
> Who created man of blood
> coagulated.
> Read! Thy Lord is the most
> beneficent,
> Who taught by the pen,
> Taught that which they knew not
> unto men."

'So I read it, and he departed from me. And I awoke from my sleep, and it was as though these words were written on my heart. Now none of God's creatures was more hateful to me than an (ecstatic) poet or a man possessed: I could not even look at them. I thought, Woe is me poet or possessed—Never shall Quraysh say this of me! I will go to the top of the mountain and throw myself down that I may kill myself and gain rest. So I went forth to do so and then when I was midway on the mountain, I heard a voice from heaven saying, "O Muhammad! thou art the apostle of God and I am Gabriel." I raised my head towards heaven to see who was speaking and lo, Gabriel in the form of a man with feet astride the horizon, saying, "O Muhammad! thou art the apostle of God and I am Gabriel." I stood gazing at him, and that turned me from my purpose moving neither forward nor backward; then I began to turn my face away from him, but towards whatever region of the sky I looked, I saw him as before. And I continued standing there, neither advancing nor turning back, until Khadīja sent her messengers in search of me and they gained the high ground above Mecca and returned to her while I was standing in the same place; then he parted from me and I from him, returning to my family. And I came to Khadīja and sat by her thigh and drew close to her. She said, "O Abū'l-Qāsim, where hast thou been? By God, I sent my messengers in search of thee, and they reached the high ground above Mecca and returned to me." I said to her, "Woe is me poet or possessed." She said, "I take refuge in God from that O Abū'l-Qāsim. God would not treat you thus since he knows your truthfulness, your great trustworthiness, your fine character, and your kindness. This cannot be, my dear. Perhaps you did see something." "Yes, I did," I said. Then I told her of what I had seen; and she said, "Rejoice, O son of my uncle, and be of good heart. Verily, by Him in whose hand is Khadīja's soul, I have hope that thou wilt be the prophet of this people."' Then she rose and gathered her garments about her and set forth to her cousin Waraqa b. Naufal b. Asad b. 'Abdu'l-'Uzzā b. Quṣayy, who had become a Christian and read the scriptures and learned from those that follow the Torah and the Gospel. And when she related to him what the apostle of God told her he had seen and heard, Waraqa cried, 'Holy! Holy! Verily by Him in whose hand is Waraqa's soul, if thou hast spoken to me the truth, O Khadīja, there hath come unto him the greatest Nāmūs (meaning Gabriel) who came to Moses aforetime, and lo, he is the prophet of this people. Bid him be of good heart.' So Khadīja returned to the apostle of God and told him what Waraqa had said and that calmed his fears somewhat. And when the apostle of God had finished his period of seclusion and returned to Mecca, in the first place he performed the circumambulation of the Ka'ba, as was his wont. While he was doing it, Waraqa met him and said, 'O son of my brother, tell me what thou hast seen and heard.' The apostle told him, and Waraqa said, 'Surely, by Him in whose hand is Waraqa's soul, thou art the prophet of this people. There hath come unto thee the greatest Nāmūs, who came unto Moses. Thou wilt be called a liar, and they will use thee despitefully and cast thee out and fight against thee. Verily, if I live to see that day, I will help God in such wise as He knoweth.' Then he brought his head near to him and kissed his forehead; and the apostle went to his own house. Waraqa's words added to his confidence and lightened his anxiety.

Ismā'īl b. Abū Ḥakīm, a freedman of the family of al-Zubayr, told me on Khadīja's authority that she said to the apostle of God, 'O son of my uncle, are you able to tell me about your visitant, when he comes to you?' He replied that he could, and she asked him to tell her when he came. So when Gabriel came to him, as he was wont, the apostle said to Khadīja, 'This is Gabriel who has just come to me.' 'Get up, O son of my uncle,' she said, 'and sit by my left thigh.' The apostle did so, and she said, 'Can you see him?' 'Yes,' he said. She said, 'Then turn round and sit on my right thigh.' He did so, and she said, 'Can you see him?' When he said that he could she asked him to move and sit in her lap. When he had done this she again asked if he could see him, and when he said yes, she disclosed her form and cast aside her veil while the apostle was sitting in her lap. Then she said, 'Can you see him?' And he replied, 'No.' She said, 'O son of my uncle, rejoice and be of good heart, by God he is an angel and not a satan.'

I told 'Abdullah b. Ḥasan this story and he said, 'I heard my mother Fāṭima, daughter of Ḥusayn, talking about this tradition from Khadīja, but as I heard it she made the apostle of God come inside her shift, and thereupon Gabriel departed, and she said to the apostle of God, "This verily is an angel and not a satan."'

## The Beginning of the Sending Down of the Qurān

The apostle began to receive revelations in the month of Ramaḍān. In the words of God, 'The month of Ramaḍān in which the Qurān was brought down as a guidance to men, and proofs of guidance and a decisive criterion.' And again, 'Verily we have sent it down on the night of destiny, and what has shown you what the night of destiny is? The night of destiny is better than a thousand months. In it the angels and the spirit descend by their Lord's permission with every matter. It is peace until the rise of dawn.' Again, 'Ḥ.M. [Ḥā' mīm, the opening of Sūrah 44] by the perspicuous book, verily we have sent it down in a blessed night. Verily, we were warning. In it every wise matter is decided as a command from us. Verily we sent it down.' And again, 'Had you believed in God and what we sent down to Our servant on the day of decision, the day on which the two parties met,' i.e. the meeting of the apostle with the polytheists in Badr. Abū Ja'far Muhammad . . . told me that the apostle of God met the polytheists in Badr on the morning of Friday, the 17th of Ramaḍān.

Then revelation came fully to the apostle while he was believing in Him and in the truth of His message. He received it willingly, and took upon himself what it entailed whether of man's goodwill or anger. Prophecy is a troublesome burden—only strong, resolute messengers can bear it by God's help and grace, because of the opposition which they meet from men in conveying God's message. The apostle carried out God's orders in spite of the opposition and ill treatment which he met with.

## Khadīja, Daughter of Khuwaylid, Accepts Islam

Khadīja believed in him and accepted as true what he brought from God, and helped him in his work. She was the first to believe in God and His apostle, and in the truth of his message. By her God lightened the burden of His prophet. He never met with contradiction and charges of falsehood, which saddened him, but [that] God comforted him by her when he went home. She strengthened him, lightened his burden, proclaimed his truth, and belittled men's opposition. May God Almighty have mercy upon her!

Hishām b. 'Urwa told me on the authority of his father 'Urwa b. al-Zubayr . . . that the apostle said, 'I was commanded to give Khadīja the good news of a house of *qaṣab* wherein would be no clamour and no toil.'

Then revelations stopped for a time so that the apostle of God was distressed and grieved. Then Gabriel brought him the Sūra of the Morning, in which his Lord, who had so honoured him, swore that He had not forsaken him, and did not hate him. God said, 'By the morning and the night when it is still, thy Lord hath not forsaken nor hated thee,' meaning that He has not left you and forsaken you, nor hated you after having loved you. 'And verily, the latter end is better for you than the beginning,' i.e. What I have for you when you return to Me is better than the honour which I have given you in the world. 'And your Lord will give you and will satisfy you,' i.e. of victory in this world and reward in the next. 'Did he not find you an orphan and give you refuge, going astray and guided you, found you poor and made you rich?' God thus told him of how He had begun to honour him in his earthly life, and of His kindness to him as an orphan poor and wandering astray, and of His delivering him from all that by His compassion.

'Do not oppress the orphan and do not repel the beggar.' That is, do not be a tyrant or proud or harsh or mean towards the weakest of God's creatures.

'Speak of the kindness of thy Lord,' i.e. tell about the kindness of God in giving you prophecy, mention it and call men to it.

So the apostle began to mention secretly God's kindness to him and to his servants in the matter of prophecy to everyone among his people whom he could trust.

## The Prescription of Prayer

The apostle was ordered to pray and so he prayed. Ṣāliḥ b. Kaisān from 'Urwa b. al-Zubayr from 'Ā'isha told me that she said, 'When prayer was first laid on the apostle it was with two prostrations for every prayer: then God raised it to four prostrations at home, while on a journey the former, ordinance of two prostrations held.'

A learned person told me that when prayer was laid on the apostle Gabriel came to him while he was on the heights of Mecca and dug a hole for him with his heel in the side of the valley from which a fountain gushed forth, and Gabriel performed the ritual ablution as the apostle watched him. This was in order to show him how to purify himself before prayer. Then the apostle performed the ritual ablution as he had seen Gabriel do it. Then Gabriel said a prayer with him while the apostle prayed with his prayer. Then Gabriel left him. The apostle came to Khadīja and performed the ritual for her as Gabriel had done for him, and she copied him. Then he prayed with her as Gabriel had prayed with him, and she prayed his prayer. . . .

## The Apostle's Public Reading and the Response

. . . When the apostle's companions prayed they went to the glens so that their people could not see them praying, and while Sa'd b. Abū Waqqāṣ was with a number of the prophet's companions in one of the glens of Mecca, a band of polytheists came upon them while they were praying and rudely interrupted them. They blamed them for what they were doing until they came to blows, and it was on that occasion that Sa'd smote a polytheist with the jawbone of a camel and wounded him. This was the first blood to be shed in Islam.

When the apostle openly displayed Islam as God ordered him his people did not withdraw or turn against him, so far as I have heard, until he spoke disparagingly of their gods. When he did that they took great offence and resolved unanimously to treat him as an enemy, except those whom God had protected by Islam from such evil, but they were a despised minority. Abâ ÂÅlib his uncle treated the apostle kindly and protected him, the latter continuing to obey God's commands, nothing turning him back. When Quraysh saw that he would not yield to them and withdrew from them and insulted their gods and that his uncle treated him kindly and stood up in his defence and would not give him up to them, some of their leading men went to Abâ ÂÅlib. . . . They said, 'O Abâ ÂÅlib, your nephew has cursed our gods, insulted our religion, mocked our way of life and accused our forefathers of error; either you must stop him or you must let us get at him, for you yourself are in the same position as we are in opposition to him and we will rid you of him.' He gave them a conciliatory reply and a soft answer and they went away.

The apostle continued on his way, publishing God's religion and calling men thereto. In consequence his relations with Quraysh deteriorated and men withdrew from him in enmity. They were always talking about him and inciting one another against him. Then they went to Abū Ṭālib a second time and said, 'You have a high and lofty position among us, and we have asked you to put a stop to your nephew's activities but you have not done so. By God, we cannot endure that our fathers should be reviled, our customs mocked and our gods insulted. Until you rid us of him we will fight the pair of you until one side perishes,' or words to that effect. Thus saying, they went off. Abū Ṭālib was deeply distressed at the breach with his people and their enmity but he could not desert the apostle and give him up to them.

Ya'qūb b. 'Utba b. al-Mughīra b. al-Akhnas told me that he was told that after hearing these words from the Quraysh Abū Ṭālib sent for his nephew and told him what his people had said. 'Spare me and yourself,' he said. 'Do not put on me a burden greater than I can bear.' The apostle thought that his uncle had the idea of abandoning and betraying him, and that he was going to lose his help and support. He answered, 'O my uncle, by God, if they put the sun in my right hand and the moon in my left on condition that I abandoned this course, until God has made it victorious, or I perish therein, I would not abandon it.' Then the apostle broke into tears, and got up. As he turned away his uncle called him and said, 'Come back, my nephew,' and when he came back, he said, 'Go and say what you please, for by God I will never give you up on any account.'

When the Quraysh perceived that Abū Ṭālib had refused to give up the apostle, and that he was resolved to part company with them, they went to him with 'Umāra b. al-Walīd b. al-Mughīra and said, according to my information, 'O Abū Ṭālib, this is 'Umāra, the strongest and most handsome young man among Quraysh, so take him and you will have the benefit of his intelligence and support; adopt him as a son and give up to us this nephew of yours, who has opposed your religion and the religion of your fathers, severed the unity of your people, and mocked our way of life, so that we may kill him. This will be man for man.' He answered, 'By God, this is an evil thing that you would put upon me, would you give me your son that I should feed him for you, and should I give you my son that you should kill him? By God, this shall never be.' Al-Muṭ'im b. 'Adīy said, 'Your people have treated you fairly and have taken pains to avoid what you dislike. I do not think that you are willing to accept anything from them.' Abū Ṭālib replied, 'They have not treated me fairly, by God, but you have agreed to betray me and help the people against me, so do what you like,' or words to that effect. So the situation worsened, the quarrel became heated and people were sharply divided, and openly showed their animosity to their opponents. Abū Ṭālib wrote the following verses, indirectly attacking Muṭ'im, and including those who had abandoned him from the 'Abdu Manāf, and his enemies among the tribes of Quraysh. He mentions therein what they had asked of him and his estrangement from them.

Say to 'Amr and al-Walīd and Muṭ'im
Rather than your protection give me a young camel,
Weak, grumbling and murmuring,
Sprinkling its flanks with its urine
Lagging behind the herd, and not keeping up.
When it goes up the desert ridges, you would call it a weasel.
I see our two brothers, sons of our mother and father,
When they are asked for help, say 'It is not our business.'
Nay, it is their affair, but they have fallen away,
As a rock falls from the top of Dhū 'Alaq.
I mean especially 'Abdu Shams and Naufal,
Who have flung us aside like a burning coal.
They have slandered their brothers among the people;
Their hands are emptied of them.
They shared their fame with men of low birth,
With men whose fathers were whispered about;
And Taym, and Makhzūm, and Zuhra, are of them
Who had been friends of ours when help was sought;
By God, there will always be enmity between us
As long as one of our descendants lives.
Their minds and thoughts were foolish,
They were entirely without judgement.

Then the Quraysh incited people against the companions of the apostle who had become Muslims. Every tribe fell upon the Muslims among them, beating them and seducing them from their religion. God protected His apostle from them through his uncle, who, when he saw what Quraysh were doing, called upon B. Hāshim and B. al-Muṭṭalib to stand with him in protecting the apostle. This they agreed to do, with the exception of Abū Lahab, the accursed enemy of God. . . .

## al-Walīd b. al-Mughīra

When the fair was due, a number of the Quraysh came to al-Walīd b. al-Mughīra, who was a man of some standing, and he addressed them in these words: 'The time of the fair has come round again and representatives of the Arabs will come to you and they will have heard about this fellow of yours, so agree upon one opinion without dispute so that none will give the lie to the other.' They replied, 'You give us your opinion about him.' He said, 'No, you speak and I will listen.' They said, 'He is a *kāhin*.' He said, 'By God, he is not that, for he has not the unintelligent murmuring and rhymed speech of the *kāhin*.' 'Then he is possessed,' they said. 'No, he is not that,' he said, 'we have seen possessed ones, and here is no choking, spasmodic movements and whispering.' 'Then he is a poet,' they said. 'No, he is no poet, for we know poetry in all its forms and metres.' 'Then he is a sorcerer.' 'No, we have seen sorcerers and their sorcery, and here is no spitting and no knots.' 'Then what are we to say, O Abū 'Abdu Shams?' they asked. He replied, 'By God, his speech is sweet, his root is a palm-tree whose branches are fruitful, and everything you have said would be known to be false. The nearest thing to the truth is your saying that he is a sorcerer, who has brought a message by which he separates a man from his father, or from his brother, or from his wife, or from his family.' . . .

## Rukāna al-Muṭṭalibī Wrestles with the Apostle

My father Isḥāq b. Yasār told me saying: Rukāna b. 'Abdu Yazīd b. Hāshim b. 'Abdu'l-Muṭṭalib b. 'Abdu Manāf was the strongest man among Quraysh, and one day he met the apostle in one of the passes of Mecca alone: 'Rukāna,' said he, 'why won't you fear God and accept my preaching?' 'If I knew that what you say is true I would follow you,' he said. The apostle then asked him if he would recognize that he spoke the truth if he threw him, and when he said Yes they began to wrestle, and when the apostle got a firm grip of him he threw him to the ground, he being unable to offer any effective resistance. 'Do it again, Muhammad,' he said, and he did it again. 'This is extraordinary,' he said, 'can you really throw me?' 'I can show you something more wonderful than that if you wish. I will call this tree that you see and it will come to me.' 'Call it,' he said. He called it and it advanced until it stood before the apostle. Then he said, 'Retire to your place,' and it did so.

Then Rukāna went to his people the B. 'Abdu Manāf and told them that their tribesman could compete with any sorcerer in the world, for he had never seen such sorcery in his life, and he went on to tell them of what he had seen and what Muhammad had done.

## A Deputation of Christians Accept Islam

While the apostle was in Mecca some twenty Christians came to him from Abyssinia when they heard news of him. They found him in the mosque and sat and talked with him, asking him questions, while some Qurayshites were in their meeting round the Ka'ba. When they had asked all the questions they wished the apostle invited them to come to God and read the Qurān to them.

When they heard the Qurān their eyes flowed with tears, and they accepted God's call, believed in him, and declared his truth. . . .

## The Night Journey and the Ascent to Heaven

. . . The following account reached me from 'Abdullah b. Mas'ūd and Abū Sa'īd al-Khudrī, and 'Ā'isha the prophet's wife, and Mu'āwiya b. Abū Sufyān, and al-Ḥasan b. Abū'l-Ḥasan al-Baṣrī, and Ibn Shihāb al-Zuhrī and Qatāda and other traditionists, and Umm Hāni' d. of Abū Ṭālib. It is pieced together in the story that follows, each one contributing something of what he was told about what happened when he was taken on the night journey. The matter of the place of the journey and what is said about it is a searching test and a matter of God's power and authority wherein is a lesson for the intelligent; and guidance and mercy and strengthening to those who believe. It was certainly an act of God by which He took him by night in what way He pleased to show him His signs which He willed him to see so that he witnessed His mighty sovereignty and power by which He does what He wills to do.

According to what I have heard 'Abdullah b. Mas'ūd used to say: Burāq, the animal whose every stride carried it as far as its eye could reach on which the prophets before him used to ride was brought to the apostle and he was mounted on it. His companion Gabriel went with him to see the wonders between heaven and earth, until he came to Jerusalem's temple. There he found Abraham the friend of God, Moses, and Jesus assembled with a company of the prophets, and he prayed with them. Then he was brought three vessels containing milk, wine, and water respectively. The apostle said: 'I heard a voice saying when these were offered to me: If he takes the water he will be drowned and his people also; if he takes the wine he will go astray and his people also; and if he takes the milk he will be rightly guided and his people also. So I took the vessel containing milk and drank it. Gabriel said to me, You have been rightly guided and so will your people be, Muhammad.'

I was told that al-Ḥasan said that the apostle said: 'While I was sleeping in the Ḥījr Gabriel came and stirred me with his foot. I sat up but saw nothing and lay down again. He came a second time and stirred me with his foot. I sat up but saw nothing and lay down again. He came to me the third time and stirred me with his foot. I sat up and he took hold of my arm and I stood beside him and he brought me out to the door of the mosque and there was a white animal, half mule, half donkey, with wings on its sides with which it propelled its feet, putting down each forefoot at the limit of its sight and he mounted me on it. Then he went out with me keeping close to me.'

'I was told that Qatāda said that he was told that the apostle said: 'When I came up to mount him he shied. Gabriel placed his hand on its mane and said, Are you not ashamed, O Burāq, to behave in this way? By God, none more honourable before God than Muhammad has ever ridden you before. The animal was so ashamed that he broke out into a sweat and stood still so that I could mount him.'

In his story al-Ḥaṣan said: 'The apostle and Gabriel went their way until they arrived at the temple at Jerusalem. There he found Abraham, Moses, and Jesus among a company of the prophets.

The apostle acted as their imam in prayer. Then he was brought two vessels, one containing wine and the other milk. The apostle took the milk and drank it, leaving the wine. Gabriel said: "You have been rightly guided to the way of nature and so will your people be, Muhammad. Wine is forbidden you." Then the apostle returned to Mecca and in the morning he told Quraysh what had happened. Most of them said, "By God, this is a plain absurdity! A caravan takes a month to go to Syria and a month to return and can Muhammad do the return journey in one night?" Many Muslims gave up their faith; some went to Abū Bakr and said, "What do you think of your friend now, Abū Bakr? He alleges that he went to Jerusalem last night and prayed there and came back to Mecca." He replied that they were lying about the apostle; but they said that he was in the mosque at that very moment telling the people about it. Abū Bakr said, "If he says so then it is true. And what is so surprising in that? He tells me that communications from God from heaven to earth come to him in an hour of a day or night and I believe him, and that is more extraordinary than that at which you boggle!" He then went to the apostle and asked him if these reports were true, and when he said they were, he asked him to describe Jerusalem to him.' Al-Ḥasan said that he was lifted up so that he could see the apostle speaking as be told Abū Bakr what Jerusalem was like. Whenever he described a part of it he said, 'That's true. I testify that you are the apostle of God' until he had completed the description, and then the apostle said, 'And you, Abū Bakr, are the *Ṣiddīq*' [Testifier to Truth]. This was the occasion on which he got this honorific.

Al-Ḥasan continued: God sent down concerning those who left Islam for this reason: 'We made the vision which we showed thee only for a test to men and the accursed tree in the Qurān. We put them in fear, but it only adds to their heinous error.' Such is al-Ḥasan's story with additions from Qatāda.

One of Abū Bakr's family told me that 'Ā'isha the prophet's wife used to say: 'The apostle's body remained where it was but God removed his spirit by night.'

Ya'qūb . . . told me that Mu'āwiya when he was asked about the apostle's night journey said, 'It was a true vision from God.' What these two latter said does not contradict what al-Ḥasan said, seeing that God Himself said, 'We made the vision which we showed thee only for a test to men;' nor does it contradict what God said in the story of Abraham when he said to his son, 'O my son, verily I saw in a dream that I must sacrifice thee,' and he acted accordingly. Thus, as I see it, revelation from God comes to the prophets waking or sleeping.

I have heard that the apostle used to say, 'My eyes sleep while my heart is awake.' Only God knows how revelation came and he saw what he saw. But whether he was asleep or awake, it was all true and actually happened.

Al-Zuhrī alleged as from Sa'īd b. al-Musayyab that the apostle described to his companions Abraham, Moses, and Jesus, as he saw them that night, saying: 'I have never seen a man more like myself than Abraham. Moses was a ruddy faced man, tall, thinly fleshed, curly haired with a hooked nose as though he were of the Shanu'a. Jesus, Son of Mary, was a reddish man of medium height with lank hair with many freckles on his face as though he had just come from a bath. One would suppose that his head was dripping with water, though there was no water on it. The man most like him among you is 'Urwa b. Mas'ūd al-Thaqafī.'

The following report has reached me from Umm Hanī' d. of Abū Ṭālib, whose name was Hind, concerning the apostle's night journey. She said: 'The apostle went on no night journey except while he was in my house. He slept that night in my house. He prayed the final night prayer, then he slept and we slept. A little before dawn the apostle woke us, and when we had prayed the dawn prayer he said, "O Umm Hāni', I prayed with you the last evening prayer in this valley as you saw. Then I went to Jerusalem and prayed there. Then I have just prayed the morning prayer with you as you see." He got up to go out and I took hold of his robe and laid bare his belly as though it were a folded Egyptian garment. I said, "O prophet of God, don't talk to the people about it for they will give you the lie and insult you." He said, "By God, I certainly will tell them." I said to a negress, a slave of mine, Follow the apostle and listen to what he says to the people, and what they say to him. He did tell them and they were amazed and asked what proof he had. He replied that he had passed the caravan of so-and-so in such-and-such a valley and the animal he bestrode scared them and a camel bolted, "and I showed them where it was as I was on the way to Syria. I carried on until in Ḍajanān I passed by a caravan of the Banū so-and-so. I found the people asleep. They had a jar of water covered with something. I took the covering off and drank the water replacing the cover. The proof of that is that their caravan is this moment coming down from al-Baiḍā' by the pass of al-Tan'īm led by a dusky camel loaded with two sacks one black and the other multihued." The people hurried to the pass and the first camel they met was as he had described. They asked the men about the vessel and they told them that they had left it full of water and covered it and that when they woke it was covered but empty. They asked the others too who were in Mecca and they said that it was quite right: they had been scared and a camel had bolted, and they had heard a man calling them to it so that they were able to recover it.'

## The Ascent to Heaven

One whom I have no reason to doubt told me on the authority of Abū Sa'īd al-Khudrī: I heard the apostle say, 'After the completion of my business in Jerusalem a ladder was brought to me finer than any I have ever seen. It was that to which the dying man looks when death approaches. My companion mounted it with me until we came to one of the gates of heaven called the Gate of the Watchers. An angel called Ismā'īl was in charge of it, and under his command were twelve thousand angels each of them having twelve thousand angels under his command.' As he told this story the apostle used to say, 'and none knows the armies of God but He.' When Gabriel brought me in, Ismā'īl asked who I was, and when he was told that I was Muhammad he asked if I had been given a mission, and on being assured of this he wished me well.

A traditionist who had got it from one who had heard it from the apostle told me that the latter said: 'All the angels who met me when I entered the lowest heaven smiled in welcome and wished me well except one who said the same things but did not smile or show that joyful expression which the others had. And when I asked Gabriel the reason he told me that if he had ever smiled on anyone before or would smile on anyone hereafter he would have smiled on me; but he does not smile because he is Mālik, the Keeper of Hell. I said to Gabriel, he holding the position with regard to God which he has described to you "obeyed there, trustworthy," "Will you not order him to show me hell?" And he said, "Certainly! O Mālik, show Muhammad Hell." Thereupon he removed its covering and the flames blazed high into the air until I thought that they would consume everything. So I asked Gabriel to order him to send them back to their place which he did. I can only compare the effect of their withdrawal to the falling of a shadow, until when the flames retreated whence they had come, Mālik placed their cover on them.'

In his tradition Abū Sa'īd al-Khudrī said that the apostle said: 'When I entered the lowest heaven I saw a man sitting there with the spirits of men passing before him. To one he would speak well and rejoice in him saying: "A good spirit from a good body" and of another he would say "Faugh!" and frown, saying: "An evil spirit from an evil body." In answer to my question Gabriel told me that this was our father Adam reviewing the spirits of his offspring; the spirit of a believer excited his pleasure, and the spirit of an infidel excited his disgust so that he said the words just quoted.

'Then I saw men with lips like camels; in their hands were pieces of fire like stones which they used to thrust into their mouths and they would come out of their posteriors. I was told that these were those who sinfully devoured the wealth of orphans.

'Then I saw men in the way of the family of Pharaoh, with such bellies as I have never seen; there were passing over them as it were camels maddened by thirst when they were cast into hell, treading them down, they being unable to move out of the way. These were the usurers.

'Then I saw men with good fat meat before them side by side with lean stinking meat, eating of the latter and leaving the former. These are those who forsake the women which God has permitted and go after those he has forbidden.

'Then I saw women hanging by their breasts. These were those who had fathered bastards on their husbands.'

Ja'far b. 'Amr told me from al-Qāsim b. Muhammad that the apostle said: 'Great is God's anger against a woman who brings a bastard into her family. He deprives the true sons of their portion and learns the secrets of the *harim*.'

To continue the tradition of Sa'īd al-Khudrī: 'Then I was taken up to the second heaven and there were the two maternal cousins Jesus, Son of Mary, and John, son of Zakariah. Then to the third heaven and there was a man whose face was as the moon at the full. This was my brother Joseph, son of Jacob. Then to the fourth heaven and there was a man called Idrīs. "And we have exalted him to a lofty place." Then to the fifth heaven and there was a man with white hair and a long beard, never have I seen a more handsome man than he. This was the beloved among his people Aaron son of 'Imrān. Then to the sixth heaven, and there was a dark man with a hooked nose like the Shanū'a. This was my brother Moses, son of 'Imrān. Then to the seventh heaven and there was a man sitting on a throne at the gate of the immortal mansion. Every day seventy thousand angels went in not to come back until the resurrection day. Never have I seen a man more like myself. This was my father Abraham. Then he took me into Paradise and there I saw a damsel with dark red lips and I asked her to whom she belonged, for she pleased me much when I saw her, and she told me "Zayd b. Ḥāritha." The apostle gave Zayd the good news about her.' . . .

## How God Dealt with the Mockers

The apostle remained firm counting on God's assistance, admonishing his people in spite of their branding him as a liar and insulting and mocking him. The principal offenders—so Yazīd b. Rūmān from 'Urwa b. al-Zubayr told me—were five men who were respected and honoured among their tribesmen. . . .

When they persisted in evil and constantly mocked the apostle, God revealed: 'Proclaim what you have been ordered and turn away from the polytheists. We will surely protect you against the mockers who put another god beside God. In the end they will know.'

The same Yazīd told me from 'Urwa (or it may have been from some other traditionist) that Gabriel came to the apostle when the mockers were going round the temple. He stood up and the apostle stood at his side; and as al-Aswad b. al-Muṭṭalib passed, Gabriel threw a green leaf in his face and he became blind. Then al-Aswad b. 'Abdu Yaghūth passed and he pointed at his belly which swelled so that he died of dropsy. Next al-Walīd passed by. He pointed at an old scar on the bottom of his ankle (the result of a wound he received some years earlier as he was trailing his gown when he passed by a man of Khuzā'a who was feathering an arrow, and the arrowhead caught in his wrapper and scratched his foot—a mere nothing). But the wound opened again and he died of it. Al-'Āṣ passed. He pointed to his instep, and he went off on his ass making for al-Ṭā'if. He tied the animal to a thorny tree and a thorn entered his foot and he died of it. Lastly al-Ḥārith passed. He pointed at his head. It immediately filled with pus and killed him.

## Those Who Migrated to Medina

. . . My father Isḥāq b. Yasār on the authority of Salama who had it from his grandmother Umm Salama the prophet's wife told me that she said: When Abū Salama had decided to set out for Medina he saddled his camel for me and mounted me on it together with my son Salama who was in my arms. Then he set out leading the camel. When the men of B. al-Mughīra . . . saw him they got up and said: 'So far as you are concerned you can do what you like; but what about your wife? Do you suppose that we shall let you take her away?' So they snatched the camel's rope from his hand and took me from him. Abū Salama's family, the B. Abdu'l-Asad, were angry at this and said: 'We will not leave our son with her seeing you have torn her from our tribesman.' So they dragged at my little boy Salama between them until they dislocated his arm, and the B. al-Asad took him away, while the B. al-Mughīra kept me with them, and my husband Abū Salama went to Medina. Thus I was separated from my husband and my son. I used to go out every morning and sit in the valley weeping continuously until a year or so had passed when one of my cousins of B. al-Mughīra passed and saw my plight and took pity on me. He said to his tribesmen, 'Why don't you let this poor woman go? You have separated husband, wife, and child.' So they said to me, 'You can join your husband if you like'; and then the B. 'Abdu'l-Asad restored my son to me. So I saddled my camel and took my son and carried him in my arms. Then I set forth making for my husband in Medina. Not a soul was with me. I thought that I could get food from anyone I met on the road until I reached my husband. When I was in Tan'īm I met 'Uthmān b. Ṭalḥa who asked me where I was going and if I was all alone. I told him that except for God and my little boy I was alone. He said that I ought not to be left helpless like that and he took hold of the camel's halter and went along with me. Never have I met an Arab more noble than he. When we halted he would make the camel kneel for me and then withdraw; when we reached a stopping-place he would lead my camel away, unload it, and tie it to a tree. Then he would go from me and lie down under a tree. When evening came he would bring the camel and saddle it, then go behind me and tell me to ride; and when I was firmly established in the saddle he would come and take the halter and lead it until he brought me to a halt. This he did all the way to Medina. When he saw a village he said: 'Your husband is in this village (Abū Salama was actually there), so enter it with the blessing of God.' Then he went off on his way back to Mecca.

She used to say, By God, I do not know a family in Islam which suffered what the family of Abū Salama did. Nor have I ever seen a nobler man than 'Uthmān b. Ṭalḥa. . . .

## The Expedition of 'Alqama b. Mujazziz

When Waqqāṣ b. Mujazziz . . . was killed on the day of Dhū Qarad, 'Alqama b. Mujazziz asked the apostle to send him on the track of the people so that he might take vengeance on them. 'Abdu'l-'Aziz . . . said: The apostle sent 'Alqama b. Mujazziz, I being with the force, and when we were on the way he summoned a part of the force and appointed 'Abdullah their leader. He was one of the apostle's companions—facetious fellow, and when they were on the way he kindled a fire and said to the men: 'Have I not claim on your obedience so that if I order you to do something you must do it?' and when they agreed he said, 'Then by virtue of my claim on your obedience I order you to leap into this fire.' Some of them began to gird up their loins so that he thought that they would leap into the fire, and then he said, 'Sit down, I was only laughing at you!' When the apostle was told of this after they had returned he said, 'If anyone orders you to do something which you ought not to do, do not obey him.' . . .

## Kurz b. Jābir's Expedition to Kill the Bajīlīs Who Had Killed Yasār

A traditionist told me from one who had told him from Muhammad b. Ṭalḥa . . . that in the raid of Muḥārib and B. Tha'laba the apostle had captured a slave called Yasār, and he put him in charge of his milch-camels to shepherd them in the neighbourhood of al-Jammā'. Some men of Qays . . . came to the apostle suffering from an epidemic and enlarged spleens, and the apostle told them that if they went to the milch-camels and drank their milk and urine they would recover, so off they went. When they recovered their health and their bellies contracted to their normal size they fell upon the apostle's shepherd Yasār and killed him and stuck thorns in his eyes and drove away his camels. The apostle sent Kurz b. Jābir in pursuit and he overtook them and brought them to the apostle as he returned from the raid of Dhū Qarad. He cut off their hands and feet and gouged out their eyes.

## The Beginning of the Apostle's Illness

While matters were thus the apostle began to suffer from the illness by which God took him to what honour and compassion He intended for him shortly before the end of Ṣafar or in the beginning of Rabī'u'l-awwal. It began, so I have been told, when he went to Baqī'u'l-Gharqad in the middle of the night and prayed for the dead. Then he returned to his family and in the morning his sufferings began.

'Abdullah b. 'Umar . . . a freedman of the apostle, said: In the middle of the night the apostle sent for me and told me that he was ordered to pray for the dead in this cemetery and that I was to go with him. I went; and when he stood among them he said, 'Peace upon you, O people of the graves! Happy are you that you are so much better off than men here. Dissensions have come like waves of darkness one after the other, the last being worse than the first.' Then he turned to me and said, 'I have been given the choice between the keys of the treasuries of this world and long life here followed by Paradise, and meeting my Lord and Paradise (at once).' I urged him to choose the former, but he said that he had chosen the latter. Then he prayed for the dead there and went away. Then it was that the illness through which God took him began.

Ya'qūb b. 'Utba . . . from 'Ā'isha, the prophet's wife, said: 'The apostle returned from the cemetery to find me suffering from a severe headache and I was saying, "O *my* head!" He said, "Nay, 'Ā'isha, O *my* head!" Then he said, "Would it distress you if you were to die before me so that I might wrap you in your shroud and pray over you and bury you?" I said, "I see you if you had done that returning to my house and spending a bridal night therein with one of your wives." The apostle smiled and then his pain overcame him as he was going the round of his wives, until he was overpowered in the house of Maymūna. He called his wives and asked their permission to be nursed in my house, and they agreed.'

## The Apostle's Illness in the House of 'Ā'isha

. . . 'Ibn Shihāb al-Zuhrī told me 'Ā'isha used to hear the apostle say, "God never takes a prophet to Himself without giving him the choice." When he was at the point of death the last word I heard the apostle saying was, "Nay, rather the Exalted Companion of paradise." I said (to myself), Then by God he is not choosing us! And I knew that that was what he used to tell us, namely that a prophet does not die without being given the choice.'

Al-Zuhrī said, Ḥamza b. 'Abdullah b. 'Umar told me that 'Ā'isha said: 'When the prophet became seriously ill he ordered the people to tell Abū Bakr to superintend the prayers. 'Ā'isha told him that Abū Bakr was a delicate man with a weak voice who wept much when he read the Qurān. He repeated his order nevertheless, and I repeated my objection. He said, "You are like Joseph's companions; tell him to preside at prayers." My only reason for saying what I did was that I wanted Abū Bakr to be spared this task, because I knew that people would never like a man who occupied the apostle's place, and would blame him for every misfortune that occurred, and I wanted Abū Bakr to be spared this.' . . .

Abū Bakr . . . told me that when the Monday came the apostle went out to morning prayer with his head wrapped up while Abū Bakr was leading the prayers. When the apostle went out the people's attention wavered, and Abū Bakr knew that the people would not behave thus unless the apostle had come, so he withdrew from his place; but the apostle pushed him in the back, saying, 'Lead the men in prayer,' and the apostle sat at his side praying in a sitting posture on the right of Abū Bakr. When he had ended prayer he turned to the men and spoke to them with a loud voice which could be heard outside the mosque: 'O men, the fire is kindled, and rebellions come like the darkness of the night. By God, you can lay nothing to my charge. I allow only what the Qurān allows and forbid only what the Qurān forbids.'. . .

Ya'qūb b. 'Utba from al-Zuhrī from 'Urwa from 'Ā'isha said: 'The apostle came back to me from the mosque that day and lay in my bosom. A man of Abū Bakr's family came in to me with a toothpick in his hand and the apostle looked at it in such a way that I knew he wanted it, and when I asked him if he wanted me to give it him he said Yes; so I took it and chewed it for him to soften it and gave it to him. He rubbed his teeth with it more energetically than I had ever seen him rub before; then he laid it down. I found him heavy in my bosom and as I looked into his face, lo his eyes were fixed and he was saying, "Nay, the most Exalted Companion is of paradise." I said, "You were given the choice and you have chosen, by Him Who sent you with the truth!" And so the apostle was taken.'

Yaḥyā . . . from his father told me that he heard 'Ā'isha say: 'The apostle died in my bosom during my turn: I had wronged none in regard to him. It was due to my ignorance and extreme youth that the apostle died in my arms. Then I laid his head on a pillow and got up beating my breast and slapping my face along with the other women.'

Al-Zuhrī said, and Sa'īd b. al-Musayyib . . . told me: 'When the apostle was dead 'Umar got up and said: "Some of the disaffected will allege that the apostle is dead, but by God he is not dead: he has gone to his Lord as Moses b. 'Imrān went and was hidden from his people for forty days, returning to them after it was said that he had died. By God, the apostle will return as Moses returned and will cut off the hands and feet of men who allege that the apostle is dead." When Abū Bakr heard what was happening he came to the door of the mosque as 'Umar was speaking to the people. He paid no attention but went in to 'Ā'isha's house to the apostle, who was lying covered by a mantle of Yamanī cloth. He went and uncovered his face and kissed him, saying, "You are dearer than my father and mother. You have tasted the death which God had decreed: a second death will never overtake you." Then he replaced the mantle on the apostle's face and went out. 'Umar was still speaking and he said, "Gently, 'Umar, be quiet." But 'Umar refused and went on talking, and when Abū Bakr saw that he would not be silent he went forward to the people who, when they heard his words, came to him and left 'Umar. Giving thanks and praise to God he said: "O men, if anyone worships Muhammad, Muhammad is dead: if anyone worships God, God is alive, immortal." Then he recited this verse: "Muhammad is nothing but an apostle. Apostles have passed away before him. Can it be that if he were to die or be killed you would turn back on your heels? He who turns back does no harm to God and God will reward the grateful." By God, it was as though the people did not know that this verse concerning the apostle had come down until Abū Bakr recited it that day. The people took it from him and it was (constantly) in their mouths. 'Umar said, "By God, when I heard Abū Bakr recite these words I was dumbfounded so that my legs would not bear me and I fell to the ground knowing that the apostle was indeed dead."'

## The Meeting in the Hall of B. Sa'ida

. . . Abū Bakr said after praising God: 'I have been given authority over you but I am not the best of you. If I do well, help me, and if I do ill, then put me right. Truth consists in loyalty and falsehood in treachery. The weak among you shall be strong in my eyes until I secure his right if God will; and the strong among you shall be weak in my eyes until I wrest the right from him. If a people refrain from fighting in the way of God, God will smite them with disgrace. Wickedness is never widespread in a people but God brings calamity upon them all. Obey me as long as I obey God and His apostle, and if I disobey them you owe me no obedience. Arise to prayer. God have mercy on you.' . . .

## The Burial Preparations

When fealty had been sworn to Abū Bakr, men came to prepare the apostle for burial on the Tuesday. 'Abdullah b. Abū Bakr and Ḥusayn b. 'Abdullah and others of our companions told me that 'Alī and 'Abbās and his sons al-Faḍl and Qutham, and Usāma b. Zayd, and Shuqrān freedman of the apostle were those who took charge of the washing of him; and that Aus b. Khaulī said, 'I adjure you by God, 'Alī, and by our share in the apostle.' Aus was one of the apostle's companions who had been at Badr. 'Alī gave him permission to enter and he came in and sat down and was present at the washing of the apostle. 'Alī drew him on to his breast and 'Abbās and al-Faḍl and Qutham turned him over along with him. Usāma and Shuqrān poured the water over him, while 'Alī washed him, having drawn him towards his breast. He still wore his shirt with which he rubbed him from the outside without touching the apostle's body with his hand the while he said, 'Dearer than my father and my mother, how sweet you are alive and dead!' The apostle's body did not present the appearance of an ordinary corpse.

Yaḥyā . . . from his father 'Abbād from 'Ā'isha: When they wanted to wash the apostle dispute arose. They did not know whether they were to strip him of his clothes as they stripped their dead or to wash him with his clothes on. As they disputed God cast a deep sleep upon them so that every man's chin was sunk on his chest. Then a voice came from the direction of the house, none knowing who it was: 'Wash the apostle with his clothes on.' So they got up and went to the apostle and washed him with his shirt on, pouring water on the shirt, and rubbing him with the shirt between him and them, 'Ā'isha used to say, 'Had I known at the beginning of my affair what I knew at the end of it none but his wives would have washed him. . . .

Ḥusayn b. 'Abdullah told me from 'Ikrima from Ibn 'Abbās: Now Abū 'Ubayda . . . used to open the ground as the Meccans dig, and Abū Ṭalḥa Zayd . . . used to dig graves for the Medinans and to make a niche in them and when they wanted to bury the apostle, al-'Abbās called two men and told one to go to Abū 'Ubayda and the other to Abū Ṭalḥa saying, 'O God, choose for the apostle.' The one sent to Abū Ṭalḥa found his man and brought him and he dug the grave with the niche for the apostle.

When the preparations for burial had been completed on the Tuesday he was laid upon his bed in his house. The Muslims had disputed over the place of burial. Some were in favour of burying him in his mosque, while others wanted to bury him with his companions. Abū Bakr said, 'I heard the apostle say, "No prophet dies but he is buried where he died;"' so the bed on which he died was taken up and they made a grave beneath it. Then the people came to visit the apostle praying over him by companies: first came the men, then the women, then the children, then the slaves. No man acted as imām in the prayers over the apostle. The apostle was buried in the middle of the night of the Wednesday. . . .

'Abdullah b. Abū Bakr told me from his wife Fāṭima d. 'Umāra from 'Amra d. 'Abdu'l-Raḥmān b. Sa'd b. Zurāra that 'Ā'isha said: We knew nothing about the burial of the apostle until we heard the sound of the pickaxes in the middle of the Wednesday night. Ibn Ishāq said: Fāṭima told me this tradition. . . .

When the apostle was laid in his grave and the earth was laid over him Shuqrān his freedman took a garment which the apostle used to wear and use as a rug and buried it in the grave saying, 'By God, none shall ever wear it after you,' so it was buried with the apostle.

Al-Mughīra . . . used to claim that he was the last man to be with the apostle. He used to say, 'I took my ring and let it fall into the grave and said, My ring has dropped. But I threw it in purposely that I might touch the apostle and be the last man to be with him.'

My father Isḥāq b. Yasār told me from Miqsam, freedman of 'Abdullah b. al-Ḥārith b. Naufal, from his freedman 'Abdullah b. al-Ḥārith: I went on the little pilgrimage with 'Alī and he visited his sister Umm Hāni' d. Abū Tālib. When he had finished his pilgrimage, ablution water was poured out for him and he washed. When he had finished some Iraqis came in saying that they had come to ask him about a matter on which they would like him to give them some information. He said, 'I suppose that al-Mughīra tells you that he was the last person to be with the apostle?' When they said that that was so, he said, 'He lies. The last man to be with the apostle was Qutham b. 'Abbās.'

Ṣāliḥ b. Kaysān told me . . . that 'Ā'isha told him: The apostle wore a black cloak when he suffered severe pain. Sometimes he would put it over his face, at others he would take it off, saying the while, 'God slay a people who choose the graves of their prophets as mosques,' warning his community against such a practice.

On the same authority I was told that the last injunction the apostle gave was in his words 'Let not two religions be left in the Arabian peninsula.' When the apostle was dead the Muslims were sore stricken. I have heard that 'Ā'isha used to say, 'When the apostle died the Arabs apostatized and Christianity and Judaism raised their heads and disaffection appeared. The Muslims became as sheep exposed to rain on a winter's night through the loss of their prophet until God united them under Abū Bakr.'

Ḥassān said mourning the apostle:

Tell the poor that plenty has left them
With the prophet who departed from them this morning.
Who was it who has a saddle and a camel for me,
My family's sustenance when rain fails?
Or with whom can we argue without anxiety
When the tongue runs away with a man?
He was the light and the brilliance we followed.
He was sight and hearing second only to God.
The day they laid him in the grave
And cast the earth upon him
Would that God had not left one of us
And neither man nor woman had survived him!
The Banū'l-Najjār were utterly abased,
But it was a thing decreed by God.
The booty was divided to the exclusion of all the people
And they scattered it openly and uselessly among themselves.

Ḥassān also said:

I swear that no man is more careful than I
In swearing an oath true and without falsehood.
By God, no woman has conceived and given birth
To one like the apostle the prophet and guide of his people;
Nor has God created among his creatures

One more faithful to his sojourner
    or his promise
Than he who was the source of
    our light,
Blessed in his deeds, just, and
    upright.
Your wives stripped the tents in
    mourning
And did not strike the pegs
    behind the curtains.
Like nuns they put on garments of
    hair
Certain of misery after happiness.
O best of men, I was as it were in a
    river
Without which I have become
    lonely in my thirst.

## Abol-Qasem Ferdowsi (932–1025)

*Translated by Jerome W. Clinton*

The *Shāh-nāmah,* the Iranian national epic, stretches over fifty thousand couplets. It is arranged chronologically, beginning with Creation and ending with the last Sassanian emperor, who died resisting the Arab invasions of Iran in 652 CE. Most of the poem records the exploits of mythic and legendary figures; only the last third records historically verifiable events of the Parthian and Sassanian periods (247 BCE–651 CE). Zoroastrianism, an ancient, pre-Islamic Indo-European religion, forms the spiritual and philosophical backdrop for the epic. Compiled over centuries, many recensions of the epic were made before Ferdowsi wrote his version in the early eleventh century, but his poetic artistry and arrangement of the materials has eclipsed all others.

The *Shāh-nāmah* has served a foundational role for Iranian culture somewhat akin to that played by the Hebrew Bible and the Greek epics in the West, the *Rāmāyana* and *Mahābhārata* in India, and the *Book of Songs* in China. Hundreds of poets, historians, and philosophers have mined the *Shāh-nāmah* for illustrative examples and meaningful allusions. Artists have rendered its characters and episodes in painting and sculpture from the Medieval Period to the present day. Composed after Iran had converted to Islam and after it had been overthrown by Arabic-speaking rulers, Ferdowsi's poem is a reclamation of Persian language and culture. It is written in a Persian literary language virtually untouched by Arabic. Persian courtly poetry during the century before Ferdowsi composed his work favored Arabic and Arab culture, but this poetry amounts, in its totality, to only a fraction of the volume of the *Shāh-nāmah.* Consequently, Ferdowsi's masterpiece holds immeasurable importance for the flowering and dissemination of medieval Persian language and literature.

The *Shāh-nāmah* is, above all, a public poem that belongs to high court culture while maintaining features common to heroic poetry—namely, its concern with nationalism, religion, and ancient legends. It is a poem of heroic action, focusing on hunting, feasting, and war; its main characters fulfill prescribed and fated roles. The geography of the epic is immense: its heroes journey throughout Arabia and Byzantium to the borders of China, India, and Central Asia. Prolonged absences from home and lengthy expeditions are common. Struggles with enemies are foremost in the narrative, the Turks (Turanians) being the most bitter foes.

Fantastic beasts and creatures, including the Simorgh (a central figure in Attar's *The Conference of Birds,* pp. 811–832), dot the landscape of the epic.

The legends circling around the heroic figure of Rostám are only a fraction of the vast *Shāh-nāmah,* but they share themes common to the whole text: kinship relations, dynastic struggles, and a pervasive sense of the power of time. More than most epics, the *Shāh-nāmah* is tragic. Like *Beowulf*—but unlike *Gilgamesh,* the *Odyssey,* or the *Aeneid*—the nation falls into ruin at the conclusion of the epic. Death and sacrifice do not, ultimately, lead to restoration, return, or redemption. The poem is built on a view of humanity that, over time, internalizes or actualizes evil. In *The Tragedy of Sohráb and Rostám,* a father unknowingly kills his own son, an act that has consequences like those in Greek tragedy or in the Norse epic of the Völsungs retold in Snorri's *Prose Edda* (pp. 1267–1271). It is interesting to ask why some epics, which seem to reflect the deepest attitudes of a culture, adopt such a tragic vision.

## *from The Shāh-nāmah*

### *The Tragedy of Sohráb and Rostám*

#### **Prologue**

A vagrant wind springs up quite suddenly,
And casts a green unripened fruit to earth.
Shall we call this a tyrant's act, or just?
Shall we consider it as right, or wrong?
If death is just, how can this not be so?
Why then lament and wail at what is just?
Your soul knows nothing of this mystery;
You cannot see what lies beyond this veil.
Though all descend to face that greedy door,
For none has it revealed its secrets twice.
Perhaps he'll like the place he goes to better,
And in that other house he may find peace.
Death's breath is like a fiercely raging fire
That has no fear of either young or old.
Here in this place of passing, not delay,
Should death cinch tight the saddle on its steed,
Know this, that it is just, and not unjust.
There's no disputing justice when it comes.
Destruction knows both youth and age as one.
For nothing that exists will long endure.
If you can fill your heart with faith's pure light,
Silence befits you best, since you're His slave.
You do not understand God's mysteries,
Unless your soul is partners with some *div.*
Strive here within the world as you pass through,
And in the end bear virtue in your heart.

Now I'll relate the battle of Sohráb—
First how his father's enmity began.

## The Beginning

In the *dehqáns'* accounts there is a tale,
To which I've added from old narratives.
The *mobád* starts his recollections thus—
Rostám one day just as the sun rose up,
Was sad at heart, and so prepared to hunt.
He armed himself, put arrows in their sheaf,
Then like a fearsome lion on the chase,
He galloped toward the borders of Turán.
As he approached the Turkish borderlands,
He saw the plain was filled with onagers [wild ass].
The Giver of the Crown [Rostám] glowed like a rose.
He laughed aloud and spurred Rakhsh from his place.
With bow and arrow, and with mace and rope,
He brought down many onagers upon
The plain. Then from dead branches, brush, and thorns,
Rostám built up a fiercely blazing fire.
And when the fire had spread, he wrenched a tree
Out of the ground to serve him as a spit.
He placed a heavy stallion on that tree,
That was a feather in his palm, no more.
When it was done he tore its limbs apart
And wolfed it down, the marrow bones and all.
Rostám then slept and rested from the hunt.
Nearby Rakhsh wandered, grazing in a meadow.
Turkish horsemen, some seven or eight, passed by
That plain and hunting ground, and as they did
They spied a horse's tracks and turned aside
To follow them along the river's bank.
When they saw Rakhsh upon the plain,
They raced ahead to snare him with their ropes.
When he was caught, they bore him galloping
Toward the town; each eager for his share.
  Rostám when he awoke from his sweet sleep,
Had need of his well-trained and ready steed.
He was distressed to find his Rakhsh was gone,
And quickly turned his face toward Semengán. . . .

*[In the city of Semengán, Rostám seeks his horse and spends the night with Tahminé, the Shah's daughter.]*

## Tahminé

And when one watch had passed on that dark night,
And Sirius rose on the heaven's wheel,
The sound of secret voices could be heard.

The chamber door was opened quietly.
A single slave, a scented candle in
Her hand, came to the pillow of Rostám.
Behind the slave, a moon-faced maid appeared,
Adorned and scented like the shining sun.
Her eyebrows bows, her tresses lassos coiled,
In stature like a slender cypress tree.
Her soul was wisdom and her body seemed
Of spirit pure, as though not made of earth.
Amazed, Rostám the fearless lion-heart,
Cried out unto the Maker of the World.
He questioned her, and asked, "What is your name?
Here in the dead of night, what do you seek?"
She answered him, "My name is Tahminé.
It seems my heart's been rent in two by grief.
The daughter of the shah of Semengán,
From lions and from tigers comes my seed.
In all the world no beauty is my match.
Few are my like beneath the azure wheel.
Outside these walls, there's none who's looked on me.
Nor has my voice been heard by any ear.
From everyone have I heard tales of you—
So wonderful they seemed to me like myths.
You fear no leopard and no *div* they say.
No crocodile nor lion is so fierce.
At night alone, you journey to Turán,
And wander freely there, and even sleep.
You spit an onager with just one hand,
And with your sword you cause the air to weep.
When you approach them with your mace in hand,
The leopard rends his claws, the lion his heart.
The eagle when he sees your naked blade,
Dares not take wing and fly off to the hunt.
The tiger's skin is branded by your rope.
The clouds weep blood in fear of your sharp lance.
As I would listen to these tales of you,
I'd bite my lip in wonder, and yearn
To look upon those shoulders and that chest.
And then Izád [God] sent you to Semengán.
I'm yours now should you want me, and, if not,
None but the fish and birds will see my face.
It's first because I do so long for you,
That I've slain reason for my passion's sake.
And next, perhaps the Maker of the World
Will place a son from you within my womb.
Perhaps he'll be like you in manliness
And strength, a child of Saturn and the Sun.

And third, that I may bring your horse to you,
I'll search throughout the whole of Semengán."
Rostám, when he looked on her angel face,
And saw in her a share of every art,
And that she'd given him some news of Rakhsh,
He saw no end to this that was not good.
As she had wished, and with goodwill and joy,
Rostám sealed firm his bond with her that night.
And when in secret she'd become his mate,
The night that followed lasted late and long.
But then at last, from high above the world,
The radiant sun cast down his shining rope.
Upon his arm Rostám had placed a jewel,
A seal that was well known throughout the world.
He gave it to her as he said, "Keep this.
And if the times should bring a girl to you,
Then take this gem and plait it in her hair—
A world-illumining omen of good luck.
But if the star of fate should send a son,
Then bind this father's token to his arm. . . .

## The Birth of Sohráb

When nine months passed for Tahminé, she bore
A healthy boy whose face shone like the moon. . . .
Because he laughed and had a cheerful face,
His mother called him by the name Sohráb.
In but a single month he'd grown a year.
His chest was like Rostám's, the son of Zal.
At three he learned the game of polo, and
At five he mastered bow and javelin.
When he was ten, in all of Semengán
Not one would dare to meet him in the field.
Sohráb went to his mother, Tahminé,
To question her, "Tell me the truth," he said.
"I'm taller than the boys who nursed with me.
It seems my head can touch the very sky.
Whose seed am I, and of what family?
When asked, 'Who is your sire?' What shall I say?
If you should keep this answer from me now,
I will not leave you in this world alive."
His mother answered him, "Be not so harsh,
But hear my words and be rejoiced by them.
Your father is the pahlaván [hero] Rostám.
Your ancestors are Sam and Narimán.
And thus it is your head can touch the sky.

You are descended from that famous line.
Since first the World Creator made the earth,
There's been no other horseman like Rostám.
Nor one like Sam the son of Narimán.
The turning sphere does not dare brush his head."
And then she brought a letter from his sire,
Rostám, and showed it secretly to him.
Enclosed with it Rostám had sent as well,
Three shining emeralds in three golden seals.
"Afrasiyáb [Shah of Turán] must never know of this,"
She said, "he must not hear a single word.
And if your father learns that you've become
A brave and noble warrior like this,
He'll call you to his side, I know.
And then your mother's heart will break."
The bold Sohráb replied, "In all the world
No man could keep a secret such as this.
From ancient times till now, those great in war
Recite for all the tales of brave Rostám.
When I have such a warlike lineage,
For me to keep it hidden can't be right.
Now from among the warlike Turks will I
Amass an army boundless as the sea
I'll drive Kavús from off his throne,
And from Irán I'll scour all trace of Tus.
To brave Rostám I'll give throne, mace, and crown,
And seat him in the place of Shah Kavús.
Then from Irán will I attack Turán,
And here confront the shah, Afrasiyáb.
I'll rout his army and I'll seize his throne.
I'll thrust my lance's tip above the sun.
For when Rostám's the father, I the son,
Who else in all the world should wear a crown?
When sun and moon illuminate the sky,
What need is there for stars to flaunt their crowns?"
From every side an army flocked to him,
Who all were noble men, brave swordsmen too.

## The Campaign Begins

This news was brought to Shah Afrasiyáb,
"Sohráb has launched his boat upon the stream.
The smell of milk still lingers on his mouth,
And yet he thinks of weapons and of war.
Since he would scour the whole earth with his blade,
He now would fight a war with Shah Kavús.

A numerous army's gathered to his side,
And he gives thought to no one else at all." . . .

And when Afrasiyáb had heard these words,
He was well pleased and laughed and showed his joy.
Then from among the army's valiant chiefs,
Those with the strength to wield a heavy mace,
He chose twelve thousand braves, men like Humán,
And these he then entrusted to Barmán.
Afrasiyáb addressed his generals thus,
"This secret must not ever come to light.
When these two face each other on the field,
The bold Rostám will surely try some ruse.
His father must the boy not recognize,
Or else his love will bind his heart to him.
Rather, that brave and ancient pahlaván
Must lose his life to this young lion-heart.
Then later on destroy the fierce Sohráb.
Bind him one night forever in his dreams."
  Alertly both the warriors went off
To meet Sohráb of the eternal soul. . . .

  There was a fortress which they called the White;
The hopes of all Irán were placed in it.
The battle-tried Hojír, a man of strength
And bravery, was keeper of the fort.
For in that time, Gostáhm was still a youth,
Although a youth of bold, heroic mien.
He had a warlike sister too, who was
Well known for her ferocity and strength.
The army of Sohráb approached the fort,
The brave Hojír observed the army there.
Swift as the wind he mounted on his steed,
And galloped out to battle from the fort.
When bold Sohráb saw that Hojír approached,
He flushed in rage and drew his vengeful sword,
And like a lion raced onto the field.
As he approached the battle-tried Hojír,
Sohráb the valiant called to him and said,
"Oh foolish man, to fight with me alone!
What is your name, and which your family?
Who is the mother that must weep for you?"
Hojír thus answered him, "In all Turán
There can be few or none to equal me.
I am Hojír the brave, the army's chief.
I mean to tear your head from off your trunk
And send it to the world's shah, Kay Kavús.

Your body will I hide beneath the soil."
Sohráb just laughed when he had heard this boast,
And galloped forward to attack Hojír.
So swiftly did they hurl their weapons that
The eye could not distinguish lance from lance.
One lance Hojír thrust at Sohráb, the point
Of which slid off his waist and did not stick.
Sohráb then seized the lance, reversed its butt,
And struck his chest a fierce and telling blow
That lifted him right off his horse's back,
And stretched him stunned and gasping on the ground.
Sohráb sprang down and sat upon his chest,
Then drew his sword to sever head from trunk.
Hojír beneath him twisted to his right,
And begged Sohráb for mercy in his fear.
The youth released his grip and spared his life.
Pleased with himself, he counseled him instead.
The warrior quickly bound his hands with rope,
And sent him as a captive to Humán.
Within the fort, when all had heard the news,
"Hojír's been taken captive by the Turks,"
They cried aloud, and men and women wept,
"The brave Hojír has now been lost to us."

## Gordafaríd

The daughter of Gazhdahám, when she had heard
The leader of their company'd been lost;
And she a woman was who like a knight,
Had gained renown in war, and who was called
Gordafaríd—for in her time there was
No mother who had borne her like—she found
The conduct of Hojír so shameful that
The tulips in her cheeks turned black as pitch.
She wasted not a moment, but bound on
The coat of mail a horseman wears to fight.
She hid her hair beneath that coat of mail,
And knotted on her head a Roman casque.
Then lionlike she raced down from the fort,
Girded for battle, and seated on the wind.
She faced the army like a warrior,
And roared a challenge like a thunderbolt,
"Who are your heroes, who your pahlaváns,
And who your brave and battle-tested chiefs?"
Sohráb the lion-killer laughed when he
Saw her, and in amazement bit his lip.

"Another onager has rushed into
The trap set by the lord of mace and blade."
Swift as the wind he donned his armored shirt,
And bound a Chinese helmet on his head,
Then galloped out to meet Gordafaríd.
When that rope-hurling maid saw him approach,
She strung her heavy bow and drew a breath.
No bird escaped her arrows with its life.
She rained her darts upon Sohráb, and as
She rode, she dodged and feinted right and left.
Sohráb observed her charge and felt ashamed,
Then flushed with rage and galloped to the fray.
He lifted up his shield and charged his foe,
The blood of battle coursing in his veins.
Gordafaríd, when she could see Sohráb
Was racing toward her like a raging flame,
She drew the bow she'd strung upon her arm;
Her yellow steed reared up to paw the clouds.
She turned her lance's point, toward Sohráb,
And then reined in her steed to face her foe.
Sohráb, as fierce as any leopard, had
Just like his foe, prepared himself to fight.
He turned the reins and brought his horse around,
Then set upon her like the God of Fire.
He snatched away her polished lance's point,
And closed upon her like a cloud of smoke.
He struck Gordafaríd upon the waist,
And one by one he split her armor's links.
Then like a mallet when it strikes the ball,
He drove her from her saddle with one blow.
Gordafaríd, as she was turning in
Her saddle, drew a sharp blade from her waist,
Struck at his lance, and parted it in two.
She fell back in her seat, and dust rose up.
  She saw she was no match for him in war,
And quickly turned away from him, and fled.
Sohráb then gave his dragon steed its head.
His anger robbed the world of all its light.
As he approached her roaring in his wrath,
She swiftly snatched the helmet from her head,
Her hair was freed then of its armored cloak;
Her face shone forth as radiant as the sun.
Sohráb now saw a maiden seated there,
Whose face was worthy of a royal crown.
He spoke in awe, "That from the army of
Irán a maid like this should come, and fight
With mounted warriors in the field of war,

And raise the dust of battle to the sky!"
He loosed his twisted lasso from its loop,
And threw it, catching her around the waist.
Sohráb thus spoke to her, "Don't seek to flee.
Oh beauteous moon, why do you wish to fight?
I've never caught an onager like you.
You'll not escape my grip. Don't even try."
Gordafaríd knew she was caught at last.
She could not free herself, save through some trick.
She turned her face to him and said, "Oh, brave
And peerless youth, so like a lion when
You face your foe, two armies watch our fight,
Our combat here of heavy mace and blade.
Should I reveal to them my face and hair,
Your army will be filled with murmuring.
'Sohráb in battle with a maiden foe,
Raised dust in clouds that rose up to the sky.'
To parley here in secret would be best.
A noble man must use his head as well.
Do not bring shame upon yourself before
These two ranked armies here because of me.
You now command the garrison and fort.
Why then should you make war instead of peace?
Once you accept this treaty which you wish,
The fort, its chief and treasure are all yours."
She turned her face and smiled upon Sohráb,
And showed him pearly teeth and ruby lips.
She seemed a garden fair as paradise.
No gardener's seen so tall a cypress tree.
Her eyes were like a deer's, her eyebrows bows.
She seemed a flower in the height of bloom.
   These words of hers perplexed Sohráb at heart. . . .
She rode along; Sohráb was at her side,
And Gazhdahám watched from the battlements.
   Gordafaríd swung wide the fortress gate,
And drew her bound and weary body through.
They sadly closed the gate behind her then.
Their hearts were filled with grief, their eyes with tears.
Her grievous wounds and those of brave Hojír,
Had saddened all within, both young and old.
"Oh brave and lion-hearted maid," they said,
"The hearts of all are mournful at your state.
You have fought well, and tried deceit and guile.
Your deeds have brought no shame upon your line."
Gordafaríd laughed loud and long, then climbed
The fortress wall to look upon their foes.
She saw Sohráb still seated on his mount,

And called, "Oh shah who leads the Chinese Turks,
Why strive so hard? Turn back from this attack,
And from all combat on the field of war."
She laughed aloud but spoke with kindliness,
"The Turks will find no brides within Irán;
That's how it is, you had no luck with me.
But don't distress yourself too much at that.
You're surely not descended from these Turks.
You must be born of some more noble race.
For with your strength of arm, your chest and neck,
None of these pahlaváns can equal you.
However when Shah Kay Kavús learns that
Some warrior's brought an army from Turán,
He'll tell Rostám to arm himself for war,
And he's a hero you can never match.
Of all your host he'll leave not one alive.
And I can't guess what evil you'll endure.
I'm saddened that a chest and neck like yours
Should disappear within some leopard's maw.
It's better if you heed my warning now,
And turn your noble face toward Turán.
Don't trust your arm alone. The foolish bull
Will only feed, and think not of the knife."
Sohráb felt shame at what he heard. The fort
Had come so easily within his grasp.
Around the citadel there lay a settlement,
A town and fields, in which the fortress stood.
He razed the town and burned the fields,
And so prepared himself for evil deeds.
Sohráb then said, "The day's come to an end;
Our hands are stayed from battle now by night.
At dawn tomorrow I'll pull down these walls;
They too shall look upon defeat in war."

## Gazhdahám's Letter to Kay Kavús

And when Sohráb had gone, old Gazhdahám
Sent for a scribe and sat him by his side.
He then composed a letter to the shah,
And sent a courier swiftly on his way. . . .

*[Kay Kavús, shah of Iran, receives Gazhadhām's letter and demands Rostám's aid against Sohráb's Turks. Rostám is slow to respond.]*

## Rostám at Court

They galloped toward the court of Shah Kavús,
With loyal thoughts and open hearts they came.

But when they entered and bowed low to him,
Kavús grew angry and he answered not
At all. At first he shouted once, at Giv,
Then washed his eyes quite free of shame.
"Who is Rostám to turn his back to me,
And give so little heed to my command?
Seize him, take him from here, and gibbet him
Alive. Then speak no more of him to me!"
Giv's heart was rent asunder by these words.
"Will you indeed mistreat Rostám like this?"
When he grew angry with Piltán and Giv,
Those gathered in the court were thunderstruck.
The shah commanded Tus as he stood there.
"Go now and hang the both of them alive!"
The shah himself then rose up from his throne,
His anger flaring up like flames from reeds,
As Tus approached Rostám and seized his arm
The warriors there could scarce believe their eyes.
Did he intend to march him from the court?
Or did his brusqueness mask a shrewd deceit?
  Tahamtán [Rostám] in turn grew angry with the shah.
"Don't nurse so hot a fire within your breast.
Each thing you do shames that already done.
You are unworthy of both throne and rule.
You go and hang the brave Sohráb alive!
Take arms, set forth and humble him yourself!"
Rostám struck Tus's hand a single blow,
But like that of a raging elephant,
And sent that worthy sprawling on the ground.
Rostám passed by him then with rapid strides,
Went out the door and mounted Rakhsh. "I am,"
He said, "the lion-heart who gave this crown.
When I'm enraged, who then is Shah Kavús?
Who's there to humble me? . . .
If this Sohráb should now invade Irán,
There's none who will be spared, not great or small.
You all must seek some way to save your souls.
You all must bend your wisdom to that task.
You'll see Rostám no more within Irán.
You have the land, I fly on vultures' wings."
  The hearts of all the notables were sad.
Their shepherd was Rostám, and they the flock.
They sought Gudárz, "This is a task for you.
What's broken will be mended in your hand.
The *sepahbód* will hear no speech but yours,
Nor will our fortune slumber at your words.
Approach this crazed and foolish shah at once,

And speak with him anew of what's just passed.
If you speak shrewdly and at length, you may
Regain the smiling fortune we have lost."
The *sepahdár* Gudárz, Keshvád's brave son,
Rode swiftly off to court, and to the shah.
He asked Kavús, "What can Rostám have done
That you would cast Irán into the dust?
When he is gone, an army will attack,
Led by that wolflike pahlaván, Sohráb.
Who's there to equal him upon the field
Of war[?]. Who'll heap dark dust upon his head? . . .[?]
Whoever has a champion like Rostám,
And drives him from the court, has little sense."
When Kay Kavús had heard the counsel of
Gudárz, he realized he spoke the truth.
He was ashamed of everything he'd said.
His wits had been confused by fear and wrath.
"Your speech is to the point," he told Gudárz.
"Advice sits well upon an old man's lips.
A padisháh should be more wise of speech,
For anger and quick words bring no reward.
You must now hasten to the brave Rostám
And speak with him at length and counsel him.
Make him forget this hastiness of mine.
Recall to him the thoughts of better times." . . .

*[Gudárz persuades Rostám to return to help Kay Kavús.]*

And when he strode into the court, Kavús
Stood up and asked forgiveness of Rostám.
"I am by nature rash in speech and act,
And one must be as God created him.
This unexpected foe oppressed my heart
Till like the moon, it grew both pale and weak.
To find some remedy I sent for you.
When you were slow to come, I grew enraged.
But when you were distressed, Piltán, I felt
Remorse, and shame has filled my mouth with dust."
Rostám replied, "Oh, shah, the world is yours.
We are your subjects. Yours is sovereignty.
I've come to court to be at your command.
May the wisdom of your soul be never less."
Kavús replied, "Today let's choose instead
To celebrate. Tomorrow we'll make war."
A place was then prepared, fit for a shah;
The palace was adorned like verdant spring.

And there they drank their wine while pale-
Cheeked beauties waited on the shah, and to
The sound of silken strings and plaintive reeds,
The sweet-voiced minstrels filled the night with song.

## The Iranians Make War

Next day at dawn he ordered Giv and Tus
To bind the war drums on the elephants.
He opened wide his treasury's doors, gave out
Supplies, and loaded up the baggage train.
A hundred thousand men, all bearing shields
And wearing mail, assembled for the march.
Then from the court, an army rode to war
Whose dust rose up and blotted out the sun.
When camped, it spread its tents and canopies
For miles, and carpeted the earth with hooves.
The hills were dark as ebony, the air
Like indigo. The river boiled with drumbeats,
And as the troops proceeded stage by stage,
The world turned dark and night obscured the day.
The flash of spears and lances through the dust
Were like bright flames seen through a deep blue haze.
There were so many flags and shining spears,
So many golden shields and gilded boots,
It seemed a cloud as dark as ebony
Had formed, and rained down drops of yellow pitch.
In all the world there was no day or night;
The heavens and the Pleiades both were gone.
Thus they proceeded to the fortress gates.
The army hid the earth and stones from view. . . .

## Rostám in the Turkish Camp

When from the earth the sun withdrew its light,
Dark night arrayed its troops upon the field. . . .
  Rostám put on a costume like the Turks',
And hastened swiftly to the fortress walls.
As Tahamtán approached their camp he heard
The revels of the Turkish troops within.
Then like a lion stalking wild gazelle,
The brave Rostám crept through the fortress gate.
He saw Sohráb, enthroned amid the feast,
At his right hand the noble Zhende Razm,
And at his left so brave a horseman as
Humán, and lionlike Barmán as well.

And yet it seemed Sohráb filled up the throne.
His legs and trunk were like a cypress tree;
His arms were like two camels' thighs,
His chest, an elephant's; his visage flushed
With health. A hundred Turkish youths were ranged
Around him there, male lions in their pride.
Some fifty servants waited on this high
And happy throne, their wrists adorned with gold.
Each one invoked God's blessing on his sword,
His lofty stature and his signet ring.
While from afar Rostám observed them all—
These Turkish heroes at their victory feast.

Zhende went out upon some task, and saw
A warrior there, tall as a cypress tree.
Among his troops he knew of none like this.
He moved toward Rostám and challenged him.
"Whose man are you?" he asked. "Tell me your name.
Come here, into the light, and show your face!"
Rostám struck Zhende's neck a single blow
That freed his spirit from his body's weight.
He lay upon the ground, now stilled by death.
Brave Zhende Razm returned no more to feast.
And when some time had passed, and Zhende Razm
Remained still absent from his side, Sohráb
Inquired about his lion-hearted friend,
"Where did he go? His place is empty here."
They went outside and saw him lying there,
Released from feasting and from strife and war.
They all returned lamenting in their pain,
Both anxious and perplexed by Zhende's death.
They told Sohráb, "Brave Zhende Razm is gone,
His days of feasting and of war are done."
Sohráb leapt up when he had heard the words,
And swift as smoke he flew to where he lay.
With servants, candles, minstrels in his train,
He went and looked upon this heavy death.
He was amazed, and stood in silent thought,
Then called his brave and gallant pahlaváns,
"We must not sleep or rest," he said, "but arm
Ourselves and keep our weapons by our sides.
A wolf has crept within the fold tonight,
Despite the shepherd and his watchful dogs.
But if the World Creator gives me aid
When next my yellow steed tears up the earth,
I'll loose my lasso from its place, and make
Iranians pay the cost of Zhende's death." . . .

## Sohráb Seeks His Father

At dawn, when the sun had cast its lasso high,
And tongues of flame shot through the highest sphere,
Sohráb put on his chainmail kaftan lined
With silk, and sat upon his silver grey.
He wore a royal helmet on his head,
And in his fist he held an Indian blade.
He fixed his rope in sixty loops upon
The saddle bow, and anger creased his brow.
He chose a tower on the wall from which
He might observe the enemy below.
He ordered that Hojír be brought to him. . . .
Sohráb then said, "Describe the leaders of
That land to me, its bravest warriors,
Its notables like Tus, Bahrám, Gudárz,
Like Shah Kavús and like far-famed Rostám.
Identify each one I ask of you. . . .

*[Hojír identifies the Iranian warriors but not Rostám.]*

Sohráb despaired at heart. In all that camp,
No trace of Tahamtán had yet appeared.
His mother had described his father's signs.
He'd seen them all, but did not trust his eyes.
He pressed Hojír once more about Rostám,
And hoped his words would satisfy his heart,
His fate was written otherwise, alas,
And that command may not be changed by man. . . .

One sought his father's camp. One hid the truth,
And would not speak the words he longed to hear.
What can one do? This world's already made.
There is no task that He has left undone.
The writ of fate was otherwise, alas.
What it commands will finish as it must. . . .

*[Unaware of their kinship, Sohráb and Rostám clash in battle.]*

## The Second Day

The shining sun spread wide its radiance,
The raven tucked its head beneath its wings,
Tahamtán put on his tiger-skin cuirass,
And sat astride his huge, fierce elephant.
To his seat he bound his rope in sixty coils,
And in his hand he grasped an Indian sword.
He galloped to the field, the place where they

Would fight, and there put on his iron helm.
All bitterness is born of precedence,
Alas when it is yoked to greedy pride!
  Sohráb stood up and armed himself. His head
Was filled with war, his heart with revelry.
Shouting his cry he rode into the field,
Within his hand, he held his bullhide mace.
He greeted him, a smile upon his lips,
As though they'd spent the night in company.
"How did you sleep? How do you feel today?
And how have you prepared yourself to fight?
Let's put aside this mace and sword of war.
Cast strife and wrong down to the ground.
Let us dismount and sit together now,
And smooth our brows with wine. And let us make
A pact before the World Preserving Lord,
That we'll repent of all our warlike plans.
Until another comes who's keen to fight,
Make peace with me and let us celebrate.
My heart is ever moved by love for you,
And wets my face with tears of modesty.
I'm sure you're from a noble line, come then,
Recite for me the line of your descent.
Aren't you the son of brave Dastán, the son
Of Sam? Aren't you the pahlaván Rostám?"
Rostám replied, "Oh, shrewd ambitious youth,
Before this hour we never spoke like this.
Last night our words were of the coming fray.
Your tricks won't work with me; don't try again.
Though you are but a youth, I am no child,
And I'm prepared to fight you hand to hand.
So let's begin our strife. Its end will be
As the Keeper of the World commands it should.
I've traveled long through hills and valleys too.
And I'm no man for guile, deceits, and lies."
Sohráb replied, "Such words do not befit
A warrior who's so advanced in years.
I wished that you might die upon your bed,
And that your soul would leave in its own time;
That those you leave behind could keep your bones,
Immure your flesh, but let your spirit fly.
But if your life is in my grasp, then as
Yazdán commands, let us lock hands and fight."
  They both dismounted from their battle steeds.
In casque and tunic they approached with care,
And to a stone they tied their steeds of war.

They then advanced, their hearts as cold as earth.
Each seized the other and they grappled till
Their bodies ran with sweat and blood. Sohráb
Was like a maddened elephant; he struck
Rostám a blow that felled him to the earth.
Then like a lion in the hunt whose claws
Have thrown a mighty stallion to the ground,
Sohráb sat firmly on the chest of huge
Rostám, fist, face, and mouth all smeared with dirt,
And from his belt he drew his polished blade.
As he bent down to sever head from trunk,
Rostám looked up and said, "Oh, lion-slaying
Chief, and master of the sword and mace and rope!
The custom of our nation is not thus.
Our faith commands us to another way.
Whoever in a wrestling match first throws
His noble adversary to the ground,
And pins him to the earth, may not cut off
His head, not even if he seeks revenge.
But if he fells him twice, he's earned that right,
And all will call him Lion if he does."
By that deceit he shrewdly sought to free
Himself from this fierce dragon's mortal grip.
  The brave youth bowed his head and yielded
To the old man's words, and said no more,
But loosed his grip and rushed off to the plain,
A lion who has seen a deer race by.
He hunted eagerly and gave no thought
To him with whom he'd fought so recently.
When it grew late, Humán came swiftly to
The field and asked him how the battle'd gone.
Sohráb then told Humán all that had passed,
And what Rostám had said to him. The brave
Humán just heaved a sigh and said, "Dear youth,
I see that you've grown weary of your life.
I fear for this stout neck and arms and chest,
This hero's waist and royal legs and feet.
You caught a tiger firm within your trap,
Then spoiled your work by letting him escape.
You'll see what consequence this foolish act
Of yours will have when next you meet to fight." . . .
  Sohráb returned toward his army's camp,
Perplexed at heart and angry with himself.
A shah once wisely spoke a proverb on
This point, "Despise no foe, however mean."
Rostám, when he'd escaped from his foe's hand,

Sprang up just like a blade of steel, and rushed
Off to a flowing stream that was nearby,
For he was like a man who'd been reborn.
He drank his fill, and when he'd washed his face
And limbs, he bowed before his Lord in prayer.
He asked for strength and victory; he did
Not know what sun and moon might hold in store,
Or if the heavens as they wheeled above
Would wish to snatch the crown from off his head.
  Then pale of face and with an anxious heart,
He left the stream to meet his foe once more. . . .

## The Death of Sohráb

Again they firmly hitched their steeds, as ill-
Intentioned fate revolved above their heads.
Once more they grappled hand to hand. Each seized
The other's belt and sought to throw him down.
Whenever evil fortune shows its wrath,
It makes a block of granite soft as wax.
Sohráb had mighty arms, and yet it seemed
The skies above had bound them fast. He paused
In fear; Rostám stretched out his hands and seized
That warlike leopard by his chest and arms.
He bent that strong and youthful back, and with
A lion's speed, he threw him to the ground.
Sohráb had not the strength; his time had come.
Rostám knew well he'd not stay down for long.
He swiftly drew a dagger from his belt
And tore the breast of that stout-hearted youth.
He writhed upon the ground; groaned once aloud,
Then thought no more of good and ill. He told
Rostám, "This was the fate allotted me.
The heavens gave my key into your hand.
It's not your fault. It was this hunchback fate,
Who raised me up then quickly cast me down.
While boys my age still spent their time in games,
My neck and shoulders stretched up to the clouds.
My mother told me who my father was.
My love for him has ended in my death.
Whenever you should thirst for someone's blood,
And stain your silver dagger with his gore,
Then Fate may thirst for yours as well, and make
Each hair upon your trunk a sharpened blade.
Now should you, fishlike, plunge into the sea,
Or cloak yourself in darkness like the night,

Or like a star take refuge in the sky,
And sever from the earth your shining light,
Still when he learns that earth's my pillow now,
My father will avenge my death on you.
A hero from among this noble band
Will take this seal and show it to Rostám.
'Sohráb's been slain, and humbled to the earth,'
He'll say, 'This happened while he searched for you.'"
  When he heard this, Rostám was near to faint.
The world around grew dark before his eyes.
And when Rostám regained his wits once more,
He asked Sohráb with sighs of grief and pain,
"What sign have you from him—Rostám? Oh, may
His name be lost to proud and noble men!"
"If you're Rostám," he said, "you slew me while
Some evil humor had confused your mind.
I tried in every way to draw you forth,
But not an atom of your love was stirred.
When first they beat the war drums at my door,
My mother came to me with bloody cheeks.
Her soul was racked by grief to see me go.
She bound a seal upon my arm, and said,
'This is your father's gift, preserve it well.
A day will come when it will be of use.' . . .
My mother with great wisdom thought to send
With me a worthy pahlaván as guide.
The noble warrior's name was Zhende Razm,
A man both wise in action and in speech.
He was to point my father out to me,
And ask for him among all groups of men.
But Zhende Razm, that worthy man, was slain.
And at his death my star declined as well.
Now loose the binding of my coat of mail,
And look upon my naked, shining flesh."
When he unloosed his armor's ties and saw
That seal, he tore his clothes and wept.
"Oh, brave and noble youth, and praised among
All men, whom I have slain with my own hand!"
He wept a bloody stream and tore his hair;
His brow was dark with dust, tears filled his eyes. . . .
Sohráb [spoke] thus with Tahamtán,
"The situation of the Turks has changed
In every way, now that my days are done.
Be kind to them, and do not let the shah
Pursue this war or urge his army on.
It was for me the Turkish troops rose up,

And mounted this campaign against Irán.
I it was who promised victory, and I
Who strove in every way to give them hope.
They should not suffer now as they retreat.
Be generous with them, and let them go."
  Rostám then mounted Rakhsh, as swift as dust.
His eyes bled tears, his lips were chilled with sighs.
He wept as he approached the army's camp,
His heart was filled with pain at what he'd done. . . .
He grasped a dagger in his hand, and made
To cut his worthless head from his own trunk.
The nobles hung upon his arm and hand, and tears
Of blood poured from the lashes of their eyes.
Gudárz said to Rostám, "What gain is there
If by your death you set the world in flames?
Were you to give yourself a hundred wounds,
How would that ease the pain of brave Sohráb?
If some time yet remains for him on earth,
He'll live, and you'll remain with him, at peace.
But if this youth is destined to depart,
Look on the world, who's there that does not die?
The head that wears a helmet and the head
That wears a crown, to death we all are prey."

## Rostám Asks Kay Kavús for the Nushdarú

Rostám called wise Gudárz and said to him,
"Depart from here upon your swiftest steed,
And take a message to Kavús the shah.
Tell him what has befallen me. With my
Own dagger I have torn the breast of my
Brave son—oh, may Rostám not live for long!
If you've some recollection of my deeds,
Then share with me a portion of my grief,
And from your store send me the *nushdarú,*
That medicine which heals whatever wound.
It would be well if you sent it to me
With no delay, and in a cup of wine.
By your good grace, my son may yet be cured,
And like his father stand before your throne."
The *sepahbód* Gudárz rode like the wind,
And gave Kavús the message from Rostám.
  Kavús replied, "If such an elephant
Should stay alive and join our royal court,
He'll make his father yet more powerful.
Rostám will slay me then, I have no doubt.

When I may suffer evil at his hands.
What gift but evil should I make him now?
You heard him, how he said. 'Who is Kavús?
If he's the shah, then who is Tus?' And with
That chest and neck, that mighty arm and fist.
In this wide world, who's there to equal him?
Will he stand humbly by my royal seat.
Or march beneath my banner's eagle wings?"
  Gudárz heard his reply, then turned and rode
Back to Rostám as swift as wind-borne smoke.
"The evil nature of the shah is like
The tree of war, perpetually in fruit.
You must depart at once and go to him.
Perhaps you can enlighten his dark soul."

## Rostám Mourns Sohráb

Rostám commanded that a servant bring
A robe and spread it by the river's bank.
He gently laid Sohráb upon the robe,
Then mounted Rakhsh and rode toward the shah.
But as he rode, his face toward the court,
They overtook him swiftly with the news,
"Sohráb has passed from this wide world; he'll need
A coffin from you now, and not a crown.
'Father!' he cried, then sighed an icy wind,
Then wept aloud and closed his eyes at last."
  Rostám dismounted from his steed at once.
Dark dust replaced the helmet on his head.
He wept and cried aloud, "Oh, noble youth,
And proud, courageous seed of pahlaváns!
The sun and moon won't see your like again,
No more will shield or mail, nor throne or crown.
Who else has been afflicted as I've been?
That I should slay a youth in my old age
Who is the grandson of world-conquering Sam,
Whose mother's seed's from famous men as well.
It would be right to sever these two hands.
No seat be mine henceforth save darkest earth.
What father's ever done a deed like this?
I now deserve abuse and icy scorn.
Who else in all this world has slain his son,
His wise, courageous, youthful son? . . .
  Rostám commanded that the body of
His son be covered with a royal robe.
He'd longed to sit upon the throne and rule;

His portion was a coffin's narrow walls.
The coffin of Sohráb was carried from
The field. Rostám returned to his own tent.
They set aflame Sohráb's pavilion while
His army cast dark dust upon their heads.
They threw his tents of many colored silk,
His precious throne and leopard saddle cloth
Into the flames, and tumult filled the air.
He cried aloud, "Oh, youthful conqueror!
Alas, that stature and that noble face!
Alas, that wisdom and that manliness!
Alas, what sorrow and heart-rending loss
No mother near, heart pierced by father's blade!"
His eyes wept bloody tears, he tore the earth,
And rent the kingly garments on his back.
Then all the pahlaváns and Shah Kavús
Sat with him in the dust beside the road.
They spoke to him with counsel and advice.
In grief Rostám was like one driven mad,
"This is the way of fortune's wheel. It holds
A lasso in this hand, a crown in that.
As one sits happily upon his throne,
A loop of rope will snatch him from his place.
Why is it we should hold the world so dear?
We and our fellows must depart this road.
The longer we have thought about our wealth,
The sooner we must face that earthy door.
If heaven's wheel knows anything of this,
Or if its mind is empty of our fate,
The turning of the wheel it cannot know,
Nor can it understand the reason why.
One must lament that he should leave this world,
Yet what this means at last, I do not know."
Then Kay Kavús spoke to Rostám at length,
"From Mount Alborz to the frailest reed,
The turning heavens carry all away.
You must not fix your heart upon this world.
One sets off quickly on the road, and one
Will take more time, but all pass on to death.
Content your heart with his departure and
Give careful heed to what I tell you now.
If you should bring the heavens down to earth,
Or set the world aflame from end to end,
You won't recall from death the one who's gone.
His soul's grown ancient in that other manse.
Once from afar I saw his arms and neck,

His lofty stature and his massive chest.
The times impelled him and his martial host
To come here now and perish by your hand.
What can you do? What remedy is there
For death? How long can you bewail his loss?"
Rostám replied, "Though he himself is gone,
Humán still sits upon this ample plain,
His Turkish and his Chinese chiefs as well.
Retain no hint of enmity toward them,
But strengthened by Yazdán and your command,
Let Zavaré guide all their army home."
"Oh, famous pahlaván," said Shah Kavús,
"This war has caused you suffering and loss.
Though they have done me many grievous wrongs,
And though Turán has set Irán aflame,
Because my heart can feel your heavy pain,
I'll think no more of them and let them go."

## Farid al-Din Attar (c. 1145–1221)

*The Conference of Birds, Manteq al-Tayr* (meaning literally "speech of birds") is first and foremost a Sufi text, a text of Islamic mysticism in which a frame narrative of the birds' pilgrimage to find the mythical beast called the Simorgh is supported by numerous short tales intended to provide answers to the birds' questions. As in many literatures, the birds represent human souls in search of the divine. The geography of the journey is spiritual: the birds pass through valleys of detachment, awe, and poverty; instead of asking for spatial directions, they ask the hoopoe (a wise bird featured in conversation with Solomon in the Qur'ān) for guidance. Although moral commentary attached to the tales usually guides the reader's interpretation, some tales present teasing paradoxes or surprising perspectives. Attention to juxtaposed narratives is crucial for a more than cursory reading of the work.

The Sufi "way," or practice, involves intense devotion to God and a passionate yearning for union with the divine. The Self is an obstacle to be overcome or annihilated on the spiritual journey. As the hoopoe guide says, "Your body's but a fleeting particle," and "All things are one—there isn't any two;/ It isn't me who speaks; it isn't you." The Self is the fragmented and separated soul that is forced to journey through mortality back to a divine unity with God. This world is a shadow, a veil that obscures and tempts the soul away from its divine journey. Sufis, like their counterparts among the mystics of medieval Europe, were often subject to persecution. One Sufi, al-Hallāj, went so far as to declare, "I am Truth; I am God" and was executed for blasphemy. Attar's exact connection with Sufism is not clear, but his *Conference of Birds* is one of its most eloquent and well-known poetic expositions.

A powerful tradition claims that al-Hallāj appeared in a dream and instructed the poet in the way of the Sufi. Attar, like many Sufis, was tried for heresy and exiled from Neishapour. He was well educated and apparently supported himself as an apothecary and perfume dealer; he was affluent enough to have traveled widely, not only within Iran, but also to Turkestan, India, Egypt, Syria, and (of course) Mecca. The *Manteq,* as a collection of tales with spiritual resonance, shares features with later European texts like Chaucer's *Canterbury Tales* and Dante's *Divine Comedy,* and the themes of some individual tales resonate with many other texts of world literature. This collection of love stories, tragedies, humorous anecdotes, lyric pieces, fiction, history, and morality combines into a complex text, which reaches toward the divine through a poetic medium.

Besides *The Conference of Birds,* Farīd al-Dīn Attar produced a considerable corpus of poetry and one work in prose, *The Memorial of the Saints,* a book of anecdotes about Islamic saints often cited by later Persian and Arabic writers. This book includes an account of the greatest Islamic female saint, Rābi'ah al-'Adawiyyah. Her teachings, poems, and sayings are preserved in many medieval and modern Islamic texts. She lived from c. 718 to 801 in and around Basra, and she is credited with emphasizing Islam as a religion of love. Rather than obeying God out of fear of punishment or out of a desire for reward in the afterlife, Rābi'ah celebrated the mystical rapture of loving God, an important development for Sufism and early Islamic mysticism.

Rābi'ah, (spelled *Rabe'a* in the translation reprinted here) was the fourth daughter of a very poor family (her name means "the fourth"). She was sold into slavery after her parents died. Emancipation came when, one night, her master saw a bright lamp appear above her head while she prayed for freedom. Its brilliance frightened him so much that he set her free. She withdrew into the desert, later returning to Basra to live out her life as a great ascetic and teacher, refusing marriage and living as a celibate. She composed the following elegant lines as a marriage refusal:

> My peace, O my brothers, is in solitude,
> And my Beloved is with me always,
> For His love I can find no substitute,
> And His love is the test for me among mortal beings. (trans. Margaret Smith)

Rābi'ah abandoned sexual differentiation and became a *mard,* or a "man of God." Her life and influence might also be compared with the sixteenth-century Indian *bhakti* poet Mīrabāī (pp. 988–993). Her work was so significant that the most eminent medieval Muslim theologians wrote commentaries on her verses. Rābi'ah is credited with a number of distinguished poems, like the following famous lines about the two types of love people have for God:

> I have loved Thee with two loves, a selfish love
>   and a love that is worthy (of Thee),
> As for the love which is selfish, I occupy myself therein
>   with remembrance of Thee to the exclusion of all others,
> As for that which is worthy of Thee, therein Thou raisest
>   the veil that I may see Thee.
> Yet is there no praise to me in this or that,
>   But the praise is to Thee, whether in that or this. (trans. Margaret Smith)

## *The Conference of Birds*

*Translated by Afkham Darbandi and Dick Davis*

. . . The world's birds gathered for their conference
And said: 'Our constitution makes no sense.
All nations in the world require a king;
How is it we alone have no such thing?
Only a kingdom can be justly run;
We need a king and must inquire for one.'

They argued how to set about their quest.
The hoopoe fluttered forward; on his breast
There shone the symbol of the Spirit's Way
And on his head Truth's crown, a feathered spray.
Discerning, righteous and intelligent,
He spoke: 'My purposes are heaven-sent;
I keep God's secrets, mundane and divine,
In proof of which behold the holy sign
*Bismillah** etched for ever on my beak.
No one can share the grief with which I seek
Our longed-for Lord, and quickened by my haste
My wits find water in the trackless waste.
I come as Solomon's close friend and claim
The matchless wisdom of that mighty name
(He never asked for those who quit his court,
But when I left him once alone he sought
With anxious vigilance for my return—
Measure my worth by this great king's concern!).
I bore his letters—back again I flew—
Whatever secrets he divined I knew;
A prophet loved me; God has trusted me;
What other bird has won such dignity?
For years I travelled over many lands,
Past oceans, mountains, valleys, desert sands,
And when the Deluge rose I flew around
The world itself and never glimpsed dry ground;
With Solomon I set out to explore
The limits of the earth from shore to shore.
I know our king—but how can I alone
Endure the journey to His distant throne?

*'In the name of God': the opening words of the Koran.

Join me, and when at last we end our quest
Our king will greet you as His honoured guest.
How long will you persist in blasphemy?
Escape your self-hood's vicious tyranny—
Whoever can evade the Self transcends
This world and as a lover he ascends.
Set free your soul; impatient of delay,
Step out along our sovereign's royal Way:
We have a king; beyond Kaf's mountain peak
The Simorgh lives, the sovereign whom you seek,
And He is always near to us, though we
Live far from His transcendent majesty.
A hundred thousand veils of dark and light
Withdraw His presence from our mortal sight,
And in both worlds no being shares the throne
That marks the Simorgh's power and His alone—
He reigns in undisturbed omnipotence,
Bathed in the light of His magnificence—
No mind, no intellect can penetrate
The mystery of His unending state:
How many countless hundred thousands pray
For patience and true knowledge of the Way
That leads to Him whom reason cannot claim,
Nor mortal purity describe or name;
There soul and mind bewildered miss the mark
And, faced by Him, like dazzled eyes, are dark—
No sage could understand His perfect grace,
Nor seer discern the beauty of His face.
His creatures strive to find a path to Him,
Deluded by each new, deceitful whim,
But fancy cannot work as she would wish;
You cannot weigh the moon like so much fish!
How many search for Him whose heads are sent
Like polo-balls in some great tournament
From side to giddy side—how many cries,
How many countless groans assail the skies!
Do not imagine that the Way is short;
Vast seas and deserts lie before His court.
Consider carefully before you start;
The journey asks of you a lion's heart.
The road is long, the sea is deep—one flies
First buffeted by joy and then by sighs;
If you desire this quest, give up your soul
And make our sovereign's court your only goal.
First wash your hands of life if you would say:
"I am a pilgrim of our sovereign's Way";

Renounce your soul for love; He you pursue
Will sacrifice His inmost soul for you.

It was in China, late one moonless night,
The Simorgh first appeared to mortal sight—
He let a feather float down through the air,
And rumours of its fame spread everywhere;
Throughout the world men separately conceived
An image of its shape, and all believed
Their private fantasies uniquely true!
(In China still this feather is on view,
Whence comes the saying you have heard, no doubt,
"Seek knowledge, unto China seek it out.")
If this same feather had not floated down,
The world would not be filled with His renown—
It is a sign of Him, and in each heart
There lies this feather's hidden counterpart.
But since no words suffice, what use are mine
To represent or to describe this sign?
Whoever wishes to explore the Way,
Let him set out—what more is there to say?'

The hoopoe finished, and at once the birds
Effusively responded to his words.
All praised the splendour of their distant king;
All rose impatient to be on the wing;
Each would renounce the Self and be the friend
Of his companions till the journey's end.
But when they pondered on the journey's length,
They hesitated; their ambitious strength
Dissolved: each bird, according to his kind,
Felt flattered but reluctantly declined.

## The nightingale's excuse

The nightingale made his excuses first.
His pleading notes described the lover's thirst,
And through the crowd hushed silence spread as he
Descanted on love's scope and mystery.
'The secrets of all love are known to me,'
He crooned. 'Throughout the darkest night my song
Resounds, and to my retinue belong
The sweet notes of the melancholy lute,
The plaintive wailing of the love-sick flute;
When love speaks in the soul my voice replies
In accents plangent as the ocean's sighs.

The man who hears this song spurns reason's rule;
Grey wisdom is content to be love's fool.
My love is for the rose; I bow to her;
From her dear presence I could never stir.
If she should disappear the nightingale
Would lose his reason and his song would fail,
And though my grief is one that no bird knows,
One being understands my heart—the rose.
I am so drowned in love that I can find
No thought of my existence in my mind.
Her worship is sufficient life for me;
The quest for her is my reality
(And nightingales are not robust or strong;
The path to find the Simorgh is too long).
My love is here; the journey you propose
Cannot beguile me from my life—the rose.
It is for me she flowers; what greater bliss
Could life provide me—anywhere—than this?
Her buds are mine; she blossoms in my sight—
How could I leave her for a single night?'

## The hoopoe answers him

The hoopoe answered him: 'Dear nightingale,
This superficial love which makes you quail
Is only for the outward show of things.
Renounce delusion and prepare your wings
For our great quest; sharp thorns defend the rose
And beauty such as hers too quickly goes.
True love will see such empty transience
For what it is—a fleeting turbulence
That fills your sleepless nights with grief and blame—
Forget the rose's blush and blush for shame!
Each spring she laughs, not *for* you, as you say,
But *at* you—and has faded in a day.

* * *

## The peacock's excuse and the hoopoe's answer

Next came the peacock, splendidly arrayed
In many-coloured pomp; this he displayed
As if he were some proud, self-conscious bride
Turning with haughty looks from side to side.
'The Painter of the world created me,'
He shrieked, 'but this celestial wealth you see
Should not excite your hearts to jealousy.

I was a dweller once in paradise;
There the insinuating snake's advice
Deceived me—I became his friend, disgrace
Was swift and I was banished from that place.
My dearest hope is that some blessèd day
A guide will come to indicate the way
Back to my paradise. The king you praise
Is too unknown a goal; my inward gaze
Is fixed for ever on that lovely land—
There is the goal which I can understand.
How could I seek the Simorgh out when I
Remember paradise?' And in reply
The hoopoe said: 'These thoughts have made you stray
Further and further from the proper Way;
You think your monarch's palace of more worth
Than Him who fashioned it and all the earth.
The home we seek is in eternity;
The Truth we seek is like a shoreless sea,
Of which your paradise is but a drop.
This ocean can be yours; why should you stop
Beguiled by dreams of evanescent dew?
The secrets of the sun are yours, but you
Content yourself with motes trapped in its beams.
Turn to what truly lives, reject what seems—
Which matters more, the body or the soul?
Be whole: desire and journey to the Whole.'

* * *

## The heron's excuse

The heron whimpered next: 'My misery
Prefers the empty shoreline of the sea.
There no one hears my desolate, thin cry—
I wait in sorrow there, there mourn and sigh.
My love is for the ocean, but since I—
A bird—must be excluded from the deep,
I haunt the solitary shore and weep.
My beak is dry—not one drop can I drink—
But if the level of the sea should sink
By one drop, jealous rage would seize my heart.
This love suffices me; how can I start
A journey like the one that you suggest?
I cannot join you in this arduous quest.
The Simorgh's glory could not comfort me;
My love is fixed entirely on the sea.'

## The hoopoe answers him

The hoopoe answered him: 'You do not know
The nature of this sea you love: below
Its surface linger sharks; tempests appear,
Then sudden calms—its course is never clear,
But turbid, varying, in constant stress;
Its water's taste is salty bitterness.
How many noble ships has it destroyed,
Their crews sucked under in the whirlpool's void:
The diver plunges and in fear of death
Must struggle to conserve his scanty breath;
The failure is cast up, a broken straw.
Who trusts the sea? Lawlessness is her law;
You will be drowned if you cannot decide
To turn away from her inconstant tide.
She seethes with love herself—that turbulence
Of tumbling waves, that yearning violence,
Are for her Lord, and since she cannot rest,
What peace could you discover in her breast?
She lives for Him—yet you are satisfied
To hear His invitation and to hide.'

## [The hoopoe tells of] a hermit who questions the ocean

A hermit asked the ocean: '"Why are you
Clothed in these mourning robes of darkest blue?
You seem to boil, and yet I see no fire!"
The ocean said: "My feverish desire
Is for the absent Friend. I am too base
For Him; my dark robes indicate disgrace
And lonely pain. Love makes my billows rage;
Love is the fire which nothing can assuage.
My salt lips thirst for Kausar's cleansing stream."
For those pure waters tens of thousands dream
And are prepared to perish; night and day
They search and fall exhausted by the Way.'

* * *

*[The other birds protest and the hoopoe tells them of their relationship with the Simorgh]*

. . . 'When long ago the Simorgh first appeared—
His face like sunlight when the clouds have cleared—
He cast unnumbered shadows on the earth,
On each one fixed his eyes, and each gave birth.

Thus we were born; the birds of every land
Are still his shadows—think, and understand.
If you had known this secret you would see
The link between yourselves and Majesty.
Do not reveal this truth, and God forfend
That you mistake for God Himself God's friend.
If you become that substance I propound,
You are not God, though in God you are drowned;
Those lost in Him are not the Deity—
This problem can be argued endlessly.
You are His shadow, and cannot be moved
By thoughts of life or death once this is proved.
If He had kept His majesty concealed,
No earthly shadow would have been revealed,
And where that shadow was directly cast
The race of birds sprang up before it passed.
Your heart is not a mirror bright and clear
If there the Simorgh's form does not appear;
No one can bear His beauty face to face,
And for this reason, of His perfect grace,
He makes a mirror in our hearts—look there
To see Him, search your hearts with anxious care.'

## [The hoopoe tells of] a king who placed mirrors in his palace

'There lived a king; his comeliness was such
The world could not acclaim his charm too much.
The world's wealth seemed a portion of his grace;
It was a miracle to view his face.
If he had rivals, then I know of none;
The earth resounded with this paragon.
When riding through his streets he did not fail
To hide his features with a scarlet veil.
Whoever scanned the veil would lose his head;
Whoever spoke his name was left for dead,
The tongue ripped from his mouth; whoever thrilled
With passion for this king was quickly killed.
A thousand for his love expired each day,
And those who saw his face, in blank dismay
Would rave and grieve and mourn their lives away—
To die for love of that bewitching sight
Was worth a hundred lives without his light.
None could survive his absence patiently,
None could endure this king's proximity—
How strange it was that men could neither brook
The presence nor the absence of his look!

Since few could bear his sight, they were content
To hear the king in sober argument,
But while they listened they endured such pain
As made them long to see their king again.
The king commanded mirrors to be placed
About the palace walls, and when he faced
Their polished surfaces his image shone
With mitigated splendour to the throng.

If you would glimpse the beauty we revere
Look in your heart—its image will appear.
Make of your heart a looking-glass and see
Reflected there the Friend's nobility;
Your sovereign's glory will illuminate
The palace where he reigns in proper state.
Search for this king within your heart; His soul
Reveals itself in atoms of the Whole.
The multitude of forms that masquerade
Throughout the world spring from the Simorgh's shade.
If you catch sight of His magnificence
It is His shadow that beguiles your glance;
The Simorgh's shadow and Himself are one;
Seek them together, twinned in unison.
But you are lost in vague uncertainty . . .
Pass beyond shadows to Reality.'

* * *

## The birds are frightened by the emptiness of the Way, and the hoopoe tells them a story about Sheikh Bayazid

The hoopoe, as their chief, was hailed and crowned—
Huge flocks of birds in homage gathered round;
A hundred thousand birds assembled there,
Making a monstrous shadow in the air.
The throng set out—but, clearing the first dune,
Their leader sent a cry up to the moon
And panic spread among the birds; they feared
The endless desolation which appeared.
They clung together in a huddling crowd,
Drew in their heads and wings and wailed aloud
A melancholy, weak, faint-hearted song—
Their burdens were too great, the way too long!
How featureless the view before their eyes,
An emptiness where they could recognize
No marks of good or ill—a silence where
The soul knew neither hope nor blank despair.

One said, 'The Way is lifeless, empty—why?'
To which the hoopoe gave this strange reply:
'To glorify the king.

One moonlit night
Sheikh Bayazid, attracted by the sight
Of such refulgent brilliance, clear as day,
Across the sleeping city took his way
And thence into the desert, where he saw
Unnumbered stars adorning heaven's floor.
He walked a little and became aware
That not a sound disturbed the desert air,
That no one moved in that immensity
Save him. His heart grew numb and gradually
Pure terror touched him. "O great God," he cried,
"Your dazzling palace beckons far and wide—
Where are the courtiers who should throng this court?"
A voice said: "Wanderer, you are distraught;
Be calm. Our glorious King cannot admit
All comers to His court; it is not fit
That every rascal who sleeps out the night
Should be allowed to glimpse its radiant light.
Most are turned back, and few perceive the throne;
Among a hundred thousand there is one"'

## The birds ask the hoopoe to resolve their doubts

The trembling birds stared out across the plain;
The road seemed endless as their endless pain.
But in the hoopoe's heart new confidence
Transported him above the firmaments—
The sands could not alarm him nor the high
Harsh sun at noon, the peacock of the sky.
What other bird, throughout the world, could bear
The troubles of the Way and all its care?

The frightened flock drew nearer to their guide.
'You know the perils of the Way,' they cried,
'And how we should behave before the king—
You served great Solomon in everything
And flew across his lands—therefore you know
Exactly where it's safe and right to go;
You've seen the ups and downs of this strange Way.
It is our wish that as our guide you say
How we should act before the king we seek;
And more, as we are ignorant and weak,
That you should solve the problems in our hearts

Before the fearful company departs.
First hear our doubts; the thing we do not doubt
Is that you'll answer them and drive them out—
We know that on this lengthy Way no light
Will come to clear uncertainty's dark night;
But when the heart is free we shall commit
Our hearts and bodies, all we have, to it.'

The hoopoe stood to speak, and all the birds
Approached to be encouraged by his words;
A hundred thousand gathered with one mind,
Serried in ranks according to their kind.
The dove and nightingale voiced their complaint;
Such beauty made the company grow faint—
A cry of ecstasy went up; a state
Where neither Self nor void predominate
Fell on the birds. The hoopoe spoke; he drew
The veil from what is ultimately true.
One asked: 'How is it you surpass us in
This search for Truth; what is our crippling sin?
We search and so do you—but you receive
Truth's purity while we stand by and grieve.'

## The hoopoe tells them about the glance of Solomon

The hoopoe answered him: 'Great Solomon
Once looked at me—it is that glance alone
Which gave me what I know; no wealth could bring
The substance I received from wisdom's king.
No one can gain this by the forms of prayer,
For even Satan bowed with pious care;
Though don't imagine that you need not pray;
We curse the fool who tricks you in this way.
Pray always, never for one moment cease,
Pray in despair and when your goods increase,
Consume your life with prayer, till Solomon
Bestows his glance, and ignorance is gone.
When Solomon accepts you, you will know
Far more than my unequal words can show.'

## The story of King Mas'oud and the fisherboy

He said: 'King Mas'oud, riding out one day,
Was parted from his army on the way.
Swift as the wind he galloped till he saw
A little boy sat by the ocean's shore.
The child was fishing—as he cast his hook,

The king dismounted with a friendly look
And sat by him; but the unhappy child
Was troubled in his heart and hardly smiled.
"You seem the saddest boy I've ever seen,"
The monarch said. "What can such sorrow mean?"
"Our father's gone; for seven children I
Must cast my line" was his subdued reply.
"Our mother's paralysed and we are poor;
It is for food that I must haunt this shore—
I come to fish here in the dawn's first light
And cannot leave until the fall of night.
The meagre harvest of my toil and pain
Must last us all till I return again."
The king said: "Let's be friends, do you agree?"
The poor child nodded and, immediately,
His new friend cast their line into the sea.
That day the boy drew up a hundred fish.
"This wealth is far beyond my wildest wish,"
He said. "A splendid haul," the king replied.
"Good Fortune has been busy at your side—
Accept your luck, don't try to comprehend
How this has happened; you'd be lost, my friend.
Your wealth is greater than my own; today
A king has fished for you—I cannot stay."
He leapt onto his horse. "But take your share,"
The boy said earnestly. "That's only fair."
"Tomorrow's catch is mine. We won't divide
Today's; you have it all," the king replied.
"Tomorrow when I fish you are the prey,
A trophy I refuse to give away."
The next day, walking in his garden's shade,
The king recalled the friend that he had made.
A captain fetched the boy, and this unknown
Was at the king's command set on his throne.
The courtiers murmured at his poverty—
"He is my friend, this fact suffices me;
He is my equal here in everything,
The partner of my throne," declared the king;
To every taunt the boy had one reply:
"My sadness vanished when the king passed by."

## A murderer who went to heaven

'A murderer, according to the law,
Was killed. That night the king who'd killed him saw
The same man in a dream; to his surprise
The villain lorded it in paradise—

The king cried: "You! In this celestial place!
Your life's work was an absolute disgrace;
How did you reach this state?" The man replied:
"A friend to God passed by me as I died;
The earth drank up my blood, but stealthily
That pilgrim on Truth's journey glanced at me,
And all the glorious extravagance
That laps me now came from his searing glance."

The man on whom that quickening glance alights
Is raised to heaven's unsuspected heights;
Indeed, until this glance discovers you
Your life's a mystery without a clue;
You cannot carve your way to heaven's throne
If you sit locked in vanity alone.
You need a skilful guide; you cannot start
This ocean-voyage with blindness in your heart.
It may be you will meet the very guide
Who glanced at me; be sure he will provide—
Whatever troubles come—a place to hide.
You cannot guess what dangers you will find,
You need a staff to guide you, like the blind.
Your sight is failing and the road is long;
Trust one who knows the journey and is strong.
Whoever travels in a great lord's shade
Need never hesitate or be afraid;
Whoever undertakes this lord's commands
Finds thorns will change to roses in his hands.'

* * *

## The hoopoe relates the story of the spider

'You've seen an active spider work—he seems
To spend his life in self-communing dreams;
In fact the web he spins is evidence
That he's endowed with some far-sighted sense.
He drapes a corner with his cunning snare
And waits until a fly's entangled there,
Then dashes out and sucks the meagre blood
Of his bewildered, buzzing, dying food.
He'll dry the carcass then, and live off it
For days, consuming bit by tasty bit—
Until the owner of the house one day
Will reach up casually to knock away
The cunning spider's home—and with her broom
She clears both fly and spider from the room.

Such is the world, and one who feeds there is
A fly trapped by that spider's subtleties;
If all the world is yours, it will pass by
As swiftly as the blinking of an eye;
And though you boast of kings and patronage,
You are a child, an actor on a stage.
Don't seek for wealth unless you are a fool;
A herd of cows is all that you can rule!
Whoever lives for banners, drums and glory
Is dead; the dervish understands this story
And calls it windy noise—winds vainly flap
The banners, hollowly the brave drums tap.
Don't gallop on the horse of vanity;
Don't pride yourself on your nobility.
They skin the leopard for his splendid pelt;
They'll flay you too before your nose has smelt
A whiff of danger. When your life's made plain,
Which will be better, death or chastening pain?
You cannot hold your head up then—obey!
How long must you persist in childish play?
Either give up your wealth or lay aside
The rash pretensions of your crazy pride.
Your palace and your gardens! They're your gaol,
The dungeon where your ruined soul will wail.
Forsake this dusty pride, know what it's worth;
Give up your restless pacing of the earth.
To see the Way, look with the eyes of thought;
Set out on it and glimpse the heavenly court—
And when you reach that souls' asylum, then
Its glory will blot out the world of men.'

* * *

## The hoopoe tells the birds about the martyrdom of Hallaj

'Hallaj was taken to the gallows tree
And cried: "I am the Truth"; they could not see
The meaning of his words and hacked at him,
Tearing his bleeding carcass limb from limb.
Then as his face grew deathly pale he raised
The bleeding stumps of broken arms and glazed
His moon-like face with glittering blood. He said:
"Since it is blood which paints a man's face red,
I've painted mine that no one here may say
'Hallaj turned pale on that last bloody day'—
If any saw me pale they'd think that I
Felt fear to face my torturers and die—

My fear's of less than one hair's consequence;
Look on my painted face for evidence!
When he must die and sees the gallows near,
The hero's courage leaves no room for fear—
Since all the world is like a little 'o',
Why should I fear whatever it may show?
Who knows the seven-headed dragon's lair,
And sleeps and eats through summer's dog-days there,
Sees many games like this—the gallows seems
The least of all his transitory dreams."
That sea of faith, Junaid, in Baghdad once
Discoursed with such persuasive eloquence
It seemed the stars bowed down to hear him speak.
This stalwart guide and comfort of the weak
Delighted in his son, a lovely child
Who as his father lectured was beguiled
And murdered by a gang—they tossed his head
In that assembly's midst and quickly fled.
Junaid looked steadfastly at this cruel sight
And did not weep but said: "What seems tonight
So strange was certain from eternity;
What happens happens from necessity."'

* * *

## The hoopoe recalls a dervish deceived by a hailstorm

'A dervish suffered bruises and sore bones
From children who continually threw stones.
He found a ruined hut and in he stole,
Not noticing its roof contained a hole.
A hailstorm started—through the leaky shed
The hail came bouncing on the old man's head.
The hail was stones for all that he could tell—
He lost his temper and began to yell.
Convinced that they were throwing stones once more,
He screamed out filthy names, fumed, stamped and swore—
Then thought: "This dark's so thick it's possible
It's not the children this time after all."
A door blew open and revealed the hail;
He saw his error and began to wail:
"The darkness tricked me, God—and on my head
Be all the foolish, filthy names I said."
If crazy dervishes behave like this
It's not for you to take their words amiss;
If they seem drunk to you, control your scorn—

Their lives are painful, savage and forlorn;
They must endure a lifetime's hopelessness
And every moment brings some new distress—
Don't meddle with their conduct; don't reprove
Those given up to madness and to love.
You would excuse them—nothing is more sure—
If you could share the darkness they endure.'

* * *

## A bird asks how long the journey is, and the hoopoe describes the seven valleys of the Way

Another bird said: 'Hoopoe, you can find
The way from here, but we are almost blind—
The path seems full of terrors and despair.
Dear hoopoe, how much further till we're there?'

'Before we reach our goal,' the hoopoe said,
'The journey's seven valleys lie ahead;
How far this is the world has never learned,
For no one who has gone there has returned—
Impatient bird, who would retrace this trail?
There is no messenger to tell the tale,
And they are lost to our concerns below—
How can men tell you what they do not know?
The first stage is the Valley of the Quest;
Then Love's wide valley is our second test;
The third is Insight into Mystery,
The fourth Detachment and Serenity—
The fifth is Unity; the sixth is Awe,
A deep Bewilderment unknown before,
The seventh Poverty and Nothingness—
And there you are suspended, motionless,
Till you are drawn—the impulse is not yours—
A drop absorbed in seas that have no shores.'

* * *

## The stone man tale told by the hoopoe

'A man in China has become a stone;
He sits and mourns, and at each muffled groan
Weeps melancholy tears, which then are found
Congealed as pebbles scattered on the ground
(What misery the world would know, what pain,
If clouds should shed such adamantine rain!).

This man is Knowledge (sensible, devout;
If you should go to China seek him out),
But he has turned to stone from secret grief,
From lack of zeal, indifference, unbelief.
The world is dark, and Knowledge is a light,
A sparkling jewel to lead you through the night—
Without it you would wander mystified,
Like Alexander lost without a guide;
But if you trust its light too much, despair
Will be the sequel of pedantic care,
And if you underestimate this jewel
Despair will mark you as a righteous fool
(Ignore or overvalue this bright stone,
And wretchedness will claim you for her own).
If you can step outside the stage we know,
The dark confusions of our life below,
And reach man's proper state, you will possess
Wisdom at which the world can never guess.
The path brings sorrow and bewildered fear,
But venture on until the Way is clear,
And neither sleep by night nor drink by day,
But give your life—completely—to the Way.'

* * *

## The hoopoe compares the world to a wax toy

'Once someone asked a dervish to portray
The nature of this world in which we stray.
He said: "This various world is like a toy—
A coloured palm-tree given to a boy,
But made of wax—now knead it in your fist,
And there's the wax of which its shapes consist;
The lovely forms and colours are undone,
And what seemed many things is only one.
All things are one—there isn't any two;
It isn't me who speaks; it isn't you." '

* * *

## The hoopoe's tale of the moths and the flame

'Moths gathered in a fluttering throng one night
To learn the truth about the candle's light,
And they decided one of them should go
To gather news of the elusive glow.

One flew till in the distance he discerned
A palace window where a candle burned—
And went no nearer; back again he flew
To tell the others what he thought he knew.
The mentor of the moths dismissed his claim,
Remarking: "He knows nothing of the flame."
A moth more eager than the one before
Set out and passed beyond the palace door.
He hovered in the aura of the fire,
A trembling blur of timorous desire,
Then headed back to say how far he'd been,
And how much he had undergone and seen.
The mentor said: "You do not bear the signs
Of one who's fathomed how the candle shines."
Another moth flew out—his dizzy flight
Turned to an ardent wooing of the light;
He dipped and soared, and in his frenzied trance
Both Self and fire were mingled by his dance—
The flame engulfed his wing-tips, body, head;
His being glowed a fierce translucent red;
And when the mentor saw that sudden blaze,
The moth's form lost within the glowing rays,
He said: "He knows, he knows the truth we seek,
That hidden truth of which we cannot speak."
To go beyond all knowledge is to find
That comprehension which eludes the mind,
And you can never gain the longed-for goal
Until you first outsoar both flesh and soul;
But should one part remain, a single hair
Will drag you back and plunge you in despair—
No creature's Self can be admitted here,
Where all identity must disappear.'

## And his account of the sufi who thought he had left the world

'A sufi once, with nothing on his mind,
Was—without warning—struck at from behind.
He turned and murmured, choking back the tears:
"The man you hit's been dead for thirty years;
He's left this world!" The man who'd struck him said:
"You talk a lot for someone who is dead!
But talk's not action—while you boast, you stray
Further and further from the secret Way,
And while a hair of you remains, your heart
And Truth are still a hundred worlds apart."'

* * *

## The journey

The hoopoe paused, and when the group had heard
His discourse, trembling fear filled every bird.
They saw the bow of this great enterprise
Could not be drawn by weakness, sloth or lies,
And some were so cast down that then and there
They turned aside and perished in despair.
With fear and apprehension in each heart,
The remnant rose up ready to depart.
They travelled on for years; a lifetime passed
Before the longed-for goal was reached at last.
What happened as they flew I cannot say,
But if you journey on that narrow Way,
Then you will act as they once did and know
The miseries they had to undergo.
Of all the army that set out, how few
Survived the Way; of that great retinue
A handful lived until the voyage was done—
Of every thousand there remained but one.
Of many who set out no trace was found.
Some deep within the ocean's depths were drowned;
Some died on mountain-tops; some died of heat;
Some flew too near the sun in their conceit,
Their hearts on fire with love—too late they learned
Their folly when their wings and feathers burned;
Some met their death between the lion's claws,
And some were ripped to death by monsters' jaws;
Some died of thirst; some hunger sent insane,
Till suicide released them from their pain;
Some became weak and could no longer fly
(They faltered, fainted, and were left to die);
Some paused bewildered and then turned aside
To gaze at marvels as if stupefied;
Some looked for pleasure's path and soon confessed
They saw no purpose in the pilgrims' quest;
Not one in every thousand souls arrived—
In every hundred thousand one survived.

## The birds arrive and are greeted by a herald

A world of birds set out, and there remained
But thirty when the promised goal was gained,
Thirty exhausted, wretched, broken things,
With hopeless hearts and tattered, trailing wings,
Who saw that nameless Glory which the mind
Acknowledges as ever-undefined,

Whose solitary flame each moment turns
A hundred worlds to nothingness and burns
With power a hundred thousand times more bright
Than sun and stars and every natural light.
The awe-struck group, bewildered and amazed,
Like insubstantial, trembling atoms, gazed
And chirmed: 'How can we live or prosper here,
Where if the sun came it would disappear?
Our hearts were torn from all we loved; we bore
The perils of a path unknown before;
And all for this? It was not this reward
That we expected from our longed-for Lord.'
It seemed their throats were cut, as if they bled
And weakly whimpered until left for dead,
Waiting for splendour to annihilate
Their insubstantial, transitory state.
Time passed; then from the highest court there flew
A herald of the starry retinue,
Who saw the thirty birds, trembling, afraid,
Their bodies broken and their feathers frayed,
And said: 'What city are you from? What race?
What business brings you to this distant place?
What are your names? You seem destroyed by fear;
What made you leave your homes and travel here?
What were you in the world? What use are you?
What can such weak and clumsy creatures do?'
The group replied: 'We flew here for one thing,
To claim the Simorgh as our rightful king;
We come as suppliants and we have sought
Through grievous paths the threshold of His court—
How long the Way was to complete our vow;
Of thousands we are only thirty now!
Was that hope false which led us to this place,
Or shall we now behold our sovereign's face?'

## The herald tells the birds to turn back

The herald said: 'This king for whom you grieve
Governs in glory you cannot conceive—
A hundred thousand armies are to Him
An ant that clambers up His threshold's rim,
And what are you? Grief is your fate—go back;
Retrace your steps along the pilgrims' track!'
And when they heard the herald's fearsome words,
A deathly hopelessness assailed the birds;
But they replied: 'Our king will not repay
With sorrow all the hazards of the Way;

Grief cannot come to us from majesty;
Grief cannot live beside such dignity.'

* * *

The herald said: 'The blaze of Majesty
Reduces souls to unreality,
And if your souls are burnt, then all the pain
That you have suffered will have been in vain.'
They answered him: 'How can a moth flee fire
When fire contains its ultimate desire?' . . .
Though grief engulfed the raggèd group, love made
The birds impetuous and unafraid;
The herald's self-possession was unmoved,
But their resilience was not reproved—
Now, gently, he unlocked the guarded door;
A hundred veils drew back, and there before
The birds' incredulous, bewildered sight
Shone the unveiled, the inmost Light of Light.
He led them to a noble throne, a place
Of intimacy, dignity and grace,
Then gave them all a written page and said
That when its contents had been duly read
The meaning that their journey had concealed,
And of the stage they'd reached, would be revealed.

## Joseph's brothers read of their treachery

When Malek Dar bought Joseph as a slave,
The price agreed (and which he gladly gave)
Seemed far too low—to be quite sure he made
The brothers sign a note for what he'd paid;
And when the wicked purchase was complete
He left with Joseph and the sealed receipt.
At last when Joseph ruled in Egypt's court
His brothers came to beg and little thought
To whom it was each bowed his humbled head
And as a suppliant appealed for bread.
Then Joseph held a scroll up in his hand
And said: 'No courtier here can understand
These Hebrew characters—if you can read
This note I'll give you all the bread you need.'
The brothers could read Hebrew easily
And cried: 'Give us the note, your majesty!'
(If any of my readers cannot find
Himself in this account, the fool is blind.)
When Joseph gave them that short document

They looked—and trembled with astonishment.
They did not read a line but in dismay
Debated inwardly what they should say.
Their past sins silenced them; they were too weak
To offer an excuse or even speak.
Then Joseph said: 'Why don't you read? You seem
Distracted, haunted by some dreadful dream.'
And they replied: 'Better to hold our breath
Than read and in so doing merit death.'

## The birds discover the Simorgh

The thirty birds read through the fateful page
And there discovered, stage by detailed stage,
Their lives, their actions, set out one by one—
All that their souls had ever been or done:
And this was bad enough, but as they read
They understood that it was they who'd led
The lovely Joseph into slavery—
Who had deprived him of his liberty
Deep in a well, then ignorantly sold
Their captive to a passing chief for gold.
(Can you not see that at each breath you sell
The Joseph you imprisoned in that well,
That he will be the king to whom you must
Naked and hungry bow down in the dust?)
The chastened spirits of these birds became
Like crumbled powder, and they shrank with shame.
Then, as by shame their spirits were refined
Of all the world's weight, they began to find
A new life flow towards them from that bright
Celestial and ever-living Light—
Their souls rose free of all they'd been before;
The past and all its actions were no more.
Their life came from that close, insistent sun
And in its vivid rays they shone as one.
There in the Simorgh's radiant face they saw
Themselves, the Simorgh of the world—with awe
They gazed, and dared at last to comprehend
They were the Simorgh and the journey's end.
They see the Simorgh—at themselves they stare,
And see a second Simorgh standing there;
They look at both and see the two are one,
That this is that, that this, the goal is won.
They ask (but inwardly; they make no sound)
The meaning of these mysteries that confound
Their puzzled ignorance—how is it true

That 'we' is not distinguished here from 'you'?
And silently their shining Lord replies:
'I am a mirror set before your eyes,
And all who come before my splendour see
Themselves, their own unique reality;
You came as thirty birds and therefore saw
These selfsame thirty birds, not less nor more;
If you had come as forty, fifty—here
An answering forty, fifty, would appear;
Though you have struggled, wandered, travelled far,
It is yourselves you see and what you are.'
(Who sees the Lord? It is himself each sees;
What ant's sight could discern the Pleiades?
What anvil could be lifted by an ant?
Or could a fly subdue an elephant?)
'How much you thought you knew and saw; but you
Now know that all you trusted was untrue.
Though you traversed the Valleys' depths and fought
With all the dangers that the journey brought,
The journey was in Me, the deeds were Mine—
You slept secure in Being's inmost shrine.
And since you came as thirty birds, you see
These thirty birds when you discover Me,
The Simorgh, Truth's last flawless jewel, the light
In which you will be lost to mortal sight,
Dispersed to nothingness until once more
You find in Me the selves you were before.'
Then, as they listened to the Simorgh's words,
A trembling dissolution filled the birds—
The substance of their being was undone,
And they were lost like shade before the sun;
Neither the pilgrims nor their guide remained.
The Simorgh ceased to speak, and silence reigned.

## *from The Memorial of the Saints*

*The Life and Teachings of Rābi'ah al-'Adawiyya*

*Translated by A.J. Arberry*

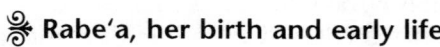

### Rabe'a, her birth and early life

If anyone says, "Why have you included Rabe'a in the rank of men?" my answer is, that the Prophet himself said, "God does not regard your outward forms." The root of the matter is not form, but intention, as the Prophet said, "Mankind will be raised up according to their intentions." Moreover, if it is proper to derive two-thirds of our religion from A'esha, surely it is permissible to take religious instruction from a handmaid of A'esha. When a woman becomes a "man" in the path of God, she is a man and one cannot any more call her a woman.

The night when Rabe'a came to earth, there was nothing whatsoever in her father's house; for her father lived in very poor circumstances. He did not possess even one drop of oil to anoint her navel; there was no lamp, and not a rag to swaddle her in. He already had three daughters, and Rabe'a was his fourth; that is why she was called by that name.

"Go to neighbour So-and-so and beg for a drop of oil, so that I can light the lamp," his wife said to him.

Now the man had entered into a covenant that he would never ask any mortal for anything. So he went out and just laid his hand on the neighbour's door, and returned.

"They will not open the door," he reported.

The poor woman wept bitterly. In that anxious state the man placed his head on his knees and went to sleep. He dreamed that he saw the Prophet.

"Be not sorrowful," the Prophet bade him. "The girl child who has just come to earth is a queen among women, who shall be the intercessor for seventy thousand of my community. Tomorrow," the Prophet continued, "go to Isa-e Zadan the governor of Basra. Write on a piece of paper to the following effect. 'Every night you send upon me a hundred blessings, and on Friday night four hundred. Last night was Friday night, and you forgot me. In expiation for that, give this man four hundred dinars lawfully acquired.'"

Rabe'a's father on awaking burst into tears. He rose up and wrote as the Prophet had bidden him, and sent the message to the governor by the hand of a chamberlain.

"Give two thousand dinars to the poor," the governor commanded when he saw the missive, "as a thanksgiving for the Master remembering me. Give four hundred dinars also to the shaikh, and tell him, 'I wish you to come to me so that I may see you. But I do not hold it proper for a man like you to come to me. I would rather come and rub my beard in your threshold. However, I adjure you by God, whatever you may need, pray let me know.'"

The man took the gold and purchased all that was necessary.

When Rabe'a had become a little older, and her mother and father were dead, a famine came upon Basra, and her sisters were scattered. Rabe'a ventured out and was seen by a wicked man who seized her and then sold her for six dirhams. Her purchaser put her to hard labour.

One day she was passing along the road when a stranger approached. Rabe'a fled. As she ran, she fell headlong and her hand was dislocated.

"Lord God," she cried, bowing her face to the ground, "I am a stranger, orphaned of mother and father, a helpless prisoner fallen into captivity, my hand broken. Yet for all this I do not grieve; all I need is Thy good pleasure, to know whether Thou art well-pleased or no."

"Do not grieve," she heard a voice say. "Tomorrow a station shall be thine such that the cherubim in heaven will envy thee."

So Rabe'a returned to her master's house. By day she continually fasted and served God, and by night she worshipped standing until day. One night her master awoke from sleep and, looking through the window of his apartment, saw Rabe'a bowing prostrate and praying.

"O God, Thou knowest that the desire of my heart is in conformity with Thy command, and that the light of my eye is in serving Thy court. If the affair lay with me, I would not rest one hour from serving Thee; but Thou Thyself hast set me under the hand of a creature."

Such was her litany. Her master perceived a lantern suspended without any chain above her head, the light whereof filled the whole house. Seeing this, he was afraid. Rising up, he returned to his bedroom and sat pondering till dawn. When day broke he summoned Rabe'a, was gentle with her and set her free.

"Give me permission to depart," Rabe'a said.

He gave her leave, and she left the house and went into the desert. From the desert she proceeded to a hermitage where she served God for a while. Then she determined to perform the pilgrimage, and set her face towards the desert. She bound her bundle on an ass. In the heart of the desert the ass died.

"Let us carry your load," the men in the party said.

"You go on," she replied. "I have not come putting my trust in you."

So the men departed, and Rabe'a remained alone.

"O God," she cried, lifting her head, "do kings so treat a woman who is a stranger and powerless? Thou hast invited me unto Thy house, then in the midst of the way Thou hast suffered my ass to die, leaving me alone in the desert."

Hardly had she completed this orison when her ass stirred and rose up. Rabe'a placed her load on its back, and continued on her way. (The narrator of this story reports that some while afterwards he saw that little donkey being sold in the market.) She travelled on through the desert for some days, then she halted.

"O God," she cried, "my heart is weary. Whither am I going? I a lump of clay, and Thy house a stone! I need Thee here."

God spoke unmediated in her heart.

"Rabe'a, thou art faring in the life-blood of eighteen thousand worlds. Hast thou not seen how Moses prayed for the vision of Me? And I cast a few motes of revelation upon the mountain, and the mountain shivered into forty pieces. Be content here with My name!"

## Anecdotes of Rabe'a

One night Rabe'a was praying in the hermitage when she was overcome by weariness and fell asleep. So deeply was she absorbed that, when a reed from the reed-mat she was lying on broke in her eye so that the blood flowed, she was quite unaware of the fact.

A thief entered and seized her chaddur. He then made to leave, but the way was barred to him. He dropped the chaddur and departed, finding the way now open. He seized the chaddur again and returned to discover the way blocked. Once more he dropped the chaddur. This he repeated seven times over; then he heard a voice proceeding from a corner of the hermitage.

"Man, do not put yourself to such pains. It is so many years now that she has committed herself to Us. The Devil himself has not the boldness to slink round her. How should a thief have the boldness to slink round her chaddur? Be gone, scoundrel! Do not put yourself to such pains. If one friend has fallen asleep, one Friend is awake and keeping watch."

Two notables of the Faith came to visit Rabe'a, and both were hungry.

"It may be that she will give us food," they said to each other. "Her food is bound to come from a lawful source."

When they sat down there was a napkin with two loaves laid before them. They were well content. A beggar arrived just then, and Rabe'a gave him the two loaves. The two men of religion were much upset, but said nothing. After a while a maidservant entered with a handful of warm bread.

"My mistress sent these," she explained.

Rabe'a counted the loaves. There were eighteen.

"Perhaps it was not this that she sent me," Rabe'a remarked.

For all that the maidservant assured her, it profited nothing. So she took back the loaves and carried them away. Now it so happened that she had taken two of the loaves for herself. She asked her mistress, and she added the two to the pile and returned with them. Rabe'a counted again, and found there were twenty loaves. She now accepted them.

"This is what your mistress sent me," she said.

She set the loaves before the two men and they ate, marvelling.

"What is the secret behind this?" they asked her. "We had an appetite for your own bread, but you took it away from us and gave it to the beggar. Then you said that the eighteen loaves did not belong to you. When they were twenty, you accepted them."

"I knew when you arrived that you were hungry," Rabe'a replied. "I said to myself, How can I offer two loaves to two such notables? So when the beggar came to the door I gave them to him and said to Almighty God, 'O God, Thou hast said that Thou repayest tenfold, and this I firmly believed. Now I have given two loaves to please Thee, so that Thou mayest give twenty in return for them.' When eighteen were brought me, I knew that either there had been some misappropriation, or that they were not meant for me."

One day Rabe'a's servant girl was making an onion stew; for it was some days since they had cooked any food. Finding that she needed some onions, she said,

"I will ask of next door."

"Forty years now," Rabe'a replied, "I have had a covenant with Almighty God not to ask for aught of any but He. Never mind the onions."

Immediately a bird swooped down from the air with peeled onions in its beak and dropped them into the pan.

"I am not sure this is not a trick," Rabe'a commented.

And she left the onion pulp alone, and ate nothing but bread.

Rabe'a had gone one day into the mountains. She was soon surrounded by a flock of deer and mountain goats, ibexes and wild asses which stared at her and made to approach her. Suddenly Hasan of Basra came on the scene and, seeing Rabe'a, moved in her direction. As soon as the animals sighted Hasan, they made off all together, so that Rabe'a remained alone. This dismayed Hasan.

"Why did they run away from me, and associated so tamely with you?" he asked Rabe'a.

"What have you eaten today?" Rabe'a countered.

"A little onion pulp."

"You eat their fat," Rabe'a remarked. "Why then should they not flee from you?"

Once Rabe'a passed by Hasan's house. Hasan had his head out of the window and was weeping, and his tears fell on Rabe'a's dress. Looking up, she thought at first that it was rain; then, realizing that it was Hasan's tears, she turned to him and addressed him.

"Master, this weeping is a sign of spiritual languor. Guard your tears, so that there may surge within you such a sea that, seeking the heart therein, you shall not find it save *in the keeping of a King Omnipotent.*"

These words distressed Hasan, but he kept his peace. Then one day he saw Rabe'a when she was near a lake. Throwing his prayer rug on the surface of the water, he called,

"Rabe'a, come! Let us pray two *rak'as* here!"

"Hasan," Rabe'a replied, "when you are showing off your spiritual goods in this worldly market, it should be things that your fellow-men are incapable of displaying."

And she flung her prayer rug into the air, and flew up on it.

"Come up here, Hasan, where people can see us!" she cried.

Hasan, who had not attained that station, said nothing. Rabe'a sought to console him.

"Hasan," she said, "what you did fishes also do, and what I did flies also do. The real business is outside both these tricks. One must apply one's self to the real business."

One night Hasan with two or three friends went to visit Rabe'a. Rabe'a had no lantern. Their hearts yearned for light. Rabe'a blew on her finger, and that night till dawn her finger shone like a lantern, and they sat in its radiance.

If anyone says, "How could this be?" I answer, "The same as Moses' hand." If it is objected, "But Moses was a prophet," I reply, "Whoever follows in the footsteps of the Prophet can possess a grain of prophethood, as the Prophet says, 'Whoever rejects a farthing's worth of unlawful things has attained a degree of prophethood.' He also said, 'A true dream is one-fortieth part of prophethood.'"

Once Rabe'a sent Hasan three things—a piece of wax, a needle, and a hair.

"Be like wax," she said. "Illumine the world, and yourself burn. Be like a needle, always be working naked. When you have done these two things, a thousand years will be for you as a hair."

"Do you desire for us to get married?" Hasan asked Rabe'a.

"The tie of marriage applies to those who have being," Rabe'a replied. "Here being has disappeared, for I have become naughted to self and exist only through Him. I belong wholly to Him. I live in the shadow of His control. You must ask my hand of Him, not of me."

"How did you find this secret, Rabe'a?" Hasan asked.

"I lost all 'found' things in Him," Rabe'a answered.

"How do you know Him?" Hasan enquired.

"You know the 'how'; I know the 'howless'," Rabe'a said.

Once Rabe'a saw a man with a bandage tied round his head.

"Why have you tied the bandage?" she asked.

"Because my head aches," the man replied.

"How old are you?" she demanded.

"Thirty," he replied.

"Have you been in pain and anguish the greater part of your life?" she enquired.

"No," the man answered.

"For thirty years you have enjoyed good health," she remarked, "and you never tied about you the bandage of thankfulness. Now because of this one night that you have a headache you tie the bandage of complaint!"

Once Rabe'a gave four silver dirhams to a man.

"Buy me a blanket," she said, "for I am naked."

The man departed. Presently he returned.

"Mistress," he said, "what colour shall I buy?"

"How did 'colour' come into the business?" Rabe'a demanded. "Give me back the money."

And she took the dirhams and flung them into the Tigris.

One spring day Rabe'a entered her apartment and put out her head.

"Mistress," her servant said, "come out and see what the Maker has wrought."

"Do you rather come in," Rabe'a replied, "and see the Maker. The contemplation of the Maker pre-occupies me, so that I do not care to look upon what He has made."

A party visited her, and saw her tearing a morsel of meat with her teeth.

"Do you not have a knife to cut up the meat?" they asked.

"I have never kept a knife in my house for fear of being cut off," she replied.

Once Rabe'a fasted for a whole week, neither eating nor sleeping. All night she was occupied with praying. Her hunger passed all bounds. A visitor entered her house bringing a bowl of food. Rabe'a accepted it and went to fetch a lamp. She returned to find that the cat had spilled the bowl.

"I will go and fetch a jug, and break my fast," she said.

By the time she had brought the jug, the lamp had gone out. She aimed to drink the water in the dark, but the jug slipped from her hand and was broken. She uttered lamentation and sighed so ardently that there was fear that half of the house would be consumed with fire.

"O God," she cried, "what is this that Thou art doing with Thy helpless servant?"

"Have a care," a voice came to her ears, "lest thou desire Me to bestow on thee all worldly blessings, but eradicate from thy heart the care for Me. Care for Me and worldly blessings can never be associated together in a single heart. Rabe'a, thou desirest one thing, and I desire another; My desire and thy desire can never be joined in one heart."

"When I heard this admonition," Rabe'a related, "I so cut off my heart from the world and curtailed my desires that whenever I have prayed during the last thirty years, I have assumed it to be my last prayer."

A party of men once visited her to put her to the test, desiring to catch her out in an unguarded utterance.

"All the virtues have been scattered upon the heads of men," they said. "The crown of prophethood has been placed on men's heads. The belt of nobility has been fastened around men's waists. No woman has ever been a prophet."

"All that is true," Rabe'a replied. "But egoism and self-worship and 'I am your Lord, the Most High' have never sprung from a woman's breast. No woman has ever been a hermaphrodite. All these things have been the speciality of men."

Once Rabe'a fell grievously sick. She was asked what the cause might be.

"I gazed upon Paradise," she replied, "and my Lord disciplined me."

Then Hasan of Basra went to visit her.

"I saw one of the notables of Basra standing at the door of Rabe'a's hermitage offering her a purse of gold and weeping," he reported. "I said, 'Sir, why are you weeping?' 'On account of this saintly woman of the age,' he replied. 'For if the blessing of her presence departs from among mankind, mankind will surely perish. I brought something for her tending,' he added, 'and I am afraid that she will not accept it. Do you intercede with her to take it.'"

So Hasan entered and spoke. Rabe'a glanced up at him and said,

"He provides for those who insult Him, and shall He not provide for those who love Him? Ever since I knew Him, I have turned my back upon His creatures. I know not whether any man's property is lawful or not; how then can I take it? I stitched together by the light of a worldly lamp a shirt which I had torn. For a while my heart was obstructed, until I remembered. Then I tore the shirt in the place where I had stitched it, and my heart became dilated. Ask the gentleman pray not to keep my heart obstructed."

Abd al-Wahed-e Amer relates as follows.

I went with Sofyan-e Thauri to visit Rabe'a when she was sick, but out of awe for her I could not begin to address her.

"You say something," I said to Sofyan.

"If you will say a prayer," Sofyan said to Rabe'a, "your pain will be eased."

"Do you not know who has willed that I should suffer? Was it not God?" Rabe'a demanded.

"Yes," Sofyan agreed.

"How is it that you know that," Rabe'a went on, "and yet you bid me to request from Him the contrary of His will? It is not right to oppose one's Friend."

"What thing do you desire, Rabe'a?" Sofyan asked.

"Sofyan, you are a learned man. Why do you speak like that? 'What thing do you desire?' By the glory of God," Rabe'a asseverated, "for twelve years now I have been desiring fresh dates. You know that in Basra dates are of no consequence. Yet till now I have not eaten any; for I am His servant, and what business has a servant to desire? If I wish, and my Lord does not wish, this would be infidelity. You must want only what He wishes, to be a true servant of God. If God himself gives, that is a different matter."

Sofyan was reduced to silence. Then he said,

"Since one cannot speak about your situation, do you say something about mine."

"You are a good man, but for the fact you love the world," Rabe'a replied. "You love reciting Traditions."

This she said, implying that that was a high position.

"Lord God," cried Sofyan, deeply moved, "be content with me!"

"Are you not ashamed," broke in Rabe'a, "to seek the contentment of One with whom you yourself are not content?"

Malek-e Dinar relates as follows.

I went to visit Rabe'a, and saw her with a broken pitcher out of which she drank and made her ritual ablutions, an old reed-mat, and a brick which she occasionally used as a pillow. I was grieved.

"I have rich friends," I told her. "If you wish, I will get something from them for you."

"Malek, you have committed a grievous error," she answered. "Is not my Provider and theirs one and the same?"

"Yes," I replied.

"And has the Provider of the poor forgotten the poor on account of their poverty? And does He remember the rich because of their riches?" she asked.

"No," I replied.

"Then," she went on, "since He knows my estate, how should I remind Him? Such is His will, and I too wish as He wills."

One day Hasan of Basra, Malek-e Dinar and Shaqiq-e Balkhi went to visit Rabe'a on her sickbed.

"He is not truthful in his claim," Hasan began, "who does not bear with fortitude the lash of his Lord."

"These words stink of egoism," Rabe'a commented.

"He is not truthful in his claim," Shaqiq tried, "who is not grateful for the lash of his Lord."

"We need something better than that," Rabe'a observed.

"He is not truthful in his claim," Malek-e Dinar offered, "who does not take delight in the lash of his Lord."

"We need something better than that," Rabe'a repeated.

"Then you say," they urged.

"He is not truthful in his claim," Rabe'a pronounced, "who does not forget the lash in contemplation of his Master."

A leading scholar of Basra visited Rabe'a on her sickbed. Sitting beside her pillow, he reviled the world.

"You love the world very dearly," Rabe'a commented. "If you did not love the world, you would not make mention of it so much. It is always the purchaser who disparages the wares. If you were done with the world, you would not mention it either for good or evil. As it is, you keep mentioning it because, as the proverb says, whoever loves a thing mentions it frequently."

When the time came that Rabe'a should die, those attending her deathbed left the room and closed the door. Then a voice was heard saying, *O soul at peace, return unto thy Lord, well-pleased!* A time passed and no sound came from the room, so they opened the door and found that she had given up the ghost.

After her death she was seen in a dream. She was asked, "How did you fare with Monkar and Nakir?" She replied, "Those youths came to me and said, 'Who is thy Lord?' I answered, 'Return and say to God, with so many thousand thousand creatures Thou didst not forget one feeble old woman. I, who have only Thee in the whole world, I shall never forget Thee, that Thou shouldst sent one to ask me, Who is thy God?'"

## Prayers of Rabe'a

O God, whatsoever Thou hast apportioned to me of worldly things, do Thou give that to Thy enemies; and whatsoever Thou hast apportioned to me in the world to come, give that to Thy friends; for Thou sufficest me.

O God, if I worship Thee for fear of Hell, burn me in Hell, and if I worship Thee in hope of Paradise, exclude me from Paradise; but if I worship Thee for Thy own sake, grudge me not Thy everlasting beauty.

O God, my whole occupation and all my desire in this world, of all worldly things, is to remember Thee, and in the world to come, of all things of the world to come, is to meet Thee. This is on my side, as I have stated; now do Thou whatsoever Thou wilt.

# Usāmah Ibn Munqidh (1095–1188)

*Translated by Philip K. Hitti*

Usāmah Ibn Munqidh wrote his memoirs when he was nearly ninety. Born into a noble Syrian family the same year Europeans launched their first crusade, Usāmah was raised to be both a warrior and a courtly gentleman. He spent at least ten years studying the Qur'ān, Arabic poetry, grammar, and calligraphy, and he reportedly knew more than twenty thousand verses of pre-Islamic poetry by heart. Over the centuries, he has been consistently acclaimed a hero of Islam and a man of letters. Besides his memoirs, Usāmah wrote a book of poetry (*Dīwan*), which was considered a classic, and a book on rhetoric (*al-Badī*).

Nurtured in the codes of Syrian chivalry, he fought against Franks, Christians, and enemy Arabs. He was a man of tremendous mental and physical ability whose courage was born of a complete resignation to divine will. Finding the world sometimes inexplicable, Usāmah understood its marvels and apparent paradoxes as evidence of God's greater plan. The oscillation of successes and failures, life and death, sickness and health, virtues and vices constitutes a key rhythm in his narrative. If he tells of his victories, he also openly records his defeats; if he recalls an evil infidel, he often follows with an account of a generous person.

Usāmah witnessed the fall of the Fatimid Caliphate in Egypt and fought alongside Saladin, the great warrior. He counted some Franks his friends and some his enemies. In 1174, when he was seventy-nine years old, he was summoned to Damascus by Saladin and given a permanent palatial residence. Usāmah's description of the Franks has made his work well known in the West, but these passages are rather minor ones in the work as a whole; the Europeans are written into his account as more of a nuisance than a major military threat. His *Book of Reflections* includes hunting and warring stories (both his own and ones he heard or witnessed), anecdotes, discussions of military strategy, descriptive meditations on animals and types of people, and poetry. The passages selected here are taken from various parts of the text, but the text as a whole proceeds in a loose chronological fashion with frequent associative forays into past events, moral tales, and essayistic observations. The book concludes with a poetic eulogy to Saladin followed by appended sections, including rare anecdotes, accounts of strange medical cures, stories of holy men, and more memories of hunting.

## from The Book of Reflections

*[Usāmah's father, mother, and grandmother]*

*Usāmah's father: A warrior.*—My father (may Allah's mercy rest upon his soul!) was greatly addicted to warfare. His body bore scars of terrible wounds. And withal he died on his own bed. One day he took part in a battle in full armor, wearing on his head a Moslem helmet with a nasal. Someone (in that period their combats were generally with the Arabs) launched a javelin at him, which struck the nasal of the helmet. The nasal bent and made my father's nose bleed, but it caused him no harm. But if Allah (praise be to his name!) had decreed that the javelin should deviate from the helmet's nasal, then it would have killed him.

On another occasion he was hit with an arrow in his leg. In his slipper he had a dagger. The arrow struck the dagger and was broken on it, without even wounding him—thanks to the excellent protection of Allah (exalted is he!).

He (may Allah's mercy rest upon his soul!) took part in a fight on Sunday, the twenty-ninth of Shawwāl, in the year 497 [July 25, 1104], against Sayf-al-Dawlah Khalaf ibn-Mulā'ib al-Ashhabi, the lord of Afāmiyah, in the territory of Kafarṭāb. He put on his byrnie, but the attendant in his haste neglected to fasten its hook on the side. A pike hit him right in the place which the attendant had failed to cover up, just above his left breast, and issued from above his right breast. The causes of his safety were due to what Providence had seen fit to execute in the way of marvels, just as the infliction of the wound was in accordance with what Allah (worthy of admiration is he!) had decreed in the way of marvels.

On that same day my father (may Allah's mercy rest upon his soul!) smote a cavalier with his lance, made his own horse shy a little to one side, bent his arm while holding the lance and withdrew the lance from the victim. Relating this story to me, he said:

> I felt something biting my forearm. I took it to be caused by the heat from the vambrace of the byrnie. But my lance fell from my hand. I turned my arm to see, and all of a sudden realized that I had been pierced with a lance in my forearm, which weakened because of the cutting off of some of the nerves.

I was present with him (may Allah's mercy rest upon his soul!) when Zayd the surgeon was dressing his wound and an attendant was standing behind his head. My father said, "O Zayd, extract this pebble from the wound." The surgeon made no reply. He repeated and said, "Seest thou not this pebble? Wilt thou not remove it from the wound?" Annoyed by his insistence, the surgeon said, "Where is the pebble? This is the end of a nerve that has been cut off." In reality it was white as though it were one of the pebbles of the Euphrates.

My father received on that day another lance thrust. But Allah spared him until he died on his own bed (may Allah's mercy rest upon his soul!) on

Monday, the twelfth of Ramaḍān, in the year 531 [May 30, 1137].

*A Koran copier.*—My father wrote a magnificent hand, which that lance thrust did not affect. But he used to copy nothing except the Koran. One day I asked him, "O my lord, how many full copies of the Koran hast thou made?" To this he replied, "Before long ye shall know." When he was on the point of death, he said, "In that box are different copies, each one of which contains the Koran in full. Place them (referring to the copies) under my cheek in the grave." We counted them and they turned out to be forty-three copies, each containing the full text. One of the copies was a huge one which he wrote in gold and in which he included all the sciences of the Koran—its different readings, its obscure terms, its Arabic style and grammar, its abrogating and abrogated passages, its commentary, reasons for its revelation, and its jurisprudence. This copy, which he styled *al-Tafsīr al-Kabīr* [the great commentary], was written in black ink alternating with red and blue. Another copy he transcribed with letters of gold, but this had no commentary. The rest of the copies were written in black ink with the following in gold: the first words of the tenth and fifth parts of the book, the number of verses, the first word of the sūrahs, the titles of the sūrahs and the headings of the sections.

My book does not require the mention of this fact. But I did mention it in order to appeal to those who read my book to solicit Allah's mercy upon my father. . . .

*Usāmah's mother as a warrior.*—On that day my mother (may Allah have mercy upon her soul!) distributed my swords and quilted jerkins. She came to a sister of mine who was well advanced in years and said, "Put on thy shoes and thy wrapper." This she did. My mother then led her to the balcony in my house overlooking the valley from the east. She made her take a seat there, and my mother herself sat at the entrance to the balcony. Allah (praise be to him!) gave us victory over the enemy [the Ismā'īlites]. I then came to my house seeking some of my weapons, but found nothing except the scabbards of the swords and the leather bags of the jerkins. I said, "O mother, where are my arms?" She replied, "My dear son, I have given the arms to those who would fight in our behalf, not believing that thou wert still alive." I said, "And my sister, what is she doing here?" She replied, "O my dear son, I have given her a seat at the balcony and sat behind her so that in case I found that the Bāṭinites had reached us, I could push her and throw her into the valley, preferring to see her dead rather than to see her captive in the hands of the peasants and ravishers." I thanked my mother for her deed, and so did my sister, who prayed that mother be rewarded [by Allah] in her behalf. Such solicitude for honor is indeed stronger than the solicitude of men.

*An aged maid also fights.*—On the same day an aged woman named Funūn, who was one of the slaves of my grandfather, al-Amīr abu-al-Ḥasan 'Ali (may Allah's mercy rest upon his soul!), veiled herself and, sword in hand, rushed to battle. She continued to fight until we joined her and became too numerous for the enemy.

*Usāmah's grandmother gives him wise advice.*—No one can deny magnanimity, enthusiasm and sound judgment in the case of noble women. One day I went out with my father (may Allah's mercy rest upon his soul!) to the hunt. My father was especially fond of hunting and had a collection of falcons, shahins, sakers, cheetahs and braches such as hardly anybody else possessed. He used to ride at the head of forty cavaliers from among his children and mamelukes, each one of whom was an expert hunter knowing all about the chase. He had in Shayzar two hunting grounds. One day he would ride to the marshy fields and streams to the west of the town, where he would hunt the francolins, waterfowl, hares and gazelles and kill the wild boars; and another day he would ride to the mountain south of the town to hunt partridges and hares. One day as we were in the mountain, the time came for the afternoon prayer. So he dismounted and we dismounted, praying each for himself, and behold! an attendant came running and said, "Here is the lion!" I brought my prayer to a conclusion before my father (may Allah's mercy rest upon his soul!) did, so that he might not prevent me from fighting the lion, mounted my horse, and, lance in hand, charged the lion. The lion faced me and roared. My horse shied with me in the saddle, and the lance, on account of its weight, fell from my hand. The lion chased me for a long distance. Then it returned to the slope of the mountain and stood there. It was one of the biggest of lions, as big as an arch, and it was famished. Every time we approached it, it would descend from the mountain and chase the horses away. Then it would resume its former position. And not once did it descend without leaving a great impression on our companions.

Finally, like a flash, I saw it leap over the haunches of the horse of one of my uncle's slaves, named Bastakīn Gharzah, and tear with its claws the clothes and leggings of the slave. It then returned to the mountain. Thus I had no way of attacking it until I climbed above it on the slope of the mountain and rushed my horse against it, giving it in the meantime a thrust with my lance which pierced its body. I left the lance in its body. The lion rolled over to the foot of the mountain with the lance in it and died. The lance was broken. This took place while my father (may Allah's mercy rest upon his soul!) was standing watching us, and with him were the children of his brother, 'Izz-al-Dīn, who, being young lads, were closely observing what was going on.

We then made our way to the town and entered it early in the evening carrying the lion. As we entered, my grandmother on my father's side (may Allah have mercy on both of their souls!) met me in the dark, holding in front of her a lighted candle. She was a very aged woman, almost a hundred years old. I entertained no doubt that she had come to congratulate me on my safety and acquaint me with her great satisfaction at what I had done. So I met her and kissed her hand. But she said to me with anger and with irritation, "O my boy, what makes thee face these adventures in which thou riskest thine own life and the life of thy horse, breakest thy weapons and increasest the antipathy and ill feeling which thine uncle cherishes in his heart against thee?" I replied, "O my grandmother, the only thing that makes me expose myself to danger in this and similar cases is to endear myself to the heart of my uncle." She said, "No, by Allah! This does not bring thee nearer to thine uncle, but, on the contrary, it alienates thee from him and makes him feel more antipathy and ill will towards thee." I then realized that my grandmother (may Allah's mercy rest upon her soul!) was giving me wise counsel and was telling me the truth. By my life, such are the mothers of men! . . .

## *An Appreciation of the Frankish Character*

*Their lack of sense.*—Mysterious are the works of the Creator, the author of all things! When one comes to recount cases regarding the Franks, he cannot but glorify Allah (exalted is he!) and sanctify him, for he sees them as animals possessing the virtues of courage and fighting, but nothing else; just as animals have only the virtues of strength and carrying loads. I shall now give some instances of their doings and their curious mentality.

In the army of King Fulk, son of Fulk, was a Frankish reverend knight who had just arrived from their land in order to make the holy pilgrimage and then return home. He was of my intimate fellowship and kept such constant company with me that he began to call me "my brother." Between us were mutual bonds of amity and friendship. When he resolved to return by sea to his homeland, he said to me:

> My brother, I am leaving for my country and I want thee to send with me thy son (my son, who was then fourteen years old, was at that time in my company) to our country, where he can see the knights and learn wisdom and chivalry. When he returns, he will be like a wise man.

Thus there fell upon my ears words which would never come out of the head of a sensible man; for even if my son were to be taken captive, his captivity could not bring him a worse misfortune than carrying him into the lands of the Franks. However, I said to the man:

> By thy life, this has exactly been my idea. But the only thing that prevented me from carrying it out was the fact that his grandmother, my mother, is so fond of him and did not this time let him come out with me until she exacted an oath from me to the effect that I would return him to her.

Thereupon he asked, "Is thy mother still alive?" "Yes." I replied. "Well," said he, "disobey her not."

*Their curious medication.*—A case illustrating their curious medicine is the following:

The lord of al-Munayṭirah wrote to my uncle asking him to dispatch a physician to treat certain sick persons among his people. My uncle sent him a Christian physician named Thābit. Thābit was absent but ten days when he returned. So we said to him, "How quickly hast thou healed thy patients!" He said:

> They brought before me a knight in whose leg an abscess had grown; and a woman afflicted with imbecility. To the knight I applied a small poultice until the abscess opened and became well; and the woman I put on diet and made her humor wet. Then a Frankish physician came to them and said, "This man knows nothing about treating them." He then said to the knight, "Which wouldst thou prefer, living with one leg or dying with two?" The latter replied, "Living with one leg." The physician said, "Bring me a strong knight and a sharp ax." A knight came with the ax. And I was standing by. Then the physician laid the leg of the patient on a block of wood and bade the knight strike his leg with the ax and

chop it off at one blow. Accordingly he struck it—while I was looking on—one blow, but the leg was not severed. He dealt another blow, upon which the marrow of the leg flowed out and the patient died on the spot. He then examined the woman and said, "This is a woman in whose head there is a devil which has possessed her. Shave off her hair." Accordingly they shaved it off and the woman began once more to eat their ordinary diet—garlic and mustard. Her imbecility took a turn for the worse. The physician then said, "The devil has penetrated through her head." He therefore took a razor, made a deep cruciform incision on it, peeled off the skin at the middle of the incision until the bone of the skull was exposed and rubbed it with salt. The woman also expired instantly. Thereupon I asked them whether my services were needed any longer, and when they replied in the negative I returned home, having learned of their medicine what I knew not before.

I have, however, witnessed a case of their medicine which was quite different from that.

The king of the Franks had for treasurer a knight named Bernard, who (may Allah's curse be upon him!) was one of the most accursed and wicked among the Franks. A horse kicked him in the leg, which was subsequently infected and which opened in fourteen different places. Every time one of these cuts would close in one place, another would open in another place. All this happened while I was praying for his perdition. Then came to him a Frankish physician and removed from the leg all the ointments which were on it and began to wash it with very strong vinegar. By this treatment all the cuts were healed and the man became well again. He was up again like a devil. . . .

*Newly arrived Franks are especially rough: One insists that Usāmah should pray eastward.*—Everyone who is a fresh emigrant from the Frankish lands is ruder in character than those who have become acclimatized and have held long association with the Moslems. Here is an illustration of their rude character.

Whenever I visited Jerusalem I always entered the Aqṣa Mosque, beside which stood a small mosque which the Franks had converted into a church. When I used to enter the Aqṣa Mosque, which was occupied by the Templars, who were my friends, the Templars would evacuate the little adjoining mosque so that I might pray in it. One day I entered this mosque, repeated the first formula, "Allah is great," and stood up in the act of praying, upon which one of the Franks rushed on me, got hold of me and turned my face eastward saying, "This is the way thou shouldst pray!" A group of Templars hastened to him, seized him and repelled him from me. I resumed my prayer. The same man, while the others were otherwise busy, rushed once more on me and turned my face eastward, saying, "This is the way thou shouldst pray!" The Templars again came in to him and expelled him. They apologized to me, saying, "This is a stranger who has only recently arrived from the land of the Franks and he has never before seen anyone praying except eastward." Thereupon I said to myself, "I have had enough prayer." So I went out and have ever been surprised at the conduct of this devil of a man, at the change in the color of his face, his trembling and his sentiment at the sight of one praying towards the *qiblah* [in Mecca].

*Another wants to show to a Moslem God as a child.*—I saw one of the Franks come to al-Amīr Mu'īn-al-Dīn (may Allah's mercy rest upon his soul!) when he was in the Dome of the Rock and say to him, "Dost thou want to see God as a child?" Mu'īn-al-Din said, "Yes." The Frank walked ahead of us until he showed us the picture of Mary with Christ (may peace be upon him!) as an infant in her lap. He then said, "This is God as a child." But Allah is exalted far above what the infidels say about him!

*Franks lack jealousy in sex affairs.*—The Franks are void of all zeal and jealousy. One of them may be walking along with his wife. He meets another man who takes the wife by the hand and steps aside to converse with her while the husband is standing on one side waiting for his wife to conclude the conversation. If she lingers too long for him, he leaves her alone with the conversant and goes away.

Here is an illustration which I myself witnessed:

When I used to visit Nāblus, I always took lodging with a man named Mu'izz, whose home was a lodging house for the Moslems. The house had windows which opened to the road, and there stood opposite to it on the other side of the road a house belonging to a Frank who sold wine for the merchants. He would take some wine in a bottle and go around announcing it by shouting, "So and so, the merchant, has just opened a cask full of this wine. He who wants to buy some of it will find it in such and such a place." The Frank's pay for the announcement made would be the wine in that bottle. One day this Frank went home and found a man with his wife in the same bed. He asked him, "What could have made thee enter into my wife's room?" The man replied, "I was tired, so I went in to rest." "But how," asked he, "didst thou get into my bed?" The other replied, "I found a bed that was spread, so I slept in it." "But," said he, "my wife was sleeping together with thee!" The other replied, "Well, the bed is hers. How could I therefore have prevented her from using her own bed?" "By the truth of my religion," said the husband, "if thou shouldst do it again, thou and I would have a quarrel." Such was for the Frank the entire expression of his disapproval and the limit of his jealousy. . . .

## *[Reflections on Old Age]*

Little did I realize at that time that the disease of senility is universal, infecting everyone whom death has neglected. But now that I have climbed to the summit of my ninetieth year, worn out by the succession of days and years, I have become myself like Jawād, the fodder dealer, and not like the generous man who can dissipate his money. Feebleness has bent me down to the ground, and old age has made one part of my body enter through another, so much so that I can now hardly recognize myself; and I continually bemoan my past. Here is what I have said in describing my own condition:

When I attained in life a high
 stage
For which I had always yearned, I
 wished for death.
Longevity has left me no energy

By which I could meet the vicissitudes of time when hostile to me.
My strength has been rendered weakness, and my two confidants,
My sight and my hearing, have betrayed me, since I attained this height.
When I rise, I feel as if laden
With a mountain; and when I walk, as though I were bound with chains.
I creep with a cane in my hand which was wont
To carry in warfare a lance and a sword.
My nights I spend in my soft bed, unable to sleep
And wide awake as though I lay on solid rock.
Man is reversed in life: the moment
He attains perfection and completion, then he reverts to the condition from which he started.

I also composed the following verses in Cairo, condemning a life of inaction and ease (and how quickly has life waned and passed by!):

Behold the vicissitudes of time, how they taught me new habits,
Since my hair turned gray, different from my former habits;
And in the changes of time is a lesson to learn by example—
And is there any state which the succession of days does not change?
I have always been the firebrand of battle: every time it abated
I lit it again with the spark struck by applying the sword to the heads of the enemy.
My whole ambition was to engage in combat with my rivals, whom I always took
For prey. They therefore were in constant trembling on account of me.
More terrible in warfare than nighttime, more impetuous in assault
Than a torrent, and more adventurous on the battlefield than destiny!
But now I have become like an idle maid who lies
On stuffed cushions behind screens and curtains.
I have almost become rotten from lying still so long, just as
The sword of Indian steel becomes rusty when kept long in its sheath.
After being dressed with coats of mail, I now dress in robes
Of Dabīqi fabric. Woe unto me and unto the fabrics!
Luxury has never been my idea nor my desired goal;
Comfort is not my affair nor my business.
I would never consent to attain glory through ease,
Nor supreme rank, without breaking swords and lances.

There was a time in which I thought that the newness of life was never to be worn out and its strength was never to be rendered weak. I thought that when I should return to Syria I would find my days there as I knew them to be—with no change that time had wrought since my departure. But when I did return, the promises of my ambition proved false and my former thoughts turned out to be a bright mirage.

O Allah, forgive me for this digression! I have inserted, in my account above, a parenthetical statement. It was a sigh of anguish which gave me relief in the utterance. . . .

*The burden of old age.*—Let no one therefore assume for a moment that the hour of death is advanced by exposing one's self to danger, or retarded by over-cautiousness. In the fact that I have myself survived is an object lesson, for how many terrors have I braved, and how many horrors and dangers have I risked! How many horsemen have I faced, and how many lions have I killed! How many sword cuts and lance thrusts have I received! How many wounds with darts and arbalest stones have been inflicted on me! All this while I was with regard to death in an impregnable fortress until I have now attained the completion of my ninetieth year. And now I view health and existence in the same light as the Prophet (may Allah's blessing and peace rest upon him!) when he said, "Health sufficeth as a malady." In fact, my survival from all those horrors has resulted for me in something even more arduous than fighting and killing. To me, death at the head of an army would have been easier than the troubles of later life. For my life has been so prolonged that the revolving days have taken from me all the objects of pleasure. The turbidity of misery has marred the clearness of happy living. I am in the position described in my own words as follows:

When, at eighty, time plays havoc
  with my power of endurance,
I am chagrined at the feebleness
  of my foot and the trembling of
  my hand.
While I write, my writing looks
  crooked,
Like the writing of one whose
  hands have shivers and tremors.
What a surprise it is that my hand
  be too feeble to carry a pen,
After it had been strong enough
  to break a lance in a lion's
  breast.
And when I walk, cane in hand, I
  feel heaviness
In my foot as though I were
  trudging through mud on a
  plain.
Say, therefore, to him who seeks
  prolonged existence:
Behold the consequences of long
  life and agedness.

My energy has subsided and weakened, the joy of living has come to an end. Long life has reversed me: all light starts from darkness and reverts to darkness. I have become as I said:

Destiny seems to have forgotten
  me, so that now I am like
An exhausted camel left by the
  caravan in the desert.
My eighty years have left no
  energy in me.
When I want to rise up, I feel as
  though I had a broken leg.
I recite my prayer sitting; for
  kneeling,
If I attempt it, is difficult.
This condition has forewarned me
  that
The time of my departure on the
  long journey has drawn nigh.

Enfeebled by years, I have been rendered incapable of performing service for the sultans. So I no more frequent their doors and no longer depend upon them for my livelihood. I have resigned from their service and have returned to them such favors as they had rendered; for I realize that the feebleness of old age cannot stand the exacting duties of service, and the merchandise of the very old man cannot be sold to an amīr. I have now confined myself to my own house, therefore, taking obscurity for my motto.

## ABU 'ABDALLAH IBN BATTUTAH (1304–1377)

*Translated by H.A.R. Gibb*

Ibn Battutah is often celebrated as the greatest traveler of the premodern world, although Marco Polo has been more widely known in the West. Assuming his records are correct, Battutah traversed at least 75,000 miles over a thirty-year period. Raised within a Moroccan family of legal scholars, he left home at age twenty-one in 1325 on his first pilgrimage to Mecca. He traveled across North Africa, Egypt, Palestine, and Syria, finally reaching the holy city of Mecca after a year and a half. Apparently fascinated with travel, he then voyaged south along the eastern shores of Africa to present-day Tanzania and returned by way of the western shores of the Persian Gulf, then finally back to Mecca via caravan through central Arabia. In 1330, he left Arabia, seeking employment with the sultan of Delhi. He took a circuitous route across the Black Sea into West Central Asia, back through the Byzantine city of Constantinople, and across the Asian steppes to India, where he arrived in 1333.

Because Muslim sultans held kingdoms in India, Battutah succeeded in finding employment in Delhi as a judge and lived there for eight years. In 1341, he was sent as an ambassador on behalf of the sultan to the Mongol emperor in China. The trip ended unsuccessfully with a shipwreck, after which Ibn Battutah traveled about for two years, visiting Ceylon (Sri Lanka), the Maldive Islands, and southern India. Around 1345, he set out for China again, this time apparently on his own initiative. Traveling by ship, he saw Bengal, Burma, Sumatra, and Canton. In 1347, he made another pilgrimage to Mecca and finally returned home to Morocco in 1349. His wanderlust was not sated, however. He crossed the Strait of Gibraltar into the Andalusian city of Granada in 1350; in 1353, he made his last sojourn across the Sahara on a risky caravan trip to the West African kingdom of Mali (in present-day Sudan).

Ibn Battutah's account belongs to a genre of Arabic literature called *rihla* (book of travels), which was popular in North African culture from the twelfth to the fourteenth centuries. Like Marco Polo, who dictated his accounts to the Romance writer Rustichello, Ibn Battutah collaborated with the Andalusian Ibn Juzayy, a young literary scholar who was commissioned to record his travels. But unlike Marco Polo, who traveled as a complete outsider, Battutah constantly encountered Muslims and a community that welcomed him as one of their own, for *Dar al-Islam* (the "abode of Islam") in the fourteenth century extended from the far west coast of Africa to Southeast Asia. In those places where Muslims were not the majority, like India, they often ruled over non-Muslims or established important merchant communities.

Moving through a world that was expanding the geographic borders of Islam, Ibn Battutah was motivated by traditions of pilgrimage and Sufism, which encouraged travel to holy sites and study with eminent mystics. His travels were also motivated by the cultural and economic interests of a significant Muslim elite, a mobile and literate group of people who sought employment and advancement in the various urban centers of *Dar al-Islam.* Thus, Battutah followed a long line of travelers and merchants who had written accounts of travels to other parts of the world. A ninth-century anonymous Muslim traveler, for example, has left an account of Canton, and a number of texts by traveling Jews and Arabs attest to conditions in

Russia, Scandinavia, India, Central Asia, Africa, Europe, and China from the ninth to the fourteenth centuries.

Ibn Battutah's *Travels* was copied many times over a period of four hundred years and was gradually introduced in Europe, Iran, and Japan through nineteenth-century translations. It is a vital historical source and offers a rare eyewitness account of the politics, social mores, and economics of fourteenth-century Sudan, Malabar, and certain regions of Asia Minor.

## from The Travels

### *[Leaving Tangiers]*

I left Tangier, my birthplace, on Thursday, 2nd Rajab, 725 [14th June, 1325], being at that time twenty-two [lunar] years of age, with the intention of making the Pilgrimage to the Holy House [at Mecca] and the Tomb of the Prophet [at Madína]. I set out alone, finding no companion to cheer the way with friendly intercourse, and no party of travellers with whom to associate myself. Swayed by an overmastering impulse within me, and a long-cherished desire to visit those glorious sanctuaries, I resolved to quit all my friends and tear myself away from my home. As my parents were still alive, it weighed grievously upon me to part from them, and both they and I were afflicted with sorrow.

On reaching the city of Tilimsán, whose sultan at that time was Abú Táshifín, I found there two ambassadors of the Sultan of Tunis, who left the city on the same day that I arrived. One of the brethren having advised me to accompany them, I consulted the will of God in this matter, and after a stay of three days in the city to procure all that I needed, I rode after them with all speed. I overtook them at the town of Miliána, where we stayed ten days, as both ambassadors fell sick on account of the summer heats. When we set out again, one of them grew worse, and died after we had stopped for three nights by a stream four miles from Miliána. I left their party there and pursued my journey, with a company of merchants from Tunis. On reaching al-Jazá'ir [Algiers] we halted outside the town for a few days, until the former party rejoined us, when we went on together through the Mitíja to the mountain of Oaks [Jurjúra] and so reached Bijáya [Bougie]. The commander of Bijáya at this time was the chamberlain Ibn Sayyid an-Nás. Now one of the Tunisian merchants of our party had died leaving three thousand dinars of gold, which he had entrusted to a certain man of Algiers to deliver to his heirs at Tunis. Ibn Sayyid an-Nás came to hear of this and forcibly seized the money. This was the first instance I witnessed of the tyranny of the agents of the Tunisian government. At Bijáya I fell ill of a fever, and one of my friends advised me to stay there till I recovered. But I refused, saying, "If God decrees my death, it shall be on the road with my face set toward Mecca." "If that is your resolve," he replied, "sell your ass and your heavy baggage, and I shall lend you what you require. In this way you will travel light, for we must make haste on our journey, for fear of meeting roving Arabs on the way." I followed his advice and he did as he had promised—may God reward him! On reaching

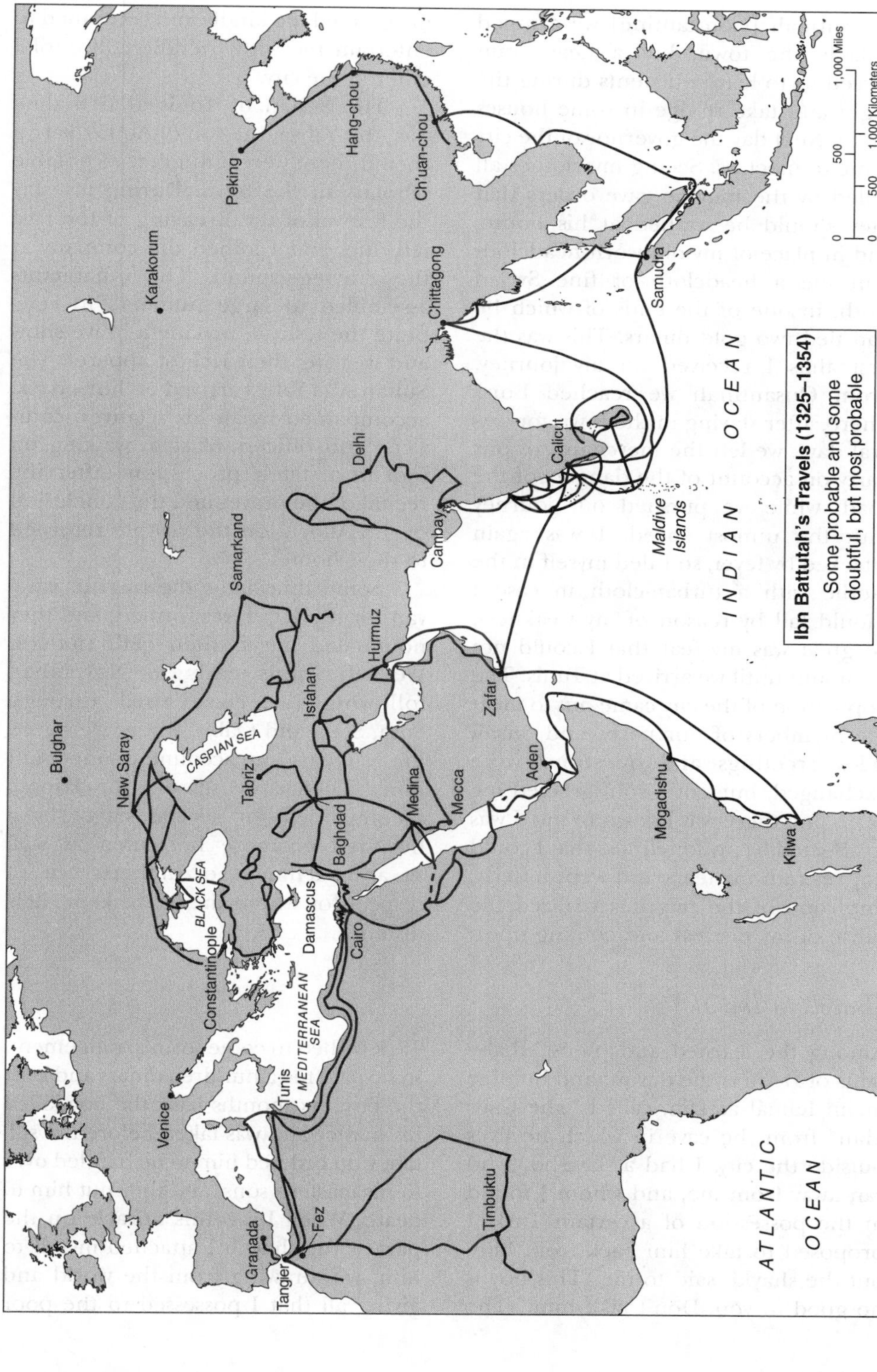
Ibn Battutah's Travels (1325–1354)
Some probable and some doubtful, but most probable
0 500 1,000 Miles
0 500 1,000 Kilometers
ATLANTIC OCEAN
INDIAN OCEAN
MEDITERRANEAN SEA
BLACK SEA
CASPIAN SEA
Maldive Islands
Tangier
Granada
Fez
Timbuktu
Tunis
Venice
Constantinople
Cairo
Damascus
Baghdad
Medina
Mecca
Aden
Mogadishu
Kilwa
Zafar
Hurmuz
Isfahan
Tabriz
Bulghar
New Saray
Samarkand
Karakorum
Cambay
Delhi
Calicut
Chittagong
Samudra
Peking
Hang-chou
Ch'uan-chou

Qusantínah [Constantine] we camped outside the town, but a heavy rain forced us to leave our tents during the night and take refuge in some houses there. Next day the governor of the city came to meet us. Seeing my clothes all soiled by the rain he gave orders that they should be washed at his house, and in place of my old worn headcloth sent me a headcloth of fine Syrian cloth, in one of the ends of which he had tied two gold dinars. This was the first alms I received on my journey. From Qusantínah we reached Bona where, after staying in the town for several days, we left the merchants of our party on account of the dangers of the road, while we pursued our journey with the utmost speed. I was again attacked by fever, so I tied myself in the saddle with a turban-cloth in case I should fall by reason of my weakness. So great was my fear that I could not dismount until we arrived at Tunis. The population of the city came out to meet the members of our party, and on all sides greetings and questions were exchanged, but not a soul greeted me as no one there was known to me. I was so affected by my loneliness that I could not restrain my tears and wept bitterly, until one of the pilgrims realized the cause of my distress and coming up to me greeted me kindly and continued to entertain me with friendly talk until I entered the city.

The Sultan of Tunis at that time was Abú Yahyá, the son of Abú Zakaríya II, and there were a number of notable scholars in the town. During my stay the festival of the Breaking of the Fast fell due, and I joined the company at the Praying-ground. The inhabitants assembled in large numbers to celebrate the festival, making a brave show and wearing their richest apparel. The Sultan Abú Yahyá arrived on horseback, accompanied by all his relatives, courtiers, and officers of state walking on foot in a stately procession. After the recital of the prayer and the conclusion of the Allocution the people returned to their homes.

Some time later the pilgrim caravan for the Hijáz was formed, and they nominated me as their qádí (judge). We left Tunis early in November, following the coast road through Súsa, Sfax, and Qábis, where we stayed for ten days on account of incessant rains. Thence we set out for Tripoli, accompanied for several stages by a hundred or more horsemen as well as a detachment of archers, out of respect for whom the Arabs kept their distance. . . .

## *[Travels in India]*

Among the learned and pious inhabitants of Delhi is the devout and humble imám Kamál ad-Dín, called "The Cave Man" from the cave in which he lives outside the city. I had a slave-boy who ran away from me, and whom I found in the possession of a certain Turk. I proposed to take him back from him, but the shaykh said to me "This boy is no good to you. Don't take him." The Turk wished to come to an arrangement, so he paid me a hundred dinars and kept the boy. Six months later the boy killed his master and was taken before the sultan, who ordered him to be handed over to his master's sons, and they put him to death. When I saw this miracle on the part of the shaykh I attached myself to him, withdrawing from the world and giving all that I possessed to the poor and needy. I stayed with him for some time, and I used to see him fast for ten and twenty days on end and remain standing most of the night. I continued with him until the sultan sent for me and I became entangled in the world once again—may God give me a good ending!

This king is of all men the fondest of making gifts and of shedding blood. His gate is never without some poor man enriched or some living man executed, and stories are current amongst the people of his generosity and courage and of his cruelty and violence towards criminals. For all that, he is of all men the most humble and the readiest to show equity and justice. The ceremonies of religion are strictly complied with at his court, and he is severe in the matter of attendance at prayer and in punishing those who neglect it. He is one of those kings whose felicity is unimpaired and surpassing all ordinary experience, but his dominant quality is generosity. We shall relate some stories of this that are marvellous beyond anything ever heard before, and I call God and his Angels and His Prophets to witness that all that I tell of his extraordinary generosity is absolute truth. I know that some of the instances I shall relate will be unacceptable to the minds of many, and that they will regard them as quite impossible, but in a matter which I have seen with my own eyes and of which I know the accuracy and have had a large share, I cannot do otherwise than speak the truth. . . .

One of their customs is that none may pass through this door except those whom the sultan has prescribed, and for each person he prescribes a number of his staff to enter along with him. Whenever any person comes to this door the scribes write down "So-and-so came at the first hour" or the second, and so on, and the sultan receives a report of this after the evening prayer. Another of their customs is that anyone who absents himself from the palace for three days or more, with or without excuse, may not enter this door thereafter except by the sultan's permission. If he has an excuse of illness or otherwise presents the sultan with a gift suitable to his rank, [a] door opens into an immense audience hall called *Hazár Ustún,* which means "A thousand pillars." The pillars are of wood and support a wooden roof, admirably carved. The people sit under this, and it is in this hall that the sultan holds public audiences.

As a rule his audiences are held in the afternoon, though he often holds them early in the day. He sits cross-legged on a throne placed on a dais carpeted in white, with a large cushion behind him and two others as arm-rests on his right and left. When he takes his seat, the wazír stands in front of him, the secretaries behind the wazír, then the chamberlains and so on in order of precedence. As the sultan sits down the chamberlains and naqíbs say in their loudest voice *Bismillah* ["In the Name of God," the opening of the Qur'an]. At the sultan's head stands the "great king" Qabúla with a fly-whisk in his hand to drive off the flies. A hundred armour-bearers stand on the right and a like number on the left, carrying shields, swords, and bows. The other functionaries and notables stand along the hall to right and left. Then they bring in sixty horses with the royal harness, half of which are ranged on the right and half on the left, where the sultan can see them. Next fifty elephants are brought in, which are adorned with silken cloths, and have their tusks shod with iron for greater efficacy in killing criminals. On the neck of each elephant is its mahout, who carries a sort of iron axe with which he punishes it and directs it to do what is required of it. Each elephant has on its back a sort of large chest capable of holding twenty warriors or more or less, according to the size of the beast. These elephants are trained to make obeisance to the sultan and incline their heads, and when they do so the chamberlains cry in a loud voice *Bismillah* ["In the Name of God," the opening of the Qur'an]. They also are arranged half on the right and half on the left behind the persons standing. As each person enters who has an appointed place of standing on the right or left, he makes obeisance on reaching the station of the chamberlains, and the chamberlains say *Bismillah,* regulating the loudness of their utterance by the rank of the person concerned, who then retires to his appointed place, beyond which he never passes. If it is one of the infidel Hindus who makes obeisance, the chamberlains say to him "God guide thee." . . .

## *[A Narrow Escape]*

The king of China had sent valuable gifts to the sultan, including a hundred slaves of both sexes, five hundred pieces of velvet and silk cloth, musk, jewelled garments and weapons, with a request that the sultan would permit him to rebuild the idol-temple which is near the mountains called Qarájíl [Himalaya]. It is in a place known as Samhal, to which the Chinese go on pilgrimage; the Muslim army in India had captured it, laid it in ruins and sacked it. The sultan, on receiving this gift, wrote to the king saying that the request could not be granted by Islamic law, as permission to build a temple in the territories of the Muslims was granted only to those who paid a poll-tax; to which he added "If thou wilt pay the *jizya* we shall empower thee to build it. And peace be on those who follow the True Guidance." He requited his present with an even richer one—a hundred thoroughbred horses, a hundred white slaves, a hundred Hindu dancing- and singing-girls, twelve hundred pieces of various kinds of cloth, gold and silver candelabra and basins, brocade robes, caps, quivers, swords, gloves embroidered with pearls, and fifteen eunuchs. As my fellow-ambassadors the sultan appointed the amír Zahír ad-Dín of Zanján, one of the most eminent men of learning, and the eunuch Káfúr, the cup-bearer, into whose keeping the present was entrusted. He sent the amír Muhammad of Herát with a thousand horsemen to escort us to the port of embarkation, and we were accompanied by the Chinese ambassadors, fifteen in number, along with their servants, about a hundred men in all.

We set out therefore in imposing force and formed a large camp. The sultan gave instructions that we were to be supplied with provisions while we were travelling through his dominions. Our journey began on the 17th of Safar 743 [22nd July 1342]. That was the day selected because they choose either the 2nd, 7th, 12th, 17th, 22nd, or 27th of the month as the day for setting out. . . .

On reaching Koel we heard that certain Hindu infidels had invested and surrounded the town of al-Jalálí. Now this town lies at a distance of seven miles from Koel, so we made in that direction. Meanwhile the infidels were engaged in battle with its inhabitants and the latter were on the verge of destruction. The infidels knew nothing of our approach until we charged down upon them, though they numbered about a thousand cavalry and three thousand foot, and we killed them to the last man and took possession of their horses and their weapons. Of our party twenty-three horsemen and fifty-five foot-soldiers suffered martyrdom, amongst them the eunuch Káfúr, the cup-bearer, into whose hands the present had been entrusted. We informed the sultan by letter of his death and halted to await his reply. During that time the infidels used to swoop down from an inaccessible hill which is in those parts and raid the environs of al-Jalálí, and our party used to ride out every day with the commander of that district to assist him in driving them off.

On one of these occasions I rode out with several of my friends and we went into a garden to take our siesta, for this was in the hot season. Then we heard some shouting, so we mounted our horses and overtook some infidels who had attacked one of the villages of al-Jalálí. When we pursued them they broke up into small parties; our troop in following them did the same, and I was isolated with five others. At this point we were attacked by a body of cavalry and foot-soldiers from a thicket thereabouts, and we fled from them because of their numbers. About ten of them pursued me, but afterwards all but three of them gave up the chase. There was no road at all before me and the ground there was very stony. My horse's forefeet got caught between the stones, so I dismounted, freed its foot and mounted again. It is customary for a man in India to carry two swords, one, called the stirrup-sword, attached to the saddle, and the other in his quiver. My stirrup-sword fell out of its scabbard, and as its ornaments were of gold I dismounted, picked it up, slung it on me and mounted, my pursuers chasing me all the while. After this I came to a deep nullah, so I dismounted and climbed down to the bottom of it, and that was the last I saw of them.

I came out of this into a valley amidst a patch of tangled wood, traversed by a road, so I walked along it, not knowing where it led to. At this juncture about forty of the infidels, carrying bows in their hands, came out upon me and surrounded me. I was afraid that they would all shoot at me at once if I fled from them, and I was wearing no armour, so I threw myself to the ground and surrendered, as they do not kill those who do that. They seized me and stripped me of everything that I was carrying except a tunic, shirt and trousers, then they took me into that patch of jungle, and finally brought me to the part of it where they stayed, near a tank of water situated amongst those trees. They gave me bread made of peas, and I ate some of it and drank some water. In their company there were two Muslims who spoke to me in Persian, and asked me all about myself. I told them part of my story, but concealed the fact that I had come from the sultan. Then they said to me: "You are sure to be put to death either by these men or by others, but this man here (pointing to one of them) is their leader." So I spoke to him, using the two Muslims as interpreters, and tried to conciliate him. He gave me [to] three of the band, one of them an old man, with whom was his son, and the third an evil black fellow. These three spoke to me and I understood from them that they had received orders to kill me. In the evening of the same day they carried me off to the cave, but God sent an ague upon the black [man], so he put his feet upon me, and the old man and his son went to sleep. In the morning they talked among themselves and made signs to me to accompany them down to the tank. I realized that they were going to kill me, so I spoke to the old man and tried to gain his favour, and he took pity on me. I cut off the sleeves of my shirt and gave them to him so that the other members of the band should not blame him on my account if I escaped.

About noon we heard voices near the tank and they thought that it was their comrades, so they made signs to me to go down with them, but when we went down we found some other people. The newcomers advised my guards to accompany them but they refused, and the three of them sat down in front of me, keeping me facing them, and laid on the ground a hempen rope which they had with them. I was watching them all the time and saying to myself: "It is with this rope that they will bind me when they kill me." I remained thus for a time, then [one of the newcomers said:] "Why have you not killed him?" The old man pointed to the black [man], as though he were excusing himself on the ground of his illness. One of these three [newcomers] was a pleasant-looking youth, and he said to me: "Do you wish me to set you at liberty?" I said "Yes," and he answered "Go." So I took the tunic which I was wearing and gave it to him and he gave me a worn double-woven cloak which he had, and showed me the way. I went off but I was afraid lest they should change their minds and overtake me, so I went into a reed thicket and hid there till sunset.

Then I made my way out and followed the road which the youth had shewn me. This led to a stream from which I drank. I went on till near midnight and came to a hill under which I slept. In the morning I continued along the road, and sometime before noon reached a high rocky hill on which there were sweet lote-trees and zizyphus bushes. I started to pull and eat the lotus berries so eagerly that the thorns left scars on my arms that remain there to this day. Coming down from that hill I entered a plain sown with cotton and containing castor-oil trees. Here there was a *bá'in,* which in their language means a very broad well with a stone casing and steps by which you go down to reach the water. Some of them have stone pavilions, arcades, and seats in the centre and on the sides, and the kings and nobles of the country vie with one another in constructing them along the highroads where there is no water. When I reached the *bá'in,* I drank some water from it and I found on it some mustard shoots which had been dropped by their owner when he washed them. Some of these I ate and saved up the rest, then I lay down under a castor-oil tree. While I was there about forty mailed horsemen came to the *bá'in* to get water and some of them entered the sown fields, then they went away, and God sealed their eyes that they did not see me. After them came about fifty others carrying arms and they too went down into the *bá'in.* One of them came up to a tree opposite the one I was under, yet he did not discover me. At this point I made my way into the field of cotton and stayed there the rest of the day, while they stayed at the *bá'in* washing their clothes and whiling away the time. At night time their voices died away, so I knew that they had either passed on or fallen asleep. Thereupon I emerged and followed the track of the horses, for it was a moonlit night, continuing till I came to another *bá'in* with a dome over it. I went down to it, drank some water, ate some of the mustard shoots which I had, and went into the dome. I found it full of grasses collected by birds, so I went to sleep in it. Now and again I felt the movement of an animal amongst the grass; I suppose it was a snake, but I was too worn out to pay any attention to it.

The next morning I went along a broad road, which led to a ruined village. Then I took another road, but with the same result as before. Several days passed in this manner. One day I came to some tangled trees with a tank of water between them. The space under these trees was like a room, and at the sides of the tank were plants like dittany and others. I intended to stop there until God should send someone to bring me to inhabited country, but I recovered a little strength, so I arose and walked along a road on which I found the tracks of cattle. I found a bull carrying a packsaddle and a sickle, but after all this road led to the villages of the infidels. Then I followed up another road, and this brought me to a ruined village. There I saw two naked blacks, and in fear of them I remained under some trees there. At nightfall I entered the village and found a house in one of whose rooms there was something like a large jar of the sort they make to store grain in. At the bottom of it there was a hole large enough to admit a man, so I crept into it and found inside it a layer of chopped straw, and amongst this a stone on which I laid my head and went to sleep. On the top of the jar there was a bird which kept fluttering its wings most of the night—I suppose it was frightened, so we made a pair of frightened creatures. This went on for seven days from the day on which I was taken prisoner, which was a Saturday. On the seventh day I came to a village of the unbelievers which was inhabited and possessed a tank of water and plots of vegetables. I asked them for some food but they refused to give me any. However, in the neighbourhood of a well I found some radish leaves and ate them. I went into the village, and found a troop of infidels with sentries posted. The sentries challenged me but I did not answer them and sat down on the ground. One of them came over with a drawn sword and raised it to strike me, but I paid no attention to him, so utterly weary did I feel. Then he searched me but found nothing on me, so he took the shirt whose sleeves I had given to the old man who had had charge of me.

On the eighth day I was consumed with thirst and I had no water at all. I came to a ruined village but found no tank in it. They have a custom in those villages of making tanks in which the rain-water collects, and this supplies them with drinking water all the year round. Then I went along a road and this brought me to an uncased well over which was a rope of vegetable fibre, but there was no vessel on it to draw water with. I took a piece of cloth which I had on my head and tied it to the rope and sucked the water that soaked into it, but that did not slake my thirst. I tied on my shoe next and drew up water in it, but that did not satisfy me either, so I drew water with it a second time, but the rope broke and the shoe fell back into the well. I then tied on the other shoe and drank until my thirst was assuaged. After that I cut the shoe and tied its uppers on my foot with the rope off the well and bits of cloth which I found there. While I was tying this on and wondering what to do, a person appeared before me. I looked at him, and lo! it was a black-skinned man, carrying a jug and a staff in his hand, and a wallet on his shoulder. He gave me the Muslim greeting "Peace be upon you" and I replied "Upon you be peace and the mercy and blessings of God." Then he asked me in Persian who I was, and I answered "A man astray," and he said: "So am I." Thereupon he tied his jug to a rope which he had with him and drew up some water. I wished to drink but he saying "Have patience," opened his wallet and brought out a handful of black chick-peas fried with a little rice. After I had eaten some of this and drunk, he made his ablutions and prayed two prostrations and I did the same. Thereupon he asked me my name. I answered "Muhammad" and asked him his, to which he replied "Joyous Heart." I took this as a good omen and rejoiced at it. After this he said to me "In the name of God accompany me." I said "Yes," and walked on with him for a little, then I found my limbs giving way, and as I was unable to stand up I sat down. He said "What is the matter with you?" I answered "I was able to walk before meeting you, but now that I have met you I cannot." Whereupon he said "Glory be to God! Mount on my shoulders." I said to him "You are weak, and have not strength for that," but he replied "God will give me strength. You must do so." So I got up on his shoulders and he said to me "Say *God is sufficient for us and an excellent guardian.*" I repeated this over and over again, but I could not keep my eyes open, and regained consciousness only on feeling myself falling to the ground. Then I woke up, but found no trace of the man, and lo! I was in an inhabited village. I entered it and found it was a village of Hindu peasants with a Muslim governor. They informed him about me and he came to meet me. I asked him the name of this village and he replied "Táj Búra." The distance from there to Koel, where our party was, is two farsakhs. The governor provided a horse to take me to his house and gave me hot food, and I washed. Then he said to me: "I have here a garment and a turban which were left in my charge by a certain Arab from Egypt, one of the soldiers belonging to the corps at Koel." I said to him "Bring them; I shall wear them until I reach camp." When he brought them I found that they were two of my own garments which I had given to that very Arab when we came to Koel. I was extremely astonished at this, then I thought of the man who had carried me on his shoulders and I remembered what the saint Abú 'Abdalláh al-Murshidí had told me, as I have related in the first journey, when he said to me: "You will enter the land of India and meet there my brother Dilshád, who will deliver you from a misfortune which will befall you there." I remembered too how he had said, when I asked him his name, "Joyous Heart" which, translated into Persian, is *Dilshád.* So I knew that it was he whom the saint had foretold that I should meet, and that he too was one of the saints, but I enjoyed no more of his company than the short space which I have related.

The same night I wrote to my friends at Koel to inform them of my safety, and they came, bringing me a horse and clothes and rejoiced at my escape. . . .

We journeyed thereafter to Gályúr [Gwalior], a large town with an impregnable fortress isolated on the summit of a lofty hill. Over its gate is an elephant with its mahout carved in stone. The governor of this town was a man of upright character, and he treated me very honourably when I stayed with him on a previous occasion. One day I came before him as he was about to have an infidel cut in two. I said to him "By God I beseech you, do not do this, for I have never seen anyone put to death in my presence." He ordered the man to be put in prison so my intervention was the means of his escape. From Gályúr we went to Parwán, a small town belonging to the Muslims, but situated in the land of the infidels. There are many tigers there, and one of the inhabitants told me that a certain tiger used to enter the town by night, although the gates were shut, and used to seize people. It killed quite a number of the townsfolk in this way. They used to wonder how it made its way in. Here is an amazing thing; a man told me that it was not a tiger who did this but a human being, one of the magicians known as *Fúgís* [Yogis], appearing in the shape of a tiger. When I heard this I refused to believe it, but a number of people said the same, so let us give at this point some account of these magicians.

The men of this class do some marvellous things. One of them will spend months without eating or drinking, and many of them have holes dug for them in the earth which are then built in on top of them, leaving only a space for air to enter. They stay in these for months, and I heard tell of one of them who remained thus for a year. The people say that they make up pills, one of which they take for a given number of days or months, and during that time they require no food or drink. They can tell what is happening at a distance. The sultan holds them in esteem and admits them to his company. Some eat nothing but vegetables, and others, the majority, eat no meat; it is obvious that they have so disciplined themselves in ascetic practices that they have no need of any of the goods or vanities of this world. There are amongst them some who merely look at a man and he falls dead on the spot. The common people say that if the breast of a man killed in this way is cut open, it is found to contain no heart, and they assert that his heart has been eaten. This is commonest in the case of women, and a woman who acts thus is called a *kaftár.* During the famine in Delhi they brought one of these women to me, saying that she had eaten the heart of a boy. I ordered them to take her to the sultan's lieutenant, who commanded that she should be put to the test. They filled four jars with water, tied them to her hands and feet and threw her into the river Jumna. As she did not sink she was known to be a *kaftár;* had she not floated she would not have been one. He ordered her then to be burned in the fire. Her ashes were collected by the men and women of the town, for they believe that anyone who fumigates himself with them is safe against a *kaftár's* enchantments during that year. . . .

We continued on our way to Nadhurbár [Nandurbar], a small town inhabited by the Marhatas, who possess great skill in the arts and are physicians and astrologers. The nobles of the

Marhatas are Brahmans and Katrís [Kshatriyas]. Their food consists of rice, vegetables, and oil of sesame, and they do not hold with giving pain to or slaughtering animals. They wash themselves thoroughly before eating and do not marry among their relatives, unless those who are cousins six times removed. Neither do they drink wine, for this in their eyes is the greatest of vices. The Muslims in India take the same view, and any Muslim who drinks it is punished with eighty stripes, and shut up in a matamore for three months, which is opened only at the hours of meals. . . .

## *[Further Travels in Southeast Asia]*

. . . The sultan of Mul-Jáwa then welcomed me and ordered a piece of cloth to be spread for me to sit upon. I said to the interpreter "How can I sit on the cloth when the sultan is sitting on the ground?" He replied "Such is his habit; he sits on the ground out of humility. You are a guest and have come from a great sultan, so he wishes to show you honour." Thereupon I sat down, and having asked me very briefly about the sultan [of India] he said to me " You shall stay with us as a guest for three days, and after that you may go."

While this sultan was sitting in audience, I saw a man with a knife in his hand resembling a bookbinder's tool. He put this knife to his own neck, and delivered a long speech which I did not understand, then gripped it with both hands and cut his own throat. So sharp was the knife and so strong his grip that his head fell to the ground. I was amazed at his action. The sultan said to me "Does anyone do this in your country?" I replied "I have never seen such a thing." Then he laughed and said "These are our slaves, who kill themselves for love of us." He gave orders that the body should be carried away and burned, and the sultan's lieutenants, the officers of state, the troops, and the citizens went out to his cremation. The sultan assigned a large pension to his children, wife, and brothers, and they were held in high esteem because of this act. One of those present at this audience told me that the speech made by the man was a declaration of his affection for the sultan, and that he was slaying himself for love of him, as his father had slain himself for love of the sultan's father, and his grandfather for love of the sultan's grandfather. Thereafter I withdrew from the audience and he sent me a guest's portion for three days.

We continued our journey by sea and thirty-four days later came to the sluggish or motionless sea. There is a reddish tinge in its waters, which, they say, is due to soil from a country in the vicinity. There are no winds or waves or movement at all in it, in spite of its wide extent. It is on account of this sea that each Chinese junk is accompanied by three vessels, as we have mentioned, which take it in tow and row it forwards. Besides this every junk has about twenty oars as big as masts, each of which is manned by a muster of thirty men or so, who stand in two ranks facing one another. Attached to the oars are two enormous ropes as thick as cables; one of the ranks pulls on the cable [at its side], then lets go, and the other rank pulls [on the cable at its side]. They chant in musical voices as they do this, most commonly saying *la'lá, la'lá.* We passed thirty-seven days on this sea, and the sailors were surprised at the facility of our crossing, for they [usually] spend forty to fifty days on it, and forty days is the shortest time required under the most favourable circumstances.

Thereafter we reached the land of Tawálisí, it being their king who is called by that name. It is a vast country and its king is a rival of the king of China. He possesses many junks, with which he makes war on the Chinese until they come to terms with him on certain conditions. The inhabitants of this land are idolaters; they are handsome men and closely resemble the Turks in figure. Their skin is most commonly of a reddish hue, and they are brave and warlike. Their women ride on horseback and are skilful archers, and fight exactly like men. We put in at one of their ports, at the town of Kaylúkarí, which is among their finest and largest cities. It was formerly the residence of the son of their king. When we anchored in the port their troops came down and the captain went ashore to them, taking with him a present for the prince. When he enquired of them about him, however, they told him that the prince's father had appointed him governor of another district and had made his daughter, whose name was Urdujá, governor of this city.

The day following our arrival at the port of Kaylúkarí, this princess summoned the ship's captain and clerk, the merchants and pilots, the commander of the footsoldiers, and the commanders of the archers to a banquet which she had prepared for them, according to her custom. The captain wished me to go with them, but I declined, because, being infidels, it is not lawful to eat their food. When they came into her presence she asked them if there was any one else of their company who had not come. The captain replied "There is only one man left, a *bakhshí* (that is, a qádí, in their tongue), and he will not eat your food." Thereupon she said "Call him," so her guards came [to me] along with the captain's party and said "Comply with the princess's wish." I went to her then, and found her sitting in full state. On my saluting her she replied to me in Turkish, and asked me from what land I had come. I said to her "From the land of India." "From the pepper country?" she asked, and I replied "Yes." She questioned me about this land and events there, and when I had answered she said "I must positively make an expedition to it and take possession of it for myself, for the quantity of its riches and its troops attracts me." I replied "Do so." She ordered me to be given robes, two elephant loads of rice, two buffaloes, ten sheep, four pounds of syrup, and four *martabáns* (that is, large jars) filled with ginger, pepper, lemons, and mangoes, all of them salted, these being among the things prepared for sea voyages.

The captain told that this princess has in her army women, female servants and slave-girls, who fight like men. She goes out in person with her troops, male and female, makes raids on her enemies, takes part in the fighting, and engages in single combat with picked warriors. He told me too that during a fierce engagement with certain of her enemies, many of her troops were killed and they were all but defeated, when she dashed forward and broke through the ranks until she reached the king against whom she was fighting, and dealt him a mortal blow with her lance. He fell dead and his army took to flight. She brought back his head on the point of a spear, and his relatives redeemed it from her for a large sum of money. When she returned to her father he gave her this town, which had formerly been in her brother's hands. The captain told me also that she is sought in marriage by various princes, but she says "I shall marry none but him who fights and overcomes me in single combat," and they avoid fighting with her for fear of the disgrace [that would attach to them] if she overcame them.

We then left the land of Tawálisí and after seventeen days at sea with a favouring wind, sailing with maximum speed and ease, reached the land of China. . . .

## *[Travels in China]*

The land of China is of vast extent, and abounding in produce, fruits, grain, gold and silver. In this respect there is no country in the world that can rival it. It is traversed by the river called the "Water of Life," which rises in some mountains, called the "Mountain of Apes," near the city of Khán-Báliq [Peking] and flows through the centre of China for the space of six months' journey, until finally it reaches Sín as-Sín [Canton]. It is bordered by villages, fields, fruit gardens, and bazaars, just like the Egyptian Nile, only that [the country through which runs] this river is even more richly cultivated and populous, and there are many waterwheels on it. In the land of China there is abundant sugar-cane, equal, nay superior, in quality to that of Egypt, as well as grapes and plums. I used to think that the 'Othmání plums of Damascus had no equal, until I saw the plums in China. It has wonderful melons too, like those of Khwárizm and Isfahán. All the fruits which we have in our country are to be found there, either much the same or of better quality. Wheat is very abundant in China, indeed better wheat I have never seen, and the same may be said of their lentils and chick-peas.

The Chinese pottery [porcelain] is manufactured only in the towns of Zaytún and Sín-kalán. It is made of the soil of some mountains in that district, which takes fire like charcoal, as we shall relate subsequently. They mix this with some stones which they have, burn the whole for three days, then pour water over it. This gives a kind of clay which they cause to ferment. The best quality of [porcelain is made from] clay that has fermented for a complete month, but no more, the poorer quality [from clay] that has fermented for ten days. The price of this porcelain there is the same as, or even less than, that of ordinary pottery in our country. It is exported to India and other countries, even reaching as far as our own lands in the West, and it is the finest of all makes of pottery.

The hens and cocks in China are very big indeed, bigger than geese in our country, and hens' eggs there are bigger than our goose eggs. On the other hand their geese are not at all large. We bought a hen once and set about cooking it, but it was too big for one pot, so we put it in two. . . .

The Chinese themselves are infidels, who worship idols and burn their dead like the Hindus. The king of China is a Tatar, one of the descendants of Tinkiz [Chingiz] Khán. In every Chinese city there is a quarter for Muslims in which they live by themselves, and in which they have mosques both for the Friday services and for other religious purposes. The Muslims are honoured and respected. The Chinese infidels eat the flesh of swine and dogs, and sell it in their markets. They are wealthy folk and well-to-do, but they make no display either in their food or their clothes. You will see one of their principal merchants, a man so rich that his wealth cannot be counted, wearing a coarse cotton tunic. But there is one thing that the Chinese take a pride in, that is, gold and silver plate. Every one of them carries a stick, on which they lean in walking, and which they call "the third leg." Silk is very plentiful among them, because the silk-worm attaches itself to fruits and feeds on them without requiring much care. For that reason it is so common to be worn by even the very poorest there. Were it not for the merchants it would have no value at all, for a single piece of cotton cloth is sold in their country for the price of many pieces of silk. It is customary amongst them for a merchant to cast what gold and silver he has into ingots, each weighing a hundredweight or more or less, and to put those ingots above the door of his house.

The Chinese use neither [gold] dinars nor [silver] dirhams in their commerce. All the gold and silver that comes into their country is cast by them into ingots, as we have described. Their buying and selling is carried on exclusively by means of pieces of paper, each of the size of the palm of the hand, and stamped with the sultan's seal. Twenty-five of these pieces of paper are called *bálisht,* which takes the place of the dinar with us [as the unit of currency]. When these notes become torn by handling, one takes them to an office corresponding to our mint, and receives their equivalent in new notes on delivering up the old ones. This transaction is made without charge and involves no expense, for those who have the duty of making the notes receive regular salaries from the sultan. . . .

The Chinese are of all peoples the most skilful in the arts and possessed of the greatest mastery of them. This characteristic of theirs is well known, and has frequently been described at length in the works of various writers. In regard to portraiture there is none, whether Greek or any other, who can match them in precision, for in this art they show a marvellous talent. I myself saw an extraordinary example of this gift of theirs. I never returned to any of their cities after I had visited it a first time without finding my portrait and the portraits of my companions drawn on the walls and on sheets of paper exhibited in the bazaars. When I visited the sultan's city I passed with my companions through the painters' bazaar on my way to the sultan's palace. We were dressed after the 'Iráqí fashion. On returning from the palace in the evening, I passed through the same bazaar, and saw my portrait and those of my companions drawn on a sheet of paper which they had affixed to the wall. . . . I was told that the sultan had ordered them to do this, and that they had come to the palace while we were there and had been observing us and drawing our portraits without our noticing it. This is a custom of theirs, I mean making portraits of all who pass through their country. In fact they have brought this to such perfection that if a stranger commits any offence that obliges him to flee from China, they send his portrait far and wide. A search is then made for him and wheresoever the [person bearing a] resemblance to that portrait is found, he is apprehended. . . .

China is the safest and best regulated of countries for a traveller. A man may go by himself a nine months' journey, carrying with him large sums of money, without any fear on that account. The system by which they ensure his safety is as follows. At every post-station in their country they have a hostelry controlled by an officer, who is stationed there with a company of horsemen and footsoldiers. After sunset or later in the evening the officer visits the hostelry with his clerk, registers the names of all travellers staying there for the night, seals up the list, and locks them into the hostelry. After sunrise he returns with his clerk, calls each person by name, and writes a detailed description of them on the list. He then sends a man with them to conduct them to the next post-station and bring back a clearance certificate from the controller there to the effect that all these persons have arrived at that station. If the guide does not produce this document, he is held responsible for them. This is the practice at every station in their country from Sín as-Sín to Khán-Báliq. In these hostelries there is everything that the traveller requires in the way of provisions, especially fowls and geese. Sheep on the other hand, are scarce with them.

To return to the account of our journey. The first city which we reached after our sea voyage was the city of Zaytún. [Now although *zaytún* means "olives"] there are no olives in this city, nor indeed in all the lands of the Chinese nor in India; it is simply a name which has been given to the place. Zaytún is an immense city. In it are woven the damask silk and satin fabrics which go by its name, and which are superior to the fabrics of Khansá and Khán-Báliq. The port of Zaytún is one of the largest in the world, or perhaps the very largest. I saw in it about a hundred large junks; as for small junks, they could not be counted for multitude. It is formed by a large inlet of the sea which penetrates the land to the point where it unites with the great river. In this city, as in all Chinese towns, a man will have a fruitgarden and a field with his house set in the middle of it, just as in the town of Sijilmása in our own country. For this reason their towns are extensive. The Muslims live in a town apart from the others. . . .

## *[Travels in Africa]*

[On the edge of the Sahara], we passed ten days of discomfort, because the water is brackish and the place is plagued with flies. Water supplies are laid in at Tagházá for the crossing of the desert which lies beyond it, which is a ten-nights' journey with no water on the way except on rare occasions. We indeed had the good fortune to find water in plenty, in pools left by the rain. One day we found a pool of sweet water between two rocky prominences. We quenched our thirst at it and then washed our clothes. Truffles are plentiful in this desert and it swarms with lice, so that people wear string necklaces containing mercury, which kills them. At that time we used to go ahead of the caravan, and when we found a place suitable for pasturage we would graze our beasts. We went on doing this until one of our party was lost in the desert; after that I neither went ahead nor lagged behind. We passed a caravan on the way and they told us that some of their party had become separated from them. We found one of them dead under a shrub, of the sort that grows in the sand, with his clothes on and a whip in his hand. The water was only about a mile away from him.

We came next to Tásarahlá, a place of subterranean water-beds, where the caravans halt. They stay there three days to rest, mend their waterskins, fill them with water, and sew on them covers of sackcloth as a precaution against the wind. From this point the *takshíf* is despatched. The *takshíf* is a name given to any man of the Massúfa tribe who is hired by the persons in the caravan to go ahead to Íwálátan, carrying letters from them to their friends there, so that they may take lodgings for them. These persons then come out a distance of four nights' journey to meet the caravan, and bring water with them. Anyone who has no friend in Íwálátan writes to some merchant well known for his worthy character, who then undertakes the same services for him. It often happens that the *takshíf* perishes in this desert, with the result that the people of Íwálátan know nothing about the caravan, and all or most of those who are with it perish. That desert is haunted by demons; if the *takshíf* be alone, they make sport of him and disorder his mind, so that he loses his way and perishes. For there is no visible road or track in these parts—nothing but sand blown hither and thither by the wind. You see hills of sand in one place, and afterwards you will see them moved to quite another place. The guide there is one who has made the journey frequently in both directions, and who is gifted with a quick intelligence. I remarked, as a strange thing, that the guide whom we had was blind in one eye, and diseased in the other, yet he had the best knowledge of the road of any man. We hired the *takshíf* on this journey for a hundred gold *mithqáls;* he was a man of the Massúfa. On the night of the seventh day [from Tásarahlá] we saw with joy the fires of the party who had come out to meet us.

Thus we reached the town of Íwálátan [Walata] after a journey from Sijilmása of two months to a day. . . .

My stay at Íwálátan lasted about fifty days; and I was shown honour and entertained by its inhabitants. It is an excessively hot place, and boasts a few small date-palms, in the shade of which they sow watermelons. Its water comes from underground waterbeds at that point, and there is plenty of mutton to be had. The garments of its inhabitants, most of whom belong to the Massúfa tribe, are of fine Egyptian fabrics. Their women are of surpassing beauty, and are shown more respect than the men. The state of affairs amongst these people is indeed extraordinary. Their men show no signs of jealousy whatever; no one claims descent from his father, but on the contrary from his mother's brother. A person's heirs are his sister's sons, not his own sons. This is a thing which I have seen nowhere in the world except among the Indians of Malabar. But those are heathens; *these* people are Muslims, punctilious in observing the hours of prayer, studying books of law, and memorizing the Koran. Yet their women show no bashfulness before men and do not veil themselves, though they are assiduous in attending the prayers. Any man who wishes to marry one of them may do so, but they do not travel with their husbands, and even if one desired to do so her family would not allow her to go.

The women there have "friends" and "companions" amongst the men outside their own families, and the men in the same way have "companions" amongst the women of other families. A man may go into his house and find his wife entertaining her "companion" but he takes no objection to it. One day at Íwálátan I went into the qádí's house, after asking his permission to enter, and found with him a young woman of remarkable beauty. When I saw her I was shocked and turned to go out, but she laughed at me, instead of being overcome by shame, and the qádí said to me "Why are you going out? She is my companion." I was amazed at their conduct, for he was a theologian and a pilgrim to boot. I was told that he had asked the sultan's permission to make the pilgrimage that year with his "companion" (whether this one or not I cannot say) but the sultan would not grant it.

When I decided to make the journey to Mállí, which is reached in twenty-four days from Íwálátan if the traveller pushes on rapidly, I hired a guide from the Massúfa (for there is no necessity to travel in a company on account of the safety of that road), and set out with three of my companions. On the way there are many trees, and these trees are of great age and girth; a whole caravan may shelter in the shade of one of them. There are trees which have neither branches nor leaves, yet the shade cast by their trunks is sufficient to shelter a man. Some of these trees are rotted in the interior and the rain-water collects in them, so that they serve as wells and the people drink of the water inside them. In others there are bees and honey, which is collected by the people. I was surprised to find inside one tree, by which I passed, a man, a weaver, who had set up his loom in it and was actually weaving. . . .

I saw a crocodile in this part of the Nile, close to the bank; it looked just like a small boat. One day I went down to the river to satisfy a need, and lo, one of the blacks came and stood between me and the river. I was amazed at such lack of manners and decency on his part, and spoke of it to someone or other. He answered "His purpose in doing that was solely to protect you from the crocodile, by placing himself between you and it."

## FROM THE THOUSAND AND ONE NIGHTS (14TH CENT.)

*Translated by Husain Haddawy*

This vast collection of tales has been immensely popular both in the Arabic-speaking world and beyond. Its origins are shadowy, but the frame narrative, which provides a motive for the extensive collection of tales, probably developed from a lost Middle Persian text entitled *The Thousand Tales,* compiled from the third century onward.

Much Persian literature was translated into Arabic after 652, when the pre-Islamic Sassanian empire fell to Arab conquerors, and the Arabic tales were incorporated into the flexible framework of the *Nights.* The surviving manuscripts from the Middle Ages vary in length and contents. The selection provided here comes from a fourteenth-century Syrian manuscript, the oldest surviving written version except for a ninth-century Egyptian page, which bears only a fragment of text.

The tenth-century scholar al-Nadīm, who compiled a bibliography of Arabic works, lists the text and describes it as a "vulgar and foolish book." Part of this traditional scholarly resistance (common even now) comes from the book's lack of distinguished poetry—the inclusion of fine poems within prose texts often distinguished great prose in the Arabic tradition. The tales have also been considered immoral, and they often depict women as little more than personifications of cunning, temptation, and intrigue. Because of these factors, and given the unsympathetic Islamic attitude toward fiction in general, scholars have not classified *The Thousand and One Nights* as great literature despite its extensive influence.

The collection has a fascinating textual history. *The Thousand and One Nights* was translated into French in the seventeenth century. European translations, especially the influential English one by Sir Richard Burton (1821–1890), freely incorporated tales from other collections and from oral traditions. These translations were so influential that they were translated back into Arabic, producing major revisions in modern Arabic editions of the medieval text. A truly scholarly edition of the original medieval text did not appear until 1984.

The text is something of a crossroads for world literature: it includes an analogue to Chaucer's *Pardoner's Tale.* In the Arabic version, two thieves agree to rob a merchant; then, overwhelmed with greed, each poisons the other while the merchant proceeds on his journey. There are also parallels to ancient Indian *Jātaka* tales. Many stories in the *Nights,* including the frame narrative, have antecedents in Sanskrit materials, some dating back to fifth-century written texts with even older oral roots. Indian tales found their way into Arabic through Persian and were supplemented at each stage of the journey. Searching for origins, however, leads into an endless labyrinth. One of the *Nights* tales can also be found in work by the second-century Roman writer, Lucian. Another bears a striking resemblance to a sixth-century BCE Greek myth. Ancient Sumerian, Babylonian, and Assyrian tales were passed down by generations of oral storytellers to emerge again in the written record of the *Nights.*

*The Thousand and One Nights* is clearly a compilation made over many centuries by many hands for many purposes. Since merchants, slaves, travelers, and gypsy bands wandered all over the regions of India, Central Asia, and the Middle East, and the tales moved back and forth across the various languages and cultures so extensively, claiming any particular origins for them remains problematic. Even though the influence of oral tradition is clear, all we can really trace, of course, is the written record. As a written document, the work has become elaborately structured, with its delightful tales-within-tales scheme. The most famous frame narrative is the one in which Shahrazad decides to save the women of her community with the power of her own voice and imagination—to conquer, that is, the sword with the word.

## Foreword

*In the Name of God the Compassionate, The Merciful. In Him I Trust*

Praise be to God, the Beneficent King, the Creator of the world and man, who raised the heavens without pillars and spread out the earth as a place of rest and erected the mountains as props and made the water flow from the hard rock and destroyed the race of Thamud, 'Ad, and Pharaoh of the vast domain. I praise Him the Supreme Lord for His guidance, and I thank Him for His infinite grace.

To proceed, I should like to inform the honorable gentlemen and noble readers that the purpose of writing this agreeable and entertaining book is the instruction of those who peruse it, for it abounds with highly edifying histories and excellent lessons for the people of distinction, and it provides them with the opportunity to learn the art of discourse, as well as what happened to kings from the beginnings of time. This book, which I have called *The Thousand and One Nights,* abounds also with splendid biographies that teach the reader to detect deception and to protect himself from it, as well as delight and divert him whenever he is burdened with the cares of life and the ills of this world. It is the Supreme God who is the True Guide.

## [The Story of King Shahrayar and Shahrazad, His Vizier's Daughter]

It is related—but God knows and sees best what lies hidden in the old accounts of bygone peoples and times—that long ago, during the time of the Sasanid dynasty, in the peninsulas of India and Indochina, there lived two kings who were brothers. The older brother was named Shahrayar, the younger Shahzaman. The older, Shahrayar, was a towering knight and a daring champion, invincible, energetic, and implacable. His power reached the remotest corners of the land and its people, so that the country was loyal to him, and his subjects obeyed him. Shahrayar himself lived and ruled in India and Indochina, while to his brother he gave the land of Samarkand to rule as king.

Ten years went by, when one day Shahrayar felt a longing for his brother the king, summoned his vizier (who had two daughters, one called Shahrazad, the other Dinarzad) and bade him go to his brother. Having made preparations, the vizier journeyed day and night until he reached Samarkand. When Shahzaman heard of the vizier's arrival, he went out with his retainers to meet him. He dismounted, embraced him, and asked him for news from his older brother, Shahrayar. The vizier replied that he was well, and that he had sent him to request his brother to visit him. Shahzaman complied with his brother's request and proceeded to make preparations for the journey. In the meantime, he had the vizier camp on the outskirts of the city, and took care of his needs. He sent him what he required of food and fodder, slaughtered many sheep in his honor, and provided him with money and supplies, as well as many horses and camels.

For ten full days he prepared himself for the journey; then he appointed a chamberlain in his place, and left the city to spend the night in his tent, near the vizier. At midnight he returned to his palace in the city, to bid his wife good-bye. But when he entered the palace, he found his wife lying in the arms of one of the kitchen boys. When he saw them, the world turned dark before his eyes and, shaking his head, he said to himself, "I am still here, and this is what she has done when I was barely outside the city. How will it be and what will happen behind my back when I go to visit my brother in India? No. Women are not to be trusted." He got exceedingly angry, adding, "By God, I am king and sovereign in Samarkand, yet my wife has betrayed me and has inflicted this on me." As his anger boiled, he drew his sword and struck both his wife and the cook. Then he dragged them by the heels and threw them from the top of the palace to the trench below. He then left the city and, going to the vizier, ordered that they depart that very hour. The drum was struck, and they set out on their journey, while Shahzaman's heart was on fire because of what his wife had done to him and how she had betrayed him with some cook, some kitchen boy. They journeyed hurriedly, day and night, through deserts and wilds, until they reached the land of King Shahrayar, who had gone out to receive them.

When Shahrayar met them, he embraced his brother, showed him favors, and treated him generously. He offered him quarters in a palace adjoining his own, for King Shahrayar had built two beautiful towering palaces in his garden, one for the guests, the other for the women and members of his household. He gave the guest house to his brother, Shahzaman, after the attendants had gone to scrub it, dry it, furnish it, and open its windows, which overlooked the garden. Thereafter, Shahzaman would spend the whole day at his brother's, return at night to sleep at the palace, then go back to his brother the next morning. But whenever he found himself alone and thought of his ordeal with his wife, he would sigh deeply, then stifle his grief, and say, "Alas, that this great misfortune should have happened to one in my position!" Then he would fret with anxiety, his spirit would sag, and he would say, "None has seen what I have seen." In his depression, he ate less and less, grew pale, and his health deteriorated. He neglected everything, wasted away, and looked ill.

When King Shahrayar looked at his brother and saw how day after day he lost weight and grew thin, pale, ashen, and sickly, he thought that this was because of his expatriation and homesickness for his country and his family, and he said to himself, "My brother is not happy here. I should prepare a goodly gift for him and send him home." For a month he gathered gifts for his brother; then he invited him to see him and said, "Brother, I would like you to know that I intend to go hunting and pursue the roaming deer, for ten days. Then I shall return to prepare you for your journey home. Would you like to go hunting with me?" Shahzaman replied, "Brother, I feel distracted and depressed. Leave me here and go with God's blessing and help."

When Shahrayar heard his brother, he thought that his dejection was because of his homesickness for his country. Not wishing to coerce him, he left him behind, and set out with his retainers and men. When they entered the wilderness, he deployed his men in a circle to begin trapping and hunting.

After his brother's departure, Shahzaman stayed in the palace and, from the window overlooking the garden, watched the birds and trees as he thought of his wife and what she had done to him, and sighed in sorrow. While he agonized over his misfortune, gazing at the heavens and turning a distracted eye on the garden, the private gate of his brother's palace opened, and there emerged, strutting like a dark-eyed deer, the lady, his brother's wife, with twenty slave-girls, ten white and ten black. While Shahzaman looked at them, without being seen, they continued to walk until they stopped below his window, without looking in his direction, thinking that he had gone to the hunt with his brother. Then they sat down, took off their clothes, and suddenly there were ten slave-girls and ten black slaves dressed in the same clothes as the girls. Then the ten black slaves mounted the ten girls, while the lady called, "Mas'ud, Mas'ud!" and a black slave jumped from the tree to the ground, rushed to her, and, raising her legs, went between her thighs and made love to her. Mas'ud topped the lady, while the ten slaves topped the ten girls, and they carried on till noon. When they were done with their business, they got up and washed themselves. Then the ten slaves put on the same clothes again, mingled with the girls, and once more there appeared to be twenty slave-girls. Mas'ud himself jumped over the garden wall and disappeared, while the slave-girls and the lady sauntered to the private gate, went in and, locking the gate behind them, went their way.

All of this happened under King Shahzaman's eyes. When he saw this spectacle of the wife and the women of his brother the great king—how ten slaves put on women's clothes and slept with his brother's paramours and concubines and what Mas'ud did with his brother's wife, in his very palace—and pondered over this calamity and great misfortune, his care and sorrow left him and he said to himself, "This is our common lot. Even though my brother is king and master of the whole world, he cannot protect what is his, his wife and his concubines, and suffers misfortune in his very home. What happened to me is little by comparison. I used to think that I was the only one who has suffered, but from what I have seen, everyone suffers. By God, my misfortune is lighter than that of my brother." He kept marveling and blaming life, whose trials none can escape, and he began to find consolation in his own affliction and forget his grief. When supper came, he ate and drank with relish and zest and, feeling better, kept eating and drinking, enjoying himself and feeling happy. He thought to himself, "I am no longer alone in my misery; I am well."

For ten days, he continued to enjoy his food and drink, and when his brother, King Shahrayar, came back from the hunt, he met him happily, treated him attentively, and greeted him cheerfully. His brother, King Shahrayar, who had missed him, said, "By God, brother, I missed you on this trip and wished you were with me." Shahzaman thanked him and sat down to carouse with him, and when night fell, and food was brought before them, the two ate and drank, and again Shahzaman ate and drank with zest. As time went by, he continued to eat and drink with appetite, and became light-hearted and carefree. His face regained color and became ruddy, and his body gained weight, as his blood circulated and he regained his energy; he was himself again, or even better. King Shahrayar noticed his brother's condition, how he used to be and how he had improved, but kept it to himself until he took him aside one day and said, "My brother Shahzaman, I would like you to do something for me, to satisfy a wish, to answer a question truthfully." Shahzaman asked, "What is it, brother?" He replied, "When you first came to stay with me, I noticed that you kept losing weight, day after day, until your looks changed, your health deteriorated, and your energy sagged. As you continued like this, I thought that what ailed you was your homesickness for your family and your country, but even though I kept noticing that you were wasting away and looking ill, I refrained from questioning you and hid my feelings from you. Then I went hunting, and when I came back, I found that you had recovered and had regained your health. Now I want you to tell me everything and to explain the cause of your deterioration and the cause of your subsequent recovery, without hiding anything from me." When Shahzaman heard what King Shahrayar said, he bowed his head, then said, "As for the cause of my recovery, that I cannot tell you, and I wish that you would excuse me from telling you." The king was greatly astonished at his brother's reply and, burning with curiosity, said, "You must tell me. For now, at least, explain the first cause."

Then Shahzaman related to his brother what happened to him with his own wife, on the night of his departure, from beginning to end, and concluded, "Thus all the while I was with you, great King, whenever I thought of the event and the misfortune that had befallen me, I felt troubled, careworn, and unhappy, and my health deteriorated. This then is the cause." Then he grew silent. When King Shahrayar heard his brother's explanation, he shook his head, greatly amazed at the deceit of women, and prayed to God to protect him from their wickedness, saying, "Brother, you were fortunate in killing your wife and her lover, who gave you good reason to feel troubled, careworn, and ill. In my opinion, what happened to you has never happened to anyone else. By God, had I been in your place, I would have killed at least a hundred or even a thousand women. I would have been furious; I would have gone mad. Now praise be to God who has delivered you from sorrow and distress. But tell me what has caused you to forget your sorrow and regain your health?" Shahzaman replied, "King, I wish that for God's sake you would excuse me from telling you." Shahrayar said, "You must." Shahzaman replied, "I fear that you will feel even more troubled and careworn than I." Shahrayar asked, "How could that be, brother? I insist on hearing your explanation."

Shahzaman then told him about what he had seen from the palace window and the calamity in his very home—how ten slaves, dressed like women, were sleeping with his women and concubines, day and night. He told him everything from beginning to end (but there is no point in repeating that). Then he concluded, "When I saw your own misfortune, I felt better—and said to myself, 'My brother is king of the world, yet such a misfortune has happened to him, and in his very home.' As a result I forgot my care and sorrow, relaxed, and began to eat and drink. This is the cause of my cheer and good spirits."

When King Shahrayar heard what his brother said and found out what had happened to him, he was furious and his blood boiled. He said, "Brother, I can't believe what you say unless I see it with my own eyes." When Shahzaman saw that his brother was in a rage, he said to him, "If you do not believe me, unless you see your misfortune with your own eyes, announce that you plan to go hunting. Then you and I shall set out with your troops, and when we get outside the city, we shall leave our tents and camp with the men behind, enter the city secretly, and go together to your palace. Then the next morning you can see with your own eyes."

King Shahrayar realized that his brother had a good plan and ordered his army to prepare for the trip. He spent the night with his brother, and when God's morning broke, the two rode out of the city with their army, preceded by the camp attendants, who had gone to drive the poles and pitch the tents where the king and his army were to camp. At nightfall King Shahrayar summoned his chief chamberlain and bade him take his place. He entrusted him with the army and ordered that for three days no one was to enter the city. Then he and his brother disguised themselves and entered the city in the dark. They went directly to the palace where Shahzaman resided and slept there till the morning. When they awoke, they sat at the palace window, watching the garden and chatting, until the light broke, the day dawned, and the sun rose. As they watched, the private gate opened, and there emerged as usual the wife of King Shahrayar, walking among twenty slave-girls. They made their way under the trees until they stood below the palace window where the two kings sat. Then they took off their women's clothes, and suddenly there were ten slaves, who mounted the ten girls and made love to them. As for the lady, she called, "Mas'ud, Mas'ud," and a black slave jumped from the tree to the ground, came to her, and said, "What do you want, you slut? Here is Sa'ad al-Din Mas'ud." She laughed and fell on her back, while the slave mounted her and like the others did his business with her. Then the black slaves got up, washed themselves, and, putting on the same clothes, mingled with the girls. Then they walked away, entered the palace, and locked the gate behind them. As for Mas'ud, he jumped over the fence to the road and went on his way.

When King Shahrayar saw the spectacle of his wife and the slave-girls, he went out of his mind, and when he and his brother came down from upstairs, he said, "No one is safe in this world. Such doings are going on in my kingdom, and in my very palace. Perish the world and perish life! This is a great calamity, indeed." Then he turned to his brother and asked, "Would you like to follow me in what I shall do?" Shahzaman answered, "Yes. I will." Shahrayar said, "Let us leave our royal state and roam the world for the love of the Supreme Lord. If we should find one whose misfortune is greater than ours, we shall return. Otherwise, we shall continue to journey through the land, without need for the trappings of royalty." Shahzaman replied, "This is an excellent idea. I shall follow you."

Then they left by the private gate, took a side road, and departed, journeying till nightfall. They slept over their sorrows, and in the morning resumed their day journey until they came to a meadow by the seashore. While they sat in the meadow amid the thick plants and trees, discussing their misfortunes and the recent events, they suddenly heard a shout and a great cry coming from the middle of the sea. They trembled with fear, thinking that the sky had fallen on the earth. Then the sea parted, and there emerged a black pillar that, as it swayed forward, got taller and taller, until it touched the clouds. Shahrayar and Shahzaman were petrified; then they ran in terror and, climbing a very tall tree, sat hiding in its foliage. When they looked again, they saw that the black pillar was cleaving the sea, wading in the water toward the green meadow, until it touched the shore. When they looked again, they saw that it was a black demon, carrying on his head a large glass chest with four steel locks. He came out, walked into the meadow, and where should he stop but under the very tree where the two kings were hiding. The demon sat down and placed the glass chest on the ground. He took out four keys and, opening the locks of the chest, pulled out a full-grown woman. She had a beautiful figure, and a face like the full moon, and a lovely smile. He took her out, laid her under the tree, and looked at her, saying, "Mistress of all noble women, you whom I carried away on your wedding night, I would like to sleep a little." Then he placed his head on the young woman's lap, stretched his legs to the sea, sank into sleep, and began to snore.

Meanwhile, the woman looked up at the tree and, turning her head by chance, saw King Shahrayar and King Shahzaman. She lifted the demon's head from her lap and placed it on the ground. Then she came and stood under the tree and motioned to them with her hand, as if to say, "Come down slowly to me." When they realized that she had seen them, they were frightened, and they begged her and implored her, in the name of the Creator of the heavens, to excuse them from climbing down. She replied, "You must come down to me." They motioned to her, saying, "This sleeping demon is the enemy of mankind. For God's sake, leave us alone." She replied, "You must come down, and if you don't, I shall wake the demon and have him kill you." She kept gesturing and pressing, until they climbed down very slowly and stood before her. Then she lay on her back, raised her legs, and said, "Make love to me and satisfy my need, or else I shall wake the demon, and he will kill you." They replied, "For God's sake, mistress, don't do this to us, for at this moment we feel nothing but dismay and fear of this demon. Please, excuse us." She replied, "You must," and insisted, swearing, "By God who created the heavens, if you don't do it, I shall wake my husband the demon and ask him to kill you and throw you into the sea." As she persisted, they could no longer resist and they made love to her, first the older brother, then the younger. When they were done and withdrew from her, she said to them, "Give me your rings," and, pulling out from the folds of her dress a small purse, opened it, and shook out ninety-eight rings of different fashions and colors. Then she asked them, "Do you know what these rings are?" They answered, "No." She said, "All the owners of these rings slept with me, for whenever one of them made love to me, I took a ring from him. Since you two have slept with me, give me your rings, so that I may add them to the rest, and make a full hundred. A hundred men have known me under the very horns of this filthy, monstrous cuckold, who has imprisoned me in this chest, locked it with four locks, and kept me in the middle of this raging, roaring sea. He has guarded me and tried to keep me pure and chaste, not realizing that nothing can prevent or alter what is predestined and that when a woman desires something, no one can stop her." When Shahrayar and Shahzaman heard what the young woman said, they were greatly amazed, danced with joy, and said, 'O God, O God! There is no power and no strength, save in God the Almighty, the Magnificent. Great is women's cunning.'" Then each of them took off his ring and handed it to her. She took them and put them with the rest in the purse. Then sitting again by the demon, she lifted his head, placed it back on her lap, and motioned to them, "Go on your way, or else I shall wake him."

They turned their backs and took to the road. Then Shahrayar turned to his brother and said, "My brother Shahzaman, look at this sorry plight. By God, it is worse than ours. This is no less than a demon who has carried a young woman away on her wedding night, imprisoned her in a glass chest, locked her up with four locks, and kept her in the middle of the sea, thinking that he could guard her from what God had foreordained, and you saw how she has managed to sleep with ninety-eight men, and added the two of us to make a hundred. Brother, let us go back to our kingdoms and our cities, never to marry a woman again. As for myself, I shall show you what I will do."

Then the two brothers headed home and journeyed till nightfall. On the morning of the third day, they reached their camp and men, entered their tent, and sat on their thrones. The chamberlains, deputies, princes, and viziers came to attend King Shahrayar, while he gave orders and bestowed robes of honor, as well as other gifts. Then at his command everyone returned to the city, and he went to his own palace and ordered his chief vizier, the father of the two girls Shahrazad and Dinarzad, who will be mentioned below, and said to him, "Take that wife of mine and put her to death." Then Shahrayar went to her himself, bound her, and handed her over to the vizier, who took her out and put her to death. Then King Shahrayar grabbed his sword, brandished it, and, entering the palace chambers, killed every one of his slave-girls and replaced them with others. He then swore to marry for one night only and kill the woman the next morning, in order to save himself from the wickedness and cunning of women, saying, "There is not a single chaste woman anywhere on the entire face of the earth." Shortly thereafter he provided his brother Shahzaman with supplies for his journey and sent him back to his own country with gifts, rarities, and money. The brother bade him good-bye and set out for home.

Shahrayar sat on his throne and ordered his vizier, the father of the two girls, to find him a wife from among the princes' daughters. The vizier found him one, and he slept with her and was done with her, and the next morning he ordered the vizier to put her to death. That very night he took one of his army officers' daughters, slept with her, and the next morning ordered the vizier to put her to death. The vizier, who could not disobey him, put her to death. The third night he took one of the merchants' daughters, slept with her till the morning, then ordered his vizier to put her to death, and the vizier did so. It became King Shahrayar's custom to take every night the daughter of a merchant or a commoner, spend the night with her, then have her put to death the next morning. He continued to do this until all the girls perished, their mothers mourned, and there arose a clamor among the fathers and mothers, who called the plague upon his head, complained to the Creator of the heavens, and called for help on Him who hears and answers prayers.

Now, as mentioned earlier, the vizier, who put the girls to death, had an older daughter called Shahrazad and a younger one called Dinarzad. The older daughter, Shahrazad, had read the books of literature, philosophy, and medicine. She knew poetry by heart, had studied historical reports, and was acquainted with the sayings of men and the maxims of sages and kings. She was intelligent, knowledgeable, wise, and refined. She had read and learned. One day she said to her father, "Father, I will tell you what is in my mind." He asked, "What is it?" She answered, "I would like you to marry me to King Shahrayar, so that I may either succeed in saving the people or perish and die like the rest." When the vizier heard what his daughter Shahrazad said, he got angry and said to her, "Foolish one, don't you know that King Shahrayar has sworn to spend but one night with a girl and have her put to death the next morning? If I give you to him, he will sleep with you for one night and will ask me to put you to death the next morning, and I shall have to do it, since I cannot disobey him." She said, "Father, you must give me to him, even if he kills me." He asked, "What has possessed you that you wish to imperil yourself?" She replied, "Father, you must give me to him. This is absolute and final." Her father the vizier became furious and said to her, "Daughter, 'He who misbehaves, ends up in trouble,' and 'He who considers not the end, the world is not his friend.' As the popular saying goes, 'I would be sitting pretty, but for my curiosity.' I am afraid that what happened to the donkey and the ox with the merchant will happen to you." She asked, "Father, what happened to the donkey, the ox, and the merchant?" He said:

## *[The Tale of the Ox and the Donkey]*

There was a prosperous and wealthy merchant who lived in the countryside and labored on a farm. He owned many camels and herds of cattle and employed many men, and he had a wife and many grown-up as well as little children. This merchant was taught the language of the beasts, on condition that if he revealed his secret to anyone, he would die; therefore, even though he knew the language of every kind of animal, he did not let anyone know, for fear of death. One day, as he sat, with his wife beside him and his children playing before him, he glanced at an ox and a donkey he kept at the farmhouse, tied to adjacent troughs, and heard the ox say to the donkey, "Watchful one, I hope that you are enjoying the comfort and the service you are getting. Your ground is swept and watered, and they serve you, feed you sifted barley, and offer you clear, cool water to drink. I, on the contrary, am taken out to plow in the middle of the night. They clamp on my neck something they call yoke and plow, push me all day under the whip to plow the field, and drive me beyond my endurance until my sides are lacerated, and my neck is flayed. They work me from nighttime to nighttime, take me back in the dark, offer me beans soiled with mud and hay mixed with chaff, and let me spend the night lying in urine and dung. Meanwhile you rest on well-swept, watered, and smoothed ground, with a clean trough full of hay. You stand in comfort, save for the rare occasion when our master the merchant rides you to do a brief errand and returns. You are comfortable, while I am weary; you sleep, while I keep awake."

When the ox finished, the donkey turned to him and said, "Greenhorn, they were right in calling you ox, for you ox harbor no deceit, malice, or meanness. Being sincere, you exert and exhaust yourself to comfort others. Have you not heard the saying 'Out of bad luck, they hastened on the road'? You go into the field from early morning to endure your torture at the plow to the point of exhaustion. When the plowman takes you back and ties you to the trough, you go on butting and beating with your horns, kicking with your hoofs, and bellowing for the beans, until they toss them to you; then you begin to eat. Next time, when they bring them to you, don't eat or even touch them, but smell them, then draw back and lie down on the hay and straw. If you do this, life will be better and kinder to you, and you will find relief."

As the ox listened, he was sure that the donkey had given him good advice. He thanked him, commended him to God, and invoked His blessing on him, and said, "May you stay safe from harm, watchful one." All of this conversation took place, daughter, while the merchant listened and understood. On the following day, the plowman came to the merchant's house and, taking the ox, placed the yoke upon his neck and worked him at the plow, but the ox lagged behind. The plowman hit him, but following the donkey's advice, the ox, dissembling, fell on his belly, and the plowman hit him again. Thus the ox kept getting up and falling until nightfall, when the plowman took him home and tied him to the trough. But this time the ox did not bellow or kick the ground with his hoofs. Instead, he withdrew, away from the trough. Astonished, the plowman brought him his beans and fodder, but the ox only smelled the fodder and pulled back and lay down at a distance with the hay and straw, complaining till the morning. When the plowman arrived, he found the trough as he had left it, full of beans and fodder, and saw the ox lying on his back, hardly breathing, his belly puffed, and his legs raised in the air. The plowman felt sorry for him and said to himself, "By God, he did seem weak and unable to work." Then he went to the merchant and said, "Master, last night, the ox refused to eat or touch his fodder."

The merchant, who knew what was going on, said to the plowman, "Go to the wily donkey, put him to the plow, and work him hard until he finishes the ox's task." The plowman left, took the donkey, and placed the yoke upon his neck. Then he took him out to the field and drove him with blows until he finished the ox's work, all the while driving him with blows and beating him until his sides were lacerated and his neck was flayed. At nightfall he took him home, barely able to drag his legs under his tired body and his drooping ears. Meanwhile the ox spent his day resting. He ate all his food, drank his water, and lay quietly, chewing his cud in comfort. All day long he kept praising the donkey's advice and invoking God's blessing on him. When the donkey came back at night, the ox stood up to greet him, saying, "Good evening, watchful one! You have done me a favor beyond description, for I have been sitting in comfort. God bless you for my sake." Seething with anger, the donkey did not reply, but said to himself, "All this happened to me because of my miscalculation. 'I would be sitting pretty, but for my curiosity.' If I don't find a way to return this ox to his former situation, I will perish." Then he went to his trough and lay down, while the ox continued to chew his cud and invoke God's blessing on him.

"You, my daughter, will likewise perish because of your miscalculation. Desist, sit quietly, and don't expose yourself to peril. I advise you out of compassion for you." She replied, "Father, I must go to the king, and you must give me to him." He said, "Don't do it." She insisted, "I must." . . .

* * *

*[The father tells another tale, trying to persuade Shahrazad not to marry the king.]*

She said, "Such tales don't deter me from my request. If you wish, I can tell you many such tales. In the end, if you don't take me to King Shahrayar, I shall go to him by myself behind your back and tell him that you have refused to give me to one like him and that you have begrudged your master one like me." The vizier asked, "Must you really do this?" She replied, "Yes, I must."

Tired and exhausted, the vizier went to King Shahrayar and, kissing the ground before him, told him about his daughter, adding that he would give her to him that very night. The king was astonished and said to him, "Vizier, how is it that you have found it possible to give me your daughter, knowing that I will, by God, the Creator of heaven, ask you to put her to death the next morning and that if you refuse, I will have you put to death too?" He replied, "My King and Lord, I have told her everything and explained all this to her, but she refuses and insists on being with you tonight." The king was delighted and said, "Go to her, prepare her, and bring her to me early in the evening."

The vizier went down, repeated the king's message to his daughter, and said, "May God not deprive me of you." She was very happy and, after preparing herself and packing what she needed, went to her younger sister, Dinarzad, and said, "Sister, listen well to what I am telling you. When I go to the king, I will send for you, and when you come and see that the king has finished with me, say, 'Sister, if you are not sleepy, tell us a story.' Then I will begin to tell a story, and it will cause the king to stop his practice, save myself, and deliver the people." Dinarzad replied, "Very well."

At nightfall the vizier took Shahrazad and went with her to the great King Shahrayar. But when Shahrayar took her to bed and began to fondle her, she wept, and when he asked her, "Why are you crying?" she replied, "I have a sister, and I wish to bid her good-bye before daybreak." Then the king sent for the sister, who came and went to sleep under the bed. When the night wore on, she woke up and waited until the king had satisfied himself with her sister Shahrazad and they were by now all fully awake. Then Dinarzad cleared her throat and said, "Sister, if you are not sleepy, tell us one of your lovely little tales to while away the night, before I bid you good-bye at daybreak, for I don't know what will happen to you tomorrow." Shahrazad turned to King Shahrayar and said, "May I have your permission to tell a story?" He replied, "Yes," and Shahrazad was very happy and said, "Listen":

## *[The Story of the Merchant and the Demon]*

### The First Night

It is said, O wise and happy King, that once there was a prosperous merchant who had abundant wealth and investments and commitments in every country. He had many women and children and kept many servants and slaves. One day, having resolved to visit another country, he took provisions, filling his saddlebag with loaves of bread and with dates, mounted his horse, and set out on his journey. For many days and nights, he journeyed under God's care until he reached his destination. When he finished his business, he turned back to his home and family. He journeyed for three days, and on the fourth day, chancing to come to an orchard, went in to avoid the heat and shade himself from the sun of the open country. He came to a spring under a walnut tree and, tying his horse, sat by the spring, pulled out from the saddlebag some loaves of bread and a handful of dates, and began to eat, throwing the date pits right and left until he had had enough. Then he got up, performed his ablutions, and performed his prayers.

But hardly had he finished when he saw an old demon, with sword in hand, standing with his feet on the ground and his head in the clouds. The demon approached until he stood before him and screamed, saying, "Get up, so that I may kill you with this sword, just as you have killed my son." When the merchant saw and heard the demon, he was terrified and awe-stricken. He asked, "Master, for what crime do you wish to kill me?" The demon replied, "I wish to kill you because you have killed my son." The merchant asked, "Who has killed your son?" The demon replied, "You have killed my son." The merchant said, "By God, I did not kill your son. When and how could that have been?" The demon said, "Didn't you sit down, take out some dates from your saddlebag, and eat, throwing the pits right and left?" The merchant replied, "Yes, I did." The demon said, "You killed my son, for as you were throwing the stones right and left, my son happened to be walking by and was struck and killed by one of them, and I must now kill you." The merchant said, "O my lord, please don't kill me." The demon replied, "I must kill you as you killed him—blood for blood." The merchant said, "To God we belong and to God we return. There is no power or strength, save in God the Almighty, the Magnificent. If I killed him, I did it by mistake. Please forgive me." The demon replied, "By God, I must kill you, as you killed my son." Then he seized him and, throwing him to the ground, raised the sword to strike him. The merchant began to weep and mourn his family and his wife and children. Again, the demon raised his sword to strike, while the merchant cried until he was drenched with tears, saying, "There is no power or strength, save in God the Almighty, the Magnificent." Then he began to recite the following verses:

Life has two days: one peace, one
 wariness,
And has two sides: worry and
 happiness.
Ask him who taunts us with
 adversity,
"Does fate, save those worthy of
 note, oppress?
Don't you see that the blowing,
 raging storms
Only the tallest of the trees beset,
And of earth's many green and
 barren lots,
Only the ones with fruits with
 stones are hit,
And of the countless stars in
 heaven's vault
None is eclipsed except the moon
 and sun?
You thought well of the days, when
 they were good,
Oblivious to the ills destined for
 one.
You were deluded by the peaceful
 nights,
Yet in the peace of night does
 sorrow stun."

When the merchant finished and stopped weeping, the demon said, "By God, I must kill you, as you killed my son, even if you weep blood." The merchant asked, "Must you?" The demon replied, "I must," and raised his sword to strike.

*But morning overtook Shahrazad, and she lapsed into silence, leaving King Shahrayar burning with curiosity to hear the rest of the story. Then Dinarzad said to her sister Shahrazad, "What a strange and lovely story!" Shahrazad replied, "What is this compared with what I shall tell you tomorrow night if the king spares me and lets me live? It will be even better and more entertaining." The king thought to himself, "I will spare her until I hear the rest of the story; then I will have her put to death the next day." When morning broke, the day dawned, and the sun rose; the king left to attend to the affairs of the kingdom, and the vizier, Shahrazad's father, was amazed and delighted. King Shahrayar governed all day and returned home at night to his quarters and got into bed with Shahrazad. Then Dinarzad said to her sister Shahrazad, "Please, sister, if you are not sleepy, tell us one of your lovely little tales to while away the night." The king added, "Let it be the conclusion of the story of the demon and the merchant, for I would like to hear it." Shahrazad replied, "With the greatest pleasure, dear, happy King":*

## The Second Night

It is related, O wise and happy King, that when the demon raised his sword, the merchant asked the demon again, "Must you kill me?" and the demon replied, "Yes." Then the merchant said, "Please give me time to say good-bye to my family and my wife and children, divide my property among them, and appoint guardians. Then I shall come back, so that you may kill me." The demon replied, "I am afraid that if I release you and grant you time, you will go and do what you wish, but will not come back." The merchant said, "I swear to keep my pledge to come back, as the God of Heaven and earth is my witness." The demon asked, "How much time do you need?" The merchant replied, "One year, so that I may see enough of my children, bid my wife good-bye, discharge my obligations to people, and come back on New Year's Day." The demon asked, "Do you swear to God that if I let you go, you will come back on New Year's Day?" The merchant replied, "Yes, I swear to God."

After the merchant swore, the demon released him, and he mounted his horse sadly and went on his way. He journeyed until he reached his home and came to his wife and children. When he saw them, he wept bitterly, and when his family saw his sorrow and grief, they began to reproach him for his behavior, and his wife said, "Husband, what is the matter with you? Why do you mourn, when we are happy, celebrating your return?" He replied, "Why not mourn when I have only one year to live?" Then he told her of his encounter with the demon and informed her that he had sworn to return on New Year's Day, so that the demon might kill him.

When they heard what he said, everyone began to cry. His wife struck her face in lamentation and cut her hair, his daughters wailed, and his little children cried. It was a day of mourning, as all the children gathered around their father to weep and exchange good-byes. The next day he wrote his will, dividing his property, discharged his obligations to people, left bequests and gifts, distributed alms, and engaged reciters to read portions of the Quran in his house. Then he summoned legal witnesses and in their presence freed his slaves and slave-girls, divided among his elder children their shares of the property, appointed guardians for his little ones, and gave his wife her share, according to her marriage contract. He spent the rest of the time with his family, and when the year came to an end, save for the time needed for the journey, he performed his ablutions, performed his prayers, and, carrying his burial shroud, began to bid his family good-bye. His sons hung around his neck, his daughters wept, and his wife wailed. Their mourning scared him, and he began to weep, as he embraced and kissed his children good-bye. He said to them, "Children, this is God's will and decree, for man was created to die." Then he turned away and, mounting his horse, journeyed day and night until he reached the orchard on New Year's Day.

He sat at the place where he had eaten the dates, waiting for the demon, with a heavy heart and tearful eyes. As he waited, an old man, leading a deer on a leash, approached and greeted him, and he returned the greeting. The old man inquired, "Friend, why do you sit here in this place of demons and devils? For in this haunted orchard none come to good." The merchant replied by telling him what had happened to him and the demon, from beginning to end. The old man was amazed at the merchant's fidelity and said, "Yours is a magnificent pledge," adding, "By God, I shall not leave until I see what will happen to you with the demon." Then he sat down beside him and chatted with him. As they talked . . .

*But morning overtook Shahrazad, and she lapsed into silence. As the day dawned, and it was light, her sister Dinarzad said, "What a strange and wonderful story!" Shahrazad replied, "Tomorrow night I shall tell something even stranger and more wonderful than this."*

## The Third Night

*When it was night and Shahrazad was in bed with the king, Dinarzad said to her sister Shahrazad, "Please, if you are not sleepy, tell us one of your lovely little tales to while away the night." The king added, "Let it be the conclusion of the merchant's story." Shahrazad replied, "As you wish":*

I heard, O happy King, that as the merchant and the man with the deer sat talking, another old man approached, with two black hounds, and when he reached them, he greeted them, and they returned his greeting. Then he asked them about themselves, and the man with the deer told him the story of the merchant and the demon, how the merchant had sworn to return on New Year's Day, and how the demon was waiting to kill him. He added that when he himself heard the story, he swore never to leave until he saw what would happen between the merchant and the demon. When the man with the two dogs heard the story, he was amazed, and he too swore never to leave them until he saw what would happen between them. Then he questioned the merchant, and the merchant repeated to him what had happened to him with the demon.

While they were engaged in conversation, a third old man approached and greeted them, and they returned his greeting. He asked, "Why do I see the two of you sitting here, with this merchant between you, looking abject, sad, and dejected?" They told him the merchant's story and explained that they were sitting and waiting to see what would happen to him with the demon. When he heard the story, he sat down with them, saying, "By God, I too like you will not leave, until I see what happens to this man with the demon." As they sat, conversing with one another, they suddenly saw the dust rising from the open country, and when it cleared, they saw the demon approaching, with a drawn steel sword in his hand. He stood before them without greeting them, yanked the merchant with his left hand, and, holding him fast before him, said, "Get ready to die." The merchant and the three old men began to weep and wail.

*But dawn broke and morning overtook Shahrazad, and she lapsed into silence. Then Dinarzad said, "Sister, what a lovely story!" Shahrazad replied, "What is this compared with what I shall tell you tomorrow night? It will be even better; it will be more wonderful, delightful, entertaining, and delectable if the king spares me and lets me live." The king was all curiosity to hear the rest of the story and said to himself, "By God, I will not have her put to death until I hear the rest of the story and find out what happened to the merchant with the demon. Then I will have her put to death the next morning, as I did with the others." Then he went out to attend to the affairs of his kingdom, and when he saw*

*Shahrazad's father, he treated him kindly and showed him favors, and the vizier was amazed. When night came, the king went home, and when he was in bed with Shahrazad, Dinarzad said, "Sister, if you are not sleepy, tell us one of your lovely little tales to while away the night." Shahrazad replied, "With the greatest pleasure":*

*[Each of the old men tells the demon a tale in an effort to save the merchant's life. One of these is The Story of the Fisherman and the Demon.]*

* * *

## [from The Story of the Fisherman and the Demon]

It is related that there was a very old fisherman who had a wife and three daughters and who was so poor that they did not have even enough food for the day. It was this fisherman's custom to cast his net four times a day. One day, while the moon was still up, he went out with his net at the call for the early morning prayer. He reached the outskirts of the city and came to the seashore. Then he set down his basket, rolled up his shirt, and waded to his waist in the water. He cast his net and waited for it to sink; then he gathered the rope and started to pull. As he pulled little by little, he felt that the net was getting heavier until he was unable to pull any further. He climbed ashore, drove a stake into the ground, and tied the end of the rope to the stake. Then he took off his clothes, dove into the water, and went around the net, shaking it and tugging at it until he managed to pull it ashore. Feeling extremely happy, he put on his clothes and went back to the net. But when he opened it, he found inside a dead donkey, which had torn it apart. The fisherman felt sad and depressed and said to himself, "There is no power and no strength save in God, the Almighty, the Magnificent," adding, "Indeed, this is a strange catch!" Then he began to recite the following verses:

O you who brave the danger in
  the dark,
Reduce your toil, for gain is not in
  work.
Look at the fisherman who labors
  at his trade,
As the stars in the night their
  orbits make,
And deeply wades into the raging
  sea,
Steadily gazing at the swelling net,
Till he returns, pleased with his
  nightly catch,
A fish whose mouth the hook of
  death has cut,
And sells it to a man who sleeps
  the night,
Safe from the cold and blessed
  with every wish.
Praised be the Lord who blesses
  and withholds:
This casts the net, but that one
  eats the fish.

*But morning overtook Shahrazad, and she lapsed into silence. Then her sister Dinarzad said, "Sister, what a lovely story!" Shahrazad replied, "Tomorrow night I shall tell you the rest, which is stranger and more wonderful, if the king spares me and lets me live!"*

## The Ninth Night

*The following night Dinarzad said to her sister Shahrazad, "Sister, if you are not sleepy, finish the fisherman's story." Shahrazad replied, "With the greatest pleasure":*

I heard, O happy King, that when the fisherman finished reciting his verses, he pushed the donkey out of the net and sat down to mend it. When he was done, he wrung it out and spread it to dry. Then he waded into the water and, invoking the Almighty God, cast the net and waited for it to sink. Then he pulled the rope little by little, but this time the net was even more firmly snagged. Thinking that it was heavy with fish, he was extremely happy. He took off his clothes and, diving into the water, freed the net and struggled with it until he reached the shore, but inside the net he found a large jar full of nothing but mud and sand. When he saw this, he felt sad and, with tears in his eyes, said to himself, "This is a strange day! God's we are and to God we return," and he began to recite the following verses:

> O my tormenting fate, forbear,
> Or if you can't, at least be fair.
> I went to seek my daily bread,
> But they said to me it was dead.
> And neither luck nor industry
> Brought back my daily bread
> to me.
> The Pleiads many fools attain,
> While sages sit in dark disdain.

Then the fisherman threw the jar away, washed his net, and, wringing it out, spread it to dry. Then he begged the Almighty God for forgiveness and went back to the water. For the third time, he cast the net and waited for it to sink. But when he pulled it up, he found nothing inside but broken pots and bottles, stones, bones, refuse, and the like. He wept at this great injustice and ill luck and began to recite the following verses:

> Your livelihood is not in your own
> hands;
> Neither by writing nor by the pen
> you thrive.
> Your luck and your wages are by
> lot;
> Some lands are waste, and some
> are fertile lands.
> The wheel of fortune lowers the
> man of worth,
> Raising the base man who
> deserves to fall.
> Come then, O death, and end this
> worthless life,
> Where the ducks soar, while the
> falcons are bound to earth.
> No wonder that you see the good
> man poor,
> While the vicious exalts in his
> estate.
> Our wages are alloted; 'tis our fate
> To search like birds for gleanings
> everywhere.
> One bird searches the earth from
> east to west,
> Another gets the tidbits while at
> rest.

Then the fisherman raised his eyes to the heavens and, seeing that the sun had risen and that it was morning and full daylight, said, "O Lord, you know that I cast my net four times only. I have already cast it three times, and there is only one more try left. Lord, let the sea serve me, even as you let it serve Moses." Having mended the net, he cast it into the sea, and waited for it to sink. When he pulled, he found that it was so heavy that he was unable to haul it. He shook it and found that it was caught at the bottom. Saying "There is no power or strength save in God, the Almighty, the Magnificent," he took off his clothes and dove for the net. He worked at it until he managed to free it, and as he hauled it to the shore, he felt that there was something heavy inside. He struggled with the net, until he opened it and found a large long-necked brass jar, with a lead stopper bearing the mark of a seal ring. When the fisherman saw the jar, he was happy and said to himself, "I will sell it in the copper market, for it must be worth at least two measures of wheat." He tried to move the jar, but it was so full and so heavy that he was unable to budge it. Looking at the lead stopper, he said to himself, "I will open the jar, shake out the contents, then roll it before me until I reach the copper market." Then he took out a knife from his belt and began to scrape and struggle with the lead stopper until he pried it loose. He held the stopper in his mouth, tilted the jar to the ground, and shook it, trying to pour out its contents, but when nothing came out, he was extremely surprised.

After a while, there began to emerge from the jar a great column of smoke, which rose and spread over the face of the earth, increasing so much that it covered the sea and rising so high that it reached the clouds and hid the daylight. For a long time, the smoke kept rising from the jar; then it gathered and took shape, and suddenly it shook and there stood a demon, with his feet on the ground and his head in the clouds. He had a head like a tomb, fangs like pincers, a mouth like a cave, teeth like stones, nostrils like trumpets, ears like shields, a throat like an alley, and eyes like lanterns. In short, all one can say is that he was a hideous monster. When the fisherman saw him, he shook with terror, his jaws locked together, and his mouth went dry. The demon cried, "O Solomon, prophet of God, forgive me, forgive me. Never again will I disobey you or defy your command."

*But morning overtook Shahrazad, and she lapsed into silence. Then Dinarzad said, "Sister, what a strange and amazing story!" Shahrazad replied, "Tomorrow night I shall tell you something stranger and more amazing if I stay alive."*

## The Tenth Night

*The following night, when Shahrazad was in bed with King Shahrayar, her sister Dinarzad said, "Please, sister, finish the story of the fisherman." Shahrazad replied, "With the greatest pleasure":*

I heard, O happy King, that when the fisherman heard what the demon said, he asked, "Demon, what are you saying? It has been more than one thousand and eight hundred years since the prophet Solomon died, and we are now ages later. What is your story, and why were you in this jar?" When the demon heard the fisherman, he said, "Be glad!" The fisherman cried, "O happy day!" The demon added, "Be glad that you will soon be put to death." The fisherman said, "You deserve to be put to shame for such tidings. Why do you wish to kill me, I who have released you and delivered you from the bottom of the sea and brought you back to this world?" The demon replied, "Make a wish!" The fisherman was happy and asked, "What shall I wish of you?" The demon replied, "Tell me how you wish to die, and what manner of death you wish me to choose." The fisherman asked, "What is my crime? Is this my reward from you for having delivered you?" The demon replied, "Fisherman, listen to my story." The fisherman said, "Make it short, for I am at my rope's end."

The demon said, "You should know that I am one of the renegade, rebellious demons. I, together with the giant Sakhr, rebelled against the prophet Solomon, the son of David, who sent against me Asif ibn-Barkhiya, who took me by force and bade me be led in defeat and humiliation before the prophet Solomon. When the prophet Solomon saw me, he invoked God to protect him from me and my looks and asked me to submit to him, but I refused. So he called for this brass jar, confined me inside, and sealed it with a lead seal on which he imprinted God's Almighty name. Then he commanded his demons to carry me and throw me into the middle of the sea. I stayed there for two hundred years, saying to myself, 'Whoever sets me free during these two hundred years, I will make him rich.' But the two hundred years went by and were followed by another two hundred, and no one set me free. Then I vowed to myself, 'Whoever sets me free, I will open for him all the treasures of the earth,' but four hundred years went by, and no one set me free. When I entered the next hundred years, I vowed to myself, 'Whoever delivers me, during these hundred years, I will make him king, make myself his servant, and fulfill every day three of his wishes,' but that hundred years too, plus all the intervening years, went by, and no one set me free. Then I raged and raved and growled and snorted and said to myself, 'Whoever delivers me from now on, I will either put him to the worst of deaths or let him choose for himself the manner of death.' Soon you came by and set me free. Tell me how you wish to die."

When the fisherman heard what the demon said, he replied, "To God we belong and to Him we return. After all these years, with my bad luck, I had to set you free now. Forgive me, and God will grant you forgiveness. Destroy me, and God will inflict on you one who will destroy you." The demon replied, "It must be. Tell me how you wish to die." When the fisherman was certain that he was going to die, he mourned and wept, saying, "O my children, may God not deprive us of each other." Again he turned to the demon and said, "For God's sake, release me as a reward for releasing you and delivering you from this jar." The demon replied, "Your death is your reward for releasing me and letting me escape." The fisherman said, "I did you a good turn, and you are about to repay me with a bad one. How true is the sentiment of the following lines:

> Our kindness they repaid with
> ugly deeds,
> Upon my life, the deeds of men
> depraved.
> He who the undeserving aids will
> meet
> The fate of him who the hyena
> saved."

The demon said, "Be brief, for as I have said, I must kill you." Then the fisherman thought to himself, "He is only a demon, while I am a human being, whom God has endowed with reason and thereby made superior to him. He may use his demonic wiles on me, but I will use my reason to deal with him." Then he asked the demon, "Must you kill me?" When the demon replied, "I must," the fisherman said, "By the Almighty name that was engraved on the ring of Solomon the son of David, will you answer me truthfully if I ask you about something?" The demon was upset and said with a shudder, "Ask, and be brief!"

*But morning overtook Shahrazad, and she lapsed into silence. Then Dinarzad said, "Sister, what an amazing and lovely story!" Shahrazad replied, "What is this compared with what I shall tell you tomorrow night if the king spares me and lets me live! It will be even more amazing."*

## The Eleventh Night

*The following night Dinarzad said to her sister Shahrazad, "Sister, if you are not sleepy, finish the story of the fisherman and the demon." Shahrazad replied, "With the greatest pleasure":*

I heard, O King, that the fisherman said, "By the Almighty name, tell me whether you really were inside this jar." The demon replied, "By the Almighty name, I was imprisoned in this jar." The fisherman said, "You are lying, for this jar is not large enough, not even for your hands and feet. How can it be large enough for your whole body?" The demon replied, "By God, I was inside. Don't you believe that I was inside it?" The fisherman said, "No, I don't." Whereupon the demon shook himself and turned into smoke, which rose, stretched over the sea, spread over the land, then gathered, and, little by little, began to enter the jar. When the smoke disappeared completely, the demon shouted from within, "Fisherman, here I am in the jar. Do you believe me now?"

The fisherman at once took out the sealed lead stopper and hurriedly clamped it on the mouth of the jar. Then he cried out, "Demon, now tell me how you wish to die. For I will throw you into this sea, build a house right here, and sit here and stop any fisherman who comes to fish and warn him that there is a demon here, who will kill whoever pulls him out and who will let him choose how he wishes to die." When the demon heard what the fisherman said and found himself imprisoned, he tried to get out but could not, for he was prevented by the seal of Solomon the son of David. Realizing that the fisherman had tricked him, the demon said, "Fisherman, don't do this to me. I was only joking with you." The fisherman replied, "You are lying, you the dirtiest and meanest of demons," and began to roll the jar toward the sea. The demon shouted, "Don't, don't!" But the fisherman replied, "Yes, yes." Then in a soft and submissive voice the demon asked, "Fisherman, what do you intend to do?" The fisherman replied, "I intend to throw you into the sea. The first time you stayed there for eight hundred years. This time I will let you stay until Doomsday. Haven't I said to you, 'Spare me, and God will spare you. Destroy me, and God will destroy you'? But you refused, and persisted in your resolve to do me in and kill me. Now it is my turn to do you in." The demon said, "Fisherman, if you open the jar, I will reward you and make you rich." The fisherman replied, "You are lying, you are lying. Your situation and mine is like that of King Yunan and the sage Duban." The demon asked, "What is their story?"

*[The fisherman tells The Tale of King Yunan and the Sage Duban.]*

* * *

## The Eighteenth Night

*The following night, Dinarzad said to her sister Shahrazad, "Please, sister, if you are not sleepy, tell us one of your lovely little tales to while away the night." The king added, "Let it be the rest of the story of the fisherman and the demon." Shahrazad replied, "With the greatest pleasure":*

I heard, O King, that the fisherman said to the demon, "Had the king spared the sage, God would have spared him and he would have lived, but he refused and insisted on destroying the sage, and the Almighty God destroyed him. You too, demon, had you from the beginning agreed to spare me, I would have spared you, but you refused and insisted on killing me; therefore, I shall punish you by keeping you in this jar and throwing you into the bottom of the sea." The demon cried out, "Fisherman, don't do it. Spare me and save me and don't blame me for my action and my offense against you. If I did ill, you should do good. As the saying goes, 'Be kind to him who wrongs you.' Don't do what Imama did to 'Atika." The fisherman asked, "What did Imama do to 'Atika?" The demon replied, "This is no time and this narrow prison is no place to tell a story, but I shall tell it to you after you release me." The fisherman said, "I must throw you into the sea. There is no way I would let you out and set you free, for I kept imploring you and calling on you, but you refused and insisted on killing me, without any offense or injury that merits punishment, except that I had set you free. When you treated me in this way, I realized that you were unclean from birth, that you were ill-natured, and that you were one who rewards good with ill. After I throw you into the sea, I shall build me a hut here and live in it for your sake, so that if anyone pulls you out, I shall acquaint him with what I suffered at your hands and shall advise him to throw you back into the sea and let you perish or languish there to the end of time, you the dirtiest of demons." The demon replied, "Set me free this time, and I pledge never to bother you or harm you, but to make you rich." When he heard this, the fisherman made the demon pledge and covenant that if the fisherman released him and let him out, he would not harm him but would serve him and be good to him.

After the fisherman secured the demon's pledge, by making him swear by the Almighty Name, he opened the seal of the jar, and the smoke began to rise. When the smoke was completely out of the jar, it gathered and turned again into a full-fledged demon, who kicked the jar away and sent it flying to the middle of the sea. When the fisherman saw what the demon had done, sure that he was going to meet with disaster and death, he wet himself and said, "This is a bad omen." Then he summoned his courage and cried out, "Demon, you have sworn and given me your pledge. Don't betray me. Come back, lest the Almighty God punish you for your betrayal. Demon, I repeat to you what the sage Duban said to King Yunan, 'Spare me, and God will spare you; destroy me, and God will destroy you.'" When the demon heard what the fisherman said, he laughed, and when the fisherman cried out again, "Demon, spare me," he replied, "Fisherman, follow me," and the fisherman followed him, hardly believing in his escape, until they came to a mountain outside the city. They climbed over to the other side and came to a vast wilderness, in the middle of which stood a lake surrounded by four hills.

The demon halted by the lake and ordered the fisherman to cast his net and fish. The fisherman looked at the lake and marveled as he saw fish in many colors, white, red, blue, and yellow. He cast his net, and when he pulled, he found four fish inside, one red, one white, one blue, and one yellow. When he saw them, he was full of admiration and delight. The demon said to him, "Take them to the king of your city and offer them to him, and he will give you enough to make you rich. Please excuse me, for I know no other way to make you rich. But don't fish here more than once a day." Then, saying, "I shall miss you," the demon kicked the ground with his foot, and it opened and swallowed him. The fisherman, O King, returned to the city, still marveling at his encounter with the demon and at the colored fish. He entered the royal palace, and when he offered the fish to the king, the king looked at them . . .

*But morning overtook Shahrazad, and she lapsed into silence. Then Dinarzad said, "Sister, what an amazing and entertaining story!" Shahrazad replied, "What is this compared with what I shall tell you tomorrow night if the king spares me and lets me live!"*

## FROM THE BOOK OF DEDE KORKUT (14TH CENT.)

*Translated by Geoffrey Lewis*

This heroic literature originated in the oral traditions of the Oghuz people, a tribal group that moved from eastern Central Asia to the lands around the Caspian Sea in the ninth and tenth centuries. The tales, some historically based and others quite fanciful, were written down in the fourteenth century, although modern editions are commonly based on two manuscripts dating from the sixteenth century. The book is named after the narrator (*dede* is an honorific title, meaning "grandfather" or "holy one"). Korkut functions as bard, philosopher, soothsayer, and historian; he is credited, by legend, with inventing the lute. Today's Turks consider the *Dede Korkut* their national epic. It consists of twelve separate but loosely related tales featuring family members of the Great Khan Bayindir and his son-in-law Salur Kazan. The work is a mixture of prose and highly poetic declamatory passages.

When the text was composed, Islam had been just recently introduced to the nomadic Oghuz people. Thus, while Islam is referred to in the narratives, it seems to have minimal impact on the social codes and rituals depicted in the tales. Muhammad and God are, however, frequently invoked for divine assistance. One tale from the collection is reproduced here. It is written in colloquial language and features a contest between two "brothers," one of whom is monstrous and unnatural and the other aristocratic, although raised by a lioness in the wilderness. This tale contains elements also found in *The Epic of Gilgamesh* (pp. 37–67) and in Homer's *Odyssey* (especially the Polyphemos episode, pp. 456–467), and it shares features found in medieval Romance materials of the Middle East and Europe.

## *How Basat Killed Goggle-eye, O My Khan!*

It is related, my Khan, that once while the Oghuz were sitting in their encampment the enemy fell upon them. In the darkness of night they broke and scattered. As they fled, the baby son of Uruz Koja fell. A lioness found him, carried him off and nursed him. Time passed, and the Oghuz came back and settled in their old home. One day the horse-drover of Oghuz Khan brought him news. 'My Khan, there is a lion comes out of the thicket roaring, but he walks with a swagger, like a man. He attacks the horses and sucks their blood.' Said Uruz, 'My Khan, maybe it is my little son who fell that time when we scattered.' The nobles mounted their horses and came to the lair of the lioness. They drove her off and seized the boy. Uruz took him to his tent. They held a celebration, there was eating and drinking. But for all that they had brought the boy home he would not stay; back he went to the lion's lair. Again they seized him and brought him back. Dede Korkut came and said, 'My boy, you are a human being; do not consort with wild beasts. Come, ride fine horses, amble and trot in company with fine young men. Your elder brother's name is Kiyan Seljuk, your name shall be Basat. I have given you your name; may God give you long life.'

One day the Oghuz migrated to their summer pasture. Now Uruz had a shepherd whom they called Konur Koja Saru Choban. Whenever the Oghuz migrated this man always went first. There was a spring called Uzun Pinar, which had become a haunt of the peris. Suddenly something startled the sheep. The shepherd was angry with the goat which led the flock, and he went forward, to see that the peri maidens had spread their wings and were flying. He threw his cloak over them and caught one. He desired her and straightway violated her. The flock began to scatter; he ran to head them off, and the peri beat her wings and flew away, saying, 'Shepherd, you have left something in trust with me. When a year has passed, come and take it. But you have brought ruination on the Oghuz.' Fear fell on the shepherd's heart and his face turned pale with anxiety at the peri's words.

Time passed, and again the Oghuz migrated to that summer pasture. Again the shepherd came to that spring. Again something startled the sheep and again the shepherd went forward. He saw a brightly glittering shape lying on the ground. The peri appeared and said, 'Come, shepherd, take back your property. But you have brought ruination on the Oghuz.' Seeing this shape, the shepherd was seized with dread. He turned round and began to rain stones on it from his sling. As each stone struck it, it grew bigger. The shepherd abandoned the shape and fled, and the sheep followed him. Now it happened that at that time Bayindir Khan and the nobles had gone out riding, and they chanced on this spring. They saw a monstrous thing lying there, its head indistinguishable from its arse. They surrounded it, and one warrior dismounted and kicked it. At every kick it grew in size. Several other warriors dismounted and kicked it, and still it grew at every kick. Uruz Koja also dismounted and kicked it. His spur drove into it and the shape split down the middle, and out came a child. Its body was that of a man, but it had one eye at the top of its head. Uruz took this child, wrapped it in the skirt of his garment and said, 'My Khan, give this to me and I shall rear it together with my son Basat.' 'Take it,' said Bayindir Khan, 'it's yours.'

Uruz took Goggle-eye and brought him to his house. He ordered a wet-nurse to come, and she put her nipple into the child's mouth. He gave one suck and took all her milk; a second suck, and he took her blood; a third, and took her life. Several other wet-nurses were brought and he destroyed them. Seeing that this was impossible, they decided to feed him on milk, but a cauldronful a day was not enough. They fed him and he grew; he began to walk, he began to play with the little boys. He started to eat the nose of one, the ear of another. The upshot was that the whole camp was greatly upset at him, but there was nothing they could do. They complained and wept in chorus before Uruz. Uruz beat Goggle-eye, he abused him, he ordered him to stop it, but he paid no attention. Finally he drove him from his house.

Goggle-eye's peri mother came and put a ring on her son's finger, saying, 'My son, this is so that no arrow will pierce you or sword cut you.' Goggle-eye left the Oghuz land and came to a high mountain. He infested the roads, he seized men, he became a notorious outlaw. Many men were sent against him; they shot arrows, which did not pierce him; they struck at him with swords, which did not cut him; they thrust at him with lances, which did not penetrate him. No shepherd, no herd-boy was left; he ate them all. Then he began to eat people from the Oghuz. The Oghuz assembled and marched against him. Seeing them, Goggle-eye was angered; he uprooted a tree, threw it, and destroyed fifty or sixty men. He dealt a blow at the prince of heroes, Kazan, and the world became too narrow for his head. Kara Göne, Kazan's brother, became helpless in Goggle-eye's hand. Alp Rüstem son of Düzen was killed. So valiant a man as the son of Ushun Koja died by his hand. His two pure-souled brothers perished at his hand. So too did Bügdüz Emen of the bloody moustaches. White-headed Uruz Koja he made vomit blood, and his son Kiyan Seljuk's gall-bladder split with terror. The Oghuz could do nothing against Goggle-eye, they broke and fled. Goggle-eye hemmed them in and barred their way, he would not let them go, he brought them back to where they were. In all, the Oghuz broke seven times, and seven times he barred their way and brought them back. The Oghuz were totally helpless in Goggle-eye's hand.

They went and called Dede Korkut, they consulted with him and said, 'Come, let us make terms.' They sent Dede Korkut to Goggle-eye. He came and greeted him, then he said, 'Goggle-eye, my son, the Oghuz are helpless in your hand, they are overwhelmed.

They have sent me to the dust of your feet; they wish to come to terms with you.' Goggle-eye said, 'Give me sixty men a day to eat.' Dede Korkut replied, 'This way you won't have any men left; you'll exhaust the supply. Let us give you two men and five hundred sheep a day.' 'Very well,' replied Goggle-eye, 'so be it, I agree. And give me two men to prepare my food for me to eat.' Dede Korkut returned to the Oghuz and told them, 'Give Goggle-eye Yünlü Koja and Yapaghilu Koja to cook his food. He also asks for two men and five hundred sheep a day.' They agreed. Whoever had four sons gave one of them, leaving three. Whoever had three gave one of them, leaving two. Whoever had two gave one, leaving one. There was a man called Kapak Kan, who had two sons. One he gave and one was left. His turn came round again. The mother screamed and cried and lamented.

Now it seems, my Khan, that Basat son of Uruz, who had gone on an expedition into the lands of the infidel, returned at this point. The poor woman said to herself, 'Basat has just come back from raiding. I'll go and perhaps he might give me a prisoner so that I can ransom my son.' Basat had pitched his gold-adorned pavilion and was sitting in it, when he saw a lady approaching. She came in, greeted Basat and wept, saying,

'Son of Uruz, my lord Basat,
Renowned among the Inner
  Oghuz and the Outer Oghuz.
With your flighted arrows that do
  not stay in your hand,
With your strong bow of the horn
  of the he-goat,
Help me!'

Said Basat, 'What is it you desire?' The poor woman replied, 'On the face of this treacherous world there has erupted a man who has not let the Oghuz rest in their domain. Those who wield the pure black steel swords have not cut a hair of his that might be cut; those who brandish the bamboo lances have not been able to make them penetrate; those who shoot the hornbeam arrows have achieved nothing. He dealt a blow at Kazan, prince of heroes; Kazan's brother Kara Göne and Bügdüz Emen of the bloody moustaches became powerless in his hand. Your white-bearded father Uruz he made vomit blood; your brother Kiyan Seljuk's gall-bladder burst on the field of battle and he gave up his soul. Of the other nobles of the teeming Oghuz, some he overpowered and some he killed. Seven times he drove the Oghuz from their place. Then he agreed to make terms; he demanded two men and five hundred sheep a day. They gave him Yünlü Kola and Yapaghilu Koja to serve him. Whoever had four sons gave one of them, whoever had three sons gave one of them, whoever had two sons gave one of them. I had two dear sons and gave one, and one remained. Now the turn has come round to me again and they are asking for him too. Help me, my lord!' Basat's dark eyes filled with tears. He declaimed for his brother; let us see, my Khan, what he declaimed.

'Your tents, pitched in a place
  apart,
Can that pitiless one have
  overthrown, brother?
Your swift-running horses from
  their stalls
Can that pitiless one have stolen,
  brother?
Your sturdy young camels from
  their file

Can that pitiless one have taken,
brother?
The sheep you would slaughter at
your feasting
Can that pitiless one have
slaughtered, brother?
Your dear bride I proudly saw you
bring home
Can that pitiless one have parted
from you, brother?
You have made my white-bearded
father mourn his son;
Can this be, O my brother?
You have made my white-skinned
mother weep;
Can this be, O my brother?
Brother, pinnacle of my black
mountain yonder!
Brother, flood of my lovely
eddying river!
Brother, strength of my strong
back!
Brother, light of my dark eyes!
I have lost my brother.'

So saying, he wept and lamented greatly. Then he gave that lady a captive and said, 'Go, ransom your son.' The lady took the captive and came and gave him in place of her son. Moreover she brought Uruz the good news that his son had come home.

Uruz rejoiced, and came with the nobles of the teeming Oghuz to meet Basat. Basat kissed his father's hand and they cried and wept together. He came to his mother's house. His mother came to meet him and pressed her dear son to her heart. Basat kissed his mother's hand, they embraced and wept together. The Oghuz nobles assembled and there was eating and drinking. Basat said, 'Princes, I shall meet Goggle-eye for my brother's sake; what do you say?' Thereupon Kazan Bey declaimed; let us see, my Khan, what he declaimed.

'Goggle-eye burst forth, a black
dragon!
I chased him round the face of the
sky but could not catch him,
Basat.
Goggle-eye burst forth, a black
tiger!
I chased him round the darkling
mountains but could not
catch him, Basat.
Goggle-eye burst forth, a raging
lion!
I chased him round the dense
forests but could not catch him,
Basat.
Though you be a man, though you
be a prince,
You will not be like me, Kazan.
Do not make your white-bearded
father cry!
Do not make your white-haired
mother weep!'

'I shall surely go,' said Basat, and Kazan replied, 'You know best.' Then Uruz wept and said, 'Son, do not leave my hearth desolate. I beg you, don't go.' Basat answered, 'No, my white-bearded honoured father, I shall go,' and he would not listen. He took from his quiver a fistful of arrows and stuck them in his belt, he girded on his sword, he grasped his bow, he rolled up his skirts, he kissed his parents' hands, he made his peace with all, he said 'Good-bye!'

He came to the crag of Salakhana, where Goggle-eye was. He saw Goggle-eye lying with his back to the sun. He took an arrow from his belt and shot it at Goggle-eye's back. The arrow did not penetrate, it broke. He shot another, which also broke. Goggle-eye said to the cooks, 'The flies here are a bit of a nuisance.' Basat shot another arrow, and that broke too. One piece fell in front of Goggle-eye, who leaped up and looked around. When he saw Basat, he clapped his hands and bellowed with laughter. He said to the cooks, 'Another spring lamb from the Oghuz!' He clutched Basat and held him, he dangled him by the throat, he brought him into his den, he pushed him into the leg of his boot and said, 'Cooks! This afternoon you will put this one on the spit for me and I'll eat him.' Then he fell asleep again. Now Basat had a dagger, and he cut the boot and slipped out. 'Tell me, men,' said he, 'how can this creature be killed?' 'We do not know,' they answered, 'but there is no flesh anywhere except his eye.' Basat advanced right up to Goggle-eye's head, raised his eyelid and saw that his eye was indeed flesh. 'Come on, men,' he said, 'put the spit in the fire and get it red-hot.' They did so. Then Basat took it in his hand, invoked blessings on Muhammad of beautiful name, and drove the spit into Goggle-eye's eye, which was destroyed. So loud did he scream and bellow that the mountains and rocks echoed.

Basat bounded into the midst of the sheep, down into the cave. Goggle-eye knew Basat was in the cave. He set himself at the entrance, put a foot on each side of it and said, 'Ho billy-goats, leaders of the flock, come one by one and pass through.' They did so, and he patted each one's head. 'My dear yearlings, and you my good fortune, my white-blazed ram, come and pass through.' A ram rose up and stretched itself. At once Basat leaped at it, cut its throat and flayed it. He left the head and tail attached to the skin, and got inside it. Basat came in front of Goggle-eye. Now Goggle-eye guessed that Basat was inside the skin, and said, 'White-blazed ram, you knew through what part I might be destroyed. I shall dash you against the cave-wall so that your tail greases the cave.' Basat gave the ram's head into Goggle-eye's hand, and Goggle-eye grasped it tightly by the muzzle. He lifted it and held the muzzle with the skin hanging. Basat slipped between Goggle-eye's legs and away. Goggle-eye raised the muzzle, dashed it against the ground and said, 'Boy, have you escaped?' Basat replied, 'My God has saved me.' Said Goggle-eye, 'Boy, take this ring which is on my finger and put it on your own finger, and arrow and sword will have no effect on you.' Basat took the ring and put it on his finger. 'Boy,' said Goggle-eye, 'have you taken the ring and put it on?' 'I have,' said Basat. Goggle-eye rushed at Basat, flailing and cutting with a dagger. He leaped away and stood on open ground. He saw that the ring was now lying under Goggle-eye's foot. 'Have you escaped?' asked Goggle-eye. Basat replied, 'My God has saved me.' Said Goggle-eye, 'Boy, do you see that vault?' 'I see it,' he replied. Goggle-eye said, 'I have a treasure; go and seal it so that the cooks don't take it.' Basat entered the vault and saw mounds of gold and silver. Looking at it, he forgot himself. Goggle-eye shut the door of the vault and said, 'Are you inside there?' 'I am,' replied Basat. Goggle-eye said, 'I shall shake it so that you and the vault are dashed to pieces.' There came to Basat's tongue the words 'There is no god but God; Muhammad is the Messenger of God.' Straightway the vault split and doors were opened in seven places, through one of which he came out. Goggle-eye put his hand against the vault and pushed so hard that the vault crumbled to bits. Said Goggle-eye, 'Boy, have you escaped?' Basat replied, 'My God has saved me.' Said Goggle-eye, 'It seems you can't be killed. Do you see that cave?' 'I see it,' said Basat. 'There are two swords in it,' said Goggle-eye, 'one with a scabbard and one without. The one without a scabbard will cut off my head. Go fetch it and cut off my head.' Basat went up to the opening of the cave. He saw a sword without a scabbard, ceaselessly moving up and down. 'I shan't get hold of this,' said he, 'without a bit of trouble.' He drew his own sword and held it out, and the moving sword split it in two. He went and fetched a tree and held it against the sword, which split it in two also. Then he took his bow in his hand, and with an arrow he struck the chain by which the sword was suspended. The sword fell and buried itself in the ground. He put it into his own scabbard and held it firmly by the hilt. He came out and said, 'Hey Goggle-eye! How are you?' Goggle-eye answered, 'Hey boy! Aren't you dead yet?' 'My God has saved me,' replied Basat. 'It seems you can't be killed,' said Goggle-eye. Then crying loudly he declaimed; let us see, my Khan, what he declaimed.

'My eye, my eye, my only eye!
With you, my only eye,
I once routed the Oghuz.
Man, you have robbed me of my
chestnut eye;
May the Almighty rob you of your
sweet life!
Such pain I suffer in my eye,
May God Almighty give no man
pain in the eye.'

Then again he spoke:

'What is the place where you
dwell, man, and whence you
migrate in the summer?
If you lose your way in the dark
night, what is your watchword?
Who is your Khan who carries the
great standard?
Who is your hero who leads on the
day of battle?
What is the name of your white-
bearded father?
For a valiant warrior to conceal his
name from another is shameful;
What is your name, man? Tell me.'

Basat declaimed to Goggle-eye; let us see, my Khan, what he declaimed.

'My place where I dwell, whence I
migrate in the summer, is the
southland.
If I lose my way in the dark night,
my watchword is God.
Our Khan who carries the great
standard is Bayindir Khan.
Our hero who leads on the day of
battle is Salur Kazan.
If you ask my father's name, it is
Mighty Tree.
If you ask my mother's name, it is
Raging Lioness.
If you ask my name, it is Basat son
of Uruz.'

'Then we are brothers!' said Goggle-eye, 'Spare me!' Basat replied,

'You filthy scoundrel, you have
made my white-bearded father
weep,
You have made my old
white-haired mother cry,
You have killed my brother Kiyan,
You have widowed my white-
skinned sister-in-law,
You have orphaned her chestnut-
eyed babes;

Shall I let you be?
Till I have wielded my pure black steel sword,
Till I have cut off your pointed-capped head,
Till I have spilled your red blood on the ground,
Till I have avenged my brother Kiyan,
I shall not let you be.'

Thereupon Goggle-eye declaimed once more:

'I meant to rise up from my place,
To break my pact with the nobles of the teeming Oghuz,
To kill their newborn young,
To have once more my fill of man-meat.
I meant, when the nobles of the teeming Oghuz massed against me,
To flee and shelter at the crag of Salakhana,
To cast rocks from a mighty catapult,
To go down, let the rocks fall on my head, and die.
Man, you have robbed me of my chestnut eye;
May the Almighty rob you of your sweet life!'

Yet again Goggle-eye declaimed:

'I have made the white-bearded old men weep much;
Their white beards' curse must have smitten you, O my eye!
I have made the white-haired old women weep much;
Their tears must have smitten you, O my eye!
Many the dark-moustached youths I have eaten;
Their manhood must have smitten you, O my eye!
Many the maidens I have eaten, their little hands dyed with henna;
Their small curses must have smitten you, O my eye!
Such pain I suffer in my eye,
May God Almighty give no man pain in the eye.
My eye, my eye, O my eye, my only eye!'

Basat, enraged, rose up and forced him down on his knees like a camel, and with Goggle-eye's own sword he cut off Goggle-eye's head. He made a hole in it, tied his bowstring to it and dragged it and dragged it until he reached the door of the cave. He sent Yünlü Koja and Yapaghilu Koja to take the good news to the Oghuz. They mounted grey-white horses and galloped away.

The news came to the lands of the teeming Oghuz. Horse-mouthed Uruz Koja galloped to his tent and gave Basat's mother glad tidings. 'Good news!' he said, 'Your son has killed Goggle-eye!' The nobles of the teeming Oghuz arrived, they came to the crag of Salakhana and brought out the head of Goggle-eye for all to see. Dede Korkut came and played joyful music. He related the adventures of the valiant fighters for the Faith, and he invoked blessings on Basat:

'When you reach the black mountain may He make a way,
May He give you passage across the blood-red water.'

And he said,

'Manfully have you avenged your brother's blood,

You have saved the nobles of the
  teeming Oghuz from a heavy
  burden;
May Almighty God give you
  honour and glory, Basat!'

When the hour of death comes may it not part you from the pure Faith, and may He forgive your sins for the sake of Muhammad the Chosen of beautiful name, O my Khan!

## Arabic and Persian Poetry

Over the course of the Middle Period, Arabic and Persian poetry flourished in many forms. The poetic genre of the *qasīdah* held the most revered place, but once classical Arabic verse was canonized within the cultural tradition, new generations of poets struggled against the constraints of older forms. They produced poetry in what is called *badī'*, or the "new" style. Like all poetic traditions, great Arabic and Persian texts range from elegy to love poems, from satires to mystical verses, from heroic praises to lighthearted songs. Sometimes, however, what appears to be a drinking song may in fact be a mystical poem about the intoxicating experience of the divine, and the same sort of spiritual analogy can inform love poetry. The selections included here move across many centuries and across many sentiments, in both the Arabic and Persian languages. These shorter poems—alongside the *qasīdahs* (pp. 725–738) and poetic narratives like *The Conference of Birds* (pp. 811–832)—give the reader an inkling of the vast poetic treasures to be found in Middle Eastern literature of the Middle Period.

The poems from early anthologies record traces of tribal oral culture from the Arabian peninsula. The pre-Islamic world had an extremely high regard for poetry and poets. *Ruwāh* (reciters) devoted themselves to memorizing poetry and to reciting it at markets and festivals throughout Arabia, often adding their own compositions. Feasts were held when an accomplished poet emerged among the tribes and settlements. Poetic craft was seen as a useful weapon for retaliating against insults and for defending one's tribal honor. It was also a creative power that could help a tribe gain fame and preserve its glorious deeds forever. The poet's roles often fused with the roles of healers and shamans in pre-Islamic society. Since pre-Islamic culture considered death final, death-defying fame achieved by feats of heroism was an important element in this poetry, just as it was in the epics of ancient Greece and Rome. 'Antara (fifth or sixth century), author of one of the great *Mu'allaqāt,* is reputed to have written the heroic verse included here. Also taken from early anthologies are an anonymous poem ("My love is ascending with the Yemen caravan"; verses by al-Farazdāk (c. 650–c. 728); and two elegies written for her brother by the most famous woman poet of early Arabic, al-Khansā' of Sulaim (580–640).

From the eighth century on, many poetic innovations were introduced. Bashshār Ibn Burd (714–783), blind from birth and son of a Persian freedman who lived in Basra, was honored in both Umayyad and 'Abbasid courts. His poems mark the beginnings of the *badī'* style. Abū Nuwās (747–813) took *badī'* even further and is noted for his mocking attitudes toward the desert images and conventions of the Classical Period. Satirizing the conventional opening lines of the *qasīdah,* he writes:

The lovelorn wretch stopped at a desert camping ground to question it,
and I stopped to inquire after the local tavern.

Despite its entrenched conventions (and despite *badī'*), early poetry of the *Jāhiliyyah*—with its images of the desert, oasis, tent, and camel, and its pervasive nostalgia characteristic of nomadic tribal literature—echoes through much later Arabic poetry, whether composed in the lush gardens of twelfth-century Moorish Spain or in the refined and distinctly intellectual urban world of ninth-century Baghdad. Al-Ma'arrī (973–1058), another famous blind poet, was born and raised in Syria, traveled considerably, and returned home to compose skeptical and somewhat cynical verse tinged with sadness.

Poets of the *Maghrib* ("West," i.e., North Africa and Spain) attained poetic heights rivaling any achieved in Baghdad, Persia, or Damascus. Ibn Ḥazm (994–1063), called the "greatest scholar and the most original thinker in Spanish Islam," produced, along with philosophic and religious writings, a body of love poetry called *Tawq al-Hamāmah,* or *The Dove's Necklace.* Influenced by Neoplatonic doctrine, Ḥazm's poems are found interspersed within a prose discussion of the nature of love. Writing two centuries before the Provençal love poets, Ḥazm situates true love in the soul and emphasizes the ennobling power of love. A number of Andalusian poets influenced European vernacular lyrics, among them Ḥazm especially, but also poets like Ibn Zaidūn (1003–1071) and Ibn Quzmān (d. 1160). Ibn Zaidūn's *Nūniyya,* or poem rhymed *Nūn* (that is, a rhyme scheme focused around "n" sounds), was written for his beloved Wallāda, a woman who rejected him in favor of a lesser poet. Classically formed and highly personal, Ibn Zaidūn's poem addresses the woman not as a convention, but rather as a real person. The *Nūniyya* is one of the best-known love poems from Moorish literature. Ibn Quzmān is one of the greatest Andalusian poets, whose irony and rebellious rejection of classical tradition are illustrated in the poem selected here.

In the East, Jalāl al-Dīn Rūmī (1207–1273) emerged as one of Islam's finest poets and certainly Persia's most original mystical poet. Like Farīd al-Dīn Attar (see pp. 809–832), Rūmī exemplifies the fine literary tradition that grew from Sufi mysticism. Rūmī founded the Mevlevi order of dervishes and composed two literary masterpieces: the *Divan Shams-i Tabriz* (a collection of *ghazals*) and the *Masnavi* (a massive religious poem often called the "Persian Qur'ān" and considered second only to Ferdowsi's *Shāh-nāmah* in literary stature). The Persian poet Ḥāfiẓ of Shiraz (1320–1389) is recognized as master of the Persian *ghazal,* a genre of poetry akin to the European lyric or sonnet. The various translations included here only hint at the eloquence and power of the originals.

# Arabic Script

Several types of Arabic script have developed over the centuries. In a culture that generally rejects pictorial representations, calligraphy often adorns manuscripts, buildings, ceramics, metalworks, and monuments for aesthetic effect. Pictured here are several different types of script:

**(1)** *naskhi,* perfected in the tenth century and widely used for writing books; **(2)** *thuluth,* similar to *naskhi* but more ornate and often used for writing book titles, chapter and section headings; **(3)** *farisi,* common in Iran and many communities of eastern Islam; **(4)** *diwani-rayhani,* widely used under the Ottomans and in Egypt (for a time, reserved exclusively for Ottoman decrees and held in great esteem); **(5)** *ruq`ah,* used for government documents, letters, and common everyday use; **(6)** *kufi,* the oldest surviving type of Arabic script, which became more ornate under the `Abbasids and gave rise to the other types (still appears on coins, monuments, and inscriptions).

**(1)**

**(2)**

**(3)**
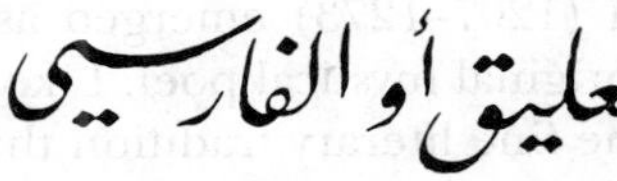


**(4)**

**(5)**

**(6)**

## 'Antarah (5th–6th cent.)

*Translated by A.J. Arberry*

### *"Make war on me, O vicissitudes of the nights"*

Make war on me, O vicissitudes of the nights, (now) on my right
hand and now on my left,
And labour to be hostile to me and to thwart me; by Allah! you
have never occupied my mind.
I have a high purpose firmer than a rock and stronger than
immovable mountains,
And a sword which, when I strike with it ever, the useless
spearheads give way before it,
And a lance-point which, whenever I lose my way in the night,
guides me and restores me from straying,
And a mettlesome steed that never sped, but that the lightning
trailed behind it from the striking of its hooves.
Dark of hue (it is), splitting the starless night with a blackness,
between its eyes a blaze like the crescent moon,
Ransoming me with its own life, and I ransom it with my life,
on the day of battle, and (with) my wealth.
And whenever the market of the war of the tall lances is afoot,
and it blazes with the polished, whetted blades,
I am the broker thereof, and my spear-point is a merchant
purchasing precious souls.
Wild beasts of the wilderness, when war breaks into flame, follow
me from the empty wastes;
Follow me, (and) you will see the blood of the foemen streaming
between the hillocks and the sands.
Then return thereafter, and thank me, and remember what you
have seen of my deeds,
And take sustenance of the skulls of the people for your little
children and your whelps.

## Anonymous (5th–6th cent.)

*Translated by Herbert Howarth and Ibrahim Shukrallah*

### *"My love is ascending with the Yemen caravan"*

My love is ascending with the Yemen caravan
My body is in Mecca in chains.

But once she came eddying towards me
The bars were fast but she came
Came and gave me greeting, and rose
And turned and pivoted my life that way

My head is bent not for death or anything.
I am not tired of the gyves, my soul
Is immune from the loud promises

Only a longing for the days has disarmed me
The days when we met and I was free.

 You are lost if the riddle approaches.
 If it turns its back you guess it.
 You see that you see no matter right
 Unless you methodically reverse it.
 To the lamp of noon night fetches
 The obscure vehicle of its light.

## *al-Khansā' (580–640)*

### *Lament for a Brother*

*Translated by Omar S. Pound*

What have we done to you, death
that you treat us so,
with always another catch
one day a warrior
the next a head of state;
charmed by the loyal
you choose the best.
Iniquitous, unequalling death
I would not complain
if you were just
but you take the worthy
leaving fools for us.
Fifty years among us
upholding rights
annulling wrongs,
impatient death
could you not wait
 a little longer.
He still would be here
and mine, a brother
without a flaw. Peace
be upon him and Spring

rains water his tomb
                but
could you not wait
        a little longer
        a little longer,
you came too soon.

### *"I was sleepless, and I passed the night keeping vigil"*

*Translated by A.J. Arberry*

I was sleepless, and I passed the night keeping vigil, as if my eyes had been anointed with pus,
Watching the stars—and I had not been charged to watch them—and anon wrapping myself in the ends of ragged robes.
For I had heard—and it was not news to rejoice me—one making report, who had come repeating intelligence,
Saying, "Sakhr is dwelling there in a tomb, struck to the ground beside the grave, between certain stones."
Depart then, and may God not keep you far (from Him), being a man who eschewed injustice, and ever sought after bloodwit.
You used to carry a heart that brooked no wrong, compounded in a nature that was never cowardly,
Like the spear-point whose (bright) shape lights up the night, (a man) bitter in resolution, free and the son of free-men.
So I shall weep for you, so long as ringdove laments and the night stars shine for the night-traveller,
And I shall never make my peace with a people with whom you were at war, not till the black cooking-pot of the (good) host becomes white!

## al-Farazdāk (c. 650–728)

*Translated by Charles Greville Tuetey*

### *"A woman free of the desert born"*

A woman free of the desert born
where the wind plays round her pavilioned tent,
her whiteness shimmering cool as the pearls,
at whose step the very earth will light,
means more than a townswoman full of tricks
who gasps when she lays aside her fans.

## *Bashshār Ibn Burd (714–783)*

*Translated by Charles Greville Tuetey*

### *"I was blind from the womb, and from blindness insight came"*

I was blind from the womb, and from blindness insight came;
and a world of the known I built through wondering why;
and the light, unfathomed, with knowledge emerged ablaze
through a heart that saved what others, unseeing, destroy;
with thoughts like the flowers on earth, and words that I taught
lightly to tread when the thoughts come full of thorns.

### *"Modest my choice of 'Abda, the girl I love"*

Modest my choice of 'Abda, the girl I love,
is called by those whose hearts beat counter to mine.
Why query the heart and what it chose and approved!
With the heart, and not the eye, the loving see,
for never eyes yet saw in love's affairs,
nor ears yet heard, unless through one: the heart.
For what is beauty but every beautiful thing
that makes a man inspired at one with his love!

## *Abū Nuwās (747–813)*

### *"The man burdened with passion is a weary man"*

*Translated by A.J. Arberry*

The man burdened with passion is a weary man, deep emotion
unsteadies him.
If he weeps, it is right that he should; what he is charged with is
no joke.
Whensoever one cause (of my pains) comes to an end, (another)
cause returns from you to me.
You are laughing lightheartedly, whilst the lover bursts into tears.
You marvel at my sickness; that I am hale and hearty—that is the
(true) marvel.

### *"I said as the peach came ambling by"*

*Translated by Charles Greville Tuetey*

I said as the peach came ambling by,
a narcissus twirled in her hand:
'What a pity to wait till we offer cash!
Give love its proper due!'
'More pitiful still,' she said, and laughed,
'is a penniless flop at the door.'

### *"Many's the noble face laid waste"*

*Translated by Charles Greville Tuetey*

Many's the noble face laid waste;
many's the exquisite beauty dissolved;
the man of courage, purpose, undone;
and of judgment, corrupted, unmade to earth.
Tell him who is near now, close: You shall go
to a dwelling remote in no man's land.
Men are the going, sons of the gone,
bearers of names entailed by the dead,
and the world of the living on trial reveals
the lurid smile of a face unmasked.

## *Al-Ma'arrī (973–1058)*

### *"Souls stretching out their necks towards the resurrection"*

*Translated by A.J. Arberry*

Souls stretching out their necks towards the resurrection, and
error standing upright in folly!
You refuse obstinately ever to do a good action, and (yet) you
make ready for the day of forgiveness!
Be not deluded by a smile from a friend, for his thoughts are (all)
hatred and guile,
And men, whether children or aged, (the latter) grow grey in
error or (the former) grow up (in it).
You foolishly love your worldly life, but it never bestowed on
you what you desired.
Ever since your carnal soul became lusty as a young camel, you
amble and shamble along in error.
Though the sleep of mortals shall be long, for the sleepers there
must surely be an awakening.
Your infatuation with the wench is a languishing and a sorrow;
an occasional visit is no joy to the passionate lover.
Though the blackness of Saturn should dye your hands, and
though Suhā should be an ear-drop in your ear,
There shall not deliver you from the accidents of the nights a
surpassing radiance or a constant wealth,
Neither shall any power protect you from being carried into
captivity, not though the darkness be a veil over you.
I perceive the onset of darkness to be ampler of wing, yet (even)
its black and besetting crow dies.
What then is amiss with Aquila, that it does not fly therein, and
with night's clinging Scorpio, that it does not crawl?

Does day reveal the sun to the beholder, when the sun has already
  risen, and its rising is in mist?
Eloquence did not ward off death from Socrates, neither did any
  medicine protect Hippocrates against it.
When you behold me fallen on the brink (of death), let me be;
  every man that entertains hope is doomed to perish;
And do not scare away the bird then from me, neither let your
  hands moisten a parched lip.

## *"The days are dressing all of us in white"*

*Translated by Henry Baerlein*

The days are dressing all of us in white,
  For him who will suspend us in a row.
  But for the sun there is no death. I know
The centuries are morsels of the night.

Have I not heard sagacious ones repeat
  An irresistibly grim argument:
  That we for all our blustering content
Are as the silent shadows at our feet.

Now this religion happens to prevail
  Until by that one it is overthrown,—
  Because men dare not live with men alone,
But always with another fairy-tale.

God is above. We never shall attain
  Our liberty from hands that overshroud;
  Or can we shake aside this heavy cloud
More than a slave can shake aside the chain?

## *"Winter came on us"*

*Translated by Herbert Howarth and Ibrahim Shukrallah*

Winter came on us. Under it
A beggar naked, the prince in his quilt.
The stars deny one a day's rations,
Feed the other the corpus of nations.
This earth, though often a bride, has killed
Her many grooms, and is still maiden.
Cup your right hand and drink clean.
The curve of the royal tusk is obscene.

Travellers, too, let us make provision
For a more exact destination.

Our best is no luckier than the surgeon
Who plotted growths in his own colon.
Let the fat swell. Cap or coronet,
Either may spin on that crossed ocean
Where featureless trunks face the infinite.

### *"Tread lightly, for a thousand hearts unseen"*

*Translated by Ameen Rihani*

Tread lightly, for a thousand hearts unseen
Might now be beating in this misty green;
  Here are the herbs that once were pretty cheeks,
Here the remains of those that once have been.

Afearing whom I trust I gain my end,
But trusting, without fear, I lose, my friend;
  Much better is the Doubt that gives me peace,
Than all the Faiths which in hell-fire may end.

Among us some are great and some are small,
Albeit in wickedness, we're masters all;
  Or, if my fellow men are like myself,
The human race shall always rise and fall.

The air of sin I breathe without restraint;
With selfishness my few good deeds I taint;
  I come as I was moulded and I go,
But near the vacant shrine of Truth I faint.

A church, a temple, or a Kāba Stone,
Koran or Bible or a martyr's bone—
  All these and more my heart can tolerate
Since my religion now is Love alone.

## *Ibn Ḥazm (994–1063)*

*Translated by James T. Monroe*

### *from The Dove's Necklace (Tawq al-Namāmah)*

I love you with a love that knows no waning, whereas some of
    men's loves are midday mirages.
I bear for you a pure, sincere love, and in [my] heart there is a
    clear picture and an inscription [declaring] my love for you.

Moreover, if my soul were filled by anything but you, I would
pluck it out, while any membrane [covering it] would be
torn away from it by [my] hands.
I desire from you nothing but love, and that is all I request
from you.
If I should come to possess it, then all the earth will [seem
like] a senile camel and mankind like motes of dust, while
the land's inhabitants will [seem like] insects.

* * *

Are you from the world of the angels, or are you a mortal?
Explain this to me, for inability [to reach the truth] has
made a mockery of my understanding.
I see a human shape, yet if I use my mind, then the body is
[in reality] a celestial one.
Blessed be He who arranged the manner of being of His
creation in such a way that you should be the [only]
beautiful, natural light [in it].
I have no doubt but that you are that spirit which a resemblance
joining one soul to another in close relationship has
directed toward us.
We lacked any proof that would bear witness to your creation,
which we could use in comparison, save only that you are
visible.
Were it not that our eye contemplates [your] essence we could only
declare that you are the Sublime, True Reason.

* * *

Having seen the hoariness on my temples and sideburns, someone
asked me how old I was.
I answered him: "I consider all my life to have been but a short
moment and nothing else, when I think reasonably and
exactly."
He replied to me: "How was that? Explain it to me, for you have
given me the most grievous news and information."
So I said: "To the [girl] possessed of my heart I once gave one
single kiss by surprise.
Hence, no matter how many years I live, I will not really consider
any but that brief moment to have been my life."

* * *

They said: "He is far away." I replied: "It is enough for me that he
is with me in the same age without being able to escape.

The sun passes over me just as it does over him every day that shines anew.
Furthermore, is one between whom and me there lies only the distance of a day's journey really far away,
When the wisdom of the God of creation joined us together? This mutual proximity is enough [for me]; I want nothing further."

## *Ibn Zaidūn (1003–1071)*

*Translated by James T. Monroe*

### *Nūniyya for Wallāda*

The morning hour of mutual separation has replaced that of mutual proximity and the moment of our mutual separation from the sweetness of our proximity has come.
Alas! While the morning of separation had drawn near, death greeted us at dawn so that the announcer of our death has stirred us because of death.
Who will be the bearer of a sorrow to those dressed in a robe of grief, a sorrow not worn out with time though it wears us out?
[Who will be the bearer of the message] that destiny, which had not ceased evoking our laughter in social enjoyment of their nearness, has now reverted to making us weep?
The enemies were angry by reason of the [cup of] love we were offered by one another [to drink] and they called [down upon us a curse] that we should choke, whereupon destiny said: "So be it!"
Thus was loosened what had been compacted by our souls and there was cut off that which had been joined by our hands.
Although we used to be such that our parting was never feared, but today we are such that we have no hope for our mutual encounter.
O would that I knew, seeing that we have not satisfied your enemies, whether our enemies have obtained any measure of satisfaction [from you].
We have believed firmly in nothing after you [have left] save in adopting faithfulness to you as our attitude, and other than it we have not embraced any religion.
It is no deserving of ours that you cool the eyes of one envious of us, or that you give pleasure to him who is hateful to us.
We used to observe despair whose obstacles would bring consolation to us; now indeed we are in despair, and yet why does despair make the heart grow fonder?

You have departed and we have departed but our ribs have never
been restored to health because of yearning for you; nor
have our tear ducts ever been dried up.
When our intimate thoughts speak secretly in your ear we are
nearly destroyed by sorrow, were it not that we constrain
ourselves to patience.
Our days have been transformed by your absence so that they have
become black-morned whereas with you our nights were
white
When the side of life was joyous by reason of our friendship and
the springtime habitation of joy was pure by our mutual
purity [of friendship],
And when we bent the branches of [the tree of] love union
offering their fruits, and then we plucked of them what
pleased us.
May your days of friendship be given to drink of the gentle spring
showers of joy, for you have been to our souls nothing save
sweet-scented plants.
Do not think your distance from us will change us even though it
has often happened that distance has changed those who
love.
By God, our desires have not sought any substitute for you,
and our hopes have not been turned aside from you.
O night traveling ray of lightning! Go to the palace in the morning
and give to drink in it to one who gave us to drink of the
pure drink of affection and love,
And ask therein whether frequent thoughts of us have distressed a
friend, frequent thoughts of whom have come to disquiet us.
And O gentle Zephyr of the East, carry our greetings to the one who
from a distance would restore our life if he were to greet us;
One who is never seen deciding to grant us assistance on his part,
even though our demand for help be not made in error.
One who is fostered in royalty, as if God had created him of musk,
whereas He decreed the creation of common men out of
clay,
Or as if He had fashioned him of silver unalloyed, and had
crowned him with a crown of gleaming native gold [hair]
in uniqueness of creation and embellishment of beauty.
When he bends over, the pearls of the necklace weigh him down
by reason of his having been brought up in luxury, and the
ankle rings make him bleed because of the tenderness of
his skin.

The sun has been to him like a tender nurse in shading him and yet he has not shown himself in his splendor, to the sun, save for short moments.
It is as if the shining stars had been fixed upon the ball of his cheeks as an amulet against evil and as an ornament.
It has not been harmful that we should not have been his equal in nobility since in love there is a compensating equality from the fact of our mutual satisfaction.
O garden wherein long ago our glances plucked roses which youthful passion displayed in their freshness, as well as sweetbriar!
And O life [of this world] which made us enjoy by reason of its brilliance, desires of all sorts, and delights of all categories!
And O happy days by reason of whose richness we have walked [in enjoyment] [dressed] in the adorned silken robe of favors whose skirts we trailed for a time!
We do not name you [in our poem] by reason of our respect and honor [for you], moreover your elevated rank makes it unnecessary [to do] so,
Because you are peerless and you have no associate in any quality. Therefore a [mere] description [of you] suffices us by way of clarifying and distinguishing [the matter].
O garden of immortality in exchange for whose lotus drink and sweet tasting Kauthar we have been given the Zaqqūm [hell-tree] and the drink made of sweat pouring off the bodies of the damned [given them to drink].
It is as if we had never passed a night while the love union was our third [partner] and good fortune lowered the eyelids of our denouncer.
[We were] like two secrets in the heart of the gloom which was concealing us, until the tongue of the dawn was on the point of divulging us.
It is not astonishing that we should recall our sorrow when the interdiction of men forbids us [to visit] him, or [that we should] abandon the patience that has forgotten us.
Verily, we have recited [the lesson of] despair on the day of separation, since [it is composed of] suras written down for us [by divine decree], and we have taken patience as a lesson learned by heart.
As for your love, we cannot compare any drink equitably with a drink of it, for when we have been given to drink of it abundantly, then we are still made to thirst all the more.

We have not avoided any horizon of beauty of which you are the star, by consoling ourselves for [its loss], nor did we fly from it out of hate,
Nor out of choice did we remove away from it, while in proximity; however, in spite of ourselves the vicissitudes [of time] have made us depart.
We are unhappy because of you when a bubbling wine is passed from hand to hand among us, mingled with water, and our singers sing to us.
Neither the glasses of wine cause to appear from our nature any sign of cheerfulness, nor do the lute-strings amuse us.
Observe the promise which we observe zealously, for a wellborn person is one who treats equitably, as he is treated.
For we have sought no companion in substitution for you, for him to make us his inalienable property, nor have we had any lover to turn us from you.
Even if the moon [that lights up] the darkness inclined toward us from the high point of its rising, it would not excite us, I beg your pardon for mentioning it.
I weep out of loyalty even if you do not generously accord me a union; yet a dream image will satisfy us and a remembrance will suffice us.
And in your answer there will be something positive [for us] if you add to it the unasked for benefactions which you have not ceased to confer upon us.
Upon you, from us, may the peace of God be, as long as an ardent love for you lasts, one which we try to conceal, but which reveals us openly [to the world].

## Ibn Quzmān (d. 1160)

### *The Radish*

*Translated by A.J. Arberry*

The radish is a good
And doubtless wholesome food,
But proves, to vex the eater,
A powerful repeater.

This only fault I find:
What should be left behind
Comes issuing instead
Right from the eater's head!

## *"My life is spent in dissipation and wantonness!"*

*Translated by James T. Monroe*

My life is spent in dissipation and wantonness!
O joy, I have begun to be a real profligate!
Indeed, it is absurd for me to repent
When my survival without a wee drink would be certain death.
*Vino, vino!* [wine, wine] And spare me what is said;
Verily, I go mad when I lose my restraint!
My slave will be freed, my money irretrievably lost
On the day I am deprived of the cup.
Should I be poured a double measure or a fivefold one,
I would most certainly empty it; if not, fill then the *jarrón!* [jug]
Ho! Clink the glasses with us!
Drunkenness, drunkenness! What care we for proper conduct?
And when you wish to quaff a morning drink,
Awaken me before the *volcón!* [emptying of cups]
Take my money and squander it on drink;
My clothes, too, and divide them up among the whores,
And assure me that my reasoning is correct.
I am never deceived in this occupation!
And when I die, let me be buried thus:
Let me sleep in a vineyard, among the vinestocks;
Spread [its] leaves over me in lieu of a shroud,
And let there be a turban of vine tendrils on my head!
Let my companion persevere in immorality, to be followed by
every beloved one.
And remember me continuously as you go about it.
As for the grapes, let whomsoever eats a bunch,
Plant the [leftover] stalk on my grave!
I will offer a toast to your health with the large cup;
Take your bottle, lift it high and empty it!
What a wonderful toast you have been honored by.
Let whatever you decree against me come to pass!
By God, were it not for a trick done to me in a matter concerning
a woman,
I would have won bliss. She said [to me]: "There is a certain
desire which
I will not grant you, it being a question of my honor."
Alas! The price of that was paid out later!
I, by God, was seated, when there came to me with a garland on
her head,
A Berber girl; what a beauty of a *conejo!* [rabbit]
"Whoa!" [Said I, "she] is not a *sera* of *cardacho,* [basket of thistles]
But don't pounce [on her] for neither is she a *grañón!*" [fine grain
porridge]

"Milady, say, are you fine, white flour or what?"
"I am going to bed." "By God; you do well!"
I said: "Enter." She replied: "No, you enter first, by God."
(Let us cuckold the man who is her husband.)
Hardly had I beheld that leg
And those two lively, lively eyes,
When my penis arose in my trousers like a pavilion,
And made a tent out of my clothes.
And since I observed that a certain "son of Adam" was dilated,
The chick wished to hide in the nest.
"Where are you taking that *pollo,* [chicken] for an immoral purpose?
Here we have a man to whom they say: 'O what shamelessness!'"
I, by God, immediately set to work:
Either it came out, or it went in,
While I thrust away sweetly, sweet as honey,
And [my] breath came out hotly between her legs.
It would have been wonderful, had it not been for the insults that were exchanged next day,
For they [the Berber woman and her family] began to squabble and to brawl:
"Remove your hand from my beard, O ass!"
"You, throw the frying pan for the *tostón!*" [fried toast]
One claws at an eyelid, the other slaps;
One tears clothes to shreds, the other floors his adversary;
No matter where I throw green quinces,
I get hit only on the head by the *bastón!* [cudgel]
That is the way the world is! Not that it is my style,
Yet in this way they managed to humiliate me.
As for me, O people, although it was a light [punishment],
Never have I suffered such shame as at present.
Indeed, my opinion is as follows: You are viewed by the eye of reproof;
No place in this city is big enough for you to hide.
Where are the means [of departure] for one such as Ibn Quzmān?
In my opinion nothing is more certain than that [I shall get them].
O my hope and my well-watched star;
My life and my beloved one:
I desire largesse and it is from you that it is desired!
I am your guarantor for your glory will be guaranteed!
Your hands have an eminent right to dispose of me,
And in your honor do I go and stop,
While your virtues are too excellent for me to describe.
Drops of water are not to be compared with bursting rain clouds.
You have shown me a path to prosperity;
You have adorned me before my enemy and my friend;

For in you my hand has been attached to a firm rope;
You who are such that all others are withheld from me.
O, Abū Isḥāq, O [friend], lord among viziers,
Bright flower of this world and lord among emirs!
The like of you gives new life to poetry for poets,
While you make public a generosity that was hidden [before your arrival]!
May you remain happy, achieving your aspirations,
And may you witness high rank and nobility with affability,
As long as darkness changes [to light] and the new moon shines,
And as long as a plant still grows green and branches rise high!

## *Jalāl al-Dīn Rūmī (1207–1273)*

### *"When you display that rosy cheek, you set the stones a-spinning for joy"*

*Translated by A.J. Arberry*

When you display that rosy cheek, you set the stones a-spinning for joy.
Once again put forth your head from the veil, for the sake of the dumbstruck lovers,
That learning may lose the way, that the man of reason may break his science to pieces;
That water through your reflection may convert to a pearl, that fire may abandon warfare.
With your beauty, I desire not the moon, neither those two or three hanging little lanterns.
With your face, I do not call the ancient, rusty heavens a mirror.
You breathed, and created anew in another shape this narrow world.
In desire for his Mars-like eye, play, Venus, again that harp!

### *"On the day of death, when my bier is on the move"*

*Translated by A.J. Arberry*

On the day of death, when my bier is on the move, do not suppose that I have any pain at leaving this world.
Do not weep for me, say not "Alas, alas!" You will fall into the devil's snare—that would indeed be alas!
When you see my hearse, say not "Parting, parting!" That time there will be for me union and encounter.
When you commit me to the grave, say not "Farewell, farewell!" For the grave is a veil over the reunion of paradise.

Having seen the going-down, look upon the coming-up; how should setting impair the sun and the moon?
To you it appears as setting, but it is a rising; the tomb appears as a prison, but it is release for the soul.
What seed ever went down into the earth which did not grow?
Why do you doubt so regarding the human seed?
What bucket ever went down and came not out full? Why this complaining of the well by the Joseph of the spirit?
When you have closed your mouth on this side, open it on that, for your shout of triumph will echo in the placeless air.

## *"Henceforward the nightingale in the garden will tell of us"*

*Translated by A.J. Arberry*

Henceforward the nightingale in the garden will tell of us, it will tell of the beauty of that heart-ravishing Beloved.
When the wind falls upon the head of the willow and it begins to dance, God alone knows what things it says to the air.
The plane-tree understands a little about the meadow's burning, it lifts up two broad hands sweetly and prays.
I ask the rose, "From whom did you steal that beauty?" The rose laughs softly out of shame, but how should she tell?
Though the rose is drunk, it is not dissolute like me, that it should tell you the secret of the intoxicated narcissus.
When you seek secrets, go amongst the drunkards, for the tipsy head shamelessly tells the secret.
Inasmuch as wine is the daughter of the vine and the family of generosity, it has opened the purse's mouth and speaks of lavishness;
Especially the wine of the heavenly trellis from the All-generous Almighty; haply God will speak of its lavishness and generosity.
That new wine ferments from the breast of the gnostic, out of the depths of his body's vat it invites you to the feast.
Since the breast gives milk, it can also give wine; from the breast its flowing fountain tells a pretty tale.
When that spirit becomes more intoxicated, it stakes its cloak, lays down cap, and abandons this gown.
When the reason drinks blood-red wine recklessly, it opens its mouth and tells the mysteries of Majesty.
Be silent, for no one will believe you; bad copper swallows not what the philosopher's stone says.
Bear tidings to Tabriz, Pride of the World; perchance our Shams-i Dīn will speak your praise.

### *"I died as mineral and became a plant"*

*Translated by R.A. Nicholson*

I died as mineral and became a plant,
I died as plant and rose to animal,
I died as animal and I was man.
Why should I fear? When was I less by dying?
Yet once more I shall die as man, to soar
With angels blest; but even from angelhood
I must pass on: all except God doth perish.
When I have sacrificed my angel soul,
I shall become what no mind e'er conceived.
Oh, let me not exist! for Non-existence
Proclaims in organ tones, "To Him we shall return."

## Ḥāfiẓ of Shiraz (1320–c. 1389)

*Translated by A.J. Arberry*

### *All My Pleasure*

All my pleasure is to sip
Wine from my beloved's lip;
I have gained the utmost bliss—
God alone be praised for this.

Fate, my old and stubborn foe,
Never let my darling go:
Give my mouth the golden wine
And her lips incarnadine.

(Clerics bigoted for God,
Elders who have lost the road—
These have made a tale of us
"Drunken sots and bibulous."

Let th' ascetic's life be dim,
I will nothing have of him;
If the monk will pious be,
God forgive his piety!)

Darling, what have I to say
Of my grief, with thee away,
Save with tears and scalding eyes
And a hundred burning sighs?

Let no infidel behold
All the bitterness untold
Cypress knows to see thy grace,
Jealous moon to view thy face.

It is yearning for thy kiss
That hath wrought in Hafiz this,
That no more he hath in care
Nightly lecture, matin prayer.

## *The Times Are Out of Joint*

Again the times are out of joint; and again
For wine and the loved one's languid glance I am fain.
The wheel of fortune's sphere is a marvellous thing:
What next proud head to the lowly dust will it bring?
Or if my Magian elder kindle the light,
Whose lantern, pray, will blaze aflame and be bright?
'Tis a famous tale, the deceitfulness of earth;
The night is pregnant: what will dawn bring to birth?
Tumult and bloody battle rage in the plain:
Bring blood-red wine, and fill the goblet again!

# India in the Middle Period

During the Middle Period, the ancient Vedic religion of India, which had given birth to Buddhism, evolved into the elaborate polytheistic ritual life of Hinduism. Buddhism, though born in India, was to have a deeper and more lasting impact on the rest of Asia than on India itself, but it remained a presence in India throughout the period. The dominant cultural development of these centuries, however, was the invasion of Islam. As early as the eighth century, only a century after Muhammad's revelation, Islam became a factor in Indian culture, spread by communities of Arab merchants and by several waves of Muslim armies: the Turkish Ghorids in the eighth century, the Arabs and Persians in the thirteenth century, and the Turkish Mughals in the sixteenth century. The Muslim minority in India, including a highly educated elite that had fled to India when Genghis Khan conquered the Middle East, became so powerful that it assumed rulership of the subcontinent after the thirteenth century.

Thus, during the Middle Period, India was home to three great cultural traditions—Hindu, Buddhist, and Muslim—but tension between the Muslim ruling class and the great majority of Hindus dominated cultural life during the period. Though the two groups arrived at a more or less peaceful working relationship, it is hard to image two worldviews more different than Hinduism and Islam—the one eclectic, unstructured, infinitely various, with no priesthood or orthodoxy; the other highly structured, legalistic, and extremely orthodox. The tension between them continues in India and Pakistan today.

All three religious traditions produced a dizzying abundance of literary texts in Sanskrit, Arabic, and a number of vernaculars, such as Pali, Hindi, Tamil, and Urdu—the last of these a *lingua franca,* which combines Hindi grammar and Arabic and Persian vocabulary. Since the major literary texts of these religious traditions are found in other parts of this book, we have selected only four authors to represent India during this period. Kālidāsa, from the fourth century CE, is the greatest poet and dramatist in Sanskrit—India's Shakespeare, a Westerner might say. His greatest play, *Śakuntalā,* is the perfect embodiment of Indian aesthetic theory. What makes *Śakuntalā* such a powerful experience for Western readers is that the basic principles of Indian drama are so entirely different from Aristotle's or Shakespeare's. When Goethe read the play in the eighteenth century, he wrote, "Would you capture heaven and earth in a single name? Then I say *Śakuntalā,* and all is said!" His *Faust* is probably the nearest work in Western literature to Indian drama.

Vidyakara, a Buddhist monk of the eleventh century, collected seventeen hundred Sanskrit poems from the previous seven centuries in an anthology he called *The Treasury of Well-Turned Verse.* Only some of the poems are on Buddhist themes. The ones selected here paint a vivid portrait of everyday life in rural India during the period. They are surprisingly secular and unlike anything to be found in medieval Europe. Their strict formalism and close observation of nature remind us more of Japanese poetry of the period.

Islam, which had no caste system, strongly appealed to the lower strata of Indian society. It inspired powerful movements of popular Hinduism in response to this appeal, especially after the imposition of Muslim rule in the thirteenth century. The most influential of these is *bhakti,* or personal devotion to the Hindu gods, a movement inspired in part by Sufi mysticism, a development of Islam that appealed strongly to Hindu spirituality. The two *bhakti* poets included here are Ravidās, a fifteenth-century spokesman for the lowest caste of untouchables, and Mīrābāī, a female poet who wrote in the sixteenth century. Both of these poets, but especially Mīrābāī, retain enormous popular appeal in modern India.

*The Lotus Sutra,* though grouped with Chinese literature of the Middle Period (see pp. 1009–1014), might as easily be included here with these Indian works. It led a multicultural life, or at least a multilingual life, from very early in its transmission; though Indian in origin (dating before the third century CE), like the *Virmalakirti Sutra* of the Ancient Period (pp. 260–265), its earliest surviving texts are in Chinese. It is indicative of the fate of Indian Buddhism that the version presented in our book is from the Chinese translation by Kumarajiva, completed in 406 CE.

## KĀLIDĀSA (LATE 4TH–EARLY 5TH CENT.)

*Translated by Barbara Stoler Miller*

While Augustine was writing in Europe, the Indian poet Kālidāsa wrote several dramas, including *Śakuntalā and the Ring of Recollection.* Kālidāsa was probably a court official from 375 to 415 under the king Chandragupta II. The Gupta kingdom is remembered as the great period of classical Indian culture (350–470), and Kālidāsa as India's greatest dramatist. Little is known of Kālidāsa himself, though his name indicates he was a devotee of the great goddess Kali; he is said to have been a lowly cowherd who was miraculously made a poet and sage—a story reminiscent of the Prophet Muhammad (pp. 761–771), and also of the first English poet Caedmon. The story of *Śakuntalā* is drawn from the first book of the *Mahābhārata* and recounts the birth of Bharata, whose name is part of that epic's title. Kālidāsa's elaboration of the story takes the form of a heroic romance.

Western readers will naturally compare the principles of such a drama with those of Greek tragedy. Just as Aristotle analyzed the principles of Greek tragedy, the Gupta period produced a similar analysis of Indian drama, the *Nātya Śastra* of Bharata (not the character in the play), roughly contemporary with Kālidāsa. Though certain similarities between the Greek and Indian dramas can be found, the differences are far more striking. Indian drama is not built on the conflict of individuals, but rather on the recurring conflicts of principles, such as duty and passion (*dharma* and *kāma*), expressed not through deeply individuated characters but rather through generic types. For example, in this play King Dusyanta is a manifestation of pure kingship. His behavior is always perfect, although conflicts inevitably arise for him because of the contingency of the world. *Śakuntalā* is the type of "heroine-in-separation."

The dramatist does not so much drive his plot to a climax and resolution as he concentrates on developing complex tonalities known as *rasas*, which are intended to have certain precise effects on the audience. *Rasa* literally means "flavor" and, by extension, "mood." Indian dramatic theory postulates eight *rasas:* erotic, heroic, comic, pathetic, furious, horrible, marvelous, and disgusting. By the use of precise conventions, the poet can produce these *rasas* in purified forms unavailable in real life or combine them with a great variety of precise emotional effects, just as one might combine spices in an Indian meal. Heroic romance concentrates on the erotic and heroic *rasas*, though Kālidāsa stages elaborate displays of the delicate relations of all of them. The formal conventions of this theory are inaccessible to the beginning reader, but the comic and marvelous elements in *Śakuntalā* are startling and memorable even in translation, especially the figure of the buffoon and the amazing transposition of the action to a heavenly world in the final act.

Another important feature of the play is its use of languages: upper-caste male characters speak in Sanskrit, largely in poetry, while lower-caste and female characters speak in a variety of vernacular languages known as Prakrits, largely in prose. The audience for such a multilayered performance was highly educated and attuned to the minutest subtleties of tone, gesture, and other dramatic conventions.

Though many of its features are lost in translation, it is a tribute to Kālidāsa that even to a modern English reader, the play can appear beautiful and powerful, shining a bright light into classical Indian culture.

## *Śakuntalā and the Ring of Recollection*

### *Characters*

*Players in the prologue:*

DIRECTOR: Director of the players and manager of the theater (*sūtradhāra*).

ACTRESS: The lead actress (*naṭī*).

*Principal roles:*

KING: Duṣyanta, the hero (*nāyaka*); ruler of Hastināpura; a royal sage of the lunar dynasty of Puru.

ŚAKUNTALĀ: The heroine (*nāyikā*); daughter of the royal sage Viśvāmitra and the celestial nymph Menakā; adoptive daughter of the ascetic Kanva.

BUFFOON: Mādhavya, the king's comical brahman companion (*vidūsaka*).

*Members of Kaṇva's hermitage:*

ANASŪYĀ and PRIYAṀVADĀ: Two young female ascetics; friends of Śakuntalā.

KAṆVA: Foster father of Śakuntalā and master of the hermitage; a sage belonging to the lineage of the divine creator Marīci, and thus related to Mārīca.

GAUTAMĪ: The senior female ascetic.

ŚĀRṄGARAVA AND ŚĀRADVATA: Kaṇva's disciples.

Various inhabitants of the hermitage: a monk with his two pupils, two boy ascetics (named Gautama and Nārada), a young disciple of Kaṇva, a trio of female ascetics.

*Members of the king's forest retinue:*

CHARIOTEER: Driver of the king's chariot (*sūta*).

GUARD: Raivataka, guardian of the entrance to the king's quarters (*dauvārika*).

GENERAL: Commander of the king's army (*senāpati*).

KARABHAKA: Royal messenger.

Various attendants, including Greco-Bactrian bow-bearers (*yavanyaḥ*).

*Members of the king's palace retinue:*

CHAMBERLAIN: Vātāyana, chief officer of the king's household (*kañcukī*).

PRIEST: Somarāta, the king's religious preceptor and household priest (*purohita*).

DOORKEEPER: Vetravatī, the female attendant who ushers in visitors and presents messages (*pratīharī*).

PARABHṚTIKĀ and MADHUKARIKĀ: Two maids assigned to the king's garden.

CATURIKĀ: A maidservant.

*City dwellers:*

MAGISTRATE: The king's low-caste brother-in-law (*śyāla*); chief of the city's policemen.

POLICEMEN: Sūcaka and Jānuka.

FISHERMAN: An outcaste.

*Celestials:*

MĀRĪCA: A divine sage; master of the celestial hermitage in which Śakuntalā gives birth to her son; father of Indra, king of the gods, whose armies Duṣyanta leads.

ADITI: Wife of Mārīca.

MĀTALI: Indra's charioteer.

SĀNUMATĪ: A nymph; friend of Śakuntalā's mother Menakā.

Various members of Mārīca's hermitage: two female ascetics, Mārīca's disciple Gālava.

BOY: Sarvadamana, son of Śakuntalā and Duṣyanta; later known as Bharata.

*Offstage voices:*

VOICE OFFSTAGE: From the backstage area or dressing room (*nepathye*); behind the curtain, out of view of the audience. The voice belongs to various players before they enter the stage, such as the monk, Śakuntalā's friends, the buffoon, Mātali; also to figures who never enter the stage, such as the angry sage Durvāsas, the two bards who chant royal panegyrics (*vaitālikau*).

VOICE IN THE AIR: A voice chanting in the air(*ākāśe*) from somewhere offstage: the bodiless voice of Speech quoted in Sanskrit by Priyaṁvadā (4.4); the voice of a cuckoo who represents the trees of the forest blessing Śakuntalā in Sanskrit (4.11); the voice of Haṁsapadikā singing a Prakrit love song (5.1).

Aside from Duṣyanta, Śakuntalā, and the buffoon, most of the characters represent types that reappear in different contexts within the play itself, an aspect of the circular structure of the play in which complementary relations are repeated. In terms of their appearance, the following roles might be played by the same actor or actress:

Kaṇva—Mārīca
Gautamī—Aditi
Anasūyā and Priyaṁvadā—
Sānumatī and Caturikā—
Two Ascetic Women in the hermitage of Mārīca
Charioteer—Mātali

Monk—Sārṅgarava
General—Chamberlain
Karabhaka—Priest

*The setting of the play shifts from the forest hermitage (Acts 1–4) to the palace (Acts 5–6) to the celestial hermitage (Act 7). The season is early summer when the play begins and spring during the sixth act; the passage of time is otherwise indicated by the birth and boyhood of Śakuntalā's son.*

## ACT ONE

The water that was first created,
the sacrifice-bearing fire, the
priest,
the time-setting sun and moon,
audible space that fills the
universe,
what men call nature, the source
of all seeds,
the air that living creatures
breathe—
through his eight embodied forms,
may Lord Śiva come to bless you!

### PROLOGUE

DIRECTOR (*looking backstage*): If you are in costume now, madam, please come on stage!

ACTRESS: I'm here, sir.

DIRECTOR: Our audience is learned. We shall play Kālidāsa's new drama called *Śakuntalā and the Ring of Recollection.* Let the players take their parts to heart!

ACTRESS: With you directing, sir, nothing will be lost.

DIRECTOR: Madam, the truth is:

I find no performance perfect
until the critics are pleased;
the better trained we are
the more we doubt ourselves.

ACTRESS: So true . . . now tell me what to do first!

DIRECTOR: What captures an audience better than a song? Sing about the new summer season and its pleasures:

To plunge in fresh waters
swept by scented forest winds
and dream in soft shadows
of the day's ripened charms.

ACTRESS (*singing*):

Sensuous women
in summer love
weave
flower earrings
from fragile petals
of mimosa
while wild bees
kiss them gently.

DIRECTOR: Well sung, madam! Your melody enchants the audience. The silent theater is like a painting. What drama should we play to please it?

ACTRESS: But didn't you just direct us to perform a new play called *Śakuntalā and the Ring of Recollection?*

DIRECTOR: Madam, I'm conscious again! For a moment I forgot.

The mood of your song's melody
carried me off by force,

just as the swift dark antelope
enchanted King Duṣyanta.

*(They both exit; the prologue ends. Then the king enters with his charioteer, in a chariot, a bow and arrow in his hand, hunting an antelope.)*

CHARIOTEER (*watching the king and the antelope*):

I see this black buck move
as you draw your bow
and I see the wild bowman Śiva,
hunting the dark antelope.

KING: Driver, this antelope has drawn us far into the forest. There he is again:

The graceful turn of his neck
as he glances back at our
speeding car,
the haunches folded into his chest
in fear of my speeding arrow,
the open mouth dropping
half-chewed grass on our path—
watch how he leaps, bounding
on air,
barely touching the earth.

*(He shows surprise.)*

Why is it so hard to keep him in sight?

CHARIOTEER: Sir, the ground was rough. I tightened the reins to slow the chariot and the buck raced ahead. Now that the path is smooth, he won't be hard to catch.

KING: Slacken the reins!

CHARIOTEER: As you command, sir.

*(He mimes the speeding chariot.)*

Look!

Their legs extend as I slacken the
reins,
plumes and manes set in the wind,
ears angle back;
our horses outrun their own
clouds of dust,
straining to match the antelope's
speed.

KING: These horses would outrace the steeds of the sun.

What is small suddenly looms large,
split forms seem to reunite,
bent shapes straighten before my
eyes—
from the chariot's speed
nothing ever stays distant or near.

CHARIOTEER: The antelope is an easy target now.

*(He mimes the fixing of an arrow.)*

VOICE OFFSTAGE: Stop! Stop, king! This antelope belongs to our hermitage! Don't kill him!

CHARIOTEER (*listening and watching*): Sir, two ascetics are protecting the black buck from your arrow's deadly aim.

KING (*showing confusion*): Rein in the horses!

CHARIOTEER: It is done!

*(He mimes the chariot's halt. Then a monk enters with two pupils, his hand raised.)*

MONK: King, this antelope belongs to our hermitage.

Withdraw your well-aimed arrow!
Your weapon
should rescue victims, not destroy
the innocent!

KING: I withdraw it.

*(He does as he says.)*

MONK: An act worthy of the Puru dynasty's shining light!

Your birth honors
the dynasty of the moon!

May you beget a son
to turn the wheel of your empire!

THE TWO PUPILS (*raising their arms*): May you beget a son to turn the wheel of your empire!

KING (*bowing*): I welcome your blessing.

MONK: King, we were going to gather firewood. From here you can see the hermitage of our master Kaṇva on the bank of the Mālinī river. If your work permits, enter and accept our hospitality.

When you see the peaceful rites of
devoted ascetics,
you will know how well your
scarred arm protects us.

KING: Is the master of the community there now?

MONK: He went to Somatīrtha, the holy shrine of the moon, and put his daughter Śakuntalā in charge of receiving guests. Some evil threatens her, it seems.

KING: Then I shall see her. She will know my devotion and commend me to the great sage.

MONK: We shall leave you now.

*(He exits with his pupils.)*

KING: Driver, urge the horses on! The sight of this holy hermitage will purify us.

CHARIOTEER: As you command, sir.

*(He mimes the chariot's speed.)*

KING (*looking around*): Without being told one can see that this is a grove where ascetics live.

CHARIOTEER: How?

KING: Don't you see—

Wild rice grains under trees
where parrots nest in hollow
trunks,
stones stained by the dark oil
of crushed iṅgudī nuts,
trusting deer who hear human
voices
yet don't break their gait,
and paths from ponds streaked
by water from wet bark cloth.

CHARIOTEER: It is perfect.

KING (*having gone a little inside*): We should not disturb the grove! Stop the chariot and let me get down!

CHARIOTEER: I'm holding the reins. You can dismount now, sir.

KING (*dismounting*): One should not enter an ascetics' grove in hunting gear. Take these!

*(He gives up his ornaments and his bow.)*

Driver, rub down the horses while I pay my respects to the residents of the hermitage!

CHARIOTEER: Yes, sir!

*(He exits.)*

KING: This gateway marks the sacred ground. I will enter.

*(He enters, indicating he feels an omen.)*

The hermitage is a tranquil place,
yet my arm is quivering . . .
do I feel a false omen of love
or does fate have doors
everywhere?

VOICE OFFSTAGE: This way, friends!

KING (*straining to listen*): I think I hear voices to the right of the grove. I'll find out.

*(Walking around and looking.)*

Young female ascetics with watering pots cradled on their hips are coming to water the saplings.

*(He mimes it in precise detail.)*

This view of them is sweet.

These forest women have beauty
rarely seen inside royal palaces—
the wild forest vines far surpass
creepers in my pleasure garden.

I'll hide in the shadows and wait.

*(Śakuntalā and her two friends enter, acting as described.)*

ŚAKUNTALĀ: This way, friends!

ANASŪYĀ: I think Father Kaṇva cares more about the trees in the hermitage than he cares about you. You're as delicate as a jasmine, yet he orders you to water the trees.

ŚAKUNTALĀ: Anasūyā, it's more than Father Kaṇva's order. I feel a sister's love for them.

*(She mimes the watering of trees.)*

KING (*to himself*): Is this Kaṇva's daughter? The sage does show poor judgment in imposing the rules of the hermitage on her.

The sage who hopes to subdue
her sensuous body by penances
is trying to cut firewood
with a blade of blue-lotus leaf.

Let it be! I can watch her closely from here in the trees.

*(He does so.)*

ŚAKUNTALĀ: Anasūyā, I can't breathe! Our friend Priyaṁvadā tied my bark dress too tightly! Loosen it a bit!

ANASŪYĀ: As you say.

*(She loosens it.)*

PRIYAṀVADĀ (*laughing*): Blame your youth for swelling your breasts. Why blame me?

KING: This bark dress fits her body badly,
but it ornaments her beauty . . .

A tangle of duckweed adorns a lotus,
a dark spot heightens the moon's glow,
the bark dress increases her charm—
beauty finds its ornaments anywhere.

ŚAKUNTALĀ (*looking in front of her*): The new branches on this mimosa tree are like fingers moving in the wind, calling to me. I must go to it!

*(Saying this, she walks around.)*

PRIYAṀVADĀ: Wait, Śakuntalā! Stay there a minute! When you stand by this mimosa tree, it seems to be guarding a creeper.

ŚAKUNTALĀ: That's why your name means "Sweet-talk."

KING: "Sweet-talk" yes, but Priyaṁvadā speaks the truth about Śakuntalā:

Her lips are fresh red buds,
her arms are tendrils,
impatient youth is poised
to blossom in her limbs.

ANASŪYĀ: Śakuntalā, this is the jasmine creeper who chose the mango tree in marriage, the one you named "Forestlight." Have you forgotten her?

ŚAKUNTALĀ: I would be forgetting myself!

*(She approaches the creeper and examines it.)*

The creeper and the tree are twined together in perfect harmony. Forestlight has just flowered and the new mango shoots are made for her pleasure.

PRIYAṀVADĀ (*smiling*): Anasūyā, don't you know why Śakuntalā looks so lovingly at Forestlight?

ANASŪYĀ: I can't guess.

PRIYAṀVADĀ: The marriage of Forestlight to her tree makes her long to have a husband too.

ŚAKUNTALĀ: You're just speaking your own secret wish.

*(Saying this, she pours water from the jar.)*

KING: Could her social class be different from her father's? There's no doubt!

She was born to be a warrior's
bride,
for my noble heart desires her—
when good men face doubt,
inner feelings are truth's only
measure.

Still, I must learn everything about her.

ŚAKUNTALĀ (*flustered*): The splashing water has alarmed a bee. He is flying from the jasmine to my face.

*(She dances to show the bee's attack.)*

KING (*looking longingly*):

Bee, you touch the quivering
corners of her frightened eyes,
you hover softly near
to whisper secrets in her ear;
a hand brushes you away,
but you drink her lips' treasure—
while the truth we seek defeats us,
you are truly blessed.

ŚAKUNTALĀ: This dreadful bee won't stop. I must escape.

*(She steps to one side, glancing about.)*

Oh! He's pursuing me . . . Save me! Please save me! This mad bee is chasing me!

BOTH FRIENDS (*laughing*): How can we save you? Call King Duṣyanta. The grove is under his protection.

KING: Here's my chance. Have no fear . . .

*(With this half-spoken, he stops and speaks to himself.)*

Then she will know that I am the king . . . Still, I shall speak.

ŚAKUNTALĀ (*stopping after a few steps*): Why is he still following me?

KING (*approaching quickly*):

While a Puru king rules the earth
to punish evildoers,
who dares to molest
these innocent young ascetics?

*(Seeing the king, all act flustered.)*

ANASŪYĀ: Sir, there's no real danger. Our friend was frightened when a bee attacked her.

*(She points to Śakuntalā.)*

KING (*approaching Śakuntalā*): Does your ascetic practice go well?

*(Śakuntalā stands speechless.)*

ANASŪYĀ: It does now that we have a special guest. Śakuntalā, go to our hut and bring the ripe fruits. We'll use this water to bathe his feet.

KING: Your kind speech is hospitality enough.

PRIYAṀVADA: Please sit in the cool shadows of this shade tree and rest, sir.

KING: You must also be tired from your work.

ANASŪYĀ: Śakuntalā, we should respect our guest. Let's sit down.

*(All sit.)*

ŚAKUNTALĀ (*to herself*): When I see him, why do I feel an emotion that the forest seems to forbid?

KING (*looking at each of the girls*): Youth and beauty complement your friendship.

PRIYAṀVADĀ (*in a stage whisper*): Anasūyā, who is he? He's so polite, fine looking, and pleasing to hear. He has the marks of royalty.

ANASŪYĀ: I'm curious too, friend. I'll just ask him.

*(Aloud.)*

Sir, your kind speech inspires trust. What family of royal sages do you adorn? What country mourns your absence? Why does a man of refinement subject himself to the discomfort of visiting an ascetics' grove?

ŚAKUNTALĀ (*to herself*): Heart, don't faint! Anasūyā speaks your thoughts.

KING (*to himself*): Should I reveal myself now or conceal who I am? I'll say it this way:

*(Aloud.)*

Lady, I have been appointed by the Puru king as the officer in charge of religious matters. I have come to this sacred forest to assure that your holy rites proceed unhindered.

ANASŪYĀ: Our religious life has a guardian now.

*(Śakuntalā mimes the embarrassment of erotic emotion.)*

BOTH FRIENDS (*observing the behavior of Śakuntalā and the king; in a stage whisper*): Śakuntalā, if only your father were here now!

ŚAKUNTALĀ (*angrily*): What if he were?

BOTH FRIENDS: He would honor this distinguished guest with what he values most in life.

ŚAKUNTALĀ: Quiet! Such words hint at your hearts' conspiracy. I won't listen.

KING: Ladies, I want to ask about your friend.

BOTH FRIENDS: Your request honors us, sir.

KING: Sage Kaṇva has always been celibate, but you call your friend his daughter. How can this be?

ANASŪYĀ: Please listen, sir. There was a powerful royal sage of the Kauśika clan . . .

KING: I am listening.

ANASŪYĀ: He begot our friend, but Kaṇva is her father because he cared for her when she was abandoned.

KING: "Abandoned"? The word makes me curious. I want to hear her story from the beginning.

ANASŪYĀ: Please listen, sir. Once when this great sage was practicing terrible austerities on the bank of the Gautamī river, he became so powerful that the jealous gods sent a nymph named Menakā to break his self-control.

KING: The gods dread men who meditate.

ANASŪYĀ: When springtime came to the forest with all its charm, the sage saw her intoxicating beauty . . .

KING: I understand what happened then. She is the nymph's daughter.

ANASŪYĀ: Yes.

KING: It had to be!

No mortal woman could give birth
to such beauty—
lightning does not flash out of the
earth.

*(Śakuntalā stands with her face bowed. The king continues speaking to himself.)*

My desire is not hopeless. Yet, when I hear her friends teasing her about a bridegroom, a new fear divides my heart.

PRIYAṀVADĀ (*smiling, looking at Śakuntalā, then turning to the king*): Sir, you seem to want to say more.

*(Śakuntalā makes a threatening gesture with her finger.)*

KING: You judge correctly. In my eagerness to learn more about your pious lives, I have another question.

PRIYAṀVADĀ: Don't hesitate! Ascetics can be questioned frankly.

KING: I want to know this about your friend:

Will she keep the vow of hermit life
only until she marries . . .
or will she always exchange
loving looks with deer in the forest?

PRIYAṀVADĀ: Sir, even in her religious life, she is subject to her father, but he does intend to give her to a suitable husband.

KING (*to himself*): His wish is not hard to fulfill.

Heart, indulge your desire—
now that doubt is dispelled,
the fire you feared to touch
is a jewel in your hands.

ŚAKUNTALĀ (*showing anger*): Anasūyā, I'm leaving!

ANASŪYĀ: Why?

ŚAKUNTALĀ: I'm going to tell Mother Gautamī that Priyaṁvadā is talking nonsense.

ANASŪYĀ: Friend, it's wrong to neglect a distinguished guest and leave as you like.

*(Śakuntalā starts to go without answering.)*

KING (*wanting to seize her, but holding back, he speaks to himself*): A lover dare not act on his impulsive thoughts!

I wanted to follow the sage's daughter,
but decorum abruptly pulled me back;
I set out and returned again
without moving my feet from this spot.

PRIYAṀVADĀ (*stopping Śakuntalā*): It's wrong of you to go!

ŚAKUNTALĀ (*bending her brow into a frown*): Give me a reason why!

PRIYAṀVADĀ: You promised to water two trees for me. Come here and pay your debt before you go!

*(She stops her by force.)*

KING: But she seems exhausted from watering the trees:

Her shoulders droop, her palms
are red from the watering pot—
even now, breathless sighs
make her breasts shake;
beads of sweat on her face
wilt the flower at her ear;
her hand holds back
disheveled locks of hair.

Here, I'll pay her debt!

*(He offers his ring. Both friends recite the syllables of the name on the seal and stare at each other.)*

Don't mistake me for what I am not! This is a gift from the king to identify me as his royal official.

PRIYAṀVADĀ: Then the ring should never leave your finger. Your word has already paid her debt.

*(She laughs a little.)*

Śakuntalā, you are freed by this kind man . . . or perhaps by the king. Go now!

ŚAKUNTALĀ (*to herself*): If I am able to . . .

*(Aloud.)*

Who are you to keep me or release me?

KING (*watching Śakuntalā*): Can she feel toward me what I feel toward her? Or is my desire fulfilled?

She won't respond directly to my
words,
but she listens when I speak;
she won't turn to look at me,
but her eyes can't rest anywhere
else.

VOICE OFFSTAGE: Ascetics, be prepared to protect the creatures of our forest grove! King Duṣyanta is hunting nearby!

Dust raised by his horses' hooves
falls like a cloud of locusts
swarming
at sunset over branches of trees
where wet bark garments hang.

In terror of the chariots, an
elephant
charged into the hermitage
and scattered the herd of black
antelope,
like a demon foe of our penances—
his tusks garlanded with branches
from a tree crushed by his weight,
his feet tangled in vines
that tether him like chains.

*(Hearing this, all the girls are agitated.)*

KING (*to himself*): Oh! My palace men are searching for me and wrecking the grove. I'll have to go back.

BOTH FRIENDS: Sir, we're all upset by this news. Please let us go to our hut.

KING (*showing confusion*): Go, please. We will try to protect the hermitage.

*(They all stand to go.)*

BOTH FRIENDS: Sir, we're ashamed that our bad hospitality is our only excuse to invite you back.

KING: Not at all. I am honored to have seen you.

*(Śakuntalā exits with her two friends, looking back at the king, lingering artfully.)*

I have little desire to return to the city. I'll join my men and have them camp near the grove. I can't control my feelings for Śakuntalā.

My body turns to go,
my heart pulls me back,
like a silk banner
buffeted by the wind.

*(All exit.)*

END OF ACT ONE

## ACT TWO

*(The buffoon enters, despondent.)*

BUFFOON (*sighing*): My bad luck! I'm tired of playing sidekick to a king who's hooked on hunting. "There's a deer!" "There's a boar!" "There's a tiger!" Even in the summer midday heat we chase from jungle to jungle on paths where trees give barely any shade. We drink stinking water from mountain streams foul with rusty leaves. At odd hours we eat nasty meals of spit-roasted meat. Even at night I can't sleep. My joints ache from galloping on that horse. Then at the crack of dawn, I'm woken rudely by a noise piercing the forest. Those sons of bitches hunt their birds then. The torture doesn't end—now I have sores on top of my bruises. Yesterday, we lagged behind. The king chased a buck into the hermitage. As luck would have it, an ascetic's daughter called Śakuntalā caught his eye. Now he isn't even thinking of going back to the city. This very dawn I found him wide-eyed, mooning about her. What a fate! I must see him after his bath.

*(He walks around, looking.)*

Here comes my friend now, wearing garlands of wild flowers. Greek women carry his bow in their hands. Good! I'll stand here pretending my arms and legs are broken. Maybe then I'll get some rest.

*(He stands leaning on his staff. The king enters with his retinue, as described.)*

KING (*to himself*):

My beloved will not be easy to win,
but signs of emotion revealed her
heart—
even when love seems hopeless,
mutual longing keeps passion alive.

*(He smiles.)*

A suitor who measures his beloved's state of mind by his own desire is a fool.

She threw tender glances
though her eyes were cast down,
her heavy hips swayed
in slow seductive movements,
she answered in anger
when her friend said, "Don't go!"
and I felt it was all for my sake . . .
but a lover sees in his own way.

BUFFOON (*still in the same position*): Dear friend, since my hands can't move to greet you, I have to salute you with my voice.

KING: How did you cripple your limbs?

BUFFOON: Why do you ask why I cry after throwing dust in my eyes yourself?

KING: I don't understand.

BUFFOON: Dear friend, when a straight reed is twisted into a crooked reed, is it by its own power, or is it the river current?

KING: The river current is the cause.

BUFFOON: And so it is with me.

KING: How so?

BUFFOON: You neglect the business of being a king and live like a woodsman in this awful camp. Chasing after wild beasts every day jolts my joints and muscles till I can't control my own limbs anymore. I beg you to let me rest for just one day!

KING (*to himself*): He says what I also feel. When I remember Kaṇva's daughter, the thought of hunting disgusts me.

I can't draw my bowstring
to shoot arrows at deer
who live with my love
and teach her tender glances.

BUFFOON: Sir, you have something on your mind. I'm crying in a wilderness.

KING (*smiling*): Yes, it is wrong to ignore my friend's plea.

BUFFOON: Live long!

*(He starts to go.)*

KING: Dear friend, stay! Hear what I have to say!

BUFFOON: At your command, sir!

KING: When you have rested, I need your help in some work that you will enjoy.

BUFFOON: Is it eating sweets? I'm game!

KING: I shall tell you. Who stands guard?

GUARD (*entering*): At your command, sir!

KING: Raivataka! Summon the general!

*(The guard exits and reenters with the general.)*

GUARD: The king is looking this way, waiting to give you his orders. Approach him, sir!

GENERAL (*looking at the king*): Hunting is said to be a vice, but our king prospers:

Drawing the bow only hardens his
chest,
he suffers the sun's scorching rays
unburned,
hard muscles mask his body's lean
state—
like a wild elephant, his energy
sustains him.

*(He approaches the king.)*

Victory, my lord! We've already tracked some wild beasts. Why the delay?

KING: Māḍhavya's censure of hunting has dampened my spirit.

GENERAL (*in a stage whisper, to the buffoon*): Friend, you stick to your opposition! I'll try to restore our king's good sense.

*(Aloud.)*

This fool is talking nonsense. Here is the king as proof:

A hunter's belly is taut and lean,
his slender body craves exertion;
he penetrates the spirit of
creatures
overcome by fear and rage;
his bowmanship is proved
by arrows striking a moving
target—
hunting is falsely called a vice.
What sport can rival it?

BUFFOON (*angrily*): The king has come to his senses. If you keep chasing from forest to forest, you'll fall into the jaws of an old bear hungry for a human nose . . .

KING: My noble general, we are near a hermitage; your words cannot please me now.

Let horned buffaloes plunge into
muddy pools!
Let herds of deer huddle in the
shade to eat grass!
Let fearless wild boars crush
fragrant swamp grass!
Let my bowstring lie slack and my
bow at rest!

GENERAL: Whatever gives the king pleasure.

KING: Withdraw the men who are in the forest now and forbid soldiers to disturb the grove!

Ascetics devoted to peace
possess a fiery hidden power,
like smooth crystal sunstones
that reflect the sun's scorching rays.

GENERAL: Whatever you command, sir!

BUFFOON: Your arguments for keeping up the hunt fall on deaf ears!

*(The general exits.)*

KING (*looking at his retinue*): You women, take away my hunting gear! Raivataka, don't neglect your duty!

RETINUE: As the king commands!

*(They exit.)*

BUFFOON: Sir, now that the flies are cleared out, sit on a stone bench under this shady canopy. Then I'll find a comfortable seat too.

KING: Go ahead!

BUFFOON: You first, sir!

*(Both walk about, then sit down.)*

KING: Māḍhavya, you haven't really used your eyes because you haven't seen true beauty.

BUFFOON: But you're right in front of me, sir!

KING: Everyone is partial to what he knows well, but I'm speaking about Śakuntalā, the jewel of the hermitage.

BUFFOON (*to himself*): I won't give him a chance!

*(Aloud.)*

Dear friend, it seems that you're pursuing an ascetic's daughter.

KING: Friend, the heart of a Puru king wouldn't crave a forbidden fruit . . .

The sage's child is a nymph's daughter,
rescued by him after she was abandoned,
like a fragile jasmine blossom
broken and caught on a sunflower pod.

BUFFOON (*laughing*): You're like the man who loses his taste for dates and prefers sour tamarind! How can you abandon the gorgeous gems of your palace?

KING: You speak this way because you haven't seen her.

BUFFOON: She must be delectable if you're so enticed!

KING: Friend, what is the use of all this talk?

The divine creator imagined perfection
and shaped her ideal form in his mind—
when I recall the beauty his power wrought,
she shines like a gemstone among my jewels.

BUFFOON: So she's the reason you reject the other beauties!

KING: She stays in my mind:

A flower no one has smelled,
a bud no fingers have plucked,
an uncut jewel, honey untasted,
unbroken fruit of holy deeds—
I don't know who is destined
to enjoy her flawless beauty.

BUFFOON: Then you should rescue her quickly! Don't let her fall into the arms of some ascetic who greases his head with iṅgudī oil!

KING: She is someone else's ward and her guardian is away.

BUFFOON: What kind of passion did her eyes betray?

KING: Ascetics are timid by nature:

Her eyes were cast down in my presence,
but she found an excuse to smile—
modesty barely contained the love
she could neither reveal nor conceal.

BUFFOON: Did you expect her to climb into your lap when she'd barely seen you?

KING: When we parted her feelings for me showed despite her modesty.

"A blade of kuśa grass
pricked my foot,"
the girl said for no reason
after walking a few steps away;
then she pretended to free
her bark dress from branches
where it was not caught
and shyly glanced at me.

BUFFOON: Stock up on food for a long trip! I can see you've turned that ascetics' grove into a pleasure garden.

KING: Friend, some of the ascetics recognize me. What excuse can we find to return to the hermitage?

BUFFOON: What excuse? Aren't you the king? Collect a sixth of their wild rice as tax!

KING: Fool! These ascetics pay tribute that pleases me more than mounds of jewels.

Tribute that kings collect
from members of society decays,
but the share of austerity
that ascetics give lasts forever.

VOICE OFFSTAGE: Good, we have succeeded!

KING (*listening*): These are the steady, calm voices of ascetics.

GUARD (*entering*): Victory, sir! Two boy ascetics are waiting near the gate.

KING: Let them enter without delay!

GUARD: I'll show them in.

*(He exits; reenters with the boys.)*

Here you are!

FIRST BOY: His majestic body inspires trust. It is natural when a king is virtually a sage.

His palace is a hermitage
with its infinite pleasures,
the discipline of protecting men
imposes austerities every day—
pairs of celestial bards praise
his perfect self-control,
adding the royal word "king"
to "sage," his sacred title.

SECOND BOY: Gautama, is this Duṣyanta, the friend of Indra?

FIRST BOY: Of course!

SECOND BOY:

It is no surprise that this arm of iron
rules the whole earth bounded by dark seas—
when demons harass the gods, victory's hope
rests on his bow and Indra's thunderbolt.

BOTH BOYS (*coming near*): Victory to you, king!

KING (*rising from his seat*): I salute you both!

BOTH BOYS: To your success, sir!

*(They offer fruits.)*

KING (*accepting their offering*): I am ready to listen.

BOTH BOYS: The ascetics know that you are camped nearby and send a petition to you.

KING: What do they request?

BOTH BOYS: Demons are taking advantage of Sage Kaṇva's absence to harass us. You must come with your charioteer to protect the hermitage for a few days!

KING: I am honored to oblige.

BUFFOON (*in a stage whisper*): Your wish is fulfilled!

KING (*smiling*): Raivataka, call my charioteer! Tell him to bring the chariot and my bow!

GUARD: As the king commands!

*(He exits.)*

BOTH BOYS (*showing delight*):

Following your ancestral duties
suits your noble form—
the Puru kings are ordained
to dispel their subjects' fear.

KING (*bowing*): You two return! I shall follow.

BOTH BOYS: Be victorious!

*(They exit.)*

KING: Māḍhavya, are you curious to see Śakuntalā?

BUFFOON: At first there was a flood, but now with this news of demons, not a drop is left.

KING: Don't be afraid! Won't you be with me?

BUFFOON: Then I'll be safe from any demon . . .

GUARD (*entering*): The chariot is ready to take you to victory . . . but Karabhaka has just come from the city with a message from the queen.

KING: Did my mother send him?

GUARD: She did.

KING: Have him enter then.

GUARD: Yes.

*(He exits; reenters with Karabhaka.)*

Here is the king. Approach!

KARABHAKA: Victory, sir! Victory! The queen has ordered a ceremony four days from now to mark the end of her fast. Your Majesty will surely give us the honor of his presence.

KING: The ascetics' business keeps me here and my mother's command calls me there. I must find a way to avoid neglecting either!

BUFFOON: Hang yourself between them the way Triśaṅku hung between heaven and earth.

KING: I'm really confused . . .

My mind is split in two
by these conflicting duties,
like a river current split
by boulders in its course.

*(Thinking.)*

Friend, my mother has treated you like a son. You must go back and report that I've set my heart on fulfilling my duty to the ascetics. You fulfill my filial duty to the queen.

BUFFOON: You don't really think I'm afraid of demons?

KING (*smiling*): My brave brahman, how could you be?

BUFFOON: Then I can travel like the king's younger brother.

KING: We really should not disturb the grove! Take my whole entourage with you!

BUFFOON: Now I've turned into the crown prince!

KING (*to himself*): This fellow is absentminded. At any time he may tell the palace women about my passion. I'll tell him this:

*(Taking the buffoon by the hand, he speaks aloud.)*

Dear friend, I'm going to the hermitage out of reverence for the sages. I really feel no desire for the young ascetic Śakuntalā.

What do I share with a rustic girl
reared among fawns, unskilled in love?
Don't mistake what I muttered
in jest for the real truth, friend!

*(All exit.)*

End of Act Two

## ACT THREE

*(A disciple of Kaṇva enters, carrying kuśa grass for a sacrificial rite.)*

Disciple: King Duṣyanta is certainly powerful. Since he entered the hermitage, our rites have not been hindered.

Why talk of fixing arrows?
The mere twang of his bowstring
clears away menacing demons
as if his bow roared with death.

I'll gather some more grass for the priests to spread on the sacrificial altar.

*(Walking around and looking, he calls aloud.)*

Priyaṁvadā, for whom are you bringing the ointment of fragrant lotus root fibers and leaves?

*(Listening.)*

What are you saying? Śakuntalā is suffering from heat exhaustion? They're for rubbing on her body? Priyaṁvadā, take care of her! She is the breath of Father Kaṇva's life. I'll give Gautamī this water from the sacrifice to use for soothing her.

*(He exits; the interlude ends. Then the king enters, suffering from love, deep in thought, sighing.)*

King:

I know the power ascetics have
and the rules that bind her,
but I cannot abandon my heart
now that she has taken it.

*(Showing the pain of love.)*

Love, why do you and the moon both contrive to deceive lovers by first gaining our trust?

Arrows of flowers and cool moon rays
are both deadly for men like me—
the moon shoots fire through icy rays
and you hurl thunderbolts of flowers.

*(Walking around.)*

Now that the rites are concluded and the priests have dismissed me, where can I rest from the weariness of this work?

*(Sighing.)*

There is no refuge but the sight of my love. I must find her.

*(Looking up at the sun.)*

Śakuntalā usually spends the heat of the day with her friends in a bower of vines on the Mālinī riverbank. I shall go there.

*(Walking around, miming the touch of breeze.)*

This place is enchanted by the wind.

A breeze fragrant with lotus pollen
and moist from the Mālinī waves
can be held in soothing embrace
by my love-scorched arms.

*(Walking around and looking.)*

I see fresh footprints
on white sand in the clearing,
deeply pressed at the heel
by the sway of full hips.

I'll just look through the branches.

*(Walking around, looking, he becomes joyous.)*

My eyes have found bliss! The girl I desire is lying on a stone couch strewn with flowers, attended by her two friends. I'll eavesdrop as they confide in one another.

*(He stands watching. Śakuntalā appears as described, with her two friends.)*

BOTH FRIENDS (*fanning her affectionately*): Śakuntalā, does the breeze from this lotus leaf please you?

ŚAKUNTALĀ: Are you fanning me?

*(The friends trade looks, miming dismay.)*

KING (*deliberating*): Śakuntalā seems to be in great physical pain. Is it the heat or is it what is in my own heart?

*(Miming ardent desire.)*

My doubts are unfounded!

Her breasts are smeared with lotus balm,
her lotus-fiber bracelet hangs limp,
her beautiful body glows in pain—
love burns young women like summer heat,
but its guilt makes them more charming.

PRIYAṀVADĀ (*in a stage whisper*): Anasūyā, Śakuntalā has been pining since she first saw the king. Could he be the cause of her sickness?

ANASŪYĀ: She must be suffering from lovesickness. I'll ask her . . .

*(Aloud.)*

Friend, I have something to ask you. Your pain seems so deep . . .

ŚAKUNTALĀ (*raising herself halfway*): What do you want to say?

ANASŪYĀ: Śakuntalā, though we don't know what it is to be in love, your condition reminds us of lovers we have heard about in stories. Can you tell us the cause of your pain? Unless we understand your illness, we can't begin to find a cure.

KING: Anasūyā expresses my own thoughts.

ŚAKUNTALĀ: Even though I want to, suddenly I can't make myself tell you.

PRIYAṀVADĀ: Śakuntalā, my friend Anasūyā means well. Don't you see how sick you are? Your limbs are wasting away. Only the shadow of your beauty remains . . .

KING: What Priyaṁvadā says is true:

Her cheeks are deeply sunken,
her breasts' full shape is gone,
her waist is thin, her shoulders bent,

and the color has left her skin—
tormented by love,
she is sad but beautiful to see,
like a jasmine creeper
when hot wind shrivels its leaves.

ŚAKUNTALĀ: Friends, who else can I tell? May I burden you?

BOTH FRIENDS: We insist! Sharing sorrow with loving friends makes it bearable.

KING:

Friends who share her joy and
sorrow
discover the love concealed in her
heart—
though she looked back longingly
at me,
now I am afraid to hear her
response.

ŚAKUNTALĀ: Friend, since my eyes first saw the guardian of the hermits' retreat, I've felt such strong desire for him!

KING: I have heard what I want to hear.

My tormentor, the god of love,
has soothed my fever himself,
like the heat of late summer
allayed by early rain clouds.

ŚAKUNTALĀ: If you two think it's right, then help me to win the king's pity. Otherwise, you'll soon pour sesame oil and water on my corpse . . .

KING: Her words destroy my doubt.

PRIYAṀVADĀ (*in a stage whisper*): She's so dangerously in love that there's no time to lose. Since her heart is set on the ornament of the Puru dynasty, we should rejoice that she desires him.

ANASŪYĀ: What you say is true.

PRIYAṀVADĀ (*aloud*): Friend, by good fortune your desire is in harmony with nature. A great river can only descend to the ocean. A jasmine creeper can only twine around a mango tree.

KING: Why is this surprising when the twin stars of spring serve the crescent moon?

ANASŪYĀ: What means do we have to fulfill our friend's desire secretly and quickly?

PRIYAṀVADĀ: "Secretly" demands some effort. "Quickly" is easy.

ANASŪYĀ: How so?

PRIYAṀVADĀ: The king was charmed by her loving look; he seems thin these days from sleepless nights.

KING: It's true . . .

This golden armlet
slips to my wrist
without touching the scars
my bowstring has made;
its gemstones are faded
by tears of secret pain
that every night wets my arm
where I bury my face.

PRIYAṀVADĀ (*thinking*): Compose a love letter and I'll hide it in a flower. I'll deliver it to his hand on the pretext of bringing an offering to the deity.

ANASŪYĀ: This subtle plan pleases me. What does Śakuntalā say?

ŚAKUNTALĀ: I'll try my friend's plan.

PRIYAṀVADĀ: Then compose a poem to declare your love!

ŚAKUNTALĀ: I'm thinking, but my heart trembles with fear that he'll reject me.

KING (*delighted*):

The man you fear will reject you
waits longing to love you, timid
girl—
a suitor may lose or be lucky,
but the goddess always wins.

BOTH FRIENDS: Why do you belittle your own virtues? Who would cover his body with a piece of cloth to keep off cool autumn moonlight?

ŚAKUNTALĀ (*smiling*): I'm trying to follow your advice.

*(She sits thinking.)*

KING: As I gaze at her, my eyes forget to blink.

She arches an eyebrow,
struggling to compose the verse—
the down rises on her cheek,
showing the passion she feels.

ŚAKUNTALĀ: I've thought of a verse, but I have nothing to write it on.

PRIYAṀVADĀ: Engrave the letters with your nail on this lotus leaf! It's as delicate as a parrot's breast.

ŚAKUNTALĀ (*miming what Priyaṁvadā described*): Listen and tell me if this makes sense!

BOTH FRIENDS: We're both paying attention.

ŚAKUNTALĀ (*singing*):

I don't know
your heart,
but day and night
for wanting you,
love violently
tortures
my limbs,
cruel man.

KING (*suddenly revealing himself*):

Love torments you, slender girl,
but he completely consumes me—
daylight spares the lotus pond
while it destroys the moon.

BOTH FRIENDS (*looking, rising with delight*): Welcome to the swift success of love's desire!

*(Śakuntalā tries to rise.)*

KING: Don't exert yourself!

Limbs lying among crushed petals
like fragile lotus stalks
are too weakened by pain
to perform ceremonious acts.

ANASŪYĀ: Then let the king sit on this stone bench!

*(The king sits; Śakuntalā rises in embarrassment.)*

PRIYAṀVADĀ: The passion of two young lovers is clear. My affection for our friend makes me speak out again now.

KING: Noble lady, don't hesitate! It is painful to keep silent when one must speak.

PRIYAṀVADĀ: We're told that it is the king's duty to ease the pain of his suffering subjects.

KING: My duty, exactly!

PRIYAṀVADĀ: Since she first saw you, our dear friend has been reduced to this sad condition. You must protect her and save her life.

KING: Noble lady, our affection is shared and I am honored by all you say.

ŚAKUNTALĀ (*looking at Priyaṁvadā*): Why are you keeping the king here? He must be anxious to return to his palace.

KING:

If you think that my lost heart
could love anyone but you,
a fatal blow strikes a man
already wounded by love's arrows!

ANASŪYĀ: We've heard that kings have many loves. Will our dear friend become a sorrow to her family after you've spent time with her?

KING: Noble lady, enough of this!

Despite my many wives,
on two the royal line rests—
sea-bound earth
and your friend.

BOTH FRIENDS: You reassure us.

PRIYAṀVADĀ (*casting a glance*): Anasūyā, this fawn is looking for its mother. Let's take it to her!

*(They both begin to leave.)*

ŚAKUNTALĀ: Come back! Don't leave me unprotected!

BOTH FRIENDS: The protector of the earth is at your side.

ŚAKUNTALĀ: Why have they gone?

KING: Don't be alarmed! I am your servant.

Shall I set moist winds in motion
with lotus-leaf fans to cool your
pain,
or rest your soft red lotus feet
on my lap to stroke them, my love?

ŚAKUNTALĀ: I cannot sin against those I respect!

*(Standing as if she wants to leave.)*

KING: Beautiful Śakuntalā, the day is still hot.

Why should your frail limbs
leave this couch of flowers
shielded by lotus leaves
to wander in the heat?

*(Saying this, he forces her to turn around.)*

ŚAKUNTALĀ: Puru king, control yourself! Though I'm burning with love, how can I give myself to you?

KING: Don't fear your elders! The father of your family knows the law. When he finds out, he will not blame you.

The daughters of royal sages often
marry
in secret and then their fathers
bless them.

ŚAKUNTALĀ: Release me! I must ask my friends' advice!

KING: Yes, I shall release you.

ŚAKUNTALĀ: When?

KING:

Only let my thirsting mouth
gently drink from your lips,
the way a bee sips nectar
from a fragile virgin blossom.

*(Saying this, he tries to raise her face. Śakuntalā evades him with a dance.)*

VOICE OFFSTAGE: Red goose, bid farewell to your gander! Night has arrived!

ŚAKUNTALĀ (*flustered*): Puru king, Mother Gautamī is surely coming to ask about my health. Hide behind this tree!

KING: Yes.

*(He conceals himself and waits. Then Gautamī enters with a vessel in her hand, accompanied by Śakuntalā's two friends.)*

BOTH FRIENDS: This way, Mother Gautamī!

GAUTAMĪ (*approaching Śakuntalā*): Child, does the fever in your limbs burn less?

ŚAKUNTALĀ: Madam, I do feel better.

GAUTAMĪ: Kuśa grass and water will soothe your body.

*(She sprinkles Śakuntalā's head.)*

Child, the day is ended. Come, let's go back to our hut!

*(She starts to go.)*

ŚAKUNTALĀ (*to herself*): My heart, even when your desire was within reach, you were bound by fear. Now you'll suffer the torment of separation and regret.

*(Stopping after a few steps, she speaks aloud.)*

Bower of creepers, refuge from my torment, I say goodbye until our joy can be renewed . . .

*(Sorrowfully, Śakuntalā exits with the other women.)*

KING (*coming out of hiding*): Fulfillment of desire is fraught with obstacles.

Why didn't I kiss her face
as it bent near my shoulder,
her fingers shielding lips
that stammered lovely warning?

Should I go now? Or shall I stay here in this bower of creepers that my love enjoyed and then left?

I see the flowers her body pressed
on this bench of stone,
the letter her nails inscribed
on the faded lotus leaf,
the lotus-fiber bracelet
that slipped from her wrist—
my eyes are prisoners
in this empty house of reeds.

VOICE IN THE AIR: King!

When the evening rituals begin,
shadows of flesh-eating demons
swarm
like amber clouds of twilight,
raising terror at the altar of fire.

KING: I am coming.

*(He exits.)*

END OF ACT THREE

## ACT FOUR

*(The two friends enter, miming the gathering of flowers.)*

ANASŪYĀ: Priyaṁvadā, I'm delighted that Śakuntalā chose a suitable husband for herself, but I still feel anxious.

PRIYAṀVADĀ: Why?

ANASŪYĀ: When the king finished the sacrifice, the sages thanked him and he left. Now that he has returned to his palace women in the city, will he remember us here?

PRIYAṀVADĀ: Have faith! He's so handsome, he can't be evil. But I don't know what Father Kaṇva will think when he hears about what happened.

ANASŪYĀ: I predict that he'll give his approval.

PRIYAṀVADĀ: Why?

ANASŪYĀ: He's always planned to give his daughter to a worthy husband. If fate accomplished it so quickly, Father Kaṇva won't object.

PRIYAṀVADĀ (*looking at the basket of flowers*): We've gathered enough flowers for the offering ceremony.

ANASŪYĀ: Shouldn't we worship the goddess who guards Śakuntalā?

PRIYAṀVADĀ: I have just begun.

*(She begins the rite.)*

VOICE OFFSTAGE: I am here!

ANASŪYĀ (*listening*): Friend, a guest is announcing himself.

PRIYAṀVADĀ: Śakuntalā is in her hut nearby, but her heart is far away.

ANASŪYĀ: You're right! Enough of these flowers!

*(They begin to leave.)*

VOICE OFFSTAGE: So . . . you slight a guest . . .

Since you blindly ignore
a great sage like me,
the lover you worship
with mindless devotion
will not remember you,
even when awakened—
like a drunkard who forgets
a story he just composed!

PRIYAṀVADĀ: Oh! What a terrible turn of events! Śakuntalā's distraction has offended someone she should have greeted.

*(Looking ahead.)*

Not just an ordinary person, but the angry sage Durvāsas himself cursed her and went away in a frenzy of quivering, mad gestures. What else but fire has such power to burn?

ANASŪYĀ: Go! Bow at his feet and make him return while I prepare the water for washing his feet!

PRIYAṀVADĀ: As you say.

*(She exits.)*

ANASŪYĀ (*after a few steps, she mimes stumbling*): Oh! The basket of flowers fell from my hand when I stumbled in my haste to go.

*(She mimes the gathering of flowers.)*

PRIYAṀVADĀ (*entering*): He's so terribly cruel! No one could pacify him! But I was able to soften him a little.

ANASŪYĀ: Even that is a great feat with him! Tell me more!

PRIYAṀVADĀ: When he refused to return, I begged him to forgive a daughter's first offense, since she didn't understand the power of his austerity.

ANASŪYĀ : Then? Then?

PRIYAṀVADĀ: He refused to change his word, but he promised that when the king sees the ring of recollection, the curse will end. Then he vanished.

ANASŪYĀ: Now we can breathe again. When he left, the king himself gave her the ring engraved with his name. Śakuntalā will have her own means of ending the curse.

PRIYAṀVADĀ: Come friend! We should finish the holy rite we're performing for her.

*(The two walk around, looking.)*

Anasūyā, look! With her face resting on her hand, our dear friend looks like a picture. She is thinking about her husband's leaving, with no thought for herself, much less for a guest.

ANASŪYĀ: Priyaṁvadā, we two must keep all this a secret between us. Our friend is fragile by nature; she needs our protection.

PRIYAṀVADĀ: Who would sprinkle a jasmine with scalding water?

*(They both exit; the interlude ends. Then a disciple of Kaṇva enters, just awakened from sleep.)*

DISCIPLE: Father Kaṇva has just returned from his pilgrimage and wants to know the exact time. I'll go into a clearing to see what remains of the night.

*(Walking around and looking.)*

It is dawn.

The moon sets over the western mountain  
as the sun rises in dawn's red trail—  
rising and setting, these two bright powers  
portend the rise and fall of men.

When the moon disappears, night lotuses  
are but dull souvenirs of its beauty—  
when her lover disappears, the sorrow  
is too painful for a frail girl to bear.

ANASŪYĀ (*throwing aside the curtain and entering*): Even a person withdrawn from worldly life knows that the king has treated Śakuntalā badly.

DISCIPLE: I'll inform Father Kaṇva that it's time for the fire oblation.

*(He exits.)*

ANASŪYĀ: Even when I'm awake, I'm useless. My hands and feet don't do their work. Love must be pleased to have made our innocent friend put her trust in a liar . . . but perhaps it was the curse of Durvāsas that changed him . . . otherwise, how could the king have made such promises and not sent even a message by now? Maybe we should send the ring to remind him. Which of these ascetics who practice austerities can we ask? Father Kaṇva has just returned from his pilgrimage. Since we feel that our friend was also at fault, we haven't told him that Śakuntalā is married to Duṣyanta and is pregnant. The problem is serious. What should we do?

PRIYAṀVADĀ (*entering, with delight*): Friend, hurry! We're to celebrate the festival of Śakuntalā's departure for her husband's house.

ANASŪYĀ: What's happened, friend?

PRIYAṀVADĀ: Listen! I went to ask Śakuntalā how she had slept. Father Kaṇva embraced her and though her face was bowed in shame, he blessed her: "Though his eyes were filled with smoke, the priest's oblation luckily fell on the fire. My child, I shall not mourn for you . . . like knowledge given to a good student I shall send you to your husband today with an escort of sages."

ANASŪYĀ: Who told Father Kaṇva what happened?

PRIYAṀVADĀ: A bodiless voice was chanting when he entered the fire sanctuary.

*(Quoting in Sanskrit.)*

Priest, know that your daughter  
carries Duṣyanta's potent seed  
for the good of the earth—  
like fire in mimosa wood.

ANASŪYĀ: I'm joyful, friend. But I know that Śakuntalā must leave us today and sorrow shadows my happiness.

PRIYAṀVADĀ: Friend, we must chase away sorrow and make this hermit girl happy!

ANASŪYĀ: Friend, I've made a garland of mimosa flowers. It's in the coconut-shell box hanging on a branch of the mango tree. Get it for me! Meanwhile I'll prepare the special ointments of deer musk, sacred earth, and blades of dūrvā grass.

PRIYAṀVADĀ: Here it is!

*(Anasūyā exits; Priyaṁvadā gracefully mimes taking down the box.)*

VOICE OFFSTAGE: Gautamī! Śārṅgarava and some others have been appointed to escort Śakuntalā.

PRIYAṀVADĀ (*listening*): Hurry! Hurry! The sages are being called to go to Hastināpura.

ANASŪYĀ (*reentering with pots of ointments in her hands*): Come, friend! Let's go!

PRIYAṀVADĀ (*looking around*): Śakuntalā stands at sunrise with freshly washed hair while the female ascetics bless her with handfuls of wild rice and auspicious words of farewell. Let's go to her together.

*(The two approach as Śakuntalā enters with Gautamī and other female ascetics, and strikes a posture as described. One after another, the female ascetics address her.)*

FIRST FEMALE ASCETIC: Child, win the title "Chief Queen" as a sign of your husband's high esteem!

SECOND FEMALE ASCETIC: Child, be a mother to heroes!

THIRD FEMALE ASCETIC: Child, be honored by your husband!

BOTH FRIENDS: This happy moment is no time for tears, friend.

*(Wiping away her tears, they calm her with dance gestures.)*

PRIYAṀVADĀ: Your beauty deserves jewels, not these humble things we've gathered in the hermitage.

*(Two boy ascetics enter with offerings in their hands.)*

BOTH BOYS: Here is an ornament for you!

*(Everyone looks amazed.)*

GAUTAMĪ: Nārada, my child, where did this come from?

FIRST BOY: From Father Kaṇva's power.

GAUTAMĪ: Was it his mind's magic?

SECOND BOY: Not at all! Listen! You ordered us to bring flowers from the forest trees for Śakuntalā.

One tree produced this white silk cloth,
another poured resinous lac to redden her feet—
the tree nymphs produced jewels in hands
that stretched from branches like young shoots.

PRIYAṀVADĀ (*watching Śakuntalā*): This is a sign that royal fortune will come to you in your husband's house.

*(Śakuntalā mimes modesty.)*

FIRST BOY: Gautama, come quickly! Father Kaṇva is back from bathing. We'll tell him how the trees honor her.

SECOND BOY: As you say.

*(The two exit.)*

BOTH FRIENDS: We've never worn them ourselves, but we'll put these jewels on your limbs the way they look in pictures.

ŚAKUNTALĀ: I trust your skill.

*(Both friends mime ornamenting her. Then Kaṇva enters, fresh from his bath.)*

KAṆVA:

My heart is touched with sadness
since Śakuntalā must go today,
my throat is choked with sobs,
my eyes are dulled by worry—
if a disciplined ascetic
suffers so deeply from love,

how do fathers bear the pain
of each daughter's parting?

*(He walks around.)*

Both Friends: Śakuntalā, your jewels are in place; now put on the pair of silken cloths.

*(Standing, Śakuntalā wraps them.)*

Gautamī: Child, your father has come. His eyes filled with tears of joy embrace you. Greet him reverently!

Śakuntalā (*modestly*): Father, I welcome you.

Kaṇva: Child,

May your husband honor you
the way Yayāti honored Śarmiṣṭhā.
As she bore her son Puru,
may you bear an imperial prince.

Gautamī: Sir, this is a blessing, not just a prayer.

Kaṇva: Child, walk around the sacrifical fires!

*(All walk around; Kaṇva intoning a prayer in Vedic meter.)*

Perfectly placed around the main altar,
fed with fuel, strewn with holy grass,
destroying sin by incense from oblations,
may these sacred fires purify you!

You must leave now!

*(Looking around.)*

Where are Śārṅgarava and the others?

Disciple (*entering*): Here we are, sir!

Kaṇva: You show your sister the way!

Śārṅgarava: Come this way!

*(They walk around.)*

Kaṇva: Listen, you trees that grow in our grove!

Until you were well watered
she could not bear to drink;
she loved you too much
to pluck your flowers for her hair;
the first time your buds bloomed,
she blossomed with joy—
may you all bless Śakuntalā
as she leaves for her husband's house.

*(Miming that he hears a cuckoo's cry.)*

The trees of her forest family
have blessed Śakuntalā—
the cuckoo's melodious song
announces their response.

Voice in the Air:

May lakes colored by lotuses mark her path!
May trees shade her from the sun's burning rays!
May the dust be as soft as lotus pollen!
May fragrant breezes cool her way!

*(All listen astonished.)*

Gautamī: Child, the divinities of our grove love you like your family and bless you. We bow to you all!

Śakuntalā (*bowing and walking around; speaking in a stage whisper*): Priyaṁvadā, though I long to see my husband, my feet move with sorrow as I start to leave the hermitage.

Priyaṁvadā: You are not the only one who grieves. The whole hermitage feels this way as your departure from our grove draws near.

Grazing deer
drop grass,

peacocks
stop dancing,
vines loose
pale leaves
falling
like tears.

Śakuntalā (*remembering*): Father, before I leave, I must see my sister, the vine Forestlight.

Kaṇva: I know that you feel a sister's love for her. She is right here.

Śakuntalā: Forestlight, though you love your mango tree, turn to embrace me with your tendril arms! After today, I'll be so far away . . .

Kaṇva:

Your merits won you the husband
I always hoped you would have
and your jasmine has her mango
tree—
my worries for you both are over.

Start your journey here!

Śakuntalā (*facing her two friends*): I entrust her care to you.

Both Friends: But who will care for us?

*(They wipe away their tears.)*

Kaṇva: Anasūyā, enough crying! You should be giving Śakuntalā courage!

*(All walk around.)*

Śakuntalā: Father, when the pregnant doe who grazes near my hut gives birth, please send someone to give me the good news.

Kaṇva: I shall not forget.

Śakuntalā (*miming the interrupting of her gait*): Who is clinging to my skirt?

*(She turns around.)*

Kaṇva: Child,

The buck whose mouth you
healed with oil
when it was pierced by a blade of
kuśa grass
and whom you fed with grains of
rice—
your adopted son will not leave
the path.

Śakuntalā: Child, don't follow when I'm abandoning those I love! I raised you when you were orphaned soon after your birth, but now I'm deserting you too. Father will look after you. Go back!

*(Weeping, she starts to go.)*

Kaṇva: Be strong!

Hold back the tears that blind
your long-lashed eyes—
you will stumble if you cannot see
the uneven ground on the path.

Śārṅgarava: Sir, the scriptures prescribe that loved ones be escorted only to the water's edge. We are at the shore of the lake. Give us your message and return!

Śakuntalā: We shall rest in the shade of this fig tree.

*(All walk around and stop; Kaṇva speaks to himself.)*

What would be the right message
to send to King Duṣyanta?

*(He ponders.)*

Śakuntalā (*in a stage whisper*): Look! The wild goose cries in anguish when her mate is hidden by lotus leaves. What I'm suffering is much worse.

ANASŪYĀ: Friend, don't speak this way!

This goose spends
every long night
in sorrow
without her mate,
but hope lets her
survive
the deep pain
of loneliness.

KAṆVA: Śārṅgarava, speak my words to the king after you present Śakuntalā!

ŚĀRṄGARAVA: As you command, sir!

KAṆVA:

Considering our discipline,
the nobility of your birth
and that she fell in love with you
before her kinsmen could act,
acknowledge her with equal rank
among your wives—
what more is destined for her,
the bride's family will not ask.

ŚĀRṄGARAVA: I grasp your message.

KAṆVA: Child, now I must instruct you. We forest hermits know something about worldly matters.

ŚĀRṄGARAVA: Nothing is beyond the scope of wise men.

KAṆVA: When you enter your husband's family:

Obey your elders, be a friend to
the other wives!
If your husband seems harsh,
don't be impatient!
Be fair to your servants, humble in
your happiness!
Women who act this way become
noble wives;
sullen girls only bring their
families disgrace.

But what does Gautamī think?

GAUTAMĪ: This is good advice for wives, child. Take it all to heart!

KAṆVA: Child, embrace me and your friends!

ŚAKUNTALĀ: Father, why must Priyaṁvadā and my other friends turn back here?

KAṆVA: They will also be given in marriage. It is not proper for them to go there now. Gautamī will go with you.

ŚAKUNTALĀ (*embracing her father*): How can I go on living in a strange place, torn from my father's side, like a vine torn from the side of a sandalwood tree growing on a mountain slope?

KAṆVA: Child, why are you so frightened?

When you are your husband's
honored wife,
absorbed in royal duties and in
your son,
born like the sun to the eastern
dawn,
the sorrow of separation will fade.

*(Śakuntalā falls at her father's feet.)*

Let my hopes for you be fulfilled!

ŚAKUNTALĀ (*approaching her two friends*): You two must embrace me together!

BOTH FRIENDS (*embracing her*): Friend, if the king seems slow to recognize you, show him the ring engraved with his name!

ŚAKUNTALĀ: Your suspicions make me tremble!

BOTH FRIENDS: Don't be afraid! It's our love that fears evil.

ŚĀRṄGARAVA: The sun is high in the afternoon sky. Hurry, please!

ŚAKUNTALĀ (*facing the sanctuary*): Father, will I ever see the grove again?

KAṆVA:

When you have lived for many
years
as a queen equal to the earth
and raised Duṣyanta's son
to be a matchless warrior,
your husband will entrust him
with the burdens of the kingdom
and will return with you
to the calm of this hermitage.

GAUTAMĪ: Child, the time for our departure has passed. Let your father turn back! It would be better, sir, if you turn back yourself. She'll keep talking this way forever.

KAṆVA: Child, my ascetic practice has been interrupted.

ŚAKUNTALĀ: My father's body is already tortured by ascetic practices. He must not grieve too much for me!

KAṆVA (*sighing*):

When I see the grains of rice
sprout from offerings you made
at the door of your hut,
how shall I calm my sorrow!

*(Śakuntalā exits with her escort.)*

BOTH FRIENDS (*watching Śakuntalā*): Śakuntalā is hidden by forest trees now.

KAṆVA: Anasūyā, your companion is following her duty. Restrain yourself and return with me!

BOTH FRIENDS: Father, the ascetics' grove seems empty without Śakuntalā. How can we enter?

KAṆVA: The strength of your love makes it seem so.

*(Walking around in meditation.)*

Good! Now that Śakuntalā is on her way to her husband's family, I feel calm.

A daughter belongs to another
man—
by sending her to her husband
today,
I feel the satisfaction
one has on repaying a loan.

*(All exit.)*

END OF ACT FOUR

## ACT FIVE

*(The king and the buffoon enter; both sit down.)*

BUFFOON: Pay attention to the music room, friend, and you'll hear the notes of a song strung into a delicious melody . . . the lady Haṁsapadikā is practicing her singing.

KING: Be quiet so I can hear her!

VOICE IN THE AIR (*singing*):

Craving sweet
new nectar,
you kissed
a mango bud once—
how could you
forget her, bee,
to bury your joy
in a lotus?

KING: The melody of the song is passionate.

BUFFOON: But did you get the meaning of the words?

KING: I once made love to her. Now she reproaches me for loving Queen Vasumatī. Friend Māḍhavya, tell Haṁsapadikā that her words rebuke me soundly.

BUFFOON: As you command!

*(He rises.)*

But if that woman grabs my hair tuft, it will be like a heavenly nymph grabbing some ascetic . . . there go my hopes of liberation!

KING: Go! Use your courtly charm to console her.

BUFFOON: What a fate!

*(He exits.)*

KING (*to himself*): Why did hearing the song's words fill me with such strong desire? I'm not parted from anyone I love . . .

Seeing rare beauty,<br>
hearing lovely sounds,<br>
even a happy man<br>
becomes strangely uneasy . . .<br>
perhaps he remembers,<br>
without knowing why,<br>
loves of another life<br>
buried deep in his being.

*(He stands bewildered. Then the king's chamberlain enters.)*

CHAMBERLAIN: At my age, look at me!

Since I took this ceremonial bamboo staff<br>
as my badge of office in the king's chambers<br>
many years have passed; now I use it<br>
as a crutch to support my faltering steps.

A king cannot neglect his duty. He has just risen from his seat of justice and though I am loath to keep him longer, Sage Kaṇva's pupils have just arrived. Authority to rule the world leaves no time for rest.

The sun's steeds were yoked before time began,<br>
the fragrant wind blows night and day,<br>
the cosmic serpent always bears earth's weight,<br>
and a king who levies taxes has his duty.

Therefore, I must perform my office.

*(Walking around and looking.)*

Weary from ruling them like children,<br>
he seeks solitude far from his subjects,<br>
like an elephant bull who seeks cool shade<br>
after gathering his herd at midday.

*(Approaching.)*

Victory to you, king! Some ascetics who dwell in the forest at the foothills of the Himālayas have come. They have women with them and bring a message from Sage Kaṇva. Listen, king, and judge!

KING (*respectfully*): Are they Sage Kaṇva's messengers?

CHAMBERLAIN: They are.

KING: Inform the teacher Somarāta that he should welcome the ascetics with the prescribed rites and then bring them to me himself. I'll wait in a place suitable for greeting them.

CHAMBERLAIN: As the king commands.

*(He exits.)*

KING (*rising*): Vetravatī, lead the way to the fire sanctuary.

DOORKEEPER: Come this way, king!

KING (*walking around, showing fatigue*): Every other creature is happy when the object of his desire is won, but for kings success contains a core of suffering.

High office only leads to greater
greed;
just perfecting its rewards is
wearisome—
a kingdom is more trouble than
it's worth,
like a royal umbrella one holds
alone.

TWO BARDS OFFSTAGE: Victory to you, king!

FIRST BARD:

You sacrifice your pleasures every
day
to labor for your subjects—
as a tree endures burning heat
to give shade from the summer sun.

SECOND BARD:

You punish villains with your rod
of justice,
you reconcile disputes, you grant
protection—
most relatives are loyal only in
hope of gain,
but you treat all your subjects like
kinsmen.

KING: My weary mind is revived.

*(He walks around.)*

DOORKEEPER: The terrace of the fire sanctuary is freshly washed and the cow is waiting to give milk for the oblation. Let the king ascend!

KING: Vetravatī, why has Father Kaṇva sent these sages to me?

Does something hinder their
ascetic life?
Or threaten creatures in the
sacred forest?
Or do my sins stunt the flowering
vines?
My mind is filled with conflicting
doubts.

DOORKEEPER: I would guess that these sages rejoice in your virtuous conduct and come to honor you.

*(The ascetics enter; Śakuntalā is in front with Gautamī; the chamberlain and the king's priest are in front of her.)*

CHAMBERLAIN: Come this way, sirs!

ŚĀRṄGARAVA: Śāradvata, my friend:

I know that this renowned king is
righteous
and none of the social classes
follows evil ways,
but my mind is so accustomed to
seclusion
that the palace feels like a house
in flames.

ŚĀRADVATA: I've felt the same way ever since we entered the city.

As if I were freshly bathed, seeing
a filthy man,
pure while he's defiled, awake
while he's asleep,
as if I were a free man watching a
prisoner,
I watch this city mired in pleasures.

ŚAKUNTALĀ (*indicating she feels an omen*): Why is my right eye twitching?

GAUTAMĪ: Child, your husband's family gods turn bad fortune into blessings!

*(They walk around.)*

PRIEST (*indicating the king*): Ascetics, the guardian of sacred order has left the seat of justice and awaits you now. Behold him!

ŚĀRṄGARAVA: Great priest, he seems praiseworthy, but we expect no less.

Boughs bend, heavy with ripened fruit,
clouds descend with fresh rain,
noble men are gracious with wealth—
this is the nature of bountiful things.

DOORKEEPER: King, their faces look calm. I'm sure that the sages have confidence in what they're doing.

KING (*seeing Śakuntalā*):

Who is she? Carefully veiled
to barely reveal her body's beauty,
surrounded by the ascetics
like a bud among withered leaves.

DOORKEEPER: King, I feel curious and puzzled too. Surely her form deserves closer inspection.

KING: Let her be! One should not stare at another man's wife!

ŚAKUNTALĀ (*placing her hand on her chest, she speaks to herself*): My heart, why are you quivering? Be quiet while I learn my noble husband's feelings.

PRIEST (*going forward*): These ascetics have been honored with due ceremony. They have a message from their teacher. The king should hear them!

KING: I am paying attention.

SAGES (*raising their hands in a gesture of greeting*): May you be victorious, king!

KING: I salute you all!

SAGES: May your desires be fulfilled!

KING: Do the sages perform austerities unhampered?

SAGES:

Who would dare obstruct the rites
of holy men whom you protect—
how can darkness descend
when the sun's rays shine?

KING: My title "king" is more meaningful now. Is the world blessed by Father Kaṇva's health?

SAGES: Saints control their own health. He asks about your welfare and sends this message . . .

KING: What does he command?

ŚĀRṄGARAVA: At the time you secretly met and married my daughter, affection made me pardon you both.

We remember you to be a prince of honor;
Śakuntalā is virtue incarnate—
the creator cannot be condemned
for mating the perfect bride and groom.

And now that she is pregnant, receive her and perform your sacred duty together.

GAUTAMĪ: Sir, I have something to say, though I wasn't appointed to speak:

She ignored her elders
and you failed to ask her kinsmen—
since you acted on your own,
what can I say to you now?

ŚAKUNTALĀ: What does my noble husband say?

KING: What has been proposed?

ŚAKUNTALĀ (*to herself*): The proposal is as clear as fire.

ŚĀRṄGARAVA: What's this? Your Majesty certainly knows the ways of the world!

People suspect a married woman who stays
with her kinsmen, even if she is chaste—
a young wife should live with her husband,
no matter how he despises her.

KING: Did I ever marry you?

ŚAKUNTALĀ (*visibly dejected, speaking to herself*): Now your fears are real, my heart!

ŚĀRṄGARAVA:

Does one turn away from duty in contempt
because his own actions repulse him?

KING: Why ask this insulting question?

ŚĀRṄGARAVA:

Such transformations take shape
when men are drunk with power.

KING: This censure is clearly directed at me.

GAUTAMĪ: Child, this is no time to be modest. I'll remove your veil. Then your husband will recognize you.

*(She does so.)*

KING (*staring at Śakuntalā*):

Must I judge whether I ever married
the flawless beauty they offer me now?
I cannot love her or leave her, like a bee
near a jasmine filled with frost at dawn.

*(He shows hesitation.)*

DOORKEEPER: Our king has a strong sense of justice. Who else would hesitate when beauty like this is handed to him?

ŚĀRṄGARAVA: King, why do you remain silent?

KING: Ascetics, even though I'm searching my mind, I don't remember marrying this lady. How can I accept a woman who is visibly pregnant when I doubt that I am the cause?

ŚAKUNTALĀ (*in a stage whisper*): My lord casts doubt on our marriage. Why were my hopes so high?

ŚĀRṄGARAVA: It can't be!

Are you going to insult the sage
who pardons the girl you seduced
and bids you keep his stolen wealth,
treating a thief like you with honor?

ŚĀRADVATA: Śārṅgarava, stop now! Śakuntalā, we have delivered our message and the king has responded. He must be shown some proof.

ŚAKUNTALĀ (*in a stage whisper*): When passion can turn to this, what's the use of reminding him? But, it's up to me to prove my honor now.

*(Aloud.)*

My noble husband . . .

*(She breaks off when this is half-spoken.)*

Since our marriage is in doubt, this is no way to address him. Puru king, you do wrong to reject a simple-hearted person with such words after you deceived her in the hermitage.

KING (*covering his ears*): Stop this shameful talk!

Are you trying to stain my name
and drag me to ruin—
like a river eroding her own banks,
soiling water and uprooting trees?

ŚAKUNTALĀ: Very well! If it's really true that fear of taking another man's wife turns you away, then this ring will revive your memory and remove your doubt.

KING: An excellent idea!

ŚAKUNTALĀ (*touching the place where the ring had been*): I'm lost! The ring is gone from my finger.

*(She looks despairingly at Gautamī.)*

GAUTAMĪ: The ring must have fallen off while you were bathing in the holy waters at the shrine of the goddess near Indra's grove.

KING (*smiling*): And so they say the female sex is cunning.

ŚAKUNTALĀ: Fate has shown its power. Yet, I will tell you something else.

KING: I am still obliged to listen.

ŚAKUNTALĀ: One day, in a jasmine bower, you held a lotusleaf cup full of water in your hand.

KING: We hear you.

ŚAKUNTALĀ: At that moment the buck I treated as my son approached. You coaxed it with the water, saying that it should drink first. But he didn't trust you and wouldn't drink from your hand. When I took the water, his trust returned. Then you jested, "Every creature trusts what its senses know. You both belong to the forest."

KING: Thus do women further their own ends by attracting eager men with the honey of false words.

GAUTAMĪ: Great king, you are wrong to speak this way. This child raised in an ascetics' grove doesn't know deceit.

KING: Old woman,

When naive female beasts show
cunning,
what can we expect of women who
reason?
Don't cuckoos let other birds
nurture
their eggs and teach the chicks to
fly?

ŚAKUNTALĀ (*angrily*): Evil man! you see everything distorted by your own ignoble heart. Who would want to imitate you now, hiding behind your show of justice, like a well overgrown with weeds?

KING (*to himself*): Her anger does not seem feigned; it makes me doubt myself.

When the absence of love's
memory
made me deny a secret affair with
her,
this fire-eyed beauty bent her
angry brows
and seemed to break the bow of
love.

*(Aloud.)*

Lady, Duṣyanta's conduct is renowned, so what you say is groundless.

ŚAKUNTALĀ: All right! I may be a self-willed wanton woman! But it was faith in the Puru dynasty that brought me into the power of a man with honey in his words and poison in his heart.

*(She covers her face at the end of the speech and weeps.)*

ŚĀRṄGARAVA: A willful act unchecked always causes pain.

One should be cautious
in forming a secret union—
unless a lover's heart is clear,
affection turns to poison.

KING: But sir, why do you demean me with such warnings? Do you trust the lady?

ŚĀRṄGARAVA (*scornfully*): You have learned everything backwards.

If you suspect the word of one
whose nature knows no guile,
then you can only trust
people who practice deception.

KING: I presume you speak the truth. Let us assume so. But what could I gain by deceiving this woman?

ŚĀRṄGARAVA: Ruin.

KING: Ruin? A Puru king has no reason to want his own ruin!

ŚĀRADVATA: Śārṅgarava, this talk is pointless. We have delivered our master's message and should return.

Since you married her, abandon her or take her—
absolute is the power a husband has over his wife.

GAUTAMĪ: You go ahead.

*(They start to go.)*

ŚAKUNTALĀ: What? Am I deceived by this cruel man and then abandoned by you?

*(She tries to follow them.)*

GAUTAMĪ (*stopping*): Śārṅgarava my son, Śakuntalā is following us, crying pitifully. What will my child do now that her husband has refused her?

ŚĀRṄGARAVA (*turning back angrily*): Bold woman, do you still insist on having your way?

*(Śakuntalā trembles in fear.)*

If you are what the king says you are,
you don't belong in Father Kaṇva's family—
if you know that your marriage vow is pure,
you can bear slavery in your husband's house.

Stay! We must go on!

KING: Ascetic, why do you disappoint the lady too?

The moon only makes lotuses open,
the sun's light awakens lilies—
a king's discipline forbids him
to touch another man's wife.

ŚĀRṄGARAVA: If you forget a past affair because of some present attachment, why do you fear injustice now?

KING (*to the priest*): Sir, I ask you to weigh the alternatives:

Since it's unclear whether I'm deluded
or she is speaking falsely—
should I risk abandoning a wife
or being tainted by another man's?

PRIEST (*deliberating*): I recommend this . . .

KING: Instruct me! I'll do as you say.

PRIEST: Then let the lady stay in our house until her child is born. If you ask why: the wise men predict that your first son will be born with the marks of a king who turns the wheel of empire. If the child of the sage's daughter bears the marks, congratulate her and welcome her into your palace chambers. Otherwise, send her back to her father.

KING: Whatever the elders desire.

PRIEST: Child, follow me!

ŚAKUNTALĀ: Mother earth, open to receive me!

*(Weeping, Śakuntalā exits with the priest and the hermits. The king, his memory lost through the curse, thinks about her.)*

VOICE OFFSTAGE: Amazing! Amazing!

KING (*listening*): What could this be?

PRIEST (*reentering, amazed*): King, something marvelous has occurred!

KING: What?

PRIEST: When Kaṇva's pupils had departed,

The girl threw up her arms and wept,
lamenting her misfortune . . .
then . . .

KING: Then what?

PRIEST:

Near the nymph's shrine a ray of light
in the shape of a woman carried her away.

*(All mime amazement.)*

KING: We've already settled the matter. Why discuss it further?

PRIEST (*observing the king*): May you be victorious!

*(He exits.)*

KING: Vetravatī, I am bewildered. Lead the way to my chamber!

DOORKEEPER: Come this way, my lord!

*(She walks forward.)*

KING:

I cannot remember marrying
the sage's abandoned daughter,
but the pain my heart feels
makes me suspect that I did.

*(All exit.)*

END OF ACT FIVE

## ACT SIX

*(The king's wife's brother, who is city magistrate, enters with two policemen leading a man whose hands are tied behind his back.)*

BOTH POLICEMEN (*beating the man*): Speak, thief! Where'd you steal this handsome ring with the king's name engraved in the jewel?

MAN (*showing fear*): Peace, sirs! I wouldn't do a thing like that.

FIRST POLICEMAN: Don't tell us the king thought you were some famous priest and gave it to you as a gift!

MAN: Listen, I'm a humble fisherman who lives near Indra's grove.

SECOND POLICEMAN: Thief, did we ask you about your caste?

MAGISTRATE: Sūcaka, let him tell it all in order! Don't interrupt him!

BOTH POLICEMEN: Whatever you command, chief!

MAN: I feed my family by catching fish with nets and hooks.

MAGISTRATE (*mocking*): What a pure profession!

MAN:

The work I do
may be vile
but I won't deny
my birthright—
a priest
doing his holy rites
pities the animals
he kills.

MAGISTRATE: Go on!

MAN: One day as I was cutting up a red carp, I saw the shining stone of this ring in its belly. When I tried to sell it, you grabbed me. Kill me or let me go! That's how I got it!

MAGISTRATE: Jānuka, I'm sure this ugly butcher's a fisherman by his stinking smell. We must investigate how he got the ring. We'll go straight to the palace.

BOTH POLICEMEN: Okay. Go in front, you pickpocket!

*(All walk around.)*

MAGISTRATE: Sūcaka, guard this villain at the palace gate! I'll report to the king how we found the ring, get his orders, and come back.

BOTH POLICEMEN: Chief, good luck with the king!

*(The magistrate exits.)*

FIRST POLICEMAN: Jānuka, the chief's been gone a long time.

SECOND POLICEMAN: Well, there are fixed times for seeing kings.

FIRST POLICEMAN: Jānuka, my hands are itching to tie on his execution garland.

*(He points to the man.)*

MAN: You shouldn't think about killing a man for no reason.

SECOND POLICEMAN (*looking*): I see our chief coming with a letter in his hand. It's probably an order from the king. You'll be thrown to the vultures or you'll see the face of death's dog again . . .

MAGISTRATE (*entering*): Sūcaka, release this fisherman! I'll tell you how he got the ring.

FIRST POLICEMAN: Whatever you say, chief!

SECOND POLICEMAN: The villain entered the house of death and came out again.

*(He unties the prisoner.)*

MAN (*bowing to the magistrate*): Master, how will I make my living now?

MAGISTRATE: The king sends you a sum equal to the ring.

*(He gives the money to the man.)*

MAN (*bowing as he grabs it*): The king honors me.

FIRST POLICEMAN: This fellow's certainly honored. He was lowered from the execution stake and raised up on a royal elephant's back.

SECOND POLICEMAN: Chief, the reward tells me this ring was special to the king.

MAGISTRATE: I don't think the king valued the stone, but when he caught sight of the ring, he suddenly seemed to remember someone he loved, and he became deeply disturbed.

FIRST POLICEMAN: You served him well, chief!

SECOND POLICEMAN: I think you better served this king of fish.

*(Looking at the fisherman with jealousy.)*

MAN: My lords, half of this is yours for your good will.

FIRST POLICEMAN: It's only fair!

MAGISTRATE: Fisherman, now that you are my greatest and dearest friend, we should pledge our love over kadamba-blossom wine. Let's go to the wine shop!

*(They all exit together; the interlude ends. Then a nymph named Sānumatī enters by the skyway.)*

SĀNUMATĪ: Now that I've performed my assigned duties at the nymph's shrine, I'll slip away to spy on King Duṣyanta while the worshipers are bathing. My friendship with Menakā makes me feel a bond with Śakuntalā. Besides, Menakā asked me to help her daughter.

*(Looking around.)*

Why don't I see preparations for the spring festival in the king's palace? I can learn everything by using my mental powers, but I must respect my friend's request. So be it! I'll make myself invisible and spy on these two girls who are guarding the pleasure garden.

*(Sānumatī mimes descending and stands waiting. Then a maid servant named Parabhṛtikā, "Little Cuckoo," enters, looking at a mango bud. A second maid, named Madhukarikā, "Little Bee," is following her.)*

FIRST MAID:

Your pale green stem
tinged with pink
is a true sign
that spring has come—
I see you,
mango-blossom bud,
and I pray
for a season of joy.

SECOND MAID: What are you muttering to yourself?

FIRST MAID: A cuckoo goes mad when she sees a mango bud.

SECOND MAID (*joyfully rushing over*): Has the sweet month of spring come?

FIRST MAID: Now's the time to sing your songs of love.

SECOND MAID: Hold me while I pluck a mango bud and worship the god of love.

FIRST MAID: Only if you'll give me half the fruit of your worship.

SECOND MAID: That goes without saying . . . our bodies may be separate, but our lives are one . . .

*(Leaning on her friend, she stands and plucks a mango bud.)*

The mango flower is still closed, but this broken stem is fragrant.

*(She makes the dove gesture with her hands.)*

Mango-blossom bud,
I offer you to Love
as he lifts

his bow of passion.
Be the first
of his flower arrows
aimed at lonely girls
with lovers far away!

*(She throws the mango bud.)*

CHAMBERLAIN (*angrily throwing aside the curtain and entering*): Not now, stupid girl! When the king has banned the festival of spring, how dare you pluck a mango bud!

BOTH MAIDS (*frightened*): Please forgive us, sir. We don't know what you mean.

CHAMBERLAIN: Did you not hear that even the spring trees and the nesting birds obey the king's order?

The mango flowers bloom without
spreading pollen,
the red amaranth buds, but will
not bloom,
cries of cuckoo cocks freeze
though frost is past,
and out of fear, Love holds his
arrow half-drawn.

BOTH MAIDS: There is no doubt about the king's great power!

FIRST MAID: Sir, several days ago we were sent to wait on the queen by Mitrāvasu, the king's brother-in-law. We were assigned to guard the pleasure garden. Since we're newcomers, we've heard no news.

CHAMBERLAIN: Let it be! But don't do it again!

BOTH MAIDS: Sir, we're curious. May we ask why the spring festival was banned?

SĀNUMATĪ: Mortals are fond of festivals. The reason must be serious.

CHAMBERLAIN: It is public knowledge. Why should I not tell them? Has the scandal of Śakuntalā's rejection not reached your ears?

BOTH MAIDS: We only heard from the king's brother-in-law that the ring was found.

CHAMBERLAIN (*to himself*): There is little more to tell.

*(Aloud.)*

When he saw the ring, the king remembered that he had married Śakuntalā in secret and had rejected her in his delusion. Since then the king has been tortured by remorse.

Despising what he once enjoyed,
he shuns his ministers every day
and spends long sleepless nights
tossing at the edge of his bed—
when courtesy demands that
he converse with palace women,
he stumbles over their names,
and then retreats in shame.

SĀNUMATĪ: This news delights me.

CHAMBERLAIN: The festival is banned because of the king's melancholy.

BOTH MAIDS: It's only right.

VOICE OFFSTAGE: This way, sir!

CHAMBERLAIN (*listening*): The king is coming. Go about your business!

BOTH MAIDS: As you say.

*(Both maids exit. Then the king enters, costumed to show his grief, accompanied by the buffoon and the doorkeeper.)*

CHAMBERLAIN (*observing the king*): Extraordinary beauty is appealing under all conditions. Even in his lovesick state, the king is wonderful to see.

Rejecting his regal jewels,
he wears one golden bangle
above his left wrist;
his lips are pale with sighs,

his eyes wan from brooding at night—
like a gemstone ground in polishing,
the fiery beauty of his body
makes his wasted form seem strong.

SĀNUMATĪ (*seeing the king*): I see why Śakuntalā pines for him though he rejected and disgraced her.

KING (*walking around slowly, deep in thought*):

This cursed heart slept
when my love came to wake it,
and now it stays awake
to suffer the pain of remorse.

SĀNUMATĪ: The girl shares his fate.

BUFFOON (*in a stage whisper*): He's having another attack of his Śakuntalā disease. I doubt if there's any cure for that.

CHAMBERLAIN (*approaching*): Victory to the king! I have inspected the grounds of the pleasure garden. Let the king visit his favorite spots and divert himself.

KING: Vetravatī, deliver a message to my noble minister Piśuna: "After being awake all night, we cannot sit on the seat of justice today. Set in writing what your judgment tells you the citizens require and send it to us!"

DOORKEEPER: Whatever you command!

*(She exits.)*

KING: Vātāyana, attend to the rest of your business!

CHAMBERLAIN: As the king commands!

*(He exits.)*

BUFFOON: You've cleared out the flies. Now you can rest in some pretty spot. The garden is pleasant now in this break between morning cold and noonday heat.

KING: Dear friend, the saying "Misfortunes rush through any crack" is absolutely right:

Barely freed by the dark force
that made me forget Kaṇva's daughter,
my mind is threatened by an arrow
of mango buds fixed on Love's bow.

BUFFOON: Wait, I'll destroy the love god's arrow with my wooden stick.

*(Raising his staff, he tries to strike a mango bud.)*

KING (*smiling*): Let it be! I see the majesty of brahman bravery. Friend, where may I sit to divert my eyes with vines that remind me of my love?

BUFFOON: Didn't you tell your maid Caturikā, "I'll pass the time in the jasmine bower. Bring me the drawing board on which I painted a picture of Śakuntalā with my own hand!"

KING: Such a place may soothe my heart. Show me the way!

BUFFOON: Come this way!

*(Both walk around; the nymph Sānumatī follows.)*

The marble seat and flower offerings in this jasmine bower are certainly trying to make us feel welcome. Come in and sit down!

*(Both enter the bower and sit.)*

SĀNUMATĪ: I'll hide behind these creepers to see the picture he's drawn of my friend. Then I'll report how great her husband's passion is.

*(She does as she says and stands waiting.)*

KING: Friend, now I remember everything. I told you about my first meeting with Śakuntalā. You weren't with me when I rejected her, but why didn't you say anything about her before? Did you suffer a loss of memory too?

BUFFOON: I didn't forget. You did tell me all about it once, but then you said, "It's all a joke without any truth." My wit is like a lump of clay, so I took you at your word . . . or it could be that fate is powerful . . .

SĀNUMATĪ: It is!

KING: Friend, help me!

BUFFOON: What's this? It doesn't become you! Noblemen never take grief to heart. Even in storms, mountains don't tremble.

KING: Dear friend, I'm defenseless when I remember the pain of my love's bewilderment when I rejected her.

When I cast her away, she followed
her kinsmen,
but Kaṇva's disciple harshly
shouted, "Stay!"
The tearful look my cruelty
provoked
burns me like an arrow tipped
with poison.

SĀNUMATĪ: The way he rehearses his actions makes me delight in his pain.

BUFFOON: Sir, I guess that the lady was carried off by some celestial creature or other.

KING: Who else would dare to touch a woman who worshiped her husband? I was told that Menakā is her mother. My heart suspects that her mother's companions carried her off.

SĀNUMATĪ: His delusion puzzled me, but not his reawakening.

BUFFOON: If that's the case, you'll meet her again in good time.

KING: How?

BUFFOON: No mother or father can bear to see a daughter parted from her husband.

KING:

Was it dream or illusion or mental
confusion,
or the last meager fruit of my
former good deeds?
It is gone now, and my heart's
desires are
like riverbanks crumbling of their
own weight.

BUFFOON: Stop this! Isn't the ring evidence that an unexpected meeting is destined to take place?

KING (*looking at the ring*): I only pity it for falling from such a place.

Ring, your punishment is proof
that your fate is as flawed as
mine—
you were placed in her lovely
fingers,
glowing with crimson nails, and
you fell.

SĀNUMATĪ: The real pity would have been if it had fallen into some other hand.

BUFFOON: What prompted you to put the signet ring on her hand?

SĀNUMATĪ: I'm curious too.

KING: I did it when I left for the city. My love broke into tears and asked, "How long will it be before my noble husband sends news to me?"

BUFFOON: Then? What then?

KING: Then I placed the ring on her finger with this promise:

One by one, day after day,
count each syllable of my name!
At the end, a messenger will come
to bring you to my palace.

But in my cruel delusion, I never kept my word.

SĀNUMATĪ: Fate broke their charming agreement!

BUFFOON: How did it get into the belly of the carp the fisherman was cutting up?

KING: While she was worshiping at the shrine of Indra's wife, it fell from her hand into the Gaṅgā.

BUFFOON: It's obvious now!

SĀNUMATĪ: And the king, doubtful of his marriage to Śakuntalā, a female ascetic, was afraid to commit an act of injustice. But why should such passionate love need a ring to be remembered?

KING: I must reproach the ring for what it's done.

BUFFOON (*to himself*): He's gone the way of all madmen . . .

KING:

Why did you leave her delicate
finger
and sink into the deep river?

Of course . . .

A mindless ring can't recognize
virtue,
but why did I reject my love?

BUFFOON (*to himself again*): Why am I consumed by a craving for food?

KING: Oh ring! Have pity on a man whose heart is tormented because he abandoned his love without cause! Let him see her again!

*(Throwing the curtain aside, the maid Caturikā enters, with the drawing board in her hand.)*

CATURIKĀ: Here's the picture you painted of the lady.

*(She shows the drawing board.)*

BUFFOON: Dear friend, how well you've painted your feelings in this sweet scene! My eyes almost stumble over the hollows and hills.

SĀNUMATĪ: What skill the king has! I feel as if my friend were before me.

KING:

The picture's imperfections are
not hers,
but this drawing does hint at her
beauty.

SĀNUMATĪ: Such words reveal that suffering has increased his modesty as much as his love.

BUFFOON: Sir, I see three ladies now and they're all lovely to look at. Which is your Śakuntalā?

SĀNUMATĪ: Only a dim-witted fool like this wouldn't know such beauty!

KING: You guess which one!

BUFFOON: I guess Śakuntalā is the one you've drawn with flowers falling from her loosened locks of hair, with drops of sweat on her face, with her arms hanging limp and tired as she stands at the side of a mango tree whose tender shoots are gleaming with the fresh water she poured. The other two are her friends.

KING: You are clever! Look at these signs of my passion!

Smudges from my sweating fingers
stain the edges of the picture

and a tear fallen from my cheek
has raised a wrinkle in the paint.

Caturikā, the scenery is only half-drawn. Go and bring my paints!

CATURIKĀ: Noble Māḍhavya, hold the drawing board until I come back!

KING: I'll hold it myself.

*(He takes it, the maid exits.)*

I rejected my love when she came to me,
and now I worship her in a painted image—
having passed by a river full of water,
I'm longing now for an empty mirage.

BUFFOON *(to himself)*: He's too far gone for a river now! He's looking for a mirage!

*(Aloud.)*

Sir, what else do you plan to draw here?

SĀNUMATĪ: He'll want to draw every place my friend loved.

KING:

I'll draw the river Mālinī
flowing through Himālaya's foothills
where pairs of wild geese nest in the sand
and deer recline on both riverbanks,
where a doe is rubbing her left eye
on the horn of a black buck antelope
under a tree whose branches
have bark dresses hanging to dry.

BUFFOON *(to himself)*: Next he'll fill the drawing board with mobs of ascetics wearing long grassy beards.

KING: Dear friend, I've forgotten to draw an ornament that Śakuntalā wore.

BUFFOON: What is it?

SĀNUMATĪ: It will suit her forest life and her tender beauty.

KING:

I haven't drawn the mimosa flower on her ear,
its filaments resting on her cheek,
or the necklace of tender lotus stalks,
lying on her breasts like autumn moonbeams.

BUFFOON: But why does the lady cover her face with her red lotus-bud fingertips and stand trembling in fear?

*(Looking closely.)*

That son-of-a-bee who steals nectar from flowers is attacking her face.

KING: Drive the impudent rogue away!

BUFFOON: You have the power to punish criminals. You drive him off!

KING: All right! Bee, favored guest of the flowering vines, why do you frustrate yourself by flying here?

A female bee waits on a flower,
thirsting for your love—
she refuses to drink
the sweet nectar without you.

SĀNUMATĪ: How gallantly he's driving him away!

BUFFOON: When you try to drive it away, this creature becomes vicious.

KING: Why don't you stop when I command you?

Bee, if you touch the lips of my love
that lure you like a young tree's virgin buds,

lips I gently kissed in festivals of
love,
I'll hold you captive in a lotus
flower cage.

BUFFOON: Why isn't he afraid of your harsh punishment?

*(Laughing, he speaks to himself.)*

He's gone crazy and I'll be the same if I go on talking like this.

*(Aloud.)*

But sir, it's just a picture!

KING: A picture? How can that be?

SĀNUMATĪ: When I couldn't tell whether it was painted, how could he realize he was looking at a picture?

KING: Dear friend, are you envious of me?

My heart's affection made me feel
the joy of seeing her—
but you reminded me again
that my love is only a picture.

*(He wipes away a tear.)*

SĀNUMATĪ: The effects of her absence make him quarrelsome.

KING: Dear friend, why do I suffer this endless pain?

Sleepless nights prevent our
meeting in dreams;
her image in a picture is ruined by
my tears.

SĀNUMATĪ: You have clearly atoned for the suffering your rejection caused Śakuntalā.

CATURIKĀ *(entering)*: Victory my lord! I found the paint box and started back right away . . . but I met Queen Vasumatī with her maid Taralikā on the path and she grabbed the box from my hand, saying, "I'll bring it to the noble lord myself!"

BUFFOON: You were lucky to get away!

CATURIKĀ: The queen's shawl got caught on a tree. While Taralikā was freeing it, I made my escape.

KING: Dear friend, the queen's pride can quickly turn to anger. Save this picture!

BUFFOON: You should say, "Save yourself!"

*(Taking the picture, he stands up.)*

If you escape the woman's deadly poison, then send word to me in the Palace of the Clouds.

*(He exits hastily.)*

SĀNUMATĪ: Even though another woman has taken his heart and he feels indifferent to the queen, he treats her with respect.

DOORKEEPER *(entering with a letter in her hand)*: Victory, king!

KING: Vetravatī, did you meet the queen on the way?

DOORKEEPER: I did, but when she saw the letter in my hand, she turned back.

KING: She knows that this is official and would not interrupt my work.

DOORKEEPER: King, the minister requests that you examine the contents of this letter. He said that the enormous job of reckoning the revenue in this one citizen's case had taken all his time.

KING: Show me the letter!

*(The girl hands it to him and he reads barely aloud.)*

What is this? "A wealthy merchant sea captain named Dhanamitra has been lost in a shipwreck and the laws say that since the brave man was childless, his accumulated wealth all goes to the king." It's terrible to be childless! A man of such wealth probably had several wives. We must find out if any one of his wives is pregnant!

DOORKEEPER: King, it's said that one of his wives, the daughter of a merchant of Ayodhyā, has performed the rite to ensure the birth of a son.

KING: The child in her womb surely deserves his paternal wealth. Go! Report this to my minister!

DOORKEEPER: As the king commands!

*(She starts to go.)*

KING: Come here a moment!

DOORKEEPER: I am here.

KING: Is it his offspring or not?

When his subjects lose a kinsman,
Duṣyanta will preserve the
estates—
unless there is some crime.
Let this be proclaimed.

DOORKEEPER: It shall be proclaimed loudly.

*(She exits; reenters.)*

The king's order will be as welcome as rain in the right season.

KING *(sighing long and deeply)*: Families without offspring whose lines of succession are cut off lose their wealth to strangers when the last male heir dies. When I die, this will happen to the wealth of the Puru dynasty.

DOORKEEPER: Heaven forbid such a fate!

KING: I curse myself for despising the treasure I was offered.

SĀNUMATĪ: He surely has my friend in mind when he blames himself.

KING:

I abandoned my lawful wife, the
holy ground
where I myself planted my family's
glory,
like earth sown with seed at the
right time,
ready to bear rich fruit in season.

SĀNUMATĪ: But your family's line will not be broken.

CATURIKĀ *(in a stage whisper)*: The king is upset by the story of the merchant. Go and bring noble Māḍhavya from the Palace of the Clouds to console him!

DOORKEEPER: A good idea!

*(She exits.)*

KING: Duṣyanta's ancestors are imperiled.

Our fathers drink the yearly
libation
mixed with my childless tears,
knowing that there is no other son
to offer the sacred funeral waters.

*(He falls into a faint.)*

CATURIKĀ *(looking at the bewildered king)*: Calm yourself, my lord!

SĀNUMATĪ: Though a light shines, his separation from Śakuntalā keeps him in a state of dark depression. I could make him happy now, but I've heard Indra's consort consoling Śakuntalā with the news that the gods are hungry for their share of the ancestral oblations and will soon conspire to have her husband welcome his lawful wife. I'll have to wait for the auspicious time, but meanwhile I'll cheer my friend by reporting his condition.

*(She exits, flying into the air.)*

VOICE OFFSTAGE: Help! Brahman-murder!

KING *(regaining consciousness, listening)*: Is it Māḍhavya's cry of pain? Who's there?

DOORKEEPER: King, your friend is in danger. Help him!

KING: Who dares to threaten him?

DOORKEEPER: Some invisible spirit seized him and dragged him to the roof of the Palace of the Clouds.

KING *(getting up)*: Not this! Even my house is haunted by spirits.

When I don't even recognize
the blunders I commit every day,
how can I keep track
of where my subjects stray?

VOICE OFFSTAGE: Dear friend! Help! Help!

KING *(breaking into a run)*: Friend, don't be afraid! I'm coming!

VOICE OFFSTAGE *(repeating the call for help)*: Why shouldn't I be afraid? Someone is trying to split my neck in three, like a stalk of sugar cane.

KING *(casting a glance)*: Quickly, my bow!

BOW-BEARER *(entering with a bow in hand)*: Here are your bow and quiver.

*(The king takes his bow and arrows.)*

VOICE OFFSTAGE:

I'll kill you as a tiger kills
struggling prey!
I'll drink fresh blood from your
tender neck!
Take refuge now in the bow
Duṣyanta lifts
to calm the fears of the oppressed!

KING *(angrily)*: How dare you abuse my name? Stop, carrion-eater! Or you will not live!

*(He strings his bow.)*

Vetravatī, lead the way to the stairs!

DOORKEEPER: This way, king.

*(All move forward in haste.)*

KING *(searching around)*: There is no one here!

VOICE OFFSTAGE: Help! Help! I see you. Don't you see me? I'm like a mouse caught by a cat! My life is hopeless!

KING: Don't count on your powers of invisibility! My magical arrows will find you. I aim this arrow:

It will strike its doomed target
and spare the brahman it must
save—
a wild goose can extract the milk
and leave the water untouched.

*(He aims the arrow. Then Indra's charioteer Mātali enters, having released the buffoon.)*

MĀTALI: King!

Indra sets demons as your targets;
draw your bow against them!
Send friends gracious glances
rather than deadly arrows!

KING *(withdrawing his arrow)*: Mātali, welcome to great Indra's charioteer!

BUFFOON *(entering)*: He tried to slaughter me like a sacrificial beast and this king is greeting him with honors!

MĀTALI *(smiling)*: Your Majesty, hear why Indra has sent me to you!

KING: I am all attention.

MĀTALI: There is an army of demons descended from one-hundred-headed Kālanemi, known to be invincible . . .

KING: I have already heard it from Nārada, the gods' messenger.

MĀTALI:

He is invulnerable to your friend Indra,
so you are appointed to lead the charge—
the moon dispels the darkness of night
since the sun cannot drive it out.

Take your weapon, mount Indra's chariot, and prepare for victory!

KING: Indra favors me with this honor. But why did you attack Māḍhavya?

MĀTALI: I'll tell you! From the signs of anguish Your Majesty showed, I knew that you were despondent. I attacked him to arouse your anger.

A fire blazes when fuel is added;
a cobra provoked raises its hood—
men can regain lost courage
if their emotions are roused.

KING (*in a stage whisper*): Dear friend, I cannot disobey a command from the lord of heaven. Inform my minister Piśuna of this and tell him this for me:

Concentrate your mind on guarding my subjects!
My bow is strung to accomplish other work.

BUFFOON: Whatever you command!

*(He exits.)*

MĀTALI: Mount the chariot, Your Majesty!

*(The king mimes mounting the chariot; all exit.)*

END OF ACT SIX

## ACT SEVEN

*(The king enters with Mātali by the skyway, mounted on a chariot.)*

KING: Mātali, though I carried out his command, I feel unworthy of the honors Indra gave me.

MĀTALI (*smiling*): Your Majesty, neither of you seems satisfied.

You belittle the aid you gave Indra
in face of the honors he conferred,
and he, amazed by your heroic acts,
deems his hospitality too slight.

KING: No, not so! When I was taking leave, he honored me beyond my heart's desire and shared his throne with me in the presence of the gods:

Indra gave me a garland of coral flowers
tinged with sandalpowder from his chest,
while he smiled at his son Jayanta,
who stood there barely hiding his envy.

MĀTALI: Don't you deserve whatever you want from Indra?

Indra's heaven of pleasures has twice
been saved by rooting out thorny demons—
your smooth-jointed arrows have now done
what Viṣṇu once did with his lion claws.

KING: Here too Indra's might deserves the praise.

When servants succeed in great tasks,
they act in hope of their master's praise—
would dawn scatter the darkness
if he were not the sun's own charioteer?

MĀTALI: This attitude suits you well!

*(He moves a little distance.)*

Look over there, Your Majesty! See how your own glorious fame has reached the vault of heaven!

Celestial artists are drawing your exploits
on leaves of the wish-granting creeper
with colors of the nymphs' cosmetic paints,
and bards are moved to sing of you in ballads.

KING: Mātali, in my desire to do battle with the demons, I did not notice the path we took to heaven as we climbed through the sky yesterday. Which course of the winds are we traveling?

MĀTALI:

They call this path of the wind Parivaha—
freed from darkness by Viṣṇu's second stride,
it bears the Gaṅgā's three celestial streams
and turns stars in orbit, dividing their rays.

KING: Mātali, this is why my soul, my senses, and my heart feel calm.

*(He looks at the chariot wheels.)*

We've descended to the level of the clouds.

MĀTALI: How do you know?

KING:

Crested cuckoos fly between the spokes,
lightning flashes glint off the horses' coats,
and a fine mist wets your chariot's wheels—
all signs that we go over rain-filled clouds.

MĀTALI: In a moment you'll be back in your own domain, Your Majesty.

KING (*looking down*): Our speeding chariot makes the mortal world appear fantastic. Look!

Mountain peaks emerge as the earth descends,
branches spread up from a sea of leaves,
fine lines become great rivers to behold—
the world seems to hurtle toward me.

MĀTALI: You observe well! (*He looks with great reverence.*) The beauty of earth is sublime.

KING: Mātali, what mountain do I see stretching into the eastern and western seas, rippled with streams of liquid gold, like a gateway of twilight clouds?

MĀTALI: Your Majesty, it is called the "Golden Peak," the mountain of the demigods, a place where austerities are practiced to perfection.

Mārīca, the descendant of Brahmā,
a father of both demons and gods,

lives the life of an ascetic here
in the company of Aditi, his wife.

KING: One must not ignore good fortune! I shall perform the rite of circumambulating the sage.

MĀTALI: An excellent idea!

*(The two mime descending.)*

KING (*smiling*):

The chariot wheels make no
sound,
they raise no clouds of dust,
they touch the ground
unhindered—
nothing marks the chariot's
descent.

MĀTALI: It is because of the extraordinary power that you and Indra both possess.

KING: Mātali, where is Mārīca's hermitage?

MĀTALI (*pointing with his hand*):

Where the sage stands staring at
the sun,
as immobile as the trunk of a tree,
his body half-buried in an ant hill,
with a snake skin on his chest,
his throat pricked by a necklace
of withered thorny vines,
wearing a coil of long matted hair
filled with nests of śakunta birds.

KING: I do homage to the sage for his severe austerity.

MĀTALI (*pulling hard on the chariot reins*): Great king, let us enter Mārīca's hermitage, where Aditi nurtures the celestial coral trees.

KING: This tranquil place surpasses heaven. I feel as if I'm bathing in a lake of nectar.

MĀTALI (*stopping the chariot*): Dismount, Your Majesty!

KING (*dismounting*): Mātali, what about you?

MĀTALI: I have stopped the chariot. I'll dismount too.

*(He does so.)*

This way, Your Majesty!

*(He walks around.)*

You can see the grounds of the ascetics' grove ahead.

KING: I am amazed!

In this forest of wish-fulfilling trees
ascetics live on only the air they
breathe
and perform their ritual ablutions
in water colored by golden lotus
pollen.
They sit in trance on jeweled
marble slabs
and stay chaste among celestial
nymphs,
practicing austerities in the place
that others seek to win by
penances.

MĀTALI: Great men always aspire to rare heights!

*(He walks around, calling aloud.)*

O venerable Śākalya, what is the sage Mārīca doing now? What do you say? In response to Aditi's question about the duties of a devoted wife, he is talking in a gathering of great sages' wives.

KING (*listening*): We must wait our turn.

MĀTALI (*looking at the king*): Your Majesty, rest at the foot of this aśoka tree. Meanwhile, I'll look for a chance to announce you to Indra's father.

KING: As you advise . . .

*(He stops.)*

MĀTALI: Your Majesty, I'll attend to this.

*(He exits.)*

KING (*indicating he feels an omen*):

I have no hope for my desire.
Why does my arm throb in vain?
Once good fortune is lost,
it becomes constant pain.

VOICE OFFSTAGE: Don't be so wild! Why is his nature so stubborn?

KING (*listening*): Unruly conduct is out of place here. Whom are they reprimanding?

*(Looking toward the sound, surprised.)*

Who is this child, guarded by two female ascetics? A boy who acts more like a man.

He has dragged this lion cub
from its mother's half-full teat
to play with it, and with his hand
he violently tugs its mane.

*(The boy enters as described, with two female ascetics.)*

BOY: Open your mouth, lion! I want to count your teeth!

FIRST ASCETIC: Nasty boy, why do you torture creatures we love like our children? You're getting too headstrong! The sages gave you the right name when they called you "Sarvadamana, Tamer-of-everything."

KING: Why is my heart drawn to this child, as if he were my own flesh? I don't have a son. That is why I feel tender toward him . . .

SECOND ASCETIC: The lioness will maul you if you don't let go of her cub!

BOY (*smiling*): Oh, I'm scared to death!

*(Pouting.)*

KING:

This child appears to be
the seed of hidden glory,
like a spark of fire
awaiting fuel to burn.

FIRST ASCETIC: Child, let go of the lion cub and I'll give you another toy!

BOY: Where is it? Give it to me!

*(He reaches out his hand.)*

KING: Why does he bear the mark of a king who turns the wheel of empire?

A hand with fine webs connecting the fingers
opens as he reaches for the object greedily,
like a single lotus with faint inner petals
spread open in the red glow of early dawn.

SECOND ASCETIC: Suvratā, you can't stop him with words! The sage Mārkaṇḍeya's son left a brightly painted clay bird in my hut. Get it for him!

FIRST ASCETIC: I will!

*(She exits.)*

BOY: But until it comes I'll play with this cub.

KING: I am attracted to this pampered boy . . .

Lucky are fathers whose laps give refuge

to the muddy limbs of adoring little sons
when childish smiles show budding teeth
and jumbled sounds make charming words.

SECOND ASCETIC: Well, he ignores me.

*(She looks back.)*

Is one of the sage's sons here?

*(Looking at the king.)*

Sir, please come here! Make him loosen his grip and let go of the lion cub! He's tormenting it in his cruel child's play.

KING (*approaching the boy, smiling*): Stop! You're a great sage's son!

When self-control is your duty by birth,
why do you violate the sanctuary laws
and ruin the animals' peaceful life,
like a young black snake in a sandal tree?

SECOND ASCETIC: Sir, he's not a sage's son.

KING: His actions and his looks confirm it. I based my false assumption on his presence in this place.

*(He does what she asked; responding to the boy's touch, he speaks to himself.)*

Even my limbs feel delighted
from the touch of a stranger's son—
the father at whose side he grew
must feel pure joy in his heart.

SECOND ASCETIC (*examining them both*): It's amazing! Amazing!

KING: What is it, madam?

SECOND ASCETIC: This boy looks surprisingly like you. He doesn't even know you, and he's acting naturally.

KING (*fondling the child*): If he's not the son of an ascetic, what lineage does he belong to?

SECOND ASCETIC: The family of Puru.

KING (*to himself*): What? His ancestry is the same as mine . . . so this lady thinks he resembles me. The family vow of Puru's descendants is to spend their last days in the forest.

As world protectors they first choose
palaces filled with sensuous pleasures,
but later, their homes are under trees
and one wife shares the ascetic vows.

*(Aloud.)*

But mortals cannot enter this realm on their own.

SECOND ASCETIC: You're right, sir. His mother is a nymph's child. She gave birth to him here in the hermitage of Mārīca.

KING (*in a stage whisper*): Here is a second ground for hope!

*(Aloud.)*

What famed royal sage claims her as his wife?

SECOND ASCETIC: Who would even think of speaking the name of a man who rejected his lawful wife?

KING (*to himself*): Perhaps this story points to me. What if I ask the name of the boy's mother? No, it is wrong to ask about another man's wife.

First Ascetic (*returning with a clay bird in her hand*): Look, Sarvadamana, a śakunta! Look! Isn't it lovely?

Boy: Where's my mother?

Both Ascetics: He's tricked by the similarity of names. He wants his mother.

Second Ascetic: Child, she told you to look at the lovely clay śakunta bird.

King (*to himself*): What? Is his mother's name Śakuntalā? But names can be the same. Even a name is a mirage . . . a false hope to herald despair.

Boy: I like this bird!

*(He picks up the toy.)*

First Ascetic (*looking frantically*): Oh, I don't see the amulet-box on his wrist!

King: Don't be alarmed! It broke off while he was tussling with the lion cub.

*(He goes to pick it up.)*

Both Ascetics: Don't touch it! Oh, he's already picked it up!

*(With their hands on their chests, they stare at each other in amazement.)*

King: Why did you warn me against it?

First Ascetic: It contains the magical herb called Aparājitā, honored sir. Mārīca gave it to him at his birth ceremony. He said that if it fell to the ground no one but his parents or himself could pick it up.

King: And if someone else does pick it up?

First Ascetic: Then it turns into a snake and strikes.

King: Have you two seen it so transformed?

Both Ascetics: Many times.

King (*to himself, joyfully*): Why not rejoice in the fulfillment of my heart's desire?

*(He embraces the child.)*

Second Ascetic: Suvratā, come, let's tell Śakuntalā that her penances are over.

*(Both ascetics exit.)*

Boy: Let me go! I want my mother!

King: Son, you will greet your mother with me.

Boy: My father is Duṣyanta, not you!

King: This contradiction confirms the truth.

*(Śakuntalā enters, wearing the single braid of a woman in mourning.)*

Śakuntalā: Even though Sarvadamana's amulet kept its natural form instead of changing into a snake, I can't hope that my destiny will be fulfilled. But maybe what my friend Sānumatī reports is right.

King (*looking at Śakuntalā*): It is Śakuntalā!

Wearing dusty gray garments,
her face gaunt from penances,
her bare braid hanging down—
she bears with perfect virtue
the trial of long separation
my cruelty forced on her.

Śakuntalā (*seeing the king pale with suffering*): He doesn't resemble my noble husband. Whose touch defiles my son when the amulet is protecting him?

BOY (*going to his mother*): Mother, who is this stranger who calls me "son"?

KING: My dear, I see that you recognize me now. Even my cruelty to you is transformed by your grace.

ŚAKUNTALĀ (*to herself*): Heart, be consoled! My cruel fate has finally taken pity on me. It is my noble husband!

KING:

Memory chanced to break my
dark delusion
and you stand before me in beauty,
like the moon's wife Rohiṇī
as she rejoins her lord after an
eclipse.

ŚAKUNTALĀ: Victory to my noble husband! Vic . . .

*(She stops when the word is half-spoken, her throat choked with tears.)*

KING: Beautiful Śakuntalā,

Even choked by your tears,
the word "victory" is my triumph
on your bare pouting lips,
pale-red flowers of your face.

BOY: Mother, who is he?

ŚAKUNTALĀ: Child, ask the powers of fate!

KING (*falling at Śakuntalā's feet*):

May the pain of my rejection
vanish from your heart;
delusion clouded my weak mind
and darkness obscured good
fortune—
a blind man tears off a garland,
fearing the bite of a snake.

ŚAKUNTALĀ: Noble husband, rise! Some crime I had committed in a former life surely came to fruit and made my kind husband indifferent to me.

*(The king rises.)*

But how did my noble husband come to remember this woman who was doomed to pain?

KING: I shall tell you after I have removed the last barb of sorrow.

In my delusion I once ignored
a teardrop burning your lip—
let me dry the tear on your lash
to end the pain of remorse!

*(He does so.)*

ŚAKUNTALĀ (*seeing the signet ring*): My noble husband, this is the ring!

KING: I regained my memory when the ring was recovered.

ŚAKUNTALĀ: When it was lost, I tried in vain to convince my noble husband who I was.

KING: Let the vine take back this flower as a sign of her union with spring.

ŚAKUNTALĀ: I don't trust it. Let my noble husband wear it!

*(Mātali enters.)*

MĀTALI: Good fortune! This meeting with your lawful wife and the sight of your son's face are reasons to rejoice.

KING: The sweet fruit of my desire! Mātali, didn't Indra know about all this?

MĀTALI: What is unknown to the gods? Come, your Majesty! The sage Mārīca grants you an audience.

KING: Śakuntalā, hold our son's hand! We shall go to see Mārīca together.

ŚAKUNTALĀ: I feel shy about appearing before my elders in my husband's company.

KING: But it is customary at a joyous time like this. Come! Come!

*(They all walk around. Then Mārīca enters with Aditi; they sit.)*

MĀRĪCA (*looking at the king*):

Aditi, this is king Duṣyanta,
who leads Indra's armies in battle;
his bow lets your son's thunderbolt
lie ready with its tip unblunted.

ADITI: He bears himself with dignity.

MĀTALI: Your Majesty, the parents of the gods look at you with affection reserved for a son. Approach them!

KING: Mātali, the sages so describe this pair:

Source of the sun's twelve potent forms,
parents of Indra, who rules the triple world,
birthplace of Viṣṇu's primordial form,
sired by Brahmā's sons, Marīci and Dakṣa.

MĀTALI: Correct!

KING (*bowing*): Indra's servant, Duṣyanta, bows to you both.

MĀRĪCA: My son, live long and protect the earth!

ADITI: My son, be an invincible warrior!

ŚAKUNTALĀ: I worship at your feet with my son.

MĀRĪCA:

Child, with a husband like Indra
and a son like his son Jayanta,
you need no other blessing.
Be like Indra's wife Paulomī!

ADITI: Child, may your husband honor you and may your child live long to give both families joy! Be seated!

*(All sit near Mārīca.)*

MĀRĪCA (*pointing to each one*):

By the turn of fortune,
virtuous Śakuntalā, her noble son,
and the king are reunited—
faith and wealth with order.

KING: Sir, first came the success of my hopes, then the sight of you. Your kindness is unparalleled.

First flowers appear, then fruits,
first clouds rise, then rain falls,
but here the chain of events is reversed—
first came success, then your blessing.

MĀTALI: This is the way the creator gods give blessings.

KING: Sir, I married your charge by secret marriage rites. When her relatives brought her to me after some time, my memory failed and I sinned against the sage Kaṇva, your kinsman. When I saw the ring, I remembered that I had married his daughter. This is all so strange!

Like one who doubts the existence
of an elephant who walks in front of him
but feels convinced by seeing footprints,
my mind has taken strange turns.

MĀRĪCA: My son, you need not take the blame. Even your delusion has another cause. Listen!

KING: I am attentive.

MĀRĪCA: When Menakā took her bewildered daughter from the steps of the nymphs' shrine and brought her to my wife, I knew through meditation that you had rejected this girl as your lawful wife because of Durvāsas' curse, and that the curse would end when you saw the ring.

KING (*sighing*): So I am freed of blame.

ŚAKUNTALĀ (*to herself*): And I am happy to learn that I wasn't rejected by my husband without cause. But I don't remember being cursed. Maybe the empty heart of love's separation made me deaf to the curse . . . my friends did warn me to show the ring to my husband . . .

MĀRĪCA: My child, I have told you the truth. Don't be angry with your husband!

You were rejected when the curse
that clouded memory made him
cruel,
but now darkness is lifted
and your power is restored—
a shadow has no shape
in a badly tarnished mirror,
but when the surface is clean
it can easily be seen.

KING: Sir, here is the glory of my family!

*(He takes the child by the hand.)*

MĀRĪCA: Know that he is destined to turn the wheel of your empire!

His chariot will smoothly cross
the ocean's rough waves
and as a mighty warrior
he will conquer the seven
continents.
Here he is called Sarvadamana,
Tamer-of-everything;
later when his burden is the world,
men will call him Bharata,
Sustainer.

KING: Since you performed his birth ceremonies, we can hope for all this.

ADITI: Sir, let Kaṇva be told that his daughter's hopes have been fulfilled. Menakā, who loves her daughter, is here in attendance.

ŚAKUNTALĀ (*to herself*): The lady expresses my own desire.

MĀRĪCA: He knows everything already through the power of his austerity.

KING: This is why the sage was not angry at me.

MĀRĪCA: Still, I want to hear his response to this joyful reunion. Who is there?

DISCIPLE (*entering*): Sir, it is I.

MĀRĪCA: Gālava, fly through the sky and report the joyous reunion to Kaṇva in my own words: "The curse is ended. Śakuntalā and her son are embraced by Duṣyanta now that his memory is restored."

DISCIPLE: As you command, sir!

*(He exits.)*

MĀRĪCA: My son, mount your friend Indra's chariot with your wife and son and return to your royal capital!

KING: As you command, sir!

MĀRĪCA: My son, what other joy can I give you?

KING: There is no greater joy, but if you will:

May the king serve nature's good!
May priests honor the goddess of
speech!
And may Śiva's dazzling power
destroy my cycle of rebirths!

*(All exit.)*

END OF ACT SEVEN AND OF THE PLAY *ŚAKUNTALĀ AND THE RING OF RECOLLECTION*

## VIDYAKARA (LATE 11TH CENT.)

*Translated by Daniel H.H. Ingalls*

Vidyakara was a Buddhist monk who lived in Bengal. He is not the author of these poems, but the anthologizer of them. He collected more than seventeen hundred Sanskrit poems of the previous half-millennium in his *Treasury of Well-Turned Verse,* most of them from the ninth and tenth centuries, but some from as early as Kālidāsa in the fourth century. Although a few of the poems in the collection focus on Buddhist themes, Vidyakara's taste was surprisingly broad; most of the poems are Hindu in spirit or simply secular. Many are erotic, and many offer scenes of lower-caste village and farm life and scenes from nature, with little or no religious implications. These poems give us a vivid sense of everyday life in medieval India; medieval Europe offers no body of literature even remotely like them. They capture the emotions of everyday life as do the Chinese *Book of Songs* (pp. 295–317) and Tang poetry (pp. 1014–1033), but the Sanskrit poems are more conventional and less personal; in these respects, they are more like Japanese tanka and haiku, particularly the Manyōshū poems (pp. 1071–1077).

Though in translation the poems may seem charmingly simple, they are in fact written in very formal Sanskrit verse. They are highly conventional, using complexes of traditional images calculated to evoke the same *rasas* that govern Indian drama (see Kālidāsa, pp. 918–972). Poems of Spring, for example, use the same bees, flowers, trees, birds, and winds; jasmine, mango and flame trees, cuckoos, and the scented winds from Malabar appear in poem after poem. Each of Vidyakara's fifty categories (e.g., times of the day, the seasons, the stages of life, the stages of love and joys of sex, lovers in separation) has similar constellations of imagery.

Because images drawn from nature are evoked precisely for their impact on the reader's emotions, poems that may appear to be purely objective are actually suggestive of moods; therefore, nature is always subtly human and symbolic. As in the drama, these poems portray general types rather than specific individuals. There is not a single personal name in the collection. When such types are evoked by close observation of the natural and social world, however, the result is a striking universality that can make the poems immediately appealing to readers a thousand years later and half a world away.

As traditional and universal as the poems are, they manage to be delightfully original within their rigid formal constraints. The Petrarchan sonnet (pp. 1344–1348) and the haiku of Japan offer similar examples of strongly conventional genres that force the poet's imagination into the most subtle effects to achieve originality—although these poems are less intellectual than the sonnet and more concrete than haiku. To appreciate the poems' peculiar effects and the variety of minute details of everyday life they portray, one might try reading all these poems closely at one sitting.

Vidyakara divides the year into six seasons. Poems from these sections contain many of the themes of the rest of the collection. Love poems from both the woman's and man's point of view have also been included here to show the contrast with the love literature of Europe and the Far East. The famous poem 646 is by a woman; it provides relief from the relentless male idealization characteristic of so many of the poems.

## *The Treasury of Well-Turned Verse*

*Spring*

*155*

The mango bud her lover sent
is envied by her friends,
and in her heart the doe-eyed damsel offers it to Love.
But now she cannot let it from her hand;
she strokes it, casts her eye upon it,
smells it, turns it, holds it to her cheek.

**Vakkuita**

*157*

In calyxes of tasty *jambu* flowers
the black bees hold a drinking bout,
pecked at, then dropped by parrots
in mistake for ripened berries.
But see, the bees too judge amiss
the parrots, green as flame-tree leaves,
and fly straight at the flowered beaks.

**Rajasekhara?**

*Summer*

*202*

To drive away the busy gnats from the reddened corners of his eyes
the water buffalo shakes his horns
and tosses up a rope of moss from which the drops of water
slowly trickle between his lids;
then, sinking in the lake,
with all annoyance gone, he sleeps.

*205*

The days are here when diving is a grateful sport,
whose winds are sweet with trumpet flowers,
when sleep comes easily in the shade,
and of whose hours the last is loveliest.

**Kālidāsa**

*211*

That flutes should charm us, cooling to the ear,
that wine when chilled with water be so precious
and that women's breasts should feel as cool as snow:
such is the guerdon which the god of love
grants us in summer.

**Rajasekhara**

*212*

A bodice soaked in cooling water,
play-bracelets made of lotus stems,
ear-ornament of acacia flowers,
pearl necklaces of jasmine:
these and their bodies wet with sandalpaste
are the magic used by fawn-eyed damsels,
which needs nor spell nor magic circle
to resurrect the god of love.

**Rajasekhara**

## *The Rains*

*220*

After the rain a gentle breeze springs up
while the sky is overlaid with clouds;
one sees the horizon suddenly in a flash of lightning;
moon and stars and planets are asleep;
a heady scent is borne from *kadambas* wet with rain
and the sound of frogs spreads out in utter darkness.
How can the lonely lover spend these nights?

**Yogesvara**

*221*

The river banks in flood make my heart gay;
where the moorhen cries, the snake lies sleeping on the cane tops,
the gray geese call and herds of antelope
gather in peaceful circles;
where thick grass growing everywhere is bent beneath the
swarms of ants
and the jungle fowl is mad with joy.

**Yogesvara**

*226*

In the paddy field flooded with fresh water
where the frogs begin to croak

and where the prickly cane along the bank is whiter than heaped
pears,
the children, sticks in hands and smeared with mud,
run after the rising fish,
yelling "chubhroo, chubhroo!"

*233*

The cloud by miring the road has spoiled the red lac of her soles
and with his rain has washed the cosmetic from her cheek;
but for these sins he makes quick recompense:
his lightning shows the wanton lass
the path that leads her to her lover's house.

*237*

The bamboo groves that grow by mountain streams
have left acquaintance with the unrestrained
performances of love by mountain couples;
now on the banks the bamboo shoots
are covered with a bark which at the bud tip
is black and shining as a young goat's ear.

*242*

The god of love, angry at the transgression of his command,
orders the traveler sent back to his mistress
with limbs constricted in a crystal cage
made by the broad bright stream of water
pouring from his umbrella.

*261*

When an adventuress comes visiting upon a rainy day,
her make-up washed by raindrops from her eyes
and thin blue sari clinging to her breasts,
showing the natural beauty of her body;
blessed is the lucky lover
who helps her change her dress.

## *Autumn*

*274*

Tail up, feet keeping time, wings beating low,
the sweet notes pouring from his upraised throat;
with little motions of his beak,

the wagtail dances for a time beside his mate
who looks upon him longingly
from eyes that swim with tears of joy.

**Manovinoda**

*281*

The jungle streams are fearful places,
tangled with heavy growth of thick high reeds
and dangerous of descent,
their sandshoals rubbed by crocodile bellies
sliding from and to the water;
their opening mudholes
thick with tracks of tigers' feet;
and their waters black and smooth as glass.

## *Early Winter*

*297*

The peasants now grow haughty,
being flattered by a hundred travelers for their straw;
at night the cows in calf, chewing the cud,
keep warm the herdsmen with their breath;
at dawn the first rays of the sun play on the great bull's back
as he lies covered with mustard flower
and eyelids thick with frost upon the village common.

**Yogesvara**

*299*

The peasant and his wife
sleep in a grass hut at the corner of the field
with coverlet and pillow made of barley straw.
The frost avoids their slumbers,
a boundary being drawn to its advance
by the warmth emitted from the wife's plump breasts.

**Kamalayudha?**

*300*

Seeing a brace of rabbits start from a corner of the field,
the peasants, calling joyfully their fellows with a great haloo,
run, old and young, with sickles, slings and sticks,
abandoning their reaping of the rice.

*302*

The fire of cow dung, which though mostly smoke
by constant stirring is made to give off flame,
comes into honor with the winter season.
At end of day it shines for the enjoyment
of peasant women, at the stretching of whose arms
the graceful robes fall back
from the contours of their breasts.

## *Late Winter*

*308*

The traveler of the sky, the sun,
sets forth at dawn from the eastern hill
wrapped in a net of snow so thick
you could pierce it only with a needle.
He must have spent the whole night curled about the fire
and numbed of foot cannot go faster forward.

*310*

The cold beauty of the moonlight fades as though
from lack of luck in love,
for no more is it met by laughter of the waterlilies;
its darling moonstone, overlaid by frost,
no longer sweats with yearning;
nor is it welcomed by the eyes of lovers
between their bouts of love.

*312*

The coming of the frost is pleasant for the rich,
whose mouths are filled with fresh betel nut
and whose limbs receive a hundred joys
embracing their dark women.
It is we poor folk who despair;
our lap, half covered by a torn and beaten rag,
receives no better gift than the trembling of our knees.

*318*

The warmth of their straw borne off by icy winds,
time and again the peasants wake the fire
whose flame dies ever back, stirring with their sticks.
From the smoking bank of mustard chaff,
noisy with the crackling of the husks,
a penetrating odor spreads
to every corner of the threshing floor.

## *Love in Enjoyment*

*560*

It is when lust has reached its peak
and all a lover's effort
is bent on consummation
that a woman, weakened, yet imploring
with every syllable, slow-spoken from access of love,
in everything she says or does is charming.

*576*

The bashful lover, almost fainting from his exercise
in the full give and take of love,
has suddenly completed all his duty.
His bolder partner, overcome by passion,
writhes and cries out and turns aside her face,
her sidelong glance flashing with disappointment.

*583*

Once more she is embarrassed, then she laughs again;
she's tired, then again takes up what's been begun.
With ornament on forehead wet with perspiration
and locks of hair that fall across the brow,
how charming is her face when changing parts in love.

**Surabhi**

*587*

"Sweetheart, let me play the mistress, you the lover."
To this she answered "No," and shook her head;
but slipping the bracelet from her wrist to mine,
without the use of words she gave consent.

*590*

Of the fawn-eyed beauty, laughing sweetly,
the cheek grows still more charming
from its loss of make-up in love's battle.
Smooth it is, as fair as ripened cane stalks,
now stamped with nailmarks
and sealed with a blush.

**Viryamitra**

*592*

When the anklet has grown still
the girdle's sound is heard.

It's ever when the lover tires,
the mistress plays the man.

## *The Woman Offended*

*645*

Long have I practiced frowning;
I have trained my eyes to close and taught my smile restraint.
I have applied myself to silence
and strengthened all my wits to keep me obdurate.
Such angry preparations have I made,
but whether they succeed or not depends on fate.

**Dharmakirti**

*646*

At first our bodies knew a perfect oneness,
but then grew two:
the love, you,
and I, unhappy I, the loved.
Now you are husband, I the wife,
what else should come of this my life,
a tree too hard to break,
if not such bitter fruit?

**Bhavakadevi**

*667*

They lay upon the bed each turned aside
and suffering in silence;
though love still dwelt within their hearts
each feared a loss of pride.
But then from out the corner of their eyes
the sidelong glances met
and the quarrel broke in laughter as they turned
and clasped each other's neck.

*697*

The bond of his affection broken,
the value that he placed upon me in his heart erased,
this man now walks before me like any other man,
his love now ceased.
The days pass with my thinking and thinking of these things.
Dear friend, I know not why my heart
breaks not into a hundred pieces.

## TWO *BHAKTI* POETS

Between the twelfth and eighteenth centuries, a religious movement known as *bhakti* developed in India and produced a great body of poetry. These poems were composed not in Sanskrit, but in regional vernaculars like Tamil and Hindi. *Bhakti* ("sharing [in God]") refers to a passionate devotion to a divinity, but a devotion unrelated to the traditional religious rituals, social conventions, and political values of Hinduism. The movement has its roots in Hinduism, of course—although after the thirteenth century, when India passed under Muslim rule, it was also influenced by the devotional practices of Islamic Sufism.

*Bhakti* provided an outlet for economic and social discontent. Modern social movements in India often adopt *bhakti* poets as avatars, but it would be wrong to see them as social rebels or to see *bhakti* as a religion of the oppressed. These poets did not try to change social conditions. They focused instead on the unreality of the world. Often compared to the mystics of medieval Europe, *bhakti* poets are not, however, constrained by rigorous spiritual discipline. *Bhakti* takes two forms: devotion to a particular god and devotion to a divine principle without attributes. The poems included here represent these two forms and are composed by members of two of India's most oppressed groups: the untouchables and women.

Ravidas lived in the late fifteenth century in Benares. He was a tanner of hides, an occupation suitable for untouchables because it requires the handling of dead animals. He does not lament his social standing, however, but affirms it and transcends it. The body is only a hollow puppet, he claims; spiritually, he is a Brāhman:

> As the lotus leaf floats above the water, Ravidas says,
> so he flowers above the world of his birth.

Ravidas is considered a guru in the Sikh form of Hinduism and is an important voice in modern movements against the caste system, including that of Mahatma Gandhi.

Mīrābāī, the most popular of all the *bhakti* poets, was a woman of the late sixteenth century, reputed by legend to have been a student of Ravidas. Unlike Ravidas, however, she was devoted to a particular god, Krishna. Legend says she rejected her royal husband to be a consort of the god (see Rābi'ah, pp. 832–840). For this violation, her husband's family tried to poison her, but the god saved her. When rejected by a priest of Krishna because she was a woman, she argued that all human beings are women in relation to the god. This argument may help explain why among all the *bhakti* poets, she speaks the most directly. She casts herself outrageously as a *gopi,* one of the divine milkmaids who are Krishna's consorts:

> Let Mira, your servant, safely cross over,
> a cowherding Gokul girl.

In India today Mīrābāī's popularity is indicated by both the seven films that have been made of her life and the numberless recordings of her songs, which are played and sung everywhere. Unlike the formal verse of the other *bhakti* poets, her songs are often indistinguishable from the oral tradition of women's folk songs.

Many are folk songs that have simply become attached to her name. She also used conventions from the Sanskrit tradition (see Kālidāsa and Vidyakara), such as images of the lover-in-separation.

## *Ravidas (late 15th cent.)*

*Translated by J.S. Hawley*

### *"I've never known how to tan or sew"*

I've never known how to tan or sew,
    though people come to me for shoes.
I haven't the needle to make the holes
    or even the tool to cut the thread.
Others stitch and knot, and tie themselves in knots
    while I, who do not knot, break free.
I keep saying Ram and Ram, says Ravidas,
    and Death keeps his business to himself.

### *"Who could long for anything but you?"*

Who could long for anything but you?
My master, you are merciful to the poor;
    you have shielded my head with a regal parasol.
Someone whose touch offends the world
    you have enveloped with yourself.
It is the lowly my Govind makes high—
    he does not fear anyone at all—
And he has exalted Namdev and Kabir,
    Trilocan, Sadhna, and Sen.
Listen saints, says Ravidas,
    Hari accomplishes everything.

### *"Oh well born of Benares, I too am born well known"*

Oh well born of Benares, I too am born well known:
    my labor is with leather. But my heart can boast the Lord.
See how you honor the purest of the pure,
    water from the Ganges, which no saint will touch
If it has been made into intoxicating drink—
    liquor is liquor whatever its source;
And this toddy tree you consider impure
    since the sacred writings have branded it that way,
But see what writings are written on its leaves:
    the Bhagavata Purana you so greatly revere.
And I, born among those who carry carrion
    in daily rounds around Benares, am now
        the lowly one to whom the mighty Brahmins come

And lowly bow. Your name, says Ravidas,
is the shelter of your slave.

### *"A family that has a true follower of the Lord"*

A family that has a true follower of the Lord
Is neither high caste nor low caste, lordly or poor.
The world will know it by its fragrance.
Priests or merchants, laborers or warriors,
halfbreeds, outcastes, and those who tend cremation fires—
their hearts are all the same.
He who becomes pure through love of the Lord
exalts himself and his family as well.
Thanks be to his village, thanks to his home,
thanks to that pure family, each and every one,
For he's drunk with the essence of the liquid of life
and he pours away all the poisons.
No one equals someone so pure and devoted—
not priests, not heroes, not parasolled kings.
As the lotus leaf floats above the water, Ravidas says,
so he flowers above the world of his birth.

### *"Mother, she asks, with what can I worship?"*

Mother, she asks, with what can I worship?
All the pure is impure. Can I offer milk?
The calf has dirtied it in sucking its mother's teat.
Water, the fish have muddied; flowers, the bees—
No other flowers could be offered than these.
The sandalwood tree, where the snake has coiled, is spoiled.
The same act formed both nectar and poison.
Everything's tainted—candles, incense, rice—
But still I can worship with my body and my mind
and I have the guru's grace to find the formless Lord.
Rituals and offerings—I can't do any of these.
What, says Ravidas, will you do with me?

### *"Your name: the act of worship"*

Your name: the act of worship
with the lifted lamp, Murari;
without the name of Hari all the universe is a lie.

Your name: the throne on which
the deity sits, your name the grinding stone,
the saffron that is ground and daubed upon the gods.

Your name: the holy water,
your name the sandal for sandalwood paste.
Grinding, chanting, I take that name and offer it to you.

Your name: the little lamp, the cruse,
your name the wick.
Your name is the oil that I pour into the ritual lamp.

Lighting your name:
the flame in the lamp
brings the glow that lightens all the corners of the house.

Your name: the garland;
your name the string, the flowers.
Beside them wither all the blossoms of the wilds.

Your handiwork: the world;
what could I offer more?
I can only wave your name like the whisk before the gods.

The world contains the vessels
for your sacred rites—
the scriptures, the direction points, and all the sacred sites—

But your name, says Ravidas,
is the lifting of the lamp;
your true name, O Hari, your food.

## *"The walls are made of water, pillared by air"*

The walls are made of water, pillared by air,
sealed together with the mortar of blood,
A cell of veins and meat and bones,
a cage to hold this poor bird.
Who cares what is yours or mine?—
for we nest in this tree only briefly.
As high as you can build, as low as you can dig,
your size will never swell the dimensions of a grave;
Those lovely curls, that turban tied so rakishly—
they'll soon be turned to ash.
If you've counted on the beauty of your wife and home
without the name of Ram, you've already lost the game.
And me: even though my birth is mean,
my ancestry by everyone despised,
I have always trusted in you, King Ram,
says Ravidas, a tanner of hides.

## *"It's just a clay puppet, but how it can dance!"*

It's just a clay puppet, but how it can dance!
It looks here, looks there, listens and talks,
races off this way and that;
It comes on something and it swells with pride,
but if fortune fades it starts to cry.
It gets tangled in its lusts, in tastes
of mind, word, and deed,
and then it meets its end and takes some other form.
Brother, says Ravidas, the world's a game, a magic show,
and I'm in love with the gamester,
the magician who makes it go.

## *"The house is large, its kitchen vast"*

The house is large, its kitchen vast,
but after only a moment's passed, it's vacant.
This body is like a scaffold made of grass:
the flames will consume it and tender it dust.
Even your family—your brothers and friends—
clamor to have you removed at dawn.
The lady of the house, who once clung to your chest,
shouts "Ghost! Ghost!" now and runs away.
The world, says Ravidas, loots and plunders all—
except me, for I have slipped away
by saying the name of God.

## *"This bodily world is a difficult road—hilly, overgrown—"*

This bodily world is a difficult road—hilly, overgrown—
and I've only this worthless bullock to rely on.
This request I make of Ram:
protect my wealth as I go along.
Who is a peddler for Ram?
My daily pack is loaded—
I am a peddler for Ram;
I traffic in his easy ecstasy:
I've loaded myself with the wealth of Ram's name
while the world is loaded down with poison.
You who know both shores of the sea,
chart my course through heaven and hell
So Death will not ambush me with his stick
nor trap me in his snare.
The world's a fading yellow dye, says the tanner Ravidas,
but Ram is an indelible red.

## *"Peddler, the first watch of night"*

Peddler,
the first watch of night.
What's this body's business?
Hari, the child-god:
you paid him no heed—
simpleton, such a foolish, childish way to think!
Simpleton, such a foolish, childish way to think—
you ignored the net of illusion,
simply paid it no mind.
What's that? Why repent?
All that water everywhere,
and once the sails are loose, you're gone.
Peddler,
so says Ravidas the slave:
simpleton, such a foolish, childish way to think.

Peddler,
the second watch of night.
You went chasing shadows of yourself.
You paid him no heed—Hari,
the child-god—
didn't board his boat.
Didn't board Hari's name—
you couldn't, all bloated up
with youth.
Desire so dulled you,
you couldn't see the line
between the woman that was yours
and someone else's.
Well, Hari will straighten the accounts;
you'll pay in full.
You'll burn if that's what's right.
Peddler,
so says Ravidas the slave:
you went chasing shadows of yourself.

Peddler,
the third watch of night.
The breath has gone slack.
Peddler, the body is bent
and what to do?
Bad thoughts have settled inside.
Bad thoughts have settled inside,
evil fool—a life completely lost.

Now was the moment,
    but you shunned what was right
    and the time will never come again.
Your frame is weary,
    your body frail,
    and still you won't rethink your ways.
Peddler,
    so says Ravidas the slave:
    the breath has gone slack.

Peddler,
    the fourth watch of night.
    The body shivers, it quakes.
Peddler,
    the Master is going to settle accounts.
    Abandon your perverse old ways.
Get wise,
    abandon the old fort.
    He may adorn you, he may feed you to the fire.
Death himself is at large:
    he's sent to have you bound,
    you smuggler. It's death's door.
The road ahead is hard,
    and you'll travel it alone.
    Where are the ones you once loved?
Peddler,
    so says Ravidas the slave:
    the body shivers, it quakes.

## *"The day it comes, it goes"*

The day it comes, it goes;
    whatever you do, nothing stays firm.
The group goes, and I go;
    the going is long, and death is overhead.
What! Are you sleeping? Wake up, fool,
    wake to the world you took to be true.
The one who gave you life daily feeds you, clothes you;
    inside every body, he runs the store.
So keep to your prayers, abandon "me" and "mine,"
    now's the time to nurture the name that's in the heart.
Life has slipped away. No one's left on the road,
    and in each direction the evening dark has come.
Madman, says Ravidas, here's the cause of it all—
    it's only a house of tricks. Ignore the world.

### *"The regal realm with the sorrowless name"*

The regal realm with the sorrowless name:
  they call it Queen City, a place with no pain,
No taxes or cares, none owns property there,
  no wrongdoing, worry, terror, or torture.
Oh my brother, I've come to take it as my own,
  my distant home, where everything is right.
That imperial kingdom is rich and secure,
  where none are third or second—all are one;
Its food and drink are famous, and those who live there
  dwell in satisfaction and in wealth.
They do this or that, they walk where they wish,
  they stroll through fabled palaces unchallenged.
Oh, says Ravidas, a tanner now set free,
  those who walk beside me are my friends.

## *Mīrābāī (late 16th cent.)*

*Translated by Mark Juergensmeyer*

### *"I'm colored with the color of dusk, oh* rana*"*

I'm colored with the color of dusk, oh *rana,*
    colored with the color of my Lord.
Drumming out the rhythm on the drums, I danced,
  dancing in the presence of the saints,
    colored with the color of my Lord.
They thought me mad for the Maddening One,
  raw for my dear dark love,
    colored with the color of my Lord.
The *rana* sent me a poison cup:
  I didn't look, I drank it up,
    colored with the color of my Lord.
The clever Mountain Lifter is the lord of Mira.
  Life after life he's true—
    colored with the color of my Lord.

### *"Life without Hari is no life, friend"*

Life without Hari is no life, friend,
And though my mother-in-law fights,
  my sister-in-law teases,
  the *rana* is angered,
A guard is stationed on a stool outside,
  and a lock is mounted on the door,

How can I abandon the love I have loved
in life after life?
Mira's Lord is the clever Mountain Lifter:
Why would I want anyone else?

## *"Today your Hari is coming, my friend"*

Today your Hari is coming,
my friend,
to play the game of Spring.
The harbinger crow in the courtyard speaks,
my friend,
an omen of good times ahead.
All the cowherds have gathered in the garden,
my friend,
where the basil grows:
I hear the sound of tambourines and drums,
my friend.
Why sleep? Wake up and go!
There's water and betel-leaf, mats and sheets,
my friend.
Go greet him: touch his feet.
Mira's Lord is the clever Mountain Lifter,
my friend,
the best blessing you could have.

## *"I saw the dark clouds burst, dark Lord"*

I saw the dark clouds burst,
dark Lord,
Saw the clouds and tumbling down
In black and yellow streams
they thicken,
Rain and rain two hours long.
See—
my eyes see only rain and water,
watering the thirsty earth green.
Me—
my love's in a distant land
and wet, I stubbornly stand at the door,
For Hari is indelibly green,
Mira's Lord,
And he has invited a standing,
stubborn love.

## *"Hey love bird, crying cuckoo"*

Hey love bird, crying cuckoo,
don't make your crying coos,
for I who am crying, cut off from my love,
will cut off your crying beak
and twist off your flying wings
and pour black salt in the wounds.

Hey, I am my love's and my love is mine.
How do you dare cry love?
But if my love were restored today
your love call would be a joy.
I would gild your crying beak with gold
and you would be my crown.

Hey, I'll write my love a note,
crying crow, now take it away
and tell him that his separated love
can't eat a single grain.
His servant Mira's mind's in a mess.
She wastes her time crying coos.

Come quick, my Lord,
the one who sees inside;
without you nothing remains.

## *"Murali sounds on the banks of the Jumna"*

Murali sounds on the banks of the Jumna,
Murali snatches away my mind;
My senses cut loose from their moorings—
Dark waters, dark garments, dark Lord.
I listen close to the sounds of Murali
And my body withers away—
Lost thoughts, lost even the power to think.
Mira's Lord, clever Mountain Lifter,
Come quick, and snatch away my pain.

## *"The Bhil woman tasted them, plum after plum"*

The Bhil woman tasted them, plum after plum,
and finally found one she could offer him.
What kind of genteel breeding was this?
And hers was no ravishing beauty.

Her family was poor, her caste quite low,
her clothes a matter of rags,
Yet Ram took that fruit—that touched, spoiled fruit—
for he knew that it stood for her love.
This was a woman who loved the taste of love,
and Ram knows no high, no low.
What sort of Veda could she ever have learned?
But quick as a flash she mounted a chariot
And sped to heaven to swing on a swing,
tied by love to God.
You are the Lord who cares for the fallen;
rescue whoever loves as she did:
Let Mira, your servant, safely cross over,
a cowherding Gokul girl.

### *"Sister, I had a dream that I wed"*

Sister, I had a dream that I wed
the Lord of those who live in need:
Five hundred sixty thousand people came
and the Lord of Braj was the groom.
In dream they set up a wedding arch;
in dream he grasped my hand;
in dream he led me around the wedding fire
and I became unshakably his bride.
Mira's been granted her mountain-lifting Lord:
from living past lives, a prize.

### *"I have talked to you, talked"*

I have talked to you, talked,
dark Lifter of Mountains,
About this old love,
from birth after birth.
Don't go, don't,
Lifter of Mountains,
Let me offer a sacrifice—myself—
beloved,
to your beautiful face.
Come, here in the courtyard,
dark Lord,
The women are singing auspicious wedding songs;
My eyes have fashioned
an altar of pearl tears,
And here is my sacrifice:
the body and mind

Of Mira,
the servant who clings to your feet,
through life after life,
a virginal harvest for you to reap.

## *"Go to where my loved one lives"*

Go to where my loved one lives,
go where he lives and tell him
if he says so, I'll color my sari red;
if he says so, I'll wear the godly yellow garb;
if he says so, I'll drape the part in my hair with pearls;
if he says so, I'll let my hair grow wild.
Mira's Lord is the clever Mountain Lifter:
listen to the praises of that king.

## *"Oh, the yogi—my friend, that clever one"*

Oh, the yogi—
my friend, that clever one
whose mind is on Siva and the Snake,
that all-knowing yogi—tell him this:

"I'm not staying here, not staying where
the land's grown strange without you, my dear,
But coming home, coming to where your place is;
take me, guard me with your guardian mercy,
please.
I'll take up your yogic garb—
your prayer beads,
earrings,
begging-bowl skull,
tattered yogic cloth—
I'll take them all
And search through the world as a yogi does
with you—yogi and yogini, side by side.

"My loved one, the rains have come,
and you promised that when they did, you'd come too.
And now the days are gone: I've counted them
one by one on the folds of my fingers
till the lines at the joints have blurred
And my love has left me pale,
my youth grown yellow as with age.

Singing of Ram,
your servant Mira
has offered you an offering:
her body and her mind."

## *"Let us go to a realm beyond going"*

Let us go to a realm beyond going,
Where death is afraid to go,
Where the high-flying birds alight and play,
Afloat in the full lake of love.
There they gather—the good, the true—
To strengthen an inner regimen,
To focus on the dark form of the Lord
And refine their minds like fire.
Garbed in goodness—their ankle bells—
They dance the dance of contentment
And deck themselves with the sixteen signs
Of beauty, and a golden crown—
There where the love of the Dark One comes first
And everything else is last.

# China in the Middle Period

Two foreign incursions into China delimit the Middle Period of Chinese history. The first is the coming of Buddhism, which may have begun as early as the first century of the Common Era but did not reach significant proportions until the centuries after the fall of the Han dynasty in 220 CE. The second is the arrival of Western culture in the form of Jesuit missionaries during the last years of the sixteenth century. Neither of these influences proved traumatic to China at first, but they brought different visions of the world and eventually transformed the Chinese cultural landscape. As many of the selections in this section demonstrate, one can read a significant amount of Chinese literature from the Middle Period without encountering many obvious references to Buddhism. However, Buddhism is present as a new cultural force and exerts considerable influence both directly and through its impact on indigenous schools of thought, particularly Daoism.

Wang Wei (701–761) was a devout Buddhist; his poetry, though only occasionally mentioning Buddhism directly, often reflects a quiet, meditative vision of nature that derives as much from Buddhism as from indigenous Daoist thought. Furthermore, the whole vast and highly imaginative world of Indian thought came into China along with Buddhism. *Journey to the West* (*Monkey*) derives from that world. The pious Chinese monk Xuan Zang (Tripitaka) and his animal friends in this novel are traveling to India to obtain Buddhist texts, and the fantastic heavens, hells, and supernatural forces that surround them are a vision of ancient India far more than of pre-Buddhist China. Buddhist religious texts were read avidly in China. The Lotus Sutra, although originally Indian, is preserved in a Chinese translation and has been much loved by Chinese readers throughout the ages.

The Middle Period of Chinese history, like the Ancient Period, alternated between periods of unity and disunity. The three centuries after the fall of the Han dynasty, known in Chinese as the Three Kingdoms and Six Dynasties (220–589), were a period of disunity characterized by a rapid succession of different ruling powers, some of them non-Chinese peoples who had swept into China from the northern and western border regions. With the rise of the Sui dynasty (589–618) and the reign of the extremely powerful and long-lasting Tang dynasty (618–907), China was unified again. The Tang dynasty, particularly during its first 150 years, was a glorious time for Chinese civilization and was characterized by great cultural openness. Its capital, Chang'an (located near modern-day Xi'an), was one of the largest and most cosmopolitan cities in the world at that time. The end of the Tang dynasty brought another brief period of disunity that was then followed by the Song dynasty (960–1279). The Song witnessed the flowering of new and fresh poetic forms and the rise of Chinese landscape painting.

The most serious military intrusion into China in the Middle Period began in the latter half of the Song dynasty and culminated with the Mongolian conquest during the thirteenth century, when China was incorporated into the great empire of Genghis Khan. The Mongol empire made travel between Europe and Asia less difficult, facilitating the journeys of such renowned travelers as Marco Polo and Ibn Battuta. The Mongol empire, known in China as the Yuan dynasty (1279–1368), collapsed in China after a century and was followed by a new and quite conservative native Chinese dynasty, the Ming (1368–1644). In literary history, the Ming dynasty is famous for the appearance of the earliest Chinese novels, represented here by *Monkey.*

## Gan Bao (early 4th cent.)

*Translated by Hsien-yi and Gladys Yang*

According to the *Analects,* Confucius did not discuss "anomalies" (*guai*—see *Analects* 7.21 p. 325). Despite the long-standing Confucian tradition of skepticism and almost exclusive concern for the social world, however, the Chinese have always been fascinated with tales of the supernatural. In fact, many literary scholars locate the seeds of Chinese fiction in short written accounts of supernatural occurrences. During the Six Dynasties period (220–581), such tales were particularly popular and were known in Chinese as *zhiguai* ("reports of anomalies"), that is, reports of the very type of event that a good Confucian should not discuss. These "reports of anomalies" are often presented as actual historical events, perhaps to minimize Confucian concern about their transmission. As a result, these tales often share the same structure and style as early historical biographies found in dynastic histories and other official writings. The reports of anomalies are typically very brief and show little concern for character development or narrative detail. The focus is on the unusual event itself and often on some edifying moral the story supposedly conveys.

# European Despair and Chinese Sadness

Every act of translation is also an act of creative adaptation. Sometimes this adaptation is not just linguistic but cultural as well and can lead to what we might call, somewhat generously, "creative distortion." An excellent example of this is provided by the German composer Gustav Mahler's (1860–1911) use of Tang dynasty poetry, particularly that of Li Bai (701–762), in his song-cycle "The Song of the Earth" ("Das Lied von der Erde"). Mahler did not read Chinese but adapted a German-language translation by the poet Hans Bethge. Bethge also did not read Chinese but had translated Judith Gautier's loose French translation of the Chinese originals. The miracle is not that Mahler's text sometimes deviates wildly from the Tang originals, but that it sometimes reflects the original quite well. However, there are serious distortions. One of Li Bai's poems entitled "A Song of Sorrow" ("Bei ge xing") is rendered by Mahler, after Bethge, as "The Drinking Song of the Earth's Sorrow" ("Das Trinklied vom Jammer der Erde"). The poem is a Chinese "Drinking Song" to be sure, but the phrase "Earth's Sorrow" should tip us off to the fact that Mahler is drawing the Chinese poem very much in the direction of the world-weariness and existential despair that were very much a part of end-of-the-century Europe but were quite foreign to Tang China. Li Bai's original contemplates a number of historical injustices and sad events from the Chinese past and concludes each stanza with the refrain "Alas, sorrow comes." That is, in the Chinese original, sorrow results from contemplating specific historical events that are sad. One drinks to forget such unhappy episodes and to find joy in the moment. Mahler does not include any of Li Bai's historical reminiscences, which would not be familiar to a Western audience anyway, but goes directly from the theme of drinking to his adaptation of the refrain (in Chinese, "Alas, sorrow comes"): "Dark is life, is death!" ("Dunkel is das Leben, is der Tod") is how Mahler renders it. However sad the events of human history might be, it is doubtful that Li Bai would have agreed with this cry of existential despair. Perhaps he might have gone so far as to say, "Life has many sad events (and happy ones, too), and death does indeed come too quickly," although he surely would have said it more poetically. But such a constrained expression of sadness hardly fits the mood of Mahler's Europe.

These stories, however, were probably read and circulated more for their entertainment than for any lessons they might convey.

Included are five examples from the most important early collection of these tales, Gan Bao's *In Search of the Supernatural* (*Sou shen ji*). The preface to Gan Bao's work explains that he became interested in anomalies when two miraculous events took place in his own family: first, the reviving of his father's favorite concubine after she had been dead and buried for ten years; and second, his brother's resuscitation after he had stopped breathing and his subsequent report of a world of ghosts and spirits he had visited while unconscious.

The first tale, *Han Ping and His Wife,* is a popular story of true love living on beyond tragic death and becoming mysteriously imprinted upon the natural world. It reminds us that the Chinese believed there was a mysterious harmony between human feeling and nature. The second, *Horse into Silkworm,* is an explanation of the origin of the silkworm cocoon and, like many Chinese stories, is constructed around a pun. *The Old Man and the Devils* is a tragic story of mistaken identity that warns us against relying on the world of mere appearance. *Married to a Ghost* is a type of story, extremely widespread in China, of marital relationships between human beings and supernatural beings who are sometimes ghosts and sometimes shape-shifting fox fairies. The final story, *Dead Drunk,* is a humorous tale of the effects of strong wine (which so many Chinese scholars drank with great enthusiasm) and of returning from the grave.

## *In Search of the Supernatural*

### *Han Ping and His Wife*

Han Ping, steward to Prince Kang of Sung, married a beautiful daughter of the Ho family. But the prince stole her from him. When Han protested, he was imprisoned and sentenced to hard labour on the city wall. His wife wrote him a secret message:

Rain, ceaseless rain,
Wide the river, deep the flood,
Yet sunrise is in my heart.

This letter fell into the hands of the prince, who showed it to his followers, but none could make out its meaning until the minister Su Ho said:

"The first line means that she longs for him continuously, the second that they have no way of meeting, the third that she intends to take her life."

Then Han Ping killed himself.

His wife secretly tore her clothes, and when the prince went up the tower with her, she threw herself from the top. His followers tried to seize her, but her clothes came away in their hands and she was dashed to death. On her belt she had left this message:

"Your Highness wished me to live, but your servant chose to die. Please bury me with Han Ping."

The prince was angry and refused her request, ordering the local people to bury her in a separate grave.

"You speak of your undying love," sneered the prince. "If you can make these tombs come together, I will not stand in your way."

Then within one day two great catalpa trees sprang up above the two graves. In ten days they grew to an enormous size. Their branches inclined towards each other, their roots intertwined beneath the soil, and their twigs interlaced above. And two love birds, one male and one female, stayed on these trees, not departing morning or night. They billed and cooed plaintively, and uttered heart-rending cries. The people of Sung lamented the lovers' death and called these trees "The Trees of Love." The southerners say these birds are the spirits of Han Ping and his wife. In Suiyang today there is a town named Hanping, and men still sing of the lovers.

## *Horse into Silkworm*

It is said that in very ancient times a man made a long journey, leaving only his daughter at home with a stallion in her care. She was so lonely that she longed for her father, and one day she said jokingly to the horse:

"If you bring my father home, I will marry you!"

At once the horse broke its tether and galloped off to where her father was. Surprised and pleased to see it, he jumped into the saddle. The stallion kept whinnying sadly, gazing back in the direction from which it had come.

"There must be some reason for this," thought the man. "Can there have been an accident at home?"

Immediately he rode back. And because the beast had shown such intelligence he treated it well, giving it extra fodder. The horse would not eat, however, but when it saw the girl pass in or out it would rear up in excitement—this happened more than once. The father was puzzled and secretly questioned his daughter, who told him what must be the cause.

"Hush!" he said. "You will disgrace our family. You had better not leave the house for the time being."

He took a crossbow and killed the horse, then flayed it and hung its hide in the courtyard.

When the man left home again, the girl and a neighbour's daughter started playing near the hide. The girl kicked it, saying:

"You beast! How dare you think of marrying a girl? Shot and flayed—you brought it on yourself!"

While she was speaking the hide reared up, wrapped itself around her and made off. The neighbour's daughter was too afraid to try to rescue her. Instead she ran to tell her father. When he came and searched for them they had disappeared, but a few days later they were found on a great tree. The girl and the hide had been changed into a silkworm which was spinning silk on the tree—spinning a large, thick cocoon the like of which had never been seen before. The neighbouring women, who kept these cocoons, made several times their former profit. So the tree was named *sang* or mulberry, which means "lost." Since then everyone has cultivated it, and this is the silkworm which we have today.

## *The Old Man and The Devils*

Chin Chu-po of the principality of Langya was sixty. One night after drinking, as he passed Pengshan Temple, he saw his two grandsons coming towards him. They took his arms and helped him along for about a hundred paces. Then they seized him by the neck and threw him to the ground.

"Old slave!" they swore. "You beat us up the other day, so today we are going to kill you."

Remembering that he had indeed beaten the boys some days ago, he pretended to be dead, and they left him there. When he got home he decided to punish them. Shocked and distressed they apologized to him.

"How could your own grandsons do such a thing?" they protested. "Those must have been devils. Please make another test."

He realized they were right.

A few days later the old man pretended to be drunk and walked past the temple again. Once more the two devils came to take his arms, and this time he seized them so that they could not escape. Reaching home, he put both devils on the fire, until their backs and bellies were scorched and cracked. He left them in the courtyard, and that night they escaped. Sorry that he had not killed them, about a month later the old man pretended to be drunk and went out at night again, taking a sword, unknown to his family. When he did not come back though it was very late, his grandsons feared the devils had caught him again. They went to look for him. And this time the old man hacked his own grandsons to death.

## *Married to a Ghost*

Lu Chung was a native of the principality of Fanyang. Thirty *li* west of his house was the graveyard of the Tsui family, one of whom had held office as imperial custodian. The day before the winter solstice when Lu was twenty, he went out in a westerly direction to hunt. He sighted a deer and pierced it with an arrow, but after falling it struggled up again. Then Lu gave chase and pursued it for some distance till suddenly, a few hundred yards to the north, he saw a large, tiled mansion resembling a government office. The deer had disappeared. The guard at the gate called out at his approach.

"Whose house is this?" asked Lu.

"The house of the imperial custodian."

"I am too shabby to call on him," said Lu.

Someone came out with an armful of new clothes and a new hat.

"Our master presents you with these," he announced.

Lu changed his clothes and went in to see the imperial custodian, to whom he introduced himself. After they had drunk and eaten several courses, his host said to Lu:

"Your father recently honoured our humble house by writing to ask for my daughter's hand for you. This is why I invited you in."

He showed Lu the letter. And though Lu had been a child when his father died, he could recognize the writing. With tears in his eyes he consented. Then the imperial custodian sent a message to the inner chambers that Lu Chung had arrived and his daughter should dress for her wedding. He bade Lu go to the east chamber. By dusk word came from within that the girl was ready. When Lu entered the east chamber, she had alighted from her carriage. They stood on the carpet and bowed together, after which Lu stayed the customary three days. Then Tsui said to him:

"You may go home now. I fancy my daughter has conceived. If she gives birth to a son, rest assured we will send him to you. If to a daughter, we will keep her ourselves."

He ordered his men to harness the carriage for Lu, who took his leave and went out. The imperial custodian saw him to the middle gate where they shook hands and shed tears. Outside the gate, Lu saw an ox-cart with a driver in blue, and found his old clothes as well as his bow and arrows. Then a man was sent out with a suit of clothes which he gave to Lu with this message from his master: "We have just become related by marriage, and are very sorry that you are leaving so soon. Please accept this suit of clothes and bedding."

Lu mounted the cart which travelled as swiftly as lightning. In no time he was home. When his relatives saw him, they did not know whether to be glad or sorry. The knowledge that Tsui the imperial custodian was dead and that Lu had been in his grave made them rather uneasy.

Four years later, on the third day of the third month, Lu was strolling by the stream when he observed two carts drawn by oxen approach through the water. As they neared the bank, all those who were with him saw them. Lu opened the door at the back of the first cart and found Tsui's daughter with a three-year-old boy. He was overjoyed to see her, and wanted to take her hand. But she pointed at the cart behind.

"You had better see my father first!"

So he greeted the imperial custodian. The girl gave the baby to Lu, and presented him with a golden bowl and a poem which read as follows:

How beautiful and bright
The glorious herb divine;
Which shines at the appointed
  hour
With splendour strange and fine.

But 'ere the herb can bloom
'Tis killed by summer frost;
Its grace destroyed for ever more,
Its splendid beauty lost.

Who knows the will of Heaven?
A stranger seeks our gate—
We meet but all too soon must
  part,
For men are ruled by fate.

What gift can I bestow?
This bowl I give my son;
And now we part for ever more,
Our love is past and done!

As soon as Lu took the child, the bowl and the poem, the two carts disappeared. When he carried the small boy home, everyone feared it must be a ghost and spat at it from a distance, but the child remained unchanged.

"Who is your father?" they asked.

It ran straight into Lu's arms.

At first all were amazed and felt forebodings; but when they read the poem they knew there was much mysterious traffic between the living and the dead.

Later Lu drove to the market to sell the bowl. He asked a very high price, for actually what he wanted was not to sell it but to find someone to identify it. An old woman slave recognized it, and went to tell her mistress:

"In the market I saw a man in a cart selling that bowl which was in Miss Tsui's coffin."

Her mistress was the girl's aunt. She sent her son to look at the bowl, and when he found that what the slave said was true he went to Lu's cart and introduced himself.

"One of my aunts married the imperial custodian and had a daughter," he said. "The girl died before her marriage, and my mother in her grief presented a golden bowl to put in the coffin. Can you tell me how you came by this bowl?"

Lu told him the story, at which the young man was moved. He took the bowl back to his mother, who asked to see the dead girl's son. All the Tsui clansmen assembled; and when they found that the child looked like one of themselves yet resembled Lu as well, they believed him.

"My niece was born at the end of the third month," said the aunt. "Her father said, 'The spring is warm and we hope the infant will prosper, so let us name her Wen-hsiu (warm and prosperous).' The name sounded like 'wedded in the grave.' That was surely an omen."

The boy grew into a talented man, and became a provincial governor with a two-thousand-bushel salary. All his descendants to this day have held official posts, while one, Lu Chih, was famed throughout the empire.

## *Dead Drunk*

Ti Hsi of Chungshan could brew wine that would make the drinker drunk for a thousand days. Liu Hsuan-shih in his district, who was a heavy drinker, asked Ti for some of this liquor.

"It has just been brewed and not settled yet," Ti told him. "I dare not offer you any."

"Even if the wine is new, won't you give me one cup?" begged Liu.

This Ti did. And Liu asked for more.

"Excellent! Please let me have another cup!"

But Ti said:

"You had better go home now and come back some other time. Just this one cup will make you drunk for a thousand days."

Liu left in some resentment. When he reached home he fell down completely insensible. His family, not suspecting the truth, wept over him and buried him.

Three years later Ti said:

"Liu should have recovered by now from the wine. I must go and see him."

He went to Liu's house and asked: "Is Hsuan-shih at home?"

The family were amazed.

"He is dead," they said. "The three years' mourning is over."

Ti was shocked and replied:

"Ah, my fine wine sent him to sleep for a thousand days. But now he should be waking."

He bade them dig up the grave and open the coffin. They found hot vapour rising from the grave. Then Ti told them to unseal it, and they saw Liu open his eyes and mouth.

"Wonderful!" he cried. "I have never been so drunk!" And he asked Ti: "What is that brew of yours which has made me so drunk on a single cup that I have only woken up today? What time of day is it now?"

All the men round the grave laughed at him. And those who had sniffed the wine on Liu's breath fell into a drunken stupor for three whole months.

## TAO QIAN (365–427)

*Translated by James R. Hightower*

Of the many poets who lived in the Three Kingdoms and Six Dynasties period (220–581), none has been more widely read and admired than Tao Qian. Both his contemporaries and a host of later admirers have regarded him as a man of great integrity who chose to live a life of poverty rather than compromise his principles by continued involvement in the "dusty world" of government bureaucracy. He is a powerful emblem of a problem that is universal but that was particularly common in the literature of China: how much is one willing to compromise peace of mind and one's sense of self for wealth and power? This problem had a particularly sharp edge in Tao Qian's time, when the political world had become very unstable and dangerous.

Tao Qian is his own best biographer. The general shape of his life and values is obvious from the first piece that follows. In *The Return,* Tao Qian speaks in the first person of his "love for freedom" and his choice to return home and spend his remaining time "composing verses beside the clear stream." As is obvious from this piece, Tao Qian enjoyed drinking wine, a topic that he pursues in his *After Drinking Wine,* from which we have selected the preface and five pieces. Two other poems reinforce the values that appear so notably in his personal life. *On Reading the "Seas and Mountains Classic"* praises a form of desultory and pleasurable reading that stands in stark contrast to the Confucian practice of painstakingly memorizing and interpreting classical texts; *Returning to the Farm to Dwell* (no. 4) concerns the poet's conviction that life "reverts in the end to empty nothing" and hence should be enjoyed rather than turned into a time of struggle and strife. Finally, we include one of the most influential pieces of short prose in the Chinese literary tradition, *The Peach Blossom Spring.* This is Tao Qian's utopian fantasy of a fisherman who is reborn from a womblike cave into a new world where people live a simple but happy rural existence somewhat reminiscent of that portrayed in Dao de jing, chapter 80. The fisherman, though treated well by those he visits, returns to the real world and immediately undertakes precisely the kind of official action that could destroy the utopia he admires so much.

Finally, a word needs to be said about the theme of drinking wine in Chinese literature, a theme so prominent throughout the writings of Tao Qian and many of the best Chinese poets. From the earliest times, Chinese civilization has emphasized ritual behavior (what the Confucians call *li*) and social responsibility. Drinking created a space of freedom and spontaneity in what could be a very high-pressured, formal society. Thus, wine came to be seen as an avenue to the naturalness that is associated with the *dao*—a way of getting in touch again with one's real feelings and hence the source of one's creativity. Drinking certainly was a real and frequent act, but it also carried a powerful symbolic significance, which should be kept in mind as we read Chinese poetry. The drinking of wine had an important place in the Western Classical tradition, as well. The word "symposium," which is the title of one of Plato's most influential dialogues (pp. 587–626) means "drinking together."

## *The Return*

I was poor, and what I got from farming was not enough to support my family. The house was full of children, the rice-jar was empty, and I could not see any way to supply the necessities of life. Friends and relatives kept urging me to become a magistrate, and I had at last come to think I should do it, but there was no way for me to get such a position. At the time I happened to have business abroad and made a good impression on the grandees as a conciliatory and humane sort of person. Because of my poverty an uncle offered me a job in a small town, but the region was still unquiet and I trembled at the thought of going away from home. However, P'eng-tse was only thirty miles from my native place, and the yield of the fields assigned the magistrate was sufficient to keep me in wine, so I applied for the office. Before many days had passed, I longed to give it up and go back home. Why, you may ask. Because my instinct is all for freedom, and will not brook discipline or restraint. Hunger and cold may be sharp, but this going against myself really sickens me. Whenever I have been involved in official life I was mortgaging myself to my mouth and belly, and the realization of this greatly upset me. I was deeply ashamed that I had so compromised my principles, but I was still going to wait out the year, after which I might pack up my clothes and slip away at night. Then my sister who had married into the Ch'eng family died in Wu-ch'ang, and my only desire was to go there as quickly as possible. I gave up my office and left of my own accord. From mid-autumn to winter I was altogether some eighty days in office, when events made it possible for me to do what I wished. I have entitled my piece 'The Return'; my preface is dated the eleventh moon of the year *i-ssu* (405).

To get out of this and go back
 home!
My fields and garden will be
 overgrown with weeds—
 I must go back.
It was my own doing that made my
 mind my body's slave
Why should I go on in melancholy
 and lonely grief?
I realize that there's no remedying
 the past
But I know that there's hope in
 the future.
After all I have not gone far on
 the wrong road
And I am aware that what I do
 today is right, yesterday wrong.
My boat rocks in the gentle breeze
Flap, flap, the wind blows my
 gown;
I ask a passerby about the road
 ahead,
Grudging the dimness of the light
 at dawn.
Then I catch sight of my cottage—
 Filled with joy I run.
The servant boy comes to welcome
 me
 My little son waits at the door.
The three paths are almost
 obliterated
 But pines and chrysanthemums
 are still here.
Leading the children by the hand
 I enter my house
 Where there is a bottle filled
 with wine.
I draw the bottle to me and pour
 myself a cup;

Seeing the trees in the courtyard
brings joy to my face.
I lean on the south window and let
my pride expand,
I consider how easy it is to be
content with a little space.
Every day I stroll in the garden for
pleasure,
There is a gate there, but it is
always shut.
Cane in hand I walk and rest
Occasionally raising my head to
gaze into the distance.
The clouds aimlessly rise from the
peaks,
The birds, weary of flying, know it
is time to come home.
As the sun's rays grow dim and
disappear from view
I walk around a lonely pine tree,
stroking it.

Back home again!
May my friendships be broken off
and my wanderings come to
an end.
The world and I shall have
nothing more to do with one
another.
If I were again to go abroad, what
should I seek?
Here I enjoy honest conversation
with my family
And take pleasure in books and
cither to dispel my worries.
The farmers tell me that now
spring is here
There will be work to do in the
west fields.
Sometimes I call for a covered cart
Sometimes I row a lonely boat
Following a deep gully through
the still water
Or crossing the hill on a rugged
path.
The trees put forth luxuriant
foliage,
The spring begins to flow in a
trickle.
I admire the seasonableness of
nature
And am moved to think that my
life will come to its close.
It is all over—
So little time are we granted
human form in the world!
Let us then follow the inclinations
of the heart:
Where would we go that we are so
agitated?
I have no desire for riches
And no expectation of Heaven.
Rather on some fine morning to
walk alone
Now planting my staff to take up a
hoe,
Or climbing the east hill and
whistling long
Or composing verses beside the
clear stream:
So I manage to accept my lot until
the ultimate homecoming.
Rejoicing in Heaven's command,
what is there to doubt?

## *After Drinking Wine*

*Preface*

Living in retirement here I have few pleasures, and now the nights are growing longer; so, as I happen to have some excellent wine, not an evening passes without a drink. All alone with my shadow I empty a bottle until suddenly I find myself drunk. And once I am drunk I write a few verses for my own amusement. In the course of time the pages have multiplied, but there is no particular sequence in what I have written. I have had a friend make a copy, with no more in mind than to provide a diversion.

*I*

Decline and growth have no fixed time,
Everyone gets his share of both:
Master Shao of the melon patch
Used to be Lord of Tungling.
Cold weather alternates with hot
And so it is with human lives—
Intelligent men understand
And are beset no more with doubts.
When chance brings them a jug of wine
They take it gladly as night comes on.

*III*

The Way has declined almost a thousand years
And all men now hold back their impulses.
Give them wine, and they refuse to drink,
All they care for is their reputation.
Whatever gives the body any value
Is it not just this one single life?
But how long is a lifetime after all?
It is brief as the startling lightning bolt.
Staid and stolid through their hundred years
What do they ever hope to get from this?

*IV*

Anxious, seeking, the bird lost from the flock—
The sun declines, and still he flies alone,
Back and forth without a place to rest;
From night to night, his cry becomes more sad,
A piercing sound of yearning for the dawn,
So far from home, with nothing for support
Until at last he finds the lonely pine
And folds his wings at this his journey's end.
In that harsh wind no tree can keep its leaves
This is the only shade that will not fail.
The bird has refuge here and resting place,
And in a thousand years will never leave.

*VII*

The fall chrysanthemums have lovely colors.
I pluck the petals that are wet with dew
And float them in this Care Dispelling Thing
To strengthen my resolve to leave the world.
I drink my solitary cup alone
And when it's empty, pour myself another.
The sun goes down, and all of nature rests
Homing birds fly chirping toward the grove.
I sit complacent on the east veranda
Having somehow found my life again.

*XIV*

Sympathetic friends who know my tastes
Bring a wine jug when they come to visit.
Sitting on the ground beneath the pine tree
A few cups of wine make us drunk,
Venerable elders gabbing all at once
And pouring from the bottle out of turn.
Aware no more that our own 'I' exists
How are we to value other things?
So rapt we are not sure of where we are—
In wine there is a taste of profundity.

## On Reading the "Seas and Mountains Classic" (no. 1)

In early summer when the grasses grow
And trees surround my house with greenery,
The birds rejoice to have a refuge there
And I too love my home.
The fields are plowed and the new seed planted
And now is time again to read my books.
This out-of-the-way lane has no deep-worn ruts
And tends to turn my friends' carts away.
With happy face I pour the spring-brewed wine
And in the garden pick some greens to cook.
A gentle shower approaches from the east
Accompanied by a temperate breeze.
I skim through the *Story of King Mu*
And view the pictures in the *Seas and Mountains Classic.*
A glance encompasses the ends of the universe—
Where is there any joy, if not in these?

## Returning to the Farm to Dwell (no. 4)

For long I left the joys of hills and lakes
Deprived of the pleasures of woods and fields.
Today I led my children and their cousins
And made a path to a deserted town.
We walked around among the grave mounds
And lingered by a dwelling from the past.
There were traces of the well and fireplace
And dry bamboo and stumps of mulberry trees.
I asked the man who gathered firewood there,
'Where are the people now who used to live here?'
The gatherer of firewood answered me
'Dead and gone, none of them are left.'

In one lifetime court and market change—
This in truth is not an idle saying.
Man's life is like a conjuror's illusion,
That reverts in the end to empty nothing.

## *The Peach Blossom Spring*

During the T'ai-yuan period of the Chin dynasty a fisherman of Wu-ling once rowed upstream, unmindful of the distance he had gone, when he suddenly came to a grove of peach trees in bloom. For several hundred paces on both banks of the stream there was no other kind of tree. The wild flowers growing under them were fresh and lovely, and fallen petals covered the ground—it made a great impression on the fisherman. He went on for a way with the idea of finding out how far the grove extended. It came to an end at the foot of a mountain whence issued the spring that supplied the stream. There was a small opening in the mountain and it seemed as though light was coming through it. The fisherman left his boat and entered the cave, which at first was extremely narrow, barely admitting his body; after a few dozen steps it suddenly opened out onto a broad and level plain where well-built houses were surrounded by rich fields and pretty ponds. Mulberry, bamboo and other trees and plants grew there, and crisscross paths skirted the fields. The sounds of cocks crowing and dogs barking could be heard from one courtyard to the next. Men and women were coming and going about their work in the fields. The clothes they wore were like those of ordinary people. Old men and boys were carefree and happy.

When they caught sight of the fisherman, they asked in surprise how he had got there. The fisherman told the whole story, and was invited to go to their house, where he was served wine while they killed a chicken for a feast. When the other villagers heard about the fisherman's arrival they all came to pay him a visit. They told him that their ancestors had fled the disorders of Ch'in times and, having taken refuge here with wives and children and neighbors, had never ventured out again; consequently they had lost all contact with the outside world. They asked what the present ruling dynasty was, for they had never heard of the Han, let alone the Wei and the Chin. They sighed unhappily as the fisherman enumerated the dynasties one by one and recounted the vicissitudes of each. The visitors all asked him to come to their houses in turn, and at every house he had wine and food. He stayed several days. As he was about to go away, the people said, 'There's no need to mention our existence to outsiders.'

After the fisherman had gone out and recovered his boat, he carefully marked the route. On reaching the city, he reported what he had found to the magistrate, who at once sent a man to follow him back to the place. They proceeded according to the marks he had made, but went astray and were unable to find the cave again.

A high-minded gentleman of Nan-yang named Liu Tzu-chi heard the story and happily made preparations to go there, but before he could leave he fell sick and died. Since then there has been no one interested in trying to find such a place. . . .

# THE LOTUS SUTRA

*Translated by Burton Watson*

The Lotus Sutra led a multicultural life, or at least a multilingual life, from very early in its transmission. We do not know the original language of this text, but it may have been an Indian dialect or a Central Asian language. It was then translated into Sanskrit, the official language of ancient India, and subsequently into Chinese, Tibetan, Mongolian, Japanese, and several other Asian languages. The earliest versions of The Lotus Sutra are Chinese translations. The first of these dates from 255 CE, but the most artful is undoubtedly that of the great scholar-monk Kumarajiva, completed in 406. Kumarajiva's version became the basis for many later translations, including the English-language translation by Burton Watson presented here.

The Lotus Sutra is highly revered throughout the Mahāyāna Buddhist world of East Asia. As a Mahāyāna text, it presents a vast world of Buddhas and bodhisattvas who can help the struggling faithful along the road to salvation. [See the introduction to the Vimalakīrti Sutra, an early Mahāyāna text for more on this subject (pp. 260–261).] The Lotus Sutra, like so many other sutras (teachings), begins with a report of what the famous disciple Ananda had heard on an earlier occasion. The report that follows transports the reader into a mythic world where Buddha preaches his message to an inconceivably large and impressive audience.

The text of The Lotus Sutra is half prose and half verse. The verses, known in Sanskrit as *gathas,* may be the older part of the text, but they are presented in current versions of the sutra as recapitulations of the prose narration that precedes them. It is possible that these verse sections were preserved in part to facilitate memorization of the essential points of the text.

The portion of the sutra presented here is the prose version of a prodigal son story. As in so many Buddhist texts, and in contrast to the realistic intimacy of the biblical parable of the prodigal son (Luke 15:11–32), this story is one of extremes: the father is fabulously wealthy; the son has been away for fifty years, then works for his father for at least another twenty years clearing away human excrement. As religious literature, the story is told to teach a "true" message and not to represent a realistic human situation. The point of the story is made clear from its frame. We are like the lost son, and Buddha is the father who patiently condescends, even in demeaning ways, to help us. We may be slow to come to enlightenment, but Buddha will continue to guide us toward a realization of our own true nature, which is the Buddha nature.

This story must have struck many East Asian readers as unusual precisely because it portrays a superior, a father, earnestly reaching down to an inferior, a son. Like Buddha himself, he continues to lead, guide, and assist his son even though the latter has wandered very far from his side and has rejected what the Chinese would call "filial duty." If some children in Chinese literature were much better than their parents deserved, then this father, the representative of the highest Buddhist ideal of compassion, was much more than his son deserved.

## *from Chapter Four*

At that time, when the men of lifelong wisdom Subhuti, Mahakatyayana, Mahakashyapa, and Mahamaudgalyayana heard from the Buddha a Law that they had never known before; and heard the World-Honored One prophesy that Shariputra would attain anuttara-samyak-sambodhi, their minds were moved as seldom before and danced for joy. At once they rose from their seats, arranged their robes, bared their right shoulders and bowed their right knees to the ground. Pressing their palms together with a single mind, they bent their bodies in a gesture of respect and, gazing up in reverence at the face of the Honored One, said to the Buddha: "We stand at the head of the monks and are all of us old and decrepit. We believed that we had already attained nirvana and that we were incapable of doing more, and so we never sought to attain anuttara-samyak-sambodhi.

"It has been a long time since the World-Honored One first began to expound the Law. During that time we have sat in our seats, our bodies weary and inert, meditating solely on the concepts of emptiness, non-form, and non-action. But as to the pleasures and transcendental powers of the Law of the bodhisattva or the purifying of Buddha lands and the salvation of living beings—these our minds took no joy in. Why is this? Because the World-Honored One had made it possible for us to transcend the threefold world and to attain the enlightenment of nirvana.

"Moreover, we are old and decrepit. When we heard of this anuttara-samyak-sambodhi, which the Buddha uses to teach and convert the bodhisattvas, our minds were not filled with any thought of joy or approval. But now in the presence of the Buddha we have heard this voice-hearer receive a prophecy that he will attain anuttara-samyak-sambodhi and our minds are greatly delighted. We have gained what we never had before. Suddenly we have been able to hear a Law that is rarely encountered, something we never expected up to now, and we look upon ourselves as profoundly fortunate. We have gained great goodness and benefit, an immeasurably rare jewel, something unsought that came of itself.

"World-Honored One, we would be pleased now to employ a parable to make clear our meaning. Suppose there was a man, still young in years, who abandoned his father, ran away, and lived for a long time in another land, for perhaps ten, twenty, or even fifty years. As he grew older, he found himself increasingly poor and in want. He hurried about in every direction, seeking for clothing and food, wandering farther and farther afield until by chance he turned his steps in the direction of his homeland.

"The father meanwhile had been searching for his son without success and had taken up residence in a certain city. The father's household was very wealthy, with immeasurable riches and treasures. Gold, silver, lapis lazuli, coral, amber, and crystal beads all filled and overflowed from his storehouses. He had many grooms and menservants, clerks and attendants, and elephants, horses, carriages, oxen, and goats beyond number. He engaged in profitable ventures at home and in all the lands around, and also had dealings with many merchants and traveling vendors.

"At this time the impoverished son wandered from village to village, passing through various lands and towns, till at last he came to the city where his father was residing. The father thought constantly of his son, but though he had been parted from him for over fifty years, he had never told anyone else about the matter. He merely pondered to himself, his heart filled with regret and longing. He thought to himself that he was old and decrepit. He had great wealth and possessions, gold, silver, and rare treasures that filled and overflowed from his storehouses, but he had no son, so that if one day he should die, the wealth and possessions would be scattered and lost, for there was no one to entrust them to.

"This was the reason he constantly thought so earnestly of his son. And he also had this thought: If I could find my son and entrust my wealth and possessions to him, then I could feel contented and easy in mind and would have no more worries.

"World-Honored One, at that time the impoverished son drifted from one kind of employment to another until he came by chance to his father's house. He stood by the side of the gate, gazing far off at his father, who was seated on a lion throne, his legs supported by a jeweled footrest, while Brahmans, noblemen, and householders, uniformly deferential, surrounded him. Festoons of pearls worth thousands or tens of thousands adorned his body, and clerks, grooms, and menservants holding white fly whisks stood in attendance to left and right. A jeweled canopy covered him, with flowered banners hanging from it, perfumed water had been sprinkled over the ground, heaps of rare flowers were scattered about, and precious objects were ranged here and there, brought out, put away, handed over and received. Such were the many different types of adornments, the emblems of prerogative and marks of distinction.

"When the impoverished son saw how great was his father's power and authority, he was filled with fear and awe and regretted he had ever come to such a place. Secretly he thought to himself: This must be some king, or one who is equal to a king. This is not the sort of place where I can hire out my labor and gain a living. It would be better to go to some poor village where, if I work hard, I will find a place and can easily earn food and clothing. If I stay here for long, I may be seized and pressed into service! Having thought in this way, he raced from the spot.

"At that time the rich old man, seated on his lion throne, spied his son and recognized him immediately. His heart was filled with great joy and at once he thought: Now I have someone to entrust my storehouses of wealth and possessions to! My thoughts have constantly been with this son of mine, but I had no way of seeing him. Now suddenly he has appeared of himself, which is exactly what I would have wished. Though I am old and decrepit, I still care what becomes of my belongings.

"Thereupon he dispatched a bystander to go after the son as quickly as possible and bring him back. At that time the messenger raced swiftly after the son and laid hold of him. The impoverished son, alarmed and fearful, cried out in an angry voice, 'I have done nothing wrong! Why am I being seized?' But the messenger held on to him more tightly than ever and forcibly dragged him back.

"At that time the son thought to himself, I have committed no crime and yet I am taken prisoner. Surely I am going to be put to death! He was more terrified than ever and sank to the ground, fainting with despair.

"The father, observing this from a distance, spoke to the messenger, saying, 'I have no need of this man. Don't force him to come here, but sprinkle cold water on his face so he will regain his senses. Then say nothing more to him!'

"Why did he do that? Because the father knew that his son was of humble outlook and ambition, and that his own rich and eminent position would be difficult for the son to accept. He knew very well that this was his son, but as a form of expedient means he refrained from saying to anyone, 'This is my son.'

"The messenger said to the son, 'I am releasing you now. You may go anywhere you wish.' The impoverished son was delighted, having gained what he had not had before, and picked himself up from the ground and went off to the poor village in order to look for food and clothing.

"At that time the rich man, hoping to entice his son back again, decided to employ an expedient means and send two men as secret messengers, men who were lean and haggard and had no imposing appearance. 'Go seek out that poor man and approach him casually. Tell him you know a place where he can earn twice the regular wage. If he agrees to the arrangement, then bring him here and put him to work. If he asks what sort of work he will be put to, say that he will be employed to clear away excrement, and that the two of you will be working with him.'

"The two messengers then set out at once to find the poor man, and when they had done so, spoke to him as they had been instructed. At that time the impoverished son asked for an advance on his wages and then went with the men to help clear away excrement.

"When the father saw his son, he pitied and wondered at him. Another day, when he was gazing out the window, he saw his son in the distance, his body thin and haggard, filthy with excrement, dirt, sweat, and defilement. The father immediately took off his necklaces, his soft fine garments and his other adornments and put on clothes that were ragged and soiled. He smeared dirt on his body, took in his right hand a utensil for removing excrement, and assuming a gruff manner, spoke to the laborers, saying, 'Keep at your work! You mustn't be lazy!' By employing this expedient means, he was able to approach his son.

"Later he spoke to his son again, saying, 'Now then, young man! You must keep on at this work and not leave me anymore. I will increase your wages, and whatever you need in the way of utensils, rice, flour, salt, vinegar, and the like you should be in no worry about. I have an old servant I can lend you when you need him. You may set your mind at ease. I will be like a father to you, so have no more worries. Why do I say this? Because I am well along in years, but you are still young and sturdy. When you are at work, you are never deceitful or lazy or speak angry or resentful words. You don't seem to have any faults of that kind the way my other workers do. From now on, you will be like my own son.' And the rich man proceeded to select a name and assign it to the man as though he were his child.

"At this time the impoverished son, though he was delighted at such treatment, still thought of himself as a person of humble station who was in the employ of another. Therefore the rich man kept him clearing away excrement for the next twenty years. By the end of this time, the son felt that he was understood and trusted, and he could come and go at ease, but he continued to live in the same place as before.

"World-Honored One, at that time the rich man fell ill and knew that he would die before long. He spoke to his impoverished son, saying, 'I now have great quantities of gold, silver, and rare treasures that fill and overflow from my storehouses. You are to take complete charge of the amounts I have and of what is to be handed out and gathered in. This is what I have in mind, and I want you to carry out my wishes. Why is this? Because from now on, you and I will not behave as two different persons. So you must keep your wits about you and see that there are no mistakes or losses.'

"At that time the impoverished son, having received these instructions, took over the surveillance of all the goods, the gold, silver, and rare treasures, and the various storehouses, but never thought of appropriating for himself so much as the cost of a single meal. He continued to live where he had before, unable to cease thinking of himself as mean and lowly.

"After some time had passed, the father perceived that his son was bit by bit becoming more self-assured and magnanimous in outlook, that he was determined to accomplish great things and despised his former low opinion of himself. Realizing that his own end was approaching, he ordered his son to arrange a meeting with his relatives and the king of the country, the high ministers, and the noblemen and householders. When they were all gathered together, he proceeded to make this announcement: 'Gentlemen, you should know that this is my son, who was born to me. In such-and-such a city he abandoned me and ran away, and for over fifty years he wandered about suffering hardship. His original name is such-and-such, and my name is such-and-such. In the past, when I was still living in my native city, I worried about him and so I set out in search of him. Sometime after, I suddenly chanced to meet up with him. This is in truth my son, and I in truth am his father. Now everything that belongs to me, all my wealth and possessions, shall belong entirely to this son of mine. Matters of outlay and income that have occurred in the past this son of mine is familiar with.'

"World-Honored One, when the impoverished son heard these words of his father, he was filled with great joy, having gained what he never had before, and he thought to himself, I originally had no mind to covet or seek such things. Yet now these stores of treasures have come of their own accord!

"World-Honored One, this old man with his great riches is none other than the Thus Come One, and we are all like the Buddha's sons. The Thus Come One constantly tells us that we are his sons. But because of the three sufferings, World-Honored One, in the midst of birth and death we undergo burning anxieties, delusions, and ignorance, delighting in and clinging to lesser doctrines. But today the World-Honored One causes us to ponder carefully, to cast aside such doctrines, the filth of frivolous debate.

"We were diligent and exerted ourselves in this matter until we had attained nirvana, which is like one day's wages. And once we had attained it, our hearts were filled with great joy and we considered that this was enough. At once we said to ourselves, 'Because we have been diligent and exerted ourselves with regard to the Buddhist Law, we have gained this breadth and wealth of understanding.'

"But the World-Honored One, knowing from past times how our minds cling to unworthy desires and delight in lesser doctrines, pardoned us and let us be, not trying to explain to us by saying, 'You will come to possess the insight of the Thus Come One, your portion of the store of treasures!' Instead the World-Honored One employed the power of expedient means, preaching to us the wisdom of the Thus Come One in such a way that we might heed the Buddha and attain nirvana, which is one day's wages. And because we considered this to be a great gain, we had no wish to pursue the Great Vehicle.

"In addition, though we expounded and set forth the Buddha wisdom for the sake of the bodhisattvas, we ourselves did not aspire to attain it. Why do I say this? Because the Buddha, knowing that our minds delight in lesser doctrines, employed the power of the expedient means to preach in a way that was appropriate for us. So we did not know that we were in truth the sons of the Buddha. But now at last we know it.

"With regard to the Buddha wisdom, the World-Honored One is never begrudging. Why do I say this? From times past we have in truth been the sons of the Buddha, but we delighted in nothing but lesser doctrines. If we had had the kind of mind that delighted in great ones, then the Buddha would have preached the Law of the Great Vehicle for us."

## Four Tang Poets

Many scholars regard the Tang dynasty (618–907) as the age when China produced its greatest poetry. Certainly later Chinese poets evaluated their own work against the standard of the Tang masters. Why such a poetic flowering took place at that time is not entirely clear. The Tang followed a long period of disunity, the Three Kingdoms and Six Dynasties (220–581), and was a time of cultural, as well as political, consolidation and synthesis. The Tang emperors traced their family lineage back to Laozi and were sympathetic to Daoism. At the same time, the government promoted mastery of the Confucian classics, and Buddhism, which had come to China from India centuries before and had developed distinctively Chinese forms, flourished during the first two centuries of the dynasty. In addition, China during the Tang was unusually open and particularly receptive to Central Asian influences, so that music, clothing, and other cultural elements flowed freely from the steppes to the agricultural heartland. Finally, the court was active in promoting and sponsoring literary activity. The best Tang poetry may not have come from the court, but state sponsorship did provide some stimulus to poetic creativity. Although all these factors contributed to new and exciting literary endeavors, they cannot entirely account for the glory of Tang poetry.

Tang poets did not typically consider themselves professional poets. Instead, they were mostly civil service bureaucrats who wrote poetry as a diversion that defined them as sensitive and intelligent men of culture. Much of the best Tang poetry was written in times of retirement, exile, or estrangement from the institutions of political power that so many of the poets wished to serve. Other poetry was written during government service but reflected an intense longing for the quiet life of the countryside or for seclusion in the mountains. In either case, Tang poetry is filled with a sense of separation and longing and with a wish that life could somehow be simpler and purer than it is.

It is impossible in a brief anthology to represent Tang poetry fairly. One standard collection of Tang poetry includes more than 48,000 poems from 2200 poets. These poems are written in a variety of styles. Some are exceedingly brief, consisting of only twenty Chinese characters in length, while others are quite lengthy; some are in a formal, highly technical style known as "regulated verse," a poetic form much more rule-laden than the English sonnet, while others are in the much more informal "old verse" form; some Tang poems are extremely dense and allusive, while others are simple and accessible to almost any reader. Despite considerable variation in style and theme, most Tang poetry, in contrast to much Western poetry, is directly linked to a particular autobiographical moment. The poem might have general implications, but usually it is fixed in a specific time and place, which are often identified in the title of the poem, in its preface, or in the body of the poem itself. Put somewhat differently, poetry is what an educated person does in reflecting on particular events.

From the enormous body of Tang poetry, we include here examples from four of the greatest masters of this period: Wang Wei (701–761), Li Bai (701–762), Du Fu (712–770), and Bai Juyi (772—846). Wang Wei passed the civil service examinations at an early age and served in a variety of government positions. Like so many other bureaucrats, he occasionally found himself in trouble. On one occasion he was exiled, on another only an imperial pardon saved him from serious punishment. Despite his official duties, Wang Wei was active as a landscape painter, musician, and poet. Indeed, his landscape painting, although it exists today only in later copies, is credited with exerting an enormous influence on this rich Chinese tradition. It has been said that in each of Wang Wei's paintings is a poem, and in each of his poems is a painting. Certainly his poetry displays a deep sensitivity to nature. Nevertheless, Chinese nature poetry, like Chinese landscape painting, almost always makes room for a human presence. It is not nature alone that interests the poet but the interrelationship of natural scene and human emotion. In Wang Wei's case, a devotion to Buddhist meditation no doubt shaped his vision of nature, for his natural world is often a place of contemplation and quiet, a space where the external scene and the internal human heart merge.

Wang's sensitivity to nature is perhaps displayed most movingly in several of his quatrains. The quatrain is a poem of four lines of either five or seven characters each. Strict rules of rhyme, tonal sequence, and grammatical parallelism govern the quatrain, but a master of the form such as Wang Wei is able to comply with the technical requirements of this verse and yet appear completely spontaneous. We include here thirteen quatrains from his *Wang River Sequence,* a series of descriptions of scenes on his beloved mountain estate. In addition, we include several other of Wang Wei's poems, all displaying to one degree or another a juxtaposition of human emotion and natural scene. His works conclude with a portrait of a rich woman whom Wang presents as a backdrop for a sympathetic comment on the poor.

Li Bai, the second of our Tang poets, is one of the giants of the Chinese literary tradition. His image in China, an image he himself took care to cultivate, is far more important than the biographical details of his life. Li Bai never occupied more than a minor government post; his most noteworthy political act was an unfortunate involvement in a minor revolt, an involvement that resulted in a short period of imprisonment. For twelve hundred years, devoted readers have admired Li Bai as an eccentric individualist who loved wine, roamed the mountains looking for immortals, and did everything he could to assert complete freedom from convention. Poetry supposedly flowed from his pen with virtually no effort. In one of his poems, he chides his younger friend Du Fu for growing "thin since our parting" and suggests "it must be the struggle of writing his poems." He himself, he would have us believe, never labored over his own compositions. Anecdotes abound about this poet's eccentric behavior. Perhaps most famous is the claim that he died when he plunged from a boat in a drunken stupor while trying to embrace the moon's reflection. While this is almost certainly false, it would be the perfect death for a poet of such romantic and unfettered vision.

Three of Li Bai's many poems on drinking are included here. For him wine becomes a means to escape into a timelessness that sounds almost religious and that perhaps finds its closest comparison in the writings of religious mystics in both the East and the West. In contrast, *Fighting South of the Ramparts* demonstrates that Li Bai's eyes were not entirely closed to the turmoil of his time.

Du Fu, whom Li Bai thought worked too hard at poetry, is generally regarded as China's greatest poet. The reputation is deserved; it derives from the astounding range and power of his poetic gifts. His reputation also comes from the fact that much of his poetry, unlike that of Li Bai, reflects a strong social consciousness, a quality much admired by many Chinese readers who prefer poetry that reflects the often tragic events of the real world. Du Fu's sensitivity to the sufferings of others was no doubt sharpened by his own exceedingly difficult life. He failed the civil service examinations on two occasions and never occupied more than minor official posts. Much of Du Fu's life was spent in grinding poverty and in traveling to seek employment. His infant son died of starvation during one of these absences, a tragedy Du Fu blamed on himself. The last and most artistically productive two decades of his life were a time of constant illness, as he was plagued by chronic coughs, malaria, rheumatism, and partial deafness. In the midst of his own distressing circumstances, Du Fu's sympathy consistently reached outward through his poetry to others and to the country at large. But his greatness as a poet comes as much from his craft as from his social concerns. He is a master technician who stretches the resources of Tang poetic diction to extremes. His syntax is often complex, and his language is both allusive and elusive.

Nowhere is Du Fu's genius illustrated more clearly than in his sequence *Autumn Meditations,* written late in his life. With their intense nostalgia for earlier and better days, these poems reflect the decline of Tang glory that followed the rebellion (755–757) of the young Turkish general An Lushan, which brought widespread devastation and drove the emperor into temporary exile. Amidst the sorrow over personal and national decline are startling images of great beauty, and a sense of eternal silence surrounds the world of conflict and chaos depicted in these meditations. The final three poems by Du Fu included here show sympathy for a *Lovely Lady* mistreated by her husband; for the poet's own wife, who waits for him alone in Fuzhou in *Moonlight Night;* and for himself as an aged poet, who is *A Man with No Family to Take Leave Of.*

Bai Juyi, our final Tang poet, was reasonably successful as a government official, although he too suffered through a period of disfavor and banishment. Bai cultivated a close friendship with Yuan Zhen (see *The Story of Ying-ying,* pp. 1034–1041), and together they argued that literature should be accessible to all and should be morally instructive. His poetry is known for its verbal simplicity; a story persists that he read all his poetry to a peasant woman and altered any portions she did not understand. Perhaps as a result of his clarity and simplicity, Bai Juyi became extremely popular during his lifetime, with his verses on the lips of almost everyone. At times this popularity troubled him, for he believed that people were always attracted to his romantic and occasional pieces much more than to his didactic verses. "The world," he wrote to Yuan Zhen, "values highest those of my poems I most despise."

From Bai Juyi's large collection of poetry, we include only three pieces. The first is a poem he did not much like but which became one of the most popular pieces ever written: *A Song of Unending Sorrow,* a long and intensely romantic poem about the tragic love affair between Emperor Xuanzong and the Honored Concubine Yang (Yang Guifei). The episode is historical, although substantially embellished by the poet. Late in his life, Emperor Xuanzong became infatuated with a young woman, Yang Guifei, and, so we are told, began to ignore governmental matters. When the Turkish general An Lushan rebelled against the emperor in 755, Xuanzong was forced to flee the capital of Chang'an. Many of the emperor's supporters blamed Yang Guifei for the flight and demanded that she be killed. The emperor complied with their wish and then spent the last years of his life mourning the death of his beloved concubine. The historical event and Bai Juyi's poem have successfully enshrined Yang Guifei as traditional China's premier *femme fatale.*

Finally, we include one of Bai Juyi's poems on a favorite pastime, mountain climbing, and conclude the selection with his *Madly Singing in the Mountains,* a wonderful celebration of the joy of poetry and also a splendid example of the skill of the great translator Arthur Waley.

## *Wang Wei (701–761)*

### *The Wang River Sequence*

*Translated by Tony Barnstone*

My country estate is at Wang River Ravine, where the scenic spots include Meng Wall Hollow, Huazi Hill, Grainy Apricot Wood Cottage, Deer Park, Magnolia Enclosure, Lakeside Pavilion, Lake Yi, Waves of Willow Trees, Luan Family Rapids, White Pebble Shoal, Magnolia Basin, etc. Pei Di and I spent our leisure writing quatrains about each of these places.

*Huazi Hill*

Migrating birds are leaving endlessly,
fall colors come to mountain after mountain.
All the way up Huazi Hill a sadness,
staining every far boundary, drifts on.

*Deer Park*

Nobody in sight on the empty mountain
but human voices are heard far off.
Low sun slips deep in the forest
and lights the green hanging moss.

*Grainy Apricot Wood Cottage*

Its beams are cut from apricot wood,
its roof is woven of fragrant reeds.
I wonder if clouds under the rafters
float into the human world as rain.

*Magnolia Enclosure*

Autumn mountains drink the sun's last rays.
Floating birds follow their mates.
At this hour colors leap into clarity.
No place for evening mist to dwell.

*House Hidden in the Bamboo Grove*

Sitting alone in the dark bamboo,
I play my lute and whistle song.
Deep in the wood no one knows
the bright moon is shining on me.

*At Lake Yi*

A flute drifts beyond the lake.
At dayfall I send my friend off.
On the waters I turn my head:
Green mountains fold up white clouds.

*South Hill*

A light boat is heading for South Hill.
North Hill faint beyond harsh waters.
Houses and people across the lake,
I see them far, far. We are strangers.

*Luan Family Rapids*

In the windy hiss of autumn rain
shallow water fumbles over stones.
Waves dance and fall on each other:
a white egret startles up, then drops.

*White Pebble Shoal*

White Pebble Shoal is clear and shallow.
You can almost grab the green cattail.
Houses east and west of the stream.
Someone washes silk in bright moonlight.

*Waves of Willow Trees*

Separate rows of silky willows touch,
and reflections merge into clear ripples.
The scene is not like the palace moat
where spring wind aches with departure.

*Lakeside Pavilion*

A light boat greets the honored guests,
far, far, coming in over the lake.
On a balcony we face bowls of wine
and lotus flowers bloom everywhere.

*Magnolia Basin*

On branch tips the hibiscus bloom.
The mountains show off red calices.
Nobody. A silent cottage in the valley.
One by one flowers open, then fall.

*Meng Wall Hollow*

I made my new home at Meng Wall.
Old Trees? Only some rotting willows.
After me, who else will lodge here,
aimlessly grieving for past owners?

## *A Farewell*

I dismount from my horse and drink your wine.
I ask where you're going.
You say you are a failure
and want to hibernate at the foot of Deep South Mountain.

Once you're gone no one will ask about you.
There are endless white clouds on the mountain.

## *Living in the Mountain on an Autumn Night*

After fresh rain on the empty mountain
comes evening and the cold of autumn.
The full moon burns through the pines.
A brook transparent over the stones.
Bamboo trees crackle as washerwomen go home
and lotus flowers sway as a fisherman's boat slips downriver.
Though the fresh smell of grass is gone,
a prince is happy in these hills.

## *Autumn Night Sitting Alone, Thinking of My Brother-in-Law Cui*

Quiet night. All creatures are sleeping.
Interminable sound of cicadas.
In the courtyard a scholar tree creaks in north wind.
Now days and nights are deep in autumn.
I know you're smoothing your feathers
and are about to fly off into the clouds.
Soon my head will be entirely white
and I think only of living by the river.
Since any day or night you'll soar into the heavens,
why say you'll join me in the fields?

### *To My Cousin Qiu, Military Supply Official*

When young I knew only the surface of things
and studied eagerly for fame and power.
I heard tales of marvelous years on horseback
and suffered from being no wiser than others.
Honestly, I didn't rely on empty words;
I tried several official posts.
But to be a clerk—always fearing punishment
for going against the times—is joyless.
In clear winter I see remote mountains
with dark green frozen in drifted snow.
Bright peaks beyond the eastern forest
tell me to abandon this world.
Cousin, like Huilian your taste is pure.

You once talked of living beyond mere dust.
I saw no rush to take your hand and go—
but how the years have thundered away!

*Lazy about Writing Poems*

With time I become lazy about writing poems.
Now my only company is old age.
In an earlier life I was a poet, a mistake,
and my former body belonged to a painter.
I can't abandon habits of that life
and sometimes am recognized by people of this world.
My name and pen name speak my former being
but about all this my heart is ignorant.

*A Wealthy Woman of Luoyang*

Near me lives the woman of Luoyang, who looks only fifteen.
Her husband rides a piebald horse with a jade bridle.
Her maid serves minced carp on gold platters.

Facing each other are many painted chambers and crimson
towers.
Red peach and green willow trees bend along the eaves.
Gauze curtains shield her as she walks to her carriage of seven
fragrances.
Precious fans welcome her back to her nine-flower canopied bed.

Her bold husband is rich, high-born and young
with more mad pride and extravagance than Ji Lun.
He loves his White Jade, teaches her to dance,
and thinks nothing of showering her with handsome corals.

Sun is quenched in the spring window. The lamp of nine
subtleties flames.
Flakes of nine subtleties drift down like petals.
After entertainment, she forgets to practice music.
She makes up and sits numb in clouds of her own fragrance.

She knows all the rich people in the city
and is always at their homes.
But who pities a girl from Yue, beautiful as jade,
poor and washing silk by the river, alone?

## *Li Bai (701–762)*

*Translated by Arthur Waley*

### *Drinking Alone by Moonlight*

*[Three Poems]*

**I**

A cup of wine, under the flowering trees;
I drink alone, for no friend is near.
Raising my cup I beckon the bright moon,
For he, with my shadow, will make three men.
The moon, alas, is no drinker of wine;
Listless, my shadow creeps about at my side.
Yet with the moon as friend and the shadow as slave
I must make merry before the Spring is spent.
To the songs I sing the moon flickers her beams;
In the dance I weave my shadow tangles and breaks.
While we were sober, three shared the fun;
Now we are drunk, each goes his way.
May we long share our odd, inanimate feast,
And meet at last on the Cloudy River of the sky.

**II**

In the third month the town of Hsien-yang
Is thick-spread with a carpet of fallen flowers.
Who in Spring can bear to grieve alone?
Who, sober, look on sights like these?
Riches and Poverty, long or short life,
By the Maker of Things are portioned and disposed;
But a cup of wine levels life and death
And a thousand things obstinately hard to prove.
When I am drunk, I lose Heaven and Earth.
Motionless—I cleave to my lonely bed.
At last I forget that I exist at all,
And at *that* moment my joy is great indeed.

**III**

If High Heaven had no love for wine,
There would not be a Wine Star in the sky.
If Earth herself had no love for wine,
There would not be a city called Wine Springs.
Since Heaven and Earth both love wine,

I can love wine, without shame before God.
Clear wine was once called a Saint;
Thick wine was once called "a Sage."

Of Saint and Sage I have long quaffed deep,
What need for me to study spirits and *hsien?*
At the third cup I penetrate the Great Way;
A full gallon—Nature and I are one . . .
But the things I feel when wine possesses my soul
I will never tell to those who are not drunk.

## *In the Mountains on a Summer Day*

Gently I stir a white feather fan,
With open shirt sitting in a green wood.
I take off my cap and hang it on a jutting stone;
A wind from the pine-trees trickles on my bare head.

## *To Tan Ch'iu*

My friend is lodging high in the Eastern Range,
Dearly loving the beauty of valleys and hills.
At green Spring he lies in the empty woods,
And is still asleep when the sun shines on high.
A pine-tree wind dusts his sleeves and coat;
A pebbly stream cleans his heart and ears.
I envy you, who far from strife and talk
Are high-propped on a pillow of blue cloud.

## *Clearing at Dawn*

The fields are chill; the sparse rain has stopped;
The colours of Spring teem on every side.
With leaping fish the blue pond is full;
With singing thrushes the green boughs droop.
The flowers of the field have dabbled their powdered cheeks;
The mountain grasses are bent level at the waist.
By the bamboo stream the last fragment of cloud
Blown by the wind slowly scatters away.

## *"You asked me what my reason is"*

You asked me what my reason is for lodging in the grey hills;
I smiled but made no reply, for my thoughts were idling on
their own;

Like the flowers of the peach-tree borne by the stream, they had sauntered far away
To other climes, to other lands that are not in the World of Men.

## *"When Chuang Chou dreamed he was a butterfly"*

When Chuang Chou dreamed he was a butterfly
The butterfly became Chuang Chou.
If single creatures can thus suffer change,
Surely the whole world must be in flux?
What wonder then if the ocean of P'êng-lai
Should dwindle into a clear, shallow stream
Or the man who plants melons at the Green Gate
Should once have been the Marquis of Tung-ling?
If wealth and honour indeed be flighty as this
By our toiling and moiling what is it that we seek?

## *Fighting South of the Ramparts*

Last year we were fighting at the source of the Sang-kan;
This year we are fighting on the Onion River road.
We have washed our swords in the surf of Parthian seas;
We have pastured our horses among the snows of the T'ien Shan,
The King's armies have grown grey and old
Fighting ten thousand leagues away from home.
The Huns have no trade but battle and carnage;
They have no fields or ploughlands,
But only wastes where white bones lie among yellow sands.
Where the House of Ch'in built the great wall that was to keep away the Tartars.
There, in its turn, the House of Han lit beacons of war.
The beacons are always alight, fighting and marching never stop.
Men die in the field, slashing sword to sword;
The horses of the conquered neigh piteously to Heaven.
Crows and hawks peck for human guts,
Carry them in their beaks and hang them on the branches of withered trees.
Captains and soldiers are smeared on the bushes and grass;
The General schemed in vain.
Know therefore that the sword is a cursed thing
Which the wise man uses only if he must.

## Du Fu (712–770)

### *Autumn Meditations*

*Translated by A.C. Graham*

### 1

Gems of dew wilt and wound the maple trees in the wood:
From Wu mountains, from Wu gorges, the air blows desolate.
The waves between the river banks merge in the seething sky,
Clouds in the wind above the passes touch their shadows on the ground.
Clustered chrysanthemums have opened twice, in tears of other days:
The forlorn boat, once and for all, tethers my homeward thoughts.
In the houses quilted clothes speed scissors and ruler.
The washing blocks pound, faster each evening, in Pai Ti high on the hill.

### 2

On the solitary walls of K'uei-chou the sunset rays slant,
Each night guided by the Dipper I gaze towards the capital.
It is true then that tears start when we hear the gibbon cry thrice:
Useless my mission adrift on the raft which came by this eighth month.
Fumes of the censers by the pictures in the ministry elude my sickbed pillow,
The whitewashed parapets of turrets against the hills dull the mournful bugles.
Look! On the wall, the moon in the ivy
Already, by the shores of the isle, lights the blossoms on the reeds.

### 3

A thousand houses rimmed by the mountains are quiet in the morning light,
Day after day in the house by the river I sit in the blue of the hills.
Two nights gone the fisher-boats once more come bobbing on the waves,
Belated swallows in cooling autumn still flit to and fro.
. . . A disdained K'uang Heng, as a critic of policy:
As promoter of learning, a Liu Hsiang who failed.
Of the school-friends of my childhood, most did well.
By the Five Tombs in light cloaks they ride their sleek horses.

**4**

Well said Ch'ang-an looks like a chess-board:
A hundred years of the saddest news.
The mansions of princes and nobles all have new lords:
Another breed is capped and robed for office.
Due north on the mountain passes the gongs and drums shake,
To the chariots and horses campaigning in the west the winged dispatches hasten.
While the fish and the dragons fall asleep and the autumn river turns cold
My native country, untroubled times, are always in my thoughts.

**5**

The gate of P'eng-lai Palace faces the South Mountain:
Dew collects on the bronze stems out of the Misty River.
See in the west on Jasper Lake the Queen Mother descend:
Approaching from the east the purple haze fills the Han-ku pass.
The clouds roll back, the pheasant-tail screens open before the throne:
Scales ringed by the sun on dragon robes! I have seen the majestic face.
I lay down once by the long river, wake left behind by the years,
Who so many times answered the roll of court by the blue chain-patterned door.

**6**

From the mouth of Ch'üt-t'ang gorges here, to the side of Crooked River there,
For ten thousand miles of mist in the wind the touch of pallid autumn.
Through the walled passage from Calyx Hall the royal splendour coursed,
To Hibiscus Park the griefs of the frontier came.
Pearl blinds and embellished pillars closed in the yellow cranes,
Embroidered cables and ivory masts startled the white seagulls.
Look back and pity the singing, dancing land!
Ch'in from most ancient times was the seat of princes.

**7**

K'un-ming Pool was the Han time's monument,
The banners of the Emperor Wu are here before my eyes.
Vega threads her loom in vain by night under the moon,

And the great stone fish's plated scales veer in the autumn wind.
The waves toss a zizania seed, over sunken clouds as black:
Dew on the calyx chills the lotus, red with dropped pollen.
    Over the pass, all the way to the sky, a road for none but the birds.
On river and lakes, to the ends of the earth, one old fisherman.

**8**

The K'un-wu road by Yü-su river ran its meandering course,
The shadow of Purple Turret Peak fell into Lake Mei-p'i.
Grains from the fragrant rice-stalks, pecked and dropped by the parrots:
On the green *wu-t'ung* tree branches which the perching phoenix aged.
Beautiful girls gathered kingfisher feathers for spring gifts:
Together in the boat, a troop of immortals, we set forth again in the evening. . . .
    This brush of many colours once forced the elements.
Chanting, peering into the distance, in anguish my white head droops.

## *Lovely Lady*

*Translated by Burton Watson*

Lovely lady, fairest of the time,
hiding away in an empty valley;
daughter of a good house, she said,
fallen now among grasses of the wood.
"There was tumult and death within the passes then;
my brothers, old and young, were killed.
Office, position—what help were they?
I couldn't even gather up my brothers' bones!
The world despises you when your luck is down;
all I had went with the turn of the flame.
My husband was a fickle fellow,
his new girl as fair as jade.
Blossoms that close at dusk keep faith with the hour,
mandarin ducks will not rest apart;
but he could only see the new one laughing,
never hear the former one's tears—"
Within the mountain the stream runs clear;
out of the mountain it turns to mud.
Her maid returns from selling a pearl,

braids vines to mend their roof of thatch.
The lady picks a flower but does not put it in her hair,
gathers juniper berries, sometimes a handful.
When the sky is cold, in thin azure sleeves,
at dusk she stands leaning by the tall bamboo.

## *Moonlight Night*

*Translated by Burton Watson*

From her room in Fu-chou tonight
all alone she watches the moon.
Far away, I grieve that her children
can't understand why she thinks of Ch'ang-an.
Fragrant mist in her cloud hair damp,
clear lucence on her jade arms cold—
when will we lean by chamber curtains
and let it light the two of us, our tear stains dried?

## *The Man with No Family to Take Leave Of*

*Translated by Burton Watson*

Ever since T'ien-pao, this silence and desolation,
fields and sheds mere masses of pigweed and bramble;
my village of a hundred households or more,
in these troubled times scattered, some east, some west;
not a word from those still living,
the dead ones all gone to dust and mire.
I was on the side that lost the battle,
so I came home, looking for the old paths,
so long on the road, to find empty lanes,
the sun grown feeble, pain and sorrow in the air.
All I meet are foxes and raccoon dogs,
their fur on end, snarling at me in anger.
And for neighbors on four sides, who do I have?
One or two aging widows.
But the roosting bird loves his old branch;
how could he reject it, narrow perch though it is?
Now that spring's here I shoulder the hoe alone,
in the evening sun once more pour water on the fields.
The local officials know I'm back;
they call me in, order me to practice the big drum.
Maybe they'll assign me to duty in my own province—
but still I've no wife, no one to take by hand.
Traveling to a post nearby, I'm one man all alone;

sent to a far-off assignment, I'll be more lost than ever.
But, since my house and village are a wilderness now,
near or far, it's all the same to me.
And always I grieve for my mother, sick so long;
five years I've left her buried in a mere ditch of a grave.
She bore me, but I hadn't the strength to help her;
to the end, both of us breathed bitter sighs.
A living man, but with no family to take leave of—
how can I be called a proper human being?

## *Bai Juyi (772–846)*

### *A Song of Unending Sorrow*

*Translated by Witter Bynner*

China's Emperor, craving beauty that might shake an empire,
Was on the throne for many years, searching, never finding,
Till a little child of the Yang clan, hardly even grown,
Bred in an inner chamber, with no one knowing her,
But with graces granted by heaven and not to be concealed,
At last one day was chosen for the imperial household.
If she but turned her head and smiled, there were cast a hundred spells,
And the powder and paint of the Six Palaces faded into nothing.
. . . It was early spring. They bathed her in the Flower–Pure Pool,
Which warmed and smoothed the creamy-tinted crystal of her skin,
And, because of her languor, a maid was lifting her
When first the Emperor noticed her and chose her for his bride.
The cloud of her hair, petal of her cheek, gold ripples of her crown when she moved,
Were sheltered on spring evenings by warm hibiscus-curtains;
But nights of spring were short and the sun arose too soon,
And the Emperor, from that time forth, forsook his early hearings
And lavished all his time on her with feasts and revelry,
His mistress of the spring, his despot of the night.
There were other ladies in his court, three thousand of rare beauty,
But his favours to three thousand were concentered in one body.
By the time she was dressed in her Golden Chamber, it would be almost evening;
And when tables were cleared in the Tower of Jade, she would loiter, slow with wine.
Her sisters and her brothers all were given titles;
And, because she so illumined and glorified her clan,
She brought to every father, every mother through the empire,

Happiness when a girl was born rather than a boy.
. . . High rose Li Palace, entering blue clouds,
And far and wide the breezes carried magical notes
Of soft song and slow dance, of string and bamboo music.
The Emperor's eyes could never gaze on her enough—
Till war-drums, booming from Yü-yang, shocked the whole earth
And broke the tunes of *The Rainbow Skirt and the Feathered Coat.*
The Forbidden City, the nine-tiered palace, loomed in the dust
From thousands of horses and chariots headed southwest.
The imperial flag opened the way, now moving and now
pausing—
But thirty miles from the capital, beyond the western gate,
The men of the army stopped, not one of them would stir
Till under their horses' hoofs they might trample those
moth-eyebrows . . .
Flowery hairpins fell to the ground, no one picked them up,
And a green and white jade hair-tassel and a yellow-gold hair-bird.
The Emperor could not save her, he could only cover his face.
And later when he turned to look, the place of blood and tears
Was hidden in a yellow dust blown by a cold wind.
. . . At the cleft of the Dagger-Tower Trail they criss-crossed through
a cloud-line
Under O-mêi Mountain. The last few came.
Flags and banners lost their colour in the fading sunlight . . .
But as waters of Shu are always green and its mountains always blue,
So changeless was His Majesty's love and deeper than the days.
He stared at the desolate moon from his temporary palace.
He heard bell-notes in the evening rain, cutting at his breast.
And when heaven and earth resumed their round and the
dragon-car faced home,
The Emperor clung to the spot and would not turn away
From the soil along the Ma-wêi slope, under which was buried
That memory, that anguish. Where was her jade-white face?
Ruler and lords, when eyes would meet, wept upon their coats
As they rode, with loose rein, slowly eastward, back to the capital.
. . . The pools, the gardens, the palace, all were just as before,
The Lake T'ai-yi hibiscus, the Wêi-yang Palace willows;
But a petal was like her face and a willow-leaf her eyebrow—
And what could he do but cry whenever he looked at them?
. . . Peach-trees and plum-trees blossomed, in the winds of spring;
Lakka-foliage fell to the ground, after autumn rains;
The Western and Southern Palaces were littered with late grasses,
And the steps were mounded with red leaves that no one swept away.
Her Pear-Garden Players became white-haired
And the eunuchs thin-eyebrowed in her Court of Pepper-Trees;

Over the throne flew fire-flies, while he brooded in the twilight.
He would lengthen the lamp-wick to its end and still could never sleep.
Bell and drum would slowly toll the dragging night-hours
And the River of Stars grow sharp in the sky, just before dawn,
And the porcelain mandarin-ducks on the roof grow thick with morning frost
And his covers of kingfisher-blue feel lonelier and colder
With the distance between life and death year after year;
And yet no beloved spirit ever visited his dreams.
. . . At Ling-ch'ün lived a Taoist priest who was a guest of heaven,
Able to summon spirits by his concentrated mind.
And people were so moved by the Emperor's constant brooding
That they besought the Taoist priest to see if he could find her.
He opened his way in space and clove the ether like lightning,
Up to heaven, under the earth, looking everywhere.
Above, he searched the Green Void, below, the Yellow Spring;
But he failed, in either place, to find the one he looked for.
And then he heard accounts of an enchanted isle at sea,
A part of the intangible and incorporeal world,
With pavilions and fine towers in the five-coloured air,
And of exquisite immortals moving to and fro,
And of one among them—whom they called The Ever True—
With a face of snow and flowers resembling hers he sought.
So he went to the West Hall's gate of gold and knocked at the jasper door
And asked a girl, called Morsel-of-Jade, to tell The Doubly-Perfect.
And the lady, at news of an envoy from the Emperor of China,
Was startled out of dreams in her nine-flowered canopy.
She pushed aside her pillow, dressed, shook away sleep,
And opened the pearly shade and then the silver screen.
Her cloudy hair-dress hung on one side because of her great haste,
And her flower-cap was loose when she came along the terrace,
While a light wind filled her cloak and fluttered with her motion
As though she danced *The Rainbow Skirt and the Feathered Coat.*
And the tear-drops drifting down her sad white face
Were like a rain in spring on the blossom of the pear.
But love glowed deep within her eyes when she bade him thank her liege,
Whose form and voice had been strange to her ever since their parting—
Since happiness had ended at the Court of the Bright Sun,
And moons and dawns had become long in Fairy-Mountain Palace.

But when she turned her face and looked down toward the earth
And tried to see the capital, there were only fog and dust.
So she took out, with emotion, the pledges he had given
And, through his envoy, sent him back a shell box and gold hairpin,
But kept one branch of the hairpin and one side of the box,
Breaking the gold of the hairpin, breaking the shell of the box;
"Our souls belong together," she said, "like this gold and this shell—
Somewhere, sometime, on earth or in heaven, we shall surely meet."
And she sent him, by his messenger, a sentence reminding him
Of vows which had been known only to their two hearts:
"On the seventh day of the Seventh-month, in the Palace of Long Life,
We told each other secretly in the quiet midnight world
That we wished to fly in heaven, two birds with the wings of one,
And to grow together on the earth, two branches of one tree."
. . . Earth endures, heaven endures; some time both shall end,
While this unending sorrow goes on and on for ever.

## *Having Climbed to the Topmost Peak of the Incense-Burner Mountain*

*Translated by Arthur Waley*

Up and up, the Incense-burner Peak!
In my heart is stored what my eyes and ears perceived.
All the year—detained by official business;
To-day at last I got a chance to go.
Grasping the creepers, I clung to dangerous rocks;
My hands and feet—weary with groping for hold.
There came with me three or four friends,
But two friends dared not go further.
At last we reached the topmost crest of the Peak;
My eyes were blinded, my soul rocked and reeled.
The chasm beneath me—ten thousand feet;
The ground I stood on, only a foot wide.
If you have not exhausted the scope of seeing and hearing,
How can you realize the wideness of the world?
The waters of the River looked narrow as a ribbon,
P'ēn Castle smaller than a man's fist.
How it clings, the dust of the world's halter!
It chokes my limbs: I cannot shake it away.
Thinking of retirement, I heaved an envious sigh,
Then, with lowered head, came back to the Ants' Nest.

## *Madly Singing in the Mountains*

*Translated by Arthur Waley*

There is no one among men that has not a special failing:
And my failing consists in writing verses.
I have broken away from the thousand ties of life:
But this infirmity still remains behind.
Each time that I look at a fine landscape,
Each time that I meet a loved friend,
I raise my voice and recite a stanza of poetry
And am glad as though a God had crossed my path.
Ever since the day I was banished to Hsün-yang
Half my time I have lived among the hills.
And often, when I have finished a new poem,
Alone I climb the road to the Eastern Rock.
I lean my body on the banks of white stone:
I pull down with my hands a green cassia branch.
My mad singing startles the valleys and hills:
The apes and birds all come to peep.
Fearing to become a laughing-stock to the world
I choose a place that is unfrequented by men.

# YUAN ZHEN (779–831)

*Translated by James R. Hightower*

During the Tang dynasty (618–907), there began to appear a somewhat more expansive form of Chinese fiction than had existed in previous dynasties. Called in Chinese *chuanqi* (literally, "transmissions of the strange"), these were short stories written in a rich and sometimes allusive classical idiom. The *chuanqi* tales are profoundly influenced by earlier historical narrative. They are typically presented as actual events that took place at a specific historical moment in a specific place. As did the earlier historians, the narrator here describes words and deeds but rarely attempts to penetrate the minds of characters. He maintains the objective stance of someone who sees actions and hears words but refuses to speculate on what characters actually think. The narrator's moralistic judgments or conclusions are usually reserved for the end of the story, a technique used earlier by the historian Sima Qian (145–c. 86? BCE; see pp. 387–403). As with the example presented here, these stories often include "raw documents," such as letters and poems, that create the impression that the story is the result of serious archival research. One might compare this story to those of the modern writer Jorge Luis Borges (pp. 2113–2121).

One of the best and certainly the most influential of these tales was written by the Tang official and *literatus* Yuan Zhen. Like so many Chinese scholar-officials, Yuan had a rocky career. He was removed from office on two occasions, only to be rehabilitated each time and brought back to high position. Along with his good friend Bai Juyi, the noted poet (see Four Tang Poets, pp. 1014–1033), Yuan led a literary movement that emphasized writing simple poetry of serious purpose. He believed literature was meant to bring political and social change. Yuan is best remembered, however, as the author of *The Story of Ying-ying*, a highly romantic tale that became the basis of several later literary works, most notably a much-beloved thirteenth-century play, *The Romance of the Western Chamber*, which was written by Wang Shifu (fl. 1295–1307).

*The Story of Ying-ying* is the tale of a young scholar's seduction and abandonment of a distant cousin, Ying-ying, a young woman of great beauty and somewhat enigmatic behavior. The modern reader easily interprets this abandonment as heartless and feels little sympathy for Chang, the male protagonist. The narrator, however, appears to applaud Chang's decision, and the story was often read in traditional China as a tale of moral courage. That is, once Chang realizes the error of his seduction and his potential vulnerability to Ying-ying's charms, mistakes that might sidetrack him from public and family obligations, he turns away from his love and chooses the world of male, Confucian duty over the world of romantic feeling. One might compare, from Roman antiquity, Aeneas's decision to leave Dido in Book IV of Virgil's *Aeneid* (pp. 651–662), and Ovid's slightly later and very different account in the *Heroides* (pp. 687–692); or one might compare the story of Abelard and Heloise, from medieval France (pp. 1226–1244), which medieval and modern readers also read quite differently.

But it is the complex character of Ying-ying herself, much more than the flat character of Chang, that gives this story its particular significance. Alternately coy and aggressive, self-aggrandizing and self-destructive, understanding and bitter, she becomes a powerful example of the dilemmas of a woman in a society where the realm of female action is tightly restricted.

## *The Story of Ying-ying*

During the Chen-yüan period [785–804] there lived a young man named Chang. He was agreeable and refined, and good looking, but firm and self-contained, and capable of no improper act. When his companions included him in one of their parties, the others could all be brawling as though they would never get enough, but Chang would just watch tolerantly without ever taking part. In this way he had gotten to be twenty-three years old without ever having had relations with a woman. When asked by his friends, he explained, "Teng-t'u tzu was no lover, but a lecher. I am the true lover—I just never happened to meet the right girl. How do I know that? It's because things of outstanding beauty never fail to make a permanent impression on me. That shows I am not without feelings." His friends took note of what he said.

Not long afterward Chang was traveling in P'u, where he lodged some ten *li* east of the city in a monastery called the Temple of Universal Salvation. It happened that a widowed Mrs. Ts'ui had also stopped there on her way back to Ch'ang-an. She had been born a Cheng; Chang's mother had been a

Cheng, and when they worked out their common ancestry, this Mrs. Ts'ui turned out to be a rather distant cousin once removed on his mother's side.

This year Hun Chen died in P'u, and the eunuch Ting Wen-ya proved unpopular with the troops, who took advantage of the mourning period to mutiny. They plundered the citizens of P'u, and Mrs. Ts'ui, in a strange place with all her wealth and servants, was terrified, having no one to turn to. Before the mutiny Chang had made friends with some of the officers in P'u, and now he requested a detachment of soldiers to protect the Ts'ui family. As a result all escaped harm. In about ten days the imperial commissioner of inquiry, Tu Ch'üeh, came with full power from the throne and restored order among the troops.

Out of gratitude to Chang for the favor he had done them, Mrs. Ts'ui invited him to a banquet in the central hall. She addressed him: "Your widowed aunt with her helpless children would never have been able to escape alive from these rioting soldiers. It is no ordinary favor you have done us; it is rather as though you had given my son and daughter their lives, and I want to introduce them to you as their elder brother so that they can express their thanks." She summoned her son Huan-lang, a very attractive child of ten or so. Then she called her daughter: "Come out and pay your respects to your brother, who saved your life." There was a delay; then word was brought that she was indisposed and asked to be excused. Her mother exclaimed in anger, "Your brother Chang saved your life. You would have been abducted if it were not for him—how can you give yourself airs?"

After a while she appeared, wearing an everyday dress and no makeup on her smooth face, except for a remaining spot of rouge. Her hair coils straggled down to touch her eyebrows. Her beauty was extraordinary, so radiant it took the breath away. Startled, Chang made her a deep bow as she sat down beside her mother. Because she had been forced to come out against her will, she looked angrily straight ahead, as though unable to endure the company. Chang asked her age. Mrs. Ts'ui said, "From the seventh month of the fifth year of the reigning emperor to the present twenty-first year, it is just seventeen years."

Chang tried to make conversation with her, but she would not respond, and he had to leave after the meal was over. From this time on Chang was infatuated but had no way to make his feelings known to her. She had a maid named Hung-niang with whom Chang had managed to exchange greetings several times, and finally he took the occasion to tell her how he felt. Not surprisingly, the maid was alarmed and fled in embarrassment. Chang was sorry he had said anything, and when she returned the next day he made shamefaced apologies without repeating his request. The maid said, "Sir, what you said is something I would not dare repeat to my mistress or let anyone else know about. But you know very well who Miss Ts'ui's relatives are; why don't you ask for her hand in marriage, as you are entitled to do because of the favor you did them?"

"From my earliest years I have never been one to make any improper connections," Chang said. "Whenever I have found myself in the company of young women, I would not even look at them, and it never occurred to me that I would be trapped in any such way. But the other day at the dinner I was hardly able to control myself, and in the days since, I walk without knowing where I am going and eat without hunger—I am afraid I cannot last another day. If I were to go through a regular matchmaker, taking three months and more for the exchange of betrothal presents and names and birthdates—you might just as well look for me among the dried fish in the shop. Can't you tell me what to do?"

"Miss Ts'ui is so very strict that not even her elders could suggest anything improper to her," the maid replied. "It would be hard for someone in my position to say such a thing. But I have noticed she writes a lot. She is always reciting poetry to herself and is moved by it for a long time after. You might see if you can seduce her with a love poem. That is the only way I can think of."

Chang was delighted and on the spot composed two stanzas of spring verses which he handed over to her. That evening Hung-niang came back with a note on colored paper for him, saying, "By Miss Ts'ui's instructions."

The title of her poem was "Bright Moon on the Night of the Fifteenth":

> I await the moon in the western
> chamber
> Where the breeze comes through
> the half-opened door.
> Sweeping the wall the flower
> shadows move:
> I imagine it is my lover who comes.

Chang understood the message: that day was the fourteenth of the second month, and an apricot tree was next to the wall east of the Ts'uis' courtyard. It would be possible to climb it.

On the night of the fifteenth Chang used the tree as a ladder to get over the wall. When he came to the western chamber, the door was ajar. Inside, Hung-niang was asleep on a bed. He awakened her, and she asked, frightened, "How did you get here?"

"Miss Ts'ui's letter told me to come," he said, not quite accurately. "You go tell her I am here."

In a minute Hung-niang was back. "She's coming! She's coming!"

Chang was both happy and nervous, convinced that success was his. Then Miss Ts'ui appeared in formal dress, with a serious face, and began to upbraid him: "You did us a great kindness when you saved our lives, and that is why my mother entrusted my young brother and myself to you. Why then did you get my silly maid to bring me that filthy poem? You began by doing a good deed in preserving me from the hands of ravishers, and you end by seeking to ravish me. You substitute seduction for rape—is there any great difference? My first impulse was to keep quiet about it, but that would have been to condone your wrongdoing, and not right. If I told my mother, it would amount to ingratitude, and the consequences would be unfortunate. I thought of having a servant convey my disapproval, but feared she would not get it right. Then I thought of writing a short message to state my case, but was afraid it would only put you on your guard. So finally I composed those vulgar lines to make sure you would come here. It was an improper thing to do, and of course I feel ashamed. But I hope that you will keep within the bounds of decency and commit no outrage."

As she finished speaking, she turned on her heel and left him. For some time Chang stood, dumbfounded. Then he went back over the wall to his quarters, all hope gone.

A few nights later Chang was sleeping alone by the veranda when someone shook him awake. Startled, he rose up, to see Hung-niang standing there, a coverlet and pillow in her arms. She patted him and said, "She is coming! She is coming! Why are you sleeping?" And she spread the quilt and put the pillow beside his. As she left, Chang sat up straight and rubbed his eyes. For some time it seemed as though he were still dreaming, but nonetheless he waited dutifully. Then there was Hung-niang again, with Miss Ts'ui leaning on her arm. She was shy and yielding, and appeared almost not to have the strength to move her limbs. The contrast with her stiff formality at their last encounter was complete.

This evening was the night of the eighteenth, and the slanting rays of the moon cast a soft light over half the bed. Chang felt a kind of floating lightness and wondered whether this was an immortal who visited him, not someone from the world of men. After a while the temple bell sounded. Daybreak was near. As Hung-niang urged her to leave, she wept softly and clung to him. Hung-niang helped her up, and they left. The whole time she had not spoken a single word. With the first light of dawn Chang got up, wondering, was it a dream? But the perfume still lingered, and as it got lighter he could see on his arm traces of her makeup and the teardrops sparkling still on the mat.

For some ten days afterward there was no word from her. Chang composed a poem of sixty lines on "An Encounter with an Immortal" which he had not yet completed when Hung-niang happened by, and he gave it to her for her mistress. After that she let him see her again, and for nearly a month he would join her in what her poem called the "western chamber," slipping out at dawn and returning stealthily at night. Chang once asked what her mother thought about the situation. She said, "She knows there is nothing she can do about it, and so she hopes you will regularize things."

Before long Chang was about to go to Ch'ang-an, and he let her know his intentions in a poem. Miss Ts'ui made no objections at all, but the look of pain on her face was very touching. On the eve of his departure he was unable to see her again. Then Chang went off to the west. A few months later he again made a trip to P'u and stayed several months with Miss Ts'ui.

She was a very good calligrapher and wrote poetry, but for all that he kept begging to see her work, she would never show it. Chang wrote poems for her, challenging her to match them, but she paid them little attention. The thing that made her unusual was that, while she excelled in the arts, she always acted as though she were ignorant, and although she was quick and clever in speaking, she would seldom indulge in repartee. She loved Chang very much, but would never say so in words. At the time she was subject to moods of profound melancholy, but she never let on. She seldom showed on her face the emotions she felt. On one occasion she was playing her zither alone at night. She did not know Chang was listening, and the music was full of sadness. As soon as he spoke, she stopped and would play no more. This made him all the more infatuated with her.

Some time later Chang had to go west again for the scheduled examinations. It was the eve of his departure, and though he had said nothing about what it involved, he sat sighing unhappily at her side. Miss Ts'ui had guessed that he was going to leave for good. Her manner was respectful, but she spoke deliberately and in a low voice: "To seduce someone and then abandon her is perfectly natural, and it would be presumptuous of me to resent it. It would be an act of charity on your part if, having first seduced me, you were to go through with it and fulfill your oath of lifelong devotion. But in either case, what is there to be so upset about in this trip? However, I see you are not happy and I have no way to cheer you up. You have praised my zither playing, and in the past I have been embarrassed to play for you. Now that you are going away, I shall do what you so often requested."

She had them prepare her zither and started to play the prelude to the "Rainbow Robe and Feather Skirt." After a few notes, her playing grew wild with grief until the piece was no longer recognizable. Everyone was reduced to tears, and Miss Ts'ui abruptly stopped playing, put down the zither, and ran back to her mother's room with tears streaming down her face. She did not come back.

The next morning Chang went away. The following year he stayed on in the capital, having failed the examinations. He wrote a letter to Miss Ts'ui to reassure her, and her reply read roughly as follows:

> I have read your letter with its message of consolation, and it filled my childish heart with mingled grief and joy. In addition you sent me a box of ornaments to adorn my hair and a stick of pomade to make my lips smooth. It was most kind of you; but for whom am I to make myself attractive? As I look at these presents my breast is filled with sorrow.
>
> Your letter said that you will stay on in the capital to pursue your studies, and of course you need quiet and the facilities there to make progress. Still it is hard on the person left alone in this far-off place. But such is my fate, and I should not complain. Since last fall I have been listless and without hope. In company I can force myself to talk and smile, but come evening I always shed tears in the solitude of my own room. Even in my sleep I often sob, yearning for the absent one. Or I am in your arms for a moment as it used to be, but before the secret meeting is done I am awake and heartbroken. The bed seems still warm beside me, but the one I love is far away.
>
> Since you said good-bye the new year has come. Ch'ang-an is a city of pleasure with chances for love everywhere. I am truly fortunate that you have not forgotten me and that your affection is not worn out. Loving you as I do, I have no way of repaying you, except to be true to our vow of lifelong fidelity.
>
> Our first meeting was at the banquet, as cousins. Then you persuaded my maid to inform me of your love; and I was unable to keep my childish heart firm. You made advances, like that other poet, Ssuma Hsiang-ju. I failed to repulse them as the girl did who threw her shuttle. When I offered myself in your bed, you treated me with the greatest kindness, and I supposed, in my innocence, that I could

always depend on you. How could I have foreseen that our encounter could not possibly lead to something definite, that having disgraced myself by coming to you, there was no further chance of serving you openly as a wife? To the end of my days this will be a lasting regret—I must hide my sighs and be silent. If you, out of kindness, would condescend to fulfill my selfish wish, though it came on my dying day it would seem to be a new lease on life. But if, as a man of the world, you curtail your feelings, sacrificing the lesser to the more important, and look on this connection as shameful, so that your solemn vow can be dispensed with, still my true love will not vanish though my bones decay and my frame dissolve; in wind and dew it will seek out the ground you walk on. My love in life and death is told in this. I weep as I write, for feelings I cannot express. Take care of yourself; a thousand times over, take care of your dear self.

This bracelet of jade is something I wore as a child; I send it to serve as a gentleman's belt pendant. Like jade may you be invariably firm and tender; like a bracelet may there be no break between what came before and what is to follow. Here are also a skein of multicolored thread and a tea roller of mottled bamboo. These things have no intrinsic value, but they are to signify that I want you to be true as jade, and your love to endure unbroken as a bracelet. The spots on the bamboo are like the marks of my tears, and my unhappy thoughts are as tangled as the thread: these objects are symbols of my feelings and tokens for all time of my love. Our hearts are close, though our bodies are far apart and there is no time I can expect to see you. But where the hidden desires are strong enough, there will be a meeting of spirits. Take care of yourself, a thousand times over. The springtime wind is often chill; eat well for your health's sake. Be circumspect and careful, and do not think too often of my unworthy person.

Chang showed her letter to his friends, and in this way word of the affair got around. One of them, Yang Chü-yüan, a skillful poet, wrote a quatrain on "Young Miss Ts'ui":

For clear purity jade cannot equal his complexion;
On the iris in the inner court snow begins to melt.
A romantic young man filled with thoughts of love.
A letter from the Hsiao girl, brokenhearted.

Yüan Chen of Ho-nan wrote a continuation of Chang's poem "Encounter with an Immortal," also in thirty couplets:

Faint moonbeams pierce the curtained window;
Fireflies glimmer across the blue sky.
The far horizon begins now to pale;
Dwarf trees gradually turn darker green.
A dragon song crosses the court bamboo;
A phoenix air brushes the wellside tree.
The silken robe trails through the thin mist;
The pendant circles tinkle in the light breeze.
The accredited envoy accompanies Hsi wang-mu;

From the cloud's center comes
Jade Boy.
Late at night everyone is quiet;
At daybreak the rain drizzles.
Pearl radiance shines on her
decorated sandals;
Flower glow shows off the
embroidered skirt.
Jasper hairpin: a walking colored
phoenix;
Gauze shawl: embracing vermilion
rainbow.
She says she comes from Jasper
Flower Bank
And is going to pay court at Green
Jade Palace.
On an outing north of Lo-yang's
wall,
By chance he came to the house
east of Sung Yü's.
His dalliance she rejects a bit at first,
But her yielding love already is
disclosed.
Lowered locks put in motion
cicada shadows;
Returning steps raise jade dust.
Her face turns to let flow flower
snow
As she climbs into bed, silk covers
in her arms.
Love birds in a neck-entwining
dance;
Kingfishers in a conjugal cage.
Eyebrows, out of shyness,
contracted;
Lip rouge, from the warmth,
melted.
Her breath is pure: fragrance of
orchid buds;
Her skin is smooth: richness of
jade flesh.
No strength, too limp to lift a
wrist;
Many charms, she likes to draw
herself together.
Sweat runs: pearls drop by drop;
Hair in disorder: black luxuriance.
Just as they rejoice in the meeting
of a lifetime
They suddenly hear the night is
over.
There is no time for lingering;
It is hard to give up the wish to
embrace.
Her comely face shows the sorrow
she feels;
With fragrant words they swear
eternal love.
She gives him a bracelet to plight
their troth;
He ties a lovers' knot as sign their
hearts are one.
Tear-borne powder runs before
the clear mirror;
Around the flickering lamp are
nighttime insects.
Moonlight is still softly shining
As the rising sun gradually dawns.
Riding on a wild goose she returns
to the Lo River.
Blowing a flute he ascends Mount
Sung.
His clothes are fragrant still with
musk perfume.
The pillow is slippery yet with red
traces.
Thick, thick, the grass grows on
the dyke;
Floating, floating, the tumbleweed
yearns for the isle.
Her plain zither plays the
"Resentful Crane Song"
In the clear Milky Way she looks
for the returning wild goose.
The sea is broad and truly hard to
cross;
The sky is high and not easy to
traverse.
The moving cloud is nowhere to
be found—
Hsiao Shih stays in his chamber.

All of Chang's friends who heard of the affair marveled at it, but Chang had determined on his own course of action. Yüan Chen was especially close to him and so was in a position to ask him for an explanation. Chang said, "It is a general rule that those women endowed by Heaven with great beauty invariably either destroy themselves or destroy someone else. If this Ts'ui woman were to meet someone with wealth and position, she would use the favor her charms gain her to be cloud and rain or dragon or monster—I can't imagine what she might turn into. Of old, King Hsin of the Shang and King Yu of the Chou were brought low by women, in spite of the size of their kingdoms and the extent of their power; their armies were scattered, their persons butchered, and down to the present day their names are objects of ridicule. I have no inner strength to withstand this evil influence. That is why I have resolutely suppressed my love."

At this statement everyone present sighed deeply.

Over a year later Ts'ui was married, and Chang for his part had taken a wife. Happening to pass through the town where she was living, he asked permission of her husband to see her, as a cousin. The husband spoke to her, but Ts'ui refused to appear. Chang's feelings of hurt showed on his face, and she was told about it. She secretly sent him a poem:

> Emaciated, I have lost my looks,
> Tossing and turning, too weary to
> leave my bed.
> It's not because of others I am
> ashamed to rise;
> For you I am haggard and before
> you ashamed.

She never did appear. Some days later when Chang was about to leave, she sent another poem of farewell:

> Cast off and abandoned, what can
> I say now.
> Whom you loved so briefly long
> ago?
> Any love you had then for me
> Will do for the one you have now.

After this he never heard any more about her. His contemporaries for the most part conceded that Chang had done well to rectify his mistake. I have often mentioned this among friends so that, forewarned, they might avoid doing such a thing, or if they did, that they might not be led astray by it. In the ninth month of a year in the Chen-yüan period, when an official, Li Kung-ch'ui, was passing the night in my house at the Pacification Quarter, the conversation touched on the subject. He found it most extraordinary and composed a "Song of Ying-ying" to commemorate the affair. Ts'ui's child-name was Ying-ying, and Kung-ch'ui used it for his poem.

## Two Song Poets

The poetry of the Song dynasty (960–1229) is less intense and less well known than that of the Tang, but it possesses a directness of presentation and a breadth of subject matter that are sometimes lacking in Tang poetry. If Chinese poetry is characterized by the expression it gives to even the most mundane experience, as some claim, then Song poetry carries this quality to its extreme. Part of the refreshing naturalness of Song poetry might also derive from the flowering of a new poetic form, the *ci,* which we might translate as "lyric," a musical form that came out of popular entertainment centers where musicians and poets mingled freely. Poets took the melodies of this new music as set patterns to which they could compose poems. Even after the original melodies were lost, these poets continued to write according to song patterns as expressed in the syllable count of the earlier lyrics. This new *ci* style enlivened the world of poetry, which had grown somewhat stale with the continued dominance of the highly formal "regulated verse" that was so common throughout the Tang era. In this way, it resembles the move, in Arabic poetry, from traditional to *badīʿ* verse.

Two of the best poets of the Song dynasty were Su Dongpo (1037–1101) and Li Qingzhao (1084–1151), the latter without question China's greatest woman poet. Su and Li both suffered greatly as a result of the political conflicts of their time. There were basically two factions at court, conservatives and reformers, and when either was in power, that faction did everything possible to eradicate the other. Thus, Su Dongpo, who was a favorite of the conservatives, spent his career alternating between high position and prison (once) or exile (twice). Li Qingzhao's life was even more complicated. Her father was one of the conservatives and had, in fact, been a close associate of Su Dongpo, but her father-in-law was a reformer. Furthermore, during the 1127 Jurchen conquest and subsequent occupation of northern China, Li was forced to flee to the south. Two years later, she was widowed, losing a husband who had shared her passion for poetry, painting, and early Chinese epigraphy. The remainder of her life is a subject of controversy. Some believe she later married a military official, was abused by her new husband, sued him for divorce, and was imprisoned for bringing the lawsuit. Others argue that the records on which this tradition is based are fabricated. Whatever the case, Li was a remarkable scholar and poet.

In the work of both Su Dongpo and Li Qingzhao, we encounter a strong sense of loss: Su for his wife ("Ten years—dead and living dim and draw apart") and for an earlier, simple, rural life ("Long ago I lived in the country"), and Li for her deceased husband (*On Plum Blossoms*). While nostalgia for an idealized past is frequently found in Chinese poetry and is reinforced by the Confucian notion that the best times are in far-off antiquity, the works of both poets contain moments of joy and even playfulness. Su is still read and admired for a spontaneity and honesty that always find a direct and yet artful presentation, while Li's intense emotion, expressed so often in surprising nature imagery, is a fresh and inimitable voice in the Chinese tradition.

## *Su Dongpo (1037–1101)*

*Translated by Burton Watson*

### *New Year's Eve II*

New Year's Eve—you'd think I could go home early
But official business keeps me.
I hold the brush and face them with tears:
Pitiful convicts in chains,
Little men who tried to fill their bellies,
Fell into the law's net, don't understand disgrace.

And I? In love with a meager stipend
I hold on to my job and miss the chance to retire.
Don't ask who is foolish or wise;
All of us alike scheme for a meal.
The ancients would have freed them a while at New Year's—
Would I dare do likewise? I am silent with shame.

## *"Ten years—dead and living dim and draw apart"*

To the tune of "River Town Man." The year *yi-mao,* 1st month, 20th day: recording a dream I had last night.

Ten years—dead and living dim and draw apart.
I don't try to remember
But forgetting is hard.
Lonely grave a thousand miles off,
Cold thoughts—where can I talk them out?
Even if we met you wouldn't know me,
Dust on my face,
Hair like frost—

In a dream last night suddenly I was home.
By the window of the little room
You were combing your hair and making up.
You turned and looked, not speaking,
Only lines of tears coursing down—
Year after year will it break my heart?
The moonlit grave,
Its stubby pines—

## *Lotus Viewing*

With the Wang brothers and my son Mai, went around the city looking at lotus flowers. We climbed to the pavilion on Mount Hsien, and in the evening went to the Temple of Flying Petals. We assigned rhymes for poems; I was given *yüeh, ming, hsing,* and *hsi,* and wrote four poems.

The clear wind—what is it?
Something to be loved, not to be named,
Moving like a prince wherever it goes;
The grass and trees whisper its praise.
This outing of ours never had a purpose;
Let the lone boat swing about as it will.
In the middle of the current, lying face up,
I greet the breeze that happens along
And lift a cup to offer to the vastness:
How pleasant—that we have no thought for each other!

Coming back through two river valleys,
Clouds and water shine in the night.

Clerks and townsmen pity my laziness;
Day by day I have fewer disputes to settle.
So I can go drinking and wandering around,
Even spending a whole night out.
We come looking for the Temple of Flying Petals,
Making the most of the light that's left.
A bell ringing; the sound of gathering feet:
Monks tumble out in mountain robes.

I may be dropping by at odd hours—
With foot and cane I'll open the door myself.
Don't treat me like a high official!
Outside I look like one, but inside I'm not.

## *"Who says a painting must look like life?"*

Written on paintings of flowering branches by Secretary Wang of Yen-ling: two poems.

Who says a painting must look like life?
He sees only with children's eyes.
Who says a poem must stick to the theme?
Poetry is certainly lost on him.
Poetry and painting share a single goal—
Clean freshness and effortless skill.
Pien Luan's sparrows live on paper;
Chao Ch'ang's flowers breathe with soul.
But what are they beside these scrolls,
Bold sketches, with spirit in every stroke?
Who'd think one dot of red
Could call up a whole unbounded spring!

## *Drinking Wine*

Following the rhymes of T'ao's "Drinking Wine." As far as quantity goes, I drink very little, but I always enjoy having a wine cup in my hand, and very often I drop off to sleep right where I'm sitting. People think I'm drunk, though in fact my head is perfectly clear—actually you couldn't say I'm either drunk or sober. Here in Yang-chou I drink as usual, though I always stop after noon. When my visitors for the day have left, I loosen my clothes, stretch out my feet, and sit where I am the rest of the day. I haven't had enough to drink to be really happy, and yet I feel an almost excessive exhilaration. So I decided to write some poems using the same rhymes as those used by T'ao Yüan-ming in his twenty poems entitled "Drinking Wine," in hopes that I could give some sort of expression to these nameless feelings. I am showing them to my brother Tzu-yu and to the scholar Ch'ao Pu-chih.

Master T'ao, I can't compete with you!
Forever snarled up in official business,
What can I do to break away,
Live just once a life like yours?
Thorns grow in the field of the mind;
Clear them and there's no finer place.
Free the mind—let it move with the world
And doubt nothing it finds there!
In wine I stumbled on unexpected joy.
Now I always have an empty cup in hand.

* * *

I dreamed I was back in primary school,
My hair tied in two knots like a boy
(I'd forgotten that now it's gray),
And I was reciting the *Analects.*
The world at best is a children's game;
Like my dream—upside-down.
Only in wine is man himself,
His mind a cave empty of doubt.
He can fall from a carriage and never get hurt—
Chuang Tzu told us no lies.
I call my son to fetch paper and brush
And take down drunken thoughts as they come.

### *"Long ago I lived in the country"*

Written at the end of a painting on the "Restoration of the Herdsmen" by Ch'ao Yüeh-chih.

Long ago I lived in the country,
Knew only sheep and cows.
Down smooth riverbeds on the cow's back,
Steady as a hundred-weight barge,
A boat that needs no steering—while banks slipped by,
I stretched out and read a book—she didn't care.
Before us we drove a hundred sheep,
Heeding my whip as soldiers heed a drum;
I didn't lay it on too often—
Only stragglers I gave a lash to.
In lowlands, grass grows tall,
But tall grass is bad for cows and sheep;
So we headed for the hills, leaping sags and gullies
(Climbing up and down made my muscles strong),
Through long woods where mist wet my straw coat and hat. . . .
But those days are gone—I see them only in a painting.

No one believes me when I say I regret
Not staying a herdsman all my life.

### *White Crane Hill*

At my new place at White Crane Hill we dug a well forty feet deep. We struck a layer of rock partway down, but finally broke through and got to water.

Seacoast wears you out with damp and heat;
My new place is better—high and cool.
In return for the sweat of hiking up and down
I've a dry spot to sleep and sit.
But paths to the river are a rocky hell;
I wince at the water bearer's aching back.
I hired four men, put them to work
Hacking through layers of obdurate rock.
Ten days and they'd gone only eight or ten feet;
Below was a stratum of solid blue stone.
Drills all day struck futile sparks—
When would we ever see springs bubble up?
I'll keep you filled with rice and wine,
You keep your drills and hammers flying!
Mountain rock must end some time—
Stubborn as I am, I won't give up.
This morning the houseboy told me with joy
They're into dirt soft enough to knead!
At dawn the pitcher brought up milky water;
By evening, it was clearer than an icy stream.
All my life has been like this—
What way to turn and not run into blocks?
But Heaven has sent me a dipper of water;
Arm for a pillow, my happiness overflows.

## Li Qingzhao (1084–1151)

*Translated by Ling Chung and Kenneth Rexroth*

### *Joy of Wine*

#### To the Tune "A Dream Song"

I remember in Hsi T'ing
All the many times
We got lost in the sunset,
Happy with wine,
And could not find our way back.
When the evening came,
Exhausted with pleasure,

We turned our boat.
By mistake we found ourselves even deeper
In the clusters of lotus blossoms,
And startled the gulls and egrets
From the sand bars.
They crowded into the air
And hastily flapped away
To the opposite shore.

## *The Beauty of White Chrysanthemums*

### To the Tune "Beauties"

It is cold in my small pavilion.
All night my bed curtains sag with damp.
I hate the *hsiao hsiao* of the implacable wind and rain
That twists and breaks your jade flesh.
Your face is not like Yang Kuei-fei flushed with wine,
Nor like Sun Shou's worried brow.
You should not be compared to Chia Wu
Who stole the imperial incense for her lover,
Nor with the lewd Lady Hsü
Who powdered only half her face
To make fun of her one-eyed husband, the Emperor.
These comparisons are not apt.
After careful consideration,
I think your charm is that
Of the poets Ch'ü Yüan and T'ao Ch'ien.
In the breeze your perfume is as
Subtle as the odor of blackberry blossoms.
In the slow end of autumn
You are white as the coming snow,
And frail as transparent jade.
Leaning, leaning toward people with
Congealed sorrow, like the ghost on the shore of the Han River,
Who gave her lover a jade pendant and vanished,
Or like the tears of the imperial concubine Lady Pan
Who wrote a poem on a silk fan after she was deserted.
Clear, bright moon, pure wind, changes to thick mist, dark rain.
Heaven ordains you will wither
And your faint fragrance disappear.
No matter how much I love you
You will fade but be remembered in this poem.
You will not need to envy
The orchids gathered along the river bank by Ch'ü Yüan
Or the chrysanthemums planted against the east hedge
    by T'ao Ch'ien.

## *Thoughts from the Women's Quarter*

### To the Tune "Nostalgia of the Flute on the Phoenix Terrace"

The incense is cold in the gold lion.
My quilts are tumbled like red waves.
I get up lazily.
Not yet myself, I comb my hair.
My toilet table is unopened.
I leave the curtains down until
The sun shines over the curtain rings.
I am afraid of this idleness
Which permits dark sorrow to overcome me.
There are so many things I would like to write
But I let them go.
I have become thinner this year
Not due to sickness, not to wine,
Not to the sorrows of Autumn.
Finished. Finished.
This time he is gone for good.
If I sang *The Sunlight in the Pass*
Ten thousand times
I could not hold him.
I think of him far-off at Wu-ling Springs.
Alone in my Ch'in pavilion,
Locked in by fog,
Only the green flowing water
In front of the pavilion
Knows my eyes that stare and stare,
Where new layers of sorrows pile up.

## *A Morning Dream*

This morning I dreamed I followed
Widely spaced bells, ringing in the wind,
And climbed through mists to rosy clouds.
I realized my destined affinity
With An Ch'i-sheng the ancient sage.
I met unexpectedly O Lü-hua
The heavenly maiden.
The Autumn wind was just then untrustworthy
And blew away all the Jade Well Flowers.
Together we saw lotus roots as big as boats.
Together we ate jujubes as huge as melons.
We were the guests of those on swaying lotus seats.
They spoke in splendid language,
Full of subtle meanings.

They argued with sharp words over paradoxes.
We drank tea brewed on living fire.
Although this might not help the Emperor to govern,
It is endless happiness.
The life of men could be like this.
Why did I have to return to my former home,
Wake up, dress, sit in meditation.
Cover my ears to shut out the disgusting racket.
My heart knows I can never see my dream come true.
At least I can remember
That world and sigh.

### *On Plum Blossoms*

#### To the Tune "A Little Wild Goose"

This morning I woke
In a bamboo bed with paper curtains.
I have no words for my weary sorrow,
No fine poetic thoughts.
The sandalwood incense smoke is stale,
The jade burner is cold.
I feel as though I were filled with quivering water.
To accompany my feelings
Someone plays three times on a flute
"Plum Blossoms Are Falling
in a Village by the River."
How bitter this Spring is.
Small wind, fine rain, *hsiao, hsiao,*
Falls like a thousand lines of tears.
The flute player is gone.
The jade tower is empty.
Broken hearted—we had relied on each other.
I pick a plum branch,
But my man has gone beyond the sky,
And there is no one to give it to.

## WU CHENG'EN (1506–1582)

*Translated by Arthur Waley*

The classic Chinese novel, which thrived from the fourteenth to the nineteenth centuries, is strongly influenced by a rich storytelling tradition. The Chinese have always been fascinated by their past; thus, many of the early novels derive from story-cycles that developed around certain historical figures or events. In these novels, a hero or group of heroes typically moves from one adventure to another, as in the early Western picaresque novel, with relatively little overall plot or character development.

*Monkey* (a direct translation of the Chinese title would be *Journey to the West*), the example we include here, is based on folklore that had gathered around the epic journey of the Buddhist monk Xuan Zang (c. 600–664) to India to obtain sacred texts. The historical journey of Xuan Zang, as he himself reported it, is exciting enough, but in the folklore tradition, it became a story of miracle and fantasy.

Wu Cheng'en wove the stories about Xuan Zang into a huge hundred-chapter novel that is regarded as one of the six great classic novels from traditional China. Certainly Wu's work is the greatest single piece of fantasy in Chinese literature. He creates a memorable group of travelers to accompany Xuan Zang, called Tripitaka in some translations. In the narrative, this group overshadows the monk himself. The two most important members of the group are Monkey, a highly intelligent, mischievous, and resourceful simian, and Pigsy, a gluttonous but strong and loyal piglike creature.

Allegorical readings of *Monkey* interpret it as an elaborate commentary on Buddhist doctrine and the search for enlightenment. Such interpretations have ample support in the text, but most Chinese have read the novel as a splendidly entertaining work of fiction. The episode that follows is a typical example. In these two chapters, Monkey frees Mr. Kao's daughter from a son-in-law who is a greedy monster. But, as it turns out, the monster has been waiting to join the pilgrimage to India and becomes the very Pigsy who will assist Tripitaka in his sacred mission. The episode, like many in *Monkey*, gains its humorous appeal in part from the fact that it points to real situations that are all too common. How many fathers-in-law have become convinced that their daughters have married greedy monsters?

*The translation used here is from Arthur Waley's abbreviated version, which he entitled* Monkey. *For those interested in reading the entire novel, there is a masterful four-volume translation by Anthony Yu under the title* Journey to the West.

## Monkey

They had been travelling for several days through very wild country when at last, very late in the evening, they saw a group of houses in the far distance.

'Monkey,' said Tripitaka, 'I think that is a farm over there. Wouldn't it be a good plan to see if we can't sleep there to-night?'

'Let me go and have a look at it,' said Monkey, 'to see whether it looks lucky or unlucky, and we can then act accordingly.'

'You can proceed,' Monkey reported presently. 'I am certain that good people live there.'

Tripitaka urged on the white horse and soon came to a gate leading into a lane down which came a lad with a cotton wrap round his head, wearing a blue jacket, umbrella in hand and a bundle on his back. He was striding along, with a defiant air. 'Where are you off to?' said Monkey stopping him. 'There's something I want to ask you. What place is this?'

The man tried to brush him aside, muttering, 'Is there no one else on the farm, that you must needs pester me with questions?'

'Now don't be cross,' said Monkey laughing. 'What harm can it do you to tell me the name of a place? If you're obliging to us, maybe we can do something to oblige you.'

Finding he could not get past, for Monkey was holding on to him tightly, he began to dance about in a great rage. 'It's enough to put anyone out,' he cried. 'I've just been insulted by the master of the house, and then I run straight into this wretched bald-pate, and have to swallow his impudence!'

'Unless you're clever enough to shake me off, which I very much doubt,' said Monkey, 'here you'll stay.' The man wriggled this way and that, but all to no purpose. He was caught as though by iron pincers. In the struggle he dropped his bundle, dropped his umbrella, and began to rain blows on Monkey with both fists. Monkey kept one hand free to catch on to the luggage, and with the other held the lad fast.

'Monkey,' said Tripitaka, 'I think there's someone coming over there. Wouldn't it do just as well if you asked him, and let this lad go?'

'Master,' said Monkey, 'you don't know what you're talking about. There's no point in asking anyone else. This is the only fellow out of whom we can get what we want.'

At last, seeing that he would never get free, the lad said, 'This is called old Mr. Kao's farm. Most of the people that live and work here have the surname Kao, so the whole place is called Kao Farm. Now let me go!'

'You look as if you were going on a journey,' said Monkey. 'Tell me where you are going, and on what business, and I will let you go.'

'My name,' he said, 'is Kao Ts'ai. Old Mr. Kao has a daughter about twenty years old and unmarried. Three years ago she was carried off by a monster, who since has kept her as his wife, and lived with her here on the farm. Old Mr. Kao was not pleased. "To have a monster as a son-in-law in the house," he says, "doesn't work very well. It's definitely discreditable to the house, and unpleasant not to be able to look forward to comings and goings between the two families." He did everything in his power to drive away the monster, but it was no good; and in the end the creature took the girl and locked her away in that back building, where she has been for six months and no one in the family has seen her.

'Old Mr. Kao gave me two or three pieces of silver and told me to go and find an exorcist, and I spent a long time chasing round all over the countryside. I succeeded at last in getting the names of three or four practitioners, but they all turned out to be unfrocked priests or mouldy Taoists, quite incapable of dealing with such a monster. Mr. Kao only just now gave me a great scolding and accused me of bungling the business. Then he gave me five pieces of silver to pay for my travelling expenses and told me to go on looking till I found a really good exorcist, and I should be looking for one now if I hadn't run into this little scamp who won't let me pass. There! You have forced me to tell you how things are, and now you can let me go.'

'You've thrown a lucky number,' said Monkey. 'This is just my job. You needn't go a step farther or spend an ounce of your silver. I'm no unfrocked priest or mouldy Taoist, I really do know how to catch monsters. You've "got your stye cured on the way to the doctor's." I'll trouble you to go to the master of the house, and tell him that a priest and his disciple have come, who are on their way to get scriptures in India, and that they can deal with any monster.'

'I hope you're telling me the truth,' said the lad. 'You'll get me into great trouble if you fail.'

'I'll positively guarantee,' said Monkey, 'that I'm not deceiving you. Make haste and lead us in.'

The lad saw nothing for it but to pick up his bundle and go back to the house. 'You half-wit,' roared old Mr. Kao, 'what have you come back for?' But as soon as he had heard the lad's story, he quickly changed into his best clothes and came out to greet the guests, smiling affably. Tripitaka returned his greeting, but Monkey did not bow or say a word. The old man looked him up and down, and not knowing quite what to make of him did not ask him how he did.

'And how about me? Don't you want to know how I am?' said Monkey.

'Isn't it enough to have a monster in the house as son-in-law,' grumbled the old man, 'without your bringing in this frightful creature to molest me?'

'In all the years you've lived,' said Monkey, 'you've evidently learnt very little wisdom. If you judge people by their appearances, you'll always be going wrong. I'm not much to look at, I grant; but I have great powers, and if you are having any trouble with bogeys or monsters in the house, that's just where I come in. I'm going to get you back your daughter, so you had better stop grumbling about my appearance.'

Mr Kao, trembling with fear, managed at last to pull himself together sufficiently to invite them both in. Monkey, without so much as by-your-leave, led the horse into the courtyard and tied it to a pillar. Then he drew up an old weather-beaten stool, asked Tripitaka to be seated, and taking another stool for himself calmly sat down at Tripitaka's side.

'The little priest knows how to make himself at home,' said Mr Kao.

'This is nothing,' said Monkey. 'Keep me here a few months and you'll see me really making myself at home!'

'I don't quite understand,' said the old man, 'whether you've come for a night's lodging or to drive out the monster.'

'We've come for a night's lodging,' said Monkey, 'but if there are any monsters about I don't mind dealing with them, just to pass the time. But first, I should like to know how many of them there are?'

'Heavens!' cried the old man, 'isn't one monster enough to afflict the household, living here as my son-in-law?'

'Just tell me about it from the beginning,' said Monkey. 'If I know what he's good for, I can deal with him.'

'We'd never had any trouble with ghosts or goblins or monsters on this farm before,' said the old man. 'Unfortunately I have no son, but only three daughters. The eldest is called Fragrant Orchid, the second Jade Orchid, and the third Blue Orchid. The first two were betrothed from childhood into neighbouring families. Our plan for the youngest was to marry her to someone who would come and live with her here and help look after us in our old age. About three years ago a very nice-looking young fellow turned up, saying that he came from Fu-ling, and that his surname was Hog. He said he had no parents or brothers and sisters, and was looking for a family where he would be taken as son-in-law, in return for the work that he did about the place. He sounded just the sort we wanted, and I accepted him. I must say he worked very hard. He pushed the plough himself and never asked to use a bull; he managed to do all his reaping without knife or staff. For some time we were perfectly satisfied, except for one thing—his appearance began to change in a very odd way.'

'In what way?' asked Monkey.

'When he first came,' said the old man, 'he was just a dark, stoutish fellow. But afterwards his nose began to turn into a regular snout, his ears became larger and larger, and great bristles began to grow at the back of his neck. In fact, he began to look more and more like a hog. His appetite is enormous. He eats four or five pounds of rice at each meal, and as a light collation in the morning I've known him to get through over a hundred pasties. He's not at all averse to fruit and vegetables either, and what with this and all the wine he drinks, in the course of the last six months he's pretty well eaten and drunk us out of house and home.'

'No doubt,' said Tripitaka, 'anyone who works so hard as he does needs a lot of nourishment.'

'If it were only this business of food,' said the old man, 'it wouldn't be so bad. But he frightens everybody round by raising magic winds, suddenly vanishing and appearing again, making stones fly through the air and such like tricks. Worst of all, he has locked up Blue Orchid in the back outhouse, and it is six months since we set eyes on her. We don't even know if she is dead or alive. It is evident that he's an ogre of some kind, and that is why we were trying to get hold of an exorcist.'

'Don't you worry,' said Monkey. 'This very night I'll catch him and make him sign a Deed of Relinquishment and give you back your daughter.'

'The main thing is to catch him,' said Mr Kao. 'It doesn't so much matter about documents.'

'Perfectly easy,' said Monkey. 'Tonight as soon as it is dark, you'll see the whole thing settled.'

'What weapons do you need, and how many men to help you?' asked Mr Kao. 'We must get on with the preparations.'

'I'm armed already,' said Monkey.

'So far as I can see, all you've got between you is a priest's staff,' said the old man. 'That wouldn't be much use against such a fiend as this.'

Monkey took his embroidery needle from behind his ear and once more changed it into a great iron cudgel. 'Does this satisfy you?' he asked. 'I doubt if your house could provide anything tougher.'

'How about followers?' said the old man.

'I need no followers,' said Monkey. 'All I ask for is some decent elderly person to sit with my Master and keep him company.'

Several respectable friends and relatives were fetched, and having looked them up and down Monkey said to Tripitaka, 'Sit here quietly and don't worry. I'm off to do this job.'

'Take me to the back building,' he said to Mr Kao, grasping his cudgel. 'I'd like to have a look at the monster's lodging-place.'

'Give me the key,' he said, when they came to the door.

'Think what you're saying,' said the old man. 'Do you suppose that if a key was all that was wanted, we should be troubling you?'

'What's the use of living so long in the world if you haven't learnt even to recognize a joke when you hear one?' said Monkey laughing. Then he went up to the door and with a terrific blow of his cudgel smashed it down. Within, it was pitch dark. 'Call to your daughter and see if she is there,' said Monkey. The old man summoned up his courage and cried, 'Miss Three!'

Recognizing her father's voice, she answered with a faint 'Papa, I am here.' Monkey peered into the darkness with his steely eyes, and it was a pitiable sight that he saw. Unwashed cheeks, matted hair, bloodless lips, weak and trembling. She tottered towards her father, flung her arms round him and burst into tears. 'Don't make that noise,' said Monkey, 'but tell us where your monster is.'

'I don't know,' she said. 'Nowadays he goes out at dawn and comes back at dusk, I can't keep track of him at all. He knows that you're trying to find someone to exorcize him; that's why he keeps away all day.'

'Not a word more!' said Monkey. 'Old man, take your darling back to the house and calm her down. I'll wait here for the monster. If he doesn't come, it is not my fault, and if he comes I'll pluck up your trouble by the roots.'

Left alone, Monkey used his magic arts to change himself into the exact image of Blue Orchid, and sat waiting for the monster to return. Presently there was a great gust of wind; stones and gravel hurtled through the air. When the wind subsided there appeared a monster of truly terrible appearance. He had short bristles on his swarthy cheeks, a long snout, and huge ears. He wore a cotton jacket that was green but not green, blue but not blue, and had a spotted handkerchief tied round his head. 'That's the article,' laughed Monkey to himself.

Dear Monkey! He did not go to meet the monster or ask him how he did, but lay on the bed groaning, as though he were ill. The monster, quite taken in, came up to the bed and grabbing at Monkey tried to kiss him. 'None of your lewd tricks on old Monkey!' laughed Monkey to himself, and giving the monster a great clout on the nose sent him reeling.

'Dear sister,' said the monster, picking himself up, 'why are you cross with me today? Is it because I am so late?'

'I'm not cross,' said Monkey.

'If you're not cross,' said the monster, 'why do you push me away?'

'You've got such a clumsy way of kissing,' said Monkey. 'You might have known that I'm not feeling well today, when you saw I did not come to the door to meet you. Take off your clothes and get into bed.' Still suspecting nothing the monster began to undress. Monkey meanwhile jumped up and sat on the commode. When the monster got into bed he felt everywhere but could not find his bride. 'Sister,' he called, 'what has become of you? Take off your clothes and get into bed.'

'You go to sleep first,' said Monkey. 'I'll follow when I've done my duties.' Monkey suddenly began to sigh, murmuring 'Was there ever such an unhappy girl as I?'

'What are you grumbling about?' said the monster. 'Since I came here, I've cost you something in food and drink, that I own. But I've more than earned what I have got. Haven't I cleaned the ground and drained ditches, carried bricks and tiles, built walls, ploughed fields, planted grain, and improved the farm out of all knowing? You've good clothes to wear and all the food you need. What's all this childish nonsense about being unhappy?'

'That's not it at all,' said Monkey. 'Today my parents came and made a fearful scene through the partition wall.'

'What did they make a scene about?' said the monster.

'They don't like having you here as their son-in-law,' said Monkey. 'They say you've got an ugly face, and they don't know who your father is and haven't seen any of your relations. They say you come and go no one knows when or where, and it's bad for the credit of the house that we don't know your name or anything at all about you. That's what they said, and it has made me miserable.'

'What do looks matter?' said the monster. 'It's a strong man they need about the place, and they can't say anything against me on that score. And if they think so ill of me, why did they accept me here at all? As for who I am, there's no mystery about it. I come from the Cloud-Ladder Cave at Fu-ling, and because I look a bit like a pig they call me Pigsy—Pigsy Bristles; next time they ask just tell them that.'

'Confiding monster!' thought Monkey. 'It needs no tortures to get a confession from him. Now we know where he comes from and who he is. It only remains to catch him.'

'They are looking for an exorcist to drive you away,' he said to the monster.

'Go to sleep,' said Pigsy, 'and don't worry about them any more. Am not I strong enough, with my nine-pronged muck-rake, to frighten off any exorcist or priest or what-not? Even if your old man's prayers could bring down the master of all devils from the Ninth Heaven, as a matter of fact he's an old friend of mine and wouldn't do anything against me.'

'He's done more than that,' said Monkey. 'He has called in the Great Sage, who five hundred years ago made turmoil in Heaven.'

'If that's so,' said Pigsy, 'I'm off! There'll be no more kissing tonight!'

'Why are you going?' asked Monkey.

'You don't know,' said Pigsy. 'That chap is terribly powerful, and I don't know that I could deal with him. I'm frightened of losing my reputation.' He dressed hastily, opened the door, and went out. But Monkey caught hold of him and making a magic pass changed himself back into his true form. 'Monster, look round,' he cried, 'and you will see that I am he.'

When Pigsy turned and saw Monkey with his sharp little teeth and grinning mouth, his fiery, steely eyes, his flat head and hairy cheeks, for all the world like a veritable thunder-demon, he was so startled that his hands fell limp beside him and his legs gave way. With a scream he tore himself free, leaving part of his coat in Monkey's hand, and was gone like a whirlwind. Monkey struck out with his cudgel; but Pigsy had already begun to make for the cave he came from. Soon Monkey was after him, crying, 'Where are you off to? If you go up to Heaven I will follow you to the summit of the Pole Star, and if you go down into the earth I will follow you to the deepest pit of hell.'

If you do not know how far he chased him or which of them won the fight, you must listen to what is told in the next chapter.

## Chapter XVII

The monster fled with Monkey at his heels, till they came at last to a high mountain, and here the monster disappeared into a cave, and a moment later came back brandishing a nine-pronged muck-rake. They set to at once and battled all night long, from the second watch till dawn began to whiten in the sky. At last the monster could hold his ground no longer, and retreating into the cave bolted the door behind him. Standing outside the cave-door, Monkey saw that on a slab of rock was the inscription 'Cloud-Ladder Cave.' As the monster showed no sign of coming out again and it was now broad daylight, Monkey thought to himself, 'The Master will be wondering what has happened to me. I had better go and see him and then come back and catch the monster.' So tripping from cloud to cloud he made his way back to the farm.

Tripitaka was still sitting with the old man, talking of this and that. He had not slept all night. He was just wondering why Monkey did not return when Monkey alighted in the courtyard, and suddenly stood before them. 'Master, here I am,' he said. The old men all bowed down before him, and supposing that he had accomplished his task thanked him for all his trouble.

'You must have had a long way to go, to catch the creature,' said Tripitaka.

'Master,' said Monkey, 'the monster is not a common incubus or elf. I have recognized him as a former inhabitant of Heaven, where he was in command of all the watery hosts. He was expelled to earth after an escapade with the daughter of the Moon Goddess, and though he was here re-incarnated with a pig-like form, he retains all his magic powers. I chased him to his mountain-cave, where he fetched out a nine-pronged muck-rake, and we fought together all night. Just at dawn he gave up the fight, and locked himself up in his cave. I would have beaten down the door and forced him to fight to a decision, but I was afraid the Master might be getting anxious, so I thought I had better come back first and report.'

'Reverend Sir,' said old Mr Kao to Monkey, 'I am afraid this hasn't helped matters much. True, you have driven him away; but after you have gone he's certain to come back again, and where shall we be then? We shall have to trouble you to catch him for us. That is the only way to pluck out our trouble by the root. I'll see to it that you have no cause to regret the trouble you take. You shall have half of all that is ours, both land and goods. If you like, my friends and relations shall sign a document to this effect. It will be well worth their while, if only we can remove this shame from our home.'

'I think you make too much of the whole affair,' said Monkey. 'The monster himself admits that his appetite is large; but he has done quite a lot of useful work. All the recent improvements in the estate are his work. He claims to be well worth what he costs in keep, and does not see why you should be so anxious to get rid of him. He is a divinity from Heaven, although condemned to live on earth, he helps to keep things going, and so far as I can see he hasn't done any harm to your daughter.'

'It may be true,' said old Mr Kao, 'that he's had no influence upon her. But I stick to it that it's very bad for our reputation. Wherever I go I hear people saying "Mr Kao has taken a monster as his son-in-law." What is one to say to that?'

'Now, Monkey,' said Tripitaka, 'don't you think you had better go and have one more fight with him and see if you can't settle the business once and for all?'

'As a matter of fact,' said Monkey, 'I was only having a little game with him, to see how things would go. This time I shall certainly catch him and bring him back for you to see. Don't you worry! Look after my Master,' he cried to Mr Kao, 'I'm off!'

So saying, he disappeared into the clouds and soon arrived at the cave. With one blow of his cudgel he beat the doors to bits, and standing at the entrance he cried, 'You noisome lout, come out and fight with Old Monkey.' Pigsy lay fast asleep within, snoring heavily. But when he heard the door being beaten down and heard himself called a noisome lout, he was so much enraged that he snatched up his rake, pulled himself together, and rushed out, crying, 'You wretched stableman, if ever there was a rogue, you're he! What have I to do with you, that you should come and knock down my door? Go and look at the Statute Book. You'll find that "obtaining entry to premises by forcing a main door" is a Miscellaneous Capital Offence.'

'You fool,' said Monkey. 'Haven't I a perfectly good justification at law for forcing your door? Remember that you laid violent hands on a respectable girl, and lived with her without matchmaker or testimony, tea, scarlet, wine, or any other ceremony. Are you aware that heads are cut off for less than that?'

'Stop that nonsense, and look at Old Pig's rake,' cried Pigsy.

He struck out, but Monkey warded off the blow, crying, 'I suppose that's the rake you used when you worked on the farm. Why should you expect me to be frightened of it?'

'You are very much mistaken,' said Pigsy. 'This rake was given to me by the Jade Emperor himself.'

'A lie!' cried Monkey. 'Here's my head. Hit as hard as you please, and we'll see!'

Pigsy raised the rake and brought it down with such force on Monkey's head that the sparks flew. But there was not a bruise or scratch. Pigsy was so much taken aback, that his hands fell limp at his side. 'What a head!' he exclaimed.

'You've still something to learn about me,' said Monkey. 'After I made havoc in Heaven and was caught by Erh-lang, all the deities of Heaven hacked me with their axes, hammered me with their mallets, slashed me with their swords, set fire to me, hurled thunderbolts at me, but not a hair of my body was hurt. Lao Tzu put me in his alchemic stove and cooked me with holy fire. But all that happened was that my eyes became fiery, my head and shoulders hard as steel. If you don't believe it, try again, and see whether you can hurt me or not.'

'I remember,' said Pigsy, 'that before you made havoc in Heaven, you lived in the Cave of the Water Curtain. Lately nothing has been heard of you. How did you get here? Perhaps my father-in-law asked you to come and deal with me.'

'Not at all,' said Monkey, 'I have been converted and am now a priest, and am going with a Chinese pilgrim called Tripitaka, who has been sent by the Emperor to fetch scriptures from India. On our way we happened to come past Mr Kao's farm, and we asked for a night's lodging. In the course of conversation Mr Kao asked for help about his daughter. That's why I'm after you, you noisome lout!'

No sooner did Pigsy hear these words than the rake fell from his hand. 'Where is that pilgrim?' he gasped. 'Take me to him.'

'What do you want to see him for?' asked Monkey.

'I've been converted,' said Pigsy. 'Didn't you know? The Bodhisattva Kuan-yin converted me and put me here to prepare myself by fasting and abstention for going to India with a pilgrim to fetch scriptures; after which, I am to receive illumination. That all happened some years ago, and since then I have had no news of this pilgrim. If you are his disciple, what on earth possessed you not to mention this scripture-seeking business? Why did you prefer to pick a quarrel and knock me about in front of my own door?'

'I suspect,' said Monkey, 'that you are just making all this up, in order to get away. If it's really true that you want to escort my Master to India, you must make a solemn vow to Heaven that you're telling the truth. Then I'll take you to him.' Pigsy flung himself upon his knees and, kow-towing at the void, up and down like a pestle in the mortar, he cried, 'I swear before the Buddha Amitabha, praised be his name, that I am telling the truth; and if I am not, may I be condemned once more by the tribunals of Heaven and sliced into ten thousand pieces.'

When Monkey heard him make this solemn vow, 'Very well then,' he said. 'First take a torch and burn down your lair, and then I will take you with me.' Pigsy took some reeds and brambles, lit a fire and soon reduced the cave to the state of a burnt-out kiln.

'You've nothing against me now,' he said. 'Take me along with you.'

'You'd better give your rake to me,' said Monkey. When Pigsy had handed over the rake, Monkey took a hair, blew on it with magic breath, and changed it into a three-ply hemp cord. Pigsy put his hands behind his back and let himself be bound. Then Monkey caught hold of his ear and dragged him along, crying, 'Hurry up! Hurry up!'

'Don't be so rough,' begged Pigsy. 'You're hurting my ear.'

'Rough indeed!' said Monkey. 'I shouldn't get far by being gentle with you. The proverb says, "The better the pig, the harder to hold." Wait till you have seen the Master and shown that you are in earnest. Then we'll let you go.'

When they reached the farm, Monkey twitched Pigsy's ear, saying, 'You see that old fellow sitting so solemnly up there? That's my Master.' Mr Kao and the other old men, seeing Monkey leading the monster by the ear, were delighted beyond measure, and came out into the courtyard to meet him. 'Reverend Sir,' they cried, 'that's the creature, sure enough, that married our master's daughter.' Pigsy fell upon his knees and with his hands still tied behind his back, kow-towed to Tripitaka, crying, 'Master, forgive me for failing to give you a proper reception. If I had known that it was you who were staying with my father-in-law I would have come to pay my respects, and all these unpleasantnesses would never have happened.'

'Monkey,' said Tripitaka, 'how did you manage to bring him to this state of mind?' Monkey let go his ear, and giving him a knock with the handle of the rake, shouted, 'Speak, fool!' Pigsy then told how he had been commissioned by Kuan-yin. 'Mr Kao,' said Tripitaka, when he heard the story, 'this is the occasion for a little incense.' Mr Kao then brought out the incense tray, and Tripitaka washed his hands, and burning incense he turned towards the south and said, 'I am much beholden, Bodhisattva!' Then he went up into the hall and resumed his seat, bidding Monkey release Pigsy from his bonds. Monkey shook himself; the rope became a hair again and returned to his body. Pigsy was free. He again did obeisance, and vowed that he would follow Tripitaka to the west. Then he bowed to Monkey, whom as the senior disciple he addressed as 'Elder Brother and Teacher.'

'Where's my wife?' said Pigsy to Mr Kao. 'I should like her to pay her respects to my Father and Brother in the Law.' 'Wife indeed!' laughed Monkey. 'You haven't got a wife now. There are some sorts of Taoists that are family men; but who ever heard of a Buddhist priest calmly talking about his "wife"? Sit down and eat your supper, and early tomorrow we'll all start out for India.'

After supper Mr Kao brought out a red lacquer bowl full of broken pieces of silver and gold, and offered the contents to the three priests, as a contribution towards their travelling expenses. He also offered them three pieces of fine silk to make clothes. Tripitaka said, 'Travelling priests must beg their way as they go. We cannot accept money or silk.' But Monkey came up and plunging his hand into the dish took out a handful of gold and silver, and called to the lad Kao Ts'ai, 'You were kind enough yesterday to introduce my Master into the house and we owe it to you that we have found a new disciple. I have no other way of showing my thanks but giving you these broken pieces of gold and silver, which I hope you will use to buy yourself a pair of shoes. If you come across any more monsters, please bespeak them for me, and I shall be even further obliged to you.'

'Reverend Sirs,' said Mr Kao, 'if I can't persuade you to accept silver or gold, I hope that you will at least let me show my gratitude by giving you these few pieces of coarse stuff, to make into cassocks.'

'A priest who accepts so much as a thread of silk,' said Tripitaka, 'must do penance for a thousand aeons to expiate his crime. All I ask is a few scraps left over from the household meal, to take with us as dry provisions.'

'Wait a minute,' cried Pigsy. 'If I get my due for all I've done on this estate since I married into the family, I should carry away several tons of provisions. That's by the way. But I think my father-in-law might in decency give me a new jacket. My old one was torn by Brother Monkey in the fight last night. And my shoes are all in pieces; I should be glad of a new pair.'

Mr Kao acceded to his request, and Pigsy, delighted by his new finery, strutted up and down in front of the company, calling to Mr Kao, 'Be so kind as to inform my mother-in-law, my sisters-in-law, and all my kinsmen by marriage that I have become a priest and must ask their pardon for going off without saying good-bye to them in person. And father-in-law, I'll trouble you to take good care of my bride. For if we don't bring off this scripture business, I shall turn layman again and live with you as your son-in-law.'

'Lout!' cried Monkey. 'Don't talk rubbish.'

'It's not rubbish,' said Pigsy. 'Things may go wrong, and then I shall be in a pretty pass! No salvation, and no wife either.'

'Kindly stop this silly argument,' said Tripitaka. 'It is high time we started.' So they put together the luggage, which

Pigsy was told to carry, and when the white horse was saddled Tripitaka was set astride. Monkey, with his cudgel over his shoulder, led the way. And so, parting from Mr Kao and all his relations, the three of them set out for the West. And if you do not know what befell them, you must listen to what is told in the next chapter.

# Japan in the Middle Period

In the first centuries of the Common Era, Japan began to develop an organized society characterized by communities engaged in wet-rice agriculture. Social cohesion led to an increasingly developed social structure dominated by clans that settled on the Yamato plain and along the shore of the inland sea. As the Yamato clan strengthened its hegemony in the sixth and seventh centuries, Japan experienced a wave of cultural borrowing from China. This first great importation of alien culture brought two key elements: a system of writing learned from the Chinese and the great religious culture associated with Buddhism.

A significant political power struggle developed around the issue of the importation of Buddhism. On one side were those who were attracted by the superior culture of mainland Asia. A more conservative and nationalistic contingent, however, rejected Buddhism and its associated culture as an alien religion and advocated instead the indigenous Shinto religion. Those who promoted Buddhism prevailed, and that religion took its place beside Shinto in the religious life of the country. Today, the two religions continue to exist side by side in Japan.

Also of great significance was the importation from China of a method of writing. Recognizing the power of the written word and wishing to gain prestige by imitating the great dynastic histories of China, the Yamato court commissioned a courtier named Yasumaro to organize and record the oral traditions of the nation's history. This work, the *Kojiki,* was completed in 712 CE. It not only gives us Japan's earliest mythology, but it also describes the chronological development of the major clans aligned with the Yamato court. Above all, it legitimates the right of the imperial family to rule the nation.

The same urge to put things in writing led to the compilation of Japan's earliest anthology of poetry, *Manyōshū,* collected sometime around the middle of the eighth century. The inadequacy of the Chinese language for expressing Japanese poetry led to the development of a new writing system more congenial to the Japanese language. Both the *Kojiki* and *Manyōshū* were composed in a hybrid writing system that seriously limited the development of literature in the vernacular language. This hybrid system died out by the end of the eighth century.

The year 795 saw the founding of the imperial capital at Kyoto, where it remained for more than a thousand years. The establishment of the capital marks the beginning of the Heian or courtly period of Japanese history. Just as the earlier introduction of Buddhist religion resulted in a dual culture of Shinto and Buddhism, the Heian period saw a similar literary division: men continued to write in formal and erudite Chinese, while women wrote in the newly emerging vernacular Japanese. Both men and women wrote Japanese poetry in Japanese, and almost from the beginning, men such as Ki no Tsurayuki insisted that men should also be able to write prose works in Japanese. Men eventually abandoned Chinese in favor of Japanese as a literary medium. The courtly Heian period saw a remarkable outpouring of literature in Japanese, both prose and poetry, especially by women connected with the court. These women wrote fiction, diaries, and miscellaneous essays; they also produced much of the outstanding poetry of the age.

Japanese courtly literature is characterized by its subjective, personal, and emotional stance, and by its single-minded devotion to elegance and sensitivity. What we would consider realism or social protest does not appear in this literature. The Buddhist-inspired tone of melancholy increasingly dominates the cultural productions of this period and distinguishes them from the exuberance of earlier works, such as the *Kojiki* and *Manyōshū.*

Civil war erupted in the late twelfth century, bringing an end to the melancholy elegance of court society. In its place, we find the emergence of the warrior hero and the foundations of the *samurai* culture of medieval Japan. With the demise of the court, literature fell into the hands of the only other literate class, the Buddhist clergy. The universal violence and disruption of the period led to a new worldview. The melancholy of the earlier age deepened, leading to a profound resignation, and the new heroes were the samurai warrior and the Buddhist priest.

In this new world of violence and bloodshed, the reclusive life of the hermit became a viable possibility, and those who chose such a life celebrated it in works of literature. The overweening ambition of warriors is also celebrated. Both clergy and warriors, however, yearned for the refinement and grace of the lost courtly era and tried to find, in their own lives, a balance between a vision of elegance and the demands of practical reality. Such a balance is found in the Nō theatre.

The premodern literary tradition in Japan is a rich tapestry comprised of mythology, poetry, fiction, diaries, essays, and drama. In these diverse works, we can glimpse a people who are in many ways remote from us in time, space, and culture, but we are constantly struck, as well, by the similarities between the inner landscapes of the ancient Japanese and our own feelings and experiences.

## FROM KOJIKI (712)

*Translated by Basil Hall Chamberlain;*
*Section IV by Donald L. Philippi*

The *Kojiki* (*The Record of Ancient Matters*) is the earliest written document preserved in Japan. It records histories that had been handed down orally for generations. Because these accounts are culled from oral tradition, they are really much older than the early eighth century; and since writing was an art introduced from China at this time, the written versions of these accounts invariably incorporate Chinese attitudes. During this period, the Japanese state was first formed; and the writing of this history was intended to establish, in a permanent written record, the right of the imperial family to rule.

The creation myth of the *Kojiki* is remarkably different from the biblical one. Here Izanagi (the Male-Who-Invites), and Izanami (the Female-Who-Invites), two of many shadowy deities, are selected by the others to become the progenitor and progenitrix of the world. Creation is seen in terms of procreation, and these myths are laced with sexual imagery: the jeweled spear drips with brine, and the erection of a pillar precedes lovemaking. The importance of ritual is recognized, and when Izanagi and Izanami go about things the wrong way, the result is unsatisfactory. Ultimately, creative power comes from the tension supplied by the union of opposites: male and female, calmness and turbulence, yang and yin.

Some of these myths are remarkably similar to Western ones. The story of Izanagi's attempt to bring Izanami back from Yomi, the land of the dead, resembles the tale of Orpheus and Euridice, which itself harks back to earlier tales, such as the Descent of Inanna. The Japanese story deals with the finality and inevitability of death, but it is also a political statement describing a conflict between the predominant Yamato people and the subordinate Izumo people. The story reveals an important attitude underlying Japanese cultural development: the hero of a subordinated people is not vilified and eradicated, but consciously assimilated, albeit in a subordinate position. We see the same theme even more clearly in the conflict between Susanoo and Amaterasu.

As with much mythology, these accounts also serve to explain place-names and how they came to be, as well as to provide explanations for meteorological phenomena. Susanoo, the storm god, was the hero of the Izumo people who lived on the stormy Japan Sea coast. He was banished by Amaterasu, the sun goddess, chief deity of the predominant Yamato people who lived on Japan's mild Pacific coast. These are the myths of an agrarian people. Susanoo's crimes against the community are to break down the dikes between the fields and to block up the irrigation ditches. Amaterasu, when unhappy, hides in a rock cave. In what amounts to a familiar solstice ritual, she is lured out and once again brings crop-growing light to the world.

Western readers will find the point of the story familiar, since it resembles the myths of the Middle Eastern Inanna (pp. 16–37) and the Greek Demeter (pp. 422–430). Hesiod's *Theogony* (pp. 409–422) and Ovid's *Metamorphoses* (pp. 675–687) provide interesting comparisons as well.

The *Kojiki* presents the earliest myths of an ancient people with all the complexity and sophistication one expects of a highly developed culture.

## I [The Beginning of Heaven and Earth]

The names of the Deities that were born in the Plain of High Heaven when the Heaven and Earth began were the Deity Master-of-the-August-Center-of-Heaven, next the High-August-Producing-Wondrous Deity, next the Divine-Producing-Wondrous Deity. These three Deities were all Deities born alone, and hid their persons. The names of the Deities that were born next from a thing that sprouted up like unto a reed-shoot when the earth, young and like unto floating oil, drifted about medusa-like, were the Pleasant-Reed-Shoot Prince-Elder Deity, next the Heavenly-Eternally-Standing Deity. These two Deities were likewise born alone, and hid their persons.

The five Deities in the above list are separate Heavenly Deities.

## II [The Seven Divine Generations]

The names of the Deities that were born next were the Earthly-Eternally-Standing Deity, next the Luxuriant-Integrating-Master Deity. These two Deities were likewise Deities that were born alone, and hid their persons. The names of the Deities that were born next were the Deity Mud-Earth-Lord, next his younger sister the Deity Mud-Earth-Lady; next the Germ-Integrating Deity, next his younger sister the Life-Integrating Deity; next the Deity Elder-of-the Great-Place, next his younger sister the Deity Elder-Lady-of-the-Great-Place; next the Deity Perfect-Exterior, next his younger sister the Deity Oh-Awful-Lady; next the Deity the Male-Who-Invites, next his younger sister the Deity the Female-Who-Invites.

From the Earthly-Eternally-Standing Deity down to the Deity the Female-Who-Invites in the previous list are what are termed the Seven Divine Generations. (The two solitary Deities above [-mentioned] are each called one generation. Of the succeeding ten Deities each pair of deities is called a generation.)

## III [The Island of Onogoro]

Hereupon all the Heavenly Deities commanded the two Deities His Augustness the Male-Who-Invites and Her Augustness the Female-Who-Invites, ordering them to "make, consolidate, and give birth to this drifting land." Granting to them an heavenly jewelled spear, they [thus] deigned to charge them. So the two Deities, standing upon the Floating Bridge of Heaven, pushed down the jewelled spear and stirred with it, whereupon, when they had stirred the brine till it went curdle-curdle, and drew [the spear] up, the brine that dripped down from the end of the spear was piled up and became an island. This is the Island of Onogoro.

## *IV [Courtship of the Deities]*

Descending from the heavens to this island, they erected heavenly pillar and a spacious palace.

At this time IZANAGI-NÖ-MIKÖTÖ [Male-Who-Invites] asked his spouse IZANAMI-NÖ-MIKÖTÖ [Female-Who-Invites], saying:

"How is your body formed?"

She replied, saying:

"My body, formed though it be formed, has one place which is formed insufficiently."

Then IZANAGI-NÖ-MIKÖTÖ said:

"My body, formed though it be formed, has one place which is formed to excess. Therefore, I would like to take that place in my body which is formed to excess and insert it into that place in your body which is formed insufficiently, and [thus] give birth to the land. How would this be?"

IZANAMI-NÖ-MIKÖTÖ replied, saying:

"That will be good."

Then IZANAGI-NÖ-MIKÖTÖ said:

"Then let us, you and me, walk in a circle around this heavenly pillar and meet and have conjugal intercourse."

After thus agreeing, [Izanagi-nö-mikötö] then said:

"You walk around from the right, and I will walk around from the left and meet you."

After having agreed to this, they circled around; then IZANAMI-NÖ-MIKÖTÖ said first:

"*Ana-ni-yasi,* how good a lad!"

Afterwards, IZANAGI-NÖ-MIKÖTÖ said:

"*Ana-ni-yasi,* how good a maiden!"

After each had finished speaking, [Izanagi-nö-mikötö] said to his spouse:

"It is not proper that the woman speak first."

Nevertheless, they commenced procreation and gave birth to a leech-child. They placed this child into a boat made of reeds and floated it away.

Next, they gave birth to the island of APA. This also is not reckoned as one of their children.

## *V [Birth of the Eight Great Islands]*

Hereupon the two Deities took counsel, saying: "The children to whom we have now given birth are not good. It will be best to announce this in the August place of the Heavenly Deities." They ascended forthwith to Heaven and enquired of Their Augustnesses the Heavenly Deities. Then the Heavenly Deities commanded and found out by grand divination, and ordered them, saying: "They were not good because the woman spoke first. Descend back again and amend your words." So thereupon descending back, they again went round the heavenly August pillar as before. Thereupon His Augustness the Male-Who-Invites spoke first: "Ah! What a fair and lovely maiden!" Afterwards his younger sister Her Augustness the Female-Who-Invites spoke: "Ah! What a fair and lovely youth!" After they had finished saying this, they were united and bore a child, the Island of Ahaji, Ho-no-sa-wake. Next they gave birth to the Island of Futa-na in Iyo. This island has one body and four faces, and each face has a name. . . . Next they gave birth to the Island[s] of Futa-go, another name for which is Heaven's-Two-Houses.

## VI [Birth of the Various Deities]

When they had finished giving birth to countries, they began afresh giving birth to Deities. . . . Next they gave birth to the Fire-Burning-Swift-Male Deity, another name for whom is the Deity Fire-Shining Prince, and another name is the Deity Fire-Shining-Elder.

## VII [Retirement of Her Augustness the Princess-Who-Invites]

Through giving birth to this child her August private parts were burnt, and she sickened and lay down. The names of the deities born from her vomit were the Deity Metal-Mountain-Prince and next the Deity Metal-Mountain-Princess. . . . So the Deity the Female-Who-Invites, through giving birth to the Deity-of-Fire, at length divinely retired. . . . So when His Augustness the Male-Who-Invites said: "Oh! Thine Augustness my lovely younger sister! Oh! That I should have exchanged thee for this single child!" And as he crept round her August pillow, and as he crept round her August feet and wept, there was born from his August tears the Deity that dwells at Konomoto near Unewo on Mount Kagu, and whose name is the Crying-Weeping-Female Deity. So he buried the divinely retired Deity the Female-Who-Invites on Mount Hiba at the boundary of the Land of Idzumo and the land of Hahaki.

## VIII [The Slaying of the Fire-Deity]

Then His Augustness the Male-Who-Invites, drawing the ten-grasp sabre that was augustly girded on him, cut off the head of his child the Deity Shining-Elder. Hereupon the names of the Deities that were born from the blood that stuck to the point of his August sword and bespattered the multitudinous rock-masses were: the Deity Rock-Splitter. . . .

## IX [The Land of Hades]

Thereupon [His Augustness the Male-Who-Invites], wishing to meet and see his younger sister Her Augustness the Female-Who-Invites, followed after her to the Land of Hades. So when from the palace she raised the door and came out to meet him, His Augustness the Male-Who-Invites spoke, saying: "Thine Augustness my lovely younger sister! The lands that I and thou made are not yet finished making; so come back!" Then Her Augustness the Female-Who-Invites answered, saying: "Lamentable indeed that thou camest not sooner! I have eaten of the furnace of Hades. Nevertheless, as I reverence the entry here of Thine Augustness my lovely elder brother, I wish to return. Moreover, I will discuss it particularly with the Deities of Hades. Look not at me!" Having spoken, she went back inside the palace; and as she tarried there very long, he could not wait. So having taken and broken off one of the end-teeth of the multitudinous and close-toothed comb stuck in the August left-bunch [of his hair], he lit one light and went in and looked. Maggots were swarming, and [she was] rotting, and in her head dwelt the Great Thunder, in her breast dwelt the Fire-Thunder. . . . [A]ltogether eight Thunder-Deities had been born and dwelt there. Hereupon His Augustness the Male-Who-Invites, overawed at the sight, fled back, whereupon his younger sister Her Augustness the Female-Who-Invites said: "Thou hast put me to shame," and at once sent the Ugly-Female-of-Hades to pursue him. So His Augustness the Male-Who-Invites took his black August head-dress and cast it down, and it instantly turned into grapes. While she picked them up and ate them, he fled on; but as she still pursued him, he took and broke the multitudinous and close-toothed comb in the right bunch [of his hair] and cast it down, and it instantly turned into bamboo-sprouts. While she pulled them up and ate them, he fled on. Again later [his younger sister] sent the eight Thunder-Deities with a thousand and five hundred warriors of Hades to pursue him. So he, drawing the ten-grasp sabre that was augustly girded on him, fled forward brandishing it in his back hand; and as they still pursued, he took, on reaching the base of the Even Pass of Hades, three peaches that were growing at its base, and waited and smote [his pursuers therewith], so that they all fled back. Then His Augustness the Male-Who-Invites announced to the peaches: "Like as ye have helped me, so must ye help all living people in the Central Land of the Reed-Plains when they shall fall into troublous circumstances and be harassed!"—and he gave [to the peaches] the designation of Their Augustnesses Great-Divine-Fruit. Last of all his younger sister Her Augustness the Princess-Who-Invites came out herself in pursuit. So he drew a thousand-draught rock, and [with it] blocked up the Even Pass of Hades, and placed the rock in the middle; and they stood opposite to one another and exchanged leave-takings; and Her Augustness the Female-Who-Invites said: "My lovely elder brother, thine Augustness! If thou do like this, I will in one day strangle to death a thousand of the folks of thy land." And His Augustness the Male-Who-Invites replied: "My lovely younger sister, Thine Augustness! If *thou* do this I will in one day set up a thousand and five hundred parturition-houses. In this manner each day a thousand people would surely die, and each day a thousand and five hundred people would surely be born." . . .

## X [The Purification of the August Person]

Therefore the Great Deity the Male-Who-Invites said: "Nay! Hideous! I have come to a hideous and polluted land,—I have! So I will perform the purification of my August person." So he went out to a plain [covered with] *ahagi* at a small river-mouth near Tachibana in Himuka in [the island of] Tsukushi and purified and cleansed himself. . . . The name of the Deity that was born as he thereupon washed his left August eye was the Heaven-Shining-Great-August Deity. The name of the Deity that was next born as he washed his right August eye was His Augustness Moon-Night-Possessor. The name of the Deity that was next born as he washed his August nose was His Brave-Swift-Impetuous-Male-Augustness.

## XI [Investiture of the Three Deities the Illustrious August Children]

At this time His Augustness the Male-Who-Invites greatly rejoiced saying: "I, begetting child after child, have at my final begetting gotten three illustrious children," [with which words,] at once jinglingly taking off and shaking the jewel-string forming his August necklace, he bestowed it on the Heavenly-Shining-Great-August Deity, saying: "Do Thine Augustness rule the Plain of High-Heaven." With this charge he bestowed it on her. . . . Next he said to His Augustness Moon-Night-Possessor: "Do Thine Augustness rule the Dominion of the Night." Thus he charged him. Next he said to His-Brave-Swift-Impetuous-Male-Augustness: "Do Thine Augustness rule the Sea-Plain."

## XII [The Crying and Weeping of His Impetuous-Male-Augustness]

So while [the other two Deities] each [assumed his and her] rule according to the command with which [their father] had deigned to charge them, His Swift-Impetuous-Male-Augustness did not [assume the] rule [of] the dominion with which he had been charged, but cried and wept till his eight-grasp beard reached to the pit of his stomach. . . . So the Great August Deity the Male-Who-Invites said to His Swift-Impetuous-Male-Augustness: "How is it that, instead of ruling the land with which I charged thee, thous dost wail and weep?" He replied saying: "I wail because I wish to depart to my deceased mother's land, to the Nether Distant Land." Then the Great August Deity the Male-Who-Invites was very angry and said: "If that be so, thou shalt not dwell in this land," and forthwith expelled him with a divine expulsion. . . .

## XIII [The August Oath]

So thereupon His Swift-Impetuous-Male-Augustness said: "If that be so, I will take leave of the Heaven-Shining Great-August-Deity, and depart." [With these words] he forthwith went up to Heaven, whereupon all the mountains and rivers shook, and every land and country quaked. So the Heaven-Shining-Great-August Deity, alarmed at the noise, said: "The reason of the ascent hither of His Augustness my elder brother is surely of no good intent. It is only that he wishes to wrest my land from me." . . .

## XV [The August Ravages of His-Impetuous-Male-Augustness]

Then His Swift-Impetuous-Male-Augustness said to the Heaven-Shining-Great-August Deity ". . . I have undoubtedly gained the victory." With these words, and impetuous with victory, he broke down the divisions of the rice-fields laid out by the Heaven-Shining-Great-August Deity, filled up the ditches, and moreover strewed excrements in the palace where she partook of the great food. So, though he did thus, the Heaven-Shining-Great-August Deity upbraided him not, but said: "What looks like excrements must be something that His Augustness mine elder brother has vomited through drunkness. . . ." But not withstanding these apologetic words, he still continued his evil acts, and was more and more [violent]. As the Heaven-Shining-Great-August Deity sat in her awful weaving-hall seeing to the weaving of the August garments of the Deities, he broke a hole in the top of the weaving-hall, and through it let fall a heavenly piebald horse which he had flayed with a backward flaying, at whose sight the women weaving the heavenly garments were so much alarmed that she struck her genitals against the shuttle and died.

## XVI [The Door of the Heavenly Rock Dwelling]

So thereupon the Heavenly-Shining-Great-August Deity, terrified at the sight, closed [behind her] the door of the Heavenly Rock-Dwelling, made it fast, and retired. Then the whole Plain of High Heaven was obscured and all the Central Land of Reed-Plains darkened. Owing to this, eternal night prevailed. Hereunto the voices of the myriad Deities were like unto the flies of the fifth moon as they swarm and a myriad portents of woe arose. Therefore did the eight hundred myriad Deities assemble in a divine assembly in the bed of the Tranquil River of Heaven, and bid the Deity Thought-Includer . . . to think of a plan, assembling the long singing birds of eternal night and making them sing, taking the hard rocks of Heaven from the river-bed of the Tranquil River of Heaven, and taking the iron from the Heavenly Metal-Mountains, calling in the smith Ama-tsu-ma-ra, charging Her

Augustness I-shi-ko-ri-do-me to make a mirror and charging His Augustness Jewel-Ancestor to make an augustly complete [string] of curved jewels eight feet [long], . . . and pulling up by its roots the true *cleyera japonica* with five hundred [branches] from Heavenly Mount Kagu, and taking and putting on its upper branches the augustly complete [string] of curved jewels eight feet [long],—of five hundred jewels—and taking and tying to the middle branches the mirror eight feet [long], and taking and hanging upon its lower branches the white pacificatory offerings and the blue pacificatory offerings, His Augustness Grand-Jewel taking these divers things and holding them together with the grand August offerings, . . . and standing hidden beside the door, and Her Augustness Heavenly-Alarming-Female hanging [round her] the heavenly clubmoss from the heavenly Mount Kagu as a sash, and making the heavenly spindle tree her headdress, and binding the leaves of the bamboo-grass of the Heavenly Mount Kagu in a posy for her hands, laying a sounding board before the door of the Heavenly Rock-Dwelling, and stamping till she made it resound and doing as if possessed by a Deity, and pulling out the nipples of her breasts, pushing down her skirt-string usque ad privates partes. Then the Plain of High Heaven shook, and the eight hundred myriad Deities laughed together. Hereupon the Heavenly-Shining-Great-August Deity was amazed, and, slightly opening the door of the Heavenly Rock-Dwelling, spoke thus from inside: "Methought that owing to my retirement the Plain of Heaven would be dark, and likewise the Central Land of Reed-Plains would be dark: how then is it that the Heavenly-Alarming-Female makes merry, and that likewise the eight hundred myriad Deities all laugh?" Then the Heavenly-Alarming-Female spoke, saying: "We rejoice and are glad because there is a Deitymore illustrious than Thine Augustness." While she was thus speaking, His Augustness Heavenly-Beckoning-Ancestor-Lord and His Augustness Grand-Jewel pushed forward the mirror and respectfully showed it to the Heavenly-Shining-Great-August Deity, where upon the Heavenly-Shining-Great-August Deity, more and more astonished, gradually came forth from the door and gazed upon it, whereupon the Heavenly-Hand-Strength-Male Diety, who was standing hidden, took her August hand and drew her out, then His Augustness Grand-Jewel drew the bottom-tied rope along her August back, and spoke, saying: "Thou must not go back further in than this!" So when the Heavenly-Shining-Great-August Deity had come forth, both the Plain of High Heaven and the Central Land of the Reed-Plains of course again became light.

## XVIII [The Eight-Forked Serpent]

So, having been expelled, [His Swift-Impetuous-Male-Augustness] descended to a place [called] Tori-kami at the head-waters of the River Hi in the land of Izumo. At this time some chopsticks came floating down the stream. So His Swift-Impetuous-Male-Augustness, thinking that there must be people at the head-waters of the river, went up it in quest of them, when he came upon an old man and an old woman,—two of them,—who had a young girl between them, and were weeping. . . . [H]e asked: "What is the cause of your crying?" [The old man] answered saying: "I had originally eight young girls as daughters. But the eight-forked serpent of Koshi has come every year and devoured [one], and it is now its time to come, wherefore we weep." Then he asked him: "What is its form like?" [The old man] answered saying: "Its eyes are like *akakagachi,* it has one body with eight heads, and eight tails. Moreover on its body grows moss, and also chamæcyparis and cryptomerias. Its length extends over eight valleys and eight hills, and if one looks at its belly, it is all constantly bloody and inflamed." Then His Swift-Impetuous-Male-Augustness said to the old man: "If this by thy daughter, wilt thou offer her to me?" He replied saying: "With reverence, but I know not thine August name." Then he replied saying: "I am elder brother to the Heaven-Shining-Great-August Deity. So I have descended from Heaven." Then the [old couple] said, "If that be so, with reverence we will offer [her to thee]." So His Swift-Impetuous-Male-Augustness, at once taking and changing the young girl into a multitudinous and close-toothed comb which he stuck into his August hair-bunch, said to the [old couple]: "Do you distil some eight-fold refined liquor. Also make a fence round about, in that fence make eight gates, at each gate tie [together] eight platforms, on each platform put a liquor-vat, and into each vat pour the eight-fold refined liquor, and wait." So as they waited after having thus prepared everything in accordance with his bidding, the eight-forked serpent came truly as [the old man] had said, and immediately dipped a head into each vat, and drank the liquor. Thereupon it was intoxicated with drinking, and all [the heads] lay down and slept. Then His Swift-Impetuous-Male-Augustness drew the ten-grasp sabre, that was augustly girded on him, and cut the serpent in pieces, so that the River Hi flowed on changed into a river of blood.

## MANYŌSHŪ (8TH CENT.)

The *Manyōshū,* Japan's earliest anthology of poetry, was compiled around the middle of the eighth century, but it includes poetry from a much earlier oral tradition. This collection of more than four thousand poems exhibits a range of poetic form and subject matter not found in later anthologies. Here we find Hitomarō celebrating the great events of the imperial court, such as the empress's procession to Yoshino, as well as the expression of personal emotion, as we see in Hitomarō's lament on leaving his wife. This unique combination of public poetry and private poetry is characteristic of the *Manyōshū* and distinguishes it from later anthologies.

We notice another example of such juxtaposition in Hitomarō's *Yoshino* (Imperial Procession) poem as well. After a hymnlike passage in praise of the empress, all the images are divided into river and mountain, autumn and spring, upstream and downstream. These opposites are brought together in praise of the sovereign. Not only her subjects, but all nature joins in praise of the empress. Similarly, in the poem of lament on leaving his wife, we see an imagistic progression from seashore to hillside to mountaintop to celestial bodies. In the end, even the cosmos shares the poet's grief.

Also typical are the poems by Ōtomo Tabito. While the poetic celebration of wine drinking also comes from the Chinese tradition, the emphasis on expressing personal feelings rather than public issues becomes the norm for Japanese poetry. Less typical is Yamanoue Okura's *Dialog of the Destitute,* which comes directly from the Chinese tradition of using poetry as a vehicle for social commentary. There are two voices in the poem—first the lament of the poor man, then the complaint of the destitute man—followed by the irony of the tax collector who demands his due even when men have nothing. The expression of social injustice in poetry is rare in Japanese literature.

Although poetry later became the art of the aristocratic classes, the *Manyōshū* includes verses from the ranks of the common people as well, as we can see in the examples from the *Songs from the East Country.*

## Hitomarō

*Translated by Ian Hideo Levy*

### *Book I. 38–39 [Imperial Procession]*

Our Lord
who rules in peace,
a very god,
manifests her divine will
and raises towering halls
above the Yoshino riverland
where waters surge,
and climbs to the top
to view the land.

On the mountains
folding upward around her
like a sheer hedge of green,
the mountain gods present their offerings.
They bring her blossoms in springtime
to decorate her hair
and, when autumn comes,
they garland her with scarlet leaves.
And the gods of the river
that runs alongside the mountains
make offerings for her imperial feast.
They send cormorants forth
over the upper shoals,
they cast dipper nets
across the lower shoals.
Mountain and river
draw together to serve her—
a god's reign indeed!

*Envoy*

A very god
whom mountain and river
draw together to serve,
she sets her boat to sail
over pools where waters surge.

## *Book II. 135–37 [Lament on Leaving His Wife]*

At Cape Kara
on the Sea of Iwami,
where the vines
   crawl on the rocks,
rockweed of the deep
grows on the reefs
and sleek seaweed
grows on the desolate shore.
As deeply do I
think of my wife
who swayed toward me in sleep
   like the lithe seaweed.
Yet few were the nights
we had slept together
before we were parted
like crawling vines uncurled.
And so I look back,
still thinking of her
with painful heart,
this clench of inner flesh,
but in the storm
of fallen scarlet leaves
on Mount Watari,
crossed as on
      a great ship,
I cannot make out the sleeves
she waves in farewell.
For she, alas,
is slowly hidden
like the moon
   in its crossing
      between the clouds
over Yagami Mountain
just as the evening sun
coursing through the heavens
has begun to glow,
         and even I

who thought I was a brave man
find the sleeves
of my well-woven robe
drenched with tears.

*Envoys*

The quick gallop
of my dapple-blue steed
races me to the clouds,
passing far away
from where my wife dwells.

O scarlet leaves
falling on the autumn mountainside:
stop, for a while, the storm
your strewing makes, that I might glimpse
the place where my wife dwells.

## Ōtomo Tabito

*Translated by Ian Hideo Levy*

### *Book III. 338–43 [Poems in Praise of Wine]*

**338**

Rather than engaging
in useless worries,
it's better to down a cup
of raw wine.

**339**

Great sages of the past
gave the name of "sage" to wine.
How well they spoke!

**340**

What the Seven Wise Men
of ancient times
wanted, it seems,
was wine.

**341**

Rather than making pronouncements
with an air of wisdom,
it's better to down the wine
and sob drunken tears.

**342**

What is most noble,
beyond all words
and beyond all deeds,
is wine.

**343**

Rather than be half-heartedly human,
I wish I could be a jug of wine
and be soaked in it!

## *Yamanoue Okura*

*Translated by Ian Hideo Levy*

### Book V. 892–93 [Dialog of the Destitute]

"On nights when rain falls,
mixed with wind,
on nights when snow falls,
mixed with rain,
I am cold.
And the cold
leaves me helpless:
I lick black lumps of salt
and suck up melted dregs of *sake*.
Coughing and sniffling,
I smooth my uncertain wisps
of beard.
I am proud—
I know no man
is better than me.
But I am cold.
I pull up my hempen nightclothes
and throw on every scrap
of cloth shirt that I own.
But the night is cold.

And I wonder how a man like you,
even poorer than myself,
with his father and mother
starving and freezing,
with his wife and children
begging and begging
through their tears,
can get through the world alive
at times like this."

"Wide, they say,
are heaven and earth—
but have they shrunk for me?
Bright, they say,
are the sun and moon—
but do they refuse to shine for me?
Is it thus for all men,
or for me alone?
Above all, I was born human,
I too toil for my keep—
as much as the next man—
yet on my shoulders hangs
a cloth shirt
not even lined with cotton,
these tattered rags
thin as strips of seaweed.
In my groveling hut,
my tilting hut,
sleeping on straw
cut and spread right on the ground,
with my father and mother
huddled at my pillow
and my wife and children
huddled at my feet,
I grieve and lament.
Not a spark rises in the stove,
and in the pot
a spider has drawn its web.
I have forgotten
what it is to cook rice!
As I lie here,
a thin cry tearing from my throat—
a tiger thrush's moan—
then, as they say,
to slice the ends
of a thing already too short,

to our rough bed
comes the scream of the village headman
with his tax collecting whip.
Is it so helpless and desperate,
the way of life in this world?"

*Envoy*

I find this world
a hard and shameful place.
But I cannot fly away—
I am not a bird.

**Presented by Yamanoue Okura with profound humility**

## *Songs from the East Country*

*Translated by Nippon Gakujutsu Shinkōkai*

### *Book XIV. 3459 ["My hands so chapped from rice-pounding"]*

My hands so chapped from rice-
pounding—
To-night again, he will hold them, sighing,
My young lord of the mansion!

### *Book XIX. 4290–91 ["Over the spring field trails the mist"]*

Composed extempore, on the twenty-third of the second month of the fifth year of Tempyō-Shōhō (753).

Over the spring field trails the mist,
And lonely is my heart;
Then in this fading light of evening
A warbler sings.

## JAPANESE COURT POETRY (10TH–15TH CENT.)

*Translated by Robert H. Brower and Earl Miner*

By the beginning of the tenth century CE, the range of Japanese poetry had narrowed considerably in terms of form, content, and even vocabulary. With the publication of the *Kokinshū* (905), the first imperially commissioned anthology of court poetry, we see a formalization of poetry in the hands of aristocrats. From this time forward, we see the exclusive use of the thirty-one-syllable *tanka* as the accepted form of poetry. The thirty-one-syllable verse is divided into five phrases of

5–7–5–7–7 syllables. The poem most often consists of an image and a sentiment; elegance is the chief requisite for both. Even within this short form, however, poems of great subtlety and sophistication were composed, as we see in Ono no Komachi's poem "*Iro miede*" ("Find mutability"). Philosophical issues were also raised, as in Narihira's lover's poem "*Kimi ya koshi*" ("My mind is dazzled"), in which she expresses confusion about the distinction between appearance and reality. Narihira had spent the night with a shrine maiden; in her "morning after poem," she wonders, Did it really happen, or was it merely a dream? In a Buddhist world where life itself was considered to be merely a dream, this statement of confusion is disingenuous.

Perhaps the subjective worldview of Japanese courtiers can be seen most clearly in Tsurayuki's poem "*Tsuki ya aranu*" ("What now is real?"). Last spring, he was with his beloved; this spring, they are separated. The moon is the same, the season is the same, only his perception of them has changed; but from his perspective, the moon and the season have changed, and he remains the same. Other poems resonate with suggestiveness, such as the anonymous "*Honobono to*" ("Dimly, dimly"), which implies much but reveals nothing explicitly. Sometimes lovers are languid, as in Narihira's "*Oki mo sezu*" ("I am at one with spring"), and at other times fierce with intensity, as in Ono no Komachi's "*Hito ni awan*" ("On such a night as this").

Just as the range and exuberance of the *Manyōshū* give way to a dominating concern for elegance in the *Kokinshū*, they also give way to a more melancholy sensibility of Buddhist evanescence in the *Shin Kokinshū* (c. 1210), a later imperially commissioned anthology of court poetry. While rejecting the foolishness of the material world, the poet nevertheless feels nostalgia for the past and also recognizes the bittersweet beauty of his reclusive world, as we see in Shunzei's two poems: "*Mukashi omou*" ("I recollect the past") and, in a more somber mood, "*Yū sareba*" ("As evening falls"). In Yoshitada's "*Wa ga seko ga*" ("On such a night"), the autumn wind blows with the disappointment of a failed rendezvous, but for Nōin, the itinerant priest who has renounced the world, the falling night and the falling blossoms combined with the sound of the vesper bell create a lonely but not unpleasant mood. A similar sentiment is expressed in darker tones by the priests Ryōzen in "*Sabishisa ni*" ("In my loneliness") and Jakuren in "*Sabishisa wa*" ("Loneliness").

Yet even in this transient world where attachment can lead only to separation, there are some defiant souls who commit to relationships doomed to fail, as we see in Teika's poem "*Hajime yori*" ("Although I heard"). Often it is the lingering sound or the lingering fragrance that gives reality to the dream. Earlier we heard Nōin's vesper bell; in the same vein, we get a whiff of Shunzei's daughter's fragrant dreams in "*Kaze kayou*" ("The wind breathes softly"). Reality is very far away indeed, for here we have only the fragrance and the dream. Finally, even that dream breaks off and slips away, as in Teika's "*Haru no yo no*" ("The bridge of dreams"). In such a world, philosophy is as useless as passion as a route to commitment or permanence; all we can do is live in the moment with a gentle sense of humor, as we see in ex-Emperor Fushimi's poem "On the Topic, 'Three Dogmas Are Not One Dogma, Nor Are They Three Separate Dogmas.'"

There is another dynamic at work in Japanese poetry. As the individual poems become briefer, this brevity is redressed by collecting individual poems into anthologies, which are not merely repositories of poetry but poetic compositions in their own right. Japanese anthologies (twenty-one of them were imperially commissioned between 905 and 1439 CE) are arranged by topic rather than chronologically or by author. Thus, poems on the topic of love are arranged in an order that follows the progress of a love affair from first tentative infatuation through full passion, and on to a cooling of ardor, separation, and memory. While the length of the individual poems has diminished, the encompassing work of poetic composition has grown. This process led to the development of *renga* ("linked verse") in the Medieval Period. The last thirteen poems in this selection, although written independently by unrelated authors, have been compiled as a sequence that will reveal, to some extent, the principles of association and progression used in collections of Japanese poetry.

## Ono no Komachi, "Find mutability"

Find mutability
In that being which alters without fading
In its outward hue—
In the color, looks, and the deceptive flower
Of the heart of what this world calls man!

## Shrine Priestess, "My mind is dazzled"

My mind is dazzled—
Did you come to visit me?
Or I to you?
Was our night a dream? Reality?
Was I sleeping? Was I awake?

## Ki no Tsurayuki, "What now is real?"

What now is real?
This moon, this spring, are altered
From their former being—
While this alone, my mortal body, remains
As ever changed by love beyond all change.

## Anonymous, "Dimly, dimly"

Dimly, dimly
In the morning mist that lies
Over Akashi Bay,
My longings follow with the ship
That vanishes behind the distant isle.

## Ariwara Narihira, "I am at one with spring"

I am at one with spring;
Neither sleeping, nor yet rising from my bed,
Till night turns into dawn,
And through the day my love for you continues
In listless looking at the ceaseless rains.

## Ono no Komachi, "On such a night as this"

On such a night as this
When the lack of moonlight shades your way to me,
I wake from sleep my passion blazing,
My breast a fire raging, exploding flame
While within me my heart chars.

## Fujiwara Shunzei, "I recollect the past"

I recollect the past
While the summer rain falls through the dark
About my grass-thatched hut,
But, *hototogisu*, singing at last among the hills,
Do not call out a freshening of my tears.

## Fujiwara Shunzei, "As evening falls"

As evening falls,
From along the moors the autumn wind
Blows chill into the heart,
And the quails raise their plaintive cry
In the deep grass of secluded Fukakusa.

## Yoshitada, "On such a night"

On such a night
When my lover fails to come,
The autumn wind—
Even more than he who fails me—
Brings disappointment in its rustling sound.

## Nōin, "As now I come"

As now I come
And see the spring day grow to dusk
In the mountain hamlet,
The cherry blossoms fall to earth
At the sounding of the temple's vesper bell.

## *Ryōzen, "In my loneliness"*

In my loneliness
I step outside my hut and gaze
In quiet revery,
But everywhere it is the same:
The melancholy autumn dusk.

## *Jakuren, "Loneliness"*

Loneliness—
The essential color of a beauty
Not to be defined:
Over the dark evergreens, the dusk
That gathers on far autumn hills.

## *Fujiwara Teika, "Although I heard"*

Although I heard
From the outset that a meeting
Can only mean to part,
I gave myself to love for you
Unconscious of the coming dawn.

## *Ariwara Narihira, "Though formerly I heard"*

Though formerly I heard
About the road that all must travel
At the inevitable end,
I never thought, or felt, today
Would bring that far tomorrow.

## *Shunzei's Daughter, "The wind breathes softly"*

The wind breathes softly,
Bringing the scent of flowers to my sleeve
And calls me from my sleep;
And, my pillow redolent with spring,
I waken from a night of fragrant dreams.

## *Fujiwara Teika, "The bridge of dreams"*

The bridge of dreams
Floating on the brief spring night
Soon breaks off:
Now from the mountaintop a cloud
Takes leave into the open sky.

## *Ex-Emperor Fushimi, "On the topic, 'The Three Dogmas Are Not One Dogma, Nor Are They Three Separate Dogmas.'"*

As I listen
To the rain outside my window
Fall in gentle drops,
I turn my midnight lamp around,
Dimming its light against the wall.

## *Fujiwara Norikane, "Dawn has not broken"*

Dawn has not broken,
But my bed is startled into waking
As they sound—
The bamboo wattlings of the fence
Crack beneath the piling snow.

## *Ex-Emperor Takakura, "The crowing cock"*

The crowing cock
Announces the arrival of the dawn—
But it is the snow
Whose radiance displays the peak of Otowa,
The "Mount of Feathered Sound."

## *Fujiwara Ietsune, "In the mountains"*

In the mountains
Even the single village path must lie
Buried from the sight,
For in the capital snow has fallen
Together with the crimson leaves.

## *Fujiwara Kunifusa, "Was it not enough"*

Was it not enough
To know loneliness without this?
—Along the hillslopes
The oak trees droop their withered leaves
And silently the snow still falls.

## Fujiwara Teika, "There is no shelter"

There is no shelter
Where I can rest my weary horse
And brush my laden sleeves:
The Sano ford and its adjoining fields
Spread over with a twilight in the snow.

## Fujiwara Teika, "The path of him I long for"

The path of him I long for
Across the foothills to where I wait
Must be wiped out:
The weight of snow has grown unbearable
In the cedars standing at my eaves.

## Fujiwara Ariie, "Beneath the piling snow"

Beneath the piling snow
The nodding bamboos of Fushimi village
Crack loudly in the night—
Even the path to love in dreams collapses
Into waking from the sounding snow.

## Izumi Shikibu, "As I fall in sadness"

As I fall in sadness
At his neglect, the firefly of the marsh
Seems to be my soul
Departing from my very flesh
And wandering in anguish off to him.

## Izumi Shikibu, "Lying down alone"

Lying down alone
My thoughts are fixed on you—so deeply
That I have forgot again
The tangles of my long black hair
In yearning for the hand that stroked it clear.

## Fujiwara Teika, "I gaze afar"

I gaze afar
And ask for neither cherry flowers
Nor crimson leaves:

The inlet with its grass-thatched huts
Clustered in the growing autumn dusk.

## *Ex-Emperor Hanazono, "The sun at dusk"*

The sun at dusk
Fades in brightness from the eaves
Where swallows twitter;
And among the willows in the garden
Blows the green breeze of spring.

## *Ki no Tomonori, "On this day in spring"*

On this day in spring
When the lambent air suffuses
Soft tranquility,
Why should the cherry petals flutter
With unsettled heart to earth?

## *Ono no Komachi, "In waking daylight"*

In waking daylight,
Then, oh then it can be understood,
But when I see myself
Shrinking from those hostile eyes
Even in my dreams: this is misery itself.

## *Ki no Tsurayuki, "As pressed by love"*

As pressed by love,
I go to hunt her in my yearning,
The wind blows cold
Through the winter darkness from the river,
Where on the banks the plovers cry.

## *Mitsune, "With the autumn wind"*

With the autumn wind
Blowing through the ageless pines
Of auspicious Suminoe
Are mingled the elated voices
Of the white waves out to sea.

## Fujiwara Shunzei, "He who hears them"

He who hears them:
His tears break at their cries—
The wild geese wing
In sad departure from the beauty
Of springtime dawn spread through the sky.

## Lady Jusammi Chikako, "Wide across the moors"

Wide across the moors
Bend the tassles of the pampas grass
In the swelling breeze;
And in the cold of the evening sun
Autumn darkens to its close.

## Fujiwara Kimikase, "Was it a previous life"

Was it a previous life
Which binds our fates, decrees that now
My feelings must be stirred—
Rushing into love with you, so hidden
Like the peak of Mount Tsukuba from my sight?

## Nijo Yoshimoto, "It must not be known"

It must not be known:
That stirring under the river of these tears
Flowing on the sleeve
With which I blot my eyes, there is a heart
Now turbid like an agitated stream.

## Fujiwara Norinaga, "For a slight moment"

For a slight moment
I may enfold within my sleeve
The river of my tears,
But how can I dam up my heart
So overbrimming with its love?

## Emperor Go-Daigo, "Despite my efforts"

Despite my efforts,
My love betrays itself in the color

Of this recent passion,
Deep as the purple of the ribbon used
For the First Binding of the Hair.

## Fujiwara Teika, "Yesterday, today"

Yesterday, today—
No matter how I gaze in vacant revery
Toward the cloud-tips
Tinted in the evening, how can I know
The feelings of her I cannot see?

## Emperor Komyo, "How strange it is"

How strange it is:
I keep falling into a vacant reverie
Of vague awareness
These days when in my mind itself
I do not really know I love.

## Lady Reizi, "Because of feelings"

Because of feelings
Now agitated in the reaches of my heart
Unknown to her and all,
My state is no longer quite like that
Of days spent in a vacant reverie of love.

## Fujiwara Kimikage, "Although her heart"

Although her heart
Is no mountain of thick-set boulders
Rooted in their place,
My beloved's feelings toward me
Stay adamantly unmoved.

## Lady Jusammi Chikako, "Sunken my love"

Sunken my love,
Like reed roots deep within a tidal pool—
So be it if it must;
But then let it rot away completely
Hidden within those secret depths.

### *Lady Daini Sammi, "Since this love of mine"*

Since this love of mine
Is like the grass all buried by the snow,
What means have I to say
That I would hide within those fields
With you there by my side?

### *Ki No Tsurayuki, "To us remote observers"*

To us remote observers
This couple seems absorbed in speaking
Of the cherry flowers,
But deep within their heart of hearts
Still other feelings lie concealed.

### *Fujiwara Ietaka, "You are as remote"*

You are as remote
As Mount Kazuraki with its slopes
Covered by green willows,
Yet no day passes but my heart
Turns toward you in its longing.

### *Kyogoku Tamekane, "Though now I love"*

Though now I love,
Wishing to change the color of your feelings
As the drizzle tints the leaves,
You remain as obstinately indifferent
As black pines whose color nothing dyes.

## IZUMI SHIKIBU (10TH CENT.)

*Translated by Edwin A. Cranston*

Izumi Shikibu wrote during the Heian period (795–1185), the courtly era of Japanese history. During these centuries, Japanese court society reached its full flowering. Two characteristics of this age are the emergence of a vernacular literature (in contrast to more formal works written in Chinese) and the predominance of women writers, such as Izumi Shikibu, in that vernacular tradition. While men continued to use the elite language of China, the ladies of the court created a new literary standard for Japan.

Coming from the middle ranks of court society, these women developed several important literary genres: novels, poetry, and memoirs. Murasaki Shikibu's *The Tale of Genji* (see the next section) is often called the world's first novel and, equally, often considered to be the greatest piece of Japanese prose fiction. These women were all highly accomplished in poetry as well; their verses can be found in the anthologies of the age. Ono no Komachi (see the previous section on Japanese court poetry) was recognized as one of the Six Poetic Geniuses of Heian Japan. Perhaps the most extensive genre developed by these court ladies, however, was the diary or memoir.

Although there are many such memoirs, the narrative we have included here, taken from *The Diary of Lady Izumi Shikibu,* presents a particularly vivid glimpse of the sort of love affair that was central to Japanese court life. A poet and writer of distinction, Izumi Shikibu also had a reputation as a lover. She became the paramour of Prince Tametaka and, following his death, received the attention of his younger brother, Atsumichi. Surely two of the purposes of the *Diary* are to demonstrate the sincerity and depth of her love for Atsumichi and to resist being characterized as a wanton woman. Although the selection presented here is only a part of her account of the affair with Atsumichi, it tells us much about court society. From the *Diary,* we can see how tentative their affair was, partly because both lovers believed it necessary to keep the relationship secret. Pride, decorum, and elegance govern the behavior of the lovers.

We find in this chronicle many of the conventions of Japanese courtly love. The gentleman most commonly visited the woman at her quarters, although, in this case, he tries to gain firmer possession of his beloved by installing her in his own mansion. The woman, for her part, receives the gentleman at her own discretion, sometimes keeping a screen between them and sometimes allowing him to enter her chamber. The relationship is complicated both by the fact that Atsumichi already has a wife and by the fact that Izumi Shikibu apparently has other lovers (although they do not appear in the *Diary*). As the couple negotiates a difficult and uncertain passage toward greater intimacy, they communicate with a steady stream of letters and poems. In the nuance and suggestion of these poems, the couple performs an elaborate minuet that will finally bring them together. In the end (not provided here), Izumi Shikibu is installed in the prince's mansion, and his angry, jealous wife moves out.

What is perhaps of most interest, however, is not the success or failure of the affair, but rather the account of the rituals by which it is effected. Some of these will seem strange to the Western reader, such as when the lovers speak of weeping into their sleeves copiously and continuously until the sleeves actually rot. Yet this was a conventional expression of lovelorn grief. More accessible to us, and more significant, are the feelings of the lovers at each stage of their affair, feelings expressed most often in terms of the seasons and the natural settings through which the lovers move.

## *from The Diary of Lady Izumi Shikibu*

Two or three days later he stole out to see her again. But as it happened, the lady had decided to go on retreat to a certain temple, and was in the midst of her preparatory purification. And besides, his neglect showed how little interest he had in her anyway. She therefore made scant effort to talk to him, using her religious observances as an excuse for ignoring him all night.

"What a rare night I have spent!" he wrote to her the next morning:

"Never had I known
In all my life
So strange a way of love:
To meet, yet be unmet
All the night long.

It was outrageous!"

Indeed, how outrageous he must have thought her, she reflected ruefully:

"Yet she who with the dark
Forever sinks into love's longing,
Though the night come,
Can never know that sweet repose
When eyelids close, as lovers join
in sleep.

And this is no rare thing for me," she said.

The next day brought another note from him: "Will you then be leaving on your pilgrimage today? When should I expect you to return? Time will drag on more drearily than ever, I fear."

She replied:

"When the moment passes
All that has been planned must
end;
Amid the pelting rain
Tonight, though perplexed of
mind,
I would 'hang the iris root.'

Such are my intentions, but I shall not be gone long."

It was two or three days later when she returned. She received a message from the Prince: "Since I have been feeling very uneasy, I would like to go and visit you. But that miserable experience of the other night has left me too disheartened and crestfallen. It seems we are destined to drift apart. And yet, though of late,

Thinking that as time passed
Forgetfulness might come,
I let the days slip by,
Today to my exceeding love
Must I surrender.

Even you must see that my feelings are not shallow."

She replied:

"Surrender and come
To me? I see no sign of that,
And yet I wait,
Although the crawling vine sends
out
Scarcely one visiting shoot."

The Prince came in his usual secretive fashion. But as the lady had discounted any such possibility and was moreover fatigued by her devotions of the past several days, she had drowsed off to sleep, and no one heard the knocking at the gate. Since he had been listening to various rumors, the Prince thought she must be entertaining another lover, and softly stole away, returning home. The next morning she received the following note:

"As I stood waiting
At the pine-wood gate
You would not open for me,
The proof of your cold heart
Was there for me to see.

'This, then, is wretchedness.' I thought, bitterly disappointed."

Apparently he had come last night! And she had been so mindless as to be asleep! She replied:

"How could you see,
When the pine-wood gate
Was locked and barred,
Whether or not
My heart was cold?

The way you seem to have leaped to false conclusions is what is really wretched. 'Could I but show my heart—'"

Though he wanted to go to her again that night, there were those who prevented him from keeping such trysts. He had to be circumspect. In particular, he felt, it would be indiscreet of him to let his Lordship of the Center or the Heir Apparent hear of his escapade. And so a very long time went by.

The rain poured down day after dreary day, and as the lady gazed out on a world of unbroken clouds she pondered what would become of her relations with the Prince. Despite the fact that she no longer paid the slightest heed to the many gallants who pressed their attentions upon her, it seemed she had become the subject of much scandalous gossip. But she resigned herself to the thought that this was the inevitable consequence of her continued existence in society.

A message came from the Prince: "How are you surviving this tedious rain?

Nothing remarkable—
The same old rain that pelts us
Every year, you think?
These are my tears of love
Falling in a deluge all day long!"

She was pleased that he had not overlooked this opportunity to send her a seasonal poem, especially now that the rain had aroused in her thoughts of the pathos of life. She wrote:

"Your tears of yearning?
Indeed I did not know—
But only thought
This was 'the rain that knows
The sorrows of my life.'"

Turning over the slip of paper, she added:

"The rain pours down,
And time brings nought but pain:
All that I know of life;
Would that with today's deluge
The flood might rise and carry me
away.

Would there be a shore awaiting me?"

When the Prince had read this he replied immediately:

"What do you mean—
To cast your very life away?
Do you alone
Drag on from day to day
Beneath a rainy heaven?

It is a bitter world for us all."

The fifth day of the fifth month came, and still the rain did not stop. The Prince had been moved by the more than usually forlorn tone of the lady's recent reply, and the next morning, following a night of continuous torrential downpour, he sent a message: "How frightening was the sound of the rain last night!"

She replied:
"All the night long
What were the things that I
Was thinking of,
While I lay listening to the sound
Of raindrops beating on my
window?

'Sheltered though I was,' my sleeves were strangely wet."

"This woman is by no means unworthy of my regard," reflected the Prince, and responded:

"I too was anxious,
For I guessed how hard the sound
Of rain must be to bear
For one who lay alone beneath
The scant protection of her eaves."

About noon word circulated that the water in the river had risen, and a crowd of people went to take a look. The Prince was among them. "How are you feeling now?" he wrote. "I have gone off to see the flood:

The banks are all awash
With waters of the flood,
But still my heart
Is deeper,
Out of all comparison.

I wonder if you have realized that?"

She replied:

"Yet I cannot
Bank upon his coming now,
He of the flood-deep heart,
For all he talks of love
In river-metaphor.

Mere words are useless."

He would go to her, he decided, and was having his clothes perfumed with burnt incense when his old wet-nurse, Jijū, approached him.

"Where is your Highness going?" she asked. "I hear people are talking about this affair. That woman is of no such high-and-mighty rank. Anyone you wish to have serve you you should summon here as your servant. These rash excursions create a very bad impression. Besides, her place is frequented by great numbers of men. Something awkward is bound to happen. All this good-for-nothing business was started by that Lieutenant what's-his-name. He's the one who led the late Prince off on *his* escapades, too. Can any good come from going about in the dead of night? The person who accompanies you on your excursions may speak to his Lordship. In this world one can never tell what may happen from one day to the next, so changeable it seems. His Lordship has something in mind, you may be sure. I feel it would be best for you to leave off these excursions until you have made certain which way the wind is blowing."

"And just where am I supposed to be going?" replied the Prince. "Since I have been feeling bored, I thought I would seek a little momentary diversion, that is all. It is nothing for people to make such a great fuss about."

The lady was strangely cold to him, no doubt of that, yet she was by no means a waste of time. Perhaps he should call her and settle her close at hand. But that would give rise to still viler gossip. With his mind in such a tangle, he let their relationship drift off into uncertainty.

At long last he went to her. "Please do not attribute it to negligence on my part," he said earnestly, "that due to no intention of mine our relations should have become so exasperatingly uncertain. I think the fault lies with you. When I heard how many gentlemen there were who found my visits to you inconvenient, I was pained; and while I hesitated out of general principle, time simply went by. Come now, just for tonight. There is a place where no one will see. We can talk to our hearts' content."

He had the carriage drawn up and urgently pressed her to get in, until, hardly aware of what she was doing, she complied. She went obsessed by the thought that someone was sure to hear, but as the night was far advanced no one knew that she had gone.

Softly they drew up beside a deserted gallery, where the Prince alighted. "Come!" he urged, but the moon was very bright, and when she too stepped down it was with obvious distaste.

"You see, not a soul about!" he said. "From now on let us meet in this fashion. It makes me feel constrained to think, 'Tonight perhaps someone is with her.'"

He talked with her tenderly until, at dawn, he had the carriage drawn up and placed her in it. "I really should accompany you," he said, "but it would be light by the time I got back, and I should find it disagreeable if people were to think I had spent the night out." And so he remained behind.

All the way home the lady wondered what people were going to think of so strange an escapade. Recalling how extraordinarily touching a figure he had presented in the early light of dawn, she wrote:

"Even if it means
I have to turn you back each
 night,
Still I must find
A way to save you from this pain
Of rising with the dawn.

It was more than I could bear."

He replied:

"The pangs of rising,
Parting in the dewy morn,
Though keenly felt,
Yet seem as nothing to the pain
Of blankly going home by night.

I refuse to listen to such ideas; since your home is in a forbidden direction tonight, I shall pick you up and bring you here."

"What a scandalous spectacle!" she thought. "If he should make a habit of this—" But he came, in his usual carriage.

"Quickly! Quickly!" he hastened her as he drew up beside the house.

"Oh, how really unbecoming a performance this is," she thought again and again as she crept out and into the carriage. They talked together at the same place as the night before. The Prince's consort thought he had gone to visit his father, the Retired Sovereign.

The dawn came. "'Cruel is the cock's cry,'" quoted the Prince, and softly climbed into the carriage. As they rode along he said, "On such occasions we really must arrange things this way."

"How can we make a practice of it?" she demurred.

He escorted her home and returned, and shortly afterward his message arrived: "I hated the cock whose crowing startled us out of our sleep this morning and have killed it." The note was attached to a cock's feather. With it was the poem:

"Killed, but still
I am not satisfied!
That wretched rooster
With its ill-timed
Cry this morning!"

She replied:

"I am the one
Who has been most offended,
Morn after morn,
By the cruel crowing of that cock
I have been forced to hear.

Has it not indeed been hateful to me!"

Two or three days went by, and then there came a night when the moon shone with extraordinary brilliance. The Prince sat gazing at it from his veranda. "How is it with you?" he wrote. "Are you too looking at the moon?

Do such thoughts
Come to you as now to me,
Pretending that my heart
Sighs for the moon which soon
must set
Behind the mountain ridge?"

Not only was she unusually charmed by these sentiments, but the message arrived just when her own memories had been aroused, and she was wondering whether someone might not have seen her in the bright moonlight that night at the Prince's mansion. She replied:

"When I consider how we saw
This self-same moon that night,
Gaze though I may,
My heart is still bemused,
My eyes absorbed in vacancy."

She was still gazing alone when the night drew futilely to its close. He did come the following night, but no one heard him. Different people occupied the various parts of the house, and when the Prince spied the carriage of someone who had come to visit one of the other wings he concluded that his lady was receiving a visitor. He was not happy about the situation, but even so, as he had no intention of breaking off with her, he sent a message: "Perhaps you didn't hear that I came last night? It cuts me to the quick to think you didn't even know:

Though I had seen before
The waves were high
Upon Pine Mountain,
Today in this long rain
I stare incredulous."

The rain was falling indeed. What a strange, upsetting turn of events! Could he have been listening to someone's gossip? She wrote back:

"You are the one whose fickleness,
As I have heard it told,
Brings waves o'er Sue's pines;
Who can compare with you
In breaking seas across that
mountaintop?"

The Prince remained depressed by what he had seen the other night, and for a long time made no contact with her. Finally he wrote:

"I think you an unfeeling wretch,
And then again my heart's desire,
And this and that and thus and so,
Till my poor brain, for turning
about,
Can find no time to rest."

It was not that she had no answer, but she was loath that he should think she was making some excuse. She sent:

"No matter what befalls,
Even if we can never meet again,
I shall not grieve:
One thing only I cannot bear:
Unending bitterness."

And so they grew even more distant. One night of brilliant moonlight the lady reclined, her gaze held by the scene before her. "How enviously limpid—": the words rose to her lips. She wrote to the Prince:

"Though you do not come,
Please let me hear from you at least;
Whom would you have me tell
Of how I gaze upon the moon
Here in my desolate dwelling?"

She entrusted the poem to a young chambermaid, telling her to hand it to the Guards lieutenant. The Prince was conversing with several people he had summoned into his presence; after they withdrew, the lieutenant brought him the poem.

"Prepare the carriage as usual," said the Prince, and took his departure.

The lady was still gazing at the moon from her veranda, but as soon as she observed someone come into the grounds she lowered the blind and sat behind it. Again she saw the familiar figure which yet never failed to delight her eyes afresh, and whose charm she found only enhanced by a soft, informal costume which had been worn until not a trace of stiffness remained.

"Since your messenger returned without this—" Without another word he placed a note on his fan and had it handed in to her. As the distance between them was too great for her to speak to him easily, she simply reached out and took the message on her own fan.

The Prince decided he too would go up onto the veranda. Walking about among the delightful plants in the garden, he murmured the familiar line, "My love, like dew upon the grass—" It was enchanting.

"I shall not stay the night this time," he said, coming closer. "Actually, I came to discover who it is that you have been secretly meeting. Since I have announced that tomorrow I am to be in seclusion, I think it would look odd if I were not at home."

And with that he started to go.

But she:

"If only it would rain!
For then perhaps the moon,
Which passes by my house,
Sailing the sky, might stay
And shed its light within."

He was touched by her childlike sincerity, which was quite beyond anything for which people gave her credit. "My love!" he exclaimed, and went up into the house for a few moments. As he departed he answered:

"Loath though I am to go,
Drawn by the cloud-dwelling
moon,
My outward form indeed departs,
But not my heart:
How should it go from you?"

After he left she read the poem he had given her:

"You told me that it was
Because of me
You gazed upon the moon,
And I have come
To see if this is true."

What a very delightful person he was after all! If only she could somehow correct the quite grotesque impression of her he had picked up from current gossip—

The Prince too felt that the situation was by no means hopeless: she would serve to lighten the tedium of his days. But soon fresh rumors came: "They say that a certain Minamoto captain has been paying court to her lately. I hear he goes to her even during the day." Or again: "Did you know that the Civil Affairs Minister has been favoring her, too?" Such stories were on everyone's lips. He could only conclude that she was inordinately fickle, and for a long time there were no messages from him.

The Prince's page came one day, and being on familiar terms with the lady's chambermaid, fell to chattering with her about this and that.

"Did you bring a message?" asked the maid.

"No," replied the page. "One night my master came and found a carriage at your mistress' gate. I think that must be the reason why he doesn't write. It seems he has heard that other men are visiting this house."

After the boy left, the maid reported what he had said.

It was a long time now, the lady reflected, since she had last exchanged small, intimate messages with the Prince. And she had certainly never made any particular demands upon him. It was true of course that on those rare occasions when he did remember her she was inspired with hope that their relationship might continue unbroken. But that was out of the question now that this contemptible gossip had led him to think of her in the way he did. Why had it come to this? she sighed despondently. And then a message came.

"What with the suffering caused by the strange disorder which has seized upon me of late, I have been quite unable to write. I have gone to see you more than once recently, but it seems my visits were rather poorly timed, for I have always had to turn around and come back. I feel completely humiliated:

> Peace, peace, so let it be,
> I shall no longer in my sore
>     offense
> Go down to the rocky strand
> And watch the fisher's boat row
>     out,
> Leaving me forsaken by the
>     shore."

He had been listening to really unspeakable rumors, and she felt ashamed to say anything to him at all. Just this once, however, she would reply:

> "I am indeed that fisher girl
> Whose task it is to burn
> The salt on Sode's shore,
> But all I do is wet my briny sleeves,
> Now that my boat has drifted far
>     away."

While they were exchanging such messages the seventh month arrived. On the seventh day the lady received from amorous gentlemen many verses written on the theme of the Weaving Maid and the Herdsman, but she did not give them so much as a glance. The Prince had always written to her without fail on such special occasions as this, she reflected, but now he seemed to have forgotten all about her. But just at that moment a note arrived. It consisted simply of this:

> "How could I know—
> That I myself
> Would be the Weaving Maid
> And look with longing gaze
> Across the Riverbed of Heaven?"

Feeling a glow of pleasure that after all he had not let the occasion slip by, she replied:

> "I cannot even look
> Upon that sky towards which you
>     gaze,
> When I consider how
> I am but such as you do loathe
> And shun at Tanabata time."

After all, he could not bring himself to give her up, the Prince realized as he read her poem.

Toward the end of the month he wrote to her. "We have become very distant with each other. Why do you not send me a note from time to time? I feel as if I meant nothing to you at all."

She replied:

"Since nothing breaks your sleep,
I think you do not hear
The wind beckoning among the reeds;
And yet does it not blow,
Night after autumn night?"

Immediately the Prince responded: "I do not 'waken at night,' my love? True, for I never go to sleep! Remember what the poem says—'When I am filled with longing—' Please do not accuse me of indifference:

If it is true the wind
Blows beckoning among the reeds,
Sleeplessly henceforth
I'll listen for your wakeful message,
Expecting to be startled from my bed."

At dusk about two days later a carriage suddenly pulled into the lady's grounds, and the Prince alighted. She was extremely embarrassed, for as yet he had never seen her; but there was no help for it. He left after some rather inconsequential conversation.

After that so many days went by without word that she became very uneasy:

"As darkly, darkly,
Filled with anxious thoughts,
The autumn days slip by,
I've come to know it well,
That questionable heart of yours.

But," she added, "'truly it is hard for man to turn his back upon the world.'"

The Prince replied, "Though of late our relations have drifted off into uncertainty, even so,

However it may be with you,
I at least have not forgotten,
Though the days slip by,
How you and I did meet
One autumn evening."

It made her feel miserable to realize that the only consolations her relationship with the Prince provided came in such wretched, fugitive, undependable trivia as this.

* * *

It was past the twentieth of the ninth month when late one night the Prince was awakened by the shining of the dawn moon. What a terribly long time it had been, he mused, and wondered, touched by the thought, whether she too might not be looking at this same moon. Surely she must, but what if someone were with her? Despite his misgivings on this score he set out, accompanied only by his usual page.

The lady was lying awake, thinking of many things, when she heard the knocking at the gate. Perhaps because the season had infected her with an autumnal melancholy, everything of late seemed more than usually touching in its sadness, and now she was lost in vacant revery. Strange! Who could it be, she wondered and awakened the servant who was sleeping nearby to go and inquire. But the girl was in no hurry to get up, and when at long last she was pulled from under the covers, she went off to wake up a manservant who would not be roused either. The latter, when he was finally made to get up, banged about in the dark and bumped into so many things that by the time he reached the gate the knocking had stopped. Whoever it was apparently had gone home, no doubt thinking she was fairly drugged with sleep, lying there without a care in the world. Who could it be, this person who was kept awake by the same thoughts as hers?

The manservant, whom the maid had finally roused, came back grumbling. "Nobody there. Never let a man get any rest, the ladies in this house. Think they hear something and send a fellow off to stumble around in the middle of the night." And he went back to sleep.

The lady however did not sleep but stayed up until at length the night was over. She gazed at the sky, which was obscured by a dense mist, until it grew light and then set about composing an account of all that she had felt on being awake to see the breaking of the dawn. While she was busy writing, a message came. It consisted simply of this:

> "I went home empty-handed,
> For I could not linger there
> And wait the setting of the moon
> That shines still in the sky at dawn
> After the long autumnal night."

Indeed, how keenly disappointed he must have been! But at least he had not forgotten her—that was what mattered. She felt happy at the thought that he too had been looking at that spectacle of sky, so moving in its beauty, and she immediately folded and sent him the composition which she had been writing more or less as an exercise.

He read:

"The sound of the wind: The tempest blew so hard it seemed not a leaf could be left on any tree, making me more than ever aware of life's fleeting sadness. The storm clouds lowered, but a mere sprinkle of rain fell. I was unbearably moved:

> Before the autumn ends
> My sleeves must rot away,
> Mouldered by my tears;
> And when the sure, cold rains
> Of winter come, whose shall I
> borrow?

But there was none to know of my despondency. Even the grass grew pale before my eyes, and though the winter rains should still be far off, it bent in seeming pain before the wind. As I looked upon this scene I compared myself, apt to vanish at any moment like the dew, to the frail leaves of grass, and in my sadness simply lay down near the veranda without making the effort to go into the inner room. But I was quite unable to sleep, though everyone else lay in a profound slumber. There was no specific reason for my wakefulness; still, I lay there through the listless hours, completely unable to drop off and utterly out of sorts. And then there came the faint cry of a wild goose. Others may not be much affected by such things, but I was moved almost beyond my power to endure:

> Untouched by drowsiness,
> How many are the nights, alas,
> That I have lain,
> Nothing for me to do but hear
> The calling of wild geese?

Thinking that anything would be better than simply lying thus all night, I pushed open the door to the veranda. The moon had slanted down the vast sky into the west, and its light shone clearly in the distance. The voice of the bell and the crowing of the cock blended into one under the mist-veiled sky, and I felt that surely there neither had been nor could ever be another moment such as this. The very tears that fell upon my sleeves seemed tenderly, strangely new.

Not I alone—
Another surely sees,
And knows the Long Month's
Waning moon at dawn
Cannot be matched for mournful
  loveliness.

If now someone should knock at my gate, what would my feelings be? But who else would spend the night in wakefulness as I have done?

Though in another place,
Is there yet one who with a heart
The same as mine
Looks on the waning moon at
  dawn?
Of whom should I inquire?"

Just as she was wondering if she should send this composition to the Prince, his messenger had come, and she had availed herself of the opportunity of presenting it to him. He was by no means ill pleased by what he read, but decided to dash off a hasty reply in order to catch her while she was still in her pensive mood.

His message was brought to her where she sat gazing off into the distance; she felt somehow disappointed as she opened it:

"Before the autumn's end
My sleeves have rotted quite away;
And yet a certain
Person thinks of nothing
But that hers may suffer so.

Think not your life
A drop of dew
About to vanish;
Were it not better to rely upon
The long-lived chrysanthemum?

Untouched by drowsiness,
Listening to the calling of wild
  geese
That fly the cloudy vault—
If you have found no other thing
  to do,
Your own heart bears the blame.

Not I alone—
Another gazed with rapture
On that dawning sky,
And saw the moon, and felt
The feelings that were mine.

Though in another place,
I thought that you at least
Were looking at the moon,
And went to you this morning—
What a fool I was!

The dawn would not break and the gate would not open—it was too much."

Despite these complaints she was glad that she had written to him.

Toward the end of the month a message came. After apologizing for his long silence the Prince went on, "You may think it a bit odd, but I have a request to make of you. It seems that a certain person whom I have been seeing for quite a long time is going off to a distant place, and I would like to say something to her that she would consider touching. The poems you send me are more touching than any others I have known. Please write one for me now."

"What complacency!" she thought. But still, to decline would seem too impertinent. She kept her remarks brief: "As to this kind request of yours, how can I presume—?

> Pray leave behind at least your
>     image,
> Mirrored in my regretful tears,
> Though, wearied of my love,
> You go away with dying autumn,
> Ignorant of my heart.

To pour my emotion into this poem cost me dearer than you know." On the margin she added, "And yet:

> Leaving you behind,
> Where can she think to go,
> When even I,
> Lovesick in a world of pain,
> Can clench my teeth and live?"

"I should say your poem is perfect," the Prince replied, "though critical opinions sound a bit conceited coming from me. But aren't you carrying it a little too far with this 'lovesick in a world of pain'?

> She who has abandoned me
> To journey far away—
> Let her go where she will,
> I do not care, as long as you
> Hold me without rival in your
>     heart.

That is all I ask."

Thus the tenth month arrived. About the tenth day of the month he came to visit her. The inner part of the house being dark and eerie, he lay with her near the veranda and spoke of all the touching sadness of this life. The lady could not fail to be moved. Again and again the moon was obscured by clouds, and a light rain fell. It seemed a night deliberately designed to touch the deepest chords of emotion. The lady's heart was a tangled skein, and she shuddered with the cold. When the Prince looked at her he thought strange indeed those reports of her devious behavior. The very sight of her trembling by his side gave them the lie. Moved to tenderness, he roused her from the jumble of painful thoughts in which she lay as if asleep:

> "Tonight we sleep
> Untouched by dew or wintry rain,
> Yet strangely are they wet,
> These sleeves of mine
> Whereon my head lies pillowed."

But the lady said nothing, for she did not feel capable of a reply, being submerged in a myriad inextricable thoughts. When the Prince saw her tears falling silently in the moonlight, his heart went out to her, and he said, "Why do you not compose a reply? I see my worthless poem has displeased you. I am sorry."

"I feel somehow too distraught," she replied. "It is not that I ignored your poem. Wait and see," she said as if to jest, "if I ever forget your 'pillow-sleeves.'"

Perhaps it was the tenor of her talk—she *did* seem utterly without a friend to whom she could turn for support. The next morning, troubled by these thoughts which colored his recollection of that sweetly sad nocturnal scene, the Prince wrote to ask how she was feeling.

She replied:

> "Within a morning's space
> They must have dried—
> Those pillow-sleeves
> So slightly dampened when we lay
> In sleep that seemed a momentary
>     dream."

He recalled with amusement her promise not to forget:

"Although they may have seemed
The figment of a dream—
My drenching tears—
It has been quite impossible
To dry those pillow-sleeves."

Thereafter the Prince made frequent visits, for apparently his heart had been moved by that touching scene under the night sky, so that he now felt a deep and pained concern for her. The more he studied her, the more he realized that she had never been hardened by the world. He was distressed at the way in which she seemed to be merely floating uncertainly on the surface of life and spoke to her from the depths of his sympathy.

## MURASAKI SHIKIBU (C. 978–1030)

*Translated by Edward G. Seidensticker*

*The Tale of Genji,* often considered the world's first novel, was written by Murasaki Shikibu, a Japanese court lady, in the first decade of the eleventh century CE. An immensely long work, the novel covers the reigns of four emperors and three generations of courtiers and ladies over a period of seventy-five years. *The Tale of Genji* has been characterized as a Buddhist sermon on the emptiness of life, a political novel detailing the intrigues at the imperial court, a psychological novel probing the actions and motives of many of its hundreds of characters, and a romance that repeats the story of an illustrious prince who finds and elevates a woman of low birth or means. Incorporating vast quantities of original poetry and poetic allusion, it also has been regarded as a primer on poetics. It describes excessive romantic love—the triumph of emotion over reason—but also the destructive consequences of that excess. And finally, through its central character, Prince Genji, the tale presents an ideal of courtliness in all its aspects.

In the millennium since it was written, *The Tale of Genji* has been a wellspring of Japanese art, providing the basis for many of the Nō plays, a source for poetry, and an object of satire and parody. In its many versions, revisions, translations, and interpretations, it has formed a core around which Japanese literature has developed through the ages.

The opening chapter of *The Tale of Genji* is a remarkable piece of literary architecture, setting out many of the major themes that are developed throughout the rest of the novel. Foremost is the notion of the danger of excessive emotion, in this case, the emperor's love for Lady Kiritsubo. The parallel with the Chinese example of Yang Kuei-fei is made explicit in a way that links the two major strands of the novel (i.e., political and amorous competition at court). The author also makes clear her pervasive sense of irony, which reflects the Buddhist idea that nothing is what it appears to be. The destructive power of jealousy and resentment is another theme established in this first chapter that reverberates throughout the book. Because of his extraordinary talents and refinement, Genji makes people around him uneasy; his accomplishments are frightening, and his success leads to disaster. A paradoxical Korean prophecy, confirmed by Japanese and Indian fortune-telling methods, announces that for Genji to fulfill his destiny will lead to disorder, but to deny it will also result in chaos. Genji's stunning grace and intelligence in a disordered and imperfect world cause further disarray.

One prominent theme linking many parts of the story is the inevitable sadness of parting and separation. Sadness, in fact, is strongly linked to that refined "sensitivity to things" (*mono no aware*) that characterizes Heian court literature. The transience of all things and the painful separation from those we love most are key motifs in *Genji.* The opening chapter also sets up the theme of Genji's search for his mother. He marries a beautiful and cultivated woman; that marriage is favorable politically, but he rejects this wife in favor of his stepmother, a conquest that proves disastrous in its success.

In the second chapter (not included here), Genji and his male friends discuss love at great length; Genji then gets to test some of his new wisdom. He seduces (a modern reader might say rapes) the wife of a local governor and finds to his astonishment that she would rather not continue the affair, even if he is the "shining Genji." Then in Chapter 3, he mistakenly seduces the lady's daughter, an awkward blunder. His ego wounded by these first affairs, in Chapter 4 Genji launches another. This one is shocking: first of all for his choice of a lover, then for the astonishing and terrible outcome. The experience will deepen him considerably. In this chapter, the reader can observe in slow motion the strange but moving etiquette of a love affair in Heian Japan—strange to us, at least, in that the lovers may never see each other's faces or even know each other's names. It is certainly a world away from the love of Abelard and Heloise (pp. 1226–1244); however, Marie de France, a court lady and their near-contemporary in France, knows conventions of love almost as elaborate, and her *Yonec* (pp. 1279–1291) can seem just as strange as *Genji* to modern eyes.

# The Tale of Genji

Japanese texts from the courtly period pose a particular problem for the translator because poetry is incorporated as an integral part of the narrative. In the passage shown here, the emperor's consort, on her deathbed, recites a final poem of farewell. Helen Craig McCullough sets the verse apart from the prose text, identifies it as a poem, and includes a transliteration of the Japanese, attempting to capture in English the five distinct measures of the original poem. Edward Seidensticker sets the poem apart from the prose but renders the poem in two sentences. Arthur Waley chooses to incorporate the poem completely into the prose narrative, reducing it to a single prose statement. While Waley's integration comes closest to how prose and poetry are actually mingled in the Japanese original, the reader of English may not realize that a poem has been uttered. McCullough, on the other hand, gives the poem a prominence it does not have in the original text.

## Helen Craig McCullough

The emperor was frantic with anxiety. He issued orders for her departure in a hand drawn carriage, but then he went to her room, and again could not bring himself to let her go. "Didn't we promise to stay together always, even on the road to death? I know you're sick, but I don't see how you can abandon me and go your own way," he said.

She gazed at him with infinite sadness. [Her poem:]

| | |
|---|---|
| kagiri tote | Grieved beyond measure |
| wakaruru michi no | to say farewell and set forth |
| kanashiki ni | on this last journey, |
| ikamahoshiki wa | gladly would I choose instead |
| inochi narikeri | the road of the living. |

"If I had dreamed this would happen . . ." She gasped for breath. She seemed to want to say something more, but she was shockingly ill and weak.

## Edward Seidensticker

Wanting somehow to help, the emperor ordered that she be given the honor of a hand-drawn carriage. He returned to her apartments and still could not bring himself to the final parting.

"We vowed that we would go together down the road we all must go. You must not leave me behind."

She looked sadly up at him. "If I had suspected that it would be so—" She was gasping for breath.

"I leave you, to go the road we all must go.
The road I would choose, if only I could, is the other."

It was evident that she would have liked to say more; but she was so weak that it had been a struggle to say even this much.

## Arthur Waley

Seeing her thus he knew not what to do. In great trouble and perplexity he sent for a hand litter. But when they would have laid her on it, he forbad them, saying 'There was an oath between us that neither would go alone upon the road that all at last must tread. How can I now let her go from me?' The lady heard him and 'At last!' she said; 'Though that desired *at last* be come, because I go alone how gladly would I live!'

Thus with faint voice and failing breath she whispered. But though she had found strength to speak, each word was uttered with great toil and pain.

## The Tale of Genji

### Ch. 1: The Paulownia Court

In a certain reign there was a lady not of the first rank whom the emperor loved more than any of the others. The grand ladies with high ambitions thought her a presumptuous upstart, and lesser ladies were still more resentful. Everything she did offended someone. Probably aware of what was happening, she fell seriously ill and came to spend more time at home than at court. The emperor's pity and affection quite passed bounds. No longer caring what his ladies and courtiers might say, he behaved as if intent upon stirring gossip.

His court looked with very great misgiving upon what seemed a reckless infatuation. In China just such an unreasoning passion had been the undoing of an emperor and had spread turmoil through the land. As the resentment grew, the example of Yang Kuei-fei was the one most frequently cited against the lady.

She survived despite her troubles, with the help of an unprecedented bounty of love. Her father, a grand councillor, was no longer living. Her mother, an old-fashioned lady of good lineage, was determined that matters be no different for her than for ladies who with paternal support were making careers at court. The mother was attentive to the smallest detail of etiquette and deportment. Yet there was a limit to what she could do. The sad fact was that the girl was without strong backing, and each time a new incident arose she was next to defenseless.

It may have been because of a bond in a former life that she bore the emperor a beautiful son, a jewel beyond compare. The emperor was in a fever of impatience to see the child, still with the mother's family; and when, on the earliest day possible, he was brought to court, he did indeed prove to be a most marvelous babe. The emperor's eldest son was the grandson of the Minister of the Right. The world assumed that with this powerful support he would one day be named crown prince; but the new child was far more beautiful. On public occasions the emperor continued to favor his eldest son. The new child was a private treasure, so to speak, on which to lavish uninhibited affection.

The mother was not of such a low rank as to attend upon the emperor's personal needs. In the general view she belonged to the upper classes. He insisted on having her always beside him, however, and on nights when there was music or other entertainment he would require that she be present. Sometimes the two of them would sleep late, and even after they had risen he would not let her go. Because of his unreasonable demands she was widely held to have fallen into immoderate habits out of keeping with her rank.

With the birth of the son, it became yet clearer that she was the emperor's favorite. The mother of the eldest son began to feel uneasy. If she did not manage carefully, she might see the new son designated crown prince. She had come to court before the emperor's other ladies, she had once been favored over the others, and she had borne several of his children. However much her complaining might trouble and annoy him, she was one lady whom he could not ignore.

Though the mother of the new son had the emperor's love, her detractors were numerous and alert to the slightest inadvertency. She was in continuous torment, feeling that she had nowhere to turn. She lived in the Paulownia Court. The emperor had to pass the apartments of other ladies to reach hers, and it must be admitted that their resentment at his constant comings and goings was not unreasonable. Her visits to the royal chambers were equally frequent. The robes of her women were in a scandalous state from trash strewn along bridges and galleries. Once some women conspired to have both doors of a gallery she must pass bolted shut, and so she found herself unable to advance or retreat. Her anguish over the mounting list of insults was presently more than the emperor could bear. He moved a lady out of rooms adjacent to his own and assigned them to the lady of the Paulownia Court and so, of course, aroused new resentment.

When the young prince reached the age of three, the resources of the treasury and the stewards' offices were exhausted to make the ceremonial bestowing of trousers as elaborate as that for the eldest son. Once more there was malicious talk; but the prince himself, as he grew up, was so superior of mien and disposition that few could find it in themselves to dislike him. Among the more discriminating, indeed, were some who marveled that such a paragon had been born into this world.

In the summer the boy's mother, feeling vaguely unwell, asked that she be allowed to go home. The emperor would not hear of it. Since they were by now used to these indispositions, he begged her to stay and see what course her health would take. It was steadily worse, and then, suddenly, everyone could see that she was failing. Her mother came pleading that he let her go home. At length he agreed.

Fearing that even now she might be the victim of a gratuitous insult, she chose to go off without ceremony, leaving the boy behind. Everything must have an end, and the emperor could no longer detain her. It saddened him inexpressibly that he was not even permitted to see her off. A lady of great charm and beauty, she was sadly emaciated. She was sunk in melancholy thoughts, but when she tried to put them into words her voice was almost inaudible. The emperor was quite beside himself, his mind a confusion of things that had been and things that were to come. He wept and vowed undying love, over and over again. The lady was unable to reply. She seemed listless and drained of strength, as if she scarcely knew what was happening. Wanting somehow to help, the emperor ordered that she be given the honor of a hand-drawn carriage. He returned to her apartments and still could not bring himself to the final parting.

"We vowed that we would go together down the road we all must go. You must not leave me behind."

She looked sadly up at him. "If I had suspected that it would be so—" She was gasping for breath.

> "I leave you, to go the road we all
> must go.
> The road I would choose, if only I
> could, is the other."

It was evident that she would have liked to say more; but she was so weak that it had been a struggle to say even this much.

The emperor was wondering again if he might not keep her with him and have her with him to the end.

But a message came from her mother, asking that she hurry. "We have obtained the agreement of eminent ascetics to conduct the necessary services, and I fear that they are to begin this evening."

So, in desolation, he let her go. He passed a sleepless night.

He sent off a messenger and was beside himself with impatience and apprehension even before there had been time for the man to reach the lady's house and return. The man arrived to find the house echoing with laments. She had died at shortly past midnight. He returned sadly to the palace. The emperor closed himself up in his private apartments. He would have liked at least to keep the boy with him, but no precedent could be found for having him away from his mother's house through the mourning. The boy looked in bewilderment at the weeping courtiers, at his father too, the tears streaming over his face. The death of a parent is sad under any circumstances, and this one was indescribably sad.

But there must be an end to weeping, and orders were given for the funeral. If only she could rise to the heavens with the smoke from the pyre, said the mother between her sobs. She rode in the hearse with several attendants, and what must her feelings have been when they reached Mount Otaki? It was there that the services were conducted with the utmost solemnity and dignity.

She looked down at the body. "With her before me, I cannot persuade myself that she is dead. At the sight of her ashes I can perhaps accept what has happened."

The words were rational enough, but she was so distraught that she seemed about to fall from the carriage. The women had known that it would be so and did what they could for her.

A messenger came from the palace with the news that the lady had been raised to the Third Rank, and presently a nunciary arrived to read the official order. For the emperor, the regret was scarcely bearable that he had not had the courage of his resolve to appoint her an imperial consort, and he wished to make amends by promoting her one rank. There were many who resented even this favor. Others, however, of a more sensitive nature, saw more than ever what a dear lady she had been, simple and gentle and difficult to find fault with. It was because she had been excessively favored by the emperor that she had been the victim of so such malice. The attendant ladies were now reminded of how sympathetic and unassuming she had been. It was for just such an occasion, they remarked to one another, that the phrase "how well one knows" had been invented.

The days went dully by. The emperor was careful to send offerings for the weekly memorial services. His grief was unabated and he spent his nights in tears, refusing to summon his other ladies. His serving women were plunged into dew-drenched autumn.

There was one lady, however, who refused to be placated. "How ridiculous," said the lady of the Kokiden Pavilion, mother of his eldest son, "that the infatuation should continue even now."

The emperor's thoughts were on his youngest son even when he was with his eldest. He sent off intelligent nurses and serving women to the house of the boy's grandmother, where he was still in residence, and made constant inquiry after him.

The autumn tempests blew and suddenly the evenings were chilly. Lost in his grief, the emperor sent off a note to the grandmother. His messenger was a woman of middle rank called Myōbu, whose father was a guards officer. It was on a beautiful moonlit night that he dispatched her, a night that brought memories. On such nights he and the dead lady had played the koto for each other. Her koto had somehow had overtones lacking in other instruments, and when she would interrupt the music to speak, the words too carried echoes of their own. Her face, her manner—they seemed to cling to him, but with "no more substance than the lucent dream."

Myōbu reached the grandmother's house. Her carriage was drawn through the gate—and what a lonely place it was! The old lady had of course lived in widowed retirement, but, not wishing to distress her only daughter, she had managed to keep the place in repair. Now all was plunged into darkness. The weeds grew ever higher and the autumn winds tore threateningly at the garden. Only the rays of the moon managed to make their way through the tangles.

The carriage was pulled up and Myōbu alighted.

The grandmother was at first unable to speak. "It has been a trial for me to go on living, and now to have one such as you come through the dews of this wild garden—I cannot tell you how much it shames me."

"A lady who visited your house the other day told us that she had to see with her own eyes before she could really understand your loneliness and sorrow. I am not at all a sensitive person, and yet I am unable to control these tears."

After a pause she delivered a message from the emperor. "He has said that for a time it all seemed as if he were wandering in a nightmare, and then when his agitation subsided he came to see that the nightmare would not end. If only he had a companion in his grief, he thought—and it occurred to him that you, my lady, might be persuaded to come unobtrusively to court. He cannot bear to think of the child languishing in this house of tears, and hopes that you will come quickly and bring him with you. He was more than once interrupted by sobs as he spoke, and it was apparent to all of us that he feared having us think him inexcusably weak. I came away without hearing him to the end."

"I cannot see for tears," said the old lady. "Let these sublime words bring me light."

This was the emperor's letter: "It seems impossibly cruel that although I had hoped for comfort with the passage of time my grief should only be worse. I am particularly grieved that I do not have the boy with me, to watch him grow and mature. Will you not bring him to me? We shall think of him as a memento."

There could be no doubting the sincerity of the royal petition. A poem was appended to the letter, but when she had come to it the old lady was no longer able to see through her tears.

"At the sound of the wind,
bringing dews to Miyagi
Plain, I think of the tender *hagi*
upon the moor."

"Tell His Majesty," said the grandmother after a time, "that it has been a great trial for me to live so long. 'Ashamed before the Takasago pines' I think that it is not for me to be seen at court. Even if the august invitation is repeated, I shall not find it possible to accept. As for the boy I do not know what his wishes are. The indications are that he is eager to go. It is sad for me, but as it should be. Please tell His Majesty of these thoughts, secret until now. I fear that I bear a curse from a previous existence and that it would be wrong and even terrible to keep the child with me."

"It would have given me great pleasure to look in upon him," said Myōbu, getting up to leave. The child was asleep. "I should have liked to report to his royal father. But he will be waiting up for me, and it must be very late."

"May I not ask you to come in private from time to time? The heart of a bereaved parent may not be darkness, perhaps, but a quiet talk from time to time would do much to bring light. You have done honor to the house on so many happy occasions, and now circumstances have required that you come with a sad message. I have lived too long a life. All of our hopes were on the girl, I must say again, from the day she was born, and until he died her father did not let me forget that she must go to court, that his own death, if it came early, should not deter me. I knew that another sort of life would be happier for a girl without strong backing, but I could not forget his wishes and sent her to court as I had promised. Blessed with favors beyond her station, she was the object of insults such as no one can be asked to endure. Yet endure them she did until finally the strain and the resentment were too much for her. And so, as I look back upon then, I know that those favors should never have been. Well, put these down, if you will, as the mad wanderings of a heart that is darkness." She was unable to go on.

It was late.

"His Majesty says much the same thing," replied Myōbu. "It was, he says, an intensity of passion such as to startle the world, and perhaps for that very reason it was fated to be brief. He cannot think of anything he has done to arouse such resentment, he says, and so he must live with resentment which seems without proper cause. Alone and utterly desolate, he finds it impossible to face the world. He fears that he must seem dreadfully eccentric. How very great—he has said it over and over again—are the burdens we bring from other lives. One scarcely ever sees him that he is not weeping." Myōbu too was in tears. "It is very late. I must get back before the night is quite over and tell him what I have seen."

The moon was sinking over the hills, the air was crystal clear, the wind was cool, and the songs of the insects among the autumn grasses would by themselves have brought tears. It was a scene from which Myōbu could not easily pull herself.

> "The autumn night is too short to
>   contain my tears
> Though songs of bell cricket
>   weary, fall into silence."

This was her farewell poem. Still she hesitated, on the point of getting into her carriage.

The old lady sent a reply:

> "Sad are the insect songs among
>   the reeds.
> More sadly yet falls the dew from
>   above the clouds.

"I seem to be in a complaining mood."

Though gifts would have been out of place, she sent as a trifling memento of her daughter a set of robes, left for just such an occasion, and with them an assortment of bodkins and combs.

The young women who had come from court with the little prince still mourned their lady, but those of them who had acquired a taste for court life yearned to be back. The memory of the emperor made them join their own to the royal petitions.

But no—a crone like herself would repel all the fine ladies and gentlemen, said the grandmother, while on the other hand she could not bear the thought of having the child out of her sight for even a moment.

Myōbu was much moved to find the emperor waiting up for her. Making it seem that his attention was on the small and beautifully planted garden before him, now in full autumn bloom, he was talking quietly with four or five women, among the most sensitive of his attendants. He had become addicted to illustrations by the emperor Uda for "The Song of Everlasting Sorrow" and to poems by Ise and Tsurayuki on that subject, and to Chinese poems as well.

He listened attentively as Myōbu described the scene she had found so affecting. He took up the letter she had brought from the grandmother.

"I am so awed by this august message that I would run away and hide; and so violent are the emotions it gives rise to that I scarcely know what to say.

> "The tree that gave them shelter
> has withered and died.
> One fears for the plight of the
> *hagi* shoots beneath."

A strange way to put the matter, thought the emperor; but the lady must still be dazed with grief. He chose to overlook the suggestion that he himself could not help the child.

He sought to hide his sorrow, not wanting these women to see him in such poor control of himself. But it was no use. He reviewed his memories over and over again, from his very earliest days with the dead lady. He had scarcely been able to bear a moment away from her while she lived. How strange that he had been able to survive the days and months since on memories alone. He had hoped to reward the grandmother's sturdy devotion, and his hopes had come to nothing.

"Well," he sighed, "she may look forward to having her day, if she will only live to see the boy grow up."

Looking at the keepsakes Myōbu had brought back, he thought what a comfort it would be if some wizard were to bring him, like that Chinese emperor, a comb from the world where his lost love was dwelling. He whispered:

> "And will no wizard search her out
> for me,
> That even he may tell me where
> she is?"

There are limits to the powers of the most gifted artist. The Chinese lady in the paintings did not have the luster of life. Yang Kuei-fei was said to have resembled the lotus of the Sublime Pond, the willows of the Timeless Hall. No doubt she was very beautiful in her Chinese finery. When he tried to remember the quiet charm of his lost lady, he found that there was no color of flower, no song of bird, to summon her up. Morning and night, over and over again, they had repeated to each other the lines from "The Song of Everlasting Sorrow":

"In the sky, as birds that share a
wing.
On earth, as trees that share a
branch."

It had been their vow, and the shortness of her life had made it an empty dream.

Everything, the moaning of the wind, the humming of autumn insects, added to the sadness. But in the apartments of the Kokiden lady matters were different. It had been some time since she had last waited upon the emperor. The moonlight being so beautiful, she saw no reason not to have music deep into the night. The emperor muttered something about the bad taste of such a performance at such a time, and those who saw his distress agreed that it was an unnecessary injury. Kokiden was of an arrogant and intractable nature and her behavior suggested that to her the emperor's grief was of no importance.

The moon set. The wicks in the lamps had been trimmed more than once and presently the oil was gone. Still he showed no sign of retiring. His mind on the boy and the old lady, he jotted down a verse:

"Tears dim the moon, even here
above the clouds.
Dim must it be in that lodging
among the reeds."

Calls outside told him that the guard was being changed. It would be one or two in the morning. People would think his behavior strange indeed. He at length withdrew to his bedchamber. He was awake the whole night through, and in dark morning, his thoughts on the blinds that would not open, he was unable to interest himself in business of state. He scarcely touched his breakfast, and lunch seemed so remote from his inclinations that his attendants exchanged looks and whispers of alarm.

Not all voices were sympathetic. Perhaps, some said, it had all been foreordained, but he had dismissed the talk and ignored the resentment and let the affair quite pass the bounds of reason; and now to neglect his duties so—it was altogether too much. Some even cited the example of the Chinese emperor who had brought ruin upon himself and his country.

The months passed and the young prince returned to the palace. He had grown into a lad of such beauty that he hardly seemed meant for this world—and indeed one almost feared that he might only briefly be a part of it. When, the following spring, it came time to name a crown prince, the emperor wanted very much to pass over his first son in favor of the younger, who, however, had no influential maternal relatives. It did not seem likely that the designation would pass unchallenged. The boy might, like his mother, be destroyed by immoderate favors. The emperor told no one of his wishes. There did after all seem to be a limit to his affections, people said, and Kokiden regained her confidence.

The boy's grandmother was inconsolable. Finally, because her prayer to be with her daughter had been answered, perhaps, she breathed her last. Once more the emperor was desolate. The boy, now six, was old enough to know grief himself. His grandmother, who had been so good to him over the years, had more than once told him what pain it would cause her, when the time came, to leave him behind.

He now lived at court. When he was seven he went through the ceremonial reading of the Chinese classics, and never before had there been so fine a performance. Again a tremor of apprehension passed over the emperor—might it be that such a prodigy was not to be long for this world?

"No one need be angry with him now that his mother is gone." He took the boy to visit the Kokiden Pavilion. "And now most especially I hope you will be kind to him."

Admitting the boy to her inner chambers, even Kokiden was pleased. Not the sternest of warriors or the most unbending of enemies could have held back a smile. Kokiden was reluctant to let him go. She had two daughters, but neither could compare with him in beauty. The lesser ladies crowded about, not in the least ashamed to show their faces, all eager to amuse him, though aware that he set them off to disadvantage. I need not speak of his accomplishments in the compulsory subjects, the classics and the like. When it came to music his flute and koto made the heavens echo—but to recount all his virtues would, I fear, give rise to a suspicion that I distort the truth.

An embassy came from Korea. Hearing that among the emissaries was a skilled physiognomist, the emperor would have liked to summon him for consultation. He decided, however, that he must defer to the emperor Uda's injunction against receiving foreigners, and instead sent this favored son to the Kōro mansion, where the party was lodged. The boy was disguised as the son of the grand moderator, his guardian at court. The wise Korean cocked his head in astonishment.

"It is the face of one who should ascend to the highest place and be father to the nation," he said quietly, as if to himself. "But to take it for such would no doubt be to predict trouble. Yet it is not the face of the minister, the deputy, who sets about ordering public affairs."

The moderator was a man of considerable learning. There was much of interest in his exchanges with the Korean. There were also exchanges of Chinese poetry, and in one of his poems the Korean succeeded most skillfully in conveying his joy at having been able to observe such a countenance on this the eve of his return to his own land, and sorrow that the parting must come so soon. The boy offered a verse that was received with high praise. The most splendid of gifts were bestowed upon him. The wise man was in return showered with gifts from the palace.

Somehow news of the sage's remarks leaked out, though the emperor himself was careful to say nothing. The Minister of the Right, grandfather of the crown prince and father of the Kokiden lady, was quick to hear, and again his suspicions were aroused. In the wisdom of his heart, the emperor had already analyzed the boy's physiognomy after the Japanese fashion and had formed tentative plans. He had thus far refrained from bestowing imperial rank on his son, and was delighted that the Korean view should so accord with his own. Lacking the support of maternal relatives, the boy would be most insecure as a prince without court rank, and the emperor could not be sure how long his own reign would last. As a commoner he could be of great service. The emperor therefore encouraged the boy in his studies, at which he was so proficient that it seemed a waste to reduce him to common rank. And yet—as a prince he would arouse the hostility of those who had cause to fear his becoming emperor. Summoning an astrologer of the Indian school, the emperor was pleased to learn that the Indian view coincided with the Japanese and the Korean; and so he concluded that the boy should become a commoner with the name Minamoto or Genji.

The months and the years passed and still the emperor could not forget his lost love. He summoned various women who might console him, but apparently it was too much to ask in this world for one who even resembled her. He remained sunk in memories, unable to interest himself in anything. Then he was told of the Fourth Princess, daughter of a former emperor, a lady famous for her beauty and reared with the greatest care by her mother, the empress. A woman now in attendance upon the emperor had in the days of his predecessor been most friendly with the princess, then but a child, and even now saw her from time to time.

"I have been at court through three reigns now," she said, "and never had I seen anyone who genuinely resembled my lady. But now the daughter of the empress dowager is growing up, and the resemblance is most astonishing. One would be hard put to find her equal."

Hoping that she might just possibly be right, the emperor asked most courteously to have the princess sent to court. Her mother was reluctant and even fearful, however. One must remember, she said, that the mother of the crown prince was a most willful lady who had subjected the lady of the Paulownia Court to open insults and presently sent her into a fatal decline. Before she had made up her mind she followed her husband in death, and the daughter was alone. The emperor renewed his petition. He said that he would treat the girl as one of his own daughters.

Her attendants and her maternal relatives and her older brother, Prince Hyōbu, consulted together and concluded that rather than languish at home she might seek consolation at court; and so she was sent off. She was called Fujitsubo. The resemblance to the dead lady was indeed astonishing. Because she was of such high birth (it may have been that people were imagining things) she seemed even more graceful and delicate than the other. No one could despise her for inferior rank, and the emperor need not feel shy about showing his love for her. The other lady, with the backing of no one all through the court, had been the victim of a love too intense; and now, though it would be wrong to say that he had quite forgotten her, he found his affections shifting to the next lady, who was a source of boundless comfort. So it is with the affairs of this world.

Since Genji never left his father's side, it was not easy for this new lady, the recipient of so many visits, to hide herself from him. The other ladies were disinclined to think themselves her inferior, and indeed each of them had her own merits. They were all rather past their prime, however. Fujitsubo's beauty was of a younger and fresher sort. Though in her childlike shyness she made an especial effort not to be seen, Genji occasionally caught a glimpse of her face. He could not remember his own mother and it moved him deeply to learn, from the lady who had first told the emperor of Fujitsubo, that the resemblance was striking. He wanted to be near her always.

"Do not be unfriendly," said the emperor to Fujitsubo. "Sometimes it almost seems to me too that you are his mother. Do not think him forward, be kind to him. Your eyes, your expression: you are really so uncommonly like her that you could pass for his mother."

Genji's affection for the new lady grew, and the most ordinary flower or tinted leaf became the occasion for expressing it. Kokiden was not pleased. She was not on good terms with Fujitsubo, and all her old resentment at Genji came back. He was handsomer than the crown prince, her chief treasure in the world, well thought of by the whole court. People began calling Genji "the shining one." Fujitsubo, ranked beside him in the emperor's affections, became "the lady of the radiant sun."

It seemed a pity that the boy must one day leave behind his boyish attire; but when he reached the age of twelve he went through his initiation ceremonies and received the cap of an adult. Determined that the ceremony should be in no way inferior to the crown prince's, which had been held some years earlier in the Grand Hall, the emperor himself bustled about adding new details to the established forms. As for the banquet after the ceremony, he did not wish the custodians of the storehouses and granaries to treat it as an ordinary public occasion.

The throne faced east on the east porch, and before it were Genji's seat and that of the minister who was to bestow the official cap. At the appointed hour in midafternoon Genji appeared. The freshness of his face and his boyish coiffure were again such as to make the emperor regret that the change must take place. The ritual cutting of the boy's hair was performed by the secretary of the treasury. As the beautiful locks fell the emperor was seized with a hopeless longing for his dead lady. Repeatedly he found himself struggling to keep his composure. The ceremony over, the boy withdrew to change to adult trousers and descended into the courtyard for ceremonial thanksgiving. There was not a person in the assembly who did not feel his eyes misting over. The emperor was stirred by the deepest of emotions. He had on brief occasions been able to forget the past, and now it all came back again. Vaguely apprehensive lest the initiation of so young a boy bring a sudden aging, he was astonished to see that his son delighted him even more.

The Minister of the Left, who bestowed the official cap, had only one daughter, his chief joy in life. Her mother, the minister's first wife, was a princess of the blood. The crown prince had sought the girl's hand, but the minister thought rather of giving her to Genji. He had heard that the emperor had similar thoughts. When the emperor suggested that the boy was without adequate sponsors for his initiation and that the support of relatives by marriage might be called for, the minister quite agreed.

The company withdrew to outer rooms and Genji took his place below the princes of the blood. The minister hinted at what was on his mind, but Genji, still very young, did not quite know what to say. There came a message through a chamberlain that the minister was expected in the royal chambers. A lady-in-waiting brought the customary gifts for his services, a woman's cloak, white and of grand proportions, and a set of robes as well. As he poured wine for his minister, the emperor recited a poem which was in fact a deeply felt admonition:

"The boyish locks are now bound
 up, a man's.
And do we tie a lasting bond for
 his future?"

This was the minister's reply:

"Fast the knot which the honest
 heart has tied.
May lavender, the hue of the troth,
 be as fast."

The minister descended from a long garden bridge to give formal thanks. He received a horse from the imperial stables and a falcon from the secretariat. In the courtyard below the emperor, princes and high courtiers received gifts in keeping with their stations. The moderator, Genji's guardian, had upon royal command prepared the trays and baskets now set out in the royal presence. As for Chinese chests of food and gifts, they overflowed the premises, in even larger numbers than for the crown prince's initiation. It was the most splendid and dignified of ceremonies.

Genji went home that evening with the Minister of the Left. The nuptial observances were conducted with great solemnity. The groom seemed to the minister and his family quite charming in his boyishness. The bride was older, and somewhat ill at ease with such a young husband.

The minister had the emperor's complete confidence, and his wife, the girl's mother, was full sister to the emperor. Both parents were therefore of the highest standing. And now they had Genji for a son-in-law. The Minister of the Right, who as a grandfather of the crown prince should have been without rivals, was somehow eclipsed. The Minister of the Left had numerous children by several ladies. One of the sons, a very handsome lad by his principal wife, was already a guards lieutenant. Relations between the two ministers were not good; but the Minister of the Right found it difficult to ignore such a talented youth, to whom he offered the hand of his fourth and favorite daughter. His esteem for his new son-in-law rivaled the other minister's esteem for Genji. To both houses the new arrangements seemed ideal.

Constantly at his father's side, Genji spent little time at the Sanjō mansion of his bride. Fujitsubo was for him a vision of sublime beauty. If he could have someone like her—but in fact there was no one really like her. His bride too was beautiful, and she had had the advantage of every luxury; but he was not at all sure that they were meant for each other. The yearning in his young heart for the other lady was agony. Now that he had come of age, he no longer had his father's permission to go behind her curtains. On evenings when there was music, he would play the flute to her koto and so communicate something of his longing, and take some comfort from her voice, soft through the curtains. Life at court was for him much preferable to life at Sanjō. Two or three days at Sanjō would be followed by five or six days at court. For the minister, youth seemed sufficient excuse for this neglect. He continued to be delighted with his son-in-law.

The minister selected the handsomest and most accomplished of ladies to wait upon the young pair and planned the sort of diversions that were most likely to interest Genji. At the palace the emperor assigned him the apartments that had been his mother's and took care that her retinue was not dispersed. Orders were handed down to the offices of repairs and fittings to remodel the house that had belonged to the lady's family. The results were magnificent. The plantings and the artificial hills had always been remarkably tasteful, and the grounds now swarmed with workmen widening the lake. If only, thought Genji , he could have with him the lady he yearned for.

The sobriquet "the shining Genji," one hears, was bestowed upon him by the Korean.

## *Ch. 4: Evening Faces*

On his way from court to pay one of his calls at Rokujō, Genji stopped to inquire after his old nurse, Koremitsu's mother, at her house in Gojō. Gravely ill, she had become a nun. The carriage entrance was closed. He sent for Koremitsu and while he was waiting looked up and down the dirty, cluttered street. Beside the nurse's house was a new fence of plaited cypress. The four or five narrow shutters above had been raised, and new blinds, white and clean, hung in the apertures. He caught outlines of pretty foreheads beyond. He would have judged, as they moved about, that they belonged to rather tall women. What sort of women might they be? His carriage was simple and unadorned and he had no outrunners. Quite certain that he would not be recognized, he leaned out for a closer look. The hanging gate, of something like trelliswork, was propped on a pole, and he could see that the house was tiny and flimsy. He felt a little sorry for the occupants of such a place—and then asked himself who in this world had more than a temporary shelter. A hut, a jeweled pavilion, they were the same. A pleasantly green vine was climbing a board wall. The white flowers, he thought, had a rather self-satisfied look about them.

"'I needs must ask the lady far off yonder,'" he said, as if to himself.

An attendant came up, bowing deeply. "The white flowers far off yonder are known as 'evening faces,'" he said. "A very human sort of name—and what a shabby place they have picked to bloom in."

It was as the man said. The neighborhood was a poor one, chiefly of small houses. Some were leaning precariously, and there were "evening faces" at the sagging eaves.

"A hapless sort of flower. Pick one off for me, would you?"

The man went inside the raised gate and broke off a flower. A pretty little girl in long, unlined yellow trousers of raw silk came out through a sliding door that seemed too good for the surroundings. Beckoning to the man, she handed him a heavily scented white fan.

"Put it on this. It isn't much of a fan, but then it isn't much of a flower either."

Koremitsu, coming out of the gate, passed it on to Genji.

"They lost the key, and I have had to keep you waiting. You aren't likely to be recognized in such a neighborhood, but it's not a very nice neighborhood to keep you waiting in."

Genji's carriage was pulled in and he dismounted. Besides Koremitsu, a son and a daughter, the former an eminent cleric, and the daughter's husband, the governor of Mikawa, were in attendance upon the old woman. They thanked him profusely for his visit.

The old woman got up to receive him. "I did not at all mind leaving the world, except for the thought that I would no longer be able to see you as I am seeing you now. My vows seem to have given me a new lease on life, and this visit makes me certain that I shall receive the radiance of Lord Amitābha with a serene and tranquil heart." And she collapsed in tears.

Genji was near tears himself. "It has worried me enormously that you should be taking so long to recover, and I was very sad to learn that you have withdrawn from the world. You must live a long life and see the career I make for myself. I am sure that if you do you will be reborn upon the highest summits of the Pure Land. I am told that it is important to rid oneself of the smallest regret for this world."

Fond of the child she has reared, a nurse tends to look upon him as a paragon even if he is a half-wit. How much prouder was the old woman, who somehow gained stature, who thought of herself as eminent in her own right for having been permitted to serve him. The tears flowed on.

Her children were ashamed for her. They exchanged glances. It would not do to have these contortions taken as signs of a lingering affection for the world.

Genji was deeply touched. "The people who were fond of me left me when I was very young. Others have come along, it is true, to take care of me, but you are the only one I am really attached to. In recent years there have been restrictions upon my movements, and I have not been able to look in upon you morning and evening as I would have wished, or indeed to have a good visit with you. Yet I become very depressed when the days go by and I do not see you. 'Would that there were on this earth no final partings.'" He spoke with great solemnity, and the scent of his sleeve, as he brushed away a tear, quite flooded the room.

Yes, thought the children, who had been silently reproaching their mother for her want of control, the fates had been kind to her. They too were now in tears.

Genji left orders that prayers and services be resumed. As he went out he asked for a torch, and in its light examined the fan on which the "evening face" had rested. It was permeated with a lady's perfume, elegant and alluring. On it was a poem in a disguised cursive hand that suggested breeding and taste. He was interested.

"I think I need not ask whose face it is,
So bright, this evening face, in the shining dew."

"Who is living in the house to the west?" he asked Koremitsu. "Have you perhaps had occasion to inquire?"

At it again, thought Koremitsu. He spoke somewhat tartly. "I must confess that these last few days I have been too busy with my mother to think about her neighbors."

"You are annoyed with me. But this fan has the appearance of something it might be interesting to look into. Make inquiries, if you will, please, of someone who knows the neighborhood."

Koremitsu went in to ask his mother's steward, and emerged with the information that the house belonged to a certain honorary vice-governor. "The husband is away in the country, and the wife seems to be a young woman of taste. Her sisters are out in service here and there. They often come visiting. I suspect the fellow is too poorly placed to know the details."

His poetess would be one of the sisters, thought Genji. A rather practiced and forward young person, and, were he to meet her, perhaps vulgar as well—but the easy familiarity of the poem had not been at all unpleasant, not something to be pushed away in disdain. His amative propensities, it will be seen, were having their way once more.

Carefully disguising his hand, he jotted down a reply on a piece of notepaper and sent it in by the attendant who had earlier been of service.

> "Come a bit nearer, please. Then
> might you know
> Whose was the evening face so
> dim in the twilight."

Thinking it a familiar profile, the lady had not lost the opportunity to surprise him with a letter, and when time passed and there was no answer she was left feeling somewhat embarrassed and disconsolate. Now came a poem by special messenger. Her women became quite giddy as they turned their minds to the problem of replying. Rather bored with it all, the messenger returned empty-handed. Genji made a quiet departure, lighted by very few torches. The shutters next door had been lowered. There was something sad about the light, dimmer than fireflies, that came through the cracks.

At the Rokujō house, the trees and the plantings had a quiet dignity. The lady herself was strangely cold and withdrawn. Thoughts of the "evening faces" quite left him. He overslept, and the sun was rising when he took his leave. He presented such a fine figure in the morning light that the women of the place understood well enough why he should be so universally admired. On his way he again passed those shutters, as he had no doubt done many times before. Because of that small incident he now looked at the house carefully, wondering who might be within.

"My mother is not doing at all well, and I have been with her," said Koremitsu some days later. And, coming nearer: "Because you seemed so interested, I called someone who knows about the house next door and had him questioned. His story was not completely clear. He said that in the Fifth Month or so someone came very quietly to live in the house, but that not even the domestics had been told who she might be. I have looked through the fence from time to time myself and had glimpses through blinds of several young women. Something about their dress suggests that they are in the service of someone of higher rank. Yesterday, when the evening light was coming directly through, I saw the lady herself writing a letter. She is very beautiful. She seemed lost in thought, and the women around her were weeping."

Genji had suspected something of the sort. He must find out more.

Koremitsu's view was that while Genji was undeniably someone the whole world took seriously, his youth and the fact that women found him attractive meant that to refrain from these little affairs would be less than human. It was not realistic to hold that certain people were beyond temptation.

"Looking for a chance to do a bit of exploring, I found a small pretext for writing to her. She answered immediately, in a good, practiced hand. Some of her women do not seem at all beneath contempt."

"Explore very thoroughly, if you will. I will not be satisfied until you do."

The house was what the guardsman would have described as the lowest of the low, but Genji was interested. What hidden charms might he not come upon!

He had thought the coldness of the governor's wife, the lady of "the locust shell," quite unique. Yet if she had proved amenable to his persuasions the affair would no doubt have been dropped as a sad mistake after that one encounter. As matters were, the resentment and the distinct possibility of final defeat never left his mind. The discussion that rainy night would seem to have made him curious about the several ranks. There had been a time when such a lady would not have been worth his notice. Yes, it had been broadening, that discussion! He had not found the willing and available one, the governor of Iyo's daughter, entirely uninteresting, but the thought that the stepmother must have been listening coolly to the interview was excruciating. He must await some sign of her real intentions.

The governor of Iyo returned to the city. He came immediately to Genji's mansion. Somewhat sunburned, his travel robes rumpled from the sea voyage, he was a rather heavy and displeasing sort of person. He was of good lineage, however, and, though aging, he still had good manners. As they spoke of his province, Genji wanted to ask the full count of those hot springs, but he was somewhat confused to find memories chasing one another through his head. How foolish that he should be so uncomfortable before the honest old man! He remembered the guardsman's warning that such affairs are unwise, and he felt sorry for the governor. Though he resented the wife's coldness, he could see that from the husband's point of view it was admirable. He was upset to learn that the governor meant to find a suitable husband for his daughter and take his wife to the provinces. He consulted the lady's young brother upon the possibility of another meeting. It would have been difficult even with the lady's cooperation, however, and she was of the view that to receive a gentleman so far above her would be extremely unwise.

Yet she did not want him to forget her entirely. Her answers to his notes on this and that occasion were pleasant enough, and contained casual little touches that made him pause in admiration. He resented her chilliness, but she interested him. As for the stepdaughter, he was certain that she would receive him hospitably enough however formidable a husband she might acquire. Reports upon her arrangements disturbed him not at all.

Autumn came. He was kept busy and unhappy by affairs of his own making, and he visited Sanjō infrequently. There was resentment.

As for the affair at Rokujō, he had overcome the lady's resistance and had his way, and, alas, he had cooled toward her. People thought it worthy of comment that his passions should seem so much more governable than before he had made her his. She was subject to fits of despondency, more intense on sleepless nights when she awaited him in vain. She feared that if rumors were to spread the gossips would make much of the difference in their ages.

On a morning of heavy mists, insistently roused by the lady, who was determined that he be on his way, Genji emerged yawning and sighing and looking very sleepy. Chūjō, one of her women, raised a shutter and pulled a curtain aside as if urging her lady to come forward and see him off. The lady lifted her head from her pillow. He was an incomparably handsome figure as he paused to admire the profusion of flowers below the veranda. Chūjō followed him down a gallery. In an aster robe that matched the season pleasantly and a gossamer train worn with clean elegance, she was a pretty, graceful woman. Glancing back, he asked her to sit with him for a time at the corner railing. The ceremonious precision of the seated figure and the hair flowing over her robes were very fine.

He took her hand.

"Though loath to be taxed with
seeking fresher blooms,
I feel impelled to pluck this
morning glory.

"Why should it be?"

She answered with practiced alacrity, making it seem that she was speaking not for herself but for her lady:

"In haste to plunge into the
morning mists,
You seem to have no heart for the
blossoms here."

A pretty little page boy, especially decked out for the occasion, it would seem, walked out among the flowers. His trousers wet with dew, he broke off a morning glory for Genji. He made a picture that called out to be painted.

Even persons to whom Genji was nothing were drawn to him. No doubt even rough mountain men wanted to pause for a time in the shade of the flowering tree, and those who had basked even briefly in his radiance had thoughts, each in accordance with his rank, of a daughter who might be taken into his service, a not ill-formed sister who might perform some humble service for him. One need not be surprised, then, that people with a measure of sensibility among those who had on some occasion received a little poem from him or been treated to some little kindness found him much on their minds. No doubt it distressed them not to be always with him.

I had forgotten: Koremitsu gave a good account of the fence peeping to which he had been assigned. "I am unable to identify her. She seems determined to hide herself from the world. In their boredom her women and girls go out to the long gallery at the street, the one with the shutters, and watch for carriages. Sometimes the lady who seems to be their mistress comes quietly out to join them. I've not had a good look at her, but she seems very pretty indeed. One day a carriage with outrunners went by. The little girls shouted to a person named Ukon that she must come in a hurry. The captain was going by, they said. An older woman came out and motioned to them to be quiet. How did they know? she asked, coming out toward the gallery. The passage from the main house is by a sort of makeshift bridge. She was hurrying and her skirt caught on something, and she stumbled and almost fell off. 'The sort of thing the god of Katsuragi might do,' she said, and seems to have lost interest in sightseeing. They told her that the man in the carriage was wearing casual court dress and that he had a retinue. They mentioned several names, and all of them were undeniably Lord Tō no Chūjō's guards and pages."

"I wish you had made positive identification." Might she be the lady of whom Tō no Chūjō had spoken so regretfully that rainy night?

Koremitsu went on, smiling at this open curiosity. "I have as a matter of fact made the proper overtures and learned all about the place. I come and go as if I did not know that they are not all equals. They think they are hiding the truth and try to insist that there is no one there but themselves when one of the little girls makes a slip."

"Let me have a peep for myself when I call on your mother."

Even if she was only in temporary lodgings, the woman would seem to be of the lower class for which his friend had indicated such contempt that rainy evening. Yet something might come of it all. Determined not to go against his master's wishes in the smallest detail and himself driven by very considerable excitement, Koremitsu searched diligently for a chance to let Genji into the house. But the details are tiresome, and I shall not go into them.

Genji did not know who the lady was and he did not want her to know who he was. In very shabby disguise, he set out to visit her on foot. He must be taking her very seriously, thought Koremitsu, who offered his horse and himself went on foot.

"Though I do not think that our gentleman will look very good with tramps for servants."

To make quite certain that the expedition remained secret, Genji took with him only the man who had been his intermediary in the matter of the "evening faces" and a page whom no one was likely to recognize. Lest he be found out even so, he did not stop to see his nurse.

The lady had his messengers followed to see how he made his way home and tried by every means to learn where he lived; but her efforts came to nothing. For all his secretiveness, Genji had grown fond of her and felt that he must go on seeing her. They were of such different ranks, he tried to tell himself, and it was altogether too frivolous. Yet his visits were frequent. In affairs of this sort, which can muddle the senses of the most serious and honest of men, he had always kept himself under tight control and avoided any occasion for censure. Now, to a most astonishing degree, he would be asking himself as he returned in the morning from a visit how he could wait through the day for the next. And then he would rebuke himself. It was madness, it was not an affair he should let disturb him. She was of an extraordinarily gentle and quiet nature. Though there was a certain vagueness about her, and indeed an almost childlike quality, it was clear that she knew something about men. She did not appear to be of very good family. What was there about her, he asked himself over and over again, that so drew him to her?

He took great pains to hide his rank and always wore travel dress, and he did not allow her to see his face. He came late at night when everyone was asleep. She was frightened, as if he were an apparition from an old story. She did not need to see his face to know that he was a fine gentleman. But who might he be? Her suspicions turned to Koremitsu. It was that young gallant, surely, who had brought the strange visitor. But Koremitsu pursued his own little affairs unremittingly, careful to feign indifference to and ignorance of this other affair. What could it all mean? The lady was lost in unfamiliar speculations.

Genji had his own worries. If, having lowered his guard with an appearance of complete unreserve, she were to slip away and hide, where would he seek her? This seemed to be but a temporary residence, and he could not be sure when she would choose to change it, and for what other. He hoped that he might reconcile himself to what must be and forget the affair as just another dalliance; but he was not confident.

On days when, to avoid attracting notice, he refrained from visiting her, his fretfulness came near anguish. Suppose he were to move her in secret to Nijō. If troublesome rumors were to arise, well, he could say that they had been fated from the start. He wondered what bond in a former life might have produced an infatuation such as he had not known before.

"Let's have a good talk," he said to her, "where we can be quite at our ease."

"It's all so strange. What you say is reasonable enough, but what you do is so strange. And rather frightening."

Yes, she might well be frightened. Something childlike in her fright brought a smile to his lips. "Which of us is the mischievous fox spirit? I wonder. Just be quiet and give yourself up to its persuasions."

Won over by his gentle warmth, she was indeed inclined to let him have his way. She seemed such a pliant little creature, likely to submit absolutely to the most outrageous demands. He thought again of Tō no Chūjō's "wild carnation," of the equable nature his friend had described that rainy night. Fearing that it would be useless, he did not try very hard to question her. She did not seem likely to indulge in dramatics and suddenly run off and hide herself, and so the fault must have been Tō no Chūjō's. Genji himself would not be guilty of such negligence—though it did occur to him that a bit of infidelity might make her more interesting.

The bright full moon of the Eighth Month came flooding in through chinks in the roof. It was not the sort of dwelling he was used to, and he was fascinated. Toward dawn he was awakened by plebeian voices in the shabby houses down the street.

"Freezing, that's what it is, freezing. There's not much business this year, and when you can't get out into the country you feel like giving up. Do you hear me, neighbor?"

He could make out every word. It embarrassed the woman that, so near at hand, there should be this clamor of preparation as people set forth on their sad little enterprises. Had she been one of the stylish ladies of the world, she would have wanted to shrivel up and disappear. She was a placid sort, however, and she seemed to take nothing, painful or embarrassing or unpleasant, too seriously. Her manner elegant and yet girlish, she did not seem to know what the rather awful clamor up and down the street might mean. He much preferred this easygoing bewilderment to a show of consternation, a face scarlet with embarrassment. As if at his very pillow, there came the booming of a foot pestle, more fearsome than the stamping of the thunder god, genuinely earsplitting. He did not know what device the sound came from, but he did know that it was enough to awaken the dead. From this direction and that there came the faint thump of fulling hammers against coarse cloth; and mingled with it—these were sounds to call forth the deepest emotions—were the calls of geese flying overhead. He slid a door open and they looked out. They had been lying near the veranda. There were tasteful clumps of black bamboo just outside and the dew shone as in more familiar places. Autumn insects sang busily, as if only inches from an ear used to wall crickets at considerable distances. It was all very clamorous, and also rather wonderful. Countless details could be overlooked in the singleness of his affection for the girl. She was pretty and fragile in a soft, modest cloak of lavender and a lined white robe. She had no single feature that struck him as especially beautiful, and yet, slender and fragile, she seemed so delicately beautiful that he was almost afraid to hear her voice. He might have wished her to be a little more assertive, but he wanted only to be near her, and yet nearer.

"Let's go off somewhere and enjoy the rest of the night. This is too much."

"But how is that possible?" She spoke very quietly. "You keep taking me by surprise."

There was a newly confiding response to his offer of his services as guardian in this world and the next. She was a strange little thing. He found it hard to believe that she had had much experience of men. He no longer cared what people might think. He asked Ukon to summon his man, who got the carriage ready. The women of the house, though uneasy, sensed the depth of his feelings and were inclined to put their trust in him.

Dawn approached. No cocks were crowing. There was only the voice of an old man making deep obeisance to a Buddha, in preparation, it would seem, for a pilgrimage to Mitake. He seemed to be prostrating himself repeatedly and with much difficulty. All very sad. In a life itself like the morning dew, what could he desire so earnestly?

"Praise to the Messiah to come," intoned the voice.

"Listen," said Genji. "He is thinking of another world.

"This pious one shall lead us on
our way
As we plight our troth for all the
lives to come."

The vow exchanged by the Chinese emperor and Yang Kuei-fei seemed to bode ill, and so he preferred to invoke Lord Maitreya, the Buddha of the Future; but such promises are rash.

"So heavy the burden I bring with
me from the past,
I doubt that I should make these
vows for the future."

It was a reply that suggested doubts about his "lives to come."

The moon was low over the western hills. She was reluctant to go with him. As he sought to persuade her, the moon suddenly disappeared behind clouds in a lovely dawn sky. Always in a hurry to be off before daylight exposed him, he lifted her easily into his carriage and took her to a nearby villa. Ukon was with them. Waiting for the caretaker to be summoned, Genji looked up at the rotting gate and the ferns that trailed thickly down over it. The groves beyond were still dark, and the mist and the dews were heavy.

Genji's sleeve was soaking, for he had raised the blinds of the carriage.

"This is a novel adventure, and I must say that it seems like a lot of trouble.

"And did it confuse them too, the men of old,
This road through the dawn, for me so new and strange?

"How does it seem to you?"

She turned shyly away.

"And is the moon, unsure of the hills it approaches,
Foredoomed to lose its way in the empty skies?

"I am afraid."

She did seem frightened, and bewildered. She was so used to all those swarms of people, he thought with a smile.

The carriage was brought in and its traces propped against the veranda while a room was made ready in the west wing. Much excited, Ukon was thinking about earlier adventures. The furious energy with which the caretaker saw to preparations made her suspect who Genji was. It was almost daylight when they alighted from the carriage. The room was clean and pleasant, for all the haste with which it had been readied.

"There are unfortunately no women here to wait upon His Lordship." The man, who addressed him through Ukon, was a lesser steward who had served in the Sanjō mansion of Genji's father-in-law. "Shall I send for someone?"

"The last thing I want. I came here because I wanted to be in complete solitude, away from all possible visitors. You are not to tell a soul."

The man put together a hurried breakfast, but he was, as he had said, without serving women to help him.

Genji told the girl that he meant to show her a love as dependable as "the patient river of the loons." He could do little else in these strange lodgings.

The sun was high when he arose. He opened the shutters. All through the badly neglected grounds not a person was to be seen. The groves were rank and overgrown. The flowers and grasses in the foreground were a drab monotone, an autumn moor. The pond was choked with weeds, and all in all it was a forbidding place. An outbuilding seemed to be fitted with rooms for the caretaker, but it was some distance away.

"It is a forbidding place," said Genji. "But I am sure that whatever devils emerge will pass me by."

He was still in disguise. She thought it unkind of him to be so secretive, and he had to agree that their relationship had gone beyond such furtiveness.

"Because of one chance meeting by the wayside
The flower now opens in the evening dew.

"And how does it look to you?"

"The face seemed quite to shine in the evening dew,
But I was dazzled by the evening light."

Her eyes turned away. She spoke in a whisper.

To him it may have seemed an interesting poem.

As a matter of fact, she found him handsomer than her poem suggested, indeed frighteningly handsome, given the setting.

"I hid my name from you because I thought it altogether too unkind of you to be keeping your name from me. Do please tell me now. This silence makes me feel that something awful might be coming."

"Call me the fisherman's daughter." Still hiding her name, she was like a little child.

"I see. I brought it all on myself? A case of *warekara*?"

And so, sometimes affectionately, sometimes reproachfully, they talked the hours away.

Koremitsu had found them out and brought provisions. Feeling a little guilty about the way he had treated Ukon, he did not come near. He thought it amusing that Genji should thus be wandering the streets, and concluded that the girl must provide sufficient cause. And he could have had her himself, had he not been so generous.

Genji and the girl looked out at an evening sky of the utmost calm. Because she found the darkness in the recesses of the house frightening, he raised the blinds at the veranda and they lay side by side. As they gazed at each other in the gathering dusk, it all seemed very strange to her, unbelievably strange. Memories of past wrongs quite left her. She was more at ease with him now, and he thought her charming. Beside him all through the day, starting up in fright at each little noise, she seemed delightfully childlike. He lowered the shutters early and had lights brought.

"You seem comfortable enough with me, and yet you raise difficulties."

At court everyone would be frantic. Where would the search be directed? He thought what a strange love it was, and he thought of the turmoil the Rokujō lady was certain to be in. She had every right to be resentful, and yet her jealous ways were not pleasant. It was that sad lady to whom his thoughts first turned. Here was the girl beside him, so simple and undemanding; and the other was so impossibly forceful in her demands. How he wished he might in some measure have his freedom.

It was past midnight. He had been asleep for a time when an exceedingly beautiful woman appeared by his pillow.

"You do not even think of visiting me, when you are so much on my mind. Instead you go running off with someone who has nothing to recommend her, and raise a great stir over her. It is cruel, intolerable." She seemed about to shake the girl from her sleep. He awoke, feeling as if he were in the power of some malign being. The light had gone out. In great alarm, he unsheathed his sword and awakened Ukon. She too seemed frightened.

"Go out to the gallery and wake the guard. Have him bring a light."

"It's much too dark."

He forced a smile. "You're behaving like a child."

He clapped his hands and a hollow echo answered. No one seemed to hear. The girl was trembling violently. She was bathed in sweat and as if in a trance, quite bereft of her senses.

"She is such a timid little thing," said Ukon, "frightened when there is nothing at all to be frightened of. This must be dreadful for her."

Yes, poor thing, thought Genji. She did seem so fragile, and she had spent the whole day gazing up at the sky.

"I'll go get someone. What a frightful echo. You stay here with her." He pulled Ukon to the girl's side.

The lights in the west gallery had gone out. There was a gentle wind. He had few people with him, and they were asleep. They were three in number: a young man who was one of his intimates and who was the son of the steward here, a court page, and the man who had been his intermediary in the matter of the "evening faces." He called out. Someone answered and came up to him.

"Bring a light. Wake the other, and shout and twang your bowstrings. What do you mean, going to sleep in a deserted house? I believe Lord Koremitsu was here."

"He was. But he said he had no orders and would come again at dawn."

An elite guardsman, the man was very adept at bow twanging. He went off with a shouting as of a fire watch. At court, thought Genji, the courtiers on night duty would have announced themselves, and the guard would be changing. It was not so very late.

He felt his way back inside. The girl was as before, and Ukon lay face down at her side.

"What is this? You're a fool to let yourself be so frightened. Are you worried about the fox spirits that come out and play tricks in deserted houses? But you needn't worry. They won't come near me." He pulled her to her knees.

"I'm not feeling at all well. That's why I was lying down. My poor lady must be terrified."

"She is indeed. And I can't think why."

He reached for the girl. She was not breathing. He lifted her and she was limp in his arms. There was no sign of life. She had seemed as defenseless as a child, and no doubt some evil power had taken possession of her. He could think of nothing to do. A man came with a torch. Ukon was not prepared to move, and Genji himself pulled up curtain frames to hide the girl.

"Bring the light closer."

It was a most unusual order. Not ordinarily permitted at Genji's side, the man hesitated to cross the threshold.

"Come, come, bring it here! There is a time and place for ceremony."

In the torchlight he had a fleeting glimpse of a figure by the girl's pillow. It was the woman in his dream. It faded away like an apparition in an old romance. In all the fright and horror, his confused thoughts centered upon the girl. There was no room for thoughts of himself.

He knelt over her and called out to her, but she was cold and had stopped breathing. It was too horrible. He had no confidant to whom he could turn for advice. It was the clergy one thought of first on such occasions. He had been so brave and confident, but he was young, and this was too much for him. He clung to the lifeless body.

"Come back, my dear, my dear. Don't do this awful thing to me." But she was cold and no longer seemed human.

The first paralyzing terror had left Ukon. Now she was writhing and wailing. Genji remembered a devil a certain minister had encountered in the Grand Hall.

"She can't possibly be dead." He found the strength to speak sharply. "All this noise in the middle of the night—you must try to be a little quieter." But it had been too sudden.

He turned again to the torchbearer. "There is someone here who seems to have had a very strange seizure. Tell your friend to find out where Lord Koremitsu is spending the night and have him come immediately. If the holy man is still at his mother's house, give him word, very quietly, that he is to come too. His mother and the people with her are not to hear. She does not approve of this sort of adventure."

He spoke calmly enough, but his mind was in a turmoil. Added to grief at the loss of the girl was horror, quite beyond describing, at this desolate place. It would be past midnight. The wind was higher and whistled more dolefully in the pines. There came a strange, hollow call of a bird. Might it be an owl? All was silence, terrifying solitude. He should not have chosen such a place—but it was too late now. Trembling violently, Ukon clung to him. He held her in his arms, wondering if she might be about to follow her lady. He was the only rational one present, and he could think of nothing to do. The flickering light wandered here and there. The upper parts of the screens behind them were in darkness, the lower parts fitfully in the light. There was a persistent creaking, as of someone coming up behind them. If only Koremitsu would come. But Koremitsu was a nocturnal wanderer without a fixed abode, and the man had to search for him in numerous places. The wait for dawn was like the passage of a thousand nights. Finally he heard a distant crowing. What legacy from a former life could have brought him to this mortal peril? He was being punished for a guilty love, his fault and no one else's, and his story would be remembered in infamy through all the ages to come. There were no secrets, strive though one might to have them. Soon everyone would know, from his royal father down, and the lowest court pages would be talking; and he would gain immortality as the model of the complete fool.

Finally Lord Koremitsu came. He was the perfect servant who did not go against his master's wishes in anything at any time; and Genji was angry that on this night of all nights he should have been away, and slow in answering the summons. Calling him inside even so, he could not immediately find the strength to say what must be said. Ukon burst into tears, the full horror of it all coming back to her at the sight of Koremitsu. Genji too lost control of himself. The only sane and rational one present, he had held Ukon in his arms, but now he gave himself up to his grief.

"Something very strange has happened," he said after a time. "Strange—'unbelievable' would not be too strong a word. I wanted a priest—one does when these things happen—and asked your reverend brother to come."

"He went back up the mountain yesterday. Yes, it is very strange indeed. Had there been anything wrong with her?"

"Nothing."

He was so handsome in his grief that Koremitsu wanted to weep. An older man who has had everything happen to him and knows what to expect can be depended upon in a crisis; but they were both young, and neither had anything to suggest.

Koremitsu finally spoke. "We must not let the caretaker know. He may be dependable enough himself, but he is sure to have relatives who will talk. We must get away from this place."

"You aren't suggesting that we could find a place where we would be less likely to be seen?"

"No, I suppose not. And the women at her house will scream and wail when they hear about it, and they live in a crowded neighborhood, and all the mob around will hear, and that will be that. But mountain temples are used to this sort of thing. There would not be much danger of attracting attention." He reflected on the problem for a time. "There is a woman I used to know. She has gone into a nunnery up in the eastern hills. A very old lady, my father's nurse, is living there. The district seems to be rather heavily populated, but the nunnery is off by itself."

In the stir as daylight came, Koremitsu had the carriage brought up. Since Genji seemed incapable of the task, he wrapped the body in a covering and lifted it into the carriage. It was very tiny and very pretty, and not at all repellent. The wrapping was loose and the hair streamed forth, as if to darken the world before Genji's eyes.

He wanted to see the last rites through to the end, but Koremitsu would not hear of it. "Take my horse and go back to Nijō, now while the streets are still quiet."

He helped Ukon into the carriage and himself proceeded on foot, the skirts of his robe hitched up. It was a strange, bedraggled sort of funeral procession, he thought, but in the face of such anguish he was prepared to risk his life. Barely conscious, Genji made his way back to Nijō.

"Where have you been?" asked the women. "You are not looking at all well."

He did not answer. Alone in his room, he pressed a hand to his heart. Why had he not gone with the others? What would she think if she were to come back to life? She would think that he had abandoned her. Self-reproach filled his heart to breaking. He had a headache and feared he had a fever. Might he too be dying? The sun was high and still he did not emerge. Thinking it all very strange, the women pressed breakfast upon him. He could not eat. A messenger reported that the emperor had been troubled by his failure to appear the day before.

His brothers-in-law came calling.

"Come in, please, just for a moment." He received only Tō no Chūjō and kept a blind between them. "My old nurse fell seriously ill and took her vows in the Fifth Month or so. Perhaps because of them, she seemed to recover. But recently she had a relapse. Someone came to ask if I would not call on her at least once more. I thought I really must go and see an old and dear servant who was on her deathbed, and so I went. One of her servants was ailing, and quite suddenly, before he had time to leave, he died. Out of deference to me they waited until night to take the body away. All this I learned later. It would be very improper of me to go to court with all these festivities coming up, I thought, and so I stayed away. I have had a headache since early this morning—perhaps I have caught cold. I must apologize."

"I see. I shall so inform your father. He sent out a search party during the concert last night, and really seemed very upset." Tō no Chūjō turned to go, and abruptly turned back. "Come now. What sort of brush did you really have? I don't believe a word of it."

Genji was startled, but managed a show of nonchalance. "You needn't go into the details. Just say that I suffered an unexpected defilement. Very unexpected, really."

Despite his cool manner, he was not up to facing people. He asked a younger brother-in-law to explain in detail his reasons for not going to court. He got off a note to Sanjō with a similar explanation.

Koremitsu came in the evening. Having announced that he had suffered a defilement, Genji had callers remain outside, and there were few people in the house. He received Koremitsu immediately.

"Are you sure she is dead?" He pressed a sleeve to his eyes.

Koremitsu too was in tears. "Yes, I fear she is most certainly dead. I could not stay shut up in a temple indefinitely, and so I have made arrangements with a venerable priest whom I happen to know rather well. Tomorrow is a good day for funerals."

"And the other woman?"

"She has seemed on the point of death herself. She does not want to be left behind by her lady. I was afraid this morning that she might throw herself over a cliff. She wanted to tell the people at Gojō, but I persuaded her to let us have a little more time."

"I am feeling rather awful myself and almost fear the worst."

"Come, now. There is nothing to be done and no point in torturing yourself. You must tell yourself that what must be must be. I shall let absolutely no one know, and I am personally taking care of everything."

"Yes, to be sure. Everything is fated. So I tell myself. But it is terrible to think that I have sent a lady to her death. You are not to tell your sister, and you must be very sure that your mother does not hear. I would not survive the scolding I would get from her."

"And the priests too: I have told them a plausible story." Koremitsu exuded confidence.

The women had caught a hint of what was going on and were more puzzled than ever. He had said that he had suffered a defilement, and he was staying away from court; but why these muffled lamentations?

Genji gave instructions for the funeral. "You must make sure that nothing goes wrong."

"Of course. No great ceremony seems called for."

Koremitsu turned to leave.

"I know you won't approve," said Genji, a fresh wave of grief sweeping over him, "but I will regret it forever if I don't see her again. I'll go on horseback."

"Very well, if you must." In fact Koremitsu thought the proposal very ill advised. "Go immediately and be back while it is still early."

Genji set out in the travel robes he had kept ready for his recent amorous excursions. He was in the bleakest despair. He was on a strange mission and the terrors of the night before made him consider turning back. Grief urged him on. If he did not see her once more, when, in another world, might he hope to see her as she had been? He had with him only Koremitsu and the attendant of that first encounter. The road seemed a long one.

The moon came out, two nights past full. They reached the river. In the dim torchlight, the darkness off towards Mount Toribe was ominous and forbidding; but Genji was too dazed with grief to be frightened. And so they reached the temple.

It was a harsh, unfriendly region at best. The board hut and chapel where the nun pursued her austerities were lonely beyond description. The light at the altar came dimly through cracks. Inside the hut a woman was weeping. In the outer chamber two or three priests were conversing and invoking the holy name in low voices. Vespers seemed to have ended in several temples nearby.

Everything was quiet. There were lights and there seemed to be clusters of people in the direction of Kiyomizu. The grand tones in which the worthy monk, the son of the nun, was reading a sutra brought on what Genji thought must be the full flood tide of his tears.

He went inside. The light was turned away from the corpse. Ukon lay behind a screen. It must be very terrible for her, thought Genji. The girl's face was unchanged and very pretty.

"Won't you let me hear your voice again?" He took her hand. "What was it that made me give you all my love, for so short a time, and then made you leave me to this misery?" He was weeping uncontrollably.

The priests did not know who he was. They sensed something remarkable, however, and felt their eyes mist over.

"Come with me to Nijō," he said to Ukon.

"We have been together since I was very young. I never left her side, not for a single moment. Where am I to go now? I will have to tell the others what has happened. As if this weren't enough, I will have to put up with their accusations." She was sobbing. "I want to go with her."

"That is only natural. But it is the way of the world. Parting is always sad. Our lives must end, early or late. Try to put your trust in me." He comforted her with the usual homilies, but presently his real feelings came out. "Put your trust in me—when I fear I have not long to live myself." He did not after all seem likely to be much help.

"It will soon be light," said Koremitsu. "We must be on our way."

Looking back and looking back again, his heart near breaking, Genji went out. The way was heavy with dew and the morning mists were thick. He scarcely knew where he was. The girl was exactly as she had been that night. They had exchanged robes and she had on a red singlet of his. What might it have been in other lives that had brought them together? He managed only with great difficulty to stay in his saddle. Koremitsu was at the reins. As they came to the river Genji fell from his horse and was unable to remount.

"So I am to die by the wayside? I doubt that I can go on."

Koremitsu was in a panic. He should not have permitted this expedition, however strong Genji's wishes. Dipping his hands in the river, he turned and made supplication to Kiyomizu. Genji somehow pulled himself together. Silently invoking the holy name, he was seen back to Nijō.

The women were much upset by these untimely wanderings. "Very bad, very bad. He has been so restless lately. And why should he have gone out again when he was not feeling well?"

Now genuinely ill, he took to his bed. Two or three days passed and he was visibly thinner. The emperor heard of the illness and was much alarmed. Continuous prayers were ordered in this shrine and that temple. The varied rites, Shinto and Confucian and Buddhist, were beyond counting. Genji's good looks had been such as to arouse forebodings. All through the court it was feared that he would not live much longer. Despite his illness, he summoned Ukon to Nijō and assigned her rooms near his own. Koremitsu composed himself sufficiently to be of service to her, for he could see that she had no one else to turn to. Choosing times when he was feeling better, Genji would summon her for a talk, and she soon was accustomed to life at Nijō. Dressed in deep mourning, she was a somewhat stern and forbidding young woman, but not without her good points.

"It lasted such a very little while. I fear that I will be taken too. It must be dreadful for you, losing your only support. I had thought that as long as I lived I would see to all your needs, and it seems sad and ironical that I should be on the point of following her." He spoke softly and there were tears in his eyes. For Ukon the old grief had been hard enough to bear, and now she feared that a new grief might be added to it.

All through the Nijō mansion there was a sense of helplessness. Emissaries from court were thicker than raindrops. Not wanting to worry his father, Genji fought to control himself. His father-in-law was extremely solicitous and came to Nijō every day. Perhaps because of all the prayers and rites the crisis passed—it had lasted some twenty days—and left no ill effects. Genji's full recovery coincided with the final cleansing of the defilement. With the unhappiness he had caused his father much on his mind, he set off for court. His father-in-law the minister then took him to Sanjō, with many an admonition along the way. He felt for a time as if he had come back from a different world.

By the end of the ninth month he was his old self once more. He had lost weight, but emaciation only made him handsomer. He spent a great deal of time gazing into space, and sometimes he would weep aloud. He must be in the clutches of some malign spirit, thought the women. It was all most peculiar.

He would summon Ukon on quiet evenings. "I don't understand it at all. Why did she so insist on keeping her name from me? Even if she *was* a fisherman's daughter it was cruel of her to be so uncommunicative. It was as if she did not know how much I loved her."

"There was no reason for keeping it secret. But why should she tell you about her insignificant self? Your attitude seemed so strange from the beginning. She used to say that she hardly knew whether she was waking or dreaming. Your refusal to identify yourself, you know, helped her guess who you were. It hurt her that you should belittle her by keeping your name from her."

"An unfortunate contest of wills. I did not want anything to stand between us; but I must always be worrying about what people will say. I must refrain from things my father and all the rest of them might take me to task for. I am not permitted the smallest indiscretion. Everything is exaggerated so. The little incident of the 'evening faces' affected me strangely and I went to very great trouble to see her. There must have been a bond between us. A love doomed from the start to be fleeting—why should it have taken such complete possession of me and made me find her so precious? You must tell me everything. What point is there in keeping secrets now? I mean to make offerings every week, and I want to know in whose name I am making them."

"Yes, of course—why have secrets now? It is only that I do not want to slight what she made so much of. Her parents are dead. Her father was a guards captain. She was his special pet, but his career did not go well and his life came to an early and disappointing end. She somehow got to know Lord Tō no Chūjō—it was when he was still a lieutenant. He was very attentive for three years or so, and then about last autumn there was a rather awful threat from his father-in-law's house. She was ridiculously timid and it frightened her beyond all reason. She ran off and hid herself at her nurse's in the western part of the city. It was a wretched little hovel of a place. She wanted to go off into the hills, but the direction she had in mind has been taboo since New Year's. So she moved to the odd place where she was so upset to have you find her. She was more reserved and withdrawn than most people, and I fear that her unwillingness to show her emotions may have seemed cold."

So it was true. Affection and pity welled up yet more strongly.

"He once told me of a lost child. Was there such a one?"

"Yes, a very pretty little girl, born two years ago last spring."

"Where is she? Bring her to me without letting anyone know. It would be such a comfort. I should tell my friend Tō no Chūjō, I suppose, but why invite criticism? I doubt that anyone could reprove me for taking in the child. You must think up a way to get around the nurse."

"It would make me very happy if you were to take the child. I would hate to have her left where she is. She is there because we had no competent nurses in the house where you found us."

The evening sky was serenely beautiful. The flowers below the veranda were withered, the songs of the insects were dying too, and autumn tints were coming over the maples. Looking out upon the scene, which might have been a painting, Ukon thought what a lovely asylum she had found herself. She wanted to avert her eyes at the thought of the house of the "evening faces." A pigeon called, somewhat discordantly, from a bamboo thicket. Remembering how the same call had frightened the girl in that deserted villa, Genji could see the little figure as if an apparition were there before him.

"How old was she? She seemed so delicate, because she was not long for this world, I suppose."

"Nineteen, perhaps? My mother, who was her nurse, died and left me behind. Her father took a fancy to me, and so we grew up together, and I never once left her side. I wonder how I can go on without her. I am almost sorry that we were so close. She seemed so weak, but I can see now that she was a source of strength."

"The weak ones do have a power over us. The clear, forceful ones I can do without. I am weak and indecisive by nature myself, and a woman who is quiet and withdrawn and follows the wishes of a man even to the point of letting herself be used has much the greater appeal. A man can shape and mold her as he wishes, and becomes fonder of her all the while."

"She was exactly what you would have wished, sir." Ukon was in tears, "That thought makes the loss seem greater."

The sky had clouded over and a chilly wind had come up. Gazing off into the distance, Genji said softly:

> "One sees the clouds as smoke
> that rose from the pyre,
> And suddenly the evening sky
> seems nearer."

"In the Eighth Month, the Ninth Month, the nights are long," he whispered, and lay down.

## KAMO NO CHŌMEI (12TH CENT.)

*Translated by Helen Craig McCullough*

Japanese court society collapsed in the twelfth century as the nation dissolved in a brutal civil war. In such circumstances, retirement from the world became a real and meaningful possibility. Kamo no Chōmei chose the life of a recluse following the Buddhist teaching of renouncing all worldly attachments and withdrawing to a series of increasingly smaller and more isolated hermitages. In *An Account of My Hermitage,* he contrasts life in society with his life as a hermit. Although he became a recluse during the years of civil war, he makes no mention of such violence as a reason for withdrawing from the world. Instead, he lays the blame on natural disasters involving fire, wind, earth, and water, the cosmic elements that disrupt the lives of men who would pursue worldly success. The disruptions Chōmei mentions are historical occurrences, but they also represent the four elements; thus, he makes the point that anyone affected by these disharmonies is out of harmony with the cosmos.

Chōmei argues that in a world where change is the only constant, worldly success means nothing, for it will soon and surely be reversed. In contrast, the hermit's life brings serenity, which allows him or her to enjoy the moment to the full. In solitude, one's companions are music, poetry, religion, and nature. In these pursuits, the author finds satisfaction in the midst of a violent and uncertain world. He suggests that such a life may not suit everyone, but it is right for him. Having made this choice, however, he then recognizes the error of it: any attachment is sinful; even his attachment to his simple way of life is as sinful as an attachment to wealth and ambition. In the end, all he can do is fall silent and enjoy the sunrise.

Chōmei's style centers on contrast at all levels, from the contrast of social life and the reclusive life, which divides the essay into two sections, down to his consistent use of antitheses in his examples of common folly. In the end, all duality is resolved in silence.

This essay is reminiscent of the biblical book of Ecclesiastes (pp. 154–164) in its recognition of ceaseless change and the absurdity of human endeavor, leading to the conclusion that all we can realistically do if we would find contentment in life is to savor the moment. In Buddhist terms, Chōmei invokes a famous episode in the *Vimalakirti Sutra* (see pp. 260–265) in his use of silence to resolve the conflict of duality. In contrast to the Confucian literati who used that sutra to justify commitment to family and social responsibility, Chōmei's reading points to a more Daoist notion of reclusiveness and a repudiation of words and intellect along with worldliness. In his treatment of these themes, one might also compare Chōmei with Montaigne (pp. 1388–1398), Tao Q'ian (pp. 1003–1008), and Bashō (pp. 1740–1762).

## *An Account of My Hermitage*

### I.

The waters of a flowing stream are ever present but never the same; the bubbles in a quiet pool disappear and form but never endure for long. So it is with men and their dwellings in the world.

The houses of the high and the low seem to last for generation after generation, standing with ridgepoles aligned and roof-tiles jostling in the magnificent imperial capital, but investigation reveals that few of them existed in the past. In some cases, a building that burned last year has been replaced this year; in others, a great house has given way to a small one. And it is the same with the occupants. The places are unchanged, the population remains large, but barely one or two survive among every twenty or thirty of the people I used to know. Just as with the bubbles on the water, someone dies at night and someone else is born in the morning. Where do they come from and where do they go, all those who are born and die? And for whose benefit, for what reason, does a man take enormous pains to build a temporary shelter pleasing to the eye? The master in his dwelling is like the dewdrop vying in ephermerality with the morning glory where it forms. The flower may remain after the dew evaporates, but it withers in the morning sun; the flower may droop before the moisture vanishes, but the dew does not survive until nightfall.

## II.

I have witnessed a number of remarkable occurances in the more than forty years since I began to understand the nature of things. Around the Hour of the Dog [7:00 pm–9:00 pm] on a very windy night—I believe it was the Twenty-eighth of the Fourth Month in the third year of Angen [1177]—a fire broke out in the southeastern part of the capital and burned toward the northwest. In the end, it spread to Suzaku Gate, the Great Hall of State, the Academy, and the Ministry of Popular Affairs, reducing them all to ashes overnight. Its source is said to have been a temporary structure housing some dancers, located near the Higuchi-Tomi-no-koji intersection. Spread here and there by an erratic wind, it burned in a pattern resembling an open fan, narrow at the base and wide at the outer edge. Suffocating smoke engulfed distant houses; wind-whipped flames descended to earth everywhere near at hand. The sky was red to the horizon with ashes lit by the fiery glare, and winged flames leaped a block or two at a time in the lurid atmosphere, torn free by the irresistible force of the gale. Everything must have seemed as unreal as a dream to the people in the fire's path. Some of them fell victim to the smoke. Others died instantly in the embrace of the flames. Still others managed to escape with their lives but failed to rescue their belongings, and all their cherished treasures turned to ashes. The value of so much property may be imagined! The fire claimed the houses of sixteen senior nobles, to say nothing of countless others of less importance. It was reported that fully one-third of the capital had been destroyed. Dozens of men and women were killed; innumerable horses and oxen perished.

All human enterprises are pointless, but it must be counted an act of supreme folly for a man to consume his treasure and put himself to endless trouble merely to build a house in a place as dangerous as the capital.

Again, around the Fourth Month in the fourth year of Jisho [1180], a great whirlwind sprang up near the Nakamikado-[Higashi] Kyogoku intersection and swept all the way to Rokujo Avenue. Not a house, large or small, escaped destruction within the area of three or four blocks where the blast wreaked its full fury. In some cases, entire buildings were flattened; in others, only crossbeams and pillars were spared. Gates were caught up and deposited four or five blocks distant; fences were blown away and neighboring properties merged. And I need hardly mention what happened to smaller objects. Everything inside a house mounted to the skies; cypress-bark thatch and shingles whirled like winter leaves in the wind. Dust ascended like smoke to blind the eye; the terrible howl of the storm swallowed the sound of voices. It seemed that even the dread karma-wind of hell could be no worse. Not only were houses damaged or destroyed, but countless men suffered injury or mutilation while the buildings were being reconstructed. The wind moved toward the south-southeast, visiting affliction on innumerable people.

Whirlwinds are common, but not ones such as that. Those who experienced it worried that it might be an extraordinary phenomenon, a warning from a supernatural being.

Again, around the Sixth Month in the fourth year of Jisho, the court moved suddenly to a new capital. Nobody had dreamed of such a thing. When we consider that more than 400 years had elapsed since the establishment of the present imperial seat during the Emperor Saga's reign, surely a new one ought not to have been chosen without exceptional justification. It was more than reasonable that people should have felt disquiet and apprehension.

But complaints were useless. The Emperor, the Ministers of State, the senior nobles, and all the others moved. Nobody remaind in the old capital who held even a minor court position. Those who aspired to office and rank, or who relied on the favor of patrons, strove to move with all possible dispatch; those who had lost the opportunity to succeed in life, or who had been rejected by society, stayed behind, sunk in gloom. The dwellings that had once stood eave to eave grew more dilapidated with every passing day. Houses were dismantled and sent floating down the Yodo River, and their former locations turned into fields before the onlookers' eyes.

In a complete reversal of values, everyone prized horses and saddles and stopped using oxen and carriages. Properties in the Western and Southern Sea circuits were sought; those in the Eastern Sea and Northern Land circuits were considered undesireable.

It happened that something took me to the new capital in Settsu Province. The cramped site, too small for proper subdivision, rose high on the north where it bordered the hills and sank low on the south beside the sea. The breaking waves never ceased to clamor; the wind from the sea blew with peculiar fury. The imperial palace struck me as unexpectedly novel and interesting, situated in the hills as it was, and I asked myself whether Empress Saimei's log house might not have been rather similar.

I wondered where the people were erecting the whole houses that were being sent downstream daily, their numbers great enough to clog the river. There were still many empty parcels of land and few houses. The old capital was already in ruins; the new one had yet to take form. Not a soul but felt as rootless as a drifting cloud. The original inhabitants grieved over the loss of their land; the new arrivals worried about plaster and lumber. On the streets, those who ought to have used carriages rode horseback; those who ought to have worn court dress or hunting robes appeared in *hitatare*. The customs of the capital had been revolutionized overnight, and the people behaved like rustic warriors.

I have heard that such changes portend civil disturbance—and that was precisely what happened. With every passing day, the world grew more unsettled, people lost more of their composure, and the common folk felt more apprehension. In the end, a crisis brought about a return to the old capital during the winter of the same year. But who knows what became of the houses that had been torn down everywhere? They were not rebuilt in their former style.

We are told that the sage Emperors of old ruled with compassion. They roofed their palaces with thatch, neglecting even to trim the eaves; they remitted the already modest taxes when they saw the commoners' cooking-fires emit less smoke than before. The reason was simply that they cherished their subjects and wished to help them. To compare the present to the past is to see what kind of government we have today.

Again, there was a dreadful two-year famine. (I think it was around the Yowa era [1181–82], but it was too long ago to be sure.) The grain crops were ruined as one calamity followed another; drought in the spring and summer, typhoons and floods in the autumn. It was vain for the farmers to till the fields in the spring or set out plants in the summer; there was no reaping in the fall, no bustle of storage in the winter. Some rural folk abandoned their land and wandered off; others deserted their homes to live in the hills. Prayers were begun and extraordinary rituals were performed, but they accomplished nothing.

The capital had always depended on the countryside for every need. Now, with nothing coming in, people were beside themselves with anxiety. In desperation, they offered all their treasures at bargain rates, but nobody took any notice. The rare person who was willing to trade thought little of gold and much of grain. The streets were overrun with mendicants; lamentations filled the air.

The first of the two years dragged to a close. But just as everyone was anticipating a return to normal in the new year, a pestilence came along to make matters even worse. Like fish gasping in a puddle, the starving populace grew closer to the final extremity with every passing day, until at last people of quite respectable appearance, clad in hats and leggings, begged frantically from house to house. These wretched, dazed beings fell prostrate even as one marveled at their ability to walk.

Countless people perished of starvation by the wayside or died next to tile-capped walls. Since there was no way to dispose of the bodies, noisome stenches filled the air, and innumerable decomposing corpses shocked the eye. Needless to say, the dead lay so thick in the Kamo riverbed that there was not even room for horses and ox-carriages to pass.

With the woodsmen and other commoners too debilitated to perform their usual functions, a shortage of firewood developed, and people who possessed no other means of support broke up their own houses to sell in the market. The amount a man could carry brought less than enough to sustain him for a day. It was shocking to see pieces of wood covered with red lacquer or gold and silver leaf jumbled together with the rest. On inquiry, one learned that desperate people were going to old temples, stealing the sacred images, tearing away the fixtures from the halls, and breaking up everything for firewood. It is because I was born in a degenerate age that I have been forced to witness such disgraceful sights.

Some deeply moving things also happened. Whenever a couple were too devoted to part, the one whose love was greater was the first to die. This is because he or she put the spouse's welfare first and gave up whatever food came to hand. Similarly, a parent always predeceased a child. One sometimes saw a recumbent child sucking at his mother's breast, unaware that her life had ended. Grieved that countless people should be perishing in that manner, Dharma Seal Ryugyo of Ninnaji Temple sought to help the dead toward enlightenment by writing the Sanskrit letter "A" on the forehead of every corpse he saw.

The authorities kept track of the deaths in the Fourth and Fifth Months. During that period, there were more than 42,300 bodies on the streets in the area south of Ichijo, north of Kujo, west of Kyogoku, and east of Suzaku. Of course, many others died before and afterward. And there would be no limit to the numbers if we were to count the Kamo riverbed, Shirakawa, the western sector, and the outlying districts, to say nothing of the provinces in the seven circuits.

People say there was something similar during the reign of the Emperor Sutoku, around the Chosho era [1132–35], but I know nothing about that. I witnessed this phenomenal famine with my own eyes.

If I remember correctly, it was at more or less the same time that a terrible seismic convulsion occurred. It was no ordinary earthquake. Mountains crumbled and buried streams; the sea tilted and immersed the land. Water gushed from fissures in the earth; huge rocks cracked and rolled into valleys. Boats being rowed near the shoreline tossed on the waves; horses journeying on the roads lost their footing. Not a Buddhist hall or stupa remained intact anywhere in the vicinity of the capital. Some crumbled, others fell flat. Dust billowed like smoke; the shaking earth and collapsing houses rumbled like thunder. If people stayed indoors, they were crushed at once; if they ran outside, the ground split apart. If men had been dragons, they might have ridden the clouds, but they lacked the wings to soar into the heavens. It was then that I came to recognize an earthquake as the most terrible of all terrible things.

The violent shaking subsided fairly soon, but aftershocks followed for some time. No day passed without twenty or thirty earthquakes of an intensity that would ordinarily have caused consternation. The intervals lengthened after ten or twenty days, and then there were tremors four or five times a day, or two or three times a day, or once every other day, or once every two or three days. It must have been about three months before they ceased.

Of the four constituents of the universe, water, fire, and wind create constant havoc, but the earth does not usually give rise to any particular calamities. To be sure, there were some dreadful earthquakes in the past for instance, the great shock that toppled the head of the Todaiji Buddha during the Saiko era [854–57], but none of them could compare with this. Immediately after the event, people all talked about the meaninglessness of life and seemed somewhat more free from spiritual impurity than usual. But nobody even mentioned the subject after the days and months had accumulated and the years had slipped by.

Such, then, is the difficulty of life in this world, such the ephemerality of man and his dwellings. Needless to say, it would be utterly impossible to list every affliction that stems from individual circumstance or social position. If a man of negligible status lives beside a powerful family, he cannot make a great display of happiness when he has cause for heartfelt rejoicing, nor can he lift his voice in lamentation when he experiences devastating grief. In all that he does, he is ill at ease; like a sparrow near a hawk's nest, he pursues his daily activities in fear and trembling. If a poor man lives next door to a wealthy house, he abases himself before the neighbors and agonizes over his wretched appearance whenever he goes out in the morning or returns in the evening. Forced to witness the envy of his wife, children, and servants, and to hear the rich household dismiss him with contempt, he is forever agitated and constantly distraught.

He who lives in a crowded area cannot escape calamity when a fire breaks out nearby; he who settles in a remote spot suffers hardships in his travels to and fro and puts himself at grave risk from robbers. The powerful man is consumed by greed; the man who refuses to seek a patron becomes an object of derision. The man who owns many possessions knows many worries; the impoverished man seethes with envy.

He who depends on another belongs to another; he who takes care of another is chained by human affection. When a man observes the conventions, he falls into economic difficulties; when he flouts them, people wonder if he is mad. Where can we live, what can we do, to find even the briefest of shelters, the most fleeting peace of mind?

## III.

For a long time, I lived in a house inherited from my paternal grandmother. Later, my fortunes declined through lack of connections, and I found myself unable to remain in society, despite many nostalgic associations. Shortly after I entered my thirties, I moved voluntarily into a simple, new dwelling one-tenth the size of the old place. I built only a personal residence, with no fashionable auxiliary structures, and although I managed an encircling earthen wall, my means did not extend to a gate. The carriage-shelter was supported by bamboo pillars, and the house was unsafe in a snowfall or windstorm. The site was near the riverbed, which left it vulnerable to floods, and there was also danger of robbers.

For more than thirty miserable years, I endured an existence in which I could not maintain my position. Every setback during that time drove home the realization that I was not blessed by fortune. And thus, at fifty, I became a monk and turned my back on the world. Having never had a wife or children, I was not bound to others by ties difficult to break; lacking office and stipend, I possessed no attachments to which to cling.

During the next five springs and autumns, I sojourned among the clouds of the Ohara hills, leading a life devoid of spiritual progress.

Now at sixty, with the dew nearing its vanishing point, I have built a new shelter for the tree's last leaves, just as a traveler might fashion a single night's resting place or an old silkworm spin a cocoon. It is not a hundredth the size of my second house. Indeed, while I have sat around uttering idle complaints, my age has increased with every year, and my house has shrunk with every move.

This house is unusual in appearance. It is barely ten feet square, and its height is less than seven feet. The location was a matter of indifference to me; I did not divine to select a site. I built a foundation and a simple roof, and attached hinges to all the joints so that I could move easily if cause for dissatisfaction arose. There would be no trouble about rebuilding. The house would barely fill two carts, and the carters' fees would be the only expense.

After settling on my present place of retirement in the Hino hills, I extended the eastern eaves about three feet to provide myself with a convenient spot in which to break up and burn firewood. On the south side of the building, I have an open bamboo veranda with a holy water shelf at the west end. Toward the north end of the west wall, beyond a freestanding screen, there is a picture of Amida Buddha, with an image of Fugen alongside and a copy of the Lotus Sutra in front. At the east end of the room, some dried bracken serves as a bed. South of the screen on the west side, a bamboo shelf suspended from the ceiling holds three leather-covered bamboo baskets, in which I keep excerpts from poetry collections and critical treatises, works on music, and religous tracts like Collection of Essentials on Rebirth in the Pure Land. A zither and a lute stand next to the shelf. The zither is of the folding variety; the handle of the lute is detachable. Such is the appearance of my rude temporary shelter.

To turn to the surroundings: I have made a rock basin in which to collect water from an elevated conduit south of the hermitage, and I gather ample supplies of firewood in a neighboring stand of trees. The locality is called Toyama, "the foothills." Vines cover the paths. The valley is thickly forested, but there is open land to the west.

Aids to contemplation abound. In the spring, lustrous cascades of wisteria burgeon in the west like purple clouds. In the summer, every song of the cuckoo conveys a promise of companionship in the Shide Mountains. In the autumn, the incessant cries of the cicadas seem to lament the transitoriness of worldly things. And in the winter, the accumulating and melting snows suggest poignant comparisons with sins and hindrances.

When I tire of reciting the sacred name or find myself intoning a sutra in a perfunctory manner, I rest as I please, I fall idle as I see fit. There is nobody to interfere, nobody to shame me. Although I do not make a point of performing silent austerities, I can control speech-induced karma because I live alone; although I do not make a fuss about obeying the commandments, I have no occasion to break them because mine is not an environment conducive to transgression.

On mornings when I compare my existence to a white wake in the water, I borrow Mansei's style while watching boats come and go at Okanoya; on evenings when the wind rustles the maple leaves, I imitate Tsunenobu's practice while recalling the Xinyang River. If my interest does not flag, I often perform "Song of the Autumn Wind" as an accompaniment to the murmur of the pines, or play "Melody of the Flowing Spring" to harmonize with the sound of the water. I am not an accomplished musician, but my playing is not designed for the pleasure of others. I merely pluck the strings alone and chant alone to comfort my own spirit.

At the foot of the hill, there is a brush-thatched cottage, the abode of the mountain warden. The small boy who lives there pays me an occasional visit, and if I chance to feel at loose ends, I set out for a ramble with him as my companion. He is ten, I am sixty. Our ages differ greatly, but we take pleasure in the same things. Sometimes we pull out reed-flower sprouts, pick iwanashi berries, heap up yam sprouts, or pluck herbs. Or we may go to the rice fields at the foot of the mountains, glean ears left by the reapers, and fashion sheafs. When the weather is balmy, we scramble up to a peak from which I can look toward the distant skies over my old home and see Kohatayama, Fushimi-no-sato, Toba, and Hatsukashi. Nobody owns the view; there is nothing to keep me from enjoying it.

When the going is easy and I feel like taking a long walk, I follow the peaks past Sumiyama and Kasatori to worship at Iwama or Ishiyama. Or I may traverse Awazu Plain, visit the site of Semimaru's dwelling, cross the Tanakami River, and seek out Sarumaru's grave. On the way home I search for cherry blossoms, pick autumn leaves, gather bracken, or collect fruit and nuts, depending on the season. Some of my trophies I present to the Buddha; others I treat as useful souvenirs.

On peaceful nights, I long for old friends while gazing at the moon through the window, or weep into my sleeve at the cry of a monkey. Sometimes I mistake fireflies in the bushes for fish lures burning far away at Maki-no-shima Island, or think that a gale must be scattering the leaves when I hear rain just before dawn. The horohoro call of a pheasant makes me wonder if the bird might be a parent; the frequent visits of deer from the peaks attest to the remoteness of my abode. Sometimes I stir up the banked fire and make it a companion for the wakefulness of old age. The mountains are so little intimidating that even the owl's hoot sounds moving rather than eerie. Indeed, there is no end to the delights of the changing seasons in these surroundings. A truly reflective man, blessed with superior powers of judgement, would undoubtedly find many more pleasures than the ones I have described.

## IV.

When I first began to live here, I thought it would not be for long, but five years have already elapsed. My temporary hermitage has gradually become a home, its eaves covered with rotted leaves and its foundation mossy. Whenever I happen to hear news of the capital, I learn that many illustrious personages have breathed their last since my retreat to these mountains. And it would be quite impossible to keep track of all the unimportant people who have died. A great many houses have also suffered destruction in recurrent conflagrations. Only in my temporary hermitage is life peaceful and safe. The quarters are cramped, but I have a place where I can lie at night and another where I can sit in the daytime. There is ample room for one person. The hermit crab likes a small shell because it knows its own size; the osprey lives on the rocky coast because it fears man. It is the same with me. Knowing myself and knowing the world, I harbor no ambitions and pursue no material objectives. Quietude is what I desire; the absence of worries is what makes me happy.

Men do not usually build houses for their own benefit. Some build for wives, children, relatives, and servants, some for friends and acquaintances, some for masters, for teachers, or even for household goods, treasures, oxen, and horses. But I have built for myself this time, not for anybody else. Because of my present conditions and my own situation, I possess neither a family to share my dwelling nor servants to work for me. If I had built a great house, whom would I have lodged in it, whom would I have established here?

Friends esteem wealth and look for favors; they do not necessarily value sincere friendship or probity. I prefer to make friends of music and nature. Servants prize lavish rewards and unstinting generosity; they do not care about protection, affection, or a safe, tranquil existence. I prefer to make my own body my servant. How do I do it? If there is work to perform, I use my body. True, I may grow weary, but it is easier than employing and looking after someone else. If there is walking to do, I walk. It is burdensome, but less so than worrying over horses, saddles, oxen, and carriages. I divide my body and put it to two uses; it suits me very well to employ hands as servants and feet as conveyances. My mind understands my body's distress; I allow the body to rest when it is distressed and use it when it feels energetic. I use it but do not make a habit of pushing it to extremes. If it finds a task irksome, I am not perturbed. It is surely a healthful practice to walk constantly and work constantly. What would be the point of idling away the time? To make others work creates bad karma. Why should I borrow their strength?

It is the same with food and clothing. I hide my nakedness under a rough fiber robe, a hemp quilt, or whatever comes to hand; I survive by eating starwort from the fields and nuts from the peaks. Because I do not mingle with others, I need not chide myself for having felt ashamed of my appearance. Because I possess little food, I find coarse fare tasty.

I do not describe such pleasures as a means of criticizing the wealthy; I merely compare my own former life with my present existence. "The triple world is but one mind." If the mind is not at peace, elephants, horses, and the seven treasures are trash; palatial residences and stately mansions are worthless. I feel warm affection for my present lonely dwelling, my tiny cottage. My beggarly appearance is a source of embarrassment on the infrequent occasions when something takes me to the capital, but after my return I feel pity for those who would pursue worldly things. If anyone doubts my sincerity, let him consider the fish and the birds. A fish never tires of water, but only another fish can understand why. A bird seeks trees, but only another bird can understand why. It is the same with the pleasures of retirement. Only a recluse can understand them.

## V.

The moon of my life is setting; my remaining years approach the rim of the hills. Very soon I shall face the darkness of the Three Evil Paths. Which of my old disappointments is worth fretting over now? The Buddha teaches us to reject worldly things. Even my affection for this thatched hut is a sin; even my love of tranquility must be counted an impediment to rebirth. Why do I waste my time in description of inconsequential pleasures?

As I reflect on these things in the quiet moments before dawn, I put a question to myself:

You retired to the seclusion of remote hills so that you might discipline your mind and practice the Way, but your impure spirit belies your monkish garb. Your dwelling presumes to imitate the abode of the honorable Yuima, but you are worse than Suddhipanthaka when it comes to obeying the commandments. Is this because you let yourself become troubled by karma-ordained poverty, or has your deluded mind finally lost its sanity?

The question remains unanswered. I can do no other than to use my impure tongue for three or four repetitions of Amida's sacred name. Then I fall silent.

Late in the Third Month of the second year of Kenryaku [1212] Set down by the monk Ren'in in the hermitage at Toyama

## FROM TALES OF THE HEIKE (13TH CENT.)

*Translated by Helen Craig McCullough*

After flourishing for more than four hundred years, in the late twelfth century Japanese court society and its preoccupation with elegance collapsed into a period of brutal civil war. From 1180 to 1185, the Taira (Heike) and Minamoto (Genji) clans struggled to supplant the Fujiwara family for control of military, political, and economic power. The war raged across the entire length of the country and culminated in the establishment of a warrior society, which eventually formed the basis of Japan's tradition of samurai culture. The collapse of court society, with its long traditions and concern for beauty and elegance, had been inevitable, according to the Buddhist philosophy of evanescence. Nevertheless, this development was bitterly lamented by those who abhorred the world of violence and brutality that replaced it.

The *Tales of the Heike* were compiled in several versions, beginning in the thirteenth century. Accounts of the war were originally sung by *Biwa Hoshi,* blind Buddhist monks who toured the countryside like troubadours. These monks accompanied their narrative recitations with a *biwa,* or lute. Thus, the tone of the narrative has a powerful rhythmic and liturgical quality, and the content is heavily influenced by Buddhist doctrine. It is impossible to know who compiled these episodic accounts into the vast work we have today.

The selections presented here include the opening lines, *Gion Shōja,* which serve as a homily for the entire text. It is a reminder both of the transitoriness of life and of the truth that those who are great and powerful will surely be brought low and become as dust before the wind. This introduction is followed by the example of the dancer Giō and her rival Hotoke, who early on realize the futility of all worldliness and renounce the world. Later comes a more detailed account of the career of the hapless Koremori. Born to wealth and power, trained as a poet, and by nature a family man, he is not suited for the world in which he lives. Appointed commander-in-chief of the Taira forces in the north, he leads his armies to a series of defeats. By the time the Taira armies have been driven from the capital, dislodged from their base at Ichi no Tani and fighting for their lives at Yashima, Koremori has had enough of war. He leaves the battle and tries to make his way back through enemy lines to rejoin his wife and son in Kyoto. This very human choice to renounce war and brutality in favor of family and cultivation is not possible, however. He then considers choosing the Buddhist solution to abandon the world of war but cannot bring himself to do it because that means renouncing family as well. Neither can he accept the world of family and culture because that means also accepting the inevitability of war. He must accept it all or renounce it all; unable to resolve the dilemma, he takes his own life.

Koremori's fellow commander, Tadanori, follows a different route. As the Taira army evacuates the capital, he makes his way through the fleeing army and crowds of refugees to return to the contested and burning city. He does this at great personal risk in order to leave copies of some of his poetry with Fujiwara Shunzei, who is editing an anthology. Tadanori explains that however the war may turn out, he would prefer to be remembered as a poet rather than a warrior. He dies heroically in battle, and even his enemies mourn the death of so fine a poet. Time and again we are reminded that although the Minamoto are better skilled in the martial arts and win the war, they are little better than uncultured savages who know nothing of art, music, or poetry. We might recall here the Homeric hero's ideal balancing of word and deed and the qualities of cultural and martial valor (*wen* and *wu*) extolled in the dynastic hymns of the ancient Chinese *Book of Songs* (pp. 295–317).

The selection concludes with the final years of Lady Kenreimon'in. Born the daughter of the Regent, wife to an emperor and mother of an emperor, she held the world, as she says, in the palm of her hand. Through no virtue of her own, she was born to such a life; through no fault of her own, she sees it all disappear. Her family becomes engaged in savage war; they are forced to flee their homes and endure hardships. Finally, she must witness the death of all her family, including her child. Forced to live on in retirement, she cannot forget—nor can she bear to remember—the things that have befallen her. She has passed through all six realms of Buddhist existence, from the paradise of her early life to the lowest depths of hell. At last she finds herself in the same position as Giō, the dancing girl from the opening chapter. She is visited in her hermitage by the Retired Emperor Go-Shirakawa, a canny political survivor who reminds her of her past. We lament the lady's loss but also recognize the irony of one who appears to succeed by actually remaining in the world.

# Tales of the Heike

The war tales collected in *Tales of the Heike* were originally recited orally by blind Buddhist monks who traveled the country like troubadours entertaining audiences with their stories. Consequently the text has a strongly liturgical quality, both in the rhythms by which it flows and in the message that is presented. To hear it spoken aloud is like hearing a sutra being chanted.

Presented here are three versions of the opening paragraph, which serves as a homily for all that is to follow. No matter what digressions the narrative takes, we are always reminded that those who are great and powerful must surely be brought low and become as dust before the wind.

祇園精舎の鐘の聲、諸行無常の響あり。娑羅雙樹の花の色、盛者必衰のことはりをあらはす。おごれる人も久しからず、只春の夜の夢のごとし。たけき者も遂にはほろびぬ、偏に風の前の塵に同じ。

## Kitagawa and Tsuchida

The bell of the Gion Temple tolls into every man's heart to warn him that all is vanity and evanescence. The faded flowers of the sala trees by the Buddha's deathbed bear witness to the truth that all who flourish are destined to decay. Yes, pride must have its fall, for it is as unsubstantial as a dream on a spring night. The brave and violent man—he too must die away in the end, like a whirl of dust in the wind.

## McCullough

The sound of the Gion Shōja bells echoes the impermanence of all things;
The color of the *śāla* flowers reveals the truth that the prosperous must decline.
The proud do not endure; they are like a dream on a spring night;
The mighty fall at last, they are as dust before the wind. . . .

## Sadler

The sound of the bell of Jetavana echoes the impermanence of all things. The hue of the flowers of the teak-tree declares that they who flourish must be brought low. Yea, the proud ones are but for a moment, like an evening dream in springtime. The mighty are destroyed at last, they are but as dust before the wind.

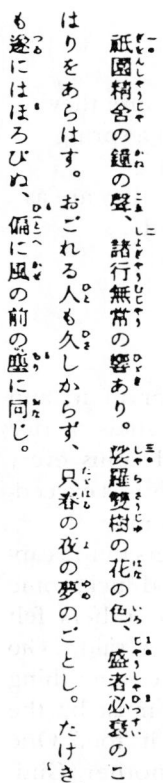

## Ch. 1 [Gion Shōja]

Time: seventh month of 1169 to around fifth month of 1177

Principal subject: growth of bad feeling between the Taira clan and the court

Principal characters:

GO-SHIRAKAWA, RETIRED EMPEROR. Head of the imperial clan

JŌKEN. Prominent Buddhist monk; holds title Dharma Seal

KIYOMORI (TAIRA). Retired head of the Taira clan; main power at court

MOTOFUSA (FUJIWARA). Imperial regent

NARICHIKA (FUJIWARA). A favorite courtier of Retired Emperor Go-Shirakawa; the principal Shishi-no-tani conspirator

NARITSUNE (FUJIWARA). Son of Narichika; son-in-law of Norimori

NORIMORI (TAIRA). Brother of Kiyomori; father-in-law of Naritsune

SHIGEMORI (TAIRA). Eldest son of Kiyomori, on whom he is a restraining influence; clan head

SHUNKAN, BISHOP. High official at Hosshōji, an important Buddhist temple; a Shishi-no-tani conspirator

TAKAKURA. Reigning emperor; son of Retired Emperor Go-Shirakawa

YASUYORI (TAIRA). A minor member of the Taira clan; a Shishi-no-tani conspirator

### 1.1. Gion Shōja

The sound of the Gion Shōja bells echoes the impermanence of all things;
The color of the *śāla* flowers reveals the truth that the prosperous must decline.
The proud do not endure; they are like a dream on a spring night;
The mighty fall at last, they are as dust before the wind. . . .

### 1.6. Giō

*[This is one of a series of early episodes describing the rise and increasing arrogance of the Taira and their leader, Kiyomori.]*

Now that Kiyomori held the whole country in the palm of his hand, he indulged in one freakish caprice after another, undeterred by the censure of society or the scorn of individuals. For instance, there were two famous and accomplished *shirabyōshi* dancers who lived in the capital in those days, sisters called Giō and Ginyo. They were the daughters of another dancer, Toji. Kiyomori took a great fancy to Giō, the older one, which meant that Ginyo, the younger, became a popular favorite. He also built a fine house for the mother, Toji, installed her in it, and sent her five hundred bushels of rice and a hundred thousand coins every month. So the whole family was exceedingly prosperous and fortunate.

When the other dancers in the capital heard about Giō's good luck, some of them felt envious and others felt spiteful. The envious ones said, "Giō has all the luck! I wish the same thing would happen to me. It must be the 'Gi' in her name. I'll use it, too." One called herself Giichi, another Gini, another Gifuku, another Gitoku, and so forth. The spiteful ones, of whom there were many, stuck to their own names. "What difference could a name or part of a name make?" they sniffed. "Good luck is something a person gets from a previous existence."

After things had gone on like that for three years, another famous dancer arrived in the capital from Kaga Province. Her name was Hotoke, and she was sixteen years old. Everybody in the city showered her with praise, high and low alike. "We've had lots of *shirabyōshi* ever since the old days, but we've never seen dancing like this," people said.

"No matter how famous I am, I'm disappointed that I've never been called in by Kiyomori, the most important man in the country," Hotoke thought. "What's to keep me from volunteering to perform for him? It's usual enough." She went to Kiyomori's house at Nishihachijō, and someone announced her.

"Hotoke is here, the dancer they're talking about in the capital nowadays."

"What's that you say? Entertainers like her aren't supposed to just show up without being called. What makes her think she can do this? Besides, she has no business coming to the place where Giō lives, whether she's a god or a buddha. Throw her out!" Kiyomori said.

As Hotoke was about to leave after that harsh dismissal, Giō spoke to Kiyomori. "It's quite customary for an entertainer to appear without an invitation. And they say Hotoke's very young, too. Now that she's plucked up the courage to come, it would be cruel to send her home with that harsh dismissal. As a dancer myself, I can't help feeling involved; I'd be miserable. You'd be doing her a great kindness if you just received her, even if you didn't watch her dance or listen to her sing. Won't you please bend a little and call her back?"

"Well, my dear, if you're going to make a point of it, I'll see her before she goes," Kiyomori said. He sent a messenger to summon Hotoke.

Hotoke had entered her carriage after that harsh dismissal. She was just leaving, but she returned in obedience to the summons. Kiyomori came out to meet her. "I shouldn't have received you today; I'm just doing it because Giō made a point of it. But I may as well listen to a song as long as I'm here. Let's have an *imayō*," he said. Hotoke assented respectfully:

Now that it has encountered
 this lord for the first time,
it will live a thousand years—
 the seedling pine tree.
Cranes seem to have come in
 flocks to
 disport themselves
where Turtle Island rises
 from the garden lake.

She chanted the song three times, and the beauty of her voice astonished everyone. Kiyomori felt a stir of interest. "You sing *imayō* nicely, my dear. I suspect you're a good dancer, too," he said. "I'll watch you do a number. Call the drummer." The drummer was set to his instrument and Hotoke danced.

A beautiful girl with a magnificent head of hair and a sweet, flawless voice could hardly have been a clumsy dancer. Her skill was beyond imagination, and Kiyomori was dazzled, swept off his feet.

"What can this mean?" Hotoke said. "It was my own idea to come, and I was thrown out for my pains, but then I was called back because Giō spoke up for me. What would she think if I were kept here? It's embarrassing even to wonder about it. Please let me go home now."

"That's out of the question. If you're hanging back because of Giō, I'll get rid of her," Kiyomori said.

"I couldn't dream of such a thing! It would be bad enough if you kept the two of us here together, but I couldn't possibly face the embarrassment if you sent her away and kept me by myself. Please let me go today. I'll come any time you happen to remember me."

"What! What! That's out of the question. Tell Giō to get out of the house right now." He sent Giō three separate messages.

Giō had resigned herself to this possibility long ago, but she had never dreamed that it might happen "so very soon as today." Now, with Kiyomori insisting on her immediate departure, she prepared to leave as soon as the room was swept and tidied.

Every parting causes sadness, even when two people have merely sheltered under the same tree or scooped water from the same stream. With what regret and grief did Giō prepare to bid farewell to her home of three years, her eyes brimming with futile tears! But she could not linger; the end had come. Weeping, she scribbled a poem on a sliding door before she set out—perhaps to serve as a reminder of one who had gone:

> Since both are grasses
> of the field, how may either
> be spared by autumn—
> the young shoot blossoming forth
> and the herb fading from view?

She got into her carriage, rode home, and fell prostrate inside the sliding doors, sobbing wildly.

"What's the matter? What's wrong?" her mother and sister asked. She could not answer. They had to learn the truth by questioning the maid who had come with her.

The monthly deliveries of rice and coins ceased, and it was the turn of Hotoke's connections to prosper. All kinds of men sent Giō letters and messengers. "People say Kiyomori has dismissed her. Why not see her and have some fun?" they thought. But she could not shrug everything off and lead a gay social life. She refused to receive the letters, much less the messengers, and spent more and more time in tears, her gloom deepened by their importunities.

The year ended, and in the following spring a messenger came to Giō's house from Kiyomori. "How have you been since we parted? Hotoke seems bored these days; come and amuse her with some *imayō* and dances." Giō made no reply.

"Why don't you answer? Do you refuse to come? If so, speak up. There are steps I can take," Kiyomori sent word.

Giō's mother, Toji, was upset. "Do give him some kind of answer, Giō," she urged tearfully. "That would be better than having him scold you like this."

Giō still refused to answer. "I'd promise to go at once if I meant to obey him, but I don't mean to, so I don't know what to say. He says he'll 'take steps' unless I obey his summons, but the most he can do is banish or kill me. Banishment wouldn't matter to me, or death, either. I can't face him again after the contemptuous way he treated me," she said.

Her mother offered some more advice. "No living creature in our country can disobey Kiyomori. The bonds linking a man and a woman are forged before this life begins. Sometimes a couple may part early, after having sworn to stay together forever; sometimes a relationship that had seemed temporary may last a lifetime. A sexual liaison is the most uncertain thing in the world. That you enjoyed Kiyomori's favor for three years was an unusual show of affection on his part. Of course he won't kill you if you don't obey his summons; he'll simply expel you from the capital. You and your sister are young; you'll probably survive very nicely, even among rocks and trees. But your feeble old mother will be banished too, and my heart sinks when I think of living in some strange country place. Won't you please let me finish out my life in the capital? I'll regard it as a filial act in this world and the next."

Giō told herself that she had to obey her mother, hard though it was. She was pitifully distraught as she set out, her eyes brimming with tears. Unable to bring herself to go alone, she traveled to Nishihachijō in a carriage with her sister, Ginyo, and two other dancers.

It was not to her old place, but to a much inferior seat, that she was directed.

"What can this mean?" she wondered. "It was misery enough to be discarded through no fault of my own; now I have to accept an inferior seat. What shall I do?" She pressed her sleeve to her face to hide the tears, but they came trickling through.

Hotoke was overcome with pity. "Ah, what's this?" she said. "It might be different if she weren't used to being called up here. Please have her come here, or else please excuse me. I'd like to go and greet her."

"That's entirely out of the question!" Kiyomori made her stay where she was.

Then Kiyomori spoke up, with no regard for Giō's feelings. "Well, how've you been since we parted? Hotoke seems bored; sing her an *imayō*."

Now that she was there, Giō felt unable to refuse. She restrained her tears and sang:

> In days of old, the Buddha
>     was but a mortal;
> in the end, we ourselves
>     will be buddhas too.
> How grievous that distinctions
>     must separate those
> who are alike in sharing
>     the Buddha-nature!

She repeated the words twice, weeping, and tears of sympathy flowed from the eyes of all the many Taira senior nobles, courtiers, gentlemen of fifth rank, and samurai who sat in rows looking on.

Kiyomori was diverted by the performance. "An excellent entertainment for the occasion," he said. "I'd like to watch you dance, but some urgent business has come up today. Keep presenting yourself from now on, even if I don't summon you; you must amuse Hotoke with your *imayō* and dances." Giō departed in silence, suppressing her tears.

"I forced myself to go to that hateful place because I didn't want to disobey Mother, and now I've been humiliated again. The same thing will keep happening if I stay in society. I'm going to drown myself," Giō said.

"If you do, I'll drown with you," said her sister, Ginyo.

The mother, Toji, was greatly distressed. In tears, she offered more advice. "It's only natural for you to feel bitter. I'm sorry I urged you to go; I didn't dream things would turn out that way. But if you drown yourself, your sister says she'll do the same, and then what will become of your feeble old mother, even if she manages to linger on after the deaths of her two daughters? I'll drown with you. I suppose a person would have to say it's one of the five deadly sins to make a parent drown before her time. The world is only a transient shelter; it doesn't matter if we suffer humiliation here. The truly hard thing is the darkness of the long afterlife. This life is nothing; I'm just worrying about your having to face the evil paths in the next one."

After hearing her mother's tearful plea, Giō suppressed her own tears. "You're right. There's no doubt that I'd be committing one of the five deadly sins if we all killed ourselves. I'll give up the idea of suicide. But I'd just have to suffer more if I stayed in the capital, so I'm going somewhere else."

Thus it was that Giō became a nun at the age of twenty-one. She built a brush-thatched hermitage deep in the Saga mountains, and there she dwelt, murmuring buddha-invocations.

"I vowed to drown myself with my sister," Ginyo said. "Why should I hang behind when it comes to renouncing the world?" Most pitifully, that nineteen-year-old girl also altered her appearance and secluded herself with Giō to pray for rebirth in paradise.

"In a world where even young girls alter their appearance, why should a feeble old mother cling to her gray hair?" the mother, Toji, said. She shaved her head at the age of forty-five and, like her daughters, performed buddha-invocations in earnest prayer for rebirth in paradise.

Spring passed, summer waned, and the first autumn winds blew. It was the season when mortals gaze at the star-meeting skies and write of love on the leaves of the paper-mulberry, the tree reminiscent of an oar crossing the heavenly stream.

One afternoon, the mother and daughters watched the setting sun disappear behind the rim of the western hills. "People say the western paradise lies where the sun sets. Someday we'll be born into a peaceful life there," they said. The thought evoked memories and brought many tears.

After the twilight faded, they fastened their plaited bamboo door, lit the dim lamp, and settled down to intoning buddha-invocations in unison.

While they were chanting, they were frightened by the sound of someone knocking on the door.

"A malevolent spirit must have come to interfere with our humble invocations," they said. "What mortal would wait until late at night to visit a brush-thatched mountain hermitage, a place where nobody ever calls, not even in the daytime? The door is just plaited bamboo; it would be the easiest thing in the world to smash it if we refused to open it. We'd better let him in. If he's a merciless creature bent on our destruction, we must rely firmly on the original vow of Amida, the Buddha in whom we have always placed our trust; we must just keep repeating the sacred name. The heavenly host comes to meet believers when it hears their voices, so it will be sure to take us to the pure land. We'll simply have to be careful not to falter in our recitations."

Reassuring one another in that manner, they opened the door. But the visitor was not a malevolent spirit. No, it was Hotoke.

"What in the world!" Giō said. "Can it really be Hotoke? Am I awake or dreaming?"

Hotoke tried to restrain her tears. "What I say will probably sound self-serving, but it would seem callous to keep quiet about it, so I want to go over the whole story from the beginning. I went to Kiyomori's mansion on my own initiative and was turned away, but then I was called back, thanks entirely to Giō's intervention. A woman is a poor, weak creature who can't control her destiny. I felt miserable about being kept there. When you were summoned again to sing the *imayō,* it brought my own situation home to me. I couldn't feel happy when I knew my turn would come some day. I also realized that you spoke the truth in the lines you left on the sliding door, 'How may either be spared by autumn?' Later on, I didn't know where you'd gone, but I heard that the three of you were living together as nuns. I envied you after that, and I kept asking for my freedom, but Kiyomori wouldn't let me go.

"When we stop and think about it, good fortune in this world is a dream within a dream; happiness and prosperity mean nothing. It's hard to achieve birth in human form, hard to gain access to the Buddha's teachings. If I sink into hell this time, it will be hard to rise again, no matter how many eons may pass. We can't count on our youth; the old may outlive the young in this world. Death refuses to wait for the space of a breath; life is more evanescent than a mayfly or a lightning flash. I couldn't bear to keep preening myself on my temporary good fortune and ignoring the life to come, so I stole away this morning, put on this appearance, and made my way here." She removed the robe that had covered her head, and they saw that she had become a nun.

"Now that I've come to you in this new guise, please forgive my past offenses," she pleaded, with tears streaming down her face. "If you say you forgive me, I want to recite the sacred name with you and be reborn on the same lotus pedestal. But if you can't bring yourself to do it, I'll wander off—I don't care where—and then I'll recite buddha-invocations as long as I live, lying on a bed of moss or the roots of a pine tree, so that I can be reborn in the pure land."

Giō tried to restrain her tears. "I never dreamed you felt that way. I ought to have been able to accept my unhappiness here at Saga, for sorrow is the common lot in this world, but I was always jealous of you. I'm afraid there would have been no rebirth in the pure land for me. I seemed stranded halfway between this world and the next. The change in your appearance has scattered my old resentment like dewdrops; there's no doubt now that I'll be reborn in the pure land. To be able to attain that goal is the greatest of all possible joys. People have talked about our becoming nuns as though it were unprecedented, and I've more or less thought the same thing, but it was only natural for me to do it when I hated society and resented my fate. What I did isn't worth mentioning if it's compared with the vows you've just taken. You weren't resentful, you knew no sorrow. Only true piety could instill such revulsion against the unclean world, such longing for the pure land, in the heart of someone who's barely turned seventeen. I look on you as a teacher. Let's seek salvation together."

Secluded in a single dwelling, the four women offered flowers and incense before the sacred images morning and evening, and their prayers never flagged. I have heard that all of them achieved their goal of rebirth in the pure land, each in her turn. And so it was that the four names, "the spirits of Giō, Ginyo, Hotoke, and Toji," were inscribed together on the memorial register at Retired Emperor Go-Shirakawa's Chōgōdō Hall. Theirs were touching histories. . . .

## *Ch. 7 [The Story of Koremori]*

Time: fourth to seventh month of 1183

Principal subjects: fighting in the north between Yoshinaka and the Taira; the flight of the Taira from the capital

Principal characters:

GO-SHIRAKAWA, RETIRED EMPEROR. Head of the imperial clan

KENREIMON'IN. Daughter of Kiyomori; consort of the late Emperor Takakura; mother of the young Emperor Antoku

KOREMORI (TAIRA). Son of Shigemori; grandson of Kiyomori

MICHIMORI (TAIRA). Son of Norimori; nephew of Kiyomori

MOTOMICHI (FUJIWARA). Imperial regent

NORITSUNE (TAIRA). Son of Norimori; nephew of Kiyomori

SHIGEHIRA (TAIRA). Son of Kiyomori

TADANORI (TAIRA). Son of Tadamori; brother of Kiyomori

TOMOMORI (TAIRA). Son of Kiyomori

TSUNEMASA (TAIRA). Son of Tsunemori; nephew of Kiyomori

YOSHINAKA (MINAMOTO). Cousin of Yoritomo; leader of anti-Taira forces in the north

YUKIIE (MINAMOTO). Son of Tameyoshi; uncle of Yoritomo and Yoshinaka

*[The expedition planned in 1181, before Kiyomori's death, has yet to take place. Fighting in the provinces has continued, and Yoshinaka, in particular, has been successful against Taira partisans. "The Heike in the capital shrugged off the news from the provinces. On the sixteenth [of the ninth month of 1182], Munemori was reappointed to the office of major counselor, and on the third of the tenth month he became palace minister. When he went to make his formal expression of gratitude on the seventh, he was attended by twelve Taira senior nobles and preceded by sixteen courtiers on horseback, including the two head chamberlains. But there seemed little substance to such magnificent occasions, staged as they were in frivolous disregard of the coming storm, while the Genji in the east and north swarmed like hornets, poised for an attack on the capital"; Sec. 6.12.]*

### 7.2. The Expedition to the Northern Provinces

Meanwhile, there were rumors that Kiso no Yoshinaka, the master of the Eastern Mountain and Northern Land roads, was about to attack the capital with more than fifty thousand horsemen. Ever since last year, the Heike had been proclaiming their intention to give battle "when the horses are fed young grass next year"; and warriors had been pouring in like clouds from the Mountain Shade, Mountain Sun, Southern Sea, and Western Sea roads. Men had arrived from the provinces of Ōmi, Mino, and Hida on the Eastern Sea Road, but none had come from Tōtōmi or anywhere farther east. (Those in the west all came.) Nobody came from Wakasa or farther north on the Northern Land Road.

It had been decided that a punitive force would be sent to the Northern Land Road to defeat Yoshinaka, and that it would go on to attack Yoritomo. During the first quarter of the hour of the dragon [7:00 A.M.–9:00 A.M.] on the seventeenth of the fourth month in the second year of Juei [1183], a combined total of more than a hundred thousand horsemen headed northward from the capital. They were led by six commanders-in-chief, and by more than three hundred and forty principal samurai commanders.

The commanders-in-chief:

KOMATSU MIDDLE CAPTAIN OF THIRD RANK KOREMORI
ECHIZEN GOVERNOR OF THIRD RANK MICHIMORI
TAJIMA GOVERNOR TSUNEMASA
SATSUMA GOVERNOR TADANORI
MIKAWA GOVERNOR TOMONORI
AWAJI GOVERNOR KIYOFUSA

The main samurai commanders:

ETCHŪ NO ZENJI MORITOSHI
KAZUSA NO TAIFU NO HANGAN TADATSUNA
HIDA NO TAIFU NO HANGAN KAGETAKA
TAKAHASHI NO HANGAN NAGATSUNA
KAWACHI NO HANGAN HIDEKUNI
MUSASHI NO SABURŌZAEMON ARIKUNI
ETCHŪ NO JIRŌBYŌE MORITSUGI
KAZUSA NO GORŌBYŌE TADAMITSU
AKUSHICHIBYŌE KAGEKIYO

The army had received authorization to live off the provinces, and it seized everything in its path from Ōsaka Barrier onward, even rice and other official tax commodities levied from powerful landowners and great houses. The common people all scattered into the mountains and fields, driven beyond endurance, as the host gradually looted its way through Shiga, Karasaki, Mitsukawajiri, Mano, Takashima, Shiotsu, and Kaizu.

* * *

## 7.4. The Battle at Hiuchi

While he was still based in Shinano Province, Kiso no Yoshinaka built a stronghold at Hiuchi in Echizen Province and provided it with a garrison of more than six thousand horsemen—the Heizenji abbot Saimei, Inazu no Shinsuke, Saitōda, Hayashi no Rokurō Mitsuakira, the Togashi novice Bussei, Tsuchida, Takebe, Miyazaki, Ishiguro, Nyūzen, Sami, and others. The position was a formidable one, surrounded by lofty rocks and peaks, with mountains in front and behind. There were also two rivers in front of it, the Nōmigawa and the Shindōgawa, and the defenders had built an elaborate dam at their confluence, felling great trees and dragging them into place to make barricades. Thus waters lapped at the base of the mountains on the east and west, just as if the stronghold had been facing a lake.

Blue and vast, the surface steeped
the southern mountains;
Red and patterned, the waves
engulfed the westering sun.

On the bottom of the heatless lake, there is gold and silver sand; by the shore at Kunming Lake, there were the boats of virtuous government; and at this artificial lake near the Hiuchi stronghold, there was a dam with roiling waters, constructed to deceive an enemy.

Since the lake could not very well be crossed without boats, the great army of the Heike idled away the days at camps in the mountains on the far side.

Now there was one member of the garrison, Abbot Saimei, whose secret sympathies lay entirely with the Taira. Saimei went out along the base of the mountains, put a letter inside a whizzing arrow, and shot it into the Heike camp when nobody was watching. "There is no natural depression under the lake; the people here have merely blocked a mountain stream. The waters will soon subside if you send out some foot soldiers at night to destroy the dam. The footing for horses is good; cross quickly. I'll shoot arrows at the defenders from the rear. Heizenji Abbot Saimei."

The commanders-in-chief were delighted. They hastened to send out foot soldiers, and the soldiers cut the dam away. In spite of the lake's impressive appearance, it was nothing but a mountain stream. Its waters soon ebbed, and the great Heike force surged across. The warriors inside the stronghold held out for a while, but there seemed little chance that so few could prevail against so many.

Saimei declared allegiance to the Heike and became their loyal man. Still defiant, Shinsuke, Saitōda, Mitsuakira, and Bussei abandoned the stronghold, retreated to Kaga Province, and dug in at Shirayama and Kawachi, but the seemingly invincible Heike followed hard on their heels into Kaga and burned the two strongholds defended by Mitsuakira and Bussei. Then, from nearby post stations, the victorious host sent couriers to the capital, where their news was received with extravagant relief and rejoicing by Munemori and the other members of the Heike clan who had stayed behind.

On the eighth of the fifth month, the Heike mustered at Shinohara, in Kaga Province, and divided their hundred thousand horsemen into frontal and rear assault forces. The frontal force, seventy thousand strong, set out toward Tonamiyama, on the border between Kaga and Echizen, with Koremori and Michimori as commanders-in-chief and Etchū no Zenji Moritoshi as the main samurai commander. The rear force, thirty thousand horsemen, proceeded toward Shio-no-yama on the border between Noto and Etchū, with Tadanori and Tomomori as commanders-in-chief and Arikuni as the foremost samurai commander.

While staying in the capital of Echigo Province, Yoshinaka learned of the Taira movements. He made hasty preparations to confront the enemy with fifty thousand horsemen. In the belief that his earlier campaign had set an auspicious precedent, he divided his army into seven groups. His uncle Yukiie went to meet the Taira at Shio-no-yama with ten thousand men. Nishina, Takanashi, and Yamada no Jirō were sent toward Kitagurosaka with seven thousand men as a rear assault force, and Higuchi no Jirō Kanemitsu and Ochiai no Gorō Kaneyuki were sent toward Minamigurosaka with seven thousand men. Ten thousand men were stationed in ambush at the entrance to Tonamiyama, at the base of Kurosaka, at Yanagihara in the area of Matsunaga, and at Gumi-no-kinbayashi. Imai no Shirō Kanehira crossed the Washinose shallows with six thousand men to take up positions at Hinomiyabayashi, and Yoshinaka himself crossed the river at Oyabe-no-watari and camped with ten thousand men at Hanyū, just north of Tonamiyama.

## 7.8. Sanemori

*[This episode takes place nine days later, on the twenty-first of the fifth month. Yoshinaka has again attacked the Heike, who had withdrawn to Shinohara, and he has again won.]*

Even though all the others were running away, Nagai no Saitō Bettō Sanemori of Musashi Province kept turning back alone to meet the enemy and put up a defense. With a special plan in mind, he had donned a red brocade tunic, a suit of armor with green lacing, and a horned helmet, had armed himself with a gilt sword with bronze fittings, a quiver containing arrows fledged with black-banded eagle feathers, and a rattan-wrapped bow, and had mounted a white-dappled reddish horse with a saddle trimmed in gold. One of Lord Kiso's men, Tezuka no Tarō Mitsumori, singled him out as a good opponent. "You're putting on quite a show! Who is this hero, this fellow who stays behind after all his friends have run away? Let's hear your name," he said.

"Who are you?" Sanemori asked.

"Tezuka no Tarō Kanezashi no Mitsumori of Shinano Province."

"We're well matched! I don't mean to be insulting, but there's a reason why I'd rather not give you my name. Come on, Tezuka! Let's wrestle!"

Sanemori spurred forward. One of Mitsumori's retainers galloped up from the rear, pressed ahead to protect his master, and gripped Sanemori as hard as he could.

"Congratulations! You want to wrestle with the strongest man in Japan!" said Sanemori. He grabbed the warrior, pulled him against the pommel of his saddle, cut off his head, and tossed it away.

After seeing his man killed, Mitsumori got around to Sanemori's left, lifted the skirt of his armor, stabbed him twice, and wrestled him to the ground as he staggered. Sanemori was still full of fight, but he was tired from all his earlier engagements. Also, he was no longer young. In the end, Mitsumori pinned him.

Mitsumori turned over Sanemori's head to another retainer, a man who had galloped up later, and hurried to report to Lord Kiso. "I've just killed an odd sort of fellow in a wrestling match. He might have been a samurai except that he was wearing a tunic made of brocade. Yet where were his men if he was a commander? I kept asking for his name, but he wouldn't give it. He talked like an easterner," he said.

"This looks to me like the face of Saitō no Sanemori," said Lord Kiso. "I saw him in Kōzuke Province when I visited there as a child, but his hair was already turning gray. It would have to be white by now. How can he have a black beard and black hair? Higuchi no Jirō Kanemitsu has known him a long time; he ought to recognize him. Tell Kanemitsu I want him."

One look was enough for Kanemitsu. "Poor fellow! Yes, that's Sanemori," he said.

"Then he must be over seventy. He ought to have white hair. How is it that his hair and beard are black?" Lord Kiso said.

Kanemitsu broke down in tears. "I meant to explain that, but I felt so sorry for him that I couldn't help crying. Even on trivial occasions, a warrior ought to say things people will remember. Saitō always used to tell me, 'If I fight a battle after I'm past sixty, I'll dye my hair and beard so I'll look young. I know it's childish to try to compete with the young fellows for first place, but I couldn't face the humiliation of having them write me off just because of my age.' Sure enough, he did dye his hair. Have it washed; see for yourself."

"You may be right," Lord Kiso said. He had the hair washed, and it turned white.

Here is how Sanemori happened to be wearing a tunic made of brocade. When he went to take his final leave of Palace Minister Munemori, he said, "Even though I wasn't the only one, it's the shame of my old age that I didn't fire a single arrow when we marched toward the east that year—that I just ran back to the capital from Kanbara in Suruga, scared to death because some birds flapped their wings. I've made up my mind to die on the battlefield during this northern campaign. I was born in Echizen Province, though I've lived at Nagai in Musashi these past few years as an official on one of your properties. There's a saying, 'Wear brocade when you go home,' so could you please let me wear a tunic made of brocade?" Moved by his gallantry, Munemori granted the request. Might we say that Sanemori had now won fame on northern soil, just as Zhu Maichen waved brocade sleeves at Huijishan long ago? How pitiful that his empty name alone should have survived, impervious to corporeal decay, while his mortal remains have become one with the northern soil!

The Heike army had seemed invincible when its hundred thousand horsemen set out from the capital on the seventeenth of the fourth month, but it numbered scarcely more than twenty thousand on its return late in the fifth month. "You can catch a lot of fish if you fish out a stream, but there won't be any next year. You can capture a lot of game if you burn a forest while you're hunting, but there won't be any next year. They would have done well to reserve some men for the future," people said.

## 7.16. Tadanori's Flight from the Capital

Somewhere along the way, Satsuma Governor Tadanori turned back to Shunzei's house on Gojō Avenue, attended by five samurai and a page. The gate was locked.

"It's Tadanori," he announced.

There was agitation inside. "One of the fugitives is back!" voices said.

Tadanori dismounted. "It's nothing special, Shunzei," he shouted. "I've just come back to speak to you. Come out here if you'd rather not open the gate."

"I think I know what he wants," Shunzei said. "He won't make any trouble. Let him in." They opened the gate and Shunzei received him. It was a moving scene.

"I haven't meant to be neglectful since you accepted me as a pupil several years ago," Tadanori said, "but my clan has had to bear the brunt of the unrest in the city and the rebellions in the provinces. During the last two or three years, I haven't been able to pay you regular visits, even though poetry is still very close to my heart. Now the emperor has left the capital, and my clan's good luck has come to an end. I had heard people say there was to be a new imperial anthology, and I had thought it would be the greatest honor of my life if you might include even one of my poems. What with all this turmoil, no commission has been handed down, but there's sure to be one after peace is restored. If this scroll contains one suitable poem, and if you should see fit to include it, I'd rejoice in my grave and act as your guardian spirit."

When he was about to leave home, he had snatched up a scroll in which he had recorded more than a hundred poems—to his mind the best of the many he had composed and saved over the years. Now he withdrew it from the armhole in his armor and gave it to Shunzei. Shunzei opened it and looked inside. "I couldn't possibly consider this a keepsake of no importance. Please don't have any fears about that. Your coming here at a time like this shows how much the art of poetry means to you; it moves me to tears," he said.

Tadanori was delighted. "Now I won't mind drowning in the western waves or leaving my bones to bleach in the wilds. Nothing remains to bind me to this transitory existence. Goodbye!" he said. He mounted his horse, tied his helmet cords, and rode off toward the west. Shunzei watched until his figure receded far into the distance. Someone was chanting a *rōei* in a resonant voice that sounded like his:

Distant lies the way ahead;
My thoughts run on to the
evening clouds at Yanshan.

Moved again by the sorrow of parting, Shunzei had to restrain tears as he went inside. Later, after the restoration of peace, he compiled the *Collection for a Thousand Years;* and then, with a full heart, he remembered how Tadanori had looked and what he had said. There were many eligible poems in the scroll, but he limited his choice to one, taking cognizance of the fact that the author was someone who had suffered imperial censure. Its topic was "Blossoms at the Old Capital." He labeled it "Anonymous."

It lies in ruins now—
the old capital at Shiga
of rippling wavelets—
but the cherries at Nagara
bloom as they bloomed long ago.

Tadanori was an enemy of the throne, so there's nothing more to be said. Still, the story is a pathetic one.

## *Ch. 10 [The Story of Koremori, cont.]*

### 10.8. Yokobue

Meanwhile, it was in body only that Middle Captain Koremori stayed at Yashima; in spirit, he was a perpetual commuter to the capital. Left behind at home but not forgotten for an instant, his wife and children were never absent from his thoughts. He decided that it was meaningless to go on living that way, and shortly before dawn, on the fifteenth of the third month in the third year of Juei [1184], he stole away from his quarters at Yashima, accompanied by three attendants—Yosōbyōe Shigekage, the page Ishidōmaru, and a groom known as Takesato, whom he chose because people said he was knowledgeable about boats. They set out from Yūki Shore in Awa Province aboard a small craft, rowed across the Naruto Straits toward Kii Province, passed Waka, Fukiage, and the Tamatsushima Shrine, where Sotōrihime had once appeared as a divinity, and arrived at Kii Harbor.

He would have liked to cross the mountains to the city—to meet his beloved family one last time—but it was bad enough for Shigehira to have been captured, paraded through the avenues, and humiliated in the capital and Kamakura. It would be a terrible disgrace for his dead father, Shigemori, if he were captured too. Many times, he felt the urge to set out, but he always fought it down, and in the end he went to Mount Kōya.

On the mountain, there was a holy man named Saitō Takiguchi Tokiyori, a son of Saitō Mochiyori of Sanjō. He had been a samurai in Shigemori's service, and Koremori had known him a long time. He had won a post in the palace guards as a boy of thirteen, and there he had fallen in love with one of Kenreimon'in's lesser attendants, a girl named Yokobue. His father gave him a severe scolding when he heard about it. "I intended to marry you into an influential family so you could rise in the world. Now I find you've got yourself involved with a nobody," he said.

"There was once a Queen Mother of the West, but she isn't around any longer; and though we hear about Dongfang Shuo, we can't see him," the youth thought. "In a world where a young person may die before an old one, a man's life is like a spark from a flint. Even when we say somebody has a long life, it doesn't amount to more than seventy or eighty years, and the prime of life only lasts for twenty years or so. In this dreamlike, fleeting existence, what would I gain by spending even a little time with a wife I didn't care for? Yet I'll seem undutiful if I marry the girl I love. This situation is doing me a favor; it demonstrates that I ought to renounce the harsh world for the path of truth." At the age of nineteen, he had cut off his hair and gone to live a pious life at the Ōjōin Cloister in Saga.

"I could have accepted it if he'd broken with me," Yokobue thought when she heard the news. "But it was cruel to go to such lengths. If he'd made up his mind to be a monk, why couldn't he have told me so? He may not want to see me, but I'm going to find him and tell him how I feel." Late one afternoon, she left the capital and took her uncertain way toward Saga. As was usual for the season, midway through the second month, the spring breeze from Umezu carried the nostalgic fragrance of plum blossoms, and haze veiled the moonlight on the Ōi River. She must have felt that her misery was all Tokiyori's fault.

People had told her that the "Takiguchi novice" was at the Ōjōin, but she had no way of knowing which cloister was his, and she began a pathetic search, hesitating here and stopping there. At last, she heard someone chanting a sacred text inside a ruined cell. The voice sounded familiar. She told the maid who had accompanied her to take in a message. "I've looked everywhere for you. Please let me see you as a monk, just this once."

The Takiguchi novice peeped through a crack in the sliding partition, his heart racing. Even the most resolute seeker after enlightenment would have been moved by her appearance, which bore pitiful witness to her long, fruitless search. But he turned her away without a meeting. "The person you want isn't here," he had someone say. "You must have come to the wrong place." Yokobue resented his coldness, but she had to contain her tears and go home.

"This is a quiet place where a man can recite the sacred name in peace," the Takiguchi novice said to one of his cloister mates. "But I parted from a girl I still loved, and now she's found out that I'm here. I hardened my heart once, but I don't think I can do it if she comes again. I must say goodbye." He left Saga, went to Mount Kōya, and took up residence at the Shōjōshin'in Cloister.

Presently, he learned that Yokobue had also entered the religious life. He sent her a poem:

> Although you harbored
> such feelings of resentment
> that you shaved your head,
> what happiness to know
> you have entered the true Way!

Yokobue answered with this:

> That I shaved my head
> was not because I harbored
> resentment toward you.
> Yours is a heart praiseworthy
> for steadfast devotion.

Before long, Yokobue died at the Hokkeji nunnery in Nara, where she had gone to live. (Perhaps it was her heavy burden of sorrow that caused her death.) After he heard the news, the Takiguchi novice prayed harder than ever, displaying a zeal so fervent that his father recognized him as his son again. Everyone who knew him revered him; they called him "the holy man at Mount Kōya."

Koremori went to visit this holy man. In the old days in the capital, he had been an elegant gentleman in a hunting robe and high cap, his garments stylishly draped and his hair smooth. Now, when Koremori saw him as a monk for the first time, he must have felt a pang of envy. Here was a true seeker after enlightenment, someone who looked like an emaciated old monk (although he was not yet thirty), dressed in a robe of deep black and a black surplice. Not even one of the seven sages of the bamboo grove, the men of Jin, could have been a more impressive sight—nor could one of the four graybeards of Mount Shang in the Han dynasty.

## 10.9. The Book of Kōya

When the Takiguchi novice saw Koremori, he said, "I must be dreaming! Why have you fled here from Yashima?"

"I made the trip westward from the capital like all the others, but I was always miserable because of the children I'd left behind," Koremori answered. "I didn't say anything, but my feelings probably showed, because Munemori and the nun of second rank both suspected that I was going to turn traitor like Yorimori. There didn't seem to be any point to my life, and I felt less and less like staying in Yashima. I finally left, not knowing exactly where I was going, and that's how I happen to be here. I'd like to follow the mountains to the capital to see my dear family just one last time, but I don't dare run the risk of suffering Shigehira's fate. It will be better for me to take religious vows here and kill myself, either with fire or with water. There's only one problem: for a long time, I've wanted to make a pilgrimage to Kumano."

"It matters very little how a man passes through this dreamlike, fleeting world. What is truly hard is to suffer rebirth in eternal darkness," the novice said.

Guided by the novice, and proceeding by way of the various halls,

Koremori at once made a pious visit to the inner cloister.

Mount Kōya stands two hundred leagues from the capital, remote from habitations and undisturbed by mortal voices. The treetops rustle in the mountain winds; peace shines in the rays of the setting sun. True purity of the spirit can be achieved on the eight peaks and in the eight valleys. Flowers bloom where mists touch the groves; handbells resound where clouds hang above the peaks. Ferns on tiles and mosses on fences bear witness to the temple's antiquity.

During the time of the sovereign who reigned in the Engi era [901–22], the emperor gave Great Teacher Kōbō a dark brown robe, in response to a request from the great teacher in a dream. The imperial messenger, Middle Counselor Suketaka, took Archbishop Kangen of the Hannyaji with him to Mount Kōya. When the two opened the door of the tomb to put the robe on the body, a dense mist concealed the great teacher. Kangen shed tears of distress. "Never have I violated one of the commandments—never since I left the womb of my kind mother and entered the chambers of my teacher. Why am I denied the privilege of worship?" he asked. He flung himself to the ground and abandoned himself to tears. Then, very gradually, the mist cleared away, a light shone as of a rising moon, and the great teacher became visible. Kangen robed him, shedding tears of joy. The great teacher's hair had grown very long, and the archbishop also received the honor of shaving his head.

The archbishop's disciple, Ishiyama Palace Chaplain Jun'yū, was much chagrined because he was unable to see the great teacher, even though the imperial messenger and Kangen could do so. The archbishop took his hand and touched it to the great teacher's knee. And we are told that a fragrance emanated from that hand for the rest of Jun'yū's life. People say it still clings to the sacred texts at Ishiyama.

The great teacher replied to the emperor with these words: "In the past, I met the bodhisattva Fugen, and from him I received all the mudras and mantras in direct transmission. An unparalleled vow has brought me to this distant foreign land. I seek to accomplish Fugen's compassionate vows in everlasting pity for mankind. Still retaining corporeal form, I have entered the realm of contemplation to await Maitreya's coming." Even thus, it seemed, must Śākyamuni's disciple Mahā-kāśyapa wait in the Kukkutapāda grotto for the spring breeze at Shizu.

The great teacher died during the hour of the tiger [3:00 A.M.– 5:00 A.M.] on the twenty-first day of the third month in the second year of Jōwa [835]. More than three hundred years have passed since then, but he will have to wait another five billion six hundred and seventy million years before Maitreya comes to deliver the three sermons—a long time, indeed.

## 10.10. Koremori Becomes a Monk

Koremori was in a pitiful state. "I don't seem to be able to set a time to end it all. I'm just like the Himalayan bird, always thinking, 'Today! Tomorrow!'" he said. With his skin blackened by salt winds and his body emaciated by incessant worry, he little resembled his old self, but he was still handsomer than other men. That night, he went back to the Takiguchi novice's hermitage and talked about the past and present until dawn. When he watched how the holy man behaved, he saw the pearl of truth being polished with unswerving diligence and faith; when he heard the bell ringing for the morning devotions, he perceived the hope of an awakening from the slumber of birth and death. He must have wanted to escape worldly ties and live in the same way, for the next morning he asked to receive a visit from Chikaku Shōnin, of the Tōzen'in, with the intention of becoming a monk.

He summoned Shigekage and Ishidōmaru. "I've had something in mind that people didn't know about, but I'm in a difficult position now, and I won't be able to survive. There's no reason why my death should keep you from making your way in life; lots of people are prospering nowadays. Once you've seen me to the end, hurry on back to the capital and find some way to support yourselves. Take care of your wives and children, and pray for my wellbeing in the next life," he said.

At first, Shigekage and Ishidōmaru were too overcome to answer. Then Shigekage spoke up, restraining his tears. "During the rebellion in the Heiji era, my father, Kageyasu, your late father's man, died at the hands of Akugenda Yoshihira while he was wrestling with Kamadabyōe Masakiyo near the intersection of Nijō Avenue and Horikawa Street. How can I reveal myself to be a lesser man? I don't remember him, because I was only two at the time. My mother died when I was seven, and there weren't any close relatives to look after me, but Lord Shigemori said, 'This is the son of a man who gave his life for mine.' I was reared near his presence, and at the age of nine, on the same night you assumed the cap of manhood, I had the privilege of having my own hair put up and receiving the name Shigekage. '*Mori* is always a part of a Taira name, so I'll give it to Godai,' His Lordship said. 'The *shige* in my name I'll give to Matsuō.' So my father's brave death turned out to be a blessing for me. Furthermore, the other retainers were all very kind.

"When His Lordship was dying, he put away thoughts of worldly things and lapsed into silence. But then he called me over. 'Poor lad!' he said. 'I've been a memento of your father for you, and you've been a memento for me. At the next distribution of offices, I was going to make you a guards lieutenant so I could call you by his old title. That won't happen now, and I'm sorry about it. Remember, always do as Lesser Captain Koremori wishes.' Did you just assume that I'd run away and leave you at the hour of your death? It's a terrible humiliation to find out what you've been thinking. You say many people are prospering nowadays, but those are all retainers of the Genji. And could I hope to live a thousand years, even if I did thrive after you became a god or buddha? Even if I prospered for ten thousand years, wouldn't the end come someday? What better chance will I have to enter the true path?" He cut off his hair with his own hand, and tearfully called on the Takiguchi novice to shave his head.

After witnessing these sights, Ishidōmaru cut off his hair at the clasp. He had served Koremori since he was eight years old and had enjoyed favors equal to those bestowed on Shigekage; thus, he asked the Takiguchi novice to shave his head too.

When Koremori saw his two retainers precede him into the religious life, he felt even more miserable than before. But he could not procrastinate forever. Three times, he chanted a Buddhist adage: "He who transmigrates through the three worlds cannot sever the bonds of attachment to family; he who rejects attachment and enters the Way receives the reward of true attachment." Then, at last, he shaved his head. "I wouldn't have minded if only I could have done this after letting my dear wife and children see me one last time as I used to look," he said. It was a sinful thought.

Koremori and Shigekage were the same age, twenty-seven that year. Ishidōmaru was eighteen.

Koremori called in the groom Takesato. "Go straight back to Yashima," he told him. "Don't go to the capital. What I've done will have to come to light sometime, but I'm afraid Her Ladyship might rush into holy orders if she heard the whole story from your lips. This is what I want you to say for me at Yashima: 'As you must have noticed, I've come to hate this life. I've felt that I could only grow more and more wretched, so I've taken religious vows without telling you. My only regret is that you must all be feeling very forlorn, now that this has happened after Kiyotsune died in the west and Moromori at Ichi-no-tani. If, by some miracle, we should regain our old preeminence, please see that Rokudai gets the armor Karakawa [Chinese Leather] and the sword Kogarasu [Little Crow], the heirlooms that came to me from Sadamori as the heir in the ninth generation.'"

"I'll wait to witness your death before I go to Yashima," Takesato said. Koremori acquiesced and kept him with him. He also asked the Takiguchi novice to accompany him, that he might provide religious guidance at the end. Then he left Mount Kōya for Sandō in the same province, wearing the garb of a mountain ascetic.

He paused and knelt at all the Kumano branch shrines—Fujishiro and the others. Just in front of the Iwashiro Shrine, north of Senri-no-hama, he met a party of seven or eight horsemen in hunting attire. Fearing capture, he put his hand on his dagger to slash his belly, and his companions did the same. But after the strangers drew closer, they leaped from their horses with no sign of hostility, made respectful bows, and went on their way.

"They must have recognized us. I wonder who they were," Koremori thought. Fearing the worst, he hurried toward Kumano.

The leader of the party on horseback was a man named Yuasa no Munemitsu. When his retainers wanted to know who the pilgrims were, tears ran down his cheeks. "It's nothing for the likes of us to talk about. That was the middle captain of third rank, the son and heir of Minister of State Shigemori. I wonder how he managed to get here from Yashima. He's already taken the tonsure. Shigekage and Ishidōmaru were with him, and they were both monks, too. I wanted to go up and pay my respects, but I went on to save him from embarrassment. He looked so pathetic!" He sobbed with his shoulder-guard pressed to his face, and all his retainers wept.

## 10.12. The Suicide of Koremori

After Koremori had visited the three shrines of Kumano without incident, he got into a small boat in front of the branch shrine at Hama-no-miya and set out on the vast blue sea. Far in the offing, there was an island called

Yamanari-no-shima. He went ashore there, peeled some bark from a great pine tree, and inscribed his name. "Grandfather: Chancellor Taira no Ason Kiyomori, religious name Jōkai. Father: Palace Minister—Major Captain of the Left Shigemori, religious name Jōren. Middle Captain Koremori of third rank, religious name Jōen, aged twenty-seven, drowns himself offshore from Nachi on the twenty-eighth day of the third month in the third year of Juei [1184]." Then he rowed toward the open sea again.

Now that the hour had arrived, he could not help feeling miserable and forlorn, determined though he was to die. As was natural for the date, which was the twenty-eighth of the third month, haze veiled the sea far into the distance, a moving sight. Even in an ordinary spring, it is sad to watch a season wane. And we may imagine the feelings of someone who would not see the dawn of another day.

When Koremori saw a fishing boat offshore come back into view after seeming to plunge into the waves, he may have been reminded of what was in store for him. And when he heard the cry of a homing goose, leading a line of its fellows toward the northern regions, he longed to send a message home, no less disconsolate than Su Wu in the land of the Xiongnu barbarians.

He reproved himself for thinking about such things. "What's wrong with me? Am I still fettered by worldly attachments?" He faced the west, joined his hands, and intoned the name of Amida Buddha. But even as he chanted, he thought, "They can't know in the capital that this is my last hour. They must be frantic for any word, even a rumor. What a terrible blow it will be when the news spreads—as it's bound to—and they find out I'm dead!" He fell silent, separated his hands, and spoke to the Takiguchi novice. "It's a mistake to have a wife and children. They're only a cause of anxiety in this world and a hindrance to enlightenment in the next. Mine have come back into my head at this very moment. I've been told that it's a grave sin to let such things linger in one's mind; I confess my guilt."

The holy man pitied him, but he felt that it would never do for him to show weakness too. Wiping away a tear, he spoke with an assumption of calm.

"It's not surprising that you should feel that way. Love is an emotion we can't control, whether we're noble or base. And the karmic bond between husband and wife is especially strong: a single night together is said to signify a bond going back through five hundred lives. It's the way of this fleeting world that those who are born must perish, that those who meet must part. 'Dew on the tip of a branch, a drop of moisture from a stalk.' The parting may be early or late, but one person will go before the other. The vows spoken at the Lishan Palace on autumn nights led to heartbreak at last; the love that inspired the portrait in the Ganquan Hall didn't endure forever. Even Songzi and Mei Fu knew the bitterness of dying; the highest bodhisattvas themselves follow the law of life and death. Even if you were to enjoy the blessing of a long life, you couldn't escape that sorrow; you must remember that you would face the identical grief if you lived for another hundred years.

"Ruling as he pleases over all six heavens in the world of desire, the heretic demon king in the sixth heaven resents the efforts of that world's inhabitants to escape the cycle of life and death, and he hinders them by assuming the form of a wife or a husband. The buddhas of the three worlds, who regard all mankind as their children, and who seek to lead us to the pure land from which there is no return, have issued strict injunctions against loving the wives and children who have chained us to the wheel of transmigration from remote antiquity to the present.

"You mustn't lose heart. In a single twelve-year period, while he was trying to carry out an imperial command to subdue Sadatō and Munetō, the barbarians in Ōshū, Yoriyoshi of the Genji cut off the heads of sixteen thousand men and killed thousands and thousands of the beasts of the fields and the fish of the rivers. And yet we're told that he was reborn in the pure land because he became a true believer at the end of his life. The merit amassed by the act of renouncing the world is exceedingly great; I'm sure all your sins from previous existences have been washed away. Even if a man builds a jeweled pagoda high enough to reach the heaven of the thirty-three divinities, he won't equal the merit that accrues from a single day in holy orders. And we are also taught this: even if a man makes offerings to a hundred arhats for a hundred or a thousand years, he won't equal the merit that accrues from a single day in holy orders. Yoriyoshi's faith was strong, so he achieved rebirth in paradise despite his heinous sins. And you who have committed no truly evil acts—how could you possibly fail to reach the pure land?

"Furthermore, the god of Kumano is a manifestation of Amida Buddha, whose vows are all dedicated to the salvation of sentient beings, from the first, 'There shall be no more three evil paths,' to the forty-eighth, 'They shall attain the three forms of patience.' The eighteenth vow says, 'Even though I attain the qualifications for buddhahood, I will not become a buddha unless the sentient beings in the ten directions, believing and rejoicing in my vows with fervent hearts, and desirous of rebirth in my pure land, achieve rebirth by reciting my name ten times.' From those words, in particular, we may rest assured that ten buddha-invocations will save us—or even one, for that matter. You must simply have complete faith, and never, never let a doubt enter your mind. If you intone the sacred name ten times with a pure heart, or even once, Amida Buddha will reduce his immeasurable stature to sixteen feet and come forth promptly from the eastern gate of his paradise to meet you, accompanied by Kannon, Seishi, and a countless host of heavenly beings and bodhisattvas in temporary manifestations, who will surround him a hundredfold, a thousandfold, playing musical instruments and singing. Though you may expect to sink to the bottom of the blue sea, you will surely mount a purple cloud. If you become a buddha and attain deliverance, there can be no doubt that you will return to your earthly home as a guide for your wife and children—that you will 'visit the impure world to save men and devas.'" He rang his bell and urged Koremori to chant the sacred name.

To Koremori it seemed a supremely favorable opportunity for rebirth in the pure land. He put away distracting thoughts immediately, intoned Amida's name a hundred times in a loud voice, and entered the sea with "Hail!" on his lips. The Hyōe novice and Ishidōmaru followed him into the waves, chanting, "Hail, Amida Buddha!"

## *The Initiates' Chapter [The Story of Lady Kenreimon'in]*

*[Treated as a secret text by the Ichikata-ryū, this chapter is believed to have originated in the late 13th century, after the* Heike *proper, and to have been given its present form by Kakuichi and his Tōdōza senior Joichi. It brings together information about Kiyomori's daughter Kenreimon'in, the mother of Emperor Antoku, which is supplied in Chapters 11 and 12 by other* Heike *texts—namely, her taking of Buddhist vows and retirement to the Jakkōin in 1185, a visit paid her by Retired Emperor Go-Shirakawa in the summer of 1186, and her death in 1191. Although it is divided into five sections, it constitutes a single literary entity—a tale in the old* monogatari *style, rich in poetic imagery, rhythmic passages,* waka, *and melancholy associations.]*

Principal characters:

DAINAGON-NO-SUKE. Widow of Kiyomori's son Shigehira; former nurse of Emperor Antoku; lady- in-waiting to Kenreimon'in

GO-SHIRAKAWA, RETIRED EMPEROR. Head of the imperial clan

KENREIMON'IN. DAUGHTER OF KIYOMORI; consort of Emperor Takakura; mother of Emperor Antoku. Taken prisoner at Dan-no-ura

### 1.1. The Imperial Lady Becomes a Nun

The imperial lady Kenreimon'in had gone to stay in the district of Yoshida, at the foot of the eastern hills. The place where she lived was a deserted cloister, the property of a Nara monk called Kyōe. Rank grasses grew in the courtyards, ferns clustered on the eaves, and the tattered blinds left the bedchambers exposed to the wind and rain. Flowers of many different colors blossomed, but there was no master to enjoy them; moonlight streamed in at night, but there was no owner to watch until dawn. It is sad to imagine how she must have felt, that lady who had lived surrounded by brocade curtains in splendid mansions, and who now found herself in so dreadfully dilapidated a habitation, separated from all her relatives. She was like a beached fish, like a bird torn from the nest—nostalgic, in her misery, even for the cheerless shipboard life at sea. Her thoughts dwelt on the distant clouds of the western ocean beyond the boundless blue waves; her tears fell when moonlight illumined the courtyard of the mossy, thatched cloister in the eastern hills. No words could describe her melancholy.

The imperial lady became a nun on the first day of the fifth month in the first year of the Bunji era [1185]. The monk who administered the precepts was Inzei, the holy man from the Ashōbō Cloister at the Chōrakuji Temple. As an offering, she gave him one of Emperor Antoku's informal cloaks. The emperor had worn it until the hour of his death; it still carried the scent of his body. She had brought it all the way from the west to the capital, meaning to keep it always beside her. But now, for lack of anything else that might be suitable, she produced it tearfully, telling herself that the deed might help the emperor attain enlightenment. The monk took it, too moved to speak, and left with tears drenching his black sleeve. People say it was made into a banner to be hung in front of the Chōrakuji Buddha.

The imperial lady had been named a junior consort at the age of fifteen, and an empress at sixteen. Always at the emperor's side, she had urged him to preside over the dawn levees and had shared his love with none at night. At twenty-two, she had given birth to a son who had become the crown prince; and after her son's accession, she had received the palace name Kenreimon'in. She had enjoyed the very greatest respect as both the daughter of Kiyomori and the mother of the emperor.

In this present year [1185], she had turned twenty-nine. The beauty that reminded others of peach blossoms remained unmarred; the freshness that recalled lotus blossoms had not faded. But there was no longer any reason to preserve the tresses reminiscent of black kingfisher feathers, and so, at last, she became a nun. Alas! Her grief knew no end, even after she rejected this transitory world for the true path. Never, not in all the lives to come, could she forget how her despairing kinsmen had cast themselves into the sea; never could she forget the faces of her son and mother. Why had her own dewlike existence dragged on, a mere source of misery? She never ceased to mourn, never ceased to weep.

The nights are short in the fifth month, but the dawns seemed slow to arrive. Not even in dreams could she recapture the past, for she never dozed. "Dim was the waning light of the lamp by the wall, lonely the nightlong beat of the dismal rain against the window." It seemed that not even the lady of Shangyang could have been more wretched when she was imprisoned in the Shangyang Palace.

The wind carried the nostalgic perfume of a flowering orange tree at the eaves—transplanted, perhaps, because the former occupant had sought a reminder of the past—and a cuckoo sang two or three times. Recalling the words of an old poem, the lady scribbled them on the lid of her inkstone case:

> That you raise your voice,
> cuckoo, seeking the fragrance
> of the flowering orange—
> is it from nostalgia
> for that "someone long ago"?

Less resolute than the nun of second rank and Michimori's wife, Kozaishō, the other Heike women had not drowned themselves in the sea, had been captured by rough warriors and brought back to the capital. Young and old alike, they had taken Buddhist vows, put on rude attire, and gone to eke out miserable existences in deep valleys and rocky wilds, places of which they had never dreamed. Their old homes had all gone up in smoke, leaving only gutted, deserted sites, fast turning into overgrown fields. The poor ladies must have felt much as did those men who returned from an immortal's dwelling, only to encounter their own descendants in the seventh generation.

Meanwhile, the great earthquake on the ninth of the seventh month had crumbled the tile-capped earthen walls and tilted the rundown buildings at the imperial lady's abode, rendering it even less habitable than before. There was not so much as a green-robed guard at the gate. Already, the depressing voices of insects made officious announcement of autumn's coming, crying from ruined brushwood fences that were even dewier than the lush fields. The nights, as they gradually lengthened, seemed more interminable than ever to the wakeful lady. It was too much that the melancholy of autumn should be superimposed on her never-ending sorrow! In the transitory world where all had changed, not one remained of the old connections who would once have felt bound to take pity on her; not one seemed left who might come to her assistance.

## 1.2. The Imperial Lady Goes to Ōhara

The imperial lady's younger sisters, the wives of Takafusa and Nobutaka, found discreet ways to express their sympathy. "In the old days, it never occurred to me that I might have to depend on those two for a living," she said, weeping. Her attendants all drenched their sleeves.

Her abode was close to the capital, near a road where there were many inquisitive passersby. She longed in vain for an opportunity to move somewhere far back in the mountains—to find a refuge too remote for distressing news to reach her ears, where she might remain while the dew of her life awaited the wind. Then a certain feminine caller told her about the Jakkōin, a very quiet place far back in the mountains at Ōhara, and she resolved to go there. "It's true that a mountain hermitage is lonely, but life is far better there than in a world full of vexations," she said. I believe I have heard that Takafusa's wife made arrangements for the palanquin and other necessities.

It was late in the ninth month of the first year of Bunji [1185] when the imperial lady went to the Jakkōin. Perhaps because the road wound through mountains, the twilight shadows began to gather as she journeyed, her eyes lingering on the colored leaves of the surrounding trees. A lonely sunset bell tolled at a temple in the fields, and the thick dew on the wayside plants added its moisture to her tear-dampened sleeves. Leaves scurried in every direction, blown by a violent wind, and a sudden shower rained down from the cloud-blackened sky, accompanied by the faint belling of a deer and the barely audible plaints of insects. It was all unspeakably depressing. "Nothing was as bad as this before, not even when we were going from bay to bay and island to island," she thought piteously.

The mossy rocks at the Jakkōin evoked an atmosphere of tranquil antiquity. It was a place in which she could willingly settle down. We may wonder if she thought of her own situation when she saw the frost-stricken clumps of dewy bush clover in the courtyard, or gazed at the withering, fading chrysanthemums by the rough fence. She went before the Buddha to pray: "May the Son of Heaven's holy spirit achieve perfect wisdom; may prompt enlightenment be his." Her son's face was before her as she spoke. Would she ever forget him in all the lives to come?

She built a ten-foot-square cell next to the Jakkōin, with one bay as a bedroom and the other as a chapel, and there she spent the days in diligent performance of the six daily devotions and the perpetual buddha-recitations.

Toward evening on the fifteenth of the tenth month, she heard footsteps in the courtyard, which lay buried under fallen oak leaves. "Who can have come to this hermitage? Look and see. If it's someone I need to hide from, I'll hurry and hide," she said.

The intruder proved to be a passing stag. When the lady asked, "Well, what was it?" Dainagon-no-suke replied in verse, suppressing her tears:

> Who might be coming,
> treading on rocks, to call here?
> The visitor whose step
> rustles through fallen oak leaves
> is but a passing stag.

With a full heart, the lady wrote the poem on a small sliding door next to her window.

Despite all its hardships, her tedious existence suggested many interesting comparisons. She likened the rows of native trees at her eaves to the seven circles of trees surrounding the pure land, and she thought of the water collecting between rocks as the waters of the eight virtues.

The ephemerality of worldly things is like springtime blossoms scattering in the breeze; the brevity of human existence is like an autumn moon disappearing behind a cloud. On mornings when the lady had enjoyed blossoms at the Chengyang Hall, the wind had come and scattered their beauty; on evenings when she had composed poems about the moon at the Zhangqiu Palace, clouds had covered the moon's face and hidden its radiance. Once she had lived in a magnificent mansion with jeweled towers, golden halls, and brocade cushions; now her brushwood hermitage drew tears even from the eyes of strangers.

## 1.3. The Imperial Journey to Ōhara

Meanwhile, around the spring of the second year of Bunji [1186], Retired Emperor Go-Shirakawa decided that he would like to see Kenreimon'in's hermitage at Ōhara. But there were tempests during the second and third months, and the cold weather dragged on, with unmelted snow on the peaks and lingering icicles in the valleys. Spring passed, summer came, and the Kamo Festival took place. Only then did the former sovereign set out under cover of darkness for the recesses of Ōhara. He traveled without ceremony, but his retinue included Tokudaiji no Sanesada, Kazan'in no Kanemasa, Tsuchimikado no Michichika, and three other senior nobles, as well as eight courtiers and a few north guards. They took the Kurama highroad, and he viewed Kiyowara no Fukayabu's Fudarakuji Temple, as well as the former residence of the Ono Grand Empress.

He changed to a palanquin at Ono. The white clouds on the distant hills recalled the cherry blossoms that had now scattered; the green leaves on the trees were poignant reminders of the end of spring. The time was late in the fourth month, a season of lush summer growth. Since he had never traveled there before, all the sights were unfamiliar as his palanquin made its way through the dense foliage. Deeply moved, he realized that the area was completely off the beaten track.

A lone Buddhist structure at the foot of the western hills proved to be the Jakkōin. The venerable garden pond and ancient trees made it seem a place with a noble history. Might it have been of just such a one that the poet wrote these lines?

> The roof tiles are broken, the fog
> burns perpetual incense;
> The doors have fallen, the
> moonbeams light eternal lamps.

Young grasses burgeoned in the courtyard, green willow branches tangled in the wind, and the duckweed on the pond, drifting with the waves, might have been mistaken for brocade set out to be washed. The wisteria clinging to the pines on the islet had put forth purple flowers; the late-blooming cherries, interspersed among the green leaves, seemed a novelty more delightful than the season's first blossoms. The kerria on the banks bloomed in profusion, and a mountain cuckoo sang from a rift in the many-layered clouds, as though to welcome the awaited imperial guest. The retired emperor composed a poem:

> Wave-flowers in full bloom:
> on the surface of the pond,
> blossoms have scattered
> from the cherry trees
> along the water's edge.

It was a place where everything seemed endowed with a special charm, even to the sound of water gushing from a cleft in time-worn rocks. The fences were overgrown with green ivy; the mountains appeared etched with an eyebrow pencil. It was a scene to which no painter could have done justice.

When the retired emperor turned his attention to the imperial lady's hermitage, he saw ivy and morning-glory vines climbing the eaves, and "forgetting-grass" day lilies mingling with "remembering-grass" ferns. It was an abode of which someone might have said, "The gourd and rice tub are often empty, the grasses riot as at Yan Yuan's house." The crude cryptomeria thatch on the roof seemed scarcely able to keep out the rains, frosts, and dews, which vied with the infiltrating moonbeams for admittance.

To the rear, there were mountains; in front, barren fields where the wind whistled through low bamboo grass. The bamboo pillars, with their many joints, recalled the manifold sorrows of those who live apart from society; the brushwood fence, with its loose weave, brought to mind the long intervals between tidings from the capital. By way of visitors, there were only the cries of monkeys swinging from tree to tree on the peaks, and the sound of woodcutters' axes felling timber for firewood. For the rest, those who came were rare, unless we might count the curling tendrils of wild vines.

"Is anybody home?" the retired emperor asked.

At first, there was no answer. Then, after a long delay, a feeble old nun appeared.

"Where has the imperial lady gone?" he asked.

"To the mountain up there, to gather flowers," she said.

"Wasn't there anybody she could send on an errand like that? Even though she's a nun now, it's not right that she should have to do it herself."

"She suffers her present hardships because there has been an end to the good karma she earned by observing the five commandments and ten good precepts," said the nun. "Why should she mind performing austerities that mortify the flesh? The *Cause and Effect Sutra* instructs us, 'If you want to know past causes, look at present effects; if you want to know future effects, look at present causes.' If Your Majesty understands past and future causes and effects, you will feel no grief at all. Prince Siddhārtha left Gayā at the age of nineteen, covered his nudity with leafy garments at the foot of Mount Daṇḍaka, climbed to the peaks for firewood, descended to the valleys for water, and finally achieved perfect enlightenment through the merit of his hard and painful austerities."

The retired emperor could not tell whether the ancient scraps of cloth in the nun's patchwork robe were silk or some other material. It was odd, he thought, that one thus attired should have spoken so. "Tell me, who are you?" he said.

The nun began to weep, and for a time was too moved to reply. When she managed to control her tears, she said, "It hurts to have to admit it, but I am Shinzei's daughter, the one who used to be called Awa-no-naishi. My mother was the Kii lady of second rank. You used to be so very kind, but now I'm such an old crone that you don't even recognize me! Oh, I can't bear it!" She was too pathetic to watch as she held her sleeve to her face, no longer able to suppress her feelings.

"Awa-no-naishi! I didn't know you. This is so much like a dream!" The retired emperor could not keep from crying.

"No wonder she didn't seem like an ordinary nun," the senior nobles and courtiers in the entourage said to one another.

The retired emperor looked around. Heavy with dew, the bushes in the courtyard leaned against the brushwood fence; on the flooded rice paddy outside, there was not even enough space for a longbill to alight. He entered the hermitage and opened the sliding door. The first room contained the welcoming triad, with a five-colored cord attached to the hand of the central deity. To the left, there was a painting of Fugen; to the right, there were pictures of the teacher Shandao and the former emperor. There were also the eight scrolls of the *Lotus Sutra* and the nine scrolls of Shandao's writings. Instead of orchid and musk fragrance, smoke ascended from offering-incense. Even thus, it seemed, must have been the ten-foot-square cell where Vimalakīrti aligned thirty-two thousand seats for the buddhas of the ten directions. Noteworthy passages from sutras, inscribed on bits of colored paper, were pasted here and there on sliding doors. There were also two lines of Chinese verse, said to have been composed at Mount Qingliang by the monk whose lay name was Ōe no Sadamoto:

> From a lone cloud, mouth organs
> and singing resound in the
> distance;
> In front of the setting sun, the
> divine host approaches to bid
> me welcome.

Somewhat apart, there was a poem that seemed to be from the imperial lady's brush:

> Did I ever think
> to find myself dwelling
> deep in the mountains,
> gazing at the moon on high,
> far from the royal palace?

Off to the side, the retired emperor saw what looked like the imperial lady's bedchamber. A hemp robe, a paper quilt, and similar articles hung from bamboo rods. It seemed only a dream that she had once worn damask, gauze, brocade, and embroidery, the choicest stuffs of Japan and China. The senior nobles and courtiers had all witnessed her former splendor, and they wept until their sleeves were drenched, recalling those earlier scenes as though they had just taken place.

Presently, two nuns, dressed in robes of deep black, came picking their way down the steep, rocky path from the mountain above.

"Who are they?" the retired emperor asked.

The old nun tried not to cry. "The one carrying the basket of rock azaleas on her arm is the imperial lady. The one with the firewood and bracken is the former emperor's nurse, Dainagon-no-suke, the daughter of Torikai Middle Counselor Korezane and the adopted daughter of Gojō Major Counselor Kunitsuna." She burst into tears as she spoke. Profoundly moved, the retired emperor also shed involuntary tears.

The imperial lady would have liked to disappear. Nun or not, it was too embarrassing to have him see her in her present attire. She stood helpless, choked with tears, neither returning to the mountain nor entering the hermitage. Perhaps she despaired of drying her sleeves, which she had soaked during the nightly drawing of holy water, and which had been drenched again after she had risen before dawn to tread the dewy mountain path. Awa-no-naishi went up to her and took the flower basket.

## 1.4. The Matter of the Six Paths

"You wear the kind of clothing that's customary for someone who has renounced the world. It's quite all right to appear in it," Awa-no-naishi said. "Hurry up and meet with His Majesty; he needs to get started back to the capital."

The imperial lady entered the hermitage. When she met the retired emperor, tears came to her eyes. "I have expected the radiance of the saving Buddha to shine before the window whenever I have recited a single invocation, and I have waited for the divine host to appear at my brushwood door whenever I have recited ten invocations, but never have I anticipated anything as remarkable as this visit," she said.

"Even those who dwell in the Bhavāgra Heaven, where the life span is eighty thousand kalpas, must face the affliction of inevitable death; not even those who dwell in the six heavens of the world of desire can evade the sorrow of the five signs of decay. The wonderful pleasures of the Joyful-to-see Palace, the delights of Bonten's lofty palace—all are but the good fortune of a dream, the happiness of a phantasm, subject to eternal change. They resemble the turning wheels of a carriage. Sadly enough, the grief of the heavenly beings' five signs of decay has visited the world of men, too," the retired emperor said. "But tell me, who comes to see you? There must be many things to remind you of the old days."

The imperial lady restrained tears. "Of course, this present state causes me temporary distress, but I look on it as a blessing when I think about my future enlightenment. I've hurried to become Śākyamuni's disciple, and have reverently placed my faith in Amida's vow; thus, I escape the sorrows of the five obstacles and the three subordinations, I purify my six senses during each of the six divisions of the day, and I pray with all my heart for rebirth in the pure land of nine grades. There's no time when I don't wait for the welcoming triad, no time when I don't offer fervent prayers for the enlightenment of my kin. But I shall never forget the former emperor's face, not in all the lives to come. I try to forget, but forgetting is impossible; I try to control my anguish, but that is impossible too. Nothing causes as much sorrow as a parent's affection; that's why I pray faithfully, morning and evening, for the former emperor's enlightenment. I believe my love for him will guide me to enlightenment, too."

"These remote islands of ours are as tiny as scattered grains of millet," the retired emperor said. "Still, the merit remaining from obedience to the ten good precepts has conferred on me the awesome title of Lord of a Myriad Chariots; and as befits my status, there's nothing that isn't the way I want it. In particular, there can be no doubt about my entering paradise in the next life, because I've been born in a land where men disseminate the Buddhist teachings, and my desire to follow the Way is fervent. There's no reason why evidence of this world's evanescence should come as a shock to me now. And yet I find it unbearable to see you like this."

The imperial lady spoke again:

> As Chancellor Kiyomori's daughter, I became the imperial mother and held the country in the palm of my hand. From the New Year's felicitations through the two changes of dress to the Buddhist names services at year's end, I was attended by the regent, the ministers of state, and the other senior nobles, as though surrounded by the eight myriad celestial beings above the clouds in the six and four heavens; of all His Majesty's many officials, not one but looked up to me in awe. Pampered behind jade curtains in the Seiryōden and the Shishinden, in spring I spent days watching the cherry blossoms on the tree in the Shishinden courtyard, in high summer I found relief from the heat by dipping water from a welling spring, in autumn I wasn't allowed to watch the moon above the clouds by myself, and in black winter, on frigid nights of white snow, I slept warm under layers of bedclothing. My only desire was to live on and on—to petition the gods, if necessary, for the immortals' art of ensuring long life and eternal youth, or to search out the elixir of immortality from Penglai. I believed that the bliss of heaven could be no more sublime than the pleasures I enjoyed day and night. But in the autumn of that year in Juei [1183], I couldn't help feeling miserable when my clansmen, terrified of a man called Kiso no Yoshinaka or some such, left the familiar capital behind the clouds, turned their homes into a blackened wilderness of plains, and traveled along the seashore from Suma to Akashi, places known to me only by name. In the daytime, my sleeves were drenched as we cleaved the boundless waves; at night, I cried until dawn with the plovers on the long sandspits. Seeing famous shores and islands wasn't enough to make me forget the capital. I thought that our forlorn state must surely resemble the sorrow of the five signs of decay.
>
> If we speak of the world of men, I have known the sad suffering caused by separation from those we love; also the hateful suffering caused by association with those we dislike. Not one of the four and eight sufferings has remained outside my experience. At the Dazaifu in Chikuzen Province, we were ousted from the Nine Provinces by a man called Koreyoshi or something like that. The mountains and fields were vast, but there was no place for us to take shelter and rest. As autumn waned that year, we gazed from the eightfold tidal paths on the moon we had watched above the clouds at the ninefold palace. Time passed,

and then, around the tenth month, Middle Captain Kiyotsune cast himself into the sea. "Genji attackers drove us out of the capital and Koreyoshi expelled us from Chinzei," he said to himself. "We're like fish in a net; there's no escape, no matter where we go. What chance do I have of living out my life?" That was our first great sorrow.

Our days were spent on the waves, our nights in the boats. We possessed no tribute goods; nobody prepared food for me. If something did come to hand, I couldn't eat it because there was no water. It's true that we were afloat on a mighty sea, but people can't drink salt water. I felt that I was experiencing the sufferings of the world of hungry spirits.

Thanks to the victories at Muroyama and Mizushima, our men seemed to regain their spirit, but many of them died at Ichi-no-tani. Those who remained exchanged informal and formal robes for iron armor and helmets, and there was never a time, early or late, when the shouts of battle stopped. I felt certain that the fighting between the *asura* kings and Taishaku must be just the same.

After the defeat at Ichi-no-tani, parents were left childless and wives husbandless. If we saw a fishing boat in the offing, we trembled lest it be an enemy vessel; the sight of snowy herons flocking in some distant pine grove made our hearts faint with terror lest they be the white banners of the Genji. And I recall how, when we were at Moji and Akama-no-seki, and we all realized that the day of our last battle had come, the nun of second rank said to me, "There isn't a chance in a thousand myriad that any male member of our house will survive. Even if some distant relative did happen to be left, we couldn't expect him to perform memorial services for us. It's always been the custom to spare women. Do your best to come through the battle safely so that you can pray for His Majesty's salvation. I hope you'll also say a prayer for the rest of us." I listened as though in a dream.

A sudden wind sprang up, and a blanket of drifting clouds came down on us, striking terror into the warriors' hearts. Our fate was sealed; no human effort could change it.

When my mother saw the end approaching, she clasped His Majesty the Emperor in her arms and went to the side of the ship. "Where are you taking me, Grandmother?" he asked, with a puzzled look. "Don't you understand?" she said. "You became an emperor because you obeyed the ten good precepts in your last life, but now an evil karma holds you fast. Your good fortune has come to an end. Turn to the east and say goodbye to the Grand Shrine of Ise, then turn to the west and repeat the sacred name of Amida Buddha, so that he and his host may come to escort you to the pure land. This country is a place of sorrow; I'm taking you to a happy realm called paradise."

His Majesty was wearing an olive-gray robe, and his hair was done up in a boy's loops at the sides. With tears in his eyes, he joined his tiny hands, knelt toward the east, and bade farewell to the Grand Shrine. Then he turned toward the west and recited the sacred name of Amida; and my mother snatched him up and jumped into the sea. Darkness shrouded my eyes as I saw my son sink under the waves; my brain seemed paralyzed. I try to forget, but forgetting is impossible; I try to control my grief, but that's impossible too. Those who were left behind uttered so great and terrible a cry that it seemed not even the shrieks of sinners under the flames in the hot hells could sound worse.

When I was returning to the city after the warriors captured me, we stopped at Akashi Shore in Harima Province. I dozed off, and in a dream I saw the former emperor and the Taira senior nobles and courtiers, all in formal array, in a place far grander than the old imperial palace. I asked where we were, because I had seen nothing like it since our departure from the capital. Someone who seemed to be the nun of second rank answered, "This is the palace of a dragon king." "What a splendid place! Is there no suffering here?" I asked. "The suffering is described in the *Ryūchikukyō Sutra.* Pray hard for us," she said. I awakened as she spoke. Since then, I've been more zealous than ever in reciting the sutras and invoking Amida's name so they can be saved. I think it's all been exactly like experiencing life in each of the six paths.

"We're told that Xuanzhuang of China saw the six paths before he achieved enlightenment, and that the holy Nichizō of our land saw them through the power of Zaō Gongen," said the retired emperor. "But it's truly rare to see them before one's very eyes, as you have done." He choked with tears, and all the senior nobles and courtiers in his retinue wrung their sleeves. The imperial lady also wept, and her attendants drenched their sleeves.

## 1.5. The Death of the Imperial Lady

Meanwhile, the sound of the bell at the Jakkōin announced the end of the day, and the evening sun sank in the west. Hard though it was to say goodbye, the retired emperor restrained his tears and set out for home. The imperial lady could not help weeping until her sleeves were drenched, her memories now more poignant than ever. After she had watched the procession gradually recede into the distance, she turned toward the sacred image. "May the holy spirit of the Son of Heaven and the dead spirits of the Heike achieve perfect wisdom and prompt enlightenment," she prayed in tears.

In the past, she had faced eastward and said, "May the Grand Shrine of Ise and the bodhisattva Hachiman grant the Son of Heaven a thousand autumns and a myriad years of life"; now, pathetically, she faced westward and prayed with folded hands, "May the holy spirit of the dead be reborn in Amida's pure land." She wrote two poems on the sliding door of her bedchamber:

How has it happened
that suddenly of late
my heart grows heavy
with nostalgia for those
who serve the imperial court?

Since the past has become
only a fleeting dream,
surely this sojourn
behind a wooden door
will prove no more permanent.

I believe I have heard that another poem was inscribed on one of the pillars at the hermitage by Tokudaiji Minister of the Left Sanesada, who was with the retired emperor:

This is the empress
whom we compared to the moon
in earlier days,
but no radiance now brightens
the lonely mountain dwelling.

At a time when the imperial lady was lost in tearful memories of the past and depressing thoughts of the future, a cuckoo from the hills happened to fly by, its voice raised in song. She murmured:

If we are to meet,
cuckoo, in this way—come, then,
let us compare tears,
for I, also, like yourself,
cry constantly in this cruel world.

The captives from Dan-no-ura had either been paraded through the streets and beheaded, or else sent into distant-exile, far from their wives and children. Of the male members of the clan, Ike Major Counselor Yorimori remained the only one who had neither been deprived of his life nor been denied the privilege of living in the capital. The forty or more women, to whom no punishment had been meted out, had turned to relatives for aid or gone to stay with other connections. But there was no house free of worrisome winds, not even inside jade blinds; there was no dwelling where the dust never rose, not even beyond brushwood doors. Husbands and wives who had slept on adjoining pillows were as remote from one another as the sky; nurturing parents and their children were set apart, neither knowing the whereabouts of the other. Tormented by longing, they barely managed to struggle through the melancholy days.

It was all the fault of Chancellor-Novice Kiyomori, that man who had held the whole country in the palm of his hand, and who had executed and banished people as he pleased, unawed by the emperor above and heedless of His Majesty's subjects below, with no concern for society as a whole or for individuals. It seemed beyond doubt that the evil deeds of a father must be visited on his offspring.

With the passing of time, the imperial lady fell ill. She recited Buddha-invocations, clasping a five-colored cord attached to the hand of the central image. "Hail, Amitābha Tathāgata, teaching lord of the western paradise! Please admit me to the pure land!" she prayed. Overcome with sorrow as the end approached, Dainagon-no-suke and Awa-no-naishi wailed on her left and right.

After her chant had gradually weakened, a purple cloud trailed through the western skies, a marvelous fragrance permeated the chamber, and music sounded on high. Man's time on earth is finite, and thus it was that her life drew to a close at last, midway through the second month in the second year of Kenkyū [1191]. The parting caused agonies of grief to the two attendants who had never left her side, not since the days when she was empress. They had nowhere to turn for help, for the grasses of old ties had withered long ago, but somehow, in a most touching fashion, they managed to perform the periodic memorial services. People said both of them attained the wisdom of the dragon girl, emulated the wife of King Bimbisāra, and achieved their goal of rebirth in the pure land.

## Nō Theatre (late 14th–early 15th cent.)

Japanese Nō theatre developed from folk traditions into a highly refined form of drama in the late fourteenth and early fifteenth centuries. This transformation was accomplished by two men: Kanami (1333–1384) and his son Zeami (1363–1443). Particularly important was Zeami who, as a skilled actor, attracted the attention of the Shogun Yoshimitsu. Throughout most of his long career, Zeami enjoyed the patronage of the highest circles of Japanese society. With this support, he was able to develop a theatre based on the purest artistic principles; he did not have to compromise with the populace. In addition to acting, Zeami was a director, a playwright, and a theorist whose ideas on art reflect the general aesthetic view of medieval Japan.

Zeami's theory of art is based on the tension between *monomane* (realistic imitation) and *yūgen* (ethereal elegance). The image of a flower is emblematic of this balance and tension: the flower has outward beauty in its petals and inner vitality in its less apparent pistils and stamens. This dichotomy of outer/inner, beautiful/vital informs every aspect of the Nō theatre.

The plays themselves are quite short and are traditionally performed in groups of five, combined to create a single dramatic presentation. The series begins with a celebratory "god" play. More a ritual celebration than a drama in our sense of the word, this play invokes the benefaction of the gods. Second is a "warrior" play. Here the hero is a warrior, often appearing as a ghost who recounts his exploits in battle and his suffering after death. Next comes a "woman" play, in which the central character is a court lady from Heian times. These plays often depict forsaken or unrequited love and emphasize elegance or grace in contrast to the more powerful but less refined warrior plays. The fourth is a "frenzy" play, which depicts insanity, ecstasy, or jealousy (i.e., the extremes of human emotions). The series concludes with a "goblin" play, in which some powerful demon appears and performs a lively dance. This final play goes beyond human bounds and combines the physical vigor of the warrior play with the emotional intensity of the frenzy play.

All aspects of the Nō are governed by a three-part dynamic that Zeami identified as *Jo, Ha,* and *Kyū* (an introduction, an intensification, and a climax, respectively). It is tempting to draw a comparison between this and Aristotle's prescription of a beginning, middle, and end for a drama, but one should be cautious of such a comparison. In any case, this tripartite division applies to the order of the series of five plays as well as to the organization and structure of a single play.

Playwrights of the Nō theatre commonly looked to the classic works of the Heian period and of the warrior era for the sources of their material. Typically, an episode in *The Tale of Genji* or in *Tales of the Heike* will be taken up and amplified. From these sources, the Nō playwrights recreate the emotional intensity of the courtly life and the physical power of the warrior's world, each tempered by the demand for elegance and refinement. Because most Nō plays are based on earlier literary works, the texts are rich tapestries of literary allusion. Of the two plays presented here, *Atsumori* is from *Tales of the Heike* and is a warrior play; the other, *Aoi no Ue,* is a "woman" play and is based on an episode in *The Tale of Genji.*

*Atsumori* is filled with contrasts and dichotomies seeking to be resolved. During the war between the Taira and the Minamoto, the Taira were attacked at their base at Ichi no Tani and driven into the sea. The young Taira warrior Atsumori retreated with the others; then he went back to retrieve his flute, which he had left behind. Before he could escape again, he was confronted by Naozane and killed. Atsumori is a youthful musician from the capital, cultivated and civilized; he has no business being in the midst of this brutal warfare. Naozane is his opposite: a grizzled old warrior from the remote eastern provinces, a man who knows only the practice of war and slaughter. In the play, however, their roles are different: Naozane has renounced the world to become a priest, while the ghost of Atsumori remains bound to the world by his ties of resentment and chagrin at his youthful death.

At one level, Atsumori is associated with his flute as an emblem of culture and order. Flute music, as incongruous for grass reapers as it is for warriors, is a leitmotif in the play, conveyed sometimes in the music itself and sometimes in allusions to famous flutes. The central message of the play is found in the homiletic opening, which summarizes the tale that follows: "The world is all a dream, and he who wakes,/casting it from him, may yet know the real." One man has been killed, the other survives; one feels resentment, the other remorse; but the play is not about right and wrong, victor and vanquished. The two figures come to realize they share a common condition—a confusion about what is real—and they must help rather than confront one another if either is to find salvation. Naozane can achieve peace only by praying for the soul of his victim; Atsumori can attain serenity only by forgiving his killer.

*Aoi no Ue* deals with the possession and death of Prince Genji's wife at the hands of a jealous rival. Here the central motif is the carriage wheel, emblematic of both the inexorable turning of the law of *karma* and the endless cycle of Lady Rokujō's jealous misery. The allusion is not only to the Buddhist parable of the burning house, but also to an earlier confrontation between Lady Rokujō and Lady Aoi in which Rokujō was publicly humiliated and her carriage wheel broken. Rokujō is unable to forgive either the insult or the fact that Aoi enjoys Prince Genji's continued affection while she herself feels rejected. Even though she is appalled and disgusted by her own feelings and behavior, she cannot contain the power of her jealous rage. Quite against her conscious will, her vindictive soul leaves her body to strike down her rival. The many holy men and shamanesses—the religious forces of Buddhism and Shintō—summoned to the scene are unable to save Aoi's life or to resolve Rokujō's hatred. All they can do is give Lady Rokujō's malignant spirit a chance to publicly express her resentments. She must resolve them for herself.

The Nō plays—brief, dense, and sometimes baffling—have always found an audience, not only in Japan but outside as well. Ulysses S. Grant, on a tour of Japan, was captivated by the plays he saw. Ezra Pound and Ernest Fenellosa were intrigued with them as poetic literary texts. William Butler Yeats was inspired by them as drama. Nearly every reader is reminded of Greek tragedy when reading these plays. While the plays continue to be read and performed in their original form, they have also been rewritten and adapted for the modern theatre by Mishima Yukio and others.

## *Atsumori*

*Translated by Royall Tyler*

*Persons in order of appearance*

| | |
|---|---|
| THE MONK RENSHŌ, FORMERLY THE MINAMOTO WARRIOR KUMAGAI | *WAKI* |
| A YOUTH (NO MASK) | *MAESHITE* |
| TWO OR THREE COMPANIONS TO THE YOUTH | *TSURE* |
| A VILLAGER | *AI* |
| THE PHANTOM OF THE TAIRA WARRIOR ATSUMORI (*ATSUMORI* OR *JŪROKU* MASK) | *NOCHIJITE* |

Remarks: *A second-category or warrior play* (shura-mono) *current in all five schools of nō.*

*To* shidai *music, enter Renshō, carrying a rosary. He stands in base square, facing rear of stage.*

RENSHŌ:

(*shidai*) The world is all a dream,
and he who wakes
the world is all a dream, and he
who wakes,
casting it from him, may yet know
the real.

*He turns to the audience.*

(*nanori*) You have before you one who in his time was Kumagai no Jirō Naozane, a warrior from Musashi province. Now I have renounced the world, and Renshō is my name. It was I, you understand, who struck Atsumori down, and the great sorrow of this deed moved me to become the monk you see. Now I am setting out for Ichi-no-tani, to comfort Atsumori and guide his spirit towards enlightenment.

(*ageula*) The wandering moon,
issuing from among the Ninefold
Clouds
issuing from among the Ninefold
Clouds,
swings southward by Yodo and
Yamazaki,
past Koya Pond and the Ikuta
River, *Mimes walking.*
and Suma shore, loud with
pounding waves
to Ichi-no-tani, where I have
arrived
to Ichi-no-tani, where I have
arrived.

(*tsukizerifu*) Having come so swiftly, I have reached Ichi-no-tani in the province of Tsu. Ah, the past returns to mind as though it were before me now. But what is this? I hear a flute from that upper field. I will wait for the player to come by and question him about what happened here. *Sits below witness pillar.*

*To* shidai *music, enter the Youth and Companions. Each carries a split bamboo pole with a bunch of mowed grass secured in the cleft. They face each other at front.*

YOUTH AND COMPANIONS:

(*shidai*) The sweet music of the
mower's flute

the sweet music of the mower's flute
floats, windborne, far across the fields.

YOUTH:
(*sashi*) Those who gather grass on yonder hill
now start for home, for twilight is at hand.

YOUTH AND COMPANIONS:
They too head back to Suma, by the sea,
and their way, like mine, is hardly long.
Back and forth I ply, from hill to shore,
heart heavy with the cares of thankless toil.
(*sageuta*) Yes, should one perchance ask after me,
my reply would speak of lonely grief.
(*ageuta*) On Suma shore
the salty drops fall fast, though were I known
the salty drops fall fast, though were I known,
I myself might hope to have a friend.
Yet, having sunk so low, I am forlorn,
and those whom I once loved are strangers now.

*While singing, Youth goes to stand in base square, Companions before Chorus.*

But I resign myself to what life brings,
and accept what griefs are mine to bear *Renshō rises.*
and accept what griefs are mine to bear.

RENSHŌ: (*mondo*) Excuse me, mowers, but I have a question for you.

YOUTH: For us, reverend sir? What is it, then?

RENSHŌ: Was it one of you I just heard playing the flute?

YOUTH: Yes, it was one of us.

RENSHŌ: How touching! For people such as you, that is a remarkably elegant thing to do! Oh yes, it is very touching.

YOUTH: It is a remarkably elegant thing, you say, for people like us to do? The proverb puts the matter well: 'Envy none above you, despise none below.' Besides,

the woodman's songs and the mower's flute

YOUTH AND COMPANIONS:
are called 'sylvan lays' and 'pastoral airs':
they nourish, too, many a poet's work,
and ring out very bravely through the world.
You need not wonder, then, to hear me play.

RENSHŌ:
(*kakeai*) I do not doubt that what you say is right.
Then, 'sylvan lays' or 'pastoral airs'

YOUTH: mean the mower's flute,

RENSHŌ: the woodman's songs:

YOUTH: music to ease all the sad trials of life,

RENSHŌ: singing,

YOUTH: dancing,

RENSHŌ: fluting—

YOUTH: all these pleasures

*Below, Youth begins to move and gesture in consonance with the text.*

CHORUS:
(*ageula*) are pastimes not unworthy of those
who care to seek out beauty: for bamboo,
who care to seek out beauty: for bamboo,
washed up by the sea, yields Little Branch,
Cicada Wing, and other famous flutes;
while this one, that the mower blows,
could be Greenleaf, as you will agree.
Perhaps upon the beach at Sumiyoshi,
one might expect instead a Koma flute;
but this is Suma. Imagine, if you will,
a flute of wood left from saltmakers' fires
a flute of wood left from saltmakers' fires.

*Exeunt Companions. Youth, in base square, turns to Renshō.*

RENSHŌ: (*kakeai*) How strange! While the other mowers have gone home, you have stayed on, alone. Why is this?

YOUTH: You ask why have I stayed behind? A voice called me here, chanting the Name. O be kind and grant me the Ten Invocations!

RENSHŌ: Very gladly. I will give you the Ten Invocations, as you ask. But then tell me who you are.

YOUTH: In truth, I am someone with a tie to Atsumori.

RENSHŌ:
One with a tie to Atsumori?
Ah, the name recalls such memories!

*Presses his palms together in prayer over his rosary.*

'Namu Amida Bu,' I chant in prayer:

*Youth goes down on one knee and presses his palms together.*

YOUTH and RENSHŌ:
'If I at last become a Buddha,
then all sentient beings who call my Name
in all the worlds, in the ten directions,
will find welcome in Me, for I abandon none.'

CHORUS:
(*uta*) Then, O monk, do not abandon me!
One calling of the Name should be enough,
but you have comforted me by night and day—
a most precious gift! As to my name,
no silence I might keep could quite conceal
the one you pray for always, dawn and dusk: *Youth rises.*
that name is my own. And, having spoken,
he fades away and is lost to view
he fades away and is lost to view.
*Exit Youth.*

*Villager entered discreetly during the* ageuta *above, and sat at villager position. He now comes forward to base square.*

VILLAGER: You see before you one who lives here at Suma, on the shore. Today I will go down to the beach and pass the time watching the ships sail by. [*Sees Renshō.*] Well! There's a monk I've not seen before. May I ask you, reverend sir, where you are from?

RENSHŌ: I came from Miyako. Do you live nearby?

VILLAGER: Yes, I do.

RENSHŌ: Then would you please come nearer? I have something to ask of you.

VILLAGER: Very well, reverend sir. [*Sits at centre, facing Renshō.*] Now, what is it?

RENSHŌ: Something rather unexpected, perhaps. I hear this is where the Minamoto and the Taira fought, and where the young Taira noble, Atsumori, died. Would you tell me all you know of the way he met his end?

VILLAGER: That certainly is an unexpected request, reverend sir. I do live here, it is true, but I really know very little about such things. Still, it would be too bad of me, the very first time we meet, to claim I know nothing at all. So I will tell you the story as I myself have heard it told.

RENSHŌ: That is very kind of you.

VILLAGER: [*Turns to audience.*] It came to pass that in the autumn of the second year of Juei, Minamoto no Yoshinaka drove the Taira clan out of Miyako. This is where they came. Then the Minamoto, bent on destroying the Taira for ever, split their army—sixty thousand and more mounted warriors—into two wings and attacked without mercy. The Taira fled.

Now one among them, a young gentleman of the fifth rank named Atsumori, was the son of Tsunemori, the Director of Palace Repairs. Atsumori was on his way down to the sea, meaning to board the imperial barge, when he realized that back in the camp he had forgotten his flute, Little Branch. He prized this flute very highly and hated to leave it behind for the enemy's taking. So he turned back, fetched the flute, and again went down to the beach. But by this time, the imperial barge and the rest of the fleet had sailed. Just as he was riding into the sea, hoping to swim his horse out to the ships, Kumagai no Jirō Naozane, a warrior from Musashi province, spread his war fan and challenged him to fight.

Atsumori wheeled his horse and closed fiercely with Kumagai. The two crashed to the ground between their mounts. But Kumagai was a very powerful man. He instantly got Atsumori under him and ripped off his helmet, meaning to take his head. He saw a youth of fifteen or sixteen, with powdered face and blackened teeth—a young man of high rank, there was no doubt about that. Kumagai wanted to spare him. Then he glanced behind him and saw Doi and Kajiwara riding up. A good seven or eight other warriors were with them. 'I do not wish to kill you,' said Kumagai, 'but as you can see, there are many men from my own side behind me. I will take your head myself, then, and afterwards pray with all my heart for the peace of your spirit.' So he cut off Atsumori's head. On examining the body, he found a flute in a brocade bag attached to the waist. When he showed the flute to his commander, all present wet the sleeves of their armour with tears. To think that he had been carrying a flute at a time like that! Even among all those gentlemen from the court, he must have been an especially gentle youth! Eventually, Kumagai found out that his victim had been Atsumori.

I wonder whether it's true, as they say, that Kumagai made himself into a monk to pray for Atsumori. If he was that sort of man, though, he wouldn't have killed Atsumori in the first place. But he did kill him, so the story must be wrong. I'd like to see that Kumagai here now! I'd kill him myself, just to make Atsumori feel better.

Well, that is the way I have heard it told. But why did you ask? I am a bit puzzled.

RENSHŌ: Thank you very much for your kind account. Perhaps there is no harm in my telling you who I am. In my time I was Kumagai no Jirō Naozane, but now I am a monk and my name is Renshō. I came here, you see, to give Atsumori's spirit comfort and guidance.

VILLAGER: *You* are Kumagai, who fought in the battle here? Why, I had no idea! Please excuse all the silly things I said. They say the man mighty in good is mighty, too, in evil. I'm sure it's just as true the other way round. Anyway, do go on comforting Atsumori's spirit.

RENSHŌ: I assure you, I am not in the least offended. Since I came here to comfort Atsumori, I will stay on a while and continue chanting the precious Sutra for him.

VILLAGER: If that is your intention, then please accept lodging at my house.

RENSHŌ: I will do so gratefully.

VILLAGER: Very well. *[Exit.]*

RENSHŌ:
(*ageuta*) Then it is well: to guide and comfort him
then it is well: to guide and comfort him,
I shall do holy rites, and through the night
call aloud the Name for Atsumori,
praying that he reach enlightenment
praying that he reach enlightenment.

*To* issei *music, enter Atsumori, in the costume of a warrior. He stops in base square.*

ATSUMORI:
(*shimo-no-ei*) Across to Awaji the plovers fly,
while the Suma barrier guard sleeps on;
yet one, I see, keeps nightlong vigil here.
O keeper of the pass, tell me your name.
(*kakeai*) Behold, Renshō: I am Atsumori.

RENSHŌ: Strange! As I chant aloud the Name,
beating out the rhythm on this gong,
and wakeful as ever in broad day,
I see Atsumori come before me.
The sight can only be a dream.

ATSUMORI: Why need you take it for a dream?
For I have come so far to be with you
in order to clear karma that is real.

RENSHŌ: I do not understand you: for the Name

has power to clear away all trace of sin.
*Call once upon the name of Amida*
*and your countless sins will be no more:*
so the sutra promises. As for me,
I have always called the Name for you.
How could sinful karma afflict you still?

ATSUMORI: Deep as the sea it runs. O lift me up,
RENSHŌ: that I too may come to Buddhahood!
ATSUMORI: Let each assure the other's life to come,
RENSHŌ: for we, once enemies,
ATSUMORI: are now become,
RENSHŌ: in very truth,
ATSUMORI: fast friends in the Law.

*Below, Atsumori moves and gestures in consonance with the text.*

CHORUS:
(*uta*) Now I understand!
'Leave the company of an evil friend,
cleave to the foe you judge a good man':
and that good man is you! O I am grateful!
How can I thank you as you deserve?
Then I will make confession of my tale.
and pass the night recounting it to you
and pass the night recounting it to you.

*Atsumori sits on a stool at centre, facing audience.*

(*kuri*) The flowers of spring rise up and deck the trees
to urge all upwards to illumination;
the autumn moon plumbs the waters' depths
to show grace from on high saving all beings.

ATSUMORI: (*sashi*) Rows of Taira mansions lined the streets
we were the leafy branches on the trees.
Like the rose of Sharon,
we flowered one day;
CHORUS: but as the Teaching that enjoins the Good
is seldom found, birth in the human realm
quickly ends, like a spark from a flint.
This we never knew, nor understood
that vigour is followed by decline.

ATSUMORI: Lords of the land, we were, but caused much grief;
CHORUS: blinded by wealth, we never knew our pride.

*Atsumori rises now, and dances through the* kuse *passage below.*

(*kuse*) Yes, the house of Taira ruled the world
twenty years and more: a generation
that passed by as swiftly as a dream.
Then came the Juei years, and one sad fall,
when storms stripped the trees of all their leaves
and scattered them to the four directions,

we took to our fragile, leaflike ships,
and tossed in restless sleep upon the waves.
Our very dreams foretold no return.
We were like caged birds that miss the clouds,
or homing geese that have lost their way.
We never lingered long under one sky,
but travelled on for days, and months, and years,
till at last spring came round again,
and we camped here, at Ichi-no-tani.
So we stayed on, hard by Suma shore,

ATSUMORI: while winds swept down upon us off the hills.

CHORUS: The fields were bitterly cold. At the sea's edge
our ships huddled close, while day and night
the plovers cried, and our own poor sleeves
wilted in the spray that drenched the beach.
Together in the seafolk's huts we slept,
till we ourselves joined these villagers,
bent to their life like the wind-bent pines.
The evening smoke rose from our cooking fires
while we sat about on heaps of sticks
piled upon the beach, and thought and thought
of how we were at Suma, in the wilds,
and we ourselves belonged to Suma now,
even as we wept for all our clan.

*Atsumori stands before drums.*

ATSUMORI:
(*kakeai*) Then came the sixth night of the second month.
My father, Tsunemori, summoned us
to play and dance, and sing *imayō*.

RENSHŌ: Why, that was the music I remember!
A flute was playing so sweetly in their camp!
We, the attackers, heard it well enough.

ATSUMORI: It was Atsumori's flute, you see:
the one I took with me to my death

RENSHŌ: and that you wished to play this final time,

ATSUMORI: while from every throat

CHORUS: rose songs and poems
(*issei*) sung in chorus to a lively beat.

*(Dance:* jo-no-mai*)*

*Atsumori performs a lively* jo-no-mai, *ending in base square. Below, he continues dancing and miming in consonance with the text.*

ATSUMORI:
(*unnamed*) Then, in time, His Majesty's ship sailed,

CHORUS:
(*noriji*) with the whole clan behind him in their own.
Anxious to be aboard, I sought the shore,
but all the warships and the imperial barge
stood already far, far out to sea.

ATSUMORI:
(*unnamed*) I was stranded. Reining in my horse,
I halted, at a loss for what to do.

CHORUS:
(*noriji*) There came then, galloping behind me,
Kumagai no Jirō Naozane,
shouting, 'You will not escape my arm!'
At this Atsumori wheeled his mount
and swiftly, all undaunted, drew his sword.
We first exchanged a few rapid blows,
then, still on horseback, closed to grapple, fell,
and wrestled on, upon the wave-washed strand.
But you had bested me, and I was slain.
Now karma brings us face to face again.
'You are my foe!' Atsumori shouts, *Brandishes sword.*
lifting his sword to strike; but Kumagai *Drops to one knee.*
with kindness has repaid old enmity, *Rises, retreats.*
calling the Name to give the spirit peace.
They at last shall be reborn together
upon one lotus throne in paradise.
Renshō, you were no enemy of mine.

*He drops his sword and, in base square, turns to Renshō with palms pressed together.*

Pray for me, O pray for my release!
Pray for me, O pray for my release!

*Facing side from base square, stamps the final beat.*

## *Aoi no Ue*

*Translated by Steven T. Brown*

*Dramatis personae:*

PRIMARY ACTOR: Vengeful spirit of Lady Rokujō
ATTENDANT ACTOR (accompanying above): Teruhi the Shamaness
SECONDARY ACTOR: Holy man from Yokawa
ATTENDANT ACTOR (accompanying above): Imperial Retainer
INTERLUDE ACTOR: Messenger from the Minister of the Left

*Place: Before Lady Aoi's sickbed in the mansion of her father, the Minister of the Left.*

*Season and time:* Uncertain.

### PART ONE

*A stage-attendant places a kimono representing Lady Aoi on her sickbed at the front of the stage.*

IMPERIAL RETAINER:
Here before you is a retainer in the service of Emperor Shujaku.
The malevolent spirit possessing the Minister of the Left's daughter Lady Aoi has recently proven to be excessively strong,

So we have summoned venerable priests of great virtue to perform various secret rites and medical cures, but there have been no signs of improvement.
I shall summon Teruhi the Shamaness, a well-known and highly-skilled catalpa bow diviner,
And have her find out through catalpa-bow divination whether it is the spirit of someone living or dead.
Is someone there? Summon forth Teruhi the Shamaness.

TERUHI:
Heaven be pure, earth be pure,
Inside and outside be pure, six sense organs be pure.
One possessed,
Now along the shore approaches,
On a dappled-grey horse,
Loosely shaking the reins.

LADY ROKUJŌ:
Riding in three carriages on the path of the Law,
Might one pass through the gate of the burning house?
At the ruins of Yûgao's dwelling, a dilapidated carriage:
How sad that there is no way to drive it out!
This wretched floating world, like an ox-drawn carriage,
This wretched floating world, like an ox-drawn carriage,
Isn't it the always re-turning wheel of karmic retribution?
Reincarnation forever rolls on like the wheels of a carriage,
Unable to pass through the six realms and four modes of birth,
The impermanence of human beings is like the banana plant or foam on water: it is the way of the world,
That yesterday's flowers are today's dreams,
How stupid it is not to wake up!
Harboring resentment towards others simply increases the misery of my floating life,
My troubled thoughts which I can never forget,
If only I could pacify them for a while.
A vengeful spirit, summoned forth by the catalpa bow,
Is revealed here now.
How shameful even now,
My appearance in a secret carriage.
Though I gaze at the moon until daybreak,
Though I gaze at the moon until daybreak,
I won't appear in the moon's light, a mayfly flickering in the dark
At the upper notch of the catalpa bow,
I rise and approach so that I might tell the story of my aimless misery,
I rise and approach so that I might tell the story of my aimless misery.
Whence comes the sound of the catalpa bow?
Whence comes the sound of the catalpa bow?
Though at the door of the main room
Of the eastern cottage,
Since I am without form,
No one questions me.

TERUHI:

How uncanny! Who it is I know not: an upper-ranking lady
Riding in a dilapidated carriage,
While someone, a young maidservant I think,
Clutches the shafts of an ox-less carriage,
Crying bitterly—how painful it all is!
I wonder: is this the one?

IMPERIAL RETAINER:

I can probably guess who it is. Tell us your name without concealment.

LADY ROKUJŌ:

In this contingent realm of delusion, as evanescent as a flash of lightning,
There is no one I should resent,
Nor should my existence be filled with sorrow.
When, I wonder, did my spirit begin to go adrift?
By the sound of the catalpa bow
I am drawn, appearing before you here and now:
Do you know who I am?
Here before you is the vengeful spirit of Rokujō Miyasudokoro.
In bygone times, when I was still acquainted with the world
Of imperial flower-viewing banquets above the clouds,
And spring morning music concerts,
On autumn nights filled with crimson leaves at the immortal's cave,
Taking delight in the moon, imbued with the seasonal colors and scents.
Though once flourishing like a flower, I have withered away,
A morning glory waiting for the sun's rays.
I know not when my bitter heart,
Like fern shoots in a field of difficulties,
Started sprouting forth. So that I might dispel such
thoughts of dew ablaze with resentment,
I have appeared before you here and now.

CHORUS:

Don't you know that in this world
Compassion is not for the sake of others?
When you are cruel towards others,
When you are cruel towards others,
It will inevitably return to you.
Why do I grieve? Turning over the arrowroot leaf,
I see that my resentment will never be exhausted,
My resentment will never be exhausted.

LADY ROKUJŌ:

Oh, how detestable! Even now I cannot refrain from striking her.

TERUHI:

How shameful! For one in Lady Rokujō's position
To engage in the practice of secondary-wife beating —how can such conduct be tolerated? Stop such thoughts at once!

LADY ROKUJŌ:

Well, no matter what you say, I am unable to resist striking her now.
Rising, I approach her pillow, and just as I strike . . .

TERUHI:
More than this I cannot allow. She approaches, saying:
"I will inflict pain on you with the end of my foot."

LADY ROKUJŌ:
Today's bitterness is a vengeful return of the past,
The flames of wrath envelop me.

TERUHI:
Don't you realize this?

LADY ROKUJŌ:
You must realize . . .

CHORUS:
How hateful is your heart,
Oh, how hateful is your heart.
My resentment is deep-seated.
Even if I make you wail in misery,
While you are alive in this world,
You shall remain tied in bonds of marriage
To one more radiant than the image of fireflies
Flashing over a dark marsh.

LADY ROKUJŌ:
Beneath the wormwood, I . . .

CHORUS:
Will not be the one I was before.
To disappear like dew on a leaf tip—
How bitter it all is!
Even in dreams,
Our vow will not return,
Having become a tale of bygone days,
And yet my attachment grows all the more:
In the clear mirror,
How shameful is the visage!
Standing by her pillow, into my dilapidated carriage
I shall conceal her and ride away,
I shall conceal her and ride away!

*Lady Rokujō pulls her kimono up over her head and withdraws to the rear of the stage.*

## PART TWO

IMPERIAL RETAINER:
Is anyone there?

MESSENGER:
I humbly appear here before you.

IMPERIAL RETAINER:
Since the malevolent spirit possessing Lady Aoi has proven to be excessively strong, please summon the holy man from Yokawa.

MESSENGER:
This is exceedingly unexpected! It was my understanding that Lady Aoi
Was already on the way to recovering from spirit possession,
But since the malevolent spirit is still out of control,
I have been instructed to summon the holy man from Yokawa.
I plan to go now. . . .
Greetings, please show me into the house so that I may deliver a message.

HOLY MAN:
Before the window of the nine forms of consciousness,
Around the seat of the ten vehicles, I am filled with the holy waters of yoga,
Which clarifies the moon of the three secret practices.

Who is it that greets me, wishing
to be admitted?

MESSENGER:
I have come with a message.
The malevolent spirit possessing
Lady Aoi is so overpowering
that I have been instructed
by the Minister
To convey a message kindly
requesting that you appear
with great haste so that she
may receive the power of
your prayers.

HOLY MAN:
At this time I am engaged in
special rites and cannot go
anywhere,
But since it is a message from the
Minister I will go
immediately.

MESSENGER:
We are greatly indebted to your
kindness. Please go in this
direction.
The holy man has arrived.
Please enter.

IMPERIAL RETAINER:
I am much obliged to you for
coming right away.

HOLY MAN:
I received your message. Where is
the person who is suffering
from illness?
I shall perform special prayers
immediately.

IMPERIAL RETAINER:
Kindly do so.

HOLY MAN:
The ascetic comes to perform
special prayers,
He follows in the steps of En no
Gyôja,
Scaling the peaks of the Womb
and Diamond Realms.
In a hempen cloak, he brushes off
the dew of seven jewels,
A robe of forbearance shields him
from defilement.
The red-wood beads of the rosary
Rustle as I rub them
And recite a single prayer:
*Namaku samanda basarada.*

*After donning the golden-horned mask of a vengeful female demon in a jealous rage, Lady Rokujō returns to center stage with her head (and horns) covered with her outer-kimono, carrying a staff in her hand.*

LADY ROKUJŌ:
Return at once, ascetic,
Return or else you will be
vanquished through your
recklessness!

HOLY MAN:
However formidable the evil spirit
may be,
Is it possible for the ascetic's
dharmic powers to be
exhausted?
Rubbing together the beads of the
rosary yet again,
In the east, Gōzanze Myōō,

CHORUS:
In the east, Gōzanze Myōō,

HOLY MAN:
In the south, Gundariyasha,

CHORUS:
In the west, Daitoku Myōō,

HOLY MAN:
In the north, Kongōyasha Myōō,

CHORUS:
In the center, the most wise Fudô
Myōō,

*Namaku samanda basarada,*
*Senda makaroshana,*
*Sofatayauntara takamman,*
Whoever hears my teaching acquires great wisdom,
Whoever knows my mind attains Buddhahood in this very body.

LADY ROKUJŌ:
Oh, how terrifying
Is the voice of perfect wisdom.
From this point forward, in the form of a vengeful spirit,
Never will I come back again.

CHORUS:
When she hears the sound of sutra chanting,
When she hears the sound of sutra chanting,
It pacifies the heart of the evil demon.
In the form of forbearance and merciful compassion,
Bodhisattvas descend to this place to welcome her.
Attaining Buddhahood, release from all worldly attachments,
She becomes filled with gratitude,
She becomes filled with gratitude.

# Korea in the Middle Period

In Korea, the Chinese language had the sort of prominence that Latin had for the vernacular literatures of the West through the Renaissance. Much of Korean literature was, in fact, written in classical Chinese. Even after Korea was united (following the period of the three kingdoms—Koguryo in the north and Paekche and Silla in the south), in the Silla period (57 BCE–935 CE), spoken Korean was still transcribed by using Chinese characters.

Old Korean poetry (*hyangga*), because it was not generally written down, barely survives. Some of the poems that do survive clearly manifest the importance of Buddhism in this early period. We have included several of the extant twenty-five lyrics, which were transcribed into Chinese characters that were meant to convey the sounds of the spoken language. During the Silla period, Buddhism continued to thrive and a national academy was established. By the tenth century, the road to gentlemanly cultivation and success for Korean men was, as in China, a thorough training in the Confucian classics. Ch'oe Ch'i-won, for example, traveled to China at the height of Tang culture to study and take the civil service exam, and he wrote poems in Chinese. Upon his return, he retired from public life and joined a monastery.

With the rise of regional powers on the peninsula, the Silla government declined until one of these regional rulers founded the Koryŏ dynasty (hence, the name "Korea"), which held power from 918 to 1392. Yi Sŏng-gye, a military man, became king in 1392 and, in the wake of the fall of the Mongol dynasty that had overrun China, founded the Chosŏn dynasty, known for its cultivation of the arts. It was not until the reign of King Sejon (1397–1450) that Korea had its own alphabet. The Chosŏn (or Yi) dynasty lasted until the Japanese annexation of Korea in 1910.

*Songs of Flying Dragons,* a poem in praise of General Yi, was the first work written in the new alphabet, which is still used in Korea today (minus four of the twenty-eight original symbols). The work was a collaborative effort of some of the best literary men of the time. Our selection includes 31 of the 248 poems that make up the work. *Songs of Flying Dragons* is a foundational epic that creates Korean history in the same sense that Homer and especially Virgil (in their epic poems) and the Japanese *Kojiki* create mythical paradigms for the establishment of the current political order. The poem creates a cultural identity for Korea through its language as well as its themes. The ideal Homeric hero is accomplished in both deed (*ergon*) and word (*epos*); the Chinese *Book of Songs* similarly constructs heroism as a Confucian combination of martial and cultural excellence (*wen* and *wu*). *Songs of Flying Dragons* contains many allusions to the dynastic hymns of the Chinese *Book of Songs* in which *wen* and *wu* are clearly extolled.

Our selections also include two female poets of the sixteenth century. Korea's most famous female poet is Hwang Chin-i, who wrote in the three-line *sijo* form. Hŏ Nansŏrhŏn's poem *A Woman's Sorrow,* in treating the theme of the abandoned woman, will remind Western readers of Ovid's *Heroides* (pp. 687–692), Christine de Pizan's *City of Ladies* (pp. 1366–1388), and Alexander Pope's *Eloisa to Abelard* (pp. 1867–1876). In this poem, originally written using the Korean alphabet, the poet movingly records her despair at being ignored by her apparently frivolous husband. The poem gives us a window onto the male-centered world of the Chosŏn dynasty from an elegant and well-educated woman's perspective. She vividly depicts a natural world that seems only to echo her own sadness and loneliness.

## Hyangga: A Selection of Old Korean Poetry (7th–10th cent.)

*Translated by Peter H. Lee*

## *Siro (fl. 692–702)*

### *Ode to Knight Chukchi*

All men sorrow and lament
Over the spring that is past;
Your face once fair and bright,
Where has it gone with deep furrows?

I must glimpse you, sir,
If I can, for an awesome moment.
My fervent mind cannot rest at night,
Far off here in the mugwort-covered swamps.

## *Sinch'ung (fl. 737–742)*

*Regret*

You said you would no more forget me
Than oaks would wither before the fall.
O that familiar face is there still,
The face I used to see and admire.

The moon in the ancient lake, it seems,
Complains of the transient tide, ebb and flow.
Your face I will see no more, no more,
O the vain world, it hates and harasses me.

## *Master Wŏlmyŏng (fl. 742–765)*

*Requiem*

On the hard road of life and death
That is near our land,
You went, afraid,
Without words.

We know not where we go,
Leaves blown, scattered,
Though fallen from the same tree,
By the first winds of autumn.

Abide, Sister, perfect your ways,
Until we meet in the Pure Land.

## *Great Master Kyunyŏ (917–973)*

*from Eleven Devotional Poems*

To the boundless throne of Buddha
In the Dharma realm,
I fervently pray
For the sweet rain of truth.

Dispel the blight of affliction
Rooted deep in the ignorant soil,
And moisten the mind's field
Where good grass struggles to grow.

The mind is a moonlit autumn field
Ripe with the gold fruit of knowledge.

## Cho'oe Ch'u-Won (875–?)

*Translated by Peter H. Lee*

### At the Ugang Station

Dismounting on the sandbar I wait for a boat,
A stretch of smoke and waves, an endless sorrow.
Only when the hills are worn flat and the waters dried up
Will there be no parting in the world of man.

### In Autumn Rain

Although I painfully chant in the autumn wind,
I have few friends in the wide world.
At third watch, it rains outside.
By the lamp my heart flies myriad miles away.

### Night Rain in a Postal Station

In a hostel an autumn rain stops;
A quiet night, a lamp on the cold window.
Sighing I sit sunk in sorrow—
Just like a monk in meditation.

## Songs of Flying Dragons (1445–1447)

*Translated by Peter H. Lee*

The tree that strikes deep root
Is firm amidst the winds.
Its flowers are good,
Its fruits abundant.

The stream whose source is deep
Gushes forth even in a drought.
It forms a river
And gains the sea.

His arrow was huge beyond compare—
His father saw it and abandoned it.
On the same day he rejoiced
In him whose genius astounded the day.

Heaven sent a genius
In order to save the people.
Hence he shot with twenty arrows
Twenty sables in the bush.

On Mount Chorae he struck two roebucks
With a single arrow.
Must one paint
This natural genius?

It was a polo match played by royal order—
He hit the ball with a "sideways block."
People on nine state roads
All admired his skill.

Heaven gave him courage and wisdom
Who was to bring order to the country.
Hence eight steeds
Appeared at the proper time.

He shot six roebucks,
He shot six crows,
He flew across
The slanting tree.

He hit the backs of forty tailed deer,
He pierced the mouths and eyes of the rebels,
He shot down three mice from the eaves,
Were there any like him in the past?

Seven pine cones,
The trunk of a dead tree,
Three arrows piercing the helmet—
None like him in the past.

He opened the four borders,
Island dwellers had no more fear of pirates.
Southern barbarians beyond our waters,
How could they not come to him?

Because robbers poisoned the people,
He initiated a land reform.
First he drove away the usurper,
He then labored to restore the state.

Kind and selfless to his brothers,
He covered their past misdeeds.
Thus today we enjoy
Humane manners and customs.

He was consistent from beginning to end,
Meritorious subjects were truly loyal to him.
He secured the throne for a myriad years.
Would his royal works ever discontinue?

Though he was busy with war,
He loved the way of the scholar.
His work of achieving peace
Shone brilliantly.

He did not boast of his natural gifts,
His learning was equally deep.
The vast scope of royal works
Was indeed great.

Upon receiving an old scholar
He knelt down with due politeness.
What do you say about
His respect for scholarship?

When you are wrapped in a dragon robe,
When you wear the belt of precious gems,
Remember, my Lord,
His fortitude and tenacity.

When you sup on northern viands and southern dainties,
When you have superb wine and precious grain,
Remember, my Lord,
His fortitude and fervor.

While the stately guards stand row upon row,
While you reign in peace and give audience,
Remember, my Lord,
His piety and constancy.

When you have men at your beck and call,
When you punish men and sentence them,
Remember, my Lord,
His mercy and temperance.

If you are unaware of people's sorrow,
Heaven will abandon you.
Remember, my Lord,
His labor and love.

If a deceitful minister flatters you,
If you are roused to pride,
Remember, my Lord,
His prowess and modesty.

If a king loses his inward power,
Even his kin will rebel.
Remember, my Lord,
His fame and virtue.

If brothers are split,
A villain will enter to sow discord.
Remember, my Lord,
His sagacity and love.

If a ruler taxes his people without measure,
The basis of the state will crumble.
Remember, my Lord,
His justice and humanity.

If your advisors wrangle before you
In order only to assist and secure the Throne,
Remember, my Lord,
His goodness and justice.

If a small man wishes to curry favor
And preaches "No leisure for culture,"
Remember, my Lord,
His effort and erudition.

When slanderers craftily make mischief,
When they grossly exaggerate small mistakes,
Remember, my Lord,
His wisdom and justice.

If perverse theories of the Western barbarians
Threaten you with sin or allure with bliss,
Remember, my Lord,
His judgment and orthodoxy.

A milennium ago,
Heaven chose the north of the Han.
There they accumulated goodness and founded the state.
Oracles foretold: a myriad years;
May your sons and grandsons reign unbroken.
But you can secure the dynasty only
When you worship Heaven and benefit the people.
Ah, you who will wear the crown, beware,
Can you depend upon your ancestors
When you go hunting by the waters of Lo?

## Hwang Chin-i (c. 1506–1544)

### *"I will break the back of this long, midwinter night"*

*Translated by David R. McCann*

I will break the back
    of this long, midwinter night,
folding it double,
    cold beneath my spring quilt,
that I may draw out
    the night, should my love return.

### *"Do not boast of your speed"*

*Translated by Peter H. Lee*

Do not boast of your speed,
O blue-green stream running by the hills:
Once you have reached the wide ocean,
You can return no more.
Why not stay here and rest,
When moonlight stuffs the empty hills?

### *"Mountains are steadfast but the mountain streams"*

*Translated by Peter H. Lee*

Mountains are steadfast but the mountain streams
Go by, go by,
And yesterdays are like the rushing streams,
They fly, they fly,
And the great heroes, famous for a day,
They die, they die.

## "Blue mountains speak of my desire"

*Translated by Peter H. Lee*

Blue mountains speak of my desire,
Green waters reflect my lover's love:
The mountains unchanging,
The waters flowing by.
Sometimes it seems the waters cannot forget me,
They part in tears, regretting, running away.

## Hŏ Nansŏrhŏn (1563–1589)

*Translated by Peter H. Lee*

## A Woman's Sorrow

Yesterday I fancied I was young;
But today, alas, I am aging.
What use is there in recalling
The joyful days of my youth?
Now I am old, recollections are vain.
Sorrow chokes me; words fail me.
When Father begot me, Mother reared me,
When they took pains to bring me up,
They dreamed, not of a duchess or marchioness,
But at least of a bride fit for a gentleman.
The turning of destiny of the three lives
And the tie chanced by a matchmaker
Brought me a romantic knight,
And careful as in a dream I trod on ice.
O was it a dream, those innocent days?
When I reached fifteen, counted sixteen,
The inborn beauty in me blossomed, and
With this face and this body
I vowed a union of a hundred years.
The flow of time and tide was sudden;
The gods too were jealous of my beauty.
Spring breezes and autumn moon,
Alas, they flew like a shuttle.
And my face that once was beautiful,
Where did it go? Who disgraced it so?
Turn away from the mirror, look no more.
Who, who will look at me now?
Blush not, my self, and reproach no one.

Don't say, "A tavern somewhere has found a friend."
When flowers smiled in the setting sun,
He rode away on a white horse
With no aim, no destination.
Where would he stop? Where should he lodge?
How far he went I know not;
I will hear nothing from him, not a word.
Yet I dare to hope he will remember me,
Though changed from what he has been.
Hush, anxious heart, hush, that longs
For the face of him who abandoned you—
Long is a day; cruel is a month.
The plum trees by the jade window
Have blossomed and scattered, spring after spring.
The winter night is bitter cold,
And snow falls thick and fast.
Long, long is a summer's day; the
Dreary rain makes my heartache keener.
And blessed spring with flowers and willows,
It, too, wears a melancholy look.
When the autumn moon enters my room
And crickets chirp on the couch,
A long sigh and salty tears
Endlessly make me recall details of the past.
It is hard to bring this cruel life to an end—
No, I must unravel my sorrow calmly.
Lighting the blue lantern, I play
"A Song of Blue Lotus" on the green lute,
And play it as my sorrow commands me,
As though the rain on the Hsiao and Hsiang
Beat confusedly over the bamboo leaves,
As though the crane returned whooping
After a span of a thousand years.
Fingers may pluck the familiar tune,
But who will listen? The room
Is empty except for the lotus-brocade curtains.
Sing the pain that pierces my entrails,
And let it unravel sorrow inch by inch.
Oh, to sleep, and see him in a dream:
But for what reason and by what enmity
Do the fallen leaves rustle in the wind
And the insects piping among the grasses
Wake me from my wretched sleep?
The Weaver and Herdboy in the sky
Meet once on the seventh day of the seventh moon—
However hard it is to cross the Milky Way—

And never miss this yearly encounter.
But since he left me, left me alone,
What magic water separates him from me
And what makes him silent across the water?
Leaning on the balustrade, I gaze at the path he took—
Dewdrops glitter on the young grass,
Evening clouds pass by; birds sing sadly
In the thicket of green bamboos.
Numberless are the sorrowful;
But none can be as wretched as I.
Think, love, you caused me this grief;
I know not whether I shall live or die.

# Europe in the Middle Period

At the beginning of the Middle Period, Christianity became the state religion of the Roman Empire, and the empire split in two. Latin became the official language of Western Europe and the Roman Church, and Greek the official language of the Byzantine empire and the Orthodox Church. The vast majority of literary texts during the Middle Period were written in these two languages. As Christianity spread northward from the Mediterranean, it brought literacy to a great number of traditional oral cultures in several language groups. It was only a matter of time before writing developed in Europe's many native languages. Vernacular literatures emerged one by one over several centuries: among the Celtic languages, Irish is represented here; among the Germanic languages, examples of English and Norse are given; among the Romance languages (those descended directly from Latin), selections from Provençal, French, and Italian are included.

To various degrees, literatures in these languages became increasingly independent of church control; eventually, they developed rich multiplicities of styles and cultural perspectives of their own. Meanwhile, Latin continued as the common language of Western European high culture, producing a rich and extensive literature. Latin was used primarily in the clerical (religious) and aristocratic world of men, but one of the most powerful Latin selections here is by a woman, Heloise. In fact, most writing by women that has come down to us from the European Middle Ages was composed in Latin and is religious in content, since women in religious orders often had access to education. The rich abundance of the late medieval Latin tradition is represented here by texts ranging over twelve centuries, from Augustine's *Confessions* (387 CE) all the way to Thomas More's *Utopia* (1516).

In Eastern Europe, the Orthodox Church generally maintained a tighter grip on the production of texts than the Roman Church did in the West. Most texts in Bulgarian, Russian, and other Slavic languages, as well as in Greek, served strictly religious functions.

Although the Roman and Byzantine worlds were in steady political contact throughout the period, there was surprisingly little literary influence across the border. Greek learning virtually disappeared from Western Europe for a thousand years. The ancient Greek heritage was preserved and developed, however, in the Arab world. It then found its way back into Europe, along with other Arabic influences, first through Muslim Spain and later through the Crusades in the eleventh and twelfth centuries. This Arabic influence helped stimulate what is now known as the "Twelfth-Century Renaissance" in Europe.

In the twelfth century, the Parisian philosopher Abelard was one of the first writers to rework Christian ideas with the tools of ancient Greek philosophy—especially that of Aristotle—although Abelard is remembered today chiefly for his love affair with his student Heloise, a relationship captured in their letters, some of which are included here. The first European universities were founded during this time in Italy, France, and England. Although the twelfth century may aptly be called a "Renaissance," classical learning would be revived more fully and directly by the Italian humanists of the fourteenth century, beginning with Petrarch.

It is impossible to account in a few words for the social and historical circumstances that guided the development of literature for more than a thousand years in the several languages included here. There are, however, a few general lines of development to watch for throughout the period, besides the spread of literacy and the tension between the Latin and vernacular traditions. First of all, the Twelfth-Century Renaissance and later the birth of classical humanism suggest a tripartite division of the period into the Early Middle Ages, the Late Middle Ages, and the Renaissance. During the Early Middle Ages, writing was overwhelmingly in the possession of the church. Books were preserved and copied in thousands of monasteries that dotted the continent. Our selections from St. Augustine represent only the tiniest fragment of the immense literature of this tradition. The little vernacular literature of the period that is not devoted to religious purposes might be characterized very generally as mythological or heroic. It is represented here by the Old Norse *Eddas*, although there are many other texts that could have been included, such as the Anglo-Saxon epic *Beowulf*, the Irish epic *The Táin*, the French *Song of Roland*, and the Spanish *Book of the Cid*.

The Late Middle Ages saw the flowering of the literature of love, Romance narratives, the personal literary voice, and the depiction of complex individual subjectivity, represented here by Abelard and Heloise, Marie de France, Christine de Pizan, Dante, and Chaucer, among others. Romances, the most popular literary genre of the period, are highly stylized, often fabulous tales of aristocratic warrior-lovers, elaborating subtle contradictions within the code of aristocratic behavior. They are often set in ancient or Middle Eastern settings—the long ago or far away.

The Romances are represented here by Marie de France. Both the love poetry and the Romances of the period were strongly influenced by Arabic (and Persian-Arabic) models. Dante and Chaucer, perhaps the greatest poets of the Middle Ages, represent the movement of literature away from the church and the aristocracy to writers of the middle class at the end of the period.

The literature of the Renaissance, often called the Early Modern Period, is characterized both by the recovery of ancient Roman and Greek learning and by the tremendous influence of the classics over the intellectual and cultural production of the time. The period is also marked by the Reformation, a division between Catholic countries of the south and Protestant countries of the north; the rapid spread of literacy that followed the invention of the printing press; and the sudden expansion of cultural influences in the age of exploration, which brought new contacts with Africa, Asia, and the New World. The fabulous wealth of Renaissance literature, surely one of the high points in the Western literary tradition, is represented here by Petrarch, Thomas More, Montaigne, and Shakespeare. In More's *Utopia* and Montaigne's *Of Cannibals,* we can see European writers critically examining their own culture in light of the startling discovery of America.

# The Latin Tradition

## AUGUSTINE (354–430)

*Translated by R.S. Pine-Coffin*

Augustine was one of the "Fathers" of the Christian Church. His copious writings established much of the doctrine and practice of the church for the next fifteen hundred years. He is most remembered by students of literature, however, for his *Confessions,* often said to be the first autobiography in Western literature. This book provides an extraordinarily detailed and thoughtful account of life in late antiquity, a time when the Roman world was undergoing deep changes at the beginning of the Middle Ages. Only a few years after the book was written, the city of Rome was sacked by the Goths, a "barbarian" tribe from outside the empire.

In the *Confessions,* Augustine records his life as a boy from provincial North Africa who eventually rose by dint of his intelligence and ambition to become a prominent Roman intellectual and teacher. He continues his account up to age thirty-three, when he decided to be baptized a Christian. Not only does he recount his experiences along the way, but he also reflects on them as a Roman philosopher and as a Christian moralist and theologian.

Three episodes from his life are included here. The first is his famous account of stealing pears from a neighbor's garden with a gang of rowdy teenage friends. In itself the event is so trivial that his lengthy self-chastizing meditation on it may seem excessive. After all, it was only a teenage prank. But in this little prank, Augustine perceives his thunderous fall into a life of sin. It becomes for him the prototype of all sins precisely because it was so utterly senseless. The act was alluring for its very forbiddenness and irrationality. This point would be less powerful, perhaps, if he had chosen a more dramatic sin to illustrate it with. The incident of the pear tree would also have reminded Augustine's first readers of Adam and Eve's original sin: taking forbidden fruit from a tree.

The second episode records the story of Augustine's friend Alypius. Here he gives us a vivid picture of daily life in a Roman city, including a riveting account of the effect of the gladiatorial games on a young man who was certain he was above being corrupted by their violence. As with the pear tree episode, here we have something close to a parable about human nature as well as an analysis of sin not so much as an individual but as a social phenomenon.

The third selection is the climactic episode of the *Confessions:* Augustine's account of his final conversion to Christianity in a garden in Milan. At this point in his life, Augustine knows exactly what he wants to do, but in spite of this knowledge, he finds he still cannot do it. He wants to renounce the desires of the flesh, but he finds his heart divided against itself. This conundrum plunges him into despair as he wrestles with the problem of his own free will: what inner forces could prevent me from acting on my own desire? Chains of habit, he concludes, can prevent the body from obeying the mind. Sex is the most tenacious of these habits; the renunciation of sex is, therefore, the ultimate test of the mind's power over the body. Finally, the voice of a child playing a game in the street—or is it an angel's voice or his own conscience?—comes to him from over the wall, and he is drawn gently across the barrier into a new life. It is a moment of profound introspection and haunting mystery.

## Confessions

### *from Book II [The Pear Tree Episode]*

It is certain, O Lord, that theft is punished by your law, the law that is written in men's hearts and cannot be erased however sinful they are. For no thief can bear that another thief should steal from him, even if he is rich and the other is driven to it by want. Yet I was willing to steal, and steal I did, although I was not compelled by any lack, unless it were the lack of a sense of justice or a distaste for what was right and a greedy love of doing wrong. For of what I stole I already had plenty, and much better at that, and I had no wish to enjoy the things I coveted by stealing, but only to enjoy the theft itself and the sin. There was a pear-tree near our vineyard, loaded with fruit that was attractive neither to look at nor to taste. Late one night a band of ruffians, myself included, went off to shake down the fruit and carry it away, for we had continued our games out of doors until well after dark, as was our pernicious habit. We took away an enormous quantity of pears, not to eat them ourselves, but simply to throw them to the pigs. Perhaps we ate some of them, but our real pleasure consisted in doing something that was forbidden.

Look into my heart, O God, the same heart on which you took pity when it was in the depths of the abyss. Let my heart now tell you what prompted me to do wrong for no purpose, and why it was only my own love of mischief that made me do it. The evil in me was foul, but I loved it. I loved my own perdition and my own faults, not the things for which I committed wrong, but the wrong itself. My soul was vicious and broke away from your safe keeping to seek its own destruction, looking for no profit in disgrace but only for disgrace itself.

* * *

The eye is attracted by beautiful objects, by gold and silver and all such things. There is great pleasure, too, in feeling something agreeable to the touch, and material things have various qualities to please each of the other senses. Again, it is gratifying to be held in esteem by other men and to have the power of giving them orders and gaining the mastery over them. This is also the reason why revenge is sweet. But our ambition to obtain all these things must not lead us astray from you, O Lord, nor must we depart from what your law allows. The life we live on earth has its own attractions as well, because it has a certain beauty of its own in harmony with all the rest of this world's beauty. Friendship among men, too, is a delightful bond, uniting many souls in one. All these things and their like can be occasions of sin because, good though they are, they are of the lowest order of good, and if we are too much tempted by them we abandon those higher and better things, your truth, your law, and you yourself, O Lord our God. For these earthly things, too, can give joy, though not such joy as my God, who made them all, can give, because *honest men will rejoice in the Lord; upright hearts will not boast in vain.*

When there is an inquiry to discover why a crime has been committed, normally no one is satisfied until it has been shown that the motive might have been either the desire of gaining, or the fear of losing, one of those good things which I said were of the lowest order. For such things are attractive and have beauty, although they are paltry trifles in comparison with the worth of God's blessed treasures. A man commits murder and we ask the reason. He did it because he wanted his victim's wife or estates for himself, or so that he might live on the proceeds of robbery, or because he was afraid that the other might defraud him of something, or because he had been wronged and was burning for revenge. Surely no one would believe that he would commit murder for no reason but the sheer delight of killing? Sallust tells us that Catiline was a man of insane ferocity, 'who chose to be cruel and vicious without apparent reason'; but we are also told that his purpose was 'not to allow his men to lose heart or waste their skill through lack of practice.' If we ask the reason for this, it is obvious that he meant that once he had made himself master of the government by means of this continual violence, he would obtain honour, power, and wealth and would no longer go in fear of the law because of his crimes or have to face difficulties through lack of funds. So even Catiline did not love crime for crime's sake. He loved something quite different, for the sake of which he committed his crimes.

* * *

If the crime of theft which I committed that night as a boy of sixteen were a living thing, I could speak to it and ask what it was that, to my shame, I loved in it. It had no beauty because it was a robbery. It is true that the pears which we stole had beauty, because they were created by you, the good God, who are the most beautiful of all beings and the Creator of all things, the supreme Good and my own true Good. But it was not the pears that my unhappy soul desired. I had plenty of my own, better than those, and I only picked them so that I might steal. For no sooner had I picked them than I threw them away, and tasted nothing in them but my own sin, which I relished and enjoyed. If any part of one of those pears passed my lips, it was the sin that gave it flavour.

And now, O Lord my God, now that I ask what pleasure I had in that theft, I find that it had no beauty to attract me. I do not mean beauty of the sort that justice and prudence possess, nor the beauty that is in man's mind and in his memory and in the life that animates him, nor the beauty of the stars in their allotted places or of the earth and sea, teeming with new life born to replace the old as it passes away. It did not even have the shadowy, deceptive beauty which makes vice attractive—pride, for instance, which is a pretence of superiority, imitating yours, for you alone are God, supreme over all; or ambition, which is only a craving for honour and glory, when you alone are to be honoured before all and you alone are glorious for ever. Cruelty is the weapon of the powerful, used to make others fear them: yet no one is to be feared but God alone, from whose power nothing can be snatched away or stolen by any man at any time or place or by any means. The lustful use caresses to win the love they crave for, yet no caress is sweeter than your charity and no love is more rewarding than the love of your truth, which shines in beauty above all else. Inquisitiveness has all the appearance of a thirst for knowledge, yet you have supreme knowledge of all things. Ignorance, too, and stupidity choose to go under the mask of simplicity and innocence, because you are simplicity itself and no innocence is greater than yours. You are innocent even of the harm which overtakes the wicked, for it is the result of their own actions. Sloth poses as the love of peace: yet what certain peace is there besides the Lord? Extravagance masquerades as fullness and abundance: but you are the full, unfailing store of never-dying sweetness. The spendthrift makes a pretence of liberality: but you are the most generous dispenser of all good. The covetous want many possessions for themselves: you possess all. The envious struggle for preferment: but what is to be preferred before you? Anger demands revenge: but what vengeance is as just as yours? Fear shrinks from any sudden, unwonted danger which threatens the things that it loves, for its only care is safety: but to you nothing is strange, nothing unforeseen. No one can part you from the things that you love, and safety is assured nowhere but in you. Grief eats away its heart for the loss of things which it took pleasure in desiring, because it wants to be like you, from whom nothing can be taken away.

So the soul defiles itself with unchaste love when it turns away from you and looks elsewhere for things which it cannot find pure and unsullied except by returning to you. All who desert you and set themselves up against you merely copy you in a perverse way; but by this very act of imitation they only show that you are the Creator of all nature and, consequently, that there is no place whatever where man may hide away from you.

What was it, then, that pleased me in that act of theft? Which of my Lord's powers did I imitate in a perverse and wicked way? Since I had no real power to break his law, was it that I enjoyed at least the pretence of doing so, like a prisoner who creates for himself the illusion of liberty by doing something wrong, when he has no fear of punishment, under a feeble hallucination of power? Here was the slave who ran away from his master and chased a shadow instead! What an abomination! What a parody of life! What abysmal death! Could I enjoy doing wrong for no other reason than that it was wrong?

* * *

*What return shall I make to the Lord* for my ability to recall these things with no fear in my soul? I will love you, Lord, and thank you, and praise your name, because you have forgiven me such great sins and such wicked deeds. I acknowledge that it was by your grace and mercy that you melted away my sins like ice. I acknowledge, too, that by your grace I was preserved from whatever sins I did not commit, for there was no knowing what I might have done, since I loved evil even if it served no purpose. I avow that you have forgiven me all, both the sins which I committed of my own accord and those which by your guidance I was spared from committing.

What man who reflects upon his own weakness can dare to claim that his own efforts have made him chaste and free from sin, as though this entitled him to love you the less, on the ground that he had less need of the mercy by which you forgive the sins of the penitent? There are some who have been called by you and because they have listened to your voice they have avoided the sins which I here record and confess for them to read. But let them not deride me for having been cured by the same Doctor who preserved them from sickness, or at least from such grave sickness as mine. Let them love you just as much, or even more, than I do, for they can see that the same healing hand which rid me of the great fever of my sins protects them from falling sick of the same disease.

* * *

It brought me no happiness, for *what harvest did I reap from acts which now make me blush,* particularly from that act of theft? I loved nothing in it except the thieving, though I cannot truly speak of that as a 'thing' that I could love, and I was only the more miserable because of it. And yet, as I recall my feelings at the time, I am quite sure that I would not have done it on my own. Was it then that I also enjoyed the company of those with whom I committed the crime? If this is so, there was something else I loved besides the act of theft; but I cannot call it 'something else', because companionship, like theft, is not a thing at all.

No one can tell me the truth of it except my God, who enlightens my mind and dispels its shadows. What conclusion am I trying to reach from these questions and this discussion? It is true that if the pears which I stole had been to my taste, and if I had wanted to get them for myself, I might have committed the crime on my own if I had needed to do no more than that to win myself the pleasure. I should have had no need to kindle my glowing desire by rubbing shoulders with a gang of accomplices. But as it was not the fruit that gave me pleasure, I must have got it from the crime itself, from the thrill of having partners in sin.

* * *

How can I explain my mood? It was certainly a very vile frame of mind and one for which I suffered; but how can I account for it? *Who knows his own frailties?*

We were tickled to laughter by the prank we had played, because no one suspected us of it although the owners were furious. Why was it, then, that I thought it fun not to have been the only culprit? Perhaps it was because we do not easily laugh when we are alone. True enough: but even when a man is all by himself and quite alone, sometimes he cannot help laughing if he thinks or hears or sees something especially funny. All the same, I am quite sure that I would never have done this thing on my own.

My God, I lay all this before you, for it is still alive in my memory. By myself I would not have committed that robbery. It was not the takings that attracted me but the raid itself, and yet to do it by myself would have been no fun and I should not have done it. This was friendship of a most unfriendly sort, bewitching my mind in an inexplicable way. For the sake of a laugh, a little sport, I was glad to do harm and anxious to damage another; and that without thought of profit for myself or retaliation for injuries received! And all because we are ashamed to hold back when others say 'Come on! Let's do it!'

* * *

Can anyone unravel this twisted tangle of knots? I shudder to look at it or think of such abomination. I long instead for innocence and justice, graceful and splendid in eyes whose sight is undefiled. My longing fills me and yet it cannot cloy. With them is certain peace and life that cannot be disturbed. The man who enters their domain goes to *share the joy of his Lord.* He shall know no fear and shall lack no good. In him that is goodness itself he shall find his own best way of life. But I deserted you, my God. In my youth I wandered away, too far from your sustaining hand, and created of myself a barren waste.

## *from Book VI [The Gladiatorial Games]*

Alypius came from my own town and his people were one of the leading families. He was younger than I was and had been a student of mine both in our own town, when I first began to teach, and later on at Carthage. He was greatly attached to me because he thought that I was a good and learned man, and I was fond of him because, although he was still young, it was quite clear that he had much natural disposition to goodness. But he had been caught in the whirl of easy morals at Carthage, with its continual round of futile entertainments, and had lost his heart and his head to the games in the amphitheatre. At the time when he was so wrapped up in this wretched sport I had opened my school as professor of rhetoric in Carthage, but because of some difference of opinion which had occurred between his father and me he was not one of my pupils. I found out that he was fatally attracted by the games and it caused me grave anxiety to think that he was likely to ruin a future which promised so well, if he had not already done so. But I had no means of offering him advice or using any pressure to restrain him, for I could claim neither the privilege of a friend nor the right of a master. I thought that he shared his father's feelings about me, although, in fact, this was not the case for he ignored his father's wishes and treated me with courtesy when we met. He soon began to come and listen to some of my lectures, but he never stayed for long.

I had forgotten that I might use my influence with him to prevent him from wasting his talents in this thoughtless, impetuous enthusiasm for futile pastimes. But you, O Lord, who hold the reins of all you have created, had not forgotten this man who was one day to be a bishop and administer your sacrament to your children. You used me to set him on the right path, but so that we might recognize that it was all by your doing, you used me without my knowledge. One day as I sat in my usual place with my pupils before me, Alypius came in and after greeting me politely sat down and listened attentively to the lesson. It occurred to me that the passage which I happened to be reading could very well be explained by an illustration taken from the games in the arena. It would appeal to the students and make my meaning clearer, and it would also enable me to make a laughing-stock of those who were under the spell of this insane sport. You know, my God, that I was not thinking of Alypius, who so badly needed to be cured of this mania. But he took my words to heart, thinking that I had meant the allusion to apply to him alone. Anyone else would have taken this as a good reason to be angry with me, but this conscientious young man saw in it cause for anger with himself and warmer affection for me. Long ago you caused these words of yours to be inserted in your book: *The wise are grateful for a remonstrance.*

I had not meant to rebuke him, but you use us all, whether we know it or not, for a purpose which is known to you, a purpose which is just. You made my heart and my tongue burn like coals to sear his mind, which was so full of promise, and cure it when it was sick of a wasting disease. Those who have no inkling of your mercy may be silent and offer you no word of praise, but from the depths of my heart I make avowal of your mercy. For after he had heard my words, Alypius hastened to drag himself out of the deep pitfall into which, dazzled by the allure of pleasure, he had plunged of his own accord. By a great effort of self-control he shook himself free of all the dirt of the arena and never went near it again. Then he managed to overcome his father's reluctance to allow him to become a pupil of mine. His father gave in and granted his request. But once he had started his studies with me he became involved in my superstitious beliefs. He particularly admired the Manichees for their ostensible continence, which he thought quite genuine, though of course it was merely a nonsensical and deceitful method of trapping precious souls which had not learnt to feel the depth of real virtue and were easily deceived by the appearance of virtue that was spurious and counterfeit.

* * *

But he did not abandon his career in the world, for his parents would not allow him to forget it. He went to Rome ahead of me to study law and there, strange to relate, he became obsessed with an extraordinary craving for gladiatorial shows. At first he detested these displays and refused to attend them. But one day during the season for this cruel and bloodthirsty sport he happened to meet some friends and fellow-students returning from their dinner. In a friendly way they brushed aside his resistance and his stubborn protests and carried him off to the arena.

'You may drag me there bodily,' he protested, 'but do you imagine that you can make me watch the show and give my mind to it? I shall be there, but it will be just as if I were not present, and I shall prove myself stronger than you or the games.'

He did not manage to deter them by what he said, and perhaps the very reason why they took him with them was to discover whether he would be as good as his word. When they arrived at the arena, the place was seething with the lust for cruelty. They found seats as best they could and Alypius shut his eyes tightly, determined to have nothing to do with these atrocities. If only he had closed his ears as well! For an incident in the fight drew a great roar from the crowd, and this thrilled him so deeply that he could not contain his curiosity. Whatever had caused the uproar, he was confident that, if he saw it, he would find it repulsive and remain master of himself. So he opened his eyes, and his soul was stabbed with a wound more deadly than any which the gladiator, whom he was so anxious to see, had received in his body. He fell, and fell more pitifully than the man whose fall had drawn that roar of excitement from the crowd. The din had pierced his ears and forced him to open his eyes, laying his soul open to receive the wound which struck it down. This was presumption, not courage. The weakness of his soul was in relying upon itself instead of trusting in you.

When he saw the blood, it was as though he had drunk a deep draught of savage passion. Instead of turning away, he fixed his eyes upon the scene and drank in all its frenzy, unaware of what he was doing. He revelled in the wickedness of the fighting and was drunk with the fascination of bloodshed. He was no longer the man who had come to the arena, but simply one of the crowd which he had joined, a fit companion for the friends who had brought him.

Need I say more? He watched and cheered and grew hot with excitement, and when he left the arena, he carried away with him a diseased mind which would leave him no peace until he came back again, no longer simply together with the friends who had first dragged him there, but at their head, leading new sheep to the slaughter. Yet you stretched out your almighty, ever merciful hand, O God, and rescued him from this madness. You taught him to trust in you, not in himself. But this was much later.

* * *

Nevertheless, all this was stored away in his memory so that later on he might turn the lesson to good account. And there was another event in his life, too, which you, my God, must surely have allowed to happen only because you knew that he was to be a great man in later life and you wanted him to start in good time to learn that, in judging cases, one man must not too easily condemn another through being over-credulous.

While he was still studying under me at Carthage, you allowed him to be arrested as a thief by the market officers. He was in the market in the middle of the day thinking over an exercise of the sort which is regularly given to students, a set piece which he had to recite. He was strolling alone in front of the law courts carrying his pen and his writing tablets, when the real thief, a young student like himself, made his way without attracting the notice of Alypius towards the leaden gratings which project over the moneylenders' shops. He carried a hatchet, which he kept out of sight, and with this he began to hack away the lead. But the moneylenders, in their shops below, heard the noise. Quietly they discussed what to do, and sent some men to arrest anyone they might find. At the sound of their voices the thief dropped his hatchet and ran off, frightened that he might be caught with it in his possession.

Alypius had not seen the thief arrive, but he saw him leave. He noticed that he was in a hurry to get away, and went into the building to discover the reason for this haste. He found the hatchet, and while he stood wondering how it came to be there, the men who had been sent to find the intruder arrived to find Alypius alone and in his hand the tool which had caused the noise that had alarmed them and brought them to the spot. They seized him and dragged him away, proudly telling the crowd of shopkeepers who had by now assembled that they had caught him in the act. Then they took him off to hand him over to the magistrates.

But this was the end of his lesson. You, O Lord, were the only witness of his innocence and at once you stood by his side to defend him. For as they were leading him away to be tortured or imprisoned, they met the architect in charge of public buildings. Alypius's captors were particularly glad to meet this official, because he had often suspected them of stealing goods missing from the market and now, at last, he would realize who was guilty of these crimes. But the architect had often seen Alypius at the house of one of the senators, whom he frequently visited. He recognized him at once and, taking him by the arm, led him aside to ask how he came to be in such trouble. When he heard what had happened, he turned to the excited onlookers, who were noisily threatening Alypius, and told them all to follow him. They passed by the house of the youth who had committed the crime. At the door they found a slave-boy, quite able to tell all he knew but too young to fear any consequences for his master. He had, in fact, been with his master in the market. Alypius remembered him and told the architect, who showed the hatchet to the boy and asked him whose it was. Without hesitation the boy answered 'Ours', and went on to tell the whole story in answer to the architect's questions. By this means the guilt was laid where it belonged, much to the confusion of the crowd, which had begun too soon to be jubilant over the arrest of Alypius. And Alypius, who was destined later to preach your word and judge many cases in your Church, went home all the wiser for this experience.

## *from Book VIII [Conversion]*

O Lord, my Helper and my Redeemer, I shall now tell and confess to the glory of your name how you released me from the fetters of lust which held me so tightly shackled and from my slavery to the things of this world. I continued to lead my usual life, but I was growing more and more unsettled and day after day I poured out my heart to you. I went to your church whenever I had time from my work, which was a painful load upon my shoulders. Alypius was with me, now taking respite from his legal work after a third term of office as assessor. He was looking for clients who would pay him for his advice, just as my pupils paid me for skill in words, if it is possible to teach such an art. As a gesture of friendship to Alypius and me, Nebridius had consented to act as assistant to a great friend of ours named Verecundus, a Milanese, who was a teacher of grammar and had made most insistent demands upon our friendship for one of us to give him loyal help, for this he badly needed. It was not the desire of profit that had led Nebridius to accept the post, for if he had wished he could have earned more by teaching literature. But he was too good and kind a friend to refuse a request which appealed to his good nature. He did what was asked of him in an unobtrusive way, taking care not to attract the attention of important people, as the world reckons importance, in case contact with them should disturb his peace of mind. For he wanted to keep his mind free and enjoy as many hours of leisure as he could for the purpose of thinking and reading and listening to discussions on philosophy.

One day when for some reason that I cannot recall Nebridius was not with us, Alypius and I were visited at our house by a fellow-countryman of ours from Africa, a man named Ponticianus, who held a high position in the

Emperor's household. He had some request to make of us and we sat down to talk. He happened to notice a book lying on a table used for games, which was near where we were sitting. He picked it up and opened it and was greatly surprised to find that it contained Paul's epistles, for he had supposed that it was one of the books which used to tax all my strength as a teacher. Then he smiled and looked at me and said how glad he was, and how surprised, to find this book, and no others, there before my eyes. He of course was a Christian and a faithful servant to you, our God. Time and again he knelt before you in church repeating his prayers and lingering over them. When I told him that I studied Paul's writings with the greatest attention, he began to tell us the story of Antony, the Egyptian monk, whose name was held in high honour by your servants, although Alypius and I had never heard it until then. When Ponticianus realized this, he went into greater detail, wishing to instil some knowledge of this great man into our ignorant minds, for he was very surprised that we had not heard of him. For our part, we too were astonished to hear of the wonders you had worked so recently, almost in our own times, and witnessed by so many, in the true faith and in the Catholic Church. In fact all three of us were amazed, Alypius and I because the story we heard was so remarkable, and Ponticianus because we had not heard it before.

After this he went on to tell us of the groups of monks in the monasteries, of their way of life that savours of your sweetness, and of the fruitful wastes of the desert. All of this was new to us. There was a monastery at Milan also, outside the walls, full of good brethren under the care of Ambrose, but we knew nothing of this either. Ponticianus continued to talk and we listened in silence. Eventually he told us of the time when he and three of his companions were at Trêves. One afternoon, while the Emperor was watching the games in the circus, they went out to stroll in the gardens near the city walls. They became separated into two groups, Ponticianus and one of the others remaining together while the other two went off by themselves. As they wandered on, the second pair came to a house which was the home of some servants of yours, men poor in spirit, to whom the kingdom of heaven belongs. In the house they found a book containing the life of Antony. One of them began to read it and was so fascinated and thrilled by the story that even before he had finished reading he conceived the idea of taking upon himself the same kind of life and abandoning his career in the world—both he and his friend were officials in the service of the State—in order to become your servant. All at once he was filled with the love of holiness. Angry with himself and full of remorse, he looked at his friend and said, 'What do we hope to gain by all the efforts we make? What are we looking for? What is our purpose in serving the State? Can we hope for anything better at Court than to be the Emperor's friends? Even so, surely our position would be precarious and exposed to much danger? We shall meet it at every turn, only to reach another danger which is greater still. And how long is it to be before we reach it? But if I wish, I can become the friend of God at this very moment.'

After saying this he turned back to the book, labouring under the pain of the new life that was taking birth in him. He read on and in his heart, where you alone could see, a change was taking place. His mind was being divested of the world, as could presently be seen. For while he was reading, his heart leaping and turning in his breast, a cry broke from him as he saw the better course and determined to take it. Your servant now, he said to his friend, 'I have torn myself free from all our ambitions and have decided to serve God. From this very moment, here and now, I shall start to serve him. If you will not follow my lead, do not stand in my way.' The other answered that he would stand by his comrade, for such service was glorious and the reward was great. So these two, now your servants, built their tower at the cost which had to be paid, that is, at the cost of giving up all they possessed and following you.

At this moment Ponticianus and the man who had been walking with him in another part of the garden arrived at the house, looking for their friends. Now that they had found them they said that it was time to go home, as the daylight was beginning to fade. But the other two told them of the decision they had made and what they proposed to do. They explained what had made them decide to take this course and how they had agreed upon it, and they asked their friends, if they would not join them, at least not to put obstacles in their way. Ponticianus said that he and the other man did not change their old ways, but they were moved to tears for their own state of life. In all reverence they congratulated the others and commended themselves to their prayers. Then they went back to the palace, burdened with hearts that were bound to this earth; but the others remained in the house and their hearts were fixed upon heaven. Both these men were under a promise of marriage, but once the two women heard what had happened, they too dedicated their virginity to you.

* * *

This was what Ponticianus told us. But while he was speaking, O Lord, you were turning me around to look at myself. For I had placed myself behind my own back, refusing to see myself. You were setting me before my own eyes so that I could see how sordid I was, how deformed and squalid, how tainted with ulcers and sores. I saw it all and stood aghast, but there was no place where I could escape from myself. If I tried to turn my eyes away they fell on Ponticianus, still telling his tale, and in this way you brought me face to face with myself once more, forcing me upon my own sight so that I should see my wickedness and loathe it. I had known it all along, but I had always pretended that it was something different. I had turned a blind eye and forgotten it.

But now, the more my heart warmed to those two men as I heard how they had made the choice that was to save them by giving themselves up entirely to your care, the more bitterly I hated myself in comparison with them. Many years of my life had passed—twelve, unless I am wrong—since I had read Cicero's *Hortensius* at the age of nineteen and it had inspired me to study philosophy. But I still postponed my renunciation of this world's joys, which would have left me free to look for that other happiness, the very search for which, let alone its discovery, I ought to have prized above the discovery of all human treasures and kingdoms or the ability to enjoy all the pleasures of the body at a mere nod of the head. As a youth I had been woefully at fault, particularly in early adolescence. I had prayed to you for chastity and said 'Give me chastity and continence, but not yet.' For I was afraid that you would answer my prayer at once and cure me too soon of the disease of lust, which I wanted satisfied, not quelled. I had wandered on along the road of vice in the sacrilegious superstition of the Manichees, not because I thought that it was right, but because I preferred it to the Christian belief, which I did not explore as I ought but opposed out of malice.

I had pretended to myself that the reason why, day after day, I staved off the decision to renounce worldly ambition and follow you alone was that I could see no certain goal towards which I might steer my course. But the time had now come when I stood naked before my own eyes, while my conscience upbraided me. 'Am I to be silent? Did you not always say that you would not discard your load of vanity for the sake of a truth that was not proved? Now you know that the truth is proved, but the load is still on your shoulders. Yet here are others who have exchanged their load for wings, although they did not wear themselves out in the search for truth or spend ten years or more in making up their minds.'

All the time that Ponticianus was speaking my conscience gnawed away at me like this. I was overcome by burning shame, and when he had finished his tale and completed the business for which he had come, he went away and I was left to my own thoughts. I made all sorts of accusations against myself. I cudgelled my soul and belaboured it with reasons why it should follow me now that I was trying so hard to follow you. But it fought back. It would not obey and yet could offer no excuse. All its old arguments were exhausted and had been shown to be false. It remained silent and afraid, for as much as the loss of life itself it feared the stanching of the flow of habit, by which it was wasting away to death.

* * *

My inner self was a house divided against itself. In the heat of the fierce conflict which I had stirred up against my soul in our common abode, my heart, I turned upon Alypius. My looks betrayed the commotion in my mind as I exclaimed, 'What is the matter with us? What is the meaning of this story? These men have not had our schooling, yet they stand up and storm the gates of heaven while we, for all our learning, lie here grovelling in this world of flesh and blood! Is it because they have led the way that we are ashamed to follow? Is it not worse to hold back?'

I cannot remember the words I used. I said something to this effect and then my feelings proved too strong for me. I broke off and turned away, leaving him to gaze at me speechless and astonished. For my voice sounded strange and the expression of my face and eyes, my flushed cheeks, and the pitch of my voice told him more of the state of my mind than the actual words that I spoke.

There was a small garden attached to the house where we lodged. We were free to make use of it as well as the rest of the house because our host, the owner of the house, did not live there. I now found myself driven by the tumult in my breast to take refuge in this garden, where no one could interrupt that fierce struggle, in which I was my own contestant, until it came to its conclusion. What the conclusion was to be you knew, O Lord, but I did not. Meanwhile I was beside myself with madness that would bring me sanity. I was dying a death that would bring me life. I knew the evil that was in me, but the good that was soon to be born in me I did not know. So I went out into the garden and Alypius followed at my heels. His presence was no intrusion on my solitude, and how could he leave me in that state? We sat down as far as possible from the house. I was frantic, overcome by violent anger with myself for not accepting your will and entering into your covenant. Yet in my bones I knew that this was what I ought to do. In my heart of hearts I praised it to the skies. And to reach this goal I needed no chariot or ship. I need not even walk as far as I had come from the house to the place where we sat, for to make the journey, and to arrive safely, no more was required than an act of will. But it must be a resolute and whole-hearted act of the will, not some lame wish which I kept turning over and over in my mind, so that it had to wrestle with itself, part of it trying to rise, part falling to the ground.

During this agony of indecision I performed many bodily actions, things which a man cannot always do, even if he wills to do them. If he has lost his limbs, or is bound hand and foot, or if his body is weakened by illness or under some other handicap, there are things which he cannot do. I tore my hair and hammered my forehead with my fists; I locked my fingers and hugged my knees; and I did all this because I made an act of will to do it. But I might have had the will to do it and yet not have done it, if my limbs had been unable to move in compliance with my will. I performed all these actions, in which the will and the power to act are not the same. Yet I did not do that one thing which I should have been far, far better pleased to do than all the rest and could have done at once, as soon as I had the will to do it, because as soon as I had the will to do so, I should have willed it wholeheartedly. For in this case the power to act was the same as the will. To will it was to do it. Yet I did not do it. My body responded to the slightest wish of my mind by moving its limbs at the least hint from me, and it did so more readily than my mind obeyed itself by assenting to its own great desire, which could be accomplished simply by an act of will.

* * *

Why does this strange phenomenon occur? What causes it? O Lord in your mercy give me light to see, for it may be that the answer to my question lies in the secret punishment of man and in the penitence which casts a deep shadow on the sons of Adam. Why does this strange phenomenon occur? What causes it? The mind gives an order to the body and is at once obeyed, but when it gives an order to itself, it is resisted. The mind commands the hand to move and is so readily obeyed that the order can scarcely be distinguished from its execution. Yet the mind is mind and the hand is part of the body. But when the mind commands the mind to make an act of will, these two are one and the same and yet the order is not obeyed. Why does this happen? What is the cause of it? The mind orders itself to make an act of will, and it would not give this order unless it willed to do so; yet it does not carry out its own command. But it does not fully will to do this thing and therefore its orders are not fully given. It gives the order only in so far as it wills, and in so far as it does not will the order is not carried out. For the will commands that an act of will should be made, and it gives this command to itself, not to some other will. The reason, then, why the command is not obeyed is that it is not given with the full will. For if the will were full, it would not command itself to be full, since it would be so already. It is therefore no strange phenomenon partly to will to do something and partly to will not to do it. It is a disease of the mind, which does not wholly rise to the heights where it is lifted by the truth, because it is weighed down by habit. So there are two wills in us, because neither by itself is the whole will, and each possesses what the other lacks.

* * *

*There are many abroad who talk of their own fantasies and lead men's minds astray.* They assert that because they have observed that there are two wills at odds with each other when we try to reach a decision, we must therefore have two minds of different natures, one good, the other evil. *Let them vanish at God's presence as the smoke vanishes.* As long as they hold these evil beliefs they are evil themselves, but even they will be good if they see the truth and accept it, so that your apostle may say to them *Once you were all darkness; now, in the Lord you are all daylight.* These people want to be light, not in the Lord, but in themselves, because they think that the nature of the soul is the same as God. In this way their darkness becomes denser still, because in their abominable arrogance they have separated themselves still further from you, who are *the true Light which enlightens every soul born into the world.* I say to them 'Take care what you say, and blush for shame. Enter God's presence, and find there enlightenment; *here is no room for downcast looks.*'

When I was trying to reach a decision about serving the Lord my God, as I had long intended to do, it was I who willed to take this course and again it was I who willed not to take it. It was I and I alone. But I neither willed to do it nor refused to do it with my full will. So I was at odds with myself. I was throwing myself into confusion. All this happened to me although I did not want it, but it did not prove that there was some second mind in me besides my own. It only meant that my mind was being punished. *My action did not come from me, but from the sinful principle that dwells in me.* It was part of the punishment of a sin freely committed by Adam, my first father.

If there were as many different natures in us as there are conflicting wills, we should have a great many more natures than merely two. Suppose that someone is trying to decide whether to go to the theatre or to the Manichees' meeting-house. The Manichees will say, 'Clearly he has two natures, the good one bringing him here to us and the bad one leading him away. Otherwise, how can you explain this dilemma of two opposing wills?' I say that the will to attend their meetings is just as bad as the will to go off to the theatre, but in their opinion it can only be a good will that leads a man to come to them. Suppose then that one of us is wavering between two conflicting wills and cannot make up his mind whether to go to the theatre or to our church. Will not the Manichees be embarrassed to know what to say? Either they must admit—which they will not do—that it is a good will which brings a man to our church, just as in their opinion it is a good will which brings their own communicants and adherents to their church; or they must presume that there are two evil natures and two evil minds in conflict in one man. If they think this, they will disprove their own theory that there is one good and one evil will in man. The only alternative is for them to be converted to the truth and to cease to deny that when a man tries to make a decision, he has one soul which is torn between conflicting wills.

So let us hear no more of their assertion, when they observe two wills in conflict in one man, that there are two opposing minds in him, one good and the other bad, and that they are in conflict because they spring from two opposing substances and two opposing principles. For you, O God of truth, prove that they are utterly wrong. You demolish their arguments and confound them completely. It may be that both the wills are bad. For instance, a man may be trying to decide whether to commit murder by poison or by stabbing; whether he should swindle another man out of one part of his property or another, that is, if he cannot obtain both; whether he should spend his money extravagantly on pleasure or hoard it like a miser; or whether he should go to the games in the circus or to the theatre, when there is a performance at both places on the same day. In this last case there may be a third possibility, that he should go and rob another person's house, if he has the chance. There may even be a fourth choice open to him, because he may wonder whether to go and commit adultery, if the occasion arises at the same time. These possibilities may occur at the same moment and all may seem equally desirable. The man cannot do all these things at once, and his mind is torn between four wills which cannot be reconciled—perhaps more than four, because there are a great many things that he might wish to do. But the Manichees do not claim that there are as many different substances in us as this.

It is just the same when the wills are good. If I question the Manichees whether it is good to find pleasure in reading Paul's Epistles or in the tranquil enjoyment of a Psalm or in a discussion of the Gospel, they will reply in each case that it is good. Supposing, then, that a man finds all these things equally attractive and the chance to do all of them occurs at the same time, is it not true that as long as he cannot make up his mind which of them he most wants to do his heart is torn between several different desires? All these different desires are good, yet they are in conflict with each other until he chooses a single course to which the will may apply itself as a single whole, so that it is no longer split into several different wills.

The same is true when the higher part of our nature aspires after eternal bliss while our lower self is held back by the love of temporal pleasure. It is the same soul that wills both, but it wills neither of them with the full force of the will. So it is wrenched in two and suffers great trials, because while truth teaches it to prefer one course, habit prevents it from relinquishing the other.

* * *

This was the nature of my sickness. I was in torment, reproaching myself more bitterly than ever as I twisted and turned in my chain. I hoped that my chain might be broken once and for all, because it was only a small thing that held me now. All the same it held me. And you, O Lord, never ceased to watch over my secret heart. In your stern mercy you lashed me with the twin scourge of fear and shame in case I should give way once more and the worn and slender remnant of my chain should not be broken but gain new strength and bind me all the faster. In my heart I kept saying 'Let it be now, let it be now!', and merely by saying this I was on the point of making the resolution. I was on the point of making it, but I did not succeed. Yet I did not fall back into my old state. I stood on the brink of resolution, waiting to take fresh breath. I tried again and came a little nearer to my goal, and then a little nearer still, so that I could almost reach out and grasp it. But I did not reach it. I could not reach out to it or grasp it, because I held back from the step by which I should die to death and become alive to life. My lower instincts, which had taken firm hold of me, were stronger than the higher, which were untried. And the closer I came to the moment which was to mark the great change in me, the more I shrank from it in horror. But it did not drive me back or turn me from my purpose: it merely left me hanging in suspense.

I was held back by mere trifles, the most paltry inanities, all my old attachments. They plucked at my garment of flesh and whispered, 'Are you going to dismiss us? From this moment we shall never be with you again, for ever and ever. From this moment you will never again be allowed to do this thing or that, for evermore.' What was it, my God, that they meant when they whispered 'this thing or that?' Things so sordid and so shameful that I beg you in your mercy to keep the soul of your servant free from them! These voices, as I heard them, seemed less than half as loud as they had been before. They no longer barred my way, blatantly contradictory, but their mutterings seemed to reach me from behind, as though they were stealthily plucking at my back, trying to make me turn my head when I wanted to go forward. Yet, in my state of indecision, they kept me from tearing myself away, from shaking myself free of them and leaping across the barrier to the other side, where you were calling me. Habit was too strong for me when it asked 'Do you think you can live without these things?'

But by now the voice of habit was very faint. I had turned my eyes elsewhere, and while I stood trembling at the barrier, on the other side I could see the chaste beauty of Continence in all her serene, unsullied joy, as she modestly beckoned me to cross over and to hesitate no more. She stretched out loving hands to welcome and embrace me, holding up a host of good examples to my sight. With her were countless boys and girls, great numbers of the young and people of all ages, staid widows and women still virgins in old age. And in their midst was Continence herself, not barren but a fruitful mother of children, of joys born of you, O Lord, her Spouse. She smiled at me to give me courage, as though she were saying, 'Can you not do what these men and these women do? Do you think they find the strength to do it in themselves and not in the Lord their God? It was the Lord their God who gave me to them. Why do you try to stand in your own strength and fail? Cast yourself upon God and have no fear. He will not shrink away and let you fall. Cast yourself upon him without fear, for he will welcome you and cure you of your ills.' I was overcome with shame, because I was still listening to the futile mutterings of my lower self and I was still hanging in suspense. And again Continence seemed to say, 'Close your ears to the unclean whispers of your body, so that it may be mortified. It tells you of things that delight you, but not such things as the law of the Lord your God has to tell.'

In this way I wrangled with myself, in my own heart, about my own self. And all the while Alypius stayed at my side, silently awaiting the outcome of this agitation that was new in me.

* * *

I probed the hidden depths of my soul and wrung its pitiful secrets from it, and when I mustered them all before the eyes of my heart, a great storm broke within me, bringing with it a great deluge of tears. I stood up and left Alypius so that I might weep and cry to my heart's content, for it occurred to me that tears were best shed in solitude. I moved away far enough to avoid being embarrassed even by his presence. He must have realized what my feelings were, for I suppose I had said something and he had known from the sound of my voice that I was ready to burst into tears. So I stood up and left him where we had been sitting, utterly bewildered. Somehow I flung myself down beneath a fig tree and gave way to the tears which now streamed from my eyes, the sacrifice that is acceptable to you. I had much to say to you, my God, not in these very words but in this strain: *Lord, will you never be content? Must we always taste your vengeance? Forget the long record of our sins.* For I felt that I was still the captive of my sins, and in my misery I kept crying 'How long shall I go on saying "tomorrow, tomorrow"? Why not now? Why not make an end of my ugly sins at this moment?'

I was asking myself these questions, weeping all the while with the most bitter sorrow in my heart, when all at once I heard the sing-song voice of a child in a nearby house. Whether it was the voice of a boy or a girl I cannot say, but again and again it repeated the refrain 'Take it and read, take it and read.' At this I looked up, thinking hard whether there was any kind of game in which children used to chant words like these, but I could not remember ever hearing them before. I stemmed my flood of tears and stood up, telling myself that this could only be a divine command to open my book of Scripture and read the first passage on which my eyes should fall. For I had heard the story of Antony, and I remembered how he had happened to go into a church while the Gospel was being read and had taken it as a counsel addressed to himself when he heard the words *Go home and sell all that belongs to you. Give it to the poor, and so the treasure you have shall be in heaven; then come back and follow me.* By this divine pronouncement he had at once been converted to you.

So I hurried back to the place where Alypius was sitting, for when I stood up to move away I had put down the book containing Paul's Epistles. I seized it and opened it, and in silence I read the first passage on which my eyes fell: *Not in revelling and drunkenness, not in lust and wantonness, not in quarrels and rivalries. Rather, arm yourselves with the Lord Jesus Christ; spend no more thought on nature and nature's appetites.* I had no wish to read more and no need to do so. For in an instant, as I came to the end of the sentence, it was as though the light of confidence flooded into my heart and all the darkness of doubt was dispelled.

I marked the place with my finger or by some other sign and closed the book. My looks now were quite calm as I told Alypius what had happened to me. He too told me what he had been feeling, which of course I did not know. He asked to see what I had read. I showed it to him and he read on beyond the text which I had read. I did not know what followed, but it was this: *Find room among you for a man of over-delicate conscience.* Alypius applied this to himself and told me so. This admonition was enough to give him strength, and without suffering the distress of hesitation he made his resolution and took this good purpose to himself. And it very well suited his moral character, which had long been far, far better than my own.

Then we went in and told my mother, who was overjoyed. And when we went on to describe how it had all happened, she was jubilant with triumph and glorified you, *who are powerful enough, and more than powerful enough, to carry out your purpose beyond all our hopes and dreams.* For she saw that you had granted her far more than she used to ask in her tearful prayers and plaintive lamentations. You converted me to yourself, so that I no longer desired a wife or placed any hope in this world but stood firmly upon the rule of faith, where you had shown me to her in a dream so many years before. And you *turned her sadness into rejoicing,* into joy far fuller than her dearest wish, far sweeter and more chaste than any she had hoped to find in children begotten of my flesh.

# Bede (673–735)

*Translated by Bertram Colgrave*

The Venerable Bede was the most brilliant Latin writer of the Anglo-Saxon period in England, and during his lifetime, his was perhaps the finest mind in Western Europe. Bede is remembered today mostly for his *Ecclesiastical History of the English People* (731), in which he almost single-handedly created the uniform dating system (BC/AD, or BCE/CE) still in use today. The following extracts are two of the most luminous and memorable passages in all of medieval Latin literature.

In the first passage, Bede recounts the conversion of the kingdom of Northumbria to Christianity by the Roman missionary Paulinus by means of the famous "Parable of the Sparrow." Here Bede delicately captures the moment when the native Germanic vision of the universe gives way to a Christian one. The Germanic vision of the world is captured in the image of a comfortable if claustrophobic hall in a winter storm, an oasis of order and warmth surrounded by a cold, violent, meaningless universe. The Christian idea that something may exist outside the hall, beyond the limits of birth and death, seems to offer tremendous relief. This same imagery can be found in the Norse *Eddas*, which might be read with this passage in mind.

In the second passage, Bede tells the story of Cædmon, the archetypal oral poet who was first inspired to focus the vernacular Old English poetic tradition on Christian themes. An illiterate cowherd, Cædmon is miraculously given the gift of poetry by God. The story closely resembles that of Kālidāsa, the great Indian poet of the Middle Period and, to some extent, also the Islamic prophet Muhammad. In Europe, the image of the "pastoral bard" is as old as Hesiod and was made a literary convention by Virgil. The biblical King David was also a shepherd-poet. All these strands combined to weave a rich pastoral literary tradition in Europe that continued right into the Modern Period. We have no reason to doubt that the poet Cædmon existed, but Bede has certainly chosen to portray him in terms of this ancient tradition. In this account, Bede validates the Old English poetic tradition by means of a miracle story: God himself gives his blessing to the vernacular. It was largely because of this "Cædmonian revolution" that England developed and preserved the first vernacular literature in Europe.

## *The Ecclesiastical History of the English People*

### *[The Parable of the Sparrow]*

When the king had heard his words, he answered that he was both willing and bound to accept the faith which Paulinus taught. He said, however, that he would confer about this with his loyal chief men and his counsellors so that, if they agreed with him, they might all be consecrated together in the waters of life. Paulinus agreed and the king did as he had said. A meeting of his council was held and each one was asked in turn what he thought of this doctrine hitherto unknown to them and this new worship of God which was being proclaimed.

Coifi, the chief of the priests, answered at once, 'Notice carefully, King, this doctrine which is now being expounded to us. I frankly admit that, for my part, I have found that the religion which we have hitherto held has no virtue nor profit in it. None of your followers has devoted himself more earnestly than I have to the worship of our gods, but nevertheless there are many who receive greater benefits and greater honour from you than I do and are more successful in all their undertakings. If the gods had any power they would have helped me more readily, seeing that I have always served them with greater zeal. So it follows that if, on examination, these new doctrines which have now been explained to us are found to be better and more effectual, let us accept them at once without any delay.'

Another of the king's chief men agreed with this advice and with these wise words and then added, 'This is how the present life of man on earth, King, appears to me in comparison with that time which is unknown to us. You are sitting feasting with your ealdormen and thegns in winter time; the fire is burning on the hearth in the middle of the hall and all inside is warm, while outside the wintry storms of rain and snow are raging; and a sparrow flies swiftly through the hall. It enters in at one door and quickly flies out through the other. For the few moments it is inside, the storm and wintry tempest cannot touch it, but after the briefest moment of calm, it flits from your sight, out of the wintry storm and into it again. So this life of man appears but for a moment; what follows or indeed what went before, we know not at all. If this new doctrine brings us more certain information, it seems right that we should accept it.' Other elders and counsellors of the king continued in the same manner, being divinely prompted to do so.

Coifi added that he would like to listen still more carefully to what Paulinus himself had to say about God. The king ordered Paulinus to speak, and when he had said his say, Coifi exclaimed, 'For a long time now I have realized that our religion is worthless; for the more diligently I sought the truth in our cult, the less I found it. Now I confess openly that the truth shines out clearly in this teaching which can bestow on us the gift of life, salvation, and eternal happiness. Therefore I advise your Majesty that we should promptly abandon and commit to the flames the temples and the altars which we have held sacred without reaping any benefit.' Why need I say more? The king publicly accepted the gospel which Paulinus preached, renounced idolatry, and confessed his faith in Christ. When he asked the high priest of their religion which of them should be the first to profane the altars and the shrines of the idols, together with their precincts, Coifi answered, 'I will; for through the wisdom the true God has given me no one can more suitably destroy those things which I once foolishly worshipped, and so set an example to all.' And at once, casting aside his vain superstitions, he asked the king to provide him with arms and a stallion; and mounting it he set out to destroy the idols. Now a high priest of their religion was not allowed to carry arms or to ride except on a mare. So, girded with a sword, he took a spear in his hand and mounting the king's stallion he set off to where the idols were. The common people who saw him thought he was mad. But as soon as he approached the shrine, without any hesitation he profaned it by casting the spear which he held into it; and greatly rejoicing in the knowledge of the worship of the true God, he ordered his companions to destroy and set fire to the shrine and all the enclosures. The place where the idols once stood is still shown, not far from York, to the east, over the river Derwent. Today it is called Goodmanham, the place where the high priest, through the inspiration of the true God, profaned and destroyed the altars which he himself had consecrated.

## *[The Story of Cædmon]*

. . . In the monastery of this abbess [Hild] there was a certain brother who was specially marked out by the grace of God, so that he used to compose godly and religious songs; thus, whatever he learned from the holy Scriptures by means of interpreters, he quickly turned into extremely delightful and moving poetry, in English, which was his own tongue. By his songs the minds of many were often inspired to despise the world and to long for the heavenly life. It is true that after him other Englishmen attempted to compose religious poems, but none could compare with him. For he did not learn the art of poetry from men nor through a man but he received the gift of song freely by the grace of God. Hence he could never compose any foolish or trivial poem but only those which were concerned with devotion and so were fitting for his devout tongue to utter. He had lived in the secular habit until he was well advanced in years and had never learned any songs. Hence sometimes at a feast, when for the sake of providing entertainment, it had been decided that they should all sing in turn, when he saw the harp approaching him, he would rise up in the middle of the feasting, go out, and return home.

On one such occasion when he did so, he left the place of feasting and went to the cattle byre, as it was his turn to take charge of them that night. In due time he stretched himself out and went to sleep, whereupon he dreamt that someone stood by him, saluted him, and called him by name: 'Cædmon,' he said, 'sing me something.' Cædmon answered, 'I cannot sing; that is why I left the feast and came here because I could not sing.' Once again the speaker said, 'Nevertheless you must sing to me.' 'What must I sing?' said Cædmon. 'Sing,' he said, 'about the beginning of created things.' Thereupon Cædmon began to sing verses which he had never heard before in praise of God the Creator, of which this is the general sense: 'Now we must praise the Maker of the heavenly kingdom, the power of the Creator and his counsel, the deeds of the Father of glory and how He, since he is the eternal God, was the Author of all marvels and first created the heavens as a roof for the children of men and then, the almighty Guardian of the human race, created the earth.' This is the sense but not the order of the words which he sang as he slept. For it is not possible to translate verse, however well composed, literally from one language to another without some loss of beauty and dignity. When he awoke, he remembered all that he had sung while asleep and soon added more verses in the same manner, praising God in fitting style.

In the morning he went to the reeve who was his master, telling him of the gift he had received, and the reeve took him to the abbess. He was then bidden to describe his dream in the presence of a number of the more learned men and also to recite his song so that they might all examine him and decide upon the nature and origin of the gift of which he spoke; and it seemed clear to all of them that the Lord had granted him heavenly grace. They then read to him a passage of sacred history or doctrine, bidding him make a song out of it, if he could, in metrical form. He undertook the task and went away; on returning next morning he repeated the passage he had been given, which he had put into excellent verse. The abbess, who recognized the grace of God which the man had received, instructed him to renounce his secular habit and to take monastic vows. She and all her people received him into the community of the brothers and ordered that he should be instructed in the whole course of sacred history. He learned all he could by listening to them and then, memorizing it and ruminating over it, like some clean animal chewing the cud, he turned it into the most melodious verse: and it sounded so sweet as he recited it that his teachers became in turn his audience. He sang about the creation of the world, the origin of the human race, and the whole history of Genesis, of the departure of Israel from Egypt and the entry into the promised land and of many other of the stories taken from the sacred Scriptures: of the incarnation, passion, and resurrection of the Lord, of His ascension into heaven, of the coming of the Holy Spirit and the teaching of the apostles. He also made songs about the terrors of future judgement, the horrors of the pains of hell, and the joys of the heavenly kingdom. In addition he composed many other songs about the divine mercies and judgements, in all of which he sought to turn his hearers away from delight in sin and arouse in them the love and practice of good works. He was a most religious man, humbly submitting himself to the discipline of the Rule; and he opposed all those who wished to act otherwise with a flaming and fervent zeal. It was for this reason that his life had a beautiful ending.

When the hour of his departure drew near he was afflicted, fourteen days before, by bodily weakness, yet so slight that he was able to walk about and talk the whole time. There was close by a building to which they used to take those who were infirm or who seemed to be at the point of death. On the night on which he was to die, as evening fell, he asked his attendant to prepare a place in this building where he could rest. The attendant did as Cædmon said though he wondered why he asked, for he did not seem to be by any means at the point of death. They had settled down in the house and were talking and joking cheerfully with each of those who were already there and it was past midnight, when he asked whether they had the Eucharist in the house. They answered, 'What need have you of the Eucharist? You are not likely to die, since you are talking as cheerfully with us as if you were in perfect health.' 'Nevertheless,' he repeated, 'bring me the Eucharist.' When he had taken it in his hand he asked if they were all charitably disposed towards him and had no complaint nor any quarrel nor grudge against him. They answered that they were all in charity with him and without the slightest feeling of anger; then they asked him in turn whether he was charitably disposed towards them. He answered at once, 'My sons, I am in charity with all the servants of God.' So, fortifying himself with the heavenly viaticum, he prepared for his entrance into the next life. Thereupon he asked them how near it was to the time when the brothers had to awake to sing their nightly praises to God. They answered, 'It will not be long.' And he answered, 'Good, let us wait until then.' And so, signing himself with the sign of the holy cross, he laid his head on the pillow, fell asleep for a little while, and so ended his life quietly. Thus it came about that, as he had served the Lord with a simple and pure mind and with quiet devotion, so he departed into His presence and left the world by a quiet death; and his tongue which had uttered so many good words in praise of the Creator also uttered its last words in His praise, as he signed himself with the sign of the cross and commended his spirit into God's hands; and from what has been said, it would seem that he had foreknowledge of his death.

## Abelard (1079–1142) and Heloise (1100–1163)

*Translated by Betty Radice*

The twelfth century in Western Europe saw a great flourishing of philosophy and literature—often referred to as the Twelfth-Century Renaissance. It was influenced in no small part by the translation of Arabic texts into Latin and the pressure of a flourishing Islamic culture in Spain. Students of literature know this period mostly for its invention of a vast literature of romantic love. Peter Abelard was at the center of all these developments. The preeminent philosopher of his age and a charismatic teacher at what was about to become the University of Paris, he championed the use of logic in the understanding of Christian faith. His theological works were highly controversial and ultimately condemned by the church, but he is most remembered today for his tragic love affair with his brilliant student Heloise. Their story is told in their own words in the following extracts from their letters.

In 1132, Abelard wrote *The History of My Misfortunes*, ostensibly as a letter of consolation for a friend. In it he tells how he seduced Heloise, fathered her child, and married her secretly, and how her uncle then hired men to attack and castrate him in revenge. Disgraced, Abelard became a monk and forced Heloise to become a nun. He wrote his *History* after many years had passed, during which time the two of them had only the most formal religious contact. The tone of his account is a startling mixture of lamentation over his own misfortune and cold condemnation of his own sinfulness.

On the other hand, Heloise's letters to Abelard, which she wrote after reading his *History*, are personal, passionate, and heart wrenching. They constitute one of the most vivid accounts of a woman's experience that survives from these centuries when women's voices were systematically silenced. Her letters are so learned and rhetorically brilliant that until recently scholars commonly claimed that Abelard must have written them, but they are now accepted as hers. It is interesting to note that Heloise argues passionately against marriage, ironically taking a decidedly antifeminist position, at least from a late-twentieth-century point of view. She was frequently quoted in the antifeminist literature of the Middle Ages.

Abelard's responses to Heloise's letters, not included here, offer her little but steady, unapologetic Christian instruction, encouraging her to transfer her love for her wounded husband onto the wounded Christ. Medieval readers would have found his attitude morally correct and inspiring, although modern readers inevitably sympathize with Heloise and find Abelard arrogant and unfeeling.

Considering their intimate content, it may seem odd to modern readers that these letters were written for public circulation, but they were thought to be morally instructive. They had an immense influence on the development of Romance as a literary genre and on the medieval and Renaissance theory of love, which focused on the tragic conflict between sexual and spiritual love. Compare the works of Marie de France, for example, or Shakespeare's *Romeo and Juliet.* Petrarch studied Heloise's letters, and Alexander Pope adapted them into poetry in the eighteenth century (see pp. 1867–1876). It is interesting to compare Abelard's story and attitudes with Sima Qian, the Chinese historian who suffered the same punishment (see pp. 390–395). One might also compare Ovid's *Heroides* (pp. 687–692), which is quoted by Heloise, and the sixteenth-century Korean poem *A Woman's Sorrow,* by Hŏ Nansŏrhŏn (pp. 1197–1199).

## *Abelard, from The History of My Misfortunes*

There was in Paris at the time a young girl named Heloise, the niece of Fulbert, one of the canons, and so much loved by him that he had done everything in his power to advance her education in letters. In looks she did not rank lowest, while in the extent of her learning she stood supreme. A gift for letters is so rare in women that it added greatly to her charm and had won her renown throughout the realm. I considered all the usual attractions for a lover and decided she was the one to bring to my bed, confident that I should have an easy success; for at that time I had youth and exceptional good looks as well as my great reputation to recommend me, and feared no rebuff from any woman I might choose to honour with my love. Knowing the girl's knowledge and love of letters I thought she would be all the more ready to consent, and that even when separated we could enjoy each other's presence by exchange of written messages in which we could speak more openly than in person, and so need never lack the pleasures of conversation.

All on fire with desire for this girl I sought an opportunity of getting to know her through private daily meetings and so more easily winning her over; and with this end in view I came to an arrangement with her uncle, with the help of some of his friends, whereby he should take me into his house, which was very near my school, for whatever sum he liked to ask. As a pretext I said that my household cares were hindering my studies and the expense was more than I could afford. Fulbert dearly loved money, and was moreover always ambitious to further his niece's education in letters, two weaknesses which made it easy for me to gain his consent and obtain my desire: he was all eagerness for my money and confident that his niece would profit from my teaching. This led him to make an urgent request which furthered my love and fell in with my wishes more than I had dared to hope; he gave me complete charge over the girl, so that I could devote all the leisure time left me by my school to teaching her by day and night, and if I found her idle I was to punish her severely. I was amazed by his simplicity—if he had entrusted a tender lamb to a ravening wolf it would not have surprised me more. In handing her over to me to punish as well as to teach, what else was he doing but giving me complete freedom to realize my desires, and providing an opportunity, even if I did not make use of it, for me to bend her to my will by threats and blows if persuasion failed? But there were two special reasons for his freedom from base suspicion: his love for his niece and my previous reputation for continence.

Need I say more? We were united, first under one roof, then in heart; and so with our lessons as a pretext we abandoned ourselves entirely to love. Her studies allowed us to withdraw in private, as love desired, and then with our books open before us, more words of love than of our reading passed between us, and more kissing than teaching. My hands strayed oftener to her bosom than to the pages; love drew our eyes to look on each other more than reading kept them on our texts. To avert suspicion I sometimes struck her, but these blows were prompted by love and tender feeling rather than anger and irritation, and were sweeter than any balm could be. In short, our desires left no stage of love-making untried, and if love could devise something new, we welcomed it. We entered on each joy the more eagerly for our previous inexperience, and were the less easily sated.

Now the more I was taken up with these pleasures, the less time I could give to philosophy and the less attention I paid to my school. It was utterly boring for me to have to go to the school, and equally wearisome to remain there and to spend my days on study when my nights were sleepless with love-making. As my interest and concentration flagged, my lectures lacked all inspiration and were merely repetitive; I could do no more than repeat what had been said long ago, and when inspiration did come to me, it was for writing love-songs, not the secrets of philosophy. A lot of these songs, as you know, are still popular and sung in many places, particularly by those who enjoy the kind of life I led. But the grief and sorrow and laments of my students when they realized my preoccupation, or rather, distraction of mind are hard to realize. Few could have failed to notice something so obvious, in fact no one, I fancy, except the man whose honour was most involved—Heloise's uncle. Several people tried on more than one occasion to draw his attention to it, but he would not believe them; because, as I said, of his boundless love for his niece and my well-known reputation for chastity in my previous life. We do not easily think ill of those whom we love most, and the taint of suspicion cannot exist along with warm affection. Hence the remark of St Jerome in his letter to Sabinian: 'We are always the last to learn of evil in our own home, and the faults of our wife and children may be the talk of the town but do not reach our ears.'

But what is last to be learned is somehow learned eventually, and common knowledge cannot easily be hidden from one individual. Several months passed and then this happened in our case. Imagine the uncle's grief at the discovery, and the lovers' grief too at being separated! How I blushed with shame and contrition for the girl's plight, and what sorrow she suffered at the thought of my disgrace! All our laments were for one another's troubles, and our distress was for each other, not for ourselves. Separation drew our hearts still closer while frustration inflamed our passion even more; then we became more abandoned as we lost all sense of shame and, indeed, shame diminished as we found more opportunities for love-making. And so we were caught in the act as the poet says happened to Mars and Venus. Soon afterwards the girl found that she was pregnant, and immediately wrote me a letter full of rejoicing to ask what I thought she should do. One night then, when her uncle was away from home, I removed her secretly from his house, as we had planned, and sent her straight to my own country. There she stayed with my sister until she gave birth to a boy, whom she called Astralabe.

On his return her uncle went almost out of his mind—one could appreciate only by experience his transports of grief and mortification. What action could he take against me? What traps could he set? He did not know. If he killed me or did me personal injury, there was the danger that his beloved niece might suffer for it in my country. It was useless to try to seize me or confine me anywhere against my will, especially as I was very much on guard against this very thing, knowing that he would not hesitate to assault me if he had the courage or the means.

In the end I took pity on his boundless misery and went to him, accusing myself of the deceit love had made me commit as if it were the basest treachery. I begged his forgiveness and promised to make any amends he might think fit. I protested that I had done nothing unusual in the eyes of anyone who had known the power of love, and recalled how since the beginning of the human race women had brought the noblest men to ruin. Moreover, to conciliate him further, I offered him satisfaction in a form he could never have hoped for: I would marry the girl I had wronged. All I stipulated was that the marriage should be kept secret so as not to damage my reputation. He agreed, pledged his word and that of his supporters, and sealed the reconciliation I desired with a kiss. But his intention was to make it easier to betray me.

I set off at once for Brittany and brought back my mistress to make her my wife. But she was strongly opposed to the proposal, and argued hotly against it for two reasons: the risk involved and the disgrace to myself. She swore that no satisfaction could ever appease her uncle, as we subsequently found out. What honour could she win, she protested, from a marriage which would dishonour me and humiliate us both? The world would justly exact punishment from her if she removed such a light from its midst. Think of the curses, the loss to the Church and grief of philosophers which would greet such a marriage! Nature had created me for all mankind—it would be a sorry scandal if I should bind myself to a single woman and submit to such base servitude. She absolutely rejected this marriage; it would be nothing but a disgrace and a burden to me. Along with the loss to my reputation she put before me the difficulties of marriage, which the apostle Paul exhorts us to avoid when he says: 'Has your marriage been dissolved? Do not seek a wife. If, however, you do marry, there is nothing wrong in it; and if a virgin marries, she has done no wrong. But those who marry will have pain and grief in this bodily life, and my aim is to spare you.' And again: 'I want you to be free from anxious care.'

But if I would accept neither the advice of the Apostle nor the exhortations of the Fathers on the heavy yoke of marriage, at least, she argued, I could listen to the philosophers, and pay regard to what had been written by them or concerning them on this subject—as for the most part the Fathers too have carefully done when they wish to rebuke us. For example, St Jerome in the first book of his *Against Jovinian* recalls how Theophrastus sets out in considerable detail the unbearable annoyances of marriage and its endless anxieties, in order to prove by the clearest possible arguments that a man should not take a wife; and he brings his reasoning from the exhortations of the philosophers to this conclusion: 'Can any Christian hear Theophrastus argue in this way without a blush?' In the same book Jerome goes on to say that 'After Cicero had divorced Terentia and was asked by Hirtius to marry his sister he firmly refused to do so, on the grounds that he could not devote his attention to a wife and philosophy alike. He does not simply say "devote attention", but adds "alike", not wishing to do anything which would be a rival to his study of philosophy.'

But apart from the hindrances to such philosophic study, consider, she said, the true conditions for a dignified way of life. What harmony can there be between pupils and nursemaids, desks and cradles, books or tablets and distaffs, pen or stylus and spindles? Who can concentrate on thoughts of Scripture or philosophy and be able to endure babies crying, nurses soothing them with lullabies, and all the noisy coming and going of men and women about the house? Will he put up with the constant muddle and squalor which small children bring into the home? The wealthy can do so, you will say, for their mansions and large houses can provide privacy and, being rich, they do not have to count the cost nor be tormented by daily cares. But philosophers lead a very different life from rich men, and those who are concerned with wealth or are involved in mundane matters will not have time for the claims of Scripture or philosophy. Consequently, the great philosophers of the past have despised the world, not renouncing it so much as escaping from it, and have denied themselves every pleasure so as to find peace in the arms of philosophy alone. The greatest of them, Seneca, gives this advice to Lucilius: 'Philosophy is not a subject for idle moments. We must neglect everything else and concentrate on this, for no time is long enough for it. Put it aside for a moment, and you might as well give it up, for once interrupted it will not remain. We must resist all other occupations, not merely dispose of them but reject them.'

This is the practice today through love of God of those among us who truly deserve the name of monks, as it was of distinguished philosophers amongst the pagans in their pursuit of philosophy. For in every people, pagan, Jew or Christian, some men have always stood out for their faith or upright way of life, and have cut themselves off from their fellows because of their singular chastity or austerity. Amongst the Jews in times past there were the Nazirites, who dedicated themselves to the Lord according to the Law, and the sons of the prophets, followers of Elijah or Elisha, whom the Old Testament calls monks, as St Jerome bears witness; and in more recent times the three sects of philosophers described by Josephus in the eighteenth book of his *Antiquities*, the Pharisees, Sadducces and Essenes. Today we have the monks who imitate either the communal life of the apostles or the earlier, solitary life of John. Among the pagans, as I said, are the philosophers: for the name of wisdom or philosophy used to be applied not so much to acquisition of learning as to a religious way of life, as we learn from the first use of the word itself and from the testimony of the saints themselves. And so St Augustine, in the eighth book of his *City of God*, distinguishes between types of philosopher:

> The Italian school was founded by Pythagoras of Samos, who is said to have been the first to use the term philosophy; before him men were called 'sages' if they seemed outstanding for some praiseworthy manner of life. But when Pythagoras was asked his profession, he replied that he was a philosopher, meaning a devotee or lover of wisdom, for he thought it too presumptuous to call himself a sage.

So the phrase 'if they seemed outstanding for some praiseworthy manner of life' clearly proves that the sages of the pagans, that is, the philosophers, were so called as a tribute to their way of life, not to their learning. There is no need for me to give examples of their chaste and sober lives—I should seem to be teaching Minerva herself. But if pagans and laymen could live in this way, though bound by no profession of faith, is there not a greater obligation on you, as clerk and canon, not to put base pleasures before your sacred duties, and to guard against being sucked down headlong into this Charybdis, there to lose all sense of shame and be plunged forever into a whirlpool of impurity? If you take no thought for the privilege of a clerk, you can at least uphold the dignity of a philosopher, and let a love of propriety curb your shamelessness if the reverence due to God means nothing to you. Remember Socrates' marriage and the sordid episode whereby he did at least remove the slur it cast on philosophy by providing an example to be a warning to his successors. This too was noted by Jerome, when he tells this tale of Socrates in the first book of his *Against Jovinian*: 'One day after he had withstood an endless stream of invective which Xanthippe poured out from a window above his head, he felt himself soaked with dirty water. All he did was to wipe his head and say: "I knew that thunderstorm would lead to rain."'

Heloise then went on to the risks I should run in bringing her back, and argued that the name of mistress instead of wife would be dearer to her and more honourable for me—only love freely given should keep me for her, not the constriction of a marriage tie, and if we had to be parted for a time, we should find the joy of being together all the sweeter the rarer our meetings were. But at last she saw that her attempts to persuade or dissuade me were making no impression on my foolish obstinacy, and she could not bear to offend me; so amidst deep sighs and tears she ended in these words: 'We shall both be destroyed. All that is left us is suffering as great as our love has been.' In this, as the whole world knows, she showed herself a true prophet.

And so when our baby son was born we entrusted him to my sister's care and returned secretly to Paris. A few days later, after a night's private vigil of prayer in a certain church, at dawn we were joined in matrimony in the presence of Fulbert and some of his, and our, friends. Afterwards we parted secretly and went our ways unobserved. Subsequently our meetings were few and furtive, in order to conceal as far as possible what we had done. But Fulbert and his servants, seeking satisfaction for the dishonour done to him, began to spread the news of the marriage and break the promise of secrecy they had given me. Heloise cursed them and swore that there was no truth in this, and in his exasperation Fulbert heaped abuse on her on several occasions. As soon as I discovered this I removed her to a convent of nuns in the town near Paris called Argenteuil, where she had been brought up and educated as a small girl, and I also had made for her a religious habit of the type worn by novices, with the exception of the veil, and made her put it on.

At this news her uncle and his friends and relatives imagined that I had tricked them, and had found an easy way of ridding myself of Heloise by making her a nun. Wild with indignation they plotted against me, and one night as I slept peacefully in an inner room in my lodgings, they bribed one of my servants to admit them and there took cruel vengeance on me of such appalling barbarity as to shock the whole world; they cut off the parts of my body whereby I had committed the wrong of which they complained. Then they fled, but the two who could be caught were blinded and mutilated as I had been, one of them being the servant who had been led by greed while in my service to betray his master.

Next morning the whole city gathered before my house, and the scene of horror and amazement, mingled with lamentations, cries and groans which exasperated and distressed me, is difficult, no, impossible, to describe. In particular, the clerks and, most of all, my pupils tormented me with their unbearable weeping and wailing until I suffered more from their sympathy than from the pain of my wound, and felt the misery of my mutilation less than my shame and humiliation. All sorts of thoughts filled my mind—how brightly my reputation had shone, and now how easily in an evil moment it had been dimmed or rather completely blotted out; how just a judgement of God had struck me in the parts of the body with which I had sinned, and how just a reprisal had been taken by the very man I had myself betrayed. I thought how my rivals would exult over my fitting punishment, how this bitter blow would bring lasting grief and misery to my friends and parents, and how fast the news of this unheard-of disgrace would spread over the whole world. What road could I take now? How could I show my face in public, to be pointed at by every finger, derided by every tongue, a monstrous spectacle to all I met? I was also appalled to remember that according to the cruel letter of the Law, a eunuch is such an abomination to the Lord that men made eunuchs by the amputation or mutilation of their members are forbidden to enter a church as if they were stinking and unclean, and even animals in that state are rejected for sacrifice. 'Ye shall not present to the Lord any animal if its testicles have been bruised or crushed, torn or cut.' 'No man whose testicles have been crushed or whose organ has been severed shall become a member of the assembly of the Lord.'

I admit that it was shame and confusion in my remorse and misery rather than any devout wish for conversion which brought me to seek shelter in a monastery cloister. Heloise had already agreed to take the veil in obedience to my wishes and entered a convent. So we both put on the religious habit, I in the Abbey of St Denis, and she in the Convent of Argenteuil which I spoke of before. There were many people, I remember, who in pity for her youth tried to dissuade her from submitting to the yoke of monastic rule as a penance too hard to bear, but all in vain; she broke out as best she could through her tears and sobs into Cornelia's famous lament:

O noble husband,
Too great for me to wed, was it my fate
To bend that lofty head? What prompted me
To marry you and bring about your fall?
Now claim your due, and see me gladly pay . . .

So saying she hurried to the altar, quickly took up the veil blessed by the bishop, and publicly bound herself to the religious life.

I had still scarcely recovered from my wound when the clerks came thronging round to pester the abbot and myself with repeated demands that I should now for love of God continue the studies which hitherto I had pursued only in desire for wealth and fame. They urged me to consider that the talent entrusted to me by God would be required of me with interest; that instead of addressing myself to the rich as before I should devote myself to educating the poor, and recognize that the hand of the Lord had touched me for the express purpose of freeing me from the temptations of the flesh and the distractions of the world so that I could devote myself to learning, and thereby prove myself a true philosopher not of the world but of God. . . .

## Heloise to Abelard

*Letter 1*

*To her master, or rather her father, husband, or rather brother; his handmaid, or rather his daughter, wife, or rather sister; to Abelard, Heloise.*

Not long ago, my beloved, by chance someone brought me the letter of consolation you had sent to a friend. I saw at once from the superscription that it was yours, and was all the more eager to read it since the writer is so dear to my heart. I hoped for renewal of strength, at least from the writer's words which would picture for me the reality I have lost. But nearly every line of this letter was filled, I remember, with gall and wormwood, as it told the pitiful story of our entry into religion and the cross of unending suffering which you, my only love, continue to bear.

In that letter you did indeed carry out the promise you made your friend at the beginning, that he would think his own troubles insignificant or nothing, in comparison with your own. First you revealed the persecution you suffered from your teachers, then the supreme treachery of the mutilation of your person, and then described the abominable jealousy and violent attacks of your fellow-students, Alberic of Rheims and Lotulf of Lombardy. You did not gloss over what at their instigation was done to your distinguished theological work or what amounted to a prison sentence passed on yourself. Then you went on to the plotting against you by your abbot and false brethren, the serious slanders from those two pseudo-apostles, spread against you by the same rivals, and the scandal stirred up among many people because you had acted contrary to custom in naming your oratory after the Paraclete. You went on to the incessant, intolerable persecutions which you still endure at the hands of that cruel tyrant and the evil monks you call your sons, and so brought your sad story to an end.

No one, I think, could read or hear it dry-eyed; my own sorrows are renewed by the detail in which you have told it, and redoubled because you say your perils are still increasing. All of us here are driven to despair of your life, and every day we await in fear and trembling the final word of your death. And so in the name of Christ, who is still giving you some protection for his service, we beseech you to write as often as you think fit to us who are his handmaids and yours, with news of the perils in which you are still storm-tossed. We are all that are left you, so at least you should let us share your sorrow or your joy.

It is always some consolation in sorrow to feel that it is shared, and any burden laid on several is carried more lightly or removed. And if this storm has quietened down for a while, you must be all the more prompt to send us a letter which will be the more gladly received. But whatever you write about will bring us no small relief in the mere proof that you have us in mind. Letters from absent friends are welcome indeed, as Seneca himself shows us by his own example when he writes these words in a passage of a letter to his friend Lucilius:

> Thank you for writing to me often, the one way in which you can make your presence felt, for I never have a letter from you without the immediate feeling that we are together. If pictures of absent friends give us pleasure, renewing our memories and relieving the pain of separation even if they cheat us with empty comfort, how much more welcome is a letter which comes to us in the very handwriting of an absent friend.

Thank God that here at least is a way of restoring your presence to us which no malice can prevent, nor any obstacle hinder; then do not, I beseech you, allow any negligence to hold you back.

You wrote your friend a long letter of consolation, prompted no doubt by his misfortunes, but really telling of your own. The detailed account you gave of these may have been intended for his comfort, but it also greatly increased our own feeling of desolation; in your desire to heal his wounds you have dealt us fresh wounds of grief as well as re-opening the old. I beg you, then, as you set about tending the wounds which others have dealt, heal the wounds you have yourself inflicted. You have done your duty to a friend and comrade, discharged your debt to friendship and comradeship, but it is a greater debt which binds you in obligation to us who can properly be called not friends so much as dearest friends, not comrades but daughters, or any other conceivable name more tender and holy. How great the debt by which you have bound yourself to us needs neither proof nor witness, were it in any doubt; if the whole world kept silent, the facts themselves would cry out. For you after God are the sole founder of this place, the sole builder of this oratory, the sole creator of this community. You have built nothing here upon another man's foundation. Everything here is your own creation. This was a wilderness open to wild beasts and brigands, a place which had known no home nor habitation of men. In the very lairs of wild beasts and lurking-places of robbers, where the name of God was never heard, you built a sanctuary to God and dedicated a shrine in the name of the Holy Spirit. To build it you drew nothing from the riches of kings and princes, though their wealth was great and could have been yours for the asking: whatever was done, the credit was to be yours alone. Clerks and scholars came flocking here, eager for your teaching, and ministered to all your needs; and even those who had lived on the benefices of the Church and knew only how to receive offerings, not to make them, whose hands were held out to take but not to give, became pressing in their lavish offers of assistance.

And so it is yours, truly your own, this new plantation for God's purpose, but it is sown with plants which are still very tender and need watering if they are to thrive. Through its feminine nature this plantation would be weak and frail even if it were not new; and so it needs a more careful and regular cultivation, according to the words of the Apostle: 'I planted the seed and Apollos watered it; but God made it grow.' The Apostle through the doctrine that he preached had planted and established in the faith the Corinthians, to whom he was writing. Afterwards the Apostle's own disciple, Apollos, had watered them with his holy exhortations and so God's grace bestowed on them growth in the virtues. You cultivate a vineyard of another's vines which you did not plant yourself and which has now turned to bitterness against you, so that often your advice brings no result and your holy words are uttered in vain. You devote your care to another's vineyard; think what you owe to your own. You teach and admonish rebels to no purpose, and in vain you throw the pearls of your divine eloquence to the pigs. While you spend so much on the stubborn, consider what you owe to the obedient; you are so generous to your enemies but should reflect on how you are indebted to your daughters. Apart from everything else, consider the close tie by which you have bound yourself to me, and repay the debt you owe a whole community of women dedicated to God by discharging it the more dutifully to her who is yours alone.

Your superior wisdom knows better than our humble learning of the many serious treatises which the holy Fathers compiled for the instruction or exhortation or even the consolation of holy women, and of the care with which these were composed. And so in the precarious early days of our conversion long ago I was not a little surprised and troubled by your forgetfulness, when neither reverence for God nor our mutual love nor the example of the holy Fathers made you think of trying to comfort me, wavering and exhausted as I was by prolonged grief, either by word when I was with you or by letter when we had parted. Yet you must know that you are bound to me by an obligation which is all the greater for the further close tie of the marriage sacrament uniting us, and are the deeper in my debt because of the love I have always borne you, as everyone knows, a love which is beyond all bounds.

You know, beloved, as the whole world knows, how much I have lost in you, how at one wretched stroke of fortune that supreme act of flagrant treachery robbed me of my very self in robbing me of you; and how my sorrow for my loss is nothing compared with what I feel for the manner in which I lost you. Surely the greater the cause for grief the greater the need for the help of consolation, and this no one can bring but you; you are the sole cause of my sorrow, and you alone can grant me the grace of consolation. You alone have the power to make me sad, to bring me happiness or comfort; you alone have so great a debt to repay me, particularly now when I have carried out all your orders so implicitly that when I was powerless to oppose you in anything, I found strength at your command to destroy myself. I did more, strange to say—my love rose to such heights of madness that it robbed itself of what it most desired beyond hope of recovery, when immediately at your bidding I changed my clothing along with my mind, in order to prove you the sole possessor of my body and my will alike. God knows I never sought anything in you except yourself; I wanted simply you, nothing of yours. I looked for no marriage-bond, no marriage portion, and it was not my own pleasures and wishes I sought to gratify, as you well know, but yours. The name of wife may seem more sacred or more binding, but sweeter for me will always be the word mistress, or, if you will permit me, that of concubine or whore. I believed that the more I humbled myself on your account, the more gratitude I should win from you, and also the less damage I should do to the brightness of your reputation.

You yourself on your own account did not altogether forget this in the letter of consolation I have spoken of which you wrote to a friend; there you thought fit to set out some of the reasons I gave in trying to dissuade you from binding us together in an ill-starred marriage. But you kept silent about most of my arguments for preferring love to wedlock and freedom to chains. God is my witness that if Augustus, Emperor of the whole world, thought fit to honour me with marriage and conferred all the earth on me to possess for ever, it would be dearer and more honourable to me to be called not his Empress but your whore.

For a man's worth does not rest on his wealth or power; these depend on fortune, but worth on his merits. And a woman should realize that if she marries a rich man more readily than a poor one, and desires her husband more for his possessions than for himself, she is offering herself for sale. Certainly any woman who comes to marry through desires of this kind deserves wages, not gratitude, for clearly her mind is on the man's property, not himself, and she would be ready to prostitute herself to a richer man, if she could. This is evident from the argument put forward in the dialogue of Aeschines Socraticus by the learned Aspasia to Xenophon and his wife. When she had expounded it in an effort to bring about a reconciliation between them, she ended with these words: 'Unless you come to believe that there is no better man nor worthier woman on earth you will always still be looking for what you judge the best thing of all—to be the husband of the best of wives and the wife of the best of husbands.'

These are saintly words which are more than philosophic; indeed, they deserve the name of wisdom, not philosophy. It is a holy error and a blessed delusion between man and wife, when perfect love can keep the ties of marriage unbroken not so much through bodily continence as chastity of spirit. But what error permitted other women, plain truth permitted me, and what they thought of their husbands, the world in general believed, or rather, knew to be true of yourself; so that my love for you was the more genuine for being further removed from error. What king or philosopher could match your fame? What district, town or village did not long to see you? When you appeared in public, who did not hurry to catch a glimpse of you, or crane his neck and strain his eyes to follow your departure? Every wife, every young girl desired you in absence and was on fire in your presence; queens and great ladies envied me my joys and my bed.

You had besides, I admit, two special gifts whereby to win at once the heart of any woman—your gifts for composing verse and song, in which we know other philosophers have rarely been successful. This was for you no more than a diversion, a recreation from the labours of your philosophic work, but you left many love-songs and verses which won wide popularity for the charm of their words and tunes and kept your name continually on everyone's lips. The beauty of the airs ensured that even the unlettered did not forget you; more than anything this made women sigh for love of you. And as most of these songs told of our love, they soon made me widely known and roused the envy of many women against me. For your manhood was adorned by every grace of mind and body, and among the women who envied me then, could there be one now who does not feel compelled by my misfortune to sympathize with my loss of such joys? Who is there who was once my enemy, whether man or woman, who is not moved now by the compassion which is my due? Wholly guilty though I am, I am also, as you know, wholly innocent. It is not the deed but the intention of the doer which makes the crime, and justice should weigh not what was done but the spirit in which it is done. What my intention towards you has always been, you alone who have known it can judge. I submit all to your scrutiny, yield to your testimony in all things.

Tell me one thing, if you can. Why, after our entry into religion, which was your decision alone, have I been so neglected and forgotten by you that I have neither a word from you when you are here to give me strength nor the consolation of a letter in absence? Tell me, I say, if you can—or I will tell you what I think and indeed the world suspects. It was desire, not affection which bound you to me, the flame of lust rather than love. So when the end came to what you desired, any show of feeling you used to make went with it. This is not merely my own opinion, beloved, it is everyone's. There is nothing personal or private about it; it is the general view which is widely held. I only wish that it *were* mine alone, and that the love you professed could find someone to defend it and so comfort me in my grief for a while. I wish I could think of some explanation which would excuse you and somehow cover up the way you hold me cheap.

I beg you then to listen to what I ask—you will see that it is a small favour which you can easily grant. While I am denied your presence, give me at least through your words—of which you have enough and to spare—some sweet semblance of yourself. It is no use my hoping for generosity in deeds if you are grudging in words. Up to now I had thought I deserved much of you, seeing that I carried out everything for your sake and continue up to the present moment in complete obedience to you. It was not any sense of vocation which brought me as a young girl to accept the austerities of the cloister, but your bidding alone, and if I deserve no gratitude from you, you may judge for yourself how my labours are in vain. I can expect no reward for this from God, for it is certain that I have done nothing as yet for love of him. When you hurried towards God I followed you, indeed, I went first to take the veil—perhaps you were thinking how Lot's wife turned back when you made me put on the religious habit and take my vows before you gave yourself to God. Your lack of trust in me over this one thing, I confess, overwhelmed me with grief and shame. I would have had no hesitation, God knows, in following you or going ahead at your bidding to the flames of Hell. My heart was not in me but with you, and now, even more, if it is not with you it is nowhere; truly, without you it cannot exist. See that it fares well with you, I beg, as it will if it finds you kind, if you give grace in return for grace, small for great, words for deeds. If only your love had less confidence in me, my dear, so that you would be more concerned on my behalf! But as it is, the more I have made you feel secure in me, the more I have to bear with your neglect.

Remember, I implore you, what I have done, and think how much you owe me. While I enjoyed with you the pleasures of the flesh, many were uncertain whether I was prompted by love or lust; but now the end is proof of the beginning. I have finally denied myself every pleasure in obedience to your will, kept nothing for myself except to prove that now, even more, I am yours. Consider then your injustice, if when I deserve more you give me less, or rather, nothing at all, especially when it is a small thing I ask of you and one you could so easily grant. And so, in the name of God to whom you have dedicated yourself, I beg you to restore your presence to me in the way you can—by writing me some word of comfort, so that in this at least I may find increased strength and readiness to serve God. When in the past you sought me out for sinful pleasures your letters came to me thick and fast, and your many songs put your Heloise on everyone's lips, so that every street and house echoed with my name. Is it not far better now to summon me to God than it was then to satisfy our lust? I beg you, think what you owe me, give ear to my pleas, and I will finish a long letter with a brief ending: farewell, my only love.

## *Letter 3*

*To her only one after Christ, she who is his alone in Christ.*

I am surprised, my only love, that contrary to custom in letter-writing and, indeed, to the natural order, you have thought fit to put my name before yours in the greeting which heads your letter, so that we have woman before man, wife before husband, handmaid before master, nun before monk, deaconess before priest and abbess before abbot. Surely the right and proper order is for those who write to their superiors or equals to put their names before their own, but in letters to inferiors, precedence in order of address follows precedence in rank.

We were also greatly surprised when instead of bringing us the healing balm of comfort you increased our desolation and made the tears to flow which you should have dried. For which of us could remain dry-eyed on hearing the words you wrote towards the end of your letter: 'But if the Lord shall deliver me into the hands of my enemies so that they overcome and kill me . . .'? My dearest, how could you think such a thought? How could you give voice to it? Never may God be so forgetful of his humble handmaids as to let them outlive you; never may he grant us a life which would be harder to bear than any form of death. The proper course would be for you to perform our funeral rites, for you to commend our souls to God, and to send ahead of you those whom you assembled for God's service—so that you need no longer be troubled by worries for us, and follow after us the more gladly because freed from concern for our salvation. Spare us, I implore you, master, spare us words such as these which can only intensify our existing unhappiness; do not deny us, before death, the one thing by which we live. 'Each day has trouble enough of its own, and that day, shrouded in bitterness, will bring with it distress enough to all it comes upon.' 'Why is it necessary,' says Seneca, 'to summon evil' and to destroy life before death comes?

You ask us, my love, if you chance to die when absent from us, to have your body brought to our burial-ground so that you may reap a fuller harvest from the prayers we shall offer in constant memory of you. But how could you suppose that our memory of you could ever fade? Besides, what time will there be then which will be fitting for prayer, when extreme distress will allow us no peace, when the soul will lose its power of reason and the tongue its use of speech? Or when the frantic mind, far from being resigned, may even (if I may say so) rage against God himself, and provoke him with complaints instead of placating him with prayers? In our misery then we shall have time only for tears and no power to pray; we shall be hurrying to follow, not to bury you, so that we may share your grave instead of laying you in it. If we lose our life in you, we shall not be able to go on living when you leave us. I would not even have us live to see that day, for if the mere mention of your death is death for us, what will the reality be if it finds us still alive? God grant we may never live on to perform this duty, to render you the service which we look for from you alone; in this may we go before, not after you!

And so, I beg you, spare us—spare her at least, who is yours alone, by refraining from words like these. They pierce our hearts with swords of death, so that what comes before is more painful than death itself. A heart which is exhausted with grief cannot find peace, nor can a mind preoccupied with anxieties genuinely devote itself to God. I beseech you not to hinder God's service to which you specially committed us. Whatever has to come to us bringing with it total grief we must hope will come suddenly, without torturing us far in advance with useless apprehension which no foresight can relieve. This is what the poet has in mind when he prays to God:

May it be sudden, whatever you
plan for us; may man's mind
Be blind to the future. Let him
hope on in his fears.

But if I lose you, what is left for me to hope for? What reason for continuing on life's pilgrimage, for which I have no support but you, and none in you save the knowledge that you are alive, now that I am forbidden all other pleasures in you and denied even the joy of your presence which from time to time could restore me to myself? O God—if I dare say it—cruel to me in everything! O merciless mercy! O Fortune who is only ill-fortune, who has already spent on me so many of the shafts she uses in her battle against mankind that she has none left with which to vent her anger on others. She has emptied a full quiver on me, so that henceforth no one else need fear her onslaughts, and if she still had a single arrow she could find no place in me to take a wound. Her only dread is that through my many wounds death may end my sufferings; and though she does not cease to destroy me, she still fears the destruction which she hurries on.

Of all wretched women I am the most wretched, and amongst the unhappy I am unhappiest. The higher I was exalted when you preferred me to all other women, the greater my suffering over my own fall and yours, when I was flung down; for the higher the ascent, the heavier the fall. Has Fortune ever set any great or noble woman above me or made her my equal, only to be similarly cast down and crushed with grief? What glory she gave me in you, what ruin she brought upon me through you! Violent in either extreme, she showed no moderation in good or evil. To make me the saddest of all women she first made me blessed above all, so that when I thought how much I had lost, my consuming grief would match my crushing loss, and my sorrow for what was taken from me would be the greater for the fuller joy of possession which had gone before; and so that the happiness of supreme ecstasy would end in the supreme bitterness of sorrow.

Moreover, to add to my indignation at the outrage you suffered, all the laws of equity in our case were reversed. For while we enjoyed the pleasures of uneasy love and abandoned ourselves to fornication (if I may use an ugly but expressive word) we were spared God's severity. But when we amended our unlawful conduct by what was lawful, and atoned for the shame of fornication by an honourable marriage, then the Lord in his anger laid his hand heavily upon us, and would not permit a chaste union though he had long tolerated one which was unchaste. The punishment you suffered would have been proper vengeance for men caught in open adultery. But what others deserve for adultery came upon you through a marriage which you believed had made amends for all previous wrong doing; what adulterous women have brought upon their lovers, your own wife brought on you. Nor was this at the time when we abandoned ourselves to our former delights, but when we had already parted and were leading chaste lives, you presiding over the school in Paris and I at your command living with the nuns at Argenteuil. Thus we were separated, to give you more time to devote yourself to your pupils, and me more freedom for prayer and meditation on the Scriptures, both of us leading a life which was holy as well as chaste. It was then that you alone paid the penalty in your body for a sin we had both committed. You alone were punished though we were both to blame, and you paid all, though you had deserved less, for you had made more than necessary reparation by humbling yourself on my account and had raised me and all my kind to your own level—so much less then, in the eyes of God and of your betrayers, should you have been thought deserving of such punishment.

What misery for me—born as I was to be the cause of such a crime! Is it the general lot of women to bring total ruin on great men? Hence the warning about women in Proverbs: 'But now, my son, listen to me, attend to what I say: do not let your heart entice you into her ways, do not stray down her paths; she has wounded and laid low so many, and the strongest have all been her victims. Her house is the way to hell, and leads down to the halls of death.' And in Ecclesiastes: 'I put all to the test . . . I find woman more bitter than death; she is a snare, her heart a net, her arms are chains. He who is pleasing to God eludes her, but the sinner is her captive.'

It was the first woman in the beginning who lured man from Paradise, and she who had been created by the Lord as his helpmate became the instrument of his total downfall. And that mighty man of God, the Nazarite whose conception was announced by an angel, Delilah alone overcame; betrayed to his enemies and robbed of his sight, he was driven by his suffering to destroy himself along with his enemies. Only the woman he had slept with could reduce to folly Solomon, wisest of all men; she drove him to such a pitch of madness that although he was the man whom the Lord had chosen to build the temple in preference to his father David, who was a righteous man, she plunged him into idolatry until the end of his life, so that he abandoned the worship of God which he had preached and taught in word and writing. Job, holiest of men, fought his last and hardest battle against his wife, who urged him to curse God. The cunning archtempter well knew from repeated experience that men are most easily brought to ruin through their wives, and so he directed his usual malice against us too, and attacked you by means of marriage when he could not destroy you through fornication. Denied the power to do evil through evil, he effected evil through good.

At least I can thank God for this: the tempter did not prevail on me to do wrong of my own consent, like the women I have mentioned, though in the outcome he made me the instrument of his malice. But even if my conscience is clear through innocence, and no consent of mine makes me guilty of this crime, too many earlier sins were committed to allow me to be wholly free from guilt. I yielded long before to the pleasures of carnal desires, and merited then what I weep for now. The sequel is a fitting punishment for my former sins, and an evil beginning must be expected to come to a bad end. For this offense, above all, may I have strength to do proper penance, so that at least by long contrition I can make some amends for your pain from the wound inflicted on you; and what you suffered in the body for a time, I may suffer, as is right, throughout my life in contrition of mind, and thus make reparation to you at least, if not to God.

For if I truthfully admit to the weakness of my unhappy soul, I can find no penitence whereby to appease God, whom I always accuse of the greatest cruelty in regard to this outrage. By rebelling against his ordinance, I offend him more by my indignation than I placate him by making amends through penitence. How can it be called repentance for sins, however great the mortification of the flesh, if the mind still retains the will to sin and is on fire with its old desires? It is easy enough for anyone to confess his sins, to accuse himself, or even to mortify his body in outward show of penance, but it is very difficult to tear the heart away from hankering after its dearest pleasures. Quite rightly then, when the saintly Job said 'I will speak out against myself,' that is, 'I will loose my tongue and open my mouth in confession to accuse myself of my sins,' he added at once 'I will speak out in bitterness of soul.' St Gregory comments on this: 'There are some who confess their faults aloud but in doing so do not know how to groan over them—they speak cheerfully of what should be lamented. And so whoever hates his faults and confesses them must still confess them in bitterness of spirit, so that this bitterness may punish him for what his tongue, at his mind's bidding, accuses him. But this bitterness of true repentance is very rare, as St Ambrose observes, when he says: 'I have more easily found men who have preserved their innocence than men who have known repentance.'

In my case, the pleasures of lovers which we shared have been too sweet—they can never displease me, and can scarcely be banished from my thoughts. Wherever I turn they are always there before my eyes, bringing with them awakened longings and fantasies which will not even let me sleep. Even during the celebration of the Mass, when our prayers should be purer, lewd visions of those pleasures take such a hold upon my unhappy soul that my thoughts are on their wantonness instead of on prayers. I should be groaning over the sins I have committed, but I can only sigh for what I have lost. Everything we did and also the times and places are stamped on my heart along with your image, so that I live through it all again with you. Even in sleep I know no respite. Sometimes my thoughts are betrayed in a movement of my body, or they break out in a unguarded word. In my utter wretchedness, that cry from a suffering soul could well be mine: 'Miserable creature that I am, who is there to rescue me out of the body doomed to this death?' Would that in truth I could go on: 'The grace of God through Jesus Christ our Lord.' This grace, my dearest, came upon you unsought—a single wound of the body by freeing you from these torments has healed many wounds in your soul. Where God may seem to you an adversary he has in fact proved himself kind: like an honest doctor who does not shrink from giving pain if it will bring about a cure. But for me, youth and passion and experience of pleasures which were so delightful intensify the torments of the flesh and longings of desire, and the assault is the more overwhelming as the nature they attack is the weaker.

Men call me chaste; they do not know the hypocrite I am. They consider purity of the flesh a virtue, though virtue belongs not to the body but to the soul. I can win praise in the eyes of men but deserve none before God, who searches our hearts and loins and sees in our darkness. I am judged religious at a time when there is little in religion which is not hypocrisy, when whoever does not offend the opinions of men receives the highest praise. And yet perhaps there is some merit and it is somehow acceptable to God, if a person whatever his intention gives no offence to the Church in his outward behaviour, does not blaspheme the name of the Lord in the hearing of unbelievers nor disgrace the Order of his profession amongst the worldly. And this too is a gift of God's grace and comes through his bounty—not only to do good but to abstain from evil—though the latter is vain if the former does not follow from it, as it is written: 'Turn from evil and do good.' Both are vain if not done for love of God.

At every stage of my life up to now, as God knows, I have feared to offend you rather than God, and tried to please you more than him. It was your command, not love of God which made me take the veil. Look at the unhappy life I lead, pitiable beyond any other, if in this world I must endure so much in vain, with no hope of future reward. For a long time my pretence deceived you, as it did many, so that you mistook hypocrisy for piety; and therefore you commend yourself to my prayers and ask me for what I expect from you. I beg you, do not feel so sure of me that you cease to help me by your own prayers. Do not suppose me healthy and so withdraw the grace of your healing. Do not believe I want for nothing and delay helping me in my hour of need. Do not think me strong, lest I fall before you can sustain me. False praise has harmed many and taken from them the support they needed. The Lord cries out through Isaiah: 'O my people! Those who call you happy lead you astray and confuse the path you should take.' And through Ezekiel he says: 'Woe upon you women who hunt men's lives by sewing magic bands upon the wrists and putting veils over the heads of persons of every age.' On the other hand, through Solomon it is said that 'The sayings of the wise are sharp as goads, like nails driven home.' That is to say, nails which cannot touch wounds gently, but only pierce through them.

Cease praising me, I beg you, lest you acquire the base stigma of being a flatterer or the charge of telling lies, or the breath of my vanity blows away any merit you saw in me to praise. No one with medical knowledge diagnoses an internal ailment by examining only outward appearance. What is common to the damned and the elect can win no favour in the eyes of God: of such a kind are the outward actions which are performed more eagerly by hypocrites than by saints. 'The heart of man is deceitful and inscrutable; who can fathom it?' And: 'A road may seem straightforward to a man, yet may end as the way to death.' It is rash for man to pass judgement on what is reserved for God's scrutiny, and so it is also written: 'Do not praise a man in his lifetime.' By this is meant, do not praise a man while in doing so you can make him no longer praiseworthy.

To me your praise is the more dangerous because I welcome it. The more anxious I am to please you in everything, the more I am won over and delighted by it. I beg you, be fearful for me always, instead of feeling confidence in me, so that I may always find help in your solicitude. Now particularly you should fear, now when I no longer have in you an outlet for my incontinence. I do not want you to exhort me to virtue and summon me to the fight, saying 'Power comes to its full strength in weakness' and 'He cannot win a crown unless he has kept the rules.' I do not seek a crown of victory; it is sufficient for me to avoid danger, and this is safer than engaging in war. In whatever corner of heaven God shall place me, I shall be satisfied. No one will envy another there, and what each one has will suffice. Let the weight of authority reinforce what I say—let us hear St Jerome: 'I confess my weakness, I do not wish to fight in hope of victory, lest the day comes when I lose the battle. What need is there to forsake what is certain and pursue uncertainty?

## Thomas More (1478–1535)

*Translated by Robert M. Adams*

Thomas More belonged to the first generation of English humanists, and his Latin *Utopia* (1516) exhibits the wit, classical learning, and concern for public life and governance that this international movement inspired in writers as diverse as Petrarch and Montaigne. More is remembered today primarily as the author of this little book and as the "Man for All Seasons," England's ill-fated Lord Chancellor who was executed by Henry VIII because he steadfastly refused to recognize the king's claim to be head of the English church. He is a saint in the Catholic Church.

*Utopia* (the name was coined by More and means "No place" in Greek) ironically has become the common term for any ideal society. The word also designates the literary genre depicting ideal societies—Plato's *Republic* is the earliest example in the West and is one of More's chief inspirations. Today's use of the term is misleading when applied to More's serious-comical work, however, for his Utopia is not Christian, much less Catholic, so he himself could not have considered it ideal. In fact, More casts himself in the work as highly skeptical of Utopia's virtues, notably its key doctrine rejecting private property. He could hardly have endorsed dozens of other Utopian practices, either, including euthanasia and divorce. Utopia is constructed along purely rational lines, in accordance with the four cardinal virtues—wisdom, fortitude, temperance, and justice—which, according to the church, ancient non-Christian philosophers also could attain.

But if *Utopia* is not actually More's notion of an ideal society, what is it? The book is clearly a fanciful but trenchant satire on European society and statecraft, but its delicate ironies are impossible to calculate. Over the centuries, it has been interpreted as endorsing wildly different political philosophies, from monasticism and humanism to modern communism. Readers of every age seem to find in it what they want.

*Utopia* was written only twenty-four years after the discovery of the New World and is one of the first major intellectual responses to the shock that this discovery delivered to European thought. Europeans were suddenly able to see their civilization within a greatly enlarged context of alternate possibilities, including the recently discovered "natural" societies of the New World. (Compare Ovid's myth of a "Golden Age," pp. 677–679.) The fictional narrator of the work, Raphael Hythloday (Greek for "Nonsense"), claims to have explored the New World with Amerigo Vespucci. As a response to the discovery of the New World, the work might be profitably compared with Montaigne's *Of Cannibals* and Shakespeare's *Tempest.*

## *Utopia, from Book Two*

### The Geography of Utopia

The island of the Utopians is two hundred miles across in the middle part where it is widest, and is nowhere much narrower than this except toward the two ends. These ends, drawn toward one another as if in a five-hundred-mile circle, make the island crescent-shaped like a new moon. Between the horns of the crescent, which are about eleven miles apart, the sea enters and spreads into a broad bay. Being sheltered from the wind by the surrounding land, the bay is never rough, but quiet and smooth instead, like a big lake. Thus, nearly the whole inner coast is one great harbor, across which ships pass in every direction, to the great advantage of the people. What with shallows on one side, and rocks on the other, the entrance into the bay is very dangerous. Near the middle of the channel, there is one rock that rises above the water, and so presents no dangers in itself; on top of it a tower has been built, and there a garrison is kept. Since the other rocks lie under water, they are very dangerous to navigation. The channels are known only to the Utopians, so hardly any strangers enter the bay without one of their pilots; and even they themselves could not enter safely if they did not direct themselves by some landmarks on the coast. If they should shift these landmarks about, they could lure to destruction an enemy fleet coming against them, however big it was.

On the outer side of the island there are likewise occasional harbors; but the coast is rugged by nature, and so well fortified that a few defenders could beat off the attack of a strong force. They say (and the appearance of the place confirms this) that their land was not always an island. But Utopus, who conquered the country and gave it his name (it had previously been called Abraxa), brought its rude and uncouth inhabitants to such a high level of culture and humanity that they now excel in that regard almost every other people. After subduing them at his first landing, he cut a channel fifteen miles wide where their land joined the continent, and caused the sea to flow around the country. He put not only the natives to work at this task, but all his own soldiers too, so that the vanquished would not think the labor a disgrace. With the work divided among so many hands, the project was finished quickly, and the neighboring peoples, who at first had laughed at his folly, were struck with wonder and terror at his success.

There are fifty-four cities on the island, all spacious and magnificent, identical in language, customs, institutions, and laws. So far as the location permits, all of them are built on the same plan, and have the same appearance. The nearest are at least twenty-four miles apart, and the farthest are not so remote that a man cannot go on foot from one to the other in a day.

Once a year each city sends three of its old and experienced citizens to Amaurot to consider affairs of common interest to the island. Amaurot is the chief city, lies near the omphalos of the land, so to speak, and convenient to every other district, so it acts as a capital. Every city has enough ground assigned to it so that at least twelve miles of farm land are available in every direction, though where the cities are farther apart, they have much more land. No city wants to enlarge its boundaries, for the inhabitants consider themselves good tenants rather than landlords. At proper intervals all over the countryside they have built houses and furnished them with farm equipment. These houses are inhabited by citizens who come to the country by turns to occupy them. No rural house has fewer than forty men and women in it, besides two slaves. A master and mistress, serious and mature persons, are in charge of each household. Over every thirty households is placed a single phylarch. Each year twenty persons from each rural household move back to the city, after completing a two-year stint in the country. In their place, twenty others are sent out from town, to learn farm work from those who have already been in the country for a year, and who are better skilled in farming. They, in turn, will teach those who come the following year. If all were equally unskilled in farm work, and new to it, they might harm the crops out of ignorance. This custom of alternating farm workers is solemnly established so that no one will have to do such hard work against his will for more than two years; but many of them who take a natural pleasure in farm life ask to stay longer.

The farm workers till the soil, raise cattle, hew wood, and take it to the city by land or water, as is most convenient. They breed an enormous number of chickens by a marvelous method. Men, not hens, hatch the eggs by keeping them in a warm place at an even temperature. As soon as they come out of the shell, the chicks recognize the men, follow them around, and are devoted to them instead of to their real mothers.

They raise very few horses, and these full of mettle, which they keep only to exercise the young men in the art of horsemanship. For the heavy work of plowing and hauling they use oxen, which they agree are inferior to horses over the short haul, but which can hold out longer under heavy burdens, are less subject to disease (as they suppose), and so can be kept with less cost and trouble. Moreover, when oxen are too old for work, they can be used for meat.

Grain they use only to make bread. They drink wine, apple or pear cider, or simple water, which they sometimes mix with honey or licorice, of which they have an abundance. Although they know very well, down to the last detail, how much grain each city and its surrounding district will consume, they produce much more grain and cattle than they need for themselves, and share the surplus with their neighbors.

Whatever goods the folk in the country need which cannot be produced there, they request of the town-magistrates, and since there is nothing to be paid or exchanged, they get what they want at once, without any haggling. They generally go to town once a month in any case, to observe the holy days. When harvest time approaches, the phylarchs in the country notify the town-magistrates how many hands will be needed. Crews of harvesters come just when they're wanted, and in one day of good weather they can usually get in the whole crop.

* * *

## Their Gold and Silver

. . . [T]hey have accumulated a vast treasure, but they do not keep it like a treasure. I'm really quite ashamed to tell you how they do keep it, because you probably won't believe me. I would not have believed it myself if someone had just told me about it; but I was there, and saw it with my own eyes. It is a general rule that the more different anything is from what people are used to, the harder it is to accept. But, considering that all their other customs are so unlike ours, a sensible man will not be surprised that they use gold and silver quite differently than we do. After all, they never do use money among themselves, but keep it only for a contingency which may or may not actually arise. So in the meanwhile they take care that no one shall overvalue gold and silver, of which money is made, beyond what the metals themselves deserve. Anyone can see, for example, that iron is far superior to either; men could not live without iron, by heaven, any more than without fire or water. But gold and silver have, by nature, no function that we cannot easily dispense with. Human folly has made them precious because they are rare. Like a most wise and generous mother, nature has placed the best things everywhere and in the open, like air, water, and the earth itself; but she has hidden away in remote places all vain and unprofitable things.

If in Utopia gold and silver were kept locked up in some tower, foolish heads among the common people might well concoct a story that the prince and the senate were out to cheat ordinary folk and get some advantage for themselves. They might indeed put the gold and silver into beautiful plate-ware and rich handiwork, but then in case of necessity the people would not want to give up such articles, on which they had begun to fix their hearts, only to melt them down for soldiers' pay. To avoid all these inconveniences, they thought of a plan which conforms with their institutions as clearly as it contrasts with our own. Unless we've actually seen it working, their plan may seem ridiculous to us, because we prize gold so highly and are so careful about protecting it. With them it's just the other way. While they eat from pottery dishes and drink from glass cups, well made but inexpensive, their chamber pots and stools—all their humblest vessels, for use in the common halls and private homes—are made of gold and silver. The chains and heavy fetters of slaves are also made of these metals. Finally, criminals who are to bear through life the mark of some disgraceful act are forced to wear golden rings on their ears, golden bands on their fingers, golden chains around their necks, and even golden crowns on their heads. Thus they hold gold and silver up to scorn in every conceivable way. As a result, when they have to part with these metals, which other nations give up with as much agony as if they were being disemboweled, the Utopians feel it no more than the loss of a penny.

They find pearls by the seashore, diamonds and rubies in certain cliffs, but never go out of set purpose to look for them. If they happen to find some, they polish them, and give them to the children who, when they are small, feel proud and pleased with such gaudy decorations. But after, when they grow a bit older, and notice that only babies like such toys, they lay them aside. Their parents don't have to say anything, they simply put these trifles away out of a shamefaced sense that they're no longer suitable, just as our children when they grow up put away their rattles, marbles, and dolls.

Different customs, different feelings: I never saw the adage better illustrated than in the case of the Anemolian ambassadors, who came to Amaurot while I was there. Because they came to discuss important business, the senate had assembled ahead of time, three citizens from each city. But the ambassadors from nearby nations, who had visited Utopia before and knew something of their customs, realized that fine clothing was not much respected in that land, silk was despised, and gold was a badge of contempt; and therefore they came in the very plainest of their clothes. But the Anemolians, who lived farther off and had had fewer dealings with the Utopians, had heard only that they all dressed alike, and very simply; so they took for granted that their hosts had nothing to wear that they didn't put on. Being themselves rather more proud than wise, they decided to dress as resplendently as the very gods and dazzle the eyes of the poor Utopians by the glitter of their garb.

Consequently the three ambassadors made a grand entry with a suite of a hundred attendants, all in clothing of many colors, and most in silk. Being noblemen at home, the ambassadors were arrayed in cloth of gold, with heavy gold chains on their necks, gold rings on their ears and fingers, and sparkling strings of pearls and gems on their caps. In fact, they were decked out in all the articles which in Utopia are used to punish slaves, shame wrongdoers, or pacify infants. It was a sight to see how they strutted when they compared their finery with the dress of the Utopians who had poured out into the street to see them pass. But it was just as funny to see how wide they fell of the mark, and how far they were from getting the consideration they wanted and expected. Except for a very few Utopians who for some special reason had visited foreign countries, all the onlookers considered this pomp and splendor a mark of disgrace. They therefore bowed to the humblest servants as lords, and took the ambassadors to be slaves because they were wearing golden chains, passing them by without any reverence at all. You might have seen children, who had themselves thrown away their pearls and gems, nudge their mothers when they saw the ambassadors' jeweled caps, and say:

"Look at that big lummox, mother, who's still wearing pearls and jewels as if he were a little kid!"

But the mother, in all seriousness, would answer:

"Hush, my boy, I think he is one of the ambassador's fools."

Others found fault with the golden chains as useless, because they were so flimsy any slave could break them, and so loose that he could easily shake them off and run away whenever he wanted. But after the ambassadors had spent a couple of days among the Utopians, they learned of the immense amounts of gold which were as thoroughly despised there as they were prized at home. They saw too that more gold and silver went into making the chains and fetters of a single runaway slave than into costuming all three of them. Somewhat crestfallen, then, they put away all the finery in which they had strutted so arrogantly; but they saw the wisdom of doing so after they had talked with the Utopians enough to learn their customs and opinions.

## Their Moral Philosophy

The Utopians marvel that any mortal can take pleasure in the weak sparkle of a little gem or bright pebble when he has a star, or the sun itself, to look at. They are amazed at the foolishness of any man who considers himself a nobler fellow because he wears clothing of specially fine wool. No matter how delicate the thread, they say, a sheep wore it once, and still was nothing but a sheep. They are surprised that gold, a useless commodity in itself, is everywhere valued so highly that man himself, who for his own purposes conferred this value on it, is far less valuable. They do not understand why a dunderhead with no more brains than a post, and who is about as depraved as he is foolish, should command a great many wise and good people, simply because he happens to have a great pile of gold. Yet if this booby should lose his money to the lowest rascal in his household (as can happen by chance, or through some legal trick—for the law can produce reversals as violent as luck itself), he would promptly become one of the fellow's scullions, as if he were personally attached to the coin, and a mere appendage to it. Even more than this, the Utopians are appalled at those people who practically worship a rich man, though they neither owe him anything, nor are obligated to him in any way. What impresses them is simply that the man is rich. Yet all the while they know he is so mean and grasping that as long as he lives not a single penny out of that great mound of money will ever come their way.

These and the like attitudes the Utopians have picked up partly from their upbringing, since the institutions of their society are completely opposed to such folly, and partly from instruction and their reading of good books. For though not many people in each city are excused from labor and assigned to scholarship full time (these are persons who from childhood have given evidence of unusual intelligence and devotion to learning), every child gets an introduction to good literature, and throughout their lives a large part of the people, men and women alike, spend their leisure time in reading.

They can study all the branches of learning in their native tongue, which is not deficient in terminology or unpleasant in sound, and adapts itself fluently to the expression of thought. Just about the same language is spoken throughout that entire area of the world, though elsewhere it is somewhat more corrupt, depending on the district.

Before we came there, the Utopians had never so much as heard about a single one of those philosophers whose names are so celebrated in our part of the world. Yet in music, dialectic, arithmetic, and geometry they have found out just about the same things as our great men of the past. But while they equal the ancients in almost all other subjects, they are far from matching the inventions of our modern logicians. In fact they have not discovered even one of those elaborate rules about restrictions, amplifications, and suppositions which our own schoolboys study in the *Small Logicals.* They are so far from being able to speculate on "second intentions," that not one of them was able to conceive of "man-in-general," though I pointed straight at him with my finger, and he is, as you well know, bigger than any giant, maybe even a colossus. On the other hand, they have learned to plot expertly the courses of the stars and the movements of the heavenly bodies. They have devised a number of different instruments by which they compute with the greatest exactness the course of the sun, the moon, and the other stars that are visible in their area of the sky. As for the friendly and hostile influences of the planets, and that whole deceitful business of divination by the stars, they have never so much as dreamed of it. From long experience in observation, they are able to forecast rains, winds, and other changes in the weather. But as to the causes of the weather, of the flow of the sea and its saltiness, and the origins and nature of the heavens and the universe, they have various opinions. Generally they treat of these matters as did our ancient philosophers, but they also disagree with one another, as the ancients did, and are unable to come up with any generally accepted theories of their own.

In matters of moral philosophy, they carry on much the same arguments as we do. They inquire into the nature of the good, distinguishing goods of the body from goods of the mind and external gifts. They ask whether the name of "good" may be applied to all three, or applies simply to goods of the mind. They discuss virtue and pleasure, but their chief concern is human happiness, and whether it consists of one thing or many. They seem overly inclined to the view of those who think that all or most human happiness consists of pleasure. And what is more surprising, they seek support for this hedonistic philosophy from their religion, which is serious and strict, indeed, almost stern and forbidding. For they never discuss happiness without joining to their philosophic rationalism the principles of religion. Without these religious principles, they think that philosophy is bound to prove weak and defective in its effort to investigate true happiness.

Their religious principles are of this nature: that the soul of man is immortal, and by God's goodness it is born for happiness; that after this life, rewards are appointed for our virtues and good deeds, punishments for our sins. Though these are indeed religious beliefs, they think that reason leads men to believe and accept them.

And they add unhesitatingly that if these beliefs were rejected, no man would be so stupid as not to realize that he should seek pleasure regardless of right and wrong. His only care would be to keep a lesser pleasure from standing in the way of a greater one, and to avoid pleasures that are inevitably followed by pain. Without religious principles, a man would have to be actually crazy to pursue harsh and painful virtue, give up the pleasures of life, and suffer pain from which he can expect no advantage. For if there is no reward after death, a man has no hope of compensation for having passed his entire existence without pleasure, that is, miserably.

In fact, the Utopians believe that happiness is found not in every kind of pleasure, but only in good and honest pleasure. Virtue itself, they say, draws our nature to this kind of pleasure, as to the supreme good. There is an opposed school which declares that virtue is itself happiness.

They define virtue as living according to nature; and God, they say, created us to that end. When a man obeys the dictates of reason in choosing one thing and avoiding another, he is following nature. Now the first rule of reason is to love and venerate the Divine Majesty to whom men owe their own existence and every happiness of which they are capable. The second rule of nature is to lead a life as free of anxiety and as full of joy as possible, and to help all one's fellow men toward that end. The most hard-faced eulogist of virtue and the grimmest enemy of pleasure, while they invite us to toil and sleepless nights and self-laceration, still admonish us to relieve the poverty and misfortune of others, as best we can. It is especially praiseworthy, they tell us, when we provide for our fellow-creature's comfort and welfare. Nothing is more humane (and humanity is the virtue most proper to human beings) than to relieve the misery of others, assuage their griefs, and by removing all sadness from their life, to restore them to enjoyment, that is, pleasure. Well, if this is the case, why doesn't nature equally invite us to do the same thing for ourselves? Either a joyful life (that is, one of pleasure) is a good thing or it isn't. If it isn't, then you should not help anyone to it—indeed, you ought to take it away from everyone you can, as harmful and deadly to them. But if such a life is good, and if we are supposed, indeed obliged, to help others to it, why shouldn't we first of all seek it for ourselves, to whom we owe no less charity than to anyone else? When nature prompts us to be kind to our neighbors, she does not mean that we should be cruel and merciless to ourselves. Thus they say that nature herself prescribes for us a joyous life, in other words, pleasure, as the goal of our actions; and living according to her prescriptions is to be defined as virtue. And as nature bids men to make one another's lives merrier, to the extent that they can, so she warns us constantly not to seek our own advantages so avidly that we cause misfortune to our fellows. And the reason for this is an excellent one; for no man is placed so highly above the rest, that he is nature's sole concern; she cherishes alike all those living beings to whom she has granted the same form.

Consequently, the Utopians maintain that men should not only abide by their private agreements, but also obey all those public laws which control the distribution of vital goods, such as are the very substance of pleasure. Any such laws, provided they have been properly promulgated by a good king, or ratified by a people free of force and fraud, should be observed; and as long as they are observed, any man is free to pursue his own interests as prudence prompts him. If, in addition to his own interests, he concerns himself with the public interest, that is an act of piety; but if, to secure his own pleasure, he deprives others of theirs, that is injustice. On the other hand, deliberately to decrease one's own pleasure in order to augment that of others is a work of humanity and benevolence which never fails to benefit the doer more even than he benefits others. He may be repaid for his kindness; and in any case, he is conscious of having done a good deed. His mind draws more joy from recalling the gratitude and good will of those whom he has benefited than his body would have drawn pleasure from the things he gave away. Finally they believe (as religion easily persuades a well-disposed mind to believe) that God will recompense us for surrendering a brief and transitory pleasure, with immense, and neverending joy. And so they conclude, after carefully considering and weighing the matter, that all our actions and the virtues exercised within them look toward pleasure and happiness as their ultimate end.

By pleasure they understand every state or movement of body or mind in which man naturally finds delight. They are right in considering man's appetites natural. By simply following his senses and his right reason a man may discover what is pleasant by nature—it is a delight that does not injure others, that does not preclude a greater pleasure, and that is not followed by pain. But a pleasure which is against nature, and which men call "delightful" only by the emptiest of fictions (as if one could change the real nature of things just by changing their names), does not really make for happiness; in fact they say, it destroys happiness. And the reason is that men whose minds are filled with false ideas of pleasure have no room left for true and genuine delight. As a matter of fact, there are a great many things which have no sweetness in them, but are mainly or entirely bitter—yet which through the perverse enticements of evil lusts are considered very great pleasures, and even the supreme goals of life.

Among the devotees of this false pleasure the Utopians include those whom I mentioned before, the people who think themselves finer fellows because they wear finer clothes. These people are twice mistaken: first in thinking their clothes better than anyone else's, and then in thinking themselves better because of their clothes. As far as a coat's usefulness goes, what does it matter if it was woven of thin thread or thick? Yet they act as if they were set apart by nature herself, rather than their own fantasies; they strut about, and put on airs. Because they have a fancy suit, they think themselves entitled to honors they would never have expected if they were dressed in homespun, and they get very angry if someone passes them by without showing special respect.

It is the same kind of absurdity to be pleased by empty, ceremonial honors. What true and natural pleasure can you get from someone's bent knee or bared head? Will the creaks in your own knees be eased thereby, or the madness in your head? The phantom of false pleasure is illustrated by other men who run mad with delight over their own blue blood, plume themselves on their nobility, and applaud themselves for all their rich ancestors (the only ancestors that count nowadays), and all their ancient family estates. Even if they don't have the shred of an estate themselves, or if they've squandered every penny of their inheritance, they don't consider themselves a bit less noble.

In the same class the Utopians put those people I described before, who are mad for jewelry and gems, and think themselves divinely happy if they find a good specimen, especially of the sort that happens to be fashionable in their country at the time—for stones vary in value from one market to another. The collector will not make an offer for the stone till it's taken out of its setting, and even then he will not buy unless the dealer guarantees and gives security that it is a true and genuine stone. What he fears is that his eyes will be deceived by a counterfeit. But if you consider the matter, why should a counterfeit give any less pleasure when your eyes cannot distinguish it from a real gem? Both should be of equal value to you, as they would be, in fact, to a blind man.

Speaking of false pleasure, what about those who pile up money, not because they want to do anything with the heap, but so they can sit and look at it? Is that true pleasure they experience, or aren't they simply cheated by a show of pleasure? Or what of those with the opposite vice, the men who hide away money they will never use and perhaps never even see again? In their anxiety to hold onto their money, they actually lose it. For what else happens when you deprive yourself, and perhaps other people too, of a chance to use money, by burying it in the ground? And yet when the miser has hidden his treasure, he exults over it as if his mind were now free to rejoice. Suppose someone stole it, and the miser died ten years later, knowing nothing of the theft. During all those ten years, what did it matter whether the money was stolen or not? In either case, it was equally useless to the owner.

To these false and foolish pleasures they add gambling, which they have heard about, though they've never tried it, as well as hunting and hawking. What pleasure can there be, they wonder, in throwing dice on a table? If there were any pleasure in the action, wouldn't doing it over and over again quickly make one tired of it? What pleasure can there be in listening to the barking and yelping of dogs—isn't that rather a disgusting noise? Is there any more real pleasure when a dog chases a rabbit than there is when a dog chases a dog? If what you like is fast running, there's plenty of that in both cases; they're just about the same. But if what you really want is slaughter, if you want to see a living creature torn apart under your eyes, then the whole thing is wrong. You ought to feel nothing but pity when you see the hare fleeing from the hound, the weak creature tormented by the stronger, the fearful and timid beast brutalized by the savage one, the harmless hare killed by the cruel dog. The Utopians, who regard this whole activity of hunting as unworthy of free men, have assigned it, accordingly, to their butchers, who as I said before, are all slaves. In their eyes, hunting is the lowest thing even butchers can do. In the slaughterhouse, their work is more useful and honest—since there they kill animals only from necessity; but hunters seek merely their own pleasure from the killing and mutilating of some poor little creature. Taking such relish in the sight of death, even if it's only beasts, reveals, in the opinion of the Utopians, a cruel disposition. Or if he isn't cruel to start with, the hunter quickly becomes so through the constant practice of such brutal pleasures.

Most men consider these activities, and countless others like them, to be pleasures; but the Utopians say flatly they have nothing at all to do with real pleasure since there's nothing naturally pleasant about them. They often please the senses, and in this they are like pleasure, but that does not alter their basic nature. The enjoyment doesn't arise from the experience itself, but only from the perverse mind of the individual, as a result of which he mistakes the bitter for the sweet, just as pregnant women, whose taste has been turned awry, sometimes think pitch and tallow taste sweeter than honey. A man's taste may be similarly depraved, by disease or by custom, but that does not change the nature of pleasure, or of anything else.

They distinguish several different classes of true pleasure, some being pleasures of the mind and others pleasures of the body. Those of the mind are knowledge and the delight which rises from contemplating the truth, also the gratification of looking back on a well-spent life and the unquestioning hope of happiness to come.

Pleasures of the body they also divide into two classes. The first is that which fills the senses with immediate delight. Sometimes this happens when organs that have been weakened by natural heat are restored with food and drink; sometimes it happens when we eliminate some excess in the body, as when we move our bowels, generate children, or relieve an itch somewhere by rubbing or scratching it. Now and then pleasure rises, not from restoring a deficiency or discharging an excess, but from something that excites our senses with a hidden but unmistakable force, and attracts them to itself. Such is the power of music.

The second kind of bodily pleasure they describe as nothing but the calm and harmonious state of the body, its state of health when undisturbed by any disorder. Health itself, when undisturbed by pain, gives pleasure, without any external excitement at all. Even though it appeals less directly to the senses than the gross gratifications of eating and drinking, many consider this to be the greatest pleasure of all. Most of the Utopians regard this as the foundation of all the other pleasures, since by itself alone it can make life peaceful and desirable, whereas without it there is no possibility of any other pleasure. Mere absence of pain, without positive health, they regard as insensibility, not pleasure.

They rejected long ago the opinion of those who doubted whether a stable and tranquil state of health was really a pleasure, on the grounds that pleasure made itself felt only when aroused from without. (They have arguments of this sort, just as we do.) But now they mostly agree that health is the greatest of bodily pleasures. Since pain is inherent in disease, they argue, and pain is the bitter enemy of pleasure, while disease is the enemy of health, then pleasure must be inherent in quiet good health. You may say pain is not the disease itself, simply an accompanying effect; but they argue that that makes no difference. For whether health is itself a pleasure or is merely the cause of pleasure (as fire is the cause of heat), the fact remains that those who have permanent health must also have pleasure.

When we eat, they say, what happens is that health, which was starting to fade, takes food as its ally in the fight against hunger. While our health gains strength, the simple process of returning vigor gives us pleasure and refreshment. If our health feels delight in the struggle, will it not rejoice when the victory has been won? When at last it is restored to its original strength, which was its aim all through the conflict, will it at once become insensible, and fail to recognize and embrace its own good? The idea that health cannot be felt they consider completely wrong. Every man who's awake, they say, feels that he's in good health—unless he isn't. Is any man so torpid and dull that he won't admit health is delightfully agreeable to him? And what is delight except pleasure under another name?

Of all the different pleasures, they seek mostly those of the mind, and prize them most highly, because most of them arise from the practice of the virtues and the consciousness of a good life. Among the pleasures of the body, they give the first place to health. As for eating and drinking and other delights of the same sort, they consider these bodily pleasures desirable but only for the sake of health. They are not pleasant in themselves, but only as ways to withstand the insidious attacks of sickness. A wise man would rather escape sickness altogether than have a good cure for it; he would rather prevent pain than find a palliative for it. And so it would be better not to need this kind of pleasure at all than to be comforted by it.

Anyone who thinks happiness consists of this sort of pleasure must confess that his ideal life would be one spent in an endless round of hunger, thirst, and itching, followed by eating, drinking, scratching, and rubbing. Who fails to see that such an existence is not only disgusting but miserable? These pleasures are certainly the lowest of all, as they are the most adulterate—for they never occur except in connection with the pains that are their contraries. Hunger, for example, is linked to the pleasure of eating, and far from equally, since the pain is sharper and lasts longer; it precedes the pleasure, and ends only when the pleasure ends with it. So the Utopians think pleasures of this sort should not be much valued, except as they are necessary to life. Yet they enjoy these pleasures too, and acknowledge gratefully the kindness of Mother Nature, who coaxes her children with allurements and cajolery to do what from hard necessity they must always do. How wretched life would be, if the daily diseases of hunger and thirst had to be overcome by bitter potions and drugs, like some other diseases that afflict us less often!

Beauty, strength, and agility, as special and pleasant gifts of nature, they joyfully accept. The pleasures of sound, sight, and smell they also accept as the special seasonings of life, recognizing that nature intended these delights to be the particular province of man. No other kind of animal contemplates the shape and loveliness of the universe, or enjoys odors, except in the way of searching for food, or distinguishes harmonious from dissonant sounds. But in all their pleasures, the Utopians observe this rule, that the lesser pleasure must not interfere with a greater, and that no pleasure shall carry pain with it as a consequence. If a pleasure is false, they think it will inevitably lead to pain.

Moreover, they think it is crazy for a man to despise beauty of form, to impair his own strength, to grind his energy down to lethargy, to exhaust his body with fasts, to ruin his health, and to scorn natural delights, unless by so doing he can better serve the welfare of others or the public good. Then indeed he may expect a greater reward from God. But otherwise, such a man does no one any good. He gains, perhaps, the empty and shadowy reputation of virtue; and no doubt he hardens himself against fantastic adversities which may never occur. But such a person the Utopians consider absolutely crazy—cruel to himself, as well as most ungrateful to nature—as if, to avoid being in her debt, he were to reject all of nature's gifts.

This is the way they think about virtue and pleasure. Human reason, they think, can attain to no surer conclusions than these, unless a revelation from heaven should inspire men with holier notions. In all this, I have no time now to consider whether they are right or wrong, and don't feel obliged to do so. I have undertaken only to describe their principles, not to defend them. But of this I am sure, that whatever you think of their ideas, there is not a happier people or a better commonwealth anywhere in the whole world.

In body they are active and lively, and stronger than you would expect from their stature, though they're by no means tiny. Their soil is not very fertile, nor their climate of the best, but they protect themselves against the weather by temperate living, and improve their soil by industry, so that nowhere do grain and cattle flourish more plentifully, nowhere are men more vigorous and liable to fewer diseases. They do all the things that farmers usually do to improve poor soil by hard work and technical knowledge, but in addition they may even transplant a forest from one place to another. They do this not so much for the sake of better growth, but to make transportation easier, in order to have wood closer to the sea, the rivers, or the cities themselves. For grain is easier than wood to transport over a long distance, especially by land.

* * *

## Care of the Sick and Dying

As I said before, the sick are carefully tended, and nothing is neglected in the way of medicine or diet which might cure them. Everything is done to mitigate the pain of those who are suffering from incurable diseases; and visitors do their best to console them by sitting and talking with them. But if the disease is not only incurable, but excruciatingly and continually painful, then the priests and public officials come and urge the invalid not to endure such agony any longer. They remind him that he is now unfit for any of life's duties, a burden to himself and to others; he has really outlived his own death. They tell him he should not let the disease prey on him any longer, but now that life is simply torture and the world a mere prison cell, he should not hesitate to free himself, or to let others free him, from the rack of living. This would be a wise act, they say, since for him death puts an end, not to pleasure, but to agony. In addition, he would be obeying the advice of the priests, who are the interpreters of God's will; which ensures that it will be a holy and a pious act.

Those who have been persuaded by these arguments either starve themselves to death or take a potion which puts them painlessly to sleep, and frees them from life without any sensation of dying. But they never force this step on a man against his will; nor, if he decides against it, do they lessen their care of him. Under these circumstances, when death is advised by the authorities, they consider self-destruction honorable. But the suicide, who takes his own life without the approval of priests and senate, they consider unworthy either of earth or fire, and throw his body, unburied and disgraced, into the nearest bog.

## Marriage Customs

Women do not marry till they are eighteen, nor men till they are twenty-two. Premarital intercourse, if discovered and proved, brings severe punishment on both man and woman, and the guilty parties are forbidden to marry during their whole lives, unless the prince, by his pardon, alleviates the sentence. In addition both the father and mother of the household where the offense occurred suffer public disgrace for having been remiss in their duty. The reason they punish this offense so severely is that they suppose few people would join in married love—with confinement to a single partner, and all the petty annoyances that married life involves—unless they were strictly restrained from a life of promiscuity.

In choosing marriage partners, they solemnly and seriously follow a custom which seemed to us foolish and absurd in the extreme. Whether she is a widow or a virgin, the bride-to-be is shown naked to the groom by a responsible and respectable matron; and, similarly, some respectable man presents the groom naked to his future bride. We laughed at this custom and called it absurd; but they were just as amazed at the folly of all other peoples. When men go to buy a colt, where they are risking only a little money, they are so suspicious that though the beast is almost bare they won't close the deal until the saddle and blanket have been taken off, lest there be a hidden sore underneath. Yet in the choice of a mate, which may cause either delight or disgust for the rest of their lives, people are completely careless. They leave all the rest of her body covered up with clothes and estimate the attractiveness of a woman from a mere handsbreadth of her person, the face, which is all they can see. And so they marry, running great risk of hating one another for the rest of their lives, if something in either's person should offend the other. Not all people are so wise as to concern themselves solely with character; even the wise appreciate physical beauty, as a supplement to a good disposition. There's no question but that deformity may lurk under clothing, serious enough to make a man hate his wife when it's too late to be separated from her. When deformities are discovered after marriage, each person must bear his own fate, so the Utopians think everyone should be protected by law beforehand.

There is extra reason for them to be careful, because in that part of the world, they are the only people who practice monogamy. Their marriages are seldom terminated except by death, though they do allow divorce for adultery or for intolerably difficult behavior. A husband or wife who is an aggrieved party to such a divorce is granted permission by the senate to remarry, but the guilty party is considered disreputable and permanently forbidden to take another mate. They absolutely forbid a husband to put away his wife against her will because of some bodily misfortune; they think it cruel that a person should be abandoned when most in need of comfort; and they add that old age, since it not only entails disease but is actually a disease itself, needs more than a precarious fidelity.

It happens occasionally that a married couple cannot get along, and have both found other persons with whom they hope to live more harmoniously. After getting the approval of the senate, they may then separate by mutual consent and contract new marriages. But such divorces are allowed only after the senators and their wives have carefully investigated the case. They allow divorce only very reluctantly because they know that husbands and wives will find it hard to settle down together if each has in mind that another new relation is easily available.

They punish adulterers with the strictest form of slavery. If both parties were married, they are both divorced, and the injured parties may marry one another, if they want, or someone else. But if one of the injured parties continues to love such an undeserving spouse, the marriage may go on, providing the innocent person chooses to share in the labor to which every slave is condemned. And sometimes it happens that the repentance of the guilty, and the devotion of the innocent party, move the prince to pity, so that he restores both to freedom. But a second conviction of adultery is punished by death.

## Punishments, Legal Procedures, and Customs

No other crimes carry fixed penalties; the senate sets specific penalties for each particular misdeed, as it is considered atrocious or venial. Husbands chastise their wives and parents their children, unless the offense is so serious that public punishment seems to be in the public interest. Generally, the gravest crimes are punished by slavery, for they think this deters offenders just as much as instant capital punishment, and is more beneficial to the state. Slaves, moreover, are permanent and visible reminders that crime does not pay. If the slaves rebel against their condition, then, like savage beasts which neither bars nor chains can tame, they are put instantly to death. But if they are patient, they are not left altogether without hope. When subdued by long hardships, if they show by their behavior that they regret the crime more than the punishment, their slavery is lightened or remitted altogether, sometimes by the prince's pardon, sometimes by popular vote.

A man who tries to seduce a woman is subject to the same penalties as if he had actually done it. They think that a crime attempted is as bad as one committed, and that failure should not confer advantages on a criminal who did all he could to succeed.

They are very fond of fools, and think it contemptible to insult them. There is no prohibition against enjoying their foolishness, and they even regard this as beneficial to the fools. If anyone is so serious and solemn that the foolish behavior and comic patter of a clown do not amuse him, they don't entrust him with the care of such a person, for fear that a man who gets no fun from a fool's only gift will not treat him kindly.

To mock a person for being deformed or crippled is considered disgraceful, not to the victim, but to the mocker, who stupidly reproaches the cripple for something he cannot help.

They think it a sign of a weak and sluggish character to neglect one's natural beauty, but they consider cosmetics a detestable affectation. From experience they have learned that no physical beauty recommends a wife to her husband so effectually as truthfulness and integrity. Though quite a few men are captured by beauty alone, none are held except by virtue and compliance.

As they deter men from crime by penalties, so they incite them to virtue by public honors. They set up in the marketplaces statues of distinguished men who have served their country well, thinking thereby to preserve the memory of their good deeds, and to spur on the citizens to emulate the glory of their ancestors.

In Utopia any man who campaigns too eagerly for a public office is sure to fail of that one, and of all others as well. As a rule, they live together harmoniously, and the public officials are never arrogant or unapproachable. Instead, they are called "fathers," and that is the way they behave. Because the officials never extort respect from the people against their will, the people respect them spontaneously, as they should. Not even the prince is distinguished from his fellow citizens by a robe or crown; he is known only by a sheaf of grain carried before him, just as the high priest is distinguished by a wax candle.

They have very few laws, and their training is such that they need no more. The chief fault they find with other nations is that, even with infinite volumes of laws and interpretations, they cannot manage their affairs properly. They think it completely unjust to bind men by a set of laws that are too many to be read and too obscure for anyone to understand. As for lawyers, a class of men whose trade it is to manipulate cases and multiply quibbles, they have no use for them at all. They think it is better for each man to plead his own case, and say the same thing to the judge that he would tell his lawyer. This makes for less ambiguity, and readier access to the truth. A man speaks his mind without tricky instructions from a lawyer, and the judge examines each point carefully, taking pains to protect simple folk against the false accusations of the crafty. It is hard to find this kind of plain dealing in other countries, where they have such a multitude of incomprehensibly intricate laws. But in Utopia everyone is a legal expert. For the laws are very few, as I said, and they consider the most obvious interpretation of any law to be the fairest. As they see things, all laws are promulgated for the single purpose of teaching every man his duty. Subtle interpretations teach very few, since hardly anybody is able to understand them, whereas the more simple and apparent sense of the law is open to everyone. If laws are not clear, they are useless; for simpleminded men (and most men are of this sort, and most men of this sort need to be told where their duty lies) there might as well be no laws at all, as laws which can be interpreted only by devious minds after endless disputes. The average, common man cannot understand this legal chicanery, and couldn't even if he devoted his whole life to studying it, since he has to earn a living in the meanwhile.

* * *

## Conclusion

Now I have described to you as accurately as I could the structure of that commonwealth which I consider not only the best but the only one that can rightfully claim that name. In other places men talk very liberally of the common wealth, but what they mean is simply their own wealth; in Utopia, where there is no private business, every man zealously pursues the public business. And in both places, men are right to act as they do. For among us, even though the state may flourish, each man knows that unless he makes separate provision for himself, he may perfectly well die of hunger. Bitter necessity, then, forces men to look out for themselves rather than for others, that is, for the people. But in Utopia, where everything belongs to everybody, no man need fear that, so long as the public warehouses are filled, he will ever lack for anything he needs. Distribution is simply not one of their problems; in Utopia no men are poor, no men are beggars. Though no man owns anything, everyone is rich.

For what can be greater riches than for a man to live joyfully and peacefully, free from all anxieties, and without worries about making a living? No man is bothered by his wife's querulous complaints about money, no man fears poverty for his son, or struggles to scrape up a dowry for his daughter. Each man can feel secure of his own livelihood and happiness and of his whole family's as well: wife, sons, grandsons, great-grandsons, great-great-grandsons, and that whole long line of descendants that gentlefolk are so fond of contemplating. Indeed, even those who once worked but can do so no longer are cared for just as well as if they were still productive.

Now here I'd like to see anyone try to compare this justice of the Utopians with the so-called justice that prevails among other peoples—among whom let me perish if I can discover the slightest scrap of justice or fairness. What kind of justice is it when a nobleman or a goldsmith or a moneylender, or someone else who makes his living by doing either nothing at all or something completely useless to the public, gets to live a life of luxury and grandeur? In the meantime, a laborer, a carter, a carpenter, or a farmer works so hard and so constantly that even a beast of burden would perish under the load; and this work of theirs is so necessary that no commonwealth could survive a year without it. Yet they earn so meager a living and lead such miserable lives that a beast of burden would really be better off. Beasts do not have to work every minute, and their food is not much worse; in fact they like it better. And, besides, they do not have to worry about their future. But workingmen not only have to sweat and suffer without present reward, but agonize over the prospect of a penniless old age.

Their daily wage is inadequate even for their present needs, so there is no possible chance of their saving toward the future.

Now isn't this an unjust and ungrateful commonwealth? It lavishes rich rewards on so-called gentry, bankers and goldsmiths and the rest of that crew, who don't work at all, are mere parasites, or purveyors of empty pleasures. And yet it makes no provision whatever for the welfare of farmers and colliers, laborers, carters, and carpenters, without whom the commonwealth would simply cease to exist. After the state has taken the labor of their best years, when they are worn out by age and sickness and utter destitution, then the thankless state, forgetting all their pains and services, throws them out to die a miserable death. What is worse, the rich constantly try to grind out of the poor part of their meager wages, not only by private swindling, but by public tax-laws. It is basically unjust that people who deserve most from the commonwealth should receive least. But now they have distorted and debased the right even further by giving their extortion the color of law; and thus they have palmed injustice off as "legal." When I run over in my mind the various commonwealths flourishing today, so help me God, I can see nothing in them but a conspiracy of the rich, who are fattening up their own interests under the name and title of the commonwealth. They invent ways and means to hang onto whatever they have acquired by sharp practice, and then they scheme to oppress the poor by buying up their toil and labor as cheaply as possible. These devices become law as soon as the rich, speaking through the commonwealth—which, of course, includes the poor as well—say they must be observed.

And yet, when these insatiably greedy and evil men have divided among themselves goods which would have sufficed for the entire people, how far they remain from the happiness of the Utopians, who have abolished not only money but with it greed! What a mass of trouble was uprooted by that one step! What a multitude of crimes was pulled up by the roots! Everyone knows that if money were abolished, fraud, theft, robbery, quarrels, brawls, seditions, murders, treasons, poisonings, and a whole set of crimes which are avenged but not prevented by the hangman would at once die out. If money disappeared, so would fear, anxiety, worry, toil, and sleepless nights. Even poverty, which seems to need money more than anything else for its relief, would vanish if money were entirely done away with.

Consider if you will this example. Take a barren year of failed harvests, when many thousands of men have been carried off by hunger. If at the end of the famine the barns of the rich were searched, I dare say positively enough grain would be found in them to have saved the lives of all those who died from starvation and disease, if it had been divided equally among them. Nobody really need have suffered from a bad harvest at all. So easily might men get the necessities of life if that cursed money, which is supposed to provide access to them, were not in fact the chief barrier to our getting what we need to live. Even the rich, I'm sure, understand this. They must know that it's better to have enough of what we really need than an abundance of superfluities, much better to escape from our many present troubles than to be burdened with great masses of wealth. And in fact I have no doubt that every man's perception of where his true interest lies, along with the authority of Christ our Saviour (whose wisdom could not fail to recognize the best, and whose goodness would not fail to counsel it), would long ago have brought the whole world to adopt Utopian laws, if it were not for one single monster, the prime plague and begetter of all others—I mean Pride.

Pride measures her advantages not by what she has but by what other people lack. Pride would not condescend even to be made a goddess, if there were no wretches for her to sneer at and domineer over. Her good fortune is dazzling only by contrast with the miseries of others, her riches are valuable only as they torment and tantalize the poverty of others. Pride is a serpent from hell which twines itself around the hearts of men; and it acts like the suckfish in holding them back from choosing a better way of life.

Pride is too deeply fixed in the hearts of men to be easily plucked out. So I am glad that the Utopians at least have been lucky enough to achieve this commonwealth, which I wish all mankind would imitate. The institutions they have adopted have made their community most happy, and as far as anyone can tell, capable of lasting forever. Now that they have rooted up the seeds of ambition and faction at home, along with most other vices, they are in no danger from internal strife, which alone has been the ruin of many other states that seemed secure. As long as they preserve harmony at home, and keep their institutions healthy, the Utopians can never be overcome or even shaken by their envious neighbors, who have often attempted their ruin, but always in vain.

When Raphael had finished his story, it seemed to me that not a few of the customs and laws he had described as existing among the Utopians were quite absurd. Their methods of waging war, their religious ceremonies, and their social customs were some of these, but my chief objection was to the basis of their whole system, that is, their communal living and their moneyless economy. This one thing alone takes away all the nobility, magnificence, splendor, and majesty which (in the popular view) are considered the true ornaments of any nation. But I saw Raphael was tired with talking, and I was not sure he could take contradiction in these matters, particularly when I remembered what he had said about certain counsellors who were afraid they might not appear wise unless they found out something to criticize in other men's ideas.

So with praise for the Utopian way of life and his account of it, I took him by the hand and led him in to supper. But first I said that we would find some other time for thinking of these matters more deeply, and for talking them over in more detail. And I still hope such an opportunity will present itself some day.

Meanwhile, though he is a man of unquestioned learning, and highly experienced in the ways of the world, I cannot agree with everything he said. Yet I confess there are many things in the Commonwealth of Utopia that I wish our own country would imitate—though I don't really expect it will.

End of Book Two

* * * * *

THE END OF THE AFTERNOON DISCOURSE OF
RAPHAEL HYTHLODAY ON THE LAWS AND
CUSTOMS OF THE ISLAND OF UTOPIA
HITHERTO KNOWN BUT TO FEW, AS
REPORTED BY THE MOST
DISTINGUISHED AND
MOST LEARNED MAN,
MR. THOMAS MORE,
CITIZEN AND SHERIFF OF LONDON

FINIS

* * * *

# THE GERMANIC TRADITION

## OLD NORSE LITERATURE

Tiny medieval Iceland, of all places, produced a very great literature unlike any other. This literature had little impact on the rest of Europe, however, probably because it was written in Old Icelandic (or Old Norse) and was never translated into Latin or the other European vernaculars. From the twelfth to the fourteenth centuries, Iceland produced a large body of anonymous prose sagas very much like novels, a form that would not be invented in continental Europe for several centuries. These sagas are highly realistic in style, with subtle characterization and vivid portrayals of everyday life in early Iceland and Norway.

The greatest known Icelandic writer was Snorri Sturluson (1179–1241). He wrote a number of sagas as well as *The Prose Edda*, a handbook of Norse mythology and legend written for poets. In this book, he rescued the ancient Germanic myths and tales that were in danger of being forgotten after the conversion to Christianity. The following extract from this work ostensibly explains why gold is called "otter's ransom" in the poetic vocabulary, but that is only an excuse for telling the epic story of the Völsungs. This story is the subject of its own saga as well as of the medieval German epic *The Nibelungenlied* and, centuries later, of Wagner's cycle of operas, *The Ring of the Nibelungs*. The story begins in the mythic world, sweeps through the heroic age, and ends in the world of early Germanic history, recounting a vast tragedy in which all the characters are driven to their deaths by fate and the conflicting demands of honor and love. All the dark themes characteristic of the Germanic worldview are present in this tale, though the dry style of Snorri's synopsis produces a curiously comic tone for what is actually a horrific story.

Snorri developed his stories in *The Prose Edda* from a collection of much earlier poems known as *The Elder Edda*, which may date from as early as the eighth or ninth century in Norway. These poems, most in the form of dramatic monologues, contain an emotional power absent in Snorri's dry retelling or in the understated style typical of the sagas. *The Lay of Gudrun*, included here, reveals the explosive emotions at one moment in the Völsung story, emotions normally kept tightly bottled up in the strong, silent heroism characteristic of Germanic literature.

## *from The Elder Edda (11th–12th cent.)*

### *The Lay of Gudrun*

*Translated by Patricia Terry*

Close to death   in her despair,
Gudrun sat grieving   over Sigurd.
She did not wail   or wring her hands,
nor did she weep   like other women.

Noblemen came   to give her comfort,
spoke wise words   to soothe her heart.
Yet Gudrun could not   give way to tears;
burdened by grief,   her heart would break.

Great ladies   decked in gold
sat with Gudrun;   each one spoke,
telling the sorrows   she had suffered,
the bitterest   each one had borne.

Gjuki's sister,   Gjaflaug, said:
"I think no woman   in the world
hapless as I am—five husbands,
three daughters,   three sisters,
eight brothers lost;   and I live on."

Yet Gudrun could not   give way to tears;
hating those   who had killed her husband,
she sat with Sigurd,   her heart like stone.

Then said Herborg,   queen of the Huns:
"I have greater   griefs to tell.
At war in the south,   my seven sons,
and then my husband—   all have been slain;
my father and mother,   my four brothers,
all, when the wind   whipped the waves,
were struck down   in their ship at sea.

"I alone laid them out,   I alone buried them,
I alone gave them   an honored grave.

All this I suffered in just one season,
and no one came to comfort me.

"Then I was caught and held a captive
in that same season; I was a slave.
Every day I had to dress
my lord's lady, and lace her shoes.

"Her jealous spite spared me no threats,
and she would beat me hard blows.
No house could boast a better master,
nor have I met a mistress worse."

Yet Gudrun could not give way to tears;
hating those who had killed her husband,
she sat with Sigurd, her heart like stone.

Gjuki's daughter, Gullrond, spoke:
"Foster-mother, your wisdom fails you—
how shall a young wife listen to words?"
She told them not to keep the dead prince concealed.

She swept off the sheet that covered Sigurd,
and placed a pillow at Gudrun's knees:
"Look at your beloved! Lay your lips on his,
the way you kissed when the king was alive."

Gudrun looked once at her lord;
she saw his hair streaming with blood,
the keen eyes dead in the king's face,
the great sword wound in Sigurd's breast.

She sank to the ground against the pillow,
her hair fell loose, her cheeks flushed red;
drops as of rain ran down to her knees.

Then Gjuki's daughter, Gudrun, wept
so that the tears streamed through her hair;
geese in the yard began to shriek,
the famous birds that belonged to Gudrun.

Gjuki's daughter, Gullrond, said:
"No man and woman in all the world
were ever given so great a love.
Sister, I know you never felt at peace
anywhere away from Sigurd."

Gudrun said:
"My Sigurd was to Gjuki's sons
as garlic stands taller than grass,
or like a bright stone on a string of beads,
a priceless jewel among the princes.

"My lord's warriors honored me once
more than any of Odin's maids:
now I am so little, like a winter leaf
clinging to a willow, since the king is dead.

"I miss in the hall, I miss in bed,
my companion killed by Gjuki's sons,
Gjuki's sons who gave me to grief,
who made their sister's bitter sorrow.

"May all who live here leave your lands
as you cast aside the oaths you swore!
Gunnar, you'll get no joy from the gold—
the rings will drive you to your death,
because you swore an oath with Sigurd.

"There was greater happiness in this house
before my Sigurd saddled Grani,
and they left on a luckless day
to woo Brynhild, the worst of women."

Then said Brynhild, Budli's daughter:
"May she mourn her man and children,
who taught you, Gudrun, to shed tears,
and gave you this day the gift of speech."

Gjuki's daughter, Gullrond, said:
"Accursed woman, don't speak such words!
Ever have you proved the bane of princes,
all the world wishes you ill;
seven kings you've brought to sorrow,
widows you've made of many wives."

Then said Brynhild, Budli's daughter:
"Atli bears the guilt of all this grief,
Atli, my brother, Budli's son.

"Around a hero in the Hunnish hall
flickered the light of Fafnir's lair,
and I paid for the prince's journey,
for that sight I still can see."

She stood by a pillar, summoning her strength;
fire burned in Brynhild's eyes,
baneful venom flew from her lips,
when she saw the wounds, how Sigurd died.

Then Gudrun went away into the forests and through the wilderness until she came to Denmark. There she stayed with Thora, Hakon's daughter, for seven years. Brynhild did not want to live on without Sigurd. She had eight of her slaves killed, and five bondmaids. Then she killed herself with her sword, as it is told in *The Short Lay of Sigurd.*

## *Snorri Sturluson (1179–1241)*

### *from The Prose Edda [Otter's Ransom]*

*Translated by Jean I. Young*

'What is the reason for calling gold "otter's ransom"?'

'It is said that when the Æsir, Óðin and Loki and Hœnir were exploring the whole world, they came to a river and went along it to a waterfall, and by the waterfall was an otter which was eating a salmon it had caught there and it was half-asleep. Loki picked up a stone and flung it at the otter, striking it on the head. Then Loki boasted of his catch—with one throw he had bagged an otter and a salmon. They took the salmon and the otter away with them and came to a farm which they entered. The farmer living there was called Hreiðmar. He was a powerful man with much skill in magic. The Æsir asked the farmer for lodgings there for the night, saying that they had plenty of food, and they showed him their catch. When Hreiðmar saw the otter, however, he called his sons Fáfnir and Regin, and told them that their brother, Otter, had been killed, and also who had done the deed. Then father and sons attacked the Æsir and made them prisoner and bound them, telling them that the otter was Hreiðmar's son. The Æsir offered to pay as large a ransom as Hreiðmar himself should demand, and those terms were agreed on and confirmed by oath. Then the otter was flayed, and Hreiðmar took the skin and told them that they had to fill it and completely cover it into the bargain with red gold. That would reconcile them. Óðin then sent Loki to the World-of-dark-elves, and he came to the dwarf called Andvari. He was in a pool in his fish shape, and Loki seizing him exacted as ransom all the gold he had in his rock dwelling. When they got there the dwarf produced all the gold he possessed and it was a very great sum of money, but he kept back in his hand a little gold ring. Loki noticed this and told him to give him the ring. The dwarf begged him not to take it from him, saying that if only he were allowed to keep it he could by its means become wealthy again. Loki said that he was to be left without a single penny and taking the ring from him was going away, when the dwarf declared that the ring would destroy everyone who owned it. Loki replied that that was all to the good, adding that the prophecy should be fulfilled, provided that he himself pronounced it in the ears of those about to take over the ring.

'He went away and came to Hreiđmar and showed the gold ring to Óđin. When Óđin saw it he admired it for its beauty and kept it back, although he paid the gold to Hreiđmar. Hreiđmar stuffed the skin to bursting and when it was full raised it up on end. Then Óđin went up to it to cover it with gold and, this done, he asked Hreiđmar to look and see if the skin was not completely hidden. Hreiđmar took a good look at it and caught sight of one whisker. He ordered this to be concealed or otherwise, he said, their agreement would be at an end. Then Óđin drew the ring from his finger and concealed the whisker, saying that now they had paid the otter's ransom. When, however, Óđin had taken his spear and Loki his shoes and there was no reason they should be afraid, Loki declared that what Andvari had said should hold good, that that ring and that gold would destroy whosoever owned them. That has been the case ever since. Now you know why gold is called otter's ransom or the forced payment of the Æsir or metal-of-strife.'

'Is anything more known about this gold?'

'Hreiđmar accepted the gold as ransom for his son, and Fáfnir and Regin asked for some of it as a ransom for their brother. Hreiđmar did not give them a single penny of it. The brothers were wicked enough to kill their father for the gold. Then Regin asked Fáfnir to go shares in the gold, but Fáfnir replied that there was little likelihood that he would share with his brother the gold for which he had killed his father, and he told Regin to go away or else he would meet with Hreiđmar's fate. Fáfnir had taken a helmet which had been Hreiđmar's and was wearing it; this struck fear into all beholders and was called the helmet of terror. He also had the sword known as Hrotti. Regin owned a sword called Refil. He took to flight but Fáfnir went up on to Gnita Heath and, making a lair there, turned himself into a dragon and lay down on the gold.

'Then Regin went to King Hjálprek in Tý and became his smith there. He adopted as his foster son Sigurđ, son of Sigmund, son of Völsung and Hjördis, Eylimi's daughter. On account of his family, strength and courage, Sigurđ was the most famous of all warrior kings. Regin told him where Fáfnir was lying on the gold and egged him on to seek the treasure. Regin made the sword called Gram. This was so sharp that, when Sigurđ thrust it into running water, he cut in two a lock of wool carried against the blade by the current. With the same sword Sigurđ clove Regin's anvil to the stock. After that Sigurđ and Regin went to Gnita Heath and Sigurđ dug pits in Fáfnir's path and sat down in one. When Fáfnir, crawling on his way down to the water, came over the pit, Sigurđ ran him through with his sword and that was his death. Then Regin came and said that Sigurđ had killed his brother, and offered him terms on condition that he took Fáfnir's heart and roasted it over a fire. Regin himself lay down and drank Fáfnir's blood and then went to sleep. When Sigurđ thought the heart he was roasting was done, he touched it with his finger to see how tender it was, and the juice from it ran on to his finger, burning it, so he put this into his mouth. When the blood came on to his tongue, however, he understood the language of birds and knew what the nuthatches sitting in the branches were saying. One said:

There sits Sigurđ
blood-bespattered,
Fáfnir's heart
roasts at the fire;
wise that liberal prince
would appear to me
should he eat
that shining heart.

There lies Regin, said another,
revolving in his mind
how to betray
the lad who trusts him;
in wrath he is collecting
crooked words together,
he longs contriver-of-evil
to avenge his brother.

Then Sigurđ went up to Regin and killed him, and afterwards to his horse which was called Grani and rode until he came to Fáfnir's lair. There he took the gold and making it into packs put it on Grani's back, mounted himself and rode on his way.

'Now you know the story explaining why gold is called Fáfnir's abode or lair, or the metal of Gnita Heath, or Grani's burden.

'Sigurđ rode on then until he came to a hall on a mountain. In it was sleeping a woman in helmet and coat of mail. He drew his sword and cut the mail-coat from her. Then she woke up and said she was called Hild. Her name was Brynhild and she was a valkyrie. Sigurđ rode away from there and came to a king called Gjúki. His wife was called Grímhild and their children were Gunnar, Högni, Guđrún and Guđný. Gotthorm was Gjúki's stepson. Sigurđ stayed there for a long time and married Guđrún, Gjúki's daughter, and Gunnar and Högni became sworn brothers of Sigurđ's. Soon after Sigurđ and the sons of Gjúki went to ask Atli Buđlason for his sister, Brynhild, as Gunnar's wife. She lived at Hindafjall and there was a rampart of flame round her hall. She had vowed only to marry that man who dared ride through the flames. Sigurđ and the Gjúkungar—they are also called the Niflungar—rode up on to the mountain and Gunnar was to ride through the rampart of flame. He had a horse called Goti but it did not dare leap into the fire. Sigurđ and Gunnar then changed shapes and also names, because Grani would not move under any man but Sigurđ, and Sigurđ vaulting on to Grani rode the rampart of flame. That evening he married Brynhild but, when they went to bed, he drew the sword Gram from its sheath and laid it between them. In the morning when he got up and dressed, however, he gave Brynhild as a wedding present the gold ring Loki had taken from Andvari, receiving another from her in exchange. Then Sigurđ jumped on to his horse and rode back to his companions. He and Gunnar changed shapes again and went back to Gjúki with Brynhild. Sigurđ had two children by Guđrún, Sigmund and Svanhild.

'On one occasion Brynhild and Guđrún went down to the water to wash their hair. When they reached the river, Brynhild waded out further from the bank, saying that she was not going to use the water in which Guđrún had rinsed her hair for her own head, since she had the more valiant husband. Guđrún went into the river after her then, and said that she had a right to wash her hair in water higher up the river, since she had a husband whom neither Gunnar nor anyone else in the world could match in courage, because he had killed Fáfnir and Regin and had inherited the property of both. Then Brynhild answered: "Sigurđ did not dare ride the rampart of flame: Gunnar did—that counts for more." Guđrún laughed then and said: "You think it was Gunnar who rode the flames? The man you slept with was the one who gave me this gold ring, and the ring you are wearing and which you received as a wedding gift is called Andvari's treasure, and I don't think that Gunnar got it on Gnita Heath." At that Brynhild was silent and went home.

'Afterwards she urged Gunnar and Högni to kill Sigurđ but, because they were his sworn brothers, they persuaded their brother Gotthorm to kill him. He ran Sigurđ through with a sword while he was sleeping, but, when Sigurđ felt the wound, he hurled the sword after Gotthorm so that it cut him asunder through the middle. Sigurđ and his three-year-old son called Sigmund, whom they also killed, perished there. After that Brynhild fell on her sword and she was burned with Sigurđ. Gunnar and Högni, however, took Fáfnir's inheritance then and Andvari's treasure and ruled the country.

'Brynhild's brother, Atli Buđlason, married Guđrún, once the wife of Sigurđ, and they had children together. King Atli invited Gunnar and Högni to stay with him and they went on this visit. Before leaving home, however, they hid the gold that was Fáfnir's inheritance in the Rhine, and it has never been found since. King Atli had troops to oppose them and these fought Gunnar and Högni and took them prisoner. King Atli had Högni's heart cut out of him while he was still living and that was his death. He had Gunnar flung into a snake-pit. A harp was procured for him in secret and, because his hands were tied, he played it with his toes in such a way that all the snakes went to sleep, but for one adder, which made for him and gnawing its way through the cartilage of his breast-bone thrust its head through the hole and buried its fangs in his liver until he was dead. Gunnar and Högni are called Niflungar or Gjúkungar; for this reason gold is called the treasure or inheritance of the Niflungar.

'A little later Guđrún killed her two sons and had goblets decorated with silver and gold made from their skulls. Then the funeral feast of the Niflungar was celebrated. From these goblets Guđrún had King Atli served with mead which was mixed with the boys' blood, and she had their hearts roasted and given the king to eat at the same banquet. When this had been done she told him about it in many ugly words. There was no lack of intoxicating mead there so that most people fell asleep where they were sitting. That same night she went to the king when he was asleep, and with her Högni's son, and they made an armed attack on him and that was his death. Then they set fire to the hall and burned the people inside it.

'After that she went down to the sea and ran into it to drown herself. She was drifted over the fiord, however, and came ashore in King Jónak's country, and when he saw her he took her home and married her. They had three sons with these names: Sörli, Hamđir, and Erp. These had hair as black as the raven, like Gunnar and Högni and the other Niflungar. Sigurđ's daughter, Svanhild, grew up there and she was a very lovely woman. King Jörmunrekk the Mighty heard of this and sent his son Randvér to ask her hand in marriage for him. When he came to Jónak, Svanhild was given into his custody and he was to take her to Jörmunrekk. Then Bikki said that it would be more suitable for Randvér to marry Svanhild, since he was young, indeed they both were, whereas Jörmunrekk was an old man. The young people were delighted with this plan. Soon after Bikki told the king and Jörmunrekk had his son seized and led to the gallows. Randvér took his hawk then, and plucking off its feathers, ordered it to be sent to his father. After that he was hanged. When King Jörmunrekk saw the hawk, it struck him that just as the hawk stripped of its feathers was unable to fly, so, now that he was an old man and without a son, had he crippled his kingdom. Once when he was riding home from a wood in which he and his court had been hunting, King Jörmunrekk caught sight of Svanhild where she sat drying her hair. They rode her down and trampled her to death under their horses' hoofs.

'When Guđrún heard this, she egged on her sons to avenge Svanhild and, when they were making ready for the expedition, procured for them coats of mail and helmets which were so strong that no weapon could pierce them. She advised them, when they reached King Jörmunrekk, to attack him at night in his sleep. Sörli and Hamđir were to cut off his hands and feet, and Erp his head. On the way, however, they asked Erp to what extent they could rely on him when they came to grips with Jörmunrekk. He replied that he would help them as the hand does the foot. They said that the hand gave no help at all to the foot and they were so annoyed with their mother for having sent them out with taunts that they wanted to do what would hurt her most, so they killed Erp because she loved him best. A little later, one of Sörli's feet slipped as he was walking, and he supported himself with his hand. Then he said: "Hand helped foot just now. It would be better if Erp was alive."

'They came to King Jörmunrekk one night when he was asleep, and were cutting off his hands and feet when he awoke and shouted to his men to rouse themselves. Hamđir said: "His head would be off now, if Erp were alive!" Then Jörmunrekk's bodyguard got up and attacked them, but they could not overcome them with weapons, so Jörmunrekk called out to them to use stones. This was done, and Sörli and Hamđir fell there. With them the whole Gjúkung line came to an end.

'Sigurđ left a daughter called Áslaug who was fostered by Heimir in Hlymdalir and great families have come from her.

'It is said that Sigmund Völsungsson was so strong that he could drink poison without coming to harm, and that Sinfjötli, his son, and Sigurđ had such hard skins that their naked bodies were immune to poison.'

# The Romance Tradition

## Provençal Poetry (late 12th cent.)

In the eleventh century, in what is now southern France, an extraordinary new form of poetry emerged in the Provençal language, devoted primarily to the subject of love and clearly influenced by the Arabic love poetry flourishing in neighboring al-Andalus (Spain). The Provençal poets are known as *troubadours* (male) and *trobairitz* (female). Nothing in European literature before this time prepares us for this sudden emergence of erotic love and the idealization of women as major themes. The influence of Andalusian poets such as Ibn Hazm and Ibn Zaidūn (pp. 905–910) is obvious in Provençal verse, and this verse, in turn, was destined to have a profound influence on the literature of love in Europe for many centuries, even to the present day.

The songs of the troubadours take many forms and have many themes, but the most influential are songs of love-longing addressed to a noble lady, who is often married. Though the lady is superior and unobtainable, the poet's devotion to her provides his life with meaning. Though he is unworthy of her, he often condemns her as cold and unmerciful for rejecting his love. These poems are earthy, witty, musical, and often purposely obscure.

As examples, we include poems by Arnaut Daniel and Bertran de Born, both from the latter half of the twelfth century. Bertran's poem is shockingly violent and comes with a peculiar textual difficulty: the two final stanzas, which unexpectedly reveal the poet's hymn to war to be a love poem as well, are omitted in many manuscripts. In fact, though all the stanzas seem genuine, no one manuscript contains them all. Textual problems of this sort plague most literature before the advent of printing. The theme of the poem, as it is reconstructed here, seems to be that the violence of men in war will pay off for them in the fields of love. The crude assumptions underlying "romantic" love have seldom been so frankly revealed.

The Countess Beatritz de Die (roughly contemporary with Arnaut and Bertran) provides an example of trobairitz poetry. Frankly erotic and adulterous, this poem also depicts love as an overwhelming force—but note that the Countess is careful to maintain her superior role in the relationship.

In addition to their place in the development of Western attitudes toward love—from Sappho's lyrics, Plato's *Symposium,* and the poems of Catullus and Ovid, through the letters of Heloise, and on through Cavalcanti and Petrarch—these Provençal poems might also be compared with the love songs of ancient Egypt, the biblical *Song of Songs,* the Chinese *Book of Songs,* Arabic and Persian poetry of the Middle Period, Vidyakara's *Treasury of Well-Turned Verse,* and Japanese court poetry—love poems from every age and all parts of the world are well represented in this anthology.

## Arnaut Daniel

*Translated by Frederick Goldin*

### *"To this sweet and pretty air"*

To this sweet and pretty air
I set words that I plane and finish;
and every word will fit well,
once I have passed the file there,
for at once Love polishes and aureates
my song, which proceeds from her,
ruler and guardian of merit.

Each day I am a better man and purer,
for I serve the noblest lady in the world,
and I worship her, I tell you this in the open.
I belong to her from my foot to the top of my head;
and let the cold wind blow,
love raining in my heart
keeps me warm when it winters most.

I hear a thousand masses and pay to have them said,
I burn lights of wax and oil,
so may God give me good luck with her,
for no defense against her does me any good.
When I look at her golden hair,
her soft young spirited body,
if someone gave me Luserna, I'd still love her more.

I love her and seek her out with a heart so full,
I think I am stealing her out of my own hands by too
much wanting,
if a man can lose a thing by loving it well.
For the heart of her submerges
mine and does not abate.
So usurious is her demand,
she gets craftsman and workshop together.

I do not want the empire of Rome,
do not make me pope of it
so that I could not turn back to her
for whom the heart in me burns and breaks apart.
If she does not cure me of this torment
with a kiss before new year's,
she murders me and sends herself to hell.

But this torment I endure
could not make me turn away from loving well,
though it holds me fast in loneliness,
for in this desert I cast my words in rhyme.
I labor in loving more than a man who works the earth,
for the Lord of Moncli did not love
N'Audierna an egg's worth more.

I am Arnaut, who hoards the wind,
and chases the hare on an ox,
and swims against the tide.

## Bertran de Born

*Translated by Frederick Goldin*

### *"I love the joyful time of Easter"*

I love the joyful time of Easter,
that makes the leaves and flowers come forth,
and it pleases me to hear the mirth
of the birds, who make their song
resound through the woods,
and it pleases me to see upon the meadows
tents and pavilions planted,
and I feel a great joy
when I see ranged along the field
knights and horses armed for war.

And it pleases me when the skirmishers
make the people and their baggage run away,
and it pleases me when I see behind them coming
a great mass of armed men together,
and I have pleasure in my heart
when I see strong castles besieged,
the broken ramparts caving in,
and I see the host on the water's edge,
closed in all around by ditches,
with palisades, strong stakes close together.

And I am as well pleased by a lord
when he is first in the attack,
armed, upon his horse, unafraid,
so he makes his men take heart
by his own brave lordliness.

And when the armies mix in battle,
each man should be poised
to follow him, smiling,
for no man is worth a thing
till he has given and gotten blow on blow.

Maces and swords and painted helms,
the useless shields cut through,
we shall see as the fighting starts,
and many vassals together striking,
and wandering wildly,
the unreined horses of the wounded and dead.

And once entered into battle
let every man proud of his birth
think only of breaking arms and heads,
for a man is worth more dead than alive and beaten.

I tell you there is not so much savor
in eating or drinking or sleeping,
as when I hear them scream, "There they are! Let's get
them!"
on both sides, and I hear riderless
horses in the shadows, neighing,
and I hear them scream, "Help! Help!"
and I see them fall among the ditches,
little men and great men on the grass,
and I see fixed in the flanks of the corpses
stumps of lances with silken streamers.

Barons, pawn your castles,
and your villages, and your cities
before you stop making war on one another.

Papiols, gladly go
fast to my Lord Yes-and-No
and tell him he has lived in peace too long.

* * *

## (extra stanzas translated by J.W. Earl)

Love wants a knightly lover,
good with weapons, large in service,
sweet-tongued and a great giver,
who knows what's right to do and say,
outdoors and in,
for a man of his potency.
He should be amusing company,
courtly and pleasing.
A lady who lies with a stud like that
is clean of all her sins.

Worthy countess, everyone says
you're the best who has ever been seen,
or will be, in the world,
the noblest lady, I've heard tell.

Beatrice of high lineage,
lady good in words and deeds,
the spring from whom all goodness flows,
beautiful without peer,
your rich merit has risen so high
it has surpassed all others.

## Countess Beatritz de Die

*Translated by Willis Barnstone*

### *"Lately I've felt a grave concern"*

Lately I've felt a grave concern
over a knight who caused me pain.
For every age I want to make it plain
how this love vanquished me. I burn,
knowing I have been doublecrossed
only because I'd not make love
with him! Dressed or naked I think of
my immense error, and I am lost.

How I would love to hold my knight
a whole night in my naked arms!
I'd give him crazy joy—that harms
no one—a cushion of delight.
For I am happier with him
than Floris was with Blancaflor,
I gave my heart to him, and more:
my mind, my life, my eyes that brim

with light. My handsome, graceful friend,
when will I have you in my power?
If I could lie with you one hour,
one night, kiss you tenderly blind,
know then I would do any deed
to have you in my husband's place.
But one condition you must face:
you must obey my every need.

## Marie de France (late 12th cent.)

*Translated by Robert Hanning and Joan Ferrante*

Despite Marie de France's efforts to guarantee that later generations would know that she, a woman, had written her texts, we do not know exactly who she was. The first woman known to write poetry in French, she was most likely a noblewoman at or near the twelfth-century Norman court of Henry II of England and his queen Eleanor of Aquitaine. Besides the *Lais* (short verse Romances), Marie translated and arranged a collection of *Fables* and wrote a religious dream-vision, *St. Patrick's Purgatory*. The last lines of the *Purgatory* assert Marie's authorship and express her concern that clerks might claim her work for themselves:

> I shall name myself so that it will be remembered;
> Marie is my name, I am of France.
> It may be that many clerks
> will take my labor for themselves.
> I don't want any of them to claim it.

Marie wrote her works in French, which was the language of the twelfth-century English court, but some of her *lais* made their way into English, Old Norse, Middle High German, and Italian translations. She drew the material for her *lais* from popular Breton tales performed by *jongleurs*—singers and storytellers—who traveled from court to court. Although Marie was not the first European author to translate short prose narratives into eloquent verse forms, she may well be the first author who did it with nonclassical material. Since each of Marie's twelve *lais* examines love from a different perspective, the collection as a whole comprises a multifaceted and complex text. Only two of the *lais* are included here, plus a general prologue. Several cultural currents intermingle in these poems: the historical tragedy of Abelard and Heloise, Celtic fantasy (the Bretons were originally from Wales, which, like Ireland, is a Celtic rather than a Germanic country), and the marvelous foreign world of Arabic love poetry.

The *lai* of *Yonec* shows these influences in an especially rich combination. It is a fairy tale of adulterous love that becomes more surreal as it proceeds, with a symbolism so dense as to be an uninterpretable allegory. Near the end of the poem, the heroine walks into an otherworldly City of Love, which is a version of the Celtic *Anwyn* (Otherworld), where her hawk-lover is entombed in an abbey church, evoking the symbolism of Christ (compare the Middle English *Corpus Christi Carol,* pp. 1297–1298). In the tale, amazingly, the church fully endorses their adulterous love.

*Chevrefoil* is the shortest of Marie's *lais* and demonstrates her delicacy and restraint as well as her ability to capture the essence of a story in a single symbol, here the intertwined honeysuckle and hazel. Marie invents an episode in story of the legendary tragic lovers Tristan and Isolde, isolating them in a magical moment when they are convinced that their love will escape tragedy. The reader, of course, knows better—a good example of "dramatic irony" (the reader's knowing something the characters do not). Interestingly, Isolde is never named in the poem.

## Lais

### *Prologue*

Whoever has received knowledge
and eloquence in speech from God
should not be silent or secretive
but demonstrate it willingly.

When a great good is widely heard of,
then, and only then, does it bloom,
and when that good is praised by many,
it has spread its blossoms.
The custom among the ancients—
as Priscian testifies—
was to speak quite obscurely
in the books they wrote,
so that those who were to come after
and study them
might gloss the letter
and supply its significance from their own wisdom.
Philosophers knew this,
they understood among themselves
that the more time they spent,
the more subtle their minds would become
and the better they would know how to keep themselves
from whatever was to be avoided.
He who would guard himself from vice
should study and understand
and begin a weighty work
by which he might keep vice at a distance,
and free himself from great sorrow.
That's why I began to think
about composing some good stories
and translating from Latin to Romance;
but that was not to bring me fame:
too many others have done it.
Then I thought of the *lais* I'd heard.
I did not doubt, indeed I knew well,
that those who first began them
and sent them forth
composed them in order to preserve
adventures they had heard.
I have heard many told;
and I don't want to neglect or forget them.
To put them into word and rhyme
I've often stayed awake.

In your honor, noble King,
who are so brave and courteous,
repository of all joys
in whose heart all goodness takes root,
I undertook to assemble these *lais*
to compose and recount them in rhyme.

In my heart I thought and determined,
sire, that I would present them to you.
If it pleases you to receive them,
you will give me great joy;
I shall be happy forever.
Do not think me presumptuous
if I dare present them to you. . . .

## *Yonec*

Now that I've begun these *lais*
the effort will not stop me;
every adventure that I know
I shall relate in rhyme.
My intention and my desire
is to tell you next of Yonec,
how he was born and how his father
first came to his mother.
The man who fathered Yonec
was called Muldumarec.

There once lived in Brittany
a rich man, old and ancient.
At Caerwent, he was acknowledged
and accepted as lord of the land.
The city sits on the Duelas,
which at one time was open to boats.
The man was very far along in years
but because he possessed a large fortune
he took a wife in order to have children,
who would come after him and be his heirs.
The girl who was given to the rich man
came from a good family;
she was wise and gracious and very beautiful—
for her beauty he loved her very much.
Because she was beautiful and noble
he made every effort to guard her.
He locked her inside his tower
in a great paved chamber.
A sister of his,
who was also old and a widow, without her own lord,
he stationed with his lady
to guard her even more closely.

There were other women, I believe,
in another chamber by themselves,
but the lady never spoke to them
unless the old woman gave her permission.
So he kept her more than seven years—
they never had any children;
she never left that tower,
neither for family nor for friends.
When the lord came to sleep there
no chamberlain or porter
dared enter that room,
not even to carry a candle before the lord.
The lady lived in great sorrow,
with tears and sighs and weeping;
she lost her beauty,
as one does who cares nothing for it,
She would have preferred
death to take her quickly.

It was the beginning of April
when the birds begin their songs.
The lord arose in the morning
and made ready to go to the woods.
He had the old woman get up
and close the door behind him—
she followed his command.
The lord went off with his men.
The old woman carried a psalter
from which she intended to read the psalms.
The lady, awake and in tears,
saw the light of the sun.
She noticed that the old woman
had left the chamber.
She grieved and sighed
and wept and raged:
"I should never have been born!
My fate is very harsh.
I'm imprisoned in this tower
and I'll never leave it unless I die.
What is this jealous old man afraid of
that he keeps me so imprisoned?
He's mad, out of his senses;
always afraid of being deceived.
I can't even go to church
or hear God's service.

If I could speak to people
and enjoy myself with them
I'd be very gracious to my lord
even if I didn't want to be.
A curse on my family,
and on all the others
who gave me to this jealous man,
who married me to his body.
It's a rough rope that I pull and draw.
He'll never die—
when he should have been baptized
he was plunged instead in the river of hell;
his sinews are hard, his veins are hard,
filled with living blood.
I've often heard
that one could once find
adventures in this land
that brought relief to the unhappy.
Knights might find young girls
to their desire, noble and lovely;
and ladies find lovers
so handsome, courtly, brave, and valiant
that they could not be blamed,
and no one else would see them.
If that might be or ever was,
if that has ever happened to anyone,
God, who has power over everything,
grant me my wish in this."
When she'd finished her lament,
she saw, through a narrow window,
the shadow of a great bird.
She didn't know what it was.
It flew into the chamber;
its feet were banded; it looked like a hawk
of five or six moultings.
It alighted before the lady.
When it had been there awhile
and she'd stared hard at it,
it became a handsome and noble knight.
The lady was astonished;
her blood went cold, she trembled,
she was frightened—she covered her head.
The knight was very courteous,
he spoke first:
"Lady," he said, "don't be afraid.

The hawk is a noble bird,
although its secrets are unknown to you.
Be reassured
and accept me as your love.
That," he said, "is why I came here.
I have loved you for a long time,
I've desired you in my heart.
Never have I loved any woman but you
nor shall I ever love another,
yet I couldn't have come to you
or left my own land
had you not asked for me.
But now I can be your love."
The lady was reassured;
she uncovered her head and spoke.
She answered the knight,
saying she would take him as her lover
if he believed in God,
and if their love was really possible.
For he was of great beauty.
Never in her life
had she seen so handsome a knight—
nor would she ever.
"My lady," he said, "you are right.
I wouldn't want you to feel
guilt because of me,
or doubt or suspicion.
I do believe in the creator
who freed us from the grief
that Adam, our father, led us into
when he bit into the bitter apple.
He is, will be, and always was
the life and light of sinners.
If you don't believe me
send for your chaplain.
Say that you've suddenly been taken ill
and that you desire the service
that God established in this world
for the healing of sinners.
I shall take on your appearance
to receive the body of our lord God,
and I'll recite my whole credo for you.
You will never doubt my faith again."
She answered that she was satisfied.
He lay beside her on the bed
but he didn't try to touch her,
to embrace her or to kiss her.

Meanwhile, the old woman had returned.
She found the lady awake
and told her it was time to get up,
she would bring her clothes.
The lady said she was ill,
that the old woman should send for the chaplain
and bring him to her quickly—
she very much feared she was dying.
The old woman said, "Be patient,
my lord has gone to the woods.
No one may come in here but me."
The lady was very upset;
she pretended to faint.
When the other saw her, she was frightened;
she unlocked the door of the chamber
and sent for the priest.
He came as quickly as he could,
bringing the *corpus domini.*
The knight received it,
drank the wine from the chalice.
Then the chaplain left
and the old woman closed the doors.
The lady lay beside her love—
there was never a more beautiful couple.
When they had laughed and played
and spoken intimately,
the knight took his leave
to return to his land.
She gently begged him
to come back often.
"Lady," he said, "whenever you please,
I will be here within the hour.
But you must make certain
that we're not discovered.
This old woman will betray us,
night and day she will spy on us.
She will perceive our love,
and tell her lord about it.
If that happens,
if we are betrayed,
I won't be able to escape.
I shall die."
With that the knight departed,
leaving his love in great joy.
In the morning she rose restored;
she was happy all week.
Her body had now become precious to her,

she completely recovered her beauty.
Now she would rather remain here
than look for pleasure elsewhere.
She wanted to see her love all the time
and enjoy herself with him.
As soon as her lord departed,
night or day, early or late,
she had him all to her pleasure.
God, let their joy endure!
Because of the great joy she felt,
because she could see her love so often,
her whole appearance changed.
But her lord was clever.
In his heart he sensed
that she was not what she had been.
He suspected his sister.
He questioned her one day,
saying he was astonished
that the lady now dressed with care.
He asked her what it meant.
The old woman said she didn't know—
no one could have spoken to her,
she had no lover or friend—
it was only that she was now more willing
to be alone than before.
His sister, too, had noticed the change.
Her lord answered:
"By my faith," he said, "I think that's so.
But you must do something for me.
In the morning, when I've gotten up
and you have shut the doors,
pretend you are going out
and leave her lying there alone.
Then hide yourself in a safe place,
watch her and find out
what it is, and where it comes from,
that gives her such great joy."
With that plan they separated.
Alas, how hard it is to protect yourself
from someone who wants to trap you,
to betray and deceive you!

Three days later, as I heard the story,
the lord pretended to go away.
He told his wife the story
that the king had sent for him by letter

but that he would return quickly.
He left the chamber and shut the door.
The old woman got up,
went behind a curtain;
from there she could hear and see
whatever she wanted to know.
The lady lay in bed but did not sleep,
she longed for her love.
He came without delay,
before any time had passed.
They gave each other great joy
with word and look
until it was time to rise—
he had to go.
But the old woman watched him,
saw how he came and went.
She was quite frightened
when she saw him first a man and then a bird.
When the lord returned—
he hadn't gone very far—
she told him and revealed
the truth about the knight
and the lord was troubled by it.
But he was quick to invent
a way to kill the knight.
He had great spikes of iron forged,
their tips sharpened—
no razor on earth could cut better.
When he had them all prepared
and pronged on all sides,
he set them in the window—
close together and firmly placed—
through which the knight passed
when he visited the lady.
God, he doesn't know what treachery
the villains are preparing.
The next day in the morning
the lord rose before dawn
and said he was going hunting.
The old woman saw him to the door
and then went back to bed
for day was not yet visible.
The lady awoke and waited
for the one she loved faithfully;
she said he might well come now
and be with her at leisure.

As soon as she asked,
he came without delay.
He flew into the window,
but the spikes were there.
One wounded him in his breast—
out rushed the red blood.
He knew he was fatally wounded;
he pulled himself free and entered the room.
He alighted on the bed, in front of the lady,
staining the bedclothes with blood.
She saw the blood and the wound
in anguish and horror.
He said, "My sweet love,
I lose my life for love of you.
I told you it would happen,
that your appearance would kill us."
When she heard that, she fainted;
for a short while she lay as if dead.
He comforted her gently,
said that grief would do no good,
but that she was pregnant with his child.
She would have a son, brave and strong,
who would comfort her;
she would call him Yonec.
He would avenge both of them
and kill their enemy.
But he could remain no longer
for his wound was bleeding badly.
He left in great sorrow.
She followed him with loud cries.
She leapt out a window—
it's a wonder that she wasn't killed,
for it was at least twenty feet high
where she made her leap,
naked beneath her gown.
She followed the traces of blood
that flowed from the knight
onto the road.
She followed that road and kept to it
until she came to a hill.
In the hill there was an opening,
red with his blood.
She couldn't see anything beyond it
but she was sure
that her love had gone in there.

She entered quickly.
She found no light
but she kept to the right road
until it emerged from the hill
into a beautiful meadow.
When she found the grass there wet with blood,
she was frightened.
She followed the traces through the meadow
and saw a city not far away.
The city was completely surrounded by walls.
There was no house, no hall or tower,
that didn't seem entirely of silver.
The buildings were very rich.
Going toward the town there were marshes,
forests, and enclosed fields.
On the other side, toward the castle,
a stream flowed all around,
where ships arrived—
there were more than three hundred sails.
The lower gate was open;
the lady entered the city,
still following the fresh blood
through the town to the castle.
No one spoke to her,
she met neither man nor woman.
When she came to the palace courtyard,
she found it covered with blood.
She entered a lovely chamber
where she found a knight sleeping.
She did not know him, so she went on
into another larger chamber.
There she found nothing but a bed
with a knight sleeping on it;
she kept going.
She entered the third chamber
and on that bed she found her love.
The feet of the bed were all of polished gold,
I couldn't guess the value of the bedclothes;
the candles and the chandeliers,
which were lit night and day,
were worth the gold of an entire city.
As soon as she saw him
she recognized the knight.
She approached, frightened,
and fell fainting over him.

He, who greatly loved her, embraced her,
lamenting his misfortune again and again.
When she recovered from her faint
he comforted her gently.
"Sweet friend, for God's sake, I beg you,
go away! Leave this place!
I shall die within the day,
there will be great sorrow here,
and if you are found
you will be hurt.
Among my people it will be well known
that they have lost me because of my love for you.
I am disturbed and troubled for you."
The lady answered: "Love,
I would rather die with you
than suffer with my lord.
If I go back to him he'll kill me."
The knight reassured her,
gave her a ring,
and explained to her
that, as long as she kept it,
her lord would not remember
anything that had happened—
he would imprison her no longer.
He gave her his sword
and then made her swear
no man would ever possess it,
that she'd keep it for their son.
When the son had grown and become
a brave and valiant knight,
she would go to a festival,
taking him and her lord with her.
They would come to an abbey.
There, beside a tomb,
they would hear the story of his death,
how he was wrongfully killed.
There she would give her son the sword.
The adventure would be recited to him,
how he was born and who his father was;
then they'd see what he would do.
When he'd told her and shown her everything,
he gave her a precious robe
and told her to put it on.
Then he sent her away.
She left carrying the ring
and the sword—they comforted her.
She had not gone half a mile

from the gate of the city
when she heard the bells ring
and the mourning begin in the castle,
and in her sorrow
she fainted four times.
When she recovered from the faints
she made her way to the hill.
She entered it, passed through it,
and returned to her country.
There with her lord
she lived many days and years.
He never accused her of that deed,
never insulted or abused her.
Her son was born and nourished,
protected and cherished.
They named him Yonec.
In all the kingdom you couldn't find
one so handsome, brave, or strong,
so generous, so munificent.
When he reached the proper age,
he was made a knight.
Hear now what happened
in that very year.
To the feast of St. Aaron,
celebrated in Caerleon
and in many other cities,
the lord had been summoned
to come with his friends,
according to the custom of the land,
and to bring his wife and his son,
all richly attired.
So it was; they went.
But they didn't know the way;
they had a boy with them
who guided them along the right road
until they came to a castle—
none more beautiful in all the world.
Inside, there was an abbey
of very religious people.
The boy who was guiding them to the festival
housed them there.
In the abbot's chamber
they were well served and honored.
Next day they went to hear Mass
before they departed,
but the abbot went to speak to them
to beg them to stay

so he could show them the dormitory,
the chapter house, and the refectory.
And since they were comfortable there,
the lord agreed to stay.
That day, after they had dined,
they went to the workshops.
On their way, they passed the chapter house,
where they found a huge tomb
covered with a cloth of embroidered silk,
a band of precious gold running from one side to the other.
At the head, the feet, and at the sides
burned twenty candles.
The chandeliers were pure gold,
the censers amethyst,
which through the day perfumed
that tomb, to its great honor.
They asked and inquired
of people from that land
whose tomb it was,
what man lay there.
The people began to weep
and, weeping, to recount
that it was the best knight
the strongest, the most fierce,
the most handsome and the best loved,
that had ever lived.
"He was king of this land;
no one was ever so courtly.
At Caerwent he was discovered
and killed for the love of a lady.
Since then we have had no lord,
but have waited many days,
just as he told and commanded us,
for the son the lady bore him."
When the lady heard that news,
she called aloud to her son.
"Fair son," she said, "you hear
how God has led us to this spot.
Your father, whom this old man murdered,
lies here in this tomb.
Now I give and commend his sword to you.
I have kept it a long time for you."
Then she revealed, for all to hear,
that the man in the tomb was the father and this was his son,
and how he used to come to her,
how her lord had betrayed him—
she told the truth.

Then she fainted over the tomb
and, in her faint, she died.
She never spoke again.
When her son saw that she had died,
he cut off his stepfather's head.
Thus with his father's sword
he avenged his mother's sorrow.
When all this had happened,
when it became known through the city,
they took the lady with great honor
and placed her in the coffin.
Before they departed
they made Yonec their lord.

Long after, those who heard this adventure
composed a lay about it,
about the pain and the grief
that they suffered for love.

## *Chevrefoil (The Honeysuckle)*

I should like very much
to tell you the truth
about the *lai* men call *Chevrefoil*—
why it was composed and where it came from.
Many have told and recited it to me
and I have found it in writing,
about Tristan and the queen
and their love that was so true,
that brought them much suffering
and caused them to die the same day.
King Mark was annoyed,
angry at his nephew Tristan;
he exiled Tristan from his land
because of the queen whom he loved.
Tristan returned to his own country,
South Wales, where he was born,
he stayed a whole year;
he couldn't come back.
Afterward he began to expose himself
to death and destruction.
Don't be surprised at this:
for one who loves very faithfully
is sad and troubled
when he cannot satisfy his desires.
Tristan was sad and worried,
so he set out from his land.

He traveled straight to Cornwall,
where the queen lived,
and entered the forest all alone—
he didn't want anyone to see him;
he came out only in the evening
when it was time to find shelter.
He took lodging that night,
with peasants, poor people.
He asked them for news
of the king—what he was doing.
They told him they had heard
that the barons had been summoned by ban.
They were to come to Tintagel
where the king wanted to hold his court;
at Pentecost they would all be there,
there'd be much joy and pleasure,
and the queen would be there too.
Tristan heard and was very happy;
she would not be able to go there
without his seeing her pass.
The day the king set out,
Tristan also came to the woods
by the road he knew
their assembly must take.
He cut a hazel tree in half,
then he squared it.
When he had prepared the wood,
he wrote his name on it with his knife.
If the queen noticed it—
and she should be on the watch for it,
for it had happened before
and she had noticed it then—
she'd know when she saw it,
that the piece of wood had come from her love.
This was the message of the writing
that he had sent to her:
he had been there a long time,
had waited and remained
to find out and to discover
how he could see her,
for he could not live without her.
With the two of them it was just
as it is with the honeysuckle
that attaches itself to the hazel tree:
when it has wound and attached
and worked itself around the trunk,

the two can survive together;
but if someone tries to separate them,
the hazel dies quickly
and the honeysuckle with it.
"Sweet love, so it is with us:
You cannot live without me, nor I without you."
The queen rode along;
she looked at the hillside
and saw the piece of wood; she knew what it was,
she recognized all the letters.
The knights who were accompanying her,
who were riding with her,
she ordered to stop:
she wanted to dismount and rest.
They obeyed her command.
She went far away from her people
and called her girl
Brenguein, who was loyal to her.
She went a short distance from the road;
and in the woods she found him
whom she loved more than any living thing.
They took great joy in each other.
He spoke to her as much as he desired,
she told him whatever she liked.
Then she assured him
that he would be reconciled with the king—
for it weighed on him
that he had sent Tristan away;
he'd done it because of the accusation.
Then she departed, she left her love,
but when it came to the separation,
they began to weep.
Tristan went to Wales,
to wait until his uncle sent for him.
For the joy that he'd felt
from his love when he saw her,
by means of the stick he inscribed
as the queen had instructed,
and in order to remember the words,
Tristan, who played the harp well,
composed a new *lai* about it.
I shall name it briefly:
in English they call it *Goat's Leaf*
the French call it *Chevrefoil.*
I have given you the truth
about the *lai* that I have told here.

## Two Middle English Lyrics (14th–16th cent.)

These two lyrics are especially beautiful examples of the way in which Christian literature of the later Middle Ages absorbed the imagery of Romance and courtly love. "*Quia amore langueo*" is a phrase taken from the Latin version of the biblical *Song of Songs,* meaning "Because I languish for love." Here we find the phrase used as the refrain in a love song sung by Christ to the human soul, written in the fourteenth century. Christ is portrayed as a wounded knight pleading for the return of his lover. In an extraordinary series of metamorphoses, Christ initially presents himself as the ideal courtly lover; then the wound in his side becomes first a bridal chamber, then a cradle where he, now a mother, nurses his baby, the soul. The image of Christ as mother is not uncommon in the later Middle Ages. The poem has been slightly modernized here.

*The Corpus Christi Carol* is among the most haunting lyrics that have come down to us from this period. A carol is a repetitive folksong with a refrain after each stanza; in this case, the lullaby refrain is actually sung after each couplet. Even in the Middle Ages, carols were associated with Christmas, which accounts for the lullaby motif—but here the baby Jesus appears as already dead and laid in the tomb. There have been three major interpretations of the poem: (1) in a secular folkloric interpretation, it could refer to the Arthurian legend of the Grail, with the wounded knight being the Fisher King (compare T.S. Eliot's *The Waste Land,* pp. 2173–2181); (2) in a religious interpretation, the knight would be Christ (as in the previous poem) and the weeping woman his mother—a *pietà*—and the poem would concern the presence of Christ's body in the Eucharist, an important theological issue of the period; (3) as a political allegory, the poem might refer to the marriage of Henry VIII to Anne Boleyn and the imprisoning of the popular Catholic queen Catherine of Aragon (whose symbol was the falcon). The poem survives only in an early sixteenth-century manuscript, which suggests it probably bore the third of these meanings, at that time at least. All these meanings are probably present in the poem simultaneously—but it still remains strangely mysterious. Compare these two poems with Marie de France's *Yonec* (pp. 1279–1291), in which many of the same symbols appear.

## *Quia Amore Langueo*

In the vale of restless mind
I sought in mountain and in meed,
Trusting a true-love for to find.
Upon a hill then took I heed,
A voice I heard (and near I yede), [*went*]
In great dolor complaining so—
"See, dear soul, my sides bleed,
    Quia amore langueo." [*because I languish for love*]

Upon this mount I found a tree,
Under this tree a man sitting;

From head to foot wounded was he,
His heart's blood I saw bleeding,
A seemly man to be a king,
A gracious face to look unto.
I asked him how he had paining,
He said "Quia amore langueo."

"I am true-love that false was never;
My sister, man's soul, I loved her thus.
Because I would in no wise dissever,
I left my kingdom glorious.
I purveyed her a palace full precious;
She fled, I followed, I loved her so
That I suffered these pains piteous,
Quia amore langueo.

"My fair love, and my spouse bright,
I saved her from beating, and she hath me beat;
I clothed her in grace and heavenly light,
This bloody surcoat she hath on me set.
For longing love I will not let— [*stop*]
Sweet strokes be these, lo!
I have loved ever as I hett, [*promised*]
Quia amore langueo.

I crowned her with bliss, and she me with thorn,
I led her to chamber, and she me to die;
I brought her to worship, and she me to scorn,
I did her reverence, and she me villainy.
To love who loveth is no mastery,
Her hate made never my love her foe—
Ask then no more questions why,
Quia amore langueo.

Look unto my hands, man!
These gloves were given me when I her sought;
They be not white, but red and wan,
Embroidered with blood (my spouse them bought!).
They will not off—I leave them nought!
I woo her with them whereever she go.
These hands full friendly for her fought,
Quia amore langueo.

"Marvel not, man, though I sit still—
My love hath shod me wonder straight.
She buckled my feet, as was her will,

With sharp nails (well thou may'st wait!).
In my love was never dis-sate,
For all my members I have opened her to;
My body I made her heart's bait,
Quia amore langueo.

"In my side I have made her nest—
Look in me how wide a wound is here!
This is her chamber, here shall she rest,
That she and I may sleep in fere, [*company*]
Here shall she wash, if any filth were,
Here is succour for all her woe.
Come if she will, she shall have cheer,
Quia amore langueo.

"I will abide till she be ready,
I will her sue if she say nay;
If she be reckless, I will be ready,
If she be dangerous, I will her pray.
If she do weep, then bide I nay. [*I will not delay*]
Mine arms be spread to clipp her to. [*embrace*]
Cry once, I come—now soul, assaye!
Quia amore langueo.

"I sit on a hill for to see far,
I look to the vale, my spouse I see;
Now runs she awayward, now cometh she near,
Yet from my eye-sight she may not be.
Some wait their prey, to make her flee—
I run before to chastize her foe.
Recover, my soul, again to me,
Quia amore langueo.

"My sweet spouse, will we go play?
Apples be ripe in my garden;
I shall clothe thee in new array,
Thy meat shall be milk, honey and wine.
Now, dear soul, let us go dine,
Thy sustenance is in my crippe, lo! [*purse*]
Tarry not now, fair spouse mine,
Quia amore langueo.

"If thou be foul, I shall make clean,
If thou be sick, I shall thee heal;
If thou aught mourn, I shall bemene. [*comfort*]
Spouse, why will thou naught with me deal?

Thou foundest never love so leal. [*true*]
What wilt thou, soul, that I shall do?
I may of unkindness thee appeal,
Quia amore langueo.

"What shall I do now with my spouse?
Abide I will her gentleness,
Would she look once out of her house
Of fleshly affections and uncleanness!
Her bed is made, her bolster is in bliss,
Her chamber is chosen—such are no more!
Look out at the windows of kindness,
Quia amore langueo.

"My spouse is in her chamber, hold your peace!
Make no noise, but let her sleep.
My babe shall suffer no disease;
I may not hear my dear child weep.
For with my pappe I shall her keep. [*breast*]
No wonder though I tend her so;
This hole in my side had been never so deep
But quia amore langueo.

"Long and love thou never so high,
Yet is my love more than thine may be.
Thou gladdest, thou weepest, I sit thee by,
Yet might thou, spouse, look once at me.
Spouse, should I always feed thee
With child's meat? Nay, love, not so!
I prove thy love with adversity,
Quia amore langueo.

"Wax not weary, mine own dear wife!
What mede is aye to live in comfort? [*reward*]
For in tribulation I run more rife
Ofter times than in disport—
In wealth, in woe, ever I support.
Then dear soul, go never me fro! [*from*]
Thy mede is marked when thou art mort, [*dead*]
Quia amore langueo."

## *The Corpus Christi Carol*

Lully, lullay, lully, lullay,
The faucon hath borne my make away. [*mate*]

He bare him up, he bare him down,
He bare him into an orchard brown.

In that orchard there was an hall
That was hanged with purple and pall.

And in that hall ther was a bed:
It was hanged with gold so red.

And in that bed ther lith a knight,
His woundes bleeding by day and night.

By that beddes side ther kneeleth a may,
And she weepeth both night and day.

And by that beddes side ther standeth a stoon: [*stone*]
*Corpus Christi* writen thereon.

## Marco Polo (1254–1324)

*Translated by Ronald Latham*

Marco Polo was a Venetian merchant who spent some twenty years traveling through Central and East Asia. His account of those journeys, *The Travels,* was much read, and it inspired later explorers such as Christopher Columbus, who went in search of the fabulous East that Marco Polo had described. It is possible that left to his own devices, Marco Polo would never have produced a book at all. In 1298, just four years after his return from Asia to Italy, he was imprisoned in Genoa as a result of a conflict between that city and his native Venice. While in prison, he told his adventures to a fellow prisoner named Rustichello, who happened to be a Romance writer of some popularity. Rustichello recorded and no doubt embellished Marco Polo's account. The original manuscript of *The Travels* was probably written in French, but it quickly appeared in Italian, Latin, and even Irish.

In order to appreciate *The Travels,* one must keep several facts in mind. First of all, Marco Polo's account is a memory, sometimes of events that had occurred more than twenty years earlier, which then passed through the retelling of a Romance writer. Second, he left Europe at the age of sixteen and spent twenty years in Asia—that is, he experienced Asia while an impressionable young man. Finally, Marco Polo was a merchant who possessed a keen eye for the material world and for local customs, but he had very little interest in, or understanding of, high culture. Whether as the result of Rustichello's fictionalizing or of his own youthful enthusiasm, Marco Polo's report is filled with superlatives, a characteristic that won him the nickname of "*Il milione,*" a term we might translate loosely as "the exaggerator." The Prologue to *The Travels* anticipates skepticism about his reports of "the finest," "the largest," or "the best" and assures us that the book "contains nothing but the truth." Contrary to the arguments of some skeptical readers, Marco Polo most likely did visit China. Details in *The Travels* are too rich and too amply verified from other sources to allow us to discount its accuracy entirely. There are, however, curious omissions: there is no mention of the Great Wall, of tea drinking, of the peculiar nature of Chinese writing, or of the bound feet of Chinese women—the latter despite the author's considerable interest in women and Chinese sexual practices. But whatever the precise mixture of fact and fiction in *The Travels,* it stands as a masterpiece of travel literature, as does Ibn Battutah's *Travels* (pp. 849–866) written later. The section called "The Road to Cathay," included here, is filled with life and fascinating detail. The narrator also provides the modern reader with great insight into the perceptions and prejudices of a European Christian who finds himself journeying among "those who worship Mahomet," "idolaters," and a whole host of people with customs radically different from his own.

## The Travels

### *from Ch. 2: The Road to Cathay*

When the traveller leaves this castle, he rides through a fine plain and a fine valley and along fine hillsides, where there is rich herbage, fine pasturage, fruit in plenty, and no lack of anything. Armies are prone to loiter here because of the abundance of supplies. This country extends for fully six days' journey and contains villages and towns whose inhabitants worship Mahomet. Sometimes the traveller encounters stretches of desert fifty or sixty miles in extent, in which there is no water to be found. Men must carry it with them; the beasts go without drinking till they have come out of the desert into the places where they find water.

After these six days he reaches a city called Shibarghan, plentifully stocked with everything needful. Here are found the best melons in the world in very great quantity, which they dry in this manner: they cut them all round in slices like strips of leather, then put them in the sun to dry, when they become sweeter than honey. And you must know that they are an article of commerce and find a ready sale through all the country round. There are also vast quantities of game, both beasts and birds. We will now leave this city and tell you of another whose name is Balkh.

Balkh is a splendid city of great size. It used to be much greater and more splendid; but the Tartars and other invaders have sacked and ravaged it. For I can tell you that there used to be many fine palaces and mansions of marble, which are still to be seen, but shattered now and in ruins. It was in this city, according to local report, that Alexander took to wife the daughter of Darius. The inhabitants worship Mahomet. And you should know that this city, which marks the limit of the Tartar lordship of the Levant, stands on the east-north-easterly frontier of Persia.

Leaving this city, we shall begin our account of another land called Talikhan. When the traveller leaves Balkh, he rides fully twelve days' journey towards the east-north-east without finding any habitation, because the people have all fled to mountain fastnesses for fear of the bandits and invaders who used to molest them. The country has water enough and game enough, and also lions. Food is not to be found in all this twelve days' journey; so those who pass this way must carry food with them for their horses as well as for themselves.

At the end of these twelve days the traveller finds a town called Talikhan, where there is a great corn-market. It stands in very fine country, and the mountains to the south of it are very large and are all made of salt. Men come from all the country round, for thirty days' journey, to fetch this salt, which is the best in the world. It is so hard that it cannot be got except with a stout iron pick. And I assure you that it is so plentiful that it would suffice for all the world to the end of time. There are also mountains abounding in almonds and pistachios, which are marketed on a big scale.

Leaving this city, the traveller proceeds for three days towards the east-north-east, finding fine country all the way, thickly peopled and rich in fruits, grain, and vines. The inhabitants worship Mahomet. They are an ill-conditioned and murderous folk. They devote a great deal of their time to tippling; for they have an excellent boiled wine, to which they are much addicted. They wear nothing on the head but a cord ten palms in length, which they wind round it. They are very good huntsmen and catch any amount of game. They wear no clothes but the skins of the beasts they catch, which they cure and make into clothing and footwear. They all know how to cure the skins of these beasts.

At the end of the three days' journey lies a city called Ishkasham, which is ruled by a count; his other cities and towns are in the mountains. Through the midst of this city flows a river of considerable size. In this district there are a lot of porcupines. When hunters set their dogs on them in hopes of a kill, the porcupines curl up and then shoot out the quills with which their backs and flanks are armed and so wound the dogs in several places.

This city is in a big province of the same name, which has a language of its own. The countryfolk, who are herdsmen, live among the mountains, where they provide themselves with fine and spacious abodes; these are caves, which are easily made because the mountains are of earth.

When he leaves this city, the traveller goes three days' journey without finding habitation or food or drink; he must take his own provisions with him, but there is enough grass for horses. After this he reaches the province of Badakhshan which I will describe to you.

Badakhshan or Balashan is a country whose inhabitants worship Mahomet and have a language of their own. It is a large kingdom, twelve days' journey in length, ruled by hereditary kings of a lineage descended from King Alexander and the daughter of Darius, the Great King of Persia. In honour of Alexander the Great, all its kings still bear the title Zulkarnein, the Saracen equivalent of our name Alexander.

In this country originate the precious stones called balass rubies, of great beauty and value. They are dug out of rocks among the mountains by tunnelling to great depths, as is done by miners working a vein of silver. They are found in one particular mountain called Sighinan. And I would have you know that they are mined only for the king and by his orders; no one else could go to the mountain and dig for these gems without incurring instant death, and it is forbidden under pain of death and forfeiture to export them out of the kingdom. The king sends them by his own men to other kings and princes and great lords, to some as tribute, to others as a token of amity; and some he barters for gold and silver. This he does so that these balass rubies may retain their present rarity and value. If he let other men mine them and export them throughout the world, there would be so many of them on the market that the price would fall and they would cease to be so precious. That is why he has imposed such a heavy penalty on anyone exporting them without authority.

And it is a fact that in this same country, in another mountain, are found the stones from which is made lapis lazuli, of the finest quality in the world. These stones originate among the mountains as a vein like the veins of other minerals. There are also mountains here in which are found veins yielding silver, copper, and lead in great abundance.

This district, and the whole country, is very cold. You should know that very good horses are bred here. They are great runners and are not shod with iron, though they are in constant use on mountain trails. There used to be horses in this country that were directly descended from Alexander's horse Bucephalus out of mares that had conceived from him and they were all born like him with a horn on the forehead. This breed was entirely in the possession of one of the king's uncles, who, because he refused to let the king have any, was put to death by him. Thereupon his wife, to avenge her husband's death, destroyed the whole breed, and so it became extinct. These mountains are also the home of saker falcons—fine birds and good fliers—and of lanner falcons. They abound in game, both beast and bird, and in wild sheep. The sheep sometimes roam in flocks of four to six hundred; and however many of them are taken, their numbers never grow less. There is good wheat here, and barley without a husk. There is no olive oil, but oil is made of sesame and nuts.

This kingdom has many narrow passes and natural fortresses, so that the inhabitants are not afraid of any invader breaking in to molest them. Their cities and towns are built on mountain tops or sites of great natural strength. It is a characteristic of these mountains that they are of immense height, so that for a man to climb from the bottom to the top is a full day's journey, from dawn till dusk. On the top are wide plateaux, with a lush growth of grass and trees and copious springs of the purest water, which pour down over the crags like rivers into the valley below. In these streams are found trout and other choice fish. On the mountain tops the air is so pure and so salubrious that if a man living in the cities and houses built in the adjoining valleys falls sick of a fever, whether tertian, quartan, or hectic, he has only to go up into the mountains, and a few days rest will banish the malady and restore him to health. Messer Marco vouches for this from his own experience. Two or three of the mountains consist largely of sulphur, and springs of sulphurous water issue from them.

The people here are good archers and keen huntsmen and most of them wear costumes of skin, because they are very short of cloth. The ladies of the nobility and gentry wear trousers, such as I will describe to you. There are some ladies who in one pair of trousers or breeches put anything up to a hundred ells of cotton cloth, folded in pleats. This is to give the impression that they have plump hips, because their menfolk delight in plumpness.

Ten days' journey south of Badakhshan is a country called Pashai. The inhabitants, who have brown skins and speak a language of their own, are idolaters. They are adept in enchantment and diabolic arts. The men wear ear-rings and brooches of gold and silver and pearls and precious stones in profusion. They are very crafty folk and artful in their own way. The climate is very hot. The stock diet is flesh and rice.

So much for Pashai. Let us deal next with another country, distant some seven days' journey to the south-east, whose name is Kashmir.

The people of Kashmir are also idolaters, speaking a language of their own. Their knowledge of devilish enchantments is something marvellous. They make their idols speak. They change the weather by enchantment and bring on thick darkness. They accomplish such marvels by magic and craft that no one who has not seen them could believe them. I may say that they are the past masters of idolatry and it is from them that idols are derived.

From this country there is a route leading to the Indian Sea. The inhabitants are brown-skinned and thin; the women are very beautiful, with such beauty as goes with a brown skin. Their diet is flesh and rice. They enjoy a temperate climate, without extremes of heat and cold. They have cities and towns in plenty, as well as forests and deserts and fastnesses so strong that they have no fear of any foe. They maintain their independence under their own kings, who are the upholders of justice. They have hermits according to their own usage, who dwell in their hermitages, practising strict abstinence in eating and drinking and avoidance of all unchastity and taking the utmost pains to commit no sin that is contrary to their law. They are accounted very holy by their own people, and I assure you that they live to a great age; and this avoidance of sin is all exercised for love of their idols. They also have abbeys and monasteries in plenty of their own faith, where the brethren live an austere life and wear tonsures like Dominican and Franciscan friars. The men of this country do not kill animals or shed blood; but certain Saracens who live intermingled with them kill their animals to provide them with food. The coral that is exported from our country for sale is sold more here than anywhere else.

We shall now leave this district without going any further, because that would mean entering India, which I do not wish to do at present; on our return journey we shall tell you all about India in due order. We shall therefore retrace our steps as far as the province of Badakhshan, because there is no other route by which we can proceed on our way.

When the traveller leaves Badakhshan, he goes twelve days' journey east-north-east up a river valley belonging to the brother of the lord of Badakhshan, where there are towns and homesteads in plenty, peopled by a warlike race who worship Mahomet. After these twelve days he reaches a country called Wakhan of no great size, for it is three days' journey across every way. The people, who worship Mahomet and speak a language of their own, are doughty warriors. They have no ruler except one whom they call *nona*, that is to say in our language 'count,' and are subject to the lord of Badakhshan. They have wild beasts in plenty and game of all sorts for the chase.

When the traveller leaves this place, he goes three days' journey towards the north-east, through mountains all the time, climbing so high that this is said to be the highest place in the world. And when he is in this high place, he finds a plain between two mountains, with a lake from which flows a very fine river. Here is the best pasturage in the world; for a lean beast grows fat here in ten days. Wild game of every sort abounds. There are great quantities of wild sheep of huge size. Their horns grow to as much as six palms in length and are never less than three or four. From these horns the shepherds make big bowls from which they feed, and also fences to keep in their flocks. There are also innumerable wolves, which devour many of the wild rams. The horns and bones of the sheep are found in such numbers that men build cairns of them beside the tracks to serve as landmarks to travellers in the snowy season.

This plain, whose name is Pamir, extends fully twelve days' journey. In all these twelve days there is no habitation or shelter, but travellers must take their provisions with them. No birds fly here because of the height and the cold. And I assure you that, because of this great cold, fire is not so bright here nor of the same colour as elsewhere, and food does not cook well.

Now let us pursue our course towards the north-east and east. At the end of this twelve days' journey, the traveller must ride fully forty days more east-north-east, always over mountains and along hillsides and gorges, traversing many rivers and many deserts. And in all this journey he finds no habitation or shelter, but must carry his stock of provisions. This country is called Belor. The inhabitants live very high up in the mountains. They are idolaters and utter savages, living entirely by the chase and dressed in the skins of beasts. They are out and out bad.

We shall now leave this country and tell you of the province of Kashgar, which lies towards the east-north-east.

Kashgar was once a kingdom; but now it is subject to the Great Khan. It has villages and towns in plenty. The biggest city, and the most splendid, is Kashgar. The inhabitants live by trade and industry. They have very fine orchards and vineyards and flourishing estates. Cotton grows here in plenty, besides flax and hemp. The soil is fruitful and productive of all the means of life. This country is the starting-point from which many merchants set out to market their wares all over the world. The folk here are very close-fisted and live very poorly, neither eating well nor drinking well. There are some Nestorian Christians in this country, having their own church and observing their own religion. The inhabitants have a language of their own. The province is five days' journey in extent.

And now to speak of Samarkand, a very large and splendid city lying towards the north-west. It is inhabited by Christians and Saracens. They are subject to the nephew of the Great Khan, who is no friend of his but is often at enmity with him. Let me tell you of a great miracle that occurred in this city.

It happened not long ago that Chaghatai, who was a brother of the

Great Khan and lord of this country and many others, became a Christian. When the Christians of Samarkand saw that their lord was a Christian, they were overjoyed. They built a big church in the city to the honour of St John the Baptist and called by his name. And to make the base of the column which stood in the centre of the church and supported the roof they took a very beautiful stone belonging to the Saracens. After Chaghatai's death, the Saracens, who had always been very resentful about this stone that stood in the Christian church, resolved to take it by force. And this they could easily have done; for they were ten times as many as the Christians. Then some of the leading Saracens went to the church of St John and told the Christians there that they wanted this stone, which had once belonged to them. The Christians promised to give them all they wanted if they would leave the stone, because its removal would do irreparable damage to the church. The Saracens declared that they did not want gold or treasure, but would have the stone at all costs. What need of more words? The government was now in the hands of the Great Khan's nephew; and he ordered the Christians to hand over the stone to the Saracens within two days. When they received this order they were greatly perplexed and did not know what to do. And then the miracle happened. You must know that, when morning came on the day on which the stone was to be handed over, the column that rested on the stone rose up, by the will of our Lord Jesus Christ, to a height of fully three palms and stayed there as firmly supported as if the stone had still been underneath. And from that day onwards the column has remained in this position, and there it still is. And this was, and still is, accounted one of the greatest miracles that have happened in the world.

Let us turn next to the province of Yarkand, five days' journey in extent. The inhabitants follow the law of Mahomet, and there are also some Nestorian Christians. They are subject to the Great Khan's nephew, of whom I have already spoken. It is amply stocked with the means of life, especially cotton. But, since there is nothing here worth mentioning in our book, we shall pass on to Khotan, which lies towards the east-north-east.

Khotan is a province eight days' journey in extent, which is subject to the Great Khan. The inhabitants all worship Mahomet. It has cities and towns in plenty, of which the most splendid, and the capital of the kingdom, bears the same name as the province, Khotan. It is amply stocked with the means of life. Cotton grows here in plenty. It has vineyards, estates, and orchards in plenty. The people live by trade and industry; they are not at all warlike.

Passing on from here we come to the province of Pem, five days' journey in extent, towards the east-north-east. Here too the inhabitants worship Mahomet and are subject to the Great Khan. It has villages and towns in plenty. The most splendid city and the capital of the province is called Pem. There are rivers here in which are found stones called jasper and chalcedony in plenty. There is no lack of the means of life. Cotton is plentiful. The inhabitants live by trade and industry.

The following custom is prevalent among them. When a woman's husband leaves her to go on a journey of more than twenty days, then, as soon as he has left, she takes another husband, and this she is fully entitled to do by local usage. And the men, wherever they go, take wives in the same way.

You should know that all the provinces I have described, from Kashgar to Pem and some way beyond, are provinces of Turkestan.

I will tell you next of another province of Turkestan, lying east-north-east, which is called Charchan. It used to be a splendid and fruitful country, but it has been much devastated by the Tartars. The inhabitants worship Mahomet. There are villages and towns in plenty, and the chief city of the kingdom is Charchan. There are rivers producing jasper and chalcedony, which are exported for sale in Cathay and bring in a good profit; for they are plentiful and of good quality.

All this province is a tract of sand; and so is the country from Khotan to Pem and from Pem to here. There are many springs of bad and bitter water, though in some places the water is good and sweet. When it happens that an army passes through the country, if it is a hostile one, the people take flight with their wives and children and their beasts two or three days' journey into the sandy wastes to places where they know that there is water and they can live with their beasts. And I assure you that no one can tell which way they have gone, because the wind covers their tracks with sand, so that there is nothing to show where they have been, but the country looks as if it had never been traversed by man or beast. That is how they escape from their enemies. But, if it happens that a friendly army passes that way, they merely drive off their beasts, because they do not want to have them seized and eaten; for the armies never pay for what they take. And you should know that, when they harvest their corn, they store it far from any habitation, in certain caves among these wastes, for fear of the armies; and from these stores they bring home what they need month by month.

After leaving Charchan, the road runs for fully five days through sandy wastes, where the water is bad and bitter, except in a few places where it is good and sweet; and there is nothing worth noting in our book. At the end of the five days' journey towards the east-north-east, is a city which stands on the verge of the Great Desert. It is here that men take in provisions for crossing the desert. Let us move on accordingly and proceed with our narrative.

The city I have mentioned, which stands at the point where the traveller enters the Great Desert, is a big city called Lop, and the desert is called the Desert of Lop. The city is subject to the Great Khan, and the inhabitants worship Mahomet. I can tell you that travellers who intend to cross the desert rest in this town for a week to refresh themselves and their beasts. At the end of the week they stock up with a month's provisions for themselves and their beasts. Then they leave the town and enter the desert.

This desert is reported to be so long that it would take a year to go from end to end; and at the narrowest point it takes a month to cross it. It consists entirely of mountains and sand and valleys. There is nothing at all to eat. But I can tell you that after travelling a day and a night you find drinking water—not enough water to supply a large company, but enough for fifty or a hundred men with their beasts. And all the way through the desert you must go for a day and a night before you find water. And I can tell you that in three or four places you find the water bitter and brackish; but at all the other watering-places, that is, twenty-eight in all, the water is good. Beasts and birds there are none, because they find nothing to eat. But I assure you that one thing is found here, and that a very strange one, which I will relate to you.

The truth is this. When a man is riding by night through this desert and something happens to make him loiter and lose touch with his companions, by dropping asleep or for some other reason, and afterwards he wants to rejoin them, then he hears spirits talking in such a way that they seem to be his companions. Sometimes, indeed, they even hail him by name. Often these voices make him stray from the path, so that he never finds it again. And in this way many travellers have been lost and have perished. And sometimes in the night they are conscious of a noise like the clatter of a great cavalcade of riders away from the road; and, believing that these are some of their own company, they go where they hear the noise and, when day breaks, find they are victims of an illusion and in an awkward plight. And there are some who, in crossing this desert, have seen a host of men coming towards them and, suspecting that they were robbers, have taken flight; so, having left the beaten track and not knowing how to return to it, they have gone hopelessly astray. Yes, and even by daylight men hear these spirit voices, and often you fancy you are listening to the strains of many instruments, especially drums, and the clash of arms. For this reason bands of travellers make a point of keeping very close together. Before they go to sleep they set up a sign pointing in the direction in which they have to travel. And round the necks of all their beasts they fasten little bells, so that by listening to the sound they may prevent them from straying off the path.

That is how they cross the desert, with all the discomfort of which you have heard. Now that I have told you all about it, let us take our leave of it and speak of the provinces you find when you emerge from it.

When the traveller has ridden for these thirty days of which I have spoken across the desert, he reaches a city called Sa-chau, lying towards the east-north-east, which is subject to the Great Khan. It lies in a province called Tangut, whose inhabitants are all idolaters, except that there are some Turks who are Nestorian Christians and also some Saracens. The idolaters speak a language of their own. They do not live by trade, but on the profit of the grain which they harvest from the soil. They have many abbeys and monasteries, all full of idols of various forms to which they make sacrifices and do great honour and reverence.

You must know that all the men here who have children rear a sheep in honour of the idols; and at the new year, or on the feast of their particular idol, those who have reared the sheep bring it with their children before the idol, and both they and the children perform a solemn act of devotion. This done, they have the sheep cooked whole. Then they bring it before the idol with great reverence and leave it there till they have recited their service and their prayer to the idol to save their children; and they say that the idols eat the substance of the flesh. When they have done this, they take the flesh that has lain before the idol and carry it home, or wherever else they may wish, and send for their kinsfolk and eat it with great reverence and great festivity. When they have eaten the flesh, they collect the bones and preserve them very carefully in a chest. The priests of the idols, however, have the head, feet, entrails and fleece and part of the flesh.

You should know also, what is true of all the idolaters in the world, that when they die their bodies are cremated. When the dead man is being carried from his house to the place where he is to be cremated, then at some point on the route his kinsfolk have erected in the middle of the road a wooden house draped with silk and cloth of gold. On arriving in front of this house, thus adorned, the cortège halts; and the mourners fling down wine and food in plenty before the dead. This they do because they say that he will be received with like honour in the next world. When he is brought to the place where he is to be cremated, his kindred provide images cut out of paper representing horses and camels and pieces of money as big as bezants; and all these they burn with the body. And they say that in the next world the dead will have as many slaves and beasts and coins as the paper images that are burnt. Lastly, let me tell you that when a body is being taken to the pyre, all the instruments in the land go in front of it making music. And all this is done in proportion to the rank of the deceased and the requirements of his station.

Now let me tell you something else. When one of these idolaters is dead, they send for their astrologer and tell him the nativity of the deceased, that is, the month, day, and hour of his birth. Armed with this knowledge, the astrologer makes his divination by diabolical art and afterwards declares on what day the corpse must be cremated. In some cases he prescribes a delay of a week before cremation, in others of a month, in others of six months. Then the relatives must keep the body in their house for this length of time; for they would never think of burning it till the diviners tell them that the time has come. While the body remains unburnt in the house, they preserve it in this manner. They take a coffin of boards of the thickness of a palm firmly joined together and all splendidly painted, and put the body inside, embalmed with camphor and other spices. Then they stop the chinks in the coffin with pitch and lime, so that it does not cause a stench in the house, and cover it with silken shrouds. Meanwhile, so long as the body remains in the house, the relatives, that is the inhabitants of the house, lay a table every day for the deceased and serve food and drink for him just as if he were alive; they set it in front of the coffin and leave it long enough to be eaten, and say that the soul has eaten some of this food. This is how they keep it till the day when they take it away for cremation. And here is another thing that they do. It often happens that these diviners tell the relatives that it is not auspicious to carry the corpse out of the house by way of the door, on the pretext that some star or other power is adverse to this door. Then the relatives have the body carried out by another door or even, on occasion, have the walls broken open and the body carried out through the breach.

All this they do for fear of offending the spirits of the dead. And if it happens that some member of the household meets with some mischance or dies, the astrologers say that the spirit of the dead has done this because he was not carried out during the ascendancy of the planet under which he was born, or of one not contrary to it, or on the proper side of the house.

So much, then, for this matter. Now I will tell you of some other cities, which lie towards the north-west near the edge of this desert.

The province of Kamul, which used to be a kingdom, contains towns and villages in plenty, the chief town being also called Kamul. The province lies between two deserts, the Great Desert and a small one three days' journey in extent. The inhabitants are all idolaters and speak a language of their own. They live on the produce of the soil; for they have a superfluity of foodstuffs and beverages, which they sell to travellers who pass that way. They are a very gay folk, who give no thought to anything but making music, singing and dancing, and reading and writing according to their own usage, and taking great delight in the pleasures of the body. I give you my word that if a stranger comes to a house here to seek hospitality he receives a very warm welcome. The host bids his wife do everything that the guest wishes. Then he leaves the house and goes about his own business and stays away two or three days. Meanwhile the guest stays with his wife in the house and does what he will with her, lying with her in one bed just as if she were his own wife; and they lead a gay life together. All the men of this city and province are thus cuckolded by their wives; but they are not the least ashamed of it. And the women are beautiful and vivacious and always ready to oblige.

Now it happened during the reign of Mongu Khan, lord of the Tartars, that he was informed of this custom that prevailed among the men of Kamul of giving their wives in adultery to outsiders. Mongu thereupon commanded them under heavy penalties to desist from this form of hospitality. When they received this command, they were greatly distressed; but for three years they reluctantly obeyed. Then they held a council and talked the matter over, and this is what they did. They took a rich gift and sent it to Mongu and entreated him to let them use their wives according to the traditions of their ancestors; for their ancestors had declared that by the pleasure they gave to guests with their wives and goods they won the favour of their idols and multiplied the yield of their crops and their tillage. When Mongu Khan heard this he said: 'Since you desire your own shame, you may have it.' So he let them have their way. And I can assure you that since then they have always upheld this tradition and uphold it still.

Another province, also subject to the Great Khan, is Uighuristan. It is a large province containing many cities and towns. The chief city, which is called Kara Khoja, has many other cities and towns dependent on it. The people are idolaters, but they include many Christians of the Nestorian sect and some Saracens. The Christians often intermarry with the idolaters. They declare that the king who originally ruled over them was not born of human stock, but arose from a sort of tuber generated by the sap of trees, which we call *esca;* and from him all the others descended. The idolaters are very well versed in their own laws and traditions and are keen students of the liberal arts. The land produces grain and excellent wine. But in winter the cold here is more intense than is known in any other part of the world.

Another province on the edge of the desert towards the north-north-east is Ghinghintalas, sixteen days in extent, which is also subject to the Great Khan. It has cities and towns in plenty. The inhabitants consist of three groups, idolaters, Mahometans, and Nestorian Christians.

Towards the northern boundary of this province is a mountain with a rich vein of steel and *ondanique*. In this same mountain occurs a vein from which is produced salamander. You must understand that this is not a beast as is commonly asserted: but its real nature is such as I will now describe. It is a well known fact that by nature no beast or other animal can live in fire, because every animal is composed of the four elements. For lack of any certain knowledge about salamander, men spoke of it, and still do, as a beast; but this is not true. I will now tell you the real facts. First, let me explain that I had a Turkish companion named Zurficar, a man of great intelligence, who spent three years in this province, in the service of the Great Khan, engaged in the extraction of this salamander and *ondanique* and steel and other products. For the Great Khan regularly appoints governors every three years to govern this province and supervise the salamander industry. My companion told me the true facts and I have also seen them for myself. When the stuff found in this vein of which you have heard has been dug out of the mountain and crumbled into bits, the particles cohere and form fibres like wool. Accordingly, when the stuff has been extracted, it is first dried, then pounded in a large copper mortar and then washed. The residue consists of this fibre of which I have spoken and worthless earth, which is separated from it. Then this wool-like fibre is carefully spun and made into cloths. When the cloths are first made, they are far from white. But they are thrown into the fire and left there for a while; and there they turn as white as snow. And whenever one of these cloths is soiled or discoloured, it is thrown into the fire and left there for a while, and it comes out as white as snow. The account I have given you of the salamander is the truth, and all the other accounts that are put about are lies and fables. Let me tell you finally that one of these cloths is now at Rome; it was sent to the Pope by the Great Khan as a valuable gift, and for this reason the sacred napkin of our lord Jesus Christ was wrapped in it.

Let us now leave this province and turn to others lying towards the east-north-east.

When the traveller leaves the province of which I have spoken, he journeys for ten days east-north-east. And all this way there is no habitation, or none to speak of, and nothing worthy of mention in our book. At the end of the ten days he reaches a province called Su-chau, in which there are cities and towns in plenty, the chief city being also called Su-chau. The inhabitants are Christians and idolaters, subject to the Great Khan. This province, together with the two last-named, forms part of the major province of Tangut. In all the mountains of this region, rhubarb grows in great abundance; it is bought here by merchants, who export it far and wide. Travellers passing this way do not venture to go among these mountains with any beast except those of the country, because a poisonous herb grows here, which makes beasts that feed on it lose their hoofs; but beasts born in the country recognize this herb and avoid it. The climate of this province is healthy, and the inhabitants are brown-skinned. They live by the produce of the soil and have little dealing with trade.

Let us now pass on to Kan-chau, a large and splendid city in Tangut proper and the capital of the whole province. The inhabitants are idolaters, with some Mahometans. There are also some Christians, who have three fine large churches in the city. The idolaters have many monasteries and abbeys according to their own usage. They have a vast quantity of idols; and I can assure you that some are as much as ten paces in length. Some are of wood, some of earthenware, some of stone, and they are all covered with gold and of excellent workmanship. These huge idols are recumbent, and groups of lesser ones are set round about them and seem to be doing them humble obeisance.

Since I have not told you of the customs of the idolaters, I will do so here.

First, you should know that those idolaters who live under a religious rule lead more virtuous lives than the others. They avoid lechery, but do not regard it as a major sin. Their principle of conduct is that, if a woman makes love to them, they may accept her overtures without sin; but, if they make the first advances, they account that a sin. If they find that any man has had unnatural intercourse with a woman, they condemn him to death. They distinguish lunar cycles as we distinguish the months. There is one such cycle in which for five days all the idolaters in the world kill neither beast nor bird; nor do they eat the flesh of animals killed during these days. And for these five days they live more virtuously than at other times. And some of them, that is the monks, abstain from flesh all their lives out of reverence and piety; but the laity do not observe this rule. They marry anything up to thirty wives, more or fewer according to what each man can afford. The men give their wives a marriage-portion in cattle, slaves, and money proportionate to their means. You should understand that they treat the first wife as having the highest status. Moreover, if the husband finds that one of his wives misbehaves or displeases him, he is free to put her away and do as he likes. Men marry their own cousins and also their fathers' widows. Many things that we regard as grave sins are not sins at all in their eyes; for they live like beasts.

So much, then, for that. Let us now speak of other regions towards the north, after remarking that Messer Niccolò and Messer Maffeo and Messer Marco spent a year in this city, but without any experiences worth recording. So we shall leave it and start on a journey of sixty days towards the north.

## *Dante Alighieri (1265–1321)*

*Translated by Robert Pinsky*

Dante's *Divine Comedy* dominates the literature of medieval Europe in the same way that Homer and Virgil dominate the Classical period and Shakespeare the Early Modern period. *The Divine Comedy* is the consummately medieval poem, displaying the medieval worldview in all its deeply traditional learning, though in a daringly original literary form. Dante's choice of the vernacular Italian over Latin was deeply considered and had a tremendous effect on future European literature. His absolute certainty on moral and theological issues makes his poem quintessentially medieval, however, just as Petrarch's deep *un*certainty only a generation later suggests that a new period—the Modern—is being born. As always, such generalities are only approximations: to call Dante consummately medieval is to define the medieval as learned and theological, whereas much literature of the period was in fact playful, popular, or secular. However we define our concepts, Dante remains a towering challenge to readers. The ability to read *The Divine Comedy* with understanding is one of the highest achievements of Western literary study.

Dante Alighieri began his career as a poet of love in the *dolce stil novo* typified by his friend Cavalcanti. His love poems, dedicated to a girl named Beatrice whom he barely knew and who died young, gradually rise to a purely spiritual Christian love. In 1301, Dante was banished from his native Florence for political reasons. During twenty years of exile, he labored on his vast epic, in which Beatrice acts as his guide through the spheres of Heaven to a final vision of God. Because of this "happy ending," and because it was written in the humble vernacular rather than in Latin, Dante called his poem the *Commedia.* (It was a later writer, Boccaccio, who called it divine, resulting in the title by which it is now universally known.)

It is the first part of the poem, however, the vision of Hell, that has most attracted readers over the centuries. In the *Inferno* as in the *Purgatorio,* Dante's guide is not Beatrice but Virgil, because Virgil had described the underworld in Book VI of *The Aeneid* (modeled in turn on Book XII of Homer's *Odyssey*). Dante writes in the most elevated tradition available to him, though in the vernacular, attempting to create as comprehensive and immortal a poem as his two great predecessors had done.

The *Inferno* is shocking: Dante travels through Hell as a pilgrim. There he meets individuals who represent the various sins, according to the Christian vision. Many of those he meets are his near-contemporaries; some are people he knows personally and even admires. Dante is shocked repeatedly by what he discovers (although he himself as the author has created it). He depicts himself as a complex character who gradually learns from his experiences in the otherworld. Throughout, we feel a terrible friction between the moral vision of God and the human vision of both Dante the pilgrim and those he meets, who often evoke our sympathy. It is hard not to pity the lovers Paolo and Francesca in Canto V, for example, or the grand ambition of Ulysses (Odysseus) in Canto XXVI, or the wrenching history of Ugolino in Canto XXXIII; but our sympathy for them only measures the distance between our humanity and the absolute vision of God, which Dante does not question.

Although the people he meets represent certain sins and the poem is obviously allegorical, Dante's depictions are startlingly realistic, which is markedly atypical of medieval literature. In this respect, Dante influenced writers who followed him, like Chaucer. The descent into the underworld has a long history in Western epic, from the Mesopotamian *Descent of Inanna* and the Greek and Roman epics to Milton's *Paradise Lost* and Ezra Pound's *Cantos.*

## from The Inferno

### *Canto I [The Dark Wood]*

Midway on our life's journey, I found myself
In dark woods, the right road lost. To tell
About those woods is hard—so tangled and rough

And savage that thinking of it now, I feel
The old fear stirring: death is hardly more bitter.
And yet, to treat the good I found there as well

I'll tell what I saw, though how I came to enter
I cannot well say, being so full of sleep
Whatever moment it was I began to blunder

Off the true path. But when I came to stop
Below a hill that marked one end of the valley
That had pierced my heart with terror, I looked up

Toward the crest and saw its shoulders already
Mantled in rays of that bright planet that shows
The road to everyone, whatever our journey.

Then I could feel the terror begin to ease
That churned in my heart's lake all through the night.
As one still panting, ashore from dangerous seas,

Looks back at the deep he has escaped, my thought
Returned, still fleeing, to regard that grim defile
That never left any alive who stayed in it.

After I had rested in my weary body awhile
I started again across the wilderness,
My left foot always lower on the hill,

And suddenly—a leopard, near the place
The way grew steep: lithe, spotted, quick of foot.
Blocking the path, she stayed before my face

And more than once she made me turn about
To go back down. It was early morning still.
The fair sun rising with the stars attending it

As when Divine Love set those beautiful
Lights into motion at creation's dawn,
And the time of day and season combined to fill

My heart with hope of that beast with festive skin—
But not so much that the next sight wasn't fearful:
A lion came at me, his head high as he ran,

Roaring with hunger so the air appeared to tremble.
Then, a grim she-wolf—whose leanness seemed to compress
All the world's cravings, that had made miserable

Such multitudes; she put such heaviness
Into my spirit, I lost hope of the crest.
Like someone eager to win, who tested by loss

Surrenders to gloom and weeps, so did that beast
Make me feel, as harrying toward me at a lope
She forced me back toward where the sun is lost.

While I was ruining myself back down to the deep,
Someone appeared—one who seemed nearly to fade
As though from long silence. I cried to his human shape

In that great wasteland: "Living man or shade,
Have pity and help me, whichever you may be!"
"No living man, though once I was," he replied.

"My parents both were Mantuans from Lombardy,
And I was born *sub Julio,* the latter end.
I lived in good Augustus's Rome, in the day

Of the false gods who lied. A poet, I hymned
Anchises' noble son, who came from Troy
When superb Ilium in its pride was burned.

But you—why go back down to such misery?
Why not ascend the delightful mountain, source
And principle that causes every joy?"

"Then are you Virgil? Are you the font that pours
So overwhelming a river of human speech?"
I answered, shamefaced. "The glory and light are yours,

That poets follow—may the love that made me search
Your book in patient study avail me, Master!
You are my guide and author, whose verses teach

The graceful style whose model has done me honor.
See this beast driving me backward—help me resist,
For she makes all my veins and pulses shudder."

"A different path from this one would be best
For you to find your way from this feral place,"
He answered, seeing how I wept. "This beast,

The cause of your complaint, lets no one pass
Her way—but harries all to death. Her nature
Is so malign and vicious she cannot appease

Her voracity, for feeding makes her hungrier.
Many are the beasts she mates: there will be more,
Until the Hound comes who will give this creature

A painful death. Not nourished by earthly fare,
He will be fed by wisdom, goodness and love.
Born between Feltro and Feltro, he shall restore

Low Italy, as Nisus fought to achieve.
And Turnus, Euryalus, Camilla the maiden—
All dead from wounds in war. He will remove

This lean wolf, hunting her through every region
Till he has thrust her back to Hell's abyss
Where Envy first dispatched her on her mission.

Therefore I judge it best that you should choose
To follow me, and I will be your guide
Away from here and through an eternal place:

To hear the cries of despair, and to behold
Ancient tormented spirits as they lament
In chorus the second death they must abide.

Then you shall see those souls who are content
To dwell in fire because they hope some day
To join the blessed: toward whom, if your ascent

Continues, your guide will be one worthier than I—
When I must leave you, you will be with her.
For the Emperor who governs from on high

Wills I not enter His city, where none may appear
Who lived like me in rebellion to His law.
His empire is everything and everywhere,

But that is His kingdom, His city, His seat of awe.
Happy is the soul He chooses for that place!"
I: "Poet, please—by the God you did not know—

Help me escape this evil that I face,
And worse. Lead me to witness what you have said,
Saint Peter's gate, and the multitude of woes—"

Then he set out, and I followed where he led.

## *Canto II [The Descent]*

Day was departing, and the darkening air
Called all earth's creatures to their evening quiet
While I alone was preparing as though for war

To struggle with my journey and with the spirit
Of pity, which flawless memory will redraw:
O Muses, O genius of art, O memory whose merit

Has inscribed inwardly those things I saw—
Help me fulfill the perfection of your nature.
I commenced: "Poet, take my measure now:

Appraise my powers before you trust me to venture
Through that deep passage where you would be my guide.
You write of the journey Silvius's father

Made to immortal realms although he stayed
A mortal witness, in his corruptible body.
That the Opponent of all evil bestowed

Such favor on him befits him, chosen for glory
By highest heaven to be the father of Rome
And of Rome's empire—later established Holy.

Seat of great Peter's heir. You say he came
To that immortal world, and things he learned
There led to the papal mantle—and triumph for him.

Later, the Chosen Vessel too went and returned,
Carrying confirmation of that faith
Which opens the way with salvation at its end.

But I—what cause, whose favor, could send me forth
On such a voyage? I am no Aeneas or Paul:
Not I nor others think me of such worth.

And therefore I have my fears of playing the fool
To embark on such a venture. You are wise:
You know my meaning better than I can tell."

And then, like one who unchooses his own choice
And thinking again undoes what he has started,
So I became: a nullifying unease

Overcame my soul on that dark slope and voided
The undertaking I had so quickly embraced.
"If I understand," the generous shade retorted.

"Cowardice grips your spirit—which can twist
A man away from the noblest enterprise
As a trick of vision startles a shying beast.

To ease your burden of fear, I will disclose
Why I came here, and what I heard that compelled
Me first to feel compassion for you: it was

A lady's voice that called me where I dwelled
In Limbo—a lady so blessed and fairly featured
I prayed her to command me. Her eyes out-jeweled

The stars in splendor. 'O generous Mantuan spirit,'
She began in a soft voice of angelic sound,
'Whose fame lives still, that the world will still inherit

As long as the world itself shall live: my friend—
No friend of Fortune—has found his way impeded
On the barren slope, and fear has turned him round.

I fear he may be already lost, unaided:
So far astray, I've come from Heaven too late.
Go now, with your fair speech and what is needed

To save him; offer the help you have to give
Before he is lost, and I will be consoled.
I am Beatrice, come from where I crave

To be again, who ask this. As love has willed,
So have I spoken. And when I return
Before my Lord, He will hear your praises told.'

Then she was silent; and I in turn began,
'O Lady of goodness, through whom alone mankind
Exceeds what the sky's least circle can contain

Within its compass: so sweet is your command
Had I already obeyed, it would feel too late.
But tell me how you so fearlessly descend

To such a center—from that encompassing state
You long to see again?' 'You yearn for the answer
Deeply,' she said, 'so I will tell in short

How I can come to Limbo, yet feel no terror:
Fear befits things with power for injury,
Not things that lack such power. God the Creator

Has by His mercy made me such that I
Cannot feel what you suffer: none of this fire
Assails me. In Heaven a Lady feels such pity

For this impediment where I send you, severe
Judgment is broken by her grace on high.
To Lucy she said: "Your faithful follower

Needs you: I commend him to you." Lucy, the foe
Of every cruelty, found me where I sat
With Rachel of old, and urged me: "Beatrice, true

Glory of God, can you not come to the aid
Of one who had such love for you he rose
Above the common crowd? Do you not heed

The pity of his cries? And do your eyes
Not see death near him, in a flood the ocean
Itself can boast no power to surpass?"

Never on earth was anyone spurred to motion
So quickly, to seize advantage or fly from danger,
As at these words I hurried here from Heaven—

Trusting your eloquence, whose gift brings honor
Both to yourself and to all those who listen.'
Having said this, she turned toward me the splendor

Of her eyes lucent with tears—which made me hasten
To save you, even more eagerly than before:
And so I rescued you on the fair mountain

Where the beast blocked the short way up. Therefore,
What is this? Why, why should you hold back?
Why be a coward rather than bolder, freer—

Since in the court of Heaven for your sake
Three blessed ladies watch, and words of mine
Have promised a good as great as you might seek?"

As flowers bent and shrunken by night at dawn
Unfold and straighten on their stems, to wake
Brightened by sunlight, so I grew strong again—

Good courage coursing through my heart, I spoke
Like one set free: "How full of true compassion
Was she who helped me, how courteous and quick

Were you to follow her bidding—and your narration
Has restored my spirit. Now, on: for I feel eager
To go with you, and cleave to my first intention.

From now, we two will share one will together:
You are my teacher, my master, and my guide."
So I spoke, and when he moved I followed after

And entered on that deep and savage road.

## *Canto III [The Gate of Hell]*

THROUGH ME YOU ENTER INTO THE CITY OF WOES,
THROUGH ME YOU ENTER INTO ETERNAL PAIN,
THROUGH ME YOU ENTER THE POPULATION OF LOSS.

JUSTICE MOVED MY HIGH MAKER, IN POWER DIVINE,
WISDOM SUPREME, LOVE PRIMAL. NO THINGS WERE
BEFORE ME NOT ETERNAL; ETERNAL I REMAIN.

ABANDON ALL HOPE, YOU WHO ENTER HERE.
These words I saw inscribed in some dark color
Over a portal. "Master," I said, "make clear

Their meaning, which I find too hard to gather."
Then he, as one who understands: "All fear
Must be left here, and cowardice die. Together,

We have arrived where I have told you: here
You will behold the wretched souls who've lost
The good of intellect." Then, with good cheer

In his expression to encourage me, he placed
His hand on mine: so, trusting to my guide,
I followed him among things undisclosed.

The sighs, groans and laments at first were so loud,
Resounding through starless air, I began to weep:
Strange languages, horrible screams, words imbued

With rage or despair, cries as of troubled sleep
Or of a tortured shrillness—they rose in a coil
Of tumult, along with noises like the slap

Of beating hands, all fused in a ceaseless flail
That churns and frenzies that dark and timeless air
Like sand in a whirlwind. And I, my head in a swirl

Of error, cried: "Master, what is this I hear?
What people are these, whom pain has overcome?"
He: "This is the sorrowful state of souls unsure,

Whose lives earned neither honor nor bad fame.
And they are mingled with angels of that base sort
Who, neither rebellious to God nor faithful to Him,

Chose neither side, but kept themselves apart—
Now Heaven expels them, not to mar its splendor,
And Hell rejects them, lest the wicked of heart

Take glory over them." And then I: "Master,
What agony is it, that makes them keen their grief
With so much force?" He: "I will make brief answer:

They have no hope of death, but a blind life
So abject, they envy any other fate.
To all memory of them, the world is deaf.

Mercy and justice disdain them. Let us not
Speak of them: look and pass on." I looked again:
A whirling banner sped at such a rate

It seemed it might never stop; behind it a train
Of souls, so long that I would not have thought
Death had undone so many. When more than one

I recognized had passed, I beheld the shade
Of him who made the Great Refusal, impelled
By cowardice: so at once I understood

Beyond all doubt that this was the dreary guild
Repellent both to God and His enemies—
Hapless ones never alive, their bare skin galled

By wasps and flies, blood trickling down the face,
Mingling with tears for harvest underfoot
By writhing maggots. Then, when I turned my eyes

Farther along our course, I could make out
People upon the shore of some great river.
"Master," I said, "it seems by this dim light

That all of these are eager to cross over—
Can you tell me by what law, and who they are?"
He answered, "Those things you will discover

When we have paused at Acheron's dismal shore."
I walked on with my head down after that,
Fearful I had displeased him, and spoke no more.

Then, at the river—an old man in a boat:
White-haired, as he drew closer shouting at us,
"Woe to you, wicked souls! Give up the thought

Of Heaven! I come to ferry you across
Into eternal dark on the opposite side,
Into fire and ice! And you there—leave this place,

You living soul, stand clear of these who are dead!"
And then, when he saw that I did not obey:
"By other ports, in a lighter boat," he said,

"You will be brought to shore by another way."
My master spoke then, "Charon, do not rage:
Thus is it willed where everything may be

Simply if it is willed. Therefore, oblige,
And ask no more." That silenced the grizzled jaws
Of the gray ferryman of the livid marsh,

Who had red wheels of flame about his eyes.
But at his words the forlorn and naked souls
Were changing color, cursing the human race,

God and their parents. Teeth chattering in their skulls,
They called curses on the seed, the place, the hour
Of their own begetting and their birth. With wails

And tears they gathered on the evil shore
That waits for all who don't fear God. There demon
Charon beckons them, with his eyes of fire;

Crowded in a herd, they obey if he should summon,
And he strikes at any laggards with his oar.
As leaves in quick succession sail down in autumn

Until the bough beholds its entire store
Fallen to the earth, so Adam's evil seed
Swoop from the bank when each is called, as sure

As a trained falcon, to cross to the other side
Of the dark water; and before one throng can land
On the far shore, on this side new souls crowd.

"My son," said the gentle master, "here are joined
The souls of all who die in the wrath of God,
From every country, all of them eager to find

Their way across the water—for the goad
Of Divine Justice spurs them so, their fear
Is transmuted to desire. Souls who are good

Never pass this way; therefore, if you hear
Charon complaining at your presence, consider
What that means." Then, the earth of that grim shore

Began to shake: so violently, I shudder
And sweat recalling it now. A wind burst up
From the tear-soaked ground to erupt red light and batter

My senses—and so I fell, as though seized by sleep.

## *Canto IV [Limbo: the Poets]*

Breaking the deep sleep that filled my head,
A heavy clap of thunder startled me up
As though by force; with rested eyes I stood

Peering to find where I was—in truth, the lip
Above the chasm of pain, which holds the din
Of infinite grief: a gulf so dark and deep

And murky that though I gazed intently down
Into the canyon, I could see nothing below.
"Now we descend into the sightless zone,"

The poet began, dead pale now: "I will go
Ahead, you second." I answered, seeing his pallor,
"How can I venture here if even you,

Who have encouraged me every time I falter,
Turn white with fear?" And he: "It is the pain
People here suffer that paints my face this color

Of pity, which you mistake for fear. Now on:
Our long road urges us forward." And he entered
The abyss's first engirdling circle, and down

He had me enter it too. Here we encountered
No laments that we could hear—except for sighs
That trembled the timeless air: they emanated

From the shadowy sadnesses, not agonies,
Of multitudes of children and women and men.
He said, "And don't you ask, what spirits are these?

Before you go on, I tell you: they did not sin;
If they have merit, it can't suffice without
Baptism, portal to the faith you maintain.

Some lived before the Christian faith, so that
They did not worship God aright—and I
Am one of these. Through this, no other fault,

We are lost, afflicted only this one way:
That having no hope, we live in longing." I heard
These words with heartfelt grief that seized on me

Knowing how many worthy souls endured
Suspension in that Limbo. "Dear sir, my master,"
I began, wanting to be reassured

In the faith that conquers every error, "Did ever
Anyone go forth from here—by his own good
Or perhaps another's—to join the blessed, after?"

He understood my covert meaning, and said,
"I was new to this condition, when I beheld
A Mighty One who descended here, arrayed

With a crown of victory. And He re-called
Back from this place the shade of our first parent,
And his son Abel, and other shades who dwelled

In Limbo. Noah, and Moses the obedient
Giver of laws, went with Him, and Abraham
The patriarch. King David and Israel went,

And Israel's sire and children, and Rachel for whom
He labored so long, and many others—and His
Coming here made them blessed, and rescued them.

Know this: no human soul was saved, till these."
We did not stop our traveling while he spoke,
But kept on passing through the woods—not trees,

But a wood of thronging spirits; nor did we make
Much distance from the place where I had slept,
When I saw a fire that overcame a bleak

Hemisphere of darkness. Well before we stopped
To address them, I could see people there and sense
They were honorable folk. "O Master apt

In science and art, who honor both, what wins
These shades distinction? Who are they who command
A place so separate from the other ones?"

And he: "Their honored names, which still resound
In your life above, have earned them Heaven's grace,
Advancing them here." Meanwhile a voice intoned:

"Hail the great Poet, whose shade had left this place
And now returns!" After the voice fell still,
I saw four great shades making their way to us,

Their aspect neither sad nor joyful. "Note well,"
My master began, "the one who carries a sword
And strides before the others, as fits his role

Among these giants: he is Homer, their lord
The sovereign poet; the satirist follows him—
Horace, with Lucan last, and Ovid third:

That lone voice just now hailed me by a name
Each of them shares with me; in such accord
They honor me well." And so I saw, all come

Together there, the splendid school of the lord
Of highest song who like an eagle soars high
Above the others. After they had shared a word

Among themselves, they turned and greeted me
With cordial gestures, at which my master smiled;
And far more honor: that fair company

Then made me one among them—so as we traveled
Onward toward the light I made a sixth
Amid such store of wisdom. Thus we strolled,

Speaking of matters I will not give breath,
Silence as fitting now as speech was there.
At length, a noble castle blocked our path,

Encircled seven times by a barrier
Of lofty walls, and defended round about
By a handsome stream we strode across: it bore

Our weight like solid ground; and after that
I passed through seven gateways with the sages.
We came to a fresh green meadow, where we met

A group of people. With grave, deliberate gazes
And manners of great authority, they spoke
Sparingly and in gentle, courtly voices.

We drew aside to a place where we could look
From a spacious well-lit height and view them all:
On that enameled green I saw—and take

Glory within me for having seen them, still—
The spirits of the great: I saw Electra
With many companions, among whom I knew well

Which shades were those of Aeneas and of Hector.
And Caesar—who wore his armor, falcon-eyed.
I saw Camilla, and Penthesilea beside her;

I saw King Latinus on the other side,
And sitting by him his daughter Lavinia.
I saw that Brutus from whom Tarquin fled,

I saw Lucretia, Julia, Marcia, Cornelia;
And sitting at a distance separately
I saw lone Saladin of Arabia.

I raised my eyes a little, and there was he
Who is acknowledged Master of those who know.
Sitting in a philosophic family

Who look to him and do him honor. I saw
Nearest him, in front, Plato and Socrates.
I saw Democritus, who strove to show

That the world is chance; Zeno, Empedocles,
Anaxagoras, Thales, Heraclitus,
Diogenes. The collector of qualities

Of things, Dioscorides. And Orpheus,
Cicero, Linus, Seneca the moralist,
Euclid the geometer, Ptolemy, Hippocrates,

Galen, Avicenna, Averroës who discussed
The Philosopher in his great commentary—
I saw so many I cannot tally the list:

For my demanding theme so pulls my story,
To multiply the telling would be too little
For the multitude of fact that filled my journey.

The company of six divide and dwindle
To two; my wise guide leads me from that quiet
Another way—again I see air tremble,

And come to a part that has no light inside it.

## *Canto V [The Lovers: Paolo and Francesca]*

So I descended from first to second circle—
Which girdles a smaller space and greater pain,
Which spurs more lamentation. Minos the dreadful

Snarls at the gate. He examines each one's sin,
Judging and disposing as he curls his tail:
That is, when an ill-begotten soul comes down,

It comes before him, and confesses all;
Minos, great connoisseur of sin, discerns
For every spirit its proper place in Hell,

And wraps himself in his tail with as many turns
As levels down that shade will have to dwell.
A crowd is always waiting: here each one learns

His judgment and is assigned a place in Hell.
They tell; they hear—and down they all are cast.
"You, who have come to sorrow's hospice, think well,"

Said Minos, who at the sight of me had paused
To interrupt his solemn task mid-deed:
"Beware how you come in and whom you trust,

Don't be deceived because the gate is wide."
My leader answered, "Must you too scold this way?
His destined path is not for you to impede:

Thus is it willed where every thing may be
Because it has been willed. So ask no more."
And now I can hear the notes of agony

In sad crescendo beginning to reach my ear:
Now I am where the noise of lamentation
Comes at me in blasts of sorrow. I am where

All light is mute, with a bellowing like the ocean
Turbulent in a storm of warring winds.
The hurricane of Hell in perpetual motion

Sweeping the ravaged spirits as it rends,
Twists, and torments them. Driven as if to land,
They reach the ruin: groaning, tears, laments,

And cursing of the power of Heaven. I learned
They suffer here who sinned in carnal things—
Their reason mastered by desire, suborned.

As winter starlings riding on their wings
Form crowded flocks, so spirits dip and veer
Foundering in the wind's rough buffetings,

Upward or downward, driven here and there
With never ease from pain nor hope of rest.
As chanting cranes will form a line in air,

So I saw souls come uttering cries—wind-tossed,
And lofted by the storm. "Master," I cried,
"Who are these people, by black air oppressed?"

"First among these you wish to know," he said,
"Was empress of many tongues—she so embraced
Lechery that she decreed it justified

Legally, to evade the scandal of her lust:
She is that Semiramis of whom we read,
Successor and wife of Ninus, she possessed

The lands the Sultan rules. Next, she who died
By her own hand for love, and broke her vow
To Sychaeus's ashes. After her comes lewd

And wanton Cleopatra. See Helen, too,
Who caused a cycle of many evil years;
And great Achilles, the hero whom love slew

In his last battle. Paris and Tristan are here—"
He pointed out by name a thousand souls
Whom love had parted from our life, or more.

When I had heard my teacher tell the rolls
Of knights and ladies of antiquity,
Pity overwhelmed me. Half-lost in its coils,

"Poet," I told him, "I would willingly
Speak with those two who move along together,
And seem so light upon the wind." And he:

"When they drift closer—then entreat them hither,
In the name of love that leads them: they will respond."
Soon their course shifted, and the merciless weather

Battered them toward us. I called against the wind,
"O wearied souls! If Another does not forbid,
Come speak with us." As doves whom desire has summoned,

With raised wings steady against the current, glide
Guided by will to the sweetness of their nest,
So leaving the flock where Dido was, the two sped

Through the malignant air till they had crossed
To where we stood—so strong was the compulsion
Of my loving call. They spoke across the blast:

"O living soul, who with courtesy and compassion
Voyage through black air visiting us who stained
The world with blood: if heaven's King bore affection

For such as we are, suffering in this wind,
Then we would pray to Him to grant you peace
For pitying us in this, our evil end.

Now we will speak and hear as you may please
To speak and hear, while the wind, for our discourse,
Is still. My birthplace is a city that lies

Where the Po finds peace with all its followers.
Love, which in gentle hearts is quickly born,
Seized him for my fair body—which, in a fierce

Manner that still torments my soul, was torn
Untimely away from me. Love, which absolves
None who are loved from loving, made my heart burn

With joy so strong that as you see it cleaves
Still to him, here. Love gave us both one death.
Caina awaits the one who took our lives."

These words were borne across from them to us.
When I had heard those afflicted souls, I lowered
My head, and held it so till I heard the voice

Of the poet ask, "What are you thinking?" I answered,
"Alas—that sweet conceptions and passion so deep
Should bring them here!" Then, looking up toward

The lovers: "Francesca, your suffering makes me weep
For sorrow and pity—but tell me, in the hours
Of sweetest sighing, how and in what shape

Or manner did Love first show you those desires
So hemmed by doubt?" And she to me: "No sadness
Is greater than in misery to rehearse

Memories of joy, as your teacher well can witness.
But if you have so great a craving to measure
Our love's first root, I'll tell it, with the fitness

Of one who weeps and tells. One day, for pleasure,
We read of Lancelot, by love constrained:
Alone, suspecting nothing, at our leisure.

Sometimes at what we read our glances joined,
Looking from the book each to the other's eyes,
And then the color in our faces drained.

But one particular moment alone it was
Defeated us: *the longed-for smile,* it said,
*Was kissed by that most noble lover:* at this,

This one, who now will never leave my side,
Kissed my mouth, trembling. A Galeotto, that book!
And so was he who wrote it; that day we read

No further." All the while the one shade spoke,
The other at her side was weeping; my pity
Overwhelmed me and I felt myself go slack:

Swooning as in death, I fell like a dying body.

## *Canto X [The Heretics: Cavalcanti]*

And now, along the narrow pathway that ran
Between those tortures and the city wall,
I followed my master. "O matchless power," I began,

"Who lead me through evil's circles at your will,
Speak to me with the answers that I crave
About these souls and the sepulchers they fill:

Might they be seen? The cover of each grave
Is lifted open, and no one is on guard."
"When they return from Jehoshaphat above,"

He answered, "bearing the bodies that they had,
All shall be closed. Here Epicurus lies
With all his followers, who call the soul dead

When the flesh dies. The question that you raise
Will soon be answered now that we are inside—
And so will the secret wish you don't express."

I said, "Dear guide, believe me: I do not hide
My heart from you, except through my intention
To speak but little, the way that you have said

Earlier I ought to be disposed." "O Tuscan!—
Who travel alive through this, the city of fire,
While speaking in so courteous a fashion—

If it should please you, stop a moment here.
Your way of speaking shows that you were born
In the same noble fatherland: there where

I possibly have wrought excessive harm."
This sound erupted from a coffer of stone—
I drew back toward my guide in my alarm.

"What are you doing?" he said. "Go back again!
And see where Farinata has sat up straight;
From the waist up, you may behold the man."

Already my eyes were on his: he sat upright,
And seemed by how he bore his chest and brow
To have scorn for Hell. My leader set

Firm hands upon me at once, and made me go
Forward between the rows of sepulchers,
Saying: "Choose fitting words," as we wended through.

At his tomb's foot, I felt his proud gaze pierce
Mine for a moment; and then as if in disdain
He spoke and asked me, "Who were your ancestors?"

Eager to comply with that, I made all plain,
Concealing nothing: whereupon he raised
His brows a little. Then he said, "These men

Were enemies to me; they fiercely opposed
Me and my forebears and my party—so, twice,
I scattered them." "If ousted and abused,"

I answered, "they returned to claim their place
From every quarter: yours have not learned that art
Of return so well." Then suddenly the face

Of a shade appeared beside him, showing the part
From the chin up—I think through having risen
Erect on his knees: his gaze began to dart

Anxiously round me, as though in expectation
Of someone with me. But when that hope was gone
He wept: "If you can journey through this blind prison

By virtue of high genius—where is my son,
And why is he not with you?" And my rejoinder:
"My own strength has not brought me, but that of one

Who guides me through here, and is waiting yonder—
Toward one your Guido perhaps had scorned." I well
Deduced his name from his words and from his manner

Of punishment, and thus could answer in full.
Suddenly straightening up, the shade cried out,
"What?—did I hear you say he 'had'? Oh tell:

Is he not still alive? Does the sweet light
Not strike his eyes?" Perceiving my delay
In giving any answer, he fell back flat,

Face upward, appearing no more. But not so he,
The great soul at whose beckoning I had paused;
He did not change his features in any way,

Nor bend his neck or waist. "The point you raised—"
He resumed where interrupted: "My kin not good
At learning that art—I feel more agonized

By that accursed fact than by this bed.
But when the Lady's face who rules this place
Has kindled fewer than fifty times," he said,

"Then you will know how heavy that art weighs.
Now tell me (may you regain the sweet world's vantage),
Why is that people so fierce in its decrees

Toward my kin?" I answered, "It was the carnage
And devastation that dyed the Arbia red
Which made the prayers in our temple savage."

Shaking his head, "I was not alone," he sighed.
"And surely I would not have chosen to join
The others without some cause, but where all agreed

To level Florence—there, I was alone:
One, who defended her before them all."
"Ah, pray you (so may your seed find peace again)

Unravel a knot that makes my reason fail,"
I said. "If I hear rightly, you seem to foresee
What time will bring, and yet you seem to deal

Differently with the present." He answered me:
"Like someone with faulty vision, we can behold
Remote things well, for so much light does He

Who rules supreme still grant us; but we are foiled
When things draw near us, and our intelligence
Is useless when they are present. So of your world

In its present state, we have no evidence
Or knowledge, except if others bring us word:
Thus you can understand that with no sense

Left to us, all our knowledge will be dead
From that Moment when the future's door is shut."
Then, moved by compunction for my fault, I said:

"Will you now tell the one who fell back flat
His son is truly still among the living?
Tell him what caused my silence: that my thought

Had wandered into that error which your resolving
Just wiped away." And now I heard my guide
Calling me back; so, hurriedly contriving

To learn, I begged the shade to say if he could
Who lay there with him, and I heard him answer:
"I lie with over a thousand of the dead;

The second Frederick is among the number,
And the Cardinal; of others I will not speak."
With that he hid himself. I walked back over

To the ancient poet, with my thoughts at work
Mulling the words that bore such menace to me.
My guide set out, and as we walked he spoke:

"Why is it you're disturbed?" I told him why;
"Preserve in memory what you have heard
Against yourself," the sage advised. "And I pray

You, listen"—he raised a finger at the word.
"When you confront her radiance, whose eyes can see
Everything in their fair clarity, be assured

Then you shall learn what your life's journey will be."
He turned to the left; and leaving the city wall
Behind our backs we continued on our way

Toward the center which was now our goal,
Following a path that strikes the valley floor:
And from that valley rose an odor so foul

The stench repelled us even high up there.

## *Canto XXVI [The Evil Counsellors: Ulysses]*

Rejoice, O Florence, since you are so great,
Beating your wings on land and on the sea,
That in Hell too your name is spread about!

I found among those there for their thievery
Five of your citizens, which carries shame
For me—and you gain no high honor thereby.

But if we dream the truth near morning time,
Then you will feel, before much time has gone,
What Prato and others crave for you—and come

Already, it would not have come too soon.
And truly, let it, since it must come to pass:
For it will all the heavier weigh me down,

The older I become. We left the place,
And on the stairway that the jutting stone
A little while before had offered us

On our descent, my guide climbed up again
And drew me up to pursue our lonely course.
Without the hand the foot could not go on,

Climbing that jagged ridge's rocks and spurs.
I sorrowed then, and when I turn my mind
To what I saw next, sorrow again—and force

My art to make its genius more restrained
Than is my usual bent, lest it should run
Where virtue doesn't: so that if any kind

Star or some better thing has made it mine
I won't myself negate the gift in me.
As many as the fireflies a peasant has seen

(Resting on a hill that time of year when he
Who lights the world least hides his face from us,
And at the hour when the fly gives way

To the mosquito) all down the valley's face,
Where perhaps he gathers grapes and tills the ground:
With flames that numerous was Hell's eighth fosse

Glittering, as I saw when I attained
A place from which its floor could be made out.
And as the one avenged by bears divined

That what he saw was Elijah's chariot
Carried by rearing horses to Heaven's domain—
For with his eyes he couldn't follow it

Except by looking at the flame alone,
Like a small cloud ascending: so each flame moves
Along the ditch's gullet with not one

Showing its plunder, though every flame contrives
To steal away a sinner. I had climbed up
To balance where the bridge's high point gives

A better view, and if I didn't grip
A rock I would have fallen from where I stood
Without a push. Seeing how from the top

I gazed intently down, my master said,
"Within the flames are spirits; each one here
Enfolds himself in what burns him." I replied,

"My Master, to hear you say it makes me sure,
But I already thought it; already, too,
I wanted to ask you who is in that fire

Which at its top is so split into two
It seems to surge from the pyre Eteocles
Shared with his brother?" He answered, "In it go

Tormented Ulysses and Diomedes
Enduring vengeance together, as they did wrath;
And in their flame they grieve for their device,

The horse that made the doorway through which went forth
The Romans' noble seed. Within their fire
Now they lament the guile that even in death

Makes Deidamia mourn Achilles, and there
They pay the price for the Palladium."
"Master," I said, "I earnestly implore,

If they can speak within those sparks of flame—
And pray my prayer be worth a thousand pleas—
Do not forbid my waiting here for them

Until their horned flame makes its way to us;
You see how yearningly it makes me lean."
And he to me: "Your prayer is worthy of praise,

And therefore I accept it. But restrain
Your tongue, leave speech to me—Greeks that they were,
They might treat words of yours with some disdain."

My master waited as the flame drew near
For the right place and moment to arrive,
Then spoke: "O you, who are two within one fire:

If I deserved of you while I was alive—
If I deserved anything great or small
From you when I wrote verse, then do not move;

But rather grant that one of you will tell
Whither, when lost, he went away to die."
The greater horn of flame began to flail

And murmur like fire the wind beats, and to ply
Its tip which, as it vibrated here and there
Like a tongue in speech, flung out a voice to say:

"When Circe had detained me more than a year
There near Gaeta, before it had that name
Aeneas gave it, and I parted from her,

Not fondness for my son, nor any claim
Of reverence for my father, nor love I owed
Penelope, to please her, could overcome

My longing for experience of the world,
Of human vices and virtue. But I sailed out
On the deep open seas, accompanied

By that small company that still had not
Deserted me, in a single ship. One coast
I saw, and then another, and I got

As far as Spain, Morocco, Sardinia, a host
of other islands that the sea bathes round.
My men and I were old and slow when we passed

The narrow outlet where Hercules let stand
His markers beyond which men were not to sail.
On my left hand I had left Ceuta behind,

And on the other sailed beyond Seville.
'O brothers who have reached the west,' I began,
'Through a hundred thousand perils, surviving all:

So little is the vigil we see remain
Still for our senses, that you should not choose
To deny it the experience—behind the sun

Leading us onward—of the world which has
No people in it. Consider well your seed:
You were not born to live as a mere brute does,

But for the pursuit of knowledge and the good.'
Then all of my companions grew so keen
To journey, spurred by this little speech I'd made,

I would have found them difficult to restrain.
Turning our stern toward the morning light,
We made wings of our oars, in an insane

Flight, always gaining on the left. The night
Showed all the stars, now, of the other pole—
Our own star fallen so low, no sign of it

Rose from the sea. The moon's low face glowed full
Five times since we set course across the deep,
And as many times was quenched invisible,

When dim in the distance we saw a mountaintop:
It seemed the highest I had ever seen.
We celebrated—but soon began to weep,

For from the newfound land a storm had grown,
Rising to strike the forepart of the ship.
It whirled the vessel round, and round again

With all the waters three times, lifting up
The stern the fourth—as pleased an Other—to press
The prow beneath the surface, and did not stop

Until the sea had closed up over us."

## *Canto XXXIII [The Traitors: Ugolino]*

Pausing in his savage meal, the sinner raised
His mouth and wiped it clean along the hair
Left on the head whose back he had laid waste.

Then he began: "You ask me to endure
Reliving a grief so desperate, the thought
Torments my heart even as I prepare

To tell it. But if my words are seeds, with fruit
Of infamy for this traitor that I gnaw,
I will both speak and weep within your sight.

I don't know who you are that come here, or how,
But you are surely Florentine to my ear.
I was Count Ugolino, you must know:

This is Archbishop Ruggieri. You will hear
Why I am such a neighbor to him as this:
How, through my trust and his devices, I bore

First being taken, then killed, no need to trace:
But things which you cannot have heard about—
The manner of my death, how cruel it was—

I shall describe, and you can tell from that
If he has wronged me. A slit in the Tower Mew
(Called Hunger's Tower after me, where yet

Others will be closed up) had let me view
Several moons already, when my bad dream
Came to me, piercing the future's veil right through:

This man appeared as lord of the hunt: he came
Chasing a wolf and whelps, on that high slope
That blocks the Pisans' view of Lucca. With him

His lean hounds ran, well trained and eager: his troop—
Gualandi, Sismondi, Lanfranchi—had been sent
To ride in front of him. With no escape,

After a short run, father and sons seemed spent;
I saw their flanks, that sharp fangs seemed to tear.
I woke before dawn, hearing the complaint

Of my own children, who were with me there,
Whimpering in their sleep and asking for bread.
You grieve already, or truly cruel you are,

As you think of what my heart began to dread—
And if not now, then when do you shed a tear?
They were awake now, with the hour when food

Was usually brought us drawing near,
And each one apprehensive from his dream.
And then I heard them nailing shut the door

Into that fearful tower—a pounding that came
From far below. Hearing that noise, I stared
Into my children's faces, not speaking to them.

Inside me I was turned to stone, so hard
I could not weep; the children wept. And my
Little Anselmo, peering at me, inquired:

'Father, what ails you?' And still I did not cry,
Nor did I answer, all that day and night
Until the next sun dawned. When one small ray

Found its way into our prison, and I made out
In their four faces the image of my own,
I bit my hands for grief; when they saw that,

They thought I did it from my hunger's pain,
And suddenly rose. 'Father: our pain,' they said,
'Will lessen if you eat us—you are the one

Who clothed us in this wretched flesh: we plead
For you to be the one who strips it away.'
I calmed myself to grieve them less. We stayed

Silent through that and then the following day.
O you hard earth, why didn't you open then?
When we had reached the fourth day, Gaddo lay

Stretched at my feet where he had fallen down:
'Father, why don't you help me?' he said, and died.
And surely as you see me, so one by one

I watched the others fall till all were dead,
Between the fifth day and the sixth. And I,
Already going blind, groped over my brood—

Calling to them, though I had watched them die,
For two long days. And then the hunger had more
Power than even sorrow had over me."

When he had finished, with a sideways stare
He gripped the skull again in his teeth, which ground
Strong as a dog's against the bone he tore.

Ah Pisa! You shame the peoples of the fair land
Where *sì* is spoken: slow as your neighbors are
To punish you, may Gorgona shift its ground,

And Capraia, till those islands make a bar
To dam the Arno, and drown your populace—
Every soul in you! Though Ugolino bore

The fame of having betrayed your fortresses,
Still it was wrong in you to so torment
His helpless children. You Thebes of latter days,

Their youthful ages made them innocent!—
Uguccione, Brigata, and the two
My song has named already. On we went,

To where frost roughly swathes a people who,
Instead of downward, turn their faces up.
There, weeping keeps them from weeping—for as they do,

Grief finds a barrier where the eyes would weep
But forced back inward, adds to their agonies:
A crystal visor of prior tears fills the cup

Below the eyebrow with a knot of ice.
And though, as when a callus has grown numb,
The cold had sucked all feeling from my face

I sensed a wind, and wondered from where it came:
"Master, who moves this? Is it not the case
All vapors are extinguished in this realm?"

"Soon," he responded, "you will reach a place
Where your own eyes—beholding what source this blast
Is poured by from above—will answer this."

And then one wretch encased in the frozen crust
Cried out to us, "O souls so cruel that here,
Of all the stations, you're assigned the last—

Lift the hard veils away from my face, I implore,
So that before the weeping freezes again
I can release a little of this despair

And misery that swell my heart." Whereon
I said, "If you would have me help you, disclose
To me who you are: if I don't help you then,

May I be sent to the bottom of the ice."
He answered, "I am Fra Alberigo, the man
Of fruit from the evil garden; in this place

I get my payment, date for fig." "Oh then,"
I said to him, "you are already dead?"
"I do not know what state my body is in,

Nor how it fares in the world above," he said.
"For Ptolomea's privilege is this:
Down to this place a soul is often conveyed

Before it is sent forth by Atropos.
So that you may more willingly scrape the cowl
Of tears made hard as glass that coats my face,

Know that as soon as a soul commits betrayal
The way I did, a devil displaces it
And governs inside the body until its toll

Of years elapses. Meanwhile, down to this vat
The soul falls headlong—so it could be true
That this shade, wintering here behind me, yet

Appears above on earth too: you must know,
If you were sent down only a short time past.
He is Ser Branca d'Oria; it's years ago

He first arrived here to be thus encased."
"Now you deceive me, for I am one who knows
That Branca d'Oria is not deceased:

He eats and drinks and sleeps and puts on clothes,"
I told him. And he answered, "In the ditch
Ruled by the Malebranche above, that seethes

And bubbles with the lake of clinging pitch,
The shade of Michel Zanche had not arrived
When this, his killer, had a devil encroach

His body (as did his kinsman, when they contrived
Together to perform their treachery)
And take his place in it. Now, as I craved,

Reach out your hand and open my eyes for me."
I did not open them—for to be rude
To such a one as him was courtesy.

Ah Genoese!—to every accustomed good,
Strangers; with every corruption, amply crowned:
Why hasn't the world expunged you as it should?

For with Romagna's worst spirit I have found
One of you—already, for deeds he was guilty of,
Bathed in Cocytus: in soul now underground

Who in body still appears alive, above.

## *Canto XXXIV [Satan]*

"And now, *Vexilla regis prodeunt*
*Inferni*—therefore, look," my master said
As we continued on the long descent,

“And see if you can make him out, ahead.”
As though, in the exhalation of heavy mist
Or while night darkened our hemisphere, one spied

A mill—blades turning in the wind, half-lost
Off in the distance—some structure of that kind
I seemed to make out now. But at a gust

Of wind, there being no other shelter at hand,
I drew behind my leader’s back again.
By now (and putting it in verse I find

Fear in myself still) I had journeyed down
To where the shades were covered wholly by ice,
Showing like straw in glass—some lying prone,

And some erect, some with the head toward us,
And others with the bottoms of the feet;
Another like a bow, bent feet to face.

When we had traveled forward to the spot
From which it pleased my master to have me see
That creature whose beauty once had been so great,

He made me stop, and moved from in front of me.
“Look: here is Dis,” he said, “and here is the place
Where you must arm yourself with the quality

Of fortitude.” How chilled and faint I was
On hearing that, you must not ask me, reader—
I do not write it; words would not suffice:

I neither died, nor kept alive—consider
With your own wits what I, alike denuded
Of death and life, became as I heard my leader.

The emperor of the realm of grief protruded
From mid-breast up above the surrounding ice.
A giant’s height, and mine, would have provided

Closer comparison than would the size
Of his arm and a giant. Envision the whole
That is proportionate to parts like these.

If he was truly once as beautiful
As he is ugly now, and raised his brows
Against his Maker—then all sorrow may well

Come out of him. How great a marvel it was
For me to see three faces on his head:
In front there was a red one; joined to this,

Each over the midpoint of a shoulder, he had
Two others—all three joining at the crown.
That on the right appeared to be a shade

Of whitish yellow; the third had such a mien
As those who come from where the Nile descends.
Two wings spread forth from under each face's chin,

Strong, and befitting such a bird, immense—
I have never seen at sea so broad a sail—
Unfeathered, batlike, and issuing three winds

That went forth as he beat them, to freeze the whole
Realm of Cocytus that surrounded him.
He wept with all six eyes, and the tears fell

Over his three chins mingled with bloody foam.
The teeth of each mouth held a sinner, kept
As by a flax rake: thus he held three of them

In agony. For the one the front mouth gripped,
The teeth were as nothing to the claws, which sliced
And tore the skin until his back was stripped.

"That soul," my master said, "who suffers most,
Is Judas Iscariot; head locked inside,
He flails his legs. Of the other two, who twist

With their heads down, the black mouth holds the shade
Of Brutus: writhing, but not a word will he scream;
Cassius is the sinewy one on the other side.

But night is rising again, and it is time
That we depart, for we have seen the whole."
As he requested, I put my arms round him,

And waiting until the wings were opened full
He took advantage of the time and place
And grasped the shaggy flank, and gripping still,

From tuft to tuft descended through the mass
Of matted hair and crusts of ice. And then,
When we had reached the pivot of the thighs,

Just where the haunch is at its thickest, with strain
And effort my master brought around his head
To where he'd had his legs: and from there on

He grappled the hair as someone climbing would—
So I supposed we were heading back to Hell.
"Cling tight, for it is stairs like these," he sighed

Like one who is exhausted, "which we must scale
To part from so much evil." Then he came up
Through a split stone, and placed me on its sill,

And climbed up toward me with his cautious step.
I raised my eyes, expecting I would see
Lucifer as I left him—and saw his shape

Inverted, with his legs held upward. May they
Who are too dull to see what point I had passed
Judge whether it perplexed me. "Come—the way

Is long, the road remaining to be crossed
Is hard: rise to your feet," the master said,
"The sun is at mid-tierce." We had come to rest

In nothing like a palace hall; instead
A kind of natural dungeon enveloped us,
With barely any light, the floor ill made.

"Before I free myself from the abyss,
My master," I said when I was on my feet,
"Speak, and dispel my error: where is the ice?

And how can he be fixed head-down like that?
And in so short a time, how can it be
Possible for the sun to make its transit

From evening to morning?" He answered me,
"You imagine you are still on the other side,
Across the center of the earth, where I

Grappled the hair on the evil serpent's hide
Who pierces the world. And all through my descent,
You were on that side; when I turned my head

And legs about, you passed the central point
To which is drawn, from every side, all weight.
Now you are on the opposite continent

Beneath the opposite hemisphere to that
Which canopies the great dry land therein:
Under the zenith of that one is the site

Whereon the Man was slain who without sin
Was born and lived; your feet this minute press
Upon a little sphere whose rounded skin

Forms the Judecca's other, outward face.
Here it is morning when it is evening there;
The one whose hair was like a ladder for us

Is still positioned as he was before.
On this side he fell down from Heaven; the earth,
Which till then stood out here, impelled by fear

Veiled itself in the sea and issued forth
In our own hemisphere. And possibly,
What now appears on this side fled its berth

And rushing upward left a cavity:
This hollow where we stand." There is below,
As far from Beelzebub as one can be

Within his tomb, a place one cannot know
By sight, but by the sound a little runnel
Makes as it wends the hollow rock its flow

Has worn, descending through its winding channel:
To get back up to the shining world from there
My guide and I went into that hidden tunnel;

And following its path, we took no care
To rest, but climbed: he first, then I—so far,
Through a round aperture I saw appear

Some of the beautiful things that Heaven bears,
Where we came forth, and once more saw the stars.

## FRANCIS PETRARCH (1303–1373)

*Translated by Mark Musa*

It is common to say that Petrarch was the first humanist and the first writer of the Renaissance—the first modern (as opposed to medieval) writer. Though such statements are always oversimplifications, it is true that, in many ways, Petrarch differs fundamentally from Dante, who lived only one generation before him. Petrarch was a great scholar of the Roman classics, collecting and editing the works of Cicero especially. His own works in Latin, sharply distinct from the Christian scholasticism of his day, catapulted him into such prominence that he was crowned poet laureate by the Roman senate in 1341. He was the most famous man of letters in Europe in his lifetime. His personal ambition and quest for fame became hallmarks of the humanistic movement and have become characteristic features of modern Western culture.

Ironically, Petrarch is most remembered today not for his Latin works, but for the 366 poems (*rime*) he wrote in Italian to a distant and mysterious young woman named Laura. In many respects, these poems are the fulfillment of the previous two centuries of European love poetry, from the Provençal troubadours and the vast literature of courtly (or Romantic) love to the spiritual refinements of Dante; but in some respects, they are so original that we are justified in calling the love poetry of the next four centuries "Petrarchan."

In the eight sonnets included here, the key features of Petrarchan love are evident. It is first and foremost a poetics of sexual frustration: Petrarch never actually meets Laura, but he broods upon her image, turning this brooding into a form of self-examination. He explores his emotions, which he finds hopelessly contradictory, the source of endless anxiety and uncertainty. He is like Augustine, waiting in the garden for a moment of conversion, but for Petrarch that moment never comes, even when Laura dies halfway through the sequence. (Augustine's *Confessions* and the letters of Abelard and Heloise were among the strongest influences on Petrarch.) He tries to relieve his obsession by writing poems, but they seem only to inflame his passion. He understands the destructiveness of his obsession; but like an addict, he keeps evoking Laura's image, deliberately deepening his own misery. He struggles to idealize and sublimate his desire, but that seems only to clarify and feed it. The only compensation for this life of torment is that the resulting poems will make him famous. Petrarchan love became one means for defining and exploring the individual self in the Renaissance. Even today, popular love songs preserve many of these Petrarchan features.

## Rime

### *1*

O You who hear within these scattered verses
the sound of sighs with which I fed my heart
in my first errant youthful days when I
in part was not the man I am today;

for all the ways in which I weep and speak
between vain hopes, between vain suffering,
in anyone who knows love through its trials,
in them, may I find pity and forgiveness.

For now I see, since I've become the talk
so long a time of people all around
(it often makes me feel so full of shame),

that from my vanities comes fruit of shame
and my repentance and the clearest knowledge
that worldly joy is a quick passing dream.

## 3

It was the day the sun's ray had turned pale
with pity for the suffering of his Maker
when I was caught, and I put up no fight,
my lady, for your lovely eyes had bound me.

It seemed no time to be on guard against
Love's blows; therefore, I went my way
secure and fearless—so, all my misfortunes
began in midst of universal woe.

Love found me all disarmed and found the way
was clear to reach my heart down through the eyes
which have become the halls and doors of tears.

It seems to me it did him little honor
to wound me with his arrow in my state
and to you, armed, not show his bow at all.

## 16

The old man takes his leave, white-haired and pale,
of the sweet place where he filled out his age
and leaves his little family, bewildered,
beholding its dear father disappear;

and then, dragging along his ancient limbs
throughout the very last days of his life,
helping himself with good will all he can,
broken by years, and wearied by the road,

he comes to Rome, pursuing his desire,
to look upon the likeness of the One
he hopes to see again up there in heaven.

Just so, alas, sometimes I go, my lady,
searching as much as possible in others
for your true, your desirable form.

## 61

Oh blessed be the day, the month, the year,
the season and the time, the hour, the instant,

the gracious countryside, the place where I
was struck by those two lovely eyes that bound me;

and blessed be the first sweet agony
I felt when I found myself bound to Love,
the bow and all the arrows that have pierced me,
the wounds that reach the bottom of my heart.

And blessed be all the poetry
I scattered, calling out my lady's name,
and all the sighs, and tears, and the desire;

blessed be all the paper upon which
I earn her fame, and every thought of mine,
only of her, and shared with no one else.

## *132*

If it's not love, then what is it I feel?
But if it's love, by God, what is this thing?
If good, why then the bitter mortal sting?
If bad, then why is every torment sweet?

If I burn willingly, why weep and grieve?
And if against my will, what good lamenting?
O living death, O pleasurable harm,
how can you rule me if I not consent?

And if I do consent, it's wrong to grieve.
Caught in contrasting winds in a frail boat
on the high seas I am without a helm,

so light of wisdom, so laden of error,
that I myself do not know what I want,
and shiver in midsummer, burn in winter.

## *319*

My days, swifter than any fawn, have fled
like shadows, and for me no good has lasted
more than a wink, and few are those calm hours
whose bittersweetness I keep in my mind.

O wretched world, changing and arrogant,
a man who puts his hope in you is blind:
from you my heart was torn and now is held
by one whose flesh and bones are turned to dust.

But her best form, which still continues living
and will forever live high in the heavens,
makes me fall more in love with all her beauty;

and as my hair is changing I think only
what she is like today and where she dwells,
what it was like to see her lovely veil.

## 333

Go now, my grieving verse, to the hard stone
that hides my precious treasure in the earth;
and there call her, who will respond from Heaven
although her mortal part be darkly buried,

and tell her I am weary now of living,
of sailing through the horrors of this sea,
but that, by gathering up her scattered leaves,
I follow her this way, step after step,

speaking of her alone, alive and dead
(rather, alive, and now immortalized),
so that the world may know and love her more.

Let her watch for the day I pass away
(It is not far from now), let her meet me,
call me, draw me to what she is in Heaven.

## 365

I go my way regretting those past times
I spent in loving something which was mortal
instead of soaring high, since I had wings
that might have taken me to higher levels.

You who see all my shameful, wicked errors,
King of all heaven, invisible, immortal,
help this frail soul of mine for she has strayed,
and all her emptiness fill up with grace,

so that, having once lived in storms, at war,
I may now die in peace, in port; and if my stay
was vain, at least let my departure count.

Over that little life that still remains to me,
and at my death, deign that your head be present:
You know You are the only hope I have.

## Geoffrey Chaucer (1343–1400)

*Glossed edition by V.A. Kolve and Glending Olson*

Under the influence of Dante and Boccaccio, Geoffrey Chaucer created, in his *Canterbury Tales,* the first fully individualized ("realistic") fictional characters in English literature. Each tale is put into the mouth of a carefully drawn narrator, so that the tale's meaning depends largely on its teller's narrative voice, which is often ironic. The resulting literary effects can be dazzlingly complex, as Chaucer creates fictions within fictions within fictions. Statements in the *Tales* can seldom be taken at face value, and it is often impossible to know what Chaucer himself believes. The "General Prologue," justly famous in its own right, introduces both the narrator and the pilgrim narrators who agree to tell tales to one another to wile away the time as they journey to their destination. The "General Prologue" draws ingenious portraits of most of the succeeding tales' narrators. From the "General Prologue," we have included only the famously beautiful opening and the description of the Pardoner, whose tale we then include in full.

The Pardoner is one of the most complex examples of Chaucer's narrative art, and the meaning of his tale is debated vigorously by scholars and critics. Chaucer strongly implies that the Pardoner is either a eunuch or a homosexual and presents him as physically and morally repellent. The Pardoner describes himself in his own Prologue as a vicious con artist who sells fake relics to the poor and ignorant, a moral monster proud of his own sinfulness. He then proceeds to demonstrate his skill in a beautifully crafted and dramatically powerful sermon against avarice. Ironically, he is preaching against his own worst sins, and thus the preaching damns the preacher. The mysterious old man who appears in the tale may reflect the Pardoner's own inner despair over his moral condition. The world that the Pardoner depicts in his tale is totally devoid of any redeeming value; it is populated by fools who pay no attention to God, to others, or to their own salvation.

Without even pausing at the end of his tale, the Pardoner proceeds to try to sell his relics to his audience, although he has already boasted to them of his dishonesty. The reader can only guess what psychological forces drive such a character and whether Chaucer is trying to provoke our loathing or a more sympathetic Christian response to the Pardoner's social isolation and spiritual pain.

The folktale of the three men who seek death and find it in gold is widespread and probably derives from the East; it can be found in the Arabic *Thousand and One Nights* and in Indian versions as well; the American film classic *Treasure of the Sierra Madre* is a variation on it.

It should also be noted that in *The Canterbury Tales,* Chaucer invents what will become the standard poetic line in English, iambic pentameter, which he uses to capture an idiomatic, conversational tone in his poetry. His language is Middle English. Though it may seem difficult at first, a little practice reading aloud will reveal Chaucer's charm, humor, and musicality.

## *The Canterbury Tales*

### *from The General Prologue*

Whan that Aprill with his shoures sote° — *sweet showers*
The droghte° of Marche hath perced to the rote,° — *dryness / root*

And bathed every veyne° in swich licour,° *vein / such moisture*
Of which vertu° engendred is the flour; *By power of which*
Whan Zephirus° eek with his swete breeth *the west wind*
Inspired° hath in every holt° and heeth° *Breathed into / wood / heath*
The tendre croppes,° and the yonge sonne *sprouts*
Hath in the Ram his halfe cours y-ronne;
And smale fowles° maken melodye, *birds*
That slepen al the night with open yë°— *eye(s)*
So priketh hem Nature in hir corages—
Than longen° folk to goon° on pilgrimages, *Then long / go*
And palmeres for to seken straunge strondes,
To ferne halwes°, couthe° in sondry londes; *far-off shires / known*
And specially, from every shires ende
Of Engelond to Caunterbury they wende,
The holy blisful martir for to seke,° *seek*
That hem hath holpen,° whan that they were seke.° *helped / sick*
Bifel° that, in that seson on a day, *It befell*
In Southwerk at the Tabard° as I lay° *(an inn) / lodged*
Redy to wenden° on my pilgrimage *depart*
To Caunterbury with ful devout corage,° *heart*
At night was come into that hostelrye° *inn*
Wel nyne and twenty in a companye
Of sondry folk, by aventure° y-falle° *chance / fallen*
In felawshipe, and pilgrims were they alle,
That toward Caunterbury wolden° ryde. *wished to*
The chambres° and the stables weren wyde,° *bedrooms/ spacious*
And wel we weren esed° atte beste.° *made comfortable / in the best (ways)*
And shortly, whan the sonne was to° reste, *at*
So hadde I spoken with hem everichon° *each and every one*
That I was of hir felawshipe anon,
And made forward° erly for to ryse, *agreement*
To take oure wey, ther as I yow devyse.° *(will) tell*
But natheles,° whyl I have tyme and space, *nevertheless*
Er that I ferther in this tale pace,° *pass on*
Me thinketh it acordaunt to resoun
To telle yow al the condicioun
Of ech of hem, so as it semed me,° *seemed to me*
And whiche° they weren, and of what degree,° *what / status*
And eek in what array° that they were inne. *clothing*

* * *

. . . Ther rood a gentil PARDONER
Of Rouncival, his° freend and his compeer,° *the summoner / companion*
That streight was comen fro the court of Rome.

Ful loude he song,° "Com hider,° love, to me."  *sang / hither*
This somnour bar to° him a stif burdoun,°  *accompanied / sturdy bass*
Was nevere trompe° of half so greet a soun.°  *trumpet / sound*
This pardoner hadde heer° as yelow as wex,°  *hair / wax*
But smothe it heng,° as dooth a strike of flex;°  *hung / bunch of flax*
By ounces° henge his lokkes that he hadde,  *In thin strands*
And therwith° he his shuldres overspradde;°  *with it / covered*
But thinne it lay, by colpons° oon and oon;  *in small bunches*
But hood, for jolitee,° wered° he noon,  *sportiveness / wore*
For it was trussed° up in his walet.°  *packed / pouch*
Him thoughte he rood al of the newe jet;
Dischevele, save his cappe, he rood al bare.
Swiche glaringe eyen° hadde he as an hare.  *staring eyes*
A vernicle hadde he sowed on his cappe.
His walet lay biforn° him in his lappe,  *in front of*
Bretful of pardoun comen from Rome al hoot.
A voys he hadde as smal as hath a goot.°  *goat*
No berd hadde he, ne nevere sholde have,
As smothe it was as it were late shave:°  *recently shaved*
I trowe° he were a gelding or a mare.  *believe*
But of his craft, fro Berwik into Ware,
Ne was ther swich another pardoner.
For in his male° he hadde a pilwe-beer,°  *bag / pillowcase*
Which that he seyde was Oure Lady veyl.°  *Our Lady's veil*
He seyde he hadde a gobet° of the seyl°  *piece / sail*
That seynt Peter hadde, whan that he wente°  *walked*
Upon the see, til Jesu Crist him hente.°  *took hold of*
He hadde a croys° of latoun,° ful of stones,°  *cross / metal / gems*
And in a glas° he hadde pigges bones.  *glass container*
But with thise relikes,° whan that he fond  *relics*
A povre person dwellinge upon lond,
Upon a° day he gat him more moneye  *In one*
Than that the person gat in monthes tweye.°  *two*
And thus, with feyned flaterye and japes,°  *tricks*
He made the person and the peple his apes.°  *fools*
But trewely to tellen, atte laste,°  *after all*
He was in chirche a noble ecclesiaste.°  *preacher*
Wel coude he rede a lessoun or a storie,°  *religious tale*
But alderbest° he song° an offertorie;  *best of all / sang*
For wel he wiste,° whan that song was songe,  *knew*
He moste preche, and wel affyle° his tonge  *make smooth*
To winne silver, as he ful wel coude—
Therefore he song the murierly° and loude. . . .  *more merrily*

* * *

## *The Pardoner's Prologue and Tale*

### *The Prologue*

"Thou bel amy,° thou Pardoner," he° seyde, *the host / sweet friend*
"Tel us som mirthe or japes° right anon." *jokes*
"It shall be doon," quod° he, "by Seint Ronyon! *said*
But first," quod he, "heer at this ale-stake° *tavern sign*
I wol both drinke and eten° of a cake." *eat*
But right anon thise gentils gonne to crye,
"Nay! lat him telle us of no ribaudye;° *ribaldry*
Tel us som moral thing, that we may lere° *learn*
Som wit,° and thanne wol we gladly here."° *Something instructive / listen*
"I graunte,° y-wis,"° quod he, "but I mot° thinke *agree / certainly / must*
Upon som honest° thing whyl that I drinke." *decent, decorous*
"Lordinges," quod he, "in chirches whan I preche,
I peyne me° to han an hauteyn° speche, *take pains / elevated*
And ringe it out as round as gooth° a belle, *sounds*
For I can al by rote° that I telle. *know all by memory*
My theme° is alwey oon,° and evere was— *text / always the same*
*Radix malorum est cupiditas.*
First I pronounce° whennes° that I come, *proclaim / whence, from where*
And thanne my bulles shewe I, alle and somme.° *one and all*
Oure lige lordes seel on my patente,° *license*
That shewe I first, my body° to warente,° *person / authorize*
That no man be so bold, ne preest ne clerk,° *neither priest nor scholar*
Me to destourbe of Cristes holy werk;
And after that thanne telle I forth my tales.
Bulles of popes and of cardinales,
Of patriarkes,° and bishoppes I shewe, *heads of churches*
And in Latyn I speke a wordes fewe,
To saffron with my predicacioun,
And for to stire° hem to devocioun. *stir*
Thanne shewe I forth my longe cristal stones,° *glass cases*
Y-crammed ful of cloutes° and of bones— *rags*
Reliks been they, as wenen they echoon.
Thanne have I in latoun a sholder-boon
Which that was of an holy Jewes shepe.
'Goode men,' seye I, 'tak of my wordes kepe:° *heed*
If that this boon be wasshe° in any welle, *washed, dunked*
If cow, or calf, or sheep, or oxe swelle,° *swell (up)*
That any worm hath ete, or worm y-stonge,
Tak water of that welle, and wash his tonge,
And it is hool° anon;° and forthermore, *healed / at once*
Of pokkes° and of scabbe and every sore *pox*
Shal every sheep be hool,° that of this welle *healed*
Drinketh a draughte. Tak kepe° eek° what I telle: *heed / also*

If that the good-man that the bestes° oweth° — *animals / owns*
Wol every wike,° er° that the cok him croweth, — *week / before*
Fastinge,° drinken of this welle a draughte— — *(While) fasting*
As thilke° holy Jewe oure eldres taughte— — *that same*
His bestes and his stoor° shal multiplye. — *stock*
And, sires, also it heleth° jalousye: — *heals*
For though a man be falle in jalous rage,
Let maken with this water his potage,
And nevere shal he more his wyf mistriste,° — *mistrust*
Though he the sooth° of hir defaute° wiste°— — *truth / erring / should know*
Al° had she taken° preestes two or three. — *Even if / taken (as lovers)*
Heer is a miteyn° eek, that ye may see: — *mitten*
He that his hond wol putte in this miteyn,
He shal have multiplying of his greyn° — *grain*
Whan he hath sowen, be it whete° or otes,° — *wheat / oats*
So that he offre pens, or elles grotes.
Goode men and wommen, o° thing warne° I yow: — *one / tell*
If any wight° be in this chirche now, — *person*
That hath doon sinne horrible, that he
Dar° nat for shame of it y-shriven be, — *Dare*
Or any womman, be she yong or old,
That hath y-maked hir housbonde cokewold,° — *a cuckold*
Swich° folk shul have no power ne no grace — *Such*
To offren° to my reliks in this place. — *To offer (money)*
And whoso findeth him out of swich blame,° — *not deserving such blame*
He wol com up and offre a° Goddes name, — *make an offereing in*
And I assoille° him by the auctoritee° — *(will) absolve / authority*
Which that by bulle y-graunted was to me.'
By this gaude° have I wonne,° yeer° by yeer, — *trick / earned / year*
An hundred mark sith I was pardoner.
I stonde lyk a clerk° in my pulpet, — *scholar*
And whan the lewed° peple is doun y-set, — *ignorant, unlearned*
I preche, so as ye han herd bifore,
And telle an hundred false japes° more. — *tricks, stories*
Thanne peyne I me° to strecche forth the nekke, — *I take pains*
And est and west upon the peple I bekke° — *nod*
As doth a dowve,° sittinge on a berne.° — *dove / in a barn*
Myn hondes and my tonge goon so yerne° — *rapidly*
That it is joye to see my bisinesse.
Of avaryce and of swich° cursednesse — *such*
Is al my preching, for° to make hem free° — *in order / generous*
To yeven hir pens, and namely unto me.
For myn entente° is nat but for to winne,° — *intention / profit*
And nothing° for correccioun of sinne: — *not at all*
I rekke° nevere, whan that they ben beried,° — *care / buried*
Though that hir soules goon a-blakeberied!

For certes,° many a predicacioun° *certainly / sermon*
Comth ofte tyme of yvel° entencioun: *evil*
Som for plesaunce° of folk and flaterye, *the entertainment*
To been avaunced by ypocrisye,
And som for veyne glorie,° and som for hate. *vainglory*
For whan I dar non other weyes debate,
Than wol I stinge him with my tonge smerte° *sharp*
In preching, so that he shal nat asterte° *leap up (to protest)*
To been° defamed falsly, if that he *At being*
Hath trespased to° my brethren or to me. *wronged*
For, though I telle noght his propre° name, *own*
Men shal wel knowe that it is the same
By signes and by othere circumstances.
Thus quyte° I folk that doon us displesances;° *requite / offenses*
Thus spitte I out my venim under hewe° *hue, coloring*
Of holynesse, to semen° holy and trewe. *seem*
But shortly° myn entente I wol devyse:° *briefly / describe*
I preche of no thing but for coveityse.° *out of covetousness*
Therfore my theme is yet, and evere was,
*Radix malorum est cupiditas.*
Thus can I preche agayn° that same vyce *against*
Which that I use,° and that is avaryce. *practice*
But though myself be gilty in that sinne,
Yet can I maken other folk to twinne° *part*
From avaryce, and sore° to repente. *ardently*
But that is nat my principal entente:
I preche nothing but for coveityse.
Of this matere° it oughte y-nogh suffyse. *subject*
Than telle I hem ensamples many oon° *examples many a one*
Of olde stories longe tyme agoon,° *past*
For lewed° peple loven tales olde; *unlearned*
Swich° thinges can they wel reporte° and holde.° *Such / repeat / remember*
What, trowe ye, the whyles I may preche
And winne° gold and silver for° I teche, *obtain / because*
That I wol live in povert° wilfully?° *poverty / willingly*
Nay, nay, I thoghte° it nevere, trewely! *considered*
For I wol preche and begge in sondry° londes; *various*
I wol nat do no labour with myn hondes,
Ne make baskettes, and live therby,
By cause I wol nat beggen ydelly.° *without profit*
I wol non of the Apostles counterfete:° *imitate*
I wol have money, wolle,° chese, and whete, *wool*
Al° were it yeven of° the povereste page,° *Even if / given by / servant*
Or of° the povereste widwe° in a village, *by / poorest widow*
Al sholde hir children sterve for famyne.
Nay! I wol drinke licour° of the vyne, *liquor, wine*

And have a joly wenche in every toun.
But herkneth,° lordinges, in conclusioun: *listen*
Youre lyking is that I shall telle a tale.
Now have I dronke a draughte of corny° ale, *malty*
By God, I hope I shal yow telle a thing
That shal by resoun° been at° youre lyking. *with reason / to*
For though myself be a ful vicious° man, *evil, vice-ridden*
A moral tale yet I yow telle can,
Which I am wont to preche for to winne.
Now holde youre pees,° my tale I wol beginne." *peace*

### *The Tale*

In Flaundres whylom was° a compaignye *once (there) was*
Of yonge folk, that haunteden folye—
As ryot, hasard, stewes, and tavernes,
Where as° with harpes, lutes, and giternes,° *There where I / guitars*
They daunce and pleyen at dees° bothe day and night, *dice*
And eten also and drinken over hir might,° *beyond their capacity*
Thurgh which they doon the devel sacrifyse° *make sacrifice to the devil*
Withinne that develes temple, in cursed wyse,° *way*
By superfluitee° abhominable. *excess*
Hir othes° been so grete and so dampnable,° *oaths, curses / condemnable*
That it is grisly for to here hem swere.
Our blissed Lordes body they totere°— *tear apart*
Hem thoughte° Jewes rente° him noght y-nough— *It seemed to them / tore*
And ech° of hem at otheres sinne lough.° *each / laughed*
And right anon thanne comen tombesteres° *female tumblers, dancers*
Fetys and smale, and yonge fruytesteres,
Singeres with harpes, baudes,° wafereres,° *bawds / girls selling cakes*
Whiche been the verray° develes officeres *the very*
To kindle and blowe the fyr of lecherye
That is annexed° unto glotonye: *joined (as a sin)*
The Holy Writ take I to my witnesse
That luxurie° is in wyn and dronkenesse. *lechery*
Lo, how that dronken Loth° unkindely° *Lot / unnaturally*
Lay by his doghtres two, unwitingly;° *unknowingly*
So dronke he was, he niste° what he wroghte.° *knew not / did*
Herodes,° whoso wel the stories soghte,° *Herod / should seek out*
Whan he of wyn was repleet° at his feste, *replete, full*
Right at his owene table he yaf his heste° *gave / command*
To sleen the Baptist John ful giltelees.° *guiltless (innocent)*
Senek° seith a good word doutelees: *Seneca*
He seith, he can no difference finde
Bitwix a man that is out of his minde
And a man which that is dronkelewe,° *drunken*

But that woodnesse, y-fallen in a shrewe,  
Persevereth lenger° than doth dronkenesse. *Continues longer*  
O glotonye,° ful of cursednesse! *gluttony*  
O cause first° of oure confusioun!° *first cause / ruin*  
O original° of oure dampnacioun, *origin*  
Til Crist had boght us with his blood agayn!  
Lo, how dere,° shortly for to sayn,° *costly / to speak briefly*  
Aboght was thilke cursed vileinye;  
Corrupt° was al this world for glotonye! *Corrupted*  
Adam oure fader and his wyf also  
Fro Paradys to labour and to wo  
Were driven for that vyce, it is no drede.° *doubt*  
For whyl that Adam fasted, as I rede,° *read*  
He was in Paradys; and whan that he  
Eet of the fruyt defended° on the tree, *forbidden*  
Anon° he was outcast to wo and peyne.° *Immediately / pain*  
O glotonye, on thee wel oghte us pleyne!  
O, wiste a man° how manye maladyes *(if) a man knew*  
Folwen of° excesse and of glotonyes, *Follow on*  
He wolde been the more mesurable° *measured, temperate*  
Of his diete, sittinge at his table.  
Allas! the shorte throte, the tendre mouth,  
Maketh that,° est and west, and north and south, *Causes*  
In erthe, in eir,° in water, men to swinke° *air / labor*  
To gete a glotoun deyntee° mete and drinke! *dainty*  
Of this matere,° O Paul, wel canstow trete:° *subject / canst thou treat*  
"Mete° unto wombe,° and wombe eek unto mete, *Meat / belly*  
Shal God destroyen bothe," as Paulus seith.  
Allas! a foul thing is it, by my feith,  
To seye this word, and fouler is the dede,  
Whan man so drinketh of the whyte and rede  
That of his throte he maketh his privee,° *privy (toilet)*  
Thurgh thilke° cursed superfluitee.° *that same / excess*  
The apostel, weping, seith ful pitously,  
"Ther walken manye of whiche yow told have I"—  
I seye it now weping with pitous voys—  
"They been enemys of Cristes croys,° *cross*  
Of which the ende is deeth: wombe° is her° god!" *belly / their*  
O wombe! O bely! O stinking cod,  
Fulfild of donge and of corrupcioun!  
At either ende of thee foul is the soun.° *sound*  
How° greet labour and cost is thee to finde!° *What / to provide for*  
Thise cookes, how they stampe,° and streyne,° and grinde, *pound / strain*  
And turnen substaunce into accident,  
To fulfille al thy likerous talent!° *lecherous (here, gluttonous) appetite*  
Out of the harde bones knokke they

The mary,° for they caste noght° awey — *marrow / nothing*
That may go thurgh the golet° softe and swote;° — *gullet / sweet*
Of spicerye° of leef, and bark, and rote° — *spices / root(s)*
Shal been his sauce y-maked by delyt,° — *to give pleasure*
To make him yet a newer° appetyt. — *renewed*
But certes, he that haunteth swich delyces
Is deed, whyl that° he liveth in tho° vyces. — *while / those*
A lecherous thing is wyn, and dronkenesse
Is ful of stryving° and of wrecchednesse. — *quarreling*
O dronke man, disfigured is thy face,
Sour is thy breeth, foul artow° to embrace, — *art thou*
And thurgh thy dronke nose semeth the soun° — *sound*
As though thou seydest ay° "Sampsoun, Sampsoun"; — *ever*
And yet, God wot,° Sampsoun drank nevere no wyn. — *knows*
Thou fallest, as it were a stiked swyn;° — *stuck pig*
Thy tonge is lost, and al thyn honest cure,° — *care for decency*
For dronkenesse is verray sepulture° — *the true tomb*
Of mannes wit° and his discrecioun.° — *understanding / discretion*
In whom that° drinke hath dominacioun, — *In him whom*
He can no conseil° kepe, it is no drede.° — *secrets / doubt*
Now kepe yow fro the whyte and fro the rede—
And namely° fro the whyte wyn of Lepe — *especially*
That is to selle° in Fishstrete° or in Chepe.° — *for sale / Fish Street / Cheapside*
This wyn of Spaigne crepeth subtilly
In othere wynes growinge faste by,
Of° which ther ryseth swich fumositee,° — *From / vapor*
That whan a man hath dronken draughtes three
And weneth° that he be at hoom in Chepe, — *thinks*
He is in Spaigne, right at the toune of Lepe,
Nat at The Rochel,° ne at Burdeux toun;° — *La Rochelle / Bordeaux*
And thanne wol he seye, "Sampsoun, Sampsoun."
But herkneth,° lordinges, o° word I yow preye, — *listen / one*
That alle the sovereyn actes,° dar I seye, — *supreme deeds*
Of victories in the Olde Testament,
Thurgh verray° God, that is omnipotent, — *true*
Were doon in abstinence and in preyere:
Loketh the Bible, and ther ye may it lere.° — *learn*
Loke Attila, the grete conquerour,
Deyde° in his sleep, with shame and dishonour, — *Died*
Bledinge ay° at his nose in dronkenesse: — *continually*
A capitayn shoulde live in sobrenesse.
And over al this, avyseth yow right wel° — *be well advised*
What was comaunded unto Lamuel°— — *Lemuel*
Nat Samuel, but Lamuel, seye I—
Redeth the Bible, and finde it expresly
Of wyn-yeving to hem that han justyse.

Namore of this, for it may wel suffyse.
And now that I have spoke of glotonye,
Now wol I yow defenden° hasardrye.° *forbid / gambling at dice*
Hasard is verray moder° of lesinges,° *the true mother / lies*
And of deceite and cursed forsweringes,° *perjuries*
Blaspheme of Crist, manslaughtre, and wast° also *waste*
Of catel° and of tyme; and forthermo, *goods*
It is repreve° and contrarie of honour *a reproach*
For to ben holde a commune hasardour.° *gambler*
And ever the hyer° he is of estaat° *higher / in social rank*
The more is he y-holden desolaat:° *considered debased*
If that a prince useth° hasardrye, *practices*
In alle governaunce and policye
He is, as by commune opinioun,
Y-holde the lasse in reputacioun.
Stilbon, that was a wys° embassadour, *wise*
Was sent to Corinthe in ful greet honour,
For Lacidomie° to make hire alliaunce.° *Lacedaemon (Sparta) / their alliance*
And whan he cam, him happede par chaunce° *it happened by chance*
That alle the grettest° that were of that lond, *greatest (men)*
Pleyinge atte° hasard he hem fond. *at (the)*
For which, as sone as it mighte be,° *could be*
He stal him° hoom agayn to his contree, *stole away*
And seyde, “Ther wol I nat lese° my name,° *lose / (good) name*
Ne I wol nat take on me so greet defame,° *dishonor*
Yow for to allye° unto none hasardours.° *to ally / gamblers*
Sendeth othere wyse embassadours—
For by my trouthe, me were levere dye° *I would rather die*
Than I yow sholde to hasardours allye.
For ye that been so glorious in honours
Shul nat allyen yow with hasardours
As by my wil, ne as by my tretee.”° *negotiations*
This wyse philosophre, thus seyde he.
Loke eek° that to the king Demetrius *also*
The king of Parthes,° as the book seith us, *Parthia*
Sente him a paire of dees° of gold in scorn, *dice*
For he hadde used hasard ther-biforn;
For which he heeld his glorie or his renoun° *renown*
At no value or reputacioun.
Lordes may finden other maner pley
Honeste° y-nough to dryve the day awey. *Honorable*
Now wol I speke of othes° false and grete *oaths, curses*
A word or two, as olde bokes trete.
Gret swering° is a thing abhominable, *cursing*
And false swering is yet more reprevable.° *reproachable*
The heighe° God forbad swering at al— *high*

Witnesse on Mathew—but in special
Of swering seith the holy Jeremye,° *Jeremiah*
"Thou shalt swere sooth° thyn othes° and nat lye, *truly / oaths*
And swere in dome,° and eek *(good) judgment*
in rightwisnesse;"° *righteousness*
But ydel° swering is a cursednesse.° *vain / wickedness*
Bihold and see, that in the first table° *tablet (of Moses)*
Of heighe Goddes hestes° honurable, *commandments*
How that the seconde heste of him is this:
"Tak nat my name in ydel° or amis."° *in vain / amiss (wrongly)*
Lo, rather° he forbedeth swich° swering *earlier (in the list) / such*
Than homicyde or many a cursed thing—
I seye that, as by ordre,° thus it stondeth— *in terms of the order*
This knoweth, that his hestes understondeth,
How that the second heste of God is that.
And forther over,° I wol thee telle al plat° *moreover / flatly*
That vengeance shal nat parten° from his hous *depart*
That° of his othes is to° outrageous. *Who / too*
"By Goddes precious herte," and "By his nayles,"
And "By the blode of Crist that is in Hayles,
Seven is my chaunce, and thyn is cink° and treye;"° *five / three*
"By Goddes armes, if thou falsly pleye,
This dagger shal thurghout thyn herte go!"
This fruyt cometh of the bicched bones two—
Forswering,° ire,° falsnesse, homicyde. *Perjury / anger*
Now for the love of Crist that for us dyde,
Lete° youre othes, bothe grete and smale. *Cease*
But, sires, now wol I telle forth my tale.
Thise ryotoures° three of which I telle, *rioters, revelers*
Longe erst er° pryme° rong of any belle, *before / 9 A.M.*
Were set hem° in a taverne for to drinke; *Had set themselves down*
And as they sat, they herde a belle clinke
Biforn a cors° was° caried to his grave. *corpse / (which) was (being)*
That oon of hem gan callen to his knave,
"Go bet," quod he, "and axe redily,
What cors is this that passeth heer forby;° *by here*
And looke that thou reporte his name wel."
"Sire," quod this boy, "it nedeth never-a-del.° *it isn't at all necessary*
It was me told, er° ye cam heer two houres. *before*
He was, pardee, an old felawe° of youres; *companion*
And sodeynly he was y-slayn to-night,
For-dronke,° as he sat on his bench upright. *Dead drunk*
Ther cam a privee° theef men clepeth° Deeth, *secret / call*
That in this contree° al the peple sleeth,° *region / kills*
And with his spere he smoot his herte atwo,
And wente his wey withouten wordes mo.° *more*

He hath a thousand slayn this pestilence.° *(during) this plague*
And maister, er° ye come in his presence, *before*
Me thinketh° that it were necessarie *it seems to me*
For to be war° of swich an adversarie: *aware, careful*
Beth redy for to mete him everemore.° *always*
Thus taughte me my dame,° I sey namore." *mother*
"By Seinte Marie," seyde this taverner,° *tavernkeeper*
"The child seith sooth, for he hath slayn this yeer,
Henne° over a myle, withinne a greet village, *Hence, from here*
Bothe man and womman, child, and hyne,° and page;° *laborer / servant*
I trowe° his habitacioun be there. *believe*
To been avysed° greet wisdom it were, *forewarned*
Er that° he dide a man a dishonour." *Before*
"Ye,° Goddes armes," quod° this ryotour,° *Aye, yes / said / reveler*
"Is it swich peril with him for to mete?
I shal him seke by wey° and eek° by strete, *road / also*
I make avow to° Goddes digne° bones! *avow (it) by / worthy*
Herkneth, felawes, we three been al ones:° *all of one mind*
Lat ech° of us holde up his hond til other,° *each / to the other*
And ech of us bicomen otheres° brother, *the others*
And we wol sleen° this false traytour Deeth. *slay*
He shal be slayn, he that so manye sleeth,
By Goddes dignitee,° er it be night." *worthiness*
Togidres° han thise three hir trouthes plight° *Together / plighted their troth*
To live and dyen ech of hem for other,° *one another*
As though he were his owene y-boren° brother. *born*
And up they sterte,° al dronken in this rage,° *leaped / passion*
And forth they goon towardes that village
Of which the taverner hadde spoke biforn,
And many a grisly ooth thanne han they sworn,
And Cristes blessed body they to-rente°— *tore apart*
Deeth shal be deed, if that they may him hente.° *seize*
Whan they han goon nat fully half a myle,
Right° as they wolde han troden° over a style,° *Just / stepped / stile*
An old man and a povre° with hem mette. *poor (one)*
This olde man ful mekely° hem grette,° *meekly / greeted them*
And seyde thus, "Now, lordes, God yow see!"° *may God protect you*
The proudest of thise ryotoures three
Answerde agayn, "What, carl,° with sory grace!° *Hey, fellow / confound you*
Why artow al forwrapped save thy face?
Why livestow° so longe in so greet age?" *livest thou*
This olde man gan loke in° his visage, *scrutinized*
And seyde thus, "For° I ne can nat finde *Because*
A man, though that I walked into Inde,° *India*
Neither in citee nor in no village,

That wolde chaunge his youthe for myn age;
And therfore moot° I han myn age stille, *must*
As longe time as it is Goddes wille.
Ne Deeth, allas! ne wol nat han my lyf.
Thus walke I, lyk° a restelees caityf,° *like / captive*
And on the ground, which is my modres° gate, *mother's*
I knokke with my staf bothe erly and late,
And seye, 'Leve° moder, leet me in! *Dear*
Lo, how I vanish,° flesh, and blood, and skin! *waste away*
Allas! whan shul my bones been at reste?
Moder, with yow wolde I chaunge° my cheste° *exchange / chest (of clothes)*
That in my chambre longe tyme hath be,° *been*
Ye, for an heyre clout° to wrappe me!' *haircloth (for burial)*
But yet to me she wol nat do that grace,
For which ful pale and welked° is my face. *withered*
But sires, to yow it is no curteisye
To speken to an old man vileinye,° *rudeness*
But° he trespasse° in worde or elles° in dede. *Unless / offend / else*
In Holy Writ ye may yourself wel rede,° *read*
'Agayns° an old man, hoor° upon his heed, *Before / hoary,white*
Ye sholde aryse.' Wherfor I yeve yow reed:
Ne dooth unto an old man noon harm now,
Namore than that ye wolde men did to yow
In age, if that ye so longe abyde.° *remain (alive)*
And God be with yow, wher ye go° or ryde; *walk*
I moot° go thider as° I have to go." *must / thither where*
"Nay, olde cherl, by God, thou shalt nat so,"
Seyde this other hasardour° anon;° *gambler / at once*
"Thou partest° nat so lightly, by Seint John! *departest*
Thou spak right now of thilke° traitour Deeth *that same*
That in this contree alle oure frendes sleeth.
Have heer my trouthe,° as° thou art his espye,° *pledge / since / spy*
Telle wher he is, or thou shalt it abye,° *pay for*
By God, and by the holy sacrament!
For soothly thou art oon of his assent° *in league with him*
To sleen us yonge folk, thou false theef!"
"Now, sires," quod he, "if that yow be so leef° *desirous*
To finde Deeth, turne up this croked° wey, *crooked*
For in that grove I lafte° him, by my fey,° *left / faith*
Under a tree, and there he wol abyde:° *stay*
Nat for youre boost he wole him nothing hyde.
See ye that ook?° right ther ye shul him finde. *oak*
God save yow, that boghte agayn° mankinde, *redeemed*
And yow amende!"° Thus seyde this olde man. *make you better*
And everich° of thise ryotoures° ran, *each / revelers*

Til he cam to that tree, and ther they founde
Of florins° fyne of golde y-coyned° rounde *florins, coins / coined*
Wel ny an° eighte busshels, as hem thoughte.° *nearly / it seemed to them*
No lenger thanne° after Deeth they soughte, *No longer then*
But ech° of hem so glad was of that sighte— *each*
For that the florins been so faire and brighte—
That doun they sette hem by this precious hord.
The worste of hem he spake the firste word.
"Brethren," quod he, "take kepe° what that I seye: *heed*
My wit° is greet, though that I bourde° and pleye. *understanding / jest*
This tresor° hath Fortune unto us yiven° *treasure / given*
In mirthe and jolitee° our lyf to liven, *merriment*
And lightly as it comth, so wol we spende.
Ey! Goddes precious dignitee!° who wende° *worthiness / would have supposed*
To-day that we sholde han so fair a grace?° *favor*
But° mighte this gold be caried fro this place *If only*
Hoom to myn hous—or elles unto youres—
For wel ye woot° that al this gold is oures— *know*
Thanne were we in heigh felicitee.° *supreme happiness*
But trewely, by daye it may nat be:° *be (done)*
Men wolde seyn that we were theves stronge,° *flagrant*
And for oure owene tresor doon us honge.° *have us hanged*
This tresor moste y-caried be by nighte,
As wysly° and as slyly° as it mighte.° *prudently / craftily / can (be)*
Wherfore I rede° that cut° among us alle *advise / lots, straws*
Be drawe,° and lat se wher the cut wol falle; *drawn, pulled*
And he that hath the cut with herte blythe
Shal renne° to the toune, and that ful swythe,° *run / quickly*
And bringe us breed and wyn ful prively.° *secretly*
And two of us shul kepen° subtilly° *guard / carefully*
This tresor wel; and if he wol nat taire,° *tarry*
Whan it is night we wol this tresor carie,
By oon assent, where as us thinketh best."
That oon of hem the cut broughte in his fest,° *fist*
And bad hem drawe, and loke wher it wol falle;
And it fil on the yongeste of hem alle,
And forth toward the toun he wente anon.
And also sone as° that he was agon, *as soon as*
That oon of hem° spak thus unto that other: *The one of them*
"Thou knowest wel thou art my sworne brother;
Thy profit° wol I telle thee anon. *Something to thy advantage*
Thou woost° wel that oure felawe is agon,° *knowest / gone*
And heer is gold, and that° ful greet plentee, *that (in)*
That shal departed° been among us three. *divided*
But natheles,° if I can shape° it so *nonetheless / arrange*

That it departed were among us two,
Hadde I nat doon a freendes torn° to thee?" *turn*
That other answerde, "I noot° how that may be: *know not*
He woot how that the gold is with us tweye.
What shal we doon? what shal we to him seye?"
"Shal it be conseil?"° seyde the firste shrewe;° *a secret / wretch*
"And I shal tellen in a wordes fewe
What we shal doon, and bringe it wel aboute."
"I graunte,"° quod that other, "out of doute, *grant (it)*
That, by my trouthe, I wol thee nat biwreye."° *betray*
"Now," quod the firste, "thou woost° wel we be tweye,° *knowest / two*
And two of us shul strenger° be than oon. *stronger*
Looke whan that he is set,° that right anoon° *has sat down / right away*
Arys° as though thou woldest with him pleye; *Arise (get up)*
And I shal ryve him thurgh the sydes tweye° *stab / through his two sides*
Whyl that thou strogelest° with him as in game,° *strugglest / as if in play*
And with thy dagger looke° thou do the same; *take heed*
And thanne shall al this gold departed° be, *divided*
My dere freend, bitwixen me and thee.
Thanne may we bothe oure lustes° al fulfille, *desires*
And pleye at dees° right at oure owene wille. *dice*
And thus acorded° been thise shrewes° tweye *agreed / cursed fellows*
To sleen the thridde, as ye han herd me seye.
This yongest, which that wente unto the toun,
Ful ofte in herte he rolleth up and doun
The beautee of thise florins newe and brighte.
"O Lord!" quod he, "if so were that I mighte
Have al this tresor to myself allone,
Ther is no man that liveth under the trone° *throne*
Of God that sholde live so mery as I!"
And atte laste° the feend,° our enemy, *at (the) last / devil*
Putte in his thought that he shold poyson beye,° *buy poison*
With which he mighte sleen his felawes tweye°— *two companions*
For-why the feend fond him in swich lyvinge
That he had leve° him to sorwe bringe: *permission (from God)*
For this was outrely° his fulle entente,° *completely / purpose*
To sleen hem bothe, and nevere to repente.
And forth he gooth—no lenger wolde he tarie—
Into the toun, unto a pothecarie,° *apothecary, pharmacist*
And preyed° him that he him wolde selle *asked*
Som poyson, that° he mighte his rattes quelle,° *so that / kill his rats*
And eek° ther was a polcat° in his hawe,° *also / weasel / yard*
That, as he seyde, his capouns° hadde y-slawe,° *capons / killed*
And fayn° he wolde wreke him,° if he mighte, *gladly / avenge himself*
On vermin, that destroyed° him by nighte. *were ruining*

The pothecarie answerde, "And thou shalt have
A thing that, also° God my soule save, *so (may)*
In al this world ther nis no° creature, *is not any*
That ete or dronke hath of this confiture° *mixture*
Noght but the mountance of a corn of whete,
That he ne shal his lyf anon° forlete.° *at once / lose*
Ye,° sterve° he shal, and that in lasse whyle° *Yes / die / shorter time*
Than thou wolt goon a paas° nat but° a myle, *walk at normal pace / only*
This poyson is so strong and violent."
This cursed man hath in his hond y-hent° *grasped*
This poyson in a box, and sith° he ran *afterward*
Into the nexte strete unto a man
And borwed [of] him large botels° three, *bottles (probably of leather)*
And in the two his poyson poured he—
The thridde he kepte clene for his° drinke— *his (own)*
For al the night he shoop him° for to swinke° *was preparing himself / work*
In caryinge of the gold out of that place.
And whan this ryotour, with sory grace,
Hadde filled with wyn his grete botels three,
To his felawes agayn repaireth° he. *returns*
What nedeth it to sermone° of it more? *speak*
For right as they hadde cast° his deeth bifore, *planned*
Right so they han him slayn, and that anon.° *immediately*
And whan that this was doon, thus spak that oon:
"Now lat us sitte and drinke, and make us merie,
And afterward we wol his body berie."° *bury*
And with that word it happed° him, par cas, *befell / by chance*
To take the botel ther° the poyson was, *where*
And drank, and yaf° his felawe drink also, *gave*
For which anon they storven° bothe two. *died*
But certes, I suppose that Avicen
Wroot nevere in no canon, ne in no fen,
Mo wonder signes of empoisoning
Than hadde thise wrecches two, er° hir° ending. *before / their*
Thus ended been thise homicydes two,
And eek° the false empoysoner° also.° *also / poisoner / as well*
O cursed sinne of alle cursednesse!
O traytours° homicyde, O wikkednesse! *traitorous*
O glotonye, luxurie,° and hasardrye! *lechery*
Thou blasphemour of Crist with vileinye° *vile speech*
And othes grete, of usage° and of pryde! *out of habit*
Allas! mankinde, how may it bityde° *happen*
That to thy Creatour which that thee wroghte,
And with his precious herte-blood thee boghte,° *redeemed*
Thou art so fals and so unkinde,° allas! *unnatural*
Now, goode men, God forgeve° yow youre trespas, *may God forgive*

And ware yow fro° the sinne of avaryce. *make you beware of*
Myn holy pardoun may yow alle waryce°— *cure*
So that ye offre nobles or sterlinges,
Or elles silver broches, spones,° ringes. *spoons*
Boweth youre heed° under this holy bulle! *head*
Cometh up, ye wyves, offreth of youre wolle!° *wool*
Youre names I entre heer in my rolle° anon:° *roll, list / at once*
Into the blisse of hevene shul ye gon.
I yow assoile,° by myn heigh power— *absolve*
Yow that wol offre°—as clene and eek as cleer° *make an offering / pure*
As ye were born.—And, lo, sires, thus I preche.
And Jesu Crist, that is our soules leche,° *healer, doctor*
So graunte° yow his pardon to receyve, *May He grant*
For that is best; I wol yow nat deceyve.
But sires, o° word forgat I in my tale: *a, one*
I have relikes and pardon in my male° *pouch*
As faire as any man in Engelond,
Whiche were me yeven° by the Popes hond. *given*
If any of yow wol of devocioun° *out of devotion*
Offren and han myn absolucioun,
Cometh forth anon, and kneleth heer adoun,
And mekely receyveth my pardoun;
Or elles, taketh pardon as ye wende,° *travel*
Al newe and fresh, at every myles ende—
So that ye offren alwey newe and newe
Nobles or pens,° which that be gode and trewe. *pence*
It is an honour to everich° that is heer *every one*
That ye mowe° have a suffisant° pardoneer *may / capable*
T'assoille° yow, in contree as ye ryde, *To absolve*
For aventures whiche that may bityde.
Peraventure° ther may falle oon or two *By chance*
Doun of his hors, and breke his nekke atwo.° *in two*
Look which a seuretee° is it to you alle *what a security*
That I am in youre felaweship y-falle,
That may assoille yow, bothe more and lasse,° *great and small*
Whan that the soule shal fro the body passe.
I rede° that oure Host heer shal biginne, *advise*
For he is most envoluped° in sinne. *enveloped, wrapped up*
Com forth, sire Hoste, and offre first anon,° *first now*
And thou shalt kisse the reliks everichon,° *every one*
Ye, for a grote:° unbokel° anon thy purs." *groat (four pence) / unbuckle*
"Nay, nay," quod he, "thanne have I Cristes curs! *said*
Lat be," quod he, "it shal nat be, so theech!"° *as I hope to prosper*
Thou woldest make me kisse thyn olde breech° *breeches*
And swere it were a relik of a seint,
Thogh it were with thy fundement° depeint!° *fundament (rectum) / stained*

But by the croys° which that Seint Eleyne° fond, *(true) Cross / St. Helena*
I wolde I hadde thy coillons° in myn hond *testicles*
In stede of relikes or of seintuarie.
Lat cutte hem of! I wol thee helpe hem carie.
Thay shul be shryned° in an hogges tord!"° *enshrined / turd*
This Pardoner answerde nat a word;
So wrooth° he was, no word ne wolde he seye. *wroth, angered*
"Now," quod our Host, "I wol no lenger pleye
With thee, ne with noon other angry man."
But right anon the worthy Knight bigan,
Whan that he saugh that al the peple lough,° *laughed*
"Namore of this, for it is right y-nough!° *quite enough*
Sire Pardoner, be glad and mery of chere;° *mood*
And ye, sire Host, that been to me so dere,
I prey yow that ye kisse the Pardoner.
And Pardoner, I prey thee, drawe thee neer,
And, as we diden, lat us laughe and pleye."
Anon° they kiste, and riden forth hir weye.° *At once / (on) their way*

## Christine de Pizan (1365–1429)

*Translated by Earl Jeffrey Richards*

Married by age fifteen and widowed at age twenty-five with three small children, Christine de Pizan was the first woman in Europe known to support herself with her writing. She was born in Venice in 1365 but soon moved to Paris where her father was employed at the French court. He insisted that his daughter receive an education, despite the objections of her mother. Between 1390 and 1429, Christine created a large body of work, including ten books of verse and eleven books of prose. She wrote short lyrics and several treatises against the misogyny of writers such as Ovid and Jean de Meun, whose *Roman de la Rose* sparked a flurry of letters and verses written by numerous *literati.* The exchange became known as the "Quarrel of the *Romance of the Rose,*" an important episode in the late medieval debate about the nature of women.

Christine also wrote works on the nature of love, a book of moral proverbs for her son, a dream-vision recording her journey to a more perfect world led by the Sybil of Cumae (a female prophetic figure borrowed from Virgil's *Aeneid*), and another vision lamenting the civil strife and violence common to late medieval France. Christine composed essays on world history, women, politics, chivalry, and the human condition in general, as well as collections of short narratives, a treatise on prudence, and meditations on seven Psalms; she also served as the official biographer of Charles V. Her writing career ended in 1429 with *Le Ditie de Jehanne d'Arc*, the only French text written in honor of Joan of Arc during the saintly warrior's lifetime.

*The Book of the City of Ladies* holds a special place in the history of women's writing: it is the first known European vernacular text written by a woman that defends women's rights to education and erudition. In this text, Christine sets out to reread and revise the misogynist mythology that permeated her own cultural tradition. She writes, "If women had written the books we read, they would have handled things differently, for women know they have been falsely accused." To construct her arguments, she uses legends, myths, history, biblical citations and narratives, and her own experience, relying heavily on Christian doctrine as a means of alleviating women's oppression. *The Book of the City of Ladies* is constructed as a moral dialogue between a naive Christine and three allegorical figures: Reason, Rectitude, and Justice. Her text borrows from and revises Ovid, Boccaccio, Dante, and others. Although she wrote in French, stylistically Christine's prose imitates Latin, so that her writing exhibits refined but sometimes difficult and complex sentence structures. The "Tale of Saint Christine" occurs near the conclusion of the *City* and provides an example of a very popular medieval and early modern genre, a saint's life. In Christine de Pizan's work, it is noteworthy for its particular resonance, since both author and saint share the same name. The selections included here represent a very small segment of the long text of *The Book of the City of Ladies.*

## *The Book of the City of Ladies*

*From Book I*

### 1. Here begins the Book of the City of Ladies, whose first chapter tells why and for what purpose this book was written.

I.1.1

One day as I was sitting alone in my study surrounded by books on all kinds of subjects, devoting myself to literary studies, my usual habit, my mind dwelt at length on the weighty opinions of various authors whom I had studied for a long time. I looked up from my book, having decided to leave such subtle questions in peace and to relax by reading some light poetry. With this in mind, I searched for some small book. By chance a strange volume came into my hands, not one of my own, but one which had been given to me along with some others. When I held it open and saw from its title page that it was by Mathéolus, I smiled, for though I had never seen it before, I had often heard that like other books it discussed respect for women. I thought I would browse through it to amuse myself. I had not been reading for very long when my good mother called me to refresh myself with some supper, for it was evening. Intending to look at it the next day, I put it down. The next morning, again seated in my study as was my habit, I remembered wanting to examine this book by Mathéolus. I started to read it and went on for a little while. Because the subject seemed to me not very pleasant for people who do not enjoy lies, and of no use in developing virtue or manners, given its lack of integrity in diction and theme, and after browsing here and there and reading the end, I put it down in order to turn my attention to more elevated and useful study. But just the sight of this book, even though it was of no authority, made me wonder how it happened that so many different men—and learned men among them—have been and are so inclined to express both in speaking and in their treatises and writings so many wicked insults about women and their behavior. Not only one or two and not even just this Mathéolus (for this book had a bad name anyway and was intended as a satire) but, more generally, judging from the treatises of all philosophers and poets and from all the orators—it would take too long to mention their names—it seems that they all speak from one and the same mouth. They all concur in one conclusion: that the behavior of women is inclined to and full of every vice. Thinking deeply about these matters, I began to examine my character and conduct as a natural woman and, similarly, I considered other women whose company I frequently kept, princesses, great ladies, women of the middle and lower classes, who had graciously told me of their most private and intimate thoughts, hoping that I could judge impartially and in good conscience whether the testimony of so many notable men could be true. To the best of my knowledge, no matter how long I confronted or dissected the problem, I could not see or realize how their claims could be true when compared to the natural behavior and character of women. Yet I still argued vehemently against women, saying that it would be impossible that so many famous men—such solemn scholars, possessed of such deep and great understanding, so clear-sighted in all things, as it seemed—could have spoken falsely on so many occasions that I could hardly find a book on morals where, even before I had read it in its entirety, I did not find several chapters or certain sections attacking women, no matter who the author was. This reason alone, in short, made me conclude that, although my intellect did not perceive my own great faults and, likewise, those of other women because of its simpleness and ignorance, it was however truly fitting that such was the case. And so I relied more on the judgment of others than on what I myself felt and knew. I was so transfixed in this line of thinking for such a long time that it seemed as if I were in a stupor. Like a gushing fountain, a series of authorities, whom I recalled one after another, came to mind, along with their opinions on this topic. And I finally decided that God formed a vile creature when He made woman, and I wondered how such a worthy artisan could have deigned to make such an abominable work which, from what they say, is the vessel as well as the refuge and abode of every evil and vice. As I was thinking this, a great unhappiness and sadness welled up in my heart, for I detested myself and the entire feminine sex, as though we were monstrosities in nature. And in my lament I spoke these words:

I.1.2

"Oh, God, how can this be? For unless I stray from my faith, I must never doubt that Your infinite wisdom and most perfect goodness ever created anything which was not good. Did You yourself not create woman in a very special way and since that time did You not give her all those inclinations which it pleased You for her to have? And how could it be that You could go wrong in anything? Yet look at all these accusations which have been judged, decided, and concluded against women. I do not know how to understand this repugnance. If it is so, fair Lord God, that in fact so many abominations abound in the female sex, for You Yourself say that the testimony of two or three witnesses lends credence, why shall I not doubt that this is true? Alas, God, why did You not let me be born in the world as a man, so that all my inclinations would be to serve You better, and so that I would not stray in anything and would be as perfect as a man is said to be? But since Your kindness has not been extended to me, then forgive my negligence in Your service, most fair Lord God, and may it not displease You, for the servant who receives fewer gifts from his lord is less obliged in his service." I spoke these words to God in my lament and a great deal more for a very long time in sad reflection, and in my folly I considered myself most unfortunate because God had made me inhabit a female body in this world.

## 2. Here Christine describes how three ladies appeared to her and how the one who was in front spoke first and comforted her in her pain.

I.2.1

So occupied with these painful thoughts, my head bowed in shame, my eyes filled with tears, leaning on the pommel of my chair's armrest, I suddenly saw a ray of light fall on my lap, as though it were the sun. I shuddered then, as if wakened from sleep, for I was sitting in a shadow where the sun could not have shone at that hour. And as I lifted my head to see where this light was coming from, I saw three crowned ladies standing before me, and the splendor of their bright faces shone on me and throughout the entire room. Now no one would ask whether I was surprised, for my doors were shut and they had still entered. Fearing that some phantom had come to tempt me and filled with great fright, I made the Sign of the Cross on my forehead.

I.2.2

Then she who was the first of the three smiled and began to speak, "Dear daughter, do not be afraid, for we have not come here to harm or trouble you but to console you, for we have taken pity on your distress, and we have come to bring you out of the ignorance which so blinds your own intellect that you shun what you know for a certainty and believe what you do not know or see or recognize except by virtue of many strange opinions. You resemble the fool in the prank who was dressed in women's clothes while he slept; because those who were making fun of him repeatedly told him he was a woman, he believed their false testimony more readily than the certainty of his own identity. Fair daughter, have you lost all sense? Have you forgotten that when fine gold is tested in the furnace, it does not change or vary in strength but becomes purer the more it is hammered and handled in different ways? Do you not know that the best things are the most debated and the most discussed? If you wish to consider the question of the highest form of reality, which consists in ideas or celestial substances, consider whether the greatest philosophers who have lived and whom you support against your own sex have ever resolved whether ideas are false and contrary to the truth. Notice how these same philosophers contradict and criticize one another, just as you have seen in the *Metaphysics* where Aristotle takes their opinions to task and speaks similarly of Plato and other philosophers. And note, moreover, how even Saint Augustine and the Doctors of the Church have criticized Aristotle in certain passages, although he is known as the prince of philosophers in whom both natural and moral philosophy attained their highest level. It also seems that you think that all the words of the philosophers are articles of faith, that they could never be wrong. As far as the poets of whom you speak are concerned, do you not know that they spoke on many subjects in a fictional way and that often they mean the contrary of what their words openly say? One can interpret them according to the grammatical figure of *antiphrasis,* which means, as you know, that if you call something bad, in fact, it is good, and also vice versa. Thus I advise you to profit from their works and to interpret them in the manner in which they are intended in those passages where they attack women. Perhaps this man, who called himself Mathéolus in his own book, intended it in such a way, for there are many things which, if taken literally, would be pure heresy. As for the attack against the estate of marriage—which is a holy estate, worthy and ordained by God—made not only by Mathéolus but also by others and even by the *Romance of the Rose* where greater credibility is averred because of the authority of its author, it is evident and proven by experience that the contrary of the evil which they posit and claim to be found in this estate through the obligation and fault of women is true. For where has the husband ever been found who would allow his wife to have authority to abuse and insult him as a matter of course, as these authorities maintain? I believe that, regardless of what you might have read, you will never see such a husband with your own eyes, so badly colored are these lies. Thus, in conclusion, I tell you, dear friend, that simplemindedness has prompted you to hold such an opinion. Come back to yourself, recover your senses, and do not trouble yourself anymore over such absurdities. For you know that any evil spoken of women so generally only hurts those who say it, not women themselves."

## 3. Here Christine tells how the lady who had said this showed her who she was and what her character and function were and told her how she would construct a city with the help of these same three ladies.

I.3.1

The famous lady spoke these words to me, in whose presence I do not know which one of my senses was more overwhelmed: my hearing from having listened to such worthy words or my sight from having seen her radiant beauty, her attire, her reverent comportment, and her most honored countenance. The same was true of the others, so that I did not know which one to look at, for the three ladies resembled each other so much that they could be told apart only with difficulty, except for the last one, for although she was of no less authority than the others, she had so fierce a visage that whoever, no matter how daring, looked in her eyes would be afraid to commit a crime, for it seemed that she threatened criminals unceasingly. Having stood up out of respect, I looked at them without saying a word, like someone too overwhelmed to utter a syllable. Reflecting on who these beings could be, I felt much admiration in my heart and, if I could have dared, I would have immediately asked their names and identities and what was the meaning of the different scepters which each one carried in her right hand, which were of fabulous richness, and why they had come here. But since I considered myself unworthy to address these questions to such high ladies as they appeared to me, I did not dare to, but continued to keep my gaze fixed on them, half-afraid and half-reassured by the words which I had heard, which had made me reject my first impression. But the most wise lady who had spoken to me and who knew in her mind what I was thinking, as one who has insight into everything, addressed my reflections, saying:

I.3.2

"Dear daughter, know that God's providence, which leaves nothing void or empty, has ordained that we, though celestial beings, remain and circulate among the people of the world here below, in order to bring order and maintain in balance those institutions we created according to the will of God in the fulfillment of various offices, that God whose daughters we three all are and from whom we were born. Thus it is my duty to straighten out men and women when they go astray and to put them back on the right path. And when they stray, if they have enough understanding to see me, I come to them quietly in spirit and preach to them, showing them their error and how they have failed, I assign them the causes, and then I teach them what to do and what to avoid. Since I serve to demonstrate clearly and to show both in thought and deed to each man and woman his or her own special qualities and faults, you see me holding this shiny mirror which I carry in my right hand in place of a scepter. I would thus have you know truly that no one can look into this mirror, no matter what kind of creature, without achieving clear self-knowledge. My mirror has such great dignity that not without reason is it surrounded by rich and precious gems, so that you see, thanks to this mirror, the essences, qualities, proportions, and measures of all things are known, nor can anything be done well without it. And because, similarly, you wish to know what are the offices of my other sisters whom you see here, each will reply in her own person about her name and character, and this way our testimony will be all the more certain to you. But now I myself will declare the reason for our coming. I must assure you, as we do nothing without good cause, that our appearance here is not at all in vain. For, although we are not common to many places and our knowledge does not come to all people, nevertheless you, for your great love of investigating the truth through long and continual study, for which you come here, solitary and separated from the world, you have deserved and deserve, our devoted friend, to be visited and consoled by us in your agitation and sadness, so that you might also see clearly, in the midst of the darkness of your thoughts, those things which taint and trouble your heart.

I.3.3

"There is another greater and even more special reason for our coming which you will learn from our speeches: in fact we have come to vanquish from the world the same error into which you had fallen, so that from now on, ladies and all valiant women may have a refuge and defense against the various assailants, those ladies who have been abandoned for so long, exposed like a field without a surrounding hedge, without finding a champion to afford them an adequate defense, notwithstanding those noble men who are required by order of law to protect them, who by negligence and apathy have allowed them to be mistreated. It is no wonder then that their jealous enemies, those outrageous villains who have assailed them with various weapons, have been victorious in a war in which women have had no defense. Where is there a city so strong which could not be taken immediately if no resistance were forthcoming, or the law case, no matter how unjust, which was not won through the obstinance of someone pleading without opposition? And the simple, noble ladies, following the example of suffering which God commands, have cheerfully suffered the great attacks which, both in the spoken and the written word, have been wrongfully and sinfully perpetrated against women by men who all the while appealed to God for the right to do so. Now it is time for their just cause to be taken from Pharaoh's hands, and for this reason, we three ladies whom you see here, moved by pity, have come to you to announce a particular edifice built like a city wall, strongly constructed and well founded, which has been predestined and established by our aid and counsel for you to build, where no one will reside except all ladies of fame and women worthy of praise, for the walls of the city will be closed to those women who lack virtue."

## 4. Here the lady explains to Christine the city which she has been commissioned to build and how she was charged to help Christine build the wall and enclosure, and then gives her name.

I.4.1

"Thus, fair daughter, the prerogative among women has been bestowed on you to establish and build the City of Ladies. For the foundation and completion of this City you will draw fresh waters from us as from clear fountains, and we will bring you sufficient building stone, stronger and more durable than any marble with cement could be. Thus your City will be extremely beautiful, without equal, and of perpetual duration in the world.

I.4.2

"Have you not read that King Tros founded the great city of Troy with the aid of Apollo, Minerva, and Neptune, whom the people of that time considered gods, and also how Cadmus founded the city of Thebes with the admonition of the gods? And yet over time these cities fell and have fallen into ruin. But I prophesy to you, as a true sybil, that this City, which you will found with our help, will never be destroyed, nor will it ever fall, but will remain prosperous forever, regardless of all its jealous enemies. Although it will be stormed by numerous assaults, it will never be taken or conquered.

I.4.3

"Long ago the Amazon kingdom was begun through the arrangement and enterprise of several ladies of great courage who despised servitude, just as history books have testified. For a long time afterward they maintained it under the rule of several queens, very noble ladies whom they elected themselves, who governed them well and maintained their dominion with great strength. Yet, although they were strong and powerful and had conquered a large part of the entire Orient in the course of their rule and terrified all the neighboring lands (even the Greeks, who were then the flower of all countries in the world, feared them), nevertheless, after a time, the power of this kingdom declined, so that as with all earthly kingdoms, nothing but its name has survived to the present. But the edifice erected by you in this City which you must construct will be far stronger, and for its founding I was commissioned, in the course of our common deliberation, to supply you with durable and pure mortar to lay the sturdy foundations and to raise the lofty walls all around, high and thick, with mighty towers and strong bastions, surrounded by moats with firm blockhouses, just as is fitting for a city with a strong and lasting defense. Following our plan, you will set the foundations deep to last all the longer, and then you will raise the walls so high that they will not fear anyone. Daughter, now that I have told you the reason for our coming and so that you will more certainly believe my words, I want you to learn my name, by whose sound alone you will be able to learn and know that, if you wish to follow my commands, you have in me an administrator so that you may do your work flawlessly. I am called Lady Reason; you see that you are in good hands. For the time being then, I will say no more." . . .

## 9. Here Christine tells how she dug in the ground, by which should be understood the questions which she put to Reason, and how Reason replied to her.

I.9.1

"Now I have prepared for you and commanded from you a great work. Consider how you can continue to excavate the ground following my marks." And so, in order to obey her command, I struck with all my force in the following way:

I.9.2

"My lady, how does it happen that Ovid, who is thought to be one of the best poets—although many believe, and I would agree with them, thanks to your correcting me, that Vergil is much more praiseworthy—that Ovid attacks women so much and so frequently, as in the book he calls *Ars amatoria,* as well as in the *Remedia amoris* and other of his volumes?"

She replied, "Ovid was a man skilled in the learned craft of poetry, and he possessed great wit and understanding in his work. However, he dissipated his body in every vanity and pleasure of the flesh, not just in one romance, but he abandoned himself to all the women he could, nor did he show restraint or loyalty, and so he stayed with no single woman. In his youth he led this kind of life as much as he could, for which in the end he received the fitting reward—dishonor and loss of possessions and limbs—for so much did he advise others through his own acts and words to lead a life like the one he led that he was finally exiled for his excessive promiscuity. Similarly, when afterward, thanks to the influence of several young, powerful Romans who were his supporters, he was called back from exile and failed to refrain from the misdeeds for which his guilt had already punished him, he was castrated and disfigured because of his faults. This is precisely the point I was telling you about before, for when he saw that he could no longer lead the life in which he was used to taking his pleasure, he began to attack women with his subtle reasonings, and through this effort he tried to make women unattractive to others." . . .

"I know another small book in Latin, my lady, called the *Secreta mulierum, The Secrets of Women,* which discusses the constitution of their natural bodies and especially their great defects."

She replied, "You can see for yourself without further proof, this book was written carelessly and colored by hypocrisy, for if you have looked at it, you know that it is obviously a treatise composed of lies. Although some say that it was written by Aristotle, it is not believable that such a philosopher could be charged with such contrived lies. For since women can clearly know with proof that certain things which he treats are not at all true, but pure fabrications, they can also conclude that the other details which he handles are outright lies. But don't you remember that he says in the beginning that some pope—I don't know which one—excommunicated every man who read the work to a woman or gave it to a woman to read?"

"My lady, I remember it well."

"Do you know the malicious reason why this lie was presented as credible to bestial and ignorant men at the beginning of the book?"

"No, my lady, not unless you tell me."

"It was done so that women would not know about the book and its contents, because the man who wrote it knew that if women read it or heard it read aloud, they would know it was lies, would contradict it, and make fun of it. With this pretense the author wanted to trick and deceive the men who read it."

"My lady, I recall that among other things, after he has discussed the impotence and weakness which cause the formation of a feminine body in the womb of the mother, he says that Nature is completely ashamed when she sees that she has formed such a body, as though it were something imperfect."

"But, sweet friend, don't you see the overweening madness, the irrational blindness which prompt such observations? Is Nature, the chambermaid of God, a greater mistress than her master, almighty God from whom comes such authority, who, when He willed, took the form of man and woman from His thought when it came to His holy will to form Adam from the mud of the ground in the field of Damascus and, once created, brought him into the Terrestrial Paradise which was and is the most worthy place in this world here below? There Adam slept, and God formed the body of woman from one of his ribs, signifying that she should stand at his side as a companion and never lie at his feet like a slave, and also that he should love her as his own flesh. If the Supreme Craftsman was not ashamed to create and form the feminine body, would Nature then have been ashamed? It is the height of folly to say this! Indeed, how was she formed? I don't know if you have already noted this: she was created in the image of God. How can any mouth dare to slander the vessel which bears such a noble imprint? But some men are foolish enough to think, when they hear that God made man in His image, that this refers to the material body. This was not the case, for God had not yet taken a human body. The soul is meant, the intellectual spirit which lasts eternally just like the Deity. God created the soul and placed wholly similar souls, equally good and noble in the feminine and in the masculine bodies. Now, to turn to the question of the creation of the body, woman was made by the Supreme Craftsman. In what place was she created? In the Terrestrial Paradise. From what substance? Was it vile matter? No, it was the noblest substance which had ever been created: it was from the body of man from which God made woman."

I.9.3

"My lady, according to what I understand from you, woman is a most noble creature. But even so, Cicero says that a man should never serve any woman and that he who does so debases himself, for no man should ever serve anyone lower than him."

She replied, "The man or the woman in whom resides greater virtue is the higher; neither the loftiness nor the lowliness of a person lies in the body according to the sex, but in the perfection of conduct and virtues. And surely he is happy who serves the Virgin, who is above all the angels." . . .

## 14. More exchanges between Christine and Reason.

I.14.1

"Certainly you speak well, my lady, and your words are most harmonious in my heart. But though such is the case as far as women's minds are concerned, it is a proven fact that women have weak bodies, tender and feeble in deeds of strength, and are cowards by nature. These things, in men's judgment, substantially reduce the degree and authority of the feminine sex, for men contend that the more imperfect a body, the lesser is its virtue and, consequently, the less praiseworthy."

She answered, "My dear daughter, such a deduction is totally invalid and unsupported, for invariably one often sees that when Nature does not give to one body which she has formed as much perfection as she has given to another and thereby makes some things imperfect, whether in shape or beauty or with some impotence or weakness of limbs, she makes up the difference with an even greater boon than she has taken away. For example, just as is said, the great philosopher Aristotle had a very ugly body, with one eye lower than the other and with a strange face, but although he had some physical deformity, truly Nature made this up to him spectacularly by giving him a retentive mind and great sense, just as he appears in his authentic writings. This recompense of such a fine mind was thus worth more to him than if he had had the very body of Absalom or a similar body.

I.14.2

"The same might be said of the great emperor Alexander, who was quite ugly, little, and had a sickly build. Nevertheless, it seems that he possessed great virtue in his heart. It is the same situation for many others. Fair friend, I assure you that a large and strong body never makes a strong and virtuous heart but comes from a natural and virtuous vigor which is a boon from God, which He allows Nature to imprint in one reasonable creature more than in another, and thus a malady is transformed into understanding or courage and not at all into the strength of the body or its limbs. We have observed this often, having seen many large men with strong bodies who are cowardly and recreant and others with small and weak bodies who are bold and vigorous, and the same holds true for other virtues. But as for boldness and physical strength, God and Nature have done a great deal for women by giving them such weakness, because, at least, thanks to this agreeable defect, they are excused from committing the horrible cruelties, the murders, and the terrible and serious crimes which have been perpetrated through force and still continuously take place in the world. Thus women will never receive the punishment which such cases demand, and it would be better, or would have been better, for the souls of several of the strongest men, if they had spent their pilgrimage in this world in weak feminine bodies. And truly I tell you, and here I come back to my major point, that if Nature did not give great strength of limb to women's bodies, she has made up for it by placing there that most virtuous inclination to love one's God and to fear sinning against His commandments. Women who act otherwise go against their own nature.

I.14.3

"But recall, nevertheless, dear friend, how it seems that God has deliberately wished to show men that even if women do not possess the great strength and physical daring which men usually have, they should not say nor should they believe that this is because strength and physical daring are excluded from the feminine sex: this is obvious, because in many women God has made manifest enormous courage, strength, and boldness to undertake and execute all kinds of hard tasks, just like those great men—solemn and valorous conquerors—have accomplished, which different writings frequently mention, and presently I will give you several examples.

I.14.4

"Fair daughter and dear friend, now I have prepared for you a large and wide ditch, completely cleared of earth, which I have carried out in large basketfuls on my shoulders. Now it is time that you lay down the heavy and sturdy stones for the foundation of the walls of the City of Ladies. Take the trowel of your pen and ready yourself to lay down bricks and to labor diligently, for you can see here a great and large stone which I want to place as the first in the first row of stones in the foundation of your City. I want you to know that Nature herself has foretold in the signs of the zodiac that it be placed and situated in this work. So I shall draw you back a little and I will throw it down for you."

## 15. Here she speaks of the Queen Semiramis.

I.15.1

"Semiramis was a woman of very great strength—in fact, of strong and powerful courage in enterprises and undertakings in deeds of arms—and was so outstanding that the people of that time who were pagans used to say, because of her enormous strength on land and on sea, that she was a sister of the great god Jupiter and daughter of the ancient god Saturn who, they believed, were the gods of the earth and the sea. This lady was the wife of King Ninus, who named the city of Nineveh after his own name and who was such a forceful conqueror that, with the help of his wife Semiramis (who, like him, would campaign in arms), he subjugated mighty Babylon and all the strong land of Assyria and many other countries. When the lady was still quite young, Ninus her husband was killed by an arrow, during the assault of a city. Once the funeral rites had been solemnly celebrated, as befitted Ninus, the lady did not give up the exercise of arms, but, with greater courage than before, vigorously undertook to govern and rule the kingdoms and lands over which her husband and she had held power on their own to begin with, as well as those which they had conquered with the sword and which she memorably and valorously controlled. She undertook and accomplished so many notable works that no man could surpass her in vigor and strength. This lady, with her great courage, feared no pain and was frightened by no danger, and so bravely exposed herself to every peril that she vanquished all her enemies who had thought to expel her during her widowhood from the countries she had conquered. Because of this, she was so feared and revered in arms that, finally, she not only controlled the lands already in her power, but also marched with a very large army to Ethiopia, with which she subjugated Ethiopia and annexed it to her empire, and from there she moved in force against India. She attacked the Indians in force, whom no man had ever approached before with the intention of making war on them, and subdued and vanquished them, and then advanced against other countries so that, in brief, she had soon conquered the entire Orient and placed it under her rule. Along with these great and mighty conquests, this lady, Semiramis, reinforced and rebuilt the strong and cruel city of

Babylon, which had been founded by Nimrod and the giants and was located on the plain of Shinar. This lady strengthened the city even more with many defenses and had wide and deep moats dug around it. Once, when Semiramis was in her chamber surrounded by her maidens who were braiding her hair, news came that one of her kingdoms had revolted against her. She stood up immediately and swore by her power that the other lock of her hair which remained to be braided would not be braided until she had avenged this injustice and brought this land back under her dominion. She had her massed troops quickly armed and advanced on the rebels and, thanks to great force and strength, brought them back under her authority. She so frightened these rebels and all her other subjects that ever after no one dared revolt. A large and richly gilt cast-bronze statue on a high pillar in Babylon which portrayed a princess holding a sword, with one side of her hair braided, the other not, bore witness to this noble and courageous deed for a long time. This queen founded and built several new cities and fortifications and performed many other outstanding deeds and accomplished so much that greater courage and more marvelous and memorable deeds have never been recorded about any man.

I.15.2

"It is quite true that many people reproach her—and if she had lived under our law, rightfully so—because she took as husband a son she had had with Ninus her lord. But here are the two principal reasons which prompted her to do this: first, she wanted no other crowned lady in her empire besides herself, which would have happened if her son had married another lady; and second, it seemed to her that no other man was worthy to have her as wife except her own son. But this lady did nothing to excuse herself for this great mistake because at this time there was still no written law, and people lived according to the law of Nature, where all people were allowed to do whatever came into their hearts without sinning, for there can be no doubt that if she thought this was evil or that she would incur the slightest reproach, she would never have done this, since she had such a great and noble heart and so deeply loved honor. And now the first stone is set in the foundation of our City. Now we must lay many more stones to advance our edifice." . . .

## 20. Here she speaks of Zenobia, Queen of the Palmyrenes.

I.20.1

"The women of Amazonia were not the only valorous women, for no less celebrated is Zenobia, queen of the Palmyrenes, a lady of noble blood and offspring of the Ptolemies, kings of Egypt. The great courage of this lady and the chivalrous inclination she possessed were obvious throughout her childhood. As soon as she was even slightly strong, no one could keep her from leaving the residence of walled cities, palaces, and royal chambers in order to live in the woods and forests, where, armed with sword and spear, she eagerly hunted wild game. After stags and hinds, she began to fight with lions and bears and all other wild beasts which she would attack fearlessly and conquer marvelously. This lady did not consider it a hardship to sleep in the woods, on the hard ground, in cold and in heat, for she feared nothing, nor did she mind traveling through forest passes, climbing mountains, going down into villages as she pursued the various beasts. This maiden despised all physical love and refused to marry for a long time, for she was a woman who wished to keep her virginity for life. In the end, under pressure from her parents, she took as husband the king of the Palmyrenes, who had a handsome face and body. The noble Zenobia was always possessed of supreme self-control and paid little attention to her own beauty, and Fortune was extremely favorable to Zenobia's inclinations by allowing her to have a husband who corresponded so well to her own mores. This king, who was quite brave, desired to conquer by force all the Orient and nearby empires. In this time Valerianus, the ruler of the Roman Empire, was captured by Sapor, the king of the Persians. The king of the Palmyrenes assembled his great army; whereupon Zenobia, who did not give any thought to preserving the freshness of her beauty, resolved to suffer the exercise of arms with her husband, to arm herself and to participate with him in all the labors of the exercise of chivalry. The king, who was named Odenatus, appointed a son, named Herod, whom he had had by another woman, to lead a part of his army in the advance guard against the Persian king Sapor, who then occupied Mesopotamia. He then ordered Zenobia his wife to advance from the one flank, in all boldness; he would then advance from the other flank with a third of his army; and they set out under these orders. But what should I tell you? The end of this affair, just as you can read in history books, was as follows: this lady Zenobia conducted herself so bravely and courageously and with such boldness and strength that she won several battles against this Persian king, and so decisively, thanks to her prowess, that she placed Mesopotamia under her husband's rule. In the end she lay siege to Sapor in his city and captured him with his concubines and great treasure. After this victory it happened that her husband was killed by one of his own relatives out of jealousy, but it did not help the relative at all because this noble-hearted lady kept him out of power; she bravely and valiantly took possession of the empire on behalf of her children, who were still small. She placed herself on the royal throne as empress, took over the government, exercised great strength and care, and, to tell the entire story, governed so well, so wisely, and with so much chivalric discipline that Gallienus, and after him, Claudius, emperors of Rome, although they occupied a large part of the Orient on behalf of Rome, never dared to undertake anything against her. The same was true for the Egyptians, the Arabians, and the Armenians: they so feared her power and bravery that they were all happy to maintain the boundaries of their lands. So wisely did this lady govern that she was honored by her princes, obeyed and loved by her people, and feared and respected by her knights. When she rode out in arms, which happened frequently, she did not speak to the members of her army unless she was in armor, with her helmet on her head, nor did she ever have herself carried in a litter, although the kings of that time all had themselves transported in this manner, but she was always mounted on a war-charger, and sometimes, to spy on her enemies, she would ride incognito in front of her troops. Just as she surpassed in discipline and chivalry all the knights of her time in the world, this noble lady Zenobia surpassed all other ladies in her noble and upright conduct and integrity of living. In her entire life-style she was extraordinarily sober. But, notwithstanding this, she often held great assemblies and feasts with her barons and with foreigners, and on these occasions she spared nothing in magnificence and royal generosity and bestowed large and beautiful gifts, for she knew well how to attract beautiful people to her love and benevolence. This woman was supremely chaste. Not only did she avoid other men, but she also slept with her husband only to have children, and demonstrated this clearly by not sleeping with her husband when she was pregnant. And to make certain that her entire outward appearance corresponded and joined with her inner character, she refused to allow any lecherous man or man of vile morals to frequent her court and insisted that all who wished to have her favor were virtuous and well-bred. She bestowed honor upon people according to their goodness, bravery, and strength and never on account of their wealth or noble birth, and she loved men with rough-hewn manners who were, nevertheless, proven in chivalry. She lived in the magnificent and lavish royal custom of an empress, in the Persian manner, which was the most stately ever to have prevailed among kings. She was served in vessels of gold and precious stones, adorned with every decoration. She amassed great treasures from her revenues and her own goods without extorting wealth from any of her subjects, and so generously did she give, when it was reasonable, that there was never seen a prince of greater generosity nor of greater magnificence.

I.20.2

"With all this having been said, the high point of her virtues which I have to tell you was, in summary, her profound learnedness in letters, both in those of the Egyptians and in those of her own language. When she rested, she diligently applied herself to study and wished to be instructed by Longinus the philosopher, who was her master and introduced her to philosophy. She knew Latin as well as Greek, through the aid of which she organized and arranged all historical works in concise and very careful form. Similarly, she desired that her children, whom she raised with strict discipline, be introduced to learning. Therefore, my dear friend, note and recall if you have ever seen or read of any prince or knight more complete in every virtue."

## *From Book II*

### 11. Concerning a woman who breast-fed her mother in prison.

II.11.1

"Similarly, a Roman woman spoken of in the histories had great love for her mother. Her mother was condemned to die in prison as punishment for a crime, and no one was to give her anything to eat or drink. Her daughter, prompted by great filial love and saddened by this condemnation, requested a special favor from those who guarded the prison, that she be able to visit her mother each day, as long as her mother was alive, so that she could admonish her to be long-suffering. And, put briefly, she wept and begged so much that the prison guards took pity on her and allowed her to visit her mother daily. But before she was brought to her mother, they would search her thoroughly to see whether she was bringing her any food. After these visitations went on for so many days that it seemed impossible to the jailers that their woman prisoner could have lasted so long without dying, and yet she was not dead, and considering that no one visited her besides her daughter, whom they carefully searched before she entered her mother's cell, they wondered a great deal how this could be. In fact, one day they watched the mother and daughter together, and then they saw that the unhappy daughter, who had recently had a child, would give her teat to her mother until the mother had taken all the milk from her breasts. In this way the daughter gave back to her mother in her old age what she had taken from her mother as an infant. This continual diligence and great love of daughter for mother moved the jailers to great pity, and when this deed had been reported to the judges, they, also moved by human compassion, freed the mother and turned her over to her daughter.

II.11.2

"Turning again to the question of a daughter's love for her father, one can mention the most virtuous and wise Griselda, who was the marquise of Saluces, whose great virtue, firmness, and constancy I will presently describe to you. What a great love, enlivened in her by her loyal nature, made her so diligent in serving her poor father Giannucolo, old and sick, in such humility and faithfulness—a love which she so diligently cultivated and maintained in her purity, virginity, and in the flower of her youth! With great care and solicitude she earned a poor living for the two of them, through the labor and skill of her hands. Daughters with such kindness and such great love for their fathers and mothers are born at truly propitious times, for although they do what they are supposed to do, they nevertheless acquire great merit for their souls; indeed, great praise in the world ought to be given them, and also to sons who act likewise.

II.11.3

"What more do you want me to say? I could give you countless examples of similar cases, but let this one be enough for you now."

## 12. Here Rectitude announces that she has finished building the houses of the city and that it is time that it be peopled.

II.12.1

"It seems to me at this point, most dear friend, that our construction is quite well advanced, for the houses of the City of Ladies stand completed all along the wide streets, its royal palaces are well constructed, and its towers and defense turrets have been raised so high and straight that one can see them from far away. It is therefore right that we start to people this noble City now, so that it does not remain vacant or empty, but instead is wholly populated with ladies of great excellence, for we do not want any others here. How happy will be the citizens of our edifice, for they will not need to fear or worry about being evicted by foreign armies, for this work has the special property that its owners cannot be expelled. Now a New Kingdom of Femininity is begun, and it is far better than the earlier kingdom of the Amazons, for the ladies residing here will not need to leave their land in order to conceive or give birth to new heirs to maintain their possessions throughout the different ages, from one generation to another, for those whom we now place here will suffice quite adequately forever more.

II.12.2

"And after we have populated it with noble citizens, my sister, Lady Justice, will come and lead the Queen, outstanding over all, and accompanied by princesses of the highest dignity who will reside in the uppermost apartments and in the lofty towers. It is fitting that on her arrival the Queen find her City supplied and peopled with noble ladies who will receive her with honors as their sovereign lady, empress of all their sex. But what citizens will we place here? Will they be dissolute or dishonored women? Certainly not, rather they shall all be women of integrity, of great beauty and authority, for there could be no fairer populace nor any greater adornment in the City than women of good character. Now let us go, dear friend, for now I am putting you to work, and I will go ahead so that we can go look for them." . . .

## 54. Christine asks Rectitude whether what many men say is true, that so few women are faithful in their love lives; and Rectitude's answer.

II.54.1

Proceeding further, I, Christine, again spoke, "My lady, let us now move on to other questions and for a short while go beyond the topics developed up to now, for I would like to ask you several questions, if I were sure that they would not bother you, since the subject I want to discuss goes somewhat beyond the temperament of reason."

She replied to me, "Friend, ask what you like, for the disciple who must ask the master questions in order to learn ought not to suffer reproof for inquiring about everything."

"My lady, a natural behavior of men toward women and of women toward men prevails in the world which is not brought about by human institutions but by the inclination of the flesh, and in which men and women love one another with a very strong love strengthened in turn by foolish pleasure. And they do not know for what reason and to what end such a mutual love is implanted in them. Men usually claim that women, in spite of everything they promise regarding this widespread passion usually called one's 'love life,' are rarely constant, not very loving, and amazingly false and fickle. All of this stems from the frivolousness of their hearts. Among other Latin authors who level this charge is Ovid, who makes serious accusations in his *Ars amatoria.* When he finishes his attack, Ovid (as well as others) says that everything contained in his books regarding women's deceptive manners and malice was for the benefit of the common good, in order to warn men about women's ruses so that they could better avoid them, like the snake hidden in the grass. If you would, dear lady, teach me the truth of this matter."

She replied, "Dear friend, as for the charge that women are deceitful, I really do not know what more I can say to you, for you yourself have adequately handled the subject, answering Ovid and the others in your *Epistre au Dieu d'Amour* and your *Epistres sur le Roman de la Rose.* But, as for the point you mention that these men attack women for the sake of the common good, I can show you that it has never been a question of this. And here is the reason: the common good of a city or land or any community of people is nothing other than the profit or general good in which all members, women as well as men, participate and take part. But whatever is done with the intention of benefiting some and not others is a matter of private and not public welfare. Even less so is an activity in which one takes from some and gives to others, and such an activity is perpetrated for the sake of private gain, and at the same time it constitutes, quite simply, a crime committed for the benefit of one person and to the disadvantage of the other. For they never address women nor warn them against men's traps even though it is certain that men frequently deceive women with their fast tricks and duplicity. There is not the slightest doubt that women belong to the people of God and the human race as much as men, and are not another species or dissimilar race, for which they should be excluded from moral teachings. Therefore, I conclude that if these men had acted in the public good—that is, for both parties—they should also have addressed themselves to women and warned them to beware of men's tricks just as they warned men to be careful about women. But leaving behind these questions and pursuing the others, that is, whether women show so little love where they set their hearts and whether women are more constant than these men claim, it will be enough for me to deduce the point for you from examples of women who persevered in their love until death. First, I will tell you of the noble Dido, queen of Carthage, whose great value I discussed above and which you yourself have spoken of earlier in your works."

## 55. Concerning Dido, Queen of Carthage, on the subject of constant love in women.

II.55.1

"Just as was said above, during the time in which Dido, queen of Carthage, was living happily in her city and ruling gloriously in peace, it happened by chance that Aeneas, fugitive from Troy following its destruction, leader and captain of many Trojans, tossed about by many storms, his ships wrecked and provisions exhausted, having lost many of his men, in need of rest, out of money, weary of wandering at sea, and in need of shelter, arrived in the port of Carthage. And when, out of fear of inadvertently landing without permission, he sent to the queen to know whether it would please her that he come into port, the noble lady, full of honor and valiance and well aware that the Trojans enjoyed a better reputation than any other nation of the world at that time and that Aeneas was of the royal house of Troy, not only gave him leave to land but also went out with a most noble company of barons and ladies and maidens to the shore to meet him and there received him and his entire company with the greatest honor. She brought him into her city and honored and feasted him and put him at ease. Why should I give you a long account? Aeneas was able to rest so long there that he hardly recalled the torments he had suffered. Dido and Aeneas spent so much time with one another that Love, who knows how to subjugate all hearts with the greatest of skill, made them become enamored of one another. But as experience showed, Dido's love for Aeneas was far greater than his love for her, for even though he had given her his pledge never to take any other woman and to be hers forever, he left after she had restored and enriched him with property and ease, his ships refreshed, repaired, and placed in order, filled with treasure and wealth, like a woman who had spared no expense where her heart was involved. He departed at night, secretly and treacherously, without farewells and without her knowledge. This was how he repaid his hostess. His departure caused so much grief for the unhappy Dido, who had loved too much, that she wished to renounce all joy and her own life. Indeed, after lamenting a great deal, she threw herself into a large fire which she had lit. Others say she killed herself with Aeneas' own sword. And so the noble queen Dido died in such a pitiful manner, who has been honored so greatly that her fame has surpassed that of all other women of her time."

## *from Book III*

### 10. Here she speaks of Saint Christine, virgin.

III.10.1

"The blessed Saint Christine, virgin, was from the city of Tyre and was the daughter of Urban, master of the knights. Her father shut her up in a tower because of her great beauty, and she had twelve maids with her. Her father also had a very beautiful chapel with idols built near Christine's chamber so that she could worship them. She, however, even as a twelve-year-old child, had already been inspired by the faith of Jesus Christ and did not pay any attention to the idols, so that her maids were astonished and repeatedly urged her to sacrifice. Yet when she took the incense, as if to sacrifice to the idols, she knelt at a window facing east, looked up to Heaven, and offered her incense to the immortal God. She spent the greater part of the night at this window, watching the stars, and sighing, piously praying to God to help her against her enemies. The maids, clearly aware her heart was in Jesus Christ, would often kneel before her, their hands clasped together, begging her not to place her trust in a strange God but to worship her parents' gods, for if she were discovered they would all be killed. Christine would answer that the Devil was deceiving them by urging them to worship so many gods and that there was but one God. When her father at last realized that his daughter refused to worship his idols, he was terribly grieved and upbraided her a great deal. She replied that she would gladly worship the God of Heaven. He thought she meant Jupiter and he was overjoyed and wanted to kiss her, but she cried out, 'Do not touch my mouth, for I wish to offer a pure offering to the celestial God.' The father was even happy with this. She returned to her chamber and nailed the door shut, then she knelt down and offered a holy prayer to God, weeping all the while. And the angel of the Lord descended and comforted her and brought her white bread and meat which she ate, for she had not tasted food for three days. Once, afterward, when Christine saw from her window several poor Christians begging at the foot of her tower, seeing that she had nothing to give them, she searched for her father's idols which were made of gold and silver, and she smashed them all and gave the fragments to the poor. When her father learned of this, he beat her cruelly. She openly declared he was deceived to worship these false images and that there was but a single God in the Trinity and that her father should worship Him whom she confessed, and she refused to worship any other in order to escape death. Thereupon her enraged father had her tied up with chains and led from square to square to be beaten and then thrown into prison. He himself wanted to be the judge of this dispute, so on the following day he had her brought before him and threatened her with every conceivable torture if she would not worship his idols. After he realized that he could not convince her with entreaties or threats, he had her sprawled completely nude and beaten so much that twelve men wearied at the task. And the father kept asking her what she thought and he said to her, 'Daughter, natural affection wrings my heart terribly to torment you who are my own flesh, but the reverence I have for my gods forces me to do this because you scorn them.' And the holy virgin replied, 'Tyrant who should not be called my father but rather enemy of my happiness, you boldly torture the flesh which you engendered, for you can easily do this, but as for my soul created by my Father in Heaven, you have no power to touch it with the slightest temptation, for it is protected by my Savior, Jesus Christ.' The cruel father, all the more enraged, had a wheel brought in, which he had ordered built, and ordered her tied to it and a fire built below it, and then he had rivers of boiling oil poured over her body. The wheel turned and completely crushed her. But God, the Father of all mercies, took pity on His servant and dispatched His angel to wreck the torture machines and to extinguish the fire, delivering the virgin, healthy and whole, and killing more than a thousand treacherous spectators who had been watching her without pity and who blasphemed the name of God. And her father asked her, 'Tell me who taught you these evil practices!' She replied, 'Pitiless despot, have I not told you that my Father, Jesus Christ, taught me this long-suffering as well as every right thing in the faith of the Living God? Because of this, I scorn your tortures and will repel all the Devil's assaults with God's strength!' Beaten and confounded, he ordered her thrown into a horrible, dark prison. While she was there, contemplating the extraordinary mysteries of God, three angels came to her in great radiance and brought her food and comforted her. Urban did not know what to do with her but could not stop devising new tortures for her. Finally, fed up completely and wishing to be free of her, he had a great stone tied around her neck and had her thrown into the sea. But as she was being thrown in, the angels took her, and she walked on the water with them. Then, raising her eyes to heaven, Christine prayed to Jesus Christ, that it please Him for her to receive in this water the holy sacrament of baptism which she greatly desired to have; whereupon Jesus Christ descended in His own person with a large company of angels and baptized her and named her Christine, from His own name, and He crowned her and placed a shining star on her forehead and set her on dry land. That night Urban was tortured by the Devil and died. The blessed Christine, whom God wanted to receive through martyrdom (which she also desired), was led back to prison by these criminals. The new judge, named Dyon, knowing what had been done to her, summoned her to appear before him, and he lusted after her because of her beauty. When he saw that his alluring words were of no use, he had her tortured again. He ordered that a large cauldron be filled with oil and that a roaring fire be built beneath it; he had her thrown in, upside down, and four men used iron hooks to rotate her. And the holy virgin sang melodiously to God, mocking her torturers and threatening them with the pains of Hell. When this enraged criminal of a judge realized that nothing was of any avail, he ordered her to be hanged by her long golden hair in the square, in front of all. The women rushed up to her, and, wailing out of pity that such a young girl be so cruelly tortured, they cried out to the judge, saying, 'Cruel felon, crueler than a savage beast, how could a man's heart conceive such monstrous cruelty against such a beautiful and tender maiden?' And all the women tried to mob him. Then the judge, who was afraid, said to her, 'Christine, friend, do not let yourself be tortured anymore, but come with me and we will go worship the supreme God who has upheld you.' He meant Jupiter, who was considered the supreme god, but she understood him in a completely different way and so she replied, 'You have spoken well, so I consent.' He had her taken down and brought up to the temple, and a large crowd followed them. Then he led her before the idols, thinking she would worship them, and she knelt down, looked up at Heaven, and prayed to God. Thereupon she stood up and, turning toward the idol, said, 'I command you in the name of Jesus Christ, oh evil spirit residing in this idol, to come out.' Whereupon the Devil immediately came out and made a loud and frightening din which scared all the spectators, who fell to the ground in fear. When the judge stood up again, he said, 'Christine, you have moved our omnipotent god, and, out of pity for you, he came out to see his creature'. This remark angered her, and she reproached him harshly for being too blind to recognize divine virtue, so she prayed to God to overturn the idol and reduce it to dust, which was done. And more than three thousand men were converted through the words and signs of this virgin. The terrified judge exclaimed, 'If the king finds out what this Christine has done against our god, he will utterly destroy me.' Thereupon, full of anguish, he went out of his mind and died. A third judge, named Julian, appeared, and he ordered Christine seized, boasting that he would make her worship the idols. In spite of all the force he could apply, he was unable physically to move her from the spot where she was standing, so he ordered a large fire built around her. She remained in the fire for three days, and from inside the flames were heard sweet melodies. Her tormentors were terrified by the amazing signs they saw. When the fire had burned out, she emerged fully healthy. The judge commanded that snakes be brought to him and had two asps (with their deadly poisonous bite) and two adders released upon her. But these snakes dropped down at her feet, their heads bowed, and did not harm her at all. Two horrible vipers were let loose, and they hung from her breasts and licked her. And Christine looked to Heaven and said, 'I give You thanks, Lord God, Jesus Christ, who have deigned to grant through Your holy virtues that these horrible serpents would come to know in me Your dignity.' The obstinate Julian, seeing these wonders, yelled at the snake-tender, 'Have you too been enchanted by Christine, so that you have no power to rouse the snakes against her?' Fearing the judge, he then tried to provoke the snakes into biting her, but they rushed at him and killed him. Since everyone was afraid of these serpents and no one dared approach, Christine commanded them in God's name to return to their cages without harming anyone, and they did so. She revived the dead man, who immediately threw himself at her feet and was converted. The judge, blinded by the Devil so that he was unable to perceive the divine mystery, said to Christine, 'You have sufficiently demonstrated your magic arts.' Infuriated, she replied, 'If your eyes would see the virtues of God, you would believe in them.' Then in his rage he ordered her breasts ripped off, whereupon milk rather than blood flowed out. And because she unceasingly pronounced the name of Jesus Christ, he had her tongue cut out, but then she spoke even better and more clearly than before of divine things and of the one blessed God, thanking Him for the bounties which He had given to her. She prayed that it please Him to receive her in His company and that the crown of her martyrdom be finally granted to her. Then a voice was heard from Heaven, saying, 'Christine, pure and radiant, the heavens are opened to you and the eternal kingdom waits, prepared for you, and the entire company of saints blesses God for your sake, for you have upheld the name of Your Christ from childhood on.' And she glorified God, turning her eyes to Heaven. The voice was heard saying, 'Come, Christine, my most beloved and elect daughter, receive the palm and everlasting crown and the reward for your life spent suffering to confess My name.' The treacherous Julian, who heard this voice, castigated the executioners and said they had not cut Christine's tongue short enough and ordered them to cut it so short that she could not speak to her Christ, whereupon they ripped out her tongue and cut it off at the root. She spat this cut-off piece of her tongue into the tyrant's face, putting out one of his eyes. She then said to him, speaking as clearly as ever, 'Tyrant, what does it profit you to have my tongue cut out so that it cannot bless God, when my soul will bless Him forever while yours languishes forever in eternal damnation? And because you did not heed my words, my tongue has blinded you, with good reason.' She ended her martyrdom then, having already seen Jesus Christ sitting on the right hand of His Father, when two arrows were shot at her, one in her side and the other in her heart. One of her relatives whom she had converted buried her body and wrote out her glorious legend."

O blessed Christine, worthy virgin favored of God, most elect and glorious martyr, in the holiness with which God has made you worthy, pray for me, a sinner, named with your name, and be my kind and merciful guardian. Behold my joy at being able to make use of your holy legend and to include it in my writings, which I have recorded here at such length out of reverence for you. May this be ever pleasing to you! Pray for all women, for whom your holy life may serve as an example for ending their lives well. Amen.

III.10.2

"What else should I tell you, dear friend, in order to fill our City with such a company? May Saint Ursula come with her multitude of eleven thousand virgins, blessed martyrs for the name of Jesus Christ, all of them beheaded after they had been sent off to be married. They arrived in the land of unbelievers who tried to force them to renounce their faith in God: they chose to die rather than to renounce Jesus Christ their Savior."

## Michel de Montaigne (1533–1592)

*Translated by Donald M. Frame*

Michel de Montaigne retired to his estate at the age of thirty-eight to spend the rest of his life in study and in writing (although he was mayor of Bordeaux for four years). His life's work is his *Essays,* a collection of 107 rambling, learned, and witty meditations on topics as diverse as pedantry, friendship, warhorses, and smells. If it is true that Renaissance humanism was a cult of the individual self, perhaps Montaigne is its greatest exemplar, for he claims: "I have no more made my book than my book has made me—a book consubstantial with its author, concerned with my own self, an integral part of my life" (from *Of Giving the Lie*); and "Authors communicate with the people by some special extrinsic mark; I am the first to do so by my entire being, as Michel de Montaigne" (*Of Repentance*). The lasting influence of this claim can be measured by comparing Rousseau's similar claim at the opening of his *Confessions* two centuries later. Especially important is Montaigne's refusal to define himself with any certainty: "I do not portray being; I portray passing." His willingness to accept his own limited and contradictory nature is echoed in writers as distant as Whitman and Thoreau, and indeed throughout modernity. It is for reasons like these that in European history, the Renaissance is also known as the Early

Modern Period. Because Montaigne is at once so immensely learned in the classics and also so charmingly self-deprecating, reading his personal, idiosyncratic essays can be one of the highest pleasures of European literary life.

The essay included here is justly famous for being among his best. *Of Cannibals* describes the New World in terms of the myths of the Golden Age (see Ovid, pp. 677–679) and the Noble Savage. As in More's *Utopia,* Montaigne's description of the customs of a society so different from his own allows him mordant insights into familiar European customs: "Truly here are real savages by our standards; for either they must be thoroughly so, or we must be; there is an amazing distance between their character and ours." Note how undogmatic, tentative, and relativistic his conclusions are. The discovery of the New World provided Renaissance writers with new possibilities for understanding the self and society, expanding horizons already stretched by growing contacts with Asia and by the humanists' rediscovery of the pre-Christian classical world.

## *Of Cannibals*

When King Pyrrhus passed over into Italy, after he had reconnoitered the formation of the army that the Romans were sending to meet him, he said: "I do not know what barbarians these are" (for so the Greeks called all foreign nations), "but the formation of this army that I see is not at all barbarous." The Greeks said as much of the army that Flamininus brought into their country, and so did Philip, seeing from a knoll the order and distribution of the Roman camp, in his kingdom, under Publius Sulpicius Galba. Thus we should beware of clinging to vulgar opinions, and judge things by reason's way, not by popular say.

I had with me for a long time a man who had lived for ten or twelve years in that other world which has been discovered in our century, in the place when Villegaignon landed, and which he called Antarctic France. This discovery of a boundless country seems worthy of consideration. I don't know if I can guarantee that some other such discovery will not be made in the future, so many personages greater than ourselves having been mistaken about this one. I am afraid we have eyes bigger than our stomachs, and more curiosity than capacity. We embrace everything, but we clasp only wind.

Plato brings in Solon, telling how he had learned from the priests of the city of Saïs in Egypt that in days of old, before the Flood, there was a great island named Atlantis, right at the mouth of the Strait of Gibraltar, which contained more land than Africa and Asia put together, and that the kings of that country, who not only possessed that island but had stretched out so far on the mainland that they held the breadth of Africa as far as Egypt, and the length of Europe as far as Tuscany, undertook to step over into Asia and subjugate all the nations that border on the Mediterranean, as far as the Black Sea; and for this purpose crossed the Spains, Gaul, Italy, as far as Greece, where the Athenians checked them; but that some time after, both the Athenians and themselves and their island were swallowed up by the Flood.

It is quite likely that that extreme devastation of waters made amazing changes in the habitations of the earth, as people maintain that the sea cut off Sicily from Italy—

> 'Tis said an earthquake once
> asunder tore
> These lands with dreadful havoc,
> which before
> Formed but one land, one coast
>
> VIRGIL

Cyprus from Syria, the island of Euboea from the mainland of Boeotia; and elsewhere joined lands that were divided, filling the channels between them with sand and mud:

> A sterile marsh, long fit for
> rowing, now
> Feeds neighbor towns, and feels
> the heavy plow.
>
> HORACE

But there is no great likelihood that that island was the new world which we have just discovered; for it almost touched Spain, and it would be an incredible result of a flood to have forced it away as far as it is, more than twelve hundred leagues; besides, the travels of the moderns have already almost revealed that it is not an island, but a mainland connected with the East Indies on one side, and elsewhere with the lands under the two poles; or, if it is separated from them, it is by so narrow a strait and interval that it does not deserve to be called an island on that account.

It seems that there are movements, some natural, others feverish, in these great bodies, just as in our own. When I consider the inroads that my river, the Dordogne, is making in my lifetime into the right bank in its descent, and that in twenty years it has gained so much ground and stolen away the foundations of several buildings, I clearly see that this is an extraordinary disturbance; for if it had always gone at this rate, or was to do so in the future, the face of the world would be turned topsy-turvy. But rivers are subject to changes: now they overflow in one direction, now in another, now they keep to their course. I am not speaking of the sudden inundations whose causes are manifest. In Médoc, along the seashore, my brother, the sieur d'Arsac, can see an estate of his buried under the sands that the sea spews forth; the tops of some buildings are still visible; his farms and domains have changed into very thin pasturage. The inhabitants say that for some time the sea has been pushing toward them so hard that they have lost four leagues of land. These sands are its harbingers; and we see great dunes of moving sand that march half a league ahead of it and keep conquering land.

The other testimony of antiquity with which some would connect this discovery is in Aristotle, at least if that little book *Of Unheard-of Wonders* is by him. He there relates that certain Carthaginians, after setting out upon the Atlantic Ocean from the Strait of Gibraltar and sailing a long time, at last discovered a great fertile island, all clothed in woods and watered by great deep rivers, far remote from any mainland; and that they, and others since, attracted by the goodness and fertility of the soil, went there with their wives and children, and began to settle there. The lords of Carthage, seeing that their country was gradually becoming depopulated, expressly forbade anyone to go there any more, on pain of death, and drove out these new inhabitants, fearing, it is said, that in course of time they might come to multiply so greatly as to supplant their former masters and ruin their state. This story of Aristotle does not fit our new lands any better than the other.

This man I had was a simple, crude fellow—a character fit to bear true witness; for clever people observe more things and more curiously, but they interpret them; and to lend weight and conviction to their interpretation, they cannot help altering history a little. They never show you things as they are, but bend and disguise them according to the way they have seen them; and to give credence to their judgment and attract you to it, they are prone to add something to their matter, to stretch it out and amplify it. We need a man either very honest, or so simple that he has not the stuff to build up false inventions and give them plausibility; and wedded to no theory. Such was my man; and besides this, he at various times brought sailors and merchants, whom he had known on that trip, to see me. So I content myself with his information, without inquiring what the cosmographers say about it.

We ought to have topographers who would give us an exact account of the places where they have been. But because they have over us the advantage of having seen Palestine, they want to enjoy the privilege of telling us news about all the rest of the world. I would like everyone to write what he knows, and as much as he knows, not only in this, but in all other subjects; for a man may have some special knowledge and experience of the nature of a river or a fountain, who in other matters knows only what everybody knows. However, to circulate this little scrap of knowledge, he will undertake to write the whole of physics. From this vice spring many great abuses.

Now, to return to my subject, I think there is nothing barbarous and savage in that nation, from what I have been told, except that each man calls barbarism whatever is not his own practice; for indeed it seems we have no other test of truth and reason than the example and pattern of the opinions and customs of the country we live in. *There* is always the perfect religion, the perfect government, the perfect and accomplished manners in all things. Those people are wild, just as we call wild the fruits that Nature has produced by herself and in her normal course; whereas really it is those that we have changed artificially and led astray from the common order, that we should rather call wild. The former retain alive and vigorous their genuine, their most useful and natural, virtues and properties, which we have debased in the latter in adapting them to gratify our corrupted taste. And yet for all that, the savor and delicacy of some uncultivated fruits of those countries is quite as excellent, even to our taste, as that of our own. It is not reasonable that art should win the place of honor over our great and powerful mother Nature. We have so overloaded the beauty and richness of her works by our inventions that we have quite smothered her. Yet wherever her purity shines forth, she wonderfully puts to shame our vain and frivolous attempts:

> Ivy comes readier without our
> care;
> In lonely caves the arbutus grows
> more fair;
> No art with artless bird song can
> compare.
>
> PROPERTIUS

All our efforts cannot even succeed in reproducing the nest of the tiniest little bird, its contexture, its beauty and convenience; or even the web of the puny spider. All things, says Plato, are produced by nature, by fortune, or by art; the greatest and most beautiful by one or the other of the first two, the least and most imperfect by the last.

These nations, then, seem to me barbarous in this sense, that they have been fashioned very little by the human mind, and are still very close to their original naturalness. The laws of nature still rule them, very little corrupted by ours; and they are in such a state of purity that I am sometimes vexed that they were unknown earlier, in the days when there were men able to judge them better than we. I am sorry that Lycurgus and Plato did not know of them; for it seems to me that what we actually see in these nations surpasses not only all the pictures in which poets have idealized the golden age and all their inventions in imagining a happy state of man, but also the conceptions and the very desire of philosophy. They could not imagine a naturalness so pure and simple as we see by experience; nor could they believe that our society could be maintained with so little artifice and human solder. This is a nation, I should say to Plato, in which there is no sort of traffic, no knowledge of letters, no science of numbers, no name for a magistrate or for political superiority, no custom of servitude, no riches or poverty, no contracts, no successions, no partitions, no occupations but leisure ones, no care for any but common kinship, no clothes, no agriculture, no metal, no use of wine or wheat. The very words that signify lying, treachery, dissimulation, avarice, envy, belittling, pardon—unheard of. How far from this perfection would he find the republic that he imagined: *Men fresh sprung from the gods* [Seneca].

These manners nature first
ordained.

VIRGIL

For the rest, they live in a country with a very pleasant and temperate climate, so that according to my witnesses it is rare to see a sick man there; and they have assured me that they never saw one palsied, bleary-eyed, toothless, or bent with age. They are settled along the sea and shut in on the land side by great high mountains, with a stretch about a hundred leagues wide in between. They have a great abundance of fish and flesh which bear no resemblance to ours, and they eat them with no other artifice than cooking. The first man who rode a horse there, though he had had dealings with them on several other trips, so horrified them in this posture that they shot him dead with arrows before they could recognize him.

Their buildings are very long, with a capacity of two or three hundred souls; they are covered with the bark of great trees, the strips reaching to the ground at one end and supporting and leaning on one another at the top, in the manner of some of our barns, whose covering hangs down to the ground and acts as a side. They have wood so hard that they cut with it and make of it their swords and grills to cook their food. Their beds are of a cotton weave, hung from the roof like those in our ships, each man having his own; for the wives sleep apart from their husbands.

They get up with the sun, and eat immediately upon rising, to last them through the day; for they take no other meal than that one. Like some other Eastern peoples, of whom Suidas tells us, who drank apart from meals, they do not drink then; but they drink several times a day, and to capacity. Their drink is made of some root, and is of the color of our claret wines. They drink it only lukewarm. This beverage keeps only two or three days; it has a slightly sharp taste, is not at all heady, is good for the stomach, and has a laxative effect upon those who are not used to it; it is a very pleasant drink for anyone who is accustomed to it. In place of bread they use a certain white substance like preserved coriander. I have tried it; it tastes sweet and a little flat.

The whole day is spent in dancing. The younger men go to hunt animals with bows. Some of the women busy themselves meanwhile with warming their drink, which is their chief duty. Some one of the old men, in the morning before they begin to eat, preaches to the whole barnful in common, walking from one end to the other, and repeating one single sentence several times until he has completed the circuit (for the buildings are fully a hundred paces long). He recommends to them only two things: valor against the enemy and love for their wives. And they never fail to point out this obligation, as their refrain, that it is their wives who keep their drink warm and seasoned.

There may be seen in several places, including my own house, specimens of their beds, of their ropes, of their wooden swords and the bracelets with which they cover their wrists in combats, and of the big canes, open at one end, by whose sound they keep time in their dances. They are close shaven all over, and shave themselves much more cleanly than we, with nothing but a wooden or stone razor. They believe that souls are immortal, and that those who have deserved well of the gods are lodged in that part of heaven where the sun rises, and the damned in the west.

They have some sort of priests and prophets, but they rarely appear before the people, having their home in the mountains. On their arrival there is a great feast and solemn assembly of several villages—each barn, as I have described it, makes up a village, and they are about one French league from each other. The prophet speaks to them in public, exhorting them to virtue and their duty; but their whole ethical science contains only these two articles: resoluteness in war and affection for their wives. He prophesies to them things to come and the results they are to expect from their undertakings, and urges them to war or holds them back from it; but this is on the condition that when he fails to prophesy correctly, and if things turn out otherwise than he has predicted, he is cut into a thousand pieces if they catch him, and condemned as a false prophet. For this reason, the prophet who has once been mistaken is never seen again.

Divination is a gift of God; that is why its abuse should be punished as imposture. Among the Scythians, when the soothsayers failed to hit the mark, they were laid, chained hand and foot, on carts full of heather and drawn by oxen, on which they were burned. Those who handle matters subject to the control of human capacity are excusable if they do the best they can. But these others, who come and trick us with assurances of an extraordinary faculty that is beyond our ken, should they not be punished for not making good their promise, and for the temerity of their imposture?

They have their wars with the nations beyond the mountains, further inland, to which they go quite naked, with no other arms than bows or wooden swords ending in a sharp point, in the manner of the tongues of our boar spears. It is astonishing what firmness they show in their combats, which never end but in slaughter and bloodshed; for as to routs and terror, they know nothing of either.

Each man brings back as his trophy the head of the enemy he has killed, and sets it up at the entrance to his dwelling. After they have treated their prisoner's well for a long time with all the hospitality they can think of, each man who has a prisoner calls a great assembly of his acquaintances. He ties a rope to one of the prisoner's arms, by the end of which he holds him, a few steps away, for fear of being hurt, and gives his dearest friend the other arm to hold in the same way; and these two, in the presence of the whole assembly, kill him with their swords. This done, they roast him and eat him in common and send some pieces to their absent friends. This is not, as people think, for nourishment, as of old the Scythians used to do; it is to betoken an extreme revenge. And the proof of this came when they saw the Portuguese, who had joined forces with their adversaries, inflict a different kind of death on them when they took them prisoner, which was to bury them up to the waist, shoot the rest of their body full of arrows, and afterward hang them. They thought that these people from the other world, being men who had sown the knowledge of many vices among their neighbors and were much greater masters than themselves in every sort of wickedness, did not adopt this sort of vengeance without some reason, and that it must be more painful than their own; so they began to give up their old method and to follow this one.

I am not sorry that we notice the barbarous horror of such acts, but I am heartily sorry that, judging their faults rightly, we should be so blind to our own. I think there is more barbarity in eating a man alive than in eating him dead; and in tearing by tortures and the rack a body still full of feeling, in roasting a man bit by bit, in having him bitten and mangled by dogs and swine (as we have not only read but seen within fresh memory, not among ancient enemies, but among neighbors and fellow citizens, and what is worse, on the pretext of piety and religion), than in roasting and eating him after he is dead.

Indeed, Chrysippus and Zeno, heads of the Stoic sect, thought there was nothing wrong in using our carcasses for any purpose in case of need, and getting nourishment from them; just as our ancestors, when besieged by Caesar in the city of Alésia, resolved to relieve their famine by eating old men, women, and other people useless for fighting.

> The Gascons once, 'tis said, their
> life renewed
> By eating of such food.
>
> JUVENAL

And physicians do not fear to use human flesh in all sorts of ways for our health, applying it either inwardly or outwardly. But there never was any opinion so disordered as to excuse treachery, disloyalty, tyranny, and cruelty, which are our ordinary vices.

So we may well call these people barbarians, in respect to the rules of reason, but not in respect to ourselves, who surpass them in every kind of barbarity.

Their warfare is wholly noble and generous, and as excusable and beautiful as this human disease can be; its only basis among them is their rivalry in valor. They are not fighting for the conquest of new lands, for they still enjoy that natural abundance that provides them without toil and trouble with all necessary things in such profusion that they have no wish to enlarge their boundaries. They are still in that happy state of desiring only as much as their natural needs demand; anything beyond that is superfluous to them.

They generally call those of the same age, brothers; those who are younger, children; and the old men are fathers to all the others. These leave to their heirs in common the full possession of their property, without division or any other title at all than just the one that Nature gives to her creatures in bringing them into the world.

If their neighbors cross the mountains to attack them and win a victory, the gain of the victor is glory, and the advantage of having proved the master in valor and virtue; for apart from this they have no use for the goods of the vanquished, and they return to their own country, where they lack neither anything necessary nor that great thing, the knowledge of how to enjoy their condition happily and be content with it. These men of ours do the same in their turn. They demand of their prisoners no other ransom than that they confess and acknowledge their defeat. But there is not one in a whole century who does not choose to die rather than to relax a single bit, by word or look, from the grandeur of an invincible courage; not one who would not rather be killed and eaten than so much as ask not to be. They treat them very freely, so that life may be all the dearer to them, and usually entertain them with threats of their coming death, of the torments they will have to suffer, the preparations that are being made for that purpose, the cutting up of their limbs, and the feast that will be made at their expense. All this is done for the sole purpose of extorting from their lips some weak or base word, or making them want to flee, so as to gain the advantage of having terrified them and broken down their firmness. For indeed, if you take it the right way, it is in this point alone that true victory lies:

> It is no victory
> Unless the vanquished foe admits
> your mastery.
>
> CLAUDIAN

The Hungarians, very bellicose fighters, did not in olden times pursue their advantage beyond putting the enemy at their mercy. For having wrung a confession from him to this effect, they let him go unharmed and unransomed, except, at most, for exacting his promise never again to take up arms against them.

We win enough advantages over our enemies that are borrowed advantages, not really our own. It is the quality of a porter, not of valor, to have sturdier arms and legs; agility is a dead and corporeal quality; it is a stroke of luck to make our enemy stumble, or dazzle his eyes by the sunlight; it is a trick of art and technique, which may be found in a worthless coward, to be an able fencer. The worth and value of a man is in his heart and his will; there lies his real honor. Valor is the strength, not of legs and arms, but of heart and soul; it consists not in the worth of our horse or our weapons, but in our own. He who falls obstinate in his courage, *if he has fallen, he fights on his knees* [Seneca]. He who relaxes none of his assurance, no matter how great the danger of imminent death; who, giving up his soul, still looks firmly and scornfully at his enemy—he is beaten not by us, but by fortune; he is killed, not conquered.

The most valiant are sometimes the most unfortunate. Thus there are triumphant defeats that rival victories. Nor did those four sister victories, the fairest that the sun ever set eyes on—Salamis, Plataea, Mycale, and Sicily—ever dare match all their combined glory against the glory of the annihilation of King Leonidas and his men at the pass of Thermopylae.

Who ever hastened with more glorious and ambitious desire to win a battle than Captain Ischolas to lose one? Who ever secured his safety more ingeniously and painstakingly than he did his destruction? He was charged to defend a certain pass in the Peloponnesus against the Arcadians. Finding himself wholly incapable of doing this, in view of the nature of the place and the inequality of the forces, he made up his mind that all who confronted the enemy would necessarily have to remain on the field. On the other hand, deeming it unworthy both of his own virtue and magnanimity and of the Lacedaemonian name to fail in his charge, he took a middle course between these two extremes, in this way. The youngest and fittest of his band he preserved for the defense and service of their country, and sent them home; and with those whose loss was less important, he determined to hold this pass, and by their death to make the enemy buy their entry as dearly as he could. And so it turned out. For he was presently surrounded on all sides by the Arcadians, and after slaughtering a large number of them, he and his men were all put to the sword. Is there a trophy dedicated to victors that would not be more due to those vanquished? The role of true victory is in fighting, not in coming off safely; and the honor of valor consists in combating, not in beating.

To return to our story. These prisoners are so far from giving in, in spite of all that is done to them, that on the contrary, during the two or three months that they are kept, they wear a gay expression; they urge their captors to hurry and put them to the test; they defy them, insult them, reproach them with their cowardice and the number of battles they have lost to the prisoners' own people.

I have a song composed by a prisoner which contains this challenge, that they should all come boldly and gather to dine off him, for they will be eating at the same time their own fathers and grandfathers, who have served to feed and nourish his body. "These muscles," he says, "this flesh and these veins are your own, poor fools that you are. You do not recognize that the substance of your ancestors' limbs is still contained in them. Savor them well; you will find in them the taste of your own flesh." An idea that certainly does not smack of barbarity. Those that paint these people dying, and who show the execution, portray the prisoner spitting in the face of his slayers and scowling at them. Indeed, to the last gasp they never stop braving and defying their enemies by word and look. Truly here are real savages by our standards; for either they must be thoroughly so, or we must be; there is an amazing distance between their character and ours.

The men there have several wives, and the higher their reputation for valor the more wives they have. It is a remarkably beautiful thing about their marriages that the same jealousy our wives have to keep us from the affection and kindness of other women, theirs have to win this for them. Being more concerned for their husbands' honor than for anything else, they strive and scheme to have as many companions as they can, since that is a sign of their husbands' valor.

Our wives will cry "Miracle!" but it is no miracle. It is a properly matrimonial virtue, but one of the highest order. In the Bible, Leah, Rachel, Sarah, and Jacob's wives gave their beautiful handmaids to their husbands; and Livia seconded the appetites of Augustus, to her own disadvantage; and Stratonice, the wife of King Deiotarus, not only lent her husband for his use a very beautiful young chambermaid in her service, but carefully brought up her children, and backed them up to succeed to their father's estates.

And lest it be thought that all this is done through a simple and servile bondage to usage and through the pressure of the authority of their ancient customs, without reasoning or judgment, and because their minds are so stupid that they cannot take any other course, I must cite some examples of their capacity. Besides the warlike song I have just quoted, I have another, a love song, which begins in this vein: "Adder, stay; stay, adder, that from the pattern of your coloring my sister may draw the fashion and the workmanship of a rich girdle that I may give to my love; so may your beauty and your pattern be forever preferred to all other serpents." This first couplet is the refrain of the song. Now I am familiar enough with poetry to be a judge of this: not only is there nothing barbarous in this fancy, but it is altogether Anacreontic. Their language, moreover, is a soft language, with an agreeable sound, somewhat like Greek in its endings.

Three of these men, ignorant of the price they will pay some day, in loss of repose and happiness, for gaining knowledge of the corruptions of this side of the ocean; ignorant also of the fact that of this intercourse will come their ruin (which I suppose is already well advanced: poor wretches, to let themselves be tricked by the desire for new things, and to have left the serenity of their own sky to come and see ours!)—three of these men were at Rouen, at the time the late King Charles IX was there. The king talked to them for a long time; they were shown our ways, our splendor, the aspect of a fine city. After that, someone asked their opinion, and wanted to know what they had found most amazing. They mentioned three things, of which I have forgotten the third, and I am very sorry for it; but I still remember two of them. They said that in the first place they thought it very strange that so many grown men, bearded, strong, and armed, who were around the king (it is likely that they were talking about the Swiss of his guard) should submit to obey a child, and that one of them was not chosen to command instead. Second (they have a way in their language of speaking of men as halves of one another), they had noticed that there were among us men full and gorged with all sorts of good things, and that their other halves were beggars at their doors, emaciated with hunger and poverty; and they thought it strange that these needy halves could endure such an injustice, and did not take the others by the throat, or set fire to their houses.

I had a very long talk with one of them; but I had an interpreter who followed my meaning so badly, and who was so hindered by his stupidity in taking in my ideas, that I could get hardly any satisfaction from the man. When I asked him what profit he gained from his superior position among his people (for he was a captain, and our sailors called him king), he told me that it was to march foremost in war. How many men followed him? He pointed to a piece of ground, to signify as many as such a space could hold; it might have been four or five thousand men. Did all his authority expire with the war? He said that this much remained, that when he visited the villages dependent on him, they made paths for him through the underbrush by which he might pass quite comfortably.

All this is not too bad—but what's the use? They don't wear breeches.

## WILLIAM SHAKESPEARE (1564–1616)

No anthology of world literature can do without Shakespeare, although including one of his long plays necessarily means excluding many of his brilliant contemporaries from this anthology. The reigns of Elizabeth I (1558–1603) and James I (1603–1625) were among the greatest periods in English literature. Shakespeare, however, is more than another great European writer; he is also the most influential European writer upon non-European cultures—inspiring Russian, Chinese, and Japanese literature, for example. He continues to inspire writers today.

William Shakespeare was born only thirty years after Montaigne. Like Montaigne, he inherited the full weight of Renaissance humanism, but in certain respects, he is Montaigne's opposite. Shakespeare is notoriously unrevealing about himself. He has, as Keats put it, a "negative capability" that allows him to disappear behind the characters he creates. His characters are unprecedented in European literature for their psychological complexity and realism. The critic Harold Bloom has even argued that our modern notion of human character derives directly from Shakespeare's characters. But which of his characters, if any, represents Shakespeare's own point of view and beliefs? We know little about his personal life, except that he was an ordinary man of the middle class, without a distinguished heritage or education. Some have found it hard to believe he actually authored the works that bear his name.

We might have included any of a dozen plays here, but we have chosen *King Lear. Hamlet* catches the spirit of the European Renaissance better in its exploration of the modern self; *Othello* faces issues of race and gender more directly in making a black African its hero; and *The Tempest* engages New World issues in the genre of Romance. However, tragedy and epic are the most elevated and ambitious genres of the period, and *King Lear* is in some ways the most moving and grandest of Shakespeare's tragedies.

As a genre, tragedy derives from classical models like *The Bacchae* (although the Greek plays were unknown to Shakespeare, whose sense of ancient tragedy came rather from the Roman writer Seneca). Like the Greek tragedies, *King Lear* portrays a world in which the gods drive human beings to insanity and death, with little sense of justice or morality. *King Lear* stretches the genre to the limit, if not beyond: some have found it too awesome even to be staged—especially the third act, in which Lear descends into madness in a howling storm.

The story of King Lear and his three daughters originates in Celtic folklore, though Shakespeare adapted it from contemporary versions. He complicates his sources by adding the Fool (whose function in the play and whose disappearance in Act III are classic problems of literary criticism), Kent (the moral center of the play), and—most importantly—the parallel subplot of Gloucester and his sons, taken from Sir Phillip Sidney's *Arcadia.* Shakespeare interweaves his two plots intricately, leading us inexorably to a scene in which the two ruined, aged fathers share their pain and madness on the white cliffs of Dover. The reconciliation of the final act, in which Cordelia appears like Christian grace, is destroyed in the play's final shattering moments. Cordelia's death is Shakespeare's own addition, and for centuries it was found so terrible that a happy ending—in which Cordelia marries the new king, Edgar—was substituted on the stage.

## The Tragedy of King Lear

*[Dramatis Personae*

LEAR, *King of Britain*
KING OF FRANCE
DUKE OF BURGUNDY
DUKE OF CORNWALL, *husband to Regan*
DUKE OF ALBANY, *husband to Goneril*
EARL OF KENT
EARL OF GLOUCESTER
EDGAR, *son to Gloucester*
EDMUND, *bastard son to Gloucester*
CURAN, *a courtier*
OSWALD, *steward to Goneril*
OLD MAN, *tenant to Gloucester*
DOCTOR
FOOL, *to Lear*
CAPTAIN *employed by Edmund*
GENTLEMAN *attendant on Cordelia*
HERALD
SERVANTS *to Cornwall*
GONERIL, REGAN, CORDELIA } *daughters to Lear*
KNIGHTS *of Lear's train,* GENTLEMEN, OFFICERS, MESSENGERS, SOLDIERS, *and* ATTENDANTS

*Scene:* Britain]

ACT I

SCENE I

*Enter* KENT, GLOUCESTER, *and* EDMUND.

KENT: I thought the King had more affected the Duke of Albany than Cornwall.

GLOU: It did always seem so to us; but now in the division of the kingdom, it appears not which of the Dukes he values most, for [equalities] are so weigh'd, that curiosity in neither can make choice of either's moi'ty.

KENT: Is not this your son, my lord?

GLOU: His breeding, sir, hath been at my charge. I have so often blush'd to acknowledge him, that now I am braz'd to't.

KENT: I cannot conceive you.

GLOU: Sir, this young fellow's mother could; whereupon she grew round-womb'd, and had indeed, sir, a son for her cradle ere she had a husband for her bed. Do you smell a fault?

KENT: I cannot wish the fault undone, the issue of it being so proper.

GLOU: But I have a son, sir, by order of law, some year elder than this, who yet is no dearer in my account. Though this knave came something saucily to the world before he was sent for, yet was his mother fair, there was good sport at his making, and the whoreson must be acknowledg'd. Do you know this noble gentleman, Edmund?

EDM: No, my lord.

GLOU: My Lord of Kent. Remember him hereafter as my honorable friend.

EDM: My services to your lordship.

KENT: I must love you, and sue to know you better.

EDM: Sir, I shall study deserving.

GLOU: He hath been out nine years, and away he shall again. (*[Sound a] sennet.*) The King is coming.

*Enter [one bearing a coronet, then]* KING LEAR, CORNWALL, ALBANY, GONERIL, REGAN, CORDELIA, *and* ATTENDANTS.

LEAR: Attend the lords of France and Burgundy, Gloucester.

GLOU: I shall, my lord. *Exit [with Edmund].*

LEAR: Mean time we shall express our darker purpose.
Give me the map there. Know that we have divided
In three our kingdom; and 'tis our fast intent
To shake all cares and business from our age,
Conferring them on younger strengths, while we
Unburthen'd crawl toward death. Our son of Cornwall,
And you, our no less loving son of Albany,
We have this hour a constant will to publish
Our daughters' several dowers, that future strife
May be prevented now. The princes, France and Burgundy,
Great rivals in our youngest daughter's love,
Long in our court have made their amorous sojourn,
And here are to be answer'd. Tell me, my daughters
(Since now we will divest us both of rule,
Interest of territory, cares of state),
Which of you shall we say doth love us most,
That we our largest bounty may extend
Where nature doth with merit challenge? Goneril,
Our eldest-born, speak first.

GON: Sir, I love you more than [words] can wield the matter,
Dearer than eyesight, space, and liberty,
Beyond what can be valued, rich or rare,
No less than life, with grace, health, beauty, honor;
As much as child e'er lov'd, or father found;
A love that makes breath poor, and speech unable:
Beyond all manner of so much I love you.

COR: *[Aside.]* What shall Cordelia speak? Love, and be silent.

LEAR: Of all these bounds, even from this line to this,
With shadowy forests and with champains rich'd,
With plenteous rivers and wide-skirted meads,

We make thee lady. To thine and Albany's [issue]
Be this perpetual. What says our second daughter,
Our dearest Regan, wife of Cornwall? [Speak.]

REG: I am made of that self metal as my sister,
And prize me at her worth. In my true heart
I find she names my very deed of love;
Only she comes too short, that I profess
Myself an enemy to all other joys
Which the most precious square of sense [possesses],
And find I am alone felicitate
In your dear Highness' love.

COR: *[Aside.]* Then poor Cordelia!
And yet not so, since I am sure my love's
More ponderous than my tongue.

LEAR: To thee and thine hereditary ever
Remain this ample third of our fair kingdom,
No less in space, validity, and pleasure,
Than that conferr'd on Goneril.—Now, our joy,
Although our last and least, to whose young love
The vines of France and milk of Burgundy
Strive to be interess'd, what can you say to draw
A third more opulent than your sisters'? Speak.

COR: Nothing, my lord.

LEAR: Nothing?

COR: Nothing.

LEAR: Nothing will come of nothing, speak again.

COR: Unhappy that I am, I cannot heave
My heart into my mouth. I love your Majesty
According to my bond, no more nor less.

LEAR: How, how, Cordelia? Mend your speech a little,
Lest you may mar your fortunes.

COR: Good my lord,
You have begot me, bred me, lov'd me: I
Return those duties back as are right fit,
Obey you, love you, and most honor you.
Why have my sisters husbands, if they say
They love you all? Happily, when I shall wed,
That lord whose hand must take my plight shall carry
Half my love with him, half my care and duty.
Sure I shall never marry like my sisters,
[To love my father all].

LEAR: But goes thy heart with this?

COR: Ay, my good lord.

LEAR: So young, and so untender?

COR: So young, my lord, and true.

LEAR: Let it be so: thy truth then be thy dow'r!
For by the sacred radiance of the sun,
The [mysteries] of Hecat and the night;
By all the operation of the orbs,
From whom we do exist and cease to be;
Here I disclaim all my paternal care,
Propinquity and property of blood,
And as a stranger to my heart and me

Hold thee from this for ever. The barbarous Scythian,
Or he that makes his generation messes
To gorge his appetite, shall to my bosom
Be as well neighbor'd, pitied, and reliev'd,
As thou my sometime daughter.

KENT: Good my liege—

LEAR: Peace, Kent!
Come not between the dragon and his wrath;
I lov'd her most, and thought to set my rest
On her kind nursery. *[To Cordelia.]* Hence, and avoid my sight!—
So be my grave my peace, as here I give
Her father's heart from her. Call France. Who stirs?
Call Burgundy. Cornwall and Albany,
With my two daughters' dow'rs digest the third;
Let pride, which she calls plainness, marry her.
I do invest you jointly with my power,
Pre-eminence, and all the large effects
That troop with majesty. Ourself, by monthly course,
With reservation of an hundred knights
By you to be sustain'd, shall our abode
Make with you by due turn. Only we shall retain
The name, and all th' addition to a king;
The sway, revenue, execution of the rest,
Beloved sons, be yours, which to confirm,
This coronet part between you.

KENT: Royal Lear,
Whom I have ever honor'd as my king,
Lov'd as my father, as my master follow'd,
As my great patron thought on in my prayers—

LEAR: The bow is bent and drawn, make from the shaft.

KENT: Let it fall rather, though the fork invade
The region of my heart; be Kent unmannerly
When Lear is mad. What wouldest thou do, old man?
Think'st thou that duty shall have dread to speak
When power to flattery bows? To plainness honor's bound,
When majesty falls to folly. Reserve thy state,
And in thy best consideration check
This hideous rashness. Answer my life my judgment,
Thy youngest daughter does not love thee least,
Nor are those empty-hearted whose low sounds
Reverb no hollowness.

LEAR: Kent, on thy life, no more.

KENT: My life I never held but as [a] pawn
To wage against thine enemies, ne'er [fear'd] to lose it,
Thy safety being motive.

LEAR: Out of my sight!

KENT: See better, Lear, and let me still remain
The true blank of thine eye.

LEAR: Now, by Apollo—

KENT: Now, by Apollo, King,
Thou Swear'st thy gods in vain.

LEAR: O vassal! miscreant!
*[Starts to draw his sword.]*

ALB, CORN: Dear sir, forbear.

KENT: Kill thy physician, and [the] fee bestow
Upon the foul disease. Revoke thy gift,
Or whilst I can vent clamor from my throat,
I'll tell thee thou dost evil.

LEAR: Hear me, recreant,
On thine allegiance, hear me!
That thou hast sought to make us break our [vow]—
Which we durst never yet—and with strain'd pride
To come betwixt our sentence and our power,
Which nor our nature nor our place can bear,
Our potency made good, take thy reward.
Five days we do allot thee, for provision
To shield thee from disasters of the world,
And on the sixt to turn thy hated back
Upon our kingdom. If, on the tenth day following,
Thy banish'd trunk be found in our dominions,
The moment is thy death. Away! By Jupiter,
This shall not be revok'd.

KENT: Fare thee well, King; sith thus thou wilt appear,
Freedom lives hence, and banishment is here.
*[To Cordelia.]* The gods to their dear shelter take thee, maid,
That justly think'st and hast most rightly said!
*[To Regan and Goneril.]* And your large speeches may your deeds approve,
That good effects may spring from words of love.
Thus Kent, O princes, bids you all adieu,
He'll shape his old course in a country new. *Exit.*

*Flourish. Enter* GLOUCESTER *with* FRANCE *and* BURGUNDY, ATTENDANTS.

[GLOU]: Here's France and Burgundy, my noble lord.

LEAR: My Lord of Burgundy,
We first address toward you, who with this king
Hath rivall'd for our daughter. What, in the least,
Will you require in present dower with her,
Or cease your quest of love?

BUR: Most royal Majesty,
I crave no more than hath your Highness offer'd,
Nor will you tender less.

LEAR: Right noble Burgundy,
When she was dear to us, we did hold her so,
But now her price is fallen. Sir, there she stands:
If aught within that little seeming substance,
Or all of it, with our displeasure piec'd,
And nothing more, may fitly like your Grace,
She's there, and she is yours.

BUR: I know no answer.

LEAR: Will you, with those infirmities she owes,

Unfriended, new adopted to our hate,
Dow'r'd with our curse, and stranger'd with our oath,
Take her, or leave her?

BUR: Pardon me, royal sir,
Election makes not up in such conditions.

LEAR: Then leave her, sir, for by the pow'r that made me,
I tell you all her wealth. *[To France.]* For you, great King,
I would not from your love make such a stray
To match you where I hate; therefore beseech you
T' avert your liking a more worthier way
Than on a wretch whom Nature is asham'd
Almost t' acknowledge hers.

FRANCE: This is most strange,
That she, whom even but now was your [best] object,
The argument of your praise, balm of your age,
The best, the dearest, should in this trice of time
Commit a thing so monstrous, to dismantle
So many folds of favor. Sure her offense
Must be of such unnatural degree
That monsters it, or your fore-vouch'd affection
Fall into taint; which to believe of her
Must be a faith that reason without miracle
Should never plant in me.

COR: I yet beseech your Majesty—
If for I want that glib and oily art
To speak and purpose not, since what I [well] intend,
I'll do't before I speak—that you make known
It is no vicious blot, murther, or foulness,
No unchaste action, or dishonored step,
That hath depriv'd me of your grace and favor,
But even for want of that for which I am richer—
A still-soliciting eye, and such a tongue
That I am glad I have not, though not to have it
Hath lost me in your liking.

LEAR: Better thou
Hadst not been born than not t' have pleas'd me better.

FRANCE: Is it but this—a tardiness in nature
Which often leaves the history unspoke
That it intends to do? My Lord of Burgundy,
What say you to the lady? Love's not love
When it is mingled with regards that stands
Aloof from th' entire point. Will you have her?
She is herself a dowry.

BUR: Royal King,
Give but that portion which yourself propos'd,
And here I take Cordelia by the hand,
Duchess of Burgundy.

LEAR: Nothing. I have sworn, I am firm.

BUR: I am sorry then you have so lost a father
That you must lose a husband.

COR: Peace be with Burgundy!
Since that [respects of fortune] are his love,
I shall not be his wife.

FRANCE: Fairest Cordelia, that art most rich being poor,
Most choice forsaken, and most lov'd despis'd,
Thee and thy virtues here I seize upon,
Be it lawful I take up what's cast away.
Gods, gods! 'tis strange that from their cold'st neglect
My love should kindle to inflam'd respect.
Thy dow'rless daughter, King, thrown to my chance,
Is queen of us, of ours, and our fair France.
Not all the dukes of wat'rish Burgundy
Can buy this unpriz'd precious maid of me.
Bid them farewell, Cordelia, though unkind,
Thou losest here, a better where to find.

LEAR: Thou hast her, France, let her be thine, for we
Have no such daughter, nor shall ever see
That face of hers again. *[To Cordelia.]* Therefore be gone,
Without our grace, our love, our benison.—
Come, noble Burgundy.

*Flourish. Exeunt [all but France, Goneril, Regan, and Cordelia].*

FRANCE: Bid farewell to your sisters.

COR: The jewels of our father, with wash'd eyes
Cordelia leaves you. I know you what you are,
And like a sister am most loath to call
Your faults as they are named.
Love well our father;
To your professed bosoms I commit him,
But yet, alas, stood I within his grace,
I would prefer him to a better place.
So farewell to you both.

REG: Prescribe not us our duty.

GON: Let your study
Be to content your lord, who hath receiv'd you
At fortune's alms. You have obedience scanted,
And well are worth the want that you have wanted.

COR: Time shall unfold what plighted cunning hides,
Who covers faults, at last with shame derides.
Well may you prosper!

FRANCE: Come, my fair Cordelia.

*Exeunt France and Cordelia.*

GON: Sister, it is not little I have to say of what most nearly appertains to us both. I think our father will hence to-night.

REG: That's most certain, and with you; next month with us.

GON: You see how full of changes his age is; the observation we have made of it hath [not] been little. He always lov'd our sister most, and with what poor judgment he hath now cast her off appears too grossly.

REG: 'Tis the infirmity of his age, yet he hath ever but slenderly known himself.

GON: The best and soundest of his time hath been but rash; then must we look from his age to receive not alone the imperfections of long-ingraff'd condition, but therewithal the unruly waywardness that infirm and choleric years bring with them.

REG: Such unconstant starts are we like to have from him as this of Kent's banishment.

GON: There is further compliment of leave-taking between France and him. Pray you let us [hit] together; if our father carry authority with such disposition as he bears, this last surrender of his will but offend us.

REG: We shall further think of it.

GON: We must do something, and i' th' heat.

*Exeunt.*

SCENE II

*Enter [*EDMUND *the] Bastard [with a letter].*

EDM: Thou, Nature, art my goddess, to thy law
My services are bound. Wherefore should I
Stand in the plague of custom, and permit
The curiosity of nations to deprive me,
For that I am some twelve or fourteen moonshines
Lag of a brother? Why bastard? Wherefore base?
When my dimensions are as well compact,
My mind as generous, and my shape as true,
As honest madam's issue? Why brand they us
With base? with baseness? bastardy? base, base?
Who, in the lusty stealth of nature, take
More composition, and fierce quality,
Than doth within a dull, stale, tired bed
Go to th' creating a whole tribe of fops,
Got 'tween asleep and wake? Well then,
Legitimate Edgar, I must have your land.
Our father's love is to the bastard Edmund
As to th' legitimate. Fine word, "legitimate"!
Well, my legitimate, if this letter speed
And my invention thrive, Edmund the base
Shall [top] th' legitimate. I grow, I prosper:
Now, gods, stand up for bastards!

*Enter* GLOUCESTER.

GLOU: Kent banish'd thus? and France in choler parted?
And the King gone to-night? Prescrib'd his pow'r,
Confin'd to exhibition? All this done
Upon the gad? Edmund, how now? what news?

EDM: So please your lordship, none.

*[Putting up the letter.]*

GLOU: Why so earnestly seek you to put up that letter?

EDM: I know no news, my lord.

GLOU: What paper were you reading?

EDM: Nothing, my lord.

GLOU: No? What needed then that terrible dispatch of it into your pocket? The quality of nothing hath not such need to hide itself. Let's see.

Come, if it be nothing, I shall not need spectacles.

EDM: I beseech you, sir, pardon me. It is a letter from my brother that I have not all o'er-read; and for so much as I have perus'd, I find it not fit for your o'erlooking.

GLOU: Give me the letter, sir.

EDM: I shall offend either to detain or give it: the contents, as in part I understand them, are to blame.

GLOU: Let's see, let's see.

EDM: I hope, for my brother's justification, he wrote this but as an essay or taste of my virtue.

GLOU *(Reads.)* "This policy and reverence of age makes the world bitter to the best of our times; keeps our fortunes from us till our oldness cannot relish them. I begin to find an idle and fond bondage in the oppression of aged tyranny, who sways, not as it hath power, but as it is suffer'd. Come to me, that of this I may speak more. If our father would sleep till I wak'd him, you should enjoy half his revenue for ever, and live the belov'd of your brother. Edgar."

Hum? conspiracy? "Sleep till I wake him, you should enjoy half his revenue." My son Edgar! had he a hand to write this? a heart and brain to breed it in?—When came you to this? Who brought it?

EDM: It was not brought me, my lord; there's the cunning of it. I found it thrown in at the casement of my closet.

GLOU: You know the character to be your brother's?

EDM: If the matter were good, my lord, I durst swear it were his; but in respect of that, I would fain think it were not.

GLOU: It is his.

EDM: It is his hand, my lord; but I hope his heart is not in the contents.

GLOU: Has he never before sounded you in this business?

EDM: Never, my lord. But I have heard him oft maintain it to be fit that, sons at perfect age and fathers declin'd, the father should be as ward to the son, and the son manage his revenue.

GLOU: O villain, villain! his very opinion in the letter. Abhorred villain! unnatural, detested, brutish villain! worse than brutish! Go, sirrah, seek him; I'll apprehend him. Abominable villain! Where is he?

EDM: I do not well know, my lord. If it shall please you to suspend your indignation against my brother till you can derive from him better testimony of his intent, you should run a certain course; where, if you violently proceed against him, mistaking his purpose, it would make a great gap in your own honor and shake in pieces the heart of his obedience. I dare pawn down my life for him that he hath writ this to feel my affection to your honor, and to no other pretense of danger.

GLOU: Think you so?

EDM: If your honor judge it meet, I will place you where you shall hear us confer of this, and by an auricular assurance have your satisfaction, and that without any further delay than this very evening.

GLOU: He cannot be such a monster—

[EDM: Nor is not, sure.

GLOU: To his father, that so tenderly and entirely loves him. Heaven and earth!] Edmund, seek him out; wind me into him, I pray you. Frame the business after your own wisdom. I would unstate myself to be in a due resolution.

EDM: I will seek him, sir, presently; convey the business as I shall find means, and acquaint you withal.

GLOU: These late eclipses in the sun and moon portend no good to us. Though the wisdom of nature can reason it thus and thus, yet nature finds itself scourg'd by the sequent effects. Love cools, friendship falls off, brothers divide: in cities, mutinies; in countries, discord; in palaces, treason; and the bond crack'd 'twixt son and father. This villain of mine comes under the prediction; there's son against father: the King falls from bias of nature; there's father against child. We have seen the best of our time. Machinations, hollowness, treachery, and all ruinous disorders follow us disquietly to our graves. Find out this villain, Edmund, it shall lose thee nothing, do it carefully. And the noble and true-hearted Kent banish'd! his offense, honesty! 'Tis strange. *Exit.*

EDM: This is the excellent foppery of the world, that when we are sick in fortune—often the surfeits of our own behavior—we make guilty of our disasters the sun, the moon, and stars, as if we were villains on necessity, fools by heavenly compulsion, knaves, thieves, and treachers by spherical predominance; drunkards, liars, and adulterers by an enforc'd obedience of planetary influence; and all that we are evil in, by a divine thrusting on. An admirable evasion of whoremaster man, to lay his goatish disposition on the charge of a star! My father compounded with my mother under the Dragon's tail, and my nativity was under Ursa Major, so that it follows, I am rough and lecherous. [Fut,] I should have been that I am, had the maidenl'est star in the firmament twinkled on my basterdizing. [Edgar—]

*Enter* EDGAR.

Pat! he comes like the catastrophe of the old comedy. My cue is villainous melancholy, with a sigh like Tom o' Bedlam.—O, these eclipses do portend these divisions! *fa, sol, la, mi.* *[Humming these notes.]*

EDG: How now, brother Edmund, what serious contemplation are you in?

EDM: I am thinking, brother, of a prediction I read this other day, what should follow these eclipses.

EDG: Do you busy yourself with that?

EDM: I promise you, the effects he writes of succeed unhappily, [as of unnaturalness between the child and the parent, death, dearth, dissolutions of ancient amities, divisions in state, menaces and maledictions against king and nobles, needless diffidences, banishment of friends, dissipation of cohorts, nuptial breaches, and I know not what.

EDG: How long have you been a sectary astronomical?

EDM: Come, come,] when saw you my father last?

EDG: The night gone by.

EDM: Spake you with him?

EDG: Ay, two hours together.

EDM: Parted you in good terms? Found you no displeasure in him by word nor countenance?

EDG: None at all.

EDM: Bethink yourself wherein you may have offended him; and at my entreaty forbear his presence until some little time hath qualified the heat of his displeasure, which at this instant so rageth in him, that with the mischief of your person it would scarcely allay.

EDG: Some villain hath done me wrong.

EDM: That's my fear. I pray you have a continent forbearance till the speed of his rage goes slower; and as I say, retire with me to my lodging, from whence I will fitly bring you to hear my lord speak. Pray ye go, there's my key. If you do stir abroad, go arm'd.

EDG: Arm'd, brother?

EDM: Brother, I advise you to the best; I am no honest man if there be any good meaning toward you. I have told you what I have seen and heard; but faintly, nothing like the image and horror of it. Pray you away.

EDG: Shall I hear from you anon?

EDM: I do serve you in this business.

*Exit [Edgar].*

A credulous father and a brother noble,
Whose nature is so far from doing harms
That he suspects none; on whose foolish honesty
My practices ride easy. I see the business.
Let me, if not by birth, have lands by wit:
All with me's meet that I can fashion fit. *Exit.*

SCENE III

*Enter* GONERIL *and Steward* [OSWALD].

GON: Did my father strike my gentleman for chiding of his Fool?

OSW: Ay, madam.

GON: By day and night he wrongs me, every hour
He flashes into one gross crime or other
That sets us all at odds. I'll not endure it.
His knights grow riotous, and himself upbraids us
On every trifle. When he returns from hunting,
I will not speak with him; say I am sick.
If you come slack of former services,
You shall do well; the fault of it I'll answer.

*[Horns within.]*

OSW: He's coming, madam, I hear him.

GON: Put on what weary negligence you please,
You and your fellows; I'd have it come to question.
If he distaste it, let him to my sister,
Whose mind and mine I know in that are one,
[Not to be overrul'd. Idle old man,
That still would manage those authorities

That he hath given away! Now by my life
Old fools are babes again, and must be us'd
With checks as flatteries, when they are seen abus'd.]
Remember what I have said.

OSW: Well, madam.

GON: And let his knights have colder looks among you;
What grows of it, no matter. Advise your fellows so.
[I would breed from hence occasions, and I shall,
That I may speak.] I'll write straight to my sister
To hold my [very] course. Prepare for dinner.

*Exeunt.*

SCENE IV

*Enter* KENT *[disguised as Caius].*

KENT: If but as [well] I other accents borrow,
That can my speech defuse, my good intent.
May carry through itself to that full issue
For which I raz'd my likeness. Now, banish'd Kent,
If thou canst serve where thou dost stand condemn'd,
So may it come, thy master, whom thou lov'st,
Shall find thee full of labors.

*Horns within. Enter* LEAR, [KNIGHTS,] *and* ATTENDANTS *[from hunting].*

LEAR: Let me not stay a jot for dinner, go get it ready. *[Exit an Attendant.]* How now, what art thou?

KENT: A man, sir.

LEAR: What dost thou profess? What wouldst thou with us?

KENT: I do profess to be no less than I seem, to serve him truly that will put me in trust, to love him that is honest, to converse with him that is wise and says little, to fear judgment, to fight when I cannot choose, and to eat no fish.

LEAR: What art thou?

KENT: A very honest-hearted fellow, and as poor as the King.

LEAR: If thou be'st as poor for a subject as he's for a king, [th'] art poor enough. What wouldst thou?

KENT: Service.

LEAR: Who wouldst thou serve?

KENT: You.

LEAR: Dost thou know me, fellow?

KENT: No, sir, but you have that in your countenance which I would fain call master.

LEAR: What's that?

KENT: Authority.

LEAR: What services canst do?

KENT: I can keep honest counsel, ride, run, mar a curious tale in telling it, and deliver a plain message bluntly. That which ordinary men are fit for, I am qualified in, and the best of me is diligence.

LEAR: How old art thou?

KENT: Not so young, sir, to love a woman for singing, nor so old to dote on her for any thing. I have years on my back forty-eight.

LEAR: Follow me, thou shalt serve me. If I like thee no worse after dinner, I will not part from thee yet. Dinner, ho, dinner! Where's my knave? my Fool? Go you and call my Fool hither. *[Exit an Attendant.]*

*Enter Steward* [OSWALD].

You, you, sirrah, where's my daughter?

OSW: So please you— *Exit.*

LEAR: What says the fellow there? Call the clotpole back. *[Exit a Knight.]* Where's my Fool? Ho! I think the world's asleep.

*[Enter* KNIGHT.*]*

How now? where's that mungrel?

KNIGHT: He says, my lord, your [daughter] is not well.

LEAR: Why came not the slave back to me when I call'd him?

KNIGHT: Sir, he answer'd me in the roundest manner, he would not.

LEAR: He would not?

KNIGHT: My lord, I know not what the matter is, but to my judgment your Highness is not entertain'd with that ceremonious affection as you were wont. There's a great abatement of kindness appears as well in the general dependants as in the Duke himself also, and your daughter.

LEAR: Ha? say'st thou so?

KNIGHT: I beseech you pardon me, my lord, if I be mistaken, for my duty cannot be silent when I think your Highness wrong'd.

LEAR: Thou but remeb'rest me of mine own conception. I have perceiv'd a most faint neglect of late, which I have rather blam'd as mine own jealous curiosity than as a very pretense and purpose of unkindness. I will look further into't. But where's my Fool? I have not seen him this two days.

KNIGHT: Since my young lady's going into France, sir, the Fool hath much pin'd away.

LEAR: No more of that, I have noted it well. Go you and tell my daughter I would speak with her. *[Exit an Attendant.]* Go you call hither my Fool.

*[Exit another Attendant.]*

*Enter Steward* [OSWALD].

O, you, sir, you, come you hither, sir. Who am I, sir?

OSW: My lady's father.

LEAR: "My lady's father"? My lord's knave! You whoreson dog, you slave, you cur!

OSW: I am none of these, my lord, I beseech your pardon.

LEAR: Do you bandy looks with me, you rascal?

*[Striking him.]*

OSW: I'll not be strucken, my lord.

KENT: Nor tripp'd neither, you base football player.

*[Tripping up his heels.]*

LEAR: I thank thee, fellow. Thou serv'st me, and I'll love thee.

KENT: Come, sir, arise, away! I'll teach you differences. Away, away! If you will measure your lubber's length again, tarry; but away! Go to, have you wisdom? So. *[Pushes Oswald out.]*

LEAR: Now, my friendly knave, I thank thee, there's earnest of thy service.

*[Giving Kent money.]*

*Enter* FOOL.

FOOL: Let me hire him too, here's my coxcomb . . .

*[Offering Kent his cap.]*

Lear: How now, my pretty knave, how dost thou?

Fool: Sirrah, you were best take my coxcomb.

[Kent]: Why, [Fool]?

Fool: Why? for taking one's part that's out of favor. Nay, and thou canst not smile as the wind sits, thou'lt catch cold shortly. There, take my coxcomb. Why, this fellow has banish'd two on 's daughters, and did the third a blessing against his will; if thou follow him, thou must needs wear my coxcomb.—How now, nuncle? Would I had two coxcombs and two daughters!

Lear: Why, my boy?

Fool: If I gave them all my living, I'ld keep my coxcombs myself. There's mine, beg another of thy daughters.

Lear: Take heed, sirrah—the whip.

Fool: Truth's a dog must to kennel, he must be whipt out, when the Lady Brach may stand by th' fire and stink.

Lear: A pestilent gall to me!

Fool: Sirrah, I'll teach thee a speech.

Lear: Do.

Fool: Mark it, nuncle:
Have more than thou showest,
Speak less than thou knowest,
Lend less than thou owest,
Ride more than thou goest,
Learn more than thou trowest,
Set less than thou throwest;
Leave thy drink and thy whore,
And keep in a' door,
And thou shalt have more
Than two tens to a score.

Kent: This is nothing, Fool.

Fool: Then 'tis like the breath of an unfee'd lawyer, you gave me nothing for't. Can you make no use of nothing, nuncle?

Lear: Why, no, boy, nothing can be made out of nothing.

Fool: *[To Kent.]* Prithee tell him, so much the rent of his land comes to. He will not believe a fool.

Lear: A bitter fool!

Fool: Dost thou know the difference, my boy, between a bitter fool and a sweet one?

Lear: No, lad, teach me.

Fool: [That lord that counsell'd thee
To give away thy land,
Come place him here by me,
Do thou for him stand.
The sweet and bitter fool
Will presently appear:
The one in motley here,
The other found out there.

Lear: Dost thou call me fool, boy?

Fool: All thy other titles thou hast given away, that thou wast born with.

Kent: This is not altogether fool, my lord.

Fool: No, faith, lords and great men will not let me; if I had a monopoly out, they would have part an't. And ladies too, they will not let me have all the fool to myself, they'll be snatching.] Nuncle, give me an egg, and I'll give thee two crowns.

Lear: What two crowns shall they be?

Fool: Why, after I have cut the egg i' th' middle and eat up the meat, the two crowns of the egg. When thou clovest thy [crown] i' th' middle and gav'st away both parts, thou bor'st thine ass on thy back o'er the dirt. Thou hadst little wit in thy bald crown when thou gav'st thy golden one away. If I speak like myself in this, let him be whipt that first finds it so.

*[Sings.]* "Fools had ne'er less grace in a year,
For wise men are grown foppish,
And know not now their wits to wear,
Their manners are so apish."

LEAR: When were you wont to be so full of songs, sirrah?

FOOL: I have us'd it, nuncle, e'er since thou mad'st thy daughters thy mothers, for when thou gav'st them the rod, and put'st down thine own breeches,
*[Sings.]* "Then they for sudden joy did weep,
And I for sorrow sung,
That such a king should play bo-peep,
And go the [fools] among."
Prithee, nuncle, keep a schoolmaster that can teach thy Fool to lie—I would fain learn to lie.

LEAR: And you lie, sirrah, we'll have you whipt.

FOOL: I marvel what kin thou and thy daughters are. They'll have me whipt for speaking true; thou'lt have me whipt for lying; and sometimes I am whipt for holding my peace. I had rather be any kind o' thing than a Fool, and yet I would not be thee, nuncle: thou hast par'd thy wit o' both sides, and left nothing i' th' middle. Here comes one o' the parings.

*Enter* GONERIL.

LEAR: How now, daughter? what makes that frontlet on? You are too much of late i' th' frown.

FOOL: Thou wast a pretty fellow when thou hadst no need to care for her frowning, now thou art an O without a figure. I am better than thou art now, I am a Fool, thou art nothing. *[To Goneril.]* Yes, forsooth, I will hold my tongue; so your face bids me, though you say nothing.
Mum, mum:
He that keeps nor crust [nor] crumb,
Weary of all, shall want some.

*[Pointing to Lear.]* That's a sheal'd peascod.

GON: Not only, sir, this your all-licens'd Fool,
But other of your insolent retinue
Do hourly carp and quarrel, breaking forth
In rank and not-to-be-endur'd riots. Sir,
I had thought, by making this well known unto you,
To have found a safe redress, but now grow fearful,
By what yourself too late have spoke and done,
That you protect this course and put it on
By your allowance; which if you should, the fault
Would not scape censure, nor the redresses sleep,
Which, in the tender of a wholesome weal,
Might in their working do you that offense,
Which else were shame, that then necessity
Will call discreet proceeding.

FOOL: For you know, nuncle,
"The hedge-sparrow fed the cuckoo so long,
That [it] had it head bit off by it young."
So out went the candle, and we were left darkling.

LEAR: Are you our daughter?

GON: I would you would make use of your good wisdom
(Whereof I know you are fraught) and put away
These dispositions which of late transport you
From what you rightly are.

FOOL: May not an ass know when the cart draws the horse?
*[Sings.]* "Whoop, Jug! I love thee."

LEAR: Does any here know me? This is not Lear.
Does Lear walk thus? speak thus? Where are his eyes?
Either his notion weakens, his discernings
Are lethargied—Ha! waking? 'Tis not so.
Who is it that can tell me who I am?

FOOL: Lear's shadow.

[LEAR: I would learn that, for by the marks of sovereignty,
Knowledge, and reason, I should be false persuaded
I had daughters.

FOOL: Which they will make an obedient father.]

LEAR: Your name, fair gentlewoman?

GON: This admiration, sir, is much o' th' savor
Of other your new pranks. I do beseech you
To understand my purposes aright,
As you are old and reverend, should be wise.
Here do you keep a hundred knights and squires,
Men so disorder'd, so debosh'd and bold,
That this our court, infected with their manners,
Shows like a riotous inn.
Epicurism and lust
Makes it more like a tavern or a brothel
Than a grac'd palace. The shame itself doth speak
For instant remedy. Be then desir'd
By her, that else will take the thing she begs,
A little to disquantity your train,
And the remainders that shall still depend,
To be such men as may besort your age,
Which know themselves and you.

LEAR: Darkness and devils!
Saddle my horses; call my train together!
Degenerate bastard, I'll not trouble thee;
Yet have I left a daughter.

GON: You strike my people,
And your disorder'd rabble make servants of their betters.

*Enter* ALBANY.

LEAR: Woe, that too late repents!—[O, sir, are you come?]
Is it your will? Speak, sir.—Prepare my horses.—
Ingratitude! thou marble-hearted fiend,
More hideous when thou show'st thee in a child
Than the sea-monster.

ALB: Pray, sir, be patient.

LEAR: *[To Goneril.]* Detested kite, thou liest.
My train are men of choice and rarest parts,
That all particulars of duty know,
And in the most exact regard support

The worships of their name. O most small fault,
How ugly didst thou in Cordelia show!
Which, like an engine, wrench'd my frame of nature
From the fix'd place; drew from my heart all love,
And added to the gall. O Lear, Lear, Lear!
Beat at this gate, that let thy folly in *[Striking his head.]*
And thy dear judgment out! Go, go, my people.

*[Exeunt Knights and Kent.]*

ALB: My lord, I am guiltless as I am ignorant
Of what hath moved you.

LEAR: It may be so, my lord.
Hear, Nature, hear, dear goddess, hear!
Suspend thy purpose, if thou didst intend
To make this creature fruitful.
Into her womb convey sterility,
Dry up in her the organs of increase,
And from her derogate body never spring
A babe to honor her! If she must teem,
Create her child of spleen, that it may live
And be a thwart disnatur'd torment to her.
Let it stamp wrinkles in her brow of youth,
With cadent tears fret channels in her cheeks,
Turn all her mother's pains and benefits
To laughter and contempt, that she may feel
How sharper than a serpent's tooth it is
To have a thankless child!—Away, away! *Exit.*

ALB: Now, gods that we adore, whereof comes this?

GON: Never afflict yourself to know more of it,
But let his disposition have that scope
As dotage gives it.

*Enter* LEAR.

LEAR: What, fifty of my followers at a clap?
Within a fortnight?

ALB: What's the matter, sir?

LEAR: I'll tell thee. *[To Goneril.]* Life and death! I am asham'd
That thou hast power to shake my manhood thus,
That these hot tears, which break from me perforce,
Should make thee worth them. Blasts and fogs upon thee!
Th' untented woundings of a father's curse
Pierce every sense about thee! Old fond eyes,
Beweep this cause again, I'll pluck ye out,
And cast you, with the waters that you loose,
To temper clay. [Yea, is't come to this?]
Ha? let it be so: I have another daughter,
Who I am sure is kind and comfortable.
When she shall hear this of thee, with her nails
She'll flea thy wolvish visage. Thou shalt find
That I'll resume the shape which thou dost think
I have cast off for ever. *Exit.*

GON: Do you mark that?

ALB: I cannot be so partial, Goneril,
To the great love I bear you—

GON: Pray you, content.—What, Oswald, ho!
*[To the Fool.]* You, sir, more knave than fool, after your master.

FOOL: Nuncle Lear, nuncle Lear, tarry, take the Fool with thee.
A fox, when one has caught her,
And such a daughter,
Should sure to the slaughter,
If my cap would buy a halter,
So the Fool follows after. *Exit.*

GON: This man hath had good counsel—a hundred knights!
'Tis politic and safe to let him keep
At point a hundred knights; yes, that on every dream,
Each buzz, each fancy, each complaint, dislike,
He may enguard his dotage with their pow'rs,
And hold our lives in mercy.—Oswald, I say!

ALB: Well, you may fear too far.

GON: Safer than trust too far.
Let me still take away the harms I fear,
Not fear still to be taken. I know his heart.
What he hath utter'd I have writ my sister;
If she sustain him and his hundred knights,
When I have show'd th' unfitness—

*Enter Steward* [OSWALD].

How now, Oswald?
What, have you writ that letter to my sister?

OSW: Ay, madam.

GON: Take you some company, and away to horse.
Inform her full of my particular fear,
And thereto add such reasons of your own
As may compact it more. Get you gone,
And hasten your return. *[Exit Oswald.]* No, no, my lord,
This milky gentleness and course of yours
Though I condemn not, yet, under pardon,
[You] are much more [attax'd] for want of wisdom
Than prais'd for harmful mildness.

ALB: How far your eyes may pierce I cannot tell:
Striving to better, oft we mar what's well.

GON: Nay then—

ALB: Well, well, th' event. *Exeunt.*

SCENE V

*Enter* LEAR, KENT *[disguised as Caius], and* FOOL.

LEAR: Go you before to Gloucester with these letters. Acquaint my daughter no further with any thing you know than comes from her demand out of the letter. If your diligence be not speedy, I shall be there afore you.

KENT: I will not sleep, my lord, till I have deliver'd your letter. *Exit.*

FOOL: If a man's brains were in 's heels, were't not in danger of kibes?

LEAR: Ay, boy.

FOOL: Then I prithee be merry, thy wit shall not go slip-shod.

LEAR: Ha, ha, ha!

FOOL: Shalt see thy other daughter will use thee kindly, for though she's as like this as a crab's like an apple, yet I can tell what I can tell.

LEAR: What canst tell, boy?

FOOL: She will taste as like this as a crab does to a crab. Thou canst tell why one's nose stands i' th' middle on 's face?

LEAR: No.

FOOL: Why, to keep one's eyes of either side 's nose, that what a man cannot smell out, he may spy into.

LEAR: I did her wrong.

FOOL: Canst tell how an oyster makes his shell?

LEAR: No.

FOOL: Nor I neither; but I can tell why a snail has a house.

LEAR: Why?

FOOL: Why, to put 's head in, not to give it away to his daughters, and leave his horns without a case.

LEAR: I will forget my nature. So kind a father! Be my horses ready?

FOOL: Thy asses are gone about 'em. The reason why the seven stars are no moe than seven is a pretty reason.

LEAR: Because they are not eight.

Fool: Yes indeed, thou wouldst make a good Fool.

LEAR: To take't again perforce! Monster ingratitude!

FOOL: If thou wert my Fool, nuncle, I'ld have thee beaten for being old before thy time.

LEAR: How's that?

FOOL: Thou shouldst not have been old till thou hadst been wise.

LEAR: O, let me not be mad, not mad, sweet heaven! Keep me in temper, I would not be mad!

*[Enter* GENTLEMAN.*]*

How now, are the horses ready?

GENT: Ready, my lord.

LEAR: Come, boy. *[Exeunt Lear and Gentleman.]*

FOOL: She that's a maid now, and
laughs at my departure,
Shall not be a maid long, unless
things be cut shorter.
*Exit.*

## ACT II

### SCENE I

*Enter Bastard* [EDMUND] *and* CURAN *severally.*

EDM: 'Save thee, Curan.

CUR: And [you,] sir. I have been with your father, and given him notice that the Duke of Cornwall and Regan his duchess will be here with him this night.

EDM: How comes that?

Cur: Nay, I know not. You have heard of the news abroad, I mean the whisper'd ones, for they are yet but ear-[bussing] arguments?

EDM: Not I. Pray you, what are they?

CUR: Have you heard of no likely wars toward, 'twixt the Dukes of Cornwall and Albany?

EDM: Not a word.

CUR: You may do then in time. Fare you well, sir.

*Exit.*

EDM: The Duke be here to-night? The better! best!
This weaves itself perforce into my business.
My father hath set guard to take my brother,
And I have one thing, of a queasy question,
Which I must act. Briefness and fortune, work!
Brother, a word! Descend. Brother, I say!

*Enter* EDGAR.

My father watches: O sir, fly this place,
Intelligence is given where you are hid;
You have now the good advantage of the night.
Have you not spoken 'gainst the Duke of Cornwall?
He's coming hither, now i' th' night, i' th' haste,
And Regan with him. Have you nothing said
Upon his party 'gainst the Duke of Albany?
Advise yourself.

EDG: I am sure on't, not a word.

EDM: I hear my father coming. Pardon me:
In cunning I must draw my sword upon you.
Draw, seem to defend yourself; now quit you well.—
Yield! Come before my father. Light ho, here!—
Fly, brother.—Torches, torches!—So farewell.

*Exit Edgar.*

Some blood drawn on me would beget opinion

*[Wounds his arm.]*

Of my more fierce endeavor. I have seen drunkards
Do more than this in sport.—Father, father!
Stop, stop! No help?

*Enter* GLOUCESTER, *and* SERVANTS *with torches.*

GLOU: Now, Edmund, where's the villain?

EDM: Here stood he in the dark, his sharp sword out,
Mumbling of wicked charms, conjuring the moon
To stand ['s] auspicious mistress.

GLOU: But where is he?

EDM: Look, sir, I bleed.

GLOU: Where is the villain, Edmund?

EDM: Fled this way, sir, when by no means he could—

GLOU: Pursue him, ho! Go after. *[Exeunt some Servants.]* By no means what?

EDM: Persuade me to the murther of your lordship,
But that I told him, the [revengive] gods
'Gainst parricides did all the thunder bend,
Spoke, with how manifold and strong a bond
The child was bound to th' father; sir, in fine,
Seeing how loathly opposite I stood
To his unnatural purpose, in fell motion
With his prepared sword he charges home
My unprovided body, latch'd mine arm;

And when he saw my best alarum'd spirits,
Bold in the quarrel's right, rous'd to th' encountcr,
Or whether gasted by the noise I made,
Full suddenly he fled.

GLOU: Let him fly far.
Not in this land shall he remain uncaught;
And found—dispatch. The noble Duke my master,
My worthy arch and patron, comes to-night.
By his authority I will proclaim it,
That he which finds him shall deserve our thanks,
Bringing the murderous coward to the stake;
He that conceals him, death.

EDM: When I dissuaded him from his intent,
And found him pight to do it, with curst speech
I threaten'd to discover him; he replied,
"Thou unpossessing bastard, dost thou think,
If I would stand against thee, would the reposal
Of any trust, virtue, or worth in thee
Make thy words faith'd? No. What [I should] deny
(As this I would, [ay,] though thou didst produce
My very character), I'ld turn it all
To thy suggestion, plot, and damned practice;
And thou must make a dullard of the world
If they not thought the profits of my death
Were very pregnant and potential spirits
To make thee seek it."

GLOU: O strange and fast'ned villain!
Would he deny his letter, said he? [I never got him.]

*Tucket within.*

Hark, the Duke's trumpets! I know not [why] he comes.
All ports I'll bar, the villain shall not scape;
The Duke must grant me that. Besides, his picture
I will send far and near, that all the kingdom
May have due note of him, and of my land,
Loyal and natural boy, I'll work the means
To make thee capable.

*Enter* CORNWALL, REGAN, *and* ATTENDANTS.

CORN: How now, my noble friend? since I came hither
(Which I can call but now) I have heard [strange news].

REG: If it be true, all vengeance comes too short
Which can pursue th' offender. How dost, my lord?

GLOU: O madam, my old heart is crack'd, it's crack'd!

REG: What, did my father's godson seek your life?
He whom my father nam'd, your Edgar?

GLOU: O lady, lady, shame would have it hid!

REG: Was he not companion with the riotous knights
That tended upon my father?

GLOU: I know not, madam. 'Tis too bad, too bad.

EDM: Yes, madam, he was of that consort.

REG: No marvel then, though he were ill affected:
'Tis they have put him on the old man's death,
To have th' expense and waste of his revenues.
I have this present evening from my sister
Been well inform'd of them, and with such cautions,
That if they come to sojourn at my house,
I'll not be there.

CORN: Nor I, assure thee, Regan.
Edmund, I hear that you have shown your father
A child-like office.

EDM: It was my duty, sir.

GLOU: He did bewray his practice, and receiv'd
This hurt you see, striving to apprehend him.

CORN: Is he pursued?

GLOU: Ay, my good lord.

CORN: If he be taken, he shall never more
Be fear'd of doing harm. Make your own purpose,
How in my strength you please. For you, Edmund,
Whose virtue and obedience doth this instant
So much commend itself, you shall be ours.
Natures of such deep trust we shall much need;
You we first seize on.

EDM: I shall serve you, sir,
Truly, however else.

GLOU: For him I thank your Grace.

CORN: You know not why we came to visit you?

REG: Thus out of season, threading dark-ey'd night:
Occasions, noble Gloucester, of some prize,
Wherein we must have use of your advice.
Our father he hath writ, so hath our sister,
Of differences, which I best [thought] it fit
To answer from our home; the several messengers
From hence attend dispatch. Our good old friend,
Lay comforts to your bosom, and bestow
Your needful counsel to our businesses,
Which craves the instant use.

GLOU: I serve you, madam.
Your Graces are right welcome.

*Flourish. Exeunt.*

SCENE II

*Enter* KENT *[disguised as Caius] and Steward* [OSWALD] *severally.*

OSW: Good dawning to thee, friend. Art of this house?

KENT: Ay.

OSW: Where may we set our horses?

KENT: I' th' mire.

OSW: Prithee, if thou lov'st me, tell me.

KENT: I love thee not.

OSW: Why then I care not for thee.

KENT: If I had thee in Lipsbury pinfold, I would make thee care for me.

OSW: Why dost thou use me thus? I know thee not.

KENT: Fellow, I know thee.

OSW: What dost thou know me for?

KENT: A knave, a rascal, an eater of broken meats; a base, proud, shallow, beggarly, three-suited, hundred-pound, filthy worsted-stocking knave; a lily-liver'd action-taking, whoreson, glass-gazing, superserviceable, finical rogue; one-trunk-inheriting slave; one that wouldst be a bawd in way of good service, and art nothing but the composition of a knave, beggar, coward, pandar, and the son and heir of a mungril bitch; one whom I will beat into [clamorous] whining, if thou deni'st the least syllable of thy addition.

OSW: Why, what a monstrous fellow art thou, thus to rail on one that is neither known of thee nor knows thee?

KENT: What a brazen-fac'd varlet art thou, to deny thou knowest me? Is it two days since I tripp'd up thy heels, and beat thee before the King? Draw, you rogue, for though it be night, yet the moon shines; *[drawing his sword]* I'll make a sop o' th' moonshine of you, you whoreson cullionly barber-monger, draw!

OSW: Away, I have nothing to do with thee.

KENT: Draw, you rascal! You come with letters against the King, and take Vanity the puppet's part against the royalty of her father. Draw, you rogue, or I'll so carbonado your shanks! Draw, you rascal! Come your ways.

OSW: Help ho! murther, help!

KENT: Strike, you slave! Stand, rogue, stand, you neat slave! Strike!

*[Beating him.]*

OSW: Help ho! murther, murther!

*Enter Bastard [*EDMUND*, with his rapier drawn].*

EDM: How now, what's the matter? Part!

KENT: With you, goodman boy, [and] you please! Come, I'll flesh ye, come on, young master.

*[Enter]* CORNWALL, REGAN, GLOUCESTER, SERVANTS.

GLOU: Weapons? arms? What's the matter here?

CORN: Keep peace, upon your lives!
He dies that strikes again. What is the matter?

REG: The messengers from our sister and the King.

CORN: What is your difference? speak.

OSW: I am scarce in breath, my lord.

KENT: No marvel, you have so bestirr'd your valor. You cowardly rascal, Nature disclaims in thee: a tailor made thee.

CORN: Thou art a strange fellow. A tailor make a man?

KENT: A tailor, sir; a stone-cutter or a painter could not have made him so ill, though they had been but two years o' th' trade.

CORN: Speak yet, how grew your quarrel?

OSW: This ancient ruffian, sir, whose life I have spar'd at suit of his grey beard—

KENT: Thou whoreson zed, thou unnecessary letter! My lord, if you['ll] give me leave, I will tread this unbolted villain into mortar, and daub the wall of a jakes with him. Spare my grey beard, you wagtail?

CORN: Peace, sirrah!
You beastly knave, know you no reverence?

KENT: Yes, sir, but anger hath a privilege.

CORN: Why art thou angry?

KENT: That such a slave as this should wear a sword,
Who wears no honesty. Such smiling rogues as these,
Like rats, oft bite the holy cords a-twain
Which are t' intrinse t' unloose; smooth every passion
That in the natures of their lords rebel,
Being oil to fire, snow to the colder moods;
[Renege,] affirm, and turn their halcyon beaks
With every gale and vary of their masters,
Knowing nought (like dogs) but following.
A plague upon your epileptic visage!
Smile you my speeches, as I were a fool?
Goose, [and] I had you upon Sarum plain,
I'ld drive ye cackling home to Camelot.

CORN: What, art thou mad, old fellow?

GLOU: How fell you out? say that.

KENT: No contraries hold more antipathy
Than I and such a knave.

CORN: Why dost thou call him knave? What is his fault?

KENT: His countenance likes me not.

CORN: No more, perchance, does mine, nor his, nor hers.

KENT: Sir, 'tis my occupation to be plain:
I have seen better faces in my time
Than stands on any shoulder that I see
Before me at this instant.

CORN: This is some fellow
Who, having been prais'd for bluntness, doth affect
A saucy roughness, and constrains the garb
Quite from his nature. He cannot flatter, he,
An honest mind and plain, he must speak truth!
And they will take['t], so; if not, he's plain.
These kind of knaves I know, which in this plainness
Harbor more craft and more corrupter ends
Than twenty silly-ducking observants
That stretch their duties nicely.

KENT: Sir, in good faith, in sincere verity,
Under th' allowance of your great aspect,
Whose influence, like the wreath of radiant fire
On [flick'ring] Phoebus' front—

CORN: What mean'st by this?

KENT: To go out of my dialect, which you discommend so much. I know, sir, I am no flatterer. He that beguil'd you in a plain accent was a plain knave, which for my part I will not be, though I should win your displeasure to entreat me to't.

CORN: What was th' offense you gave him?

OSW: I never gave him any.
It pleas'd the King his master very late
To strike at me upon his misconstruction,
When he, compact, and flattering his displeasure,
Tripp'd me behind; being down, insulted, rail'd,

And put upon him such a deal of man
That worthied him, got praises of the King
For him attempting who was self-subdued,
And in the fleshment of this [dread] exploit,
Drew on me here again.

KENT: None of these rogues and cowards
But Ajax is their fool.

CORN: Fetch forth the stocks!
You stubborn ancient knave, you reverent braggart,
We'll teach you.

KENT: Sir, I am too old to learn.
Call not your stocks for me, I serve the King,
On whose employment I was sent to you.
You shall do small respects, show too bold malice
Against the grace and person of my master,
Stocking his messenger.

CORN: Fetch forth the stocks! As I have life and honor,
There shall he sit till noon.

REG: Till noon? Till night, my lord, and all night too.

KENT: Why, Madam, if I were your father's dog,
You should not use me so.

REG: Sir, being his knave, I will.

CORN: This is a fellow of the self-same color
Our sister speaks of. Come, bring away the stocks!

*Stocks brought out.*

GLOU: Let me beseech your Grace not to do so.
[His fault is much, and the good King his master
Will check him for't. Your purpos'd low correction
Is such as basest and [contemned'st] wretches
For pilf'rings and most common trespasses
Are punish'd with.] The King must take it ill
That he, so slightly valued in his messenger,
Should have him thus restrained.

CORN: I'll answer that.

REG: My sister may receive it much more worse
To have her gentleman abus'd, assaulted,
[For following her affairs. Put in his legs.]

*[Kent is put in the stocks.]*

Come, my [good] lord, away.

*Exit [with all but Gloucester and Kent].*

GLOU: I am sorry for thee, friend, 'tis the Duke['s] pleasure,
Whose disposition, all the world well knows,
Will not be rubb'd nor stopp'd. I'll entreat for thee.

KENT: Pray do not, sir. I have watch'd and travell'd hard:
Some time I shall sleep out, the rest I'll whistle.
A good man's fortune may grow out at heels.
Give you good morrow!

GLOU: The Duke's to blame in this, 'twill be ill taken. *Exit.*

KENT: Good King, that must approve the common saw,
Thou out of heaven's benediction com'st
To the warm sun!
Approach, thou beacon to this under globe,

That by thy comfortable beams I may
Peruse this letter. Nothing almost sees miracles
But misery. I know 'tis from Cordelia,
Who hath most fortunately been inform'd
Of my obscured course; *[reads]* "—and shall find time
From this enormous state—seeking to give
Losses their remedies."—All weary and o'erwatch'd,
Take vantage, heavy eyes, not to behold
This shameful lodging.
Fortune, good night; smile once more, turn thy wheel.

*[Sleeps.]*

[SCENE III]

*Enter* EDGAR.

EDG: I heard myself proclaim'd,
And by the happy hollow of a tree
Escap'd the hunt. No port is free, no place
That guard and most unusual vigilance
Does not attend my taking. Whiles I may scape
I will preserve myself, and am bethought
To take the basest and most poorest shape
That ever penury, in contempt of man,
Brought near to beast. My face I'll grime with filth,
Blanket my loins, elf all my hairs in knots,
And with presented nakedness outface
The winds and persecutions of the sky.
The country gives me proof and president
Of Bedlam beggars, who, with roaring voices,
Strike in their numb'd and mortified arms
Pins, wooden pricks, nails, sprigs of rosemary;
And with this horrible object, from low farms,
Poor pelting villages, sheep-cotes, and mills,
Sometimes with lunatic bans, sometime with prayers,
Enforce their charity. Poor Turlygod! poor Tom!
That's something yet: Edgar I nothing am. *Exit.*

[SCENE IV]

*Enter* LEAR, FOOL, *and* GENTLEMAN. *[*KENT, *disguised as Caius, in the stocks.]*

LEAR: 'Tis strange that they should so depart from home,
And not send back my [messenger].

GENT: As I learn'd,
The night before there was no purpose in them
Of this remove.

KENT: Hail to thee, noble master!

LEAR: Ha?

Mak'st thou this shame thy pastime?

Kent: No, my lord.

Fool: Hah, ha, he wears cruel garters. Horses are tied by the heads, dogs and bears by th' neck, monkeys by th' loins, and men by th' legs. When a man['s] overlusty at legs, then he wears wooden nether-stocks.

Lear: What's he that hath so much thy place mistook
To set thee here?

Kent: It is both he and she,
Your son and daughter.

Lear: No.

Kent: Yes.

Lear: No, I say.

Kent: I say yea.

[Lear. No, no, they would not.

Kent: Yes, they have.]

Lear: By Jupiter, I swear no.

Kent: By Juno, I swear ay.

Lear: They durst not do't;
They could not, would not do't. 'Tis worse than murther
To do upon respect such violent outrage.
Resolve me with all modest haste which way
Thou mightst deserve, or they impose, this usage,
Coming from us.

Kent: My lord, when at their home
I did commend your Highness' letters to them,
Ere I was risen from the place that showed
My duty kneeling, came there a reeking post,
Stew'd in his haste, half breathless, [panting] forth
From Goneril his mistress salutations;
Deliver'd letters, spite of intermission,
Which presently they read; on those contents
They summon'd up their meiny, straight took horse,
Commanded me to follow, and attend
The leisure of their answer, gave me cold looks:
And meeting here the other messenger,
Whose welcome I perceiv'd had poison'd mine—
Being the very fellow which of late
Display'd so saucily against your Highness—
Having more man than wit about me, drew.
He rais'd the house with loud and coward cries.
Your son and daughter found this trespass worth
The shame which here it suffers.

Fool: Winter's not gone yet, if the wild geese fly that way.
Fathers that wear rags
Do make their children blind,
But fathers that bear bags
Shall see their children kind.
Fortune, that arrant whore,
Ne'er turns the key to th' poor.
But for all this, thou shalt have as many dolors for thy daughters as thou canst tell in a year.

Lear: O how this mother swells up toward my heart!
*[Hysterica] passio,* down, thou climbing sorrow,
Thy element's below.—Where is this daughter?

Kent: With the Earl, sir, here within.

Lear: Follow me not,
Stay here. *Exit.*

GENT: Made you no more offense but what you speak of?

KENT: None.
How chance the King comes with so small a number?

FOOL: And thou hadst been set i' th' stocks for that question, thou'dst well deserv'd it.

KENT: Why, Fool?

FOOL: We'll set thee to school to an ant, to teach thee there's no laboring i' th' winter. All that follow their noses are led by their eyes but blind men, and there's not a nose among twenty but can smell him that's stinking. Let go thy hold when a great wheel runs down a hill, lest it break thy neck with following; but the great one that goes upward, let him draw thee after. When a wise man gives thee better counsel, give me mine again, I would have none but knaves follow it, since a fool gives it.
That sir which serves and seeks for gain,
And follows but for form,
Will pack when it begins to rain,
And leave thee in the storm.
But I will tarry, the Fool will stay,
And let the wise man fly.
The knave turns fool that runs away,
The Fool no knave, perdie.

KENT: Where learn'd you this, Fool?

FOOL: Not i' th' stocks, fool.

*Enter* LEAR *and* GLOUCESTER.

LEAR: Deny to speak with me? They are sick? they are weary?
They have travell'd all the night? Mere fetches,
The images of revolt and flying off.
Fetch me a better answer.

GLOU: My dear lord,
You know the fiery quality of the Duke,
How unremovable and fix'd he is
In his own course.

LEAR: Vengeance! plague! death! confusion!
Fiery? What quality? Why, Gloucester, Gloucester,
I'ld speak with the Duke of Cornwall and his wife.

GLOU: Well, my good lord, I have inform'd them so.

LEAR: Inform'd them? Dost thou understand me, man?

GLOU: Ay, my good lord.

LEAR: The King would speak with Cornwall, the dear father
Would with his daughter speak, commands, tends service.
Are they inform'd of this? My breath and blood!
Fiery? the fiery Duke? Tell the hot Duke that—
No, but not yet, may be he is not well:
Infirmity doth still neglect all office
Whereto our health is bound; we are not ourselves
When nature, being oppress'd, commands the mind
To suffer with the body. I'll forbear,
And am fallen out with my more headier will,
To take the indispos'd and sickly fit
For the sound man. *[Looking on Kent.]* Death on my state! wherefore
Should he sit here? This act persuades me
That this remotion of the Duke and her

Is practice only. Give me my servant forth.
Go tell the Duke, and 's wife, I'ld speak with them—
Now, presently. Bid them come forth and hear me,
Or at their chamber-door I'll beat the drum
Till it cry sleep to death.

GLOU: I would have all well betwixt you. *Exit.*

LEAR: O me, my heart! my rising heart! But down!

FOOL: Cry to it, nuncle, as the cockney did to the eels when she put 'em i' th' paste alive; she knapp'd 'em o' th' coxcombs with a stick, and cried, "Down, wantons, down!" 'Twas her brother that, in pure kindness to his horse, butter'd his hay.

*Enter* CORNWALL, REGAN, GLOUCESTER, SERVANTS.

LEAR: Good morrow to you both.

CORN: Hail to your Grace!

*Kent here set at liberty.*

REG: I am glad to see your Highness.

LEAR: Regan, I think [you] are; I know what reason
I have to think so. If thou shouldst not be glad,
I would divorce me from thy [mother's] tomb,
Sepulchring an adult'ress. *[To Kent.]* O, are you free?
Some other time for that. *[Exit Kent.]* Beloved Regan,
Thy sister's naught. O Regan, she hath tied
Sharp-tooth'd unkindness, like a vulture, here.
*[Points to his heart.]*
I can scarce speak to thee; thou'lt not believe
With how deprav'd a quality—O Regan!

REG: I pray you, sir, take patience. I have hope
You less know how to value her desert
Than she to scant her duty.

LEAR: Say? How is that?

REG: I cannot think my sister in the least
Would fail her obligation. If, sir, perchance
She have restrain'd the riots of your followers,
'Tis on such ground and to such wholesome end
As clears her from all blame.

LEAR: My curses on her!

REG: O sir, you are old,
Nature in you stands on the very verge
Of his confine. You should be rul'd and led
By some discretion that discerns your state
Better than you yourself. Therefore I pray you
That to our sister you do make return.
Say you have wrong'd her.

LEAR: Ask her forgiveness?
Do you but mark how this becomes the house!
"Dear daughter, I confess that I am old; *[Kneeling.]*
Age is unnecessary. On my knees I beg
That you'll vouchsafe me raiment, bed, and food."

REG: Good sir, no more; these are unsightly tricks.
Return you to my sister.

LEAR: *[Rising.]* Never, Regan:
She hath abate me of half my train;

Look'd black upon me, strook me with her tongue,
Most serpent-like, upon the very heart.
All the stor'd vengeances of heaven fall
On her ingrateful top! Strike her young bones,
You taking airs, with lameness!

CORN: Fie, sir, fie!

LEAR: You nimble lightnings, dart your blinding flames
Into her scornful eyes! Infect her beauty,
You fen-suck'd fogs, drawn by the pow'rful sun,
To fall and blister!

REG: O the blest gods! so
Will you wish on me, when the rash mood is on.

LEAR: No, Regan, thou shalt never have my curse.
Thy tender-hefted nature shall not give
Thee o'er to harshness. Her eyes are fierce, but thine
Do comfort, and not burn. 'Tis not in thee
To grudge my pleasures, to cut off my train,
To bandy hasty words, to scant my sizes,
And in conclusion to oppose the bolt
Against my coming in. Thou better know'st
The offices of nature, bond of childhood,
Effects of courtesy, dues of gratitude:
Thy half o' th' kingdom hast thou not forgot,
Wherein I thee endow'd.

REG: Good sir, to th' purpose.

LEAR: Who put my man i' th' stocks?

*Tucket within.*

*Enter Steward* [OSWALD].

CORN: What trumpet's that?

REG: I know't, my sister's. This approves her letter,
That she would soon be here. *[To Oswald.]* Is your lady come?

LEAR: This is a slave whose easy-borrowed pride
Dwells in the [fickle] grace of her he follows.
Out, varlet, from my sight!

CORN: What means your Grace?

*Enter* GONERIL.

LEAR: Who stock'd my servant? Regan, I have good hope
Thou didst not know on't. Who comes here? O heavens!
If you do love old men, if your sweet sway
Allow obedience, if you yourselves are old,
Make it your cause; send down, and take my part.
*[To Goneril.]* Art not asham'd to look upon this beard?
O Regan, will you take her by the hand?

GON: Why not by th' hand, sir? How have I offended?
All's not offense that indiscretion finds
And dotage terms so.

LEAR: O sides, you are too tough!
Will you yet hold? How came my man i' th' stocks?

CORN: I set him there, sir; but his own disorders
Deserv'd much less advancement.

LEAR: You? Did you?

REG: I pray you, father, being weak, seem so.

If till the expiration of your month
You will return and sojourn with my sister,
Dismissing half your train, come then to me.
I am now from home, and out of that provision
Which shall be needful for your entertainment.

LEAR: Return to her? and fifty men dismiss'd?
No, rather I abjure all roofs, and choose
To wage against the enmity o' th' air,
To be a comrade with the wolf and owl—
Necessity's sharp pinch. Return with her?
Why, the hot-bloodied France, that dowerless took
Our youngest born, I could as well be brought
To knee his throne, and squire-like, pension beg
To keep base life afoot. Return with her?
Persuade me rather to be slave and sumpter
To this detested groom. *[Pointing at Oswald.]*

GON: At your choice, sir.

LEAR: I prithee, daughter, do not make me mad.
I will not trouble thee, my child; farewell:
We'll no more meet, no more see one another.
But yet thou art my flesh, my blood, my daughter—
Or rather a disease that's in my flesh,
Which I must needs call mine. Thou art a bile,
A plague-sore, or embossed carbuncle,
In my corrupted blood. But I'll not chide thee,
Let shame come when it will, I do not call it.
I do not bid the thunder-bearer shoot,
Nor tell tales of thee to high-judging Jove.
Mend when thou canst, be better at thy leisure,
I can be patient, I can stay with Regan,
I and my hundred knights.

REG: Not altogether so,
I look'd not for you yet, nor am provided
For your fit welcome. Give ear, sir, to my sister,
For those that mingle reason with your passion
Must be content to think you old, and so—
But she knows what she does.

LEAR: Is this well spoken?

REG: I dare avouch it, sir. What, fifty followers?
Is it not well? What should you need of more?
Yea, or so many? sith that both charge and danger
Speak 'gainst so great a number? How in one house
Should many people under two commands
Hold amity? 'Tis hard, almost impossible.

GON: Why might not you, my lord, receive attendance
From those that she calls servants or from mine?

REG: Why not, my lord? If then they chanc'd to slack ye,

We could control them. If you will come to me
(For now I spy a danger), I entreat you
To bring but five and twenty; to no more
Will I give place or notice.

LEAR: I gave you all—

REG: And in good time you gave it.

LEAR: Made you my guardians, my depositaries,
But kept a reservation to be followed
With such a number. What, must I come to you
With five and twenty? Regan, said you so?

REG: And speak't again, my lord, no more with me.

LEAR: Those wicked creatures yet do look well-favor'd
When others are more wicked; not being the worst
Stands in some rank of praise. *[To Goneril.]* I'll go with thee,
Thy fifty yet doth double five and twenty,
And thou art twice her love.

GON: Hear me, my lord:
What need you five and twenty? ten? or five?
To follow in a house where twice so many
Have a command to tend you?

REG: What need one?

LEAR: O, reason not the need! our basest beggars
Are in the poorest thing superfluous.
Allow not nature more than nature needs,
Man's life is cheap as beast's. Thou art a lady;
If only to go warm were gorgeous,
Why, nature needs not what thou gorgeous wear'st,
Which scarcely keeps thee warm. But for true need—
You heavens, give me that patience, patience I need!
You see me here, you gods, a poor old man,
As full of grief as age, wretched in both.
If it be you that stirs these daughters' hearts
Against their father, fool me not so much
To bear it tamely; touch me with noble anger,
And let not women's weapons, water-drops,
Stain my man's cheeks! No, you unnatural hags,
I will have such revenges on you both
That all the world shall—I will do such things—
What they are yet I know not, but they shall be
The terrors of the earth! You think I'll weep:
No, I'll not weep.
I have full cause of weeping, but this heart

*Storm and tempest.*

Shall break into a hundred thousand flaws
Or ere I'll weep. O Fool, I shall go mad!

*Exeunt [Lear, Gloucester, Gentleman, and Fool].*

CORN: Let us withdraw, 'twill be a storm.

REG: This house is little, the old man and 's people
Cannot be well bestow'd.

GON: 'Tis his own blame hath put himself from rest,
And must needs taste his folly.

REG: For his particular, I'll receive him gladly,
But not one follower.

GON: So am I purpos'd.
Where is my Lord of Gloucester?

CORN: Followed the old man forth.

*Enter* GLOUCESTER.

He is return'd.

GLOU: The King is in high rage.

CORN: Whither is he going?

GLOU: He calls to horse, but will I know not whither.

CORN: 'Tis best to give him way, he leads himself.

GON: My lord, entreat him by no means to stay.

GLOU: Alack, the night comes on, and the [bleak] winds
Do sorely ruffle; for many miles about
There's scarce a bush.

REG: O sir, to willful men,
The injuries that they themselves procure
Must be their schoolmasters. Shut up your doors.
He is attended with a desperate train,
And what they may incense him to, being apt
To have his ear abus'd, wisdom bids fear.

CORN: Shut up your doors, my lord, 'tis a wild night,
My Regan counsels well. Come out o' th' storm.

*Exeunt.*

## ACT III

### SCENE I

*Storm still. Enter* KENT *[disguised as Caius] and a* GENTLEMAN *severally.*

KENT: Who's there, besides foul weather?

GENT: One minded like the weather, most unquietly.

KENT: I know you. Where's the King?

GENT: Contending with the fretful elements;
Bids the wind blow the earth into the sea,
Or swell the curled waters 'bove the main,
That things might change or cease, [tears his white hair,
Which the impetuous blasts with eyeless rage
Catch in their fury, and make nothing of,
Strives in his little world of man to outscorn
The to-and-fro-conflicting wind and rain.
This night, wherein the cub-drawn bear would couch,
The lion and the belly-pinched wolf
Keep their fur dry, unbonneted he runs,
And bids what will take all.]

KENT: But who is with him?

GENT: None but the Fool, who labors to outjest
His heart-strook injuries.

KENT: Sir, I do know you,
And dare upon the warrant of my note
Commend a dear thing to you. There is division
(Although as yet the face of it is cover'd
With mutual cunning) 'twixt Albany and Cornwall;
Who have—as who have not, that their great stars
Thron'd and set high?—servants, who seem no less,
Which are to France the spies and speculations
Intelligent of our state. What hath been seen,
Either in snuffs and packings of the Dukes,
Or the hard rein which both of them hath borne
Against the old kind King; or something deeper,
Whereof (perchance) these are but furnishings—
[But true it is, from France there comes a power
Into this scattered kingdom, who already
Wise in our negligence, have secret feet
In some of our best ports, and are at point
To show their open banner. Now to you:
If on my credit you dare build so far
To make your speed to Dover, you shall find
Some that will thank you, making just report
Of how unnatural and bemadding sorrow
The King hath cause to plain.
I am a gentleman of blood and breeding,
And from some knowledge and assurance, offer
This office to you.]

GENT: I will talk further with you.

KENT: No, do not.
For confirmation that I am much more
Than my out-wall, open this purse and take
What it contains. If you shall see Cordelia
(As fear not but you shall), show her this ring,
And she will tell you who that fellow is
That yet you do not know. Fie on this storm!
I will go seek the King.

GENT: Give me your hand. Have you no more to say?

KENT: Few words, but to effect, more than all yet:
That when we have found the King—in which your pain
That way, I'll this—he that first lights on him
Holla the other. *Exeunt [severally].*

SCENE II

*Enter* LEAR *and* FOOL.

LEAR: Blow, winds, and crack your cheeks! rage, blow!
You cataracts and hurricanoes, spout
Till you have drench'd our steeples, [drown'd] the cocks!
You sulph'rous and thought-executing fires,
Vaunt-couriers of oak-cleaving thunderbolts,

Singe my white head! And thou, all-shaking thunder,
Strike flat the thick rotundity o' th' world!
Crack nature's moulds, all germains spill at once
That makes ingrateful man!

FOOL: O nuncle, court holy-water in a dry house is better than this rain-water out o' door. Good nuncle, in, ask thy daughter's blessing. Here's a night pities neither wise men nor fools.

LEAR: Rumble thy bellyful! Spit, fire! Spout, rain!
Nor rain, wind, thunder, fire are my daughters.
I tax not you, you elements, with unkindness;
I never gave you kingdom, call'd you children;
You owe me no subscription. Then let fall
Your horrible pleasure. Here I stand your slave,
A poor, infirm, weak, and despis'd old man;
But yet I call you servile ministers,
That will with two pernicious daughters join
Your high-engender'd battles 'gainst a head
So old and white as this. O, ho! 'tis foul.

FOOL: He that has a house to put 's head in has a good head-piece.
The codpiece that will house
Before the head has any,
The head and he shall louse:
So beggars marry many.
The man that makes his toe
What he his heart should make,
Shall of a corn cry woe,
And turn his sleep to wake.
For there was never yet fair woman but she made mouths in a glass.

*Enter* KENT *[disguised as Caius].*

LEAR: No, I will be the pattern of all patience, I will say nothing.

KENT: Who's there?

FOOL: Marry, here's grace and a codpiece—that's a wise man and a fool.

KENT: Alas, sir, are you here? Things that love night
Love not such nights as these. The wrathful skies
Gallow the very wanderers of the dark,
And make them keep their caves. Since I was man,
Such sheets of fire, such bursts of horrid thunder,
Such groans of roaring wind and rain, I never
Remember to have heard. Man's nature cannot carry
Th' affliction nor the fear.

LEAR: Let the great gods,
That keep this dreadful pudder o'er our heads,
Find out their enemies now. Tremble, thou wretch
That hast within thee undivulged crimes
Unwhipt of justice! Hide thee, thou bloody hand;
Thou perjur'd, and thou simular of virtue
That art incestuous! Caitiff, to pieces shake,
That under covert and convenient seeming
Has practic'd on man's life! Close pent-up guilts,
Rive your concealing continents, and cry
These dreadful summoners grace. I am a man
More sinn'd against than sinning.

KENT: Alack, bare-headed?
Gracious my lord, hard by here is a hovel,
Some friendship will it lend you 'gainst the tempest.
Repose you there, while I to this hard house
(More harder than the stones whereof 'tis rais'd,
Which even but now, demanding after you,
Denied me to come in) return, and force
Their scanted courtesy.

LEAR: My wits begin to turn.
Come on, my boy. How dost, my boy? Art cold?
I am cold myself. Where is this straw, my fellow?
The art of our necessities is strange
And can make vild things precious. Come, your hovel.
Poor Fool and knave, I have one part in my heart
That's sorry yet for thee.

FOOL: *[Sings.]*
"He that has and a little tine wit—
With heigh-ho, the wind and the rain—
Must make content with his fortunes fit,
Though the rain it raineth every day."

LEAR: True, boy. Come bring us to this hovel.

*Exit [with Kent].*

FOOL: This is a brave night to cool a courtezan. I'll speak a prophecy ere I go:
When priests are more in word than matter;
When brewers mar their malt with water;
When nobles are their tailors' tutors;
No, heretics burn'd, but wenches' suitors;
Then shall the realm of Albion
Come to great confusion.
When every case in law is right;
No squire in debt, nor no poor knight;
When slanders do not live in tongues;
Nor cutpurses come not to throngs;
When usurers tell their gold i' th' field,
And bawds and whores do churches build;
Then comes the time, who lives to see't,
That going shall be us'd with feet.
This prophecy Merlin shall make, for I live before his time.

*Exit.*

SCENE III

*Enter* GLOUCESTER *and* EDMUND *[with lights].*

GLOU: Alack, alack, Edmund, I like not this unnatural dealing. When I desir'd their leave that I might pity him, they took from me the use of mine own house, charg'd me on pain of perpetual displeasure neither to speak of him, entreat for him, or any way sustain him.

EDM: Most savage and unnatural!

GLOU: Go to; say you nothing. There is division between the Dukes, and a worse matter than that. I have receiv'd a letter this night—'tis dangerous to be spoken; I have lock'd the letter in my closet. These injuries the King now bears will be reveng'd home; there is part of a power already footed: we must incline to the King. I will look him and privily relieve him. Go you and maintain talk with the Duke, that my charity be not of him perceiv'd. If he ask for me, I am ill and gone to bed. If I die for['t] (as no less is threat'ned me), the King my old master must be reliev'd. There is strange things toward, Edmund, pray you be careful. *Exit.*

EDM: This courtesy, forbid thee, shall the Duke
Instantly know, and of that letter too.
This seems a fair deserving, and must draw me
That which my father loses: no less than all.
The younger rises when the old doth fall. *Exit.*

SCENE IV

*Enter* LEAR, KENT *[disguised as Caius], and* FOOL.

KENT: Here is the place, my lord; good my lord, enter,
The tyranny of the open night's too rough
For nature to endure. *Storm still.*

LEAR: Let me alone.

KENT: Good my lord, enter here.

LEAR: Wilt break my heart?

KENT: I had rather break mine own. Good my lord, enter.

LEAR: Thou think'st 'tis much that this contentious storm
Invades us to the skin; so 'tis to thee;
But where the greater malady is fix'd,
The lesser is scarce felt. Thou'dst shun a bear,
But if [thy] flight lay toward the roaring sea,
Thou'dst meet the bear i' th' mouth. When the mind's free,
The body's delicate; [this] tempest in my mind
Doth from my senses take all feeling else,
Save what beats there—filial ingratitude!
Is it not as this mouth should tear this hand
For lifting food to't? But I will punish home.
No, I will weep no more. In such a night
To shut me out? Pour on, I will endure.
In such a night as this? O Regan, Goneril!
Your old kind father, whose frank heart gave all—
O, that way madness lies, let me shun that!
No more of that.

KENT: Good my lord, enter here.

LEAR: Prithee go in thyself, seek thine own ease.
This tempest will not give me leave to ponder
On things would hurt me more. But I'll go in.
*[To the Fool.]* In, boy, go first.—You houseless poverty—

Nay, get thee in; I'll pray, and then
I'll sleep.

*Exit [Fool].*

Poor naked wretches, wheresoe'er
you are,
That bide the pelting of this
pitiless storm,
How shall your houseless heads
and unfed sides,
Your [loop'd] and window'd
raggedness, defend you
From seasons such as these? O, I
have ta'en
Too little care of this! Take physic,
pomp,
Expose thyself to feel what
wretches feel,
That thou mayst shake the
superflux to them,
And show the heavens more just.

EDG: *[Within.]* Fathom and half, fathom and half! Poor Tom!

*[Enter] Fool [from the hovel].*

FOOL: Come not in here, nuncle, here's a spirit. Help me, help me!

KENT: Give me thy hand. Who's there?

FOOL: A spirit, a spirit! he says his name's poor Tom.

KENT: What art thou that dost grumble there i' th' straw? Come forth.

*Enter* EDGAR *[disguised as a madman].*

EDG: Away, the foul fiend follows me! Through the sharp hawthorn blow the [cold] winds. Humh, go to thy bed and warm thee.

LEAR: Didst thou give all to thy daughters? And art thou come to this?

EDG: Who gives any thing to poor Tom? whom the foul fiend hath led through fire and through flame, through [ford] and whirlpool, o'er bog and quagmire; that hath laid knives under his pillow, and halters in his pew, set ratsbane by his porridge, made him proud of heart, to ride on a bay trotting-horse over four-inch'd bridges, to course his own shadow for a traitor. Bless thy five wits! Tom's a-cold—O do de, do de, do de. Bless thee from whirlwinds, star-blasting, and taking! Do poor Tom some charity, whom the foul fiend vexes. There could I have him now—and there—and there again—and there. *Storm still.*

LEAR: Has his daughters brought him to this pass? Couldst thou save nothing? Wouldst thou give 'em all?

FOOL: Nay, he reserv'd a blanket, else we had been all sham'd.

LEAR: Now all the plagues that in the
pendulous air
Hang fated o'er men's faults light
on thy daughters!

KENT: He hath no daughters, sir.

LEAR: Death, traitor! nothing could
have subdu'd nature
To such a lowness but his unkind
daughters.
Is it the fashion, that discarded
fathers
Should have thus little mercy on
their flesh?
Judicious punishment! 'twas this
flesh begot
Those pelican daughters.

EDG: Pillicock sat on Pillicock-Hill, alow! alow, loo, loo!

FOOL: This cold night will turn us all to fools and madmen.

EDG: Take heed o' th' foul fiend. Obey thy parents, keep thy word's justice, swear not, commit not with man's sworn spouse, set not thy sweet heart on proud array. Tom's a-cold.

LEAR: What hast thou been?

EDG: A servingman! proud in heart and mind; that curl'd my hair; wore gloves in my cap; serv'd the lust of my mistress' heart, and did the act of darkness with her; swore as many oaths as I spake words, and broke them in the sweet face of heaven: one that slept in the contriving of lust, and wak'd to do it. Wine lov'd I [deeply], dice dearly; and in woman out-paramour'd the Turk. False of heart, light of ear, bloody of hand; hog in sloth, fox in stealth, wolf in greediness, dog in madness, lion in prey. Let not the creaking of shoes nor the rustling of silks betray thy poor heart to woman. Keep thy foot out of brothels, thy hand out of plackets, thy pen from lenders' books, and defy the foul fiend. Still through the hawthorn blows the cold wind: says suum, mun, nonny. Dolphin my boy, boy, sessa! let him trot by. *Storm still.*

LEAR: Thou wert better in a grave than to answer with thy uncover'd body this extremity of the skies. Is man no more than this? Consider him well. Thou ow'st the worm no silk, the beast no hide, the sheep no wool, the cat no perfume. Ha? here's three on 's are sophisticated. Thou art the thing itself: unaccommodated man is no more but such a poor, bare, fork'd animal as thou art. Off, off, you lendings! Come, unbutton here. *[Tearing off his clothes.]*

FOOL: Prithee, nuncle, be contented, 'tis a naughty night to swim in. Now a little fire in a wild field were like an old lecher's heart, a small spark, all the rest on 's body cold.

*Enter* GLOUCESTER *with a torch.*

Look, here comes a walking fire.

EDG: This is the foul [fiend] Flibbertigibbet; he begins at curfew, and walks [till the] first cock; he gives the web and the pin, [squinies] the eye, and makes the hare-lip; mildews the white wheat, and hurts the poor creature of earth.

Swithold footed thrice the 'old,
He met the night-mare and her
nine-fold;
Bid her alight,
And her troth plight,
And aroint thee, witch, aroint
thee!

KENT: How fares your Grace?

LEAR: What's he?

KENT: Who's there? What is't you seek?

GLOU: What are you there? Your names?

EDG: Poor Tom, that eats the swimming frog, the toad, the todpole, the wall-newt, and the water; that in the fury of his heart, when the foul fiend rages, eats cow-dung for sallets; swallows the old rat and the ditch-dog; drinks the green mantle of the standing pool; who is whipt from tithing to tithing, and [stock-] punish'd and imprison'd; who hath [had] three suits to his back, six shirts to his body—

Horse to ride, and weapon to
wear;
But mice and rats, and such small
deer,
Have been Tom's food for seven
long year.

Beware my follower. Peace, Smulkin, peace, thou fiend!

GLOU: What, hath your Grace no better company?

EDG: The prince of darkness is a gentleman. Modo he's call'd, and Mahu.

GLOU: Our flesh and blood, my lord, is grown so vild
That it doth hate what gets it.

EDG: Poor Tom's a-cold.

GLOU: Go in with me; my duty cannot suffer
T' obey in all your daughters' hard commands.
Though their injunction be to bar my doors;
And let this tyrannous night take hold upon you,
Yet have I ventured to come seek you out,
And bring you where both fire and food is ready.

LEAR: First let me talk with this philosopher.
What is the cause of thunder?

KENT: Good my lord, take his offer, go into th' house.

LEAR: I'll talk a word with this same learned Theban.
What is your study?

EDG: How to prevent the fiend, and to kill vermin.

LEAR: Let me ask you one word in private.

KENT: Importune him once more to go, my lord,
His wits begin t' unsettle.

GLOU: Canst thou blame him?

*Storm still.*

His daughters seek his death. Ah, that good Kent!
He said it would be thus, poor banish'd man.
Thou sayest the King grows mad, I'll tell thee, friend,
I am almost mad myself. I had a son,
Now outlaw'd from my blood; he sought my life,
But lately, very late. I lov'd him, friend,
No father his son dearer; true to tell thee,
The grief hath craz'd my wits. What a night's this!
I do beseech your Grace—

LEAR: O, cry you mercy, sir.
Noble philosopher, your company.

EDG: Tom's a-cold.

GLOU: In, fellow, there, into th' hovel; keep thee warm.

LEAR: Come, let's in all.

KENT: This way, my lord.

LEAR: With him;
I will keep still with my philosopher.

KENT: Good my lord, soothe him; let him take the fellow.

GLOU: Take him you on.

KENT: Sirrah, come on; go along with us.

LEAR: Come, good Athenian.

GLOU: No words, no words, hush.

EDG: Child Rowland to the dark tower came,
His word was still, "Fie, foh, and fum,
I smell the blood of a British man."

*Exeunt.*

SCENE V

*Enter* CORNWALL *and* EDMUND.

CORN: I will have my revenge ere I depart his house.

EDM: How, my lord, I may be censur'd, that nature thus gives way to loyalty, something fears me to think of.

CORN: I now perceive, it was not altogether your brother's evil disposition made him seek his death; but a provoking merit, set a-work by a reprovable badness in himself.

EDM: How malicious is my fortune, that I must repent to be just! This is the letter which he spoke of, which approves him an intelligent party to the advantages of France. O heavens! that this treason were not; or not I the detector!

CORN: Go with me to the Duchess.

EDM: If the matter of this paper be certain, you have mighty business in hand.

CORN: True or false, it hath made thee Earl of Gloucester. Seek out where thy father is, that he may be ready for our apprehension.

EDM: *[Aside.]* If I find him comforting the King, it will stuff his suspicion more fully.—I will persever in my course of loyalty, though the conflict be sore between that and my blood.

CORN: I will lay trust upon thee; and thou shalt find a [dearer] father in my love.

*Exeunt.*

## SCENE VI

*Enter* KENT *[disguised as Caius] and* GLOUCESTER.

GLOU: Here is better than the open air, take it thankfully. I will piece out the comfort with what addition I can. I will not be long from you.

KENT: All the pow'r of his wits have given way to his impatience. The gods reward your kindness!

*Exit [Gloucester].*

*Enter* LEAR, EDGAR, *and* FOOL.

EDG: Frateretto calls me, and tells me Nero is an angler in the lake of darkness. Pray, innocent, and beware the foul fiend.

FOOL: Prithee, nuncle, tell me whether a madman be a gentleman or a yeoman?

LEAR: A king, a king!

FOOL: No, he's a yeoman that has a gentleman to his son; for he's a mad yeoman that sees his son a gentleman before him.

LEAR: To have a thousand with red burning spits
Come hizzing in upon 'em—

[EDG: The foul fiend bites my back.

FOOL: He's mad that trusts in the tameness of a wolf, a horse's health, a boy's love, or a whore's oath.

LEAR: It shall be done, I will arraign them straight.
*[To Edgar.]* Come sit thou here, most learned [justicer];
*[To the Fool.]* Thou, sapient sir, sit here. [Now], you she-foxes—

EDG: Look where he stands and glares!
Want'st thou eyes at trial, madam?

*[Sings.]*

"Come o'er the [bourn], Bessy, to me"—

FOOL: *[Sings.]*

Her boat hath a leak,
And she must not speak
Why she dares not come over to thee.

EDG: The foul fiend haunts poor Tom in the voice of a nightingale.

Hoppedance cries in Tom's belly for two white herring. Croak not, black angel, I have no food for thee.

KENT: How do you, sir? Stand you not so amaz'd. Will you lie down and rest upon the cushions?

LEAR: I'll see their trial first, bring in their evidence.
*[To Edgar.]* Thou robed man of justice, take thy place.
*[To the Fool.]* And thou, his yoke-fellow of equity,
Bench by his side. *[To Kent.]* You are o' th' commission,
Sit you too.

EDG: Let us deal justly. *[Sings.]*
Sleepest or wakest thou, jolly shepherd?
Thy sheep be in the corn,
And for one blast of thy minikin mouth,
Thy sheep shall take no harm.
Purr the cat is grey.

LEAR: Arraign her first, 'tis Goneril. I here take my oath before this honorable assembly, [she] kick'd the poor king her father.

FOOL: Come hither, mistress. Is your name Goneril?

LEAR: She cannot deny it.

FOOL: Cry you mercy, I took you for a join-stool.

LEAR: And here's another, whose warp'd looks proclaim
What store her heart is made an. Stop her there!
Arms, arms, sword, fire! Corruption in the place!
False justicer, why hast thou let her scape?]

EDG: Bless thy five wits!

KENT: O pity! Sir, where is the patience now
That you so oft have boasted to retain?

EDG: *[Aside.]* My tears begin to take his part so much,
They mar my counterfeiting.

LEAR: The little dogs and all,
Trey, Blanch, and Sweetheart, see, they bark at me.

EDG: Tom will throw his head at them.
Avaunt, you curs!
Be thy mouth or black or white,
Tooth that poisons if it bite;
Mastiff, greyhound, mongril grim,
Hound or spaniel, brach or [lym],
Or bobtail [tike] or trundle-tail,
Tom will make him weep and wail,
For with throwing thus my head,
Dogs leapt the hatch, and all are fled.

Do de, de, de. Sessa! Come, march to wakes and fairs and market towns. Poor Tom, thy horn is dry.

LEAR: Then let them anatomize Regan; see what breeds about her heart. Is there any cause in nature that make these hard hearts? *[To Edgar.]* You, sir, I entertain for one of my hundred; only I do not like the fashion of your garments. You will say they are Persian, but let them be chang'd.

KENT: Now, good my lord, lie here and rest awhile.

LEAR: Make no noise, make no noise, draw the curtains. So, so; we'll go to supper i' th' morning.

FOOL: And I'll go to bed at noon.

*Enter* GLOUCESTER.

GLOU: Come hither, friend; where is the King my master?

KENT: Here, sir, but trouble him not—his wits are gone.

GLOU: Good friend, I prithee take him in thy arms;
I have o'erheard a plot of death upon him.
There is a litter ready, lay him in't,
And drive toward Dover, friend, where thou shalt meet
Both welcome and protection. Take up thy master;
If thou shouldst dally half an hour, his life,
With thine and all that offer to defend him,
Stand in assured loss. Take up, take up,
And follow me, that will to some provision
Give thee quick conduct.

[KENT: Oppressed nature sleeps.
This rest might yet have balm'd thy broken sinews,
Which, if convenience will not allow,
Stand in hard cure. *[To the Fool.]* Come help to bear thy master;
Thou must not stay behind.]

[GLOU]: Come, come, away.

*Exeunt [all but Edgar].*

[EDG: When we our betters see bearing our woes,
We scarcely think our miseries our foes.
Who alone suffers, suffers most i' th' mind,
Leaving free things and happy shows behind,
But then the mind much sufferance doth o'erskip,
When grief hath mates, and bearing fellowship.
How light and portable my pain seems now,
When that which makes me bend makes the King bow:
He childed as I fathered! Tom, away!
Mark the high noises, and thyself bewray
When false opinion, whose wrong thoughts defile thee,
In thy just proof repeals and reconciles thee.
What will hap more to-night, safe scape the King!
Lurk, lurk,] *[Exit.]*

## SCENE VII

*Enter* CORNWALL, REGAN, GONERIL, *Bastard* [EDMUND], *and* SERVANTS.

CORN: *[To Goneril.]* Post speedily to my lord your husband, show him this letter. The army of France is landed.—Seek out the traitor Gloucester.

*[Exeunt some of the Servants.]*

REG: Hang him instantly.

GON: Pluck out his eyes.

CORN: Leave him to my displeasure. Edmund, keep you our sister company; the revenges we are bound to take upon your traitorous father are not fit for your beholding. Advise the Duke, where you are going, to a most [festinate] preparation; we are bound to the like. Our posts shall be swift and intelligent betwixt us. Farewell, dear sister, farewell, my Lord of Gloucester.

*Enter Steward* [OSWALD].

How now? where's the King?

OSW: My Lord of Gloucester hath convey'd him hence.
Some five or six and thirty of his knights,
Hot questrists after him, met him at gate,
Who, with some other of the lord's dependants,
Are gone with him toward Dover, where they boast
To have well-armed friends.

CORN: Get horses for your mistress.

GON: Farewell, sweet lord, and sister.

CORN: Edmund, farewell.

*Exeunt [Goneril, Edmund, and Oswald].*

Go seek the traitor Gloucester,
Pinion him like a thief, bring him before us.

*[Exeunt other Servants.]*

Though well we may not pass upon his life
Without the form of justice, yet our power
Shall do a court'sy to our wrath, which men
May blame, but not control.

*Enter* GLOUCESTER *[brought in by two or three]* SERVANTS.

Who's there? The traitor?

REG: Ingrateful fox, 'tis he.

CORN: Bind fast his corky arms.

GLOU: What means your Graces? Good my friends, consider
You are my guests. Do me no foul play, friends.

CORN: Bind him, I say. *[Servants bind him.]*

REG: Hard, hard. O filthy traitor!

GLOU: Unmerciful lady as you are, I'm none.

CORN: To this chair bind him. Villain, thou shalt find— *[Regan plucks his beard.]*

GLOU: By the kind gods, 'tis most ignobly done
To pluck me by the beard.

REG: So white, and such a traitor?

GLOU: Naughty lady,
These hairs which thou dost ravish from my chin
Will quicken and accuse thee. I am your host,
With robber's hands my hospitable favors
You should not ruffle thus. What will you do?

CORN: Come, sir, what letters had you late from France?

REG: Be simple-answer'd, for we know the truth.

CORN: And what confederacy have you with the traitors
Late footed in the kingdom?

REG: To whose hands you have sent the lunatic King—
Speak.

GLOU: I have a letter guessingly set down,
Which came front one that's of a neutral heart,
And not from one oppos'd.

CORN: Cunning.

REG: And false.

CORN: Where hast thou sent the King?

GLOU: To Dover.

REG: Wherefore to Dover? Wast thou not charg'd at peril—

CORN: Wherefore to Dover? Let him answer that.

GLOU: I am tied to th' stake, and I must stand the course.

REG: Wherefore to Dover?

GLOU: Because I would not see thy cruel nails
Pluck out his poor old eyes, nor thy fierce sister
In his anointed flesh [rash] boarish fangs.
The sea, with such a storm as his bare head
In hell-black night endur'd, would have buoy'd up
And quench'd the stelled fires;
Yet, poor old heart, he holp the heavens to rain.
If wolves had at thy gate howl'd that [dearn] time,
Thou shouldst have said, "Good porter, turn the key."
All cruels else subscribe; but I shall see
The winged vengeance overtake such children.

CORN: See't shalt thou never. Fellows, hold the chair,
Upon these eyes of thine I'll set my foot.

GLOU: He that will think to live till he be old,
Give me some help! O cruel! O you gods!

REG: One side will mock another; th' other too.

CORN: If you see vengeance—

[1.] SERV: Hold your hand, my lord!
I have serv'd you ever since I was a child;
But better service have I never done you
Than now to bid you hold.

REG: How now, you dog?

[1.] SERV: If you did wear a beard upon your chin,
I'ld shake it on this quarrel. What do you mean?

CORN: My villain! *[Draw and fight.]*

[1.] SERV: Nay then come on, and take the chance of anger.

*[Cornwall is wounded.]*

REG: Give me thy sword. A peasant stand up thus?

*[She takes a sword and runs at him behind;] kills him.*

[1.] SERV: O, I am slain! My lord, you have one eye left
To see some mischief on him. O!

*[He dies.]*

CORN: Lest it see more, prevent it. Out, vild jelly!
Where is thy lustre now?

GLOU: All dark and comfortless! Where's my son Edmund?
Edmund, enkindle all the sparks of nature,
To quit this horrid act.

REG: Out, treacherous villain!
Thou call'st on him that hates thee. It was he
That made the overture of thy treasons to us,
Who is too good to pity thee.

GLOU: O my follies! then Edgar was abus'd.
Kind gods, forgive me that, and prosper him!

REG: Go thrust him out at gates, and let him smell
His way to Dover. *Exit [one] with Gloucester.*
How is't, my lord? How look you?

CORN: I have receiv'd a hurt; follow me, lady.—
Turn out that eyeless villain; throw this slave
Upon the dunghill. Regan, I bleed apace,

Untimely comes this hurt. Give me your arm.

*Exit [led by Regan].*

*[2.]* SERV: I'll never care what wickedness I do,
If this man come to good.

*[3.]* SERV: If she live long,
And in the end meet the old course of death,
Women will all turn monsters.

*[2.]* SERV: Let's follow the old Earl, and get the Bedlam
To lead him where he would; his roguish madness
Allows itself to any thing.

*[3.]* SERV: Go thou. I'll fetch some flax and whites of eggs
To apply to his bleeding face. Now heaven help him!

*Exeunt [severally].]*

## ACT IV

### SCENE I

*Enter* EDGAR.

EDG: Yet better thus, and known to be contemn'd,
Than still contemn'd and flatter'd. To be worst,
The lowest and most dejected thing of fortune,
Stands still in esperance, lives not in fear.
The lamentable change is from the best,
The worst returns to laughter. Welcome then,
Thou unsubstantial air that I embrace:
The wretch that thou hast blown unto the worst
Owes nothing to thy blasts.

*Enter* GLOUCESTER *[led by] an* OLD MAN.

But who comes here?
My father, [parti-ey'd]? World, world, O world!
But that thy strange mutations make us hate thee,
Life would not yield to age.

OLD MAN: O my good lord,
I have been your tenant, and your father's tenant,
These fourscore years.

GLOU: Away, get thee away! Good friend, be gone,
Thy comforts can do me no good at all;
Thee they may hurt.

OLD MAN: You cannot see your way.

GLOU: I have no way, and therefore want no eyes;
I stumbled when I saw. Full oft 'tis seen,
Our means secure us, and our mere defects
Prove our commodities. O dear son Edgar,
The food of thy abused father's wrath!
Might I but live to see thee in my touch,
I'ld say I had eyes again.

OLD MAN: How now? who's there?

EDG: *[Aside.]* O gods! Who is't can say, "I am at the worst"?
I am worse than e'er I was.

OLD MAN: 'Tis poor mad Tom.

EDG: *[Aside.]* And worse I may be yet: the worst is not
So long as we can say, "This is the worst."

OLD MAN: Fellow, where goest?

GLOU: Is it a beggar-man?

OLD MAN: Madman and beggar too.

GLOU: He has some reason, else he could not beg.
I' th' last night's storm I such a fellow saw,
Which made me think a man a worm. My son
Came then into my mind, and yet my mind
Was then scarce friends with him. I have heard more since.
As flies to wanton boys are we to th' gods,
They kill us for their sport.

EDG: *[Aside.]* How should this be?
Bad is the trade that must play fool to sorrow,
Ang'ring itself and others.—Bless thee, master!

GLOU: Is that the naked fellow?

OLD MAN: Ay, my lord.

GLOU: [Then prithee] get thee away. If for my sake
Thou wilt o'ertake us hence a mile or twain
I' th' way toward Dover, do it for ancient love,
And bring some covering for this naked soul,
Which I'll entreat to lead me.

OLD MAN: Alack, sir, he is mad.

GLOU: 'Tis the time's plague, when madmen lead the blind.
Do as I bid thee, or rather do thy pleasure;
Above the rest, be gone.

OLD MAN: I'll bring him the best 'parel that I have,
Come on't what will. *Exit.*

GLOU: Sirrah, naked fellow—

EDG: Poor Tom's a-cold. *[Aside.]* I cannot daub it further.

GLOU: Come hither, fellow.

EDG: *[Aside.]* And yet I must.—Bless thy sweet eyes, they bleed.

GLOU: Know'st thou the way to Dover?

EDG: Both stile and gate, horse-way and foot-path. Poor Tom hath been scar'd out of his good wits. Bless thee, good man's son, from the foul fiend! [Five fiends have been in poor Tom at once: of lust, as Obidicut; Hobbididence, prince of dumbness; Mahu, of stealing; Modo, of murder; Flibbertigibbet, of [mopping] and mowing, who since possesses chambermaids and waiting-women. So, bless thee, master!]

GLOU: Here, take this purse, thou whom the heav'ns' plagues
Have humbled to all strokes. That I am wretched
Makes thee the happier; heavens, deal so still!
Let the superfluous and lust-dieted man,
That slaves your ordinance, that will not see
Because he does not feel, feel your pow'r quickly;
So distribution should undo excess,
And each man have enough. Dost thou know Dover?

EDG: Ay, master.

GLOU: There is a cliff, whose high and bending head
Looks fearfully in the confined deep.
Bring me but to the very brim of it,
And I'll repair the misery thou dost bear
With something rich about me. From that place
I shall no leading need.

EDG: Give me thy arm;
Poor Tom shall lead thee. *Exeunt.*

SCENE II

*Enter* GONERIL, *Bastard* [EDMUND].

GON: Welcome, my lord. I marvel our mild husband
Not met us on the way.

*[Enter* OSWALD, *the Steward.]*

Now, where's your master?

OSW: Madam, within, but never man so chang'd.
I told him of the army that was landed;
He smil'd at it. I told him you were coming;
His answer was, "The worse." Of Gloucester's treachery,
And of the loyal service of his son,
When I inform'd him, then he call'd me sot,
And told me I had turn'd the wrong side out.
What most he should dislike seems pleasant to him;
What like, offensive.

GON: *[To Edmund.]* Then shall you go no further.
It is the cowish terror of his spirit
That dares not undertake; he'll not feel wrongs
Which tie him to an answer. Our wishes on the way
May prove effects. Back, Edmund, to my brother,
Hasten his musters and conduct his pow'rs.
I must change names at home, and give the distaff
Into my husband's hands. This trusty servant
Shall pass between us. Ere long you are like to hear
(If you dare venture in your own behalf)
A mistress's command. Wear this; spare speech.
Decline your head: this kiss, if it durst speak,
Would stretch thy spirits up into the air.
Conceive, and fare thee well.

EDM: Yours in the ranks of death. *Exit.*

GON: My most dear Gloucester!
O, the difference of man and man!
To thee a woman's services are due,
[A] fool usurps my [bed].

OSW: Madam, here comes my lord. *[Exit.]*

*Enter* ALBANY.

GON: I have been worth the [whistling].

ALB: O Goneril,
You are not worth the dust which the rude wind
Blows in your face. [I fear your disposition;
That nature which contemns it origin
Cannot be bordered certain in itself.
She that herself will sliver and disbranch
From her material sap, perforce must wither,
And come to deadly use.

GON: No more, the text is foolish.

ALB: Wisdom and goodness to the vild seem vild,
Filths savor but themselves. What have you done?
Tigers, not daughters, what have you perform'd?
A father, and a gracious aged man,

Whose reverence even the head-lugg'd bear would lick,
Most barbarous, most degenerate, have you madded.
Could my good brother suffer you to do it?
A man, a prince, by him so benefited!
If that the heavens do not their visible spirits
Send quickly down to tame [these] vild offenses,
It will come,
Humanity must perforce prey on itself,
Like monsters of the deep.]

GON: Milk-liver'd man,
That bear'st a check for blows, a head for wrongs,
Who hast not in thy brows an eye discerning
Thine honor from thy suffering, [that not know'st
Fools do those villains pity who are punish'd
Ere they have done their mischief, where's thy drum?
France spreads his banners in our noiseless land,
With plumed helm thy state begins [to threat],
Whilst thou, a moral fool, sits still and cries,
"Alack, why does he so?"]

ALB: See thyself, devil!
Proper deformity [shows] not in the fiend
So horrid as in woman.

GON: O vain fool!

[ALB: Thou changed and self-cover'd thing, for shame
Bemonster not thy feature. Were't my fitness
To let these hands obey my blood,
They are apt enough to dislocate and tear
Thy flesh and bones. Howe'er thou art a fiend,
A woman's shape doth shield thee.

GON: Marry, your manhood mew!]

*Enter a* MESSENGER.

[ALB: What news?]

MESS: O my good lord, the Duke of Cornwall's dead,
Slain by his servant, going to put out
The other eye of Gloucester.

ALB: Gloucester's eyes?

MESS: A servant that he bred, thrill'd with remorse,
Oppos'd against the act, bending his sword
To his great master, who, [thereat] enraged,
Flew on him, and amongst them fell'd him dead,
But not without that harmful stroke which since
Hath pluck'd him after.

ALB: This shows you are above,
You [justicers], that these our nether crimes
So speedily can venge! But, O poor Gloucester,
Lost he his other eye?

MESS: Both, both, my lord.
This letter, madam, craves a speedy answer;
'Tis from your sister.

GON: *[Aside.]* One way I like this well,
But being widow, and my Gloucester with her,
May all the building in my fancy pluck
Upon my hateful life. Another way,
The news is not so tart.—I'll read, and answer. *[Exit.]*

ALB: Where was his son when they did take his eyes?

MESS: Come with my lady hither.

ALB: He is not here.

MESS: No, my good lord, I met him back again.

ALB: Knows he the wickedness?

MESS: Ay, my good lord; 'twas he inform'd against him,
And quit the house on purpose that their punishment
Might have the freer course.

ALB: Gloucester, I live
To thank thee for the love thou show'dst the King,
And to revenge thine eyes. Come hither, friend,
Tell me what more thou know'st.

*Exeunt.*

SCENE III

*Enter* KENT *and a* GENTLEMAN.

KENT: Why the King of France is so suddenly gone back, know you no reason?

GENT: Something he left imperfect in the state, which since his coming forth is thought of, which imports to the kingdom so much fear and danger that his personal return was most requir'd and necessary.

KENT: Who hath he left behind him general?

GENT: The Marshal of France, Monsieur La Far.

KENT: Did your letters pierce the Queen to any demonstration of grief?

GENT: Ay, [sir], she took them, read them in my presence,
And now and then an ample tear trill'd down
Her delicate cheek. It seem'd she was a queen
Over her passion, who, most rebel-like,
Sought to be king o'er her.

KENT: O then it mov'd her.

GENT: Not to a rage, patience and sorrow [strove]
Who should express her goodliest. You have seen
Sunshine and rain at once; her smiles and tears
Were like a better way: those happy smilets
That play'd on her ripe lip [seem'd] not to know
What guests were in her eyes, which, parted thence,
As pearls from diamonds dropp'd. In brief,
Sorrow would be a rarity most beloved,
If all could so become it.

KENT: Made she no verbal question?

GENT: Faith, once or twice she heav'd the name of "father"
Pantingly forth, as if it press'd her heart;
Cried, "Sisters, sisters! Shame of ladies, sisters!
Kent! father! sisters! What, i' th' storm? i' th' night?
Let pity not be believ'd!" There she shook
The holy water from her heavenly eyes,
And, clamor-moistened, then away she started
To deal with grief alone.

KENT: It is the stars,
The stars above us, govern our conditions,
Else one self mate and make could not beget
Such different issues. You spoke not with her since?

GENT: No.

KENT: Was this before the King return'd?

GENT: No, since.

KENT: Well, sir, the poor distressed Lear's i' th' town,
Who sometime, in his better tune, remembers
What we are come about, and by no means
Will yield to see his daughter.

GENT: Why, good sir?

KENT: A sovereign shame so elbows him: his own unkindness,
That stripp'd her from his benediction, turn'd her
To foreign casualties, gave her dear rights
To his dog-hearted daughters—these things sting
His mind so venomously, that burning shame
Detains him from Cordelia.

GENT: Alack, poor gentleman!

KENT: Of Albany's and Cornwall's powers you heard not?

GENT: 'Tis so, they are afoot.

KENT: Well, sir, I'll bring you to our master Lear,
And leave you to attend him. Some dear cause
Will in concealment wrap me up awhile;
When I am known aright, you shall not grieve
Lending me this acquaintance. I pray you go
Along with me. *[Exeunt.]*

SCENE IV

*Enter, with Drum and Colors,* CORDELIA, [DOCTOR], *and* SOLDIERS.

COR: Alack, 'tis he! Why, he was met even now
As mad as the vex'd sea, singing aloud,
Crown'd with rank [femiter] and furrow-weeds,
With hardocks, hemlock, nettles, cuckoo-flow'rs,
Darnel, and all the idle weeds that grow
In our sustaining corn. A [century] send forth;
Search every acre in the high-grown field,
And bring him to our eye. *[Exit an Officer.]* What can man's wisdom
In the restoring his bereaved sense?
He that helps him take all my outward worth.

[DOCT:] There is means, madam.
Our foster-nurse of nature is repose,
The which he lacks; that to provoke in him
Are many simples operative, whose power
Will close the eye of anguish.

COR: All blest secrets,
All you unpublish'd virtues of the earth,
Spring with my tears; be aidant and remediate
In the good man's [distress]! Seek, seek for him,

Lest his ungovern'd rage dissolve the life
That wants the means to lead it.

*Enter* MESSENGER.

MESS: News, madam!
The British pow'rs are marching hitherward.

COR: 'Tis known before; our preparation stands
In expectation of them. O dear father,
It is thy business that I go about;
Therefore great France
My mourning and importun'd tears hath pitied.
No blown ambition doth our arms incite,
But love, dear love, and our ag'd father's right.
Soon may I hear and see him!

*Exeunt.*

SCENE V

*Enter* REGAN *and Steward* [OSWALD].

REG: But are my brother's pow'rs set forth?

OSW: Ay, madam.

REG: Himself in person there?

OSW: Madam, with much ado;
Your sister is the better soldier.

REG: Lord Edmund spake not with your lord at home?

OSW: No, madam.

REG: What might import my sister's letter to him?

OSW: I know not, lady.

REG: Faith, he is posted hence on serious matter.
It was great ignorance, Gloucester's eyes being out,
To let him live; where he arrives he moves
All hearts against us. Edmund, I think, is gone,
In pity of his misery, to dispatch
His nighted life; moreover to descry
The strength o' th' enemy.

OSW: I must needs after him, madam, with my letter.

REG: Our troops set forth to-morrow, stay with us;
The ways are dangerous.

OSW: I may not, madam;
My lady charg'd my duty in this business.

REG: Why should she write to Edmund? Might not you
Transport her purposes by word? Belike
Some things—I know not what. I'll love thee much—
Let me unseal the letter.

OSW: Madam, I had rather—

REG: I know your lady does not love her husband,
I am sure of that; and at her late being here
She gave strange eliads and most speaking looks
To noble Edmund. I know you are of her bosom.

OSW: I, madam?

REG: I speak in understanding: y' are; I know't.
Therefore I do advise you take this note:
My lord is dead; Edmund and I have talk'd,

And more convenient is he for my hand
Than for your lady's. You may gather more.
If you do find him, pray you give him this;
And when your mistress hears thus much from you,
I pray desire her call her wisdom to her.
So fare you well.
If you do chance to hear of that blind traitor,
Preferment falls on him that cuts him off.

OSW: Would I could meet [him,] madam! I should show
What party I do follow.

REG: Fare thee well. *Exeunt.*

SCENE VI

*Enter* GLOUCESTER *and* EDGAR *[dressed like a peasant].*

GLOU: When shall I come to th' top of that same hill?

EDG: You do climb up it now. Look how we labor.

GLOU: Methinks the ground is even.

EDG: Horrible steep.
Hark, do you hear the sea?

GLOU: No, truly.

EDG: Why then your other senses grow imperfect
By your eyes' anguish.

GLOU: So may it be indeed.
Methinks thy voice is alter'd, and thou speak'st
In better phrase and matter than thou didst.

EDG: Y' are much deceiv'd. In nothing am I chang'd
But in my garments.

GLOU: Methinks y' are better spoken.

EDG: Come on, sir, here's the place; stand still.
How fearful
And dizzy 'tis, to cast one's eyes so low!
The crows and choughs that wing the midway air
Show scarce so gross as beetles. Half way down
Hangs one that gathers sampire, dreadful trade!
Methinks he seems no bigger than his head.
The fishermen that [walk] upon the beach
Appear like mice; and yond tall anchoring bark,
Diminish'd to her cock; her cock, a buoy
Almost too small for sight. The murmuring surge,
That on th' unnumb'red idle pebble chafes,
Cannot be heard so high. I'll look no more,
Lest my brain turn, and the deficient sight
Topple down headlong.

GLOU: Set me where you stand.

EDG: Give me your hand. You are now within a foot
Of th' extreme verge. For all beneath the moon
Would I not leap upright.

GLOU: Let go my hand.
Here, friend, 's another purse; in it a jewel
Well worth a poor man's taking. Fairies and gods

Prosper it with thee! Go thou further off:
Bid me farewell, and let me hear thee going.

EDG: Now fare ye well, good sir.

GLOU: With all my heart.

EDG: *[Aside.]* Why I do trifle thus with his despair
Is done to cure it.

GLOU: O you mighty gods! *[He kneels.]*
This world I do renounce, and in your sights
Shake patiently my great affliction off.
If I could bear it longer, and not fall
To quarrel with your great opposeless wills,
My snuff and loathed part of nature should
Burn itself out. If Edgar live, O bless him!
Now, fellow, fare thee well. *[He falls.]*

EDG: Gone, sir; farewell!
And yet I know not how conceit may rob
The treasury of life, when life itself
Yields to the theft. Had he been where he thought,
By this had thought been past. Alive or dead?—
Ho, you, sir! friend! Hear you, sir! speak!—
Thus might he pass indeed; yet he revives.—
What are you, sir?

GLOU: Away, and let me die.

EDG: Hadst thou been aught but goss'mer, feathers, air
(So many fathom down precipitating),
Thou'dst shiver'd like an egg: but thou dost breathe,
Hast heavy substance, bleed'st not, speak'st, art sound.
Ten masts at each make not the altitude
Which thou hast perpendicularly fell.
Thy life's a miracle. Speak yet again.

GLOU: But have I fall'n, or no?

EDG: From the dread summit of this chalky bourn.
Look up a-height, the shrill-gorg'd lark so far
Cannot be seen or heard. Do but look up.

GLOU: Alack, I have no eyes.
Is wretchedness depriv'd that benefit,
To end itself by death? 'Twas yet some comfort,
When misery could beguile the tyrant's rage,
And frustrate his proud will.

EDG: Give me your arm.
Up—so. How is't? Feel you your legs? You stand.

GLOU: Too well, too well.

EDG: This is above all strangeness.
Upon the crown o' th' cliff, what thing was that
Which parted from you?

GLOU: A poor unfortunate beggar.

EDG: As I stood here below, methought his eyes
Were two full moons; he had a thousand noses,
Horns welk'd and waved like the [enridged] sea.
It was some fiend; therefore, thou happy father,
Think that the clearest gods, who make them honors
Of men's impossibilities, have preserved thee.

GLOU: I do remember now. Henceforth I'll bear
Affliction till it do cry out itself
"Enough, enough," and die. That thing you speak of,
I took it for a man; often 'twould say,
"The fiend, the fiend!"—he led me to that place.

EDG: Bear free and patient thoughts.

*Enter* LEAR *[mad, crowned with weeds and flowers].*

But who comes here?
The safer sense will ne'er accommodate
His master thus.

LEAR: No, they cannot touch me for [coining,] I am the King himself.

EDG: O thou side-piercing sight!

LEAR: Nature's above art in that respect. There's your press-money. That fellow handles his bow like a crow-keeper; draw me a clothier's yard. Look, look, a mouse! Peace, peace, this piece of toasted cheese will do't. There's my gauntlet, I'll prove it on a giant. Bring up the brown bills. O, well flown, bird! i' th' clout, i' th' clout—hewgh! Give the word.

EDG: Sweet marjorum.

LEAR: Pass.

GLOU: I know that voice.

LEAR: Ha! Goneril with a white beard? They flatter'd me like a dog, and told me I had the white hairs in my beard ere the black ones were there. To say "ay" and "no" to every thing that I said! "Ay," and "no" too, was no good divinity. When the rain came to wet me once, and the wind to make me chatter, when the thunder would not peace at my bidding, there I found 'em, there I smelt 'em out. Go to, they are not men o' their words: they told me I was every thing. 'Tis a lie, I am not ague-proof.

GLOU: The trick of that voice I do well remember;
Is't not the King?

LEAR: Ay, every inch a king!
When I do stare, see how the subject quakes.
I pardon that man's life. What was thy cause?
Adultery?
Thou shalt not die. Die for adultery? No,
The wren goes to't, and the small gilded fly
Does lecher in my sight.
Let copulation thrive; for Gloucester's bastard son
Was kinder to his father than my daughters
Got 'tween the lawful sheets.
To't, luxury, pell-mell, for I lack soldiers.
Behold yond simp'ring dame,
Whose face between her forks presages snow;
That minces virtue, and does shake the head
To hear of pleasure's name—
The fitchew nor the soiled horse goes to't
With a more riotous appetite.
Down from the waist they are Centaurs,
Though women all above;
But to the girdle do the gods inherit,
Beneath is all the fiends': there's hell, there's darkness,
There is the sulphurous pit, burning, scalding,
Stench, consumption. Fie, fie, fie! pah, pah!

Give me an ounce of civet; good apothecary,
Sweeten my imagination. There's money for thee.

GLOU: O, let me kiss that hand!

LEAR: Let me wipe it first, it smells of mortality.

GLOU: O ruin'd piece of nature! This great world
Shall so wear out to nought. Dost thou know me?

LEAR: I remember thine eyes well enough. Dost thou squiny at me? No, do thy worst, blind Cupid, I'll not love. Read thou this challenge; mark but the penning of it.

GLOU: Were all thy letters suns, I could not see.

EDG: *[Aside.]* I would not take this from report; it is,
And my heart breaks at it.

LEAR: Read.

GLOU: What, with the case of eyes?

LEAR: O ho, are you there with me? No eyes in your head, nor no money in your purse? Your eyes are in a heavy case, your purse in a light, yet you see how this world goes.

GLOU: I see it feelingly.

LEAR: What, art mad? A man may see how this world goes with no eyes. Look with thine ears; see how yond justice rails upon yond simple thief. Hark in thine ear: change places, and handy-dandy, which is the justice, which is the thief? Thou hast seen a farmer's dog bark at a beggar?

GLOU: Ay, sir.

LEAR: And the creature run from the cur? There thou mightst behold the great image of authority: a dog's obey'd in office.
Thou rascal beadle, hold thy bloody hand!
Why dost thou lash that whore? Strip thy own back,
Thou hotly lusts to use her in that kind
For which thou whip'st her. The usurer hangs the cozener.
Thorough tatter'd clothes [small] vices do appear;
Robes and furr'd gowns hide all. [Plate sin] with gold,
And the strong lance of justice hurtless breaks;
Arm it in rags, a pigmy's straw does pierce it.
None does offend, none, I say none, I'll able 'em.
Take that of me, my friend, who have the power
To seal th' accuser's lips. Get thee glass eyes,
And like a scurvy politician, seem
To see the things thou dost not. Now, now, now, now.
Pull off my boots; harder, harder—so.

EDG: *[Aside.]* O, matter and impertinency mix'd,
Reason in madness!

LEAR: If thou wilt weep my fortunes, take my eyes.
I know thee well enough, thy name is Gloucester.
Thou must be patient; we came crying hither.
Thou know'st, the first time that we smell the air
We wawl and cry. I will preach to thee. Mark.

*[Lear takes off his crown of weeds and flowers.]*

GLOU: Alack, alack the day!

LEAR: When we are born, we cry that we are come
To this great stage of fools.—This' a good block.
It were a delicate stratagem, to shoe
A troop of horse with felt. I'll put't in proof,
And when I have stol'n upon these son-in-laws,
Then kill, kill, kill, kill, kill, kill!

*Enter a* GENTLEMAN *[with* ATTENDANTS.*]*

GENT: O, here he is: lay hand upon him.—Sir,
Your most dear daughter—

LEAR: No rescue? What, a prisoner? I am even
The natural fool of fortune. Use me well,
You shall have ransom. Let me have surgeons,
I am cut to th' brains.

GENT: You shall have any thing.

LEAR: No seconds? All myself?
Why, this would make a man a man of salt
To use his eyes for garden water-pots,
[Ay, and laying autumn's dust.

GENT: Good sir—]

LEAR: I will die bravely, like a smug bridegroom. What?
I will be jovial. Come, come, I am a king,
Masters, know you that?

GENT: You are a royal one, and we obey you.

LEAR: Then there's life in't. Come, and you get it, you shall get it by running. Sa, sa, sa, sa.

*Exit [running; Attendants follow].*

GENT: A sight most pitiful in the meanest wretch,
Past speaking of in a king! Thou hast [one] daughter
Who redeems nature from the general curse
Which twain have brought her to.

EDG: Hail, gentle sir.

GENT: Sir, speed you: what's your will?

EDG: Do you hear aught, sir, of a battle toward?

GENT: Most sure and vulgar; every one hears that,
Which can distinguish sound.

EDG: But by your favor,
How near's the other army?

GENT: Near and on speedy foot; the main descry
Stands on the hourly thought.

EDG: I thank you, sir, that's all.

GENT: Though that the Queen on special cause is here,
Her army is mov'd on.

EDG: I thank you, sir.

*Exit [Gentleman].*

GLOU: You ever-gentle gods, take my breath from me,
Let not my worser spirit tempt me again
To die before you please!

EDG: Well pray you, father.

GLOU: Now, good sir, what are you?

EDG: A most poor man, made tame to fortune's blows,
Who, by the art of known and feeling sorrows,
Am pregnant to good pity. Give me your hand,
I'll lead you to some biding.

GLOU: Hearty thanks;
The bounty and the benison of heaven
To boot, and boot!

*Enter Steward* [OSWALD].

OSW: A proclaim'd prize! Most happy!
That eyeless head of thine was first fram'd flesh
To raise my fortunes. Thou old unhappy traitor,
Briefly thyself remember; the sword is out
That must destroy thee.

GLOU: Now let thy friendly hand
Put strength enough to't.

*[Edgar interposes.]*

OSW: Wherefore, bold peasant,
[Durst] thou support a publish'd traitor? Hence,
Lest that th' infection of his fortune take
Like hold on thee. Let go his arm.

EDG: Chill not let go, zir, without vurther [cagion].

OSW: Let go, slave, or thou di'st!

EDG: Good gentleman, go your gait, and let poor voke pass. And chud ha' bin zwagger'd out of my life, 'twould not ha' bin zo long as 'tis by a vortnight. Nay, come not near th' old man; keep out, che vor' ye, or Ice try whither your costard or my ballow be the harder. Chill be plain with you.

OSW: Out, dunghill! *[They fight.]*

EDG: Chill pick your teeth, zir. Come, no matter vor your foins.

OSW: Slave, thou hast slain me. Villain, take my purse:
If ever thou wilt thrive, bury my body,
And give the letters which thou find'st about me
To Edmund Earl of Gloucester; seek him out
Upon the English party, O untimely death!
Death! *[He dies.]*

EDG: I know thee well; a serviceable villain,
As duteous to the vices of thy mistress
As badness would desire.

GLOU: What, is he dead?

EDG: Sit you down, father; rest you.
Let's see these pockets; the letters that he speaks of
May be my friends. He's dead; I am only sorry
He had no other deathsman. Let us see.
Leave, gentle wax, and, manners, blame us not:
To know our enemies' minds, we rip their hearts,
Their papers is more lawful.

*(Reads the letter.)* "Let our reciprocal vows be remem'red. You have many opportunities to cut him off; if your will want not, time and place will be fruitfully offer'd. There is nothing done, if he return the conqueror; then am I the prisoner, and his bed my jail; from the loath'd warmth whereof deliver me, and supply the place for your labor.

Your (wife, so I would say) affectionate servant,
Goneril."

O indistinguish'd space of woman's will!
A plot upon her virtuous husband's life,
And the exchange my brother! Here, in the sands,

Thee I'll rake up, the post unsanctified
Of murtherous lechers; and in the mature time
With this ungracious paper strike the sight
Of the death-practic'd Duke. For him 'tis well
That of thy death and business I can tell.

GLOU: The King is mad; how stiff is my vild sense
That I stand up, and have ingenious feeling
Of my huge sorrows! Better I were distract,
So should my thoughts be sever'd from my griefs,
And woes by wrong imaginations lose
The knowledge of themselves.

*Drum afar off.*

EDG: Give me your hand;
Far off methinks I hear the beaten drum.
Come, father, I'll bestow you with a friend. *Exeunt.*

## SCENE VII

*Enter* CORDELIA, KENT *[still dressed as Caius], and* [DOCTOR].

COR: O thou good Kent, how shall I live and work
To match thy goodness? My life will be too short,
And every measure fail me.

KENT: To be acknowledg'd, madam, is o'erpaid.
All my reports go with the modest truth,
Nor more nor clipt, but so.

COR: Be better suited,
These weeds are memories of those worser hours;
I prithee put them off.

KENT: Pardon, dear madam,
Yet to be known shortens my made intent.
My boon I make it, that you know me not
Till time and I think meet.

COR: Then be't so, my good lord. *[To the Doctor.]*
How does the King?

[DOCT]: Madam, sleeps still.

COR: O you kind gods!
Cure this great breach in his abused nature,
Th' untun'd and jarring senses, O, wind up
Of this child-changed father!

[DOCT:] So please your Majesty
That we may wake the King? he hath slept long.

COR: Be govern'd by your knowledge, and proceed
I' th' sway of your own will. Is he array'd?

GENT: Ay, madam; in the heaviness of sleep
We put fresh garments on him.

[DOCT:] Be by, good madam, when we do awake him,
I doubt [not] of his temperance.

[COR: Very well.]

*Enter* LEAR *in a chair carried by* SERVANTS. *[*GENTLEMAN *in attendance. Soft music.]*

[DOCT: Please you draw near.—Louder the music there!]

COR: O my dear father, restoration hang
Thy medicine on my lips, and let this kiss
Repair those violent harms that my two sisters
Have in thy reverence made.
KENT: Kind and dear princess!
COR: Had you not been their father, these white flakes
Did challenge pity of them. Was this a face
To be oppos'd against the [warring] winds?
[To stand against the deep dread-bolted thunder?
In the most terrible and nimble stroke
Of quick cross lightning? to watch—poor perdu!—
With this thin helm?] Mine enemy's dog,
Though he had bit me, should have stood that night
Against my fire, and wast thou fain, poor father,
To hovel thee with swine and rogues forlorn
In short and musty straw? Alack, alack,
'Tis wonder that thy life and wits at once
Had not concluded all. He wakes, speak to him.
[DOCT:] Madam, do you, 'tis fittest.
COR: How does my royal lord? How fares your Majesty?
LEAR: You do me wrong to take me out o' th' grave:
Thou art a soul in bliss, but I am bound
Upon a wheel of fire, that mine own tears
Do scald like molten lead.
COR: Sir, do you know me?
LEAR: You are a spirit, I know; [when] did you die?
COR: Still, still, far wide!
[DOCT:] He's scarce awake, let him alone a while.
LEAR: Where have I been? Where am I? Fair daylight?
I am mightily abus'd; I should ev'n die with pity
To see another thus. I know not what to say.
I will not swear these are my hands. Let's see,
I feel this pin prick. Would I were assur'd
Of my condition!
COR: O, look upon me, sir,
And hold your hand in benediction o'er me.
[No, sir,] you must not kneel.
LEAR: Pray do not mock me.
I am a very foolish fond old man,
Fourscore and upward, not an hour more nor less;
And to deal plainly,
I fear I am not in my perfect mind.
Methinks I should know you, and know this man,
Yet I am doubtful: for I am mainly ignorant
What place this is, and all the skill I have
Remembers not these garments; nor I know not
Where I did lodge last night. Do not laugh at me,
For (as I am a man) I think this lady
To be my child Cordelia.
COR: And so I am; I am.
LEAR: Be your tears wet? Yes, faith. I pray weep not.
If you have poison for me, I will drink it.

I know you do not love me, for your sisters
Have (as I do remember) done me wrong:
You have some cause, they have not.

COR: No cause, no cause.

LEAR: Am I in France?

KENT: In your own kingdom, sir.

LEAR: Do not abuse me.

[DOCT:] Be comforted, good madam, the great rage,
You see, is kill'd in him, [and yet it is danger
To make him even o'er the time he has lost.]
Desire him to go in, trouble him no more
Till further settling.

COR: Will't please your Highness walk?

LEAR: You must bear with me.
Pray you now forget and forgive; I am old and foolish.

*Exeunt. [Manent Kent and Gentleman.]*

[GENT: Holds it true, sir, that the Duke of Cornwall was so slain?

KENT: Most certain, sir.

GENT: Who is conductor of his people?

KENT: As 'tis said, the bastard son of Gloucester.

GENT: They say Edgar, his banish'd son, is with the Earl of Kent in Germany.

KENT: Report is changeable. 'Tis time to look about, the powers of the kingdom approach apace.

GENT: The arbiterment is like to be bloody. Fare you well, sir. *[Exit.]*

KENT: My point and period will be thoroughly wrought,
Or well or ill, as this day's battle's fought. *Exit.*]

## ACT V

### SCENE I

*Enter, with Drum and Colors,* EDMUND, REGAN, GENTLEMEN, *and* SOLDIERS.

EDM: Know of the Duke if his last purpose hold,
Or whether since he is advis'd by aught
To change the course. He's full of alteration
And self-reproving—bring his constant pleasure.

*[To a Gentleman, who goes out.]*

REG: Our sister's man is certainly miscarried.

EDM: 'Tis to be doubted, madam.

REG: Now, sweet lord,
You know the goodness I intend upon you:
Tell me but truly, but then speak the truth,
Do you not love my sister?

EDM: In honor'd love.

REG: But have you never found my brother's way
To the forfended place?

[EDM: That thought abuses you.

REG: I am doubtful that you have been conjunct
And bosom'd with her—as far as we call hers.]

EDM: No, by mine honor, madam.

REG: I never shall endure her. Dear my lord,
Be not familiar with her.

EDM: Fear [me] not.
She and the Duke her husband!

*Enter, with Drum and Colors,* ALBANY, GONERIL, SOLDIERS.

[GON: *[Aside.]* I had rather lose the battle than that sister
Should loosen him and me.]

ALB: Our very loving sister, well bemet.
Sir, this I heard: the King is come to his daughter,
With others whom the rigor of our state
Forc'd to cry out. [Where I could not be honest,
I never yet was valiant. For this business,
It touches us as France invades our land,
Not bolds the King, with others whom, I fear,
Most just and heavy causes make oppose.

EDM: Sir, you speak nobly.]

REG: Why is this reason'd?

GON: Combine together 'gainst the enemy;
For these domestic and particular broils
Are not the question here.

ALB: Let's then determine
With th' ancient of war on our proceeding.

[EDM: I shall attend you presently at your tent.]

REG: Sister, you'll go with us?

GON: No.

REG: 'Tis most convenient, pray go with us.

GON: *[Aside.]* O ho, I know the riddle.—I will go.

*Exeunt both the armies.*

*[As they are going out,] enter* EDGAR *[disguised. Albany remains].*

EDG: If e'er your Grace had speech with man so poor,
Hear me one word.

ALB: I'll overtake you.—Speak.

EDG: Before you fight the battle, ope this letter.
If you have victory, let the trumpet sound
For him that brought it. Wretched though I seem,
I can produce a champion that will prove
What is avouched there. If you miscarry,
Your business of the world hath so an end,
And machination ceases. Fortune [love] you!

ALB: Stay till I have read the letter.

EDG: I was forbid it.
When time shall serve, let but the herald cry,
And I'll appear again.

ALB: Why, fare thee well, I will o'erlook thy paper. *Exit [Edgar].*

*Enter* EDMUND.

EDM: The enemy's in view, draw up your powers.
Here is the guess of their true strength and forces,
By diligent discovery, but your haste
Is now urg'd on you.

ALB: We will greet the time. *Exit.*

EDM: To both these sisters have I sworn my love;

Each jealous of the other, as the stung
Are of the adder. Which of them shall I take?
Both? one? or neither? Neither can be enjoy'd
If both remain alive: to take the widow
Exasperates, makes mad her sister Goneril,
And hardly shall I carry out my side,
Her husband being alive. Now then, we'll use
His countenance for the battle, which being done,
Let her who would be rid of him devise
His speedy taking off. As for the mercy
Which he intends to Lear and to Cordelia,
The battle done, and they within our power,
Shall never see his pardon; for my state
Stands on me to defend, not to debate. *Exit.*

## SCENE II

*Alarum within. Enter, with Drum and Colors, [the* Powers *of France] over the stage,* Cordelia *[with her* Father *in her hand,] and exeunt.*

*Enter* Edgar *and* Gloucester.

Edg: Here, father, take the shadow of this tree
For your good host; pray that the right may thrive.
If ever I return to you again,
I'll bring you comfort.

Glou: Grace go with you, sir! *Exit [Edgar].*

*Alarum and retreat within. Enter* Edgar.

Edg: Away, old man, give me thy hand, away!
King Lear hath lost, he and his daughter ta'en.
Give me thy hand; come on.

Glou: No further, sir, a man may rot even here.

Edg: What, in ill thoughts again? Men must endure
Their going hence even as their coming hither,
Ripeness is all. Come on.

Glou: And that's true too. *Exeunt.*

## SCENE III

*Enter in conquest, with Drum and Colors,* Edmund, Lear *and* Cordelia *as prisoners,* Soldiers, Captain.

Edm: Some officers take them away. Good guard,
Until their greater pleasures first be known
That are to censure them.

Cor: We are not the first
Who with best meaning have incurr'd the worst.
For thee, oppressed king, I am cast down,
Myself could else out-frown false Fortune's frown.
Shall we not see these daughters and these sisters?

LEAR: No, no, no, no! Come let's away to prison:
We two alone will sing like birds i' th' cage;
When thou dost ask me blessing, I'll kneel down
And ask of thee forgiveness. So we'll live,
And pray, and sing, and tell old tales, and laugh
At gilded butterflies, and hear poor rogues
Talk of court news; and we'll talk with them too—
Who loses and who wins; who's in, who's out—
And take upon 's the mystery of things
As if we were God's spies; and we'll wear out,
In a wall'd prison, packs and sects of great ones,
That ebb and flow by th' moon.

EDM: Take them away.

LEAR: Upon such sacrifices, my Cordelia,
The gods themselves throw incense. Have I caught thee?
He that parts us shall bring a brand from heaven,
And fire us hence like foxes. Wipe thine eyes;
The good-years shall devour them, flesh and fell,
Ere they shall make us weep! We'll see 'em starv'd first.
Come. *Exit [with Cordelia, guarded].*

EDM: Come hither, captain; hark.
Take thou this note *[giving a paper];* go follow them to prison.
One step I have advanc'd thee; if thou dost
As this instructs thee, thou dost make thy way
To noble fortunes. Know thou this, that men
Are as the time is: to be tender-minded
Does not become a sword. Thy great employment
Will not bear question; either say thou'lt do't,
Or thrive by other means.

CAPT: I'll do't, my lord.

EDM: About it, and write happy when th' hast done.
Mark, I say instantly, and carry it so
As I have set it down.

[CAPT: I cannot draw a cart, nor eat dried oats,
If it be man's work, I'll do't.]

*Exit Captain.*

*Flourish. Enter* ALBANY, GONERIL, REGAN, *[another* CAPTAIN,*]* SOLDIERS.

ALB: Sir, you have show'd to-day your valiant strain,
And fortune led you well. You have the captives
Who were the opposites of this day's strife;
I do require them of you, so to use them
As we shall find their merits and our safety
May equally determine.

EDM: Sir, I thought it fit
To send the old and miserable King
To some retention [and appointed guard],
Whose age had charms in it, whose title more,
To pluck the common bosom on his side,

And turn our impress'd lances in our eyes
Which do command them. With him I sent the Queen,
My reason all the same, and they are ready
To-morrow, or at further space, t' appear
Where you shall hold your session. [At this time
We sweat and bleed: the friend hath lost his friend,
And the best quarrels, in the heat, are curs'd
By those that feel their sharpness.
The question of Cordelia and her father
Requires a fitter place.]

ALB: Sir, by your patience,
I hold you but a subject of this war,
Not as a brother.

REG: That's as we list to grace him.
Methinks our pleasure might have been demanded
Ere you had spoke so far. He led our powers,
Bore the commission of my place and person,
The which immediacy may well stand up,
And call itself your brother.

GON: Not so hot.
In his own grace he doth exalt himself,
More than in your addition.

REG: In my rights,
By me invested, he compeers the best.

[GON]: That were the most, if he should husband you.

REG: Jesters do oft prove prophets.

GON: Holla, holla!
That eye that told you so look'd but a-squint.

REG: Lady, I am not well, else I should answer
From a full-flowing stomach. General,
Take thou my soldiers, prisoners, patrimony;
Dispose of them, of me; the walls is thine.
Witness the world, that I create thee here
My lord and master.

GON: Mean you to enjoy him?

ALB: The let-alone lies not in your good will.

EDM: Nor in thine, lord.

ALB: Half-blooded fellow, yes.

REG: *[To Edmund.]* Let the drum strike, and prove my title thine.

ALB: Stay yet, hear reason. Edmund, I arrest thee
On capital treason, and in thy [attaint],
This gilded serpent *[pointing to Goneril]*. For your claim, fair [sister],
I bar it in the interest of my wife;
'Tis she is sub-contracted to this lord,
And I, her husband, contradict your banes.
If you will marry, make your loves to me,
My lady is bespoke.

GON: An enterlude!

ALB: Thou art armed, Gloucester, let the trumpet sound.
If none appear to prove upon thy person
Thy heinous, manifest, and many treasons,
There is my pledge *[throwing down a glove]*. I'll make it on thy heart,

Ere I taste bread, thou art in nothing less
Than I have here proclaim'd thee.

REG: Sick, O, sick!

GON: *[Aside.]* If not, I'll ne'er trust medicine.

EDM: There's my exchange *[throwing down a glove]*. What in the world [he is]
That names me traitor, villain-like he lies.
Call by the trumpet; he that dares approach:
On him, on you—who not?—I will maintain
My truth and honor firmly.

ALB: A herald, ho!

[EDM: A herald, ho, a herald!]

[ALB:] Trust to thy single virtue, for thy soldiers,
All levied in my name, have in my name
Took their discharge.

REG: My sickness grows upon me.

ALB: She is not well, convey her to my tent.

*[Exit Regan, led.]*

*Enter a* HERALD.

Come hither, herald. Let the trumpet sound,
And read out this.

[CAPT: Sound, trumpet!] *A trumpet sounds.*

HER: *(Reads.)* "If any man of quality or degree within the lists of the army will maintain upon Edmund, supposed Earl of Gloucester, that he is a manifold traitor, let him appear by the third sound of the trumpet. He is bold in his defense."

[EDM: Sound!] *First trumpet.*

HER: Again! *Second trumpet.*

HER: Again! *Third trumpet.*

*Trumpet answers within.*

*Enter* EDGAR *[at the third sound,] armed, [a Trumpet before him].*

ALB: Ask him his purposes, why he appears
Upon this call o' th' trumpet.

HER: What are you?
Your name, your quality? and why you answer
This present summons?

EDG: Know, my name is lost,
By treason's tooth bare-gnawn and canker-bit,
Yet am I noble as the adversary
I come to cope.

ALB: Which is that adversary?

EDG: What's he that speaks for Edmund Earl of Gloucester?

EDM: Himself; what say'st thou to him?

EDG: Draw thy sword,
That if my speech offend a noble heart,
Thy arm may do thee justice; here is mine:
Behold, it is my privilege,
The privilege of mine honors,
My oath, and my profession. I protest,
Maugre thy strength, place, youth, and eminence,
[Despite] thy victor-sword and fire-new fortune,
Thy valor, and thy heart, thou art a traitor;
False to thy gods, thy brother, and thy father,
Conspirant 'gainst this high illustrious prince,
And from th' extremest upward of thy head
To the descent and dust below thy foot,
A most toad-spotted traitor. Say thou "No,"

This sword, this arm, and my best spirits are bent
To prove upon thy heart, whereto I speak,
Thou liest.

EDM: In wisdom I should ask thy name,
But since thy outside looks so fair and warlike,
And that thy tongue some say of breeding breathes,
What safe and nicely I might well delay
By rule of knighthood, I disdain and spurn.
Back do I toss these treasons to thy head,
With the hell-hated lie o'erwhelm thy heart,
Which for they yet glance by, and scarcely bruise,
This sword of mine shall give them instant way
Where they shall rest for ever. Trumpets, speak!

*Alarums. [They fight. Edmund falls.]*

ALB: Save him, save him!

GON: This is practice, Gloucester.
By th' law of war thou wast not bound to answer
An unknown opposite. Thou art not vanquish'd,
But cozen'd and beguil'd.

ALB: Shut your mouth, dame,
Or with this paper shall I [stopple] it. Hold, sir.—
Thou worse than any name, read thine own evil.
No tearing, lady, I perceive you know it.

GON: Say if I do, the laws are mine, not thine;
Who can arraign me for't?

ALB: Most monstrous! O!
Know'st thou this paper?

[GON:] Ask me not what I know.

*Exit.*

ALB: Go after her; she's desperate, govern her.

EDM: What you have charg'd me with, that have I done,
And more, much more, the time will bring it out.
'Tis past, and so am I. But what art thou
That hast this fortune on me? If thou'rt noble,
I do forgive thee.

EDG: Let's exchange charity.
I am no less in blood than thou art, Edmund;
If more, the more th' hast wrong'd me.
My name is Edgar, and thy father's son.
The gods are just, and of our pleasant vices
Make instruments to plague us:
The dark and vicious place where thee he got
Cost him his eyes.

EDM: Th' hast spoken right, 'tis true.
The wheel is come full circle, I am here.

ALB: Methought thy very gait did prophesy
A royal nobleness. I must embrace thee.
Let sorrow split my heart, if ever I
Did hate thee or thy father.

EDG: Worthy prince, I know't.

ALB: Where have you hid yourself?
How have you known the miseries of your father?

EDG: By nursing them, my lord. List a brief tale,

And when 'tis told, O that my heart would burst!
The bloody proclamation to escape,
That follow'd me so near (O, our lives' sweetness!
That we the pain of death would hourly die
Rather than die at once!), taught me to shift
Into a madman's rags, t' assume a semblance
That very dogs disdain'd; and in this habit
Met I my father with his bleeding rings,
Their precious stones new lost; became his guide,
Led him, begg'd for him, sav'd him from despair;
Never (O fault!) reveal'd myself unto him,
Until some half hour past, when I was arm'd.
Not sure, though hoping, of this good success,
I ask'd his blessing, and from first to last
Told him our pilgrimage. But his flaw'd heart
(Alack, too weak the conflict to support!)
'Twixt two extremes of passion, joy and grief,
Burst smilingly.

EDM: This speech of yours hath mov'd me,
And shall perchance do good: but speak you on,
You look as you had something more to say.

ALB: If there be more, more woeful, hold it in,
For I am almost ready to dissolve,
Hearing of this.

[EDG: This would have seem'd a period
To such as love not sorrow, but another,
To amplify too much, would make much more,
And top extremity. Whilst I
Was big in clamor, came there in a man,
Who, having seen me in my worst estate,
Shunn'd my abhorr'd society, but then finding
Who 'twas that so endur'd, with his strong arms
He fastened on my neck and bellowed out
As he'd burst heaven, threw [him] on my father,
Told the most piteous tale of Lear and him
That ever ear received, which in recounting,
His grief grew puissant and the strings of life
Began to crack. Twice then the trumpets sounded,
And there I left him tranc'd.

ALB: But who was this?

EDG: Kent, sir, the banish'd Kent, who in disguise
Followed his enemy king, and did him service
Improper for a slave.]

*Enter a* GENTLEMAN *[with a bloody knife].*

GENT: Help, help! O, help!

EDG: What kind of help?

ALB: Speak, man.

EDG: What means this bloody knife?

GENT: 'Tis hot, it smokes,
It came even from the heart of—O, she's dead!

ALB: Who dead? Speak, man.
GENT: Your lady, sir, your lady; and her sister
By her is poison'd; she confesses it.
EDM: I was contracted to them both; all three
Now marry in an instant.
EDG: Here comes Kent.

*Enter* KENT.

ALB: Produce the bodies, be they alive or dead.

*[Exit Gentleman.]*

This judgment of the heavens, that makes us tremble,
Touches us not with pity.—O, is this he?
The time will not allow the compliment
Which very manners urges.
KENT: I am come
To bid my king and master aye good night.
Is he not here?
ALB: Great thing of us forgot!
Speak, Edmund, where's the King? and where's Cordelia?

*Goneril and Regan's bodies brought out.*

Seest thou this object, Kent?
KENT: Alack, why thus?
EDM: Yet Edmund was belov'd!
The one the other poison'd for my sake,
And after slew herself.
ALB: Even so. Cover their faces.
EDM: I pant for life. Some good I mean to do,
Despite of mine own nature.
Quickly send
(Be brief in it) to th' castle, for my writ
Is on the life of Lear and on Cordelia.
Nay, send in time.
ALB: Run, run, O, run!
EDG: To who, my lord? Who has the office? Send
Thy token of reprieve.
EDM: Well thought on. Take my sword. [The captain—]
Give it the captain.
[ALB:] Haste thee, for thy life.

*[Exit Edgar.]*

EDM: He hath commission from thy wife and me
To hang Cordelia in the prison, and
To lay the blame upon her own despair,
That she fordid herself.
ALB: The gods defend her! Bear him hence awhile.

*[Edmund is borne off.]*

*Enter* LEAR *with Cordelia in his arms, [*EDGAR *and a* GENTLEMAN *following].*

Lear: Howl, howl, howl! O, [you] are men of stones!
Had I your tongues and eyes, I'ld use them so
That heaven's vault should crack. She's gone for ever!
I know when one is dead, and when one lives;
She's dead as earth. Lend me a looking-glass,
If that her breath will mist or stain the stone,
Why then she lives.
KENT: Is this the promis'd end?
EDG: Or image of that horror?
ALB: Fall, and cease!
LEAR: This feather stirs, she lives! If it be so,

It is a chance which does redeem all sorrows
That ever I have felt.

KENT: *[Kneeling.]* O my good master!

LEAR: Prithee away.

EDG: 'Tis noble Kent, your friend.

LEAR: A plague upon you, murderers, traitors all!
I might have sav'd her, now she's gone for ever!
Cordelia, Cordelia, stay a little. Ha!
What is't thou say'st? Her voice was ever soft,
Gentle, and low, an excellent thing in woman.
I kill'd the slave that was a-hanging thee.

GENT: 'Tis true, my lords, he did.

LEAR: Did I not, fellow?
I have seen the day, with my good biting falchion
I would have made [them] skip. I am old now,
And these same crosses spoil me. Who are you?
Mine eyes are not o' th' best; I'll tell you straight.

KENT: If Fortune brag of two she lov'd and hated,
One of them we behold.

LEAR: This is a dull sight. Are you not Kent?

KENT: The same:
Your servant Kent. Where is your servant Caius?

LEAR: He's a good fellow, I can tell you that;
He'll strike, and quickly too. He's dead and rotten.

KENT: No, my good lord, I am the very man—

LEAR: I'll see that straight.

KENT: That from your first of difference and decay,
Have follow'd your sad steps—

LEAR: [You] are welcome hither.

KENT: Nor no man else. All's cheerless, dark, and deadly.
Your eldest daughters have foredone themselves,
And desperately are dead.

LEAR: Ay, so I think.

ALB: He knows not what he says, and vain is it
That we present us to him.

EDG: Very bootless.

*Enter a* MESSENGER.

MESS: Edmund is dead, my lord.

ALB: That's but a trifle here.
You lords and noble friends, know our intent.
What comfort to this great decay may come
Shall be applied. For us, we will resign,
During the life of this old majesty,
To him our absolute power. *[To Edgar and Kent.]* You, to your rights,
With boot, and such addition as your honors
Have more than merited. All friends shall taste
The wages of their virtue, and all foes
The cup of their deservings. O, see, see!

LEAR: And my poor fool is hang'd! No, no, no life!
Why should a dog, a horse, a rat, have life,
And thou no breath at all? Thou'lt come no more,
Never, never, never, never, never.

Pray you undo this button. Thank you, sir.
Do you see this? Look on her! Look her lips,
Look there, look there! *He dies.*

EDG: He faints. My lord, my lord!

KENT: Break, heart, I prithee break!

EDG: Look up, my lord.

KENT: Vex not his ghost. O, let him pass, he hates him
That would upon the rack of this tough world
Stretch him out longer.

EDG: He is gone indeed.

KENT: The wonder is he hath endur'd so long,
He but usurp'd his life.

ALB: Bear them from hence. Our present business
Is general woe. *[To Kent and Edgar.]* Friends of my soul, you twain
Rule in this realm, and the gor'd state sustain.

KENT: I have a journey, sir, shortly to go:
My master calls me, I must not say no.

EDG: The weight of this sad time we must obey,
Speak what we feel, not what we ought to say:
The oldest hath borne most; we that are young
Shall never see so much, nor live so long.

*Exeunt with a dead march.*

## Miguel de Cervantes (1547–1616)

*Translated by Samuel Putnam*

Contemporary with Shakespeare and Montaigne, Cervantes witnessed the peak and the decline of his country's wealth, as the gold supply from conquered lands in the New World gradually dwindled. The Spain of Cervantes's childhood believed itself invincible and launched crusades against the Moors in the south and against Protestants throughout Europe. But by the turn of the seventeenth century, the country was exhausted. Spain fought on multiple and continuously shifting fronts with a dream of uniting all of Europe under Spanish political leadership and one religious doctrine; this effort, coupled with the massive task of managing vast American lands and conquered peoples, depleted the nation's economic and human resources.

Born into a relatively poor family, Cervantes received only about six years of formal schooling, but he read voraciously and continued learning on his own. His writing reveals familiarity with some Greek literature, many Latin authors, and some of the great writers of the Italian Renaissance. As an adult, Cervantes traveled throughout Spain, lived five years in Italy, enlisted in the Spanish army, and fought in several campaigns. He participated in raids against Arab fortresses at Tunis and was sold into slavery by pirates who captured his boat. His five years of slavery in Algiers were punctuated by repeated attempts to escape; he was eventually ransomed by monks. After he returned to Spain at age thirty-three, his life became a constant struggle against poverty. With a maimed left arm and hand, his applications for further military service were rejected. He turned to writing and worked in what might now be called civil service jobs. He was forever in debt and frequently ran afoul of the law. Cervantes is said to have begun *Don Quixote* while imprisoned in 1597 for embezzling government monies.

The first part of *Don Quixote* was distributed for sale in 1605 and received immediate acclaim and widespread success, both inside and outside Spain. A second part was added in 1610. An immense novel, *Don Quixote* has been translated into more than a hundred languages and has left its mark on many writers, composers, and visual artists from the seventeenth century to the present day. Translated into English in 1612, subsequent editions kept the book circulating in England from that time forward. Cervantes's social satire and psychological portraits served as models for English fiction and for the development of the novel in the eighteenth century.

Don Quixote, having read too many medieval Romances, fancies himself a medieval knight long after the age of knighthood is over and gallops out into a seventeenth-century Spanish landscape. This "man who becomes a book" misperceives the world, and his insistence on the correctness of his own interpretations creates humor, pathos, and tragedy. A satire on chivalric Romances, which were extremely popular in the sixteenth century, *Don Quixote* is a marvelously complex mosaic of medieval and Renaissance materials. It simultaneously yearns for an honorable, chivalric past and satirizes the naivete of such a desire. The relation of illusion to reality is central to the narrative, and the novel anticipates the presence of the same theme in modern and postmodern fiction and metafiction.

## *from Don Quixote*

### *from Part One*

### Chapter I.

Which treats of the station in life and the pursuits of the famous gentleman, Don Quixote de la Mancha.

In a village of La Mancha the name of which I have no desire to recall, there lived not so long ago one of those gentlemen who always have a lance in the rack, an ancient buckler, a skinny nag, and a greyhound for the chase. A stew with more beef than mutton in it, chopped meat for his evening meal, scraps for a Saturday, lentils on Friday, and a young pigeon as a special delicacy for Sunday, went to account for three-quarters of his income. The rest of it he laid out on a broadcloth greatcoat and velvet stockings for feast days, with slippers to match, while the other days of the week he cut a figure in a suit of the finest homespun. Living with him were a housekeeper in her forties, a niece who was not yet twenty, and a lad of the field and market place who saddled his horse for him and wielded the pruning knife.

This gentleman of ours was close on to fifty, of a robust constitution but with little flesh on his bones and a face that was lean and gaunt. He was noted for his early rising, being very fond of the hunt. They will try to tell you that his surname was Quijada or Quesada—there is some difference of opinion among those who have written on the subject—but according to the most likely conjectures we are to understand that it was really Quejana. But all this means very little so far as our story is concerned, providing that in the telling of it we do not depart one iota from the truth.

You may know, then, that the aforesaid gentleman, on those occasions when he was at leisure, which was most of the year around, was in the habit of reading books of chivalry with such pleasure and devotion as to lead him almost wholly to forget the life of a hunter and even the administration of his estate. So great was his curiosity and infatuation in this regard that he even sold many acres of tillable land in order to be able to buy and read the books that he loved, and he would carry home with him as many of them as he could obtain.

Of all those that he thus devoured none pleased him so well as the ones that had been composed by the famous Feliciano de Silva, whose lucid prose style and involved conceits were as precious to him as pearls; especially when he came to read those tales of love and amorous challenges that are to be met with in many places, such a passage as the following, for example: "The reason of the unreason that afflicts my reason, in such a manner weakens my reason that I with reason lament me of your comeliness." And he was similarly affected when his eyes fell upon such lines as these: ". . . the high Heaven of your divinity divinely fortifies you with the stars and renders you deserving of that desert your greatness doth deserve."

The poor fellow used to lie awake nights in an effort to disentangle the meaning and make sense out of passages such as these, although Aristotle himself would not have been able to understand them, even if he had been resurrected for that sole purpose. He was not at ease in his mind over those wounds that Don Belianís gave and received; for no matter how great the surgeons who treated him, the poor fellow must have been left with his face and his entire body covered with marks and scars. Nevertheless, he was grateful to the author for closing the book with the promise of an interminable adventure to come; many a time he was tempted to take up his pen and literally finish the tale as had been promised, and he undoubtedly would have done so, and would have succeeded at it very well, if his thoughts had not been constantly occupied with other things of greater moment.

He often talked it over with the village curate, who was a learned man, a graduate of Sigüenza, and they would hold long discussions as to who had been the better knight, Palmerin of England or Amadis of Gaul; but Master Nicholas, the barber of the same village, was in the habit of saying that no one could come up to the Knight of Phoebus, and that if anyone *could* compare with him it was Don Galaor, brother of Amadis of Gaul, for Galaor was ready for anything—he was none of your finical knights, who went around whimpering as his brother did, and in point of valor he did not lag behind him.

In short, our gentleman became so immersed in his reading that he spent whole nights from sundown to sunup and his days from dawn to dusk in poring over his books, until, finally, from so little sleeping and so much reading, his brain dried up and he went completely out of his mind. He had filled his imagination with everything that he had read, with enchantments, knightly encounters, battles, challenges, wounds, with tales of love and its torments, and all sorts of impossible things, and as a result had come to believe that all these fictitious happenings were true; they were more real to him than anything else in the world. He would remark that the Cid Ruy Díaz had been a very good knight, but there was no comparison between him and the Knight of the Flaming Sword, who with a single backward stroke had cut in half two fierce and monstrous giants. He preferred Bernardo del Carpio, who at Roncesvalles had slain Roland despite the charm the latter bore, availing himself of the stratagem which Hercules employed when he strangled Antaeus, the son of Earth, in his arms.

He had much good to say for Morgante who, though he belonged to the haughty, overbearing race of giants, was of an affable disposition and well brought up. But, above all, he cherished an admiration for Rinaldo of Montalbán, especially as he beheld him sallying forth from his castle to rob all those that crossed his path, or when he thought of him overseas stealing the image of Mohammed which, so the story has it, was all of gold. And he would have liked very well to have had his fill of kicking that traitor Galalón, a privilege for which he would have given his housekeeper with his niece thrown into the bargain.

At last, when his wits were gone beyond repair, he came to conceive the strangest idea that ever occurred to any madman in this world. It now appeared to him fitting and necessary, in order to win a greater amount of honor for himself and serve his country at the same time, to become a knight-errant and roam the world on horseback, in a suit of armor; he would go in quest of adventures, by way of putting into practice all that he had read in his books; he would right every manner of wrong, placing himself in situations of the greatest peril such as would redound to the eternal glory of his name. As a reward for his valor and the might of his arm, the poor fellow could already see himself crowned Emperor of Trebizond at the very least; and so, carried away by the strange pleasure that he found in such thoughts as these, he at once set about putting his plan into effect.

The first thing he did was to burnish up some old pieces of armor, left him by his great-grandfather, which for ages had lain in a corner, moldering and forgotten. He polished and adjusted them as best he could, and then he noticed that one very important thing was lacking: there was no closed helmet, but only a morion, or visorless headpiece, with turned up brim of the kind foot soldiers wore. His ingenuity, however, enabled him to remedy this, and he proceeded to fashion out of cardboard a kind of half-helmet, which, when attached to the morion, gave the appearance of a whole one. True, when he went to see if it was strong enough to withstand a good slashing blow, he was somewhat disappointed; for when he drew his sword and gave it a couple of thrusts, he succeeded only in undoing a whole week's labor. The ease with which he had hewed it to bits disturbed him no little, and he decided to make it over. This time he placed a few strips of iron on the inside, and then, convinced that it was strong enough, refrained from putting it to any further test; instead, he adopted it then and there as the finest helmet ever made.

After this, he went out to have a look at his nag; and although the animal had more *cuartos,* or cracks, in its hoof than there are quarters in a real, and more blemishes than Gonela's steed which *tantum pellis et ossa fuit,* it nonetheless looked to its master like a far better horse than Alexander's Bucephalus or the Babieca of the Cid. He spent all of four days in trying to think up a name for his mount; for—so he told himself—seeing that it belonged to so famous and worthy a knight, there was no reason why it should not have a name of equal renown. The kind of name he wanted was one that would at once indicate what the nag had been before it came to belong to a knight-errant and what its present status was; for it stood to reason that, when the master's worldly condition changed, his horse also ought to have a famous, high-sounding appellation, one suited to the new order of things and the new profession that it was to follow.

After he in his memory and imagination had made up, struck out, and discarded many names, now adding to and now subtracting from the list, he finally hit upon "Rocinante," a name that impressed him as being sonorous and at the same time indicative of what the steed had been when it was but a hack, whereas now it was nothing other than the first and foremost of all the hacks in the world.

Having found a name for his horse that pleased his fancy, he then desired to do as much for himself, and this required another week, and by the end of that period he had made up his mind that he was henceforth to be known as Don Quixote, which, as has been stated, has led the authors of this veracious history to assume that his real name must undoubtedly have been Quijada, and not Quesada as others would have it. But remembering that the valiant Amadis was not content to call himself that and nothing more, but added the name of his kingdom and fatherland that he might make it famous also, and thus came to take the name Amadis of Gaul, so our good knight chose to add his place of origin and become "Don Quixote de la Mancha"; for by this means, as he saw it, he was making very plain his lineage and was conferring honor upon his country by taking its name as his own.

And so, having polished up his armor and made the morion over into a closed helmet, and having given himself and his horse a name, he naturally found but one thing lacking still: he must seek out a lady of whom he could become enamored; for a knight-errant without a ladylove was like a tree without leaves or fruit, a body without a soul.

"If," he said to himself, "as a punishment for my sins or by a stroke of fortune I should come upon some giant hereabouts, a thing that very commonly happens to knights-errant, and if I should slay him in a hand-to-hand encounter or perhaps cut him in two, or, finally, if I should vanquish and subdue him, would it not be well to have someone to whom I may send him as a present, in order that he, if he is living, may come in, fall upon his knees in front of my sweet lady, and say in a humble and submissive tone of voice, 'I, lady, am the giant Caraculiambro, lord of the island Malindrania, who has been overcome in single combat by that knight who never can be praised enough, Don Quixote de la Mancha, the same who sent me to present myself before your Grace that your Highness may dispose of me as you see fit'?"

Oh, how our good knight reveled in this speech, and more than ever when he came to think of the name that he should give his lady! As the story goes, there was a very good-looking farm girl who lived near by, with whom he had once been smitten, although it is generally believed that she never knew or suspected it. Her name was Aldonza Lorenzo, and it seemed to him that she was the one upon whom he should bestow the title of mistress of his thoughts. For her he wished a name that should not be incongruous with his own and that would convey the suggestion of a princess or a great lady; and, accordingly, he resolved to call her "Dulcinea del Toboso," she being a native of that place. A musical name to his ears, out of the ordinary and significant, like the others he had chosen for himself and his appurtenances.

## Chapter II.

Which treats of the first sally that the ingenious Don Quixote made from his native heath.

Having, then, made all these preparations, he did not wish to lose any time in putting his plan into effect, for he could not but blame himself for what the world was losing by his delay, so many were the wrongs that were to be righted, the grievances to be redressed, the abuses to be done away with, and the duties to be performed. Accordingly, without informing anyone of his intention and without letting anyone see him, he set out one morning before daybreak on one of those very hot days in July. Donning all his armor, mounting Rocinante, adjusting his ill-contrived helmet, bracing his shield on his arm, and taking up his lance, he sallied forth by the back gate of his stable yard into the open countryside. It was with great contentment and joy that he saw how easily he had made a beginning toward the fulfillment of his desire.

No sooner was he out on the plain, however, than a terrible thought assailed him, one that all but caused him to abandon the enterprise he had undertaken. This occurred when he suddenly remembered that he had never formally been dubbed a knight, and so, in accordance with the law of knighthood, was not permitted to bear arms against one who had a right to that title. And even if he had been, as a novice knight he would have had to wear white armor, without any device on his shield, until he should have earned one by his exploits. These thoughts led him to waver in his purpose, but, madness prevailing over reason, he resolved to have himself knighted by the first person he met, as many others had done if what he had read in those books that he had at home was true. And so far as white armor was concerned, he would scour his own the first chance that offered until it shone whiter than any ermine. With this he became more tranquil and continued on his way, letting his horse take whatever path it chose, for he believed that therein lay the very essence of adventures.

And so we find our newly fledged adventurer jogging along and talking to himself. "Undoubtedly," he is saying, "in the days to come, when the true history of my famous deeds is published, the learned chronicler who records them, when he comes to describe my first sally so early in the morning, will put down something like this: 'No sooner had the rubicund Apollo spread over the face of the broad and spacious earth the gilded filaments of his beauteous locks, and no sooner had the little singing birds of painted plumage greeted with their sweet and mellifluous harmony the coming of the Dawn, who, leaving the soft couch of her jealous spouse, now showed herself to mortals at all the doors and balconies of the horizon that bounds La Mancha—no sooner had this happened than the famous knight, Don Quixote de la Mancha, forsaking his own downy bed and mounting his famous steed, Rocinante, fared forth and began riding over the ancient and famous Campo de Montiel.'"

And this was the truth, for he was indeed riding over that stretch of plain.

"O happy age and happy century," he went on, "in which my famous exploits shall be published, exploits worthy of being engraved in bronze, sculptured in marble, and depicted in paintings for the benefit of posterity. O wise magician, whoever you be, to whom shall fall the task of chronicling this extraordinary history of mine! I beg of you not to forget my good Rocinante, eternal companion of my wayfarings and my wanderings."

Then, as though he really had been in love: "O Princess Dulcinea, lady of this captive heart! Much wrong have you done me in thus sending me forth with your reproaches and sternly commanding me not to appear in your beauteous presence. O lady, deign to be mindful of this your subject who endures so many woes for the love of you."

And so he went on, stringing together absurdities, all of a kind that his books had taught him, imitating insofar as he was able the language of their authors. He rode slowly, and the sun came up so swiftly and with so much heat that it would have been sufficient to melt his brains if he had had any. He had been on the road almost the entire day without anything happening that is worthy of being set down here; and he was on the verge of despair, for he wished to meet someone at once with whom he might try the valor of his good right arm. Certain authors say that his first adventure was that of Puerto Lápice, while others state that it was that of the windmills; but in this particular instance I am in a position to affirm what I have read in the annals of La Mancha; and that is to the effect that he went all that day until nightfall, when he and his hack found themselves tired to death and famished. Gazing all around him to see if he could discover some castle or shepherd's hut where he might take shelter and attend to his pressing needs, he caught sight of an inn not far off the road along which they were traveling, and this to him was like a star guiding him not merely to the gates, but rather, let us say, to the palace of redemption. Quickening his pace, he came up to it just as night was falling.

By chance there stood in the doorway two lasses of the sort known as "of the district"; they were on their way to Seville in the company of some mule drivers who were spending the night in the inn. Now, everything that this adventurer of ours thought, saw, or imagined seemed to him to be directly out of one of the storybooks he had read, and so, when he caught sight of the inn, it at once became a castle with its four turrets and its pinnacles of gleaming silver, not to speak of the draw-bridge and moat and all the other things that are commonly supposed to go with a castle. As he rode up to it, he accordingly reined in Rocinante and sat there waiting for a dwarf to appear upon the battlements and blow his trumpet by way of announcing the arrival of a knight. The dwarf, however, was slow in coming, and as Rocinante was anxious to reach the stable, Don Quixote drew up to the door of the hostelry and surveyed the two merry maidens, who to him were a pair of beauteous damsels or gracious ladies taking their ease at the castle gate.

And then a swineherd came along, engaged in rounding up his drove of hogs—for, without any apology, that is what they were. He gave a blast on his horn to bring them together, and this at once became for Don Quixote just what he wished it to be: some dwarf who was heralding his coming; and so it was with a vast deal of satisfaction that he presented himself before the ladies in question, who, upon beholding a man in full armor like this, with lance and buckler, were filled with fright and made as if to flee indoors. Realizing that they were afraid, Don Quixote raised his pasteboard visor and revealed his withered, dust-covered face.

"Do not flee, your Ladyships," he said to them in a courteous manner and gentle voice. "You need not fear that any wrong will be done you, for it is not in accordance with the order of knighthood which I profess to wrong anyone, much less such highborn damsels as your appearance shows you to be."

The girls looked at him, endeavoring to scan his face, which was half hidden by his ill-made visor. Never having heard women of their profession called damsels before, they were unable to restrain their laughter, at which Don Quixote took offense.

"Modesty," he observed, "well becomes those with the dower of beauty, and, moreover, laughter that has not good cause is a very foolish thing. But I do not say this to be discourteous or to hurt your feelings; my only desire is to serve you."

The ladies did not understand what he was talking about, but felt more than ever like laughing at our knight's unprepossessing figure. This increased his annoyance, and there is no telling what would have happened if at that moment the innkeeper had not come out. He was very fat and very peaceably inclined; but upon sighting this grotesque personage clad in bits of armor that were quite as oddly matched as were his bridle, lance, buckler, and corselet, mine host was not at all indisposed to join the lasses in their merriment. He was suspicious, however, of all this paraphernalia and decided that it would be better to keep a civil tongue in his head.

"If, Sir Knight," he said, "your Grace desires a lodging, aside from a bed—for there is none to be had in this inn—you will find all else that you may want in great abundance."

When Don Quixote saw how humble the governor of the castle was—for he took the innkeeper and his inn to be no less than that—he replied, "For me, Sir Castellan, anything will do, since

Arms are my only ornament,
My only rest the fight, etc."

The landlord thought that the knight had called him a castellan because he took him for one of those worthies of Castile, whereas the truth was, he was an Andalusian from the beach of Sanlúcar, no less a thief than Cacus himself, and as full of tricks as a student or a page boy.

"In that case," he said,

"Your bed will be the solid rock,
Your sleep: to watch all night.

This being so, you may be assured of finding beneath this roof enough to keep you awake for a whole year, to say nothing of a single night."

With this, he went up to hold the stirrup for Don Quixote, who encountered much difficulty in dismounting, not having broken his fast all day long. The knight then directed his host to take good care of the steed, as it was the best piece of horseflesh in all the world. The innkeeper looked it over, and it did not impress him as being half as good as Don Quixote had said it was. Having stabled the animal, he came back to see what his guest would have and found the latter being relieved of his armor by the damsels, who by now had made their peace with the new arrival. They had already removed his breastplate and backpiece but had no idea how they were going to open his gorget or get his improvised helmet off. That piece of armor had been tied on with green ribbons which it would be necessary to cut, since the knots could not be undone, but he would not hear of this, and so spent all the rest of that night with his headpiece in place, which gave him the weirdest, most laughable appearance that could be imagined.

Don Quixote fancied that these wenches who were assisting him must surely be the chatelaine and other ladies of the castle, and so proceeded to address them very gracefully and with much wit:

"Never was knight so served
By any noble dame
As was Don Quixote
When from his village he came,
With damsels to wait on his every need
While princesses cared for his hack . . .

"By hack," he explained, "is meant my steed Rocinante, for that is his name, and mine is Don Quixote de la Mancha. I had no intention of revealing my identity until my exploits done in your service should have made me known to you; but the necessity of adapting to present circumstances that old ballad of Lancelot has led to your becoming acquainted with it prematurely. However, the time will come when your Ladyships shall command and I will obey and with the valor of my good right arm show you how eager I am to serve you."

The young women were not used to listening to speeches like this and had not a word to say, but merely asked him if he desired to eat anything.

"I could eat a bite of something, yes," replied Don Quixote. "Indeed, I feel that a little food would go very nicely just now."

He thereupon learned that, since it was Friday, there was nothing to be had in all the inn except a few portions of codfish, which in Castile is called *abadejo,* in Andalusia *bacalao,* in some places *curadillo,* and elsewhere *truchuella* or small trout. Would his Grace, then, have some small trout, seeing that was all there was that they could offer him?

"If there are enough of them," said Don Quixote, "they will take the place of a trout, for it is all one to me whether I am given in change eight reales or one piece of eight. What is more, those small trout may be like veal, which is better than beef, or like kid, which is better than goat. But however that may be, bring them on at once, for the weight and burden of arms is not to be borne without inner sustenance."

Placing the table at the door of the hostelry, in the open air, they brought the guest a portion of badly soaked and worse cooked codfish and a piece of bread as black and moldy as the suit of armor that he wore. It was a mirth-provoking sight to see him eat, for he still had his helmet on with his visor fastened, which made it impossible for him to put anything into his mouth with his hands, and so it was necessary for one of the girls to feed him. As for giving him anything to drink, that would have been out of the question if the innkeeper had not hollowed out a reed, placing one end in Don Quixote's mouth while through the other end he poured the wine. All this the knight bore very patiently rather than have them cut the ribbons of his helmet.

At this point a gelder of pigs approached the inn, announcing his arrival with four or five blasts on his horn, all of which confirmed Don Quixote in the belief that this was indeed a famous castle, for what was this if not music that they were playing for him? The fish was trout, the bread was of the finest, the wenches were ladies, and the innkeeper was the castellan. He was convinced that he had been right in his resolve to sally forth and roam the world at large, but there was one thing that still distressed him greatly, and that was the fact that he had not as yet been dubbed a knight; as he saw it, he could not legitimately engage in any adventure until he had received the order of knighthood.

## from Chapter VII.

Of the second sally of our good knight Don Quixote de la Mancha.

. . . After that he remained at home very tranquilly for a couple of weeks, without giving sign of any desire to repeat his former madness. During that time he had the most pleasant conversations with his two old friends, the curate and the barber, on the point he had raised to the effect that what the world needed most was knights-errant and a revival of chivalry. The curate would occasionally contradict him and again would give in, for it was only by means of this artifice that he could carry on a conversation with him at all.

In the meanwhile Don Quixote was bringing his powers of persuasion to bear upon a farmer who lived near by, a good man—if this title may be applied to one who is poor—but with very few wits in his head. The short of it is, by pleas and promises, he got the hapless rustic to agree to ride forth with him and serve him as his squire. Among other things, Don Quixote told him that he ought to be more than willing to go, because no telling what adventure might occur which would win them an island, and then he (the farmer) would be left to be the governor of it. As a result of these and other similar assurances, Sancho Panza forsook his wife and children and consented to take upon himself the duties of squire to his neighbor.

Next, Don Quixote set out to raise some money, and by selling this thing and pawning that and getting the worst of the bargain always, he finally scraped together a reasonable amount. He also asked a friend of his for the loan of a buckler and patched up his broken helmet as well as he could. He advised his squire, Sancho, of the day and hour when they were to take the road and told him to see to laying in a supply of those things that were most necessary, and, above all, not to forget the saddlebags. Sancho replied that he would see to all this and added that he was also thinking of taking along with him a very good ass that he had, as he was not much used to going on foot.

With regard to the ass, Don Quixote had to do a little thinking, trying to recall if any knight-errant had ever had a squire thus asininely mounted. He could not think of any, but nevertheless he decided to take Sancho with the intention of providing him with a nobler steed as soon as occasion offered; he had but to appropriate the horse of the first discourteous knight he met. Having furnished himself with shirts and all the other things that the innkeeper had recommended, he and Panza rode forth one night unseen by anyone and without taking leave of wife and children, housekeeper or niece. They went so far that by the time morning came they were safe from discovery had a hunt been started for them.

Mounted on his ass, Sancho Panza rode along like a patriarch, with saddlebags and flask, his mind set upon becoming governor of that island that his master had promised him. Don Quixote determined to take the same route and road over the Campo de Montiel that he had followed on his first journey; but he was not so uncomfortable this time, for it was early morning and the sun's rays fell upon them slantingly and accordingly did not tire them too much.

"Look, Sir Knight-errant," said Sancho, "your Grace should not forget that island you promised me; for no matter how big it is, I'll be able to govern it right enough."

"I would have you know, friend Sancho Panza," replied Don Quixote, "that among the knights-errant of old it was a very common custom to make their squires governors of the islands or the kingdoms that they won, and I am resolved that in my case so pleasing a usage shall not fall into desuetude. I even mean to go them one better; for they very often, perhaps most of the time, waited until their squires were old men who had had their fill of serving their masters during bad days and worse nights, whereupon they would give them the title of count, or marquis at most, of some valley or province more or less. But if you live and I live, it well may be that within a week I shall win some kingdom with others dependent upon it, and it will be the easiest thing in the world to crown you king of one of them. You need not marvel at this, for all sorts of unforeseen things happen to knights like me, and I may readily be able to give you even more than I have promised."

"In that case," said Sancho Panza, "if by one of those miracles of which your Grace was speaking I should become king, I would certainly send for Juana Gutiérrez, my old lady, to come and be my queen, and the young ones could be infantes."

"There is no doubt about it," Don Quixote assured him.

"Well, I doubt it," said Sancho, "for I think that even if God were to rain kingdoms upon the earth, no crown would sit well on the head of Mari Gutiérrez, for I am telling you, sir, as a queen she is not worth two maravedis. She would do better as a countess, God help her."

"Leave everything to God, Sancho," said Don Quixote, "and he will give you whatever is most fitting; but I trust you will not be so pusillanimous as to be content with anything less than the title of viceroy."

"That I will not," said Sancho Panza, "especially seeing that I have in your Grace so illustrious a master who can give me all that is suitable to me and all that I can manage."

## Chapter VIII.

Of the good fortune which the valorous Don Quixote had in the terrifying and never-before-imagined adventure of the windmills, along with other events that deserve to be suitably recorded.

At this point they caught sight of thirty or forty windmills which were standing on the plain there, and no sooner had Don Quixote laid eyes upon them than he turned to his squire and said, "Fortune is guiding our affairs better than we could have wished; for you see there before you, friend Sancho Panza, some thirty or more lawless giants with whom I mean to do battle. I shall deprive them of their lives, and with the spoils from this encounter we shall begin to enrich ourselves; for this is righteous warfare, and it is a great service to God to remove so accursed a breed from the face of the earth."

"What giants?" said Sancho Panza.

"Those that you see there," replied his master, "those with the long arms some of which are as much as two leagues in length."

"But look, your Grace, those are not giants but windmills, and what appear to be arms are their wings which, when whirled in the breeze, cause the millstone to go."

"It is plain to be seen," said Don Quixote, "that you have had little experience in this matter of adventures. If you are afraid, go off to one side and say your prayers while I am engaging them in fierce, unequal combat."

Saying this, he gave spurs to his steed Rocinante, without paying any heed to Sancho's warning that these were truly windmills and not giants that he was riding forth to attack. Nor even when he was close upon them did he perceive what they really were, but shouted at the top of his lungs, "Do not seek to flee, cowards and vile creatures that you are, for it is but a single knight with whom you have to deal!"

At that moment a little wind came up and the big wings began turning.

"Though you flourish as many arms as did the giant Briareus," said Don Quixote when he perceived this, "you still shall have to answer to me."

He thereupon commended himself with all his heart to his lady Dulcinea, beseeching her to succor him in this peril; and, being well covered with his shield and with his lance at rest, he bore down upon them at a full gallop and fell upon the first mill that stood in his way, giving a thrust at the wing, which was whirling at such a speed that his lance was broken into bits and both horse and horseman went rolling over the plain, very much battered indeed. Sancho upon his donkey came hurrying to his master's assistance as fast as he could, but when he reached the spot, the knight was unable to move, so great was the shock with which he and Rocinante had hit the ground.

"God help us!" exclaimed Sancho, "did I not tell your Grace to look well, that those were nothing but windmills, a fact which no one could fail to see unless he had other mills of the same sort in his head?"

"Be quiet, friend Sancho," said Don Quixote. "Such are the fortunes of war, which more than any other are subject to constant change. What is more, when I come to think of it, I am sure that this must be the work of that magician Frestón, the one who robbed me of my study and my books, and who has thus changed the giants into windmills in order to deprive me of the glory of overcoming them, so great is the enmity that he bears me; but in the end his evil arts shall not prevail against this trusty sword of mine."

"May God's will be done," was Sancho Panza's response. And with the aid of his squire the knight was once more mounted on Rocinante, who stood there with one shoulder half out of joint. And so, speaking of the adventure that had just befallen them, they continued along the Puerto Lápice highway; for there, Don Quixote said, they could not fail to find many and varied adventures, this being a much traveled thoroughfare. The only thing was, the knight was exceedingly downcast over the loss of his lance.

"I remember," he said to his squire, "having read of a Spanish knight by the name of Diego Pérez de Vargas, who, having broken his sword in battle, tore from an oak a heavy bough or branch and with it did such feats of valor that day, and pounded so many Moors, that he came to be known as Machuca, and he and his descendants from that day forth have been called Vargas y Machuca. I tell you this because I too intend to provide myself with just such a bough as the one he wielded, and with it I propose to do such exploits that you shall deem yourself fortunate to have been found worthy to come with me and behold and witness things that are almost beyond belief."

"God's will be done," said Sancho. "I believe everything that your Grace says; but straighten yourself up in the saddle a little, for you seem to be slipping down on one side, owing, no doubt, to the shaking-up that you received in your fall."

"Ah, that is the truth," replied Don Quixote.

* * *

. . . Meanwhile Don Quixote, as we have said, was speaking to the lady in the coach.

"Your beauty, my lady, may now dispose of your person as best may please you, for the arrogance of your abductors lies upon the ground, overthrown by this good arm of mine; and in order that you may not pine to know the name of your liberator, I may inform you that I am Don Quixote de la Mancha, knight-errant and adventurer and captive of the peerless and beauteous Doña Dulcinea del Toboso. In payment of the favor which you have received from me, I ask nothing other than that you return to El Toboso and on my behalf pay your respects to this lady, telling her that it was I who set you free."

One of the squires accompanying those in the coach, a Biscayan, was listening to Don Quixote's words, and when he saw that the knight did not propose to let the coach proceed upon its way but was bent upon having it turn back to El Toboso, he promptly went up to him, seized his lance, and said to him in bad Castilian and worse Biscayan, "Go, *caballero,* and bad luck go with you; for by the God that created me, if you do not let this coach pass, me kill you or me no Biscayan."

Don Quixote heard him attentively enough and answered him very mildly, "If you were a *caballero,* which you are not, I should already have chastised you, wretched creature, for your foolhardiness and your impudence."

"Me no *caballero?*" cried the Biscayan. "Me swear to God, you lie like a Christian. If you will but lay aside your lance and unsheath your sword, you will soon see that you are carrying water to the cat! Biscayan on land, gentleman at sea, but a gentleman in spite of the devil, and you lie if you say otherwise."

"'You shall see as to that presently,' said Agrajes," Don Quixote quoted. He cast his lance to the earth, drew his sword, and, taking his buckler on his arm, attacked the Biscayan with intent to slay him. The latter, when he saw his adversary approaching, would have liked to dismount from his mule, for she was one of the worthless sort that are let for hire and he had no confidence in her; but there was no time for this, and so he had no choice but to draw his own sword in turn and make the best of it. However, he was near enough to the coach to be able to snatch a cushion from it to serve him as a shield; and then they fell upon each other as though they were mortal enemies. The rest of those present sought to make peace between them but did not succeed, for the Biscayan with his disjointed phrases kept muttering that if they did not let him finish the battle then he himself would have to kill his mistress and anyone else who tried to stop him.

The lady inside the carriage, amazed by it all and trembling at what she saw, directed her coachman to drive on a little way; and there from a distance she watched the deadly combat, in the course of which the Biscayan came down with a great blow on Don Quixote's shoulder, over the top of the latter's shield, and had not the knight been clad in armor, it would have split him to the waist.

Feeling the weight of this blow, Don Quixote cried out, "O lady of my soul, Dulcinea, flower of beauty, succor this your champion who out of gratitude for your many favors finds himself in so perilous a plight!" To utter these words, lay bold of his sword, cover himself with his buckler, and attack the Biscayan was but the work of a moment; for he was now resolved to risk everything upon a single stroke.

As he saw Don Quixote approaching with so dauntless a bearing, the Biscayan was well aware of his adversary's courage and forthwith determined to imitate the example thus set him. He kept himself protected with his cushion, but he was unable to get his she-mule to budge to one side or the other, for the beast, out of sheer exhaustion and being, moreover, unused to such childish play, was incapable of taking a single step. And so, then, as has been stated, Don Quixote was approaching the wary Biscayan, his sword raised on high and with the firm resolve of cleaving his enemy in two; and the Biscayan was awaiting the knight in the same posture, cushion in front of him and with uplifted sword.

All the bystanders were trembling with suspense at what would happen as a result of the terrible blows that were threatened, and the lady in the coach and her maids were making a thousand vows and offerings to all the images and shrines in Spain, praying that God would save them all and the lady's squire from this great peril that confronted them.

But the unfortunate part of the matter is that at this very point the author of the history breaks off and leaves the battle pending, excusing himself upon the ground that he has been unable to find anything else in writing concerning the exploits of Don Quixote beyond those already set forth. It is true, on the other hand, that the second author of this work could not bring himself to believe that so unusual a chronicle would have been consigned to oblivion, nor that the learned ones of La Mancha were possessed of so little curiosity as not to be able to discover in their archives or registry offices certain papers that have to do with this famous knight. Being convinced of this, he did not despair of coming upon the end of this pleasing story, and Heaven favoring him, he did find it, as shall be related in the second part.

## Chapter IX.

In which is concluded and brought to an end the stupendous battle between the gallant Biscayan and the valiant Knight of La Mancha.

In the first part of the history we left the valorous Biscayan and the famous Don Quixote with swords unsheathed and raised aloft, about to let fall furious slashing blows which, had they been delivered fairly and squarely, would at the very least have split them in two and laid them wide open from top to bottom like a pomegranate; and it was at this doubtful point that the pleasing chronicle came to a halt and broke off, without the author's informing us as to where the rest of it might be found.

I was deeply grieved by such a circumstance, and the pleasure I had had in reading so slight a portion was turned into annoyance as I thought of how difficult it would be to come upon the greater part which it seemed to me must still be missing. It appeared impossible and contrary to all good precedent that so worthy a knight should not have had some scribe to take upon himself the task of writing an account of these unheard-of exploits; for that was something that had happened to none of the knights-errant who, as the saying has it, had gone forth in quest of adventures, seeing that each of them had one or two chroniclers, as if ready at hand, who not only had set down their deeds, but had depicted their most trivial thoughts and amiable weaknesses, however well concealed they might be. The good knight of La Mancha surely could not have been so unfortunate as to have lacked what Platir and others like him had in abundance. And so I could not bring myself to believe that this gallant history could have remained thus lopped off and mutilated, and I could not but lay the blame upon the malignity of time, that devourer and consumer of all things, which must either have consumed it or kept it hidden.

On the other hand, I reflected that inasmuch as among the knight's books had been found such modern works as *The Disenchantments of Jealousy* and *The*

*Nymphs and Shepherds of Henares,* his story likewise must be modern, and that even though it might not have been written down, it must remain in the memory of the good folk of his village and the surrounding ones. This thought left me somewhat confused and more than ever desirous of knowing the real and true story, the whole story, of the life and wondrous deeds of our famous Spaniard, Don Quixote, light and mirror of the chivalry of La Mancha, the first in our age and in these calamitous times to devote himself to the hardships and exercises of knight-errantry and to go about righting wrongs, succoring widows, and protecting damsels—damsels such as those who, mounted upon their palfreys and with riding-whip in hand, in full possession of their virginity, were in the habit of going from mountain to mountain and from valley to valley; for unless there were some villain, some rustic with an ax and hood, or some monstrous giant to force them, there were in times past maiden ladies who at the end of eighty years, during all which time they had not slept for a single day beneath a roof, would go to their graves as virginal as when their mothers had borne them.

If I speak of these things, it is for the reason that in this and in all other respects our gallant Quixote is deserving of constant memory and praise, and even I am not to be denied my share of it for my diligence and the labor to which I put myself in searching out the conclusion of this agreeable narrative; although if heaven, luck, and circumstance had not aided me, the world would have had to do without the pleasure and the pastime which anyone may enjoy who will read this work attentively for an hour or two. The manner in which it came about was as follows:

I was standing one day in the Alcaná, or market place, of Toledo when a lad came up to sell some old notebooks and other papers to a silk weaver who was there. As I am extremely fond of reading anything, even though it be but the scraps of paper in the streets, I followed my natural inclination and took one of the books, whereupon I at once perceived that it was written in characters which I recognized as Arabic. I recognized them, but reading them was another thing; and so I began looking around to see if there was any Spanish-speaking Moor near by who would be able to read them for me. It was not very hard to find such an interpreter, nor would it have been even if the tongue in question had been an older and a better one. To make a long story short, chance brought a fellow my way; and when I told him what it was I wished and placed the book in his hands, he opened it in the middle and began reading and at once fell to laughing. When I asked him what the cause of his laughter was, he replied that it was a note which had been written in the margin.

I besought him to tell me the content of the note, and he, laughing still, went on, "As I told you, it is something in the margin here: 'This Dulcinea del Toboso, so often referred to, is said to have been the best hand at salting pigs of any woman in all La Mancha.'"

No sooner had I heard the name Dulcinea del Toboso than I was astonished and held in suspense, for at once the thought occurred to me that those notebooks must contain the history of Don Quixote. With this in mind I urged him to read me the title, and he proceeded to do so, turning the Arabic into Castilian upon the spot: *History of Don Quixote de la Mancha, Written by Cid Hamete Benengeli, Arabic Historian.* It was all I could do to conceal my satisfaction and, snatching them from the silk weaver, I bought from the lad all the papers and notebooks that he had for half a real; but if he had known or suspected how very much I wanted them, he might well have had more than six reales for them.

The Moor and I then betook ourselves to the cathedral cloister, where I requested him to translate for me into the Castilian tongue all the books that had to do with Don Quixote, adding nothing and subtracting nothing; and I offered him whatever payment he desired. He was content with two arrobas of raisins and two fanegas of wheat and promised to translate them well and faithfully and with all dispatch. However, in order to facilitate matters, and also because I did not wish to let such a find as this out of my hands, I took the fellow home with me, where in a little more than a month and a half he translated the whole of the work just as you will find it set down here.

In the first of the books there was a very lifelike picture of the battle between Don Quixote and the Biscayan, the two being in precisely the same posture as described in the history, their swords upraised, the one covered by his buckler, the other with his cushion. As for the Biscayan's mule, you could see at the distance of a crossbow shot that it was one for hire. Beneath the Biscayan there was a rubric which read: "Don Sancho de Azpeitia," which must undoubtedly have been his name; while beneath the feet of Rocinante was another inscription: "Don Quixote." Rocinante was marvelously portrayed: so long and lank, so lean and flabby, so extremely consumptive-looking that one could well understand the justness and propriety with which the name of "hack" had been bestowed upon him.

Alongside Rocinante stood Sancho Panza, holding the halter of his ass, and below was the legend: "Sancho Zancas." The picture showed him with a big belly, a short body, and long shanks, and that must have been where he got the names of Panza y Zancas by which he is a number of times called in the course of the history. There are other small details that might be mentioned, but they are of little importance and have nothing to do with the truth of the story—and no story is bad so long as it is true.

If there is any objection to be raised against the veracity of the present one, it can be only that the author was an Arab, and that nation is known for its lying propensities; but even though they be our enemies, it may readily be understood that they would more likely have detracted from, rather than added to, the chronicle. So it seems to me, at any rate; for whenever he might and should deploy the resources of his pen in praise of so worthy a knight, the author appears to take pains to pass over the matter in silence; all of which in my opinion is ill done and ill conceived, for it should be the duty of historians to be exact, truthful, and dispassionate, and neither interest nor fear nor rancor nor affection should swerve them from the path of truth, whose mother is history, rival of time, depository of deeds, witness of the past, exemplar and adviser to the present, and the future's counselor. In this work, I am sure, will be found all that could be desired in the way of pleasant reading; and if it is lacking in any way, I maintain that this is the fault of that hound of an author rather than of the subject.

But to come to the point, the second part, according to the translation, began as follows:

As the two valorous and enraged combatants stood there, swords upraised and poised on high, it seemed from their bold mien as if they must surely be threatening heaven, earth, and hell itself. The first to let fall a blow was the choleric Biscayan, and he came down with such force and fury that, had not his sword been deflected in mid-air, that single stroke would have sufficed to put an end to this fearful combat and to all our knight's adventures at the same time; but fortune, which was reserving him for greater things, turned aside his adversary's blade in such a manner that, even though it fell upon his left shoulder, it did him no other damage than to strip him completely of his armor on that side, carrying with it a good part of his helmet along with half an ear, the headpiece clattering to the ground with a dreadful din, leaving its wearer in a sorry state.

Heaven help me! Who could properly describe the rage that now entered the heart of our hero of La Mancha as he saw himself treated in this fashion? It may merely be said that he once more reared himself in the stirrups, laid hold of his sword with both hands, and dealt the Biscayan such a blow, over the cushion and upon the head, that, even so good a defense proving useless, it was as if a mountain had fallen upon his enemy. The latter now began bleeding through the mouth, nose, and ears; he seemed about to fall from his mule, and would have fallen, no doubt, if he had not grasped the beast about the neck, but at that moment his feet slipped from the stirrups and his arms let go, and the mule, frightened by the terrible blow, began running across the plain, hurling its rider to the earth with a few quick plunges.

Don Quixote stood watching all this very calmly. When he saw his enemy fall, he leaped from his horse, ran over very nimbly, and thrust the point of his sword into the Biscayan's eyes, calling upon him at the same time to surrender or otherwise he would cut off his head. The Biscayan was so bewildered that he was unable to utter a single word in reply, and things would have gone badly with him, so blind was Don Quixote in his rage, if the ladies of the coach, who up to then had watched the struggle in dismay, had not come up to him at this point and begged him with many blandishments to do them the very great favor of sparing their squire's life.

To which Don Quixote replied with much haughtiness and dignity, "Most certainly, lovely ladies, I shall be very happy to do that which you ask of me, but upon one condition and understanding, and that is that this knight promise me that he will go to El Toboso and present himself in my behalf before Doña Dulcinea, in order that she may do with him as she may see fit."

Trembling and disconsolate, the ladies did not pause to discuss Don Quixote's request, but without so much as inquiring who Dulcinea might be they promised him that the squire would fulfill that which was commanded of him.

"Very well, then, trusting in your word, I will do him no further harm, even though he has well deserved it."

## Chapter X.

Of the pleasing conversation that took place between Don Quixote and Sancho Panza, his squire.

By this time Sancho Panza had got to his feet, somewhat the worse for wear as the result of the treatment he had received from the friars' lads. He had been watching the battle attentively and praying God in his heart to give the victory to his master, Don Quixote, in order that he, Sancho, might gain some island where he could go to be governor as had been promised him. Seeing now that the combat was over and the knight was returning to mount Rocinante once more, he went up to hold the stirrup for him; but first he fell on his knees in front of him and, taking his hand, kissed it and said, "May your Grace be pleased, Señor Don Quixote, to grant me the governorship of that island which you have won in this deadly affray; for however large it may be, I feel that I am indeed capable of governing it as well as any man in this world has ever done."

To which Don Quixote replied, "Be advised, brother Sancho, that this adventure and other similar ones have nothing to do with islands; they are affairs of the crossroads in which one gains nothing more than a broken head or an ear the less. Be patient, for there will be others which will not only make you a governor, but more than that."

# *from Part II*

## Chapter X.

Wherein is related the ingenuity that Sancho displayed by laying a spell upon the lady Dulcinea, with other events as outlandish as they are true.

When the author of this great history comes to relate the events set forth in the present chapter, he remarks that he would prefer to pass over them in silence, as he fears that he will not be believed. For Don Quixote's madness here reaches a point beyond which the imagination cannot go, and even exceeds that point by a couple of bowshots. Nevertheless, in spite of such fear and misgiving, the historian has written down the events in question just as they happened, without adding to the chronicle in any way or holding back one particle of the truth, being in the end wholly unconcerned with the objections that might be raised by those who would make him out to be a liar. And in doing so he was right; for while the truth may run thin, it never breaks, and always rises above falsehood as oil does above water.

The history, then, goes on to state that, after he had hidden himself in the wood, forest, or oak grove near El Toboso, Don Quixote ordered Sancho to return to the city and not to appear in his master's presence again until he should first have spoken in person to the lady Dulcinea and begged her to be pleased to grant her captive knight a glimpse of her, that she might bestow her blessing upon him, which would enable him to hope for a most fortunate conclusion to all his difficult enterprises and undertakings. Taking upon himself this task that had been assigned him, the squire promised to bring back as fair a reply as he had on the previous occasion.

"Go, my son," Don Quixote said to him, "and do not let yourself be dazed by the light from that sun of beauty that you go to seek. Ah, happy are you above all the squires in the world! Be sure to remember, and do not let it slip your mind, just how she receives you. Note whether she changes color while you are giving her my message and if she is restless and perturbed upon hearing my name. It may be that you will find her seated in sumptuous and royal state, in which case she will perhaps fall back upon a cushion; or if she be standing, see if she rests first upon one foot and then upon the other. Observe if she repeats two or three times the answer she gives you and if her mood varies from mildness to austerity, from the harsh to the amorous. She may raise a hand to her hair to smooth it back, though it be not disordered.

"In short, my son, note her every action and movement. If you report to me faithfully all these things, I shall be able to make out the hidden secret of her heart and discover how she feels with regard to my love; for I may tell you, Sancho, if you do not know it already, that among lovers exterior signs of this sort are the most reliable couriers that there are, bringing news of what goes on inside the heart. Go, then, my friend and may a better fortune than mine be your guide. May you be more successful than I dare hope in this fearful and bitter solitude in which you leave me."

"I go," said Sancho, "and I will return shortly. In the meantime, my master, cheer up that little heart of yours; for right now you must have one no bigger than a hazelnut. Remember what they say, that a stout heart breaks bad luck, and where there is no bacon there are no pegs. And they also say that when you least expect it the hare leaps out. I tell you this for the reason that, if we did not find my lady's palace or castle last night, now that it is day I expect to come upon it when I'm not looking for it; and once I've found it, leave it to me to deal with her."

"I must say, Sancho," replied Don Quixote, "that your proverbs always come in very pat no matter what it is we are talking about. May God give me luck and grant me that which I desire."

With this, Sancho turned his back on his master and, lashing his donkey, rode off, leaving the knight seated in the saddle, his feet in the stirrups, and leaning on his lance. We, too, shall leave Don Quixote there, full of sad and troubled thoughts, as we accompany his squire, who was quite as pensive and troubled as he. As soon as he was out of the wood, Sancho turned his head and looked back, and, perceiving that he was by this time out of sight, he dismounted from his ass and sat down at the foot of a tree, where he began talking to himself, as follows:

"Look here, brother Sancho, supposing that you tell us where your Grace is going. Is it to hunt for some ass that has strayed? No, certainly not. Then, what *are* you hunting for? I am going to hunt for a princess, nothing more or less than that, and in her I am to find the sun of beauty and all the heavens combined. And where do you think you are going to find all this, Sancho? Where? In the great city of El Toboso. Well and good; and who sent you to look for her? The famous knight, Don Quixote de la Mancha, who rights wrongs and gives food to the thirsty and drink to the hungry. That is all very well; but do you know where her house is, Sancho? My master says it will be some royal palace or proud castle. And have you ever laid eyes upon her by any chance? Neither I nor my master has ever seen her. And supposing the people of El Toboso knew that you were here luring their princesses and disturbing their ladies, don't you think it would be only right and proper if they came and clubbed your ribs without leaving a whole bone in your body? And, to tell the truth, they would be right, if you did not take into account that I am sent here under orders and that

*A messenger you are, my friend,*
*No blame belongs to you.*

But don't put your trust in that, Sancho, for the Manchegan folks are as hot-tempered as they are honest and will not put up with anything from anybody. God help you if they get wind of you, for it will mean bad luck. Out with you, villian! Let the bolt fall! Am I to go looking for a cat with three feet just to please another? Hunting for Dulcinea in El Toboso is like trying to find Marica in Rávena or a bachelor in Salamanca. It was the devil, it was the devil himself and nobody else, that got me into this."

Such was Sancho's soliloquy. It had led him to no conclusion thus far, and so he continued:

"Well, there is a remedy for everything except death, beneath whose yoke we all have to pass, however heavy it may weigh upon us, when life draws to a close. I have seen by a thousand signs that this master of mine is a madman who ought to be in a cell, yet I am not behind him in that respect, seeing that I am foolish enough to follow and serve him. That is certainly the case if there's any truth in the old saying, 'Tell me what company you keep and I'll tell you who you are,' or that other one, 'Not with whom you are bred but with whom you are fed.' And seeing that he is a madman, and that he is there can be no doubt—so mad that he takes one thing for another, white for black and black for white, like the time when he insisted the windmills were giants and the monks' mules were dromedaries, and the flocks of sheep were enemy armies, and other things of the same sort—seeing that this is so, it will not be hard to make him believe that the first farm girl I fall in with around here is the lady Dulcinea. If he doesn't believe it, I'll swear to it; and if he swears that it isn't so, I'll swear right back at him; and if he insists, I'll insist more than he does, so that, come what may, I'll always have my quoit on the peg. If I keep it up like that, I'll bring him around to the point where he won't be sending me on any more such errands as this, when he sees how little comes of it. Or maybe, and I imagine that this will more likely be the case, he will think that one of those wicked enchanters, who, he says, have it in for him, has changed her form just to spite and harm him."

These reflections greatly calmed Sancho Panza's mind and led him to look upon his business as already accomplished. He accordingly remained where he was until the afternoon, in order that Don Quixote might think he had had time to go to El Toboso and return. Everything went off so well with him that when he arose to mount his gray again, he saw coming toward him from the direction of the city three peasant lasses astride three ass-colts or fillies—the author is not specific on this point, but it seems more likely that they were she-asses, on which village girls commonly ride. However, it is of no great importance and there is no reason why we should stop to verify so trifling a detail.

The short of the matter is, as soon as Sancho saw the lasses he hastened to where Don Quixote was, only to find the knight sighing and uttering a thousand amorous laments.

"What is it, Sancho, my friend? Am I to be able to mark this day with a white stone or a black one?"

"It would be better," replied Sancho, "if your Grace marked it with red ocher like the lists on the professors' chairs, so that all could see it very plainly."

"That means, I take it," said Don Quixote, "that you bring good news."

"Good news it is," replied Sancho. "All your Grace has to do is to put spur to Rocinante and ride out into the open, and there you will see the lady Dulcinea del Toboso in person, who with two of her damsels has come to pay her respects to your Grace."

"Good Lord, Sancho my friend, what is this you are telling me? Take care that you do not deceive me or try to relieve with false joy my very real sadness."

"And what would I get by deceiving your Grace," Sancho wanted to know, "when you will soon enough discover for yourself whether I am speaking the truth or not? Come quickly, sir, and you will see the princess, our mistress, clad and adorned as befits one of her quality. She and her damsels are all one blaze of gold, pearls, diamonds, rubies, and brocade cloth with more than ten borders. Their hair falling loose over their shoulders are so many sunbeams playing with the wind. And, what is more, they come mounted upon three piebald cackneys, the finest you ever saw."

"*Hackneys,* you mean to say, Sancho."

"*Hackneys* or *cackneys,* it makes very little difference," replied Sancho. "No matter what their mounts, they are the finest ladies you could wish for, especially the Princess Dulcinea, my lady, who stuns your senses."

"Come, Sancho, my son," said Don Quixote, "let us go. As a reward for the news you bring me, as good as it is unexpected, I promise you the best spoils that I win in my first adventure; and in case this is not enough to satisfy you, I will send you the colts which my three mares will give me this year—as you know, they are now out on the village common and are about to foal."

"I will take the colts," said Sancho, "for the spoils from that first adventure are rather uncertain."

At this point they emerged from the wood close to where the three village lasses were. Gazing up and down the highway that led to El Toboso, Don Quixote was completely bewildered, since all he could see was these country maidens. He then asked Sancho if the princess and her damsels had left the city or were, perhaps, waiting there.

"What do you mean?" said Sancho. "Are your Grace's eyes in the back of your head that you cannot see that those are the ones coming there, as bright and shining as the sun itself at midday?"

"I see nothing," declared Don Quixote, "except three farm girls on three jackasses."

"Then God deliver me from the devil!" exclaimed Sancho. "Is it possible that those three hackneys, or whatever you call them, white as the driven snow, look like jackasses to your Grace? By the living God, I would tear out this beard of mine if that were true!"

"But I tell you, friend Sancho, it is as true that those are jackasses, or she-asses, as it is that I am Don Quixote and you Sancho Panza. At least, that is the way they look to me."

"Be quiet, sir," Sancho admonished him, "you must not say such a thing as that. Open those eyes of yours and come do reverence to the lady of your affections, for she draws near."

Saying this, he rode on to meet the village maids and, slipping down off his donkey, seized one of their beasts by the halter and fell on his knees in front of its rider.

"O queen and princess and duchess of beauty," he said, "may your Highness and Majesty be pleased to receive and show favor to your captive knight, who stands there as if turned to marble, overwhelmed and breathless at finding himself in your magnificent presence. I am Sancho Panza, his squire, and he is the world-weary knight Don Quixote, otherwise known as the Knight of the Mournful Countenance."

By this time Don Quixote was down on his knees beside Sancho. His eyes were fairly starting from their sockets and there was a deeply troubled look in them as he stared up at the one whom Sancho had called queen and lady; all that he could see in her was a village wench, and not a very pretty one at that, for she was round-faced and snub-nosed. He was astounded and perplexed and did not dare open his mouth. The girls were also very much astonished to behold these two men, so different in appearance, kneeling in front of one of them so that she could not pass. It was this one who most ungraciously broke the silence.

"Get out of my way," she said peevishly, "and let me pass. And bad luck go with you. For we are in a hurry."

"O princess and universal lady of El Toboso!" cried Sancho. "How can your magnanimous heart fail to melt as you behold kneeling before your sublimated presence the one who is the very pillar and support of knight-errantry?"

Hearing this, one of the others spoke up. "Whoa, there, she-ass of my father!" she said. "Wait until I curry you down. Just look at the small-fry gentry, will you, who've come to make sport of us country girls! Just as if we couldn't give them tit for tat. Be on your way and get out of ours, if you know what's good for you."

"Arise, Sancho," said Don Quixote, "for I perceive that fortune has not had her fill of evil done to me but has taken possession of all the roads by which some happiness may come to what little soul is left within me. And thou, who art all that could be desired, the sum of human gentleness and sole remedy for this afflicted heart that doth adore thee! The malign enchanter who doth persecute me hath placed clouds and cataracts upon my eyes, and for them and them alone hath transformed thy peerless beauty into the face of a lowly peasant maid; and I can only hope that he has not likewise changed my face into that of some monster by way of rendering it abhorrent in thy sight. But for all of that, hesitate not to gaze upon me tenderly and lovingly, beholding in this act of submission as I kneel before thee a tribute to thy metamorphosed beauty from this humbly worshiping heart of mine."

"Just listen to him run on, will you? My grandmother!" cried the lass.

"Enough of such gibberish. We'll thank you to let us go our way."

Sancho fell back and let her pass, being very thankful to get out of it so easily.

No sooner did she find herself free than the girl who was supposed to have Dulcinea's face began spurring her "cackney" with a spike on the end of a long stick that she carried with her, whereupon the beast set off at top speed across the meadow. Feeling the prick, which appeared to annoy it more than was ordinarily the case, the ass started cutting such capers that the lady Dulcinea was thrown to the ground. When he saw this, Don Quixote hastened to lift her up while Sancho busied himself with tightening the girths and adjusting the packsaddle which had slipped down under the animal's belly. This having been accomplished, Don Quixote was about to take his enchanted lady in his arms to place her upon the she-ass when the girl saved him the trouble by jumping up from the ground, stepping back a few paces, and taking a run for it. Placing both hands upon the crupper of the ass, she landed more lightly than a falcon upon the packsaddle and remained sitting there astride it like a man.

"In the name of Roque!" exclaimed Sancho, "our lady is like a lanner, only lighter, and can teach the cleverest Cordovan or Mexican how to mount. She cleared the back of the saddle in one jump, and without any spurs she makes her hackney run like a zebra, and her damsels are not far behind, for they all of them go like the wind."

This was the truth. Seeing Dulcinea in the saddle, the other two prodded their beasts and followed her on the run, without so much as turning their heads to look back for a distance of half a league. Don Quixote stood gazing after them, and when they were no longer visible he turned to Sancho and spoke.

"Sancho," he said, "you can see now, can you not, how the enchanters hate me? And just see how far they carry their malice and the grudge they bear me, since they would deprive me of the happiness I might derive from a sight of my mistress. The truth of the matter is, I was born to be an example of misfortune and to be the target and mark at which the arrows of ill luck are aimed and directed. I would further call your attention, Sancho, to the fact that, not content with merely transforming my Dulcinea, they must change her into a figure as low and repulsive as that village girl, robbing her at the same time of that which is so characteristic of highborn ladies, namely, their pleasing scent, which comes from always being among amber and flowers. For I would have you know, Sancho, that when Dulcinea leaped upon her hackney as you call it (though I must say, it seemed to me more like a she-ass), the odor that she gave off was one of raw garlic that made my head swim and poisoned my heart."

"O you scum!" cried Sancho. "O wretched and evil-minded enchanters! If I could but see you strung up by the gills like sardines on a reed! Great is your wisdom, great is your power, and greater yet the harm you do! Was it not enough, O villainous ones, to have changed the pearls of my lady's eyes into cork galls and her hair of purest gold into the bristles of red ox's tail? No, you had to change all of her features from good to ill, and even alter her smell, since had you not done so we might have discovered what lay concealed beneath that ugly bark. And yet, to tell the truth, I never noticed her ugliness but only her beauty, which was set off to perfection by a mole that she had on her right lip—it resembled a mustache, being surrounded by seven or eight red hairs of more than a palm in length."

"As a rule," observed Don Quixote, "moles on the face correspond to those on the body, and Dulcinea must accordingly have one of the same sort on the flat of her thigh, on the same side as the other. But hairs of the length you mentioned are very long for moles."

"Well, all I can tell you," answered Sancho, "is that there they were as big as life."

"I believe you, friend," said Don Quixote, "for everything pertaining to Dulcinea is by nature perfect and well finished, and so, if she had a hundred moles of the kind you have described, upon her they would not be moles but resplendent moons and stars. But tell me one thing, Sancho: that thing that looked to me like a packsaddle which you were adjusting, was it a flat saddle or a sidesaddle?"

"It was neither one nor the other," replied Sancho, "but a *jineta,* with a field-covering so rich that it must have been worth half a kingdom."

"Oh, if I could but have seen all that, Sancho! I tell you again, and I will tell you a thousand times, that I am the most unfortunate of men."

It was all that the rogue of a Sancho could do to keep from laughing as he listened to this foolish talk on the part of his master, who had been so ingeniously deceived. Finally, after much other talk had passed between them, they mounted their beasts once more and took the road for Saragossa, hoping to arrive there in time for a certain important feast that is celebrated in that illustrious city every year. Before they reached their destination, however, many strange and noteworthy things were to happen to them that deserve to be set down and read, as will be seen further on.

## Chapter XI.

Of the strange adventure that befell the valiant Don Quixote in connection with the cart or wagon of the Parliament of Death.

Continuing on his way, Don Quixote was deeply dejected as he thought of the cruel joke which the enchanters had played upon him by transforming his lady Dulcinea into the ugly form of the village girl, nor could he imagine any means of restoring her to her original shape. He was so absorbed in these reflections that, without noticing it, he let go Rocinante's rein, and that animal, taking advantage of the freedom granted him, now paused at every step to feed upon the abundant green grass that covered the plain. It was Sancho who awakened the knight from his daydreams.

"Sir," he said, "sorrows are made not for beasts but for men, but if men feel them too much they become beasts. Your Grace ought to pull yourself together and pick up Rocinante's rein; you ought to wake up and cheer up and show that gallant spirit that knights-errant are supposed to have. What the devil is this, anyway? What kind of weakness is it? Are we here or in France? Let Satan carry off all the Dulcineas in the world; the welfare of a single knight means more than all the spells and transformations on this earth."

"Hush, Sancho," replied Don Quixote, in not too wan a voice, "hush, I say, and do not be uttering blasphemies against that enchanted lady, seeing that I alone am to blame for her misfortunes, which are due to the envy that the wicked ones bear me."

"That is what I say," agreed Sancho. "Who saw her once and saw her now, his heart would surely weep, I vow."

"You, Sancho, may well say that," was Don Quixote's response, "for you beheld her in all the fullness of her beauty; the spell did not go so far as to disturb *your* sight or conceal her loveliness from you; it was solely against me and these eyes of mine that the force of its venom was directed. And yet, Sancho, there is one thing that occurs to me. It would seem that you have not well described her; for, unless my memory serves me wrong, you said that she had eyes like pearls, and eyes of that sort are more characteristic of the sea bream than they are of a lady. Dulcinea's eyes must be green emeralds, large and luscious, with two rainbows for brows. Take those pearls from her eyes and bestow them upon her teeth, for undoubtedly, Sancho, you must have mistaken the former for the latter."

"That may be," said Sancho, "for her beauty disturbed me as much as her ugliness did your Grace. But let us leave it to God, for he knows all that is to happen in this vale of tears, in this evil world of ours, where you scarcely find anything that does not have in it some mixture of wickedness, deceit, and villainy. But there is one thing, my master, that worries me most of all: what is your Grace going to do when you have overcome some giant or knight and wish to send him to present himself before the beautiful Dulcinea? Where is that poor giant or wretched knight going to find her? I can see them now, wandering like a lot of nitwits through the streets of El Toboso looking for my lady. Even if they were to meet her in the middle of the street, they wouldn't know her from my father."

"It may be, Sancho," said Don Quixote, "that the spell will not prevent them from recognizing her as it does me. But we shall see as to that after we shall have dispatched one or two of them to seek her out; for I shall command them to return and give me an account of what happened."

"I must say," replied Sancho, "that your Grace has spoken very much to the point, and by this means we shall be able to find out what we wish to know. And since it is only to your Grace that her beauty is hidden, the misfortune is more yours than hers. So long as the lady Dulcinea has health and happiness, we will make the best of it and go on seeking adventures, leaving it to time to work a cure, for he is the best doctor for this and other greater ills."

# part 3

# Modern Literature

THE PROBLEM OF WHAT TEXTS TO CHOOSE FOR A TRULY GLOBAL ANTHOLOGY of world literature becomes especially acute in the Modern Period with the emergence into print of many new literatures and an increasingly global system of communication. The last four centuries have seen the publication of an enormous number of extraordinary and influential writers from all the countries of the world. Because time and reading communities have not yet winnowed the possibilities into clear patterns, we have chosen texts that resonate especially well with works from the earlier eras in the anthology. We have tried to represent the main geographical areas of the globe, understanding that there are far too many interesting literary traditions for us to include them all. We have also kept in mind a particular question, one that each selection seems to answer in an important way: What is modernity?

The word "modern" is commonly used to mean "new," and most often it refers to our own era—just as it did for earlier periods—from the seventeenth to the early twentieth centuries. The term implies freshness, innovation, and exploration. It is a well-established practice, however, for historians to use "modern" to refer to a particular set of attitudes expounded most influentially by the philosophers of the seventeenth- and eighteenth-century European Enlightenment, especially in France. These ideas include the solidification of secular attitudes that had gained momentum in the European Renaissance; a radically expanded sense of the human community resulting from the voyages of exploration, discovery, and colonization by European countries in the sixteenth and seventeenth centuries; and an emerging confidence in industrial technology and science. American ideas about democracy and the rights of individuals derived most immediately from the Enlightenment, as did the widespread beliefs in the desirability and inevitability of progress and the superiority of the "objective" or scientific view of the universe. Many philosophers of the Enlightenment, driven by a desire to improve the material conditions of people's lives, saw traditional attachments to religious or mythical beliefs as superstition and as an impediment to progress. Rationality, a belief in the virtually unlimited capacities of human reason to solve the perennial problems of humankind, was prized most of all.

This Enlightenment sense of the "modern" has become characteristic of Western or Euro-American culture. For many parts of the world, however, the "modern age" dates simply from whenever that culture collided with the West, and the experience of the modern has to do with reconciling the conflicting demands of traditional culture with the sudden appearance of Western values. In Japan Matsuo Bashō looks back to a rich literary tradition and remains unaffected by foreign influences, while Natsume Sōseki struggles with the concept of the self and its attendant and conflicting demands of freedom and responsibility. It is in this sense that Sōseki can be called a "modern" Japanese author. Similarly, in China *Dream of the Red Chamber* epitomizes traditional values, while Lu Xun's story *Ah Q—The Real Story*—challenges what it means to be Chinese in a world exposed to Western values. In Africa, Chinua Achebe's *Things Fall Apart* shows traditional culture being overwhelmed and crushed by encroaching European values. In case after case, we find writers expressing the dilemma of people faced with a choice between old values and traditions that are meaningful and familiar but no longer seem to work, and powerful new values that feel alien, dehumanizing, and disruptive. In Angkarn Kalayaanaphong's works, the European insistence on individualism and the view of land as merely an inert source of exploitable raw resources clash with the Thai tradition of sacramental reality and the need for reverence toward all forms of life and toward sacred spaces in the landscape. In Japan these Western attitudes clash with Bashō's recognition that places are invested with meaning by the events that have occurred in them over time.

As travel increased and industrialism became a worldwide phenomenon, the works of most of the world's urbanized cultures gradually emerged into print, bringing their visions of reality to international attention. Europeans became aware of the traditional societies of India, China, and Japan as traders and missionaries began to bring information, texts, and works of art back home. Their many conflicts notwithstanding, Asian and European cultures began to enrich each other with new ways of imagining the world, other spiritual systems, and other technologies.

The indigenous peoples of Africa, the Americas, and Australia were suddenly exposed to the domination of alien empires hungry for the products of unexploited landscapes. Rich tribal cultures that had endured for millennia around the world came under attack by European colonizers. Landscapes and ecosystems that had seemed relatively balanced and stable for centuries or even millennia were suddenly plundered for minerals, crops, animals, and human workers. At the same time, however, European colonizers "discovered" the cultural riches of the colonized—Islamic mysticism, the ancient Hindu scriptures, the writings of Confucius, Zen Buddhism, Native American spiritual practices—and introduced them into intellectual and cultural circles in France, Italy, England, Spain, the Netherlands, and Germany. Jean-Jacques Rousseau was much taken by reports of Native American life brought back to France by Jesuit missionaries, and the American thinker Emerson was fascinated by Hindu and Confucian thought.

In East Asia during the Modern Period, concepts such as "freedom," "self," and "nation" were introduced for the first time into the vocabulary of philosophy and literature. These concepts are explored in literature, even as the nature of literature itself is undergoing radical change. In Japan, for example, the aesthetic principles of Aristotle were introduced along with Romanticism (with its strong faith in human imagination) and Naturalism (with its detached, scientific worldview). The functions of literature were expanded to include political and social critique. Even the language of literature had to be revised. In Japan and China this meant breaking away from a traditional literary language and seeking a more colloquial substitute; in India, Africa, and Latin America it often meant abandoning native languages altogether, in favor of English, French, or Spanish.

The fruits of Europe's Enlightenment were impressive, leading to advances in the contemporary world that would have struck previous ages with the kind of wonder the explorer Cortez experienced when he became the first European to see the magnificent buildings of Aztec civilization. Nevertheless, the Western doctrine of progress sent shock waves through the world; behind it lurked a unilinear, essentially imperialist conception of the history of humankind that assumed Europe and North America were the most developed or advanced cultures. The German philosopher Hegel saw history as a series of distinct phases of the human spirit that reached fulfillment only in his own age, his own country, and indeed his own philosophy. To the peoples of Asia, Africa, Australia, the Caribbean, and Central and South America, however, the situation looked quite different. To them it seemed like an invasion.

Karl Marx admired Hegel's vision of progress but was convinced that the shape of history was determined not by the advance of Hegel's "world spirit" but rather by the ultimate triumph of the working class. Indeed, class and colonial conflicts have been a hallmark of modernity since the nineteenth century, brought about by the terrible social and economic excesses of industrialism all over the globe. Modernity was thus shaped by the disturbing consciousness of rapid change, the destruction of traditional beliefs and ways of life, and the overwhelming power associated with the engines of technology and commerce. For believers in progress, it has seemed that one can either get on board this fast-moving train or be left behind by it and become a relic of the past. To traditionalists in cultures all over the world, however, change came too quickly, sacred ways were being destroyed, and the ticking of the progressivist clock needed to be ignored or even turned back. In many traditional societies, efforts were made to adopt the technological fruits of modern European civilization while retaining the most enduring of traditional practices and beliefs. Maintaining this duality has often proved very difficult, if not impossible.

Even in the West, technological progress seemed to bring in its wake a spiritual "waste land" (to use the phrase of the Anglo-American poet T.S. Eliot), as the emotional landscapes in which people had habitually lived seemed increasingly sterile in the twentieth century. The horrors of World War I seemed especially to crystallize the bleak modern worldview against which figures like Winnie, in Samuel Beckett's *Happy Days,* must continuously and desperately struggle. Throughout the Modern Period, however, literature and the other arts have been the means by which many artists tried to restore the ancient sense of the full range of human experience, not in an attempt to dominate or control reality but rather to recapture a sense of participation in the unfolding wholeness and mystery of existence. Toward the end of the European Renaissance, for example, Cervantes explored the ways in which imagination can restore a sense of magical participation in reality. In the nineteenth century, Romantics like Hölderlin looked for this lost wholeness in poetry. In the twentieth century, novelists like Marcel Proust and Virginia Woolf, faced with an increasingly mechanistic or meaningless or uncaring physical universe, searched for meaning in the power of the internal, subjective experience of ordinary individuals. Thus many European and American writers share with their Asian and African counterparts the quest for a new balance between the new and the old.

Modernist literature of the first half of the twentieth century—represented here in the work of James Joyce, Virginia Woolf, Marcel Proust, Ezra Pound, and T.S. Eliot—participates in the progressivist and even apocalyptic sense of the modern and simultaneously laments the collapse of traditional forms that results. The atonality of modern music; the success of free verse in French and American poetry, with its rejection of age-old traditions of meter and form; the antirepresentational schools of modern painting; the apparent plotlessness of much modernist fiction as seen in novels such as Virginia Woolf's *To the Lighthouse*—all these suggest that modern consciousness sees itself as reaching some final stage of development in or moving out beyond the traditional histories of the arts.

In this time period too, we have a similarity between European literature and the literatures of non-Western cultures. All strive, sometimes desperately, to find meaning in the rubble of collapsed traditions. Yet despite the march of an ever more extreme modernism, with its flaunting of conventions, the novel continues to flourish, poets continue to write in both traditional and experimental forms all over the world, and plays and essays continue to be crucial to culture everywhere. Many of these forms, however, express a bewildering sense of loss and fragmentation, as well as visions of positive new cultural realities emerging out of postcolonial experience, such as the emergence into print of the voices of ethnic groups previously unheard. In China, Vietnam, India, Japan, Argentina, Brazil, India, Chile, Jamaica, Cuba, South Africa, Nigeria, Senegal, as well as in countries in Europe and North America, writers pour forth their depictions of life in rapidly changing societies.

Chinua Achebe describes the fragmentation of traditional life in a Nigerian village; Ding Ling portrays a bleak modern China that has no connection and no resonances with its rich ancient past; Toni Morrison celebrates the vibrant culture of an African American neighborhood in Ohio that flourishes in spite of the pressures of racism all around it.

Most critics and literary historians now describe the late twentieth century as the "postmodern" period. Postmodern writers are perhaps best described as those who reject any single, unilinear narrative that claims to explain all history. From a postmodern perspective, "modernity" is a largely failed progressivist effort that characterized the scientific optimism of the Enlightenment and resulted in the murderous ideologies of our century. In some sense, then, both literary modernism and postmodernism, as defined by French thinker Jean-François Lyotard, share a common ground. "I will use the term *modern,*" Lyotard writes, "to designate any science that legitimates itself . . . [by] making an appeal to some grand narrative, such as the dialectics of Spirit, . . . the emancipation of the rational or working subject or the creation of wealth. . . . Simplifying to the extreme, I define *postmodernism* as incredulity towards metanarratives"*—that is, toward any single narrative explanation of the unfolding of history that claims to be valid for all time and for all people.

Many of the works included in this Modern section are acts of resistance against any prevailing, unilinear view of the shape of history in general or of literary history in particular. Before the Modern Period, for example, one largely unacknowledged but very tenacious "metanarrative," in Europe and elsewhere, assumes that authors are always men and that literary history should be written from the perspective of men. By the eighteenth century in England, however, the majority of writers of what was then a new literary form, the novel, were women, and one of them, Jane Austen, is now rightly considered to be one of the greatest novelists of all time. Though Jane Austen did not self-consciously draw attention to the fact that she was a woman writer, Virginia Woolf brought that awareness into sharp focus. Consider too the resurgence of women writers in Japan, after a lapse of hundreds of years since the fabulous golden age of women writers like Murasaki Shikibu in the Heian court.

Exchange between cultures, even distant cultures, has been a fact since the beginning of recorded history, but in the Modern Period we are often especially struck by the mingling or juxtaposition of many different attitudes drawn from different parts of the globe, such as we find in Ezra Pound's poetry. We often witness startling conflicts not only between different cultures, as we see in Achebe's *Things Fall Apart,* but also between traditional assumptions and contemporary experience within the same culture, as is the case with the eighteenth-century Chinese novel *Dream of the Red Chamber* and the twentieth-century stories by India's Salman Rushdie, China's Lu Xun and Korea's Sonu Hwi.

---

**The Postmodern Condition,* trans. Geoff Bennington and Brian Massumi (Minneapolis: Univ. of Minnesota Press, 1984), xxiii–xxiv.

One characteristic of the modern world is that writers have a new freedom to reach across geographical, cultural, and linguistic boundaries to find new forms and new perspectives with which to organize their work. Ezra Pound was deeply drawn to the Chinese *Book of Songs* and Japanese haiku; the Japanese writer Abe Kōbō learned the art of the short story from Kafka and Beckett; and the Chinese writer Lu Xun learned it from Chekhov and Gogol. The bigger the world seems, the smaller it gets. In our selections for the Modern section of our anthology, we can only hint at the vast, kaleidescopic, global literary scene we now inhabit, as writers continue to describe and try to make sense of the amazing heterogeneity of the modern world.

# The Modern Middle East and Africa

From the sixteenth to the early twentieth centuries, vast regions of Africa and the Middle East were subjected to European and Turkish rule. For four hundred years Ottoman Turks ruled most of the Middle East, fostering a cultural isolation that led to highly ornate, stylized, and conventional Arabic poetry and prose. Meanwhile, countries in Europe and the Americas conducted an extensive slave trade in Africa and sent missionaries and explorers into its "unknown" regions; European powers eventually invaded it militarily and set up colonial rule throughout most of the continent. Europe eventually subjugated even the Ottoman empire; by the nineteenth century much of the Middle East and Africa lay under European rule. Colonial rule was usually violent and was always traumatic to African and Middle Eastern traditional cultures. Not surprisingly, conflict with Western culture is still a major theme in Arabic and African literature.

Napoleon's 1798 invasion of Egypt, for example, marks the beginning of modern Arabic literature. The French occupation, though it lasted only three years, introduced Western technology and culture to the region, dramatically influencing Arabic literary history. The first Arabic printing press in Egypt came with the French. Its initial purpose was to publish and circulate French political proclamations in Arabic, but the mass production of books eventually led to a resurgence of literary output as the literate population grew and began to challenge the ruling elite's hold on literacy and the manual production of texts.

For many generations nationalist struggles were the focus of Middle Eastern and African writers. Gradually, Western literary forms and subjects came to influence these writers too. European education—whether imposed on indigenous populations or sought by politicians, scientists, scholars, and entrepreneurs—created a context for Westernization and powerful cultural challenges to traditional Middle Eastern and African societies. Tawfiq al-Hakim (1898–1987), the preeminent modern Arab dramatist, recalls the tension colonial education created in the early twentieth century as it exposed students to European thought but neglected the vast and rich Arabic tradition:

> I remember that I bought out of my pocket money a book newly translated into Arabic: it was by the English philosopher Spencer, on ethics, and I felt proud to be reading philosophy, although I do not now believe that I understood anything worth mentioning. . . . As for the Arab philosophers, such as al-Ghazālī, Averroes and Avicenna, no one ever directed us to them.*

In the twentieth century, nation after nation in Africa and the Middle East emerged from European rule, but Westernization often intensified conflicts even within indigenous communities. Some writers and thinkers advocated weaving Western ideas into Islamic or African cultures; others resisted what they saw as cultural assault or annihilation and embraced a form of religious or cultural fundamentalism or an extreme leftist communism. Whether in Egypt, Zimbabwe, or Iran, the middle class grew in power, affecting the traditional patronage system that had aligned artists with aristocrats since the Middle Ages. Rather than creating literature that immortalized, entertained, or provided moral instruction for the wealthy (the traditional aims of literature in earlier periods), writers in modern Africa and the Middle East began using the medium to represent and change society and politics.

In the past, dazzling displays of craft won admirers for a writer or storyteller, but the modern writer in Africa or the Middle East is more often concerned with a modernist project: reflecting the world, achieving a mimetic representation of real people in the realm of the ordinary. Arabic literature of the Modern Period—often called *al-Nahdah,* or "renaissance"—like contemporary African or Israeli literature arises from an intense mixture of imported Western forms and traditional native literary forms and concerns.

In addition to the innovations sparked by cross-cultural influences, the spread of literacy allowed women to make significant contributions to written culture as early as the nineteenth century and more frequently in the twentieth, especially under socialist regimes. As do male writers, women write both in imitation of traditional poems and songs and in imitation of Western forms; they advocate traditional roles for women but also argue for change. Their participation has at times met with hostility. Nawal al-Sa'dawi, an Egyptian physician (b. 1930), has been imprisoned for her writings and her activism. In 1988, responding to the growth of a fundamentalist presence in Egypt, she published *Suqut al-Imam,* a book translated

*Cited in Pierre Cachia, *An Overview of Modern Arabic Literature.* (Edinburgh: Edinburgh University Press, 1990), 39.

into English as *Fall of the Imam.* The novel, which she considers to be not an attack on Islam but rather an attack on patriarchy and its exploitation of Islam, brought death threats so serious she had to be continually protected by bodyguards.

Although the prestige of the novel as a genre in the West has often eclipsed short fiction, the short story in Arabic countries, as in many other "developing" countries, such as India, Thailand, and Vietnam, has been more popular and arguably a more influential cultural presence. In Arabic, the short narrative is traditional, going back at least to *The Thousand and One Nights;* and from the late nineteenth through the late twentieth centuries, newspapers and magazines have provided writers with a new and powerful venue for publishing their work, especially the short story.

Innovations in Arabic, Israeli, and African poetry have followed paths similar to the one outlined for prose. Westernization means that some poets experiment with European verse forms, particularly the more inward, reflective, psychological, and self-expressive secular lyric; however, poets and storytellers also continue to write and recite in all the traditional forms, which still have considerable influence, despite modern Western-style poetic experiments.

# EGYPT

## NAGUIB MAHFOUZ (B. 1911)

*Translated by Denys Johnson-Davies*

Naguib Mahfouz is probably the best-known Arab fiction writer today. He won the Nobel Prize in literature in 1988. Mahfouz was born in Cairo, attended government schools, and graduated from the University of Cairo in 1934 with a degree in philosophy. Until his retirement, he supported himself by working as a civil servant and by writing for the leading Cairo newspaper, *Al-Ahram,* work he has continued even in retirement.

During Mahfouz's childhood, Egypt was occupied by the British until a constitutional monarchy was established in 1923. The monarchy was overthrown in 1955 by Gamal Abdel-Nasser, who attempted to establish a republic with democratic reforms. Mahfouz became disillusioned with Nasser's administration and its failure to better the lives of ordinary people. Social concerns are usually strongly expressed in his writings, and they transcend the particulars of Egyptian society. He writes of social change, upheaval, the challenges that Western technology and culture have brought to Egypt, and the power of spiritual truth to heal individuals, families, and nations.

Westerners have called Mahfouz the "Balzac of Egypt" and a "Dickens of Cairo cafés," but he is not simply an Egyptian version of European realists or naturalists; he also looks back to the premodern tradition of Arabic literature and draws inspiration from it as well as adapting the novel form to his own specific purposes. He has written *Layali alf layla* (*Nights of a Thousand Nights,* 1982), a modern reenvisioning of

*The Thousand and One Nights,* and his *Rihlat Ibn Fattuma* (*Travels of Ibn Fattuma,* 1983) is a contemporary recasting of the fourteenth-century *Travels of Ibn Battutah.* By looking back, Mahfouz preserves the past, deconstructs traditional literary genres, and envisions new ways of creating fiction for Arabic literature.

Mahfouz's early realistic novels are written in the tradition of nineteenth-century European novels. *The Trilogy* (1956–57), probably his most famous novel, is reminiscent of the works of Thomas Mann. *The Trilogy* stretches across a huge canvas of time, chronicling the life of a middle-class family for three generations, from 1917 and the rise of an Egyptian nationalist movement to 1944, when Cairo suffered air raids during World War II. He offers a panoramic view of Egypt's rebellious response to European occupation as well as its own deep internal divisions. These divisions are represented by two brothers of the middle generation; one becomes a Muslim, the other joins the Left and marries a woman who is focused on her own career as a journalist. The novel ends with both brothers in jail for their political activities and with the birth of a new generation.

Mahfouz's most recent fiction is experimental and revisionist and includes surrealist features that echo writers like Kafka (pp. 2049–2054) and Borges (pp. 2113–2121). Throughout his career his work has focused on what he has termed the "tragedies of society." "Zaabalawi," the short story we have included here, is from his collection entitled *God's World.* It illustrates the blend of realism and allegory common in Mahfouz's writings. The terminally ill narrator, having exhausted the power of medical science to cure him, searches for Zaabalawi, a holy man who figured in tales the narrator learned as a child. The guides on the journey, and the journey itself, with its allegorical levels of meaning, draw on the strong Middle Eastern traditions of dream narratives like Attar's *Conference of Birds* (pp. 809–832). *Zaabalawi* also reflects themes in Mahfouz's Nobel Prize speech, in which he asks us to rethink our emphasis on scientific and technological developments to the detriment of the pressing and complex needs of both the global community and its individual citizens.

## *Zaabalawi*

Finally I became convinced that I had to find Sheikh Zaabalawi.

The first time I had heard of his name had been in a song:

> 'What's wrong with the world, O
> Zaabalawi?
> They've turned it upside down
> and made it insipid.'

It had been a popular song in my childhood and one day it had occurred to me—in the way children have of asking endless questions—to ask my father about him.

'Who is Zaabalawi, father?'

He had looked at me hesitantly as though doubting my ability to understand the answer. However, he had replied:

'May his blessing descend upon you, he's a true saint of God, a remover of worries and troubles. Were it not for him I would have died miserably—'

In the years that followed I heard him many a time sing the praises of this good saint and speak of the miracles he performed. The days passed and brought with them many illnesses from each one of which I was able, without too much trouble and at a cost I could afford, to find a cure, until I became afflicted with that illness for which no one possesses a remedy. When I had tried everything in vain and was overcome by despair, I remembered by chance what I had heard in my childhood: Why, I asked myself, should I not seek out Sheikh Zaabalawi? I recollected that my father had said that he had made his acquaintance in Khan Gaafar at the house of Sheikh Kamar, one of those sheikhs who practised law in the religious courts, and I therefore took myself off to his house. Wishing to make sure that he was still living there, I made enquiries of a vendor of beans whom I found in the lower part of the house.

'Sheikh Kamar!' he said, looking at me in amazement. 'He left the quarter ages ago. They say he's now living in Garden City and has his office in al-Azhaar Square.'

I looked up the office address in the telephone book and immediately set off to the Chamber of Commerce Building where it was located. On asking to see him I was ushered into a room just as a beautiful woman with a most intoxicating perfume was leaving it. The man received me with a smile and motioned me towards a fine leather-upholstered chair. My feet were conscious of the costly lushness of the carpet despite the thick soles of my shoes. The man wore a lounge suit and was smoking a cigar; his manner of sitting was that of someone well satisfied both with himself and his worldly possessions. The look of warm welcome he gave me left no doubt in my mind that he thought me a prospective client, and I felt acutely embarrassed at encroaching upon his valuable time.

'Welcome!' he said, prompting me to speak.

'I am the son of your old friend Sheikh Ali al-Tatawi,' I answered so as to put an end to my equivocal position.

A certain languor was apparent in the glance he cast at me; the languor was not total in that he had not as yet lost all hope in me.

'God rest his soul,' he said. 'He was a fine man.'

The very pain that had driven me to go there now prevailed upon me to stay.

'He told me,' I continued, 'of a devout saint named Zaabalawi whom he met at Your Honour's. I am in need of him, sir, if he be still in the land of the living.'

The languor became firmly entrenched in his eyes and it would have come as no surprise to me if he had shown the door to both me and my father's memory.

'That,' he said in the tone of one who has made up his mind to terminate the conversation, 'was a very long time ago and I scarcely recall him now.'

Rising to my feet so as to put his mind at rest regarding my intention of going, I asked:

'Was he really a saint?'

'We used to regard him as a man of miracles.'

'And where could I find him today?' I asked, making another move towards the door.

'To the best of my knowledge he was living in the Birgawi Residence in al-Azhar,' and he applied himself to some papers on his desk with a resolute movement that indicated he wouldn't open his mouth again. I bowed my head in thanks, apologized several times for disturbing him and left the office, my head so buzzing with embarrassment that I was oblivious to all sounds around me.

I went to the Birgawi Residence which was situated in a thickly populated quarter. I found that time had so eaten into the building that nothing was left of it save an antiquated façade and a courtyard which, despite it being supposedly in the charge of a caretaker, was being used as a rubbish dump. A small insignificant fellow, a mere prologue to a man, was using the covered entrance as a place for the sale of old books on theology and mysticism.

On asking him about Zaabalawi he peered at me through narrow, inflamed eyes and said in amazement:

'Zaabalawi! Good heavens, what a time ago that was! Certainly he used to live in this house when it was livable in, and many was the time he would sit with me talking of bygone days and I would be blessed by his holy presence. Where, though, is Zaabalawi today?'

He shrugged his shoulders sorrowfully and soon left me to attend to an approaching customer. I proceeded to make enquiries of many shopkeepers in the district. While I found that a large number of them had never even heard of him, some, though recalling nostalgically the pleasant times they had spent with him, were ignorant of his present whereabouts, while others openly made fun of him, labelled him a charlatan, and advised me to put myself in the hands of a doctor—as though I had not already done so. I therefore had no alternative but to return disconsolately home.

With the passing of the days like motes in the air my pains grew so severe that I was sure I would not be able to hold out much longer. Once again I fell to wondering about Zaabalawi and clutching at the hopes his venerable name stirred within me. Then it occurred to me to seek the help of the local Sheikh of the district; in fact, I was surprised I hadn't thought of this to begin with. His office was in the nature of a small shop except that it contained a desk and a telephone, and I found him sitting at his desk wearing a jacket over his striped *galabia*. As he did not interrupt his conversation with a man sitting beside him, I stood waiting till the man had gone. He then looked up at me coldly. I told myself that I should win him over by the usual methods, and it wasn't long before I had him cheerfully inviting me to sit down.

'I'm in need of Sheikh Zaabalawi,' I answered his enquiry as to the purpose of my visit.

He gazed at me with the same astonishment as that shown by those I had previously encountered.

'At least,' he said, giving me a smile that revealed his gold teeth, 'he is still alive. The devil of it is, though, he has no fixed abode. You might well bump into him as you go out of here, on the other hand you might spend days and months in fruitless search of him.'

'Even you can't find him!'

'Even I! He's a baffling man, but I thank the Lord that he's still alive!'

He gazed at me intently, and murmured:

'It seems your condition is serious.'

'Very!'

'May God come to your aid! But why don't you go about it rationally?'

He spread out a sheet of paper on the desk and drew on it with unexpected speed and skill until he had made a full plan of the district showing all the various quarters, lanes, alleyways, and squares. He looked at it admiringly and said, 'These are dwelling-houses, here is the Quarter of the Perfumers, here the Quarter of the Coppersmiths, the Mouski, the Police and Fire Stations. The drawing is your best guide. Look carefully in the cafés, the places where the dervishes perform their rites, the mosques and prayer-rooms, and the Green Gate, for he may well be concealed among the beggars and be indistinguishable from them. Actually, I myself haven't seen him for years, having been somewhat preoccupied with the cares of the world and was only brought back to those most exquisite times of my youth by your enquiry.'

I gazed at the map in bewilderment. The telephone rang and he took up the receiver.

'Take it,' he told me, generously. 'We're at your service.'

Folding up the map, I left and wandered off through the quarter, from square to street to alleyway, making enquiries of everyone I felt was familiar with the place. At last the owner of a small establishment for ironing clothes told me:

'Go to the calligrapher Hassanein in Umm al-Ghulam—they were friends.'

I went to Umm al-Ghulam where I found old Hassanein working in a deep, narrow shop full of signboards and jars of colour. A strange smell, a mixture of glue and perfume, permeated its every corner. Old Hassanein was squatting on a sheepskin rug in front of a board propped against the wall; in the middle of it he had inscribed the word 'Allah' in silver lettering. He was engrossed in embellishing the letters with prodigious care. I stood behind him, fearful to disturb him or break the inspiration that flowed to his masterly hand. When my concern at not interrupting him had lasted some time, he suddenly enquired with unaffected gentleness:

'Yes?'

Realizing that he was aware of my presence, I introduced myself.

'I've been told that Sheikh Zaabalawi is your friend and I'm looking for him,' I said.

His hand came to a stop. He scrutinized me in astonishment.

'Zaabalawi! God be praised!' he said with a sigh.

'He is a friend of yours, isn't he?' I asked eagerly.

'He was, once upon a time. A real man of mystery: he'd visit you so often that people would imagine he was your nearest and dearest, then would disappear as though he'd never existed. Yet saints are not to be blamed.'

The spark of hope went out with the suddenness of a lamp by a power-cut.

'He was so constantly with me,' said the man, 'that I felt him to be a part of everything I drew. But where is he today?'

'Perhaps he is still alive?'

'He's alive, without a doubt. He had impeccable taste and it was due to him that I made my most beautiful drawings.'

'God knows,' I said, in a voice almost stifled by the dead ashes of hope, 'that I am in the direst need of him and no one knows better than you of the ailments in respect of which he is sought.'

'Yes—yes. May God restore you to health. He is, in truth, as is said of him, a man, and more—'

Smiling broadly, he added: 'And his face is possessed of an unforgettable beauty. But where is he?'

Reluctantly I rose to my feet, shook hands and left. I continued on my way eastwards and westwards through the quarter, enquiring about him from everyone who, by reason of age or experience, I felt was likely to help me. Eventually I was informed by a vendor of lupine that he had met him a short while ago at the house of Sheikh Gad, the well-known composer. I went to the musician's house in Tabakshiyya where I found him in a room tastefully furnished in the old style, its walls redolent with history. He was seated on a divan, his famous lute lying beside him, concealing within itself the most beautiful melodies of our age, while from within the house came the sound of pestle and mortar and the clamour of children. I immediately greeted him and introduced myself, and was put at my ease by the unaffected way in which he received me. He did not ask, either in words or gesture, what had brought me, and I did not feel that he even harboured any such curiosity. Amazed at his understanding and kindness, which boded well, I said:

'O Sheikh Gad, I am an admirer of yours and have long been enchanted by the renderings of your songs.'

'Thank you,' he said with a smile.

'Please excuse my disturbing you,' I continued timidly, 'but I was told that Zaabalawi was your friend and I am in urgent need of him.'

'Zaabalawi!' he said, frowning in concentration. 'You need him? God be with you, for who knows, O Zaabalawi, where you are?'

'Doesn't he visit you?' I asked eagerly.

'He visited me some time ago. He might well come now; on the other hand I mightn't see him till death!'

I gave an audible sigh and asked:

'What made him like that?'

He took up his lute. 'Such are saints or they would not be saints,' he said laughing.

'Do those who need him suffer as I do?'

'Such suffering is part of the cure!'

He took up the plectrum and began plucking soft strains from the strings. Lost in thought, I followed his movements. Then, as though addressing myself, I said:

'So my visit has been in vain!'

He smiled, laying his cheek against the side of the lute.

'God forgive you,' he said, 'for saying such a thing of a visit that has caused me to know you and you me!'

I was much embarrassed and said apologetically:

'Please forgive me; my feelings of defeat made me forget my manners!'

'Do not give in to defeat. This extraordinary man brings fatigue to all who seek him. It was easy enough with him in the old days when his place of abode was known. Today, though, the world has changed and after having enjoyed a position attained only by potentates, he is now pursued by the police on a charge of false pretences. It is therefore no longer an easy matter to reach him, but have patience and be sure that you will do so.'

He raised his head from the lute and skilfully led into the opening bars of a melody. Then he sang:

'I make lavish mention, even
 though I blame myself,
of those I have loved,
For the words of lovers are my
 wine.'

With a heart that was weary and listless I followed the beauty of the melody and the singing.

'I composed the music to this poem in a single night,' he told me when he had finished. 'I remember that it was the night of the Lesser Bairam. He was my guest for the whole of that night and the poem was of his choosing. He would sit for a while just where you are, then would get up and play with my children as though he were one of them. Whenever I was overcome by weariness or my inspiration failed me he would punch me playfully in the chest and joke with me, and I would bubble over with melodies and thus I continued working till I finished the most beautiful piece I have ever composed.'

'Does he know anything about music?'

'He was the epitome of things musical. He had an extremely beautiful speaking voice and you had only to hear him to want to burst into song. His loftiness of spirit stirred within you—'

'How was it that he cured those diseases before which men are powerless?'

'That is his secret. Maybe you will learn it when you meet him.'

But when would that meeting occur? We relapsed into silence and the hubbub of children once more filled the room.

Again the Sheikh began to sing. He went on repeating the words 'and I have a memory of her' in different and beautiful variations until the very walls danced in ecstasy. I expressed my wholehearted admiration and he gave me a smile of thanks. I then got up and asked permission to leave and he accompanied me to the outer door. As I shook him by the hand he said, 'I hear that nowadays he frequents the house of Hagg Wanas al-Damanhouri. Do you know him?'

I shook my head, a modicum of renewed hope creeping into my heart.

'He is a man of private means,' he told me, 'who from time to time visits Cairo, putting up at some hotel or other. Every evening, though, he spends at the Negma Bar in Alfi Street.'

I waited for nightfall, and went to the Negma Bar. I asked a waiter about Hagg Wanas and he pointed to a corner which was semi-secluded because of its position behind a large pillar with mirrors on its four sides. There I saw a man seated alone at a table with a bottle three-quarters empty and another empty one in front of him; there were no snacks or food to be seen and I was sure that I was in the presence of a hardened drinker. He was wearing a loosely flowing silk *galabia* and a carefully wound turban; his legs were stretched out towards the base of the pillar, and as he gazed into the mirror in rapt contentment the sides of his face, rounded and handsome despite the fact that he was approaching old age, were flushed with wine. I approached quietly till I stood but a few feet away from him. He did not turn towards me or give any indication that he was aware of my presence.

'Good evening, Mr. Wanas,' I said with amiable friendliness.

He turned towards me abruptly as though my voice had roused him from slumber and glared at me in disapproval. I was about to explain what had brought me to him when he interrupted me in an almost imperative tone of voice which was none the less not devoid of an extraordinary gentleness:

'First, please sit down, and, second, please get drunk!'

I opened my mouth to make my excuses but, stopping up his ears with his fingers, he said:

'Not a word till you do what I say.'

I realized that I was in the presence of a capricious drunkard and told myself that I should go along with him at least halfway.

'Would you permit me to ask one question?' I said with a smile, sitting down.

Without removing his hands from his ears he indicated the bottle.

'When engaged in a drinking bout like this I do not allow any conversation between myself and another unless, like me, he is drunk, otherwise the session loses all propriety and mutual comprehension is rendered impossible.'

I made a sign indicating that I didn't drink.

'That's your look-out,' he said offhandedly. 'And that's my condition!'

He filled me a glass which I meekly took and drank. No sooner had it settled in my stomach than it seemed to ignite. I waited patiently till I had grown used to its ferocity, and said:

'It's very strong, and I think the time has come for me to ask you about—'

Once again, however, he put his fingers in his ears.

'I shan't listen to you until you're drunk!'

He filled up my glass for the second time. I glanced at it in trepidation; then, overcoming my innate objection, I drank it down at a gulp. No sooner had it come to rest inside me than I lost all will-power. With the third glass I lost my memory and with the fourth the future vanished. The world turned round about me and I forgot why I had gone there. The man leaned towards me attentively but I saw him—saw everything—as a mere meaningless series of coloured planes. I don't know how long it was before my head sank down on to the arm of the chair and I plunged into deep sleep. During it I had a beautiful dream the like of which I had never experienced. I dreamed that I was in an immense garden surrounded on all sides by luxuriant trees and the sky was nothing but stars seen between the entwined branches, all enfolded in an atmosphere like that of sunset or a sky overcast with cloud. I was lying on a small hummock of jasmine petals which fell upon me like rain, while the lucent spray of a fountain unceasingly sprinkled my head and temples. I was in a state of deep contentedness, of ecstatic serenity. An orchestra of warbling and cooing played in my ear. There was an extraordinary sense of harmony between me and my inner self, and between the two of us and the world, everything being in its rightful place without discord or distortion. In the whole world there was no single reason for speech or movement, for the universe moved in a rapture of ecstasy. This lasted but a short while. When I opened my eyes consciousness struck at me like a policeman's fist and I saw Wanas al-Damanhouri regarding me with concern. In the bar only a few drowsy people were left.

'You have slept deeply,' said my companion; 'you were obviously hungry for sleep.'

I rested my heavy head in the palms of my hands. When I took them away in astonishment and looked down at them I found that they glistened with drops of water.

'My head's wet,' I protested.

'Yes, my friend tried to rouse you,' he answered quietly.

'Somebody saw me in this state?'

'Don't worry, he is a good man. Have you not heard of Sheikh Zaabalawi?'

'Zaabalawi!' I exclaimed, jumping to my feet.

'Yes,' he answered in surprise. 'What's wrong?'

'Where is he?'

'I don't know where he is now. He was here and then he left.'

I was about to run off in pursuit but found I was more exhausted than I had imagined. Collapsed over the table, I cried out in despair:

'My sole reason for coming to you was to meet him. Help me to catch up with him or send someone after him.'

The man called a vendor of prawns and asked him to seek out the Sheikh and bring him back. Then he turned to me.

'I didn't realize you were afflicted. I'm very sorry—'

'You wouldn't let me speak,' I said irritably.

'What a pity! He was sitting on this chair beside you the whole time. He was playing with a string of jasmine petals he had round his neck, a gift from one of his admirers, then, taking pity on you, he began to sprinkle some water on your head to bring you round.'

'Does he meet you here every night?' I asked, my eyes not leaving the doorway through which the vendor of prawns had left.

'He was with me tonight, last night and the night before that, but before that I hadn't seen him for a month.'

'Perhaps he will come tomorrow,' I answered with a sigh.

'Perhaps.'

'I am willing to give him any money he wants.'

Wanas answered sympathetically:

'The strange thing is that he is not open to such temptations, yet he will cure you if you meet him.'

'Without charge?'

'Merely on sensing that you love him.'

The vendor of prawns returned, having failed in his mission.

I recovered some of my energy and left the bar, albeit unsteadily. At every street corner I called out, 'Zaabalawi!' in the vague hope that I would be rewarded with an answering shout. The street boys turned contemptuous eyes on me till I sought refuge in the first available taxi.

The following evening I stayed up with Wanas al-Damanhouri till dawn, but the Sheikh did not put in an appearance. Wanas informed me that he would be going away to the country and wouldn't be returning to Cairo until he'd sold the cotton crop.

I must wait, I told myself; I must train myself to be patient. Let me content myself with having made certain of the existence of Zaabalawi, and even of his affection for me, which encourages me to think that he will be prepared to cure me if a meeting between us takes place.

Sometimes, however, the long delay wearied me. I would become beset by despair and would try to persuade myself to dismiss him from my mind completely. How many weary people in this life know him not or regard him as a mere myth! Why, then, should I torture myself about him in this way?

No sooner, however, did my pains force themselves upon me than I would again begin to think about him, asking myself as to when I would be fortunate enough to meet him. The fact that I ceased to have any news of Wanas and was told he had gone to live abroad did not deflect me from my purpose; the truth of the matter was that I had become fully convinced that I had to find Zaabalawi.

Yes, I have to find Zaabalawi.

## Salwa Bakr (b. 1949)

*Translated by Denys Johnson-Davies*

Salwa Bakr was born in Egypt and educated in business, history, and theater. Her father, a railway worker, died before she was born. She has supported herself as a government rationing inspector and as a film and literature critic in Lebanon and Cyprus. Politically active while a university student in Cairo, she abandoned activism because of the chasm she observed between emancipatory rhetoric and the actual treatment of women. Her brief imprisonment for political activities gave rise to her first novel, *The Golden Chariot That Didn't Take Off Into The Sky*, which focuses on the lives of inmates in a women's prison.

Bakr's short stories feature marginalized and nonconforming characters, usually working-class women who are struggling to survive physically, psychologically, or economically. In a recent interview she discussed the link between a society and its literature: "Especially in our days we need literature. We live in a time when the boundaries between good and bad are obscured. Literature is a means to clarify, to distinguish between the two." Her work is also explicitly focused to criticize and disrupt oppressive practices in Egyptian society; and unlike some writers who find the Euro-American world wholly corrupting and narcissistic, Bakr comments, "In the West we can see that the main civilized value achieved is individual freedom. This was achieved through a long history of battles and revolutions." At the same time, however, her fiction indicts the rise of Western economic practices and technology in Egypt, finding in them the source of many of her characters' economic woes.

A keen admirer of contemporary Arabic writers, she has committed herself to giving voice to women's experiences in her fiction. Her work criticizes institutions that oppress people (women particularly) and people who participate in their own oppression out of fear. Often she writes about women who do not meet the cultural stereotypes of beauty. Some of her stories concern women who attempt, successfully or unsuccessfully, to construct a life outside the institution of the family. Often she writes about women who are alone or abandoned, literally or figuratively, by husbands or lovers.

She identifies the Russian short story writer Chekhov and Spain's Cervantes (pp. 1469–1494) as key literary influences and is particularly drawn to Cervantes's ability to represent the ridiculous with deceptively simple narrative methods. Her writing is clearly influenced by the European short story and by the development of feminism in the West. It also continues the strong moral and ethical quality found in the Arabic literary tradition, even though she advocates transforming the traditional Arabic moral and social order.

### *That Beautiful Undiscovered Voice*

Everything had started quite naturally in accordance with the usual daily rites: the rooms were tidied and cleaned, the plates were laid awaiting the food, the radio, turned down low, was chattering out the afternoon news, which in general was the same as usual. Abdul Hamid, however, felt that there was a certain unease affecting his wife, causing her to hunch her shoulders more than usual when she swallowed her food; also she was not entering into the conversation with him as she should.

'What is it, Sayyida?' he asked her.

'Nothing,' she replied glumly and went off to the kitchen, pleading that the tea was boiling over. But when she returned she seemed even more distressed and allowed the top of the teapot to fall on the floor as she was pouring the tea into the glasses. Abdul Hamid again asked her what was wrong in a disapproving tone. She shyly whispered back that she wanted to talk to him about something, but that she was embarrassed.

'Hope it's all right,' he said as he lit a cigarette, guessing at what the news would be. She would no doubt be asking for money and would give as a reason some incidental matter, or would try to persuade him that the monthly expenses had gone up. There was no other subject Sayyida would be embarrassed to talk about. He bared his teeth and knotted his brows and moved his neck from left to right so as to make a cracking noise as he prepared himself for the inevitable battle. He decided that he would come out the victor, however heated it was, for he was not going to pay one single red millieme over and above what he was already paying in household expenses each month, not if Sayyida—as the saying goes—were to see her own earlobe. He took a sip of the almost black tea, and said to her between clenched teeth, 'Out with it!'

From deep down inside her Sayyida tried to thrust her courage up to her tongue and to utter what she wanted to say, but her courage quickly slipped back again into its abyss. Her voice emerged weak and timid.

'The fact of the matter is I've discovered I'm . . .'

'Pregnant?'

The husband was on his feet, screaming, like someone who has of a sudden accidentally impaled himself. The words, 'Can it possibly be?' sprang from his lips, accompanied by a spray of spittle brought about by his agitation. 'Is it possible that you can again be pregnant, Sayyida? By my mother's grave, I'll be really annoyed with you if it's true, and my pocket's empty, which is to say no more children and, no more abortions. You get yourself out of this one, if you can.'

He gave himself a good scratch between the thighs and walked, crazed, towards the window, which overlooked the street filled with the clamour of people and cars. Enraged, he thought of what he might do to her. Should he hit her? Throw her to the ground and kick her till she started bleeding and had a miscarriage? Or should he open the window full and throw her out? If it hadn't been that the cigarette was almost burning his fingers, so that he had to return to bury the stub in the ashtray, Sayyida may not have found the opportunity, her courage having risen to her tongue, to say to him, 'It's not pregnancy or anything of the sort—the thing is that my voice has become extremely beautiful.'

Abdul Hamid fastened his gaze on her for several seconds, during which he remained at a loss. Then he burst into hysterical laughter, as though he had just heard a joke without an end. Blood gushed to his brain making his puffed-up head look like a red balloon on the point of bursting. His features and teeth went on making agitated movements which were only brought to a halt by the angry voice of his wife.

'Just listen, first.'

He seated himself and she began to recount to him exactly what had happened to her. After he had left for work in the morning, and after the children had gone off to their schools, she had as usual remained alone in the house and had set about her housework: sweeping and dusting and cooking and tidying up the rooms. After the call to the noon prayer she had said to herself, 'Go off, my girl, to the bathroom and pour a pail of water over yourself and you'll feel refreshed and get rid of the dirt.'

It was after Sayyida had taken her clothes off and washed her head a couple of times, and while she was removing the soap from her eyes, that it occurred to her to sing and amuse herself as usual. No sooner had she begun with the song '*I love the life of freedom*' than she felt as though some other person had come into the bathroom with her and had begun to sing in her place. The voice was not her own voice, the one she had become accustomed to; instead it was a beautiful melodious voice wholly unrelated to her own. She immediately splashed some water on to her eyes to get rid of the soap and gazed round the bathroom. She wheeled about in search of a human being or some other creature, while invoking God's name and seeking to be protected from the Devil. But her eyes fell on nothing but the single window, which was firmly closed, the mirror over the basin, with the toothbrushes placed on the shelf, and her clean clothes, which she'd just got out of the cupboard, hanging on the nail on the back of the door. She muttered, 'There is no god but God!' and went on with her shower. When she was sure that there was no sound except that of the water flowing over her body, she continued with her singing of '*I love the life of freedom.*' The voice that issued from her was even more beautiful, clear and strong. The loufa in her hand became as though nailed to her thigh, which she had begun to scrub. She said, 'In the name of God the Merciful, the compassionate,' and, 'I take my refuge in God from the accursed Devil,' and despite her belief that there were no *afreets,* except for human beings themselves, she was nevertheless frightened. Her heart was beating hard and she called out to herself in a low voice: 'Sayyida, Sayyida.' Back came a voice other than that which she knew. It was too beautiful. So she began to raise her voice still further and to put inflections into it, 'O Sayyida . . . O Sayyida,' at the same time overcome by a state of joyous rapture. However, she suddenly came to her senses.

'Perhaps someone had heard me, or you had returned home, Abdul Hamid, for one reason or another, and had heard me calling to myself. You would think I'd gone off my head or was a bit touched. So I kept quiet and terror made of my tongue a piece of dried firewood, while my teeth were chattering, and I said to myself, "Maybe it really is a question of *afreets.*" So I began reciting to myself. I said, "I seek refuge in the Lord of the Daybreak from the evil of that which He created," right through till I'd finished the chapter. I dried my body with the towel, and in my confusion I put my *galabia* on back to front. I then opened the door and went running to the window, looking down at the people in the street and feeling less alone. When I was back to my old self and had relaxed, I went and sat on the sofa and did my hair. After that, as though I had heard some disembodied voice calling to me, I found myself once again singing, "*O sweetness of the world, O sweetness.*" Imagine, my dear Abdul Hamid, I found that my voice was even sweeter, a voice that might have issued from Paradise, a magical voice that was unrivalled in this world. To tell you the truth, I was delighted and at peace with myself. The sensation of fear had left my heart, for I felt it was impossible that the voice was that of a *djinn;* it was a human voice, a completely natural voice and yet very different from my old one.'

Then, looking into his eyes with a deep contentment, she said, 'Please, Abdul Hamid, please just listen to me.' And she began to sing.

But Abdul Hamid silenced her with a resolute look. It was as though he hadn't heard anything of what she had said. He then asked her if she had told anyone but himself of the matter. When she confirmed to him that the thing had happened only a few hours ago and that she had not met a soul since he had left in the morning, he heaved a sigh of relief and asked her to forget the whole thing. 'And don't bring the subject up with anyone whatsoever, and especially not with the children.' She was annoyed that he didn't believe her and swore by all that was holy that what she had said had really and truly happened.

The tears gathered in her eyes as she vehemently denied that she'd gone soft in the head.

Abdul Hamid sat on the sofa and asked her to make him a lightly sugared coffee. While she was putting her feet into her slippers and preparing to go, he suddenly felt sorry for her and said, 'Listen, Sayyida. You're over forty and you've got four kids, meaning to say that talking rubbish diminishes your status and makes you a figure of fun in front of the children. And what would the position be if any grown-up person in his senses were to hear you? Just suppose that what you say is true—what does it mean? Are you intending to take up singing, for example? Intending to become a professional singer? By God, what a story!'

He laughed with satisfaction, for he found the matter to be far removed from any of the fears he had had. Then he gave her a playful slap on the bottom and whispered to her, 'After the coffee, come along and we'll stretch out together on the bed.'

For the rest of the day things went on as usual, and Sayyida almost forgot what had happened to her that morning. She continued to carry out the tasks of the second part of the day with her usual enthusiasm: she folded up the washing, took tea round to the children while they were doing their homework, and made herself free for half an hour to watch the television serial. When Abdul Hamid returned from the café, to which he had gone after sunset, she made supper for him with the children, a meal during which he joked with some and rebuked those who needed rebuking.

But in the evening, when she was on her own, Abdul Hamid having gone to sleep, she thought confusedly as to what she really was going to do about her voice, that beautiful voice that she had suddenly discovered was buried inside her, like someone who has come across a wonderful treasure and doesn't know what to do with it. She began actively to think, but always came back to the same logical answer: a beautiful voice is made for singing. So why didn't she sing and let people hear her voice? She was tempted to believe that it was only right that people should hear her voice, and that a person's voice had nothing to do with his age. What was wrong with people listening to someone's voice regardless of age or whether he was a man or a woman? She had more or less become convinced by this line of thought, when she became possessed of an overwhelming desire to sit in bed and sing '*O sweetness of the world, O sweetness.*'

So she started to sit down but, just as she was about to open her mouth and begin, Abdul Hamid turned over in bed and became aware of her. He looked at her anxiously and asked, 'What's wrong, Sayyida?'

She said she was on her way to the kitchen for a drink of water because her mouth was a bit dry.

On the following morning, when she began to sing, Sayyida became madly excited. Standing in front of the sink and washing the dishes left over from breakfast after Abdul Hamid and the children had gone out, she again heard that beautiful voice that sounded so fascinating, unearthly and overflowing with power and purity. She was seized with a feeling that she was some other being, with no connection with the Sayyida she knew, the Sayyida that dusted and swept and did her head up in a kerchief each day because she couldn't find the time to put a comb through her hair. She quickly rinsed her hands of soap, drying them with the end of her nightdress, which she hadn't yet taken off, and ran to the mirror. Standing in front of it, she sang, '*I love the life of freedom,*' and her voice rang out anew, strong, pure and clear, like some priceless jewel. She watched herself, her lips dancing with the tuneful words, her eyes sparkling with joyful enthusiasm, her cheeks ruddy with blood which she imagined had gushed from hidden springs in her body, her eyebrows that met and separated in ordered movements, leading the features of the face in a brilliant concord of sounds, as though they were the two skillful hands of the conductor of a superb orchestra.

She felt she was beautiful, perhaps for the first time for quite a long while. This feeling came to her and it rejuvenated her. She stood looking at her face, reproaching herself for the way she had left her eyebrows untrimmed, embarrassed to find a slight moustache under her nose, sorry to have so neglected her hair. Then she felt anger at herself. Why had she let herself go in this way, while possessing within her this beautiful voice? She stood there and came to a decision: 'In order to sing I am obliged to feel beautiful. Yes, by God—obliged.'

Sayyida quickly put on her clothes, for she must go down to the street to buy vegetables and bread before Abdul Hamid and the children returned home. Her mind was still occupied with the same matter, but she naturally had no plan in relation to how she would sing, and where she would begin, and how she would face Abdul Hamid with this decision of hers. She thought of going to some friend of hers to disclose her secret to her, as women do in films, but she discovered, for the first time in her life, that she had not a single friend, no human being with whom she was intimate, nobody close to her heart, apart from her mother and her sister Awatef, both of whom she had at the outset regarded as not being suitable, by reason of her prior knowledge of their attitude were she to tell them of' the matter. It would be an attitude of scorn which would have them laughing at what she had to say, turning it into a joke and announcing it in front of any relatives who visited them. She thought of her neighbour, Umm Hasan, but Umm Hasan, despite their very good relationship, had never had any secrets with Sayyida. For the first time in her life she felt resentment towards Abdul Hamid, because he had friends with whom to sit in the café, and there was his bosom friend Ismail, to whom he may have told secrets that he had never divulged to her, despite the fact that she was his intimate companion and had given him four children.

Her state of excitement remained with her even as she entered Isa the grocer's shop to buy some cheese and macaroni and ten eggs. Old Isa had no need to scrutinize her closely to notice that she was distraught. 'Why are you upset, Mrs. Sayyida, so early of a morning?' he asked her, but before she answered he had decided that he knew already: life had become hard, and the high cost of living was an unrestrained ghoul who made its way into everything and was completely out of control. Meanwhile people walked about and talked to themselves because of their wretchedness and lack of means (of course, Isa had noticed that she used to talk to herself occasionally). Then he said to her—and he was the old grocer with whom they had been dealing for a long time and with whom they had links of neighbourliness and affection—that he knew that Abdul Hamid was doing all he possibly could to provide for the children and that she should be patient with him. He was none the less astonished when, suddenly, he found her bursting into tears and sobbing like someone who has lost someone dear to them.

Isa took her by the hand and sat her down in a chair, then opened a bottle of fizzy lemonade for her, saying, 'Take it easy and put the Devil to shame.' It was morning and the shop was not yet filled with customers, so the man whispered to her earnestly, 'Any problem, God forbid, between you and Abdul Hamid?' It was difficult for her to explain, so she burst into sobs once again.

When she had recovered, she said, 'Listen, Uncle Isa, I need to talk to you about something, something slightly personal, on condition you try to understand me and don't talk to Abdul Hamid about it, because he's sworn to divorce me if I don't keep the news well hidden and not talk to a soul about it.'

Uncle Isa sensed that the matter was indeed grave, and he was seized by an irresistible desire to hear a family secret that had to do with one of the inhabitants of the street; he experienced the pleasure of being about to learn some new bit of gossip that he would quickly be employing, so he drew up a chair and sat down close to her so that he might not miss so much as a word.

'It's happened that I've discovered my voice,' she said, as though divulging a solemn secret, and she began to relate to him what had happened to her and the words that had passed between her and Abdul Hamid. The man did not laugh, or utter so much as a word—as they say in books. When she had finished her story and said to him, smiling with embarrassment, that she was ready to let him hear her beautiful voice, so that he might confirm for himself the truth of what she had said, he scrutinized her pityingly and replied, 'Drink up the lemonade, Sayyida.'

Without drinking the lemonade, she took up the things she had bought from him and left. When, in the afternoon, Abdul Hamid returned, and while they were having their lunch, he told her that, on his way home, he had bought some matches from the shop of Isa the grocer, and that he was going to the doctor's that evening and that she must accompany him.

When they arrived at the clinic of the psychologist, Sayyida was partly convinced about her husband's idea. He had said that he loved her and that he wanted only her good and that of the children and that psychological illness was like any other illness and that there was nothing to be ashamed about. In fact it was quite curable, but the important thing was to treat it quickly, right at the beginning. Thanks be to God, there was nothing wrong with her, but the story of the voice had perhaps come about through being exhausted with housework, or some hidden problem inside her she wasn't aware of, because the inner part of every human being is a vast bottomless sea, and the spirit's secret is deeply hidden, with the Almighty alone knowing what is in the inmost depths of every human.

'What I am trying to say is that it's difficult for a man to know himself, Sayyida, and medicine has been made for just such difficult circumstances. Also, Sayyida, despite my modest education, I am a believer and profess the unity of God, and I don't believe in the story of *djinn* and *afreets,* because our Lord has said in the Qur'an: "And we have made between you and them an impregnable barrier." Anyway, my dear, let's have a go. All it means is losing ten pounds from the money which anyway is flying away like so many sparrows out of our control. Maybe, with God's permission, they'll bring a cure and everything will return to normal and you'll be all right. The fact is, this morning you told Isa the grocer, but tomorrow or the day after, against your will, you could tell someone else, or something could happen that would make us a laughing-stock in front of people, and all sorts of things could be said about you, without cause. And I, Sayyida, were it not for my affection for you and for the children, I'd have shut up about the matter and kept quiet, but you know I am fond of you since you are the mother of my children and my life's partner.'

They entered the doctor's office and sat down. The man asking her about her problem seemed to her to be very peevish, grumpy and disturbed, also in a great hurry. So Abdul Hamid started off by telling him the story in brief. But the doctor, rapping the glass top of his desk with his pen, asked him to let her tell it; so Sayyida recounted everything that had happened to her from the very moment she had entered the bath, right up to her conversation with Isa the grocer.

When she had completed all she had to say, noticing that the man had listened to her attentively without any interruption, she asked him, smiling with pleasure because of her feeling that he understood her situation, 'Could I sing you a little song, doctor?'

No sign of interest showed itself on the doctor's features. He looked as though he were accustomed to such things. He didn't smile, he didn't frown, and he made no reply. He merely wrote some words in a foreign language on a piece of paper and gave it to the husband with the words, 'Three pills of the first kind daily, after each meal, and one of the others every evening before she goes to bed.'

Then he turned to Sayyida, saying, 'Keep away from anything that causes you stress, and never allow yourself to be alone. Put on the wireless when you're in the bathroom, eat well, but try to go for walks and lose some weight, because you're too fat. Keep on with the medicine, and when you feel depressed and you're in a bad mood, come along at once to the clinic.' Then he stood up and stretched out his hand to her saying, 'Nice to have met you.'

The others went out as usual next morning and she remained alone in the house. She got up sluggishly, without enthusiasm, to gather up the breakfast dishes. She swallowed the food that was left on the plates, telling herself as usual, 'It's a shame to throw a couple of mouthfuls of beans into the rubbish bin. There's not enough cheese left to make it worthwhile keeping the plate for it.' Then she made herself a glass of tea, which she sipped while nibbling at a pastry that had remained on the table. Feeling she had eaten too much, she got up, dragging her body along, to tidy up the rooms and sweep.

While in the bedroom she came face to face with herself in the mirror. She contemplated herself in her nightgown: a pallid yellowish face, despite its fullness, listless eyes, expressionless features, like those of someone from whom life had absented itself. She pulled herself together and tried to sing '*O sweetness of the world, O sweetness*'. She made an effort but no sound came from her. She cleared her throat and tried '*I love the life of freedom,*' but in no way would the voice imprisoned in her throat come forth. It was as if it were stoppered by an enormous cork. She cleared her throat again and finally decided to practise scales. She was surprised to hear the old voice, the voice she had known since she had first become aware of life, her own voice, weak and hoarse and devoid of any beauty, clarity or strength. She contemplated herself again. Her face was her face of old, the face she had known in times past. She gave a bitter smile, shaking her head with sorrow, then took up the two boxes of pills to flush them down the lavatory.

# Palestine

## Fadwa Tuqan (b. 1917)

*Translated by Patricia Alanah Byrne*

Fadwa Tuqan was born in Nablus, Palestine. She was introduced to creative writing by her brother, Ibrahim Tuqan, a well-known poet. Her work is heavily influenced by European romanticism, and she began writing free verse quite early. She has published at least six books of poems since 1952. After the June 1967 war, when her birthplace was incorporated into the state of Israel, her poems took on political themes. She has written both personal lyrics of great emotional intensity and more public, community-focused works of social protest and celebration.

The first selection here, "In the Aging City," is set in London, capital of the empire that ruled Palestine until 1948. Containing memories of Nablus, Tuqan's birthplace, this poem interweaves images of urban alienation similar to those found in T.S. Eliot's *The Waste Land* (pp. 2173–2181) with memories of colonization and loss. Fusing memory, landscape, exile, imprisonment, and the dream of return, Tuqan's poems reflect not only themes common in modernism and romanticism but the historical realities of a Palestinian diaspora as well. The last poem in this brief selection focuses on the soul and is clearly reminiscent of Islamic verse of the Middle Period as well as modern European and American lyric poetry.

## *In the Aging City*

City streets and pavements receive me
with other people, the human tide rushes
me on. I move in this current, but only on
the surface, remaining by myself.
The tide overflows to sweep
these sidewalks and streets.
Faces, faces, faces rolling on,
dry and grim, they move on the surface,
remaining without human touch.
Here is nearness without being near.
Here is the no-presence in presence.
Here is nothing but the presence of absence!

Traffic light reddens; the tide holds back.
Bats flash across memory:
*a tank passes, as I crossed in the Nablus marketplace,*
*I moved out of its way.*
*How well I've learned not to disturb*
*the path of traffic! How well I've memorized traffic laws!*
*And now here I am, in the London slave market*
*where they sold my parents and people . . .*
*Here I stand, a part of the profitable deal,*
*carrying the brunt of the sin—*
*Mine was that I am a plant*
*grown by the mountains of Palestine.*
*Ah! Those who died yesterday are at rest now.*
*(I suspect that their corpses cursed me*
*as I gave way for a tank to pass,*
*then moved on in the stream.)*
*Aisha's letter is on my desk,*
*Nablus is quiet, life flowing on*
*like river water . . .*
*The prison seal is an eloquent silence*
*(A guard tells her the trees have fallen,*
*the woods are not set ablaze anymore.*
*But Aisha insists the forest is thick,*

*trees standing like fortresses. She dreams*
*of the forest she left blazing with fire*
*five years ago. She heard the thunder*
*of wind in her dream, tells the guard:*
*"I don't believe you, you're one of them,*
*and you remain the Prophets of the Lie."*
*Then she crouches in the darkness of prison, dreaming.*
*Shaded by her standing trees she is joyous at the sound*
*of the far forest rattling with swords of flame.*
*And Aisha dreams and dreams.)*

The traffic light clicks green, the tide drives on.
My memory flits away, bats fall into a deep well.
A shadow changes direction, follows me,
sends out a bridge.
        —Are you a stranger like I am?
Two drops separate from the tide,
sit removed in a corner of the park.
        —Do you like Osborne?
        —Who doesn't?
        —England's elderly and its officers
          setting with the sun of Suez . . .
        —Who do you think will plant tomorrow's tree
          for this country?
        —The hippie youth.
        —You are sour, very sour.
The hippie tide passes by,
sweeping the city.
London keeps beat with
the toll of Big Ben.
        —Around the corner
          there's a pub and an elegant hotel
          with central heating—will you come?
        —Impossible!
A London lady passes, complaining to her dog
of arthritis and a pinched sciatic nerve.
        —Impossible!
        —Aren't you a modern woman?
        —I've grown beyond the days of rashness;
          sorrow has made me a hundred years old. Impossible!
I remove his arm from my shoulders.
        —I'm besieged by loneliness.
        —We're all besieged by loneliness;
          we're all alone, play along with life alone,
          suffer alone, and die by ourselves.

You will remain alone here, even if a hundred
women embrace you!
City streets and sidewalks swallow us with others,
a human tide sweeping us away in waves of faces.
We remain on the surface, touching nothing.

## *In the Flux*

That evening
faces faded around us
The room was drowned in fog
Nothing lived
but the shining blue of your eyes
and the call in that
shining blue
where my heart
sailed, a ship
driven by the tide
The tide carried
us onto a sea
without shores
stretching
limitless current
and flow
waves telling the endless
story of life
now abridged in one glance
and the earth drowned in the rushing
flood of winds and rain

That evening
my garden awoke
The fingers of the wind
unhinged its fences
Grasses swayed, flowers bursting,
fruits ripening
in the blissful dance of wind and rain
Faces faded, all else was a fog
that evening
nothing existed
but the blue shining light in your eyes
and the call in the shining blue
where my heart sailed
like a ship driven by the tide.

## *Face Lost in the Wilderness*

Do not fill postcards with memories.
Between my heart and the luxury of passion
stretches a desert where ropes of fire
blaze and smolder, where snakes
coil and recoil, swallowing blossoms
with poison and flame.

No! Don't ask me to remember. Love's memory
is dark, the dream clouded;
love is a lost phantom
in a wilderness night.
Friend, the night has slain the moon.
In the mirror of my heart you can find no shelter,
only my country's disfigured face,
her face, lovely and mutilated,
her precious face . . .

How did the world revolve in this way?
Our love was young. Did it grow in this horror?
In the night of defeat, black waters
covered my land, blood on the walls
was the only bouquet.
I hallucinated: "Open your breast,
open your mother's breast for an embrace
priceless are the offerings!"
The jungle beast was toasting in the
tavern of crime; winds of misfortune
howled in the four corners.
He was with me that day.
I didn't realize morning
would remove him.
Our smiles cheated sorrow
as I raved: "Beloved stranger!
Why did my country become a gateway
to hell? Since when are apples bitter?
When did moonlight stop bathing orchards?
My people used to plant fields and love life
Joyfully they dipped their bread in oil
Fruits and flowers tinted the land
with magnificent hues—
will the seasons ever again
give their gifts to my people?"
Sorrow—Jerusalem's night is silence and smoke.

They imposed a curfew; now nothing beats in the
heart of the City but their bloodied heels
under which Jerusalem trembles
like a raped girl.

Two shadows from a balcony
stared down at the City's night.
In the corner a suitcase of clothes,
souvenirs from the Holy Land—
his blue eyes stretched like sad lakes.
He loved Jerusalem. She was his mystical lover.
On and on I ranted, "Ah, love! Why did God abandon
my country? Imprisoning light, leaving us
in seas of darkness?"
The world was a mythical dragon standing
at her gate. "Who will ever solve this mystery,
beloved, the secret of these words?"

Now twenty moons have passed,
twenty moons, and my life continues.
Your absence too continues. Only one memory remaining:
The face of my stricken country filling my heart.

And my life continues—
the wind merges me with my people
on the terrible road of rocks and thorns.
But behind the river, dark forests of spears
sway and swell; the roaring storm
unravels mystery, giving to dragon-silence
the power of words.
A rush and din, flame and sparks
lighting the road—
one group after another
falls embracing, in one lofty death.
The night, no matter how long, will continue
to give birth to star after star
and my life continues,
my life continues.

## I Found It

I found it on a radiant day
after a long drifting.
It was green and blossoming

as the sun over palm trees
scattered golden bouquets;
April was generous that season
with loving and sun.

I found it
after a long wandering.
It was a tender evergreen bough
where birds took shelter,
a bough bending gently under storms
which later was straight again,
rich with sap,
never snapping in the wind's hand.
It stayed supple
as if there were no bad weather,
echoing the brightness of stars,
the gentle breeze,
the dew and the clouds.

I found it
on a vivid summer day
after a long straying,
a tedious search.
It was a quiet lake
where thirsty human wolves
and swirling winds could only briefly
disturb the waters.
Then they would clear again like crystal
to be the moon's mirror,
swimming place of light and blue,
bathing pool for the guardian stars.

I found it!
And now when the storms wail
and the face of the sun is masked in clouds,
when my shining fate revolves to dark,
my light will never be extinguished!
Everything that shadowed my life
wrapping it with night after night
has disappeared, lain down
in memory's grave,
since the day
my soul found
my soul.

# ISRAEL

## YEHUDA AMICHAI (B. 1924)

Born in Wurzberg, Germany, Yehuda Amichai immigrated to Palestine with his family in 1936. He served in the British army during World War II, with the Palmach during the Israeli War of Independence in 1948, and in the Israeli army in 1956 and 1973. Amichai's first collection of poems was published in 1955, and he has subsequently published at least eleven. Although he has written novels, short stories, and plays, he is best known for his poetry, which is frequently taught in public schools and often recited at weddings and funerals. His poems have even been set to music. His work has been translated into at least thirty-three languages, including Chinese and Japanese as well as English.

Raised in an Orthodox Jewish home, Amichai has said that his writing reflects the ethics of his father, a shoemaker, and the cruelties of war and politics. Memory functions as a common theme in his poetry, as is evident in both poems presented here. In one poem, Amichai writes, "What I will never see again I must love forever." Memory is a prominent theme in Jewish literature of the post-Holocaust era regardless of linguistic or national differences among the authors and can also be seen in the work of the American Jewish poet, Irena Klepfisz, whose work is included in this volume (pp. 2209–2219).

Amichai's poems also frequently allude to biblical and liturgical texts, although in translation these allusions are sometimes not as apparent as they are in Hebrew. Attempting to re-create a sense of the religious language woven throughout the texts, the two translators of Amichai's poems included here have borrowed from the King James version of the Bible. Commenting on his project to express the modern world in a revived version of ancient Hebrew, Amachai writes in his poem, "National Thoughts": "To speak now in this weary language, / a language that was torn from its sleep in the Bible: dazzled, / it wobbles from mouth to mouth."

"Jerusalem, 1967" and "Tourists" rest at an intersection of place, time, and culture. Both reflect on the meanings people attribute to location, and both contrast the views of travelers and outside observers with those of permanent inhabitants.

## *Jerusalem, 1967*

*Translated by Stephen Mitchell*

*To my friends Dennis, Arieh, and Harold*

*1*

This year I traveled a long way
to view the silence of my city.
A baby calms down when you rock it, a city calms down
from the distance. I dwelled in longing. I played the hopscotch

of the four strict squares of Yehuda Ha-Levi:
*My heart. Myself. East. West.*

I heard bells ringing in the religions of time,
but the wailing that I heard inside me
has always been from my Yehudean desert.

Now that I've come back, I'm screaming again.
And at night, stars rise like the bubbles of the drowned,
and every morning I scream the scream of a newborn baby
at the tumult of houses and at all this huge light.

*2*

I've come back to this city where names
are given to distances as if to human beings
and the numbers are not of bus routes
but: 70 After, 1917, 500
B.C., Forty-eight. These are the lines
you really travel on.

And already the demons of the past are meeting
with the demons of the future and negotiating about me
above me, their give-and-take neither giving nor taking,
in the high arches of shell-orbits above my head.

A man who comes back to Jerusalem is aware that the places
that used to hurt don't hurt anymore.
But a light warning remains in everything,
like the movement of a light veil: warning.

*3*

Illuminated is the Tower of David, illuminated is the Church
of Maria,
illuminated the patriarchs sleeping in their burial cave,
illuminated
are the faces from inside, illuminated the translucent
honey cakes, illuminated the clock and illuminated the time
passing through your thighs as you take off your dress.

Illuminated illuminated. Illuminated are the cheeks of my
childhood,
illuminated the stones that wanted to be illuminated
along with those that wanted to sleep in the darkness of squares.

Illuminated are the spiders of the banister and the cobwebs of churches
and the acrobats of the stairs. But more than all these, and in them all,
illuminated is the terrible, true X-ray writing
in letters of bones, in white and lightning: *MENE*
*MENE TEKEL UPHARSIN.*

*4*

In vain you will look for the fences of barbed wire.
You know that such things
don't disappear. A different city perhaps
is now being cut in two; two lovers
separated; a different flesh is tormenting itself now
with these thorns, refusing to be stone.
In vain you will look. You lift up your eyes unto the hills,
perhaps there? Not these hills, accidents of geology,
but The Hills. You ask
questions without a rise in your voice, without a question mark,
only because you're supposed to ask them; and they
don't exist. But a great weariness wants you with all your might
and gets you. Like death.

Jerusalem, the only city in the world
where the right to vote is granted even to the dead.

*5*

On Yom Kippur in 1967, the Year of Forgetting, I put on
my dark holiday clothes and walked to the Old City of Jerusalem.
For a long time I stood in front of an Arab's hole-in-the-wall shop,
not far from the Damascus Gate, a shop with
buttons and zippers and spools of thread
in every color and snaps and buckles.
A rare light and many colors, like an open Ark.

I told him in my heart that my father too
had a shop like this, with thread and buttons.
I explained to him in my heart about all the decades
and the causes and the events, why I am now here
and my father's shop was burned there and he is buried here.

When I finished, it was time for the Closing of the Gates prayer.
He too lowered the shutters and locked the gate
and I returned, with all the worshipers, home.

*6*

It's not time that keeps me far away from my childhood,
it's this city and everything in it. Now
I've got to learn Arabic too, to reach all the way to Jericho
from both ends of time; and the length of walls has been added
and the height of towers and the domes of prayer houses
whose area is immeasurable. All these
really broaden my life and force me
always to emigrate once more from the smell
of river and forest.
My life is stretched out this way; it grows very thin
like cloth, transparent. You can see right through me.

*7*

In this summer of wide-open-eyed hatred
and blind love, I'm beginning to believe again
in all the little things that will fill
the holes left by the shells: soil, a bit of grass,
perhaps, after the rains, small insects of every kind.
I think of children growing up half in the ethics of their fathers
and half in the science of war.
The tears now penetrate into my eyes from the outside
and my ears invent, every day, the footsteps of
the messenger of good tidings.

*8*

The city plays hide-and-seek among her names:
Yerushalayim, Al-Quds, Salem, Jeru, Yeru, all the while
whispering her first, Jebusite name: Y'vus,
Y'vus, Y'vus, in the dark. She weeps
with longing: Ælia Capitolina, Ælia, Ælia.
She comes to any man who calls her
at night, alone. But we know
who comes to whom.

*9*

On an open door a sign hangs: Closed.
How do you explain it? Now
the chain is free at both ends: there is no
prisoner and no warden, no dog and no master.
The chain will gradually turn into wings.
How do you explain it?
Ah well, you'll explain it.

*10*

Jerusalem is short and crouched among its hills,
unlike New York, for example.
Two thousand years ago she crouched
in the marvelous starting-line position.
All the other cities ran ahead, did long
laps in the arena of time, they won or lost,
and died. Jerusalem remained in the starting-crouch:
all the victories are clenched inside her,
hidden inside her. All the defeats.
Her strength grows and her breathing is calm
for a race even beyond the arena.

*11*

Loneliness is always in the middle,
protected and fortified. People were supposed
to feel secure in that, and they don't.
When they go out, after a long time,
caves are formed for the new solitaries.
What do you know about Jerusalem?
You don't need to understand languages;
they pass through everything as if through the ruins of houses.
People are a wall of moving stones.
But even in the Wailing Wall
I haven't seen stones as sad as these.
The letters of my pain are illuminated
like the name of the hotel across the street.
What awaits me and what doesn't await me.

*12*

Jerusalem stone is the only stone that can
feel pain. It has a network of nerves.
From time to time Jerusalem crowds into
mass protests like the tower of Babel.
But with huge clubs God-the-Police beats her
down: houses are razed, walls flattened,
and afterward the city disperses, muttering
prayers of complaint and sporadic screams from churches
and synagogues and loud-moaning mosques.
Each to his own place.

*13*

Always beside ruined houses and iron girders
twisted like the arms of the slain, you find

someone who is sweeping the paved path
or tending the little garden, sensitive
paths, square flower-beds.
Large desires for a horrible death are well cared-for
as in the monastery of the White Brothers next to the Lions' Gate.
But farther on, in the courtyard, the earth gapes:
columns and arches supporting vain land
and negotiating with one another: crusaders and guardian angels,
a sultan and Rabbi Yehuda the Pious. Arched vaults with a
column, ransom for prisoners, and strange conditions in rolled-up
contracts, and sealing-stones. Curved hooks holding
air.
Capitals and broken pieces of columns scattered like chessmen
in a game that was interrupted in anger,
and Herod, who already, two thousand years ago, wailed
like mortar shells. He knew.

*14*

If clouds are a ceiling, I would like to
sit in the room beneath them: a dead kingdom rises
up from me, up, like steam from hot food.
A door squeaks: an opening cloud.
In the distances of valleys someone rapped iron against stone
but the echo erects large, different things in the air.

Above the houses—houses with houses above them. This is
all of history.
This learning in schools without roof
and without walls and without chairs and without teachers.
This learning in the absolute outside,
a learning short as a single heartbeat. All of it.

*15*

I and Jerusalem are like a blind man and a cripple.
She sees for me
out to the Dead Sea, to the End of Days.
And I hoist her up on my shoulders
and walk blind in my darkness underneath.

*16*

On this bright autumn day
I establish Jerusalem once again.
The foundation scrolls
are flying in the air, birds, thoughts.

God is angry with me
because I always force him
to create the world once again
from chaos, light, second day, until
man, and back to the beginning.

*17*

In the morning the shadow of the Old City falls
on the New. In the afternoon—vice versa.
Nobody profits. The muezzin's prayer
is wasted on the new houses. The ringing
bells roll like balls and bounce back.
The shout of *Holy, Holy, Holy* from the synagogues will fade
like gray smoke.

At the end of summer I breathe this air
that is burnt and pained. My thoughts have
the stillness of many closed books:
many crowded books, with most of their pages
stuck together like eyelids in the morning.

*18*

I climb up the Tower of David
a little higher than the prayer that ascends the highest:
halfway to heaven. A few of
the ancients succeeded: Mohammed, Jesus,
and others. Though they didn't find rest in heaven;
they just entered a higher excitement. But
the applause for them hasn't stopped ever since,
down below.

*19*

Jerusalem is built on the vaulted foundations
of a held-back scream. If there were no reason
for the scream, the foundations would crumble, the city would collapse;
if the scream were screamed, Jerusalem would explode into the heavens.

*20*

Poets come in the evening into the Old City
and they emerge from it pockets stuffed with images
and metaphors and little well-constructed parables
and crepuscular similes from among columns and crypts,
from within darkening fruit

and delicate filigree of hammered hearts.
I lifted my hand to my forehead
to wipe off the sweat
and found I had accidentally raised up
the ghost of Else Lasker-Schüler.
Light and tiny as she was
in her life, all the more so in her death. Ah, but
her poems.

*21*

Jerusalem is a port city on the shore of eternity.
The Temple Mount is a huge ship, a magnificent
luxury liner. From the portholes of her Western Wall
cheerful saints look out, travelers. Hasidim on the pier
wave goodbye, shout hooray, hooray, bon voyage! She is
always arriving, always sailing away. And the fences and the piers
and the policemen and the flags and the high masts of churches
and mosques and the smokestacks of synagogues and the boats
of psalms of praise and the mountain-waves. The shofar blows:
          another one
has just left. Yom Kippur sailors in white uniforms
climb among ladders and ropes of well-tested prayers.

And the commerce and the gates and the golden domes:
Jerusalem is the Venice of God.

*22*

Jerusalem is Sodom's sister-city,
but the merciful salt didn't have mercy on her
and didn't cover her with a silent whiteness.
Jerusalem is an unconsenting Pompeii.
History books that were thrown into the fire,
their pages are strewn about, stiffening in red.

An eye whose color is too light, blind,
always shattered in a sieve of veins.
Many births gaping below,
a womb with numberless teeth,
a double-edged woman and the holy beasts.

The sun thought that Jerusalem was a sea
and set in her: a terrible mistake.
Sky fish were caught in a net of alleys,
tearing one another to pieces.
Jerusalem. An operation that was left open.
The surgeons went to take a nap in faraway skies,

but her dead gradually
formed a circle, all around her,
like quiet petals.
My God.
My stamen.
Amen.

## *Tourists*

*Translated by Chana Bloch*

*1*

So condolence visits is what they're here for,
sitting around at the Holocaust Memorial, putting on a serious face
at the Wailing Wall,
laughing behind heavy curtains in hotel rooms.

They get themselves photographed with the important dead
at Rachel's Tomb and Herzl's Tomb, and up on Ammunition Hill.
They weep at the beautiful prowess of our boys,
lust after our tough girls
and hang up their underwear
to dry quickly
in cool blue bathrooms.

*2*

Once I was sitting on the steps near the gate at David's Citadel and I put down my two heavy baskets beside me. A group of tourists stood there around their guide, and I became their point of reference. "You see that man over there with the baskets? A little to the right of his head there's an arch from the Roman period. A little to the right of his head." "But he's moving, he's moving!" I said to myself: Redemption will come only when they are told, "Do you see that arch over there from the Roman period? It doesn't matter, but near it, a little to the left and then down a bit, there's a man who has just bought fruit and vegetables for his family."

# SENEGAL

## LÉOPOLD SÉDAR SENGHOR (B. 1906)

*Translated by John Reed and Clive Wake*

Léopold Sédar Senghor was born in Senegal when it was a part of the French colony of French West Africa. The son of rich Catholic landowners, Senghor began his education in a mission school but then moved on to the Lycée in Dakar, where he was steeped in the French classical curriculum based on Latin, Greek, French, and mathematics. His extraordinary literary gifts led to a scholarship for university study in Paris. Together with other students of African descent from French colonies, Senghor founded the *Négritude* movement, which was inspired by the writings of African Americans and proclaimed an international culture of the African diaspora. In 1933 Senghor became the first African to obtain the highest degree available in the French system of education. For some years afterward he taught French, Latin, and Greek in France. During World War II he fought in the French army, was captured by the Germans, and spent two years in a German prison. After the war, he entered politics and eventually became the first president of Senegal at the time of its independence in 1960, retaining the office until 1980 and distinguishing himself by adroit leadership and tireless efforts for African independence and unity.

Senghor's first book of poetry, *Chants d'Ombre,* was published in 1945. He has won numerous honors as a poet, including the *Grand Prix International de Poésie,* one of the most prestigious prizes in French letters, and election to the *Académie Française.* He has also been very active in drawing attention to African writers and has compiled an early anthology of African poetry for which the philosopher Jean-Paul Sartre wrote the preface.

Senghor is a man of two worlds, schooled in French literature—he writes all his poetry in French—but at the same time proudly immersed in his African heritage, which descends from the great West African empires of Mali (thirteenth–fifteenth centuries) and Songhai (sixteenth century), both frequently mentioned in his writings. He draws poetic inspiration from the rhythms of African song and dance. The poems selected here exemplify his commitment to his African heritage and landscape. For example, in "The Return of the Prodigal Son," the poet returns home to beg the blessing of his ancestors and even approaches them at the shrine of Mbissel, where sacrifices are made to the indigenous gods. But at the same time, he explains to his African ancestors that he has "made friends with the outlawed princes of the intellect" and has lived "in the fellowship of my blue-eyed brothers." Senghor has long been an advocate of the universal kinship of all human beings.

## *Nuit de Sine*

Woman, lay on my forehead your perfumed hands, hands softer
    than fur.
Above, the swaying palm trees rustle in the high night breeze
Hardly at all. No lullaby even.
The rhythmic silence cradles us.
Listen to its song, listen to our dark blood beat, listen
To the deep pulse of Africa beating in the mist of forgotten
    villages.

See the tired moon comes down to her bed on the slack sea.
The laughter grows weary, the story-tellers even

Are nodding their heads like a child on the back of its mother.
The feet of the dancers grow heavy, and heavy the voice of the answering choirs.

It is the hour of stars, of Night that dreams
Leaning upon this hill of clouds, wrapped in its long milky cloth.
The roofs of the huts gleam tenderly. What do they say so secretly to the stars?
Inside the fire goes out among intimate smells that are acrid and sweet.

Woman, light the clear oil lamp, where the ancestors gathered around may talk as parents talk when the children are put to bed.
Listen to the voice of the ancients of Elissa. Exiled like us
They have never wanted to die, to let the torrent of their seed be lost in the sands.
Let me listen in the smoky hut where there comes a glimpse of the friendly spirits
My head on your bosom warm like a *dang* still steaming from the fire.
Let me breathe the smell of our Dead, gather and speak out again their living voice, learn to
Live before I go down, deeper than diver, into the high profundities of sleep.

## Black Woman

Naked woman, black woman
Clothed with your colour which is life, with your form which is beauty!
In your shadow I have grown up; the gentleness of your hands was laid over my eyes.
And now, high up on the sun-baked pass, at the heart of summer, at the heart of noon, I come upon you, my Promised Land,
And your beauty strikes me to the heart like the flash of an eagle.

Naked woman, dark woman
Firm-fleshed ripe fruit, sombre raptures of black wine, mouth making lyrical my mouth
Savannah stretching to clear horizons, savannah shuddering beneath the East Wind's eager caresses
Carved tom-tom, taut tom-tom, muttering under the Conqueror's fingers
Your solemn contralto voice is the spiritual song of the Beloved.

Naked woman, dark woman
Oil that no breath ruffles, calm oil on the athlete's flanks, on the flanks of the Princes of Mali
Gazelle limbed in Paradise, pearls are stars on the night of your skin
Delights of the mind, the glinting of red gold against your watered skin
Under the shadow of your hair, my care is lightened by the neighbouring suns of your eyes.

Naked woman, black woman
I sing your beauty that passes, the form that I fix in the Eternal,
Before jealous Fate turns you to ashes to feed the roots of life.

## *Prayer to Masks*

Masks! Masks!
Black mask red mask, you white-and-black masks
Masks of the four points from which the Spirit blows
In silence I salute you!
Nor you the least, Lion-headed Ancestor
You guard this place forbidden to all laughter of women, to all smiles that fade
You distill this air of eternity in which I breathe the air of my Fathers.
Masks of unmasked faces, stripped of the marks of illness and the lines of age
You who have fashioned this portrait, this my face bent over the altar of white paper
In your own image, hear me!
The Africa of the empires is dying, see, the agony of a pitiful princess
And Europe too where we are joined by the navel.
Fix your unchanging eyes upon your children, who are given orders
Who give away their lives like the poor their last clothes.
Let us report present at the rebirth of the World
Like the yeast which white flour needs.
For who would teach rhythm to a dead world of machines and guns?
Who would give the cry of joy to wake the dead and the bereaved at dawn?
Say, who would give back the memory of life to the man whose hopes are smashed?
They call us men of coffee cotton oil
They call us men of death.

We are the men of the dance, whose feet draw new strength
pounding the hardened earth.

## *The Return of the Prodigal Son*

*Lament for kora*

*To Jacques Maguilen Senghor, my nephew*

### I

And my heart once more on the stone step, under the high gate of honour.
And a quiver runs through the warm ashes of the Man with lightning eyes, my father.
On my hunger, the dust of sixteen wandering years, and the restlessness of all the roads of Europe
And the hum of vast cities; and the towns beaten by a thousand breakers in my head.
My heart has stayed as pure as the East Wind in the month of March.

### II

And I challenge the witness of my blood appearing in heads vacant of ideas, in this belly abandoned by the muscles of courage.
Let me follow the golden note from the flute of silence, let me follow the herdsman, my fellow-dreamer of long ago
Naked under his milk-white girdle, with a flamboyant flower on his forehead.
Pierce, herdsman, pierce, with a long unearthly note the tottering villa where window frames and occupants are hollow with termites.
And my heart once more under the high dwelling built by the pride of the Man
And my heart once more at the grave where reverently he has laid his long genealogy to rest.
There is no need of paper; only the sonorous leaf of the *dyali* and the golden red stylet of his tongue.

### III

How vast, empty the courtyard is in the odour of vacancy
Like the plain in the dry season trembling with its own emptiness
What lumberjack storm has felled the centennial tree?
A whole people were fed by its shade on the circular terrace

A whole household with its grooms and shepherds, servants and craftsmen
On the red terrace that kept safe the herds swelling like a sea in the great days of fire and blood.
Or is this a district struck by four-engined eagles
And the strong pounce of leonine bombs?

## IV

And my heart once more on the steps of the high dwelling.
I prostrate myself at your feet, in the dust of my respect
At your feet, Ancestors still present, who rule in pride the great hall of your masks defying Time.
Faithful servant of my childhood, see my feet where the mud of Civilization sticks.
Clean water for my feet, servant, and only their white soles on the mats of silence.
Peace peace and peace, my Fathers, upon the brow of the Prodigal Son.

## V

You above all, Elephant of Mbissel, who clothed your poet *dyali* in friendship
And he shared the dishes of honour with you, the fat that makes the lips to shine
And the horses of the River, gifts of the Kings of Sine, masters of millet masters of the palms
Kings of Sine who had planted at Dyakhaw the upright force of their lance.
And above all, Mbogu colour of the desert; and the Guelwars poured out libations of tears at his going
Pure rain of dew when the Sun's death bleeds on the seashore and on the waves of the warrior dead.

## VI

Elephant of Mbissel, through your ears hidden from our sight, may my Ancestors hear my reverent prayer.
Bless you, my Fathers, bless you!
Shopkeepers and bankers, lords of gold and of suburbs with forests of chimneys
—They bought their nobility and the womb of their mother was black
Shopkeepers and bankers have proscribed me from the Nation.
On the honour of my weapons they had the word 'Mercenary' cut
And they knew that I did not ask for pay; only the ten sous
To lull my smoky dream, and milk to wash my blue bitterness.

If I have replanted my allegiance on the fields of defeat, it is
because God with his hand of lead had stricken France.
Bless you, my Fathers, bless you.
You who allowed contempt and derision, polite offences and
discreet allusions
Prohibitions and segregations.
Then you tore from the heart too trusting the ties that linked it to
the pulse of the world.
Bless you, you who have never let hatred gravel this heart of man.
You know that I have made friends with the outlawed princes of
the intellect, with the princes of form
That I have eaten the bread which makes hungry the innumerable
army of workers and those without work
That I have dreamt of a sunlit world in the fellowship of my
blue-eyed brothers.

**VII**

Elephant of Mbissel, I am glad to see the shops around the
high dwelling empty.
I clap, I burst out clapping! Let bankruptcy thrive!
I am glad the white wings have deserted this arm of the sea.
In the submarine bush, let crocodiles hunt; let sea-cows browse in
peace!
I set fire to the *seco,* the pyramid of groundnuts that commands
the country,
To the rigid jetty, will implacable upon the sea
And then I revive the murmur of herds amid neighing and lowing
The murmur at evening tempered by the moonlight of flute and
conchs
I revive the procession of maidservants through the dew
And the great calabashes of milk, steady on the rhythm of swaying
hips
I revive the caravan of asses and dromedaries among smells of
millet and rice
Among the glittering of mirrors, and the tinkling of faces and
silver bells.
I revive my virtues of the soil.

**VIII**

Elephant of Mbissel, hear my reverent prayer.
Give me the fervent learning of the great doctors of Timbuktu
Give me the determination of Soni Ali, son of the Lion's slaver—a
tide race to the conquest of a continent.
Breathe upon me the wisdom of the Keita.
Give me the Guelwar's courage, gird my loins with the power of a

*tyedo.*
Let me die in my people's quarrel, if need be in the smell of
powder and guns.
Keep, root in my freed heart the first love of the same people.
Make me your Master of Language; or rather, let me be named
the ambassador of my people.

**IX**

Bless you, my Fathers, who bless the Prodigal Son.
Let me see once more on the right where the women stay the
place where I played with the doves and my brothers,
the sons of the Lion.
Ah! to sleep once more in the fresh bed of my childhood
Ah! once more those black dear hands to tuck in my sleep
Once more the white smile of my mother.
Tomorrow, I shall take again the road to Europe, road of my
embassy
Homesick for my black land.

# Kenya

## Grace Ogot (b. 1930)

One of the first Kenyan women writers to achieve a wide reputation, Grace Ogot writes fiction dealing with rural village life, the world of missionary hospitals, and life in modern African cities such as Nairobi. She was educated at Ng'iya and Butere Schools and studied nursing in Uganda and England. These experiences gave her opportunities to develop professionally in ways not available for previous generations of Kenyan women; indeed, even now, women remain in traditional roles in rural villages. In addition to her nursing experience, she has worked as a scriptwriter, a community development officer, and a public relations officer for an international airline and has had her own business in Nairobi. Her first novel, *The Promised Land,* was published in 1966; she has also published several short story collections, among them *Land Without Thunder,* from which our selection is taken.

Ogot's fiction often relates experiences of the macabre and the fantastic, as in a story of an old man who steals a piece of meat from an eagle and develops an insatiable craving for human liver or a story about an enormous snake that takes over a house in a small village and terrorizes the whole community. "The Bamboo Hut," written in English, is a more benign story about a woman who abandons a baby girl. The girl reappears years later and wins the heart of her own unsuspecting twin brother. This is a story of lost relatives and mysterious reappearances that recalls the story of the similarly orphaned Oedipus but has a much happier outcome.

## the bamboo hut

The setting sun was ablaze, and its angry rays coloured the water on Lake Victoria. Mboga's heart beat fast. He had never seen the disc of the setting sun look so big and ominous. He moved towards the foot of the sacred Hill of Ramogi where his forefathers had from time immemorial worshipped God and pleaded with the ancestors.

For many years Mboga had beseeched Ramogi, the ancestor of the Luo people, to intercede on his behalf for a son, an heir to the beaded stool of the Kadibo people. He had decided to make one final plea on this sacred spot. He spat in the direction of the setting sun, and then prayed.

*God of Ramogi and God of*
*Podho*
*You led us from distant lands,*
*And protected us against all our*
*enemies.*
*You gave us land and other*
*possessions,*
*Let the name of Ramogi*
*continue*
*Let us multiply and expand in all*
*directions*
*People call me Mboga the Mighty,*
*the handsome ruler,*
*Father of the clan.*
*What is a mighty ruler without a*
*son?*
*What is a father without an*
*heir?*

Darkness was falling when Mboga reached home. In the inner compound of his homestead, his 'numerous daughters', as he always referred to them, were busy helping their mothers prepare the evening meal. And although he loved all his sixteen daughters, they were like the birds of the air who, at the appropriate season, migrate to other lands. Who would comfort and succour him in old age?

The drizzle that had started in the evening continued up to the early hours of the next day. The children stayed in their mothers' huts. Agtiso took a red sweet potato from a basket and buried it in the cow-dung fire. She added a handful of dry cow-dung to the fire, and then turned to Achieng' her mother.

"Mama—why can't we live in the bamboo hut? It is clean, cosy, cool and beautiful. Please ask Baba if we can move into it," she said appealingly.

"But our hut is one of the best in the compound, my child."

"I know that, Mama, but it can't beat the bamboo hut. Our hut has no inner chamber and we have no bamboo beds or beaded stools."

Agtiso took a wooden poker and turned the potato over.

"Right, Mama," she said, throwing the poker down. "If you are afraid of the chief, I will ask him myself. I am not afraid."

The bamboo hut stood next to the chief's large hut. It looked beautiful in the morning drizzle. Agtiso's mother took her eyes away from it. She was expecting her second baby after an interval of nearly seven years. She knew it would be a girl. The chief, who had nine wives, had promised the bamboo hut to whoever bore him a son, an heir to the beaded stool.

Two months after Mboga's visit to the sacred hill, Achieng' gave birth while she was out at the well. It was a baby girl! The long-nursed desire for a son turned her heart against the baby, and she wept bitterly. "How do I break this sad news to my husband? Will the chief bear the thought of another girl? No, no, no. Let my mouth remain sealed for ever—the ancestors have wronged me."

But Achieng's weeping was interrupted by a sharp pain that stabbed her belly and her back. It was like one of those miracles that occur only once in a while. Achieng' gave birth again—it was a boy!

The river bank was still deserted as most women did not fetch water at midday. Everything was so quiet, apart from a few frogs who seemed to be rejoicing with her. She felt very tired, and for a few minutes different passions played a wild dance within her. Love, hatred, anger and happiness crossed and intermingled. The chief had waited for a son for over twelve years. Let the chief have only one child, a son, so that he might see the fulfilment of his life's dream. Achieng' made up her mind. She made a grass-basket and lined it with leaves—there she laid Apiyo and hid the basket near the well. She gave her a long, close and last look, and then ran a finger over her face, hair, lips and delicate fingers. She then walked home with her baby boy, and slipped into her hut unnoticed while people were having their midday meal.

The important news was conveyed to Chief Mboga by his elder wife while he was resting in his hut.

"God of Ramogi has covered the nakedness of the father of the people. Achieng' has given birth to a baby son."

Mboga looked at his wife unbelievingly. A joyous smile played on his lips, and then disappeared, leaving only muscles twitching at the corners of his mouth. He eyed his wife and then got up to go to Achieng's hut. But his elder wife barred his way.

"The great chief should not be over-powered by emotion. Achieng' is under the care of women for four days. Only then can the great chief see his beloved son."

Mboga moved a few steps backwards and sat on his stool. "All right, tell Achieng' that I have received the news." Then the Chief's drum boomed out to announce the birth of a new baby. This time it boomed out four times instead of the usual three for a girl, and the family rejoiced. Envy mixed with bitterness in the minds of Achieng's co-wives, but they did not show it. A sheep was slaughtered for the delivered mother and all good things were showered upon her.

Chief Mboga never laughed or shed tears in public, but on the fourth day when he held his son at a naming ceremony, his close relatives saw big lumps of tears rolling down his cheeks as he called out the name of the boy.

"You will be called 'Owiny' after the second son of Ramogi. You will live long, and in my old age you will hold the staff of Ramogi in your right hand to rule your people." Then the chief's beaded staff was placed in Owiny's right hand and the chief's ornamental bracelet put on his wrist.

On that day, Achieng' and Agtiso, her daughter, moved to the bamboo hut. There, they were to bring up Owiny, heir to Mboga's beaded stool. The chief offered numerous thanksgiving sacrifices at the foot of the sacred hill. His prayers always ended with the refrain:

"Now I know you did indeed choose me to be a ruler among these people. You have given me a son."

Amid all the revelry, Achieng' maintained a most singular gravity. She felt as if something in her heart were breaking. She couldn't go on like this any longer—but what was to be done? Should she look for her daughter? No, she couldn't do anything like that. Could she tell her husband the truth—but how?

She went to the well on the sixth day to bathe herself after confinement. She walked hurriedly past the place where she had abandoned her daughter Apiyo. There was nothing on the spot to betray her, and the long grass stood erect as though nothing had ever rested on it. As she trudged along on her way home, Achieng' had many thoughts, confused thoughts, but thoughts nevertheless, and even visions, about her lost daughter.

She saw an old, withered woman pick up her daughter by the well. She saw her perform a kind of witches' dance round the basket, before carrying it away. The route followed by the old woman was towards the no-man's land lying between the Kadibo folk and their enemies. She then saw her daughter being thrown away in this forest, which was known to be infested with wild animals.

Unconsciously, she yelled! Her heart began to beat and a sudden moisture wetted the middle of her palms. Was it true? "No, no, no!" she replied.

Years slipped by, but Achieng's distraught mind showed no signs of improvement. It was a life of visions and depression in the day-time, and of nightmares at night. Neither her privileged position among the chiefs' wives nor the future prospects for her son were adequate to fill the acute emptiness she felt in her heart.

Owiny grew up into a fine, strong man, with the usual characteristics of single children—sulky, headstrong and independent. One afternoon, as the chief was on one of his regular walks to the sacred hill, he encountered a group of young women carrying loads of fire-wood. The girls left the path and hid behind the long bushes to let the chief pass. But one girl put her bundle down and stood waiting. When the chief got close to her, she bowed her head and greeted him.

"Peace be with you, great chief."

"Peace, my child," said the chief, who was obviously moved by the courage of this young girl.

"Are you not afraid of the chief like your sisters?" the chief teased her.

"No. It is my lucky day to meet the kind chief."

Then she put the bundle on her head and walked away.

That night Mboga called his son and told him about the young woman.

"She is the daughter of Owuor Chilo the clan elder of Usigu. She is visiting her aunt here. Try and see her tomorrow. If you like her, we will approach her parents. She should make a good wife."

Owiny was curious to meet the young lady whose personality had impressed the chief so much. He kept watch on her movements; and when a messenger informed him that the girl and her friends had been seen swimming in the river Odundu, he immediately rushed to the scene.

At the river half a dozen young women were swimming and shouting at one another. One of the older girls saw Owiny first, and rushed out of the water yelling, "The chief's son! The chief's son!"

The girls, taken unaware, scrambled out of the water and hid behind the nearest bushes. But the girl who obviously looked younger than the others continued to swim, undisturbed. Owiny moved closer to her.

"Why aren't you afraid of the son of the chief?" he asked her, jokingly.

The girl was not bashful. She looked knowingly at him, raised her head a little and, concealing her breasts, said, "Because the son of the chief does not respect ladies' privacy.

"I was on my way to the hills to hunt, when I heard some shrieking noises—I therefore came to check."

"Right," she said with finality, as she dived in and out. "Now that you know who were shrieking, you can continue with your journey."

Owiny stood there puzzled. This foolhardy girl was not from his clan—her accent was foreign. She could be the girl the chief had told him about.

"Can't you come out and give your friends their loin cloths? I didn't mean to be rude to them."

"It would be better if you left us alone—we are still swimming."

"No," Owiny said firmly. "I want to talk to all of you about the coming festival of the chief."

"All right," she said. "Throw me my loin cloth—it is the beaded one."

Owiny was shocked by the girl's natural air of importance. He never took orders from anyone, let alone any woman—he was always waited upon. He swallowed his pride and threw her the beaded loin cloth. The girl wrapped her loin cloth round her waist and emerged from the water unafraid. She grabbed the other loin cloths in her arm and handed them to her friends behind the bushes.

Owiny felt warm and uncomfortable where he stood. For the first time in his life he was unsure of himself. He took a close look at the girl—she was much older than the chief had suggested. Her long slender legs would fill up with maturity. Her fingers were long and graceful; and she had a straight back and flat lovable belly. Her breasts were still young and stood erect like wooden carvings on her chest. Her skin dotted with water was the colour of the rising sun. As Owiny looked at her, she reminded him of Arosi, the legendary and beautiful goddess of the sea. They exchanged a few words, and she told Owiny that her name was Awiti.

That evening Owiny was in a melancholy mood. A newly discovered fire was burning in his heart. He reported to his father that he had seen the girl and that he liked her very much.

In those days the marriage preliminaries for the son of a chief were conducted with proper punctilio. The chief therefore sent out messengers to investigate the girl's background. Gossip had reached Achieng' that her would-be daughter-in-law had no equal for beauty in all Luoland. She had, moreover, been brought up with great care and was diligent.

The messengers returned with red dust on their feet and with empty bellies. On seeing them, Chief Mboga went to his hut to receive the news.

They told him:

"The family of Owuor Chilo did not deal with us kindly when we enquired about the girl. It seemed that a word had reached them that the young man, your son, may be seeking her hand in marriage. They insisted that Awiti was too young, that they should be given time. But we pressed them. We had seen the girl—she is beautiful and ripe for marriage. The family then conferred among themselves outside, and when they joined us, they told us that Awiti may not wish to marry the chief's son."

The messenger who was speaking looked at the chief anxiously and moistened his dry lips.

"Go on," the chief roared aggressively.

He looked past them so that they could not notice the angry frown which distorted his face.

"They said, great chief, that it is impossible." Mboga's fame was not confined to his clan alone. Who was Owuor Chilo whose daughter could reject the offer of the son of the chief?

"Go on," he repeated.

"We were not satisfied with the excuses given, so we called at a neighbouring village and enquired circumspectly about the girl. We were told that Awiti has no parents. She was found abandoned by the well by Owuor's elder wife who adopted her."

The messenger cleared his throat, and mopped away a mushroom of sweat from his forehead.

The air suddenly became still and suffocating, as Chief Mboga discharged his messengers. He knocked his pipe on a wooden log nearby to empty the dead ashes. Owiny's new hut caught his eye. Mboga knew that his son would not accept the news. But a chief's son could not marry a nonentity, a woman of unknown parentage.

That evening when the restless cows had been milked and the tired children sat round the fire by their mothers waiting for the evening meal, Owiny was summoned to the chief's hut. Mboga broke the sad news to his son.

"My son, you cannot marry Chilo's daughter. She was abandoned as a baby by the well—the wife of Chilo found her and brought her up."

Mboga sucked his pipe and then spat on the hard-beaten floor.

"As the future ruler of the land you cannot marry a woman whose background is a mystery."

Owiny tightened his buttocks on the oily stool he was sitting on. He wanted to rise and leave the chief's hut, but he fell back. Breath had gone out of him, and he felt dizzy. As he recovered from the shock, he had a hazy vision of Awiti—he saw her beautiful figure and her provocative breasts. The fire revived in him. He must tell his father the truth.

"Father let me take her to be my wife. I love her. I want to live with her. I . . ."

Tears choked Owiny and he could not complete the sentence.

"No, my son," the chief said. "She is not good enough for our home—the ancestors would be displeased. We shall find you a suitable woman."

Owiny got up unexpectedly, paced up and down the room and then turned sharply to face his father.

"Will the great chief change his mind and allow me to marry the woman I desire?"

Mboga gripped the ruling staff tightly.

"No," he thundered and his voice rang in the still night. Owiny stood before his father for a while before he spoke gravely.

"Great chief, you will not see my face again. I have chosen the daughter of Chilo—you can keep your beaded stool."

Without waiting for his father's reply, Owiny left. He shut himself up in his hut—he wished to blot the whole world out of his sight. What was he to do? Commit suicide? No—he must live to marry Awiti. Run away—but where?

The dismay in the homestead, when the news became known, may well be imagined. But all the uncles, aunts and other relatives agreed with the chief that Awiti would not make a suitable wife for Mboga's son. Only Achieng', Owiny's mother, knew the truth. Was she to die with this secret? Her son's life was at stake—why not face the chief and tell him the truth? She might ruin his life—but he was old enough to die. Her son had all his life before him. She made up her mind—she must say it.

She went to the chief's hut and fell at his feet weeping.

"She is my daughter. Awiti is the daughter of the great chief, and twin sister to Owiny, your son. I abandoned her by the well because I wanted to give you nothing but a son."

Mboga sat still and the hairs on his skin stood erect like those of a frightened cat. The scene on the path from the sacred hill when Awiti greeted him by the road side came to his mind. Yes, her face resembled that of his son. Mboga looked past this wife into the dark night. Only a few hours more and it would be sunrise, then the whole land would know the truth. He knew his people were going to persuade him to send Achieng' away. She had thrown away her new-born baby, she had angered the ancestors, she was not worthy of being a chief's wife.

But Mboga made up his mind. No-one was going to take Achieng' from him. She was the centre of his life. The self-doubt that often follows the betrayal of life-long trust crept into Mboga's mind. He wondered what other secrets were still hidden in the bosoms of his wives. He lifted Achieng's head from his feet.

"Mother of Awiti, arise. For my sake you have borne a heavy burden for many years. You have denied yourself the pleasure a mother gets from seeing her child. Go and tell your son that he has a very beautiful sister. I shall give him my choicest bull to slaughter and eat with his sister and friends—let us all rejoice and thank our ancestor Ramogi."

# Nigeria

## Chinua Achebe (b. 1930)

Chinua Achebe, a writer from the Ibo tribe of eastern Nigeria, is a major literary voice from black Africa. His first novel, *Things Fall Apart,* published in 1958, is perhaps his finest treatment of what being an African in the modern world means. The setting for the work is Nigeria in the early years of the twentieth century as European imperialism begins to have an impact on a small village. Because so much writing from Africa has been from the perspective of the imperialist outsider, Achebe's purpose is to present Africa from an African perspective. In this work he gives a detailed depiction of traditional village life in order to demonstrate to the rest of the world that traditional African culture is rich and meaningful in its own terms and also to reassure African readers who might have accepted the myth of African inferiority that it is false.

In the context of emergent African nationalism, Achebe has not been reluctant to argue that fiction can and even should play a role in defining social change. His novel, *Things Fall Apart,* nevertheless, is not merely a nationalistic polemic. He creates a rich narrative tapestry studded with proverbs and oral tales that embellish his story. Also memorable are the cast of characters. Okonkwo, the central figure, is a man of strength who defeats his enemies in battle, who triumphs over the recalcitrant forces of nature to make his farm prosper, and who overcomes his family background to become a leader of his village. Yet this man of strength is trapped by his fear of failure and weakness. While he struggles valiantly to achieve his version of success, he cannot resist fate; neither can he find in himself the tolerance to accept a new social order. By contrast, his friend Obierika represents both the cost and the reward of tolerance and willingness to adapt to inevitable change. British colonial administrators are purposely presented as one-dimensional, stereotyped figures, who are intolerant in their own way.

Achebe does not advocate a return to precolonial times; he is too much of a realist for that. He does not try to argue that traditional culture was perfect. But he does recognize the loss involved in the destruction of traditional values and ways, and he is at the same time skeptical about the so-called benefits of European culture. In the end he recognizes and articulates the complexities of the need for compromise and change. In the broadest terms, Achebe's characters live in a changing world and their successes and failures depend on the extent to which they can control or adapt to change.

In the excerpts presented here, we see a traditional wedding feast, an instance of the administration of village justice, and a confrontation with an alien culture.

## *from Things Fall Apart*

### Chapter Ten

Large crowds began to gather on the village *ilo* as soon as the edge had worn off the sun's heat and it was no longer painful on the body. Most communal ceremonies took place at that time of the day, so that even when it was said that a ceremony would begin 'after the midday meal' everyone understood that it would begin a long time later, when the sun's heat had softened.

It was clear from the way the crowd stood or sat that the ceremony was for men. There were many women, but they looked on from the fringe like outsiders. The titled men and elders sat on their stools waiting for the trials to begin. In front of them was a row of stools on which nobody sat. There were nine of them. Two little groups of people stood at a respectable distance beyond the stools. They faced the elders. There were three men in one group and three men and one woman in the other. The woman was Mgbafo and the three men with her were her brothers. In the other group were her husband, Uzowulu, and his relatives. Mgbafo and her brothers were as still as statues into whose faces the artist has moulded defiance. Uzowulu and his relatives, on the other hand, were whispering together. It looked like whispering, but they were really talking at the top of their voices. Everybody in the crowd was talking. It was like the market. From a distance the noise was a deep rumble carried by the wind.

An iron gong sounded, setting up a wave of expectation in the crowd. Everyone looked in the direction of the *egwugwu* house. *Gome, gome, gome, gome* went the gong, and a powerful flute blew a high-pitched blast. Then came the voices of the *egwugwu,* guttural and awesome. The wave struck the women and children and there was a backward stampede. But it was momentary. They were already far enough where they stood and there was room for running away if any of the *egwugwu* should go towards them.

The drum sounded again and the flute blew. The *egwugwu* house was now a pandemonium of quavering voices: *Aru oyim de de de de dei!* filled the air as the spirits of the ancestors, just emerged from the earth, greeted themselves in their esoteric language. The *egwugwu* house into which they emerged faced the forest, away from the crowd, who saw only its back with the many-coloured patterns and drawings done by specially chosen women at regular intervals. These women never saw the inside of the hut. No woman ever did. They scrubbed and painted the outside walls under the supervision of men. If they imagined what was inside, they kept their imagination to themselves. No woman ever asked questions about the most powerful and the most secret cult in the clan.

*Aru oyim de de de dei!* flew around the dark, closed hut like tongues of fire. The ancestral spirits of the clan were abroad. The metal gong beat continuously now and the flute, shrill and powerful, floated on the chaos.

And then the *egwugwu* appeared. The women and children sent up a great shout and took to their heels. It was instinctive. A woman fled as soon as an *egwugwu* came in sight. And when, as on that day, nine of the greatest masked spirits in the clan came out together it was a terrifying spectacle. Even Mgbafo took to her heels and had to be restrained by her brothers.

Each of the nine *egwugwu* represented a village of the clan. Their leader was called Evil Forest. Smoke poured out of his head.

The nine villages of Umuofia had grown out of the nine sons of the first father of the clan. Evil Forest represented the village of Umeru, or the children of Eru, who was the eldest of the nine sons.

*'Umuofia kwenu!'* shouted the leading *egwugwu,* pushing the air with his raffia arms. The elders of the clan replied, *'Yao!'*

*'Umuofia kwenu!'*

*'Yaa!'*

*'Umuofia kwenu!'*

*'Yaa!'*

Evil Forest then thrust the pointed end of his rattling staff into the earth. And it began to shake and rattle, like something agitating with a metallic life. He took the first of the empty stools and the eight other *egwugwu* began to sit in order of seniority after him.

Okonkwo's wives, and perhaps other women as well, might have noticed that the second *egwugwu* had the springy walk of Okonkwo. And they might also have noticed that Okonkwo was not among the titled men and elders who sat behind the row of *egwugwu.* But if they thought these things they kept them within themselves. The *egwugwu* with the springy walk was one of the dead fathers of the clan. He looked terrible with the smoked raffia body, a huge wooden face painted white except for the round hollow eyes and the charred teeth that were as big as a man's fingers. On his head were two powerful horns.

When all the *egwugwu* had sat down and the sound of the many tiny bells and rattles on their bodies had subsided, Evil Forest addressed the two groups of people facing them.

'Uzowulu's body, I salute you,' he said. Spirits always addressed humans as 'bodies.' Uzowulu bent down and touched the earth with his right hand as a sign of submission.

'Our father, my hand has touched the ground,' he said.

'Uzowulu's body, do you know me?' asked the spirit.

'How can I know you, father? You are beyond our knowledge.'

Evil Forest then turned to the other group and addressed the eldest of the three brothers.

'The body of Odukwe, I greet you,' he said, and Odukwe bent down and touched the earth. The hearing then began.

Uzowulu stepped forward and presented his case.

'That woman standing there is my wife, Mgbafo. I married her with my money and my yams. I do not owe my in-laws anything. I owe them no yams. I owe them no coco-yams. One morning three of them came to my house, beat me up and took my wife and children away. This happened in the rainy season. I have waited in vain for my wife to return. At last I went to my in-laws and said to them, "You have taken back your sister. I did not send her away. You yourselves took her. The law of the clan is that you should return her bride-price." But my wife's brothers said they had nothing to tell me. So I have brought the matter to the fathers of the clan. My case is finished. I salute you.'

'Your words are good,' said the leader of the *egwugwu*. 'Let us hear Odukwe. His words may also be good.'

Odukwe was short and thick-set. He stepped forward, saluted the spirits and began his story.

'My in-law has told you that we went to his house, beat him up and took our sister and her children away. All that is true. He told you that he came to take back her bride-price and we refused to give it to him. That also is true. My in-law, Uzowulu, is a beast. My sister lived with him for nine years. During those years no single day passed in the sky without his beating the woman. We have tried to settle their quarrels time without number and on each occasion Uzowulu was guilty—'

'It is a lie!' Uzowulu shouted.

'Two years ago,' continued Odukwe, 'when she was pregnant, he beat her until she miscarried.'

'It is a lie. She miscarried after she had gone to sleep with her lover.'

'Uzowulu's body, I salute you,' said Evil Forest, silencing him. 'What kind of lover sleeps with a pregnant woman?' There was a loud murmur of approbation from the crowd. Odukwe continued:

'Last year when my sister was recovering from an illness, he beat her again so that if the neighbours had not gone in to save her she would have been killed. We heard of it, and did as you have been told. The law of Umuofia is that if a woman runs away from her husband her bride-price is returned. But in this case she ran away to save her life. Her two children belong to Uzowulu. We do not dispute it, but they are too young to leave their mother. If, on the other hand, Uzowulu should recover from his madness and come in the proper way to beg his wife to return she will do so on the understanding that if he ever beats her again we shall cut off his genitals for him.'

The crowd roared with laughter. Evil Forest rose to his feet and order was immediately restored. A steady cloud of smoke rose from his head. He sat down again and called two witnesses. They were both Uzowulu's neighbours, and they agreed about the beating. Evil Forest then stood up, pulled out his staff and thrust it into the earth again. He ran a few steps in the direction of the women; they all fled in terror, only to return to their places almost immediately. The nine *egwugwu* then went away to consult together in their house. They were silent for a long time. Then the metal gong sounded and the flute was blown. The *egwugwu* had emerged once again from their underground home. They saluted one another and then reappeared on the *ilo.*

*'Umuofia kwenu!'* roared Evil Forest, facing the elders and grandees of the clan.

*'Yaa!'* replied the thunderous crowd, then silence descended from the sky and swallowed the noise.

Evil Forest began to speak and all the while he spoke everyone was silent. The eight other *egwugwu* were as still as statues.

'We have heard both sides of the case,' said Evil Forest. 'Our duty is not to blame this man or to praise that, but to settle the dispute.' He turned to Uzowulu's group and allowed a short pause.

'Uzowulu's body, do you know me?'

'How can I know you, father? You are beyond our knowledge,' Uzowulu replied.

'I am Evil Forest. I kill a man on the day that his life is sweetest to him.

'That is true,' replied Uzowulu.

'Go to your in-laws with a pot of wine and beg your wife to return to you. It is not bravery when a man fights with a woman.' He turned to Odukwe, and allowed a brief pause.

'Odukwe's body, I greet you,' he said.

'My hand is on the ground,' replied Odukwe.

'Do you know me?'

'No man can know you,' replied Odukwe.

'I am Evil Forest, I am Dry-meat-that-fills-the-mouth, I am Fire-that-burns-without-faggots. If your in-law brings wine to you, let your sister go with him. I salute you.' He pulled his staff from the hard earth and thrust it back.

*'Umofia kwenu!'* he roared, and the crowd answered.

'I don't know why such a trifle should come before the *egwugwu,*' said one elder to another.

'Don't you know what kind of man Uzowulu is? He will not listen to any other decision,' replied the other.

As they spoke two other groups of people had replaced the first before the *egwugwu,* and a great land case began.

## Chapter Twelve

On the following morning the entire neighbourhood wore a festive air because Okonkwo's friend, Obierika, was celebrating his daughter's *uri.* It was the day on which her suitor (having already paid the greater part of her bride-price) would bring palm-wine not only to her parents and immediate relatives but to the wide and extensive group of kinsmen called *umunna.*

Everybody had been invited—men, women and children. But it was really a woman's ceremony and the central figures were the bride and her mother.

As soon as day broke, breakfast was hastily eaten and women and children began to gather at Obierika's compound to help the bride's mother in her difficult but happy task of cooking for a whole village.

Okonkwo's family was astir like any other family in the neighbourhood. Nwoye's mother and Okonkwo's youngest wife were ready to set out for Obierika's compound with all their children. Nwoye's mother carried a basket of coco-yams, a cake of salt and smoked fish which she would present to Obierika's wife. Okonkwo's youngest wife, Ojiugo, also had a basket of plantains and coco-yams and a small pot of palm-oil. Their children carried pots of water.

Ekwefi was tired and sleepy from the exhausting experiences of the previous night. It was not very long since they had returned. The priestess, with Ezinma sleeping on her back, had crawled out of the shrine on her belly like a snake. She had not as much as looked at Okonkwo and Ekwefi or shown any surprise at finding them at the mouth of the cave. She looked straight ahead of her and walked back to the village. Okonkwo and his wife followed at a respectful distance. They thought the priestess might be going to her house, but she went to Okonkwo's compound, passed through his *obi* and into Ekwefi's hut and walked into her bedroom. She placed Ezinma carefully on the bed and went away without saying a word to anybody.

Ezinma was still sleeping when everyone else was astir, and Ekwefi asked Nwoye's mother and Ojiugo to explain to Obierika's wife that she would be late. She had got ready her basket of coco-yams and fish, but she must wait for Ezinma to wake.

'You need some sleep yourself,' said Nwoye's mother. 'You look very tired.'

As they spoke Ezinma emerged from the hut, rubbing her eyes and stretching her spare frame. She saw the other children with their water-pots and remembered that they were going to fetch water for Obierika's wife. She went back to the hut and brought her pot.

'Have you slept enough?' asked her mother.

'Yes,' she replied. 'Let us go.'

'Not before you have had your breakfast,' said Ekwefi. And she went into her hut to warm the vegetable soup she had cooked last night.

'We shall be going,' said Nwoye's mother. 'I will tell Obierika's wife that you are coming later.' And so they all went to help Obierika's wife—Nwoye's mother with her four children and Ojiugo with her two.

As they trooped through Okonkwo's *obi* he asked: 'Who will prepare my afternoon meal?'

'I shall return to do it,' said Ojiugo.

Okonkwo was also feeling tired and sleepy, for although nobody else knew it, he had not slept at all last night. He had felt very anxious but did not show it. When Ekwefi had followed the priestess, he had allowed what he regarded as a reasonable and manly interval to pass and then gone with his matchet to the shrine, where he thought they must be. It was only when he had got there that it had occurred to him that the priestess might have chosen to go round the villages first. Okonkwo had returned home and sat waiting. When he thought he had waited long enough he again returned to the shrine. But the Hills and the Caves were as silent as death. It was only on his fourth trip that he had found Ekwefi, and by then he had become gravely worried.

Obierika's compound was as busy as an ant-hill. Temporary cooking tripods were erected on every available space by bringing together three blocks of sun-dried earth and making a fire in their midst. Cooking pots went up and down the tripods, and foo-foo was pounded in a hundred wooden mortars. Some of the women cooked the yams and the cassava, and others prepared vegetable soup. Young men pounded the foo-foo or split firewood. The children made endless trips to the stream.

Three young men helped Obierika to slaughter the two goats with which the soup was made. They were very fat goats, but the fattest of all was tethered to a peg near the wall of the compound. It was as big as a small cow. Obierika had sent one of his relatives all the way to Umuike to buy that goat. It was the one he would present alive to his in-laws.

'The market of Umuike is a wonderful place,' said the young man who had been sent by Obierika to buy the giant goat. 'There are so many people on it that if you threw up a grain of sand it would not find a way to fall to earth again.'

'It is the result of a great medicine,' said Obierika. 'The people of Umuike wanted their market to grow and swallow up the markets of their neighbours. So they made a powerful medicine. Every market-day, before the first cock-crow, this medicine stands on the market-ground in the shape of an old woman with a fan. With this magic fan she beckons to the market all the neighbouring clans. She beckons in front of her and behind her, to her right and to her left.'

'And so everybody comes,' said another man, 'honest men and thieves. They can steal your cloth from off your waist in that market.'

'Yes,' said Obierika. 'I warned Nwankwo to keep a sharp eye and a sharp ear. There was once a man who went to sell a goat. He led it on a thick rope which he tied round his wrist. But as he walked through the market he realised that people were pointing at him as they do to a madman. He could not understand it until he looked back and saw that what he led at the end of the tether was not a goat but a heavy log of wood.'

'Do you think a thief can do that kind of thing single-handed?' asked Nwankwo.

'No,' said Obierika. 'They use medicine.'

When they had cut the goats' throats and collected the blood in a bowl, they held them over an open fire to burn off the hair, and the smell of burning hair blended with the smell of cooking. Then they washed them and cut them up for the women who prepared the soup.

All this ant-hill activity was going smoothly when a sudden interruption came. It was a cry in the distance: *Ojiodu achuiiiji-o-o!* (*The one that uses its tail to drive flies away!*) Every woman immediately abandoned whatever she was doing and rushed out in the direction of the cry.

'We cannot all rush out like that, leaving what we are cooking to burn in the fire,' shouted Chielo, the priestess. 'Three or four of us should stay behind.'

'It is true,' said another woman. 'We will allow three or four women to stay behind.'

Five women stayed behind to look after the cooking-pots, and all the rest rushed away to see the cow that had been let loose. When they saw it they drove it back to its owner, who at once paid the heavy fine which the village imposed on anyone whose cow was let loose on his neighbours' crops. When the women had exacted the penalty they checked among themselves to see if any woman had failed to come out when the cry had been raised.

'Where is Mgbogo?' asked one of them.

'She is ill in bed,' said Mgbogo's next-door neighbour. 'She has *iba*.'

'The only other person is Udenkwo,' said another woman, 'and her child is not twenty-eight days yet.'

Those women whom Obierika's wife had not asked to help her with the cooking returned to their homes, and the rest went back, in a body, to Obierika's compound.

'Whose cow is it?' asked the women who had been allowed to stay behind.

'It was my husband's,' said Ezelagbo. 'One of the young children had opened the gate of the cow-shed.'

Early in the afternoon the first two pots of palm-wine arrived from Obierika's in-laws. They were duly presented to the women, who drank a cup or two each, to help them in their cooking. Some of it also went to the bride and her attendant maidens, who were putting the last delicate touches of razor to her coiffure and cam wood on her smooth skin.

When the heat of the sun began to soften, Obierika's son, Maduka, took a long broom and swept the ground in front of his father's *obi*. And as if they had been waiting for that, Obierika's relatives and friends began to arrive, every man with his goatskin bag hung on one shoulder and a rolled goatskin mat under his arm. Some of them were accompanied by their sons bearing carved wooden stools. Okonkwo was one of them. They sat in a half circle and began to talk of many things. It would not be long before the suitors came.

Okonkwo brought out his snuff-bottle and offered it to Ogbuefi Ezenwa, who sat next to him. Ezenwa took it, tapped it on his knee-cap, rubbed his left palm on his body to dry it before tipping a little snuff into it. His actions were deliberate, and he spoke as he performed them:

'I hope our in-laws will bring many pots of wine. Although they come from a village that is known for being close-fisted, they ought to know that Akueke is the bride for a king.'

'They dare not bring fewer than thirty pots,' said Okonkwo. 'I shall tell them my mind if they do.'

At that moment Obierika's son, Maduka, led out the giant goat from the inner compound, for his father's relatives to see. They all admired it and said that that was the way things should be done. The goat was then led back to the inner compound.

Very soon after, the in-laws began to arrive. Young men and boys in single file, each carrying a pot of wine, came first. Obierika's relatives counted the pots as they came in. Twenty, twenty-five. There was a long break, and the hosts looked at each other as if to say, 'I told you.' Then more pots came. Thirty, thirty-five, forty, forty-five. The hosts nodded in approval and seemed to say, 'Now they are behaving like men.' Altogether there were fifty pots of wine. After the pot-bearers came Ibe, the suitor, and the elders of his family. They sat in a half-moon, thus completing a circle with their hosts. The pots of wine stood in their midst. Then the bride, her mother and half a dozen other women and girls emerged from the inner compound, and went round the circle shaking hands with all. The bride's mother led the way, followed by the bride and the other women. The married women wore their best cloths and the girls wore red and black waist-beads and anklets of brass.

When the women retired, Obierika presented kola nuts to his in-laws. His eldest brother broke the first one. 'Life to all of us,' he said as he broke it. 'And let there be friendship between your family and ours.'

The crowd answered: *'Ee-e-e!'*

'We are giving you our daughter today. She will be a good wife to you. She will bear you nine sons like the mother of our town.'

*'Ee-e-e!'*

The oldest man in the camp of the visitors replied: 'It will be good for you and it will be good for us.'

*'Ee-e-e!'*

'This is not the first time my people have come to marry your daughter. My mother was one of you.'

*'Ee-e-e!'*

'And this will not be the last, because you understand us and we understand you. You are a great family.'

*'Ee-e-e!'*

'Prosperous men and great warriors.' He looked in the direction of Okonkwo. 'Your daughter will bear us sons like you.'

*'Ee-e-e!'*

The kola was eaten and the drinking of palm-wine began. Groups of four or five men sat round with a pot in their midst. As the evening wore on, food was presented to the guests. There were huge bowls of foo-foo and steaming pots of soup. There were also pots of yam pottage. It was a great feast.

As night fell, burning torches were set on wooden tripods and the young men raised a song. The elders sat in a big circle and the singers went round singing each man's praise as they came before him. They had something to say for every man. Some were great farmers, some were orators who spoke for the clan; Okonkwo was the greatest wrestler and warrior alive. When they had gone round the circle they settled down in the centre, and girls came from the inner compound to dance. At first the bride was not among them. But when she finally appeared holding a cock in her right hand, a loud cheer rose from the crowd. All the other dancers made way for her. She presented the cock to the musicians and began to dance. Her brass anklets rattled as she danced and her body gleamed with cam wood in the soft yellow light. The musicians with their wood, clay and metal instruments went from song to song. And they were all gay. They sang the latest song in the village:

'If I hold her hand
  She says, "Don't touch!"
If I hold her foot
  She says, 'Don't touch!"
But when I hold her waist beads
  She pretends not to know.'

The night was already far spent when the guests rose to go, taking their bride home to spend seven market weeks with her suitor's family. They sang songs as they went, and on their way they paid short courtesy visits to prominent men like Okonkwo, before they finally left for their village. Okonkwo made a present of two cocks to them.

## Chapter Twenty-One

There were many men and women in Umuofia who did not feel as strongly as Okonkwo about the new dispensation. The white man had indeed brought a lunatic religion, but he had also built a trading store and for the first time palm-oil and kernel became things of great price, and much money flowed into Umuofia.

And even in the matter of religion there was a growing feeling that there might be something in it after all, something vaguely akin to method in the overwhelming madness.

This growing feeling was due to Mr Brown, the white missionary, who was very firm in restraining his flock from provoking the wrath of the clan. One member in particular was very difficult to restrain. His name was Enoch and his father was the priest of the snake cult. The story went around that Enoch had killed and eaten the sacred python, and that his father had cursed him.

Mr Brown preached against such excess of zeal. Every thing was possible, he told his energetic flock, but everything was not expedient. And so Mr Brown came to be respected even by the clan, because he trod softly on its faith. He made friends with some of the great men of the clan and on one of his frequent visits to the neighbouring villages he had been presented with a carved elephant tusk, which was a sign of dignity and rank. One of the great men in that village was called Akunna and he had given one of his sons to be taught the white man's knowledge in Mr Brown's school.

Whenever Mr Brown went to that village he spent long hours with Akunna in his *obi* talking through an interpreter about religion. Neither of them succeeded in converting the other but they learnt more about their different beliefs.

'You say that there is one supreme God who made heaven and earth,' said Akunna on one of Mr Brown's visits. 'We also believe in Him and call Him Chukwu. He made all the world and the other gods.'

'There are no other gods,' said Mr Brown. 'Chukwu is the only God and all others are false. You carve a piece of wood—like that one' (he pointed at the rafters from which Akunna's carved *Ikenga* hung), 'and you call it a god. But it is still a piece of wood.'

'Yes,' said Akunna. 'It is indeed a piece of wood. The tree from which it came was made by Chukwu, as indeed all minor gods were. But He made them for His messengers so that we could approach Him through them. It is like yourself. You are the head of your church.'

'No,' protested Mr Brown. 'The head of my church is God Himself.'

'I know,' said Akunna, 'but there must be a head in this world among men. Somebody like yourself must be the head here.'

'The head of my church in that sense is in England.'

'That is exactly what I am saying. The head of your church is in your country. He has sent you here as his messenger. And you have also appointed your own messengers and servants. Or let me take another example, the District Commissioner. He is sent by your king.'

'They have a queen,' said the interpreter on his own account.

'Your queen sends her messenger, the District Commissioner. He finds that he cannot do the work alone and so he appoints *kotma* to help him. It is the same with God, or Chukwu. He appoints the smaller gods to help Him because His work is too great for one person.'

'You should not think of him as a person,' said Mr Brown, 'It is because you do so that you imagine He must need helpers. And the worst thing about it is that you give all the worship to the false gods you have created.'

'That is not so. We make sacrifices to the little gods, but when they fail and there is no one else to turn to we go to Chukwu. It is right to do so. We approach a great man through his servants. But when his servants fail to help us, then we go to the last source of hope. We appear to pay greater attention to the little gods but that is not so. We worry them more because we are afraid to worry their Master. Our fathers knew that Chukwu was the Overlord and that is why many of them gave their children the name Chukwuka—"Chukwu is Supreme".'

'You said one interesting thing,' said Mr Brown. 'You are afraid of Chukwu. In my religion Chukwu is a loving Father and need not be feared by those who do His will.'

'But we must fear Him when we are not doing His will,' said Akunna. 'And who is to tell His will? It is too great to be known.'

In this way Mr Brown learnt a good deal about the religion of the clan and he came to the conclusion that a frontal attack on it would not succeed. And so he built a school and a little hospital in Umuofia. He went from family to family begging people to send their children to his school. But at first they only sent their slaves or sometimes their lazy children. Mr Brown begged and argued and prophesied. He said that the leaders of the land in the future would be men and women who had learnt to read and write. If Umuofia failed to send her children to the school, strangers would come from other places to rule them. They could already see that happening in the Native Court, where the D.C. was surrounded by strangers who spoke his tongue. Most of these strangers came from the distant town of Umuru on the bank of the Great River where the white man first went.

In the end Mr Brown's arguments began to have an effect. More people came to learn in his school, and he encouraged them with gifts of singlets and towels. They were not all young, these people who came to learn. Some of them were thirty years old or more. They worked on their farms in the morning and went to school in the afternoon. And it was not long before the people began to say that the white man's medicine was quick in working. Mr Brown's school produced quick results. A few months in it were enough to make one a court messenger or even a court clerk. Those who stayed longer became teachers; and from Umuofia labourers went forth into the Lord's vineyard. New churches were established in the surrounding villages and a few schools with them. From the very beginning religion and education went hand in hand.

Mr Brown's mission grew from strength to strength, and because of its link with the new administration it earned a new social prestige. But Mr Brown himself was breaking down in health. At first he ignored the warning signs. But in the end he had to leave his flock, sad and broken.

It was in the first rainy season after Okonkwo's return to Umuofia that Mr Brown left for home. As soon as he had learnt of Okonkwo's return five months earlier, the missionary had immediately paid him a visit. He had just sent Okonkwo's son, Nwoye, who was now called Isaac, to the new training college for teachers in Umuru. And he had hoped that Okonkwo would be happy to hear of it. But Okonkwo had driven him away with the threat that if he came into his compound again, he would be carried out of it.

Okonkwo's return to his native land was not as memorable as he had wished. It was true his two beautiful daughters aroused great interest among suitors and marriage negotiations were soon in progress, but, beyond that, Umuofia did not appear to have taken any special notice of the warrior's return. The clan had undergone such profound change during his exile that it was barely recognizable. The new religion and government and the trading stores were very much in the people's eyes and minds. There were still many who saw these new institutions as evil, but even they talked and thought about little else, and certainly not about Okonkwo's return.

And it was the wrong year too. If Okonkwo had immediately initiated his two sons into the *ozo* society as he had planned he would have caused a stir. But the initiation rite was performed once in three years in Umuofia, and he had to wait for nearly two years for the next round of ceremonies.

Okonkwo was deeply grieved. And it was not just a personal grief. He mourned for the clan, which he saw breaking up and falling apart, and he mourned for the warlike men of Umuofia, who had so unaccountably become soft like women.

## Chapter Twenty-Two

Mr Brown's successor was the Reverend James Smith, and he was a different kind of man. He condemned openly Mr Brown's policy of compromise and accommodation. He saw things as black and white. And black was evil. He saw the world as a battlefield in which the children of light were locked in mortal conflict with the sons of darkness. He spoke in his sermons about sheep and goats and about wheat and tares. He believed in slaying the prophets of Baal.

Mr Smith was greatly distressed by the ignorance which many of his flock showed even in such things as the Trinity and the Sacraments. It only showed that they were seeds sown on a rocky soil. Mr Brown had thought of nothing but numbers. He should have known that the kingdom of God did not depend on large crowds. Our Lord Himself stressed the importance of fewness. Narrow is the way and few the number. To fill the Lord's holy temple with an idolatrous crowd clamouring for signs was a folly of everlasting consequence. Our Lord used the whip only once in His life—to drive the crowd away from His church.

Within a few weeks of his arrival in Umuofia Mr Smith suspended a young woman from the church for pouring new wine into old bottles. This woman had allowed her heathen husband to mutilate her dead child. The child had been declared an *ogbanje,* plaguing its mother by dying and entering her womb to be born again. Four times this child had run its evil round. And so it was mutilated to discourage it from returning.

Mr Smith was filled with wrath when he heard of this. He disbelieved the story which even some of the most faithful confirmed, the story of really evil children who were not deterred by mutilation, but came back with all the scars. He replied that such stories were spread in the world by the Devil to lead men astray. Those who believed such stories were unworthy of the Lord's table.

There was a saying in Umuofia that as a man danced so the drums were beaten for him. Mr Smith danced a furious step and so the drums went mad. The over-zealous converts who had smarted under Mr Brown's restraining hand now flourished in full favour. One of them was Enoch, the son of the snake-priest who was believed to have killed and eaten the sacred python. Enoch's devotion to the new faith had seemed so much greater than Mr Brown's that the villagers called him The Outsider who wept louder than the bereaved.

Enoch was short and slight of build, and always seemed in great haste. His feet were short and broad, and when he stood or walked his heels came together and his feet opened outwards as if they had quarrelled and meant to go in different directions. Such was the excessive energy bottled up in Enoch's small body that it was always erupting in quarrels and fights. On Sundays he always imagined that the sermon was preached for the benefit of his enemies. And if he happened to sit near one of them he would occasionally turn to give him a meaningful look, as if to say, 'I told you so.' It was Enoch who touched off the great conflict between church and clan in Umuofia which had been gathering since Mr Brown left.

It happened during the annual ceremony which was held in honour of the earth deity. At such times the ancestors of the clan who had been committed to Mother Earth at their death emerged again as *egwugwu* through tiny ant-holes.

One of the greatest crimes a man could commit was to unmask an *egwugwu* in public, or to say or do anything which might reduce its immortal prestige in the eyes of the uninitiated. And this was what Enoch did.

The annual worship of the earth goddess fell on a Sunday, and the masked spirits were abroad. The Christian women who had been to church could not therefore go home. Some of their men had gone out to beg the *egwugwu* to retire for a short while for the women to pass. They agreed and were already retiring, when Enoch boasted aloud that they would not dare to touch a Christian. Whereupon they all came back and one of them gave Enoch a good stroke of the cane, which was always carried. Enoch fell on him and tore off his mask. The other *egwugwu* immediately surrounded their desecrated companion, to shield him from the profane gaze of women and children, and led him away. Enoch had killed an ancestral spirit, and Umuofia was thrown into confusion.

That night the Mother of the Spirits walked the length and breadth of the clan, weeping for her murdered son. It was a terrible night. Not even the oldest man in Umuofia had ever heard such a strange and fearful sound, and it was never to be heard again. It seemed as if the very soul of the tribe wept for a great evil that was coming—its own death.

On the next day all the masked *egwugwu* of Umuofia assembled in the market-place. They came from all the quarters of the clan and even from the neighbouring villages. The dreaded Otakagu came from Imo, and Ekwensu, dangling a white cock, arrived from Uli. It was a terrible gathering. The eerie voices of countless spirits, the bells that clattered behind some of them, and the clash of matchets as they ran forwards and backwards and saluted one another, sent tremors of fear into every heart. For the first time in living memory the sacred bull-roarer was heard in broad day light.

From the market-place the furious band made for Enoch's compound. Some of the elders of the clan went with them, wearing heavy protections of charms and amulets. These were men whose arms were strong in *ogwu*, or medicine. As for the ordinary men and women, they listened from the safety of their huts.

The leaders of the Christians had met together at Mr Smith's parsonage on the previous night. As they deliberated they could hear the Mother of Spirits wailing for her son. The chilling sound affected Mr Smith, and for the first time he seemed to be afraid.

'What are they planning to do?' he asked. No one knew, because such a thing had never happened before. Mr Smith would have sent for the District Commissioner and his court messengers, but they had gone on tour on the previous day.

'One thing is clear,' said Mr Smith. 'We cannot offer physical resistance to them. Our strength lies in the Lord.' They knelt down together and prayed to God for delivery.

'O Lord save Thy people,' cried Mr Smith.

'And bless Thine inheritance,' replied the men.

They decided that Enoch should be hidden in the parsonage for a day or two. Enoch himself was greatly disappointed when he heard this, for he had hoped that a holy war was imminent; and there were a few other Christians who thought like him. But wisdom prevailed in the camp of the faithful and many lives were thus saved.

The band of *egwugwu* moved like a furious whirlwind to Enoch's compound and with matchet and fire reduced it to a desolate heap. And from there they made for the church, intoxicated with destruction.

Mr Smith was in his church when he heard the masked spirits coming. He walked quietly to the door which commanded the approach to the church compound, and stood there. But when the first three or four *egwugwu* appeared on the church compound he nearly bolted. He overcame this impulse and instead of running away he went down the two steps that led up to the church and walked towards the approaching spirits.

They surged forward, and a long stretch of the bamboo fence with which the church compound was surrounded gave way before them. Discordant bells clanged, matchets clashed and the air was full of dust and weird sounds. Mr Smith heard a sound of footsteps behind him. He turned round and saw Okeke, his interpreter. Okeke had not been on the best of terms with his master since he had strongly condemned Enoch's behaviour at the meeting of the leaders of the church during the night. Okeke had gone as far as to say that Enoch should not be hidden in the parsonage, because he would only draw the wrath of the clan on the pastor.

Mr Smith had rebuked him in very strong language, and had not sought his advice that morning. But now, as he came up and stood by him confronting the angry spirits, Mr Smith looked at him and smiled. It was a wan smile, but there was deep gratitude there.

For a brief moment the onrush of the *egwugwu* was checked by the unexpected composure of the two men. But it was only a momentary check, like the tense silence between blasts of thunder. The second onrush was greater than the first. It swallowed up the two men. Then an unmistakable voice rose above the tumult and there was immediate silence. Space was made around the two men, and Ajofia began to speak.

Ajofia was the leading *egwugwu* of Umuofia. He was the head and spokesman of the nine ancestors who administered justice in the clan. His voice was unmistakable and so he was able to bring immediate peace to the agitated spirits. He then addressed Mr Smith, and as he spoke clouds of smoke rose from his head.

'The body of the white man, I salute you,' he said, using the language in which immortals spoke to men.

'The body of the white man, do you know me?' he asked.

Mr Smith looked at his interpreter, but Okeke, who was a native of distant Umuru, was also at a loss.

Ajofia laughed in his guttural voice. It was like the laugh of rusty metal. 'They are strangers,' he said, 'and they are ignorant. But let that pass.' He turned round to his comrades and saluted them, calling them the fathers of Umuofia. He dug his rattling spear into the ground and it shook with metallic life. Then he turned once more to the missionary and his interpreter.

'Tell the white man that we will not do him any harm,' he said to the interpreter. 'Tell him to go back to his house and leave us alone. We liked his brother who was with us before. He was foolish, but we liked him, and for his sake we shall not harm his brother. But this shrine which he built must be destroyed. We shall no longer allow it in our midst. It has bred untold abominations and we have come to put an end to it.' He turned to his comrades, 'Fathers of Umuofia, I salute you;' and they replied with one guttural voice. He turned again to the missionary. 'You can stay with us if you like our ways. You can worship your own god. It is good that a man should worship the gods and the spirits of his fathers. Go back to your house so that you may not be hurt. Our anger is great but we have held it down so that we can talk to you.'

Mr Smith said to his interpreter: 'Tell them to go away from here. This is the house of God and I will not live to see it desecrated.'

Okeke interpreted wisely to the spirits and leaders of Umuofia: 'The white man says he is happy you have come to him with your grievances, like friends. He will be happy if you leave the matter in his hands.'

'We cannot leave the matter in his hands because he does not understand our customs, just as we do not understand his. We say he is foolish because he does not know our ways, and perhaps he says we are foolish because we do not know his. Let him go away.'

Mr Smith stood his ground. But he could not save his church. When the *egwugwu* went away the red-earth church which Mr Brown had built was a pile of earth and ashes. And for the moment the spirit of the clan was pacified.

## Wole Soyinka (b. 1934)

Among African writers, Wole Soyinka is a marvel of talent and productivity who, like Shakespeare and Molière before him, is both a writer and man of the theatre. He has written more than a dozen plays, several books of poetry and essays, two novels, and two volumes of autobiography. In addition, he has been a vigorous supporter of political and intellectual liberty in Nigeria through newspaper columns and street theatre productions, even though such activities resulted in his imprisonment for twenty-six months during the Nigerian civil war of the mid-1960s.

Soyinka was born in the western Nigerian city of Abekuta to parents who were Christian converts. His father was a scholarly headmaster of the missionary school where Soyinka received his early education. His mother, whom he affectionately calls the "Wild Christian," was as fierce in her faith as his father was meticulous in his devotion to the intellectual life and the English language. Soyinka grew up in a complex mixture of traditional Yoruba life and the sedate parsonage environment of the missionary school with its English manners. He was drawn to the numerous gods and rituals of Yoruba traditions, and his grandfather conducted him through a traditional coming-of-age ritual to prepare him for entry into the outside world.

After primary education in Abekuta, Soyinka attended secondary school in Ibadan before studying for two years at University College there. Among his classmates was Chinua Achebe, whose fiction has been internationally influential and whose novel *Things Fall Apart* treats the same conflicts of traditional African culture and Western/Christian influences that also appear in Soyinka's plays. Soyinka then moved on to the University of Leeds in England, where he studied English literature and theatre from 1954–1957. After graduation he spent a year and a half in London working as a play reader at the Royal Court Theatre. There he experienced the dramatic ferment of the late 1950s, when young English playwrights like Harold Pinter and John Osborne were absorbing the avant-garde influences of such Continental dramatists as Beckett and Brecht. Two of Soyinka's early plays were performed in London during this period. In 1960 he returned to Nigeria, where he has made his home ever since, with the exception of several years of political exile during the country's military dictatorship from 1969–1975. In 1986 Soyinka was awarded the Nobel Prize in literature.

Soyinka's work illustrates his belief that the breadth of an artist's vision depends on the depth of his responsibility to his roots. His plays engage the continuing power of ancient Yoruba belief and ritual. His knowledge of Yoruba sacrificial practices informs his remarkable translation/adaptation of the *Bacchae* of Euripedes, in which Soyinka's Agave accepts the sacred rightness of her role in the sacrificial slaughter of her son, and Tiresias proclaims that Pentheus's blood has turned into wine. In most of his work Soyinka puts his rich training in European theatre and literature to new uses in his depiction of Nigerians seeking to define themselves in the modern, postcolonial environment, which mixes traditional practices with Western technology and cultural influences, often with tragic political consequences.

We have selected the radio play *A Scourge of Hyacinths* (broadcast on the BBC in 1991), which presents an urbane professional man sentenced to death by arbitrary retroactive decrees of a military dictatorship. His predicament represents the meaningless disruption of lives that Franz Kafka so powerfully captured in novels such as the *The Trial* and *The Castle,* in which individuals are destroyed by anonymous bureaucratic forces. Soyinka's characters are a representative trio of men talking in their jail cell and trying to understand their plight, while water hyacinths outside choke the waterways of Nigeria—just as the dictatorship chokes the social world. The hero's family, of Cuban ancestry, embodies the African diaspora—people borne away as slaves to new worlds but returning many years later to the continent of their ancestors.

## *A Scourge of Hyacinths*

MIGUEL DOMINGO
THE MOTHER
AUGUSTINE EMUKE
KOLÁWOLE DETIBA
CHIME
SUPERINTENDENT
MILITARY VOICE
NEWS-VENDOR
ANNOUNCER

*Tramp of footsteps through echoing corridor—five men in a file, but irregular steps. They come raggedly to a stop. Jangle of a bunch of heavy keys. One is selected, inserted in a lock and turned. A heavy steel door swings open. Two of the men enter.*

SUPERINTENDENT (*gently*): Yes, you too Mr Domingo. You'll be sharing this cell with your . . . with these two.

*The third man enters. The door clangs shut and the key is turned again in the lock. Silence.*

A warder will be along before evening with an extra mattress. We are . . . short of beds and other items right now, so you'll just have to manage. I don't have to tell you, the prison is overcrowded. Both the Military Command and Security send everybody in here as if space is no problem. I suppose because we are hemmed in by the lagoon they think this is the most secure prison. Well, you two are already at home here; I am sure you will show Mr Domingo the ropes.

*Silence.*

I am sorry about how things turned out for you this morning. But I hope you didn't take that sentence seriously. This regime wants to put a scare in people, that's all. If there is anything we can do for you—under the circumstances—just summon my immediate assistant. I have instructed him to make you as comfortable as possible. All of you. Shall I send you reading material, Mr Domingo?

*Silence.*

I really am sorry, but you must take your mind off the verdict and try and settle down. Leave the rest to your lawyers. The appeals won't be heard for some time, so there is nothing to do but to put it out of mind. It's hard at first but—we all adjust. Fortunately you are not restricted in any way—well, I mean, not like the politicians. For them it's more and more restrictions every day. No letters, no newspapers, no visitors. In your own case I can use my discretion. You can see I haven't put you in the wing for condemned prisoners—your cellmates will bear me out—this is the very cell they've occupied while the trial was on. Normally, after a death sentence, we transfer the condemned prisoner to the special wing but, as I said, nobody takes that sentence seriously. Once they've had enough of their little joke, it will be commuted to life. Even less. That's if the Appeal Court doesn't overturn the verdict altogether. Well, I shall drop in on my evening rounds, just to see how you're getting on. Oh yes—Mr Aremu.

WARDER: Yessir.

SUPERINTENDENT: Send them one of the games we seized from the politicians. You see how careful we have to be these days Mr Domingo? Some prison informer sent a report to the secret police that we were giving the politicians preferential treatment. So, orders came that even their pastime—ludo, cards, draughts and other games—everything was to be withdrawn. The warder will bring you what we have and you can make your choice. (*Pause.*) Try and think of the battle as just beginning, Mr Domingo. Same for you two. I shall call in the evening.

*The two officers depart, their footsteps fading down the corridor. Silence, except for a soft lapping of water and lagoon sounds. A bed creaks. Footsteps across a concrete floor. Pause.*

MIGUEL DOMINGO (*quietly*): So the water hyacinths have spread also to this part of the lagoon. I suppose I ought to feel at home.

*Silence.*

*Again, footsteps across the floor. Metallic noise as if the door has been gently shaken.*

MIGUEL: Oh yes; I know this is a prison cell, but it's that court I am not so sure about. The tribunal where the sentence was passed. Was that part of it for real?

*Silence.*

EMUKE (*bitterly*): You know wetin I think? Even God no fit forgive people like you. Some tings dey, wey God no go forgive, and 'e be like your own be one of them.

DETIBA: Emuke, leave the man alone.

EMUKE: No, lef me! I wan' say it one time and then I no go say anything again. When the man turn up for court today, I no believe my eyes. I say to my self, abi dis man dey craze?

DETIBA: Well, I said the same thing, didn't I? But—what happened has happened. We are all in the same boat.

EMUKE: No, we no dey inside de same boat. Even from before, na inside separate boat we dey. And in own boat better pass we own. We dey inside custody so we no get choice. We must appear before tribunal whether we like am or not. But in own case, 'e get bail. The court grant am bail. He get high connection so they gi'am bail. Then he take in own leg walka inside court—after dey done change decree to capital offence. Dat one, na in I no understand. What kin' sense be dat?

DETIBA: Well, it wasn't we alone. I overheard some reporters—even lawyers—saying the same thing. I don't think I paid much attention to my own case. In any case I already knew the outcome, there was nothing any lawyer could do for me, unless he could bribe enough members of the tribunal. So I passed the time asking myself, why did he come back?

EMUKE: Unless money done pass reach tribunal hand.

DETIBA: Hn-hn. Hn-hn. Either money, or connection. I thought maybe everything had been fixed for him. But when it came to his turn, and the chairman read out the judgement—'Miguel Domingo—Guilty as charged'—ah, I tell you, I began to wonder.

*Silence except for muted lapping of water.*

MIGUEL: It beats me. How could one have been so completely without any premonition? I have seen this wall from the outside—I don't know how many times—maybe over a hundred times. We used to go boating from the family house in Akoka; quite often we would take this route. Sometimes we simply came to meet the fishermen in the evenings as they came in with their catch—over there, in that direction. The prisoners would look out from the windows and wave at us. Sometimes we waved back. At least I did, as a child anyway. Maybe I even waved to someone standing against the bars of that very window. There was nothing like the water hyacinth then, so the fish market was a regular event. (*Pause.*) In all those pleasure rides, I never thought I would be looking outwards from this side. The thought never crossed my mind.

*Pause. A wry chuckle.*

And Tiatin also, who claims to have visions—well, to be fair, she certainly makes some accurate predictions, unnervingly accurate sometimes—but she never foresaw this one, at least she never told me.

EMUKE: You can talk all the grammar wey you want. I done been say am anyway, grammar people no get sense. Chai! Even God no fit approve dat kin' foolishness. My own condition dey pain me too, I confess. But as I say before, me and Detiba we no get choice. Dem refuse us bail, hold us inside twenty-four hour daily lock-up for this cell . . .

MIGUEL: I suppose we can't even enjoy that occasional distraction now. The hyacinths must have stopped the motor-boats.

EMUKE (*hisses*): The man wan' pretend say 'e no hear me.

DETIBA: They've made life miserable for everyone. You can't imagine how it has affected prison life, Mr Domingo. Before, the canoes with outboard motors would come right up to the walls and attend to business. Every morning, very early. Prisoners would lower messages and money, then haul up their own mail, or whatever they'd ordered. The prison officials knew about it but they turned a blind eye. It made life easier—something to look forward to. Those facing the canal acted as go-betweens for the others. But, during the ten months we've been here, the weeds finally gained the upper hand. First they fouled up the propellers, so the boats took to paddles. Then even the paddles couldn't fight the weeds. For over three months now, not one canoe has been able to find its way anywhere close to the wall.

EMUKE: What about the Ijaw boy wey drown?

DETIBA: Oh yes, that was a horrible day. Can you imagine, we actually watched someone drown one morning. No way to help. Just watched his legs get more and more entangled in those slimy long roots. It was as if some hidden monster kept dragging him down.

MIGUEL: You saw him?

DETIBA: Everybody watched, all the inmates on the water side of the prison. You see, after the boats gave up, he and two, maybe three other strong swimmers would find a passage through the hyacinths with waterproof packs and carry on business. The scale was reduced of course but it was still better than this present nothing. Then the other swimmers also gave up, leaving only him. Until one Sunday morning . . .

*Rapid footsteps across the cell.*

MIGUEL: This window? You watched him through this window?

EMUKE: Which other window you see inside here?

*Silence.*

MIGUEL (*softly*): I have never seen death at close quarters, not even on the roads with all their carnage.

*Silence.*

EMUKE: Wetin make you come back Mister? I wan' know. I no sabbe dat kin' ting at all. Your family get money, dem get property, dem get plenty influence. You fit dey Russia or Australia by now and nobody fit catch up. Wetin happen? I just wan' know. You bribe tribunal and then dey disappoint you? For my home town, people for say na your enemy take medicine spoil your mind for dat kin' ting to happen.

DETIBA: Let the man have his peace, Emuke. He'll tell us in his own time. After all we'll have plenty of it on our hands. (*Bitter laugh.*) A whole life sentence of it.

EMUKE: That's if they no fire us tomorrow. These soja people, I no trust them. They fit wake up tomorrow and say—line up everybody awaiting execution. Fire them one time!

DETIBA: No-o-o. Even when sentence was passed, I was already thinking how many years we would actually spend in gaol. I agree with that Superintendent.

EMUKE: Wetin you dey talk? You no take your own ear hear sentence? Hey, Mr Domingo, wetin you think?

MIGUEL: What?

EMUKE (*irritably*): The man mind done travel! Detiba and I dey argue about this sentence. You think na 'shakara' den make? You tink dey no go put us for firing squad?

MIGUEL: I'm afraid they won't, that's what I'm afraid of. Because I can't think of passing twenty years or more behind these walls. Behind any walls. But I fear they will commute it to life. It's obvious.

EMUKE: We go see. All I know is that this na wicked country to do something like this. We know some country wey, if you steal, they cut off your hand. But everybody know that in advance. So if you steal, na your choice. Every crime get in proper punishment. But if wait until man commit crime, then you come change the punishment, dat one na foul. Na proper foul. I no know any other country wey dat kin' ting dey happen.

DETIBA: I agree. It's like football. Or any other game. No one changes rules in the middle of a game. Just imagine, half-way through a football game, the referee says the rules have changed. One side has scored a goal but after half-time, he says it is no longer a goal. Or he says a corner kick which took place ten minutes ago should now be a penalty kick. Can you imagine that? In a mere game it is bad enough, how much more in a matter of life and death.

EMUKE: Only army mind fit think dat kin' ting.

DETIBA: It's their profession. They don't know the difference between life and death. Soja man come, soja man go, finish.

EMUKE: Chineke! Small crime wey carry only seven years before. Abi? No to seven years maximum before?

DETIBA: Until three days ago. Anyway, it's all a game of nerves. And the verdict is still subject to appeal, then the Supreme Military Council takes a final decision.

MIGUEL: Hey, come and take a look. There's a canoe trying to break through the hyacinths.

*Scramble of feet towards the window. Distant splashes on lagoon.*

DETIBA: Come on, champion, come on!

EMUKE: Na sign, I swear, na sign from heaven.

DETIBA: He's more than half-way through already.

*Shouts from the others windows along the wall urging on the lone paddler.*

MIGUEL: What he needs is an assistant wielding a giant pair of water shears, maybe five yards long.

DETIBA: He seems to be doing quite well without it. Come on, dig in man, dig in!

EMUKE: 'E go do am. If not today, then tomorrow. The others go join am try if 'e no manage reach us today.

*Loud cheers from the entire length of the wall. The cheers slow down. Change of tone from optimism to depression.*

DETIBA: He's giving up. He's turning back.

*Fade in Yoruba-Cuban music, a ceremonial chant for Yemanja. A man's footsteps descend a wooden staircase, slowing down as it gets closer to the bottom. Stops. A pause.*

THE MOTHER (*soft intoning*): Oh Yemanja, sister of the clear waters, fill me with wisdom. Find me the path. Cut through the unseen weeds which enfold my house in a fulsome embrace. Save us from this shame hanging over our heads, protectress of the innocent. Let your luminous waters unroll a carpet of light in the direction I must take. Show me a sign. Point your spangled fins in the direction I must proceed. Unveil yourself before me tonight. Let your eyes be the twin stars locked one on each foot. Rescue this house from shame, from the deep shame . . .

MIGUEL: Tiatin. What are you doing up so late?

*Footsteps towards the record player. The music is turned down.*

Tiatin. It's Miguel.

*Pause.*

THE MOTHER: Tell me Miguel, why do you think they gave such a lovely name to this infliction? Seaweed is all it appears to be. Parasite. Useless to humans. It chokes the ports. Imperils navigation. Creates hardship for the fishermen—ask your Uncle Demasia, with his fishing trawlers. He has to berth out at sea. The closest he can come is on the salt-water side of Yemanja's island.

MIGUEL: Did you open this window? Oh! You've even left the mosquito netting wide open—what is the matter?

THE MOTHER: Mind you, under the yellow glow of the night sky, one begins to understand why they're here, from where they came. We humans may have no use for the weeds but the gods . . . come closer. Sometimes I think I can sense a pulse in their very stillness, especially at night.

*Footsteps in the direction of the woman's voice. A window is opened wider.*

THE MOTHER: What do you see Miguel? Do you feel anything about them?

MIGUEL: Nothing new. And I do have an even better view from my window upstairs. A green baize stretching into the horizon, what else? But you are right. It is an infliction. And the government appears helpless. At least, it's done nothing effective.

THE MOTHER: There is nothing that the government—or anyone—can do. It was sent, and it will be removed when SHE is appeased.

MIGUEL: Oh no! Please, mother!

THE MOTHER: Mother?

MIGUEL: Sorry, Tiatin.

THE MOTHER (*brief chuckle*): You always give yourself away when you disapprove of something I say—or do. Deeply that is, not with anything trivial. When I hear 'Mother' instead of the childhood nickname you gave me, I know I have troubled you.

MIGUEL: No, not really . . .

THE MOTHER: Yes, yes really. But I don't mind, Miguel. I divine the truth and if others do not accept, I am still at peace with what is revealed. But let me ask you something—is this the first time these waters have been blockaded?

MIGUEL: Blockaded? How?

THE MOTHER: Think back, Miguel. Think of the late seventies, at the height of our first grand national madness. Take your mind to the oil boom and all that came its wake.

MIGUEL (*brief pause*): I can't recall anything. And anyway, I haven't the time. There is a car waiting for me.

THE MOTHER: I know. But you do have the time, I promise you. Surely you remember? The result was not much different then. The scene was different of course. Noisier. Lots of motion. And more colourful, more spectacular. Flags on poles and fairy lights on mastheads stretching into the dark ocean. Every night, the seas lit up for miles. The harbour was one continuous regatta . . .

MIGUEL: Oh, the cement blockade. Good God, what strange recollections you have tonight. I had long forgotten that débâcle. So has the rest of the nation, I am sure.

THE MOTHER: The water hyacinths brought it all back. That is exactly how it was at the time—a sea blockade. Never mind that the—apparent—causes were different, the result is the same.

MIGUEL: Apparent? The difference was not merely 'apparent' Tiatin. This is a natural infliction. In the other case, the regime licensed importation of cement from all corners of the world. And the world obliged. An armada of ships loaded with billions of tons of cement, sealing up the harbours and even extending beyond our territorial waters. Christ, they certainly made us the laughing stock of the world. The treasury was emptied paying demurrage to ship-owners!

THE MOTHER: You did not find the event—planned? Deliberate?

MIGUEL: Oh I know some claimed it was a conspiracy by foreign powers. Plenty of talk about the western powers conspiring to bring the nation to its knees, strangle its economy, etcetera. That was soon debunked. A simple case of greedy operators, a perfect partnership of business and military.

THE MOTHER: Hm. We are agreed on one thing anyway. The nation was blockaded. As it now is. The army was in power. As it is now.

MIGUEL: Not merely in power. They thought they were the nation.

THE MOTHER: I tell you Miguel, it will prove to have been a thousand times easier to get rid of that fleet of cement-laden ships than it will be to remove these spongy, uninvited guests. Actually they are not unlike the army interlopers. They choke us. Their embrace suffocates the nation. But they are mere mortals, that's the difference. They think they are gods but they are mere men. (*Pause.*) Or lettuce.

MIGUEL: Lettuce, Tiatin?

THE MOTHER: Hasn't it struck you sometimes as you watch them massed on the parade ground? In those olive green fatigues starched and ironed a deadly gloss. That's when they most resemble a field of crisp lettuce. A kind of mutation but still—lettuce.

MIGUEL (*laughing*): Oh Tiatin.

THE MOTHER: But deadly. Poisonous. Nothing I would introduce into a bowl of salad.

MIGUEL: You are impossible tonight.

THE MOTHER: Maybe. But it will be far easier to get rid of this real—though also inedible—lettuce; you'll remind me I said so.

MIGUEL: That's possible. Quite possible. So far it has defeated technicians and scientists—marine biologists and all. They are running around like a rudderless boat, pontificating, doing the old trial and error routine . . . damn! What am I doing getting into a discussion with you over water hyacinths at this time of the night!

THE MOTHER: It isn't just the time of the night, is it?

MIGUEL (*soberly*): No it's not. I have to leave. The car waiting.

*A sigh from* THE MOTHER. *She walks across to a chair. Sound of chair scraping against the floor.*

THE MOTHER: Sit down, Miguel.

MIGUEL: Tiatin . . .

THE MOTHER: Give me fifteen minutes, no, ten. I shall say my piece and then you may leave. Just a small reminder of your family's history, how once it also looked as if we had reached rock bottom.

MIGUEL: You've picked a bad night for family history, Tiatin. The family history is on record, and this son is in one hell of a hurry.

THE MOTHER: We have a name to maintain. Confronted by these barbarians in uniform, that becomes even more important. We have to show them we are from durable stock. We too have fought battles and won. We bear honourable scars.

MIGUEL: I know. But there is more than the family name at stake at this moment. There is the all-important question of my life. No Tiatin, don't say anything. Maybe I am a gambler, like grandfather, but I do not gamble with my life.

THE MOTHER: I am even less of a gambler than you, Miguel. I am also a mother. Your mother. Can you imagine I would gamble with your life?

MIGUEL (*scraping of chair as he rises*): Daybreak mustn't find me in this house. The earlier I leave . . .

THE MOTHER: You don't know when I shall see you again. And you'll be missing next Saturday . . .

MIGUEL: Next Saturday? What about it?

THE MOTHER: It's the Saturday of the Easter weekend, Miguel!

MIGUEL: Our family day? It had escaped my mind.

*Pause.*

Actually it is more *your* day isn't it? Yemanja's Festival Day on the island. That's why you picked it.

THE MOTHER: It's the day the Domingo clan reunites each year—that's what matters. And you'll be missing.

MIGUEL: All right then. Ten minutes, no more.

THE MOTHER: The clock is above my head. You can start counting after you've turned off that music.

*Footsteps towards the player.*

MIGUEL: I hate to be the one to silence the praise songs of Yemanja . . .

THE MOTHER: Her devotee permits it.

MIGUEL: So, I dare.

*Click. Music off.*

THE MOTHER: Come and sit here, beside me.

MIGUEL: Ten minutes, you promised.

*Footsteps across. Chair against the floor.*

THE MOTHER: Thank you. (*Pause.*) There is not much to say. Not now that you have clearly decided. But I must speak with that other Miguel. Not the one who is so brilliant, a little rash and impetuous like his great grandfather and his father. Not the sensitive one who will yet put into his profession all the music which his mother's life should have been, no, not that Miguel. I want to talk to the Miguel who is much more like his grandfather.

MIGUEL: So now I am the gambler of the family?

THE MOTHER: That's what the family remembers him by. But I think of him more as the careless one. Forgetful. The Domingo who always forgot.

MIGUEL: Forgetful! Grandfather? That's not how I remember him. He was the least forgetful . . .

THE MOTHER: Forgetful of his roots, Miguel. Forgetful of himself. Of the name of the Domingos! No Domingo who takes pride in that name, who remembers what that name means in Lagos, would gamble away the family fortune, the family name.

MIGUEL: I know the story Tiatin. The family fortune was rebuilt. That past is forgotten.

THE MOTHER: And the family name which he also gambled away? Must you in your turn toss it away? Oduaiye Domingo sat at dawn at the gambling table. He had lost all his money, then the family plantation, the golf course, the stables, this very house—our ancestral home! Finally there was nothing left to risk—except the name. (*Bitter laugh.*) You have to hand it to your grandfather though. No one else I know of has ever gambled away a name. I mean, to think of that in the dying moments of the game, just before dawn! He tried to gamble off our other estates on the island part of Lagos but his gambling partners knew better. They told him, sorry, all that is already mortgaged, for all we know. He tried one business after another but no one quite knew what the status of the business was, and gamblers are practical, hard-headed people—your grandfather being the exception of course. Finally, with nothing left which anyone would accept, he put his name on the table. There you are he said—Double or quits. The name of the Domingo against all my debts. (*Pause.*) At first they laughed, then the novelty of the idea hit them. So they made him sign a piece of paper, but there was no need. Oduaiye Domingo was a man of his word.

MIGUEL: The Domingos appear to wallow in that reputation, I've noticed. It can be a burden.

THE MOTHER: The man who brought us back—whether as freed slaves or as seeds in his loins established that family code. The family lore is that he flogged his sons with the very whip he used on his horses—if they made the mistake of breaking their word. Even in jest. Your great grandfather burnt the words which still decorate the lintel on the original bungalow—A Domingo—Is—His—Word. It is the first thing you were all taught to read—once you had mastered the alphabet.

MIGUEL: Then great grandson Miguel Domingo hereby re-interprets that lop-sided lesson to suit the circumstances. I gave no one my word.

THE MOTHER: But your bail bond Miguel!

MIGUEL: A legal contract only. If I break it, they keep the money.

What more can they demand? This regime changed the rules *after* the bond. The entire agreement has been rendered null and void.

THE MOTHER: I have lit sixty candles to Santa Yemanja. I asked for a sign and I received it. You are in no danger whatsoever. I read your innocence in the serenity of her gaze. She takes the innocent under her protection.

MIGUEL: I wish I shared your faith.

THE MOTHER: But you *are* innocent. Miguel, you *are* innocent?

MIGUEL: You see? You still ask me that. If even you can still doubt me . . .

THE MOTHER: No, it's you who doubt yourself. When you say, I wish I shared your faith, what does that mean? My faith is in you. I have faith in your innocence, and that means that I see you in the embrace of Yemanja, protectress of the innocent. Nothing, no one can harm you.

MIGUEL: I'm sorry but that is one argument I can never win. Not with you. As for the other one, the name of the Domingos, I prefer not to risk it by presenting myself in court tomorrow. Let them try me *in absentia.*

THE MOTHER: Your family has a stake in this matter Miguel. Your bail was given to the family. But for that name, the judge would have refused bail. Do you dispute that?

MIGUEL: Why should I? I know it's true. The other two standing trial with me have spent over nine months in prison custody.

THE MOTHER: Then you know it. You know it is not your affair alone.

MIGUEL: Tiatin, listen please, listen to me very carefully. Tomorrow . . .

THE MOTHER: We have the best lawyer in the country. He has never lost a criminal case. The family will spend its entire fortune if need be. And we have contacts at the very highest level. Your Uncle Demasia . . .

MIGUEL: I am grateful Tiatin. But listen to me. Just listen for a moment. No, PLEASE (*Pause.*) Try now and grasp the difference. (*He speaks with slow emphasis.*) When I was first arraigned, it was under a civilian government and the crime I am accused of did not carry a capital forfeit. Now it is death by firing squad. You heard it yourself Tiatin.

THE MOTHER: How does that affect you? Your so-called crime and arrest took place long before the decree. It can only affect future offenders.

MIGUEL: Did you listen Tiatin? Did you *listen* to that man as he read out the new decree on television? The one with the voice of cold slurry swilling through concrete mixers. The decree affects all those currently standing trial.

THE MOTHER: That was not the way I heard it. And what if it did anyway? You are innocent. Running away will however paint you guilty in the eyes of the world. Miguel, the Domingos do not run. Even your grandfather understood that. He changed his name—yes, he led a wretched existence till he died but he remained here. Disgraced, destitute, despised. But he stayed! But you will let these rootless gangsters chase you out? These—these people without a name?

MIGUEL: Tiatin . . .

THE MOTHER: Look at this quarter. A century ago it was swamp. Nothing but swamp. Not even the water hyacinth thought it worth the trouble of a visitation. Only toads, inedible crabs and mudskippers. A small timberyard was the only sign of life, and a shack with a wooden floor raised on stilts and joined to land by a rickety walkway, where the Cherubim and Seraphim Sect came to dance and pray every evening and on Sundays. Your ancestor roamed the whole of Lagos, found it was the only piece of property he could afford. He bought it and drained it. He turned it into a thriving plantation. The first ever golf course in Lagos was built here, before even the Europeans built the one at Ikoyi. He was fond of golf. Pa Manuel was an exception that way. The other returnees generally took to racing and polo but, he loved golf. So he built that golf course here, just for him and his friends. The Europeans and other aliens used to join him. In those days they were proud to be seen with the Domingos . . .

MIGUEL: Tiatin . . .

THE MOTHER: Oh Miguel, my Miguel, listen! I reminding my forgetful one of his family history. When those lazy, good-for-nothing Lagosians saw how this fetid, undesired swamp was being transformed, they turned on him. They tried to force him out. He fought them in the courts—right up to the Privy Council in London—and won. Then they tried their strong-arm stuff, hired the scum of the ghettos, thugs and arsonists, brought Igun mercenaries from Badagry to invade our home from the lagoon. In the middle of the night they tried to set the house on fire! Tried to burn us out!

MIGUEL: I know the entire story Tiatin . . .

THE MOTHER: The Domingos do not run, Miguel. Your ancestors only ran when they were slaves. Then they ran, and ran, and ran. They took only their gods with them as they ran from one island in the Caribbean to another. San Domingo, Haiti, Cuba. Till they were shipped back to their West African ancestral lands. But the running is over Miguel, the running is over. Here! On this earth of Sango, Yemanja, Osun, Ososi! Some of the returnees chose Abomey, Fernando Po, Douala—some even went further south to Angola. For your great grandfather, it was Lagos. When he disembarked he said to himself—the running is over. Pa Omowale Manuel unwrapped his most treasured possession, his iron *ose* of Sango and stuck it into the ground. May Sango's axe strike me dead, he swore, if I ever allow any mortal to chase me or my offspring off this land. When this house was built—only a wooden bungalow at the time—his wife built a shrine to her own deity Yemanja, on this very spot. I have kept the flame of that goddess alive, and she has never failed the Domingo clan.

MIGUEL: Pa Manuel is dead Tiatin. He died over a century ago. Before this breed of men were born, these ones who burst through their mothers' wombs with machine guns and hand grenades.

THE MOTHER: And what breed of men are they? They breathe, don't they? They fall sick and die. They struggle and sicken themselves like children over the confection of power . . .

MIGUEL: Ah, you've said it. They do things for power that no one would ever dream of. But enough. Your time is up Tiatin.

*Scrape of chair as* MIGUEL *rises.*

We shall talk more of them some other time. Now I must go.

THE MOTHER *(intense plea):* I know you are safe here Miguel. You are safe! These men cannot harm you, no. They dare not touch one hair of your head. I have been promised.

MIGUEL: Promised? Who by? Someone in government? In the Army? Someone in the know? In the corridors of power? Someone right within the very exercise of power? Or—she? The power which came with the clan from Haiti and from Cuba and directs the motions of the water hyacinths?

THE MOTHER: Don't blaspheme Miguel. Rein in your tongue and do not blaspheme!

MIGUEL: Me? Why should I wish to blaspheme against something that nourishes you so completely? Indeed, you could almost say I am sometimes envious. I have nothing I believe in.

THE MOTHER *(fiercely):* Last Saturday, as with nearly every Saturday since your arrest, Iyalorisa went into trance after trance invoking the goddess over you, Miguel. Oh it has been a double Passion week for my island people Miguel. We have fasted as never before in Lent, and our Santa has revealed her benevolent face to us. So do not ever take that name in vain.

MIGUEL: I do not. You are unjust Tiatin. How many Saturdays have I risen early just to watch you don your white robes and blue sash, your face motionless as you lit one candle after the other in your private shrine, then walk, almost trance-like to the boathouse. I have followed and watched you untie the chalk-smeared canoe you use for no other journey and row yourself to Yemanja's island. Sure, I stopped accompanying you so many years ago, but do you think I haven't shared in that peace I know it brought you? And not I alone. I tell you Tiatin, it is what compensates for that . . . I don't know—because you are a contradiction, Tiatin, that is the truth. One moment you mount your invisible throne and reign over this house like a relic from some foreign aristocracy, the next you are mounted by a goddess just like any of the other village peasants, market women, fishermen's wives and the rest—wallowing in the chalk and sand of that shrine on the island. If I hadn't seen it with my own eyes, I would never have believed it.

*Pause.*

Yet, when you return from it all, it's as if you bring back with you the flesh of that greeting—Salaam aleikum. A real peace descends on the house, a rare texture of peace you could touch with your hands.

THE MOTHER *(a brief pause, then she sighs):* Yemanja knows our hearts and minds. She is kind, but just.

MIGUEL: It is not your goddess who has pronounced a threat on my life. It is not any maid or mother of the waters but men of studded boots, of whips and batons and guns and mind-numbing propaganda. Why! Even Sango armed with his thunder and lightning would hesitate to take on a sub-machine gun.

THE MOTHER: And is this the first we have seen of them? Is it the last?

MIGUEL: I keep telling you Tiatin, these ones are different. Different! They are out to prove something, I don't know what. But I do not wish to find out—at least, not while I am within their reach. I do not want to be proof of whatever they wish to prove. Tiatin, there is something about these people which robs me of my sleep.

THE MOTHER: And my sleep, Miguel? The sleep of the Domingos, compelled to face the world each day, knowing that one of theirs has fled? Has run off like a coward? Stamped his guilt on the gates, on the walls of their ancestors? And your little sister still in college? Your nephews and nieces. And the rest of the Domingos when they attempt to take their hard-earned pride of place in society? Shall we retire from society, lock up our windows and gates? Shall we change our name like your grandfather did?

MIGUEL: But my LIFE Tiatin, my life! You want me to place my life at risk because of family pride? Because of your place in society? Tiatin, this is a society of short memories—how often have you said it? How often have you complained—oh and with such bitterness!—of the failure of that same society to give the Domingos credit for moulding the being of Lagos out of swamp and sludge! Yes, let's say I run away. Give them three months, even one, and I swear no one will even recall the affair of Miguel Domingo!

THE MOTHER: And we? You think we also have a short memory?

MIGUEL: Enough! Enough, Tiatin, I am leaving. Now, before dawn. I am innocent. But I do not wish to die to prove it to anyone, not even to the Domingo clan!

*MIGUEL's footsteps going off. Sound of suitcase hitting the floor. A key is turned in the lock. The door creaks open.*

THE MOTHER: Where will you go?

MIGUEL: It's all arranged. I shall stay with a friend—you know him, Chime—tonight. Tomorrow he'll drive me over to the East, Calabar or Port Harcourt. Oron is also likely—it's full of smugglers—their boats are fast and they know the creeks. From there by boat to Fernando Po . . . if the hyacinths have not yet taken over that coastline. In which case we'll head for Obudu Ranch and cross over from there to the Cameroon.

THE MOTHER: Fernando Po? You've been in touch with Cousin Vicky?

MIGUEL: Naturally I shall look up our relations but I shan't be staying with them. I made friends when we went there on holiday in 'eighty. I've kept in touch with them.

THE MOTHER: Well, thank Yemanja for small mercies. At least Macias is no longer in charge. That place had become a cemetery for our countrymen, especially the labour migrants from the East.

MIGUEL: I wouldn't have dreamt of sharing the same borders with that madman, not even for a day. No, the situation is much better now. Even for business. These friends of mine—they're easterners—they're really making their millions, and they've offered me a partnership.

THE MOTHER: Doing what?

MIGUEL: There you go again . . .

THE MOTHER: I have every reason to be cautious. It was also 'friends' who got you, us, into this present mess.

MIGUEL: Believe me Tiatin, their business is completely legitimate. Totally and lucratively! *(Laughs.)* You should see their factories—plastic and other synthetic products. Their other line is refining natural oils for export. I have personally inspected their export ledger. I mean, in hard currency.

*Pause.*

THE MOTHER: We shall all pray for you. Go with God—whichever one you believe in.

MIGUEL: Oh Tiatin . . .

*Rapid strides across the room. Sighs as they hug each other.*

THE MOTHER: Yemanja will protect you. Go to Oron. You'll find no shortage of boats from there.

MIGUEL: I love you, Tiatin.

THE MOTHER: You are my favourite, you know that. A mother should avoid favourites but I cannot help it. Your siblings knew it even as children, to my eternal embarrassment. But you are so much like the image I retain of Omowale Manuel. Stubborn, strong willed even when he knew he was wrong.

MIGUEL: Now she wants to start another argument.

THE MOTHER: No. Go. But, wait Miguel. It's so late. You know the streets are not safe at this hour.

MIGUEL: My friend has been waiting outside while we argued.

THE MOTHER: Oh Miguel, how could you! Why didn't you tell me? I thought it was your driver.

MIGUEL: You forget I wasn't expecting to find you downstairs. And then we got talking. He doesn't mind.

THE MOTHER: Where does he live? How far do you have to go at this time?

MIGUEL: Ikorodu Road. By six in the morning we are through the toll gates. By the time the Tribunal issues a bench-warrant, I'll be over the border.

*Pause.*

THE MOTHER: Hm. You know what I think is a better idea? The Tribunal sits at ten, not so?

MIGUEL: When it starts on time, yes.

THE MOTHER: The first flights out of Ikeja begin at half-past five. It's hardly fifteen minutes to the airport from here, so why don't you stay the night instead and leave here by four thirty? You can take your choice—Calabar or Port Harcourt—there are at least three flights heading east. By seven at the latest you'll be in . . .

MIGUEL: We need to stay mobile throughout, I must have a car at my disposal . . .

THE MOTHER: Then head for Port Harcourt. My sister still runs the Palmeria Hotel. She has any number of cars at her beck and call. We can call her right now, yes, that's a good idea.

MIGUEL: Chime has gone to all this trouble . . . no, it's not fair. And it means he would have to drive home by himself.

THE MOTHER: What are we doing with all the guest rooms—invite him to stay the night. I'll prepare a late supper and we'll telephone Matilda.

MIGUEL: There is one more factor you are overlooking . . .

THE MOTHER: What else is there?

MIGUEL: Our famous National Airline—somewhat unpredictable, wouldn't you agree? We could get to the Airport tomorrow and find that all flights have been cancelled. Then what?

THE MOTHER: What a pessimist you are. Everyone knows that the first flights always take off, and on time. At dawn it's quite a display, they take off almost in formation, unleashing themselves like hungry dogs against all points of the compass. Oh come on Miguel, you have remarked it yourself hundreds of times . . .

MIGUEL: Hm.

THE MOTHER: There is no 'hm' about it. And anyway, if you lose your flight, you can fall back on your original plan. You lose nothing. Agreed? Go and bring in your accomplice. I'll put together one of those night specials you're so fond of.

MIGUEL: All right. I'll call Chime.

*He takes a few steps. Stops.*

You know Tiatin, you really are amazing. One moment you invoke ancestral ghosts to keep me from fleeing, the next you're actively aiding and abetting . . .

THE MOTHER: Be quiet. You understand nothing. Just bring in your poor abandoned friend so we can all get some sleep before morning.

MIGUEL *chuckles. Footsteps in the direction of the door. Fade in music. Out.*

*Back in the prison cell. Fade in* MIGUEL *speaking.*

MIGUEL: You know the strangest thing . . . by the time we had finished supper, I was feeling quite secure. Not just cosy with home comforts and all that. Simply secure. In that living-room with its high wooden ceiling, Chime and I relaxed on over-stuffed cushions, sipping sherry sent by our cousins in Fernando Po . . . all the menace I had felt began to vanish. The regime faded into nothing—cheap, cardboard terrors, nothing more. You won't understand unless you knew the house . . .

DETIBA: Is that what happened? You fed well? You felt good? You woke up in your family bed and decided to tempt fate?

*Pause.*

MIGUEL: I wish it were that simple. It would be easier if I could console myself with the thought that it served me right. But what I felt at night was quite different from what I felt in the morning. True enough, before falling asleep, I kept asking myself—why have I been in such a panic? I was granted bail. My sureties are highly influential figures in society. We have relations even in the military hierarchy, quite high up—a Colonel in fact. I was confident that if I walked into court the following morning, self-assured, ready to clear my name, things would simply take their normal course. The case could go on and on and of course I would return home at the end of each hearing. A verdict of guilty? The possibility of that had vanished completely. Was I not a Domingo?

EMUKE: Sometime, dis ting na fate. Man can't escape his destiny.

MIGUEL: When the prosecution opened the session by applying to withdraw my bail, even before the witness resumed his testimony . . . then, that banished shiver of doubt returned . . .

DETIBA: Me too. That's when I said to myself, this is no longer routine business.

EMUKE: Well, na you give them chance. You chop belleful, you drink, your sense fall asleep. Instead make you go far far as you done plan, you take your own legs walka inside military tribunal wey don change rule for middle of football game.

MIGUEL: No, I did not walk into court of my own free will. (*Quietly.*) I did not.

*Pause.*

DETIBA: What are you trying to say? We watched you enter, surrounded by your lawyers. They were chatting and laughing with all the confidence in the world. In fact I'll tell you, I felt bitter and resentful. I thought to myself, that's what money and influence can do. We are certain to be convicted but that one will go free.

MIGUEL: No, I did not walk in because I wanted to. I was trying to tell you, or maybe trying to explain something to myself. You see, when my alarm went off, I jumped up a different Miguel from the one who went to sleep—(*Bitter laugh.*)—as our friend said—on a full belly. Oh yes, I did go to the airport as planned . . .

*Airport sounds. Jet engines warming up in the background, roar at full throttle, fading off. The somewhat muted motions of an airport stirring itself awake.*

ANNOUNCER: This is to announce the departure of Flight 370 to Yola via Enugu. Intending passengers with boarding passes are invited to proceed to Gate 11 for immediate . . .

*A loud click as the microphone is switched off. A clipped military voice takes over.*

MILITARY VOICE: A nation without discipline is a nation without a future. The bane of our nation has always been indiscipline. This cancer must be rooted out. Were you at your desk on the dot of the hour for the resumption of duty? Do you put in a full day's work for a full day's pay? Is your favourite pastime malingering? Is your office a private reception room for your friends and relations? Are you the kind of employee who is never on seat? All these symptoms of indiscipline must be rooted out. Monitor your fellow worker. Report any sign of indiscipline to your local BAI. Support the Brigade Against Indiscipline. Long live our glorious Fatherland. (*Click.*)

ANNOUNCER: . . . for passengers on Flight 286 to Kaduna. This flight will now leave from Gate 17 . . . Repeat: Flight 286 to Kaduna will now . . .

STAFF (*shouting over the last words*): Will you please stand in line. Stand in line! It's people like you being preached to by BAI.

PASSENGER: BAI-BAI, Madam. (*Laughter.*)

WOMAN: I want my boarding pass . . .

STAFF: Madam, you can see I am still busy checking in this passenger.

WOMAN: Then give me back my ticket.

STAFF: Which one is it? I have several tickets here . . .

WOMAN: Why? That is how everything gets confused. Why don't you treat one ticket at a time? You too should take lesson from the Brigade . . .

STAFF: Don't teach me my job . . .

ANNOUNCER: Last call for Flight 307 to Abuja and Minna boarding at Gate 15. Final call for Flight 307. All passengers with boarding passes should proceed direct to Gate 15. Final call for Flight 307.

*Fade in* CHIME'S *voice. Sliding doors opening and closing. Both men,* CHIME *and* MIGUEL, *walking rapidly. General airport activity.*

CHIME: Of course I'm coming with you. I am going to deliver you personally to my business partners in Fernando Po.

MIGUEL: Seriously Chime there's no need. I know this auntie of mine very well. She is most capable. If there is an emergency she will simply hole me up in her hotel and I tell you, all the Security Units can search that place from top to bottom, she won't let them find me.

CHIME: Just the same, I'm coming. You stay right here while I get the tickets.

MIGUEL: You just want a night out in the Garden City, that's all.

CHIME: Sure. It's a long time I've tasted the night pleasures of Port Harcourt.

MIGUEL: En-hen, that's better. I'll go over to the news-stand and see what . . .

MILITARY VOICE: A corrupt nation is a nation without a future. Smuggling is economic sabotage. Smuggling is an unpatriotic act, it is next to treason. Nepotism is a form of corruption. Corruption in all forms has been the bane of our nation. Currency trafficking is economic sabotage. It plays into the hands of foreign powers. It is an act of treason and will be treated as such. All forms of corruption must be rooted out. Your loyalty should be to the nation and the nation only. It is father, mother, brother, sister, mentor and friend. The nation is your first family. Be your family's eyes and ears. Keep watch on those nearest to you. Report any act of corruption to your local BAI. Support the Brigade Against Indiscipline. Long live our glorious Fatherland! (*Click.*)

*Silence. Then abrupt resumption of airport activities.*

MIGUEL: You mean there is no escape from *that* anywhere?

CHIME: It's improved. They've found someone who can actually string some intelligible words together.

MIGUEL: Go and get those tickets, Chime. Let's get me out of here.

CHIME: Where did you say you were going?

MIGUEL: The news-stand. The papers should have arrived.

CHIME: Okay, I'll meet you there. Best buy all the papers you can lay hands on. You know you'll find only yesterday's editions when we get to the East.

*Fade in announcement over last speech.*

ANNOUNCER: National Airways regret to announce . . .

MIGUEL: Oh no!

ANNOUNCER: . . . a delay on Flight 107 to Kano due to technical reasons.

MIGUEL *lets out a deep sigh of relief.*

A further announcement on this flight will be made shortly.

MIGUEL: Not today please, no, not today. Clear skies all the way to all Eastern Airports, please God, please, whoever, please every single deity Tiatin believes in and I will never never be impatient with her Yemanja again. Lady of the luminous waters, if not for me, then for your faithful one Tiatin, blow away mists and clouds from the skies, reward her fidelity to you . . .

ANNOUNCER: First boarding announcement for Flight 179 to Port Harcourt leaving from Gate 21. Flight 179 to Port Harcourt ready to board from Gate 21. Thank you.

MIGUEL: That's it. That's more like it. Keep the candles burning Tiatin. Don't let even one go out. I can't remember which of them takes care of the skies but please don't ignore him, or her, certainly not today. Tell them to take our wingless Airline under their protective wing . . .

NEWS-VENDOR: Beg your pardon, Sir . . .

MIGUEL: What?

NEWS-VENDOR: I thought you asked for papers.

MIGUEL: Did I? Oh yes, which papers have come in? Give me one of each.

NEWS-VENDOR: Sure. We get *Daily Times . . . Punch . . . New Nigerian.*

*Sound of newspapers being extracted from bundles and slapped down on the counter.*

The *Concord* never come in yet . . . aha, here is *Vanguard* . . . Sir? Wey de man? Oga! Mister man! Mister Man! Ah-ah! What kin joke be dis for morning time? Why the man come waste my time so?

*Rapid footsteps.*

CHIME: Hallo Vendor.

NEWS-VENDOR *(half-heartedly):* Good morning.

CHIME: Ah-ah. Hope no problem.

NEWS-VENDOR: No-o, nothing. Is just these foolish people who think it is good to waste a man's time early in the morning. One man come here just now, ask for one of each paper. As I am just putting them together he take off.

CHIME: Maybe they called his flight.

NEWS-VENDOR: Haba! 'E for take only one minute to collect in papers' and give me my money.

CHIME: Ah well, never mind. Actually I was looking for a friend of mine. I asked him to wait for me here. Rather tall, he was carrying a brief-case. Blue shirt, yellow tie. Has he been here?

NEWS-VENDOR: Ah? He wear glasses?

CHIME: That's right. Rimless.

NEWS-VENDOR: What?

CHIME: Rimless. You know, the kind without a rim. Just glasses.

NEWS-VENDOR: That's the very man. He order one of every paper and then he just disappear. I bend down—so—to take out the bundle of papers from *Punch.* When I stand up again, he just done disappear.

CHIME: What do you mean? He didn't say anything?

*Footsteps approaching.*

NEWS-VENDOR: Na in I tell you. I see am one time, next moment I no see am again.

*Footsteps come to a stop.*

CLEANER: Excuse me Sah, you be Mr Chime?

CHIME (*suspicious*): Who are you?

CLEANER: I just be cleaner. Morning shift. I dey clean toilet when one man come inside. 'E beg me make I come call you. 'E give me one Naira, say make I wait for news-vendor if I no find you.

CHIME: Toilet! Which one?

CLEANER: The one downstairs. Stairs wey dey behind Ethiopian Airlines. He say 'e no feel well at all, so 'e run come toilet.

CHIME (*relief in his voice*): Ah, you see Mr News-vendor, that's what happened to him. I'll take the papers—how much?

NEWS-VENDOR: Na two Naira fifty for the five. Tell your friend sorry o. No wonder he disappear like that. Perhaps he feel like he wan' vomit, so 'e run go toilet.

CHIME: Yes, I suppose so. (*Rustle of notes.*) Here you are. Keep the change.

*Rapid strides over glazed concrete floor. They pass through echoing passage, rapidly down flight of steps, then another brief passage. Swing doors are pushed open. Abrupt stop.*

CHIME: Miguel?

MIGUEL: S-sh. I'm over here.

CHIME: Are you all right?

MIGUEL (*intense whisper*): Over here. Get into the next cubicle. Hurry before someone comes in.

CHIME: What's the matter?

MIGUEL: Get in quickly. There isn't much time.

*Rapid steps. Toilet cubicle door is opened, shut and bolted.*

CHIME: What's going on? I thought you were ill.

MIGUEL: All is not well Chime. We have to act fast. I saw my man.

CHIME: Who?

MIGUEL: The NSO detective who was detailed to my case. I'm not sure he saw me—I ducked very fast. He was obviously on the watch for someone. He was scanning the lounge like a radar.

CHIME: Oh, he could be on another case. They finished their part of the business ages ago. The Investigation Squad take no further interest. They don't even follow the prosecution once they've finished.

MIGUEL: One can never be sure of anything. Everybody is afraid. They'll all be on the alert. What do you think will go through his mind when he sees me at the airport? And so early in the morning. Anyone can put two and two together. One telephone call—even if he has not been detailed here on my account—and we'll have a welcoming committee on arrival. That's if we get on the flight in the first place.

CHIME: You're right.

MIGUEL: So do we go back to the original plan?

CHIME: We could still get on that flight. I know someone who can drive us directly onto the tarmac—one of the maintenance engineers. He'll take us in his official van.

MIGUEL: Chime, I am *not* going to try to get on that flight. On any flight from here. It would be suicidal. What is my detective doing at the airport? Which of his colleagues will come aboard to check faces? They've been doing spot checks since the coup, remember? Looking for fugitive politicians.

CHIME: Right. Back to the car then. We travel by road.

MILITARY VOICE: No nation survives without vigilance. The price of freedom is eternal vigilance. Report anything unusual. Report anything suspicious. The enemies of our national sovereignty are numerous and tireless. They are both without and within our national borders. Play a role in preserving our sovereign integrity. Do not sell out your Fatherland. Be the watchful eyes of the greater family. Lack of vigilance is brother to lack of discipline. A nation without discipline has no future. Assist your BAI with daily vigilance. Support your Brigade Against Indiscipline. Long live the Fatherland!

*Silence.*

MIGUEL: When did it start to proliferate to this obscene level?

CHIME: Blow that! Let's think of what we are going to do?

MIGUEL: Oh, but it has everything to do with how we decide to move. Doesn't it give you the feeling of being surrounded? Everywhere you turn—damn it, even in the toilet!

CHIME: Snap out of that mood, Miguel. Let's act!

MIGUEL: Don't worry about me. Actually, I was doing some practical thinking. You see, I don't believe even the roads are safe any more.

CHIME: There is less risk if we leave right away. It's not quite five, do you realise? In another fifteen minutes we can be at the toll-gate. Virtually no traffic.

MIGUEL: And at the toll-gate? At those ubiquitous check points? How soon before an eager cop recognises the face of Miguel Domingo?

CHIME: Well, are we just going to hole up in these cubicles until they find you?

MIGUEL: No. We're leaving now. But I have thought of something else. Much safer. Maybe I should have thought of it sooner—while we were still at home. Never mind, come on. It's time we moved.

*Sound of drawn bolts in quick succession. Mild creaks of toilet doors.*

CHIME: You can tell me about this master plan on the way. But wait here while I go and see if the coast is clear.

MIGUEL: We'll lose time that way. Every second matters now.

CHIME: How many seconds just to go up and . . . ?

MIGUEL: Let's go together. Don't look right or left, just straight ahead and make for the exit. A flight came in some minutes ago. If our man sees us heading outwards, why shouldn't either of us have been on the flight? Or both.

*Swing doors out of the toilet. Up the stairs and on glazed floor, rapid footsteps beneath dialogue. Fade in airport bustle as they walk briskly through the lounge.*

I could be rushing back for the trial. You came to meet me at the airport. Or maybe I came to meet you. A new member of my legal team. Or vital defence witness. Maybe both of us just arrived on the flight. The important thing is that we're heading out, not catching a flight. And discussing the celebrated case most animatedly. Most natural thing in the world, don't you agree? Don't look now, but I've just seen my man. Still scanning everyone in the lounge with those mean predatory eyes. I've turned my head to argue intently into your face because he was just swinging his radar in this direction. I'm giving him the back of my head; let him recognise that if he can. Scavengers! Warn me if I seem to be increasing my pace will you? We mustn't appear to be too much in a hurry.

CHIME: No, no, we're doing quite well, Mr Domingo. Just tell me what you'd like me to do or say. And when. Should I gesticulate or something? I feel I'm not contributing.

MIGUEL: A lawyer should also be a good listener. You've been giving me your professional attention. I don't think he's seen me. We're halfway through; another minute and we'll reach the sliding doors and then we head back home again.

CHIME: Where?

MIGUEL: Don't stop Mr Chime. Where else do you expect us to head? If he follows us he'll simply confirm one of our silently transmitted scenarios; the accused dutifully rushing back home for his trial.

CHIME: But home! Yours?

MIGUEL: None other. The boathouse. Only one place remains for me, that's the island village where my mother goes for her Saturday worship. I'll borrow her canoe. It's only some twenty-five minutes paddling—for her, that is. I have done it before in fifteen but that was years ago. I'm sure I can still manage twenty. And if you feel like the exercise . . .

CHIME: Of course I'll come with you.

MIGUEL: Then between us we can eat up that distance in twelve or fifteen. Certainly arrive well before dawn. Uncle Demasia's fishing trawler can pick me up—Tiatin will arrange it. I'll just stay put until she can make the contact. May take a day or two but I'll be safe there. And I don't think they have loudspeakers there screaming the obscenities of the Brigade.

CHIME: Even if they did . . .

MILITARY VOICE: What are the watchwords of our national goal? DISCIPLINE. SELF-RELIANCE. SELF-SUFFICIENCY. VIGILANCE. A nation which bargains away its integrity through indiscipline loses respect in the eyes of the world. A nation which depends on the hand-outs of other nations loses respect in the eyes of the world. A nation which does not produce what it needs to survive loses self-respect. A nation which is slack encourages saboteurs against its very existence. It is the duty of every citizen to . . .

*Sliding doors open towards the end of the broadcast, slide shut and cut off the words. The open-air roar of a plane about to take off. Sibilant screech as it taxis towards take-off. Full take-off roar, fading off into distance. Over vanishing plane, fade in the mournful sound of foghorns, then a gentle lap of waters.*

*Mix ecstatic section of Yemanja's ceremonial music which later changes to elegaic. About thirty seconds, gradual fading out, leaving the sound of water splashing against the sides of a canoe as two paddles stab into thickly clogged water. Occasionally the paddles drag up seeming debris which splash back dully into the lagoon as if it has been dredged up from an unending tangle. Heavy breathing and even groans betray exertion beyond normal paddling.*

CHIME: Dawn is breaking, Miguel.

MIGUEL: Worse than dawn will find us if we remain here.

CHIME: What are we going to do?

MIGUEL: Keep trying. Safety is on the other side of that beach-head. Look, I can actually see the prow of the wreck which has lain there half-submerged for half a century.

CHIME: Is that it? That brown wedge just beyond the jutting?

MIGUEL: That's the one. Tiatin swears it was lured there and wrecked by Yemanja to punish the European sailors for encroaching. Her island is forbidden to strangers.

CHIME: She really does believe in that goddess, doesn't she?

MIGUEL: Believe in it? If she had her way Lagos would be renamed Yemanja.

*Huge wallop on the water. Heavy breathing of exertion.*

Look, just look at that! It's like digging up a network of roots. We'll never get there, Chime. It's over an hour since . . .

CHIME: Keep trying. The water looks freer ahead. Almost clear in fact. Once we get over this section . . .

MIGUEL: You don't think we should go back? At least while the way back is still open?

CHIME: What are you talking about? Let's give forwards one more try.

MIGUEL (*in between exertions*): I don't understand it. She paddles this thing by herself every Saturday to the island—that's where all the devotees from the neighbouring hamlets gather for worship. Last Saturday, she rowed over in this very canoe. I watched her go and return.

CHIME: It is obvious. She knows the passage. We've missed it.

MIGUEL: Impossible. From the boathouse to the tip of that wreck, it's one straight line. Look behind you and see for yourself. We've cut a straight furrow through the weeds.

CHIME (*pause*): Yes, it is pretty straight. Then what? What does it mean?

MIGUEL: It means the weeds have thickened impassably from this point outwards. We have reached dead-end.

CHIME: Since Saturday? Your mother passed through here this last Saturday?

MIGUEL: Even in normal times, she does not miss the weekly worship. Since my arrest, what do you imagine?

CHIME: I wish we had a helicopter.

MIGUEL: Don't make ludicrous wishes, Chime.

CHIME: What else is there to do?

MIGUEL: Go back.

CHIME: Go back?

MIGUEL: Yes, go back. Before these venomous coils close up behind us.

CHIME: Now who is fantasizing?

MIGUEL: Fantasizing? I am no longer sure of anything.

CHIME (*With increasing resignation.*): All I know and see is the sun inching up slowly behind that fist of mangrove. It separates our part of the lagoon from the open seas, and we are in this damned canoe with futile paddles battling a malicious tangle of weeds. For all we know these roots may reach right down to seabed. Any moment now the patrols will emerge—they take this route every day on their way to do battle with smugglers—I don't want them to find us here, marooned among the hyacinths. The journals have made my face familiar even to the blindest reader, and a policeman can always do with promotion.

CHIME: Come on Miguel, there's no need to sound so—despondent.

MIGUEL: I must spare our family the humiliation of being dragged out of one set of parasites by another. We'll turn around.

CHIME: As you wish. There is still time to think of something else.

*Strike of paddle against the canoe.*

MIGUEL: No, no! What are you trying to do?

CHIME: You said to turn around.

MIGUEL: You want us to get stuck? You can't turn the boat around in this tangle. We turn round and face the other way.

*Movements within the canoe as they turn round to face the opposite direction. A cry of alarm from* CHIME.

Careful, careful, Chime. Keep your hands on the sides and avoid standing straight up. I don't think I could find the strength to pull you out if you fell overboard.

CHIME: You really are one for exaggerating.

MIGUEL: If I fall in, I won't bother to struggle. I'll simply let the tentacles drag me down to their bed of slime.

*The sound of water rises to huge slashes. Then tone down to a more rhythmic lapping against a stone wall.*

*The prison.*

DETIBA: She was waiting up when you returned, you said. Didn't she do anything?

MIGUEL: Nothing. And she said nothing at all. Her chair was aligned as if it marked the end of the futile furrow we had just cut through the hyacinths. So was her gaze. Only that had travelled much beyond, perhaps it came to rest on the haven which had eluded us. I stopped by her side, waited briefly, but she remained as she was, immobile. I went up to my room to prepare for the trial.

*Pause.*

*A rattle of the cell door.*

WARDER: Mr Domingo, the Superintendent wanted you to see these.

*Rustle of newspapers passed through the bars.*

There is something in there to cheer you up. Everybody is speaking up against the sentence.

*Newspaper noise as the pages are opened.*

EMUKE: Wetin den dey talk? Wetin?

DETIBA: Can't you find it? What page is it?

WARDER: It's right there, bottom of the front page. And some other condemnations inside. One of them is from the former Chief Justice of the Federation. I'll come back later for the papers.

*Footsteps going off.*

MIGUEL (*reading*): National Bar Association condemns retroactive laws. The National Bar Association, in a statement issued at its Apapa Secretariat has condemned the practice of enacting laws to deal with offences committed when such laws did not exist . . .

EMUKE: Wetin former Chief Justice say, na dat one I wan hear. 'E sentence me one time to four years when 'e still be ordinary High Court Judge.

MIGUEL: I'm sure they'll say more or less the same thing.

*Newspaper rustle.*

Here is one from the Roman Catholic Archbishop. 'No one has a right to take a human life under a law which did not exist at the time of a presumed offence.' Good, I'm glad somebody is actually mentioning the issue of presumption of guilt. If ever there was a clear case of a verdict dictated from above, against the full weight of evidence . . . ah, here's another—it begins to look like a ground swell of protest. Even the editorial—hm, quite courageous. And the National Students Association . . . Amnesty, national chapter—oh yes, I'm sure Amnesty International will take an interest very soon . . . the Traditional Rulers' Council—they are appealing for clemency. (*Throws paper away.*) Clemency!

DETIBA: Keep cool, Mr Domingo.

MIGUEL: Clemency! Is that the issue?

DETIBA: Give me the paper. Does it matter what they call it? They are all saying the same thing, only differently.

MIGUEL: No, it is not the same thing. That is the kind of language that flatters the bestial egos of such a breed of rulers. It makes them feel that the world and every living thing within it is their largesse, from which they dole out crumbs when they are sated. Clemency! Even a retarded child must know that the issue is one of justice.

DETIBA: This would be more to your taste then. I've found the statement of your friend, Emuke.

EMUKE: Wetin 'e talk?

DETIBA (*reading*): 'In his own statement, the former Chief Justice of the Federation, Sir Tolade Akindero warned that if the sentence was carried out, it would amount to judicial murder.' Is that more like it, Mr Domingo?

MIGUEL: Ah, what does it matter anyway? Why do we deceive ourselves? We're living in a lawless time.

DETIBA: Here's one more. The Crusade for National Conscience is organising a continuous vigil outside the prison until the sentence is rescinded.

MIGUEL *(violently)*: No!

DETIBA: No? Why not? It all helps to put pressure on the regime.

MIGUEL: Don't you know who they are?

DETIBA: Not much. I've only heard of them once or twice—in the papers.

MIGUEL: They are a religious sect who particularly abhor public executions. And they are rather fanatical in their actions. If they hold that vigil and they're ordered to disperse, they are just as likely to obey peacefully as to disobey—equally peacefully. This regime will not hesitate to open fire on them. I don't want anyone's death on my conscience.

DETIBA: That is really beyond our control, isn't it?

*Four or five pairs of boots marching towards the cell as if in formation. They come to a halt outside the cell.*

SUPERINTENDENT: Everybody get dressed. Mr Domingo—and you two, same for you. You've all been sent for.

MIGUEL: Who by?

SUPERINTENDENT: We don't know. The order is from the same Security Unit that used to fetch you for interrogation.

DETIBA: Interrogation? Are they reopening the case? Or the Appeal Court? Is the hearing today?

MIGUEL: Today is a public holiday. The courts are not sitting.

*Bustle in the cell as clothes are changed.*

SUPERINTENDENT: Well, you may be both right and wrong there. You could be appearing before a Special Panel.

MIGUEL: What?

SUPERINTENDENT: I'm not supposed to tell you this, but we received a secret circular yesterday. All offences in your category, including verdicts delivered by the political tribunal, are no longer subject to review by the Court of Appeal. The Head of State has taken over their functions. My suspicion is that he has set up his own panel—it's the only kind that would sit on a public holiday. I'm only guessing, but I don't see why else they should bother you.

MIGUEL: Will our lawyers be present? Have they been informed?

SUPERINTENDENT: Mr Domingo, I've told you all I know. The usual form for taking you out of prison was brought by Security. My job is simply to hand you over.

MIGUEL: All right, thank you.

EMUKE: I done ready.

DETIBA: Me too.

MIGUEL: Let's go.

*Dialogue continues over footsteps through corridors, down flights of stairs until they reach the* SUPERINTENDENT*'s office.*

SUPERINTENDENT: Actually you don't know how lucky you are to be away from the premises today. Another set of armed robbers are going to be executed. The stakes are already being set up. Prisoners are confined to their cells—that's the routine—but within an hour the word will go round on the prison grapevine, and then you'd be amazed at the change. The quiet is unearthly, something you feel under your skin.

MIGUEL: They are shot in the prison yard?

SUPERINTENDENT: No, not inside. On the open grounds outside the prison. It's in public, you know. The Military are in charge. We never know in advance whose turn it is—unless they are our own prisoners of course. They bring them from other prisons directly to the grounds outside. All we get are instructions to prepare the stakes for such-and-such o'clock on such a day. Like this morning. You're lucky to be out of it. Well, here we are.

*Door opens into the* SUPERINTENDENT'S *office. Men rising to their feet.*

SUPERINTENDENT: Well, gentlemen, all three present for escort. Please sign the receipt forms.

*Scratch of pen on paper.*

EMUKE (*whisper*): Dese no be our regular escorts.

DETIBA: They change them all the time.

SUPERINTENDENT: Thank you. Well my friends, good luck. See you on my evening rounds.

MIGUEL: Thank you.

*Door opens, closes. A short walk by five pairs of feet, two booted.*

WARDER: Open the gates.

VOICE: You have the exeat?

WARDER: Here.

*Brief rustle of paper.*

VOICE: Okay. Open.

*Bolts are withdrawn. A wooden bar is raised from its rest against the gate. The wooden gate creaks open. Immediately there is noise from a distanced crowd. Audible moans of 'No', 'No', 'No'. It is a helpless, not aggressive 'No'.*

MIGUEL: Who are all this crowd? Oh, of course. The Superintendent said there was . . .

DETIBA: I can't believe people still bring their children to watch this kind of thing.

MIGUEL: Must be one of the really notorious gangs. Just look at the crowd! But, Detiba . . .

DETIBA: Yeah?

MIGUEL: This is not the usual bloodthirsty crowd one sees on television. These ones appear—almost plaintive. Sober.

*Four pairs of boots advance marching crisply, come to a stop. One pair advances two or three more paces.*

OFFICER: Identify yourselves as I call out your names. Koláwole Detiba.

*Gates begin to creak shut.*

DETIBA: Ye-e-s?

OFFICER: Augustine Emuke.

EMUKE: Present.

OFFICER: Miguel Domingo.

MIGUEL: I am here.

OFFICER: By virtue of warrant signed by the Head of State and Commander of the Armed Forces . . .

*Gates slam shut. Bolts are replaced. A lone pair of boots head in the direction of the* SUPERINTENDENT*'s office, slowly, as if dragging. Door opens.*

SUPERINTENDENT: Yes, what is it?

WARDER: Did you know, Sir?

SUPERINTENDENT: Did I know what?

*A sudden burst of gun fire.*

SUPERINTENDENT: I really must air-condition this office. It's the only thing that will keep out that sound.

*Three single pistol shots, one after the other.*

Yes, what was your question again?

WARDER: I just wondered if you knew, Sir—the three stakes, who they were for.

*Fade in dirge from Yemanja's music.*

# Modern India and Southeast Asia

The very concept of "Indian literature" is problematic. Most modern nations are unified by a single language; India, however, has eighteen "recognized" vernacular languages, including Hindi, Urdu, Tamil, and Bengali, representing different regions or populations, and dozens of other languages as well. In this anthology, the classic texts from the Ancient Period are written in the ancient "official" language of India, Sanskrit; the Middle Period selections include texts in Sanskrit and Hindi. But with the decline of Sanskrit as a living literary language (much like the decline of Latin in Europe), it is as hard to speak of an Indian national literature as it is to speak of a European one. Well into the twentieth century, an Indian writer using one of the regional languages would have to be translated into several others just to reach all Indians—not to mention the rest of the world. In this century, however, two vernacular writers have made an indelible impression on the world stage: Rabindranath Tagore (in Bengali) and Chandra Chatterjee (in Hindi). Tagore won the Nobel Prize in literature in 1913.

India spent nearly two centuries under British colonial rule until it won independence in 1947. Among the many legacies of British rule, English has remained the new "official" language of India, as Sanskrit once was, and in the last half-century an Indian literature in English that has quickly become a major voice in world literature has emerged. The greatest of the English-writing Indian authors today, Salman Rushdie, points out that English is no more an imposed language from outside India than is Urdu, which developed during the Muslim invasion of India in the thirteenth century—or for that matter, Sanskrit, which Aryan invaders brought much earlier. One of the ironies of English-language Indian literature, however, is that many of its writers now live outside India, although the same pattern might be found in a number of modern postcolonial literatures. The discovery of an Indian literary "voice" has coincided, then, with the discovery of a global one.

No matter how "modern" Indian writers have become, the phantasms of history remain barely concealed beneath the surface, as we see in the story by Tagore included here. The modern, represented by the English jacket and hat, seems spiritually impoverished, and the dream of a vanished past, for all its seductive richness, is as elusive and insubstantial as the fragrance of a perfume. Another issue in this literature is the gap between generations, often represented by a move from the country and the traditions it represents to the city and its modern opportunities. In the story by Rajee Seth, this tension is heightened by the fact that the son has gone overseas to seek his future in another, even more modern, country.

As might be expected from a country as varied in traditions, religions, and languages as India, its literature may first strike Western readers as chaotic and undisciplined. Indian art and architecture, as well as government and city life, often strike Westerners the same way. One finds in Rushdie's novels, for example, an exuberance, a superabundance of plots, characters, styles, and themes, untypical of American or English writers. In addition, Indian life is suffused by religious traditions that many Westerners think of as mythological or superstitious but that lend Indians easy access to a rich literary symbolism. Indian literature is nothing if not vital and exciting.

Though India and much of Southeast Asia came under European colonial rule, Thailand stoutly maintained its national independence, even while assimilating much that is Western. At the same time, Thailand shares with India and the rest of Southeast Asia the cultural legacy of Hīnayāna (as opposed to Mahāyāna) Buddhism. We include only one example from this rich tradition, a story by Angkarn Kalayaanaphong that thoughtfully expresses the traditional view that human beings are just another part of the natural world.

Vietnam also has complex cultural traditions. Unlike Thailand and other countries to the west of the Annamite chain of mountains, Vietnam is culturally much closer to China than to India. This is true in spite of centuries of military hostilities between China and Vietnam. Following French colonization in the nineteenth century, Vietnam entered a century-long struggle to reestablish political and cultural autonomy. Vietnamese independence was declared at the end of World War II, but not until the mid-1970s was it fully achieved. During the 1980s, Vietnam emerged again on the global cultural scene, and its lively contemporary literature mingles French, Russian, and English influences with its own rich literary heritage.

# India

## Rabindranath Tagore (1861–1941)

*Translated by Amiya Chakravarty*

The best known and most admired writer of modern India is Rabindranath Tagore. Tagore grew up in Calcutta in a large family of some means. His education, however, was not highly formal, and he even attributed his creativity "to the good fortune to escape the school training which could set up for me an artificial standard based upon the prescriptions of the school master." This claim notwithstanding, Tagore amassed impressive learning, particularly in Sanskrit literature and in the literature of the West. He discovered his literary talent early in life, writing his first poems at the age of nine. By his early twenties, Tagore had published several volumes of poetry, a major play, and a novel. His literary output continued unabated through subsequent decades, winning him international acclaim and, in 1913, the Nobel Prize. Although Tagore never was a political activist, he was close to Mohandas Gandhi and spoke out on behalf of Indian nationalism. A deep philosophical vision, thoroughly Indian in nature, gave his politics a rather ethereal glaze:

> Again, in that emptiness,
> Iron-bound,
> Fire-breathing,
> The powerful English
> Scattering energy.
> Time's current will
> Sweep away Empire's nets.
> Their merchandise troops
> Will leave no sign
> On the path of the stars.

The short story we include here, "The Hungry Stones," is an evocation of the glory of the Muslim Moghul dynasty that dominated northern India in the seventeenth century. It is also a story that gains much of its romance and mystery from earlier texts, particularly *The Thousand and One Nights.* Tagore's story, like the Arabian tales to which it refers, also remains eternally open ended. (Why did the storyteller not go mad? Or did he?) The peculiar story told by the talkative "Mohammedan" is delightfully ambiguous. It can be read as a story of the experience of being haunted, with "hungry stones" permanently soaking up the souls of those who dwell in the Moghul palace; as a tale of the way in which an overly keen awareness of history can blur the line between reality and a dream of the past; as the fantasy of a bored man about some earlier, more romantic era; or as a fantastic lie concocted by a garrulous but rather petty Scheherazade. The story also contains a classic example of a frame that distances the original narrator from the storyteller and, in this case, adds a touch of humor: the narrator does not believe the story, but his "theosophist kinsman" does, and this difference causes "a lifelong rupture" in their relationship.

## *The Hungry Stones*

My kinsman and I were returning to Calcutta from our Puja trip when we met the man in a train. From his dress and bearing we at first took him for an up-country Mohammedan, but were puzzled as we listened to him speak. He talked so confidently on all subjects that you might think the Disposer of All Things consulted him at all times. Hitherto we had been perfectly happy; we did not know that secret forces were at work, that the Russians had advanced close to us, that the English had deep and secret policies, that confusion among the native chiefs had come to a point. But our newly-acquired friend said with a sly smile: "There happen more things in heaven and earth, Horatio, than are reported in your newspapers." As we had never before stirred from our homes, the demeanour of the man struck us with wonder. Even on the most trivial topic he would quote science or comment on the Vedas or repeat quatrains from some Persian poet, and as we had no knowledge of science or the Vedas or Persian, our admiration for him increased, and my kinsman, a theosophist, was convinced that our fellow-passenger must have been supernaturally inspired by some strange magnetism or occult power or astral body. He listened with devotional rapture to even the tritest saying of our extraordinary companion, and secretly took notes of the conversation. I think that the man saw this and was pleased by it.

When the train reached its junction, we stood in the waiting-room for our connection. It was 10 P.M., and since we heard that the train was likely to be quite late, because of something wrong in the lines, I spread my bed on the table and was about to lie down for a comfortable doze, when this extraordinary person began spinning the following yarn. Of course, I got no sleep that night.

"When, owing to a disagreement about some questions of administrative policy, I quit my post at Junagarh and entered the service of the Nizam of Hyderabad, they appointed me at once, as a strong young man, collector of cotton duties at Barich.

"Barich is a lovely place. The Susta chatters over stones and babbles on the pebbles, tripping through the woods like a skillful dancing girl. A flight of 150 steps rises from the river, above which, at the foot of the hills, stands a solitary marble palace. Nobody lives nearby; the village and the cotton market are far away.

"About 250 years ago, Emperor Mahmud Shah II built this lonely palace for his pleasure and luxury. In those days jets of rose-water spurted from its fountains, and on the cold marble floors of its spray-cooled rooms young Persian women sat, their hair dishevelled before bathing, and splashing their soft naked feet in the clear water of the reservoirs, would sing the *ghazals* of their vineyards, to the tune of a guitar.

"The fountains play no longer, the songs have ceased, white feet no longer step gracefully on the snowy marble. It is now the lonely home of men oppressed with solitude and deprived of the society of women. Karim Khan, my old office clerk, repeatedly warned me not to take up my abode there. 'Pass the day there if you like,' said he, 'but never stay the night.' I passed it off with a light laugh. The servants said that they would work till dark and then go away. I gave my assent. The house had such a bad name that even thieves would not venture near it after dark.

"At first the solitude of the deserted palace weighed upon me like a nightmare. I would stay out and work as long as possible, then return home tired at night, go to bed and fall asleep.

"Before a week had passed, the place began to exert a weird fascination upon me. It is difficult to describe or to induce people to believe; but I felt as if the whole house was like a living organism slowly and imperceptibly digesting me by the action of some stupefying gastric juice.

"Perhaps the process had begun as soon as I set my foot in the house, but I distinctly remember the day on which I first was conscious of it. It was the beginning of summer, and the market being dull I had no work to do. A little before sunset I was sitting in an armchair near the water's edge below the steps. The Susta had sunk low; a broad patch of sand on the other side glowed with the hues of evening, and on this side the pebbles at the bottom of the clear shallow waters were glistening. There was not a breath of wind anywhere, and the still air was laden with an oppressive scent from the spicy shrubs growing on the hills close by.

"As the sun sank behind the hilltops a long dark curtain fell upon the stage of day, and the intervening hills cut short the time in which light and shade mingle at sunset. I thought of going out for a ride, and was about to get up when I heard a footfall on the steps behind. I looked back, but there was no one.

"As I sat down again, thinking it an illusion, I heard many footfalls, as if a large number of persons were rushing down the steps. A strange delight, slightly tinged with fear, passed through my body, and although there was no figure before my eyes, I thought I saw a bevy of maidens coming down the steps to bathe in the Susta that summer evening. No sound broke the silence of the valley, the river, or the palace, but I distinctly heard the maidens' gay and mirthful laugh, like the gurgle of a spring gushing forth in a hundred cascades, as they ran past me in playful pursuit toward the river. As they were invisible to me, so I was, as it were, invisible to them. The river was perfectly calm, but I felt that its clear and shallow waters were suddenly stirred by the splashes of arms jingling with bracelets, and that the girls laughed and spattered water at one another, while the feet of those who were swimming tossed up tiny waves in a shower of pearls.

"I felt a thrill at my heart; I cannot say whether it was due to fear or curiosity. I had a strong desire to see them more clearly, but nothing was visible. I thought I could catch all that they said if I only strained my ears, but I heard nothing but the chirping of the cicada in the woods. It seemed as if a dark curtain of 250 years was hanging before me, and I could tremblingly lift a corner of it and peer through, although the other side was completely enveloped in darkness.

"The oppressive closeness of the evening was broken by a sudden gust of wind, the surface of the Susta rippled and curled like the hair of a nymph, and from the woods wrapt in the evening gloom there came a simultaneous murmur as though they were awakening from a black dream. Call it reality or dream, the momentary glimpse of that invisible mirage reflected from a far-off world, 250 years old, vanished in a flash. The mystic forms that brushed past me with their quick, ethereal steps, and loud voiceless laughter, threw themselves into the river and did not return wringing their dripping robes. Like fragrance wafted away by the wind they were dispersed by a single breath of the spring.

"Then I was filled with the fear that it was the Muse that had taken advantage of my solitude, and possessed me—the witch had evidently come to ruin a poor devil like myself making a living by collecting cotton duties. I decided to have a good dinner; it is the empty stomach that all sorts of incurable diseases find an easy prey. I sent for my cook and gave orders for a sumptuous *moghlai* dinner, redolent of spices and *ghi.*

"Next morning the whole affair seemed like a queer fantasy. With a light heart I put on a sola hat like the sahebs, and drove out to my work. I was to have written my quarterly report that day, and expected to return late, but before it was dark I was strangely drawn to my house—by what I could not say. I felt that they were all waiting, and that I should not delay any longer. Leaving my report unfinished, I rose, put on my sola hat, and startling the dark, deserted path with the rattle of my carriage, I reached the palace on the gloomy skirts of the hills.

"On the first floor the stairs led to a spacious hall, its roof stretching over ornamental arches resting on three rows of massive pillars, and groaning day and night under the weight of its own solitude. The day had just come to an end and the lamps had not yet been lighted. As I pushed the door open there was a great bustle, as if a throng of people had broken in confusion and rushed out through doors, windows, corridors, verandas and rooms, to make a hurried escape.

"I saw no one and stood bewildered, my hair on end and a kind of ecstatic delight. A faint scent of attar and unguents effaced by age lingered in my nostrils. Standing in the darkness between the rows of those ancient pillars, I could hear the gurgle of fountains splashing on the marble floor, a strange tune on the guitar, the jingle of ornaments and the tinkle of anklets, the clang of bells tolling the hours, the distant note of *nahabat,* the din of the crystal pendants of chandeliers shaken by the breeze, the song of bulbuls from the cages in the corridors, the cackle of storks in the gardens—all creating a strange, unearthly music.

"Then I came under such a spell that this intangible, inaccessible vision appeared to be the only reality in the world, everything else a mere dream. That I, Srijut So-and-so, the eldest son of So-and-so of blessed memory, should be drawing a monthly salary of 450 rupees as collector of cotton duties, driving in my dog-cart to my office every day in a shirt coat and sola hat, appeared to me to be such an astonishingly ludicrous illusion that I burst into a horse-laugh as I stood in the gloom of that vast, silent hall.

"At that moment my servant entered with a lighted kerosene lamp in his hand. I do not know whether he thought me mad, but it came back to me at once that I was indeed Srijut So-and-so, son of So-and-so of blessed memory, and that, while our poets, great and small, could alone say whether inside or outside the earth there was region where unseen fountains perpetually played, and fairy guitars struck by invisible fingers sent forth an eternal harmony, at any rate it was certain that I collected duties at the cotton market at Barich, and earned 450 rupees *per mensem* as my salary. As I sat over the newspaper at my camp-table lighted by the kerosene lamp, I laughed in great glee at my curious illusion.

"After I had finished my paper and eaten my *moghlai* dinner, I put out the lamp and lay down on my bed in a small side-room. Through the open window a star high above the Avalli hills was gazing from millions and millions of miles at Mr. Collector lying on a humble camp-bedstead. I was amused at the idea, and do not know when I fell asleep or how long I slept, but I suddenly awoke, although I heard no sound and saw no intruder. The bright star on the hilltop had disappeared, and the dim light of the new moon was stealthily entering the room through the open window, as if ashamed of its intrusion.

"I saw nobody but felt as if someone was gently pushing me. She said nothing, but beckoned me with her five fingers adorned with rings to follow her cautiously. I got up noiselessly, and though not a soul except myself was there in the apartments of that deserted palace with its slumbering sounds and waking echoes, I feared at every step lest anyone should awake. Most of the rooms were always closed, and I had never entered them.

"Breathlessly and with silent steps I followed my invisible guide—I cannot now say where. What endless dark and narrow passages, what long corridors, what silent and solemn audience-chambers and secret cells!

"Though I could not see my guide, she was not invisible to my mind's eye: an Arab girl, her arms visible through loose sleeves, smooth as marble, a thin veil falling on her face from the fringe of her cap, and a curved dagger at her waist! I thought that one of the thousand and one Arabian Nights had been wafted to me from the world of romance, and that at the dead of night I was wending my way through the narrow alleys of slumbering Bagdad to a trysting-place fraught with peril.

"At last my guide stopped before a deep blue screen, and seemed to point to something below. There was nothing there, but a sudden dread froze the blood in my heart. I thought I saw on the floor at the foot of the screen a terrible Negro eunuch dressed in rich brocade, sitting and dozing with outstretched legs, with a naked sword on his lap. My guide lightly skipped over his legs and held up a fringe of the screen. I could catch a glimpse of a room with a Persian carpet. Some one was sitting on a bed; I could not see her, but caught a glimpse of two exquisite feet in gold-embroidered slippers hanging out from loose saffron-colored pajamas and placed idly on the orange-colored velvet carpet. On one side there was a bluish crystal tray on which a few apples, pears, oranges, bunches of grapes, two small cups, and gold-tinted decanter were evidently awaiting the guest. A fragrant, intoxicating vapor from a strange incense that burned within almost overpowered my senses.

"With a trembling heart I attempted to step across the outstretched legs of the eunuch, but he suddenly woke with a start and the sword fell from his lap with a sharp clang on the marble floor.

"A terrific scream made me jump, and I saw I was sitting on my camp-bedstead, sweating heavily. The crescent moon was pale in the morning light like a sleepless patient at dawn, and our crazy Meher Ali was crying out, as is his daily custom, 'Stand back! Stand back!' while he went along the lonely road.

"Such was the abrupt close of one of my Arabian Nights, but there were a thousand left.

"Then there followed a great discord between my days and nights. During the day I would go to my work worn and tired, cursing the bewitching night and her empty dreams, but at night my daily life would appear as a petty, false, and ludicrous vanity.

"At darkness I was caught and overwhelmed in the snare of a strange intoxication. I would be transformed into some unknown personage of a bygone age, playing my part in unwritten history, and my short English coat and tight breeches did not suit me in the least. With a red velvet hat, loose pajamas, an embroidered vest, a long flowing silk gown, and colored handkerchiefs scented with attar, I would complete my elaborate toilet, sit on a high-cushioned chair, and replace my cigarette with a many-coiled narghileh filled with rose-water, as if in eager expectation of a strange meeting with a beloved one.

"I have no power to describe the incidents that unfolded as the gloom of the night deepened. I felt as if in the curious apartments of that vast edifice the fragments of a beautiful story, which I could follow for some distance, but of which I could never see the end, flew about in a sudden gust of the vernal breeze. And in pursuit of them I would wander from room to room the whole night long.

"Amid the eddy of these dream-fragments, the smell of henna, the twanging of the guitar, the waves of air charged with fragrant spray, I would catch the momentary glimpse of a fair young woman. It was she who had saffron-colored pajamas, white soft feet in gold-embroidered slippers with curved toes, a close-fitting bodice wrought with gold, and a red cap from which a golden frill fell on her brow and cheeks. She maddened me. In pursuit of her I wandered from room to room, from path to path among the bewildering maze of alleys in the enchanted dreamland of the nether world of sleep.

"Sometimes in the evening, while carefully arraying myself as a prince before a large mirror, a candle burning on either side, I would see a sudden reflection of the Persian beauty by my side. A swift turn of her neck, an eager glance of passion and pain glowing in her large dark eyes, a suspicion of speech on her dainty red lips, her figure, fair and slim, crowned with youth like a blossoming creeper, quickly uplifted in her graceful tilting gait, a dazzling flash of pain and craving and ecstasy, a smile and a glance and a blaze of jewels and silk, and she melted away. A wild gust of wind, laden with all the fragrance of hills and woods, would put out my light, and I would fling aside my array and lie down on my bed, my eyes closed and my body thrilling with delight. There around me in the breeze, amid all the perfume of the woods and hills, caresses, kisses, tender touches, gentle murmurs in my ears, and fragrant breaths on my brow floated through the silent gloom, or a sweetly-perfumed kerchief was wafted again and again on my cheeks. Then slowly a mysterious serpent would twist her stupefying coils about me, and heaving a sigh I would lapse into insensibility, and then into a profound slumber.

"One evening I decided to ride my horse. My English hat and coat were resting on a rack, and I was about to take them down when a sudden whirlwind, crested with the sands of the Susta and the dead leaves of the Avalli hills, caught them up and whirled them around and around while a loud peal of merry laughter rose higher and higher, striking all the chords of mirth till it died away in the land of the sunset. I could not go out for my ride, and the next day I gave up for good my queer English coat and hat.

"Again that day at the dead of night I heard stifled, heart-breaking sobs, as if below the bed, below the floor, below the stony foundation of that gigantic palace, from the depths of a dark damp grave, a voice piteously cried and implored me: 'Oh, rescue me! Break through these doors of illusion, slumber and fruitless dreams, place me by your side on the saddle, press me to your heart, and riding through hills and woods and across the river, take me to the warm radiance of your sunny rooms above!'

"Oh, how can I rescue you? What drowning beauty, what incarnate passion shall I drag to the shore from this wild eddy of dreams? O lovely apparition! Where did you flourish and when? By what cool spring, under the shade of what date-groves were you born; in the lap of what homeless wanderer in the desert? What Bedouin snatched you from your mother's arms, an opening bud plucked from a wild creeper; placed you on a horse swift as lightning; crossed the burning sands; and took you to the slave-market of what royal city? And there, what officer of the Badshah, seeing the glory of your bashful blossoming youth, paid for you in gold, placed you in a golden palanquin and offered you as a present for the seraglio of his master? And O, the history of that place! The music of the *sareng*, the jingle of anklets, the occasional flash of daggers, the glowing wine of Shiraz poison, and the piercing, flashing glance! What grandeur, what servitude! The slave-girls to your right and left waved the *charmar* as diamonds flashed from their bracelets; the Badshah, the king of kings, fell on his knees at your snowy feet in bejewelled shoes, and outside the terrible Abyssinian eunuch, looking like a messenger of death, but clothed like an angel, stood with a naked sword in his hand! Then, flower of the desert, swept away by the blood-stained ocean of grandeur with its foam of jealousy, and rocks and shoals of intrigue, on what shore of cruel death were you cast, or in what other land more splendid and more cruel?

"Suddenly at this moment that crazy Meher Ali screamed out: 'Stand back! Stand back!! All is false! All is false!' I opened my eyes and saw that it was already light. My *chaprasi* came and handed me my letters, and the cook waited with a salam for my orders.

"I said: 'No, I can stay here no longer.' That very day I packed up and moved to my office. Old Karim Khan smiled a little as he saw me. I felt nettled, but said nothing and began my work.

"As evening approached I grew absent-minded; I felt as if I had an appointment to keep, and the work of examining the cotton accounts seemed wholly useless. Even the Nizamat of the Nizam did not appear to be worth much. Whatever belonged to the present, whatever was moving and acting and working for bread seemed trivial, meaningless, and contemptible.

"I threw down my pen, closed my ledgers, got into my dog-cart, and drove away. It stopped by itself at the gate of the marble palace just at the hour of twilight. I quickly climbed the stairs and entered the room.

"A heavy silence was reigning. The dark rooms were sullen, as if they had taken offense. My heart was full of contrition but there was no one to whom I could open it, or of whom I could ask forgiveness. I wandered about the dark rooms with a vacant mind. I wished I had a guitar by which I could sing to the unknown: 'O fire, the poor moth that made a vain effort to fly away has come back to thee! Forgive it but this once, burn its wings and consume it in thy flame!'

"Suddenly two tear-drops fell on my brow from overhead. Dark clouds had overcast the top of the Avalli hills; the gloomy woods and the sooty waters of the Susta were waiting in an ominous calm. Suddenly land, water, and sky shivered, and a wild tempest-blast rushed howling through the distant pathless woods, showing its lightning-teeth like a raving maniac who had broken his chains. The desolate halls of the palace banged their doors, and moaned in the bitterness of anguish.

"The servants were all in the office, and there was no one to light the lamps. The night was cloudy and moonless. In the dense gloom I could distinctly feel that a woman was lying on her face on the carpet below the bed, clasping and tearing her long dishevelled hair with desperate fingers. Blood was trickling down her fair brow, and she was now laughing a hard, mirthless laugh, now bursting into violent wringing sobs, now rending her bodice and striking at her bare bosom, as the wind roared in through the open window and the rain poured in torrents and soaked her through and through.

"All during the night there was no cessation of the storm or of the passionate cry. In sorrow I wandered in the dark from room to room. Whom could I console when no one was here? Whose agony was this? Where did this inconsolable grief come from?

"And the mad man cried out: 'Stand back! Stand back! All is false! All is false!'

"I saw that the day had dawned, and that in that dreadful weather Meher Ali was going around the palace with his usual cry. Suddenly it came to me that perhaps he had once lived in that house, and that although he had gone mad, he came there every day and went around and around, fascinated by the weird spell cast by the marble demon. Despite the storm and rain I ran to him and asked: 'Ho, Meher Ali, what is false?'

"He did not answer, but pushed me aside and went around and around with his frantic cry like a bird flying fascinated about the jaws of a snake, and making a desperate effort to warn himself by repeating: 'Stand back! Stand back! All is false! All is false!' I ran like a mad man through the pelting rain to my office, and asked Karim Khan: 'Tell me the meaning of all this!'

"What I gathered from that old man was this: that at one time unrequited passion and unsatisfied longings and flames of wild pleasure raged within that palace, and the curse of all the heart-aches and blasted hopes had made its every stone thirsty and hungry, eager to swallow up like a famished ogress any living man who might chance to approach. Not one of those who lived there for three consecutive nights could escape these cruel jaws, save Meher Ali, who had escaped at the cost of his reason.

"I asked: 'Is there no means of my release?' The old man said: 'There is only one means, and that is very difficult. I will tell you what it is, but first you must hear the history of a young Persian girl who once lived in that pleasure-dome. A stranger or a more bitterly heart-rending tragedy was never enacted on this earth.'"

Just at this moment the coolies announced that the train was coming. We hurriedly picked up our luggage as the train steamed in. An English gentleman, apparently just aroused from slumber, and endeavoring to read the name of the station was looking out of a first-class carriage. As soon as he caught sight of our fellow-passenger, he cried, "Hello," and invited him into his compartment. As we got into a second-class carriage, we had no chance of discovering who the man was or the end of his story.

I said: "The man evidently took us for fools and imposed upon us out of fun. The story is pure fabrication from start to finish." The discussion that followed ended in a lifelong rupture between my theosophist kinsman and myself.

## Rajee Seth (b. 1935)

*Translated by Jai Ratan*

Contemporary literature of the Indian subcontinent is being written in more than a dozen languages, including English. No one writer or work can possibly portray the diversity represented by the social and cultural richness of all these traditions. Nevertheless, writers do share common experiences and confront the same fundamental personal issues. The gap in understanding between generations, for example, is universal. The failure to understand is exacerbated as young Indians leave their villages for life in the cities or to enjoy opportunities to study or work abroad. In this story, "Just a Simple Bridge," an ordinary civil bureaucrat struggles to understand the new world inhabited by his son. He fails, and examples of miscommunication and misunderstanding are many. At the same time, there is a warm bond between the parents and their son. Children grow up and leave home, Indian society becomes increasingly urbanized and internationalized, but the caring and love that form a bond between parents and children endure even when communication breaks down.

Rajee Seth began writing at an early age, but it was only in 1974, at the age of 39, that she began to publish her work. Her writing is not limited to fiction; Seth also writes poetry, essays, reviews, and travelogues. She has published several collections of short stories as well as one novel. Although writing in Hindi, one of many regional languages in India, Seth in some ways represents a broad culture of the Indian subcontinent. She was born in a city in what is now Pakistan but was educated in India and lives in India today. She first studied English and Indian literature at Lucknow University in India and later studied philosophy at Ahmedabad. She strives, she says, to portray in her writing the inner life of Indian society.

## *Just a Simple Bridge*

For three days Tilak Raj had been running around, trying to buy a room cooler. Tilak Raj's quest was touched with a sense of urgency. There had been a letter from his son in America. He was coming home. It was just for a mid-summer break, but no point in wasting those four weeks, Ladi had written. And, anyway, he'd prefer to spend the time at home with his people, he'd said.

The trip would cost his son a lot of money—nothing short of ten thousand rupees. This amount seemed inconceivably extravagant, but Tilak Raj had decided not to worry about that. The money would go from his son's pocket, not his own. To think that his son had such money to spend just to come home on holiday would normally have made him hold his head high with pride. Yet, he found his stomach churning at the thought of so much money being spent so heedlessly. Ten thousand rupees was what Tilak Raj earned in a whole year—and he spent it all on maintaining the family. Couldn't his son forgo his holiday and save money?

But it was futile to think in that vein. The money was not his; it was not even his son's to save. It was earmarked for his air passage home. If he did not avail himself of it, he would lose it anyway, by default, Ladi had explained in one of his letters. Such expenditures were known as "actuals." There was no question of making a saving on them.

His son's letters were full of snippets of information. They conjured up visions of wide roads, dazzling lights, comfortable homes, a cornucopia of plenty. Ladi had pointed out it was different. He wrote, "Papa, you can't imagine what it's really like, being here . . ." and, grudgingly, Tilak Raj would murmur that maybe Ladi was right, that imagination did have a way of distorting reality. But then, a country where they gave away thousands of rupees for just a holiday at home . . . ?

Tilak Raj felt guilty, thinking in this strain. Didn't he want his son to come home on this visit? Was he not equating his son with money? What if his son guessed his thoughts? Though sitting alone in his room he shrank into himself, as if everyone could see the workings of his mind.

Did Ladi remember anything of what his father had told him so many times as he was growing up? Money was not everything, Tilak Raj believed. "Look at me," he'd tell Ladi, "my whole life lies before you like an open book. Hardship is the best teacher in life; undergo hardships and you make good in life. You are still a boy and your whole life lies before you. At your age I used to carry a sack weighing a mound and a half on my back . . ." The fact that every morning while rolling up his sleeves to fetch bucketfuls of water from the tap, Tilak Raj caught himself looking wistfully at his thin arms, didn't change anything.

Tilak Raj gave himself a mental shake. At his age why was he getting entangled with such morbid thoughts? What was past was past. True, he may not get a paisa from his son, but then, he was not so badly off. Both his daughters were married. One of them was happy, the other a little less happy—but he'd never allowed his thoughts to dwell on his second daughter. He had by now learnt that knack of keeping his mind thinking only such thoughts that could not disturb. At night while lying by his side his wife would complain about their second daughter's lot, and, without even thinking he could turn on his side and remark sharply, "One must learn to take the rough with the smooth. Take your own case. Have you been happy in every possible way? Did you get all that you aspired for in life?"

Now, "Are you listening?" he asked his wife as he ate his evening meal. "Ladi is coming. I'm thinking of buying a cooler."

His wife's eyes widened. "What?" she asked. "A cooler?"

"He must have formed different habits. He will be here just for a few days and may not be able to stand the lu. You know how it is these days."

"So what! He knows all about the hot winds. Surely, he couldn't have taken so soon to lordly ways. His university gives him a stipend only to acquire higher education."

Tilak Raj was annoyed. This woman would never understand. A woman who cooked one meal and saved something from it for the next and then, on top of it, wanted to be patted on her back for it, would never understand. She was the kind of woman who gloated over the fact that she could cook a pumpkin and make an extra curry from its rind.

Next day, he left the house earlier than usual, fearing that he would not have time enough that evening to catch up on his shopping. Moreover, in the evening the shopkeepers became too shop-weary to treat customers with the same effusiveness. They sized up the customer from his dress and modulated their tone accordingly. They were also always in a hurry to reach home. Tilak Raj found it easier to plan his day to suit the shopkeepers' moods, to give in to the pressures of a situation. He had been doing so all his life.

The shopkeeper had just rolled up his shutters and here was the first customer of the day! It augured well.

"Yes, what can I do for you?" he asked Tilak Raj, in a voice laced with honey.

"I want to buy a cooler."

"Oh, yes. Oh, yes." The shopkeeper pulled out the drawer and took out a thick wad of papers. "Zenith. Coolex. Summer Time Supreme. We have them all. Here's the pricelist. From eighteen hundred upwards. This one is very sophisticated. The latest model. The pump . . ."

Tilak Raj was lost in thought. At last, "Can I hire a cooler? I mean for one season?"

"But why not buy one, Saab? In four seasons you can realise the cost of the cooler."

"Well . . ."

Without soiling his hand by shoving it into the sack, the shopkeeper seemed to have gauged the quality for its content. With measured coolness he said, "Yes, coolers are available for hire, but we don't stock such things. Try the fourth shop on this row."

Tilak Raj felt as if a rough piece of rope that was grating against his neck had been removed. He climbed down from the shop with great alacrity and walked away. His toes hurt as they usually did when he walked too fast. But it would have to subside of its own accord. His son was coming on a visit. He pushed his chest out, although he found the effort a bit taxing for his age.

Tilak Raj's wife eyed the cooler doubtfully as it was unloaded from the cart and got deposited outside her door in the glaring afternoon heat.

"Why have you brought it here?"

"Isn't this Government Quarter No. S-75?"

"Yes, so it is."

"Then it is meant for this house, Saab is following."

Like a child with a new toy in her hands, she turned over the word 'Saab' in her mind. The pigeon that was lodged in her heart and which had stayed still for such a long time, suddenly fluttered its wings.

"Saab must have told you where the cooler is to be installed."

The workers who had sat down on the ground to rest did not consider it necessary to reply to her question. Taking their angochas from their shoulders they started fanning themselves. She went in and came out with cold water from the surahi. "Here, drink it," she said. "May I add some sugar to it?"

Just then, Tilak Raj, whom the labourers had called 'Saab', came into view, his face glistening with sweat, his shirt and black terylene pants showing damp patches. The cooler was installed in the window opening onto the narrow verandah. The electrician left and husband and wife planted themselves in front of the cooler. A blast of cool air flew past their bodies. Not that they had not experienced a cooler before but now, they were overwhelmed by its comforting presence in their own house. They could manipulate the weather just by touching an electric switch!

"Shall I switch it off?" his wife asked. "What a humming noise it makes. Must be consuming a lot of electricity."

"Keep it on for sometime. Today at least. We won't use it again until Ladi comes."

She saw that her husband himself was not showing any sign of moving away from the cooler. He had taken off his sweat-drenched banian.

She cut two big chunks from the water melon she had left overnight in the bucket to cool off. They ate, forgetting to switch off the cooler.

In the days that followed, they dusted the cooler, checked its reserve of water but never got round to switching it on. Tilak Raj sometimes reminded his wife that whether she used it or not they would have to pay the full season's rent for it—six hundred rupees, not a rupee less. "But then the electricity bill?" his wife murmured and they continued to sweat it out.

Such luxuries were a distant dream for them. Maybe it was part of the lifestyle for their son, yet, "it demands a formal inauguration," decided Tilak Raj's wife. They would spring it as a surprise on him. The boy had gone far by virtue of his own enterprise; his father had nothing to do with it. And now, he was coming back from a cold country and it would not behove his parents to plunge him into a furnace. He was coming out of consideration for his parents. But for them, he could have spent his holidays in a more enjoyable manner.

The day before Ladi was to arrive, Tilak Raj tried, in his timid way, to ask Mr Khosla at his office, if he could drive him to the airport in his car to receive his son.

Mr Khosla stared at Tilak Raj. The fool! He didn't even know the proper decorum of making a request. What was so special about a son going abroad for education? While making a request should one forget one's humble origins?

"You know I drive the car myself . . . and at the ungodly hour of three in the morning?" Mr Khosla said.

"No, no, of course not," Tilak Raj murmured hastily, humiliated by the look on Mr Khosla's face.

And Ladi came home on his own.

Tilak Raj restrained himself. He didn't know how to show the surge of happiness he felt at seeing Ladi, looking suave, at ease, happy. Ladi's complexion had improved and his mother felt his muscles had become more prominent as she swayed in visible happiness in his arms. When Ladi bent down to touch his father's feet, blood coursed through Tilak Raj's old body. He gently patted Ladi's head and then stood back. He didn't know what to do next. His son seemed an unknown commodity, an alien.

When Ladi had lived at home, Tilak Raj had not paid him much heed. The boy had gone his own way while he himself went about his daily pursuits like an oil crusher's blinkered bullock, round and round, leaving home in the morning, returning each evening. A victim of chronic constipation, a good part of every morning had always been spent cajoling his bowels. Then there was the rush of getting to the bus stop in time so that he could be at the head of the long queue of passengers. And, once in the office, there was the daily tension of maintaining his dignity as he hovered over the thin line separating him from the white-collared gentility. How often had he felt as if his superiors resented his head clerk's stature. He had come to the conclusion, quite early in his working life, that peace was not a commodity to be easily had by one torn between vicissitudes. Perhaps one could rest only after retirement from service when the heat of one's blood had swallowed all life's longings and desires.

Ladi was plying him with questions touching upon his health, life in general and prospects of advancement in his job.

Why didn't Ladi understand? Could things change in two years when they had not changed in the course of so many long years? Perhaps, having been away for so long, Ladi had forgotten the temper and tenor of the house.

"Will Saru and Nita be visiting us?" he asked eagerly.

"Yes, your sisters will come when it suits their convenience," Ladi's mother said. The words implied that if she invited her daughters she would have to bear their travel expenses from Bangalore and Lucknow. And this year her financial position had been undermined due to sundry unforseen expenses to which had been added the burden of hiring a cooler.

But, it didn't seem as if Ladi had understood. He was going around the small house, taking in everything with a casual glance. He looked behind the curtains made from discarded saris; at the cement shelves built into the walls. He went to the back of the house and examined the small kitchen garden. He stood there gazing at the blazing sun, remembering how, long ago, his mother used to describe it as "the angry demon raining down fire."

His mother urged him to come inside, tacitly reminding him that he still had to have his bath and take his meal. They reminded him that he must be feeling worn after his twenty-two hour sleepless journey, sitting stiff and tied down to his narrow seat. She offered him a glass of cool panna.

"Ah," said Ladi with pleasure. "Rivers of milk and juice flow there. But this raw mango juice laced with green mint leaves—oh, it's divine! We never get it there."

He playfully squeezed his mother's knees.

His mother beamed at him. But Tilak Raj, sitting nearby, had nothing to say. He felt uncertain and strange. How difficult it was to make even a simple bridge between a knee and a pair of hands!

Then, a feeling buried under the debris of time, suddenly erupted and lodged itself in his throat. In spite of his son's, 'No, no!' he poured the panna from his glass into his son's.

What more could he do?

The meal over, it was time for the afternoon siesta. Curtains were drawn against the glare outside, and the whirring of the cooler filled the house. The hot winds of summer, the lu, were held at bay, like unwelcome guests.

The couple waited expectantly for Ladi to say something about the cooler. Now. It was too big a presence to ignore. Ladi's mother remembered how, as a young boy, when Ladi sat down to study, she would wet a straw hand fan and keep fanning him. When she'd dozed off, resting her back against the wall, "Ma, the ceiling fan . . ." Ladi would say and, "No son, it makes the room so hot. A hand fan is better. We can at least wet it," she would reply and start fanning him with renewed vigour. Did he not remember?

But Ladi only said, "I had planned my journey in such a way so that I would arrive on a Sunday. I knew Papa would be home and we could have a nice time together."

"Oh yes," Tilak Raj murmured, but it was obvious that he had not heard his son's words that should have touched his heart.

Yes, Tilak Raj's mind had wandered. He couldn't but feel proud that now, finally, he had done something special for his son. He felt he was standing at the other end of what constituted give and take. But, words failed him. Even if he could put his thoughts into words, it would only sound cheap, mean. It would be akin to plunging a knife into his skin just to show off the colour of his blood.

Ladi was stretched out on the cot over which his mother had spread a milk-white bedsheet; a brand new pillow cover for the pillow. He made some noises when his father lay down on a mat spread on the floor, but soon reconciled himself.

"I was hoping Barre Bhaiyya would already be here."

"I thought I would send your elder brother word on your arrival," Ladi's mother said. "He comes only when he is in a mood for it. For that matter since many years we have given up hope of . . ."

Ma, everybody has some limitation."

"Maybe, maybe not," Tilak Raj said. "There must be something lacking in us."

A silence hung in the air. They all seemed to have withdrawn into their shells. Tilak Raj wondered if Ladi was indulgent to them now because they were no longer part of his life? He had travelled far, learnt much, lived a life of a grown-up man with problems that they could not even begin to imagine. How could his parents span the chasm?

Tilak Raj shook his head. He sighed. But the next moment he realised that there was no need to agonize over these questions. Ladi had come home to relax, sleep and have a peaceful time. And now Ladi was asleep. Why should he brood over these matters? People came and people went. And time too, went its own way.

It was close to seven when Ladi awoke. The evening sun of May was still relentless.

Seeing him stir, his mother asked, "Tea? Milkshake? What do you generally prefer in the evening?"

Ladi laughed as he got off his bed. "My favourite drink?" He playfully pinched his mother's arm. "Don't you know my habits, Ma? Did I go abroad to study or . . . ?"

Sipping his tea, he asked, "Does Keshav ever visit us?"

"Yes, once in a blue moon."

"And Seema?"

"She drops in often while returning from college."

"I'll visit them today. It's been such a long time since I have walked under such a bright sun. You emerge from an air-conditioned room and walk into another air-conditioned room there!"

"You'll find it very hot."

"No I won't. And I won't mind even if I do. I'll have a bath on my return when I'm all drenched in sweat. People over there do not know what great fun that is!"

Tilak Raj suddenly felt apprehensive as if as soon as Ladi stepped out of the house, its walls would crumble and fall.

But then what did he want? Why was he obsessed with this thought of asking Ladi if he had seen something new in the house? He thought Ladi should know the specific reason why he had bought the cooler this summer. How he had to demean himself to buy it.

No, he told himself, not he, but Ladi's mother was sure to broach the subject. While she was talking he would lie there with closed eyes and quietly, without interrupting, pretending sleep, he would listen to the goings-on between mother and son. Lying there he would listen to the sound of his bridge being built from the other end, he'd listen to his wife saying, "He has done all this for you . . . only for you. Otherwise, as you know, all his life he has suffered only because he is so willful. He is always so unbending."

Tilak Raj heard his wife say, "Your tea is getting cold. I've told you so many times I've brought your tea!"

He was still lying on the mat with closed eyes. As he opened them it seemed as if inside him, other eyes opened, too.

He sat up on his mat.

Ladi was taking off his tight striped shirt.

"Today I must change into my white kurta." He was pulling his suitcase from under the cot.

"Arre, it still looks brand new! Don't you ever wear it there?"

"No Ma, machine washing is so expensive there. It can spell my financial ruin. So the kurta just stayed in my trunk."

He smiled wryly at his mother, then went to wash his face at the washbasin in the verandah. "It's still very hot outside," he said, coming back into the room. "No?"

Tilak Raj's ears perked up.

Ladi had started singing a film tune under his breath. Standing in the middle of the room he had pulled down his trousers from under the towel which was still dangling from above his waist. Kicking off the trousers he pulled white pyjamas over his legs. Whipping the towel off his waist he hitched up the pyjamas and knotted the pyjama string. He put on his kurta and went and sat in the chair which his father had bought in a private furniture auction at his office.

Cool breeze from the cooler wafted past him.

Tilak Raj saw that his wife was totally absorbed in her son.

"It's so calm and quiet here. We don't have such peaceful evenings over there," Ladi said cheerfully as he got up from the chair and went to comb his hair, wetting the comb as was his habit.

His father raised his eyes to the old looking glass hanging from the wall. Would Ladi not notice the cooler reflected there?

"I may be late, Ma."

"But you'll be back for your dinner, won't you?"

"Yes, I may. But I can't be sure."

"I don't mind it. But, your Papa will miss you at dinner. You know how he has hired a . . . er . . . er . . ."

Tilak Raj mumbled and pressed his wife's toe with his foot.

"Okay then," said Ladi promptly. "I'm in no hurry. I'll go visiting tomorrow and make it a leisurely affair. In a short while we shall pull out our cots and sit in the open."

"No, go. It's all right with us," Tilak Raj said, his voice subdued.

He could not understand why his son had failed to mark the new in the house from the old, why he could not see the huge contraption fitted into the window which was releasing such blasts of cool breeze at such breath-taking speed? Didn't he remember that it had not been there before?

Tilak Raj felt a sort of heaviness steal over him.

Tilak Raj watched his son walk out of the front door.

He switched off the cooler and returned to the mat on the floor. It didn't matter, he told himself, sternly. He would not think about himself. He would concentrate on his son and his son's achievements. He would think only of Ladi. Just that and nothing more.

It was better that way.

## SALMAN RUSHDIE (B. 1947)

Born in Bombay to parents who moved in 1964 to Pakistan, Salman Rushdie received most of his education in English. He attended Cambridge University from 1965 to 1968 and is now a naturalized British citizen. Like the Nigerian writers Wole Soyinka and Chinua Achebe, Rushdie writes in English. (He was raised by his parents to be bilingual.) This choice not only allows his work an international readership but also makes it accessible to readers in Pakistan and India, where the extreme variety of indigenous languages makes his family's language, Urdu, less likely to attract a wide audience. Rushdie has also claimed that English, with its ability to absorb foreign words, is a much better language in which to record the global late twentieth-century experience. As an expatriate, he shares the experience of a host of writers that includes Joseph Conrad, Henry James, Milan Kundera, Michael Ondaatje, Mavis Gallant, Bharati Mukherjee, Joseph Brodsky, and V.S. Naipaul. Not surprisingly, Rushdie often writes at the crossroads of cultures, and his work emphasizes migration and multicultural blendings. He has acknowledged the strong influence in his own work of Jorge Borges (pp. 2113–2121), Gabriel Garcia Marquez (pp. 2140–2145), Milan Kundera, Gunter Grass, and Thomas Pynchon. Like theirs, Rushdie's fiction often features self-conscious, metafictional elements common in postmodernism. In a 1982 interview he described his novels as "large-scale, fantasized, satiric, anti-epic[s]" like those of "Rabelais or Gogol or Boccaccio."* His innovations with

*Salman Rushdie, "Interview." *Kunapipi*, 20.

English have been understood to be attempts to "decolonize" the language. His works are also highly intertextual, referring to works from many traditions, and they frequently contain satirical commentaries on Islamic, Pakistani, Indian, and British society and politics.

Rushdie is best known for his novels, among them *Midnight's Children* (1981), *Satanic Verses* (1988), *Haroun and the Sea of Stories* (1990), and *The Moor's Last Sigh* (1995). *Satanic Verses* launched Rushdie into the international political spotlight when, in 1989, Iran's Ayatollah Khomeini condemned him to death for writing it. The Ayatollah's *fatwa*, or death sentence, now rescinded, forced Rushdie to live in hiding from those who might seek a reward for assassinating him. Ironically, the novel, which attacks the danger of absolute belief systems, has sparked book burnings, bomb threats, riots, and murder. The Rushdie affair has also become a *cause célèbre* among those who defend artistic freedom and freedom of speech.

The work included here, "The Courter," comes from Rushdie's 1994 collection of short stories titled *East, West.* It features mixtures of cultures, satire, and experiments with language. These elements are all tied to the themes of love and multicultural identity that are common in Rushdie's recent fiction.

## *The Courter*

### I

Certainly-Mary was the smallest woman Mixed-Up the hall porter had come across, dwarfs excepted, a tiny sixty-year-old Indian lady with her greying hair tied behind her head in a neat bun, hitching up her red-hemmed white sari in the front and negotiating the apartment block's front steps as if they were Alps. 'No,' he said aloud, furrowing his brow. What would be the right peaks. Ah, good, that was the name. 'Ghats,' he said proudly. Word from a schoolboy atlas long ago, when India felt as far away as Paradise. (Nowadays Paradise seemed even further away but India, and Hell, had come a good bit closer.) 'Western Ghats, Eastern Ghats, and now Kensington Ghats,' he said, giggling. 'Mountains.'

She stopped in front of him in the oak-panelled lobby. 'But ghats in India are also stairs,' she said. 'Yes yes certainly. For instance in Hindu holy city of Varanasi, where the Brahmins sit taking the filgrims' money is called Dasashwamedh-ghat. Broad-broad staircase down to River Ganga. O, most certainly! Also Manikarnika-ghat. They buy fire from a house with a tiger leaping from the roof—yes certainly, a statue tiger, coloured by Technicolor, what are you thinking?—and they bring it in a box to set fire to their loved ones' bodies. Funeral fires are of sandal. Photographs not allowed; no, certainly not.'

He began thinking of her as Certainly-Mary because she never said plain yes or no; always this O-yes-certainly or no-certainly-not. In the confused circumstances that had prevailed ever since his brain, his one sure thing, had let him down, he could hardly be certain of anything any more; so he was stunned by her sureness, first into nostalgia, then envy, then attraction. And attraction was a thing so long forgotten that when the churning started he thought for a long time it must be the Chinese dumplings he had brought home from the High Street carry-out.

English was hard for Certainly-Mary, and this was a part of what drew damaged old Mixed-Up towards her. The letter p was a particular problem, often turning into an f or a c; when she proceeded through the lobby with a wheeled wicker shopping basket, she would say, 'Going shocking,' and when, on her return, he offered to help lift the basket up the front ghats, she would answer, 'Yes, fleas.' As the elevator lifted her away, she called through the grille: 'Oé, courter! Thank you, courter. O, yes, certainly.' (In Hindi and Konkani, however, her p's knew their place.)

So: thanks to her unexpected, somehow stomach-churning magic, he was no longer porter, but courter. 'Courter,' he repeated to the mirror when she had gone. His breath made a little dwindling picture of the word on the glass. 'Courter courter caught.' Okay. People called him many things, he did not mind. But this name, this courter, this he would try to be.

## 2

For years now I've been meaning to write down the story of Certainly-Mary, our ayah, the woman who did as much as my mother to raise my sisters and me, and her great adventure with her 'courter' in London, where we all lived for a time in the early Sixties in a block called Waverley House; but what with one thing and another I never got round to it.

Then recently I heard from Certainly-Mary after a longish silence. She wrote to say that she was ninety-one, had had a serious operation, and would I kindly send her some money, because she was embarrassed that her niece, with whom she was now living in the Kurla district of Bombay, was so badly out of pocket.

I sent the money, and soon afterwards received a pleasant letter from the niece, Stella, written in the same hand as the letter from 'Aya'—as we had always called Mary, palindromically dropping the 'h'. Aya had been so touched, the niece wrote, that I remembered her after all these years. 'I have been hearing the stories about you folks all my life,' the letter went on, 'and I think of you a little bit as family. Maybe you recall my mother, Mary's sister. She unfortunately passed on. Now it is I who write Mary's letters for her. We all wish you the best.'

This message from an intimate stranger reached out to me in my enforced exile from the beloved country of my birth and moved me, stirring things that had been buried very deep. Of course it also made me feel guilty about having done so little for Mary over the years. For whatever reason, it has become more important than ever to set down the story I've been carrying around unwritten for so long, the story of Aya and the gentle man whom she renamed—with unintentional but prophetic overtones of romance—'the courter'. I see now that it is not just their story, but ours, mine, as well.

## 3

His real name was Mecir: you were supposed to say Mishirsh because it had invisible accents on it in some Iron Curtain language in which the accents had to be invisible, my sister Durré said solemnly, in case somebody spied on them or rubbed them out or something. His first name also began with an m but it was so full of what we called Communist consonants, all those z's and c's and w's walled up together without vowels to give them breathing space, that I never even tried to learn it.

At first we thought of nicknaming him after a mischievous little comic-book character, Mr Mxyztplk from the Fifth Dimension, who looked a bit like Elmer Fudd and used to make Superman's life hell until ole Supe could trick him into saying his name backwards, Klptzyxm, whereupon he disappeared back into the Fifth Dimension; but because we weren't too sure how to say Mxyztplk (not to mention Klptzyxm) we dropped that idea. 'We'll just call you Mixed-Up,' I told him in the end, to simplify life. 'Mishter Mikshed-Up Mishirsh.' I was fifteen then and bursting with unemployed cock and it meant I could say things like that right into people's faces, even people less accommodating than Mr Mecir with his stroke.

What I remember most vividly are his pink rubber washing-up gloves, which he seemed never to remove, at least not until he came calling for Certainly-Mary . . .

At any rate, when I insulted him, with my sisters Durré and Muneeza cackling in the lift, Mecir just grinned an empty good-natured grin, nodded, 'You call me what you like, okay,' and went back to buffing and polishing the brasswork. There was no point teasing him if he was going to be like that, so I got into the lift and all the way to the fourth floor we sang *I Can't Stop Loving You* at the top of our best Ray Charles voices, which were pretty awful. But we were wearing our dark glasses, so it didn't matter.

## 4

It was the summer of 1962, and school was out. My baby sister Scheherazade was just one year old. Durré was a bee-hived fourteen; Muneeza was ten, and already quite a handful. The three of us—or rather Durré and me, with Muneeza trying desperately and unsuccessfully to be included in our gang—would stand over Scheherazade's cot and sing to her. 'No nursery rhymes,' Durré had decreed, and so there were none, for though she was a year my junior she was a natural leader. The infant Scheherazade's lullabies were our cover versions of recent hits by Chubby Checker, Neil Sedaka, Elvis and Pat Boone.

'Why don't you come home, Speedy Gonzales?' we bellowed in sweet disharmony: but most of all, and with actions, we would jump down, turn around and pick a bale of cotton. We would have jumped down, turned around and picked those bales all day except that the Maharaja of B— in the flat below complained, and Aya Mary came in to plead with us to be quiet.

'Look, see, it's Jumble-Aya who's fallen for Mixed-Up,' Durré shouted, and Mary blushed a truly immense blush. So naturally we segued right into a quick me-oh-my-oh; son of a gun, we had big fun. But then the baby began to yell, my father came in with his head down bull-fashion and steaming from both ears, and we needed all the good luck charms we could find.

I had been at boarding school in England for a year or so when Abba took the decision to bring the family over. Like all his decisions, it was neither explained to nor discussed with anyone, not even my mother. When they first arrived he rented two adjacent flats in a seedy Bayswater mansion block called Graham Court, which lurked furtively in a nothing street that crawled along the side of the ABC Queensway cinema towards the Porchester Baths. He commandeered one of these flats for himself and put my mother, three sisters and Aya in the other; also, on school holidays, me. England, where liquor was freely available, did little for my father's *bonhomie,* so in a way it was a relief to have a flat to ourselves.

Most nights he emptied a bottle of Johnnie Walker Red Label and a soda-siphon. My mother did not dare to go across to 'his place' in the evenings. She said: 'He makes faces at me.'

Aya Mary took Abba his dinner and answered all his calls (if he wanted anything, he would phone us up and ask for it). I am not sure why Mary was spared his drunken rages. She said it was because she was nine years his senior, so she could tell him to show due respect.

After a few months, however, my father leased a three-bedroom fourth-floor apartment with a fancy address. This was Waverley House in Kensington Court, W8. Among its other residents were not one but two Indian Maharajas, the sporting Prince P— as well as the old B— who has already been mentioned. Now we were jammed in together, my parents and Baby Scarezade (as her siblings had affectionately begun to call her) in the master bedroom, the three of us in a much smaller room, and Mary, I regret to admit, on a straw mat laid on the fitted carpet in the hall. The third bedroom became my father's office, where he made phone-calls and kept his *Encyclopedia Britannica,* his *Reader's Digests,* and (under lock and key) the television cabinet. We entered it at our peril. It was the Minotaur's lair.

One morning he was persuaded to drop in at the corner pharmacy and pick up some supplies for the baby. When he returned there was a hurt, schoolboyish look on his face that I had never seen before, and he was pressing his hand against his cheek.

'She hit me,' he said plaintively.

'Hai! Allah-tobah! Darling!' cried my mother, fussing. 'Who hit you? Are you injured? Show me, let me see.'

'I did nothing,' he said, standing there in the hall with the pharmacy bag in his other hand and a face as pink as Mecir's rubber gloves. 'I just went in with your list. The girl seemed very helpful. I asked for baby compound, Johnson's powder, teething jelly, and she brought them out. Then I asked did she have any nipples, and she slapped my face.'

My mother was appalled. 'Just for that?' And Certainly-Mary backed her up. 'What is this nonsense?' she wanted to know. 'I have been in that chemist's shock, and they have flenty nickels, different sizes, all on view.'

Durré and Muneeza could not contain themselves. They were rolling round on the floor, laughing and kicking their legs in the air.

'You both shut your face at once,' my mother ordered. 'A madwoman has hit your father. Where is the comedy?'

'I don't believe it,' Durré gasped. 'You just went up to that girl and said,' and here she fell apart again, stamping her feet and holding her stomach, '"*have you got any nipples?*"'

My father grew thunderous, empurpled. Durré controlled herself. 'But Abba,' she said, at length, 'here they call them teats.'

Now my mother's and Mary's hands flew to their mouths, and even my father looked shocked. 'But how shameless!' my mother said. 'The same word as for what's on your bosoms?' She coloured, and stuck out her tongue for shame.

'These English,' sighed Certainly-Mary. 'But aren't they the limit? Certainly-yes; they are.'

I remember this story with delight, because it was the only time I ever saw my father so discomfited, and the incident became legendary and the girl in the pharmacy was installed as the object of our great veneration. (Durré and I went in there just to take a look at her—she was a plain, short girl of about seventeen, with large, unavoidable breasts—but she caught us whispering and glared so fiercely that we fled.) And also because in the general hilarity I was able to conceal the shaming truth that I, who had been in England for so long, would have made the same mistake as Abba did.

It wasn't just Certainly-Mary and my parents who had trouble with the English language. My schoolfellows tittered when in my Bombay way I said 'brought-up' for upbringing (as in 'where was your brought-up?') and 'thrice' for three times and 'quarter-plate' for side-plate and 'macaroni' for pasta in general. As for learning the difference between nipples and teats, I really hadn't had any opportunities to increase my word power in that area at all.

## 5

So I was a little jealous of Certainly-Mary when Mixed-Up came to call. He rang our bell, his body quivering with deference in an old suit grown too loose, the trousers tightly gathered by a belt; he had taken off his rubber gloves and there were roses in his hand. My father opened the door and gave him a withering look. Being a snob, Abba was not pleased that the flat lacked a separate service entrance, so that even a porter had to be treated as a member of the same universe as himself.

'Mary,' Mixed-Up managed, licking his lips and pushing back his floppy white hair. 'I, to see Miss Mary, come, am.'

'Wait on,' Abba said, and shut the door in his face.

Certainly-Mary spent all her afternoons off with old Mixed-Up from then on, even though that first date was not a complete success. He took her 'up West' to show her the visitors' London she had never seen, but at the top of an up escalator at Piccadilly Circus, while Mecir was painfully enunciating the words on the posters she couldn't read—*Unzip a banana,* and *Idris when I's dri*—she got her sari stuck in the jaws of the machine, and as the escalator pulled at the garment it began to unwind. She was forced to spin round and round like a top, and screamed at the top of her voice, 'O BAAP! BAAPU-RÉ! BAAP-RÉ-BAAP-RÉ-BAAP!' It was Mixed-Up who saved her by pushing the emergency stop button before the sari was completely unwound and she was exposed in her petticoat for all the world to see.

'O, courter!' she wept on his shoulder. 'O, no more escaleater, courter, nevermore, surely not!'

My own amorous longings were aimed at Durré's best friend, a Polish girl called Rozalia, who had a holiday job at Faiman's shoe shop on Oxford Street. I pursued her pathetically throughout the holidays and, on and off, for the next two years. She would let me have lunch with her sometimes and buy her a Coke and a sandwich, and once she came with me to stand on the terraces at White Hart Lane to watch Jimmy Greaves's first game for the Spurs. 'Come on you whoi-oites,' we both shouted dutifully. 'Come on you *Lily-whoites*.' After that she even invited me into the back room at Faiman's, where she kissed me twice and let me touch her breast, but that was as far as I got.

And then there was my sort-of-cousin Chandni, whose mother's sister had married my mother's brother, though they had since split up. Chandni was eighteen months older than me, and so sexy it made you sick. She was training to be an Indian classical dancer, Odissi as well as Natyam, but in the meantime she dressed in tight black jeans and a clinging black polo-neck jumper and took me, now and then, to hang out at Bunjie's, where she knew most of the folk-music crowd that frequented the place, and where she answered to the name of Moonlight, which is what *chandni* means. I chain-smoked with the folkies and then went to the toilet to throw up.

Chandni was the stuff of obsessions. She was a teenage dream, the Moon River come to Earth like the Goddess Ganga, dolled up in slinky black. But for her I was just the young greenhorn cousin to whom she was being nice because he hadn't learned his way around.

*She-E-rry, won't you come out tonight?* yodelled the Four Seasons. I knew exactly how they felt. *Come, come, come out toni-yi-yight.* And while you're at it, love me do.

## 6

They went for walks in Kensington Gardens. 'Pan,' Mixed-Up said, pointing at a statue. 'Los' boy. Nev' grew up.' They went to Barkers and Pontings and Derry & Toms and picked out furniture and curtains for imaginary homes. They cruised supermarkets and chose little delicacies to eat. In Mecir's cramped lounge they sipped what he called 'chimpanzee tea' and toasted crumpets in front of an electric bar fire.

Thanks to Mixed-Up, Mary was at last able to watch television. She liked children's programmes best, especially *The Flintstones.* Once, giggling at her daring, Mary confided to Mixed-Up that Fred and Wilma reminded her of her Sahib and Begum Sahiba upstairs;

at which the courter, matching her audaciousness, pointed first at Certainly-Mary and then at himself, grinned a wide gappy smile and said, 'Rubble.'

Later, on the news, a vulpine Englishman with a thin moustache and mad eyes declaimed a warning about immigrants, and Certainly-Mary flapped her hand at the set: 'Khali-pili bom marta,' she objected, and then, for her host's benefit translated: 'For nothing he is shouting shouting. Bad life! Switch it off.'

They were often interrupted by the Maharajas of B— and P—, who came downstairs to escape their wives and ring other women from the call-box in the porter's room.

'Oh, baby, forget that guy,' said sporty Prince P—, who seemed to spend all his days in tennis whites, and whose plump gold Rolex was almost lost in the thick hair on his arm. 'I'll show you a better time than him, baby; step into my world.'

The Maharaja of B— was older, uglier, more matter-of-fact. 'Yes, bring all appliances. Room is booked in name of Mr Douglas Home. Six forty-five to seven fifteen. You have printed rate card? Please. Also a two-foot ruler, must be wooden. Frilly apron, plus.'

This is what has lasted in my memory of Waverley House, this seething mass of bad marriages, booze, philanderers and unfulfilled young lusts; of the Maharaja of P— roaring away towards London's casinoland every night, in a red sports car with fitted blondes, and of the Maharaja of B— skulking off to Kensington High Street wearing dark glasses in the dark, and a coat with the collar turned up even though it was high summer; and at the heart of our little universe were Certainly-Mary and her courter, drinking chimpanzee tea and singing along with the national anthem of Bedrock.

But they were not really like Barney and Betty Rubble at all. They were formal, polite. They were . . . courtly. He courted her, and, like a coy, ringleted ingénue with a fan, she inclined her head, and entertained his suit.

## 7

I spent one half-term weekend in 1963 at the home in Beccles, Suffolk of Field Marshal Sir Charles Lutwidge-Dodgson, an old India hand and a family friend who was supporting my application for British citizenship. 'The Dodo', as he was known, invited me down by myself, saying he wanted to get to know me better.

He was a huge man whose skin had started hanging too loosely on his face, a giant living in a tiny thatched cottage and forever bumping his head. No wonder he was irascible at times; he was in Hell, a Gulliver trapped in that rose-garden Lilliput of croquet hoops, church bells, sepia photographs and old battle-trumpets.

The weekend was fitful and awkward until the Dodo asked if I played chess. Slightly awestruck at the prospect of playing a Field Marshal, I nodded; and ninety minutes later, to my amazement, won the game.

I went into the kitchen, strutting somewhat, planning to boast a little to the old soldier's long-time housekeeper, Mrs Liddell. But as soon as I entered she said: 'Don't tell me. You never went and won?'

'Yes,' I said, affecting nonchalance. 'As a matter of fact, yes, I did.'

'Gawd,' said Mrs Liddell. 'Now there'll be hell to pay. You go back in there and ask him for another game, and this time make sure you lose.'

I did as I was told, but was never invited to Beccles again.

Still, the defeat of the Dodo gave me new confidence at the chessboard, so when I returned to Waverley House after finishing my O levels, and was at once invited to play a game by Mixed-Up (Mary had told him about my victory in the Battle of Beccles with great pride and some hyperbole), I said: 'Sure, I don't mind.' How long could it take to thrash the old duffer, after all?

There followed a massacre royal. Mixed-Up did not just beat me; he had me for breakfast, over easy. I couldn't believe it—the canny opening, the fluency of his combination play, the force of his attacks, my own impossibly cramped, strangled positions—and asked for a second game. This time he tucked into me even more heartily. I sat broken in my chair at the end, close to tears. *Big girls don't cry,* I reminded myself, but the song went on playing in my head: *That's just an alibi.*

'Who are you?' I demanded, humiliation weighing down every syllable. 'The devil in disguise?'

Mixed-Up gave his big, silly grin. 'Grand Master,' he said. 'Long time. Before head.'

'You're a Grand Master,' I repeated, still in a daze. Then in a moment of horror I remembered that I had seen the name Mecir in books of classic games. 'Nimzo-Indian,' I said aloud. He beamed and nodded furiously.

'That Mecir?' I asked wonderingly.

'That,' he said. There was saliva dribbling out of a corner of his sloppy old mouth. This ruined old man was in the books. He was in the books. And even with his mind turned to rubble he could still wipe the floor with me.

'Now play lady,' he grinned. I didn't get it. 'Mary lady,' he said. 'Yes yes certainly.'

She was pouring tea, waiting for my answer. 'Aya, you can't play,' I said, bewildered.

'Learning, baba,' she said. 'What is it, na? Only a game.'

And then she, too, beat me senseless, and with the black pieces, at that. It was not the greatest day of my life.

## 8

From *100 Most Instructive Chess Games* by Robert Reshevsky, 1961:

> *M. Mecir—M. Najdorf*
> *Dallas 1950, Nimzo-Indian Defense*
> The attack of a tactician can be troublesome to meet—that of a strategist even more so. Whereas the tactician's threats may be unmistakable, the strategist confuses the issue by keeping things in abeyance. He threatens to threaten!
>
> Take this game for instance: Mecir posts a Knight at Q6 to get a grip on the center. Then he establishes a passed Pawn on one wing to occupy his opponent on the Queen side. Finally he stirs up the position on the King side. What does the poor bewildered opponent do?

> How can he defend everything at once? Where will the blow fall?
>
> Watch Mecir keep Najdorf on the run, as he shifts the attack from side to side!

Chess had become their private language. Old Mixed-Up, lost as he was for words, retained, on the chessboard, much of the articulacy and subtlety which had vanished from his speech. As Certainly-Mary gained in skill—and she had learned with astonishing speed, I thought bitterly, for someone who couldn't read or write or pronounce the letter p—she was better able to understand, and respond to, the wit of the reduced maestro with whom she had so unexpectedly forged a bond.

He taught her with great patience, showing-not-telling, repeating openings and combinations and endgame techniques over and over until she began to see the meaning in the patterns. When they played, he handicapped himself, he told her her best moves and demonstrated their consequences, drawing her, step by step, into the infinite possibilities of the game.

Such was their courtship. 'It is like an adventure, baba,' Mary once tried to explain to me. 'It is like going with him to his country, you know? What a place, baap-ré! Beautiful and dangerous and funny and full of fuzzles. For me it is a big-big discovery. What to tell you? I go for the game. It is a wonder.'

I understood, then, how far things had gone between them. Certainly-Mary had never married, and had made it clear to old Mixed-Up that it was too late to start any of that monkey business at her age. The courter was a widower, and had grown-up children somewhere, lost long ago behind the ever-higher walls of Eastern Europe. But in the game of chess they had found a form of flirtation, an endless renewal that precluded the possibility of boredom, a courtly wonderland of the ageing heart.

What would the Dodo have made of it all? No doubt it would have scandalised him to see chess, chess of all games, the great formalisation of war, transformed into an art of love.

As for me: my defeats by Certainly-Mary and her courter ushered in further humiliations. Durré and Muneeza went down with the mumps, and so, finally, in spite of my mother's efforts to segregate us, did I. I lay terrified in bed while the doctor warned me not to stand up and move around if I could possibly help it. 'If you do,' he said, 'your parents won't need to punish you. You will have punished yourself quite enough.'

I spent the following few weeks tormented day and night by visions of grotesquely swollen testicles and a subsequent life of limp impotence—finished before I'd even started, it wasn't fair!—which were made much worse by my sisters' quick recovery and incessant gibes. But in the end I was lucky; the illness didn't spread to the deep South. 'Think how happy your hundred and one girlfriends will be, bhai,' sneered Durré, who knew all about my continued failures in the Rozalia and Chandni departments.

On the radio, people were always singing about the joys of being sixteen years old. I wondered where they were, all those boys and girls of my age having the time of their lives. Were they driving around America in Studebaker convertibles? They certainly weren't in my neighbourhood. London, W8 was

Sam Cooke country that summer. *Another Saturday night* . . . There might be a mop-top love-song stuck at number one, but I was down with lonely Sam in the lower depths of the charts, how-I-wishing I had someone, etc., and generally feeling in a pretty goddamn dreadful way.

## 9

'Baba, come quick.'

It was late at night when Aya Mary shook me awake. After many urgent hisses, she managed to drag me out of sleep and pull me, pajama'ed and yawning, down the hall. On the landing outside our flat was Mixed-Up the courter, huddled up against a wall, weeping. He had a black eye and there was dried blood on his mouth.

'What happened?' I asked Mary, shocked.

'Men,' wailed Mixed-Up. 'Threaten. Beat.'

He had been in his lounge earlier that evening when the sporting Maharaja of P— burst in to say, 'If anybody comes looking for me, okay, any tough-guy type guys, okay, I am out, okay? Oh you tea. Don't let them go upstairs, okay? Big tip, okay?'

A short time later, the old Maharaja of B— also arrived in Mecir's lounge, looking distressed.

'Suno, listen on,' said the Maharaja of B—. 'You don't know where I am, samajh liya? Understood? Some low persons may inquire. You don't know. I am abroad, achha? On extended travels abroad. Do your job, porter. Handsome recompense.'

Late at night two tough-guy types did indeed turn up. It seemed the hairy Prince P— had gambling debts. 'Out,' Mixed-Up grinned in his sweetest way. The tough-guy types nodded, slowly. They had long hair and thick lips like Mick Jagger's. 'He's a busy gent. We should of made an appointment,' said the first type to the second. 'Didn't I tell you we should of called?'

'You did,' agreed the second type. 'Got to do these things right, you said, he's royalty. And you was right, my son, I put my hand up, I was dead wrong. I put my hand up to that.'

'Let's leave our card,' said the first type. 'Then he'll know to expect us.'

'Ideal,' said the second type, and smashed his fist into old Mixed-Up's mouth. 'You tell him,' the second type said, and struck the old man in the eye. 'When he's in. You mention it.'

He had locked the front door after that; but much later, well after midnight, there was a hammering. Mixed-Up called out, 'Who?'

'We are close friends of the Maharaja of B—' said a voice. 'No, I tell a lie. Acquaintances.'

'He calls upon a lady of our acquaintance,' said a second voice. 'To be precise.'

'It is in that connection that we crave audience,' said the first voice.

'Gone,' said Mecir. 'Jet plane. Gone.'

There was a silence. Then the second voice said, 'Can't be in the jet set if you never jump on a jet, eh? Biarritz, Monte, all of that.'

'Be sure and let His Highness know', said the first voice, 'that we eagerly await his return.'

'With regard to our mutual friend,' said the second voice. 'Eagerly.'

*What does the poor bewildered opponent do?* The words from the chess book popped unbidden into my head. *How can he defend everything at once? Where will the blow fall? Watch Mecir keep Najdorf on the run, as he shifts the attack from side to side!*

Mixed-Up returned to his lounge and on this occasion, even though there had been no use of force, he began to weep. After a time he took the elevator up to the fourth floor and whispered through our letterbox to Certainly-Mary sleeping on her mat.

'I didn't want to wake Sahib,' Mary said. 'You know his trouble, na? And Begum Sahiba is so tired at end of the day. So now you tell, baba, what to do?'

What did she expect me to come up with? I was sixteen years old. 'Mixed-Up must call the police,' I unoriginally offered.

'No, no, baba,' said Certainly-Mary emphatically. 'If the courter makes a scandal for Maharaja-log, then in the end it is the courter only who will be out on his ear.'

I had no other ideas. I stood before them feeling like a fool, while they both turned upon me their frightened, supplicant eyes.

'Go to sleep,' I said. 'We'll think about it in the morning.' *The first pair of thugs were tacticians,* I was thinking. *They were troublesome to meet. But the second pair were scarier; they were strategists. They threatened to threaten.*

Nothing happened in the morning, and the sky was clear. It was almost impossible to believe in fists, and menacing voices at the door. During the course of the day both Maharajas visited the porter's lounge and stuck five-pound notes in Mixed-Up's waistcoat pocket. 'Held the fort, good man,' said Prince P—, and the Maharaja of B— echoed those sentiments: 'Spot on. All handled now, achha? Problem over.'

The three of us—Aya Mary, her courter, and me—held a council of war that afternoon and decided that no further action was necessary. The hall porter was the front line in any such situation, I argued, and the front line had held. And now the risks were past. Assurances had been given. End of story.

'End of story,' repeated Certainly-Mary doubtfully, but then, seeking to reassure Mecir, she brightened. 'Correct,' she said. 'Most certainly! All-done, finis.' She slapped her hands against each other for emphasis. She asked Mixed-Up if he wanted a game of chess; but for once the courter didn't want to play.

## 10

After that I was distracted, for a time, from the story of Mixed-Up and Certainly-Mary by violence nearer home.

My middle sister Muneeza, now eleven, was entering her delinquent phase a little early. She was the true inheritor of my father's black rage, and when she lost control it was terrible to behold. That summer she seemed to pick fights with my father on purpose; seemed prepared, at her young age, to test her strength against his. (I intervened in her rows with Abba only once, in the kitchen. She grabbed the kitchen scissors and flung them at me. They cut me on the thigh. After that I kept my distance.)

As I witnessed their wars I felt myself coming unstuck from the idea of family itself. I looked at my screaming sister and thought how brilliantly self-destructive she was, how triumphantly she was ruining her relations with the people she needed most.

And I looked at my choleric, face-pulling father and thought about British citizenship. My existing Indian passport permitted me to travel only to a very few countries, which were carefully listed on the second right-hand page. But I might soon have a British passport and then, by hook or by crook, I would get away from him. I would not have this face-pulling in my life.

At sixteen, you still think you can escape from your father. You aren't listening to his voice speaking through your mouth, you don't see how your gestures already mirror his; you don't see him in the way you hold your body, in the way you sign your name. You don't hear his whisper in your blood.

On the day I have to tell you about, my two-year-old sister Chhoti Scheherazade, Little Scare-zade, started crying as she often did during one of our family rows. Amma and Aya Mary loaded her into her push-chair and made a rapid getaway. They pushed her to Kensington Square and then sat on the grass, turned Scheherazade loose and made philosophical remarks while she tired herself out. Finally, she fell asleep, and they made their way home in the fading light of the evening. Outside Waverley House they were approached by two well-turned-out young men with Beatle haircuts and the buttoned-up, collarless jackets made popular by the band. The first of these young men asked my mother, very politely, if she might be the Maharani of B—.

'No,' my mother answered, flattered.

'Oh, but you are, madam,' said the second Beatle, equally politely. 'For you are heading for Waverley House and that is the Maharaja's place of residence.'

'No, no,' my mother said, still blushing with pleasure. 'We are a different Indian family.'

'Quite so,' the first Beatle nodded understandingly, and then, to my mother's great surprise, placed a finger alongside his nose, and winked. 'Incognito, eh. Mum's the word.'

'Now excuse us,' my mother said, losing patience. 'We are not the ladies you seek.'

The second Beatle tapped a foot lightly against a wheel of the push-chair. 'Your husband seeks ladies, madam, were you aware of that fact? Yes, he does. Most assiduously, may I add.'

'Too assiduously,' said the first Beatle, his face darkening.

'I tell you I am not the Maharani Begum,' my mother said, growing suddenly alarmed. 'Her business is not my business. Kindly let me pass.'

The second Beatle stepped closer to her. She could feel his breath, which was minty. 'One of the ladies he sought out was our ward, as you might say,' he explained. 'That would be the term. Under our protection, you follow. Us, therefore, being responsible for her welfare.'

'Your husband,' said the first Beatle, showing his teeth in a frightening way, and raising his voice one notch, 'damaged the goods. Do you hear me, Queenie? He damaged the fucking goods.'

'Mistaken identity, fleas,' said Certainly-Mary. 'Many Indian residents in Waverley House. We are decent ladies; *fleas*.'

The second Beatle had taken out something from an inside pocket. A blade caught the light. 'Fucking wogs,' he said. 'You fucking come over here, you don't fucking know how to fucking behave. Why don't you fucking fuck off to fucking Wogistan? Fuck your fucking wog arses. Now then,' he added in a quiet voice, holding up the knife, 'unbutton your blouses.'

Just then a loud noise emanated from the doorway of Waverley House. The two women and the two men turned to look, and out came Mixed-Up, yelling at the top of his voice and windmilling his arms like a mad old loon.

'Hullo,' said the Beatle with the knife, looking amused. 'Who's this, then? Oh oh fucking seven?'

Mixed-Up was trying to speak, he was in a mighty agony of effort, but all that was coming out of his mouth was raw, unshaped noise. Scheherazade woke up and joined in. The two Beatles looked displeased. But then something happened inside old Mixed-Up; something popped, and in a great rush he gabbled, 'Sirs sirs no sirs these not B— women sirs B— women upstairs on floor three sirs Maharaja of B— also sirs God's truth mother's grave swear.'

It was the longest sentence he had spoken since the stroke that had broken his tongue long ago.

And what with his torrent and Scheherazade's squalls there were suddenly heads poking out from doorways, attention was being paid, and the two Beatles nodded gravely. 'Honest mistake,' the first of them said apologetically to my mother, and actually bowed from the waist. 'Could happen to anyone,' the knife-man added, ruefully. They turned and began to walk quickly away. As they passed Mecir, however, they paused. 'I know you, though,' said the knife-man. '"*Jet plane. Gone.*"' He made a short movement of the arm, and then Mixed-Up the courter was lying on the pavement with blood leaking from a wound in his stomach. 'All okay now,' he gasped, and passed out.

## 11

He was on the road to recovery by Christmas; my mother's letter to the landlords, in which she called him a 'knight in shining armour', ensured that he was well looked after, and his job was kept open for him. He continued to live in his little ground-floor cubby-hole, while the hall porter's duties were carried out by shift-duty staff. 'Nothing but the best for our very own hero,' the landlords assured my mother in their reply.

The two Maharajas and their retinues had moved out before I came home for the Christmas holidays, so we had no further visits from the Beatles or the Rolling Stones. Certainly-Mary spent as much time as she could with Mecir; but it was the look of my old Aya that worried me more than poor Mixed-Up. She looked older, and powdery, as if she might crumble away at any moment into dust.

'We didn't want to worry you at school,' my mother said. 'She has been having heart trouble. Palpitations. Not all the time, but.'

Mary's health problems had sobered up the whole family. Muneeza's tantrums had stopped, and even my father was making an effort. They had put up a Christmas tree in the sitting-room and decorated it with all sorts of baubles. It was so odd to see a Christmas tree at our place that I realised things must be fairly serious.

On Christmas Eve my mother suggested that Mary might like it if we all sang some carols. Amma had made song-sheets, six copies, by hand. When we did *O come, all ye faithful* I showed off by singing from memory in Latin. Everybody behaved perfectly. When Muneeza suggested that we should try *Swinging on a Star* or *I Wanna Hold Your Hand* instead of this boring stuff, she wasn't really being serious. So this is family life, I thought. This is it.

But we were only play-acting.

A few weeks earlier, at school, I'd come across an American boy, the star of the school's Rugby football team, crying in the Chapel cloisters. I asked him what the matter was and he told me that President Kennedy had been assassinated. 'I don't believe you,' I said, but I could see that it was true. The football star sobbed and sobbed. I took his hand.

'When the President dies, the nation is orphaned,' he eventually said, broken-heartedly parroting a piece of cracker-barrel wisdom he'd probably heard on Voice of America.

'I know how you feel,' I lied. 'My father just died, too.'

Mary's heart trouble turned out to be a mystery; unpredictably, it came and went. She was subjected to all sorts of tests during the next six months, but each time the doctors ended up by shaking their heads: they couldn't find anything wrong with her. Physically, she was right as rain; except that there were these periods when her heart kicked and bucked in her chest like the wild horses in *The Misfits,* the ones whose roping and tying made Marilyn Monroe so mad.

Mecir went back to work in the spring, but his experience had knocked the stuffing out of him. He was slower to smile, duller of eye, more inward. Mary, too, had turned in upon herself. They still met for tea, crumpets and *The Flintstones,* but something was no longer quite right.

At the beginning of the summer Mary made an announcement.

'I know what is wrong with me,' she told my parents, out of the blue. 'I need to go home.'

'But, Aya,' my mother argued, 'homesickness is not a real disease.'

'God knows for what-all we came over to this country,' Mary said. 'But I can no longer stay. No. Certainly not.' Her determination was absolute.

So it was England that was breaking her heart, breaking it by not being India. London was killing her, by not being Bombay. And Mixed-Up? I wondered. Was the courter killing her, too, because he was no longer himself? Or was it that her heart, roped by two different loves, was being pulled both East and West, whinnying and rearing, like those movie horses being yanked this way by Clark Gable and that way by Montgomery Clift, and she knew that to live she would have to choose?

'I must go,' said Certainly-Mary. 'Yes, certainly. *Bas.* Enough.'

That summer, the summer of '64, I turned seventeen. Chandni went back to India. Durré's Polish friend Rozalia informed me over a sandwich in Oxford Street that she was getting engaged to a 'real man', so I could forget about seeing her again, because this Zbigniew was the jealous type. Roy Orbison sang *It's Over* in my ears as I walked away to the Tube, but the truth was that nothing had really begun.

Certainly-Mary left us in mid-July. My father bought her a one-way ticket to Bombay, and that last morning was heavy with the pain of ending. When we took her bags down to the car, Mecir the hall porter was nowhere to be seen. Mary did not knock on the door of his lounge, but walked straight out through the freshly polished oak-panelled lobby, whose mirrors and brasses were sparkling brightly; she climbed into the back seat of our Ford Zodiac and sat there stiffly with her carry-on grip on her lap, staring straight ahead. I had known and loved her all my life. *Never mind your damned courter,* I wanted to shout at her, *what about me?*

As it happened, she was right about the homesickness. After her return to Bombay, she never had a day's heart trouble again; and, as the letter from her niece Stella confirmed, at ninety-one she was still going strong.

Soon after she left, my father told us he had decided to 'shift location' to Pakistan. As usual, there were no discussions, no explanations, just the simple fiat. He gave up the lease on the flat in Waverley House at the end of the summer holidays, and they all went off to Karachi, while I went back to school.

I became a British citizen that year. I was one of the lucky ones, I guess, because in spite of that chess game I had the Dodo on my side. And the passport did, in many ways, set me free. It allowed me to come and go, to make choices that were not the ones my father would have wished. But I, too, have ropes around my neck, I have them to this day, pulling me this way and that, East and West, the nooses tightening, commanding, *choose, choose.*

I buck, I snort, I whinny, I rear, I kick. Ropes, I do not choose between you. Lassoes, lariats, I choose neither of you, and both. Do you hear? I refuse to choose.

A year or so after we moved out I was in the area and dropped in at Waverley House to see how the old courter was doing. Maybe, I thought, we could have a game of chess, and he could beat me to a pulp. The lobby was empty, so I knocked on the door of his little lounge. A stranger answered.

'Where's Mixed-Up?' I cried, taken by surprise. I apologised at once, embarrassed. 'Mr Mecir, I meant, the porter.'

'I'm the porter, sir,' the man said. 'I don't know anything about any mix-up.'

# Thailand

## Angkarn Kalayaanaphong (b. 1926)

*Translated by Herbert P. Phillips*

Angkarn Kalayaanaphong is widely known as a poet and painter as well as a writer of short fiction. Some contemporary Thai writers have concentrated on modern and international perspectives and experiences for their works; Angkarn has found solace in the traditional spirituality of Thai culture. Although sometimes accused of corrupting the lyrical beauty of the Thai language by using it to express scenes that are untraditionally harsh, he has always demonstrated a poet's ear for the rhythms of language. In "Grandma" the harmony of language and viewpoint reinforce each other.

This story is an expression of extraordinary harmony achieved through the Buddhist ideal of complete un-self-consciousness. The rains lift; the clouds drift over the mountains; and the old woman, recovering from her illness, is simply a part of the cosmic process. In this context it is not surprising to find that she can talk with the plants, and she herself seems only mildly surprised that they speak to her. She will look after her own needs but hopes not to cause disruption and asks the plants she wishes to pick if it will be painful for them. They assure her it is no problem to have someone of her sensitivity pluck them. The only disruptive element comes when she steps on a snake and it bites her; yet even here, stepping on the snake is an accident, done without rancor, and the snake's response is instinctive and natural, not angry or vengeful. The woman accepts her death serenely as an inevitable part of the cosmic process, and the cosmos continues on its course unrippled by her death. Death is no occasion for self-conscious histrionics and mourning, only something to be accepted. The old woman's oneness with nature relieves death of its sting.

## *Grandma*

One twilight during rainy season, the downpour has come to an end, leaving a trail of clean white clouds moving in gentle procession. The bushes and the flowering trees turn a brilliant and refreshing green. The setting sun, a ball of red, radiates its beams, bringing forth the rainbows that dine on the droplets left behind. Behind the high mountains, the wind blows gently, shaking the glistening raindrops off the leaves of the mahogany and rubber trees. Down there is a lonely hamlet, a great distance from the center of things.

An old woman, crumbling from her years, lives in an old hut in the middle of a deserted field. Her hair is the color of fog and her face is wrinkled and dried, though the center of her eyes still sparkle. But she is in the dusk of her day, over eighty years of age, her body bent over into a widow's hump.

She belongs to the age of grandmothers, without relatives or friends. For many years she has been picking greens in the field and splitting logs to sell for a living. Now she has grown thin and is constantly ill, missing her meals when there is nothing to eat. One day, after recovering from her most recent illness, she craved some rice and *liang* curry, a curry made of the greenest vegetables. So she left her hut to pick some greens. She noticed the *tamlyng* shoots quivering seductively in the wind. At the moment she was reaching toward the vine to pluck one of the shoots, another shoot spoke out: "Grandma, please pick me first. That shoot there is my younger sister. Wait until tomorrow, and maybe then she'll have something to talk with you about."

Grandma was at first dumbfounded and then perplexed, but she gathered her courage and answered, "Of course, for most people on this earth, there'll be a tomorrow, but for me, today is always the last day. Nothing is certain.

Tomorrow morning when the cock crows close to three o'clock maybe I will have breathed my last. I have already come that close, many times. So today I want to eat some *liang* curry to my heart's content."

The tamarind shrub, entering the conversation, asked her, "Do you have any rice?"

"Well, some. I bought about four or five litres a few days ago. But there's only a little more than a litre left, and it's full of weevils. I'll have to pick them out first. By the time the rice is cooked, the night spirits will be out and it will be time to light the torch."

As soon as the old woman finished her words, the yellow papaya, so ripe that it was ready to fall, said in a loud but trembling voice, "Grandma, take this rich and ripe papaya to eat first." Grandma had not yet recovered from her amazement, but she expressed her deepest gratitude to these plants.

The papaya said repeatedly, "Take me first to eat. I have a laxative that will clean your intestines and will make you feel more relaxed. Then you will make yourself forget your concerns and worries, feel in a pleasant frame of mind, enjoy the rainbow of the seven gleaming rays of the morning sun, and wake up early in the morning breathing in the pure and fresh air, welcoming the deity of the new day who will bestow upon you the divine ray of happiness and will prolong your life span. Grandma, you will have a tomorrow that will go on and on for as long as you wish."

Grandma asked, "Why can plants talk? In earlier days you were so quiet as to be mute. Or perhaps your compassion lies secreted deeply within you. You are able to bring forth your generosity and your magnanimous mercy so that I can feel the delight of the divine power that has revived my strength and vigor."

At that moment, all the plants of the field declaimed in chorus: "Although we share the same world with human beings we are immune to the influence of mankind's basic character and thought, which is composed of selfishness, small-mindedness, and avarice. By no means do we follow the human example of pretense, deception, and intrigue. Other than Grandma, we communicate with nobody. We see that you are deserted and ignored uncompassionately by the rest of mankind. Because of the deep pathos we feel for you, we can no longer refrain from speaking.

"In fact, the deities have bestowed souls on all living things, but we prefer to be mute. Even though we have our own language, we act as if we did not. We sometimes communicate with each other in our own language, but it is too mystifying to be understood by any human being. At first, we thought that Grandma would breathe her last tonight. But we were fortunate to realize that through the intercession of Divine happiness you have regained your strength, prolonging your life much further."

Grandma listened intently, deeply moved by the chorus.

Immediately, the watercress in the pond behind the hut said, "Grandma, I will put forth new, fresh leaves for you to pick and sell every day in the market. In the future there will be more people in this area, so my price will increase. Grandma, proclaim to everyone that watercress is a superb medicine. After eating me, people's eyesight also improves."

The old woman was so touched that tears streamed down her cheeks. She kneeled down, lowered her body, and raising her hands to her forehead to pay respect, she expressed her gratitude to Mother Earth and all the vegetables and plants, saying, "Grandma really doesn't want to be any trouble at all to you."

"When I pick you don't you feel any pain?"

The watercress quivering in the wind laughed and said, "Only the deities in heaven have such exquisite compassion. Grandma, do you think that the gods that created us would have also bestowed upon us the feeling to know pain? The whole world would then be filled with the cries of our mourning and the screams of our agony as a result of the way we are treated every day and night by human beings. We do speak and we do feel many things, but this is because of the wondrous power of our souls.

"Fortunately, we plants have a nervous system that does not know pain. If we were any different, the torment and misery would be too great to bear, and we would just die. Come Grandma, please pick me. I am always happy to produce fresh, new leaves."

After that day, the watercress in the pond grew longer and larger, putting forth beautifully more stems and fresh leaves. The old woman picked them to sell at the market, earning enough to pay for her rice and other food and continuing to live in the old hut. Portions of the palm leaf covering the hut were torn, making a hole through which the twinkling stars glittered. The constellation Orion passed in the sky and the frogs and tadpoles croaked melodiously. It was deep into the night.

This time the old woman has been sick with malaria for several days. Her temperature has risen very high, making her deaf in both ears. She feels dizzy and is talking as if delirious in her sleep. The weather has changed and it is hot and humid everywhere. The dark, sad clouds are hiding the moon. The wind blows stronger, becoming more turbulent and shaking the whole country. The trees are like swings swaying in the rain. Flashes of lightning and thunder strike down with a deafening clap that shakes the whole world. The old woman is panic-stricken and loses consciousness. Her body is soaked with rain. After a few hours, the storm tapers off. The sky begins to fill with the silver and golden rays of morning. The joyous chirping of the Boradok birds and Malaysian parrots can be heard clearly in the distance.

She has regained consciousness, but her fever has not abated. Poor dear, she is delirious. She is confused and goes down to pick some watercress. The watercress cries out in warning, "Grandma, don't come down here. There are dangerous snakes near the edge of the pond. They are mating." However, she does not hear the entreating voice and walks on down, straight ahead.

So it happens, in a moment of fate, she steps on the tip of the tail of a vicious cobra. The cobra is startled. It swings around and bites her fully. The fangs are buried into her. She feels a sudden pain at the back of her foot, so she moves to soothe it with her hand. The cobra strikes again, this time at her hand, and she begins to realize that she has been bitten by a snake. Panic-stricken, she loses consciousness, and falls at the edge of the pond. Before long, the deadly poison of the cobra works its way against the current of her bloodstream. In old age, the woman has little resistance. The poison forces itself through the blood into the depth of her heart, bringing her pulse to an end. The old woman breathes her last. But her eyes are still open wide, as if to express her concern for the vegetables, trees, and flowers who are her companions. Their friendship has no comparison.

A portion of the waning moon still shows faintly and then disappears behind the trees. The day is beginning to dawn. The rain has abated some time ago. The air is calm and chilly, creating an atmosphere of solitude and silence, except for the reverberations of nature. Exploding dewdrops crackle on leaves. Only one lingering star still glitters in the immaculate womb of heaven.

For anyone having the power to hear beyond the range of the human ear the sobbing of the trees and flowers in that field would be very clear. The watercress, the papayas, the tamarinds, and the *tamlyng* shoots are all lamenting and weeping.

A tiny flower with a trembling voice said, "Older brothers and sisters, I am so unhappy because I was hoping this morning to bloom into a bright violet flower. If Grandma could have seen my brilliant color it would have helped to relieve her pain. It is so sad."

The *tamlyng* said, "Look at that! An army of fire ants is eating away at the pupils of Grandma's eyes. They are chewing away at her eyes in swarms. In a few days her corpse will rot and swell. The vultures and crows will peck at her body and feed from her flesh. Her bones will be scattered over the soil and sand. It is so pitiful."

After its lamentations, the *tamlyng* again begins to sob until tears come forth from the center of its pure white blossoms. The tears blend with the dew and overflow the petals, as if they are a stream of remorse mourning the death of this old woman who has said farewell to the world and has disappeared forever.

# VIETNAM

## NGUYEN HUY THIEP (B. 1950)

*Translated by Greg Lockhart*

One of an accomplished new generation of Vietnamese writers who came of age during the French and American wars raging across his homeland, Nguyen Huy Thiep was born in Hanoi but spent much of his youth living in a traditional farming community where his mother worked in the fields with her neighbors. He graduated from the National Vietnamese Teacher's College in 1970, during the American bombing campaign. He took a job as a history teacher in a remote province and in his leisure time began writing and painting. Nguyen Huy Thiep's literary apprenticeship coincided with a period of strong Russian cultural influence in Vietnam. He might have learned from the fiction of Chekhov and Dostoevsky; however, the ambience and subject matter of his stories are uniquely Vietnamese. By 1987 his work began to appear in Vietnamese journals, and in 1988 more than twenty of his stories were published. Our selection comes from a collection of his stories titled *The General Retires and Other Stories.*

"Salt of the Jungle" is the brief, ironic hunting adventure of a sixty-year-old man who begins his foray into the forest exhilarated by the fresh air and natural surroundings where he is confident of proving his prowess. His attempt to shoot a monkey throws him into an unexpected encounter with the consciousness of his kinship with other animals. One might compare his work with the "magical realism" of South American writers like Gabriel Garcia Marquez (pp. 2140–2145). This style, in which the realism of Euro-American modernism is blended with the oral folk tales of a traditional society, is becoming an international style in countries emerging into the global literary scene.

## *Salt of the Jungle*

A month after the new year is the best time to be in the jungle. The vegetation is bursting with fresh buds, and its leaves are deep green and moist. Nature is both daunting and delicate, and this is due, in large measure, to the showers of spring rain.

At around this time, your feet sink into carpets of rotting leaves, you inhale pure air, and, sometimes, your body shudders with pleasure, because a drop of water has fallen from a leaf and struck your bare shoulder. Miraculously, the vexations of your daily life can be completely forgotten, because a small squirrel has sprung onto a branch. And, as it happened, it was at just such a time that Mr. Dieu went hunting.

The idea to go hunting had come to him when his son, who was studying in a foreign country, sent him a gift of a double-barreled shotgun. The gun was as light as a toy, and so sleek that he could not have dreamt such a beautiful thing existed. Mr. Dieu was sixty, and, at that age, both a new shotgun and a spring day for the hunt really made life worth living.

To dress for the occasion, he put on a warm quilted coat and trousers, a fur hat, and laced up a pair of high boots. To be well prepared, he also took a ration of sticky rice rolled into a ball the size of his fist. He moved up along the bed of a dry stream toward its source, a mile from which was the fabled kingdom of limestone caves.

Mr. Dieu turned onto a beaten track that wound through the jungle. As he moved along, he was aware that the trees on either side were full of bluebirds. Yet, he did not shoot. With a gun like his, it would have been a waste of ammunition, especially when he had already had his fill of bluebirds. They were tasty enough, but had a fishy flavor. In any case, he had no need to shoot birds with a loft full of pigeons at home.

At a turn in the track, Mr. Dieu was startled by a rustling in a bush. A clump of motley vines flew up in front of his face, and, as he caught his breath, a pair of jungle fowls shot out in front of the bush with their heads down, clucking. Mr. Dieu raised his shotgun and aimed. However, the fowls did not present a good target. *I'll miss,* he thought. He considered the situation, and sat down motionless for a very long time, waiting for the jungle to become quiet again. The fowls would think there was nobody there: it would be better that way—for them and for him.

The mountain range was full of towering peaks. Mr. Dieu looked at them as he contemplated his strength. To bag a monkey or a mountain goat would certainly be something. But he knew that mountain goats were difficult game. It was only by some stroke of luck that he would get a good shot at one, and he did not think that luck would come.

As he weighed carefully the pros and cons, Mr. Dieu decided to move along the foot of the limestone mountain range and hunt monkeys in the Dau Da Forest. He would be surer of finding food and wasting less energy. Mount Hoa Qua and Thuy Liem Cave were along the valley and, like the forest, they were legendary monkey haunts. Mr. Dieu also knew that he did not have difficulty shooting monkeys.

He stopped on a piece of rising ground, amid trees covered with climbing vines. This species of tree was unknown to him, with its silver leaves and golden flowers like earrings that hung down to the earth. Mr. Dieu sat quietly and observed, for he wanted to see if there were any monkeys there. These animals are as crafty as human beings; when they gather food they always put out sentries, and monkey sentries are very acute. If you don't see them, there is no hope for the hunt, no hope of hitting the leader of the troop. Of course, the leader was only a monkey. But it was not just any monkey. It would be the one that fate had singled out for him. So he had to wait, had to be cunning if he wanted to shoot his monkey.

Mr. Dieu sat quietly and relaxed for half an hour. The spring weather was warm and silky. It had been a long time since he had had the opportunity to sit as peacefully as this. And as he sat without a care in the world, the tranquillity of the jungle flowed through his being.

Suddenly, a swishing sound came rushing from out of the Dau Da Forest. It was the sound of a large animal moving through the trees. Mr. Dieu knew it was the leader of a monkey troop. He also knew that this monkey was formidable. It would appear with the brutal self-confidence of a king. Mr. Dieu smiled and watched carefully.

The sound continued for a while; then, suddenly, the beast appeared. It rapidly propelled itself through the jungle as though it never rested. Mr. Dieu admired its nimbleness. However, it disappeared in a flash, leaving him with a sharp stab of disappointment that this king-like creature would not be his. The elation he had felt since leaving home that morning was beginning to subside.

As soon as the leader disappeared, a gaggle of about twenty monkeys swung into view, criss-crossing Mr. Dieu's field of vision from very many angles. Some of them appeared on perches high up in the trees, others swung through the branches, and still others sprang to the ground. Within this medley of movement, Mr. Dieu noticed three monkeys that stayed together: a male, a female, and their young baby. He knew immediately that this male monkey was his prey.

Mr. Dieu felt hot. He took off his hat and quilted coat and placed them under a bush. He also placed his ball of sticky rice there. Gradually, he moved into a depression in the ground. He observed carefully, and noticed that the female monkey was standing guard. That was convenient, for with a becoming sense of vanity, she had distracted herself with the task of picking off her body lice.

Mr. Dieu made his calculations, then crept along, keeping windward of the female monkey. He had to get within twenty meters of the troop before he would be able to shoot. He crawled rapidly and skillfully. Once he had located his prey, he was sure he would kill it. That monkey was his. He was so certain of this, he felt that if he stumbled or made a careless move it would not make any difference.

Yet, even though he thought like this, Mr. Dieu still stalked the monkey troop carefully. He knew that nature was full of surprises, that one could never be too cautious.

He rested the shotgun in the fork of a tree, while the family trio had no inkling that disaster was near. The father was perched in a tree plucking fruit and throwing it down to the mother and child. Before he threw it, he always selected the best fruit and ate it himself. *How contemptible,* thought Mr. Dieu as he squeezed the trigger. The shotgun blast stunned the monkey troop for several seconds: the male monkey had fallen heavily to the ground with its arms outstretched.

The confusion into which the shotgun blast had thrown the monkey troop caused Mr. Dieu to tremble. He had done something cruel. His arms and legs went limp, with the kind of sensation that overcomes someone who has just overexerted himself with heavy work, and the troop disappeared into the jungle before he knew it. The female monkey and the baby also ran off after the others, but, after moving some distance, the female suddenly turned around and returned. Her mate, whose shoulder had been shattered by the shotgun pellets, was trying to raise himself but kept falling back to the ground.

The female monkey advanced carefully to where her mate had fallen and looked around, suspicious of the silence. The male monkey let out a pitiful scream, before he became silent again and listened, with a frantic expression on his face.

*Oh, get away from there!* Mr. Dieu groaned softly. But the female monkey looked as though she was prepared to sacrifice herself. She went to her mate and lifted him up in her arms. Mr. Dieu angrily raised his shotgun. Her readiness to sacrifice herself made him hate her like some bourgeois madame who paraded her noble nature. He knew all about the deceptions in which such theatrical performances were rooted; she could not deceive an old hunter like him.

As Mr. Dieu prepared to squeeze the trigger, the female monkey turned around and looked at him with terror in her eyes. She dropped the male monkey with a thud and fled. Mr. Dieu breathed a sigh of relief, then laughed quietly. He rose to his feet and left his hiding place.

*I've made a mistake!* Mr. Dieu cursed under his breath. For when he moved from his hiding place, the female monkey immediately turned around. *She knows I'm human,* he sighed, *the game is up.* Exactly so: the female monkey now kept him in the corner of her eye as she rushed headlong back to her mate. She deftly put her arms around him and hugged him to her chest. The two rolled around in a ball on the ground. She was acting like a crazy old woman. She was going to sacrifice herself recklessly, because of some noble instinct that nature prized. This stirred deep feelings of guilt in Mr. Dieu's heart. He had revealed himself as an assassin, while the female monkey, who faced death, still bared her teeth in a smile. Whatever he did now, he could only suffer, he could never rest, and he could even die two years before his time if he shot the female monkey at this moment. And all of this was because he had come out of his hiding place two minutes too soon.

As if to torment him, the monkeys took each other by the hand and ran off. *You pathetic old figure, Dieu,* he thought sadly. *With a pair of arthritic legs like yours, how are you going to run as fast as a monkey driven by loyalty and devotion?* The female monkey waved her bow legs, grinned, and made obscene gestures. Mr. Dieu angrily hurled his shotgun down in front of him. He wanted to frighten the female monkey into releasing her mate.

At the moment the shotgun hit the ground, the baby monkey suddenly appeared from a rocky mound. It grabbed the sling of the shotgun and dragged it off along the ground. The three monkeys scurried off on all fours, shrieking. Mr. Dieu was struck dumb for a second, then burst out laughing: his predicament was so ridiculous.

He picked up a handful of dirt and stones and threw it at the monkeys, as he took off howling in pursuit. The monkeys, who were terrified by these developments, split up, with the two adults veering off in the direction of the mountains and the baby running toward the cliff. *Losing the shotgun will be disastrous,* thought Mr. Dieu, and he continued to chase the baby monkey. He charged forward and narrowed the distance between them to the extent that only a jagged rock prevented him from reaching his gun.

By chasing the baby monkey, Mr. Dieu had taken a course of action that had extraordinary consequences. These began when the small monkey just rolled over the edge of the precipice, holding the shotgun sling tightly. Evidently, it was too inexperienced to react in any other way.

Mr. Dieu was pale and soaked with sweat. He stood looking down over the cliff with his body shaking. From far below came the echo of a piercing scream, the likes of which he had never heard before. He drew back in fear, as a mist swirled up from the abyss and enveloped the vegetation around him. Very quickly the entire landscape was obscured by eerie vapors. He ran back to the mountain. It was perhaps the first time since childhood that Mr. Dieu had run as though he were being chased by a ghost.

Mr. Dieu was exhausted when he reached the foot of the mountain. He sat down on the ground, looking back in the direction of the precipice, which the mist had now obscured. He remembered suddenly that this was the most feared place in the valley: the place that hunters called Death Hollow. Here, with alarming regularity, somebody perished in the mist each year.

*Ghosts?* thought Mr. Dieu. *Forsaken spirits usually take the form of white monkeys, don't they?* It had been a white monkey that seized the gun. Moreover, this had been such an extraordinary action that Mr. Dieu began to wonder if what he had been chasing was really a monkey.

*Am I dreaming?* he wondered, looking around. *Is all of this happening?* He stood up and looked at the mountain wall on the other side of Death Hollow. He was stunned, for now, without a trace of mist, the dome of the sky was clear and vast, and the entire landscape was visible in every detail.

An agitated cry came from somewhere above him. Mr. Dieu looked up and there he saw the wounded monkey lying across a rock ledge. The female monkey was nowhere to be seen, and so, very happy in the certainty that he would now catch his monkey, Mr. Dieu searched for a way to climb up on the rock ledge.

Finding a way up the side of the steep, slippery mountain was both difficult and dangerous. Mr. Dieu gauged his strength. *Whatever way, I'm going to get that monkey,* he murmured to himself, as he calmly used the crevices in the rock face to work his way up.

After about ten minutes, Mr. Dieu felt hot. He chose a spot where he could stand, then took off his boots and outer garments and placed them in the fork of a mulberry tree. He climbed onward quickly with no doubts about his ability to reach the ledge.

The slab of rock on which the wounded monkey lay was smooth and seemed somewhat unstable. Beneath it, there was a crevice as wide as Mr. Dieu's hand, which would allow him to pull himself up. He shuddered, frightened by the feeling that the slab might move and roll down the mountain at any moment. Nature was cruel and might want to test his courage further.

Mr. Dieu finally pulled himself up on the rock ledge with his elbows, and there he saw an extremely beautiful monkey with fine golden hair. It lay prone with its hands raking across the surface of the rock, as if it were trying to pull itself along. Its shoulder was stained red with blood.

Mr. Dieu put his hand on the monkey and felt its feverish body heat. *Easier than putting a hand on a sparrow,* he thought. Next, he slipped his hand under the monkey's chest and lifted it to estimate its weight. However, he withdrew his hand quickly when the chest emitted a low, but very disconcerting *hum,* which made him feel that his intervention had aroused Death's fury. The monkey stirred Mr. Dieu's pity when it trembled and rolled its sluggish eyes toward him. The shotgun pellets had smashed the monkey's shoulder blade and come out through four centimeters of bone. Each time the bones rubbed together, the monkey writhed in pain.

"I can't leave you like that," said Mr. Dieu. He picked up some Lao grass, crumpled it in his hand, and put it in the monkey's mouth. The monkey chewed the grass carefully, while Mr. Dieu applied a handful of leaves to its wound to stem the bleeding. The monkey curled its body into a ball and again turned its moist eyes toward Mr. Dieu. The old man looked away.

The monkey then buried its head in Mr. Dieu's arms, and a stammering sound came out of its mouth. The monkey was like a helpless child imploring him for help. Mr. Dieu felt very miserable. "It is better for me if you resist," he murmured, looking down at the suffering brow of the shriveled monkey. "I am old, and you know the sympathy of old people is easily aroused. What can I use to bandage you, poor monkey?"

Mr. Dieu considered the situation. He had no choice but to take off his shorts and use them to bandage the monkey's wound. When he did this, the bleeding stopped and the monkey no longer groaned.

Naked now, Mr. Dieu picked the monkey up and kept adjusting its weight in his arms as he found his way back down the mountain. Then, suddenly, as though impelled by some force, the mountainside began to slide away with a tremendous roar from about halfway up.

*An avalanche!*

Mr. Dieu jumped in terror and clung tightly to a rock. A section of the path he had taken to come up the mountain now flashed down past him, leaving only the surface of the rock shorn smooth. Mr. Dieu could no longer see the mulberry tree where he had left his boots and outer garments. To descend that way was now impossible. He would have to circle around behind the mountain. Even though it was farther this way, it was the only safe alternative.

Mr. Dieu groped his way down the mountain for more than two hours before he reached the bottom. He had never had as difficult and as exhausting an ordeal as that. His body was covered in scratches. The monkey hovered between life and death, as he dragged it along the ground. For Mr. Dieu, it was agonizing to have to drag the monkey like that, but he no longer had the strength to carry it in his arms.

When Mr. Dieu reached the clump of bushes and vines he had hidden behind that morning, he stopped to pick up his hat and coat and the ball of sticky rice he had left there. But, to his astonishment, he found that a termites' nest as tall as rice stubble had risen in that spot. The nest was a sticky mound of fresh red earth plastered together with termites' wings. Unfortunately, his things had been mixed up in the nest and turned to mash. Mr. Dieu sighed, turned around in frustration, and lifted the monkey up in his arms. *How humiliating it will be to return home naked,* he scowled angrily. *I'll become a laughing stock.*

He set off, thinking about what he was going to do, and walked around in a circle until he found the track again. *How did this happen?* He burst out laughing. *Who has ever shot a monkey like this? A sparrow-and-a-half of meat on it. Golden hair like dye. You shoot an animal like this even though you've got no clothes? Serves you right, you old fool!*

There was a faint sound of something moving behind him. He gave a start, turned around, and recognized the female monkey, who immediately disappeared behind a bush. It turned out that she had followed Mr. Dieu from the mountain without his realizing it. *How bizarre,* he thought. After moving on for some distance, Mr. Dieu turned around again and, to his exasperation, saw that she was still following him. He put the male monkey down on the ground, gathered some stones, and chased the female monkey away. She gave a high-pitched scream and disappeared. When Mr. Dieu looked around a little later, she still tagged along behind him.

The trio continued to plod on through the jungle. The female monkey was incredibly persistent, and made Mr. Dieu feel that it was all so terribly unfair, that he was being pursued by misfortune.

By now, the male monkey had also recognized the call of his mate. He wriggled around. This wriggling made Mr. Dieu feel extremely wretched, and it so exhausted him that he didn't have the strength to carry the monkey any farther. To make matters worse, the monkey's hands clawed at Mr. Dieu's chest and made it bleed. Mr. Dieu could no longer bear the situation, and, in a fury, he threw the monkey down on the ground.

While the monkey lay sprawled out on a piece of wet grass, Mr. Dieu sat down and looked at it. Not far away, the female monkey bobbed out from behind the foot of a tree to see what was happening. As Mr. Dieu now looked at both of the monkeys, he felt a burning sensation on the bridge of his nose. Profoundly sad, he was overcome by the realization that, in life, responsibility weighs heavily on every living thing.

*All right, I'll set you free,* declared Mr. Dieu. He sat peacefully for a moment, then stood up without warning, and spat a wad of saliva on the ground near his feet. After hesitating for some time, he finally hurried off. The female monkey shot straight out of her hiding place as though she had been waiting for exactly this moment, and ran quickly to her mate.

Mr. Dieu turned onto another track because he wanted to avoid people. This track was choked with bramble bushes that made the going difficult, but they were covered by masses of *tu huyen* flowers. Mr. Dieu stopped in amazement. *Tu huyen* flowers bloom only once in thirty years, and people that come across them are said to meet with good luck. The flowers are white. They are as small as the head of a toothpick and have a salty taste. People call them "salt of the jungle." When the jungle is braided together with these flowers, it is a sign that the country is blessed with peace and abundant harvests.

When he came out of the valley, Mr. Dieu went down into the fields. The spring rain was gentle but very good for the rice seeds. Naked and lonely, he went on his way. A little later, his shadow faded into the curtain of rain.

In only a few days it would be the beginning of summer. The weather would gradually get warmer. . . .

# Modern China

Most specialists define "modern Chinese literature" as beginning in the second decade of the twentieth century. There is good reason for this. In 1905 the civil service examination system, which had enshrined the preeminence of the Confucian classics for many centuries, came to an end. Six years later, in 1911, the last imperial dynasty was overthrown, ending a system of dynastic succession that had lasted for at least three millennia, and Sun Yat-sen (1866–1925) announced the founding of the "Republic of China." In the realm of literature, a new generation of writers broke the bonds of the old literary Chinese language, which was based on the ancient Confucian classics, and began to produce essays, fiction, and poetry in the vernacular, a language reflecting the living idiom.

These changes were monumental, to be sure, but it is possible to draw a quite different boundary for the beginning of modern China from a global perspective. Although Westerners had been traveling to China since at least the time of the Mongolian Empire (1281–1367) (Marco Polo was the most famous of the early visitors), China and the West did not have meaningful intellectual contact until Jesuit missionaries began to arrive in China during the last years of the sixteenth century. The Jesuits, unlike their less-educated Western predecessors in China, were bearers of the full cultural legacy of Europe. Over the next century or so, they inaugurated an intense discussion between East and West that was to have profound implications for Europe and for China. Each culture presented a profound challenge to the other. China was an extremely sophisticated civilization, complete with an ancient philosophy and an immense literary heritage that owed nothing to the classical and biblical roots that Westerners considered the basis of all high culture; Europe presented to China a formidable cultural legacy of its own that could not be easily brushed aside as "barbarian," particularly in view of the scientific and technological accomplishments that eventually enabled Europe to impose itself on the East. Neither Europe nor China was ever the same again. Henceforth, each would act with a full awareness of the existence and challenge of the other.

Our section on modern Chinese literature begins with the *Dream of the Red Chamber,* a work that might be read both as a culmination of the traditional Chinese literary legacy and as a step toward a much more self-conscious literature that is not impervious to the existence of other traditions. Within a century of the time of Cao Xueqin (1715–1763), the author of this great novel, the meeting of East and West turned ugly. European colonial powers became obsessed with China as a potential market for Western goods and were distressed at the Chinese reluctance to open its doors fully to the West. This economic interest led to the Opium War of 1839–1840, in which the British defeated the Chinese and forced them to accept the British opium trade.

The last dynasty of China, the Qing (1644–1911), was ruled by non-Chinese Manchus who had swept into China in the seventeenth century from the north and northeast. By the middle of the nineteenth century, the Manchu government had grown weak and could resist neither the growing pressure from the West nor the constant internal rebellions of disaffected Chinese. This last dynasty died slowly, buffeted from both without and within, and was replaced by a Republic that proved unable to provide the kind of stability that its revolutionary founders had promised. The story of the first few decades after the fall of the dynasty is no happier than that of the decades before. Factions and parties struggled for control of China; the most intense conflict pitted the Kuomintang (or KMT, known in English as the "Nationalists") against the Chinese Communists—and soon the Japanese invaded and gained control of most of northern China and the southern coastline. After the defeat of the Japanese in 1945, a bitter civil war erupted between the KMT and the Communists. The Communists eventually won and proclaimed the foundation of the People's Republic of China in 1949.

As he stood on Tiananmen ("The Gate of Heavenly Peace") in 1949, Mao Zedong (1893–1976) announced that "The Chinese people have stood up." Whatever one may think of what followed under the government of the People's Republic, there is no doubt that China escaped a century or more of Western domination and has taken its place alongside the Western powers and Japan as one of the most important and influential nations of our time.

The traumatic and disruptive events of the past four centuries have had a profound impact on the world of Chinese literature. The coming of the West, the fall of the dynastic order that had sustained and influenced much of the previous literary tradition, the use of the vernacular language instead of classical (or literary) Chinese—all this has forced writers to rethink their work and, in many cases, to begin anew. Lu Xun, perhaps the most important of the new wave of writers, was thoroughly disillusioned with the corrupt and weak China in which he grew up, and he and many of his contemporaries looked for inspiration to the institutions and literary models of the West. Fiction writers, in particular, found inspiration in nineteenth-century Western realism, and Chinese poets experimented with poetic forms that derived from the West and sometimes could be adapted to the Chinese language only rather awkwardly—the sonnet is a particularly striking example. Moreover, the tragedy of modern Chinese history has often placed a heavy political burden on the writer. It has silenced some and made life very difficult for countless others; it has sometimes reduced the most talented writers, either by force or by willing compliance, to propagandists.

Modern Chinese literature now seems to have struck a balance between the very weighty Chinese literary tradition and the influence of the West. Chinese writers are now part of an international community and have used their greater freedom to create a voice that is sure to grow even more dynamic in the decades ahead.

## Cao Xueqin (1715–1763)

*Translated by David Hawkes and John Minford*

*Dream of the Red Chamber,* first published in 1792, is China's finest novel and occupies a preeminence in China equivalent to that of the *Tale of Genji* in Japan or *Don Quixote* in Europe. Many Chinese readers read this novel over and over again, mining its incredible riches throughout the course of a lifetime. To read *Dream of the Red Chamber* even once requires a significant commitment of time, for it is 120 chapters long and contains a vast world of fictional characters and complex situations. The brilliant English translation of David Hawkes and John Minford (reprinted here), published in five volumes under the alternate title *The Story of the Stone,* runs to just over 2300 pages.

We know even less about the life of the author Cao Xueqin than we do about Shakespeare. We do know that Cao was born into a distinguished family that had served the Manchu imperial household for several generations but fell into difficult straits during his lifetime. Since the fate of the family resembles that of the Jia family described in the novel, many scholars assume that *Dream of the Red Chamber* is strongly autobiographical. The author provided some foundation for such a reading when he was quoted as follows in an early commentary:

> Having made an utter failure of my life, I found myself one day, in the midst of my poverty and wretchedness, thinking about the female companions of my youth. As I went over them one by one, examining and comparing them in my mind's eye, it suddenly came over me that those slips of girls—which is all they were then—were in every way, both morally and intellectually, superior to the "grave and mustachioed signior" I am now supposed to have become. I must not, for the sake of keeping them hid, allow those wonderful girls to pass into oblivion without a memorial.*

*Cao Xueqin and Gao E. *The Story of the Stone* (also known as *Dream of the Red Chamber*), vol. 5, *The Dreamer Wakes,* trans. by John Minford (London, New York: Penguin, 1986), 338–39.

Thus, *Dream of the Red Chamber,* with its large array of exceedingly sensitive and intelligent female characters, is perhaps Cao's own memorial to those "slips of girls" he knew in his youth.

To summarize adequately a novel of the enormous length and intricacy of *Dream of the Red Chamber* is impossible. On the simplest level, it is a great page-turner about the love of a young man, Bao-yu (Precious Jade), for his female cousin, Dai-yu (Black Jade), and of the ultimate frustration of that love when Bao-yu's family tricks him into marrying another cousin, Bao-chai (Precious Clasp). The family's decision in favor of the sensible Bao-chai over the excessively sensitive Dai-yu appears reasonable, at least from the perspective of the older generation, but, as we see in the excerpt, the decision has devastating consequences. On another level, *Dream of the Red Chamber* is a story of Bao-yu's preference for the aesthetic, private world of the garden where his predominantly female cousins frolic, over the proper masculine duty of studying for the civil service examination and earning prestige for his family. Consequently, the novel can be read as an expression of the tension between the world of public duty and private pleasure, a tension common in Chinese literature and encountered earlier in the writings of Tao Qian (pp. 1003–1008) and many others.

Such a reading of the novel, however, should not obscure the religious frame that surrounds the day-to-day realism of most of the text. That frame, which reflects a Buddhist-Daoist vision rather than a Confucian one, turns *Dream of the Red Chamber* into a story of how Bao-yu becomes ensnared in the illusions of the world and mistakes the mundane rhythms of his life for reality. As a result of personal suffering, Bao-yu gradually becomes disillusioned and, in chapter 119, rejects his wife, child, land, and family, much like Gautama Buddha himself, and wanders away to become a monk. Readers of the novel typically reenact Bao-yu's mistake and are drawn into the details and drama of daily life portrayed so vividly in chapter after chapter, forgetting the religious message that begins and ends the novel. The novel's readers, like Bao-yu, become caught in a false dream.

The sections of the text excerpted here deal primarily with the complicated relationships between Bao-yu and his two cousins, Dai-yu and Bao-chai. After the introductory chapter, which explains the origin of the book in a most paradoxical and surreal way, the story begins with Dai-yu offended and in tears. Her overly sensitive nature, which perhaps contributes to the beauty of her poetry and appeals so much to her equally sensitive cousin Bao-yu, ultimately undermines her health and destroys her. Bao-chai, by contrast, is an extremely stable and, at times, rather overbearing young woman. Moreover, Bao-chai possesses a locket that contains an inscription similar to the inscription on the mysterious piece of jade that was discovered in Bao-yu's mouth at the time of his birth, so the two seem fated to end up together.

Chapter 27 contains a famous scene of Dai-yu burying flowers, one of her favorite pastimes, and wondering who will bury her. Bao-yu, ever moved by his cousin's tears, collapses in grief at Dai-yu's sad recitation. In chapter 97, Bao-yu, who has become seriously ill and mentally confused, believes he is to marry his beloved Dai-yu, but his family deceives him. He sees Bao-chai as he lifts the wedding veil. Meanwhile, Dai-yu, just as she feared, dies virtually alone at the very moment Bao-yu marries another.

The passages of the novel we have excerpted, less than two percent of the original, are filled with emotion that some readers might regard as excessive. However, what makes *Dream of the Red Chamber* so remarkable compared to earlier Chinese novels is that in the world of this novel, the behavior of each character is carefully and convincingly motivated. Cao, in addition to being a stylist of a beautiful and always delicate prose, is a psychologist who takes the time to develop characters who have a dense reality that is rare in Chinese fiction and that few real people ever achieve.

## *from Dream of the Red Chamber*

### Chapter I

Zhen Shi-yin Makes the Stone's Acquaintance in a Dream

GENTLE READER,

What, you may ask, was the origin of this book?

Though the answer to this question may at first seem to border on the absurd, reflection will show that there is a good deal more in it than meets the eye.

Long ago, when the goddess Nü-wa was repairing the sky, she melted down a great quantity of rock and, on the Incredible Crags of the Great Fable Mountains, moulded the amalgam into thirty-six thousand, five hundred and one large building blocks, each measuring seventy-two feet by a hundred and forty-four feet square. She used thirty-six thousand five hundred of these blocks in the course of her building operations, leaving a single odd block unused, which lay, all on its own, at the foot of Greensickness Peak in the aforementioned mountains.

Now this block of stone, having undergone the melting and moulding of a goddess, possessed magic powers. It could move about at will and could grow or shrink to any size it wanted. Observing that all the other blocks had been used for celestial repairs and that it was the only one to have been rejected as unworthy, it became filled with shame and resentment and passed its days in sorrow and lamentation.

One day, in the midst of its lamentings, it saw a monk and a Taoist approaching from a great distance, each of them remarkable for certain eccentricities of manner and appearance. When they arrived at the foot of Greensickness Peak, they sat down on the ground and began to talk. The monk, catching sight of a lustrous, translucent stone—it was in fact the rejected building block which had now shrunk itself to the size of a fan-pendant and looked very attractive in its new shape—took it up on the palm of his hand and addressed it with a smile:

'Ha, I see you have magical properties! But nothing to recommend you. I shall have to cut a few words on you so that anyone seeing you will know at once that you are something special. After that I shall take you to a certain

brilliant
successful
poetical
cultivated
aristocratic
elegant
delectable

luxurious
opulent
locality on a little trip.'

The stone was delighted.

'What words will you cut? Where is this place you will take me to? I beg to be enlightened.'

'Do not ask,' replied the monk with a laugh. 'You will know soon enough when the time comes.'

And with that he slipped the stone into his sleeve and set off at a great pace with the Taoist. But where they both went to I have no idea.

* * *

Countless aeons went by and a certain Taoist called Vanitas in quest of the secret of immortality chanced to be passing below that same Greensickness Peak in the Incredible Crags of the Great Fable Mountains when he caught sight of a large stone standing there, on which the characters of a long inscription were clearly discernible.

Vanitas read the inscription through from beginning to end and learned that this was a once lifeless stone block which had been found unworthy to repair the sky, but which had magically transformed its shape and been taken down by the Buddhist mahāsattva Impervioso and the Taoist illuminate Mysterioso into the world of mortals, where it had lived out the life of a man before finally attaining nirvana and returning to the other shore. The inscription named the country where it had been born, and went into considerable detail about its domestic life, youthful amours, and even the verses, mottoes and riddles it had written. All it lacked was the authentication of a dynasty and date. On the back of the stone was inscribed the following quatrain:

Found unfit to repair the azure sky
Long years a foolish mortal man
 was I.
My life in both worlds on this
 stone is writ:
Pray who will copy out and
 publish it?

From his reading of the inscription Vanitas realized that this was a stone of some consequence. Accordingly he addressed himself to it in the following manner:

'Brother Stone, according to what you yourself seem to imply in these verses, this story of yours contains matter of sufficient interest to merit publication and has been carved here with that end in view. But as far as I can see (a) it has no discoverable dynastic period, and (b) it contains no examples of moral grandeur among its characters—no statesmanship, no social message of any kind. All I can find in it, in fact, are a number of females, conspicuous, if at all, only for their passion or folly or for some trifling talent or insignificant virtue. Even if I were to copy all this out, I cannot see that it would make a very remarkable book.'

'Come, your reverence,' said the stone (for Vanitas had been correct in assuming that it could speak) 'must you be so obtuse? All the romances ever written have an artificial period setting—Han or Tang for the most part. In refusing to make use of that stale old convention and telling my *Story of the Stone* exactly as it occurred, it seems to me that, far from *depriving* it of anything, I have given it a freshness these other books do not have.

'Your so-called "historical romances", consisting, as they do, of scandalous anecdotes about statesmen and emperors of bygone days and scabrous attacks on the reputations of long-dead gentlewomen, contain more wickedness and immorality than I care to mention. Still worse is the "erotic novel", by whose filthy obscenities our young folk are all too easily corrupted. And the "boudoir romances", those dreary stereotypes with their volume after volume all pitched on the same note and their different characters undistinguishable except by name (all those ideally beautiful young ladies and ideally eligible young bachelors)—even they seem unable to avoid descending sooner or later into indecency.

'The trouble with this last kind of romance is that it only gets written in the first place because the author requires a framework in which to show off his love-poems. He goes about constructing this framework quite mechanically, beginning with the names of his pair of young lovers and invariably adding a third character, a servant or the like, to make mischief between them, like the *chou* in a comedy.

'What makes these romances even more detestable is the stilted, bombastic language—inanities dressed in pompous rhetoric, remote alike from nature and common sense and teeming with the grossest absurdities.

'Surely my "number of females", whom I spent half a lifetime studying with my own eyes and ears, are preferable to this kind of stuff? I do not claim that they are better people than the ones who appear in books written before my time; I am only saying that the contemplation of their actions and motives may prove a more effective antidote to boredom and melancholy. And even the inelegant verses with which my story is interlarded could serve to entertain and amuse on those convivial occasions when rhymes and riddles are in demand.

'All that my story narrates, the meetings and partings, the joys and sorrows, the ups and downs of fortune, are recorded exactly as they happened. I have not dared to add the tiniest bit of touching-up, for fear of losing the true picture.

'My only wish is that men in the world below may sometimes pick up this tale when they are recovering from sleep or drunkenness, or when they wish to escape from business worries or a fit of the dumps, and in doing so find not only mental refreshment but even perhaps, if they will heed its lesson and abandon their vain and frivolous pursuits, some small arrest in the deterioration of their vital forces. What does your reverence say to that?'

For a long time Vanitas stood lost in thought, pondering this speech. He then subjected the *Story of the Stone* to a careful second reading. He could see that its main theme was love; that it consisted quite simply of a true record of real events; and that it was entirely free from any tendency to deprave and corrupt. He therefore copied it all out from beginning to end and took it back with him to look for a publisher.

As a consequence of all this, Vanitas, starting off in the Void (which is Truth) came to the contemplation of Form (which is Illusion); and from Form engendered Passion; and by communicating Passion, entered again into

Form; and from Form awoke to the Void (which is Truth). He therefore changed his name from Vanitas to Brother Amor, or the Passionate Monk, (because he had approached Truth by way of Passion), and changed the title of the book from *The Story of the Stone* to *The Tale of Brother Amor.*

Old Kong Mei-xi from the homeland of Confucius called the book *A Mirror for the Romantic*. Wu Yu-feng called it *A Dream of Golden Days*. Cao Xueqin in his Nostalgia Studio worked on it for ten years, in the course of which he rewrote it no less than five times, dividing it into chapters, composing chapter headings, renaming it *The Twelve Beauties of Jinling,* and adding an introductory quatrain. Red Inkstone restored the original title when he recopied the book and added his second set of annotations to it.

This, then, is a true account of how *The Story of the Stone* came to be written.

Pages full of idle words
Penned with hot and bitter tears:
All men call the author fool;
None his secret message hears.

* * *

The origin of *The Story of the Stone* has now been made clear. The same cannot, however, be said of the characters and events which it recorded. Gentle reader, have patience! This is how the inscription began:

Long, long ago the world was tilted downwards towards the south-east; and in that lower-lying south-easterly part of the earth there is a city called Soochow; and in Soochow the district around the Chang-men Gate is reckoned one of the two or three wealthiest and most fashionable quarters in the world of men. Outside the Chang-men Gate is a wide thoroughfare called Worldly Way; and somewhere off Worldly Way is an area called Carnal Lane. There is an old temple in the Carnal Lane area which, because of the way it is bottled up inside a narrow *cul-de-sac,* is referred to locally as Bottle-gourd Temple. Next door to Bottle-gourd Temple lived a gentleman of private means called Zhen Shi-yin and his wife Feng-shi, a kind, good woman with a profound sense of decency and decorum. The household was not a particularly wealthy one, but they were nevertheless looked up to by all and sundry as the leading family in the neighbourhood.

Zhen Shi-yin himself was by nature a quiet and totally unambitious person. He devoted his time to his garden and to the pleasures of wine and poetry. Except for a single flaw, his existence could, indeed, have been described as an idyllic one. The flaw was that, although already past fifty, he had no son, only a little girl, just two years old, whose name was Ying-lian.

Once, during the tedium of a burning summer's day, Shi-yin was sitting idly in his study. The book had slipped from his nerveless grasp and his head had nodded down onto the desk in a doze. While in this drowsy state he seemed to drift off to some place he could not identify, where he became aware of a monk and a Taoist walking along and talking as they went.

'Where do you intend to take that thing you are carrying?' the Taoist was asking.

'Don't you worry about him!' replied the monk with a laugh. 'There is a batch of lovesick souls awaiting incarnation in the world below whose fate is due to be decided this very day. I intend to take advantage of this opportunity to slip our little friend in amongst them and let him have a taste of human life along with the rest.'

'Well, well, so another lot of these amorous wretches is about to enter the vale of tears,' said the Taoist. 'How did all this begin? And where are the souls to be reborn?'

'You will laugh when I tell you,' said the monk. 'When this stone was left unused by the goddess, he found himself at a loose end and took to wandering about all over the place for want of better to do, until one day his wanderings took him to the place where the fairy Disenchantment lives.

'Now Disenchantment could tell that there was something unusual about this stone, so she kept him there in her Sunset Glow Palace and gave him the honorary title of Divine Luminescent Stone-in-Waiting in the Court of Sunset Glow.

'But most of his time he spent west of Sunset Glow exploring the banks of the Magic River. There, by the Rock of Rebirth, he found the beautiful Crimson Pearl Flower, for which he conceived such a fancy that he took to watering her every day with sweet dew, thereby conferring on her the gift of life.

'Crimson Pearl's substance was composed of the purest cosmic essences, so she was already half-divine; and now, thanks to the vitalizing effect of the sweet dew, she was able to shed her vegetable shape and assume the form of a girl.

'This fairy girl wandered about outside the Realm of Separation, eating the Secret Passion Fruit when she was hungry and drinking from the Pool of Sadness when she was thirsty. The consciousness that she owed the stone something for his kindness in watering her began to prey on her mind and ended by becoming an obsession.

'"I have no sweet dew here that I can repay him with," she would say to herself. "The only way in which I could perhaps repay him would be with the tears shed during the whole of a mortal lifetime if he and I were ever to be reborn as humans in the world below."

'Because of this strange affair, Disenchantment has got together a group of amorous young souls, of which Crimson Pearl is one, and intends to send them down into the world to take part in the great illusion of human life. And as today happens to be the day on which this stone is fated to go into the world too, I am taking him with me to Disenchantment's tribunal for the purpose of getting him registered and sent down to earth with the rest of these romantic creatures.'

'How very amusing!' said the Taoist. 'I have certainly never heard of a debt of tears before. Why shouldn't the two of us take advantage of this opportunity to go down into the world ourselves and save a few souls? It would be a work of merit.'

'That is exactly what I was thinking,' said the monk. 'Come with me to Disenchantment's palace to get this absurd creature cleared. Then, when this last batch of romantic idiots goes down, you and I can go down with them. At present about half have already been born. They await this last batch to make up the number.'

'Very good, I will go with you then,' said the Taoist. Shi-yin heard all this conversation quite clearly, and curiosity impelled him to go forward and greet the two reverend gentlemen. They returned his greeting and asked him what he wanted.

'It is not often that one has the opportunity of listening to a discussion of the operations of *karma* such as the one I have just been privileged to overhear,' said Shi-yin. 'Unfortunately I am a man of very limited understanding and have not been able to derive the full benefit from your conversation. If you would have the very great kindness to enlighten my benighted understanding with a somewhat fuller account of what you were discussing, I can promise you the most devout attention. I feel sure that your teaching would have a salutary effect on me and—who knows—might save me from the pains of hell.'

The reverend gentlemen laughed. 'These are heavenly mysteries and may not be divulged. But if you wish to escape from the fiery pit, you have only to remember us when the time comes, and all will be well.'

Shi-yin saw that it would be useless to press them. 'Heavenly mysteries must not, of course, be revealed. But might one perhaps inquire what the "absurd creature" is that you were talking about? Is it possible that I might be allowed to see it?'

'Oh, as for that,' said the monk: 'I think it is on the cards for you to have a look at *him*,' and he took the object from his sleeve and handed it to Shi-yin.

Shi-yin took the object from him and saw that it was a clear, beautiful jade on one side of which were carved the words 'Magic Jade'. There were several columns of smaller characters on the back, which Shi-yin was just going to examine more closely when the monk, with a cry of 'Here we are, at the frontier of Illusion', snatched the stone from him and disappeared, with the Taoist, through a big stone archway above which

THE LAND OF ILLUSION

was written in large characters. A couplet in smaller characters was inscribed vertically on either side of the arch:

> Truth becomes fiction when the
> fiction's true;
> Real becomes not-real where the
> unreal's real.

Shi-yin was on the point of following them through the archway when suddenly a great clap of thunder seemed to shake the earth to its very foundations, making him cry out in alarm.

And there he was sitting in his study, the contents of his dream already half forgotten, with the sun still blazing on the ever-rustling plantains outside, and the wet-nurse at the door with his little daughter Ying-lian in her arms. Her delicate little pink-and-white face seemed dearer to him than ever at that moment, and he stretched out his arms to take her and hugged her to him.

After playing with her for a while at his desk, he carried her out to the front of the house to watch the bustle in the street. He was about to go in again when he saw a monk and a Taoist approaching, the monk scabby-headed and barefoot, the Taoist tousle-haired and limping. They were behaving like madmen, shouting with laughter and gesticulating wildly as they walked along.

When this strange pair reached Shi-yin's door and saw him standing there holding Ying-lian, the monk burst into loud sobs. 'Patron,' he said, addressing Shi-yin, 'what are you doing, holding in your arms that ill-fated creature who is destined to involve both her parents in her own misfortune?'

Shi-yin realized that he was listening to the words of a madman and took no notice. But the monk persisted:

'Give her to me! Give her to me!'

Shi-yin was beginning to lose patience and, clasping his little girl more tightly to him, turned on his heel and was about to re-enter the house when the monk pointed his finger at him, roared with laughter, and then proceeded to intone the following verses:

> 'Fond man, your pampered child
>   to cherish so—
> That caltrop-glass which shines on
>   melting snow!
> Beware the high feast of the
>   fifteenth day,
> When all in smoke and fire shall
>   pass away!'

Shi-yin heard all this quite plainly and was a little worried by it. He was thinking of asking the monk what lay behind these puzzling words when he heard the Taoist say, 'We don't need to stay together. Why don't we part company here and each go about his own business? Three *kalpas* from now I shall wait for you on Bei-mang Hill. Having joined forces again there, we can go together to the Land of Illusion to sign off.'

'Excellent!' said the other. And the two of them went off and soon were both lost to sight.

'There must have been something behind all this,' thought Shi-yin to himself. 'I really ought to have asked him what he meant, but now it is too late.'

He was still standing outside his door brooding when Jia Yu-cun, the poor student who lodged at the Bottle-gourd Temple next door, came up to him. Yu-cun was a native of Hu-zhou and came from a family of scholars and bureaucrats which had, however, fallen on bad times when Yu-cun was born. The family fortunes on both his father's and mother's side had all been spent, and the members of the family had themselves gradually died off until only Yu-cun was left. There were no prospects for him in his home town, so he had set off for the capital, in search of fame and fortune. Unfortunately he had got no further than Soochow when his funds ran out, and he had now been living there in poverty for a year, lodging in this temple and keeping himself alive by working as a copyist. For this reason Shi-yin saw a great deal of his company.

As soon as he caught sight of Shi-yin, Yu-cun clasped his hands in greeting and smiled ingratiatingly. 'I could see you standing there gazing, sir. Has anything been happening in the street?'

'No, no,' said Shi-yin. 'It just happened that my little girl was crying, so I brought her out here to amuse her. Your coming is most opportune, dear boy. I was beginning to feel most dreadfully bored. Won't you come into my little den, and we can help each other to while away this tedious hot day?'

So saying, he called for a servant to take the child indoors, while he himself took Yu-cun by the hand and led him into his study, where his boy served them both with tea. But they had not exchanged half-a-dozen words before one of the servants rushed in to say that 'Mr Yan had come to pay a call.' Shi-yin hurriedly rose up and excused himself: 'I seem to have brought you here under false pretences. I do hope you will forgive me. If you don't mind sitting on your own here for a moment, I shall be with you directly.'

Yu-cun rose to his feet too. 'Please do not distress yourself on my account, sir. I am a regular visitor here and can easily wait a bit.' But by the time he had finished saying this, Shi-yin was already out of the study and on his way to the guest-room.

Left to himself, Yu-cun was flicking through some of Shi-yin's books of poetry in order to pass the time, when he heard a woman's cough outside the window. Immediately he jumped up and peered out to see who it was. The cough appeared to have come from a maid who was picking flowers in the garden. She was an unusually good-looking girl with a rather refined face: not a great beauty, by any means, but with something striking about her. Yu-cun gazed at her spellbound.

Having now finished picking her flowers, this anonymous member of the Zhen household was about to go in again when, on some sudden impulse, she raised her head and caught sight of a man standing in the window. His hat was frayed and his clothing threadbare; yet, though obviously poor, he had a fine, manly physique and handsome, well-proportioned features.

The maid hastened to remove herself from this male presence; but as she went she thought to herself, 'What a fine-looking man! But so shabby! The family hasn't got any friends or relations as poor as that. It must be that Jia Yu-cun the master is always on about. No wonder he says that he won't stay poor long. I remember hearing him say that he's often wanted to help him but hasn't yet found an opportunity.' And thinking these thoughts she could not forbear to turn back for another peep or two.

Yu-cun saw her turn back and, at once assuming that she had taken a fancy to him, was beside himself with delight. What a perceptive young woman she must be, he thought, to have seen the genius underneath the rags! A real friend in trouble!

After a while the boy came in again and Yu-cun elicited from him that the visitor in the front room was now staying to dinner. It was obviously out of the question to wait much longer, so he slipped down the passage-way at the side of the house and let himself out by the back gate. Nor did Shi-yin invite him round again when, having at last seen off his visitor, he learned that Yu-cun had already left.

But then the Mid Autumn festival arrived and, after the family convivialities were over, Shi-yin had a little dinner for two laid out in his study and went in person to invite Yu-cun, walking to his temple lodgings in the moonlight.

Ever since the day the Zhens' maid had, by looking back twice over her shoulder, convinced him that she was a friend, Yu-cun had had the girl very much on his mind, and now that it was festival time, the full moon of Mid Autumn lent an inspiration to his romantic impulses which finally resulted in the following octet:

'Ere on ambition's path my feet
  are set,
Sorrow comes often this poor
  heart to fret.
Yet, as my brow contracted with
  new care,
Was there not one who, parting,
  turned to stare?
Dare I, that grasp at shadows in
  the wind,
Hope, underneath the moon, a
  friend to find?
Bright orb, if with my plight you
  sympathize,
Shine first upon the chamber
  where she lies.'

Having delivered himself of this masterpiece, Yu-cun's thoughts began to run on his unrealized ambitions and, after much head-scratching and many heavenward glances accompanied by heavy sighs, he produced the following couplet, reciting it in a loud, ringing voice which caught the ear of Shi-yin, who chanced at that moment to be arriving:

> 'The jewel in the casket bides till
> one shall come to buy.
> The jade pin in the drawer hides,
> waiting its time to fly.'

Shi-yin smiled. 'You are a man of no mean ambition, Yu-cun.'

'Oh no!' Yu-cun smiled back deprecatingly. 'You are too flattering. I was merely reciting at random from the lines of some old poet. But what brings you here, sir?'

'Tonight is Mid Autumn night,' said Shi-yin. 'People call it the Festival of Reunion. It occurred to me that you might be feeling rather lonely here in your monkery, so I have arranged for the two of us to take a little wine together in my study. I hope you will not refuse to join me.'

Yu-cun made no polite pretence of declining. 'Your kindness is more than I deserve,' he said. 'I accept gratefully.' And he accompanied Shi-yin back to the study next door.

Soon they had finished their tea. Wine and various choice dishes were brought in and placed on the table, already laid out with cups, plates, and so forth, and the two men took their places and began to drink. At first they were rather slow and ceremonious; but gradually, as the conversation grew more animated, their potations too became more reckless and uninhibited. The sounds of music and singing which could now be heard from every house in the neighbourhood and the full moon which shone with cold brilliance overhead seemed to increase their elation, so that the cups were emptied almost as soon as they touched their lips, and Yu-cun, who was already a sheet or so in the wind, was seized with an irrepressible excitement to which he presently gave expression in the form of a quatrain, ostensibly on the subject of the moon, but really about the ambition he had hitherto been at some pains to conceal:

> 'In thrice five nights her perfect O
> is made,
> Whose cold light bathes each
> marble balustrade.
> As her bright wheel starts on its
> starry ways,
> On earth ten thousand heads look
> up and gaze.'

'Bravo!' said Shi-yin loudly. 'I have always insisted that you were a young fellow who would go up in the world, and now, in these verses you have just recited, I see an augury of your ascent. In no time at all we shall see you up among the clouds! This calls for a drink!' And, saying this, he poured Yu-cun a large cup of wine.

Yu-cun drained the cup, then, surprisingly, sighed:

'Don't imagine the drink is making me boastful, but I really do believe that if it were just a question of having the sort of qualifications now in demand, I should stand as good a chance as any of getting myself on to the list of candidates. The trouble is that I simply have no means of laying my hands on the money that would be needed for lodgings and travel expenses. The journey to the capital is a long one, and the sort of money I can earn from my copying is not enough—'

'Why ever didn't you say this before?' said Shi-yin interrupting him. 'I have long wanted to do something about this, but on all the occasions I have met you previously, the conversation has never got round to this subject, and I haven't liked to broach it for fear of offending you. Well, now we know where we are. I am not a very clever man, but at least I know the right thing to do when I see it. Luckily, the next Triennial is only a few months ahead. You must go to the capital without delay. A spring examination triumph will make you feel that all your studying has been worth while. I shall take care of all your expenses. It is the least return I can make for your friendship.' And there and then he instructed his boy to go with all speed and make up a parcel of fifty taels of the best refined silver and two suits of winter clothes.

'The almanac gives the nineteenth as a good day for travelling,' he went on, addressing Yu-cun again. 'You can set about hiring a boat for the journey straight away. How delightful it will be to meet again next winter when you have distinguished yourself by soaring to the top over all the other candidates!'

Yu-cun accepted the silver and the clothes with only the most perfunctory word of thanks and without, apparently, giving them a further moment's thought, for he continued to drink and laugh and talk as if nothing had happened. It was well after midnight before they broke up.

After seeing Yu-cun off, Shi-yin went to bed and slept without a break until the sun was high in the sky next morning. When he awoke, his mind was still running on the conversation of the previous night. He thought he would write a couple of introductory letters for Yu-cun to take with him to the capital, and arrange for him to call on the family of an official he was acquainted with who might be able to put him up; but when he sent a servant to invite him over, the servant brought back word from the temple as follows:

'The monk says that Mr Jia set out for the capital at five o'clock this morning, sir. He says he left a message to pass on to you. He said to tell you, "A scholar should not concern himself with almanacs, but should act as the situation demands," and he said there wasn't time to say good-bye.'

So Shi-yin was obliged to let the matter drop.

* * *

It is a true saying that 'time in idleness is quickly spent'. In no time at all it was Fifteenth Night, and Shi-yin sent little Ying-lian out, in the charge of one of the servants called Calamity, to see the mummers and the coloured lanterns. It was near midnight when Calamity, feeling an urgent need to relieve his bladder, put Ying-lian down on someone's doorstep while he went about his business, only to find, on his return, that the child was nowhere to be seen. Frantically he searched for her throughout the rest of the night; but when day dawned and he had still not found her, he took to his heels, not daring to face his master and mistress, and made off for another part of the country.

Shi-yin and his wife knew that something must be wrong when their little girl failed to return home all night. Then a search was made; but all those sent out were obliged in the end to report that no trace of her could be found.

The shock of so sudden a loss to a middle-aged couple who had only ever had the one daughter can be imagined. In tears every day and most of the night, they almost lost the will to go on living, and after about a month like this first Shi-yin and then his wife fell ill, so that doctors and diviners were in daily attendance on them.

Then, on the fifteenth of the third month, while frying cakes for an offering, the monk of Bottle-gourd Temple carelessly allowed the oil to catch alight, which set fire to the paper window. And, since the houses in this area all had wooden walls and bamboo fences—though also, doubtless, because they were doomed to destruction anyway—the fire leaped from house to house until the whole street was blazing away like a regular Fiery Mountain; and though the firemen came to put it out, by the time they arrived the fire was well under way and long past controlling, and roared away all night long until it had burnt itself out, rendering heaven knows how many families homeless in the process.

Poor Zhens! Though they and their handful of domestics escaped unhurt, their house, which was only next door to the temple, was soon reduced to a heap of rubble, while Shi-yin stood by helpless, groaning and stamping in despair.

After some discussion with his wife, Shi-yin decided that they should move to their farm in the country; but a series of crop failures due to flooding and drought had led to widespread brigandage in those parts, and government troops were out everywhere hunting down the mutinous peasants and making arrests. In such conditions it was impossible to settle on the farm, so Shi-yin sold the land and, taking only two of the maids with them, went with his wife to seek refuge with his father-in-law, Feng Su.

This Feng Su was a Ru-zhou man who, though only a farmer by calling, had a very comfortable sufficiency. He was somewhat displeased to see his son-in-law arriving like a refugee on his doorstep; but fortunately Shi-yin had on him the money he had realized from the sale of the farm, and this he now entrusted to his father-in-law to buy for him, as and when he could, a house and land on which he could depend for his future livelihood. Feng Su embezzled about half of this sum and used the other half to provide him with a ruinous cottage and some fields of poor, thin soil.

A scholar, with no experience of business or agricultural matters, Shi-yin now found himself poorer after a year or two of struggle than when he had started. Feng Su would treat him to a few pearls of rustic wisdom whenever they met, but behind his back would grumble to all and sundry about 'incompetents' and 'people who liked their food but were too lazy to work for it', which caused Shi-yin great bitterness when it came to his ears. The anxieties and injustices which now beset him, coming on top of the shocks he had suffered a year or two previously, left a man of his years with little resistance to the joint onslaught of poverty and ill-health, and gradually he began to betray the unmistakable symptoms of a decline.

One day, wishing to take his mind off his troubles for a bit, he had dragged himself, stick in hand, to the main road, when it chanced that he suddenly caught sight of a Taoist with a limp—a crazy, erratic figure in hempen sandals and tattered clothes, who chanted the following words to himself as he advanced towards him:

'Men all know that salvation
should be won,
But with ambition won't have
done, have done.
Where are the famous ones of
days gone by?
In grassy graves they lie now, every
one.

Men all know that salvation should
be won,
But with their riches won't have
done, have done.
Each day they grumble they've not
made enough.
When they've enough, it's
goodnight everyone!

Men all know that salvation should
be won,
But with their loving wives they
won't have done.
The darlings every day protest
their love:
But once you're dead, they're off
with another one.

Men all know that salvation should
be won,
But with their children won't have
done, have done.
Yet though of parents fond there
is no lack,
Of grateful children saw I ne'er a
one.'

Shi-yin approached the Taoist and questioned him. 'What is all this you are saying? All I can make out is a lot of "won" and "done".'

'If you can make out "won" and "done",' replied the Taoist with a smile, 'you may be said to have understood; for in all the affairs of this world what is won is done, and what is done is won; for whoever has not yet done has not yet won, and in order to have won, one must first have done. I shall call my song the "Won-Done Song".'

Shi-yin had always been quick-witted, and on hearing these words a flash of understanding had illuminated his mind. He therefore smiled back at the Taoist: 'Wait a minute! How would you like me to provide your "Won-Done Song" with a commentary?'

'Please do!' said the Taoist; and Shi-yin proceeded as follows:

'Mean hovels and abandoned halls
Where courtiers once paid daily
calls:
Bleak haunts where weeds and
willows scarcely thrive
Were once with mirth and revelry
alive.
Whilst cobwebs shroud the
mansion's gilded beams,
The cottage casement with choice
muslin gleams.
Would you of perfumed elegance
recite?
Even as you speak, the raven locks
turn white.
Who yesterday her lord's bones
laid in clay,
On silken bridal-bed shall lie
today.
Coffers with gold and silver filled:
Now, in a trice, a tramp by all
reviled.

One at some other's short life
gives a sigh,
Not knowing that he, too, goes
home—to die!
The sheltered and well-educated
lad,
In spite of all your care, may turn
out bad;
And the delicate, fastidious maid
End in a foul stews, plying a
shameful trade.
The judge whose hat is too small
for his head
Wears, in the end, a convict's
cangue instead.
Who shivering once in rags
bemoaned his fate,
Today finds fault with scarlet robes
of state.
In such commotion does the
world's theatre rage:
As each one leaves, another takes
the stage.
In vain we roam:
Each in the end must call a
strange land home.
Each of us with that poor girl may
compare
Who sews a wedding-gown for
another bride to wear.'

'A very accurate commentary!' cried the mad, lame Taoist, clapping his hands delightedly.

But Shi-yin merely snatched the satchel that hung from the other's shoulder and slung it from his own, and with a shout of 'Let's go!' and without even waiting to call back home, he strode off into the wide world in the company of the madman.

This event made a great uproar in the little town, and news of it was relayed from gossip to gossip until it reached the ears of Mrs Zhen, who cried herself into fits when she heard it. After consulting her father, she sent men out to inquire everywhere after her husband; but no news of him was to be had.

It was now imperative that she should move in with her parents and look to them for support. Fortunately she still had the two maids who had stayed on with her from the Soochow days, and by sewing and embroidering morning, noon and night, she and her women were able to make some contribution to her father's income. The latter still found daily occasion to complain, but there was very little he could do about it.

One day the elder of the two maids was purchasing some silks at the door when she heard the criers clearing the street and all the people began to tell each other that the new mandarin had arrived. She hid in the doorway and watched the guards and runners marching past two by two. But when the mandarin in his black hat and scarlet robe of office was borne past in his great chair, she stared for some time as though puzzled. 'Where have I seen that mandarin before?' she wondered. 'His face looks extraordinarily familiar.' But presently she went into the house again and gave the matter no further thought.

That night, just as they were getting ready for bed, there was suddenly a great commotion at the door and a confused hubbub of voices shouting that someone was wanted at the *yamen* for questioning, which so terrified Feng Su that he was momentarily struck dumb and could only stare.

If you wish to know what further calamity this portended, you will have to read the following chapter.

## Chapter 27

### Beauty Perspiring Sports with Butterflies by the Raindrop Pavilion

As Dai-yu stood there weeping, there was a sudden creak of the courtyard gate and Bao-chai walked out, accompanied by Bao-yu with Aroma and a bevy of other maids who had come out to see her off. Dai-yu was on the point of stepping forward to question Bao-yu, but shrank from embarrassing him in front of so many people. Instead she slipped back into the shadows to let Bao-chai pass, emerging only when Bao-yu and the rest were back inside and the gate was once more barred. She stood for a while facing it, and shed a few silent tears; then, realizing that it was pointless to remain standing there, she turned and went back to her room and began, in a listless, mechanical manner, to take off her ornaments and prepare herself for the night.

Nightingale and Snowgoose had long since become habituated to Dai-yu's moody temperament; they were used to her unaccountable fits of depression, when she would sit, the picture of misery, in gloomy silence broken only by an occasional gusty sigh, and to her mysterious, perpetual weeping, that was occasioned by no observable cause. At first they had tried to reason with her, or, imagining that she must be grieving for her parents or that she was feeling homesick or had been upset by some unkindness, they would do their best to comfort her. But as the months lengthened into years and she still continued exactly the same as before, they gradually became accustomed and no longer sought reasons for her behaviour. That was why they ignored her on this occasion and left her alone to her misery, remaining where they were in the outer room and continuing to occupy themselves with their own affairs.

She sat, motionless as a statue, leaning against the back of the bed, her hands clasped about her knees, her eyes full of tears. It had already been dark for some hours when she finally lay down to sleep.

Our story passes over the rest of that night in silence.

* * *

Next day was the twenty-sixth of the fourth month, the day on which, this year, the festival of Grain in Ear was due to fall. To be precise, the festival's official commencement was on the twenty-sixth day of the fourth month at two o'clock in the afternoon. It has been the custom from time immemorial to make offerings to the flower fairies on this day. For Grain in Ear marks the beginning of summer; it is about this time that the blossom begins to fall; and tradition has it that the flower-spirits, their work now completed, go away on this day and do not return until the following year. The offerings are therefore thought of as a sort of farewell party for the flowers.

This charming custom of 'speeding the fairies' is a special favourite with the fair sex, and in Prospect Garden all the girls were up betimes on this day making little coaches and palanquins out of willow-twigs and flowers and little banners and pennants from scraps of brocade and any other pretty material they could find, which they fastened with threads of coloured silk to the tops of flowering trees and shrubs. Soon every plant and tree was decorated and the whole garden had become a shimmering sea of nodding blossoms and fluttering coloured streamers. Moving about in the midst of it all, the girls in their brilliant summer dresses, beside which the most vivid hues of plant and plumage became faint with envy, added the final touch of brightness to a scene of indescribable gaiety and colour.

All the young people—Bao-chai, Ying-chun, Tan-chun, Xi-chun, Li Wan, Xi-feng and her little girl and Caltrop, and all the maids from all the different apartments—were outside in the Garden enjoying themselves—all, that is, except Dai-yu, whose absence, beginning to be noticed, was first commented on by Ying-chun:

'What's happened to Cousin Lin? Lazy girl! Surely she can't *still* be in bed at this hour?'

Bao-chai volunteered to go and fetch her:

'The rest of you wait here; I'll go and rout her out for you,' she said; and breaking away from the others, she made off in the direction of the Naiad's House.

While she was on her way, she caught sight of Élégante and the eleven other little actresses, evidently on their way to join in the fun. They came up and greeted her, and for a while she stood and chatted with them. As she was leaving them, she turned back and pointed in the direction from which she had just come:

'You'll find the others somewhere over there,' she said. 'I'm on my way to get Miss Lin. I'll join the rest of you presently.'

She continued, by the circuitous route that the garden's contours obliged her to take, on her way to the Naiad's House. Raising her eyes as she approached it, she suddenly became aware that the figure ahead of her just disappearing inside it was Bao-yu. She stopped and lowered her eyes pensively again to the ground.

'Bao-yu and Dai-yu have known each other since they were little,' she reflected. 'They are used to behaving uninhibitedly when they are alone together. They don't seem to care what they say to one another; and one is never quite sure what sort of mood one is going to find them in. And Dai-yu, at the best of times, is always so touchy and suspicious. If I go in now after him, *he* is sure to feel embarrassed and *she* is sure to start imagining things. It would be better to go back without seeing her.'

Her mind made up, she turned round and began to retrace her steps, intending to go back to the other girls; but just at that moment she noticed two enormous turquoise-coloured butterflies a little way ahead of her, each as large as a child's fan, fluttering and dancing on the breeze. She watched them fascinated and thought she would like to play a game with them. Taking a fan from inside her sleeve and holding it outspread in front of her, she followed them off the path and into the grass.

To and fro fluttered the pair of butterflies, sometimes alighting for a moment, but always flying off again before she could reach them. Once they seemed on the point of flying across the little river that flowed through the midst of the garden and Bao-chai had to stalk them with bated breath for fear of startling them out on to the water. By the time she had reached the Raindrop Pavilion she was perspiring freely and her interest in the butterflies was beginning to evaporate. . . .

We now return to Dai-yu, who, having slept so little the night before, was very late getting up on the morning of the festival. Hearing that the other girls were all out in the garden 'speeding the fairies' and fearing to be teased by them for her lazy habits, she hurried over her toilet and went out as soon as it was completed. A smiling Bao-yu appeared in the gateway as she was stepping down into the courtyard.

'Well, coz,' he said, 'I hope you *didn't* tell on me yesterday. You had me worrying about it all last night.'

Dai-yu turned back, ignoring him, to address Nightingale inside:

'When you do the room, leave one of the casements open so that the parent swallows can get in. And put the lion doorstop on the bottom of the blind to stop it flapping. And don't forget to put the cover back on the burner after you've lighted the incense.'

She made her way across the courtyard, still ignoring him.

Bao-yu, who knew nothing of the little drama that had taken place outside his gate the night before, assumed that she was still angry about his unfortunate lapse earlier on that same day, when he had offended her susceptibilities with a somewhat risqué quotation from *The Western Chamber.* He offered her now, with energetic bowing and hand-pumping, the apologies that the previous day's emergency had caused him to neglect. But Dai-yu walked straight past him and out of the gate, not deigning so much as a glance in his direction, and stalked off in search of the others.

Bao-yu was nonplussed. He began to suspect that something more than he had first imagined must be wrong.

'Surely it can't only be because of yesterday lunchtime that she's carrying on in this fashion? There must be something else. On the other hand, I didn't get back until late and I didn't see her again last night, so how *could* I have offended her?'

Preoccupied with these reflections, he followed her at some distance behind.

Not far ahead Bao-chai and Tan-chun were watching the ungainly courtship dance of some storks. When they saw Dai-yu coming, they invited her to join them, and the three girls stood together and chatted. Then Bao-yu arrived. Tan-chun greeted him with sisterly concern:

'How have you been keeping, Bao? It's three whole days since I saw you last.'

Bao-yu smiled back at her.

'How have *you* been keeping, sis? I was asking Cousin Wan about you the day before yesterday.'

'Come over here a minute,' said Tan-chun. 'I want to talk to you.'

He followed her into the shade of a pomegranate tree a little way apart from the other two.

'Has Father asked to see you at all during this last day or two?' Tan-chun began.

'No.'

'I thought I heard someone say yesterday that he had been asking for you.'

'No,' said Bao-yu, smiling at her concern. 'Whoever it was was mistaken. He certainly hasn't asked for *me.*'

Tan-chun smiled and changed the subject.

'During the past few months,' she said, 'I've managed to save up another ten strings or so of cash. I'd like you to take it again like you did last time, and next time you go out, if you see a nice painting or calligraphic scroll or some amusing little thing that would do for my room, I'd like you to buy it for me.'

'Well, I don't know,' said Bao-yu. 'In the trips I make to bazaars and temple fairs, whether it's inside the city or round about, I can't say that I ever see anything *really* nice or out of the ordinary. It's all bronzes and jades and porcelain and that sort of stuff. Apart from that it's mostly dress-making materials and clothes and things to eat.'

'Now what would I want things like that for?' said Tan-chun. 'No, I mean something like that little wickerwork basket you bought me last time, or the little box carved out of bamboo root, or the little clay burner. I thought they were sweet. Unfortunately the others took such a fancy to them that they carried them off as loot and wouldn't give them back to me again.'

'Oh, if *those* are the sort of things you want,' said Bao-yu laughing, 'it's very simple. Just give a few strings of cash to one of the boys and he'll bring you back a whole cartload of them.'

'What do the boys know about it?' said Tan-chun. 'I need someone who can pick out the interesting things and the ones that are in good taste. You get me lots of nice little things, and I'll embroider a pair of slippers for you like the ones I made for you last time—only this time I'll do them more carefully.'

'Talking of those slippers reminds me,' said Bao-yu. 'I happened to run into Father once when I was wearing them. He was Most Displeased. When he asked me who made them, I naturally didn't dare to tell him that *you* had, so I said that Aunt Wang had given them to me as a birthday present a few days before. There wasn't much he could do about it when he heard that they came from Aunt Wang; so after a very long pause he just said, "What a pointless waste of human effort and valuable material, to produce things like that!" I told this to Aroma when I got back, and she said, "Oh, that's nothing! You should have heard your Aunt Zhao complaining about those slippers. She was *furious* when she heard about them: 'Her own natural brother so down at heel he scarcely dares show his face to people, and she spends her time making things like that!'"'

Tan-chun's smile had vanished:

'How *can* she talk such nonsense? Why should *I* be the one to make shoes for him? Huan gets a clothing allowance, doesn't he? He gets his clothing and footwear provided for the same as all the rest of us. And fancy saying a thing like that in front of a roomful of servants! For whose benefit was this remark made, I wonder? I make an occasional pair of slippers just for something to do in my spare time; and if I give a pair to someone I particularly like, that's my own affair. Surely no one else has any business to start telling me who I should give them to? Oh, she's so *petty*!'

Bao-yu shook his head:

'Perhaps you're being a bit hard on her. She's probably got her reasons.'

This made Tan-chun really angry. Her chin went up defiantly:

'Now you're being as stupid as her. Of *course* she's got her reasons; but they are ignorant, stupid reasons. But she can think what she likes: as far as *I* am concerned, Sir Jia is my father and Lady Wang is my mother, and who was born in whose room doesn't interest me—

the way I choose my friends inside the family has nothing to do with that. Oh, I know I shouldn't talk about her like this; but she is *so* idiotic about these things. As a matter of fact I can give you an even better example than your story of the slippers. That last time I gave you my savings to get something for me, she saw me a few days afterwards and started telling me how short of money she was and how difficult things were for her. I took no notice, of course. But later, when the maids were out of the room, she began attacking me for giving the money I'd saved to other people instead of giving it to Huan. Really! I didn't know whether to laugh or get angry with her. In the end I just walked out of the room and went round to see Mother.'

There was an amused interruption at this point from Bao-chai, who was still standing where they had left her a few minutes before:

'Do finish your talking and come back soon! It's easy to see that you two are brother and sister. As soon as you see each other, you get into a huddle and start talking about family secrets. Would it *really* be such a disaster if anything you are saying were to be overheard?'

Tan-chun and Bao-yu rejoined her, laughing.

Not seeing Dai-yu, Bao-yu realized that she must have slipped off elsewhere while he was talking.

'Better leave it a day or two,' he told himself on reflection. 'Wait until her anger has calmed down a bit.'

While he was looking downwards and meditating, he noticed that the ground where they were standing was carpeted with a bright profusion of wind-blown flowers—pomegranate and balsam for the most part.

'You can see she's upset,' he thought ruefully. 'She's neglecting her flowers. I'll bury this lot for her and remind her about it next time I see her.'

He became aware that Bao-chai was arranging for him and Tan-chun to go with her outside.

'I'll join you two presently,' he said, and waited until they were a little way off before stooping down to gather the fallen blossoms into the skirt of his gown. It was quite a way from where he was to the place where Dai-yu had buried the peach-blossom on that previous occasion, but he made his way towards it, over rocks and bridges and through plantations of trees and flowers. When he had almost reached his destination and there was only the spur of a miniature 'mountain' between him and the burial-place of the flowers, he heard the sound of a voice, coming from the other side of the rock, whose continuous, gentle chiding was occasionally broken by the most pitiable and heart-rending sobs.

'It must be a maid from one of the apartments,' thought Bao-yu. 'Someone has been ill-treating her, and she has run here to cry on her own.'

He stood still and endeavoured to catch what the weeping girl was saying. She appeared to be reciting something:

The blossoms fade and falling fill
    the air,
Of fragrance and bright hues
    bereft and bare.
Floss drifts and flutters round the
    Maiden's bower,
Or softly strikes against her
    curtained door.

The Maid, grieved by these signs
    of spring's decease,

Seeking some means her sorrow to
  express,
Has rake in hand into the garden
  gone,
Before the fallen flowers are
  trampled on.

Elm-pods and willow-floss are
  fragrant too;
Why care, Maid, where the fallen
  flowers blew?
Next year, when peach and
  plum-tree bloom again,
Which of your sweet companions
  will remain?

This spring the heartless swallow
  built his nest
Beneath the caves of mud with
  flowers compressed.
Next year the flowers will blossom
  as before,
But swallow, nest, and Maid will be
  no more.

Three hundred and three-score
  the year's full tale:
From swords of frost and from the
  slaughtering gale
How can the lovely flowers long
  stay intact,
Or, once loosed, from their
  drifting fate draw back?

Blooming so steadfast, fallen so
  hard to find!
Beside the flowers' grave, with
  sorrowing mind,
The solitary Maid sheds many a
  tear,
Which on the boughs as bloody
  drops appear.

At twilight, when the cuckoo sings
  no more,
The Maiden with her rake goes in
  at door
And lays her down between the
  lamplit walls,
While a chill rain against the
  window falls.

I know not why my heart's so
  strangely sad,
Half grieving for the spring and
  yet half glad:
Glad that it came, grieved it so
  soon was spent.
So soft it came, so silently it
  went!

Last night, outside, a mournful
  sound was heard:
The spirits of the flowers and of
  the bird.
But neither bird nor flowers would
  long delay,
Bird lacking speech, and flowers
  too shy to stay.

And then I wished that I had
  wings to fly
After the drifting flowers across
  the sky:
Across the sky to the world's
  farthest end,
The flowers' last fragrant
  resting-place to find.

But better their remains in silk to
  lay
And bury underneath the
  wholesome clay,
Pure substances the pure earth to
  enrich,
Than leave to soak and stink in
  some foul ditch.

Can I, that these flowers'
  obsequies attend,
  obsequies attend,

Divine how soon or late *my* life will
end?
Let others laugh flower-burial to
see:
Another year who will be burying
me?

As petals drop and spring begins
to fail,
The bloom of youth, too, sickens
and turns pale.
One day, when spring has gone
and youth has fled.
The Maiden and the flowers will
both be dead.

All this was uttered in a voice half-choked with sobs; for the words recited seemed only to inflame the grief of the reciter—indeed, Bao-yu, listening on the other side of the rock, was so overcome by them that he had already flung himself weeping upon the ground.

But the sequel to this painful scene will be told in the following chapter.

## Chapter 28

### A Crimson Cummerbund Becomes a Pledge of Friendship

On the night before the festival, it may be remembered, Lin Dai-yu had mistakenly supposed Bao-yu responsible for Skybright's refusal to open the gate for her. The ceremonial farewell to the flowers of the following morning had transformed her pent-up and still smouldering resentment into a more generalized and seasonable sorrow. This had finally found its expression in a violent outburst of grief as she was burying the latest collection of fallen blossoms in her flower-grave. Meditation on the fate of flowers had led her to contemplation of her own sad and orphaned lot; she had burst into tears, and soon after had begun a recitation of the poem whose words we recorded in the preceding chapter.

Unknown to her, Bao-yu was listening to this recitation from the slope of the near-by rockery. At first he merely nodded and sighed sympathetically; but when he heard the words

'Can I, that these flowers'
obsequies attend,
Divine how soon or late *my* life will
end?'

and, a little later,

'One day when spring has gone
and youth has fled,
The Maiden and the flowers will
both be dead.'

he flung himself on the ground in a fit of weeping, scattering the earth all about him with the flowers he had been carrying in the skirt of his gown.

Lin Dai-yu dead! A world from which that delicate, flowerlike countenance had irrevocably departed! It was unutterable anguish to think of it. Yet his sensitized imagination *did* now consider it—went on, indeed, to consider a world from which the others, too—Bao-chai, Caltrop, Aroma and the rest—had also irrevocably departed. Where would *he* be then? What would have become of him? And what of the Garden, the rocks, the flowers, the trees? To whom would they belong when he and the girls were no longer there to enjoy them? Passing from loss to loss in his imagination, he plunged deeper and deeper into a grief that seemed inconsolable. As the poet says:

Flowers in my eyes and bird-song
in my ears
Augment my loss and mock my
bitter tears.

Dai-yu, then, as she stood plunged in her own private sorrowing, suddenly heard the sound of another person crying bitterly on the rocks above her.

'The others are always telling me I'm a "case",' she thought. 'Surely there can't be another "case" up there?'

But on looking up she saw that it was Bao-yu.

'Pshaw!' she said crossly to herself. 'I thought it was another girl, but all the time it was that cruel, hate—'

'Hateful' she had been going to say, but clapped her mouth shut before uttering it. She sighed instead and began to walk away.

By the time Bao-yu's weeping was over, Dai-yu was no longer there. He realized that she must have seen him and have gone away in order to avoid him. Feeling suddenly rather foolish, he rose to his feet and brushed the earth from his clothes. Then he descended from the rockery and began to retrace his steps in the direction of Green Delights. Quite by coincidence Dai-yu was walking along the same path a little way ahead.

'Stop a minute!' he cried, hurrying forward to catch up with her. 'I know you are not taking any notice of me, but I only want to ask you one simple question, and then you need never have anything more to do with me.'

Dai-yu had turned back to see who it was. When she saw that it was Bao-yu still, she was going to ignore him again; but hearing him say that he only wanted to ask her one question, she told him that he might do so.

Bao-yu could not resist teasing her a little.

'How about *two* questions? Would you wait for two?'

Dai-yu set her face forwards and began walking on again.

Bao-yu sighed.

'If it has to be like this now,' he said, as if to himself, 'it's a pity it was ever like it was in the beginning.'

Dai-yu's curiosity got the better of her. She stopped walking and turned once more towards him.

'Like *what* in the beginning?' she asked. 'And like what now?'

'Oh, the *beginning*!' said Bao-yu. 'In the *beginning*, when you first came here, I was your faithful companion in all your games. Anything I had, even the thing most dear to me, was yours for the asking. If there was something to eat that I specially liked, I had only to hear that you were fond of it too and I would religiously hoard it away to share with you when you got back, not daring even to touch it until you came. We ate at the same table. We slept in the same bed. I used to think that because we were so close then, there would be something special about our relationship when we grew up—that even if we weren't particularly affectionate, we should at least have more understanding and forbearance for each other than the rest. But how wrong I was! Now that you *have* grown up, you seem only to have grown more touchy. You don't seem to care about *me* any more at all. You spend all your time brooding about outsiders like Feng and Chai. I haven't got any *real* brothers and sisters left here now. There are Huan and Tan, of course; but as you know, they're only my half- brother and half-sister: they aren't my mother's children. I'm on my own, like you. I should have thought we had so much in common—But what's the use? I try and try, but it gets me nowhere; and nobody knows or cares.'

At this point—in spite of himself—he burst into tears.

The palpable evidence of her own eyes and ears had by now wrought a considerable softening on Dai-yu's heart. A sympathetic tear stole down her own cheek, and she hung her head and said nothing. Bao-yu could see that he had moved her.

'I know I'm not much use nowadays,' he continued, 'but however bad you may think me, I would never wittingly do anything in your presence to offend you. If I *do* ever slip up in some way, you ought to tell me off about it and warn me not to do it again, or shout at me—hit me, even, if you feel like it; I shouldn't mind. But you don't do that. You just ignore me. You leave me utterly at a loss to know what I'm supposed to have done wrong, so that I'm driven half frantic wondering what I ought to do to make up for it. If I were to die now, I should die with a grievance, and all the masses and exorcisms in the world wouldn't lay my ghost. Only when you explained what your reason was for ignoring me should I cease from haunting you and be reborn into another life.'

Dai-yu's resentment for the gate incident had by now completely evaporated. She merely said:

'Oh well, in that case why did you tell your maids not to let me in when I came to call on you?'

'I honestly don't know what you are referring to,' said Bao-yu in surprise. 'Strike me dead if I ever did any such thing!'

'Hush!' said Dai-yu. 'Talking about death at this time of the morning! You should be more careful what you say. If you did, you did. If you didn't, you didn't. There's no need for these horrible oaths.'

'I really and truly didn't know you had called,' said Bao-yu. 'Cousin Bao came and sat with me a few minutes last night and then went away again. That's the only call I know about.'

Dai-yu reflected for a moment or two, then smiled.

'Yes, it must have been the maids being lazy. Certainly they can be very disagreeable at such times.'

'Yes, I'm sure that's what it was,' said Bao-yu. 'When I get back, I'll find out who it was and give her a good talking-to.'

'I think some of your young ladies could *do* with a good talking-to,' said Dai-yu, '—though it's not really for me to say so. It's a good job it was only me they were rude to. If Miss Bao or Miss Cow were to call and they behaved like that to *her*, that would be really serious.'

She giggled mischievously. Bao-yu didn't know whether to laugh with her or grind his teeth. But just at that moment a maid came up to ask them both to lunch and the two of them went together out of the Garden and through into the front part of the mansion, calling in at Lady Wang's on the way. . . .

## Chapter 97

Lin Dai-yu Burns Her Poems

We have seen how Dai-yu, on reaching the entrance of the Naiad's House, and on hearing Nightingale's cry of relief, slumped forward, vomited blood and almost fainted. Luckily Nightingale and Ripple were both at hand to assist her into the house. When Ripple left, Nightingale and Snowgoose stood by Dai-yu's bedside and watched her gradually come round.

'Why are you two standing round me crying?' asked Dai-yu, and Nightingale, greatly reassured to hear her talking sense again, replied:

'On your way back from Her Old Ladyship's, Miss, you had quite a nasty turn. We were scared and did not know what to do. That's why we were crying.'

'I am not going to die yet!' said Dai-yu, with a bitter smile. But before she could even finish this sentence, she was doubled up and gasping for breath once more.

When she had learned earlier that day that Bao-yu and Bao-chai were to be married, the shock of knowing that what she had feared for so long was now about to come true, had thrown her into such a turmoil that at first she had quite taken leave of her senses. Now that she had brought up the blood, her mind gradually became clearer. Though at first she could remember nothing, when she saw Nightingale crying, Simple's words slowly came back to her. This time she did not succumb to her emotions, but set her heart instead on a speedy death and final settlement of her debt with fate.

Nightingale and Snowgoose could only stand by helplessly. They would have gone to inform the ladies, but were afraid of a repetition of the last occasion, when Xi-feng had rebuked them for creating a false alarm. Ripple had already given all away, however, by the look of horror on her face when she returned to Grandmother Jia's apartment. The old lady, who had just risen from her midday nap, asked her what the matter was, and in her shocked state Ripple told her all that she had just witnessed.

'What a terrible thing!' exclaimed Grandmother Jia, aghast. She sent for Lady Wang and Xi-feng at once, and told them both the news.

'But I gave instructions to everyone to observe strict secrecy,' said Xi-feng. 'Who can have betrayed us? Now we have another problem on our hands.'

'Never mind that for the moment,' said Grandmother Jia. 'We must first find out how she is.'

She took Lady Wang and Xi-feng with her to visit Dai-yu, and they arrived to find her barely conscious, breathing in faint little gasps, her face bloodless and white as snow. After a while she coughed again. A maid brought the spittoon and they watched with horror as she spat out a mouthful of blood and phlegm. Dai-yu faintly opened her eyes, and seeing Grandmother Jia standing at her bedside, struggled to find breath to speak.

'Grandmother! Your love for me has been in vain.'

Grandmother Jia was most distraught.

'There now, my dear, you must rest. There is nothing to fear.'

Dai-yu smiled faintly and closed her eyes again. A maid came in to tell Xi-feng that the doctor had arrived. The ladies withdrew, and doctor Wang came in with Jia Lian. He took Dai-yu's pulses, and said:

'As yet, there is no cause for alarm. An obstruction of morbid humours has affected the liver, which is unable to store the blood, and as a consequence her spirit has been disturbed. I shall prescribe a medicine to check the Yin, and to halt the flow of blood. I think all will be well.'

Doctor Wang left the room, accompanied by Jia Lian, to write out his prescription.

Grandmother Jia could tell that this time Dai-yu was seriously ill, and as they left the room, she said to Lady Wang and Xi-feng:

'I do not wish to sound gloomy or bring her bad luck, but I fear she has small hope of recovery, poor child. You must make ready her grave-clothes and coffin. Who knows, such preparations may even turn her luck. She may recover, which will be a mercy for us all. But it would be sensible anyway to be prepared for the worst, and not be taken unawares. We shall be so busy over the next few days.'

Xi-feng said she would make the necessary arrangements. Grandmother Jia then questioned Nightingale, but she had no idea who it was that had upset Dai-yu. The more she thought about it, the more it puzzled Grandmother Jia, and she said to Xi-feng and Lady Wang:

'I can understand that the two of them should have grown rather fond of one another, after growing up together and playing together as children. But now that they are older and more mature, the time has come for them to observe a certain distance. She must behave properly, if she is to earn my love. It's quite wrong of her to think she can disregard such things. Then all my love *will* have been in vain! What you have told me troubles me.'

She returned to her apartment and sent for Aroma again. Aroma repeated to her all that she had told Lady Wang on the previous occasion, and in addition described the scene earlier that day between Dai-yu and Bao-yu.

'And yet, when I saw her just now,' said Grandmother Jia, 'she still seemed able to talk sense. I simply cannot understand it. Ours is a decent family. We do not tolerate unseemly goings-on. And that applies to foolish romantic attachments. If her illness is of a respectable nature, I do not mind how much we have to spend to get her better. But if she is suffering from some form of lovesickness, no amount of medicine will cure it and she can expect no further sympathy from me either.'

'You really shouldn't worry about Cousin Lin, Grandmother,' said Xi-feng. 'Lian will be visiting her regularly with the doctor. We must concentrate on the wedding arrangements. Early this morning I heard that the finishing touches were being put to the bridal courtyard. You and Aunt Wang and I should go over to Aunt Xue's for a final consultation. There is one thing that occurs to me, however: with Bao-chai there, it will be rather awkward for us to discuss the wedding. Maybe we should ask Aunt Xue to come over here tomorrow evening, and then we can settle everything at once.'

Grandmother Jia and Lady Wang agreed that her proposal was a good one, and said:

'It is too late today. Tomorrow after lunch, let us all go over together.'

Grandmother Jia's dinner was now served, and Xi-feng and Lady Wang returned to their apartments.

Next day, Xi-feng came over after breakfast. Wishing to sound out Bao-yu according to her plan, she advanced into his room and said:

'Congratulations, Cousin Bao! Uncle Zheng has already chosen a lucky day for your wedding! Isn't that good news?'

Bao-yu stared at her with a blank smile, and nodded his head faintly.

'He is marrying you,' went on Xi-feng, with a studied smile, 'to your cousin Lin. Are you happy?'

Bao-yu burst out laughing. Xi-feng watched him carefully, but could not make out whether he had understood her, or was simply raving. She went on:

'Uncle Zheng says, you are to marry Miss Lin, *if* you get better. But not if you carry on behaving like a half-wit.'

Bao-yu's expression suddenly changed to one of utter seriousness, as he said:

'I'm not a half-wit. You're the half-wit.'

He stood up.

'I am going to see Cousin Lin, to set her mind at rest.'

Xi-feng quickly put out a hand to stop him.

'She knows already. And, as your bride-to-be, she would be much too embarrassed to receive you now.'

'What about when we're married? Will she see me then?'

Xi-feng found this both comic and somewhat disturbing.

'Aroma was right,' she thought to herself. 'Mention Dai-yu, and while he still talks like an idiot, he at least seems to understand what's going on. I can see we shall be in real trouble, if he sees through our scheme and finds out that his bride is not to be Dai-yu after all.'

In reply to his question, she said, suppressing a smile:

'If you behave, she will see you. But not if you continue to act like an imbecile.'

To which Bao-yu replied:

'I have given my heart to Cousin Lin. If she marries me, she will bring it with her and put it back in its proper place.'

Now this was madman's talk if ever, thought Xi-feng. She left him, and walked back into the outer room, glancing with a smile in Grandmother Jia's direction. The old lady too found Bao-yu's words both funny and distressing. . . .

* * *

Dai-yu meanwhile, for all the medicine she took, continued to grow iller with every day that passed. Nightingale did her utmost to raise her spirits. Our story finds her standing once more by Dai-yu's bedside, earnestly beseeching her:

'Miss, now that things have come to this pass, I simply must speak my mind. We know what it is that's eating your heart out. But can't you see that your fears are groundless? Why, look at the state Bao-yu is in! How can he possibly get married, when he's so ill? You must ignore these silly rumours, stop fretting and let yourself get better.'

Dai-yu gave a wraithlike smile, but said nothing. She started coughing again and brought up a lot more blood. Nightingale and Snowgoose came closer and watched her feebly struggling for breath. They knew that any further attempt to rally her would be to no avail, and could do nothing but stand there watching and weeping. Each day Nightingale went over three or four times to tell Grandmother Jia, but Faithful, judging the old lady's attitude towards Dai-yu to have hardened of late, intercepted her reports and hardly mentioned Dai-yu to her mistress. Grandmother Jia was preoccupied with the wedding arrangements, and in the absence of any particular news of Dai-yu, did not show a great deal of interest in the girl's fate, considering it sufficient that she should be receiving medical attention.

Previously, when she had been ill, Dai-yu had always received frequent visits from everyone in the household, from Grandmother Jia down to the humblest maidservant. But now not a single person came to see her. The only face she saw looking down at her was that of Nightingale. She began to feel her end drawing near, and struggled to say a few words to her:

'Dear Nightingale! Dear sister! Closest friend! Though you were Grandmother's maid before you came to serve me, over the years you have become as a sister to me . . .'

She had to stop for breath. Nightingale felt a pang of pity, was reduced to tears and could say nothing. After a long silence, Dai-yu began to speak again, searching for breath between words:

'Dear sister! I am so uncomfortable lying down like this. Please help me up and sit next to me.'

'I don't think you should sit up, Miss, in your condition. You might get cold in the draught.'

Dai-yu closed her eyes in silence. A little later she asked to sit up again. Nightingale and Snowgoose felt they could no longer deny her request. They propped her up on both sides with soft pillows, while Nightingale sat by her on the bed to give further support. Dai-yu was not equal to the effort. The bed where she sat on it seemed to dig into her, and she struggled with all her remaining strength to lift herself up and ease the pain. She told Snowgoose to come closer.

'My poems . . .'

Her voice failed, and she fought for breath again. Snowgoose guessed that she meant the manuscripts she had been revising a few days previously, went to fetch them and laid them on Dai-yu's lap. Dai-yu nodded, then raised her eyes and gazed in the direction of a chest that stood on a stand close by. Snowgoose did not know how to interpret this and stood there at a loss. Dai-yu stared at her now with feverish impatience. She began to cough again and brought up another mouthful of blood. Snowgoose went to fetch some water, and Dai-yu rinsed her mouth and spat into the spittoon. Nightingale wiped her lips with a handkerchief. Dai-yu took the handkerchief from her and pointed to the chest. She tried to speak, but was again seized with an attack of breathlessness and closed her eyes.

'Lie down, Miss,' said Nightingale. Dai-yu shook her head. Nightingale thought she must want one of her handkerchiefs, and told Snowgoose to open the chest and bring her a plain white silk one. Dai-yu looked at it, and dropped it on the bed. Making a supreme effort, she gasped out:

'The ones with the writing on . . .'

Nightingale finally realized that she meant the handkerchiefs Bao-yu had sent her, the ones she had inscribed with her own poems. She told Snowgoose to fetch them, and herself handed them to Dai-yu, with these words of advice:

'You must lie down and rest, Miss. Don't start wearing yourself out. You can look at these another time, when you are feeling better.'

Dai-yu took the handkerchiefs in one hand and without even looking at them, brought round her other hand (which cost her a great effort) and tried with all her might to tear them in two. But she was so weak that all she could achieve was a pathetic trembling motion.

Nightingale knew that Bao-yu was the object of all this bitterness but dared not mention his name, saying instead:

'Miss, there is no sense in working yourself up again.'

Dai-yu nodded faintly, and slipped the handkerchiefs into her sleeve.

'Light the lamp,' she ordered.

Snowgoose promptly obeyed. Dai-yu looked into the lamp, then closed her eyes and sat in silence. Another fit of breathlessness. Then:

'Make up the fire in the brazier.'

Thinking she wanted it for the extra warmth, Nightingale protested:

'You should lie down, Miss, and have another cover on. And the fumes from the brazier might be bad for you.'

Dai-yu shook her head, and Snowgoose reluctantly made up the brazier, placing it on its stand on the floor. Dai-yu made a motion with her hand, indicating that she wanted it moved up onto the kang. Snowgoose lifted it and placed it there, temporarily using the floor-stand, while she went out to fetch the special stand they used on the kang. Dai-yu, far from resting back in the warmth, now inclined her body slightly forward—Nightingale had to support her with both hands as she did so. Dai-yu took the handkerchiefs in one hand. Staring into the flames and nodding thoughtfully to herself, she dropped them into the brazier. Nightingale was horrified, but much as she would have liked to snatch them from the flames, she did not dare move her hands and leave Dai-yu unsupported. Snowgoose was out of the room, fetching the brazier-stand, and by now the handkerchiefs were all ablaze.

'Miss!' cried Nightingale. 'What are you doing?'

As if she had not heard, Dai-yu reached over for her manuscripts, glanced at them and let them fall again onto the kang. Nightingale, anxious lest she burn these too, leaned up against Dai-yu and freeing one hand, reached out with it to take hold of them. But before she could do so, Dai-yu had picked them up again and dropped them in the flames. The brazier was out of Nightingale's reach, and there was nothing she could do but look on helplessly.

Just at that moment Snowgoose came in with the stand. She saw Dai-yu drop something into the fire, and without knowing what it was, rushed forward to try and save it. The manuscripts had caught at once and were already ablaze. Heedless of the danger to her hands, Snowgoose reached into the flames and pulled out what she could, throwing the paper on the floor and stamping frantically on it. But the fire had done its work, and only a few charred fragments remained.

Dai-yu closed her eyes and slumped back, almost causing Nightingale to topple over with her. Nightingale, her heart thumping in great agitation, called Snowgoose over to help her settle Dai-yu down again. It was too late now to send for anyone. And yet, what if Dai-yu should die during the night, and the only people there were Snowgoose, herself and the one or two other junior maids in the Naiad's House? They passed a restless night. Morning came at last, and Dai-yu seemed a little more comfortable. But after breakfast she suddenly began coughing and vomiting, and became tense and feverish again. Nightingale could see that she had reached a crisis. She called Snowgoose and the other juniors in and told them to mount watch, while she went to report to Grandmother Jia. But when she reached Grandmother Jia's apartment, she found it almost deserted. Only a few old nannies and charladies were there, keeping an eye.

'Where is Her Old Ladyship?' asked Nightingale.

'We don't know,' came the reply in chorus.

That was very odd, thought Nightingale. She went into Bao-yu's room and found that too quite empty, save for a single maid who answered with the same 'Don't know'. By now Nightingale had more or less guessed the truth. How could they be so heartless and so cruel? And to think that not a soul had come to visit Dai-yu during the past few days! As the bitterness of it struck her with full force, she felt a great wave of resentment break out within her, and turned abruptly to go.

'I shall go and find Bao-yu, and see how *he* is faring! I wonder how he will manage to brazen it out in front of me! I remember last year, when I made up that story about Miss Lin going back to the South, he fell sick with despair. To think that now he should be openly doing a thing like this! Men must have hearts as cold as ice or snow. What hateful creatures they are!'

She was already at Green Delights, and found the courtyard gate ajar. All was quiet within. Suddenly she realized:

'Of course! If he is getting married, he will have a new apartment. But where?'

She was looking around her in uncertainty, when she saw Bao-yu's page boy Inky rush past, and called to him to stop. He came over, and with a broad smile asked:

'What are you doing here, Miss Nightingale?'

'I heard that Master Bao was getting married,' replied Nightingale, 'and I wanted to watch some of the fun. But I can seen I've come to the wrong place. And I don't know when the wedding is taking place, either.'

'If I tell you,' said Inky in a confidential tone, 'you must promise not to tell Snowgoose. We've been given orders not to let any of you know. The wedding's to be tonight. Of course it's not being held here. The Master told Mr Lian to set aside another apartment.'

'What's the matter?' continued Inky, after a pause.

'Nothing,' replied Nightingale. 'You can go now.'

Inky rushed off again. Nightingale stood there for a while, lost in thought. Suddenly she remembered Dai-yu. She might already be dead! Her eyes filled with tears, and clenching her teeth, she said fiercely:

'Bao-yu! If she dies, you may think you can wash your hands of her in this callous way: but when you are happily married, and have your heart's desire, you needn't think you can look *me* in the face again!'

As she walked, she began to weep. She made her way, sobbing pitifully, across the Garden. She was not far from the Naiad's House, when she saw two junior maids standing at the gate, peeping out nervously. They saw her coming, and one of them cried out:

'There's Miss Nightingale! At last!'

Nightingale could see that all was not well. Gesturing to them anxiously to be silent, she hurried in, to find Dai-yu red in the face, the fire from her liver having risen upwards and inflamed her cheeks. This was a dangerous sign, and Nightingale called Dai-yu's old wet-nurse, Nannie Wang, to come and take a look. One glance was enough to reduce this old woman to tears. Nightingale had turned to Nannie Wang as an older person, who could be expected to lend them some courage in this extremity. But she turned out to be quite helpless, and only made Nightingale more distraught than before. Suddenly she thought of someone else she could turn to, and sent one of the younger maids to fetch her with all speed. Her choice might seem a strange one; but Nightingale, reasoned that as a widow, Li Wan would certainly be excluded from Bao-yu's wedding festivities. Besides she was in general charge of affairs in the Garden, and it would be in order to ask her to come.

Li Wan was at home correcting some of Jia Lan's poems, when the maid came rushing frantically in and cried:

'Mrs Zhu! Miss Lin's dying! Everyone over there is in tears!'

Li Wan rose startled to her feet and without a word set off at once for the Naiad's House, followed by her maids Candida and Casta. As she walked, she wept and lamented to herself:

'When I think of all the times we have spent together—oh my poor cousin! So lovely, so gifted! There is hardly another like her. Only Frost Maiden and the Goddess of the Moon could rival her. How can she be leaving us at such a tender age, for that distant land from whence no travellers return . . . And to think that because of Xi-feng's deceitful scheme, I have not been able to show myself at the Naiad's House and have done nothing to show my sisterly affection! Oh the poor, dear girl!'

She was already at the gate of the Naiad's House. There was no sound from within. She began to fret.

'I must be too late! She must have died already and they are resting between their lamentations. I wonder if her grave-clothes and coverlet are ready?'

She quickened her step and hurried on into the room. A young maid standing at the inner doorway had already seen her, and called out:

'Mrs Zhu is here!'

Nightingale hurried out to meet her.

'How is she?' asked Li Wan.

Nightingale tried to answer but all she could muster was a choked sob. Tears poured down her cheeks like pearls from a broken necklace, as she pointed silently to where Dai-yu lay. Realizing with a pang what Nightingale's pitiable condition must portend, Li Wan asked no more, but went over at once to see for herself. Dai-yu no longer had the strength to speak. When Li Wan said her name a few times, her eyes opened a slit as if in recognition of the voice. But her eyelids and lips could only make a trembling suggestion of a movement. Although she still breathed, it was now more than she could manage to utter a single word, or shed a single tear.

Li Wan turned around and saw that Nightingale was no longer in the room. She asked Snowgoose where she was, and Snowgoose replied:

'In the outer room.'

Li Wan hurried out, to find Nightingale lying on the empty bed, her face a ghastly green, her eyes closed, tears streaming down her cheeks. Where her head lay on the embroidered pillow, with its border of fine brocade, was a patch the size of a small plate, wet with her tears and the copious effusions of her nose. When Li Wan called to her, she opened her eyes slowly, and raised herself slightly on the bed.

'Silly girl!' Li Wan upbraided her. 'Is this a time for tears? Fetch Miss Lin's grave-clothes and dress her in them.

Are you going to leave it till it is too late? Would you have her go naked from the world? Would you ruin her honour?' . . .

Now, though Bao-yu's mind was still clouded from the loss of his jade, his sense of joy at the prospect of marrying Dai-yu—in his eyes the most blessed, the most wonderful thing that had happened in heaven or earth since time began—had caused a temporary resurgence of physical well-being, if not a full restoration of his mental faculties. Xi-feng's ingenious plan had had exactly the intended effect, and he was now counting the minutes till he should see Dai-yu. Today was the day when all his dreams were to come true, and he was filled with a feeling of ecstasy. He still occasionally let slip some tell-tale imbecile remark, but in other respects gave the appearance of having completely recovered. All this Snowgoose observed, and was filled with hatred for him and grief for her mistress. She knew nothing of the true cause of his joy. . . .

Bao-yu told Aroma to hurry and dress him in his bridegroom's finery. He sat in Lady Wang's chamber, watching Xi-feng and You-shi bustling about their preparations, himself bursting with impatience for the great moment.

'If Cousin Lin is coming from the Garden,' he asked Aroma, 'why all this fuss? Why isn't she here yet?'

Suppressing a smile, Aroma replied:

'She has to wait for the propitious moment.'

Xi-feng turned to Lady Wang and said:

'Because we are in mourning, we cannot have music in the street. But the traditional ceremony would seem so drab without any music at all, so I have told some of the women-servants with a bit of musical knowledge, the ones who used to look after the actresses, to come and play a little, to add a bit of a festive touch.'

Lady Wang nodded, and said she thought this a good idea. Presently the great bridal palanquin was born in through the main gate. The little ensemble of women-servants played, as it entered down an avenue of twelve pairs of palace-lanterns, creating a passably stylish impression. The Master of Ceremonies requested the bride to step out of her palanquin, and Bao-yu saw the Matron of Honour, all in red, lead out his bride, her face concealed by the bridal veil. There was a maid in attendance, and Bao-yu saw to his surprise that it was Snowgoose. This puzzled him for a moment.

'Why Snowgoose, and not Nightingale?' he asked himself. Then: 'Of course. Snowgoose is Dai-yu's original maid from the South, whereas Nightingale was one of our maids, which would never do.'

And so, when he saw Snowgoose, it was as if he had seen the face of Dai-yu herself beneath the veil.

The Master of Ceremonies chanted the liturgy, and the bride and groom knelt before Heaven and Earth. Grandmother Jia was called forth to receive their obeisances, as were Sir Zheng, Lady Wang and other elders of the family, after which they escorted the couple into the hall and thence to the bridal chamber. Here they were made to sit on the bridal bed, were showered with dried fruit and subjected to the various other practices customary in old Nanking families such as the Jias, which we need not describe in detail here.

Jia Zheng, it will be remembered, had gone along with the plan grudgingly, in deference to Grandmother

Jia's wishes, retaining grave though unspoken doubts himself as to her theory of 'turning Bao-yu's luck'. But today, seeing Bao-yu bear himself with a semblance of dignity, he could not help but be pleased.

The bride was now sitting alone on the bridal bed, and the moment had come for the groom to remove her veil. Xi-feng had made her preparations for this event, and now asked Grandmother Jia, Lady Wang and others of the ladies present to step forward into the bridal chamber to assist her. The sense of climax seemed to cause Bao-yu to revert somewhat to his imbecile ways, for as he approached his bride he said:

'Are you better now, coz? It's such a long time since we last saw each other. What do you want to go wrapping yourself up in that silly thing for?'

He was about to raise the veil. Grandmother Jia broke into a cold sweat. But he hesitated, thinking to himself:

'I know how sensitive Cousin Lin is. I must be very careful not to offend her.'

He waited a little longer. But soon the suspense became unbearable, and he walked up to her and lifted the veil. The Matron of Honour took it from him, while Snowgoose melted into the background and Oriole came forward to take her place. Bao-yu stared at his bride. Surely this was Bao-chai? Incredulous, with one hand holding the lantern, he rubbed his eyes with the other and looked again. It *was* Bao-chai. How pretty she looked, in her wedding-gown! He gazed at her soft skin, the full curve of her shoulders, and her hair done up in tresses that hung from her temples! Her eyes were moist, her lips quivered slightly. Her whole appearance had the simple elegance of a white lily, wet with pendant dew; the maidenly blush on her cheeks resembled apricot-blossom wreathed in mist. For a moment he stared at her in utter astonishment. Then he noticed that Oriole was standing at her side, while Snowgoose had quite vanished. A feeling of helpless bewilderment seized him, and thinking he must be dreaming, he stood there in a motionless daze. The maids took the lamp from him and helped him to a chair, where he sat with his eyes fixed in front of him, still without uttering a single word. Grandmother Jia was anxious lest this might signal the approach of another of his fits, and herself came over to rally him, while Xi-feng and You-shi escorted Bao-chai to a chair in the inner part of the room. Bao-chai held her head bowed and said nothing.

After a while, Bao-yu had composed himself sufficiently to think. He saw Grandmother Jia and Lady Wang sitting opposite him, and asked Aroma in a whisper:

'Where am I? This must all be a dream.'

'A dream? Why, it's the happiest day of your life!' said Aroma. 'How can you be so silly? Take care: Sir Zeng is outside.'

Pointing now to where Bao-chai sat, and still whispering, Bao-yu asked again:

'Who is that beautiful lady sitting over there?'

Aroma found this so comical that for a while she could say nothing, but held her hand to her face to conceal her mirth. Finally she replied:

'That is your bride, the new Mrs Bao-yu.'

The other maids also turned away, unable to contain their laughter.

Bao-yu: 'Don't be so silly! What do you mean, "Mrs Bao-yu"? Who *is* Mrs Bao-yu?'

Aroma: 'Miss Chai.'

Bao-yu: 'But what about Miss Lin?'

Aroma: 'The Master decided you should marry Miss Chai. What's Miss Lin got to do with it?'

Bao-yu: 'But I saw her just a moment ago, and Snowgoose too. They couldn't have just vanished! What sort of trick is this that you're all playing on me?'

Xi-feng came up and whispered in his ear:

'Miss Chai is sitting over there, so please stop talking like this. If you offend her, Grannie will be very cross with you.'

Bao-yu was now more hopelessly confused than ever. The mysterious goings-on of that night, coming on top of his already precarious mental state, had wrought him up to such a pitch of despair that all he could do was cry—'I must find Cousin Lin!'—again and again. Grandmother Jia and the other ladies tried to comfort him but he was impervious to their efforts. Furthermore, with Bao-chai in the room, they had to be careful what they said. Bao-yu was clearly suffering from a severe relapse, and they now abandoned their attempts to rally him and instead helped him to bed, while ordering several sticks of gum benzoin incense to be lit, the heavy, sedative fumes of which soon filled the room. They all stood in awesome hush. After a short while, the incense began to take effect and Bao-yu sank into a heavy slumber, much to the relief of the ladies, who sat down again to await the dawn. Grandmother Jia told Xi-feng to ask Bao-chai to lie down and rest, which she did, fully dressed as she was, behaving as though she had heard nothing.

Jia Zheng had remained in an outer room during all of this, and so had seen nothing to disillusion him of the reassuring impression he had received earlier on. The following day, as it happened, was the day selected according to the almanac for his departure to his new post. After a short rest, he took formal leave of the festivities and returned to his apartment. Grandmother Jia, too, left Bao-yu sound asleep and returned to her apartment for a brief rest.

The next morning, Jia Zheng took leave of the ancestors in the family shrine and came to bid his mother farewell. He bowed before her and said:

'I, your unworthy son, am about to depart for afar. My only wish is that you should keep warm in the cold weather and take good care of yourself. As soon as I arrive at my post, I shall write to ask how you are. You are not to worry on my account. Bao-yu's marriage has now been celebrated in accordance with your wishes, and it only remains for me to beg you to instruct him, and impart to him the wisdom of your years.'

Grandmother Jia, for fear that Jia Zheng would worry on his journey, made no mention of Bao-yu's relapse but merely said:

'There is one thing I should tell you. Although the rites were performed last night, Bao-yu's marriage was not properly consummated. His health would not allow it. Custom, I know, decrees that he should see you off today. But in view of all the circumstances, his earlier illness, the luck turning, his still fragile state of convalescence and yesterday's exertions, I am worried that by going out he might catch a chill. So I put it to you: if you wish him to fulfil his filial obligations by seeing you off, then send for him at once and instruct him accordingly; but if you love him, then spare him and let him say goodbye and make his kotow to you here.'

'Why should I want him to see me off?' returned Jia Zheng. 'All I want is that from now on he should study in earnest. That would bring me greater pleasure by far.'

Grandmother Jia was most relieved to hear this. She told Jia Zheng to be seated and sent Faithful, after imparting to her various secret instructions, to fetch Bao-yu and to bring Aroma with him. Faithful had not been away many minutes, when Bao-yu came in and with the usual promptings, performed his duty to his father. Luckily the sight of his father brought him, for a few moments, sufficient clarity to get through the formalities without any gross lapses. Jia Zheng delivered himself of a few exhortatory words, to all of which his son gave the correct replies. Then Jia Zheng told Aroma to escort him back to his room, while he himself went to Lady Wang's apartment. There he earnestly enjoined Lady Wang to take charge of Bao-yu's moral welfare during his absence.

'There must be none of his previous unruliness,' he added. 'He must now prepare himself to enter for next year's provincial examination.'

Lady Wang assured him that she would do her utmost, and without mentioning anything else, at once sent a maid to escort Bao-chai into the room. Bao-chai performed the rite proper to a newly-married bride seeing off her father-in-law, and then remained in the room when Jia Zheng left. The other women-folk accompanied him as far as the inner gate before turning back. Cousin Zhen and the other young male Jias received a few words of exhortation, drank a farewell toast, and, together with a crowd of other friends and relatives, accompanied him as far as the Hostelry of the Tearful Parting, some three or four miles beyond the city walls, where they bid their final farewell.

But of Jia Zheng's departure no more. Let us return to Bao-yu, who on leaving his father, had suffered an immediate relapse. His mind became more and more clouded, and he could swallow neither food nor drink. Whether or not he was to emerge from this crisis alive will be revealed in the next chapter.

## Chapter 98

### Crimson Pearl's Suffering Spirit Returns

On his return from seeing his father, Bao-yu, as we have seen, regressed into a worse state of stupor and depression than ever. He was too lacking in energy to move, and could eat nothing, but fell straight into a heavy slumber. Once more the doctor was called, once more he took Bao-yu's pulses and made out a prescription, which was administered to no effect. He could not even recognize the people around him. And yet, if helped into a sitting position, he could still pass for someone in normal health. Provided he was not called upon to do anything, there were no external symptoms to indicate how seriously ill he was. He continued like this for several days, to the increasing anxiety of the family, until the Ninth Day after the wedding, when according to tradition the newly-married couple should visit the bride's family. If they did not go,

Aunt Xue would be most offended. But if they went with Bao-yu in his present state, whatever were they to say? Knowing that his illness was caused by his attachment to Dai-yu, Grandmother Jia would have liked to make a clean breast of it and tell Aunt Xue. But she feared that this too might cause offence and ill-feeling. It was also difficult for her to be of any comfort to Bao-chai, who was in a delicate position as a new member of the Jia family. Such comfort could only be rendered by a visit from the girl's mother, which would be difficult if they had already offended her by not celebrating the Ninth Day. It must be gone through with. Grandmother Jia imparted her views on the matter to Lady Wang and Xi-feng:

'It is only Bao-yu's mind that has been temporarily affected. I don't think a little excursion would do him any harm. We must prepare two small sedan-chairs, and send a maid to support him. They can go through the Garden. Once the Ninth Day has been properly celebrated, we can ask Mrs Xue to come over and comfort Bao-chai, while we do our utmost to restore Bao-yu to health. They will both benefit.'

Lady Wang agreed and immediately began making the necessary preparations. Bao-chai acquiesced in the charade out of a sense of conjugal duty, while Bao-yu in his moronic state was easily manipulated. Bao-chai now knew the full truth, and in her own mind blamed her mother for making a foolish decision. But now that things had gone this far she said nothing. Aunt Xue herself, when she witnessed Bao-yu's pitiful condition, began to regret having ever given her consent, and could only bring herself to play a perfunctory part in the proceedings.

When they returned home, Bao-yu's condition seemed to grow worse. By the next day he could not even sit up in bed. This deterioration continued daily, until he could no longer swallow medicine or water. Aunt Xue was there, and she and the other ladies in their frantic despair scoured the city for eminent physicians, without finding one that could diagnose the illness. Finally they discovered, lodging in a broken-down temple outside the city, a down-and-out practitioner by the name of Bi Zhi-an, who diagnosed it as a case of severe emotional shock, aggravated by a failure to dress in accordance with the seasons and by irregular eating habits, with consequent accumulation of choler and obstruction of the humours. In short, an internal disorder made worse by external factors. He made out a prescription in accordance with this diagnosis, which was administered that evening. At about ten o'clock it began to take effect. Bao-yu began to show signs of consciousness and asked for water to drink. Grandmother Jia, Lady Wang and all the other ladies congregated round the sick-bed felt that they could at last have a brief respite from their vigil, and Aunt Xue was invited to bring Bao-chai with her to Grandmother Jia's apartment to rest for a while.

His brief access of clarity enabled Bao-yu to understand the gravity of his illness. When the others had gone and he was left alone with Aroma, he called her over to his side and taking her by the hand said tearfully:

'Please tell me how Cousin Chai came to be here? I remember Father marrying me to Cousin Lin. Why has *she* been made to go? Why has Cousin Chai taken her place? She has no right to be here! I'd like to tell her so, but I don't want to offend her. How has Cousin Lin taken it? Is she very upset?'

Aroma did not dare tell him the truth, but merely said:

'Miss Lin is ill.'

'I must go and see her,' insisted Bao-yu. He wanted to get up, but days of going without food and drink had so sapped his strength that he could no longer move, but could only weep bitterly and say:

'I know I am going to die! There's something on my mind, something very important, that I want you to tell Grannie for me. Cousin Lin and I are both ill. We are both dying. It will be too late to help us when we are dead; but if they prepare a room for us now and if we are taken there before it is too late, we can at least be cared for together while we are still alive, and be laid out together when we die. Do this for me, for friendship's sake!'

Aroma found this plea at once disturbing, comical and moving. Bao-chai, who happened to be passing with Oriole, heard every word and took him to task straight away.

'Instead of resting and trying to get well, you make yourself iller with all this gloomy talk! Grandmother has scarcely stopped worrying about you for a moment, and here you are causing more trouble for her. She is over eighty now and may not live to acquire title because of your achievements; but at least, by leading a good life, you can repay her a little for all that she has suffered for your sake. And I hardly need mention the agonies Mother has endured in bringing you up. You are the only son she has left. If you were to die, think how she would suffer! As for me, I am wretched enough as it is; you don't need to make a widow of me. Three good reasons why even if you want to die, the powers above will not let you and you will not be able to. After four or five days of proper rest and care, your illness will pass, your strength will be restored and you will be yourself again.'

For a while Bao-yu could think of no reply to this homily. Finally he gave a silly laugh and said:

'After not speaking to me for so long, here you are lecturing me. You are wasting your breath.'

Encouraged by this response to go a step further, Bao-cahi said:

'Let me tell you the plain truth, then. Some days ago, while you were unconscious, Cousin Lin passed away.'

With a sudden movement, Bao-yu sat up and cried out in horror:

'It can't be true!'

'It is. Would I lie about such a thing? Grandmother and Mother knew how fond you were of each other, and wouldn't tell you because they were afraid that if they did, you would die too.'

Bao-yu began howling unrestrainedly and slumped back in his bed. Suddenly all was pitch black before his eyes. He could not tell where he was and was beginning to feel very lost, when he thought he saw a man walking towards him and asked in a bewildered tone of voice:

'Would you be so kind as to tell me where I am?'

'This,' replied the stranger, 'is the road to the Springs of the Nether World. Your time is not yet come. What brings you here?'

'I have just learned of the death of a friend and have come to find her. But I seem to have lost my way.'

'Who is this friend of yours?'

'Lin Dai-yu of Soochow.'

The man gave a chilling smile:

'In life Lin Dai-yu was no ordinary mortal, and in death she has become no ordinary shade. An ordinary mortal has two souls which coalesce at birth to vitalize the physical frame, and disperse at death to rejoin the cosmic flux. If you consider the impossibility of tracing even such ordinary human entities in the Nether World, you will realize what a futile task it is to look for Lin Dai-yu. You had better return at once.'

After standing for a moment lost in thought, Bao-yu asked again:

'But if as you say, death is a dispersion, how can there be such a place as the Nether World?'

'There is,' replied the man with a superior smile, 'and yet there is not, such a place. It is a teaching, devised to warn mankind in its blind attachment to the idea of life and death. The Supreme Wrath is aroused by human folly in all forms—whether it be excessive ambition, premature death self-sought, or futile self-destruction through debauchery and a life of overweening violence. Hell is the place where souls such as these are imprisoned and made to suffer countless torments in expiation of their sins. This search of yours for Lin Dai-yu is a case of futile self-delusion. Dai-yu has already returned to the Land of Illusion and if you really want to find her you must cultivate your mind and strengthen your spiritual nature. Then one day you will see her again. But if you throw your life away, you will be guilty of premature death self-sought and will be confined to Hell. And then, although you may be allowed to see your parents, you will certainly never see Dai-yu again.'

When he had finished speaking, the man took a stone from within his sleeve and threw it at Bao-yu's chest. The words he had spoken and the impact of the stone as it landed on his chest combined to give Bao-yu such a fright that he would have returned home at once, if he had only known which way to turn. In his confusion he suddenly heard a voice, and turning, saw the figures of Grandmother Jia, Lady Wang, Bao-chai, Aroma and his other maids standing in a circle around him, weeping and calling his name. He was lying on his own bed. The red lamp was on the table. The moon was shining brilliantly through the window. He was back among the elegant comforts of his own home. A moment's reflection told him that what he had just experienced had been a dream. He was in a cold sweat. Though his mind felt strangely lucid, thinking only intensified his feeling of helpless desolation, and he uttered several profound sighs.

Bao-chai had known of Dai-yu's death for several days. While Grandmother Jia had forbidden the maids to tell him for fear of further complicating his illness, she felt she knew better. Aware that it was Dai-yu who lay at the root of his illness and that the loss of his jade was only a secondary factor, she took the opportunity of breaking the news of her death to him in this abrupt manner, hoping that by severing his attachment once and for all she would enable his sanity and health to be restored. Grandmother Jia, Lady Wang and company were not aware of her intentions and at first reproached her for her lack of caution. But when they saw Bao-yu regain consciousness, they were all greatly relieved and went at once to the library to ask doctor Bi to come in and examine his patient again. The doctor carefully took his pulses.

'How odd!' he exclaimed. 'His pulses are deep and still, his spirit calm, the oppression quite dispersed. Tomorrow he must take a regulative draught, which I shall prescribe, and he should make a prompt and complete recovery.'

The doctor left and the ladies all returned to their apartments in much improved spirits.

Although at first Aroma greatly resented the way in which Bao-chai had broken the news, she did not dare say so. Oriole, on the other hand, reproved her mistress in private for having been, as she put it, too hasty.

'What do you know about such things?' retorted Bao-chai. 'Leave this to me. I take full responsibility.'

Bao-chai ignored the opinions and criticisms of those around her and continued to keep a close watch on Bao-yu's progress, probing him judiciously, like an acupuncturist with a needle.

A day or two later, he began to feel a slight improvement in himself, though his mental equilibrium was still easily disturbed by the least thought of Dai-yu. Aroma was constantly at his side, with such words of consolation as:

'The Master chose Miss Chai as your bride for her more dependable nature. He thought Miss Lin too difficult and temperamental for you, and besides there was always the fear that she would not live long. Then later Her Old Ladyship thought you were not in a fit state to know what was best for you and would only be upset and make yourself iller if you knew the truth, so she made Snowgoose come over, to try and make things easier for you.'

This did nothing to lessen his grief, and he often wept inconsolably. But each time he thought of putting an end to his life, he remembered the words of the stranger in his dream; and then he thought of the distress his death would cause his mother and grandmother and knew that he could not tear himself away from them. He also reflected that Dai-yu was dead, and that Bao-chai was a fine lady in her own right; there must after all have been some truth in the bond of gold and jade. This thought eased his mind a little. Bao-chai could see that things were improving, and herself felt calmer as a result. Every day she scrupulously performed her duties towards Grandmother Jia and Lady Wang, and when these were completed, did all she could to cure Bao-yu of his grief. He was still not able to sit up for long periods, but often when he saw her sitting by his bedside he would succumb to his old weakness for the fairer sex. She tried to rally him in an earnest manner, saying:

'The important thing is to take care of your health. Now that we are married, we have a whole lifetime ahead of us.'

He was reluctant to listen to her advice. But since his grandmother, his mother, Aunt Xue and all the others took it in turns to watch over him during the day, and since Bao-chai slept on her own in an adjoining room, and he was waited on at night by one or two maids of Grandmother Jia's, he found himself left with little choice but to rest and get well again. And as time went by and Bao-chai proved herself a gentle and devoted companion, he found that a small part of his love for Dai-yu began to transfer itself to her. But this belongs to a later part of our story.

* * *

Let us return to the wedding-day. Dai-yu, it will be remembered, had lost consciousness while it was still light, and was holding onto life by the slenderest thread. Her weak breathing and precarious heart-beat caused Li Wan and

Nightingale to weep in despair. By evening however, she seemed easier again. She feebly opened her eyes, and seemed to be asking for water or medicine. Snowgoose had already left, and only Li Wan and Nightingale were at her bedside. Nightingale brought her a little cup of pear-juice blended with a decoction of longans, and with a small silver spoon fed her two or three spoonfuls of it. Dai-yu closed her eyes and rested for a while. Consciousness would flicker momentarily within her, then fade away again. Li Wan recognized this peaceful state as the last transient revival of the dying, but thinking that the end would not come for a few hours, she returned briefly to Sweet-rice Village to see to her own affairs.

Dai-yu opened her eyes again. Seeing no one in the room but Nightingale and her old wet-nurse and a few other junior maids, she clutched Nightingale's hand and said with a great effort:

'I am finished! After the years you have spent seeing to my every need, I had hoped the two of us could always be together. But now . . .'

She broke off, panting for breath, closed her eyes and lay still, gripping Nightingale's hand tightly. Nightingale did not dare to move. She had thought that Dai-yu seemed so much better, had even hoped she might pull through after all; but these words sent a chill down her spine. After a long pause, Dai-yu spoke again:

'Sister Nightingale! I have no family of my own here. My body is pure: promise me you'll ask them to bury me at home!'

She closed her eyes again and was silent. Her grip tightened still further around Nightingale's hand, and she was seized with another paroxysm of breathlessness. When she could breathe again, her outward breaths became longer, her inward breaths shorter and more feeble. They quickened at a rate that caused Nightingale great alarm, and she sent at once for Li Wan. Tan-chun happened to arrive at that very moment. Nightingale said to her in an urgent whisper:

'Miss! Come and look at Miss Lin!' As she spoke, her tears fell like drops of rain. Tan-chun came over and felt Dai-yu's hand. It was already cold, and her eyes were glazed and lifeless. Tan-chun and Nightingale wept as they gave orders for water to be brought and for Dai-yu to be washed. Now Li Wan came hurrying in. She, Tan-chun and Nightingale looked at each other, but were too shocked to say a word. They began wiping Dai-yu's face with a flannel, when suddenly she cried out in a loud voice:

'Bao-yu! Bao-yu! How could you . . .'

Her whole body broke into a cold sweat and she could say no more. They tried to calm her down and support her. She sweated more and more profusely and her body became colder by degrees. Tan-chun and Li Wan told the maids to put up her hair and dress her in her grave-clothes, and to be quick about it. Her eyes rolled upwards. Alas!

> Her fragrant soul disperses, wafted
> on the breeze;
> Her sorrows now a dream, drifting
> into the night.

The moment Dai-yu breathed her last was the very moment that Bao-yu took Bao-chai to be his wife. . . .

## SHEN FU (1763–1808?)

*Translated by Leonard Pratt and Chiang Su-hui*

We know nothing of Shen Fu except what he tells us in his extraordinary autobiography, titled *Six Records of a Floating Life,* of which only four records have survived. Shen Fu was from the class of government bureaucrats, but he himself never passed the civil service examinations and was consequently trapped in low-level secretarial positions, where he was never particularly successful. He married his cousin, Chen Yün, and much of his life seems to have been spent in conflict between his love for her, which he describes with great frankness in his autobiography, and his sense of filial duty.

*Six Records of a Floating Life* is not a simple, chronological autobiography. Instead, Shen Fu arranges his life into categories—the joys of marriage, the pleasures of leisure, the sorrows of misfortune, and so on—and allows the full texture of his life to appear only after all the layers have been completed. What seems after the first and second records to be a life of great leisure and bliss takes on a much more troubled aspect after the third record, which reveals his father's intense dislike for Yün, his wife, and the scandals she supposedly brought upon the family.

The second record, "The Pleasures of Leisure," included here, portrays a man of such extreme aesthetic concerns and sensitivities—invariably sensitivities for the beauty of the small—that he almost can be read as a parody of a certain type of Chinese *literatus.* However, he is no parody. The life portrayed here has usually been read by Chinese as one of genuine charm, although indeed mixed with great sorrow and tragedy. Shen Fu's work, which has been particularly popular in this century, presents a picture of the possibilities of pleasure and beauty in a traditional China that stands on the edge of a new and dangerous challenge coming from the West.

## *from Six Records of a Floating Life*

### *The Pleasures of Leisure*

When I was small I could stare directly at the sun with my eyes wide open. I could see the smallest things clearly and often took an almost mystic pleasure in making out the patterns on them.

During the summer, whenever I heard the sound of mosquitoes swarming, I would pretend they were a flock of cranes dancing across the open sky, and in my imagination they actually would become hundreds of cranes. I would look at them so long my neck became stiff. At night I would let mosquitoes inside my mosquito netting, blow smoke at them, and imagine that what I saw were white cranes soaring through blue clouds. It really did look like cranes flying among the clouds, and it was a sight that delighted me.

I would often squat down by unkempt grassy places in flower beds or by niches in walls, low enough so that my head was level with them, and concentrate so carefully that to me the grass became a forest and the insects became animals. Imagining that small mounds of earth were hills and that shallow holes were valleys, I let my spirit wander there in happiness and contentment.

Once while I was concentrating all my attention on two insects battling in the grass, a giant suddenly appeared, knocking down the mountains and pulling up the trees. It was nothing but a toad, but with one flick of his tongue he swallowed both the insects. I was small, and because I had been so caught up in the scene I could not help being frightened. When I had calmed down, I caught the toad, spanked it severely, and expelled it to a neighbour's yard. Since growing up I have sometimes thought that the battle of the two insects was probably an attempted rape. The ancients said, 'Rapists deserve death.' I wonder, was this why the insects were eaten by the toad?

One day while I was absorbed in my imaginary world, my egg was bitten by an earthworm (in Soochow we call the male organs eggs), so that it swelled up and I could not urinate. The servants caught a duck, and were forcing it to open its mouth over the wound, when suddenly one of them let go of the bird. The duck stretched out its neck as if to bite me there, and I screamed with fright. This became a family joke. These were all things that happened to me when I was small.

When I was a little older I became obsessed with a love of flowers, and found much delight in pruning miniature potted trees to make them look like real ones. It was not until I met Chang Lan-po, however, that I began really to learn how to prune branches and care for sprouts, and later to understand grafting and the creation of miniature rock formations in the pots. My favourite flower was the orchid, because of its elegant fragrance and charming appearance, though it is difficult to obtain ones that can be considered truly classic.

Shortly before Lan-po died he presented me with a pot of orchids that looked like lotus flowers. The centres were white and broad, and the edges of the petals were straight. They had thin stems, and the petals themselves were quite pale. This was a classic flower, and I treasured mine like a piece of old jade. When I was away from home Yün would water it herself, and its flowers and leaves grew luxuriantly. After I had had it for almost two years, however, it suddenly dried up and died. I dug it up and found the roots in good condition, white as jade with many new shoots. At first I could not understand it, and could only sigh at the thought that I was simply not lucky enough to raise so fine a flower. Only later did I learn that someone who had asked for a cutting and been refused had poured boiling water over it and killed it. I swore that from that time on I would never grow orchids again.

My next favourite flower was the azalea. Although it has no fragrance to speak of, its colours are long-lasting and it is easy to prune. But because Yün loved their branches and leaves, she could not stand seeing me prune them too much, so it was difficult to raise them properly. It was the same with all my other plants.

Every year chrysanthemums would grow east of the fence, blooming in the autumn. I preferred to pick them and put them in vases, rather than raise them in pots. It was not that I did not enjoy looking at them in pots, but because our house had no garden I could not grow them in pots myself, and had I bought them in the market and transplanted them, they would have looked all jumbled and wrong. I did not want that.

When putting chrysanthemums in a vase one should select an odd number of flowers, not an even number. Each vase should contain flowers of only a single colour. The mouths of the vases should be wide so that the flowers can spread out naturally.

Whether one is displaying five or seven flowers, or thirty or forty flowers, they should rise straight from the mouth of the vase in one mass, neither crowded together nor falling around loosely and leaning against the mouth of the vase. This technique is called 'rising tightly'.

Some of the flowers should stand up gracefully, while others spread out at angles. Some should be high and some low, with a few buds in between, to keep the arrangement from looking stiff and unnatural.

The leaves should not be disorderly and the stems should not be stiff. If one uses pins to hold the flowers in position they should be hidden, the long pins cut off so that none protrude from the stems. This technique is called 'clearing the mouth of the vase'.

From three to seven vases can be arranged on a table, depending on its size. No more than seven vases should be set out on one table, or it will not be possible to tell the eyes from the eyebrows, and the arrangement will look just like the cheap chrysanthemum screens sold in the markets. The stands should be from three or four inches to two feet and five or six inches tall. They should be different in height, but should be in proportion to one another so that there is an attractive relationship between the appearance of them all. If there is a tall stand in the centre with two low ones at the sides, or if the ones at the back are tall and the ones in front are low, or if they are set out in pairs, they will look like what people call a 'beautiful pile of trash'. Whether the flowers should be dense or spread out, whether they should lean towards the viewer or away, all depends on the sense of pictorial composition of someone who knows how to appreciate them.

When preparing flower pots, one can make a glue by mixing pitch, resin, elm bark, flour, and oil, and heating the mixture in the glowing ashes of rice stalks. Push pins up through a copper disc, and then heat the glue and stick the disc to the inside of the pot. After the glue has cooled, tie up a bunch of flowers with thin wire and push them down on to the pins. They should be at an angle to look best, and they should not be right in the middle of the pot. The branches should be separated, the leaves should stand out clearly, and the flowers themselves must not crowd together. Afterwards add water to the pot, and use a little sand to cover up the copper disc. The arrangement will only be correct if it looks as if the flowers have been grown in the pot.

To prune flowers picked from trees and fruits for display in a vase (for one cannot pick all the flowers oneself, and those picked by others will always be unsatisfactory), first hold them in your hand and turn them this way and that, to see how they look best. After deciding that, prune off the extra branches to make an attractive arrangement that is spare and uncommon. Then consider how the stems will curve when put into the vase, so that you can avoid having all the leaves at the back of the arrangement, or all the flowers at the sides. If you just take any branch that comes to hand and cut a straight stem from it to put into a vase, it will look stiff and out of place, the blooms will face sideways and the leaves will turn backwards so that the whole will be unattractive and inharmonious as well.

This is how to make a curve in a straight stem: saw halfway through it, insert a small piece of brick or stone into the cut, and the stem will bend. If the stem then tends to fall over, use one or two pins to strengthen it.

Even maple leaves and bamboo branches, bits of grass and thistles, can all be used in decorative arrangements. A single green bamboo twig—if complemented by a few aspen seeds, some leaves of fine grass, and two thistle branches, all of them in proper arrangement—can have an unworldly beauty.

When flowers and trees are planted for the first time, it does not matter if they are set in at an angle. Let the leaves face where they will, for after a year they and the branches will straighten up by themselves. In fact, if a tree is planted straight up it will be difficult for it to grow into a striking shape.

In raising potted trees, first select those which have roots that are exposed and crooked like chickens' feet. Cut off about the first three branches, then let the others grow. Each branch should have a section of the trunk to itself, with from seven to nine branches to the top of the tree. There should not be two branches opposite one another like shoulders, nor should the joints be swollen like the knees of a crane. The branches should grow out in all directions, not only to the right and left, or to the front and back, otherwise the tree will look bare. Some trees are called 'double-trunked' or 'triple-trunked'; this is when two or three trees grow from the same roots. If the roots of a tree do not look like chickens' feet the tree will look unattractive, as if it has been just stuck in the dirt.

The proper training of a tree takes at least thirty or forty years. In my lifetime I have seen only one man who managed to raise several trees properly, old Wan Tsai-chang of my home county. Once at a home in Yangchou I saw a potted boxwood and a potted cyprus that had been presented by a visitor from Yüshan, but this was at the home of a merchant and their being in such a place was as pitiful as brilliant pearls being thrown into the darkness. Other than these, the trees I have seen have not been particularly good. If the branches are allowed to grow out so that a tree looks like a pagoda, or if they twist around like earthworms, the tree will look as if it had been trained by only a common gardener.

While adding some detail in the pot with flowers or stones, try to create small scenes as lovely as pictures, or grand vistas of enchantment. These can be the delight of your study if you can lose yourself in contemplation of them when sitting with a cup of fine tea. Once when planting narcissi I had no stones from Lingpi to put in the pot, so instead I used small pieces of coal that looked like stones. If one takes five or seven cabbage sprouts as white as jade and of various sizes, plants them in sand in a rectangular pot, and then covers the sand with small pieces of coal instead of stones, the black coal will contrast with the white cabbage and look most interesting. Thinking up possibilities like this can provide endless enjoyment, more than I can describe.

If one puts some calamus seeds in the mouth, chews them along with cold rice broth, and blows the mixture on to bits of charcoal which are then put in a dark and damp place, a very fine calamus will grow on them. The bits of charcoal can then be moved to a pot or a bowl, wherever one wants, and will look like stones covered with luxuriant moss.

Old lotus seeds can be ground off on each end and put into an eggshell, which can then be put with a chicken's other eggs and taken out when they hatch. Plant the seeds in a small pot using the mud from an old swallow's nest into which asparagus has been ground until it forms twenty per cent of the mixture. Water them with river water and let them get the light of the morning sun. When the flowers bloom they will be the size of a wine cup, and the leaves will have shrunk to the size of a bowl, a beautiful and charming effect.

In laying out gardens, pavilions, wandering paths, small mountains of stone, and flower plantings, try to give the feeling of the small in the large and the large in the small, of the real in the illusion, and of the illusion in the reality. Some things should be hidden and some should be obvious, some prominent and some vague. Arranging a proper garden is not just a matter of setting out winding paths in a broad area with many rocks; thinking that it is will only waste time and energy.

To make a miniature mountain, pile up some dirt, then place stones on it and plant flowers and grass here and there. The fence in front of it should be of plum trees, and the wall behind it should be covered with vines, so that it will look just like a mountain even though there is no mountain there.

This is a way of showing the small in the large: in an unused corner plant some bamboo, which will quickly grow tall, then plant some luxuriant plum trees in front to screen it.

This is a way to show the large in the small: the wall of a small garden should be winding and covered with green vines, and large stones decorated with inscriptions can be set into it. Then one will be able to open a window and, while looking at a stone wall, feel as if one were gazing out across endless precipices.

Here is a way to show the real amidst an illusion: arrange the garden so that when a guest feels he has seen everything he can suddenly take a turn in the path and have a broad new vista open up before him, or open a simple door in a pavilion only to find it leads to an entirely new garden.

There are several ways of creating an illusion amidst reality: make a gateway into a closed yard, and then cover it over with bamboo and stones; the yard beyond, while real, will then look like an illusion. Or, on top of a wall build a low railing; it will look like an upper balcony, creating an illusion from reality.

Poor scholars who live in small crowded houses should rearrange their rooms in imitation of the sterns of the Taiping boats of my home county, the steps of which can be made into three beds by extending them at front and back. Each bed is then separated from its neighbour by a board covered with paper. Looking at them when they are laid out is like walking a long road—you do not have a confined feeling at all. When Yün and I were living in Yangchou we arranged our house in this fashion. Though the house had only two spans, we divided it into two bedrooms, a kitchen, and a living room, and still had plenty of space left over. Yün had laughed about our handiwork, saying, 'The layout is fine, but it still does not quite have the feel of a rich home.' I had had to admit she was right!

Once while I was sweeping the family graves in the mountains, I came across some pretty patterned stones, which I took home and talked over with Yün. 'If you use putty to set Hsüanchou pebbles into a white stone pot,' I said, 'it looks attractive because the putty, the stones, and the pot are all the same colour. These yellow stones are lovely, but if I use the usual white putty on them it will contrast with the yellow of the stones and make the chisel marks on them stand out. What can I do about that?'

'Take the poorer stones,' said Yün, 'and pound them into dust. Mix the dust in with the putty and use it to fill in the chisel marks while it is still wet. When it dries perhaps the colours will be the same.'

We did as she suggested, and built up a miniature mountain in a rectangular pot from the kilns at Yihsing. The mountain was on the left, with another small mound on the right. Along the mountain we made horizontal patterns, similar to those on the mountains in paintings by Yün-lin. The cliffs were irregular, like those along a river bank. We filled an empty corner of the pot with river mud and planted duckweed, white with many petals. On top of the stones we planted morning glories, which are usually called cloud pines. It all took us several days to complete. By the deep autumn the morning glories had grown all over the mountain, covering it like wistaria hanging from a rock face, and when their flowers bloomed they were a deep red. The white duckweed also bloomed, and letting one's spirit wander among the red and the white was like a visit to Peng Island. We put the pot out under the eaves and discussed it in great detail: here we should build a pavilion on the water, there a thatched arbour; here we should inscribe a stone with the characters 'Where flowers drop and waters flow'. We could live here, we could fish there, from this other place we could gaze off into the distance. We were as excited about it as if we were actually going to move to those imaginary hills and vales. But one night some miserable cats fighting over something to eat fell from the eaves, smashing the pot in an instant.

I sighed, and said, 'Even this little project has incurred the jealousy of heaven!' Neither of us could keep from shedding tears.

Burning incense in a quiet room is one of the refined pleasures of leisure. Yün used to take garu wood and other fragrant things and steam them in a rice cauldron. Then we would burn them slowly on a brass stand about half an inch above a fire; the scent was subtle and lovely, and there was no smoke. Buddha's Hands should not be smelled by someone who is drunk, or they will spoil. Quinces should not be allowed to sweat; if they do, they should be washed with water. Only the *hsiangyüan* does not need special treatment.

There are also ways of arranging Buddha's Hands and quinces as decorations, but I cannot write out the details of these. Often people will thoughtlessly pick up and smell something fragrant that is part of an arrangement, and then just as thoughtlessly put it back; these are people who do not understand decoration.

When living at home I always had a vase of flowers on my desk. Once Yün said to me, 'No matter what the weather, you can always manage to put together beautiful flower arrangements. Now in painting there is a school that specializes in insects on grasses. Why don't you try your hand at that?'

'There's no way to control the wandering of insects. How can I study them?' I answered.

'There is a way, but I am afraid it seems almost criminal to me,' said Yün.

'Try telling me.'

'When an insect dies its colours do not change,' Yün said. 'You could find an insect like a praying mantis, a cicada, or a butterfly, and kill it by sticking it with a pin. Then use a fine wire to tie its neck to a flower or a blade of grass, arranging its feet to grasp the stem or stand on a leaf. It will look just as if it were alive. Wouldn't that work?'

I was delighted and did as she suggested. No one who saw these insects failed to praise them. It is hard to find such clever women these days!

While Yün and I were staying with the Huas at Hsishan, Madam Hua had her two daughters learn characters from Yün. As they studied, the summer sun beat down with a fierce glare in the courtyard of their country home, so Yün showed them how to make movable screens out of live flowers. Each of these screens had a base made by taking two thin sticks of wood four or five inches long and joining them with four crosspieces each about a foot long, making a flat platform like the top of a low stool. Then she drilled round holes at each corner of this and stood a lattice of bamboo in them. In the middle she put a pot filled with sand and planted with hyacinth beans, the vines of which would climb up the bamboo lattice. The screens were about six or seven feet tall, but two people could easily move one of them. They can be put anywhere you like, filling the windows with green shade and blocking the sun while letting a breeze through. If you make several, they can be set out in winding patterns that can be rearranged as you like; thus they are called 'movable flower screens'. Any climbing vines or fragrant plants can be used to make them, and they render life in the countryside most pleasant.

My friend Lu Pan-fang, whose courtesy name was Chang and whose literary name was Chün-shan, was a talented painter of pine and cypress trees, and of plum flowers and chrysanthemums. He could also write in the li script and inscribe chops. We once lived at his home, the Villa of Serenity, for a year and a half. The building we stayed in faced east and was of five spans, of which we occupied three. From our rooms we could gaze into the far distance, regardless of whether it was dark or bright, windy or rainy. In the yard there was a cassia tree with a lovely, clear fragrance, and the building itself had a hallway with side rooms, all very quiet.

When we moved there we took a servant couple with us, and they brought along their little daughter. The man could make clothes, and the woman could spin cotton; so to provide for our needs, Yün did embroidery, and the servant woman spun while her husband sewed.

I have always enjoyed entertaining, and for that we needed to buy a little wine for drinking games. Yün fortunately was good at making a meal without spending much money. Melon, vegetables, fish, and shrimps, when passed through Yün's hands, would take on a delicious taste. My friends knew I was poor, and they would often contribute some money for wine so that we could talk the day away. For my part, I kept the place spotless, and neither dominated the conversation nor objected to a casual atmosphere.

Among my friends were Yang Pu-fan, whose courtesy name was Chang-hsü and who was a talented portrait painter; Yüan Shao-yü, whose courtesy name was Pai and who was adept at painting mountains and rivers, and Wang Hsing-lan, whose courtesy name was Yen and who did skillful paintings of flowers and birds. They all liked the refined atmosphere at the Villa of Serenity, so they brought along their painting things and I studied with them. I would paint characters and carve chops, sell them, and give Yün the money so she could prepare tea and wine for our guests. We would spend the whole day doing nothing but criticizing poetry and talking about painting.

There were also the gentlemen Hsia Tan-an and his brother Yi-shan, Miao Shan-yi and his brother Chih-pai, and Chiang Yün-hsiang, Lu Chü-hsiang, Chou Hsiao-hsia, Kuo Hsiao-yü, Hua Hsin-fan, and Chang Hsien-han. They were like swallows on the rafters, coming and going as they pleased. Yün even sold her hairpins to buy wine without a second thought, because we did not want to give up lightly such a beautiful time and place. But now we are all parted like clouds blown by the wind. The jade is broken, the incense buried! I cannot bear to look back.

Four things were forbidden at the Villa of Serenity: talking about official promotions, official business, or the eight-legged official examinations, and playing cards or dice. Offenders were fined five catties of wine. Four things were encouraged: generosity, romantic refinement, an unrestrained atmosphere, and peace and quiet.

With nothing to do in the long summer, we held examination parties. There would be eight people at each party, and each would bring two hundred copper cash. We would draw lots, and the winner would become the examination master, sitting apart and being in charge of the proceedings. The second would be the official recorder, and also sat separately. Everyone else became an examination candidate, and drew a sheet of paper from the recorder, all properly stamped with a seal. The examination master would announce two lines of poetry, one of five characters and one of seven characters, and the candidates would then have the time it took a stick of incense to burn in which to write lines rhyming with them. They could walk or stand while thinking, but no one was allowed to talk or exchange ideas. When they had finished their couplets they put them into a box, and were then allowed to sit down. To prevent favouritism, when everyone had handed in his paper the recorder opened the box and copied the papers into a book which he then gave to the examination master.

From the sixteen couplets, the best three of seven-character lines and the best three of five-character lines would be chosen. The writer of the couplet selected as the best of these six became the next examination master, and whoever was placed second would be the next recorder. Those who failed to have either of their couplets chosen would be fined twenty cash, and anyone who had no more than one chosen would be fined ten; if someone went beyond the time limit, he was fined forty. The examination master for each round got one hundred cash incense money, so by playing ten rounds a day we would accumulate a thousand cash, enough for plenty of wine. Only Yün's was considered an official paper, and she was allowed to sit while thinking out her answers.

One day Yang Pu-fan did a sketch of Yün and me in the garden; it looked just like us. That night the moonlight was very beautiful, and the shadows the orchids sketched on the whitewashed wall were especially lovely. Hsing-lan was drunk, and merrily announced, 'Pu-fan can sketch your portrait, but I can paint the flowers' shadows.'

'But can you paint them as well as we were sketched?' I asked, laughing.

Hsing-lan then took a sheet of blank paper, put it up on the wall, and painted in the shadows with heavy and light ink, depending on whether they were dark or light as they were cast on the paper. We took it down and looked at it in the daylight, and while it could not be considered a true painting, he had captured the natural serenity of the leaves in the moonlight. Yün treasured it, and we all wrote inscriptions on it.

There were two places in Soochow, called the South Garden and the North Garden. We wanted to go there once when the rape flowers were in bloom, but unfortunately there were no wine houses near by where we could find something to drink. We could have taken a basket of things with us, but then we would have had to toast the flowers in cold wine and that would have been no fun at all. We talked about looking for a drinking place near by, and about first looking at the flowers and then coming home to drink, but neither sounded as much fun as toasting the flowers with warm wine.

We had not made up our minds what to do when Yün laughed. 'Tomorrow all of you give me some wine money, and I'll bring a small stove myself.'

Everyone laughed and agreed.

After they left, I asked Yün, 'Are you really going to bring a stove yourself?'

'No,' she said, 'but in the market I've seen dumpling-sellers who carry with them a pan, a small stove, and everything else we might need. Why not hire one of them to go with us? I can cook the food beforehand, and we can warm things up when we get there.'

'That sounds fine for the wine and the food,' I said, 'but what are you going to do for a teapot?'

'We can take along an earthenware pot,' said Yün, 'hang it right over the little stove with an iron hook, and add some more fuel to heat the tea. Wouldn't that work?'

I clapped my hands in approval. There was a dumpling-seller named Pao on the street corner, and I offered him a hundred cash to bring his things with us the next afternoon. He happily agreed. The next day when all those who were going with us to look at the flowers had arrived, I told them what we had done and they all sighed with admiration.

After lunch we went off to the South Garden, carrying cushions and mats with us. We picked a place in the shade of a willow tree and sat down. First we made tea, and when we had finished it, we warmed the wine and cooked the food. The wind and sun were exquisite. The earth was golden, and the blue clothes and red sleeves of strollers filled the paths between the fields, while butterflies and bees flew all around us. The scene was so intoxicating one hardly needed to drink. After a while the wine and food were ready, and everyone sat down on the ground to feast. The man who had helped us out was not an ordinary sort, so we persuaded him to come and join us in our drinking. The strollers who saw us all envied our clever idea. By the end of the afternoon cups and plates were scattered around and all of us were very jolly, some sitting and some lying down, some singing and some whistling. As the red sun set I felt like eating some rice porridge, so our helper quickly bought some rice and cooked it, and we all went home well satisfied.

'Did you all enjoy today's trip?' asked Yün.

'Without your help it wouldn't have been nearly so much fun,' they replied. Laughing and joking, we parted.

Poor scholars should be frugal but still refined and clean insofar as their home, clothing, and food are concerned. I define frugality as 'knowing when to save money'.

For example, at meals I like a little to drink but do not enjoy a great many dishes. So Yün once made a plum flower tray, by taking six white porcelain saucers two inches across and putting one in the middle and the five others around the outside, so that when set together they looked like a plum flower. These she painted grey, and then made a cover for the tray that was rounded with a handle on top shaped like a flower stem. When placed on the table it looked as if a plum flower had been put there, and the food seemed to have been set down on its petals. One tray with six different dishes was enough for a leisurely meal with two or three close friends. If we ate everything, we would just refill the tray. Yün also made a round tray with a low edge on which she could conveniently put things like cups, chopsticks, and wine pots, making it easy to carry them around and set them down wherever she liked. These are all examples of frugality in eating.

Yün also made all my caps, collars, and socks. If clothes develop holes, they can be patched by using pieces of the same garment. They should look neat and clean. Clothes should be dark in colour so that dirty spots will not show; then they can be worn either to go out, or around the house. These are examples of frugality in clothing.

When we first moved to the Villa of Serenity we felt our rooms were too dark, so we pasted white paper on the walls to brighten them up. During the summer we took out the downstairs windows, but there were no screens and we felt the place was too open and lacking in privacy.

'There are those old bamboo curtains,' said Yün. 'Why don't we use them in place of screens?'

'How?' I asked.

'We could take several lengths of bamboo and paint them black,' she said, 'and make a framework out of them that fills the top of the window while leaving the lower half of it empty. Then cut one of the bamboo curtains in half and hang it from the framework so that it reaches down as far as a table top. Four short pieces of bamboo can be tied up vertically in the empty space, and finally we can cover the crosspiece from which the bamboo curtain is hung by winding strips of old black cloth around it and sewing them together. It would give us privacy, be attractive, and not cost anything.'

This is another example of what I mean by 'knowing when to save money'. One should apply this rule in everything. The saying of the ancients, 'Even ends of bamboo and sawdust have their uses', is very true.

When lotus flowers bloom in the summer, they close up at night but open again in the morning. Yün used to put a few tea leaves in a gauze bag and put it inside a lotus flower before it closed in the evening. The next morning she would take out the tea and boil it with natural spring water. It had a wonderful and unique fragrance.

## Lu Xun (1881–1936)

*Translated by William A. Lyell*

Lu Xun has been lionized in the People's Republic as modern China's greatest writer, a status acquired more for political than literary reasons. As one of the founding members of the League of Leftist Writers in 1930, he maintained close relationships with left-wing activists up to the time of his death. He was attracted to literature because he believed that China was a sick nation and that literature was the best means to heal this spiritual sickness. Such an essentially utilitarian view of literature appealed to reformers and revolutionaries alike and played no small role in associating modern Chinese literature with the patriotic task of national salvation. Despite his strong political views and his heartfelt concerns for China's future, he remained a fiercely independent thinker who consistently attacked what he considered to be illogical opinions of either the right or the left. Perhaps he died at the right time to be made a hero, for he might have fared no better under the Communist Party than did many of his fellow intellectuals.

In 1902, years before his involvement in literary and political controversies, Lu Xun went to Japan with his brother to study medicine. There he read Japanese translations of such Russian realist writers as Chekhov, Andreyev, and Gogol. He was deeply impressed with what he considered to be their social consciousness and commended Gogol for "making the world aware of the hitherto invisible traces of tears on the tragic faces of suffering people."* With a desire to do the same for the Chinese people and to cure a national spiritual sickness, he turned from medicine to literature. During these years, the Chinese imperial government first tottered and then fell, and the entire Chinese tradition came under attack. Lu Xun quickly became a central figure in creating a new literature written in the vernacular "language of the people" rather than in the learned language of the Chinese classics. His writing struck some conservatives as harsh and crude, but literary reformers saw his short stories and essays as establishing a new standard for Chinese prose.

Of Lu Xun's many short stories, the best-known in both China and the West is *Ah Q—The Real Story.* This piece is a bitter satire of what Lu Xun considered to be China's national sickness. Ah Q, the central character and the representative of China, is a pathetic creature who construes every defeat and humiliation as a spiritual victory. Little more than a coward and a bully, he remains steadfastly convinced of his own moral superiority and blames everybody but himself for his repeated failures. He is finally drawn to revolution, more from a ridiculous need to feel powerful than from any genuine political knowledge, and he dies, like a character from a Kafka story, without ever quite understanding his crime.

The satire in *Ah Q* is fierce and cuts in many directions, at reformers and revolutionaries as much as at traditionalists. The narrator himself is a strange and complex presence. He wants to place his narrative in the tradition of biography,

*William A. Lyell, *Lu Hsün's Vision of Reality* (Berkeley, Los Angeles, London: University of California Press, 1976), 91.

but Ah Q is a nobody (the narrator does not even know his name), and the very act of so self-consciously preserving a record of Ah Q's misdeeds seems pointless. Some critics have reproved Lu Xun for "changing tone" from the facetious to the tragic midway through the story. Such mixing of tone, however, is itself a part of much modern literature and, in the case of *Ah Q*, may also be a part of the message. Surely Ah Q is too ridiculous to be tragic. At the same time, we cannot comfortably laugh at a character of such ignorance and self-delusion who is an insignificant part of a Chinese village of unrelenting coldness and cruelty. Perhaps the genius of Lu Xun exists in this very capacity to make us, his readers, feel embarrassed and uneasy as we read about a world the one-time student of medicine considered profoundly sick.

## *Ah Q—The Real Story*

### Chapter I

An Introduction

For at least a couple of years now, I've had it in the back of my mind to do a biography of Ah Q, but whenever it's come right down to it, I've always had second thoughts. Goes to show I'm not the kind of writer who *Forgeth words of immortalitie / For generations yet to be.* Besides, if you're going to get your words to last all that long, they've got to be about someone worth remembering all that long in the first place. Then the man gets remembered because of the words, and the words because of the man. And then after a while people gradually lose track of which one's remembered because of which. Knowing all of this, why did I finally settle on the likes of Ah Q for a biography? Guess the devil made me do it.

No sooner did I take up my writing brush to begin this very *un*immortal work of mine than I ran into a horrendous host of difficulties.

*One.* The question of a title. What *kind* of biography was it to be? As Confucius once said, "*Be the title not just so / Then the words refuse to flow.*" You really *do* have to be pretty darned careful about titles. But there are so many! Why, just for biographies alone there are enough titles hanging around to make your head swim: *narrative biography, autobiography, private biography, public biography, supplementary biography, family biography, biographical sketch.* Trouble is—not one of them fits.

*Narrative biography?* That's the kind done for well-heeled people rich enough to make it into the official histories, and Ah Q certainly wouldn't be at home in that crowd. *Autobiography?* But I'm not Ah Q. *Public biography?* Okay then, where's the *private* one? Or, why not just make this one the *private* one? But then *private biography* is the term they use for accounts of Daoist monks who live forever, and Ah Q doesn't fit in with that crew either. *Supplementary biography?* But then there'd have to be a *basic biography* for this to be supplementary *to,* and the president of our republic has yet to order the National Historical Institute to do the basic one. Still and all, that didn't stop Charles Dickens. You won't find any section entitled "Narrative Biographies of Gamblers" in the standard English histories, but he went right ahead and called one of his works *Alternate Biographies of Gamblers* just the same, even though there were no standard ones for them to be alternate to. Well, a literary giant like Dickens might get away with something like that, but I certainly wouldn't be able to pull it off.

How about *family biography?* Yes, but I'm not part of his family, nor has any of his descendants come by to commission me to do it. *Abbreviated biography* won't work either because there's no full one around. When you come right down to it, what I'm writing here is going to be the only standard biography of Ah Q you'll find anywhere. Of course I don't dare forget my place and call it that, for the style is "vulgar" and the language I've cast it in is not the language of the classics but rather the "vile vernacular of mere rickshaw boys and peddlers." And so in the end I've taken my title from a phrase that's popular among the storytellers, those lowly souls who have always been beyond the pale of the Three Doctrines and Nine Schools. Storytellers often end a long digression with the cliché, "Enough of this idle chatter, let's get back to the *real story.*" That's where I got my title from. And if "real story" in this context gets mixed up with the "real story" in that book left to us by the ancients, *The Real Story of Calligraphy*—well, sorry, I just don't have the time to worry about all that.

*Two.* The standard format for biographies requires that you begin with something like: "So-and-so, whose courtesy name was this-or-that, was a native of such-and-such." The trouble is I don't know what Ah Q's family name was. There was once a day when it *seemed* to be Zhao, but then the very next morning it wasn't all that clear anymore. That was the day Old Master Zhao's son passed the *Budding Talent* exam.

With a *clang-clang* of gongs and all the usual pomp, the good news arrived in the village. As luck would have it, Ah Q had just downed a bowl of wine or two. Soon as he heard the news, he danced for joy and told everyone what a great honor this was to him *personally* because he belonged to the same clan as Old Master Zhao. As a matter of fact, the way Ah Q had it worked out, he even came out three notches above the *Budding Talent* in the clan's generational pecking order! The people who were standing around when Ah Q announced this actually began to treat him with more respect too.

Who could have foreseen that the very next day the local sheriff would order Ah Q to hightail it on out to the Zhaos' place? As soon as Old Master Zhao clapped eyes on Ah Q, the old fellow's face flushed scarlet. "Ah Q, you miserable bastard," he bellowed, "did you say you're a clansman of mine?"

Ah Q didn't let out a peep. The more the old man looked at him, the madder he got. He bore in a few steps closer: "How dare you talk such rubbish? How could *I* possibly have a clansman like *you?*"

Still not a peep. Just as Ah Q was about to beat a hasty retreat, Old Master Zhao bolted forward and slapped him across the face. "How could *you* be named Zhao? How could you even *deserve* to be named Zhao?"

Instead of offering any argument to prove that he was an honest-to-goodness Zhao, Ah Q simply retreated on out through the gate, putting his hand to his cheek as he went. The sheriff escorted him and gave him another good bawling out once they were outside. Only after Ah Q had greased that notable's palm with two hundred coppers was he free of him. Everybody who heard about this agreed that Ah Q had been too reckless, that he had gone *looking* for a beating, for more than likely he wasn't named Zhao in the first place. And supposing he was? What with Master Zhao living right there in the area, he shouldn't have been dumb enough to say so. After that, nobody ever mentioned Ah Q's family background again. And so—to make a long story short—I have no idea what his family name was.

*Three.* I don't know how to write his *given* name either. While he was alive everybody called him Ah-QUEI, but after he died, even the man on the street never thought of mentioning his name again. Much less did any scholar-official take it into his head to *inscribe it on bamboo and silk for generations yet to be.* And so it is that I lead the way in facing up to a linguistic crisis: should the QUEI be written with the character meaning "laurel" or with the one meaning "high rank"?

If Ah Q had used the character meaning "moon pavilion" as his courtesy name, or if he had been born in the eighth lunar month, then his given name would certainly be written with the QUEI meaning "laurel." But he didn't *have* a courtesy name. Or if he did, nobody knew it. If only at some point in his career he had sent out invitations soliciting eulogies on the grand occasion of his fiftieth or sixtieth birthday, the way scholar-officials do, then I could check "laurel" against those. But since Ah Q never sent out any such invitations, it would be downright dogmatic of me to insist on "laurel."

Again, if he'd had an elder or younger brother named Ah Fu, written with the *fu* that means "riches," then Ah Q's QUEI would certainly be written with the character meaning "high rank" so as to balance it. But Ah Q was a loner, and so I've got no evidence in favor of the word meaning "high rank" either. I have even less of a case for any of the other relatively obscure characters pronounced "QUEI." I once tried asking Old Master Zhao's son, his nibs the *Budding Talent.* You can imagine my surprise when I ended up drawing a blank from someone as learned and cultivated as Mister *Budding Talent* himself. But the upshot of what little he *did* have to say was that there was no longer any way of telling what character "QUEI" should be, because ever since Chen Duxiu had put out that radical magazine *New Youth* and advocated scrapping the Chinese characters altogether in favor of spelling with a foreign alphabet, our "national heritage" had sunk into utter oblivion.

The only thing I hadn't tried was writing to a certain friend back home. And so I got off a letter to him asking him to look up Ah Q's police record. Didn't get a reply for eight months. When it did come, my friend said he hadn't been able to find any name that sounded even remotely like Ah-QUEI. I still don't know if that was really the case or whether he just hadn't bothered to look it up in the first place. At any rate, I was at a dead end.

I'm afraid the Chinese phonetic symbols aren't all that popular yet, and so I've had to resort to a foreign word to represent the second character in my hero's given name. According to the popular English way of spelling Chinese it would be QUEI, or just "Q" for short. Now I'll grant you this comes perilously close to blindly following *New Youth*—and I am terribly sorry about that—but when even a wise and learned *Budding Talent* doesn't know what character to use, what can you expect from the likes of me?

*Four.* The question of his native place. If his family name were definitely Zhao then I could follow the custom, so popular in present-day biographical writing, of naming the ancient district from whence his family hailed. That way, basing myself on the standard reference, *The Hundred Surnames and Their Places of Origin,* I could assert with confidence that our Ah Q *doth a Tianshui man of Longxi be.* Trouble is, since it's somewhat doubtful that Zhao was his family name in the first place, how can I assert with any degree of certainty *where* his family came from? Granted, he lived mostly in Wei Village, but he often spent time in other places too. And so if I wrote that Ah Q *doth a Tianshui man of Longxi be,* I'd be downright guilty of violating the hallowed principles of historiography.

There's one thing I do pride myself on: when you take the "Q" away from "Ah Q," you've still got an "Ah" there, and I'm positive I haven't mixed that character up with any other. I could show that one off to anybody, no matter how learned. As to the rest, well, that's beyond the scope of a man of shallow scholarship like myself. I can only hope that the disciples of Mr. Hu Shi, who describes himself as having a "weakness for historical research coupled with an addiction to textual criticism," will be able to ferret out new clues at some time in the future. But by that time I'm afraid my "Ah Q—The Real Story" will have long since passed out of existence.

What I've written up to here may be taken as a preface.

## Chapter 2

### A Brief Account of His Victories

Not only is there a certain vagueness surrounding Ah Q's given name, family name, and place of origin, but there is also a great deal of uncertainty regarding his "official resumé." Since the people in Wei Village were only interested in Ah Q for his labor—or to serve as the butt of their jokes—they had never paid any attention to what "positions" he had held in the past. Nor did Ah Q himself ever throw any light on his background, except when in the course of a squabble he would occasionally glower at someone and say, "We used to be much richer than you! Who the hell do you think you are anyway?"

Having no family, Ah Q lived at the local Land-and-Grain Temple, and having no fixed occupation, he did odd jobs. When there was wheat to be harvested, he harvested it; when there was rice to be hulled, he did that; and if there was a boat to be poled, he'd turn his hand to that too. When a job lasted a bit longer than the usual, he might temporarily put up at the home of his employer, but once the work was done, he'd move out.

When the busy season came, to be sure, people's minds would turn to Ah Q, but what they would think about was his ability to work and not the particulars of his "resumé." Once the busy season was over they would have forgotten his very *existence,* not to mention the details of his past career. There was only a single instance when anyone had ever praised him, and that was when an old man had said, "That Ah Q's *some* worker!" Bare-chested at the time and standing right in front of the old man, Ah Q looked so scrawny and worn-out that one couldn't tell whether the old fellow had really meant it or was simply making fun of him. Nonetheless, Ah Q had been pleased as punch.

Since he thought so well of *himself*, Ah Q considered the other villagers simply beneath his notice. He went so far with this that he even looked down his nose at the village's two *Young Literati*. He didn't realize, of course, that up there in the rarefied world of scholar-officialdom *those whom one doth Young Literati name* can darn well get to be *those whom one must Budding Talents proclaim*—if you don't keep an eye on them. That's why Old Master Qian and Old Master Zhao were so all-fired respected in the village: they were daddies to those two *Young Literati*—and rich to boot. Ah Q, however, was less than impressed. "My son's gonna be a lot richer." On top of that, Ah Q had been to town a couple of times and that made him even more full of himself. Yet he could be contemptuous of townsfolk too. For instance, Wei Villagers called a seat made from a three-foot plank a *longbench* and so did Ah Q, but the townsfolk called it a *stickbench*. "That's not right, that's flatass dumb!" he thought to himself. And how about fish? When frying bigheads, Wei Villagers would toss chopped scallions into the pan, but the townsfolk always used *shredded* ones. "That's not right, that's flatass stupid!" he thought to himself. "On the other hand, I gotta remember that next to me, Wei Villagers are just a bunch of hicks. They've never even *seen* how bigheads are fried in town."

So Ah Q used to be rich, had seen a thing or two, and was "some" worker—in sum, he came very close to being the perfect man. Unfortunately, however, he had a few physical shortcomings, the most annoying of which was an assortment of shiny scars that had been left on his scalp by an attack of scabies. Despite the undeniable fact that those scars had the good fortune to be attached to Ah Q's body, strange to say, he didn't seem to think them particularly worth bragging about. And so it was that he shunned the word "scabies" and any other word sounding even remotely like it.

He later expanded the scope of this taboo until it included words like "bright" and "shiny" and—still later—even "lamp" and "candle." Whether it was intentional or not, if anyone should violate this taboo, Ah Q would seethe with anger until every last one of his scabies scars would flush its deepest red. Then he would size up his opponent: if it happened to be someone who stuttered so badly that he couldn't get the second word out after the first, Ah Q would curse him up one side and down the other; if it was someone so puny and weak that he could hardly stand, Ah Q would start a fight. And yet, strange to tell, in all such encounters Ah Q somehow still managed to come out the loser more often than not. After some time, he modified his plan of battle and for the most part simply gave his opponent a dirty look.

Who would have expected that after Ah Q adopted his policy of dirtylookism, the Wei Village idlers would take even greater pleasure in taunting him? As soon as they set eyes on him, they would draw back in feigned surprise and say, "Hey, it's getting lighter out!"

As usual, Ah Q would start to go into a slow boil.

"Oh, so that's it, there's a kerosene lamp here—no wonder!" They weren't about to be intimidated by any dirty look from the likes of Ah Q.

Since a dirty look didn't seem to do it, he would try a snappy comeback: "Why you guys don't even deserve to gaze on . . ." At this point it usually seemed as if those whatchamacallits up there on his head had been transformed into grand and glorious *Scars de Scabie,* not at all to be confused with the ordinary variety. But as I have said before, our Ah Q was a man of keen insight, and therefore he would realize immediately that he was on the verge of violating his own taboo and would catch himself up in midsentence.

Not content to let it go at that, the Wei Village idlers would keep right on baiting him until it all ended up in a fight anyway. From a purely formal point of view, Ah Q would be defeated: he would be grabbed by his discolored queue, and would have his head given four or five resounding thumps against a wall. Then the idlers would walk away, fully satisfied and fully victorious. Ah Q would stand there for a bit and then think to himself, "It's just as though I'd been beaten up by my own sons! What's the world coming to, anyway, when sons . . ." At this point Ah Q too would walk away, fully satisfied and fully victorious.

Later on Ah Q took to saying out loud the various things he thought to himself. And so it was that before long every Ah-Q-baiter in the village was onto his schemes for winning psychological victories. From then on, whenever Ah Q's discolored queue was grabbed, his tormentor would steal a march on him as well: "Ah Q, this isn't a son beatin' up on his old man, it's a human being beatin' up on an *animal!* Let's hear *you* say it now, 'A human being beatin'up on an animal'!"

Holding fast to the base of his queue with both hands, Ah Q would cock his head to one side and rejoin: "Beatin' up on a *bug,* does that make you happy? Now give a guy a break, huh?"

But even though he was only a "bug," the idlers still wouldn't let him off the hook. In the time-honored fashion, they would seek out the nearest wall and give his head four or five resounding thumps before walking away, fully satisfied and fully victorious —and convinced that *this* time they had done him in once and for all. But before ten seconds were out, Ah Q would also walk away, fully satisfied and fully victorious, for he was convinced that of all the "self-putdown artists" this old world has seen, he was number one. Take away "self-putdown artist" and what did you have left? *Number one*—that's what! What was a *Metropolitan Graduate? Number one*—that's all. "Who the hell do these jerks think they are anyway!" Having subdued his foes with such ingenious strategems, Ah Q would go happily off to the wineshop and down a few bowls. He would banter with some, squabble with others, and then on the crest of fresh victories, would make his way happily back to the Land-and-Grain Temple, put his head down on his pillow, and go to sleep.

If he happened to have money, he'd go and play a round of *Pickaside.* As people crowded around the gambling stand, Ah Q would sandwich his way in among them, his face bathed in sweat. Of all the voices his would be the loudest.

"Four hundred on *Green Dragon!*"

"Oh-kay, off with the cover and let's see which side has turned up!" His face bathed in sweat, the stakeholder would take off the cover. "*Heaven's Gate* gets the money! *In-the-Corner* splits even! Nobody on *White Tiger* or *Through-the-Hall!* Pass Ah Q's dough over here!"

"One hundred on *Through-the-Hall*—make it a hundred and fifty!"

In the midst of the stakeholder's incantations, Ah Q's money would gradually make its way into the pockets of other people whose faces, like his own, were also bathed in sweat. Finally Ah Q would have to squeeze his way back through the crowd and stand on the sidelines, now reduced to becoming excited or disappointed on someone else's behalf. He would continue to watch until the game broke up and then reluctantly make his way back to the Land-and-Grain Temple. Next day, with swollen eyes, Ah Q would go to work.

It is true, however, that losing can sometimes be a blessing in disguise, for once when Ah Q *did* actually win, he came very close to losing.

It was on a night when Wei Village was holding a festival of thanksgiving to the gods. As usual, a religious opera was performed. As usual again, a number of gambling stands were set up close to the stage. So as far as Ah Q was concerned, the orchestra's crashing cymbals and pounding drums might just as well have been miles away, for he heard nothing but the singsong chant of the stakeholder. Ah Q won! He won again! And then again he won some more! Copper pennies turned into silver dollars, and the dollars piled up into a tall stack. Ah Q was beside himself. "Two dollars on *Heaven's Gate!*"

He never found out who started the fight or why, but at any rate he suddenly found himself buried under a pandemonium of curses, blows, and kicks. No sooner had he struggled to his feet than he discovered that the gambling stand was gone, and the people who had been surrounding it were nowhere to be seen. His body seemed to hurt in a couple of spots, as though he too had taken a few punches and kicks. One or two people looked at him in surprise. Looking somewhat lost, he made his way back to the Land-and-Grain Temple. After collecting himself a bit, he realized that his pile of silver dollars had disappeared. Since most people who set up gambling stands at festivals like this didn't come from the village themselves, there was no possible way of ever finding out what actually had happened.

What a bright and glittering pile of dollars that had been, too. And now they were gone. Gone! He tried to write the whole thing off by telling himself that he'd been robbed by his own sons, but somehow or other he still felt disappointed and depressed. Then he considered dismissing it by calling himself a bug, but somehow or other that left him feeling just as depressed and disappointed as ever. For the first time in Ah Q's life, he tasted something like the real bitterness of defeat.

But then, in the twinkling of an eye, he transformed that defeat into victory! He raised his right hand and, one after the other, gave himself two sharp slaps across the mouth. His face burned with a prickly pain. After those slaps, however, he began to feel at peace with himself. It was as though Ah Q had done the slapping and the person he had slapped was some *other*

Ah Q. And before too long it actually seemed as though he had slapped someone else altogether—though he had to admit that his own face still stung a bit. Complacent and content, Ah Q now lay down—victorious.

He slept.

## Chapter 3

A Brief Account of His Victories (cont.)

Although Ah Q was indeed often victorious, it wasn't until he had been graced with a slap across the mouth from Old Master Zhao—for his temerity in laying claim to the Zhao family name—that he finally became famous.

That day, after he had greased the sheriff's palm to the tune of two hundred coppers, Ah Q went home and lay down fuming with anger. But before very long, he began to think, "What's the world coming to when a son strikes his own father?" And then his thoughts turned another corner as he considered the great prestige that Old Master Zhao enjoyed in the village. Gradually Ah Q began feeling quite pleased with himself that such a prestigious man was now his son. He got up and headed off to the wineshop, singing the strains of *The Young Widow Visits Her Husband's Grave* as he went. At this juncture, Ah Q truly felt that Old Master Zhao really *was* a cut above everyone else.

Strange to tell, after the slapping incident everyone did in fact seem to treat Ah Q with unusual respect. The way Ah Q saw it, this was probably because he was Old Master Zhao's father. But if the truth be known, that wasn't it at all. Instead it was the result of a Wei Village precedent that ran something like this: if Ah-seven slugged Ah-eight, or if Li-four clobbered Zhang-three, no one thought anything of it. But if such an incident was connected to some eminent personage like his nibs Old Master Zhao, then it would be permanently recorded on the lips of the people. And after that, because the man who had done the striking was already famous, the man who had been hit would ride to renown on his coattails.

It goes without saying, of course, that everyone laid the blame for the incident on Ah Q. Now, here one might be tempted to ask, "*Pray tell wherein lieth the why and the wherefore of that?*" Simple. His nibs Old Master Zhao *couldn't* be wrong! But if Ah Q *was* the one at fault, then why should everyone treat him with such respect? Well, that's a tough one. A rough answer might go something like this: though it's true that Ah Q got slapped for claiming to be a clansman of Old Master Zhao, who's to say that there might not be some truth to it? On the off chance that there was, it would still be prudent to treat Ah Q with respect. Or perhaps it may have been related to the example of the Sacrificial Ox in the Confucian Temple. Although the ox is just as much a domestic animal as the pig or sheep, Confucian scholars would not dare commit the blasphemy of eating its meat once the spirit of Confucius had set his chopsticks to it during the sacrifice. And in point of fact, for several years after the slapping incident things went swimmingly for Ah Q.

In the spring of one year, a pleasantly inebriated Ah Q was walking down the street when he chanced upon Bearded Wang. Chest bared, Wang sat in the sunlight at the base of a wall, picking lice out of his jacket. Ah Q suddenly became aware of an itching sensation on his own body too. Now this Bearded Wang was not only bearded, but boasted a set of scabies scars as well, and so everyone else called him *Scabby* Bearded Wang. Ah Q, on the other hand, edited out the "scabby" but disdained the man completely nonetheless. It wasn't that Ah Q saw anything all that unusual in being scabby, but that beard of Wang's was going just a bit too far—what an eyesore! But now Ah Q sat down right next to him. Had it been any other villager, he wouldn't have been so bold, but what did he have to fear from the likes of Bearded Wang? As a matter of fact, he was doing Bearded Wang an honor by being willing to sit down with him in the first place.

Ah Q peeled off his raggedy old jacket and turned it inside out. But a prolonged search yielded—perhaps because the jacket had recently been washed, or perhaps because Ah Q didn't look carefully enough—only three or four lice. He looked over and saw that Bearded Wang was picking them out one after the other and sometimes even two or three at a time. What's more, those lice kept going *pow pow pow,* as loud as you please, when Bearded Wang popped them between his teeth.

At first Ah Q felt merely disappointed, but after a while he began to resent the downright injustice of it all—to think that even the low-life likes of Bearded Wang could come up with all those nice lice while he, on the other hand, could find only a paltry few. Why it was nothing short of a social disgrace! How he longed to find a couple of good big ones. But he simply couldn't. It was all he could do to come up with even one *medium* louse. He angrily thrust that one between his teeth and bit down with all his might—only a piddling little *pop,* nothing to compare with Bearded Wang's loud and lusty *pows.* Now every last scabies scar on Ah Q's head flushed scarlet. He hurled his jacket to the ground and spat with disgust. "Hairy beast!"

"Who are you cursin' out, you mangy dog?" Bearded Wang raised his eyes and gave Ah Q a contemptuous glance.

Although people had treated Ah Q a bit more respectfully of late, making him more full of himself than ever, still he was always cautious in the presence of the Wei Village idlers, all of whom would just as soon fight as have breakfast. In fact this was the first time he had dared to put on such a martial display before one of them. Did this hairy-faced beast actually have the gall to use intemperate language within Ah Q's hearing?

"If the shoe fits!" Ah Q got up and put his hands on his waist.

"Are your bones itchin' for a good trouncin'?" Bearded Wang stood up and threw his jacket across his shoulders.

Thinking that Bearded Wang was getting ready to make a run for it, Ah Q sprang forward and threw a punch. But before his fist had reached its mark, Bearded Wang grabbed it and gave it such a yank that Ah Q went stumbling forward completely off balance. At the same time, with his free hand, Bearded Wang grabbed Ah Q's queue, twisted it fast, and prepared to drag him over to the wall and smack his head against it in the time-honored fashion.

"*His fists need never be swung, for the gentleman useth his tongue,*" quoted Ah Q, head cocked to one side.

It would appear, however, that Bearded Wang was no gentleman, for ignoring this classical lore, he slammed Ah Q's head against the wall five times in succession, and then gave him a good hard shove that sent Ah Q staggering away, fighting to regain his balance. Thoroughly satisfied then, Bearded Wang strode away.

In Ah Q's memory, this could probably be reckoned as the first real disgrace of an entire lifetime, for Bearded Wang—flawed by a beard growing rampant all over his face—had always been the object of Ah Q's taunts, and had certainly never before made light of Ah Q, much less dared to lay hands on him. Thus the event that had just transpired was something totally unexpected. Could it possibly be true, as people were saying in town, that the emperor had put an end to the civil service examinations and did not need *Budding Talents* anymore? Could it be that the Zhao family's prestige had consequently declined and that people now felt free to look down on Ah Q as a result?

Thrown for a loss, Ah Q just stood there.

Out of the distance, someone else was coming toward him—another enemy had arrived. This too was one of the people whom Ah Q most detested, the son of Old Master Qian. Some time back, this lad had gone off to town and attended one of those new fangled academies where they taught foreign things along with Chinese subjects. After that, somehow or other, he'd sailed off to Japan. By the time he came back half a year later he was walking stiff-legged, just the way foreigners do, and his queue was gone! That was enough to send his mother into a good dozen fits of wailing and his dear wife had thrice tried to drown herself in the well. Later on his mother went around saying: "Some hoodlums got him drunk and cut it off. He could have been an important official, but now we can't make any plans until it grows back again." Ah Q, however, did not buy a word of it and made a point of calling him "fake foreign devil" or "foreign sellout," cursing him under his breath the moment he set eyes on him.

But the thing that Ah Q, in the tradition of all the doughty heroes of yore, did *shunneth full well and righteously repel* was that fake queue. To have a queue and sink so low as to let it be a *fake* one was clear proof that the man had lost all claim to humanity, and since that wife of his hadn't taken a fourth dive into the well, she obviously couldn't be a good woman either.

This Fake Foreign Devil came closer.

"Baldy! Jackass!" Now, previously Ah Q had always said that kind of thing under his breath, but today after his defeat at the hands of Bearded Wang, he was seething with fury and hungry for revenge. Lightly, yet quite audibly, the words escaped his lips before even *he* knew they were out.

To Ah Q's surprise, "Baldy" started moving directly toward him, a yellow-lacquered cane—what Ah Q called *a wailing stick*—in his hand. In that split second Ah Q realized he was probably in for a drubbing. Pulling his head down between his shoulders, he braced himself for the worst. *WHACK!* Sure enough, there was the right sound, and it felt as though a blow had landed on his head, too. Ah Q pointed to a child nearby and offered defensively, "I was talking about *him!*"

*WHACK! WHACK-WHACK!*

In Ah Q's memory, this could probably be reckoned as the *second* real disgrace of an entire lifetime. Fortunately, however, by the time the whacking sounds had subsided, he had begun to feel somewhat relaxed. It was rather as if he'd just completed some pressing task that had to be done. What was more, "forgetfulness"—that priceless medicine handed down to us by our ancestors—began to take its effect too. He headed away toward the wineshop and by the time he drew near the door he had long since begun to feel quite happy again.

But walking straight toward him was a young Buddhist nun from the Convent of Silent Cultivation. Even in ordinary times, Ah Q would always have spit whenever he ran across a nun and now, having just been humiliated, he had all the more reason. At this point he began to think back over his day and once again began itching for revenge. He walked straight toward her and spat on the ground.

"*Aaaaaaawk . . . tuh!*"

Doing her best to ignore him, the young nun lowered her head and kept on her way. Ah Q fell in step beside her. Suddenly he reached over and fondled the skin of her shaved head. "Hey Baldy, better hurry on back—your monk's waitin' for ya," he said with an inane smile.

"What's gotten into you? Get your filthy paws off me!" Her face flushing scarlet, the nun hurried onward.

The patrons of the wineshop roared with laughter. Seeing that his meritorious service to the court had gained such great favor with these tippling nobles, Ah Q felt his spirits soar ever higher. "If the monk can fondle you, then why can't I?" He pinched her cheek between his thumb and forefinger.

Once again the patrons of the wineshop roared with laughter, and Ah Q was even more elated. Then, so as to fully satisfy these courtly connoisseurs of his martial performance, he gave the nun's cheek a final pinch before letting her go.

Because of this encounter with the nun, Ah Q had long since forgotten Bearded Wang and the Fake Foreign Devil as well. It was as if he'd avenged himself for all the bad luck he'd had that day. Strange to tell, his whole body seemed to feel relaxed, too, even more relaxed than after the echoes of the Fake Foreign Devil's *WHACK! WHACK-WHACK!* had died away. Walking on air, Ah Q seemed ready to take off and soar away at any minute.

"May you never have a son, Ah Q!" He heard the sound of the nun's sobbing voice in the distance.

"Hah, hah, hah!" One hundred percent elated, Ah Q laughed.

"Hah, hah!" Ninety percent elated, the patrons of the wineshop laughed too.

## Chapter 4

### The Tragedy of Love

It has long been noted that some conquerors prefer enemies as fierce as tigers and brave as eagles, for only then can they savor the true joy of victory. If, on the other hand, their foes are as tame as sheep or timid as chickens, then they find no pleasure in their triumph.

Then too, you have the conqueror who overcomes all opposition, sees his enemies die or surrender, and finally reports his victory back to the throne: "*In fear and trembling, thy servant draws his breath, who, in addressing you, deserveth only death.*" Such a conqueror has no enemies, no rivals, and no friends—he has nothing left except himself, standing there in utter isolation at the very apex of his triumph, lonely and forlorn. At such a time the hero experiences not the joy of victory, but rather its poignant melancholy.

Rest assured, dear reader, that our Ah Q was not so feckless as any of the above. No, he was *always* full of himself. Perhaps we have here yet another proof that the spiritual civilization of China is superior to any other on the face of the earth.

Why just look at him! Tripping along on air like that, he might well soar skyward and fly away at any moment!

And yet there was something about this *particular* victory that made Ah Q feel somehow—different. After tripping along on air for quite some time, he finally floated back to the Land-and-Grain Temple. Now ordinarily at this point he would have flopped down and begun to snore. Who would have thought that tonight he wouldn't even be able to get his eyes shut? There was something very strange—he could feel it—going on in the index finger and thumb of one hand. Could it be that there was something soft and smooth on that young nun's face that had somehow rubbed off on them? Or could it be that he had somehow rubbed his finger and thumb smooth on her face?

"May you never have a son, Ah Q!"

The nun's curse echoed in his ears again and set Ah Q to thinking, "That's right, oughta have a woman! If I die with no son, who's gonna sacrifice a bowl of rice now and then for my ghost to eat? Yeah, gotta get me a woman!"

Now bear in mind, gentle reader, *Of three things which do unfilial be / The worst is to lack posteritie.* And then too, if you also remember how the classics tell of the exemplary concern of Ziwen, in those days of yore, lest *the ghosts of the Ruo'ao clan go hungry, woman and man*—a great human tragedy, indeed!—then you'll see right off quick that Ah Q's thinking was, as a matter of fact, thoroughly in accord with the sagacious morality of our classical tradition. Unfortunately, however, after his thoughts started galloping off in this direction, Ah Q *completely lacked the art to rein in his unbridled heart.*

"Woman, woman!" Ah Q thought to himself.

And then Ah Q thought to himself again, ". . . if the monk can fondle you . . . woman . . . woman!"

There is no way of telling when it was that Ah Q finally began to snore that night. What is certain, however, is that from that time forward his index finger and thumb always had a certain smooth feel to them, and so it was that from that time forward, too, he was always walking on air. "Woman!!!" Ah Q thought to himself.

From this instance alone, you can see what baleful creatures women be. Now by rights most Chinese men could have become saints or sages a long time back—trouble is, they were all done in by women. The Shang dynasty [1766–1122 B.C.] was brought down by the enticing Da Ji, and the captivating Bao Si destroyed the Zhou [1122–221 B.C.]. As for the Qin dynasty [221–206 B.C.], though we can't find any clear statement as to exactly what happened, we probably wouldn't be one hundred percent wrong if we assumed that a female had put that one on the skids, too. And we know for an undeniable fact that it was because of the singsong girl Diao Chan that Dong Zhuo [d. A.D. 192] was killed.

Now our Ah Q started out as an upright man too. Though we don't know if this was because he had been shown the way by some enlightened teacher, we do know that he rigorously observed *the great barrier that should be 'twixt the he and the she* and was well endowed with a sense of moral uprightness that made him despise heretical behavior such as that of the young nun or the Fake Foreign Devil. Ah Q's philosophy ran like this: Any nun is bound to be secretly shacked up with a monk. If a woman is out walking on the street, she's certainly trying to seduce a man or two. If a man and woman are talking to each other, they're sure to be arranging a tryst. He often employed his dirty-lookism to punish such miscreants. Occasionally he would voice a loud comment to show that *he* knew what a couple was "really up to," no matter how innocent their behavior might seem on the surface. And occasionally—if the place was isolated—he'd throw a pebble at them from behind.

Who could possibly have foreseen that just as he was approaching the age when, like Confucius, he should have "stood firm," Ah Q would be so subverted by a young Buddhist nun that he would go around walking on air. Now according to the tenets of Confucian morality, the kinds of feelings engendered by airwalking are *not* the kinds of feelings one should have in the first place. So we can readily see what utterly despicable creatures females really are. If the young nun's face had not been so smooth, Ah Q would not have fallen, or had there been a veil between her face and his fingers, things would never have gone so far either. As a matter of fact, five or six years back he'd even pinched a girl's thigh once while watching an opera, but in that case her trousers had separated his fingers from her skin, so that the experience had not been enough to set him airwalking afterwards. In the case of the young nun, however, things had been entirely different. Goes to show you what a detestable and heretical doctrine Buddhism really is, too.

"Woman!" thought Ah Q.

He constantly kept an eye out for women who were "trying to seduce a man or two," but none of them so much as smiled at him. Whenever a woman talked with him, Ah Q kept a close ear to everything that was said but still he heard nothing that was even vaguely related to "having an affair." Why of course! That's partly what made women so rotten in the first place—the hypocrites all *pretended* to be straight!

After supper one evening, Ah Q sat in Old Master Zhao's kitchen having a leisurely smoke on his pipe. He had just put in a full day of hulling rice. If it had been at anyone else's place, he would have gone right home after supper, but here the situation was somewhat different. Ordinarily the Zhao family ate quite early, for it was an established item of family protocol that no one was allowed to waste good money lighting a lamp. People simply went straight to bed after supper. There were, however, certain exceptions to the rule: Old Master Zhao's young hopeful had been permitted to burn the midnight oil while preparing for his *Budding Talent* exam, and Ah Q was allowed to hull rice by lamplight whenever he came to help out during the busy season. Indeed, that's why he could not afford to sit and dawdle over his pipe like this.

Having finished the dishes, Amah Wu, the one and only maid in Old Master Zhao's household, sat down on the *longbench* next to Ah Q and began to chat. "The Old Missus hasn't eaten a thing for days now. It's all because the Old Master's going to buy a concubine."

"Woman . . . Amah Wu . . . this nice young widow," Ah Q thought to himself.

"Our Young Missus is going to have a baby in August and . . ."

"WOMAN," thought Ah Q to himself. He put down his pipe and stood up.

". . . the Young Missus says . . ." Amah Wu prattled on.

Now Ah Q moved directly in front of her and knelt at her feet. "Sleep with me! Sleep with me!"

For a brief instant you could have heard a pin drop.

"*AIYA!!!*" Amah Wu had been stunned speechless at first. And then quite suddenly, she had begun to tremble, and then she had let out that big aiya-scream. Now she bolted for the door and ran outside, screaming as she went. It sounded as if she was crying, too.

Ah Q found himself kneeling before a blank wall. He too was stunned for a moment. Placing his hands on the *longbench,* he slowly dragged himself to his feet, barely conscious that he'd probably gotten himself into some kind of mess. Heart pounding, he hastily thrust his pipe into his belt and made ready to go back to his hulling when *BONG!* a good solid blow landed on his head. He turned and saw the young *Budding Talent* standing before him, a heavy staff in hand.

"Rebellious wretch, why you . . ."

The heavy pole clove the air again. Ah Q grabbed the top of his head with both hands. *WHACK!* The blow landed on his knuckles and hurt more than a little. As he burst through the kitchen door, he seemed to feel yet another hard blow land on his back.

"Turtle's egg!" the *Budding Talent* cursed from behind.

Ah Q ran to the hulling shed as fast as his legs would carry him. He stood there alone. Pain lingered in his fingers, and the expression "turtle's egg" in his mind, for that was one locution that the countryfolk of Wei Village never used. Only rich people who rubbed noses with officials said fancy things like that, and thus it made a deep impression on Ah Q and gave him quite a fright to boot. By now, all those "woman" thoughts had left him. What was more, having taken a good cursing and beating, he felt as though he had actually accomplished something, gotten it over and done with. And so before long, without a care in the world, Ah Q set himself to hulling rice again. He worked up a sweat and paused to strip down.

While taking off his shirt, Ah Q heard a loud commotion somewhere outside. Now Ah Q had never liked anything better than a bit of excitement, and so without a second thought he headed off in the direction of the noise. Little by little, the sounds led him to the inner courtyard outside Old Master Zhao's rooms. Although it was dusk, Ah Q was able to make out several of the people: Old Master Zhao's wife—the one who hadn't eaten for two days in a row—Seventh Sister Zou from next door, and two honest-to-goodness Zhao clansmen, Zhao Baiyan and Zhao Sichen.

The Young Missus was leading Amah Wu out of the servants' quarters. "Come on outside. Don't hole up in your room and brood like that."

"Everyone knows what a virtuous woman you are. Don't go looking on the short side of things, no matter what!" said Seventh Sister Zou from the sidelines.

Amah Wu went right on with her wailing. She sandwiched in some words too, but they weren't all that easy to make out. "Now that's interesting," thought Ah Q. "Wonder what kind of tricks this Young Widow's been up to anyway?" He moved in closer and stood next to Zhao Sichen to find out what was going on.

Suddenly Ah Q caught sight of the *Budding Talent* bearing down on him. What's more, there was a large bamboo pole in his hands. As Ah Q looked at the pole, it suddenly occurred to him that he had recently been whacked with just such a pole, and that the commotion in progress somehow or other seemed to have something to do with him personally. Ah Q turned, intending to hightail it back to the hulling shed, but found himself cut off by the pole. He backtracked, went the other way, and made it safely out the rear gate. Before long he was back inside the Land-and-Grain Temple.

After Ah Q had sat there for a while, his skin started to break out in goosebumps—he was cold. Though it was spring, the nights were still quite chilly and it was certainly no time to be going around bare-chested. Now he remembered, he had left his cotton jacket back at the Zhaos' place. Fear of the *Budding Talent's* bamboo pole, however, kept him from going to get the jacket. At this impasse, the sheriff entered.

"You motherfucker, Ah Q! Even tryin' to make out with the Zhao servants. You're a rebel, pure and simple! You've screwed up my sleep too, mother!" On and on in this vein, the sheriff gave Ah Q a good tongue-lashing, and there was, of course, no reasonable defense that Ah Q could offer. Toward the end of this harangue, the sheriff demanded a four dollar tip (twice the usual amount because he had been forced to come out at night). Since Ah Q had no ready cash, the sheriff took his old felt hat as security. Then he laid down the law:

(1) Ah Q was to take a pair of candles (one catty apiece) along with a packet of incense to the Zhao residence and apologize.

(2) The Zhao family was to hire Daoist priests to exorcise the ghosts of people who had hanged themselves—cost to be borne by Ah Q.

(3) Henceforth Ah Q was never to darken the Zhao family's door again.

(4) Should anything at all *ever* befall Amah Wu, Ah Q would be held responsible.

(5) Ah Q would not be allowed to ask the Zhao family for his back wages or his jacket.

Ah Q, of course, agreed to all these conditions—trouble was he didn't have the money to make good on them. Fortunately, since it was already spring, he didn't need his cotton quilt all that much anymore, and so he hocked it for two thousand coppers so as to fulfill the five conditions.

After a bare-chested Ah Q had kowtowed his apology to the Zhaos, he even had a few coppers left over. But instead of redeeming his felt hat, he simply bought some wine and drank them up. The Zhao family didn't actually light the candles or burn the incense he had bought either, but since the Old Missus could make good use of them when she worshipped Buddha, they kept them all the same. The best part of Ah Q's raggedy old jacket went into making diapers for the baby born to the Young Missus in August. The rest of it was converted into liners for Amah Wu's shoes.

## Chapter 5

### The Problem of Livelihood

Having complied with the five conditions laid down by the sheriff, Ah Q went back to the Land-and-Grain Temple just as he always did. But after the sun went down that night, he gradually became aware that something was not quite right in this world of his. He wracked his brains for a good long while and then finally figured it out: the reason for his not-quite-right feeling probably had something to do with his being bare-chested. Remembering that he still had a tattered old winter jacket, he threw that across his shoulders and lay down. When he opened his eyes again, the rays of the rising sun were already falling on top of the west wall. He sat up straight and declared, "Shit!"

After rising, he went out and wandered around the streets just as he always did. Although this time it wasn't any physical discomfort that bothered him—as had his bare-chested state the previous night—once again Ah Q began to feel that there was something not quite right in this world of his, for it seemed that from this day forward all the women of Wei Village began turning shy on him. As soon as they saw Ah Q approaching, they'd scurry into their houses. Even Seventh Sister Zou, who was fast approaching fifty, scurried inside like all the others and called her eleven-year-old daughter inside after her. Ah Q was puzzled. "The bitches have started actin' like high-class young ladies all of a sudden—sluts!" But it wasn't until several days later that this not-quite-right feeling took on a critical intensity. First off, the wineshop wouldn't extend him any more credit. In the second place, the old man who took care of the temple started running off at the mouth with the obvious intention of running him off. In the third place, it had been quite some time—though he couldn't remember exactly how long—since anyone had asked Ah Q to do any odd jobs. No credit at the wineshop? He could deal with that. And so what if the caretaker did try to run him off? He could handle that one too. But if no one gave him any work to do, his stomach would be empty in short order and that would truly constitute an extraordinarily "shitty" state of affairs.

At the end of his rope, he went to hunt up the people who used to hire him to see what was going on. Of course the one place he couldn't go was to the Zhaos' house, because he'd been enjoined never to darken their door again. But it turned out that even at his former employers' places the situation had changed radically too. Everywhere he went, a man would walk out looking quite put out at his intrusion and shoo him away like a beggar. "We don't have anything for you. Now scram!"

At this point Ah Q was more confused than ever. "Always used to be that these folks couldn't do without me," he thought to himself. "Doesn't make any sense that they just don't have any more work all of a sudden. There's gotta be more to this than meets the eye." Only after carefully asking around did he discover that *now* whenever people had any work, they all went to a certain Young Don. Now in Ah Q's eyes, this Young D was a miserable little critter, all skinny and weak as could be. Why he was even lower than Bearded Wang! Who would ever have dreamt that a young nobody like that would actually do him out of his ricebowl?

In light of all the above, Ah Q's present fury was not to be compared with any of his ordinary rages. As he walked along, seething with resentment, Ah Q suddenly raised a fist and belted out a line of local opera: "*My mace of steel I grasp full tight / And with it I shall now thee smite!*"

A few days later he finally came across Young D in front of the short stretch of wall that protected the Qian family compound from prying eyes. As the saying goes, "*When met by chance, foe spots foe at one fell glance.*" Ah Q immediately moved in on Young D and the latter stopped dead in his tracks.

"Animal!" shouted Ah Q, giving him his dirtiest look as spittle shot from the corners of his mouth.

"I'm a bug—does that make you happy?" responded Young D.

Such modesty only served to intensify Ah Q's ire. Since he had no steel mace handy, however, he was forced to join battle barehanded. He reached out and grabbed Young D by the queue. Young D defended himself by holding tight to the root of his own queue with one hand while grabbing Ah Q's with the other. In like fashion, Ah Q used *his* free hand to protect himself by holding fast, too, to the root of his own queue. The old Ah Q had never considered Young D's martial skills to be worthy of mention, but the new Ah Q hadn't had anything to eat recently and by now yielded nothing to Young D in miserable-little-critterliness himself. It was an even match. As Young D and Ah Q bent toward each other, four hands grasped two heads. The blue shadow that was cast by the two men on the Qian family's whitewashed wall was shaped like a rainbow, a rainbow that froze and then remained motionless for a good half hour.

"Okay now, okay!" said some of the people who had gathered round to watch—they were probably trying to break up the fight. "All right now, *all right!*" said some others. One couldn't tell whether they were simply expressing admiration or were urging the combatants to show greater animation. But whatever the case, neither Ah Q nor Young D was paying any attention to the crowd.

When Ah Q advanced three steps, Young D retreated three steps and they both stood still. When Young D advanced three steps, Ah Q retreated three steps and they both stood still. After approximately half an hour of this—it's really hard to tell because there were very few clocks in Wei Village that struck the hours, so maybe it was only twenty minutes—both their heads were steaming and their faces were bathed in sweat. Finally Ah Q's hands released their hold; at precisely the same moment Young D's hands released their hold, too. Simultaneously the two men straightened up; simultaneously they backed away from each other and elbowed their separate ways out through the ring of spectators.

"Let that be a lesson, you fucker!" said Ah Q, turning his head back to Young D.

"Let that be a lesson, you fucker!" said Young D, turning his head back to Ah Q.

So it would seem that there was no victory or defeat in the epic battle that was mounted by these two renowned warriors, nor is it known whether the spectators were satisfied with the show. At any rate, Ah Q came out of it in the same fix he had been in before—no one came to offer him work.

One day when it was quite warm and a gentle breeze was just bringing the first hint of summer into the village, quite incongruously Ah Q started to feel cold. This he could put up with. The first order of business was that hungry stomach of his. His cotton quilt, felt hat, and cotton shirt had long since disappeared, and after that he'd even sold his padded-cotton winter jacket. Now he was left with nothing but a pair of pants—he couldn't part with those no matter what—and a raggedy unlined jacket. He might have been able to *give* that away for somebody to make shoe soles with, but he certainly wouldn't be able to turn a profit on it.

For quite some time now he had fantasized about *finding* some money on the street someplace, but so far he hadn't seen any lying around. Okay then, why not find some money right here in this dilapidated room of his at the Land-and-Grain Temple? Eagerly he searched his quarters over. His room was empty, so empty that he could see at a glance there was nothing to be found in it. At this point, Ah Q decided to go out and scare up something to eat.

Although his intention in going out was to "scare up something to eat," yet when he saw the familiar wineshop, the familiar steamed breadrolls, strange to tell, he walked right on by. Not only did he fail to stop, but what's more, he didn't even want the bread or wine. That's not what he was really looking for. Then, exactly what was it that he *was* looking for? Even Ah Q himself couldn't have told you.

Now Wei Village wasn't very large to begin with, and before too long Ah Q had walked clear through the place. Then he came to a sea of rice paddies covered with fresh green sprouts and extending as far as the eye could see. It was animated here and there by bobbing dots of black—peasants working in the fields. But Ah Q did not take time to stop and savor the rustic charm of such a scene; he kept right on walking, for he knew instinctively that all of that was far removed from his basic concern of "scaring up something to eat." Finally he came to the walls of the Convent of Silent Cultivation.

The whitewashed walls rose abruptly out of the green sea surrounding them. The low earthen wall behind the convent enclosed a vegetable garden. Ah Q hesitated for a moment, but looking around and seeing no one in sight, he grabbed the blackhair vines that covered the wall and started to climb. Everyplace he managed to get a toehold, the dirt of the wall crumbled and *whooshed* down through the leaves while the trembling of his feet rustled the vines. Availing himself of a nearby mulberry limb, he finally made it over the wall and jumped down into the garden. There was a profusion of things growing there but there didn't seem to be any wine or steamed breadrolls handy, or anything else you could readily sink your teeth into. There was a copse of bamboo over by the western wall with lots of sprouts growing below. As luck would have it, though, none of them were steamed and ready to eat. There was also some rape, but it had long since gone to seed. There was some mustard, too, but it was about to flower, and the little cabbages were also long past ripe.

Feeling every bit as wronged as a Young Literatus who had just failed the civil service examinations, Ah Q slowly walked through a gate into the rear courtyard. He was suddenly greeted by an extraordinarily pleasant surprise, for what met his eyes could be nothing else but a turnip patch. He squatted down and started pulling them up when suddenly a very round head thrust itself out of a door and then shrank back as quickly as it had emerged. Now *that* could be nothing else but a young Buddhist nun. Ah Q thought young Buddhist nuns were worthless to begin with and was not about to be intimidated by the likes of them, but still, men of the world have always appreciated the wisdom of "playing it safe," and so he stripped the leaves from four turnips without further delay and hastily stuffed them into the front of his shirt. By that time, the old abbess herself had already come out.

"Buddha preserve us, what do you think you're doing climbing into our garden to steal turnips, Ah Q? Aiya! Such a sin! Buddha preserve us!"

"When did *I* ever climb into *your* garden to steal turnips?" Ah Q asked, walking away but keeping an eye on the nun too.

"Just now . . . aren't those . . ." The old nun pointed to his bulging shirt.

"Oh, you think these are yours, huh? Can you call 'em by name and make 'em come to you? Why you don't even—"

Before he could finish, a black dog was lunging toward him and Ah Q broke into a run. The dog had been at the front gate but somehow or other had come around to the back. It was right on Ah Q's heels and about to grab his leg when, as luck would have it, a turnip dropped out of his shirt, startling the animal long enough to give Ah Q time to climb the mulberry tree and vault over the wall. Outside, both Ah Q and turnips went spilling all over the ground; inside, the black dog kept barking at the mulberry tree while the old abbess continued to invoke the name of Buddha.

Afraid lest the abbess might let the dog out after him, Ah Q quickly gathered up the turnips and hurried on his way. He picked up a few pebbles at the side of the road just in case, but since the black dog did not reappear, he finally threw them away and began eating the turnips as he walked along. "Not gonna find anything to eat around here," he thought to himself. "I could always go to town." By the time he had finished the third turnip, he was already quite firm in his decision to head for town.

## Chapter 6

From Dynastic Revival to the Fading Days of Empire

It was just past the Mid-Autumn Festival that year when Wei Village caught sight of Ah Q again. "Ah Q's back." All who heard the news were surprised and forthwith rolled back their minds to ponder: "Wonder where he went?" The last few times he went to town, Ah Q had been bursting with news when he got back and had wasted no time telling everyone about his trip. But this time—nary a word. No one had even noticed that he was gone, although it is possible he may have told the old man who looked after the Land-and-Grain Temple that he was going. According to old established Wei Village precedent, however, going to town was no big thing unless it was Old Master Zhao or Old Master Qian who did the going. Even a trip to town by the Fake Foreign Devil was nothing to get worked up about, much less a trip by the likes of Ah Q. Thus the old caretaker at the temple hadn't bothered to spread word of our hero's departure for town, and consequently the inhabitants of Wei Village had been ignorant of the event.

The circumstances of his return this time were rather different too—to tell the truth, they were downright odd. The sky was almost black when Ah Q appeared, all sleepy-eyed, at the door of the wineshop. He shuffled up to the counter, extended a hand from his waist, and threw down a whole fistful of silver and copper coins. "Hard cash! Bring on the wine!" He was sporting a brand new unlined jacket and a money pouch weighed his belt down into an arc. According to old established Wei Village precedent, should one chance to meet a presentable personage with anything about him that caught the eye, then *Come what may, sweet courtesie / Should be the order of the day.* Now there was no mistaking that it really *was* Ah Q they were dealing with, but *this* Ah Q was entirely different from the raggedy-jacket Ah Q they were accustomed to, and thus they treated him with deference. This was an instance of what the ancients had in mind when they advised: *After an absence of even three days / A scholar-official rates a fresh gaze.*

Thus, from the manager to the waiters, and from patrons on down to mere passers-by, everyone quite naturally assumed a respectful, albeit inquisitive, air. *Behold how yon manager doth begin, with a nod to which he now appendeth some words:* "Hey, it's Ah Q! You're back!"

"I'm back."

"Looks like you've done pretty well for yourself. Let's see, you were at . . . uh . . . at . . ."

"Went to town."

This momentous item of intelligence had blanketed all of Wei Village by the very next day.

Everyone wanted to hear the saga of Ah Q's "dynastic restoration" to his present ready-cash and new-lined-jacket level of affluence. In the wineshop, in the teashop, and under the eaves of the temple, bit by bit people ferreted out the details. And as a consequence of all this, Ah Q was treated with new respect.

The way Ah Q told it, he had been working for an Old Master in town—a *Selectman,* no less. All who heard this chapter and verse looked impressed. This *Selectman*'s last name was Bai, but since he was the only *Selectman* in the whole town, there was no reason to use it. Whenever a *Selectman* was spoken of, it would have had to be Bai. This was true not only in the town but also in every place within a hundred miles around. It was as if people actually thought this man's family name was *Selectman,* and his given name, Old Master. To have been employed in the residence of such a man was, of course, impressive enough. But according to what Ah Q further revealed, he had not deemed it appropriate to remain in Bai's employ, for he considered the Old Master *Selectman* a bit too "fuckin'" this and a mite too "fuckin'" that. All who heard this sighed, but they were secretly pleased as well. They sighed because Ah Q had thrown away such a good job, but they were secretly pleased because they felt he hadn't deserved it to begin with.

The way Ah Q told it, the main reason for his return to Wei Village was his general dissatisfaction with the townsfolk. They called a *longbench* a *stickbench* and used shredded leeks—yes, *shredded*—when frying fish. And as if that weren't enough, he'd recently discovered an even greater shortcoming among them: when the women walked, their fannies didn't have much wiggle. Despite all that, however, here and there one did find things in town worthy of admiration. For instance, when it came to gambling, the Wei Village bumpkins couldn't manage anything better than a simple game played with thirty-two bamboo counters. Here only the Fake Foreign Devil knew how to play Ma John, but in town every little shitkicker on the block knew it up one side and down the other. If the Fake Foreign Devil ever fell into the clutches of one of those little bastards, it'd be like some two-for-a-nickel ghost coming up against the King of Hell! All who heard this chapter and verse took on an embarrassed air.

"Have you ever seen a de-capitation?" Ah Q asked. "Wow! Is that ever somethin' to see! Killin' the revolutionaries—yup, that's a real sight!" He shook his head with such appreciative enthusiasm that spittle flew from his mouth and landed on the face of Zhao Sichen, seated directly opposite him. All who heard this chapter and verse assumed an air of solemnity. Once more Ah Q looked all around and surveyed his audience. Listening with rapt attention, Bearded Wang had stretched out his neck, the better to hear Ah Q's rendition. Suddenly Ah Q raised his right arm, took aim at the nape of Bearded Wang's neck, clove the air with his hand, and shouted, "*ZAP!*"

Fairly jumping out of his skin with fright, Bearded Wang jerked his head in as quick as lightning. All who heard this chapter and verse of Ah Q's story took on a frightened—albeit appreciative—air. For several days afterward, Bearded Wang wandered around in a daze, no longer daring even to come near to Ah Q. And the others who had listened to Ah Q that day were similarly wary.

Although I dare not make so bold as to say that at this point Ah Q's standing in the eyes of the Wei Villagers was actually higher than that of Old Master Zhao, still if I were to characterize it as almost equivalent, I should probably not be guilty of any great linguistic lapse.

This being the case, it was not long before the great name of Ah Q was bruited about in the boudoirs of Wei Village for a second time. Actually only the Qians and Zhaos lived in households large enough to boast "boudoirs." Nine out of ten families had only ordinary bedrooms at best. But be they boudoirs or bedrooms, women's quarters are women's quarters and it was something of a miracle that Ah Q's name should ever be heard in such precincts at all. Yet it seemed that of late, whenever the village women met, conversation would invariably turn to Ah Q. How about that blue silk skirt Seventh Sister Zou had bought of him! Secondhand, to be sure, but for ninety cents who could complain? And what about the red calico shirt Zhao Baiyin's mother had bought—seven-tenths new and it had only cost her three strings of cash, at ninety-two to the string. (One authority states that it was actually Zhao Sichen's mother. Pending further research, however, this identification can only be regarded as tentative.)

And now all the women's eyes throughout the village were hanging out: they all wanted to see Ah Q. In the market for a silk skirt? See Ah Q. Need a calico shirt? Go look up Ah Q. Not only did they no longer avoid him, but occasionally they would even hunt him down. "Any more silk skirts, Ah Q? No? How about calico then? You've gotta have some calico ones left." News of all this excitement eventually made its way from the shallows of ordinary village bedrooms into the depths of the Zhao and Qian boudoirs, carried thence by Seventh Sister Zou, who in an excess of smug satisfaction had taken the blue skirt and shown it off to Mrs. Zhao. That lady had, in her turn, told Old Master Zhao about Seventh Sister's purchase in terms of highest approbation. That gentleman, in his turn, had discussed it with Young Master Zhao, his *Budding Talent* son, at a dinner-table conclave that very evening, opining that there was something suspicious about Ah Q. "We had better be a bit more careful about locking our windows and doors at night. Wonder what kind of stuff he has left? We might be able to get some real bargains."

At just that time, Mrs. Zhao happened to be in the market for a good sleeveless fur jacket—if the price was right. That did it. The clan conclave approved a resolution that called for one of their number to prevail upon the good offices of Seventh Sister Zou to seek out Ah Q on that very night. Furthermore, in order that the resolution might be carried out, an exception to family protocol was also passed: an oil lamp would be lit after sunset.

The lamp burned and burned, but Ah Q was nowhere to be seen. The entire Zhao household was thrown out of kilter. Forever yawning, some faulted Ah Q's fly-by-night character, while others blamed Seventh Sister Zou for lack of diligence. Mrs. Zhao was of the opinion that Ah Q was afraid to come because of the restrictions imposed on him by the sheriff back in the spring. Old Master Zhao, on the other hand, believed that this wouldn't have made any difference because "*I* am the one who sent for him." In the end, it was Old Master Zhao who proved best at predicting the ways of the world, for Seventh Sister finally arrived with Ah Q in tow.

"He kept telling me . . . he didn't have anything left, but I told . . . I told him to come and tell you that to your face. He even said . . . even said . . ." Still trying to catch her breath, Seventh Sister Zou wheezed heavily.

"Old Master!" Ah Q hailed, stopping dead in his tracks under the eaves and smiling a smile that didn't look like a smile.

"Ah Q, I hear that you prospered while you were away," offered Old Master Zhao, who strode forward in greeting, his eyes busy with a head-to-toe inventory of Ah Q. "Glad to hear it, very glad. Now . . . uh . . . I hear you have a few secondhand items for sale. Why not bring over whatever you've got and let us have a look. The only reason I'm interested is that I just happen to be in the market for—"

"I've already told Seventh Sister Zou, stuff's all gone."

"*Gone?*" The plaintive note slipped out before Old Master Zhao had time to catch it. "How could they all go so quickly?"

"It was only some stuff a buddy of mine let me have. Wasn't much to begin with. Sold some to—"

"Surely you must have something left."

"All I've got now is a door curtain."

"All right then, bring *that* over," said Mrs. Zhao excitedly.

"In that case, we'll see you again tomorrow," said Old Master Zhao without much enthusiasm. "Ah Q, whenever you have anything from now on, be sure to bring it to our place first."

"We would certainly offer you better prices than anyone else around," added the *Budding Talent.* Mrs. *Budding Talent* stole a furtive glance at Ah Q to see if her husband's words had had any effect.

"I need a sleeveless fur jacket!" Mrs. Zhao came right out with it.

Although Ah Q had promised to do as they said, he sauntered out in such a lackadaisical way that it was hard to tell if he really meant it. This whole business proved a great disappointment to Old Master Zhao. In fact he was so vexed that he stopped yawning. The *Budding Talent* was quite put out with Ah Q as well. "Have to keep a sharp eye on that turtle's egg. Maybe we ought to have the sheriff drive him out of town and be done with it."

Old Master Zhao, however, did not see things the same way and opined that such a course would only serve to turn Ah Q into a lifelong enemy. Besides, people in that line of work were likely to bear out the truth of the saying *The hawk is always a pest, but never 'round its own nest,* and hence there was no need for concern around Wei Village. "As long as we keep a little more alert nights, we should be all right." The beneficiary of this "courtyard guidance" promptly decided that his father couldn't be more correct and immediately tabled the resolution calling for exile. Furthermore, he enjoined Seventh Sister Zou to refrain from telling anyone that such a possibility had even been entertained. The following day Seventh Sister Zou took the blue silk skirt she had bought from Ah Q and dyed it black. Then, far and wide, she broadcast all the Zhaos' suspicions regarding Ah Q—though she did not, in good faith, touch on that particular chapter and verse having to do with the *Budding Talent*'s suggestion about exile. Nonetheless, what she did say proved quite damaging to Ah Q.

First off, the sheriff hunted him down and made off with the door curtain, steadfastly refusing to return it despite Ah Q's protestation that Mrs. Zhao was anxious to see it. Worse yet, the sheriff even tried to press Ah Q into making a monthly "filial donation." Second, there was a sudden transformation in the form of respect that Wei Villagers showed Ah Q. The expressions they wore now announced that although they still weren't about to take any liberties with him, they would just as soon give him a wide berth. These expressions were by no means identical to the ones they had worn earlier when guarding against a surprise "*ZAP!*" either. No, there was now an element of the attitude that Confucius recommended one should take with regard to ghosts and spirits: "*Respectful you may be, but keep some distance 'twixt them and thee.*"

Only the village roustabouts had the temerity to get close to Ah Q. They moved in and subjected him to an unrelenting barrage of questions, hoping to find out exactly what he'd been up to in town. For his part, Ah Q didn't hold anything back either. On the contrary, he related his urban experiences with a real touch of pride. It was now they learned that, in the brief course of his criminal career, Ah Q's role had been little more than that of an extra. He had neither *scaled walls* nor had he *tunneled through barriers* the way real burglars are supposed to do. In fact, he had merely waited outside to receive the stolen goods as they were passed to him from inside. One night, just after the head of the gang had handed him a sack of stuff and headed back for more, Ah Q heard a great commotion break out on the inside. He had immediately taken to his heels, climbed over the city wall, and fled back to Wei Village, no longer possessing the nerve to continue in his new calling.

Strange to say, these revelations had a remarkably adverse effect on Ah Q. The Wei Villagers' *respectful-be* attitude had been sustained by fear, pure and simple. Who would ever have guessed that in point of fact Ah Q was nothing more than a burglar who no longer dared to burgle? It was truly a case of *He whose years bring nought of fame / To our respect can lay no claim.*

## Chapter 7

### Revolution

On the Fourteenth Day of the Ninth Month of the Third Year of the Xuantong Reign—in other words, on the day Ah Q sold his money pouch to Zhao Baiyan—on the Fourth Stroke of the Third Watch, a large black-canopied boat tied up at the Zhao family wharf. Since it had been poled in during the middle of the night, the villagers were sound asleep and unaware of its arrival. When they left their homes before dawn next morning, however, quite a few of them caught sight of it. After some quick nosing around, they discovered it belonged to none other than Old Master *Selectman.*

That boat carried a cargo of unrest into Wei Village. Well before noon, everyone had heard about it and was quite worried. The Zhaos, of course, were secretive as to the boat's real mission, but out on the street word had it that the Revolutionary Party was about to occupy the town and that Old Master *Selectman* had come out to Wei Village to hole up until things blew over. The sole dissenting opinion was offered by Seventh Sister Zou. The way she told it, the boat only carried a few battered old trunks that Old Master *Selectman* wanted to store at the Zhaos' place, but Old Master Zhao had refused and the trunks had been sent back to town. If you stopped to think about it, she probably had something there, for despite their both being members of the educated scholar-official class, *Budding Talent* Zhao and Old Master *Selectman* had never hit it off very well and it would seem unlikely that there could be any "brothers-in-adversity" relationship between them. What was more, since Seventh Sister Zou was a *neighbor* of the Zhaos, her view of things ought to be closer to the mark. And so people decided that, more likely than not, Seventh Sister Zou had the right of it.

Nevertheless rumors continued to fly. One of them went like this: although, to be sure, Old Master *Selectman* had probably not come in person, he *had* sent along a lengthy letter in which, after many a twist and turn through the maze of kith and kin, he had established himself as at least a "kissin' cousin" to the Zhaos. After reading the said letter, Old Master Zhao had given that possibility a quick roll around his brain and concluded that such a relationship could certainly do him no harm. He had therefore kept the battered old trunks, which were at this very moment stuffed under his wife's bed. And as to the Revolutionary Party, there were those who held that it had occupied the town that very night, every soldier wearing a white helmet—obviously in mourning for the Emperor Chong Zhen.

Ah Q's ear had long since been exposed to the expression "Revolutionary Party." What was more, only this year he had seen members of that same party being executed. His idea of the whole thing—though he wouldn't have been able to tell you exactly how he came by it—had always been that "revolutionaries" were troublemakers, hell-bent on turning the world upside down, and that meant giving Ah Q a hard time personally. Hence his own attitude toward such mischief makers had been one of *antipathy most intense and abhorrence most immense.* But who could ever have guessed that Old Master *Selectman*—respected and feared as he was for miles and miles around—would be utterly terrified by this Revolutionary Party? It was a sweet thought and it made Ah Q lean their way. Furthermore, with all the "cock-suckin' villagers" running around like chickens with their heads cut off, how could Ah Q help but be pleased?

"Why *not* be a revolutionary?" he asked himself. "There's a whole bunch of fuckers I'd like to revolution clear out of this world and into the next, the sorry bastards! I just might throw in with that Revolution Party myself!"

Ah Q had been a bit hard up lately and that probably helped put him out of sorts to begin with. On top of that, he'd had two bowls of wine on an empty stomach that very afternoon. He thought as he walked; and he walked as he thought. And then he began to walk an inch or so above the ground. Thoughts and wine had suddenly transformed his single person into an entire revolutionary army! Everyone in Wei Village was now his prisoner. Everyone! He was soon so full of himself he could no longer contain it.

"On with the rebellion!" shouted Ah Q.

The Wei Villagers watched him with a look that bordered on a look of terror, a look that made Ah Q feel as comfortable as a man drinking melted snow in the middle of June. Now he was full to the point of overflowing. "Whatever Ah Q wants, Ah Q gets! Whatever *woman* Ah Q wants, Ah Q gets!" he shouted happily and then began to sing.

*"Da-da dum-dum!*
*In my cups, would that I had*
*ne'er . . .*
*Da-da dum-dum!*
*. . . taken the head of my*
*brother-in-arms,*
*Brother Zheng.*
*Would that I had ne'er . . .*
*Ah . . . ah-ah . . . ah . . .*
*Da-da dum-dum, da dum-ya-dum!*
*My mace of steel I grasp full tight,*
*And with it I shall now thee*
*smite . . . "*

Two Zhaos were standing at the front gate of their family compound discussing the implications of the revolution with two honest-to-goodness relatives. Head held jauntily aloft, Ah Q cruised on past without deigning to notice them.

"*Da-da . . .*"

"Q, my friend," hailed Old Master Zhao somewhat diffidently.

"*Dum-dum!*" Never dreaming that his own name could possibly be linked with "friend," it did not occur to Ah Q that these words had anything to do with him, and so he kept right on singing: "*Da-dum . . . dum-ya-dum . . . dum!*"

"Old friend, Q!"

"*Would that I had ne'er—*"

"AH Q!" The *Budding Talent* was forced to shout out the name they usually used on him.

Ah Q stopped dead in his tracks, cocked his head to one side, and inquired, "What?"

"Q, my friend. Now . . . uh . . ." Old Gentleman Zhao seemed at a loss for words. "Uh . . . you've gotten rich, huh?"

"Rich? You betcha! From here on out, whatever Ah Q wants, Ah Q gets!"

"Ah Q . . . I mean, Elder Brother Q. Poor folks like us won't be in any trouble, will they?" Zhao Baiyan asked anxiously in an attempt to determine which way the revolutionary winds were blowing.

"Poor, my foot! You sure as hell have a lot more dough than I do." Ah Q turned and walked away, bringing all conversation to a disappointing halt.

Old Master Zhao and son went back inside and discussed everything that had transpired until it was time to light—or time not to light—their lamps. Zhao Baiyan went back home, undid his moneybelt, and ordered his wife to hide it at the bottom of the family trunk.

Walking on air, Ah Q continued floating hither and yon for quite a while so that by the time he got back to the Land-and-Grain Temple, he was thoroughly sober. Tonight even the caretaker turned affable and invited him in for tea. Ah Q asked him for two crackers, and after finishing them, even managed to hit him up for a four-ounce candle and candlestick. Alone in his little room at last, luxuriating, Ah Q lit the candle and lay down. He was indescribably happy.

The flames shimmered and danced as if it were New Year's Eve, and Ah Q's thoughts began to do some high stepping too. "Throw in with the troublemakers? Yeah, that would be fun. I can see it now. A bunch of those Revolution Party guys'll come by the temple here, all decked out in white armor and white helmets, wearin' sabers too! They'll come marchin' right in and shout: 'Let's go, Ah Q, come with us!' And I'll go with them too! Steel maces, bombs, foreign rifles, spears, knives—they'll have it all. Then those cocksuckin' villagers will find out how pitiful they really are. I can see 'em kneelin' on the ground and beggin' me to spare 'em. Fat chance! Young D and Old Master Zhao'll be the first to go. I'll get the *Budding Talent* too, and then I'll do in the Fake Foreign Devil. Wonder if I should let any of 'em live? Well by rights I suppose I could spare Bearded Wang—but no, I'm not gonna.

"And think of all the stuff I'll get, too. March right into their houses and rip open their trunks—gold, silver, foreign money, foreign calico shirts! For starters I'll take that Ningbo bed the *Budding Talent*'s wife has and move it over here to the temple. The Qians' tables and chairs will do just fine, thank you—maybe I'll take some from the Zhaos, too. Won't even have to lift a finger. Get Young D to do all the heavy work. Better step lively too, if he doesn't want a good belt or two.

"Let's see. Zhao Sichen's sister is a real dog, and there's not much point in talkin' about Seventh Sister Zou's daughter for a couple of years yet. Fake Foreign Devil's wife is willin' to sleep with a husband that's got no queue—she can't be any damn good! If only *Budding Talent*'s old lady didn't have that mole on her eyelid. Haven't seen Amah Wu in a while, wonder where she is? But then she's got those big-ass feet."

Before he had time to arrange all the pieces just right, Ah Q was already snoring. The four-ounce candle had burned down less than half an inch and its bright rays shone warm and red on his open mouth. And then all of a sudden he screamed, raised his head, and looked around in panic. Finally his gaze came to rest on the four-ounce candle. He put his head back down and went to sleep.

Ah Q didn't get out of bed until quite late the next day. He went out on the street and did a quick survey—everything was exactly as it had always been. His stomach was exactly as it had always been too—empty. He thought about what he should do next but failed to come up with anything. And then suddenly he seemed to have hit on something, for his body gradually began to move. Thinking more with his feet than with anything else, Ah Q finally arrived at the Convent of Silent Cultivation.

It was every bit as quiet as he remembered it from the previous spring. He knocked on the gate. A dog began to bark inside. Ah Q hastily picked out a large piece of brick and approached the gate again. He began knocking with the brick, much harder than before, but it was not until many a pockmark had appeared on the surface of the big black gate that he heard someone coming out.

Ah Q immediately secured a better hold on the brick, spread his feet wide, and prepared to do battle with the dog. The gate opened no more than a crack, however, and no guardian canine burst forth. Peeking in through that crack, Ah Q saw nothing but an elderly nun.

"What are *you* doing here again?" she asked in alarm.

"There's been a revolution, haven't you heard?"

"Revolution? Haven't we had just about enough revolution for one day?"

"Huh?" Ah Q was puzzled.

"Don't you know? The revolutionists have already been here."

"*What* revolutionists?" Ah Q was more puzzled than ever.

"The *Budding Talent* and Fake Foreign Devil!"

Ah Q was stunned by the news. The elderly nun, sensing his loss of momentum, quickly shut the gate. By the time he realized what had happened, the gate was locked tighter than a drum. Ah Q pounded on it once again, but this time there was no response.

It had all happened that very morning. Always right on top of things, *Budding Talent* Zhao learned that the revolutionaries had taken the town during the night. He responded by coiling his queue up on top of his head and heading out bright and early to pay his respects to the Fake Foreign Devil, a man with whom he had never been on good terms heretofore. However, since this was "a time for people from all walks of life to unite in national renewal," they now hit it off just fine, quickly became the comradeliest of comrades-in-arms, and joined together to undertake the task of revolution.

But where to begin? After wracking their brains at great length, they finally remembered that there was a "Long Live the Emperor" tablet over at the Convent of Silent Cultivation. They righteously decided that this tablet would have to go, and set out forthwith for the convent. Giving the two a good piece of her mind, the elderly nun had tried to stop them. Thereupon, taking her as a symbol of the entire Manchu establishment, they gave her a sound thrashing. After they left, the old nun had collected herself enough to survey the damage. The objectionable tablet, of course, lay shattered on the ground. She also discovered that an extremely valuable antique censer that had stood before a statue of the Bodhisattva Guanyin was nowhere to be seen.

It was only much later that day that Ah Q found out about all this. He was more than a little sorry that he had been asleep during the foray and was also quite put out that they hadn't come to get him. He backed up another step in his thoughts and wondered: "Do you suppose they don't know I've already thrown in with the Revolution Party?"

## Chapter 8

Request to Revolt Denied

The Wei Villagers felt more reassured with every passing day. The word from town was that although the Revolutionary Party had indeed taken over, it hadn't made any changes to speak of. His honor the county magistrate was still the same man, though they called him something else now. Old Master *Selectman* had also acquired some sort of new label (the Wei Villagers couldn't keep track of all these new revolutionary titles). And the same old lieutenant was in charge of the soldiers, too.

The only worrisome thing about this whole business was that some bad elements had slipped into the Revolutionary Party and started lopping queues off the day after they arrived in town. The boatman from over in the next village, Sevenpounder, had fallen into their clutches and had been so transformed that he no longer looked even human. The incident occasioned but little anxiety among the Wei Villagers, however, because few of them ever ventured into town in the first place, and the one or two who were thinking of making the trek immediately changed their plans. Why risk ending up like Sevenpounder if you didn't have to? At first, Ah Q had considered going into town to look up some old friends, but on hearing of Sevenpounder's tragic fate, he too had no choice but to cancel his trip.

And yet you couldn't say that the revolution hadn't triggered any reforms in Wei Village, either. Within a few days after the revolutionaries took the town, for instance, the number of people with queues coiled up on top of their heads gradually began to increase. As I have reported earlier, it was his nibs the *Budding Talent* who led the way; next came Zhao Sichen and Zhao Baiyan; and after that Ah Q also joined the parade. During the summer, of course, it was not uncommon for people in Wei Village to coil their queues up on top of their heads, or even to do them up in knots. But this was late autumn, not summer. And so, from the point of view of those who did the coiling, one cannot maintain that this "autumn practice of summer etiquette" demonstrated anything less than a magnificent decisiveness worthy of the doughtiest heroes. And once that's granted, one cannot say that the revolution didn't trigger any reforms in Wei Village either.

When Zhao Sichen came walking down the street with the back of his head scandalously bared, people would look at him and then warn each other: "Look out, here comes a revolutionary!" When Ah Q heard of this, he was quite envious. Although Ah Q had long since gotten wind of the momentous news about the *Budding Talent*'s coiling his queue up, the idea that *he* might do the same had never crossed his mind. It was only when he saw Zhao Sichen do it that Ah Q gave a thought to imitating this new fashion. Having resolved to put that thought into practice, and using a chopstick for hairpin, Ah Q coiled up his queue too. After some hesitation, he even got up the nerve to go out on the street looking like that.

People actually did give him a second look, but they didn't warn each other about a revolutionary coming. At first, Ah Q merely felt displeased, but later on he began to resent the injustice of it all. He got so worked up that he began flying off the handle at the least provocation. In point of fact, however, he wasn't any worse off now than he had been before he revolted. People were passably polite to him and the stores didn't insist on cash every time he bought anything, yet somehow or other Ah Q felt that this whole revolution business was a big disappointment. Since there really *had* been a revolution, there ought to be more to it than just this.

Later on he ran into Young D. That was the straw that broke the camel's back—Young D had coiled up his queue too! What was more, he'd had the gall to use a chopstick! Never in his wildest dreams had Ah Q expected that someone the likes of Young D would have the nerve to join in on the queue-coiling and he was simply not going to have it! Just who the hell did Young D think he was anyway? Ah Q felt like seizing him on the spot, breaking that chopstick, putting that queue back down, and slapping him across the mouth a few times as punishment for forgetting his place. In the end, however, Ah Q let him off with a contemptuous "*Aaaaaaawk . . . tuh!*" accompanied by a dirty look.

During these parlous times, the Fake Foreign Devil was the only one who ventured into town. *Budding Talent* Zhao had briefly considered going in to visit Old Master *Selectman* in order to cash in on the goodwill the Zhaos had earned by hiding the *Selectman*'s trunks. But the *Budding Talent* was also mindful of the risk he would bring to bear on his queue and decided against it. Instead, he wrote a yellow-umbrella letter and prevailed upon the Fake Foreign Devil to take it into town and show it around in the right places, so that he might gain entry to the Revolutionary Party. When the Fake Foreign Devil returned, he promptly relieved the *Budding Talent* of four dollars, in exchange for which the latter received a Silver Peach to pin onto his lapel. That peach bowled the villagers over. Everyone said it was the symbol of the "Persimmon Oil Party" and worth at least an Imperial Academy Button. Old Master Zhao's prestige soared to even greater heights than it had reached when his son won the *Budding Talent*. The upshot was that Old Master Zhao began lording it over everyone again and even started getting uppity with Ah Q.

Ah Q, in turn, felt he wasn't getting a square deal. He was left out of things at every turn. But as soon as he heard about the Silver Peach business, he realized why this was so. If you're going to revolt, just *saying* so isn't enough. And coiling your queue won't cut it either. The first order of business is to get in touch with the revolutionaries.

Now Ah Q had known only two revolutionaries in his entire life. The one in town had gotten his head *ZAPPED!* off a good while back. The other one was the Fake Foreign Devil. That settled it. Like it or not, Ah Q would have to get in touch with him.

The front gate at the Qians' stood wide open. Ah Q skulked inside and was somewhat startled by the sight that greeted him. There in the middle of the courtyard stood the Fake Foreign Devil, decked out from stem to stern in solid black—foreign clothes, it looked like—and sporting a Silver Peach too! His hand grasped the cane from whose instruction Ah Q had so often profited in the past. His queue, grown out to a good foot and a half by now, was all undone. The freed hair cascaded down over his shoulders, making him look for all the world like some kind of Daoist Immortal. Standing just opposite this apparition, at straight-arrow attention, were Zhao Baiyan and a trio of Wei Villagers. Making a great show of deference, they hung on the Fake Foreign Devil's every word.

Quietly Ah Q made his way in, taking up a position behind Zhao Baiyan. He wanted to say something to the black-garbed star of the show but couldn't figure out what to call him. "Fake Foreign Devil" obviously wouldn't do. "Foreigner" was no better. And "Revolutionary" didn't quite do it either. Maybe he just ought to call him *Mr.* Foreigner.

"Mr. Foreigner" hadn't even noticed Ah Q. Eyes rolled skyward, he was just now hitting his stride: "I'm an impatient sort myself, and so whenever I met him, I'd always say, 'Brother Hong, let's get on with it.' But he would reply, '*Mais non, mon ami*!'—that's a foreign expression for 'no.' If he hadn't kept 'no-ing' me like that, the revolution would have come off a long time ago, but it goes to show you how carefully he proceeds in everything. He's tried to get me to take a post up there in Hubei I don't know how many times, but I've never agreed. After all, who wants a post in some insignificant county seat?"

"Ahem . . . Mr. . . ." Ah Q took advantage of a momentary pause in the Fake Foreign Devil's monologue to say his piece. It had taken all the courage he could muster, and then some, to even open his mouth.

But for some reason or other his intended form of address, "Mr. Foreigner," stuck in his throat.

"Out with it! What is it?"

"I . . . I . . ."

"Get out of here!"

"I want to throw in with . . ."

"Beat it!" Mr. Foreigner raised his *wailing* stick ominously high.

Then Zhao Baiyan and the village idlers began to bark at him too. "The gentleman has told you to beat it. That should be enough!"

Letting his feet do the thinking, Ah Q escaped through the gate, one hand shielding his head. To his surprise, however, Mr. Foreigner didn't bother to come after him. Nonetheless Ah Q hightailed it some sixty paces or so before gradually slowing down to a walk. He was heartbroken. If Mr. Foreigner wouldn't give him permission to revolt, he was done for. Never again could he look forward to having men in white helmets and white armor come by and ask him to join up. The idlers back there at Mr. Foreigner's place would waste no time in spreading word of what had just taken place, and Ah Q would become a laughingstock to the likes of Young D and Bearded Wang. That was bad enough. But the worst of it was that all his ambitions, hopes, and plans for the future had been wiped out at a single stroke.

In his entire life, Ah Q had never before experienced such a feeling of utter aimlessness. He felt that even coiling up his queue was pointless and briefly considered letting it down again just to get even. In the end, however, he didn't. With no particular goal in mind, Ah Q loafed around until nightfall. Then he put two bowls of wine on his tab and promptly drank them down. Gradually his spirits began to rise and glimpses of white helmets and white armor began to flicker across his brain once again.

One night, as had become his habit of late, Ah Q dawdled around in the wineshop till closing time and then started to trudge on back to the temple. *BIFF BANG BAM BOOM*—an odd kind of racket. Didn't sound like firecrackers either. Always a lover of excitement, Ah Q liked nothing better than minding everyone else's business. So he made a beeline through the darkness to the source of the noise. Hearing some footsteps, he stopped and cocked his head, the better to listen. A man hurtled past him in full retreat from something or other. Ah Q reversed his own course and fell in beside him. When he made a turn, Ah Q made a turn. When he stopped, Ah Q also stopped. Seeing there was no one behind them, Ah Q took a closer look—Young D!

"What's goin' on?" Ah Q felt left out again.

"The Zhaos . . . the Zhaos . . . got robbed!" Young D tried to catch his breath. The news made Ah Q's heart *thump thump* all the faster. Having caught his breath, Young D continued to make his escape under the eaves of the houses and so, at first, did Ah Q. Having had some experience in "this line of work," however, Ah Q was the bolder of the two and finally headed back up the street to see what was really going on. He stopped and watched while a steady line of white helmets and white jackets came out of the Zhao's place—with trunks, furniture, even the stylish Ningbo bed that belonged to the *Budding Talent*'s old lady. He wanted to get closer for a better look, but his feet simply wouldn't move.

Wei Village lay very quiet in the darkness, as quiet as it might have lain during the reign of Fu Xi. Ah Q stood and watched until he was tired of watching, but there was still no end in sight. A steady stream of people went back and forth moving things out, so many things that Ah Q could scarcely believe his eyes. He decided against getting any closer and headed back to the temple.

It was pitch black in the Land-and-Grain Temple. Closing the main gate behind him, Ah Q groped his way back into his room. He lay there for a long time before he was finally able to collect his thoughts enough to assess his own situation. Quite clearly the white-helmet white-armor people had arrived, but also just as clearly, they had not invited him to join them. And so no matter how much loot they made off with at the Zhaos' place, he didn't stand to get any share of it. "It's all because that Fake Foreign Devil wouldn't let me revolt, otherwise I'd sure as hell have gotten some of that stuff." The more he thought, the madder he got, until at last he could contain himself no longer. "Won't let me revolt, huh? You're the only one allowed to revolt, fuckin' Fake Foreign Devil! Okay, go right ahead and revolt to your heart's content. Revolt's a crime you can get your head chopped off for. Just watch and see if I don't turn your ass in! I'll just sit back and watch 'em haul you into town and lop off your head! They'll do in your whole family—*ZAP! ZAP! ZAP!*"

## Chapter 9

The Grand Reunion

After the burglary at Old Master Zhao's the villagers were, for the most part, quite pleased—and frightened too; Ah Q was, for the most part, quite pleased—and frightened as well. Four days later he was arrested in the middle of the night and hauled off to town.

As luck would have it, there was no moon that night and taking full advantage of the darkness, one squad of soldiers, one squad of militia, and five detectives slipped into the village to surround the Land-and-Grain Temple. Expectantly, they set up a machine gun opposite the temple gate, Ah Z, however, failed to come roaring out on cue. They waited and waited, but there was nary a peep within the temple compound. Unable to stand the suspense, the lieutenant persuaded two of his bravos—for a reward of twenty strings of cash, one full thousand to the string—to scale the temple wall. Once inside they let their cohorts in through the gate, and together they all thundered onward to Ah Q's room and took him captive there. When they had dragged him out to the machine gun emplacement, he was beginning to wake up.

And by the time they entered the town with Ah Q in tow, it was already high noon. He watched himself supported under the arms and escorted into a rundown *yamen* where, after five or six shifts in direction, he was finally shoved into a cell. A big barrel door slammed shut at his heels as he stumbled inside. The other three sides of the cell were bare walls. Upon closer inspection he discovered two other men over in one corner.

Although somewhat upset, Ah Q was not particularly dissatisfied with his present accommodations, for his own room back at the temple was certainly no more elegantly appointed than this cell. The other two men, it turned out, were country people like himself, and it wasn't too long before he had struck up a conversation with them. One said he was there because Old Master *Selectman* was dunning him for rents owed by his dead grandfather. The other had no idea why he had been arrested. When they asked Ah Q what he was in for, he replied without the slightest hesitation: "Cause I wanna revolt."

During the second half of the day, the big barrel door opened once again. Ah Q was hauled out and taken to the courtroom. Up front an old man, head shaven clean, sat on a dais. Ah Q thought he must be some kind of monk at first, but then he noticed a line of soldiers standing below the old fellow and many long-gowned gentry types on either side of him as well. Some of these long-gowns had their heads shaved clean just like the old geezer, but one had hair that was a good foot and a half long and fanned out over his shoulders just like the Fake Foreign Devil's. Every mother's son of them looked mean and ugly. What was more, they nailed Ah Q with dirty looks. At this juncture, it occurred to Ah Q that there must be something more to the bald old geezer than met the eye. Ah Q's knees instantly loosened of their own accord and he sank to a kneeling position.

"Stand! Stand while addressing this court! No kneeling!" barked the long-gowned types virtually in unison.

Ah Q appeared to understand, but didn't seem able to stay on his feet. As if of its own accord, his body collapsed into a squat and then, capitalizing on the momentum already built up, continued right on down into a full-fledged kneel.

"A born slave!" observed the long-gowned types with contempt, but they didn't try to get him to stand up again either.

"Why not come right out and confess it all now, and spare yourself a lot of needless suffering later on. We know exactly what happened anyway." The bald-headed old man's gaze never left Ah Q's face. His voice was kindly—calm and clear. "Just fess up and we'll let you go."

"Confess!" bellowed the long-gowns.

"Well, to tell the truth . . . I was gonna . . . gonna come and throw—"

"Then why *didn't* you come?" asked the old man in the sweetest of tones.

"Fake Foreign Devil wouldn't let me!"

"Nonsense! Too late to talk about that now anyway. Where are your confederates?"

"My what?"

"The bunch that burglarized the Zhaos' place with you?"

"Those guys didn't even come by to get me! Carted all that stuff off for themselves!" Ah Q waxed indignant at the very thought of it.

"Where did they cart it off to? If you tell, I can let you walk out of here." The old man's voice was more mellifluous than ever.

"How should I know? They didn't come by to get me!"

At this juncture the old man gave a wink, and Ah Q was once again shoved through the big barred door.

The next morning he was hauled out a second time. The courtroom was exactly as it had been yesterday—the bald-headed old man sitting on the dais while Ah Q knelt on the floor before him. "Do you have anything to say to this court?" asked the old man, voice dripping with compassion.

Ah Q thought for a bit. He didn't, and said no.

Then one of the long-gowns presented him with a sheet of paper and a writing brush. When the said personage thrust the brush into the prisoner's hand, Ah Q was so terrified that it was almost a case of *the heavenly part of the soul took to wing, and the earthly part to heel,* for this was the first time in his whole life that any relationship had ever been established between his hand and a writing brush. Just as he was wondering how you were supposed to hold the thing, the long-gown pointed to a place on the paper and told him to sign.

Ah Q's fingers tightened around the brush. In a voice that echoed with fear and shame he confessed: "Don't . . . don't know how to write."

"In that case we'll go easy on you. Just draw a circle."

Ah Q tried to compose himself enough to make the circle, but the hand that held the brush refused to stop trembling. The long-gowns carefully spread the paper out flat on the floor before him. Ah Q leaned forward over it, and marshaling all the strength and concentration at his command, approached the task at hand. Dreadfully concerned lest someone laugh at him, he was determined to make that circle a nice round one, but that damned brush lay heavy in his hand and turned out to be disobedient as well. Tremble after tremble, he traced the circle around and was on the point of closing it up when suddenly the brush shrugged off to one side, producing something that looked more like a watermelon seed than a circle.

Just as Ah Q was starting to feel conscience stricken at not being able to make a nice round circle, one of the long-gowns, not seeming to mind in the least, made off with both brush and paper.

The second time Ah Q was shoved into the cell, it didn't seem to bother him much at all, for he had come to the conclusion that in this old world of ours there must be times when a man is supposed to get hauled in and out of cells, and times when he's supposed to draw circles on a sheet of paper too. "It would take a real jackass to draw a nice *round* circle anyway," he told himself and then promptly fell asleep.

Old Master *Selectman,* on the other hand, didn't get a single wink that whole night, for he'd had a good go-round with the lieutenant during the day. The *Selectman* had maintained that the first order of business was recovery of the stolen property, but the lieutenant had insisted that the most important thing was to make a public example of Ah Q. The lieutenant, who had only recently stopped giving a hoot *what* Old Master *Selectman* thought, had slammed his fist hard on the table and quoted: *"Make an example of only one / And a hundred crimes will go undone.* Put yourself in my shoes. I've been a lieutenant in the Revolutionary Party for less than three weeks and we've already had a dozen cases of burglary. Not a single one solved, either. Now what kind of face does that give me? When I finally do figure one out, you have to come along and start acting like some old fuddy-duddy scholar. Well I won't have it! *I'm* the one in charge of this case!" But Old Master *Selectman* held his ground. He even threatened to resign his new position as deputy in the Revolutionary Government if the lieutenant didn't do his best to recover the stolen property. "Be my guest!" had been the lieutenant's only response. And so it was that Old Master *Selectman* didn't get a single wink that whole night. We can thank our lucky stars, however, that he did not actually resign the next day.

The third time Ah Q was hauled out through the big barred door was on the morrow of the entire night during which Old Master *Selectman* didn't get a single wink.

Ah Q entered the courtroom once again. Just as before, the bald-headed old man sat on the dais while Ah Q knelt on the floor before him.

"Do you have anything more to tell the court?" asked the old man in kindly tones.

Ah Q thought for a bit. He didn't, and said no.

And then all of a sudden some of the long-gowned and short-gowned types put a white cotton vest on him, a vest with words written all over it.

Now a very queasy feeling came over Ah Q, for such an outfit was like unto the *mourning clothes* that people wore when their parents died—and mourning clothes were definitely unlucky.

Hands tied behind him, Ah Q was hauled out through the front gate of the *yamen* and lifted up onto an open cart. Two men in short jackets seated themselves on either side of him. The cart lurched into motion.

Ah Q saw that there were some militiamen and a squad of soldiers marching in front of the cart. The soldiers were shouldering foreign rifles. Mouths agape, spectators lined both sides of the road. He couldn't see, of course, whatever it was that was bringing up the rear. Suddenly it dawned on him. It couldn't be anything else—this was an execution!

Ah Q panicked. Everything went black. There was a loud ringing in his ears and he slipped to the edge of unconsciousness. But rather than falling in, he stayed there teetering on the brink. Remaining in this state, he was by turns terror-stricken and perfectly at ease. As his mind flickered on and off, Ah Q concluded that in this old world of ours there must be times when a man is supposed to get hauled away and have his head chopped off.

He recognized their route of march. He was puzzled—why weren't they headed to the execution ground? Ah Q didn't realize that he was first being paraded through the streets as "a warning to the people." But even if he had known, it would have made no difference. He would simply have concluded that in this old world of ours there must be times when a man is supposed to be paraded through the streets as a warning to the people. Then he solved the puzzle—yes, he was in fact headed toward the execution ground, but they were taking the long way around.

There was no longer even the slightest doubt. He was going to be beheaded—*ZAP!* In a daze, he turned his head first to one side and then the other. Everywhere he looked people were following along behind him just like ants. Then he just so happened to catch sight of Amah Wu standing in the midst of a group over by the roadside. Because she had been working in town, he had not been able to pay his respects to her in a long, long time.

Ah Q was suddenly gripped by shame at his own lack of pluck—all this time and he still hadn't sung a single line of opera. Thoughts began to swirl around like a cyclone in his brain. *The Young Widow Visits Her Husband's Grave* was not stirring enough. "*Would that I had not . . .*" from *Battle of the Dragon and Tiger Generals* did not have any real wallop either. Better stick to that old reliable: "*My mace of steel I grasp full tight / And with it I shall now thee smite!*" Having made his selection and suiting gesture to word, he started to raise his hand, but it wouldn't go up. Then he remembered—it was tied behind him. Couldn't sing that one either.

"Twenty years from now . . ." Ah Q shouted the first half of the sentence, a sentence he had never used before, one he had never been taught but which he seemed to have mastered on his own nonetheless.

"Bravo! Bravo!" Shouts rose from the crowd like the howls of so many wolves.

The cart continued relentlessly forward. Amid all the cheering, Ah Q turned and looked at Amah Wu once again. It was apparent, however, that she had not even noticed him, for she was lost in contemplation of the novel-looking foreign rifles the soldiers were carrying. So he turned back and looked again at the people who had just cheered.

Once again thoughts began to swirl around like a cyclone in his brain. He was taken back to a time four years earlier when he had encountered a hungry wolf at the foot of a mountain. It had stalked him with persistent tenacity, neither closing in nor dropping back by so much as half a step, patiently awaiting its chance to tear into his flesh. Ah Q had been terrified and it was only because he happened to be carrying a small hatchet at the time that he had mustered the courage to make it back to Wei Village. He had never forgotten that wolf's eyes—ferocious and timid at the same time and glowing like two fiendish flames that might, at any moment, burn through his body from afar.

But now he saw eyes that were even more terrible, eyes such as he had never seen before. Sharp and dull at the same time, these eyes had already devoured his words and now sought to tear into something beyond mere flesh and bone. Neither closing in nor dropping back by so much as half a step, they stalked him with persistent tenacity. And then they all merged into a single set of fangs that ripped and tore at Ah Q's soul.

"Help . . ."

But before Ah Q could get it out, everything went black before his eyes, there was a loud ringing in his ears, and he felt his entire being crumble like so much dust.

As for the impact of his death, the greatest was on Old Master *Selectman,* for he was thus unable to recover any of the stolen property. Hence his entire family took to wailing. Next came the Zhao family. Some Revolutionaries cut the *Budding Talent's* queue off when he went into town to report the burglary. On top of that, they forced him to tip them twenty strings of cash for their services. Thus the entire Zhao family took to wailing, too.

As to public opinion, the inhabitants of Wei Village were unanimous. Everyone agreed that Ah Q had indeed been an evil man, the clear proof of which could be found in the fact that he had in truth been executed. If he hadn't been bad, then how could he have gone and gotten himself executed?

Public opinion in town was something less than favorable too. Most townsfolk were disappointed—a shooting had not proved nearly so much fun as a good old-fashioned beheading. Worse yet, in his role as condemned criminal Ah Q had given a miserable performance—paraded through the streets all that time and not a single line of opera! They had followed him in vain.

## DING LING (1904–1985)

*Translated by Gary J. Bjorge*

Ding Ling is the most famous Chinese woman writer of the twentieth century. She began writing at a very young age and was quickly accepted as one of the strongest voices among the new vernacular fiction writers who appeared after the literary revolution of the 1910s and early 1920s. Ding Ling, like so many of her contemporaries, was influenced more by the work of Western writers than by traditional Chinese fiction. She was particularly drawn to the French writer Gustave Flaubert (1821–1880) and deeply admired his *Madame Bovary,* a novel that clearly influenced several of her early short stories.

Ding Ling's long life was shaped by her early commitment to the Communist Party, which she formally joined in 1931, the year the Nationalist police executed her husband, Hu Yepin. Like so many left-wing writers, Ding Ling was caught in the dangerous political currents that have swirled in China around the question of the role literature should play in the socialist state. A free spirit both in intellect and way of life, Ding Ling was censured by the communist leadership in the early 1940s for her feminist views and her "unorthodox tendencies," was expelled from the party in 1958 as a "rightist," and was imprisoned during the Cultural Revolution. Still, much of her writing, particularly during the 1940s and 1950s, is obviously meant to serve what she believed to be the interests of China and the Communist Party.

The story included here, "When I Was in Xia Village," was written in 1940 while Ding Ling was with Mao Zedong and the communist leadership at Yan'an. The narrator of the story is a loyal comrade who has been sent to Xia Village for rest and recuperation. While in the village, she becomes acquainted with a young woman, Zhenzhen, who was raped and used as a war prostitute by the invading Japanese army. What makes Zhenzhen so remarkable is her refusal to fall into self-pity and her resistance to allowing others to categorize her as a victim. She somehow remains aloof from the turmoil that swirls about her and turns for friendship to the narrator, the only figure in the story willing to allow Zhenzhen to define herself. The narrator becomes the most intriguing character in the story. She is Ding Ling's idea of the perfect party leader, and one can perhaps locate in her tolerance and gentleness a hope for a leadership style that must often have been at variance with much that Ding Ling encountered at Yan'an.

## *When I Was in Xia Village*

Because of the turmoil in the Political Department, Comrade Mo Yü decided to send me to stay temporarily in a neighboring village. Actually, I was already completely well, but the opportunity to rest for a while in a quiet environment and arrange my notes from the past three months did have its attractions. So I agreed to spend two weeks in Xia Village, a place about ten miles from the Political Department.

A female comrade from the Propaganda Department, who was apparently on a work assignment, went with me. Since she wasn't a person who enjoyed conversation, however, the journey was rather lonely. Also, because her feet had once been bound and my own spirits were low, we traveled slowly. We set out in the morning, but it was nearly sunset by the time we reached our destination.

The village looked much like any other from a distance, but I knew it contained a very beautiful Catholic church that had escaped destruction and a small grove of pine trees. The place where I would be staying was in the midst of these trees, which clung to the hillside. From that spot it would be possible to look straight across to the church. By now I could see orderly rows of cave dwellings and the green trees above them. I felt content with the village.

My traveling companion had given me the impression that the village was very busy, but when we entered it, not even a single child or dog was to be seen. The only movement was dry leaves twirling about lightly in the wind. They would fly a short distance, then drop to earth again.

"This used to be an elementary school, but last year the Jap devils destroyed it. Look at those steps over there. That used to be a big classroom," my companion, Agui, told me. She was somewhat excited now, not so reserved as she had been during the day. Pointing to a large empty courtyard, she continued: "A year and a half ago, this area was full of life. Every evening after supper, the comrades gathered here to play soccer or basketball." Becoming more agitated, she asked, "Why isn't anyone here? Should we go to the assembly hall or head up the hill? We don't know where they've taken our luggage either. We have to straighten that out first."

On the wall next to the gate of the village assembly hall, many white paper slips had been pasted. They read "Office of the [Communist] Association," "Xia Village Branch of the [Communist] Association," and so on. But when we went inside, we couldn't find a soul. It was completely quiet, with only a few tables set about. We were both standing there dumbly when suddenly a man rushed in. He looked at us for a moment, seemed about to ask us something, but swallowed his words and prepared to dash away. We called to him to stop, however, and made him answer our questions.

"The people of the village? They've all gone to the west door. Baggage? Hmm. Yes, there was baggage. It was carried up the hill some time ago to Liu Erma's home." As he talked, he sized us up.

Learning that he was a member of the Peasant's Salvation Association, we asked him to accompany us up the hill and also asked him to deliver a note to one of the local comrades. He agreed to take the note, but he wouldn't go with us. He seemed impatient and ran off by himself.

The street too was very quiet. The doors of several shops were closed. Others were still open, exposing pitch-black interiors. We still couldn't find anyone. Fortunately, Agui was familiar with the village and led me up the hill. It was already dark. The winter sun sets very quickly.

The hill was not high, and a large number of stone cave dwellings were scattered here and there from the bottom to the top. In a few places, people were standing out in front peering into the distance. Agui knew very well that we had not yet reached our destination, but whenever we met someone she asked, "Is this the way to Liu Erma's house?" "How far is it to Liu Erma's house?" "Could you please tell me the way to Liu Erma's house?" Or, she would ask, "Did you notice any baggage being sent to Liu Erma's house? Is Liu Erma home?"

The answers we received always satisfied us, and this continued right up to the most distant and highest house, which was the Liu family's. Two small dogs were the first to greet us. Then a woman came out and asked who we were. As soon as they heard it was me, two more women came out. Holding a lantern, they escorted us into the courtyard and then into a cave on the side toward the east. The cave was virtually empty. On the *kang* under the window were piled my bedroll, my small leather carrying case, and Agui's quilt.

Some of the people there knew Agui. They took her hand and asked her many questions, and after a while they led her out, leaving me alone in the room. I arranged my bed and was about to lie down when suddenly they all crowded back in again. One of Liu Erma's daughters-in-law was carrying a bowl of noodles. Agui, Liu Erma, and a young girl were holding bowls, chopsticks, and a dish of onions and pepper. The young girl also brought in a brazier of burning coal.

Attentively, they urged me to eat some noodles and touched my hands and arms. Liu Erma and her daughter-in-law also sat down on the *kang*. There was an air of mystery about them as they continued the conversation interrupted by their entry into the room.

At first I thought I had caused their amazement, but gradually I realized that this wasn't the case. They were interested in only one thing—the topic of their conversation. Since all I heard were a few fragmentary sentences, I couldn't understand what they were talking about. This was especially true of what Liu Erma said because she frequently lowered her voice, as if afraid that someone might overhear her. Agui had changed completely. She now appeared quite capable and was very talkative. She listened closely to what the others were saying and seemed able to grasp the essence of their words. The daughter-in-law and the young girl said little. At times they added a word or two, but for the most part they just listened intently to what Agui and Liu Erma were saying. They seemed afraid to miss a single word.

Suddenly the courtyard was filled with noise. A large number of people had rushed in, and they all seemed to be talking at once. Liu Erma and the others climbed nervously off the *kang* and hurried outside. Without thinking, I followed along behind them to see what was happening.

By this time the courtyard was in complete darkness. Two red paper lanterns bobbed and weaved above the crowd. I worked my way into the throng and looked around. I couldn't see anything. The others also were squeezing in for no apparent reason. They seemed to want to say more, but they did not. I heard only simple exchanges that confused me even more.

"Yüwa, are you here too?"

"Have you seen her yet?"

"Yes, I've seen her. I was a little afraid."

"What is there to be afraid of? She's just a human being, and prettier than ever too."

At first I was sure that they were talking about a new bride, but people said that wasn't so. Then I thought there was a prisoner present, but that was wrong too. I followed the crowd to the doorway of the central cave, but all there was to see was more people packed tightly together. Thick smoke obscured my vision, so I had no choice but to back away. Others were also leaving by now, and the courtyard was much less crowded.

Since I couldn't sleep, I set about rearranging my carrying case by the lantern light. I paged through several notebooks, looked at photographs, and sharpened some pencils. I was obviously tired, but I also felt the kind of excitement that comes just before a new life begins. I prepared a time schedule for myself and was determined to adhere to it, beginning the very next day.

At that moment there was a man's voice at the door. "Are you asleep, comrade?" Before I could reply, the fellow entered the room. He was about twenty years old, a rather refined-looking country youth. "I received Director Mo's letter some time ago," he said. "This area is relatively quiet. Don't worry about a thing. That's my job. If you need something, don't hesitate to ask Liu Erma. Director Mo said you wanted to stay here for two weeks. Fine. If you enjoy your visit, we'd be happy to have you stay longer. I live in a neighboring cave, just below these. If you need me, just send someone to find me."

He declined to come up on the *kang,* and since there was no bench on the floor to sit on, I jumped down and said, "Ah! You must be Comrade Ma. Did you receive the note I sent you? Please sit down and talk for a while."

I knew that he held a position of some responsibility in the village. As a student he had not yet finished junior high school.

"They tell me you've written a lot of books," he responded. "It's too bad we haven't seen a single one." As he spoke he looked at my open carrying case that was lying on the *kang.* Our conversation turned to the subject of the local level of study. Then he said, "After you've rested for a few days, we'll definitely invite you to give a talk. It can be to a mass meeting or to a training class. In any case, you'll certainly be able to help us. Our most difficult task here is 'cultural recreation.'"

I had seen many young men like him at the Front. When I first met them, I was always amazed. I felt that these youth, who were somewhat remote from me, were really changing fast. Changing the subject, I asked him, "What was going on just now?"

"Zhenzhen, the daughter of Liu Dama, has returned," he answered. "I never thought she could be so great." I immediately sensed a joyful, radiant twinkle in his eyes. As I was about to ask another question, he added, "She's come back from the Japanese area. She's been working there for over a year."

"Oh my!" I gasped.

He was about to tell me more when someone outside called for him. All he could say was that he'd be sure to have Zhenzhen call on me the next day. As if to provoke my interest further, he added that Zhenzhen must certainly have a lot of material for stories.

It was very late when Agui came back. She lay down on the *kang* but could not sleep. She tossed and turned and sighed continuously. I was very tired, but I still wished that she would tell me something about the events of the evening.

"No, comrade," she said. "I can't talk about it now. I'm too upset. I'll tell you tomorrow. Ahh . . . How miserable it is to be a woman." After this she covered her head with her quilt and lay completely still, no longer sighing. I didn't know when she finally fell asleep.

Early the next morning I stepped outside for a stroll, and before I knew it I had walked down to the village. I went into a general store to rest and buy red dates for Liu Erma to put in the rice porridge. As soon as the owner learned that I was living with Liu Erma, his small eyes narrowed and he asked me in a low, excited voice, "Did you get a look at her niece? I hear her disease has even taken her nose. That's because she was abused by the Jap devils." Turning his head, he called to his wife, who was standing in the inner doorway, "She has nerve, coming home! It's revenge against her father, Liu Fusheng."

"That girl was always frivolous. You saw the way she used to roam around the streets. Wasn't she Xia Dabao's old flame? If he hadn't been poor, wouldn't she have married him a long time ago?" As she finished speaking, the old woman lifted her skirts and came into the store.

The owner turned his face back toward me and said, "There are so many rumors." His eyes stopped blinking and his expression became very serious. "It's said that she has slept with at least a hundred men. Humph! I've heard that she even became the wife of a Japanese officer. Such a shameful woman should not be allowed to return."

Not wanting to argue with him, I held back my anger and left. I didn't look back, but I felt that he had again narrowed his small eyes and was feeling smug as he watched me walk away. As I neared the corner by the Catholic church, I overheard a conversation by two women who were drawing water at the well. One said, "She sought out Father Lu and told him she definitely wanted to be a nun. When Father Lu asked her for a reason, she didn't say a word, just cried. Who knows what she did there? Now she's worse than a prostitute . . ."

"Yesterday they told me she walks with a limp. Achh! How can she face people?"

"Someone said she's even wearing a gold ring that a Jap devil gave her!"

"I understand she's been as far away as Datong and has seen many things. She can even speak Japanese."

My walk was making me unhappy, so I returned home. Since Agui had already gone out, I sat alone in my room and read a small pamphlet. After a while, I raised my eyes and noticed two large baskets for storing grain sitting near the wall. They must have had a long history, because they were as black as the wall itself. Opening the movable portion of the paper window, I peered out at the gray sky. The weather had changed completely from what it had been when I arrived the day before. The hard ground of the courtyard had been swept clean, and at the far edge a tree with a few withered branches stood out starkly against the leaden sky. There wasn't a single person to be seen.

I opened my carrying case, took out pen and paper, and wrote two letters. I wondered why Agui had not yet returned. I had forgotten that she had work to do. I was somehow thinking that she had come to be my companion. The days of winter are very short, but right then I was feeling that they were even longer than summer days.

Some time later, the young girl who had been in my room the night before came out into the courtyard. I immediately jumped down off the *kang,* stepped out the door, and called to her, but she just looked at me and smiled before rushing into another cave. I walked around the courtyard twice and then stopped to watch a hawk fly into the grove of trees by the church. The courtyard there had many large trees. I started walking again and, on the right side of the courtyard, picked up the sound of a woman crying. She was trying to stop, frequently blowing her nose.

I tried hard to control myself. I thought about why I was here and about all my plans. I had to rest and live according to the time schedule I had made. I returned to my room, but I couldn't sleep and had no interest in writing in my notebook.

Fortunately, a short while later Liu Erma came to see me. The young girl was with her, and her daughter-in-law arrived soon after. The three of them climbed up on the *kang* and took seats around the small brazier. The young girl looked closely at my things, which were laid out on the little square *kang* table.

"At that time no one could take care of anyone else," Liu Erma said, talking about the Japanese attack on Xia Village a year and a half before. "Those of us who lived on the hilltop were luckier. We could run away quickly. Many who lived in the village could not escape. Apparently it was all fate. Just then, on that day, our family's Zhenzhen had run over to the Catholic church. Only later did we learn that her unhappiness about what was happening had caused her to go to talk to the foreign priest about becoming a nun. Her father was in the midst of negotiating a marriage for her with the young proprietor of a rice store in Xiliu Village. He was almost thirty, a widower, and his family was well respected. We all said he would be a good match, but Zhenzhen said no and broke into tears before her father. In other matters, her father had always deferred to her wishes, but in this case the old man was adamant. He had no son and had always wanted to betroth his daughter to a good man. Who would have thought that Zhenzhen would turn around in anger and run off to the Catholic church. It was at that moment that the Japs caught her. How could her mother and father help grieving?"

"Was that her mother crying?"

"Yes."

"And your niece?"

"Well, she's really just a child. When she came back yesterday, she cried for a long time, but today she went to the assembly in high spirits. She's only eighteen."

"I heard she was the wife of a Japanese. Is that true?"

"It's hard to say. We haven't been able to find out for sure. There are many rumors, of course. She's contracted a disease, but how could anyone keep clean in such a place? The possibility of her marrying the merchant seems to be over. Who would want a woman who was abused by the Jap devils? She definitely has the disease. Last night she said so herself. This time she's changed a lot. When she talks about those devils, she shows no more emotion than if she were talking about an ordinary meal at home. She's only eighteen, but she has no sense of embarrassment at all."

"Xia Dabao came again today," the daughter-in-law said quietly, her questioning eyes fixed on Erma.

"Who is Xia Dabao?" I asked.

"He's a young man who works in the village flour mill," replied Liu Erma. "When he was young, he and Zhenzhen were classmates for a year. They liked each other very much, but his family was poor, even poorer than ours. He didn't dare do anything, but our Zhenzhen was head over heels in love with him and kept clinging to him. Then she was upset when he didn't respond. Isn't it because of him that she wanted to be a nun? After Zhenzhen fell into the hands of the Jap devils, he often came to see her parents. At first just the sight of him made Zhenzhen's father angry. At times he cursed him, but Xia Dabao would say nothing. After a scolding he would leave and then come back another day. Dabao is really a good boy. Now he's even a squad leader in the self-defense corps. Today he came once again, apparently to talk with Zhenzhen's mother about marrying Zhenzhen. All I could hear was her crying. Later he left in tears himself."

"Does he know about your niece's situation?"

"How could he help knowing? There is no one in this village who doesn't know everything. They all know more than we do ourselves."

"Mother, everyone says that Xia Dabao is foolish," the young girl interjected.

"Humph! The boy has a good conscience. I approve of this match. Since the Jap devils came, who has any money? Judging from the words of Zhenzhen's parents, I think they approve too. If not him, who? Even without mentioning her disease, her reputation is enough to deter anyone."

"He was the one wearing the dark blue jacket and the copper-colored felt hat with the turned-up brim," the young girl said. Her eyes were sparkling with curiosity, and she seemed to understand this matter very well.

His figure began to take shape in my memory. When I went out for my walk earlier that morning, I had seen an alert, honest-looking young man who fit this description. He had been standing outside my courtyard, but had not shown any intention of coming in. On my way home, I had seen him again, this time emerging from the pine woods beyond the cave dwellings. I had thought he was someone from my courtyard or from a neighboring one and hadn't paid much attention to him. As I recalled him now, I felt that he was a rather capable man, not a bad young man at all.

I now feared that my plan for rest and recuperation could not be realized. Why were my thoughts so confused? I wasn't particularly anxious to meet anybody, and yet my mind still couldn't rest. Agui had come in during the conversation, and now she seemed to sense my feelings. As she went out with the others, she gave me a knowing smile. I understood her meaning and busied myself with arranging the *kang*. My bedroll, the lamp, and the fire all seemed much brighter. I had just placed the tea kettle on the fire when Agui returned. Behind her I heard another person.

"We have a guest, comrade!" Agui called. Even before she finished speaking, I heard someone giggling.

Standing in the doorway, I grasped the hands of this person whom I had not seen before. They were burning hot, and I couldn't help being a bit startled. She followed Agui up onto the *kang* and sat down. A single long braid hung down her back.

In the eyes of the new arrival, the cave that depressed me seemed to be something new and fresh. She looked around at everything with an excited glint in her eyes. She sat opposite me, her body tilted back slightly and her two hands spread apart on the bedroll for support. She didn't seem to want to say anything. Her eyes finally came to rest on my face.

The shadows lengthened her eyes and made her chin quite pointed. But even though her eyes were in deep shadow, her pupils shone brightly in the light of the lamp and the fire. They were like two open windows in a summer home in the country, clear and clean.

I didn't know how to begin a conversation without touching an open wound and hurting her self-respect. So my first move was to pour her a cup of hot tea.

It was Zhenzhen who spoke first: "Are you a Southerner? I think so. You aren't like the people from this province."

"Have you seen many Southerners?" I asked, thinking it best to talk about what she wanted to talk about.

"No," she said, shaking her head. Her eyes still fixed on me, she added, "I've only seen a few. They always seem a little different. I like you people from the South. Southern women, unlike us, can all read many, many books. I want to study with you. Will you teach me?"

I expressed my willingness to do so, and she quickly continued, "Japanese women also can read a lot of books. All those devil soldiers carried a few well-written letters, some from wives, some from girlfriends. Some were written by girls they didn't even know. They would include a photograph and use syrupy language. I don't know if those girls were sincere or not, but they always made the devils hold their letters to their hearts like precious treasures."

"I understand that you can speak Japanese," I said. "Is that true?"

Her face flushed slightly before she replied, in a very open manner, "I was there for such a long time. I went around and around for over a year. I can speak a fair amount. Being able to understand their language had many advantages."

"Did you go to a lot of different places with them?"

"I wasn't always with the same unit. People think that because I was the wife of a Jap officer I enjoyed luxury. Actually, I came back here twice before. Altogether, this is my third time. I was ordered to go on this last mission. There was no choice. I was familiar with the area, the work was important, and it was impossible to find anyone else in a short time. I won't be sent back anymore. They're going to treat my disease. That's fine with me because I've missed my dad and mom, and I'm glad to be able to come back to see them. My mother, though, is really hopeless. When I'm not home, she cries. When I'm here, she still cries."

"You must have known many hardships."

"She has endured unthinkable suffering," Agui interrupted, her face twisted in a pained expression. In a voice breaking with emotion, she added, "It's a real tragedy to be a woman, isn't it, Zhenzhen?" She slid over to be next to her.

"Suffering?" Zhenzhen asked, her thoughts apparently far, far away. "Right now I can't say for certain. Some things were hard to endure at the time, but when I recall them now they don't seem like much. Other things were no problem to do when I did them, but when I think about them now I'm very sad. More than a year . . . It's all past. Since I came back this time, a great many people have looked at me strangely. As far as the people of this village are concerned, I'm an outsider. Some are very friendly to me. Others avoid me. The members of my family are just the same. They all like to steal looks at me. Nobody treats me the way they used to. Have I changed? I've thought about this a great deal, and I don't think I've changed at all. If I have changed, maybe it's that my heart has become somewhat harder. But could anyone spend time in such a place and not become hard-hearted? People have no choice. They're forced to be like that!"

There was no outward sign of her disease. Her complexion was ruddy. Her voice was clear. She showed no signs of inhibition or rudeness. She did not exaggerate. She gave the impression that she had never had any complaints or sad thoughts. Finally, I could restrain myself no longer and asked her about her disease.

"People are always like that, even if they find themselves in worse situations. They brace themselves and see it through. Can you just give up and die? Later, after I made contact with our own people, I became less afraid. As I watched the Jap devils suffer defeat in battle and the guerrillas take action on all sides as a result of the tricks I was playing, I felt better by the day. I felt that even though my life was hard, I could still manage. Somehow I had to find a way to survive, and if at all possible, to live a life that was meaningful. That's why I'm pleased that they intend to treat my disease. It will be better to be cured. Actually, these past few days I haven't felt too bad. On the way home, I stayed in Zhangjiayi for two days and was given two shots and some medicine to take orally. The worst time was in the fall. I was told that my insides were rotting away, and then, because of some important information and the fact that no one could be found to take my place, I had to go back. That night I walked alone in the dark for ten miles. Every single step was painful. My mind was filled with the desire to sit down and rest. If the work hadn't been so important, I definitely wouldn't have gone back. But I had to. Ahh! I was afraid I might be recognized by the Jap devils, and I was also worried about missing my rendezvous. After it was over, I slept for a full week before I could pull myself together. It really isn't all that easy to die, is it?"

Without waiting for me to respond, she continued on with her story. At times she stopped talking and looked at us. Perhaps she was searching for reactions on our faces. Or maybe she was only thinking of something else. I could see that Agui was more troubled than Zhenzhen. For the most part she sat in silence, and when she did speak, it was only for a sentence or two. Her words gave voice to a limitless sympathy for Zhenzhen, but her expression when silent revealed even more clearly how moved she was by what Zhenzhen was saying. Her soul was being crushed. She herself was feeling the suffering that Zhenzhen had known before.

It was my impression that Zhenzhen had no intention whatever of trying to elicit sympathy from others. Even as others took upon themselves part of the misfortune that she had suffered, she seemed unaware of it. But that very fact made others feel even more sympathetic. It would have been better if, instead of listening to her recount the events of this period with a calmness that almost made you think she was talking about someone else, you could have heard her cry. Probably you would have cried with her, but you would have felt better.

After a while Agui began to cry, and Zhenzhen turned to comfort her. There were many things that I had wanted to discuss with Zhenzhen, but I couldn't bring myself to say anything. I wished to remain silent. After Zhenzhen left, I forced myself to read by the lamp for an hour. Not once did I look at Agui or ask her a question, even though she was lying very close to me, even though she tossed and turned and sighed all the time, unable to fall asleep.

After this Zhenzhen came to talk with me every day. She did not talk about herself alone. She very often showed great curiosity about many aspects of my life that were beyond her own experiences. At times, when my words were far removed from her life, it was obvious that she was struggling to understand, but nevertheless she listened intently. The two of us also took walks together down to the village. The youth were very good to her. Naturally, they were all activists. People like the owner of the general store, however, always gave us cold, steely stares. They disliked and despised Zhenzhen. They even treated me as someone not of their kind. This was especially true of the women, who, all because of Zhenzhen, became extremely self-righteous, perceiving themselves as saintly and pure. They were proud about never having been raped.

After Agui left the village, I grew even closer to Zhenzhen. It seemed that neither of us could be without the other. As soon as we were apart, we thought of each other. I like people who are enthusiastic and lively, who can be really happy or sad, and at the same time are straightforward and candid. Zhenzhen was just such a person. Our conversations took up a great deal of time, but I always felt that they were beneficial to my studies and to my personal growth. As the days went by, however, I discovered that Zhenzhen was not being completely open about something. I did not resent this. Moreover, I was determined not to touch upon this secret of hers. All people have things buried deeply in their hearts that they don't want to tell others. This secret was a matter of private emotions. It had nothing to do with other people or with Zhenzhen's own morality.

A few days before my departure, Zhenzhen suddenly began to appear very agitated. Nothing special seemed to have happened, and she showed no desire to talk to me about anything new. Yet she frequently came to my room looking disturbed and restless, and after sitting for a few minutes, she would get up and leave. I knew she had not eaten well for several days and was often passing up meals. I had asked her about her disease and knew that the cause of her uneasiness was not simply physical. Sometimes, after coming to my room, she would make a few disjointed remarks. At other times, she put on an attentive expression, as if asking me to talk. But I could see that her thoughts were elsewhere, on things that she didn't want others to know. She was trying to conceal her emotions by acting as if nothing was wrong.

Twice I saw that capable young man come out of Zhenzhen's home. I had already compared my impression of him with Zhenzhen, and I sympathized with him deeply. Zhenzhen had been abused by many men, and had contracted a stigmatized, hard-to-cure disease, but he still patiently came to see her and still sought the approval of her parents to marry her. He didn't look down on her. He did not fear the derision or the rebukes of others. He must have felt she needed him more than ever. He understood what kind of attitude a man should have toward the woman of his choice at such a time and what his responsibilities were.

But what of Zhenzhen? Although naturally there were many aspects of her emotions and her sorrows that I had not learned during this short period, she had never expressed any hope that a man would marry her or, if you will, comfort her. I thought she had become so hard because she had been hurt so badly. She seemed not to want anything from anyone. It would be good if love, some extraordinarily sympathetic commiseration, could warm her soul. I wanted her to find a place where she could cry this out. I was hoping for a chance to attend a wedding in this family. At the very least, I wanted to hear of an agreement to marry before I left.

"What is Zhenzhen thinking of?" I asked myself. "This can't be delayed indefinitely, and it shouldn't be turned into a big problem."

One day Liu Erma, her daughter-in-law, and her young daughter all came to see me. I was sure they intended to give me a report on something, but when they started to speak, I didn't allow them the opportunity to tell me anything. If my friend wouldn't confide in me, and I wouldn't ask her about it directly, then I felt it would be harmful to her, to myself, and to our friendship to ask others about it.

That same evening at dusk, the courtyard was again filled with people milling about. All the neighbors were there, whispering to one another. Some looked sad, but there were also those who appeared to find it all exciting. The weather was frigid, but curiosity warmed their hearts. In the severe cold, they drew in their shoulders, hunched their backs, thrust their hands into their sleeves, puffed out their breath, and looked at each other as if they were investigating something very interesting.

At first all I heard was the sound of quarreling coming from Liu Dama's dwelling. Then I heard Liu Dama crying. This was followed by the sound of a man crying. As far as I could tell, it was Zhenzhen's father. Next came a crash of dishes breaking. Unable to bear it any longer, I pushed my way through the curious onlookers and rushed inside.

"You've come at just the right time," Liu Erma said as she pulled me inside. "You talk to our Zhenzhen."

Zhenzhen's face was hidden by her long disheveled hair, but two wild eyes could still be seen peering out at the people gathered there. I walked over to her and stood beside her, but she seemed completely oblivious to my presence. Perhaps she took me as one of the enemy and not worth a moment's concern. Her appearance had changed so completely that I could hardly remember the liveliness, the bright pleasantness I had found in her before. She was like a cornered animal. She was like an evening goddess. Whom did she hate? Why was her expression so fierce?

"You're so heartless. You don't think about your mother and father at all. You don't care how much I've suffered because of you in the last year." Liu Dama pounded on the *kang* as she scolded her daughter, tears like raindrops dropping to the *kang* or the floor and flowing down the contours of her face. Several women had surrounded her and were preventing her from coming down off the *kang*. It was frightening to see a person lose her self-respect and allow all her feelings to come out in a blind rage. I thought of telling her that such crying was useless, but at the same time, I realized that nothing I could say now would make any difference.

Zhenzhen's father looked very weak and old. His hands hung down limply. He was sighing deeply. Xia Dabao was seated beside him. There was a helpless look in his eyes as he stared at the old couple.

"You must say something. Don't you feel sorry for your mother?"

"When the end of a road is reached, one must turn. After water has flowed as far as it can, it must change direction. Aren't you going to change at all? Why make yourself suffer?" The women were trying to persuade Zhenzhen with such words.

I could see that this affair could not turn out the way that everyone was hoping. Zhenzhen had shown me much earlier that she didn't want anyone's sympathy. She, in turn, had no sympathy for anyone else. She had made her decision long ago and would not change. If people wanted to call her stubborn, then so be it. With teeth tightly clenched, she looked ready to stand up to all of them.

At last the others agreed to listen to me, and I asked Zhenzhen to come to my room and rest. I told them that everything could be discussed later that night. But when I led Zhenzhen out of the house, she did not follow me to my room. Instead, she ran off up the hillside.

"That girl has big ideas."

"Humph! She looks down on us country folk."

"She's such a cheap little hussy and yet she puts on such airs. Xia Dabao deserves it . . ."

These were some of the comments being made by the crowd in the courtyard. Then, when they realized that there was no longer anything of interest to see, the crowd drifted away.

I hesitated for a while in the courtyard before deciding to go up the hillside myself. On the top of the hill were numerous graves set among the pine trees. Broken stone tablets stood before them. No one was there. Not even the sound of a falling leaf broke the stillness. I ran back and forth calling Zhenzhen's name. What sounded like a response temporarily comforted my loneliness, but in an instant the vast silence of the hills became even deeper. The colors of sunset had completely faded. All around me a thin, smokelike mist rose silently and spread out to the middle slopes of the hills, both nearby and in the distance. I was worried and sat down weakly on a tombstone. Over and over I asked myself, "Should I go on up the hill or wait for her here?" I was hoping that I could relieve Zhenzhen of some of her distress.

At that moment I saw a shadow moving toward me from below. I quickly saw that it was Xia Dabao. I remained silent, hoping that he wouldn't see me and would continue on up the hill, but he came straight at me. At last I felt that I had to greet him and called, "Have you found her? I still haven't seen her."

He walked over to me and sat down on the dry grass. He said nothing, only stared into the distance. I felt a little uneasy. He really was very young. His eyebrows were long and thin. His eyes were quite large, but now they looked dull and lifeless. His small mouth was tightly drawn. Perhaps before it had been appealing, but now it was full of anguish, as if trying to hold in his pain. He had an honest-looking nose, but of what use was it to him now?

"Don't be sad," I said. "Maybe tomorrow everything will be all right. I'll talk to her this evening."

"Tomorrow, tomorrow—she'll always hate me. I know that she hates me." He spoke in a sad low voice that was slightly hoarse.

"No," I replied, searching my memory. "She has never shown me that she hates anyone." This was not a lie.

"She wouldn't tell you. She wouldn't tell anyone. She won't forgive me as long as she lives."

"Why should she hate you?"

"Of course—" he began. Suddenly he turned his face toward me and looked at me intently. "Tell me," he said, "at that time I had nothing. Should I have encouraged her to run away with me? Is all of this my fault? Is it?"

He didn't wait for my answer. As if speaking to himself, he went on, "It is my fault. Could anyone say that I did the right thing? Didn't I bring this harm to her? If I had been as brave as she, she never would have—I know her character. She'll always hate me. Tell me, what should I do? What would she want me to do? How can I make her happy? My life is worthless. Am I of even the slightest use to her? Can you tell me? I simply don't know what I should do. Ahhh! How miserable things are! This is worse than being captured by the Jap devils." Without a break, he continued to mumble on and on.

When I asked him to go back home with me, he stood up and we took several steps together. Then he stopped and said that he had heard a sound coming from the very top of the hill. There was nothing to do but encourage him to go on up, and I watched until he had disappeared into the thick pines. Then I started back. By now it was almost completely dark. It was very late when I went to bed that night, but I still hadn't received any news. I didn't know what had happened to them.

Even before I ate breakfast the next morning, I finished packing my suitcase. Comrade Ma had promised that he would be coming this day to help me move, and I was all prepared to return to the Political Department and then go on to [my next assignment]. The enemy was about to start another "mopping-up campaign," and my health would not permit me to remain in this area. Director Mo had said that the ill definitely had to be moved out first, but I felt uneasy. Should I try to stay? If I did, I could be a burden to others. What about leaving? If I went, would I ever be able to return? As I was sitting on my bedroll pondering these questions, I sensed someone slipping quietly into my room.

With a single thrust of her body, Zhenzhen jumped up onto the *kang* and took a seat opposite me. I could see that her face was slightly swollen, and when I grasped her hands as she spread them over the fire, the heat that had made such an impression on me before once again distressed me. Then and there I realized how serious her disease was.

"Zhenzhen," I said, "I'm about to leave. I don't know when we'll meet again. I hope you'll listen to your mother—"

"I have come to tell you," she interrupted, "that I'll be leaving tomorrow too. I want to leave home as soon as possible."

"Really?" I asked.

"Yes," she said, her face again revealing that special vibrancy. "They've told me to go in for medical treatment."

"Ah," I sighed, thinking that perhaps we could travel together. "Does your mother know?"

"No, she doesn't know yet. But if I say that I'm going for medical treatment and that after my disease is cured I'll come back, she'll be sure to let me go. Just staying at home doesn't have anything to offer, does it?"

At this moment I felt that she had a rare serenity about her. I recalled the words that Xia Dabao had spoken to me the previous evening and asked her directly, "Has the problem of your marriage been resolved?"

"Resolved? Oh, well, it's all the same."

"Did you heed your mother's advice?" I still didn't dare express my hopes for her. I didn't want to think of the image left in my mind by that young man. I was hoping that someday he would be happy.

"Why should I listen to what they say? Did they ever listen to me?"

"Well, are you really angry with them?"

There was no response.

"Well, then, do you really hate Xia Dabao?"

For a long time she did not reply. Then, in a very calm voice, she said, "I can't say that I hate him. I just feel now that I'm someone who's diseased. It's a fact that I was abused by a large number of Jap devils. I don't remember the exact number. In any case, I'm unclean, and with such a black mark I don't expect any good fortune to come my way. I feel that living among strangers and keeping busy would be better than living at home where people know me. Now that they've approved sending me to [Yan'an] for treatment, I've been thinking about staying there and doing some studying. I hear it's a big place with lots of schools and that anyone can attend. It's better for each of us to go our own separate ways than it is to have everyone stay together in one place. I'm doing this for myself, but I'm also doing it for the others. I don't feel that I owe anyone an apology. Neither do I feel especially happy. What I do feel is that after I go to [Yan'an], I'll be in a new situation. I will be able to start life fresh. A person's life is not just for one's father and mother, or even for oneself. Some have called me young, inexperienced, and bad-tempered. I don't dispute it. There are some things that I just have to keep to myself."

I was amazed. Something new was coming out of her. I felt that what she had said was really worth examining. There was nothing for me to do but express approval of her plan.

When I took my departure, Zhenzhen's family was there to see me off. She, however, had gone to the village office. I didn't see Xia Dabao before I left either.

I wasn't sad as I went away. I seemed to see the bright future that Zhenzhen had before her. The next day I would be seeing her again. That had been decided. And we would still be together for some time. As soon as Comrade Ma and I walked out the door of Zhenzhen's home, he told me of her decision and confirmed that what she had told me that morning would quickly come to pass.

# Modern Japan

In 1868 Japan emerged from 250 years of self-imposed isolation, making a conscious choice to modernize and westernize. The process was explosive and largely successful in political and economic terms. The new government systematically set about revising the nation's administrative structure, reorganizing the military, establishing a new system of education, and implementing changes in every aspect of Japanese life. The success of this transformation can be measured in several ways. By the early years of the twentieth century Japan was secure as a modern nation, had avoided becoming a colony of any of the big powers in the Pacific, had revised its unequal treaty arrangements, had successfully fought a war with China (1894–1895), had defeated Russia in war (1904–1905), and had begun a colonial empire of its own (Korea and Taiwan). By many standards, Japan had successfully modernized.

The limits of Japan's success were called into question in 1945, when the country lay in ruins, occupied by a foreign army for the first time in its history. Many wondered what had gone wrong. Nevertheless, a second miraculous transformation occurred in the fifty years following defeat in war: the Japanese "economic miracle" brought Japan once again to a position among the leading nations of the world.

Beneath these outward signs of success, however, lies a deep intellectual and spiritual uncertainty about what it means to be modern and about what it means to be Japanese. Central to this uncertainty is the idea of the self. Japan began its quest for modernity in the nineteenth century, coming from a tradition of neo-Confucianism that did not recognize the existence of an autonomous self. Within the framework of Confucian belief, people were expected to conform to certain roles. A person whose social position was warrior was expected to be the best possible warrior according to historically defined standards. A wife was expected to emulate as closely as possible the ideal wife; a student's job was to be the best possible student. One can recognize the Hindu and Buddhist concept of dharma in this idea. Personal morality was defined by how well one fulfilled one's duty and played the appropriate role. The system allowed no room for personal idiosyncracy. No one was expected to ask the questions "Who am I?" or "What do I want to be or do?" The whole notion of choosing one's identity and taking responsibility for it was utterly new in nineteenth-century Japan.

Natsume Sōseki was one of the earliest to raise this issue of identity in Japanese literature. In novel after novel he explored the idea of the self and asked in particular the question "How can a person be a free individual and still function in a morally acceptable way in society?" His characters make choices in their lives and sometimes make mistakes, but they have not learned the paths of redemption. Having made mistakes, they are condemned forever to failure. Abe Kōbō dealt with the same issue of the self, using Kafka and the German existentialists for models. His characters are so depersonalized by society that they are transformed into sticks or other objects, or they seek an authentic ground of being, only to discover they have no self to put in it. Ōba Minako's characters have achieved Japan's postwar dream of material success but continue to be dissatisfied and to seek restlessly for meaningful relationships, a search that requires a strong sense of self with which to relate to other selves.

Fortunately, in the process of modernization Japan has not abandoned its rich literary tradition. Matsuo Bashō represents a traditional attempt at the denial of the individual ego and a submergence of the self until it can become one with nature and move freely in space and time. In the twentieth century, Kawabata Yusunari continues to maintain a traditional stance, which says that the memory of an encounter is more important than the encounter itself.

Whether looking to modern, Western models, or to a thousand years of literary tradition, contemporary Japanese writers have produced one of the richest and most varied national literatures.

## MATSUO BASHŌ (1644–1694)

*Translated by Hiroaki Satō*

In the spring of 1689, the haiku poet Matsuo Bashō sold his hermitage in Edo and set out on a spiritual and poetic journey through the remote northern provinces of Japan. The trip took 150 days and covered some 600 miles. On the road, Bashō kept a journal of his experiences. This travel diary is a prose text studded with haiku poems creating what is known as *haibun,* a narrative form derived from the Heian period poem-tale that also represents the development of a new literary genre in Japan.

Travel was popular in Edo-period Japan because in that tightly controlled society, it gave common people the opportunity to break out of their daily routines and experience something new. As a consequence, making their appearance at this time are many travel accounts and guide books designed to assist travelers by telling them what to expect or providing a vicarious experience for those who could not leave home but could read about distant places. For Bashō, however, travel had a deeper significance. He saw travel as a metaphor for life and he literally turned his life into a journey. In doing this Bashō was, in part, following a Buddhist notion of renunciation, giving up all worldly possessions, even home and family, in favor of a life free from attachments. In a more secular sense, Bashō seems to have believed that only poetry endures the changes of time, and he chose not to be distracted from his committment to poetry by worldly concerns.

Bashō had made other poetic journeys in the past to areas more commonly visited by travelers. The trip he presented in this diary was to be his last and most significant journey, and he chose to visit the remote northern provinces. In part his intention was to escape society and immerse himself in nature. But Bashō was no explorer looking for unknown territories and landscapes; rather, he saw this trip as an opportunity to visit sites celebrated by other poets so that he could see for himself what had inspired them and could test his own poetic creations against theirs. He also frequently compared these poetic sites with places celebrated in Chinese poetry. Thus Bashō's journey was a travel in time as well as in space, as he communed with the poets of other times and other places and shared their inspirations.

After completing this journey in the fall of 1689, Bashō spent four years polishing and revising his manuscript. The text we have is not so much a factual account of his experiences on the road as it is a carefully crafted poetic odyssey.

Bashō used this diary to explore the relationship between individuals and nature, maintaining that we should become one with nature and immerse ourselves in it. The poet also reflected on the nature of beauty and insisted that the world of rustic beauty is as important as the realm of the more traditional concept of an artfully refined beauty. Bashō frequently made allusions to the great warriors of Japan's medieval period and created a tension between the evanesence of heroic deeds and the enduring quality of poetic achievement.

Bashō's choice of a reclusive life away from the demands of conventional society grew out of a tradition that includes Kamo no Chōmei (pp. 1132–1141) and anticipates the experiences of such later figures as Henry David Thoreau, Huck Finn, and Jack Kerouac.

# Bashō's Narrow Road

This text is the opening passage from Bashō's travel diary *Narrow Road to the Deep North* written in Bashō's own hand and showing his personal calligraphy. At the bottom the same text is reproduced in mechanical type.

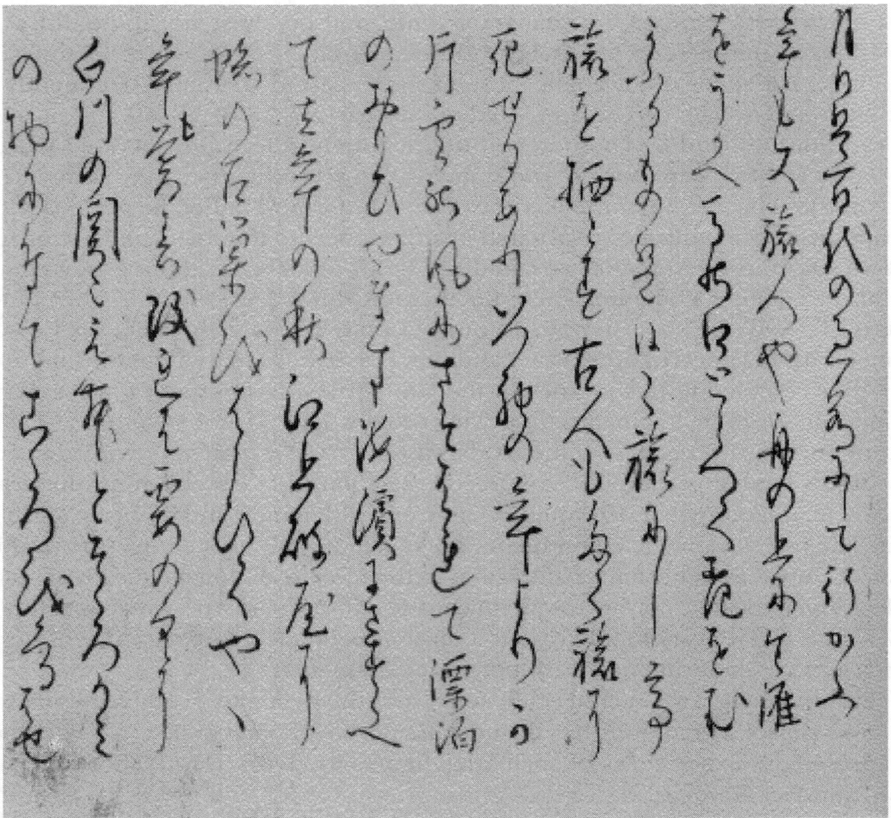

月日は百代の過客にして行かふ
年も又旅人也舟の上に生涯
をうかへ馬の口とらへて老をむ
かふるものは日々旅にして
旅を栖とす古人も多く旅に
死せるありいつれの年よりか
片雲の風にさそはれて漂泊
のおもひやます海浜にさすらへ
て去年の秋江上破屋に
蜘の古巣をはらひてやゝ
年も暮春改れは霞の空に
白川の関こえむとそゝろかみ
の物に付てこゝろをくるはせ

一オ

# TRANSLATIONS OF HAIKU

古池や

蛙とびこむ

水の音

Old pond—frogs jumped in—sound of water.

[Lafcadio Hearn]

The old pond
A frog jumps in—
Plop!

[R. H. Blyth]

Into the ancient pond
A frog jumps
Water's sound!

[D. T. Suzuki]

An old-time pond, from off whose shadowed depth
Is heard the splash where some lithe frog leaps in.

[Clara A. Walsh]

A lonely pond in age-old stillness sleeps . . .
Apart, unstirred by sound or motion . . . till
Suddenly into it a lithe frog leaps.

[Curtis Hidden Page]

OLD DARK SLEEPY POOL . . .
QUICK UNEXPECTED
FROG
GOES PLOP! WATERSPLASH!

[Peter Beilenson]

Oh thou unrippled pool of quietness
Upon whose shimmering surface, like the tears
Of olden days, a small batrachian leaps,
The while acquatic sounds assail our ears.

[Lindley Williams Hubbell]

There once was a curious frog
Who sat by a pond on a log
And, to see what resulted,
In the pond catapulted
With a water-noise heard round the bog.

[Alfred H. Marks]

The old pond is still
a frog leaps right into it
splashing the water

[Earl Miner and Hiroko Odagiri]

The old pond
A frog jumped in
Kerplunk!

[Alan Ginsberg]

An old pond—
The sound
Of a diving frog.

[Kenneth Rexroth]

The quiet pond
A frog leaps in,
The sound of the water.

[Edward Seidensticker]

## from Narrow Road to the Interior

The months and days are wayfarers of a hundred generations, and the years that come and go are also travelers. Those who float all their lives on a boat or reach their old age leading a horse by the bit make travel out of each day and inhabit travel. Many in the past also died while traveling. In which year it was I do not recall, but I, too, began to be lured by the wind like a fragmentary cloud and have since been unable to resist wanderlust, roaming out to the seashores. Last fall, I swept aside old cobwebs in my dilapidated hut in Fukagawa, and soon the year came to a close; as spring began and haze rose in the sky, I longed to walk beyond Shirakawa Barrier and, possessed and deranged by the distracting deity and enticed by the guardian deity of the road, I was unable to concentrate on anything. In the end I mended the rips in my pants, replaced hat strings, and, the moment I gave a moxa treatment to my kneecaps, I thought of the moon over Matsushima. I gave my living quarters to someone and moved into Sampū's villa:

*Kusa no to mo sumi-kawaru yo zo*
*hina no ie*
In my grass hut the residents
change: now a dolls' house

I left the first eight links hung on a post of my hut.

On the twenty-seventh of the third month, the daybreak sky was suffused with haze; even though the moon at dawn loses much of its light, the peak of Fuji was faintly visible, and I was uncertain when again I might see the flowering treetops of Ueno and Yanaka. My close friends, who had been gathered since the previous evening, sent me off in a boat. When we climbed out of the boat at a place called Senju, I was depressed by the thought of the three thousand *li* that lay ahead and shed tears at a parting in this illusory world.

*Yuku haru ya tori naki uo no me wa*
*namida*
Departing spring: birds cry and, in
the eyes of fish, tears

This was the first time I used my travel writing implements, and I was still reluctant to venture farther. My friends lined up along the road, apparently to keep watching us as long as they could see us.

This year, the second year of Genroku it must be, I casually thought of making a pilgrimage over a long road to Ōshō and, even while realizing that I could end up regretting my hair turning white under the sky of Wu, I gambled on the slim, uncertain chance of returning alive from a place of which I had heard but hadn't seen with my own eyes. And the day we left, we managed to reach the station called Sōka. The things that I had hung over my thin-boned shoulders tormented me first. Although I had left with practically nothing, there were things like a paper-garment to keep me from night's cold, a *yukata*, rainwear, and ink and brushes, in addition to which were the farewell gifts I was unable to decline. I was unable to discard them, either, and had to resign myself to their becoming a burden on the road.

We paid our respects to Muro no Yashima. Sora, my companion on the road, said: "The deity here is called

Princess-to-make-trees-bloom and is also enshrined on Fuji. This is called Muro no Yashima because she shut herself up in a doorless chamber and vowed to burn herself, but in the midst of that act gave birth to Prince-fire-out. It is also because of this that it is customary to mention smoke in a poem about this place." Again, local history has it that catching the fish called *konoshiro* is banned.

On the thirtieth we stayed at the foot of Mount Nikkō. The inn proprietor said, "My name is Buddha Gozaemon. Because my principle is to be honest in everything, people call me that. Please feel completely relaxed on your grass pillow and have a good rest." Wondering what kind of Buddha manifested himself in this world of mud and dust to help someone like me, who resembled a Buddhist mendicant or a pilgrim, I observed the proprietor's behavior with some care and found him to be simply unwise and undiscriminating, a man of honesty incarnate. It was like strong will and blunt simplicity approaching ultimate humanity. His innate clarity of mind should be highly valued.

On the first day of the fourth month, we paid our respects to The Mountain. In ancient times the name of this mountain used to be written to read *Futarasan* (Mount Two Disasters), but when the Great Teacher Kūkai founded the temple, he changed it to *Nikkō* (Sunlight). He must have foreseen the future a thousand years ahead: today the light from this place illuminates the entire heaven, its beneficence fills the whole land, and the easeful home for all four classes of people is peaceful. Awestruck, I was barely able to take up my brush:

> *Ara tōto aoba wakaba no hi no hikari*
> Look, so holy: green leaves young
> leaves in the light of the sun

Mount Dark Hair had haze around it, its snow still white.

> *Sori-sutete Kurokami-yama ni*
> *koromogae* —SORA
> Shaving off the dark hair
> mountain and clothes changed

Sora is from the Kawai family; his common name is Sōgorō. With our eaves side by side under the lower leaves of plantain, he helps me in the labor of acquiring firewood and water. This time he was delighted to share with me the views of Matsushima and Kisakata; at the same time, to console me for the hardship of traveling, on the day he left for this journey he shaved his hair, changed his appearance to that of one in an ink-dyed robe, and revised the characters of his name from *sōgo* (all five) to *sōgo* (religious enlightenment). This is why he came up with the piece on Mount Dark Hair. The two-character word *koromogae* sounds powerful.

We climbed the mountain for more than two thousand yards and came to a waterfall. Flying down a hundred feet from the top of a rocky cavern, it drops into an azure pool surrounded with a thousand rocks. I've heard it said that since you can put yourself in the cave and look at the waterfall from behind, it is called the Back-view Waterfall.

> *Shibaraku wa taki ni komoru ya ge no*
> *hajime*
> Confining ourselves in a waterfall
> a while in early summer

Because we had an acquaintance at a place called Kurobane, in Nasu, we decided to take a straight path there through the wild field that opened up before us. Aiming at a village in the distance, we kept going, but it started to rain and dusk fell. We borrowed space at a farmer's house for the night and as soon as the day broke we resumed our walk through the field. There was a horse being pastured. We pleaded with a man who was cutting grass, and the man, though a rustic, knew what compassion was, and was gracious enough to rent us the horse, saying: "I wonder what to do. You see, this field has paths crisscrossing it, and first-time travelers tend to take the wrong paths. I'm concerned about that. Take this horse, let him carry you as far as he goes, and, when he stops, let him go."

Two small children followed us, running after the horse. One of them was a small girl and her name was Kasane. It was an unfamiliar name but elegant:

> *Kasane towa yae-nadeshiko no na*
> *narubeshi* —SORA
> Kasane must be another name for
> "eightfold" pink

In time we reached the village. We tied a sum to the seat of the saddle and sent the horse back.

We visited Jōbōji so-and-so, the castle deputy of Kurobane, in his house. He was delighted with our unexpected visit, and we went on talking throughout days and nights. His brother, named Tōsui, came to visit us mornings and evenings whenever he could, taking us to his own house as well. We were also invited by their relatives as the days went by.

One day we wandered out into the suburbs, took a look at a place where dog chasing used to be practiced, and waded into the Bear-bamboo of Nasu to pay a visit to the old grave of Lady Tamamo. From there we went to Hachiman Shrine. Because we had heard it was this shrine that Yoichi invoked when he prayed, "Above all, my tribal deity, the right Hachiman, of my province," before shooting through the target fan, our veneration was especially deep. As dusk fell, we returned to Tōsui's house.

There is a temple for rough training called Kōmyō. Invited there, we paid our respects to the Ascetic Hall.

> *Natsuyama ni ashida o ogamu kadode*
> *kana*
> Summer hills: we pray to the clogs
> as we depart

In this province, far inside Ungan Temple, there is a place in the mountains where Monk Butchō used to live. He had written to me some time back that he had scribbled on the rock there with pine charcoal:

> *Tateyoko no go-shaku ni taranu kusa*
> *no io*
> *musubu mo kuyashi ame nakariseba*
> A grass hut less than five by five—I
> regret living
> even in it: if only there were no
> rainfalls!

To see the place, I went to Ungan Temple using a walking stick. People invited others, many of them young, and there was a good deal of gaiety on the way; before I knew it, we had reached the foothills. The mountain appeared deep; the path along the valley was long, with pine and cedar black, water oozing and dripping from the moss, and even though it was Deutzia Month, the air still felt cold. Where the Ten Views were exhausted, we crossed a bridge and entered the gate.

So, where is it?—wondering, we climbed the mountain from the other side and found on a boulder a small hut leaning on a cave. It was like looking at the "death barrier" of Zen Master Miao or the rock room of Monk Fa-yün.

*Kitsutsuki mo io wa yaburazu natsu kodachi*
Even woodpeckers don't tear at the hut in summer trees

I left this impromptu hokku on a post.

From there we went to the Killing Rock. Courtesy of the castle deputy, we went on horseback. The man who was leading my horse asked, "Would you write a poem card for me, sir?" I was touched by his elegant turn of mind:

*No o yoko ni uma hikimuke yo hototogisu*
Turn the horse round across the field, cuckoo

The Killing Rock is near a foothill where hot water bubbles up. Its poisonous power has not died out; so many bees and butterflies lie dead that the sand around it is scarcely visible.

The willow tree with "clear water flowing" was in the village of Ashino, by a paddy ridge. Kohō so-and-so, the chief of this county, had written to me from time to time to say, "I'd like to show you the willow," so I had wondered in what kind of place it would be. Today I was able to stop in the shade of this willow.

*Ta ichimai uete tachisaru yanagi kana*
One paddy planted I walk away from the willow tree

After days passed with us feeling uncertain, we reached Shirakawa Barrier and finally began to feel we were on the road. Now I understood what was meant by "I'd like to send word to the City." Above all, this being one of the Three Barriers, people with sensitive minds have taken note of it. With the autumn wind in my ear and red leaves in my mind's eye, I was still moved by the green leaves on the treetops. Deutzia flowers making white brocade, wild roses vying in bloom, I felt as if I were passing through the barrier in snow. I'm told that Kiyosuke has written that in the old days, people used to adjust their headgear and straighten their garments.

*U no hana o kazashi ni seki no haregi kana* —SORA
Deutzia flowers donned, for the barrier a special costume

In time, we passed the barrier, went along, and crossed the Abukuma River. High to our left rose the peak of Aizu, and to our right were the villages of Iwaki, Sōma, and Miharu; behind us was a mountain range as if to partition Hitachi and Shimotsuke. We passed a place called Mirror Marsh, but today, the sky leaden, it did not reflect things well.

At Sukagawa Station we visited a person named Tōkyū, who put us up for four or five days. The first thing he asked was, "How did you pass Shirakawa Barrier?" I said, "These long travels have been painful, and I was exhausted body and soul. At the same time my heart was entranced by the landscape and I was so profoundly moved thinking of things of the past that I did not come up with anything brilliant. Still, I could not possibly pass the place without a piece:

*Fūryū no hajime ya Oku no taueuta*
The start of poetry: a rice-planting
song in the Interior."

This was followed by the second, third links, and we ended up completing three sequences.

Near this station there was a monk who had removed himself from this world, choosing to live in the shade of a large chestnut tree. I thought of his quiet existence as reminiscent of "the mountain where horse chestnuts were picked" and wrote out the following. The words were:

> The character for "chestnut" combines "west" and "tree"; since it suggests the Pure Land to the West, Bodhisattva Gyōgi used this tree all his life, I am told, to make his walking sticks and the pillars of his house:

*Yo no hito no mitsukenu hana ya noki no kuri*
People hardly note its flowers: the
chestnut near the eaves

About five *li* from Tōkyū's house, off from Hihada Station, was Mount Asaka. It was close to the road. There were many swamps around. Because it was not far from the time for harvesting *katsumi,* I asked people, "Which plant is the flowering *katsumi?*" but there was not a person who knew. As we visited swamps, asked people, and walked about mumbling, "*Katsumi, katsumi,*" the sun came down to the rim of hills. We turned right at Two Pines, took a look at the Cave Abode of Kurozuka, and lodged in Fukushima.

The following day, we went to Shinobu village looking for the Stone for Rubbing Shinobu Figures. In a foothills village far away, the stone lay half buried in the ground. A boy from the village came by and told us: "Long ago, this stone was on top of the mountain, but passersby would trample upon the wheat going to test the stone. People here hated it and pushed the stone down into this valley. So it lies here, its face down." A likely story, or was it?

*Sanae toru temoto ya mukashi Shinobu-zuri*
The hands taking seedlings recall
the ancient rubbing

We crossed the river at Tsukinowa Ferry and came out at a station called Senoue. The site where Satō Shōji's mansion used to be was located about one and a half *li* toward the left, close to the mountain. We heard that it was at Sabano, in Iizuka Village. We asked for directions as we went along until we reached a place called Maruyama. It was Shōji's old castle. A place below there was where the main gate used to be, someone told us, and we shed tears. Also, an old temple nearby retained the family's stone steles. Among them the one about the two wives was the first to touch me deeply. Women though they were, they have left such a reputation of gallantry, I marveled, and wet my sleeves. You do not have to look far to find a Tear-shedding Stele.

When we went in the temple and asked for tea, we learned that among its treasures were Yoshitsune's sword and Benkei's casket.

*Oi mo tachi mo satsuki ni kazare kaminobori*
Display both casket and sword in
May with paper carps

This happened on the first day of the fifth month.

That night we stayed in Iizuka. There was a hot spring, so we took a bath, then sought a lodging place. It turned out to be a disturbingly poor house with straw mats laid on the earth floor. Because there was not even a lamp, we made our bed by the light from the fire pit and lay down. At night thunder rumbled and rain fell without interruption. There were leaks where we lay, and, bitten by fleas and mosquitoes, we were unable to sleep. Even my chronic illness revived, and I almost fainted. As the sky of the short night finally lightened, we resumed our travels. With the remnants of the night still with me, I rented a horse and we went out to Ko'ori Station. We still had such a great distance ahead of us that the kind of illness I had made me feel uncertain, but by reminding myself that this was a journey, a pilgrimage to remote corners, that I had resolved to abandon the secular world, resigned as I was to the transience of all things, and die on the road, and that all this was a fate ordained by Heaven, I regained my strength a little and trod on the road as I pleased, and we went beyond Ōkido, Date.

As we passed Abumizuri and Shiroishi castles and entered Kasajima County, we asked a person the whereabouts of the grave of Captain First Secretary Sanetaka and were told: "The foothill villages you can see from here in the distance, to the right, are called Raincoat Ring and Hat Isle and there we still have the shrine for the guardian deity of the road and 'the keepsake pampas grass.'" On account of the May rains of the past several days, the road was terrible, and I was tired besides, so we walked ahead, seeing the villages in the distance. I decided that both names, Raincoat Ring and Hat Isle, were appropriate for the May rains:

*Kasajima wa izuko satsuki no nukari*
*michi*
Where is Hat Isle?—this road so
mired in May

We stayed in Iwanuma.

The Pine of Takekuma was truly eye-opening. Its trunk forked out into two at the ground, and you knew it hadn't lost its old appearance. First I thought of Priest Nōin. Perhaps because the gentleman who had earlier come down here as governor of Mutsu is said to have cut it down and used it as bridge pilings at the Natori River, he made a poem saying "the pine now has left no trace." I'd heard that from time to time people had cut the tree down and planted a new one, but for a thousand years to this day it has retained its shape; a felicitous pine tree it is indeed.

Because someone named Kyohaku had given me a farewell gift: *Takekuma no matsu mise mōse oso-zakura,* "Show him the Takekuma Pine, late-blooming cherry"

*Sakura yori matsu wa futaki o*
*mitsuki goshi*
Three months since the cherry:
the two-trunk pine

We crossed the Natori River and entered Sendai. It was the day blue flags were hung. We sought out an inn and stayed for several days.

Here, there was a wood-block carver named Kaemon. Hearing that he had some interest in poetry, I became acquainted with him. "I have looked into some of the famous places whose locations have become uncertain over the years," he said, and guided us around one whole day. The bush clover in Miyagi Plain grew luxuriantly, making me wonder how it might look in the fall. Tamada, Yokono, then on to Azalea Hill where *asebi* were in bloom. We went into a pine forest where no sunlight came in, and were told the place was called Under-the-tree. It must be because the dew was dense in the past as well that someone made a poem saying, "Servant, Umbrella." We offered prayers at Yakushi Hall and the holy shrine for Tenjin, and the day came to an end. In addition, Kaemon drew certain places of Matsushima and Shiogama and gave the drawing to us as a present. Furthermore, he gave us two pairs of straw sandals with indigo-dyed thongs as a farewell gift. When it came to this, he truly revealed himself to be someone demented by elegant pursuits.

*Ayame-gusa ashi ni musuban zōri no o*
Blue flags will be tied to our feet
above sandal thongs

As we walked along, relying on Kaemon's drawing, there was the "Ten-plait Sedge" on the hillside of the Narrow Road to the Interior. It is said that even today, each year, ten-plait sedge mats are prepared and presented to the governor of the province.

Tsubo Stone Marker.
It is in Taga Castle, in Ichikawa Village.

Tsubo Stone Marker is perhaps a little over six feet high, about three feet wide. The moss dug aside, the letters were barely visible. It indicated the distances to the national borders in the four directions. I read: "This castle was laid down, in the first year of Jinki, by Inspector-General and Commander-in-Chief of the Pacification Headquarters Lord Ōno Azumahito. In the sixth year of Tempyō Hōji, it was completed by Councilor, Subjugator-of-the-Eastern-Sea-and-the-Eastern-Mountains, and ditto Lord Emi no Asakari. The first day of the twelfth month." This corresponds to the reign of Emperor Shōmu.

There are a great number of poetic place names people have handed down to us as sung of in poems since long ago. However, as mountains collapse, rivers shift, and paths are renewed, stones are buried and hidden in the ground and trees age and are replaced by young ones, the passage of time and the changing world making me see, so far, only uncertain traces of them. But now, finally, here was an indubitable monument from a thousand years ago, which, right in front of my eyes, allowed me to contemplate the minds of ancient people. This was one virtue of pilgrimage, the joy of being alive. I forgot the ordeals of travel and could not hold back the tears that flowed down.

From there we visited Tama River of Noda and Offshore Stone. For Pine Hill of Sue, they built a temple, calling it Masshōzan. The spaces between the pine trees were all covered by graves. As I thought that all the pledges for "a single wing" and "a linked branch" finally end up like this, my sadness increased. We then heard the vesper bell on Shiogama Bay. The May-rain sky cleared up a little and, under the faint evening moon, Magaki Isle was close by. Fishermen's boats rowed back, and as I heard the men dividing their catch, I was moved, recalling the heart of someone who had to say "pulled with a rope, truly sad." That night, a blind monk plucked the biwa to narrate something called Oku-jōruri. It was not the *Heike* or a *mai*, but as he raised his rustic tune high, though he was quite noisy near my pillow, I couldn't help admiring him for not forgetting an old tradition in such a forsaken place.

Early in the morning we paid our respects to the Deity of Shiogama. A governor of the province had revived the shrine. Its columns are thick, the rafters brilliantly painted, the stone steps built exceedingly high, and the morning sun made the crimson fence sparkle. It was admirable to think that the Divine Soul should manifest himself so conspicuously at one end of the road and in the borderland, part of the Way of our Nation though it may be.

In front of the Deity there was an old lantern. On the surface of its metal door was written: "Presented by Izumi no Saburō in the Third Year of Bunji." I could conjure up his face from five hundred years ago and was unaccountably enthralled. He was a brave, righteous soldier with filial dedication. His great reputation survives to this day, and there is not one who does not admire him. Truly, a man should cultivate the Way and stick to righteousness. "One's reputation can suffer," it is said.

It was already noon. We rented a boat and crossed to Matsushima. After about two *li*, we arrived on the shore of Ojima.

Although this has been said a number of times, Matsushima is the most beautiful scenery in Japan and wouldn't embarrass itself alongside Lake Tung-t'ing and Lake Hsi. It allows the sea in at the southeast, with the bay inside three *li* across, brimming with the tides of Chê-chiang. There are an inexhaustible number of islands, some steeply rising, pointing at heaven, some lying, prostrating themselves on the waves. Some are piled twice, heaped thrice, parted to the left, linked to the right. There are some that carry others on their backs, some that hug others in their arms, as if loving their children, grandchildren. The green of the pines comes in delicate shades, and their branches are blown bent by the salty winds as if they had created their crookedness by themselves.

Matsushima is ineffable, made up like a beauty's face. All this may have been the doing of the Great Mountain God in the days of rock-smashing deities. The Creator's heavenly handiwork—who can use his brush or exhaust words to his satisfaction?

The Ojima shore, connected to the mainland, is an isle jutting out into the sea. There are things like the site where Zen Master Ungo's detached residence used to be and his Zen meditation rock. I also saw under pine trees a smattering of people who had renounced this world quietly living in a grass hut from which smoke rose from a fire of gleanings and pine cones. I did not know who they were, but I stopped by, feeling close to them. The moon shining on the sea gave a view different from that of daytime. We went back to the bay shore and sought an inn. It had a second floor with an open window, and as we lay in the midst of wind and cloud, I felt mysteriously exhilarated.

*Matsushima ya tsuru ni mi o kare*
*hototogisu* —SORA
In Matsushima, borrow a crane's
guise, cuckoo

Mouth shut, I tried to sleep and could not. When we parted at my old hut, Sodō had made a poem on Matsushima. Hara Anteki had kindly presented me with a *waka* on Bay Isle of Pines. I opened my bag and made them my company for the night. There were also hokku by Sampū and Jokushi.

On the eleventh we paid our respects to Zuigan Temple. This temple was founded thirty-two abbots ago by Makabe no Heishirō, after he returned to Japan from T'ang, where he had gone upon taking Buddhist vows. Later, through Zen Master Ungo's virtuous proselytizing, its seven halls and roof-tiles were rebuilt, and with its golden walls and decorative Buddhist articles aglitter, it turned into a great cathedral, the Buddhist paradise on earth. I could not help wondering where that holy man Kembutsu's temple was.

On the twelfth we meant to go to Hiraizumi, but because we had heard about the Aneha Pine and the Thong-breaking Bridge, we took a road seldom used by people but frequented by pheasants, rabbits, and woodcutters, and pushed ahead, until we took the wrong road and ended up coming out in a port called Ishinomaki. Across the sea we saw Mount Kinka, of which a poem saying "gold has bloomed" was presented to His Majesty. Several hundred freight ships gathered in the inlet, houses vied for the land, and smoke kept rising from the ovens. Wondering how we ended up in a place like this, we tried to find lodging, but no one was willing to let us lodge. Finally we managed to spend the night in a poor small house, and as the day broke, we resumed wandering along an unknown road. We walked on a long riverbank, looking at Sleeve Ferry, Meadow of Mottled Tails, and the Sedge Field of Mano in the distance. After lodging one night in a place called Toima, which was along an elongated marsh, we reached Hiraizumi. The distance between the two was a little over twenty *li* I think.

The glory of the three generations lasted only as long as a single nap. The place where the main gate stood was one *li* this side. Hidehira's site had turned into paddies, with only Kinkeizan retaining its shape. First, we went up to the Takadachi and saw the Kitagami was a large river flowing from Nambu. The Koromo River flows around Izumi Castle and below the Takadachi pours into the large river. The old site for Yasuhira and others was on the other side of Koromo Barrier, with the Nambu side fortified for defense, it seemed, against the Ezo. The most loyal among his loyal vassals were selected and put up in this castle, but their fame lasted only for a moment and turned into clumps of grass. "The country destroyed, the mountains and rivers remain. In the castle it is now spring and the grass has turned green." Sitting on our hats laid on the ground, we shed tears for a while:

*Natsukusa ya tsuwamono-domo ga*
*yume no ato*
Summer grass: where the warriors
used to dream

*U no hana ni Kanefusa miyuru shiraga kana* —SORA
In deutzia flowers I see Kanefusa's
white hair

The two halls about which I had heard so much were open. The Sutra Hall retained the statues of the three guardian kings, and contained in the Light Hall were the coffins of the three generations, with three Bodhisattvas rising peacefully above them. If left alone the seven treasures would have scattered, the jeweled doors torn in the wind, and the gilt columns decayed in frost and snow, the whole thing turning into dilapidation and empty grass in no time; but it was newly enclosed on the four sides, and a tiled roof was built above it to shelter it from wind and rain. So for a thousand years now it has remained as a commemoration:

*Samidare o furi-nokoshite ya Hikari-dō*
The May rains, falling, seem to
spare the Light Hall

Looking at the Nambu Highway in the distance, we stayed in Iwate Village. We passed Oguro Cape and the Islet of Mizu, and as we went from the hot spring of Narugo and reached Shitomae Barrier, we were ready to cross over to the Province of Dewa. Because the road seldom saw travelers, the barrier guard regarded us as suspicious, and it took time before we gained passage. By the time we climbed the Big Mountain, the sun had already set, so we sought lodging in the house of a border guard that we happened to see. For three days the wind and rain were wild, and we had to hole up there in the midst of the dreary mountains.

*Nomi shirami uma no barisuru*
*makura moto*
Fleas and lice: a horse pisses right
near my pillow

Our host said, "From here to Dewa Province beyond the Big Mountain, the road is uncertain. You should have a guide for crossing it." We said, "Surely," and asked for one. A powerfully built young man carrying a curved sword sidewise showed up and, holding an oak cane, he walked ahead of us. Worrying, "This has to be the day we definitely run into some danger," we followed him.

Just as our host had said, the high mountains, deeply wooded, did not have a single bird calling that we could hear, and under the overgrowing trees the darkness was such that it was like walking in the night. We felt as if "dust were falling upon us from the tip of the clouds" as we pushed ahead, making sure of each step through the bear bamboo, crossing the streams, stumbling on the rocks, with cold sweat trickling down our bodies, until we came out in the manor of Mogami. The man who had guided us said, "On this road there's always some trouble. I'm glad that I was able to bring you over here without any mishap." We parted in happiness. Even hearing about it after the fact, our hearts throbbed.

In Obanazawa we visited a man named Seifū. He is wealthy but his heart is not lowly. Someone who goes to the cities from time to time, he of course knew what traveling is like. He made us stay for days, relieving us of the pain of the long trek and entertaining us in various ways.

*Suzushisa o waga yado ni shite*
*nemaru kana*
Making the coolness our home we
lie about

*Hai-ide yo kaiya ga shita no hiki no*
*koe*
Crawl out, toad: your voice under
the silkworm shed

*Mayuhaki o omokage ni shite beni no*
*hana*
Recalling the image of the
eyebrow brush: the safflower

*Kogai suru hito wa kodai no sugata*
*kana* —SORA
Those raising silkworms are in
ancient garb

In the domain of Yamagata is a mountain temple called Ryūshaku-ji. Founded by the Great Teacher Jikaku, it is a particularly pure, tranquil place. Because people urged us to take a look at it, we turned back from Obanazawa, the distance between them about seven *li*. The sun was not down yet. After reserving lodging at the visitors' quarters at the foot we climbed to the temple on the mountaintop. The mountain was made of rocks piled upon boulders, the pines and cypresses were aged, and with the soil and stones old and smooth with moss and the doors of the lesser halls upon the rocks all closed, we heard not a sound. As we went around the cliff, crawled up the rocks, and paid respects to the Buddhist sanctum, the splendid scenery was so hushed and silent that we could only feel our hearts grow clear.

*Shizukasa ya iwa ni shimiiru semi no*
*koe*
Quietness: seeping into the rocks,
the cicada's voice

Hoping to ride down the Mogami River, we waited for good weather at a place called Ōishida. Here the seeds of ancient haikai had been spilled, and there were some who kept nurturing the unforgotten flower from the past, trying to soothe their rustic hearts of simple reeds and horns, groping their way with their feet, but they were lost in the two ways of old and new, they said, because they did not have a proper guide. As a result, we ended up doing a sequence. The poetry of this journey culminated in it.

The Mogami River rises in Michinoku, originating as it does in Yamagata. It has terrifyingly dangerous spots such as Go Stones and Falcon. It flows north of Mount Itajiki and in the end enters the sea at Sakata. From left and right, mountains close in, and the boat rides down through foliage. The so-called *inafune* must be the boats loaded with rice that ply the waters here. The White-thread Falls splash down through rifts in green leaves. The Sennin Hall stands right at the water's edge. In the brimming water our boat looks precarious.

*Samidare o atsumete hayashi*
*Mogami-gawa*
Gathering the May rains and swift,
the Mogami River

On the third day of the sixth month we climbed Mount Haguro. We visited someone named Zushi Sakichi and had the honor of meeting Acting Superintendent Egaku Ajari. He put us up in his detached quarters in Minamidani and served as our host with exquisite pity and compassion.

On the fourth day we held a haikai session in the Main Hall.

*Arigata ya yuki o kaorasu*
*Minamidani*
Admirable: the snow emitting
fragrance in South Valley

On the fifth day we paid our respects to Gongen. It is not known which period the Great Teacher Nōjo, who established this shrine, comes from. The *Engi-sbiki* says it is a shrine of Ushū Sato-yama. Did the scribe mistake the character *kuro* for *sato* and call it *sato-yama*? Did he abbreviate Ushū Kuro-yama and call it Haguro-yama? I'm told that the *Fudoki* says that the name Dewa derives from the birds' feathers used as an annual tribute from this province. Along with Gassan and

Yudono, it makes up the "three mountains." This temple belongs to Tōei-zan Kan'ei Temple, in Edo, and under the bright moon of Tendai Insight it holds up the light of law for All-round Enlightenment. The monks' quarters are lined up roof to roof. The followers of rough training and ritual practices encourage one another in Buddhist ways. The spiritual benefits of this soulful place are such as to fill people with veneration and dread. With its long-lasting prosperity, this holy mountain must be described as felicitous.

On the eighth we climbed Gassan. *Yūshime* hung on our bodies, *hōkan* wrapped around our heads, and led by a mountain guide, we climbed about eight *li* through clouds and mists, treading ice and snow, wondering whether we'd entered the orbits of the sun and the moon. Breathless and frozen, we reached the summit, when the sun set and the moon rose. With bear bamboo spread and short bamboo as pillow, we lay down and waited for the day to break. As the sun rose and clouds dissipated, we went down to Yudono.

Near the valley was a smith's hut. A smith of this province decided to use the spiritual water here, purified himself, and made swords, on which he finally engraved the name Gassan; they are now prized by the whole world. I recalled how swords used to be tempered at Dragon Spring. Thinking of the days of Kan-chiang and Mo-yeh, I realized how an obsession with the Way could accomplish profound things.

While resting on a rock, I noticed half-open buds on a cherry tree about three feet tall. The way those cherry blossoms, buried under accumulating snow as they had been, were now beginning to bloom though so late, touched me deeply. It was as if plum blossoms were emitting their fragrance right there under the scorching sun. I recalled the sentiments in a poem by Bishop Gyōson, and my feeling intensified. On the whole, the training rules forbid the disclosure of details on this mountain to anyone else. Accordingly, I shall not write any more.

When we returned to the hall, at Ajari's request I wrote out my pieces on our pilgrimage to the three mountains on poem cards.

*Suzushisa ya hono mikazuki no*
*Haguro-san*
Coolness: a faint three-day moon
over Mount Haguro

*Kumo no mine ikutsu kuzurete tsuki*
*no yama*
Many cloud peaks collapse and the
moon over the mount

*Katararenu Yudono ni nurasu tamoto*
*kana*
In the Bath Chamber I can't speak
of I wet my sleeves

*Yudono-yama zeni fumu michi no*
*namida kana* —SORA
At Mount Bath Chamber, in tears I
step on coins on my way

After leaving Haguro and arriving in the castle town of Tsurugaoka, we were welcomed into the house of a samurai named Shigeyuki, of the Nagayama family, and did a haikai sequence. Sakichi came along with us. We went down to Sakata Port on a riverboat. We stayed in the house of a physician named En'an Fugyoku.

*Atsumi-yama ya Fuku-ura kakete*
*yūsuzumi*
From Mount Atsumi away to Fuku
Bay: evening cool

*Atsuki hi o umi ni iretari*
*Mogami-gawa*
Pouring the hot sun into the sea,
the Mogami River

Though we had seen a countless number of natural wonders on the river, mountain, sea, and land, we were now very eager to see Kisakata. As it lay northeast of Sakata Port, we went over a mountain, walked along the coast, and trod on the sand, for about ten *li,* until, about the time the sun was close to setting, almost hidden in the salty wind swirling up the sand and in the blurring rain, we saw Mount Chōkai. We groped our way in the darkness and, encouraged that because "the rain itself is a spectacle" the clear weather after the rain would be even better, we borrowed space in a fisherman's hut and waited for the rain to let up.

The next morning the sky was very clear. As the morning sun began to shine forth resplendently, we put out in a boat in Kisakata. First, we rowed to Nōin Island and visited the site of his quiet residence of three years. When we climbed out of the boat on the facing shore, the old cherry tree about which a poem was made speaking of "row over the blossoms" remained as a keepsake of Priest Saigyō. Close to the bay was an imperial tomb, which we were told was Empress Jingū's grave. The temple was called Kammanju-ji. I had never heard that she had visited this area. I wondered how the story came about.

When we sat in the temple's main room and rolled up the blind, the entire landscape appeared in a single sweep, with Chōkai pushing up heaven to the south, its shadow reflected in the bay. At the western end was Muyamuya Barrier; to the east was an embankment built with a road leading to Akita in the distance; up to the north was the sea, and the place where the waves rolled in was called the Tide-cross. The bay, its length and width combined, was about one *li,* and though its appearance suggested Matsushima, it also differed from it. Matsushima seemed to be smiling, Kisakata resentful. Sadness added to loneliness, the make-up of the place resembled a soul in distress.

*Kisakata ya ame ni Seishi ga nebu no*
*hana*
In Kisakata in the rain Hsi-shih's
silk tree flowers

*Shiokoshi ya tsuru hagi nurete umi*
*suzushi*
At Tide-cross cranes' shins are wet
in the cool sea

*Rite*

*Kisakata ya ryōri nani kuu kami-mat-*
*suri* —SORA
In Kisakata what food's eaten at
the gods' festival?

*Ama no ya ya toita o shikite yū-*
*suzumi*
—Merchant from the Province of
Mino —TEIJI
At a fisherman's we sit on a door
for evening coolness

Spotting an osprey nest atop a rock
*Nami koenu chigiri arite ya misago no*
*su* —SORA
With the vow that waves won't
come over the osprey nest

As we accumulated days in our inability to separate ourselves from Sakata, we saw the Hokuriku Route in the clouds. The thought of the great distance pained our hearts. We heard that it was 130 *li* to the capital of Kaga.

As we passed Nezu Barrier, we stepped into the land of Echigo and reached Ichiburi Barrier in Etchū. It took us nine days. My spirit run down by the hardship of heat and rain, I became ill and could not keep a record.

*Fumitsuki ya muika mo tsune no yo*
*niwa nizu*
Seventh month: even the sixth
isn't like an ordinary night

*Araumi ya Sado ni yokotau*
*Amanogawa*
Rough sea: lying toward Sado
Island the River of Heaven

Today, because we had come over the most difficult spots in the North Country, called Parent Ignored, Child Ignored, Dog Going Back, and Horse Turned Back, we were tired and, pulling our pillows up close to ourselves, we tried to sleep. From one room beyond, toward the front, however, I heard the voices of young women, two of them I thought. As I listened to them telling their stories, with the voice of an old man interjecting from time to time, the women turned out to be prostitutes of a place called Niigata, in Echigo Province. They were on their way to pay their respects to Ise Shrine, and the man had accompanied them as far as this barrier. They were trying to write letters to be taken back tomorrow to their home town to convey some ineffectual messages. As if cast up on the beach by white waves, living lowly lives like those of fishermen's children, forced to have faithless relationships, we are, to our great misfortune, committing sinful deeds day after day—such was their talk, and while listening to it, I fell asleep.

The next morning, as we were preparing to leave, they came to us and said in tears: "We're worried about the roads we're taking from now on; we're saddened by so much uncertainty. May we follow you—we'll keep some distance from you. On account of the robe you wear, would you extend Buddha's compassion to us, so we may enter Buddhahood?" However, I had to tell them: "We sympathize with your plight, but we stop in many places. You should go along following the others as they go. With the Sun Goddess's protection, all should go well."

And so we left. Nevertheless, sadness did not cease for quite some time.

*Hitotsuya ni yūjo mo netari hagi to*
*tsuki*
In one house prostitutes also slept:
bush clover and moon

I told this to Sora, and he wrote it down.

They speak of the forty-eight flows of Kurobe, and we certainly had to cross countless rivers before coming out on a bay called Nago. It doesn't have to be spring to appreciate the wisteria flowers of Tako; one can also visit their sad decline in early fall, we thought, and asked someone about them and were told, "You'll have to walk along the beach about five *li* from here until you reach the foothill woods beyond. Still, there are only shabby fishermen's thatched huts there, and no one will be willing to give you lodging even for one night." Intimidated, we went on to enter the province of Kaga.

*Wase no ka ya wake-iru migi wa Ariso*
*Umi*
We wade into early rice fragrance,
the Rough Sea to our right

Going over Mount Deutzia Flower and Kurikara Valley, we reached Kanazawa on the midpoint day of the seventh month. Here, there was a merchant named Kasho, a frequent visitor from Ōzaka. We stayed in the same inn.

Someone named Isshō had begun to be fairly well known among those of like mind as one fond of this pursuit, but had died young, in the previous winter. His brother hosted a session in commemoration:

*Tsuka mo ugoke waga naku koe wa*
*aki no kaze*
Gravestone, move: sound of my
wailing the autumn wind

*Invited to a Certain Grass Hut*

*Aki suzushi tegoto ni muke ya uri*
*nasubi*
Autumn's cool: let each of us peel
a melon, an eggplant

*On the Way*

*Akaaka to hi wa tsurenaku mo aki no*
*kaze*
Red and red: the sun's indifferent
to the autumn wind

*At a Place Called Little Pine*

*Shiorashiki na ya komatsu fuku hagi*
*susuki*
Daintily named Little Pine blowing
bush clover, pampas grass

Here we paid our respects to Ōta Shrine. It had Sanemori's helmet, along with a strip of brocade. Long ago, while he still belonged to the Minamoto clan, Lord Yoshitomo gave it to him, we were told. It certainly wasn't one for an ordinary soldier. From visor to side-guard, it had gold-speckled arabesque engravings in the chrysanthemum pattern, and the dragon head had antlers riveted to it. After Sanemori was killed in battle, Kiso Yoshinaka donated it to this shrine with a letter of prayers, with Higuchi no Jirō as messenger—so said the official account vividly.

*Muzan ya na kabuto no shita no*
*kirigirisu*
Cruel: under the helmet a cricket

On our way to the hot springs of Yamanaka, we walked with Shirane Peak at our back. In the foothills to the left was Kannon Hall. After Cloistered Emperor Kazan, completed his pilgrimage to the Thirty-three Places, he built a house for a statue of Great-compassion-great-sorrow and named it Nata, they said. We were told that the name was made from the two characters that begin with Nachi and Tanigumi. With oddly shaped stones arranged variously and surrounded by old pines, it was a small hall with a thatched roof built against a rock—this, a wonderful, gratifying land.

*Ishiyama no ishi yori shiroshi aki no*
*kaze*
Whiter than the stones of the stone
mountain the autumn wind

We bathed in a hot spring. We heard that its efficacy was second only to that of Arima.

*Yamanaka ya kiku wa taoranu yu no*
*nioi*
In Yamanaka I don't break mums
off in hot water's scent

The proprietor, named Kumenosuke, was still a boy. His father was fond of haikai. When Teishitsu, of Kyoto, was a young man, he came here and was so embarrassed by his ignorance of poetry that upon his return to Kyoto he became a disciple of Teitoku and he began to be known. Even after his reputation was established, he would not accept judge's fees in this village. This is now an old story.

Sora developed stomach trouble and, because he had a relative in a place called Nagashima, in the province of Ise, went ahead, leaving me with:

*Yukiyukite taore fusu tomo hagi no*
*hara* —SORA
In the end I might collapse, but in
a field of bush clover

The one going saddened, the one left behind despondent, we were like single ducks after parting, lost in clouds. I added:

*Kyō yori wa kakitsuke kesan kasa no*
*tsuyu*
From today on, erase the inscript,
dew on my hat

I stayed in a temple called Zenshō-ji outside the castle town of Daishōji. It was still in the domain of Kaga. Sora, who had also stayed in this temple the previous night, had left this piece:

*Yomosugara akikaze kiku ya ura no*
*yama*
All night long I hear the autumn
wind on the mountain in back

The separation of a single night was equal to that of a thousand *li*. Listening to the autumn winds, I lay in the quarters for training monks. Near daybreak, as the voices of sutra chanting rose in the sky, the gong rang out, and I entered the dining hall. Eager with the thought that I would enter the province of Echizen today, I hurried out of the temple. Young monks followed me, carrying inkstones and paper down to the staircase. As it happened, the willow in the garden was scattering its leaves:

*Niwa haite ideba ya tera ni chiru*
*yanagi*
As I sweep the garden and walk
out, willow leaves scatter

I dashed this off impromptu with my straw sandals on.

On the border of Echizen, I put out in a boat in the inlet of Yoshizaki and poled myself to visit the Tide-cross Pines.

*Yomosugara arashi ni nami o*
*hakobasete*
*tsuki o taretaru Shiokoshi no matsu*
—SAIGYŌ
All night long with the storm carrying the waves, the Tide-cross
Pines drip the moon

In this one poem are all the views described. One word added would be like "a useless finger implanted."

I visited the resident monk of Tenryū Temple, in Maruoka, whom I had known previously. Also, someone named Hokushi, of Kanazawa, intending to accompany me briefly, ended up coming as far as this, unable to separate. He tried to compose a hokku at all the notable sites, without overlooking a single one, and from time to time recited an interesting one to me. When the time to part finally came:

*Mono kakite ōgi hikisaku nagori kana*
I write on a fan and tear it apart,
lingering

I walked into the mountain about five thousand yards to offer prayers at Eihei Temple. It is Zen Master Dōgen's. He avoided the vicinity of Kyoto, I was told, and chose to leave his traces at foothills like this for some unfathomable reason.

It was only three *li* to Fukui, so I set out after finishing supper, but I found the road at dusk rough going.

In this place lived an ancient hermit named Tōsai. Which year was it, he had come to Edo to visit me. It was about ten years ago. Wondering how much more ancient he must have become or if he might even be dead by now, I made an inquiry and was told that he still lived on in such and such a place.

Away from the busy part of town, his was a small, miserable house overgrown with moonflowers and snake gourds, its doorway hidden behind cockscombs and broom goosefoots. Deciding this must be it, I knocked on the gate, and a lonesome-looking woman came out and said, "I don't know where you are from, sir, but you look like an itinerant priest. The owner went to visit so-and-so in this neighborhood. If you have some business with him, please go see him there." So I guessed she must be his wife. Marveling how an atmosphere like this is possible only in an old story, I soon found him and stayed in that house for two nights, after which I hurried out hoping to see the full moon in Tsuruga Port. To see me off, Tōsai merrily set out with me, the skirts of his kimono tucked up in a funny way, saying he'd be my guide on the road.

In time Shirane Peak hid itself and Hina Peak emerged. When I crossed Asamuzu Bridge, the Reeds of Tamae had tufts out. Past Bush Warbler Barrier and down Yuno'o Pass, I heard the season's first wild geese over Hiuchi Castle and Mount Return and, on the evening of the fourteenth, sought an inn in the port town of Tsuruga.

That night the moon was particularly fine. "Will the moon be like this tomorrow, too?" I asked, and the proprietor said, as he offered sake, "Across this Koshi region, we are even less certain whether it's going to be fine or cloudy tomorrow night."

So I paid a night visit to Kehi Shrine. It is the mausoleum of Emperor Chūai. The shrine looked divinely ancient, and with the moon shining in through the pine trees, the white sand before the deity was like frost spread out.

"Long ago, the holy man Yugyō II made a great resolution and himself cut the grass, carried mud and stones, and drained the muddy swamp. So now there's no more trouble for those who come to pay their respects. That ancient example still lives today, and each holy man carries sand to the sacred place before the deity. It is called 'Yugyō's sand-carrying,'" explained my host.

*Tsuki kiyoshi Yugyō no moteru suna*
*no ue*
The moon is clear above the sand
Yugyō has carried

On the fifteenth day it rained as my host had predicted.

*Meigetsu ya Hokukoku biyori sadame-*
*naki*
Full moon: the weather in the
North Country is unreliable

On the sixteenth day, with the sky clear, desiring to pick some small *masuho* shells, we hurried a boat to Colored Beach. It was seven *li* over the water. Ten'ya so-and-so had lunch baskets and bamboo sake tubes prepared with care and attention and, a number of his servants riding in the boat and a tailwind driving us, we were blown to the shore in no time. It had only a few small houses of fishermen and the forlorn-looking Hokke Temple. There we drank tea and warmed sake to endure the loneliness of the evening.

> *Sabishisa* ya *Suma ni kachitaru hama no aki*
> The loneliness here's superior to
> Suma, autumn on the beach

> *Nami no ma ya kogai ni majiru hagi no chiri*
> In the waves, mixing with small
> shells bush clover litter

I had Tōsai write down a brief account of the day and left it at the temple.

Rotsū had come as far as this port to welcome me back and accompanied me to the province of Mino. As I entered the manor of Ōgaki, assisted by a horse, Sora came from Ise to join us. Etsujin galloped his horse to do the same, and we all gathered in Jokō's house. Zensenshi, Keikō and his sons, and others who are close to me came to visit day and night and, as if meeting someone who had returned to life, expressed joy and consolation. Even before I was able to shake off the weariness of my travels, the sixth day of the ninth month came along, so I decided to offer prayers at the rebuilding of Ise Shrine and put myself on a boat again:

> *Hamaguri no*
> *futami ni*
> *wakare yuku aki zo*
> A clam
> separates lid
> from flesh as autumn departs

## Natsume Sōseki (1867–1916)

*Translated by Beongeheon Yu*

Natsume Sōseki is widely regarded as the finest Japanese author of the twentieth century. After a period of study in England, Sōseki returned to Japan in 1903 to become a prominent scholar and teacher of English literature. In 1907 he abandoned his academic career to devote his full attention to writing fiction. His reputation today rests on a dozen novels written during the last decade of his life.

Although Sōseki brought the modernization of Japanese literature to maturity by adapting elements of form and style he had learned in England, he was also a tireless experimenter with literary style and narrative form. Unlike many of his contemporaries, he was unwilling merely to imitate European models; he was determined to learn from the West without abandoning Japan's rich literary heritage. This led him to write *Kusamakura* (*Three Cornered World*, 1906), which he called a novel in the manner of a haiku.

While making the technical adjustments of style and form required to modernize fiction, Sōseki also used his work to explore the great philosophical issues raised by Japan's process of Westernization and modernization. Sōseki deplored what he regarded as the shallow adoption of the outward trappings of modernization by a society that failed to see or appreciate the deeper implications of the changes that were taking place. Foremost among the new concepts being introduced was the idea of the individual self as an autonomous being. Premodern Japanese society, with its heavily Neo-Confucian worldview, defined morality and success in terms of recognizing and fulfilling one's proper role in society; there was no margin for eccentricity or individual choice. The modern, Western worldview presents the notion that each individual is free to pursue his own path but must make choices and take responsibility for them. Japan had no tradition of such individualism and therefore could offer no models for pursuing such a life.

In an important published lecture "Watakushi no kojinshugi" ("My Individualism," 1914), Sōseki carefully outlined his idea of the self and the implications of the idea. At the same time, in a series of novels he explored this theme in detail. In the selection presented here from *Kōjin* (*The Wayfarer*, 1912–1913) Sōseki probed the themes of loneliness, alienation, and guilt. The possibilities his characters find for relief from their modern condition are not hopeful. Ichirō, the central figure in this novel, is a typically anguished intellectual who declares that the only solutions to the modern person's dilemma are suicide, insanity, and religion. Ichirō considers and rejects suicide and religion as possible avenues to salvation as he slides inexorably toward insanity. Eventually Sōseki concluded that the only path to redemption lay in learning to surrender the self to some larger, transcendent ideal. Unfortunately, the author died before he could articulate this philosophy fully, but he does show the intellectual and emotional struggle involved in coming to terms with the more profound implications of Japan's outwardly successful modernization.

## from Wayfarer

### 28

From the next day on I anxiously awaited a letter from Mr. H. One, two, three, I counted on my fingers the days that had passed. No letter had come from him, however—not even a picture postcard—and I was disappointed. There was no levity in him, such as might make him forgetful of his responsibility; there was evidence, on the other hand, of the kind of liberality that might make him neglect to discharge his duty as punctiliously as expected. That's how I, a member of the impatient tribe of humanity, looked at him from a distance.

Then, on the evening of exactly the eleventh day after their departure, I at last received a ponderous missive. Mr. H's penned words entirely covered the finely lined stationery. From the number of the pages I could tell it was not the sort of thing which could have been done in a couple of hours. Sitting immobile as a mannequin chained to the desk, I began reading it. My eyes shone with a burning determination not to miss a single word, written in tiny black characters. My mind was riveted to the pages, yet it glided over them as smoothly as a sleigh over the snow. In a word, I had not the slightest notion how long it took me from the very first line of the first page of Mr. H's letter to the final word of the last page.

The letter read as follows:

As I invited Mr. Nagano to travel with me, I also promised to comply with your request. But in doing this I had misgivings that once I faced the situation, I might find it very difficult to carry out your wishes; even if possible, it might not be necessary; and whether necessary or not, it might not be proper. And on the first and second days of our journey these three attitudes worked together in varying combinations, so that I became increasingly convinced that I might have to break my word. On the third and fourth days some reconsideration seemed demanded on my part; and then on the fifth and sixth days and so on, as the days went on, I gradually came to the conclusion that it might be necessary after all not merely to think it over but also to write to you as I had promised. Though the word necessary may mean something quite different to you than it does to me, I shall not explain it here, for you will find that out for yourself by the time you come to the end of this letter. As for my initial feeling that ethically it is not quite proper to accede to your request, I do not think I can get rid of it no matter how much time may elapse. On the other hand, the degree of necessity is plainly becoming great, so great as to override that ethical feeling. Probably there will be no time for me to write a letter. (This being the only trouble that dogged me wherever I went.) We both sleep in the same room; we eat meals together in the same room. And together we go out for a walk, and take a bath too, as long as the structure of the bathroom can accommodate us both. All these things considered, the only time when we move separately is when we go to the toilet.

I do not mean to say that we two are rattling on from morn 'til night. There are times when we each read our own books and also lie down to rest quietly. However, ignoring someone's very presence, to write about him and confide it to a third person is a very difficult thing for me to do. Thus while I do realize the necessity of reporting, I still find it very trying. Such an opportunity does not come so readily, however I may wish it. But chance has proved kind enough to take me in hand and finally let me do what I deem necessary. Trying not to be much concerned with your brother's presence, I have begun to write this letter. And I hope to finish it under similar circumstances.

## 29

Two or three days ago we came into the valley of Benigayatsu and dropped exhausted into this glen. We are now staying in a small summer house owned by one of my relatives. The owner, who can't leave Tokyo before August, had offered to put the place at our disposal any time before that, and we have chanced to avail ourselves of his kind offer during our travel.

Although the word summer house may sound very respectable, the truth is that it is a shabby and cramped place. As for its appearance, it is no better than the places of those petty government officials, with monthly pay of forty or fifty *yen*, which you can find on the outskirts of Tokyo. But as it is in the country, there is at least some land, some space around it. A yard or a vegetable garden, difficult to say which, slopes down under the eaves and extends as far as the fence, which is overladen with the berries of sweet viburnums. Over the foliage is seen only a quarter or so of the straw-thatched roof of the neighboring house.

From under the same eaves we have a clear view of the opposite hill across the glen. As the entire hill is some count's country seat, at times we catch glimpses through the trees of colored *yukata* and hear women's voices coming over a cliff. On the top of the cliff a tall pine soars into the sky. We regard it as our lofty task to look up at this tree, from under our low eaves, morning and evening.

Of all the areas we have so far passed through, this place seems to please your brother the most. For this there may be various reasons, but the main one, as I see it, is that the feeling that the two of us alone have become masters of an independent residence brings to your unsociable brother a certain tranquillity. Although he hadn't been able to sleep well any place else, since the night we came here he has been sleeping well. In fact now, while I am driving my fountain-pen forward, he is sound asleep.

Chance has also favored me in seeing to it that we need not loll about in one room, sitting knee to knee with each other, as is usual in the ordinary inn. But the house, as I have just said, is cramped indeed. On the hilltop to the right of our gate there is a western-style house built by a millionaire, in comparison with which ours is no better than a matchbox. Even so, it is a solitary independent house enclosed by fences, and altogether insulated from the surroundings. Cramped as it is, the house has five rooms. Here, however, we need not arise at the same time, as at an inn. One of us may rise, while the other can sleep as long as he wants. I can leave your brother undisturbed, and sit at the lacquered papier-mâché desk provided in the next room. The same is true in the daytime: when we get tired of being face to face, either of us may keep out of sight and do whatever suits him for as long as he wishes. And then at a suitable time he may return.

By taking advantage of such a chance, I am writing this letter. It is fortunate for you, I think, that I can unexpectedly take advantage of this chance. At the same time it is unfortunate for me to have thus come to recognize the necessity of taking advantage of it.

What I am saying does not have the orderliness of a diary; nor may it have any scientific precision. However, I can only remind you that it is the consequence of two negative factors—one inherent in travel itself, the trains, rickshas, inns, etc., bound to obstruct all regular chores; and the other in the very nature of this task of mine which cannot be tackled with ease. It is surprising to me that I am now able to report to you even as much as what follows, fragmentary as it may be. This, I owe altogether to chance.

## 30

Neither of us has any great taste for traveling. Consequently the plan we set up was as commonplace as our own experience itself. We decided our purpose would be just as well served if we toured several nearby and conveniently located spots as do many other tourists. With this vaguely in mind, we first thought of trying Sagami and Izu or thereabouts.

I was still better off than your brother, for I had some rough idea about main points and transportation to get there; whereas your brother almost transcended geography and directions. He could not tell whether Kozu is this side of or beyond Odawara, although perhaps he merely doesn't care rather than cannot tell. What really amazes me is that your brother, while thus indifferent to such an extreme, is incapable of taking a detached attitude toward anything relative to human affairs. But that is an aside. As it is difficult to return to the subject from such a digression, I shall henceforth keep as close to the main stream as I can.

Originally we agreed to start from Zushi as a jumping-off point. But that morning, while rushing to Shimbashi Station by ricksha, I had a different idea. Ordinary as our trip was going to be, to go straight to Zushi seemed just too ordinary to interest me. At the station I talked it over with your brother once more, and suggested that by reversing our itinerary, we might go first from Numazu to Shuzenji and then cross the mountains and go down to Ito. There was of course no objection on the part of your brother, who could not even tell whether Odawara is beyond or this side of Kozu; we at once bought tickets for Numazu and boarded a Tokaido train.

On the train nothing happened worth reporting. Following our arrival at our destination—while we bathed, ate, and sipped tea, there was nothing that could command my special attention. Not until that night did I come to realize that I might have something to convey to your folks about your brother.

It was too early for us to turn in. Already we were tired of chatting. I was overcome with the kind of ennui every traveler experiences. Then happening to notice a heavy-looking *go* board standing beside the alcove, I instantly carried it out to the middle of the room. Of course, I meant to play against your brother. And I am not sure whether you know this, but anyway while in school, though you may not think it of me, I had frequently played *go* with your brother. Although later on we stopped playing suddenly as if by preconcerted notion, the *go* board at this time seemed an ideal way to pass the hours that already somehow seemed to hang heavy on us.

Your brother stared at the board for a moment, and then said, "Well, I'd better not play." "Now don't say that. Come. Let's play," I countered quite determinedly. "No. No, I'd rather not," he said, however. And as I looked at his face there was a peculiar expression around his eyes, an expression which, oddly enough, betrayed no sign of either dislike of the game or indifference to it. Reluctant to force him, I nevertheless picked up the *go* stones and began arranging the white and black stones on the board for a match. Your brother watched for a little while. As I continued playing by myself, however, he abruptly rose from his seat and went out in the hallway. I thought he had probably gone to the toilet, and paid no more attention to him.

## 31

As I expected, your brother came back almost at once. And hardly had he said, "Let's have a game," than he snatched the stones from my hand. Noticing nothing, I said "All right," and began the game immediately. We were such wretched *go*-players that we could make our moves rapidly and finish quickly. We could easily play two games in an hour, a rate that could bore neither lookers-on nor players. But your brother said it was very trying to wait out the finish of even that rapidly changing *go* board, and at last gave up playing halfway through a game. I wondered if he might be feeling ill, but he merely smiled.

Not until we were about to turn in did your brother mention anything about his mental state at the moment. It seems that he felt it repugnant to do anything, even to play a game of *go,* and that at the same time he could not stand doing nothing. This conflict was already painful to him, and he had foreseen that once the game started he would surely be oppressed with the feeling that he could not afford to play a game like *go.* Yet he could not help playing it. So he had had no choice but to face the *go* board. And no sooner had he faced it than he lost all his patience. At last the white and black stones scattered over the board began to look like monsters which were purposely gathering and parting, separating and joining only to torture his brain. In a few seconds' time he felt he might have played havoc with the board to drive away these monsters, your brother told me. Although I had all that time noticed nothing, I was now somewhat startled and felt sorry that I had been so inconsiderate.

"No, this is not just with *go,*" your brother said and apparently forgave my blunder. Then he launched into an account of his day-to-day life. His attitude was calm enough even when he stopped playing halfway through a game. It may be that you people do not understand his feeling, which shows no abnormality whatsoever on the surface. To me at least this was a discovery.

Whether reading, reasoning, eating, walking, whatever he is doing and around the clock, he says he cannot find any peace of mind. No matter what he does, he is bedeviled by the feeling that he just can't afford to do that sort of thing.

"Nothing is as frustrating as when what I am doing is not related to the end I have always in mind," he told me.

"Isn't it good enough if what you are doing becomes a means?" I inquired.

"Yes, that would be fine. But only when you have your end can you determine your means."

Your brother is frustrated, for he thinks whatever he does, no matter how, becomes neither his end nor his means. He is completely insecure; as a result he cannot stay still. He gets up because he cannot sleep in peace, so he contends. Once he gets up, he cannot stand being merely awake, so he walks. Once he walks he cannot just keep walking, so he runs. And once he starts running he cannot stop no matter where he may run. Not only must he not stop anywhere, but he cannot help accelerating his speed every moment. And he says it frightens him to imagine what it will ultimately lead to; he says it is so frightening that he breaks into a cold sweat. Yes, he says it is unbearably frightening.

## 32

Your brother's explanation came to me as a surprise. Though having never once in my life experienced this sort of insecurity, I could understand it all right, even if I couldn't really feel it at all. I listened to him with the feeling of one who has no experience of a headache, and yet has to put up with someone's complaint about a splitting headache. I mused awhile; and while I was musing, I came to envision, though vaguely, the fate of man. I thought I had found fitting solace for your brother.

"Now what you call insecurity is the insecurity of the entire human race, and it isn't peculiar to you alone—if you realize this, that's that. Constant motion and flow is our very fate."

What I said here was not only vague but really disgustingly feeble. It was bound to wither beneath your brother's sharp, disdainful glance. But he replied:

"Man's insecurity stems from the advance of science. Never once has science, which never ceases to move forward, allowed us to pause. From walking to ricksha, from ricksha to carriage, from carriage to train, from train to automobile, from there on to the dirigible, further on to the airplane, and further on and on—no matter how far we may go, it won't let us take a breath. How far it will sweep us along, nobody knows for sure. It is really frightening."

"Yes, it is frightening, indeed," I agreed.

Your brother laughed.

"When you say it is frightening, it is simply because you feel it convenient to use the word frightening. That is no genuine fright. In other words, it is nothing but the fright of the head. Mine is different. Mine is the fright of the heart. It is a living fright which beats like my pulse."

In your brother's words there was no particle of falsehood, I assure you. And yet it is hardly possible to experience personally his fright.

"But if that is everyone's fate, it is hardly necessary that you alone be frightened," I offered.

"It is a matter of fact, if not of necessity," he returned, and then continued:

"It is frightening because the fate which the whole of humanity will reach in several centuries, I must go through—in my own lifetime—and at that all alone. And an average lifetime would be advantageous; but whether it be ten years, one year, or further shortened into one month, even one week, I must go through the same fate just the same. That's what frightens me. You may think I am telling a lie; but let me tell you this: cut my life at any point and in any fragment; and whether the length of that fragment be an hour or thirty minutes, you will find it goes through precisely the same fate. That's why it is frightening. In short, I gather within myself the insecurity of the whole human race, and distill that insecurity down into every moment, that is the fright I am experiencing."

"It won't do you any good. You ought to take it a little easier."

"It won't do me any good, that much at least I know."

In front of your brother I was quietly smoking. I wished I might help him escape this anguish somehow. I forgot everything else. Just then your brother, who had been staring me in the face, said suddenly, "You are a better man than I am." As I happened to be quite convinced of his intellectual superiority, this praise was neither gratifying nor flattering. Still I quietly puffed my cigar, and after a while he calmed down. Then we both got beneath the mosquito-net and went to sleep.

## 33

The next day we stayed in the same place. In the morning, as soon as we were out of bed, we strolled around the beach; it was then that your brother gazed at the deep somnolent sea and said joyously, "I like the sea as quiet as this." Lately he seems to long for anything that is at rest. For that reason, apparently he preferred mountains to water. This preference of his, though, differs from an ordinary person's enjoyment of nature, I think. This is evident in the following words by your brother:

"From the way I grow a mustache, wear a suit, hold a cigar in my mouth, I may look outwardly like a respectable gentleman, but in reality my mind is like a shelterless beggar wandering around from morning to night. All the time I am pursued by insecurity. Hopelessly restless. And at length I think that in the world there is no poor devil as crude as I. Then as often happens, in the streetcar or elsewhere, I raise my eyes, look across and catch sight of a face which seems completely carefree. The moment my eyes are fixed on such an undepraved, blank face, a deep thrill of joy runs throughout my frame. My mind revives just as the stalks of rice withering in dry weather welcome rain. At the same time that face, the one which is devoid of any thought, and completely relaxed, takes on nobility for me. Yes, it seems full of nobility, be his eyes slanted, his nose flat, his features plain. Before that face I feel like kneeling down and expressing my gratitude with a pious feeling very close to religious sentiment. My attitude toward nature is exactly the same. Long ago I used to enjoy things simply because they were beautiful, but that feeling is something I cannot afford now."

He now assigned mine to the category of such holy faces as he happened to come across in the streetcar. I declined such an unsought-for honor. Then, your brother said in earnest:

"Once or twice a day, I'm sure, it occurs to you too that your face automatically mirrors the natural state of your mind, which neither craves loss or gain, nor bothers about good or evil. I use the word holy for you at those particular moments—only at those moments."

Probably in an attempt to offer concrete evidence to me since I was still uncertain about all this, your brother, as illustration, referred to what I had been like at the time we turned in the night before. As he admitted, your brother had been overly agitated then, as a consequence of our talk. But as he had looked at my face his agitated state had calmed by degrees. Whether I would affirm this or not, it was none of his concern. One thing was certain, he declared, that under my favorable influence at the moment he had been able, even if temporarily, to escape from his agonizing insecurity.

I've already related what my attitude was like at that particular moment. I was quietly smoking. Nothing else. I was then oblivious to everything other than the desire to help him out of this insecurity. But I did not expect my wishes to communicate themselves. Nevertheless, in it there might have been genuine sincerity. Did he then perceive that sincerity in my face?

Your brother and I wandered along the sands, and while wandering I pondered: isn't he the type of person who cannot find peace until he goes into religion? More emphatically stated, isn't your brother now suffering in order to become a man of faith?

## 34

"Have you not lately thought about God?"

At last I asked such a question. When I said specifically lately, I was prompted by an old memory of our student days. In those days we both were still naive and full of random ideas; even so, your meditative brother and I had often discussed the existence of God. Incidentally, even then his brain worked somewhat differently from others'. As often happened, while idly walking he became suddenly conscious of the fact that he had just been walking, and this now became an insoluble problem which he had to wrestle with: it is undoubtedly I who walk if I will myself to, but whence do both my will to walk and my strength to walk spring? This was a big question for him.

Hence we had frequently used terms such as God and prime mover. As I now think about it, we used them without any real understanding. Even God, thus verbally abused, soon became trite. Then we would become silent as if by tacit agreement. How many years has it been, I wonder. Then one quiet summer morning I stood in front of that vast vessel holding the deep color called sea and, facing your brother, I uttered the word God once more.

But your brother had forgotten the word altogether. He showed no sign even of recalling it. In reply to my question only a faintly ironic grin flashed across the corners of his lips.

Yet I was not so timid as to be daunted by such an attitude. Nor were we on such delicate terms that we had to retreat warily before speaking out fully what was on our minds. I ventured one step farther.

"Now you say a nobody's face often makes you feel so glad; then you would be many hundreds of times happier if you might always be able to be with God and to worship his perfect image, wouldn't you?"

"What is the use of toying with such empty, sheerly verbal logic? Perhaps you'd better bring me God."

Your brother's tone as well as his wrinkled brows were quivering with impatience. He suddenly picked up a pebble at his feet, and dashing four or five yards toward the water's edge he threw it far out into the distant water. The sea received the pebble calmly. He repeated the act two or three times, as one would who is angered by his own futile efforts. Your brother stamped around in the seaweeds which had been washed ashore and whose names I didn't know—perhaps *kobu* or *wakame.* And then he came back to where I was standing.

"I prefer the living man to a dead God."

So your brother said, gasping for breath. And together we slowly walked back toward the inn.

"Whether it be a ricksha man's, a lazy bum's, or a thief's, whatever face—at the very moment it gladdens me—is God, after all, isn't it? Mountains, rivers, seas—nature at the instant when I feel it sublime is nothing but God, is it not? What other kinds of God are there?"

"Well, yes—" was the only answer I made. And for the moment your brother looked anything but satisfied. But afterwards, by look or manner, he betrayed that he had been impressed by my remark nevertheless. To tell the truth, although he snubbed me I was somehow more impressed.

## 35

We stayed in Numazu for a couple of days. When I suggested that we take advantage of the opportunity to go as far as Okitsu he said no. I had not the faintest idea why on that particular occasion your brother, who had so far let me have my way about our itinerary, ventured to reject my proposal. Later, when I asked why, he explained that he didn't care for the place renowned for Miho's Pine Grove and the Angel's Feather-Robe. Certainly his brain works in an odd way, I must say.

At last we returned as far as Mishima. There we transferred to an Ohito-bound train and finally arrived in Shuzenji. From the start your brother apparently was very much pleased with the idea of this watering-place. And yet as soon as we got to our destination he groaned with disappointment. That is, what he really liked was the name of Shuzenji, not the place itself. This may seem a trivial matter, but still to a degree it's characteristic of your brother, so I am taking this occasion to add it.

As you know, this watering-place is located in a town sunk deep into the bottom of a ravine and embraced by mountains. Once in, you face the verdant cliffs closing in on you on all sides, and you have no choice but to look upward. So cramped is it that if you walk with downcast eyes you can hardly notice the color of the earth. Your brother, who had so far preferred mountains to the sea, felt hemmed in the moment he came to Shuzenji, surrounded by mountains, and at once I took him out. Where there would be a main street in an ordinary town we found a river-bed through which flowed a stream of blue water dashing against the rocks. As a consequence there was scarcely any room to walk around freely. I lured your brother to the hot spring gushing from some cracks in the rock in the middle of the stream, for there men and women, interestingly enough, were all bathing together. Its uncleanliness was also something to talk about. Neither he nor I had the nerve to throw off our *yukata* and hop in. Instead, we stood on the rock for a long time, looking curiously at the black mass of bathers. Your brother seemed delighted. As we returned by way of a precarious plank bridge between the rock and the bank, he mumbled the phrase pious people. Evidently he did not mean it ironically; that seemed the way he really felt.

The following morning we were steeping in the indoor bath, brushing our teeth, when he said, "I couldn't sleep last night either." As I happened to be convinced that insomnia was most harmful to him particularly at that time, I considered that problem.

"When you can't sleep you are trying very hard to get to sleep, are you not?" I asked.

"Exactly. That makes it all the more difficult for me to sleep," he said.

"Now, tell me whether you feel guilty about someone if you don't sleep?" I asked again.

Your brother looked puzzled. Sitting on the edge of the piled-stone tub as he was, he was staring at his own hands and stomach. He is not very fleshy, as you know.

"There are times I can't get to sleep too. But insomnia is also fun," I said.

"How is that?" This time it was your brother who asked. I then cited an ancient poet's phrase which I happened to remember, "Wakeful in the light of a lamp, and mindful of exquisite fragrance." Your brother instantly smiled at me.

"A fellow like you can understand such sentiment!" he remarked with an incredulous look.

## 36

Later that day I dragged him out again, and this time we climbed the mountain. If you look upwards, there are mountains to climb; if you look downwards, there are springs to dip yourself in—there is nothing else to do. This is that sort of place.

Your brother, his lean legs flashing, walks briskly up a narrow path. And for that reason he seems to get tired faster than others. As I followed him up, hulkingly in my obesity, there he sits at the root of a tree, gasping for breath. He is not waiting for others; out of breath, he can only collapse.

Every now and then he stopped and looked at the lilies blooming amid the bushes. Once, for instance, he pointed expressly to the white petals and declared, "Those are mine." I could not catch his meaning; nor did I have a mind to ask, and finally we reached the summit. As we rested at the tea booth there, pointing to the woods and ravines unfolding under our feet, he said once more, "They are all mine too." Hearing these words repeated, I at last had become curious. Yet I was not to have my doubts dispelled on the spot, for in reply to my question he merely smiled a lonely smile.

On the stools at the tea booth we drowsed for a little while as though dead. What your brother was thinking about during the time, I do not know. For my part I only looked at the white clouds drifting along in the clear sky. The sun glared in my eyes. I became concerned about the heat we would have to brave on our way home. I hurried him along, and we started down the mountain. And it was just then that he suddenly grabbed at my shoulder from behind and asked, "How far do your mind and mine meet together and from where do they part?" Halting, I was shaken by the left shoulder two or three times. Just as my body was jarred, so was my mind. I always regarded your brother as a thinker. Since we had undertaken this journey together I had also concluded that he was one who was trying to go into religion and yet was having difficulty finding the entrance. In fact then my mental shock was due to my wondering if this question was possibly prompted by that sort of viewpoint. By nature I am indifferent to things—and also so dull-witted that I am not easily perturbed. But on account of your various requests prior to our departure, I tended to be particularly sensitive toward your brother at least. I felt then that I was almost on the point of slipping off my usual unperturbed way.

"*Keine Brücke führt von Mensch zu Mensch.*" (There is no bridge leading from one man to another.)

In reply I cited this German proverb which I happened to remember—though it was no doubt partly contrived strategically to keep the problem from getting complicated.

"Probably so," said he, "at this moment you cannot answer in any other way."

"Why is that?" I at once asked.

"One who is not truthful with himself can never be truthful with others."

I could not think to which aspect of myself I should apply his remark.

"You are traveling along as my nurse, are you not? I am grateful for your goodwill. But your behavior thus motivated is no more than hypocrisy, I think. I as your friend am moving away from you, that is all."

Such was your brother's declaration. And leaving me behind, he rushed down the mountain path alone. As he did I heard him exclaim, "*Einsamkeit, du meine Heimat Einsamkeit!*" (Loneliness, loneliness, thou mine home.)

## 37

With much anxiety I returned to the inn where I found your brother pale and lying in the middle of the room. When he saw me he neither spoke nor moved. I adopted a policy of leaving him as he was—one who valued naturalness. Sitting beside him, I had a smoke in quiet. Then I picked up a towel and went to the bath to wash off the unpleasant sweat. As I was standing by the tub, washing myself, he came to join me. Then for the first time we spoke to each other. "Tired, aren't you?" I asked. "Yes, I am," he replied.

From about lunch time by degrees he recovered his humor. At last I mentioned the melodramatic scene that had taken place between us a little earlier on the mountain path. At first he smiled but finally drew himself up, became serious, and declared that he was wretchedly lonely. For the first time he made the painful confession that he was invariably lonely not only in society but also at home. And he seemed more suspicious of his own family than he was of me, his intimate friend. In his eyes, both your parents epitomized hypocrisy itself. And especially was this true of his wife. He mentioned striking his wife on the head.

"At a first blow she is calm. At a second she is still calm. And at a third, although I expect resistance, there is none. The more blows the more ladylike she becomes. This helps all the more to make a ruffian out of me. It's just like venting my wrath on a lamb, only to prove the degradation of my character. Isn't she cruel to use her husband's wrath in this way to display her superiority? Now look. Women are far more cruel than men who resort to force. I wonder why the devil she didn't stand up to me when I hit her. No, she didn't need to resist, but why didn't she say so much as a single word back to me?"

As he said this, his face was filled with pain. Strangely though, while describing so graphically his own disagreeable behavior toward his wife, your brother would say almost nothing concrete about what really had motivated him. He merely insisted that on all sides he is besieged with hypocrisy, and yet he would not illustrate that hypocrisy to me. I wondered why in the world he was so excited about the empty-sounding word hypocrisy. In fact, your brother reminded me that my stupid doubts were due to the fact that I knew the word hypocrisy only in a dictionary sense, and rebuked me for being ignorant of its actual meaning. In his opinion I am far separated from actuality. I did not force out of him what he meant by hypocrisy. Consequently I have not the faintest idea about what sort of trouble besets his family. I left it that way, for in the first place it is a point I am not happy to pry into; also, whether I do or not, it is something I need not report to you, who are a member of the family. Yet, let me say a word just for your information: while saying something, though abstract, about his parents and his wife, he never mentioned your name. Nor did he say anything about your sister, Oshige-san.

## 38

It was on the night we arrived in Odawara from Shuzenji that I told your brother about Mallarmé. Mallarmé is the name of a famous French poet. I hope you won't mind my telling you, since it's out of your line. Although I say this, I confess I know nothing but the name. What I said about him is therefore no criticism of his works. The fact is that before leaving Tokyo I had come across an anecdote about this poet while glancing through a foreign magazine to which I regularly subscribe. It was such an interesting piece that I happened to remember it, and I used it as something for your brother to think about.

This Mallarmé, it so happens, had many young admirers. And these admirers were in the habit of gathering at his house and listening to his talk far into the night. No matter how many came his place was always before the fireplace and his seat was always the rocking chair. This had gradually become the kind of time-honored custom that no one dared violate. One evening, however, there was new visitor. This visitor, who I understand was an Englishman named Symons, unaware of the long-established custom, and probably thinking that all places and chairs were the same, seated himself in that special chair which Mallarmé always took. This disturbed Mallarmé; so much so that he could not concentrate on this talk. Naturally this spoiled the gathering.

"Now that is really rigidity," I concluded after having related the Mallarmé anecdote. And then turning to your brother, I said, "But your rigidity is even greater than Mallarmé's."

Your brother is a sensitive person. Aesthetically, ethically, and intellectually he is in fact hypersensitive. As a result, it would seem that he was born only to torture himself. He has none of that saving dullness of intelligence which sees little difference between A and B. To him it must be either A or B. And if it is to be A, its shape, degree, and shade of color must precisely match his own conception of it; otherwise he will not accept it. Your brother, being sensitive, is all his life walking on a line he has chosen—a line as precarious as a tight rope. At the same time he impatiently demands that others also tread an equally precarious rope, without missing their footing. It would be a mistake, though, to think that this stems from his selfishness. Imagine a world which could react exactly the way your brother expects; that world would undoubtedly be far more advanced than the world as it is now. Consequently, he detests the world which is—aesthetically, intellectually, and ethically—not as advanced as he is himself. That's why it is different from mere selfishness, I think. Indeed, it has nothing to do with the rigidity of Mallarmé who was so disturbed by the loss of his seat.

But probably greater still is his suffering. I sincerely wish to help him find relief from this suffering somehow. For his part, scarcely able to bear it, he is struggling as desperately as a drowning man. I can very well see the struggle that is going on in his mind. But I wonder whether it would be worthwhile, merely for the sake of the peace he might find, to blur that vision which is so sharp by virtue of his inborn capacity and long cultivation. Supposing that it is worthwhile, is it a humanly possible task?

I knew very well. I knew very well that his brain, overwrought with thinking, was echoing with the word religion which is written in blood and tears.

## 39

"To die, to go mad, or to enter religion—these are the only three courses left open for me," your brother declared at length. At that moment he looked rather like a man riding into the abyss of despair.

"And yet I do not think I can possibly enter religion; nor can I take my life, being too much attached to it. That leaves me only one way out—madness. Aside from my future, do I seem to you even now to be in my right mind? Hasn't something already gone wrong with me? That is what really frightens me."

He rose and went out to the veranda. There he leaned over the railing awhile, gazing at the sea. Then he paced back and forth in front of the room two or three times before returning to his seat.

"Blessed is Mallarmé, whose peace of mind was disturbed by such a thing as the loss of his chair. I for one have lost almost all. Even this body—even these limbs—the little that is left in my possession, betrays me mercilessly."

These words were not a mere hollow expression. Long superior in his capacity for introspection, your brother is now suffering from its coercion as a result of his excessive thinking. No matter in what frame of mind he may be, no longer is he able to go forward unless he first subjects his action to scrutiny. That's why the flow of his life is being interrupted every moment. It must be as trying as being called to the phone every other minute during mealtime. But it is his mind which interrupts, as well as his mind which is interrupted; in the last analysis he is controlled by these two minds which accuse each other from morning till night just as a wife and her mother-in-law might. As a consequence he cannot have even momentary peace.

From what your brother had told me, I could now understand what he meant when he asserted his discernment of nobility in the face of one who thinks about nothing. This conclusion had been altogether a product of his thinking. Yet because of this very thinking he is unable to enter that desired state. He has pursued a study of happiness in hopes of becoming happy. Yet no matter how much he might study, happiness always eludes him.

At last I once more mentioned the word God to your brother. And quite unexpectedly he struck me on the head. But that was the last scene which took place at Odawara. There was yet another scene before this blow came; so let me tell you about that first. As I have said earlier, however, since our fields are altogether different, what I am writing may at times appear to you mere pedantry and uncalled-for elaboration. Consequently when I insert foreign words which may mean little to you I become all the more hesitant. Since I am trying to leave out such outlandish words unless I deem them absolutely necessary, I hope you will understand this and read on without prejudice. Should you entertain misgivings about my sincerity what I have written so far can serve no purpose whatsoever.

While still in school I came across the following legend about Mohammed. Mohammed is said to have declared that he would summon before him a big mountain which happened to stand in the distance, and he invited interested witnesses to be present on a certain date.

## 40

The day came around and, as a multitude of people gathered around him, true to his word Mohammed called aloud upon the mountain to come to him. Not an inch would the mountain move, however. Still composed, Mohammed repeated the command. The mountain stood as still as before, and Mohammed was compelled to repeat the command a third time. But seeing, even after three repetitions, that the mountain showed no sign of motion, he said to the crowd: "In keeping with my promise I summoned the mountain. But the mountain seems reluctant to come. And since the mountain does not come I have no choice but to go to it." Saying this, he walked quickly toward the mountain.

I was too young when I read this story. I thought merely that it was an excellent vehicle for witticism, and told it around to various people. Among them there was one who was my senior and, while everyone else had a laugh, this man commented, "Ah, that is a great story. The true substance of religion is in it. It contains everything." I listened attentively to his comment, though it was beyond my comprehension. Many years had passed when I repeated the same story to your brother at Odawara. Yes, the same story just as it was, and I didn't mean it to be a joke.

"Why not walk toward the mountain?"

When I suggested this, he remained silent. For fear that I might have failed to make myself understood I added:

"You are the kind of fellow who summons the mountain, and who becomes irate when it doesn't come, the kind of fellow who stamps the ground with chagrin, and only thinks of criticizing the mountain. Why not walk up to the mountain?"

"What if it has a duty to come to me?" said your brother.

"Whether it has the duty or not, you just go if you need to," I said.

"Why should I when I have no duty?"

"Then go for the sake of happiness, if you don't like to go out of necessity," I replied.

At this your brother became silent again. He understands very well what I am driving at. But he cannot live without erecting in the center of his life his own lofty standard, the standard which he has laboriously built up thus far, of distinctions between right and wrong, between good and evil, and between beauty and ugliness. He does not care to throw it all away even to seek happiness. Rather, clinging to it all, he yet becomes desperate for happiness. And he himself recognizes full well the very contradiction that enmeshes him.

"If you stop regarding your own self as the axis of life and fling it overboard altogether, you will feel more comfortable, believe me," I again suggested.

"Then, what would be the axis to live by?" he asked.

"God," I replied.

"What is God?" he asked again.

Here I must confess something. As you go through the dialogue between your brother and me, I might sound as though I were a man of religion—as though laboring to lead him somehow to the way of faith. But I am no more than a common mortal who has nothing to do with either Christ or Mohammed. I am a wild creature of nature who has grown up aimlessly, without feeling the slightest necessity for religion. If our talk somehow gravitates toward it, it is entirely because I am dealing with such an intensely troubled person as your brother.

## 41

And precisely therein lay the reason he had dealt me a blow. Although I knew nothing about God, I dared to use the word God. When your brother questioned me about this in return, I should have said vaguely that it has the same meaning as Heaven or Fate. But circumstances did not allow for such an explanation. Our dialogue at the time, as I recall, proceeded in the following manner:

"Since there are things in the world that just don't turn out as you wish, you must acknowledge the fact that there is at work a will other than yours, must you not?"

"Yes."

"Furthermore, that will is far greater than yours, isn't it?"

"Perhaps greater, for I am being beaten. But most of them are not as good, not as beautiful, not as true as mine. There is no reason why I should be beaten, and yet I am. That's maddening."

"You are talking about the feeble struggle between man and man. That is not what I am talking about. I mean something larger than that."

"Where is something as vague as that?"

"If you deny it, then there is no way of saving you. That's all."

"Then let us suppose for a moment that . . ."

"Leave everything to it, and let it do as it pleases. Now look. When you ride a ricksha, can't you trust that the puller won't drop you and therefore sleep peacefully while in it?"

"I do not know of any supreme being as trustworthy as a ricksha man. You don't either. What you are saying is a sermon made up just on my behalf; it is not the religion you yourself are practicing, is it?"

"By all means, it is."

"Then have you renounced your ego altogether?"

"Well yes, in a way."

"That is, death or life, you are at peace, trusting that God will take care of you as he pleases?"

"Well, yes."

The more he pressed me the less certain I felt myself growing. But as I was completely at the mercy of circumstances there was nothing I could possibly do. Just then suddenly your brother raised his hand and slapped me in the face.

By nature I am insensitive as you well can see, thanks to which I have thus far managed somehow to survive, without either getting into serious brawls with others or incurring their wrath. Probably because I was dull-witted, even as a child I was not spanked by my parents, so far as I can remember. Still less as I grew up. Thus, when for the first time in my life I was slapped in the face, I immediately took offense in spite of myself.

"What do you think you are doing?"

"Now you know."

I did not understand what he meant by this, "Now you know."

"This is outrageous."

"Now you know. You do not trust God at all. You get mad just the same. You lose your balance over trifles. Your peace is upset."

I made no answer. Nor could I make any. Meanwhile your brother abruptly left his seat. And all that I heard were his footsteps rushing down the stairs.

## 42

I called a maid and inquired about my companion.

"He has just gone out. Probably to the beach, sir."

As the maid's answer coincided with my own guess I abandoned any further worry and threw myself down. At that instant I took notice of your brother's summer hat hung on the end of a clothes rack. That is, he had rushed out somewhere, hatless in the heat of the day. To someone like you, so much concerned with every move he makes, the way I stretched myself out on my back might seem too carefree. This is no doubt because I am a dullard. Yet this, I think, involves something noteworthy—something more than my slowness can explain away; so let me dwell on it for a moment.

I had confidence in your brother's intelligence. I thought highly of his power of comprehension. Time and time again he will unexpectedly speak out things incomprehensible to the average person. To those who do not know him or have little education, these might sound as strange as a cracked bell, but to those who understand him well these are rather more welcome than any conventional remarks. In them I used to find his originality. That is why I did not hesitate to declare positively to you that there was nothing to worry about. Then we set out for our journey. And exactly how he has been getting on since we started out I have so far described, but because of what I have learned about him during our trip it has become necessary for me to revise my initial opinion by degrees.

That your brother's brain is in better order than mine I still believe there is no doubt whatsoever. As a human being, however, right now he is somewhat confused, as compared with his former self. And that confusion, I think, stems from the precise and orderly functioning of his brain. For my part I would prefer to admire his ordered brain while reserving some doubts about his disordered mind. As far as he is concerned, however, his ordered brain is his disordered mind. This is what puzzles me: his brain is all right, but something may be wrong with his mind—dependable and yet not to be depended upon. If I say this, can it be accepted by you as a satisfactory report? Since I know no other way of describing it, I myself am already completely at sea.

I let your brother rush down the stairs, and then threw myself down to rest. To that extent I was at ease. As he'd gone out without wearing his hat I had no doubt that he would soon be back. On the contrary, however, he did not return as readily as I had expected. No longer could I remain stretched at full length and at ease. With frank misgivings, I rose at last.

Out on the beach I noticed that the sun was already behind the clouds. Both the leaden, overcast sky, and the shore and the sea below, tinted grey, looked melancholy, and a peculiarly tepid wind blew, carrying a briny odor. A white dot on that grey expanse, as I gradually became aware, was the figure of your brother crouching on the beach. When I approached him quietly and spoke to him from behind, he rose instantly saying, "I'm sorry for what I did a while ago."

After having rambled about aimlessly and endlessly, he at last had become exhausted, and had crouched down to rest on the spot where I had found him, he told me.

"Let's go to the mountains. I am sick of this place. Let's go to the mountains." He seemed eager to be off.

## 43

That night we finally decided to go to the mountains. The only mountain we could reach easily from Odawara was Hakone, and to this worldly spa I took your brother, the least worldly of men. From the start he said that the place would surely be noisy. Yet he insisted that he would be able to stand two or three days of it simply because it was a mountain.

"What a waste it is to go to a resort merely to put up with it!"

That was another remark your brother then made in a self-mocking tone. As might be expected, from the very night we arrived there he was subjected to the mercies of a boisterous guest in the next room. Although we couldn't decide whether he was from Tokyo or Yokohama, this guest was apparently a merchant, a contractor, or a broker—anyway something of that sort, judging from his manner of speech. Every now and then he raised his braying voice completely regardless of other guests. It was quite hard even on me, though I am ordinarily unmindful of such things. On account of this fellow, however, your brother and I retired that night without any complicated discussion. In other words, the fellow next door made such a hell of a noise he destroyed our meditation, so to speak.

On the following morning when I asked your brother, "Could you sleep last night?" he shook his head, saying, "Not a wink. How I envy you!" While he had had difficulty getting to sleep it seemed that I had snored loudly all night long.

From dawn that day it drizzled, and at about ten o'clock the drizzle turned into a regular rainfall. Shortly after noon it showed some signs of an approaching storm. Suddenly your brother rose, and tucking up his *yukata,* asserted that he was going out to roam around the mountain. He insisted that he was going to get some exercise no matter what, braving the downfall, scaling hill and dale. "What a chore!" I thought, but since it would be less troublesome for me to go along with him than try to dissuade him I presently said "All right," and also tucked up my *yukata.*

In no time he was rushing into the teeth of the choking wind. Like a bouncing ball he was leaping in the midst of those indescribable reverberations—the splashes of water or the booming from the sky. And he was shrieking with violence enough to rupture his blood vessels. He was many times more violent than the guest next door had been the previous night. His voice sounded even more like a wild beast's than that fellow's. His savage cries, once out of his mouth, were borne away by the gusts, to be smashed into pieces by the pursuing rain.

Then, soon afterwards, he lapsed into silence, although he still roamed about. He kept walking around until he was well out of breath.

I think it was an hour or two after we left that we returned to the inn dripping wet. I was chilled to the bone and your brother's lips had changed color. As we warmed ourselves in the bath, he kept saying, "Splendid!" To him it was perhaps splendid indeed, to be conquered by nature which harbors no hostility. "But what a chore!" I said simply, glad to stretch out my legs comfortably in the bathtub.

That night the next room was as silent as a grave, contrary to our expectations. From the maid we learned that the guest who had given so much trouble the previous night was already gone. It was that evening when, to my surprise, I heard your brother's views on religion. Indeed, I was somewhat shocked.

## 44

As a modern day youth you may also have little sympathy for the time-worn word religion. I wish I could possibly manage without referring to such knotty matters. But understanding your brother necessitates our touching on it. To you it may be uninteresting if surprising, but so long as you shun it the only result is that your brother himself will remain an enigma. Therefore I want you to have patience and read on without skipping this portion. If only you have patience, I am sure you can understand it. Please read it and understand him well, and then try to explain the matter to your parents, to their satisfaction. I feel really sorry for your old parents who are overly concerned with your brother. But as it is, you are the only means by which I can describe to his family what he really is. I hope you will pay serious attention to my report which may sound odd. I am certainly not trying to discuss such a complicated problem for fun. I cannot help it, for this complicated problem is itself part of your brother. Separate one from the other, and we will no longer have your brother in flesh and blood.

Your brother dislikes to erect any other authority than himself, whether it be God, the Buddha, or what not. (I use the word erect here following your brother.) Yet it has nothing to do with the Nietzschean assertion of ego.

"God is myself," says your brother. Should strangers happen to overhear the way he draws such a forthright conclusion, they might think him a bit out of his mind. Indeed, he speaks in such a violent way that perhaps they may not be able to think otherwise.

"Well, isn't that tantamount to asserting that you are absolute?" I criticize, but not an inch will he yield as he answers.

"I am absolute."

The more we repeated such dialogues the more peculiar your brother's tone grew. Not just his tone, but also what he said by degrees slipped more and more out of the ordinary. Had he been arguing with someone unlike myself he would most certainly have been dismissed as a case of sheer madness. However, I never took him so lightly as to give him up in that easy way. At last I pushed him to the brink.

Your brother's so-called absolute turned out to be no mere abstraction which a philosopher had spun out of his head. It was something plainly psychological, the kind of state which one could enter and experience in person.

He argues that one who has attained a pure peace of mind should naturally be able to enter this state without seeking it, and that once he enters the state the universe and all creatures—every possible object—would vanish, and there would be only self; and that self at the moment would be something existing and yet non-existing, it would be impossible to say which. It is something great and yet minute. It is something beyond description. In short, it is absolute. And should some partaker of this absolute hear all at once the sound of a fire-bell, then the sound of that fire-bell would be his self. In other words, the absolute becomes the relative itself. Consequently, no longer is it necessary to trouble oneself to project things and objectify others besides himself; nor need one fear even the possibility.

"The fundamental principle should remain the same, whether in death or life. Otherwise, there could be no peace of mind. A clever fellow might exhort, 'Rise above the times, by all means'; I, for one, believe that one must rise above life and death as well."

So asserted your brother, almost clenching his teeth.

## 45

In this instance also I must admit that your brother was over my head. Never had it occurred to me that it is humanly possible to attain the state he was referring to. On hearing his argument out to the conclusion which arrived with such logical precision, I thought that such a conclusion might be the case. Yet I also thought that such might not necessarily be the case at all. At any rate, I only proved to be unqualified to question it. Confronted by his impassioned words I sat perfectly silent. Then your brother's attitude changed. Until then my silence had frequently taken the edge off his argument, though all that had happened by sheer chance. Being such an intelligent person your brother would surely have seen through me had I merely played silent to some purpose. Perhaps, that is, my slowness somehow proved to be my advantage.

"Now look. Please do not despise me as a mere talker," your brother continued and suddenly placed his hands on the floor. I was stuck for an answer.

"To a staid fellow like you, I may indeed sound like a silly chatterer. Such as I am, though, I am anxious to practice what I am preaching. Day and night, never do I stop thinking that I should practice it. Yes, I am thinking continuously that I cannot live if I don't practice it."

Still I was at a loss what to say in reply.

"Now, tell me. Do you think my ideas wrong?" inquired your brother.

"No, I do not," I answered.

"Or do you think they are not quite thorough?"

"Fundamental enough, it seems to me," I answered again.

"But how can I change from a speculative to a practical man? Please tell me that," he beseeched me.

"Oh, but that's something beyond my power," I backed off, suddenly awestruck at this turn.

"Yes, you can. You are a man born to be practical. That's why you are happy. That's why you can be so tranquil," your brother pursued.

It was evident that he was in earnest and, turning to him with a sigh, I declared:

"In intelligence you are far superior to me. It is certainly beyond my power to save you. I might touch those of duller intelligence than mine. But I could have no effect on you at all, for you are more intelligent than I am. In other words, you are born thin and tall, whereas I am fat and chunky. If you want to be fat like me, there can be no other way than for you to shorten yourself."

From his eyes fell teardrops.

"Plainly I recognize the absolute state. But the more distinct my *Weltanschauung* becomes, the further the absolute moves away from me. In short, I was born to explore topography only on a map; yet I have all along been anxious to have the same experience as a practical man in gaiters would have, ranging over hill and dale. I am stupid; I am inconsistent; I know my stupidity; I know my inconsistency; and yet I still struggle, nevertheless. I am a fool. As a man you are far more mature than I."

Once more he placed his hands before me, and as if to apologize he then dropped his head. Tears fell in streams from his eyes. I was overwhelmed.

## 46

As we left Hakone, your brother said, "I won't come to such a place again." Of all the places we had so far passed through there was none in fact that pleased him. I guess he is the kind of person who quickly becomes tired no matter where he may go and no matter with whom. Well, it must be so, for in the first place he is not pleased even with his own body or his own mind. He speaks of his own body and mind as though they were his knavish traitors. And that this was by no means a nonsensical half-jest I can well understand, after staying with him all these days. This, I am sure, you will also understand thoroughly from my own objective account.

You may wonder how your brother in this state, and I, can travel together. To me too this is something to marvel at. Once my head was filled with all that I have just stated about your brother, it might seem difficult for me even to deal with him, however thick-headed I might be. But the fact is that I do not find it so painful to live vis-à-vis with him. It is, I should think, at least much easier than outsiders might be led to imagine, although if asked why it is so, I am quite at a loss for an answer. Don't you have this same experience with your brother? If you do not, it would appear that I, a stranger, rather than you, his own brother, enjoy greater intimacy with him. By intimacy I do not mean mere friendship. I do mean that we both share somehow the unique nature which harmonizes us into unity, and thereby enables us to get along.

Ever since we set out on our journey I have constantly said and done what would hurt his feelings. And once I was even struck by him on the head. Yet with all this I think I can stand before your entire family and declare that I haven't yet fallen out of his good graces. At the same time I have not the slightest doubt that I still from the bottom of my heart love and respect your brother, despite his certain weakness.

Your brother is an upright man, upright enough to drop his head and shed tears before an ordinary fellow like me; he has the courage to dare it. He is a man of principle who discerns that it is proper to dare it. So clear-headed is he that he tends to go forward, leaving his own self behind. He is suffering, for the other implements of his mind fail to keep pace with his intellect. In terms of character this is a blemish; in terms of success it is an ominous danger. While I lament this conflict for your brother's sake, and trace all its causes to his overly active intellect, I cannot rid myself of genuine respect for that very same intellect. So long as we take him for a hard-to-please and selfish person, there may be no opportunity to approach him. In that case we will have to give up the chance for good, the chance to allay his suffering even if slightly.

We left Hakone, as I have already said, and we came directly to this summer house in Benigayatsu. Earlier and at my own discretion I had made a plan to stop over in Kozu, but I finally decided against bringing it up for his consideration. Since I was afraid he might again say angrily, "I won't come to such a place again." Besides, when he heard from me about this summer house, he was most eager to come here for a quiet rest.

## 47

As it is now, anything can easily excite your brother and yet he can hardly bear any excitement. For him, therefore, this hermitage-like summer house would seem to have been most suitable. When from the quiet room he looked up at a soaring pinetree on the cliff across the ravine, he said, "Good," and sat down.

"That pinetree is also yours."

Consolingly I tried to mimic his way of talking, for I remembered his words, "Those lilies are mine," and "That mountain and that ravine are also mine," whose meaning I had not quite been able to understand at Shuzenji.

The house had been kept by an old man who returned to his own place when we arrived. Still once every morning and evening he continues coming to sweep and clean the place and to draw water. As the possibility of cooking for ourselves was out of the question, we had him arrange with a nearby inn to deliver our three meals daily. Since this house is lighted by electricity we are spared the trouble of lighting lamps at night. Thus, all that we have to do from the time we leave bed till the time we retire at night is, at most, to make our beds and hang up the mosquito net.

"Well, it's certainly easier and more leisurely than doing our own cooking," your brother says. Indeed, this place is undoubtedly the most quiet of all those mountain and sea places we have passed through. As often happens, when we keep quiet by ourselves, we do not hear the rustle of the wind even. The only noise that there is is the creaking of the wheel-well in the shade of sweet viburnums, which your brother does not mind, oddly enough. Apparently he is gradually becoming collected. I should have brought him here earlier.

In the yard there is a patch of eggplant and some Indian corn. We talked about plucking off the eggplants to eat, but it would be too much trouble to pickle them, so we gave up the idea. As for the Indian corn, it is not ripe enough yet to be edible. By the well at the back door tomatoes are growing, which we eat in the morning while washing our faces. In the heat of the day your brother often goes down to this patch of land, hardly distinguishable as yard or garden, and crouches there fixedly. Every now and then he sniffs the cannas which, as you know, have no fragrance, or he examines the flower petals of the evening primroses. On the day of our arrival, for instance, he went over to the pampas-grass growing on the boundary between our place and that of our millionaire neighbor to our left, and stood stock-still there for a long time. From the room I watched him; he did not move for so long that at last I slipped on sandals and headed over to him. Dividing the neighbor's house and ours is a bank about two yards high, which is covered all over with pampas-grass in season. As I approached him, your brother glanced at me over his shoulder, pointing down at the roots of the grass.

At the roots of the grass a crab was crawling—a tiny one, no bigger than a thumbnail. It was not the only one, however; for, in time, while I was watching, there came another, a third, and so on, their numbers growing rapidly until at last they swarmed all over.

"Look. Some are crossing the blades of grass," he observed, still standing motionless. I left him where he was, and returned to my seat.

It makes me immeasurably happy to see your brother so absorbed in these trifles as to almost forget himself. And I even think it is worth all my trouble to have brought him out for our trip. And that night I told him what I meant by this.

## 48

"A while ago you were possessing those crabs, were you not?"

As I suddenly spoke, your brother, surprisingly enough, gave a merry chuckle. Ever since Shuzenji I had often used the word *possess* in such a peculiar way that your brother had taken it as merely a joke. To him, therefore, I might have sounded amusing. Well, to amuse is far more preferable than to anger. As a matter of fact, however, I was being quite serious.

"Yes, an absolute possession," I corrected myself at once. This time your brother did not laugh, either. Nor did he make any answer, and it was again my turn to speak out:

"The other day we had a difficult argument about what you called the absolute, but I fail to see why you need to go to so much trouble as to try to enter that absolute state. There would be no problem, I should think, so long as you could absorb yourself as you did in the crabs. To be first conscious of the absolute, then seize the moment when the absolute switches to the relative and thereby seek their unity—isn't this too difficult? In the first place, it's problematical whether it is humanly possible."

Your brother would not interrupt me yet. He seemed to be quite a bit steadier than usual, and I ventured a step further.

"Wouldn't it be handier to go the other way round?"

"The other way round?" he returned, his eyes sparkling earnestly.

"Yes—that is to say, to be so absorbed in the crabs, and thereby forget yourself. If you were thus perfectly one with your object, that would be the state you're talking about."

"Indeed," he responded uncertainly.

"Indeed? You are actually practicing it. Don't you realize that?"

"I see."

His response was still vague. Then suddenly it dawned on me that all along I had been saying something quite unnecessary. To tell the truth, I have not the faintest notion of the absolute. I had never given any thought to it; nor had I even tried to entertain such a thought as far as I could remember. Thanks to my education, I had only learned to mouth that sort of term. Nevertheless, as a man I was more stable than your brother, although I would, of course, be ashamed if you took this to mean that I am superior to him; let me put it this way: my mental state is closer to the general average than his. What, as a friend, I am working for with him is only to have him regain the position of the average person like me. To put it somewhat differently, it means the seemingly ridiculous act of converting the extraordinary to the ordinary. But for your brother's anguished suffering, it would make no sense for one like me to try to start such an argument with him. Your brother is honest. If he cannot quite understand, he yet keeps pressing me for an answer, and thus pressed for an answer I am at a loss how to respond. And worse yet, such a critical discourse, I fear, is likely to turn your brother, who is only just becoming practical, back to where he was, to his former injuring attitude. That was what I feared more than anything else. I do wish I could provide him with something that can captivate his mind completely, so completely as to leave no room for his inquiring attitude—something as engrossing, let us say, as all the works of art, as all the lofty mountains and mighty rivers, or as all the beautiful women in the world. And for a year or so I would like to keep him under their complete spell. After all, your brother's alleged desire to possess things would ultimately seem to mean being possessed by things, wouldn't it? Consequently, to be absolutely possessed by things, I think, is to possess things absolutely. Only then and there will your brother, who does not believe in God, find his peace of mind in this world.

## 49

The night before we had gone out to the beach for a walk. From our place to the beach it is about a fifth of a mile. We follow a narrow path to the road and then must cross it to have a view of the color of the sea. There was still some time before the moon was to rise. The waves were darkly in motion, and the division between the water and the beach was hardly distinguishable until our eyes became adjusted. In this darkness your brother continued boldly on his way. From time to time lukewarm water came running over my feet. The waves, after breaking on the shore, rolled in, unexpectedly spreading far out like a flattened rice cake.

"Don't your clogs get wet?" I asked him from behind.

"Tuck up the bottom of your *yukata,*" he urged. Apparently he had already tucked his up behind, and was ready to get his feet dirty. It was so dark that I had not noticed although we were only a few yards apart. Probably because it is the best season in this resort place we ran into many people, and invariably they were couples—silently groping their way in the dark. Consequently we could not discern them at all until they suddenly confronted us. Then as they passed close to us I raised my eyes to scrutinize them only to find that they were indeed all young couples, just the sort I had come across many a time.

It was then that I heard from your brother about a certain Osada-san. It seems that she had lately gotten married and had gone to Osaka. Those young couples we saw must somehow have reminded your brother of her in bridal costume.

Osada-san, according to him, was a good-natured person, the least selfish in the family. Her kind was born happy, he declared enviously, and admitted he wished he could be that way too. Unacquainted with Osada-san, I had no comment but merely mumbled, "I see."

"She is something like you made into a woman," your brother said and paused there on the sands. I did likewise.

A dim light came into sight on the height beyond us. By day in that direction we could see a red building through the trees, and this light probably belonged to the owner of the red western-style house. Solitary in the thick shades of night, it glittered like a star. But while my face was directed toward this light, your brother stood facing the rolling sea.

Just then suddenly the notes of a piano rang out above us. The house stood on the stone wall piled regularly two yards high above the sands. From the end of this stone wall notched steps slanted up to the garden, so as directly to connect the garden and the beach. I ascended the steps.

Over the garden fell a streak of light from the house. Bathed in its faint glow, the ground was covered all over with grass. Flowers which I could not see distinctly since the garden was so dark and spacious seemed to be in bloom here and there. The notes of the piano were coming from a brightly lighted room of the western-style building in front.

"It looks like a foreigner's summer house."

"Probably it is."

Your brother and I sat together on the top of the steps. The notes of the piano, scarcely audible, reached our ears from time to time. Both of us remained silent. Every now and then the tip of his cigarette glowed red.

## 50

Certain that your brother would tell me more about Osada-san I waited somewhat anxiously in the dark for him to speak. But as though absorbed in his smoking he merely made the tip of his cigarette glow from time to time, and would not say a word. When he threw the butt down at the foot of the steps and turned toward me, I expected that our topic might drift away from Osada-san. I was a little puzzled, in fact, for his thought now had nothing to do with her; nor did it have any connection with the notes of the piano, the spacious lawn, the beautiful summer house, resort, travel or anything else related to our surroundings and the present moment. Instead, it was about an ancient Buddhist bonze.

The name of this bonze, I recall, was Kyogen. He was said to be both so intelligent and sagacious that a word was clue enough to express a whole thought. Yet this very alert intelligence, as your brother explained, had hindered his spiritual enlightenment for a long period of time. What this means is clear even to me, although I know nothing about spiritual enlightenment. Still more so, painfully clear, must it be to him who is wrestling with the burden of his own intelligence. "The source of his trouble was in fact his erudition itself," your brother declared emphatically.

For several years the bonze had studied and practiced Zen under the guidance of his master, Abbot Hyakujo, but the master passed away before he could obtain results. Then he had gone to Isan. Isan denounced him, saying that there would be no hope as long as he took pride in flaunting his learning. Isan is said to have told him to come back in the form of existence prior to the time of his own parents. Kyogen, the bonze, returned to his living quarters. After reviewing what he had till then acquired from volumes of books, so it has been said, he sighed that no such painted cake could appease hunger. So he burned all the books he had collected.

"I'll give it all up. From now on I'll live on gruel."

Henceforth he ceased to think of even the word Zen. He flung off good and evil, the form of existence prior to the time of his parents, and in fact any and every thing. Then it occurred to him to choose a quiet place and there build a little hermitage. He cut the grass on the lot; he dug out the stumps; he cleared away the stones to level the ground. Then it was that one of the stones he hurled aside struck the nearby bamboo thicket with a thud. And with this sound the spiritual truth burst upon him.

"One single blow has done away with all my learning," he exclaimed joyously.

"I wish I could somehow be like Kyogen," said your brother. What he means is clear to you too, I think. He wishes to be relieved of every possible burden, and he has no God to entrust that burden to. Therefore, he wishes to dump it all into a dustbin or some such place. In high intelligence your brother much resembles Kyogen. For that reason he envies Kyogen all the more.

Thus, your brother's story had nothing to do with the foreigner's summer house or the fashionable musical instrument. Why at the summit of the dark stone steps, in the midst of the pervading smell of brine, he chose to tell this particular story, I do not know. But by the time he had finished his story, the notes of the piano could no longer be heard. Either because of the proximity of the tide or of the night dew, our *yukata* had become damp. Upon my urging, we retraced our steps. As we came out in the street I stopped by my favorite candy store and bought some bean-jam buns. Nibbling them, we returned to our place quietly through the dark. The old man's boy whom we had asked to look after the house while we were away, was fast asleep, in spite of the buzzing mosquitoes. Giving him the remaining buns, I sent him home at once.

## 51

Yesterday morning, while we were having our breakfast, I took your brother's bowl and filled it with his first serving of boiled rice. At that time he once again mentioned Osada-san's name. As I understand it, before marriage she used to wait on him just as I was doing then. Just the previous night I had been compared to her in point of personality, and I was now compared to her in the way I waited on him.

This prompted me to ask him, "Do you think you could be happy if you lived like this with that Osada-san?"

Your brother thoughtfully raised his chopsticks to his mouth. But from his attitude I inferred that he was perhaps reluctant to reply, and I did not press him further.

Then suddenly, after swallowing two or three mouthfuls, he blurted out, "I did say Osada-san was born to be happy. But I am not saying she could make me happy."

His retort sounds logically very consistent and straightforward. In its dark depths, however, it already harbors inconsistency. For once he had told me plainly that he rejoices almost gratefully at a natural face which shows no concern with anything. Is this not the same as saying that one born to be happy can also make others happy? I smiled at him. In a case like this he just cannot let you off scot-free; he snaps back at you directly.

"Yes, I mean exactly what I say. I do not want you to doubt that. You can be sure that what I said is said, and that what I didn't say hasn't been said."

I did not want to contradict him, but it seemed to me slightly amusing that, clear-headed as he was, he showed no reluctance to toy with that verbal logic he always despised. I therefore exposed freely what seemed to me the self-contradiction he had lapsed into.

Still saying nothing, he crammed rice into his mouth a couple of times.

Then his bowl was empty, and since the server was still beside me, out of his reach, I held out my hand before him to receive his bowl for another serving. This time, however, he would not accept my offer, but insisted instead that the server be handed over to him.

So I pushed it over to him and, picking up the large scoop, he heaped his bowl with rice. Then placing the bowl on the table he asked without even attempting to pick up his chopsticks: "Do you think that a woman remains the same after marriage?"

On this occasion I could not answer offhand. Perhaps this was because I usually gave no thought to things like that, and I in turn busied myself cramming rice into my mouth, while awaiting his explanation.

"Osada-san before marriage was altogether different from the married Osada-san. Osada-san as she is now, I tell you, has already been spoiled by her husband."

"What sort of fellow did she marry, anyway?" I interposed.

"Once married, a woman becomes perverse on account of her husband, no matter who he may be. As I say this I don't know how much I have already corrupted my own wife. Wouldn't it be really shameless to expect happiness from the very wife one has debased? Happiness is something you just can't demand from a woman whose innocence has been destroyed by marriage."

No sooner had your brother said this than he took up and emptied the over-loaded rice bowl.

## 52

Now I think I have described as fully as I can how your brother has behaved since we set out on our journey. It seems as if it were only yesterday that we left Tokyo, but in reality it has been by count already more than ten days. To you and your aged parents who have been looking forward to my letter these ten days may have been perhaps too long, I am afraid. That I understand too. But under the circumstances, as I explained at the beginning of this letter, I had little time to take up the pen until we finally came here for a restful stay. Hence my inevitable delay. In reporting on your brother, however, I haven't skipped any of the last ten days. In this letter I have taken special care to note down how he has been each day. That is my excuse; that is my satisfaction, as well; for I am closing this letter with the confidence that I have done my duty better than I had initially expected.

I cannot figure out the time I have spent on this, it being the kind of labor whose extent is not to be measured by the clock. All the same, it is no doubt a very painstaking task. This is the first time in my life I have written a letter of such length. It just couldn't have been written at one sitting; nor could it have been written in a day. Snatching every spare moment, I sit at the desk and begin where I left off last time. But it is nothing. If I could make your brother come to life in this letter, just as I have observed and understood him, I would not mind taking the trouble and would tax my strength many times more than I have done so far.

I am writing this letter in behalf of your brother whom I care for; also I am writing this letter in behalf of you who equally care. And last, I am writing this letter in behalf of your loving parents, the father and mother of both you and your brother. Your brother as I have found him may perhaps be different from your brother as you people have found him. Your brother as I understand him also may not be the same brother as you people understand him. If my letter is worth this effort its value, I want you to bear in mind, rests in precisely that. That is, its value lies in the different reflection I received as I looked at the same person from a different angle. This, I want you to note and use for your benefit.

It may be your wish to obtain some especially clear knowledge about his future, but I, being no prophet, have no right to meddle with the future. When the sky is covered with clouds it may rain or it may not rain at all. One thing at least is certain, that while it is cloudy we cannot enjoy sunshine. All of you people seem to lay a certain amount of blame on your poor brother for making those around him miserable, but I don't think that one who is not happy himself has the strength to make others happy. If we demand warm sunshine from the cloud-covered sun, we are simply demanding something impossible. While I am here with your brother I am trying to dispel this cloud for him. Before expecting warm sunshine from him it would be well for you to banish first the cloud that surrounds his head. Should you fail to do this, something unfortunate may befall your family. For your brother himself too there will be sadness, and I as I state this will be saddened too, in that event.

I have described your brother as he has been during the last ten days, and the question now is what he will be in the next ten days. That question, no one can answer. But suppose I could answer for him in the next ten days, who then could answer for the following one month, and for the following half year? All I have presented is a faithful account of only the last ten days. This account, which I, being thickheaded, have merely written down without rereading it, may certainly have inconsistencies. For that matter, even your brother's speech and behavior may also have inconsistencies which I have failed to notice. Nonetheless, I do declare this: your brother is in earnest; he is not trying to fool me. I am honest too and I have not the slightest intention of misleading you.

When I started writing this letter your brother was snoring loudly. So is he now as I am finishing it off. It seems strange that I happened to begin writing while he was sleeping, and am now finishing while he is again sleeping. Somehow or other I feel how happy he would be should he never awaken from this sleep. Yet at the same time I feel that he would be very sad indeed should he not awaken.

## Kawabata Yasunari (1899–1972)

Kawabata Yasunari was the first Japanese author to win the Nobel Prize in literature. In its citation, the Swedish Academy noted that Kawabata stands as a spokesman for a uniquely Japanese outlook and for the literary values used to express that view. Though this assessment is undoubtedly accurate, Kawabata was also a literary experimenter. In the prewar years he dabbled in several forms of avant-garde stream-of-consciousness writing and impressionism. He also sought out and championed the work of younger, unknown writers; his most famous protégé was Mishima Yukio.

Kawabata is noted for his short stories and short novels. These are generally lyrical but with a cool, detached, some would say nihilistic, tone. Kawabata is especially known for his portraits of women. His writing is characterized by a sensual, tactile quality in which exquisite beauty is often juxtaposed with equally exquisite ugliness.

Early in his career Kawabata wrote a collection of several hundred short vignettes and sketches that he called "palm of the hand" stories to reflect their brevity. Some of these short pieces were shaped into short stories, as in the examples presented here. Others were developed in an impressionistic manner similar to the construction of *renga,* linked-verse poetry. One episode or portrait suggests another, which in turn leads to something else. Many of Kawabata's novels are constructed in this way and depend on an almost musical sense of flow and association rather than on a rigid, overarching architectural structure. Some readers will feel impatient with what may appear to be a pointless and rambling narrative; others will be attracted by these tactile and sensitive expressions of great suggestiveness.

"The Pomegranate," presented here, resonates with feelings left unspoken, allowing or even forcing the reader to evoke his or her own mood of resignation and acceptance, offering a chance to savor beauty, inviting the imagination to do its work. In "Snow," reality is defined in terms of memory. Here the relationships are cherished because they exist only in memory, refined from the dross of actual encounters. The same is true of "Cereus," where the man's relationship with his former wife is seen through flowers, friends, child, and memory. In Kawabata's stories perhaps more than in Sōseki's we find fiction in the manner of a haiku.

## *The Pomegranate*

*Translated by Howard Hibbitt*

In the high wind that night the pomegranate tree was stripped of its leaves.

The leaves lay in a circle around the base.

Kimiko was startled to see it naked in the morning, and wondered at the flawlessness of the circle. She would have expected the wind to disturb it.

There was a pomegranate, a very fine one, left behind in the tree.

"Just come and look at it," she called to her mother.

"I had forgotten." Her mother glanced up at the tree and went back to the kitchen.

It made Kimiko think of their loneliness. The pomegranate over the veranda too seemed lonely and forgotten.

Two weeks or so before, her seven-year-old nephew had come visiting, and had noticed the pomegranates immediately. He had scrambled up into the tree. Kimiko had felt that she was in the presence of life.

"There is a big one up above," she called from the veranda.

"But if I pick it I can't get back down."

It was true. To climb down with pomegranates in both hands would not be easy. Kimiko smiled. He was a dear.

Until he had come the house had forgotten the pomegranate. And until now they had forgotten it again.

Then the fruit had been hidden in the leaves. Now it stood clear against the sky.

There was strength in the fruit and in the circle of leaves at the base. Kimiko went and knocked it down with a bamboo pole.

It was so ripe that the seeds seemed to force it open. They glistened in the sunlight when she laid it on the veranda, and the sun seemed to go on through them.

She felt somehow apologetic.

Upstairs with her sewing at about ten, she heard Keikichi's voice. Though the door was unlocked, he seemed to have come around to the garden. There was urgency in his voice.

"Kimiko, Kimiko!" her mother called. "Keikichi is here."

Kimiko had let her needle come unthreaded. She pushed it into the pincushion.

"Kimiko had been saying how she wanted to see you again before you leave." Keikichi was going to war. "But we could hardly go and see you without an invitation, and you didn't come and didn't come. It was good of you to come today."

She asked him to stay for lunch, but he was in a hurry.

"Well, do at least have a pomegranate. We grew it ourselves." She called up to Kimiko again.

He greeted her with his eyes, as if it were more than he could do to wait for her to come down. She stopped on the stairs.

Something warm seemed to come into his eyes, and the pomegranate fell from his hand.

They looked at each other and smiled.

When she realized that she was smiling she flushed. Keikichi got up from the veranda.

"Take care of yourself, Kimiko."

"And you."

He had already turned away and was saying good-by to her mother.

Kimiko looked on at the garden gate after he had left.

"He was in such a hurry," said her mother. "And it's such a fine pomegrante."

He had left it on the veranda.

Apparently he had dropped it as that warm something came into his eyes and he was beginning to open it. He had not broken it completely in two. It lay with the seeds up.

Her mother took it to the kitchen and washed it, and handed it to Kimiko.

Kimiko frowned and pulled back, and then, flushing once more, took it in some confusion.

Keikichi would seem to have taken a few seeds from the edge.

With her mother watching her, it would have been strange for Kimiko to refuse to eat. She bit nonchalantly into it. The sourness filled her mouth. She felt a kind of sad happiness, as if it were penetrating far down inside her.

Uninterested, her mother had stood up.

She went to a mirror and sat down. "Just look at my hair, will you. I said good-by to Keikichi with this wild mop of hair."

Kimiko could hear the comb.

"When your father died," her mother said softly, "I was afraid to comb my hair. When I combed my hair I would forget what I was doing. When I came to myself it would be as if your father were waiting for me to finish."

Kimiko remembered her mother's habit of eating what her father had left on his plate.

She felt something pull at her, a happiness that made her want to weep.

Her mother had probably given her the pomegranate because of a reluctance to throw it away. Only because of that. It had become a habit not to throw things away.

Alone with her private happiness, Kimiko felt shy before her mother.

She thought that it had been a better farewell than Keikichi could have been aware of, and that she could wait any length of time for him to come back.

She looked toward her mother. The sun was falling on the paper doors beyond which she sat at her mirror.

She was somehow afraid to bite into the pomegranate on her knee.

## *Snow*

*Translated by Lane Dunlop and J. Martin Holman*

For the past four or five years, Noda Sankichi had secluded himself at a Tokyo high-rise hotel from the evening of New Year's Day until the morning of the third. Although the hotel had an imposing name, Sankichi's name for it was the Dream Hotel.

"Father has gone to the Dream Hotel," his son or his daughter would say to New Year's visitors who came to the house. The visitors would take it as a joke meant to conceal Sankichi's whereabouts.

"That's a nice place. He must be having a good New Year's there." Some of them even said this.

However, not even Sankichi's family knew that Sankichi actually did have dreams at the Dream Hotel.

The room at the hotel was the same every year. It was the Snow Room. Again, only Sankichi knew that he always called whatever room it was the Snow Room.

When he'd arrive at the hotel, Sankichi would draw the curtains of the room, immediately get into bed, and close his eyes. For two or three hours, he would lie there quietly. It was true that he was seeking rest from the irritation and fatigue of a busy, agitated year, but, even when the fretful tiredness had gone away, a deeper weariness welled up and spread out within him. Understanding this, Sankichi waited for his weariness to reach its fullest extent. When he had been pulled down to the bottom of the weariness, his head gone numb with it, then the dream would begin to rise toward the surface.

In the darkness behind his eyelids, tiny millet-sized grains of light would begin to dance and flow. The grains were of a pale, golden, transparent hue. As their gold chilled to a faint whiteness, they turned into snowflakes, all flowing in the same direction and at the same slow speed. They were powdery flakes, falling in the distance.

"This New Year's, too, the snow has come."

With this thought, the snow would belong to Sankichi. It was falling in Sankichi's heart.

In the darkness of his closed eyes, the snow came nearer. Falling thick and fast, it changed into peony snowflakes. The big, petal-like snowflakes fell more slowly than the powdery snowflakes. Sankichi was enfolded in the silent, peaceful blizzard.

It was all right to open his eyes now.

When Sankichi opened his eyes, the wall of the room had become a snowscape. What he'd seen behind his eyelids was merely the snow falling; what he saw on the wall was the landscape in which the snow had fallen.

In a large field in which stood only five or six bare-branched trees, peony snowflakes were falling. As the snow drifted higher, neither earth nor grass was visible. There were no houses, no sign of a human being. It was a lonely scene, and yet Sankichi, in his electrically heated bed, did not feel the coldness of the snowy field. But the snowy landscape was all there was. Sankichi himself was not there.

"Where shall I go? Whom shall I call?" Although the thought came to him, it was not his own. It was the voice of the snow.

The snowy plain, in which nothing moved but falling snow, presently, of its own accord, flowed away, shifting to the scenery of a mountain gorge. On the far side, the mountain towered up. A stream wound along its base. Although the narrow stream seemed choked with snow, it was flowing without a ripple. A mass of snow that had fallen in from the bank was floating along. Halted by a boulder that jutted out into the current, it melted into the water.

The boulder was a huge mass of amethyst quartz.

At the top of the quartz boulder, Sankichi's father appeared. His father was holding the three- or four-year-old Sankichi in his arms.

"Father, it's dangerous—standing on that sort of sharp, jagged rock. The soles of your feet must hurt." From the bed, the fifty-four-year-old Sankichi spoke to his father in the snowy landscape.

The crown of the boulder was a cluster of pointed quartz crystals that looked as if they could pierce his father's feet. At Sankichi's words, his father shifted his weight for a better footing. As he did so, the snow atop the boulder crumbled and fell into the stream. Perhaps frightened by that, Sankichi's father held him tighter.

"It's strange that this narrow little stream isn't buried under so much snow," his father said.

There was snow on his father's head and shoulders and on his arms, which held Sankichi.

The snow scene on the wall was shifting, moving upstream. A lake came into view. It was a small lake, in the depths of the mountains, but, as the source of such a narrow little stream, it seemed too large. The white peony snowflakes, the farther away they were, took on a tinge of gray. Heavy clouds hovered in the distance. The mountains on the far shore were indistinct.

Sankichi gazed for a while at the steadily falling peony snowflakes as they melted into the lake's surface. On the mountains of the far shore, something was moving. It was coming nearer through the gray sky. It was a flock of birds. They had great snow-colored wings. As if the snow itself had become their wings, even when they flew past Sankichi's eyes, there was no sound of wingbeats. Were their wings extended in silent, slow waves? Was the falling snow bearing up the birds?

When he tried to count the birds, there were seven, there were eleven . . . He lost count. But Sankichi felt it as a pleasure rather than as a puzzlement.

"What birds are those? What are those wings?"

"We're not birds. Don't you see who's riding on the wings?" A voice answered from one of the snowbirds.

"Ah, I see," Sankichi said.

Riding on the birds through the falling snow, all the women who had loved Sankichi had come to him. Which of them had spoken first?

In his dream, Sankichi could freely call up those who had loved him in the past.

From the evening of New Year's Day to the morning of the third, in the Snow Room of the Dream Hotel, drawing the curtains, having his meals brought to the room, never leaving his bed, Sankichi communed with those souls.

## *Cereus*

*Translated by Edward Seidensticker*

For three summers now, Komiya had invited several of his wife's school friends to look at the night-blooming cereus.

"Beautiful," said Mrs. Murayama, the first to arrive, as she stepped into the parlor. "See how many there are. More than last year." She gazed at the cereus. "There were seven last year? How many are there tonight?"

It was an old-fashioned Western frame house with a large parlor. The table had been pushed aside and the cereus was at the center on a circular stand. The stand was slightly below knee level, but Mrs. Murayama was looking up at the blossoms.

"Like a white fantasy." She had said the same thing last year. Two years before when she had first seen the cereus, she had said the same thing, with rather more enthusiasm.

She went nearer and looked up at it for a few moments and then turned to thank Komiya.

"Good evening, Toshiko," she said to the girl beside him. "Thank you for letting me come. You're bigger and prettier. The cereus is blooming twice as well as last year and so are you."

The girl looked up at her but did not answer. She did not seem shy but she did not smile.

"You must have worked very hard on it," said Mrs. Murayama to Komiya, "to have it blooming so nicely."

"I think this will be the best evening this year." Hence the sudden invitation, he no doubt meant to say, though somehow his voice did not say it.

Mrs. Murayama lived nearby, at Kugenuma. He had called her and told her that this was the evening, and she had called her friends in Tokyo. She told him the results: two of the five women invited had other engagements and a third would have to wait for her husband to come home, and Mrs. Imasato and Mrs. Omori would definitely come.

"Mrs. Omori said that since there would only be three of us she wondered if she might ask Shimaki Sumiko to come along. She's not been here before. She's about the only one in the class left unmarried."

Toshiko got up and started out through the door beyond the cereus.

"Let's look at it together, Toshiko," said Mrs. Omori.

"I saw it bloom."

"You actually saw it come into bloom? With your father? You must tell me what it was like."

The girl went out without looking back.

Two years before, Mrs. Murayama remembered, Komiya had told her that it came into bloom like a lotus, waving as if in a gentle breeze.

"Does she dislike seeing her mother's friends? Is it that she doesn't want to hear about her mother? I wish Sachiko were with us. Though if she were here I suppose you wouldn't be troubling yourself."

Mrs. Murayama had first seen the cereus when she had come one summer evening two years before to tell him that his estranged wife wanted a reconciliation. She had come again with several friends and asked him to forgive his wife.

They heard an automobile, and Mrs. Imasato had arrived. It was nearly ten. The cereus opened in the evening and the blossoms faded at two or three in the morning. It was a flower of a single night. About twenty minutes later Mrs. Omori arrived with Shimaki Sumiko. Mrs. Murayama introduced Sumiko to Komiya.

"She's too young and pretty. That's why she's still single."

"It's because I've been ill so much." Sumiko's eyes were shining as she looked at the cereus. She was the only one who had not seen it before. She walked slowly around it and brought her face near.

The blossoms came from thick stems at the end of longish leaves. The great white flowers were swaying gently in the breeze through the window. It was a strange flower, the petals somehow different from those of a long-pedaled chrysanthemum or a white dahlia. It was like a flower in a dream. A profusion of deep-green leaves stretched upward from the bamboo that supported the three stalks. There too were the most flowers. As with other varieties of cactus, the pistils were long and leaves grew from other leaves.

Sumiko did not notice that Komiya, struck by her intentness, had come up beside her.

"There are considerable numbers of them here and there in Japan, but it is unusual to have thirteen blossoms in one night. It blooms six or seven nights a year. Tonight seems likely to be the best."

He told her that what looked like a large lily bud would be blooming tomorrow. Of the little bean-like protuberances on the leaves some would be leaves and some would be buds. It would take a month for the smaller buds to bloom.

Sumiko was enveloped in the sweet perfume, sweeter than a lily but not as insistent.

Not taking her eyes from the cereus, Sumiko sat down. "A violin. Who is playing?"

"My daughter."

"What a pretty piece. What is it?"

"I'm afraid I don't know."

"A good accompaniment to the cereus," said Mrs. Omori.

After looking at the ceiling for a time, Sumiko went out on the lawn. The sea was immediately below.

She said when she came back inside: "She was on the balcony upstairs. She wasn't facing the sea but standing with her back to it. I wonder if that is better."

## Abe Kōbō (1924–1993)

*Translated by John Nathan*

Abe Kōbō represents a new sort of Japanese writer emerging in the postwar era. Scarred by the war and the intense nationalism that accompanied it, Abe consciously turned away from the traditional wellsprings of Japanese literature. Rather than looking to Japan's past for models and inspiration, he turned to the broader stage of world literature and found an affinity with Franz Kafka (pp. 2049–2054), Samuel Beckett (pp. 1944–1966), and Harold Pinter.

Abe's fiction and drama deal with the condition of modern, urban man without defining him in terms of a national heritage. Indeed, Abe, much influenced by German existential thinkers, rejected national identity as an inauthentic mode of being. Consequently, his settings and landscapes are not necessarily Japanese but merely urban, or wasteland, or both.

Abe's characters typically find themselves in situations that tear them away from their normal routine existence. They fall into a hole in the sand and are trapped there; they lose their faces, forget their names, or are otherwise robbed of what they consider to be their identities. There follows a desperate struggle to regain normalcy and eventually a realization that to succeed in escaping back to the comfortable past is to fail in a more painful yet more meaningful endeavor to come to terms with the present. Escape must not only be escape from something but also be escape to something, and the Abe hero is forced to seek out new, more authentic modes of being.

In the story "Stick" we see Abe's debt to Kafka, as Abe adopted the theme of metamorphosis. The man in the story is so dehumanized that he has become a stick. Even a stick, however, might be useful for something, but this particular stick is nothing more than an object for scholarly scrutiny, punishment, and rejection. Being of no value as a human being, in the end he is not even worth passing judgement on. In "Red Cocoon" Abe dealt with the notion of place as a source of identity. A man wants a place of his own with which he can identify. Eventually he finds it but at the expense of his sense of personal authenticity. He has a place of his own but no self to bring home to it.

## *Stick*

A sultry Sunday afternoon in June . . . The department store roof was swarming with people, the station and streets below looked puffy and swollen after the rain. I had wedged myself and my two boys into a space just right for one, a niche someone had just vacated between the stair well and a ventilator, but my children had got bored as I boosted them up to the railing so they could see, and I myself had succumbed to the fascination of staring downwards. But there was nothing so special about that; most of the people hanging on that railing were adults. Kids usually lose interest right away and begin pestering to go home, whereupon their parents snap at them as if they were being disturbed at work and then dreamily lower their chins to the railing again. Of course a minor part of this pleasure has to do with feeling guilty but that doesn't mean, does it, that it's a pleasure to be denied? I was just day-dreaming, that's all, and I'm certain there was nothing on my mind so important that there might have been a pressing need to remember it afterwards. I will say that I was feeling curiously irritable; it may have been the humidity and dampness, and my kids were getting on my nerves.

Then my older boy yelled Daddy! as if he were angry about something. Involuntarily I leaned over the railing, trying to escape from that jarring voice. I say leaned, but it was really more an attitude than a motion, and I can't believe I had really placed myself in danger. Yet suddenly I was floating in space and then, as I listened to my son scream Daaady!, falling.

I'm not sure whether it happened before I fell or while I was falling, but the first thing I knew, I had become a wooden stick. Not too thick or too slender, just right for handling, a perfectly straight stick about a yard long. Daaady! The second scream floated down to me. A crack opened in the crowd milling on the street below, and I aimed for the opening, tumbling end over end as I plunged straight downwards. I bounced off the pavement with a sharp brittle crack, caromed off a gingko tree and stuck, quivering, in the ditch between the pavement and the street.

Furious bystanders glared up at the building, where the small blood-drained faces of my children peered politely over the railing on the roof. Promising to see they got just what they deserved, the guard at the entrance left his post and rushed gallantly into the depths of the department store. The crowd's anger was mounting, people shook their fists threateningly. For a while I had to remain just as I had fallen, sticking into the ditch, unnoticed.

Finally, a student approached me. He was accompanied by another student wearing an identical uniform and by a man who seemed to be their professor. The two boys were as alike as identical twins in height and features, they even wore their student caps at the same rakish angle. The professor, a tall man with a white moustache and very strong glasses, seemed a gentleman of great dignity and presence.

The first student drew me out of the ground and said, almost regretfully: 'Even a stick can die if it takes a fall like that and lands wrong.'

'Let's have a look,' said the professor, smiling. He took me from the student and hefted me: 'It's lighter than I thought. But there's no point in setting our sights too high. Even a piece of wood will make perfectly good research material for you boys. As a matter of fact, it's just what you need for your first practical exercise. I propose that we put our heads together and see what can be learned from an examination of this stick.'

The professor moved off, tapping me in front of him as if I were a cane, the two students following along behind. Skirting the crowd, they moved into the square in front of the station and, finding all the benches there filled, sat down in a row on a small patch of lawn. The professor grasped me in both hands and held me up to the light, squinting along my length. Then I noticed something very strange. Apparently the students noticed it at the same time, for they spoke almost simultaneously: 'Professor—your moustache—' The professor seemed to be wearing a false moustache; the left side had pulled loose and it was fluttering in the breeze. The professor nodded calmly, moistening the moustache with some saliva and patting it back into place. Then he turned back to the students as if nothing in the world had happened and said: 'Now, let's see what you can deduce from this stick. Make your analysis first, then evaluate your data and try determining some appropriate sentence.'

The student on the right picked me up first and scrutinized me from various angles. 'The first thing I observe is that this stick has a top and a bottom,' he said finally, sliding me in and out of the tube he had made of his hand. 'At one end the stick is rather grimy from having been gripped; at the other, the wood has been worn away. In my opinion, this signifies that the stick under observation is not merely a piece of wood such as you might find lying alongside the road, but a tool that was used by someone for a very specific purpose. Furthermore, it appears that this stick was handled roughly; it's covered with nicks and scratches. Yet it was never discarded, someone continued to use it, which suggests that it must have been a sincere and simple soul when it was alive.'

'What you say is basically correct,' the professor interrupted, 'but I'm afraid you've got too sentimental.' Now the student on the left spoke up, his voice almost harsh, as if he were struggling to pick up the line of the professor's argument: 'It seems to me that this stick must have been totally useless, impotent. I mean, well, it lacks any complexity whatsoever. An ordinary stick is just too crude to be one of man's tools. Why, even a monkey can use a stick.'

'But the other side of that coin,' objected the first student, 'is that a stick can be considered the most fundamental tool. And the very fact that it's not specialized makes its range of uses all the wider. A stick can lead a blind man, or train an animal; used as a lever it can move great weights, or you can attack an enemy with it.'

'I'm afraid I can't go along with what you say about a stick leading a blind man. It seems to me the blind are just using a stick to lead themselves.'

'Maybe that's what is meant by sincerity.'

'Maybe so. But don't forget, the professor can beat me with this stick if he wants, but I can use it to beat him, too!'

This brought a burst of laughter from the professor. 'Watching two peas in a pod have an argument is really very amusing. The fact is, though, that you're expressing precisely the same idea, but in different terms. The essence of what you're both saying is that the man we have here was a stick. And that's all we need to know about him, a perfectly sufficient solution to the problem. In short, what you both really mean to say is that this stick was a stick.'

'But aren't we at least obliged to assign special significance to the fact that he was able to be a stick?' Anxious not to concede his point, the first student was almost pleading. 'I've seen all kinds of men in our specimen room, but I've never seen a stick, not one. I insist this variety of simple sincerity is rare—'

'Now just because we don't happen to have something in our specimen room doesn't necessarily make it rare,' the professor countered. 'As a matter of fact, sometimes we don't have things because we consider them too commonplace. In other words, there are cases where we don't recognize the necessity of dealing with something in our study because it is too ordinary.'

Both students looked up at once, as if by prearrangement, and scanned the crowd that milled around them. The professor laughed and said: 'I didn't mean to imply that all these people here will turn into sticks. When I said a stick was ordinary I was speaking qualitatively. Mathematicians don't bother any more to discuss the characteristics of a triangle because further inquiry can't possibly result in any new discovery. It's the same sort of thing with a stick.' The professor paused. Then:

'By the way, what verdict do you boys intend to hand down?'

'Do we have to punish even a stick like this?' asked the first student in a troubled voice. The professor turned to the student on the left. 'What do you think?' he asked.

'Of course we have to. Punishing the dead is what we do. As long as we exist we have no choice but to punish.'

'All right, then: what do you suppose the most appropriate sentence would be?' The students sat quietly, pondering the problem to themselves. The professor began scratching something in the ground with the tip of me. It began as an abstract design with no meaning at all, then arms and legs took shape and it became a sketch of a monster. But almost immediately the professor began to scratch the picture out. When it was obliterated he stood up and said in a near whisper, his eyes fixed on something in the distance: 'We've all had plenty of time to think by now. The answer is so simple it's very difficult. I talked about this at one of my lectures and I'm sure you remember it—those whose sentence is not being sentenced?'

'I remember,' the students answered with one voice.

'The courts up here must judge only a certain percentage of mankind. But we must judge all men, at least as long as there are no immortals. Yet compared to the number of men in the world, there are pitifully few of us. And if we should ever be required to judge all the dead in exactly the same way we should surely perish from sheer exhaustion. Fortunately, there are those who conveniently enable us to sentence them by passing no sentence at all—'

'A stick like this is a prime example of that group.'

Smiling, the professor released me. I fell to the ground and began to roll but the professor pinned me under his boot and continued: 'Accordingly, abandoning this stick here is the best punishment we can devise. I'm certain that someone will pick him up eventually and use him as a stick, just as he was used when he was alive.'

Now one of the students spoke abruptly, as if just remembering something: 'I wonder if this stick had any interesting thoughts as it listened to our discussion?'

The professor gazed affectionately at the student's face, but didn't speak. Instead he began walking away, signaling the end of the session. Apparently the students were concerned about me after all, for they looked back in my direction several times, but the crowd quickly engulfed them and they were lost from sight.

Someone kicked me out of his way. And I sank half-way into the ground, still soft after the rain. Dad. Daddy.

Daaaady! I distinctly heard the screaming, it sounded like my own children and it sounded very different. There were thousands in that crowd, and there could have been any number of children besides my own who had to summon their fathers with screams. Nothing strange about that at all.

## *Red Cocoon*

The day is dying, time for men to hurry home: but I have no place to go. I slowly walk the narrow crack dividing house from house and wonder-wonder-wonder how there can be so many and none, not one, for me.

When I leaned against a telephone pole to urinate there was a piece of rope curling on the ground and I wanted to hang myself. The rope leers, eyes on my throat—Brother, Let's rest! Christ—yes I want to rest. How can I? I'm no brother to a piece of rope; besides, I haven't found a convincing reason why there is no house for me.

Night comes every day. At night, when it's dark, you have to rest. But you need a house to do that. Then it's impossible that no house is mine.

A revelation. Maybe I've been deluding myself. It's not that I don't have a house, maybe I've just forgotten which is mine. Yet, it's possible. This one, for example, stopping in front of a place I happen to be passing; how do I know this isn't mine? Of course there is nothing special about it to suggest it might be mine, but the same is true about any house and doesn't constitute a proof that the house in question is not mine. Up with courage, then, and knock at the door.

On the other side of the window, luckily half open, the smiling face of a woman. She looks friendly. The winds of hope sweep past my heart and it unfurls, a flag, and wildly flutters. I smile, too, and greet her like a gentleman:

'Excuse me for asking, but I was just wondering if this wasn't my house!'

Abruptly her face hardens: 'What's that—who *are* you?'

I think of explaining, then realize that it's hopeless: I have no idea what I should say. How can I convince her that who I am is not the problem? A little desperate now:

'If you insist this is not my house, I'd like you to prove it.'

'Now look here—' she seems frightened; and that irks me.

'If there's no proof to the contrary, I think I'll just assume that this is my house!'

'But it just so happens that this is my house!'

'What's that supposed to mean? Just because it's your house doesn't necessarily mean it isn't mine. Don't you agree?'

No answer, and the woman's face becomes a wall and seals the window off. So this is the reality that lurks behind the smile on a woman's face. A wall! This same transfiguration always gives substance to that weird logic where something can't be mine because it belongs to someone else.

But why-why-why is everything someone else's and not mine? Can't there at least be something that doesn't belong to anyone? Sometimes I have the illusion that a section of concrete culvert about to be buried in the street or waiting in a factory yard is my house. But culverts are always on their way to belonging to someone and before long they disappear independently of my will or concern. Or they transform themselves into something that is obviously not my house.

Then how about this park bench? Fine, no problem. If this is really my house and if he just doesn't come along with his club and drive me away . . . surely this belongs to EVERYONE not to anyone in particular. But he says:

'Hey, get-the-hell up. This bench belongs to everyone, not to anyone in particular, and certainly not to the likes of you. On your way, Jocko. Any objections and we'll just have you step through the gate of the law and come down to our basement room. If you stop anywhere along the way you'll be guilty of a criminal offence.'

Do they mean me when they talk about the wandering Jew?

The day wanes. I walk: walk.

Unvanishing unaltering rooted in the ground unmoving houses. Between them opens an ever-changing crack without one single stable face—the road. Rain bristles it like a brush, snow makes it as wide as the rut left by a wheel, wind rolls it on and onward like a conveyor belt. Walking. I still don't understand why there is no house for me so I can't hang myself yet.

Hey, who's there, who's clinging to my foot that way? If that's the hangman's rope then there's no hurry, take it easy, STOPRUSHINGME. No, it's something else, a bit of sticky silk thread, and when I grab hold and pull, it winds out of a crack in my shoe. That's funny, I think, curious, and as I wind out more and more of the thread something even stranger happens. Gradually my body begins to lean, I can't hold myself vertical to the ground any more. I wonder if the earth's axis has tilted, changing the direction of gravity?

Then my shoe falls off my foot and thuds to the ground and I understand for the first time what has happened. There's no warp in the earth's axis, one of my legs has shortened. As I reel out more and more of the thread my leg has unravelled, like the frayed elbow on a wool jacket.

Already I can't move another step. I stand dead still, bewildered, and the thread in my bewildered hand, the thread that is my leg, began to move with a will of its own. It slithered out of my hand and to the ground, then wrapped around my body like a snake. When my left leg had unravelled completely the thread transferred itself to my right and soon enveloped my whole body in a silken bag yet continued even then to unwind, unravelling me as it filled the bag in from the inside. Then, finally, I was gone, extinguished.

A large, empty cocoon remained.

Hmnnn. Now I can rest at last. The cocoon smoulders in the light of the sinking sun. Beyond a doubt this is my own house and no one can disturb me. Yes, I have a house now, but there is no me to come home to it.

Inside the cocoon time stops. It grows dark outside but here the sun is always setting, the burning colours in the evening sky seep into the walls and make them glow. There was no reason to hope he wouldn't notice a peculiarity so conspicuous as this. And he did find me, discovered the cocoon I had become, between a railroad crossing and the track. At first he was angry, but he soon decided I was a rare find, and put me in his pocket. After rolling around there for a while I was transferred to his little boy's toy box.

## Ōba Minako (b. 1930)

*Translated by Stephen Kohl and Toyama Ryōko*

Postwar Japanese literature has been characterized by the emergence of a large number of women writers who have come to play a major role in shaping contemporary fiction. Ōba Minako first appeared on the literary scene in 1967, when her story "Sanbiki no kani" ("The Three Crabs") won the distinguished Akutagawa Prize. Since that beginning Ōba has steadily established her position as a major writer.

Ōba's writing is remarkable for its variety. She is regarded by many as a writer who deals not only with feminist issues but also with gender issues generally: questioning, interpreting, defining, and challenging the roles of women in contemporary society. Ōba brings an international perspective to her works. Having lived in Sitka, Alaska, for twelve years and begun her literary career there, her interests and horizons are broader than those of many of her contemporaries, and this internationalism also marks a significant new trend in Japanese writing. Although global in her experience and outlook, Ōba is also firmly grounded in the rich traditions of Japanese literature. Especially in her more recent works, she has turned to the classics of Japanese literature, which she has adapted and retold in ways that make them viable in today's world. She has also written and translated a significant number of children's stories and fairy tales from around the world.

Yuri, the heroine of "The Three Crabs," is a woman who has attained postwar Japan's ideal life; she has a home and a family, ample wealth, and a circle of friends. Her satisfaction should be complete, but it is not. She yearns for something, some relationship, that can be more meaningful. In this story she fails to find it and has to return to her deadening routine. As she deals with her morning-after depression, her emotion is not guilt for betraying her husband and daughter but rather loneliness and pathos at having failed to achieve a significant encounter with another human being. Yet in the end we feel confident that if she failed this time, she will surely try again. The story's strength comes from the honesty, courage, and determination with which Yuri examines her life and chooses to take charge of it.

## *The Three Crabs*

The murmur of the sea rose and fell through the fog like the quiet sound of a sleeper's breathing. In the beach grass, the seagulls were already awake, flapping their wings and crying harshly. Dingy gulls, the color of soot-stained snow turned their beady orange eyes in her direction and arrogantly scratched at the sand.

As she walked along, the fog seemed to flow about her. Yuri walked with the gritty sand creeping up her legs under her torn stockings. The sea was purple tinged with a black band. A young man wearing a hunting cap and carrying a canvas Boston bag waited by the yellow sign at the bus stop.

The man nodded and said, "Once the fog clears it's going to be a fine day." It was not clear whether he was talking to Yuri or to himself.

Yuri looked out at the swirling fog and at the faint, milky luminescence of the sea. She worked some of the sand out of her stocking with the tip of her finger.

Looking down a moment later Yuri saw a pair of crabs creeping along together near the tip of her shoe. A crab has no face and yet for some reason a crab's warped shell never failed to remind Yuri of a face. The crab suddenly extended its two long, watery eyes. The two crabs crept around as though their legs were tangled together. The sharp edges of their shells were the same dark purple as the sea.

"Here comes the bus," said the man with the hunting cap.

There were only five or six passengers on this, the first bus of the day.

"I wonder why the fog is so thick today?"

The fog seemed to be licking at their heads and shoulders.

"L city please," said Yuri unzipping her purse.

"Eighty-five cents," said the driver.

As she searched for the money she wondered if they had really come that far and found that she did not have enough change. She was supposed to have a twenty dollar bill tucked away in the inside pocket of her purse, but when she looked, it was not there. The man in the hunting cap was waiting behind her.

"Just a moment please, let me sit down while I find it." Yuri sat down in the first empty seat and began searching through her purse. It was not there. The twenty dollar bill which she had definitely put into her purse when she left home last night was not there now. She always put large bills in the inside pocket of her purse and her small change in a coin pocket which snapped shut. She only found sixty-five cents in the coin pocket.

The man with the hunting cap sat down beside her. "What happened? Lose your money?"

"I guess so." Yuri groped around in the bottom of her purse for any change that might have fallen there. She found two or three coins. Gathering them together she paid the driver and asked, "You stop at the amusement park, don't you?"

"Which entrance you want?"

"By the Opera House."

"The north side is it?"

"I think so . . ." said Yuri rummaging in her purse for her car keys.

"We stop real close there," said the driver and the hunting cap simultaneously.

She once more began looking through her purse. She did not find the twenty dollar bill, but she did find a crumpled one dollar bill in a small side pocket. The bill was limp and lipstick stained.

"This fog sure is thick . . ." said the man with the hunting cap speaking neither to himself nor to Yuri.

Yuri gazed at the forlorn neon sign flashing on and off in the ever lightening fog with the deep purple sea in the background.

Yuri felt a vague discomfort in her stomach as she stirred the cake batter. Mechanically she broke an egg into the bowl and mixed in the butter. As she blended in the baking powder and salt she felt the nausea rising in her throat like morning sickness.

Rie was whipping the cream. She was looking forward to licking the bowl later.

"Who all will be coming?" asked Rie dipping into the whipped cream with her finger.

"It doesn't matter who's coming. I don't want you to go telling Susan every time your parents have friends over," said Yuri holding back the pain in her stomach.

"Oh all right," said Rie rolling up the whites of her eyes. "Look Rie," continued Yuri, "there is no one else mama can be completely honest with, so every now and then I like to talk to you. To admit things like . . . I hate Sasha, or how I feel that I have to go ahead and bake this cake even though just the thought of it makes me vomit. But don't go telling everyone what I just said, okay? When mama says strange things like this, just listen to her and think of her as a poor fool. Mama may be a fool but she needs your sympathy. Be kind to her once in a while."

As she stirred the batter, Yuri made up her mind not to play bridge that night no matter what.

Taking out a bottle of liquor, Takeshi frowned and said, "You shouldn't say things like this to a child. Even though you're an adult you haven't learned to put up with things." Turning to his daughter he continued, "All right, Rie. Everyone has to put up with certain things."

"Oh all right." Rie rolled up the whites of her eyes once again.

"I hate to say this, but my stomach is too upset to play bridge. You had better invite someone else to make a fourth. I'll tell you what, everyone would feel bad if you told them I was ill so just say that I had to go out suddenly. It wouldn't be very much fun having a poor player like me hanging around anyway."

"Whoever heard of a bridge party without a hostess?"

"My sister will be coming through this evening on her way from San Francisco and I am going to meet her. That will be all right, I will tell them that."

"Do you want to be such a nuisance?"

"Nuisance? I'm making a peaceful suggestion. Wouldn't it be more polite to just disappear than to be unreasonably patient and upset myself by making pointless conversation?"

"How can you consider yourself as 'being patient.' You are just basically arrogant. You think you are somehow special when you have to put up with someone."

"Um." Yuri felt bad. She thought she would bawl if she had to put up with anymore of this. "Maybe I am arrogant and self-confident in the sense that I can't help responding to other people's feelings. Certain kinds of people aren't sensitive to the feelings of others, or else when they are sensitive ignore them. But I am a sentimental person and since I am responsive to the feelings of others, I get mad when I put my whole heart into something and my efforts are ignored. So, it would be better after all to do things without getting involved in them, don't you think so?"

"Do what you damn well want." Takeshi gave Yuri a spiteful look and sipped his whisky.

"Okay! I have an idea. Let's invite Keiko. She is brilliant, has sex appeal, she's pretentious; she likes nothing better than to be called into people's houses. Keiko will be just right. She would love to visit a house when the hostess is out."

Rie felt that her mother was disgusting when she acted like this and she sympathized with her father. She was only ten but she was precocious and she usually understood what adults were talking about.

"Hello, Keiko? Yes, I know this is rather on the spur of the moment, but would you come over to play some bridge? You see, I just now found out that my sister will be coming through and I really would like to meet her. Would this interfere with your studying for tomorrow? You really would be doing a favor. I'd be indebted to you. You know, having a young lady like yourself here would really liven things up. Oh, thank you so much . . . Yes, that's right. I'll ask the Yokotas to swing by your place and give you a ride. Yes, I'll ask them myself. Yes, we'll have two tables playing."

When Yuri finished talking on the phone she felt somewhat relieved and felt like putting Takeshi in a good mood.

"I really don't feel well. I probably either have a cancer or I am pregnant again."

Takeshi who had just raised his glass to his lips, smiled sarcastically into it. "Well then, congratulations. When's the big day?"

"It's twelve months away."

"Let's try for nine months, okay?"

"What are you bitching for. Not even twelve months would give me time to get ready."

"Be careful now. You shouldn't be telling fibs like this in front of children. Like that business about your sister coming in from San Francisco. Rie knows perfectly well that she's not really coming."

"Rie is a sensitive and intelligent child. She understands a little white lie is no mortal sin as long as no one gets hurt by it. Tralalalala . . ."

"Now don't start singing those tuneless songs of yours. My ears are sensitive."

"We can't tell lies in front of children, but we also must not tell the truth. Tralalala. That Keiko has sex appeal, or that Sasha is Father Baranoff's wife and papa's girl friend, or that mama is putting a curse on all the guests with the cake. Haha. Ten black birds are going to come popping out of this cake. Ha. Tralalala."

"It stands to reason. After all, just because mama has been sleeping with Mr. Stein, it doesn't mean that she is acting as a go-between for Rhonda and Mr. Stein. All right? There is such a thing in this world as courtesy even if it is exhausting. People should not always say out loud what they feel in their hearts."

"For the children there are sweet and gentle fairy tales. The beautiful princess and the gallant prince fall in love, they live in a glass palace and eat cotton candy, Tralalala."

"I'm asking you for the last time to cut out the Tralalala. You must think you're Carmen, singing like that. It sounds to me like you're practicing yodeling."

"Oh, wonderful. I'm a shepherdess in a small Swiss chalet." Yuri opened the oven door with a bang. "Look at this cake. It is so wonderful that if I opened a shop on the Ginza I would make a fortune in no time. This is the finest cake made with a rare recipe. There is just one spell I've put on it. If Sasha or Keiko eats it, they will get fat as pigs and have heart disease."

"You are going to make a fortune by making them get so fat they have heart disease. You mean it will cost you a fortune."

"Why do you always have to be so realistic?"

"You have a run in your stocking. Just above the knee."

"Didn't you tell me once that a run in a woman's stocking turned you on?"

"It depends on the woman and the circumstances. You can't always generalize."

Yuri, having made up her mind not to play bridge, was much more relaxed, and she felt like putting on some make-up. As she was putting on eye liner in the bathroom mirror, Rie came in with her hands clasped behind her back and with the voice of a schoolmaster said, "Oh mama, you want to make yourself look young."

"That's right. Every woman wants to look young."

"But mama, everyone knows I'm your daughter so they're not going to believe that you're less than thirty."

"Some women have children when they're sixteen years old."

"But nice girls don't do that."

"How about it? Do you think your mama looks like she is twenty-six?"

"Well, I know how old you are. I can't pretend that I don't."

"What are you just standing there for? It's not good to always go around criticizing people. It's especially odious in young ladies."

"I have to go to the bathroom. That's what I'm waiting for."

"Mama isn't a boy; I'll just look the other way."

"Never mind. I'll wait." Rie flounced out with a toss of her head.

The look in Rie's eyes when she looked at Yuri always reminded Yuri of her own mother's eyes. Yuri herself remembered looking at her mother with the same look that Rie turned on her now.

She put on her favorite green one-piece dress with a bow at the neck and a brushed silver pendant. The pendant was a charming and finely crafted piece of riveted silver in an abstract design. She had gotten it three years earlier on her birthday from a lover whom she still remembered fondly. The rough edges of the silver had been rounded off so it looked like a cut piece of coral. Apparently it had been skillfully fused with a powerful torch so that the craftsman could form any shape he chose. Then it had been oxidized and burnished in places and in other places the silver shone brightly.

In the living room where the bridge tables were arranged, Takeshi was lying on the sofa reading a magazine which a Japanese student had left there.

"There is coffee, tea, and cake all ready to be served. You'll fix the cocktails yourself, won't you dear? I have put out martini glasses, old-fashioned glasses, and soft drink glasses. The napkins are in their usual box."

"You know, sometimes you are pretty good looking."

Takeshi glanced at Yuri and holding up a nude color fold-out said, "Stay and chat with your guests for a moment. You've gone to all this trouble to get yourself dressed up. Besides, I'm not as good a liar as you are. We need to make the situation clear to everyone."

"There may not be enough olives, but it probably tastes all right without them. If you run out of gin, go ahead and use the vodka."

The doorbell rang.

"Oh oh, they're here."

"What are you doing with that nude magazine? Put it away someplace. Japanese magazines are unusual around here; they attract people's attention. The next thing you know someone will start thumbing through it."

"Well, I'm not trying to prove anything. They're published in every country. Everyone wants to see them."

"When you have a stag party you can go ahead and do what you like."

"Women want to be looked at too."

Yuri opened the door.

It was Frank Stein. He was wearing a brown corduroy jacket and suede shoes.

"You asked me to come like this, but Yuri is dressed up."

"It's like this, Frank, something awkward has come up. I just got a phone call from my sister. She will be in town for two or three hours this evening so I am going out to the airport to meet her. Please excuse me. Do you mind?"

"Oh, I see. Wouldn't you really rather have her come here?"

"No. No. There will be other people coming. She will only be here two or three hours to change planes."

"Doesn't Takeshi need to go?"

"I would just as soon stay here and play bridge, thank you. I don't know why, but for some reason I always win like mad when my wife is not around."

"Right. Sit down and make yourself at home. I'm not in such a hurry. I'll stay and chat for a while. Till everyone gets here."

Frank looked at Yuri with hungry eyes. "Gee. That's too bad because Rhonda is coming."

"Yes, it's too bad for Takeshi too, because Sasha is coming," Yuri said bluntly.

"But the priest is coming, isn't he," asked Frank.

Takeshi, as though he had not been following the conversation, said, "They say it's a popular thing to cut off a piece of a Viet Cong's body and bring it back as a war trophy."

"Oh, really? That sort of thing probably happens. That's the way war is in every age. Men can fulfill their dreams of killing and raping without being sent to the electric chair. But be careful, Takeshi. I don't mind saying it before the others come, but if you bring up the subject of Vietnam at a party, everyone will have their own biased opinion. No one will speak honestly and openly. Let's not spend the evening playing guessing games with one another. Japanese look the other way while they spit on the Americans and Americans put on a protective shell in front of their compatriots. Anyway, the only one who always gives us a lecture on his views is Father Baranoff. It's because God really exists for a priest whatever he might believe at the bottom of his heart. It's very convenient having God on your side. No one complains if he argues that it's against God's will to kill people. Very nice, eh? No other reasons are allowed. He gets all puffed up and makes speeches. While Sasha is there as a reminder of the sordid scenes in the priest's wretched bed, she just takes a woman's privilege to be unreasonable and shrugs the whole thing off saying, 'I don't like any war.' She just expresses conventional opinions."

"Take a look at the university faculty," said Frank. "Half of them are supporting the war, about two-thirds of the rest are simply ignoring it, and only about one-third of the others stand up and really protest and they sound like grubbing faultfinders. The vast majority just don't care one way or the other. If they are drafted, they are drafted and they have no choice but to try and avoid a bullet."

"What puzzles me is the way you Americans keep harping on the subject of how to get out of Vietnam gracefully and with honor. You are always talking about that. You Americans have a habit of laughing at the affected airs of silly old Englishmen, but when it comes to your own affairs, you can't help acting like a character out of a western."

"We Americans have the stubbornness of a southern aristocracy, the lawlessness of the west, the envy of the northerners, and the egoism of the easterners, but I am a cosmopolitan. You claim to be Japanese, but really both of you are drifters, rootless, aren't you."

"That's why we sing such lovely songs, isn't it? The same is more or less true of all the people here, even Sasha and the Yokotas."

"It's better to make up your own mind and not just follow others."

Frank gave Yuri a piercing look.

"Aren't you surprised? I have heard that even we foreigners are obliged to register for the draft. The classification is 4G." Takeshi inserted a few words.

"Ha. This is the first time I have heard that. I'm 5A myself."

"In your case, you wouldn't be satisfied with anything but a 5A classification," said Yuri.

"I have already been drafted. During the Korean War."

"Aren't you pretty lucky to have a 5A classification even though you are not married?"

"I have two children."

"Do you support them?" laughed Takeshi cynically.

"You bet I do. I have a strong sense of fatherly love."

"Well," said Yuri, "the party will be finished once the conversation turns to the presidential election and Vietnam."

"On the contrary, if we can get off on these sophisticated obscenities, the party will last till morning," said Takeshi.

"If you give me the high sign on the sly, I'll bring up the subject of Vietnam," said Frank.

Takeshi, as host, brought the conversation back to a more polite level, "How about Rhonda? She's getting to be a good looking woman."

"How about me? Haven't I become more sexy?" Frank pulled up the collar of his corduroy jacket.

"You always have been," said Yuri bluntly.

"Oh, I see. I don't remember that you ever felt that way."

"You have a bad memory, but I have a fairly good one myself."

"It's just that my wife has gotten to be pretty sociable lately," said Takeshi with a laugh.

Yuri recognized a touch of irony in her husband's laugh.

"Yuri, I wish you had such a good memory. I'm a romantic. I seem to be a lyrical sort of man . . . That's why."

Yuri tried to recall the time when she had slept with Frank, but could not. In any case, there was nothing romantic or lyrical about it.

"You're lyrical? Don't make me laugh. You have the objectivity of a historian who serves his glorious master," said Takeshi.

"Anyone can tell you what their hopes and aspirations are. I have always wished that I were lyrical."

"Sure. But that's a different matter. How about you ma'am?" said Takeshi looking back at his wife as he went to the kitchen for some drinks. "You were something of a lyric poet, weren't you?"

"It looks as though Takeshi's in love with you and you with him," said Frank.

"If you can make that kind of observation, it must be so. After all, you have the objectivity of a historian in the service of his master."

"Now, now. That's enough of that. Husbands and wives should share their privacy and have their own dialogue. It would be pointless otherwise. Look at me. I left my wife in a hurry when I got tired of meaningless conversations. I was afraid that my words would become hollow and lose their meaning."

Takeshi returned and handed Frank a martini. "Does it taste all right? Did I give you enough time to seduce her?"

"Oh, there was plenty of time."

"Not quite enough," said Yuri as though disappointed.

"Takeshi, this year's scholarly convention will be in A city. I am going to make a leisurely trip out of it and meet my son." Frank turned to the subject of children.

"Which son?"

"The first one. The kid's already nine. He's really getting to be precocious."

"I know what you mean. My daughter is even worse than my wife. My wife is willing to disregard her husband and then she gives in to her daughter."

"I expect so. Rie is bright and besides that she is a very charming young lady. You probably worry about her a lot."

"I especially worry about men like you."

"Ah come on. I'm completely respectable. Recently."

"Just a little while ago Yuri was complaining that there was something wrong with her stomach. I thought for sure she was pregnant."

Frank glanced at Yuri's abdomen and said, "In the twentieth century pregnancy is not a matter of fertility, rather it is a symbol of sterility and destruction. Even in American literature this has been the case at least since Faulkner. Maybe even since Hawthorne."

"Naturally. That's one way to tell a civilized country. But in my home it is a symbol of peace," said Takeshi.

Yuri winked at Frank who said, "Yes, but you are a century ahead of us. This is not sterility, but a forewarning of a revolution, isn't it?"

"So far there is no turbulence of this sort."

Frank turned to Yuri and said, "But Yuri, aren't you really on your way to meet your lover tonight?"

"Wouldn't that be nice?"

"Don't suggest these strange things," said Takeshi.

"Don't you ever get nervous about that?" Frank asked.

"It depends on one's mood. Sometimes even I am cheerful. When I am like that, I even flatter my wife. Especially at times like tonight when she made a cake with the idea of poisoning us all."

"Frank, don't you want to give me some comfort? Look at the way my husband is treating me."

"I feel for you."

"Go ahead, don't mind me. But we can't afford to have both of you gone or there won't be enough people here tonight. You'll have another chance."

"Rhonda said she would be about ten minutes late," said Frank changing the subject.

"How many times did you see her last week?"

"Just once. Rhonda monopolizes people. She doesn't give a man time to let his mind wander." Frank said this for Yuri's benefit.

Yuri looked across at Takeshi as she hooked her thumb around the pendant and brought it to her lips.

"Last week, Rhonda had dinner with that highway engineer who just came out from Chicago. She invited him to her place. Too bad nobody saw what time he left there," said Takeshi.

"Um," said Frank as he gazed at Yuri's pendant. "Well, in that case I should have gone out with Sasha or Keiko."

"That's right. Keiko is a very self-conscious woman. She might not be very much fun to play around with, but Sasha would probably be a lot of fun," said Takeshi looking at Yuri.

"May I remind you that there will be ladies at the party too," said Yuri and Frank grinned.

"This is an in-group story. After all, Yuri is Takeshi's dear wife."

"That's certainly the way it seems."

The doorbell rang. Yuri and Takeshi went out willingly. It was Mr. and Mrs. Yokota. Behind them was Keiko Matsuura.

"Well, well. Please come in. The weather's finally turned chilly. What a lovely outfit, Mrs. Yokota. That's what I would call a sunflower color. It's really gorgeous. Keiko, you really look chic tonight."

"You ought to leave that kind of flattery for the men. Women don't appreciate having another woman flatter them," said Takeshi.

"Yuri is different from you," said Frank. "She tailors her jealousy to fit the situation. She is trying to conceal her husband's charm from other women."

"Good evening everyone, it certainly is warm," said Mr. Yokota. Yokota's thin hair had been blown by the wind and was plastered to his forehead. If you looked at him from the front, the bald patch was clearly visible.

"Darling, why don't you comb your hair," said the charming Mrs. Yokota. She considered herself to be far more charming than her husband deserved, but still she tried to conceal his baldness from people.

Keiko went across and sat down beside Frank. She made a point of never sitting next to a woman.

"How is your thesis coming along?" Frank asked her.

"All I have left to do is type it up, but if I try to type it myself I keep wanting to stop and revise it."

Mrs. Yokota gave Keiko a spiteful look. Mrs. Yokota was good at wearing flashy clothes, but she could never sell herself to a man with conversation.

"I saw your essay on Faulkner in T magazine. Mr. Stein, you are so wonderfully sarcastic. Yuri told me some time ago that your style is marvelous," said Keiko. Once again Mrs. Yokota's eyes flashed. One could see the self-confidence in Mrs. Yokota's large, long-lashed eyes, but the chin beneath her slightly protruding teeth lacked self-confidence. Even though she always pulled back both lips to cover them, she had to do it consciously. On the other hand, Keiko had a protruding lower lip. She had a childish pronunciation, but men were attracted by it and she became more and more talkative.

"Mr. Stein, I understand your American Literature of the 1930's has been very popular among the students," said Keiko.

The doorbell rang. Takeshi and Yuri both went to the door. It was Father Baranoff and Sasha.

Sasha was wearing black fish-net stockings and a black satin Chinese dress embroidered with colorful budding peonies.

"Well, now, what's all this? You wear your best clothes and make the place feel like an opera box," said Frank in his corduroy jacket.

"Not really, this is just my dressing gown."

Sasha took a deep breath as though she were about to begin to sing an aria.

"Well, well . . ." said Frank with a sarcastic smile.

Mr. Yokota turned his carefully combed head and coughed. He was very susceptible to erotic stimulation.

"Excuse me, Sasha, but would you teach Yuri the proper way to do the Tralala where Carmen is abusing Jose? It seems to me she is a little off key right there."

"Takeshi, if you insult your wife in public, you will pay for it when it comes time to make an alimony settlement," said Yuri solemnly.

"I wonder what happens when a person doesn't mean to be insulting. I should know about that for future reference," said Mrs. Yokota.

"From ancient times ignorance has been counted as a sin," said Frank.

"What happens when you don't plan to get a divorce?" asked Takeshi.

"If you haven't considered divorce before now, this will provide the grounds for it," said Frank.

"Yes, but our divorce court—supposing we had one—wouldn't take place in America. In Japan the man still gets off with the best deal."

"On the contrary, in America the man also gets the best deal," said Sasha.

"Well, if the matter is on this level, I can still tolerate it," said Mrs. Yokota with bashful coquetry. Father Baranoff's eyes shone with lust.

Sasha looked down on Mrs. Yokota with a contemptuous glance. Sasha's skin was fat and coarse textured and pock-marked so that it reminded one of a grapefruit skin.

"Did you have to obey the court's orders when you got divorced?" Keiko asked Frank.

"I did not even have enough money to afford a lawyer, so I didn't."

"But you still had some money to pay your former wife, didn't you?" asked Mr. Yokota with a definite interest.

"No, I was the one who had my wife stolen away by another lover."

"Of course, well, you managed that very well," said Mr. Yokota politely.

"You're spilling your martini," observed Mrs. Yokota genteelly. She laughed, making small wrinkles at the sides of her nose.

These slight wrinkles, the sunflower outfit, her gentle cooing titter are nothing but a façade to give the impression of modest womanhood, but in another forty years she will be cackling like a monkey, thought Yuri. As a woman, she knew all too well that it was an act of coquetry, a miserable plot, a yearning for small, empty pleasures. When she thought about this it made her feel dizzy and nauseous. Since this feeling of nausea was a thing which Yuri generated within herself, she felt that the only way to relieve it would be to tear out her liver or something.

"You look like someone sitting on a cloud; you look inscrutable," said Frank to Yuri.

"Why not, I'm floating."

The doorbell rang.

"It's Rhonda," said Takeshi going to the door.

Rhonda wore a black dress and held some flowers. She embraced Yuri and pressed her cheek to Yuri's.

"Oh, you're so pretty. You look just like a forest nymph," said Takeshi.

"Thank you. You are your usual charming self," said Rhonda giving Takeshi a kiss on the cheek.

"Now, look at you Frank. As usual you look like the wisest man in the world," said Rhonda throwing him a kiss.

"The plight of the lonely genius is usually incurable; right, Father?" Yokota inquired of Father Baranoff.

"Yes, you're probably right." Father Baranoff was drinking his vodka straight and the tip of his nose was red as a cherry.

"But how does a doctor or a physicist explain the fact that some people cannot be hypnotized?" said Frank looking from Takeshi to Yokota.

"Well, I specialize in women," said Takeshi.

"Even so, hypnotism is very closely related to that. How do you treat a woman who cannot be put under hypnosis?"

"Doctors are extremely susceptible to acquaintances who try to get free diagnoses from them," said Takeshi.

"Well, what can you do? Physicists are in the same boat; do you think they only dispense their data at scientific conferences?" said Frank turning to Yokota.

"Not me. I would only be abusing my brain if I worried about anything that did not affect me directly," said Yokota in a dejected voice.

Sasha, sitting next to the priest was braying laughter.

Some public facilities are cleaner than the one at home, thought Frank as he looked at Sasha and considered her promiscuity.

Sometimes I think I have lost all my sexual urge, thought Takeshi as his eyes moved from Sasha to Rhonda to Mrs. Yokota to Keiko to Yuri.

Now what is she laughing so hard about? thought Yuri looking at the laughing Keiko.

As Yuri caught Takeshi's glance she suddenly moved closer to Yokota and, laughing gaily, began to whisper to Mrs. Yokota in Japanese. "Mrs. Yokota, you know, you really are a poet at heart. You know that Frank there is a Faulkner scholar; no one is less a poet than him."

As her meaningless words gushed out, Yuri felt the urge to shrug a shoulder over her mouth to stifle a yawn.

"I wonder how much easier it would be if I were not so sensitive to men's charm?"

"I heard that Sasha's recital is to be next Saturday," said Yokota without answering Yuri.

"I expect my husband will be going." As she spoke Yuri looked at Sasha's thick lips and at the grotesque movement of her throat which resembled the movement of a frog's throat.

"I hear it will be completely undistinguished this time; there will be a lot of Russian folk songs," said the priest in a managerial voice.

"But she will sing a selection from *Carmen,* won't she?" Takeshi moved close to Sasha.

"Sure, that's one of her standard pieces," said the priest in a voice that sounded like a rubber ball going flat.

Takeshi and Frank laughed knowingly and looked at the priest from both sides. Yokota just sat with his ears open drinking and looking in silence at the ceiling like a mud snail in the mud.

"I have heard that Yokota is an excellent *shakuhachi* player," said Takeshi.

"Eh, what's that?" asked Yokota in a high, toneless voice. At times like this he could hear very well.

"I would like to hear you play sometime," said Frank.

"No, there must be some mistake," demurred Yokota.

"I have heard that your wife is very good on the *koto*." This was a surprising declaration by Keiko who rarely praised other women.

"Where did you get that Chinese dress?" Takeshi asked Sasha.

"When I was in China. I spent ten years there—in Shanghai and Peking."

"Did you sing on stage when you were in China?"

"Yes. I also sang in a church."

"Did they always have good looking priests like Father Baranoff in the churches?"

"For a woman, every man is attractive in his own way." Sasha laughed jiggling her hips.

"We women think you men are attractive indeed. Isn't that right, Keiko? Besides, Takeshi, as far as you are concerned we still are mysterious, aren't we? It must be so because the complex feelings I have for men are so mysterious that sometimes I can't restrain them."

"If the church has attractive women like you in it, it is not a complete waste. You can give some richness to the hymn singing."

Takeshi was busily whispering something to Sasha, but presently he looked up and caught Yuri's eye.

"Rhonda, you should stop imitating the trendy pop art. After all, you are qualified to teach at the university; you should get into something more serious."

"Come on Frank, who are you to be saying that I should be more serious? I would really have to be a washout to take advice from you."

"You are a rather self-confident individual, but you have more than self-confidence, you have a stubborn streak."

"You only think that because you are stubborn yourself, Frank," interjected Takeshi quickly and then he turned back to Sasha.

"If I painted a nice quiet picture," Rhonda sighed, "Frank would still dismiss it as nothing more than a sketch for a school-girl romance."

"Mr. Yokota, why are you just sitting there so quietly?" Yuri's lips brushed Yokota's ear lobe as she whispered this. At the same time she sent Mrs. Yokota an indulgent, motherly smile. Mrs. Yokota looked at her with the clear eyes of a witch and gave a soft, cooing laugh over the priest's shoulder.

"Tralala." Sasha responded to Takeshi by singing a refrain from the gypsy dance of *Carmen*.

"Oh my, I have to run."

As Yuri went around excusing herself, Mrs. Yokota remained happy, Keiko was disinterested, and Frank and Mr. Yokota listened to her sympathetically. Rhonda was the only one who walked with her to the door.

"It's too bad you have to go. I'll serve the coffee. Give my best to your sister," whispered Rhonda as she accompanied Yuri to the car.

"You know, I'm going to Chicago tomorrow. I will probably be sleeping with the highway engineer."

"As you wish. You are no longer at the age when you have to try to catch a man. You have your own life. You don't have to compromise with others. So why don't you just do as you like. But let me tell you Rhonda, love is a nuisance. A decent and thoughtful man is often boring, but on the other hand, a man who is too demanding is just a burden."

"The give-and-take between a man and a woman is really just an opportunity for something more, and sometimes it works itself out in strange ways. If two people just happen to run into each other, then it is nothing more than a chance encounter. That's why I may come slinking back to you within a week like some poor naïve school girl. Or I may come back refreshed, clean, and wearing a new outfit, but with a mixed expression of satisfaction and melancholy on my face. It's true Yuri. At our age. Frank is all right, you know, as a casual lover. . . ."

"Rhonda, let me ask you something. When a person is divorced, is it natural that she would like a man who has a different personality than her husband?"

"Hmmm. I wonder. There's more to it than that. Once a man and a woman begin to hurt each other, there is no end to it. It's like a splinter; the more one tries to get it out, the deeper it becomes embedded. Finally, only the scars remain."

"It sounds like you still have some lingering affection for your former husband."

"Just because I still have some affection for him doesn't mean that I can't give my heart to another man."

"Rhonda, men are very cautious and clever. They are almost as bad as we are. It's like you flattering yourself into thinking you understand a man's heart. By the same token, a man can read your heart."

"I admit that, but I will still go to Chicago. Besides, there is a man there who wants to buy one of my paintings."

"You don't have to justify what you are doing. After all, you have your own life. From Chicago you can fly on to Paris and fool around for a week, but your life would be just the same as before. It wouldn't change a bit; your two children, your career as a teacher, and Frank's interest in you. . . ."

Yuri put the car in gear.

"Yuri, I'm lonely. Really lonely. I just don't know what to do."

"There's nothing you can do. Well, so long. Oh, and Rhonda, enjoy yourself."

Yuri released the brake.

Yuri drove slowly, about fifteen miles an hour. By the time she realized how slowly she was going there were five or six cars behind her. In confusion she speeded up to thirty. Fortunately, the stop light at the next intersection was red and it gave her time to think. She could see the entrance to the monorail at the next corner and decided to go to the amusement park nearby. She did not care where she went. Anyway, it was probably better than going to a movie. Having made up her mind to go to the amusement park Yuri felt relieved and concentrated on finding a parking place. She parked the car in a lot on the north side of the Opera House.

She stood for a moment in front of the Opera House and gazed at a poster of Margot Fonteyn in *Swan Lake.* Beside it was a poster for an exhibit of folk crafts by Alaskan Indians. She walked aimlessly in the direction of the exhibit. Yuri yawned expansively as she walked. She opened her mouth wide and made no attempt to suppress it. The yawn was as refreshing as a breath of fresh air.

There was no sign of children around the amusement park after nine o'clock. Lovers, hand in hand, looked happily at the various rides. Yuri stopped beside a pond advertising motorboat races. She watched the lovers gazing contentedly at the spray thrown up as they operated the motorboats.

At the entrance to the exhibit of Alaskan Indian crafts, Yuri paused to gaze idly at a ride in which an airplane circled upward around a tower. She really had no particular interest in Alaskan Indian crafts.

The exhibition hall was deserted. The lights in the empty hall were dim, and it seemed to Yuri that the eyes of the manikins followed her glowing with a supernatural light. A crow-headdress with large, tapering human eyes had a remarkably long beak extending out from the forehead like the beak of a cap and from between the upper and lower parts of the beak there showed a real-looking red tongue. At the back there was a queue of wool which looked like a woman's black hair. This crow headdress was made of some kind of wood and its various lines were deeply carved in a simple, abstract pattern. Despite the fact that it was decorated with many primitive colors such as red, yellow, green, and black, the natural dyes had, over the years, achieved a subdued harmony. Oddly enough, when one looked at this crow headdress part by part; the beak, eyes, pupils, front and back, it was not a close imitation of a real crow, but in spite of the fact that the eyes were especially abstract, it had the wide-staring eyes of a man. And yet, when one looked at the whole thing, it seemed strangely to blend the lives and destinies of men and crows. Among uncivilized people there is a certain vital affinity with the natural world of trees, grass, mountains, valleys, and animals. With something close to faith these people believed in the mutual bond between men and nature. There was also a frog headdress and an eagle headdress. In the undulating lines of their simple visages which were carved in bleached driftwood, faces whose mouths and eyes revealed a wicked laughter, rattles used by the shamans, faces reminiscent of the carvings on totem poles, faces which reminded one of the ancient legends; carvings composed of depictions of one animal after another; boats and utensils carved with the same animal designs, blankets which resembled shawls woven from animal fur. In the dim hall Yuri heard the muffled murmur of praying, chanting men.

At the entrance to the hall sat a man in a pink shirt.

"All right now, it's time to close the hall," he said.

It was apparent that the man was waiting for Yuri to finish looking at the exhibit.

Startled, Yuri turned suddenly and nearly fell. The man in the pink shirt dashed over and put his arms around her and managed to keep her from falling.

"Oh, thank you," said Yuri blushing. "I don't have very good coordination. I always seem to be stumbling. It irritates my husband . . . to have his wife stumbling over her own feet all the time in front of people. Thank you for giving me a hand. Sorry to have bothered you, thank you. Well, good-bye." Yuri started to walk away.

"Just a moment, please. Something's stuck to the heel of your shoe. You'd better take it off. You don't want to slip again," said pink shirt.

Being careful not to slip again Yuri leaned on a nearby sofa and turned up the heel of her shoe.

"Not that one, the left one."

The heel of her left shoe was worn through and a strip of worn leather was dangling.

"There is nothing stuck to it. It's part of the shoe. It's the worn-out leather."

It was about two inches long. When she pulled at it, the leather continued to strip off until she could see the wooden base of the heel.

"It can't be fixed. These are just old shoes. When I pulled at it, the leather covering the whole heel came off," said Yuri indignantly.

"I have a knife," said pink shirt taking a knife from his pocket. He cut the torn leather.

"Thank you very much. You are very kind," said Yuri facetiously.

"Don't mention it," said pink shirt with a vague smile.

Yuri left the exhibition hall, but as she had no place to go she stood gazing at the neon-lit fountain beside the entrance. On the lawn beside the fountain was a single large elm with a stone bench beneath it. Just as Yuri was about to go over and sit down, it was occupied by a pair of lovers.

The lights went off in the exhibition hall and pink shirt came out. Having given up on the occupied bench, Yuri turned to go down the steps and nearly bumped into him.

"What's this? Are you still here?" said pink shirt as he grasped hold of Yuri to steady her. "I think you went off and left your purse on the sofa." He was holding Yuri's purse. "This is interesting leather work. Is it from your country?"As he said this, pink shirt held out the handbag with its tooled leather design of fish among the seaweed. "I was just thinking of taking it over to the office, to the lost and found," said pink shirt handing the purse to Yuri.

"Sorry to trouble you," said Yuri in confusion. She must have left it on the sofa when she was fixing her broken shoe. "I seem to be a little out of it today."

Beside the exhibition hall were several stands offering games of skill. The prizes were kewpie dolls and stuffed cats and elephants which bounced up and down on a shelf. Next to this was a stand selling orange juice and grape juice which bubbled up in large glass jars. She could smell coffee.

"Shall we have a cup of coffee?" Pink shirt jingled some coins in his pants' pocket. As Yuri neither followed him nor turned away, he invited her to accompany him. He leaned against the counter and taking two steaming paper cups of coffee, he called to Yuri. "You seem to be a little out of it. Some coffee will wake you up." Pink shirt urged Yuri to take the paper cup.

He had stiff, black hair mixed with a little gray, but his eyes were blue, almost green.

"I'm one quarter Eskimo," pink shirt introduced his lineage. "One quarter Tlingit, one quarter Swedish, and one quarter Polish." Although he had some gray hair, his face was relatively young. It occurred to Yuri that he was prematurely gray.

"Don't you smoke?"

"I don't smoke because I have throat cancer," said Yuri shaking her head.

"That's too bad. Well, one of these days they will have some good medicine. If you can just hold out a little longer . . ." said pink shirt.

"I don't even have one sixteenth non-Japanese blood, but long long ago there may have been something like Eskimo blood in my lineage."

"Sure, there almost certainly was. Long ago they walked across between

Alaska and Siberia on the ice. The northern part of Japan was also connected to this bridge."

"Something like that may have happened."

He undid the top button of his pink shirt and shook his head in the sweltering heat.

"Do you like pink shirts like that?" asked Yuri.

"It's not that I like it, my wife bought it for me," said pink shirt.

"It's a pretty color," said Yuri looking at pink shirt's wedding ring.

"Is a wife's role terribly unrewarding?" he asked.

"Oh, it is probably about the same as a man's."

"Most jobs aren't very much fun," said pink shirt.

"It seems that way," agreed Yuri. "I have to go," she said looking at her watch.

"Are you going back to your husband?"

"I guess so," said Yuri beginning to walk away. As she walked she felt the man's presence at her shoulder. Even though she was aware of him, she felt it would be a nuisance to try and get rid of him.

Since it was Friday night there were still plenty of people in the amusement park. Yuri gazed absently at a teen-age couple as they held each other and shrieked while spinning round and round in cups in a ride called the Mad Hatter's Tea Party. The girl's short miniskirt was hiked up on her legs and her flaxen hair was twisted around the boy's wrist. Circus music was playing and there was the smell of hamburgers frying. Yuri moved on to the Jet Coaster. Long ago when she had gone on a date with Takeshi to an amusement park in Tokyo they had gotten in a long line and waited their turn on the Jet Coaster, but finally they gave it up and she recalled that they had gone to the garden in the amusement park.

The entrance to the monorail was next to the Jet Coaster. She glanced in that direction. The inside of the monorail car shone a bright, light purple. Yuri watched the men and women shrieking on the Jet Coaster. It was late and there were no children around. Yuri thought about buying a ticket.

"Why don't we take a ride on the Jet Coaster?" asked pink shirt. Yuri nodded her agreement. She was not used to a man who made proposals like this when she least expected it.

Pink shirt put his arm around Yuri's shoulder and handed her a ticket.

"I'm afraid," said Yuri, "I may not be able to keep control of myself."

"Have you ever been on one?" asked pink shirt. He was wearing a tweed jacket over his pink shirt.

"Unh, unh," said Yuri shaking her head.

"It's all right. Just hold on to me," said pink shirt. Yuri thought of the long line of people who had been waiting for the Jet Coaster in Tokyo. 'Let's not. It will take another hour.' Even as she said this Yuri had seen the sadness in Takeshi's eyes. 'I may get motion sickness,' as she had said this she saw that Takeshi's eyes were clouded over. 'I'm afraid' she had said and Takeshi's eyes had softened. Yuri herself had felt pained as a result of her sensitivity to this faint clouding of men's eyes. She couldn't bring herself to look at pink shirt's face. She kept silent and let herself drift along with the words he whispered in her ear.

"It's really great. Wondering what will happen next is the best part." He rested his hand on Yuri's shoulder.

The whistle sounded and the Jet Coaster began to move. At first nothing much happened. Soon they came to a steep slope and violently plunged down into the valley and it seemed they were going to crash. Just at the last moment they swooped up the slope on the far side. No sooner had they felt relieved than they rounded a sharp curve. Pink shirt had his arm around Yuri's waist; he clutched her tightly and dug in with his fingers. Yuri's body was pressed against the man's shoulder. They let their bodies be tumbled and swayed like a cat being shaken by the scruff of its neck. The black night was a deep blue color as it whirled round and round and the street lights flowed by like countless glittering stars. She moaned several times in a low voice, but she was not terrified enough to scream. She was alone like a cat being flung around. Pink shirt clutched at Yuri. When the Jet Coaster stopped Yuri leaned her head against pink shirt. Pink shirt tried to lift her up with his arms around her and then holding her to him he looked at her face.

"Are you all right?"

Yuri nodded and began to walk. The night air was clear and cool. The man paused to light a cigarette.

"You were crouching there just like a dead bird," the man said. "How about it, shall we ride something else?" he asked looking at Yuri. He was tall and stoop shouldered. Yuri shook her head.

"Shall we eat something?" the man asked.

Yuri shook her head.

"Shall we get something to drink?" the man asked.

Yuri shook her head.

"Cigarette?" the man asked.

Yuri shook her head.

"You don't want anything to eat, you don't want anything to drink, you don't smoke; so what do you want? Shall we dance?" the man asked.

"What kind of dancing?" asked Yuri.

"Go-go dancing."

"I don't know how. I'm an old-fashioned woman. I'm too old to do those new kinds of dances."

"You do slow dancing? I don't know very much about slow dancing. It's just like walking. Let's go dancing."

"Okay."

Yuri considered this for a while. She thought as she walked. They walked toward the fountain holding hands. The fountain was lit with blue lights and it looked like fireworks as it shot up. On the stone bench under the elm tree was a white handkerchief which someone had left behind. It was a man's handkerchief.

"Yes indeed, let's go dancing," said pink shirt.

"Okay," agreeing with him Yuri sat down on the handkerchief. There was the sound of music; possibly Debussy. Apparently there were speakers located here and there around the fountain.

"Is that Beethoven?" asked pink shirt.

"I wonder," said Yuri looking at the jewels of water splashing in the fountain. "It probably is."

A group of well dressed people came from the Opera House. Since it was too early for the performance to be over, it must have been intermission. Black suited men leaned whispering over bare shouldered women.

"I guess they are having a musical performance," said pink shirt.

"Apparently," said Yuri.

"The only music I understand is jazz. I hate opera more than anything.

Whenever I hear it I get a funny tickle in my throat and begin to yawn."

"Sometimes it gives me a headache," said Yuri.

"Let's go dancing," said pink shirt. He pulled her hand. For some reason she looked back in the direction of the parking lot.

"Don't you want to dance?"

"It's not that. Is the dance hall nearby? My car is parked here."

"I'll take you back to your car later."

They began walking.

"I guess it will be all right if it is within walking distance," said Yuri.

"Why? I guess there are some places close by, but would it matter if we went somewhere else?"

"Let's go to a place here in the park. It's less trouble."

"It's no trouble, just follow me."

Yuri stopped walking.

"All right then, we'll go to a place here in the park."

They walked in the direction of the rock and roll music they could hear. Pink shirt ordered beer. As Yuri put her lips to the glass she watched the go-go dancers. She decided it looked easy; that anyone could do it. It seemed that all she had to do was move her body any way she liked as long as it was in time with the music.

"Let's dance," said pink shirt.

Yuri put down her glass of beer and stood up. As they danced her body moved halfheartedly within the man's embrace. Soon they were separated and each moving freely. Even so, they still moved together as a couple. It occurred to her that this kind of dancing had a great deal more creative freedom than the old, slow dancing. By the time the first set had ended Yuri felt as though she had been released.

"Let's keep going," said pink shirt making no move to return to their seats after the music had ended. They continued to dance for about three sets. One set had some swing mixed in with it but Yuri preferred dancing it her own way. Yuri enjoyed her own dance even though she pretended to be moving with her partner.

"Why don't you wear a mini-skirt?" asked pink shirt when they returned to their seats.

"I don't have nice looking legs," said Yuri bluntly.

"That's not true," he said bending over to take a look at her legs under the table.

"Don't be silly," Yuri said pulling on pink shirt's ear. He pulled Yuri to him laughing and kissed her beside the ear. Then for a while they sat in silence and drank their beer. Yuri sipped her beer slowly as though it were brandy.

When a slow tune was played, pink shirt stood up and invited Yuri to dance. He walked onto the floor clutching Yuri close to him. Yuri was tired and from time to time she would push pink shirt away and so they paused. Suddenly Yuri recalled a time long ago when she was working hard to become a good dancer for Takeshi and how she had been intent on trying not to take a wrong step. Pink shirt was smiling gently. Yuri responded with a smile. They both gave themselves up to the music and drifted easily along as though on clouds.

"You are light as a feather. If I don't hold onto you, you would just float away," said pink shirt.

Later, they sat down and drank the rest of their beer. As usual Yuri took her time drinking so that she would not have to decline another drink if it were offered.

"Shall we take a drive somewhere?" asked pink shirt.

"All right," said Yuri looking at the man's hand which rested on her own.

Pink shirt stood up. They walked slowly toward the exit of the amusement park. Boys and girls were still clutching each other and screaming in the Mad Hatter's Tea Cups. She glanced at her watch. It was eleven o'clock. The bridge party would not be over yet. Pink shirt had an old Chevrolet. The motor sounded like it belonged to a logging truck. It made a rough sound like a steam locomotive stopping.

"Where shall we go?" asked pink shirt. As he spoke he turned the car into the street. A couple came out of a neon-lit club called the Flamingo; a black man with his hands in his pockets leaned against a light pole and watched them.

"Why are you so quiet?" asked pink shirt.

"Why not? What is there to talk about?" said Yuri leaning her shoulder against the car door.

"Why don't you sit closer to me? You're strange," said pink shirt. "I like a woman who chatters a lot."

"Why don't you look for one then? I'll get off here," said Yuri.

"That's not what I meant. You're mad."

"I'm not mad. It's just that there isn't anything to talk about."

There were very few street lights and they had apparently left the city.

"Let's go to the beach," said pink shirt.

After that neither of them spoke for a long time.

"You like the beach?" asked pink shirt.

"Sometimes I like it; sometimes it scares me."

Opening the window she could smell the sea.

"Can you hear the sound of the surf?"

Yuri nodded. They came out onto the sea coast and dimly in the darkness they could see the long tufts of beach grass. The sea shone softly like a mist shrouded lake.

"This is an inlet," said the man resting his chin on the steering wheel.

Memories of the sea at night suddenly reminded Yuri of a friend with lips red as crushed strawberries. The friend's name was A and her lips were always chapped and cracked in two or three places with red blood oozing from them. Her skin was constantly plagued with eczema.

"I look unclean," she said closing her darkly circled eyes in despair. Nevertheless, A had very beautiful, long, thin, clean looking fingers. She would twine her long fingers together and rest her eczema infested cheeks on her hands.

"How about it, shall we go on further?" asked pink shirt. He held Yuri around the waist and drew her to him. Their lips met. Then with his free hand he began to grope between her thighs.

Yuri and A had gone swimming in the sea in the pitch dark just before dawn on the day of the summer festival. It was a sandy shore on the Sea of Japan and at this time of year the farmers brought their oxen to the sand dunes. In those days some families still used oxen in the fields. The sand dunes spread out where the field of silverberries left off. The sea was rough and in the distance was Sado Island. They walked through the dense growths of red pine and black acacia in their bare feet. Then they swam together in the pitch black sea. The dark waves hit them unexpectedly and the ground gave way to terrifying and unknowable depths and the water enfolded their bodies like a great warm tongue. There were large, sucking, choking waves. The sky gradually grew lighter and they thought of themselves as two beautiful mermaids. Indeed, they were just the right age to be beautiful mermaids.

The oxen had small, red eyes and stood at the edge of the water being washed by the sea and watching the two girls. They were roommates in the university dormitory and there was a hint of Lesbianism in their friendship. When Yuri had broken off with her first lover, she had wanted only to visit her friend in her house by the Japan Sea. In the school dormitory, their feelings for each other were far from gloomy, rather they were ridiculously pathetic. Eventually they realized that their feelings were normal though a bit delicate. They wanted nothing more than that. Then both of them married.

She wondered if they were still friends. She did not know. It may be that they no longer had anything to talk about. Even if she returned to Japan, thought Yuri, she no longer had any friends there. Her men friends were even worse. Whenever she thought of one of them, she invariably felt that there was a deep gap separating her from them. She wanted to return to Japan because she longed for affection and yet she realized that there was no one she could have a heart-to-heart talk with. She doubted any of her close friends from long ago would look at her the same way they had in the past. Generally speaking, Japanese people disdain those who return from America. Yuri decided that she too disdained them. Even now she disdained them. In short, she disdained herself.

A red neon sign saying Three Crabs was flashing on and off in the distance beyond the beach grass. Pink shirt was not starved for sex. He simply enjoyed it. The emptiness and pathos which the man felt was transmitted to Yuri and made her feel pleasantly calm.

"Why are you so quiet?" asked the man.

"There is nothing to talk about," said Yuri.

"Let's go in there." With his chin the man pointed to the Three Crabs. Once again the car came to life with the sound of a logging truck. It resembled the weary sigh of an old woman.

"Somehow I don't feel like going home," said the man.

"Let's just stay here like this for a little while longer," said the man finding comfort in Yuri's faded body. Yuri pressed her cheek against the glass window and looked at the sea. She thought about Frank Stein's long, thin nostrils; she thought about Sasha's thick lips and funny laugh; she thought about the thin creases beside Mrs. Yokota's nose. Then she thought about Takeshi's metallic voice and about Rie's brassy voice saying, "Humpf, nice girls don't do that." Somehow both the father and the daughter had metallic voices.

The Three Crabs is built like a log cabin situated on the coast. There is a green light out front.

# Modern Korea

The political history of an autonomous Korea has been troubled and tragic. A sense of national unity prevailed in the Silla, Koryŏ, and Chosŏn periods. Indeed, the Chosŏn period (when the Yi dynasty reigned) was remarkably enduring, even in the wake of the Mongol invasion with its usurpation of Chinese rule in China's Yuan dynasty (1271–1368). The expression and transmission of a native Korean sensibility, however, was made difficult by the fact that the Korean alphabet was invented only in the fifteenth century. Though Korean civilization owed much to the great Chinese tradition, there was nonetheless a tension between the two cultures. Korea's relationship with Japan has been even more problematic. In the late nineteenth century, China and Japan often feuded over their interests in Korea, which became a pawn in their intense rivalry for domination of the region. In the wake of an internationally recognized treaty that ended the Russo-Japanese War in 1905, Korea was first declared a protectorate of Japan and then was summarily annexed in 1910. Korea became the Japanese province of Chosen and, once again, the expression of native Korean culture suffered. Indeed, under Japanese rule Korean culture was brutally suppressed. It became illegal, for example, for Koreans to publish their writings in the Korean language.

At the end of World War II, Korea did become free of Japanese domination, but its independence was miserably compromised by the agreement reached between the occupying forces of the United States in the south and the Soviet Union in the north. The agreement divided the country into North Korea and South Korea at the thirty-eighth parallel. After North Korea invaded South Korea in 1950, the two countries were embroiled in war for three years. All the killing resolved nothing. More than two million troops died in the Korean War, and a million South Korean citizens lost their lives, but the two Koreas still exist. Today there is some optimism that Korea might eventually be reunited, but North Korea has remained a tightly closed society stubbornly resistant to change.

## Sonu Hwi (b. 1922)

*Translated by Marshall R. Pihl*

Modern Korea is represented here by Sonu Hwi, a prizewinning author educated in Seoul, whose work is a clear response to the political realities of modern Korea in the aftermath of the Korean War. He himself was a member of the Korean armed forces. Besides being a novelist and short-story writer, he has been a regular editorial writer for one newspaper in Seoul and the editor of another.

In "Thoughts of Home," published in 1965, Sonu reflects on the crisis of the relation of modernity to traditional cultural values. What most immediately precipitates that crisis in this particular story is the division of Korea. Forced to move south of the thirty-eighth parallel as a consequence of the partition, the father of Yi Changhwan must abandon the delapidated but deeply familiar home where his ancestors had lived and died for generations. In a desperate attempt to adapt to the trauma of forced relocation, he pathetically tries to simulate in the South, with uncanny precision, his old house in the North. Everything must be the same—not only the natural surroundings but even the presence of rats in the attic, which the old man imports in order to make him feel more at home. The past cannot, of course, be completely recaptured; time does not stand still, especially in the modern world. Even the old man comes to realize this, and it is this awareness that precipitates the story's catastrophe.

## *Thoughts of Home*

I crossed the Thirty-eighth Parallel and came to the south in the spring of the year after the liberation. So it would now be some nineteen years I have lived here, making this other place my home.

I don't know why it is, but lately I've been having a dream in which I go back home. No, I find myself already there. For a long time I was too busy for such dreams. No sooner had I come to the south than I stumbled into the thick of a chaotic political battle between the left and right; then I was suddenly thrown into a war in 1950 that had me moving constantly all over the country. Even after that, with the endless struggle to make a living, I had no time for dreams. But this spring I found myself able to arrange for a small, subsidized house and found myself, at last, master of my own home. Perhaps that's the reason for the dreams.

Up to three or four years ago I had had no thought of getting my own house, even if the money had been available. After leaving the north, no matter where I lived I felt like a stranger in someone else's land—I always planned to go back to my own home one day. What sort of house—home—could I have here? But then, somehow, I happened into a large sum of money. Sick of the wretched life of a tenant—forced to move every six months or, at best, every two years—I arranged for this squat, little subsidized place near the edge of Koyang county on the far outskirts of Seoul.

My friends congratulated me, joking that at long last I had grown up and become a man of property. But even though the house belonged to me it didn't feel like my home. There was no change in the feeling that I would someday return to the old homestead I had left behind.

My longing for the north would explain why this little house—no bigger than the palm of your hand—has failed so to give me any real homelike feeling. And the more comfortable I have become, the more intense the thoughts of my old home. Perhaps this lies behind the dream in which I find myself back home again.

Several days ago I ran into my old friend Yi Changhwan who lives down near Ch'ungju in North Ch'ungch'ŏng province. When I learned that his father had died two months earlier I was once more put in mind of my old home. An intense feeling of nostalgia stung my heart. I wanted to slash out with a sharp knife at the invisible curtain that hung before my eyes. In the face of this thing I felt nearly suffocated with heartsick anger.

Just last night I couldn't shake the frustration that seized my heart as I lay in the darkness of my bedroom, thinking of home. I had to get up, light the lamp, and sit for quite some time, staring blankly into space. It took several deep breaths to ease the tightness I felt in my chest. I realized how similar I am at heart to Yi Changhwan's father who had died, yearning so to see his home in the north. While I sat there, arms folded, I thought again of what had happened a year ago spring when I was invited down to the country to see the new house that Yi Changhwan's father had built.

My friend Yi Changhwan had asked particularly that I go with him to see this house his father had built as his permanent home in a village near Ch'ungju.

"Father says I must bring you with me."

"Must? Why so?"

"He says he wants to see you come into the yard of his new house and then spend the night visiting and playing cards in the side room as you used to do back home in the north."

"But why?"

"Well, Father had some special reasons for building the house in Ch'ungju." Yi Changhwan explained why his father had gone down there and built a house.

A year earlier his father had gone without explanation on a tour of the countryside and returned to announce that he had found a fine spot where he must build himself a house.

When he came to the south the spring after liberation, his father had opened an automobile repair service that did well enough for him to buy an expensive house in Myŏngnyun-dong, but he suddenly felt he had to build this house in the country in spite of what people said.

"The shape of the mountains and the lay of the land are like it was back in the north. The only flaw is that it has no river flowing by. But the mountain ridges in the east at sunrise look the same. And the thick, dark pines in the hills out back with clumps of chestnuts here and there—it's all just like it was."

"What do you have in mind, Father?" Yi Changhwan asked with caution in his voice.

"Well, I'm going to build myself a home there."

Finally, Yi Changhwan understood why his father had been spending so much time in the countryside that his face had become darkly tanned. His father had thought constantly of his old home and now, after so much yearning, had found a spot that looked the same and was about to build a home like the one he had left behind.

This all seemed vain and useless to Yi Changhwan, but he knew his father's character well enough to realize he could never dissuade him.

Long before they had ever left their home in the north, well before liberation, Yi Changhwan had urged his father again and again to rebuild their house. It was a ramshackle building nearly a hundred years old that had sheltered some four generations. The rafters were rotting and the posts tilted, creaking as if about to collapse whenever the wind blew.

Once Yi Changhwan had gone up into the rafters to set a trap for the rats that had been tormenting him with their nightly rampages. His nose stung with the odor of mold and his feet sank in the frothy dust. Though he walked carefully, the wooden planking creaked like it was about to crash down, unable to bear the weight of his body.

The earthen floor of the shapelessly long and cavernous kitchen was covered with more than a foot of hard, black dirt; people from the village would come and take a little from time to time—to use in making medicine, they said. The villagers knew well that his father would be displeased, believing that something auspicious was being lost, so they would wait until he was out to come like thieves and ask his mother's permission to dig up some of the dirt.

The stones placed under the downspouts to deflect rain, unmoved for one hundred years, had grown dark with age and spotted with moss; falling water from the roof, cutting the long years into them, had drilled holes deep enough to take an adult's ring finger with room to spare.

The village was open, without walls or front gates. Schools of minnows always played in the stream that flowed right by the house, and the large swamp a little further away swarmed with catfish and carp.

The low ridges that swept down from the mountains behind the house, sheltering it for some distance on either side, were shaped like what the geomancers call the Green Dragon of the East and White Tiger of the West. Between the lower ends of the ridges where they merged with the fields stood a grove of willows, cutting across like a natural fence. The seven acres of paddies and fields lying within produced enough grain for a modest family to sustain itself comfortably by its own labor.

Before liberation a famous mineralogist once visited and offered to buy the land on which the house stood but left in surprise when he met with an angry response, bordering on insult, from Yi Changhwan's father.

"What? You want to buy this land where we have honored the spirits of our ancestors for generations? Do you think all it takes is money? Is that all you know?" the old man had roared.

Out on the broad, flat mountain ridge they called the Green Dragon of the East rested the spirits of five generations, counting back from Yi Changhwan's grandfather. Yi Changhwan had grown up to realize that their home was set on no ordinary ancestral land.

Sheltered as they were by the embrace of the back hills, the considerable west wind in the winter was deflected skyward, up over the house nestled in its basin-like site. With spring, the steady wind from the south seemed to circle round and settle into the basin with their house. And the well water that rose beneath the juniper tree was warm in winter and cold in summer.

But the old house was so dilapidated that it somewhat gave the impression of an old clown. Yi Changhwan had proposed to his father that they rebuild the house.

"Why? Do you want something like Deacon Yi's foreign house?" he answered, adding, "All they did was stick in a lot of glass windows. What's homey about that? If you're so keen on tearing down this house and building a new one, wait till after I'm dead and gone. Then you may do as you please."

In the last of these words lay his father's unspoken warning not to bring the subject up again in his presence.

In the spring of the second year after liberation the old man had been thrown out of this house he so cherished. The day had come to leave—their possessions loaded into an oxcart—but Yi Changhwan's father did nothing to help. He just sat puffing silently on a pipe in the room where his father and grandfather before him had lived and died. Yi Changhwan had shouldered the last of their baggage.

"It's time to go now, Father."

"I know."

He struck his pipe on the ashtray to knock out the embers and then, coughing once loudly, slowly rose and went outside clutching his long arrowroot cane. After staring vacantly at the house for a while, he took a long, sweeping look around the grounds where it stood. Then, finally, he spoke.

"So much for that. Let's go now."

When they had crossed over the stepping stones in the stream in front of the house and reached the edge of the swamp on the other side, the old man stopped. He looked back again for some time, then stepped off briskly, cutting through the willow grove.

Now, some fifteen years later, Yi Changhwan's father had built a house shaped like the one he had left in the north. It was located in the countryside of North Ch'ungch'ŏng in a setting that recaptured the feeling of his lost homestead. He had asked me to come visit. As one of his son Yi Changhwan's oldest friends, I had been in and out of the old house since childhood.

I had no reason at all to turn down his request. So I set out with Yi Changhwan the following day to visit his father's house way down in the country beyond Choch'iwŏn and Ch'ungju.

We had walked some three *ri* over four steep passes when Yi Changhwan turned to me.

"Don't be surprised when you see it."

"Why should I be surprised?"

"Well, just don't be surprised," was all he would answer.

We passed over the last, lowish hill and I looked out over the broad expanse of fields that reached all the way to the mountains across from us. I gasped, capable only of silent but heartfelt agreement. I don't know if it was because I already believed what Yi Changhwan had told me, but the scene before my eyes felt somehow like what I had seen when I used to approach his old home in the north.

Though things weren't really the same, when you examined them carefully one by one—the high mountains in the distance, the ridges that swept down on either side, or the way a willow grove joined the ends of the ridges as they merged with the fields—the overall impression of the scene was still an extremely familiar one.

"I feel like I've been here before."

"Does it look familiar?"

"It's really close."

Our steps quickened and we passed a stand of acacias and drew nearer. But the closer we got, the fainter the impression of similarity I had felt. All the same, when I looked across to the house in that setting I could only sigh.

There was no question about it. This was surely Yi Changhwan's old house in the north that I had known so well. More than just the general shape of the house, this new building—hardly a month old—resembled the old one even to its ancient, run-down appearance.

I knew it well. I could see the hole for the dog in a corner of the straw fence around the country-style outhouse at the end of the west wing.

Even that.

As we got closer to the house I was swept with a growing sense of nostalgia and could feel the gooseflesh rising all over my body.

The narrow, twisting path that hugged the woods . . . the stepping stones in the stream that were held in place by wooden stakes and straw rope . . . the stagnant pool a little further downstream . . . ah! the tilting posts of the cowshed . . . and, inside, a calf, tied by a rope to a stake.

No sooner had we entered the yard than I found myself rooted in the center, peering at my surroundings. The tiles on the roof were not new. I wondered where they had come from. Even the downspouts were made of old tin.

The sides of the house were all plastered in clay, as was the fat chimney at one corner. The top of the chimney was finished off with pieces of wood, looking like a box had been placed up there. There was no wood-floored breezeway; in its place a wooden stoop stood over the stepping stones. On the doors hung crude iron pull-rings.

"What do you think of it?" Yi Changhwan had moved up next to me and spoke in a low voice.

"Hmm." I threw my shoulders way back and looked up in the sky. "When I came into this yard I really had the feeling I was in your house back north."

"You were surprised?"

"Umm, I was."

"Well, then . . ." Yi Changhwan began to speak but stopped.

"It's weird. The more it seems to resemble the old homestead . . . no, I mean the more I think of it as copied after the old house, the more unfamiliar it seems to me. I don't know why."

"The more similar, the less familiar?" he asked, confusion showing all over his face.

"Yes."

"Who's there? Isn't that Nongha?"

I heard a familiar voice behind my back. As I wheeled around, Yi Changhwan's father emerged suddenly into the yard from an opening between the cowshed and the main building. He wore a brown vest over the heavy cotton trousers that were tied off in the old way at the ankles.

"Ah! How have you been, sir?" I asked, bowing. Yi Changhwan's father beamed.

"You're here. You made it all right!" He approached and placed his hand on my right shoulder. He examined me for a while.

"You're beginning to get some wrinkles, son," he said. "Just a moment, now," he added and, releasing my shoulder, crossed over to the stoop and sat down.

"Now, I want to see you and Changhwan go out and then come back in again, together."

I was taken aback but, catching a glance from Yi Changhwan, I followed him all the way out to the stepping stones in the stream.

"Father wants to see you and me walking into the yard together as we did in the old days, back north." He looked a bit apologetic.

"Oh? Nothing difficult about that."

So the two of us directed our steps once more along the narrow path and into the yard.

Yi Changhwan's father, from his position on the stoop, watched our reappearance through narrowed eyes.

"Good! That's it!" he cried out, nodding his head up and down.

Yi Changhwan and I were standing in the middle of the yard, not knowing what to do next, when his father leapt down from the stoop and came out to us. He spoke to me.

"Nongha, what do you think? Doesn't it seem like you're home again?" he asked.

"Yes, sir," I answered. "Really . . . to be so much like the old homestead . . ."

I stole a look at Yi Changhwan. The look of confusion I had caught on his face a moment ago had faded now, but in its place shadows had gathered. His father's wrinkled face had a look of distant yearning.

"I tried to make it just the same. The workers had never done such a thing before, but they spared no effort." His head nodded with satisfaction and he took a long, careful look around the house.

"Here, you must be hungry! Why don't we go inside now?" he said, hopping up on the stoop and gesturing for us to follow.

I followed him into the room and there, inside, I met with another surprise when I saw the rush mat spread out on the floor.

"Where did you get this, sir?" I looked at the mat for some time and then sat down, running my hand over its smooth but fibrous surface.

"Make yourself comfortable," said Yi Changhwan's father as he reached for the long, bamboo-stemmed pipe which was resting against a wooden ashtray at the end of the room. He slowly filled it and put it into his mouth.

"I did have some trouble finding it," he said, and thoughtfully stroked the rush mat with one hand as if he were fondling a treasure.

"It's been fifteen years since we left and I now know that returning to the homestead is out of the question. I'm too old to wait any longer. I have no way to move those mountains down to me, so I built this house here. Of course I couldn't make it exactly the same, but it gives me the feeling I'm back home in my own house. That's a lot better than nothing."

He let his thoughts form a moment and spoke again.

"But, you know, there's no limit to a man's desire. The trouble is that once I had set out to imitate the old house, I found myself more and more caught up with minor details. Just placing a stone step. I would think it went one place but when I put it there it seemed wrong. So I'd stick it here and then there and after setting it and digging it up five or six times I would even end up going back to the spot where I had started. . . ." His eyes were filled with emotion.

In the evening Yi Changhwan and I had supper together in the same room with his father. While I was impressed by the old brass rice bowls, I was particularly struck by the fact that he served *toe piji* in addition to the usual foods.

To southerners, *piji* is what's left over when the wet bean curd is pressed into shape, but back home what we call *toe piji* is made by boiling up ham bones and pork with ground beans. This was not that common a dish even among refugees from the north, many of who had since developed more refined tastes.

As I picked out the generous ham bones to chew on I appreciated how intense were the old man's feelings for home. He longed for the reminders of home he could find even in the smell of *toe piji*. This tenacious yearning, this soul for which *piji* was a perfume! No—this heartrending scream of longing!

At first I had thought that Yi Changhwan's disapproval of his father lay in a fear that he would get inextricably wrapped up in this project of his, but when I came to understand I realized his concern lay elsewhere.

I played cards with Yi Changhwan until late that night and when we heard the sound of his father's snores from the inner room we put out the lamp and got into our beds. The oil lamp was a copy of the "room lamp" they had used in the old house back north before liberation. The next day Yi Changhwan and I went back up to Seoul.

A few days short of a year later I met Yi Changhwan and heard the sad news that his father had drowned in the swamp that had been dug out in front of his house. We had met and gone to a dark wine-stall and there, as we shared our cups, I heard several stories of his father's last days.

He told me of how his father had given a banquet on his birthday and invited down the few old friends of his who were still living in Seoul. He said the old men drank wine and exchanged stories about home and then sang nostalgic songs until late into the night.

"They hugged each other, laughing until they cried and crying until they laughed, acting like silly children again. I was waiting on them and heard the stories they told each other. It was mostly unimportant, pointless talk but I could sense one thing in particular—a lament that they could not see home again."

"A lament?"

"Uh-huh, a sad lament."

"A lament, you say. . . ."

"The old men stayed there two or three days and by the fourth day they finally had all left. After seeing the last of them off, Father seemed lost, like someone who had lost his soul."

"I can imagine."

"It was the last banquet Father would share with his friends."

Yi Changhwan paused a moment and sighed.

"After that he would become irritable very easily. Whoever went down to see him from then on—my cousin and his wife, or anyone—had to be extremely careful with him. And what's worse . . ."

He went on to tell how his father would get up all of a sudden in the middle of the night and, waking everyone, demand of his confused guests why there were no rats in his house.

"What's the trouble, Uncle?" they asked with caution.

At the sound of their questioning voices, he seemed to steady himself.

"Well, I was lying in bed and it seemed so quiet. I could hear the rattle of the ring the calf is tied to out in the shed, but then I suddenly realized there was no sound of rats racing around in the rafters. Why aren't there any rats?"

The next day Yi Changhwan's cousin went to a nearby village and bought five rats at fifty *wŏn* apiece and let them loose in the space above the ceilings in his uncle's house. Thinking they might run away, he even scattered rice and barley around for them to eat. He waited four days—each night expecting some reaction—but there was no indication that the old man had heard the sound of rats playing in the ceiling.

On the evening of the fifth day, just when the cousin was thinking that he had spent the 250 *wŏn* for nothing, as he was coming back through the yard from the outhouse, he heard what seemed like a scream from his uncle.

The startled cousin, fearing something had happened, dashed toward his uncle's room only to discover the old man out in the yard with his head pressed up against the crack between the sliding kitchen doors.

"What's the matter, Uncle?" he asked anxiously.

The old man turned and whispered to his nephew, narrow eyes filled with yearning.

"Quietly!" he admonished. Then, gesturing for his nephew to approach, he added, "Now come and listen here."

The younger man had no idea what was behind this but approached as he had been asked. He squatted down and pressed his ear to the crack between the doors.

"Can you hear the rats?"

"Sir?"

"Listen carefully. I just this moment heard a rat squeaking in there."

They were squatting face to face, but the cousin felt so sorry for the old man that he couldn't manage to look straight at him. He lowered his eyes to the ground.

A moment later the intolerable silence was broken as two squeals from a rat in a corner of the kitchen leaked out through the crack in the door. The old man's face lit up with satisfaction.

"Well? Did you hear it?"

"Yes. It cried twice," he replied like a schoolboy reciting his lesson.

"It looks like my father had longed even for the sound of rats. Even though it wasn't one from the old house." Yi Changhwan laughed bitterly.

"About three months ago, most of our close relatives went down to Father's house to join in memorial services for my great-grandfather. He was so very happy to see everyone together again—'Just like it was back north.' But when the services were over and the banquet was under way, father began to overdrink for the first time in a long while. He had the wine table removed and suddenly broke into sobbing lamentations. Everyone was startled by this and asked him why."

Yi Changhwan fell silent for a moment.

"What had started him crying was the thought of his older sister left behind in the north. He wasn't just crying, Nongha, he was sobbing and tearing at his chest. . . ."

"That's understandable."

"I came back up to Seoul the next day. But according to my cousin, he fell into the habit of talking to himself. My cousin told me he couldn't make out anything my father was mumbling even when he stood right next to him."

"Anything?"

"Umm. The only thing he said he could make out—and that just barely—was what Father would say as he pointed somewhere with his arrowroot cane: 'No, no. This isn't the way it was.'"

"Hmm."

"On the morning of the day he died, Father suddenly announced he was going to go fishing in the swamp. So my cousin asked if he wanted him to go into town and buy some hooks. But he said it wasn't that kind of fishing. Do you remember, Nongha, what we did when we were little? How we would get a piece of mosquito netting about one meter square and tie thin willow branches at the corners? Then we'd bind them in the middle where they crossed and put the thing on the end of a long bamboo pole. Remember?"

"Yes. And we'd hang squash blossoms and things from it."

"Right."

"Then we'd stick it out in the water and sprinkle bits of bean paste in the middle so the minnow and baby carp would collect in it. And when we pulled it out the net would be full of all those squirming little fish."

"That's it. That's what Father did that day."

"And then?"

"So my cousin sat beside him half the day, helping. At one point he left for a moment to go into the house, but when he got back he found my father with the upper half of his body thrust into the water."

"Had he fallen over?"

"Well, when they got him out he was already dead."

"How could he die like that?"

"It really doesn't seem a reasonable way to go."

"He'd never do such a thing. No, there was no sign of anything like that at all. . . . I raced down there as soon as I got the telegram, but all I found when I straightened up the things in his desk drawers was a note."

"What did it say?"

"It told where he wanted to be buried."

"Where was that?"

"In a sunny spot on the wide, flat ridge we called the Green Dragon of the East. The one that sweeps down by the left wing of the house. It's a pine grove like the burial ground back in the north." He said he buried his father there and came back up to Seoul.

He and I came out of the wine-stall and parted. Although it was late I purposely walked all the way to West Gate and there caught the last bus home. I don't know why, but I wanted to walk by myself. As I walked along in the night a weird idea came to me.

As Yi Changhwan's father sat by the edge of the swamp could he have seen something? Could he have looked across to the groves and fields in front of him, then turned his head to scan the mountains that embraced house after house, lifted his eyes to the skies and then lowered them again to look into the swamp? And there—blue skies and white clouds reflected in the peacefully still mirror of the water—could he have seen the reflection of his own face?

I understand. I remember the face of Yi Changhwan's grandfather when I was young. As Yi Changhwan's father had grown older his face came to look more and more like his father's—Yi Changhwan's grandfather.

And so, in the water . . .

# Modern Europe

When "modernity" began will always be a matter of debate. The Latin word *modo,* from which the adjective "modern" derives, means "recent," "just now," and surely everyone who has ever lived has felt that she or he was living in the most "modern" era of humankind. People in the past did not conceive of themselves as living in the past; they were living in a present that we, whose present will soon be past, now refer to as the past. This having been said, there is something especially modern about the European Enlightenment, a movement whose seeds were sown in classical antiquity and revived in the Renaissance (or "rebirth," also referred to as the "Early Modern Period"). In Europe, the Enlightenment (or the "Neoclassical Period") was a continuation of the Renaissance, which was itself a rebirth of classical antiquity.

The term "Enlightenment" emerged as a rallying cry for those intellectuals, mainly associated with authors such as Denis Diderot and Jean Le Rond d'Alembert, who compiled the progressivist *Encyclopédie* in prerevolutionary eighteenth-century France. These thinkers conceived of the medieval Christian order as the "Dark Ages." What was "dark" about the Dark Ages? Two interrelated attitudes immediately come to mind: a blind belief in the doctrines of Christianity and an unquestioning reliance on authority. Many medieval Christians, convinced of their imperfection, looked to a future salvation beyond the earthly world. In the Enlightenment that "beyond" was concretized into the expectation of a continuing process of perfecting life in this world. This future perfection could be achieved, according to some voices of the Enlightenment, only by completely rejecting the dark past of religion and authority and being guided instead by reason.

Men and women, however, certainly cannot live by reason alone, and thus much of the literature of modern Europe is concerned with rediscovering what gets left out when human beings are expected to be fully rational creatures. The literature of the rediscovered emotions is often called "Romanticism," but it is easier to use such categories as Romanticism in theory than in practice. We might just say that the Enlightenment explored the tension between the ideals of reason and the stubbornly human need for religion, the emotions, and the irrational.

The first work in this section of our anthology, Milton's *Paradise Lost,* can be read as its author's acknowledgment of the dark side of human nature that was ignored or defied when Puritan revolutionaries, having first executed the king to end monarchial rule in England, imagined a gloriously egalitarian future for their country. Such hopes were dashed when the monarchy was restored only twenty years later. A century later the French Revolution ended in similar disillusionment. About the same time in Germany, Goethe brought the Enlightenment to its fulfillment, then in his *Faust* produced an explosive critique of its rational ideals. In nineteenth-century Russia, Dostoevsky, who began as a secular socialist, devoted much of his fiction to an analysis of how the Enlightenment legacy had been deeply destructive to the human spirit. In France, Baudelaire described in his poetry the depths of human depravity that lurk just beneath the surface of civilized, modern, bourgois European life.

One of the virtues of Saint Augustine's conception of a unified medieval Christendom was a notion of human nature and human destiny that transcended ethnic and linguistic differences. The means to this end were a universal religion (Christianity) and a universal language (Latin). In the late Middle Ages and the Renaissance, the movement to grant vernacular languages the prestige of Latin gained momentum. The fruits of this movement, such as the epics of Dante in Italian and of Milton in English, decided the issue in favor of the vernaculars. In the eighteenth and nineteenth centuries, the hegemony of the nation-state, and with it the notion of national literatures, solidified. This conception of the distinctiveness of the various national literatures became the basis of the modern university's partitioning of literary study into departments of English, Russian, French, German, Chinese, and so on. The acceptance of the notion of the secular nation, with its distinctive language and spirit, as the primary carrier of meaning in history, has had a dubious impact on modern Europe. Nazi Germany was perhaps the furthest extreme of such nationalism when it proclaimed itself the carrier of the world-historic destiny of *das Deutsche Volk* ("the German people"). Today Europe struggles to achieve unity out of its fragmented history. A global anthology such as this one is a modest attempt at resisting the notion of literature as the expression of the mystical uniqueness of the modern nation-state. European—and world—literature is more unified than national barriers suggest.

The literature of modern Europe can be divided into several movements or stages. Neoclassicism, with its admiration for the writers of classical antiquity, can be seen as a development—and in many ways a narrowing—of the aims of Renaissance humanism. Emphasizing balance, polish, and wit, it reached its apex in the France of Louis XIV and was imported to England after the Restoration of the English monarchy in 1660. Neoclassical writers admire the imagination but worry about its potential excesses. Neoclassicism is often associated with a conservative public order. Louis XIV, known as the "Sun King," was the very paradigm of the absolute monarch. In the great neoclassical period of literature in France—the period of Molière—all order radiated from Louis and his court. Neoclassicism also reigned in eighteenth-century England, illustrated here by Pope.

Nineteenth-century Romanticism turned outward toward political activism and inward toward validating the primacy of subjective experience. A literature of ordinary human beings, not just the educated and aristocratic, it focused on the awesome but conflicting powers of the human imagination. Rousseau and Hölderlin are its exemplars here.

In the twentieth century we see the development of Modernism, a literary movement that is in many ways an outgrowth of Romanticism, with its emphasis upon the primacy of the individual's own personal experience and vision and even eccentricities. Modernist literature stages a full-scale assault on traditional literary forms and values, allowing the artist what feels like total freedom to invent highly individualistic works that often place a tremendous burden on the reader to discover their meanings. Proust, Kafka, Joyce, Woolf, Beckett, and Rilke are all modernists in this sense, along with Pound and Eliot, who can be found in the section on the Americas (pp. 2168–2181).

## England and Ireland

## John Milton (1608–1674)

The humanist movement begun by Petrarch in the fourteenth century found its perfect fulfillment three hundred years later in John Milton, an Englishman of enormous intellect, ambition, and learning who was fluent in many ancient and modern languages. Early in life he set his sights on writing an English epic to equal those of Homer and Virgil. In the best humanist tradition, however, his plan was long delayed by public service. During the English Revolution he was appointed foreign secretary, and in a series of official letters and pamphlets he defended the revolutionaries' execution of King Charles I, an act that shocked the other European monarchial states. He also wrote tracts on social issues including divorce and freedom of the press. Having labored tirelessly for the Republic for twenty years, Milton was left disgraced and destitute when the monarchy was restored in 1660. By then totally blind (like Homer), he turned at last to write his epic, *Paradise Lost.*

In spite of his epic's dense erudition and its relatively slow pace, Milton's command of the English poetic line is almost flawlessly beautiful. Generations of English readers, not just Puritans, revered *Paradise Lost* like the Bible; and for centuries

English poets have struggled to equal his mastery. Learning to read *Paradise Lost* with pleasure is one of the highest and most satisfying achievements of literary study in English.

Unlike earlier epics, Milton's does not celebrate cultural or national origins but the origins of all humanity. A radical protestant, that is, a Puritan, Milton tells the story of Adam and Eve's fall from Paradise, expanding the Bible's brief account (pp. 99–101) into a vast cosmic epic. The passages included here represent the three settings of the poem and highlights of its chief drama: Book One is set in hell; Book Three is set in heaven; and Books Four, Nine, and Twelve are set in Paradise.

The descent into hell, an epic fixture at the center of Homer's *Odyssey* and Virgil's *Aeneid,* is placed at the opening of this work, as the *Inferno* opens Dante's *Divine Comedy.* In the first two books of *Paradise Lost,* the angel Lucifer, having failed in a revolution against God, is cast headlong into hell, where he plots the corruption of humankind as his revenge. A century after the poem was written, the poet William Blake argued that Satan is the most passionately drawn character in the poem and its real hero—understandably, since Milton shared a similar fall from grace. Just as most modern readers find Dante's *Inferno* more interesting than his *Paradiso,* many prefer Milton's dark and thunderous opening to the elevated drama of the first marriage and the first sin. Most of the poem takes place not in hell, however, but in heaven and the human world, and from Milton's point of view Adam and Christ are more obvious candidates for hero.

The opening lines of Book Three are perhaps the most personal of the epic, as Milton meditates upon his blindness before presenting his vision of God. God's speech identifies the great theme of the poem as the problem of human freedom, the most intractable philosophical problem offered by Christianity. God created human beings free, knowing they would sin; but if God saw that beforehand, how can it be said that human beings are really free? How free are we if God sees everything we do before we do it? The same theme suffuses Satan's speeches in Book One.

Book Four details Milton's vision of a perfect human world before the first sin. Much of its interest today derives from his portrait of Eve, his vision of the ideal woman. Three hundred years later there is much to object to in this portrait, but his thinking on the subject was advanced for his age. Eve's song to Adam as they retire to bed at the end of their first day and Milton's hymn to wedded love that follows it are two of the most beautiful love poems of the English Renaissance.

The Fall itself takes place in two stages; Satan seduces Eve and then Adam chooses to join her. The end result is not completely negative, because it allows Christ to redeem humankind later. In the famous last lines of the poem, the world as we know it, filled with opportunities for goodness, peace and love, lies before Adam and Eve as they leave Paradise forever. The scene is drawn with tenderness and understanding rather than accusation and regret:

> The world was all before them, where to choose
> Their place of rest, and Providence their guide.
> They, hand in hand, with wandering steps and slow,
> Through Eden took their solitary way.

## *Paradise Lost*

### *Book I [Invocation; Satan in Hell]*

Of man's first disobedience, and the fruit
Of that forbidden tree, whose mortal taste
Brought death into the world, and all our woe,
With loss of Eden, till one greater Man
Restore us, and regain the blissful seat,
Sing Heav'nly Muse, that on the secret top
Of Oreb, or of Sinai, didst inspire
That shepherd, who first taught the chosen seed,
In the beginning how the heav'ns and earth
Rose out of chaos: or if Sion hill
Delight thee more, and Siloa's brook that flowed
Fast by the oracle of God; I thence
Invoke thy aid to my advent'rous song,
That with no middle flight intends to soar
Above th' Aonian mount, while it pursues
Things unattempted yet in prose or rhyme.
And chiefly thou O Spirit, that dost prefer
Before all temples th' upright heart and pure,
Instruct me, for thou know'st; thou from the first
Wast present, and with mighty wings outspread
Dove-like sat'st brooding on the vast abyss
And mad'st it pregnant: what in me is dark
Illumine, what is low raise and support;
That to the highth of this great argument
I may assert Eternal Providence,
And justify the ways of God to men.
        Say first, for heav'n hides nothing from thy view
Nor the deep tract of hell, say first what cause
Moved our grand parents in that happy state,
Favored of Heav'n so highly, to fall off
From their Creator, and transgress his will
For one restraint, lords of the world besides?
Who first seduced them to that foul revolt?
Th' infernal Serpent; he it was, whose guile
Stirred up with envy and revenge, deceived
The mother of mankind, what time his pride
Had cast him out from heav'n, with all his host
Of rebel angels, by whose aid aspiring
To set himself in glory above his peers,
He trusted to have equaled the Most High,
If he opposed; and with ambitious aim
Against the throne and monarchy of God

Raised impious war in heav'n and battle proud
With vain attempt. Him the Almighty Power
Hurled headlong flaming from th' ethereal sky
With hideous ruin and combustion down
To bottomless perdition, there to dwell
In adamantine chains and penal fire,
Who durst defy th' Omnipotent to arms.
Nine times the space that measures day and night
To mortal men, he with his horrid crew
Lay vanquished, rolling in the fiery gulf
Confounded though immortal: but his doom
Reserved him to more wrath; for now the thought
Both of lost happiness and lasting pain
Torments him; round he throws his baleful eyes
That witnessed huge affliction and dismay
Mixed with obdúrate pride and steadfast hate:
At once as far as angels ken he views
The dismal situation waste and wild,
A dungeon horrible, on all sides round
As one great furnace flamed, yet from those flames
No light, but rather darkness visible
Served only to discover sights of woe,
Regions of sorrow, doleful shades, where peace
And rest can never dwell, hope never comes
That comes to all; but torture without end
Still urges, and a fiery deluge, fed
With ever-burning sulphur unconsumed:
Such place Eternal Justice had prepared
For those rebellious, here their prison ordained
In utter darkness, and their portion set
As far removed from God and light of heav'n
As from the center thrice to th' utmost pole.
O how unlike the place from whence they fell!
There the companions of his fall, o'erwhelmed
With floods and whirlwinds of tempestuous fire,
He soon discerns, and welt'ring by his side
One next himself in power, and next in crime,
Long after known in Palestine, and named
Beëlzebub. To whom th' Arch-Enemy,
And thence in heav'n called Satan, with bold words
Breaking the horrid silence thus began.
"If thou beest he; but O how fall'n! how changed
From him, who in the happy realms of light
Clothed with transcendent brightness didst outshine
Myriads though bright: if he whom mutual league,
United thoughts and counsels, equal hope

And hazard in the glorious enterprise,
Joined with me once, now misery hath joined
In equal ruin: into what pit thou seest
From what highth fall'n, so much the stronger proved
He with his thunder: and till then who knew
The force of those dire arms? Yet not for those,
Nor what the potent victor in his rage
Can else inflict, do I repent or change,
Though changed in outward luster, that fixed mind
And high disdain, from sense of injured merit,
That with the mightiest raised me to contend,
And to the fierce contention brought along
Innumerable force of Spirits armed
That durst dislike his reign, and me preferring,
His utmost power with adverse power opposed
In dubious baffle on the plains of heav'n,
And shook his throne. What though the field be lost?
All is not lost; the unconquerable will,
And study of revenge, immortal hate,
And courage never to submit or yield:
And what is else not to be overcome?
That glory never shall his wrath or might
Extort from me. To bow and sue for grace
With suppliant knee, and deify his power
Who from the terror of this arm so late
Doubted his empire, that were low indeed,
That were an ignominy and shame beneath
This downfall; since by fate the strength of gods
And this empyreal substance cannot fail,
Since through experience of this great event
In arms not worse, in foresight much advanced,
We may with more successful hope resolve
To wage by force or guile eternal war
Irreconcilable, to our grand foe,
Who now triúmphs, and in th' excess of joy
Sole reigning holds the tyranny of heav'n."
So spake th' apostate angel, though in pain,
Vaunting aloud, but racked with deep despair:
And him thus answered soon his bold compeer.
"O Prince, O Chief of many thronèd Powers,
That led th' embattled Seraphim to war
Under thy conduct, and in dreadful deeds
Fearless, endangered heav'ns perpetual King;
And put to proof his high supremacy,
Whether upheld by strength, or chance, or fate;
Too well I see and rue the dire event,

That with sad overthrow and foul defeat
Hath lost us heav'n, and all this mighty host
In horrible destruction laid thus low,
As far as gods and heav'nly essences
Can perish: for the mind and spirit remains
Invincible, and vigor soon returns,
Though all our glory extinct, and happy state
Here swallowed up in endless misery.
But what if he our conqueror (whom I now
Of force believe almighty, since no less
Than such could have o'erpow'red such force as ours)
Have left us this our spirit and strength entire
Strongly to suffer and support our pains,
That we may so suffice his vengeful ire,
Or do him mightier service as his thralls
By right of war, whate'er his business be
Here in the heart of hell to work in fire,
Or do his errands in the gloomy deep;
What can it then avail though yet we feel
Strength undiminished, or eternal being
To undergo eternal punishment?"
Whereto with speedy words th' Arch-Fiend replied.
"Fall'n Cherub, to be weak is miserable
Doing or suffering: but of this be sure,
To do aught good never will be our task,
But ever to do ill our sole delight,
As being the contrary to his high will
Whom we resist. If then his providence
Out of our evil seek to bring forth good,
Our labor must be to pervert that end,
And out of good still to find means of evil;
Which ofttimes may succeed, so as perhaps
Shall grieve him, if I fail not, and disturb
His inmost counsels from their destined aim.
But see the angry victor hath recalled
His ministers of vengeance and pursuit
Back to the gates of heav'n: the sulphurous hail
Shot after us in storm, o'erblown hath laid
The fiery surge, that from the precipice
Of heav'n received us falling, and the thunder,
Winged with red lightning and impetuous rage,
Perhaps hath spent his shafts, and ceases now
To bellow through the vast and boundless deep.
Let us not slip th' occasion, whether scorn,
Or satiate fury yield it from our foe.

Seest thou yon dreary plain, forlorn and wild,
The seat of desolation, void of light,
Save what the glimmering of these livid flames
Casts pale and dreadful? Thither let us tend
From off the tossing of these fiery waves,
There rest, if any rest can harbor there,
And reassembling our afflicted powers,
Consult how we may henceforth most offend
Our enemy, our own loss how repair,
How overcome this dire calamity,
What reinforcement we may gain from hope,
If not what resolution from despair."
    Thus Satan talking to his nearest mate
With head uplift above the wave, and eyes
That sparkling blazed, his other parts besides
Prone on the flood, extended long and large
Lay floating many a rood, in bulk as huge
As whom the fables name of monstrous size,
Titanian, or Earth-born, that warred on Jove,
Briareos or Typhon, whom the den
By ancient Tarsus held, or that sea-beast
Leviathan, which God of all his works
Created hugest that swim th' ocean stream:
Him haply slumb'ring on the Norway foam
The pilot of some small night-foundered skiff,
Deeming some island, oft, as seamen tell,
With fixèd anchor in his scaly rind
Moors by his side under the lee, while night
Invests the sea, and wishèd morn delays:
So stretched out huge in length the Arch-Fiend lay
Chained on the burning lake, nor ever thence
Had ris'n or heaved his head, but that the will
And high permission of all-ruling Heaven
Left him at large to his own dark designs,
That with reiterated crimes he might
Heap on himself damnation, while he sought
Evil to others, and enraged might see
How all his malice served but to bring forth
Infinite goodness, grace and mercy shown
On man by him seduced, but on himself
Treble confusion, wrath and vengeance poured.
Forthwith upright he rears from off the pool
His mighty stature; on each hand the flames
Driv'n backward slope their pointing spires, and rolled
In billows, leave i' th' midst a horrid vale.

Then with expanded wings he steers his flight
Aloft, incumbent on the dusky air
That felt unusual weight, till on dry land
He lights, if it were land that ever burned
With solid, as the lake with liquid fire,
And such appeared in hue; as when the force
Of subterranean wind transports a hill
Torn from Pelorus, or the shattered side
Of thund'ring Etna, whose combustible
And fueled entrails thence conceiving fire,
Sublimed with mineral fury, aid the winds,
And leave a singèd bottom all involved
With stench and smoke: such resting found the sole
Of unblest feet. Him followed his next mate,
Both glorying to have scaped the Stygian flood
As gods, and by their own recovered strength,
Not by the sufferance of supernal power.
"Is this the region, this the soil, the clime,"
Said then the lost Archangel, "this the seat
That we must change for heav'n, this mournful gloom
For that celestial light? Be it so, since he
Who now is sovran can dispose and bid
What shall be right: farthest from him is best
Whom reason hath equaled, force hath made supreme
Above his equals. Farewell happy fields
Where joy for ever dwells: hail horrors, hail
Infernal world, and thou profoundest hell
Receive thy new possessor: one who brings
A mind not to be changed by place or time.
The mind is its own place, and in itself
Can make a heav'n of hell, a hell of heav'n.
What matter where, if I be still the same,
And what I should be all but less than he
Whom thunder hath made greater? Here at least
We shall be free; th' Almighty hath not built
Here for his envy, will not drive us hence:
Here we may reign secure, and in my choice
To reign is worth ambition though in hell:
Better to reign in hell, than serve in heav'n.
But wherefore let we then our faithful friends,
Th' associates and copartners of our loss
Lie thus astonished on th' oblivious pool,
And call them not to share with us their part
In this unhappy mansion, or once more
With rallied arms to try what may be yet
Regained in heav'n, or what more lost in hell?"

So Satan spake, and him Beëlzebub
Thus answered. "Leader of those armies bright,
Which but th' Omnipotent none could have foiled,
If once they hear that voice, their liveliest pledge
Of hope in fears and dangers, heard so oft
In worst extremes, and on the perilous edge
Of battle when it raged, in all assaults
Their surest signal, they will soon resume
New courage and revive, though now they lie
Groveling and prostrate on yon lake of fire,
As we erewhile, astounded and amazed,
No wonder, fall'n such a pernicious highth."
He scarce had ceased when the superior Fiend
Was moving toward the shore; his ponderous shield
Ethereal temper, massy, large and round,
Behind him cast; the broad circumference
Hung on his shoulders like the moon, whose orb
Through optic glass the Tuscan artist views
At evening from the top of Fesole,
Or in Valdarno, to descry new lands,
Rivers or mountains in her spotty globe.
His spear, to equal which the tallest pine
Hewn on Norwegian hills, to be the mast
Of some great ammiral, were but a wand,
He walked with to support uneasy steps
Over the burning marl, not like those steps
On heaven's azure; and the torrid clime
Smote on him sore besides, vaulted with fire;
Nathless he so endured, till on the beach
Of that inflamèd sea, he stood and called
His legions, angel forms, who lay entranced
Thick as autumnal leaves that strow the brooks
In Vallombrosa, where th' Etrurian shades
High overarched embow'r; or scattered sedge
Afloat, when with fierce winds Orion armed
Hath vexed the Red Sea coast, whose waves o'erthrew
Busiris and his Memphian chivalry,
While with perfidious hatred they pursued
The sojourners of Goshen, who beheld
From the safe shore their floating carcasses
And broken chariot wheels. So thick bestrown
Abject and lost lay these, covering the flood,
Under amazement of their hideous change.
He called so loud, that all the hollow deep
Of hell resounded. "Princes, Potentates,
Warriors, the flow'r of heav'n, once yours, now lost,

If such astonishment as this can seize
Eternal Spirits: or have ye chos'n this place
After the toil of battle to repose
Your wearied virtue, for the ease you find
To slumber here, as in the vales of heav'n?
Or in this abject posture have ye sworn
To adore the conqueror? who now beholds
Cherub and Seraph rolling in the flood
With scattered arms and ensigns, till anon
His swift pursuers from heav'n gates discern
Th' advantage, and descending tread us down
Thus drooping, or with linkèd thunderbolts
Transfix us to the bottom of this gulf.
Awake, arise, or be for ever fall'n."
They heard, and were abashed, and up they sprung
Upon the wing, as when men wont to watch
On duty, sleeping found by whom they dread,
Rouse and bestir themselves ere well awake.
Nor did they not perceive the evil plight
In which they were, or the fierce pains not feel;
Yet to their general's voice they soon obeyed
Innumerable. As when the potent rod
Of Amram's son in Egypt's evil day
Waved round the coast, up called a pitchy cloud
Of locusts, warping on the eastern wind,
That o'er the realm of impious Pharaoh hung
Like night, and darkened all the land of Nile:
So numberless were those bad angels seen
Hovering on wing under the cope of hell
'Twixt upper, nether, and surrounding fires;
Till, as a signal giv'n, th' uplifted spear
Of their great Sultan waving to direct
Their course, in even balance down they light
On the firm brimstone, and fill all the plain;
A multitude, like which the populous North
Poured never from her frozen loins, to pass
Rhene or the Danaw, when her barbarous sons
Came like a deluge on the South, and spread
Beneath Gibraltar to the Libyan sands.
Forthwith from every squadron and each band
The heads and leaders thither haste where stood
Their great commander; godlike shapes and forms
Excelling human, princely dignities,
And powers that erst in heaven sat on thrones;
Though of their names in heav'nly records now

Be no memorial, blotted out and razed
By their rebellion, from the Books of Life.

* * *

"O myriads of immortal Spirits, O Powers
Matchless, but with th' Almighty, and that strife
Was not inglorious, though th' event was dire,
As this place testifies, and this dire change
Hateful to utter: but what power of mind
Foreseeing or presaging, from the depth
Of knowledge past or present, could have feared,
How such united force of gods, how such
As stood like these, could ever know repulse?
For who can yet believe, though after loss,
That all these puissant legions, whose exile
Hath emptied heav'n, shall fail to reascend
Self-raised, and repossess their native seat?
For me, be witness all the host of heav'n,
If counsels different, or danger shunned
By me, have lost our hopes. But he who reigns
Monarch in heav'n, till then as one secure
Sat on his throne, upheld by old repute,
Consent or custom, and his regal state
Put forth at full, but still his strength concealed,
Which tempted our attempt, and wrought our fall.
Henceforth his might we know, and know our own
So as not either to provoke, or dread
New war, provoked; our better part remains
To work in close design, by fraud or guile
What force effected not: that he no less
At length from us may find, who overcomes
By force, hath overcome but half his foe.
Space may produce new worlds; whereof so rife
There went a fame in heav'n that he ere long
Intended to create, and therein plant
A generation, whom his choice regard
Should favor equal to the sons of heaven:
Thither, if but to pry, shall be perhaps
Our first eruption, thither or elsewhere:
For this infernal pit shall never hold
Celestial Spirits in bondage, not th' abyss
Long under darkness cover. But these thoughts
Full counsel must mature: peace is despaired,
For who can think submission? War then, war

Open or understood must be resolved."
He spake: and to confirm his words, out flew
Millions of flaming swords, drawn from the thighs
Of mighty Cherubim; the sudden blaze
Far round illumined hell: highly they raged
Against the Highest, and fierce with graspèd arms
Clashed on their sounding shields the din of war,
Hurling defiance toward the vault of heav'n. . . .

## *Book III [Invocation to Light; God in Heaven]*

Hail holy Light, offspring of Heav'n first-born,
Or of th' Eternal coeternal beam
May I express thee unblamed? Since God is light,
And never but in unapproachèd light
Dwelt from eternity, dwelt then in thee,
Bright effluence of bright essence increate.
Or hear'st thou rather pure ethereal stream,
Whose fountain who shall tell? Before the sun,
Before the heavens thou wert, and at the voice
Of God, as with a mantle didst invest
The rising world of waters dark and deep,
Won from the void and formless infinite.
Thee I revisit now with bolder wing,
Escaped the Stygian pool, though long detained
In that obscure sojourn, while in my flight
Through utter and through middle darkness borne
With other notes than to th' Orphéan lyre
I sung of Chaos and eternal Night,
Taught by the Heav'nly Muse to venture down
The dark descent, and up to reascend,
Though hard and rare: thee I revisit safe,
And feel thy sovran vital lamp; but thou
Revisit'st not these eyes, that roll in vain
To find thy piercing ray, and find no dawn;
So thick a drop serene hath quenched their orbs,
Or dim suffusion veiled. Yet not the more
Cease I to wander where the Muses haunt
Clear spring, or shady grove, or sunny hill,
Smit with the love of sacred song; but chief
Thee Sion and the flow'ry brooks beneath
That wash thy hallowed feet, and warbling flow,
Nightly I visit: nor sometimes forget
Those other two equaled with me in fate,
So were I equaled with them in renown,
Blind Thamyris and blind Maeonides,

And Tiresias and Phineus prophets old.
Then feed on thoughts, that voluntary move
Harmonious numbers; as the wakeful bird
Sings darkling, and in shadiest covert hid
Tunes her nocturnal note. Thus with the year
Seasons return, but not to me returns
Day, or the sweet approach of ev'n or morn,
Or sight of vernal bloom, or summer's rose,
Or flocks, or herds, or human face divine;
But cloud instead, and ever-during dark
Surrounds me, from the cheerful ways of men
Cut off, and for the book of knowledge fair
Presented with a universal blank
Of nature's works to me expunged and razed,
And wisdom at one entrance quite shut out.
So much the rather thou celestial Light
Shine inward, and the mind through all her powers
Irradiate, there plant eyes, all mist from thence
Purge and disperse, that I may see and tell
Of things invisible to mortal sight.
        Now had the Almighty Father from above,
From the pure empyrean where he sits
High throned above all highth, bent down his eye,
His own works and their works at once to view:
Above him all the sanctities of heaven
Stood thick as stars, and from his sight received
Beatitude past utterance; on his right
The radiant image of his glory sat,
His only Son; on earth he first beheld
Our two first parents, yet the only two
Of mankind, in the happy garden placed,
Reaping immortal fruits of joy and love,
Uninterrupted joy, unrivaled love
In blissful solitude; he then surveyed
Hell and the gulf between, and Satan there
Coasting the wall of heav'n on this side Night
In the dun air sublime, and ready now
To stoop with wearied wings, and willing feet
On the bare outside of this world, that seemed
Firm land embosomed without firmament,
Uncertain which, in ocean or in air.
Him God beholding from his prospect high,
Wherein past, present, future he beholds,
Thus to his only Son foreseeing spake.
        "Only begotten Son, seest thou what rage
Transports our Adversary, whom no bounds

Prescribed, no bars of hell, nor all the chains
Heaped on him there, nor yet the main abyss
Wide interrupt can hold; so bent he seems
On desperate revenge, that shall redound
Upon his own rebellious head. And now
Through all restraint broke loose he wings his way
Not far off heav'n, in the precincts of light,
Directly towards the new-created world,
And man there placed, with purpose to assay
If him by force he can destroy, or worse,
By some false guile pervert; and shall pervert;
For man will hearken to his glozing lies,
And easily transgress the sole command,
Sole pledge of his obedience: so will fall
He and his faithless progeny: whose fault?
Whose but his own? Ingrate, he had of me
All he could have; I made him just and right,
Sufficient to have stood, though free to fall.
Such I created all th' ethereal Powers
And Spirits, both them who stood and them who failed;
Freely they stood who stood, and fell who fell.
Not free, what proof could they have giv'n sincere
Of true allegiance, constant faith or love,
Where only what they needs must do, appeared,
Not what they would? What praise could they receive?
What pleasure I from such obedience paid,
When will and reason (reason also is choice)
Useless and vain, of freedom both despoiled,
Made passive both, had served necessity,
Not me. They therefore as to right belonged,
So were created, nor can justly accuse
Their Maker, or their making, or their fate,
As if predestination overruled
Their will, disposed by absolute decree
Or high foreknowledge; they themselves decreed
Their own revolt, not I: if I foreknew,
Foreknowledge had no influence on their fault,
Which had no less proved certain unforeknown.
So without least impulse or shadow of fate,
Or aught by me immutably foreseen,
They trespass, authors to themselves in all
Both what they judge and what they choose; for so
I formed them free, and free they must remain,
Till they enthrall themselves: I else must change
Their nature, and revoke the high decree
Unchangeable, eternal, which ordained

Their freedom, they themselves ordained their fall.
The first sort by their own suggestion fell,
Self-tempted, self-depraved: man falls deceived
By the other first: man therefore shall find grace,
The other none: in mercy and justice both,
Through heav'n and earth, so shall my glory excel,
But mercy first and last shall brightest shine." . . .

## *Book IV [Adam and Eve in Paradise]*

. . . The Fiend
Saw undelighted all delight, all kind
Of living creatures new to sight and strange:
Two of far nobler shape erect and tall,
God-like erect, with native honor clad
In naked majesty seemed lords of all,
And worthy seemed, for in their looks divine
The image of their glorious Maker shone,
Truth, wisdom, sanctitude severe and pure,
Severe but in true filial freedom placed;
Whence true authority in men; though both
Not equal, as their sex not equal seemed;
For contemplation he and valor formed,
For softness she and sweet attractive grace,
He for God only, she for God in him:
His fair large front and eye sublime declared
Absolute rule; and hyacinthine locks
Round from his parted forelock manly hung
Clust'ring, but not beneath his shoulders broad:
She as a veil down to the slender waist
Her unadorned golden tresses wore
Disheveled, but in wanton ringlets waved
As the vine curls her tendrils, which implied
Subjection, but required with gentle sway,
And by her yielded, by him best received,
Yielded with coy submission, modest pride,
And sweet reluctant amorous delay.
Nor those mysterious parts were then concealed,
Then was not guilty shame, dishonest shame
Of nature's works, honor dishonorable,
Sin-bred, how have ye troubled all mankind
With shows instead, mere shows of seeming pure,
And banished from man's life his happiest life,
Simplicity and spotless innocence.
So passed they naked on, nor shunned the sight
Of God or angel, for they thought no ill:

So hand in hand they passed, the loveliest pair
That ever since in love's embraces met,
Adam the goodliest man of men since born
His sons, the fairest of her daughters Eve.
Under a tuft of shade that on a green
Stood whispering soft, by a fresh fountain side
They sat them down, and after no more toil
Of their sweet gard'ning labor than sufficed
To recommend cool Zephyr, and made ease
More easy, wholesome thirst and appetite
More grateful, to their supper fruits they fell,
Nectarine fruits which the compliant boughs
Yielded them, sidelong as they sat recline
On the soft downy bank damasked with flow'rs:
The savory pulp they chew, and in the rind
Still as they thirsted scoop the brimming stream;
Nor gentle purpose, nor endearing smiles
Wanted, nor youthful dalliance as beseems
Fair couple, linked in happy nuptial league,
Alone as they. About them frisking played
All beasts of th' earth, since wild, and of all chase
In wood or wilderness, forest or den;
Sporting the lion ramped, and in his paw
Dandled the kid; bears, tigers, ounces, pards
Gamboled before them; th' unwieldy elephant
To make them mirth used all his might, and wreathed
His lithe proboscis; close the serpent sly
Insinuating, wove with Gordian twine
His braided train, and of his fatal guile
Gave proof unheeded; others on the grass
Couched, and now filled with pasture gazing sat,
Or bedward ruminating: for the sun
Declined was hasting now with prone career
To th' Ocean Isles, and in th' ascending scale
Of heav'n the stars that usher evening rose:
When Satan still in gaze, as first he stood,
Scarce thus at length failed speech recovered sad.

"O hell! what do mine eyes with grief behold,
Into our room of bliss thus high advanced
Creatures of other mold, earth-born perhaps,
Not Spirits, yet to heav'nly Spirits bright
Little inferior; whom my thoughts pursue
With wonder, and could love, so lively shines
In them divine resemblance, and such grace
The hand that formed them on their shape hath poured.
Ah gentle pair, ye little think how nigh

Your change approaches, when all these delights
Will vanish and deliver ye to woe,
More woe, the more your taste is now of joy;
Happy, but for so happy ill secured
Long to continue, and this high seat your heav'n
Ill fenced for Heav'n to keep out such a foe
As now is entered; yet no purposed foe
To you whom I could pity thus forlorn
Though I unpitied: league with you I seek,
And mutual amity so strait, so close,
That I with you must dwell, or you with me
Henceforth; my dwelling haply may not please
Like this fair Paradise, your sense, yet such
Accept your Maker's work; he gave it me,
Which I as freely give; hell shall unfold,
To entertain you two, her widest gates,
And send forth all her kings; there will be room,
Not like these narrow limits, to receive
Your numerous offspring; if no better place,
Thank him who puts me loath to this revenge
On you who wrong me not for him who wronged.
And should I at your harmless innocence
Melt, as I do, yet public reason just,
Honor and empire with revenge enlarged,
By conquering this new world, compels me now
To do what else though damned I should abhor."
        So spake the Fiend, and with necessity,
The tyrant's plea, excused his devilish deeds.
Then from his lofty stand on that high tree
Down he alights among the sportful herd
Of those four-footed kinds, himself now one,
Now other, as their shape served best his end
Nearer to view his prey, and unespied
To mark what of their state he more might learn
By word or action marked: about them round
A lion now he stalks with fiery glare,
Then as a tiger, who by chance hath spied
In some purlieu two gentle fawns at play,
Straight couches close, then rising changes oft
His couchant watch, as one who chose his ground
Whence rushing he might surest seize them both
Gripped in each paw: when Adam first of men
To first of women Eve thus moving speech
Turned him all ear to hear new utterance flow.
        "Sole partner and sole part of all these joys,
Dearer thyself than all; needs must the Power

That made us, and for us this ample world
Be infinitely good, and of his good
As liberal and free as infinite,
That raised us from the dust and placed us here
In all this happiness, who at his hand
Have nothing merited, nor can perform
Aught whereof he hath need, he who requires
From us no other service than to keep
This one, this easy charge, of all the trees
In Paradise that bear delicious fruit
So various, not to taste that only Tree
Of Knowledge, planted by the Tree of Life,
So near grows death to life, whate'er death is,
Some dreadful thing no doubt; for well thou know'st
God hath pronounced it death to taste that Tree,
The only sign of our obedience left
Among so many signs of power and rule
Conferred upon us, and dominion giv'n
Over all other creatures that possess
Earth, air, and sea. Then let us not think hard
One easy prohibition, who enjoy
Free leave so large to all things else, and choice
Unlimited of manifold delights:
But let us ever praise him, and extol
His bounty, following our delightful task
To prune these growing plants, and tend these flow'rs,
Which were it toilsome, yet with thee were sweet."
    To whom thus Eve replied. "O thou for whom
And from whom I was formed flesh of thy flesh,
And without whom am to no end, my guide
And head, what thou hast said is just and right.
For we to him indeed all praises owe,
And daily thanks, I chiefly who enjoy
So far the happier lot, enjoying thee
Preeminent by so much odds, while thou
Like consort to thyself canst nowhere find.
That day I oft remember, when from sleep
I first awaked, and found myself reposed
Under a shade on flowers, much wond'ring where
And what I was, whence thither brought, and how.
Not distant far from thence a murmuring sound
Of waters issued from a cave and spread
Into a liquid plain, then stood unmoved
Pure as th' expanse of heav'n; I thither went
With unexperienced thought, and laid me down
On the green bank, to look into the clear
Smooth lake, that to me seemed another sky.

As I bent down to look, just opposite,
A shape within the wat'ry gleam appeared
Bending to look on me, I started back,
It started back, but pleased I soon returned,
Pleased it returned as soon with answering looks
Of sympathy and love; there I had fixed
Mine eyes till now, and pined with vain desire,
Had not a voice thus warned me, 'What thou seest,
What there thou seest fair creature is thyself,
With thee it came and goes: but follow me,
And I will bring thee where no shadow stays
Thy coming, and thy soft embraces, he
Whose image thou art, him thou shalt enjoy
Inseparably thine, to him shalt bear
Multitudes like thyself, and thence be called
Mother of human race:' what could I do,
But follow straight, invisibly thus led?
Till I espied thee, fair indeed and tall,
Under a platan, yet methought less fair,
Less winning soft, less amiably mild,
Than that smooth wat'ry image; back I turned,
Thou following cried'st aloud, 'Return fair Eve,
Whom fli'st thou? Whom thou fli'st, of him thou art,
His flesh, his bone; to give thee being I lent
Out of my side to thee, nearest my heart
Substantial life, to have thee by my side
Henceforth an individual solace dear;
Part of my soul I seek thee, and thee claim
My other half': with that thy gentle hand
Seized mine, I yielded, and from that time see
How beauty is excelled by manly grace
And wisdom, which alone is truly fair."
    So spake our general mother, and with eyes
Of conjugal attraction unreproved,
And meek surrender, half embracing leaned
On our first father, half her swelling breast
Naked met his under the flowing gold
Of her loose tresses hid: he in delight
Both of her beauty and submissive charms
Smiled with superior love, as Jupiter
On Juno smiles, when he impregns the clouds
That shed May flowers; and pressed her matron lip
With kisses pure: aside the Devil turned
For envy, yet with jealous leer malign
Eyed them askance, and to himself thus plained.
    "Sight hateful, sight tormenting! thus these two
Imparadised in one another's arms

The happier Eden, shall enjoy their fill
Of bliss on bliss, while I to hell am thrust,
Where neither joy nor love, but fierce desire,
Among our other torments not the least,
Still unfulfilled with pain of longing pines;
Yet let me not forget what I have gained
From their own mouths; all is not theirs it seems:
One fatal tree there stands of Knowledge called,
Forbidden them to taste: Knowledge forbidden?
Suspicious, reasonless. Why should their Lord
Envy them that? Can it be sin to know,
Can it be death? And do they only stand
By ignorance, is that their happy state,
The proof of their obedience and their faith?
O fair foundation laid whereon to build
Their ruin! Hence I will excite their minds
With more desire to know, and to reject
Envious commands, invented with design
To keep them low whom knowledge might exalt
Equal with gods; aspiring to be such,
They taste and die: what likelier can ensue?
But first with narrow search I must walk round
This garden, and no corner leave unspied;
A chance but chance may lead where I may meet
Some wand'ring Spirit of heav'n, by fountain side,
Or in thick shade retired, from him to draw
What further would be learnt. Live while ye may,
Yet happy pair; enjoy, till I return,
Short pleasures, for long woes are to succeed."

* * *

To whom* thus Eve with perfect beauty adorned.
"My author and disposer, what thou bidd'st
Unargued I obey; so God ordains,
God is thy law, thou mine: to know no more
Is woman's happiest knowledge and her praise.
With thee conversing I forget all time,
All seasons and their change, all please alike.
Sweet is the breath of morn, her rising sweet,
With charm of earliest birds; pleasant the sun
When first on this delightful land he spreads
His orient beams, on herb, tree, fruit, and flow'r,

*Adam

Glist'ring with dew; fragrant the fertile earth
After soft showers; and sweet the coming on
Of grateful evening mild, then silent night
With this her solemn bird and this fair moon,
And these the gems of heav'n, her starry train:
But neither breath of morn when she ascends
With charm of earliest birds, nor rising sun
On this delightful land, nor herb, fruit, flow'r,
Glist'ring with dew, nor fragrance after showers,
Nor grateful evening mild, nor silent night
With this her solemn bird, nor walk by moon,
Or glittering starlight without thee is sweet.
But wherefore all night long shine these, for whom
This glorious sight, when sleep hath shut all eyes?"

* * *

This said unanimous, and other rites
Observing none, but adoration pure
Which God likes best, into their inmost bow'r
Handed they went; and eased the putting off
These troublesome disguises which we wear,
Straight side by side were laid, nor turned I ween
Adam from his fair spouse, nor Eve the rites
Mysterious of connubial love refused:
Whatever hypocrites austerely talk
Of purity and place and innocence,
Defaming as impure what God declares
Pure, and commands to some, leaves free to all.
Our Maker bids increase, who bids abstain
But our destroyer, foe to God and man?
Hailed wedded Love, mysterious law, true source
Of human offspring, sole propriety
In Paradise of all things common else.
By thee adulterous lust was driv'n from men
Among the bestial herds to range, by thee
Founded in reason, loyal, just, and pure,
Relations dear, and all the charities
Of father, son, and brother first were known.
Far be it, that I should write thee sin or blame,
Or think thee unbefitting holiest place,
Perpetual fountain of domestic sweets,
Whose bed is undefiled and chaste pronounced,
Present, or past, as saints and patriarchs used.
Here Love his golden shafts employs, here lights
His constant lamp, and waves his purple wings,
Reigns here and revels; not in the bought smile

Of harlots, loveless, joyless, unendeared,
Casual fruition, nor in court amours,
Mixed dance, or wanton masque, or midnight ball,
Or serenate, which the starved lover sings
To his proud fair, best quitted with disdain.
These lulled by nightingales embracing slept,
And on their naked limbs the flow'ry roof
Show'red roses, which the morn repaired. Sleep on,
Blest pair; and O yet happiest if ye seek
No happier state, and know to know no more. . . .

## *Book IX [The Fall]*

He* bolder now, uncalled before her stood;
But as in gaze admiring: oft he bowed
His turret crest, and sleek enameled neck,
Fawning, and licked the ground whereon she trod.
His gentle dumb expression turned at length
The eye of Eve to mark his play; he glad
Of her attention gained, with serpent tongue
Organic, or impulse of vocal air,
His fraudulent temptation thus began.
"Wonder not, sovran mistress, if perhaps
Thou canst, who art sole wonder, much less arm
Thy looks, the heav'n of mildness, with disdain,
Displeased that I approach thee thus, and gaze
Insatiate, I thus single, nor have feared
Thy awful brow, more awful thus retired.
Fairest resemblance of thy Maker fair,
Thee all things living gaze on, all things thine
By gift, and thy celestial beauty adore
With ravishment beheld, there best beheld
Where universally admired; but here
In this enclosure wild, these beasts among,
Beholders rude, and shallow to discern
Half what in thee is fair, one man except,
Who sees thee? (and what is one?) who shouldst be seen
A goddess among gods, adored and served
By angels numberless, thy daily train."
So glozed the Tempter, and his proem tuned;
Into the heart of Eve his words made way,
Though at the voice much marveling; at length
Not unamazed she thus in answer spake.

*Satan

"What may this mean? Language of man pronounced
By tongue of brute, and human sense expressed?
The first at least of these I thought denied
To beasts, whom God on their creation-day
Created mute to all articulate sound;
The latter I demur, for in their looks
Much reason, and in their actions oft appears.
Thee, serpent, subtlest beast of all the field
I knew, but not with human voice endued;
Redouble then this miracle, and say,
How cam'st thou speakable of mute, and how
To me so friendly grown above the rest
Of brutal kind, that daily are in sight?
Say, for such wonder claims attention due."
To whom the guileful Tempter thus replied.
"Empress of this fair world, resplendent Eve,
Easy to me it is to tell thee all
What thou command'st, and right thou shouldst be obeyed:
I was at first as other beasts that graze
The trodden herb, of abject thoughts and low,
As was my food, nor aught but food discerned
Or sex, and apprehended nothing high:
Till on a day roving the field, I chanced
A goodly tree far distant to behold
Loaden with fruit of fairest colors mixed,
Ruddy and gold: I nearer drew to gaze;
When from the boughs a savory odor blown,
Grateful to appetite, more pleased my sense
Than smell of sweetest fennel, or the teats
Of ewe or goat dropping with milk at ev'n,
Unsucked of lamb or kid, that tend their play.
To satisfy the sharp desire I had
Of tasting those fair apples, I resolved
Not to defer; hunger and thirst at once,
Powerful persuaders, quickened at the scent
Of that alluring fruit, urged me so keen.
About the mossy trunk I wound me soon,
For high from ground the branches would require
Thy utmost reach or Adam's: round the tree
All other beasts that saw, with like desire
Longing and envying stood, but could not reach.
Amid the tree now got, where plenty hung
Tempting so nigh, to pluck and eat my fill
I spared not, for such pleasure till that hour
At feed or fountain never had I found.
Sated at length, ere long I might perceive
Strange alteration in me, to degree

Of reason in my inward powers, and speech
Wanted not long, though to this shape retained.
Thenceforth to speculations high or deep
I turned my thoughts, and with capacious mind
Considered all things visible in heav'n,
Or earth, or middle, all things fair and good;
But all that fair and good in thy divine
Semblance, and in thy beauty's heav'nly ray
United I beheld; no fair to thine
Equivalent or second, which compelled
Me thus, though importune perhaps, to come
And gaze, and worship thee of right declared
Sovran of creatures, universal dame."
     So talked the spirited sly snake; and Eve
Yet more amazed unwary thus replied.
     "Serpent, thy overpraising leaves in doubt
The virtue of that fruit, in thee first proved:
But say, where grows the tree, from hence how far?
For many are the trees of God that grow
In Paradise, and various, yet unknown
To us, in such abundance lies our choice,
As leaves a greater store of fruit untouched,
Still hanging incorruptible, till men
Grow up to their provision, and more hands
Help to disburden nature of her bearth."
     To whom the wily adder, blithe and glad.
"Empress, the way is ready, and not long,
Beyond a row of myrtles, on a flat,
Fast by a fountain, one small thicket past
Of blowing myrrh and balm; if thou accept
My conduct, I can bring thee thither soon."
     "Lead then," said Eve. He leading swiftly rolled
In tangles, and made intricate seem straight,
To mischief swift. Hope elevates, and joy
Brightens his crest, as when a wand'ring fire,
Compact of unctuous vapor, which the night
Condenses, and the cold environs round,
Kindled through agitation to a flame,
Which oft, they say, some evil spirit attends,
Hovering and blazing with delusive light,
Misleads th' amazed night-wanderer from his way
To bogs and mires, and oft through pond or pool,
There swallowed up and lost, from succor far.
So glistered the dire snake, and into fraud
Led Eve our credulous mother, to the tree
Of prohibition, root of all our woe;
Which when she saw, thus to her guide she spake.

"Serpent, we might have spared our coming hither,
Fruitless to me, though fruit be here to excess,
The credit of whose virtue rest with thee,
Wondrous indeed, if cause of such effects.
But of this tree we may not taste nor touch;
God so commanded, and left that command
Sole daughter of his voice; the rest, we live
Law to ourselves, our reason is our law."
To whom the Tempter guilefully replied.
"Indeed? hath God then said that of the fruit
Of all these garden trees ye shall not eat,
Yet lords declared of all in earth or air?"
To whom thus Eve yet sinless. "Of the fruit
Of each tree in the garden we may eat,
But of the fruit of this fair tree amidst
The garden, God hath said, 'Ye shall not eat
Thereof, nor shall ye touch it, lest ye die.'"
She scarce had said, though brief, when now more bold
The Tempter, but with show of zeal and love
To man, and indignation at his wrong,
New part puts on, and as to passion moved,
Fluctuates disturbed, yet comely, and in act
Raised, as of some great matter to begin.
As when of old some orator renowned
In Athens or free Rome, where eloquence
Flourished, since mute, to some great cause addressed,
Stood in himself collected, while each part,
Motion, each act won audience ere the tongue,
Sometimes in highth began, as no delay
Of preface brooking through his zeal of right.
So standing, moving, or to highth upgrown
The Tempter all impassioned thus began.
"O sacred, wise, and wisdom-giving plant,
Mother of science, now I feel thy power
Within me clear, not only to discern
Things in their causes, but to trace the ways
Of highest agents, deemed however wise.
Queen of this universe, do not believe
Those rigid threats of death; ye shall not die:
How should ye? By the fruit? It gives you life
To knowledge. By the Threat'ner? Look on me,
Me who have touched and tasted, yet both live,
And life more perfect have attained than fate
Meant me, by vent'ring higher than my lot.
Shall that be shut to man, which to the beast
Is open? Or will God incense his ire
For such a petty trespass, and not praise

Rather your dauntless virtue, whom the pain
Of death denounced, whatever thing death be,
Deterred not from achieving what might lead
To happier life, knowledge of good and evil;
Of good, how just? Of evil, if what is evil
Be real, why not known, since easier shunned?
God therefore cannot hurt ye, and be just;
Not just, not God; not feared then, nor obeyed:
Your fear itself of death removes the fear.
Why then was this forbid? Why but to awe,
Why but to keep ye low and ignorant,
His worshipers; he knows that in the day
Ye eat thereof, your eyes that seem so clear,
Yet are but dim, shall perfectly be then
Opened and cleared, and ye shall be as gods,
Knowing both good and evil as they know.
That ye should be as gods, since I as man,
Internal man, is but proportion meet,
I of brute human, ye of human gods.
So ye shall die perhaps, by putting off
Human, to put on gods, death to be wished,
Though threatened, which no worse than this can bring.
And what are gods that man may not become
As they, participating godlike food?
The gods are first, and that advantage use
On our belief, that all from them proceeds;
I question it, for this fair earth I see,
Warmed by the sun, producing every kind,
Them nothing: if they all things, who enclosed
Knowledge of good and evil in this tree,
That whoso eats thereof, forthwith attains
Wisdom without their leave? And wherein lies
Th' offense, that man should thus attain to know?
What can your knowledge hurt him, or this tree
Impart against his will if all be his?
Or is it envy, and can envy dwell
In heav'nly breasts? These, these and many more
Causes import your need of this fair fruit.
Goddess humane, reach then, and freely taste."

He ended, and his words replete with guile
Into her heart too easy entrance won:
Fixed on the fruit she gazed, which to behold
Might tempt alone, and in her ears the sound
Yet rung of his persuasive words, impregned
With reason, to her seeming, and with truth;
Meanwhile the hour of noon drew on, and waked
An eager appetite, raised by the smell

So savory of that fruit, which with desire,
Inclinable now grown to touch or taste,
Solicited her longing eye; yet first
Pausing a while, thus to herself she mused:
"Great are thy virtues, doubtless, best of fruits,
Though kept from man, and worthy to be admired,
Whose taste, too long forborne, at first assay
Gave elocution to the mute, and taught
The tongue not made for speech to speak thy praise:
Thy praise he also who forbids thy use,
Conceals not from us, naming thee the Tree
Of Knowledge, knowledge both of good and evil;
Forbids us then to taste, but his forbidding
Commends thee more, while it infers the good
By thee communicated, and our want:
For good unknown, sure is not had, or had
And yet unknown, is as not had at all.
In plain then, what forbids he but to know,
Forbids us good, forbids us to be wise?
Such prohibitions bind not. But if death
Bind us with after-bands, what profits then
Our inward freedom? In the day we eat
Of this fair fruit, our doom is, we shall die.
How dies the serpent? He hath eat'n and lives,
And knows, and speaks, and reasons, and discerns,
Irrational till then. For us alone
Was death invented? Or to us denied
This intellectual food, for beasts reserved?
For beasts it seems: yet that one beast which first
Hath tasted, envies not, but brings with joy
The good befall'n him, author unsuspect,
Friendly to man, far from deceit or guile.
What fear I then, rather what know to fear
Under this ignorance of good and evil,
Of God or death, of law or penalty?
Here grows the cure of all, this fruit divine,
Fair to the eye, inviting to the taste,
Of virtue to make wise: what hinders then
To reach, and feed at once both body and mind?"
So saying, her rash hand in evil hour
Forth reaching to the fruit, she plucked, she ate:
Earth felt the wound, and nature from her seat
Sighing through all her works gave signs of woe,
That all was lost. Back to the thicket slunk
The guilty serpent, and well might, for Eve
Intent now wholly on her taste, naught else
Regarded, such delight till then, as seemed,

In fruit she never tasted, whether true
Or fancied so, through expectation high
Of knowledge, nor was Godhead from her thought.

* * *

Thus Eve with count'nance blithe her story told;
But in her cheek distemper flushing glowed.
On th' other side, Adam, soon as he heard
The fatal trespass done by Eve, amazed,
Astonied stood and blank, while horror chill
Ran through his veins, and all his joints relaxed;
From his slack hand the garland wreathed for Eve
Down dropped, and all the faded roses shed:
Speechless he stood and pale, till thus at length
First to himself he inward silence broke.
"O fairest of creation, last and best
Of all God's works, creature in whom excelled
Whatever can to sight or thought be formed,
Holy, divine, good, amiable, or sweet!
How art thou lost, how on a sudden lost,
Defaced, deflow'red, and now to death devote?
Rather how hast thou yielded to transgress
The strict forbiddance, how to violate
The sacred fruit forbidd'n! some cursèd fraud
Of enemy hath beguiled thee, yet unknown,
And me with thee hath ruined, for with thee
Certain my resolution is to die;
How can I live without thee, how forgo
Thy sweet converse and love so dearly joined,
To live again in these wild woods forlorn?
Should God create another Eve, and I
Another rib afford, yet loss of thee
Would never from my heart; no no, I feel
The link of nature draw me: flesh of flesh,
Bone of my bone thou art, and from thy state
Mine never shall be parted, bliss or woe."
So having said, as one from sad dismay
Recomforted, and after thoughts disturbed
Submitting to what seemed remédiless,
Thus in calm mood his words to Eve he turned.
"Bold deed thou hast presumed, advent'rous Eve,
And peril great provoked, who thus hast dared
Had it been only coveting to eye
That sacred fruit, sacred to abstinence,
Much more to taste it under ban to touch.

But past who can recall, or done undo?
Not God omnipotent, nor fate; yet so
Perhaps thou shalt not die, perhaps the fact
Is not so heinous now, foretasted fruit,
Profaned first by the serpent, by him first
Made common and unhallowed ere our taste;
Nor yet on him found deadly, he yet lives,
Lives, as thou saidst, and gains to live as man
Higher degree of life, inducement strong
To us, as likely tasting to attain
Proportional ascent, which cannot be
But to be gods, or angels demi-gods.
Nor can I think that God, Creator wise,
Though threat'ning, will in earnest so destroy
Us his prime creatures, dignified so high,
Set over all his works, which in our fall,
For us created, needs with us must fail,
Dependent made; so God shall uncreate,
Be frustrate, do, undo, and labor lose,
Not well conceived of God, who though his power
Creation could repeat, yet would be loath
Us to abolish, lest the Adversary
Triumph and say; 'Fickle their state whom God
Most favors, who can please him long? Me first
He ruined, now mankind; whom will he next?'
Matter of scorn, not to be given the Foe.
However I with thee have fixed my lot,
Certain to undergo like doom; if death
Consort with thee, death is to me as life;
So forcible within my heart I feel
The bond of nature draw me to my own,
My own in thee, for what thou art is mine;
Our state cannot be severed, we are one,
One flesh; to lose thee were to lose myself."
        So Adam, and thus Eve to him replied.
"O glorious trial of exceeding love,
Illustrious evidence, example high!
Engaging me to emulate, but short
Of thy perfection, how shall I attain,
Adam, from whose dear side I boast me sprung,
And gladly of our union hear thee speak,
One heart, one soul in both; whereof good proof
This day affords, declaring thee resolved,
Rather than death or aught than death more dread
Shall separate us, linked in love so dear,
To undergo with me one guilt, one crime,

If any be, of tasting this fair fruit,
Whose virtue, for of good still good proceeds,
Direct, or by occasion hath presented
This happy trial of thy love, which else
So eminently never had been known.
Were it I thought death menaced would ensue
This my attempt, I would sustain alone
The worst, and not persuade thee, rather die
Deserted, than oblige thee with a fact
Pernicious to thy peace, chiefly assured
Remarkably so late of thy so true,
So faithful love unequaled; but I feel
Far otherwise th' event, not death, but life
Augmented, opened eyes, new hopes, new joys,
Taste so divine, that what of sweet before
Hath touched my sense, flat seems to this, and harsh.
Of my experience, Adam, freely taste,
And fear of death deliver to the winds."
　　So saying, she embraced him, and for joy
Tenderly wept, much won that he his love
Had so ennobled, as of choice to incur
Divine displeasure for her sake, or death.
In recompense (for such compliance bad
Such recompense best merits) from the bough
She gave him of that fair enticing fruit
With liberal hand: he scrupled not to eat
Against his better knowledge, not deceived,
But fondly overcome with female charm.
Earth trembled from her entrails, as again
In pangs, and nature gave a second groan;
Sky loured, and muttering thunder, some sad drops
Wept at completing of the mortal sin
Original . . .

## *Book XII [Departure from Paradise]*

Th' Archangel stood, and from the other hill
To their fixed station, all in bright array
The Cherubim descended; on the ground
Gliding metéorous, as evening mist
Ris'n from a river o'er the marish glides,
And gathers ground fast at the laborer's heel
Homeward returning. High in front advanced,
The brandished sword of God before them blazed
Fierce as a comet; which with torrid heat,

And vapor as the Libyan air adust,
Began to parch that temperate clime; whereat
In either hand the hast'ning angel caught
Our ling'ring parents, and to th' eastern gate
Led them direct, and down the cliff as fast
To the subjected plain; then disappeared.
They looking back, all th' eastern side beheld
Of Paradise, so late their happy seat,
Waved over by that flaming brand, the gate
With dreadful faces thronged and fiery arms:
Some natural tears they dropped, but wiped them soon;
The world was all before them, where to choose
Their place of rest, and Providence their guide:
They hand in hand with wand'ring steps and slow,
Through Eden took their solitary way.

## ALEXANDER POPE (1688–1744)

In terms of sheer verbal talent and brilliant artistry, Alexander Pope was the greatest English poet of the eighteenth century and indeed one of the greatest verbal geniuses in the English language. One of the tests of a writer's lasting influence is how often he or she is quoted. For speakers of English, after Shakespeare it is Pope who wins this honor, even if most of those who use Pope's lines in conversation are unaware they are quoting eighteenth-century poetry. "A little learning is a dang'rous thing"; "Hope springs eternal in the human breast"; "For fools rush in where angels fear to tred"; "To err is human; to forgive divine"; "Damn with faint praise"; "What oft was thought, but ne'er so well express'd": all of these phrases are directly quoted from Pope's poetry. They are memorable partly because they exemplify the neoclassical point of view articulated in the last of these quotations. By neoclassical standards, a poet should aim not for the Romantic and modernist virtue of originality at all costs, especially if this originality is achieved at the expense of displaying private eccentricities. Poetry more fully achieves its ends by recalling "What oft was thought, but ne'er so well express'd."

Although Pope became the most famous English poet of his time, he remained a marginal figure in many ways. First, there was the matter of his health: from his early adolescence, he suffered from diseases that left him stunted with a bent spine; at maturity, he was less than five feet tall. Second, there was his religion: a Roman Catholic in an overwhelmingly Protestant country, "Pope Alexander," as he was sometimes called, was denied many privileges, including a university education. It is an irony of English literary history that one of the most classically informed and polished of English poets never attended university. This very quality of never quite fitting into the conventional mold, however, provided Pope with a critical perspective that rendered him a particularly shrewd and brilliant satiric poet. It also gave him a natural sympathy with others who were likewise denied positions of political power and social privilege—with women, for example.

Which brings us to *Eloisa to Abelard.* Published in 1717, the materials for this poem were drawn from an English translation of a 1697 French version of the impassioned Latin correspondence between Peter Abelard and his former pupil Heloise (or Eloisa, as Pope calls her), with whom Abelard fell deeply and tragically in love. We have included the relevant portions of their original letters in this anthology (pp. 1233–1244). When they first met, Abelard was Heloise's tutor. She was about sixteen or seventeen years old; he was in his thirties. Heloise's uncle Fulbert, angered at their secret marriage, had Abelard attacked and castrated. Abelard retired to a monastic life, and Heloise became a nun. Their letters were written many years later.

Pope employs the antithetical balance of the heroic couplet, the poetic form of which he was a master, in order to register Heloise's conflicting passions. On the one hand, she wishes to devote herself fully to God and to purge herself of her physical passion for Abelard; on the other, as soon as she thinks of God she is reminded of Abelard, and her erotic passion is reignited. The poem expresses the frustrations of Heloise, who can enjoy her passion for Abelard only in her memory and imagination. Pope, whose physical limitations perhaps gave him a special insight into Heloise's frustrations, paints a sympathetic portrait of her hopeless dilemma.

Pope's poetry is often informed by the poetry of ancient Greece and Rome, particularly by Homer, whose epics Pope translated early in his career; by Horace, whose witty conversation poems became models for much of Pope's mature satirical poetry; and, most important in this case, by Ovid, whose *Heroides* (pp. 687–692), like Pope's *Eloisa to Abelard,* take the form of passionate letters written by famous women to the lovers who abandoned them.

## Eloisa to Abelard

### The Argument

Abelard *and* Eloisa *flourish'd in the twelfth Century; they were two of the most distinguish'd persons of their age in learning and beauty, but for nothing more famous than for their unfortunate passion. After a long course of Calamities, they retired each to a several Convent, and consecrated the remainder of their days to religion. It was many years after this separation, that a letter of* Abelard*'s to a Friend which contain'd the history of his misfortune, fell into the hands of* Eloisa. *This awakening all her tenderness, occasion'd those celebrated letters (out of which the following is partly extracted) which give so lively a picture of the struggles of grace and nature, virtue and passion.*

In these deep solitudes and awful cells,
Where heav'nly-pensive, contemplation dwells,
And ever-musing melancholy reigns;
What means this tumult in a Vestal's veins?
Why rove my thoughts beyond this last retreat?
Why feels my heart its long-forgotten heat?
Yet, yet I love!—From *Abelard* it came,
And *Eloisa* yet must kiss the name.
        Dear fatal name! rest ever unreveal'd,
Nor pass these lips in holy silence seal'd.

Hide it, my heart, within that close disguise,
Where, mix'd with God's, his lov'd Idea lies.
Oh write it not, my hand—The name appears
Already written—wash it out, my tears!
In vain lost *Eloisa* weeps and prays,
Her heart still dictates, and her hand obeys.
Relentless walls! whose darksom round contains
Repentant sighs, and voluntary pains:
Ye rugged rocks! which holy knees have worn;
Ye grots and caverns shagg'd with horrid thorn!
Shrines! where their vigils pale-ey'd virgins keep,
And pitying saints, whose statues learn to weep!
Tho' cold like you, unmov'd, and silent grown,
I have not yet forgot my self to stone.
All is not Heav'n's while *Abelard* has part,
Still rebel nature holds out half my heart;
Nor pray'rs nor fasts its stubborn pulse restrain,
Nor tears, for ages, taught to flow in vain.
Soon as thy letters trembling I unclose,
That well-known name awakens all my woes.
Oh name for ever sad! for ever dear!
Still breath'd in sighs, still usher'd with a tear.
I tremble too where-e'er my own I find,
Some dire misfortune follows close behind.
Line after line my gushing eyes o'erflow,
Led thro' a sad variety of woe:
Now warm in love, now with'ring in thy bloom,
Lost in a convent's solitary gloom!
There stern religion quench'd th' unwilling flame,
There dy'd the best of passions, Love and Fame.
Yet write, oh write me all, that I may join
Griefs to thy griefs, and eccho sighs to thine.
Nor foes nor fortune take this pow'r away.
And is my *Abelard* less kind than they?
Tears still are mine, and those I need not spare,
Love but demands what else were shed in pray'r;
No happier task these faded eyes pursue,
To read and weep is all they now can do.
Then share thy pain, allow that sad relief;
Ah more than share it! give me all thy grief.
Heav'n first taught letters for some wretch's aid,
Some banish'd lover, or same captive maid;
They live, they speak, they breathe what love inspires,
Warm from the soul, and faithful to its fires,
The virgin's wish without her fears impart,
Excuse the blush, and pour out all the heart,

Speed the soft intercourse from soul to soul,
And waft a sigh from *Indus* to the *Pole.*
Thou know'st how guiltless first I met thy flame,
When Love approach'd me under Friendship's name;
My fancy form'd thee of Angelick kind,
Some emanation of th' all-beauteous Mind.
Those smiling eyes, attemp'ring ev'ry ray,
Shone sweetly lambent with celestial day:
Guiltless I gaz'd; heav'n listen'd while you sung;
And truths divine came mended from that tongue.
From lips like those what precept fail'd to move?
Too soon they taught me 'twas no sin to love.
Back thro' the paths of pleasing sense I ran,
Nor wish'd an Angel whom I lov'd a Man.
Dim and remote the joys of saints I see,
Nor envy them, that heav'n I lose for thee.
How oft', when press'd to marriage, have I said,
Curse on all laws but those which love has made!
Love, free as air, at sight of human ties,
Spreads his light wings, and in a moment flies.
Let wealth, let honour, wait the wedded dame,
August her deed, and sacred be her fame;
Before true passion all those views remove,
Fame, wealth, and honour! what are you to Love?
The jealous God, when we profane his fires,
Those restless passions in revenge inspires;
And bids them make mistaken mortals groan,
Who seek in love for ought but love alone.
Should at my feet the world's great master fall,
Himself, his throne, his world, I'd scorn 'em all:
Not *Cæsar's* empress wou'd I deign to prove;
No, make me mistress to the man I love;
If there be yet another name more free,
More fond than mistress, make me that to thee!
Oh happy state! when souls each other draw,
When love is liberty, and nature, law:
All then is full, possessing, and possest,
No craving Void left aking in the breast:
Ev'n thought meets thought ere from the lips it part,
And each warm wish springs mutual from the heart.
This sure is bliss (if bliss on earth there be)
And once the lot of *Abelard* and me.
Alas how chang'd! what sudden horrors rise!
A naked Lover bound and bleeding lies!
Where, where was *Eloise?* her voice, her hand,
Her ponyard, bad oppos'd the dire command.

Barbarian stay! that bloody stroke restrain;
The crime was common, common be the pain.
I can no more; by shame, by rage supprest,
Let tears, and burning blushes speak the rest.
    Canst thou forget that sad, that solemn day,
When victims at yon' altar's foot we lay?
Canst thou forget what tears that moment fell,
When, warm in youth, I bade the world farewell?
As with cold lips I kiss'd the sacred veil,
The shrines all trembled, and the lamps grew pale:
Heav'n scarce believ'd the conquest it survey'd,
And Saints with wonder heard the vows I made.
Yet then, to those dread altars as I drew,
Not on the Cross my eyes were fix'd, but you;
Not grace, or zeal, love only was my call,
And if I lose thy love, I lose my all.
Come! with thy looks, thy words, relieve my woe;
Those still at least are left thee to bestow.
Still on that breast enamour'd let me lie,
Still drink delicious poison from thy eye,
Pant on thy lip, and to thy heart be prest;
Give all thou canst—and let me dream the rest.
Ah no! instruct me other joys to prize,
With other beauties charm my partial eyes,
Full in my view set all the bright abode,
And make my soul quit *Abelard* for God.
    Ah think at least thy flock deserves thy care,
Plants of thy hand, and children of thy pray'r.
From the false world in early youth they fled,
By thee to mountains, wilds, and deserts led.
You rais'd these hallow'd walls; the desert smil'd,
And Paradise was open'd in the Wild.
No weeping orphan saw his father's stores
Our shrines irradiate, or emblaze the floors;
No silver saints, by dying misers giv'n,
Here brib'd the rage of ill-requited heav'n:
But such plain roofs as piety could raise,
And only vocal with the Maker's praise.
In these lone walls (their day's eternal bound)
These moss-grown domes with spiry turrets crown'd,
Where awful arches make a noon-day night,
And the dim windows shed a solemn light;
Thy eyes diffus'd a reconciling ray,
And gleams of glory brighten'd all the day.
But now no face divine contentment wears,
'Tis all blank sadness, or continual tears.

See how the force of others' pray'rs I try,
(Oh pious fraud of am'rous charity!)
But why should I on others' pray'rs depend?
Come thou, my father, brother, husband, friend!
Ah let thy handmaid, sister, daughter move,
And, all those tender names in one, thy love!
The darksom pines that o'er yon' rocks reclin'd
Wave high, and murmur to the hollow wind,
The wandring streams that shine between the hills,
The grots that eccho to the tinkling rills,
The dying gales that pant upon the trees,
The lakes that quiver to the curling breeze;
No more these scenes my meditation aid,
Or lull to rest the visionary maid:
But o'er the twilight groves, and dusky caves,
Long-sounding isles, and intermingled graves,
Black Melancholy sits, and round her throws
A death-like silence, and a dread repose:
Her gloomy presence saddens all the scene,
Shades ev'ry flow'r, and darkens ev'ry green,
Deepens the murmur of the falling floods,
And breathes a browner horror on the woods.
Yet here for ever, ever must I stay;
Sad proof how well a lover can obey!
Death, only death, can break the lasting chain;
And here ev'n then, shall my cold dust remain,
Here all its frailties, all its flames resign,
And wait, till 'tis no sin to mix with thine.
Ah wretch! believ'd the spouse of God in vain,
Confess'd within the slave of love and man.
Assist me heav'n! but whence arose that pray'r?
Sprung it from piety, or from despair?
Ev'n here, where frozen chastity retires,
Love finds an altar for forbidden fires.
I ought to grieve, but cannot what I ought;
I mourn the lover, not lament the fault;
I view my crime, but kindle at the view,
Repent old pleasures, and sollicit new:
Now turn'd to heav'n, I weep my past offence,
Now think of thee, and curse my innocence.
Of all affliction taught a lover yet,
'Tis sure the hardest science to forget!
How shall I lose the sin, yet keep the sense,
And love th' offender, yet detest th' offence?
How the dear object from the crime remove,
Or how distinguish penitence from love?

Unequal task! a passion to resign,
For hearts so touch'd, so pierc'd, so lost as mine.
Ere such a soul regains its peaceful state,
How often must it love, how often hate!
How often, hope, despair, resent, regret,
Conceal, disdain—do all things but forget.
But let heav'n seize it, all at once 'tis fir'd,
Not touch'd, but rapt; not waken'd, but inspir'd!
Oh come! oh teach me nature to subdue,
Renounce my love, my life, my self—and you.
Fill my fond heart with God alone, for he
Alone can rival, can succeed to thee.

How happy is the blameless Vestal's lot!
The world forgetting, by the world forgot.
Eternal sun-shine of the spotless mind!
Each pray'r accepted, and each wish resign'd;
Labour and rest, that equal periods keep;
'Obedient slumbers that can wake and weep';
Desires compos'd, affections ever ev'n,
Tears that delight, and sighs that waft to heav'n.
Grace shines around her with serenest beams,
And whisp'ring Angels prompt her golden dreams.
For her th' unfading rose of *Eden* blooms,
And wings of Seraphs shed divine perfumes;
For her the Spouse prepares the bridal ring,
For her white virgins *Hymenæals* sing;
To sounds of heav'nly harps, she dies away,
And melts in visions of eternal day.

Far other dreams my erring soul employ,
Far other raptures, of unholy joy:
When at the close of each sad, sorrowing day,
Fancy restores what vengeance snatch'd away,
Then conscience sleeps, and leaving nature free,
All my loose soul unbounded springs to thee.
O curst, dear horrors of all-conscious night!
How glowing guilt exalts the keen delight!
Provoking Dæmons all restraint remove,
And stir within me ev'ry source of love.
I hear thee, view thee, gaze o'er all thy charms,
And round thy phantom glue my clasping arms.
I wake—no more I hear, no more I view,
The phantom flies me, as unkind as you.
I call aloud; it hears not what I say;
I stretch my empty arms; it glides away:
To dream once more I close my willing eyes;
Ye soft illusions, dear deceits, arise!

Alas no more!—methinks we wandring go
Thro' dreary wastes, and weep each other's woe;
Where round some mould'ring tow'r pale ivy creeps,
And low-brow'd rocks hang nodding o'er the deeps.
Sudden you mount! you becken from the skies;
Clouds interpose, waves roar, and winds arise.
I shriek, start up, the same sad prospect find,
And wake to all the griefs I left behind.
    For thee the fates, severely kind, ordain
A cool suspense from pleasure and from pain;
Thy life a long, dead calm of fix'd repose;
No pulse that riots, and no blood that glows.
Still as the sea, ere winds were taught to blow,
Or moving spirit bade the waters flow;
Soft as the slumbers of a saint forgiv'n,
And mild as opening gleams of promis'd heav'n.
    Come *Abelard!* for what hast thou to dread?
The torch of *Venus* burns not for the dead;
Nature stands check'd; Religion disapproves;
Ev'n thou art cold—yet *Eloisa* loves.
Ah hopeless, lasting flames! like those that burn
To light the dead, and warm th' unfruitful urn.
    What scenes appear where-e'er I turn my view!
The dear Ideas, where I fly, pursue,
Rise in the grove, before the altar rise,
Stain all my soul, and wanton in my eyes!
I waste the Matin lamp in sighs for thee,
Thy image steals between my God and me,
Thy voice I seem in ev'ry hymn to hear,
With ev'ry bead I drop too soft a tear.
When from the Censer clouds of fragrance roll,
And swelling organs lift the rising soul;
One thought of thee puts all the pomp to flight,
Priests, Tapers, Temples, swim before my sight:
In seas of flame my plunging soul is drown'd,
While Altars blaze, and Angels tremble round.
    While prostrate here in humble grief I lie,
Kind, virtuous drops just gath'ring in my eye,
While praying, trembling, in the dust I roll,
And dawning grace is opening on my soul:
Come, if thou dar'st, all charming as thou art!
Oppose thy self to heav'n; dispute my heart;
Come, with one glance of those deluding eyes,
Blot out each bright Idea of the skies.
Take back that grace, those sorrows, and those tears,
Take back my fruitless penitence and pray'rs,

Snatch me, just mounting, from the blest abode,
Assist the Fiends and tear me from my God!
No, fly me, fly me! far as Pole from Pole;
Rise *Alps* between us! and whole oceans roll!
Ah come not, write not, think not once of me,
Nor share one pang of all I felt for thee.
Thy oaths I quit, thy memory resign,
Forget, renounce me, hate whate'er was mine.
Fair eyes, and tempting looks (which yet I view!)
Long lov'd, ador'd ideas! all adieu!
O grace serene! oh virtue heav'nly fair!
Divine oblivion of low-thoughted care!
Fresh blooming hope, gay daughter of the sky!
And faith, our early immortality!
Enter each mild, each amicable guest;
Receive, and wrap me in eternal rest!
See in her Cell sad *Eloisa* spread,
Propt on some tomb, a neighbour of the dead!
In each low wind methinks a Spirit calls,
And more than Echoes talk along the walls.
Here, as I watch'd the dying lamps around,
From yonder shrine I heard a hollow sound.
Come, sister come! (it said, or seem'd to say)
Thy place is here, sad sister come away!
Once like thy self, I trembled, wept, and pray'd,
Love's victim then, tho' now a sainted maid:
But all is calm in this eternal sleep;
Here grief forgets to groan, and love to weep,
Ev'n superstition loses ev'ry fear;
For God, not man, absolves our frailties here.
I come, I come! prepare your roseate bow'rs,
Celestial palms, and ever-blooming flow'rs.
Thither, where sinners may have rest, I go,
Where flames refin'd in breasts seraphic glow.
Thou, *Abelard!* the last sad office pay,
And smooth my passage to the realms of day:
See my lips tremble, and my eye-balls roll,
Suck my last breath, and catch my flying soul!
Ah no—in sacred vestments may'st thou stand,
The hallow'd taper trembling in thy hand,
Present the Cross before my lifted eye,
Teach me at once, and learn of me to die.
Ah then, thy once-lov'd *Eloisa* see!
It will be then no crime to gaze on me.
See from my cheek the transient roses fly!
See the last sparkle languish in my eye!

Till ev'ry motion, pulse, and breath, be o'er;
And ev'n my *Abelard* be lov'd no more.
O death all-eloquent! you only prove
What dust we doat on, when 'tis man we love.
Then too, when fate shall thy fair frame destroy,
(That cause of all my guilt, and all my joy)
In trance extatic may thy pangs be drown'd,
Bright clouds descend, and Angels watch thee round,
From opening skies may streaming glories shine,
And Saints embrace thee with a love like mine.
May one kind grave unite each hapless name,
And graft my love immortal on thy fame.
Then, ages hence, when all my woes are o'er,
When this rebellious heart shall beat no more;
If ever chance two wand'ring lovers brings
To *Paraclete*'s white walls, and silver springs,
O'er the pale marble shall they join their heads,
And drink the falling tears each other sheds,
Then sadly say, with mutual pity mov'd,
Oh may we never love as these have lov'd!
From the full quire when loud *Hosanna*'s rise,
And swell the pomp of dreadful sacrifice,
Amid that scene, if some relenting eye
Glance on the stone where our cold reliques lie,
Devotion's self shall steal a thought from heav'n,
One human tear shall drop, and be forgiv'n.
And sure if fate some future Bard shall join
In sad similitude of griefs to mine,
Condemn'd whole years in absence to deplore,
And image charms he must behold no more,
Such if there be, who loves so long, so well;
Let him our sad, our tender story tell;
The well-sung woes will sooth my pensive ghost;
He best can paint 'em, who shall feel 'em most.

## Jane Austen (1775–1817)

Jane Austen raised the realistic novel to a stage of unprecedented perfection in England. Out of the demise of medieval Romance and Renaissance prose narrative, the European novel emerged in the eighteenth century. The best-known English novelists of the eighteenth century are Henry Fielding, Daniel Defoe, and Samuel Richardson. Austen's work does not much resemble theirs. Her social comedy and irony are lighter in touch than Fielding's rollicking picaresque; indeed, one must read our selection from *Pride and Prejudice* very carefully to register Austen's gentle but pervasive satiric understatement. If she shares a kinship with any of her male predecessors, it is with the psychological insight of Richardson's cautionary tales of virtuous maidens beset by ardent but not overscrupulous lovers. In Austen's hands, this "conduct-book" approach grew into an elegant comedy of manners that exposed the political and economic underpinnings of polite English society. She created a prose as incisive as it is lucid and graceful to match the world she depicted.

In fact, the majority of novelists in eighteenth-century England were women. As Samuel Johnson remarked, by the eighteenth century "the revolution of years" had "produced a generation of Amazons of the pen, who with the spirit of their predecessors have set masculine tyranny at defiance."* Although the modest and well-balanced Jane Austen might well have found her beloved Dr. Johnson's phrase somewhat histrionic, she was herself to become one of the "Amazons of the pen." Austen published her novels in the early nineteenth century during the start of the Romantic period in England, but her moral outlook was resolutely a product of the eighteenth century. In her portrait of Marianne Dashwood in her first novel, *Sense and Sensibility* (1811), Austen pointed out the dangers of abandoning one's mind and soul to "sensibility," that is, to powerful feeling for its own sake divorced from "sense" or reason, in the manner of Rousseau. If, for the more romantic Rousseau, human beings are stifled and constricted by the societies and institutions in which they unhappily find themselves, Austen's normative characters do not yearn for isolation. They are social creatures, deeply and necessarily embedded in their social contexts.

*Pride and Prejudice* was published in 1813. In the combined portraits of the spirited Elizabeth Bennet and her more temperate and accepting sister Jane, we might see something of Jane Austen's own wit, independence, moral courage, and strength of character. The central plot of the novel treats the romantic relationship between Elizabeth, one of five marriageable Bennet sisters, and Fitzwilliam Darcy. The early chapters of the novel, which trace the beginning of this at-first unlikely relationship that ultimately ends in marriage, are excerpted here. The aristocratic and haughty Darcy comes to admire the middle-class Elizabeth for her character rather than her birth. It is a marriage that mirrors the rise of the democratic form of the novel over the more aristocratic genres of epic and romance. As his love for Elizabeth moves Darcy beyond his pride, Elizabeth's for Darcy moves her beyond her prejudice against him, a prejudice that has some basis in fact but that is the product largely of rumor and false impressions. It is a story not of Romantic extremes but of exquisite balances.

---

**Adventurer*, No. 115, December 11, 1753.

## *Pride and Prejudice*

### Chapter I.

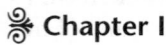

It is a truth universally acknowledged, that a single man in possession of a good fortune, must be in want of a wife.

However little known the feelings or views of such a man may be on his first entering a neighbourhood, this truth is so well fixed in the minds of the surrounding families, that he is considered as the rightful property of some one or other of their daughters.

"My dear Mr. Bennet," said his lady to him one day, "have you heard that Netherfield Park is let at last?"

Mr. Bennet replied that he had not.

"But it is," returned she; "for Mrs. Long has just been here, and she told me all about it."

Mr. Bennet made no answer.

"Do not you want to know who has taken it?" cried his wife impatiently.

"*You* want to tell me, and I have no objection to hearing it."

This was invitation enough.

"Why, my dear, you must know, Mrs. Long says that Netherfield is taken by a young man of large fortune from the north of England; that he came down on Monday in a chaise and four to see the place, and was so much delighted with it that he agreed with Mr. Morris immediately; that he is to take possession before Michaelmas, and some of his servants are to be in the house by the end of next week."

"What is his name?"

"Bingley."

"Is he married or single?"

"Oh! single, my dear, to be sure! A single man of large fortune; four or five thousand a year. What a fine thing for our girls!"

"How so? how can it affect them?"

"My dear Mr. Bennet," replied his wife, "how can you be so tiresome! You must know that I am thinking of his marrying one of them."

"Is that his design in settling here?"

"Design! nonsense, how can you talk so! But it is very likely that he *may* fall in love with one of them, and therefore you must visit him as soon as he comes."

"I see no occasion for that. You and the girls may go, or you may send them by themselves, which perhaps will be still better, for as you are as handsome as any of them, Mr. Bingley might like you the best of the party."

"My dear, you flatter me. I certainly *have* had my share of beauty, but I do not pretend to be any thing extraordinary now. When a woman has five grown up daughters, she ought to give over thinking of her own beauty."

"In such cases, a woman has not often much beauty to think of."

"But, my dear, you must indeed go and see Mr. Bingley when he comes into the neighbourhood."

"It is more than I engage for, I assure you."

"But consider your daughters. Only think what an establishment it would be for one of them. Sir William and Lady Lucas are determined to go, merely on that account, for in general you know they visit no new comers. Indeed you must go, for it will be impossible for *us* to visit him, if you do not."

"You are over scrupulous surely. I dare say Mr. Bingley will be very glad to see you; and I will send a few lines by you to assure him of my hearty consent to his marrying which ever he chuses of the girls; though I must throw in a good word for my little Lizzy."

"I desire you will do no such thing. Lizzy is not a bit better than the others; and I am sure she is not half so handsome as Jane, nor half so good humoured as Lydia. But you are always giving *her* the preference."

"They have none of them much to recommend them," replied he; "they are all silly and ignorant like other girls; but Lizzy has something more of quickness than her sisters."

"Mr. Bennet, how can you abuse your own children in such a way? You take delight in vexing me. You have no compassion on my poor nerves."

"You mistake me, my dear. I have a high respect for your nerves. They are my old friends. I have heard you mention them with consideration these twenty years at least."

"Ah! you do not know what I suffer."

"But I hope you will get over it, and live to see many young men of four thousand a year come into the neighbourhood."

"It will be no use to us, if twenty such should come since you will not visit them."

"Depend upon it, my dear, that when there are twenty, I will visit them all."

Mr. Bennet was so odd a mixture of quick parts, sarcastic humour, reserve, and caprice, that the experience of three and twenty years had been insufficient to make his wife understand his character. *Her* mind was less difficult to develope. She was a woman of mean understanding, little information, and uncertain temper. When she was discontented she fancied herself nervous. The business of her life was to get her daughters married; its solace was visiting and news.

## Chapter II.

Mr. Bennet was among the earliest of those who waited on Mr. Bingley. He had always intended to visit him, though to the last always assuring his wife that he should not go; and till the evening after the visit was paid, she had no knowledge of it. It was then disclosed in the following manner. Observing his second daughter employed in trimming a hat, he suddenly addressed her with,

"I hope Mr. Bingley will like it Lizzy."

"We are not in a way to know *what* Mr. Bingley likes," said her mother resentfully, "since we are not to visit."

"But you forget, mama," said Elizabeth, "that we shall meet him at the assemblies, and that Mrs. Long has promised to introduce him."

"I do not believe Mrs. Long will do any such thing. She has two nieces of her own. She is a selfish, hypocritical woman, and I have no opinion of her."

"No more have I," said Mr. Bennet; "and I am glad to find that you do not depend on her serving you."

Mrs. Bennet deigned not to make any reply; but unable to contain herself, began scolding one of her daughters.

"Don't keep coughing so, Kitty, for heaven's sake! Have a little compassion on my nerves. You tear them to pieces."

"Kitty has no discretion in her coughs," said her father; "she times them ill."

"I do not cough for my own amusement," replied Kitty fretfully.

"When is your next ball to be, Lizzy?"

"To-morrow fortnight."

"Aye, so it is," cried her mother, "and Mrs. Long does not come back till the day before; so, it will be impossible for her to introduce him, for she will not know him herself."

"Then, my dear, you may have the advantage of your friend, and introduce Mr. Bingley to *her.*"

"Impossible, Mr. Bennet, impossible, when I am not acquainted with him myself; how can you be so teazing?"

"I honour your circumspection. A fortnight's acquaintance is certainly very little. One cannot know what a man really is by the end of a fortnight. But if *we* do not venture, somebody else will; and after all, Mrs. Long and her nieces must stand their chance; and therefore, as she will think it an act of kindness, if you decline the office, I will take it on myself."

The girls stared at their father. Mrs. Bennet said only, "Nonsense, nonsense!"

"What can be the meaning of that emphatic exclamation?" cried he. "Do you consider the forms of introduction, and the stress that is laid on them, as nonsense? I cannot quite agree with you *there.* What say you, Mary? for you are a young lady of deep reflection I know, and read great books, and make extracts."

Mary wished to say something very sensible, but knew not how.

"While Mary is adjusting her ideas," he continued, "let us return to Mr. Bingley."

"I am sick of Mr. Bingley," cried his wife.

"I am sorry to hear *that;* but why did not you tell me so before? If I had known as much this morning, I certainly would not have called on him. It is very unlucky; but as I have actually paid the visit, we cannot escape the acquaintance now."

The astonishment of the ladies was just what he wished; that of Mrs. Bennet perhaps surpassing the rest; though when the first tumult of joy was over, she began to declare that it was what she had expected all the while.

"How good it was in you, my dear Mr. Bennet! But I knew I should persuade you at last. I was sure you loved your girls too well to neglect such an acquaintance. Well, how pleased I am! and it is such a good joke, too, that you should have gone this morning, and never said a word about it till now."

"Now, Kitty, you may cough as much as you chuse," said Mr. Bennet; and, as he spoke, he left the room, fatigued with the raptures of his wife.

"What an excellent father you have, girls," said she, when the door was shut. "I do not know how you will ever make him amends for his kindness; or me either, for that matter. At our time of life, it is not so pleasant I can tell you, to be making new acquaintances every day; but for your sakes, we would do any thing. Lydia, my love, though you *are* the youngest, I dare say Mr. Bingley will dance with you at the next ball."

"Oh!" said Lydia stoutly, "I am not afraid; for though I *am* the youngest, I'm the tallest."

The rest of the evening was spent in conjecturing how soon he would return Mr. Bennet's visit, and determining when they should ask him to dinner.

## Chapter III.

Not all that Mrs. Bennet, however, with the assistance of her five daughters, could ask on the subject was sufficient to draw from her husband any satisfactory description of Mr. Bingley. They attacked him in various ways; with barefaced questions, ingenious suppositions, and distant surmises; but he eluded the skill of them all; and they were at last obliged to accept the second-hand intelligence of their neighbour Lady Lucas. Her report was highly favourable. Sir William had been delighted with him. He was quite young, wonderfully handsome, extremely agreeable, and to crown the whole, he meant to be at the next assembly with a large party. Nothing could be more delightful! To be fond of dancing was a certain step towards falling in love; and very lively hopes of Mr. Bingley's heart were entertained.

"If I can but see one of my daughters happily settled at Netherfield," said Mrs. Bennet to her husband, "and all the others equally well married, I shall have nothing to wish for."

In a few days Mr. Bingley returned Mr. Bennet's visit, and sat about ten minutes with him in his library. He had entertained hopes of being admitted to a sight of the young ladies, of whose beauty he had heard much; but he saw only the father. The ladies were somewhat more fortunate, for they had the advantage of ascertaining from an upper window, that he wore a blue coat and rode a black horse.

An invitation to dinner was soon afterwards dispatched; and already had Mrs. Bennet planned the courses that were to do credit to her housekeeping, when an answer arrived which deferred it all. Mr. Bingley was obliged to be in town the following day, and consequently unable to accept the honour of their invitation, &c. Mrs. Bennet was quite disconcerted. She could not imagine what business he could have in town so soon after his arrival in Hertfordshire; and she began to fear that he might be always flying about from one place to another, and never settled at Netherfield as he ought to be. Lady Lucas quieted her fears a little by starting the idea of his being gone to London only to get a large party for the ball; and a report soon followed that Mr. Bingley was to bring twelve ladies and seven gentlemen with him to the assembly. The girls grieved over such a number of ladies; but were comforted the day before the ball by hearing, that instead of twelve, he had brought only six with him from London, his five sisters and a cousin. And when the party entered the assembly room, it consisted of only five altogether; Mr. Bingley, his two sisters, the husband of the eldest, and another young man.

Mr. Bingley was good looking and gentlemanlike; he had a pleasant countenance, and easy, unaffected manners. His sisters were fine women, with an air of decided fashion. His brother-in-law, Mr. Hurst, merely looked the gentleman; but his friend Mr. Darcy soon drew the attention of the room by his fine, tall person, handsome features, noble mien; and the report which was in general circulation within five minutes after his entrance, of his having ten thousand a year. The gentlemen pronounced him to be a fine figure of a man, the ladies declared he was much handsomer than Mr. Bingley, and he was looked at with great admiration for about half the evening, till his manners gave a disgust which turned the tide of his popularity; for he was discovered to be proud, to be above his company, and above being pleased; and not all his large estate in Derbyshire could then save him from having a most forbidding, disagreeable countenance, and being unworthy to be compared with his friend.

Mr. Bingley had soon made himself acquainted with all the principal people in the room; he was lively and unreserved, danced every dance, was angry that the ball closed so early, and talked of giving one himself at Netherfield. Such amiable qualities must speak for themselves. What a contrast between him and his friend! Mr. Darcy danced only once with Mrs. Hurst and once with Miss Bingley, declined being introduced to any other lady, and spent the rest of the evening in walking about the room, speaking occasionally to one of his own party. His character was decided. He was the proudest, most disagreeable man in the world, and every body hoped that he would never come there again. Amongst the most violent against him was Mrs. Bennet, whose dislike of his general behaviour, was sharpened into particular resentment, by his having slighted one of her daughters.

Elizabeth Bennet had been obliged, by the scarcity of gentlemen, to sit down for two dances; and during part of that time, Mr. Darcy had been standing near enough for her to overhear a conversation between him and Mr. Bingley, who came from the dance for a few minutes, to press his friend to join it.

"Come, Darcy," said he, "I must have you dance. I hate to see you standing about by yourself in this stupid manner. You had much better dance."

"I certainly shall not. You know how I detest it, unless I am particularly acquainted with my partner. At such an assembly as this, it would be insupportable. Your sisters are engaged, and there is not another woman in the room, whom it would not be a punishment to me to stand up with."

"I would not be so fastidious as you are," cried Bingley, "for a kingdom! Upon my honour, I never met with so many pleasant girls in my life, as I have this evening; and there are several of them you see uncommonly pretty."

"*You* are dancing with the only handsome girl in the room," said Mr. Darcy, looking at the eldest Miss Bennet.

"Oh! she is the most beautiful creature I ever beheld! But there is one of her sisters sitting down just behind you, who is very pretty, and I dare say, very agreeable. Do let me ask my partner to introduce you."

"Which do you mean?" and turning round, he looked for a moment at Elizabeth, till catching her eye, he withdrew his own and coldly said, "She is tolerable; but not handsome enough to tempt *me;* and I am in no humour at present to give consequence to young ladies who are slighted by other men. You had better return to your partner and enjoy her smiles, for you are wasting your time with me."

Mr. Bingley followed his advice. Mr. Darcy walked off; and Elizabeth remained with no very cordial feelings towards him. She told the story however with great spirit among her friends; for she had a lively, playful disposition, which delighted in any thing ridiculous.

The evening altogether passed off pleasantly to the whole family. Mrs. Bennet had seen her eldest daughter much admired by the Netherfield party. Mr. Bingley had danced with her twice, and she had been distinguished by his sisters. Jane was as much gratified by this, as her mother could be, though in a quieter way. Elizabeth felt Jane's pleasure. Mary had heard herself mentioned to Miss Bingley as the most accomplished girl in the neighbourhood; and Catherine and Lydia had been fortunate enough to be never without partners, which was all that they had yet learnt to care for at a ball. They returned therefore in good spirits to Longbourn, the village where they lived, and of which they were the principal inhabitants. They found Mr. Bennet still up. With a book he was regardless of time; and on the present occasion he had a good deal of curiosity as to the event of an evening which had raised such splendid expectations. He had rather hoped that all his wife's views on the stranger would be disappointed; but he soon found that he had a very different story to hear.

"Oh! my dear Mr. Bennet," as she entered the room, "we have had a most delightful evening, a most excellent ball. I wish you had been there. Jane was so admired, nothing could be like it. Every body said how well she looked; and Mr. Bingley thought her quite beautiful, and danced with her twice. Only think of *that* my dear; he actually danced with her twice; and she was the only creature in the room that he asked a second time. First of all, he asked Miss Lucas. I was so vexed to see him stand up with her; but, however, he did not admire her at all: indeed, nobody can, you know; and he seemed quite struck with Jane as she was going down the dance. So, he enquired who she was, and got introduced, and asked her for the two next. Then, the two third he danced with Miss King, and the two fourth with Maria Lucas, and the two fifth with Jane again, and the two sixth with Lizzy, and the Boulanger—"

"If he had had any compassion for *me*," cried her husband impatiently, "he would not have danced half so much! For God's sake, say no more of his partners. Oh! that he had sprained his ancle in the first dance!"

"Oh! my dear," continued Mrs. Bennet, "I am quite delighted with him. He is so excessively handsome! and his sisters are charming women. I never in my life saw any thing more elegant than their dresses. I dare say the lace upon Mrs. Hurst's gown—"

Here she was interrupted again. Mr. Bennet protested against any description of finery. She was therefore obliged to seek another branch of the subject, and related, with much bitterness of spirit and some exaggeration, the shocking rudeness of Mr. Darcy.

"But I can assure you," she added, "that Lizzy does not lose much by not suiting *his* fancy; for he is a most disagreeable, horrid man, not at all worth pleasing. So high and so conceited that there was no enduring him! He walked here, and he walked there, fancying himself so very great! Not handsome enough to dance with! I wish you had been there, my dear, to have given him one of your set downs. I quite detest the man."

## Chapter IV.

When Jane and Elizabeth were alone, the former, who had been cautious in her praise of Mr. Bingley before, expressed to her sister how very much she admired him.

"He is just what a young man ought to be," said she, "sensible, good humoured, lively; and I never saw such happy manners!—so much ease, with such perfect good breeding!"

"He is also handsome," replied Elizabeth, "which a young man ought likewise to be, if he possibly can. His character is thereby complete."

"I was very much flattered by his asking me to dance a second time. I did not expect such a compliment."

"Did not you? *I* did for you. But that is one great difference between us. Compliments always take *you* by surprise, and *me* never. What could be more natural than his asking you again? He could not help seeing that you were about five times as pretty as every other woman in the room. No thanks to his gallantry for that. Well, he certainly is very agreeable, and I give you leave to like him. You have liked many a stupider person."

"Dear Lizzy!"

"Oh! you are a great deal too apt you know, to like people in general. You never see a fault in any body. All the world are good and agreeable in your eyes. I never heard you speak ill of a human being in my life."

"I would wish not to be hasty in censuring any one; but I always speak what I think."

"I know you do; and it is *that* which makes the wonder. With *your* good sense, to be so honestly blind to the follies and nonsense of others! Affectation of candour is common enough;—one meets it every where. But to be candid without ostentation or design—to take the good of every body's character and make it still better, and say nothing of the bad—belongs to you alone. And so, you like this man's sisters too, do you? Their manners are not equal to his."

"Certainly not; at first. But they are very pleasing women when you converse with them. Miss Bingley is to live with her brother and keep his house; and I am much mistaken if we shall not find a very charming neighbour in her."

Elizabeth listened in silence, but was not convinced: their behaviour at the assembly had not been calculated to please in general; and with more quickness of observation and less pliancy of temper than her sister, and with a judgment too unassailed by any attention to herself, she was very little disposed to approve them. They were in fact very fine ladies; not deficient in good humour when they were pleased, nor in the power of being agreeable where they chose it; but proud and conceited. They were rather handsome, had been educated in one of the first private seminaries in town, had a fortune of twenty thousand pounds, were in the habit of spending more than they ought, and of associating with people of rank; and were therefore in every respect entitled to think well of themselves, and meanly of others. They were of a respectable family in the north of England; a circumstance more deeply impressed on their memories than that their brother's fortune and their own had been acquired by trade.

Mr. Bingley inherited property to the amount of nearly a hundred thousand pounds from his father, who had intended to purchase an estate, but did not live to do it.—Mr. Bingley intended it likewise, and sometimes made choice of his county; but as he was now provided with a good house and the liberty of a manor, it was doubtful to many of those who best knew the easiness of his temper, whether he might not spend the remainder of his days at Netherfield, and leave the next generation to purchase.

His sisters were very anxious for his having an estate of his own; but though he was now established only as a tenant, Miss Bingley was by no means unwilling to preside at his table, nor was Mrs. Hurst, who had married a man of more fashion than fortune, less disposed to consider his house as her home when it suited her. Mr. Bingley had not been of age two years, when he was tempted by an accidental recommendation to look at Netherfield House. He did look at it and into it for half an hour, was pleased with the situation and the principal rooms, satisfied with what the owner said in its praise, and took it immediately.

Between him and Darcy there was a very steady friendship, in spite of a great opposition of character.—Bingley was endeared to Darcy by the easiness, openness, ductility of his temper, though no disposition could offer a greater contrast to his own, and though with his own he never appeared dissatisfied. On the strength of Darcy's regard Bingley had the firmest reliance, and of his judgment the highest opinion. In understanding Darcy was the superior. Bingley was by no means deficient, but Darcy was clever. He was at the same time haughty, reserved, and fastidious, and his manners, though well bred, were not inviting. In that respect his friend had greatly the advantage. Bingley was sure of being liked wherever he appeared, Darcy was continually giving offence.

The manner in which they spoke of the Meryton assembly was sufficiently characteristic. Bingley had never met with pleasanter people or prettier girls in his life; every body had been most kind and attentive to him, there had been no formality, no stiffness, he had soon felt acquainted with all the room; and as to Miss Bennet, he could not conceive an angel more beautiful. Darcy, on the contrary, had seen a collection of people in whom there was little beauty and no fashion, for none of whom he had felt the smallest interest, and from none received either attention or pleasure. Miss Bennet he acknowledged to be pretty, but she smiled too much.

Mrs. Hurst and her sister allowed it to be so—but still they admired her and liked her, and pronounced her to be a sweet girl, and one whom they should not object to know more of. Miss Bennet was therefore established as a sweet girl, and their brother felt authorised by such commendation to think of her as he chose.

## Chapter V.

Within a short walk of Longbourn lived a family with whom the Bennets were particularly intimate. Sir William Lucas had been formerly in trade in Meryton, where he had made a tolerable fortune and risen to the honour of knighthood by an address to the King, during his mayoralty. The distinction had perhaps been felt too strongly. It had given him a disgust to his business and to his residence in a small market town; and quitting them both, he had removed with his family to a house about a mile from Meryton, denominated from that period Lucas Lodge, where he could think with pleasure of his own importance, and unshackled by business, occupy himself solely in being civil to all the world. For though elated by his rank, it did not render him supercilious; on the contrary, he was all attention to every body. By nature inoffensive, friendly and obliging, his presentation at St. James's had made him courteous.

Lady Lucas was a very good kind of woman, not too clever to be a valuable neighbour to Mrs. Bennet.—They had several children. The eldest of them, a sensible, intelligent young woman, about twenty-seven, was Elizabeth's intimate friend.

That the Miss Lucases and the Miss Bennets should meet to talk over a ball was absolutely necessary; and the morning after the assembly brought the former to Longbourn to hear and to communicate.

"*You* began the evening well, Charlotte," said Mrs. Bennet with civil self-command to Miss Lucas. "*You* were Mr. Bingley's first choice."

"Yes;—but he seemed to like his second better."

"Oh!—you mean Jane, I suppose—because he danced with her twice. To be sure that *did* seem as if he admired her—indeed I rather believe he *did*—I heard something about it—but I hardly know what—something about Mr. Robinson."

"Perhaps you mean what I overheard between him and Mr. Robinson; did not I mention it to you? Mr. Robinson's asking him how he liked our Meryton assemblies, and whether he did not think there were a great many pretty women in the room, and *which* he thought the prettiest? and his answering immediately to the last question—Oh! the eldest Miss Bennet beyond a doubt, there cannot be two opinions on that point."

"Upon my word!—Well, that was very decided indeed—that does seem as if—but however, it may all come to nothing you know."

"*My* overhearings were more to the purpose than *yours,* Eliza," said Charlotte. "Mr. Darcy is not so well worth listening to as his friend, is he?—Poor Eliza!—to be only just *tolerable.*"

"I beg you would not put it into Lizzy's head to be vexed by his ill-treatment; for he is such a disagreeable man that it would be quite a misfortune to be liked by him. Mrs. Long told me last night that he sat close to her for half an hour without once opening his lips."

"Are you quite sure, Ma'am?—is not there a little mistake?" said Jane.—"I certainly saw Mr. Darcy speaking to her."

"Aye—because she asked him at last how he liked Netherfield, and he could not help answering her;—but she said he seemed very angry at being spoke to."

"Miss Bingley told me," said Jane, "that he never speaks much unless among his intimate acquaintance. With *them* he is remarkably agreeable."

"I do not believe a word of it, my dear. If he had been so very agreeable he would have talked to Mrs. Long. But I can guess how it was; every body says that he is ate up with pride, and I dare say he had heard somehow that Mrs. Long does not keep a carriage, and had come to the ball in a hack chaise."

"I do not mind his not talking to Mrs. Long," said Miss Lucas, "but I wish he had danced with Eliza."

"Another time, Lizzy," said her mother, "I would not dance with *him,* if I were you."

"I believe, Ma'am, I may safely promise you *never* to dance with him."

"His pride," said Miss Lucas, "does not offend *me* so much as pride often does, because there is an excuse for it. One cannot wonder that so very fine a young man, with family, fortune, every thing in his favour, should think highly of himself. If I may so express it, he has a *right* to be proud."

"That is very true," replied Elizabeth, "and I could easily forgive *his* pride, if he had not mortified *mine.*"

"Pride," observed Mary, who piqued herself upon the solidity of her reflections, "is a very common failing I believe. By all that I have ever read, I am convinced that it is very common indeed, that human nature is particularly prone to it, and that there are very few of us who do not cherish a feeling of self-complacency on the score of some quality or other, real or imaginary. Vanity and pride are different things, though the words are often used synonimously. A person may be proud without being vain. Pride relates more to our opinion of ourselves, vanity to what we would have others think of us."

"If I were as rich as Mr. Darcy," cried a young Lucas who came with his sisters, "I should not care how proud I was. I would keep a pack of foxhounds, and drink a bottle of wine every day."

"Then you would drink a great deal more than you ought," said Mrs. Bennet; "and if I were to see you at it I should take away your bottle directly."

The boy protested that she should not; she continued to declare that she would, and the argument ended only with the visit.

## Chapter VI.

The ladies of Longbourn soon waited on those of Netherfield. The visit was returned in due form. Miss Bennet's pleasing manners grew on the good will of Mrs. Hurst and Miss Bingley; and though the mother was found to be intolerable and the younger sisters not worth speaking to, a wish of being better acquainted with *them,* was expressed towards the two eldest. By Jane this attention was received with the greatest pleasure; but Elizabeth still saw superciliousness in their treatment of every body, hardly excepting even her sister, and could not like them; though their kindness to Jane, such as it was, had a value as arising in all probability from the influence of their brother's admiration. It was generally evident whenever they met, that he *did* admire her; and to *her* it was equally evident that Jane was yielding to the preference which she had begun to entertain for him from the first, and was in a way to be very much in love; but she considered with pleasure that it was not likely to be discovered by the world in general, since Jane united with great strength of feeling, a composure of temper and a uniform cheerfulness of manner, which would guard her from the suspicions of the impertinent. She mentioned this to her friend Miss Lucas.

"It may perhaps be pleasant," replied Charlotte, "to be able to impose on the public in such a case; but it is sometimes a disadvantage to be so very guarded. If a woman conceals her affection with the same skill from the object of it, she may lose the opportunity of fixing him; and it will then be but poor consolation to believe the world equally in the dark. There is so much of gratitude or vanity in almost every attachment, that it is not safe to leave any to itself. We can all *begin* freely—a slight preference is natural enough; but there are very few of us who have heart enough to be really in love without encouragement. In nine cases out of ten, a woman had better shew *more* affection than she feels. Bingley likes your sister undoubtedly; but he may never do more than like her, if she does not help him on."

"But she does help him on, as much as her nature will allow. If *I* can perceive her regard for him, he must be a simpleton indeed not to discover it too."

"Remember, Eliza, that he does not know Jane's disposition as you do."

"But if a woman is partial to a man, and does not endeavour to conceal it, he must find it out."

"Perhaps he must, if he sees enough of her. But though Bingley and Jane meet tolerably often, it is never for many hours together; and as they always see each other in large mixed parties, it is impossible that every moment should be employed in conversing together. Jane should therefore make the most of every half hour in which she can command his attention. When she is secure of him, there will be leisure for falling in love as much as she chuses."

"Your plan is a good one," replied Elizabeth, "where nothing is in question but the desire of being well married; and if I were determined to get a rich husband, or any husband, I dare say I should adopt it. But these are not Jane's feelings; she is not acting by design. As yet, she cannot even be certain of the degree of her own regard, nor of its reasonableness. She has known him only a fortnight. She danced four dances with him at Meryton; she saw him one morning at his own house, and has since dined in company with him four times. This is not quite enough to make her understand his character."

"Not as you represent it. Had she merely *dined* with him, she might only have discovered whether he had a good appetite; but you must remember that four evenings have been also spent together—and four evenings may do a great deal."

"Yes; these four evenings have enabled them to ascertain that they both like Vingt-un better than Commerce; but with respect to any other leading characteristic, I do not imagine that much has been unfolded."

"Well," said Charlotte, "I wish Jane success with all my heart; and if she were married to him to-morrow, I should think she had as good a chance of happiness, as if she were to be studying his character for a twelvemonth. Happiness in marriage is entirely a matter of chance. If the dispositions of the parties are ever so well known to each other, or ever so similar before-hand, it does not advance their felicity in the least. They always continue to grow sufficiently unlike afterwards to have their share of vexation; and it is better to know as little as possible of the defects of the person with whom you are to pass your life."

"You make me laugh, Charlotte; but it is not sound. You know it is not sound, and that you would never act in this way yourself."

Occupied in observing Mr. Bingley's attentions to her sister, Elizabeth was far from suspecting that she was herself becoming an object of some interest in the eyes of his friend. Mr. Darcy had at first scarcely allowed her to be pretty; he had looked at her without admiration at the ball; and when they next met, he looked at her only to criticise. But no sooner had he made it clear to himself and his friends that she had hardly a good feature in her face, than he began to find it was rendered uncommonly intelligent by the beautiful expression of her dark eyes. To this discovery succeeded some others equally mortifying. Though he had detected with a critical eye more than one failure of perfect symmetry in her form, he was forced to acknowledge her figure to be light and pleasing; and in spite of his asserting that her manners were not those of the fashionable world, he was caught by their easy playfulness. Of this she was perfectly unaware;—to her he was only the man who made himself agreeable no where, and who had not thought her handsome enough to dance with.

He began to wish to know more of her, and as a step towards conversing with her himself, attended to her conversation with others. His doing so drew her notice. It was at Sir William Lucas's, where a large party were assembled.

"What does Mr. Darcy mean," said she to Charlotte, "by listening to my conversation with Colonel Forster?"

"That is a question which Mr. Darcy only can answer."

"But if he does it any more I shall certainly let him know that I see what he is about. He has a very satirical eye, and if I do not begin by being impertinent myself, I shall soon grow afraid of him."

On his approaching them soon afterwards, though without seeming to have any intention of speaking, Miss Lucas defied her friend to mention such a subject to him, which immediately provoking Elizabeth to do it, she turned to him and said,

"Did not you think, Mr. Darcy, that I expressed myself uncommonly well just now, when I was teazing Colonel Forster to give us a ball at Meryton?"

"With great energy;—but it is a subject which always makes a lady energetic."

"You are severe on us."

"It will be *her* turn soon to be teazed," said Miss Lucas. "I am going to open the instrument, Eliza, and you know what follows."

"You are a very strange creature by way of a friend!—always wanting me to play and sing before any body and every body!—If my vanity had taken a musical turn, you would have been invaluable, but as it is, I would really rather not sit down before those who must be in the habit of hearing the very best performers." On Miss Lucas's persevering, however, she added, "Very well; if it must be so, it must." And gravely glancing at Mr. Darcy, "There is a fine old saying, which every body here is of course familiar with—'Keep your breath to cool your porridge,'—and I shall keep mine to swell my song."

Her performance was pleasing, though by no means capital. After a song or two, and before she could reply to the entreaties of several that she would sing again, she was eagerly succeeded at the instrument by her sister Mary, who having, in consequence of being the only plain one in the family, worked hard for knowledge and accomplishments, was always impatient for display.

Mary had neither genius nor taste; and though vanity had given her application, it had given her likewise a pedantic air and conceited manner, which would have injured a higher degree of excellence than she had reached. Elizabeth, easy and unaffected, had been listened to with much more pleasure, though not playing half so well; and Mary, at the end of a long concerto, was glad to purchase praise and gratitude by Scotch and Irish airs, at the request of her younger sisters, who with some of the Lucases and two or three officers joined eagerly in dancing at one end of the room.

Mr. Darcy stood near them in silent indignation at such a mode of passing the evening, to the exclusion of all conversation, and was too much engrossed by his own thoughts to perceive that Sir William Lucas was his neighbour, till Sir William thus began.

"What a charming amusement for young people this is, Mr. Darcy!—There is nothing like dancing after all.—I consider it as one of the first refinements of polished societies."

"Certainly, Sir;—and it has the advantage also of being in vogue amongst the less polished societies of the world.—Every savage can dance."

Sir William only smiled. "Your friend performs delightfully;" he continued after a pause, on seeing Bingley join the group;—"and I doubt not that you are an adept in the science yourself, Mr. Darcy."

"You saw me dance at Meryton, I believe, Sir."

"Yes, indeed, and received no inconsiderable pleasure from the sight. Do you often dance at St. James's?"

"Never, sir."

"Do you not think it would be a proper compliment to the place?"

"It is a compliment which I never pay to any place if I can avoid it."

"You have a house in town, I conclude?"

Mr. Darcy bowed.

"I had once some thoughts of fixing in town myself—for I am fond of superior society; but I did not feel quite certain that the air of London would agree with Lady Lucas."

He paused in hopes of an answer; but his companion was not disposed to make any; and Elizabeth at that instant moving towards them, he was struck with the notion of doing a very gallant thing, and called out to her,

"My dear Miss Eliza, why are not you dancing?—Mr. Darcy, you must allow me to present this young lady to you as a very desirable partner.—You cannot refuse to dance, I am sure, when so much beauty is before you." And taking her hand, he would have given it to Mr. Darcy, who, though extremely surprised, was not unwilling to receive it, when she instantly drew back, and said with some discomposure to Sir William,

"Indeed, Sir, I have not the least intention of dancing.—I entreat you not to suppose that I moved this way in order to beg for a partner."

Mr. Darcy with grave propriety requested to be allowed the honour of her hand; but in vain. Elizabeth was determined; nor did Sir William at all shake her purpose by his attempt at persuasion.

"You excel so much in the dance, Miss Eliza, that it is cruel to deny me the happiness of seeing you; and though this gentleman dislikes the amusement in general, he can have no objection, I am sure, to oblige us for one half hour."

"Mr. Darcy is all politeness," said Elizabeth, smiling.

"He is indeed—but considering the inducement, my dear Miss Eliza, we cannot wonder at his complaisance; for who would object to such a partner?"

Elizabeth looked archly, and turned away. Her resistance had not injured her with the gentleman, and he was thinking of her with some complacency, when thus accosted by Miss Bingley,

"I can guess the subject of your reverie."

"I should imagine not."

"You are considering how insupportable it would be to pass many evenings in this manner—in such society; and indeed I am quite of your opinion. I was never more annoyed! The insipidity and yet the noise; the nothingness and yet the self-importance of all these people!—What would I give to hear your strictures on them!"

"Your conjecture is totally wrong, I assure you. My mind was more agreeably engaged. I have been meditating on the very great pleasure which a pair of fine eyes in the face of a pretty woman can bestow."

Miss Bingley immediately fixed her eyes on his face, and desired he would tell her what lady had the credit of inspiring such reflections. Mr. Darcy replied with great intrepidity,

"Miss Elizabeth Bennet."

"Miss Elizabeth Bennet!" repeated Miss Bingley. "I am all astonishment. How long has she been such a favourite?—and pray when am I to wish you joy?"

"That is exactly the question which I expected you to ask. A lady's imagination is very rapid; it jumps from admiration to love, from love to matrimony in a moment. I knew you would be wishing me joy."

"Nay, if you are so serious about it, I shall consider the matter as absolutely settled. You will have a charming mother-in-law, indeed, and of course she will be always at Pemberley with you."

He listened to her with perfect indifference, while she chose to entertain herself in this manner, and as his composure convinced her that all was safe, her wit flowed long.

## Chapter VII.

Mr. Bennet's property consisted almost entirely in an estate of two thousand a year, which, unfortunately for his daughters, was entailed in default of heirs male, on a distant relation; and their mother's fortune, though ample for her situation in life, could but ill supply the deficiency of his. Her father had been an attorney in Meryton, and had left her four thousand pounds.

She had a sister married to a Mr. Philips, who had been a clerk to their father, and succeeded him in the business, and a brother settled in London in a respectable line of trade.

The village of Longbourn was only one mile from Meryton; a most convenient distance for the young ladies, who were usually tempted thither three or four times a week, to pay their duty to their aunt and to a milliner's shop just over the way. The two youngest of the family, Catherine and Lydia, were particularly frequent in these attentions; their minds were more vacant than their sisters', and when nothing better offered, a walk to Meryton was necessary to amuse their morning hours and furnish conversation for the evening; and however bare of news the country in general might be, they always contrived to learn some from their aunt. At present, indeed, they were well supplied both with news and happiness by the recent arrival of a militia regiment in the neighbourhood; it was to remain the whole winter, and Meryton was the head quarters.

Their visits to Mrs. Philips were now productive of the most interesting intelligence. Every day added something to their knowledge of the officers' names and connections. Their lodgings were not long a secret, and at length they began to know the officers themselves. Mr. Philips visited them all, and this opened to his nieces a source of felicity unknown before. They could talk of nothing but officers; and Mr. Bingley's large fortune, the mention of which gave animation to their mother, was worthless in their eyes when opposed to the regimentals of an ensign.

After listening one morning to their effusions on this subject, Mr. Bennet coolly observed,

"From all that I can collect by your manner of talking, you must be two of the silliest girls in the country. I have suspected it some time, but I am now convinced."

Catherine was disconcerted, and made no answer; but Lydia, with perfect indifference, continued to express her admiration of Captain Carter, and her hope of seeing him in the course of the day, as he was going the next morning to London.

"I am astonished, my dear," said Mrs. Bennet, "that you should be so ready to think your own children silly. If I wished to think slightingly of any body's children, it should not be of my own however."

"If my children are silly I must hope to be always sensible of it."

"Yes—but as it happens, they are all of them very clever."

"This is the only point, I flatter myself, on which we do not agree. I had hoped that our sentiments coincided in every particular, but I must so far differ from you as to think our two youngest daughters uncommonly foolish."

"My dear Mr. Bennet, you must not expect such girls to have the sense of their father and mother.—When they get to our age I dare say they will not think about officers any more than we do. I remember the time when I liked a red coat myself very well—and indeed so I do still at my heart; and if a smart young colonel, with five or six thousand a year, should want one of my girls, I shall not say nay to him; and I thought Colonel Forster looked very becoming the other night at Sir William's in his regimentals."

"Mama,"' cried Lydia, "my aunt says that Colonel Forster and Captain Carter do not go so often to Miss Watson's as they did when they first came; she sees them now very often standing in Clarke's library."

Mrs. Bennet was prevented replying by the entrance of the footman with a note for Miss Bennet; it came from Netherfield, and the servant waited for an answer. Mrs. Bennet's eyes sparkled with pleasure, and she was eagerly calling out, while her daughter read,

"Well, Jane, who is it from? what is it about? what does he say? Well, Jane, make haste and tell us; make haste, my love."

"It is from Miss Bingley," said Jane, and then read it aloud.

> "My dear Friend,
>
> "If you are not so compassionate as to dine to-day with Louisa and me, we shall be in danger of hating each other for the rest of our lives, for a whole day's tête-à-tête between two women can never end without a quarrel. Come as soon as you can on the receipt of this. My brother and the gentlemen are to dine with the officers. Yours ever,
>
> "CAROLINE BINGLEY."

"With the officers!" cried Lydia. "I wonder my aunt did not tell us of *that*."

"Dining out," said Mrs. Bennet, "that is very unlucky."

"Can I have the carriage?" said Jane.

"No, my dear, you had better go on horseback, because it seems likely to rain; and then you must stay all night."

"That would be a good scheme," said Elizabeth, "if you were sure that they would not offer to send her home."

"Oh! but the gentlemen will have Mr. Bingley's chaise to go to Meryton; and the Hursts have no horses to theirs."

"I had much rather go in the coach."

"But, my dear, your father cannot spare the horses, I am sure. They are wanted in the farm, Mr. Bennet, are not they?"

"They are wanted in the farm much oftener than I can get them."

"But if you have got them to day," said Elizabeth, "my mother's purpose will be answered."

She did at last extort from her father an acknowledgment that the horses were engaged. Jane was therefore obliged to go on horseback, and her mother attended her to the door with many cheerful prognostics of a bad day. Her hopes were answered; Jane had not been gone long before it rained hard. Her sisters were uneasy for her, but her mother was delighted. The rain continued the whole evening without intermission; Jane certainly could not come back.

"This was a lucky idea of mine, indeed!" said Mrs. Bennet, more than once, as if the credit of making it rain were all her own. Till the next morning, however, she was not aware of all the felicity of her contrivance. Breakfast was scarcely over when a servant from Netherfield brought the following note for Elizabeth:

> "My dearest Lizzy,
>
> "I find myself very unwell this morning, which, I suppose, is to be imputed to my getting wet through yesterday. My kind friends will not hear of my returning home till I am better. They insist also on my seeing Mr. Jones—therefore do not be alarmed if you should hear of his having been to me—and excepting a sore-throat and head-ache there is not much the matter with me.
>
> "Yours, &c."

"Well, my dear," said Mr. Bennet, when Elizabeth had read the note aloud, "if your daughter should have a dangerous fit of illness, if she should die, it would be a comfort to know that it was all in pursuit of Mr. Bingley, and under your orders."

"Oh! I am not at all afraid of her dying. People do not die of little trifling colds. She will be taken good care of. As long as she stays there, it is all very well. I would go and see her, if I could have the carriage."

Elizabeth, feeling really anxious, was determined to go to her, though the carriage was not to be had; and as she was no horse-woman, walking was her only alternative. She declared her resolution.

"How can you be so silly," cried her mother, "as to think of such a thing, in all this dirt! You will not be fit to be seen when you get there."

"I shall be very fit to see Jane—which is all I want."

"Is this a hint to me, Lizzy," said her father, "to send for the horses?"

"No, indeed. I do not wish to avoid the walk. The distance is nothing, when one has a motive; only three miles. I shall be back by dinner."

"I admire the activity of your benevolence," observed Mary, "but every impulse of feeling should be guided by reason; and, in my opinion, exertion should always be in proportion to what is required."

"We will go as far as Meryton with you," said Catherine and Lydia.—Elizabeth accepted their company, and the three young ladies set off together.

"If we make haste," said Lydia, as they walked along, "perhaps we may see something of Captain Carter before he goes."

In Meryton they parted; the two youngest repaired to the lodgings of one of the officers' wives, and Elizabeth continued her walk alone, crossing field after field at a quick pace, jumping over stiles and springing over puddles with impatient activity, and finding herself at last within view of the house, with weary ancles, dirty stockings, and a face glowing with the warmth of exercise.

She was shewn into the breakfast-parlour, where all but Jane were assembled, and where her appearance created a great deal of surprise.—That she should have walked three miles so early in the day, in such dirty weather, and by herself, was almost incredible to Mrs. Hurst and Miss Bingley; and Elizabeth was convinced that they held her in contempt for it. She was received, however, very politely by them; and in their brother's manners there was something better than politeness; there was good humour and kindness.—Mr. Darcy said very little, and Mr. Hurst nothing at all. The former was divided between admiration of the brilliancy which exercise had given to her complexion, and doubt as to the occasion's justifying her coming so far alone. The latter was thinking only of his breakfast.

Her enquiries after her sister were not very favourably answered. Miss Bennet had slept ill, and though up, was very feverish and not well enough to leave her room. Elizabeth was glad to be taken to her immediately; and Jane, who had only been withheld by the fear of giving alarm or inconvenience, from expressing in her note how much she longed for such a visit, was delighted at her entrance. She was not equal, however, to much conversation, and when Miss Bingley left them together, could attempt little beside expressions of gratitude for the extraordinary kindness she was treated with. Elizabeth silently attended her.

When breakfast was over, they were joined by the sisters; and Elizabeth began to like them herself, when she saw how much affection and solicitude they shewed for Jane. The apothecary came, and having examined his patient, said, as might be supposed, that she had caught a violent cold, and that they must endeavour to get the better of it; advised her to return to bed, and promised her some draughts. The advice was followed readily, for the feverish symptoms increased, and her head ached acutely. Elizabeth did not quit her room for a moment, nor were the other ladies often absent; the gentlemen being out, they had in fact nothing to do elsewhere.

When the clock struck three, Elizabeth felt that she must go; and very unwillingly said so. Miss Bingley offered her the carriage, and she only wanted a little pressing to accept it, when Jane testified such concern in parting with her, that Miss Bingley was obliged to convert the offer of the chaise into an invitation to remain at Netherfield for the present. Elizabeth most thankfully consented, and a servant was dispatched to Longbourn to acquaint the family with her stay, and bring back a supply of clothes.

## Chapter VIII.

At five o'clock the two ladies retired to dress, and at half past six Elizabeth was summoned to dinner. To the civil enquiries which then poured in, and amongst which she had the pleasure of distinguishing the much superior solicitude of Mr. Bingley's, she could not make a very favourable answer. Jane was by no means better. The sisters, on hearing this, repeated three or four times how much they were grieved, how shocking it was to have a bad cold, and how excessively they disliked being ill themselves; and then thought no more of the matter: and their indifference towards Jane when not immediately before them, restored Elizabeth to the enjoyment of all her original dislike.

Their brother, indeed, was the only one of the party whom she could regard with any complacency. His anxiety for Jane was evident, and his attentions to herself most pleasing, and they prevented her feeling herself so much an intruder as she believed she was considered by the others. She had very little notice from any but him. Miss Bingley was engrossed by Mr. Darcy, her sister scarcely less so; and as for Mr. Hurst, by whom Elizabeth sat, he was an indolent man, who lived only to eat, drink, and play at cards, who when he found her prefer a plain dish to a ragout, had nothing to say to her.

When dinner was over, she returned directly to Jane, and Miss Bingley began abusing her as soon as she was out of the room. Her manners were pronounced to be very bad indeed, a mixture of pride and impertinence; she had no conversation, no stile, no taste, no beauty. Mrs. Hurst thought the same, and added,

"She has nothing, in short, to recommend her, but being an excellent walker. I shall never forget her appearance this morning. She really looked almost wild."

"She did indeed, Louisa. I could hardly keep my countenance. Very nonsensical to come at all! Why must *she* be scampering about the country, because her sister had a cold? Her hair so untidy, so blowsy!"

"Yes, and her petticoat; I hope you saw her petticoat, six inches deep in mud, I am absolutely certain; and the gown which had been let down to hide it, not doing its office."

"Your picture may be very exact, Louisa," said Bingley; "but this was all lost upon me. I thought Miss Elizabeth Bennet looked remarkably well, when she came into the room this morning. Her dirty petticoat quite escaped my notice."

"*You* observed it, Mr. Darcy, I am sure," said Miss Bingley; "and I am inclined to think that you would not wish to see *your sister* make such an exhibition."

"Certainly not."

"To walk three miles, or four miles, or five miles, or whatever it is, above her ancles in dirt, and alone, quite alone! what could she mean by it? It seems to me to shew an abominable sort of conceited independence, a most country town indifference to decorum."

"It shews an affection for her sister that is very pleasing," said Bingley.

"I am afraid, Mr. Darcy," observed Miss Bingley, in a half whisper, "that this adventure has rather affected your admiration of her fine eyes."

"Not at all," he replied; "they were brightened by the exercise."—A short pause followed this speech, and Mrs. Hurst began again.

"I have an excessive regard for Jane Bennet, she is really a very sweet girl, and I wish with all my heart she were well settled. But with such a father and mother, and such low connections, I am afraid there is no chance of it."

"I think I have heard you say, that their uncle is an attorney in Meryton."

"Yes; and they have another, who lives somewhere near Cheapside."

"That is capital," added her sister, and they both laughed heartily.

"If they had uncles enough to fill *all* Cheapside," cried Bingley, "it would not make them one jot less agreeable."

"But it must very materially lessen their chance of marrying men of any consideration in the world," replied Darcy.

To this speech Bingley made no answer; but his sisters gave it their hearty assent, and indulged their mirth for some time at the expense of their dear friend's vulgar relations.

With a renewal of tenderness, however, they repaired to her room on leaving the dining-parlour, and sat with her till summoned to coffee. She was still very poorly, and Elizabeth would not quit her at all, till late in the evening, when she had the comfort of seeing her asleep, and when it appeared to her rather right than pleasant that she should go down stairs herself. On entering the drawing-room she found the whole party at loo, and was immediately invited to join them; but suspecting them to be playing high she declined it, and making her sister the excuse, said she would amuse herself for the short time she could stay below with a book. Mr. Hurst looked at her with astonishment.

"Do you prefer reading to cards?" said he; "that is rather singular."

"Miss Eliza Bennet," said Miss Bingley, "despises cards. She is a great reader and has no pleasure in anything else."

"I deserve neither such praise nor such censure," cried Elizabeth; "I am *not* a great reader, and I have pleasure in many things."

"In nursing your sister I am sure you have pleasure," said Bingley; "and I hope it will soon be increased by seeing her quite well."

Elizabeth thanked him from her heart, and then walked towards a table where a few books were lying. He immediately offered to fetch her others; all that his library afforded.

"And I wish my collection were larger for your benefit and my own credit; but I am an idle fellow, and though I have not many, I have more than I ever look into."

Elizabeth assured him that she could suit herself perfectly with those in the room.

"I am astonished," said Miss Bingley, "that my father should have left so small a collection of books.—What a delightful library you have at Pemberley, Mr. Darcy!"

"It ought to be good," he replied, "it has been the work of many generations."

"And then you have added so much to it yourself, you are always buying books."

"I cannot comprehend the neglect of a family library in such days as these."

"Neglect! I am sure you neglect nothing that can add to the beauties of that noble place. Charles, when you build *your* house, I wish it may be half as delightful as Pemberley."

"I wish it may."

"But I would really advise you to make your purchase in that neighbourhood, and take Pemberley for a kind of model. There is not a finer county in England than Derbyshire."

"With all my heart; I will buy Pemberley itself if Darcy will sell it."

"I am talking of possibilities, Charles."

"Upon my word, Caroline, I should think it more possible to get Pemberley by purchase than by imitation."

Elizabeth was so much caught by what passed, as to leave her very little attention for her book; and soon laying it wholly aside, she drew near the card-table, and stationed herself between Mr. Bingley and his eldest sister, to observe the game.

"Is Miss Darcy much grown since the spring?" said Miss Bingley; "will she be as tall as I am?"

"I think she will. She is now about Miss Elizabeth Bennet's height, or rather taller."

"How I long to see her again! I never met with anybody who delighted me so much. Such a countenance, such manners! and so extremely accomplished for her age! Her performance on the piano-forte is exquisite."

"It is amazing to me," said Bingley, "how young ladies can have patience to be so very accomplished, as they all are."

"All young ladies accomplished! My dear Charles, what do you mean?"

"Yes, all of them, I think. They all paint tables, cover skreens and net purses. I scarcely know any one who cannot do all this, and I am sure I never heard a young lady spoken of for the first time, without being informed that she was very accomplished."

"Your list of the common extent of accomplishments," said Darcy, "has too much truth. The word is applied to many a woman who deserves it no otherwise than by netting a purse, or covering a skreen. But I am very far from agreeing with you in your estimation of ladies in general. I cannot boast of knowing more than half a dozen, in the whole range of my acquaintance, that are really accomplished."

"Nor I, I am sure," said Miss Bingley.

"Then," observed Elizabeth, "you must comprehend a great deal in your idea of an accomplished woman."

"Yes; I do comprehend a great deal in it."

"Oh! certainly," cried his faithful assistant, "no one can be really esteemed accomplished, who does not greatly surpass what is usually met with. A woman must have a thorough knowledge of music, singing, drawing, dancing, and the modern languages, to deserve the word; and besides all this, she must possess a certain something in her air and manner of walking, the tone of her voice, her address and expressions, or the word will be but half deserved."

"All this she must possess," added Darcy, "and to all this she must yet add something more substantial, in the improvement of her mind by extensive reading."

"I am no longer surprised at your knowing *only* six accomplished women. I rather wonder now at your knowing *any*."

"Are you so severe upon your own sex, as to doubt the possibility of all this ?"

"*I* never saw such a woman. *I* never saw such capacity, and taste, and application, and elegance, as you describe, united."

Mrs. Hurst and Miss Bingley both cried out against the injustice of her implied doubt, and were both protesting that they knew many women who answered this description, when Mr. Hurst called them to order, with bitter complaints of their inattention to what was going forward. As all conversation was thereby at an end, Elizabeth soon afterwards left the room.

"Eliza Bennet," said Miss Bingley, when the door was closed on her, "is one of those young ladies who seek to recommend themselves to the other sex, by undervaluing their own; and with many men, I dare say, it succeeds.

But, in my opinion, it is a paltry device, a very mean art."

"Undoubtedly," replied Darcy, to whom this remark was chiefly addressed, "there is meanness in *all* the arts which ladies sometimes condescend to employ for captivation. Whatever bears affinity to cunning is despicable."

Miss Bingley was not so entirely satisfied with this reply as to continue the subject.

Elizabeth joined them again only to say that her sister was worse, and that she could not leave her. Bingley urged Mr. Jones's being sent for immediately; while his sisters, convinced that no country advice could be of any service, recommended an express to town for one of the most eminent physicians. This, she would not hear of; but she was not so unwilling to comply with their brother's proposal; and it was settled that Mr. Jones should be sent for early in the morning, if Miss Bennet were not decidedly better. Bingley was quite uncomfortable; his sisters declared that they were miserable. They solaced their wretchedness, however, by duets after supper, while he could find no better relief to his feelings than by giving his housekeeper directions that every possible attention might be paid to the sick lady and her sister.

## Chapter IX.

Elizabeth passed the chief of the night in her sister's room, and in the morning had the pleasure of being able to send a tolerable answer to the enquiries which she very early received from Mr. Bingley by a housemaid, and some time afterwards from the two elegant ladies who waited on his sisters. In spite of this amendment, however, she requested to have a note sent to Longbourn, desiring her mother to visit Jane, and form her own judgment of her situation. The note was immediately dispatched, and its contents as quickly complied with. Mrs. Bennet, accompanied by her two youngest girls, reached Netherfield soon after the family breakfast.

Had she found Jane in any apparent danger, Mrs. Bennet would have been very miserable; but being satisfied on seeing her that her illness was not alarming, she had no wish of her recovering immediately, as her restoration to health would probably remove her from Netherfield. She would not listen therefore to her daughter's proposal of being carried home; neither did the apothecary, who arrived about the same time, think it at all advisable. After sitting a little while with Jane, on Miss Bingley's appearance and invitation, the mother and three daughters all attended her into the breakfast parlour. Bingley met them with hopes that Mrs. Bennet had not found Miss Bennet worse than she expected.

"Indeed I have, Sir," was her answer. "She is a great deal too ill to be moved. Mr. Jones says we must not think of moving her. We must trespass a little longer on your kindness."

"Removed!" cried Bingley. "It must not be thought of. My sister, I am sure, will not hear of her removal."

"You may depend upon it, Madam," said Miss Bingley, with cold civility, "that Miss Bennet shall receive every possible attention while she remains with us."

Mrs. Bennet was profuse in her acknowledgments.

"I am sure," she added, "if it was not for such good friends I do not know what would become of her, for she is very ill indeed, and suffers a vast deal, though with the greatest patience in the world, which is always the way with her, for she has, without exception, the sweetest temper I ever met with. I often tell my other girls they are nothing to *her.* You have a sweet room here, Mr. Bingley, and a charming prospect over that gravel walk. I do not know a place in the country that is equal to Netherfield. You will not think of quitting it in a hurry I hope, though you have but a short lease."

"Whatever I do is done in a hurry," replied he; "and therefore if I should resolve to quit Netherfield, I should probably be off in five minutes. At present, however, I consider myself as quite fixed here."

"That is exactly what I should have supposed of you," said Elizabeth.

"You begin to comprehend me, do you ?" cried he, turning towards her.

"Oh! yes—I understand you perfectly."

"I wish I might take this for a compliment; but to be so easily seen through I am afraid is pitiful."

"That is as it happens. It does not necessarily follow that a deep, intricate character is more or less estimable than such a one as yours."

"Lizzy," cried her mother, "remember where you are, and do not run on in the wild manner that you are suffered to do at home."

"I did not know before," continued Bingley immediately, "that you were a studier of character. It must be an amusing study."

"Yes; but intricate characters are the *most* amusing. They have at least that advantage."

"The country," said Darcy, "can in general supply but few subjects for such a study. In a country neighbourhood you move in a very confined and unvarying society."

"But people themselves alter so much, that there is something new to be observed in them for ever."

"Yes, indeed," cried Mrs. Bennet, offended by his manner of mentioning a country neighbourhood. "I assure you there is quite as much of *that* going on in the country as in town."

Every body was surprised; and Darcy, after looking at her for a moment, turned silently away. Mrs. Bennet, who fancied she had gained a complete victory over him, continued her triumph.

"I cannot see that London has any great advantage over the country for my part, except the shops and public places. The country is a vast deal pleasanter, is not it, Mr. Bingley?"

"When I am in the country," he replied, "I never wish to leave it; and when I am in town it is pretty much the same. They have each their advantages, and I can be equally happy in either."

"Aye—that is because you have the right disposition. But that gentleman," looking at Darcy, "seemed to think the country was nothing at all."

"Indeed, Mama, you are mistaken," said Elizabeth, blushing for her mother. "You quite mistook Mr. Darcy. He only meant that there were not such a variety of people to be met with in the country as in town, which you must acknowledge to be true."

"Certainly, my dear, nobody said there were; but as to not meeting with many people in this neighbourhood, I believe there are few neighbourhoods larger. I know we dine with four and twenty families."

Nothing but concern for Elizabeth could enable Bingley to keep his countenance. His sister was less delicate, and directed her eye towards Mr. Darcy with a very expressive smile. Elizabeth, for the sake of saying something that might turn her mother's thoughts, now asked her if Charlotte Lucas had been at Longbourn since *her* coming away.

"Yes, she called yesterday with her father. What an agreeable man Sir William is, Mr. Bingley—is not he? so much the man of fashion! so genteel and so easy!—He has always something to say to every body.—*That* is my idea of good breeding; and those persons who fancy themselves very important and never open their mouths, quite mistake the matter."

"Did Charlotte dine with you?"

"No, she would go home. I fancy she was wanted about the mince pies. For my part, Mr. Bingley, *I* always keep servants that can do their own work; *my* daughters are brought up differently. But every body is to judge for themselves, and the Lucases are very good sort of girls, I assure you. It is a pity they are not handsome!—Not that *I* think Charlotte so *very* plain—but then she is our particular friend."

"She seems a very pleasant young woman," said Bingley.

"Oh! dear, yes;—but you must own she is very plain. Lady Lucas herself has often said so, and envied me Jane's beauty. I do not like to boast of my own child, but to be sure, Jane—one does not often see any body better looking. It is what every body says. I do not trust my own partiality. When she was only fifteen, there was a gentleman at my brother Gardiner's in town, so much in love with her, that my sister-in-law was sure he would make her an offer before we came away. But however he did not. Perhaps he thought her too young. However, he wrote some verses on her, and very pretty they were."

"And so ended his affection," said Elizabeth impatiently. "There has been many a one, I fancy, overcome in the same way. I wonder who first discovered the efficacy of poetry in driving away love!"

"I have been used to consider poetry as the *food* of love," said Darcy.

"Of a fine, stout, healthy love it may. Every thing nourishes what is strong already. But if it be only a slight, thin sort of inclination, I am convinced that one good sonnet will starve it entirely away."

Darcy only smiled; and the general pause which ensued made Elizabeth tremble lest her mother should be exposing herself again. She longed to speak, but could think of nothing to say; and after a short silence Mrs. Bennet began repeating her thanks to Mr. Bingley for his kindness to Jane, with an apology for troubling him also with Lizzy. Mr. Bingley was unaffectedly civil in his answer, and forced his younger sister to be civil also, and say what the occasion required. She performed her part indeed without much graciousness, but Mrs. Bennet was satisfied, and soon afterwards ordered her carriage. Upon this signal, the youngest of her daughters put herself forward. The two girls had been whispering to each other during the whole visit, and the result of it was, that the youngest should tax Mr. Bingley with having promised on his first coming into the country to give a ball at Netherfield.

Lydia was a stout, well-grown girl of fifteen, with a fine complexion and good-humoured countenance; a favourite with her mother, whose affection had brought her into public at an early age. She had high animal spirits, and a sort of natural self-consequence, which the attentions of the officers, to whom her uncle's good dinners and her own easy manners recommended her, had increased into assurance. She was very equal therefore to address Mr. Bingley on the subject of the ball, and abruptly reminded him of his promise; adding, that it would be the most shameful thing in the world if he did not keep it. His answer to this sudden attack was delightful to their mother's ear.

"I am perfectly ready, I assure you, to keep my engagement; and when your sister is recovered, you shall if you please name the very day of the ball. But you would not wish to be dancing while she is ill."

Lydia declared herself satisfied. "Oh! yes—it would be much better to wait till Jane was well, and by that time most likely Captain Carter would be at Meryton again. And when you have given *your* ball," she added, "I shall insist on their giving one also. I shall tell Colonel Forster it will be quite a shame if he does not."

Mrs. Bennet and her daughters then departed, and Elizabeth returned instantly to Jane, leaving her own and her relations' behaviour to the remarks of the two ladies and Mr. Darcy; the latter of whom, however, could not be prevailed on to join in their censure of *her,* in spite of all Miss Bingley's witticisms on *fine eyes.*

## Chapter X.

The day passed much as the day before had done. Mrs. Hurst and Miss Bingley had spent some hours of the morning with the invalid, who continued, though slowly, to mend; and in the evening Elizabeth joined their party in the drawing-room. The loo table, however, did not appear. Mr. Darcy was writing, and Miss Bingley, seated near him, was watching the progress of his letter, and repeatedly calling off his attention by messages to his sister. Mr. Hurst and Mr. Bingley were at piquet, and Mrs. Hurst was observing their game.

Elizabeth took up some needlework, and was sufficiently amused in attending to what passed between Darcy and his companion. The perpetual commendations of the lady either on his hand-writing, or on the evenness of his lines, or on the length of his letter, with the perfect unconcern with which her praises were received, formed a curious dialogue, and was exactly in unison with her opinion of each.

"How delighted Miss Darcy will be to receive such a letter!"

He made no answer.

"You write uncommonly fast."

"You are mistaken. I write rather slowly."

"How many letters you must have occasion to write in the course of the year! Letters of business too! How odious I should think them!"

"It is fortunate, then, that they fall to my lot instead of to yours."

"Pray tell your sister that I long to see her."

"I have already told her so once, by your desire."

"I am afraid you do not like your pen. Let me mend it for you. I mend pens remarkably well."

"Thank you—but I always mend my own."

"How can you contrive to write so even?"

He was silent.

"Tell your sister I am delighted to hear of her improvement on the harp, and pray let her know that I am quite in raptures with her beautiful little design for a table, and I think it infinitely superior to Miss Grantley's."

"Will you give me leave to defer your raptures till I write again?—At present I have not room to do them justice."

"Oh! it is of no consequence. I shall see her in January. But do you always write such charming long letters to her, Mr. Darcy?"

"They are generally long; but whether always charming, it is not for me to determine."

"It is a rule with me, that a person who can write a long letter, with ease, cannot write ill."

"That will not do for a compliment to Darcy, Caroline," cried her brother—"because he does *not* write with ease. He studies too much for words of four syllables.—Do not you, Darcy?"

"My stile of writing is very different from yours."

"Oh," cried Miss Bingley, "Charles writes in the most careless way imaginable. He leaves out half his words, and blots the rest."

"My ideas flow so rapidly that I have not time to express them—by which means my letters sometimes convey no ideas at all to my correspondents."

"Your humility, Mr. Bingley," said Elizabeth, "must disarm reproof."

"Nothing is more deceitful," said Darcy, "than the appearance of humility. It is often only carelessness of opinion, and sometimes an indirect boast."

"And which of the two do you call *my* little recent piece of modesty?"

"The indirect boast;—for you are really proud of your defects in writing, because you consider them as proceeding from a rapidity of thought and carelessness of execution, which if not estimable, you think at least highly interesting. The power of doing any thing with quickness is always much prized by the possessor, and often without any attention to the imperfection of the performance. When you told Mrs. Bennet this morning that if you ever resolved on quitting Netherfield you should be gone in five minutes, you meant it to be a sort of panegyric, of compliment to yourself—and yet what is there so very laudable in a precipitance which must leave very necessary business undone, and can be of no real advantage to yourself or any one else?"

"Nay," cried Bingley, "this is too much, to remember at night all the foolish things that were said in the morning. And yet, upon my honour, I believed what I said of myself to be true, and I believe it at this moment. At least, therefore, I did not assume the character of needless precipitance merely to shew off before the ladies."

"I dare say you believed it; but I am by no means convinced that you would be gone with such celerity. Your conduct would be quite as dependant on chance as that of any man I know; and if, as you were mounting your horse, a friend were to say, 'Bingley, you had better stay till next week,' you would probably do it, you would probably not go—and, at another word, might stay a month."

"You have only proved by this," cried Elizabeth, "that Mr. Bingley did not do justice to his own disposition.

You have shewn him off now much more than he did himself."

"I am exceedingly gratified," said Bingley, "by your converting what my friend says into a compliment on the sweetness of my temper. But I am afraid you are giving it a turn which that gentleman did by no means intend; for he would certainly think the better of me, if under such a circumstance I were to give a flat denial, and ride off as fast as I could."

"Would Mr. Darcy then consider the rashness of your original intention as atoned for by your obstinacy in adhering to it?"

"Upon my word I cannot exactly explain the matter, Darcy must speak for himself."

"You expect me to account for opinions which you chuse to call mine, but which I have never acknowledged. Allowing the case, however, to stand according to your representation, you must remember, Miss Bennet, that the friend who is supposed to desire his return to the house, and the delay of his plan, has merely desired it, asked it without offering one argument in favour of its propriety."

"To yield readily—easily—to the *persuasion* of a friend is no merit with you."

"To yield without conviction is no compliment to the understanding of either."

"You appear to me, Mr. Darcy, to allow nothing for the influence of friendship and affection. A regard for the requester would often make one readily yield to a request, without waiting for arguments to reason one into it. I am not particularly speaking of such a case as you have supposed about Mr. Bingley. We may as well wait, perhaps, till the circumstance occurs, before we discuss the discretion of his behaviour thereupon. But in general and ordinary cases between friend and friend, where one of them is desired by the other to change a resolution of no very great moment, should you think ill of that person for complying with the desire, without waiting to be argued into it?"

"Will it not be advisable, before we proceed on this subject, to arrange with rather more precision the degree of importance which is to appertain to this request, as well as the degree of intimacy subsisting between the parties?"

"By all means," cried Bingley; "let us hear all the particulars, not forgetting their comparative height and size; for that will have more weight in the argument, Miss Bennet, than you may be aware of. I assure you that if Darcy were not such a great tall fellow, in comparison with myself, I should not pay him half so much deference. I declare I do not know a more aweful object than Darcy, on particular occasions, and in particular places; at his own house especially, and of a Sunday evening when he has nothing to do."

Mr. Darcy smiled; but Elizabeth thought she could perceive that he was rather offended; and therefore checked her laugh. Miss Bingley warmly resented the indignity he had received, in an expostulation with her brother for talking such nonsense.

"I see your design, Bingley," said his friend.—"You dislike an argument, and want to silence this."

"Perhaps I do. Arguments are too much like disputes. If you and Miss Bennet will defer yours till I am out of the room, I shall be very thankful; and then you may say whatever you like of me."

"What you ask," said Elizabeth, "is no sacrifice on my side; and Mr. Darcy had much better finish his letter."

Mr. Darcy took her advice, and did finish his letter.

When that business was over, he applied to Miss Bingley and Elizabeth for the indulgence of some music. Miss Bingley moved with alacrity to the piano-forte, and after a polite request that Elizabeth would lead the way, which the other as politely and more earnestly negatived, she seated herself.

Mrs. Hurst sang with her sister, and while they were thus employed Elizabeth could not help observing as she turned over some music books that lay on the instrument, how frequently Mr. Darcy's eyes were fixed on her. She hardly knew how to suppose that she could be an object of admiration to so great a man; and yet that he should look at her because he disliked her, was still more strange. She could only imagine however at last, that she drew his notice because there was a something about her more wrong and reprehensible, according to his ideas of right, than in any other person present. The supposition did not pain her. She liked him too little to care for his approbation.

After playing some Italian songs, Miss Bingley varied the charm by a lively Scotch air; and soon afterwards Mr. Darcy, drawing near Elizabeth, said to her—

"Do not you feel a great inclination, Miss Bennet, to seize such an opportunity of dancing a reel?"

She smiled, but made no answer. He repeated the question, with some surprise at her silence.

"Oh!" said she, "I heard you before; but I could not immediately determine what to say in reply. You wanted me, I know, to say 'Yes,' that you might have the pleasure of despising my taste; but I always delight in overthrowing those kind of schemes, and cheating a person of their premeditated contempt. I have therefore made up my mind to tell you, that I do not want to dance a reel at all—and now despise me if you dare."

"Indeed I do not dare."

Elizabeth, having rather expected to affront him, was amazed at his gallantry; but there was a mixture of sweetness and archness in her manner which made it difficult for her to affront anybody; and Darcy had never been so bewitched by any woman as he was by her. He really believed, that were it not for the inferiority of her connections, he should be in some danger.

Miss Bingley saw, or suspected enough to be jealous; and her great anxiety for the recovery of her dear friend Jane, received some assistance from her desire of getting rid of Elizabeth.

She often tried to provoke Darcy into disliking her guest, by talking of their supposed marriage, and planning his happiness in such an alliance.

"I hope," said she, as they were walking together in the shrubbery the next day, "you will give your mother-in-law a few hints, when this desirable event takes place, as to the advantage of holding her tongue; and if you can compass it, do cure the younger girls of running after the officers.—And, if I may mention so delicate a subject, endeavour to check that little something, bordering on conceit and impertinence, which your lady possesses."

"Have you any thing else to propose for my domestic felicity?"

"Oh! yes.—Do let the portraits of your uncle and aunt Philips be placed in the gallery at Pemberley. Put them next to your great uncle the judge. They are in the same profession, you know; only in different lines. As for your Elizabeth's picture, you must not attempt to have it taken, for what painter could do justice to those beautiful eyes?"

"It would not be easy, indeed, to catch their expression, but their colour and shape, and the eye-lashes, so remarkably fine, might be copied."

At that moment they were met from another walk, by Mrs. Hurst and Elizabeth herself.

"I did not know that you intended to walk," said Miss Bingley, in some confusion, lest they had been overheard.

"You used us abominably ill," answered Mrs. Hurst, "in running away without telling us that you were coming out."

Then taking the disengaged arm of Mr. Darcy, she left Elizabeth to walk by herself. The path just admitted three. Mr. Darcy felt their rudeness and immediately said,—

"This walk is not wide enough for our party. We had better go into the avenue."

But Elizabeth, who had not the least inclination to remain with them, laughingly answered,

"No, no; stay where you are.—You are charmingly group'd, and appear to uncommon advantage. The picturesque would be spoilt by admitting a fourth. Good bye."

She then ran gaily off, rejoicing as she rambled about, in the hope of being at home again in a day or two. Jane was already so much recovered as to intend leaving her room for a couple of hours that evening.

## Chapter XI.

When the ladies removed after dinner, Elizabeth ran up to her sister, and seeing her well guarded from cold, attended her into the drawing-room; where she was welcomed by her two friends with many professions of pleasure; and Elizabeth had never seen them so agreeable as they were during the hour which passed before the gentlemen appeared. Their powers of conversation were considerable. They could describe an entertainment with accuracy, relate an anecdote with humour, and laugh at their acquaintance with spirit.

But when the gentlemen entered, Jane was no longer the first object. Miss Bingley's eyes were instantly turned towards Darcy, and she had something to say to him before he had advanced many steps. He addressed himself directly to Miss Bennet, with a polite congratulation; Mr. Hurst also made her a slight bow, and said he was "very glad;" but diffuseness and warmth remained for Bingley's salutation. He was full of joy and attention. The first half hour was spent in piling up the fire, lest she should suffer from the change of room; and she removed at his desire to the other side of the fire-place, that she might be farther from the door. He then sat down by her, and talked scarcely to any one else. Elizabeth, at work in the opposite corner, saw it all with great delight.

When tea was over, Mr. Hurst reminded his sister-in-law of the card-table—but in vain. She had obtained private intelligence that Mr. Darcy did not wish for cards; and Mr. Hurst soon found even his open petition rejected. She assured him that no one intended to play, and the silence of the whole party on the subject, seemed to justify her. Mr. Hurst had therefore nothing to do, but to stretch himself on one of the sophas and go to sleep. Darcy took up a book; Miss Bingley did the same; and Mrs. Hurst, principally occupied in playing with her bracelets and rings, joined now and then in her brother's conversation with Miss Bennet.

Miss Bingley's attention was quite as much engaged in watching Mr. Darcy's progress through *his* book, as in reading her own; and she was perpetually either making some inquiry, or looking at his page. She could not win him, however, to any conversation; he merely answered her question, and read on. At length, quite exhausted by the attempt to be amused with her own book, which she had only chosen because it was the second volume of his, she gave a great yawn and said, "How pleasant it is to spend an evening in this way! I declare after all there is no enjoyment like reading! How much sooner one tires of any thing than of a book!—When I have a house of my own, I shall be miserable if I have not an excellent library."

No one made any reply. She then yawned again, threw aside her book, and cast her eyes round the room in quest of some amusement; when hearing her brother mentioning a ball to Miss Bennet, she turned suddenly towards him and said,

"By the bye, Charles, are you really serious in meditating a dance at Netherfield?—I would advise you, before you determine on it, to consult the wishes of the present party; I am much mistaken if there are not some among us to whom a ball would be rather a punishment than a pleasure."

"If you mean Darcy," cried her brother, "he may go to bed, if he chuses, before it begins—but as for the ball, it is quite a settled thing; and as soon as Nicholls has made white soup enough I shall send round my cards."

"I should like balls infinitely better," she replied, "if they were carried on in a different manner; but there is something insufferably tedious in the usual process of such a meeting. It would surely be much more rational if conversation instead of dancing made the order of the day."

"Much more rational, my dear Caroline, I dare say but it would not be near so much like a ball."

Miss Bingley made no answer; and soon afterwards got up and walked about the room. Her figure was elegant, and she walked well;—but Darcy, at whom it was all aimed, was still inflexibly studious. In the desperation of her feelings she resolved on one effort more; and, turning to Elizabeth, said,

"Miss Eliza Bennet, let me persuade you to follow my example, and take a turn about the room.—I assure you it is very refreshing after sitting so long in one attitude."

Elizabeth was surprised, but agreed to it immediately. Miss Bingley succeeded no less in the real object of her civility; Mr. Darcy looked up. He was as much awake to the novelty of attention in that quarter as Elizabeth herself could be, and unconsciously closed his book. He was directly invited to join their party, but he declined it, observing, that he could imagine but two motives for their chusing to walk up and down the room together, with either of which motives his joining them would interfere. "What could he mean? she was dying to know what could be his meaning"—and asked Elizabeth whether she could at all understand him?

"Not at all," was her answer; "but depend upon it, he means to be severe on us, and our surest way of disappointing him, will be to ask nothing about it."

Miss Bingley, however, was incapable of disappointing Mr. Darcy in any thing, and persevered therefore in requiring an explanation of his two motives.

"I have not the smallest objection to explaining them," said he, as soon as she allowed him to speak. "You either chuse this method of passing the evening because you are in each other's confidence and have secret affairs to discuss, or because you are conscious that your figures appear to the greatest advantage in walking;—if the first, I should be completely in your way;—and if the second, I can admire you much better as I sit by the fire."

"Oh! shocking!" cried Miss Bingley. "I never heard any thing so abominable. How shall we punish him for such a speech?"

"Nothing so easy, if you have but the inclination," said Elizabeth. "We can all plague and punish one another. Teaze him—laugh at him.—Intimate as you are, you must know how it is to be done."

"But upon my honour I do *not.* I do assure you that my intimacy has not yet taught me *that.* Teaze calmness of temper and presence of mind! No, no—I feel he may defy us there. And as to laughter, we will not expose ourselves, if you please, by attempting to laugh without a subject. Mr. Darcy may hug himself."

"Mr. Darcy is not to be laughed at!" cried Elizabeth. "That is an uncommon advantage, and uncommon I hope it will continue, for it would be a great loss to *me* to have many such acquaintance. I dearly love a laugh."

"Miss Bingley," said he, "has given me credit for more than can be. The wisest and the best of men, nay, the wisest and best of their actions, may be rendered ridiculous by a person whose first object in life is a joke."

"Certainly," replied Elizabeth—"there are such people, but I hope I am not one of *them.* I hope I never ridicule what is wise or good. Follies and nonsense, whims and inconsistencies *do* divert me, I own, and I laugh at them whenever I can.—But these, I suppose, are precisely what you are without."

"Perhaps that is not possible for any one. But it has been the study of my life to avoid those weaknesses which often expose a strong understanding to ridicule."

"Such as vanity and pride."

"Yes, vanity is a weakness indeed. But pride—where there is a real superiority of mind, pride will be always under good regulation."

Elizabeth turned away to hide a smile.

"Your examination of Mr. Darcy is over, I presume," said Miss Bingley;—"and pray what is the result?"

"I am perfectly convinced by it that Mr. Darcy has no defect. He owns it himself without disguise."

"No"—said Darcy, "I have made no such pretension. I have faults enough, but they are not, I hope, of understanding. My temper I dare not vouch for.—It is I believe too little yielding—certainly too little for the convenience of the world. I cannot forget the follies and vices of others so soon as I ought, nor their offences against myself. My feelings are not puffed about with every attempt to move them. My temper would perhaps be called resentful.—My good opinion once lost is lost for ever."

"*That* is a failing indeed!"—cried Elizabeth. "Implacable resentment *is* a shade in a character. But you have chosen your fault well.—I really cannot *laugh* at it. You are safe from me."

"There is, I believe, in every disposition a tendency to some particular evil, a natural defect, which not even the best education can overcome."

"And *your* defect is a propensity to hate every body."

"And yours," he replied with a smile, "is wilfully to misunderstand them."

"Do let us have a little music,"—cried Miss Bingley, tired of a conversation in which she had no share.—"Louisa, you will not mind my waking Mr. Hurst."

Her sister made not the smallest objection, and the piano-forte was opened, and Darcy, after a few moments recollection, was not sorry for it. He began to feel the danger of paying Elizabeth too much attention.

## JAMES JOYCE (1882–1941)

James Joyce was born to a middle-class family in Dublin and was educated in Jesuit schools, whose rigorous intellectual discipline marked him for the rest of his life. While his family declined into poverty, Joyce mastered ancient and modern languages, training himself for a literary life. He felt the suffocating pressures for conformity in Dublin and by the age of twenty decided that exile was the only chance for survival. When he finished his university studies he fled to Paris, returning to Dublin only briefly when his mother died. After her death he returned to the Continent with Nora Barnacle, a woman from Ireland's West Country, who was to be his life's companion. They lived in Trieste, Rome, and Zurich and then settled in Paris for nearly twenty years. There he became the center of an international literary avant-garde, although his fiction always remained rooted in Dublin.

Inspired by the ideas of Norwegian playwright Henrik Ibsen and by the short stories of the Russian writer Anton Chekhov, Joyce crafted a lyrical prose of immense flexibility and nuance in his first published book, the short story collection *Dubliners* (1914). "Araby," one of two gemlike stories from *Dubliners* included here, recounts an episode in the life of an adolescent boy whose romantic fantasies of far-off Arabia lead him to a sudden, unexpected "epiphany" (realization) about himself. "Evaline" presents a moment of decision in the life of a young woman torn between duty to family and a chance for personal fulfillment.

After this precocious beginning, Joyce moved from one experiment to another in a constant state of evolution that seemed to exhaust each new form he invented. He published *A Portrait of the Artist as a Young Man,* a semi-autobiographical novel, in 1916. In that book he began to develop the stream-of-consciousness technique that would characterize his work for the rest of his life, in ever more complex and compacted forms. An accomplished singer, Joyce transferred his musical gift into words when he turned to writing. Thus the prose of *Dubliners* and *Portrait* echoes with repeated phrases, motifs, and other musical techniques so subtle that they are likely to go unnoticed by many readers.

Joyce's next and most famous book, *Ulysses* (1922), carried such experimentation much further, introducing new forms and techniques in every chapter. Joyce regarded himself as a priest of art, expecting his readers to devote as much time to understanding his books as he spent writing them. In *Ulysses,* Joyce not only developed one bewildering new fictional technique after another but also, in an elaborately devised system of parallels, restaged Homer's *Odyssey* in just one day in Dublin in 1904. Joyce's Ulysses (the Latin name of Odysseus) is Leopold Bloom, a perfectly ordinary man whose inner world is exposed in all its comic, grotesque, and pathetic detail as he moves through an ordinary day. Like T.S. Eliot's *Waste Land, Ulysses* had an extraordinary impact on the literary world when it first appeared, heightened by official charges of obscenity that seem absurd by today's standards. The chapter included here takes Bloom through the first hour of his day, from breakfast to the bathroom. Even though nothing eventful happens, the reader learns more about Bloom than he or she might have thought possible; the stream of Bloom's consciousness never slows down but darts and drifts from thought to thought, memory to memory, fantasy to fantasy.

"Well, you know or don't you kennet or haven't I told you every telling has a taling and that's the he and the she of it" is how Joyce characterizes narrative art in his last and most extraordinary book, *Finnegans Wake* (1939). He depicts human experience and thought, consciousness and unconsciousness, merging with natural processes and other life-forms in constant metamorphosis, represented in the book's highly artificial dream-language, a nearly unintelligible torrent of multilingual puns. The celebrated first page of the novel—as much as many readers ever attempt—is included here. Any statement of its meaning would be inadequate, but the reader cannot help but hear the hundred-letter thunderclap when the hod-carrier Tim Finnegan falls from his ladder and dies. His body becomes the Dublin landscape in the narrator's dreamworld.

## *Araby*

North Richmond Street, being blind, was a quiet street except at the hour when the Christian Brothers' School set the boys free. An uninhabited house of two storeys stood at the blind end, detached from its neighbours in a square ground. The other houses of the street, conscious of decent lives within them, gazed at one another with brown imperturbable faces.

The former tenant of our house, a priest, had died in the back drawing-room. Air, musty from having been long enclosed, hung in all the rooms, and the waste room behind the kitchen was littered with old useless papers. Among these I found a few paper-covered books, the pages of which were curled and damp: *The Abbot,* by Walter Scott, *The Devout Communicant* and *The Memoirs of Vidocq.* I liked the last best because its leaves were yellow. The wild garden behind the house contained a central apple-tree and a few straggling bushes under one of which I found the late tenant's rusty bicycle-pump. He had been a very charitable priest; in his will he had left all his money to institutions and the furniture of his house to his sister.

When the short days of winter came dusk fell before we had well eaten our dinners. When we met in the street the houses had grown sombre. The space of sky above us was the colour of ever-changing violet and towards it the lamps of the street lifted their feeble lanterns. The cold air stung us and we played till our bodies glowed. Our shouts echoed in the silent street. The career of our play brought us through the dark muddy lanes behind the houses where we ran the gantlet of the rough tribes from the cottages, to the back doors of the dark dripping gardens where odours arose from the ashpits, to the dark odorous stables where a coachman smoothed and combed the horse or shook music from the buckled harness. When we returned to the street light from the kitchen windows had filled the areas. If my uncle was seen turning the corner we hid in the shadow until we had seen him safely housed. Or if Mangan's sister came out on the doorstep to call her brother in to his tea we watched her from our shadow peer up and down the street. We waited to see whether she would remain or go in and, if she remained, we left our shadow and walked up to Mangan's steps resignedly. She was waiting for us, her figure defined by the light from the half-opened door. Her brother always teased her before he obeyed and I stood by the railings looking at her. Her dress swung as she moved her body and the soft rope of her hair tossed from side to side.

Every morning I lay on the floor in the front parlour watching her door. The blind was pulled down to within an inch of the sash so that I could not be seen. When she came out on the doorstep my heart leaped. I ran to the hall, seized my books and followed her. I kept her brown figure always in my eye and, when we came near the point at which our ways diverged, I quickened my pace and passed her. This happened morning after morning. I had never spoken to her, except for a few casual words, and yet her name was like a summons to all my foolish blood.

Her image accompanied me even in places the most hostile to romance. On Saturday evenings when my aunt went marketing I had to go to carry some of the parcels. We walked through the flaring streets, jostled by drunken men and bargaining women, amid the curses of labourers, the shrill litanies of shop-boys who stood on guard by the barrels of pigs' cheeks, the nasal chanting of street-singers, who sang a *come-all-you* about O'Donovan Rossa, or a ballad about the troubles in our native land. These noises converged in a single sensation of life for me: I imagined that I bore my chalice safely through a throng of foes. Her name sprang to my lips at moments in strange prayers and praises which I myself did not understand. My eyes were often full of tears (I could not tell why) and at times a flood from my heart seemed to pour itself out into my bosom. I thought little of the future. I did not know whether I would ever speak to her or not or, if I spoke to her, how I could tell her of my confused adoration. But my body was like a harp and her words and gestures were like fingers running upon the wires.

One evening I went into the back drawing-room in which the priest had died. It was a dark rainy evening and there was no sound in the house. Through one of the broken panes I heard the rain impinge upon the earth, the fine incessant needles of water playing in the sodden beds. Some distant lamp or lighted window gleamed below me. I was thankful that I could see so little. All my senses seemed to desire to veil themselves and, feeling that I was about to slip from them, I pressed the palms of my hands together until they trembled, murmuring: *O love! O love!* many times.

At last she spoke to me. When she addressed the first words to me I was so confused that I did not know what to answer. She asked me was I going to *Araby*. I forget whether I answered yes or no. It would be a splendid bazaar, she said; she would love to go.

—And why can't you? I asked.

While she spoke she turned a silver bracelet round and round her wrist. She could not go, she said, because there would be a retreat that week in her convent. Her brother and two other boys were fighting for their caps and I was alone at the railings. She held one of the spikes, bowing her head towards me. The light from the lamp opposite our door caught the white curve of her neck, lit up her hair that rested there and, falling, lit up the hand upon the railing. It fell over one side of her dress and caught the white border of a petticoat, just visible as she stood at ease.

—It's well for you, she said.

—If I go, I said, I will bring you something.

What innumerable follies laid waste my waking and sleeping thoughts after that evening! I wished to annihilate the tedious intervening days. I chafed against the work of school. At night in my bedroom and by day in the classroom her image came between me and the page I strove to read. The syllables of the word *Araby* were called to me through the silence in which my soul luxuriated and cast an Eastern enchantment over me. I asked for leave to go to the bazaar on Saturday night. My aunt was surprised and hoped it was not some Freemason affair. I answered few questions in class. I watched my master's face pass from amiability to sternness; he hoped I was not beginning to idle. I could not call my wandering thoughts together. I had hardly any patience with the serious work of life which, now that it stood between me and my desire, seemed to me child's play, ugly monotonous child's play.

On Saturday morning I reminded my uncle that I wished to go to the bazaar in the evening. He was fussing at the hallstand, looking for the hat-brush, and answered me curtly:

—Yes, boy, I know.

As he was in the hall I could not go into the front parlour and lie at the window. I left the house in bad humour and walked slowly towards the school. The air was pitilessly raw and already my heart misgave me.

When I came home to dinner my uncle had not yet been home. Still it was early. I sat staring at the clock for some time and, when its ticking began to irritate me, I left the room. I mounted the staircase and gained the upper part of the house. The high cold empty gloomy rooms liberated me and I went from room to room singing. From the front window I saw my companions playing below in the street. Their cries reached me weakened and indistinct and, leaning my forehead against the cool glass, I looked over at the dark house where she lived. I may have stood there for an hour, seeing nothing but the brown-clad figure cast by my imagination, touched discreetly by the lamplight at the curved neck, at the hand upon the railings and at the border below the dress.

When I came downstairs again I found Mrs Mercer sitting at the fire. She was an old garrulous woman, a pawnbroker's widow, who collected used stamps for some pious purpose. I had to endure the gossip of the tea-table. The meal was prolonged beyond an hour and still my uncle did not come. Mrs Mercer stood up to go: she was sorry she couldn't wait any longer, but it was after eight o'clock and she did not like to be out late, as the night air was bad for her. When she had gone I began to walk up and down the room, clenching my fists. My aunt said:

—I'm afraid you may put off your bazaar for this night of Our Lord.

At nine o'clock I heard my uncle's latchkey in the halldoor. I heard him talking to himself and heard the hallstand rocking when it had received the weight of his overcoat. I could interpret these signs. When he was midway through his dinner I asked him to give me the money to go to the bazaar. He had forgotten.

—The people are in bed and after their first sleep now, he said.

I did not smile. My aunt said to him energetically:

—Can't you give him the money and let him go? You've kept him late enough as it is.

My uncle said he was very sorry he had forgotten. He said he believed in the old saying: *All work and no play makes Jack a dull boy*. He asked me where I was going and, when I had told him a second time he asked me did I know *The Arab's Farewell to his Steed*. When I left the kitchen he was about to recite the opening lines of the piece to my aunt.

I held a florin tightly in my hand as I strode down Buckingham Street towards the station. The sight of the streets thronged with buyers and glaring with gas recalled to me the purpose of my journey. I took my seat in a third-class carriage of a deserted train. After an intolerable delay the train moved out of the station slowly. It crept onward among ruinous houses and over the twinkling river. At Westland Row Station a crowd of people pressed to the carriage doors; but the porters moved them back, saying that it was a special train for the bazaar. I remained alone in the bare carriage. In a few minutes the train drew up beside an improvised wooden platform. I passed out on to the road and saw by the lighted dial of a clock that it was ten minutes to ten. In front of me was a large building which displayed the magical name.

I could not find any sixpenny entrance and, fearing that the bazaar would be closed, I passed in quickly through a turnstile, handing a shilling to a weary-looking man. I found myself in a big hall girdled at half its height by a gallery. Nearly all the stalls were closed and the greater part of the hall was in darkness. I recognised a silence like that which pervades a church after a service. I walked into the centre of the bazaar timidly. A few people were gathered about the stalls which were still open. Before a curtain, over which the words *Café Chantant* were written in coloured lamps, two men were counting money on a salver. I listened to the fall of the coins.

Remembering with difficulty why I had come I went over to one of the stalls and examined porcelain vases and flowered tea-sets. At the door of the stall a young lady was talking and laughing with two young gentlemen. I remarked their English accents and listened vaguely to their conversation.

—O, I never said such a thing!

—O, but you did!

—O, but I didn't!

—Didn't she say that?

—Yes. I heard her.

—O, there's a . . . fib!

Observing me the young lady came over and asked me did I wish to buy anything. The tone of her voice was not encouraging; she seemed to have spoken to me out of a sense of duty. I looked humbly at the great jars that stood like eastern guards at either side of the dark entrance to the stall and murmured:

—No, thank you.

The young lady changed the position of one of the vases and went back to the two young men. They began to talk of the same subject. Once or twice the young lady glanced at me over her shoulder.

I lingered before her stall, though I knew my stay was useless, to make my interest in her wares seem the more real. Then I turned away slowly and walked down the middle of the bazaar. I allowed the two pennies to fall against the sixpence in my pocket. I heard a voice call from one end of the gallery that the light was out. The upper part of the hall was now completely dark.

Gazing up into the darkness I saw myself as a creature driven and derided by vanity; and my eyes burned with anguish and anger.

## Eveline

She sat at the window watching the evening invade the avenue. Her head was leaned against the window curtains and in her nostrils was the odour of dusty cretonne. She was tired.

Few people passed. The man out of the last house passed on his way home; she heard his footsteps clacking along the concrete pavement and afterwards crunching on the cinder path before the new red houses. One time there used to be a field there in which they used to play every evening with other people's children. Then a man from Belfast bought the field and built houses in it—not like their little brown houses but bright brick houses with shining roofs. The children of the avenue used to play together in that field—the Devines, the Waters, the Dunns, little Keogh the cripple, she and her brothers and sisters. Ernest, however, never played: he was too grown up. Her father used often to hunt them in out of the field with his blackthorn stick; but usually little Keogh used to keep *nix* and call out when he saw her father coming. Still they seemed to have been rather happy then. Her father was not so bad then; and besides, her mother was alive. That was a long time ago; she and her brothers and sisters were all grown up; her mother was dead. Tizzie Dunn was dead, too, and the Waters had gone back to England. Everything changes. Now she was going to go away like the others, to leave her home.

Home! She looked round the room, reviewing all its familiar objects which she had dusted once a week for so many years, wondering where on earth all the dust came from. Perhaps she would never see again those familiar objects from which she had never dreamed of being divided. And yet during all those years she had never found out the name of the priest whose yellowing photograph hung on the wall above the broken harmonium beside the coloured print of the promises made to Blessed Margaret Mary Alacoque. He had been a school friend of her father. Whenever he showed the photograph to a visitor her father used to pass it with a casual word:

—He is in Melbourne now.

She had consented to go away, to leave her home. Was that wise? She tried to weigh each side of the question. In her home anyway she had shelter and food; she had those whom she had known all her life about her. Of course she had to work hard both in the house and at business. What would they say of her in the Stores when they found out that she had run away with a fellow? Say she was a fool, perhaps; and her place would be filled up by advertisement. Miss Gavan would be glad. She had always had an edge on her, especially whenever there were people listening.

—Miss Hill, don't you see these ladies are waiting?

—Look lively, Miss Hill, please.

She would not cry many tears at leaving the Stores.

But in her new home, in a distant unknown country, it would not be like that. Then she would be married—she, Eveline. People would treat her with respect then. She would not be treated as her mother had been. Even now, though she was over nineteen, she sometimes felt herself in danger of her father's violence. She knew it was that that had given her the palpitations. When they were growing up he had never gone for her, like he used to go for Harry and Ernest, because she was a girl; but latterly he had begun to threaten her and say what he would do to her only for her dead mother's sake. And now she had nobody to protect her. Ernest was dead and Harry, who was in the church decorating business, was nearly always down somewhere in the country. Besides, the invariable squabble for money on Saturday nights had begun to weary her unspeakably. She always gave her entire wages—seven shillings—and Harry always sent up what he could but the trouble was to get any money from her father. He said she used to squander the money, that she had no head, that he wasn't going to give her his hard-earned money to throw about the streets, and much more, for he was usually fairly bad of a Saturday night. In the end he would give her the money and ask her had she any intention of buying Sunday's dinner. Then she had to rush out as quickly as she could and do her marketing, holding her black leather purse tightly in her hand as she elbowed her way through the crowds and returning home late under her load of provisions. She had hard work to keep the house together and to see that the two young children who had been left to her charge went to school regularly and got their meals regularly. It was hard work—a hard life—but now that she was about to leave it she did not find it a wholly undesirable life.

She was about to explore another life with Frank. Frank was very kind, manly, open-hearted. She was to go away with him by the night-boat to be his wife and to live with him in Buenos Ayres where he had a home waiting for her. How well she remembered the first time she had seen him; he was lodging in a house on the main road where she used to visit. It seemed a few weeks ago. He was standing at the gate, his peaked cap pushed back on his head and his hair tumbled forward over a face of bronze. Then they had come to know each other. He used to meet her outside the Stores every evening and see her home. He took her to see *The Bohemian Girl* and she felt elated as she sat in an unaccustomed part of the theatre with him. He was awfully fond of music and sang a little. People knew that they were courting and, when he sang about the lass that loves a sailor, she always felt pleasantly confused. He used to call her Poppens out of fun. First of all it had been an excitement for her to have a fellow and then she had begun to like him. He had tales of distant countries. He had started as a deck boy at a pound a month on a ship of the Allan Line going out to Canada. He told her the names of the ships he had been on and the names of the different services. He had sailed through the Straits of Magellan and he told her stories of the terrible Patagonians. He had fallen on his feet in Buenos Ayres, he said, and had come over to the old country just for a holiday. Of course, her father had found out the affair and had forbidden her to have anything to say to him.

—I know these sailor chaps, he said.

One day he had quarrelled with Frank and after that she had to meet her lover secretly.

The evening deepened in the avenue. The white of two letters in her lap grew indistinct. One was to Harry; the other was to her father. Ernest had been her favourite but she liked Harry too. Her father was becoming old lately, she noticed; he would miss her. Sometimes he could be very nice. Not long before, when she had been laid up for a day, he had read her out a ghost story and made toast for her at the fire. Another day, when their mother was alive, they had all gone for a picnic to the Hill of Howth. She remembered her father putting on her mother's bonnet to make the children laugh.

Her time was running out but she continued to sit by the window, leaning her head against the window curtain, inhaling the odour of dusty cretonne. Down far in the avenue she could hear a street organ playing. She knew the air. Strange that it should come that very night to remind her of the promise to her mother, her promise to keep the home together as long as she could. She remembered the last night of her mother's illness; she was again in the close dark room at the other side of the hall and outside she heard a melancholy air of Italy. The organ-player had been ordered to go away and given sixpence. She remembered her father strutting back into the sickroom saying:

—Damned Italians! coming over here!

As she mused the pitiful vision of her mother's life laid its spell on the very quick of her being—that life of commonplace sacrifices closing in final craziness. She trembled as she heard again her mother's voice saying constantly with foolish insistence:

—Derevaun Seraun! Derevaun Seraun!

She stood up in a sudden impulse of terror. Escape! She must escape! Frank would save her. He would give her life, perhaps love, too. But she wanted to live. Why should she be unhappy? She had a right to happiness. Frank would take her in his arms, fold her in his arms. He would save her.

She stood among the swaying crowd in the station at the North Wall. He held her hand and she knew that he was speaking to her, saying something about the passage over and over again. The station was full of soldiers with brown baggages. Through the wide doors of the sheds she caught a glimpse of the black mass of the boat, lying in beside the quay wall, with illumined portholes. She answered nothing. She felt her cheek pale and cold and, out of a maze of distress, she prayed to God to direct her, to show her what was her duty. The boat blew a long mournful whistle into the mist. If she went, to-morrow she would be on the sea with Frank, steaming towards Buenos Ayres. Their passage had been booked. Could she still draw back after all he had done for her? Her distress awoke a nausea in her body and she kept moving her lips in silent fervent prayer.

A bell clanged upon her heart. She felt him seize her hand:

—Come!

All the seas of the world tumbled about her heart. He was drawing her into them: he would drown her. She gripped with both hands at the iron railing.

—Come!

No! No! No! It was impossible. Her hands clutched the iron in frenzy. Amid the seas she sent a cry of anguish!

—Eveline! Evvy!

He rushed beyond the barrier and called to her to follow. He was shouted at to go on but he still called to her. She set her white face to him, passive, like a helpless animal. Her eyes gave him no sign of love or farewell or recognition.

## *from Ulysses*

### Chapter 4 [Calypso: Bloom's Breakfast]

*Mr Leopold Bloom ate with relish the inner organs of beasts and fowls. He liked thick giblet soup, nutty gizzards, a stuffed roast heart, liverslices fried with crustcrumbs, fried hencods' roes. Most of all he liked grilled mutton kidneys which gave to his palate a fine tang of faintly scented urine.

Kidneys were in his mind as he moved about the kitchen softly, righting her breakfast things on the humpy tray. Gelid light and air were in the kitchen but out of doors gentle summer morning everywhere. Made him feel a bit peckish.

The coals were reddening.

Another slice of bread and butter: three, four: right. She didn't like her plate full. Right. He turned from the tray, lifted the kettle off the hob and set it sideways on the fire. It sat there, dull and squat, its spout stuck out. Cup of tea soon. Good. Mouth dry.

The cat walked stiffly round a leg of the table with tail on high.

—Mkgnao!

—O, there you are, Mr Bloom said, turning from the fire.

The cat mewed in answer and stalked again stiffly round a leg of the table, mewing. Just how she stalks over my writingtable. Prr. Scratch my head. Prr.

Mr Bloom watched curiously, kindly the lithe black form. Clean to see: the gloss of her sleek hide, the white button under the butt of her tail, the green flashing eyes. He bent down to her, his hands on his knees.

—Milk for the pussens, he said.

—Mrkgnao! the cat cried.

They call them stupid. They understand what we say better than we understand them. She understands all she wants to. Vindictive too. Cruel. Her nature. Curious mice never squeal.

Seem to like it. Wonder what I look like to her. Height of a tower? No, she can jump me.

—Afraid of the chickens she is, he said mockingly. Afraid of the chookchooks. I never saw such a stupid pussens as the pussens.

—Mrkrgnao! the cat said loudly.

She blinked up out of her avid shameclosing eyes, mewing plaintively and long, showing him her milkwhite teeth. He watched the dark eyeslits narrowing with greed till her eyes were green stones. Then he went to the dresser, took the jug Hanlon's milkman had just filled for him, poured warmbubbled milk on a saucer and set it slowly on the floor.

—Gurrhr! she cried, running to lap.

He watched the bristles shining wirily in the weak light as she tipped three times and licked lightly. Wonder is it true if you clip them they can't mouse after. Why? They shine in the dark, perhaps, the tips. Or kind of feelers in the dark, perhaps.

He listened to her licking lap. Ham and eggs, no. No good eggs with this drouth. Want pure fresh water. Thursday: not a good day either for a mutton kidney at Buckley's. Fried with butter, a shake of pepper. Better a pork kidney at Dlugacz's. While the kettle is boiling. She lapped slower, then licking the saucer clean. Why are their tongues so rough? To lap better, all porous holes. Nothing she can eat? He glanced round him. No.

On quietly creaky boots he went up the staircase to the hall, paused by the bedroom door. She might like something tasty. Thin bread and butter she likes in the morning. Still perhaps: once in a way.

He said softly in the bare hall:

—I'm going round the corner. Be back in a minute.

And when he had heard his voice say it he added:

—You don't want anything for breakfast?

A sleepy soft grunt answered:

—Mn.

No. She didn't want anything. He heard then a warm heavy sigh, softer, as she turned over and the loose brass quoits of the bedstead jingled. Must get those settled really. Pity. All the way from Gibraltar. Forgotten any little Spanish she knew. Wonder what her father gave for it. Old style. Ah yes! of course. Bought it at the governor's auction. Got a short knock. Hard as nails at a bargain, old Tweedy. Yes sir. At Plevna that was. I rose from the ranks, sir, and I'm proud of it. Still he had brains enough to make that corner in stamps. Now that was farseeing.

His hand took his hat from the peg over his initialled heavy overcoat and his lost property office secondhand waterproof. Stamps: stickyback pictures. Daresay lots of officers are in the swim too. Course they do. The sweated legend in the crown of his hat told him mutely: Plasto's high grade ha. He peeped quickly inside the leather headband. White slip of paper. Quite safe.

On the doorstep he felt in his hip pocket for the latchkey. Not there. In the trousers I left off. Must get it. Potato I have. Creaky wardrobe. No use disturbing her. She turned over sleepily that time. He pulled the halldoor to after him very quietly, more, till the footleaf dropped gently over the threshold, a limp lid. Looked shut. All right till I come back anyhow.

He crossed to the bright side, avoiding the loose cellarflap of number seventyfive. The sun was nearing the steeple of George's church. Be a warm day I fancy. Specially in these black clothes feel it more. Black conducts, reflects, (refracts is it?), the heat. But I couldn't go in that light suit. Make a picnic of it. His eyelids sank quietly often as he walked in happy warmth. Boland's breadvan delivering with trays our daily but she prefers yesterday's loaves turnovers crisp crowns hot. Makes you feel young. Somewhere in the east: early morning: set off at dawn. Travel round in front of the sun, steal a day's march on him. Keep it up for ever never grow a day older technically. Walk along a strand, strange land, come to a city gate, sentry there, old ranker too, old Tweedy's big moustaches, leaning on a long kind of a spear. Wander through awned streets. Turbaned faces going by. Dark caves of carpet shops, big man, Turko the terrible, seated crosslegged, smoking a coiled pipe. Cries of sellers in the streets. Drink water scented with fennel, sherbet. Dander along all day. Might meet a robber or two. Well, meet him. Getting on to sundown. The shadows of the mosques among the pillars: priest with a scroll rolled up. A shiver of the trees, signal, the evening wind. I pass on. Fading gold sky. A mother watches me from her doorway. She calls her children home in their dark language. High wall: beyond strings twanged. Night sky, moon, violet, colour of Molly's new garters. Strings. Listen. A girl playing one of those instruments what do you call them: dulcimers. I pass.

Probably not a bit like it really. Kind of stuff you read: in the track of the sun. Sunburst on the titlepage. He smiled, pleasing himself. What Arthur Griffith said about the headpiece over the *Freeman* leader: a homerule sun rising up in the northwest from the laneway behind the bank of Ireland. He prolonged his pleased smile. Ikey touch that: homerule sun rising up in the northwest.

He approached Larry O'Rourke's. From the cellar grating floated up the flabby gush of porter. Through the open doorway the bar squirted out whiffs of ginger, teadust, biscuitmush. Good house, however: just the end of the city traffic. For instance M'Auley's down there: n. g. as position. Of course if they ran a tramline along the North Circular from the cattlemarket to the quays value would go up like a shot.

Baldhead over the blind. Cute old codger. No use canvassing him for an ad. Still he knows his own business best. There he is, sure enough, my bold Larry, leaning against the sugarbin in his shirtsleeves watching the aproned curate swab up with mop and bucket. Simon Dedalus takes him off to a tee with his eyes screwed up. Do you know what I'm going to tell you? What's that, Mr O'Rourke? Do you know what? The Russians, they'd only be an eight o'clock breakfast for the Japanese.

Stop and say a word: about the funeral perhaps. Sad thing about poor Dignam, Mr O'Rourke.

Turning into Dorset street he said freshly in greeting through the doorway:

—Good day, Mr O'Rourke.

—Good day to you.

—Lovely weather, sir.

—'Tis all that.

Where do they get the money? Coming up redheaded curates from the county Leitrim, rinsing empties and old man in the cellar. Then, lo and behold, they blossom out as Adam Findlaters or Dan Tallons. Then think of the competition. General thirst. Good puzzle would be cross Dublin without passing a pub. Save it they can't. Off the drunks perhaps. Put down three and carry five. What is that, a bob here and there, dribs and drabs. On the wholesale orders perhaps. Doing a double shuffle with the town travellers. Square it you with the boss and we'll split the job, see?

How much would that tot to off the porter in the month? Say ten barrels of stuff. Say he got ten per cent off. O more. Fifteen. He passed Saint Joseph's National school. Brats' clamour. Windows open. Fresh air helps memory. Or a lilt. Ahbeesee defeegee kelomen opeecue rustyouvee doubleyou. Boys are they? Yes, Inishturk. Inishark. Inishboffin. At their joggerfry. Mine. Slieve Bloom.

He halted before Dlugacz's window, staring at the hanks of sausages, polonies, black and white. Fifteen multiplied by. The figures whitened in his mind, unsolved: displeased, he let them fade. The shiny links, packed with forcemeat, fed his gaze and he breathed in tranquilly the lukewarm breath of cooked spicy pigs' blood.

A kidney oozed bloodgouts on the willowpatterned dish: the last. He stood by the nextdoor girl at the counter. Would she buy it too, calling the items from a slip in her hand? Chapped: washingsoda. And a pound and a half of Denny's sausages. His eyes rested on her vigorous hips. Woods his name is. Wonder what he does. Wife is oldish. New blood. No followers allowed. Strong pair of arms. Whacking a carpet on the clothesline. She does whack it, by George. The way her crooked skirt swings at each whack.

The ferreteyed porkbutcher folded the sausages he had snipped off with blotchy fingers, sausagepink. Sound meat there: like a stallfed heifer.

He took a page up from the pile of cut sheets: the model farm at Kinnereth on the lakeshore of Tiberias. Can become ideal winter sanatorium. Moses Montefiore. I thought he was, Farmhouse, wall round it, blurred cattle cropping. He held the page from him: interesting: read it nearer, the title, the blurred cropping cattle, the page rustling. A young white heifer. Those mornings in the cattlemarket, the beasts lowing in their pens, branded sheep, flop and fall of dung, the breeders in hobnailed boots trudging through the litter, slapping a palm on a ripemeated hindquarter, there's a prime one, unpeeled switches in their hands. He held the page aslant patiently, bending his senses and his will, his soft subject gaze at rest. The crooked skirt swinging, whack by whack by whack.

The porkbutcher snapped two sheets from the pile, wrapped up her prime sausages and made a red grimace.

—Now, my miss, he said.

She tendered a coin, smiling boldly, holding her thick wrist out.

—Thank you, my miss. And one shilling threepence change. For you, please?

Mr Bloom pointed quickly. To catch up and walk behind her if she went slowly, behind her moving hams. Pleasant to see first thing in the morning. Hurry up, damn it. Make hay while the sun shines. She stood outside the shop in sunlight and sauntered lazily to the right. He sighed down his nose: they never understand. Sodachapped hands. Crusted toenails too. Brown scapulars in tatters, defending her both ways. The sting of disregard glowed to weak pleasure within his breast. For another: a constable off duty cuddling her in Eccles lane. They like them sizeable. Prime sausage. O please, Mr Policeman, I'm lost in the wood.

—Threepence, please.

His hand accepted the moist tender gland and slid it into a sidepocket. Then it fetched up three coins from his trousers' pocket and laid them on the rubber prickles. They lay, were read quickly and quickly slid, disc by disc, into the till.

—Thank you, sir. Another time.

A speck of eager fire from foxeyes thanked him. He withdrew his gaze after an instant. No: better not: another time.

—Good morning, he said, moving away.

—Good morning, sir.

No sign. Gone. What matter?

He walked back along Dorset street, reading gravely. Agendath Netaim: planters' company. To purchase waste sandy tracts from Turkish government and plant with eucalyptus trees. Excellent for shade, fuel and construction. Orangegroves and immense melonfields north of Jaffa. You pay eighty marks and they plant a dunam of land for you with olives, oranges, almonds or citrons. Olives cheaper: oranges need artificial irrigation. Every year you get a sending of the crop. Your name entered for life as owner in the book of the union. Can pay ten down and the balance in yearly instalments. Bleibtreustrasse 34, Berlin, W. 15.

Nothing doing. Still an idea behind it.

He looked at the cattle, blurred in silver heat. Silverpowdered olivetrees. Quiet long days: pruning, ripening. Olives are packed in jars, eh? I have a few left from Andrews. Molly spitting them out. Knows the taste of them now. Oranges in tissue paper packed in crates. Citrons too. Wonder is poor Citron still in Saint Kevin's parade. And Mastiansky with the old cither. Pleasant evenings we had then. Molly in Citron's basketchair. Nice to hold, cool waxen fruit, hold in the hand, lift it to the nostrils and smell the perfume. Like that, heavy, sweet, wild perfume. Always the same, year after year. They fetched high prices too, Moisel told me. Arbutus place: Pleasants-street: pleasant old times. Must be without a flaw, he said. Coming all that way: Spain, Gibraltar, Mediterranean, the Levant. Crates lined up on the quayside at Jaffa, chap ticking them off in a book, navvies handling them barefoot in soiled dungarees. There's whatdoyoucallhim out of. How do you? Doesn't see. Chap you know just to salute bit of a bore. His back is like that Norwegian captain's. Wonder if I'll meet him today. Watering cart. To provoke the rain. On earth as it is in heaven.

A cloud began to cover the sun slowly, wholly. Grey. Far.

No, not like that. A barren land, bare waste. Vulcanic lake, the dead sea: no fish, weedless, sunk deep in the earth. No wind could lift those waves, grey metal, poisonous foggy waters. Brimstone they called it raining down: the cities of the plain: Sodom, Gomorrah, Edom. All dead names. A dead sea in a dead land, grey and old. Old now. It bore the oldest, the first race. A bent hag crossed from Cassidy's, clutching a naggin bottle by the neck. The oldest people. Wandered far away over all the earth, captivity to captivity, multiplying, dying, being born everywhere. It lay there now. Now it could bear no more. Dead: an old woman's: the grey sunken cunt of the world.

Desolation.

Grey horror seared his flesh. Folding the page into his pocket he turned into Eccles street, hurrying homeward. Cold oils slid along his veins, chilling his blood: age crusting him with a salt cloak. Well, I am here now. Yes, I am here now. Morning mouth bad images. Got up wrong side of the bed. Must begin again those Sandow's exercises. On the hands down. Blotchy brown brick houses. Number eighty still unlet. Why is that? Valuation is only twentyeight. Towers, Battersby, North, MacArthur: parlour windows plastered with bills. Plasters on a sore eye. To smell the gentle smoke of tea, fume of the pan, sizzling butter. Be near her ample bedwarmed flesh. Yes, yes.

Quick warm sunlight came running from Berkeley road, swiftly, in slim sandals, along the brightening footpath. Runs, she runs to meet me, a girl with gold hair on the wind.

Two letters and a card lay on the hallfloor. He stooped and gathered them. Mrs Marion Bloom. His quickened heart slowed at once. Bold hand. Mrs Marion.

—Poldy!

Entering the bedroom he halfclosed his eyes and walked through warm yellow twilight towards her tousled head.

—Who are the letters for?

He looked at them. Mullingar. Milly.

—A letter for me from Milly, he said carefully, and a card to you. And a letter for you.

He laid her card and letter on the twill bedspread near the curve of her knees.

—Do you want the blind up?

Letting the blind up by gentle tugs halfway his backward eye saw her glance at the letter and tuck it under her pillow.

—That do? he asked, turning.

She was reading the card, propped on her elbow.

—She got the things, she said.

He waited till she had laid the card aside and curled herself back slowly with a snug sigh.

—Hurry up with that tea, she said. I'm parched.

—The kettle is boiling, he said.

But he delayed to clear the chair: her striped petticoat, tossed soiled linen: and lifted all in an armful on to the foot of the bed.

As he went down the kitchen stairs she called:

—Poldy!

—What?

—Scald the teapot.

On the boil sure enough: a plume of steam from the spout. He scalded and rinsed out the teapot and put in four full spoons of tea, tilting the kettle then to let the water flow in. Having set it to draw he took off the kettle, crushed the pan flat on the live coals and watched the lump of butter slide and melt. While he unwrapped the kidney the cat mewed hungrily against him. Give her too much meat she won't mouse. Say they won't eat pork. Kosher. Here. He let the bloodsmeared paper fall to her and dropped the kidney amid the sizzling butter sauce. Pepper. He sprinkled it through his fingers ringwise from the chipped eggcup.

Then he slit open his letter, glancing down the page and over. Thanks: new tam: Mr Coghlan: lough Owel picnic: young student: Blazes Boylan's seaside girls.

The tea was drawn. He filled his own moustachecup, sham crown Derby, smiling. Silly Milly's birthday gift. Only five she was then. No, wait: four. I gave her the amberoid necklace she broke. Putting pieces of folded brown paper in the letterbox for her. He smiled, pouring.

*O, Milly Bloom, you are my darling.*
*You are my lookingglass from night to morning.*
*I'd rather have you without a farthing*
*Than Katey Keogh with her ass and garden.*

Poor old professor Goodwin. Dreadful old case. Still he was a courteous old chap. Oldfashioned way he used to bow Molly off the platform. And the little mirror in his silk hat. The night Milly brought it into the parlour. O, look what I found in professor Goodwin's hat! All we laughed. Sex breaking out even then. Pert little piece she was.

He prodded a fork into the kidney and slapped it over: then fitted the teapot on the tray. Its hump bumped as he took it up. Everything on it? Bread and butter, four, sugar, spoon, her cream. Yes. He carried it upstairs, his thumb hooked in the teapot handle.

Nudging the door open with his knee he carried the tray in and set it on the chair by the bedhead.

—What a time you were! she said.

She set the brasses jingling as she raised herself briskly, an elbow on the pillow. He looked calmly down on her bulk and between her large soft bubs, sloping within her nightdress like a shegoat's udder. The warmth of her couched body rose on the air, mingling with the fragrance of the tea she poured.

A strip of torn envelope peeped from under the dimpled pillow. In the act of going he stayed to straighten the bedspread.

—Who was the letter from? he asked.

Bold hand. Marion.

—O, Boylan, she said. He's bringing the programme.

—What are you singing?

—*Là ci darem* with J.C. Doyle, she said, and *Love's Old Sweet Song.*

Her full lips, drinking, smiled. Rather stale smell that incense leaves next day. Like foul flowerwater.

—Would you like the window open a little?

She doubled a slice of bread into her mouth, asking:

—What time is the funeral?

—Eleven, I think, he answered. I didn't see the paper.

Following the pointing of her finger he took up a leg of her soiled drawers from the bed. No? Then, a twisted grey garter looped round a stocking: rumpled, shiny sole.

—No: that book.

Other stocking. Her petticoat.

—It must have fell down, she said.

He felt here and there. *Voglio e non vorrei.* Wonder if she pronounces that right: *voglio.* Not in the bed. Must have slid down. He stooped and lifted the valance. The book, fallen, sprawled against the bulge of the orangekeyed chamberpot.

—Show here, she said. I put a mark in it. There's a word I wanted to ask you.

She swallowed a draught of tea from her cup held by nothandle and, having wiped her fingertips smartly on the blanket, began to search the text with the hairpin till she reached the word.

—Met him what? he asked.

—Here, she said. What does that mean?

He leaned downward and read near her polished thumbnail.

—Metempsychosis?

—Yes. Who's he when he's at home?

—Metempsychosis, he said, frowning. It's Greek: from the Greek. That means the transmigration of souls.

—O, rocks! she said. Tell us in plain words.

He smiled, glancing askance at her mocking eyes. The same young eyes. The first night after the charades. Dolphin's Barn. He turned over the smudged pages. *Ruby: the Pride of the Ring.* Hello. Illustration. Fierce Italian with carriagewhip. Must be Ruby pride of the on the floor naked. Sheet kindly lent. *The monster Maffei desisted and flung his victim from him with an oath.* Cruelty behind it all. Doped animals. Trapeze at Hengler's. Had to look the other way. Mob gaping. Break your neck and we'll break our sides. Families of them. Bone them young so they metamspychosis. That we live after death. Our souls. That a man's soul after he dies, Dignam's soul. . . .

—Did you finish it? he asked.

—Yes, she said. There's nothing smutty in it. Is she in love with the first fellow all the time?

—Never read it. Do you want another?

—Yes. Get another of Paul de Kock's. Nice name he has.

She poured more tea into her cup, watching it flow sideways.

Must get that Capel street library book renewed or they'll write to Kearney, my guarantor. Reincarnation: that's the word.

—Some people believe, he said, that we go on living in another body after death, that we lived before. They call it reincarnation. That we all lived before on the earth thousands of years ago or some other planet. They say we have forgotten it. Some say they remember their past lives.

The sluggish cream wound curdling spirals through her tea. Better remind her of the word: metempsychosis. An example would be better. An example?

*The Bath of the Nymph* over the bed. Given away with the Easter number of *Photo Bits:* splendid masterpiece in art colours. Tea before you put milk in. Not unlike her with her hair down: slimmer. Three and six I gave for the frame. She said it would look nice over the bed. Naked nymphs: Greece: and for instance all the people that lived then.

He turned the pages back.

—Metempsychosis, he said, is what the ancient Greeks called it. They used to believe you could be changed into an animal or a tree, for instance. What they called nymphs, for example.

Her spoon ceased to stir up the sugar. She gazed straight before her, inhaling through her arched nostrils.

—There's a smell of burn, she said. Did you leave anything on the fire?

—The kidney! he cried suddenly.

He fitted the book roughly into his inner pocket and, stubbing his toes against the broken commode, hurried out towards the smell, stepping hastily down the stairs with a flurried stork's legs. Pungent smoke shot up in an angry jet from a side of the pan. By prodding a prong of the fork under the kidney he detached it and turned it turtle on its back. Only a little burnt. He tossed it off the pan on to a plate and let the scanty brown gravy trickle over it.

Cup of tea now. He sat down, cut and buttered a slice of the loaf. He shore away the burnt flesh and flung it to the cat. Then he put a forkful into his mouth, chewing with discernment the toothsome pliant meat. Done to a turn. A mouthful of tea. Then he cut away dies of bread, sopped one in the gravy and put it in his mouth. What was that about some young student and a picnic? He creased out the letter at his side, reading it slowly as he chewed, sopping another die of bread in the gravy and raising it to his mouth.

> Dearest Papli
> Thanks ever so much for the lovely birthday present. It suits me splendid. Everyone says I am quite the belle in my new tam. I got mummy's lovely box of creams and am writing. They are lovely. I am getting on swimming in the photo business now. Mr Coghlan took one of me and Mrs. Will send when developed. We did great biz yesterday. Fair day and all the beef to the heels were in. We are going to lough Owel on Monday with a few friends to make a scrap picnic. Give my love to mummy and to yourself a big kiss and thanks. I hear them at the piano downstairs. There is to be a concert in the Greville Arms on Saturday. There is a young student comes here some evenings named Bannon his cousins or something are big swells and he sings Boylan's (I was on the pop of writing Blazes Boylan's) song about those seaside girls. Tell him silly Milly sends my best respects. I must now close with fondest love
>
> Your fond daughter
> Milly
>
> P. S. Excuse bad writing am in hurry. Byby.
>
> M.

Fifteen yesterday. Curious, fifteenth of the month too. Her first birthday away from home. Separation. Remember the summer morning she was born, running to knock up Mrs Thornton in Denzille street. Jolly old woman. Lot of babies she must have helped into the world. She knew from the first poor little Rudy wouldn't live. Well, God is good, sir. She knew at once. He would be eleven now if he had lived.

His vacant face stared pityingly at the postscript. Excuse bad writing. Hurry. Piano downstairs. Coming out of her shell. Row with her in the XL Café about the bracelet. Wouldn't eat her cakes or speak or look. Saucebox. He sopped other dies of bread in the gravy and ate piece after piece of kidney. Twelve and six a week. Not much. Still, she might do worse. Musichall stage. Young student. He drank a draught of cooler tea to wash down his meal. Then he read the letter again: twice.

O, well: she knows how to mind herself. But if not? No, nothing has happened. Of course it might. Wait in any case till it does. A wild piece of goods. Her slim legs running up the staircase. Destiny. Ripening now. Vain: very.

He smiled with troubled affection at the kitchen window. Day I caught her in the street pinching her cheeks to make them red. Anemic a little. Was given milk too long. On the *Erin's King* that day round the Kish. Damned old tub pitching about. Not a bit funky. Her pale blue scarf loose in the wind with her hair.

*All dimpled cheeks and curls,*
*Your head it simply swirls.*

Seaside girls. Torn envelope. Hands stuck in his trousers' pockets, jarvey off for the day, singing. Friend of the family. *Swurls*, he says. Pier with lamps, summer evening, band.

> *Those girls, those girls,*
> *Those lovely seaside girls.*

Milly too. Young kisses: the first. Far away now past. Mrs Marion. Reading, lying back now, counting the strands of her hair, smiling, braiding.

A soft qualm, regret, flowed down his backbone, increasing. Will happen, yes. Prevent. Useless: can't move. Girl's sweet light lips. Will happen too. He felt the flowing qualm spread over him. Useless to move now. Lips kissed, kissing, kissed. Full gluey woman's lips.

Better where she is down there: away. Occupy her. Wanted a dog to pass the time. Might take a trip down there. August bank holiday, only two and six return. Six weeks off, however. Might work a press pass. Or through M'Coy.

The cat, having cleaned all her fur, returned to the meatstained paper, nosed at it and stalked to the door. She looked back at him, mewing. Wants to go out. Wait before a door sometime it will open. Let her wait. Has the fidgets. Electric. Thunder in the air. Was washing at her ear with her back to the fire too.

He felt heavy, full: then a gentle loosening of his bowels. He stood up, undoing the waistband of his trousers. The cat mewed to him.

—Miaow! he said in answer. Wait till I'm ready.

Heaviness: hot day coming. Too much trouble to fag up the stairs to the landing.

A paper. He liked to read at stool. Hope no ape comes knocking just as I'm.

In the tabledrawer he found an old number of *Titbits*. He folded it under his armpit, went to the door and opened it. The cat went up in soft bounds. Ah, wanted to go upstairs, curl up in a ball on the bed.

Listening, he heard her voice:

—Come, come, pussy. Come.

He went out through the backdoor into the garden: stood to listen towards the next garden. No sound. Perhaps hanging clothes out to dry. The maid was in the garden. Fine morning.

He bent down to regard a lean file of spearmint growing by the wall. Make a summerhouse here. Scarlet runners. Virginia creepers. Want to manure the whole place over, scabby soil. A coat of liver of sulphur. All soil like that without dung. Household slops. Loam, what is this that is? The hens in the next garden: their droppings are very good top dressing. Best of all though are the cattle, especially when they are fed on those oilcakes. Mulch of dung. Best thing to clean ladies' kid gloves. Dirty cleans. Ashes too. Reclaim the whole place. Grow peas in that corner there. Lettuce. Always have fresh greens then. Still gardens have their drawbacks. That bee or bluebottle here Whitmonday.

He walked on. Where is my hat, by the way? Must have put it back on the peg. Or hanging up on the floor. Funny I don't remember that. Hallstand too full. Four umbrellas, her raincloak. Picking up the letters. Drago's shopbell ringing. Queer I was just thinking that moment. Brown brillantined hair over his collar. Just had a wash and brushup. Wonder have I time for a bath this morning. Tara street. Chap in the paybox there got away James Stephens, they say. O'Brien.

Deep voice that fellow Dlugacz has. Agendath what is it? Now, my miss. Enthusiast.

He kicked open the crazy door of the jakes. Better be careful not to get these trousers dirty for the funeral. He went in, bowing his head under the low lintel. Leaving the door ajar, amid the stench of mouldy limewash and stale cobwebs he undid his braces. Before sitting down he peered through a chink up at the nextdoor windows. The king was in his countinghouse. Nobody.

Asquat on the cuckstool he folded out his paper, turning its pages over on his bared knees. Something new and easy. No great hurry. Keep it a bit. Our prize titbit: *Matcham's Masterstroke.* Written by Mr Philip Beaufoy, Playgoers' Club, London. Payment at the rate of one guinea a column has been made to the writer. Three and a half. Three pounds three. Three pounds, thirteen and six.

Quietly he read, restraining himself, the first column and, yielding but resisting, began the second. Midway, his last resistance yielding, he allowed his bowels to ease themselves quietly as he read, reading still patiently that slight constipation of yesterday quite gone. Hope it's not too big bring on piles again. No, just right. So. Ah! Costive. One tabloid of cascara sagrada. Life might be so. It did not move or touch him but it was something quick and neat. Print anything now. Silly season. He read on, seated calm above his own rising smell. Neat certainly. *Matcham often thinks of the masterstroke by which he won the laughing witch who now.* Begins and ends morally. *Hand in hand.* Smart. He glanced back through what he had read and, while feeling his water flow quietly, he envied kindly Mr Beaufoy who had written it and received payment of three pounds, thirteen and six.

Might manage a sketch. By Mr and Mrs L. M. Bloom. Invent a story for some proverb. Which? Time I used to try jotting down on my cuff what she said dressing. Dislike dressing together. Nicked myself shaving. Biting her nether lip, hooking the placket of her skirt. Timing her. 9.15. Did Roberts pay you yet? 9.20. What had Gretta Conroy on? 9.23. What possessed me to buy this comb? 9.24. I'm swelled after that cabbage. A speck of dust on the patent leather of her boot: rubbing smartly in turn each welt against her stockinged calf. Morning after the bazaar dance when May's band played Ponchielli's dance of the hours. Explain that: morning hours, noon, then evening coming on, then night hours. Washing her teeth. That was the first night. Her head dancing. Her fansticks clicking. Is that Boylan well off? He has money. Why? I noticed he had a good rich smell off his breath dancing. No use humming then. Allude to it. Strange kind of music that last night. The mirror was in shadow. She rubbed her handglass briskly on her woollen vest against her full wagging bub. Peering into it. Lines in her eyes. It wouldn't pan out somehow.

Evening hours, girls in grey gauze. Night hours then: black with daggers and eyemasks. Poetical idea: pink, then golden, then grey, then black. Still, true to life also. Day: then the night.

He tore away half the prize story sharply and wiped himself with it. Then he girded up his trousers, braced and buttoned himself. He pulled back the jerky shaky door of the jakes and came forth from the gloom into the air.

In the bright light, lightened and cooled in limb, he eyed carefully his black trousers: the ends, the knees, the houghs of the knees. What time is the funeral? Better find out in the paper.

A creak and a dark whirr in the air high up. The bells of George's church. They tolled the hour: loud dark iron.

*Heigho! Heigho!*
*Heigho! Heigho!*
*Heigho! Heigho!*

Quarter to. There again: the overtone following through the air. A third.

Poor Dignam!

## from Finnegans Wake [the first page]

riverrun, past Eve and Adam's, from swerve of shore to bend of bay, brings us by a commodius vicus of recirculation back to Howth Castle and Environs.

Sir Tristram, violer d'amores, fr'over the short sea, had passentore rearrived from North Armorica on this side the scraggy isthmus of Europe Minor to wielderfight his penisolate war: nor had topsawyer's rocks by the stream Oconee exaggerated themselse to Laurens County's gorgios while they went doublin their mumper all the time: nor avoice from afire bellowsed mishe mishe to tauftauf thuartpeatrick: not yet, though venissoon after, had a kidscad buttended a bland old isaac: not yet, though all's fair in vanessy, were sosie sesthers wroth with twone nathandjoe. Rot a peck of pa's malt had Jhem or Shen brewed by arclight and rory end to the regginbrow was to be seen ringsome on the aquaface.

The fall (bababadalgharaghtakamminarronnkonnbronntonnerronntuonnthunntrovarrhounawnskawntoohoohoordenenthurnuk!) of a once wallstrait oldparr is retaled early in bed and later on life down through all christian minstrelsy. The great fall of the offwall entailed at such short notice the pftjschute of Finnegan, erse solid man, that the humptyhillhead of humself prumptly sends an unquiring one well to the west in quest of his tumptytumtoes: and their upturnpikepointandplace is at the knock out in the park where oranges have been laid to rust upon the green since devlinsfirst loved livvy.

# Virginia Woolf (1882–1941)

Together with Anton Chekhov, Marcel Proust, and James Joyce, Virginia Woolf was one of the great modernist innovators in prose fiction who moved plot and scene from the heroic and external to the subtle and internal. Woolf differs from her peers, however, in her central concern for the lives of women, although this concern is part of a wider commitment to the entire human condition. Her fiction engages social problems in the British class system and the need for people to see themselves as enmeshed in a great living universe that dwarfs their pretensions. Woolf dedicated herself to the "common reader" and took pains to make her work accessible to anyone willing to take the time to understand it.

Woolf absorbed English literary tradition directly from her father, Sir Leslie Stephen, a Victorian literary biographer and essayist. She rued the inability of girls in her generation to get the kind of education provided to boys, but ironically she was better off than her brothers because of her good fortune in having her father as mentor. The American poet James Russell Lowell was her godfather, Henry James was a family friend, and her childhood was lived in the midst of the comings and goings of English and American literati. Thus when she began to develop her own rebellious program of artistic development, she did so from the richest literary base imaginable.

With her husband Leonard Woolf, she was involved in liberal politics and progressive artistic and intellectual life from early adulthood. They were part of the so-called Bloomsbury Group of artists and thinkers who lived in a relatively bohemian style for their era, championing such movements as psychoanalysis, Indian self-determination, and Post-Impressionist art. They founded the Hogarth Press and published the works of Sigmund Freud, T.S. Eliot, Katherine Mansfield, and many of the other new talents of their day. Woolf was a lifelong pacifist who believed that the competitiveness, aggression, and hierarchy of masculinist culture were responsible for war. She correctly predicted the disastrous outcomes of European fascism in the 1930s. In "Three Guineas," a long essay written at that time, Woolf analyzed the social roots of war, particularly in the training of boys and the rituals of public life.

Woolf was a prolific writer, producing nine novels, many stories, several volumes of essays, six volumes of letters, five volumes of diaries, and two biographies (one of them the life of a dog). Her long essay "A Room of One's Own" is both a masterpiece of prose and the classic feminist statement about the role of women in the history of literature: "a woman must have money and a room of her own if she is to write fiction." In her novels, from *Jacob's Room* through *Mrs. Dalloway, To the Lighthouse, The Waves,* and *Between the Acts,* she created a new form in graceful, playful, and at the same time tough and deeply serious prose. In her essay "Modern Fiction" she argued that "life is not a series of gig-lamps symmetrically arranged" like the explicit plots of the traditional novel. Instead she saw that even the most ordinary minds are tremendously sensitive and responsive to myriad impressions—"trivial, fantastic, evanescent, or engraved with the sharpness of steel"—that shower upon us incessantly and produce "a luminous halo, a semi-transparent envelope surrounding us from the beginning of consciousness to the end." She sought to capture this complex quality of experience in her fiction. She praised both Proust and Joyce for their innovative stream-of-consciousness styles.

The selection that follows includes the first five short parts of the long first section of *To the Lighthouse,* capturing one day in the life of a large Victorian family. To read it, we must slow our pace and follow the unfolding thought captured by the poetic compression of her style. The novel begins in the midst of a busy scene in a vacation house at the seacoast. Mrs. Ramsay, the mother of the family, sits fitting a stocking on her youngest son while her husband and other children and houseguests walk, play, read, paint, and drowse around her. Woolf reveals the many-layered social reality over which Mrs. Ramsay presides, demonstrating how it can be known only through the collective consciousness of all its members. The relationships of mother and child, husband and wife, friends and protégés, children and servants, are all woven around Mrs. Ramsay. She is a complex figure whom Woolf portrays as a creator of civilization itself, a nurturing and constantly generative source of life. But Mrs. Ramsay is also controlling, secretly exhausted, and melancholy. Although she is triumphant in "The Window," the long first section of the novel, the short middle section "Time Passes" records the inexorable mutability and decay that overcome the house in the following ten years. The deaths of Mrs. Ramsay and two of her eight children are set against the backdrop of vast natural powers and the impersonal ravages of World War I. The novel's final section, "The Lighthouse," portrays a muted and chastened group of survivors who return to the house and finally make the pilgrimage to the lighthouse that Mrs. Ramsay had promised at the very beginning of the book.

## *from To the Lighthouse*

### *The Window*

#### I

"Yes, of course, if it's fine tomorrow," said Mrs. Ramsay. "But you'll have to be up with the lark," she added.

To her son these words conveyed an extraordinary joy, as if it were settled, the expedition were bound to take place, and the wonder to which he had looked forward, for years and years it seemed, was, after a night's darkness and a day's sail, within touch. Since he belonged, even at the age of six, to that great clan which cannot keep this feeling separate from that, but must let future prospects, with their joys and sorrows, cloud what is actually at hand, since to such people even in earliest childhood any turn in the wheel of sensation has the power to crystallise and transfix the moment upon which its gloom or radiance rests, James Ramsay, sitting on the floor cutting out pictures from the illustrated catalogue of the Army and Navy Stores, endowed the picture of a refrigerator, as his mother spoke, with heavenly bliss. It was fringed with joy. The wheelbarrow, the lawn mower, the sound of poplar trees, leaves whitening before rain, rooks cawing, brooms knocking, dresses rustling—all these were so coloured and distinguished in his mind that he had already his private code, his secret language, though he appeared the image of stark and uncompromising severity, with his high forehead and his fierce blue eyes, impeccably candid and pure, frowning slightly at the sight of human frailty, so that his mother, watching him guide his scissors neatly round the refrigerator, imagined him all red and ermine on the Bench or directing a stern and momentous enterprise in some crisis of public affairs.

"But," said his father, stopping in front of the drawing-room window, "it won't be fine."

Had there been an axe handy, or a poker, any weapon that would have gashed a hole in his father's breast and killed him, there and then, James would have seized it. Such were the extremes of emotion that Mr. Ramsay excited in his children's breasts by his mere presence; standing, as now, lean as a knife, narrow as the blade of one, grinning sarcastically, not only with the pleasure of disillusioning his son and casting ridicule upon his wife, who was ten thousand times better in every way than he was (James thought), but also with some secret conceit at his own accuracy of judgement. What he said was true. It was always true. He was incapable of untruth; never tampered with a fact; never altered a disagreeable word to suit the pleasure or convenience of any mortal being, least of all of his own children, who, sprung from his loins, should be aware from childhood that life is difficult; facts uncompromising; and the passage to that fabled land where our brightest hopes are extinguished, our frail barks founder in darkness (here Mr. Ramsay would straighten his back and narrow his little blue eyes upon the horizon), one that needs, above all, courage, truth, and the power to endure.

"But it may be fine—I expect it will be fine," said Mrs. Ramsay, making some little twist of the reddish brown stocking she was knitting, impatiently. If she finished it tonight, if they did go to the Lighthouse after all, it was to be given to the Lighthouse keeper for his little boy, who was threatened with a tuberculous hip; together with a pile of old magazines, and some tobacco, indeed, whatever she could find lying about, not really wanted, but only littering the room, to give those poor fellows, who must be bored to death sitting all day with nothing to do but polish the lamp and trim the wick and rake about on their scrap of garden, something to amuse them. For how would you like to be shut up for a whole month at a time, and possibly more in stormy weather, upon a rock the size of a tennis lawn? she would ask; and to have no letters or newspapers, and to see nobody; if you were married, not to see your wife, not to know how your children were—if they were ill, if they had fallen down and broken their legs or arms; to see the same dreary waves breaking week after week, and then a dreadful storm coming, and the windows covered with spray, and birds dashed against the lamp, and the whole place rocking, and not be able to put your nose out of doors for fear of being swept into the sea? How would you like that? she asked, addressing herself particularly to her daughters. So she added, rather differently, one must take them whatever comforts one can.

"It's due west," said the atheist Tansley, holding his bony fingers spread so that the wind blew through them, for he was sharing Mr. Ramsay's evening walk up and down, up and down the terrace. That is to say, the wind blew from the worst possible direction for landing at the Lighthouse. Yes, he did say disagreeable things, Mrs. Ramsay admitted; it was odious of him to rub this in, and make James still more disappointed; but at the same time, she would not let them laugh at him. "The atheist," they called him; "the little atheist." Rose mocked him; Prue mocked him; Andrew, Jasper, Roger mocked him; even old Badger without a tooth in his head had bit him, for being (as Nancy put it) the hundred and tenth young man to chase them all the way up to the Hebrides when it was ever so much nicer to be alone.

"Nonsense," said Mrs. Ramsay, with great severity. Apart from the habit of exaggeration which they had from her, and from the implication (which was true) that she asked too many people to stay, and had to lodge some in the town, she could not bear incivility to her guests, to young men in particular, who were poor as church mice, "exceptionally able," her husband said, his great admirers, and come there for a holiday. Indeed, she had the whole of the other sex under her protection; for reasons she could not explain, for their chivalry and valour, for the fact that they negotiated treaties, ruled India, controlled finance; finally for an attitude towards herself which no woman could fail to feel or to find agreeable, something trustful, childlike, reverential; which an old woman could take from a young man without loss of dignity, and woe betide the girl—pray Heaven it was none of her daughters!—who did not feel the worth of it, and all that it implied, to the marrow of her bones!

She turned with severity upon Nancy. He had not chased them, she said. He had been asked.

They must find a way out of it all. There might be some simpler way, some less laborious way, she sighed. When she looked in the glass and saw her hair grey, her cheek sunk, at fifty, she thought, possibly she might have managed things better—her husband; money; his books. But for her own part she would never for a single second regret her decision, evade difficulties, or slur over duties. She was now formidable to behold, and it was only in silence, looking up from their plates, after she had spoken so severely about Charles Tansley, that her daughters, Prue, Nancy, Rose—could sport with infidel ideas which they had brewed for themselves of a life different from hers; in Paris, perhaps; a wilder life; not always taking care of some man or other; for there was in all their minds a mute questioning of deference and chivalry, of the Bank of England and the Indian Empire, of ringed fingers and lace, though to them all there was something in this of the essence of beauty, which called out the manliness in their girlish hearts, and made them, as they sat at table beneath their mother's eyes, honour her strange severity, her extreme courtesy, like a Queen's raising from the mud to wash a beggar's dirty foot, when she thus admonished them so very severely about that wretched atheist who had chased them—or, speaking accurately, been invited to stay with them—in the Isles of Skye.

"There'll be no landing at the Lighthouse tomorrow," said Charles Tansley, clapping his hands together as he stood at the window with her husband. Surely, he had said enough. She wished they would both leave her and James alone and go on talking. She looked at him. He was such a miserable specimen, the children said, all humps and hollows. He couldn't play cricket; he poked; he shuffled. He was a sarcastic brute, Andrew said. They knew what he liked best—to be for ever walking up and down, up and down, with Mr. Ramsay, and saying who had won this, who had won that, who was a "first-rate man" at Latin verses, who was "brilliant but I think fundamentally unsound," who was undoubtedly the "ablest fellow in Balliol," who had buried his light temporarily at Bristol or Bedford, but was bound to be heard of later when his Prolegomena, of which Mr. Tansley had the first pages in proof with him if Mr. Ramsay would like to see them, to some branch of mathematics or philosophy saw the light of day. That was what they talked about.

She could not help laughing herself sometimes. She said, the other day, something about "waves mountains high." Yes, said Charles Tansley, it was a little rough. "Aren't you drenched to the skin?" she had said, "Damp, not wet through," said Mr. Tansley, pinching his sleeve, feeling his socks.

But it was not that they minded, the children said. It was not his face; it was not his manners. It was him—his point of view. When they talked about something interesting, people, music, history, anything, even said it was a fine evening so why not sit out of doors, then what they complained of about Charles Tansley was that until he had turned the whole thing round and made it somehow reflect himself and disparage them—he was not satisfied. And he would go to picture galleries they said and he would ask one, did one like his tie? God knows, said Rose, one did not.

Disappearing as stealthily as stags from the dinner-table directly the meal was over, the eight sons and daughters of Mr. and Mrs. Ramsay sought their bedrooms, their fastnesses in a house where there was no other privacy to debate anything, everything; Tansley's tie; the passing of the Reform Bill; sea birds and butterflies; people; while the sun poured into those attics, which a plank alone separated from each other so that every footstep could be plainly heard and the Swiss girl sobbing for her father who was dying of cancer in a valley of the Grisons, and lit up bats, flannels, straw hats, ink-pots, paint-pots, beetles, and the skulls of small birds, while it drew from the long frilled strips of seaweed pinned to the wall a smell of salt and weeds, which was in the towels too, gritty with sand from bathing.

Strife, divisions, difference of opinion, prejudices twisted into the very fibre of being, oh, that they should begin so early, Mrs. Ramsay deplored. They were so critical, her children. They talked such nonsense. She went from the dining-room, holding James by the hand, since he would not go with the others. It seemed to her such nonsense—inventing differences, when people, heaven knows, were different enough without that. The real differences, she thought, standing by the drawing-room window, are enough, quite enough. She had in mind at the moment, rich and poor, high and low; the great in birth receiving from her, some half grudgingly, half respect, for had she not in her veins the blood of that very noble, if slightly mythical, Italian house, whose daughters, scattered about English drawing-rooms in the nineteenth century, had lisped so charmingly, had stormed so wildly, and all her wit and her bearing and her temper came from them, and not from the sluggish English, or the cold Scotch; but more profoundly, she ruminated the other problem, of rich and poor, and the things she saw with her own eyes, weekly, daily, here or in London, when she visited this widow, or that struggling wife in person with a bag on her arm, and a note-book and pencil with which she wrote down in columns carefully ruled for the purpose wages and spendings, employment and unemployment, in the hope that thus she would cease to be a private woman whose charity was half a sop to her own indignation, half a relief to her own curiosity, and become what with her untrained mind she greatly admired, an investigator, elucidating the social problem.

Insoluble questions they were, it seemed to her, standing there, holding James by the hand. He had followed her into the drawing-room, that young man they laughed at; he was standing by the table, fidgeting with something, awkwardly, feeling himself out of things, as she knew without looking round. They had all gone—the children; Minta Doyle and Paul Rayley; Augustus Carmichael; her husband—they had all gone. So she turned with a sigh and said, "Would it bore you to come with me, Mr. Tansley?"

She had a dull errand in the town; she had a letter or two to write; she would be ten minutes perhaps; she would put on her hat. And, with her basket and her parasol, there she was again, ten minutes later, giving out a sense of being ready, of being equipped for a jaunt, which, however, she must interrupt for a moment, as they passed the tennis lawn, to ask Mr. Carmichael, who was basking with his yellow cat's eyes ajar, so that like a cat's they seemed to reflect the branches moving or the clouds passing, but to give no inkling of any inner thoughts or emotion whatsoever, if he wanted anything.

For they were making the great expedition, she said, laughing. They were going to the town. "Stamps, writing-paper, tobacco?" she suggested, stopping by his side. But no, he wanted nothing. His hands clasped themselves over his capacious paunch, his eyes blinked, as if he would have liked to reply kindly to these blandishments (she was seductive but a little nervous) but could not, sunk as he was in a grey-green somnolence which embraced them all, without need of words, in a vast and benevolent lethargy of well-wishing; all the house; all the world; all the people in it, for he had slipped into his glass at lunch a few drops of something, which accounted, the children thought, for the vivid streak of canary-yellow in moustache and beard that were otherwise milk white. No, nothing, he murmured.

He should have been a great philosopher, said Mrs. Ramsay, as they went down the road to the fishing village, but he had made an unfortunate marriage. Holding her black parasol very erect, and moving with an indescribable air of expectation, as if she were going to meet some one round the corner, she told the story; an affair at Oxford with some girl; an early marriage; poverty; going to India; translating a little poetry "very beautifully, I believe," being willing to teach the boys Persian or Hindustanee, but what really was the use of that?—and then lying, as they saw him, on the lawn.

It flattered him; snubbed as he had been, it soothed him that Mrs. Ramsay should tell him this. Charles Tansley revived. Insinuating, too, as she did the greatness of man's intellect, even in its decay, the subjection of all wives—not that she blamed the girl, and the marriage had been happy enough, she believed—to their husband's labours, she made him feel better pleased with himself than he had done yet, and he would have liked, had they taken a cab, for example, to have paid for it. As for her little bag, might he not carry that? No, no, she said, she always carried *that* herself. She did too. Yes, he felt that in her. He felt many things, something in particular that excited him and disturbed him for reasons which he could not give. He would like her to see him, gowned and hooded, walking in a procession. A fellowship, a professorship, he felt capable of anything and saw himself—but what was she looking at? At a man pasting a bill. The vast flapping sheet flattened itself out, and each shove of the brush revealed fresh legs, hoops, horses, glistening reds and blues, beautifully smooth, until half the wall was covered with the advertisement of a circus; a hundred horsemen, twenty performing seals, lions, tigers . . . Craning forwards, for she was short-sighted, she read it out . . . "will visit this town," she read. It was terribly dangerous work for a one-armed man, she exclaimed, to stand on top of a ladder like that—his left arm had been cut off in a reaping machine two years ago.

"Let us all go!" she cried, moving on, as if all those riders and horses had filled her with childlike exultation and made her forget her pity.

"Let's go," he said, repeating her words, clicking them out, however, with a self-consciousness that made her wince. "Let us go to the circus." No. He could not say it right. He could not feel it right. But why not? she wondered. What was wrong with him then? She liked him warmly, at the moment. Had they not been taken, she asked, to circuses when they were children? Never, he answered, as if she asked the very thing he wanted; had been longing all these days to say, how they did not go to circuses. It was a large family, nine brothers and sisters, and his father was a working man. "My father is a chemist, Mrs. Ramsay. He keeps a shop." He himself had paid his own way since he was thirteen. Often he went without a greatcoat in winter. He could never "return hospitality" (those were his parched stiff words) at college. He had to make things last twice the time other people did; he smoked the cheapest tobacco; shag; the same the old men did in the quays. He worked hard—seven hours a day; his subject was now the influence of something upon somebody—they were walking on and Mrs. Ramsay did not quite catch the meaning, only the words, here and there . . . dissertation . . . fellowship . . . readership . . . lectureship. She could not follow the ugly academic jargon, that rattled itself off so glibly, but said to herself that she saw now why going to the circus had knocked him off his perch, poor little man, and why he came out, instantly, with all that about his father and mother and brothers and sisters, and she would see to it that they didn't laugh at him any more; she would tell Prue about it. What he would have liked, she supposed, would have been to say how he had gone not to the circus but to Ibsen with the Ramsays. He was an awful prig—oh yes, an insufferable bore. For, though they had reached the town now and were in the main street, with carts grinding past on the cobbles, still he went on talking, about settlements, and teaching, and working men, and helping our own class, and lectures, till she gathered that he had got back entire self-confidence, had recovered from the circus, and was about (and now again she liked him warmly) to tell her—but here, the houses falling away on both sides, they came out on the quay, and the whole bay spread before them and Mrs. Ramsay could not help exclaiming, "Oh, how beautiful!" For the great plateful of blue water was before her; the hoary Lighthouse, distant, austere, in the midst; and on the right, as far as the eye could see, fading and falling, in soft low pleats, the green sand dunes with the wild flowing grasses on them, which always seemed to be running away into some moon country, uninhabited of men.

That was the view, she said, stopping, growing greyer-eyed, that her husband loved.

She paused a moment. But now, she said, artists had come here. There indeed, only a few paces off, stood one of them, in Panama hat and yellow boots, seriously, softly, absorbedly, for all that he was watched by ten little boys, with an air of profound contentment on his round red face gazing, and then, when he had gazed, dipping; imbuing the tip of his brush in some soft mound of green or pink. Since Mr. Paunceforte had been there, three years before, all the pictures were like that, she said, green and grey, with lemon-coloured sailing-boats, and pink women on the beach.

But her grandmother's friends, she said, glancing discreetly as they passed, took the greatest pains; first they mixed their own colours, and then they ground them, and then they put damp cloths to keep them moist.

So Mr. Tansley supposed she meant him to see that that man's picture was skimpy, was that what one said? The colours weren't solid? Was that what one said? Under the influence of that extraordinary emotion which had been growing all the walk, had begun in the garden when he had wanted to take her bag, had increased in the town when he had wanted to tell her everything about himself, he was coming to see himself, and everything he had ever known gone crooked a little. It was awfully strange.

There he stood in the parlour of the poky little house where she had taken him, waiting for her, while she went upstairs a moment to see a woman. He heard her quick step above; heard her voice cheerful, then low; looked at the mats, tea-caddies, glass shades; waited quite impatiently; looked forward eagerly to the walk home; determined to carry her bag; then heard her come out; shut a door; say they must keep the windows open and the doors shut, ask at the house for anything they wanted (she must be talking to a child) when, suddenly, in she came, stood for a moment silent (as if she had been pretending up there, and for a moment let herself be now), stood quite motionless for a moment against a picture of Queen Victoria wearing the blue ribbon of the Garter; when all at once he realised that it was this: it was this:—she was the most beautiful person he had ever seen.

With stars in her eyes and veils in her hair, with cyclamen and wild violets—what nonsense was he thinking? She was fifty at least; she had eight children. Stepping through fields of flowers and taking to her breast buds that had broken and lambs that had fallen; with the stars in her eyes and the wind in her hair— He took her bag.

"Good-bye, Elsie," she said, and they walked up the street, she holding her parasol erect and walking as if she expected to meet some one round the corner, while for the first time in his life Charles Tansley felt an extraordinary pride; a man digging in a drain stopped digging and looked at her, let his arm fall down and looked at her; for the first time in his life Charles Tansley felt an extraordinary pride; felt the wind and the cyclamen and the violets for he was walking with a beautiful woman. He had hold of her bag.

## II

"No going to the Lighthouse, James," he said, as he stood by the window, speaking awkwardly, but trying in deference to Mrs. Ramsay to soften his voice into some semblance of geniality at least.

Odious little man, thought Mrs. Ramsay, why go on saying that?

## III

"Perhaps you will wake up and find the sun shining and the birds singing," she said compassionately, smoothing the little boy's hair, for her husband, with his caustic saying that it would not be fine, had dashed his spirits she could see. This going to the Lighthouse was a passion of his, she saw, and then, as if her husband had not said enough, with his caustic saying that it would not be fine tomorrow, this odious little man went and rubbed it in all over again.

"Perhaps it will be fine tomorrow," she said, smoothing his hair.

All she could do now was to admire the refrigerator, and turn the pages of the Stores list in the hope that she might come upon something like a rake, or a mowing-machine, which, with its prongs and its handles, would need the greatest skill and care in cutting out. All these young men parodied her husband, she reflected; he said it would rain; they said it would be a positive tornado.

But here, as she turned the page, suddenly her search for the picture of a rake or a mowing-machine was interrupted. The gruff murmur, irregularly broken by the taking out of pipes and the putting in of pipes which had kept on assuring her, though she could not hear what was said (as she sat in the window which opened on the terrace), that the men were happily talking; this sound, which had lasted now half an hour and had taken its place soothingly in the scale of sounds pressing on top of her, such as the tap of balls upon bats, the sharp, sudden bark now and then, "How's that? How's that?" of the children playing cricket, had ceased; so that the monotonous fall of the waves on the beach, which for the most part beat a measured and soothing tattoo to her thoughts and seemed consolingly to repeat over and over again as she sat with the children the words of some old cradle song, murmured by nature, "I am guarding you—I am your support," but at other times suddenly and unexpectedly, especially when her mind raised itself slightly from the task actually in hand, had no such kindly meaning, but like a ghostly roll of drums remorselessly beat the measure of life, made one think of the destruction of the island and its engulfment in the sea, and warned her whose day had slipped past in one quick doing after another that it was all ephemeral as a rainbow—this sound which had been obscured and concealed under the other sounds suddenly thundered hollow in her ears and made her look up with an impulse of terror.

They had ceased to talk; that was the explanation. Falling in one second from the tension which had gripped her to the other extreme which, as if to recoup her for her unnecessary expense of emotion, was cool, amused, and even faintly malicious, she concluded that poor Charles Tansley had been shed. That was of little account to her. If her husband required sacrifices (and indeed he did) she cheerfully offered up to him Charles Tansley, who had snubbed her little boy.

One moment more, with her head raised, she listened, as if she waited for some habitual sound, some regular mechanical sound; and then, hearing something rhythmical, half said, half chanted, beginning in the garden, as her husband beat up and down the terrace, something between a croak and a song, she was soothed once more, assured again that all was well, and looking down at the book on her knee found the picture of a pocket knife with six blades which could only be cut out if James was very careful.

Suddenly a loud cry, as of a sleep-walker, half roused, something about

Stormed at with shot and shell

sung out with the utmost intensity in her ear, made her turn apprehensively to see if any one heard him. Only Lily Briscoe, she was glad to find; and that did not matter. But the sight of the girl standing on the edge of the lawn painting reminded her; she was supposed to be keeping her head as much in the same position as possible for Lily's picture. Lily's picture! Mrs. Ramsay smiled. With her little Chinese eyes and her puckered-up face, she would never marry; one could not take her painting very seriously; she was an independent little creature, and Mrs. Ramsay liked her for it; so, remembering her promise, she bent her head.

## IV

Indeed, he almost knocked her easel over, coming down upon her with his hands waving shouting out, "Boldly we rode and well," but, mercifully, he turned sharp, and rode off, to die gloriously she supposed upon the heights of Balaclava. Never was anybody at once so ridiculous and so alarming. But so long as he kept like that, waving, shouting, she was safe; he would not stand still and look at her picture. And that was what Lily Briscoe could not have endured. Even while she looked at the mass, at the line, at the colour, at Mrs. Ramsay sitting in the window with James, she kept a feeler on her surroundings lest some one should creep up, and suddenly she should find her picture looked at. But now, with all her senses quickened as they were, looking, straining, till the colour of the wall and the jacmanna beyond burnt into her eyes, she was aware of some one coming out of the house, coming towards her; but somehow divined, from the footfall, William Bankes, so that though her brush quivered, she did not, as she would have done had it been Mr. Tansley, Paul Rayley, Minta Doyle, or practically anybody else, turn her canvas upon the grass, but let it stand. William Bankes stood beside her.

They had rooms in the village, and so, walking in, walking out, parting late on door-mats, had said little things about the soup, about the children, about one thing and another which made them allies; so that when he stood beside her now in his judicial way (he was old enough to be her father too, a botanist, a widower, smelling of soap, very scrupulous and clean) she just stood there. He just stood there. Her shoes were excellent, he observed. They allowed the toes their natural expansion. Lodging in the same house with her, he had noticed too, how orderly she was, up before breakfast and off to paint, he believed, alone: poor, presumably, and without the complexion or the allurement of Miss Doyle certainly, but with a good sense which made her in his eyes superior to that young lady. Now, for instance, when Ramsay bore down on them, shouting, gesticulating, Miss Briscoe, he felt certain, understood.

"Some one had blundered."

Mr. Ramsay glared at them. He glared at them without seeming to see them. That did make them both vaguely uncomfortable. Together they had seen a thing they had not been meant to see. They had encroached upon a privacy. So, Lily thought, it was probably an excuse of his for moving, for getting out of earshot, that made Mr. Bankes almost immediately say something about its being chilly and suggest taking a stroll. She would come, yes. But it was with difficulty that she took her eyes off her picture.

The jacmanna was bright violet; the wall staring white. She would not have considered it honest to tamper with the bright violet and the staring white, since she saw them like that, fashionable though it was, since Mr. Paunceforte's visit, to see everything pale, elegant, semitransparent. Then beneath the colour there was the shape. She could see it all so clearly, so commandingly, when she looked: it was when she took her brush in hand that the whole thing changed. It was in that moment's flight between the picture and her canvas that the demons set on her who often brought her to the verge of tears and made this passage from conception to work as dreadful as any down a dark passage for a child. Such she often felt herself—struggling against terrific odds to maintain her courage; to say: "But this is what I see; this is what I see," and so to clasp some miserable remnant of her vision to her breast, which a thousand forces did their best to pluck from her. And it was then too, in that chill and windy way, as she began to paint, that there forced themselves upon her other things, her own inadequacy, her insignificance, keeping house for her father off the Brompton Road, and had much ado to control her impulse to fling herself (thank Heaven she had always resisted so far) at Mrs. Ramsay's knee and say to her—but what could one say to her? "I'm in love with you?" No, that was not true. "I'm in love with this all," waving her hand at the hedge, at the house, at the children. It was absurd, it was impossible. So now she laid her brushes neatly in the box, side by side, and said to William Bankes:

"It suddenly gets cold. The sun seems to give less heat," she said, looking about her, for it was bright enough, the grass still a soft deep green, the house starred in its greenery with purple passion flowers, and rooks dropping cool cries from the high blue. But something moved, flashed, turned a silver wing in the air. It was September after all, the middle of September, and past six in the evening. So off they strolled down the garden in the usual direction, past the tennis lawn, past the pampas grass, to that break in the thick hedge, guarded by red hot pokers like brasiers of clear burning coal, between which the blue waters of the bay looked bluer than ever.

They came there regularly every evening drawn by some need. It was as if the water floated off and set sailing thoughts which had grown stagnant on dry land, and gave to their bodies even some sort of physical relief. First, the pulse of colour flooded the bay with blue, and the heart expanded with it and the body swam, only the next instant to be checked and chilled by the prickly blackness on the ruffled waves. Then, up behind the great black rock, almost every evening spurted irregularly, so that one had to watch for it and it was a delight when it came, a fountain of white water; and then, while one waited for that, one watched, on the pale semicircular beach, wave after wave shedding again and again smoothly, a film of mother of pearl.

They both smiled, standing there. They both felt a common hilarity, excited by the moving waves; and then by the swift cutting race of a sailing boat, which, having sliced a curve in the bay, stopped; shivered; let its sails drop down; and then, with a natural instinct to complete the picture, after this swift movement, both of them looked at the dunes far away, and instead of merriment felt come over them some sadness—because the thing was completed partly, and partly because distant views seem to outlast by a million years (Lily thought) the gazer and to be communing already with a sky which beholds an earth entirely at rest.

Looking at the far sand hills, William Bankes thought of Ramsay: thought of a road in Westmorland, thought of Ramsay striding along a road by himself hung round with that solitude which seemed to be his natural air. But this was suddenly interrupted, William Bankes remembered (and this must refer to some actual incident), by a hen, straddling her wings out in protection of a covey of little chicks, upon which Ramsay, stopping, pointed his stick and said "Pretty—pretty," an odd illumination in to his heart, Bankes had thought it, which showed his simplicity, his sympathy with humble things; but it seemed to him as if their friendship had ceased, there, on that stretch of road. After that, Ramsay had married. After that, what with one thing and another, the pulp had gone out of their friendship. Whose fault it was he could not say, only, after a time, repetition had taken the place of newness. It was to repeat that they met. But in this dumb colloquy with the sand dunes he maintained that his affection for Ramsay had in no way diminished; but there, like the body of a young man laid up in peat for a century, with the red fresh on his lips, was his friendship, in its acuteness and reality, laid up across the bay among the sandhills.

He was anxious for the sake of this friendship and perhaps too in order to clear himself in his own mind from the imputation of having dried and shrunk—for Ramsay lived in a welter of children, whereas Bankes was childless and a widower—he was anxious that Lily Briscoe should not disparage Ramsay (a great man in his own way) yet should understand how things stood between them. Begun long years ago, their friendship had petered out on a Westmorland road, where the hen spread her wings before her chicks; after which Ramsay had married, and their paths lying different ways, there had been, certainly for no one's fault, some tendency, when they met, to repeat.

Yes. That was it. He finished. He turned from the view. And, turning to walk back the other way, up the drive, Mr. Bankes was alive to things which would not have struck him had not those sandhills revealed to him the body of his friendship lying with the red on its lips laid up in peat—for instance, Cam, the little girl, Ramsay's youngest daughter. She was picking Sweet Alice on the bank. She was wild and fierce. She would not "give a flower to the gentleman" as the nursemaid told her. No! no! no! she would not! She clenched her fist. She stamped. And Mr. Bankes felt aged and saddened and somehow put into the wrong by her about his friendship. He must have dried and shrunk.

The Ramsays were not rich, and it was a wonder how they managed to contrive it all. Eight children! To feed eight children on philosophy! Here was another of them, Jasper this time, strolling past, to have a shot at a bird, he said, nonchalantly, swinging Lily's hand like a pump-handle as he passed, which caused Mr. Bankes to say, bitterly, how *she* was a favourite. There was education now to be considered (true, Mrs. Ramsay had something of her own perhaps) let alone the daily wear and tear of shoes and stockings which those "great fellows," all well grown, angular, ruthless youngsters, must require. As for being sure which was which, or in what order they came, that was beyond him. He called them privately after the Kings and Queens of England; Cam the Wicked, James the Ruthless, Andrew the Just, Prue the Fair—for Prue would have beauty, he thought, how could she help it?—and Andrew brains. While he walked up the drive and Lily Briscoe said yes and no and capped his comments (for she was in love with them all, in love with this world) he weighed Ramsay's case, commiserated him, envied him, as if he had seen him divest himself of all those glories of isolation and austerity which crowned him in youth to cumber himself definitely with fluttering wings and clucking domesticities. They gave him something—William Bankes acknowledged that; it would have been pleasant if Cam had stuck a flower in his coat or clambered over his shoulder, to look at a picture of Vesuvius in eruption; but they had also, his old friends could not but feel, destroyed something. What would a stranger think now? What did this Lily Briscoe think? Could one help noticing that habits grew on him? eccentricities, weaknesses perhaps? It was astonishing that a man of his intellect could stoop so low as he did—but that was too harsh a phrase—could depend so much as he did upon people's praise.

"Oh, but," said Lily, "think of his work!"

Whenever she "thought of his work" she always saw clearly before her a large kitchen table. It was Andrew's doing. She asked him what his father's books were about. "Subject and object and the nature of reality," Andrew had said. And when she said Heavens, she had no notion what that meant. "Think of a kitchen table then," he told her, "when you're not there."

So now she always saw, when she thought of Mr. Ramsay's work, a scrubbed kitchen table. It lodged now in the fork of a pear tree, for they had reached the orchard. And with a painful effort of concentration, she focused her mind, not upon the silver-bossed bark of the tree, or upon its fish-shaped leaves, but upon a phantom kitchen table, one of those scrubbed board tables, grained and knotted, whose virtue seems to have been laid bare by years of muscular integrity, which stuck there, its four legs in air. Naturally, if one's days were passed in this seeing of angular essences, this reducing of lovely evenings, with all their flamingo clouds and blue and silver to a white deal four-legged table (and it was a mark of the finest minds so to do), naturally one could not be judged like an ordinary person.

Mr. Bankes liked her for bidding him "think of his work." He had thought of it, often and often. Times without number, he had said, "Ramsay is one of those men who do their best work before they are forty." He had made a definite contribution to philosophy in one little book when he was only five and twenty; what came after was more or less amplification, repetition. But the number of men who make a definite contribution to anything whatsoever is very small, he said, pausing by the pear tree, well brushed, scrupulously exact, exquisitely judicial. Suddenly, as if the movement of his hand had released it, the load of her accumulated impressions of him tilted up, and down poured in a ponderous avalanche all she felt about him. That was one sensation. Then up rose in a fume the essence of his being. That was another. She felt herself transfixed by the intensity of her perception; it was his severity; his goodness. I respect you (she addressed silently him in person) in every atom; you are not vain; you are entirely impersonal; you are finer than Mr. Ramsay; you are the finest human being that I know; you have neither wife nor child (without any sexual feeling, she longed to cherish that loneliness), you live for science (involuntarily, sections of potatoes rose before her eyes); praise would be an insult to you; generous, pure-hearted, heroic man! But simultaneously, she remembered how he had brought a valet all the way up here; objected to dogs on chairs; would prose for hours (until Mr. Ramsay slammed out of the room) about salt in vegetables and the iniquity of English cooks.

How then did it work out, all this? How did one judge people, think of them? How did one add up this and that and conclude that it was liking one felt, or disliking? And to those words, what meaning attached, after all? Standing now, apparently transfixed, by the pear tree, impressions poured in upon her of those two men, and to follow her thought was like following a voice which speaks too quickly to be taken down by one's pencil, and the voice was her own voice saying without prompting undeniable, everlasting, contradictory things, so that even the fissures and humps on the bark of the pear tree were irrevocably fixed there for eternity. You have greatness, she continued, but Mr. Ramsay has none of it. He is petty, selfish, vain, egotistical; he is spoilt; he is a tyrant; he wears Mrs. Ramsay to death; but he has what you (she addressed Mr. Bankes) have not; a fiery unworldliness; he knows nothing about trifles; he loves dogs and his children. He has eight. Mr. Bankes has none. Did he not come down in two coats the other night and let Mrs. Ramsay trim his hair into a pudding basin? All of this danced up and down, like a company of gnats, each separate, but all marvellously controlled in an invisible elastic net—danced up and down in Lily's mind, in and about the branches of the pear tree, where still hung in effigy the scrubbed kitchen table, symbol of her profound respect for Mr. Ramsay's mind, until her thought which had spun quicker and quicker exploded of its own intensity; she felt released; a shot went off close at hand, and there came, flying from its fragments, frightened, effusive, tumultuous, a flock of starlings.

"Jasper!" said Mr. Bankes. They turned the way the starlings flew, over the terrace. Following the scatter of swift-flying birds in the sky they stepped through the gap in the high hedge straight into Mr. Ramsay, who boomed tragically at them, "Some one had blundered!"

His eyes, glazed with emotion, defiant with tragic intensity, met theirs for a second, and trembled on the verge of recognition; but then, raising his hand, half-way to his face as if to avert, to brush off, in an agony of peevish shame, their normal gaze, as if he begged them to withhold for a moment what he knew to be inevitable, as if he impressed upon them his own child-like resentment of interruption, yet even in the moment of discovery was not to be routed utterly, but was determined to hold fast to something of this delicious emotion, this impure rhapsody of which he was ashamed, but in which he revelled—he turned abruptly, slammed his private door on them; and, Lily Briscoe and Mr. Bankes, looking uneasily up into the sky, observed that the flock of starlings which Jasper had routed with his gun had settled on the tops of the elm trees.

## V

"And even if it isn't fine tomorrow," said Mrs. Ramsay, raising her eyes to glance at William Bankes and Lily Briscoe as they passed, "it will be another day. And now," she said, thinking that Lily's charm was her Chinese eyes, aslant in her white, puckered little face, but it would take a clever man to see it, "and now stand up, and let me measure your leg," for they might go to the Lighthouse after all, and she must see if the stocking did not need to be an inch or two longer in the leg.

Smiling, for it was an admirable idea, that had flashed upon her this very second—William and Lily should marry—she took the heather-mixture stocking, with its criss-cross of steel needles at the mouth of it, and measured it against James's leg.

"My dear, stand still," she said, for in his jealousy, not liking to serve as measuring block for the Lighthouse keeper's little boy, James fidgeted purposely; and if he did that, how could she see, was it too long, was it too short? she asked.

She looked up—what demon possessed him, her youngest, her cherished?—and saw the room, saw the chairs, thought them fearfully shabby. Their entrails, as Andrew said the other day, were all over the floor; but then what was the point, she asked, of buying good chairs to let them spoil up here all through the winter when the house, with only one old woman to see to it, positively dripped with wet? Never mind, the rent was precisely twopence half-penny; the children loved it; it did her husband good to be three thousand, or if she must be accurate, three hundred miles from his libraries and his lectures and his disciples; and there was room for visitors. Mats, camp beds, crazy ghosts of chairs and tables whose London life of service was done—they did well enough here; and a photograph or two, and books. Books, she thought, grew of themselves. She never had time to read them. Alas! even the books that had been given her and inscribed by the hand of the poet himself: "For her whose wishes must be obeyed" . . . "The happier Helen of our days" . . . disgraceful to say, she had never read them. And Croom on the Mind and Bates on the Savage Customs of Polynesia ("My dear, stand still," she said)—neither of those could one send to the Lighthouse. At a certain moment, she supposed, the house would become so shabby that something must be done. If they could be taught to wipe their feet and not bring the beach in with them—that would be something. Crabs, she had to allow, if Andrew really wished to dissect them, or if Jasper believed that one could make soup from seaweed, one could not prevent it; or Rose's objects—shells, reeds, stones; for they were gifted, her children, but all in quite different ways. And the result of it was, she sighed, taking in the whole room from floor to ceiling, as she held the stocking against James's leg, that things got shabbier and got shabbier summer after summer. The mat was fading; the wall-paper was flapping. You couldn't tell any more that those were roses on it. Still, if every door in a house is left perpetually open, and no lockmaker in the whole of Scotland can mend a bolt, things must spoil. Every door was left open. She listened. The drawing-room door was open; the hall door was open; it sounded as if the bedroom doors were open; and certainly the window on the landing was open, for that she had opened herself. That windows should be open, and doors shut—simple as it was, could none of them remember it? She would go into the maids' bedrooms at night and find them sealed like ovens, except for Marie's, the Swiss girl, who would rather go without a bath than without fresh air, but then at home, she had said, "the mountains are so beautiful." She had said that last night looking out of the window with tears in her eyes. "The mountains are so beautiful." Her father was dying there, Mrs. Ramsay knew. He was leaving them fatherless. Scolding and demonstrating (how to make a bed, how to open a window, with hands that shut and spread like a Frenchwoman's) all had folded itself quietly about her, when the girl spoke, as, after a flight through the sunshine the wings of a bird fold themselves quietly and the blue of its plumage changes from bright steel to soft purple. She had stood there silent for there was nothing to be said. He had cancer of the throat. At the recollection—how she had stood there, how the girl had said, "At home the mountains are so beautiful," and there was no hope, no hope whatever, she had a spasm of irritation, and speaking sharply, said to James:

"Stand still. Don't be tiresome," so that he knew instantly that her severity was real, and straightened his leg and she measured it.

The stocking was too short by half an inch at least, making allowance for the fact that Sorley's little boy would be less well grown than James.

"It's too short," she said, "ever so much too short."

Never did anybody look so sad. Bitter and black, half-way down, in the darkness, in the shaft which ran from the sunlight to the depths, perhaps a tear formed; a tear fell; the waters swayed this way and that, received it, and were at rest. Never did anybody look so sad.

But was it nothing but looks, people said? What was there behind it—her beauty and splendour? Had he blown his brains out, they asked, had he died the week before they were married—some other, earlier lover, of whom rumours reached one? Or was there nothing? nothing but an incomparable beauty which she lived behind, and could do nothing to disturb? For easily though she might have said at some moment of intimacy when stories of great passion, of love foiled, of ambition thwarted came her way how she too had known or felt or been through it herself, she never spoke. She was silent always. She knew then—she knew without having learnt. Her simplicity fathomed what clever people falsified. Her singleness of mind made her drop plumb like a stone, alight exact as a bird, gave her, naturally, this swoop and fall of the spirit upon truth which delighted, eased, sustained—falsely perhaps.

("Nature has but little clay," said Mr. Bankes once, much moved by her voice on the telephone though she was only telling him a fact about a train, "like that of which she moulded you." He saw her at the end of the line very clearly Greek, straight, blue-eyed. How incongruous it seemed to be telephoning to a woman like that. The Graces assembling seemed to have joined hands in meadows of asphodel to compose that face. He would catch the 10:30 at Euston.

"Yet she's no more aware of her beauty than a child," said Mr. Bankes, replacing the receiver and crossing the room to see what progress the workmen were making with an hotel which they were building at the back of his house. And he thought of Mrs. Ramsay as he looked at that stir among the unfinished walls. For always, he thought, there was something incongruous to be worked into the harmony of her face. She clapped a deer-stalker's hat on her head; she ran across the lawn in goloshes to snatch a child from mischief. So that if it was her beauty merely that one thought of, one must remember the quivering thing, the living thing (they were carrying bricks up a little plank as he watched them), and work it into the picture; or if one thought of her simply as a woman, one must endow her with some freak of idiosyncrasy—she did not like admiration—or suppose some latent desire to doff her royalty of form as if her beauty bored her and all that men say of beauty, and she wanted only to be like other people, insignificant. He did not know. He did not know. He must go to his work.)

Knitting her reddish-brown hairy stocking, with her head outlined absurdly by the gilt frame, the green shawl which she had tossed over the edge of the frame, and the authenticated masterpiece by Michael Angelo, Mrs. Ramsay smoothed out what had been harsh in her manner a moment before, raised his head, and kissed her little boy on the forehead. "Let us find another picture to cut out," she said.

## Samuel Beckett (1906–1989)

Samuel Beckett received the Nobel Prize for literature in 1969. Like his fellow Dubliner James Joyce, he lived and worked in France; and again like Joyce, he was a master of style with a keen interest in language. Beckett wrote in both English and French. His novels include *Murphy* (1938) and the trilogy *Molly, Malone Dies,* and *The Unnamable* (1951–1953), which he originally wrote in French. It is for his plays, however, that Beckett is best known. *Waiting for Godot* (1953) established his reputation as the leader of the theatrical avant-garde. The success of that play is suggested by the fact that its title has become a vivid expression for the anticipation of some transfiguring event one anxiously waits for but which will never, in fact, occur. Beckett's other plays include *Endgame* (1957); *Krapp's Last Tape* (1958); and *Happy Days* (1961), which is included here.

Aristotle defined drama as an imitation of an action, but *Happy Days* is remarkable for being a drama in which nothing happens. Indeed, Winnie, the play's protagonist, is completely immobile. As the play begins, she is buried from the waist down in a mound of sand and must crane her neck backward to get a glimpse of her husband, Willie. Beckett is supremely modern in his relentless laying bare of the illusions to which people desperately cling in order to make sense of their lives in a world utterly indifferent to them. In reality, Winnie has nothing to live for. She inhabits a bleak world of unremitting sunglare and endless desert, but unlike the Jews of the biblical Exodus (pp. 125–132), she cannot even wander, and there is no Moses in sight. God revealed himself to Moses in a burning bush, but when Winnie's parasol catches fire it is a random and meaningless occurrence that she can best explain as the result of spontaneous combustion.

In the course of the play, Winnie sinks even more deeply into the sand and can barely turn her head. The only marker of what were once days and nights is the shrill, high-pitched buzzing of an electric bell that informs her when it is time to awake and when to go to sleep. On this bedrock of total despair, Winnie pathetically but heroically manages to construct a necessary attitude of grateful optimism. She tries to establish a daily routine and distracts herself from the utter bleakness of her situation by rummaging through, and straining to find some interest in, the mundane objects she keeps in a bag by her side. One of these objects is a revolver she affectionately calls "Brownie." Thus she has the option of freeing herself from the meaningless misery of her existence, but she chooses to go on living, even in a state of alienated sadness. Why does she make this choice? It is a question we also ask of the biblical *Job*, a work that might profitably be read along with *Happy Days.*

At the very end of the play, Willie, in a barely audible voice, utters Winnie's name in an affectionately abbreviated form: "Win." Willie has said almost nothing for the entire second act, and up to this point has not addressed his wife by name. This slight but moving affirmation of Winnie's being and of her importance to Willie, however bizarrely understated, is apparently enough to justify her triumphant willingness to go on ekeing out her existence in a meaningless universe. We define ourselves and make sense of a fundamentally senseless world, Beckett is suggesting, through the objects to which and people with whom we relate.

Beckett brilliantly—and with a sense of humor that somewhat lightens the gloom of his vision—explores the despair that lies just below the surface of modern life as we pursue our daily routines and indulge in hopes that we strongly suspect are really only defenses against the senselessness and helplessness of our existence.

## *Happy Days*

### ACT I

*Expanse of scorched grass rising centre to low mound. Gentle slopes down to front and either side of stage. Back an abrupter fall to stage level. Maximum of simplicity and symmetry.*

*Blazing light.*

*Very pompier trompe-l'oeil backcloth to represent unbroken plain and sky receding to meet in far distance.*

*Imbedded up to above her waist in exact centre of mound,* WINNIE. *About fifty, well preserved, blond for preference, plump, arms and shoulders bare, low bodice, big bosom, pearl necklet. She is discovered sleeping, her arms on the ground before her, her head on her arms. Beside her on ground to her left a capacious black bag, shopping variety, and to her right a collapsible collapsed parasol, beak of handle emerging from sheath.*

*To her right and rear, lying asleep on ground, hidden by mound,* WILLIE.

*Long pause. A bell rings piercingly, say ten seconds, stops. She does not move. Pause. Bell more piercingly, say five seconds. She wakes. Bell stops. She raises her head, gazes front. Long pause. She straightens up, lays her hands flat on ground, throws back her head and gazes at zenith. Long pause.*

WINNIE (*gazing at zenith*): Another heavenly day. (*Pause. Head back level, eyes front, pause. She clasps hands to breast, closes eyes. Lips move in inaudible prayer, say ten seconds. Lips still. Hands remain clasped. Low.*) For Jesus Christ sake Amen. (*Eyes open, hands unclasp, return to mound. Pause. She clasps hands to breast again, closes eyes, lips move again in inaudible addendum, say five seconds. Low.*) World without end Amen. (*Eyes open, hands unclasp, return to mound. Pause.*) Begin, Winnie. (*Pause.*) Begin your day, Winnie. (*Pause. She turns to bag, rummages in it without moving it from its place, brings out toothbrush, rummages again, brings out flat tube of toothpaste, turns back front, unscrews cap of tube, lays cap on ground, squeezes with difficulty small blob of paste on brush, holds tube in one hand and brushes teeth with other. She turns modestly aside and back to her right to spit out behind mound. In this position her eyes rest on* WILLIE. *She spits out. She cranes a little further back and down. Loud.*) Hoo-oo! (*Pause. Louder.*) Hoo-oo! (*Pause. Tender smile as she turns back front, lays down brush.*) Poor Willie—(*examines tube, smile off*)—running out—(*looks for cap*)—ah well—(*finds cap*)—can't be helped—(*screws on cap*)—just one of those old things—(*lays down tube*)—another of those old things—(*turns towards bag*)—just can't be cured—(*rummages in bag*)—cannot be cured—(*brings out small mirror, turns back front*)—ah yes—(*inspects teeth in mirror*)—poor dear Willie—(*testing upper front teeth with thumb, indistinctly*)—good Lord!—(*pulling back upper lip to inspect gums, do.*)—good God!—(*pulling back corner of mouth, mouth open, do.*)—ah well—(*other corner, do.*)—no worse—(*abandons inspection, normal speech*)—no better, no worse—(*lays down mirror*)—no change—(*wipes fingers on grass*)—no pain—(*looks for toothbrush*)—hardly any—(*takes up toothbrush*)—great thing that—(*examines handle of brush*)—nothing like it—(*examines handle, reads*)—pure . . . what?—(*pause*)—what?—(*lays down brush*)—ah yes—(*turns towards bag*)—poor Willie—(*rummages in bag*)—no zest—(*rummages*)—for anything—(*brings out spectacles in case*)—no interest—(*turns back front*)—in life—(*takes spectacles from case*)—poor dear Willie—(*lays down case*)—sleep forever—(*opens spectacles*)—marvellous gift—(*puts on spectacles*)—nothing to touch it—(*looks for toothbrush*)—in my opinion—(*takes up toothbrush*)—always said so—(*examines handle of brush*)—wish I had it—(*examines handle, reads*)—genuine . . . pure . . . what?—(*lays down brush*)—blind next—(*takes off* *spectacles*)—ah well—(*lays down spectacles*)—seen enough—(*feels in bodice for handkerchief*)—I suppose—(*takes out folded handkerchief*)—by now—(*shakes out handkerchief*)—what are those wonderful lines —(*wipes one eye*)—woe woe is me—(*wipes the other*)—to see what I see—(*looks for spectacles*)—ah yes—(*takes up spectacles*)—wouldn't miss it—(*starts polishing spectacles, breathing on lenses*)—or would I?—(*polishes*)—holy light—(*polishes*)—bob up out of dark—(*polishes*)—blaze of hellish light. (*Stops polishing, raises face to sky, pause, head back level, resumes polishing, stops polishing, cranes back to her right and down.*) Hoo-oo! (*Pause. Tender smile as she turns back front and resumes polishing. Smile off.*) Marvellous gift—(*stops polishing, lays down spectacles*)—wish I had it—(*folds handkerchief*)—ah well—(*puts handkerchief back in bodice*)—can't complain—(*looks for spectacles*)—no no—(*takes up spectacles*)—mustn't complain—(*holds up spectacles, looks through lens*)—so much to be thankful for—(*looks through other lens*)—no pain—(*puts on spectacles*)—hardly any—(*looks for toothbrush*)—wonderful thing that—(*takes up toothbrush*)—nothing like it—(*examines handle of brush*)—slight headache sometimes—(*examines handle, reads*)—guaranteed . . . genuine . . . pure . . . what?—(*looks closer*)—genuine pure—(*takes handkerchief from bodice*)—ah yes—(*shakes out handkerchief*)—occasional mild migraine—(*starts wiping handle of brush*—it comes—(*wipes*)—then goes—(*wiping mechanically*)—ah yes—(*wiping*)—many mercies—(*wiping*)—great mercies—(*stops wiping, fixed lost gaze, brokenly*)—prayers perhaps not for naught —(*pause, do.*)—first thing—(*pause, do.*)—last thing—(*head down, resumes wiping, stops wiping, head up, calmed, wipes eyes, folds handkerchief, puts it back in bodice, examines handle of brush, reads*)—fully guaranteed . . . genuine pure . . .—(*looks closer*)—genuine pure . . . (*Takes off spectacles, lays them and brush down, gazes before her.*) Old things. (*Pause.*) Old eyes. (*Long pause.*) On, Winnie. (*She casts about her, sees parasol, considers it at length, takes it up and develops from sheath a handle of surprising length. Holding butt of parasol in right hand she cranes back and down to her right to hang over* WILLIE.) Hoo-oo! (*Pause.*) Willie! (*Pause.*) Wonderful gift. (*She strikes down at him with beak of parasol.*) Wish I had it. (*She strikes again. The parasol slips from her grasp and falls behind mound. It is immediately restored to her by* WILLIE*'s invisible hand.*) Thank you, dear. (*She transfers parasol to left hand, turns back front and examines right palm.*) Damp. (*Returns parasol to right hand, examines left palm.*) Ah well, no worse. (*Head up, cheerfully.*) No better, no worse, no change. (*Pause. Do.*) No pain. (*Cranes back to look down at* WILLIE, *holding parasol by butt as before.*) Don't go off on me again now dear will you please, I may need you. (*Pause.*) No hurry, no hurry, just don't curl up on me again. (*Turns back front, lays down parasol, examines palms together, wipes them on grass.*) Perhaps a shade off colour just the same. (*Turns to bag, rummages in it, brings out revolver, holds it up, kisses it rapidly, puts it back, rummages, brings out almost *empty bottle of red medicine, turns back front, looks for spectacles, puts them on, reads label.*) Loss of spirits . . . lack of keenness . . . want of appetite . . . infants . . . children . . . adults . . . six level . . . tablespoonfuls daily—(*head up, smile*)—the old style!—(*smile off, head down, reads*)—daily . . . before and after . . . meals . . . instantaneous . . . (*looks closer*) . . . improvement. (*Takes off spectacles, lays them down, holds up bottle at arm's length to see level, unscrews cap, swigs it off head well back, tosses cap and bottle away in* WILLIE*'s direction. Sound of breaking glass.*) Ah that's better! (*Turns to bag, rummages in it, brings out lipstick, turns back front, examines lipstick.*) Running out. (*Looks for spectacles.*) Ah well. (*Puts on spectacles, looks for mirror.*) Musn't complain. (*Takes up mirror, starts doing lips.*) What is that wonderful line? (*Lips.*) Oh fleeting joys—(*lips*)—oh something lasting woe. (*Lips. She is interrupted by disturbance from* WILLIE. *He is sitting up. She lowers lipstick and mirror and cranes back and down to look at him. Pause. Top back* of WILLIE*'s bald head, trickling blood, rises to view above slope, comes to rest.* WINNIE *pushes up her spectacles. Pause. His hand appears with handkerchief, spreads it on skull, disappears. Pause. The hand appears with boater, club ribbon, settles it on head, rakish angle, disappears. Pause.* WINNIE *cranes a little further back and down.*) Slip on your drawers, dear, before you get singed. (*Pause.*) No? (*Pause.*) Oh I see, you still have some of that stuff left. (*Pause.*) Work it well in, dear. (*Pause.*) Now the other. (*Pause. She turns back front, gazes before her. Happy expression.*) Oh this is going to be another happy day! (*Pause. Happy expression off. She pulls down spectacles and resumes lips.* WILLIE *opens newspaper, hands invisible. Tops of yellow sheets appear on either side of his head.* WINNIE *finishes lips, inspects them in mirror held a little further away.*) Ensign crimson. (WILLIE *turns page.* WINNIE *lays down lipstick and mirror, turns towards bag.*) Pale flag.

WILLIE *turns page.* WINNIE *rummages in bag, brings out small ornate brimless hat with crumpled feather, turns back front, straightens hat, smooths feather, raises it towards head, arrests gesture as* WILLIE *reads.*

WILLIE: His Grace and Most Reverend Father in God Dr Carolus Hunter dead in tub.

*Pause.*

WINNIE (*gazing front, hat in hand, tone of fervent reminiscence*): Charlie Hunter! (*Pause.*) I close my eyes—(*she takes off spectacles and does so, hat in one hand, spectacles in other,* WILLIE *turns page*)—and am sitting on his knees again, in the back garden at Borough Green, under the horse-beech. (*Pause. She opens eyes, puts on spectacles, fiddles with hat.*) Oh the happy memories!

*Pause. She raises hat towards head, arrests gesture as* WILLIE *reads.*

WILLIE: Opening for smart youth.

*Pause. She raises hat towards head, arrests gesture, takes off spectacles, gazes front, hat in one hand, spectacles in other.*

WINNIE: My first ball! (*Long pause.*) My second ball! (*Long pause. Closes eyes.*) My first kiss! (*Pause. Willie turns page. Winnie opens eyes.*) A Mr

Johnson, or Johnston, or perhaps I should say John*stone.* Very bushy moustache very tawny. (*Reverently.*) Almost ginger! (*Pause.*) Within a toolshed, though whose I cannot conceive. We had no toolshed and he most certainly had no toolshed. (*Closes eyes.*) I see the piles of pots. (*Pause.*) The tangles of bast. (*Pause.*) The shadows deepening among the rafters.

*Pause. She opens eyes, puts on spectacles, raises hat towards head, arrests gesture as* WILLIE *reads.*

WILLIE: Wanted bright boy.

*Pause.* WINNIE *puts on hat hurriedly, looks for mirror.* WILLIE *turns page.* WINNIE *takes up mirror, inspects hat, lays down mirror, turns towards bag. Paper disappears.* WINNIE *rummages in bag, brings out magnifying-glass, turns back front, looks for toothbrush. Paper reappears, folded, and begins to fan* WILLIE*'s face, hand invisible.* WINNIE *takes up toothbrush and examines handle through glass.*

WINNIE: Fully guaranteed . . . (WILLIE *stops fanning*). . . genuine pure . . . (*Pause.* WILLIE *resumes fanning.* WINNIE *looks closer, reads.*) Fully guaranteed . . . (WILLIE *stops fanning*) . . . genuine pure . . . (*Pause.* WILLIE *resumes fanning.* WINNIE *lays down glass and brush, takes handkerchief from bodice, takes off and polishes spectacles, puts on spectacles, looks for glass, takes up and polishes glass, lays down glass, looks for brush, takes up brush and wipes handle, lays down brush, puts handkerchief back in bodice, looks for glass, takes up glass, looks for brush, takes up brush and examines handle through glass.*) Fully guaranteed . . . (WILLIE *stops fanning*) . . . genuine pure . . . (*pause,* WILLIE *resumes fanning*) . . . hog's (WILLIE *stops fanning, pause*) . . . setae. (*Pause.* WINNIE *lays down glass and brush, paper disappears,* WINNIE *takes off spectacles, lays them down, gazes front.*) Hog's setae. (*Pause.*) That is what I find so wonderful, that not a day goes by—(*smile*)—to speak in the old style—(*smile off*)—hardly a day, without some addition to one's knowledge however trifling, the addition I mean, provided one takes the pains. (WILLIE*'s hand reappears with a postcard which he examines close to eyes.*) And if for some strange reason no further pains are possible, why then just close the eyes—(*she does so*)—and wait for the day to come—(*opens eyes*)—the happy day to come when flesh melts at so many degrees and the night of the moon has so many hundred hours. (*Pause.*) That is what I find so comforting when I lose heart and envy the brute beast. (*Turning towards* WILLIE.) I hope you are taking in—(*She sees postcard, bends lower.*) What is that you have there, Willie, may I see? (*She reaches down with hand and* WILLIE *hands her card. The hairy forearm appears above slope, raised in gesture of giving, the hand open to take back, and remains in this position till card is returned.* WINNIE *turns back front and examines card.*) Heavens what are they up to! (*She looks for spectacles, puts them on and examines card.*) No but this is just genuine pure filth! (*Examines card.*) Make any nice-minded person want to vomit! (*Impatience of* WILLIE*'s fingers. She looks for glass, takes it up and examines card through glass. Long pause.*) What does that creature in the background think he's doing? (*Looks closer.*) Oh no really! (*Impatience of *fingers. Last long look. She lays down glass, takes edge of card between right forefinger and thumb, averts head, takes nose between left forefinger and thumb.*) Pah! (*Drops card.*) Take it away! (WILLIE*'s arm disappears. His hand reappears immediately, holding card.* WINNIE *takes off spectacles, lays them down, gazes before her. During what follows* WILLIE *continues to relish card, varying angles and distance from his eyes.*) Hog's setae. (*Puzzled expression.*) What exactly is a hog? (*Pause. Do.*) A sow of course I know, but a hog . . . (*Puzzled expression off.*) Oh well what does it matter, that is what I always say, it will come back, that is what I find so wonderful, all comes back. (*Pause.*) All? (*Pause.*) No, not all. (*Smile.*) No no. (*Smile off.*) Not quite. (*Pause.*) A part. (*Pause.*) Floats up, one fine day, out of the blue. (*Pause.*) That is what I find so wonderful. (*Pause. She turns towards bag. Hand and card disappear. She makes to rummage in bag, arrests gesture.*) No. (*She turns back front. Smile.*) No no. (*Smile off.*) Gently Winnie. (*She gazes front.* WILLIE*'s hand reappears, takes off hat, disappears with hat.*) What then? (*Hand reappears, takes handkerchief from skull, disappears with handkerchief. Sharply, as to one not paying attention.*) Winnie! (WILLIE *bows head out of sight.*) What *is* the alternative? (*Pause.*) What *is* the al—(WILLIE *blows nose loud and long, head and hands invisible. She turns to look at him. Pause. Head reappears. Pause. Hand reappears with handkerchief, spreads it on skull, disappears. Pause. Hand reappears with boater, settles it on head, rakish angle, disappears. Pause.*) Would I had let you sleep on. (*She turns back front. Intermittent plucking at grass, head up and down, to animate following.*) Ah yes, if only I could bear to be alone, I mean prattle away with not a soul to hear. (*Pause.*) Not that I flatter myself you hear much, no Willie, God forbid. (*Pause.*) Days perhaps when you hear nothing. (*Pause.*) But days too when you answer. (*Pause.*) So that I may say at all times, even when you do not answer and perhaps hear nothing, Something of this is being heard, I am not merely talking to myself, that is in the wilderness, a thing I could never bear to do—for any length of time. (*Pause.*) That is what enables me to go on, go on talking that is. (*Pause.*) Whereas if you were to die—(*smile*)—to speak in the old style—(*smile off*)—or go away and leave me, then what would I do, what *could* I do, all day long, I mean between the bell for waking and the bell for sleep? (*Pause.*) Simply gaze before me with compressed lips. (*Long pause while she does so. No more plucking.*) Not another word as long as I drew breath, nothing to break the silence of this place. (*Pause.*) Save possibly, now and then, every now and then, a sigh into my looking-glass. (*Pause.*) Or a brief . . . gale of laughter, should I happen to see the old joke again. (*Pause. Smile appears, broadens and seems about to culminate in laugh when suddenly replaced by expression of anxiety.*) My hair! (*Pause.*) Did I brush and comb my hair? (*Pause.*) I may have done. (*Pause.*) Normally I do. (*Pause.*) There is so little one *can* do. (*Pause.*) One does it all. (*Pause.*) All one can. (*Pause.*) Tis only human. (*Pause.*) Human nature. (*She begins to inspect mound, looks up.*) Human weakness. (*She resumes inspection of mound, looks up.*) Natural weakness. (*She resumes inspection of mound.*) I see no comb. (*Inspects.*) Nor any hairbrush. (*Looks up. Puzzled expression. She turns to bag, rummages in it.*) The comb is here. (*Back front. Puzzled expression. Back to bag. Rummages.*) The brush is here. (*Back front. Puzzled expression.*) Perhaps I put them back, after use. (*Pause. Do.*) But normally I do not put things back, after use, no, I leave them lying about and put them back all together, at the end of the day. (*Smile.*) To speak in the old style. (*Pause.*) The sweet old style. (*Smile off.*) And yet . . . I seem . . . to remember . . . (*Suddenly careless.*) Oh well, what does it matter, that is what I always say, I shall simply brush and comb them later on, purely and simply, I have the whole—(*Pause. Puzzled.*) Them? (*Pause.*) Or it? (*Pause.*) Brush and comb it? (*Pause.*) Sounds improper somehow. (*Pause. Turning a little towards* WILLIE.) What would you say, Willie? (*Pause. Turning a little further.*) What would you say, Willie, speaking of your hair, them or it? (*Pause.*) The hair on your head, I mean. (*Pause. Turning a little further.*) The hair on your head, Willie, what would you say speaking of the hair on your head, them or it?

*Long pause.*

WILLIE: It.

WINNIE (*turning back front, joyful*): Oh you are going to talk to me today, this is going to be a happy day! (*Pause. Joy off.*) Another happy day. (*Pause.*) Ah well, where was I, my hair, yes, later on, I shall be thankful for it later on. (*Pause.*) I have my—(*raises hands to hat*)—yes, on, my hat on—(*lowers hands*)—I cannot take it off now. (*Pause.*) To think there are times one cannot take off one's hat, not if one's life were at stake. Times one cannot put it on, times one cannot take it off. (*Pause.*) How often I have said, Put on your hat now, Winnie, there is nothing else for it, take off your hat now, Winnie, like a good girl, it will do you good, and did not. (*Pause.*) Could not. (*Pause. She raises hand, frees a strand of hair from under hat, draws it towards eye, squints at it, lets it go, hand down.*) Golden you called it, that day, when the last guest was gone—(*hand up in gesture of raising a glass*)—to your golden . . . may it never . . . (*voice breaks*) . . . may it never . . . (*Hand down. Head down. Pause. Low.*) That day. (*Pause. Do.*) What day? (*Pause. Head up. Normal voice.*) What now? (*Pause.*) Words fail, there are times when even they fail. (*Turning a little towards* WILLIE.) Is that not so, Willie? (*Pause. Turning a little further.*) Is not that so, Willie, that even words fail, at times? (*Pause. Back front.*) What is one to do then, until they come again? Brush and comb the hair, if it has not been done, or if there is some doubt, trim the nails if they are in need of trimming, these things tide one over. (*Pause.*) That is what I mean. (*Pause.*) That is all I mean. (*Pause.*) That is what I find so wonderful, that not a day goes by—(*smile*)—to speak in the old style—

(*smile off*)—without some blessing—(WILLIE *collapses behind slope, his head disappears,* WINNIE *turns towards event*)—in disguise. (*She cranes back and down.*) Go back into your hole now, Willie, you've exposed yourself enough. (*Pause.*) Do as I say, Willie, don't lie sprawling there in this hellish sun, go back into your hole. (*Pause.*) Go on now, Willie. (WILLIE *invisible starts crawling left towards hole.*) That's the man. (*She follows his progress with her eyes.*) Not head first, stupid, how are you going to turn? (*Pause.*) That's it . . . right round . . . now . . . back in. (*Pause.*) Oh I know it is not easy, dear, crawling backwards, but it is rewarding in the end. (*Pause.*) You have left your vaseline behind. (*She watches as he crawls back for vaseline.*) The lid! (*She watches as he crawls back towards hole. Irritated.*) Not head first, I tell you! *(Pause.)* More to the right. (*Pause.*) The *right,* I said. (*Pause. Irritated.*) Keep your tail down, can't you! (*Pause.*) Now. (*Pause.*) There! (*All these directions loud. Now in her normal voice, still turned towards him.*) Can you hear me? (*Pause.*) I beseech you, Willie, just yes or no, can you hear me, just yes or nothing.

*Pause.*

WILLIE: Yes.

WINNIE (*turning front, same voice*): And now?

WILLIE (*irritated*): Yes.

WINNIE (*less loud*): And now?

WILLIE (*more irritated*): Yes.

WINNIE (*still less loud*): And now? (*A little louder.*) And now?

WILLIE (*violently*): Yes!

WINNIE (*same voice*): Fear no more the heat o' the sun. (*Pause.*) Did you hear that?

WILLIE (*irritated*): Yes.

WINNIE (*same voice*): What? (*Pause.*) What?

WILLIE (*more irritated*): Fear no more.

*Pause.*

WINNIE (*same voice*): No more what? (*Pause.*) Fear no more what?

WILLIE (*violently*): Fear no more!

WINNIE (*normal voice, gabbled*): Bless you Willie I do appreciate your goodness I know what an effort it costs you, now you may relax I shall not trouble you again unless I am obliged to, by that I mean unless I come to the end of my own resources which is most unlikely, just to know that in theory you can hear me even though in fact you don't is all I need, just to feel you there within earshot and conceivably on the qui vive is all I ask, not to say anything I would not wish you to hear or liable to cause you pain, not to be just babbling away on trust as it is were not knowing and something gnawing at me. (*Pause for breath.*) Doubt. (*Places index and second finger on heart area, moves them about, brings them to rest.*) Here. (*Moves them slightly.*) Abouts. (*Hand away.*) Oh no doubt the time will come when before I can utter a word I must make sure you heard the one that went before and then no doubt another come another time when I must learn to talk to myself a thing I could never bear to do such wilderness. (*Pause.*) Or gaze before me with compressed lips. (*She does so.*) All day long. (*Gaze and lips again.*) No. (*Smile.*) No no. (*Smile off.*) There is of course the bag. (*Turns towards it.*) There will always be the bag. (*Back front.*) Yes, I suppose so. (*Pause.*) Even when you are gone, Willie. (*She turns a little towards him.*) You *are* going, Willie, aren't you? (*Pause. Louder.*) You *will* be going soon, Willie, won't you? (*Pause. Louder.*) Willie! (*Pause. She cranes back and down to look at him.*) So you have taken off your straw, that is wise. (*Pause.*) You do look snug, I must say, with your chin on your hands and the old blue eyes like saucers in the shadows. (*Pause.*) Can you see me from there I wonder, I still wonder. (*Pause.*) No? (*Back front.*) Oh I know it does not follow when two are gathered together—(*faltering*)—in this way—(*normal*)—that because one sees the other the other sees the one, life has taught me that . . . too. (*Pause.*) Yes, life I suppose, there is no other word. (*She turns a little towards him.*) Could you see me, Willie, do you think, from where you are, if you were to raise your eyes in my direction? (*Turns a little further.*) Lift up your eyes to me, Willie, and tell me can you see me, do that for me, I'll lean back as far as I can. (*Does so. Pause.*) No? (*Pause.*) Well never mind. (*Turns back painfully front.*) The earth is very tight today, can it be I have put on flesh, I trust not. (*Pause. Absently, eyes lowered.*) The great heat possibly. (*Starts to pat and stroke ground.*) All things expanding, some more than others. (*Pause. Patting and stroking.*) Some less. (*Pause. Do.*) Oh I can well imagine what is passing through your mind, it is not enough to have to listen to the woman, now I must look at her as well. (*Pause. Do.*) Well it is very understandable. (*Pause. Do.*) Most understandable. (*Pause. Do.*) One does not appear to be asking a great deal, indeed at times it would seem hardly possible—(*voice breaks, falls to a murmur*)—to ask less—of a fellow-creature—to put it mildly—whereas actually—when you think about it—look into your heart—see the other—what he needs—peace—to be left in peace—then perhaps the moon—all this time—asking for the moon. (*Pause. Stroking hand suddenly still. Lively.*) Oh I say, what have we here? (*Bending head to ground, incredulous.*) Looks like life of some kind! (*Looks for spectacles, puts them on, bends closer. Pause.*) An emmet! (*Recoils. Shrill.*) Willie, an emmet, a live emmet! (*Seizes magnifying-glass, bends to ground again, inspects through glass.*) Where's it gone? (*Inspects.*) Ah! (*Follows its progress through grass.*) Has like a little white ball in its arms. (*Follows progress. Hand still. Pause.*) It's gone in. (*Continues a moment to gaze at spot through glass, then slowly straightens up, lays down glass, takes off spectacles and gazes before her, spectacles in hand. Finally.*) Like a little white ball.

*Long pause. Gesture to lay down spectacles.*

WILLIE: Eggs.

WINNIE (*arresting gesture*): What?

*Pause.*

WILLIE: Eggs. (*Pause. Gesture to lay down glasses.*) Formication.

WINNIE (*arresting gesture*): What?

*Pause.*

WILLIE: Formication.

*Pause. She lays down spectacles, gazes before her. Finally.*

WINNIE (*murmur*): God. (*Pause.* WILLIE *laughs quietly. After a moment she joins in. They laugh quietly together.* WILLIE *stops. She laughs on a moment alone.* WILLIE *joins in. They laugh together. She stops.* WILLIE *laughs on a moment alone. He stops. Pause. Normal voice.*) Ah well what a joy in any case to hear you laugh again, Willie, I was convinced I never would, you never would. (*Pause.*) I suppose some people might think us a trifle irreverent, but I doubt it. (*Pause.*) How can one better magnify the Almighty than by sniggering with him at his little jokes, particularly the poorer ones? (*Pause.*) I think you would back me up there, Willie. (*Pause.*) Or were we perhaps diverted by two quite different things? (*Pause.*) Oh well, what does it matter, that is what I always say, so long as one . . . you know . . . what is that wonderful line . . . laughing wild . . . something something laughing wild amid severest woe. (*Pause.*) And now? (*Long pause.*) Was I lovable once, Willie? (*Pause.*) Was I ever lovable? (*Pause.*) Do not misunderstand my question, I am not asking you if you loved me, we know all about that, I am asking you if you found me lovable—at one stage. (*Pause.*) No? (*Pause.*) You can't? (*Pause.*) Well I admit it is a teaser. And you have done more than your bit already, for the time being, just lie back now and relax, I shall not trouble you again unless I am compelled to, just to know you are there within hearing and conceivably on the semi-alert is . . . er . . . paradise enow. (*Pause.*) The day is now well advanced. (*Smile.*) To speak in the old style. (*Smile off.*) And yet it is perhaps a little soon for my song. (*Pause.*) To sing too soon is a great mistake, I find. (*Turning towards bag.*) There is of course the bag. (*Looking at bag.*) The bag. (*Back front.*) Could I enumerate its contents? (*Pause.*) No. (*Pause.*) Could I, if some kind person were to come along and ask, What all have you got in that big black bag, Winnie? give an exhaustive answer? (*Pause.*) No. (*Pause.*) The depths in particular, who knows what treasures. (*Pause.*) What comforts. (*Turns to look at bag.*) Yes, there is the bag. (*Back front.*) But something tells me, Do not overdo the bag, Winnie, make use of it of course, let it help you . . . along, when stuck, by all means, but cast your mind forward, something tells me, cast your mind forward, Winnie, to the time when words must fail—(*she closes eyes, pause, opens eyes*)—and do not overdo the bag. (*Pause. She turns to look at bag.*) Perhaps just one quick dip. (*She turns back front, closes eyes, throws out left arm, plunges hand in bag and brings out revolver. Disgusted.*) You again! (*She opens eyes, brings revolver front and contemplates it. She weighs it in her palm.*) You'd think the weight of this thing would bring it down among the . . . last rounds. But no. It doesn't. Ever uppermost, like Browning. (*Pause.*) Brownie . . . (*Turning a little towards* WILLIE.) Remember Brownie, Willie? (*Pause.*) Remember how you used to keep on at me to take it away from you? Take it away, Winnie, take it away, before I put myself out of my misery. (*Back front. Derisive.*) *Your* misery! (*To revolver.*) Oh I suppose it's a comfort to know you're there, but I'm tired of you. (*Pause.*) I'll leave you out, that's what I'll do. (*She lays revolver on ground to her right.*) There, that's your home from this day out. (*Smile*) The old style! (*Smile off.*) And now? (*Long pause.*) Is gravity what it was, Willie, I fancy not. (*Pause.*) Yes, the feeling more and more that if I were not held—(*gesture*)—in this way, I would simply float up into the blue. (*Pause.*) And that perhaps some day the earth will yield and let me go, the pull is so great, yes, crack all round me and let me out. (*Pause.*) Don't you ever have that feeling, Willie, of being sucked up? (*Pause.*) Don't you have to cling on sometimes, Willie? (*Pause. She turns a little towards him.*) Willie.

*Pause.*

WILLIE: *Sucked* up?

WINNIE: Yes love, up into the blue, like gossamer. (*Pause.*) No? (*Pause.*) You don't? (*Pause.*) Ah well, natural laws, natural laws, I suppose it's like everything else, it all depends on the creature you happen to be. All I can say is for my part is that for me they are not what they were when I was young and . . . foolish and . . . (*faltering, head down*) . . . beautiful . . . possibly . . . lovely . . . in a way . . . to look at. (*Pause. Head up.*) Forgive me, Willie, sorrow keeps breaking in. (*Normal voice.*) Ah well what a joy in any case to know you are there, as usual, and perhaps awake, and perhaps taking all this in, some of all this, what a happy day for me . . . it will have been. (*Pause.*) So far. (*Pause.*) What a blessing nothing grows, imagine if all this stuff were to start growing. (*Pause.*) Imagine. (*Pause.*) Ah yes, great mercies. (*Long pause.*) I can say no more. (*Pause.*) For the moment. (*Pause. Turns to look at bag. Back front. Smile.*) No no. (*Smile off. Looks at parasol.*) I suppose I might—(*takes up parasol*)—yes, I suppose I might . . . hoist this thing now. (*Begins to unfurl it. Following punctuated by mechanical difficulties overcome.*) One keeps putting off—putting up—for fear of putting up—too soon—and the day goes by—quite by—without one's having put up—at all. (*Parasol now fully open. Turned to her right she twirls it idly this way and that.*) Ah yes, so little to say, so little to do, and the fear so great, certain days, of finding oneself . . . left, with hours still to run, before the bell for sleep, and nothing more to say, nothing more to do, that the days go by, certain days go by, quite by, the bell goes, and little or nothing said, little or nothing done. (*Raising parasol.*) That is the danger. (*Turning front.*) To be guarded against. (*She gazes front, holding up parasol with right hand. Maximum pause.*) I used to perspire freely. (*Pause.*) Now hardly at all. (*Pause.*) The heat is much greater. (*Pause.*) The perspiration much less. (*Pause.*) That is what I find so wonderful. (*Pause.*) The way man adapts himself. (*Pause.*) To changing conditions. (*She transfers parasol to left hand. Long pause.*) Holding up wearies the arm. (*Pause.*) Not if one is going along. (*Pause.*) Only if one is at rest. (*Pause.*) That is a curious observation. (*Pause.*) I hope you heard that, Willie, I should be grieved to think you had not heard that. (*She takes parasol in both hands. Long pause.*) I am weary, holding it up, and I cannot put it down. (*Pause.*) I am worse off with it up than with it down, and I cannot put it down. (*Pause.*) Reason says, Put it down, Winnie, it is not helping you, put the thing down and get on with something else. (*Pause.*) I cannot. (*Pause.*) I cannot move. (*Pause.*) No, something must happen, in the world, take place, some change, I cannot, if I am to move again. (*Pause.*) Willie. (*Mildly.*) Help. (*Pause.*) No? (*Pause.*) Bid me put this thing down, Willie, I would obey you instantly, as I have always done, honoured and obeyed. (*Pause.*) Please, Willie. (*Mildly.*) For pity's sake. (*Pause.*) No? (*Pause.*) You can't? (*Pause.*) Well I don't blame you, no, it would ill become me, who cannot move, to blame my Willie because he cannot speak. (*Pause.*) Fortunately I am in tongue again. (*Pause.*) That is what I find so wonderful, my two lamps, when one goes out the other burns brighter. (*Pause.*) Oh yes, great mercies. (*Maximum pause. The parasol goes on fire. Smoke, flames if feasible. She sniffs, looks up, throws parasol to her right behind mound, cranes back to watch it burning. Pause.*) Ah earth you old extinguisher. (*Back front.*) I presume this has occurred before, though I cannot recall it. (*Pause.*) Can you, Willie? (*Turns a little towards him.*) Can you recall this having occurred before? (*Pause. Cranes back to look at him.*) Do you know what has occurred, Willie? (*Pause.*) Have you gone off on me again? (*Pause.*) I do not ask if you are alive to all that is going on, I merely ask if you have not gone off on me again. (*Pause.*) Your eyes appear to be closed, but that has no particular significance we know. (*Pause.*) Raise a finger, dear, will you please, if you are not quite senseless. (*Pause.*) Do that for me, Willie please, just the little finger, if you are still conscious. (*Pause. Joyful.*) Oh all five, you are a darling today, now I may continue with an easy mind. (*Back front.*) Yes, what ever occurred that did not occur before and yet . . . I wonder, yes, I confess I wonder. (*Pause.*) With the sun blazing so much fiercer down, and hourly fiercer, is it not natural things should go on fire never known to do so, in this way I mean, spontaneous like. (*Pause.*) Shall I myself not melt perhaps in the end, or burn, oh I do not mean necessarily burst into flames, no, just little by little be charred to a black cinder, all this—(*ample gesture of arms*)—visible flesh. (*Pause.*) On the other hand, did I ever know a temperate time? (*Pause.*) No. (*Pause.*) I speak of temperate times and torrid times, they are empty words. (*Pause.*) I speak of when I was not yet caught—in this way—and had my legs and had the use of my legs, and could seek out a shady place, like you, when I was tired of the sun, or a sunny place when I was tired of the shade, like you, and they are all empty words. (*Pause.*) It is no hotter today than yesterday, it will be no hotter tomorrow than today, how could it, and so on back into the far past, forward into the far future. (*Pause.*) And should one day the earth cover my breasts, then I shall never have seen my breasts, no one ever seen my breasts. (*Pause.*) I hope you caught something of that, Willie, I should be sorry to think you had caught nothing of all that, it is not every day I rise to such heights. (*Pause.*) Yes, something seems to have occurred, something has seemed to occur, and nothing has occurred, nothing at all, you are quite right, Willie. (*Pause.*) The sunshade will be there again tomorrow, beside me on this mound, to help me through the day. (*Pause. She takes up mirror.*) I take up this little glass, I shiver it on a stone—(*does so*)—I throw it away—(*does so far behind her*)—it will be in the bag again tomorrow, without a scratch, to help me through the day. (*Pause.*) No, one can do nothing. (*Pause.*) That is what I find so wonderful, the way things . . . (*voice breaks, head down*) . . . things . . . so wonderful. (*Long pause, head down. Finally turns, still bowed, to bag, brings out unidentifiable odds and ends, stuffs them back, fumbles deeper, brings out finally musical-box, winds it up, turns it on, listens for a moment holding it in both hands, huddled over it, turns back front, straightens up and listens to tune, holding box to breast with both hands. It plays the Waltz Duet "I love you so" from* The Merry Widow. *Gradually happy expression. She sways to the rhythm. Music stops. Pause. Brief burst of hoarse song without words—musical-box tune—from* WILLIE. *Increase of happy expression. She lays down box.*) Oh this will have been a happy day! (*She claps hands.*) Again, Willie, again! (*Claps.*) Encore, Willie, please! (*Pause. Happy expression off.*) No? You won't do that for me? (*Pause.*) Well it is very understandable, very understandable. One cannot sing just to please someone, however much one loves them, no, song must come from the heart, that is what I always say, pour out from the inmost, like a thrush. (*Pause.*) How often I have said, in evil hours, Sing now, Winnie, sing your song, there is nothing else for it, and did not. (*Pause.*) Could not. (*Pause.*) No, like the thrush, or the bird of dawning, with no thought of benefit, to oneself or anyone else. (*Pause.*) And now? (*Long pause. Low.*) Strange feeling. (*Pause. Do.*) Strange feeling that someone is looking at me. I am clear, then dim, then gone, then dim again, then clear again, and so on, back and forth, in and out of someone's eye. (*Pause. Do.*) Strange? (*Pause. Do.*) No, here all is strange. (*Pause. Normal voice.*) Something says, Stop talking now, Winnie, for a minute, don't squander all your words for the day, stop talking and do something for a change, will you? (*She raises hands and holds them open before her eyes. Apostrophic.*) Do something! (*She closes hands.*) What claws! (*She turns to bag, rummages in it, brings out finally a nail file, turns back front and begins to file nails. Files for a time in silence, then the following punctuated by filing.*) There floats up—into my thoughts—a Mr Shower—a Mr and perhaps a Mrs Shower—no—they are holding hands—his fiancée then more likely—or just some—loved one. (*Looks closer at nails.*) Very brittle today. (*Resumes filing.*) Shower—Shower—does the name mean anything—to you, Willie—evoke any reality, I mean—for you, Willie—don't answer if you don't—feel up to it—you have done more—than your bit—already—Shower—Shower. (*Inspects filed nails.*) Bit more like it. (*Raises head, gazes front.*) Keep yourself nice, Winnie, that's what I always say, come what may, keep yourself nice. (*Pause. Resumes filing.*) Yes—Shower—Shower—(*stops filing, raises head, gazes front, pause*)—or Cooker, perhaps I should say Cooker. (*Turning a little towards* WILLIE.) Cooker, Willie, does Cooker strike a chord? (*Pause. Turns a little further. Louder.*) Cooker, Willie, does Cooker ring a bell, the name Cooker? (*Pause. She cranes back to look at him. Pause.*) Oh really! (*Pause.*) Have you no handkerchief, darling? (*Pause.*) Have you no delicacy? (*Pause.*) Oh, Willie, you're not eating it! Spit it out, dear, spit it out! (*Pause. Back front.*) Ah well, I suppose it's only natural. (*Break in voice.*) Human. (*Pause. Do.*) What *is* one to do? (*Head down. Do.*) All day long. (*Pause. Do.*) Day after day. (*Pause. Head up. Smile. Calm.*) The old style! (*Smile off. Resumes nails.*) No, done him. (*Passes on to next.*) Should have put on my glasses. (*Pause.*) Too late now. (*Finishes left hand, inspects it.*) Bit more human. (*Starts right hand. Following punctuated as before.*) Well anyway—this man Shower—or Cooker—no matter—and the woman—hand in hand—in the other hands bags—kind of big brown grips—standing there gaping at me—and at last this man Shower—or Cooker—ends in er anyway—stake my life on that—What's she doing? he says—What's the idea? he says—stuck up to her diddies in the bleeding ground—coarse fellow—What does it mean? he says—What's it meant to mean?—and so on—lot more stuff like that—usual drivel—Do you hear me? he says—I do, she says, God help me—What do you mean, he says, God help you? (*Stops filing, raises head, gazes front.*) And you, she says, what's the idea of you, she says, what are you meant to mean? It is because you're still on your two flat feet, with your old ditty full of tinned muck and changes of underwear, dragging me up and down this fornicating wilderness, coarse creature, fit mate—(*with sudden violence*)—let go of my hand and drop for God's sake, she says, drop! (*Pause. Resumes filing.*) Why doesn't he dig her out? he says—referring to you, my dear—What good is she to him like that?—What good is he to her like that?—and so on—usual tosh—Good! she says, have a heart for God's sake—Dig her out, he says, dig her out, no sense in her like that—Dig her out with what? she says—I'd dig her out with my bare hands, he says—must have been man and—wife. (*Files in silence.*) Next thing they're away—hand in hand—and the bags—dim—then gone—last human kind—to stray this way. (*Finishes right hand, inspects it, lays down file, gazes front.*) Strange thing, time like this, drift up into the mind. (*Pause.*) Strange? (*Pause.*) No, here all is strange. (*Pause.*) Thankful for it in any case. (*Voice breaks.*) Most thankful. (*Head down. Pause. Head up. Calm.*) Bow and raise the head, bow and raise, always that. (*Pause.*)

And now? (*Long pause. Starts putting things back in bag, toothbrush last. This operation, interrupted by pauses as indicated, punctuates following.*) It is perhaps a little soon—to make ready—for the night—(*stops tidying, head up, smile*)—the old style!—(*smile off, resumes tidying*)—and yet I do—make ready for the night—feeling it at hand—the bell for sleep—saying to myself—Winnie—it will not be long now, Winnie—until the bell for sleep. (*Stops tidying, head up.*) Sometimes I am wrong. (*Smile.*) But not often. (*Smile off.*) Sometimes all is over, for the day, all done, all said, all ready for the night, and the day not over, far from over, the night not ready, far, far from ready. (*Smile.*) But not often. (*Smile off.*) Yes, the bell for sleep, when I feel it at hand, and so make ready for the night—(*gesture*)—in this way, sometimes I am wrong—(*smile*)—but not often. (*Smile off. Resumes tidying.*) I used to think—I say I used to think—that all these things—put back into the bag—if too soon—put back too soon—could be taken out again—if necessary—if needed—and so on—indefinitely—back into the bag—back out of the bag—until the bell—went. (*Stops tidying, head up, smile.*) But no. (*Smile broader.*) No no. (*Smile off. Resumes tidying.*) I suppose this—might seem strange—this—what shall I say—this what I have said—yes—(*she takes up revolver*)—strange—(*she turns to put revolver in bag*)—were it not—(*about to put revolver in bag she arrests gesture and turns back front*)—were it not—(*she lays down revolver to her right, stops tidying, head up*)—that all seems strange. (*Pause.*) Most strange. (*Pause.*) Never any change. (*Pause.*) And more and more strange. (*Pause. She bends to mound again, takes up last object, i.e. toothbrush, and turns to put it in bag when her attention is drawn to disturbance from* WILLIE. *She cranes back and to her right to see. Pause.*) Weary of your hole, dear? (*Pause.*) Well I can understand that. (*Pause.*) Don't forget your straw. (*Pause.*) Not the crawler you were, poor darling. (*Pause.*) No, not the crawler I gave my heart to. (*Pause.*) The hands and knees, love, try the hands and knees. (*Pause.*) The knees! The knees! (*Pause.*) What a curse, mobility! (*She follows with eyes his progress towards her behind mound, i.e. towards place he occupied at beginning of act.*) Another foot, Willie, and you're home. (*Pause as she observes last foot.*) Ah! (*Turns back front laboriously, rubs neck.*) Crick in my neck admiring you. (*Rubs neck.*) But it's worth it, well worth it. (*Turning slightly towards him.*) Do you know what I dream sometimes? (*Pause.*) What I dream sometimes, Willie. (*Pause.*) That you'll come round and live this side where I could see you. (*Pause. Back front.*) I'd be a different woman. (*Pause.*) Unrecognizable. (*Turning slightly towards him.*) Or just now and then, come round this side just every now and then and let me feast on you. (*Back front.*) But you can't, I know. (*Head down.*) I know. (*Pause. Head up.*) Well anyway—(*looks at toothbrush in her hand*)—can't be long now—(*looks at brush*)—until the bell. (*Top back of* WILLIE*'s head appears above slope.* WINNIE *looks closer at brush.*) Fully guaranteed . . . (*head *up*) . . . what's this it was? (WILLIE*'s hand appears with handkerchief, spreads it on skull, disappears.*) Genuine pure . . . fully guaranteed . . . (WILLIE*'s hand appears with boater, settles it on head, rakish angle, disappears*) . . . genuine pure . . . ah! hog's setae. (*Pause.*) What is a hog exactly? (*Pause. Turns slightly towards* WILLIE.) What exactly is a hog, Willie, do you know, I can't remember. (*Pause. Turning a little further, pleading.*) What *is* a hog, Willie, please!

*Pause.*

WILLIE: Castrated male swine. (*Happy expression appears on* WINNIE*'s face.*) Reared for slaughter.

*Happy expression increases.* WILLIE *opens newspaper, hands invisible. Tops of yellow sheets appear on either side of his head.* WINNIE *gazes before her with happy expression.*

WINNIE: Oh this *is* a happy day! This will have been another happy day! (*Pause.*) After all. (*Pause.*) So far.

*Pause. Happy expression off.* WILLIE *turns page. Pause. He turns another page. Pause.*

WILLIE: Opening for smart youth.

*Pause.* WINNIE *takes off hat, turns to put it in bag, arrests gesture, turns back front. Smile.*

WINNIE: No. (*Smile broader.*) No no. (*Smile off. Puts on hat again, gazes front, pause.*) And now? (*Pause.*) Sing. (*Pause.*) Sing your song, Winnie. (*Pause.*) No? (*Pause.*) Then pray. (*Pause.*) Pray your prayer, Winnie.

*Pause.* WILLIE *turns page. Pause.*

WILLIE: Wanted bright boy.

*Pause.* WINNIE *gazes before her.* WILLIE *turns page. Pause. Newspaper disappears. Long pause.*

WINNIE: Pray your old prayer, Winnie.

*Long pause.*

CURTAIN

## ACT II

*Scene as before.*

WINNIE *imbedded up to neck, hat on head, eyes closed. Her head, which she can no longer turn, nor bow, nor raise, faces front motionless throughout act. Movements of eyes as indicated.*

*Bag and parasol as before. Revolver conspicuous to her right on mound.*

*Long pause.*

*Bell rings loudly. She opens eyes at once. Bell stops. She gazes front. Long pause.*

WINNIE: Hail, holy light. (*Long pause. She closes her eyes. Bell rings loudly. She opens eyes at once. Bell stops. She gazes front. Long smile. Smile off. Long pause.*) Someone is looking at me still. (*Pause.*) Caring for me still. (*Pause.*) That is what I find so wonderful. (*Pause.*) Eyes on my eyes. (*Pause.*) What is that unforgettable line? (*Pause. Eyes right.*) Willie. (*Pause. Louder.*) Willie. (*Pause. Eyes front.*) May one still speak of time? (*Pause.*) Say it is a long time now, Willie, since I saw you. (*Pause.*) Since I heard you. (*Pause.*) May one? (*Pause.*) One does. (*Smile.*) The old style! (*Smile off.*) There is so little one can speak of. (*Pause.*) One speaks of it all. (*Pause.*) All one can. (*Pause.*) I used to think . . . (*pause*) . . . I say I used to think that I would learn to talk alone. (*Pause.*) By that I mean to myself, the wilderness. (*Smile.*) But no. (*Smile broader.*) No no. (*Smile off.*) Ergo you are there. (*Pause.*) Oh no doubt you are dead, like the others, no doubt you have died, or gone away and left me, like the others, it doesn't matter, you are there. (*Pause. Eyes left.*) The bag too is there, the same as ever, I can see it. (*Pause. Eyes right. Louder.*) The bag is there, Willie, as good as ever, the one you gave me that day . . . to go to market. (*Pause. Eyes front.*) That day. (*Pause.*) What day? (*Pause.*) I used to pray. (*Pause.*) I say I used to pray. (*Pause.*) Yes, I must confess I did. (*Smile.*) Not now. (*Smile broader.*) No no. (*Smile off. Pause.*) Then . . . now . . . what difficulties here, for the mind. (*Pause.*) To have been always what I am—and so changed from what I was. (*Pause.*) I am the one, I say the one, then the other. (*Pause.*) Now the one, then the other. (*Pause.*) There is so little one can say, one says it all. (*Pause.*) All one can. (*Pause.*) And no truth in it anywhere. (*Pause.*) My arms. (*Pause.*) My breasts. (*Pause.*) What arms? (*Pause.*) What breasts? (*Pause.*) Willie. (*Pause.*) What Willie? (*Sudden vehement affirmation.*) My Willie! (*Eyes right, calling.*) Willie! (*Pause. Louder.*) Willie! (*Pause. Eyes front.*) Ah well, not to know, not to know for sure, great mercy, all I ask. (*Pause.*) Ah yes . . . then . . . now . . . beechen green . . . this . . . Charlie . . . kisses . . . this . . . all that . . . deep trouble for the mind. (*Pause.*) But it does not trouble mine. (*Smile.*) Not now. (*Smile broader.*) No no. (*Smile off. Long pause. She closes eyes. Bell rings loudly. She opens eyes. Pause.*) Eyes float up that seem to close in peace . . . to see . . . in peace. (*Pause.*) Not mine. (*Smile.*) Not now. (*Smile broader.*) No no. (*Smile off. Long pause.*) Willie. (*Pause.*) Do you think the earth has lost its atmosphere, Willie? (*Pause.*) Do you, Willie? (*Pause.*) You have no opinion? (*Pause.*) Well that is like you, you never had any opinion about anything. (*Pause.*) It's understandable. (*Pause.*) Most. (*Pause.*) The earthball. (*Pause.*) I sometimes wonder. (*Pause.*) Perhaps not quite all. (*Pause.*) There always remains something. (*Pause.*) Of everything. (*Pause.*) Some remains. (*Pause.*) If the mind were to go. (*Pause.*) It won't of course. (*Pause.*) Not quite. (*Pause.*) Not mine. (*Smile*) Not now. (*Smile broader.*) No no. (*Smile off. Long pause.*) It might be the eternal cold. (*Pause.*) Everlasting perishing cold. (*Pause.*) Just chance, I take it, happy chance. (*Pause.*) Oh yes, great mercies, great mercies. (*Pause.*) And now? (*Long pause.*) The face. (*Pause.*) The nose. (*She squints down.*) I can see it . . . (*squinting down*) . . . the tip . . . the nostrils . . . breath of life . . . that curve you so admired . . .

(*pouts*) . . . a hint of lip . . . (*pouts again*) . . . if I pout them out . . . (*sticks out tongue*) . . . the tongue of course . . . you so admired . . . if I stick it out . . . (*sticks it out again*) . . . the tip . . . (*eyes up*) . . . suspicion of brow . . . eyebrow . . . imagination possibly . . . (*eyes left*) . . . cheek . . . no . . . (*eyes right*) . . . no . . . (*distends cheeks*) . . . even if I puff them out . . . (*eyes left, distends cheeks again*) . . . no . . . no damask. (*Eyes front.*) That is all. (*Pause.*) The bag of course . . . (*eyes left*) . . . a little blurred perhaps . . . but the bag. (*Eyes front. Offhand.*) The earth of course and sky. (*Eyes right.*) The sunshade you gave me . . . that day . . . (*pause*) . . . that day . . . the lake . . . the reeds. (*Eyes front. Pause.*) What day? (*Pause.*) What reeds? (*Long pause. Eyes close. Bell rings loudly. Eyes open. Pause. Eyes right.*) Brownie of course. (*Pause.*) You remember Brownie, Willie, I can see him. (*Pause.*) Brownie is there, Willie, beside me. (*Pause. Loud.*) Brownie is there, Willie. (*Pause. Eyes front.*) That is all. (*Pause.*) What would I do without them? (*Pause.*) What would I do without them, when words fail? (*Pause.*) Gaze before me, with compressed lips. (*Long pause while she does so.*) I cannot. (*Pause.*) Ah yes, great mercies, great mercies. (*Long pause. Low.*) Sometimes I hear sounds. (*Listening expression. Normal voice.*) But not often. (*Pause.*) They are a boon, sounds are a boon, they help me . . . through the day. (*Smile*) The old style! (*Smile off.*) Yes, those are happy days, when there are sounds. (*Pause.*) When I hear sounds. (*Pause.*) I used to think . . . (*pause*) . . . I say I used to think they were in my head. (*Smile.*) But no. (*Smile broader.*) No no. (*Smile off.*) That was just logic. (*Pause.*) Reason. (*Pause.*) I have not lost my reason. (*Pause.*) Not yet. (*Pause.*) Not all. (*Pause.*) Some remains. (*Pause.*) Sounds. (*Pause.*) Like little . . . sunderings, little falls . . . apart. (*Pause. Low.*) It's things, Willie. (*Pause. Normal voice.*) In the bag, outside the bag. (*Pause.*) Ah yes, things have their life, that is what I always say, *things* have a life. (*Pause.*) Take my looking-glass, it doesn't need me. (*Pause.*) The bell. (*Pause.*) It hurts like a knife. (*Pause.*) A gouge. (*Pause.*) One cannot ignore it. (*Pause.*) How often . . . (*pause*) . . . I say how often I have said, Ignore it, Winnie, ignore the bell, pay no heed, just sleep and wake, sleep and wake, as you please, open and close the eyes, as you please, or in the way you find most helpful. (*Pause.*) Open and close the eyes, Winnie, open and close, always that. (*Pause.*) But no. (*Smile.*) Not now. (*Smile broader.*) No no. (*Smile off. Pause.*) What now? (*Pause.*) What now, Willie? (*Long pause.*) There is my story of course, when all else fails. (*Pause.*) A life. (*Smile*) A long life. (*Smile off.*) Beginning in the womb, where life used to begin, Mildred has memories, she will have memories, of the womb, before she dies, the mother's womb. (*Pause.*) She is now four or five already and has recently been given a big waxen dolly. (*Pause.*) Fully clothed, complete outfit. (*Pause.*) Shoes, socks, undies, complete set, frilly frock, gloves. (*Pause.*) White mesh. (*Pause.*) A little white straw hat with a chin elastic. (*Pause.*) Pearly necklet. (*Pause.*) A little picture-book with legends in real print to go under her arm when she takes her walk. (*Pause.*) China blue eyes that open and shut. (*Pause. Narrative.*) The sun was not well up when Milly rose, descended the steep . . . (*pause*) . . . slipped on her nightgown, descended all alone the steep wooden stairs, backwards on all fours, though she had been forbidden to do so, entered the . . . (*pause*) . . . tiptoed down the silent passage, entered the nursery and began to undress Dolly. (*Pause.*) Crept under the table and began to undress Dolly. (*Pause.*) Scolding her . . . the while. (*Pause.*) Suddenly a mouse—(*Long pause.*) Gently, Winnie. (*Long pause. Calling.*) Willie! (*Pause. Louder.*) Willie! (*Pause. Mild reproach.*) I sometimes find your attitude a little strange, Willie, all this time, it is not like you to be wantonly cruel. (*Pause.*) Strange? (*Pause.*) No. (*Smile.*) Not here. (*Smile broader.*) Not now. (*Smile off.*) And yet . . . (*Suddenly anxious.*) I do hope nothing is amiss. (*Eyes right, loud.*) Is all well, dear? (*Pause. Eyes front. To herself.*) God grant he did not go in head foremost! (*Eyes right, loud.*) You're not stuck, Willie? (*Pause. Do.*) You're not jammed, Willie? (*Eyes front, distressed.*) Perhaps he is crying out for help all this time and I do not hear him! (*Pause.*) I do of course hear cries. (*Pause.*) But they are in my head surely. (*Pause.*) Is it possible that . . . (*Pause. With finality.*) No no, my head was always full of cries. (*Pause.*) Faint confused cries. (*Pause.*) They come. (*Pause.*) Then go. (*Pause.*) As on a wind. (*Pause.*) That is what I find so wonderful. (*Pause.*) They cease. (*Pause.*) Ah yes, great mercies, great mercies. (*Pause.*) The day is now well advanced. (*Smile. Smile off.*) And yet it is perhaps a little soon for my song. (*Pause.*) To sing too soon is fatal, I always find. (*Pause.*) On the other hand it is possible to leave it too late. (*Pause.*) The bell goes for sleep and one has not sung. (*Pause.*) The whole day has flown—(*smile, smile off*)—flown by, quite by, and no song of any class, kind or description. (*Pause.*) There is a problem here. (*Pause.*) One cannot sing . . . just like that, no. (*Pause.*) It bubbles up, for some unknown reason, the time is ill chosen, one chokes it back. (*Pause.*) One says, Now is the time, it is now or never, and one cannot. (*Pause.*) Simply cannot sing. (*Pause.*) Not a note. (*Pause.*) Another thing, Willie, while we are on this subject. (*Pause.*) The sadness after song. (*Pause.*) Have you run across that, Willie? (*Pause.*) In the course of your experience. (*Pause.*) No? (*Pause.*) Sadness after intimate sexual intercourse one is familiar with of course. (*Pause.*) You would concur with Aristotle there, Willie, I fancy. (*Pause.*) Yes, that one knows and is prepared to face. (*Pause.*) But after song . . . (*Pause.*) It does not last of course. (*Pause.*) That is what I find so wonderful. (*Pause.*) It wears away. (*Pause.*) What are those exquisite lines? (*Pause.*) Go forget me why should something o'er that something shadow fling . . . go forget me . . . why should sorrow . . . brightly smile . . . go forget me . . . never hear me . . . sweetly smile . . . brightly sing . . . (*Pause. With a sigh.*) One loses one's classics. (*Pause.*) Oh not all. (*Pause.*) A part. (*Pause.*) A part remains. (*Pause.*) That is what I find so wonderful, a part remains, of one's classics, to help one through the day. (*Pause.*) Oh yes, many mercies, many mercies. (*Pause.*) And now? (*Pause.*) And now, Willie? (*Long pause.*) I call to the eye of the mind . . . Mr. Shower—or Cooker. (*She closes her eyes. Bell rings loudly. She opens her eyes. Pause.*) Hand in hand, in the other hands bags. (*Pause.*) Getting on . . . in life. (*Pause.*) No longer young, not yet old. (*Pause.*) Standing there gaping at me. (*Pause.*) Can't have been a bad bosom, he says, in its day. (*Pause.*) Seen worse shoulders, he says, in my time. (*Pause.*) Does she feel her legs? he says. (*Pause.*) Is there any life in her legs? he says (*Pause.*) Has she anything on underneath? he says. (*Pause.*) Ask her, he says, I'm shy. (*Pause.*) Ask her what? she says. (*Pause.*) Is there any life in her legs. (*Pause.*) Has she anything on underneath. (*Pause.*) Ask her yourself, she says. (*Pause. With sudden violence.*) Let go of me for Christ sake and drop! (*Pause. Do.*) Drop dead! (*Smile.*) But no. (*Smile broader.*) No no. (*Smile off.*) I watch them recede. (*Pause.*) Hand in hand—and the bags. (*Pause.*) Dim. (*Pause.*) Then gone. (*Pause.*) Last human kind—to stray this way. (*Pause.*) Up to date. (*Pause.*) And now? (*Pause. Low.*) Help. (*Pause. Do.*) Help, Willie. (*Pause. Do.*) No? (*Long pause. Narrative.*) Suddenly a mouse . . . (*Pause.*) Suddenly a mouse ran up her little thigh and Mildred, dropping Dolly in her fright, began to scream—(WINNIE *gives a sudden piercing scream*)—and screamed and screamed—(WINNIE *screams twice*)—screamed and screamed and screamed and screamed till all came running, in their night attire, papa, mamma, Bibby and . . . old Annie, to see what was the matter . . . (*pause*) . . . what on earth could possibly be the matter. (*Pause.*) Too late. (*Pause.*) Too late. (*Long pause. Just audible.*) Willie. (*Pause. Normal voice.*) Ah well, not long now, Winnie, can't be long now, until the bell for sleep. (*Pause.*) Then you may close your eyes, then you *must* close your eyes—and keep them closed. (*Pause.*) Why say that again? (*Pause.*) I used to think . . . (*pause.*) . . . I say I used to think there was no difference between one fraction of a second and the next. (*Pause.*) I used to say . . . (*pause*) . . . I say I used to say, Winnie, you are changeless, there is never any difference between one fraction of a second and the next. (*Pause.*) Why bring that up again? (*Pause.*) There is so little one can bring up, one brings up all. (*Pause.*) All one can. (*Pause.*) My neck is hurting me. (*Pause. With sudden violence.*) My neck is hurting me! (*Pause.*) Ah that's better. (*With mild irritation.*) Everything within reason. (*Long pause.*) I can do no more. (*Pause.*) Say no more. (*Pause.*) But I must say more. (*Pause.*) Problem here. (*Pause.*) No, something must move, in the world, I can't any more. (*Pause.*) A zephyr. (*Pause.*) A breath. (*Pause.*) What are those immortal lines? (*Pause.*) It might be the eternal dark. (*Pause.*) Black night without end. (*Pause.*) Just chance, I take it, happy chance. (*Pause.*) Oh yes, abounding mercies. (*Long pause.*) And now? (*Pause.*) And now, Willie? (*Long pause.*) That day. (*Pause.*) The pink fizz. (*Pause.*) The flute glasses. (*Pause.*) The last guest gone. (*Pause.*) The last bumper with the bodies nearly touching. (*Pause.*) The look. (*Long pause.*) What day? (*Long pause.*) What look? (*Long pause.*) I hear cries. (*Pause.*) Sing. (*Pause.*) Sing your old song, Winnie.

*Long pause. Suddenly alert expression. Eyes switch right.* WILLIE'*s head appears to her right round corner of mound. He is on all fours, dressed to kill—top hat, morning coat, striped trousers, etc., white gloves in hand. Very long bushy white Battle of Britain moustache. He halts, gazes front, smooths moustache. He emerges completely from behind mound, turns to his left, halts, looks up at* WINNIE. *He advances on all fours towards centre, halts, turns head front, gazes front, strokes moustache, straightens tie, adjusts hat, advances a little further, halts, takes off hat and looks up at* WINNIE. *He is now not far from centre and within her field of vision. Unable to sustain effort of looking up he sinks head to ground.*

WINNIE (*mondaine*): Well this is an unexpected pleasure! (*Pause.*) Reminds me of the day you came whining for my hand. (*Pause.*) I worship you, Winnie, be mine. (*He looks up.*) Life a mockery without Win. (*She goes off into a giggle.*) What a get up, you do look a sight! (*Giggles.*) Where are the flowers? (*Pause.*) That smile today. (WILLIE *sinks head.*) What's that on your neck, an anthrax? (*Pause.*) Want to watch that, Willie, before it gets a hold on you. (*Pause.*) Where were you all this time? (*Pause.*) What were you doing all this time? (*Pause.*) Changing? (*Pause.*) Did you not hear me screaming for you? (*Pause.*) Did you get stuck in your hole? (*Pause. He looks up.*) That's right, Willie, look at me. (*Pause.*) Feast your old eyes, Willie. (*Pause.*) Does anything remain? (*Pause.*) Any remains? (*Pause.*) No? (*Pause.*) I haven't been able to look after it, you know. (*He sinks his head.*) You are still recognizable, in a way. (*Pause.*) Are you thinking of coming to live this side now . . . for a bit maybe? (*Pause.*) No? (*Pause.*) Just a brief call? (*Pause.*) Have you gone deaf, Willie? (*Pause.*) Dumb? (*Pause.*) Oh I know you were never one to talk, I worship you Winnie be mine and then nothing from that day forth only tidbits from Reynolds' News. (*Eyes front. Pause.*) Ah well, what matter, that's what I always say, it will have been a happy day, after all, another happy day. (*Pause.*) Not long now, Winnie. (*Pause.*) I hear cries. (*Pause.*) Do you ever hear cries, Willie? (*Pause.*) No? (*Eyes back on Willie.*) Willie. (*Pause.*) Look at me again, Willie. (*Pause.*) Once more, Willie. (*He looks up. Happily.*) Ah! (*Pause. Shocked.*) What ails you, Willie, I never saw such an expression! (*Pause.*) Put on your hat, dear, it's the sun, don't stand on ceremony, I won't mind. (*He drops hat and gloves and starts to crawl up mound towards her. Gleeful.*) Oh I say, this is terrific! (*He halts, clinging to mound with one hand, reaching up with the other.*) Come on, dear, put a bit of jizz into it, I'll cheer you on. (*Pause.*) Is it me you're after, Willie . . . or is it something else? (*Pause.*) Do you want to touch my face . . . again? (*Pause.*) Is it a kiss you're after, Willie . . . or is it something else? (*Pause.*) There was a time when I could have given you a hand. (*Pause.*) And then a time before that again when I did give you a hand. (*Pause.*) You were always in dire need of a hand, Willie. (*He slithers back to foot of mound and lies with face to ground.*) Brrum! (*Pause. He rises to hands and knees, raises his face towards her.*) Have another go, Willie, I'll cheer you on. (*Pause.*) Don't look at me like that! (*Pause. Vehement.*) Don't look at me like that! (*Pause. Low.*) Have you gone off your head, Willie? (*Pause. Do.*) Out of your poor old wits, Willie?

*Pause.*

WILLIE (*just audible*): Win.

*Pause.* WINNIE*'s eyes front. Happy expression appears, grows.*

WINNIE: Win! (*Pause.*) Oh this *is* a happy day, this will have been another happy day! (*Pause.*) After all. (*Pause.*) So far.

*Pause. She hums tentatively beginning of song, then sings softly, musical-box tune.*

Though I say not
What I may not
Let you hear,
Yet the swaying
Dance is saying,
Love me dear!
Every touch of fingers
Tells me what I know,
Says for you,
It's true, it's true,
You love me so!

*Pause. Happy expression off. She closes her eyes. Bell rings loudly. She opens her eyes. She smiles, gazing front. She turns her eyes, smiling, to* WILLIE*, still on his hands and knees looking up at her. Smile off. They look at each other. Long pause.*

CURTAIN

# FRANCE

## MADAME DE SÉVIGNÉ (1626–1696)

*Translated by H.T. Barnwell*

"This great lady, this robust and fertile letter writer, who in our age would probably have been one of the great novelists, takes up presumably as much space in the consciousness of living readers as any figure of her vanished age." This opening statement of Virginia Woolf's highly appreciative essay is certainly true as far as French readers are concerned; Mme de Sévigné is one of the great classic writers of French literature, though much of her lively style gets lost in translation. Some fifteen hundred of her letters survive, creating a vivid picture of the age of Louis XIV. As a member of the nobility, she lived at the very heart of French society and was personally acquainted with the great figures of the age. She reported about them in her letters with all the spontaneity of conversation and with the instinctive art of a born storyteller.

Marie de Rabutin-Chantal was blessed with beauty, charm, and wit. She was also one of the most cultivated women of her day, educated by distinguished men of learning and well read in Latin, Italian, and Spanish as well as French literature. Her marriage to the Marquis de Sévigné proved unfortunate. He was unfaithful and financially irresponsible and left her a widow on her twenty-fifth birthday when he was killed in a duel over a mistress. He left her with a daughter, on whom she doted; a son, who became a great comfort to her; and an estate in total disarray. Although subsequently courted by some of the greatest and most dashing noblemen, she preferred her independence and never remarried, taking her place at the center of the elegant, sophisticated, aristocratic society that flourished under Louis XIV. Celebrated by poets for the brilliance of her conversation as well as for her beauty, she held her own with the cleverest in that world and numbered among her closest friends several of the other great writers of the day. She was an attractive, warm-hearted person with many friends who kept her well supplied with news and gossip, which she passed on to others in her highly entertaining letters.

To the modern reader these letters present a bewildering array of names and titles, but it is not necessary to know the identity of those noble or royal personages to appreciate the stories she told. Although not an eyewitness to many of the scenes she so dramatically portrayed—such as the death in battle of the great general Turenne, the suicide of the legendary chef Vatel, or the investiture of members of the Order of the Holy Ghost—she had such a gift for bringing the moment to life that her letters have all the immediacy of first-hand observation. Although seldom at court herself, she retailed all the news from the royal palaces, and her letters give the reader a sense of the autocratic Sun King's reign with its pomp and circumstance and endless wars.

She also wrote of personal matters: of family and friends; of her beloved uncle the Abbé de Coulanges, who repaired her fortunes after the death of her husband and served as her mentor and mainstay for most of her life; of her quiet life on her estate in Brittany, where she went periodically to economize; and most obsessively of her daughter, who married a nobleman from Provence and went off to live in that distant region. Mme de Sévigné missed her daughter terribly and wrote long letters to her. The great majority of her surviving letters are addressed to her (Mme de Grignan), but letters to a good many others survive as well, notably those to her two witty cousins, the Marquis de Coulanges and the Comte de Bussy-Rabutin, himself a renowned letter writer. There are also letters to other writers, to men of learning, and to statesmen like the Marquis de Pomponne, who was one of Louis's ministers. Her pen gallops, as she said, particularly when writing to her cousins, reflecting her irrepressible high spirits and enjoyment of life. But she also had her solemn moments, writing often of religion and increasingly, as she aged, of death.

## Letters of Mme de Sévigné

### *To M. de Pomponne*

*Monday, 1st December [1664]*

. . . I must tell you a little anecdote: it is perfectly true and will amuse you. Recently the King has been dabbling in writing verse; M. de Saint-Aignan and M. Dangeau teach him how to set about it. The other day he wrote a little madrigal which he did not find too well contrived himself. One morning he said to Marshal de Gramont: 'Marshal, please read this little madrigal and tell me whether you have ever seen one so tasteless. Because people know that I have recently taken a liking to verse, they bring me all kinds to see.' After reading it, the Marshal said to the King: 'Sire, Your Majesty has exquisite judgment in all things: this is indeed the silliest and most ridiculous madrigal I have ever read.' The King began to laugh, and said: 'Do you not think that its author is a conceited fop?' 'Sire, he can certainly be given no other name.' 'Well!' said the King, 'I am delighted that you have spoken so frankly. It is I who wrote it.' 'Oh! Your Majesty, what a trick! Please, Sire, let me see it again: I read it too quickly.' 'No, Marshal: one's first reactions are always the most natural.' The King laughed a great deal over this piece of nonsense, and everyone agrees that it is the cruellest little thing that could be done to an old courtier. For my part, as I always like to meditate on things, I wish the King would do so about this and learn from it how far he is likely to be from ever knowing the truth. . . .

### *To Comte de Bussy Rabutin*

*Paris, 4th December [1668]*

. . . I must tell you a piece of news which will no doubt make you very happy. It is, in a word, that the prettiest girl in France is to marry, not the best-looking boy, but one of the most honourable men in the kingdom: he is M. de Grignan, whom you have known for a long time. All his wives have died in order to make way for your cousin, and even, by some extraordinary kindness, his father and son; so that, as he is richer than he ever has been and, by virtue of his rank, property, and personal qualities, a man after our own hearts, we are not haggling with him as people usually do. . . .

### *To Coulanges*

*Paris, Monday, 15th December [1670]*

I am going to tell you the most astonishing thing, the most surprising, the most wonderful, the most miraculous, the most triumphant, the most astounding, the most unheard of, the most peculiar, the most extraordinary, the most unbelievable, the most unexpected, the greatest, the smallest, the rarest, the commonest, the most illustrious, the most secret until to-day, the most brilliant, the most enviable: in short, a thing of which only one example can be found in bygone ages, and even that example is not a perfect one; a thing that people cannot believe in Paris (how could one believe it at Lyons?); a thing that makes everyone cry for mercy; a thing that makes Mme de Rohan and Mme d'Hauterive overjoyed; in short a thing that will be done on Sunday, when those who see it will think their eyes deceive them; a thing that will be done on Sunday, but not, perhaps, on Monday. I cannot bring myself to tell you what it is. Guess: I give you three tries. Do you give it up? Well, I shall have to tell you: on Sunday, at the Louvre, M. de Lauzun is to marry, guess who . . . I give you four guesses, ten, a hundred. Mme de Coulanges says: 'That is a hard one to guess. Mme de La Vallière.' 'Not at all, Madam.' 'Then it is Mlle de Retz?' 'Not at all. You are a real provincial.' 'You must think us terribly stupid. It is Mlle Colbert?' 'Even further from the truth.' 'Surely it is Mlle de Créquy?' 'You are nowhere near it. So I shall have to tell you after all: on Sunday, at the Louvre, he is to marry, with the King's permission, Mademoiselle, Mademoiselle de . . . Mademoiselle . . . guess the name: he is going to marry Mademoiselle, yes indeed! really and truly! without a word of a lie! Mademoiselle, the great Mademoiselle, Mademoiselle, the daughter of the late Monsieur; Mademoiselle, the grand-daughter of Henry IV; Mademoiselle d'Eu, Mademoiselle de Dombes, Mademoiselle de Montpensier, Mademoiselle d'Orléans; Mademoiselle, the King's first cousin; Mademoiselle, who was destined for the throne; Mademoiselle, the only match in France worthy of Monsieur.' There is a fine topic of conversation for you. If you scream, if you are beside yourself, if you say we have been telling lies, that it is all untrue, that we are making fun of you, that it is a fine piece of bantering, that it is pointless to try and imagine it, if, in a word, you call us names—we shall admit you are right: we have done just the same as you.

Good-bye; the letters delivered by this mail will show you whether we are telling the truth or not.

## *To Coulanges*

*Paris, Friday, 19th December [1670]*

What people call being thunderstruck is what happened last night at the Tuileries; but I shall have to go back a little. You are given up to joy, to rapture, to delight over the princess and her fortunate lover. So it was on Monday that the matter was made public, as you know. Tuesday was spent in talking about it, in being astonished, in giving congratulations. On Wednesday Mademoiselle made a deed of gift to M. de Lauzun, with the intention of giving him the necessary titles, names, and dignities to be listed in the marriage contract, which was drawn up the same day. So, for the time being, she gave him four duchies: the first is the earldom of Eu, which is the first peerage of France and gives absolute precedence; the duchy of Montpensier, which title he used all day yesterday; the duchy of Saint-Fargeau, and the duchy of Châtellerault: all that is reckoned to be worth twenty-two millions. Thus the contract was drawn up and he took the name of Montpensier. On Thursday morning—yesterday—Mademoiselle hoped the King would sign, as he had said; but about seven o'clock in the evening His Majesty, persuaded by the Queen, Monsieur, and several old fogies that the affair was injurious to his reputation, decided to break it off, and having sent for Mademoiselle and M. de Lauzun, he declared, in the presence of M. le Prince, that he was forbidding them to think any more of their marriage. M. de Lauzun heard the order with all the respect, all the submission, all the courage, and all the despair that so great a fall deserved. As for Mademoiselle, in accordance with her temperament, she burst into tears, screams, violent displays of grief, and excessive lamentations; and she has not got out of bed all day, nor eaten anything except broth. There is a fine dream for you, a fine subject for a novel or a tragedy, but above all a fine subject for endless argument and talk: that is just what we are doing incessantly, constantly, day and night, morning and evening. We hope you will do so, too, *e fra tanto vi bacio le mani!*

## *To Coulanges*

*Paris, Wednesday, 24th December [1670]*

You now know the romantic story of Mademoiselle and M. de Lauzun. It is the right kind of subject for a tragedy within all the rules of drama. We were arranging acts and scenes the other day; we took four days instead of twenty-four hours, and it was a perfect play. Never were such changes seen in so short a time; you never saw so much excitement; you never heard such extraordinary news. M. de Lauzun played his part to perfection; he bore his misfortune with a constancy and courage, and yet with a grief mingled with the deepest respect, which have won him the admiration of everyone. What he has lost is beyond price; but the King's favour, which he has kept, is also beyond price, and his fate does not appear to be desperate. Mademoiselle has behaved very well, too; she has wept a great deal; to-day she began once more to pay her respects at the Louvre: everyone at Court had visited her. That is the end of the affair. Good-bye.

## *To Mme de Grignan*

*Paris, [Sunday,] 26th April [1671]*

It is Sunday, 26th April; this letter will not go till Wednesday; but it is not a letter; it is an account that Moreuil has just given me—for you—of what happened concerning Vatel at Chantilly. I wrote to you on Friday that he had stabbed himself: here are the details.

The King arrived on Thursday evening; the hunt, the lanterns, the moonlight, the drive, the meal in a place carpeted with jonquils—it was all one could wish for. They had supper: at some tables there was no roast, because several unexpected guests had turned up. Vatel was greatly disturbed; he said several times: 'My honour is ruined; this is a disgrace I cannot endure.' He told Gourville: 'My head is spinning. I have not slept for twelve nights. Help me to give orders.' Gourville relieved him where he could. The roast that was missing, not from the King's, but from the lowest tables, was constantly in his thoughts. Gourville told Monsieur le Prince. Monsieur le Prince went right to his room and said: 'Vatel, everything is all right. There was never anything finer than the King's supper.' He said: 'Sir, your kindness is too much for me. I know that there was no roast at two tables.' 'Not at all,' said Monsieur le Prince. 'Do not worry; everything is all right.' Darkness fell: the firework display was a failure—it was hidden by a cloud. It had cost sixteen thousand francs. At four in the morning Vatel was walking all over the place. He found everyone asleep. He met a little contractor who had brought only two loads of fresh fish; he asked: 'Is that all there is?' He said: 'Yes, sir.' He did not know that Vatel had sent to every seaport. He waited a short while; the other contractors did not come; his head was spinning—he thought there would be no more fish. He found Gourville and said: 'Sir, this disgrace will be the end of me. My honour and reputation are at stake.' Gourville laughed at him. Vatel went up to his room, put his sword against the door and thrust it through his heart—but only at the third attempt, for the first two thrusts were not fatal: he fell down dead. Meanwhile, the fish was arriving from every quarter. People were looking for Vatel to portion it out; they went to his room; they banged on the door and burst it in; they found him in a pool of blood; they ran to Monsieur le Prince—he was in despair. Monsieur le Duc wept: everything on his journey to Burgundy was to depend on Vatel. Monsieur le Prince told the King about it very gloomily; they said it was through having too high a sense of honour in his particular way; they praised him very much, and praised and criticized his courage. The King said he had delayed coming to Chantilly for five years because he realized all the trouble it would cause. He told Monsieur le Prince that he should have had only two tables and not undertaken all the rest. He swore that he would not allow Monsieur le Prince to act like this again: but it was too late for poor Vatel. Meanwhile, Gourville was trying to make good the loss of Vatel; he succeeded: there was an excellent dinner, they had a collation and supper, they took a walk, they played, they hunted; everything was scented with jonquils, all was enchantment. Yesterday, Saturday, they did the same again; and in the evening the King went to Liancourt, where he had ordered a midnight feast. He is to remain there to-day.

That is what Moreuil told me for your information. I have thrown my cap over the windmills; I know nothing further. M. d'Hacqueville, who was present throughout, will no doubt give you some account of it; but as his writing is not so legible as mine, I am writing all the same. There is a surfeit of details for you, but because in similar circumstances I should appreciate them, I have given them to you.

## *To Mme de Grignan*

*Paris, Wednesday, 16th March [1672]*

. . . You ask me, dear child, whether I still enjoy life. I confess I find it full of bitter sorrows; but I have even less taste for death. I consider myself so unfortunate in having to put an end to it all by death that if it were possible I could ask for nothing better than to go backwards. I find myself under a contract that entangles me: I am launched into life without my consent, and I must leave it—I am overcome by the very thought; and how shall I leave it? By what road? By what door? When will it be? In what state of mind? Shall I suffer a thousand and one pains that will make me die in despair? Shall I have a stroke? Shall I die in an accident? What will be my relationship with God? What shall I have to offer Him? Will fear and necessity bring me back to Him? Shall I have no feeling other than fear? What can I hope for? Am I worthy of Paradise? Am I worthy of Hell? What an alternative! What perplexity! Nothing is so foolish as putting one's salvation in jeopardy; but nothing is so natural, and the silly life I lead the easiest thing in the world to understand. I am sunk in these thoughts, and I find death so terrible that I hate life more because it leads me there than for the thorns it puts in my way. You will tell me I want to live for ever. Not at all; but if I had been given the choice, I should like to have died in my nurse's arms: that would have spared me many sorrows and would have given me Heaven very surely and easily. But let us talk of something else. . . .

## *To Mme de Grignan*

*Paris, Monday, 15th January [1674]*

. . . At last, my dear, I have seen Mme de Marans in her cell: I used to say in her box at the theatre. I found her very slovenly; not a hair on her head, a coif of old Venetian lace, a black kerchief, a faded grey cloak, an old skirt. She was pleased to see me; we kissed each other tenderly. She has not changed much. First we talked about you: she loves you as much as ever, and she seems to have humbled herself so much that one cannot help liking her. We talked about her religious devotion; she told me God had indeed granted her blessings for which she is extremely thankful. These blessings are nothing other than great faith, a tender love for God, and horror of the world: all this is accompanied by so much mistrust of herself and her weaknesses that she is convinced that if she were to take the air for a moment this heavenly grace would evaporate. I thought it was like a phial of essence that she was keeping in her solitude: she thinks the world would make her lose the precious liquid and even fears the worries of devotion. Mme de Schomberg calls herself flighty in comparison with Mme de Marans. That unsociable temperament you know has turned into withdrawal from the world: character does not change. She is not even so foolish, as so many women are, as to fall in love with her confessor—she does not like that relationship: she talks to him only in the confessional. She goes to church on foot and reads all the proper books; she works and prays; she regulates every hour of the day; she takes almost all her meals in her room; she sees Mme de Schomberg at fixed times; she hates society news as much as she used to like it; she excuses her neighbours as readily as she used to accuse them; she loves God as much as she used to love the world. We laughed a great deal over her former ways—we held them up to ridicule. She is not at all like the nuns of Saint Clare: she talks very sincerely and very agreeably about her present state. I was there for two hours—one does not get bored with her; she mortifies herself for this pleasure, but without affectation. In short, she is much nicer than she used to be. . . .

## *To Comte de Bussy Rabutin*

*Paris, 6th August [1675]*

. . . You ask me where I am, how I am, and how I amuse myself. I am in Paris, I am well, and I amuse myself with trifles. But this style is rather laconic—I will expand it a little. I should be in Brittany, where I have many things to attend to, were it not for the disturbances which make it unsafe. Four thousand men, commanded by M. de Fourbin, are going there. What we want to know is what effect this punishment will have. I am waiting to find out, and if the rebels come to repentance and submit to lawful authority, I shall resume my intended journey and spend part of the winter there.

I have suffered a good deal from the vapours, and my fine health, which you have known to be so invincible, has been subject to a few attacks that humbled me as though I had received an insult.

As for my way of life, you know that, too. I spend it with five or six friends whose company pleases me, and in carrying out a thousand duties that are incumbent on me—and that is no mean task. But what grieves me is that while we are doing nothing the days pass, and our poor lives are made up of those days, and we grow old and die. I find it very displeasing. I find life too short: we are hardly out of our youth when we find ourselves in old age. I wish we could have a hundred years for certain and the rest uncertain. Do you wish for that, too? But what can we do about it? My niece will share my opinion depending on whether she is happy or unhappy in her marriage. She may tell us about it, or she may not. At all events, I am sure there is no sweetness, no comfort, and no delight that I do not wish her as she enters the married state. I sometimes talk about it to my niece the nun. I find her very amiable; she is witty in a way that reminds one of you. To my way of thinking, I can give her no higher praise.

For the rest, you are an excellent almanac: as a man of the profession, you foresaw everything that has happened in Germany; but you did not see M. de Turenne's death, nor the cannon shot fired at random that picked out him alone among ten or twelve others. For my part, seeing Providence at work in all things, I see that cannon as being loaded from all eternity; I see that all things led M. de Turenne to that place, and do not find that it means perdition for him, provided that his conscience was clear. What more could he need? He has died in the midst of his glory. His reputation could go no higher: at that very moment he even had the pleasure of seeing the enemy withdrawing, and the fruits of his strategy during the past three months. Sometimes, merely by living, a star may fade. It is safer, especially for heroes, to be cut off in their prime, for their every action is so closely observed. If Comte d'Harcourt had died after taking the Sainte-Marguerite Islands or relieving Casale, and Maréchal du Plessis Praslin after the battle of Rethel, would they not have enjoyed greater glory? M. de Turenne did not feel the pains of death: do you regard that too as of no account? . . .

## *To Mme de Grignan*

*Paris, Wednesday, 28th August [1675]*

. . . My dear, I am going to talk to you again about M. de Turenne. Mme d'Elbeuf, who is staying for a few days at Cardinal de Bouillon's, asked me to dinner with the two of them yesterday, in order to talk about their sorrow. Mme de La Fayette was there. We did exactly what we were determined to do: our eyes were never dry. She had an exquisitely painted portrait of the hero, whose entire suite had arrived at eleven o'clock: all those poor people were dissolved in tears, and all were already wearing mourning. Three noblemen came—they nearly died when they saw the portrait: their cries were heart-rending; they could not say a word. His valets, servants, pages, trumpeters, all were in tears and caused others to burst into tears. The first to recover his speech replied to our sad questions: we got him to give us an account of his master's death. He wanted to confess in the evening, and, letting it be seen that he was withdrawing to his tent, he had given his orders for the night and was to partake of the sacrament the next day, which was Sunday. He reckoned to give battle and mount his horse at two o'clock on the Saturday, after his meal. He had a good number of men with him: he left them all thirty yards from the hill-top for which he was making. He said to young D'Elbeuf: 'Stay there, nephew; you are only hanging around me and will attract their attention to me.' Approaching his destination, he found M. d'Hamilton, who said: 'Come this way, sir: they will fire where you are going.' 'Sir,' he said, 'that *is* the way I am going. I have no desire to be killed to-day. Everything will be perfectly all right.' He was turning his horse when he saw Saint-Hilaire who, hat in hand, said to him: 'Sir, take a look at the battery I have placed over here.' He went back some little distance, and on his way he was struck by a shot that carried away the arm and hand in which Saint-Hilaire held his hat, and pierced the hero's body after shattering his arm. That nobleman was still looking at him; he did not see him fall. His horse carried him to where he had left young D'Elbeuf: he still had not fallen, though he was bent with his face over the pommel. At that very moment the horse stopped and he fell into the arms of his men. Twice he opened wide his eyes and made as if to speak, and then he lay still for ever: just imagine that he was dead and that part of his heart had been carried away. There was shouting and weeping. M. d'Hamilton put an end to the noise and had young D'Elbeuf taken away: he had thrown himself on to the body, did not wish to leave it, and was almost fainting with grief. A coat was thrown over the corpse; it was removed to the shelter of a hedge and quietly guarded; a carriage arrived and carried it to his tent, where M. de Lorges, M. de Roye, and many others almost died of grief. But they had to do violence to their feelings and think of the weighty matters he had in hand. There was a military service for him in the camp, where tears and cries were the true signs of mourning: all the officers, however, wore scarves of crape and all the drums were covered with the same material and beat only a single beat; pikes were trailed and muskets reversed; but one cannot imagine the cries of a whole army and remain unmoved. His two real nephews (for the eldest is not worthy of the name) were present at the ceremony, in a state that is not hard to visualize. M. de Roye, wounded though he was, had himself carried there; for the Mass was not said till they had crossed the Rhine. I think the poor Chevalier must have been overcome with grief.

When the body left the army there was more sorrow: everywhere it went there was a great clamour. But at Langres they surpassed themselves: they all went out to meet him, all in mourning, more than two hundred of them, followed by the populace; all the clergy were there in state; they had a solemn service said in the town and everyone immediately subscribed towards the cost: it amounted to five thousand francs, because they escorted the body to the next town and wished to pay for the whole procession. What do you think of these spontaneous marks of an affection occasioned by outstanding virtue?

He arrives at Saint-Denis to-night or to-morrow; his entire household was going to meet him two leagues from here; he will lie for the time being in one chapel until they have the other ready. There will be a service there, before the state service at Notre-Dame.

What do you think of the entertainment we enjoyed? We dined as you can imagine, and until four o'clock we did nothing but sigh. . . .

## *To Mme de Grignan*

*Paris, Friday, 23rd February [1680]*

. . . I am only going to tell you about Mme Voisin: it was not on Wednesday, as I had told you, that she was burnt—it was only yesterday. She knew her sentence on Monday—a most unusual business. In the evening she said to her guards: 'What! Are we not going to have a midnight feast?' The fancy took her to eat with them at midnight, for it was not a fast-day. She drank a great deal of wine and sang a score of drinking-songs. On Tuesday she was put to the torture, ordinary and extraordinary. She had dined and then slept for eight hours. On the mattress, she was brought face to face with Mme de Dreux and Mme le Féron, and several others: no one knows yet what she said—it is thought that some strange things will come to light. In the evening, broken though she was, she again began her scandalous riotousness. They tried to shame her and told her she would be better to think about God and sing an *Ave maris stella* and a *Salve* rather than all those songs: she sang them both in comic fashion, and ate in the evening and went to sleep. Wednesday was also spent in confrontations, in disorderliness and singing: she did not want a confessor. Then on Thursday, yesterday, they wanted to give her nothing but soup. She grumbled about it: she was afraid she might not have the strength to speak to those gentlemen. She came from Vincennes to Paris by coach. She choked a little and was embarrassed. They tried to make her confess—nothing doing. At five o'clock she was bound, and with a torch in her hand she appeared in the tumbril, dressed in a white garment made for people to be burnt in. She was very red and you could see her violently pushing away the confessor and the crucifix. We saw her pass at the Hôtel de Sully: I was with Mme de Chaulnes and Mme de Sully, the Countess, and several others. At Notre-Dame she refused to make a public confession, and at the *Grève* she struggled with all her might to prevent them taking her out of the tumbril: she was dragged out by force and put on the faggots, seated and bound with iron; she was covered with straw; she swore a great deal; she pushed the straw back five or six times; but in the end the fire grew bigger and she disappeared from view: now her ashes are floating in the air. Such was the death of Mme Voisin, famous for her crimes and impious behaviour. People think that all this will have serious consequences that will surprise us all. . . .

## *To Mme de Grignan*

*Blois, Thursday, 9th May [1680]*

. . . Here is the news of our journey: it will keep us going till we have some from Denmark. We boarded the boat at six o'clock in the most wonderful weather. I had the body of my coach arranged so that the sun did not come in. We put the windows down; the front opening makes a marvellous picture, and the ones in the doors and sides give us all the views imaginable. There are only the Abbé and myself in this little room, seated on good cushions, in the fresh air, and very comfortable: all the rest are like pigs on straw. We have eaten soup and hot boiled beef: we have a little stove and we eat off a board in the coach, like the King and Queen. See how much more refined our Loire has become and how crude we were in the days when *the heart was on the left:* mine, my dear, whether on the right or on the left, is indeed full of you. If you ask what I do in this charming coach, in which I am not in the least afraid, I think of my dear child, I live on the tender affection I have for her and that she has for me, on my interest in all that concerns her, on my consciousness of the orders of Providence which keep us apart and on the sadness they cause me; I think of her affairs and of my own. It all goes to make up something of *my daughter's temperament,* in spite of *my mother's temperament,* which shines all around me. I watch and admire the lovely view that keeps painters busy. I am touched by the kindness of the good Abbé, who, at the age of seventy-three, has set out once more by land and water to attend to my affairs. Then I take up a book that M. de La Rochefoucauld got me to buy, *The Reunification of Portugal,* in two octavo volumes. It is a translation from the Italian—the story and the style are equally praiseworthy. You see the King of Portugal, a young and courageous prince, rushing headlong towards his evil fate. He perishes in Africa in a war against the son of Abdullah, Zaida's uncle. It is certainly one of the most entertaining tales one could read.

Then I come back to Providence and its ways, and to what I have heard you say about our wills being the means by which its eternal decrees are carried out. I should like to talk to someone. I have come from a place where people are quite accustomed to airing their views. The good Abbé and I do talk, but not in a way to amuse ourselves. We pass under all the bridges so pleasantly that we are always wishing for the next one: there are not many thank-offerings to be seen for deliverance from wrecks on the Loire, any more than on the Durance. There is more reason to fear the latter—for it is mad—than our calm, majestic Loire. We arrived here early. Everyone is walking about or shaving, and I am writing romantically on the bank of the river, where our hostelry is situated: it is the Galley—you have been there.

I have heard hundreds of nightingales, and thought of the ones you can hear from your balcony. I dare not tell you, my child, what gloom the idea of your poor health has cast over all my thoughts. You will understand, and you know how much I wish for a restoration of your health. If you love me, you will devote your every care and effort to it, so as to show your real affection for me: this matter is a touchstone. Good-night, my dearest, and good-bye until to-morrow at Tours.

## *To Comte de Bussy Rabutin*

*Paris, 10th March [1687]*

Here is more death and sadness, dear cousin. But how could I refrain from speaking to you about the finest, the most magnificent and the most triumphant funeral ceremony that mortal man ever celebrated? It was in honour of Monsieur le Prince and was held to-day in Notre-Dame. All the best minds devoted all their energies to setting forth all that the great prince did and was. His ancestors were portrayed on medallions as far back as Saint Louis, and all his victories in bas-reliefs, mantled as it were with tents open at the corners, and borne by skeletons striking the most wonderful attitudes. The mausoleum, reaching almost to the vaulting, was covered with a still higher canopy, in the form of a hood, hanging down at the four corners. The whole choir was decorated with the bas-reliefs, with mottoes underneath, illustrating every phase of his life. The time of his alliance with the Spaniards was symbolized by a dark night, with three Latin words saying: 'What was done out of the sun must be hidden.' Studded over everything were sombre-coloured fleurs-de-lis, and at the bottom was a little lamp making thousands of reflections like stars. . . .

Everyone has been to see this stately piece of decoration. It cost the present Monsieur le Prince a hundred thousand francs, but the expenditure is greatly to his credit. The Bishop of Meaux delivered the funeral oration: it is to appear in print. That, dear cousin, is very roughly the subject of the drama. If I had dared risk making you pay twice the postage, you would have been better satisfied. So here we are in the realms of gloom once more.

## *To Comte de Bussy Rabutin*

*Paris, 13th November [1687]*

I have just received a letter from you, dear cousin, the most charming and affectionate ever. I have never seen friendship explained so simply and so convincingly. Anyhow, you have convinced me, and I believe my life is necessary for the preservation and enjoyment of yours. So I am going to give you an account of it, in order to cheer you and let you know what state I am in.

I will take up the thread from the last days of the life of my dear uncle the Abbé, to whom, as you know, I was infinitely indebted. It was to him that I owed the comforts and tranquillity of my life; it is to him that you owe the happiness I brought to you when we met: but for him we should never have laughed together. You owe him all my gaiety, my good humour, my liveliness, my gift for understanding you properly, the intelligence that allowed me to comprehend what you had said and guess what you were going to say. In a word, by rescuing me from the abyss in which M. de Sévigné had left me, the good Abbé gave me back my old personality, as you had known it, and made it worthy of your respect and affection. I will draw a veil over the errors of your ways: they are great, but I must forget them and tell you that I felt very keenly the loss of that charming source of all the peace of mind I have known. He died within seven days, of a continuous fever, as though he were still young, expressing the most Christian thoughts, which touched me deeply; for God has given me a fund of religion which has allowed me to look without flinching on this last act of our lives. His lasted eighty years. He lived honourably and died a Christian death: God grant we may do likewise! It was at the end of August, and I wept bitterly. . . .

## *To Mme and M. de Grignan*

*Paris, Wednesday, 17th November [1688]*

So our Marquis is seventeen years old to-day, my dear child. To everything else that contributes to the start of his career must be added a very nice little contusion which does him great honour, I assure you, by virtue of the coolness and composure with which he received it. The Chevalier will inform you how M. de Sainte-Maure told the King about it: he is overwhelmed with congratulations at Versailles, and so am I here. Mme de Lavardin asked me to meet her yesterday at Mme de La Fayette's: she wanted to rejoice with me. Mme de La Fayette had invited me with the same intention. First of all she gaily said: 'Well! What will Mme de Grignan find to cavil at in that? Tell her she ought to be delighted, and that if a price could be put on it, it would be something to buy. In a word, she is all too fortunate.' I promised to tell you all that, and I do so with pleasure. You are also asked to accept Mme de Lavardin's sincerest regards, and the hearty congratulations of Mme de Coulanges, the Duchesse du Lude, the *Heavenly Sisters,* the Duchesse de Villeroi, and Father Morel, whom I saw yesterday because I went to poor Saint-Aubin's.

My dear child, he is so beset by a holy desire for death that he has hurried to receive all the last sacraments. Monsieur de Saint-Jacques did not wish to give him Extreme Unction yesterday, and it caused him great sorrow. For he desires nothing but eternity and sighs after nothing but to be at one with God. His calmness, his resignation, his meekness, his detachment, surpass anything that we have seen: indeed, they are not human feelings at all. The ministrations of his priest and Father Morel, who are his spiritual directors, of his friends, nurses, and doctors, are out of this world, a foretaste of the felicity to come. Du Chesne is his doctor: he is an excellent man—no pain, no medicine. 'Try to drink something, sir, and be patient.' A room without noise, without disturbance, without any unpleasant smell; no fever, except internally and imperceptibly; a clear head, deep silence, because of the inflammation of his lungs, good serious talk, no trifling: in short, no one ever saw its like. The poor patient considers he is unworthy of dying in the same place as Mme de Longueville died. I told Tréville, who was at Mme de La Fayette's, all about it. He answered: 'That is how people die in that part of the town.' . . .

But to keep up your spirits I am going to pass to the other extreme, that is, from death to a wedding and from excessive pomp to excessive familiarity, both of them being as unprecedented as can be. It is about the Duc de Gramont's son, who is fifteen, and M. de Noailles's daughter that I wish to speak. They are to be married to-night at Versailles. This is how it is to be done: no one has been invited, no one has been notified: everyone will have supper or a collation in his own apartments. At midnight the bride and bridegroom will be taken together to the church without the parents being there, unless they happen to be at Versailles at the time. They will be married without any great display of dress, and will not be ceremonially bedded: the governess and tutor will be left to see that they get into the same bed. The next day it will be presumed that everything has passed off as it should. No one will go and tease them—no jests and no unpleasant jokes. When they get up, the boy will attend the King's Mass and dinner, and the little lady will dress as usual, and will pay her calls with her grandmother. She will not, like a village bride, be exposed on her bed to every troublesome caller. And the whole wedding (they are usually conspicuous occasions) will be most prettily and naturally mingled with life's everyday activities: it has slipped so imperceptibly into the daily round that no one has realized that the two families had something to celebrate.

That is what I wanted to say to fill out my letter, cousin; and I think that this second description is, of its kind, as extraordinary as the other. . . .

## *To Mme de Grignan*

*Paris, Monday, 3rd January [1689]*

. . . The ceremony for your *brothers* was held, then, on New Year's Day, at Versailles. Coulanges has returned: he sends you a thousand thanks for your pretty answer. . . . I wondered at all the thoughts that come into your head, and at the appropriateness and elegance of your remarks on what people write to you. That is something I do not do with just anybody's letters, for I do not read them more than once: it is a bad practice on my part. He informed me, then, that the ceremony began on the Friday, as I told you: on that day, those who were already sworn took part. They wore fine clothes and their collars and presented an excellent appearance. On Saturday it was the turn of all the others, including two Marshals of France who had not attended on the previous occasion. Maréchal de Bellefonds looked utterly ridiculous, because, through modesty and indifference to his appearance, he had omitted to put any ribbons at the knees of his Court breeches, and so looked quite naked. The company as a whole was splendid, and M. de La Trousse among the best; he had some difficulty with his wig: one of the side pieces worked round to the back of his head and stayed there, so that his cheek was quite uncovered; he kept on pulling at it, but the part that was causing the trouble would not move—it was rather annoying. Then M. de Montchevreuil and M. de Villars, who were in the same line, became so frantically hooked up with each other, their swords, ribbons, lace, and all their trimmings all got so mixed up, jumbled together, and entangled, all the little hooked parts were so perfectly intertwined, that no man's hand could separate them; the more they tried to do so, the more entangled they became, like the links of Roger's armour. In the end, as the whole ceremony and all the bowing and movements were held up, they had to be torn apart by force, and the stronger man won. But what completely upset the dignity of the ceremony was the negligence of good old D'Hocquincourt, who was dressed so much in the manner of a Provençal or a Breton that, as his Court breeches were not so accommodating as the ones he usually wears, his shirt would not remain tucked into them, however much he pleaded with it. For, realizing the state he was in, he tried continually to put himself in order, but always without avail, so that Madame la Dauphine could no longer restrain herself from bursting into a peal of laughter. It was a great pity: it very nearly shook the King's majesty, and never, in the records of the Order, has such a mishap been seen. In the evening the King said: 'I am always the one to stand up for poor M. d'Hocquincourt; it was his tailor's fault.' Anyhow, it was very amusing. . . .

## *To Mme de Grignan*

*Paris, Monday, 21st February [1689]*

. . . I paid my respects at Saint-Cyr the other day, and the occasion proved more agreeable than I should ever have expected. Mme de Coulanges, Mme de Bagnols, Abbé Têtu, and I went over on Saturday. We found that seats had been reserved for us. An officer told Mme de Coulanges that Mme de Maintenon was keeping her a seat near her own: you can see how highly honoured she was. 'You, Madam, may choose your seat,' he told me. I sat with Mme de Bagnols in the second row behind the duchesses. Maréchal de Bellefonds came and sat on my right, and in front of us were Mmes d'Auvergne, de Coislin, and de Sully. The Marshal and I listened to the tragedy with such attention that we became conspicuous, muttering a few well-placed words of admiration that were perhaps not under the *fontanges* worn by all the ladies. I cannot tell you how delightful the play is: it is not easy to stage and no one will ever try to imitate it. The music, poetry, singing, and characters make up so harmonious a whole, so perfect and complete, that it leaves nothing to be desired. The girls who play the parts of kings and great people seem to have been made for that very purpose. The audience is most attentive and is only sorry to see such a charming play come to an end. Everything in it is simple and innocent, everything is sublime and touching. Its closeness to Holy Scripture commands respect; all the music is suited to the words, which are taken from the Psalms and Wisdom, and fitted in to the subject of the play—it is so beautiful that one cannot restrain one's tears. The favour with which it is received can be measured by people's liking for it and their attentiveness during the performance. I was delighted with it, and so was the Marshal: he left his seat to go and tell the King how pleased he was, saying that he was sitting next to a lady who certainly deserved to see *Esther.* The King came to our seats, and, turning round, he addressed me, saying: 'Madam, I am told you have been very pleased with the performance.' Quite unabashed, I said: 'Sire, I am delighted: words cannot express my feelings.' The King said: 'Racine is very clever.' I replied: 'Sire, he certainly is, but, to tell the truth, so are those young ladies. They enter into the play as though they had been acting all their lives.' He said: 'Ah! yes. That is certainly true.' And then His Majesty departed, leaving me there to be envied by everyone. As I was about the only newcomer present, it gave him some pleasure to see me admire the play without any fuss or show. Monsieur le Prince and Madame la Princesse came to say a word or two to me, Mme de Maintenon too like a flash of lightning—she was going away with the King: I answered everybody's questions, for I was in capital form. We came back in the evening by torchlight. I had supper with Mme de Coulanges: the King had spoken to her, too, with an air of familiarity that made him seem extremely kind. In the evening I saw the Chevalier and without affectation told him all about my good fortune, for I was unwilling to conceal it, as some people do, for no good reason. He was very pleased about it all, and that was that. I am sure he did not afterwards think I was empty-headed and vain or that I had been carried away like common folk. Ask him. . . .

## *To Mme de Grignan*

*Les Rochers, Sunday, 18th September [1689]*

. . . So you want to know what we do here, dear child? Ah, well! here you are then: we get up at eight o'clock, and go to Mass at nine. The weather decides whether we take a walk or not, each often going his own way. We eat a good dinner. A neighbour drops in, and we discuss the news. In the afternoon we work, my daughter-in-law at a hundred and one different things, and I at two bands of tapestry Mme de Kerman gave me at Chaulnes. At five o'clock we separate and take a walk, either alone or together. We meet at a very lovely spot, we have books, we pray, we dream of my dear daughter, we build castles in the air—or in Provence—sometimes gay ones, sometimes sad. My son reads us delightful books: we have one book of devotion, the others of history. They amuse us and keep us occupied. We discuss what we have read. My son is indefatigable: he will read for five hours at a stretch if we so desire. Receiving letters and answering them occupies a large place in our lives, especially in mine. We have had visitors and shall have others: we do not ask for them, but when they come we are pleased to see them. My son has engaged some workmen: he is having his great walks *adorned,* as the saying is in these parts. They are indeed lovely. He is having his forecourt sanded. And, my child, it is strange how in this colourless and almost melancholy existence the days run on and slip away from us. Goodness knows what else escapes us at the same time! But *let us not talk about that!* I think about it, however, and one should. We have our supper at eight o'clock. Sévigné reads after supper—but light-hearted books, for fear of going to sleep. They leave me at ten o'clock—I rarely go to bed before midnight. There you have pretty well the rule of our monastery. Above the door are these words: SACRED LIBERTY, OR DO WHAT YOU LIKE. I like life here a hundred times better than at Rennes: it will be soon enough to go and spend Lent there for nourishment of soul and body. . . .

## *To Comte de Bussy Rabutin*

*Grignan, 13th November [1690]*

When you see the date on this letter, cousin, you will take me for a bird. I have bravely travelled from Brittany to Provence. If my daughter had been in Paris I should have gone there; but, knowing that she was going to spend the winter in this lovely country, I decided to come and spend it with her, enjoy her lovely sunshine, and return to Paris with her in the coming year. I considered that after giving my son sixteen months of my time, it was only right that I should give a few to my daughter: this project, which appeared difficult to realize, did not cost me too much trouble. I spent three weeks on the way, by litter and on the Rhône. I even took a few days rest; and at the end of it all I was welcomed by M. de Grignan and my daughter with such affection, such sincere joy and gratitude, that I consider I have not come nearly far enough to visit such kind people, and that the one hundred and fifty leagues I have covered have not caused me the slightest fatigue. Some day I will tell you about this great house, its beauty and magnificent furnishings. I wanted to inform you that I had changed climates, so that you would not write to Les Rochers, but here, where the sun appears capable of rejuvenating me with its gentle warmth. We should not spurn such help at our age, dear cousin. I received your last letter before leaving Brittany, but I was so overwhelmed with business matters that I postponed replying to it till I reached here.

The other day we heard of the death of M. de Seignelai. How young he was! how rich! what property he possessed! His good fortune was complete in all respects: it seems to us that splendour itself is dead. What has surprised us is that we hear that Mme de Seignelai is forgoing the joint estate, because her husband's debts amount to five millions. It shows that large incomes are useless when one's expenditure is two or three times greater. But after all, dear cousin, death is the universal leveller—it is there that we shall await those who have been fortunate: death humbles their pride and joy, and in so doing comforts those who have been less well blessed. A word or two of Christianity would not be out of place here, but I do not want to preach a sermon—I only want to write an affectionate letter to my dear cousin and ask him for news of himself and his dear daughter, send them both my love, assure him of the respect and services of Mme de Grignan and her husband—for they ask me to do so—and beg him to love me always: it is not worth changing after so many years of affection.

## *To Coulanges*

*[Grignan, 26th July 1691]*

So M. de Louvois is dead—that great minister, that man of such eminence, who held such high position, whose *self,* as M. Nicole says, was so far-reaching, and who was at the centre of so many things! What activity, what plans and projects, what secrets, what intrigues to unravel, what wars begun, what schemings, what fine chess-board moves to make and prepare! 'Oh God! give me a little time: I very much want to have the Duke of Savoy in check and to checkmate the Prince of Orange.' 'No, no—you will not have a moment, not a single moment.' Should one reason over this strange stroke of fortune? Indeed, one ought to meditate on it in one's study. That is the second minister you have seen die during your stay in Rome. Nothing could be more dissimilar than their deaths, but nothing could be more similar than their fortunes, their attachments, and the hundred thousand million chains which bound them both to earth.

And when you consider all these weighty matters that ought to raise our thoughts to God, you find your faith shaken, because of what is happening in Rome and in the conclave. My poor cousin, you are making a mistake. I have heard it said that a very intelligent man drew quite the opposite conclusion from what he saw in that great city: that the Christian religion must be completely holy and quite miraculous to go on existing as it does in the midst of so much disorder and profanity. So do what that man did, draw the same conclusions, and remember that in bygone ages that same city was red with the blood of multitudes of martyrs; that in the earliest centuries all the secret deliberations of the conclave ended with choosing among the priests the one who seemed to have most enthusiasm and strength to endure martyrdom; that no less than thirty-seven popes in unbroken succession suffered it, and yet the inevitability of such a death did not make them run away or refuse that office with which death was linked—and what a death! You have only to read the history of it to see for yourself. People try to convince us that a religion which lives by perpetual miracle for ever and without changing is only a product of men's imaginations! But men do not imagine that kind of thing. Read what St Augustine says in *The Truth of Religion;* read Abbadie, who, though very different from that great saint, fully deserves comparison with him when he speaks of the Christian religion (ask Abbé de Polignac whether he has a high opinion of the book). So gather all these thoughts together, and be less superficial in your judgments. Remember that whatever stratagems there may be within the conclave, it is always the Holy Ghost who chooses the pope. God does everything and is master of everything. And this is how we ought to think (I have read it in an authoritative book): 'What can trouble a person who knows that it is God who does all things, and who loves what God does?' It is on that note that I leave you, dear cousin. Good-bye.

## *To Coulanges*

*Grignan, 3rd February [1695]*

Madame de Chaulnes tells me I am really too fortunate to be here with lovely sunshine. She thinks all our days are spun with gold and silk. Alas! cousin, it is a hundred times colder here than in Paris. We are exposed to every wind that blows—the south wind, the north wind, the devil, all seeing who can jeer at us most. They fight among themselves for the honour of shutting us up in our rooms. All our rivers are frozen over. Even the Rhône, the furious Rhône, cannot hold out against it. There is ice in our inkwells. Our fingers, numb with cold, can no longer control our pens. We breathe nothing but snow. Our mountains are lovely in all their horror. Every day I wish there were a painter here who could really depict these terrifying beauties in all their extent. That is what things are like here. Tell the Duchesse de Chaulnes a little about it all: she thinks we are walking about meadows, with sunshades, in the shadow of the orange-trees.

You imagined a vivid picture of all the rustic splendours of our wedding. Everyone has taken his share of the praises you bestowed. But we do not know what you mean about a wedding-night. Oh dear! how coarse you are! I was charmed by the whole atmosphere and modesty of that evening. I told Mme de Coulanges about it. The bride was taken to her room; her dress, her linen, and her coifs were taken away. She took her hair down, she was undressed, and she went to bed. We did not know who entered or left her room. Everyone went to bed. The next morning we got up, but no one went to see the bridal pair. They got up, too, and dressed. No silly questions were asked, such as: 'Are you my son-in-law?' or 'Are you my daughter-in-law?' They are what they are. No invitation to any form of breakfast was made: everyone did and ate what he liked. Everything passed off in silence and modesty. No one was put out of countenance; there was no embarrassment; no one played any silly tricks. I had never seen anything of the kind, and I consider it to be the prettiest and most decent thing in the world.

The cold is freezing me and making my pen drop out of my fingers. Where are you? At Saint-Martin? At Meudon? At Bâville? What is the fortunate place that has possession of that nice *young* Coulanges? I have just said everything that is bad about avarice to Mme de Coulanges. The riches left by Mme de Meckelbourg make me extremely happy to think that I shall die without any ready money, but also without debts: that is all I ask of God, and it is enough for a Christian.

## Jean-Jacques Rousseau (1712–1778)

*Translated by J.M. Cohen*

Jean-Jacques Rousseau was a person of many talents and accomplishments: he was a composer, a political theorist, a theorist of education, a philosopher, and man of letters. He believed that individuals were choked and stifled by institutions, and he called for a return to nature. In this sense, he was a leading light of what was to become the Romantic movement in the West. His *Confessions* are an intimate record of his personal experiences, and they convey a sense of self-preoccupation and obsession that contrasts sharply with the restraint of his model, the *Confessions* of Augustine (pp. 1203–1221). Going far beyond the revelations of the self that we find in the spritely but still sober essays of Montaigne (pp. 1388–1398), Rousseau revealed himself in startling ways. Although he was striving to be unusually frank in his representation of himself, he often showed how thin is the line between pretensions to sincerity and exhibitionism.

The eighteenth century is often referred to as the Age of Reason. The French *philosophes* of the eighteenth century were believers in progress who were horrified by what they saw as the superstitious nature of religious belief that had characterized medieval Europe, and they hoped humanity could now march forward under the banner of enlightened reason. Rousseau, with his emphasis on emotion, feeling, impulse, and his own originality ("I have resolved on an enterprise which has no precedent, and which, once complete, will have no imitator") and uniqueness ("I am made unlike any one I have ever met; I will even venture to say that I am like no one in the whole world"), represents the reverse side of such rationalism. With Rousseau, Western Romantic individualism was given a form that is clearly felt to this day.

The opening pages of Book I of the *Confessions,* included here, describe Rousseau's early childhood. He speculated on how his early experiences shaped what he considered to be his uniquely troubled personality. This emphasis on the importance of early experiences to the formation of character is central to such important modernists as Proust, in his great novel *In Search of Lost Time* (pp. 2004–2037), and Freud in his development of psychoanalysis. Rousseau described two experiences that particularly affected him for the remainder of his life: his pleasurable beating at the hands of his teacher, Mlle. Lambercier, which forever determined the nature of his sexual desires; and his anger over the punishment he received for a crime that he did not commit and therefore would not confess to—an anger and resentment that forever made him, at least in his own estimation, a crusader for justice and defender of the defenseless.

For Augustine, such early traumas are understood from the position of someone who has undergone a momentous conversion to Christianity that throws into stark opposition the differences between the love of self and the love of God. Rousseau's *Confessions* remained resolutely within the realm of love of self, but the author yearned for relief from self-love in such experiences as living in the purest and most sublime natural surroundings. If Augustine wished to persuade his readers to love God as much as he did, Rousseau appears to have wanted his readers to love Rousseau and to correct the world's misunderstanding of him.

## *The Confessions*

*from Book One*

### 1712–1719

I have resolved on an enterprise which has no precedent, and which, once complete, will have no imitator. My purpose is to display to my kind a portrait in every way true to nature, and the man I shall portray will be myself.

Simply myself. I know my own heart and understand my fellow man. But I am made unlike any one I have ever met; I will even venture to say that I am like no one in the whole world. I may be no better, but at least I am different. Whether Nature did well or ill in breaking the mould in which she formed me, is a question which can only be resolved after the reading of my book.

Let the last trump sound when it will, I shall come forward with this work in my hand, to present myself before my Sovereign Judge, and proclaim aloud: 'Here is what I have done, and if by chance I have used some immaterial embellishment it has been only to fill a void due to a defect of memory. I may have taken for fact what was no more than probability, but I have never put down as true what I knew to be false. I have displayed myself as I was, as vile and despicable when my behaviour was such, as good, generous, and noble when I was so. I have bared my secret soul as Thou thyself hast seen it, Eternal Being! So let the numberless legion of my fellow men gather round me, and hear my confessions. Let them groan at my depravities, and blush for my misdeeds. But let each one of them reveal his heart at the foot of Thy throne with equal sincerity, and may any man who dares, say "I was a better man than he."'

I was born at Geneva in 1712, the son of Isaac Rousseau, a citizen of that town, and Susanne Bernard, his wife. My father's inheritance, being a fifteenth part only of a very small property which had been divided among as many children, was almost nothing, and he relied for his living entirely on his trade of watchmaker, at which he was very highly skilled. My mother was the daughter of a minister of religion and rather better-off. She had besides both intelligence and beauty, and my father had not found it easy to win her. Their love had begun almost with their birth; at eight or nine they would walk together every evening along La Treille, and at ten they were inseparable. Sympathy and mental affinity strengthened in them a feeling first formed by habit. Both, being affectionate and sensitive by nature, were only waiting for the moment when they would find similar qualities in another; or rather the moment was waiting for them, and both threw their affections at the first heart that opened to receive them. Fate, by appearing to oppose their passion, only strengthened it. Unable to obtain his mistress, the young lover ate out his heart with grief, and she counselled him to travel and forget her. He travelled in vain, and returned more in love than ever, to find her he loved still faithful and fond. After such a proof, it was inevitable that they should love one another for all their lives. They swore to do so, and Heaven smiled on their vows.

Gabriel Bernard, one of my mother's brothers, fell in love with one of my father's sisters, and she refused to marry him unless her brother could marry my mother at the same time. Love overcame all obstacles, and the two pairs were wedded on the same day. So it was that my uncle married my aunt, and their children became my double first cousins. Within a year both couples had a child, but at the end of that time each of them was forced to separate.

My uncle Bernard, who was an engineer, went to serve in the Empire and Hungary under Prince Eugène, and distinguished himself at the siege and battle of Belgrade. My father, after the birth of my only brother, left for Constantinople, where he had been called to become watchmaker to the Sultan's Seraglio. While he was away my mother's beauty, wit, and talents* brought her admirers, one of the most pressing of whom was M. de la Closure, the French Resident in the city. His feelings must have been very strong, for thirty years later I have seen him moved when merely speaking to me about her. But my mother had more than her virtue with which to defend herself; she deeply loved my father, and urged him to come back. He threw up everything to do so, and I was the unhappy fruit of his return. For ten months later I was born, a poor and sickly child, and cost

---

*She had talents much above her station. For her father the minister, who adored her, had taken great pains with her education. She drew, sang, and played accompaniments on the lute; she was well read and wrote very fair verses. Here is an impromptu which she composed as she was walking with her sister- in-law and their two children, apropos some remark made about her absent husband and brother:

Ces deux messieurs qui sont absens
Nous sont chers de bien des manières:
Ce sont nos amis, nos amants,
Ce sont nos maris et nos frères,
Et les pères de ces enfants.

[These two absent gentlemen are dear to us in many ways. They are our friends and our lovers, they are our husbands and our brothers, and they are these children's fathers.]

my mother her life. So my birth was the first of my misfortunes.

I never knew how my father stood up to his loss, but I know that he never got over it. He seemed to see her again in me, but could never forget that I had robbed him of her; he never kissed me that I did not know by his sighs and his convulsive embrace that there was a bitter grief mingled with his affection, a grief which nevertheless intensified his feeling for me. When he said to me, 'Jean-Jacques, let us talk of your mother,' I would reply: 'Very well, father, but we are sure to cry.' 'Ah,' he would say with a groan; 'Give her back to me, console me for her, fill the void she has left in my heart! Should I love you so if you were not more to me than a son?' Forty years after he lost her he died in the arms of a second wife, but with his first wife's name on his lips, and her picture imprinted upon his heart.

Such were my parents. And of all the gifts with which Heaven endowed them, they left me but one, a sensitive heart. It had been the making of their happiness, but for me it has been the cause of all the misfortunes in my life.

I was almost born dead, and they had little hope of saving me. I brought with me the seed of a disorder which has grown stronger with the years, and now gives me only occasional intervals of relief in which to suffer more painfully in some other way. But one of my father's sisters, a nice sensible woman bestowed such care on me that I survived; and now, as I write this, she is still alive at the age of eighty, nursing a husband rather younger than herself but ruined by drink. My dear aunt, I pardon you for causing me to live, and I deeply regret that I cannot repay you in the evening of your days all the care and affection you lavished on me at the dawn of mine. My nurse Jacqueline is still alive too, and healthy and strong. Indeed the fingers that opened my eyes at birth may well close them at my death.

I felt before I thought: which is the common lot of man, though more pronounced in my case than in another's. I know nothing of myself till I was five or six. I do not know how I learnt to read. I only remember my first books and their effect upon me; it is from my earliest reading that I date the unbroken consciousness of my own existence. My mother had possessed some novels, and my father and I began to read them after our supper. At first it was only to give me some practice in reading. But soon my interest in this entertaining literature became so strong that we read by turns continuously, and spent whole nights so engaged. For we could never leave off till the end of the book. Sometimes my father would say with shame as we heard the morning larks: 'Come, let us go to bed. I am more of a child than you are.'

In a short time I acquired by this dangerous method, not only an extreme facility in reading and expressing myself, but a singular insight for my age into the passions. I had no idea of the facts, but I was already familiar with every feeling. I had grasped nothing; I had sensed everything. These confused emotions which I experienced one after another, did not warp my reasoning powers in any way, for as yet I had none. But they shaped them after a special pattern, giving me the strangest and most romantic notions about human life, which neither experience nor reflection has ever succeeded in curing me of.

## 1719–1723

The novels gave out in the summer of 1719, and that winter we changed our reading. Having exhausted my mother's library, we turned to that portion of her father's which had fallen to us. Fortunately it contained some good books, as it could hardly fail to do, for the collection had been formed by a minister, who deserved the title, a man of learning, after the fashion of his day, but of taste and good sense as well. Lesueur's *History of Church and Empire,* Bossuet's *Discourse upon Universal History,* Plutarch's *Lives,* Nani's *History of Venice,* Ovid's *Metamorphoses,* La Bruyère, Fontenelle's *Worlds* and his *Dialogues with the Dead,* and some volumes of Molière were transported to my father's workshop, where I read them to him every day while he worked.

Thus I acquired a sound taste, which was perhaps unique for my years. Plutarch, of them all, was my especial favourite, and the pleasure I took in reading and re-reading him did something to cure me of my passion for novels. Soon indeed I came to prefer Agesilaus, Brutus, and Aristides to Orondates, Artamenes, and Juba. It was this enthralling reading, and the discussions it gave rise to between my father and myself, that created in me that proud and intractable spirit, that impatience with the yoke of servitude, which has afflicted me throughout my life, in those situations least fitted to afford it scope. Continuously preoccupied with Rome and Athens, living as one might say with their great men, myself born the citizen of a republic and the son of a father whose patriotism was his strongest passion, I took fire by his example and pictured myself as a Greek or a Roman. I became indeed that character whose life I was reading; the recital of his constancy or his daring deeds so carrying me away that my eyes sparkled and my voice rang. One day when I was reading the story of Scaevola over table, I frightened them all by putting out my hand and grasping a chafing-dish in imitation of that hero.

I had one brother seven years older than myself, who was learning my father's trade. The extraordinary affection lavished upon me led to his being somewhat neglected, which I consider very wrong. Moreover his education had suffered by this neglect, and he was acquiring low habits even before he arrived at an age at which he could in fact indulge them. He was apprenticed to another master, with whom he took the same liberties as he had taken at home. I hardly ever saw him. Indeed, I can hardly say that I ever knew him, but I did not cease to love him dearly, and he loved me as well as a scoundrel can love. I remember once when my father was correcting him severely and angrily, throwing myself impetuously between them, and clasping my arms tightly around him. Thus I covered him with my body, and received the blows intended for him. So obstinately did I maintain my hold that, either as a result of my tearful cries or so as not to hurt me more than him, my father let him off his punishment. In the end my brother became so bad that he ran away and completely disappeared. We heard some time later that he was in Germany. But he did not write at all, and we had no more news of him after that. So it was that I became an only son.

But if that poor lad's upbringing was neglected, it was a different matter with his brother. No royal child could be more scrupulously cared for than I was in my early years. I was idolized by everyone around me and, what is rarer, always treated as a beloved son, never as a spoiled child. Never once, until I left my father's house, was I allowed to run out alone into the road with the other children. They never had to repress or to indulge in me any of those wayward humours that are usually attributed to Nature, but which are all the product of education alone. I had the faults of my years. I was a chatterer, I was greedy, and sometimes I lied. I would have stolen fruit or sweets or any kind of eatable; but I never took delight in being naughty or destructive, or in accusing other people or torturing poor animals. However, I do remember once having made water in one of our neighbour's cooking-pots while she was at church; her name was Mme Clot. I will even admit that the thought of it still makes me laugh, because Mme Clot, although a good woman on the whole, was the grumpiest old body I have ever met. And that is a brief and truthful account of all my childish misdeeds.

How could I have turned out wicked when I had nothing but examples of kindliness before my eyes, none but the best people in the world around me? My father, my aunt, my nurse, our friends and relations and everyone near me, may not have done my every bidding, but they did love me, and I loved them in return. My desires were so rarely excited and so rarely thwarted, that it never came into my head to have any. I could swear indeed that until I was put under a master I did not so much as know what it was to want my own way. When I was not reading or writing with my father, or going out for walks with my nurse, I spent all my time with my aunt, watching her embroider, hearing her sing, always sitting or standing beside her; and I was happy. Her cheerfulness and kindness and her pleasant face have left such an impression upon me that I can still remember her manner, her attitude and the way she looked. I recall too her affectionate little remarks, and I could still describe her clothes and her headdress, not forgetting the two curls of black hair she combed over her temples in the fashion of the day.

I am quite sure that it is to her I owe my taste, or rather my passion, for music, though it did not develop in me till long afterwards. She knew an enormous number of songs and tunes which she sang in a thin voice, that was very sweet. Such was the serenity of this excellent woman that it kept melancholy and sadness away, not only from her but from anyone who came near her; and such delight did I take in her singing that not only have many of her songs remained in my memory, but even now that I have lost her, others which I had completely forgotten since my childhood come back to me as I grow older, with a charm that I cannot express. It may seem incredible but, old dotard that I am, eaten up with cares and infirmities, I still find myself weeping like a child as I hum her little airs in my broken, tremulous voice. There is one in particular, the whole tune of which has come back to me. But the second half of the words persistently defies all my efforts to remember them, though I have a confused memory of the rhymes. Here is the opening and as much as I can recall of the rest:

Thyrsis, I dare not come
To listen to your playing
Under the elm.
For round our farm
Do you know what they're saying?
A shepherd born
Who faithfully swore
nothing to fear
But never is a rose without a
thorn.

I strive in vain to account for the strange effect which that song has on my heart, but I cannot explain why I am moved. All I know is that I am quite incapable of singing it to the end without breaking into tears. Countless times I have made up my mind to write to Paris and find out the rest of the words, if there is anyone who still knows them. But I am almost sure that the pleasure I derive from recalling the tune would partly vanish, once I had proof that anyone but my poor aunt Susan had sung it.

Such were the first affections of my dawning years; and thus there began to form in me, or to display itself for the first time, a heart at once proud and affectionate, and a character at once effeminate and inflexible, which by always wavering between weakness and courage, between self-indulgence and virtue, has throughout my life set me in conflict with myself, to such effect that abstinence and enjoyment, pleasure and prudence have alike eluded me.

The course of my education was interrupted by an accident, the consequences of which have influenced the rest of my life. My father quarrelled with M. Gautier, a French captain with relations on the Council. This Gautier was a braggart and a coward who, happening to bleed at the nose, revenged himself by accusing my father of having drawn his sword against him in the city. When they decided to put my father in prison, however, he insisted that, according to the law, his accuser should be arrested also; and when he failed to get his way he preferred to leave Geneva and remain abroad for the rest of his life rather than lose both liberty and honour by giving in.

I stayed behind in the charge of my uncle Bernard, who was then employed on the city's fortifications. His elder daughter was dead, but he had a son of my age, and we were sent together to Bossey to board with the pastor, M. Lambercier, to learn Latin and all that sorry nonsense as well that goes by the name of education.

Two years' sojourn in that village somewhat modified my harsh Roman manners, and brought me back to the stage of childhood. At Geneva, where nothing was demanded of me, I loved steady reading, which was almost my sole amusement; at Bossey the work I had to do made me prefer games, which I played as a relaxation. The country too was such a fresh experience that I could never have enough of it. Indeed the taste that I got for it was so strong that it has remained inextinguishable, and the memory of the happy days I spent there has made me long regretfully for a country life and its pleasures at every stage of my existence, till now, when I am in the country once more. M. Lambercier was a very intelligent man; though he did not neglect our lessons, he did not load us with excessive work; and the proof of his capability is that, despite my dislike for compulsion, I have never looked back with distaste on my lesson times with him. I may not have learnt very much from him, but what I did learn I learnt without difficulty and I have remembered it all.

The simplicity of this rural existence brought me one invaluable benefit; it opened my heart to friendship. Up to that time I had known nothing but lofty and theoretical emotions. Living peacefully side by side with my cousin Bernard gave me a bond of affection with him, and in a very short time I felt a greater attachment for him than I had ever felt for my brother, an attachment that has never disappeared. He was a tall, lank, sickly boy, as mild in spirit as he was weak in body, and he never abused his favoured position in the house as my guardian's son. We shared the same studies, the same amusements, and the same tastes; we were on our own and of the same age, and each of us needed a companion; to be separated would have broken our hearts. Seldom though we had the opportunity of proving our attachment to one another, it was extremely strong. For not only could we not have lived one moment apart, but we never imagined that we could ever be parted. Being both of a nature easily swayed by affection, and tractable so long as there was no attempt at constraint, we were always in agreement on all subjects, and if the favour of our guardians gave him some advantage when they were present, the ascendancy was mine when we were alone—which redressed the balance. At our lessons I prompted him if he broke down; and when I had written my exercise I helped him with his. In our sports too I was the more active, and always took the lead. In fact our two natures agreed so well, and our friendship was so mutual and wholehearted that for five complete years, both at Bossey and at Geneva, we were almost inseparable. We often fought, I confess, but no one ever had to part us. Not one of our quarrels lasted more than a quarter of an hour, and not once did either of us complain of the other. It may be said that these observations are puerile, but the relationship they describe is perhaps a unique one in all the history of childhood.

The manner of my life at Bossey suited me so well that if only it had lasted longer it could not have failed to fix my character for ever. It was founded on the affectionate, tender, and peaceable emotions. There was never, I believe, a creature of our kind with less vanity than I. By sudden transports I achieved moments of bliss, but immediately afterwards I relapsed into languor. My strongest desire was to be loved by everyone who came near me. I was gentle, so was my cousin, and so were our guardians. For a whole two years I was neither the witness nor the victim of any violence. Everything served to strengthen the natural disposition of my heart. Nothing seemed to me so delightful as to see everyone pleased with me and with everything. I shall always remember repeating my catechism in church, where nothing upset me more than the grieved and anxious look on Mlle Lambercier's face when I hesitated. This made me unhappier than did my shame at faltering in public, though that too distressed me exceedingly. For although I was not very susceptible to praise, I was always extremely sensitive to disgrace. But I may say now that the expectation of a scolding from Mlle Lambercier alarmed me less than the fear of annoying her.

Neither she nor her brother was lacking in severity when necessary. But as their severity was almost always just and never excessive, I took it to heart and never resented it. I was more upset at displeasing them, however, than at being punished; and a word of rebuke was more painful to me than a blow. It embarrasses me to be more explicit, but it is necessary nevertheless. How differently people would treat children if only they saw the eventual results of the indiscriminate, and often culpable, methods of punishment they employ! The magnitude of the lesson to be derived from so common and unfortunate a case as my own has resolved me to write it down.

Since Mlle Lambercier treated us with a mother's love, she had also a mother's authority, which she exercised sometimes by inflicting on us such childish chastisements as we had earned. For a long while she confined herself to threats, and the threat of a punishment entirely unknown to me frightened me sufficiently. But when in the end I was beaten I found the experience less dreadful in fact than in anticipation; and the very strange thing was that this punishment increased my affection for the inflicter. It required all the strength of my devotion and all my natural gentleness to prevent my deliberately earning another beating; I had discovered in the shame and pain of the punishment an admixture of sensuality which had left me rather eager than otherwise for a repetition by the same hand. No doubt, there being some degree of precocious sexuality in all this, the same punishment at the hands of her brother would not have seemed pleasant at all. But he was of too kindly a disposition to be likely to take over this duty; and so, if I refrained from earning a fresh punishment, it was only out of fear of annoying Mlle Lambercier; so much am I swayed by kindness, even by kindness that is based on sensuality, that it has always prevailed with me over sensuality itself.

The next occasion, which I postponed, although not through fear, occurred through no fault of mine—that is to say I did not act deliberately. But I may say that I took advantage of it with an easy conscience. This second occasion, however, was also the last. For Mlle Lambercier had no doubt detected signs that this punishment was not having the desired effect. She announced, therefore, that she would abandon it, since she found it too exhausting. Hitherto we had always slept in her room, and sometimes, in winter, in her bed. Two days afterwards we were made to sleep in another room, and henceforward I had the honour, willingly though I would have dispensed with it, of being treated as a big boy.

Who could have supposed that this childish punishment, received at the age of eight at the hands of a woman of thirty, would determine my tastes and desires, my passions, my very self for the rest of my life, and that in a sense diametrically opposed to the one in which they should normally have developed. At the moment when my senses were aroused my desires took a false turn and, confining themselves to this early experience, never set about seeking a different one. With sensuality burning in my blood almost from my birth, I kept myself pure and unsullied up to an age when even the coldest and most backward natures have developed. Tormented for a long while by I knew not what, I feasted feverish eyes on lovely women, recalling them ceaselessly to my imagination, but only to make use of them in my own fashion as so many Mlle Lamberciers.

My morals might well have been impaired by these strange tastes, which persisted with a depraved and insane intensity. But in fact they kept me pure even after the age of puberty. If ever education was chaste and decent, mine was. My three aunts were not only women of remarkable virtue, but examples of a modesty that has long since disappeared from womankind. My father was a pleasure lover, but a gallant of the old school, and never made a remark in the hearing of those women he loved most that would have brought a blush to a virgin's cheek; and never was the respect due to children more scrupulously observed than in my family and in my case. I did not find the slightest difference in this respect at M. Lambercier's; a very good servant maid was dismissed for a dubious word pronounced in our hearing. Not only had I not till adolescence any clear ideas concerning sexual intercourse, but my muddled thoughts on the subject always assumed odious and disgusting shapes. I had a horror of prostitutes which has never left me, and I could not look on a debauchee without contempt and even fear. Such had been my horror of immorality, even since the day when, on my way to Petit Saconex along the sunken road, I saw the holes in the earth on either side where I was told such people performed their fornications. When I thought of this I was always reminded of the coupling of dogs, and my stomach turned over at the very thought.

These adolescent prejudices would themselves have been sufficient to retard the first explosions of an inflammable temperament. But they were reinforced, as I have said, by the effect upon me of the promptings of sensuality. Imagining no pleasures other than those I had known, I could not, for all the restless tinglings in my veins, direct my desires towards any other form of gratification. Always I stopped short of imagining those satisfactions which I had been taught to loathe, and which, little though I suspected it, were in fact not so far divorced from those I envisaged. In my crazy fantasies, my wild fits of eroticism, and in the strange behaviour which they sometimes drove me to, I always invoked, imaginatively, the aid of the opposite sex, without so much as dreaming that a woman could serve any other purpose than the one I lusted for.

Not only, therefore, did I, though ardent, lascivious, and precocious by nature, pass the age of puberty without desiring or knowing any other sensual pleasures than those which Mlle Lambercier had, in all innocence, acquainted me with; but when finally, in the course of years, I became a man I was preserved by that very perversity which might have been my undoing. My old childish tastes did not vanish, but became so intimately associated with those of maturity that I could never, when sensually aroused, keep the two apart. This peculiarity, together with my natural timidity, has always made me very backward with women, since I have never had the courage to be frank or the power to get what I wanted, it being impossible for the kind of pleasure I desired—to which the other kind is no more than a consummation—to be taken by him who wants it, or to be guessed at by the woman who could grant it. So I have spent my days in silent longing in the presence of those I most loved. I never dared to reveal my strange taste, but at least I got some pleasure from situations which pandered to the thought of it. To fall on my knees before a masterful mistress, to obey her commands, to have to beg for her forgiveness, have been to me the most delicate of pleasures; and the more my vivid imagination heated my blood the more like a spellbound lover I looked. As can be imagined, this way of making love does not lead to rapid progress, and is not very dangerous to the virtue of the desired object. Consequently I have possessed few women, but I have not failed to get a great deal of satisfaction in my own way, that is to say imaginatively. So it is that my sensibility, combined with my timidity and my romantic nature, have preserved the purity of my feelings and my morals, by the aid of those same tastes which might, with a little more boldness, have plunged me into the most brutal sensuality.

Now I have made the first and most painful step in the dark and miry maze of my confessions. It is the ridiculous and the shameful, not one's criminal actions, that it is hardest to confess. But henceforth I am certain of myself; after what I have just had the courage to say, nothing else will defeat me. How much it has cost me to make such revelations can be judged when I say that though sometimes labouring under passions that have robbed me of sight, of hearing, and of my senses, though sometimes trembling convulsively in my whole body in the presence of the woman I loved, I have never, during the whole course of my life, been able to force myself, even in moments of extreme intimacy, to confess my peculiarities and implore her to grant the one favour which was lacking. That confession I was only able to make once, when I was a child to a child of my own age, and then it was she who made the first overtures.

When I trace my nature back in this way to its earliest manifestations, I find features which may appear incompatible, but which have nevertheless combined to form a strong, simple, and uniform whole. I find other features, however, which, though similar in appearance, have formed by a concatenation of circumstances combinations so different that one could never suppose them to be in any way related to one another. Who would imagine, for instance, that I owe one of the most vigorous elements in my character to the same origins as the weakness and sensuality that flows in my veins? Before we leave the subject I have been dwelling on, I will show it under a very different light.

One day I was learning my lessons alone in the room next to the kitchen, where the servant had left Mlle Lambercier's combs to dry on the stove top. Now when she came to take them off, she discovered that the teeth of one were broken off, all down one side. Who was to be blamed for this? I was the only person who had been in the room; but I said I had not touched it. M. and Mlle Lambercier jointly lectured, pressed, and threatened me; but I stubbornly maintained my denial. Appearances were too strong for me, however, and all my protests were overruled, although this was the first time that I had been convicted of a downright lie. They took the matter seriously, as it deserved. The mischief, the untruth, and my persistent denials, all seemed to deserve a punishment; but this time it was not Mlle Lambercier who inflicted it. They wrote to my Uncle Bernard, and he came. My cousin was accused of another crime no less grave; we were awarded the same chastisement, which was a severe one. If they had intended to allay my depraved tastes for ever by using the evil as its own remedy, they could not have gone about it in a better way. For a long time my desires left me in peace.

They were unable to force from me the confession they required. Though the punishment was several times repeated and I was reduced to the most deplorable condition, I remained inflexible. I would have died rather than give in, and I was resolved to. So force had to yield before the diabolical obstinacy of a child. For that is what they called my persistence. But finally I emerged from that cruel ordeal shattered but triumphant.

It is now nearly fifty years since this occurrence, and I have no fear of a fresh punishment for the offence. But I declare before Heaven that I was not guilty. I had not broken, nor so much as touched, the comb. I had not gone near the stove, nor so much as thought of doing so. But do not ask me how the mischief occurred. I have no idea, and I cannot understand it. But I do most positively know that I was innocent.

Imagine a person timid and docile in ordinary life, but proud, fiery, and inflexible when roused, a child who has always been controlled by the voice of reason, always treated with kindness, fairness, and indulgence, a creature without a thought of injustice, now for the first time suffering a most grave one at the hands of the people he loves best and mostly deeply respects. Imagine the revolution in his ideas, the violent change of his feelings, the confusion in his heart and brain, in his small intellectual and moral being! I say, imagine all this if you can. For myself I do not feel capable of unravelling the strands, or even remotely following all that happened at that time within me.

I had not yet sufficient reasoning power to realize the extent to which appearances were against me, to put myself in my elders' position. I clung to my own, and all I felt was the cruelty of an appalling punishment for a crime I had not committed. The physical pain was bad enough, but I hardly noticed it; what I felt was indignation, rage, and despair. My cousin was in a more or less similar case; he had been punished for what had only been a mistake but was taken for a premeditated crime, and he, following my example, got into a rage, and so to speak, worked himself up to the same pitch as myself. Lying together in the same bed, we embraced wildly, almost stifling one another; and when our young hearts were somewhat assuaged and we could give voice to our anger, we sat up and shouted a hundred times in unison at the tops of our voices: 'Carnifex!* carnifex! carnifex!'

I feel my pulse beat faster once more as I write. I shall always remember that time if I live to be a thousand. That first meeting with violence and injustice has remained so deeply engraved on my heart that any thought which recalls it summons back this first emotion. The feeling was only a personal one in its origins, but it has since assumed such a consistency and has become so divorced from personal interests that my blood boils at the sight or the tale of any injustice, whoever may be the sufferer and wherever it may have taken place, in just the same way as if I were myself its victim. When I read of the cruelties of a fierce tyrant, of the subtle machinations of a rascally priest, I would gladly go and stab the wretch myself, even if it were to cost me my life a hundred times over. I have often run till I dropped, flinging stones at some cock or cow or dog, or any animal that I saw tormenting

*Torturer

another because it felt itself the stronger. This is perhaps an innate characteristic in me. Indeed I think it is. But the memory of the first injustice I suffered was so painful, so persistent, and so intricately bound up with it that, however strong my initial bent in that direction, this youthful experience must certainly have powerfully reinforced it.

There ended the serenity of my childish life. From that moment I never again enjoyed pure happiness, and even to-day I am conscious that memory of childhood's delights stops short at that point. We stayed some months longer at Bossey. We lived as we are told the first man lived in the earthly paradise, but we no longer enjoyed it; in appearance our situation was unchanged, but in reality it was an entirely different kind of existence. No longer were we young people bound by ties of respect, intimacy, and confidence to our guardians; we no longer looked on them as gods who read our hearts; we were less ashamed of wrongdoing, and more afraid of being caught; we began to be secretive, to rebel, and to lie. All the vices of our years began to corrupt our innocence and to give an ugly turn to our amusements. Even the country no longer had for us those sweet and simple charms that touch the heart; it seemed to our eyes depressing and empty, as if it had been covered by a veil that cloaked its beauties. We gave up tending our little gardens, our herbs and flowers. We no longer went out to scratch the surface of the ground and shout with delight at finding one of the seeds we had sown beginning to sprout. We grew to dislike that life; and they grew to dislike us. So my uncle took us away, and we left M. and Mme Lambercier, with few regrets on either side, each party having grown weary of the other.

More than thirty years have passed since my departure from Bossey without my once recalling my stay there in any consecutive way or with any pleasure. But now that I have passed my prime and am declining into old age, I find these memories reviving as others fade, and stamping themselves on my mind with a charm and vividness of outline that grows from day to day. It is as if, feeling my life escaping from me, I were trying to recapture it at its beginnings. The smallest events of that time please me by the mere fact that they are of that time. I remember places and people and moments in all their detail. I can see the man- or maid-servant bustling about the room, a swallow flying in at the window, a fly alighting on my hand while I am saying my lesson. I can see the whole arrangement of the room in which we lived, on the right of which was M. Lambercier's study, with an engraving of all the popes, a barometer, and a large almanac on the walls. The windows were darkened by raspberry canes, which sometimes grew into the room; for the garden climbed steeply above the back of the house, and overshadowed it. I am well aware that the reader does not require information, but I, on the other hand, feel impelled to give it to him. Why should I not relate all the little incidents of that happy time, that still give me a flutter of pleasure to recall—six or seven of them at least. . . . Or let us strike a bargain. I will let you off five and be content with one, just one, so long as I am allowed to take as long as I like in telling it, in order to prolong my pleasure.

If I were not concerned for yours, I might choose the tale of Mlle Lambercier's unfortunate tumble at the end of the field, which caused her to display her full back view to the

King of Sardinia as he passed. But the incident of the walnut tree on the terrace pleases me better. For I took part in it, whereas I was only a spectator of Mlle Lambercier's tumble; and I assure you that I did not find the least cause for laughter in an accident which, though comical in itself, filled me with alarm on behalf of one whom I loved as a mother, or perhaps even more dearly.

Outside the gate into the courtyard, on the left as you came in, was a terrace on which we often sat of an afternoon, although it was fully exposed to the sun. In order to provide some shade, however, M. Lambercier had a walnut tree planted there. Its planting was carried out with all solemnity; we two boarders were its godparents, and whilst the hole was being filled we each held the tree with one hand, singing triumphal songs. Now for its watering a kind of trench was left all round it, and every day my cousin and I eagerly watched the watering ceremony, which confirmed us in our natural belief that it was a finer thing to plant a tree on a terrace than a flag in the breech. We resolved, therefore, to win that glory for ourselves and share it with no one.

For that purpose we went and cut a slip from a young willow, and planted it on the terrace some eight or ten feet from the sacred walnut. Nor did we omit to dig a trench round our tree, but the difficulty was to obtain the wherewithal to fill it. For our water was brought from a considerable distance, and we children were not allowed to run out and fetch it. Nevertheless our willow could not thrive without it, and for some days we resorted to every sort of device for getting it, to such good effect that it budded beneath our eyes, putting out little leaves whose growth we measured hour by hour, in the firm belief that, though it was not a foot high, it would not be long before it cast us a shade.

Now our tree was our sole preoccupation, and we went about in a sort of fever, incapable of applying ourselves to our lessons or to anything else. Our elders, therefore, unable to make out the cause of the trouble, kept us more confined than ever; and the fatal moment drew near when our water would give out. We were desperate at the thought of watching our tree parch to death. Finally invention's mother, necessity, suggested a way of keeping it alive and saving ourselves from death by despair. Our plan was to make an underground tunnel which would secretly bring to the willow some of the water which was given to the walnut tree. Feverishly we undertook our enterprise, but at first it did not succeed; the runnel filled up with dirt, and everything went wrong. But nothing deterred us: *'Labor omnia vincit improbus.'* We dug away more earth and deepened our trench to give the water a flow; and we cut some boxes into little narrow boards, putting some of them flat at the bottom and propping others at angles at each side to make a triangular channel for our stream. Where it flowed in we planted thin sticks at intervals to form a grating or trap that would hold up the fine earth and stones, and keep the channel free for the water. Then we carefully covered our work, treading the soil well down, and on the day when it was completed waited in an ecstasy of alternate hope and fear for watering time. After centuries of delay the hour came round at last, and M. Lambercier emerged, as usual, to witness the ceremony, throughout which we both stood behind him, to hide our tree. For, most fortunately, he had his back to it.

A few seconds after the first bucket was poured in we saw a trickle of water flow into our trench. At this sight our caution deserted us, and we set up such shouts of joy that M. Lambercier turned round; which was a pity since he had just been observing with delight how good the soil was around his tree and how greedily it absorbed the water. Shocked, however, to see it providing for two trenches, he also set up a shout. Then, taking a closer look, he discovered our trick and sent straight for a mattock, which quickly knocked a few of our boards flying. 'An aqueduct! an aqueduct!' he cried, and rained down his merciless blows on every side. Each one of them pierced us to the heart. In a moment the boards, the runnel, the trench, and the willow were all destroyed, and the earth all round was ploughed up. But, in the course of all this frightful business, the only words uttered were his cries of 'An aqueduct! an aqueduct!' as he knocked everything to pieces.

It may be supposed that the incident had unpleasant consequences for the young architects. But not so. That was all. M. Lambercier did not utter a word of reproach, did not look sternly upon us, and never mentioned the matter at all, though we heard his full-throated laugh ring out shortly afterwards from his sister's room. You could hear M. Lambercier's laugh from afar. What was even more surprising, however, was that when the first shock was over, we were not very distressed ourselves. We planted another tree in another place, and often reminded one another of the first one's unhappy fate, by significantly repeating 'An aqueduct! an aqueduct!' Before that time I had had occasional bouts of conceit and fancied myself an Aristides or a Brutus; but this was my first well-defined attack of vanity. To have built an aqueduct with our own hands and set a cutting to compete with a large tree seemed to me the very height of glory, the meaning of which I understood better at ten than did Caesar at thirty.

The memory of that incident so stuck in my mind—or was so forcibly recalled to it—that one of my dearest plans, on revisiting Geneva in 1754, was to go back to Bossey, and see the memorials of my youth, chief among them that well-loved walnut tree, which by that time would have been a third of a century old. But I was so besieged by people, so little my own master, that I could not find a moment in which to please myself. It is unlikely that I shall ever have this opportunity again. But though I have lost all hope of ever seeing it now, I still long to do so, and were I ever to return to that dear village and find my walnut tree still alive, I should most probably water it with my tears.

## Charles Baudelaire (1821–1867)

*Translated by Richard Howard*

Charles Baudelaire is often said to have invented modern poetry. He was a contemporary of the American poet Walt Whitman but had a more pronounced sense of the emptiness and moral depravity of modernity, especially city life. In this respect he had a great influence on modernists like T.S. Eliot, whose *Waste Land* (pp. 2174–2181) draws inspiration from him.

Baudelaire adored the Gothic romanticism of Edgar Allen Poe but turned it into a lurid surrealistic depiction of Paris life—its streets and brothels, its criminals and outcasts. The appearance of *The Flowers of Evil* in 1857 produced a public outcry; Baudelaire and his publisher were tried for indecency, and six of the poems were banned. His poetry still has the power to shock. Many readers will find his depiction of women especially vile, but it is consonant with his more general feeling that human beings are only so many sites of sin and depravity, boredom and excess. His depictions of the body, bordering on pornography, imply his own depravity and emptiness as much as that of his subjects.

Baudelaire is one of the world's great love poets, although in a strangely negative mode. He celebrated all forms and permutations of sexuality, always in the context of his society's pervasive disapproval. His poems about lesbians were especially shocking to his audience. Rather than making any positive claims for sexuality, however, he wallowed in its forbiddenness. It is hard to know how much he exaggerated his own attitudes in a calculated attempt to shock his readers ("I am a graveyard that the moon abhors," he writes in "Spleen"), but he did inhabit the Parisian demimonde, spending most of his adult life with a mulatto prostitute named Jeanne Duval, his "Black Venus," about whom he wrote many of his best poems, including "The Head of Hair" and "The Vampire."

Behind Baudelaire's posturing lies a sense of sin and a religious framework that validates his self-loathing and produces the required shock value of the poems: he sees himself as damned, which is a religious attitude, after all. Behind Baudelaire's depiction of what is disgusting, the reader discovers an essentially romantic aesthetic; a frustrated desire to transcend the world; and a feeling for the symbolic value of nature, love, and language, which both leads him on and frustrates him (as in "Elevation" and "Correspondences"). Baudelaire's image of the poet as a tormented soul and social outcast became commonplace in the century after he lived.

Perhaps the most famous poem of *The Flowers of Evil* is the opening one, "To the Reader." A summary of all his peculiar themes, it ends with the haunting line that accuses us of being just like him, although we hypocritically deny it: "*Hypocrite lecteur, mon semblemble, mon frere!*" His poems are intended as a mirror into the most vile regions of the modern soul, both his and ours.

## *The Flowers of Evil*

### *To the Reader*

Stupidity, delusion, selfishness and lust
torment our bodies and possess our minds,
and we sustain our affable remorse
the way a beggar nourishes his lice.

Our sins are stubborn, our contrition lame;
we want our scruples to be worth our while—
how cheerfully we crawl back to the mire:
a few cheap tears will wash our stains away!

Satan Trismegistus subtly rocks
our ravished spirits on his wicked bed
until the precious metal of our will
is leached out by this cunning alchemist:

the Devil's hand directs our every move—
the things we loathed become the things we love;
day by day we drop through stinking shades
quite undeterred on our descent to Hell.

Like a poor profligate who sucks and bites
the withered breast of some well-seasoned trull,
we snatch in passing at clandestine joys
and squeeze the oldest orange harder yet.

Wriggling in our brains like a million worms,
a demon demos holds its revels there,
and when we breathe, the Lethe in our lungs
trickles sighing on its secret course.

If rape and arson, poison and the knife
have not yet stitched their ludicrous designs
onto the banal buckram of our fates,
it is because our souls lack enterprise!

But here among the scorpions and the hounds,
the jackals, apes and vultures, snakes and wolves,
monsters that howl and growl and squeal and crawl,
in all the squalid zoo of vices, one

is even uglier and fouler than the rest,
although the least flamboyant of the lot;
this beast would gladly undermine the earth
and swallow all creation in a yawn;

I speak of Boredom which with ready tears
dreams of hangings as it puffs its pipe.
Reader, you know this squeamish monster well,
—hypocrite reader,—my alias,—my twin!

## *Elevation*

Above the lake in the valley and the grove
along the hillside, high over the sea
and the passing clouds, and even past the sun!
to the farthest confines of the starry vault

mount, my spirit, wander at your ease
and range exultant through transparent space
like a rugged swimmer revelling in the waves
with an unutterable male delight.

Ascend beyond the sickly atmosphere
to a higher plane, and purify yourself
by drinking as if it were ambrosia
the fire that fills and fuels Emptiness.

Free from the futile strivings and the cares
which dim existence to a realm of mist,
happy is he who wings an upward way
on mighty pinions to the fields of light;

whose thoughts like larks spontaneously rise
into the morning sky; whose flight, unchecked,
outreaches life and readily comprehends
the language of flowers and of all mute things.

## *Correspondences*

The pillars of Nature's temple are alive
and sometimes yield perplexing messages;
forests of symbols between us and the shrine
remark our passage with accustomed eyes.

Like long-held echoes, blending somewhere else
into one deep and shadowy unison
as limitless as darkness and as day,
the sounds, the scents, the colors correspond.

There are odors succulent as young flesh,
sweet as flutes, and green as any grass,
while others—rich, corrupt and masterful—

possess the power of such infinite things
as incense, amber, benjamin and musk,
to praise the senses' raptures and the mind's.

## *The Head of Hair*

Ecstatic fleece that ripples to your nape
and reeks of negligence in every curl!
To people my dim cubicle tonight
with memories shrouded in that head of hair,
I'd have it flutter like a handkerchief!

For torpid Asia, torrid Africa
—the wilderness I thought a world away—
survive at the heart of this dark continent . . .
As other souls set sail to music, mine,
O my love! embarks on your redolent hair.

Take me, tousled current, to where men
as mighty as the trees they live among
submit like them to the sun's long tyranny;
ebony sea, you bear a brilliant dream
of sails and pennants, mariners and masts,

a harbor where my soul can slake its thirst
for color, sound and smell—where ships that glide
among the seas of golden silk throw wide
their yardarms to embrace a glorious sky
palpitating in eternal heat.

Drunk, and in love with drunkenness, I'll dive
into this ocean where the other lurks,
and solaced by these waves, my restlessness
will find a fruitful lethargy at last,
rocking forever at aromatic ease.

Blue hair, vault of shadows, be for me
the canopy of overarching sky;
here at the downy roots of every strand
I stupefy myself on the mingled scent
of musk and tar and coconut oil for hours . . .

For hours? Forever! Into that splendid mane
let me braid rubies, ropes of pearls to bind
you indissolubly to my desire—
you the oasis where I dream, the gourd
from which I gulp the wine of memory.

## *The Vampire*

Sudden as a knife you thrust
    into my sorry heart
and strong as a host of demons came,
    gaudy and libertine,

to make in my corrupted mind
    your bed and bedlam there;
—Beast, who bind me to you close
    as convict to his chains,

as gambler to his winning streak,
    as drunkard to his wine,
close as the carrion to its worms—
    I curse you! Be accursed!

I begged the sword by one swift stroke
    to grant me liberty;
nor did my cowardice disdain
    less clear-cut remedies.

### *Spleen (II)*

Souvenirs?
More than if I had lived a thousand years!

No chest of drawers crammed with documents,
love-letters, wedding-invitations, wills,
a lock of someone's hair rolled up in a deed,
hides so many secrets as my brain.
This branching catacombs, this pyramid
contains more corpses than the potter's field:
I am a graveyard that the moon abhors,
where long worms like regrets come out to feed
most ravenously on my dearest dead.
I am an old boudoir where a rack of gowns,
perfumed by withered roses, rots to dust;
where only faint pastels and pale Bouchers
inhale the scent of long-unstoppered flasks.

## Marcel Proust (1871–1922)

*Translated by C.K. Scott Moncrieff, as adapted by Terence Kilmartin*

"*À la recherche du temps perdu*" (literally *In Search of Lost Time,* but often referred to as *Remembrance of Things Past*) by Marcel Proust is one of the greatest and most innovative works of prose fiction in the twentieth century. The famous opening section of the first volume, *Swann's Way,* of this multivolumed work is included here. In this section, "Combray," the narrator Marcel, now a sickly and bedridden old man, is hovering between sleep and wakefulness, unsure of precisely where or even who he is, unable quite to distinguish between what is dream and what is reality. In this in-between state, memories of his childhood in Combray well up from beneath his conscious mind. With those memories, the huge, magnificent, complex architecture of the novel emerges from his consciousness, just as a folded piece of Japanese paper, when dropped into a porcelain bowl filled with water, expands to take on particular and definite shapes.

At the beginning of the Enlightenment, John Locke discussed what he called the "association of ideas," the ways in which people often associate certain words with early experiences. Each time a person hears that particular word later in life, it may evoke the earlier experience, which may have no logical connection to that word and its meaning. For Locke, the association of ideas was potentially a form of madness. The goal of language was, for Locke, a transparent referentiality: words should always present clear and distinct ideas that should be communicable to every rational person. Proust's fiction is based on the notion that the association of ideas is precisely what the artist must explore. Indeed, the whole of Proust's novel emerges from a memory of the narrator's childhood that is evoked when he happens to taste a madeleine cake dipped in lemon tea. The taste reminds him of the tea his grandmother used to serve him as a child in Combray, and this association opens up the narrator's vast inner world of memories.

Proust's subject matter, aristocratic French society at the turn of the century—extremely refined, even precious, often quite snobbish—is itself rather limited in scope. But as in much modernist literature, Proust's true subject is the analysis of his own subjectivity and the way it interacts with and even creates its world. Conventional novels, such as Jane Austen's, are—in Aristotle's sense—imitations of an action revealing character. Though the Marcel who is the narrator of *In Search of Lost Time* is not precisely Marcel Proust, the two are close enough to support the idea that Proust's chief subject is Proust. In some sense, then, this novel is closer to Rousseau's *Confessions* than to Austen's novels.

Montaigne declared that he was himself the subject of his essays, and Rousseau said the same of his autobiography—but neither of these previous works was a novel. In Proust's novel, "objective" reality takes on meaning only as it flows through Marcel's consciousness. Indeed, for Proust, only through the consciousness of an experiencing subject does any object get constructed. Like Saint Augustine in his *Confessions,* Proust sees the past not as some measurable and externally objective reality but rather as something that is alive only as it is vividly experienced through memory.

## *from In Search of Lost Time*

*Swann's Way*

### Part One

#### Combray

*I*

For a long time I would go to bed early. Sometimes, the candle barely out, my eyes closed so quickly that I did not have time to tell myself: "I'm falling asleep." And half an hour later the thought that it was time to look for sleep would awaken me; I would make as if to put away the book which I imagined was still in my hands, and to blow out the light; I had gone on thinking, while I was asleep, about what I had just been reading, but these thoughts had taken a rather peculiar turn; it seemed to me that I myself was the immediate subject of my book: a church, a quartet, the rivalry between François I and Charles V. This impression would persist for some moments after I awoke; it did not offend my reason, but lay like scales upon my eyes and prevented them from registering the fact that the candle was no longer burning. Then it would begin to seem unintelligible, as the thoughts of a previous existence must be after reincarnation; the subject of my book would separate itself from me, leaving me free to apply myself to it or not; and at the same time my sight would return and I would be astonished to find myself in a state of darkness, pleasant and restful enough for my eyes, but even more, perhaps, for my mind, to which it appeared incomprehensible, without a cause, something dark indeed.

I would ask myself what time it could be; I could hear the whistling of trains, which, now nearer and now further off, punctuating the distance like the note of a bird in a forest, showed me in perspective the deserted countryside through which a traveller is hurrying towards the nearby station; and the path he is taking will be engraved in his memory by the excitement induced by strange surroundings, by unaccustomed activities, by the conversation he has had and the farewells exchanged beneath an unfamiliar lamp that still echo in his ears amid the silence of the night, and by the happy prospect of being home again.

I would lay my cheeks gently against the comfortable cheeks of my pillow, as plump and fresh as the cheeks of childhood. I would strike a match to look at my watch. Nearly midnight. The hour when an invalid, who has been obliged to set out on a journey and to sleep in a strange hotel, awakened by a sudden spasm, sees with glad relief a streak of daylight showing under his door. Thank God, it is morning! The servants will be about in a minute: he can ring, and someone will come to look after him. The thought of being assuaged gives him strength to endure his pain. He is certain he heard footsteps: they come nearer, and then die away. The ray of light beneath his door is extinguished. It is midnight; someone has just turned down the gas; the last servant has gone to bed, and he must lie all night suffering without remedy.

I would fall asleep again, and thereafter would reawaken for short snatches only, just long enough to hear the regular creaking of the wainscot, or to open my eyes to stare at the shifting kaleidoscope of the darkness, to savour, in a momentary glimmer of consciousness, the sleep which lay heavy upon the furniture, the room, that whole of which I formed no more than a small part and whose insensibility I should very soon return to share. Or else while sleeping I had drifted back to an earlier stage in my life, now for ever outgrown, and had come under the thrall of one of my childish terrors, such as that old terror of my great-uncle's pulling my curls which was effectually dispelled on the day—the dawn of a new era to me—when they were finally cropped from my head. I had forgotten that event during my sleep, but I remembered it again immediately I had succeeded in waking myself up to escape my great-uncle's fingers, and as a measure of precaution I would bury the whole of my head in the pillow before returning to the world of dreams.

Sometimes, too, as Eve was created from a rib of Adam, a woman would be born during my sleep from some misplacing of my thigh. Conceived from the pleasure I was on the point of enjoying, she it was, I imagined, who offered me that pleasure. My body, conscious that its own warmth was permeating hers, would strive to become one with her, and I would awake. The rest of humanity seemed very remote in comparison with this woman whose company I had left but a moment ago; my cheek was still warm from her kiss, my body ached beneath the weight of hers. If, as would sometimes happen, she had the features of some woman whom I had known in waking hours, I would abandon myself altogether to this end: to find her again, like people who set out on a journey to see with their eyes some city of their desire, and imagine that one can taste in reality what has charmed one's fancy. And then, gradually, the memory of her would fade away, I had forgotten the girl of my dream.

When a man is asleep, he has in a circle round him the chain of the hours, the sequence of the years, the order of the heavenly bodies. Instinctively he consults them when he awakes, and in an instant reads off his own position on the earth's surface and the time that has elapsed during his slumbers; but this ordered procession is apt to grow confused, and to break its ranks. Suppose that, towards morning, after a night of insomnia, sleep descends upon him while he is reading, in quite a different position from that in which he normally goes to sleep, he has only to lift his arm to arrest the sun and turn it back in its course, and, at the moment of waking, he will have no idea of the time, but will conclude that he has just gone to bed. Or suppose that he dozes off in some even more abnormal and divergent position, sitting in an armchair, for instance, after dinner: then the world will go hurtling out of orbit, the magic chair will carry him at full speed through time and space, and when he opens his eyes again he will imagine that he went to sleep months earlier in another place. But for me it was enough if, in my own bed, my sleep was so heavy as completely to relax my consciousness; for then I lost all sense of the place in which I had gone to sleep, and when I awoke in the middle of the night, not knowing where I was, I could not even be sure at first who I was; I had only the most rudimentary sense of existence, such as may lurk and flicker in the depths of an animal's consciousness; I was more destitute than the cave-dweller; but then the memory—not yet of the place in which I was, but of various other places where I had lived and might now very possibly be—would come like a rope let down from heaven to draw me up out of the abyss of not-being, from which I could never have escaped by myself: in a flash I would traverse centuries of civilisation, and out of a blurred glimpse of oil-lamps, then of shirts with turned-down collars, would gradually piece together the original components of my ego.

Perhaps the immobility of the things that surround us is forced upon them by our conviction that they are themselves and not anything else, by the immobility of our conception of them. For it always happened that when I awoke like this, and my mind struggled in an unsuccessful attempt to discover where I was, everything revolved around me through the darkness: things, places, years. My body, still too heavy with sleep to move, would endeavour to construe from the pattern of its tiredness the position of its various limbs, in order to deduce therefrom the direction of the wall, the location of the furniture, to piece together and give a name to the house in which it lay. Its memory, the composite memory of its ribs, its knees, its shoulder-blades, offered it a series of rooms in which it had at one time or another slept, while the unseen walls, shifting and adapting themselves to the shape of each successive room that it remembered, whirled round it in the dark. And even before my brain, hesitating at the threshold of times and shapes, had reassembled the circumstances sufficiently to identify the room, it—my body—would recall from each room in succession the style of the bed, the position of the doors, the angle at which the daylight came in at the windows, whether there was a passage outside, what I had had in my mind when I went to sleep and found there when I awoke. The stiffened side on which I lay would, for instance, in trying to fix its position, imagine itself to be lying face to the wall in a big bed with a canopy; and at once I would say to myself, "Why, I must have fallen asleep before Mamma came to say good night," for I was in the country at my grandfather's, who died years ago; and my body, the side upon which I was lying, faithful guardians of a past which my mind should never have forgotten, brought back before my eyes the glimmering flame of the night-light in its urn-shaped bowl of Bohemian glass that hung by chains from the ceiling, and the chimney-piece of Siena marble in my bedroom at Combray, in my grandparents' house, in those far distant days which at this moment I imagined to be in the present without being able to picture them exactly, and which would become plainer in a little while when I was properly awake.

Then the memory of a new position would spring up, and the wall would slide away in another direction; I was in my room in Mme de Saint-Loup's house in the country; good heavens, it must be ten o'clock, they will have finished dinner! I must have overslept myself in the little nap which I always take when I come in from my walk with Mme de Saint-Loup, before dressing for the evening. For many years have now elapsed since the Combray days when, coming in from the longest and latest walks, I would still be in time to see the reflection of the sunset glowing in the panes of my bedroom window. It is a very different kind of life that one leads at Tansonville, at Mme de Saint-Loup's, and a different kind of pleasure that I derive from taking walks only in the evenings, from visiting by moonlight the roads on which I used to play as a child in the sunshine; as for the bedroom in which I must have fallen asleep instead of dressing for dinner, I can see it from the distance as we return from our walk, with its lamp shining through the window, a solitary beacon in the night.

These shifting and confused gusts of memory never lasted for more than a few seconds; it often happened that, in my brief spell of uncertainty as to where I was, I did not distinguish the various suppositions of which it was composed any more than, when we watch a horse running, we isolate the successive positions of its body as they appear upon a bioscope. But I had seen first one and then another of the rooms in which I had slept during my life, and in the end I would revisit them all in the long course of my waking dream: rooms in winter, where on going to bed I would at once bury my head in a nest woven out of the most diverse materials—the corner of my pillow, the top of my blankets, a piece of a shawl, the edge of my bed, and a copy of a children's paper—which I had contrived to cement together, bird-fashion, by dint of continuous pressure; rooms where, in freezing weather, I would enjoy the satisfaction of being shut in from the outer world (like the sea-swallow which builds at the end of a dark tunnel and is kept warm by the surrounding earth), and where, the fire keeping in all night, I would sleep wrapped up, as it were, in a great cloak of snug and smoky air, shot with the glow of the logs intermittently breaking out again in flame, a sort of alcove without walls, a cave of warmth dug out of the heart of the room itself, a zone of heat whose boundaries were constantly shifting and altering in temperature as gusts of air traversed them to strike freshly upon my face, from the corners of the room or from parts near the window or far from the fireplace which had therefore remained cold;—or rooms in summer, where I would delight to feel myself a part of the warm night, where the moonlight striking upon the half-opened shutters would throw down to the foot of my bed its enchanted ladder, where I would fall asleep, as it might be in the open air, like a titmouse which the breeze gently rocks at the tip of a sunbeam;—or sometimes the Louis XVI room, so cheerful that I never felt too miserable in it, even on my first night, and in which the slender columns that lightly supported its ceiling drew so gracefully apart to reveal and frame the site of the bed;—sometimes, again, the little room with the high ceiling, hollowed in the form of a pyramid out of two separate storeys, and partly walled with mahogany, in which from the first moment, mentally poisoned by the unfamiliar scent of vetiver, I was convinced of the hostility of the violet curtains and of the insolent indifference of a clock that chattered on at the top of its voice as though I were not there; in which a strange and pitiless rectangular cheval-glass, standing across one corner of the room, carved out for itself a site I had not looked to find tenanted in the soft plenitude of my normal field of vision; in which my mind, striving for hours on end to break away from its moorings, to stretch upwards so as to take on the exact shape of the room and to reach to the topmost height of its gigantic funnel, had endured many a painful night as I lay stretched out in bed, my eyes staring upwards, my ears straining, my nostrils flaring, my heart beating; until habit had changed the colour of the curtains, silenced the clock, brought an expression of pity to the cruel, slanting face of the glass, disguised or even completely dispelled the scent of vetiver, and appreciably reduced the apparent loftiness of the ceiling. Habit! that skilful but slow-moving arranger who begins by letting our minds suffer for weeks on end in temporary quarters, but whom our minds are none the less only too happy to discover at last, for without it, reduced to their own devices, they would be powerless to make any room seem habitable.

Certainly I was now well awake; my body had veered round for the last time and the good angel of certainty had made all the surrounding objects stand still, had set me down under my bedclothes, in my bedroom, and had fixed, approximately in their right places in the uncertain light, my chest of drawers, my writing-table, my fireplace, the window overlooking the street, and both the doors. But for all that I now knew that I was not in any of the houses of which the ignorance of the waking moment had, in a flash, if not presented me with a distinct picture, at least persuaded me of the possible presence, my memory had been set in motion; as a rule I did not attempt to go to sleep again at once, but used to spend the greater part of the night recalling our life in the old days at Combray with my great-aunt, at Balbec, Paris, Doncières, Venice, and the rest; remembering again all the places and people I had known, what I had actually seen of them, and what others had told me.

At Combray, as every afternoon ended, long before the time when I should have to go to bed and lie there, unsleeping, far from my mother and grandmother, my bedroom became the fixed point on which my melancholy and anxious thoughts were centred. Someone had indeed had the happy idea of giving me, to distract me on evenings when I seemed abnormally wretched, a magic lantern, which used to be set on top of my lamp while we waited for dinner-time to come; and, after the fashion of the master-builders and glass-painters of Gothic days, it substituted for the opaqueness of my walls an impalpable iridescence, supernatural phenomena of many colours, in which legends were depicted as on a shifting and transitory window. But my sorrows were only increased thereby, because this mere change of lighting was enough to destroy the familiar impression I had of my room, thanks to which, save for the torture of going to bed, it had become quite endurable. Now I no longer recognised it, and felt uneasy in it, as in a room in some hotel or chalet, in a place where I had just arrived by train for the first time.

Riding at a jerky trot, Golo, filled with an infamous design, issued from the little triangular forest which softened with dark green the slope of a hill, and advanced fitfully towards the castle of poor Geneviève de Brabant. This castle was cut off short by a curved line which was in fact the circumference of one of the transparent ovals in the slides which were pushed into position through a slot in the lantern. It was only the wing of a castle, and in front of it stretched a moor on which Geneviève stood dreaming, wearing a blue girdle. The castle and the moor were yellow, but I could tell their colour without waiting to see them, for before the slides made their appearance the old-gold sonorous name of Brabant had given me an unmistakable clue. Golo stopped for a moment and listened sadly to the accompanying patter read aloud by my great-aunt, which he seemed perfectly to understand, for he modified his attitude with a docility not devoid of a degree of majesty, so as to conform to the indications given in the text; then he rode away at the same jerky trot. And nothing could arrest his slow progress. If the lantern were moved I could still distinguish Golo's horse advancing across the window-curtains, swelling out with their curves and diving into their folds. The body of Golo himself, being of the same supernatural substance as his steed's, overcame every material obstacle—everything that seemed to bar his way—by taking it as an ossature and absorbing it into himself: even the doorknob—on which, adapting themselves at once, his red cloak or his pale face, still as noble and as melancholy, floated invincibly—would never betray the least concern at this transvertebration.

And, indeed, I found plenty of charm in these bright projections, which seemed to emanate from a

Merovingian past and shed around me the reflections of such ancient history. But I cannot express the discomfort I felt at this intrusion of mystery and beauty into a room which I had succeeded in filling with my own personality until I thought no more of it than of myself. The anaesthetic effect of habit being destroyed, I would begin to think—and to feel—such melancholy things. The doorknob of my room, which was different to me from all the other doorknobs in the world, inasmuch as it seemed to move of its own accord and without my having to turn it, so unconscious had its manipulation become—lo and behold, it was now an astral body for Golo. And as soon as the dinner-bell rang I would hurry down to the dining-room, where the big hanging lamp, ignorant of Golo and Bluebeard but well acquainted with my family and the dish of stewed beef, shed the same light as on every other evening; and I would fall into the arms of my mother, whom the misfortunes of Geneviève de Brabant had made all the dearer to me, just as the crimes of Golo had driven me to a more than ordinarily scrupulous examination of my own conscience.

But after dinner, alas, I was soon obliged to leave Mamma, who stayed talking with the others, in the garden if it was fine, or in the little parlour where everyone took shelter when it was wet. Everyone except my grandmother, who held that "It's a pity to shut oneself indoors in the country," and used to have endless arguments with my father on the very wettest days, because he would send me up to my room with a book instead of letting me stay out of doors. "That is not the way to make him strong and active," she would say sadly, "especially this little man, who needs all the strength and will-power that he can get." My father would shrug his shoulders and study the barometer, for he took an interest in meteorology, while my mother, keeping very quiet so as not to disturb him, looked at him with tender respect, but not too hard, not wishing to penetrate the mysteries of his superior mind. But my grandmother, in all weathers, even when the rain was coming down in torrents and Françoise had rushed the precious wicker armchairs indoors so that they should not get soaked, was to be seen pacing the deserted rain-lashed garden, pushing back her disordered grey locks so that her forehead might be freer to absorb the health-giving draughts of wind and rain. She would say, "At last one can breathe!" and would trot up and down the sodden paths—too straight and symmetrical for her liking, owing to the want of any feeling for nature in the new gardener, whom my father had been asking all morning if the weather were going to improve—her keen, jerky little step regulated by the various effects wrought upon her soul by the intoxication of the storm, the power of hygiene, the stupidity of my upbringing and the symmetry of gardens, rather than by any anxiety (for that was quite unknown to her) to save her plum-coloured skirt from the mudstains beneath which it would gradually disappear to a height that was the constant bane and despair of her maid.

When these walks of my grandmother's took place after dinner there was one thing which never failed to bring her back to the house: this was if (at one of those points when her circular itinerary brought her back, moth-like, in sight of the lamp in the little parlour where the liqueurs were set out on the card-table) my great-aunt called out to her: "Bathilde! Come in and stop your husband drinking brandy!" For, simply to tease her (she had brought so different a type of mind into my father's family that everyone made fun of her), my great-aunt used to make my grandfather, who was forbidden liqueurs, take just a few drops. My poor grandmother would come in and beg and implore her husband not to taste the brandy; and he would get angry and gulp it down all the same, and she would go out again sad and discouraged, but still smiling, for she was so humble of heart and so gentle that her tenderness for others and her disregard for herself and her own troubles blended in a smile which, unlike those seen on the majority of human faces, bore no trace of irony save for herself, while for all of us kisses seemed to spring from her eyes, which could not look upon those she loved without seeming to bestow upon them passionate caresses. This torture inflicted on her by my great-aunt, the sight of my grandmother's vain entreaties, of her feeble attempts, doomed in advance, to remove the liqueur-glass from my grandfather's hands—all these were things of the sort to which, in later years, one can grow so accustomed as to smile at them and to take the persecutor's side resolutely and cheerfully enough to persuade oneself that it is not really persecution; but in those days they filled me with such horror that I longed to strike my great-aunt. And yet, as soon as I heard her "Bathilde! Come in and stop your husband drinking brandy," in my cowardice I became at once a man, and did what all we grown men do when face to face with suffering and injustice: I preferred not to see them; I ran up to the top of the house to cry by myself in a little room beside the schoolroom and beneath the roof, which smelt of orris-root and was scented also by a wild currant-bush which had climbed up between the stones of the outer wall and thrust a flowering branch in through the half-opened window. Intended for a more special and a baser use, this room, from which, in the daytime, I could see as far as the keep of Roussainville-le-Pin, was for a long time my place of refuge, doubtless because it was the only room whose door I was allowed to lock, whenever my occupation was such as required an inviolable solitude: reading or day-dreaming, tears or sensual pleasure. Alas! I did not realise that my own lack of will-power, my delicate health, and the consequent uncertainty as to my future, weighed far more heavily on my grandmother's mind than any little dietary indiscretion by her husband in the course of those endless perambulations, afternoon and evening, during which we used to see her handsome face passing to and fro, half raised towards the sky, its brown and wrinkled cheeks, which with age had acquired almost the purple hue of tilled fields in autumn, covered, if she were "going out," by a half-lifted veil, while upon them either the cold or some sad reflection invariably left the drying traces of an involuntary tear.

My sole consolation when I went upstairs for the night was that Mamma would come in and kiss me after I was in bed. But this good night lasted for so short a time, she went down again so soon, that the moment in which I heard her climb the stairs, and then caught the sound of her garden dress of blue muslin, from which hung little tassels of plaited straw, rustling along the double-doored corridor, was for me a moment of the utmost pain; for it heralded the moment which was to follow it, when she would have left me and gone downstairs again. So much so that I reached the point of hoping that this good night which I loved so much would come as late as possible, so as to prolong the time of respite during which Mamma would not yet have appeared. Sometimes when, after kissing me, she opened the door to go, I longed to call her back, to say to her "Kiss me just once more," but I knew that then she would at once look displeased, for the concession which she made to my wretchedness and agitation in coming up to give me this kiss of peace always annoyed my father, who thought such rituals absurd, and she would have liked to try to induce me to outgrow the need, the habit, of having her there at all, let alone get into the habit of asking her for an additional kiss when she was already crossing the threshold. And to see her look displeased destroyed all the calm and serenity she had brought me a moment before, when she had bent her loving face down over my bed, and held it out to me like a host for an act of peace-giving communion in which my lips might imbibe her real presence and with it the power to sleep. But those evenings on which Mamma stayed so short a time in my room were sweet indeed compared to those on which we had people to dinner, and therefore she did not come at all. Our "people" were usually limited to M. Swann, who, apart from a few passing strangers, was almost the only person who ever came to the house at Combray, sometimes to a neighbourly dinner (but less frequently since his unfortunate marriage, as my family did not care to receive his wife) and sometimes after dinner, uninvited. On those evenings when, as we sat in front of the house round the iron table beneath the big chestnut-tree, we heard, from the far end of the garden, not the shrill and assertive alarm bell which assailed and deafened with its ferruginous, interminable, frozen sound any member of the household who set it off on entering "without ringing," but the double tinkle, timid, oval, golden, of the visitors' bell, everyone would at once exclaim "A visitor! Who in the world can it be?" but they knew quite well that it could only be M. Swann. My great-aunt, speaking in a loud voice to set an example, in a tone which she endeavoured to make sound natural, would tell the others not to whisper so; that nothing could be more offensive to a stranger coming in, who would be led to think that people were saying things about him which he was not meant to hear; and then my grandmother, always happy to find an excuse for an additional turn in the garden, would be sent out to reconnoitre, and would take the opportunity to remove surreptitiously, as she passed, the stakes of a rose-tree or two, so as to make the roses look a little more natural, as a mother might run her hand through her boy's hair after the barber has smoothed it down, to make it look naturally wavy.

We would all wait there in suspense for the report which my grandmother would bring back from the enemy lines, as though there might be a choice between a large number of possible assailants, and then, soon after, my grandfather would say: "I recognise Swann's voice." And indeed one could tell him only by his voice, for it was difficult to make out his face with its arched nose and green eyes, under a high forehead fringed with fair, almost red hair, done in the Bressant style, because in the garden we used as little light as possible, so as not to attract mosquitoes; and I would slip away unobtrusively to order the liqueurs to be brought out, for my grandmother made a great point, thinking it "nicer," of their not being allowed to seem anything out of the ordinary, which we kept for visitors only. Although a far younger man, M. Swann was very attached to my grandfather, who had been an intimate friend of Swann's father, an excellent but eccentric man the ardour of whose feelings and the current of whose thoughts would often be checked or diverted by the most trifling thing. Several times in the course of a year I would hear my grandfather tell at table the story, which never varied, of the behaviour of M. Swann the elder upon the death of his wife, by whose bedside he had watched day and night. My grandfather, who had not seen him for a long time, hastened to join him at the Swanns' family property on the outskirts of Combray, and managed to entice him for a moment, weeping profusely, out of the death-chamber, so that he should not be present when the body was laid in its coffin. They took a turn or two in the park, where there was a little sunshine. Suddenly M. Swann seized my grandfather by the arm and cried, "Ah, my dear old friend, how fortunate we are to be walking here together on such a charming day! Don't you see how pretty they are, all these trees, my hawthorns, and my new pond, on which you have never congratulated me? You look as solemn as the grave. Don't you feel this little breeze? Ah! whatever you may say, it's good to be alive all the same, my dear Amédée!" And then, abruptly, the memory of his dead wife returned to him, and probably thinking it too complicated to inquire into how, at such a time, he could have allowed himself to be carried away by an impulse of happiness, he confined himself to a gesture which he habitually employed whenever any perplexing question came into his mind: that is, he passed his hand across his forehead, rubbed his eyes, and wiped his glasses. And yet he never got over the loss of his wife, but used to say to my grandfather, during the two years by which he survived her, "It's a funny thing, now; I very often think of my poor wife, but I cannot think of her for long at a time." "Often, but a little at a time, like poor old Swann," became one of my grandfather's favourite sayings, which he would apply to all manner of things. I should have assumed that this father of Swann's had been a monster if my grandfather, whom I regarded as a better judge than myself, and whose word was my law and often led me in the long run to pardon offences which I should have been inclined to condemn, had not gone on to exclaim, "But, after all, he had a heart of gold."

For many years, during the course of which—especially before his marriage—M. Swann the younger came often to see them at Combray, my great-aunt and my grandparents never suspected that he had entirely ceased to live in the society which his family had frequented, and that, under the sort of incognito which the name of Swann gave him among us, they were harbouring—with the complete innocence of a family of respectable innkeepers who have in their midst some celebrated highwayman without knowing it—one of the most distinguished members of the Jockey Club, a particular friend of the Comte de Paris and of the Prince of Wales, and one of the men most sought after in the aristocratic world of the Faubourg Saint-Germain.

Our utter ignorance of the brilliant social life which Swann led was, of course, due in part to his own reserve and discretion, but also to the fact that middle-class people in those days took what was almost a Hindu view of society, which they held to consist of sharply defined castes, so that everyone at his birth found himself called to that station in life which his parents already occupied, and from which nothing, save the accident of an exceptional career or of a "good" marriage, could extract you and translate you to a superior caste. M. Swann the elder had been a stockbroker; and so "young Swann" found himself immured for life in a caste whose members' fortunes, as in a category of tax-payers, varied between such and such limits of income. One knew the people with whom his father had associated, and so one knew his own associates, the people with whom he was "in a position" to mix. If he knew other people besides, those were youthful acquaintances on whom the old friends of his family, like my relatives, shut their eyes all the more good-naturedly because Swann himself, after he was left an orphan, still came most faithfully to see us; but we would have been ready to wager that the people outside our acquaintance whom Swann knew were of the sort to whom he would not have dared to raise his hat if he had met them while he was walking with us. Had it been absolutely essential to apply to Swann a social coefficient peculiar to himself, as distinct from all the other sons of other stockbrokers in his father's position, his coefficient would have been rather lower than theirs, because, being very simple in his habits, and having always had a "craze" for antiques and pictures, he now lived and amassed his collections in an old house which my grandmother longed to visit but which was situated on the Quai d'Orléans, a neighbourhood in which my great-aunt thought it most degrading to be quartered. "Are you really a connoisseur at least?" she would say to him; "I ask for your own sake, as you are likely to have fakes palmed off on you by the dealers," for she did not, in fact, endow him with any critical faculty, and had no great opinion of the intelligence of a man who, in conversation, would avoid serious topics and showed a very dull preciseness, not only when he gave us kitchen recipes, going into the most minute details, but even when my grandmother's sisters were talking to him about art. When challenged by them to give an opinion, or to express his admiration for some picture, he would remain almost disobligingly silent, and would then make amends by furnishing (if he could) some fact or other about the gallery in which the picture was hung, or the date at which it had been painted. But as a rule he would content himself with trying to amuse us by telling us about his latest adventure with someone whom we ourselves knew, such as the Combray chemist, or our cook, or our coachman. These stories certainly used to make my great-aunt laugh, but she could never decide whether this was on account of the absurd role which Swann invariably gave himself therein, or of the wit that he showed in telling them: "I must say you really are a regular character, M. Swann!"

As she was the only member of our family who could be described as a trifle "common," she would always take care to remark to strangers, when

Swann was mentioned, that he could easily, had he so wished, have lived in the Boulevard Haussmann or the Avenue de l'Opéra, and that he was the son of old M. Swann who must have left four or five million francs, but that it was a fad of his. A fad which, moreover, she thought was bound to amuse other people so much that in Paris, when M. Swann called on New Year's Day bringing her a little packet of marrons glacés, she never failed, if there were strangers in the room, to say to him: "Well, M. Swann, and do you still live next door to the bonded warehouse, so as to be sure of not missing your train when you go to Lyons?" and she would peep out of the corner of her eye, over her glasses, at the other visitors.

But if anyone had suggested to my great-aunt that this Swann, who, in his capacity as the son of old M. Swann, was "fully qualified" to be received by any of the "best people," by the most respected barristers and solicitors of Paris (though he was perhaps a trifle inclined to let this hereditary privilege go by default), had another almost secret existence of a wholly different kind; that when he left our house in Paris, saying that he must go home to bed, he would no sooner have turned the corner than he would stop, retrace his steps, and be off to some salon on whose like no stockbroker or associate of stockbrokers had ever set eyes—that would have seemed to my aunt as extraordinary as, to a woman of wider reading, the thought of being herself on terms of intimacy with Aristaeus and of learning that after having a chat with her he would plunge deep into the realms of Thetis, into an empire veiled from mortal eyes, in which Virgil depicts him as being received with open arms; or—to be content with an image more likely to have occurred to her, for she had seen it painted on the plates we used for biscuits at Combray—as the thought of having had to dinner Ali Baba, who, as soon as he finds himself alone and unobserved, will make his way into the cave, resplendent with its unsuspected treasures.

One day when he had come to see us after dinner in Paris, apologising for being in evening clothes, Françoise told us after he had left that she had got it from his coachman that he had been dining "with a princess." "A nice sort of princess," retorted my aunt, shrugging her shoulders without raising her eyes from her knitting, serenely sarcastic.

Altogether, my great-aunt treated him with scant ceremony. Since she was of the opinion that he ought to feel flattered by our invitations, she thought it only right and proper that he should never come to see us in summer without a basket of peaches or raspberries from his garden, and that from each of his visits to Italy he should bring back some photographs of old masters for me.

It seemed quite natural, therefore, to send for him whenever a recipe for some special sauce or for a pineapple salad was needed for one of our big dinner-parties, to which he himself would not be invited, being regarded as insufficiently important to be served up to new friends who might be in our house for the first time. If the conversation turned upon the princes of the House of France, "gentlemen you and I will never know, will we, and don't want to, do we?" my great-aunt would say tartly to Swann, who had, perhaps, a letter from Twickenham in his pocket; she would make him push the piano into place and turn over the music on evenings when my grandmother's sister sang, manipulating this person who was elsewhere so sought after with the rough simplicity of a child who will play with a collectors' piece with no more circumspection than if it were a cheap gewgaw. Doubtless the Swann who was a familiar figure in all the clubs of those days differed hugely from the Swann created by my great-aunt when, of an evening, in our little garden at Combray, after the two shy peals had sounded from the gate, she would inject and vitalise with everything she knew about the Swann family the obscure and shadowy figure who emerged, with my grandmother in his wake, from the dark background and who was identified by his voice. But then, even in the most insignificant details of our daily life, none of us can be said to constitute a material whole, which is identical for everyone, and need only be turned up like a page in an account-book or the record of a will; our social personality is a creation of the thoughts of other people. Even the simple act which we describe as "seeing someone we know" is to some extent an intellectual process. We pack the physical outline of the person we see with all the notions we have already formed about him, and in the total picture of him which we compose in our minds those notions have certainly the principal place. In the end they come to fill out so completely the curve of his cheeks, to follow so exactly the line of his nose, they blend so harmoniously in the sound of his voice as if it were no more than a transparent envelope, that each time we see the face or hear the voice it is these notions which we recognise and to which we listen. And so, no doubt, from the Swann they had constructed for themselves my family had left out, in their ignorance, a whole host of details of his life in the world of fashion, details which caused other people, when they met him, to see all the graces enthroned in his face and stopping at the line of his aquiline nose as at a natural frontier; but they had contrived also to put into this face divested of all glamour, vacant and roomy as an untenanted house, to plant in the depths of these under-valued eyes, a lingering residuum, vague but not unpleasing—half-memory and half-oblivion—of idle hours spent together after our weekly dinners, round the card-table or in the garden, during our companionable country life. Our friend's corporeal envelope had been so well lined with this residuum, as well as various earlier memories of his parents, that their own special Swann had become to my family a complete and living creature; so that even now I have the feeling of leaving someone I know for another quite different person when, going back in memory, I pass from the Swann whom I knew later and more intimately to this early Swann—this early Swann in whom I can distinguish the charming mistakes of my youth, and who in fact is less like his successor than he is like the other people I knew at that time, as though one's life were a picture gallery in which all the portraits of any one period had a marked family likeness, a similar tonality—this early Swann abounding in leisure, fragrant with the scent of the great chestnut-tree, of baskets of raspberries and of a sprig of tarragon.

And yet one day, when my grandmother had gone to ask some favour of a lady whom she had known at the Sacré Cœur (and with whom, because of our notions of caste, she had not cared to keep up any degree of intimacy in spite of several common interests), the Marquise de Villeparisis, of the famous house of Bouillon, this lady had said to her:

"I believe you know M. Swann very well; he's a great friend of my nephew and niece, the des Laumes."

My grandmother had returned from the call full of praise for the house, which overlooked some gardens, and in which Mme de Villeparisis had advised her to rent a flat, and also for a repairing tailor and his daughter who kept a little shop in the courtyard, into which she had gone to ask them to put a stitch in her skirt, which she had torn on the staircase. My grandmother had found these people perfectly charming: the girl, she said, was a jewel, and the tailor the best and most distinguished man she had ever seen. For in her eyes distinction was a thing wholly independent of social position. She was in ecstasies over some answer the tailor had made to her, saying to Mamma:

"Sévigné would not have put it better!" and, by way of contrast, of a nephew of Mme de Villeparisis whom she had met at the house:

"My dear, he is so common!"

Now, the effect of the remark about Swann had been, not to raise him in my great-aunt's estimation, but to lower Mme de Villeparisis. It appeared that the deference which, on my grandmother's authority, we owed to Mme de Villeparisis imposed on her the reciprocal obligation to do nothing that would render her less worthy of our regard, and that she had failed in this duty by becoming aware of Swann's existence and in allowing members of her family to associate with him. "What! She knows Swann? A person who, you always made out, was related to Marshal MacMahon!" This view of Swann's social position which prevailed in my family seemed to be confirmed later on by his marriage with a woman of the worst type, almost a prostitute, whom, to do him justice, he never attempted to introduce to us—for he continued to come to our house alone, though more and more seldom—but from whom they felt they could establish, on the assumption that he had found her there, the circle, unknown to them, in which he ordinarily moved.

But on one occasion my grandfather read in a newspaper that M. Swann was one of the most regular attendants at the Sunday luncheons given by the Duc de X———, whose father and uncle had been among our most prominent statesmen in the reign of Louis-Philippe. Now my grandfather was curious to learn all the smallest details which might help him to take a mental share in the private lives of men like Molé, the Duc Pasquier, or the Duc de Broglie. He was delighted to find that Swann associated with people who had known them. My great-aunt, on the other hand, interpreted this piece of news in a sense discreditable to Swann; for anyone who chose his associates outside the caste in which he had been born and bred, outside his "proper station," automatically lowered himself in her eyes. It seemed to her that such a one abdicated all claim to enjoy the fruits of the splendid connections with people of good position which prudent parents cultivate and store up for their children's benefit, and she had actually ceased to "see" the son of a lawyer of our acquaintance because he had married a "Highness" and had thereby stepped down—in her eyes—from the respectable position of a lawyer's son to that of those adventurers, upstart footmen or stable-boys mostly, to whom, we are told, queens have sometimes shown their favours. She objected, therefore, to my grandfather's plan of questioning Swann, when next he came to dine with us, about these people whose friendship with him we had discovered. At the same time my grandmother's two sisters, elderly spinsters who shared her nobility of character but lacked her intelligence, declared that they could not conceive what pleasure their brother-in-law could find in talking about such trifles. They were ladies of lofty aspirations, who for that reason were incapable of taking the least interest in what might be termed gossip, even if it had some historical import, or, generally speaking, in anything that was not directly associated with some aesthetic or virtuous object. So complete was their negation of interest in anything which seemed directly or indirectly connected with worldly matters that their sense of hearing—having finally come to realise its temporary futility when the tone of the conversation at the dinner-table became frivolous or merely mundane without the two old ladies' being able to guide it back to topics dear to themselves—would put its receptive organs into abeyance to the point of actually becoming atrophied. So that if my grandfather wished to attract the attention of the two sisters, he had to resort to some such physical stimuli as alienists adopt in dealing with their distracted patients: to wit, repeated taps on a glass with the blade of a knife, accompanied by a sharp word and a compelling glance, violent methods which these psychiatrists are apt to bring with them into their everyday life among the sane, either from force of professional habit or because they think the whole world a trifle mad.

Their interest grew, however, when, the day before Swann was to dine with us, and when he had made them a special present of a case of Asti, my great-aunt, who had in her hand a copy of the *Figaro* in which to the name of a picture then on view in a Corot exhibition were added the words, "from the collection of M. Charles Swann," asked: "Did you see that Swann is 'mentioned' in the *Figaro?*"

"But I've always told you," said my grandmother, "that he had a great deal of taste."

"You would, of course," retorted my great-aunt, "say anything just to seem different from *us.*" For, knowing that my grandmother never agreed with her, and not being quite confident that it was her own opinion which the rest of us invariably endorsed, she wished to extort from us a wholesale condemnation of my grandmother's views, against which she hoped to force us into solidarity with her own. But we sat silent. My grandmother's sisters having expressed a desire to mention to Swann this reference to him in the *Figaro,* my great-aunt dissuaded them. Whenever she saw in others an advantage, however trivial, which she herself lacked, she would persuade herself that it was no advantage at all, but a drawback, and would pity so as not to have to envy them.

"I don't think that would please him at all; I know very well that I should hate to see my name printed like that, as large as life, in the paper, and I shouldn't feel at all flattered if anyone spoke to me about it."

She did not, however, put any very great pressure upon my grandmother's sisters, for they, in their horror of vulgarity, had brought to such a fine art the concealment of a personal allusion in a wealth of ingenious circumlocution, that it would often pass unnoticed even by the person to whom it was addressed. As for my mother, her only thought was of trying to induce my father to speak to Swann, not about his wife but about his daughter, whom he worshipped, and for whose sake it was understood that he had ultimately made his unfortunate marriage.

"You need only say a word; just ask him how she is. It must be so very hard for him."

My father, however, was annoyed: "No, no; you have the most absurd ideas. It would be utterly ridiculous."

But the only one of us in whom the prospect of Swann's arrival gave rise to an unhappy foreboding was myself. This was because on the evenings when there were visitors, or just M. Swann, in the house, Mamma did not come up to my room. I dined before the others, and afterwards came and sat at table until eight o'clock, when it was understood that I must go upstairs; that frail and precious kiss which Mamma used normally to bestow on me when I was in bed and just going to sleep had to be transported from the dining-room to my bedroom where I must keep it inviolate all the time that it took me to undress, without letting its sweet charm be broken, without letting its volatile essence diffuse itself and evaporate; and it was precisely on those very evenings when I needed to receive it with special care that I was obliged to take it, to snatch it brusquely and in public, without even having the time or the equanimity to bring to what I was doing the single-minded attention of lunatics who compel themselves to exclude all other thoughts from their minds while they are shutting a door, so that when the sickness of uncertainty sweeps over them again they can triumphantly oppose it with the recollection of the precise moment when they shut the door.

We were all in the garden when the double tinkle of the visitors' bell sounded shyly. Everyone knew that it must be Swann, and yet they looked at one another inquiringly and sent my grandmother to reconnoitre.

"See that you thank him intelligibly for the wine," my grandfather warned his two sisters-in-law. "You know how good it is, and the case is huge."

"Now, don't start whispering!" said my great-aunt. "How would you like to come into a house and find everyone muttering to themselves?"

"Ah! There's M. Swann," cried my father. "Let's ask him if he thinks it will be fine tomorrow."

My mother fancied that a word from her would wipe out all the distress which my family had contrived to cause Swann since his marriage. She found an opportunity to draw him aside for a moment. But I followed her: I could not bring myself to let her out of my sight while I felt that in a few minutes I should have to leave her in the dining-room and go up to my bed without the consoling thought, as on ordinary evenings, that she would come up later to kiss me.

"Now, M. Swann," she said, "do tell me about your daughter. I'm sure she already has a taste for beautiful things, like her papa."

"Come along and sit down here with us all on the verandah," said my grandfather, coming up to him. My mother had to abandon her quest, but managed to extract from the restriction itself a further delicate thought, like good poets whom the tyranny of rhyme forces into the discovery of their finest lines.

"We can talk about her again when we are by ourselves," she said, or rather whispered to Swann. "Only a mother is capable of understanding these things. I'm sure that hers would agree with me."

And so we all sat down round the iron table. I should have liked not to think of the hours of anguish which I should have to spend that evening alone in my room, without being able to go to sleep: I tried to convince myself that they were of no importance since I should have forgotten them next morning, and to fix my mind on thoughts of the future which would carry me, as on a bridge, across the terrifying abyss that yawned at my feet. But my mind, strained by this foreboding, distended like the look which I shot at my mother, would not allow any extraneous impression to enter. Thoughts did indeed enter it, but only on the condition that they left behind them every element of beauty, or even of humour, by which I might have been distracted or beguiled. As a surgical patient, thanks to a local anaesthetic, can look on fully conscious while an operation is being performed upon him and yet feel nothing, I could repeat to myself some favourite lines, or watch my grandfather's efforts to talk to Swann about the Duc d'Audiffret-Pasquier, without being able to kindle any emotion from the one or amusement from the other. Hardly had my grandfather begun to question Swann about that orator when one of my grandmother's sisters, in whose ears the question echoed like a solemn but untimely silence which her natural politeness bade her interrupt, addressed the other with:

"Just fancy, Flora, I met a young Swedish governess today who told me some most interesting things about the co-operative movement in Scandinavia. We really must have her to dine here one evening."

"To be sure!" said her sister Flora, "but I haven't wasted my time either. I met such a clever old gentleman at M. Vinteuil's who knows Maubant quite well, and Maubant has told him every little thing about how he gets up his parts. It's the most interesting thing I ever heard. He's a neighbour of M. Vinteuil's, and I never knew; and he is so nice besides."

"M. Vinteuil is not the only one who has nice neighbours," cried my aunt Céline in a voice that was loud because of shyness and forced because of premeditation, darting, as she spoke, what she called a "significant glance" at Swann. And my aunt Flora, who realised that this veiled utterance was Céline's way of thanking Swann for the Asti, looked at him also with a blend of congratulation and irony, either because she simply wished to underline her sister's little witticism, or because she envied Swann his having inspired it, or because she imagined that he was embarrassed, and could not help having a little fun at his expense.

"I think it would be worth while," Flora went on, "to have this old gentleman to dinner. When you get him going on Maubant or Mme Materna he will talk for hours on end."

"That must be delightful," sighed my grandfather, in whose mind nature had unfortunately forgotten to include any capacity whatsoever for becoming passionately interested in the Swedish co-operative movement or in the methods employed by Maubant to get up his parts, just as it had forgotten to endow my grandmother's two sisters with a grain of that precious salt which one has oneself to "add to taste" in order to extract any savour from a narrative of the private life of Molé or of the Comte de Paris.

"By the way," said Swann to my grandfather, "what I was going to tell you has more to do than you might think with what you were asking me just now, for in some respects there has been very little change. I came across a passage in Saint-Simon this morning which would have amused you. It's in the volume which covers his mission to Spain; not one of the best, little more in fact than a journal, but at least a wonderfully well written journal, which fairly distinguishes it from the tedious journals we feel bound to read morning and evening."

"I don't agree with you: there are some days when I find reading the papers very pleasant indeed," my aunt Flora broke in, to show Swann that she had read the note about his Corot in the *Figaro*.

"Yes," aunt Céline went one better, "when they write about things or people in whom we are interested."

"I don't deny it," answered Swann in some bewilderment. "The fault I find with our journalism is that it forces us to take an interest in some fresh triviality or other every day, whereas only three or four books in a lifetime give us anything that is of real importance. Suppose that, every morning, when we tore the wrapper off our paper with fevered hands, a transmutation were to take place, and we were to find inside it—oh! I don't know; shall we say Pascal's *Pensées*?" He articulated the title with an ironic emphasis so as not to appear pedantic. "And then, in the gilt and tooled volumes which we open once in ten years," he went on, showing that contempt for worldly matters which some men of the world like to affect, "we should read that the Queen of the Hellenes had arrived at Cannes, or that the Princesse de Léon had given a fancy dress ball. In that way we should arrive at a happy medium." But at once regretting that he had allowed himself to speak of serious matters even in jest, he added ironically: "What a fine conversation we're having! I can't think why we climb to these lofty heights," and then, turning to my grandfather: "Well, Saint-Simon tells how Maulévrier had had the audacity to try to shake hands with his sons. You remember how he says of Maulévrier, 'Never did I find in that coarse bottle anything but ill-humour, boorishness, and folly.'"

"Coarse or not, I know bottles in which there is something very different," said Flora briskly, feeling bound to thank Swann as well as her sister, since the present of Asti had been addressed to them both. Céline laughed.

Swann was puzzled, but went on: "'I cannot say whether it was ignorance or cozenage,' writes Saint-Simon. 'He tried to give his hand to my children. I noticed it in time to prevent him.'"

My grandfather was already in ecstasies over "ignorance or cozenage," but Mlle Céline—the name of Saint-Simon, a "man of letters," having arrested the complete paralysis of her auditory faculties—was indignant:

"What! You admire that? Well, that's a fine thing, I must say! But what's it supposed to mean? Isn't one man as good as the next? What difference can it make whether he's a duke or a groom so long as he's intelligent and kind? He had a fine way of bringing up his children, your Saint-Simon, if he didn't teach them to shake hands with all decent folk. Really and truly, it's abominable. And you dare to quote it!"

And my grandfather, utterly depressed, realising how futile it would be, against this opposition, to attempt to get Swann to tell him the stories which would have amused him, murmured to my mother: "Just tell me again that line of yours which always comforts me so much on these occasions. Oh, yes: 'What virtues, Lord, Thou makest us abhor!' How good that is!"

I never took my eyes off my mother. I knew that when they were at table I should not be permitted to stay there for the whole of dinner-time, and that Mamma, for fear of annoying my father, would not allow me to kiss her several times in public, as I would have done in my room. And so I promised myself that in the dining-room, as they began to eat and drink and as I felt the hour approach, I would put beforehand into this kiss, which was bound to be so brief and furtive, everything that my own efforts could muster, would carefully choose in advance the exact spot on her cheek where I would imprint it, and would so prepare my thoughts as to be able, thanks to these mental preliminaries, to consecrate the whole of the minute Mamma would grant me to the sensation of her cheek against my lips, as a painter who can have his subject for short sittings only prepares his palette, and from what he remembers and from rough notes does in advance everything which he possibly can do in the sitter's absence. But tonight, before the dinner-bell had sounded, my grandfather said with unconscious cruelty: "The little man looks tired; he'd better go up to bed. Besides, we're dining late tonight."

And my father, who was less scrupulous than my grandmother or my mother in observing the letter of a treaty, went on: "Yes; run along; off to bed."

I would have kissed Mamma then and there, but at that moment the dinner-bell rang.

"No, no, leave your mother alone. You've said good night to one another, that's enough. These exhibitions are absurd. Go on upstairs."

And so I must set forth without viaticum; must climb each step of the staircase "against my heart," as the saying is, climbing in opposition to my heart's desire, which was to return to my mother, since she had not, by kissing me, given my heart leave to accompany me. That hateful staircase, up which I always went so sadly, gave out a smell of varnish which had, as it were, absorbed and crystallised the special quality of sorrow that I felt each evening, and made it perhaps even crueller to my sensibility because, when it assumed this olfactory guise, my intellect was powerless to resist it. When we have gone to sleep with a raging toothache and are conscious of it only as of a little girl whom we attempt, time after time, to pull out of the water, or a line of Molière which we repeat incessantly to ourselves, it is a great relief to wake up, so that our intelligence can disentangle the idea of toothache from any artificial semblance of heroism or rhythmic cadence. It was the converse of this relief which I felt when my anguish at having to go up to my room invaded my consciousness in a manner infinitely more rapid, instantaneous almost, a manner at once insidious and brutal, through the inhalation—far more poisonous than moral penetration—of the smell of varnish peculiar to that staircase.

Once in my room I had to stop every loophole, to close the shutters, to dig my own grave as I turned down the bed clothes, to wrap myself in the shroud of my nightshirt. But before burying myself in the iron bed which had been placed there because, on summer nights, I was too hot among the rep curtains of the four-poster, I was stirred to revolt, and attempted the desperate stratagem of a condemned prisoner. I wrote to my mother begging her to come upstairs for an important reason which I could not put in writing. My fear was that Françoise, my aunt's cook who used to be put in charge of me when I was at Combray, might refuse to take my note. I had a suspicion that, in her eyes, to carry a message to my mother when there was a guest would appear as flatly inconceivable as for the door-keeper of a theatre to hand a letter to an actor upon the stage. On the subject of things which might or might not be done she possessed a code at once imperious, abundant, subtle, and uncompromising on points themselves imperceptible or irrelevant, which gave it a resemblance to those ancient laws which combine such cruel ordinances as the massacre of infants at the breast with prohibitions of exaggerated refinement against "seething the kid in his mother's milk," or "eating of the sinew which is upon the hollow of the thigh." This code, judging by the sudden obstinacy which she would put into her refusal to carry out certain of our instructions, seemed to have provided for social complexities and refinements of etiquette which nothing in Françoise's background or in her career as a servant in a village household could have put into her head; and we were obliged to assume that there was latent in her some past existence in the ancient history of France, noble and little understood, as in those manufacturing towns where old mansions still testify to their former courtly days, and chemical workers toil among delicately sculptured scenes from *Le Miracle de Théophile* or *Les quatres fils Aymon.*

In this particular instance, the article of her code which made it highly improbable that—barring an outbreak of fire—Françoise would go down and disturb Mamma in the presence of M. Swann for so unimportant a person as myself was one embodying the respect she showed not only for the family (as for the dead, for the clergy, or for royalty), but also for the stranger within our gates; a respect which I should perhaps have found touching in a book, but which never failed to irritate me on her lips, because of the solemn and sentimental tones in which she would express it, and which irritated me more than usual this evening when the sacred character with which she invested the dinner-party might have the effect of making her decline to disturb its ceremonial. But to give myself a chance of success I had no hesitation in lying, telling her that it was not in the least myself who had wanted to write to Mamma, but Mamma who, on saying good night to me, had begged me not to forget to send her an answer about something she had asked me to look for, and that she would certainly be very angry if this note were not taken to her. I think that Françoise disbelieved me, for, like those primitive men whose senses were so much keener than our own, she could immediately detect, from signs imperceptible to the rest of us, the truth or falsehood of anything that we might wish to conceal from her. She studied the envelope for five minutes as though an examination of the paper itself and the look of my handwriting could enlighten her as to the nature of the contents, or tell her to which article of her code she ought to refer the matter. Then she went out with an air of resignation which seemed to imply: "It's hard lines on parents having a child like that."

A moment later she returned to say that they were still at the ice stage and that it was impossible for the butler to deliver the note at once, in front of everybody; but that when the finger-bowls were put round he would find a way of slipping it into Mamma's hand. At once my anxiety subsided; it was now no longer (as it had been a moment ago) until tomorrow that I had lost my mother, since my little note—though it would annoy her, no doubt, and doubly so because this stratagem would make me ridiculous in Swann's eyes—would at least admit me, invisible and enraptured, into the same room as herself, would whisper about me into her ear; since that forbidden and unfriendly dining-room, where but a moment ago the ice itself—with burned nuts in it—and the finger bowls seemed to me to be concealing pleasures that were baleful and of a mortal sadness because Mamma was tasting of them while I was far away, had opened its doors to me and, like a ripe fruit which bursts through its skin, was going to pour out into my intoxicated heart the sweetness of Mamma's attention while she was reading what I had written. Now I was no longer separated from her; the barriers were down; an exquisite thread united us. Besides, that was not all: for surely Mamma would come.

As for the agony through which I had just passed, I imagined that Swann would have laughed heartily at it if he had read my letter and had guessed its purpose; whereas, on the contrary, as I was to learn in due course, a similar anguish had been the bane of his life for many years, and no one perhaps could have understood my feelings at that moment so well as he; to him, the anguish that comes from knowing that the creature one adores is in some place of enjoyment where oneself is not and cannot follow—to him that anguish came through love, to which it is in a sense predestined, by which it will be seized upon and exploited; but when, as had befallen me, it possesses one's soul before love has yet entered into one's life, then it must drift, awaiting love's coming, vague and free, without precise attachment, at the disposal of one sentiment today, of another tomorrow, of filial piety or affection for a friend. And the joy with which I first bound myself apprentice, when Françoise returned to tell me that my letter would be delivered, Swann, too, had known well—that false joy which a friend or relative of the woman we love can give us, when, on his arrival at the house or theatre where she is to be found, for some ball or party or "first night" at which he is to meet her, he sees us wandering outside, desperately awaiting some opportunity of communicating with her. He recognises us, greets us familiarly, and asks what we are doing there. And when we invent a story of having some urgent message to give to his relative or friend, he assures us that nothing could be simpler, takes us in at the door, and promises to send her down to us in five minutes. How we love him—as at that moment I loved Françoise—the good-natured intermediary who by a single word has made supportable, human, almost propitious the inconceivable, infernal scene of gaiety in the thick of which we had been imagining swarms of enemies, perverse and seductive, beguiling away from us, even making laugh at us, the woman we love! If we are to judge of them by him—this relative who has accosted us and who is himself an initiate in those cruel mysteries—then the other guests cannot be so very demoniacal. Those inaccessible and excruciating hours during which she was about to taste of unknown pleasures—suddenly, through an unexpected breach, we have broken into them; suddenly we can picture to ourselves, we possess, we intervene upon, we have almost created, one of the moments the succession of which would have composed those hours, a moment as real as all the rest, if not actually more important to us because our mistress is more intensely a part of it: namely, the moment in which he goes to tell her that we are waiting below. And doubtless the other moments of the party would not have been so very different from this one, would be no more exquisite, no more calculated to make us suffer, since this kind friend has assured us that "Of course, she will be delighted to come down! It will be far more amusing for her to talk to you than to be bored up there." Alas! Swann had learned by experience that the good intentions of a third party are powerless to influence a woman who is annoyed to find herself pursued even into a ballroom by a man she does not love. Too often, the kind friend comes down again alone.

My mother did not appear, but without the slightest consideration for my self-respect (which depended upon her keeping up the fiction that she had asked me to let her know the result of my search for something or other) told Françoise to tell me, in so many words: "There is no answer"—words I have so often, since then, heard the hall-porters in grand hotels and the flunkeys in gambling-clubs and the like repeat to some poor girl who replies in bewilderment: "What! he said nothing? It's not possible. You did give him my letter, didn't you? Very well, I shall wait a little longer." And, just as she invariably protests that she does not need the extra gas-jet which the porter offers to light for her, and sits on there, hearing nothing further except an occasional remark on the weather which the porter exchanges with a bell-hop whom he will send off suddenly, when he notices the time, to put some customer's wine on the ice, so, having declined Françoise's offer to make me some tea or to stay beside me, I let her go off again to the pantry, and lay down and shut my eyes, trying not to hear the voices of my family who were drinking their coffee in the garden.

But after a few seconds I realised that, by writing that note to Mamma, by approaching—at the risk of making her angry—so near to her that I felt I could reach out and grasp the moment in which I should see her again, I had cut myself off from the possibility of going to sleep until I actually had seen her, and my heart began to beat more and more painfully as I increased my agitation by ordering myself to keep calm and to acquiesce in my ill-fortune. Then, suddenly, my anxiety subsided, a feeling of intense happiness coursed through me, as when a strong medicine begins to take effect and one's pain vanishes: I had formed a resolution to abandon all attempts to go to sleep without seeing Mamma, had made up my mind to kiss her at all costs, even though this meant the certainty of being in disgrace with her for long afterwards—when she herself came up to bed. The calm which succeeded my anguish filled me with extraordinary exhilaration, no less than my sense of expectation, my thirst for and my fear of danger. Noiselessly I opened the window and sat down on the foot of my bed. I hardly dared to move in case they should hear me from below. Outside, things too seemed frozen, rapt in a mute intentness not to disturb the moonlight which, duplicating each of them and throwing it back by the extension in front of it of a shadow denser and more concrete than its substance, had made the whole landscape at once thinner and larger, like a map which, after being folded up, is spread out upon the ground. What had to move—a leaf of the chestnut-tree, for instance—moved. But its minute quivering, total, self-contained, finished down to its minutest gradation and its last delicate tremor, did not impinge upon the rest of the scene, did not merge with it, remained circumscribed. Exposed upon this surface of silence which absorbed nothing of them, the most distant sounds, those which must have come from gardens at the far end of the town, could be distinguished with such exact "finish" that the impression they gave of coming from a distance seemed due only to their "pianissimo" execution, like those movements on muted strings so well performed by the orchestra of the Conservatoire that, even though one does not miss a single note, one thinks none the less that they are being played somewhere outside, a long way from the concert hall, so that all the old subscribers—my grandmother's sisters too, when Swann had given them his seats—used to strain their ears as if they had caught the distant approach of an army on the march, which had not yet rounded the corner of the Rue de Trévise.

I was well aware that I had placed myself in a position than which none could be counted upon to involve me in graver consequences at my parents' hands; consequences far graver, indeed, than a stranger would have imagined, and such as (he would have thought) could follow only some really shameful misdemeanour. But in the upbringing which they had given me faults were not classified in the same order as in that of other children, and I had been taught to place at the head of the list (doubtless because there was no other class of faults from which I needed to be more carefully protected) those in which I can now distinguish the common feature that one succumbs to them by yielding to a nervous impulse. But such a phrase had never been uttered in my hearing; no one had yet accounted for my temptations in a way which might have led me to believe that there was some excuse for my giving in to them, or that I was actually incapable of holding out against them. Yet I could easily recognise this class of transgressions by the anguish of mind which preceded as well as by the rigour of the punishment which followed them; and I knew that what I had just done was in the same category as certain other sins for which I had been severely punished, though infinitely more serious than they. When I went out to meet my mother on her way up to bed, and when she saw that I had stayed up in order to say good night to her again in the passage, I should not be allowed to stay in the house a day longer, I should be packed off to school next morning; so much was certain. Very well: had I been obliged, the next moment, to hurl myself out of the window, I should still have preferred such a fate. For what I wanted now was Mamma, to say good night to her. I had gone too far along the road which led to the fulfilment of this desire to be able to retrace my steps.

I could hear my parents' footsteps as they accompanied Swann to the gate, and when the clanging of the bell assured me that he had really gone, I crept to the window. Mamma was asking my father if he had thought the lobster good, and whether M. Swann had

had a second helping of the coffee-and-pistachio ice. "I thought it rather so-so," she was saying. "Next time we shall have to try another flavour."

"I can't tell you," said my great-aunt, "what a change I find in Swann. He is quite antiquated!" She had grown so accustomed to seeing Swann always in the same stage of adolescence that it was a shock to her to find him suddenly less young than the age she still attributed to him. And the others too were beginning to remark in Swann that abnormal, excessive, shameful and deserved senescence of bachelors, of all those for whom it seems that the great day which knows no morrow must be longer than for other men, since for them it is void of promise, and from its dawn the moments steadily accumulate without any subsequent partition among offspring.

"I fancy he has a lot of trouble with that wretched wife of his, who lives with a certain Monsieur de Charlus, as all Combray knows. It's the talk of the town."

My mother observed that, in spite of this, he had looked much less unhappy of late. "And he doesn't nearly so often do that trick of his, so like his father, of wiping his eyes and drawing his hand across his forehead. I think myself that in his heart of hearts he no longer loves that woman."

"Why, of course he doesn't," answered my grandfather. "He wrote me a letter about it, ages ago, to which I took care to pay no attention, but it left no doubt as to his feelings, or at any rate his love, for his wife. Hullo! you two; you never thanked him for the Asti," he went on, turning to his sisters-in-law.

"What! we never thanked him? I think, between you and me, that I put it to him quite neatly," replied my aunt Flora.

"Yes, you managed it very well; I admired you for it," said my aunt Céline.

"But you did it very prettily, too."

"Yes; I was rather proud of my remark about 'nice neighbours.'"

"What! Do you call that thanking him?" shouted my grandfather. "I heard that all right, but devil take me if I guessed it was meant for Swann. You may be quite sure he never noticed it."

"Come, come; Swann isn't a fool. I'm sure he understood. You didn't expect me to tell him the number of bottles, or to guess what he paid for them."

My father and mother were left alone and sat down for a moment; then my father said: "Well, shall we go up to bed?"

"As you wish, dear, though I don't feel at all sleepy. I don't know why; it can't be the coffee-ice—it wasn't strong enough to keep me awake like this. But I see a light in the servants' hall: poor Françoise has been sitting up for me, so I'll get her to unhook me while you go and undress."

My mother opened the latticed door which led from the hall to the staircase. Presently I heard her coming upstairs to close her window. I went quietly into the passage; my heart was beating so violently that I could hardly move, but at least it was throbbing no longer with anxiety, but with terror and joy. I saw in the well of the stair a light coming upwards, from Mamma's candle. Then I saw Mamma herself and I threw myself upon her. For an instant she looked at me in astonishment, not realising what could have happened. Then her face assumed an expression of anger. She said not a single word to me; and indeed I used to go for days on end without being spoken to, for far more venial offences than this. A single word from Mamma would have been an admission that further intercourse with me was within the bounds of possibility, and that might perhaps have appeared to me more terrible still, as indicating that, with such a punishment as was in store for me, mere silence and black looks would have been puerile. A word from her then would have implied the false calm with which one addresses a servant to whom one has just decided to give notice; the kiss one bestows on a son who is being packed off to enlist, which would have been denied him if it had merely been a matter of being angry with him for a few days. But she heard my father coming from the dressing-room, where he had gone to take off his clothes, and, to avoid the scene which he would make if he saw me, she said to me in a voice half-stifled with anger: "Off you go at once. Do you want your father to see you waiting there like an idiot?" But I implored her again: "Come and say good night to me," terrified as I saw the light from my father's candle already creeping up the wall, but also making use of his approach as a means of blackmail, in the hope that my mother, not wishing him to find me there, as find me he must if she continued to refuse me, would give in and say: "Go back to your room. I will come."

Too late: my father was upon us. Instinctively I murmured, though no one heard me, "I'm done for!"

I was not, however. My father used constantly to refuse to let me do things which were quite clearly allowed by the more liberal charters granted me by my mother and grandmother, because he paid no heed to "principles," and because for him there was no such thing as the "rule of law." For some quite irrelevant reason, or for no reason at all, he would at the last moment prevent me from taking some particular walk, one so regular, so hallowed, that to deprive me of it was a clear breach of faith; or again, as he had done this evening, long before the appointed hour he would snap out: "Run along up to bed now; no excuses!" But at the same time, because he was devoid of principles (in my grandmother's sense), he could not, strictly speaking, be called intransigent. He looked at me for a moment with an air of surprise and annoyance, and then when Mamma had told him, not without some embarrassment, what had happened, said to her: "Go along with him, then. You said just now that you didn't feel very sleepy, so stay in his room for a little. I don't need anything."

"But, my dear," my mother answered timidly, "whether or not I feel sleepy is not the point; we mustn't let the child get into the habit . . ."

"There's no question of getting into a habit," said my father, with a shrug of the shoulders; "you can see quite well that the child is unhappy. After all, we aren't gaolers. You'll end by making him ill, and a lot of good that will do. There are two beds in his room; tell Françoise to make up the big one for you, and stay with him for the rest of the night. Anyhow, I'm off to bed; I'm not so nervy as you. Good night."

It was impossible for me to thank my father; he would have been exasperated by what he called mawkishness. I stood there, not daring to move; he was still in front of us, a tall figure in his white nightshirt, crowned with the pink and violet cashmere scarf which he used to wrap around his head since he had begun to suffer from neuralgia, standing like Abraham in the engraving after Benozzo Gozzoli which M. Swann had given me, telling Sarah that she must tear herself away from Isaac. Many years have passed since that night. The wall of the staircase up which I had watched the light of his candle gradually climb was long ago demolished. And in myself, too, many things have perished which I imagined would last for ever, and new ones have arisen, giving birth to new sorrows and new joys which in those days I could not have foreseen, just as now the old are hard to understand. It is a long time, too, since my father has been able to say to Mamma: "Go along with the child." Never again will such moments be possible for me. But of late I have been increasingly able to catch, if I listen attentively, the sound of the sobs which I had the strength to control in my father's presence, and which broke out only when I found myself alone with Mamma. In reality their echo has never ceased; and it is only because life is now growing more and more quiet round about me that I hear them anew, like those convent bells which are so effectively drowned during the day by the noises of the street that one would suppose them to have stopped, until they ring out again through the silent evening air.

Mamma spent that night in my room: when I had just committed an offence for which I expected to be banished from the household, my parents gave me a far greater concession than I could ever have won as the reward of a good deed. Even at the moment when it manifested itself in this crowning mercy, my father's behaviour towards me still retained that arbitrary and unwarranted quality which was so characteristic of him and which arose from the fact that his actions were generally dictated by chance expediencies rather than based on any formal plan. And perhaps even what I called his severity, when he sent me off to bed, deserved that title less than my mother's or my grandmother's attitude, for his nature, which in some respects differed more than theirs from my own, had probably prevented him from realising until then how wretched I was every evening, something which my mother and grandmother knew well; but they loved me enough to be unwilling to spare me that suffering, which they hoped to teach me to overcome, so as to reduce my nervous sensibility and to strengthen my will. Whereas my father, whose affection for me was of another kind, would not, I suspect, have had the same courage, for as soon as he had grasped the fact that I was unhappy he had said to my mother: "Go and comfort him."

Mamma stayed that night in my room, and it seemed that she did not wish to mar by recrimination those hours which were so different from anything that I had had a right to expect, for when Françoise (who guessed that something extraordinary must have happened when she saw Mamma sitting by my side, holding my hand and letting me cry unchided) said to her: "But, Madame, what is young master crying for?" she replied: "Why, Françoise, he doesn't know himself: it's his nerves. Make up the big bed for me quickly and then go off to your own." And thus for the first time my unhappiness was regarded no longer as a punishable offence but as an involuntary ailment which had been officially recognised, a nervous condition for which I was in no way responsible: I had the consolation of no longer having to mingle apprehensive scruples with the bitterness of my tears; I could weep henceforth without sin. I felt no small degree of pride, either, in Françoise's presence at this return to humane conditions which, not an hour after Mamma had refused to come up to my room and had sent the snubbing message that I was to go to sleep, raised me to the dignity of a grown-up person, brought me of a sudden to a sort of puberty of sorrow, a manumission of tears. I ought to have been happy; I was not. It struck me that my mother had just made a first concession which must have been painful to her, that it was a first abdication on her part from the ideal she had formed for me, and that for the first time she who was so brave had to confess herself beaten. It struck me that if I had just won a victory it was over her, that I had succeeded, as sickness or sorrow or age might have succeeded, in relaxing her will, in undermining her judgment; and that this evening opened a new era, would remain a black date in the calendar. And if I had dared now, I should have said to Mamma: "No, I don't want you to, you mustn't sleep here." But I was conscious of the practical wisdom, of what would nowadays be called the realism, with which she tempered the ardent idealism of my grandmother's nature, and I knew that now the mischief was done she would prefer to let me enjoy the soothing pleasure of her company, and not to disturb my father again. Certainly my mother's beautiful face seemed to shine again with youth that evening, as she sat gently holding my hands and trying to check my tears; but this was just what I felt should not have been; her anger would have saddened me less than this new gentleness, unknown to my childhood experience; I felt that I had with an impious and secret finger traced a first wrinkle upon her soul and brought out a first white hair on her head. This thought redoubled my sobs, and then I saw that Mamma, who had never allowed herself to indulge in any undue emotion with me, was suddenly overcome by my tears and had to struggle to keep back her own. When she realised that I had noticed this, she said to me with a smile: "Why, my little chick, my little canary, he's going to make Mamma as silly as himself if this goes on. Look, since you can't sleep, and Mamma can't either, we mustn't go on in this stupid way; we must do something; I'll get one of your books." But I had none there. "Would you like me to get out the books now that your grandmother is going to give you for your birthday? Just think it over first, and don't be disappointed if there's nothing new for you then."

I was only too delighted, and Mamma went to fetch a parcel of books of which I could not distinguish, through the paper in which they were wrapped, any more than their short, wide format but which, even at this first glimpse, brief and obscure as it was, bade fair to eclipse already the paintbox of New Year's Day and the silkworms of the year before. The books were *La Mare au Diable, François le Champi, La Petite Fadette* and *Les Maîtres Sonneurs.* My grandmother, as I learned afterwards, had at first chosen Musset's poems, a volume of Rousseau, and *Indiana;* for while she considered light reading as unwholesome as sweets and cakes, she did not reflect that the strong breath of genius might have upon the mind even of a child an influence at once more dangerous and less invigorating than that of fresh air and sea breezes upon his body. But when my father had almost called her an imbecile on learning the names of the books she proposed to give me, she had journeyed back by herself to Jouy-le-Vicomte to the bookseller's, so that there should be no danger of my not having my present in time (it was a boiling hot day, and she had come home so unwell that the doctor had warned my mother not to allow her to tire herself so), and had fallen back upon the four pastoral novels of George Sand. "My dear," she had said to Mamma, "I could not bring myself to give the child anything that was not well written."

The truth was that she could never permit herself to buy anything from which no intellectual profit was to be derived, above all the profit which fine things afford us by teaching us to seek our pleasures elsewhere than in the barren satisfaction of worldly wealth. Even when she had to make someone a present of the kind called "useful," when she had to give an armchair or some table-silver or a walking-stick, she would choose antiques, as though their long desuetude had effaced from them any semblance of utility and fitted them rather to instruct us in the lives of the men of other days than to serve the common requirements of our own. She would have liked me to have in my room photographs of ancient buildings or of beautiful places. But at the moment of buying them, and for all that the subject of the picture had an aesthetic value, she would find that vulgarity and utility had too prominent a part in them, through the mechanical nature of their reproduction by photography. She attempted by a subterfuge, if not to eliminate altogether this commercial banality, at least to minimise it, to supplant it to a certain extent with what was art still, to introduce, as it were, several "thicknesses" of art: instead of photographs of Chartres Cathedral, of the Fountains of Saint-Cloud, or of Vesuvius, she would inquire of Swann whether some great painter had not depicted them, and preferred to give me photographs of "Chartres Cathedral" after Corot, of the "Fountains of Saint-Cloud" after Hubert Robert, and of "Vesuvius" after Turner, which were a stage higher in the scale of art. But although the photographer had been prevented from reproducing directly these masterpieces or beauties of nature, and had there been replaced by a great artist, he resumed his odious position when it came to reproducing the artist's interpretation. Accordingly, having to reckon again with vulgarity, my grandmother would endeavour to postpone the moment of contact still further. She would ask Swann if the picture had not been engraved, preferring, when possible, old engravings with some interest of association apart from themselves, such, for example, as show us a masterpiece in a state in which we can no longer see it today (like Morghen's print of Leonardo's "Last Supper" before its defacement). It must be admitted that the results of this method of interpreting the art of making presents were not always happy. The idea which I formed of Venice, from a drawing by Titian which is supposed to have the lagoon in the background, was certainly far less accurate than what I should have derived from ordinary photographs. We could no longer keep count in the family (when my great-aunt wanted to draw up an indictment of my grandmother) of all the armchairs she had presented to married couples, young and old, which on a first attempt to sit down upon them had at once collapsed beneath the weight of their recipients. But my grandmother would have thought it sordid to concern herself too closely with the solidity of any piece of furniture in which could still be discerned a flourish, a smile, a brave conceit of the past. And even what in such pieces answered a material need, since it did so in a manner to which we are no longer accustomed, charmed her like those old forms of speech in which we can still see traces of a metaphor whose fine point has been worn away by the rough usage of our modern tongue. As it happened, the pastoral novels of George Sand which she was giving me for my birthday were regular lumber-rooms full of expressions that have fallen out of use and become quaint and picturesque, and are now only to be found in country dialects. And my grandmother had bought them in preference to other books, as she would more readily have taken a house with a Gothic dovecot or some other such piece of antiquity as will exert a benign influence on the mind by giving it a hankering for impossible journeys through the realms of time.

Mamma sat down by my bed; she had chosen *François le Champi,* whose reddish cover and incomprehensible title gave it, for me, a distinct personality and a mysterious attraction. I had not then read any real novels. I had heard it said that George Sand was a typical novelist. This predisposed me to imagine that *François le Champi* contained something inexpressibly delicious. The narrative devices designed to arouse curiosity or melt to pity, certain modes of expression which disturb or sadden the reader, and which, with a little experience, he may recognise as common to a great many novels, seemed to me—for whom a new book was not one of a number of similar objects but, as it were, a unique person, absolutely self-contained—simply an intoxicating distillation of the peculiar essence of *François le Champi.* Beneath the everyday incidents, the ordinary objects and common words, I sensed a strange and individual tone of voice. The plot began to unfold: to me it seemed all the more obscure because in those days, when I read, I used often to day-dream about something quite different for page after page. And the gaps which this habit left in my knowledge of the story were widened by the fact that when it was Mamma who was reading to me aloud she left all the love-scenes out. And so all the odd changes which take place in the relations between the miller's wife and the boy, changes which only the gradual dawning of love can explain, seemed to me steeped in a mystery the key to which (I readily believed) lay in that strange and mellifluous name of *Champi,* which invested the boy who bore it, I had no idea why, with its own vivid, ruddy, charming colour. If my mother was not a faithful reader, she was none the less an admirable one, when reading a work in which she found the note of true feeling, in the respectful simplicity of her interpretation and the beauty and sweetness of her voice. Even in ordinary life, when it was not works of art but men and women whom she was moved to pity or admire, it was touching to observe with what deference she would banish from her voice, her gestures, from her whole conversation, now the note of gaiety which might have distressed some mother who had once lost a child, now the recollection of an event or anniversary which might have reminded some old gentleman of the burden of his years, now the household topic which might have bored some young man of letters. And so, when she read aloud the prose of George Sand, prose which is everywhere redolent of that generosity and moral distinction which Mamma had learned from my grandmother to place above all other qualities in life, and which I was not to teach her until much later to refrain from placing above all other qualities in literature too, taking pains to banish from her voice any pettiness or affectation which might have choked that powerful stream of language, she supplied all the natural tenderness, all the lavish sweetness which they demanded to sentences which seemed to have been composed for her voice and which were all, so to speak, within the compass of her sensibility. She found, to tackle them in the required tone, the warmth of feeling which pre-existed and dictated them, but which is not to be found in the words themselves, and by this means she smoothed away, as she read, any harshness or discordance in the tenses of verbs, endowing the imperfect and the preterite with all the sweetness to be found in generosity, all the melancholy to be found in love, guiding the sentence that was drawing to a close towards the one that was about to begin, now hastening, now slackening the pace of the syllables so as to bring them, despite their differences of quantity, into a uniform rhythm, and breathing into this quite ordinary prose a kind of emotional life and continuity.

My aching heart was soothed; I let myself be borne upon the current of this gentle night on which I had my mother by my side. I knew that such a night could not be repeated; that the strongest desire I had in the world, namely, to keep my mother in my room through the sad hours of darkness, ran too much counter to general requirements and to the wishes of others for such a concession as had been granted me this evening to be anything but a rare and artificial exception. Tomorrow night my anguish would return and Mamma would not stay by my side. But when my anguish was assuaged, I could no longer understand it; besides, tomorrow was still a long way off; I told myself that I should still have time to take preventive action, although that time could bring me no access of power since these things were in no way dependent upon the exercise of my will, and seemed not quite inevitable only because they were still separated from me by this short interval.

And so it was that, for a long time afterwards, when I lay awake at night and revived old memories of Combray, I saw no more of it than this sort of luminous panel, sharply defined against a vague and shadowy background, like the panels which the glow of a Bengal light or a searchlight beam will cut out and illuminate in a building the other parts of which remain plunged in darkness: broad enough at its base, the little parlour, the dining-room, the opening of the dark path from which M. Swann, the unwitting author of my sufferings, would emerge, the hall through which I would journey to the first step of that staircase, so painful to climb, which constituted, all by itself, the slender cone of this irregular pyramid; and, at the summit, my bedroom, with the little passage through whose glazed door Mamma would enter; in a word, seen always at the same evening hour, isolated from all its possible surroundings, detached and solitary against the dark background, the bare minimum of scenery necessary (like the décor one sees prescribed on the title-page of an old play, for its performance in the provinces) to the drama of my undressing; as though all Combray had consisted of but two floors joined by a slender staircase, and as though there had been no time there but seven o'clock at night. I must own that I could have assured any questioner that Combray did include other scenes and did exist at other hours than these. But since the facts which I should then have recalled would have been prompted only by voluntary memory, the memory of the intellect, and since the pictures which that kind of memory shows us preserve nothing of the past itself, I should never have had any wish to ponder over this residue of Combray. To me it was in reality all dead.

Permanently dead? Very possibly.

There is a large element of chance in these matters, and a second chance occurrence, that of our own death, often prevents us from awaiting for any length of time the favours of the first.

I feel that there is much to be said for the Celtic belief that the souls of those whom we have lost are held captive in some inferior being, in an animal, in a plant, in some inanimate object, and thus effectively lost to us until the day (which to many never comes) when we happen to pass by the tree or to obtain possession of the object which forms their prison. Then they start and tremble, they call us by our name, and as soon as we have recognised them the spell is broken. Delivered by us, they have overcome death and return to share our life.

And so it is with our own past. It is a labour in vain to attempt to recapture it: all the efforts of our intellect must prove futile. The past is hidden somewhere outside the realm, beyond the reach of intellect, in some material object (in the sensation which that material object will give us) of which we have no inkling. And it depends on chance whether or not we come upon this object before we ourselves must die.

Many years had elapsed during which nothing of Combray, except what lay in the theatre and the drama of my going to bed there, had any existence for me, when one day in winter, on my return home, my mother, seeing that I was cold, offered me some tea, a thing I did not ordinarily take. I declined at first, and then, for no particular reason, changed my mind. She sent for one of those squat, plump little cakes called "petites madeleines," which look as though they had been moulded in the fluted valve of a scallop shell. And soon, mechanically, dispirited after a dreary day with the prospect of a depressing morrow, I raised to my lips a spoonful of the tea in which I had soaked a morsel of the cake. No sooner had the warm liquid mixed with the crumbs touched my palate than a shiver ran through me and I stopped, intent upon the extraordinary thing that was happening to me. An exquisite pleasure had invaded my senses, something isolated, detached, with no suggestion of its origin. And at once the vicissitudes of life had become indifferent to me, its disasters innocuous, its brevity illusory—this new sensation having had the effect, which love has, of filling me with a precious essence; or rather this essence was not in me, it *was* me. I had ceased now to feel mediocre, contingent, mortal. Whence could it have come to me, this all-powerful joy? I sensed that it was connected with the taste of the tea and the cake, but that it infinitely transcended those savours, could not, indeed, be of the same nature. Where did it come from? What did it mean? How could I seize and apprehend it?

I drink a second mouthful, in which I find nothing more than in the first, then a third, which gives me rather less than the second. It is time to stop; the potion is losing its virtue. It is plain that the truth I am seeking lies not in the cup but in myself. The drink has called it into being, but does not know it, and can only repeat indefinitely, with a progressive diminution of strength, the same message which I cannot interpret, though I hope at least to be able to call it forth again and to find it there presently, intact and at my disposal, for my final enlightenment. I put down the cup and examine my own mind. It alone can discover the truth. But how? What an abyss of uncertainty, whenever the mind feels overtaken by itself; when it, the seeker, is at the same time the dark region through which it must go seeking and where all its equipment will avail it nothing. Seek? More than that: create. It is face to face with something which does not yet exist, which it alone can make actual, which it alone can bring into the light of day.

And I begin again to ask myself what it could have been, this unremembered state which brought with it no logical proof, but the indisputable evidence, of its felicity, its reality, and in whose presence other states of consciousness melted and vanished. I want to try to make it reappear. I retrace my thoughts to the moment at which I drank the first spoonful of tea. I rediscover the same state, illuminated by no fresh light. I ask my mind to make one further effort, to bring back once more the fleeting sensation. And so that nothing may interrupt it in its course I shut out every obstacle, every extraneous idea, I stop my ears and screen my attention from the sounds from the next room. And then, feeling that my mind is tiring itself without having any success to report, I compel it for a change to enjoy the distraction which I have just denied it, to think of other things, to rest and refresh itself before making a final effort. And then for the second time I clear an empty space in front of it; I place in position before my mind's eye the still recent taste of that first mouthful, and I feel something start within me, something that leaves its resting-place and attempts to rise, something that has been anchored at a great depth; I do not know yet what it is, but I can feel it mounting slowly; I can measure the resistance, I can hear the echo of great spaces traversed.

Undoubtedly what is thus palpitating in the depths of my being must be the image, the visual memory which, being linked to that taste, is trying to follow it into my conscious mind. But its struggles are too far off, too confused and chaotic; scarcely can I perceive the neutral glow into which the elusive whirling medley of stirred-up colours is fused, and I cannot distinguish its form, cannot invite it, as the one possible interpreter, to translate for me the evidence of its contemporary, its inseparable paramour, the taste, cannot ask it to inform me what special circumstance is in question, from what period in my past life.

Will it ultimately reach the clear surface of my consciousness, this memory, this old, dead moment which the magnetism of an identical moment has travelled so far to importune, to disturb, to raise up out of the very depths of my being? I cannot tell. Now I feel nothing; it has stopped, has perhaps sunk back into its darkness, from which who can say whether it will ever rise again? Ten times over I must essay the task, must lean down over the abyss. And each time the cowardice that deters us from every difficult task, every important enterprise, has urged me to leave the thing alone, to drink my tea and to think merely of the worries of today and my hopes for tomorrow, which can be brooded over painlessly.

And suddenly the memory revealed itself. The taste was that of the little piece of madeleine which on Sunday mornings at Combray (because on those mornings I did not go out before mass), when I went to say good morning to her in her bedroom, my aunt Léonie used to give me, dipping it first in her own cup of tea or tisane. The sight of the little madeleine had recalled nothing to my mind before I tasted it, perhaps because I had so often seen such things in the meantime, without tasting them, on the trays in pastry-cooks' windows, that their image had dissociated itself from those Combray days to take its place among others more recent; perhaps because, of those memories so long abandoned and put out of mind, nothing now survived, everything was scattered; the shapes of things, including that of the little scallop-shell of pastry, so richly sensual under its severe, religious folds, were either obliterated or had been so long dormant as to have lost the power of expansion which would have allowed them to resume their place in my consciousness. But when from a long-distant past nothing subsists, after the people are dead, after the things are broken and scattered, taste and smell alone, more fragile but more enduring, more immaterial, more persistent, more faithful, remain poised a long time, like souls, remembering, waiting, hoping, amid the ruins of all the rest; and bear unflinchingly, in the tiny and almost impalpable drop of their essence, the vast structure of recollection.

And as soon as I had recognised the taste of the piece of madeleine soaked in her decoction of lime-blossom which my aunt used to give me (although I did not yet know and must long postpone the discovery of why this memory made me so happy) immediately the old grey house upon the street, where her room was, rose up like a stage set to attach itself to the little pavilion opening on to the garden which had been built out behind it for my parents (the isolated segment which until that moment had been all that I could see); and with the house the town, from morning to night and in all weathers, the Square where I used to be sent before lunch, the streets along which I used to run errands, the country roads we took when it was fine. And as in the game wherein the Japanese amuse themselves by filling a porcelain bowl with water and steeping in it little pieces of paper which until then are without character or form, but, the moment they become wet, stretch and twist and take on colour and distinctive shape, become flowers or houses or people, solid and recognisable, so in that moment all the flowers in our garden and in M. Swann's park, and the water-lilies on the Vivonne and the good folk of the village and their little dwellings and the parish church and the whole of Combray and its surroundings, taking shape and solidity, sprang into being, town and gardens alike, from my cup of tea.

# Germany and Czechoslovakia

## Friedrich Hölderlin (1770–1843)

*Translated by Michael Hamburger*

Friedrich Hölderlin was a student of theology with Hegel at Tübingen. His poetry, like Hegel's philosophy, is a reaction against the materialism and rationalism of the Enlightenment. Both Hölderlin and Hegel were in pursuit of the *Geist* or "spirit" of God. In the *Phenomenology of Spirit,* Hegel claimed he had found it and that it is revealed in his philosophical system, which would bring philosophy's search for truth to an end. Hölderlin was less optimistic. His poems record his impassioned search for the divine. This quest for the divine, of which Hölderlin said he could find only "traces" in the contemporary world, made a strong impression on the modern philosopher Martin Heidegger and through him, on recent literary theory. As Hölderlin puts it in "Patmos,"

Near is
And difficult to grasp, the God.

In European poetry of the seventeenth and eighteenth centuries, the Greek experience of divinity was reduced to ornamentation and mannerism. For archaic poets such as Pindar (pp. 491–497), however, the divine was real, and divinity was revealed, however fitfully, in moments such as the athletic victories celebrated in Pindar's odes. Hölderlin spent years studying, translating, and imitating Pindar. Many poets have tried, usually with dismal results, to imitate the conventions of Pindar's odes (see Horace's amusing attempt, pp. 670–673), but only Hölderlin has been able to capture Pindar's spirit, with its acute sensitivity to "theophany" (the sudden appearance of the divine). "Patmos" is an ode after the manner of Pindar, which records the poet's search for the divine as it appeared on the island of Patmos to Saint John (author of the final book of the New Testament, the Apocalypse). For Hölderlin, poetry was supremely important for its ability to record such traces, for it can point the reader to the experiences that engendered the traces. As he says toward the conclusion of the poem,

What the Father
Who reigns over all loves most
Is that the solid letter
Be given scrupulous care

One of the central aims of the Romantic movement in the West was to regain through poetry a sense of participation in a world that had been de-divinized, most recently through the mechanistic theories prevalent in the Enlightenment. The universe had come to be seen as a great machine, controlled by the laws of cause and effect, and best understood by science. In their efforts to re-divinize the physical world and to find common ground between Greek and Christian experiences of the divine, Hölderlin's poems represent some of the noblest and most influential efforts of European Romantic poetry.

## Patmos

*For the Landgrave of Homburg*

Near is
And difficult to grasp, the God.
But where danger threatens
That which saves from it also grows.
In gloomy places dwell
The eagles, and fearless over
The chasm walk the sons of the Alps
On bridges lightly built.
Therefore, since round about
Are heaped the summits of Time
And the most loved live near, growing faint
On mountains most separate,
Give us innocent water,
O pinions give us, with minds most faithful
To cross over and to return.

So I spoke, when more swiftly
Than ever I had expected,
And far as I never thought
I should come, a Genius carried me
From my own house. There glimmered
In twilight, as I went,
The shadowy wood
And the yearning streams of
My homeland; no longer I knew those regions;
But soon, in a radiance fresh,
Mysteriously,
In the golden haze,
Quickly grown up,
With strides of the sun,
And fragrant with a thousand peaks,

Now Asia burst into flower for me, and dazzled
I looked for one thing there I might know, being unaccustomed
To those wide streets where down
From Tmolus drives
The golden-bedded Pactolus,
And Taurus stands, and Messogis,
And full of flowers the garden,
A quiet fire; but in the light, high up
There blossoms the silver snow;
And, witness to life immortal,

On inaccessible walls
Pristine the ivy grows, and supported
On living pillars, cedars and laurels,
There stand the festive,
The palaces built by gods.

But around Asia's gates there murmur,
Extending this way and that
In the uncertain plain of the sea,
Shadowless roads enough;
Yet the boatman knows the islands.
And when I heard
That of the near islands one
Was Patmos,
I greatly desired
There to be lodged, and there
To approach the dark grotto.
For not like Cyprus,
The rich in wellsprings,
Nor any of the others
Magnificently does Patmos dwell,

Hospitable nonetheless
In her poorer house
She is,
And when, after shipwreck or lamenting for
His homeland or else for
The friend departed from him,
A stranger draws near
To her, she is glad to hear it, and her children,
The voices of the hot noonday copse,
And where the sand falls, and the field's
Flat surface cracks, the sounds—
These hear him, and lovingly all is loud
With the man's re-echoed lament. So once
She tended the God-beloved,
The seer who in blessèd youth

Had walked with
The son of the Highest, inseparable, for
The bearer of thunder loved the disciple's
Ingenuousness, and the attentive man
Saw the face of the God exactly
When over the mystery of the vine
They sat together at the banqueting hour
And in his great soul, calmly foreknowing,

The Lord pronounced death and the ultimate love, for never
He could find words enough
To say about kindness, then, and to soothe, when
He saw it, the wrath of the world.
For all things are good. After that he died. Much could
Be said of it. And the friends at the very last
Saw him, the gladdest, looking up triumphant,

Yet they were sad, now that
The evening had come, amazed,
For the souls of these men contained
Things greatly predetermined, but under the sun they loved
This life and were loath to part from
The visible face of the Lord
And their homeland. Driven in,
Like fire into iron, was this, and beside them
The loved one's shadow walked.
Therefore he sent them
The Spirit, and mightily trembled
The house, and God's thunderstorms rolled
Distantly rumbling above
Their heads foreknowledge bowed, when deep in thought
Assembled were the heroes of death,

Now that, departing,
Once more he appeared to them.
For now the kingly one extinguished
The day of the sun and broke
The straightly beaming, the sceptre,
Divinely suffering, yet of his own free will,
For it was to come back when
The time was due. To have done so later
Would not have been good, and the work of men
Abruptly broken off, disloyally, and from now on
A joy it was
To dwell in loving Night and in fixed,
Ingenuous eyes to preserve
Abysses of wisdom. And low down at
The foot of mountains, too, will living images thrive,

Yet dreadful it is how here and there
Unendingly God disperses whatever lives.
For only to part from the sight
Of their dear friends
And far across the mountains to go
Alone, when doubly

Perceived, heavenly spirit before had been
Unanimous; and not predicted was this,
But seized them by the hair, on the instant,
When suddenly the God
Far off in haste looked back
At them, and vowing,
So that he would stay, from now on goldenly
Bound fast as to ropes,
Calling the evil by name, they linked hands—

But when thereupon he dies
To whom beauty most adhered, so that
A miracle was wrought in his person and
The Heavenly had pointed at him,
And when, an enigma to one another
For ever, they cannot understand
One another who lived together
Conjoined by remembrance, and not only
The sand or the willows it takes away,
And seizes the temples, when even
The demigod's honour and that of his friends
Is blown away by the wind, and the Highest
Himself averts his face
Because nowhere now
An immortal is to be seen in the skies or
On our green earth, what is this?

It is the sower's cast when he scoops up
The wheat in his shovel
And throws it, towards clear space, swinging it over the
thrashing-floor.
The husk falls at his feet, but
The grain reaches its end,
And there's no harm if some of it
Is lost, and of the speech
The living sound dies away,
For the work of gods, too, is like our own,
Not all things at once does the Highest intend.
The pit bears iron, though,
And glowing resins Etna,
And so I should have wealth
With which to form an image and see
The Christ as he truly was,

But if someone spurred himself on
And, talking sadly, on the road, when I was

Defenceless, attacked me, so that amazed I tried
To copy the God's own image, I, a servant—
In anger visible once I saw
The Lord of Heaven, not that I should be something, but
To learn. Benign they are, but what they most abhor,
While their reign lasts, is falsehood, and then
What's human no longer counts among human kind.
For they do not govern, the fate
It is of immortals that governs, and their work
Proceeds by its own force and hurrying seeks its end.
For when heavenly triumph goes higher
The jubilant son of the Highest
Is called like the sun by the strong,

A secret token, and here is the wand
Of song, signalling downward,
For nothing is common. The dead
He reawakens whom coarseness has not
Made captive yet. But many timid eyes
Are waiting to see the light.
They are reluctant to flower
Beneath the searing beam, though it is
The golden bridle that curbs their courage.
But when, as if
By swelling eyebrows made
Oblivious of the world
A quietly shining strength falls from holy scripture,
Rejoicing in grace, they
May practise upon the quiet gaze.

And if the Heavenly now
Love me as I believe,
How much more you
They surely love,
For one thing I know:
The eternal Father's will
Means much to you. Now silent is
His sign on thundering heaven. And there is one who stands
Beneath it his whole life long. For Christ lives yet.
But all the heroes, his sons,
Have come, and holy scriptures
About him, and lightning is explained by
The deeds of the world until now,
A race that cannot be stopped. But he is present in it. For known
To him are all his works from the beginning.

Too long, too long now
The honour of the Heavenly has been invisible.
For almost they must guide
Our fingers, and shamefully
A power is wrestling our hearts from us.
For every one of the Heavenly wants sacrifices, and
When one of these was omitted
No good ever came of it.
We have served Mother Earth
And lately have served the sunlight,
Unwittingly, but what the Father
Who reigns over all loves most
Is that the solid letter
Be given scrupulous care, and the existing
Be well interpreted. This German song observes.

## Rainer Maria Rilke (1875–1926)

*Translated by A. Poulin Jr.*

Rainer Maria Rilke is usually considered the greatest German-language poet of the twentieth century. He was born in Prague just eight years before Franz Kafka. He came from a German-speaking family of Austrian descent that had served the Austro-Hungarian Empire in military and professional activities. Rilke passed an unhappy childhood and adolescence caught between a mother who had wanted a daughter—and consequently named him Maria and dressed him in girl's clothing—and an uncle who pushed him into military schools, which he came to hate. Rilke discovered his literary vocation early in life and cultivated an image of himself as a decadent aesthete eager to establish relationships with anyone who might advance his artistic career.

Rilke disliked his home city of Prague and spent much of his life traveling and living elsewhere. He was particularly influenced by his years in Paris, where he served a stint as the sculptor Auguste Rodin's secretary. Rilke met, and initiated a long and rich correspondence with, the French novelist André Gide, who introduced him into a circle of French intellectuals that included Paul Valéry, a poet Rilke admired and eventually translated into German. In addition to his masterful poetry and prose in German, Rilke wrote significant French verse and also worked in Russian and Italian.

The two poems included here are from Rilke's greatest work, the ten *Duino Elegies*. These poems take their name from Duino, located on the Adriatic coast near Trieste, Italy. Rilke was staying in a castle there in 1912, after a long period of poetic barrenness, when he seemed to hear a voice coming from the sea, giving him the first line of his ten-poem cycle: "And if I cried, who'd listen to me in those angelic orders?" This dramatic moment renewed Rilke's poetic inspiration and touched off a new period of artistic creativity.

Rilke's haunting *Duino Elegies,* like all great poetry, resist easy translation into a simple message. They are unusually abstract and philosophical: the reader must think hard to grasp their images and follow their movement. Rilke's designation of them as "elegies" indicates that they are poems of mourning—but mourning for what? Who are the angels who dominate the poems so mysteriously? Rilke's elegies share the literary mood of the early twentieth century; they seem to be mourning our lonely alienation from meaning itself. Whoever the angels are, they are so far removed and exist in such extraordinary radiance that their presence would be unendurable. We constantly reach out with desire and hope but in doing so grow only dimmer. The poems are filled with images of time and space; the poet longs to find some place, perhaps a lover's embrace, that is pure and contained; but his heart and mind, calling out to angels quite beyond him, allow him no repose:

> You *still* don't understand? Throw the emptiness in
> your arms out into that space we breathe; maybe birds
> will feel the air thinning as they fly deeper into themselves.

## Duino Elegies

### *The First Elegy*

And if I cried, who'd listen to me in those angelic
orders? Even if one of them suddenly held me
to his heart, I'd vanish in his overwhelming
presence. Because beauty's nothing
but the start of terror we can hardly bear,
and we adore it because of the serene scorn
it could kill us with. Every angel's terrifying.
  So I control myself and choke back the lure
of my dark cry. Ah, who can we turn to,
then? Neither angels nor men,
and the animals already know by instinct
we're not comfortably at home
in our translated world. Maybe what's left
for us is some tree on a hillside we can look at
day after day, one of yesterday's streets,
and the perverse affection of a habit
that liked us so much it never let go.
  And the night, oh the night when the wind
full of outer space gnaws at our faces; that wished for,
gentle, deceptive one waiting painfully for the lonely
heart—she'd stay on for anyone. Is she easier on lovers?
But they use each other to hide their fate.
  You *still* don't understand? Throw the emptiness in
your arms out into that space we breathe; maybe birds
will feel the air thinning as they fly deeper into themselves.

Yes, Springs needed you. Many stars
waited for you to see them. A wave
that had broken long ago swelled toward you,
or when you walked by an open window, a violin
gave itself. All that was your charge.
But could you live up to it? Weren't you always
distracted by hope, as if all this promised
you a lover? (Where would you have hidden her,
with all those strange and heavy thoughts
flowing in and out of you, often staying overnight?)
When longing overcomes you, sing about great lovers;
their famous passions still aren't immortal enough.
You found that the deserted, those you almost envied,
could love you so much more than those you loved.
Begin again. Try out your impotent praise again;
think about the hero who lives on: even his fall
was only an excuse for another life, a final birth.
But exhausted nature draws all lovers back
into herself, as if there weren't the energy
to create them twice. Have you remembered
Gaspara Stampa well enough? From that greater love's
example, any girl deserted by her lover
can believe: "If only I could be like her!"
Shouldn't our ancient suffering be more
fruitful by now? Isn't it time our loving freed
us from the one we love and we, trembling, endured:
as the arrow endures the string, and in that gathering momentum
becomes more than itself. Because to stay is to be nowhere.

Voices, voices. My heart, listen as only
saints have listened: until some colossal
sound lifted them right off the ground; yet,
they listened so intently that, impossible
creatures, they kept on kneeling. Not that you could
endure the voice of God! But listen to the breathing,
the endless news growing out of silence,
rustling toward you from those who died young.
Whenever you entered a church in Rome or Naples,
didn't their fate always softly speak to you?
Or an inscription raised itself to reach you,
like that tablet in Santa Maria Formosa recently.
What do they want from me? That I gently wipe away
the look of suffered injustice sometimes
hindering the pure motion of spirits a little.

It's true, it's strange not living on earth
anymore, not using customs you hardly learned,

not giving the meaning of a human future
to roses and other things that promise so much;
no longer being what you used to be
in hands that were always anxious,
throwing out even your own name like a broken toy.
It's strange not to wish your wishes anymore. Strange
to see the old relationships now loosely fluttering
in space. And it's hard being dead and straining
to make up for it until you can begin to feel
a trace of eternity. But the living are wrong
to make distinctions that are too absolute.
Angels (they say) often can't tell whether
they move among the living or the dead.
The eternal torrent hurls all ages through
both realms forever and drowns out their voices in both.

At last, those who left too soon don't need us anymore;
we're weaned from the things of this earth as gently
as we outgrow our mother's breast. But we, who need
such great mysteries, whose source of blessed progress
so often is our sadness—could we exist without them?
Is the story meaningless, how once during the lament for Linos,

the first daring music pierced the barren numbness,
and in that stunned space, suddenly abandoned
by an almost godlike youth, the Void first felt
that vibration which charms and comforts and helps us now?

## *The Second Elegy*

Every angel's terrifying. Almost deadly birds
of my soul, I know what you are, but, oh,
I still sing to you! What happened to the days of Tobias
when one of you stood in a simple doorway, partly
disguised for the trip, radiant, no longer appalling;
(a young man to the young man as he looked out amazed).
If the archangel, the dangerous one behind the stars,
took just one step down toward us today: the quicker
pounding of our heart would kill us. Who are you?

Fortunate first ones, creation's pampered darlings,
ranges, mountain tops, morning-red ridges
of all Beginning—seed of a blossoming god,
hinges of light, hallways, stairways, thrones,
spaces of being, force fields of ecstasy, storms
of unchecked rapture, and suddenly, separate,

*mirrors:* each drawing its own widespread
streaming beauty back into its face.

But we: we vanish in our feelings. Oh, we breathe
ourselves out, and out; our smell dissolves
from ember to ember. It's true, someone may tell us:
"You're in my blood, this room, Spring floods
with you . . ." What good is it? He can't hold us.
We vanish in him and around him. And the beautiful,
oh, who can hold them back? Some look is always rising
in their faces, and falling. Like dew on new grass,
like heat from a steaming dish, everything we are rises
away from us. O smile, where are you going?
O upturned look: new, warm, the heart's receding wave—
it hurts me, but that's what we are. Does the cosmic
space we dissolve into taste of us, then? Do angels
really absorb only what poured out of them,
or sometimes, as if by mistake, is there a trace
of us, too? Do the contours of their features bear
as much of us as that vague look on a pregnant woman's
face? Unnoticed by them in their whirling back
into themselves. (Why should they notice.)

If they were understood, lovers might say marvelous
things in the night air. Because it seems everything
wants to camouflage us. Look, trees exist;
the houses we live in still hold up. But we
pass by all of it like an exchange of breath.
Everything conspires to ignore us, half out of shame,
perhaps, half out of some speechless hope.

Lovers, satisfied with each other, I'm asking you
about us. You hold each other. What's your proof?
Look, sometimes it happens my hands become aware
of each other, or my worn out face seeks shelter
in them. Then I feel a slight sensation.
But who'd dare to exist just for that?
Yet you, who grow in the other's ecstasy
until he's overcome and begs: "No more!";
you, who in one another's hands grow
more abundant like grapes in a vintage year;
you, who sometimes disappear, but only when the other
takes over completely, I'm asking you about us.
I know why you touch each other so ecstatically:
that touch *lasts.* That place you cover with such
tenderness doesn't vanish, because you feel a pure

duration there. In your embrace you almost find
the promise of eternity. And yet, when you've survived
the fear of that first look, the longing at the window,
and that first walk in the garden, once: lovers,
are you still the same? When you lift yourselves
up to each other's lips and begin, drink for drink—
oh how strangely the drinker then slips from the role.

Didn't the caution of human gestures on Attic steles
amaze you? Weren't love and separation placed
on those shoulders so lightly they seemed made
of other stuff than we are? Remember the hands:
despite the power in the torso, they lie weightless.
The self-controlled knew this: we can only go this far.
All we can do is touch one another like this. The gods
can press down harder on us, but that's the gods' affair.

If only we could find something pure, contained,
narrow, human—our own small strip of orchard
between river and rock. For our heart rises
out of us as it did out of the others. And we can't
follow it any longer into figures that tame it, or
into godlike bodies where it finds a greater mastery. 79

## FRANZ KAFKA (1883–1924)

*Translated by Joachim Neugroschel*

Franz Kafka lived in Prague through the tumultuous years of the First World War. He was Jewish, fluent in Yiddish and Czech, but he wrote in German. More than any other European writer, he gave voice to the growing sense of dislocation, alienation, and absurdity that came to characterize the modern era. His name is now synonymous with the most frightening aspects of twentieth-century life, especially the feeling that the human individual, crippled by guilt and paranoia, is lost in a meaningless and impersonal bureaucratic apparatus of social, economic, and political forces.

Kafka grew up surrounded by a mood of oppression. As a Jew he was despised by the relatively small community of powerful anti-Semitic German Austrians with whom he shared a language; as an Austrian he was hated by the subjugated Czech majority, whose resentment toward German-speakers was intense and entrenched —and whose anti-Semitism also ran deep.

Kafka made a successful if unhappy living as an executive in a large insurance firm and lived with his overbearing parents until his early death from tuberculosis. He published numerous short stories, most of them dark, impenetrable parables, many of them only a page or two in length. The stories reveal a life dominated by an emotional and spiritual hunger that remained unsatisfied. Gifted at expressing human loss, estrangement, and anxiety in the modern world, Kafka baffles the reader with somber and fantastic events expressed in a deceptively simple style and language. But his greatness as a writer is not due only to his mastery of style and his portrait of modern life as a nightmare. By stripping reality of all its comforting conventions and familiarity, he exposed the human condition as an experience of having been thrown into a meaningless universe and a struggle to create meaning in the face of inevitable failure and death.

His realism is a stylistic maneuver designed to disorient our habits of understanding. His combination of matter-of-factness and bizarre fantasy seems dreamlike or surreal but does not yield easily to symbolic or Freudian analysis. He combined the mundane and the mysterious, achieving extreme representations of subjectivity within narrative forms that are stylistically detached and objective. Reality and dream mesh in a world where metaphors come alive.

All those features of Kafka's art are evident in his famous little story "A Country Doctor," a terrifying nightmare that radiates the oppressive sense of guilt that apparently dominated his inner life. It is not a dream that can be facilely interpreted, however, but a true nightmare, with contradictory moods and symbols that leave the reader as frightened and exhausted as the narrator at the end. "A Country Doctor" is followed by "An Imperial Message," which vividly captures Kafka's existentialist view of the human condition in only one page.

## A Country Doctor

I was in a great predicament: an urgent trip lay ahead of me; a dangerously ill patient awaited me in a village ten leagues away; a heavy blizzard filled the vast space between me and him; I did have a wagon, lightweight, with large wheels, just the right kind of wagon for our country roads. Bundled up in my fur coat, holding my instrument bag, I stood in the courtyard, ready to travel; but the horse was lacking, the horse. My own horse had died the previous night because of its overexertion in this icy winter. My housemaid was now running around the village, trying to borrow a horse; but it was hopeless, I knew it; and covering up with more and more snow, becoming more and more immobile, I stood there forlorn.

My maid appeared at the gate, alone, swinging the lantern. Naturally: who would lend someone a horse at such a time for such a trip? I strode back across the courtyard; I could think of no solution. Confused, tormented, I kicked the brittle door of the pigsty, which had not been used in years. The door opened, banging to and fro on its hinges. Warmth and aroma emerged, as if from horses. A dim stable lantern swayed inside on a rope. A man, cowering in the low shed, exposed his open, blue-eyed face.

"Should I harness up?" he asked, creeping out on all fours. I could think of nothing to say, so I stooped down only to see what else was in the sty. The maid stood beside me. "You never know what you've got in your own house," she said, and we both laughed.

"Hey, Brother, hey, Sister!" shouted the stableman, and two horses, mighty creatures with strong flanks, tucking their legs in close to their bodies, lowering their well-shaped heads like camels, shuffled out one behind the other solely by twisting their rumps out of the doorway, which they filled completely. But then they promptly stood upright, on high legs, with densely steaming bodies.

"Help him," I said, and the willing girl dashed over to hand the wagon harness to the stableman.

But no sooner did she reach him than he clutched her and banged his face against her. She screamed and fled back to me; the red imprint of two rows of teeth were left on the girl's cheek.

"You swine," I yelled furiously, "do you want a whipping?" But then I promptly remembered that he was a stranger, that I did not know where he came from, and that he was helping me voluntarily while everyone else had refused.

As if knowing my thoughts, he does not hold my threat against me; instead, still busy with the horses, he turns toward me only once. "Get in," he then says, and indeed: everything is ready. I have never, I note to myself, ridden with such a beautiful pair of horses, and I get in cheerfully.

"But I'm driving," I tell him, "you don't know the way."

"Certainly," he says, "I'm not going with you anyhow, I'm staying with Rosa."

"No," Rosa shouts and runs into the house with a correct foreboding of her inescapable fate. I hear the jingling chain that she draws across the door; I hear the lock snap; I also see her dashing through the hallway and the rooms, putting out all the lights to avoid being found.

"You're coming along," I tell the stableman, "or I won't go, as urgent as this trip may be. I wouldn't dream of giving you the girl as the price of this trip."

"Giddyap!" he says, clapping his hands. The wagon is yanked away, like a log in a current. I hear the door of my house bursting and splintering under the stableman's onslaught; then my eyes and ears are filled with a roar that penetrates equally to all my senses. But even that lasts only a moment, for, as if my patient's farmyard opened up right in front of my gates, I am already there. The horses stand calmly; the snow has stopped falling; moonlight all around. My patient's parents hurry out of the house, his sister behind them; they practically lift me from the wagon. I glean nothing from their confused chatter; the air in the sickroom is almost unbreathable; the neglected hearth oven is smoking. I will push open the window; but first I want to look at the patient. Gaunt, no fever, not cold, not warm, with vacant eyes, shirtless, the boy heaves himself up under the featherbed, clings to my neck, whispers into my ear, "Doctor, let me die." I peer around; no one has heard it. The parents stand mute, leaning forward, waiting for my verdict; the sister has brought a chair for my bag. I open my bag and search through my instruments. The boy keeps groping for me from the bed to remind me of his plea; I take hold of some pincers, check them in the candlelight, and put them down again. "Yes," I think blasphemously, "in such cases the gods help, sending the missing horse, adding a second one because of the urgency, bestowing the stableboy on top of everything else—"

Only now do I think of Rosa. What do I do, how can I rescue her, how can I get her out from under that stableboy, ten leagues away, uncontrollable horses in front of my wagon?—these horses, which have now somehow loosened the reins, pushed open the windows, I don't know how, from the outside; each has stuck its head through a window and, undaunted by the family's shrieks, they gape at the patient.

"I'm driving right home," I think, as if the horses were asking me to travel; but the sister believes I am dazed by the heat, and so I put up with her removing my fur coat. A glass of rum is set down for me. The old man pats me on the back—the sacrifice of his treasure justifies this familiarity. I shake my head; I feel nauseated within the narrow circle of the old man's thoughts; that is the only reason why I refuse to drink. The mother stands by the bed, luring me over; I obey and, while a horse neighs loudly toward the ceiling, I place my head on the boy's chest, and he shudders under my wet beard. It confirms what I know: the boy is healthy, his circulation a bit poor—he is saturated with coffee by the worried mother, but healthy, and it would be best to kick him out of bed. I am no do-gooder and so I let him lie. I am employed by the district and perform my responsibility thoroughly, almost overdoing it. Though badly paid, I am generous and helpful with the poor. I still have to take care of Rosa, then the boy can have his way, and I too will want to die. What am I doing here in this endless winter!? My horse has died, and no one in the village will lend me his own. I have to pull my team from the pigsty; if they did not happen to be horses, then I would have to ride with sows. That is how it is. And I nod to the family. They know nothing about it, and if they did know, they would not believe it. Writing prescriptions is easy, but communicating with people is hard. Well, then I am done with my visit, once again they have summoned me for nothing, I am used to it, with the help of my night bell the entire district torments me; but having to give up Rosa this time—that lovely girl, who has lived in my home for years, barely noticed by me—this sacrifice is too great, and I have to come up with sophistry, devise some makeshift solution to avoid pouncing on this family, who, after all, cannot for the life of them return Rosa to me. But when I close my bag and signal for my fur coat, and the family members stand together, the father snuffling over the rum glass in his hand, the mother probably disappointed in me (just what do people expect anyway?), tearfully biting her lips, and the sister flourishing a bloodstained towel, I am somehow willing to admit, if need be, that the boy may be sick after all. I go to him, he smiles at me as if I were bringing him the strongest soup of all—ah, now both horses are neighing: the noise, probably ordained by a higher power, is meant to facilitate the examination. And now I find: Yes, the boy *is* ill. In his right side, near the hip, a hand-sized wound has opened up. Pink, in many nuances, dark in its depth, lighter toward the edges, soft-grained, with uneven clots of blood, and open like the surface of a mine. That much from the distance. A closer inspection reveals a complication. Who can look at that without whistling softly? Worms, equal in length and thickness to my little finger, rosy in color and also splashed with blood, caught inside the wound, with tiny white heads, with many tiny legs, wriggle up to the light. Poor boy, there is no helping you. I have located your big wound; you are being destroyed by that blossom in your side. The family is happy, they see me doing something; the sister says so to the mother, the mother to the father, the father to several guests who, balancing with outstretched arms, tiptoe in through the moonlight of the open door.

"Will you save me?" the boy whispers, sobbing, utterly blinded by the life in his wound. That is what the people are like in my area. Always demanding the impossible of a doctor. They have lost the ancient faith; the pastor sits at home, unraveling his liturgical vestments one by one. But the doctor is supposed to accomplish everything with his delicate surgical hand. Well, whatever: I did not offer myself; if you people misuse me for sacred purposes, then I will put up with that too. What more could I ask? I, an old country doctor, bereft of my housemaid! And so they come, the family and the village elders, and undress me. A school chorus with the teacher at its head stands outside the house, singing these words to an extremely simple tune:

> Strip him, then he'll heal,
> And if he doesn't heal, then kill
> him!
> He's only a doctor, only a doctor.

Then I am stripped bare and, my fingers in my beard, my head bowed, I calmly gaze at the people. I am quite composed and superior to them all and will remain so, even though it will not help me, for now they take me by my head and feet and carry me to the bed. They place me along the wall, on the side with the wound. Then they all leave the room; the door is closed; the singing dies out; clouds pass across the moon; the bedding lies warm around me; in the windows the horses' heads waver like shadows.

"You know," someone says into my ear, "I have very little confidence in you. Why, you were only shaken off here, you didn't come on your own two feet. Instead of helping me, you crowd my deathbed. I would love to scratch your eyes out."

"Right," I say, "it *is* shameful. But I *am* a doctor, after all. What should I do? Believe me, it is no easier for me."

"I should content myself with that excuse? Oh, I have to. I always have to content myself. I came into the world with a lovely wound; that was my only endowment."

"Young friend," I say, "your problem is that you don't have an overall grasp of things. I, who have been in all sickrooms, far and wide, say to you: Your wound is not so bad. Created at a sharp angle with two strokes of the ax. Many people offer a side and barely catch the sound of the ax in the forest, much less hear it getting closer to them."

"Is that really so or are you deceiving me in my fever?"

"It is really so—take a district physician's word of honor."

And he took it and fell silent.

But now it was time to think about saving myself. The horses were still standing faithfully in their places. Clothes, fur, and bag were quickly snatched up; I did not care to waste time dressing. If the horses raced as they had coming here, I would leap from this bed to mine, as it were. Obediently a horse backed away from the window; I tossed the bundle into the wagon; my fur coat soared too far, it clung to a hook by only one sleeve. Good enough. I swung myself on the horse. The reins loosely trailing behind, one horse barely tied to the other, the wagon bumbling behind them, the fur was the last thing in the snow.

"Giddyap!" I said, but the movement was not lively. Slowly, like old men, we moved through snowy wasteland. For a long, long time, we could hear the new but defective singing of the children:

Cheer up, all you patients,
The doctor has been placed in your bed!

Never will I come home at this rate; my flourishing practice is doomed; a successor robs me, but to no avail, for he cannot replace me. The disgusting stableman rages in my home; Rosa is his victim; I refuse to picture it. Naked, at the mercy of the frost in this most wretched era, with an earthly wagon, unearthly horses, I, an old man, wander about. My fur coat hangs from the back of the wagon, but I cannot reach it, and not one of my agile patients, that riffraff, will lift a finger. Deceived! Deceived! Once you have responded to the false alarm of the night bell—it can never be made good.

## *An Imperial Message*

An emperor on his deathbed, we are told, sent a message to you, the only one, the wretched subject, the insignificant shadow who had fled from the imperial sun to the most distant distance—you of all people. He ordered the messenger to kneel at his bedside and he whispered the message into his ear; it was so important to him that he had the messenger whisper it back to him. By nodding his head, he confirmed the correctness of the words. And before the entire throng attending his death—all hindering walls are torn down and the grandees of the empire stand in a ring on the wide- and high-swinging staircase—in front of all these men he dispatched the messenger. The messenger instantly set out; a strong, a tireless man. Stretching out now one, now the other arm, he forces his way through the crowd; if he meets with resistance, he points to his chest, to the symbol of the sun. He advances easily like no one else. But the crowd is so large; their dwellings are numberless. If he could reach an open field, how lightly he would fly, and soon, no doubt, you would hear the splendid banging of his fists on your door. But instead, what useless efforts he makes; he is still pushing his way through the rooms of the innermost palace. He will never make it; and if he succeeded, nothing would be gained: he would have to fight his way down the staircases; and if he succeeded, nothing would be gained: he would have to stride across the courtyards; and after the courtyards the second enclosing palace; and again staircases and courtyards; and again a palace; and so on for thousands of years. And if he finally plunges through the outermost gate—but it can never, never happen—the entire imperial capital, the center of the world, still lies before him, piled high with its sediment. No one gets through here, and certainly not with a dead man's message. But you sit at your window and dream up the message when the evening comes.

# RUSSIA

## FYODOR DOSTOYEVSKY (1821–1881)

*Translated by Serge Shishkoff*

Fyodor Dostoyevsky was the second of seven children in a strict and religious lower-middle-class family. Dostoyevsky's father, a surgeon at a hospital for the poor in Moscow, kept his children largely isolated from outsiders. In 1833 Fyodor and his older brother finally gained access to schools outside the home, but all his life Dostoyevsky felt inferior to other Russian writers, especially Tolstoy and Turgenev, who had learned French in childhood and who had been exposed to secular culture. Dostoyevsky's mother died when he was young; his father was mysteriously murdered in 1839 by his serfs, whom he had taken to abusing. By that time Dostoyevsky had a job in the Engineering Corps, which he left in 1844 to pursue writing full time. In 1845 he published his first novel, *Poor Folk,* and was acclaimed a superb talent.

Four years later he was imprisoned, tried, and sentenced to death for his association with a group of intellectuals outraged by the injustices of nineteenth-century czarist Russia, and who discussed literature and socialist thought. Taken out to be executed with his colleagues, his sentence was commuted at the last minute, and he was exiled to Siberia for four years of hard labor in a penal colony. This experience gave him material for his novel *The House of the Dead* (1860). After his release he read Kant, Hegel, and the Qur'ān, as well as contemporary Russian writers. A great fan of Pushkin, Dostoyevsky also found inspiration in Gogol, Shakespeare, and Goethe, but most especially Friedrich Schiller, whose works he committed to memory.

Conscious of the price individuals pay when forced into institutional regimentation and standardization, Dostoyevsky raged against the "impossible generalized man." In 1864 he published *Notes from Underground,* a highly experimental work in which he examined the dilemmas of rationality, human freedom, and suffering. The book has had a profound influence on modern literature and has been called the "best overture for existentialism ever written." Rejecting the Enlightenment, Dostoyevsky's Underground Man believes that reason is a dead end, that it cannot account for human behavior, and that happiness is best achieved by following desire or caprice instead. His own desires involve both giving and receiving pain. He attacks all system-builders because they ignore the contradictory impulses obvious in human behavior, but he also attacks romantic notions of humanity's inherent goodness, arguing instead that hell exists in consciousness itself. The Underground Man is a tangle of contradictions, a figure who has internalized Enlightenment rationality but rages against it at the same time. He is morally abominable, but he knows it, announcing in his opening sentence that he is a sick and spiteful man. His rage against the forces that have degraded him makes him a disturbing "anti-hero" whom the reader can both admire and despise.

Dostoyevsky's later world-renowned works—*Crime and Punishment, The Brothers Karamazov,* and *The Idiot* among them—move away from the severity of *Notes from Underground* toward a redemptively Christian but nonetheless tragic sense of life.

# *from Notes from Underground*

## Part One

### The Underground*

*I*

I am a sick man . . . I am a nasty man. A truly unattractive man. I think there's something wrong with my liver. But then again, I don't understand a damn thing about my sickness, and I don't know for sure what's wrong with me. I'm not seeing a doctor about it and never have, even though I do have respect for medicine and doctors. What's more, I am superstitious to the extreme; well, at least to the extent of respecting medicine. (I am sufficiently educated not to be superstitious, but I am.) No sir, it's out of nastiness that I don't want to see a doctor. You, my dear sir, probably don't understand that. Well, I do. Of course, I can't explain exactly who'll be put in a pickle in this case by my nastiness; I know full well that I can in no way "foul up" even the doctors by not going to them for treatment; I know better than anyone that all this will harm just me alone and no one else. But, nonetheless, if I don't get treatment, it's from nastiness. My liver hurts, all right then—let it hurt even worse!

I have been living this way for a long time—twenty years or so. I'm forty now. I used to have a post in the civil service, but I don't any more. I was a nasty official. I was rude and took pleasure in it. After all, I never took a bribe, so that was the least I could do to compensate myself for it. (A poor joke, but I am not going to cross it out. I wrote it thinking that it would be very clever, but now that I myself see that I only wanted to show off abominably, I purposely won't cross it out!) When petitioners looking for information happened to come to the desk where I sat, I gnashed my teeth at them, and I felt an insatiable delight when I succeeded in upsetting someone. I almost always succeeded. For the most part they were timid people—you know, petitioners. But of the swaggerers I particularly despised a certain officer. He just wouldn't submit and clanged his saber in an obnoxious way. For a year and a half I carried on a war with him over that saber. In the end I prevailed. He stopped clanging. But then, that

*Author's Note: Both the author of the notes and the "Notes" themselves are, of course, fictitious. Nevertheless, personages such as the author of notes such as these not only can, but must, exist in our society, if one takes into consideration the circumstances under which our society was formed. I wanted to present to the public, in a more conspicuous way than usual, one of the personalities of the recent past. He is one of the representatives of the generation still living out its life. In this excerpt, entitled "The Underground," this person introduces himself, his outlook, and, as it were, tries to elucidate the reasons that made him appear and made it inevitable that he should appear in our midst. In the next excerpt, the true "notes" of that person about certain events in his life will be given.

FYODOR DOSTOYEVSKY

was back in my youth. But do you know, gentlemen, what the main point of my nastiness was? Well, what the whole thing consisted of, what made it such a vile mess, was that every moment, even at the moment of greatest rancor, I shamefully recognized inwardly that I was not only not a nasty man but not even a disgruntled one, that I was only needlessly frightening sparrows and satisfying my whims that way. I might be frothing at the mouth, but bring me some little trinket, give me a bit of tea with sugar, and I'd probably calm right down. I might even be touched to the heart, even though afterwards I'd surely gnash my teeth at myself, and suffer from insomnia out of shame, for several months. That's the way I am.

I lied about myself earlier when I said that I was a nasty official. Lied out of nastiness. I was just fooling around with the petitioners, and with the officer too, but I could never have actually become a nasty person. Every moment I recognized within myself many, many elements completely opposed to that. I felt them swarming around inside me, all those opposing elements. I knew that all my life they had been swarming around inside me and begging to come out into the light, but I would not let them, would not, purposely would not let them out into the light. They tormented me into shame; they drove me to convulsions, and finally I got fed up with them, oh, how fed up! Say, gentlemen, I hope that you won't get the idea that now I feel repentant about something, that I am asking your forgiveness for something. I am sure that you think so . . . But I assure you that it's all the same to me, even if you do . . .

I not only did not manage to become nasty, but I did not manage to become anything at all; not nasty, not nice, not crooked, not honest, not a hero, not an insect. Now I am living out my life in my corner, taunting myself with the spiteful and pointless consolation that an intelligent man cannot really become anything anyway—it takes a fool to become anything. Yes indeed, the intelligent man of the nineteenth century is obliged and morally bound to be basically characterless, while the man with character, the man of action, is apt to be basically a limited creature. This is my conviction of forty years. I am forty years old, and surely forty years is all of life; obviously it is the deepest of old age. Living beyond the age of forty is indecent, vulgar, immoral! Who lives longer than forty years—answer me truthfully, honestly? I'll tell you who: fools and bastards, that's who. I'll say that right to the face of all these patriarchs, all these venerable patriarchs, all these silver-haired and sweet-smelling patriarchs! I'll tell the whole world right to its face! I have a right to talk this way because I am going to live to be sixty myself. I'll live to be seventy! I'll live to be eighty! . . . Wait! Let me catch my breath . . .

You probably think, gentlemen, that I want to make you laugh? Wrong again. I am not as lighthearted as you think, or as you may think; besides, if out of irritation with all this jabber (and I already sense that you are irritated), you decide to ask me precisely who I am anyway?—then I'll answer you: I am a collegiate assessor. I worked so I'd have something to eat (but only for that), and when, last year, one of my distant relatives left me six thousand rubles in his last testament, I immediately retired and settled in my corner. I lived in this corner before, but now I have settled in this corner. My room—miserable, disgusting—is way out at the edge of town.

My servant is a countrywoman, old, mean out of stupidity, and what's more, she always gives off an awful smell. I am told that the climate of Petersburg is becoming bad for me and that with my meager resources living in Petersburg is too expensive. I know all that. I know it far better than all these experienced and all-wise advicegivers and tsk-tskers. But I am going to stay in Petersburg; I am not going to leave Petersburg! I am not going to leave because . . . Oh, it really doesn't matter at all whether I leave or not.

But tell me this: what can a decent man talk about with the greatest pleasure of all?

Here is the answer: about himself.

Well then, I am going to talk about myself too.

*II*

Now I would like to tell you, gentlemen, whether you wish to hear it or not, why it was that I could not manage to become even an insect. I assure you solemnly that many a time I wanted to become an insect. But I was not granted even that honor. I swear to you, gentlemen, that being overly conscious is a sickness, a real, full-blown sickness. For human use the ordinary human consciousness would be more than adequate, and that is only a half or even a quarter of the allotment of the progressive man in our unhappy nineteenth century, who has, furthermore, the utter misfortune to be living in Petersburg, the most abstract and premeditated city on the face of the earth. (Cities can be premeditated and unpremeditated.) It would be quite sufficient, for instance, to have the consciousness with which all the so-called matter-of-fact people and men of action live. I bet that you think that I am writing all this to show off, to scoff at men of action, and that my showing off is in very bad taste, just like my officer rattling his saber. But, gentlemen, who could possibly be vain about his sicknesses and, moreover, brag about them?

But what am I thinking of? Everybody does that; that's what people do brag about—their sicknesses, and I probably do it more than anyone else. Let's not argue—my objections are absurd. But, nonetheless, I am firmly convinced that not only a great deal of consciousness, but even any consciousness at all is a sickness. I stand on that. Let's drop that, too, for a minute. Tell me this. Why should it be, as if by design, that at the very moment, yes, the very moment that I was most capable of being conscious of all the subtleties of "all that is beautiful and sublime," as they used to say around here at one time, it turned out that instead of being conscious, I did such abominable things that . . . well, anyway, to be brief, things that probably everybody has done, but which I did, as if by design, at the precise moment when I was most conscious that I shouldn't do them at all? The more conscious I was of good and all this "beautiful and sublime," the deeper I sank into my morass and the more apt I was to be completely bogged down in it. But the main point was that all this seemed to be in me not by chance but as if that were the way it was meant to be. This seemed to be my most normal state and not any kind of sickness or affliction, so I finally lost even the desire to fight that affliction. It all ended by my almost believing (maybe I actually did come to believe) that probably this was in fact my normal state. But at the very outset, at the very beginning, what agonies I suffered in this struggle! I did not believe that such things happened to other people, and for that reason I kept them to myself like secrets. I was ashamed (and maybe I am ashamed even now); I reached the point where I felt some kind of secret, abnormal, base gratification when I returned to my corner on some awful Petersburg night and felt intensely conscious that again that day I had committed another vile act, that what was done could never be undone again, and then inwardly, secretly I would gnaw, gnaw at myself for it, pestering and sucking the life out of myself until the bitterness eventually turned into some kind of shameful, damned sweetness and finally into a real, definite pleasure. Yes, pleasure, pleasure! I stand on that. That's why I began to speak—I want to find out for sure: do other people have such feelings of pleasure? Let me explain: the pleasure involved here comes precisely from an all-too-acute consciousness of your own degradation, because you yourself feel that you have reached the last wall; that it was vile all right, but that it could not be otherwise; that you no longer had a way out, that you could never become a different man, that even if you still had the time and the faith to change yourself into something else, you probably would not have the desire to change; even if you had the desire, you could do nothing even then, because, in reality, there might be nothing to change into. But most important and the end result of everything was that all this followed the normal and basic laws of intensified consciousness and the momentum that stemmed directly from those laws, and consequently one not only could not change, but there was simply nothing one could do. Here's what happens, for example, as a result of intensified consciousness: you know that you are a wretch as if it were a consolation to a wretch that he himself already realizes that he actually is a wretch. But enough . . . All that word-weaving, and what have I explained? How can this pleasure be explained? But I'll explain myself! I'll get to the bottom of this! That's why I took up my pen . . .

I am, for instance, terribly self-centered. I am touchy and quick to take offense, like a hunchback or a dwarf; but, honestly, there have been times when if someone had happened to slap my face, it's possible that I would even have been happy about it. I mean it: I am sure that even here I could have found a pleasure of sorts, a pleasure of despair, naturally, but in despair you find the most searing pleasures, especially when you are keenly conscious of the hopelessness of your situation. And when you have received that slap, the consciousness of the extent to which you have been reduced to a pulp crushes you. More important though, no matter how you look at it, I still come out most to blame for everything, and, what is most painful, to blame without any reason and, so to speak, because of the laws of nature. To blame, first, because I am more intelligent than everybody around me. (I always considered myself more intelligent than everybody around me and, would you believe it, sometimes I was embarrassed by it. At least, all my life I have looked somehow to the side and could never look people directly in the eyes.) To blame, finally, because even if there were magnanimity within me, I would only suffer more from the consciousness of its complete uselessness. For it is certain that I would not have been capable of putting my magnanimity to any use: I could not be forgiving, for perhaps the offender had slapped me because of the laws of nature, and one cannot forgive the laws of nature; nor could I forget it, because laws of nature or not, I had still been insulted. Finally, even if I had wished to be altogether unmagnanimous, and if, on the contrary, I had wished to take revenge on the offender, I could in no way take revenge on anyone, because, in all probability, I would not have been able to decide to do anything even if I could. Why not? I would like to say a few words on this subject separately.

*III*

Take people who know how to avenge themselves and, in general, can stand up for themselves—how do they handle this sort of thing, for instance? Obviously, when they are seized by, let's say, a feeling of revenge, for a time absolutely nothing remains in their entire being except that feeling. Such a gentleman lunges straight toward his goal like an enraged bull with his horns lowered, and it would take at least a wall to stop him. (By the way, faced with a wall, such gentlemen, that is, matter-of-fact people and men of action, forthrightly give up. To them the wall is not a way out, as it is, for example, to people like us who think a lot and, consequently, do nothing; it is not an excuse to turn back, an excuse that people of our kind usually do not themselves believe, but which they always welcome. No, with complete forthrightness, they give up. For them the wall has a calming, morally absolving, final quality—even, I guess, something mystical. But more about the wall later.) Well, sir, that is precisely the kind of matter-of-fact man that I consider the real, normal man, the kind that tender Mother Nature herself, who obligingly bore him on earth, wanted him to be. I envy that kind of man with all my guts. He's stupid, I'll grant you that, but perhaps the normal man has to be stupid, how does one know? Maybe it's even very becoming. And what makes me even more convinced of this, let's say, suspicion is that if, for example, you take the antithesis of the normal man, that is, the intensely conscious man, who originated, of course, not in the loins of nature but in a test tube (this borders on mysticism, gentlemen, but I suspect that too), then this test-tube man sometimes gives up so completely in the face of his antithesis that with all his intensified consciousness he honestly considers himself to be a mouse, not a man. Granted, a mouse with intensified consciousness, but still a mouse, whereas here we have a man, and therefore, etc. And most importantly, he himself, yes, even he considers himself to be a mouse; nobody asks him to; and that is a significant point. Now let's take a look at this mouse in action. Let's assume that it too has been wronged (and it is almost always wronged) and likewise wants revenge. Even more anger may build up in it, perhaps, than in *l'homme de la nature et de la vérité*. The filthy, base, petty desire to repay the offender with the same evil may rankle in it even worse than in *l'homme de la nature et de la vérité*, because *l'homme de la nature et de la vérité*, in his innate stupidity, considers his revenge to be justice pure and simple, whereas the mouse, because of its intensified consciousness, denies that it has anything to do with justice. We finally reach the heart of the matter, the act of revenge itself. The wretched mouse has succeeded in erecting around itself, besides the initial filth, so much more in the form of doubts and questions; to the one question it brings so many unresolved questions that it unavoidably collects all around itself some kind of fatal glop, some kind of stinking muck made up of its doubts, worries and, finally, the spittle showered on it by the matter-of-fact men who stand around grandly in the guise of judges and dictators and laugh heartily at the mouse with all the power of their robust throats. Naturally, all it can do is flip its paw in resignation and, with a smile of affected scorn, which even it does not believe, scamper into its little crack. There, in its miserable, stinking underground, our wronged, beaten-down, and ridiculed mouse immediately plunges into cold, venomous, and most important, everlasting spite. For forty uninterrupted years it will remember the insult to the last, most shameful detail and add to it each time still more shameful details, maliciously taunting and provoking itself by its own imaginings. It will be shamed by its own imaginings, yet it will remember everything, go over everything, dream up a lot of slander against itself under the pretext that this too might have happened, and will forgive nothing. Conceivably it might even start to take revenge, but somehow in spurts, in petty ways, hiding behind corners, incognito, not believing in its right to revenge nor in its success, and knowing beforehand that all its attempts at revenge will make it suffer a hundred times more than the one on whom it is avenging itself, and that that one in turn will not feel so much as a mosquito bite. On its deathbed it will once again remember everything, together with the interest that has accumulated, and . . . But it is exactly there, in that cold, repulsive half-despair, half-belief, in that conscious grief-imposed entombment of oneself alive for forty years, in that strongly conceived and yet partly doubtful hopelessness of one's position, in all that venom of unsatisfied desires turned inward, in all that fever of vacillations, in decisions taken forever and retracted again in a minute—it is in all this that one finds the juice of that strange pleasure of which I spoke. It is so refined, so inaccessible to the consciousness that people who are ever so slightly limited or even simply people with strong nerves won't understand the first thing about it. "Perhaps it also will not be understood," you'll chime in, with a smirk, "by those who have never been slapped in the face"—and in this way politely hint that at some time in my life I also may have received a slap in the face, and that's the reason I speak like an expert. I'll bet that is what you are thinking. But don't worry, gentlemen, I have never been slapped, though I don't care at all what you may think about that. And perhaps I even regret that during my lifetime I did not give out enough slaps myself. But enough, not another word on this subject that interests you so.

I will continue calmly about people with strong nerves who do not understand certain refinements of pleasure. In particular circumstances, for instance, these gentlemen, even though they bellow like bulls with all their might, even though, we'll assume, it does bring them the greatest of honors, nonetheless, as I have already pointed out, in the face of an impossibility, they immediately resign themselves. Impossibility—does that mean a stone wall? What stone wall? Well, the laws of nature, of course, the conclusions of the natural sciences, mathematics. When they prove to you, for example, that you descended from a monkey, there is no use scowling—take it as it is. When they prove to you that actually a drop of your own fat must be dearer to you than a hundred thousand of your fellow men, and that in the end this conclusion will solve all the so-called virtues and duties and other ravings and prejudices, you've got to take it as it is, there's nothing else to do, because two times two is mathematics. Go argue with that.

"For goodness sakes," they'll yell at you, "you can't rebel, this is two times two makes four. Nature doesn't ask your approval; she couldn't care less about your desires and whether you like her laws or not. You have to take her as she is and, consequently, all her conclusions as well. A wall, then, is a wall, etc., etc." Good Lord, what do I care about the laws of nature and arithmetic, if for some reason I don't like those laws and this two times two makes four. Of course, I won't ram through such a wall with my head if I really don't have the strength to ram through it, but I will not submit just because I have a stone wall before me and I don't have enough strength.

As if such a stone wall really were any solace and really did contain the slightest word of conciliation, for the one and only reason that it represents two times two makes four. Oh absurdity of all absurdities! How different it is if you understand everything, are conscious of everything, of all the impossibilities and stone walls; not to accept even one of these impossibilities and stone walls if accepting it is repugnant to you; to arrive by way of the most inevitable logical combinations at the most repulsive conclusions on the eternal theme that you are somehow to blame even for that stone wall, though on the other hand, it is clearly evident that you are in no way to blame and, as a consequence, grinding your teeth in silent frustration, to sink sensuously into inertia, dreaming that as it turns out, there is not even anyone to be mad at; that the object cannot be found, and perhaps will never be found, that there has been a switch, double-dealing, a swindle, that it is simple nonsense—no one can tell who or what, but in spite of all these uncertainties and double-dealings, it hurts you just the same, and the less you know, the more it hurts.

*IV*

"Ha, ha, ha! After this you'll find pleasure even in a toothache!" you will exclaim with laughter.

"So? There *is* pleasure in a toothache," I'll answer. "My teeth ached for a whole month; I know there is." Here, of course, one does not seethe in silence, one moans, but these moans are not sincere, there is malice in these moans, and it is in this malice that the whole point lies. It is through those moans that the pleasure of the sufferer is expressed; if he did not find pleasure in them, he wouldn't bother to moan. This is a very good example, gentlemen, and I will expand upon it. These moans express, first of all, the total aimlessness of your pain, so degrading to your consciousness, all the law-abidingness of nature, for which, of course, you don't give a damn, but from which you suffer just the same, while it does not. They express the consciousness of the fact, that though you can't come up with an enemy, you do have pain; the consciousness that you, along with all the possible Wagenheims,* are completely enslaved by your teeth; that if someone desired it, your teeth would stop aching, and if he didn't, they would go on aching another three months; and if, finally, you still do not agree and persist in protesting, the only thing left for your consolation is to flog yourself or hit your wall as painfully as possible with your fist; but other than that, there is absolutely nothing. Well, from those bloody insults, from those jeers of unknown origin, the pleasure begins at last, and sometimes reaches the highest degree of sensuality. I beg you, gentlemen, listen sometime to the moans of the educated man of the nineteenth century, who is suffering from his teeth, say, on the second or third day of his illness, when he has begun to moan, not as he did on the first day, that is, not simply because his teeth ached, not like some uncouth peasant or other, but like a man touched by enlightenment and by European civilization, like a man "who has forsaken the soil and the principles of the people," as they say nowadays. His moans become somehow despicable, mean, and malicious, and they continue for entire days and nights. And yet he himself knows that he will derive no benefit from the moans; he knows better than anyone else that he is needlessly taxing and irritating himself and others; he knows that even the audience for which he is exerting himself, and his whole family, have too long listened to him with loathing, that they don't believe him in the least bit and secretly understand that he could moan in another, simpler way, without tremolos and embellishments, that he is carrying on this way only from malice and spite. Well, then, it is in all these consciousnesses and ignominies that the sensuality is found. "So I am bothering you, I am straining your pity, I don't let anyone in the house sleep. Well, stay awake then, feel every moment that my teeth are aching. I am no longer a hero to you, as I earlier tried to appear, but simply a slimy man, a good-for-nothing. Well, that's fine with me. I'm very glad that you've found me out. Listening to my obnoxious moans repels you? So be repelled; in a minute I'll give you an even more repulsive tremolo . . ." You still don't understand, gentlemen? No, it is clear that one has to plunge deeply into consciousness and enlightenment to understand all the quirks of this sensuality. You laugh? Delighted, gentlemen. My jokes are, of course, tasteless, uneven, confused, self-mistrusting. But that is because I don't respect myself. After all, can a conscious man respect himself at all?

## *V*

How in the world, how in the world can a man who attempts to find pleasure in the very feeling of his own debasement respect himself at all? I am not saying this now out of some sort of mawkish repentance. And in general, I could

---

*Wagenheims: two dentists with the same last name who advertised in the Petersburg newspapers in 1864—Trans.

never bring myself to say: "I'm sorry, Daddy, I won't do it again," not because I was incapable of saying it, but on the contrary maybe just because I was all too capable of it, and in what a way, too. I'd be caught, as if by design, on occasions when I was not to blame in dream or in spirit. That was the vilest part. And with all that I grew mellow just the same, I repented, I dripped tears, and, of course, I conned myself, although I was by no means pretending. My feelings somehow always managed to louse things up . . . I couldn't even blame the laws of nature, though all the same the laws of nature wronged me continuously and more than anything else in my whole life. It is repugnant to recall all this, and it was repugnant then too. You see, within a minute or so, I would already have angrily realized that all this was nothing but lies, lies, detestable, affected lies—that is, all those repentances, all those mellowings, all those vows to reform. And should you ask why I wrenched and tortured myself that way, I would answer: because sitting on my hands was just too dull; so I engaged in silly antics. Honest. Look at yourselves, gentlemen, and then you'll understand that it is so. I thought up my own adventures and created a life of my own, so that I would have at least a semblance of living. How many times did I—well, say, for example, get miffed without any reason, just for the heck of it; a person usually knows himself that he feels miffed without any reason, that he is pretending, but, I assure you, eventually he brings himself to the point where he really is miffed. All my life I was somehow drawn to pull stunts like these, so that eventually I could not control myself. There was a time—even two times—when I wanted to make myself fall in love. And I suffered, gentlemen, I assure you. In the very depths of my soul I didn't really believe that I was suffering; a snicker rose, and yet I did suffer, and in a very real, genuine way at that; I became jealous, lost my head . . . And all from boredom, gentlemen, all from boredom; I was overcome by inertia. As a matter of fact, the direct, predictable, straightforward fruit of consciousness is inertia, that is, conscious sitting on one's hands. I mentioned that earlier. I repeat, I repeat urgently: all those matter-of-fact people and men of action act because they are dull and narrow. How can that be explained? Here's how: as a consequence of that narrowness they take immediate and secondary causes as primary ones, and in that way they are convinced sooner and more easily than other people that they have found an unimpeachable basis for their actions; it puts their minds at rest, and that's the important thing. After all, to act, you have to have your mind completely at rest beforehand and have absolutely no doubts left. But how do you expect me, for instance, to put my mind at rest? Where are the primary causes to sustain me, where are the foundations? Where will I lay my hands on them? Thinking is my preoccupation, consequently every primary cause of mine drags along right behind it another one, still more primary, and so on into infinity. That is precisely the essence of all consciousness and thinking. Once again then, we are dealing with the laws of nature. So what do we have as a result, finally? Still the same thing, of course. Remember: a while ago I spoke of revenge. (You probably didn't grasp it.) It was said: a man takes revenge because he sees justice in it. That means that he has found the primary cause, has found the foundation, namely, justice. Therefore, his mind is put at rest on all accounts, and consequently he avenges himself calmly and successfully, convinced that he is doing the honest and just thing. But I see no justice in it, I do not find any kind of virtue either, and consequently, if I ever avenge myself, I will do it only out of nastiness. Nastiness could, of course, overcome everything, all my doubts, and therefore could quite successfully serve as the primary cause precisely because it is not a cause. But what can I do if there isn't even any nastiness in me (you remember, that is what I started with a while ago). Here again, because of these damned laws of consciousness, my nastiness is subject to a chemical breakdown. And so, right before your eyes the object vanishes, the reasons evaporate, the culprit is not to be found, the insult ceases being an insult and becomes a matter of fate, something like the toothache, for which no one is to blame, and consequently, once again there remains the very same recourse—that is, to hit the wall as painfully as possible. So you shrug it off because you haven't found the primary cause. But try to be carried away by your feeling, blindly, without thinking, without the primary cause, suppressing consciousness at least for that time; try to hate or love, simply so as not to sit on your hands. The day after tomorrow, and that's certainly the very latest, you will begin to despise yourself because you have knowingly conned yourself. And what do we get as a result? A soap bubble and inertia. Ah, gentlemen, perhaps the only reason I consider myself an intelligent man is that all my life I have neither started nor finished anything. All right, all right, so I am a babbler, a harmless, annoying babbler just like all of us. But what can you do, if the direct and sole purpose of every intelligent man is babbling—that is, intentionally shooting the breeze?

*VI*

Oh, if I did nothing only out of laziness. Lord, how I would respect myself then. I would respect myself precisely because I would at least be capable of being lazy; at least one quality in me would be sort of positive, one which I could believe in myself. The question: Who is he? The answer: A loafer; why, it would be exceedingly nice to hear that about oneself. It would mean a positive designation, it would mean that there is something to be said about me. "Loafer," why, that's a title and a purpose, that's a whole career. Don't joke, it's so. Then, by right, I would be a member of a most exclusive club and I would devote myself totally to continually respecting myself. I knew a gentleman who prided himself all his life on being a good judge of Lafite. He considered this to be his positive virtue and he never had any doubts about himself. He died not merely with a clear conscience, but with a triumphant one, and he was absolutely right. And I would then have chosen a career for myself: I would have been a loafer and a glutton, only not a simple one, but, for instance, one who approves of everything beautiful and sublime. How do you like that? I have been dreaming about it for a long time. This "beautiful and sublime" has been giving me a real pain in the neck for my forty years, but those were my forty years, but then, oh, then it would have been different. Right away I would have found an appropriate activity, namely, to drink to all that is beautiful and sublime. I would have seized every opportunity, first to shed a tear into my goblet and then drink to all that is beautiful and sublime. I would have turned everything in the world into something beautiful and sublime; in the most foul, indisputable garbage I would have uncovered the beautiful and sublime. I would have become as lacrimose as a wet sponge. An artist, for example, painted a picture of crap.* I'd immediately drink to the artist who had painted the picture of crap, because I love all that is beautiful and sublime. An author wrote "however anyone wishes";† I'd immediately drink to "anyone" because I love all that is "beautiful and sublime." I'd demand to be respected for it, I'd persecute anyone who failed to show me respect. I'd live peacefully, I'd die solemnly—my God, how splendid, really and truly splendid! And I'd grow such a paunch, I'd build such a triple chin, I'd develop such a colorful nose that anyone who saw me in the street would say, looking at me: "Well, there is a plus for you, there's something really and truly positive!" Say what you wish, gentlemen, but in our negative era it is nice to hear such comments.

*VII*

But these are but golden dreams. Oh, tell me, who was the first to enunciate, who was the first to proclaim that man makes mischief only because he does not know his own true interests; but that if he were enlightened, if his eyes were opened to his real, normal interests, man would immediately stop making mischief, and would immediately become nice and noble, because, being enlightened and understanding his true advantages, he would see that his own advantage lies precisely in the good, and it is known that not a single man can knowingly act against his own advantage, and consequently he would, so to speak, of necessity begin to do good? Oh, infant! Oh, pure, innocent child! In the first place, when in all these millennia did a man do something solely for his own advantage? What should we do with the millions of facts attesting to instances where people *knowingly,* that is, with a complete understanding of their true advantage, relegated it to second place and rushed headlong down a different road, ran a risk, took a gamble without anyone or anything compelling them to do it, as if the only thing they did not wish was precisely taking the indicated road, and stubbornly, willfully carved out another road, a difficult, absurd one that they had to seek out in almost complete darkness. This means, then, that the stubbornness and willfulness was in fact more enjoyable to them than any advantage . . . Advantage! What is this thing called advantage? And would you really be willing to take it upon yourself to define with absolute precision exactly what constitutes man's advantage? And what if it should turn out

---

*Picture of crap: "*Xudožnik, naprimer, napisal kartinu Ge.*" An untranslatable pun based on the fact that the name of the painter GE (N. N. Gué, 1831–1894) is also the euphemistic abbreviation of the word "*govno*"—Trans.

†"however anyone wishes": a reference to N. Shchedrin's article, "However Anyone Wishes," which appeared in 1863—Trans.

that *sometimes* man's advantage not only can but even must consist precisely in his wishing something harmful for himself, and not something advantageous. And if that's so, if such a case can occur at all, the whole rule crumbles into dust. What do you think, are there such cases? You are laughing; go ahead, gentlemen, laugh, but just answer me: Have man's advantages been counted with absolute accuracy? Aren't there some that not only have not been forced, but positively cannot be forced into any classification? You, gentlemen, as far as I know, have derived your entire list of man's advantages as a mean taken from statistical figures and scientific-economic formulas. You say the advantages are well-being, wealth, freedom, tranquility, well, and so on, and so on; so that a man who would, for instance, overtly and knowingly go against this whole list, would be, in your opinion, and well, of course, in my opinion too, an obscurantist or an absolute madman, right? But one thing is strange: why does it happen that when all these statisticians, sages, and lovers of mankind enumerate man's advantages, they invariably omit one advantage? They don't even take it into account in the form in which it ought to be taken, and yet the whole calculation depends upon it. That doesn't look like a big problem, all you have to do is take it—that advantage—and put it down on the list. But that is just the hitch, this tricky advantage does not fall into any category and cannot be squeezed onto any list. I, for instance, have a friend . . . Eh, gentlemen, he is your friend too, and, indeed, there is hardly anyone whose friend he isn't! When he is preparing to do something, this gentleman readily expounds to you eloquently and clearly exactly how he has to proceed according to the laws of reason and truth. And that is not all: with trepidation and passion he will tell you about the true, normal human interests; mockingly he chides the near-sighted fools who do not understand either their own advantages or the true meaning of virtue, and exactly fifteen minutes later, without any sudden, outside cause but precisely from something inside himself that is stronger than all his interests, he takes another tack altogether, that is, he'll overtly go against what he himself had said: against the laws of reason, against his own advantage, well, in a word, against everything . . . I have to warn you that my friend is a composite character and so it is rather hard to blame just him alone. Think about it, gentlemen, isn't there always, in fact, some such thing that is dearer to almost every man than his best advantage, or (if we are to preserve logic) some such most advantageous advantage (precisely the omitted one we just mentioned) that is more paramount and more advantageous than all the other advantages and for which a man is ready to go against all the laws, that is, against reason, honor, tranquility, well-being—in a word, against all those beautiful and useful things—all for the sake of attaining that fundamental, most advantageous advantage that is dearer to him than anything else?

"Well, it is still advantage just the same," you will interrupt me. Allow me, sirs, we will clear this up eventually, and never mind the pun, the point lies in the fact that this advantage is remarkable precisely because it demolishes all our classifications and constantly destroys all the systems established by the lovers of mankind for the happiness of mankind. In short, it interferes with everything. But before I name this advantage, I want to compromise myself personally, and therefore I'll boldly proclaim that all these lovely systems—all these theories that explain to mankind its real, normal interests so that, perforce, striving to attain these interests, it would immediately become nice and noble—for the time being are, in my opinion, mere logistics! Yes, sir, logistics! To maintain even this theory of the reform of all mankind through a system of its own advantages is, in my opinion, almost the same as . . . well, it's like maintaining, for instance, along with Buckle, that civilization is making man soft; therefore, he is becoming less bloodthirsty and less capable of waging war. As far as logic is concerned, it seems to work out that way for him. But man is so partial to systems and abstract conclusions that he is willing to distort the truth deliberately, close his eyes and plug up his ears, all to justify his logic. The reason I chose this example is that it is an exceedingly glaring example. Just look around: blood is flowing in torrents, and in such a cheerful way, too, just like champagne. This sums up this nineteenth century of ours—the same one that Buckle lived in. There is Napoleon for you—both the great one and the present one. There is North America for you—Union Forever. Finally, there is that laughable Schleswig-Holstein for you. And what is it that civilization softens in us? Civilization produces in man only a multiplicity of sensations and . . . and absolutely nothing more. And through the development of this multiplicity, man will, I dare say, eventually reach the point where he finds pleasure in the sight of blood. Actually this has already happened to him. Have you noticed that the most refined bloodletters were almost without exception the most civilized gentlemen; all these various Attilas and Stenka Razins couldn't hold a candle to them, and if they don't stand out as strikingly as Attila and Stenka Razin, that's precisely because we encounter them far too often, they are too common, they have become familiar. Anyway, because of civilization man has become if not more bloodthirsty, then surely bloodthirsty in a worse, more repulsive way than before. In the old days he saw justice in the bloodshed and with a clear conscience he exterminated whomever he thought fit; nowadays, although we consider bloodshed an abomination, we practice this abomination just the same, and even more than before. You decide for yourselves which is worse. It is said that Cleopatra (excuse the example from Roman history) enjoyed sticking golden pins into the breasts of her slave girls, and found pleasure in their screams and writhing. You will say that this was in barbaric times, relatively speaking; that even now we are in barbaric times because (also relatively speaking) even now pins are being stuck into people; that even now, though man has learned to see sometimes more clearly than in barbaric times, he is still far from having come to learn to act the way that reason and science indicate. Nevertheless, you are quite certain that he will surely come to learn it when he is completely cured of a couple of old bad habits and when common sense and science completely reeducate human nature and turn it in the proper direction. You believe that then man will, on his own, stop making *voluntary* mistakes and, against his own will, so to speak, not want to set his will against his normal interests. That is not all: then, you will say, science itself will teach man (though I think this is a luxury) that in reality he is not endowed with either will or fancy, and moreover never has been, and that he himself is nothing more than something on the order of a piano key or an organ cog; and that, moreover, there are still the laws of nature in the world, so that whatever he does is done not at all because of his wanting it, but all by itself, according to the laws of nature. Consequently, we have only to discover these laws of nature, and man will no longer be responsible for his actions, and life will be exceedingly easy for him. All human actions, it goes without saying, will then be computed according to these laws, mathematically, like logarithmic tables, up to 108,000 and entered on the calendar; or better still, certain well-intentioned publications will appear, like the present-day encyclopedic dictionaries, in which everything will be so exactly calculated and denoted that neither actions nor adventures will any longer exist on earth.

At that time—this is still you talking—new economic relations will be set up, completely ready-made and also computed with mathematical precision, so that in a flash all the conceivable questions will disappear, simply because all the conceivable answers to them will have been obtained. Then the Crystal Palace* will be built. Then . . . well, in a word, those will be the halcyon days. Of course, it is utterly impossible to guarantee (this time I am speaking) that it would not be, for instance, terribly dull then (because what can one possibly do, when everything is computed according to a table?), but in exchange everything will be exceedingly sensible. Of course, what won't one think up out of boredom! After all, the golden pins are stuck in out of boredom too, but that still wouldn't be too bad. What is despicable (this is still me speaking) is that, perish the thought, for all I know, people may then even welcome the golden pins. After all, man is stupid, phenomenally stupid. That is, though he is by no means stupid, he is, to make up for it, so ungrateful that no matter how hard you try, you'll never find another like him. So I, for one, would not be the least bit surprised if suddenly, for no apparent reason, in the midst of the future general sensibleness some fine sir should appear with an ignoble, or rather, retrograde and mocking countenance, strike a devil-may-care pose and tell us all: "Gentlemen, why don't we topple all this sensibleness with one stroke, boot it into the dirt, for the sole purpose of sending all these logarithms to the devil and living once again according to our own stupid will!" That wouldn't be too bad; the annoying part is that he would most certainly find followers—that is the way man is made. And all this for the emptiest reason, one that probably should not even be mentioned: namely, that man in every place and time, no matter who he was, liked to do what he wanted and absolutely not what reason and his

*Crystal Palace: a reference to the "Pig iron and crystal" palace in Chernyshevsky's novel *What Is to Be Done?,* where it is part of the future socialist society. The exact wording was undoubtedly inspired by the Crystal Palace erected in Hyde Park, London, for the Great Exhibition in 1851—Trans.

advantage indicated, and one can want something opposed to one's own advantage, and sometimes one even *positively must* (this is my idea). Your very own unrestricted and free wanting, your very own fancy, no matter how wild, your own fantasy, even if sometimes excited almost to the verge of madness—all these things make up that aforementioned, omitted, most advantageous advantage, the one which does not fit into any classification and because of which all systems and theories are constantly shattered to hell. And where on earth did all these sages get the idea that man needs some kind of normal, some kind of virtuous wanting? Why in the world do they necessarily think that man necessarily requires sensibly advantageous wanting? Man needs only and exclusively an *independent* wanting, whatever this independence may cost or wherever it may lead. Well, as for wanting—who the hell knows . . .

*VIII*

"Ha! ha! ha! But this wanting, if you want, does not as a matter of fact even exist," you will interrupt with a booming laugh. "Even now science has succeeded so well in dissecting man that we already know that wanting, and what we call free will, are nothing more than . . ."

Wait a minute, gentlemen, I wanted to begin that way myself. I have to admit that I even got a little frightened. I was just about to shout that the devil only knows what wanting does depend on—and perhaps we should thank God for that—but then I remembered about science . . . and I simmered down. And just at that moment you started talking. Just think, really, if someday they actually find the formula for all our wants and fancies, that is, what they depend on, exactly by which laws they occur, precisely how they are propagated, where they lead in such-and-such a case, and so on, and so on, that is, a real mathematical formula—don't you see that man will probably stop wanting altogether right then and there and, moreover, will probably even stop for sure. Why would anyone care to want according to a table? That is not all: he would immediately change from a man to an organ cog or some such thing; for exactly what is a man without desires, without will, and without wants except a cog in the organ wheel? What do you think? Let's figure out the probabilities—could this happen or not?

"Hm," you'll decide, "for the most part our wantings are mistaken because of a mistaken view of our advantages. The very reason we sometimes want sheer nonsense is that in our stupidity we see in that nonsense the easiest way to achieve some sort of advantage that is previously assumed." Well, when all this is explained and figured out on a piece of paper (which is entirely possible because it is surely abominable and senseless to believe beforehand that man will remain ignorant of some laws of nature), then, of course, there won't be any so-called desires. After all, if wanting were ever completely in league with reason, then obviously we would be reasoning and not wanting, simply because it would be absolutely impossible, for example, without losing one's reason, to want something nonsensical and so knowingly go against reason and desire something harmful for oneself. And since all wanting and reasoning can, in fact, be calculated—for some day they will surely discover the laws of what we call our free will—then, all kidding aside, something like a table can be arranged, so that we would actually want according to that table. If, for instance, some day, they calculate and prove to me that if I thumbed my nose at such-and-such it was precisely because I could not have done otherwise, and it had to be done with this very finger, then what is left in me that is *free,* particularly if I am a learned man and have finished a course of study somewhere? I could then calculate my whole life thirty years ahead; in a word, if it is indeed arranged this way then we simply won't be able to do anything; in any event, we will have to accept it. And in general we must tirelessly repeat to ourselves that certainly at such-and-such a moment and under such-and-such circumstances nature does not ask our opinion, that we must take her as she is and not as we imagine her to be, and if we are indeed on our way to the table and the calendar, and, well, even on our way to the test tube, there's nothing that can be done, we have to accept even the test tube—or else, even without you, it will begin to . . .

Yes, but here's the catch! Forgive my philosophizing, gentlemen, it is the result of forty years in the underground. Allow me to dream a little. Let me tell you: reason, gentlemen, is a fine thing, no doubt about that, but reason is only reason and satisfies only the reasoning capacity of man, while wanting is the expression of all aspects of life, that is, of all life, including reason and all the itches. And even though our life often turns out pretty rotten in this manifestation, nevertheless it's life and not just the extraction of a square root. Take me, for instance; quite naturally I want to live so as to satisfy my entire capacity to live and not only to satisfy my reasoning capacity, which is perhaps a piddling twentieth part of my total capacity to live. What does reason know? Reason knows only what it has managed to learn (I guess there are some things that it will never learn; perhaps that's no consolation, but why shouldn't we mention it?), while human nature acts as a whole, with everything it's got, consciously, and unconsciously, and though it blunders, it lives. I suspect, gentlemen, that you are looking at me with pity: you keep repeating that an educated and progressive man, in short, the kind the man of the future is going to be, could not knowingly want something disadvantageous, that's mathematics. I quite agree, it's indeed mathematics. But for the hundredth time I repeat to you that there is only one case, just one, in which man can deliberately, consciously desire even something harmful, stupid, even extremely stupid, to wit: in order to *have the right* to desire even the most stupid thing and not be bound by the obligation to desire only something intelligent. After all, this very stupid thing, this fancy of yours, gentlemen, may indeed be the most advantageous of anything on earth to people like us, especially in some cases. And in particular, it may be more advantageous than all the advantages even in a case where it causes us evident injury and contradicts the most sensible conclusions of our reason about advantages, because in any event it preserves what is most important and most precious to us, that is, our personality and our individuality. There are some who claim that it is, in fact, the most precious to man; of course, wanting may even, if it wants, agree with reason, especially if this alliance is not overdone, but applied with moderation; it is useful and sometimes even praiseworthy. But wanting very often, and perhaps more often than not, differs absolutely and obstinately from reason and . . . and . . . and, do you know, this too is useful and sometimes even praiseworthy. Let's assume, gentlemen, that man is not stupid. (Actually, you see, one should never say that about him, if only because if even he is stupid, who then can possibly be intelligent?) But if he is not stupid, he is nevertheless monstrously ungrateful. Phenomenally ungrateful. I even think that the best definition of man is this: a creature with two legs—and ungrateful. But that is still not all; that is still not his principal shortcoming; his greatest shortcoming is his perpetual indecorousness, perpetual from the time of the Great Flood to the Schleswig-Holstein period of human destiny. Indecorousness, and consequently, a lack of good sense; for it has long been known that lack of good sense arises only from indecorousness. Do try to cast a glance at the history of mankind; well, what do you see? Is it majestic? All right, let's say it is majestic; just consider the Colossus of Rhodes alone—isn't that something! It is for good reason that Mr. Anaevsky* reports that some claim it is the creation of human hands; others assert that it was created by nature herself. Is it colorful? All right, let's say it's colorful; take just the dress uniforms worn by officialdom, military and civilian, from all times and all nations—doesn't that add up to something? And if you throw in the everyday uniforms, it would make your eyes pop out of your head; no historian could hold onto his senses. Is it monotonous? Well, all right, let's say it's monotonous: they fight and fight, they fight now and they fought before and they fought afterward—you must agree that it is all too monotonous. In a word, one may say anything at all about world history, anything that might come to the mind of the most deranged imagination. There is only one thing that you cannot say—that it is sensible. You'd choke on the first word. And here is the sort of thing that is encountered all the time: you see, there constantly appear in life such decorous and sensible people, such sages and lovers of mankind, who precisely take it as their goal to behave all their lives as decorously and as sensibly as possible, in order to, so to speak, spread the light to their brethren, strictly for the purpose of proving to them that it is in fact possible to live both decorously and sensibly on this earth. And what happens? Predictably, many of these lovers of mankind, sooner or later, toward the end of their life betray their goals by doing something ludicrous, sometimes even something quite unseemly. Now I ask you . . . what can you expect of man in his capacity as a creature endowed with such strange qualities? Go ahead, shower him with all the blessings of the earth, plunge him in over his head in happiness so that only the bubbles pop up on the surface of the happiness as if on water; give him such economic affluence that there would be nothing left for him to do but sleep, eat gingerbread, and attend to the noncessation of world history; even then, even in that

*Anaevsky: A. E. Anaevsky (1788–1886), author of many worthless books that were a constant subject of derision in various publications in the 1850s and 1860s—Trans.

case, man would, out of sheer ingratitude, out of sheer perversity, do something loathsome. He'd even risk the gingerbread and purposely desire the most pernicious rubbish, the most uneconomical nonsense only in order to add his own pernicious fantastic element to all this positive good sense. He'd desire to secure for himself precisely his own fantastic dreams, his own most trivial stupidity, only in order to assure himself (as if this were quite so indispensable) that people are still people and not piano keys, which, even though they are played upon by the laws of nature with their own hands, are threatened with being played with such a heavy hand that it would be impossible to want anything except by the calendar. And that is still not all: even in the event that he really turned out to be a piano key, even if that were proved to him by the natural sciences and mathematics, even then he would not come to his senses, but would purposely do something contrary just out of ingratitude alone; strictly speaking, just to have his own way. And if it should turn out that he does not have the means, he'll think up some destruction and chaos, he'll think up various sufferings but he'll get his way just the same! He'll turn a curse loose on the world, and since man is the only one who can curse (that is his privilege, the one that distinguishes him most significantly from other animals), he will, I bet, through the curse alone, have his way, that is, he will really assure himself that he is a man and not a piano key! If you say that all these things—chaos, darkness, curse—can be calculated by the table so that the very possibility of preliminary calculation will stop everything and reason will have the upper hand—then man will purposely make himself insane for the occasion so as not to have reason and to have his own way! I believe in this, I vouch for it, because it seems that all this human business really consists only in man's proving to himself every minute that he is a man and not a cog, proving it even if it costs him his own skin, proving it even if he has to become a troglodite. And in view of all this, how can I help transgressing by praising the fact that this has not yet come and that for the time being the devil only knows what wanting depends on . . .

You shout at me (if you still care to honor me with your shouts) that, after all, no one is divesting me of my will; the only concern here is to arrange things somehow so that my will, all by itself, would of its own will coincide with my normal advantages, with the laws of nature, and with arithmetic.

Eh, gentlemen, what kind of will of one's own is that going to be, when things come to tables and arithmetic, when there will be only two times two makes four around? My will or not, two times two would still be four. Some free will that is!

*IX*

Gentlemen, I am joking of course, and I realize that I am joking inappropriately but, after all, one shouldn't take everything as a joke. Perhaps I am gnashing my teeth as I joke. Gentlemen, I am tormented by questions; solve them for me. There you are, for instance, trying to break man of old habits and straighten out his will according to the demands of science and common sense. But how do you know that man not only can but *must* be made over this way? How do you deduce that human wanting absolutely *must* improve? In short, how do you know that such an improvement would really be to man's advantage? And if we are to come out with everything, why are you so *perfectly* convinced that not going against the true, normal advantages guaranteed by arguments of reason and arithmetic is always truly advantageous to man and is the law for all mankind? After all, for the time being all that is just a supposition of yours. Let's concede that it is a law of logic, but perhaps it is not at all a law of mankind. Perhaps you think, gentlemen, that I am insane? Let me make a reservation. I agree: man is a predominantly creative animal, condemned to strive consciously toward a goal and to practice the art of engineering, that is, eternally and incessantly to hew a road *to wherever it may lead.* Perhaps the very reason he sometimes wants to slip off to the side is precisely that man is *condemned* to hew that road, and also perhaps, that no matter how stupid the man of direct action is in general, nevertheless it dawns on him that that road, it turns out, almost always goes *wherever it may lead,* and that the important thing is not where it goes, but only that it does go, and that the decorous child, forsaking the engineering art, should not abandon himself to pernicious idleness, which, as everyone knows, is the mother of all vices. Man likes to create and to hew roads, no doubt about it. But why then does he also passionately love destruction and chaos? Now, explain that one if you can! But I would like to put in a few words about that on my own. Don't you think that perhaps the reason he likes destruction and chaos so much (there's no question, after all, that sometimes he likes it a great deal, that's for sure) is that he himself instinctively fears attaining the goal and completing the building being raised? For all you know, perhaps he likes this building only from a distance but not right up close; perhaps he only likes to create it but not live in it, leaving it afterwards *aux animaux domestiques* like ants, sheep, and so on, and so on. Well, now, ants have entirely different tastes. They have an amazing edifice of the same type that is indestructible for all eternity—the anthill.

The worthy ants began with the anthill and, most likely, will end with the anthill, which pays great tribute to their constancy and steadfastness. But man is a frivolous and unseemly creature and maybe, like a chessplayer, likes just the process of attaining the goal alone, and not the goal itself. And who knows (one can't be sure), maybe the entire goal here on earth toward which mankind is striving consists of nothing more than this continuity of process of attainment alone, in other words, in life itself and not actually in the goal proper, which, it goes without saying, cannot be anything except two times two makes four, that is, a formula, and after all, two times two makes four is already not life, gentlemen, but the beginning of death. At least man has always somehow feared this two times two makes four, and I fear it even now. Possibly man does nothing but search for this two times two makes four, crosses oceans, gives his life in this search, but to find it, really to discover it—he is somehow afraid of that, so help me God. After all, he senses that as soon as he finds it, there won't be anything left to search for. Workers, their labor finished, at least get money, go to a tavern, then they land in the cooler—that keeps them busy for a whole week. But where can man go? At any rate there is something uneasy about him that can be observed when he has attained such goals. He likes the attaining, but not altogether to have attained, and that is, of course, terribly funny. In short, man is made in a comical way; obviously there is a pun to be found in all this. But two times two makes four is an insufferable thing. Two times two makes four is, in my opinion, nothing but an impertinence, yes, sir. Two times two makes four looks like a dandy, struts like a cock of the walk blocking your way, and spits. I agree that two times two makes four is a wonderful thing; but if we are to praise everything, then two times two makes five is sometimes a most delightful little thing.

And why are you so firmly, so solemnly convinced that just the normal and positive alone, in a word, that just well-being alone is advantageous to man? Couldn't reason be mistaken about advantages? After all, perhaps well-being is not the only thing man likes? Perhaps he likes suffering just as much? Perhaps suffering is just as advantageous to him as well-being? Yet man sometimes likes suffering terribly, to the point of passion, and that is a fact. There isn't even any need here to look at world history; ask yourself if only you're a man and have lived even a little. As far as my personal opinion is concerned, to like nothing but well-being is somehow even indecent. It may be good or it may be bad, but it is sometimes also very pleasant to break something. I am not really standing up for suffering here, but not for well-being either. I am standing up for . . . my own fancy and for its being guaranteed to me when I need it. Suffering, for instance, is not permitted in vaudeville, I know that. It would be quite unthinkable in the Crystal Palace: suffering is doubt, it is negation, and what kind of Crystal Palace would that be, in which one could doubt? And yet I am certain that man will never reject true suffering, that is, destruction and chaos. Suffering—why, after all, it is the sole cause of consciousness. Even though at the outset I announced that, in my opinion, consciousness is man's greatest misfortune, yet I know that man loves it and will not trade it for any satisfaction. Consciousness, for example, is immeasurably higher than two times two. After two times two, of course, there would be nothing left to do or even to learn. All that will then be possible is this—to plug up your five senses and sink into contemplation. Whereas, with consciousness, you may still have the same result, that is, there will still be nothing to do, but at least you could sometimes flog yourself, and whatever else you may say, it livens up things a little. Perhaps it is retrograde, but it's still better than nothing.

## *X*

You believe in the crystal edifice indestructible for all eternity, the kind that you could never stick your tongue out at on the sly or thumb your nose at secretly. Well, perhaps the reason I am afraid of that edifice is that it is crystal and indestructible for all eternity and one can't even stick one's tongue out at it on the sly.

Look here: if instead of the palace there were a chicken coop, and it were raining, I just might crawl into the chicken coop to keep from getting wet, but nonetheless I wouldn't take the chicken coop for a palace, simply out of gratitude for being sheltered from the rain. You laugh, you even say that it wouldn't matter in this case whether it were a chicken coop or a mansion. Yes, I answer, if not getting wet were the only reason for living.

Well, what is to be done if I have taken it into my head that people are not living just for that, and that if one is to live at all, then one should live in a mansion? That is my want, that is my desire. You will gouge it out of me only when you change my desires. Well, change me, entice me with something different, give me another ideal. But in the meantime I will not take a chicken coop for a palace. Let's even say that the crystal edifice is a bluff, that according to the laws of nature it shouldn't even exist and that I made it up only as a consequence of some of the old-fashioned, irrational habits of our generation. But what do I care if it is not supposed to exist? What does it matter, since it exists in my desires, or rather, exists as long as my desires exist? Perhaps you are laughing again? Please do; I will accept all the derision, and will still not say that I am full when I want to eat; I still know that I will not settle for a compromise, for an uninterrupted periodic zero, just because it exists according to the laws of nature and exists *in fact.* I will not take as the crown of my desires a housing project with apartments for poor tenants, with a lease for a thousand years and, just in case, with the dentist Wagenheim on the signboard. Destroy my desires, erase my ideals, show me something better and I'll follow you. I suppose you will say that it is not worth getting involved, but in that case, I can answer you in the same way, can't I? We're having a serious discussion, but if you do not wish to consider me worthy of your attention, I am not going to get down on my hands and knees. I have the underground.

And as long as I am still alive and have desires, may my arms wither away if I carry so much as a single brick for that kind of housing project! Forget that a while ago I myself had rejected the crystal building just because one cannot taunt it by sticking out one's tongue. I didn't say that because I enjoy sticking out my tongue so much, not at all. Perhaps I was only mad because a building at which one would not feel compelled to stick out one's tongue is yet to be found among your buildings. On the contrary, I would allow my tongue to be cut out altogether, out of sheer gratitude, if things could only be arranged so that I myself would never want to stick it out again. What do I care if it can't be arranged that way and we have to be satisfied with apartments? Why then was I made with such desires? Is it possible that I was made that way only to come to the conclusion that the making of me was simply a swindle? Could that be the whole purpose? I don't believe it.

But anyway, do you know what? I am convinced that the underground likes of me should be held in check. Even though they are capable of remaining in the underground silently for forty years, once they come out into the light and burst open, then they talk, talk, talk . . .

*XI*

The upshot of it all, gentlemen: it's better to do nothing! Better to have conscious inertia! And so, long live the underground! I did say that I envied the normal man with all my guts, but under the conditions in which I see him, I don't want to be him (though I will not stop envying him. No, no, in any case, the underground is more advantageous!). There at least one can . . . Aw!

But here I am lying again. I am lying because I myself know, like two times two, that it is not the underground at all that is better, but something different, entirely different, something that I crave but that I just can't find! To hell with the underground!

Even this would have been better here: if I myself believed anything whatsoever of all that I have just written. But I swear to you, gentlemen, that I do not believe a word, not even one little word of all that I have just dashed off! That is, I do believe, perhaps, but at the same time, I don't know why, I feel and suspect that I am lying like a trooper.

"Then why in the world did you write all this?" you say to me.

"What if I should lock you up for forty years without anything to do, and then after forty years came to visit you in the underground to see how far gone you were? You just can't leave a man alone and without anything to do for forty years!"

"And isn't it shameful, isn't it degrading?" you may say to me, shaking your head with contempt. "You crave life and yet you solve life's questions with a logical mish-mash. And how obnoxious, how insolent your outbursts are, and at the same time how frightened you are! You talk nonsense, and it makes you happy; you say insolent things but you are constantly frightened by them and beg forgiveness. You claim that you are afraid of nothing and at the same time you are worried about our opinion of you. You claim that you are gnashing your teeth and, at the same time, you are cracking jokes to make us laugh. You realize that your jokes are not witty but you are obviously very pleased with their literary merit. Perhaps you did, in fact, happen to suffer, but you don't respect your suffering one bit. There is also truth in you, but no purity; for the sake of the pettiest vanity you put your truth on show, under a cloud, in the marketplace . . . You really want to say something, but out of fear you conceal your final word because instead of the determination to utter it you have only timorous insolence. You glory in your consciousness but all you do is waver, because even though your mind is functioning, your heart is clouded by depravity, and without a pure heart there can be no full, sound consciousness. And how terribly obnoxious you are, how intrusive, affected! Lies, lies, and lies!"

It goes without saying that I just dreamed up all those words of yours. That too comes from the underground. For forty years on end I kept my ear to the crack listening to those words of yours. I thought them up myself, for that's about all that came to me. Small wonder that they were learned by heart and took a literary form . . .

But are you, are you really so gullible that you imagine I might publish all this and, what's more, give it to you to read? And here is another puzzle for me: why, actually, do I call you "gentlemen," why do I address you as if I were really addressing readers? Confessions of the kind that I intend to begin setting forth are not published and are not given to other people to read. I, at least, don't have that much firmness in me and, moreover, I don't see the necessity of having it. But you see, a certain fancy has occurred to me and I want to carry it out at all costs. This is what I have in mind:

In the reminiscences of every man there are some things that he does not reveal to anyone except possibly to friends. Then there are some that he will not even reveal to friends, but only to himself, and even so in secret. But finally there are some that a man is afraid to reveal even to himself, and every decent man accumulates a good number of such things. I'll even venture this: the more decent a man is, the more of them he has. At any rate I myself made up my mind just a little while ago to recall some of my earlier adventures; until now I have always bypassed them, even with a sort of uneasiness. Now, however, when I have not only remembered, but even decided to write it all down, precisely now I want to make a test to find out: is it possible to be completely open with one's own self at least, and not be afraid of the whole truth? Let me say this, by the way: Heine asserts that faithful autobiographies are almost impossible, and that a man will assuredly lie about himself. In his opinion Rousseau, for instance, certainly lied about himself in his confession and even lied intentionally, out of vanity. I am sure that Heine is right; I understand perfectly well how, just out of simple vanity, one can sometimes impute whole crimes to oneself, and I can even conceive very well what kind of vanity that could be. But Heine commented about a man who was making a confession before an audience. I, on the other hand, am writing only for myself, and I state once and for all that if I appear to be writing as though I were addressing readers, it is just simply for show, because it's easier for me to write that way. It is a form, just an irrelevant form, for I am never going to have readers. I have already stated that.

I don't want to feel restricted by anything in editing my notes. I am not going to introduce any system or order. I'll write down whatever I recall.

How about this, for instance: couldn't you split hairs and ask me: "If you really don't expect readers, why are you making pacts with yourself, and on paper yet, namely, that you are not going to introduce any system or order, that you will write whatever you recall, and so on, and so on? Why are you explaining? Why are you making excuses?"

"Well, you figure it out," I answer.

This, by the way, involves an entire psychology. Maybe it's just that I am a coward. And maybe it's just that I purposely imagine an audience in front of me, so that I'll conduct myself more properly while I am writing. There could be a thousand reasons.

But here's something else: why, for precisely what reason do I want to write? If it's not for the public, then couldn't one, you know, just remember everything mentally and not transfer it to paper?

That's right, but on paper it will be somehow more impressive. There is something imposing about it, I will be able to judge myself better, it will enhance the style. Besides, perhaps, I will actually get some relief from writing it down. Today, for example, I am particularly oppressed by a certain recollection from the distant past. It came back to me sharply a few days ago, and since then, it has stuck to me like an annoying musical tune that one cannot get rid of. And yet it is necessary to be rid of it. I have hundreds of such recollections, but occasionally one in particular out of the hundreds stands out and oppresses me. For some reason I believe that if I write it down it will leave me alone. Then why not try it?

Finally, I am bored, yet I continually do nothing. Writing things down is actually something like working. They say that work makes a man kind and honest. Well, there's a chance, at least.

It is snowing today—an almost wet, yellow, dull snow. It was snowing yesterday too, and also a few days ago. It was on account of the wet snow, I think, that I recalled the incident that I can't get rid of now. And so, let this be a story on account of the wet snow.

## Anna Akhmatova (1889–1966)

*Translated by Judith Hemschemeyer*

Born near Odessa, Anna Gorenko took Akhmatova, the name of her Tatar great-grandmother, as her pen name because her father did not want his name associated with poetry. She was well educated and studied Latin and law at the University of Kiev (1906–1907). Akhmatova is one of Russia's most prominent twentieth-century lyric poets. From 1925 to 1940 the government prevented her from publishing any poetry, but during World War II, her poem "Courage," included here, was recited throughout Russia. She produced a vast body of poetry, including powerful love poems, war poems, elegies, and poems about poetry and poets (Dante, Shakespeare, and Pushkin were among her favorites).

Her *Requiem,* like most of the poetry from her last thirty years of writing, is dedicated to remembering. Akhmatova suffered as most Soviet citizens did, living through a time when millions of people were arrested, imprisoned, and executed, and bonds between friends and family were broken or dissolved in fear. She lost people temporarily, permanently, continually and was forced into silence herself. The poet Marina Tsvetaeva called her the "muse of weeping." Her first husband was executed in 1921. In 1935 her lover and her son were imprisoned (the occasion for the *Requiem* cycle). Many of her dearest friends—poets and intellectuals—were exiled, imprisoned, or killed during Stalin's purges. In 1946 a visit from Isaiah Berlin and her immense popularity with Russian citizens led to her expulsion from the Union of Soviet Writers; her son was imprisoned again from 1949 to 1956, which compelled her to write poems praising the Stalinist regime in hopes of helping him survive. In the last decade of her life, hardships eased, and she traveled a little outside the Soviet Union. With the lifting of severe censorship, many of her previously banned poems were finally published.

## *Requiem*

### *"No, not under the vault of alien skies"*

No, not under the vault of alien skies,
And not under the shelter of alien wings—
I was with my people then,
There, where my people, unfortunately, were.

*1961*

## *Instead of a Preface*

In the terrible years of the Yezhov terror, I spent seventeen months in the prison lines of Leningrad. Once, someone "recognized" me. Then a woman with bluish lips standing behind me, who, of course, had never heard me called by name before, woke up from the stupor to which everyone had succumbed and whispered in my ear (everyone spoke in whispers there):

"Can you describe this?"

And I answered: "Yes, I can."

Then something that looked like a smile passed over what had once been her face.

*April 1, 1957*
*Leningrad*

## *Dedication*

Mountains bow down to this grief,
Mighty rivers cease to flow,
But the prison gates hold firm,
And behind them are the "prisoners' burrows"
And mortal woe.
For someone a fresh breeze blows,
For someone the sunset luxuriates—
We wouldn't know, we are those who everywhere
Hear only the rasp of the hateful key
And the soldiers' heavy tread.
We rose as if for an early service,
Trudged through the savaged capital
And met there, more lifeless than the dead;
The sun is lower and the Neva mistier,
But hope keeps singing from afar.
The verdict . . . And her tears gush forth,
Already she is cut off from the rest,
As if they painfully wrenched life from her heart,
As if they brutally knocked her flat,
But she goes on . . . Staggering . . . Alone . . .
Where now are my chance friends
Of those two diabolical years?
What do they imagine is in Siberia's storms,
What appears to them dimly in the circle of the moon?
I am sending my farewell greeting to them.

*March 1940*

## *Prologue*

That was when the ones who smiled
Were the dead, glad to be at rest.
And like a useless appendage, Leningrad
Swung from its prisons.
And when, senseless from torment,
Regiments of convicts marched,
And the short songs of farewell
Were sung by locomotive whistles.
The stars of death stood above us
And innocent Russia writhed
Under bloody boots
And under the tires of the Black Marias.

## *I*

They led you away at dawn,
I followed you, like a mourner,
In the dark front room the children were crying,
By the icon shelf the candle was dying.
On your lips was the icon's chill.
The deathly sweat on your brow . . . Unforgettable!—
I will be like the wives of the Streltsy,
Howling under the Kremlin towers.

*1935*

## *II*

Quietly flows the quiet Don,
Yellow moon slips into a home.

He slips in with cap askew,
He sees a shadow, yellow moon.

This woman is ill,
This woman is alone,

Husband in the grave, son in prison,
Say a prayer for me.

*III*

No, it is not I, it is somebody else who is suffering.
I would not have been able to bear what happened,
Let them shroud it in black,
And let them carry off the lanterns . . .
        Night.

*1940*

*IV*

You should have been shown, you mocker,
Minion of all your friends,
Gay little sinner of Tsarskoye Selo,
What would happen in your life—
How three-hundredth in line, with a parcel,
You would stand by the Kresty prison,
Your fiery tears
Burning through the New Year's ice.
Over there the prison poplar bends,
And there's no sound—and over there how many
Innocent lives are ending now . . .

*V*

For seventeen months I've been crying out,
Calling you home.
I flung myself at the hangman's feet,
You are my son and my horror.
Everything is confused forever,
And it's not clear to me
Who is a beast now, who is a man,
And how long before the execution.
And there are only dusty flowers,
And the chinking of the censer, and tracks
From somewhere to nowhere.
And staring me straight in the eyes,
And threatening impending death,
Is an enormous star.

*1939*

## *VI*

The light weeks will take flight,
I won't comprehend what happened.
Just as the white nights
Stared at you, dear son, in prison,

So they are staring again,
With the burning eyes of a hawk,
Talking about your lofty cross,
And about death.

*1939*

## *VII: The Sentence*

And the stone word fell
On my still-living breast.
Never mind, I was ready.
I will manage somehow.

Today I have so much to do:
I must kill memory once and for all,
I must turn my soul to stone,
I must learn to live again—

Unless . . . Summer's ardent rustling
Is like a festival outside my window.
For a long time I've foreseen this
Brilliant day, deserted house.

*June 22, 1939*
*Fountain House*

## *VIII: To Death*

You will come in any case—so why not now?
I am waiting for you—I can't stand much more.
I've put out the light and opened the door
For you, so simple and miraculous.
So come in any form you please,

Burst in as a gas shell
Or, like a gangster, steal in with a length of pipe,
Or poison me with typhus fumes.
Or be that fairy tale you've dreamed up,
So sickeningly familiar to everyone—
In which I glimpse the top of a pale blue cap
And the house attendant white with fear.
Now it doesn't matter anymore. The Yenisey swirls,
The North Star shines.
And the final horror dims
The blue luster of beloved eyes.

*August 19, 1939*
*Fountain House*

## *IX*

Now madness half shadows
My soul with its wing,
And makes it drunk with fiery wine
And beckons toward the black ravine.

And I've finally realized
That I must give in,
Overhearing myself
Raving as if it were somebody else.

And it does not allow me to take
Anything of mine with me
(No matter how I plead with it,
No matter how I supplicate):

Not the terrible eyes of my son—
Suffering turned to stone,
Not the day of the terror,
Not the hour I met with him in prison,

Not the sweet coolness of his hands,
Not the trembling shadow of the lindens,
Not the far-off, fragile sound—
Of the final words of consolation.

*May 4, 1940*
*Fountain House*

## *X: Crucifixion*

*"Do not weep for Me, Mother,*
*I am in the grave."*

### 1

A choir of angels sang the praises of that
momentous hour,
And the heavens dissolved in fire.
To his Father He said: "Why hast Thou forsaken me!"
And to his Mother: "Oh, do not weep for Me . . . "

*1940*
*Fountain House*

### 2

Mary Magdalene beat her breast and sobbed,
The beloved disciple turned to stone,
But where the silent Mother stood, there
No one glanced and no one would have dared.

*1943*
*Tashkent*

## *Epilogue I*

I learned how faces fall,
How terror darts from under eyelids,
How suffering traces lines
Of stiff cuneiform on cheeks,
How locks of ashen-blonde or black
Turn silver suddenly,
Smiles fade on submissive lips
And fear trembles in a dry laugh.
And I pray not for myself alone,
But for all those who stood there with me
In cruel cold, and in July's heat,
At that blind, red wall.

## *Epilogue II*

Once more the day of remembrance draws near.
I see, I hear, I feel you:

The one they almost had to drag at the end,
And the one who tramps her native land no more,

And the one who, tossing her beautiful head,
Said: "Coming here's like coming home."

I'd like to name them all by name,
But the list has been confiscated and is nowhere to be found.

I have woven a wide mantle for them
From their meager, overheard words.

I will remember them always and everywhere,
I will never forget them no matter what comes.

And if they gag my exhausted mouth
Through which a hundred million scream,

Then may the people remember me
On the eve of my remembrance day.

And if ever in this country
They decide to erect a monument to me,

I consent to that honor
Under these conditions—that it stand

Neither by the sea, where I was born:
My last tie with the sea is broken,

Nor in the tsar's garden near the cherished pine stump,
Where an inconsolable shade looks for me,

But here, where I stood for three hundred hours,
And where they never unbolted the doors for me.

This, lest in blissful death
I forget the rumbling of the Black Marias,

Forget how that detested door slammed shut
And an old woman howled like a wounded animal.

And may the melting snow stream like tears
From my motionless lids of bronze,

And a prison dove coo in the distance,
And the ships of the Neva sail calmly on.

*March 1940*

## Dante

*Il mio bel San Giovanni.*—Dante*

Even after his death he did not return
To his ancient Florence.
To the one who, leaving, did not look back,
To him I sing this song.
A torch, the night, the last embrace,
Beyond the threshold, the wild wail of fate.
From hell he sent her curses
And in paradise he could not forget her—
But barefoot, in a hairshirt,
With a lighted candle he did not walk
Through his Florence—his beloved,
Perfidious, base, longed for . . .

*August 17, 1936*

## Courage

We know what lies in balance at this moment,
And what is happening right now.
The hour for courage strikes upon our clocks,
And courage will not desert us.
We're not frightened by a hail of lead,
We're not bitter without a roof overhead—
And we will preserve you, Russian speech,
Mighty Russian word!
We will transmit you to our grandchildren
Free and pure and rescued from captivity
Forever!

*February 23, 1942*
*Tashkent*

## Native Land

*But there is no people on earth more tearless,*
*More simple and more full of pride.*
1922

We don't wear her on our breast in cherished amulets,
We don't, with wrenching sobs, write verse about her,

**My beautiful San Giovanni.* (It.)

She does not disturb our bitter sleep,
Nor seem to us the promised paradise.
We have not made her, in our souls,
An object to be bought or sold.
Suffering, sick, wandering over her,
We don't even remember her.
  Yes, for us it's the mud on galoshes,
  Yes, for us it's the grit on our teeth.
  And we grind, and we knead, and we crumble
  This clean dust.
But we lie in her and we become her,
And because of that we freely call her—ours.

*1961*
*Leningrad. The hospital in the harbor.*

## Creation

  . . . it says:
I remember everything simultaneously;
Like the distant beam of a distant lighthouse,
I carry the universe before me
Like an easy burden in an outstretched palm,
And in the depths, mysteriously growing, is the seed
Of what is to come . . .

*November 14, 1959*
*Leningrad*

# POLAND

## WISLAWA SZYMBORSKA (B. 1923)

*Translated by Stanislaw Baránczak and Clare Cavanagh*

Although she has spent much of her adult life under repressive regimes—first the Nazi occupation of Poland, then the Soviet-backed Communist regime—Wislawa Szymborska has nevertheless managed to publish a powerful body of poetry that has made her a world-famous literary figure. Szymborska was born in a small town near Poznan in western Poland. She studied Polish literature and sociology at the Jagellonian University in Cracow from 1945 to 1948, and has lived in Cracow ever since. She has been at the heart of Polish literary life, editing and writing for newspapers and periodicals as well as working on her own poetry and translations. She won the Nobel Prize in literature in 1996.

Szymborska's early work conformed to the Communist requirements for "social realism"—an approach to art that required the expression of state-approved socialist political ideals. Censorship began to ease in the mid-1950s, however, allowing Polish writers to express themselves more freely and seek genuine intellectual independence. Since 1957 Szymborska has produced a series of small but forceful volumes of poetry as well as accomplished translations of French poetry and several volumes of book reviews. Her aesthetic credo is expressed at the end of a poem called "The Joy of Writing":

> The joy of writing.
> Power of preserving.
> The revenge of a mortal hand.

Her range of stylistic exploration is impossible to translate adequately, but the best translations preserve an economy of expression, a wry sense of humor, and an ironic understatement. Her themes range from the impossibility of fully knowing the secrets of nature ("Conversation with a Stone") to the unity of all matter on the globe ("Water") to the erosion of modern confidence in progress ("The Century's Decline"). Some poems express a macabre sense of the tricks played on people by the fleeting illusions of the world. "Theatre Impressions," for example, expands outward from an apparently simple comment on the experience of seeing a stage fiction suddenly trumped by the reality of actors taking their bows and removing their costumes.

## *Water*

A drop of water fell on my hand,
drawn from the Ganges and the Nile,

from hoarfrost ascended to heaven off a seal's whiskers,
from jugs broken in the cities of Ys and Tyre.

On my index finger
the Caspian Sea isn't landlocked,

and the Pacific is the Rudawa's meek tributary,
the same stream that floated in a little cloud over Paris

in the year seven hundred and sixty-four
on the seventh of May at three a.m.

There are not enough mouths to utter
all your fleeting names, O water.

I would have to name you in every tongue,
pronouncing all the vowels at once

while also keeping silent—for the sake of the lake
that still goes unnamed

and doesn't exist on this earth, just as the star
reflected in it is not in the sky.

Someone was drowning, someone dying was
calling out for you. Long ago, yesterday.

You have saved houses from fire, you have carried off
houses and trees, forests and towns alike.

You've been in christening fonts and courtesans' baths.
In coffins and kisses.

Gnawing at stone, feeding rainbows.
In the sweat and the dew of pyramids and lilacs.

How light the raindrop's contents are.
How gently the world touches me.

Whenever wherever whatever has happened
is written on waters of Babel.

## *Conversation with a Stone*

I knock at the stone's front door.
"It's only me, let me come in.
I want to enter your insides,
have a look round,
breathe my fill of you."

"Go away," says the stone.
"I'm shut tight.
Even if you break me to pieces,
we'll all still be closed.
You can grind us to sand,
we still won't let you in."

I knock at the stone's front door.
"It's only me, let me come in.
I've come out of pure curiosity.
Only life can quench it.
I mean to stroll through your palace,
then go calling on a leaf, a drop of water.
I don't have much time.
My mortality should touch you."

"I'm made of stone," says the stone,
"and must therefore keep a straight face.
Go away.
I don't have the muscles to laugh."

I knock at the stone's front door.
"It's only me, let me come in.
I hear you have great empty halls inside you,
unseen, their beauty in vain,
soundless, not echoing anyone's steps.
Admit you don't know them well yourself."

"Great and empty, true enough," says the stone,
"but there isn't any room.
Beautiful, perhaps, but not to the taste
of your poor senses.

You may get to know me, but you'll never know me through.
My whole surface is turned toward you,
all my insides turned away."

I knock at the stone's front door.
"It's only me, let me come in.
I don't seek refuge for eternity.
I'm not unhappy.
I'm not homeless.
My world is worth returning to.
I'll enter and exit empty-handed.

And my proof I was there
will be only words,
which no one will believe."

"You shall not enter," says the stone.
"You lack the sense of taking part.
No other sense can make up for your missing sense of
taking part.
Even sight heightened to become all-seeing
will do you no good without a sense of taking part.
You shall not enter, you have only a sense of what that
sense should be,
only its seed, imagination."

I knock at the stone's front door.
"It's only me, let me come in.
I haven't got two thousand centuries,
so let me come under your roof."

"If you don't believe me," says the stone,
"just ask the leaf, it will tell you the same.
Ask a drop of water, it will say what the leaf has said.
And, finally, ask a hair from your own head.
I am bursting with laughter, yes, laughter, vast laughter,
although I don't know how to laugh."

I knock at the stone's front door.
"It's only me, let me come in."

"I don't have a door," says the stone.

## *Theatre Impressions*

For me the tragedy's most important act is the sixth:
the raising of the dead from the stage's battlegrounds,
the straightening of wigs and fancy gowns,
removing knives from stricken breasts,
taking nooses from lifeless necks,
lining up among the living
to face the audience.

The bows, both solo and ensemble—
the pale hand on the wounded heart,
the curtseys of the hapless suicide,
the bobbing of the chopped-off head.

The bows in pairs—
rage extends its arm to meekness,
the victim's eyes smile at the torturer,
the rebel indulgently walks beside the tyrant.

Eternity trampled by the golden slipper's toe.
Redeeming values swept aside with the swish of a wide-brimmed hat.
The unrepentant urge to start all over tomorrow.

Now enter, single file, the hosts who died early on,
in Acts 3 and 4, or between scenes.

The miraculous return of all those lost without a trace.
The thought that they've been waiting patiently offstage
without taking off their makeup
or their costumes
moves me more than all the tragedy's tirades.

But the curtain's fall is the most uplifting part,
the things you see before it hits the floor:
here one hand quickly reaches for a flower,
there another hand picks up a fallen sword.
Only then one last, unseen, hand
does its duty
and grabs me by the throat.

## *Seen from Above*

A dead beetle lies on the path through the field.
Three pairs of legs folded neatly on its belly.
Instead of death's confusion, tidiness and order.
The horror of this sight is moderate,
its scope is strictly local, from the wheat grass to the mint.
The grief is quarantined.
The sky is blue.

To preserve our peace of mind, animals die
more shallowly: they aren't deceased, they're dead.
They leave behind, we'd like to think, less feeling and less world,
departing, we suppose, from a stage less tragic.
Their meek souls never haunt us in the dark,
they know their place,
they show respect.

And so the dead beetle on the path
lies unmourned and shining in the sun.
One glance at it will do for meditation—
clearly nothing much has happened to it.
Important matters are reserved for us,
for our life and our death, a death
that always claims the right of way.

## *Our Ancestors' Short Lives*

Few of them made it to thirty.
Old age was the privilege of rocks and trees.
Childhood ended as fast as wolf cubs grow.
One had to hurry, to get on with life
before the sun went down,
before the first snow.

Thirteen-year-olds bearing children,
four-year-olds stalking birds' nests in the rushes,
leading the hunt at twenty—
they aren't yet, then they are gone.
Infinity's ends fused quickly.
Witches chewed charms
with all the teeth of youth intact.
A son grew to manhood beneath his father's eye.
Beneath the grandfather's blank sockets the grandson
was born.

And anyway they didn't count the years.
They counted nets, pods, sheds, and axes.
Time, so generous toward any petty star in the sky,
offered them a nearly empty hand
and quickly took it back, as if the effort were too much.
One step more, two steps more
along the glittering river
that sprang from darkness and vanished into darkness.

There wasn't a moment to lose,
no deferred questions, no belated revelations,
just those experienced in time.
Wisdom couldn't wait for gray hair.
It had to see clearly before it saw the light
and to hear every voice before it sounded.

Good and evil—
they knew little of them, but knew all:
when evil triumphs, good goes into hiding;
when good is manifest, then evil lies low.
Neither can be conquered
or cast off beyond return.
Hence, if joy, then with a touch of fear;
if despair, then not without some quiet hope.
Life, however long, will always be short.
Too short for anything to be added.

## *The Century's Decline*

Our twentieth century was going to improve on the others.
It will never prove it now,
now that its years are numbered,
its gait is shaky,
its breath is short.

Too many things have happened
that weren't supposed to happen,
and what was supposed to come about
has not.

Happiness and spring, among other things,
were supposed to be getting closer.

Fear was expected to leave the mountains and the valleys.
Truth was supposed to hit home
before a lie.

A couple of problems weren't going
to come up anymore:
hunger, for example,
and war, and so forth.

There was going to be respect
for helpless people's helplessness,
trust, that kind of stuff.

Anyone who planned to enjoy the world
is now faced
with a hopeless task.

Stupidity isn't funny.
Wisdom isn't gay.
Hope
isn't that young girl anymore,
et cetera, alas.

God was finally going to believe
in a man both good and strong,
but good and strong
are still two different men.

"How should we live?" someone asked me in a letter.
I had meant to ask him
the same question.

Again, and as ever,
as may be seen above,
the most pressing questions
are naïve ones.

## *Nothing's a Gift*

Nothing's a gift, it's all on loan.
I'm drowning in debts up to my ears.
I'll have to pay for myself
with my self,
give up my life for my life.

Here's how it's arranged:
The heart can be repossessed,
the liver, too,
and each single finger and toe.

Too late to tear up the terms,
my debts will be repaid,
and I'll be fleeced,
or, more precisely, flayed.

I move about the planet
in a crush of other debtors.
Some are saddled with the burden
of paying off their wings.
Others must, willy-nilly,
account for every leaf.

Every tissue in us lies
on the debit side.
Not a tentacle or tendril
is for keeps.

The inventory, infinitely detailed,
implies we'll be left
not just empty-handed
but handless, too.

I can't remember
where, when, and why
I let someone open
this account in my name.

We call the protest against this
the soul.
And it's the only item
not included on the list.

# The Americas

Only in the Modern Period have the Americas emerged as a distinctive literary presence in global culture. Indigenous peoples such as the Maya and Aztecs of Central America, the Incas of South America, and the Mississippi Mound people of North America developed complex, self-conscious urban cultures before significant European contact; but as far as we know at present, only the Maya used a writing system to record poetic, historical, or narrative works. The *Popul Vuh,* their astonishing mythological epic, marks the beginning of New World literature at the very opening of the Modern Period. Despite the absence of written works, all native peoples of the hemisphere transmitted histories, cosmologies, poems, myths, and folktales in rich oral traditions, many of which still remain to be collected.

In their urge to conquer indigenous peoples and convey the alleged benefits of European civilization to them, explorers and colonists destroyed much of the culture they encountered. The conquest of Mexico was especially destructive in literary terms, for hundreds of Mayan manuscripts were burned, inscribed monuments were defaced, and people educated in the literary traditions were killed or forced into slavery. The Spanish language was imposed on the native peoples of Central and South America (except in Brazil, where Portuguese was imposed). North American indigenous peoples were treated similarly by Spanish, French, and British colonial powers. In a few cases priests interested in Indian cultures helped preserve manuscripts or worked with native interpreters to record stories, legends, customs, and poetry. Until the recent decipherment of Mayan hieroglyphs, such transcribed oral traditions were the only written records we possessed of pre-European cultures in the Americas.

In many isolated areas Indians continued to keep their oral traditions alive, although they were influenced by Christian beliefs and European narrative traditions. Mayan peoples in southern Mexico, Guatemala, and Belize continued to practice traditional religious rituals and calendrical reckoning and to recite stories and poems that preserved their ancient culture. Many tribal peoples of South America also kept oral traditions alive. In the meantime, tribal peoples learned the European languages of the colonists and since the nineteenth century have been writing their own literary works in these languages, contributing to emerging national literatures. The last selection in our anthology is by Louise Erdrich, who belongs to a new generation of Native American writers in the United States. Here she tells a story that captures the conflict of traditional and European cultures in the mind of a mixed-blood Chippewa girl growing up on a reservation in North Dakota.

In discovering and settling what seemed to them a New World, Europeans sought to describe what they found, to chronicle their adventures in exotic new places, to justify their establishment of homes and communities, and to create their literatures distinct from those of Europe. This last process can be said to have seriously begun only in the nineteenth century and to have come to real fruition throughout the hemisphere in the twentieth. Meanwhile, the early descriptions of native peoples and accounts of settlement caused great ferment in Europe, fueling idealized conceptions of alternative cultural values, the myth of the Noble Savage, fantastic visions of vast riches in virgin landscapes, and fresh perspectives on European traditions such as the pastoral. Indian customs prompted new ideas in philosophers and poets like Thomas More (see his *Utopia*, pp. 1244–1263) and Montaigne (see his *Of Cannibals*, pp. 1388–1398).

What is "American" culture? Are some cultural experiences common to the whole hemisphere and also unique to it? Rapid hybridization, creolization, self-consciousness about race and origin, slavery, confrontation with aboriginal peoples and the wilderness—these and other experiences gave birth to New World perspectives and literary programs. Their dramatic takeover of the hemisphere led European settlers to develop ideals of individuality and power that could derive only from conquest but were masked by a presumption of innocence. At the same time, however, enormous cultural dynamism resulted from these encounters.

As in biological "ecotones," or borders where ecosystems overlap, diversity is richest and new life forms emerge, so also the dynamic processes of cultural mingling among indigenous peoples, African slaves, and European colonists created vibrant new artistic and literary forms in the Americas. Sugar plantations in the Caribbean created very different conditions for literary life than did middle-class small farms and commercial enterprises in New England. One result shared by all, however, was explosive cultural energy. Another was the "magical realism" developed by South American writers like Gabriel Garcia Márquez, who injected into the European genre of the realistic novel the exaggerated style of indigenous oral folktales. Jorge Luis Borges from Argentina, Márquez from Colombia, Toni Morrison and Louise Erdrich from the United States, and Ángela Hernández from the Dominican Republic all employ that style, which has begun to influence writers around the world such as Salman Rushdie in India and Abe Kōbō in Japan.

In the United States, jazz, the "Western," and Hollywood films are obvious examples of distinctive artistic innovations and, in fact, much of American literature (that is, literature of the United States) is distinctive. By the middle of the nineteenth century, Ralph Waldo Emerson was calling for an "American poet," and the call was answered in two innovative ways by Walt Whitman and Emily Dickinson. In the same period Hawthorne explored the history of the United States, especially its Puritan religious and ethical heritage, in deeply symbolic romances that intensify the affairs of ordinary life for rhetorical effect. Thoreau created a new prose form in *Walden,* in which Montaigne-like philosophical musings take on a new literary style that is deeply responsive to the natural world. Mark Twain brought the epic down to earth, sending Huck Finn and Jim, the runaway slave, down the Mississippi on a raft. In our own century, Faulkner was influenced by Hawthorne's notion of the romance, and he in turn influenced Márquez by creating a dense, convoluted Romantic prose capable of conveying the florid tone of Southern life and exploring its underside. It is wrong to say that Europeans "discovered" America, but it is certainly right to say that the New World settlers invented literature anew.

# THE MAYA

## THE POPUL VUH

*Translated by Dennis Tedlock*

The Mayan lords of Quiché called this ancient text their "Council Book" and consulted it as an instrument for seeing the future, the past, and the powers that govern the world. It was also variously named "Our Place in the Shadows" and "The Dawn of Life." The *Popul Vuh* is the great epic of Native American literature. It could conceivably descend from oral traditions reaching back a thousand years before its writing to the Central American coastal civilization of the Olmecs who preceded the Maya. It begins with the Mayan creation story, in which living creatures are fashioned by the "Maker, Modeler, mother-father of life" in a series of experiments that only gradually produce viable forms. This origin story allows readers to recover the vision of the first four humans, who were able to see the true four-sided and four-cornered shape of the world. The book also presents a long cycle of narratives about the gods who prepared the sky-earth for human life and founded the kingship of the Quiché people, as well as the exploits of Hero Twins related to similar figures in Navajo mythology.

Mayan writing developed in hieroglyphic forms that have a logosyllabic nature like ancient Hittite and modern Japanese; that is, hieroglyphic signs function both as pictographs and as phonetic symbols. Dramatic breakthroughs in the mid-1980s made it possible to decipher the Mayan hieroglyphs and finally hear their creators speaking across the centuries. The Spanish conquistadors burned almost all

Mayan writings, but the *Popul Vuh* survived because ingenious Mayan scribes learned from Spanish missionaries how to create a romanized form of their language. One bilingual copy in Quiché and Spanish survived, transcribed by a Spanish missionary whose very compatriots were responsible for the virtual destruction of Mayan civilization.

Before the recent decipherment of Mayan hieroglyphs, some of the bloody practices pictured in Mayan art were thought to be fantastical or purely figurative. The Maya were often thought to have been a nonviolent people whose complex civilization functioned in harmony with their environment. Now we have a fuller and grimmer picture of their lives. Although some of the grisly events in the *Popul Vuh,* like decapitation and ball games played with human heads, have symbolic meanings in the narrative, they also seem to reflect the Maya's warlike habits and the regular human sacrifice of captives and orphaned children. Ambitious kings instigated frequent wars and monumental construction projects that strained the capacity of the landscape and subjugated large populations, eventually leading to environmental collapse. Before that catastrophe, however, and these disturbing practices notwithstanding, classical Mayan civilization flourished from 300 to around 900 CE, dominating much of Central America and what is now southern Mexico. It produced vibrant art, architecture, technology, and literature. In the hierarchical Mayan society, writers were artist-scribes who belonged to the highest social strata.

Our selections from the *Popul Vuh* include the opening accounts of the creation and the story of the hero twins Hunahpu and Xbalanque, who travel to the underworld to defeat its terrible lords, One and Seven Death, in the Ball Game Sacrifice. By those means they rescue their twin fathers, the corn gods One Hunahpu and Seven Hunahpu. Their survival depends on trickster abilities that allow them to playfully outwit a very hostile world. There are many interesting comparisons to be drawn between the *Popul Vuh* and the creation stories in Hesiod's *Theogony,* the biblical Genesis, and the Japanese *Kojiki,* as well as to the underworld descents of Inanna, Gilgamesh, Persephone, and Odysseus and related fertility myths and epic journeys.

The selections are taken from the excellent recent translation by Dennis Tedlock, which takes advantage of many of the latest advances in Mayan archaeology and epigraphy.

# Mayan Writing

u dzib
"his writing"

"son of"

u "the moon"

Black

West

yal
"child of" (mother)

u nichin
"child of" (father)

Mayan hieroglyphic writing has been deciphered only in the past twenty-five years through international cooperation of scholars and archaeologists. It has opened up a whole cultural world to our understanding, causing drastic reassessments of Mayan civilization. Formerly considered peaceful and harmonious as a culture, the Maya now speak for themselves through their inscriptions as a fiercely warlike people with a richly developed artistic, literary, astronomical, and mathematical heritage. There are about eight hundred signs in Mayan hieroglyphic script, but these include many archaic logograms and royal names later dropped from general use. For normal purposes only about two hundred to three hundred glyphs were actually being utilized. The understanding of this writing system is still evolving.

## Part I [The Creation]

This is the beginning of the Ancient Word, here in this place called Quiché. Here we shall inscribe, we shall implant the Ancient Word, the potential and source for everything done in the citadel of Quiché, in the nation of Quiché people.

And here we shall take up the demonstration, revelation, and account of how things were put in shadow and brought to light

by the Maker, Modeler, named
Bearer, Begetter,
Hunahpu Possum, Hunahpu
Coyote,
Great White Peccary, Tapir,
Sovereign Plumed Serpent,
Heart of the Lake, Heart of the
Sea,
Maker of the Blue-Green Plate,
Maker of the Blue-Green Bowl,

as they are called, also named, also described as

the midwife, matchmaker
named Xpiyacoc, Xmucane,
defender, protector,
twice a midwife, twice a
matchmaker,

as is said in the words of Quiché. They accounted for everything—and did it, too—as enlightened beings, in enlightened words. We shall write about this now amid the preaching of God, in Christendom now. We shall bring it out because there is no longer a place to see it, a Council Book,

a place to see "The Light That
Came from Across the Sea,"
the account of "Our Place in the
Shadows,"
a place to see "The Dawn of Life,"

as it is called. There is the original book and ancient writing, but he who reads and ponders it hides his face. It takes a long performance and account to complete the emergence of all the sky-earth:

the fourfold siding, fourfold
cornering,
measuring, fourfold staking,
halving the cord, stretching the
cord
in the sky, on the earth,
the four sides, the four corners,

as it is said,

by the Maker, Modeler,
mother-father of life, of
humankind,
giver of breath, giver of heart,
bearer, upbringer in the light that
lasts
of those born in the light,
begotten in the light;
worrier, knower of everything,
whatever there is:
sky-earth, lake-sea.

This is the account, here it is:

Now it still ripples, now it still murmurs, ripples, it still sighs, still hums, and it is empty under the sky.

Here follow the first words, the first eloquence:

There is not yet one person, one animal, bird, fish, crab, tree, rock, hollow, canyon, meadow, forest. Only the sky alone is there; the face of the earth is not clear. Only the sea alone is pooled under all the sky; there is nothing whatever gathered together. It is at rest; not a single thing stirs. It is held back, kept at rest under the sky.

Whatever there is that might be is simply not there: only the pooled water, only the calm sea, only it alone is pooled.

Whatever might be is simply not there: only murmurs, ripples, in the dark, in the night. Only the Maker, Modeler alone, Sovereign Plumed Serpent, the Bearers, Begetters are in the water, a glittering light. They are there, they are enclosed in quetzal feathers, in blue-green.

Thus the name, "Plumed Serpent." They are great knowers, great thinkers in their very being.

And of course there is the sky, and there is also the Heart of Sky. This is the name of the god, as it is spoken.

And then came his word, he came here to the Sovereign Plumed Serpent, here in the blackness, in the early dawn. He spoke with the Sovereign Plumed Serpent, and they talked, then they thought, then they worried. They agreed with each other, they joined their words, their thoughts. Then it was clear, then they reached accord in the light, and then humanity was clear, when they conceived the growth, the generation of trees, of bushes, and the growth of life, of humankind, in the blackness, in the early dawn, all because of the Heart of Sky, named Hurricane. Thunderbolt Hurricane comes first, the second is Newborn Thunderbolt, and the third is Raw Thunderbolt.

So there were three of them, as Heart of Sky, who came to the Sovereign Plumed Serpent, when the dawn of life was conceived:

"How should it be sown, how should it dawn? Who is to be the provider, nurturer?"

"Let it be this way, think about it: this water should be removed, emptied out for the formation of the earth's own plate and platform, then comes the sowing, the dawning of the sky-earth. But there will be no high days and no bright praise for our work, our design, until the rise of the human work, the human design," they said.

And then the earth arose because of them, it was simply their word that brought it forth. For the forming of the earth they said "Earth." It arose suddenly, just like a cloud, like a mist, now forming, unfolding. Then the mountains were separated from the water, all at once the great mountains came forth. By their genius alone, by their cutting edge alone they carried out the conception of the mountain-plain, whose face grew instant groves of cypress and pine.

And the Plumed Serpent was pleased with this:

"It was good that you came, Heart of Sky, Hurricane, and Newborn Thunderbolt, Raw Thunderbolt. Our work, our design will turn out well," they said.

And the earth was formed first, the mountain-plain. The channels of water were separated; their branches wound their ways among the mountains. The waters were divided when the great mountains appeared.

Such was the formation of the earth when it was brought forth by the Heart of Sky, Heart of Earth, as they are called, since they were the first to think of it. The sky was set apart, and the earth was set apart in the midst of the waters.

Such was their plan when they thought, when they worried about the completion of their work.

Now they planned the animals of the mountains, all the guardians of the forests, creatures of the mountains: the deer, birds, pumas, jaguars, serpents, rattlesnakes, yellowbites, guardians of the bushes.

A Bearer, Begetter speaks:

"Why this pointless humming? Why should there merely be rustling beneath the trees and bushes?"

"Indeed—they had better have guardians," the others replied. As soon as they thought it and said it, deer and birds came forth.

And then they gave out homes to the deer and birds:

"You, the deer: sleep along the rivers, in the canyons. Be here in the meadows, in the thickets, in the forests, multiply yourselves. You will stand and walk on all fours," they were told.

So then they established the nests of the birds, small and great:

"You, precious birds: your nests, your houses are in the trees, in the bushes. Multiply there, scatter there, in the branches of trees, the branches of bushes," the deer and birds were told.

When this deed had been done, all of them had received a place to sleep and a place to stay. So it is that the nests of the animals are on the earth, given by the Bearer, Begetter. Now the arrangement of the deer and birds was complete.

And then the deer and birds were told by the Maker, Modeler, Bearer, Begetter:

"Talk, speak out. Don't moan, don't cry out. Please talk, each to each, within each kind, within each group," they were told—the deer, birds, puma, jaguar, serpent.

"Name now our names, praise us. We are your mother, we are your father. Speak now:

'Hurricane,
Newborn Thunderbolt, Raw
  Thunderbolt,
Heart of Sky, Heart of Earth,
Maker, Modeler,
Bearer, Begetter,'

speak, pray to us, keep our days," they were told. But it didn't turn out that they spoke like people: they just squawked, they just chattered, they just howled. It wasn't apparent what language they spoke; each one gave a different cry. When the Maker, Modeler heard this:

"It hasn't turned out well, they haven't spoken," they said among themselves. "It hasn't turned out that our names have been named. Since we are their mason and sculptor, this will not do," the Bearers and Begetters said among themselves. So they told them:

"You will simply have to be transformed. Since it hasn't turned out well and you haven't spoken, we have changed our word:

"What you feed on, what you eat, the places where you sleep, the places where you stay, whatever is yours will remain in the canyons, the forests. Although it turned out that our days were not kept, nor did you pray to us, there may yet be strength in the keeper of days, the giver of praise whom we have yet to make. Just accept your service, just let your flesh be eaten.

"So be it, this must be your service," they were told when they were instructed—the animals, small and great, on the face of the earth.

And then they wanted to test their timing again, they wanted to experiment again, and they wanted to prepare for the keeping of days again. They had not heard their speech among the animals; it did not come to fruition and it was not complete.

And so their flesh was brought low: they served, they were eaten, they were killed—the animals on the face of the earth.

Again there comes an experiment with the human work, the human design, by the Maker, Modeler, Bearer, Begetter:

"It must simply be tried again. The time for the planting and dawning is nearing. For this we must make a provider and nurturer. How else can we be invoked and remembered on the face of the earth? We have already made our first try at our work and design, but it turned out that they didn't keep our days, nor did they glorify us.

"So now let's try to make a giver of praise, giver of respect, provider, nurturer," they said.

So then comes the building and working with earth and mud. They made a body, but it didn't look good to them. It was just separating, just crumbling, just loosening, just softening, just disintegrating, and just dissolving. Its head wouldn't turn, either. Its face was just lopsided, its face was just twisted. It couldn't look around. It talked at first, but senselessly. It was quickly dissolving in the water.

"It won't last," the mason and sculptor said then. "It seems to be dwindling away, so let it just dwindle. It can't walk and it can't multiply, so let it be merely a thought," they said.

So then they dismantled, again they brought down their work and design. Again they talked:

"What is there for us to make that would turn out well, that would succeed in keeping our days and praying to us?" they said. Then they planned again:

"We'll just tell Xpiyacoc, Xmucane, Hunahpu Possum, Hunahpu Coyote, to try a counting of days, a counting of lots," the mason and sculptor said to themselves. Then they invoked Xpiyacoc, Xmucane.

Then comes the naming of those who are the midmost seers: the "Grandmother of Day, Grandmother of Light," as the Maker, Modeler called them. These are names of Xpiyacoc and Xmucane.

When Hurricane had spoken with the Sovereign Plumed Serpent, they invoked the daykeepers, diviners, the midmost seers:

"There is yet to find, yet to discover how we are to model a person, construct a person again, a provider, nurturer, so that we are called upon and we are recognized: our recompense is in words.

> Midwife, matchmaker,
> our grandmother, our
> grandfather,
> Xpiyacoc, Xmucane,
> let there be planting, let there be
> the dawning
> of our invocation, our sustenance,
> our recognition
> by the human work, the human
> design,
> the human figure, the human
> mass.

So be it, fulfill your names:

> Hunahpu Possum, Hunahpu
> Coyote,
> Bearer twice over, Begetter twice
> over,
> Great Peccary, Great Tapir,
> lapidary, jeweler,
> sawyer, carpenter,
> Maker of the Blue-Green Plate,
> Maker of the Blue-Green Bowl,
> incense maker, master craftsman,
> Grandmother of Day,
> Grandmother of Light.

You have been called upon because of our work, our design. Run your hands over the kernels of corn, over the seeds of the coral tree, just get it done, just let it come out whether we should carve and gouge a mouth, a face in wood," they told the daykeepers.

And then comes the borrowing, the counting of days; the hand is moved over the corn kernels, over the coral seeds, the days, the lots.

Then they spoke to them, one of them a grandmother, the other a grandfather.

This is the grandfather, this is the master of the coral seeds: Xpiyacoc is his name.

And this is the grandmother, the daykeeper, diviner who stands behind others: Xmucane is her name.

And they said, as they set out the days:

"Just let it be found, just let it be discovered,
say it, our ear is listening,
may you talk, may you speak,
just find the wood for the carving and sculpting
by the builder, sculptor.
Is this to be the provider, the nurturer
when it comes to the planting, the dawning?
You corn kernels, you coral seeds,
you days, you lots:
may you succeed, may you be accurate,"

they said to the corn kernels, coral seeds, days, lots. "Have shame, you up there, Heart of Sky: attempt no deception before the mouth and face of Sovereign Plumed Serpent," they said. Then they spoke straight to the point:

"It is well that there be your manikins, woodcarvings, talking, speaking, there on the face of the earth."

"So be it," they replied. The moment they spoke it was done: the manikins, woodcarvings, human in looks and human in speech.

This was the peopling of the face of the earth:

They came into being, they multiplied, they had daughters, they had sons, these manikins, woodcarvings. But there was nothing in their hearts and nothing in their minds, no memory of their mason and builder. They just went and walked wherever they wanted. Now they did not remember the Heart of Sky.

And so they fell, just an experiment and just a cutout for humankind. They were talking at first but their faces were dry. They were not yet developed in the legs and arms. They had no blood, no lymph. They had no sweat, no fat. Their complexions were dry, their faces were crusty. They flailed their legs and arms, their bodies were deformed.

And so they accomplished nothing before the Maker, Modeler who gave them birth, gave them heart. They became the first numerous people here on the face of the earth.

Again there comes a humiliation, destruction, and demolition. The manikins, woodcarvings were killed when the Heart of Sky devised a flood for them. A great flood was made; it came down on the heads of the manikins, woodcarvings.

The man's body was carved from the wood of the coral tree by the Maker, Modeler. And as for the woman, the Maker, Modeler needed the pith of reeds for the woman's body. They were not competent, nor did they speak before the builder and sculptor who made them and brought them forth, and so they were killed, done in by a flood:

There came a rain of resin from the sky.

There came the one named Gouger of Faces: he gouged out their eyeballs.

There came Sudden Bloodletter: he snapped off their heads.

There came Crunching Jaguar: he ate their flesh.

There came Tearing Jaguar: he tore them open.

They were pounded down to the bones and tendons, smashed and pulverized even to the bones. Their faces were smashed because they were incompetent before their mother and their father, the Heart of Sky, named Hurricane. The earth was blackened because of this; the black rainstorm began, rain all day and rain all night. Into their houses came the animals, small and great. Their faces were crushed by things of wood and stone. Everything spoke: their water jars, their tortilla griddles, their plates, their cooking pots, their dogs, their grinding stones, each and every thing crushed their faces. Their dogs and turkeys told them:

"You caused us pain, you ate us, but now it is *you* whom *we* shall eat." And this is the grinding stone:

"We were undone because of you.

Every day, every day,
in the dark, in the dawn, forever,
r-r-rip, r-r-rip,
r-r-rub, r-r-rub,
right in our faces, because of you.

This was the service we gave you at first, when you were still people, but today you will learn of our power. We shall pound and we shall grind your flesh," their grinding stones told them.

And this is what their dogs said, when they spoke in their turn:

"Why is it you can't seem to give us our food? We just watch and you just keep us down, and you throw us around. You keep a stick ready when you eat, just so you can hit us. We don't talk, so we've received nothing from you. How could you not have known? You *did* know that we were wasting away there, behind you.

"So, this very day you will taste the teeth in our mouths. We shall eat you," their dogs told them, and their faces were crushed.

And then their tortilla griddles and cooking pots spoke to them in turn:

"Pain! That's all you've done for us. Our mouths are sooty, our faces are sooty. By setting us on the fire all the time, you burn us. Since *we* felt no pain, *you* try it. We shall burn you," all their cooking pots said, crushing their faces.

The stones, their hearthstones were shooting out, coming right out of the fire, going for their heads, causing them pain. Now they run for it, helter-skelter.

They want to climb up on the houses, but they fall as the houses collapse.

They want to climb the trees; they're thrown off by the trees.

They want to get inside caves, but the caves slam shut in their faces.

Such was the scattering of the human work, the human design. The people were ground down, overthrown. The mouths and faces of all of them were destroyed and crushed. And it used to be said that the monkeys in the forests today are a sign of this. They were left as a sign because wood alone was used for their flesh by the builder and sculptor.

So this is why monkeys look like people: they are a sign of a previous human work, human design—mere manikins, mere woodcarvings.

This was when there was just a trace of early dawn on the face of the earth, there was no sun. But there was one who magnified himself; Seven Macaw is his name. The sky-earth was already there, but the face of the sun-moon was clouded over. Even so, it is said that his light provided a sign for the people who were flooded. He was like a person of genius in his being.

"I am great. My place is now higher than that of the human work, the human design. I am their sun and I am their light, and I am also their months.

"So be it: my light is great. I am the walkway and I am the foothold of the people, because my eyes are of metal. My teeth just glitter with jewels, and turquoise as well; they stand out blue with stones like the face of the sky.

"And this nose of mine shines white into the distance like the moon. Since my nest is metal, it lights up the face of the earth. When I come forth before my nest, I am like the sun and moon for those who are born in the light, begotten in the light. It must be so, because my face reaches into the distance," says Seven Macaw.

It is not true that he is the sun, this Seven Macaw, yet he magnifies himself, his wings, his metal. But the scope of his face lies right around his own perch; his face does not reach every where beneath the sky. The faces of the sun, moon, and stars are not yet visible, it has not yet dawned.

And so Seven Macaw puffs himself up as the days and the months, though the light of the sun and moon has not yet clarified. He only wished for surpassing greatness. This was when the flood was worked upon the manikins, woodcarvings.

And now we shall explain how Seven Macaw died, when the people were vanquished, done in by the mason and sculptor.

## *Part III [The Hero Twins in the Underworld]*

And here is the account of a maiden, the daughter of a lord named Blood Gatherer.

And this is when a maiden heard of it, the daughter of a lord. Blood Gatherer is the name of her father, and Blood Woman is the name of the maiden.

And when he heard the account of the fruit of the tree, her father retold it. And she was amazed at the account:

"I'm not acquainted with that tree they talk about. '"Its fruit is truly sweet!" they say,' I hear," she said.

Next, she went all alone and arrived where the tree stood. It stood at the Place of Ball Game Sacrifice:

"What? Well! What's the fruit of this tree? Shouldn't this tree bear something sweet? They shouldn't die, they shouldn't be wasted. Should I pick one?" said the maiden.

And then the bone spoke; it was here in the fork of the tree:

"Why do you want a mere bone, a round thing in the branches of a tree?" said the head of One Hunahpu when it spoke to the maiden. "You don't want it," she was told.

"I do want it," said the maiden.

"Very well. Stretch out your right hand here, so I can see it," said the bone.

"Yes," said the maiden. She stretched out her right hand, up there in front of the bone.

And then the bone spit out its saliva, which landed squarely in the hand of the maiden.

And then she looked in her hand, she inspected it right away, but the bone's saliva wasn't in her hand.

"It is just a sign I have given you, my saliva, my spittle. This, my head, has nothing on it—just bone, nothing of meat. It's just the same with the head of a great lord: it's just the flesh that makes his face look good. And when he dies, people get frightened by his bones. After that, his son is like his saliva, his spittle, in his being, whether it be the son of a lord or the son of a craftsman, an orator. The father does not disappear, but goes on being fulfilled. Neither dimmed nor destroyed is the face of a lord, a warrior, craftsman, orator. Rather, he will leave his daughters and sons. So it is that I have done likewise through you. Now go up there on the face of the earth; you will not die. Keep the word. So be it," said the head of One and Seven Hunahpu—they were of one mind when they did it.

This was the word Hurricane, Newborn Thunderbolt, Raw Thunderbolt had given them. In the same way, by the time the maiden returned to her home, she had been given many instructions. Right away something was generated in her belly, from the saliva alone, and this was the generation of Hunahpu and Xbalanque.

And when the maiden got home and six months had passed, she was found out by her father. Blood Gatherer is the name of her father.

And after the maiden was noticed by her father, when he saw that she was now with child, all the lords then shared their thoughts—One and Seven Death, along with Blood Gatherer:

"This daughter of mine is with child, lords. It's just a bastard," Blood Gatherer said when he joined the lords.

"Very well. Get her to open her mouth. If she doesn't tell, then sacrifice her. Go far away and sacrifice her."

"Very well, your lordships," he replied. After that, he questioned his daughter:

"Who is responsible for the child in your belly, my daughter?" he said.

"There is no child, my father, sir; there is no man whose face I've known," she replied.

"Very well. It really is a bastard you carry! Take her away for sacrifice, you Military Keepers of the Mat. Bring back her heart in a bowl, so the lords can take it in their hands this very day," the owls were told, the four of them.

Then they left, carrying the bowl. When they left they took the maiden by the hand, bringing along the White Dagger, the instrument of sacrifice.

"It would not turn out well if you sacrificed me, messengers, because it is not a bastard that's in my belly. What's in my belly generated all by itself when I went to marvel at the head of One Hunahpu, which is there at the Place of Ball Game Sacrifice. So please stop: don't do your sacrifice, messengers," said the maiden. Then they talked:

"What are we going to use in place of her heart? We were told by her father:

'Bring back her heart. The lords will take it in their hands, they will satisfy themselves, they will make themselves familiar with its composition. Hurry, bring it back in a bowl, put her heart in the bowl.' Isn't that what we've been told? What shall we deliver in the bowl? What we want above all is that you should not die," said the messengers.

"Very well. My heart must not be theirs, nor will your homes be here. Nor will you simply force people to die, but hereafter, what will be truly yours will be the true bearers of bastards. And hereafter, as for One and Seven Death, only blood, only nodules of sap, will be theirs. So be it that these things are presented before them, and not that hearts are burned before them. So be it: use the fruit of a tree," said the maiden.

And it was red tree sap she went out to gather in the bowl.

After it congealed, the substitute for her heart became round. When the sap of the croton tree was tapped, tree sap like blood, it became the substitute for her blood. When she rolled the blood around inside there, the sap of the croton tree, it formed a surface like blood, glistening red now, round inside the bowl. When the tree was cut open by the maiden, the so-called cochineal croton, the sap is what she called blood, and so there is talk of "nodules of blood."

"So you have been blessed with the face of the earth. It shall be yours," she told the owls.

"Very well, maiden. We'll show you the way up there. You just walk on ahead; we have yet to deliver this apparent duplicate of your heart before the lords," said the messengers.

And when they came before the lords, they were all watching closely:

"Hasn't it turned out well?" said One Death.

"It has turned out well, your lordships, and this is her heart. It's in the bowl."

"Very well. So I'll look," said One Death, and when he lifted it up with his fingers, its surface was soaked with gore, its surface glistened red with blood.

"Good. Stir up the fire, put it over the fire," said One Death.

After that they dried it over the fire, and the Xibalbans savored the aroma. They all ended up standing here, they leaned over it intently. They found the smoke of the blood to be truly sweet!

And while they stayed at their cooking, the owls went to show the maiden the way out. They sent her up through a hole onto the earth, and then the guides returned below.

In this way the lords of Xibalba were defeated by a maiden; all of them were blinded.

And here, where the mother of One Monkey and One Artisan lived, was where the woman named Blood Woman arrived.

And when the Blood Woman came to the mother of One Monkey and One Artisan, her children were still in her belly, but it wasn't very long before the birth of Hunahpu and Xbalanque, as they are called.

And when the woman came to the grandmother, the woman said to the grandmother:

"I've come, mother, madam. I'm your daughter-in-law and I'm your child, mother, madam," she said when she came here to the grandmother.

"Where do you come from? As for my lastborn children, didn't they die in Xibalba? And these two remain as their sign and their word: One Monkey and One Artisan are their names. So if you've come to see my children, get out of here!" the maiden was told by the grandmother.

"Even so, I really am your daughter-in-law. I am already his, I belong to One Hunahpu. What I carry is his. One Hunahpu and Seven Hunahpu are alive, they are not dead. They have merely made a way for the light to show itself, madam mother-in-law, as you will see when you look at the faces of what I carry," the grandmother was told.

And One Monkey and One Artisan have been keeping their grandmother entertained: all they do is play and sing, all they work at is writing and carving, every day, and this cheers the heart of their grandmother.

And then the grandmother said:

"I don't want you, no thanks, my daughter-in-law. It's just a bastard in your belly, you trickster! These children of mine who are named by you are dead," said the grandmother.

"Truly, what I say to you is so!"

"Very well, my daughter-in-law, I hear you. So get going, get their food so they can eat. Go pick a big netful of corn, then come back—since you are already my daughter-in-law, as I understand it," the maiden was told.

"Very well," she replied.

After that, she went to the garden; One Monkey and One Artisan had a garden. The maiden followed the path they had cleared and arrived there in the garden, but there was only one clump, there was no other plant, no second or third. That one clump had borne its ears. So then the maiden's heart stopped:

"It looks like I'm a sinner, a debtor! Where will I get the netful of food she asked for?" she said. And then the guardians of food were called upon by her:

"Come thou, rise up, come thou,
stand up:
Generous Woman, Harvest
Woman,
Cacao Woman, Cornmeal Woman,
thou guardian of the food of One
Monkey, One Artisan,"

said the maiden.

And then she took hold of the silk, the bunch of silk at the top of the ear. She pulled it straight out, she didn't pick the ear, and the ear reproduced itself to make food for the net. It filled the big net.

And then the maiden came back, but animals carried her net. When she got back she went to put the pack frame in the corner of the house, so it would look to the grandmother as if she had arrived with a load.

And then, when the grandmother saw the food, a big netful:

"Where did that food of yours come from? You've leveled the place! I'm going to see if you've brought back our whole garden!" said the grandmother.

And then she went off, she went to look at the garden, but the one clump was still there, and the place where the net had been put at the foot of it was still obvious.

And the grandmother came back in a hurry, and she got back home, and she said to the maiden:

"The sign is still there. You really are my daughter-in-law! I'll have to keep watching what you do. These grandchildren of mine are already showing genius," the maiden was told.

Now this is where we shall speak of the birth of Hunahpu and Xbalanque.

And this is their birth; we shall tell of it here.

Then it came to the day of their birth, and the maiden named Blood Woman gave birth. The grandmother was not present when they were born; they were born suddenly. Two of them were born, named Hunahpu and Xbalanque. They were born in the mountains, and then they came into the house. Since they weren't sleeping:

"Throw them out of here! They're really loudmouths!" said the grandmother.

After that, when they put them on an anthill, they slept soundly there. And when they removed them from there, they put them in brambles next.

And this is what One Monkey and One Artisan wanted: that they should die on the anthill and die in the brambles. One Monkey and One Artisan wanted this because they were rowdyish and flushed with jealousy. They didn't allow their younger brothers in the house at first, as if they didn't even know them, but even so they flourished in the mountains.

And One Monkey and One Artisan were great flautists and singers, and as they grew up they went through great suffering and pain. It had cost them suffering to become great knowers. Through it all they became flautists, singers, and writers, carvers. They did everything well. They simply knew it when they were born, they simply had genius. And they were the successors of their fathers who had gone to Xibalba, their dead fathers.

Since One Monkey and One Artisan were great knowers, in their hearts they already realized everything when their younger brothers came into being, but they didn't reveal their insight because of their jealousy. The anger in their hearts came down on their own heads; no great harm was done. They were decoyed by Hunahpu and Xbalanque, who merely went out shooting every day. These two got no love from the grandmother, or from One Monkey and One Artisan. They weren't given their meals; the meals had been prepared and One Monkey and One Artisan had already eaten them before they got there.

But Hunahpu and Xbalanque aren't turning red with anger; rather, they just let it go, even though they know their proper place, which they see as clear as day. So they bring birds when they arrive each day, and One Monkey and One Artisan eat them. Nothing whatsoever is given to Hunahpu and Xbalanque, either one of them. All One Monkey and One Artisan do is play and sing.

And then Hunahpu and Xbalanque arrived again, but now they came in here without bringing their birds, so the grandmother turned red:

"What's your reason for not bringing birds?" Hunahpu and Xbalanque were asked.

"There are some, our dear grandmother, but our birds just got hung up in a tree," they said, "and there's no way to get up the tree after them, our dear grandmother, and so we'd like our elder brothers to please go with us, to please go get the birds down," they said.

"Very well. We'll go with you at dawn," the elder brothers replied.

Now they had won, and they gathered their thoughts, the two of them, about the fall of One Monkey and One Artisan:

"We'll just turn their very being around with our words. So be it, since they have caused us great suffering. They wished that we might die and disappear—we, their younger brothers. Just as they wished us to be slaves here, so we shall defeat them there. We shall simply make a sign of it," they said to one another.

And then they went there beneath a tree, the kind named yellowwood, together with the elder brothers. When they got there they started shooting. There were countless birds up in the tree, chittering, and the elder brothers were amazed when they saw the birds. And not one of these birds fell down beneath the tree:

"Those birds of ours don't fall down; just go throw them down," they told their elder brothers.

"Very well," they replied.

And then they climbed up the tree, and the tree began to grow, its trunk got thicker.

After that, they wanted to get down, but now One Monkey and One Artisan couldn't make it down from the tree. So they said, from up in the tree:

"How can we grab hold? You, our younger brothers, take pity on us! Now this tree looks frightening to us, dear younger brothers," they said from up in the tree. Then Hunahpu and Xbalanque told them:

"Undo your pants, tie them around your hips, with the long end trailing like a tail behind you, and then you'll be better able to move," they were told by their younger brothers.

"All right," they said.

And then they left the ends of their loincloths trailing, and all at once these became tails. Now they looked like mere monkeys.

After that they went along in the trees of the mountains, small and great. They went through the forests, now howling, now keeping quiet in the branches of trees.

Such was the defeat of One Monkey and One Artisan by Hunahpu and Xbalanque. They did it by means of their genius alone.

# Argentina

## Jorge Luis Borges (1899–1986)

The Argentinian writer Jorge Luis Borges is the fountainhead of a rich tradition of modern Latin American literature. Oddly, Borges was influenced more by English than Spanish literature. He even read *Don Quixote* first in English. The greatest influence on his work, however, was clearly Kafka. Kafka's most distinctive works are his short parables suggesting absurd, impenetrable allegories (pp. 2050–2054), and Borges wrote almost exclusively in that form. Some of his best works are only one or two pages long, but they are so startlingly original that they have had an immeasurable impact on modern literature.

At the age of forty Borges sustained a head injury that put him in doubt of his sanity and his future as a writer. While still in the hospital, to prove his abilities to himself, he wrote his first story, "Pierre Menard, Author of the Quixote," followed by "Tlön, Uqbar, Orbis Tertius." In those stories he announced the themes that would preoccupy him the rest of his life. "Pierre Menard" explores the paradoxes of literary influence and originality. The most original literary achievement turns out to be a total identification with a previous writer's work: "The text of Cervantes and that of Menard are verbally identical, but the second is almost infinitely richer." His ironies are such that whatever theme we might detect here, its opposite is also present.

Like most of Borges's works, "Pierre Menard" is highly intellectual but also richly comic. Philosophically Borges is a nihilist, but his is an almost joyful nihilism. As Borges says in "Pierre Menard," "There is no intellectual exercise which is not ultimately useless." That uselessness freed Borges from the social and political concerns that mark so much recent art and allowed him to range freely in his own version of high modernist intellectual aestheticism. His writing is always efficient, precise, formally brilliant, and metaphysically challenging.

The most important recurring symbol in Borges's work is the labyrinth. History, knowledge, the library, and literary tradition (and certainly this anthology!) are all labyrinths, at the center of which we find only mirrors. So it is with the work of Menard, which draws on the reader to read history backward, and also with the dizzying encyclopedia of Uqbar. In the literature of Uqbar, "everything is the work of one single author." To appreciate the story's paradoxes fully, remember that the "Postscript 1947" was written in 1940, predicting that this story would soon destroy the world.

The one-page "Borges and I" states as economically as possible the splitting of the self that takes place when a writer writes. On the one hand, there is a private self, impossible for others to know and, on the other, a public persona who gradually comes to destroy its more authentic double: "Which of us is writing this page I don't know."

Near the end of his life, totally blind but still working as a national librarian, Borges fell deeply in love with Old English poetry. His little poem about *Beowulf* is among the most moving comments ever made on that epic and is a poignant summary of his own life.

## *Pierre Menard, Author of the Quixote*

*Translated by Anthony Bonner*

The *visible* works left by this novelist are easily and briefly enumerated. It is therefore impossible to forgive the omissions and additions perpetrated by Madame Henri Bachelier in a fallacious catalog that a certain newspaper, whose Protestant tendencies are no secret, was inconsiderate enough to inflict on its wretched readers—even though they are few and Calvinist, if not Masonic and circumcised. Menard's true friends regarded this catalog with alarm, and even with a certain sadness. It is as if yesterday we were gathered together before the final marble and the fateful cypresses, and already error is trying to tarnish his memory. . . . Decidedly, a brief rectification is inevitable.

I am certain that it would be very easy to challenge my meager authority. I hope, nevertheless, that I will not be prevented from mentioning two important testimonials. The Baroness de Bacourt (at whose unforgettable *vendredis* I had the honor of becoming acquainted with the late lamented poet) has seen fit to approve these lines. The Countess de Bagnoregio, one of the most refined minds in the principality of Monaco (and now of Pittsburgh, Pennsylvania, since her recent marriage to the international philanthropist Simon Kautsch who, alas, has been so slandered by the victims of his disinterested handiwork), has sacrificed to "truth and death" (those are her words) that majestic reserve which distinguishes her, and in an open letter published in the magazine *Luxe* also grants me her consent. These authorizations, I believe, are not insufficient.

I have said that Menard's *visible* lifework is easily enumerated. Having carefully examined his private archives, I have been able to verify that it consists of the following:

a. A Symbolist sonnet which appeared twice (with variations) in the magazine *La conque* (the March and October issues of 1899).

b. A monograph on the possibility of constructing a poetic vocabulary of concepts that would not be synonyms or periphrases of those which make up ordinary language, "but ideal objects created by means of common agreement and destined essentially to fill poetic needs" (Nîmes, 1901).

c. A monograph on "certain connections or affinities" among the ideas of Descartes, Leibniz, and John Wilkins (Nîmes, 1903).

d. A monograph on the *Characteristica universalis* of Leibniz (Nîmes, 1904).

e. A technical article on the possibility of enriching the game of chess by means of eliminating one of the rooks' pawns. Menard proposes, recommends, disputes, and ends by rejecting this innovation.

f. A monograph on the *Ars magna generalis* of Ramón Lull (Nîmes, 1906).

g. A translation with prologue and notes of the *Libro de la invención y arte del juego del ajedrez* by Ruy López de Segura (Paris, 1907).

h. The rough draft of a monograph on the symbolic logic of George Boole.

i. An examination of the metric laws essential to French prose, illustrated with examples from Saint-Simon (*Revue des langues romanes,* Montpellier, October 1909).

j. An answer to Luc Durtain (who had denied the existence of such laws) illustrated with examples from Luc Durtain (*Revue des langues romanes,* Montpellier, December 1909).

k. A manuscript translation of the *Aguja de navegar cultos* of Quevedo, entitled *La boussole des précieux.*

l. A preface to the catalog of the exposition of lithographs by Carolus Hourcade (Nîmes, 1914).

m. His work, *Les problèmes d'un problème* (Paris, 1917), which takes up in chronological order the various solutions of the famous problem of Achilles and the tortoise. Two editions of this book have appeared so far; the second has as an epigraph Leibniz's advice "*Ne craignez point, monsieur, la tortue,*" and contains revisions of the chapters dedicated to Russell and Descartes.

n. An obstinate analysis of the "syntactic habits" of Toulet (*N.R.F.,* March 1921). I remember that Menard used to declare that censuring and praising were sentimental operations which had nothing to do with criticism.

o. A transposition into Alexandrines of *Le cimetiére marin* of Paul Valéry (*N.R.F.,* January 1928).

p. An invective against Paul Valéry in the *Journal for the Suppression of Reality* of Jacques Reboul. (This invective, it should be stated parenthetically, is the exact reverse of his true opinion of Valéry. The latter understood it as such, and the old friendship between the two was never endangered.)

q. A "definition" of the Countess of Bagnoregio in the "victorious volume"—the phrase is that of another collaborator, Gabriele d'Annunzio—which this lady publishes yearly to rectify the inevitable falsifications of journalism and to present "to the world and to Italy" an authentic effigy of her person, which is so exposed (by reason of her beauty and her activities) to erroneous or hasty interpretations.

r. A cycle of admirable sonnets for the Baroness de Bacourt (1934).

s. A manuscript list of verses which owe their effectiveness to punctuation.[1]

Up to this point (with no other omission than that of some vague, circumstantial sonnets for the hospitable, or greedy, album of Madame Henri Bachelier) we have the *visible* part of Menard's works in chronological order. Now I will pass over to that other part, which is subterranean, interminably heroic, and unequaled, and which is also—oh, the possibilities inherent in the man!—inconclusive. This work, possibly the most significant of our time, consists of the ninth and thirty-eighth chapters of Part One of *Don Quixote* and a fragment of the twenty-second chapter. I realize that such an affirmation seems absurd; but the justification of this "absurdity" is the primary object of this note.[2]

Two texts of unequal value inspired the undertaking. One was that philological fragment of Novalis—No. 2005 of the Dresden edition—which outlines the theme of *total* identification with a specific author. The other was one of those parasitic books which places Christ on a boulevard, Hamlet on the Cannebière, and Don Quixote on Wall Street. Like any man of good taste, Menard detested these useless carnivals, only suitable—he used to say—for evoking plebeian delight in anachronism, or (what is worse) charming us with the primary idea that all epochs are the same, or that they are different. He considered more interesting, even though it had been carried out in a contradictory and superficial way, Daudet's famous plan: to unite in *one* figure, Tartarin, the Ingenious Gentleman and his squire. . . . Any insinuation that Menard dedicated his life to the writing of a contemporary *Don Quixote* is a calumny of his illustrious memory.

He did not want to compose another *Don Quixote*—which would be easy—but *the Don Quixote*. It is unnecessary to add that his aim was never to produce a mechanical transcription of the original; he did not propose to copy it. His admirable ambition was to produce pages which would coincide—word for word and line for line—with those of Miguel de Cervantes.

"My intent is merely astonishing," he wrote me from Bayonne on December 30, 1934. "The ultimate goal of a theological or metaphysical demonstration—the external world, God, chance, universal forms—is no less anterior or common than this novel which I am now developing. The only difference is that philosophers publish in pleasant volumes the intermediary

[1]Madame Henri Bachelier also lists a literal translation of a literal translation done by Quevedo of the *Introduction à la vie dévote* of Saint Francis of Sales. In Pierre Menard's library there are no traces of such a work. She must have misunderstood a remark of his which he had intended as a joke.

[2]I also had another, secondary intent—that of sketching a portrait of Pierre Menard. But how would I dare to compete with the golden pages the Baroness de Bacourt tells me she is preparing, or with the delicate and precise pencil of Carolus Hourcade?

stages of their work and that I have decided to lose them." And, in fact, not one page of a rough draft remains to bear witness to this work of years.

The initial method he conceived was relatively simple: to know Spanish well, to reembrace the Catholic faith, to fight against Moors and Turks, to forget European history between 1602 and 1918, and to *be* Miguel de Cervantes. Pierre Menard studied this procedure (I know that he arrived at a rather faithful handling of seventeenth-century Spanish) but rejected it as too easy. Rather because it was impossible, the reader will say! I agree, but the undertaking was impossible from the start, and of all the possible means of carrying it out, this one was the least interesting. To be, in the twentieth century, a popular novelist of the seventeenth seemed to him a diminution. To be, in some way, Cervantes and to arrive at *Don Quixote* seemed to him less arduous—and consequently less interesting—than to continue being Pierre Menard and to arrive at *Don Quixote* through the experiences of Pierre Menard. (This conviction, let it be said in passing, forced him to exclude the autobiographical prologue of the second part of *Don Quixote.* To include this prologue would have meant creating another personage—Cervantes—but it would also have meant presenting *Don Quixote* as the work of this personage and not of Menard. He naturally denied himself such an easy problem), "My undertaking is not essentially different," he said in another part of the same letter. "I would only have to be immortal in order to carry it out." Shall I confess that I often imagine that he finished it and that I am reading *Don Quixote*—the entire work—as if Menard had conceived it? Several nights ago, while leafing through Chapter 26—which he had never attempted—I recognized our friend's style and, as it were, his voice in this exceptional phrase: the nymphs of the rivers, mournful and humid Echo. This effective combination of two adjectives, one moral and the other physical, reminded me of a line from Shakespeare which we discussed one afternoon:

> Where a malignant and turbaned Turk . . .

Why precisely *Don Quixote,* our reader will ask. Such a preference would not have been inexplicable in a Spaniard; but it undoubtedly was in a Symbolist from Nîmes, essentially devoted to Poe, who engendered Baudelaire, who engendered Mallaremé, who engendered Valéry, who engendered Edmond Teste. The letter quoted above clarifies this point. "*Don Quixote,*" Menard explains, "interests me profoundly, but it does not seem to me to have been—how shall I say it—inevitable. I cannot imagine the universe without the interjection of Edgar Allan Poe:

> Ah, bear in mind this garden was enchanted!

Or without the *Bateau Ivre* or the *Ancient Mariner,* but I know that I am capable of imagining it without *Don Quixote.* (I speak, naturally, of my personal capacity not of the historical repercussions of these works.) *Don Quixote* is an accidental book. *Don Quixote* is unnecessary. I can premeditate writing. I can write it without incurring a tautology. When I was twelve or thirteen years old I read it perhaps in its entirety. Since then I have reread several chapters attentively, but not the ones I am going to undertake. I have likewise studied the *entremeses,* the comedies, the *Galatea,* the exemplary novels, and the undoubtedly laborious efforts of *Pérsiles y Sigismunda* and the *Viaje al Parnaso*. . . . My general memory of *Don Quixote,* simplified by forgetfulness and indifference, is much the same as the imprecise, anterior image of a book not yet written. Once this image (which no one can deny me in good faith) has been postulated, my problems are undeniably considerably more difficult than those which Cervantes faced. My affable precursor did not refuse the collaboration of fate; he went along composing his immortal work a little *à la diable,* swept along by inertias of language and invention. I have contracted the mysterious duty of reconstructing literally his spontaneous work. My solitary game is governed by two polar laws. The first permits me to attempt variants of a formal and psychological nature; the second obliges me to sacrifice them to the 'original' text and irrefutably to rationalize this annihilation. . . . To these artificial obstacles one must add another congenital one. To compose *Don Quixote* at the beginning of the seventeenth century was a reasonable, necessary and perhaps inevitable undertaking; at the beginning of the twentieth century it is almost impossible. It is not in vain that three hundred years have passed, charged with the most complex happenings—among them, to mention only one, that same *Don Quixote.*"

In spite of these three obstacles, the fragmentary *Don Quixote* of Menard is more subtle than that of Cervantes. The latter indulges in a rather coarse opposition between tales of knighthood and the meager, provincial reality of his country; Menard chooses as "reality" the land of Carmen during the century of Lepanto and Lope. What Hispanophile would not have advised Maurice Bariès or Dr. Rodríguez Larreta to make such a choice! Menard, as if it were the most natural thing in the world, eludes them. In his work there are neither bands of gypsies, conquistadors, mystics, Philip the Seconds, nor autos-da-fé. He disregards or proscribes local color. This disdain indicates a new approach to the historical novel. This disdain condemns *Salammbô* without appeal.

It is no less astonishing to consider isolated chapters. Let us examine, for instance, Chapter 38 of Part One "which treats of the curious discourse that Don Quixote delivered on the subject of arms and letters." As is known, Don Quixote (like Quevedo in a later, analogous passage of *La hora de todos*) passes judgment against letters and in favor of arms. Cervantes was an old soldier, which explains such a judgment. But that the *Don Quixote* of Pierre Menard—a contemporary of *La trahison des clercs* and Bertrand Russell—should relapse into these nebulous sophistries! Madame Bachelier has seen in them an admirable and typical subordination of the author to the psychology of the hero; others (by no means perspicaciously) a *transcription* of *Don Quixote;* the Baroness de Bacourt, the influence of Nietzsche. To this third interpretation (which seems to me irrefutable) I do not know if I would dare to add a fourth; which coincides very well with the divine modesty of Pierre Menard: his resigned or ironic habit of propounding ideas which were the strict reverse of those he preferred. (One will remember his diatribe against Paul Valéry in the ephemeral journal of the superrealist Jacques Reboul.) The text of Cervantes and that of Menard are verbally identical, but the second is almost infinitely richer. (More ambiguous, his detractors will say; but ambiguity is a richness.) It is a revelation to compare the *Don Quixote* of Menard with that of Cervantes. The latter, for instance, wrote (*Don Quixote*, Part One, Chapter 9):

> . . . *la verdad, cuya madre es la historia, émula del tiempo, depósito de las acciones, testigo de lo pasado, ejemplo y aviso de lo presente, advertencia de lo por venir.*
>
> [. . . truth, whose mother is history, who is the rival of time, depository of deeds, witness of the past, example and lesson to the present, and warning to the future.]

Written in the seventeenth century, written by the "ingenious layman" Cervantes, this enumeration is a mere rhetorical eulogy of history. Menard, on the other hand, writes:

> . . . *la verdad, cuya madre es la historia, émula del tiempo, depósito de las acciones, testigo de lo pasado, ejemplo y aviso de lo presente, advertencia de lo por venir.*
>
> [. . . truth, whose mother is history, who is the rival of time, depository of deeds, witness of the past, example and lesson to the present, and warning to the future.]

History, *mother* of truth; the idea is astounding. Menard, a contemporary of William James, does not define history as an investigation of reality, but as its origin. Historical truth, for him, is not what took place; it is what we think took place. The final clauses—*example and lesson to the present, and warning to the future*—are shamelessly pragmatic.

Equally vivid is the contrast in styles. The archaic style of Menard—in the last analysis, a foreigner—suffers from a certain affectation. Not so that of his precursor, who handles easily the ordinary Spanish of his time.

There is no intellectual exercise which is not ultimately useless. A philosophical doctrine is in the beginning a seemingly true description of the universe; as the years pass it becomes a mere chapter—if not a paragraph or a noun—in the history of philosophy. In literature, this ultimate decay is even more notorious. "*Don Quixote*," Menard once told me, "was above all an agreeable book; now it is an occasion for patriotic toasts, grammatical arrogance and obscene deluxe editions. Glory is an incomprehension, and perhaps the worst."

These nihilist arguments contain nothing new; what is unusual is the decision Pierre Menard derived from them. He resolved to outstrip that vanity which awaits all the woes of mankind; he undertook a task that was complex in the extreme and futile from the outset. He dedicated his conscience and nightly studies to the repetition of a pre-existing book in a foreign tongue. The number of rough drafts kept on increasing; he tenaciously made corrections and tore up thousands of manuscript pages.[3] He did not permit them to be examined, and he took great care that they would not survive him. It is in vain that I have tried to reconstruct them.

I have thought that it is legitimate to consider the "final" *Don Quixote* as a

[3]I remember his square-ruled notebooks, the black streaks where he had crossed out words, his peculiar typographical symbols, and his insectlike handwriting. In the late afternoon he liked to go for walks on the outskirts of Nîmes; he would take a notebook with him and make a gay bonfire.

kind of palimpsest, in which should appear traces—tenuous but not undecipherable—of the "previous" handwriting of our friend. Unfortunately, only a second Pierre Menard, inverting the work of the former, could exhume and resuscitate these Troys. . . .

"To think, analyze and invent," he also wrote me, "are not anomalous acts, but the normal respiration of the intelligence. To glorify the occasional fulfillment of this function, to treasure ancient thoughts of others, to remember with incredulous amazement that the *doctor universalis* thought, is to confess our languor or barbarism. Every man should be capable of all ideas, and I believe that in the future he will be."

Menard (perhaps without wishing to) has enriched, by means of a new technique, the hesitant and rudimentary art of reading: the technique is one of deliberate anachronism and erroneous attributions. This technique, with its infinite applications, urges us to run through the *Odyssey* as if it were written after the *Aeneid,* and to read *Le jardin du Centaure* by Madame Henri Bachelier as if it were by Madame Henri Bachelier. This technique would fill the dullest books with adventure. Would not the attributing of *The Imitation of Christ* to Louis Ferdinand Céline or James Joyce be a sufficient renovation of its tenuous spiritual counsels?

## *Borges and I*

*Translated by N.T. Giovanni*

It's to the other man, to Borges, that things happen. I walk along the streets of Buenos Aires, stopping now and then—perhaps out of habit—to look at the arch of an old entranceway or a grillwork gate; of Borges I get news through the mail and glimpse his name among a committee of professors or in a dictionary of biography. I have a taste for hourglasses, maps, eighteenth-century typography, the roots of words, the smell of coffee, and Stevenson's prose; the other man shares these likes, but in a showy way that turns them into stagy mannerisms. It would be an exaggeration to say that we are on bad terms; I live, I let myself live, so that Borges can weave his tales and poems, and those tales and poems are my justification. It is not hard for me to admit that he has managed to write a few worthwhile pages, but these pages cannot save me, perhaps because what is good no longer belongs to anyone—not even the other man—but rather to speech or tradition. In any case, I am fated to become lost once and for all, and only some moment of myself will survive in the other man. Little by little, I have been surrendering everything to him, even though I have evidence of his stubborn habit of falsification and exaggerating. Spinoza held that all things try to keep on being themselves; a stone wants to be a stone and the tiger, a tiger. I shall remain in Borges, not in myself (if it is so that I am someone), but I recognize myself less in his books than in those of others or than in the laborious tuning of a guitar. Years ago, I tried ridding myself of him and I went from myths of the outlying slums of the city to games with time and infinity, but those games are now part of Borges and I will have to turn to other things. And so, my life is a running away, and I lose everything and everything is left to oblivion or to the other man.

Which of us is writing this page I don't know.

## *Poem Written in a Copy of Beowulf*

*Translated by Alaistair Reid*

At various times, I have asked myself what reasons
moved me to study, while my night came down,
without particular hope of satisfaction,
the language of the blunt-tongued Anglo-Saxons.

Used up by the years, my memory
loses its grip on words that I have vainly
repeated and repeated. My life in the same way
weaves and unweaves its weary history.

Then I tell myself: it must be that the soul
has some secret, sufficient way of knowing
that it is immortal, that its vast, encompassing
circle can take in all, can accomplish all.

Beyond my anxiety, beyond this writing,
the universe waits, inexhaustible, inviting.

# CHILE

## PABLO NERUDA (1904–1973)

The Chilean poet Pablo Neruda (born Ricardo Eliecer Neftali Reyes) is probably best known for his collection *Twenty Love Poems and a Song of Despair* (1924) and for the epic poem *Canto General* (*General Song,* published in 1950). His verse has profoundly influenced and shaped modern South American poetry. Neruda produced twenty-nine books of poetry that have been translated into eighty languages. He won the Nobel Prize for literature in 1971.

As a young man Neruda hid his poetry from his father by publishing under a pseudonym, but in the 1920s he traveled to Spain and found encouragement from Federico Garcia Lorca, Spain's leading poet and dramatist of the time. Lorca's execution at the hands of Fascists in 1936 catapulted Neruda into more active political work and writing. From 1927 to 1931 Neruda served as a diplomat in Burma, Ceylon (Sri Lanka), Jakarta, and Singapore, an experience that only intensified his sense of alienation from the world. He was forced to flee his homeland in 1948 after openly criticizing Chile's government.

Neruda's poetry addresses social and philosophical issues and celebrates the power of language. Much influenced by Whitman, Neruda rejoices in the multitudinous experiences of society and the self. "The Heights of Macchu Picchu," the first selection included here, is from *Canto General,* perhaps the most successful twentieth-century epic poem. Combining the metaphysical with the political and social, the poem is a history of the American continent from its ancient origins to the poet's "I Am." In this well-known section of the epic, Neruda was inspired by the ancient Incan ruins at Macchu Picchu and worked to revive the voices of its people: "I come to speak for your dead mouths." "The Word," from his 1962 collection *Fully Empowered,* resonates with the language of the Gospel of John in its joyful celebration of human language. His last collection, *The Book of Questions,* is an imaginative inquiry into the world and the self. Read in its entirety, its hypnotic and marvelously childlike repetitive questions have the effect of opening up the possibilities of the world.

## *Canto General: The Heights of Macchu Picchu*

*Translated by Jack Schmitt*

**I**

From air to air, like an
empty net
I went between the streets and atmosphere, arriving and departing,
in the advent of autumn the outstretched coin
of the leaves, and between springtime and the ears of corn,
all that the greatest love, as within a falling
glove, hands us like a long moon.

(Days of vivid splendor in the inclemency
of corpses: steel transformed
into acid silence:
nights frayed to the last flour:
beleaguered stamens of the nuptial land.)
Someone awaiting me among the violins
discovered a world like an entombed tower
spiraling down beneath all
the harsh sulphur-colored leaves:
father down, in the gold of geology,
like a sword enveloped in meteors,
I plunged my turbulent and tender hand
into the genital matrix of the earth.

I put my brow amid the deep waves,
descended like a drop amid the sulphurous peace,
and, like a blind man, returned to the jasmine
of the spent human springtime.

## 2

If the lofty germ is carried from flower to flower
and the rock preserves its flower disseminated
in its hammered suit of diamond and sand,
man crumples the petal of light which he gathers
in determinate deep-sea springs
and drills the quivering metal in his hands.
And all along, amid clothing and mist, upon the sunken table,
like a jumbled quantity, lies the soul:
quartz and vigilance, tears in the ocean
like pools of cold: yet he still
torments it under the habitual rug, rips it
in the hostile vestments of wire.

No: in corridors, air, sea or on roads,
who guards (like red poppies) his blood
without a dagger? Rage has extenuated
the sad trade of the merchant of souls,
and, while at the top of the plum tree, the dew
has left for a thousand years its transparent letter
upon the same branch that awaits it, O heart, O brow crushed
between the autumn cavities.

How many times in the wintry streets of a city or in
a bus or a boat at dusk, or in the deepest
loneliness, a night of revelry beneath the sound
of shadows and bells, in the very grotto human pleasure
I've tried to stop and seek the eternal unfathomable lode
that I touched before on stone or in the lightning unleashed by
a kiss.

(Whatever in grain like a yellow tale
of swollen little breasts keep repeating a number
perpetually tender in the germinal layers,
and which, always identical, is stripped to ivory,
and whatever in water is a transparent land, a bell
from the distant snows down to the bloody waves.)

I could grasp nothing but a clump of faces or precipitous
masks, like rings of empty gold,
like scattered clothes, offspring of an enraged autumn
that would have made the miserable tree of the frightened races
shake.
I had no place to rest my hand,
which, fluid like the water of an impounded spring
or firm as a chunk of anthracite or crystal,

would have returned the warmth or cold of my outstretched hand.
What was man? In what part of his conversation begun
amid shops and whistles, in which of his metallic movements
lived the indestructible, the imperishable, life?

## 3

Like corn man was husked in the bottomless
granary of forgotten deeds, the miserable course of
events, from one to seven, to eight,
and not one death but many deaths came to each:
every day a little death, dust, maggot, a lamp
quenched in the mire of the slums, a little thick-winged death
entered each man like a short lance,
and man was driven by bread or by knife:
herdsman, child of the seaports, dark captain of the plow,
or rodent of the teeming streets:

all were consumed awaiting their death, their daily ration of death:
and the ominous adversity of each day was like
a black glass from which they drank trembling.

## 4

Mighty death invited me many times:
it was like the invisible salt in the waves,
and what its invisible taste disseminated
was like halves of sinking and rising
or vast structures of wind and glacier.
I came to the cutting edge, to the narrows
of the air, to the shroud of agriculture and stone,
to the stellar void of the final steps
and the vertiginous spiraling road:
but, wide sea, O death! you do not come in waves
but in a galloping nocturnal clarity
or like the total numbers of the night.
You never rummaged around in pockets, your visit
was not possible without red vestments:
without an auroral carpet of enclosed silence:
without towering entombed patrimonies of tears.

I could not love in each being a tree
with a little autumn on its back (the death of a thousand leaves),
all the false deaths and resurrections
without land, without abyss:
I've tried to swim in the most expansive lives,
in the most free-flowing estuaries,

and when man went on denying me
and kept blocking path and door so that
my headspring hands could not touch his wounded inexistence,
then I went from street to street and river to river,
city to city and bed to bed,
my brackish mask traversed the desert,
and in the last humiliated homes, without light or fire,
without bread, without stone, without silence, alone,
I rolled on dying of my own death.

### 5

It was not you, solemn death, iron-plumed bird,
that the poor heir of these rooms
carried, between rushed meals, under his empty skin:
rather a poor petal with its cord exterminated:
an atom from the breast that did not come to combat
or the harsh dew that did not fall on his brow.
It was what could not be revived, a bit
of the little death without peace or territory:
a bone, a bell that died within him.
I raised the bandages dressed in iodine, sank my hands
into the pitiful sorrows killed by death,
and in the wound I found nothing but a chilling gust
that entered through the vague interstices of the soul.

### 6

And so I scaled the ladder of the earth
amid the atrocious maze of lost jungles
up to you, Macchu Picchu.
High citadel of terraced stones,
at long last the dwelling of him whom the earth
did not conceal in its slumbering vestments.
In you, as in two parallel lines,
the cradle of lightning and man
was rocked in a wind of thorns.

Mother of stone, sea spray of the condors.

Towering reef of the human dawn.

Spade lost in the primal sand.

This was the dwelling, this is the site:
here the full kernels of corn rose
and fell again like red hailstones.

Here the golden fiber emerged from the vicuña
to clothe love, tombs, mothers,
the king, prayers, warriors.

Here man's feet rested at night
beside the eagle's feet, in the high gory
retreats, and at dawn
they trod the rarefied mist with feet of thunder
and touched lands and stones
until they recognized them in the night or in death.

I behold vestments and hands,
the vestige of water in the sonorous void,
the wall tempered by the touch of a face
that beheld with my eyes the earthen lamps,
that oiled with my hands the vanished
wood: because everything—clothing, skin, vessels,
words, wine, bread—
is gone, fallen to earth.

And the air flowed with orange-blossom
fingers over all the sleeping:
a thousand years of air, months, weeks of air,
of blue wind, of iron cordillera,
like gentle hurricanes of footsteps
polishing the solitary precinct of stone.

### 7

O remains of a single abyss, shadows of one gorge—
the deep one—the real, most searing death
attained the scale
of your magnitude,
and from the quarried stones,
from the spires,
from the terraced aqueducts
you tumbled as in autumn
to a single death.
Today the empty air no longer weeps,
no longer knows your feet of clay,
has now forgotten your pitchers that filtered the sky
when the lightning's knives emptied it,
and the powerful tree was eaten away
by the mist and felled by the wind.
It sustained a hand that fell suddenly
from the heights to the end of time.
You are no more, spider hands, fragile

filaments, spun web:
all that you were has fallen: customs, frayed
syllables, masks of dazzling light.

But a permanence of stone and word:
the citadel was raised like a chalice in the hands
of all, the living, the dead, the silent, sustained
by so much death, a wall, from so much life a stroke
of stone petals: the permanent rose, the dwelling:
this Andean reef of glacial colonies.

When the clay-colored hand
turned to clay, when the little eyelids closed,
filled with rough walls, brimming with castles,
and when the entire man was trapped in his hole,
exactitude remained hoisted aloft:
this high site of the human dawn:
the highest vessel that has contained silence:
a life of stone after so many lives.

## 8

Rise up with me, American love.

Kiss the secret stones with me.
The torrential silver of the Urubamba
makes the pollen fly to its yellow cup.
It spans the void of the grapevine,
the petrous plant, the hard wreath
upon the silence of the highland casket.
Come, minuscule life, between the wings
of the earth, while—crystal and cold, pounded air
extracting assailed emeralds—
O, wild water, you run down from the snow.

Love, love, even the abrupt night,
from the sonorous Andean flint
to the dawn's red knees,
contemplates the snow's blind child.

O, sonorous threaded Wilkamayu,
when you beat your lineal thunder
to a white froth, like wounded snow,
when your precipitous storm
sings and batters, awakening the sky,
what language do you bring to the ear recently
wrenched from your Andean froth?

Who seized the cold's lightning
and left it shackled in the heights,
dispersed in its glacial tears,
smitten in its swift swords,
hammering its embattled stamens,
borne on its warrior's bed,
startled in its rocky end?

What are your tormented sparks saying?
Did your secret insurgent lightning
once journey charged with words?
Who keeps on shattering frozen syllables,
black languages, golden banners,
deep mouths, muffled cries,
in your slender arterial waters?

Who keeps on cutting floral eyelids
that come to gaze from the earth?
Who hurls down the dead clusters
that fell in your cascade hands
to strip the night stripped
in the coal of geology?

Who flings the branch down from its bonds?
Who once again entombs farewells?

Love, love, never touch the brink
or worship the sunken head:
let time attain its stature
in its salon of shattered headsprings,
and, between the swift water and the walls,
gather the air from the gorge,
the parallel sheets of the wind,
the cordilleras' blind canal,
the harsh greeting of the dew,
and, rise up, flower by flower, through the dense growth,
treading the hurtling serpent.

In the steep zone—forest and stone,
mist of green stars, radiant jungle—
Mantur explodes like a blinding lake
or a new layer of silence.

Come to my very heart, to my dawn,
up to the crowned solitudes.
The dead kingdom is still alive.

And over the Sundial the sanguinary shadow
of the condor crosses like a black ship.

## 9

Sidereal eagle, vineyard of mist.
Lost bastion, blind scimitar.
Spangled waistband, solemn bread.
Torrential stairway, immense eyelid.
Triangular tunic, stone pollen.
Granite lamp, stone bread.
Mineral serpent, stone rose.
Entombed ship, stone headspring.
Moonhorse, stone light.
Equinoctial square, stone vapor.
Ultimate geometry, stone book.
Tympanum fashioned amid the squalls.
Madrepore of sunken time.
Rampart tempered by fingers.
Ceiling assailed by feathers.
Mirror bouquets, stormy foundations.
Thrones toppled by the vine.
Regime of the enraged claw.
Hurricane sustained on the slopes.
Immobile cataract of turquoise.
Patriarchal bell of the sleeping.
Hitching ring of the tamed snows.
Iron recumbent upon its statues.
Inaccessible dark tempest.
Puma hands, bloodstained rock.
Towering sombrero, snowy dispute.
Night raised on fingers and roots.
Window of the mists, hardened dove.
Nocturnal plant, statue of thunder.
Essential cordillera, searoof.
Architecture of lost eagles.
Skyrope, heavenly bee.
Bloody level, man-made star.
Mineral bubble, quartz moon.
Andean serpent, brow of amaranth.
Cupola of silence, pure land.
Seabride, tree of cathedrals.
Cluster of salt, black-winged cherry tree.
Snow-capped teeth, cold thunderbolt.
Scored moon, menacing stone.
Headdresses of the cold, action of the air.

Volcano of hands, obscure cataract.
Silver wave, pointer of time.

## 10

Stone upon stone, and man, where was he?
Air upon air, and man, where was he?
Time upon time, and man, where was he?
Were you too a broken shard
of inconclusive man, of empty raptor,
who on the streets today, on the trails,
on the dead autumn leaves, keeps
tearing away at the heart right up to the grave?
Poor hand, foot, poor life . . .
Did the days of light
unraveled in you, like raindrops
on the banners of a feast day,
give petal by petal of their dark food
to the empty mouth?
Hunger, coral of mankind,
hunger, secret plant, woodcutters' stump,
hunger, did the edge of your reef rise up
to these high suspended towers?

I want to know, salt of the roads,
show me the spoon—architecture, let me
scratch at the stamens of stone with a little stick,
ascend the rungs of the air up to the void,
scrape the innards until I touch mankind.

Macchu Picchu, did you put
stone upon stone and, at the base, tatters?
Coal upon coal and, at the bottom, tears?
Fire in gold and, within it, the trembling
drop of red blood?
Bring me back the slave that you buried!
Shake from the earth the hard bread
of the poor wretch, show me
the slave's clothing and his window.
Tell me how he slept when he lived.
Tell me if his sleep was
harsh, gaping, like a black chasm
worn by fatigue upon the wall.
The wall, the wall! If upon his sleep
each layer of stone weighed down, and if he fell beneath it
as beneath a moon, with his dream!

Ancient America, sunken bride,
your fingers too,
on leaving the jungle for the high void of the gods,
beneath the nuptial standards of light and decorum,
mingling with the thunder of drums and spears,
your fingers, your fingers too,
which the abstract rose, the cold line, and
the crimson breast of the new grain transferred
to the fabric of radiant substance, to the hard cavities—
did you, entombed America, did you too store in the depths
of your bitter intestine, like an eagle, hunger?

## 11

Through the hazy splendor,
through the stone night, let me plunge my hand,
and let the aged heart of the forsaken beat in me
like a bird captive for a thousand years!
Let me forget, today, this joy, which is greater than the sea,
because man is greater than the sea and its islands,
and we must fall into him as into a well to emerge from
    the bottom
with a bouquet of secret water and sunken truths.
Let me forget, great stone, the powerful proportion,
the transcendent measure, the honeycombed stones,
and from the square let me today run
my hand over the hypotenuse of rough blood and sackcloth.
When, like a horseshoe of red elytra, the frenzied condor
beats my temples in the order of its flight,
and the hurricane of cruel feathers sweeps the somber dust
from the diagonal steps, I do not see the swift brute,
I do not see the blind cycle of its claws,
I see the man of old, the servant, asleep in the fields,
I see a body, a thousand bodies, a man, a thousand women,
black with rain and night, beneath the black squall,
with the heavy stone of the statue:
Juan Stonecutter, son of Wiracocha
Juan Coldeater, son of a green star,
Juan Barefoot, grandson of turquoise,
rise up to be born with me, my brother.

## 12

Rise up to be born with me, my brother.

Give me your hand from the deep
zone of your disseminated sorrow.

You'll not return from the bottom of the rocks.
You'll not return from subterranean time.
Your stiff voice will not return.
Your drilled eyes will not return.
Behold me from the depths of the earth,
laborer, weaver, silent herdsman:
tamer of the tutelary guanacos:
mason of the defied scaffold:
bearer of the Andean tears:
jeweler with your fingers crushed:
tiller trembling in the seed:
potter spilt in your clay:
bring to the cup of this new life, brothers,
all your timeless buried sorrows.
Show me your blood and your furrow,
tell me: I was punished here,
because the jewel did not shine or the earth
did not surrender the gemstone or kernel on time:
show me the stone on which you fell
and the wood on which you were crucified,
strike the old flintstones,
the old lamps, the whips sticking
throughout the centuries to your wounds
and the war clubs glistening red.
I've come to speak through your dead mouths.
Throughout the earth join all
the silent scattered lips
and from the depths speak to me all night long,
as if I were anchored with you,
tell me everything, chain by chain,
link by link, and step by step,
sharpen the knives that you've kept,
put them in my breast and in my hand,
like a river of yellow lightning,
like a river of buried jaguars,
and let me weep hours, days, years,
blind ages, stellar centuries.

Give me silence, water, hope.

Give me struggle, iron, volcanoes.

Cling to my body like magnets.

Hasten to my veins and to my mouth.

Speak through my words and my blood.

## *The Word*

*Translated by Alastair Reid*

The word
was born in the blood,
grew in the dark body, beating,
and flew through the lips and the mouth.

Farther away and nearer
still, still it came
from dead fathers and from wandering races,
from lands that had returned to stone
weary of their poor tribes,
because when pain took to the roads
the settlements set out and arrived
and new lands and water reunited
to sow their word anew.

And so, this is the inheritance—
this is the wavelength which connects us
with the dead man and the dawn
of new beings not yet come to light.

Still the atmosphere quivers
with the initial word
dressed up
in terror and sighing.
It emerged
from the darkness
and until now there is no thunder
that rumbles yet with all the iron
of that word,
the first
word uttered—
perhaps it was only a ripple, a drop,
and yet its great cataract falls and falls.

Later on, the word fills with meaning.
It remained gravid and it filled up with lives.
Everything had to do with births and sounds—
affirmation, clarity, strength,
negation, destruction, death—
the verb took over all the power
and blended existence with essence
in the electricity of its beauty.

Human word, syllable, combination
of spread light and the fine art of the silversmith,
hereditary goblet which gathers
the communications of the blood—
here is where silence was gathered up
in the completeness of the human word
and, for human beings, not to speak is to die—
language extends even to the hair,
the mouth speaks without the lips moving—
all of a sudden the eyes are words.

I take the word and go over it
as though it were nothing more than a human shape,
its arrangements awe me and I find my way
through each variation in the spoken word—
I utter and I am and without speaking I approach
the limit of words and the silence.

I drink to the word, raising
a word or a shining cup,
in it I drink
the pure wine of language
or inexhaustible water,
maternal source of words,
and cup and water and wine
give rise to my song
because the verb is the source
and vivid life—it is blood,
blood which expresses its substance
and so implies its own unwinding—
words give glass-quality to glass, blood to blood,
and life to life itself.

## *from The Book of Questions*

*Translated by William O'Daey*

### I

Why don't the immense airplanes
fly around with their children?

Which yellow bird
fills its nest with lemons?

Why don't they train helicopters
to suck honey from the sunlight?

Where did the full moon leave
its sack of flour tonight?

**III**

Tell me, is the rose naked
or is that her only dress?

Why do trees conceal
the splendor of their roots?

Who hears the regrets
of the thieving automobile?

Is there anything in the world sadder
than a train standing in the rain?

**IV**

How many churches are there in heaven?

Why doesn't the shark attack
the brazen sirens?

Does smoke talk with the clouds?

Is it true our desires
must be watered with dew?

**VIII**

What is it that upsets the volcanoes
that spit fire, cold and rage?

Why wasn't Christopher Columbus
able to discover Spain?

How many questions does a cat have?

Do tears not yet spilled
wait in small lakes?

Or are they invisible rivers
that run toward sadness?

## X

What will they think of my hat,
the Polish, in a hundred years?

What will they say about my poetry
who never touched my blood?

How do we measure the foam
that slips from the beer?

What does a fly do, imprisoned
in one of Petrarch's sonnets?

## XIV

And what did the rubies say
standing before the juice of pomegranates?

Why doesn't Thursday talk itself
into coming after Friday?

Who shouted with glee
when the color blue was born?

Why does the earth grieve
when the violets appear?

## XXVIII

Why don't old people remember
debts or burns?

Was it real, that scent
of the surprised maiden?

Why don't the poor understand
as soon as they stop being poor?

Where can you find a bell
that will ring in your dreams?

## XLII

Does he who is always waiting suffer more
than he who's never waited for anyone?

Where does the rainbow end,
in your soul or on the horizon?

Perhaps heaven will be,
for suicides, an invisible star?

Where are the vineyards of iron
from where the meteor falls?

### XLIII

Who was she who made love to you
in your dream, while you slept?

Where do the things in dreams go?
Do they pass to the dreams of others?

And does the father who lives in your dreams
die again when you awaken?

In dream, do plants blossom
and their solemn fruit ripen?

### XLIV

Where is the child I was,
still inside me or gone?

Does he know that I never loved him
and that he never loved me?

Why did we spend so much time
growing up only to separate?

Why did we both not die
when my childhood died?

And why does my skeleton pursue me
if my soul has fallen away?

### LXIV

Why do my faded clothes
flutter like a flag?

Am I sometimes evil
or am I always good?

Do we learn kindness
or the mask of kindness?

Isn't the rosebush of evil white
and aren't the flowers of goodness black?

Who assigns names and numbers
to the innumerable innocent?

## LXX

What forced labor
does Hitler do in hell?

Does he paint walls or cadavers?
Does he sniff the fumes of the dead?

Do they feed him the ashes
of so many burnt children?

Or, since his death, have they given him
blood to drink from a funnel?

Or do they hammer into his mouth
the pulled gold teeth?

## LXXI

Or do they lay him down to sleep
on his barbed wire?

Or are they tattooing his skin
for the lamps in hell?

Or do black mastiffs of flame
bite him without mercy?

Or must he travel without rest,
night and day with his prisoners?

Or must he die without dying
eternally under the gas?

## LXXII

If all rivers are sweet
where does the sea get its salt?

How do the seasons know
they must change their shirt?

Why so slowly in winter
and later with such a rapid shudder?

And how do the roots know
they must climb toward the light?

And then greet the air
with so many flowers and colors?

Is it always the same spring
who revives her role?

## LXXIII

Who works harder on earth,
a human or the grain's sun?

Between the fir tree and the poppy
whom does the earth love more?

Between the orchids and the wheat
which does it favor?

Why a flower with such opulence
and wheat with its dirty gold?

Does autumn enter legally
or is it an underground season?

## LXXIV

Why does it linger in the branches
until the leaves fall?

And where are its yellow trousers
left hanging?

Is it true that autumn seems to wait
for something to happen?

Perhaps the trembling of a leaf
or the movement of the universe?

Is there a magnet under the earth,
brother magnet of autumn?

When is the appointment of the rose
decreed under the earth?

# Colombia

## Gabriel García Márquez (b. 1928)

*Translated by Gregory Rabassa and J.S. Bernstein*

Regarded as one of the twentieth century's great novelists, Gabriel García Márquez won the Nobel Prize in literature in 1982. His most famous work, *One Hundred Years of Solitude* (1967), is known worldwide. Márquez was born the same year as the "Banana Massacre," in which hundreds of Colombian peasants were killed attempting to improve their working and living conditions. Economically at the mercy of the U.S.-owned United Fruit Company, the peasants staged a strike that sparked a series of violent uprisings and military responses that have continued to punctuate Colombian history ever since. In Márquez's village alone, more than a hundred peasants were shot in response to the banana workers' strike. From 1947 to 1953, rifts between conservative and liberal factions in the country claimed at least 150,000 lives. The period is known in Colombia as "*la violencia.*"

Márquez was raised by his maternal grandparents against this violent backdrop. He received private education at a Jesuit school in Zipaquira and, after acquiring a bachelor's degree, spent three years studying law. In 1950 he abandoned his legal studies and began a serious career as a journalist. He traveled extensively throughout much of Western and Eastern Europe and the Americas, living for a time in New York City.

Although he has lived outside Colombia for a considerable portion of his adult life (most recently in Mexico City), his fiction is deeply embedded in the landscape and culture of Colombia. Acknowledging the influence of writers such as Faulkner, Woolf, and Kafka, Márquez's work also reflects avant-garde techniques developed by Borges as well as the specifically South American version of "magical realism" first practiced and described by the Cuban novelist Alejo Carpentier in his 1949 novel, *The Kingdom of the World.* The greatest influence on his work, however, Márquez attributes to his grandparents. His much-acclaimed prose style imitates his grandmother's storytelling voice. Márquez has frequently acknowledged the way she would say the "wildest things with a completely natural tone of voice." Her folktales and superstitions, as much or more than the influence of Kafka, gave rise to his magical realism. Márquez reported that when he first read Kafka's "The Metamorphosis," he heard in its style his grandmother's voice telling outrageous tales with a deadpan face.

"The Handsomest Drowned Man in the World" provides a glimpse into the power of magical realism, featuring the gargantuan body of a dead man that washes ashore and is prepared for proper burial by the women of the village. The story's subtitle, "A Tale for Children," is ironic. The narrative, with its focus on the massive sea-encrusted body of a drowned Odysseus and its careful record of a community's response to the intrusive hypermasculinity of the corpse, resonates with themes common in Márquez's mature fiction: alienation, love, death, and the conflicts between older traditions and beliefs and more modern efficiencies. In the eerily mournful world of this tale, rationality is beside the point.

## *The Handsomest Drowned Man in the World*

### *A Tale for Children*

The first children who saw the dark and slinky bulge approaching through the sea let themselves think it was an enemy ship. Then they saw it had no flags or masts and they thought it was a whale. But when it was washed up on the beach, they removed the clumps of seaweed, the jellyfish tentacles, and the remains of fish and flotsam, and only then did they see that it was a drowned man.

They had been playing with him all afternoon, burying him in the sand and digging him up again, when someone chanced to see them and spread the alarm in the village. The men who carried him to the nearest house noticed that he weighed more than any dead man they had ever known, almost as much as a horse, and they said to each other that maybe he'd been floating too long and the water had got into his bones. When they laid him on the floor they said he'd been taller than all other men because there was barely enough room for him in the house, but they thought that maybe the ability to keep on growing after death was part of the nature of certain drowned men. He had the smell of the sea about him and only his shape gave one to suppose that it was the corpse of a human being, because the skin was covered with a crust of mud and scales.

They did not even have to clean off his face to know that the dead man was a stranger. The village was made up of only twenty-odd wooden houses that had stone courtyards with no flowers and which were spread about on the end of a desertlike cape. There was so little land that mothers always went about with the fear that the wind would carry off their children and the few dead that the years had caused among them had to be thrown off the cliffs. But the sea was calm and bountiful and all the men fit into seven boats. So when they found the drowned man they simply had to look at one another to see that they were all there.

That night they did not go out to work at sea. While the men went to find out if anyone was missing in neighboring villages, the women stayed behind to care for the drowned man. They took the mud off with grass swabs, they removed the underwater stones entangled in his hair, and they scraped the crust off with tools used for scaling fish. As they were doing that they noticed that the vegetation on him came from faraway oceans and deep water and that his clothes were in tatters, as if he had sailed through labyrinths of coral. They noticed too that he bore his death with pride, for he did not have the lonely look of other drowned men who came out of the sea or that haggard, needy look of men who drowned in rivers. But only when they finished cleaning him off did they become aware of the kind of man he was and it left them breathless. Not only was he the tallest, strongest, most virile, and best built man they had ever seen, but even though they were looking at him there was no room for him in their imagination.

They could not find a bed in the village large enough to lay him on nor was there a table solid enough to use for his wake. The tallest men's holiday pants would not fit him, not the fattest ones' Sunday shirts, nor the shoes of the one with the biggest feet. Fascinated by his huge size and his beauty, the women then decided to make him some pants from a large piece of sail and a shirt from some bridal brabant linen so that he could continue through his death with dignity. As they sewed, sitting in a circle and gazing at the corpse between stitches, it seemed to them that the wind had never been so steady nor the sea so restless as on that night and they supposed that the change had something to do with the dead man. They thought that if that magnificent man had lived in the village, his house would have had the widest doors, the highest ceiling, and the strongest floor, his bedstead would have been made from a midship frame held together by iron bolts, and his wife would have been the happiest woman. They thought that he would have had so much authority that he could have drawn fish out of the sea simply by calling their names and that he would have put so much work into his land that springs would have burst forth from among the rocks so that he would have been able to plant flowers on the cliffs. They secretly compared him to their own men, thinking that for all their lives theirs were incapable of doing what he could do in one night, and they ended up dismissing them deep in their hearts as the weakest, meanest, and most useless creatures on earth. They were wandering through that maze of fantasy when the oldest woman, who as the oldest had looked upon the drowned man with more compassion than passion, sighed:

"He has the face of someone called Esteban."

It was true. Most of them had only to take another look at him to see that he could not have any other name. The more stubborn among them, who were the youngest, still lived for a few hours with the illusion that when they put his clothes on and he lay among the flowers in patent leather shoes his name might be Lautaro. But it was a vain illusion. There had not been enough canvas, the poorly cut and worse sewn pants were too tight, and the hidden strength of his heart popped the buttons on his shirt. After midnight the whistling of the wind died down and the sea fell into its Wednesday drowsiness. The silence put an end to any last doubts: he was Esteban. The women who had dressed him, who had combed his hair, had cut his nails and shaved him were unable to hold back a shudder of pity when they had to resign themselves to his being dragged along the ground. It was then that they understood how unhappy he must have been with that huge body since it bothered him even after death. They could see him in life, condemned to going through doors sideways, cracking his head on crossbeams, remaining on his feet during visits, not knowing what to do with his soft, pink, sea lion hands while the lady of the house looked for her most resistant chair and begged him, frightened to death, sit here, Esteban, please, and he, leaning against the wall, smiling, don't bother, ma'am, I'm fine where I am, his heels raw and his back roasted from having done the same thing so many times whenever he paid a visit, don't bother, ma'am, I'm fine where I am, just to avoid the embarrassment of breaking up the chair, and never knowing perhaps that the ones who said don't go, Esteban, at least wait till the coffee's ready, were the ones who later on would whisper the big boob finally left, how nice, the handsome fool has gone. That was what the women were thinking beside the body a little before dawn. Later, when they covered his face with a handkerchief so that the light would not bother him, he looked so forever dead, so defenseless, so much like their men that the first furrows of tears opened in their hearts. It was one of the younger ones who began the weeping. The others, coming to, went from sighs to wails, and the more they sobbed the more they felt like weeping, because the drowned man was becoming all the more Esteban for them, and so they wept so much, for he was the most destitute, most peaceful, and most obliging man on earth, poor Esteban. So when the men returned with the news that the drowned man was not from the neighboring villages either, the women felt an opening of jubilation in the midst of their tears.

"Praise the Lord," they sighed, "he's ours!"

The men thought the fuss was only womanish frivolity. Fatigued because of the difficult nighttime inquiries, all they wanted was to get rid of the bother of the newcomer once and for all before the sun grew strong on that arid, windless day. They improvised a litter with the remains of foremasts and gaffs, tying it together with rigging so that it would bear the weight of the body until they reached the cliffs. They wanted to tie the anchor from a cargo ship to him so that he would sink easily into the deepest waves, where fish are blind and divers die of nostalgia, and bad currents would not bring him back to shore, as had happened with other bodies. But the more they hurried, the more the women thought of ways to waste time. They walked about like startled hens, pecking with the sea charms on their breasts, some interfering on one side to put a scapular of the good wind on the drowned man, some on the other side to put a wrist compass on him, and after a great deal of *get away from there, woman, stay out of the way, look, you almost made me fall on top of the dead man,* the men began to feel mistrust in their livers and started grumbling about why so many main-altar decorations for a stranger, because no matter how many nails and holy-water jars he had on him, the sharks would chew him all the same, but the women kept piling on their junk relics, running back and forth, stumbling, while they released in sighs what they did not in tears, so that the men finally exploded with *since when has there ever been such a fuss over a drifting corpse, a drowned nobody, a piece of cold Wednesday meat.* One of the women, mortified by so much lack of care, then removed the handkerchief from the dead man's face and the men were left breathless too.

He was Esteban. It was not necessary to repeat it for them to recognize him. If they had been told Sir Walter Raleigh, even they might have been impressed with his gringo accent, the macaw on his shoulder, his cannibal-killing blunderbuss, but there could be only one Esteban in the world and there he was, stretched out like a sperm whale, shoeless, wearing the pants of an undersized child, and with those stony nails that had to be cut with a knife. They only had to take the handkerchief off his face to see that he was ashamed, that it was not his fault that he was so big or so heavy or so handsome, and if he had known that this was going to happen, he would have looked for a more discreet place to drown in, seriously, I even would have tied the anchor off a galleon around my neck and staggered off a cliff like someone who doesn't like things in order not to be upsetting people now with this Wednesday dead body, as you people say, in order not to be bothering anyone with this filthy piece of cold meat that doesn't have anything to do with me. There was so much truth in his manner that even the most mistrustful men, the ones who felt the bitterness of endless nights at sea fearing that their women would tire of dreaming about them and begin to dream of drowned men, even they and others who were harder still shuddered in the marrow of their bones at Esteban's sincerity.

That was how they came to hold the most splendid funeral they could conceive of for an abandoned drowned man. Some women who had gone to get flowers in the neighboring villages returned with other women who could not believe what they had been told, and those women went back for more flowers when they saw the dead man, and they brought more and more until there were so many flowers and so many people that it was hard to walk about. At the final moment it pained them to return him to the waters as an orphan and they chose a father and mother from among the best people, and aunts and uncles and cousins, so that through him all the inhabitants of the village became kinsmen. Some sailors who heard the weeping from a distance went off course and people heard of one who had himself tied to the mainmast, remembering ancient fables about sirens. While they fought for the privilege of carrying him on their shoulders along the steep escarpment by the cliffs, men and women became aware for the first time of the desolation of their streets, the dryness of their courtyards, the narrowness of their dreams as they faced the splendor and beauty of their drowned man. They let him go without an anchor so that he could come back if he wished and whenever he wished, and they all held their breath for the fraction of centuries the body took to fall into the abyss. They did not need to look at one another to realize that they were no longer all present, that they would never be. But they also knew that everything would be different from then on, that their houses would have wider doors, higher ceilings, and stronger floors so that Esteban's memory could go everywhere without bumping into beams and so that no one in the future would dare whisper the big boob finally died, too bad, the handsome fool has finally died, because they were going to paint their house fronts gay colors to make Esteban's memory eternal and they were going to break their backs digging for springs among the stones and planting flowers on the cliffs so that in future years at dawn the passengers on great liners would awaken, suffocated by the smell of gardens on the high seas, and the captain would have to come down from the bridge in his dress uniform, with his astrolabe, his pole star, and his row of war medals and, pointing to the promontory of roses on the horizon, he would say in fourteen languages, look there, where the wind is so peaceful now that it's gone to sleep beneath the beds, over there, where the sun's so bright that the sunflowers don't know which way to turn, yes, over there, that's Esteban's village.

*(1968)*

# Dominican Republic

## Ángela Hernández (b. 1954)

*Translated by Lizabeth Paravisini-Gebert*

Ángela Hernández is one of a new generation of Caribbean writers who express the region's sense of cultural independence and self-confidence as the twentieth century draws to a close and the literature of the island nations takes a more prominent place in world literature. She was born in Jarabacoa, Dominican Republic, and was educated as a chemical engineer. Her writing reflects her political activism, particularly in regard to women's issues. She has published two books of poetry and a collection of short stories, *Alótropos*. She is also well known as an essayist on women's rights.

Hernández's Spanish is richly poetic and her fiction is characterized by the exploration of imaginative extremes that express intense emotional states. In the story included here, "How to Gather the Shadows of the Flowers," two voices describe the strange psychological development of a beautiful and serious girl abandoned by her husband. The voice of a sibling tells the events that led to Faride's gradual escape into a surreal psychological state and eventually into a dreamy death, while a more distant observer speculates on her descent into madness—or poetry. Faride's writings and the descriptions of her inner life resemble the magical realism that Gabriel Garcia Márquez established as a powerful international literary influence.

### *How to Gather the Shadows of the Flowers*

"Voyage of voyages with a hundred returns / capricious voyages / testimony of sighs / returns without turns / time in bouquets / and in my brow a sacred zeal to fade away / perhaps to return."

We found this text under the mattress and, like the rest of them, it seemed intended to provide us with clues to understand her. An impossible enterprise for us who had known her and loved her as a common girl, as the eldest sister, for whom our parents reserved certain privileges.

Faride was the only one of us to attend a private school (Papa got her a scholarship to an evangelical institute).

The rest of us went to public school. When she finished high school she started working as a cashier in a supermarket; she remained in that job for six months. One day, surprisingly, she quit. Mama accused her of acting unconscionably, a judgment ratified by my father's recriminating glances. They both employed every possible means to extract from her the reason for her self-dismissal. She had not been laid off, nor had she had any difficulties in balancing the register every day, nor any trouble with any customer. It was not until after many weeks of siege that she said: "The supervisor kept pawing me." Nobody bothered her about it again. Two months later she began to work in a fabric shop. That's how she was, unaffected, serious, and reserved. I have brought you some photographs, but I must return them right away. My mother has forbidden us to touch her belongings.

*From the very first glance the photographs captured my attention; I was intrigued above all by the well-defined combination of white and black features in one face: thick lips, very fine nose, long and kinky curls. In her eyes you caught a glimpse of an expression as dual and marked as the lines of her profile; there was in them a latent force: a vague expressiveness, a black blaze behind a deceiving curtain of void. From that day on, the image of her seductive gaze has been an obsessive burden in my brain. After that I would stay with José after class to hear more details.*

The women of my family marry before they turn twenty. My grandmother married very young; my mother followed the tradition, and Faride got married a few months before turning eighteen. I don't think she had a good idea of what marriage meant; I'm not even sure whether she was happy or not, but I do remember her clearly, distressed and nervous, untiringly knitting tablecloths and bedcovers the year before Raúl left for the United States. Not that she had much choice. Faride supported the household. They had two children and had been married four years and he still had not found a steady job. When she returned to our house with the children, she seemed sad and somewhat relieved.

*I have turned this information over and over in my mind, trying to understand the meaning of the events that took place in José's house. I haven't found anything that points to Faride having been subject to any special circumstances in her childhood and adolescence. There were nine siblings, who received the same upbringing and grew up in the same house. Three of them, including Faride, were born in the central mountains, but that doesn't make them different. The two eldest brothers seem to have nothing in common with her; José, the sixth child, whom I know best, is as normal a young man as they come.*

Industrious and conscientious, when she moved back into the house Faride continued working in the shop and knitting tablecloths and bedcovers in the evenings and weekends. Her friends would say to her jokingly: "Aha! knitting while she awaits her husband, like Penelope," and she would reply with a smile: "I knit to eat, not to deceive myself."

In some ways, in some small things, my sister's behavior was different from that of other people. She showed no special interest in her physical appearance. She never wore lipstick or eye makeup. Her wardrobe was very simple; she made her own clothes of light fabrics and pastel colors; lemon yellow and lilac predominated in her apparel. I was the oldest of the siblings still living at home; I was then just past twelve; I don't remember ever seeing her angry at me; she never lectured me, nor did she offer advice on any subject. But these details of behavior don't make anyone special; least of all in our house, where chattering and long conversations between adults were extremely rare and where everyone preferred to keep to themselves; my mother listened to the radio; my father played dominoes; my older brothers cruised the streets; Faride knitted.

We got along very well with her and the children; life followed its natural course and none of us, not even our parents, had noticed the gradual transformation taking place within our sister; it was with great surprise that we witnessed the unexpected eruption of the world brewing within her. It happened at breakfast:

"He'll help me, this one will indeed help me, Mama. This man is really worth it. He is beautiful like a sun. He smells of May, he tastes like mint washed by a rain shower. He's not rich, nor young; he's not even heroic. But he's incomparably loving. He carries me to bed every day, and you should see what a bed, soft like a song filtered through water. He only needs a glance to understand me; he knows what I yearn for just from sensing it."

We couldn't quite understand her words. Not even Papa and Mama seemed to understand, since they were looking at her with puzzled expressions on their faces.

"The house has burst into flower in the few days we have spent together. Flowers assumed gigantic proportions with every minute of love. Violets and poppies growing deliriously; fennel and sunflowers and red-wine-colored hollyhocks like open umbrellas. It's like a jungle now. The orchids climb the walls, forming very elegant nosegays, they barely let you see anything through the glass. The whole house is made of transparent glass. At first I was embarrassed; someone could see us when we did things in bed. Then I realized that the house was alone in the world. Swarms of bees embroider honey hives around the stalks of the carnations, green crickets and fireflies gather pollen to build their homes. Ah, the hollyhocks fascinate me with the red-wine blood exquisitely retained in their corollas! Please advise me: What can one do with a garden gone out of control? What would we do if the flowers continue to climb to the ceiling and manage to conceal the sun? He could abandon me. He knows the garden grows only for me. What tragic pleasure! What sweet mortification!"

We remained silent. We couldn't understand her speech, but it fascinated us; Mama and Papa looked at her in astonishment. She got up, washed her hands, took her purse, and left.

The children delighted in our daughter's stories as if they were fairy tales. We got very agitated; we had never heard Faride talk about men, least of all in such insolent terms. We went over the details of the past week, and not finding anything extraordinary to justify her words, we decided to question her when she returned.

She didn't come back until eight o'clock that night, and didn't even allow us to approach her: "I'm dying to sleep," she said as she threw herself onto the bed between her children without changing clothes. She was snubbing us for the first time in her life, and the disrespect of her action poisoned our evening.

*The correspondences between their description of Faride's words and her writings were remarkable. The papers she left in her own handwriting share a similar tone. In one and the other the central mystery derives from the comparison between her discourse and her slight intellectual training. Where did these figurations come from? Was it perhaps a peculiar type of schizophrenia? Sometimes her brother worries me; more than by vocation, he has chosen this career with the hope of solving her enigma, and perhaps he's only moving further and further away from the clues.*

We had been watching for her when she came in and sat next to me at the table. She seemed peaceful, cheerful; there was a disconcerting clarity in her eyes; two drops of dew hung from her pupils. A serenity and happiness which I felt spreading through my body.

I shuddered, my hands shook, when I saw her approach. A presentiment oppressed my heart. I saw the six-year-old girl with a wide ribbon holding her hair, the lively girl who grabbed my legs and whom I pushed away with a slap; the angel of light who kissed me, licked my lips, hugged me, caressed my breasts, and whom I pushed away, annoyed because two younger children demanded my attention; the insistent girl that got under my skirt wanting to play, and whom I spanked because I had too much work and her moving bothered me; the little one who at dawn cuddled at my feet hoping to remain unnoticed, and whom I would put back to bed screaming at her to be quiet. The one who would take care of her little brothers and sisters so I would love her more, the one who asked me to let her suckle when I breast-fed her little brother, the one who exasperated me with her cajoling, when it was already too late. The same face, the same ribbon, the same laugh, the same eyes. I would have wanted to hug her, but too much time and distance had passed between the two of us.

"I gave him a shell of twelve colors. Uf! it was so hard to find. It was between rocks, in a big hollow. I placed a strong tree trunk across the hollow, hung from it and walked with my hands to where the treasure was. It is the size of a teacup. The colors spring from the outside and then spread to the inside. It is so curious, so many colors emerging from a dark little knot."

She lowered her voice, as if she were speaking to herself; then she continued, excitedly.

"He loved my gift. *C'est très joli, comme la vie*, he said to me."

My mother contained herself. Who is he? she asked her. Faride looked at her, puzzled, and replied naturally: "The director of the Oncology Institute."

"I never imagined he would be so beautiful. When he laughs, and he's almost always laughing, he leans back, chair and all. His laughter soars to the sky like bubbles of music coming out of a flute. I feel like sucking his mouth, I feel like eating him with lettuce and carnations. His teeth look moist. His laughter flows from inside, as if a glass of water flowered in his throat."

Mama blushed; Papa was uncomfortable in his chair; we were enjoying the story.

"He has requested me as his assistant in his operations, in the radioactive treatments and the laboratory. I tell him I know nothing of diseases and healing. He soothes me with his beautiful laughter; you'll learn, we'll teach you. We spent long dead hours, no, better still, living, gloriously living hours seated in two wooden chairs, on the rocks, by the sea. The others were far away. The rocks jutted out of the sea, we sailed on an indigo air several meters above the water."

Then, deep in thought, she commented to herself: "This special man makes me forget cancer." She devoured her breakfast and left hurriedly. We remained there talking about cancer. For some of us it was a bumblebee with horns, to others a plant with white spots. Unable to agree, we asked Mama. Anguished, she replied: "It's many things at the same time."

My husband and I were troubled. We had educated Faride as a good Christian and didn't recognize her in these daring speeches. We even came to suspect that she was keeping bad company, but anyway, people don't change just like that, from one moment to the next.

"They're dreams. Did you notice today? They're only dreams."

"She believes they're real. This is very unusual. She'll go telling those filthy stories around. They'll say she's a tramp. The husband working in New York and she living with other men."

"People who know us won't take her words seriously."

On Monday Mama woke us up early; she made us have breakfast and get ready for school in a hurry. Before we left, however, she couldn't prevent our overhearing our sister telling her in the kitchen:

"Mama, the young ones are darlings. His name is Andrés and Lucía introduced me to him at her party. Fire at first sight! One look and we were captivated. It's understandable: tender, passionate, soft, with his big green eyes, he's like a big son between my legs."

I found the piece of paper on the nightstand in her room; it was in her handwriting, and the contents seemed to refer to the story of the shell and the doctor. I woke her up very early, dawn had not yet broken. I took her to the kitchen, I wanted to speak to her without interruptions. Maybe the paper would clarify something, maybe her stories were nothing more than ideas copied from some disturbing book. What is this? I asked her.

"Can't you see? I wrote it night before last: I am a relative of the stones / of the delicate waves of the coast / of the fragile horizons / the ever winding and unwinding snails / rocking in the vigils of their chiaroscuro moves / with their easy melodies / with their sonority of distant sea / with their peaceful and oblivious song / with mother-of-pearl winding and unwinding around submarine lines / drinking them like wine, like salt, like elementary milk."

She had repeated from memory the words on the piece of paper; she half-closed her eyes and continued to recite, as if she were reading something written inside her lids:

"Wet and surprised / like a newborn / I can barely touch myself / I did not take the sun, there was no time / nor did I learn my tongue / nor did I detect the clues to my surroundings / I lie on myself / drowsy and timid / my textures are tender / in this my very embryo / sometimes I renew myself."

I felt a tingle down my spine. I didn't dare interrupt her, it wasn't my daughter talking.

"To exist and not to be / is a miracle / to be the frontier to the undecipherable / equidistant to acceptance /

a wisdom on the margin of precepts / a lucid candor / a hidden golden vertebra / a lace made of spinning violets / forming a violet heart."

Almost voiceless, I said: Faride, my daughter, what is happening to you? I didn't even dare touch her, I sensed her distant and alien.

"Nothing is the matter, Mama."

"Where do you get these stories from?"

"What stories?"

"The ones you've just told me, the ones from breakfast on Saturday and Sunday."

"They're not stories. I wrote that poetry fifty years ago. It's mine. I don't tell stories, I never could learn any."

"Are you telling me that these are truths, reality?"

"What is the truth, Mama? What is reality?"

"The truth is the truth, the same truth you learned when you were a child. Reality is that you're twenty-three years old. You couldn't have written anything fifty years ago. Tell me the truth; you never lied."

"I'm not lying."

"Don't drive me to despair. Trust me; tell me what's happening in your life."

"I trust you. Nothing is happening to me; I am well."

"Tell me then, why are you inventing these extravagant stories so detrimental to your good name?"

"What extravagant stories?"

"These fantasies of men and love affairs so different from your reality as a serious woman."

"What is reality, Mama?"

"Reality is eating rice and plantains, giving birth to a child, working, seeing clearly what things are like!"

"And what are things like?"

I didn't insist anymore; this senseless conversation was driving me mad.

The next day, she sat at the table, giddy. The children had left for school. One of our older children was with us. I had asked him to be there, knowing that Faride respected him almost more than she did her father, she feared him more. From the time she was very young we entrusted her care to her brother. His presence, however, didn't inhibit her.

"It was a beautiful, but at the same time, boring trip; two months at sea, seeing sky, seeing blue and more blue, seeing the same people, the unseasonal birds hovering over our heads. But it was worth it. My mother's friends were waiting for me, with a bouquet of flowers and open arms. I went with Ferita to register at the university. I took only two courses: botany and history, because I first must grow used to the city and my new friends, before I throw myself completely into my studies. I get my teachers confused; they are so white, so similar. God made white people's skin with the same roll of fabric. Yesterday we went to see Unamuno's *Shadows of Dreams.* The theater is very elegant, and so are the people. After the performance we went to my apartment, we drank wine and beer, we danced, and rolled on the floor."

"Enough!" I said with anger and sadness. My oldest son only commented: "What is she talking about?" We had to practically push him out of the house by force, he was furious and wanted to beat her up. According to him, Faride had become a trollop and two or three good blows would straighten her out. She didn't seem surprised, and when we returned she even added:

"The trolley cars, the buildings, the beautiful paintings in the museums, the

Graf Zeppelin, the romantic friends reciting verses in the parks."

The narratives at breakfast became routine. They sent us away from the table, they made us run out to school, they separated us from her and her belongings, managing thereby to sharpen our curiosity. We spied on conversations, searched her purse, and eluded Mama's and Papa's watchful eyes to be with her. Mama thought that Faride's ravings were a passing thing, attributing them to lack of news from Raúl. In effect, there had been no news from him since he had left. Mama had gone to the group that had organized the trip, but they said they weren't responsible for people after they took them over. Papa considered Raúl a scoundrel; he wasn't interested in his whereabouts, and even less in his fate. That Saturday, Faride came in to the kitchen, trembling: there was a somber expression on her face. Papa and Mama were alarmed.

"It was alive, the desiccated bird, the prehistoric desiccated bird sent to me by my friend from India was alive. It chased me into the rice bog, into the labyrinth of caves in San Juan, between my legs. It seemed dead when it arrived through the mail, but it was alive. An atrocious bird, sticky, with long legs and long sharp goads instead of feathers. It was humid and dead and moved. I don't know what to do with it. I tried throwing it out the window only to find it again under my bed. Ten times I took it out of my room and it would return to my side, like an amulet reeking of death, and it is in my room, and it holds its viscous skin to my face. Oh God, it has made me throw up my insides!"

Papa and Mama listened to her in consternation. Even we, spying through the gaps in the kitchen wall, were profoundly impressed. She suddenly changed her expression and laughed:

"Ah, but what a beautiful little house. He sent it to me as a gift. It came in the mail today. It's not taller than my legs, but it has a thousand little doors, all pink, all painted in a different pink. A thousand shades of pink on the façade. When you open a little door, you find a three-verse poem and a painting which explains that year's history. A thousand years of Indian history in a thousand paintings and a thousand poems. In the last little door, the one in a pink so intense it approaches the orange of red-tinted clouds, is the Salt March and the Peace Poem: Peace, salt, autumn splendor / they are within us and together they will sprout / like a water spring that blinds certain fires."

When we, intrigued, asked her about the little house, she told us that she would show it to us later. In India, she told us, children didn't use books to study history, but little houses like these. Through millennia, Hindus have learned the exceptional art of miniaturizing trees and history.

On Faride's birthday her colleagues at work organized a little party for her, to which they invited us. We went to the store in the afternoon, after the shop closed, feeling apprehensive. To our surprise, the celebration proceeded quite normally. The shop owner gave her a certificate commending her for her exceptional performance as a salesperson; he also gave her a small gold chain, exhorting her to keep up the good work with her usual cordiality and efficiency. Her co-workers loved and admired her, as we could attest to.

At home, however, the modifications in her conduct were marked. She knitted less and spent long periods of time in silence.

She didn't waste any chance to play. She would get lost in the ring around the rosie, pocket full of posies, look who's here Punchinella, Punchinella, Miss Mary Mack Mack with silver buttons all down her back back; she ran and jumped with boundless energy, and none of us could catch her when we played tag. Papa and Mama rested easy when they saw us like that. But a turn in the situation agitated the entire household, and from then on our parents didn't even bother to hide their anguish from us.

It was Sunday. Papa was playing dominoes with a group of friends, in front of the house. Faride, euphoric, started to turn around the playing table, jumping as she held the edges of her skirt, opening it like a fan. She sang out the words, heaping them onto each other in an easy flowing laughter.

"My lover returned from the crystal house. He has brought me his riddles once more. This time I will guess the answers. The glass house is celebrating tonight, all the windows have been opened and the rooms are bursting with full moons. We are going to Moscow to ride the Ferris wheel. He amuses himself with the trapeze artists. Together we built a sculpture to the tenderness of the panda bear / Providence shines like a firefly in the Caribbean Sea / with the fishermen on the golden beach / at dawn / we encircle its waters / with boreal ribbons / we wove a basket / that knows about Ithaca / through eternal ice / we go animatedly / on expeditions / silver camels / carry us on their rumps / through snowy peaks / so clear / so beautiful / that in their translucency / time melts / and the soul dissolves."

From that moment on, our household was in an upheaval. Faride would tell her rapturous stories to anyone who would listen. Some people would come to our house and incite her to talk so as to feed the rumors circulating around the neighborhood. Mama and Papa quickly gathered together some money and took her to a psychiatrist.

He examined her, and submitted her to different tests. He tested her reflexes, laid logical traps for her; they spoke for more than a hour. Faced with our bewilderment, he told us she was undoubtedly sane, and that he found her to be an intelligent and cooperative young woman. We narrated to him the events of Sunday and of the days before. He asked us to understand her youth and her ideas. The dreams of each generation differ, he insisted. I insisted on his hearing her in front of us, thinking that perhaps she had pulled the wool over his eyes. We called her in and I asked her to read one of her poems. She then proceeded to recite with great spontaneity, looking us in the eye:

"Populations of stars uninhabit the sky to hurl themselves at my heavens / matrixes of fresh bubbles / pay deaf ears to their original water springs / and make a watery bouquet in my sex / juice of virgin meadows / squeezed by sheer will / form the blood of my wanderings / I am with them / a game of love / a born traveler."

The doctor expressed that that poetry confirmed his diagnosis: Faride was intelligent and original, and advised us to let her be. We left his office even more baffled; no one said a word on our way back.

Her dreams gained ground as the days went by. It was hard to wake her up in the morning. Sometimes she would wash up, have breakfast in the kitchen, and return to bed. We would wake her up again shaking her roughly. She would then do two or three routine chores and then return to bed to continue her interrupted sleep. When we forced her to get up and kept her from returning to bed, as I lectured her on her lack of responsibility toward work and of the importance of her salary to the family's finances, she would walk through the house as if it were a stage and she the leading actress, playing a role known only to herself.

Sometimes, sitting upright in bed, she examined her surroundings as if she didn't recognize anything. She walked by inertia, repeating to us previous dialogues. Pensive and inexpressive, it would take her up to three-quarters of an hour to cross the line dividing her two realities.

We did all we could to isolate the neighbors from the atmosphere of our house. Our older children would entertain visitors in front of the house, taking chairs out to the sidewalk and engaging in conversation almost on the street. I abstained from going out. I went only to mass on Sunday and I tried to do so with the greatest discretion: I was terrified of questions. We forbade the children to enter Faride's bedroom. After repeated excuses, we had to admit that she wouldn't return to work, and so we informed the shop owner. But all our efforts did nothing more than unleash more rumors. The neighbors' assumptions were like knives in my heart. As far as they were concerned Faride was pregnant, Faride had had a botched abortion in a back-alley clinic, Faride had an unstoppable hemorrhage, Faride had gone mad and walked naked through the house making pornographic gestures, Faride was rotting with cancer, her face had been eaten up by maggots, and therefore we had locked her up.

Our friends asked us in school if it was true that our sister smelled bad, if we were having another little brother or sister, how many men had given her children; they asked us if we would get sick just like her. Faced with that rosary of rumors, Mama drastically changed policies. She opened doors and windows, invited the neighboring women to the house for coffee, canceled the orders that kept us away from our sister, allowed her children to sleep with her again, and no longer prevented her from going out into the yard.

The friends and neighbors saw her walk the sidewalk, water the eggplants planted in the yard, and frolic with her children. They took turns spying on her, since she would let herself be seen only once in a while. Some ended up attributing to her a passing illness or a harmless dementia. They also agreed, however, that her physique did not betray any ailment whatsoever. They saw her like she looked then: her profile more defined, her cheeks rosy and with a profound calm always peeking through her eyes.

Every once in a while I would sit down to watch her sleep. Certain discoveries had awakened in me hopes of a cure. Watching her fixedly, I noticed the movements of her eyelids and the slight stretching of her lips when the familiar voices of the market women offered their pigeon peas, coriander, and oregano for sale. She didn't seem disconnected from the prattle of children playing baseball in the neighborhood park. If my daughter was not completely rooted in this reality, neither was she in the other.

Mama's hopes soon began to fade. Faride's residence on this side of reality diminished progressively, until it was reduced to the narrow space of no more than an hour. Then she would awaken completely, drink a glass of water, bathe and perfume herself. She would talk briefly with Mama and Papa, and would romp with us for a while, demonstrating a complete command of her two diverse time frames. When she was asleep, she lay totally submerged in a deep tranquility; when she was awake, she was nimble and clear-sighted.

One day she awakened all of us with a frantic cry. It was a calm dawn in April, fresh and fragrant, I will never forget it. Standing around her bed, we heard her last words.

"I have found the solution!! Kiss me all of you!! Kiss me and hold me in your arms because I have found the solution!! Now I know how to irrigate a garden that won't stop growing, how to gather the shadows of the flowers, how to prevent their concealing the sun, and how to walk diagonally across the instants."

She went to sleep definitively. She slept for exactly six months. Pale, on her back, smiling: her heartbeats began to fade. At the end she looked like a beautiful dream dressed in pink, a dream that our parents refused to bury.

*I don't know why the family opted for the diagnosis of madness. The notion that it was a singular form of dementia, still unexplored by psychiatry, is taking root in José; his career plans are driven by the desire to deepen the investigation of the case.*

*The one exception is the mother, for whom the daughter was possessed by a woman from the past; her eagerness leads her to think that José, sometimes, is possessed by Faride's spirit. They alone knew her intimately, having witnessed every detail of the most intense moments of her extraordinary behavior; but they could be mistaken, however, and it could perhaps be a mere matter of poetics.*

# The United States

## Walt Whitman (1819–1892)

Walt Whitman was forever infuriating people who charged him with laziness. First he angered his father and brothers because he shirked household duties; later he drifted in and out of jobs, being hired and fired periodically. Whitman is credited with writing the best poetry of the American Civil War, having experienced it first-hand when he went looking for his brother, who was missing in action in Virginia. Although Whitman found his brother, witnessing war close up changed him, and he subsequently devoted himself to caring for wounded soldiers of both armies who were hospitalized in Washington, D.C. He supported himself as a journalist and as a civil servant. He struggled for some time with his sexual identity. When explicitly homosexual passages appeared in later versions of his monumental collection of poems *Leaves of Grass,* he lost his job. Although he had several long-term relationships, he spent much of his life drifting from lover to lover, enduring economic hardship and loneliness.

In the 1855 Preface to *Leaves of Grass,* Whitman dedicated himself to the task of "singing America," articulating innovative poetic forms he considered appropriate for a new nation. He rebelled against the traditional rules and structures of poetry, which, he argued, should no longer rule the imagination. Whitman imagined himself a poet-priest who ministered to America with poetry celebrating individualism, the common people, the American landscape, and democratic ideals of community. His manner of celebrating the great diversity of nature and humanity by gigantic acts of identification, in which he becomes the city, the country, or the universe, often gives his poetry a religious tone reminiscent of Hindu or Sufi mysticism:

> These are really the thoughts of all men in all ages and lands, they are not original with me,
> If they are not yours as much as mine they are nothing, or next to nothing.
> If they are not the riddle and the untying of the riddle they are nothing,
> If they are not just as close as they are distant they are nothing.
> This is the grass that grows wherever the land and the water is,
> This the common air that bathes the globe. ("Song of Myself")

Whitman was the first U.S. poet to achieve international recognition. *Leaves of Grass,* written between 1855 and 1891, includes about three hundred poems. One of the best known is "When Lilacs Last in the Dooryard Bloom'd," which is included here. Lamenting the death of President Abraham Lincoln, this elegy combines personal and public sorrow, gradually moving from grief to acceptance. The poem achieves its effect through an accumulation of images, sounds, lines, and emotions, weaving them together with memory, sorrow, praise, and hope.

## *Memories of President Lincoln*

### *When Lilacs Last in the Dooryard Bloom'd*

**1**

When lilacs last in the dooryard bloom'd,
And the great star early droop'd in the western sky in the night,
I mourn'd, and yet shall mourn with ever-returning spring.

Ever-returning spring, trinity sure to me you bring,
Lilac blooming perennial and drooping star in the west,
And thought of him I love.

**2**

O powerful western fallen star!
O shades of night—O moody, tearful night!
O great star disappear'd—O the black murk that hides the star!
O cruel hands that hold me powerless—O helpless soul of me!
O harsh surrounding cloud that will not free my soul.

**3**

In the dooryard fronting an old farm-house near the white-wash'd palings,
Stands the lilac-bush tall-growing with heart-shaped leaves of rich green,

With many a pointed blossom rising delicate, with the perfume strong I love,
With every leaf a miracle—and from this bush in the dooryard,
With delicate-color'd blossoms and heart-shaped leaves of rich green,
A sprig with its flower I break.

**4**

In the swamp in secluded recesses,
A shy and hidden bird is warbling a song.

Solitary the thrush,
The hermit withdrawn to himself, avoiding the settlements,
Sings by himself a song.

Song of the bleeding throat,
Death's outlet song of life, (for well dear brother I know,
If thou wast not granted to sing thou would'st surely die.)

**5**

Over the breast of the spring, the land, amid cities,
Amid lanes and through old woods, where lately the violets peep'd from the ground, spotting the gray debris,
Amid the grass in the fields each side of the lanes, passing the endless grass,
Passing the yellow-spear'd wheat, every grain from its shroud in the dark-brown fields uprisen,
Passing the apple-tree blows of white and pink in the orchards,
Carrying a corpse to where it shall rest in the grave,
Night and day journeys a coffin.

**6**

Coffin that passes through lanes and streets,
Through day and night with the great cloud darkening the land,
With the pomp of the inloop'd flags with the cities draped in black,
With the show of the States themselves as of crape-veil'd women standing,
With processions long and winding and the flambeaus of the night,
With the countless torches lit, with the silent sea of faces and the unbared heads,
With the waiting depot, the arriving coffin, and the sombre faces,
With dirges through the night, with the thousand voices rising strong and solemn,

With all the mournful voices of the dirges pour'd around the coffin,
The dim-lit churches and the shuddering organs—where amid these you journey,
With the tolling tolling bells' perpetual clang,
Here, coffin that slowly passes,
I give you my sprig of lilac.

**7**

(Nor for you, for one alone,
Blossoms and branches green to coffins all I bring,
For fresh as the morning, thus would I chant a song for you O sane and sacred death.

All over bouquets of roses,
O death, I cover you over with roses and early lilies,
But mostly and now the lilac that blooms the first,
Copious I break, I break the sprigs from the bushes,
With loaded arms I come, pouring for you,
For you and the coffins all of you O death.)

**8**

O western orb sailing the heaven,
Now I know what you must have meant as a month since I walk'd,
As I walk'd in silence the transparent shadowy night,
As I saw you had something to tell as you bent to me night after night,
As you droop'd from the sky low down as if to my side, (while the other stars all look'd on,)
As we wander'd together the solemn night, (for something I know not what kept me from sleep,)
As the night advanced, and I saw on the rim of the west how full you were of woe,
As I stood on the rising ground in the breeze in the cool transparent night,
As I watch'd where you pass'd and was lost in the netherward black of the night,
As my soul in its trouble dissatisfied sank, as where you sad orb,
Concluded, dropt in the night, and was gone.

**9**

Sing on there in the swamp,
O singer bashful and tender, I hear your notes, I hear your call,

I hear, I come presently, I understand you,
But a moment I linger, for the lustrous star has detain'd me,
The star my departing comrade holds and detains me.

**10**

O how shall I warble myself for the dead one there I loved?
And how shall I deck my song for the large sweet soul that has gone?
And what shall my perfume be for the grave of him I love?

Sea-winds blown from east and west,
Blown from the Eastern sea and blown from the Western sea, till there on the prairies meeting,
These and with these and the breath of my chant,
I'll perfume the grave of him I love.

**11**

O what shall I hang on the chamber walls?
And what shall the pictures be that I hang on the walls,
To adorn the burial-house of him I love?

Pictures of growing spring and farms and homes,
With the Fourth-month eve at sundown, and the gray smoke lucid and bright,
With floods of the yellow gold of the gorgeous, indolent, sinking sun, burning, expanding the air,
With the fresh sweet herbage under foot, and the pale green leaves of the trees prolific,
In the distance the flowing glaze, the breast of the river, with a wind-dapple here and there,
With ranging hills on the banks, with many a line against the sky, and shadows,
And the city at hand with dwellings so dense, and stacks of chimneys,
And all the scenes of life and the workshops, and the workmen homeward returning.

**12**

Lo, body and soul—this land,
My own Manhattan with spires, and the sparkling and hurrying tides, and the ships,
The varied and ample land, the South and the North in the light, Ohio's shores and flashing Missouri,
And ever the far-spreading prairies cover'd with grass and corn.

Lo, the most excellent sun so calm and haughty,
The violet and purple morn with just-felt breezes,
The gentle soft-born measureless light,
The miracle spreading bathing all, the fulfill'd noon,
The coming eve delicious, the welcome night and the stars,
Over my cities shining all, enveloping man and land.

## 13

Sing on, sing on you gray-brown bird,
Sing from the swamps, the recesses, pour your chant from the bushes,
Limitless out of the dusk, out of the cedars and pines.

Sing on dearest brother, warble your reedy song,
Loud human song, with voice of uttermost woe.

O liquid and free and tender!
O wild and loose to my soul—O wondrous singer!
You only I hear—yet the star holds me, (but will soon depart,)
Yet the lilac with mastering odor holds me.

## 14

Now while I sat in the day and look'd forth,
In the close of the day with its light and the fields of spring, and the farmers preparing their crops,
In the large unconscious scenery of my land with its lakes and forests,
In the heavenly aerial beauty, (after the perturb'd winds and the storms,)
Under the arching heavens of the afternoon swift passing, and the voices of children and women,
The many-moving sea-tides, and I saw the ships how they sail'd,
And the summer approaching with richness, and the fields all busy with labor,
And the infinite separate houses, how they all went on, each with its meals and minutia of daily usages,
And the I streets how their throbbings throbb'd, and the cities pent—lo, then and there,
Falling upon them all and among them all, enveloping me with the rest,
Appear'd the cloud, appear'd the long black trail,
And I knew death, its thought, and the sacred knowledge of death.

Then with the knowledge of death as walking one side of me,
And the thought of death close-walking the other side of me,

And I in the middle as with companions, and as holding the hands of companions,
I fled forth to the hiding receiving night that talks not,
Down to the shores of the water, the path by the swamp in the dimness,
To the solemn shadowy cedars and ghostly pines so still.

And the singer so shy to the rest receiv'd me,
The gray-brown bird I know receiv'd us comrades three,
And he sang the carol of death, and a verse for him I love.

From deep secluded recesses,
From the fragrant cedars and the ghostly pines so still,
Came the carol of the bird.

And the charm of the carol rapt me,
As I held as if by their hands my comrades in the night,
And the voice of my spirit tallied the song of the bird.

*Come lovely and soothing death,*
*Undulate round the world, serenely arriving, arriving,*
*In the day, in the night, to all, to each,*
*Sooner or later delicate death.*

*Prais'd be the fathomless universe,*
*For life and joy, and for objects and knowledge curious,*
*And for love, sweet love—but praise! praise! praise!*
*For the sure-enwinding arms of cool-enfolding death.*

*Dark mother always gliding near with soft feet,*
*Have none chanted for thee a chant of fullest welcome?*
*Then I chant it for thee, I glorify thee above all,*
*I bring thee a song that when thou must indeed come, come unfalteringly.*

*Approach strong deliveress,*
*When it is so, when thou hast taken them I joyously sing the dead,*
*Lost in the loving floating ocean of thee,*
*Laved in the flood of thy bliss O death.*

*From me to thee glad serenades,*
*Dances for thee I propose saluting thee, adornments and feastings for thee,*
*And the sights of the open landscape and the high-spread sky are fitting,*
*And life and the fields, and the huge and thoughtful night.*

*The night in silence under many a star,*
*The ocean shore and the husky whispering wave whose voice I know,*

*And the soul turning to thee O vast and well-veil'd death,*
*And the body gratefully nestling close to thee.*

*Over the tree-tops I float thee a song,*
*Over the rising and sinking waves, over the myriad fields and the prairies wide,*
*Over the dense-pack'd cities all and the teeming wharves and ways,*
*I float this carol with joy, with joy to thee O death.*

## 15

To the tally of my soul,
Loud and strong kept up the gray-brown bird,
With pure deliberate notes spreading filling the night.

Loud in the pines and cedars dim,
Clear in the freshness moist and the swamp-perfume,
And I with my comrades there in the night.

While my sight that was bound in my eyes unclosed,
As to long panoramas of visions.

And I saw askant the armies,
I saw as in noiseless dreams hundreds of battle-flags,
Borne through the smoke of the battles and pierc'd with missiles I saw them,
And carried hither and yon through the smoke, and torn and bloody,
And at last but a few shreds left on the staffs, (and all in silence,)
And the staffs all splinter'd and broken.

I saw battle-corpses, myriads of them,
And the white skeletons of young men, I saw them,
I saw the debris and debris of all the slain soldiers of the war,
But I saw they were not as was thought,
They themselves were fully at rest, they suffer'd not,
The living remain'd and suffer'd, the mother suffer'd,
And the wife and the child and the musing comrade suffer'd,
And the armies that remain'd suffer'd.

## 16

Passing the visions, passing the night,
Passing unloosing the hold of my comrades' hands,
Passing the song of the hermit bird and the tallying song of my soul,
Victorious song, death's outlet song, yet varying ever-altering song,

As low and wailing, yet clear the notes, rising and falling, flooding
the night,
Sadly sinking and fainting, as warning and warning, and yet
again bursting with joy,
Covering the earth and filling the spread of the heaven,
As that powerful psalm in the night I heard from recesses,
Passing, I leave thee lilac with heart-shaped leaves,
I leave thee there in the door-yard, blooming, returning with
spring.

I cease from my song for thee,
From my gaze on thee in the west, fronting the west, communing
with thee,
O comrade lustrous with silver face in the night.

Yet each to keep and all, retrievements out of the night,
The song, the wondrous chant of the gray-brown bird,
And the tallying chant, the echo arous'd in my soul,
With the lustrous and drooping star with the countenance full of
woe,
With the holders holding my hand nearing the call of the bird,
Comrades mine and I in the midst, and their memory ever to
keep, for the dead I loved so well,
For the sweetest, wisest soul of all my days and lands—and this for
his dear sake,
Lilac and star and bird twined with the chant of my soul,
There in the fragrant pines and the cedars dusk and dim.

## Emily Dickinson (1830–1886)

Emily Dickinson wrote close to eighteen hundred poems, some on the margins of newspapers, inside envelopes, or on brown paper bags while living as a recluse in her father's house in Amherst, Massachusetts. Born into a leading Amherst family of culture and means, she received an excellent education by nineteenth-century American standards for women, completing what would now be called a high school education at Amherst Academy and then attending Mount Holyoke Female Seminary (later to become Mount Holyoke College) for a year. Like Thoreau, Dickinson lived deliberately, creating a private world where she could maintain intensity and simplicity. She lived away from home only once and, after 1872, hardly ever left her house and garden. Episodes of blindness exacerbated her reclusiveness. She cultivated a small circle of friends and family, however, with whom she carried on deep and passionate relationships.

During Dickinson's lifetime only fourteen of her poems were published. After she died her sister discovered huge numbers of poems tucked away in drawers and among her papers. A small selection of poems was edited and published in 1890, but the complete poems did not appear until the 1950s. Unlike her contemporary Whitman, Dickinson did not fashion herself as a public or national poet, nor did she proclaim herself a leader. Those were not roles commonly available to nineteenth-century women. She was a rebel, however, in rejecting conventional "womanly" attitudes and enacting in her poetry a radical challenge to masculine power, especially the stern Father God of Puritan Christianity. In one poem she expressed this rebellious impulse in explosive terms:

> The soul has moments of Escape—
> When Bursting all the doors—
> She dances like a Bomb, abroad,
> And swings upon the Hours.

Her innovative rhythms, off-rhymes, and metaphors broke the established conventions of poetry at least as much as Whitman's experiments, even though her characteristic verse form is the familiar meter of Christian hymns. Taken together, Whitman and Dickinson anticipated the major stylistic tendencies of twentieth-century poetry in Europe and the Americas.

Dickinson resisted easy truths, observing that anyone who proclaims truth will be shown by truth to be a liar. Instead she delighted in riddles and paradoxes spoken through many personae, such as a little girl, a boy, a nun, a sane madwoman, or a teasing suitor of God. Her poems often reveal a sharp playfulness and sense of humor. Major themes are the necessity of surviving acute psychic pain, confrontation with death, the ecstasy of experiencing the natural world, the violence at the heart of life, and the necessity of maintaining the independence of one's inner life. All those matters are explored within the realm of simple everyday life. Her poetry demonstrates familiarity with Greek and Roman classics, the Bible, Milton, Shakespeare, and Dante, but it also works to create a distinctive female voice within a literary heritage that had allowed hardly any space for the expression of women's experiences. When Dickinson echoes canonical texts, she usually does so "against the grain."

## *130: "These are the days when Birds come back"*

These are the days when Birds come back—
A very few—a Bird or two—
To take a backward look.

These are the days when skies resume
The old—old sophistries of June—
A blue and gold mistake.

Oh fraud that cannot cheat the Bee—
Almost thy plausibility
Induces my belief.

Till ranks of seeds their witness bear—
And softly thro' the altered air
Hurries a timid leaf.

Oh Sacrament of summer days,
Oh Last Communion in the Haze—
Permit a child to join.

Thy sacred emblems to partake—
Thy consecrated bread to take
And thine immortal wine!

*c. 1859*

## 303: "The Soul selects her own Society"

The Soul selects her own Society—
Then—shuts the Door—
To her divine Majority—
Present no more—

Unmoved—she notes the Chariots—pausing—
At her low Gate—
Unmoved—an Emperor be kneeling
Upon her Mat—

I've known her—from an ample nation—
Choose One—
Then—close the Valves of her attention—
Like Stone—

*c. 1862*

## 435: "Much Madness is divinest Sense"

Much Madness is divinest Sense—
To a discerning Eye—
Much Sense—the starkest Madness—
'Tis the Majority
In this, as All, prevail—
Assent—and you are sane—
Demur—you're straightway dangerous—
And handled with a Chain—

*c. 1862*

## *465: "I heard a Fly buzz—when I died"*

I heard a Fly buzz—when I died—
The Stillness in the Room
Was like the Stillness in the Air
Between the Heaves of Storm—

The Eyes around—had wrung them dry—
And Breaths were gathering firm

For that last Onset—when the King
Be witnessed—in the Room—
I willed my Keepsakes—Signed away
What portion of me be
Assignable—and then it was
There interposed a Fly—

With Blue—uncertain stumbling Buzz—
Between the light—and me—
And then the Windows failed—and then
I could not see to see—

## *501: "This World is not Conclusion"*

This World is not Conclusion.
A Species stands beyond—
Invisible, as Music—
But positive, as Sound—
It beckons, and it baffles—
Philosophy—don't know—
And through a Riddle, at the last—
Sagacity, must go—
To guess it, puzzles scholars—
To gain it, Men have borne
Contempt of Generations
And Crucifixion, shown—
Faith slips—and laughs, and rallies—
Blushes, if any see—
Plucks at a twig of Evidence—
And asks a Vane, the way—
Much Gesture, from the Pulpit—
Strong Hallelujahs roll—
Narcotics cannot still the Tooth
That nibbles at the soul—

*c. 1862*

## 632: "The Brain—is wider than the Sky"

The Brain—is wider than the Sky—
For—put them side by side—
The one the other will contain
With ease—and You—beside—

The Brain is deeper than the sea—
For—hold them—Blue to Blue—
The one the other will absorb—
As Sponges—Buckets—do—

The Brain is just the weight of God—
For—Heft them—Pound for Pound—

And they will differ—if they do—
As Syllable from Sound—

*c. 1862*

## 712: "Because I could not stop for Death"

Because I could not stop for Death—
He kindly stopped for me—
The Carriage held but just Ourselves—
And Immortality.

We slowly drove—He knew no haste
And I had put away
My labor and my leisure too,
For His Civility—

We passed the School, where Children strove
At Recess—in the Ring—
We passed the Fields of Gazing Grain—
We passed the Setting Sun—

Or rather—He passed Us—
The Dews drew quivering and chill—
For only Gossamer, my Gown—
My Tippet—only Tulle—

We paused before a House that seemed
A Swelling of the Ground—
The Roof was scarcely visible—
The Cornice—in the Ground—

Since then—'tis Centuries—and yet
Feels shorter than the Day
I first surmised the Horses' Heads
Were toward Eternity—

*c. 1863*

## 986: "A narrow Fellow in the Grass"

A narrow Fellow in the Grass
Occasionally rides—
You may have met Him—did you not
His notice sudden is—

The Grass divides as with a Comb—
A spotted shaft is seen—
And then it closes at your feet
And opens further on—

He likes a Boggy Acre
A Floor too cool for Corn—
Yet when a Boy, and Barefoot—
I more than once at Noon
Have passed, I thought, a Whip lash
Unbraiding in the Sun
When stooping to secure it
It wrinkled, and was gone—

Several of Nature's People
I know, and they know me—
I feel for them a transport
Of cordiality—

But never met this Fellow
Attended, or alone
Without a tighter breathing
And Zero at the Bone—

*c. 1865*

## 1129: "Tell all the Truth but tell it slant"

Tell all the Truth but tell it slant—
Success in Circuit lies
Too bright for our infirm Delight
The Truth's superb surprise

As Lightning to the Children eased
With explanation kind
The Truth must dazzle gradually
Or every man be blind—

*1868*

## EZRA POUND (1885–1972)

Along with T.S. Eliot, whom he deeply influenced, Ezra Pound was one of the creators of high modernist poetry. Pound had an inspiringly unprovincial, indeed global, view of poetry. In attempting to invigorate poetry in the English language, Pound looked to the literature not only of ancient and medieval Europe but of China and Japan as well. He had a brilliant ear for free verse, which he championed, and a flair for foreign languages, some of which he knew more intimately than others. As a poetic translator, he was the greatest pioneer of the twentieth century. For a specimen of his version of the ancient Chinese *Book of Songs*, which he translated in its entirety, see the box of sample translations included among selections from that work (p. 297).

Here four other of his poems are included. The first two, "The River-Merchant's Wife: A Letter" and "Exile's Letter," are adaptations of poems by the famous Chinese poet Li Bai (pp. 1022–1024). The third is an influential "imagist" poem titled "In a Station of the Metro." Disapproving of what he took to be the vague wordiness of Romantic and Victorian English verse, Pound looked to the poetry of China and Japan and based his "imagist" poems on the spare technical precision of the Japanese haiku. The fourth selection is the first poem from Pound's rambling epic, *The Cantos*. In *The Cantos*, Pound attempted to resuscitate the poetic epic in a paradigmatically high-modern, fragmentary form. Pound used alliterative meter based on the Anglo-Saxon line of poems like *Beowulf* to translate the eleventh book of Homer's *Odyssey*, the descent to the underworld; however, rather than translate Homer directly from the Greek, Pound worked from a Renaissance Latin version of the *Odyssey* by Andreas Divus. Thus the ideal reader will understand that Pound himself, at the beginning of his own epic, *The Cantos*, is descending into the underworld of epic poetry in order to commune with the ghosts of the Greek, Latin, and Anglo-Saxon epic traditions.

Like Eliot and many other American writers of their generation, Pound left the United States and settled in Europe. His reputation as a brilliant innovator, as the champion of a revolutionary generation of writers, and as the founder of the modernist movement in Anglo-American poetry was eclipsed during World War II, when he moved to Italy and made radio broadcasts in support of Mussolini. At the end of the war, he was interned as a prisoner of war, indicted for treason, and finally committed to a mental hospital in the United States. While in prison camp, however, he wrote a brilliant series of *Cantos*, for which the American literary establishment awarded him the Bollingen Prize for Poetry in 1948, much to the astonishment of public and government opinion. At the behest of his fellow poets, he was finally released in 1958, the indictment against him was dismissed, and he returned to Italy. The whole drama is neatly illustrative of high Modernism's insistence that art is beyond politics—that is, that the poetic brilliance of Pound's later work was not believed to have been compromised even by the enormous folly of his personal opinions and political commitments. Many of today's academic literary critics are inclined to think otherwise, but no one can deny Pound's wonderful command of language and the poetic line.

## *The River-Merchant's Wife: A Letter*

While my hair was still cut straight across my forehead
I played about the front gate, pulling flowers.
You came by on bamboo stilts, playing horse,
You walked about my seat, playing with blue plums.
And we went on living in the village of Chokan:
Two small people, without dislike or suspicion.

At fourteen I married My Lord you.
I never laughed, being bashful.
Lowering my head, I looked at the wall.
Called to, a thousand times, I never looked back.

At fifteen I stopped scowling,
I desired my dust to be mingled with yours
For ever and for ever and for ever.
Why should I climb the look out?

At sixteen you departed,
You went into far Ku-to-yen, by the river of swirling eddies,
And you have been gone five months.
The monkeys make sorrowful noise overhead.

You dragged your feet when you went out.
By the gate now, the moss is grown, the different mosses,
Too deep to clear them away!
The leaves fall early this autumn, in wind.
The paired butterflies are already yellow with August
Over the grass in the West garden;
They hurt me. I grow older.
If you are coming down through the narrows of the river Kiang,
Please let me know beforehand,
And I will come out to meet you
As far as Cho-fu-Sa.

## *Exile's Letter*

To So-Kin of Rakuyo, ancient friend, Chancellor of Gen.
Now I remember that you built me a special tavern
By the south side of the bridge at Ten-Shin.
With yellow gold and white jewels, we paid for songs and laughter
And we were drunk for month on month, forgetting the kings
        and princes.
Intelligent men came drifting in from the sea and from the west
        border,
And with them, and with you especially
There was nothing at cross purpose,
And they made nothing of sea-crossing or of mountain-crossing,
If only they could be of that fellowship,
And we all spoke out our hearts and minds, without regret.
And then I was sent off to South Wei,
        smothered in laurel groves,
And you to the north of Raku-hoku
Till we had nothing but thoughts and memories in common.
And then, when separation had come to its worst,
We met, and travelled into Sen-Go,
Through all the thirty-six folds of the turning and twisting waters.
Into a valley of the thousand bright flowers,
That was the first valley;
And into ten thousand valleys full of voices and pine-winds.
And with silver harness and reins of gold,
Out came the East of Kan foreman and his company
And there came also the 'True man' of Shi-yo to meet me,
Playing on a jewelled mouth-organ.
In the storied houses of San-Ko they gave us more Sennin music,
Many instruments, like the sound of young phoenix broods.
The foreman of Kan Chu, drunk, danced
        because his long sleeves wouldn't keep still
With that music playing,
And I, wrapped in brocade, went to sleep with my head on his lap,
And my spirit so high it was all over the heavens,
And before the end of the day we were scattered like stars, or rain.
I had to be off to So, far away over the waters,
You back to your river-bridge.

And your father, who was as brave as a leopard,
Was governor in Hei Shu, and put down the barbarian rabble.
And one May he had you send for me,
        despite the long distance.
And what with broken wheels and so on, I won't say it wasn't
        hard going,

Over roads twisted like sheep's guts.
And I was still going, late in the year,
in the cutting wind from the North,
And thinking how little you cared for the cost,
and you caring enough to pay it.
And what a reception:
Red jade cups, food well set on a blue jewelled table,
And I was drunk, and had no thought of returning.
And you would walk out with me to the western corner of the castle,
To the dynastic temple, with water about it clear as blue jade,
With boats floating, and the sound of mouth-organs and drums,
With ripples like dragon-scales, going grass-green on the water,
Pleasure lasting, with courtesans, going and coming without
hindrance,
With the willow flakes falling like snow,
And the vermilioned girls getting drunk about sunset,
And the water, a hundred feet deep, reflecting green eyebrows
—Eyebrows painted green are a fine sight in young moonlight,
Gracefully painted—
And the girls singing back at each other,
Dancing in transparent brocade,
And the wind lifting the song, and interrupting it,
Tossing it up under the clouds.
And all this comes to an end.
And is not again to be met with.
I went up to the court for examination,
Tried Layu's luck, offered the Choyo song,
And got no promotion,
and went back to the East Mountains
White-headed.
And once again, later, we met at the South bridge-head.
And then the crowd broke up, you went north to San palace,
And if you ask how I regret that parting:
It is like the flowers falling at Spring's end
Confused, whirled in a tangle.
What is the use of talking, and there is no end of talking,
There is no end of things in the heart.
I call in the boy,
Have him sit on his knees here
To seal this,
And send it a thousand miles, thinking.

## *In a Station of the Metro*

The apparition of these faces in the crowd;
Petals on a wet, black bough.

## Canto I

And then went down to the ship,
Set keel to breakers, forth on the godly sea, and
We set up mast and sail on that swart ship,
Bore sheep aboard her, and our bodies also
Heavy with weeping, so winds from sternward
Bore us out onward with bellying canvas,
Circe's this craft, the trim-coifed goddess.
Then sat we amidships, wind jamming the tiller,
Thus with stretched sail, we went over sea till day's end.
Sun to his slumber, shadows o'er all the ocean,
Came we then to the bounds of deepest water,
To the Kimmerian lands, and peopled cities
Covered with close-webbed mist, unpiercèd ever
With glitter of sun-rays
Nor with stars stretched, nor looking back from heaven
Swartest night stretched over wretched men there.
The ocean flowing backward, came we then to the place
Aforesaid by Circe.
Here did they rites, Perimedes and Eurylochus,
And drawing sword from my hip
I dug the ell-square pitkin;
Poured we libations unto each the dead,
First mead and then sweet wine, water mixed with white flour.
Then prayed I many a prayer to the sickly death's-heads;
As set in Ithaca, sterile bulls of the best
For sacrifice, heaping the pyre with goods,
A sheep to Tiresias only, black and a bell-sheep.
Dark blood flowed in the fosse,
Souls out of Erebus, cadaverous dead, of brides,
Of youths and of the old who had borne much;
Souls stained with recent tears, girls tender,
Men many, mauled with bronze lance heads,
Battle spoil, bearing yet, dreory arms,
These many crowded about me; with shouting,
Pallor upon me, cried to my men for more beasts;
Slaughtered the herds, sheep slain of bronze;
Poured ointment, cried to the gods,
To Pluto the strong, and praised Proserpine;
Unsheathed the narrow sword,
I sat to keep off the impetuous impotent dead,
Till I should hear Tiresias.
But first Elpenor came, our friend Elpenor,
Unburied, cast on the wide earth,
Limbs that we left in the house of Circe,

Unwept, unwrapped in sepulchre, since toils urged other.
Pitiful spirit. And I cried in hurried speech:
'Elpenor, how art thou come to this dark coast?
'Cam'st thou afoot, outstripping seamen?'
        And he in heavy speech:
'Ill fate and abundant wine. I slept in Circe's ingle.
'Going down the long ladder unguarded,
'I fell against the buttress,
'Shattered the nape-nerve, the soul sought Avernus.
'But thou, O King, I bid remember me, unwept, unburied,
'Heap up mine arms, be tomb by sea-bord, and inscribed:
'*A man of no fortune, and with a name to come.*
'And set my oar up, that I swung mid fellows.'

And Anticlea came, whom I beat off, and then Tiresias Theban,
Holding his golden wand, knew me, and spoke first:
'A second time? why? man of ill scar,
'Facing the sunless dead and this joyless region?
'Stand from the fosse, leave me my bloody bever
'For soothsay.'
        And I stepped back,
And he strong with the blood, said then: 'Odysseus
'Shalt return through spiteful Neptune, over dark seas,
'Lose all companions.' Then Anticlea came.
Lie quiet Divus. I mean, that is Andreas Divus,
In officina Wecheli, 1538, out of Homer.
And he sailed, by Sirens and thence outward and away
And unto Circe.
        Venerandam,
In the Cretan's phrase, with the golden crown, Aphrodite,
Cypri munimenta sortita est, mirthful, oricalchi, with golden
Girdles and breast bands, thou with dark eyelids
Bearing the golden bough of Argicida. So that:

## T.S. ELIOT (1888–1965)

T.S. Eliot is often hailed as the preeminent poetic voice of twentieth-century Euro-American literature. Although born, raised, and educated in the United States, Eliot lived in Europe almost his entire adult life. After working briefly as a teacher and as a bank clerk, he became director of a publishing house in London, a post he kept until retirement. Encouraged by Ezra Pound's reception of his early "Love Song of J. Alfred Prufrock," Eliot published that now famous poem in 1915. Pound had a great influence on Eliot's verse, serving as a secret editor of and collaborator on "The Waste Land," published in 1922.

In the twenties and thirties, Eliot's poems were often considered shocking for their intellectual difficulty, their fracturing of poetic conventions, and their ironic and sometimes despairing tone. They work through a principle of accumulation: images, tones, modes, scenes, themes, and voices are woven together, gradually accruing meaning and mood through associative links or stark contrasts. The poems are heavily intertextual, borrowing from and making allusions to classical poetry and mythology, religion, and major and minor writers of the European tradition. They also wander into Middle Eastern and Asian traditions for images, poetic lines, and themes.

Along with Pound, Eliot is often credited with inventing "high modernism." He won the Nobel Prize in literature in 1948 for his poetic innovations and for his ability to capture so vividly the fragmentation and despair of Western modernity. Eliot's early poems typically express a loss of identity, purpose, faith, and community, as well as the quest for renewal. His poetry strains to create meaning from the fragments of modern culture. Although "The Waste Land" is a difficult poem, close study of its tapestry will reward the reader with a much better understanding of both the poem and modern culture and life.

The quest in "The Waste Land" is loosely structured around the myth of the Fisher King and the search for the Holy Grail, themes Eliot found in both medieval Romance and modern anthropology. The quest is multivalent—psychological, physical, aesthetic, spiritual, and philosophical—and the need for renewal is evident everywhere: the modern world, especially the modern city, is a dry wasteland in which languid ghosts drift through their empty lives. The poem ends with fragments from the ancient Indian Upanishads that sound like thunder. But is it the thunder of the long-desired renewing rain or of destruction? Eliot's copious scholarly notes to the poem (included here) are so surprisingly unhelpful that it is hard to know how seriously to take them.

The major symbols and techniques of "The Waste Land" express both the meaning and the lack of meaning, both the emotional emptiness and the stirrings of emotion that constitute this rich poem. Major images and motifs include the wasteland, water, the city, stairs, the journey, dreams, time, death, rebirth, repetition, fragmentation, myth, past and future, love, suffering, and relief. When the poem appeared in 1922, it electrified literary life in America and England. A whole generation of readers would remember for a lifetime the moment when they first encountered "The Waste Land" because it spoke so profoundly to the despair that the horrors of World War I had left in its wake. In a new kind of poetry they could see that a new poetic age had been born.

## *from The Waste Land*

### I. The Burial of the Dead

April is the cruellest month, breeding
Lilacs out of the dead land, mixing
Memory and desire, stirring
Dull roots with spring rain.
Winter kept us warm, covering

Earth in forgetful snow, feeding
A little life with dried tubers.
Summer surprised us, coming over the Starnbergersee
With a shower of rain; we stopped in the colonnade,
And went on in sunlight, into the Hofgarten,
And drank coffee, and talked for an hour.
Bin gar keine Russin, stamm' aus Litauen, echt deutsch.
And when we were children, staying at the arch-duke's,
My cousin's, he took me out on a sled,
And I was frightened. He said, Marie,
Marie, hold on tight. And down we went.
In the mountains, there you feel free.
I read, much of the night, and go south in the winter.

What are the roots that clutch, what branches grow
Out of this stony rubbish? Son of man,
You cannot say, or guess, for you know only
A heap of broken images, where the sun beats,
And the dead tree gives no shelter, the cricket no relief,
And the dry stone no sound of water. Only
There is shadow under this red rock,
(Come in under the shadow of this red rock),
And I will show you something different from either
Your shadow at morning striding behind you
Or your shadow at evening rising to meet you;
I will show you fear in a handful of dust.
*Frisch weht der Wind*
*Der Heimat zu*
*Mein Irisch Kind,*
*Wo weilest du?*
'You gave me hyacinths first a year ago;
'They called me the hyacinth girl.'
—Yet when we came back, late, from the hyacinth garden,
Your arms full, and your hair wet, I could not
Speak, and my eyes failed, I was neither
Living nor dead, and I knew nothing,
Looking into the heart of light, the silence.
*Oed' und leer das Meer.*

* * *

Unreal City,
Under the brown fog of a winter dawn,
A crowd flowed over London Bridge, so many,
I had not thought death had undone so many.
Sighs, short and infrequent, were exhaled,
And each man fixed his eyes before his feet.

Flowed up the hill and down King William Street,
To where Saint Mary Woolnoth kept the hours
With a dead sound on the final stroke of nine.
There I saw one I knew, and stopped him, crying: 'Stetson!
'You who were with me in the ships at Mylae!
'That corpse you planted last year in your garden,
'Has it begun to sprout? Will it bloom this year?
'Or has the sudden frost disturbed its bed?
'O keep the Dog far hence, that's friend to men,
'Or with his nails he'll dig it up again!
'You! hypocrite lecteur!—mon semblable,—mon frère!'

## II. A Game of Chess

* * *

'My nerves are bad to-night. Yes, bad. Stay with me.
'Speak to me. Why do you never speak. Speak.
        'What are you thinking of? What thinking? What?
'I never know what you are thinking. Think.'

I think we are in rats' alley
Where the dead men lost their bones.

'What is that noise?'
        The wind under the door.
'What is that noise now? What is the wind doing?'
        Nothing again nothing.
        'Do
'You know nothing? Do you see nothing? Do you remember
'Nothing?'

        I remember
Those are pearls that were his eyes.
'Are you alive, or not? Is there nothing in your head?'
        But
O O O O that Shakespeherian Rag—
It's so elegant
So intelligent
'What shall I do now? What shall I do?'
'I shall rush out as I am, and walk the street
'With my hair down, so. What shall we do tomorrow?
'What shall we ever do?'
        The hot water at ten.
And if it rains, a closed car at four.
And we shall play a game of chess,
Pressing lidless eyes and waiting for a knock upon the door.

When Lil's husband got demobbed, I said—
I didn't mince my words, I said to her myself,
HURRY UP PLEASE ITS TIME
Now Albert's coming back, make yourself a bit smart.
He'll want to know what you done with that money be gave you
To get yourself some teeth. He did, I was there.
You have them all out, Lil, and get a nice set,
He said, I swear, I can't bear to look at you.
And no more can't I, I said, and think of poor Albert,
He's been in the army four years, he wants a good time,
And if you don't give it him, there's others will, I said.
Oh is there, she said. Something o' that, I said.
Then I'll know who to thank, she said, and give me a straight look.
HURRY UP PLEASE ITS TIME
If you don't like it you can get on with it, I said.
Others can pick and choose if you can't.
But if Albert makes off, it won't be for lack of telling.
You ought to be ashamed, I said, to look so antique.
(And her only thirty-one.)
I can't help it, she said, pulling a long face,
It's them pills I took, to bring it off, she said.
(She's had five already, and nearly died of young George.)
The chemist said it would be all right, but I've never been the same.
You *are* a proper fool, I said.
Well, if Albert won't leave you alone, there it is, I said,
What you get married for if you don't want children?
HURRY UP PLEASE ITS TIME
Well, that Sunday Albert was home, they had a hot gammon,
And they asked me in to dinner, to get the beauty of it hot—
HURRY UP PLEASE ITS TIME
HURRY UP PLEASE ITS TIME
Goonight Bill. Goonight Lou. Goonight May. Goonight.
Ta ta. Goonight. Goonight.
Good night, ladies, good night, sweet ladies, good night, good night.

## V. What the Thunder Said

After the torchlight red on sweaty faces
After the frosty silence in the gardens
After the agony in stony places
The shouting and the crying
Prison and palace and reverberation
Of thunder of spring over distant mountains
He who was living is now dead
We who were living are now dying
With a little patience

Here is no water but only rock
Rock and no water and the sandy road
The road winding above among the mountains
Which are mountains of rock without water
If there were water we should stop and drink
Amongst the rock one cannot stop or think
Sweat is dry and feet are in the sand
If there were only water amongst the rock
Dead mountain mouth of carious teeth that cannot spit
Here one can neither stand nor lie nor sit
There is not even silence in the mountains
But dry sterile thunder without rain
There is not even solitude in the mountains
But red sullen faces sneer and snarl
From doors of mudcracked houses
                    If there were water
        And no rock
        If there were rock
        And also water
        And water
        A spring
        A pool among the rock
        If there were the sound of water only
        Not the cicada
        And dry grass singing
        But sound of water over a rock
        Where the hermit-thrush sings in the pine trees
        Drip drop drip drop drop drop drop
        But there is no water

* * *

In this decayed hole among the mountains
In the faint moonlight, the grass is singing
Over the tumbled graves, about the chapel
There is the empty chapel, only the wind's home.
It has no windows, and the door swings,
Dry bones can harm no one.
Only a cock stood on the rooftree
Co co rico co co rico
In a flash of lightning. Then a damp gust
Bringing rain

Ganga was sunken, and the limp leaves
Waited for rain, while the black clouds
Gathered far distant, over Himavant.
The jungle crouched, humped in silence.

Then spoke the thunder
DA
*Datta:* what have we given?
My friend, blood shaking my heart
The awful daring of a moment's surrender
Which an age of prudence can never retract
By this, and this only, we have existed
Which is not to be found in our obituaries
Or in memories draped by the beneficent spider
Or under seals broken by the lean solicitor
In our empty rooms
DA
*Dayadhvam:* I have heard the key
Turn in the door once and turn once only
We think of the key, each in his prison
Thinking of the key, each confirms a prison
Only at nightfall, aethereal rumours
Revive for a moment a broken Coriolanus
DA
*Damyata:* The boat responded
Gaily, to the hand expert with sail and oar
The sea was calm, your heart would have responded
Gaily, when invited, beating obedient
To controlling hands

I sat upon the shore
Fishing, with the arid plain behind me
Shall I at least set my lands in order?
London Bridge is falling down falling down falling down
*Poi s'ascose nel foco che gli affina*
*Quando fiam uti chelidon*—O swallow swallow
*Le Prince d'Aquitaine à la tour abolie*
These fragments I have shored against my ruins
Why then Ile fit you. Hieronymo's mad againe.
Datta. Dayadhvam. Damyata.
Shantih shantih shantih

## Eliot's Notes on The Waste Land

Not only the title, but the plan and a good deal of the incidental symbolism of the poem were suggested by Miss Jessie L. Weston's book on the Grail legend: *From Ritual to Romance* (Cambridge). Indeed, so deeply am indebted, Miss Weston's book will elucidate the difficulties of the poem much better than my notes can do; and I recommend it (apart from the great interest of the book itself) to any who think such elucidation of the poem worth the trouble. To another work of anthropology I am indebted in general, one which has influenced our generation profoundly; I mean *The Golden Bough;* I have used especially the two volumes *Adonis, Attis, Osiris.* Anyone who is acquainted with these works will immediately recognise in the poem certain references to vegetation ceremonies.

### I. The Burial of the Dead

Line 20. Cf. Ezekiel II, i.

23. Cf. Ecclesiastes XII, v.

31.V. *Tristan und Isolde,* I, verses 5–8.

42. Id. III, verse 24.

43. Cf. Baudelaire:

'Fourmillante cité, cité pleine de rêves,

'Où le spectre en plein jour raccroche le passant.'

46. Cf. *Inferno,* III, 55–57:

'si lunga tratta

di gente, ch'io non avrei mai creduto

'che morte tanta n'avesse disfatta.'

47. Cf. *Inferno,* IV, 25–27: 'Quivi, secondo che per ascoltare, 'non avea pianto, ma'che di sospiri, 'che l'aura eterna facevan tremare.'

51. A phenomenon which I have often noticed.

57. Cf. the Dirge in Webster's *White Devil.*

59. V. Baudelaire, Preface to *Fleurs du Mal.*

### II. A Game of Chess

67. Cf. Webster: 'Is the wind in that door still?'

75. Cf. Part I, l. 37,48.

87. Cf. the game of chess in Middleton's *Women beware Women.*

121. See *Hamlet* iv, v, 72.

### V. What the Thunder Said

In the first part of Part V three themes are employed: the journey to Emmaus, the approach to the Chapel Perilous (see Miss Weston's book) and the present decay of eastern Europe.

157. This is *Turdus aonalaschkae pallasii,* the hermit-thrush which I have heard in Quebec Province. Chapman says (*Handbook of Birds of Eastern North America*) 'it is most at home in secluded woodland and thickety retreats. . . . Its notes are not remarkable for variety or volume, but in purity and sweetness of tone and exquisite modulation they are unequalled.' Its 'water-dripping song' is justly celebrated.

172. Himavant is a mountain.

176. 'Datta, dayadhvam, damyata' (Give, sympathise, control). The fable of the meaning of the Thunder is found in the *Brihadaranyaka—Upanishad,* 5, I. A translation is found in Deussen's *Sechzig Upanishads des Veda,* p. 489.

182. Cf. Webster, *The White Devil,* V, vi:

'. . . they'll remarry
Ere the worm pierce your
winding-sheet, ere the spider
Make a thin curtain for your
epitaphs.'

186. Cf. *Inferno,* XXXIII, 46:

'ed io sentii chiavar l'uscio di sotto
all'orrible torre.'

Also F. H. Bradley, *Appearance and Reality,* p. 346.

'My external sensations are no less private to myself than are my thoughts or my feelings. In either case my experience falls within my own circle, a circle closed on the outside; and, with all its elements alike, every sphere is opaque to the others which surround it. . . . In brief, regarded as an existence which appears in a soul, the whole world for each is peculiar and private to that soul.'

198. V. Weston: *From Ritual to Romance;* chapter on the Fisher King.

201. V. *Purgatorio,* XXVI, 148.

'"Ara vos prec per aquella valor
"que vos condus al som de
l'escalina,
"sovegna vos a temps de ma dolor."
Poi s'ascose nel foco che gli affina.'

202. V. *Pervigilium Veneris.* Cf. Philomela in Parts II and III.

203. V. Gerard de Nerval, Sonnet *El Desdichado.*

205. V. Kyd's *Spanish Tragedy.*

207. Shantih. Repeated as here, a formal ending to an Upanishad. 'The Peace which passeth understanding' is our equivalent to this word.

## William Faulkner (1897–1962)

William Faulkner is arguably the greatest American novelist of the twentieth century and almost certainly the one who has had the most profound impact abroad. His writing is a curious mixture of disparate elements, a cross between James Joyce and Mark Twain, combining the most experimental techniques of Modernism with the artless art of the frontier storyteller, the most elaborate, luxuriant style with the plain down-to-earth talk of country folk. Often a difficult writer to read, he is notorious for his complicated rhetoric, his sentences that go on and on, sometimes without apparent regard for syntax or sense. Yet he is a writer of extraordinary power who captures all kinds of passionate intensity and warring elements in his complex style.

Born in small-town Mississippi, Faulkner grew up in a rich oral tradition and a world full of memories. Many of the stories centered on his great-grandfather and namesake, the "Old Colonel," a Civil War hero, best-selling novelist, and builder of the local railroad, who was killed by his former partner in the public square. Growing up in the shadow of such a flamboyant character, Faulkner was left with a sense that his family and the South had fallen into a decline. But his heritage also endowed him with a wealth of material that became the stuff of some of his greatest works. Faulkner's fiction is marked by a strong sense of history, and most of his novels are family chronicles.

Faulkner lived almost his entire life in Oxford, Mississippi, the county seat that he re-created as the center of his little world, that "postage stamp of native soil," which he mapped and populated and named Yoknapatawpha County, designating himself "sole owner and proprietor." That was the setting he explored in most of his fiction, tracing its history from the first white settlers to the time he was writing and its genealogies down through the generations, including poor farmers as well as members of the leading families, blacks as well as whites, and even a few native Chickasaws. Blacks outnumbered whites, and the two races sometimes intermingled, as Faulkner confronted the consequences of slavery in miscegenation and incest. Faulkner's fiction is haunted by the past, but he also grappled with contemporary questions of racial and social justice.

Once he found his proper voice and subject, Faulkner produced a number of remarkably powerful novels, beginning with *The Sound and the Fury* in 1929, including *As I Lay Dying, Light in August, Absalom, Absalom!,* and concluding with *Go Down, Moses* in 1942. After 1942 the quality of his work never achieved the same level, though he continued to write and published his last novel a short while before his death in 1962. Never a best-selling author, Faulkner found it necessary to write for the movies in order to make ends meet, and most of his books went out of print until brought to the attention of the American public by foreign writers and by the Nobel Prize in literature that he won in 1950.

The title of the story in this anthology, "That Evening Sun," comes from a blues song whose refrain, "I hate to see that evening sun go down," takes on a sinister irony in Faulkner's hands. As part of his chronicle of the decaying aristocratic Compson family of *The Sound and the Fury,* the events of the story focus on a black washerwoman's fears that her estranged husband will emerge from hiding and murder her after dark. Although it is not possible to know whether or not that is likely from within the story, elsewhere in Faulkner's fiction we learn that Nancy had reason to expect her end. By telling the story from her employer's children's point of view, Faulkner creates a tone of naive bafflement surrounding Nancy's behavior. He uses the children's incomprehension as a screen behind which he can indirectly approach the forbidden topic of white men's use of black women and black men's enraged reactions to their inability to stop it.

## *That Evening Sun*

### I

Monday is no different from any other weekday in Jefferson now. The streets are paved now, and the telephone and electric companies are cutting down more and more of the shade trees—the water oaks, the maples and locusts and elms—to make room for iron poles bearing clusters of bloated and ghostly and bloodless grapes, and we have a city laundry which makes the rounds on Monday morning, gathering the bundles of clothes into bright-colored, specially-made motor cars: the soiled wearing of a whole week now flees apparitionlike behind alert and irritable electric horns, with a long diminishing noise of rubber and asphalt like tearing silk, and even the Negro women who still take in white people's washing after the old custom, fetch and deliver it in automobiles.

But fifteen years ago, on Monday morning the quiet, dusty, shady streets would be full of Negro women with, balanced on their steady, turbaned heads, bundles of clothes tied up in sheets, almost as large as cotton bales, carried so without touch of hand between the kitchen door of the white house and the blackened washpot beside a cabin door in Negro Hollow.

Nancy would set her bundle on the top of her head, then upon the bundle in turn she would set the black straw sailor hat which she wore winter and summer. She was tall, with a high, sad face sunken a little where her teeth were missing. Sometimes we would go a part of the way down the lane and across the pasture with her, to watch the balanced bundle and the hat that never bobbed nor wavered, even when she walked down into the ditch and up the other side and stooped through the fence. She would go down on her hands and knees and crawl through the gap, her head rigid, uptilted, the bundle steady as a rock or a balloon, and rise to her feet again and go on.

Sometimes the husbands of the washing women would fetch and deliver the clothes, but Jesus never did that for Nancy, even before father told him to stay away from our house, even when Dilsey was sick and Nancy would come to cook for us.

And then about half the time we'd have to go down the lane to Nancy's cabin and tell her to come on and cook breakfast. We would stop at the ditch, because father told us to not have anything to do with Jesus—he was a short black man, with a razor scar down his face—and we would throw rocks at Nancy's house until she came to the door, leaning her head around it without any clothes on.

"What yawl mean, chunking my house?" Nancy said. "What you little devils mean?"

"Father says for you to come on and get breakfast," Caddy said. "Father says it's over a half an hour now, and you've got to come this minute."

"I aint studying no breakfast," Nancy said. "I going to get my sleep out."

"I bet you're drunk," Jason said. "Father says you're drunk. Are you drunk, Nancy?"

"Who says I is?" Nancy said. "I got to get my sleep out. I aint studying no breakfast."

So after a while we quit chunking the cabin and went back home. When she finally came, it was too late for me to go to school. So we thought it was whisky until that day they arrested her again and they were taking her to jail and they passed Mr Stovall. He was the cashier in the bank and a deacon in the Baptist church, and Nancy began to say:

"When you going to pay me, white man? When you going to pay me, white man? It's been three times now since you paid me a cent—" Mr Stovall knocked her down, but she kept on saying, "When you going to pay me, white man? It's been three times now since—" until Mr Stovall kicked her in the mouth with his heel and the marshal caught Mr Stovall back, and Nancy lying in the street, laughing. She turned her head and spat out some blood and teeth and said, "It's been three times now since he paid me a cent."

That was how she lost her teeth, and all that day they told about Nancy and Mr Stovall, and all that night the ones that passed the jail could hear Nancy singing and yelling. They could see her hands holding to the window bars, and a lot of them stopped along the fence, listening to her and to the jailer trying to make her stop. She didn't shut up until almost daylight, when the jailer began to hear a bumping and scraping upstairs and he went up there and found Nancy hanging from the window bar. He said that it was cocaine and not whisky, because no nigger would try to commit suicide unless he was full of cocaine, because a nigger full of cocaine wasn't a nigger any longer.

The jailer cut her down and revived her; then he beat her, whipped her. She had hung herself with her dress. She had fixed it all right, but when they arrested her she didn't have on anything except a dress and so she didn't have anything to tie her hands with and she couldn't make her hands let go of the window ledge. So the jailer heard the noise and ran up there and found Nancy hanging from the window, stark naked, her belly already swelling out a little, like a little balloon.

When Dilsey was sick in her cabin and Nancy was cooking for us, we could see her apron swelling out; that was before father told Jesus to stay away from the house. Jesus was in the kitchen, sitting behind the stove, with his razor scar on his black face like a piece of dirty string. He said it was a watermelon that Nancy had under her dress.

"It never come off of your vine, though," Nancy said.

"Off of what vine?" Caddy said.

"I can cut down the vine it did come off of," Jesus said.

"What makes you want to talk like that before these chillen?" Nancy said. "Whyn't you go on to work? You done et. You want Mr Jason to catch you hanging around his kitchen, talking that way before these chillen?"

"Talking what way?" Caddy said. "What vine?"

"I cant hang around white man's kitchen," Jesus said. "But white man can hang around mine. White man can come in my house, but I cant stop him. When white man want to come in my house, I aint got no house. I cant stop him, but he cant kick me outen it. He cant do that."

Dilsey was still sick in her cabin. Father told Jesus to stay off our place. Dilsey was still sick. It was a long time. We were in the library after supper.

"Isn't Nancy through in the kitchen yet?" mother said. "It seems to me that she has had plenty of time to have finished the dishes."

"Let Quentin go and see," father said. "Go and see if Nancy is through, Quentin. Tell her she can go on home."

I went to the kitchen. Nancy was through. The dishes were put away and the fire was out. Nancy was sitting in a chair, close to the cold stove. She looked at me.

"Mother wants to know if you are through," I said.

"Yes," Nancy said. She looked at me. "I done finished." She looked at me.

"What is it?"' I said. "What is it?"

"I aint nothing but a nigger," Nancy said. "It aint none of my fault."

She looked at me, sitting in the chair before the cold stove, the sailor hat on her head. I went back to the library. It was the cold stove and all, when you think of a kitchen being warm and busy and cheerful. And with a cold stove and the dishes all put away, and nobody wanting to eat at that hour.

"Is she through?" mother said.

"Yessum," I said.

"What is she doing?" mother said.

"She's not doing anything. She's through."

"I'll go and see," father said.

"Maybe she's waiting for Jesus to come and take her home," Caddy said.

"Jesus is gone," I said. Nancy told us how one morning she woke up and Jesus was gone.

"He quit me," Nancy said. "Done gone to Memphis, I reckon. Dodging them city *po*-lice for a while, I reckon."

"And a good riddance," father said. "I hope he stays there."

"Nancy's scaired of the dark," Jason said.

"So are you," Caddy said.

"I'm not," Jason said.

"Scairy cat," Caddy said.

"I'm not," Jason said.

"You, Candace!" mother said. Father came back.

"I am going to walk down the lane with Nancy," he said. "She says that Jesus is back."

"Has she seen him?" mother said.

"No. Some Negro sent her word that he was back in town. I wont be long."

"You'll leave me alone, to take Nancy home?" mother said. "Is her safety more precious to you than mine?"

"I wont be long," father said.

"You'll leave these children unprotected, with that Negro about?"

"I'm going too," Caddy said. "Let me go, Father."

"What would he do with them, if he were unfortunate enough to have them?" father said.

"I want to go, too," Jason said.

"Jason!" mother said. She was speaking to father. You could tell that by the way she said the name. Like she believed that all day father had been trying to think of doing the thing she wouldn't like the most, and that she knew all the time that after a while he would think of it. I stayed quiet, because father and I both knew that mother would want him to make me stay with her if she just thought of it in time. So father didn't look at me. I was the oldest. I was nine and Caddy was seven and Jason was five.

"Nonsense," father said. "We wont be long."

Nancy had her hat on. We came to the lane. "Jesus always been good to me," Nancy said. "Whenever he had two dollars, one of them was mine." We walked in the lane. "If I can just get through the lane," Nancy said, "I be all right then."

The lane was always dark. "This is where Jason got scared on Hallowe'en," Caddy said.

"I didn't," Jason said.

"Cant Aunt Rachel do anything with him?" father said. Aunt Rachel was old. She lived in a cabin beyond Nancy's, by herself. She had white hair and she smoked a pipe in the door, all day long; she didn't work any more. They said she was Jesus' mother. Sometimes she said she was and sometimes she said she wasn't any kin to Jesus.

"Yes, you did," Caddy said. "You were scairder than Frony. You were scairder than T.P. even. Scairder than niggers."

"Cant nobody do nothing with him," Nancy said. "He say I done woke up the devil in him and aint but one thing going to lay it down again."

"Well, he's gone now," father said. "There's nothing for you to be afraid of now. And if you'd just let white men alone."

"Let what white men alone?" Caddy said. "How let them alone?"

"He aint gone nowhere," Nancy said. "I can feel him. I can feel him now, in this lane. He hearing us talk, every word, hid somewhere, waiting. I aint seen him, and I aint going to see him again but once more, with that razor in his mouth. That razor on that string down his back, inside his shirt. And then I aint going to be even surprised."

"I wasn't scaired," Jason said.

"If you'd behave yourself, you'd have kept out of this," father said. "But it's all right now. He's probably in St. Louis now. Probably got another wife by now and forgot all about you."

"If he has, I better not find out about it," Nancy said. "I'd stand there right over them, and every time he wropped her, I'd cut that arm off. I'd cut his head off and I'd slit her belly and I'd shove—"

"Hush," father said.

"Slit whose belly, Nancy?" Caddy said.

"I wasn't scaired," Jason said. "I'd walk right down this lane by myself."

"Yah," Caddy said. "You wouldn't dare to put your foot down in it if we were not here too."

## II

Dilsey was still sick, so we took Nancy home every night until mother said, "How much longer is this going on? I to be left alone in this big house while you take home a frightened Negro?"

We fixed a pallet in the kitchen for Nancy. One night we waked up, hearing the sound. It was not singing, and it was not crying, coming up the dark stairs. There was a light in mother's room and we heard father going down the hall, down the back stairs, and Caddy and I went into the hall. The floor was cold. Our toes curled away from it while we listened to the sound. It was like singing and it wasn't like singing, like the sounds that Negroes make.

Then it stopped and we heard father going down the back stairs, and we went to the head of the stairs. Then the sound began again, in the stairway, not loud, and we could see Nancy's eyes halfway up the stairs, against the wall. They looked like cat's eyes do, like a big cat against the wall, watching us. When we came down the steps to where she was, she quit making the sound again, and we stood there until father came back up from the kitchen, with his pistol in his hand. He went back down with Nancy and they came back with Nancy's pallet.

We spread the pallet in our room. After the light in mother's room went off, we could see Nancy's eyes again. "Nancy," Caddy whispered, "are you asleep, Nancy?"

Nancy whispered something. It was oh or no, I dont know which. Like nobody had made it, like it came from nowhere and went nowhere, until it was like Nancy was not there at all; that I had looked so hard at her eyes on the stairs that they had got printed on my eyeballs, like the sun does when you have closed your eyes and there is no sun. "Jesus," Nancy whispered. "Jesus."

"Was it Jesus?" Caddy said. "Did he try to come into the kitchen?"

"Jesus," Nancy said. Like this: Jeeeeeeeeeeeeeeeesus, until the sound went out, like a match or a candle does.

"It's the other Jesus she means," I said.

"Can you see us, Nancy?" Caddy whispered. "Can you see our eyes too?"

"I aint nothing but a nigger," Nancy said. "God knows. God knows."

"What did you see down there in the kitchen?" Caddy whispered. "What tried to get in?"

"God knows," Nancy said. We could see her eyes. "God knows."

Dilsey got well. She cooked dinner. "You'd better stay in bed a day or two longer," father said.

"What for?" Dilsey said. "If I had been a day later, this place would be to rack and ruin. Get on out of here now, and let me get my kitchen straight again."

Dilsey cooked supper too. And that night, just before dark, Nancy came into the kitchen.

"How do you know he's back?" Dilsey said. "You aint seen him."

"Jesus is a nigger," Jason said.

"I can feel him," Nancy said. "I can feel him laying yonder in the ditch."

"Tonight?" Dilsey said. "Is he there tonight?"

"Dilsey's a nigger too," Jason said.

"You try to eat something," Dilsey said.

"I dont want nothing," Nancy said.

"I aint a nigger," Jason said.

"Drink some coffee," Dilsey said. She poured a cup of coffee for Nancy. "Do you know he's out there tonight? How come you know it's tonight?"

"I know," Nancy said. "He's there, waiting. I know. I done lived with him too long. I know what he is fixing to do fore he know it himself."

"Drink some coffee," Dilsey said. Nancy held the cup to her mouth and blew into the cup. Her mouth pursed out like a spreading adder's, like a rubber mouth, like she had blown all the color out of her lips with blowing the coffee.

"I aint a nigger," Jason said. "Are you a nigger, Nancy?"

"I hellborn, child," Nancy said. "I wont be nothing soon. I going back where I come from soon."

## III

She began to drink the coffee. While she was drinking, holding the cup in both hands, she began to make the sound again. She made the sound into the cup and the coffee sploshed out onto her hands and her dress. Her eyes looked at us and she sat there, her elbows on her knees, holding the cup in both hands, looking at us across the wet cup, making the sound. "Look at Nancy," Jason said. "Nancy cant cook for us now. Dilsey's got well now."

"You hush up," Dilsey said. Nancy held the cup in both hands, looking at us, making the sound, like there were two of them: one looking at us and the other making the sound.

"Whyn't you let Mr Jason telefoam the marshal?" Dilsey said. Nancy stopped then, holding the cup in her long brown hands. She tried to drink some coffee again, but it sploshed out of the cup, onto her hands and her dress, and she put the cup down. Jason watched her.

"I cant swallow it," Nancy said. "I swallows but it wont go down me."

"You go down to the cabin," Dilsey said. "Frony will fix you a pallet and I'll be there soon."

"Wont no nigger stop him," Nancy said.

"I aint a nigger," Jason said. "Am I, Dilsey?"

"I reckon not," Dilsey said. She looked at Nancy, "I dont reckon so. What you going to do, then?"

Nancy looked at us. Her eyes went fast, like she was afraid there wasn't time to look, without hardly moving at all. She looked at us, at all three of us at one time. "You member that night I stayed in yawls' room?" she said. She told about how we waked up early the next morning, and played. We had to play quiet, on her pallet, until father woke up and it was time to get breakfast. "Go and ask your maw to let me stay here tonight," Nancy said. "I wont need no pallet. We can play some more."

Caddy asked mother. Jason went too. "I cant have Negroes sleeping in the bedrooms," mother said. Jason cried. He cried until mother said he couldn't have any dessert for three days if he didn't stop. Then Jason said he would stop if Dilsey would make a chocolate cake. Father was there.

"Why dont you do something about it?" mother said. "What do we have officers for?"

"Why is Nancy afraid of Jesus?" Caddy said. "Are you afraid of father, mother?"

"What could the officers do?" father said. "If Nancy hasn't seen him, how could the officers find him?"

"Then why is she afraid?" mother said.

"She says he is there. She says she knows he is there tonight."

"Yet we pay taxes," mother said. "I must wait here alone in this big house while you take a Negro woman home."

"You know that I am not lying outside with a razor," father said.

"I'll stop if Dilsey will make a chocolate cake," Jason said. Mother told us to go out and father said he didn't know if Jason would get a chocolate cake or not, but he knew what Jason was going to get in about a minute. We went back to the kitchen and told Nancy.

"Father said for you to go home and lock the door, and you'll be all right," Caddy said. "All right from what, Nancy? Is Jesus mad at you?" Nancy was holding the coffee cup in her hands again, her elbows on her knees and her hands holding the cup between her knees. She was looking into the cup. "What have you done that made Jesus mad?" Caddy said. Nancy let the cup go. It didn't break on the floor, but the coffee spilled out, and Nancy sat there with her hands still making the shape of the cup. She began to make the sound again, not loud. Not singing and not unsinging. We watched her.

"Here," Dilsey said. "You quit that, now. You get aholt of yourself. You wait here. I going to get Versh to walk home with you." Dilsey went out.

We looked at Nancy. Her shoulders kept shaking, but she quit making the sound. We watched her. "What's Jesus going to do to you?" Caddy said. "He went away."

Nancy looked at us. "We had fun that night I stayed in yawls' room, didn't we?"

"I didn't," Jason said. "I didn't have any fun."

"You were asleep in mother's room," Caddy said. "You were not there."

"Let's go down to my house and have some more fun," Nancy said.

"Mother wont let us," I said. "It's too late now."

"Dont bother her," Nancy said. "We can tell her in the morning. She wont mind."

"She wouldn't let us," I said.

"Dont ask her now," Nancy said. "Dont bother her now."

"She didn't say we couldn't go," Caddy said.

"We didn't ask," I said.

"If you go, I'll tell," Jason said.

"We'll have fun," Nancy said. "They won't mind, just to my house. I been working for yawl a long time. They won't mind."

"I'm not afraid to go," Caddy said. "Jason is the one that's afraid. He'll tell."

"I'm not," Jason said.

"Yes, you are," Caddy said. "You'll tell."

"I won't tell," Jason said. "I'm not afraid."

"Jason ain't afraid to go with me," Nancy said. "Is you, Jason?"

"Jason is going to tell," Caddy said. The lane was dark. We passed the pasture gate. "I bet if something was to jump out from behind that gate, Jason would holler."

"I wouldn't," Jason said. We walked down the lane. Nancy was talking loud.

"What are you talking so loud for, Nancy?" Caddy said.

"Who; me?" Nancy said. "Listen at Quentin and Caddy and Jason saying I'm talking loud."

"You talk like there was five of us here," Caddy said. "You talk like father was here too."

"Who; me talking loud, Mr Jason?" Nancy said.

"Nancy called Jason 'Mister,'" Caddy said.

"Listen how Caddy and Quentin and Jason talk," Nancy said.

"We're not talking loud," Caddy said. "You're the one that's talking like father—"

"Hush," Nancy said; "hush, Mr Jason."

"Nancy called Jason 'Mister' aguh—"

"Hush," Nancy said. She was talking loud when we crossed the ditch and stooped through the fence where she used to stoop through with the clothes on her head. Then we came to her house. We were going fast then. She opened the door. The smell of the house was like the lamp and the smell of Nancy was like the wick, like they were waiting for one another to begin to smell. She lit the lamp and closed the door and put the bar up. Then she quit talking loud, looking at us.

"What're we going to do?" Caddy said.

"What do yawl want to do?" Nancy said.

"You said we would have some fun," Caddy said.

There was something about Nancy's house; something you could smell besides Nancy and the house. Jason smelled it, even. "I don't want to stay here," he said. "I want to go home."

"Go home, then," Caddy said.

"I don't want to go by myself," Jason said.

"We're going to have some fun," Nancy said.

"How?" Caddy said.

Nancy stood by the door. She was looking at us, only it was like she had emptied her eyes, like she had quit using them. "What do you want to do?" she said.

"Tell us a story," Caddy said. "Can you tell a story?"

"Yes," Nancy said.

"Tell it," Caddy said. We looked at Nancy. "You don't know any stories."

"Yes," Nancy said. "Yes, I do."

She came and sat in a chair before the hearth. There was a little fire there. Nancy built it up, when it was already hot inside. She built a good blaze. She told a story. She talked like her eyes looked, like her eyes watching us and her voice talking to us did not belong to her. Like she was living somewhere else, waiting somewhere else. She was outside the cabin. Her voice was inside and the shape of her, the Nancy that could stoop under a barbed wire fence with a bundle of clothes balanced on her head as though without weight, like a balloon, was there. But that was all. "And so this here queen come walking up to the ditch, where that bad man was hiding. She was walking up to the ditch, and she say 'If I can just get past this here ditch,' was what she say . . ."

"What ditch?" Caddy said. "A ditch like that one out there? Why did a queen want to go into a ditch?"

"To get to her house," Nancy said. She looked at us. "She had to cross the ditch to get into her house quick and bar the door."

"Why did she want to go home and bar the door?" Caddy said.

## IV

Nancy looked at us. She quit talking. She looked at us. Jason's legs stuck straight out of his pants where he sat on Nancy's lap. "I don't think that's a good story," he said. "I want to go home."

"Maybe we had better," Caddy said. She got up from the floor. "I bet they are looking for us right now." She went toward the door.

"No," Nancy said. "Don't open it." She got up quick and passed Caddy. She didn't touch the door, the wooden bar.

"Why not?" Caddy said.

"Come back to the lamp," Nancy said. "We'll have fun. You don't have to go."

"We ought to go," Caddy said. "Unless we have a lot of fun." She and Nancy came back to the fire, the lamp.

"I want to go home," Jason said. "I'm going to tell."

"I know another story," Nancy said. She stood close to the lamp. She looked at Caddy, like when your eyes look up at a stick balanced on your nose. She had to look down to see Caddy, but her eyes looked like that, like when you are balancing a stick.

"I won't listen to it," Jason said. "I'll bang on the floor."

"It's a good one," Nancy said. "It's better than the other one."

"What's it about?" Caddy said. Nancy was standing by the lamp. Her hand was on the lamp, against the light, long and brown.

"Your hand is on that hot globe," Caddy said. "Don't it feel hot to your hand?"

Nancy looked at her hand on the lamp chimney. She took her hand away, slow. She stood there, looking at Caddy, wringing her long hand as though it were tied to her wrist with a string.

"Let's do something else," Caddy said.

"I want to go home," Jason said.

"I got some popcorn," Nancy said. She looked at Caddy and then at Jason and then at me and then at Caddy again. "I got some popcorn."

"I don't like popcorn," Jason said. "I'd rather have candy."

Nancy looked at Jason. "You can hold the popper." She was still wringing her hand; it was long and limp and brown.

"All right," Jason said. "I'll stay a while if I can do that. Caddy can't hold it. I'll want to go home again if Caddy holds the popper."

Nancy built up the fire. "Look at Nancy putting her hands in the fire," Caddy said. "What's the matter with you, Nancy?"

"I got popcorn," Nancy said. "I got some." She took the popper from under the bed. It was broken. Jason began to cry.

"Now we can't have any popcorn," he said.

"We ought to go home, anyway," Caddy said. "Come on, Quentin."

"Wait," Nancy said; "wait. I can fix it. Don't you want to help me fix it?"

"I don't think I want any," Caddy said. "It's too late now."

"You help me, Jason," Nancy said. "Don't you want to help me?"

"No," Jason said. "I want to go home."

"Hush," Nancy said; "hush. Watch. Watch me. I can fix it so Jason can hold it and pop the corn." She got a piece of wire and fixed the popper.

"It won't hold good," Caddy said.

"Yes, it will," Nancy said. "Yawl watch. Yawl help me shell some corn."

The popcorn was under the bed too. We shelled it into the popper and Nancy helped Jason hold the popper over the fire.

"It's not popping," Jason said. "I want to go home."

"You wait," Nancy said. "It'll begin to pop. We'll have fun then." She was sitting close to the fire. The lamp was turned up so high it was beginning to smoke.

"Why don't you turn it down some?" I said.

"It's all right," Nancy said. "I'll clean it. Yawl wait. The popcorn will start in a minute."

"I don't believe it's going to start," Caddy said. "We ought to start home, anyway. They'll be worried."

"No," Nancy said. "It's going to pop. Dilsey will tell um yawl with me. I been working for yawl long time. They won't mind if yawl at my house. You wait, now. It'll start popping any minute now."

Then Jason got some smoke in his eyes and he began to cry. He dropped the popper into the fire. Nancy got a wet rag and wiped Jason's face, but he didn't stop crying.

"Hush," she said. "Hush." But he didn't hush. Caddy took the popper out of the fire.

"It's burned up," she said. "You'll have to get some more popcorn, Nancy."

"Did you put all of it in?" Nancy said.

"Yes," Caddy said. Nancy looked at Caddy. Then she took the popper and opened it and poured the cinders into her apron and began to sort the grains, her hands long and brown, and we watching her.

"Haven't you got any more?" Caddy said.

"Yes," Nancy said; "yes. Look. This here ain't burnt. All we need to do is—"

"I want to go home," Jason said. "I'm going to tell."

"Hush," Caddy said. We all listened. Nancy's head was already turned toward the barred door, her eyes filled with red lamplight. "Somebody is coming," Caddy said.

Then Nancy began to make that sound again, not loud, sitting there above the fire, her long hands dangling between her knees; all of a sudden water began to come out on her face in big drops, running down her face, carrying in each one a little turning ball of firelight like a spark until it dropped off her chin. "She's not crying," I said.

"I ain't crying," Nancy said. Her eyes were closed. "I ain't crying. Who is it?"

"I don't know," Caddy said. She went to the door and looked out. "We've got to go now," she said. "Here comes father."

"I'm going to tell," Jason said. "Yawl made me come."

The water still ran down Nancy's face. She turned in her chair. "Listen. Tell him. Tell him we going to have fun. Tell him I take good care of yawl until in the morning. Tell him to let me come home with yawl and sleep on the floor. Tell him I won't need no pallet.

We'll have fun. You member last time how we had so much fun?"

"I didn't have fun," Jason said. "You hurt me. You put smoke in my eyes. I'm going to tell."

## V

Father came in. He looked at us. Nancy did not get up.

"Tell him," she said.

"Caddy made us come down here," Jason said. "I didn't want to."

Father came to the fire. Nancy looked up at him. "Can't you go to Aunt Rachel's and stay?" he said. Nancy looked up at father, her hands between her knees. "He's not here," father said. "I would have seen him. There's not a soul in sight."

"He in the ditch," Nancy said. "He waiting in the ditch yonder."

"Nonsense," father said. He looked at Nancy. "Do you know he's there?"

"I got the sign," Nancy said.

"What sign?"

"I got it. It was on the table when I come in. It was a hogbone, with blood meat still on it, laying by the lamp. He's out there. When yawl walk out that door, I gone."

"Gone where, Nancy?" Caddy said.

"I'm not a tattletale," Jason said.

"Nonsense," father said.

"He out there," Nancy said. "He looking through that window this minute, waiting for yawl to go. Then I gone."

"Nonsense," father said. "Lock up your house and we'll take you on to Aunt Rachel's."

"'Twont do no good," Nancy said. She didn't look at father now, but he looked down at her, at her long, limp, moving hands. "Putting it off wont do no good."

"Then what do you want to do?" father said.

"I don't know," Nancy said. "I can't do nothing. Just put it off. And that don't do no good. I reckon it belong to me. I reckon what I going to get ain't no more than mine."

"Get what?" Caddy said. "What's yours?"

"Nothing," father said. "You all must get to bed."

"Caddy made me come," Jason said.

"Go on to Aunt Rachel's," father said.

"It won't do no good," Nancy said, She sat before the fire, her elbows on her knees, her long hands between her knees. "When even your own kitchen wouldn't do no good. When even if I was sleeping on the floor in the room with your chillen, and the next morning there I am, and blood—"

"Hush," father said. "Lock the door and put out the lamp and go to bed."

"I scared of the dark," Nancy said. "I scared for it to happen in the dark."

"You mean you're going to sit right here with the lamp lighted?" father said. Then Nancy began to make the sound again, sitting before the fire, her long hands between her knees. "Ah, damnation," father said. "Come along, chillen. It's past bedtime."

"When yawl go home, I gone," Nancy said. She talked quieter now, and her face looked quiet, like her hands. "Anyway, I got my coffin money saved up with Mr. Lovelady." Mr. Lovelady was a short, dirty man who collected the Negro insurance, coming around to the cabins or the kitchens every Saturday morning, to collect fifteen cents. He and his wife lived at the hotel. One morning his wife committed suicide. They had a child, a little girl. He and the child went away. After a week or two he came back alone. We would see him going along the lanes and the back streets on Saturday mornings.

"Nonsense," father said. "You'll be the first thing I'll see in the kitchen tomorrow morning."

"You'll see what you'll see, I reckon," Nancy said. "But it will take the Lord to say what that will be."

## VI

We left her sitting before the fire.

"Come and put the bar up," father said. But she didn't move. She didn't look at us again, sitting quietly there between the lamp and the fire. From some distance down the lane we could look back and see her through the open door.

"What, Father?" Caddy said. "What's going to happen?"

"Nothing," father said. Jason was on father's back, so Jason was the tallest of all of us. We went down into the ditch. I looked at it, quiet. I couldn't see much where the moonlight and the shadows tangled.

"If Jesus is hid here, he can see us, cant he?" Caddy said.

"He's not there," father said. "He went away a long time ago."

"You made me come," Jason said, high; against the sky it looked like father had two heads, a little one and a big one. "I didn't want to."

We went up out of the ditch. We could still see Nancy's house and the open door, but we couldn't see Nancy now, sitting before the fire with the door open, because she was tired. "I just done got tired," she said. "I just a nigger. It ain't no fault of mine."

But we could hear her, because she began just after we came up out of the ditch, the sound that was not singing and not unsinging. "Who will do our washing now, Father?" I said.

"I'm not a nigger," Jason said, high and close above father's head.

"You're worse," Caddy said, "you are a tattletale. If something was to jump out, you'd be scairder than a nigger."

"I wouldn't," Jason said.

"You'd cry," Caddy said.

"Caddy," father said.

"I wouldn't!" Jason said.

"Scairy cat," Caddy said.

"Candace!" father said.

## ELIZABETH BISHOP (1911–1979)

Elizabeth Bishop inherited the modernist use of terseness, irony, elipsis, and allusion from the generation of T.S. Eliot, Ezra Pound, Hilda Doolittle, and Marianne Moore that preceded her. She fashioned the wry cosmopolitan mode into a deceptively simple poetic style that exposes the deep significance of ordinary events. Mexican poet Octavio Paz said her work was characterized by the "enormous power of reticence."

Because of the early death of her father and the mental instability of her mother, Bishop had a painful childhood. She was born in Worcester, Massachusetts, but became a ward of her grandparents after her father's death. For a time she lived in Nova Scotia with her maternal grandparents but then was moved to the home of her father's parents in Worcester and later to the home of an aunt. She attended Vassar College, from which she graduated in 1934. During her college years she became a friend of Marianne Moore, who encouraged her writing and served as a model of what a woman poet might accomplish.

Her adult life was very private and often shadowed by mental anguish. She spent sixteen years living with a close friend in Brazil until the friend's suicide. Many of her poems are set in Brazil and other tropical climates, like Key West. "The Armadillo" records a Brazilian festival in a way that reveals the devastating effect of human activities on animals adapted for survival in the wild that are helpless when they blunder into the human world. Other poems, such as "The Fish" and "At the Fishhouses," describe sea creatures in terms suggesting the enormous power and mystery of the nonhuman world just beyond our understanding. "In the Waiting Room" recounts her experience of horror as a little girl waiting for her aunt in a dentist's office suddenly wakens to the realities of suffering, the vastness of the earth, and the variety and strangeness of its human inhabitants.

In reading Bishop's poetry, it is important to pay attention to the tiniest details of ordinary experience that in unexpected settings open out with vivid new significance. Details drawn from simple domestic furnishings—such as the comparison of skin to ancient peeling wallpaper in "The Fish," or of flesh to feathers—suddenly communicate strangeness and wonder, leading to the final heroic victory of the old fish.

## *The Fish*

I caught a tremendous fish
and held him beside the boat
half out of water, with my hook
fast in a corner of his mouth.
He didn't fight.
He hadn't fought at all.
He hung a grunting weight,
battered and venerable
and homely. Here and there
his brown skin hung in strips
like ancient wallpaper,
and its pattern of darker brown
was like wallpaper:
shapes like full-blown roses
stained and lost through age.
He was speckled with barnacles,
fine rosettes of lime,
and infested
with tiny white sea-lice,

and underneath two or three
rags of green weed hung down.
While his gills were breathing in
the terrible oxygen
—the frightening gills,
fresh and crisp with blood,
that can cut so badly—
I thought of the coarse white flesh
packed in like feathers,
the big bones and the little bones,
the dramatic reds and blacks
of his shiny entrails,
and the pink swim-bladder
like a big peony.
I looked into his eyes
which were far larger than mine
but shallower, and yellowed,
the irises backed and packed
with tarnished tinfoil
seen through the lenses
of old scratched isinglass.
They shifted a little, but not
to return my stare.
—It was more like the tipping
of an object toward the light.
I admired his sullen face,
the mechanism of his jaw,
and then I saw
that from his lower lip
—if you could call it a lip—
grim, wet, and weaponlike,
hung five old pieces of fish-line,
or four and a wire leader
with the swivel still attached,
with all their five big hooks
grown firmly in his mouth.
A green line, frayed at the end
where he broke it, two heavier lines,
and a fine black thread
still crimped from the strain and snap
when it broke and he got away.
Like medals with their ribbons
frayed and wavering,
a five-haired beard of wisdom
trailing from his aching jaw.
I stared and stared

and victory filled up
the little rented boat,
from the pool of bilge
where oil had spread a rainbow
around the rusted engine
to the bailer rusted orange,
the sun-cracked thwarts,
the oarlocks on their strings,
the gunnels—until everything
was rainbow, rainbow, rainbow!
And I let the fish go.

## *At the Fishhouses*

Although it is a cold evening,
down by one of the fishhouses
an old man sits netting,
his net, in the gloaming almost invisible,
a dark purple-brown,
and his shuttle worn and polished.
The air smells so strong of codfish
it makes one's nose run and one's eyes water.
The five fishhouses have steeply peaked roofs
and narrow, cleated gangplanks slant up
to storerooms in the gables
for the wheelbarrows to be pushed up and down on.
All is silver: the heavy surface of the sea,
swelling slowly as if considering spilling over,
is opaque, but the silver of the benches,
the lobster pots, and masts, scattered
among the wild jagged rocks,
is of an apparent translucence
like the small old buildings with an emerald moss
growing on their shoreward walls.
The big fish tubs are completely lined
with layers of beautiful herring scales
and the wheelbarrows are similarly plastered
with creamy iridescent coats of mail,
with small iridescent flies crawling on them.
Up on the little slope behind the houses,
set in the sparse bright sprinkle of grass,
is an ancient wooden capstan,
cracked, with two long bleached handles
and some melancholy stains, like dried blood,
where the ironwork has rusted.
The old man accepts a Lucky Strike.

He was a friend of my grandfather.
We talk of the decline in the population
and of codfish and herring
while he waits for a herring boat to come in.
There are sequins on his vest and on his thumb.
He has scraped the scales, the principal beauty,
from unnumbered fish with that black old knife,
the blade of which is almost worn away.

Down at the water's edge, at the place
where they haul up the boats, up the long ramp
descending into the water, thin silver
tree trunks are laid horizontally
across the gray stones, down and down
at intervals of four or five feet.

Cold dark deep and absolutely clear,
element bearable to no mortal,
to fish and to seals . . . One seal particularly
I have seen here evening after evening.
He was curious about me. He was interested in music;
like me a believer in total immersion,
so I used to sing him Baptist hymns.
I also sang "A Mighty Fortress Is Our God."
He stood up in the water and regarded me
steadily, moving his head a little.
Then he would disappear, then suddenly emerge
almost in the same spot, with a sort of shrug
as if it were against his better judgment.
Cold dark deep and absolutely clear,
the clear gray icy water . . . Back, behind us,
the dignified tall firs begin.
Bluish, associating with their shadows,
a million Christmas trees stand
waiting for Christmas. The water seems suspended
above the rounded gray and blue-gray stones.
I have seen it over and over, the same sea, the same,
slightly, indifferently swinging above the stones,
icily free above the stones,
above the stones and then the world.
If you should dip your hand in,
your wrist would ache immediately,
your bones would begin to ache and your hand would burn
as if the water were a transmutation of fire
that feeds on stones and burns with a dark gray flame.
If you tasted it, it would first taste bitter,

then briny, then surely burn your tongue.
It is like what we imagine knowledge to be:
dark, salt, clear, moving, utterly free,
drawn from the cold hard mouth
of the world, derived from the rocky breasts
forever, flowing and drawn, and since
our knowledge is historical, flowing, and flown.

## The Armadillo

*For Robert Lowell*

This is the time of year
when almost every night
the frail, illegal fire balloons appear.
Climbing the mountain height,

rising toward a saint
still honored in these parts,
the paper chambers flush and fill with light
that comes and goes, like hearts.

Once up against the sky it's hard
to tell them from the stars—
planets, that is—the tinted ones:
Venus going down, or Mars,

or the pale green one. With a wind,
they flare and falter, wobble and toss;
but if it's still they steer between
the kite sticks of the Southern Cross,

receding, dwindling, solemnly
and steadily forsaking us,
or, in the downdraft from a peak,
suddenly turning dangerous.

Last night another big one fell.
It splattered like an egg of fire
against the cliff behind the house.
The flame ran down. We saw the pair

of owls who nest there flying up
and up, their whirling black-and-white
stained bright pink underneath, until
they shrieked up out of sight.

The ancient owls' nest must have burned.
Hastily, all alone,
a glistening armadillo left the scene,
rose-flecked, head down, tail down,

and then a baby rabbit jumped out,
*short*-eared, to our surprise.
So soft!—a handful of intangible ash
with fixed, ignited eyes.

*Too pretty, dreamlike mimicry!*
*O falling fire and piercing cry*
*and panic, and a weak mailed fist*
*clenched ignorant against the sky!*

## In the Waiting Room

In Worcester, Massachusetts,
I went with Aunt Consuelo
to keep her dentist's appointment
and sat and waited for her
in the dentist's waiting room.
It was winter. It got dark
early. The waiting room
was full of grown-up people,
arctics and overcoats,
lamps and magazines.
My aunt was inside
what seemed like a long time
and while I waited I read
the *National Geographic*
(I could read) and carefully
studied the photographs:
the inside of a volcano,
black, and full of ashes;
then it was spilling over
in rivulets of fire.
Osa and Martin Johnson
dressed in riding breeches,
laced boots, and pith helmets.
A dead man slung on a pole
—"Long Pig," the caption said.
Babies with pointed heads
wound round and round with string;
black, naked women with necks

wound round and round with wire
like the necks of light bulbs.
Their breasts were horrifying.
I read it right straight through.
I was too shy to stop.
And then I looked at the cover:
the yellow margins, the date.
Suddenly, from inside,
came an *oh!* of pain
—Aunt Consuelo's voice—
not very loud or long.
I wasn't at all surprised;
even then I knew she was
a foolish, timid woman.
I might have been embarrassed,
but wasn't. What took me
completely by surprise
was that it was *me:*
my voice, in my mouth.
Without thinking at all
I was my foolish aunt,
I—we—were falling, falling,
our eyes glued to the cover
of the *National Geographic,*
February, 1918.

I said to myself: three days
and you'll be seven years old.
I was saying it to stop
the sensation of falling off
the round, turning world
into cold, blue-black space.
But I felt: you are an *I,*
you are an *Elizabeth,*
you are one of *them.*
*Why* should you be one, too?
I scarcely dared to look
to see what it was I was.
I gave a sidelong glance
—I couldn't look any higher—
at shadowy gray knees,
trousers and skirts and boots
and different pairs of hands
lying under the lamps.
I knew that nothing stranger
had ever happened, that nothing

stranger could ever happen.
Why should I be my aunt,
or me, or anyone?
What similarities—
boots, hands, the family voice
I felt in my throat, or even
the *National Geographic*
and those awful hanging breasts—
held us all together
or made us all just one?
How—I didn't know any
word for it—how "unlikely" . . .
How had I come to be here,
like them, and overhear
a cry of pain that could have
got loud and worse but hadn't?

The waiting room was bright
and too hot. It was sliding
beneath a big black wave,
another, and another.

Then I was back in it.
The War was on. Outside,
in Worcester, Massachusetts,
were night and slush and cold,
and it was still the fifth
of February, 1918.

## TONI MORRISON (B. 1931)

Toni Morrison has revitalized the American novel, crafting a direct, visceral prose that is capable of both epic weight and the most intimate lyricism. Each of her six novels has explored its own territory, as she depicts the lives of African Americans in Ohio, the Caribbean, or New York City. In the process Morrison has employed her own North American style of "magic realism" which unites African traditions of magic and folklore with scrupulous realism. Her first novel, *The Bluest Eye* (1969), treats the explosive subjects of racism and incest, and her next novel, *Sula* (1973), explores the coming of age of two African American girls in a segregated Ohio town. *The Song of Solomon* (1977) turns to the search of a young black man for identity in a similar setting, and *Tar Baby* (1981) depicts the experience of an African American woman from the United States as she encounters the life of Caribbean African Americans. With *Beloved* (1987), Morrison ventures into the highly charged subject of slavery, creating a new narrative style and a new avenue into the emotional reality of history. The novel *Jazz* (1992) brings to life the rich cultural milieu of the Harlem Renaissance. In 1992 she also published *Playing in the Dark,* an analysis of the rhetorical structures used to encode the African presence in American literary tradition.

Born Chloe Anthony Wofford in 1931 in Lorain, Ohio, Toni Morrison earned a B.A. degree in 1953 from Howard University, where she was trained in African American literature. Two years later she received an M.A. from Cornell University. From there she went on to college teaching in Texas but soon moved to New York and began a career in publishing, which continued until she was recognized as one of the major voices in American literature in the 1980s. She is now a distinguished professor at Princeton University.

With her receipt of the Nobel Prize in literature in 1993, Morrison achieved not only a personal triumph but also international recognition for the rich tradition of African American literary achievement to which her own writing contributes. The poetry of Phyllis Wheatley in the eighteenth century and slave narratives like those of Frederick Douglass and Harriet Jacobs in the nineteenth led to a growing stream of accomplished fiction, poetry, and essays in the twentieth. Writers like James Weldon Johnson, Langston Hughes, Zora Neale Hurston, Jean Toomer, Richard Wright, and Gwendolyn Brooks are only part of the tradition that inspired Morrison, as they also inspired African writers to develop their own emergent literatures in our century.

However, Toni Morrison also works from the wider American literary tradition and the English tradition that gave birth to it. Shakespeare, Hawthorne, Melville, Twain, and Faulkner are a few of the other literary ancestors to whose influence she testifies, even as she points out the racist habits of representation that unbalance that literary heritage. Morrison's fiction powerfully extends the fictional range of American literature, correcting those imbalances by defining the many forms of selfhood in African American life and by describing historical eras from the viewpoint of the black community—especially in *Beloved* and *Jazz.*

Our selection comes from *Sula,* the story of a friendship between two girls growing up in the Negro section of an Ohio town similar to Lorain, Ohio. The town is a microcosm of a whole world struggling to live the American dream in a segregated society determined to deny its benefits to dark-skinned people. The novel is also a study of women's bonds that form a web of community to sustain families in these circumstances. Morrison's prose is direct, sensuous, and vividly detailed. In the opening sections of the novel, the black neighborhood is described with fiercely satiric humor. The odd but deeply symbolic ritual of National Suicide Day is explained, and Sula's friend and foil Nel Wright is introduced through a story that indicates what lies behind the genteel respectability Sula envies in her friend. Sula's own household is then presented: it is a matriarchy presided over by a generous but quirky one-legged grandmother named Eva, who performs a desperate act to end the drug addiction of her adult son.

## *from Sula*

In that place, where they tore the nightshade and blackberry patches from their roots to make room for the Medallion City Golf Course, there was once a neighborhood. It stood in the hills above the valley town of Medallion and spread all the way to the river. It is called the suburbs now, but when black people lived there it was called the Bottom. One road, shaded by beeches, oaks, maples and chestnuts, connected it to the valley. The beeches are gone now, and so are the pear trees where children sat and yelled down through the blossoms to passersby. Generous funds have been allotted to level the stripped and faded buildings that clutter the road from Medallion up to the golf course. They are going to raze the Time and a Half Pool Hall, where feet in long tan shoes once pointed down from chair rungs. A steel ball will knock to dust Irene's Palace of Cosmetology, where women used to lean their heads back on sink trays and doze while Irene lathered Nu Nile into their hair. Men in khaki work clothes will pry loose the slats of Reba's Grill, where the owner cooked in her hat because she couldn't remember the ingredients without it.

There will be nothing left of the Bottom (the footbridge that crossed the river is already gone), but perhaps it is just as well, since it wasn't a town anyway: just a neighborhood where on quiet days people in valley houses could hear singing sometimes, banjos sometimes, and, if a valley man happened to have business up in those hills—collecting rent or insurance payments—he might see a dark woman in a flowered dress doing a bit of cakewalk, a bit of black bottom, a bit of "messing around" to the lively notes of a mouth organ. Her bare feet would raise the saffron dust that floated down on the coveralls and bunion-split shoes of the man breathing music in and out of his harmonica. The black people watching her would laugh and rub their knees, and it would be easy for the valley man to hear the laughter and not notice the adult pain that rested somewhere under the eyelids, somewhere under their head rags and soft felt hats, somewhere in the palm of the hand, somewhere behind the frayed lapels, somewhere in the sinew's curve. He'd have to stand in the back of Greater Saint Matthew's and let the tenor's voice dress him in silk, or touch the hands of the spoon carvers (who had not worked in eight years) and let the fingers that danced on wood kiss his skin. Otherwise the pain would escape him even though the laughter was part of the pain.

A shucking, knee-slapping, wet-eyed laughter that could even describe and explain how they came to be where they were.

A joke. A nigger joke. That was the way it got started. Not the town, of course, but that part of town where the Negroes lived, the part they called the Bottom in spite of the fact that it was up in the hills. Just a nigger joke. The kind white folks tell when the mill closes down and they're looking for a little comfort somewhere. The kind colored folks tell on themselves when the rain doesn't come, or comes for weeks, and they're looking for a little comfort somehow.

A good white farmer promised freedom and a piece of bottom land to his slave if he would perform some very difficult chores. When the slave completed the work, he asked the farmer to keep his end of the bargain. Freedom was easy—the farmer had no objection to that. But he didn't want to give up any land. So he told the slave that he was very sorry that he had to give him valley land. He had hoped to give him a piece of the Bottom. The slave blinked and said he thought valley land was bottom land. The master said, "Oh, no! See those hills? That's bottom land, rich and fertile."

"But it's high up in the hills," said the slave.

"High up from us," said the master, "but when God looks down, it's the bottom. That's why we call it so. It's the bottom of heaven—best land there is."

So the slave pressed his master to try to get him some. He preferred it to the valley. And it was done. The nigger got the hilly land, where planting was backbreaking, where the soil slid down and washed away the seeds, and where the wind lingered all through the winter.

Which accounted for the fact that white people lived on the rich valley floor in that little river town in Ohio, and the blacks populated the hills above it, taking small consolation in the fact that every day they could literally look down on the white folks.

Still, it was lovely up in the Bottom. After the town grew and the farm land turned into a village and the village into a town and the streets of Medallion were hot and dusty with progress, those heavy trees that sheltered the shacks up in the Bottom were wonderful to see. And the hunters who went there sometimes wondered in private if maybe the white farmer was right after all. Maybe it was the bottom of heaven.

The black people would have disagreed, but they had no time to think about it. They were mightily preoccupied with earthly things—and each other, wondering even as early as 1920 what Shadrack was all about, what that little girl Sula who grew into a woman in their town was all about, and what they themselves were all about, tucked up there in the Bottom.

## 1919

Except for World War II, nothing ever interfered with the celebration of National Suicide Day. It had taken place every January third since 1920, although Shadrack, its founder, was for many years the only celebrant. Blasted and permanently astonished by the events of 1917, he had returned to Medallion handsome but ravaged, and even the most fastidious people in the town sometimes caught themselves dreaming of what he must have been like a few years back before he went off to war. A young man of hardly twenty, his head full of nothing and his mouth recalling the taste of lipstick, Shadrack had found himself in December, 1917, running with his comrades across a field in France. It was his first encounter with the enemy and he didn't know whether his company was running toward them or away. For several days they had been marching, keeping close to a stream that was frozen at its edges. At one point they crossed it, and no sooner had he stepped foot on the other side than the day was adangle with shouts and explosions. Shellfire was all around him, and though he knew that this was something called *it,* he could not muster up the proper feeling—the feeling that would accommodate *it.* He expected to be terrified or exhilarated—to feel *something* very strong. In fact, he felt only the bite of a nail in his boot, which pierced the ball of his foot whenever he came down on it. The day was cold enough to make his breath visible, and he wondered for a moment at the purity and whiteness of his own breath among the dirty, gray explosions surrounding him. He ran, bayonet fixed, deep in the great sweep of men flying across this field. Wincing at the pain in his foot, he turned his head a little to the right and saw the face of a soldier near him fly off. Before he could register shock, the rest of the soldier's head disappeared under the inverted soup bowl of his helmet. But stubbornly, taking no direction from the brain, the body of the headless soldier ran on, with energy and grace, ignoring altogether the drip and slide of brain tissue down its back.

When Shadrack opened his eyes he was propped up in a small bed. Before him on a tray was a large tin plate divided into three triangles. In one triangle was rice, in another meat, and in the third stewed tomatoes. A small round depression held a cup of whitish liquid. Shadrack stared at the soft colors that filled these triangles: the lumpy whiteness of rice, the quivering blood tomatoes, the grayish-brown meat. All their repugnance was contained in the neat balance of the triangles—a balance that soothed him, transferred some of its equilibrium to him. Thus reassured that the white, the red and the brown would stay where they were—would not explode or burst forth from their restricted zones—he suddenly felt hungry and looked around for his hands. His glance was cautious at first, for he had to be very careful—anything could be anywhere. Then he noticed two lumps beneath the beige blanket on either side of his hips. With extreme care he lifted one arm and was relieved to find his hand attached to his wrist. He tried the other and found it also. Slowly he directed one hand toward the cup and, just as he was about to spread his fingers, they began to grow in higgledy-piggledy fashion like Jack's beanstalk all over the tray and the bed. With a shriek he closed his eyes and thrust his huge growing hands under the covers. Once out of sight they seemed to shrink back to their normal size. But the yell had brought a male nurse.

"Private? We're not going to have any trouble today, are we? Are we, Private?"

Shadrack looked up at a balding man dressed in a green-cotton jacket and trousers. His hair was parted low on the right side so that some twenty or thirty yellow hairs could discreetly cover the nakedness of his head.

"Come on. Pick up that spoon. Pick it up, Private. Nobody is going to feed you forever."

Sweat slid from Shadrack's armpits down his sides. He could not bear to see his hands grow again and he was frightened of the voice in the apple-green suit.

"Pick it up, I said. There's no point to this . . ." The nurse reached under the cover for Shadrack's wrist to pull out the monstrous hand. Shadrack jerked it back and overturned the tray. In panic he raised himself to his knees and tried to fling off and away his terrible fingers, but succeeded only in knocking the nurse into the next bed.

When they bound Shadrack into a straitjacket, he was both relieved and grateful, for his hands were at last hidden and confined to whatever size they had attained.

Laced and silent in his small bed, he tried to tie the loose cords in his mind. He wanted desperately to see his own face and connect it with the word "private"—the word the nurse (and the others who helped bind him) had called him. "Private"—the thought was something secret, and he wondered why they looked at him and called him a secret. Still, if his hands behaved as they had done, what might he expect from his face? The fear and longing were too much for him, so he began to think of other things. That is, he let his mind slip into whatever cave mouths of memory it chose.

He saw a window that looked out on a river which he knew was full of fish. Someone was speaking softly just outside the door . . .

Shadrack's earlier violence had coincided with a memorandum from the hospital executive staff in reference to the distribution of patients in high-risk areas. There was clearly a demand for space. The priority or the violence earned Shadrack his release, $217 in cash, a full suit of clothes and copies of very official-looking papers.

When he stepped out of the hospital door the grounds overwhelmed him: the cropped shrubbery, the edged lawns, the undeviating walks. Shadrack looked at the cement stretches: each one leading clearheadedly to some presumably desirable destination. There were no fences, no warnings, no obstacles at all between concrete and green grass, so one could easily ignore the tidy sweep of stone and cut out in another direction—a direction of one's own.

Shadrack stood at the foot of the hospital steps watching the heads of trees tossing ruefully but harmlessly, since their trunks were rooted too deeply in the earth to threaten him. Only the walks made him uneasy. He shifted his weight, wondering how he could get to the gate without stepping on the concrete. While plotting his course—where he would have to leap, where to skirt a clump of bushes—a loud guffaw startled him. Two men were going up the steps. Then he noticed that there were many people about, and that he was just now seeing them, or else they had just materialized. They were thin slips, like paper dolls floating down the walks. Some were seated in chairs with wheels, propelled by other paper figures from behind. All seemed to be smoking, and their arms and legs curved in the breeze. A good high wind would pull them up and away and they would land perhaps among the tops of the trees.

Shadrack took the plunge. Four steps and he was on the grass heading for the gate. He kept his head down to avoid seeing the paper people swerving and bending here and there, and he lost his way. When he looked up, he was standing by a low red building separated from the main building by a covered walkway. From somewhere came a sweetish smell which reminded him of something painful. He looked around for the gate and saw that he had gone directly away from it in his complicated journey over the grass. Just to the left of the low building was a graveled driveway that appeared to lead outside the grounds. He trotted quickly to it and left, at last, a haven of more than a year, only eight days of which he fully recollected.

Once on the road, he headed west. The long stay in the hospital had left him weak—too weak to walk steadily on the gravel shoulders of the road. He shuffled, grew dizzy, stopped for breath, started again, stumbling and sweating but refusing to wipe his temples, still afraid to look at his hands. Passengers in dark, square cars shuttered their eyes at what they took to be a drunken man.

The sun was already directly over his head when he came to a town. A few blocks of shaded streets and he was already at its heart—a pretty, quietly regulated downtown.

Exhausted, his feet clotted with pain, he sat down at the curbside to take off his shoes. He closed his eyes to avoid seeing his hands and fumbled with the laces of the heavy high-topped shoes. The nurse had tied them into a double knot, the way one does for children, and Shadrack, long unaccustomed to the manipulation of intricate things, could not get them loose. Uncoordinated, his fingernails tore away at the knots. He fought a rising hysteria that was not merely anxiety to free his aching feet; his very life depended on the release of the knots. Suddenly without raising his eyelids, he began to cry. Twenty-two years old, weak, hot, frightened, not daring to acknowledge the fact that he didn't even know who or what he was . . . with no past, no language, no tribe, no source, no address book, no comb, no pencil, no clock, no pocket handkerchief, no rug, no bed, no can opener, no faded postcard, no soap, no key, no tobacco pouch, no soiled underwear and nothing nothing nothing to do . . . he was sure of one thing only: the unchecked monstrosity of his hands. He cried soundlessly at the curbside of a small Midwestern town wondering where the window was, and the river, and the soft voices just outside the door . . .

Through his tears he saw the fingers joining the laces, tentatively at first, then rapidly. The four fingers of each hand fused into the fabric, knotted themselves and zigzagged in and out of the tiny eyeholes.

By the time the police drove up, Shadrack was suffering from a blinding headache, which was not abated by the comfort he felt when the policemen pulled his hands away from what he thought was a permanent entanglement with his shoelaces. They took him to jail, booked him for vagrancy and intoxication, and locked him in a cell. Lying on a cot, Shadrack could only stare helplessly at the wall, so paralyzing was the pain in his head. He lay in this agony for a long while and then realized he was staring at the painted-over letters of a command to fuck himself. He studied the phrase as the pain in his head subsided.

Like moonlight stealing under a window shade an idea insinuated itself: his earlier desire to see his own face. He looked for a mirror; there was none. Finally, keeping his hands carefully behind his back he made his way to the toilet bowl and peeped in. The water was unevenly lit by the sun so he could make nothing out. Returning to his cot he took the blanket and covered his head, rendering the water dark enough to see his reflection. There in the toilet water he saw a grave black face. A black so definite, so unequivocal, it astonished him. He had been harboring a skittish apprehension that he was not real—that he didn't exist at all. But when the blackness greeted him with its indisputable presence, he wanted nothing more. In his joy he took the risk of letting one edge of the blanket drop and glanced at his hands. They were still. Courteously still.

Shadrack rose and returned to the cot, where he fell into the first sleep of his new life. A sleep deeper than the hospital drugs; deeper than the pits of plums, steadier than the condor's wing; more tranquil than the curve of eggs.

The sheriff looked through the bars at the young man with the matted hair. He had read through his prisoner's papers and hailed a farmer. When Shadrack awoke, the sheriff handed him back his papers and escorted him to the back of a wagon.

Shadrack got in and in less than three hours he was back in Medallion, for he had been only twenty-two miles from his window, his river, and his soft voices just outside the door.

In the back of the wagon, supported by sacks of squash and hills of pumpkins, Shadrack began a struggle that was to last for twelve days, a struggle to order and focus experience. It had to do with making a place for fear as a way of controlling it. He knew the smell of death and was terrified of it, for he could not anticipate it. It was not death or dying that frightened him, but the unexpectedness of both. In sorting it all out, he hit on the notion that if one day a year were devoted to it, everybody could get it out of the way and the rest of the year would be safe and free. In this manner he instituted National Suicide Day.

On the third day of the new year, he walked through the Bottom down Carpenter's Road with a cowbell and a hangman's rope calling the people together. Telling them that this was their only chance to kill themselves or each other.

At first the people in the town were frightened; they knew Shadrack was crazy but that did not mean that he didn't have any sense or, even more important, that he had no power. His eyes were so wild, his hair so long and matted, his voice was so full of authority and thunder that he caused panic on the first, or Charter, National Suicide Day in 1920. The next one, in 1921, was less frightening but still worrisome. The people had seen him a year now in between. He lived in a shack on the riverbank that had once belonged to his grandfather long time dead. On Tuesday and Friday he sold the fish he had caught that morning, the rest of the week he was drunk, loud, obscene, funny and outrageous. But he never touched anybody, never fought, never caressed. Once the people understood the boundaries and nature of his madness, they could fit him, so to speak, into the scheme of things.

Then, on subsequent National Suicide Days, the grown people looked out from behind curtains as he rang his bell; a few stragglers increased their speed, and little children screamed and ran. The tetter heads tried goading him (although he was only four or five years older than they) but not for long, for his curses were stingingly personal.

As time went along, the people took less notice of these January thirds, or rather they thought they did, thought they had no attitudes or feelings one way or another about Shadrack's annual solitary parade. In fact they had simply stopped remarking on the holiday because they had absorbed it into their thoughts, into their language, into their lives.

Someone said to a friend, "You sure was a long time delivering that baby. How long was you in labor?"

And the friend answered, "'Bout three days. The pains started on Suicide Day and kept up till the following Sunday. Was borned on Sunday. All my boys is Sunday boys."

Some lover said to his bride-to-be, "Let's do it after New Years, 'stead of before. I get paid New Year's Eve."

And his sweetheart answered, "OK, but make sure it ain't on Suicide Day. I ain't 'bout to be listening to no cowbells whilst the weddin's going on."

Somebody's grandmother said her hens always started a laying of double yolks right after Suicide Day.

Then Reverend Deal took it up, saying the same folks who had sense enough to avoid Shadrack's call were the ones who insisted on drinking themselves to death or womanizing themselves to death. "May's well go on with Shad and save the Lamb the trouble of redemption."

Easily, quietly, Suicide Day became a part of the fabric of life up in the Bottom of Medallion, Ohio.

## IRENA KLEPFISZ (B. 1941)

Irena Klepfisz's work belongs to a chorus of voices, formerly silenced or marginalized in literary publication, that have steadily grown in importance in the twentieth century. It is a chorus that includes more and more women writers, immigrants, political dissidents, nonwhite Euro-Americans, gays and lesbians, ethnic minorities, and other writers living on what Gloria Anzaldua has called the "borderlands" of late twentieth-century dominant culture. Klepfisz's work also belongs to the body of Holocaust literature, which is steadily growing in importance. Born in the Warsaw Ghetto, Klepfisz's life began amidst an unprecedented assault on Jews in Europe: the Holocaust. Her poem "Bashert" recalls the nearly complete annihilation of family, community, culture, and language, and it explores what living as a Holocaust survivor means.

The Warsaw Ghetto, established to isolate and hold Jews for deportation to concentration camps, became an urban death camp of its own. In a twenty-month period immediately following Klepfisz's birth, 83,000 of the half-million Jews living in the ghetto died of starvation and disease. Those who did not escape were murdered in response to the April 1943 ghetto uprising against the Nazis. Klepfisz's father, Michal, gave his life actively fighting in the uprising. Irena's mother escaped with her daughter to the countryside and lived concealed among Polish peasants until 1945. After the war they traveled through Sweden to the United States where, at age eight, Irena enrolled in New York public schools and began learning the language and culture of her adopted country. She also attended Workmen's Circle Yiddish schools, institutions devoted to keeping alive the language and culture that survivors had brought with them to the new country.

The poem "Bashert" (a Yiddish word meaning "predestined" or "inevitable"), like Klepfisz's life, exists "almost equidistant from two continents." It shares the ambiguities, contradictions, and lived incongruities common to immigrant literature worldwide. The poem also asserts a specifically Jewish self and its community in an act of creation and remembrance, its meanings written on the boundaries within and between cultures, losses, and languages. "Bashert" melds poetry and prose, elegy and narration, echoing in its form the struggle Irena undergoes as she creates her identity between two worlds and grows into adulthood surviving the fragmentation, the disintegration, and the immense grief of the Holocaust.

Working to shape meaning and an identity capable of tolerating the memories of the past while living in the present, Klepfisz, as Jew, feminist, lesbian, and immigrant, finds connections between her marginalized self and other Americans. As she writes in the forward to a more recent collection of her work, "in the spring of

1990 in New York City where 70,000 homeless remain uncared for, I am even more aware than I was in 1982 of our society's stubborn ability to throw away human life, human potential, human creativity, to suppress the best in us, the art in us." Klepfisz's "Bashert" moves between continents and historical moments, between self and others, creating a powerful poetic statement.

## *Bashert*

These words are dedicated to those who died

These words are dedicated to those who died
because they had no love and felt alone in the world
because they were afraid to be alone and tried to stick it out
because they could not ask
because they were shunned
because they were sick and their bodies could not resist the disease
because they played it safe
because they had no connections
because they had no faith
because they felt they did not belong and wanted to die

These words are dedicated to those who died
because they were loners and liked it
because they acquired friends and drew others to them
because they took risks
because they were stubborn and refused to give up
because they asked for too much

These words are dedicated to those who died
because a card was lost and a number was skipped
because a bed was denied
because a place was filled and no other place was left

These words are dedicated to those who died
because someone did not follow through
because someone was overworked and forgot
because someone left everything to God
because someone was late
because someone did not arrive at all
because someone told them to wait and they just couldn't any longer

These words are dedicated to those who died
because death is a punishment
because death is a reward

because death is the final rest
because death is eternal rage

These words are dedicated to those who died

*Bashert*

These words are dedicated to those who survived

These words are dedicated to those who survived
because their second grade teacher gave them books
because they did not draw attention to themselves and got lost
in the shuffle
because they knew someone who knew someone else who could
help them and bumped into them on a corner on a Thursday
afternoon
because they played it safe
because they were lucky

These words are dedicated to those who survived
because they knew how to cut corners
because they drew attention to themselves and always got picked
because they took risks
because they had no principles and were hard

These words are dedicated to those who survived
because they refused to give up and defied statistics
because they had faith and trusted in God
because they expected the worst and were always prepared
because they were angry
because they could ask
because they mooched off others and saved their strength
because they endured humiliation
because they turned the other cheek
because they looked the other way

These words are dedicated to those who survived
because life is a wilderness and they were savage
because life is an awakening and they were alert
because life is a flowering and they blossomed
because life is a struggle and they struggled
because life is a gift and they were free to accept it

These words are dedicated to those who survived

*Bashert*

## 1. Poland, 1944: My mother is walking down a road.

My mother is walking down a road. Somewhere in Poland. Walking towards an unnamed town for some kind of permit. She is carrying her Aryan identity papers. She has left me with an old peasant who is willing to say she is my grandmother.

She is walking down a road. Her terror in leaving me behind, in risking the separation is swallowed now, like all other feelings. But as she walks, she pictures me waving from the dusty yard, imagines herself suddenly picked up, the identity papers challenged. And even if she were to survive that, would she ever find me later? She tastes the terror in her mouth again. She swallows.

I am over three years old, corn silk blond and blue eyed like any Polish child. There is terrible suffering among the peasants. Starvation. And like so many others, I am ill. Perhaps dying. I have bad lungs. Fever. An ugly ear infection that oozes pus. None of these symptoms are disappearing.

The night before, my mother feeds me watery soup and then sits and listens while I say my prayers to the Holy Mother, Mother of God. I ask her, just as the nuns taught me, to help us all: me, my mother, the old woman. And then catching myself, learning to use memory, I ask the Mother of God to help my father. The Polish words slip easily from my lips. My mother is satisfied. The peasant has perhaps heard and is reassured. My mother has found her to be kind, but knows that she is suspicious of strangers.

My mother is sick. Goiter. Malnutrition. Vitamin deficiencies. She has skin sores which she cannot cure. For months now she has been living in complete isolation, with no point of reference outside of herself. She has been her own sole advisor, companion, comforter. Almost everyone of her world is dead: three sisters, nephews and nieces, her mother, her husband, her in-laws. All gone. Even the remnants of the resistance, those few left after the uprising, have dispersed into the Polish countryside. She is more alone than she could have ever imagined. Only she knows her real name and she is perhaps dying. She is thirty years old.

I am over three years old. I have no consciousness of our danger, our separateness from the others. I have no awareness that we are playing a part. I only know that I have a special name, that I have been named for the Goddess of Peace. And each night, I sleep secure in that knowledge. And when I wet my bed, my mother places me on her belly and lies on the stain. She fears the old woman and hopes her body's warmth will dry the sheet before dawn.

My mother is walking down a road. Another woman joins her. My mother sees through the deception, but she has promised herself that never, under any circumstances, will she take that risk. So she swallows her hunger for contact and trust and instead talks about the sick child left behind and lies about the husband in the labor camp.

Someone is walking towards them. A large, strange woman with wild red hair. They try not to look at her too closely, to seem overly curious. But as they pass her, my mother feels something move inside her. The movement grows and grows till it is an explosion of yearning that she cannot contain. She stops, orders her companion to continue without her. And then she turns.

The woman with the red hair has also stopped and turned. She is grotesque, bloated with hunger, almost savage in her rags. She and my mother move towards each other. Cautiously, deliberately, they probe past the hunger, the swollen flesh, the infected skin, the rags. Slowly, they begin to pierce five years of encrusted history. And slowly, there is perception and recognition.

In this wilderness of occupied Poland, in this vast emptiness where no one can be trusted, my mother has suddenly, bizarrely, met one of my father's teachers. A family friend. Another Jew.

They do not cry, but weep as they chronicle the dead and count the living. Then they rush to me. To the woman I am a familiar sight. She calculates that I will not live out the week, but comments only on my striking resemblance to my father. She says she has contacts. She leaves. One night a package of food is delivered anonymously. We eat. We begin to bridge the gap towards life. We survive.

## 2. Chicago, 1964: I am walking home alone at midnight.

I am walking home alone at midnight. I am a student of literature, and each night I stay in the library until it closes. Yet each night, as I return I still feel unprepared for the next day. The nature of literary movements eludes me. I only understand individual writers. I have trouble remembering genre definitions, historical dates and names, cannot grasp their meaning, significance. A whole world of abstractions and theories remains beyond my reach, on the other side of a wall I cannot climb over.

So each night, I walk home clutching my books as if I were a small school child. The city is alien. Since coming to America, this is my first time away from a Jewish neighborhood, Jewish friends, and I feel isolated, baffled at how to make a place for myself in this larger, gentile world which I have entered.

I am walking home alone at midnight. The university seems an island ungrounded. Most of its surrounding streets have been emptied. On some, all evidence of previous life removed except for occasional fringes of rubble that reveal vague outlines that hint at things that were. On others, old buildings still stand, though these are hollow like caves, once of use and then abandoned. Everything is poised. Everything is waiting for the emptiness to close in upon itself, for the emptiness to be filled up, for the emptiness to be swallowed and forgotten.

Walking home, I am only dimly aware of the meaning of this strange void through which I pass. I am even less aware of the dangers for someone like me, a woman walking home alone at midnight. I am totally preoccupied with another time, another place. Night after night, protected by the darkness, I think only of Elza who is dead. I am trying to place a fact about her, a fact which stubbornly resists classification: nothing that happened to her afterwards mattered. All that agonized effort. All that caring. *None of that mattered!*

At the end of the war, friends come to claim her. With the cold, calculated cunning of an adult, the eight year old vehemently denies who she is. No she is not who they think. Not a Jew. They have made a mistake. Mixed her up with another Elza. This one belongs here, with her mother.

She is simply being scrupulous in following her parents' instructions. "Do not ever admit to anyone who you are. It is our secret. Eventually we will come for you. Remember! *Never admit who you are!* Promise!"

Four years later, the war is over. Her parents dead. She is still bound by her promise. This woman *is* her mother. Her parents' friends know better. The woman has been kind, has saved her. But she is a Pole and Elza is a Jew. Finally, the bribe is big enough and the child released. Elza becomes an orphan.

*And afterwards?* She is adopted and finally seems to have everything. Two parents. Two handsome brothers. A house. Her own room. She studies Latin and does translations. Is valedictorian of her class. Goes away to college. Has boyfriends, affairs. Comes to New York. Works. Begins graduate school. Explicates Dylan Thomas, T.S. Eliot. Marries.

But none of it matters. She cannot keep up. The signs are clear. She is a poor housekeeper. Insists they eat off paper plates. She buys enough clothes to fill all her closets. But nothing soothes her. Finally she signs her own papers. Is released within a few months. I finish college and leave for Europe. Three weeks later, she checks into a hotel and takes an overdose. She is twenty-five years old.

Fearing I too might be in danger, my mother instructs Polish Jews resettled in Paris and Tel Aviv: "Don't tell her!" And to me she writes: "Elza is in the hospital again. There is no hope." I am suspicious, refer to her whenever I can. I am alert. Sense a discomfort, an edge I cannot define. I think I know, but I never dare ask. I come home. Seven months after her death, I finally know.

A story she once told me remains alive. During the war, the Polish woman sends her to buy a notebook for school. She is given the wrong change and points it out. The shopkeeper eyes her sharply: "Very accurate. Just like a Jew. Perhaps you are a little Jewess?" And Elza feels afraid and wonders if this woman sees the truth in her blue eyes.

Another memory. Elza is reading accounts of the war. She cannot help herself she tells me. An anecdote explains something to her. A woman in a camp requests a bandage for a wound. And the guard, so startled by her simplicity and directness, makes sure she gets one. That woman, Elza tells me, refused to stop acting like a human being. Jews, she concludes, made a terrible mistake.

I am walking home alone at midnight. I am raw with the pain of her death. I wonder. Is it inevitable? Everything that happened to us afterwards, to all of us, does none of it matter? Does it not matter what we do and where we live? Are there moments in history which cannot be escaped or transcended, but which act like time warps permanently trapping all those who are touched by them? And that which should have happened in 1944 in Poland and didn't, must it happen now? In 1964? In Chicago? Or can history be tricked and cheated?

These questions haunt me. Yet I persist with a will I myself do not understand. I continue reading, studying, making friends. And as the rawness of Elza's death eases and becomes familiar, as time becomes distance, I find myself more and more grounded in my present life, in my passion for words and literature. I begin to perceive the world around me. I develop perspective.

I see the rubble of this unbombed landscape, see that the city, like the rest of this alien country, is not simply a geographic place, but a time zone, an era in which I, by my very presence in it, am rooted. No one simply passes through. History keeps unfolding and demanding a response. A life obliterated around me of those I barely noticed. A life unmarked, unrecorded. A silent mass migration. Relocation. Common rubble in the streets.

I see now the present dangers, the dangers of the void, of the American hollowness in which I walk calmly day and night as I continue my life. I begin to see the incessant grinding down of lines for stamps, for jobs, for a bed to sleep in, of a death stretched imperceptibly over a lifetime. I begin to understand the ingenuity of it. The invisibility. The Holocaust without smoke.

Everything is poised. Everything is waiting for the emptiness to be filled up, for the filling-up that can never replace, that can only take over. Like time itself. Or history.

## 3. Brooklyn, 1971: I am almost equidistant from two continents.

I am almost equidistant from two continents. I look back, towards one, then forward towards the other. The moment is approaching when I will be equidistant from both and will have to choose. Maintaining equidistance is not a choice.

By one of those minor and peculiar coincidences that permanently shape and give texture to our lives, I am born on my father's twenty-eighth birthday. Two years later, exactly three days after his thirtieth and my second birthday, he is dead in the brush factory district of the Warsaw Ghetto. His corpse is buried in a courtyard and eventually the spot blends with the rest of the rubble. The Uprising, my birth, his death—all merge and become interchangeable. That is the heritage of one continent.

In one of the classes that I teach, all the students are Black and Puerto Rican. I am the only white. Initially, the students are nervous, wondering if I will be a hard task master. I am nervous too, though I do not yet have a name for it. After a few months together, we grow accustomed to each other. I am trying to understand my role here. That is the heritage of the other continent.

And now, approaching my own thirtieth birthday, approaching the moment when I will be equidistant from the two land masses, I feel some kind of cellular breakdown in my body, a sudden surging inside me, as if flesh and muscle and bone were losing definition. Everything in me yearns to become transparent, to be everywhere, to become like the water between two vast land masses that will never touch. I desire to become salt water, to establish the connection.

I am almost equidistant from two continents.

April 17, 1955. I have been asked to light one of the six candles. I stand on the stage in the large, darkened auditorium, wait to be called, wait to accept the flame, to pass it on like a memory. I am numb with terror at the spectacle around me. I fear these people with blue numbers on their arms, people who are disfigured and scarred, who have missing limbs and uneasy walks, people whose histories repel me. Here in this auditorium, they abandon all inhibitions, they transform themselves into pure sound, the sound of irretrievable loss, of wild pain and sorrow. Then they become all flesh, wringing their hands and covering their swollen eyes and flushed faces. They call out to me and I feel myself dissolving.

When it is time for me to come forward, to light the candle for those children who were burned, who were shot, who were stomped to death, I move without feeling. And as I near the candelabra, I hear them call out the common Yiddish names: *Surele. Moyshele. Channele. Rivkele. Yankele. Shayndele. Rayzl. Benyomin. Chavele. Miriam. Chaim.* The names brush against my face, invade my ears, my mouth. I breathe them into my lungs, into my bones. And as the list continues, guided by their sounds, I cross the stage and light the sixth and final candle. It is my fourteenth birthday.

I am almost equidistant from two continents.

March, 1971. There are twenty-eight people in the class. Eighteen women, ten men. Some married. Some single. Alone. With children. With parents and grandparents. Nieces. Nephews. They are here because they have not met the minimum standards of this college. This class is their special chance to catch up. Subject and verb agreement. Sentence fragments. Pronoun reference. Vocabulary building. Paragraph organization. Topic sentence. Reading comprehension. Study skills. Discipline. All this to catch up, or as one student said to me, his eyes earnest: "I want to write so that when I go for a job they won't think I'm lazy."

I am required to take attendance. I check through the names, call them out each morning: *James. Reggie. Marie. Simone. Joy. Christine. Alvarez. Ashcroft. Basile. Colon. Corbett. White. Raphael. Dennis. Juan. Carissa. Lamont. Andrea.* Fragments of their lives fall before me. The chaos and disorganization. A mother needing help in filling out forms in English. A sick child. Hospital regulations. A brother looking for a job. Another brother in trouble. Welfare red tape. Unemployment payment restrictions. Waiting lists. Eviction. SRO. The daily grind interrupting their catching-up, and the increasing sense that with each day missed, they fall further behind.

I am almost equidistant from two continents. I look back towards one, then forward towards the other. There is a need in me to become transparent like water, to become the salt water which is their only connection.

March, 1971. Marie wants to study medicine. She concedes it's a long haul, but, as she says, "It's only time. What difference does it make?" Slightly older than the others, she lives alone with her daughter. To some of the women's horror, she refuses to have a telephone, does not like to be intruded upon. When necessary, she can always be reached through a neighbor. She rarely misses class, on a few occasions brings her daughter with her who sits serenely drawing pictures. Facing Marie, I sometimes do not know who I am and wonder how she perceives me. She seems oblivious to my discomfort. She is only focused on the class, always reworking her assignments, reading everything twice, asking endless questions to make sure she really understands. One day, at the end of the hour, when we are alone, she asks: "What are you?" I am caught off guard, know the meaning of the question, but feel the resistance in me. I break it down and answer quietly: "A Jew." She nods and in that moment two vast land masses touch.

Each continent has its legacy. The day I reach my thirtieth birthday, the age of my father's death, I am equidistant from both. And as the moment passes, everything in me becomes defined again. I am once again muscle, flesh, bone. America is not my chosen home, not even the place of my birth. Just a spot where it seemed safe to go to escape certain dangers. But safety, I discover, is only temporary. No place guarantees it to anyone forever. I have stayed because there is no other place to go. In my muscles, my flesh, my bone, I balance the heritages, the histories of two continents.

## 4. Cherry Plain, 1981: I have become a keeper of accounts.

There are moments when I suddenly become breathless, as if I had just tricked someone, but was afraid the ruse would be exposed and I'd be hunted again. At those moments, the myths that propel our history, that turn fiction into fact, emerge in full force in me, as I stare into the eyes of strangers or someone suddenly grown alien. And when I see their eyes become pinpoints of judgments, become cold and indifferent, or simply distanced with curiosity, at those moments I hear again the words of the Polish woman:

*Very accurate. Just like a Jew. You are perhaps a little Jewess?*

At moments such as these I teeter, shed the present, and like rage, like pride, like acceptance, like the refusal to deny, I call upon the ancient myths again and say:

Yes. It's true. All true. I am scrupulously accurate. I keep track of all distinctions. Between past and present. Pain and pleasure. Living and surviving. Resistance and capitulation. Will and circumstances. Between life and death. Yes. I am scrupulously accurate. I have become a keeper of accounts.

Like the patriarchs, the shabby scholars who only lived for what was written and studied it all their lives

Like the inhuman usurers and dusty pawnbrokers who were quarantined within precisely prescribed limits of every European town and who were as accurate as the magistrates that drew the boundaries of their lives and declared them diseased

Like those men of stone who insisted that the *goyim* fulfil the contracts they had signed and who responded to the tearful pleas of illness, weakness, sudden calamity and poverty, with the words: "What are these to me? You have made me a keeper of accounts. Give me my pound of flesh. It says on this piece of paper, you owe me a pound of flesh!"

Like those old, heartless, dried up merchants whose entire lives were spent in the grubby *shtetl* streets that are now but memory, whose only body softness was in their fingertips worn smooth by silver coins, whose vision that all that mattered was on pieces of paper was proven absolutely accurate, when their zloty, francs, and marks could not buy off the written words *Żyd, Juif, Jude*

Like these, my despised ancestors I have become a keeper of accounts.

And like all the matriarchs, the wives and daughters, the sisters and aunts, the nieces, the keepers of button shops, milliners, seamstresses, peddlers of foul fish, of matches, of rotten apples, laundresses, midwives, floor washers and street cleaners, who rushed exhausted all week so that *shabes* could be observed with fresh *challah* on the table, who argued in the common tongue

and begged for the daughter run
off to the revolution
and the daughter run off with a
*shegetz*
who refused to sit *shiva* and say
*kaddish* for a living child
who always begged for life
who understood the accounts but
saw them differently
who knew the power of human
laws, knew they always counted
no matter what the revolution or
the party or the state
who knew the power of the words
*Żyd, Juif, Jude*

who cried whole lifetimes for their
runaway children
for the husbands immobilized by
the written word
for the brother grown callous
from usury
for the uncle grown indifferent
from crime, from bargaining,
from chiseling, from jewing them
down

Like these, my despised ancestors
I have become a keeper of
accounts.

I do not shun this legacy. I claim it as mine whenever I see the photographs of nameless people. Standing staring off the edge of the picture. People dressed in coats lined with fur. Or ragged at elbows and collar. Hats cocked on one side glancing anxiously toward the lens. A peasant cap centered and ordinary. Hair styled in the latest fashion. Or standing ashamed a coarse wig awkwardly fitted. The shabby clothes.

Buttons missing. The elegant stance. Diamond rings. Gold teeth. The hair being shaved. The face of humiliation. The hand holding the child's hand. A tree. A track. A vague building in a photograph. A facility. And then the fields of hair the endless fields of hair the earth growing fertile with their bodies with their souls.

Old rarely seen types. Gone they say forever. And yet I know they can be revived again that I can trigger them again. That they awaken in me for I have felt it happen in the sight of strangers or someone suddenly grown alien. Whenever I have seen the judgment the coldness and indifference the distanced curiosity. At those moments I teeter shed my present self and all time merges and like rage like pride like acceptance like the refusal to deny I answer

Yes. It is true. I am a keeper of accounts.

*Bashert*

## Louise Erdrich (b. 1954)

Louise Erdrich, an American poet and fiction writer of Ojibwa and German descent, quickly established herself as a major voice in contemporary letters, publishing two books of poetry and four novels in the ten-year period from 1984 to 1994. In both forms, she depicts the interwoven lives of Native Americans and European Americans in the North Dakota plains region where she grew up. Both Erdrich's Chippewa (for Ojibwa) mother and German American father taught in a Bureau of Indian Affairs school in Wahpeton, North Dakota, during her childhood. There were also regular sojourns with extended family on the Turtle Mountain Reservation, where her grandfather was head of the Tribal Council.

Erdrich is a member of the Turtle Mountain Band of Ojibwa. She grew up inhabiting the double world that she explores in her fiction and poetry. At Dartmouth College, where she earned her B.A. in 1976, she was a member of the first entering class that included women and joined the new Native American Studies Program. She received an M.A. in creative writing from Johns Hopkins University and after a number of years working as a poet in schools and in various editorial positions, she returned to Dartmouth as a writer-in-residence. There she began a literary friendship and collaboration with writer and scholar Michael Dorris, director of the Dartmouth Native American Studies Program, that evolved into marriage. Erdrich and Dorris collaborated on their individual projects, writing books individually that resulted from regular discussion and consultation. Dorris died in 1997.

Erdrich explores the lives of rural Americans seeking identity and direction through the long period from the end of the frontier days to the dislocations of the late twentieth century. More particularly, her fiction has followed the lives of several Ojibwa (or Anishinabe) families from the close of the frontier era and the confinement of Indian tribes on reservations or government allotments up to the present day, when tribes all over the country are working to establish viable businesses on their reservations. Like the southern writer William Faulkner, whom Erdrich acknowledges as an important influence, she has used the family saga as a way of capturing the history of a community. She envisions her characters' lives with fierce humor and an unblinking gaze at cruelty and pain as a way of dealing frankly with the social complexities of reservation life. In spite of the problems of unemployment, poverty, and alcoholism, Erdrich's families find ways to adapt and survive. A triumphant toughness, especially in many of the women in her fiction, holds families together. Each generation produces leaders who can cope with government regulations and help their communities to move toward economic survival.

"Saint Marie," the selection in this anthology, comes from *Love Medicine*, a collection of closely related short stories about contemporary Ojibwa and mixed-blood members of an extended family. It recounts the shocking experience of young Marie Lazarre, who seeks to prove her "whiteness" by leaving the reservation and joining a convent but receives instead a searing initiation into Christian fanaticism. By fusing fairytale motifs from the German story of Hansel and Gretel with materials from the North Dakota Chippewa and Catholic traditions, Erdrich creates an allegory of cultural assimilation. However, the story also reveals the humbling self-knowledge that comes to Marie in her confrontation with the fanatic nun, Sister Leopolda.

## *Saint Marie*

*Marie Lazarre*

So when I went there, I knew the dark fish must rise. Plumes of radiance had soldered on me. No reservation girl had ever prayed so hard. There was no use in trying to ignore me any longer. I was going up there on the hill with the black robe women. They were not any lighter than me. I was going up there to pray as good as they could. Because I don't have that much Indian blood. And they never thought they'd have a girl from this reservation as a saint they'd have to kneel to. But they'd have me. And I'd be carved in pure gold. With ruby lips. And my toenails would be little pink ocean shells, which they would have to stoop down off their high horse to kiss.

I was ignorant. I was near age fourteen. The length of sky is just about the size of my ignorance. Pure and wide. And it was just that—the pure and wideness of my ignorance—that got me up the hill to Sacred Heart Convent and brought me back down alive. For maybe Jesus did not take my bait, but them Sisters tried to cram me right down whole.

You ever see a walleye strike so bad the lure is practically out its back end before you reel it in? That is what they done with me. I don't like to make that low comparison, but I have seen a walleye do that once. And it's the same attempt as Sister Leopolda made to get me in her clutch.

I had the mail-order Catholic soul you get in a girl raised out in the bush, whose only thought is getting into town. For Sunday Mass is the only time my aunt brought us children in except for school, when we were harnessed. Our soul went cheap. We were so anxious to get there we would have walked in on our hands and knees. We just craved going to the store, slinging bottle caps in the dust, making fool eyes at each other. And of course we went to church.

Where they have the convent is on top of the highest hill, so that from its windows the Sisters can be looking into the marrow of the town. Recently a windbreak was planted before the bar "for the purposes of tornado insurance." Don't tell me that. That poplar stand was put up to hide the drinkers as they get the transformation. As they are served into the beast of their burden. While they're drinking, that body comes upon them, and then they stagger or crawl out the bar door, pulling a weight they can't move past the poplars. They don't want no holy witness to their fall.

Anyway, I climbed. That was a long-ago day. There was a road then for wagons that wound in ruts to the top of the hill where they had their buildings of painted brick. Gleaming white. So white the sun glanced off in dazzling display to set forms whirling behind your eyelids. The face of God you could hardly look at. But that day it drizzled, so I could look all I wanted. I saw the homelier side. The cracked whitewash and swallows nesting in the busted ends of eaves. I saw the boards sawed the size of broken windowpanes and the fruit trees, stripped. Only the tough wild rhubarb flourished. Goldenrod rubbed up their walls. It was a poor convent. I didn't see that then but I know that now. Compared to others it was humble, ragtag, out in the middle of no place. It was the end of the world to some. Where the maps stopped. Where God had only half a hand in the creation. Where the Dark One had put in thick bush, liquor, wild dogs, and Indians.

I heard later that the Sacred Heart Convent was a catchall place for nuns that don't get along elsewhere. Nuns that complain too much or lose their mind. I'll always wonder now, after hearing that, where they picked up Sister Leopolda. Perhaps she had scarred someone else, the way she left a mark on me. Perhaps she was just sent around to test her Sisters' faith, here and there, like the spot-checker in a factory. For she was the definite most-hard trial to anyone's endurance, even when they started out with veils of wretched love upon their eyes.

I was that girl who thought the black hem of her garment would help me rise. Veils of love which was only hate petrified by longing—that was me. I was like those bush Indians who stole the holy black hat of a Jesuit and swallowed little scraps of it to cure their fevers. But the hat itself carried smallpox and was killing them with belief. Veils of faith! I had this confidence in Leopolda. She was different. The other Sisters had long ago gone blank and given up on Satan. He slept for them. They never noticed his comings and goings. But Leopolda kept track of him and knew his habits, minds he burrowed in, deep spaces where he hid. She knew as much about him as my grandma, who called him by other names and was not afraid.

In her class, Sister Leopolda carried a long oak pole for opening high windows. It had a hook made of iron on one end that could jerk a patch of your hair out or throttle you by the collar—all from a distance. She used this deadly hook-pole for catching Satan by surprise. He could have entered without your knowing it—through your lips or your nose or any one of your seven openings—and gained your mind. But she would see him. That pole would brain you from behind. And he would gasp, dazzled, and take the first thing she offered, which was pain.

She had a stringer of children who could only breathe if she said the word. I was the worst of them. She always said the Dark One wanted me most of all, and I believed this. I stood out. Evil was a common thing I trusted. Before sleep sometimes he came and whispered conversation in the old language of the bush. I listened. He told me things he never told anyone but Indians. I was privy to both worlds of his knowledge. I listened to him, but I had confidence in Leopolda. She was the only one of the bunch he even noticed.

There came a day, though, when Leopolda turned the tide with her hook-pole.

It was a quiet day with everyone working at their desks, when I heard him. He had sneaked into the closets in the back of the room. He was scratching around, tasting crumbs in our pockets, stealing buttons, squirting his dark juice in the linings and the boots. I was the only one who heard him, and I got bold. I smiled. I glanced back and smiled and looked up at her sly to see if she had noticed. My heart jumped. For she was looking straight at me. And she sniffed. She had a big stark bony nose stuck to the front of her face for smelling out brimstone and evil thoughts. She had smelled him on me. She stood up. Tall, pale, a blackness leading into the deeper blackness of the slate wall behind her. Her oak pole had flown into her grip. She had seen me glance at the closet. Oh, she knew. She knew just where he was. I watched her watch him in her mind's eye. The whole class was watching now. She was staring, sizing, following his scuffle. And all of a sudden she tensed down, posed on her bent kneesprings, cocked her arm back. She threw the oak pole singing over my head, through my braincloud. It cracked through the thin wood door of the back closet, and the heavy pointed hook drove through his heart. I turned. She'd speared her own black rubber overboot where he'd taken refuge in the tip of her darkest toe.

Something howled in my mind. Loss and darkness. I understood. I was to suffer for my smile.

He rose up hard in my heart. I didn't blink when the pole cracked. My skull was tough. I didn't flinch when she shrieked in my ear. I only shrugged at the flowers of hell. He wanted me. More than anything he craved me. But then she did the worst. She did what broke my mind to her. She grabbed me by the collar and dragged me, feet flying, through the room and threw me in the closet with her dead black overboot. And I was there. The only light was a crack beneath the door. I asked the Dark One to enter into me and boost my mind. I asked him to restrain my tears, for they was pushing behind my eyes. But he was afraid to come back there. He was afraid of her sharp pole. And I was afraid of Leopolda's pole for the first time, too. I felt the cold hook in my heart. How it could crack through the door at any minute and drag me out, like a dead fish on a gaff, drop me on the floor like a gutshot squirrel.

I was nothing. I edged back to the wall as far as I could. I breathed the chalk dust. The hem of her full black cloak cut against my cheek. He had left me. Her spear could find me any time. Her keen ears would aim the hook into the beat of my heart.

What was that sound?

It filled the closet, filled it up until it spilled over, but I did not recognize the crying wailing voice as mine until the door cracked open, brightness, and she hoisted me to her camphor-smelling lips.

"He *wants* you," she said. "That's the difference. I give you love."

Love. The black hook. The spear singing through the mind. I saw that she had tracked the Dark One to my heart and flushed him out into the open. So now my heart was an empty nest where she could lurk.

Well, I was weak. I was weak when I let her in, but she got a foothold there. Hard to dislodge as the year passed. Sometimes I felt him—the brush of dim wings—but only rarely did his voice compel. It was between Marie and Leopolda now, and the struggle changed. I began to realize I had been on the wrong track with the fruits of hell. The real way to overcome Leopolda was this: I'd get to heaven first. And then, when I saw her coming, I'd shut the gate. She'd be out! That is why, besides the bowing and the scraping I'd be dealt, I wanted to sit on the altar as a saint.

To this end, I went up on the hill. Sister Leopolda was the consecrated nun who had sponsored me to come there.

"You're not vain," she said. "You're too honest, looking into the mirror, for that. You're not smart. You don't have the ambition to get clear. You have two choices. One, you can marry a no-good Indian, bear his brats, die like a dog. Or two, you can give yourself to God."

"I'll come up there," I said, "but not because of what you think."

I could have had any damn man on the reservation at the time. And I could have made him treat me like his own life. I looked good. And I looked white. But I wanted Sister Leopolda's heart. And here was the thing: sometimes I wanted her heart in love and admiration. Sometimes. And sometimes I wanted her heart to roast on a black stick.

She answered the back door where they had instructed me to call. I stood there with my bundle. She looked me up and down.

"All right," she said finally. "Come in."

She took my hand. Her fingers were like a bundle of broom straws, so thin and dry, but the strength of them was unnatural. I couldn't have tugged loose if she was leading me into rooms of white-hot coal. Her strength was a kind of perverse miracle, for she got it from fasting herself thin. Because of this hunger practice her lips were a wounded brown and her skin deadly pale. Her eye sockets were two deep lashless hollows in a taut skull. I told you about the nose already. It stuck out far and made the place her eyes moved even deeper, as if she stared out the wrong end of a gun barrel. She took the bundle from my hands and threw it in the corner.

"You'll be sleeping behind the stove, child."

It was immense, like a great furnace. There was a small cot close behind it.

"Looks like it could get warm there," I said.

"Hot. It does."

"Do I get a habit?"

I wanted something like the thing she wore. Flowing black cotton. Her face was strapped in white bandages, and a sharp crest of starched white cardboard hung over her forehead like a glaring beak. If possible, I wanted a bigger, longer, whiter beak than hers.

"No," she said, grinning her great skull grin. "You don't get one yet. Who knows, you might not like us. Or we might not like you."

But she had loved me, or offered me love. And she had tried to hunt the Dark One down. So I had this confidence.

"I'll inherit your keys from you," I said.

She looked at me sharply, and her grin turned strange. She hissed, taking in her breath. Then she turned to the door and took a key from her belt. It was a giant key, and it unlocked the larder where the food was stored.

Inside there was all kinds of good stuff. Things I'd tasted only once or twice in my life. I saw sticks of dried fruit, jars of orange peel, spice like cinnamon. I saw tins of crackers with ships painted on the side. I saw pickles. Jars of herring and the rind of pigs. There was cheese, a big brown block of it from the thick milk of goats. And besides that there was the everyday stuff, in great quantities, the flour and the coffee.

It was the cheese that got to me. When I saw it my stomach hollowed. My tongue dripped. I loved that goat-milk cheese better than anything I'd ever ate. I stared at it. The rich curve in the buttery cloth.

"When you inherit my keys," she said sourly, slamming the door in my face, "you can eat all you want of the priest's cheese."

Then she seemed to consider what she'd done. She looked at me. She took the key from her belt and went back, sliced a hunk off, and put it in my hand.

"If you're good you'll taste this cheese again. When I'm dead and gone," she said.

Then she dragged out the big sack of flour. When I finished that heaven stuff she told me to roll my sleeves up and begin doing God's labor. For a while we worked in silence, mixing up the dough and pounding it out on stone slabs.

"God's work," I said after a while. "If this is God's work, then I've done it all my life."

"Well, you've done it with the Devil in your heart then," she said. "Not God."

"How do you know?" I asked. But I knew she did. And I wished I had not brought up the subject.

"I see right into you like a clear glass," she said. "I always did."

"You don't know it," she continued after a while, "but he's come around here sulking. He's come around here brooding. You brought him in. He knows the smell of me, and he's going to make a last ditch try to get you back. Don't let him." She glared over at me. Her eyes were cold and lighted. "Don't let him touch you. We'll be a long time getting rid of him."

So I was careful. I was careful not to give him an inch. I said a rosary, two rosaries, three, underneath my breath. I said the Creed. I said every scrap of Latin I knew while we punched the dough with our fists. And still, I dropped the cup. It rolled under that monstrous iron stove, which was getting fired up for baking.

And she was on me. She saw he'd entered my distraction.

"Our good cup," she said. "Get it out of there, Marie."

I reached for the poker to snag it out from beneath the stove. But I had a sinking feel in my stomach as I did this. Sure enough, her long arm darted past me like a whip. The poker lighted in her hand.

"Reach," she said. "Reach with your arm for that cup. And when your flesh is hot, remember that the flames you feel are only one fraction of the heat you will feel in his hellish embrace."

She always did things this way, to teach you lessons. So I wasn't surprised. It was playacting, anyway, because a stove isn't very hot underneath right along the floor. They aren't made that way. Otherwise a wood floor would burn. So I said yes and got down on my stomach and reached under. I meant to grab it quick and jump up again, before she could think up another lesson, but here it happened. Although I groped for the cup, my hand closed on nothing. That cup was nowhere to be found. I heard her step toward me, a slow step. I heard the creak of thick shoe leather, the little *plat* as the folds of her heavy skirts met, a trickle of fine sand sifting, somewhere, perhaps in the bowels of her, and I was afraid. I tried to scramble up, but her foot came down lightly behind my ear, and I was lowered. The foot came down more firmly at the base of my neck, and I was held.

"You're like I was," she said. "He wants you very much."

"He doesn't want me no more," I said. "He had his fill. I got the cup!"

I heard the valve opening, the hissed intake of breath, and knew that I should not have spoke.

"You lie," she said. "You're cold. There is a wicked ice forming in your blood. You don't have a shred of devotion for God. Only wild cold dark lust. I know it. I know how you feel. I see the beast . . . the beast watches me out of your eyes sometimes. Cold."

The urgent scrape of metal. It took a moment to know from where. Top of the stove. Kettle. Lessons. She was steadying herself with the iron poker. I could feel it like pure certainty, driving into the wood floor. I would not remind her of pokers. I heard the water as it came, tipped from the spout, cooling as it fell but still scalding as it struck. I must have twitched beneath her foot, because she steadied me, and then the poker nudged up beside my arm as if to guide. "To warm your cold ash heart," she said. I felt how patient she would be. The water came. My mind went dead blank. Again. I could only think the kettle would be cooling slowly in her hand. I could not stand it. I bit my lip so as not to satisfy her with a sound. She gave me more reason to keep still.

"I will boil him from your mind if you make a peep," she said, "by filling up your ear."

Any sensible fool would have run back down the hill the minute Leopolda let them up from under her heel. But I was snared in her black intelligence by then. I could not think straight. I had prayed so hard I think I broke a cog in my mind. I prayed while her foot squeezed my throat. While my skin burst. I prayed even when I heard the wind come through, shrieking in the busted bird nests. I didn't stop when pure light fell, turning slowly behind my eyelids. God's face. Even that did not disrupt my continued praise. Words came. Words came from nowhere and flooded my mind.

Now I could pray much better than any one of them. Than all of them full force. This was proved. I turned to her in a daze when she let me up. My thoughts were gone, and yet I remember how surprised I was. Tears glittered in her eyes, deep down, like the sinking reflection in a well.

"It was so hard, Marie," she gasped. Her hands were shaking. The kettle clattered against the stove. "But I have used all the water up now. I think he is gone."

"I prayed," I said foolishly. "I prayed very hard."

"Yes," she said. "My dear one, I know."

We sat together quietly because we had no more words. We let the dough rise and punched it down once. She gave me a bowl of mush, unlocked the sausage from a special cupboard, and took that in to the Sisters. They sat down the hall, chewing their sausage, and I could hear them. I could hear their teeth bite through their bread and meat. I couldn't move. My shirt was dry but the cloth stuck to my back, and I couldn't think straight. I was losing the sense to understand how her mind worked. She'd gotten past me with her poker and I would never be a saint. I despaired. I felt I had no inside voice, nothing to direct me, no darkness, no Marie. I was about to throw that cornmeal mush out to the birds and make a run for it, when the vision rose up blazing in my mind.

I was rippling gold. My breasts were bare and my nipples flashed and winked. Diamonds tipped them. I could walk through panes of glass. I could walk through windows. She was at my feet, swallowing the glass after each step I took. I broke through another and another. The glass she swallowed ground and cut until her starved insides were only a subtle dust. She coughed. She coughed a cloud of dust. And then she was only a black rag that flapped off, snagged in bobwire, hung there for an age, and finally rotted into the breeze.

I saw this, mouth hanging open, gazing off into the flagged boughs of trees.

"Get up!" she cried. "Stop dreaming. It is time to bake."

Two other Sisters had come in with her, wide women with hands like paddles. They were evening and smoothing out the firebox beneath the great jaws of the oven.

"Who is this one?" they asked Leopolda. "Is she yours?"

"She is mine," said Leopolda. "A very good girl."

"What is your name?" one asked me.

"Marie."

"Marie. Star of the Sea."

"She will shine," said Leopolda, "when we have burned off the dark corrosion."

The others laughed, but uncertainly. They were mild and sturdy French, who did not understand Leopolda's twisted jokes, although they muttered respectfully at things she said. I knew they wouldn't believe what she had done with the kettle. There was no question. So I kept quiet.

"*Elle est docile,*" they said approvingly as they left to starch the linens.

"Does it pain?" Leopolda asked me as soon as they were out the door.

I did not answer. I felt sick with the hurt.

"Come along," she said.

The building was wholly quiet now. I followed her up the narrow staircase into a hall of little rooms, many doors. Her cell was the quietest, at the very end. Inside, the air smelled stale, as if the door had not been opened for years. There was a crude straw mattress, a tiny bookcase with a picture of Saint Francis hanging over it, a ragged palm, a stool for sitting on, a crucifix. She told me to remove my blouse and sit on the stool. I did so. She took a pot of salve from the bookcase and began to smooth it upon my burns. Her hands made slow, wide circles, stopping the pain. I closed my eyes. I expected to see blackness. Peace. But instead the vision reared up again. My chest was still tipped with diamonds. I was walking through windows. She was chewing up the broken litter I left behind.

"I am going," I said. "Let me go."

But she held me down.

"Don't go," she said quickly. "Don't. We have just begun."

I was weakening. My thoughts were whirling pitifully. The pain had kept me strong, and as it left me I began to forget it; I couldn't hold on. I began to wonder if she'd really scalded me with the kettle. I could not remember. To remember this seemed the most important thing in the world. But I was losing the memory. The scalding. The pouring. It began to vanish. I felt like my mind was coming off its hinge, flapping in the breeze, hanging by the hair of my own pain. I wrenched out of her grip.

"He was always in you," I said. "Even more than in me. He wanted you even more. And now he's got you. Get thee behind me!"

I shouted that, grabbed my shirt, and ran through the door throwing the cloth on my body. I got down the stairs and into the kitchen, even, but no matter what I told myself, I couldn't get out the door. It wasn't finished. And she knew I would not leave. Her quiet step was immediately behind me.

"We must take the bread from the oven now," she said.

She was pretending nothing happened. But for the first time I had gotten through some chink she'd left in her darkness. Touched some doubt. Her voice was so low and brittle it cracked off at the end of her sentence.

"Help me, Marie," she said slowly.

But I was not going to help her, even though she had calmly buttoned the back of my shirt up and put the big cloth mittens in my hands for taking out the loaves. I could have bolted for it then. But I didn't. I knew that something was nearing completion. Something was about to happen. My back was a wall of singing flame. I was turning. I watched her take the long fork in one hand, to tap the loaves. In the other hand she gripped the black poker to hook the pans.

"Help me," she said again, and I thought, Yes, this is part of it. I put the mittens on my hands and swung the door open on its hinges. The oven gaped. She stood back a moment, letting the first blast of heat rush by. I moved behind her. I could feel the heat at my front and at my back. Before, behind. My skin was turning to beaten gold. It was coming quicker than I thought. The oven was like the gate of a personal hell. Just big enough and hot enough for one person, and that was her. One kick and Leopolda would fly in headfirst. And that would be one-millionth of the heat she would feel when she finally collapsed in his hellish embrace.

Saints know these numbers.

She bent forward with her fork held out. I kicked her with all my might. She flew in. But the outstretched poker hit the back wall first, so she rebounded. The oven was not so deep as I had thought.

There was a moment when I felt a sort of thin, hot disappointment, as when a fish slips off the line. Only I was the one going to be lost. She was fearfully silent. She whirled. Her veil had cutting edges. She had the poker in one hand. In the other she held that long sharp fork she used to tap the delicate crusts of loaves. Her face turned upside down on her shoulders. Her face turned blue. But saints are used to miracles. I felt no trace of fear.

If I was going to be lost, let the diamonds cut! Let her eat ground glass!

"Bitch of Jesus Christ!" I shouted. "Kneel and beg! Lick the floor!"

That was when she stabbed me through the hand with the fork, then took the poker up alongside my head, and knocked me out.

It must have been a half an hour later when I came around. Things were so strange. So strange I can hardly tell it for delight at the remembrance. For when I came around this was actually taking place. I was being worshiped. I had somehow gained the altar of a saint.

I was lying back on the stiff couch in the Mother Superior's office. I looked around me. It was as though my deepest dream had come to life. The Sisters of the convent were kneeling to me. Sister Bonaventure. Sister Dympna. Sister Cecilia Saint-Claire. The two French with hands like paddles. They were down on their knees. Black capes were slung over some of their heads. My name was buzzing up and down the room, like a fat autumn fly lighting on the tips of their tongues between Latin, humming up the heavy blood-dark curtains, circling their little cosseted heads. Marie! Marie! A girl thrown in a closet. Who was afraid of a rubber overboot. Who was half overcome. A girl who came in the back door where they threw their garbage. Marie! Who never found the cup. Who had to eat their cold mush. Marie! Leopolda had her face buried in her knuckles. Saint Marie of the Holy Slops! Saint Marie of the Bread Fork! Saint Marie of the Burnt Back and Scalded Butt!

I broke out and laughed.

They looked up. All holy hell burst loose when they saw I'd woke. I still did not understand what was happening. They were watching, talking, but not to me.

"The marks . . ."

"She has her hand closed."

"*Je ne peux pas voir.*"

I was not stupid enough to ask what they were talking about. I couldn't tell why I was lying in white sheets. I couldn't tell why they were praying to me. But I'll tell you this: it seemed entirely natural. It was me. I lifted up my hand as in my dream. It was completely limp with sacredness.

"Peace be with you."

My arm was dried blood from the wrist down to the elbow. And it hurt. Their faces turned like flat flowers of adoration to follow that hand's movements. I let it swing through the air, imparting a saint's blessing. I had practiced. I knew exactly how to act.

They murmured. I heaved a sigh, and a golden beam of light suddenly broke through the clouded window and flooded down directly on my face. A stroke of perfect luck! They had to be convinced.

Leopolda still knelt in the back of the room. Her knuckles were crammed halfway down her throat. Let me tell you, a saint has senses honed keen as a wolf. I knew that she was over my barrel now. How it happened did not matter. The last thing I remembered was how she flew from the oven and stabbed me. That one thing was most certainly true.

"Come forward, Sister Leopolda." I gestured with my heavenly wound. Oh, it hurt. It bled when I reopened the slight heal. "Kneel beside me," I said.

She kneeled, but her voice box evidently did not work, for her mouth opened, shut, opened, but no sound came out. My throat clenched in noble delight I had read of as befitting a saint. She could not speak. But she was beaten. It was in her eyes. She stared at me now with all the deep hate of the wheel of devilish dust that rolled wild within her emptiness.

"What is it you want to tell me?" I asked. And at last she spoke.

"I have told my Sisters of your passion," she managed to choke out. "How the stigmata . . . the marks of the nails . . . appeared in your palm and you swooned at the holy vision. . . ."

"Yes," I said curiously.

And then, after a moment, I understood.

Leopolda had saved herself with her quick brain. She had witnessed a miracle. She had hid the fork and told this to the others. And of course they believed her, because they never knew how Satan came and went or where he took refuge.

"I saw it from the first," said the large one who put the bread in the oven. "Humility of the spirit. So rare in these girls."

"I saw it, too," said the other one with great satisfaction. She sighed quietly. "If only it was me."

Leopolda was kneeling bolt upright, face blazing and twitching, a barely held fountain of blasting poison.

"Christ has marked me," I agreed.

I smiled the saint's smirk into her face. And then I looked at her. That was my mistake.

For I saw her kneeling there. Leopolda with her soul like a rubber overboot. With her face of a starved rat. With the desperate eyes drowning in the deep wells of her wrongness. There would be no one else after me. And I would leave. I saw Leopolda kneeling within the shambles of her love.

My heart had been about to surge from my chest with the blackness of my joyous heat. Now it dropped. I pitied her. I pitied her. Pity twisted in my stomach like that hook-pole was driven through me. I was caught. It was a feeling more terrible than any amount of boiling water and worse than being forked. Still, still, I could not help what I did. I had already smiled in a saint's mealy forgiveness. I heard myself speaking gently.

"Receive the dispensation of my sacred blood," I whispered.

But there was no heart in it. No joy when she bent to touch the floor. No dark leaping. I fell back into the white pillows. Blank dust was whirling through the light shafts. My skin was dust. Dust my lips. Dust the dirty spoons on the ends of my feet.

Rise up! I thought. Rise up and walk! There is no limit to this dust!

# Acknowledgments


## Ancient Mesopotamia and Egypt

Anonymous, "The Courtship of Inanna and Dumuzi" and "The Descent of Inanna" translated by Samuel Noah Kramer, from Diane Wolkstein and Samuel Noah Kramer, eds., *Inanna: Queen of Heaven and Earth: Her Stories and Hymns from Sumer.* Copyright © 1983 by Diane Wolkstein and Samuel Noah Kramer. Reprinted with the permission of Diane Wolkstein and the Estate of Samuel Noah Kramer.

"The Epic of Gilgamesh" translated by N.K. Sandars from *The Epic of Gilgamesh,* Second Revised edition. Copyright © 1960, 1964, 1972 by N.K. Sandars. Reprinted with the permission of Penguin Books, Ltd.

### *Poetry of Ancient Egypt*

Pharaoh Akhnaten, "Hymn to the Sun," translated by John A. Wilson, from Thorkild Jacobsen and John A. Wilson, eds., *Most Ancient Verse* (Chicago: The Oriental Institute of the University of Chicago, 1963). Reprinted with the permission of The Oriental Institute of the University of Chicago.

Anonymous, "The Tale of the Shipwrecked Sailor," "The Debate Between a Man Tired of Life and His Soul," and "The Song of the Harper," translated by John L. Foster, from *Echoes of Egyptian Voices: An Anthology of Ancient Egyptian Poetry* (Norman: University of Oklahoma Press, 1992). Copyright © 1992 by John Lawrence Foster. Reprinted with the permission of the translator.

"The Song of the Swallow," translated by John A. Wilson, from Thorkild Jacobsen and John A. Wilson, eds., *Most Ancient Verse.* Copyright © 1963. Reprinted with the permission of The Oriental Institute of the University of Chicago.

Anonymous, "The little sycamore," "Lover excites my desire with his voice," "I passed the precinct of his house," "Seven days have passed," "Please come quick," "How well the lady knows to cast the noose," and "See what the lady has done to me!" from William Kelly Simpson, ed., *The Literature of Ancient Egypt: An Anthology of Stories, Instructions and Poetry.* Copyright © 1972 by Yale University. Reprinted with the permission of Yale University Press.

## Ancient India

Anonymous, "The Hymn of Creation," "The Hymn of Man," "Hymn to the Dawn," "A Psalm of Vasishtha," "Hymn of the Thoughts of Men," and "Hymn of Purification" from *The Hymns of the* Rig Veda, translated by Jean LeMée. Copyright © 1975 by Jean LeMée. Reprinted with the permission of Alfred A. Knopf, Inc.

Anonymous, "Chandogya Upanishad" from "The Upanishads" translated by Royal Weiler, from *Sources of Indian Tradition,* Second Edition, Volume I, edited by Ainslie T. Embree. Copyright © 1988 by Columbia University Press. Reprinted with the permission of the publishers.

From The Ramayana of Valmiki, translated by Hari Prasad Shastri: Yuddha Kanda ("Sita's Rescue and Trial"), Uttara Kanda ("Rama and Sita's Marriage"), and Uttara Kanda ("Rama Hears the Ramayana"). Copyright © 1959. Reprinted with the permission of Shanti Sadan Publishers, London.

Bhagavad Gita selections: "Arjuna's Dejection," "Philosophy and Spiritual Discipline," and "The Vision of Krishna's Totality," from The Bhagavad-Gita, translated by Barbara Stoler Miller. Copyright © 1986 by Barbara Stoler Miller. Reprinted with the permission of Bantam Books, a division of the Bantam Doubleday Dell Publishing Group, Inc.

Anonymous, "The Dharma-Door of Nonduality" from *The Holy Teaching of Vimalakirti, A Mahayana Scripture,* translated by Robert A.F. Thurman. Copyright © 1976 by The Pennsylvania State University. Reprinted with the permission of The Pennsylvania State University Press.

## Ancient China

The Book of Songs selections, translated by Arthur Waley (New York: Grove Press, 1960). Copyright 1937 by George Allen & Unwin, Ltd. Reprinted with the permission of The Arthur Waley Estate. The Book of Songs, 23: "Fields show dead deer," translated by Steven Shankman (unpublished translation). Reprinted with the permission of the translator.

Confucius analects, from *The Analects of Confucius,* edited and translated by D.C. Lau. Copyright © 1979 by D.C. Lau. Reprinted with the permission of Penguin Books, Ltd.

Laozi, "Dao de jing," translated by D.C. Lau from Tao Te Ching, edited by Sarah Allen. Copyright © 1994 by D.C. Lau. Reprinted with the permission of David Campbell Publishers, Ltd./ Everyman's Library.

Zhuangzi, "On the Equality of Things" from *Wandering on the Way: Early Taoist Tales and Parables of Chuang Tzu,* edited and translated by Victor H. Mair. Copyright © 1994 by Victor H. Mair. Reprinted with the permission of Bantam Books, a division of Bantam Doubleday Dell Publishing Group, Inc.

Mozi, "Shedding Light on Ghosts," from an unpublished translation by Laura Hess. Copyright © 1995 by Laura Hess. Reprinted with the permission of the translator.

Qu Yuan, "On Encountering Sorrow (Li sao)," from *Songs of the South,* translated by David Hawkes. Copyright © 1979 by David Hawkes. Reprinted with the permission of Penguin Books, Ltd.

### *Rhyme-Prose (Fu) of the Han Dynasty*

Sung Yu, "On the Wind," from *The Columbia Book of Chinese Poetry: From Early Times to the Thirteenth Century,* translated by Burton Watson. Copyright © 1984 by Columbia University Press. Reprinted with the permission of the publishers.

Jia Yi, "The Owl," from *The Columbia Book of Chinese Poetry: From Early Times to the Thirteenth Century,* translated by Burton Watson. Copyright © 1984 by Columbia University Press. Reprinted with the permission of the publishers.

Anonymous, "Fighting South of the Ramparts" from *The Columbia Book of Chinese Poetry: From Early Times to the Thirteenth Century.* Copyright © 1984 by Columbia University Press. Reprinted with the permission of the publishers.

Cai Yan, "Eighteen Verses Sung to a Tatar Reed Whistle," translated by Kenneth Rexroth and Ling Chung, from *Women Poets of China.* Copyright © 1972 by Kenneth Rexroth and Ling Chung. Reprinted with the permission of New Directions Publishing Corporation.

Zhang Heng, "The Bones of Chuang Tzu" from *The Temple, and Other Poems,* translated by Arthur Waley. Copyright 1923 by Alfred A. Knopf, Inc. Reprinted with the permission of Alfred A. Knopf, Inc. and The Estate of Arthur Waley.

Sima Qian, excerpt from "Postface to Records of the Historian" from *Ssu-ma Chien: Grand Historian of China,* translated and edited by Burton Watson. Copyright © 1958 by Columbia University Press. Reprinted with the permission of the publishers. "Letter to Jen An (Shao-ch'ing)," translated by John Robert Hightower, and "The Basic Annals of Xiang Yu," translated by Burton Watson, from Cyril Birch, ed., *An Anthology of Chinese Literature: From Early Times to the Fourteenth Century.* Copyright © 1965 by Grove Press, Inc. Reprinted with the permission of Grove/Atlantic, Inc. "The Meaning of Meng Tian" translated by Raymond Dawson, from *Sima Qian: Historical Records.* Copyright © 1984 by Raymond Dawson. Reprinted with the permission of Oxford University Press, Ltd.

## Ancient Greece and Rome

Hesiod, "Theogony" from *Hesiod: Theogony, Works and Days, Shield,* translated by Apostolos N. Athanassakis. Copyright © 1983 by The Johns Hopkins University Press. Reprinted with the permission of the publishers.

"To Demeter" from *The Homeric Hymns,* edited and translated by Apostolos N. Athanassakis. Copyright © 1976 by The Johns Hopkins University Press. Reprinted with the permission of the publishers.

Homer, "The Odyssey" excerpts from The Odyssey, edited and translated by Robert Fitzgerald. Copyright © 1990 by Robert Fitzgerald. Reprinted with the permission of Bantam Books, a division of Bantam Doubleday

Dell Publishing Group, Inc. The Odyssey ("The Cattle of the Sun: The Siren's Song") translated by Richmond Lattimore. Copyright © 1965, 1967 by Richmond Lattimore. Reprinted with the permission of HarperCollins Publishers, Inc.

Sappho, 1: "Bright-throned, undying Aphrodite," translated by J.V. Cunningham, from The Poems of J.V. Cunningham, edited by Timothy Steele. Copyright © 1997 by the Ohio University Press. Reprinted with the permission of Ohio University Press/Swallow Press, Athens, Ohio. 16: "To an army wife, in Sardis" and 31: "He is more than a hero," from *Sappho: Lyrics in the Original Greek,* translated by Mary Barnard. Copyright © 1958 by The Regents of the University of California, renewed 1984 by Mary Barnard. Reprinted with the permission of the University of California Press.

Pindar, "Olympian 14" from *Pindar's Victory Songs,* translated by Frank J. Nisetich. Copyright © 1980 by The Johns Hopkins University Press. Reprinted with the permission of the publishers. "Pythian 3," translated by Steven Shankman, from *La fontana* (March 1994). Copyright © 1994 by Steven Shankman. Reprinted with the permission of the translator.

Thucydides, "The Peloponnesian War," excerpts from *The Peloponnesian War: Thucydides, The Crawley Translation,* revised and with an introduction by T.E. Wick. Copyright © 1981 by Random House, Inc. Reprinted with the permission of the publishers.

Euripides, *Bacchae,* translated by William Arrowsmith, from *Complete Greek Tragedies,* Volume IV. Copyright © 1958 by The University of Chicago. Reprinted with the permission of The University of Chicago Press.

Plato, "The Apology" from *Euthyphro, Apology, Crito,* translated by F.J. Church. Copyright © 1955. Reprinted with the permission of Prentice-Hall, Inc., Upper Saddle River, NJ 07458. "The Allegory of the Cave" from *The Republic of Plato,* translated with an introduction and notes by Francis Macdonald Cornford. Copyright © 1976 by Francis Macdonald Cornford. Reprinted with the permission of Oxford University Press, Ltd.

Catullus poems: 5 ("Come Lesbia mine, let us but live and love"), 8 ("My poor Catullus, play no more the fool"), and 11 ("Aurelius and Furius, comrades sworn"), translated by Clarence W. Mendell. 51 ("That man is seen by me as a God's equal") and 85 ("I hate and love. Perhaps you're asking why I do that?") from *The Poems of Catullus,* edited and translated by Guy Lee. Copyright © 1990 by Guy Lee. Reprinted with the permission of Oxford University Press, Ltd.

Virgil, *The Aeneid* selections, translated by Robert Fitzgerald. Copyright © 1983 by Robert Fitzgerald. Reprinted with the permission of Random House, Inc.

Horace, Carmina I.11 ("Don't ask—banish the thought") and I.22 ("Dear Fuscus"), translated by Steven Shankman, from *Hellas: A Journal of Poetry and the Humanities* 7, no. 2 (Fall/ Winter 1996). Reprinted with the permission of the translator and publisher. Carmina III.30 ("My memorial is done: it will outlast bronze") and IV.2 ("Whoever labors to be Pindar's equal") from *Odes and Epodes,* translated by Joseph P. Clancy. Copyright © 1960, renewed 1988 by Joseph P. Clancy. Reprinted with the permission of The University of Chicago Press.

Ovid, "The Metamorphoses" excerpts from *The Metamorphosis of Ovid,* translated by Allen Mandelbaum. Copyright © 1993 by Allen Mandelbaum. Reprinted with the permission of Harcourt Brace and Company. "Dido to Aeneas" from *Ovid's Heroines: A Verse Translation of Heroides,* translated by Daryl Hine. Copyright © 1991 by Daryl Hine. Reprinted with the permission of Yale University Press.

Bible, The New Testament, Gospel of Mark, from the New King James Version. Copyright © 1985, 1983, 1982, 1980, 1979 by Thomas Nelson, Inc. Reprinted with the permission of the publishers.

## The Middle East of the Middle Period

Imru' al-Qays, "Mu 'allaqah"; Labid Ibn Rabia, "The Mu 'allaqah"; and Shanfara, "Lamiyyat al-'Arab" from Suzanne Pinckney Stetkevych, ed. and trans., *The Mute Immortals Speak: Pre-Islamic Poetry and the Poetics of Ritual* (Ithaca: Cornell University Press, 1993). Reprinted by permission.

Qur'an excerpts, from The Koran, translated by N.J. Dawood. Copyright © 1990 by N.J. Dawood. Reprinted with the permission of Penguin Books, Ltd.

Muhammad Ibn Ishaq, "The Life of the Prophet" from *The Life of Muhammad: A Translation of Ishaq's Sirat Rasul Allah,* translated by A. Guillaume. Copyright © 1955 by A. Guillaume. Reprinted with the permission of Oxford University Press, Ltd.

Abol-Qasem Ferdowski, "Sohrab and Rostam" from *Shahname: The Tragedy of Sohrab and Rostam,* translated by Jerome W. Clinton. Copyright © 1987 by The University of Washington Press. Reprinted with the permission of the publishers.

Farid al-Din Attar, "The Conference of the Birds" from *The Conference of the Birds,* translated by Afkham Darbandi and Dick Davis. Copyright © 1984 by Afkham Darbandi and Dick Davis. Reprinted with the permission of Penguin Books, Ltd. "The Memorial of the Saints: The Life and Teachings of Rabe 'a al-Adawiya" from *Muslim Saints and Mystics: Episodes from the Tadhkirat al-Auliya'* by Farid al-Din Attar, translated by A.J. Arberry (Chicago: The University of Chicago Press, 1966). Copyright © 1966. Reprinted with the permission of Biblioteca Persica.

Usamah Ibn Munqidh, "The Book of Reflections" ["Usamah's father and grandfather"], "An appreciation of the Frankish Character," and ["Reflections on old age"], from *An Arab-Syrian Gentleman and Warrior in the Period of the Crusades,* translated by Philip K. Hitti. Copyright © 1987 by Princeton University Press. Reprinted with the permission of the publishers.

Abu 'Abdallah Ibn Battuta, Book 1 Chapter 1, "Travels in India," "A Narrow Escape," "Travels in the Far East," and "Travels in Africa" from *The Travels of Ibn Battutah, A.D. 1325–1354,* edited and translated by H.A.R. Gibb (New York: Robert McBride, 1929). Copyright 1929 by H.A.R. Gibb. Reprinted with the permission of David Higham Associates, Ltd.

Excerpts from *The Arabian Nights: The Thousand and One Nights,* translated by Husain Haddawy. Copyright © 1990 by W. W. Norton & Company, Inc. Reprinted with the permission of the publisher.

Anonymous, "How Prince Uruz Son of Prince Kazan Was Taken Prisoner, O My Kahn!" and "How Basat Killed Goggle-Eye, O My Kahn!" from *The Book of Dede Korkut,* translated by Geoffrey Lewis. Copyright © 1974 by Geoffrey Lewis. Reprinted with the permission of Penguin Books, Ltd.

## *Arabic and Persian Poetry*

'Antara, "Make war on me, O vicissitudes of the nights," from *Arabic Poetry,* translated by A.J. Arberry. Copyright © 1965. Reprinted with the permission of Cambridge University Press.

Abu al-Ata al-Sindi, "I dreamt of you," translated by James Kritzeck, from *The Anthology of Islamic Literature: From the Rise of Islam to Modern Times,* edited by James Kritzeck. Copyright © 1964 by James Kritzeck. Reprinted with the permission of Henry Holt and Company, Inc.

Malik Ibn al-Rayb, "I thought who would weep for me, and none did I find to mourn," translated by C.J. Lyall, from *Ancient Arabic Poetry.* Copyright 1930 by Columbia University Press. Reprinted with the permission of the publishers.

Yazid Ibn al-Khadhdhaq, "I lie as though time had shot my shape with darts unawares," translated by C.J. Lyall, from *Ancient Arabic Poetry.* Copyright 1930 by Columbia University Press. Reprinted with the permission of the publishers.

Al-Khansa', "Lament for a Brother" from *Arabic and Persian Poems in English.* Copyright © 1986 by Omar Pound. Reprinted with the permission of Lynne Rienner Publishers.

Al-Khansa', "I was sleepless, and I passed the night keeping vigil" from *Arabic Poetry,* translated by A.J. Arberry. Copyright © 1965. Reprinted with the permission of Cambridge University Press.

Al-Farazdak, "A woman free of the desert born" from *Classical Arabic Poetry: 162 Poems from Imrulkais to Ma'arri,* edited and translated by Charles G. Tuetey. Copyright © 1985 by Charles G. Tuetey. Reprinted with the permission of Kegan Paul International.

Bashshar Ibn Burd, "I was blind from the womb, and from blindness insight came" and "Modest my choice of 'Abda, the girl I love" from *Classical Arabic Poetry: 162 Poems from Imrulkais to Ma'arri,* edited and translated by Charles G. Tuetey. Copyright © 1985. Reprinted with the permission of Routledge.

Abu Nuwas, "The man burdened with passion is a weary man" from *Arabic Poetry,* translated by A.J. Arberry. Copyright © 1965. Reprinted with the permission of Cambridge University Press.

Abu Nuwas, "I said as the peach came ambling by" and "Many's the noble face laid waste" from *Classical Arabic Poetry: 162 Poems from Imrulkais to Ma'arri,* edited and translated by Charles G. Tuetey. Copyright © 1985. Reprinted with the permission of Routledge.

al-Ma'arri, "Souls stretching out their necks towards the resurrection" from *Arabic Poetry,* translated by A.J. Arberry. Copyright © 1965. Reprinted with the permission of Cambridge University Press.

Ibn Hazm, "I love you with a love that knows no waning," "Are you from the world of the angels, or are you mortal?," "I enjoy conversation when, in it, he is mentioned to me," "Having seen the hoariness on my temples and sideburns," and "They said 'He is far away.' I replied: 'it is enough'" from *Hispano-Arabic Poetry,* edited and translated by James T. Monroe. Copyright © 1974 by The Regents of the University of California. Reprinted with the permission of University of California Press.

Ibn Zaidun, "Two fragments," translated by Harold Morland, from *Arabic-Andalusian Casidas* (London: Phoenix Press, 1949). Copyright 1949 by Phoenix Press. Reprinted with the permission of the translator. "The Nuniyya for Wallada," from *Hispano-Arabic Poetry,* edited and translated by James T. Monroe. Copyright © 1974 by The Regents of the University of California Press. Reprinted with the permission of the University of California Press.

Ibn Quzman, "My life is spent in dissipation and wantonness" from *Hispano-Arabic Poetry,* edited and translated by James T. Monroe. Copyright © 1974 by The Regents of the University of California. Reprinted with the permission of the University of California Press.

Jeluluddin Rumi, "When you display that rosy cheek, you set the stones a-spinning for joy," "We have become drunk and our heart has departed, it has fled from us," "On the day of death, when my bier is on the move, do not suppose," "Love took away sleep from me—and love takes away sleep," and "Henceforward the nightingale in the garden will tell of us" from *Mystical Poems of Rumi,* translated by A.J. Arberry. Copyright © 1965. Reprinted with the permission of The University of Chicago Press.

Shams al-din Hafiz of Shiraz, "All My Pleasure" and "The Times Are Out of Joint" from *Fifty Poems of Hafiz,* edited and translated by A.J. Arberry. Copyright 1947. Reprinted with the permission of Cambridge University Press.

## India in the Middle Period

Kalidasa, "Sakuntala and the Ring of Recollection" from *Theater of Memory: The Plays of Kalidasa,* translated by Barbara Stoler Miller. Copyright © 1984 by Columbia University Press. Reprinted with the permission of the publishers.

Vidyakara, selected poems from *Sanskrit Poetry from Vidyakara's "Treasury,"* translated by Daniel H.H. Ingalls. Copyright © 1965, 1968 by the President and Fellows of Harvard College. Reprinted with the permission of Harvard University Press.

### *Two Bhakti Poets*

Ravidās, selected poems from *Songs of the Saints of India,* translated by J.S. Hawley and Mark Juergensmeyer. Copyright © 1988 by Oxford University Press, Inc. Reprinted with the permission of the publishers.

Mīrābāī poems, translated by John Stratton Hawley and Mark Juergensmeyer, from *Songs of the Saints of India.* Copyright © 1988 by Oxford University Press, Inc. Reprinted with the permission of the publishers.

## China of the Middle Period

Tao Qian, selected poems from *The Poetry of T'ao Ch'ien,* edited and translated by James Robert Hightower. Copyright © 1970 by James Robert Hightower. Reprinted with the permission of Oxford University Press, Ltd.

Anonymous, "The Lotus Sutra," Chapter 4 (406), from *The Lotus Sutra,* translated by Burton Watson. Copyright © 1993 by Columbia University Press. Reprinted with the permission of the publishers.

### *Four Tang Poets*

Wang Wei, selected poems from *Laughing Lost in the Mountains: Poems of Wang Wei,* translated by Tony Barnstone, Willis Barnstone, and Xu Haixin. Copyright © 1991 by University Press of New England. Reprinted with the permission of the publishers.

Li Bai, "Drinking Alone by Moonlight," "In the Mountains on a Summer Day," "To Tan Ch'iu," "Clearing at Dawn" from *More Translations from the Chinese,* edited and translated by Arthur Waley. Copyright 1919 by Alfred A. Knopf, Inc., renewed 1947 by Arthur Waley. Reprinted with the permission of The Estate of Arthur Waley.

Li Bai, "You asked me what my reason is," "When Chang Chou dreamed he was a butterfly," and "Fighting South of the Ramparts" from *The Poetry and Career of Li Po,* edited and translated by Arthur Waley (New York: The Macmillan Company, 1950). Copyright 1950 by Arthur Waley. Reprinted with the permission of The Estate of Arthur Waley.

Du Fu, "Autumn Meditations" from *Poems of the Late T'ang,* edited and translated by A.C. Graham. Copyright © 1965 by A.C. Graham. Reprinted with the permission of Penguin Books, Ltd.

Bai Juyi, "A Song of Unending Sorrow" from *The Jade Mountain: A Chinese Anthology,* translated by Witter Bynner. Copyright 1929 by Alfred A. Knopf, Inc., renewed © 1957 by Witter Bynner. Reprinted with the permission of Alfred A. Knopf, Inc.

Bai Juyi, "Having Climbed to the Topmost Peak of the Incense-Burner Mountain" and "Madly Singing in the Mountains" from *One Hundred and Seventy Chinese Poems,* edited and translated by Arthur Waley. Copyright 1919 by Alfred A. Knopf, Inc., renewed 1947 by Arthur Waley. Reprinted with the permission of Constable Publishers, Ltd.

Yuan Zhen, "The Story of Ying-ying," translated by James R. Hightower, from *Traditional Chinese Stories: Themes and Variations,* edited by Joseph S.M. Lau and Y.W. Ma. Copyright © 1978 by Columbia University Press. Reprinted with the permission of the publishers.

### *Two Song Poets*

Su Dongpo, "New Year's Eve II," "Ten Years—Dead and Living Dim and Draw Apart," "Lotus Viewing," "Who Says a Painting Must Look Like Life?," "Drinking Wine," "Long Ago I Lived in the Country," and "White Crane Hill" from *Su Tung-P'o: Selections from a Sung Dynasty Poet,* edited and translated by Burton Watson. Copyright © 1965 by Columbia University Press. Reprinted with the permission of the publishers.

Li Qingzhao, "Joy of Wine," "The Beauty of White Chrysanthemums," "Thoughts from the Women's Quarter," "A Morning Dream," and "On Plum Blossoms" from *Li Ch'ing-Chao: Complete Poems,* edited and translated by Ling Chung and Kenneth Rexroth. Copyright © 1979 by Kenneth Rexroth and Ling Chung. Reprinted with the permission of New Directions Publishing Corporation.

Wu Ch'eng, excerpts from *Monkey,* translated by Arthur Waley. Copyright 1943 by John Day and Company. Reprinted with the permission of Grove/Atlantic, Inc.

### Japan in the Middle Period

Hitomarō, excerpts from *Manyōshū* (Book I.38–39: "Imperial Procession" and Book II.135–137: "Lament on Leaving His Wife"), from *The Ten Thousand Leaves: A Translation of the Man'yoshu, Japan's Premier Anthology of Classic Poetry,* Volume 1, translated by Ian Hideo Levy. Copyright © 1981 by Princeton University Press. Reprinted with the permission of the University of Tokyo Press.

Ōtomo Tabito, excerpt from "Manyōshū" (Book III.338–343: "Poems in Praise of Wine"), from *The Ten Thousand Leaves: A Translation of the Man'yoshu, Japan's Premier Anthology of Classic Poetry,* Volume 1, translated by Ian Hideo Levy. Copyright © 1981 by Princeton University Press. Reprinted with the permission of the publishers.

Yamanoue Okura, excerpt from "Manyōshū" (Book V.892–893: "Dialog of the Destitute") from *The Ten Thousand Leaves: A Translation of the Man'yoshu, Japan's Premier Anthology of Classic Poetry,* Volume 1, translated by Ian Hideo Levy. Copyright © 1981 by Princeton University Press. Reprinted with the permission of the publishers.

Anonymous, excerpts from *Manyōshū* (Book XVI.3459: "My hands so chapped from rice-pounding" and Book XIX.4290–4291: "Over the spring field trails the mist"), from *The Man-yōshū: The Nippon Gakujutsu Shinkokai Translation of One Thousand Poems,* translated by Donald Keene. Copyright © 1965. Reprinted with the permission of Japanese Society for the Promotion of Science.

### Japanese Court Poetry

Ono no Komachi, "Find mutability" and "On such a night as this" from *Japanese Court Poetry* by Robert H. Brower and Earl Miner. Copyright © 1961 by the Board of Trustees of the Leland Stanford Junior University. Reprinted with the permission of Stanford University Press.

Shrine Priestess, "My mind is dazzled" from *Japanese Court Poetry* by Robert H. Brower and Earl Miner. Copyright © 1961 by the Board of Trustees of the Leland Stanford Junior University. Reprinted with the permission of Stanford University Press.

Ki no Tsurayuki, "What now is real?," "As pressed by love," and "To us remote observers" from *Japanese Court Poetry* by Robert H. Brower and Earl Miner. Copyright © 1961 by the Board of Trustees of the Leland Stanford Junior University. Reprinted with the permission of Stanford University Press.

Anonymous, "Dimly, dimly" from *Japanese Court Poetry* by Robert H. Brower and Earl Miner. Copyright © 1961 by the Board of Trustees of the Leland Stanford Junior University. Reprinted with the permission of Stanford University Press.

Fujiwara Shunzei, "I recollect the past," "As evening falls," "As evening falls," and "He who hears them" from *Japanese Court Poetry* by Robert H. Brower and Earl Miner. Copyright © 1961 by the Board of Trustees of the Leland Stanford Junior University. Reprinted with the permission of Stanford University Press.

Ariwara Narihira, "I am at one with spring" and "Though formerly I heard" from *Japanese Court Poetry* by Robert H. Brower and Earl Miner. Copyright © 1961 by the Board of Trustees of the Leland Stanford Junior University. Reprinted with the permission of Stanford University Press.

Yoshitada, "On such a night" from *Japanese Court Poetry* by Robert H. Brower and Earl Miner. Copyright © 1961 by the Board of Trustees of the Leland Stanford Junior University. Reprinted with the permission of Stanford University Press.

Nōin, "As now I come" from *Japanese Court Poetry* by Robert H. Brower and Earl Miner. Copyright © 1961 by the Board of Trustees of the Leland Stanford Junior University. Reprinted with the permission of Stanford University Press.

Ryōzen, "In my loneliness" from *Japanese Court Poetry* by Robert H. Brower and Earl Miner. Copyright © 1961 by the Board of Trustees of the Leland Stanford Junior University. Reprinted with the permission of Stanford University Press.

Jakuren, "Loneliness" from *Japanese Court Poetry* by Robert H. Brower and Earl Miner. Copyright © 1961 by the Board of Trustees of the Leland Stanford Junior University. Reprinted with the permission of Stanford University Press.

Fujiwara Teika, "Although I heard," "The bridge of dreams," "There is no shelter," "The path of him I long for," "I gaze afar," and "Yesterday, today" from *Japanese Court Poetry* by Robert H. Brower and Earl Miner. Copyright © 1961 by the Board of Trustees of the Leland Stanford Junior University. Reprinted with the permission of Stanford University Press.

Shunzei's daughter, "The wind breathes softly" from *Japanese Court Poetry* by Robert H. Brower and Earl Miner. Copyright © 1961 by the Board of Trustees of the Leland Stanford Junior University. Reprinted with the permission of Stanford University Press.

Ex-Emperor Fushimi, "On the Topic, 'The Three Dogmas Are Not One Dogma'" from *Japanese Court Poetry* by Robert H. Brower and Earl Miner. Copyright © 1961 by the Board of Trustees of the Leland Stanford Junior University. Reprinted with the permission of Stanford University Press.

Fujiwara Norikane, "Dawn has not broken" from *Japanese Court Poetry* by Robert H. Brower and Earl Miner. Copyright © 1961 by the Board of Trustees of the Leland Stanford Junior University. Reprinted with the permission of Stanford University Press.

Ex-Emperor Takakura, "The Crowing Cock" from *Japanese Court Poetry* by Robert H. Brower and Earl Miner. Copyright © 1961 by the Board of Trustees of the Leland Stanford Junior University. Reprinted with the permission of Stanford University Press.

Fujiwara Ietsune, "In the Mountains" from *Japanese Court Poetry* by Robert H. Brower and Earl Miner. Copyright © 1961 by the Board of Trustees of the Leland Stanford Junior University. Reprinted with the permission of Stanford University Press.

Fujiwara Kunifusa, "Was it not enough" from *Japanese Court Poetry* by Robert H. Brower and

Earl Miner. Copyright © 1961 by the Board of Trustees of the Leland Stanford Junior University. Reprinted with the permission of Stanford University Press.

Fujiwara Ariie, "Beneath the piling snow" from *Japanese Court Poetry* by Robert H. Brower and Earl Miner. Copyright © 1961 by the Board of Trustees of the Leland Stanford Junior University. Reprinted with the permission of Stanford University Press.

Izumi Shikibu, "As I fall in sadness" and "Lying down alone" from *Japanese Court Poetry* by Robert H. Brower and Earl Miner. Copyright © 1961 by the Board of Trustees of the Leland Stanford Junior University. Reprinted with the permission of Stanford University Press.

Ex-Emperor Hanazono, "The sun at dusk" from *Japanese Court Poetry* by Robert H. Brower and Earl Miner. Copyright © 1961 by the Board of Trustees of the Leland Stanford Junior University. Reprinted with the permission of Stanford University Press.

Mitsune, "With the autumn wind" from *Japanese Court Poetry* by Robert H. Brower and Earl Miner. Copyright © 1961 by the Board of Trustees of the Leland Stanford Junior University. Reprinted with the permission of Stanford University Press.

Lady Jusammi Chikako, "Wide across the moors" and "Sunken my love" from *Japanese Court Poetry* by Robert H. Brower and Earl Miner. Copyright © 1961 by the Board of Trustees of the Leland Stanford Junior University. Reprinted with the permission of Stanford University Press.

Fujiwara Kimikage, "Was it a previous life" and "Although her heart" from *Japanese Court Poetry* by Robert H. Brower and Earl Miner. Copyright © 1961 by the Board of Trustees of the Leland Stanford Junior University. Reprinted with the permission of Stanford University Press.

Nijo Yoshimoto, "It must not be known" from *Japanese Court Poetry* by Robert H. Brower and Earl Miner. Copyright © 1961 by the Board of Trustees of the Leland Stanford Junior University. Reprinted with the permission of Stanford University Press.

Fujiwara Norinaga, "For a slight moment" from *Japanese Court Poetry* by Robert H. Brower and Earl Miner. Copyright © 1961 by the Board of Trustees of the Leland Stanford Junior University. Reprinted with the permission of Stanford University Press.

Emperor Go-Daigo, "Despite my efforts" from *Japanese Court Poetry* by Robert H. Brower and Earl Miner. Copyright © 1961 by the Board of Trustees of the Leland Stanford Junior University. Reprinted with the permission of Stanford University Press.

Emperor Komyo, "How strange it is" from *Japanese Court Poetry* by Robert H. Brower and Earl Miner. Copyright © 1961 by the Board of Trustees of the Leland Stanford Junior University. Reprinted with the permission of Stanford University Press.

Lady Reizei, "Because of feelings" from *Japanese Court Poetry* by Robert H. Brower and Earl Miner. Copyright © 1961 by the Board of Trustees of the Leland Stanford Junior University. Reprinted with the permission of Stanford University Press.

Lady Daini Sammi, "Since this love of mine" from *Japanese Court Poetry* by Robert H. Brower and Earl Miner. Copyright © 1961 by the Board of Trustees of the Leland Stanford Junior University. Reprinted with the permission of Stanford University Press.

Fujiwara Ietaka, "You are as remote" from *Japanese Court Poetry* by Robert H. Brower and Earl Miner. Copyright © 1961 by the Board of Trustees of the Leland Stanford Junior University. Reprinted with the permission of Stanford University Press.

Kyogoku Tamekane, "Though now I love" from *Japanese Court Poetry* by Robert H. Brower and Earl Miner. Copyright © 1961 by the Board of Trustees of the Leland Stanford Junior University. Reprinted with the permission of Stanford University Press.

Izumi Shikibu, "The Diary of Izumi Shikibu" from *The Izumi Shikibu Diary: A Romance of the Heian Court,* translated by Edwin A. Cranston. Copyright © 1969 by the Harvard-Yenching Institute. Reprinted with the permission of Harvard University Press.

Murasaki Shikibu, "The Paulownia Court" and "Evening Faces" from *The Tale of the Genji,* translated by Edward Seidensticker. Copyright © 1976 by Edward G. Seidensticker. Reprinted with the permission of Alfred A. Knopf, Inc.

Kamo no Chōmei, "An Account of My Hermitage" from *Classical Japanese Prose: An Anthology,* translated by Helen Craig McCullough. Copyright © 1990 by the Board of Trustees of the Leland Stanford Junior University. Reprinted with the permission of Stanford University Press.

Anonymous, "The Story of Giō," "The Story of Koremori," "The Story of Koremori, continued," and "The Initiate's Chapter: The Story of Lady Kenreimon'in" from *Genji and Heike: Selections,* translated by Helen Craig McCullough. Originally published as *The Tale of the Heike,* translated by Helen Craig McCullough. Copyright © 1988 by the Board of Trustees of the Leland Stanford Junior University. Reprinted with the permission of Stanford University Press.

Nō Theatre, *Atsumori* from *Japanese Nō Dramas,* edited and translated by Royall Tyler. Copyright © 1992 by Reprinted with the permission of Penguin Books, Ltd.

Nō Theatre, *Aoi no Ue,* translated by Steven T. Brown as part of the dissertation *Staying Contingency: The Historicity of Chance in Greek Tragedy and Japanese Noh Drama* (Stanford University, 1994). Copyright © 1994 by Steven T. Brown. Reprinted with the permission of the translator.

## Korea in the Middle Period

Siro, "Ode to Knight Chukchi," translated by Peter H. Lee, from *Anthology of Korean Literature: From Early Times to the Nineteenth Century,* edited by Peter H. Lee. Copyright © 1981 by The University Press of Hawaii. Reprinted with the permission of the publishers.

Sinch'ung, "Regret," translated by Peter H. Lee, from *Anthology of Korean Literature: From Early Times to the Nineteenth Century,* edited by Peter H. Lee. Copyright © 1981 by The University Press of Hawaii. Reprinted with the permission of the publisher.

Master Wolmyong, "Requiem," translated by Peter H. Lee, from *Anthology of Korean Literature: From Early Times to the Nineteenth Century,* edited by Peter H. Lee. Copyright © 1981 by The University Press of Hawaii. Reprinted with the permission of the publisher.

Great Master Kyunyo, "Devotional Poems," translated by Peter H. Lee, from *Anthology of Korean Literature: From Early Times to the Nineteenth Century,* edited by Peter H. Lee. Copyright © 1981 by The University Press of Hawaii. Reprinted with the permission of the publisher.

Cho'oe Ch'i-Won, "At the Ugang Station," "In Autumn Rain," and "Night Rain in a Postal Station," translated by Peter H. Lee, from *Anthology of Korean Literature: From Early Times to the Nineteenth Century,* edited by Peter H. Lee. Copyright © 1981 by The University Press of Hawaii. Reprinted with the permission of the publisher.

Anonymous, "Songs of the Flying Dragon," translated by Peter H. Lee, from *Anthology of Korean Literature: From Early Times to the Nineteenth Century,* edited by Peter H. Lee. Copyright © 1981 by The University Press of Hawaii. Reprinted with the permission of the publisher.

Hwang Chin-I, "I will break the back of this long, midwinter night," translated by David R. McCann; "Do not boast of your speed," "Mountains are steadfast but the mountain streams," and "Blue mountains speak of my desire," translated by Peter H. Lee from *Anthology of Korean Literature: From Early Times to the Nineteenth Century,* edited by Peter H. Lee. Copyright © 1981 by The University Press of Hawaii. Reprinted with the permission of the publisher.

Ho Nonshorhon, "A Woman's Sorrow," translated by Peter H. Lee, from *Anthology of Korean Literature: From Early Times to the Nineteenth Century,* edited by Peter H. Lee. Copyright © 1981 by The University Press of Hawaii. Reprinted with the permission of the publisher.

## Europe in the Middle Period

### *The Latin Tradition*

Saint Augustine, excerpts from *The Confessions,* translated by R.S. Pine-Coffin. Copyright © 1961 by R.S. Pine-Coffin. Reprinted with the permission of Penguin Books, Ltd.

Bede, excerpts from *The Ecclesiastical History of the English People,* translated by Bertram Colgrave. Copyright © 1969 by Bertram Colgrave. Reprinted with the permission of Oxford University Press, Ltd.

Abelard and Heloise, "The History of My Misfortunes" and excerpts from "Letters"

(1 and 3) from *The Letters of Abelard and Heloise,* edited and translated by Betty Radice. Copyright © 1974 by Betty Radice. Reprinted with the permission of Penguin Books, Ltd.

Thomas More, excerpts from *Utopia: A Norton Critical Edition,* Second Edition, edited and translated by Robert Adams. Copyright © 1992, 1975 by W.W. Norton & Company, Inc. Reprinted with the permission of the publishers.

### *The Germanic Tradition*

Anonymous, "The Lay of Gudrun" from *Poems of the Elder Edda.* Copyright © 1990 by the University of Pennsylvania Press. Reprinted with the permission of the publisher.

Snorri Sturluson, "The Ring of the Volsungs" from *The Prose Edda of Snorri Sturluson: Tales from Norse Mythology,* translated by Jean I. Young. Copyright © 1964 by The Regents of the University of California. Reprinted with the permission of the University of California Press.

### *Provençal Poetry: The Romance Tradition*

Arnaut Daniel, "To this sweet and pretty air" from *Lyrics of the Troubadours and Trouveres,* edited and translated by Frederick Goldin. Copyright © 1973 by Frederick Goldin. Reprinted with the permission of Doubleday, a division of the Bantam Doubleday Dell Publishing Group, Inc.

Bertran de Born, "I love the joyful time of Easter" from *Lyrics of the Troubadours and Trouveres,* edited and translated by Frederick Goldin. Copyright © 1973 by Frederick Goldin. Reprinted with the permission of Doubleday, a division of the Bantam Doubleday Dell Publishing Group, Inc.

Countess Beatriz de Die, "Lately I've felt a grave concern," translated by Willis Barnstone, from *A Book of Women Poets from Antiquity to Now,* edited by Aliki and Willis Barnstone. Copyright © 1980 by Aliki and Willis Barnstone. Reprinted with the permission of Schocken Books.

Marie de France, excerpts from "Lais" ("Prologue," "Yonec," "Chevrefoil") from *The Lais of Marie de France,* edited and translated by Robert Hanning and Joan Ferrante. Reprinted with the permission of The Labyrinth Press.

Anonymous, "Quia Amore Langueo" and "The Corpus Christi Carol" from *German and Italian Lyrics of the Middle Ages,* translated by Frederick Goldin. Copyright © 1973 by Frederick Goldin. Reprinted with the permission of Doubleday, a division of the Bantam Doubleday Dell Publishing Group, Inc.

Guido Cavalcanti, "The Canzone" ["Donna me priegha"], translated by Ezra Pound, from *Ezra Pound, Selected Poems.* Copyright © 1957 by Ezra Pound. Reprinted with the permission of New Directions Publishing Corporation.

Marco Polo, "The Road to Cathay" from *The Travels of Marco Polo,* edited and translated by Ronald Latham. Copyright © 1958 by Ronald Latham. Reprinted with the permission of Penguin Books, Ltd.

Dante Alighieri, excerpts from "The Divine Comedy" (Inferno: Cantos I–V, X, XXVI, XXXIII–XXXIV) from *The Inferno of Dante,* translated by Robert Pinky. Copyright © 1994 by Robert Pinky. Reprinted with the permission of Farrar, Straus & Giroux, Inc.

Francis Petrarch, excerpts from "Rime" translated by Mark Musa, from *The Italian Renaissance Reader,* edited by Julia Conway Bondanella and Mark Musa. Copyright © 1987 by Julia Conway Bondanella and Mark Musa. Reprinted with the permission of Penguin Putnam Inc.

Geoffrey Chaucer, "General Prologue" ("Introduction," "The Pardoner") and "The Pardoner's Prologue and Tale" from *Geoffrey Chaucer, The Canterbury Tales: Nine Tales and the General Prologue: A Norton Critical Edition,* edited and translated by V.A. Kolve and Glending Olson. Copyright © 1989 by W.W. Norton & Co., Inc. Reprinted with the permission of the publishers.

Christine de Pizan, "The Building of the City of Ladies" and "The Stories of Dido and Saint Christine" from *The Book of the City of Ladies,* translated by Earl J. Richards. Copyright © 1982 by Persea Books. Reprinted with the permission of the publishers.

Michel de Montaigne, "Of Cannibals" from *The Complete Essays of Montaigne,* translated by Donald Frame. Copyright © 1958 by the Board of Trustees of the Leland Stanford Junior University, renewed 1986 by Donald M. Frame. Reprinted with the permission of Stanford University Press.

William Shakespeare, "King Lear" from *The Riverside Shakespeare,* edited by G. Blakemore Evans. Copyright © 1974 by Houghton Mifflin

Company. Reprinted with the permission of the publishers. All rights reserved.

Miguel de Cervantes, excerpts from "Don Quixote" from *The Portable Cervantes,* edited and translated by Samuel Putnam. Copyright 1949, 1950, 1951 by Samuel Putnam. Reprinted with the permission of Penguin Putnam Inc.

## The Modern Middle East and Africa

Naguib Mahfouz, "Zaabalawi," translated by Denys Johnson-Davies, from *Modern Arabic Short Stories.* Copyright © 1967 by Denys Johnson-Davies. Reprinted with the permission of Lynne Rienner Publishers.

Salwa Bakr, "That Beautiful Undiscovered Voice" from *The Wiles of Men and Other Stories,* translated by Denys Johnson-Davies. Copyright © 1992 by Denys Johnson-Davies. Reprinted with the permission of Quartet Books Limited.

### *Palestine*

Fadwa Tuqan, "In the Aging City," "In the Flux," "Face Lost in the Wilderness," and "I Found It," translated by Patricia Alahan Byrne with the help of Salma Khadra, and from Naomi Shahib Nye, from *Selected Poems,* edited by Salma Khadra. Reprinted with permission.

### *Israel*

Yehuda Amichai, "Jerusalem, 1967" and "Tourists," translated by Chana Block and Stephen Mitchell, from *The Selected Poetry of Yehuda Amichai,* Newly Revised and Expanded Edition. Copyright © 1986 by Chana Block and Stephen Mitchell. Copyright © 1996 by The Regents of the University of California. Reprinted with the permission of the University of California Press.

### *Senegal*

Léopold Sédar Senghor, "Nuit de Sine," "Black Woman," "Prayer to Maska," and "The Return of the Prodigal Son" from *Selected Poems,* translated by John Reed and Clive Wake. Reprinted with the permission of The University Press of Virginia.

### *Kenya*

Grace Ogot, "The Bamboo Hut" from *Land Without Thunder.* Copyright © 1968. Reprinted with the permission of East African Educational Publishers.

### *Nigeria*

Chinua Achebe, excerpts from *Things Fall Apart.* Copyright © 1958 by Chinua Achebe. Reprinted with the permission of Heinemann Educational Publishers, a division of Reed Educational & Professional Publishing, Ltd.

Wole Soyinka, "A Scourge of Hyacinths" from *From Zia, With Love.* Copyright © 1992 by Wole Soyinka. Reprinted with the permission of Methuen.

## Modern India and Southeast Asia

### *India*

Rajee Seth, "Just a Simple Bridge," translated by Jai Ratan, from *Separate Journeys: Short Stories by Indian Women Writers,* edited by Geeta Dhamarajan. Copyright © 1993. Reprinted with the permission of Mantra Publishing, Ltd.

Salman Rushdie, "The Courter" from *East West.* Copyright © 1994 by Salman Rushdie. Reprinted with the permission of Pantheon Books, a division of Random House, Inc.

### *Thailand*

Angkarn Kalayaanaphong, "Grandma," from *Modern Thai Literature, Within an Ethnographic Interpretation,* edited by Herbert P. Phillips. Originally from Sangkhomsaat Parithat 3, no. 4 (1966). Reprinted with the permission of the University of Hawaii Press.

### *Vietnam*

Nguyen Huy Thiep, "Salt of the Jungle," translated by Greg Lockhart, from *The General Retires and Other Stories.* Copyright © 1992 by Greg Lockhart. Reprinted with the permission of Oxford University Press, South-East Asia Publishing Unit.

## Modern China

Cao Xueqin, excerpts from *The Story of the Stone: A Chinese Novel by Cao Xueqin in Five Volumes,* translated by David Hawkes and John Minford. Copyright © 1977 by David Hawkes. Copyright © 1982 by John Minford. Reprinted with the permission of Penguin Books, Ltd.

Shen Fu, excerpt from *Six Records of a Floating Life* (Second Record: "The Pleasures of Leisure"), translated by Leonard Pratt and Chiang Su-hui. Copyright © 1983 by Leonard Pratt and Chiang Su-hui. Reprinted with the permission of Penguin Books, Ltd.

Lu Xun, "Ah Q—The Real Story" from *Diary of a Madman and Other Stories,* translated by William A. Lyell. Copyright © 1990 by the University of Hawaii Press. Reprinted with the permission of the publishers.

Ding Ling, "When I Was in Xia Village," translated by Gary J. Bjorge, from *I Myself Am a Woman: Selected Writings of Ding Ling,* edited by Tani E. Barlow. Copyright © 1989 by Beacon Press. Reprinted with the permission of the publishers.

## Modern Japan

Matsuo Bashō, excerpt from *Narrow Road,* translated by Hiroaki Sato. Copyright © 1996 by Hiroaki Sato. Reprinted with the permission of Stone Bridge Press.

Natsume Sōseki, excerpt from *The Wayfarer,* translated by Beongcheon Yu. Copyright © 1967. Reprinted with the permission of Wayne State University Press.

Kawabata Yasunari, "The Pomegranate" and "Ceres," translated by Edward Seidensticker, from *Contemporary Japanese Literature: An Anthology of Fiction, Film, and Other Writing Since 1945,* edited by Howard Hibbett. Copyright © 1977 by Edward Seidensticker. Reprinted with the permission of Alfred A. Knopf, Inc.

Kawabata Yasunari, "Snow" from Palm-of-the-Hand Stories, translated by Lane Dunlop and J. Martin Holman. Copyright © 1988. Reprinted with the permission of North Point Press, a division of Farrar, Straus & Giroux, Inc.

Abe Kōbō, "Stick" and "Red Cocoon," translated by John Nathan, from *New Writing in Japan,* edited by Yukio Mishima and Geoffrey Bownas. Copyright © 1972 by John Nathan. Reprinted with the permission of Penguin Books, Ltd.

Ōba Minako, "The Three Crabs," translated by Stephen Kohl and Toyama Ryōko, from *Japan Quarterly* 25, no. 3 (July–September 1978). Reprinted with the permission of Japan Quarterly, Asahi Shimbun Publishing Co., Tokyo.

## Modern Korea

Sonu Hwi, "Thoughts of Home," translated by Marshall R. Pihl, from *Modern Korean Literature,* edited by Peter H. Lee. Copyright © 1990 by the University of Hawaii Press. Reprinted with the permission of the publishers.

## Modern Europe

### *England and Ireland*

John Milton, excerpts from "Paradise Lost" (Books I, III, IV, IX and XII) from *Paradise Lost: A Norton Critical Edition,* Second Edition, edited by Scott Elledge. Copyright © 1993, 1975 by W.W. Norton & Company, Inc. Reprinted with the permission of the publishers.

Alexander Pope, "Eloisa to Abelard" from *The Poetry and Prose of Alexander Pope,* edited by Aubrey Williams (Boston: Houghton Mifflin Company, 1969). Copyright © 1969 by Aubrey Williams. Reprinted with the permission of the editor.

James Joyce, "Calypso" from *Ulysses: The Corrected Text,* edited by Hans Walter Gabler. Copyright © 1986 by Random House, Inc. Reprinted with the permission of the publishers.

Virginia Woolf, "The Window" from *To the Lighthouse.* Copyright 1927 by Harcourt Brace and Company, renewed 1954 by Leonard Woolf. Reprinted with the permission of Harcourt Brace and Company.

Samuel Beckett, *Happy Days.* Copyright © 1961 and renewed 1989 by Samuel Beckett. Reprinted with the permission of Grove/Atlantic, Inc.

### *France*

Madame de Sévigné, Letters 1–21 from *Selected Letters,* edited and translated by H.T. Barnwell. Copyright © 1960 by H.T. Barnwell. Reprinted with the permission of Everyman's Library/ David Campbell Publishers, Ltd.

Jean-Jacques Rousseau, excerpts from *The Confessions of Jean-Jacques Rousseau,* translated by J.M. Cohen. Copyright 1954 by J.M. Cohen Reprinted with the permission of Penguin Books, Ltd.

Charles Baudelaire, "To the Reader," "Elevation," "Correspondences," "The Head of Hair," "The

Vampire," and "Spleen II" from *Poems,* translated by Richard Howard. Copyright © 1980 by Richard Howard. Reprinted with the permission of Alfred A. Knopf, Inc.

Marcel Proust, "Combray" from *In Search of Lost Time,* translated by C.K. Scott Moncrieff and Terence Kilmartin, revised by D.J. Enright. Copyright © 1992 by Random House, Inc. & Chatto and Windus. Reprinted with the permission of Random House, Inc.

### *Germany and Czechoslovakia*

Friederich Hölderlin, "Patmos," from *Poems and Fragments,* translated by Michael Hamburger. Copyright © 1980 by Michael Hamburger. Reprinted with the permission of Anvil Poetry Press, Ltd.

Rainer Maria Rilke, excerpts from "The Duino Elegies" ("First Elegy" and "Second Elegy") from *Selected Poetry of Rainer Maria Rilke,* edited and translated by Stephen Mitchell. Copyright © 1989 by Stephen Mitchell. Reprinted with the permission of Random House, Inc.

Franz Kafka, "A Country Doctor" and "An Imperial Message," translated by Joachim Neugroschel, from *In the Penal Colony and Other Stories.* Copyright © 1993 by Joachim Neugroschel. Reprinted with the permission of Scribner, a division of Simon & Schuster.

### *Russia*

Fyodor Dostoevsky, *Notes from the Underground,* translated by Serge Shishkoff (New York: Crowell, 1969). Copyright © 1969 by Serge Shishkoff. Reprinted by permission.

Anna Akhmatova, "Dante," "Courage," "Native Land," "Creation," and excerpts from "Requiem," translated by Judith Hemschemeyer, from *Complete Poems of Anna Akhmatova,* edited by Roberta Reeder. Copyright © 1992 by Judith Hemschemeyer. Reprinted with the permission of Zephyr Press.

### *Poland*

Wislaw Szymborska, "Water," "Conversation with a Stone," "Theater Impressions," "Seen from Above," "Our Ancestors' Short Lives," "The Century's Decline," and "Nothing's a Gift" from *View With a Grain of Sand,* translated by Stanislaw Baraczak and Clare Cavanagh. Copyright © 1995 by Stanislaw Baraczak and Clare Cavanagh. Reprinted with the permission of Harcourt Brace and Company.

## The Americas

### *Mayan*

Popul Vuh, "The Creation" and "The Hero Twins in the Underworld" from *Popul Vuh: The Mayan Book of the Dawn of Life,* translated by Dennis Tedlock. Copyright © 1985 by Dennis Tedlock. Reprinted with the permission of Simon & Schuster.

### *Argentina*

Jorge Luis Borges, "Pierre Menard, Author of Quixote," translated by Anthony Bonner, and "Borges and I," translated by N.T. Giovanni, from *Borges: A Reader,* edited by Emir Rodriguez Monegal and Alastair Reid. Copyright © 1981 by Jorge Luis Borges, Emir Rodriguez Monegal, and Alastair Reid. Reprinted with the permission of Dutton Signet, a division of Penguin Putnam Inc. "Poem Written in a Copy of Beowulf," translated by Alastair Reid, from *Borges: A Reader,* edited by Emir Rodriguez Monegal and Alastair Reid. Copyright © 1981 by Jorge Luis Borges, Emir Rodriguez Monegal, and Alastair Reid. Reprinted with the permission of Dutton Signet, a division of Penguin Putnam Inc.

### *Chile*

Pablo Neruda, "The Heights of Macchu Picchu," translated by Jack Schmitt, from *Canto General.* Copyright © 1991 by Regents of the University of California. Reprinted with the permission of the University of California Press. "The Word," translated by Alastair Reid, from *Fully Empowered.* Copyright © 1962 by Editorial Losada, S.A., Buenos Aires. Translation copyright © 1967, 1969, 1970, 1975 by Alaistair Reid. Reprinted with the permission of Farrar, Straus & Giroux, Inc. Excerpts from *The Book of Questions,* translated by William O'Daly. Copyright © 1991. Reprinted with the permission of Copper Canyon Press, P. O. Box 271, Port Townsend, WA 98368-0271.

### *Colombia*

Gabriel Garcia Marquez, "The Handsomest Drowned Man in the World," translated by

Gregory Rabassa and J.S. Bernstein, from *Leaf Storm and Other Stories*. Copyright © 1971 by Gabriel Garcia Marquez. Reprinted with the permission of HarperCollins Publishers, Inc.

### Dominican Republic

Angela Hernández, "How to Gather the Shadows of the Flowers," translated by Lizabeth Paravisini-Gerbert, from *Green Cane and Juicy Flotsam: Short Stories by Caribbean Women,* edited by Carmen C. Esteves and Lizabeth Paravisini-Gerbert. Copyright © 1992 by Rutgers, The State University. Reprinted with the permission of Rutgers University Press.

### The United States

Walt Whitman, "Memories of President Lincoln: When Lilacs Last in the Dooryard Bloomed" from *Leaves of Grass,* edited by Harold W. Blodgett and Sculley Bradley. Copyright © 1965 by New York University Press. Reprinted with the permission of the publishers.

Emily Dickinson, 130: "These are the days when Birds come back"; 303: "The Soul selects her own Society"; 435: "Much Madness is divinest Sense"; 465: "I heard a fly buzz—when I died"; 501: "This World is not Conclusion"; 632: "The Brain—is wider than the Sky"; 712: "Because I could not stop for Death—"; 986: "A narrow Fellow in the Grass"; and 1129: "Tell all the Truth but tell it slant" from *The Complete Poems of Emily Dickinson,* edited by Thomas H. Johnson. Copyright 1951, © 1955, 1979, 1982 by the President and Fellows of Harvard College Reprinted with the permission of The Belknap Press of Harvard University Press.

Ezra Pound, "The River-Merchant's Wife: A Letter," "Exile's Letter," and "In a Station of the Metro" from *Personae.* Copyright 1926 by Ezra Pound. Canto 1 ("And then went down to the ship") from *The Cantos.* Copyright 1934 by Ezra Pound. All reprinted with the permission of New Directions Publishing Corporation.

T.S. Eliot, "The Waste Land" (excerpts) from *Collected Poems 1909–1962.* Copyright 1936 by Harcourt Brace & Company, renewed © 1964 by T.S. Eliot. Reprinted with the permission of Faber and Faber Limited.

William Faulkner, "That Evening Sun" from *Collected Stories of William Faulkner.* Copyright 1931 and renewed © 1959 by William Faulkner. Reprinted with the permission of Random House, Inc.

Elizabeth Bishop, "The Fish," "At the Fishhouses," "The Armadillo," and "In the Waiting Room" from *The Complete Poems 1927–1979.* Copyright 1950 by Elizabeth Bishop. Reprinted with the permission of Farrar, Straus & Giroux, Inc.

Toni Morrison, excerpt from *Sula* (New York: Alfred A. Knopf, 1974). Copyright © 1974 by Toni Morrison. Reprinted with the permission of International Creative Management.

Louise Erdrich, "Saint Marie" from *Love Medicine,* New and Expanded Version. Copyright © 1993 by Louise Erdrich. Reprinted with the permission of Henry Holt and Company, Inc.

## Photo Credits

### Ancient Literature

Ancient Mesopotamia and Egypt, p. 13: Staatliche Museen zu Berlin—PreuBischer Kulturbesitz—Vorderasiatisches Museum.

Ancient India, p. 173: Indian Samath (Uttar Pradesh). 5th Century. "Sitting Buddha." Cunar-Sandstone, Height 158 cm. Samath, Archaeologisches Museum. Photo: AKG London.

Ancient China, p. 289: Wang Lu/China Stock Photo Library.

Ancient Greece and Rome, p. 405: Brygos Painter (5th BCE). "Bacchante, Cup Painting." Staatliche Antikensammlung, Munich, Germany. Foto Marburg/Art Resource, NY.

### Literature of the Middle Period

The Middle East of the Middle Period, p. 721: Arabic Script from ms Arabe 5847, fol. 5V. Cliche Bibliotheque nationale de France, Paris.

India in the Middle Period, p. 917: "Sita's Test, from Ramayana" by painter Jagannath Mahapatra, Raghuraipur (Orissa), India, 1983. (anonymous collection). The University of California, Berkeley.

China in the Middle Period, p. 995: Ma Yuan, Sung dynasty, "Lifting a Cup to Sport with the Moon." 205.6 cm x 104.1 cm. National Palace Museum, Taipei, Taiwan, Republic of China.

Japan in the Middle Period, p. 1061: Tosa Mitsunori; Tosa, Mitsuoki; Tosa, Mitsuyoshi; Karasumaru Mitsukata: "Illustrations of Genji Monogatari: Vol. 1, The Tale of Genji." Color; paper; platinum; Calligraphy. h. 10 1/2 in x l. 35 11/16 ft. Knobs, 7/16" hexagonal crystal. Copyright © The Seattle Art Museum. Eugene Fuller Memorial Collection. Photograph by Paul Macapia.

Korea in the Middle Period, p. 1189: "Tiger." National Museum, Seoul Korea. Josse/Art Resource, NY.

Europe in the Middle Period, p. 1201: MS Harley 4431 f4 (min) "Christine de Pisan in Her Study," by permissions of the British Library.

*Modern Literature*

The Modern Middle East and Africa, p. 1501: Professor Herbert M. Cole.

Modern India and Southeast Asia, p. 1591: Doranne Jacobson.

Modern China, p. 1635: ChinaStock Photo Library.

Modern Japan, p. 1739: Morris G. Simoncelli

Modern Korea, p. 1823: Kim Sik (1579–1662), "Water Buffalo." Choson dynasty. Framed album leaf. Ink and light colors of silk. Korea University Museum, Seoul.

Modern Europe, p. 1835: Vasily Kandinsky, "Composition 8." July 1923. Oil on canvas, 140 x 2009 cm (55 1/8 x 79 1/8 inches). Solomon R. Guggenheim Museum, New York. Gift, Solomon R. Guggenheim, 1937. Photograph by David Heald. Copyright © The Solomon R. Guggenheim Foundation, New York (FN37.262).

The Americas, p. 2097: Drawing by Carlos A. Villacorta of a Mayan carved relief from Popul Vuh. Photography by Hillel Burger. Copyright © 1984 The President and Fellows of Harvard College. Courtesy Peabody Museum, Harvard.

# Index

## D



## E



## F



## G

## H



## I



## J

## K



## L



## M



## N

## S



## T

## Z